The Contemporary Thesaurus of Search Terms and Synonyms

Editorial Review Board

The Contemporary Thesaurus of Search Terms and Synonyms

A Guide for Natural Language Computer Searching

Second Edition

Sara D. Knapp

ORYX PRESS

2000

The rare Arabian Oryx is believed to have inspired the myth of the unicorn. This desert antelope became virtually extinct in the early 1960s. At that time, several groups of international conservationists arranged to have nine animals sent to the Phoenix Zoo to be the nucleus of a captive breeding herd. Today, the Oryx population is over 1,000, and over 500 have been returned to the Middle East.

© 2000 by The Oryx Press
4041 North Central at Indian School Road
Phoenix, Arizona 85012-3397
www.oryxpress.com
Published simultaneously in Canada

Printed and bound in the United States of America

∞ The paper used in this publication meets the minimum requirements of American National Standard for Information Science—Permanence of Paper for Printed Library Materials, ANSI Z39.48, 1984.

Library of Congress Cataloging-in-Publication Data

Knapp, Sara D.
  The thesaurus of search terms and synonyms : a guide for natural language computer searching / Sara D. Knapp.—2nd ed.
    p. cm
  Includes bibliographical references and index.
  ISBN 1-57356-107-X (alk. paper)
  1. Electronic information resource searching—English-speaking countries. 2. English language—Terms and phrases. 3. Social sciences—English-speaking countries—Terminology. I. Title.

ZA4060.K58   2000
025.4'9—dc21   99-050091

For Sue and Vincent

Contents

Preface

The Contemporary Thesaurus of Search Terms and Synonyms updates and expands The Contemporary Thesaurus of Social Science Terms and Synonyms (Oryx Press, 1993). This new volume includes thousands of concepts from business and the humanities, in addition to the original social science coverage. It is designed to help users find meaningful words for searching the Internet as well as for computer searching of CD-ROM and online databases.

In recent years, we have seen an explosion of new terms representing the dynamic changes in our world. Political and social boundaries have been transcended, ethnic and cultural tensions have emerged or re-emerged. Old alliances have dissolved, new networks of power have arisen. The coalescing of economic power has fostered economic globalization. The need for rapid responses has called forth such concepts as "just-in-time" manufacturing, "virtual factories," "self-designing organizations," and "adhocracies." Business is being instantly transacted on the Internet. Economic pressures, information, and technology have fueled enormous changes. Human lives are commodified as "human resources" to be deployed economically. From reconstituted families, mobile career patterns, changing neighborhoods, downsized organizations, and merged businesses to emerging nations and ethnic cleansing, millions of people are continually uprooted by powerful forces reshaping their lives.

The world is in flux. Ideologies compete in attempting to explain and reconcile irreconcilable tensions. New words reflect new and old conceptualizations of contemporary life and times. An ever-changing vocabulary names these burgeoning developments and so this thesaurus is a lexical "slice in time." The integration of terms from the humanities, business, and the social sciences reflects the interrelationship of these disciplines in reality. At the same time that social science races to quantitatively describe and qualitatively understand what is happening, art, literature, and music reflect the myriad responses of diverse peoples to our complex and unstable world. And religion, philosophy, and other belief systems seek old and new meanings to life and ways to reaffirm the importance of being human in a sometimes inhuman world.

Because a whole new generation of students and other people are now searching online, the Thesaurus also includes a chapter on the basics of computer searching and another chapter on how to use "natural language" terms (and this thesaurus) to improve searches.

The term "thesaurus" has Greek and Latin roots and originally meant a treasury or storehouse. By the eighteenth century, it had come to mean a "storehouse of knowledge," such as a dictionary or encyclopedia (Onions, 1955). In 1852, Peter Mark Roget published his own treasure-house of knowledge, the Thesaurus of English Words and Phrases Classified and Arranged so as to Facilitate the Expression of Ideas and Assist in Literary Composition. In so doing, Roget gave a new meaning to the term "thesaurus" and since then it has been the term applied to books for finding synonyms (Laird, 1971). Although often better organized than Roget's original rather artificial classification, thesauruses of this type all provide bountiful treasuries of words.

The Contemporary Thesaurus of Search Terms and Synonyms follows in the tradition of Roget, providing an array of terms, from which the user selects those which best suit a particular need. The Thesaurus leads the user from a single word or phrase to a "treasury" of expressions, from which alternative words or a more precise term can be chosen. A search strategy is likely to be most effective when the terms searched describe as precisely as possible whatever is sought. This is particularly important in searching the World Wide Web, where huge, but not always relevant, results are often retrieved. In a landmark book on computer-based retrieval of information, F.W. Lancaster and E.G. Fayen wrote:

> The most significant cause of recall failure in a natural language system is the inability of the searcher to think of all possible approaches to retrieval. The searcher in a natural language system needs a thesaurus, or similar aid, just as much as the searcher in the controlled vocabulary system—perhaps even more so. . . . (Lancaster and Fayen, 1973)

This volume is primarily an aid to computer searching, but it may also be useful for writers and speakers seeking alternative ways to express ideas. It complements both literary and search thesauruses because it is interdisciplinary, contains a wealth of terms, and covers many new and socially relevant topics.

Scope

The Contemporary Thesaurus of Search Terms and Synonyms is broad in scope and includes more than 20,000 entries for over 8,500 concepts representing thousands of words and phrases. Subject coverage includes concepts from business and economics; from the humanities (music, art, literature, religion, philosophy, and history); and updated entries from anthropology, business, current events, education, environmental concerns, geriatrics, medicine, mental health, political science, public administration, public affairs, psychiatry, psychology, religion, sociology, social work, and women's issues. As in the first edition, for fields with technical terminology, only general aspects are covered. For example, linguistics and statistics are treated in only a general fashion. Research often cuts across traditional boundaries of scholarship, making it necessary to search the literature of one field using terminology drawn from another field. The terminology itself has been found to overlap fields. A recent study showed a high degree of overlap between subject headings in the humanities and the social sciences (Knapp, Cohen, and Juedes, 1998). For this reason, a natural language thesaurus of search terms should have broad, interdisciplinary coverage.

Sources

The concepts and terms chosen for *The Contemporary Thesaurus of Search Terms and Synonyms* were taken from actual search requests; from newspapers, sources on the World Wide Web, specialized thesauruses, databases, and subject dictionaries; or were contributed by colleagues, clients, and friends. This work is built on the foundation of many other thesauruses and dictionaries, which are listed in "Selected Sources Used to Compile This Thesaurus" at the end of the book. Concepts and terms were taken from many sources. Some of the more important sources are *The Cambridge Dictionary of Philosophy*; *The Columbia Dictionary of Modern Literary and Cultural Criticism*; *Dictionary of Business & Management*; *Dictionary of Concepts in History*; *Dictionary of Multicultural Education*; *Humanities Index*; *INFO-SOUTH*; *Latin American Information System Thesaurus*; *Medical Subject Headings, Annotated Alphabetic List*; *New Harvard Dictionary of Music*; *Newspaper Abstracts Thesaurus*; *The Oxford Dictionary of Art*; *The Oxford Dictionary of New Words*; *PAIS Subject Headings*; *Thesaurus of Aging Terminology*; *Thesaurus of ERIC Descriptors*; *Thesaurus of Psychological Index Terms*; *Thesaurus of Sociological Indexing Terms*; *Wall Street Words*; and *A Women's Thesaurus*. Many new words and concepts were taken from online sources, such as the online *New York Times* and *World Wide Words*.

Concepts and Terms

Concepts emerge from the activity of scholars seeking to understand and explain phenomena. Organizing knowledge into concepts helps not only to identify topics, but to define them, classify them, and relate them to other concepts. Without concepts, we might be unable to think (Ritter, 1986). The *Thesaurus* is organized by concepts. Each group of terms is listed alphabetically under a concept title, usually its common name or the term(s) used by dictionaries or other thesauruses. Each concept group consists of synonyms, near-synonyms, closely related terms, or specific examples illustrating that concept.

Concept titles appear in natural word order, e.g., "Information literacy," but there are cross-references from all the other significant title words, e.g., "**Literacy, information.** See *Information literacy*."

"*See also*" notes refer users to related concepts. These related concepts, from a variety of sources, illustrate the power of an interdisciplinary thesaurus. For example, for the concept "Motivation" many related concepts are listed, including, among others, "Nurturance" (from *A Women's Thesaurus*); "Sex drive"

(from *Thesaurus of Psychological Index Terms*); "Student motivation" (from *Thesaurus of ERIC Descriptors*); and "Profit motive" (from *Thesaurus of Sociological Indexing Terms*).

Some records contain lists of examples. For instance, the records on "Environmental pollutants" and "Wild animals" list examples of pollutants and animals. These lists are not intended to be authoritative or comprehensive, but rather, to suggest other avenues of approach. Similarly, the lists of cultural groups, such as "Southeast Asian cultural groups" or "Central American native cultural groups," include major cultural groups for each area, but are not intended to be authoritative or comprehensive.

Country names are listed under geographical regions, for example, "Sub-Saharan Africa" or "Central America." Brackets are used to indicate alternative or former names of countries, for example, Botswana [Bechuanaland] or Burkina Faso [Upper Volta]. The country names were as up-to-date as possible as of this writing, but in time events may change some of these entries. Brackets have also been used to indicate some other alternative names, such as the street names of drugs.

Within a record, the first word or phrase is always the concept title repeated with appropriate suffixes in parentheses. This title is usually followed by a few phrases that seem close in meaning to it. The other terms represent near-synonyms or related aspects of the concept. Select *only* those that are closely related to your topic.

Below is a sample of a complete record:

Online privacy. Online privacy. *Choose from:* online, cyber(space), electronic mail, email, e-mail, electronic fund transfer(s), internet, computerized data, computerized medical record(s), digital, e-commerce, credit file(s), web, site(s), website(s), home page(s), track(ed,ing) user(s), virtual communit(y,ies) *with:* privacy, encrypt(ed,ing,ion), cryptograph(y,ic), confidential(ity), security. *Consider also:* disabl(e,ed,ing) cookie(s). *See also* Computer crimes; Confidentiality; Digital signatures; Electronic eavesdropping; Gossip sites; Invasion of privacy; Market research; Online harassment; Online users; Privacy; Privacy laws; Right of privacy; Surveillance of citizens; Virtual reality.

The *Thesaurus* includes sexist, racist, pejorative, and slang terms that may not meet with everyone's approval. They are included, not because they are recommended, but because they may be necessary in searching various kinds of literature. For example, "handicapped" has a negative connotation. However, the term is still used in the literature and in the subject indexing for some databases. A search for this subject would miss relevant literature if it did not include "handicapped," "disabled," and (persons with) "disabilities." In another example, the editor of *A Women's Thesaurus* points out that the term "unwed mothers" defines women in terms of their relationship to men, yet the term is used in several "mainstream" thesauruses (*Thesaurus of Psychological Index Terms; Thesaurus of Sociological Indexing Terms; Thesaurus of ERIC Descriptors*) and is still used by authors. I have used "Single mothers" (which *A Women's Thesaurus* recommends) as a concept title, but have included a cross-reference to it from the commonly used phrase "Unwed mothers." More foreign terms are included in this edition than in the first. The inclusion of the humanities, particularly music, has introduced concepts frequently expressed in French, German, or Italian. The globalization of business and politics has also called for the inclusion of foreign terms now found in English-language articles, such as hajj, compadrazgo, maquiladoras, and chaebols. Diacriticals or other symbols are not included because they are generally not available for searching.

The choice of search terms should be guided by their closeness in meaning to what is being searched. Because concepts and terms are taken from many sources, some concepts overlap. I hope the redundancy will help users find needed terms.

What Is Not Included

The *Thesaurus* is not a dictionary; words are not defined. Because the *Thesaurus* provides synonyms or at least closely related terms, it omits items for which no synonyms or closely related terms could be found, for example, "econometrics." Those items for which there is only "one way to say it," such as proper names, names of tests, and many technical terms, are also omitted, except as they relate to more general concepts. And the terminology of highly technical areas is given only general coverage. In general, most slang terms and British spellings have been omitted, but information on British spelling is covered in Appendix B, "British Spellings." Also omitted are some very abstract terms (e.g., "extension in logic"), or terms that are so general they have no useful synonyms.

The Contemporary Thesaurus of Search Terms and Synonyms is directed to users performing computer searches and also to writers and speakers. It suggests words that may be used for many purposes. But purposes are unique and only those words that most closely match the subject of your search should be selected. The choice of words belongs to you. I hope that the *Thesaurus* will be helpful in making that choice.

Future Editions

The structure of our world, from new family forms to new international alliances, is rapidly changing. With these changes, our thinking and the words we use to describe the new realities are also evolving. Time and space have limited what could be included in this edition, but reference works of this kind must be revised and updated to add new terms. And a natural language thesaurus for online searching, integrating terms from many sources, is really a unique kind of reference work. For both these reasons, suggestions from users about any aspect of the book, including suggestions for concepts and terms to be included in future editions, would be especially welcome. You may e-mail comments to the editor at SK314@CNSVAX.ALBANY.EDU.

References

Audi, Robert, ed. *The Cambridge Dictionary of Philosophy*. Cambridge: Cambridge University Press, 1995.

Booth, Barbara. *Thesaurus of Sociological Indexing Terms*. San Diego: Sociological Abstracts, Inc., 1996.

Capek, Mary Ellen S., ed. *A Women's Thesaurus*. New York: Harper & Row, 1989.

Childers, Ian and Harold Osborne, eds. *The Oxford Dictionary of Art*. Oxford: The Oxford University Press, 1988.

Childers, Joseph and Gary Hentzl, eds. *The Columbia Dictionary of Modern Literary and Cultural Criticism*. New York: Columbia University Press, 1995.

Grant, Carl A. and Gloria Ladson-Billings, eds. *Dictionary of Multicultural Education*. Phoenix: Oryx Press, 1997.

Humanities Index. New York: H.W. Wilson, 1994- .

INFO-SOUTH, Latin American Information System Thesaurus. Coral Gables, FL: University of Miami, INFO-SOUTH, North-South Center, n.d.

Knapp, Sara D., Laura B. Cohen, and D.R. Juedes. "A Natural Language Thesaurus for the Humanities: The Need for a Database Search Aid." *Library Quarterly* 68 (Oct., 1998): 406-30.

Knowles, Elizabeth and Julia Elliott. *The Oxford Dictionary of New Words*. New York: Oxford University Press, 1997.

Laird, Charlton. *Webster's New World Thesaurus*. New York: New American Library, 1975.

Lancaster, F.W. and E.G. Fayen. *Information Retrieval Online*. Los Angeles: Melville, 1973.

Little, William. *The Oxford Universal Dictionary on Historical Principles*. 3rd ed. Prepared by William Little, H.W. Fowler, and J. Coulson, Revised and edited by C.T. Onions. Oxford: The Clarendon Press, 1955.

National Library of Medicine Staff. *Medical Subject Headings, Annotated Alphabetic List*. Bethesda, MD: National Library of Medicine, 1989- .

New York Times. New York: The New York Times, 1998- . Available at <http://www.nytimes.com/>.

Newspaper Abstracts Thesaurus. Ann Arbor, MI: UMI, 1988.

Public Affairs Information Service. *PAIS Subject Headings*. New York: Public Affairs Information Service, 1990.

Quinion, Michael B. *World Wide Words*. 1998- . Available at <http://www.quinion.com/words/>.

Randel, Don Michael, ed. *New Harvard Dictionary of Music*. Cambridge, MA: The Belknap Press of Harvard University Press, 1986.

Ritter, Harry. *Dictionary of Concepts in History*. Westport, CT: Greenwood Press, 1986.

Rosenberg, Jerry Martin, ed. *Dictionary of Business & Management*. New York: John Wiley, 1993.

Scott, David Logan. *Wall Street Words*. Boston: Houghton Mifflin, 1988.

Thesaurus of Aging Terminology: AgeLine Database on Middle Age and Aging. Washington, DC: American Association of Retired Persons, 1997.

Thesaurus of ERIC Descriptors. 13th ed. Phoenix: Oryx Press, 1995.

Walker, Alvin, Jr., ed. *Thesaurus of Psychological Index Terms*. Washington, DC: American Psychological Association, 1997.

Acknowledgments

In compiling this thesaurus and reviewing entries from the earlier edition, I have been fortunate in being assisted by an editorial review board of subject experts. Their command of their subject areas enabled them to suggest many excellent additional concepts and terms and to expertly review the existing work for both additions and judicious deletions. My thanks to Eleanor Gossen, Don Juedes, Paul Nudelman, Judith Place, and Mary Van Ullen. I am very appreciative of their contributions to this work.

My former colleague and sometimes collaborator, Donna R. Dolan, has contributed words, ideas, and enthusiastic support. Before the work even began, she was sending me lists of words for the next edition. Throughout the work, she was always ready for me to send her concepts to explore. She made first-rate suggestions for concepts as well as text, as she has always done. She is a true friend and a valued collaborator.

I am also very grateful to another friend, colleague, and our Libraries' Webmaster, Laura B. Cohen, who reviewed many records concerning the Internet, the World Wide Web, and related new concepts. Her fine suggestions greatly improved those records. Her award-winning Internet Tutorials <http://www.albany.edu/library/internet/> were very helpful to me in writing about the Web and I heartily recommend them. She ungrudgingly reviewed my revised chapters on searching and suggested numerous improvements relating to the Internet, the Web, and many other areas.

A very special thanks to my sister and brother-in-law, Sue and Vincent Hodgson for support, for reviewing records, for suggesting terms, and for proofreading thousands of records. I thank them even more, though it is impossible to do so adequately, for their special role in our lives in recent years.

My thanks to Arnold Patashnick for finding many excellent dictionaries and looking up numerous definitions. Thanks to him and Paul Nudelman for discussions about ideas and words. I am grateful for their willingness to pick up lexical challenges.

Thanks to Peter Rinne for suggesting some words I might never have considered. His interest and enthusiasm are appreciated.

Thank you to Kai Larsen for good suggestions in the field of management.

I am grateful to the University at Albany, State University of New York for granting me a sabbatical leave in 1997 to work on this project.

How to Use This Book

Each entry consists of a concept title plus terms and phrases that are synonymous or closely related. It has been pointed out that there are few, if any, true synonyms. Terms that are *obviously* not synonymous are included here because in computer searching they are often used as though they were. For example, "child," "children," and "childhood" certainly do not have the same meaning in ordinary usage. If you were writing or speaking, you would use only that word which meant exactly what you intended. But, in a computer search, you might use all of them. For example, to search for information about "homeless children," you might be interested in the following:

> "The **homeless child** at school."
> "The effects of **homelessness** on **children**."
> "**Childhood** experiences of **homelessness**."

Unless you use one of the new search engines (see more about them later), searches will retrieve only those items which have *exactly* the words you used in your search strategy. To retrieve the articles above, your strategy should search for the terms *"child"* OR *"children"* OR *"childhood"* AND *"homeless"* OR *"homelessness."* One way might be to use truncation to search for all words beginning with the root words "child" or "homeless."

This thesaurus also includes specific examples of general concepts. Specifics may provide excellent alternatives in a search strategy. For example, in a search for "street drugs" you might use "illegal drugs," but also including the names of specific drugs like "marijuana" or "crack cocaine" would improve the search.

Concepts may be searchable by terms that imply rather than describe them. For example, some material on "mentally ill offenders" may be found by searching for the "McNaughton Rule," a rule under which defendants plead insanity; "urban public health" may be implied by "cities" and "rat control." *The Contemporary Thesaurus of Search Terms and Synonyms* includes some meaningful words and phrases that may be useful in searching and writing, although they only imply a concept.

Words with the same spelling, but very different meanings, are listed separately. The following records on "depression" are examples:

Depression (economic). Depression. Economic(ally) depress(ed,ion,ions). Recession(s). Stock market crash(es). Financial panic(s). Deflation. Stagflation. Hard times. Bank failure(s). Black Monday. Great depression. *Choose from:* economic *with:* cris(is,es), slump(s), contraction(s), turndown(s), downward spiral(s), fall(en,ing), plung(e,es,ed,ing), meltdown(s), crash(ed,es,ing), downturn(s). *Consider also:* rust belt, bread line(s), soup kitchen(s), Works Projects Administration, WPA, Civilian Conservation Corps, CCC. *See also* Bank failures; Bankruptcy; Business cycles; Business failures; Decline; Economic conditions; Economic crises; Economic problems; Plant closings; Recession; Unemployment rates.

Depression (psychology). Depress(ed,ion,ive). Mental depression. Desponden(t,cy). Weep(y,iness). Deject(ed,ion). Gloom(y,iness). Sad(ness). Despair(ed,ing). Discourage(d,ment). Low(er,ered) mood. Defeatis(t,m). Hopeless(ness). Feeling worthless(ness). Learned helplessness. Lonel(y,iness). Lack of affect. Listless(ness). Intropunitive(ness). Unhapp(y,iness). Hypochondria(c, cal). Stupor. Weltschmerz. Dysthym(ia,ic,ics). Athym(ia,ic). Melanchol(y,ia). *Consider also:* self *with:* denial, abnegation, neglect, abuse, deprecation, depreciation, accusation, destructive. *Consider also:* suicid(e,es, al). *See also* Agitated depression; Anaclitic depression; Anhedonia; Anxiety; Bereavement; Bipolar disorder; Depressive disorder; Emotionally disturbed; Emotions; Grief; Holiday depression; Hopelessness; Involutional psychosis; Learned helplessness; Loneliness; Major depression; Neurotic depressive reaction; Pessimism; Postpartum depression; Psychopathology; Reactive depression; Sadness; Seasonal affective disorder; Self accusation.

"Choose from:" and "Consider also:" Notes

Words that can be combined as phrases are suggested in the "Choose from:" or "Consider also:" notes and linked by "with" as shown below:

Educational counseling. Educational counseling. *Choose from:* education(al), academic *with:* counsel(ing,or,ors), advis(ing,ement,or,ors), advice, guidance, mentor(s,ing). *See also* Academic aspiration; Counseling; School counseling; Vocational guidance.

You might select combinations such as "academic advisement" or "educational guidance" or combine several terms from each group. For example, "*Choose from:* education(al), academic *with:* counsel(ing,or,ors), advis(ing,ement,or,ors), advice, guidance, mentor(s,ing)" suggests the following possibilities:

educational counseling	academic counseling
educational counselors	academic counselors
educational advisement	academic advisement

educational advice	academic advice
educational guidance	academic guidance
educational mentoring	academic mentoring
educational mentors	academic mentors

Some of the terms in each group may not be suitable to combine with some of the other terms in that group. Use your own good judgment; select carefully.

Suffixes

Suffixes in parentheses suggest words that may be included for more comprehensiveness in your search. For example, "mentor(s,ed,ing)" suggests that you could search for: "mentor," "mentors," "mentored," or "mentoring," or, in this case, consider truncating "mentor" to search for all of them. Parenthetical suffixes are *not* necessarily recommended truncation points. Bab(y,ies) should be searched as "baby or babies" *never* as "bab" truncated. As in selecting terms, your judgment is essential.

A diagram of a sample entry illustrating each section of an entry is displayed inside the front cover of this book.

Hyphens and Apostrophes

Hyphens and apostrophes are searchable in some search systems, but are omitted in others. The searcher must determine the policy for the system. If in doubt about a system, it may be wise to enter terms in all possible ways. For example, *"Self esteem"* OR *"Self-esteem."*

When to Use Natural Language in Computer Searching

There are many reasons for using natural language terms in computer searches, such as when:

- searching the World Wide Web

- specificity and flexibility are needed
- comprehensiveness is required
- searching full-text databases
- databases have inadequate indexing
- databases lack descriptors
- relevant descriptors were only recently established
- descriptors don't "fit" the concept
- searching across databases

When subject indexing (controlled vocabulary) is absent or inadequate, natural language terms are essential. *The Contemporary Thesaurus of Search Terms and Synonyms* is a finding aid for such terms.

The terms contained in each record are neither recipes nor precise formulas. They are intended as springboards for the imagination of the searcher. You will *almost never* use all the terms listed, but only those terms most relevant to your topic. The words will sometimes have different meanings depending upon the database you use to search and the other words you combine with them. An example of such a word is "figurative." Combined with "art," it means "representational art"; combined with "language," it implies metaphorical expressions.

Some things are difficult to search with natural language terms. For example, to search for "children who are murderers," the terms you would use will also retrieve items about murderers *of* children. Only controlled vocabulary can assure that the two concepts will occur in a specified relationship to each other. That doesn't mean you shouldn't search with natural language terms when you need to, only that you should be aware of the possibility of this problem and edit your search results accordingly. Finally, searching is always somewhat imprecise and even the best strategies on the best systems don't retrieve 100 percent recall (everything on the topic) and 100 percent relevance (everything retrieved being relevant). Aim for an optimum balance between recall and relevance; allow for some margin of imprecision. For more on the techniques of this kind of searching, see the section in this book on "Natural Language Searching."

Basics of Computer Searching

This introduction to computer searching is intended for novices. It explains and illustrates some basic principles of searching that apply to searching the World Wide Web, searching online, and searching CD-ROM databases. Some of the features discussed include searching the World Wide Web; databases, records, and fields; "AND," "OR," and "NOT" logical operators; truncation; choosing an information source; some basic search processes; analyzing your search topic; and sample searches. This section offers a brief overview of search systems that vary greatly in detail and are constantly changing. For the particulars of any system, consult help pages or system documentation.

Online Searching

The term "online" refers to being connected, as when we say that the printer is "online," and also means communicating with another computer via telecommunications. All online searching is *interactive,* which allows you to view results and then modify your strategy to improve results. Today, most online searching is conducted over the Internet.

Searching the Internet

The Internet is a worldwide interconnected network of communications networks linking millions of sources of information, including libraries and research, governmental, educational, and commercial organizations. Through it an enormous ocean of information is available.

The World Wide Web (abbreviated as the Web, WWW, or W3) is a system of Internet servers that supports hypertext to access several Internet protocols on a single interface. The Web consists of files, called pages or home pages, containing links to documents and resources throughout the Internet. The operation of the Web relies primarily on hypertext as its means of information retrieval. Hypertext is a document containing words that connect to other documents. These words are called links and are selectable by the user (Cohen, 1999).

The Internet can be used simply as a mode of telecommunications to access a particular site, such as a library catalog or the DIALOG, Lexis-Nexis, or OCLC commercial systems. The databases on these systems can then be searched using that organization's search software. Web search engines, such as AltaVista, InfoSeek, and Northern Light, allow the user to enter keywords relating to a topic and retrieve a list of Internet sites or Web page excerpts containing those keywords.

CD-ROM Searching

CD-ROM—"compact disc, read only memory"—searching means using a computer to search a database stored on a compact disc. Many databases are available in online and CD-ROM formats and many are migrating to Windows-based Web versions. The search systems used to search CD-ROMs are typically supplied by the vendor.

Databases, Records, and Fields

A *database* is a collection of data, or information, arranged in records and files that can be sorted, searched, or manipulated by computer. Databases are often produced by one company or organization, a "database producer," but marketed by other companies, who provide the search systems used for CD-ROM searching. For example, the Sociofile database is produced by Sociological Abstracts. It is available on CD-ROM through EBSCO, NISC, OVID, and SilverPlatter, and online through DIALOG, OCLC, DIMDI, Ovid, and Cambridge Scientific Abstracts.

A *record* is the basic unit of information within a file. In a file of mailing labels, each individual mailing label constitutes one record. In a bibliographic database, each reference to a book or journal article is a record. In a full-text database, the entire article appears as a record.

A *field* is that section of each computer record that is designated for and contains a specific type of information. In a file of mailing labels, the name is stored in one field, the street address is stored in another field, and so on. Below is a sample from a mailing label database.

Field Name	Data
NAME	John Greenfield
STREET	18 King Road
CITY	Guilderland
STATE	New York
ZIP CODE	12084

Bibliographic databases have separate fields for the title of the publication, the author, the publisher, the date of publication, and other relevant information. These separate fields can be useful in searching. You can specify in your search that you want only items in which a particular word occurs in a field such as the title field. Restricting searches to specific fields is discussed further in the section on "Natural Language Searching."

The following example shows some of the fields of a record from a bibliographic database. The name of each field is shown in the left-hand column.

ERIC ACCESSION NUMBER	EJ303735.
AUTHOR	Weil, Richard H.
TITLE	International Adoptions: The Quiet Migration.
JOURNAL CITATION	International Migration Review; v18 n2 p276-93 Sum 1984. 84.
LANGUAGE	EN.
YEAR OF PUBLICATION	84.
MAJOR DESCRIPTORS	Adopted-Children. Adoption. Foreign-Countries. Immigrants.
MINOR DESCRIPTORS	Agency-Role. Government-Role. International-Relations. Laws. Public-Policy. Refugees. Social-Attitudes.
ABSTRACT	Examines patterns in the international migration of children for adoption since World War II, with emphasis on those going to Sweden, the United Kingdom, and the United States. Relates findings to political and cultural factors. . . .

The World Wide Web consists of files, called pages or home pages, containing links to documents and resources throughout the Internet. Records on the World Wide Web also have fields. Although some are quite different from those of a bibliographic database, they can be useful for searching. There are many variations of fields on the Web, but a few of the most important ones are shown below as retrieved by one popular search engine, AltaVista. Other searchable fields will be discussed later.

TITLE	Care and Feeding of Elderly Computers
URL (Uniform Resource Locator)	www.galactic.co.uk
DOMAIN	[above, the *uk* indicates document is from the U.K.]
TEXT	"I happen to have a humble collection of elderly computers. I fancy every. . . ."

The Logical Operators

The words "AND," "OR," and "NOT" are used to combine terms or exclude particular terms from your search results. These terms, which indicate the logical relationship between search terms, are called "Boolean operators." They are named for the nineteenth-century British mathematician, George Boole.

The *"AND"* Operator

Combining two terms with "AND" requires that both be present for a record to be retrieved. For example, on one database, separate searches for the words "oil" and "exploration" retrieved 235 and 450 records, respectively. A combined search for "oil *AND* exploration" retrieved only 15 records containing both words. An example of a title retrieved is "Nigeria's oil and gas exploration industry."

The *"OR"* Operator

"OR" requires that *at least one* of the terms you specify be present in a record for it to be retrieved. It is usually used to link synonyms or related terms. For example, separate searches for "Syria," "Iraq," and "Iran" retrieved 158, 243, and 356 records, respectively, but a search for "Syria *OR* Iraq *OR* Iran" yielded 572 records, those containing any one of the three terms, any two of the three, or all three. Titles of some records retrieved included "Republic of fear—The politics of modern *Iraq*," "Drugs and *Iran* after the Islamic revolution," "Cold-war and covert action-the United States and *Syria*."

The *"NOT"* Operator

"NOT" requires that one term be present in a record but that another term be excluded. For example, "dolphins *NOT* Miami" retrieves only records that contain the word "dolphins" but that do *not* contain the word "Miami." If a record contains both words, it will not be retrieved in accordance with your command to "NOT" retrieve items containing the second word. This allows you to search for dolphins, but avoid anything about the "Miami Dolphins."

Caution! Use "NOT" with great care. "NOT" excludes *all* items containing the terms to which you have applied it. Thus, in the sample above, *every record* containing the word "Miami" will be excluded, *even if* the record also contains something that you do want to see, for example, an article about dolphins swimming off Miami Beach.

Word Proximity

If you are searching for the phrase "book value," it must be searched as a phrase with the two words adjacent to each other and appearing in that order. "Book" *AND* "value" could retrieve documents in which the words appear far apart and have nothing to do with each other. Many online search systems and Internet search engines allow users to search for phrases. Some systems also allow you to specify whether the words are within or beyond some range of each other and in what order they appear. On many Web search engines, users can specify that terms be searched as a phrase by enclosing them in quotes.

Truncation

Right-hand truncation means searching any word beginning with a specified root word. Truncation enables you to use one term to search for a number of possible word endings at the same time. For example, if you truncated the word "hazard," you would also be able to search for "hazards" or "hazardous." You truncate by placing a truncation symbol (also called a "mask symbol") at the point where you wish to truncate the word. To truncate "hazard," you would put the truncation symbol after the "d." Each search system has its own symbol for truncation. Commonly used symbols include the question mark (?), the dollar sign ($), and the asterisk (*). For this example, we will use the asterisk (*). If you truncate "resettl," as *resettl**, your search will retrieve any records containing any of the following words: resettle, resettled, resettlement, resettlements, resettling, as though you had searched for resettle *or* resettled *or* resettlement *or* resettlements *or* resettling. Some newer search systems have automatic means of retrieving for plurals so that you don't need to truncate to get both singular and plural forms of a term.

Truncating saves time, but can also be disastrous! Truncating "cat" will retrieve far more than just millions of cats! It will retrieve "cattle," "categories," "catches," "cataracts," "Catholics," "catalogs," "cathartics," "cathedrals," and more. In some systems, you can limit the number of characters following a truncation symbol. Thus, if you limited "cat" to only one character following the "t," you would avoid retrieving most irrelevancies, but could still retrieve "cate," "cath," "Cato," and "Catt." On short word stems, it is often safer to *"or"* the singular and plural forms, such as "rat *or* rats." Some systems also permit left-hand truncation, that is, any word ending with a specified string of characters, for example, any word ending with "phobia." Some systems allow for "embedded mask symbols," searching for a word where the variation occurs within the word, rather than at either end. For example, "women *or* woman" can be searched as "wom?n" on one system or "wom$n" on another. If this feature is not available on your system, then *"or"* the variations: "women *or* woman."

New Search Engines

A number of vendors and some Internet search engines have developed systems for retrieval based on ranking, statistical algorithms, and other criteria. These include Westlaw (WIN), DIALOG (TARGET), Ebsco (Natural Language), and others. These systems do not require the user to specify Boolean operators, but they do work best when the request is clearly expressed in the most specific terms possible. They are especially useful in searching full-text documents.

Choosing an Information Source

Today, users have a wide variety of information sources and formats from which to choose. Some sources are available in printed, CD-ROM, and several online versions. In choosing an information source, consider the following:

- subject coverage
- time period covered
- timeliness of updates
- type of information provided
- costs to you in time and money

In deciding whether to use a printed or computer version of a source, consider that computer searches are particularly useful when:

- you need a comprehensive search
- your topic is so specific that there are no applicable subject headings in printed indexes
- your topic is so new or obscure that material is difficult to locate
- there is no printed version of the index or source
- your research involves the relationship of several subjects
- you are looking for a narrow aspect of a broad subject

If you are using a search engine to search the World Wide Web, it is also important to know the characteristics and functions of the various search engines before choosing one. Consider features such as the following:

- frequency of updates to system index
- availability of online help
- size of database
- availability of Boolean and proximity operators
- default Boolean logic, i.e., system interprets spaces between words as "OR" or "AND"
- availability of truncation or presence of automatic pluralization
- availability of field searching
- special features such as ability to sort results by broad categories
- drawbacks such as limits to the number of hits retrievable

Basic Search Process

How do computers search? Essentially, by searching the indexes of databases for any records, or indexes to the World Wide Web for any sites, containing the words you specified. Think of it as a matching process. If you search for "Sweden," you would retrieve the sample record shown earlier in this section to illustrate fields, because the word "Sweden" occurs in the abstract of that record. On the other hand, if you asked for the word "Swedish," you would not retrieve that record because "Swedish" does not appear in that record. Unless you are using one of the new enhanced search engines, you will retrieve only those records containing words that match *exactly* those words you have used in your search.

Analyzing Your Search Topic

It is a good idea to write down your search topic and analyze it before beginning your search. An example of a search request is the following:

1. I need a bibliography on African-American music.

After writing down your search topic, identify the *main* concepts. Include only the essential ideas. For example, the preceding search request could be divided into two concept groups.

Concept A	Concept B
African American	Music

Next identify synonyms or near-synonyms that can be used to express each concept. For example, some of the terms that *might* be used for this search are:

Concept A	Concept B
African American	music
African-American	music(al,ally,ian,ians)
Afro American	hymn(s)
Afro-American	work song(s)
black	spiritual(s)
Negro(es)	ballad(s)
plantation	minstrel(s)
slave(s,ry)	song(s)
Harlem	tune(s)
	jazz

The terms you choose will be the "building blocks" of your search.

The next step will be to decide which logical operators should be used to relate these "building blocks" to each other. You will use "OR" to link the terms within each concept to each other. Thus, for example, you might use "African-American *OR* Afro-American" And you will use "AND" to link the groups to each other, as shown in the sample search below.

Sample Search

In this search, we are looking for African-American music on the *Dissertation Abstracts Online* database, searched through OCLC's *FirstSearch* Advanced search. A sample strategy and results might look like the following:

Select	#	Previous Search	Results
	#1	su:(African American or Afro-American)	4557
	#2	su:(African American or Afro-American) and su:(music or song+)	325
	#3	(hymn+ or spiritual+)	9160
	#4	(#1 and #3)	215
	#5	(#2 or #4)	479

Note that in this system, you can only use two OR operators in one search and the plus sign (+) is used to retrieve plurals

Reference

Cohen, Laura B. "A Basic Guide to the Internet." University at Albany Libraries, December 1998. See <http://www.albany.edu/library/internet/internet.html>, May 3, 1999.

Natural Language Searching

When you begin a search, you start with those words that come to mind. You then "translate" your thoughts into the words that will best retrieve the information you want. For some searches, you will use subject descriptors from a controlled vocabulary; for others, you may use natural language, or a combination of the two.

What Is Controlled Vocabulary Searching?

A controlled vocabulary is a list of subject terms used to index (and retrieve) documents or records. In information science, in contrast to thesauruses of natural language terms, "thesaurus" has taken on another meaning as the published form of a controlled vocabulary. The following are examples of published controlled vocabularies: *Library of Congress Subject Headings, Thesaurus of Psychological Index Terms, Thesaurus of Sociological Indexing Terms, Thesaurus of Aging Terminology,* and *Thesaurus of ERIC Descriptors.*

As the preceding titles show, the subject terms in a controlled vocabulary are sometimes referred to as "subject headings," "index terms," or "descriptors." A descriptor in a controlled vocabulary usually has a specified meaning. This meaning allows a distinction to be made between words that are spelled the same way, but have different meanings. For example, the *Thesaurus of ERIC Descriptors* distinguishes between "identification" in the sense of "recognition" and the same word as a psychological process.

In a controlled vocabulary, cross-references lead the user from a variety of unused, non-indexed terms to the descriptors used to index records or texts. For example, in the *Thesaurus of ERIC Descriptors*, entries for "personnel administrators," "personnel managers," or "school personnel directors" direct the reader to use "personnel directors."

Descriptors that are assigned to a document describe the subject of the document even though the author of the document may not have used those words. For example, the descriptor "automobiles" could be assigned to all documents about "Fords," "Chevrolets," "Toyotas," "Lincolns," "Mercedes," and so on. This means that in a controlled-vocabulary search, the searcher only needs to search for "automobiles" to retrieve all the documents about "cars" or "motor vehicles" (if they happen to be automobiles) or specific brands of automobiles.

Database-specific, controlled vocabularies are used to index databases in many subject fields. For example, the *Thesaurus of Psychological Index Terms* covers the subjects of the *PsycINFO* online database, the *PsycLIT* CD-ROM database, and so on.

What Is Natural Language Searching?

When *The Contemporary Thesaurus of Social Science Terms and Synonyms* was published in 1993, "natural language processing" was just emerging on the online horizon. The phrase "natural language" was frequently used, as it still is, to mean "a human language" as contrasted to programing languages or controlled vocabularies (*PC Webopaedia*, 1999).

A "natural language query" has been described as "A query expressed by typing English, French or any other spoken language in a normal manner. . . . In order to allow for spoken queries, both a voice recognition system and natural language query software are required" (*TechEncyclopedia*, 1999).

"Natural language processing is a range of computational techniques for analyzing and representing naturally occurring texts at one or more levels of linguistic analysis for the purpose of achieving human-like language processing for a range of particular tasks or applications" (Liddy, 1998). These techniques applied to searching have been called "post-boolean linguistic search engines" (Quint, 1995). Yet another source defines "free text" as "The use of natural language in information retrieval" (University of Arizona, School of Information Resources and Library Science, 1998).

In subject searching of printed indexes and card catalogs, you had no choice but to look under assigned subject headings. The computer, however, now makes it possible to search for words or phrases anywhere *within* texts. This is "natural language" or "free text" searching and it means searching for the words or phrases used by authors in the natural language of documents.

In this type of searching you use all the terms an author might have used to express the idea you are searching for. Instead of retrieving everything about automobiles with the term "automobiles," in free text searching you would have to search for "automobiles" OR "cars" OR "Fords" OR "Chevrolets" OR "Toyotas" OR "Lincolns" OR "Mercedes" or any other names of cars you could think of. On the other hand, if you wanted only items about "Toyotas," you wouldn't retrieve all the documents about all the other types of cars.

The use of natural language is now more widespread than ever because the Internet has made available so much information that is *not* indexed and therefore has no assigned subject headings. The proliferation of information sources often results in searches with extremely high recall and low relevance. The remedy for this problem lies in knowing which search engine to use or which database to choose, having a good command of system and database features, and, most important, using the most descriptive and precise terms to describe the information sought. In writing about the new search software, Quint (1995) says "When it comes to search strategies, use lots of specific terms and a minimum of evaluative terms ('cause,' 'effective,' 'resulting,' etc.)."

When searching relatively small databases, or looking for obscure topics, you need to search numerous alternative terms *ORed* together to improve recall. When searching large databases or topics about which a lot has been published, you need to use precise terms and to combine terms using *AND* to focus strategies and refine results.

A list of words with similar meanings, such as the *Thesaurus*, provides the searcher with the advantages of natural language searching without having to think of many possible ways that a concept may have been expressed.

When to Use Natural Language Searching

Below are some situations that call for the of use natural language terms.

- When searching the World Wide Web. The authorship, professionalism, and sponsoring entity of sources vary all over the lot. There is no consistency in the words used by the authors of Web documents. Web search engines generally have little or no standardized subject indexing.
- When a database has no controlled vocabulary. For example, there are no controlled vocabularies for *Dissertation Abstracts International, Social SciSearch*, or the *Arts and Humanities Search* databases.
- When a thesaurus has no descriptor for a concept. For example, the *Thesaurus of Psychological Index Terms* has no descriptor for "role reversal," *PAIS Subject Headings* has no descriptor for "sustainable development," and the *Thesaurus of Sociological Indexing Terms* has no descriptor for "affordable housing."
- For new terminology such as "outsourcing," "sick building syndrome," or "doctor-assisted suicide."
- When descriptors are too new. Use natural language to search that part of the database compiled before the descriptor was established. An important example of this is the new segment of the PsycINFO and PsycLit databases which now includes references from 1887 to 1966. These references do not contain descriptors and it is important to identify and search synonyms to allow for changes in professional terminology over time (*PsycINFO News*, 1998). Another example is the new (1999) SocioFile descriptor, "Child labor." A natural language search of titles in the 10 years of the SilverPlatter SocioFile database prior to the introduction of the descriptor retrieved 214 records.
- With full-text databases. These databases contain the entire text of journal articles, books, or newspapers and often have little or no indexing. For example, use natural language to search a newspaper database for such current topics as "misconduct in office," "school violence," or "public opinion." Including synonyms in searches of a full-text newspaper database increases the number of relevant items retrieved with a negligible increase in the number of irrelevant items retrieved (Kristensen and Jarvelin, 1990).

- For subject searches on large interdisciplinary databases such as online catalogs or OCLC's WorldCat, EBSCOhost, and Academic Index. These databases require natural language terms if Library of Congress subject headings don't "fit" the subject.
- For maximum recall. Studies have shown that natural language terms combined with controlled vocabulary terms retrieve the greatest number of relevant records (Byrne, 1975; Markey, Atherton, and Newton,1980). One author has stated that "the only way to maximize return . . . was to use both controlled vocabulary terms and free text terms" (Calkins, 1980). On a database that has a descriptor "automobiles," this method would mean searching for the descriptor "automobiles" but *also* using the names of all the cars as well. To do this, you would use the Boolean operator "*OR*." On a SilverPlatter database, it might look like this: Automobile* *OR* (Chevrolet* *OR* Buick* *OR* Cadillac* *OR* Honda* *OR* Toyota* *OR* Nissan*), etc.
- For increased specificity. Combine natural language *AND* descriptors, when the descriptor retrieves too many irrelevant items. In the example above, if you wanted only Japanese cars, you might use the descriptor "automobiles" and combine it (using the Boolean *AND*) with "Japan*" and the names of specific Japanese cars like "Honda," or "Toyota" (using the Boolean *OR*). On a SilverPlatter database, it might look like this: Automobile*in de *AND* (Japan* *OR* Honda* *OR* Toyota* *OR* Nissan*) (*Note*: The "in de" restricts "Automobile" to the discriptor field.)
- For cross-database searching. On some systems, you can search several files at once or you can enter free-text terms on one database, then "save" and "execute" on another database. Since natural language is database-independent, the same natural language terms can generally be used across several databases.
- For interdisciplinary searches. Use appropriate descriptors for each database and supplement them with natural language terms for the aspects not covered by the controlled vocabulary.
- For specific topics such as "Library of Congress," "White House lawn," or "Williamsburg."

The language of standard controlled vocabularies can never be sufficiently refined, nor flexible enough, nor comprehensive enough to reflect all the needs of users dealing with a complex, interdependent, and constantly changing world. Whenever controlled vocabulary is inadequate, natural language searching is essential.

How to Use Natural Language Searching

If little has been published on your topic, cast a "broad net" to capture as much as possible of what is out there. It may be worth retrieving some irrelevant items not to miss valuable ones. View some of the titles you retrieve to determine whether your strategy needs more fine-tuning or expanding. The following techniques will help focus your search.

Context Can Determine Meaning

Meaning is conveyed, not only by words themselves, but also by the context in which they are used. The word "fast" has a different meaning when you are talking about racing than it does when you are talking about food. In ordinary conversation, such distinctions are automatically understood. In computer searching, they may need to be specified.

The searcher needs to be aware of the context from which the search request is derived as well as the context in which the terms will be searched. The broadest and most obvious search context is the database you choose for your search. For example, suppose you are searching for the psychological aspects of a disease. If you search for, say, "diabetes" on a psychological database such as *PsycINFO* (*PsycLIT* on CD-ROM), the database coverage itself ensures that most articles indexed under "diabetes" will have a psychological slant. Unless you want something more specific, it may not be necessary to specify any psychological terms because the database (context) determines that these records will have a psychological perspective.

Often, choosing the appropriate database is all you need to do to establish the right context for your search. In some instances, you will find it useful to search only a subset of a database. Searchable broad subject categories are available for *Dissertation Abstracts* [on DIALOG], *Social SciSearch, SciSearch, Arts and Humanities Search, SocioFile, PsycINFO,* and many other databases. Many databases have some type of designators to retrieve broad subject area subsets, but these designators should be used with care because most of them do not retrieve everything in the database that is related to the broad areas they describe. Similarly, many World Wide Web search engines, such as Inference Find, MetaFind, and Northern Light, have means of organizing search results by broad categories. For more about using broad subject categories in searches of particular databases and search engines and for examples, see "Appendix A: Putting Searches in Context."

Words with Multiple Meanings

Homonyms or homographs are words that have multiple meanings but the same spelling. For instance, with "strikes," you could get labor, baseball, rattlesnakes, disaster, or lightning. "Dating" could be archaeological or romantic. "Figurative" is metaphorical in literature and representational in art. How do you offset this? Often, the context, either the database or a subset of the database, will ensure that the word will have the meaning you want. Sometimes you must combine the term with other terms to eliminate irrelevant meanings. For example, the word "plant" could refer to a factory or a living organism. In a biological database, you would be unlikely to retrieve things about factories. Or if your search were for "plants" *AND* "layoffs" or for "plant closings" the chances are that you would not retrieve items about gardening.

Searching Phrases

You may need to use phrases rather than single words for freetext searching, for example, "ancestor worship," "cargo cults" or "living conditions." If you are not able to specify that these words occur adjacent to each other in that order, the search results may be much less relevant. For example, unless you can specify word order, a search for "state police" would also retrieve "police state." Most systems have methods of searching for words that are adjacent to each other. Many allow you

to specify the word order as well. For details, consult system documentation.

Searching Words Near Each Other

Sometimes it is a good idea to require that the two words be adjacent to each other, such as in "cargo cults," but in other cases it is useful to allow them to be separated by other words but to be near each other or in the same sentence. For example, in a search for "global education," if you allowed for the words to appear in the same sentence, but not necessarily adjacent to each other, you would get such hits as "Citizenship **Education** in a **Global** Age," and "**Education** for **Global** Perspectives." These titles would not have been retrieved if you had searched the exact phrase "global education," requiring the words to appear adjacent to each other.

Is a "same sentence" strategy always a good idea? Very often, but there are times when it is not precise enough. If you were looking for the "nuclear family," and didn't specify that the two words appear adjacent to each other, you might also retrieve things on the "effect on the **family** of the threat of **nuclear** warfare."

The "operators" that specify that words appear adjacent to each other, within a specified number of words of each other, within the same sentence, or within the same field are called "proximity operators." On some systems, you can specify the number of words that you will allow between two words. For example, on DIALOG, you use "*(1w)*" to require the terms to be within one word of each other, e.g., seasonal *(1w)* disorder. On the Lycos Search Engine, you use the *ONEAR/n* operator, as in Seasonal *ONEAR/1* disorder.

On many systems, including World Wide Web search engines, you can search phrases by putting them inside quotation marks. Thus, you could search "seasonal affective disorder." These strategies would retrieve items in which the terms appear together as you specified.

Restricting Searches to Specific Fields

In natural language searches, especially in full-text databases, you may want to limit the fields in which the computer will search for words or phrases. This method will retrieve fewer titles but they will be more relevant. Most frequently, you will want to limit the search to items in which the word(s) appear in the title field. For example, a search in *Dissertation Abstracts International* for the word "empowerment" in all searchable fields retrieved 355 documents compared with 92 documents when the word was searched only in the title field.

Making Searches More Specific (Narrower)**

Use the following techniques to make searches more specific:

1. **Add terms connected by AND.** For example, a search for "fires" retrieved 356 records, but "fires *and* prevention" yielded only 68 records.
2. **Add terms connected by NOT.** For example, a search for "fires" retrieved 356 records, but "fires *not* insurance" yielded only 187 records.
3. **Delete terms connected by OR.** For example, a search for "oceans *or* rivers *or* lakes" retrieved 959 records, but " rivers *or* lakes" yielded only 628 records.

4. **Require terms to be adjacent or within the same sentence**. For example, searching for "wetlands *and* preservation" finds those terms when they co-occur anywhere in the same reference. A search for this yielded 153 records; searching for "wetlands *near* preservation," which specifies that the terms must occur in the same sentence, and "wetlands preservation," which requires that the terms be adjacent, yielded 34 and 19 records, respectively.

5. **Decrease term truncation.** For example, using "danger*" resulted in 978 records, but using "dangerous*" or "dangerousness," resulted in 231 and 56 records, respectively.

6. **Add, refine, or alter classification or category codes**. Some databases have codes that can be used to restrict searches to broad subject areas. For example, searching for "assimilation" retrieved 1,331 records; using "assimilation *and* cc=sociology," where the "cc=" restricts the search to articles from sociology journals, resulted in only 304 records.

7. **Restrict search terms to specific fields**. For example, a search for "feminist spirituality" retrieved 39 hits, but using "(feminist spirituality)/TI," where "/TI" restricts the search to the title field, retrieved only 11 records.

8. **Limit by language, time period, age group, or publication type**. For example, searching for "habitat protection" retrieved 98 records, but limiting "habitat protection" to English retrieved only 85 records.

Making Searches More Inclusive (Broader)**

Use the following techniques to make searches more inclusive:

1. **Delete terms connected by AND.** For example, a search for "fires *and* prevention" retrieved only 68 records, but "fires" yielded 356 hits.

2. **Delete terms connected by NOT.** For example, a search for "fires *not* insurance" yielded only 187 records, while "fires" retrieved 356 records.

3. **Add terms or synonyms connected by OR.** For example, a search for " rivers *or* lakes" yielded only 628 records, but "oceans *or* rivers *or* lakes" retrieved 959.

4. **Move from term adjacency or same sentence to combining terms in different fields.** For example, searching for "wetlands preservation," which requires that the terms be adjacent, or "wetlands *near* preservation," which specifies that the terms must occur in the same sentence, yielded 19 and 34 records, respectively. Using "wetlands *and* preservation," which finds those terms when they co-occur anywhere in the same reference, yielded 153 records.

5. **Increase term truncation**. For example, one search using "dangerousness" resulted in 56 records, but using "dangerous*" or "danger*" resulted in 231 and 978 records, respectively.

6. **Delete or alter classification or category codes.** Some databases have codes that can be used to restrict searches to broad subject areas. For example, searching for "assimilation *and* cc=sociology," where the "cc=" restricts the search to articles from sociology journals, resulted in

only 304 records, but using just "assimilation" retrieved 1,331 records.

7. **Remove restrictions to specific fields.** For example, using "(feminist spirituality)/TI," where "/TI" restricts the search to the title field, retrieved only 11 records. However, using "feminist spirituality," which will allow searching for the term in any field, yielded 39 hits.

8. **Remove language, time period, age group, or publication type limit.** For example, using "habitat protection" *and* LG=English," where "LG=English" restricts results to items in English, retrieved only 85 records. However, using "habitat protection" retrieved 98 records.

---

*Truncation symbol, field qualifiers, and limiters vary by system. Consult your system documentation.

**Adapted from C.L. Warden (1977) and (1985).

References

Booth, Barbara. *Thesaurus of Sociological Indexing Terms*. 4th ed. San Diego: Sociological Abstracts, 1996.

Byrne, Jerry R. "Relative Effectiveness of Titles, Abstracts and Subject Headings for Machine Retrieval from the Compendex Services." *Journal of the American Society for Information Science,* August 1975, 26(4).

Calkins, Mary L. "Free Text or Controlled Vocabulary?" *Database,* June 1980, 3(53).

"Historical-File Tips and Techniques for PsycINFO, PsycLIT." *PsycINFO News*, Fall 1998.

Kristensen, Jaana and Kalervo Jarvelin. "The Effectiveness of a Searching Thesaurus in Free-Text Searching in a Full-Text Database." *International Classification*, 1990, 17(2).

Liddy, Elizabeth D. "Enhanced Text Retrieval Using Natural Language Processing." *Bulletin of the American Society for Information Science*, April/May 1998, 24(14).

Markey, Karen, Pauline Atherton, and Claudia Newton. "An Analysis of Controlled Vocabulary and Free Text Search Statements in Online Search Statements." *Online Review,* September 1980, 4(3).

National Library of Medicine Staff. *Medical Subject Headings, Annotated Alphabetic List*. Bethesda, MD: National Library of Medicine, 1989-98.

PC Webopaedia. Available at <http://www.pcwebopedia.com>, April 4, 1999.

Quint, Barbara. "The Artifices of Natural Language Searching." *Wilson Library Bulletin,* December 1994, 69(60).

——. "The New Realities of Natural Language Searching." *Wilson Library Bulletin,* January 1995, 69(63).

"Search Samples." *PsycINFO News*, March 1990, 10(1).

TechEncyclopedia. Available at <http://techweb.com/encyclopedia/>, April 4, 1999.

Thesaurus of Aging Terminology: AgeLine Database on Middle Age and Aging. 6th ed. Washington, DC: AgeLine Database, Research Databases Development Team, Research Group, American Association of Retired Persons, 1997.

Thesaurus of ERIC Descriptors, 13th ed. Phoenix: Oryx Press, 1995.

Thesaurus of Psychological Index Terms. Alvin Walker, Jr., ed. Washington, DC: American Psychological Association, 1997.

University of Arizona. School of Information Resources and Library Science. *The Information Professional's Glossary.* September 1998. Available at <http://www.sir.arizona.edu/glossary.html>, March 18, 1999.

Warden, C. L. "Modification of Online Search Strategies." *Online '85 Conference Proceedings.* New York, 1985.

——. *Online Searching of Bibliographic Databases, the Role of the Search Analyst.* Schenectady, NY: General Electric Corporate Research and Development, 1977; General Electric Technical Information Series Report No. 76CRD280.

A

Abandoned children. Abandoned child(ren). Parent(s,al) abandon(ed, ing,ment,ments). *Choose from:* desert(ed), reject(ed), abandon(ed, ing,ment,ments), neglect(ed), cast off, throw away, throwaway *with:* child(ren), infant(s), bab(y,ies), son(s), daughter(s), offspring, juvenile(s), minor(s), boy(s), girl(s). *See also* Abandonment; Anaclitic depression; Child neglect; Deadbeat parents; Failure to thrive (psychosocial); Foundlings; Homeless children; Orphans; Street children; Unwanted children; Unwanted pregnancy.

Abandoned property. Abandoned propert(y,ies). *Choose from:* abandon(ed,ing,ment), unclaimed, deserted, unoccupied, uninhabited *with:* propert(y,ies), building(s), house(s), asset(s), residence(s), residential, store(s), tenement(s). *See also* Absentee ownership; Brownfields; Condemnation of buildings; Enemy property; Land (property); Ownership; Real estate.

Abandonment. Abandon(ed,ing,ment). Desert(ed,ing,ion). Forsak(e,en,ing). Reject(ed,ing,ion). Defect(ed,ing,ion). Neglect(ed,ing). *Consider also:* parental loss, loss of significant other, emotional loss, sense of loss, given up for adoption, withdraw(n,ing,al). *See also* Abandoned children; Desertion; Loneliness.

Abatement. Abatement(s). Deduction(s). Discount(s). Rebate(s). Reduction(s). *See also* Tax deductions.

Abattoirs. See *Slaughterhouses*.

Abbeys. Abbey(s). *Consider also:* communit(y,ies) *with:* religious, nuns, brothers, monks. *Consider also:* abbess(es), abbot(s), cloister(s,ed), monaster(y,ies), friar(y,ies), convent(s), nunner(y,ies). *See also* Abbots; Asceticism; Cloisters; Religious buildings.

Abbots. Abbot(s,ship). *Choose from:* superior or head *with:* abbey(s) or monaster(y,ies). *See also* Abbeys; Religious personnel.

Abbreviations. Abbreviat(ed,ing,ion,ions). Acronym(s). Abridg(e,ed,ing,ment, ments). Shortened form(s). Initialism(s). *Consider also:* abstract(s), digest(s), overview(s), synop(sis,ses), summar(y, ies). *See also* Compendiums; Excerpts; Mnemonic learning; Written communications.

Abdication. Abdicat(e,ed,ing,ion). Cede(d,ing). Relinquish(ed,ing). Resign(ed,ing,ation). Withdraw from office. Renounc(e,ed,ing). Renunciat(ion,ive,ory). Abandon(ed, ing,ment). Step(ped,ping) down. *See also* Ceding; Disengagement; Renunciation; Resignations.

Abdomen. Abdomen(s). Abdominal(ly). Bell(y,ies). Tumm(y,ies). Gut(s). Stomach(s). *Consider also:* gastric, epigastric, umbilical region, periton(eum,eal), viscera(l), inguinal canal, groin, retroperitoneal space, umbilicus. *See also* Anatomy.

Abdominal injuries. Abdominal injur(y,ies). *Choose from:* abdominal, abdomen(s), visceral, splenic, thoracoabdominal, abdominopelvic, retroperitoneal, intestinal, peritoneal, pancreatic, gastric, stomach(es), bell(y, ies) *with:* wound(s,ed,ing), injur(e,ed, y,ies) trauma(tic,s), lesion(s), rupture(s), lesion(s), hernia(s). *See also* Abdomen; Injuries.

Abduction. Abduct(ed,ing,ion). Kidnap(ped,ping). Steal(ing). Stolen. *Consider also:* captiv(e,es,ity), hostage(s), alienation of affection(s). *See also* Child kidnapping; Kidnapping; Missing persons.

Abduction (logic). Abduct(ion,ive) logic. Abductive reasoning. Inference to the best explanation. *See also* Logic; Inference.

Abilities, mental. See *Mental abilities*.

Ability. Abilit(y,ies). Talent(ed,s). Capacit(y,ies). Capabilit(y,ies). Capable. Competen(t,ce,cy,cies). Skill(ed, fulness,s). Aptitude(s). Strength(s). Proficien(t,cy). Expertise. Gift(ed,s). Expert(ness). Dexterity. Adept(ness). Deft(ness). Hand(y,iness). Clever(ness). *See also* Ability grouping; Ability identification; Ability level; Academic ability; Academic aptitude; Achievement; Aptitude; Aspirations; Area of knowledge; Artistic ability; Capacity; Cognitive ability; Communication skills; Competence; Creativity; Gifted; Intelligence; Language proficiency; Learning ability; Leadership; Mathematical ability; Mechanical ability; Motor skills; Musical ability; Nonverbal ability; Productivity; Qualifications; Reading ability; Scientific knowledge; Skill; Social skills; Spatial ability; Verbal ability.

Ability, academic. See *Academic ability*.

Ability, artistic. See *Artistic ability*.

Ability, cognitive. See *Cognitive ability*.

Ability, creative. See *Artistic ability; Concept formation; Creativity; Divergent thinking; Gifted; Imagination; Individuality; Intelligence; Inventions; Inventors; Knowledge; Musical ability; Personality traits; Self expression*.

Ability, executive. See *Executive ability*.

Ability, influence of age on. See *Influence of age on ability*.

Ability, language. See *Verbal ability*.

Ability, learning. See *Learning ability*.

Ability, mathematical. See *Mathematical ability*.

Ability, mechanical. See *Mechanical ability*.

Ability, musical. See *Musical ability*.

Ability, nonverbal. See *Nonverbal ability*.

Ability, reading. See *Reading ability*.

Ability, social. See *Social skills*.

Ability, spatial. See *Spatial ability*.

Ability, testing for. See *Ability identification*.

Ability, verbal. See *Verbal ability*.

Ability grouping. Ability group(ed,ing,s). Tracking system(s). *Choose from:* academic, educational, school, abilit(y,ies), achievement *with:* track(s, ing), group(s,ed,ing). *See also* Ability identification; Ability level; Academic ability; Academic achievement; Nongraded schools; Tracking (education).

Ability identification. Ability identification. *Choose from:* abilit(y,ies), talent(ed,s), skill(s), proficienc(y,ies), competenc(y, ies), gifted *with:* identif(y,ied,ication), test(s,ed,ing), screen(ed,ing), assess(ed, ing,ment), measur(e,ed,ing,ment,ments), predict(ed,ing,ion,ions), indicat(e,ed,ing, or,ors,ion,ions). *See also* Ability; Ability grouping; Aptitude tests; Intelligence tests; Screening.

Ability level. Ability level(s). *Choose from:* abilit(y,ies), aptitude(s), expertise, skill(s), competenc(e,y,ies), proficienc(y, ies), talent(s) *with:* level(s), difference(s), comparison(s), rating(s). *See also* Ability; Ability grouping; Ability identification; Competence; Educational attainment; Influence of age on ability; Intelligence quotient; Knowledge level.

Abjection. Abject(ion). Miser(y,ies,able). Wretched(ness). Hopeless(ness). Pitiful(ly). Pathetic. Degrad(ed,ing). Destitut(e,ion). Squalid. Humbl(e,ed, ing). *See also* Hopelessness; Pessimism; Powerlessness.

Ablations. See *Lesions*.

Able-bodied. See *Physical fitness*.

Ableism. See *Attitudes toward handicapped; Attitudes toward physical illness; Attitudes toward physical handicaps.*

Abnormal psychology. See *Psychopathology.*

Abnormalities. See *Anomalies; Physical abnormalities.*

Abnormalities, drug induced. See *Drug induced abnormalities.*

Abnormalities, human. See *Human abnormalities.*

Abnormalities, physical. See *Physical abnormalities.*

Abolitionists. Abolition(ism,ist,ists). Anti-Slavery Society. Antislavery movement(s). *Consider also:* underground railroad, Emancipation Proclamation, slavery question. *See also* Civil war; Emancipation; Freedmen; Fugitive slaves; History; Slavery.

Aboriginal people. See *Aborigines; Indigenous populations.*

Aborigines. Aborigine(s). Aboriginal people(s). Autochthon(al,ous,ism,y, ously). *Choose from:* Australian, Australoid *with:* tribe(s), aborigin(al,e, es), race(s). Australasian(s). *Consider also:* Kariera, Murngin, Aranda, Arunta. *See also* Australoid race; Acculturation; Biculturalism; Cultural groups; Culture (anthropology); Culture change; Culture contact; Hunting and gathering societies; Indigenous populations; Oceanic cultural groups; Traditional societies.

Abortifacients. Abortifacient(s). Abortient(s), Abortigen(s). Abortion pill(s). *Choose from:* drug induced, chemical(s), steroid(s), ergot(s), lamineria *with:* abortion(s), terminat(e,ed,ing,ion) pregnanc(y,ies). *Consider also:* RU-486, mifepristone, PGE, PGF, fluprostenol, ethacridine, laminaria, prostaglandin f, prostaglandin e, carboprost, dinoprost, equimate, antigestational drug(s). *See also* Drugs; Emergency contraception; Induced abortion; Medical abortion.

Abortion. Abort(ed,ing,ion,ions). Miscarr(y,ied,iage,iages). Abortus. Aborticide. *Choose from:* induced, forced, premature *with:* deliver(y,ies), birth(s). *Choose from:* interrupt(ed, ing,ion), terminat(e,ed,ing,ion) *with:* pregnanc(y,ies). *Consider also:* problem pregnanc(y,ies), cervix incompetence. *See also* Abortifacients; Abortion applicants; Abortion clinics; Abortion counseling; Abortion laws; Abortion rights movement; Antiabortion movement; Birth control; Criminal abortion; Emotional aspects of abortion; Family planning; Induced abortion; Infanticide; Medical abortion; Miscarriages; Population policy; Pregnancy; Repro-

ductive rights; Surgery; Unwanted pregnancy.

Abortion, criminal. See *Criminal abortion.*

Abortion, emotional aspects of. See *Emotional aspects of abortion.*

Abortion, induced. See *Induced abortion.*

Abortion, legal. See *Legal abortion.*

Abortion, medical. See *Medical abortion.*

Abortion, spontaneous. See *Miscarriages.*

Abortion applicants. Abortion applicant(s). *Choose from:* abortion(s), pregnancy termination *with:* applicant(s), seek(ing, ers), demand(s,ed,ing), request(s,ed,ers, ing), appl(y,ied,ying), desir(e,es,ed,ing). *See also* Abortion; Abortion clinics; Abortion counseling; Abortion laws; Help seeking behavior; Unwanted pregnancy.

Abortion clinics. Abortion clinic(s). Abortion center(s). Abortion service(s). Abortion provider(s). Abortuar(y,ies). *See also* Abortion; Abortion counseling; Abortion applicants.

Abortion counseling. Abortion counseling. *Choose from:* abort(ed,ing,ion,ions), pre-abortion, preabortion, post abortion, postabortion, terminat(e,ed,ing,ion) pregnanc(y,ies) *with:* counsel(ed,ing, or,ors), microcounsel(ed,ing), co-counsel(ed,ing), casework, guidance, pastoral care, referral(s), supportive therap(y,ies), support group(s), group therap(y,ies), crisis center(s), crisis intervention, crisis line(s), psychotherap (y,ies). *See also* Abortion; Abortion applicants; Abortion clinics; Counseling; Criminal abortion; Emotional aspects of abortion; Feminist therapy; Induced abortion; Miscarriages; Unwanted pregnancy.

Abortion laws. Abortion law(s). *Choose from:* abortion(s), antiabortion, pregnancy terminat(e,ed,ion,ions), right to life, pro-choice, prochoice *with:* law(s,ful,suits), legal(ize,ized,izing, ization), due process, public polic(y,ies), amendment(s), bill(s), Supreme Court, statute(s). *Consider also:* Roe vs Wade. *See also* Abortion; Abortion counseling; Abortion applicants; Antiabortion movement; Abortion rights movement; Criminal abortion; Induced abortion.

Abortion pill. See *Abortifacients; Medical abortion.*

Abortion rights movement. Abortion rights movement(s). *Choose from:* abortion right(s), pro choice, reproductive right(s), reproductive freedom, pro-abortion(ist,ists,ism), legaliz(e,ed,ing, ation) abortion *with:* consciousness raising, demonstrat(or,ors,ion,ions), protester(s), protest(s), movement(s), activis(m,ts), resistance, part(y,ies), group(s), campaign(s), mobilization,

boycott(s). *Consider also:* Abortion Rights Mobilization, Catholics for a Free Choice, Committee to Defend Reproductive Rights, Religious Coalition for Abortion Rights, Voters for Choice, Planned Parenthood, Physicians for Choice, National Women's Health Network, National Abortion Rights Action League, NARAL, National Organization of Women, etc. *See also* Abortion; Antiabortion movement; Abortion laws; Civil rights organizations; Feminism; Political liberalism; Protest movements; Radical movements; Reproductive rights; Suffrage movement; Women's groups.

Abreaction. Abreaction. Psychocathar(sis, tic). Cathar(sis,tic). *Choose from:* discharg(e,ed,ing), express(ed,ing), talk(ed,ing), work(ed,ing) through, reliv(e,ing), re- experienc(e,ed,ing), reviv(e,ed,ing), releas(e,ed,ing) *with:* pain(ful), tension(s), distress(ed,es,ing), emotion(s), affect(s,ive). *See also* Catharsis; Psychoanalysis.

Abroad, Americans. See *Americans abroad.*

Abroad, study. See *International educational exchange.*

Absence. Absen(t,ce,ee,eeism). AWOL. Nonattendance. Truan(t,cy). Fail(ure) to appear. Missing. *See also* Absenteeism; Paternal deprivation; Maternal deprivation; Military desertion.

Absence, father. See *Paternal deprivation.*

Absence, leaves of. See *Leaves of absence.*

Absence, mother. See *Maternal deprivation.*

Absence, parental. See *Parental absence.*

Absence and presumption of death. Absen(t,ce) and presum(ed,ption) dea(d,th). Supposition of death. *Consider also:* kidnap(ped,ping), desaparecido(s). *See also* Missing persons; Missing in action.

Absent without leave. See *Military desertion.*

Absentee fathers. See *Paternal deprivation.*

Absentee mothers. See *Maternal deprivation.*

Absentee ownership. Absentee owner(s, ship). Absentee landlord(s). *Choose from:* absent(ee), nonmanaging, nonresident, off-premise(s), out-of-state, out-of-town *with:* owner(s,ship). *Consider also:* silent partner(s), foreign invest(or,ors,ment,ments). *See also* Abandoned property; Landlords; Land (property); Land ownership; Ownership; Real estate.

Absentee voting. Absentee vot(e,es,ers,ing). Absentee ballot(s). Absentees as voter(s). Nonresident voter(s). Absen(t, ce) voter(s). *See also* Americans abroad;

Ballots; Residence requirements; Voter participation; Voting.

Absenteeism. Absen(ce,ces,tee,teeism). Sick leave. Sickleave. Sickout. Stay(ed,ing) home. Poor attendance. Loss of work days. Truan(t,cy). Attendance problem(s). Nonattendance. *Choose from:* absen(t,ce,ces,teeism) *with:* employee(s), class(es), work, school, student(s). *Consider also:* cut(ting) class(es). *See also* Absence; Attendance (presence); Patient dropouts; School attendance; Student dropouts; Truancy.

Absenteeism, employee. See *Absenteeism.*

Absenteeism, school. See *Absenteeism.*

Absentmindedness. Absentminded(ness). Inattent(ive,ion). Preoccupied. Habitual inattention. Unaware(ness). Unmindful(ness). Unattentive. Unheeding. *See also* Attention; Attention span; Daydreaming; Fantasies (thought disturbances).

Absolute, The. See *Deities; God concepts; Religious beliefs.*

Absolute monarchy. See *Despotism.*

Absolute music. Absolute music. Absolute(n) Musik. Absolute(n) Tonkunst. Abstract music. *Consider also:* pure music. *See also* Program music; Music.

Absolution. Absolution. Absolv(e,ed,ing). Redemption. Redeem(ed,ing). Exonerat(e,ed,ing,ion,ions). Vindicat(e, ed,ing,ion,ions). Pardon(s,ed,ing). Exculpat(e,ed,ing,ion). Acquit(ted,tal). Amnesty. Forgiv(e,ing,eness). Clear(ed, ing,ance) of guilt. Purif(y,ied,ication). *See also* Acquittal; Forgiveness; Guilt; Indulgences; Shame; Sin; Pardon.

Absolutism. Absolutis(m,t,ts,tic). Ethical objectivis(m,t,ts). Universal truth(s). Objective truth(s). Universal principle(s). Moral absolut(e,es,ism). Religious absolut(e,es,ism). *Choose from:* absolute, objective, eternal, superhuman, universal, immutable, unassailable, rigid, ultraconservative *with:* standard(s), value(s), truth(s), principle(s), law(s), authority. *Consider also:* zealot(s), sovereignty, supreme(ness), absolute(ness), imperious(ness), domination, authoritarian(ism), iron rule, word of God, imperialis(m,tic), dictator(s,ship), tyrann(y,ical), totalitarian(ism), law(s) of nature. *See also* Anti-intellectualism; Categorical imperative; Conservative; Despotism; Divine right of kings; Dogma; Exclusivity (Religion); Extremism; Ideologies; Political conservatism; Relativism; Religious fundamentalism; Theocracy; Zealots.

Abstention. See *Abstinence; Drug withdrawal; Temperance.*

Abstinence. Abstinen(t,ce). Abstention. Abstain(ed,ing). Refrain(ed,ing). Nonindulgen(ce,t). Non-is(m,t,ts). Moderation. Continence. Fast(s,ed,ing). Auster(e,ity). Celiba(te,cy). Temperance. Renounc(e,ed,ing). Resist(ed,ing). Avoid(ed,ing,ance). Abstemious(ly, ness). Forbearance. Self-denial. Frugal(ity). Chast(e,ity). Ascetic(ism). Eschew(ed,ing,al). *See also* Celibacy; Drug withdrawal; Frugality; Monasticism; Religious life; Religious personnel; Renunciation; Sacrificial rites; Self control; Self sacrifice; Sexual abstinence; Sobriety; Temperance; Thriftiness; Virginity.

Abstinence, alcohol. See *Sobriety.*

Abstinence, sexual. See *Sexual abstinence.*

Abstract art. Abstract art(ist,ists,work, works). Abstract paint(er,ers,ing,ings). Abstraction in art. *Choose from:* abstract, 20th century, twentieth century, contemporary, non-representational, non-figurative, non-objective, orphism, synchronism, constructivism, rayonism, suprematism, surreal(ism) *with:* art(s,ist, ists,work,works), paint(er,ers,ing,ings), sculpt(ure,ures), *Consider also:* Alexander Calder, Willem De Kooning , Piet Mondrian, etc. *See also* Artistic styles; Abstract Expressionism; Concrete art; Constructivism; Dadaism; Genres (art); Surrealism.

Abstract expressionism. Abstract expression(ism). Action painting. Tachis(m,me,t,te). Art Informel. Art autre. Abstraction lyrique. New York School. Informalism. Lyrical Abstraction. *Consider also:* Willem de Kooning, Jackson Pollock, Hans Hofmann, Robert Motherwell, Vasily Kandinsky, etc. *See also* Abstract art; Artistic styles; Expressionism (art); Genres (art).

Abstract reasoning. See *Abstraction; Reasoning.*

Abstraction. Abstraction(s). Abstract reasoning. Generalization(s). *Choose from:* abstract(ive), theoretical, logical, conceptual *with:* reasoning, evaluation(s), process(es), coding, thinking, abilit(y,ies), thought(s). *Consider also:* conceptualization(s), generalization(s), formal operational thought, concept formation, theory building, metaphor(s,ical), simplification, deduction(s), induction(s), inference(s), inferential, analog(y,ies). *Consider also:* abstract, categorical *with:* attitude. *See also* Cognitive processes; Comprehension; Concept formation; Cognitive generalization; Deduction; Divergent thinking; Imagery; Induction; Logical thinking; Reasoning.

Abstracts. Abstract(s). Condens(ed,ing, ation,ations). Abridg(e,ed,ing,ement, ements). Synops(is,es). Summar(y,ies, ize,ized,ization,izations). *See also* Compendiums; Excerpts; Reference materials.

Absurd. Absurd(ism,ity). Senseless(ness). Meaningless(ness). Iron(y,ies,ic). Existentialis(m,t). Dada(ism). Surreal(ism). Nonsens(e,ical). Incoheren(t,ce). Irrational(ism,ity). Kafkaesque(ness). Catch-22. *See also* Alienation; Dadaism; Existentialism; Fragmentation (experience); Grotesque; Hopelessness; Impersonal; Irony; Literature; Meaninglessness; Postmodernism; Scatology.

Abuse, alcohol. See *Alcoholism; Problem drinking.*

Abuse, animal. See *Cruelty to animals.*

Abuse, cannabis. See *Substance abuse.*

Abuse, child. See *Child abuse.*

Abuse detection, substance. See *Substance abuse detection.*

Abuse, drug. See *Drug addiction; Substance abuse.*

Abuse, drugs of. See *Designer drugs; Hallucinogens; Narcotics; Street drugs; Tranquilizers.*

Abuse, elder. See *Elder abuse.*

Abuse, emotional. See *Emotional abuse.*

Abuse, generational cycle of child. See *Generational cycle of child abuse.*

Abuse, inhalant. See *Inhalant abuse.*

Abuse, marijuana. See *Substance abuse.*

Abuse, phencyclidine. See *Substance abuse.*

Abuse, physical. See *Abusive parents; Battered women; Child abuse; Corporal punishment; Cruelty; Elder abuse; Emotional abuse; Family violence; Marital rape; Police brutality; Rape; Sadism; Sexual abuse; Sexual sadism; Sexual violence; Spouse abuse; Terrorism; Torture; Violence.*

Abuse, sexual. See *Sexual abuse.*

Abuse, solvent. See *Solvent abuse.*

Abuse, spouse. See *Spouse abuse.*

Abuse, substance. See *Substance abuse.*

Abuse, verbal. See *Verbal abuse.*

Abuse, wife. See *Spouse abuse.*

Abuse of persons. See *Abusive parents; Battered women; Child abuse; Corporal punishment; Cruelty; Elder abuse; Emotional abuse; Family violence; Flagellants and flagellation; Marital rape; Police brutality; Rape; Sadism; Sexual abuse; Sexual sadism; Sexual violence; Spouse abuse; Terrorism; Torture; Violence.*

Abuse of power. Abuse(s) of power. Misuse(s) of power. Autocratic domination. Power play(s). Power and control tactic(s). Powerholder(s). *Consider also:* human rights violation(s), sexual harassment, corporate misconduct, adultis(m,t), racis(m,t), sexis(m,t). *See also* Despotism; Exploitation; Oppression; Tyranny.

Abuse of substances. See *Alcoholism; Drug addiction; Solvent abuse; Substance abuse.*

Abuse prevention, child. See *Child abuse prevention.*

Abused psychologically, men. See *Psychologically abused men.*

Abusive language. See *Invective; Verbal abuse.*

Abusive parents. Abus(ive,ing) parent(s). *Choose from:* abus(ive,ing), battering, molest(ing,er,ers), cruel(ty), punitive, harsh(ness), brutal(ity,ities) *with:* parent(s,al), mother(s), father(s), maternal, paternal. *Consider also:* parents anonymous, mothers anonymous, battered child(ren), abusive famil(y,ies). *See also* Child abuse; Child abuse prevention; Cruelty; Family violence; Incest; Molested children; Sexual abuse; Sexual harassment; Victimization.

Academic ability. Academic abilit(y,ies). Intellectual(ly) superior(ity). *Choose from:* academic, scholastic, scholarly, intellectual, learning, reasoning, writing *with:* abilit(y,ies), aptitude(s), talent(s), superior(ity), able, potential. *See also* Academic achievement; Academic aptitude; Academic aspiration; Academic skills; Achievement potential; Academically gifted; Intelligence; Scholars.

Academic achievement. Academic achievement. Student promotion. Gradepoint average. Academic status. *Choose from:* academic, student, mathematics, reading, school, educational, pupil, schol(arly,astic) *with:* success, progress, competence, development, accomplishment(s), performance, growth, underachievement, overachievement, attainment, achievement, grade(s,point), productivity, standing. *See also* Academic ability; Academic aptitude; Academic failure; Academic skills; Achievement gains; Academic overachievement; Achievement potential; Educational attainment; Knowledge level; Mathematics achievement; Reading achievement; Scholars; Scholarship; Success.

Academic achievement motivation. See *Educational motivation.*

Academic advising. Academic advis(ing, ement). *Choose from:* academic, educational, faculty, student(s) *with:* advis(ing,or,ors), adviser(s), advice. Assist(ing,ed) student(s) to select course(s). *See also* Advice; Educational counseling.

Academic aptitude. Academic aptitude. *Choose from:* academic, scholastic, scholarly, school, student(s), learner(s), intellectual *with:* aptitude(s), potential, abilit(y,ies), test performance. *See also* Academic ability; Academic achievement; Academically gifted; Academic aspiration; Intelligence; Student characteristics.

Academic aspiration. Academic aspiration(s). *Choose from:* academic, education(al), student(s), scholastic, scholarly, graduate, college, university, higher education *with:* aspiration(s), achievement motivation, plan(s), goal(s), objective(s), persistence. *See also* Academic ability; Academic achievement; Academic aptitude; Achievement need; Achievement potential; Educational motivation; Educational objectives; Student motivation.

Academic degrees. Academic degree(s). Doctorate(s). *Choose from:* academic, educational, advanced, associate, bachelors, baccalaureate, masters, college, graduate, undergraduate, doctoral, BA, AB, BS, MS, MA, PHD, earned, honorary *with:* degree(s). *Consider also:* high school diploma(s). *See also* College graduates; College students; Educational attainment; Occupational qualifications; Professional education.

Academic disciplines. Academic discipline(s). *Choose from:* academic, intellectual, scientific, university *with:* field(s), major(s), discipline(s), subject(s). *See also* Higher education; Humanities; Knowledge; Mathematics; Social sciences.

Academic education. Academic education. *Choose from:* academic, liberal, formal, college preparatory, classical, higher *with:* education, curriculum, subject(s), stud(y,ies), instruction, program(s), course(s), schooling. *See also* Academic disciplines; Higher education; Humanities.

Academic environment. Academic environment(s). *Choose from:* academic, school, learning, scholarly, educational, classroom, college(s), universit(y,ies) *with:* environment(s), setting(s), climate(s), milieu(s). *See also* Academic freedom; Adjustment (to environment); Classroom environment; Environment; Extended school year; School orientation; School schedules; Social environment.

Academic failure. Academic failure. *Choose from:* academic, scholastic, student(s), school, education(al), learning *with:* fail(ed,ing,ure,ures), unsuccessful, probation, problem(s), difficult(y,ies). *Consider also:* grade retention, academically at risk, learning deficit(s), academic probation,

underachiever(s), problem student(s), learning disabilit(y,ies), high risk student(s). *See also* Academic achievement; Academic probation; Student dropouts; Underachievement.

Academic freedom. Academic freedom(s). *Choose from:* freedom(s), autonom(y, ous), right(s) *with:* teach(ing,ers), academic, professor(s), college(s), universit(y,ies), intellectual, student(s), professional. *See also* Academic environment; Censorship; Civil rights; Faculty; Free thought; Freedom of information; Freedom of speech; Information dissemination; Intellectual life; Personal independence; Student teacher relations; Tolerance.

Academic libraries. Academic librar(y,ies). *Choose from:* academic, college(s), universit(y,ies) *with:* librar(y,ies), learning resource(s) center(s). *See also* Archives; Learning centers; Libraries.

Academic overachievement. Academic overachiev(ement,er,ers,ed,ing). School achievement syndrome. *Choose from:* academic, school, scholastic, scholarly *with:* overachiev(ement,ed,ing), overcompensat(e,ed,ing,ion), discrepant achievement, superior achiev(ement, ements,ers,ed,ing), perfection(ism,ist, ists). *Consider also:* accelerated student(s). *See also* Academic achievement; Academic aspiration; Acceleration (education).

Academic performance. See *Academic achievement.*

Academic persistence. Academic persistence. *Choose from:* academic, college, education(al), student(s), learner(s) *with:* persist(ed,ing,ence,ent). *See also* Attrition; Diligence; Persistence; School adjustment; School attendance; Student dropouts; Reentry students.

Academic probation. Academic probation. *Choose from:* academic, student(s), scholastic, school, educational *with:* probation(ary). *See also* Academic failure; Grade repetition; School attendance; Student dropouts; School expulsion; Underachievement.

Academic rank. Academic rank(s). *Choose from:* academic, faculty, professional, professor(ial) *with:* rank(s), level(s), status, standing. *See also* Employment status; Faculty; Seniority; Teachers.

Academic records. Academic record(s). *Choose from:* academic, student(s), scholastic, school, college, university, grade(s) *with:* record(s), transcript(s). *See also* Academic achievement; Grading (educational); Student records.

Academic skills. Academic skill(s). *Choose from:* academic, preacademic, reading, verbal, math(ematics), writing, English language, foreign language, native language, pre-professional *with:* skill(s), proficien(t,cy,cies), deficien(t,cy,cies), placement test(s), grade point average(s), content mastery, competen(t,cy). *See also* Academic ability; Academic achievement; Mathematics achievement; Reading achievement; Student characteristics.

Academic specialization. See *Specialization.*

Academic standards. Academic standard(s). *Choose from:* academic, accreditation, student, education(al), college, university, admission, grading, teach(er,ing), scholastic *with:* standard(s), criteria, passing grade(s). *Consider also:* minimum competenc(y, ies,e), proficiency standard(s). *See also* Academic achievement; Academic probation; Accreditation; Back to basics; Competency based education; Educational malpractice; Knowledge level; Mastery learning; School admission criteria; Selection tests.

Academic tenure. Academic tenure. Permanent appointment(s). Permanent status(es). *Choose from:* faculty, academic, professor(s), instructor(s), teacher(s) *with:* tenure(d), years of employment, permanent appointment(s), duration of employment, long term employment, longevity, seniority. *See also* Academic rank; Career goals; Career ladders; Faculty; Occupational tenure; Promotion (occupational); Seniority.

Academic underachievement. See *Underachievement.*

Academic writing. See *Scholarship.*

Academically gifted. Academically gifted. *Choose from:* gifted, superior, talented, precocious *with:* student(s), pupil(s), grader(s), academic. *See also* Academic ability; Academic achievement; Academic aptitude; Acceleration (education); Gifted; Intelligence; Scholars.

Acalculia. Acalcul(ia,ic). Anarithm(ia,ic). *Choose from:* numerical skill(s), math(ematics,ematical) *with:* difficult(y,ies), deficit(s). *Consider also:* dyscalcul(ia,ic), Gerstmann's syndrome. *See also* Aphasia; Learning disabilities.

Acceleration (education). Accelerat(e,ed, ing,ion). *Choose from:* accelerated, time shortened *with:* course(s), program(s), education, student(s). *Consider also:* three year(s) *with:* bachelors degree(s), baccalaureate. Early entrance to college. *See also* Academic ability; Academic achievement; Academic aptitude; Academically gifted; Educational placement; Extended school year.

Acceleration (speed). Accelerat(e,es,ed, ing,ion). *Choose from:* increas(e,es, ed,ing) *with:* velocity, speed. *Consider also:* G force effect(s). *See also* Acceleration effects; Flight simulation; Hurry (speed); Motion.

Acceleration effects. Acceleration effect(s). *Choose from:* accelerat(e,es,ed,ing,ion), G force *with:* effect(s), reaction(s), adapt(ed,ing,ation,ations), manifestation(s). *Consider also:* motion sickness, flight conditions. *See also* Acceleration (speed); Flight simulation; Motion; Physiological stress.

Accents. Accent(s,uation). Regional pronunciation. Speech pattern(s). *Consider also:* diphthongs, tonal phonology, inflection, articulat(e,ed,ion), inton(e,ed,ation), cadence, stress, tempo. *See also* Cadence; Dialects; Nonstandard English.

Acceptability. Acceptab(le,leness,ility,ly). Acceptable standard(s). Suitab(le,ility). Satisfactor(y,iness,ily). Sufficien(t,cy). Valid(ity). Appropriate(ly,ness). Adequacy. Adequate(ly,ness). Tolerab(le, leness,ility,ly). Respectab(le,leness,ility, ly). Admissab(le,leness,ility,ly). Passab(le,leness,ility,ly). Bearab(le, leness,ility,ly). *See also* Comfortableness; Decency; Group norms; Social approval; Social desirability.

Acceptance. Accept(ed,ing,ance). Approv(e,ed,ing,al). Recogniz(e,ed,ing). Recognition. Endors(e,ed,ing,ement). Support(ed,ing). Sanction(ed,ing). Upheld. Confirm(ed,ing,ation). Recommend(ed,ing,ation). Favorably received. Popular(ity). Fashionable. Belonging(ness). High demand. Consumer demand. *See also* Affiliation motivation; Approval; Belongingness; Brotherliness; Clearance (authorization); Confirmation; Interpersonal relations; Peer relations; Rejection (psychology); Resistance; Social acceptance; Social approval; Social attitudes; Social desirability; Social isolation; Social response.

Acceptance, social. See *Social acceptance.*

Acceptance of health care, patient. See *Patient compliance.*

Access. Access(ible,ibility,ed,ing). *Choose from:* opportunity, permission, permit(ted,ting), right, liberty, ability, freedom *with:* enter, entr(y,ance), admit(ted,ting,tance), use. *Consider also:* being included, acceptance, admit(ted,tance), admission, entrée, ingress. *See also* Access to education; Access to information; Architectural accessibility; Racial integration; School integration.

Access, solar. See *Solar access.*

Access to education. Access to education. Open admission(s). Open access. *Choose from:* access(ible,ibility), open, equal opportunity *with:* education(al), school(s), universit(y,ies), college(s). *See*

also Academic aspiration; Academic freedom; Access; Admissions; Architectural accessibility; Coeducation; Compulsory education; Distance education; Educational opportunities; Equal education; Nonsexist education; Nontraditional education; School admission criteria; School attendance; Single sex schools.

Access to information. Access to information. Free flow of information. Right to know. Free library service. Open archives. Public domain data. Freedom of information. Sunshine law. Intellectual freedom. *Choose from:* access(ible,ibility), avail(able,ability), public domain, open *with:* information, idea(s), data, file(s), database(s), record(s), medical record(s), school record(s), document(s), government information, archive(s), librar(y,ies), book(s), journal article(s), material(s), resources. *Consider also:* glasnost. *See also* Academic freedom; Access; Attribution of news; Classified information; Confidential communications; Confidential records; Confidentiality; Freedom of information; Freedom of speech; Government correspondence; Government secrecy; Home schooling; Information leaks; Information policy; Information seeking; Information services; Library censorship; News policies; Public meetings; Search strategies.

Accessibility, architectural. See *Architectural accessibility.*

Accessibility for disabled. See *Architectural accessibility.*

Acciaccatura. Acciaccatura(e,s). Accacciatura(e,s). Zusammenschlag. Simultaneous appoggiatura. *See also* Arpeggio; Embellishment (music); Music; Ornamentation (music).

Accident law. Accident law. Casualty law. Personal injury suit(s). Accident claim(s). Accident suit(s). *Consider also:* punitive damage award(s), no fault insurance, tort claim(s), automobile liability insurance. *See also* Accidents; Law (practice).

Accident prevention. Accident prevention. Safety. Smoke detect(or,ors,ion). *Choose from:* protective, warning, safety *with:* device(s), sign(s,al,als). *Choose from:* accident(al,s), disaster(s), catastrophe(s), injur(y,ies), casualt(y,ies), hazard(s,ous), unsafe *with:* prevent(ed,ing,ion), control, avoid(ed,ing,ance), reduc(e,ed,ing), reduction(s), eliminat(e,ed,ing,ion). *Consider also:* safe(ty) *with:* practice(s), regulation(s), standard(s), product(s), occupational, program(s), warning(s), workplace(s), situation(s). *See also* Accidents; Aviation safety; Equipment safety; Highway safety; Occupational safety; Product safety; Risk management; Safety; Safety devices; Water safety.

Accident proneness. Accident prone(ness). *Choose from:* accident(s), disaster(s), catastrophe(s) *with:* prone(ness), repeater(s), stress related, lack of alertness, unconsciously motivated, fatigue, likelihood, predispos(ed,ition). *Consider also:* purposive, intentional *with:* accident(s). *See also* Accidents; Accident prevention; Mental fatigue; Safety; Stress.

Accidental crisis. Accidental cris(is,es). *Consider also:* situational, unanticipated *with:* cris(is,es). *See also* Experiences (events); Stress.

Accidental falls. Accidental fall(s). Stumbl(e,ed,ing). *Choose from:* accident(al,s) *with:* fall(s,ing), fell, trip(ped,ping), slip(ped,ping), ladder(s), height(s), stairway(s), stair(s), high place(s). *Choose from:* fall(s,ing), fell *with:* down, out of bed. *Consider also:* home accident(s). *See also* Accidents; Home accidents; Injuries.

Accidental homosexuality. Accidental homosexuality. Faute de mieux. *Consider also:* situational, occasional *with:* homosexual(ity), inversion. *See also* Attitudes toward homosexuality; Bisexuality; Ego dystonic homosexuality; Homosexuality.

Accidents. Accident(al,ally,s). Drown(ed,ing). Calamit(y,ies). Mishap(s). Casualt(ies,y). Disaster(s). Auto(mobile) crash(es). Collision(s). Collid(e,ed,ing). Equipment failure(s). Misfortune(s). Catastroph(e,es,ic). Shipwreck(ed,s). Slip(s,ped,ping). Misadventure(s). Spill(s). Fall(s,ing,en). *Consider also:* safety. *See also* Accident law; Accident prevention; Accident proneness; Accidental falls; Adversity; Aviation accidents; Catastrophes; Collisions at sea; Drunk driving; Emergencies; Emergency services; Hardships; Hazards; Health; Home accidents; Industrial accidents; Injuries; Marine accidents; Nuclear accidents; Occupational safety; Pedestrian accidents; Personal injuries; Purposive accidents; Rescue; Traffic accidents; Transportation accidents; Safety; Wrecks.

Accidents, air traffic. See *Aviation accidents.*

Accidents, aviation. See *Aviation accidents.*

Accidents, home. See *Home accidents.*

Accidents, industrial. See *Industrial accidents.*

Accidents, marine. See *Marine accidents.*

Accidents, mine. See *Mine accidents.*

Accidents, motor vehicle. See *Traffic accidents.*

Accidents, nuclear. See *Nuclear accidents.*

Accidents, occupational. See *Industrial accidents.*

Accidents, pedestrian. See *Pedestrian accidents.*

Accidents, purposive. See *Purposive accidents.*

Accidents, traffic. See *Traffic accidents.*

Accidents, transportation. See *Transportation accidents.*

Acclimatization. Acclimatiz(e,ed,ing,ation). Acclimat(e,ed,ing,ion). *Consider also:* climat(e,ic), environmental condition(s), thermal, cold, heat, weather, altitude, dry(ness), damp(ness) *with:* adapt(ed, ing,ation), adjust(ed,ing,ment), response(s). *See also* Adaptability; Adaptation; Adjustment (to environment); Atmospheric conditions; Orientation; Temperature effects; Thermal acclimatization; Thermoregulation.

Acclimatization, thermal. See *Thermal acclimatization.*

Accommodation. See *Acculturation; Adaptation; Adjustment (to environment); Assimilation (cultural); Social adjustment.*

Accommodation, ocular. See *Ocular accommodation.*

Accommodation, religious. See *Religious accommodation.*

Accomodations, living. See *Housing.*

Accomplices. Accomplice(s). Partner(s) in crime. Accessor(y,ies) to crime. *Choose from:* aid(s,ed,ing), abet(s,ted,ting), assist(s,ed,ing), complicity, fail(s,ed,ing) to prevent, promot(es,ed,ing), facilitat(es,ed,ing) *with:* crime(s), felon(y,ies), offense(s), illegal(y,ities), murder(s), assault(s), kidnapping(s), etc. *Consider also:* particeps criminus, socius criminis, confederate(s), abettor(s), conspirator(s), all(y,ies). *See also* Associates; Collaboration; Collaborators; Collusion; Crime; Criminal act; Informers; Organized crime; Partners; Social contagion.

Accomplishment. See *Achievement.*

Account books. Account book(s). Ledger(s). Expense account book(s). *Consider also:* daybook(s), checkbook(s), check stub(s), volume(s) of invoice(s), cashbook(s), accounts receivable book(s), record book(s) of trust accounts, record book(s) on bonds and mortgages, financial account(s). *See also* Accounting; Cartularies.

Accountability. Accountab(le,ility). Answerab(le,ility). Responsib(le,ility, ities). Warrant(y,ies). Guarantee(s,d). Liab(le,ility,ilities). *Consider also:* audit(s,ed,ing), legal(ly) require(d,ment,

ments), obligat(ed,ing,ion,ions), quality control, regulat(ed,ing,ory), performance measure(s), performance assessment(s), program evaluation(s), self evaluation(s), quality assurance, negligence suit(s), malpractice suit(s). *See also* Authority (power); Codes of ethics; Competence; Competency based education; Consumer protection; Contracts; Cost effectiveness; Duties; Educational malpractice; Educational objectives; Evaluation; Fiduciary responsibility; Financial statements; Liability; Malpractice; Ministerial responsibility (government); Negligence; Organizational objectives; Peer review; Performance; Product liability; Productivity; Professional liability; Program evaluation; Psychotherapeutic outcomes; Quality control; Relevance; Responsibility (answerability); Supererogation.

Accountants. Accountant(s). Accounting officer(s). Controller(s). Comptroller(s). *Consider also:* certified public accountant(s), CPA(s), chartered accountant(s), bookkeeper(s), auditor(s). *See also* Accounting; Accounting standards; Financial audit; Professional personnel.

Accounting. Account(ed,ing). *Consider also:* billing, payroll, bookkeeping, financial *with:* function(s), practice(s), record(s), transaction(s), statement(s), audit(s). Account(s) payable. Account(s) receivable. *See also* Account books; Accountants; Accounting standards; Accounting systems; Accounts payable and receivable; Billing systems; Budgets; Cash flow; Cost accounting; Finance; Financial audit; Financial statements; Financial management; Government finances; Public finance.

Accounting, cost. See *Cost accounting.*

Accounting standards. Accounting standard(s). *Choose from:* accounting, financial reporting, financial statement(s), annual report(s), audit(s,ed,ing), *with:* standard(s), rule(s), principle(s), directive(s), framework(s), quality review, regulation(s), *Consider also:* certified public accountant(s), Financial Accounting Standards Board, FASB. *See also* Account books; Accountants; Accounting; Accounts payable and receivable; Financial audit; Financial statements; Financial management.

Accounting systems. Accounting system(s). *Choose from:* accountan(t,ts,cy,ting), financial management, project tracking, costing, financial application(s) *with:* system(s), software, package(s). *Consider also:* Accounting information system(s), Gain-on-Sale Accounting, GOS accounting, throughput accounting, Cash Flow Return on Investment (CFROI), Economic Value Added (EVA) approach, global management accounting, Generally Accepted Accounting Principles (GAAP), Managerial Cost Accounting (MCA), Activity-Based Costing analysis (ABC), Customer Profitability Analysis (CPA). *See also* Accounting; Billing systems; Decision support systems; Management information systems.

Accounts, personal. See *Autobiography.*

Accounts payable and receivable.
Account(s) payable and receivable. *Consider also:* debit(s), liabilit(y,ies), asset(s), credit, billing(s), bill collection(s), cash flow(s), payment(s), uncollected account(s), account(s) receivable, account(s) payable, financial status. *See also* Accounting; Accounting standards; Billing systems; Budgets; Cash flow; Financial audit; Financial management; Liquidation.

Accreditation. Accredit(ed,ing,ation). Approv(e,ed,ing,al,als). Authoriz(e, ed,ing). Certif(y,ying,ied,ication). Official recognition. Officially recognized. Credential(s,ing,ism). Licens(e,es,ed,ing). Validat(e,ed, ing,ion,ions). *See also* Academic standards; Accrediting agencies; Certificates; Certification; Credentialing; Eligibility determination; Legitimacy; Quality control.

Accrediting agencies. Accrediting agenc(y,ies). Accreditor(s). Specialty board(s). *Choose from:* accredit(ing, ation) *with:* agenc(y,ies), association(s), team(s), committee(s), board(s). *See also* Academic standards; Accreditation; Agencies; Criteria; Professional standards; Standards.

Acculturation. Acculturat(e,ed,ing,ion,ive). Americaniz(e,ed,ing,ation). Westerniz(e, ed,ing,ation). Overcom(e,ing) culture shock. Intercultural adjustment(s). Melting pot. Adopt(ed,ing) a new culture. Assimilat(e,ed,ing,ion). Naturaliz(e,ed,ing,ation). Inculturat(e,ed, ing,ion). Indegeniz(e,ed,ing,ation). *Choose from:* immigrant(s), displaced person(s), sojourner(s), newcomer(s), refugee(s) *with:* adjust(ed,ing,ment), host culture(s), adapt(ed,ing,ation). *Consider also:* biculturalism, cultural assimilation, culture contact, cultural fusion, accomodation, socialization, antagonistic acculturation, marginal acculturation, planitational acculturation, hyphenated American(s), value mutation(s). *See also* Assimilation (cultural); Biculturalism; Citizenship; Common culture; Cultural conflict; Cultural cooperation; Cultural diversity; Cultural identity; Cultural issues; Cultural maintenance; Cultural pluralism; Cultural transmission; Cultural values; Culture (anthropology); Culture change; Culture contact; Culture shock;

Ethnic groups; Ethnicity; Immigrants; Indigenous populations; Intercultural communication; Intercultural relations; Intermarriage; Language shift; National identity; Naturalization; Refugees; Social integration; Subcultures.

Accumulation. Accumulat(e,ed,ion,ions). Amass(ed,ing). Hoard(s,ed,ing). Collect(ed,ing,ion,ions). Agglomeration(s). Stockpile(s). Cache(s). Reserve(s). Acquisition(s). Acquir(e,ed,ing). *Consider also:* purchas(e,ed,ing), accru(e,ed,ing). *See also* Acquisition; Backlog; Buildup; Capital (financial); Collecting mania; Enlargement; Hoarding; Land (property); Ownership; Personal property; Property rights; Saving; Storage; Wealth.

Accuracy. Accura(te,teness,cy). Correct(ness). Exact(ness,itude). Veracity. Valid(ity). Unerring(ness). Precise(ness). Precision. Literal(ly,ness). Flawless(ness). Perfect(ion). Faultless(ness). *Consider also:* definitive(ness), factual(ity), fidelity, thorough(ness). *See also* Bias; Competence; Correctness; Errors; Excellence; Financial audit; Flawless; Judgment; Media portrayal; Perfection; Reliability; Truth; Validity; Verification.

Accuracy and fairness in reporting. See *Fairness and accuracy in reporting.*

Accusation, self. See *Self accusation.*

Accusations. See *Allegations; Blame; Scapegoating; Self accusation.*

Aches. See *Pain.*

Achievement. Achievement(s). Achiev(e,ed, er,ers,ing). Success(ful). Attain(ed,ing, ment,ments). Win(ning). Winner(s). Succeed(ed,ing). Overachiev(e,ed,ing, ement). Fulfill(ed,ing,ment). Fruition. Accomplish(ed,ing,ment,ments). Overcom(e,ing) obstacle(s). Promot(ed,ing,ion,ions). *See also* Academic achievement; Achievement gains; Achievement need; Achievement potential; Achievement potential; Achievement tests; Ascription; Aspirations; Attainment; Awards; Competence; Educational attainment; Effectiveness; Evaluation; Excellence; Failure; Goals; Honored (esteem); Improvement; Knowledge level; Mathematics achievement; Overachievement; Occupational success; Perfection; Performance; Quality; Reading achievement; Recognition (achievement); Success; Underachievement.

Achievement, academic. See *Academic achievement.*

Achievement, mathematics. See *Mathematics achievement.*

Achievement motivation, academic. See *Educational motivation.*

Achievement, occupational. See *Occupational success.*

Achievement, professional. See *Occupational success.*

Achievement, reading. See *Reading achievement.*

Achievement, scholastic. See *Academic achievement.*

Achievement, solution. See *Problem solving.*

Achievement, student. See *Academic achievement.*

Achievement gains. Achievement gain(s). *Choose from:* achievement, test retest, cognitive, comprehension, competency, proficiency *with:* gain(s,ed,ing), progress(ed,ing), increas(e,es,ed,ing), develop(ed,ing,ment), loss(es). *Consider also:* reading, arithmetic, academic, schoolwork *with:* gain(s,ed,ing), achiev(e,ed,ing), achievement(s), progress(ed,ing). *See also* Academic achievement; Achievement gains; Achievement tests; Educational attainment; Improvement; Knowledge level; Mathematics achievement; Reading achievement.

Achievement measures. See *Achievement tests.*

Achievement motivation. See *Achievement need.*

Achievement need. Achievement need. NAch. *Choose from:* achievement(s), success(es), succeed, excel, accomplishment(s) *with:* need(s), pride, orient(ed,ation), drive(s), motivat(e,ed, ing,ion), motive(s). *Consider also:* fear of failure, competitive(ness), deferred gratification. *See also* Academic aspiration; Achievement potential; Affiliation motivation; Aspirations; Compensation (defense mechanism); Competition; Deferered compensation; Educational motivation; Fear of failure; Fear of success; Goal orientation; Motivation; Protestant ethic; Status seekers; Success.

Achievement potential. Achievement potential. Potential achievement. *Choose from:* achievement, educational, school, learning, academic, occupational, creativ(e,ity), managerial, success *with:* potential, expectancy, attribution(s), predictive measure(s). *Consider also:* abilit(y,ies), aptitude, gifted. *See also* Academic ability; Academic aptitude; Achievement need; Educational motivation.

Achievement tests. Achievement test(s). *Choose from:* academic, achievement, acquired learning, arithmetic, basic(s), competency, comprehension, criterion referenced, educational, effectiveness, equivalency, knowledge, mastery, mathematics, performance, placement, proficiency, reading, skill(s) *with:* test(s), exam(s), examination(s), measur(e,es,ing,ment), evaluation method(s), assessment(s), scale(s), questionnaire(s), diagnostic(s), inventor(y,ies), instrument(s). *Consider also:* national competency test(s), Iowa test(s) of basic skills, Stanford achievement test, wide range achievement test. *See also* Academic achievement; Achievement; Achievement gains; Aptitude tests; Criterion referenced tests; Culture fair tests; Intelligence tests; Language tests; Performance tests; Reading tests; Tests.

Acid rain. Acid(ic) rain(water,fall). *Choose from:* acid(ity,ic,ification) *with:* precipitation, air pollution, watershed(s), rain(water,fall), snow. *See also* Air pollution; Atmospheric contamination; Environmental pollutants; Environmental pollution; Greenhouse effect; Industrial wastes; Water pollution; Weather.

Acmeism. Acmeis(m,t,ts,ty). Akmeis(m,t,ts,ty). *Consider also:* post-symbolism, Sergey Gorodetsky, Nikolay S. Gumilyov, Anna Akhmatova, Osip Mandelshtam. *See also* Literary movements.

Acoustics. Acoustic(s,ally). Psycho-acoustic(s,ally). Ultrasonic(s). Sonication. Aeroacoustic(s,ally). *Consider also:* sound *with:* transmission, wave(s), quality, perception, intensity, frequenc(y,ies), spectrograph(s). *See also* Architecture; Facility design and construction; Filtered noise; Noise (sounds); Noise effects; Noise levels (work areas); White noise.

Acquaintance rape. Acquaintance rape(s). Date rape(s). Campus rape(s). *Choose from:* acquaintance(s), friend(s), date(s), dating, classmate(s), fellow student(s), co-worker(s), colleague(s), boss(es), boyfriend(s), lover(s), partner(s), known assailant(s), teacher(s), professor(s) *with:* rape(s,d), raping, rapist(s), forc(e,ed,ible) sex, sexual(ly) assault(s,ed,ing,ive), sexual(ly) coerc(e,ed,ing,ion), sexual(ly) violat(e,ed,ion,ions), sexual(ly) abus(e,es,ed,ing,ive), sexual(ly) aggress(ive,iveness,ion), victimiz(e,ed,ing,ation), sodom(y,ize,ized,izing). *See also* Human courtship; Marital rape; Online harassment; Premarital sexual behavior; Rape; Rape drugs; Sex offenders; Sexual abuse; Sexual assault; Sexual coercion; Sexual consent; Sexual exploitation; Sexual foreplay; Sexual harassment; Sexual violence; Social dating; Statutory rape.

Acquaintances. Acquaintance(s). Social contact(s). Friend(s). Neighbor(s). Peer(s). Associate(s). Colleague(s). Companion(s). Schoolmate(s).

Playmate(s). Comrade(s). Patron(s). Customer(s). Client(s). Confrere(s). Fellow worker(s). Teammate(s). Co-worker(s). *Consider also:* business associate(s), coworker(s), acquaintance(ship). *See also* Contemporaries; Friendship; Neighbors; Peers; Secondary relationships; Social contact; Social life.

Acquiescence. Acquiesce(nce,nt). Tacit(ly) encourage(ment). Assent. Consent. Concur(rence,rent,ring,red). Comply(ing). Compli(ed,ance). Obedien(t,ce). Accord(ance). Conced(e,ed,ing). Concession(s). Submit(ted,ting). Submission. Nonresistance. Acknowledg(e,ed,ing). Sufferance. Willing(ness). Resignation. Acced(e,ed,ing,ence). Nonresistance. Yield(ed,ing). Capitulat(e,ed,ing,ion). Waiving right(s). Abandon(ed,ing) right(s). *Consider also:* enabler(s). *See also* Compliance; Compromises; Cooptation; Informed consent; Patient compliance.

Acquired immunodeficiency syndrome. See *AIDS.*

Acquisition. Acquisition(s,al). Acquir(e,ed,ement,ing). Accru(e,ed,ing). Addition(s). Annex(ed,ing,ation,ations). Attain(ed,ing,ment). Accession(s). Increment(s). Asset(s). Belonging(s). Possession(s). Procur(e,ed,ing,ement). Purchas(e,ed,ing). Collect(ed,ing,ion,ions). Gain(ed,ing) possession. *Choose from:* hold(ing), held, own(ed,ing), purchas(ed,ing) *with:* share(s), stock(s), securit(y,ies). *See also* Accumulation; Collecting mania; Ownership; Personal property; Purchasing.

Acquisition, language. See *Language acquisition.*

Acquisition of territory. Acquisition of territor(y,ies). Land grab(s). Forced annexation(s). Occupied territor(y,ies). *Consider also:* territorial imperative. *Choose from:* land(s), propert(y,ies), territor(y,ies) *with:* seiz(e,ed,ure), acquir(e,ed,ing), acquisition, buy(ing), bought, take possession, conquer(ed,ing), conquest, occup(y,ied). *See also* Occupancy; Territorial expansion.

Acquisitions, corporate. See *Corporate acquisitions.*

Acquisitions, library. See *Library acquisitions.*

Acquittal. Acquit(tal,tals,ting,ted). Exonerat(e,ed,ing,ion). Dismiss(ed,ing,al) charge(s). Set free. Judicial(ly) discharge(d). Release(d) from obligation(s). Release(d) from suspicion. *Choose from:* declar(e,ed,ation), find(s,ing), found *with:* innocen(t,ce). *Consider also:* absolution, absolv(e,ed,ing), suspended sentence(s), amnesty, pardon(s,ed,ing), reprieve(s,d),

vindicat(e,ed,ing,ion). exculpat(e,ed,ing,ion). *See also* Criminal proceedings; Judicial decisions; Legal procedures; Plea bargaining; Verdicts.

Acrobats. Acrobat(s,ic,ics). Gymnast(s). Tumbler(s). Trapeze artist(s). Aerialist(s). *See also* Gymnastics.

Acronyms. See *Abbreviations.*

Acrophobia. Acrophob(ia,ic). Hyposophob(ia,ic). *Choose from:* height(s), high place(s) *with:* fear(s,ful), phob(ic,ia,ias), anxiety, anxious(ness). *See also* Phobias.

Act (Philosophy). Act(s,ion,ions). Operation(s). Deed(s). Accomplishment(s). *Consider also:* middle act(s,ion,ions), negative act(s,ion,ions). *See also* Action; De facto; Philosophy.

Act, criminal. See *Criminal act.*

Acting. Act(ed,ing). Clown(s,ing). Dramatic(s). Dramatiz(e,ed,ing). Dramatic abilit(y,ies). Dramatic aptitude(s). Feign(ed,ing). Impersonat(e,ed,ing,ion,ions). Mime(s). Mimicry. Parody(ing). Stage performance(s). Playact(ing). Play rehearsal. Portray(al,ing). Psychodrama(s). Rehears(e,ed,ing) play(s). Role playing. Role simulation(s). Simulating. Sociodrama(s). Starring role(s). Vaudeville. *See also* Actors and actresses; Drama; Improvisation (acting); Method (acting); Theater.

Acting, method. See *Method (acting).*

Acting out. Act(ed,ing) out. *Consider also:* unconscious(ly) reliv(e,ing), displace(ment) of response, transference. *See also* Behavior disorders; Emotionally disturbed; Symptoms.

Action. Act(ed,ing,ion,ivity). Deed(s). Behavior. Conduct. Movement(s). Motion(s). Operat(e,ed,ing,ion,ions). Execut(e,ed,ing,ion,ions). Combat (in war). Enact(ed,ing,ments). Caus(e,ed,ing) change. Transact(ed,ing,ion,ions). React(ed,ing,ion,ions). Response(s). Work(ing). Feat(s). Performance(s). Achievement(s). Accomplishment(s). Progress. Exchange(s). Function(ed,ing). *See also* Act (Philosophy); Action research; Affirmative action; Behavior; Class action; Collective action; De facto; Enactment; Freedom (theology); Intentionality; Political action; Protest movements; Social action; Social action (sociological); Volition.

Action, activity. See *Action; Animation (Cinematography); Behavior; Energy expenditure (physical); Exercise; Restlessness; Walking; Work.*

Action, affirmative. See *Affirmative action.*

Action, collective. See *Collective action.*

Action, community. See *Activism; Citizen participation; Community involvement;*

Community support; Local politics; Protest movements; Social action.

Action, missing in. See *Missing in action.*

Action, political. See *Political action.*

Action, social. See *Social action.*

Action, social sociological. See *Social action (sociological).*

Actioncommittees, political. See *Interest groups.*

Action research. Action research. *Choose from:* action, utilitarian, applica(ble,bility), application(s), applied, practical(ity), useful(ness), practice oriented *with:* research, stud(y,ies). *See also* Evaluation; Group research; Operations research; Research; Social action.

Actions and defenses. See *Lawsuits.*

Activation. Activat(e,ed,ing,ion). Actuat(e,ed,ing,ion). Put into action. Commenc(e,ed,ing). Activiz(e,ed, ing,ion). Mobiliz(e,ed,ing,ion). *Consider also:* put on active duty, vitaliz(e,ed,ing, ion), energiz(e,ed,ing,ion), invigorat(e, ed,ing,ion), formal(ly) institut(e,ed,ion), turn(ed,ing) on. *See also* Arousal; Mobilization.

Active learning. Active learning. Critical thinking. *Choose from:* active, interactive, open-ended, student-centered, meaning-centered, discovery-based, experiential, cooperative, problem-solving, self-initiated, self directed *with:* learning, activit(y,ies), curriculum, environment(s), class discussion(s), instruction. *Consider also:* peer teaching, role playing, independent study, action learning, problem based learning. *See also* Cooperative learning; Critical thinking; Discovery learning; Humanistic education; Individualized instruction; Learning; Self education; Student motivation.

Activism. Activis(m,t,ts). Militan(t,cy). Protest(ed,er,ers,s,ing). Agitat(e,ion, or,ors). Militant community action. Dissenter(s). Dissent(ed,ing). Demonstrat(ed,ing,ion,ions). Demonstrator(s). Unrest. Reform organization(s). Social action. Reform movement(s). Advoca(cy,te,tes). Rights group(s). Radicalism. Radical movement(s). Student protest(s). Protest group(s). Civil disobedience. *Choose from:* political(ly), sociopolitical(ly) *with:* participat(e,ed,ing,ion), participant(s), protest(s), active, activit(y,ies), activism. *Choose from:* protest, militant, dissent, rights, radical, activist *with:* demonstration(s), action, participat(e,ed,ing,ion), crusade(s), march(es). *See also* Activists; Antismoking movement; Citizen participation; Civil disobedience; Civil rights organizations; Collective action;

Community power; Consciousness raising activities; Ecumenical movement; Environmentalism; Feminism; Gray power; Homosexual liberation movement; Interest groups; Labor movements; Lobbying; Militancy; Mobilization; Peace movements; Political movements; Protest movements; Radical movements; Religious movements; Social action; Social agitation; Social criticism; Social demonstrations; Social movements; Suffrage movement; Volunteers; Women's groups; Youth movements.

Activism, judicial. See *Judicial activism.*

Activism, political. See *Activism; Advocacy; Interest groups; Lobbying; Militancy; Political action; Populism; Protest movements; Social action; Social reform.*

Activism, student. See *Youth movements.*

Activists. Activist(s). Advocate(s). Reformer(s). Change agent(s). Radical(s). Labor organizer(s). Liberator(s). Demonstrator(s). Abolitionist(s). Peacenik(s). Black power. Consciousness raising group(s). Environmentalist(s). Feminist(s). Pacifist(s). Prohibitionist(s). Protester(s). Suffragist(s). Suffragette(s). Zionist(s). *See also* Activism; Civil disobedience; Civil rights organizations; Ecumenical movement; Environmentalism; Feminism; Gray power; Homosexual liberation movement; Interest groups; Labor movements; Peace movements; Peasant rebellions; Political movements; Protest movements; Radical movements; Religious movements; Social action; Social demonstrations; Social movements; Suffrage movement; Women's groups; Youth movements.

Activities, civic. See *Civic activities.*

Activities, consciousness raising. See *Consciousness raising activities.*

Activities, cultural. See *Cultural activities.*

Activities, daily. See *Activities of daily living; Everyday life.*

Activities, extracurricular. See *Extracurricular activities.*

Activities, leisure. See *Leisure activities.*

Activities, organizing. See *Organizing activities.*

Activities, outdoor. See *Camping; Recreation; Sports; Vacations.*

Activities, social. See *Social activities.*

Activities, student. See *Student activities.*

Activities of daily living. Activities of daily living. Daily activit(y,ies). Daily regimen. Independence training. *Choose from:* living, daily life *with:* activit(y,ies), skill(s). *Consider also:* dressing, eating, bathing, grooming,

personal care. *Consider also:* self *with:* care, help, management. *See also* Body care; Daily; Self care; Self neglect.

Activity (action). See *Action; Animation (Cinematography); Behavior; Energy expenditure (physical); Exercise; Restlessness; Walking; Work.*

Activity, motor. See *Motor activity.*

Activity level. Activity level(s). Energetic state(s). *Choose from:* activ(e,ity), motor behavior *with:* level(s), extent, pattern(s), high(ly), low, slow, normal(ly). *See also* Motivation; Motor activity.

Activity therapy. See *Recreation therapy.*

Activity units. Activity unit(s). Experience unit(s). *Choose from:* activity, experience, study, learning, science, biology, energy *with:* module(s), unit(s), project(s). *See also* Discovery learning.

Actors. See *Acting; Actors and actresses.*

Actors and actresses. Actor(s). Actress(es). Thespian(s). Movie star(s). Matinee idol(s). Leading lad(y,ies). Leading m(an,en). Impersonator(s). Entertainer(s). Mime(s). Movie star(s). Performer(s). Playactor(s). Stage personalit(y,ies). Performing artist(s). Theatre performer(s). *Consider also:* dramatis person(a,ae), supernumerar(y,ies). *See also* Acting; Drama; Improvisation (acting); Method (acting); Theater.

Actresses. See *Acting; Actors and actresses.*

Actresses and actors. See *Actors and actresses.*

Acts (behavior). See *Act (Philosophy); Action; Behavior; Volition.*

Acts (legal). See *Statutes.*

Acts, speech. See *Speech acts.*

Acts of omission. See *Negligence.*

Actualization, self. See *Self actualization.*

Actuarial analysis. Actuarial analy(sis,ses). *Choose from:* actuarial, risk, life expectancy, mortality, survivorship, survival *with:* analy(sis,ses), classification(s), factor(s), table(s), method(s), model(s). *Consider also:* rating system(s). *See also* Economic research; Life insurance; Mortality rates.

Acuity, visual. See *Visual acuity.*

Acupuncture. Acupuncture. Electroacupuncture. Acupuncture reflexotherapy. *Consider also:* acupressure, shiatsu, endorphin release. *See also* Alternative medicine; Chinese medicine.

Acute disease. Acute disease(s). *Choose from:* acute(ly,ness), sever(e,ity), serious(ly), intensity, critical(ly) *with:* disease(s), disorder(s), condition(s), ill(ness,nesses). *See also* Chronic disease; Infectious disorders; Severity of disorders.

Acute psychosis. Acute psychos(is,es). *Choose from:* acute(ly), severe(ly), exacerbated *with:* psychos(is,es), psychotic disorder(s), insan(e,ity), mental(ly) ill(ness,nesses), psychiatric disorder(s), schizophren(ia,ic), breakdown(s), caton(ia,ic), man(ia,ic), delirium tremens, delusion(s,al), hallucinat(e,ed,ing,ion,ions). *Consider also:* boufees delirantes. *See also* Chronic psychosis; Psychoses.

Ad hocracies. See *Adhocracies.*

Ad infinitum. See *Endlessness.*

Ad lib. Ad lib(bed,bing). Improvis(e,ed, ing,ate,ating,ation). Extemporiz(e,ed, ing,ation). *Choose from:* impromptu, spontaneous(ly) *with:* speech(es), speak(ing), spoke(n), deliver(ed). *See also* Improvisation; Improvisation (acting); Public speaking; Spontaneity.

Adages. Adage(s). Saying(s). Byword(s). Proverb(s). *Consider also:* epigram(s), maxim(s), moto(es). *See also* Aphorisms; Axioms; Dictums; Figurative language; Folklore; Metaphors.

Adaptability. Adapt(able,ability,ableness, ive,iveness). Adjust(able,ability). Flex(ible,ibility). Coping abilit(y,ies). Adaptational style(s). Versatil(e,ity). Plian(t,cy). Accomodat(e,ed,ing,ion). Obliging. Amen(able,ability). Agreeable(ness). Agree(able,ability). Compensating. Modifiab(le,ility). Able to modify. Plastic(ity). *Consider also:* inflexib(le,ility), rigid(ity). *See also* Adaptation; Coping; Personality traits.

Adaptation. Adapt(ed,ing,ation,ations). Acclimat(e,ed,ing,ion). Acclimatiz(e,ed, ing,ation). Accomodat(e,ed,ing,ion). Acculturat(e,ed,ing,ion). Accustom(ize, izing,ized). Adjust(ed,ing,ment,ments). Alter(ed,ing,ation,ations). Assimilat(e, ed,ing). Becom(e,ed,ing) attuned. Chang(e,ed,ing). Complian(t,ce). Comply(ing). Complied. Conform(ity, ing). Conversion. Counteradaptation(s). Evolv(e,ed,ing). Evolution(ary). Familiariz(e,ed,ing,ation). Familiarity. Habituat(e,ed,ing,ion). Maladapt(ed, ing,ation,ations). Maladjust(ed,ing). Maladjustment(s). Moderat(e,ed,ing, ion). Modif(y,ying,ied). Modification(s). Naturaliz(e,ed,ing,ation). Readapt(ed, ing,ation,ive,ability). Reconcil(e,ed, ing,iation). *Choose from:* adaptive *with:* response(s), behavior(s). *Consider also:* orient(ed,ing,ation), rearrang(e,ed,ing, ment). *See also* Acclimatization; Acculturation; Adaptability; Adjustment (to environment); Assimilation (cultural); Coping; Evolution; Social adjustment; Thermal acclimatization.

Adaptation, light. See *Light adaptation.*

Adaptation, psychological. See *Emotional adjustment.*

Adaptation, sensory. See *Sensory adaptation.*

Adaptation, social. See *Acculturation; Adaptation; Interpersonal relations; Social adjustment.*

Adaptation level theory. Adaptation level theory. Helson's theory. *Consider also:* judgement by subjective scales. *See also* Attention; Cognitive processes; Perception.

Adaptation syndrome, general. See *General adaptation syndrome.*

Adaptation to environment. See *Adjustment (to environment).*

Adaptations, film. See *Film adaptations.*

Adapted physical education. Adapted physical education. *Choose from:* adapted, special, individualized, exceptional, disabilit(y,ies), disabled, handicapped, retarded, obese, blind, mainstreamed, wheelchair *with:* physical education, fitness, aerobic(s), athlet(es,ics), bowling, camping, swimming, playing ball, softball, roller skating, dancing, exercis(e,es,ing), trampoline(s), fitness, sport(s). *Consider also:* special olympics. *See also* Disability; Individualized instruction; Physical education; Physically handicapped; Special education.

Addendum. Addend(a,um). Append(ed, ing,age,ages). Appendix(es). Appendices. Codicil(s). Rider(s). Supplement(s). Supplementary material. *Consider also:* epilog(s,ue,ues), sequel(s), postscript(s), afterword(s), postlude(s), coda(s). *See also* Agreement (document); Commentaries; Epilogues; Journal articles; Literature; Literary criticism; Literary errors and blunders; Professional literature.

Addicted babies. See *Drug addicted babies*

Addiction. Addict(s,ed,ion,ions,ing,ive). Compulsive craving(s). Pathological craving(s). Overdependen(t,ce). Habit(ual,s). Enslavement. Habituat(ed, ion). *Consider also:* alcohol(ic,ism), compulsive gambl(er,ers,ing), inhaling gasoline, glue sniffing, drug dependen(t,ce), drug abuse(r,rs), substance abuse(r,rs), eating disorder(s), sex addict(s,ion), smok(er,ers,ing), dipsomania, narcotic addiction, drug addiction, heroin addiction, co-dependen(ce,t,cy), addictive relationship(s), workaholi(c,cs,sm), shopaholi(c,cs,sm). *See also* Alcoholism; Behavior disorders; Co-dependency; Computer addiction; Drug addiction; Drug use; Drug withdrawal; Drugs in athletics; Eating disorders; Gateway drugs; Substance abuse; Substance dependence.

Addiction, alcohol. See *Alcoholism.*

Addiction, alcoholic. See *Alcoholism.*

Addiction, computer. See *Computer addiction.*

Addiction, cross. See *Cross addiction.*

Addiction, drug. See *Drug addiction.*

Addiction, hospital. See *Factitious disorders.*

Addiction, Internet. See *Computer addiction.*

Additives, feed. See *Food additives.*

Additives, food. See *Food additives.*

Address (location). See *Place of business; Place of residence.*

Addresses (public speaking). See *Lectures and lecturing.*

Adhocracies. Adhocra(cy,cies,tic). Ad hocrac(cy,cies,tic). Organ(ic,ismic) organization(s). Organization(s) without structure. Continuous restructuring. *Consider also:* kaizen, task culture(s), governance without government, ad hoc working group(s), task force(s), expert group(s), operating adhocra(cy,cies,tic), administrative adhocra(cy,cies,tic). *See also* Boundaryless organizations; Contracting out; Decentralization; Interorganizational networks; Just-in-time manufacturing; Management methods; Organizational structure; Subcontracting; Teaming; Virtual organizations.

Adjournment. Adjourn(ed,ing,ment). Discontinu(e,ed,ing,ance). Dissolv(e, ed,ing). Dissolution. Defer(ral,red, ring,ment). Clos(e,ed,ing,ure). Terminat(e,ed,ing). End(ed,ing). *Consider also:* suspen(d,ded,ding,sion), delay(ed,ing), postpon(e,ed,ing,ement), intermission(s), interrupt(ed,ing, ion,ions), recess(ed,es,ing). *See also* Closure; Delays; End; Ends; Epilogues; Finale; Legal procedures.

Adjudication. Adjudicat(e,ed,ing,ion, ive,or,ors). Adjudg(e,ed,ment,ing). Decree(s,d,ing). Arbitrat(e,ed,ing,ion). Litigat(e,ed,ing,ion). *Choose from:* court, judicial, judge(s), umpire(s), referee(s) *with:* opinion(s), decision(s), determination(s), decree(s,ing), ruling(s). *See also* Due process; Legal procedures.

Adjustment (to environment). Adjust(ed, ing,ment,ments) to environment. Acclimatiz(e,ed,ing,ation). Acclimat(e, ed,ing,ion). Balancing. Align(ed, ing,ment). Mak(e,ing) concession(s). Compromis(e,ed,es,ing). Maladapt(ed, ing,ion,ions). Maladjust(ed,ing, ment,ments). *Choose from:* adjust(ed, ing,ment,ments), reaction(s), survival, transition(s), orient(ed,ing,ation,ations), accept(ed,ing,ance), cop(e,ed,ing), habituat(e,ed,ing,ion,ions), readjust(ed, ing,ment,ments), accomodat(ed,ing, ation,ations), acculturat(ed,ing,ion), naturaliz(e,ed,ing,ation), familiariz(e,ed, ing,ation), personaliz(e,ed,ing,ation), evolution, evolv(e,ed,ing) *with:* environment(s,al), surrounding(s), circumstance(s), situation(s), society, social(ly), school(s), vocation(al), marital, condition(s), milieu, noise, pollution, climat(e,ic), season(s,al), winter, summer, temperature, setting(s), isolat(e,ed,ing,ion), crowd(s,ed,ing), ecology, habitat, communit(y,ies), relocation, resettlement. *See also* Acclimatization; Acculturation; Adaptation; Adjustment disorders; Birth adjustment; Childhood adjustment disorders; Conformity (personality); Cooptation; Coping; Counseling; Culture shock; Deinstitutionalization; Dyssocial reaction; Emotional adjustment; Environment; Environmental effects; Hospital environment; Life change events; Life stage transitions; Loss adjustment; Occupational adjustment; Orientation; Personal adjustment; Problems; Psychosocial readjustment; Rehabilitation; School adjustment; Social adjustment; Social conformity; Social support; Social support networks; Socialization; Stress management; Temperature effects; Well being.

Adjustment, birth. See *Birth adjustment.*

Adjustment, emotional. See *Emotional adjustment.*

Adjustment, environmental. See *Adjustment (to environment).*

Adjustment, loss. See *Loss adjustment.*

Adjustment, marital. See *Marital conflict; Marital relationship.*

Adjustment, occupational. See *Occupational adjustment.*

Adjustment, personal. See *Personal adjustment.*

Adjustment, school. See *School adjustment.*

Adjustment, social. See *Social adjustment.*

Adjustment, vocational. See *Occupational adjustment.*

Adjustment assistance, trade. See *Trade protection.*

Adjustment disorders. Adjustment disorder(s). *Choose from:* adjustment *with:* disorder(s), reaction(s). *Choose from:* reactive, reaction(s) *with:* depress(ive,ion), disorder(s). *Consider also:* maladjust(ed,ment), maladapt(ed, ation), situational disorder(s). *See also* Behavior problems; Child reactive disorders; Dyssocial reaction; Emotional adjustment; Reactive depression.

Adjustment disorders, childhood. See *Childhood adjustment disorders.*

Administration. Administrat(ive,ion,or,ors). Direct(ed,ing). Govern(ed,ing,ance). *Consider also:* management, manager(s), utilization of resource(s), management-by-objective(s), supervis(ion,ory), time management, superintend(ed,ing), management team(s), participative decision making, trustee(s,ship,ships), organizational objective(s), management information system(s), planning, polic(y,ies), coordinat(e,ed,ing,ion), direct(ed,ing, ion), quality control, quality assurance, cost benefit analys(is,es), bureaucrac(y, ies), program management. *See also* Administrative policy; Administrative problems; Administrative procedures; Administrators; Budgets; Business administration; Committees; Coordination (interpersonal); Educational administration; Governing; Governing boards; Leadership; Library administration; Management methods; Military administration; Organizational effectiveness; Participative management; Personnel management; Planning; Policy implementation; Policy making; Public administration; Quality control; Resource allocation.

Administration, business. See *Business administration.*

Administration, customs. See *Customs administration.*

Administration, educational. See *Educational administration.*

Administration, library. See *Library administration.*

Administration, military. See *Military administration.*

Administration, public. See *Public administration.*

Administration, self. See *Self administration.*

Administration of estates. Administ(er, erred,ration) of estate(s). *Choose from:* manag(e,ed,ing) administ(er,erred, ration), trustee(s), executor(s) *with:* estate(s), inheritance(s), asset(s), propert(y,ies), holding(s), belonging(s). *See also* Asset management; Estate planning; Estates (law); Inheritance; Legacies.

Administrative agencies. Administrative agenc(y,ies). Administrative unit(s). *Choose from:* management, governing, policy-making, supervisory *with:* department(s), bureau(s), organization(s), unit(s), agenc(y,ies), commission(s), board(s), division(s), corporation(s). *Consider also:* regulatory agenc(y,ies), Federal Trade Commission, Public Service Commission, etc. *See also* Administrative courts; Public administration.

Administrative courts. Administrative court(s). Administrative tribunal(s). *Consider also:* administrative judge(s). *See also* Administrative agencies; Courts.

Administrative law. Administrative law(s). Administrative adjudication. Regulatory decision(s). Regulatory act(s). *Choose from:* administrative, executive *with:* rule(making,s), interpretation(s), regulat(e,ed,ory,ion), deregulat(e,ed,ion), order(s). *See also* Administrative policy; Public policy.

Administrative policy. Administrative polic(y,ies). *Choose from:* administrative, official, executive, presidential, agency *with:* polic(y,ies), guideline(s), rule(s), principle(s), directive(s), regulation(s), order(s). *See also* Administrative law; Administrative problems; Policy implementation; Personnel policy; Policy; Policy analysis; Policy evaluation; Policy making.

Administrative problems. Administrative problem(s). *Choose from:* administrat(ion,ive), supervisor(s,y), managerial, management, executive(s), personnel *with:* problem(s), difficult(y,ies), conflict(s), issue(s), question(s), dispute(s), concern(s). *See also* Administration; Problems; Conflict; Industrial conflict.

Administrative procedure. Administrative procedure(s). Administrative proceeding(s). *Consider also:* Code of Federal Regulations. *See also* Administration; Policy implementation.

Administrative responsibility. Administrat(ive,or) responsibilit(y,ies). Administrat(ive,or) accountab(le,ity). *Choose from:* administrat(ive,or,ors), executive(s), manager(s,ial), official(s) *with:* responsibilit(y,ies), accountab(le, ity), answerab(le,ity), liab(le,ility,ilities), dut(y,ies). *See also* Administrators; Ministerial responsibility (government); Public administration.

Administrators. Administrator(s). Administrative personnel. Management personnel. Administrative staff. Executive(s). Executive officer(s). CEO(s). Chief executive officer(s). Manager(s). Supervisor(s). Boss(es). Superintendent(s). Leader(s). Authorit(y,ies). Director(ate,ship,s). Employer(s). Overseer(s). Fore(man,men). Captain(s). Commander(s). President(s). Chief(s). Governor(s). Dean(s). Chair(man,men, women,woman,person,persons). Chair person(s). Coordinator(s). Department head(s). Development officer(s). Officer(s) of the company. Managerial personnel. Administration. Officials. Top official(s). Officer(s). Principal(s). Trustee(s). Middle level manage(r,rs, ment). Top level manage(r,rs,ment).

Consider also: vice president(s), assistant principal(s), personnel director(s), comptroller(s), admissions officer(s), registrar(s), etc. *See also* Administration; Administrative problems; Administrative responsibility; Chief executive officers; Educational administrators; Executive ability; Leadership; Management functions; Managers; Nurse administrators; Personnel management; Policy making; Power structure; Presidents; Professional personnel; Supervision.

Administrators, educational. See *Educational administrators.*

Administrators, nurse. See *Nurse administrators.*

Administrators, school. See *Educational administrators.*

Admiration. Admir(e,ed,ing,ation). High(ly) regard(ed). Esteem(ed). High opinion. Venerat(e,ed,ing,ion). Rever(ed,ing,ence). Appreciat(e,ed, ing,ion). Extol(led,ling). Idoliz(e,ed, ing). Ador(e,ed,ing,ation). Approbat(e, ed,ing,ion). Prais(e,ed,ing,es). *Consider also:* philosemit(ic,ism), anglophil(e,es), philomath(ic). *See also* Charisma; Commemoration; Commendation; Eulogies; Flattery; Glory; Honored (esteem); Prestige; Recognition (achievement); Reputation; Respect; Social acceptance; Social desirability; Tribute.

Admission, patient. See *Patient admission.*

Admission criteria, school. See *School admission criteria.*

Admissions. Admission(s). Admit(tance, ted,ting). Readmit(ted,ting). Readmission(s). Entr(y,ies,ance). Reception. Access. Accept(ed,ance). *Consider also:* ingress, initiation(s), introduction(s), open door(s), inclu(de,ded,ding,sive,sion), welcom(e,ed,ing). *See also* Abortion applicants; Hospitalization; Institutionalization (persons); Intake (agency); Patient admission; Patient readmission; Psychiatric hospitalization; School admission criteria; Social acceptance.

Adobe. See *Dwellings.*

Adolescence. Adolescen(ce,t,ts). Youth. Teen(s,age,aged,ager,agers). Juvenile(s). Preadolescen(ce,t,ts). Menarche. Pubert(al,y). Young adult(s,hood). Preteen(s). Tweenie(s). Minor(s). Pubescen(ce,t). Young people. *Choose from:* junior high school, high school, secondary school *with:* student(s), freshm(an,en), sophomore(s), junior(s), senior(s). *Consider also:* 13th generation, millenial generation, specific ages or grades, under 21, age(d) 13, 14 yr old(s), 14 year(s) old, Grade 12, twelfth grade, etc. *See also* Adolescent behavior; Adolescent development; High school

students; Junior high school students; Juvenile delinquency; Parent adolescent relations; Premarital sexual behavior; Puberty; Runaways; Sexual maturation; Single mothers; Social dating; Statutory rape; Teenage fathers; Teenage mothers; Teenage suicide; Young adults; Youth culture; Youth movements; Youth organizations.

Adolescent behavior. Adolescent behavior(s). *Choose from:* adolescen(t,ts,ce), young adult(s), youth, teen(age,ager,agers), preadolescen(t,ts, ce), high school student(s) *with:* behavior(s), conduct, dating, performance, habit(s), adjustment, aggressive(ness), assertive(ness), communicat(e,ed,ing,ion), competitive(ness), cooperative(ness), demeanor, disobedien(t,ce), drinking, drug(s), group(s), peer influence(s), inhibit(ed,ion,ions), leadership, life style(s), misbehavior, sports, participat(e,ed,ing,ion), persistence, active, activit(y,ies), response(s), risk taking, self control, shy(ness), smoking, sociab(le,ility), social behavior, sex(ual,ually,uality), conformity, dominance, substance abuse(r,rs), alcohol(ic,ics,ism). *See also* Adolescence; Adolescent development; Behavior; Behavior development; Behavior patterns; Behavior problems; Family relations; Juvenile delinquency; Parent adolescent relations; Runaways; Single mothers; Social behavior disorders; Social dating; Teenage fathers; Teenage mothers; Teenage suicide; Unwanted pregnancy; Young adults; Youth culture; Youth movements; Youth organizations.

Adolescent development. Adolescent development. *Choose from:* adolescen(t, ts,ce), teen(s), teenage(r,rs), youth, high school student(s), pre-teen(s), pre-adolescent(s) *with:* develop(ing,ed, ment), matur(e,ed,ing,ation), identity formation, self actualization, growth, developmental stage(s). *See also* Adolescence; Adolescent behavior; Child development; Developmental stages; Human development; Physical development; Psychosexual development; Puberty; Sex education; Sexual maturation.

Adolescent fathers. See *Teenage fathers.*

Adolescent mothers. See *Teenage mothers.*

Adolescent parent relations. See *Parent adolescent relations.*

Adolescent pregnancy. See *Teenage mothers.*

Adolescents. See *Adolescence.*

Adopted children. Adopted child(ren). Adoptee(s). *Choose from:* adopted *with:* child(ren), adolescent(s), daughter(s), son(s), offspring, male(s), female(s),

infant(s), bab(y,ies). *Consider also:* black market bab(y,ies). *See also* Adoption; Adoptive parents; Foster children; Stepfamily.

Adoption. Adopt(ion,ed,ive,ee,ees). Permanen(t,cy) placement. *Consider also:* child placement(s), foster care, foster home(s), foster parent(s), surrogate parent(s,hood), befriend(ed, ing). *See also* Adopted children; Adoptive parents; Biological family; Child custody; Kinship; Legal procedures; Placement (of a dependent person); Stepfamily.

Adoption, interracial. See *Interethnic families.*

Adoption, mixed race. See *Interethnic families.*

Adoption, trans-racial. See *Interethnic families.*

Adoption of ideas. Adopt(ed,ing,ion) of idea(s). *Choose from:* adopt(ed,ing,ion), accept(ed,ing), incorporat(e,ed,ing,ion), acquir(e,ed,ing), assum(e,ed,ing), embrac(e,ed,ing) *with:* idea(s), concept(s), view(s,point,points), outlook(s), theor(y,ies), practice(s), innovation(s), project(s), program(s), technolog(y,ies). *See also* Attitude change; Diffusion; Diffusion of innovation; Educational innovations; Information dissemination; Innovations.

Adoptive parents. Adopt(ive,ing,ed) parent(s,hood). *Choose from:* adopt(ive,ing,ed) *with:* parent(s,hood), famil(y,ies), mother(s), father(s). *See also* Adoption; Family members; Parents; Stepfamily.

Adroitness. See *Gifted; Intelligence.*

Ads, musical. See *Musical ads.*

Adult. Adult(s,hood). Over 18. Over 21. Maturity. Prime of life. Full grown. Voting age. Age of majority. Middle aged. Mature person(s). Men. Man. Women. Woman. Childbearing age. Being of age. Grownup(s). *See also* Adult development; Adult offspring; Adult students; Age groups; Elderly; Human life cycle; Middle age; Young adults.

Adult basic education. Adult basic education. *Choose from:* adult(s,hood) *with:* basic, fundamental, remedial, literacy *with:* education, class(es), curriculum, skill(s). *See also* Adult education; Adult literacy; Basic education; Literacy programs; Primary education.

Adult child relations. See *Parent child relations.*

Adult children. See *Adult offspring.*

Adult day care. Adult day care. Partial hospitalization. *Choose from:* adult(s), geriatric, elderly *with:* day(time) *with:*

hospitaliz(ed,ation), center(s), care, hospital(s), treatment. *See also* Adult foster care; Caregivers; Dependent parents; Filial responsibility; Home visiting programs.

Adult development. Adult development. Successful aging. *Choose from:* adult(s,hood), midlife, middle aged, old age, life-span *with:* develop(ed,ing, ment), matur(ed,ing,ation), identity development, growth, self-realization, self-actualization, personality integration, integrity, passage(s), transition(s). *See also* Adult education; Aging; Developmental stages; Life stage transitions; Lifelong learning; Midlife crisis; Physiological aging; Psychological aging.

Adult education. Adult education. *Choose from:* adult(s,hood), continuing, lifelong, postsecondary, parent(ing,hood), preretirement, veteran(s) *with:* education(al), learning, class(es), instruction(al). *Consider also:* andragog(y,ical), androgog(y,ical). *See also* Adult basic education; Adult development; Adult students; Continuing education; Lifelong learning; Parent training; Professional education; Professional development; Self education.

Adult ego state. See *Emotional maturity.*

Adult entertainment. Adult entertainment. Porn(o,ographic,ography). Erotica. Centerfold(s). Sexually explicit. Explicit sexual stimuli. Hard core pornography. X-rated. Sin strip(s). Strip joint(s). Erotic club(s). Massage parlor(s). Sexually oriented advertising. Hustler magazine. Playboy. Penthouse. Pos(ed,ing) nude. Sex shop(s). Dial-a-porn. *Choose from:* obscen(e,ity), indecen(t,cy), explicit, adult, X-rated, erotic, suggestive, nude, topless, kinky, porn(o,ographic,ography), bawdy, sexually provocative, hard core *with:* picture(s), movie(s), film(s), video(s), literature, book(s,stores), show(s), magazine(s), material(s), radio, club(s), advertis(ments,ing), theater(s), theatrical performance(s), entertain(ment,er,ers). *Consider also:* escort agenc(y,ies), massage parlour(s), video-peep masturbation booth(s), porn shop(s), peep show(s), stripper(s), strip tease, strip bar(s), indecent table dancing. *See also* Bawdy songs; Belly dance; Burlesque; Cybersex; Dirty dancing; Entertainment; Entertainment industry; Images of women; Indecent communications; Nightclubs; Obscenity; Pornography; Prurience; Sexism.

Adult foster care. Adult foster care. *Choose from:* adult(s,hood), elderly, geriatric, retarded person(s), older person(s) *with:* foster care, protective service(s), boarding home(s). *See also* Adult day

care; Boardinghouses; Custodial care; Foster home care; Group homes; Homes for the elderly; Sheltered housing.

Adult games. Adult game(s). *Choose from:* adult(s), grownup(s), grown-up(s), party *with:* game(s), recreation(al), play(ed, ing), toy(s). *Consider also:* billiards, bridge, canasta, cribbage, card games, checker(s), chess, charades, dominoes, poker, bingo, Boggle, Trivial Pursuits, Monopoly, Scrabble, snooker, pool, shuffleboard, puzzle(s). *See also* Board games; Children's games ; Computer games; Electronic games; Leisure activities; Play.

Adult learning. See *Adult development; Lifelong learning.*

Adult literacy. Adult literacy. *Choose from:* adult(s,hood), universal, citizen(s), population *with:* litera(cy,te,tes), illitera(cy,te,tes). *See also* Adult basic education; Illiteracy; Information skills; Literacy programs; Reading skills; Writing.

Adult offspring. Adult offspring. Adult child(ren). Grown child(ren). Grownup child(ren). Adult son(s). Adult daughter(s). College-aged child(ren). Married daughter(s). Married son(s). *See also* Boomerang children; Caregiver burden; Dependent parents; Filial piety; Filial responsibility; Intergenerational relations; Parent child communication; Parent child relations.

Adult students. Adult student(s). Older learner(s). *Choose from:* adult(s), older, mature, elderly, reentry, nontraditional *with:* student(s), learner(s). *See also* Adult basic education; Adult education; Continuing education; Lifelong learning; Married students; Reentry students.

Adulteration, food. See *Food additives; Food contamination; Herbicides; Pesticides; Product tampering.*

Adultery. See *Extramarital relations.*

Adulthood. See *Adult.*

Adults. See *Adult.*

Adults, older. See *Aged 80 and over; Elderly.*

Adults, young. See *Young adults.*

Advance directives. Advance directive(s). Advance care planning. *Consider also:* living will(s), patient self-determination, do-not-resuscitate order(s), health care decision(s), end-of-life issue(s), durable power(s) of attorney, health care prox(y,ies). *See also* Do not resuscitate orders; Patient rights; Terminal care; Termination of treatment; Treatment withholding.

Advance organizers. Advance organizer(s). Prequestion(s). *Choose from:* advance, concept, graphic, structur(al,ed), visual, spatial, contextual *with:* organizer(s),

overview(s). *Consider also:* preview(s, ed,ing). *See also* Reading; Teaching methods.

Advanced countries. See *Developed countries.*

Advanced degrees. See *Academic degrees.*

Advanced developing countries. See *Newly industrializing economies.*

Advanced economies. See *Developed countries.*

Adventitious impairments. Adventitious impairment(s). *Choose from:* adventitious(ly), late *with:* handicap(ped,s), disabilit(y,ies), impair(ed,ment,ments), blind(ness), disabled, deaf(ness). *See also* Disability.

Adventure. Adventur(e,er,ers,ous,ism). Ventur(e,es). Tak(e,ing) risk(s). Daring enterprise(s). *See also* Quests; Risk taking.

Adventure stories. Adventure stor(y,ies). Tale(s) of adventure. *Choose from:* stor(y,ies), tale(s), yarn(s), anecdote(s), journalis(m,tic), series, fiction, account(s) *with:* adventur(e,es,ous, ousness,ly), daring, danger(s,ous, ousness), risk(s,y). *Consider also:* heroic tale(s), odyssey(s), epic novel(s), saga(s). *See also* Fiction; Heroes; Legends; Travel writing; Western fiction.

Adversarial. Adversarial. Accusatorial. Contentious(ness). Disputatious. Combative(ness). Argumentative. Quarrelsome. Contending. *See also* Personality traits.

Adversary. Adversar(y,ies). Opponent(s). Antagonist(s). Enem(y,ies). Competitor(s). Rival(s). Opposition. Combatant(s). Foe(s). Assailant(s). Contestant(s). *Consider also:* competition. *See also* Antagonism; Athletes; Competitive behavior; Enemies; Resistance.

Adverse reactions, drug. See *Drug effects.*

Adversity. Adversit(y,ies). Misfortune(s). Hardship(s). Affliction(s). Miser(y,ies). Woe(s). Bad luck. Calamit(y,ies). *Consider also:* contretemps, mischance, mishap(s), tragedy, unlucky, ruin(s,ed, ing,ation), misadventure(s), setback(s), distress(ed), suffering; depriv(ed,ation), destitut(e,ion), indigen(t,ce), poverty. *See also* Accidents; Catastrophes; Deprivation; Economic conditions; Economic problems; Hardships; Poverty; Tragedy.

Advertising. Advertis(e,ed,ing). Advertisement(s). Ad(s). Marketing. Commercial(s). Jingle(s). Infomercial(s). Advertorial(s). Publici(ty,ze). Junk mail. Retail promotion(s). Promotional material(s). Promotion campaign(s). Campaign sponsor. Handbill(s). Propagand(a,ize,izing). Counter detailing. Madison Ave. Yellow pages. TV spot(s). Billboard(s). Telemarketing. Bumper sticker(s). *Consider also:* product positioning, blurb(s), broadside(s), placard(s), handbill(s), spot announcement(s). *See also* Advertising agencies; Advertising campaigns; Brand loyalty; Classified advertising; Comparative advertising; Database marketing; Declarations; Direct mail advertising; Direct marketing; Emotional appeal; Fraudulent advertising; Global campaigns; Infomercials; Junk email; Magazine advertising; Market development; Marketing; Marketing plans; Marketing strategies; Mass media; Medical advertising; Musical ads; Newspapaer advertising; Orders (business); Outdoor advertising; Political advertising; Popular culture; Promotion (business); Propaganda; Public relations; Religious advertising; Sales; Slogans; Target marketing; Telemarketing.

Advertising, advocacy. See *Advocacy advertising.*

Advertising, classified. See *Classified advertising.*

Advertising, comparative. See *Comparative advertising.*

Advertising, direct mail. See *Direct mail advertising.*

Advertising, false. See *Fraudulent advertising.*

Advertising, fraudulent. See *Fraudulent advertising.*

Advertising, magazine. See *Magazine advertising.*

Advertising, medical. See *Medical advertising.*

Advertising, negative. See *Comparative advertising.*

Advertising, newspaper. See *Newspaper advertising.*

Advertising, opinion. See *Advocacy advertising.*

Advertising, outdoor. See *Outdoor advertising.*

Advertising, political. See *Political advertising.*

Advertising, religious. See *Religious advertising.*

Advertising agencies. Advertising agenc(y,ies). Ad agenc(y,ies). Advertising firm(s). Public relation(s) agenc(y,ies). Public relations firm(s). Advertising shop(s). Advertising industry. *See also* Advertising; Business organizations; Promotion (business).

Advertising campaigns. Advertising campaign(s). *Choose from:* advertising, ad(s), marketing, promotion(al), public relations, publicity *with:* campaign(s), drive(s), solicitation(s), operation(s), canvass(ed,ing,er,ers). *Consider also:* telemarketing, business theatre, media promotion(s). *See also* Advertising; Brand identity; Campaigns; Comparative advertising; Marketing plans; Marketing strategies; Musical ads; Promotion (business); Telemarketing.

Advertising laws. Advertising law(s). *Consider also:* Federal Trade Commission regulations. *Choose from:* advertis(e,ement,ements,ing) promotional material(s), ad(s), billboard(s) *with:* law(s), control(led,s), regulat(e,ed,ion,ions), ban(ned,s), restrict(ed,ion,ions), prohibit(ed,ing, ion,ions), code(s) of ethics. *See also* Consumer protection.

Advertising research. Advertising research. *Choose from:* advertising, commercials, promotion(s,al), publicity *with:* research, pretest(ed,ing), survey(s), stud(y,ies), evaluat(e,ed,ion,ions), assess(ed,ing, ment), compar(e,ed,ing,ison,isons). *See also* Consumer behavior; Focus groups; Market research.

Advice. Advice. Advis(e,ed,ing,ement). Recommendation(d). Counsel(ed,ing). Consult(ed,ing,ation,ations). Admonition(s). Caution(ed,ing). *Consider also:* direction(s), guidance, opinion(s), exhortation(s), instruction(s), teaching(s), forewarning(s), warning(s). *See also* Academic advising; Advisors; Consultation; Exhortation; Vocational guidance.

Advising, academic. See *Academic advising.*

Advisors. Advisor(s,y). Adviser(s). Consultant(s). Mentor(s,ing,ship). Counselor(s). Expert(s). Guru(s). *Choose from:* lawyer(s), guide(s), confidant(s,e,es), coach(es), preceptor(s, ship), support relationship(s), master(s), therapist(s) *with:* apprentice(s), student(s), patient(s), client(s). *Consider also:* advisory group(s), councillor(s), cabinet member(s), minister(s). *See also* Advice; Attorneys; Advisory committees; Consultants; Experts; Mentors; Teachers; Technical assistance; Think tanks.

Advisory committees. Advisory committee(s). *Choose from:* advisory, resident(s), worker(s), community, review, consultative, citizen(s), consumer(s), user(s), director(s), expert(s) *with:* committee(s), board(s), participation, bod(y,ies), group(s), panel(s), task force(s), commission(s), council(s). *Consider also:* cabinet member(s), privy council(s), president(ial,s) cabinet(s). *See also* Advisors; Committees; Consultants; Governing boards.

Advisory groups. See *Advisory committees.*

Advocacy. Advocacy. Advocat(e,es,ed,ing). Adopt(ed,ing) cause(s). Apologist(s). Apostle(s). Ombuds(men,man,woman, women,person,persons). Lobb(y,ies, ying). Political action committee(s). PAC(S). Speaking out. Support(ed,ing, er,ers). Back(ing,er,ers). Espous(e,ed, ing,al). Defend(ing,er,ers). Champion(ed,ing). Represent(ed,ing). Protect(ion,ing,or,ors). *Choose from:* stand(ing) up, plead(ing), take part, speak(ing) out *with:* behalf, favor(ed, ing). *Consider also:* representative(s), linkage worker(s), expediter(s), campaigner(s), exponent(s), proponent(s), sponsor(s), subsidizer(s), spokesperson(s), adherent(s), champion(s), endorser(s). *See also* Apostles; Change agents; Child advocacy; Citizen participation; Consumer organizations; Defense (verbal); Foster (promote); Interest groups; Lobbying; Ombudsmen; Patient advocacy; Political action; Promotion (business); Protest movements; Public relations; Representatives; Social action.

Advocacy, child. See *Child advocacy.*

Advocacy, patient. See *Patient advocacy.*

Advocacy advertising. Advocacy advertising. Opinion advertising. Advocacy message(s). Issue advocacy ad(s,vertising,vertisement,vertisements). Issue advocacy spending. Issue advocacy money. *Choose from:* political issue(s), advocacy group(s), issue advocacy, single-issue group(s) *with:* commercial(s), voter guide(s), direct mail, advertising campaign(s), ad(s,vertising,vertisement,vertisements). *Consider also:* cause-related marketing, public service announcement(s). *See also* Campaign finance reform; Campaign funds; Corporate image; Financial disclosure; Political campaigns; Political contributions; Promotion (business); Public relations.

Advocacy groups. See *Advocacy; Change agents; Interest groups; Lobbying; Social movements.*

Advocates. See *Advocacy.*

Advocates, consumer. See *Consumer organizations.*

Aerial bombing. See *Aerial warfare.*

Aerial reconnaissance. Aerial reconnaissance. *Choose from:* aerial, plane(s), satellite(s), flight(s) *with:* reconnaissance, observ(e,ed,ing,ation,ations, er,ers), monitor(ed,ing,s), photo(s,graph, graphs,graphy), spy(ing), spie(s,d). *Consider also:* satellite image(s). *See also* Aerial warfare; Combat; Espionage; Geographic information systems; Military airplanes; Military intelligence; Surveillance of citizens.

Aerial warfare. Aerial warfare. Air war(s,fare). Aerial war(s,fare). Air combat. Bombing mission(s). Air strike(s). Air battle(s). Air attack(s). Strategic bombing(s). Jets down warplane(s). No-fly zone violation(s). Sortie(s). Cruise missile(s). Patriot missile(s). Star war(s). *Choose from:* air, aerial, aircraft, plane(s), jet(s), warplane(s) *with:* strike(s), bomb(ed, ing), assault(s,ed,ing), attack(s,ed,ing), reconnaissance, mission(s), strateg(y, ic,ies), tactic(s,al), weapons(s), power, defense(s), force(s), war(s,fare), operation(s), exercise(s), maneuver(s), clash(es), conflict(s), skirmish(es), role(s), mission(s), tactic(s), campaign(s), battle(s), combat, bomb(ed,ing,ings), attack(s,ed,ing), action(s), movement(s), engagement(s), undertaking(s), interven(e,ed,ing, tion,tions), offensive(s). *See also* Air bases; Air power; Aircraft; Antiaircraft artillery; Assault (battle); Ballistic missiles; Combat; Military airplanes; Military operations.

Aerialists. Aerialist(s). Trapeze artist(s). Tightrope walker(s). Tightrope performer(s). High wire performer(s). *See also* Gymnastics.

Aeronautical museums. Aeronautical museum(s). Air and space museum(s). Aerospace museum(s). *See also* Aircraft; Astronauts; Exhibits; Flying machines; Museums; Trade shows.

Aeronautical sports. Aeronautical sport(s). Aerosport(s). Air sport(s). *Consider also:* hang glid(ing,er,ers), ballooning, gas balloon(s), hot air balloon(s), thermal flight(s), wave flight(s), Skydiv(ing,er,ers). *See also* Extreme sports; Sports.

Aerophagy. Aerophag(y,ia). Nervous eructation. *Choose from:* air *with:* swallow(ed,ing), drink(ing). *See also* Habits.

Aerospace industries. Aerospace industries. *Choose from:* aerospace, space, aviation, aircraft, airline(s), air travel, satellite(s), spaceflight *with:* compan(y,ies), corporat(e,ion,ions), industr(y,ies), firm(s), multinational(s), procurement, military industrial complex, Rohr, Lockheed, Boeing, Northrup, Martin Marietta, etc. *See also* Aircraft; Aircraft industry; Air transportation; Aviation safety.

Aerospace medicine. Aerospace medicine. *Choose from:* aerospace, space, aviation, flying, air travel, airline(s), altitude, decompression, acceleration *with:* medicine, sick(ness), ill(ness,nesses), disorder(s), neurasthenia. *Consider also:* aeroneurosis. *See also* Air transportation; Military medical personnel.

Aerospace personnel. Aerospace personnel. *Choose from:* aircraft, airline(s), aerospace, flight, air force, helicopter(s), inflight, jet *with:* personnel, crew(s), staff, pilot(s), copilot(s), officer(s), instructor(s), trainee(s), attendant(s). *Consider also:* air traffic controller(s), groundcrew(s), astronaut(s), aviator(s), air(man,men,women,woman,crew,crews). *See also* Astronauts; Personnel.

Aesthetic education. Aesthetic education. *Choose from:* aesthetic, esthetic, artistic, art(s), music(al), film(s) *with:* education, development, literacy, experience(s), curriculum, socialization, appreciation. *See also* Aesthetic preferences; Aesthetics; Art education; Cultural activities; Cultural events; Dance education; Music education.

Aesthetic preferences. Aesthetic preference(s). *Choose from:* aesthetic(s), esthetic(s), art(istic), music(al), film(s), poetry, sculpture, litera(ry,ture) *with:* preference(s), appreciation, sensitivity, taste(s,fulness), attitude(s), value(s), judgment(s), choice(s), development, satisfaction, discriminat(ion,ing). *See also* Aesthetic education; Aesthetics; Art appreciation; Art criticism; Designs; Music criticism; Preferences; Social values.

Aestheticism. Aestheticis(m,t,ts). Estheticis(m,t,ts). Art for art's sake. *Consider also:* Dante Gabriel Rossetti, Edward Burne-Jones, Algernon Charles Swinburne, Oscar Wilde, Walter Pater, Aubrey Beardsley, The Yellow Book. *See also* Decadence (Literary movement); Symbolist movement.

Aesthetics. Aesthetic(ally,s). Esthetic(ally,s). Art appreciation. Music appreciation. Beaut(iful,y). Good taste. Tasteful. Artistic. Classic. Simpl(e,icity). Pur(e,ity). Graceful(ness). Delicacy. Delicate(ness). Lovel(y,iness). Attractive(ness). Exquisite(ness). Polished. Discriminating. Fastidious(ness). Refined. Cultivated. Elegan(t,ce). Connoisseur. Aesthet(e,ician). Gourmet(s). *See also* Art appreciation; Art criticism; Artistic styles; Arts; Camp (aesthetics); Classic (standard); Connoisseurs; Cultural values; Decorative arts; Elegance; Form (aesthetics); Formalism; Literary criticism; Literary style; Social values.

Aetiology. See *Etiology.*

Affairs, foreign. See *Detente; Foreign policy; International relations.*

Affairs, international. See *International relations.*

Affect. Affect(ive,ivity). Mood(s). Emotion(s,al,ality). Feeling(s). Feeling tone(s). Affective process(es). Wish(es). Pleasure principle. Emotional state(s). *See also* Affective behavior; Affective disorders; Attitudes; Emotions; Morale; Psychological distress; Personality traits.

Affect hunger. See *Psychosocial deprivation.*

Affection. Affection(ate,al). Lov(e,ed,ing). Caring. Devot(ed,ing,ion). Warmhearted(ness). Friend(ly,liness, ship). Fond(ly,ness). Endear(ing,ment). Amity. Lik(e,ed,ing). *Consider also:* object attachment, bonding. *See also* Affiliation motivation; Emotions; Forms of affection; Friendliness; Interpersonal attraction; Interpersonal relations; Love.

Affection, forms of. See *Forms of affection.*

Affective behavior. Affective behavior(s). Emotion(s,ality). Affect(ivity). Affective symptom(s). Feeling(s). *Choose from:* emotional, affective *with:* state(s), behavior(s), response(s), expression(s), reciprocity, reciprocal. *Consider also:* affectionate, angry, anxious, bored, depersonalized, depressed, euphoric, excited, expressive, fearful, frustrated, grief, guilty, happy, hatred, hostile, impassioned, jealous, loving, passionate, playful, sensuous, sentimental, spontaneous, teasing *with:* behavior(s). *See also* Attachment behavior; Attitudes; Behavior; Emotional responses; Interests; Prosocial behavior.

Affective disorder, seasonal. See *Seasonal affective disorder.*

Affective disorders. Affective disorder(s). *Choose from:* affective, reactive, mani(a,c,cs), bipolar, involutional *with:* disorder(s), illness(es), depression, psychotic disorder(s), neurotic disorder(s), neuros(es,is), psychos(is,es), disturbance(s). Reactive psychotic depression. Mani(a,c,cs). Manic depress(ion,ive). *See also* Affective symptoms; Alexithymia; Anxiety disorders; Major depression; Mania; Manic disorder; Neurotic depressive reaction.

Affective education. See *Humanistic education.*

Affective symptoms. Affective symptoms. Affectivity. *Choose from:* affect(ive), emotion(s,al), neurotic, depressive *with:* symptom(s), state(s), sign(s), inappropriate, loss, ambivalen(t,ce), flat(ten, tened,tening), blunt(ed,ing), correlate(s). *Consider also:* alexithymia, depersonalization, anxiety, depression, elation, schizoaffective. *See also* Alexithymia; Depersonalization disorder; Depression (psychology); Emotionally disturbed; Mania.

Affectivity. See *Affective symptoms.*

Affidavit. Affidavit(s). Sworn statement(s). Sworn declaration(s). *Consider also:* affirmation(s), deposition(s), oath(s), pledge(s), testimony, written declaration(s), attest(ed,ing,ation), testament(s). *See also* Agreement (document); Assertions; Deposition;

Evidence; Testimony; Withholding evidence; Witness tampering; Witnesses.

Affiliation (businesses). Affiliat(e,ed,es, ion). Branch(es). Member(s,ship,ships). Associat(e,ed,ion,ions,ing). Union(s). Federat(e,ed,ing,ion,ions). Subsidiar(y, ies). Piggyback. Joint venture(s). Related corporation(s). Alliance(s). Allies. Merge(d,r,rs). Franchise(d,s). Partner(s,ship,ships). Amalgamation(s). Confederation(s). League(s). *Consider also:* populated joint venture(s), unpopulated joint venture(s), shell compan(y,ies). *See also* Alliances; Associates; Branch operations; Cartels; Consortia; Corporate networks; Federations; Interorganizational networks; Joint ventures; Mergers; Organizational affiliation; Partners; Strategic alliances; Subsidiary management; Subsidiaries; Teaming; Trade associations.

Affiliation (personal). See *Organization membership.*

Affiliation, need for. See *Affiliation motivation.*

Affiliation, organizational. See *Organizational affiliation.*

Affiliation, political. See *Political affiliation.*

Affiliation, religious. See *Religious affiliation.*

Affiliation motivation. Affiliation motivation. *Choose from:* affiliat(ive,ion), join(ing), bond(ed,ing), interdependen(t,ce), belong(ing,ingness), interaction, association(al), intimacy, social, friendship *with:* need(s), dependence, drive(s), desire(s), motiv(e,es,ation). *Consider also:* social hunger. *See also* Affection; Belongingness; Friendliness; Friendship; Group feeling; Gregariousness; Needs; Organization membership; Sociability.

Affinal. Affin(al,e,es,ity). Relat(ed,ionship) by marriage. Co-affinal. In-laws. Son in-law. Daughter in-law. Mother in-law. Father in-law. *See also* Extended family; Kinship; Marriage.

Affirmations. See *Assertions.*

Affirmative action. Affirmative action. Executive Order 11246 as amended by Executive Order 11375. *Choose from:* equity, equality, equal opportunit(y,ies), fair(ness), nondiscriminatory *with:* race(s), racial, Black(s), people of color, African American(s), Afro-American(s), Negro(es), Oriental(s), Native American(s), Hispanic(s), Spanish-speaking, minorit(y,ies), woman, women, female(s), gender, sex, ethnic(ity), disabilit(y,ies), religion(s), protected class(es), education, quota(s), employment, hiring, promotion(s). *Consider also:* race sensitive

admission(s), equal(ize,ized,izing) opportunit(y,ies), equal employment opportunities, Title IX. *See also* Comparable worth; Cultural diversity; Desegregation; Educational opportunities; Employment discrimination; Employment of persons with disabilities; Employment opportunities; Equal education; Equal job opportunities; Equity (payment); Minority groups; Nonsexist education; Nontraditional careers; Nontraditional education; Personnel policy; Personnel selection; Preferential treatment; Quotas; Racial diversity; Racial integration; Racial segregation; School integration; School segregation; Sexism; Sexual division of labor; Sexual inequality; Tokenism; Working women.

Affixes. Affix(al,ial,es). *Consider also:* suffix(es), prefix(es). *See also* Clitics (grammar); Words.

Affluence. See *Wealth.*

Affordable housing. Affordable housing. *Choose from:* affordable, low income, inexpensive, low cost, low rent(s) *with:* hous(e,es,ing), dwelling(s), residence(s), apartment(s), home(s), living quarters, flat(s). *Consider also:* government housing, council house(s), urban homesteading, homeownership project(s), Habitat for Humanity, Habitat International, tenement(s), migrant housing, rent control. *See also* Home ownership; Homeless; House buying; Housing costs; Housing market; Housing policy; Public housing; Rent control; Subsidized housing.

Afforestation. See *Tree planting.*

Africa, North. See *North Africa.*

Africa, Sub-Saharan. See *Sub-Saharan Africa.*

African American language. See *Ebonics.*

African American songs. See *Afro-American music.*

African Americans. See *Blacks.*

African bloc. See *Pan-Africanism.*

African cultural groups. African cultural group(s). *Choose from:* North Africa(n), sub-Saharan *with:* indigenous, native(s), population(s), people(s), minority group(s), ethnic group(s), populace, tribe(s), resident(s), inhabitant(s). *North African, consider also names of specific groups, for example:* Berber(s), Copt(s), Murle(s), Nubian(s), Jerbian(s), Saharan tribe(s). *Sub-Saharan, consider also names of specific groups, for example:* Acoli, Akans, Ambo, Amharas, Anang, Anuaks, Arusha, Ashantis, Atuot, Azande, Baganda, Bakongo, Bakwiri, Bangwa, Bantus, Banyang, Banyankore, Barundi, Basuto, Bayaka, Budja, Bushmen, Chaga, Chewa, Chokosi, Dinka, Dogons, Duala, Ewe, Fan, Fon,

Fulahs, Ga, Gabra, Gallas, Gbaya, Hausas, Higi, Hottentots, Ibibios, Igbo, Isoka, Kalanga, Kamba, Kapsiki, Kikuyu, Korekore, Kpelle, Kumu, Kuria, Lala, Lebou, Lozi, Lugbara, Luo, Mandingo, Mang'anja, Manzes, Mashona, Mbiem, Mongo, Mpongwe, Nama Hottentots, Ndebele, Ndembu, Nguni, Nilo-Hamitic tribe(s), Nilotic tribe(s), Nuba, Nuer, Nupe, Nyakyusa, Nzakara, Padola, Pare, Rukuba, Sarakholle, Shilluks, Sisala, Suks, Taita, Thonga, Tswana, Turkana, Vasu, Venda, Wahehe, Wambulu, Wapangwa, Wolofs, Xosa, Yorubas, Zaramo, Zulus. *See also* African empires; Benue-Niger languages; Blacks; Chad languages; Cultural groups; Culture (anthropology); Culture change; Culture contact; Ethnic groups; Hamitic languages; Hunting and gathering societies; Indigenous populations; Kwa languages; Macro-Khoisan languages; Mandingo (Mande) languages; Niger-Congo languages, Atlantic (Western); Nilo-Saharan languages; North Africa; Pan-Africanism; Semitic languages; Sub-Saharan Africa; Sudanic languages; Traditional societies; Voltaic (Gur) languages.

African empires. African empire(s). African civilization(s). *Choose from:* African, North African, sub-Saharan *with:* civilization(s), culture(s), nation(s), dynast(y,ies), kingdom(s), empire(s), world(s), chiefdom(s), tribe(s). *North Africa, consider also names of specific groups or periods, for example:* Egyptology, Pharoah(s), Empire of the Nile, Amenhotep (I-IV), Thutmose (I-IV), Tut-ankh-amen, Ramses (I-III), Tanite Dynasty, Libyan Dynasty, Nubian Dynasty, Saite Dynasty, Old Kingdom [Empire] of Egypt, Middle Kingdom [Empire] of Egypt, New Kingdom [Empire] of Egypt, Berber(s), Kharejite Muslims, Coptic Christian(s,ity), Hafsid Empire, Maghreb(i) [Maghrib(i)] or names of countries. *Sub-Saharan Africa, consider also names of specific groups, for example:* Abomey Kingdom, Akan Civilization, Ankole Kingdom, Bacwezi Dynasty, Bantu monarch(y,ies) [civilization], Buganda Kingdom, Bunyoro Kingdom, Burundi Kingdom, Ha Kingdom, Ihangiro Kingdom, Kitara Empire, Kiziba Kingdom, Kongo Kingdom, Luba Kingdom, Mshope Chiefdom, Mutasa Dynasty, Njelu Chiefdom, Ovimbundu Chiefdom, Rotse Kingdom, Rwanda Kingdom, Shona Kingdom, Solima Yalunka Kingdom, Songhay Kingdom, Yeke Kingdom, Zulu Kingdom, etc. *See also* African cultural groups; Asian empires; Benue-Niger languages; Chad languages; Civilization; Cultural history; Culture contact; Dynasties; Hamitic languages; Historical periods; Indigenous populations; Islam;

Kwa languages; Macro-Khoisan languages; Mandingo (Mande) languages; Middle East; Niger-Congo languages, Atlantic (Western); Nilo-Saharan languages; North Africa; Pre-Columbian empires; Semitic languages; Sub-Saharan Africa; Sudanic languages; Traditional societies; Voltaic (Gur) languages; Western civilization; World history .

African languages. See *Benue-Niger languages; Chad languages; Hamitic languages; Kwa languages; Macro-Khoisan languages; Mandingo (Mande) languages; Niger-Congo Atlantic (Western) languages; Nilo-Saharan languages; Semitic languages; Sudanic languages; Voltaic (Gur) languages.*

African liberation movement. See *Anti-apartheid movement.*

Afro-American music. Afro-American music. *Choose from:* Afro-American, African-American, black, Negro, plantation, slave(s,ry), Harlem *with:* music(al,ally,ian,ians), song(s), tune(s), hymn(s), work song(s), spiritual(s), ballad(s), minstrel(s). *Consider also:* field holler(s), cakewalk(s), ring shout(s), ragtime, zydeco, reggae, calypso, salsa, steel band(s), blues, barrelhouse, boogie woogie, soul music, funk, disco music, Motown, rap music, rhythm and blues, hip hop. *See also* Afro-Cuban music; Blues (music); Folk dancing; Folk music; Funk (music); Gospel music; Jazz; Music; Popular music; Rhythm and blues; Rock and roll; Rock music; Soul music.

Afro Americans. See *Blacks.*

Afro-Cuban music. Afro-Cuban music. Afro-American music. *Choose from:* Afro-Cuban, African-Cuban *with:* music(al,ally,ian,ians), song(s), tune(s), hymn(s), jazz, rhythm(s), ballad(s), minstrel(s). *Consider also:* conga(s), rumba(s), yambu(s), guaguanco(s), mambo(s), chachacha(s), danzons(s). *See also* Afro-American music; Folk dancing; Folk music; Music.

Afrocentrism. Afrocentri(c,city,sm,st). Africentri(c,city,sm,st). African worldview(s). African centered. *Consider also:* African civilization(s), Africana studies, Africanity, Africological. *See also* Black nationalism; Cultural imperialism; Ethnic identity; Ethnocentrism; Eurocentrism; Racial identity; Worldview.

After school programs. After school program(s). *Choose from:* after school, after hours, after class, extended day *with:* program(s), activit(y,ies), playgroup(s), child care, day care. *See also* Child self care; Extracurricular activities.

Aftercare. Aftercare. After care. *Choose from:* posthospital, transitional, post-release, followup *with:* care, treatment, program(s). *Consider also:* halfway house(s), patient care planning, discharge planning, home care, posthospital adjustment, outpatient program(s), rehabilitation, family care, foster care. *See also* Foster home care; Halfway houses; Outpatient treatment; Patient discharge; Patient education; Posttreatment followup; Postoperative care; Self care.

Aftereffect, figural. See *Figural aftereffect.*

Afterimage. Afterimage(s). Aftersensation(s). Visual aftereffect(s). McCollough effect. Successive contrast. *Choose from:* persisting, continuing *with:* retinal, chromatic *with:* impression(s), aftereffect(s). *See also* Illusions (perception); Perceptual disturbances.

Afterworld. Afterworld. Heaven. Hell. Purgatory. Hades. Jahannam. *Consider also:* afterlife, hereafter, paradise. *See also* Future punishment; Heaven; Hell; Immortality; Religious beliefs; Voyages to the otherworld.

Agape. See *Love.*

Age. See *Age groups.*

Age (Psychology). Age. Life stage transition(s). Future-oriented age effect(s). Age-related difference(s). *Choose from:* ag(e,ed,ing) *with:* psycholog(y,ical), emotion(s,al), cognit(ive,ion), attitud(e,es,inal), personalit(y,ies). *See also* Age groups; Developmental stages.

Age, bronze. See *Bronze age.*

Age, childbearing. See *Childbearing age.*

Age, ice. See *Glacial epoch.*

Age, influence of on ability. See *Influence of age on ability.*

Age, information. See *Information society.*

Age, marriage. See *Marriage age.*

Age, maternal. See *Maternal age.*

Age, mental. See *Mental age.*

Age, middle. See *Middle age.*

Age, middle stone. See *Mesolithic period.*

Age, old. See *Aged 80 and over; Elderly.*

Age, paternal. See *Paternal age.*

Age determination by skeleton. Age determination by skeleton. *Choose from:* bone(s), skelet(al,on) *with:* age(s), maturity, maturation *with:* measur(e,ed, ing,ement), determin(e,ed,ing,ation), estimat(e,ed,es,ing,ion), assess(ed,ing, ment,ments). *See also* Age determination by teeth; Animal remains (archaeology); Archaeological chemistry; Archaeology; Bones; Human remains (archaeology); Physical anthropology.

Age determination by teeth. Age determination by teeth. *Choose from:* teeth, tooth, dental *with:* age(s), maturity, maturation *with:* measur(e,ed,ing, ement,ements), determin(e,ed,ing,ation), estimat(e,ed,es,ing,ion), assess(ed, ing,ment). *See also* Age determination by skeleton; Animal remains (archaeology); Archaeological chemistry; Archaeology; Human remains (archaeology); Physical anthropology.

Age differences. Age difference(s). *Choose from:* age, generation(al,s), *with:* factor(s), differen(ce,ces,tial,tials), compar(itive,ison,isons,ability), varia(bility,tion,tions), relat(ed,ionship), dependent, linked, influence(s), disparit(y,ies), discrepan(t,cy,cies), inequal(ity,ities), diversity, differentiation, distinction(s), dissimilarit(y,ies), characteristic(s), correlate(s), effect(s). *See also* Age discrepant marriages; Age groups; Child development; Gender differences; Generation gap; Human development; Intergenerational relations.

Age discrepant marriages. Age discrepant marriage(s). *Choose from:* age discrepant, age differen(ce,ces,tial,tials), age heterogamous, age disparity, relative age(s), age inequalit(y,ies), older, younger *with:* marriage(s), marr(y, ied,ying), spouse(s), husband(s), wife, wives, remarr(y,ied,ying), remarriage(s). *See also* Age differences; Marriage.

Age discrimination. Age discrimination. Age bias. Age consciousness. Adultism. Ageism. *Choose from:* accept(ance,ing), anxiet(y,ies), ascription(s), attitude(s), attribution(s), belief(s), bias(es,ed), concept(s), depict(ed,ing,ion), discriminat(e,ed,ing,ion), exclusion(ary), exclud(ed,ing), fear(s), phobi(a,as,c), image(s), injustice; misinterpret(ed, ing,ation) , label(s,ed,ing), labell(ed, ing), intoleran(t,ce), misunderstood, misunderstanding, misperception(s), ostracism, ostraciz(e,ed,ing), perception(s), prejudice(d,s), public opinion, stereotype(s), unequal treatment, unfair(ly,ness), stigma(s,tized) *with:* child(ren), juvenile(s), adolescen(t, ts,ce), high school student(s), youth, young adult(s), middle age(d), aging, aged, elder(ly), senior citizen(s), old age, older people, older worker(s), old persons. *Consider also:* intergenerational relation(s,ship,ships). *See also* Attitudes toward the aged; Injustice; Oppression; Public opinion; Social discrimination; Stereotyping.

Age groups. Age group(s). Cohort(s). *Choose from:* age *with:* group(s,ed), level(s), range(s), span. *Choose from:* stage(s) *with:* life, development(al). Lifestage(s). *Consider also:* lifetime(s), generation(s). *Consider also:* aged, adult(s,hood), adolescen(t,ts,ce), childhood, infan(t,ts,cy), middle age(d), newborn, neonatal, preschool, youth, young children, older adult(s,hood), school age, advanc(ed,ing) age, advanc(ed,ing) years, girlhood, boyhood, childhood. *See also* Adult; Adolescence; Age (Psychology); Age differences; Age of majority; Aged 80 and over; Ages of man; Children; Elderly; Generations; Human life cycle; Infants; Middle age; Peers; Young adults.

Age groups, developmental. See *Age groups.*

Age of father. See *Paternal age.*

Age of majority. Age of majority. Over 21. Legal drinking age. Minimum combat age. Old enough to vote. Rights of youth. Over 18. Age of consent. *Consider also:* sui juris. *See also* Age groups; Consent (law); Parental consent; Voting rights; Young adults.

Age of mother. See *Maternal age.*

Age regression (hypnotic). Age regression. Regressive hypnotherap(y,ies). *Choose from:* hypno(sis,tic), age *with:* regress(ion,ive). *Consider also:* earl(y,iest) memor(y,ies). *See also* Early experiences; Early memories; Hypnosis; Hypnotherapy; Psychotherapeutic techniques.

Aged. See *Elderly.*

Aged, attitudes toward. See *Age discrimination; Attitudes toward the aged.*

Aged, cruelty to. See *Elder abuse.*

Aged, extreme. See *Aged 80 and over.*

Aged 80 and over. Aged 80, 85, 90, 100, etc. Very old. Octogenarian(s). Nonagenarian(s). Centenarian(s). Very elderly. Extreme age(d). Oldest old. Old old. Long-lived. Later life. *Consider also:* frail elderly, age de retour. *See also* Age groups; Elderly; Frail elderly; Physiological aging; Psychological aging.

Ageism. See *Age discrimination; Attitudes toward the aged.*

Agencies. Agenc(y,ies). Organization(s). Center(s). Clinic(s). Association(s). Bureau(s). Institution(s). Charit(y,ies). Council(s). *Consider also:* business(es), organization(s). *See also* Accrediting agencies; Charities; Clinics; Delivery of services; Employment agencies; Government agencies; International organizations; News agencies; Nongovernmental organizations; Nonprofit organizations; Private agencies; Social agencies; Services; Voluntary health agencies.

Agencies, accrediting. See *Accrediting agencies.*

Agencies, administrative. See *Administrative agencies.*

Agencies, advertising. See *Advertising agencies.*

Agencies, employment. See *Employment agencies.*

Agencies, federal. See *Government agencies.*

Agencies, government. See *Government agencies.*

Agencies, international See *International organizations.*

Agencies, news. See *News agencies.*

Agencies, private. See *Private agencies.*

Agencies, social. See *Social agencies.*

Agencies, voluntary health. See *Voluntary health agencies.*

Agenda. Agend(a,as,um,ums). Program(s). Schedule(s). *Consider also:* itinerar(y,ies), outline(s), timetable(s). *See also* Appointments and schedules; Meetings; Time utilization.

Agent (Philosophy). Agent(s). Actant(s). Agency ex nihilo. Agency in medias res. Agent-based virtue(s). *Consider also:* negative, positive *with:* agency. *See also* Intentionality.

Agents. Agent(s). Attache(s). Courier(s). Representative(s). Deput(y,ies). Intermediar(y,ies). Prox(y,ies). Delegate(s). Ambassador(s). Emissar(y,ies). Diplomat(s). Envoy(s). Functionar(y,ies). Salesperson(s). Salespeople. Sales(man,men,woman, women). Agency team(s). Broker(s). Middle(man,men). Surrogate(s). *Consider also:* advocate(s), assistant(s), attorney(s), legat(e,or,ors), messenger(s), plenipotentiar(y,ies), internuncio(s), executor(s), trustee(s). *See also* Assistants; Brokers; Delegates; Messengers; Representatives.

Agents, antidepressive. See *Antidepressive agents.*

Agents, press. See *Press agents.*

Agents, sales. See *Sales personnel.*

Agents, tranquilizing. See *Tranquilizers.*

Ages, middle. See *Middle ages.*

Ages of man. Ages of man. Man's life span. Human life cycle. *See also* Age groups; Human development.

Aggregate economics. Aggregate economics. Macroeconomics. *Choose from:* total, aggregate *with:* consumption, employment, demand, markets, goods, services. *See also* Comprehensiveness; Production consumption relationship; Supply and demand; Supply side economics.

Aggression. Aggression. Aggressive behavior(s). *Choose from:* aggressive, agonistic, assaultive, hostile, explosive, violent, destructive, dangerous,

threatening, attack, belligerent, predatory, brutal, offensive, intrusive, competitive, noxious, combative, intimiding, warlike, quarrelsome, contentious, argumentative, disruptive *with:* behavior(s), act(s,ion,ions). *Consider also:* invasion(s), violence, threat(s), abuse(s), torture(s), attack(s), mouse killing, muricide, mobbing, biting, killing(s), cruelty, homicide(s), predation, belligeren(t,ce), revenge, cannibalism, predator(s), brutality, offensiveness, intruder(s), intrusion(s), competitive(ness), vandalism, combative(ness), intimidat(ing,ion), assailant(s), encroach(ed,ing,ment, ments). *See also* Aggressiveness (trait); Air rage; Animal aggressive behavior; Antisocial behavior; Arguments; Assault (battle); Assault (personal); Assertiveness; Behavior problems; Belligerency; Challenge; Competition; Conflict; Crime; Crimes against peace; Dominance; Frustration; Hostility; Interpersonal conflict; Invasion; Juvenile delinquency; Militarism; Military readiness; Military regimes; Military strategies; Military weapons; Rape; Riots; Road rage; Social interaction; Terrorism; Threat; Threat postures; Violence; War.

Aggressive behavior, animal. See *Animal aggressive behavior.*

Aggressive driving. See *Road rage.*

Aggressive passive personality disorder. See *Passive aggressive personality disorder.*

Aggressiveness (trait). Aggress(ive, iveness,ivity). Aggressive behavior. *Choose from:* aggressive, abusive, violent, destructive, belligerent, predatory, brutal, offensive, intrusive, competitive, combative, quarrelsome, contentious, argumentative, disruptive *with:* tendenc(y,ies), trait(s), nature, personalit(y,ies). *Consider also:* hostil(e,ity), explosive(ness), destructive(ness), dangerous(ness), belligeren(t,ce), brutality, offensive(ness), intrusive(ness), competitive(ness), combative(ness), quarrelsome(ness), contentious(ness), argumentative(ness), cruel(ty), hard driving, revengeful(ness). *See also* Aggression; Assertiveness; Machismo; Personality traits.

Agility, physical. See *Physical agility.*

Aging. Aging. Aging process(es). Retirement role(s). Grow(n,ing) older. Graying. Stage(s) of life. Matur(e,ed, ing,ation). Adult develop(e,ed,ing,ment). Life change(s). Passages. Life transition(s). Midlife transition(s). Rite(s) of passage. Preretirement preparation. *Choose from:* physical, physiological, psychosocial, emotional, moral, intellectual *with:* aging, matur(ing,ation,ational), declin(e,ed, ing), development(s,al). *Consider also:* developmental stage(s), age factors, senescen(ce,t), longevity. *See also* Adult development; Age discrimination; Aged 80 and over; Attitudes toward the aged; Caregiver burden; Climacteric; Elder abuse; Elderly; Human life cycle; Influence of age on ability; Life cycle; Life experiences; Life review; Life stage transitions; Loss of function; Middle age; Midlife crisis; Physiological aging; Psychological aging.

Aging, attitudes toward. See *Age discrimination; Attitudes toward the aged.*

Aging, physical. See *Physiological aging.*

Aging, physiological. See *Physiological aging.*

Aging, psychological. See *Psychological aging.*

Aging education. Aging education. *Choose from:* aging, gerontolog(y,ical), geriatric(s), intergenerational, pre-retirement *with:* education(al), workshop(s), class(es), course(s). *See also* Age differences; Adult education.

Agitated depression. Agitated depression. Ademon(ia,ic). *See also* Depression (psychology).

Agitation. Agitat(e,ed,ion,ional). Extreme tension. Restless(ness). Overwrought. Anguish(ed). Stir(red,ring) up. Perturb(ed,ing). Arous(e,ed,ing,al). *See also* Concentration difficulties; Motor activity; Nervousness; Psychomotor agitation; Restlessness.

Agitation, emotional. See *Restlessness.*

Agitation, political. See *Social agitation.*

Agitation, psychomotor. See *Psychomotor agitation.*

Agitation, social. See *Social agitation.*

Agitators. Agitator(s). Agent(s) provocateur. Disrupter(s). Incendiar(y,ies). Instigator(s). Fomenter(s). Inciter(s). *See also* Civil disobedience; Civil disorders; Dissidents; Incitement; Malinformation; Protesters; Social agitation; Terrorism.

Agnosia. Agnos(ia,ic). Gerstmann's syndrome. Phantom limb. Autopagnos(ia,ic). Prosopagnos(ia,ic). Prosopo affective agnos(ia,ic). Capgras' syndrome. Astereognosis. Anosognos(ia, ic). Somatotopagnos(ia,ic). Ideational apraxia. Sensory apraxia. *See also* Aphasia; Perceptual disturbances.

Agnosticism. Agnostic(s,ism). Doubter(s). Skeptic(s,ism). Unbeliever(s). *Consider also:* non-theis(m,t,ts,tic). *See also* Atheism; Heresy; Irreligion; Nontheistic religion; Philosophy; Religion; Uncertainty.

Agonistic behavior. Agonistic behavior(s). Agonistic(al,ally). Agonist(s). Social

fighting. Territorial defense. Inking behavior(s). Muricide. Mouse killing. Retaliat(e,ed,ing). Retaliation(s). Struggl(e,ed,es,ing). Argumentative(ness). *See also* Aggression; Animal aggressive behavior; Territoriality.

Agoraphobia. Agoraphob(ia,ic). Territorial apprehension. Dread of open places. Fear of market place. Travel phobia. Calamity syndrome. *Consider also:* panic attack(s). *See also* Panic disorder; Phobias; Social phobia.

Agraphia. Agraph(ia,ic). Inability to write. *See also* Learning disabilities.

Agrarian societies. Agrarian societ(y,ies). Agrarian(ism). Agrarian system(s). Agricultural societ(y,ies). Nonindustrial societ(y,ies). Feudalism. Peasantry. Peasant societ(y,ies). Hacienda(s). Latifund(ia,ismo). Plantation(s). *Choose from:* agrarian, agricultural, pastoral, peasant, rural *with:* societ(y,ies), life, communit(y,ies), people(s), population. *See also* Agricultural collectives; Agriculture; Dual economy; Economic underdevelopment; Farm life; Peasants; Primitive agriculture; Traditional societies.

Agrarian structures. Agrarian structure(s). Agricultural structure(s). Agricultural institution(s). Farm(ing) structure(s). Rural social structure(s). Structure(s) of agriculture. Traditional forms of land control. Structural organization of agriculture. Feudal(ism). Manorial system(s). Common land(s). Land reform(s). Hacienda(s). Plantation(s). Green revolution. Crofting. Ayllus. Ejido(s). Homestead(ing). Sharecropp(ers,ing). Farm tenan(cy,ts). Farming system(s). *See also* Agricultural collectives; Common lands; Feudalism; Homesteading; Land ownership; Land reform; Manors; Sharecropping; Small farms.

Agreement. Agreement(s). Agree(d,ing,s). Accord(ance). Consens(ual,us). Concurr(ed,ence). Unanim(ous,ity). Assent(ed,ing). Approv(ed,al,ing). Confirm(ed,ing). Ratif(y,ying,ication). Deal(s). *See also* Agreement (document); Alliances; Communication (thought transfer); Consensus; Consent (law); Disputes; Harmonization; Informed consent; Interpersonal relations; Persuasion; Rapport; Similarity.

Agreement (document). Agreement(s). Treat(y,ies). Pact(s). Contract(s). Compact(s). Note(s). Affidavit(s). Codicil(s). Covenant(s). Guarantee(s). Warrant(y,ies). Deed(s). Lease(s). Charter(s). Bond(s). Accord(s). *Consider also:* promise(s), pledge(s). *See also* Addendum; Affidavit; Charters; Contracts; Earnest money; Guarantees; Legal documents; Promises; Treaties.

Agreements, compacts. See *Agreement (document); Contracts; Legal documents; Treaties.*

Agreements, license. See *License agreements.*

Agreements, licensing. See *License agreements.*

Agreements, trade. See *Commercial treaties.*

Agribusiness. Agribusiness(es). Agroindustr(y,ies). Agristructure(s). Rural entrepreneur(s). Capitalization of agriculture. Food compan(y,ies). Capitalist farm(s). Agricultural syndicate(s). Factory farm(s,ing). Business of agriculture. Corporat(e,ion) farm(s,ing). Food manufacturing. Soybean industry, etc. Soybean futures, etc. *Choose from:* agricultur(e,al), farm(s,ing), crop(s) *with:* price(s), marketing, manag(ers,erial), information, production, subsid(y,ies,ization), export(s), business(es), industr(y,ies,ial), compan(y,ies), corporat(e,ion,ions). *See also* Agricultural chemicals; Agricultural mechanization; Agricultural prices; Agricultural productivity; Agricultural workers; Agriculture; Animal industry; Animal products; Cattle industry; Coffee industry; Dairying; Ecological imperialism; Farm management; Farms; Farming; Food industry; Grain trade; Horse industry; Meat industry; Nut industry; Rural development.; Rural industries; Rural land; Tobacco farms.

Agricultural assistance. Agricultural assistance. *Choose from:* agricultur(e,al), rural development, farm(s,ing,er,ers), food production *with:* technology transfer, assist(ed,ing,ance), aid(s,ed,ing), help(s,ed,ing), grant(s), contribut(e,ed,ing,ion,ions), support(s,ed,ing), foundation(s). *See also* Agricultural extension; Economic assistance; Foreign aid; Rural development.

Agricultural chemicals. Agricultural chem(ical,icals,istry). Fertilizer(s). Pesticide(s). Herbicide(s). *Choose from:* agricultur(e,al), farm(s,ing,er,ers), crop(s), agribusiness *with:* chemical(s, ly), residue(s), effluen(t,ts,ce), runoff(s). *See also* Agribusiness; Agricultural pests; Carcinogens; Dioxin; Environmental pollutants; Herbicides; Organic farming; Pesticides; Soil conservation; Soil degradation; Soil fertility

Agricultural chemistry. See *Agricultural chemicals.*

Agricultural collectives. Agricultural collective(s). Collective farm(s). Kolkhoz(y,es). Moshav. Kibbutz(im). Cooperative communit(y,ies). Agricultural cooperative(s). Agricultural co-op(s). Collectivized agriculture. State farm(s,ing). Sovkhoz. Zadruga(s).

Peasant collective(s). Ayllus. *See also* Agrarian structures; Collectivism; Common lands; Common ownership; Communes; Cooperatives; Socialism.

Agricultural colonies. Agricultural colon(y,ies, ization). Grown by colon(y,ies). *Choose from:* colon(y,ies, ization) *with:* agricultur(e,al), crop(s), food(s,stuff,stuffs), farm(s,ing). *See also* Colonialism; Exploitation; World economy.

Agricultural communities. See *Agrarian societies; Rural communities.*

Agricultural credit. Agricultural credit. *Choose from:* agricultur(e,al), farm(er,ers,ing) *with:* loan(s), credit, assistance, bank(s), cooperative(s). *See also* Agricultural collectives; Consumer credit.

Agricultural diversification. Agricultural diversification. *Choose from:* agricultur(e,al), rural, farm(s,ing,er,ers), crop(s) *with:* diversif(y,ied,ies, ication,ications), diverse, diversity, rotat(e,es,ed,ing,ion,ions), vary(ing), varied, variability, alternat(e,es, ing,ive,ives). *Consider also:* new crop(s), crop introduction, multicrop, sustainable agriculture. *See also* Agricultural extension; Farm produce; Farming; Organic farming; Rural land; Soil conservation; Soil degradation; Soil fertility.

Agricultural ecology. Agricultural ecology. Organic farming. Sustainable agriculture. Stewardship of resources. *Choose from:* agricultur(e,al), crop(s), livestock, grazing, farm(s,ing), plant(s), animal(s), pest(s), soil *with:* ecolog(y,ical), biodiversity, conservation, habitat(s), organic, stewardship. *See also* Appropriate technologies; Organic farming; Phytogeography; Plant succession; Restoration ecology; Sustainable development.

Agricultural engineering. Agricultural engineer(ed,ing,s). Genetically-engineered food(s). *Choose from:* genetic(ally) engineer(ed,ing), bioengineer(ed,ing) *with:* agricultur(e, al), crop(s), food(s,stuff,stuffs). *Consider also:* irrigation, drainage engineering. *See also* Biotechnology; Earthwork; Plant genetics.

Agricultural extension. Agricultural extension. *Choose from:* cooperative, agricultural, rural, university *with:* extension service(s). *Consider also:* village level worker(s), Rural Development Act, Rural Development Policy Act, county agricultural agent(s). *See also* Agricultural assistance; Agricultural diversification; Agricultural mechanization; Rural development; Rural development.

Agricultural implements. Agricultural implement(s). Farm tool(s). Field machinery. Harvest(ing) machine(s,ry). *Consider also:* plow(s), plough(s), harrow(s), harvester(s), tractor(s), tiller(s), combine(s), reaper(s), incubator(s), threshing machine(s,ry). *Choose from:* agricultur(e,al), horticultur(e,al), farm(s,ing,er,ers) *with:* implement(s), machine(s,ry), tool(s), implement(s), equipment. *See also* Agriculture; Agricultural mechanization.

Agricultural innovations. Agricultural innovation(s). Green revolution. Agricultural reform(s). *Choose from:* agricultur(e,al), farm(s,er,ers), agrarian, rural *with:* advance(s), progress, development(s), alternative(s), adopt(ed, ing,ion) technolog(y,ical). *See also* Agriculture; Agricultural mechanization; Innovations.

Agricultural labor. See *Agricultural workers.*

Agricultural laborers. See *Agricultural workers.*

Agricultural laws and legislation. Agricultural law(s) and legislation. Grazing right(s). Farm Bill(s). Farm subsid(y,ies). Agricultural polic(y,ies). *Choose from:* agricultur(e,al), agrarian, farm(s,er,ers,ing), ranch(es,er,ers,ing), farmworker(s), crop(s), milk, wheat, sorghum *with:* law(s), legislat(ive,ion, or,ors), polic(y,ies), regulat(ed,ing, ion,ions). *Consider also:* House Agriculture Committee. *See also* Agricultural price supports; Government subsidization; Government subsidization; Right of pasture.

Agricultural machinery. See *Agricultural mechanization.*

Agricultural mechanization. Agricultural mechanization. Agricultural modernization. *Choose from:* agricultur(e,al), farm(s,ing) *with:* mechaniz(e,ed,ing, ation), technolog(y,ical), technical, machine(s,ry), tractor(s), combines, mechanical power. *Consider also:* agricultur(e,al), farm(s,ing) *with:* change(s), develop(ing,ment), implement(ed,ing,ation). *See also* Adoption of ideas; Agribusiness; Agricultural diversification; Agricultural implements; Agricultural innovations; Agriculture; Appropriate technologies; Machinery; Farm management; Farming; Innovations; Medieval technology; Rural development; Rural industries; Soil degradation; Sustainable development; Technological progress.

Agricultural pests. Agricultural pest(s). Melon blight. Cotton bollworm(s). Corn ear worm(s). Pest Plant(s). Locust(s). Moth(s). Mediteranean fruit fl(ies,y). Gnat(s). Caterpillar(s). *Consider also:* kudzu, loosestrife, cotoneaster, ligustrum sinese, heavenly bamboo, etc. *Choose from:* agricultur(e,al), farm(s, ing,er,ers), crop(s) *with:* pest(s), insect(s), vermin, weevil(s), mite(s), earworm(s), moth(s), ear wig(s). *See also* Agricultural chemicals; Insects; Pesticides.

Agricultural price supports. Agricultural price support(s). Milk price regulation. Farm income support. *Choose from:* price compact(s), price intervention, subsid(y,ies), price support(s), federal crop insurance, assist(ed,ing,ance), buying power *with:* agricultur(e,al), farm(s,ing,er,ers), agrarian, basic commodities. *See also* Agricultural laws and legislation; Agricultural prices; Agricultural productivity; Grain trade; Price control.

Agricultural prices. Agricultural price(s). Farm price(s). *Choose from:* agricultur(e,al), farm(s,ing,er,ers), crop(s), fresh produce, milk, dairy product(s), wheat, corn, rice, meat, fruit(s), vegetable(s) *with:* price(s), market value(s). *Consider also:* commodity price(s). *See also* Agribusiness; Agricultural price supports; Grain trade.

Agricultural productivity. Agricultural producti(vity,on). *Choose from:* agricultur(e,al), farm(s,ing,er,ers), food *with:* producti(vity,on), efficien(t,cy), return(s), output, yield(s), profit(s,able,ability). *Consider also:* land productivity, farm income(s). *See also* Agribusiness; Agricultural price supports.

Agricultural research. Agricultural research. Farm report(s). Agricultural news. *Choose from:* agricultur(e,al), farm(s,ing,er,ers), crop(s), fresh produce, milk, dairy product(s), wheat, corn, rice, meat, fruit(s), vegetable(s), cattle, poultry, livestock, soil *with:* stud(y,ies), research, drug trial(s), control group(s), in-vivo, experiment(s,ing,ation), test(ed,ing,s), subject(s). *See also* Animal studies; Research; Soil science; Soil surveys.

Agricultural societies. See *Agrarian societies.*

Agricultural workers. Agricultural worker(s). Farmer(s). Agricultural technician(s). Cultivator(s). Food producer(s). Migrant worker(s). Rancher(s). Sharecropper(s). Bracero(s). Cowboy(s). Cowgirl(s). *Choose from:* agricultural, farm, ranch, rural *with:* worker(s), labor, laborer(s), operator(s), personnel, hand(s). *Consider also:* village level worker(s), peasant(s), farm wives, corn gleaner(s), grape picker(s), hothouse worker(s), cattle breeder(s). *See also* Agricultural workers disease; Blacksmithing; Blue collar workers; Cowboys; Farm life; Farming; Herders; Labor unions; Labor force; Migrant workers; Part time farming; Peasants; Plantations; Rural population.

Agricultural workers disease. Agricultural workers disease(s). Farmer(s) lung. Silo fillers disease. *Choose from:* pesticide poisoning(s), health problem(s), occupational disease(s), occupational pathology, occupational hazard(s), occupational risk(s), pesticide(s), agricultural dust, insecticide residue(s) *with:* agricultural worker(s), farm worker(s), grape picker(s), swine breeding worker(s), tobacco worker(s), field worker(s), hothouse worker(s). *See also* Agricultural chemicals; Agricultural workers; Environmental pollutants; Flies; Hazardous occupations; Herbicides; Occupational diseases; Occupational exposure; Pesticides; Rural health.

Agriculture. Agricultur(e,al). Agriculturalist(s). Agronom(y,ic,ics). Agronomist(s). Agrarian. Agribusiness. Animal husbandry. Cattle breeding. Crop raising. Cropping. Dairying. Farm(ing,ers). Farm management. Harvest(ed,ing). Horticultur(e,al). Hydroponic(s). Market gardening. Pasturage. Raising livestock. Ranching. Sharecropper(s). Soil culture. Stock raising. Tillage. Truck farm(ing,er,ers). Viticulture. *See also* Agrarian societies; Agrarian structures; Agribusiness; Agricultural assistance; Agricultural chemicals; Agricultural collectives; Agricultural diversification; Agricultural extension; Agricultural implements; Agricultural innovations; Agricultural mechanization; Agricultural workers; Agricultural workers disease; Arid regions agriculture; Bee culture; Cattle industry; Crops; Cultivated Plants; Dairying; Farming; Farms; Grain; Harvesting; Land use; Life sciences; Mariculture, Plant cultivation; Plantations; Rural development; Sharecropping; Slash burn agriculture; Soil conservation; Soil fertility.

Agriculture, arid regions. See *Arid regions agriculture.*

Agriculture, cooperative. See *Agricultural collectives.*

Agriculture, ecological. See *Organic farming.*

Agriculture, prehistoric. See *Prehistoric agriculture.*

Agriculture, primitive. See *Primitive agriculture.*

Agriculture, slash burn. See *Slash burn agriculture.*

Agroforestry. See *Tree farms; Tree planting.*

Agronomy. See *Farming.*

Aid. See *Assistance.*

Aid, categorical. See *Fiscal federalism.*

Aid, foreign. See *Foreign aid.*

Aid, government. See *Government aid.*

Aid, international. See *Foreign aid.*

Aid, state. See *Government aid.*

Aid, student financial. See *Student financial aid.*

Aides, community health. See *Community health aides.*

Aides, nurses. See *Nurses aides.*

Aides, psychiatric. See *Psychiatric aides.*

AIDS. AIDS. Acquired immune deficiency syndrome. Acquired immunodeficiency syndrome. Full blown AIDS. PWA. Person with AIDS. Gay compromise syndrome. Gay plague. Gay related immune disease. Aids related complex. ARC. *Choose from:* acquired *with:* immunodeficiency, immunologic deficiency, immune deficiency, immune dysfunction, impaired cell mediated immunity. *Choose from:* immune deficien(cy,t), immunocompromised, immunodeficien(cy,t), immunodepress(ed,ion), immune dysregulation, immunosuppression, immunologic abnormalities *with:* drug abuse(rs), intravenous, Haitian(s), homosexual(ity,s), gay(s), Kaposi's sarcoma, pneumocystis carinii, pneumocystis pneumonia, hemophiliac(s). *Consider also:* HIV virus, HIV positive, HIV disease, HIV antibody seropositivity, HIV asymptomaticity, lymphadenopathy syndrome, HIV-1, HIV-2, human immunodeficiency virus, ARV, aids related virus, HTLV-III, HTLV-3, human T-cell lymphotropic virus, human T-cell lymphocyte virus, lymphocyte virus-3, LAV-1, LAV-2, lymphadenopathy associated virus. *See also* Disease; Needle sharing; Sexually transmitted diseases.

AIDS patients. See *AIDS; Patients.*

Aids, communication for disabled. See *Communication aids for handicapped.*

Aids, communication for handicapped. See *Communication aids for handicapped.*

Aids, hearing. See *Hearing aids.*

Aids, mobility. See *Mobility aids.*

Aids, visual. See *Visual aids.*

Ailurophobia. See *Cat phobia.*

Aim. See *Ambitions; Aspirations; Career goals; Educational plans; Goal orientation; Goals; Motivation; Social goals.*

Air. Air. Atmospher(e,ic). *Consider also:* ventilat(e,ed,ion), oxygen, nitrogen, gas(ses). *See also* Air pollution.

Air, swallowing. See *Swallowing air.*

Air bases. Air base(s). Military airfields(s). Naval Air Station(s). Military air base(s). Air Force base(s). Military airport(s). *Consider also:* Langley Field, Lajes Field, etc. *See also* Air defenses; Air power; Airports; Aerial warfare; Military airplanes.

Air defenses. Air defense(s). Aerospace defense(s). Missile defense(s). Defense against missile(s). Plane(s) shot down. Warplane(s). North American Aerospace Defense Command (NORAD). Radar-guided missile(s). Rescue plane(s). Air patrol(s). Strategic Defense Iniative (SDI). *See also* Air bases; Air power; Aerial warfare; Military airplanes.

Air Force personnel. Air Force personnel. Air(men,man,women,woman). Aircrew(s). *Choose from:* Air Force, Royal Air Force *with:* personnel, administrator(s), specialist(s), officer(s), enlisted, technician(s), instructor(s), student(s), personnel, supervisor(s), trainee(s), crew(s), enlistee(s), ROTC, nurse(s), cadet(s), troop(s), mission(s), team(s), member(s), reserve officers training corps. *See also* Armed forces; Military personnel.

Air freight. Air freight. Air cargo. *Choose from:* air *with:* freight, cargo(es) carrier. *Consider also:* second day delivery, same day delivery. *See also* Carriers (shipping); Freight.

Air pollution. Air pollution. Polluted air. Smog. Atmospheric contamination. Global distillation. Concentrat(ed, ion,ions) of carbon monoxide. Tobacco smoke. Automobile exhaust(s). Poor air quality. Passive smoking. Sick building(s). Acid rain. *Choose from:* air, atmospher(e,ic), carbon monoxide, sulfur dioxide, lead, crop spraying, automobile exhaust(s), aerosol(s), dust, harmful vapor(s), smoke, nuclear explosion(s), incinerat(e,ed,ing,or, ors,ion) *with:* pollut(ed,ing,ion,ant,ants), contaminat(ed,ing,ion), contaminant(s). *Consider also:* Clean Air Act. *See also* Acid rain; Air; Atmospheric contamination; Carcinogens; Ecology; Environmental impacts; Environmental pollutants; Environmental pollution; Greenhouse effect; Hazardous materials; Hazardous wastes; Industrial wastes; Medical wastes; Nuclear waste; Pollution control; Sick building syndrome; Urban health; Waste disposal; Waste to energy.

Air pollution syndrome. See *Sick building syndrome.*

Air power. Air power. Air superiority. Fire power from the air. Air Force combat capabilit(y,ies). Air capabilit(y,ies). Warplane(s). *Consider also:* air attack(s). fighter plane(s), stealth fighter(s), air raid(s), bombing campaign(s), air attack(s), air strike(s), air raid(s), U2 spy plane(s), surface-to-air missile site(s), electronic-warfare technology, fighter aircraft. *See also* Air bases; Air defenses; Aerial warfare; Military airplanes.

Air rage. Air rage(s). *Choose from:* aggress(ive,ively,or,ors), harass(ed, ing,ment), assault(ed,ing), fight(s,ing), hostile(e,ity,ities), violen(ce,t), reckless(ly), drunk(en), unrul(y,iness), threat(s,en,ened,ening), punch(ed, es,ing), kick(s,ed,ing), verbal abuse, drunken rage(s), belligerent *with:* airline(s), airplane(s), flight(s), plane(s), airport(s), air passenger(s), flier(s), flyer(s), travel(er,ers), flight attendant(s). *See also* Aggression; Anger; Antisocial behavior; Belligerency; Hostility; Resentment; Road rage; Violence.

Air safety. See *Aviation safety.*

Air traffic accidents. See *Aviation accidents.*

Air traffic control. Air traffic control. *Choose from:* air traffic, landing(s), ground approach(es), airport(s) *with:* control(ling,lers), guidance, radar. *See also* Airports; Aviation safety; Control.

Air transportation. Air transport(ation). Air carrier(s). *Choose from:* air, airline(s), aircraft, airplane(s), aerospace, plane(s), jet(s), aviation, supersonic, turboprop(s), aeronautic(s,al) *with:* transport(ation), travel, flight(s), flying, operation(s), traffic, landing(s), safety, passenger(s), express, cargo, industry, carrier(s). *Consider also:* passenger airline(s), airline business(es), airbus(es), commercial flight(s), commuter flight(s), Delta Airlines, American Airlines, Boeing 757, Boeing 737, DC-3, etc. *See also* Aerospace industries; Business travel; Carriers (shipping); Destination; Ground effect machines; Jet lag; Transport workers; Transportation.

Air travel. See *Air transportation.*

Air warfare. See *Aerial warfare.*

Aircraft. Aircraft. Helicopter(s). Airplane(s). Plane(s). Aircarrier(s). Airship(s). Aerostat(s). Aerodyne(s). Dirigible(s). Zeppelin(s). Blimp(s). Aeroplane(s). Jet(s,liner,liners). Airbus(es). Space shuttle(s). Sattelite(s). Air fleet(s). Air shuttle(s). *Choose from specific planes such as:* Boeing *with:* 707, 720, 727, 707-32C, 737; Douglas *with:* DC-8, DC-8F, DC-9, DC-10; Beechcraft *with:* T-34, 99A, etc. *See also* Aircraft industry; Aerospace industries; Aeronautical museums; Air transportation; Flight instrumentation; Flying machines; Ground effect machines.

Aircraft carriers. Aircraft carrier(s). Carrier task force(s). Carrier airwing(s). Helicopter carrier(s). Supercarrier(s). Flattop(s). *Consider also:* flight deck(s). *See also* Military airplanes; Seapower; Ships; Warships.

Aircraft industry. Aircraft industry. Aerospace industry. Aviation industry. *Choose from:* aircraft, aerospace, aviation, airplane(s), airbus(ses) *with:* industr(y,ies,ial), manufactur(er,ing,ed), compan(y,ies), produc(er,ers,tion), maker(s). *Consider also:* Cessna Aircraft, McDonnell Douglas, Boeing, etc. *See also* Aerospace industries; Aircraft.

Airlines. See *Air transportation.*

Airplane industry. See *Aircraft industry.*

Airplanes. See *Aircraft.*

Airplanes, military. See *Military airplanes.*

Airports. Airport(s). Airstation(s). Air base(s). Airdrome(s). Aerodrome(s). Air field(s). *Choose from:* air *with:* facilit(y,ies), hangar(s), runway(s), landing strip(s), installation(s). *See also* Air bases; Air traffic control; Aviation accidents; Aviation safety; Infrastructure (economics).

Akathisia. See *Restlessness.*

Alarm responses. Alarm response(s). *Choose from:* alarm(s), warning(s), startle, fear, defense, defensive, escape, distress *with:* response(s), recruitment, communicat(e,ed,ing), communication(s), note(s), effect(s), call(s), reaction(s), reflex(es). *Consider also:* escape stimulus, tonic immobility, alarm pheromone(s). *See also* Animal communication; Animal defensive behavior; Fear; Startle reaction; Tonic immobility.

Alaska natives. Alaska(n) native(s). Aleut(s). *Consider also:* Kwakiutl, Haida, Tsimshian, Nootka, Eskimo(s). *See also* Indigenous populations; Ethnic groups; Minority groups; North American native cultural groups; Traditional societies.

Albinism. Albin(ism,o,os). *Choose from:* absence, deficien(t,cy,cies) *with:* pigment(ation). *Consider also:* chediak-higashi-syndrome. *See also* Genetics; Hereditary diseases.

Alchemy. Alchem(y,ic,ical,ist,ists). Transmutation of metal(s). *Choose from:* transmut(e,ed,ing,ation) *with:* base metal(s), gold. *Consider also:* quest, search(ed,ing) *with:* elixir of life, immortality, stone of knowledge, philosopher's stone. *Consider also:* Praxis Spagyrica Philosophica, aqua regia, Bologna stone. *See also* Astrology; Magic; Medieval technology; Occultism; Transubstantiation.

Alcohol. See *Alcoholic beverages; Ethyl alcohol.*

Alcohol, ethyl. See *Ethyl alcohol.*

Alcohol, fetal syndrome. See *Fetal alcohol syndrome.*

Alcohol abstinence. See *Sobriety.*

Alcohol abuse. See *Alcoholism; Problem drinking.*

Alcohol addiction. See *Alcoholism.*

Alcohol amnestic disorder. Alcohol amnestic disorder. *Choose from:* Korsakoff(s), Korsakov(s), Wernicke(s) *with:* syndrome, psychosis, disease. *Consider also:* chronic alcoholic delirium, chronic delirium tremens, metalcoholic psychosis, alcoholic dysmnesic syndrome, alcoholic dementia. *See also* Alcoholic dementia; Alcoholic psychoses.

Alcohol consumption. See *Alcohol drinking.*

Alcohol dependency. See *Alcoholism; Problem drinking.*

Alcohol deterrents. Alcohol deterrent(s). Alcohol aversive therap(y,ies). *Consider also:* antabuse, disulfiram, disulfuram, succinylcholine, apomorphine, tetraethylthiuram disulfide, naltrexone, acamprosate, campral, Alcoholics Anonymous. *See also* Alcohol rehabilitation; Detoxification.

Alcohol detoxification. See *Detoxification.*

Alcohol drinking. Alcohol drinking. *Choose from:* alcohol(s,ic), ethanol, liquor(s), beer, wine, whiskey, rum, gin, bourbon, etc. *with:* drink(ing,er,ers), drank, drunk(en), use(rs), intake, usage, consum(e,ed,ing,ption), ingest(ed,ing, ion), crav(e,ed,ing), abus(e,er,ers,ed). *Choose from:* social, problem, controlled, dyssocial, thymogenic, escape, somatopathic *with:* drinking. *Choose from:* drinking *with:* behavior, habit(s,ual), patterns. *Consider also:* alcoholism, alcoolisation. *See also* Alcoholism; Drinking behavior; Drinking customs; Drunk driving; Problem drinking; Sobriety; Social drinking; Temperance; Temperance movements.

Alcohol drinking attitudes. Alcohol drinking attitude(s). *Choose from:* drinking, alcohol(s,ic,ism), liquor *with:* attitude(s), opinion(s), philosoph(y,ies, ic,ical), cultural pattern(s), public opinion, social norm(s), folklore, custom(s). *See also* Alcohol rehabilitation; Attitudes; Attitudes toward health; Drinking customs; Sobriety.

Alcohol education. Alcohol education. *Choose from:* drinking, drunk(en, enness), intoxication, alcohol(s,ic,ism), liquor, DWI *with:* education(al), instruction(al), communication, mass media, information(al), campaign(s), awareness. *See also* Alcoholic beverages; Drinking behavior; Drug education; Health education.

Alcohol fuels. See *Alternative energy.*

Alcohol hallucinosis. See *Alcoholic hallucinosis; Alcohol withdrawal delirium.*

Alcohol intoxication. See *Drunkenness.*

Alcohol intoxication, diagnosis of. See *Diagnosis of alcohol intoxication.*

Alcohol rehabilitation. Alcohol(ism,ic) rehabilit(ed,ing,ation). *Choose from:* alcohol(ism,ic,ics) *with:* rehab, rehabilitat(e,ed,ing,ation), detoxif(y,ied, ication), medication(s), treatment(ed, ing), social skills training, assertiveness training, total abstinence, avers(ive,ion) therap(y,ies), avers(ive,ion) treatment(s), halfway house(s), behavior therapy, counsel(ed,ing), casework, hospitaliz(e, ed,ation), psychotherap(y,ies,eutic). *Consider also:* Alcoholics Anonymous, anti-alcoholic agent(s). *See also* Alcohol deterrents; Alcohol drinking attitudes; Detoxification; Drug rehabilitation; Rehabilitation counseling; Self help groups; Sobriety.

Alcohol use. See *Alcohol drinking.*

Alcohol withdrawal delirium. Alcohol withdrawal delirium. Delirium tremens. Rum fit(s). *Choose from:* alcohol(ic,ism) *with:* withdrawal, detoxification, abstinence, cessation *with:* delirium, symptom(s), syndrome, psychos(is,es), morning shakes, nausea, malaise. *See also* Alcoholic psychoses; Alcohol rehabilitation.

Alcoholic addiction. See *Alcoholism.*

Alcoholic beverages. Alcoholic beverage(s). Liquor(s). Liqueur(s). *Choose from:* alcohol(ic) *with:* beverage(s), drink(s), cocktail(s), punch(es). *Consider also:* wine(s), beer(s), ale(s), rum, gin, whisk(y,ey,ies), vodka, bourbon, slivovitz, mead, sherr(y,ies), cognac, tequila, champagne(s), etc. *See also* Alcohol education; Beverage industry; Beverages; Brewing; Brewing industry; Distillation; Drinking behavior; Fermentation; Grapes; Illicit liquor; Liquor industry.

Alcoholic dementia. Alcoholic dementia. *Choose from:* alcohol(ic,ics,ism) *with:* dementia(s), deteriorat(e,ed,ing,ion), delusion(s), hallucinat(e,ed,ing,ion,ions). *See also* Alcohol amnestic disorder; Alcoholic hallucinosis; Alcoholic psychoses.

Alcoholic deterioration. Alcoholic deterioration. *Choose from:* alcohol(ic, ism), drinking *with:* deteriorat(e,ed, ing,ion), beta, physical complication(s), cirrhosis, polyneuropath(y,ies,ic), somatophatic, nutritional deficienc(y, ies). *See also* Alcoholic dementia; Alcoholic psychoses; Beta alcoholism; Deterioration.

Alcoholic hallucinosis. Alcohol(ic) hallucinosis. *Choose from:* alcohol(ic, ics,ism), drinking *with:* hallucinat(e,ed, ing,ory,ion,ions), hear(ing) voice(s), vision(s). *Consider also:* delirium tremens, Korsakoffs psychosis. *See also* Alcoholic dementia; Alcoholic psychoses.

Alcoholic intoxication. See *Drunkenness.*

Alcoholic psychoses. Alcohol(ic,ics,ism) psychos(is,es). *Choose from:* alcohol(ic,ics,ism), ethanol, drinking, drunk(en,enness), intoxication *with:* psychos(is,es), delirium, acute, dementia, deliria, predelirium, paranoi(a,d), hallucinosis, hallucinat(e,ed,ing, ion,ions), delusion(s,al). *Consider also:* Korsakoff(s) psychosis, alcohol amnestic disorder, alcohol withdrawal delirium, delirium tremens. *See also* Alcohol amnestic disorder; Alcoholic dementia; Alcoholic deterioration; Alcoholic hallucinosis; Organic psychoses.

Alcoholics, skid row. See *Skid row alcoholics.*

Alcoholism. Alcohol(ic,ics,ism). Chronic(ally) drunk(en,enness). Binge drink(er,ers,ing). Fetal alcohol syndrome. FAS. Delirium tremens. Heavy drinker(s). DWI. *Choose from:* alcohol, ethanol, liquor(s), beer, wine(s), drunk(en,enness), drink(ing), inebriat(ed,ion) *with:* dependen(t,cy), abuse(r,rs), misuse, long term, problem(s), tolerance, chronic(ally), habit(ual), skid row. *Consider also:* alcoholic *with:* cardiomyopathy, psychos(is,es), withdrawal, amnestic disorder, hepatitis, liver cirrhosis. *Consider also:* Korsakoffs syndrome, Wernicke's syndrome. *See also* Alcohol amnestic disorder; Alcohol deterrents; Alcohol drinking; Alcohol drinking attitudes; Alcohol education; Alcohol education; Alcohol rehabilitation; Alcohol withdrawal delirium; Alcoholic beverages; Alcoholic dementia; Alcoholic deterioration; Alcoholic hallucinosis; Alcoholic psychoses; Beta alcoholism; Delta alcoholism; Dipsomania; Drunk driving; Gamma alcoholism; Gateway drugs; Malnutrition; Nutrition disorders; Problem drinking; Social drinking; Sobriety; Substance abuse; Temperance movements.

Alcoholism, alpha. See *Problem drinking.*

Alcoholism, beta. See *Beta alcoholism.*

Alcoholism, delta. See *Delta alcoholism.*

Alcoholism, epsilon. See *Dypsomania.*

Alcoholism, gamma. See *Gamma alcoholism.*

Aleatory music. See *Chance composition.*

Aleuts. See *Alaska natives.*

Alexia. Alex(ia,ic). *Choose from:* cortical, motor, music, subcortical *with:* alex(ia,ic), blindness. *Consider also:* acquired dyslexia, sensory aphasia, word blind(ness), visual aphasia. *See also* Aphasia; Reading disabilities.

Alexithymia. Alexithym(ia,ic). Affectless(ness). *Consider also:* constricted, inexpressiv(e,ity), numb(ed,

ing) *with:* emotion(s,al,ality), affect(ive), fantas(y,ies). *Consider also:* masked depression, anhedonia. *See also* Affective disorders; Psychophysiologic disorders.

Algonquian languages. Algonquian language(s). Arapaho. Blackfoot. Ritwan. Yurok. Algonquin. Cree. Delaware. Kickapoo. Menominee. Micmac. Mohegan. Narragansett. Natick. Ojibwa (Chippewa). Penobscot. Pequot. Potawatami. Powhatan. Sac and Fox. Shawnee. Cheyenne. Salishan. Flathead. Coeur d'Alene. Bella Coola. Wakashan. Nootka. Kwakiutl. *See also* Language; Languages (as subjects); North America; North American native cultural groups.

Aliases. See *Pseudonyms.*

Alien labor. Alien labor(er,ers). *Choose from:* illegal alien(s), illegal immigra(nt,nts,tion), undocumented immigra(nt,nts,tion), slave trade(s), criminal alien(s), refugee(s), immigration control *with:* labor(er,ers,ing), work(s,ed,ing), employ(ment,er,ers,ed), temporary work(er,ers), job(s), temp(s), compan(y,ies), corporation(s), business(es). *Consider also:* Padrone system, Padron(e,i,es). *See also* Foreign labor; Foreign professional personnel; Foreign workers; Foreigners.

Alienation. Alienat(ed,ion). Estrange(d, ment). Dissociat(ed,ion). Misanthrop(e, ic). Detach(ed,ment). Outsider(s). Hopeless(ness). Meaningless(ness). False consciousness. Objectification. *Consider also:* powerless(ness), anomie, disaffiliat(ed,ion), rootless(ness), helpless(ness), irrelevan(t,ce), lonel(y, iness), psychological deprivation, depersonalization, negativism, impersonal(ity), insensitiv(e,ity), demoraliz(e,ed,ation), impotence, disillusion(ed,ment), secularization, psychological separation, disenchant(ed, ment), death of God, dispossess(ed,ion), boredom, estranged labor, social estrangement. *See also* Absurd; Anger; Anomie; Apathy; Counterrevolutions; Death of God (theology); Dehumanization; Depersonalization disorder; Disengagement; Disillusionment; Disorders; Emotions; Existentialism; Fragmentation (experience); Hostility; Impersonal; Loneliness; Marginality (sociological); Mass society; Meaninglessness; Negativism; Nihilism; Ostracism; Pessimism; Postmodernism; Potential dropouts; Professional isolation; Reification; Rejection (psychology); Resentment; Role conflict; Social attitudes; Social isolation; Social loafing; Withdrawal (defense mechanism).

Alienation, social. See *Alienation.*

Aliens. Alien(s). Exile(s). Foreigner(s). Immigrant(s). Immigration. Boat people. Green card(s). Emigre(s). Deport(ed,ing, ation). Sanctuary movement. Refugee(s). Migrant(s). McCarran-Walter Act. Worker amnesty. Amnesty Act. Illegals. Visa violator(s). Border patrol(s). Imported labor(er,ers). Guestworker(s). Migrant labor(er,ers). Wetback(s). Foreign-born. Defector(s). Expatriate(s). Immigration service. Displaced person(s). Refugee(s). Outsider(s). Outlander(s). Non-citizen(s). Nonresident(s). Undocumented worker(s). Foreign tourist(s). Denizen(s). *Consider also:* Nigerian-born, German-born, etc. *See also* Displaced persons; Foreign students; Foreign workers; Foreigners; Illegal aliens; Immigrants; Immigration; Refugees.

Aliens, illegal. See *Illegal aliens.*

Alignments. Alignment(s). Affiliat(e,ed,es, ion,ions). Associat(es,ion,ions). All(y,ies). Alliance(s). Support(ers,ing). Taking side(s). Partisan. *See also* Alliances; Coalitions; Polarization.

Alimony. Alimony. Divorce settlement(s). Obligation(s) to former spouse. Divorce planning. Divorce negotiation(s). Marital dissolution agreement(s). Divorce payment(s). Spous(e,al) support. *Consider also:* palimony, divorce decree(s). *See also* Child support; Divorce; Marriage settlements.

Alkaloids, ergot. See *Ergot alkaloids.*

All volunteer military force. See *Volunteer military personnel.*

Allegations. Allegation(s). Alleg(e,ed,ing). Accus(e,ed,ing,ation,ations). Adduc(e,ed,ing). Assert(ed,ing,ion,ions). Attest(ed,ing,ation). Avow(ed,ing,al). Imput(e,ed,ing.ation). Declar(e,ed,ing, ation,ations). Profess(ed,ing). *Consider also:* insinuat(e,ed,ing,ion,ions), affirm(ed,ing,ation,ations), depos(e,ed, ing,ition). *See also* Assertions; Blame; Complaints; Denunciation; Derogation; Indictments; Testimony.

Allegiance. See *Loyalty.*

Allegory. Allegor(y,ies,ical,ically, ize,izes,izing). *Consider also:* parable(s), fable(s), tale(s), stor(y,ies), myth(s), double meaning(s). *See also* Anecdotes; Figurative language; Folklore; Irony; Literature; Metaphors; Mythology; Personification.

Allergies. See *Hypersensitivity.*

Allergies, food. See *Food hypersensitivity.*

Alliances. Alliance(s). All(y,ies). Solidarity. Popular front(s). Entente. Coalition(s). Linkage(s). Cooperat(e,ing,ion). Union(s). League(s). Bloc(s). Alignment(s). Partner(s,ship,ships).

Military link(s). Confederation(s). Cartel(s). Consort(ia,ium,iums). Junta(s). *Consider also:* treat(y,ies), balance of power, common security interests. *See also* Affiliation (businesses); Agreement (document); Alignments; Cartels; Clubs; Coalescence; Coalitions; Collective security; Combinations; Conflict; Consortia; Corporate networks; Intergroup relations; International alliances; International cooperation; International organizations; International relations; Interorganizational networks; Organizational development; Partners; Power sharing; Shared services; Strategic alliances; Teaming; Treaties; Unification; War.

Alliances, international. See *International alliances.*

Alliances, strategic. See *Strategic alliances.*

Allied countries. See *International alliances.*

Allied health personnel. Allied health personnel. Paraprofessional health personnel. Caretaker(s). Counselor(s). Ancillary staff. Nonprofessional health personnel. Therapist(s). Professional health personnel. Health professional(s). Paramedic(al,s). Nurse practitioner(s). Corps(man,men,women,woman). Health worker(s). Health supervisor(s). Medical technician(s). Dietary assistant(s). Health officer(s). Allied medical personnel. Health specialist(s). Genetic associate(s). Medical personnel. Sanitary engineer(s). Auxiliary health personnel. Allied health profession(al,als,s). Medic(s). Dietitian(s). Denturists. Emergency squad personnel. Optometrist(s). Therapists. Medical secretar(y,ies). Medical receptionist(s). *Choose from:* dental, hospital, environmental, health, home health, medical, medical record(s), nurs(e,es,ing), occupational therapy, physical therapy, psychiatric, radiolog(y,ic), surg(ery,ical), veterinary, community health, emergency room, operating room, pharmacist(s), physician(s), ophthalmic, pediatric *with:* assistant(s), aide(s), attendant(s), auxiliar(y,ies), hygienist(s), staff, technician(s), technician(s), technologist(s). *See also* Ancillaries; Paraprofessional personnel; Professional personnel.

Alliteration. Alliterat(e,ion,ive,ing,io). Stabreim(ender Vers). *Consider also:* initial rhyme(s), head rhyme(s), polytopon, l'annomination, homoeoteleuton. *See also* Literary parallells; Poetics; Poetry.

Allocation. Allocat(e,ed,ing,ion,ions). Divid(e,ed,ing). Partition(ed,ing). Triage. Apportion(ed,ing,ment,ments). Portion(s). Subdivid(e,ed,ing). Subdivision(s). Reallocat(e,ed,ing,

ion,ions). Division of labor. Ration(ed,ing). District(ed,ing). Redistrict(ed,ing). Rational division. Who gets what. Quota(s). Allotment(s). Allot(ted). Appropriat(e,ed,ing,ion,ions). Allowance(s). Distribut(e,ed,ion,ions). Redistribut(e,ed,ing,ion,ions). *See also* Apportionment; Appropriations (set aside); Biased selection; Budgets; Cost effectiveness; Delivery of services; Economic planning; Expenditures; Health care rationing; Needs assessment; Political representation; Priorities; Rationing; Resource allocation; Resources; Triage; Waiting lists; Zoning.

Allocation, resource. See *Resource allocation.*

Allocation, time. See *Time utilization.*

Allotment. See *Allocation.*

Allusions. Allus(ion,ions,ive,ively,iveness). Allude(d). Indirect reference(s). Infer(red,ring,ence,ences). Literary referen(t,ts,ce,ces). Impl(y,ied). Hint(ed, ing,s). Implicit reference(s). *See also* Figurative language; Gothicism; Literature; Metaphors; Sex symbolism; Symbolism.

Almanacs. Almanac(k,ks,s). Chronicle(s). *Consider also:* diar(y,ies), yearbook(s), calendar(s), annual(s). *See also* Calendars; Chronicles.

Alms. Alms(giving,giver,givers). Contribution(s). Offering(s). Donation(s). Zakat. *Consider also:* tith(e,ed,ing), benefaction(s), beneficence(s), charit(y,ies). *See also* Almshouses; Baksheesh; Begging; Charity; Gifts.

Almshouses. Almshouse(s). Alms house(s). Workhouse(s). Orphan-house(s). Poor house(s). Poor asylum(s). Poor farm(s). County home(s). County farm(s). *Consider also:* poor relief, pauper(s,ism). *See also* Alms; Begging; Charities; Poverty.

Alone, fear of being. See *Autophobia.*

Alone, living. See *Living alone.*

Alopecia. Alopec(ic,ia,ias). Hair loss(es). Hypotrichosis. Bald(ing,ness). *Choose from:* hair, wool *with:* deficien(t,cy), falling, loss(es), losing, lost. *Consider also:* alopecia areata, alopecia mucinosa. *See also* Hair.

Aloud, reading. See *Oral reading.*

Alpha alcoholism. See *Problem drinking.*

Alpha rhythm. Alpha rhythm. *Choose from:* alpha *with:* rhythm, frequency, periods, occipital, EEG, activity, pattern(s), biofeedback, wave(s), interval(s), cycle(s). *Choose from:* berger *with:* rhythm, wave(s). *Consider also:* alpha state(s). *See also* Electroencephalography.

Alphabet letters. See *Letters (alphabet).*

Alphabets. Alphabet(s,ic,ical,ically, ize,ized,izing). ABCs. Letter(s). Character(s). *Choose from:* Cyrillic, Greek, Roman, Hebrew, Arabic, Devanagari, Runes, Ogham, Sequoyah, Deseret *with:* alphabet(s). *Consider also:* orthograph(y,ic), phoneme(s), hieroglyphic(s), cuneiform, Aleph Beth, logograph(y,ic,ically), logogram(s, matic), rune(s). *See also* Letters (alphabet); Vowels; Written communications

Altaic, east languages. See *East Altaic languages.*

Altered states of consciousness. Altered state(s) of consciousness. Mental state(s). *Consider also:* automatism(s), biofeedback, dream(s), hallucination(s), hypnosis, hypnotized, hypnagogic state(s), meditation, mystical state(s), religious experience(s), parapsychological phenomena, sensory deprivation, trance(s), drunk(en,enness), high on drugs, delirious(ness), disorient(ed, ation), twilight sleep, stupor(s), coma(s,tose), fugue(s), somnambulism. *See also* Arousal; Automatism; Coma; Consciousness disorders; Disorientation; Dreams; Drunkenness; Hallucinations; Hypnosis; Meditation; Parapsychology; Psychedelic experiences; Religious experience; Trance.

Alterity. See *Otherness.*

Alternating personality. See *Multiple personality.*

Alternative energy. Alternative energy. Wind power. Biomass conversion. Solar architecture. Hydroelectric. Bio-energy. Biogas. Bioethanol. Biofuel(s) Bioconversion of agricultural waste(s). Energy crop(s). Synfuel(s). Alcohol fuel(s). Gasohol. Hydropower. *Choose from:* alternat(e,ive,ives), renewable, nonconventional, soft, unconventional, solar, passive, photovoltaic, wind, biomass, hydroelectric, appropriate technolog(y,ies), geothermal, recycl(e,ed,ing,able), sun(light), windmill(s), wood burning, unusual, tide(s), tidal, waves *with:* energy, power, electric(al,ity), generat(e,ed,ing,or,ors), heat(ed,ing), cool(ed,ing). *Choose from:* sun, solar *with:* panel(s), reflector(s), collector(s), kiln(s), cooking, furnace(s), refrigerat(e,ed,ing,ion). *See also* Appropriate technologies; Energy conservation; Energy generating resources; Fuel; Natural resources; Nonrenewable resources; Recycling; Renewable resources; Solar energy; Sustainable development; Utility costs; Water power; Wind power; Zero emissions vehicles.

Alternative family forms. Alternative family form(s). *Choose from:* alternative, commun(e,es,al), diversified, kibbutz(im), unconventional, experimental, variant, open, nontraditional, changing, homosexual, emergent, emerging, reconstituted, blended, egalitarian, worksharing, father only, single parent, mother headed, dual career, polygynous, extended, utopian, stem *with:* family form(s), household(s), family lifestyle(s), life, home(s), famil(y,ies), marriage(s), marital form(s). *Consider also:* polygam(y,ous), intentionally childless, childfree, nonmarital relationship(s), nonmarital contract(s), intimate life style(s), househusband(s), trial marriage(s), shared famil(y,ies), living together, cohabitation, coupling, stepfamil(y,ies), spouse swapping, serial marriage(s). *See also* Alternative lifestyles; Extended family; Gay couples; Group marriage; Lifestyle; Marriage contracts; Nuclear family; Polygamy; Single parent family; Stepfamily.

Alternative lifestyles. Alternative lifestyle(s). *Choose from:* alternative, nontraditional, unconventional *with:* lifestyle(s), life, lives, habit(s). *See also* Alternative family forms; Alternative work patterns; Celibacy; Gay couples; Hippies; Job sharing; Lifestyle; Monasticism; Nontraditional careers; Quality of life; Status inconsistency.

Alternative medicine. Alternative medicine. Naturopathy. Health food(s). Macrobiotic diet(s). Holistic medicine. Folk remed(y,ies). Acupuncture. Iridology. Chiropractor(s). Reflexotherapy. *Choose from:* alternative, holistic, traditional, folk(lore), primitive, indigenous, native, tribal, meditation, herbal *with:* medicine(s), medical, pharmaceutical(s), medical practice(s), psychiatr(y,ic), heal(ing, er,ers), tonic(s), treatment(s), therap(y, ies,eutic), remed(y,ies). *Consider also:* therapeutic system(s), anti-psychiatry, T. Szasz, M. Foucault, R.D. Laing. *See also* Acupuncture; Alternatives to institutionalization; Ayurvedic medicine; Chinese medicine; Herbal medicine; Holistic health; Homeopathy; Massage; Naturopathy; Nostrums; Oriental medicine; Orthomolecular therapy; Pet therapy; Plant folklore; Preventive medicine; Psychotherapeutic imagery; Psychotropic plants; Quackery; Traditional medicine; Vitamin therapy.

Alternative press. Alternative press. *Choose from:* alternative, independent, underground, clandestine, little known *with:* press(es), publish(ing,er,ers), news media, news(paper,papers), periodical(s), magazine(s), material(s), source(s), publication(s). *Consider also:* samizdat. *See also* Freedom of the press; Little presses; News media; Newspapers; Publishing; Publishers; Underground.

Alternative radio broadcasting. Alternative radio broadcasting. Alternative commercial radio. Countercultural commercial radio. *Choose from:* alternative, countercultural, freeform, progressive, underground *with:* radio, broadcast(s,ing). *Consider also:* member supported, public *with:* radio, broadcast(s,ing). *See also* Broadcast journalism; Broadcasting; Broadcasting stations; Pirate radio broadcasting.

Alternative schools. See *Nontraditional education.*

Alternative services. See *Alternatives to institutionalization.*

Alternative work patterns. Alternative work pattern(s). Job sharing. *Choose from:* job(s), work, position(s), appointment(s), staff line(s), schedule(s), duties *with:* shar(e,ed,ing), part time. *Consider also:* alternative work schedule(s), shared work compensation, shortened workweek(s), compressed workweek(s), work hour reduction(s), flexible worklife, flextime, time-income tradeoff(s), phased retirement(s), part time retirement(s), alternative(s) to retirement, home based work, four-day workweek(s), ten-hour day(s), multiple job(s,holding), telecommut(ing,er,ers). *See also* Alternative lifestyles; Contract labor; Flexible retirement; Flexible workplace practices; Home based businesses; Job sharing; Moonlighting; Nontraditional careers; Overtime work; Part time employment; Part time farming; Personnel scheduling; Temporary employees; Work load; Work schedules; Workday shifts; Worktime.

Alternatives. Alternative(s). Competing view(s,points). Competing values. New approach(es). New interpretation(s). New perspective(s). Nontraditional approach(es). Holistic approach(es). Innovation(s). Option(s). Choice(s). *Consider also:* backup(s), recourse(s), replacement(s), substitute(s). *See also* Alternative energy; Alternative family forms; Alternative medicine; Alternative press; Alternative work patterns; Alternatives to incarceration; Alternatives to institutionalization; Appropriate technologies; Choices (alternatives); Innovations; Nontraditional careers; Nontraditional education.

Alternatives (choices). See *Choices (alternatives).*

Alternatives, animal testing. See *Animal testing alternatives.*

Alternatives to incarceration. Alternative(s) to incarceration. Decarcerat(e,ed,ing,ion). *Choose from:* alternative(s), lieu *with:* incarcerat(e,ed, ing,ion), custody, jail(s,ed,ing), penal system(s), correction(s,al), prison(s), imprison(ed,ing,ment), detention. *Choose from:* community based *with:*

detention, correction(al,s), restitution. *Consider also:* community service, contract probation, correctional day program(s), deinstitutionaliz(e,ed,ing, ation), parole, probation, deport(ed, ing,ation), supervised liberty, fine(s), weekend sentence(s), home detention, house arrest(s), home incarceration, community sentencing, work release, victim compensation, electronic detention, electric monitor(ing), personal telemonitoring, disincarceration. *Consider also:* open prison(s), open corrections, prison(s) without bars, punishment without walls. *See also* Alternatives to institutionalization; Criminal rehabilitation; Day reporting centers (corrections); Deinstitutionalization; Judicial decisions; Penal reform; Plea bargaining; Reparations; Restitution; Restorative justice; Sentencing; Trial (law).

Alternatives to institutionalization. Alternative(s) to institutionalization. *Choose from:* day care, domiciliary, foster, homemaker, home health, respite, supportive *with:* service(s). *Choose from:* group, independent, congregate, communal *with:* home(s), house(s), residence(s), living. *Choose from:* community *with:* plac(ed,ing,ment). *Consider also:* halfway house(s), day treatment, adult day care. *See also* Alternatives to incarceration; Consumer directed care; Coping; Deinstitutionalization; Institutional release; Psychosocial readjustment; Psychosocial rehabilitation; Social adjustment; Vocational rehabilitation.

Altitude. Altitude(s). Above sealevel. *Consider also:* elevation(s), peak(s), height(s), mountain(s,tops), Ande(s,an), Alp(s,ine), Himalaya(s,n), Rockies, summit(s). *See also* Ascent; Altitude effects; Mountaineering.

Altitude effects. Altitude effect(s). *Choose from:* altitude(s), decompression, mountain(s), Alps, Rockies, Himalaya(s,n) *with:* effect(s), acclimatization, stress(ed,es,ing), response(s), adjustment, performance, function(s), efficiency, body change(s), sick(ness), alert(ness), drows(y,iness), fatigue, short(ness) of breath. *See also* Altitude; Altitude sickness; Ascent; Environmental effects.

Altitude sickness. Altitude sickness. *Choose from:* altitude(s), high altitude(s), mountain(s) *with:* anox(ia,ic), hypox(ia,ic), risk(s), sick(ness,nesses), tolerance, syndrome, heart disease, ill(ness,nesses), medical problem(s), edema, asthma, disorder(s). *Consider also:* Acosta(s), D'Acosta(s) *with:* disease, syndrome. *See also* Altitude; Altitude effects; Environmental effects; Environmental stress; Mountaineering.

Altruism. Altruis(m,tic). Unselfish(ness). Community interest. Team spirit. Empath(y,etic). Sympath(y,etic). Affective identification. Prosocial. Social minded(ness). Social mindful(ness). Helping behavior. Generous. Generosity. Car(e,ed,ing). Shar(e,ed,ing). Philanthrop(y,ic). Humanitarian(ism). Consideration for others. Concern for others. Social commitment. Humane(ness). Kind(ness). *Consider also:* alter-ego(ism), B love, being love, brotherly love, agape. *See also* Brotherliness; Charitable behavior; Charities; Cooperation; Ethics; Favors; Generosity; Gift giving; Giving; Good samaritans; Helping behavior; Humane; Humanitarianism; Interpersonal relations; Kindness; Magnanimity; Moral attitudes; Philanthropy; Prosocial behavior; Self interest; Sharing; Social behavior; Social ethics; Social values; Unselfishness; Volunteers.

Alzheimer's disease. Alzheimer(s) disease. Alzheimer type senile dementia. Alzheimer type patient(s). *Consider also:* presenile dementia, presenile psychosis, cerebral sclerosis. *See also* Cognition disorders; Cognition disorders; Mental confusion; Senile dementia; Wandering behavior.

Amateur theatricals. Amateur theatrical(s). Amateur theater(s). School play(s). Amateur thespian(s). Parlor play(s). *Choose from:* amateur, school, community *with:* theatrical(s), play(s), musical comed(y,ies), production(s), theater(s), *See also* Amateurs; Little theater; Theater.

Amateurs. Amateur(s,ism). Nonprofessional(s). Novice(s). Amateur status. Lay(man,men,women,woman, person,persons). Laity. Neophyte(s). Apprentice(s). Beginner(s). *Consider also:* aspirant(s), dilettante(s), recruit(s). *See also* Amateur theatricals; Laymen; Leisure activities; Little theater; Novices; Sports.

Ambassadors. See *Diplomats; Representatives.*

Ambidexterity. Ambidexter(ity). Ambidextr(ism,ous,ously,ality). Bilateral writing ability. *See also* Cerebral dominance; Laterality.

Ambience. Ambien(ce,t). Ambian(ce,t). Surrounding(s). Milieu(s,x). Atmosphere. Mood. Setting(s). Environment(s). Climate(s). Mise-en-scène). Scene(s,ry). *Consider also:* circumstance(s), background(s), theatrical effect(s). *See also* Classroom environment; Context; Environment; Environmental effects; Environmental psychology.

Ambiguity. Ambiguit(y,ies). Ambiguous(ness). Role stress. Role multiplicity. Indirect duplicity.

Equivocat(e,ed,ing,ion). Pun(s). *Consider also:* abstruse(ness), hidden meaning(s), hidden agenda(s), innuendo(s), word play(s), ambivalen(t, ce), circumlocut(ion,ory), evas(ion,ive, iveness), deceptive(ness), vague(ness), obscur(e,ity). *See also* Communication (thought transfer); Definition (words); Double meanings; Meaning; Role ambiguity; Tolerance for ambiguity.

Ambiguity, role. See *Role ambiguity.*

Ambiguity, tolerance for. See *Tolerance for ambiguity.*

Ambitions. Ambition(s). Aspiration(al,s). Intent(ion,ions). Dream(s). Hope(s). Enterprising. Enthusias(m,tic). Target(s). Purpose(s). Calling(s). Aim(s). Ambitious(ness). Goal setting. Striving. Status seeker(s). *Choose from:* achievement, career, performance *with:* motivation(s), orientation(s), expectation(s). *Choose from:* academic, occupational, parent(al), educational, vocational, professional, status, career *with:* aspiration(s), ambition(s), objective(s), aim(s), goal(s). *See also* Achievement need; Ambitiousness; Aspirations; Career goals; Educational plans; Goal orientation; Goals; Motivation; Status seekers.

Ambitiousness. Ambitious(ly,ness). Aspiring. Enterprising. Emulous(ness). Enterprising. Industrious(ness). Success oriented. *Consider also:* aggressive(ness), push(y,ing), energetic, hardworking, indefatigable; utopian, visionary. *See also* Ambitions; Drive; Initiative (personal).

Ambivalence. Ambivalen(t,ce,cy,cies). Contradictory feeling(s). Internal conflict(s). Uncertain(ty,ties). Undecided. Indecisive(ness). Irresolute(ness). Unsure. Dubious(ness). Hesitant. Vacillat(ed,ing). Fickle(ness). Equivoc(al,ate,ated,ating). Love hate relationship(s). *See also* Decision making; Choice (psychology); Conflict; Conflict of interest; Emotions; Hesitancy; Indecisiveness; Internal conflict; Role ambiguity; Role conflict.

Ambulances. Ambulance(s). Mobile coronary care unit(s). Emergency medical vehicle(s). EMV(s). Mobile emergency care. Emergency helicopter(s). Mobile intensive care. Emergency lifeboat(s). *Consider also:* patient transport(ation). *See also* Assistance in emergencies; Emergencies; Emergency medicine; Emergency services; Medical care.

Ambulatory care. Ambulatory care. *Choose from:* ambulatory, outpatient, office, dispensary, walk-in *with:* care, clinic(s), surgery, service(s), procedure(s), treatment(s), anesthesia, visit(s). *Choose from:* satellite, maternal, obstetric, pediatric, geriatric, mental health, child guidance, psychiatric, medical *with:* clinic(s). *Consider also:* day hospital(s), polyclinic(s), ambulatory peritoneal dialysis. *See also* Clinics; Community health services; Outpatient treatment; Walk-in clinics.

Ambulatory surgery. Ambulatory surgery. *Choose from:* ambulatory, outpatient, day stay, office *with:* surger(y,ies), surgical, myringoplasty, operation(s). *Consider also:* surgicenter(s). *See also* Ambulatory care; Community health services; Outpatient treatment; Surgery; Walk-in clinics.

Amenities. Amenit(y,ies). Advantage(s). Enhanc(e,ed,ing,ement,ements). Enrich(ed,ing,ment,ments). Improv(e,ed, ing,ement,ements). Agreeable(ness). Pleasant(ness). Comfort(able). Convenien(t,ce). Better(ment). Excellen(t,ce). Attractive(ness). *See also* Comfortableness; Etiquette; Living standards; Luxuries; Manners.

Amenorrhea. Amenorr(hea,hoea,hoic,heic). *Consider also:* oligomenorrhea, pseudocyesis. *Choose from:* absence, suppress(ed,ing,ion), cessation *with:* menstruat(e,ed,ing,ion), menses. *See also* Menstrual disorders; Menstruation.

Amentia. See *Mental retardation.*

America, Central. See *Central America.*

America, Latin. See *Central America; South America.*

America, North. See *North America.*

America, South. See *South America.*

American Indian reservations. See *American Indian territories.*

American Indian territories. Indian territor(y,ies). *Choose from:* Indian(s), Native American(s), Inuit, or tribes by name such as Navajo(s), Blackfeet, Penobscot(s), etc. *with:* homeland(s), reservation(s), reserve(s), land(s), land claim(s), land(s) in trust, propert(y,ies), real estate, owned, territor(y,ies,ial), sacred place(s), sacred space(s), sanctura(y,ies), game preserve(s), acre(age,s). *See also* Land (property); Land ownership; Land preservation; Land tenure; Land use; North American native cultural groups.

American Indians. See *Central American native cultural groups; Indigenous populations; North American native cultural groups; South American native cultural groups.*

American Indians, Central. See *Central American native cultural groups.*

American Indians, North. See *North American native cultural groups.*

Americanization. See *Acculturation.*

Americans abroad. American(s) abroad.

U.S. Diplomat(s). American embass(y,ies). American-born. Ugly American(s). U.S. exchange student(s). Peace Corps volunteer(s). Americans living in ... Americans working in ... *Choose from:* American(s), U.S. citizen(s) *with:* overseas, stationed abroad, exchange(s), Fulbright(s), hostage(s), missionar(y,ies), tourist(s), journalist(s), expatriate(s), draft dodger(s). *See also* Absentee voting; Anti-Americanism; Culture shock; Exchange of persons; Globalization; International educational exchange; Military civilian relations; Military families; Military personnel; Multinational corporations; Neocolonialism; Tourism; Travel writing.

Americans, African. See *Blacks.*

Americans, Asian. See *Asian Americans.*

Americans, Hispanic. See *Hispanic Americans.*

Americans, hyphenated. See *Biculturalism.*

Americans, Italian. See *Italian Americans.*

Americans, Japanese. See *Japanese Americans.*

Americans, Korean. See *Korean Americans.*

Americans, Latin. See *Latin Americans.*

Americans, Mexican. See *Mexican Americans.*

Americans, native. See *Central American native cultural groups; Indigenous populations; North American native cultural groups; South American native cultural groups.*

Americans, Spanish. See *Hispanic Americans; Latin Americans.*

Americans in foreign countries. See *Americans abroad.*

Amish. See *Mennonites.*

Amnesia. Amnes(ia,ic,tia,tic). Forget(ful, ting). *Choose from:* memory, recall(ed,ing), remember(ed,ing) *with:* loss(es), los(e,ing), lost, unable, inability. *Consider also:* transient global, retrograde, anterograde, retroantero-grade, lacunar *with:* amnesia. *Consider also:* fugue reaction. *See also* Amnesic syndrome; Forgetting; Memory disorders.

Amnesic syndrome. Amnesic syndrome. Axial amnesia. Korsakoff's amnesia. *See also* Amnesia.

Amnestic disorder, alcohol. See *Alcohol amnestic disorder.*

Amnesty. Amnesty. Pardon(ed,ing). Forgiv(e,en,ing,eness). Legal(ized, ization). Free(d,ing) prisoner(s). Releas(e,ed,ing) prisoner(s). *Choose from:* eas(e,ed,ing) *with:* restriction(s),

law(s). Exonerat(e,ed,ing,ion). Reconciliation. Clemency. Show(ed,ing) mercy. Repriev(e,ed,ing). Suspend(ed, ing) sentence. Exempt(ed,ing). Safe passage. *Consider also:* compassion, concession(s), absolv(e,ed,ing), absolution, respite, lenien(t,cy). *See also* Exemption (law); Legal procedures; Mercy; Pardon.

Amortization. Amortiz(e,ed,ing,ation). *Choose from:* debt(s), cost(s), charge(s), expenditure(s), loan(s), lease(s) *with:* writ(e,ing)-off(s), written off, reduc(e,ed,ing,tion,tions), gradual(ly) extinguish(ed,ing,ment), installment(s), prorat(e,ed,ing), amortiz(e,ed,ing,ation). *Consider also:* depreciat(e,ed,ing,ion). *See also* Capital expenditures; Cost recovery; Depreciation; Expenditures.

Amount. See *Quantity.*

Amounts, reinforcement. See *Reinforcement amounts.*

Amphetamines See *Stimulants; Street drugs.*

Amphibia. Amphibia(n,ns,l). *Consider also:* tadpole(s), frog(s), caudata, axoloti, triton, triturus, apoda, urodele, caecilian(s), newt(s), anura(ns), salamander(s), bufo(nidae), xenopus, ran(a,idae), ambystom(a,idae), proteidae, necturus, urodela, notophthalmus viridescens, pleurodeles, salamandr(a, idae), pipidae, salienta, mud pupp(y,ies). *See also* Frogs; Reptiles; Vertebrates.

Amputation. Amputat(e,ed,ing,ion,ions). *Consider also:* amputee(s), phantom limb(s), stump(s), disarticulation, hemipelvectom(y,ies), mastectom(y,ies), replantation, reimplantation. *Choose from:* loss, los(e,ing,t), missing, severed *with:* limb(s), digit(s), finger(s), leg(s), arm(s), breast(s). *See also* Phantom limb; Prostheses; Surgery.

Amputees. See *Amputation.*

Amusement parks. Amusement park(s). Amusement ride(s). Merry-go-round(s). Ferris wheel(s). Roller coaster(s). *Consider also:* Sea World, Wildwater Kingdom, Disneyland, Cypress Gardens, Coney Island, etc. *See also* Carnivals; Recreation areas.

Amusements. See *Entertainment.*

Amusements, children's. See *Children's games.*

Anabaptists. Anabaptis(m,t,ts). *Consider also:* Mennonite(s), Amish, Hutterite(s). *See also* Millenarianism; Protestantism.

Anachronisms. Anachronis(m,ms,tic, tically). Anachron(ic,ous,ously). Chronological error(s). *Choose from:* chronological(ly), historical(ly) *with:* misplac(e,ed,ing), out of place, error(s), discontinuit(y,ies). *Consider also:* archais(m,t,tic), misdat(e,ed,ing), mistim(ed,ing), parachronism(s), antedat(e,ed,ing), proleps(is,es), postdat(e,ed,ing), presentism. *See also* Errors; Historical perspective; Literary errors and blunders; Obsolescence.

Anaclitic depression. Anaclitic depression. Infant hospitalism. *Consider also:* anaclinic, anaclisis. *See also* Failure to thrive (psychosocial); Maternal deprivation; Parental absence.

Anagram problem solving. Anagram problem solving. *Choose from:* anagram(s), scrambled word(s) *with:* solv(ed,ing), solution(s), performance(s), recognition. *See also* Anagrams; Cognitive processes; Problem solving; Word games.

Anagrams. Anagram(s). Bigram(s). Scrambled words. Scrambled letters. *See also* Anagram problem solving; Literary games; Vocabulary; Word games.

Anal intercourse. See *Sodomy.*

Anal personality. Anal personalit(y,ies). Anality. *Choose from:* anal *with:* personalit(y,ies), character(s). *Consider also:* compulsive(ness), obsessive(ness), frugal(ity), obstinacy, orderliness. *Choose from:* anal *with:* retentive(ness), retention, triad. *See also* Anal stage; Compulsive behavior; Orderliness; Personality traits; Thriftiness.

Anal stage. Anal stage. Anality. *Choose from:* anal *with:* stage(s), erogeneity, sadis(m,tic), erotic(ism), regress(ion, iveness), erotism, humor, expulsion, aggress(ion,iveness), phase(s), fixat(ed,ion). *See also* Anal personality; Child development; Personality development.

Analgesia. Analges(ia,ic,ics). Antinociception. Audioanalgesia. Neuroleptanalgesia. *Choose from:* pain(ful), discomfort, ache(s) *with:* insensitiv(e,ity), block(ed,ing), relief, reliev(e,ed,ing), alleviat(e,ed,ing), insensible, inhibit(ed,ing,ion), control, treatment, suppress(ed,ing,ion), management. *See also* Drug therapy; Pain perception; Prescription drugs.

Analgesics. See *Analgesia.*

Analogical reasoning. Analogical reasoning. Reasoning by analog(y,ies). *Choose from:* analog(y,ies,ical), metaphor(s,ic, ical) *with:* problem(s) solving, reason(ed,ing), task(s), transfer(s). *Consider also:* inductive reasoning. *See also* Analogy; Cognitive development; Cognitive generalization; Induction; Reasoning.

Analogy. Analog(y,ies,ue,ues,cal,ous, ousness). Simil(e,es,itude). Comparab(le,leness,ility). Parallel(s,ing, ism). Alike(ness). Likeness(es). Similar(ity,ities). Resembl(e,ed,ing, ance,ances). *Consider also:* affinit(y,ies),

correlation(s), equivalen(t,ce), homolog(y,ous), parit(y,ies), semblance(s). *See also* Analogical reasoning; Meaning; Metaphors.

Analysis. Analys(is,es). Analytic(al). Analyz(e,ed,ing). Stud(y,ies). Review(s). Explicat(e,ed,ion,ions). Interpret(ed,ing, ation,ations). Assay(s). Breakdown(s). Broken down. Clarif(y,ying,ied, ication,ications). Criticism. Critique(d). Abstract(ed). Summar(y,izing). Explanation(s). Detect(ed,ing,ion). Determin(e,ed,ing,ation,ations). Estimat(e,ed,ing,ion,ions). Valuat(e,ed, ing,ion,ions). Evaluat(e,ed,ing,ion,ions). Identif(y,ying,ied,ication,ications). *Consider also:* dissect(ed,ing,ion), examin(e,ed,ing,ation), inquir(y,ies), scrutin(y,ize,ized,izing). *See also* Actuarial analysis; Audience analysis; Class analysis; Classification; Cohort analysis; Conversational analysis; Cost analysis; Data analysis; Deciphering; Didactic analysis; Discourse analysis; Error analysis; Exegesis; Factor analysis; Ideal types; Policy analysis; Psycho-analysis; Qualitative methods; Quantitative methods; Research; Secondary analysis; Task performance and analysis; Transactional analysis.

Analysis (Philosophy). Analys(is,es). Analyz(e,ed,ing). Analytic(ally, ity). Explicat(e,ed,es,ing,ion,ions). Clarification(s). Clarif(y,ied). *Consider also:* logical analysis; meta-analysis; analytic philosoph(y,ica). *See also* Causality; Logic; Logical positivism; Philosophy.

Analysis, actuarial. See *Actuarial analysis.*

Analysis, audience. See *Audience analysis.*

Analysis, class. See *Class analysis.*

Analysis, cohort. See *Cohort analysis.*

Analysis, content. See *Content analysis.*

Analysis, conversational. See *Conversational analysis.*

Analysis, cost. See *Cost analysis.*

Analysis, cost benefit. See *Cost effectiveness.*

Analysis, data. See *Data analysis.*

Analysis, didactic. See *Didactic analysis.*

Analysis, discourse. See *Discourse analysis.*

Analysis, error. See *Error analysis.*

Analysis, factor. See *Factor analysis.*

Analysis, job. See *Job descriptions.*

Analysis, policy. See *Policy analysis.*

Analysis, qualitative. See *Qualitative methods.*

Analysis, quantitative. See *Quantitative methods.*

Analysis, risk. See *Risk assessment.*

Analysis, secondary. See *Secondary analysis.*

Analysis, spatial. See *Spatial organization.*

Analysis, subject. See *Content analysis.*

Analysis, systems. See *Systems analysis.*

Analysis, task performance and. See *Task performance and analysis.*

Analysis, transactional. See *Transactional analysis.*

Analytical psychotherapy. Analytical psychotherap(y,ies). *Choose from:* analytical(ly), psychoanalytic(ally), integrative, Freudian *with:* psychotherap(y,ies), therap(y,ies), treatment. *Consider also:* Freudian analysis. *See also* Psychoanalysis; Psychoanalytic interpretation; Psycho-analytic theory.

Anaphrodisiac. Anaphrodisiac(s). Sexual sedative(s). Sexual anesthes(ia,ias, tic,tics). *Consider also:* potassium bromide, heroin, camphor, rue, ruta graveolens. *See also* Aphrodisiacs; Drugs.

Anarchism. Anarch(ic,ism,ists,istic,y). Apolitical. Unpolitical. Nihilis(t,tic,m). Minimal state. Libertarian. Lawless(ness). Abolition of state. Bakunnis(t,m). Anarcho-syndicalism. *See also* Chaos; Libertarianism; Nihilism; Political ideologies; Political movements; Vigilantes.

Anatolian languages. Anatolian language(s). Hieroglyphic Hittite. Hittite (Kanesian). Luwian. Lycian. Lydian. Palaic. *See also* Antiquity (time); Language; Languages (as subjects); Middle East.

Anatomic models. Anatomic(al) model(s). Model(s) of the body. Replica cast(s). Anatomical wax model(s). *Consider also:* eye(s), teeth, heart(s), digestive system(s), etc. *with:* model(s), cast(s), simulat(e,ed,ing,ion,ions), replica(s). *Consider also:* manikin(s), moulage(s). *See also* Biological models; Medical education; Medical illustration; Scientific models.

Anatomical gifts. Anatomical gift(s). *Choose from:* donor(s), donat(e,ed, ing,ion), source(s), gift(s), procure(ment) *with:* organ(s), heart(s), kidney(s), tissue(s), cardiac, bone marrow. *Consider also:* conscription, draft, sale, selling, sold, distribution, supply *with:* cadaveric organ(s). *See also* Blood banks; Blood donors; Dead bodies; Living donors; Organ transplantation; Tissue banks; Tissue donors.

Anatomy. Anatom(y,ia,ist,ic,ical). Neuroanatomy. Nomina anatomica. *Consider also:* dissect(ed,ing,ion,ions), morpholog(y,ical), morphometr(y,ic).

See also Abdomen; Anatomical gifts; Back; Body covering (Anatomy); Body height; Body weight; Bones; Brain; Cardiovascular system; Chest; Digestive system; Dissection; Ear; Endocrine system; Eye; Foot; Female genitalia; Male genitalia; Hand; Heart; Human body; Nervous system; Physique; Respiratory system; Sense organs.

Ancestor worship. Ancestor worship. Ancestor practice(s). Cult of ancestor(s). Ancestor rite(s). *Choose from:* ancestor(s), ancestral, agnat(es,ic), ghost(s), dead spirit(s), genealog(y,ical) *with:* worship(ped,ping), venerat(e,ed, ing,ion), religion, religious, reverenc(e, ing), piety, cult(s). *See also* Ghosts; Reincarnation; Religions; Shintoism; Traditional societies; Voodooism.

Ancestors. Ancestor(s). Ancestral. Descent. Genealog(y,ies,ical). Geneaolog(y,ies, ical). Grandparent(s). Parent(s). Great grandparent(s). Familial. Line(s) of descent. Forbear(s). Forefather(s). Foremother(s). Progenitor(s). Primogenitor(s). Family founder(s). Founding father(s). Sire(s). Grandsire(s). *Consider also:* antecedent(s), forerunner(s), prototype(s), progenitor(s), founder(s). *See also* Creators; Extended family; Genealogy.

Ancient architecture. Ancient architecture. Pre-Hellenic architecture. Architectural Heritage. *Consider also:* Stonehenge, megalith(s,ic). *Choose from:* ancient, pre-Hellenic, mesolithic, proto-historic, Aztec(s), Inca(n), ancient Maya(n), pre-Columbian, ancient Egypt(ian), ancient Near East(ern), Mycenae(an,ans), Minoa(n,ns), Mesopotamia(n,ns), Indus Valley, Hittite(s), Etruscan(s), Judaea(n), Greco-Roman, Ur(artian), Hellenistic, bronze age, Cyprus, Ugarit(ic), etc. *with:* architecture, stonemason(ry), town planning, monument(s), tomb(s), basilica(s), ashlar mason(ry), ruin(s), synagogue(s), temple(s), building(s), pyramid(s). *See also* Ancient art; Antiquities (objects); Antiquity (time); Architectural styles; Architecture; Art history; Classical architecture; Extinct cities; Mesolithic period; Primitive architecture.

Ancient art. Ancient art(s). L'arte antica. Antike(n) Kunst(werke). L'art ancien. *Choose from:* ancient, antiquit(y,ies), pre-classical, Cypriot, Crete, ancient Persia(n), archaic Gree(k,ce), Mesopotamia(n), Anatolia(n), Sumer(ian,ians), Hittite(s), Assyria(n), ancient near east(ern) *with:* art(s), portrait(s,ure), architecture, sculpture(s), painting(s), figurine(s). *See also* Ancient architecture; Antiquities (objects); Antiquity (time); Art history; Arts; Classical art; Earthworks; Figurines; Humanities.

Ancient astronomy. Ancient astronom(y,er,ers). *Choose from:* ancient, early, prehistoric, medieval, antiquity, Mayan(s), Inca(s,n), Aztec(s), Egyptian(s), Greek(s), Roman(s) *with:* astronom(y,er,ers), eclipse(s), astrolog(er,ers,y), cosmos(es), cosmograph(y,er,ers). *Consider also:* archaeoastronom(y,ical). *See also* Astronomy; Eclipses; Nautical astronomy.

Ancient education. Ancient education. *Choose from:* ancient, antiquit(y,ies), pre-classical, ancient Persia(n), ancient Egypt(ian), archaic Gree(k,ce,cian), Confuci(us,an), ancient Sparta, Plato, Aristot(le,elian), St. Augustine, *with:* educat(e,ed,ing,ion), gymnasi(a,um), teach(ing), learn(ing), school(s,ing). *See also* Antiquity (time); Education.

Ancient geography. Ancient geography. *Choose from:* Bibl(e,ical), Roman, ancient Greece, Ancient Egypt, Alexander the Great, ancient civilization(s), antiquit(y,ies), viking(s) *with:* geograph(y,ical), geolog(y,ical), map(s,ped,ping). *Consider also:* time-slice map(s). *See also* Antiquity (time); Geography; Historical geography; World history.

Ancient goldwork. Ancient goldwork. *Choose from:* ancient, antiquit(y,ies), antique(s), early, Assyro-Babylonian, Celtic, Mycenaean, Pre-Columbian, ancient Greece, pre-Incan *with:* gold(en), precious metal(s) *with:* article(s), cup(s), ornament(s), treasure(s), relic(s), jewelry, decorat(ion,ions,ive). *See also* Ancient jewelry; Antiquities (objects); Antiquity (time); Goldwork; Treasure.

Ancient Greek music. Ancient Greek music. *Choose from:* Ancient Greek, Ancient Greece, Aristoxenus, Pythagorean(ism), Neopythag-orean(ism), Aristotelian, Dorian, Phyrigian, Lydian, Mixolydian, Hypolydian, Hyperlydian, Hypophrygian, Hyperphrygian, Locrian, Hypodorian, Hyperdorian, Hypoaeolian, Hyperaeolian, Hypomixolydian, Hypermixolydian, Ionian, Iastian *with:* ton(e,es,on,os), music(al,ally), tetrachord(s), harmon(ic,ics,iai,y,ies), tune(s), song(s), hymn(s). *Consider also:* nomos kitharodikos, nomos aulodikos. *See also* Music.

Ancient jewelry. Ancient jewelry. *Choose from:* ancient, antiquit(y,ies), antique(s), early, Assyro-Babylonian, Celtic, Mycenaean, Pre-Columbian, ancient Greece, pre-Incan *with:* jewel(s,ry), scarab(s), talisman(s), amulet(s), torque(s), bracelet(s), necklace(s), earring(s). *See also* Antiquities (objects); Ancient goldwork; Talisman.

Ancient literature. Ancient literature. Antike(n) literatur. Ancient fiction. Latin literature. Greek literature. Biblical Literature. Ancient Myth(s,ology). Dead Sea Scroll(s). *Choose from:* antiquit(y, ies), ancient Latin, Aramaic, Sumer(ian, ians), ancient Hebrew, ancient Israelite(s), ancient Egypt(ian), ancient arab(ic), classical, ancient Rom(e,an), Ovid (ian), Plutarch(ian), Pausanias, ancient Gree(k,ce), Hellenistic, Homer(ic), Pindar(ic), Aeschyl(us,ean), Sophocle(s,an), Euripede(s,an), Plato, Cicero, ancient Chin(a,ese), ancient India(n), early Christian(ity) *with:* literature, tale(s), folktale(s), inscription(s), myth(s,ology), drama(s), traged(y,ies), narrative(s), manuscript(s), letter(s), stor(y,ies), poe(m,ms,t,ts,try), writing(s). *See also* Antiquity (time); Centos; Latin drama; Latin epigrams; Latin inscriptions; Latin laudatory poetry; Latin literature; Literature; Mythology; Roman law; Scholia.

Ancillaries. Ancillar(y,ies). Auxiliar(y,ies). Subordinate(s,d). Subsidiar(y,ies). Supplement(ed,ing,ary). Accessor(y,ies). Adjuvant(s). Appurtenant(s). Collateral. Contribut(e,ed,ing,ory). Subservien(t, ce). *Consider also:* concomitan(t,ce), accompan(ied,ying), attendant(s), attend(ed,ing), collateral, incidental(ly), satellite(s). *See also* Allied health personnel; Manpower; Subsidiaries; Volunteers.

Andean-Equatorial languages. Andean-Equatorial languages. Andean: Araucanian, Mapuche. Quechu-Maran: Aymara, Quechua. Equatorial: Arawakan, Taino, Tupi-Guarani, Guarani, Lingua Geral, Tupi. Jivaroan: Jivaro. *See also* Language; Languages (as subjects); South America; South American native cultural groups.

Andragogy. See *Adult education.*

Androcentrism. Androcentri(sm,c,city). Male anthropocentri(c,city,sm). Male centered. *Choose from:* male, patriarchal, masculin(e,ity) *with:* perspective(s), point of view, obsession(s), bias(es,ed), gender based motivation(s), domination, dogma(s), gendered, gender lense(s), polarization. *See also* Machismo; Male chauvinism; Masculinity; Misogyny; Patriarchy; Sexism; Sexual inequality; Sexual oppression.

Androgyny. Androgyn(e,y,al,ic,oid, ism,eity,ization). Androgynous(ity). Androgenic. Sex role adaptability. Cross(ed,ing) sex role(s). *Consider also:* intersexual(ity), unisex, pseudo-thermaphrodit(e,es,ism), hermaphrodit(e, es,ism), bisexual(ity). *See also* Femininity; Gender differences; Gender identity; Masculinity; Sex roles.

Anecdotes. Anecdot(e,es,al). Short account(s). Yarn(s). Short stor(y,ies). Tale(s). Fable(s). Myth(s). Sketch(es). Allegor(y,ies). Narrative(s). Legend(s). *See also* Allegory; Character sketches; Folk culture; Ghost stories; Haunted houses; Mythology.

Anemia. Anem(ia,ic). Anaem(ia,ic). Low hemoglobin. Deficiency of red cell mass. Deficient in hemoglobin. *Consider also:* erythropoeisis. *See also* Illness; Nutrition; Thinness; Undernourishment.

Anesthesia, hysterical. See *Hysterical anesthesia.*

Aneuploidy. Aneuploid(y,s). *Consider also:* D trisomy, E trisomy, G trisomy, XXX superfemale, XYY, XXYY, XXY Klinefelter's syndrome, XO Turner's syndrome, unbalanced chromosomes. *See also* Hereditary diseases.

Angels. Angel(s,ic,ology). Cherub(s,im). Seraph(s,im). Archangel(s). Beneficent spirit(s). Divine messenger(s). *See also* Demons; Good spirits; Religion.

Anger. Anger(ed). Angry. Fury. Furious. Enrage(d). Ire. Wrath(ful). Resent(ful,ment,ments). Animosity. Infuriated. Mad(dened). Hostil(e,ity). Rage. *See also* Alienation; Depression (psychology); Emotions; Frustration; Hostility; Jealousy; Loneliness; Rejection (psychology); Resentment; Road rage.

Anglos. See *Whites.*

Angst. Angst. Existential anxiety. *See also* Anxiety.

Anguish. Anguish(ed). Wretched(ness). Agon(y,ies,ize,ized,izing). Torment(s, ed,ing). Worr(y,ies,ied). Heartache(s). Heartbroken. Grief. Griev(e,ed,ing). Remorse(ful). Psychological(ly) distress(ed,es). *Choose from:* psychosomatic, psychological(ly), psychophysiological(ly), psychiatric, mental(ly), emotional(ly), posttraumatic *with:* distress(ed,es,ing), stress(ed,es). *Consider also:* burnout, depression, worr(y,ied), unhappy, combat reaction(s), status insecurity, high level of stress, strain(s), malaise, bereavement, psychological stress, emotional cris(es,is). *See also* Anxiety; Depression (psychology); Distress; Psychological stress.

Anhedonia. Anhedon(ia,ic). Dystych(ia,ic). Inability to experience pleasure. Pleasure deficit. *Consider also:* hyphedon(ia,ic). *See also* Dysthymic disorder; Enjoyment; Hedonic damages; Neuroses; Pleasure; Schizophrenia.

Animal abuse. See *Cruelty to animals.*

Animal aggressive behavior. Animal aggressive behavior(s). Muricide. Mouse killing. Prey catching. *Choose from:* appetitive, predatory *with:* behavior(s),

response(s), act(s,ion,ions), signal(s). *Choose from:* aggress(ion,ive,ivity), predat(ion,ory), attack(s,ing), fight(ing), agonistic, threat(en,ening) *with:* animal(s), mammal(s), primate(s), or animals by name, such as: rat(s), mice, mouse, rabbit(s), cat(s), cockroach(es), crab(s), chicken(s), squirrel(s), bird(s), gull(s), etc. *See also* Aggression; Agonistic behavior; Animals; Birds of prey; Predatory animals.

Animal behavior. Animal behavior(s). *Choose from:* animal(s), mammal(s), primate(s), instinctive, bird(s), insect(s) or specific animals by name *with:* behavior(al,s), ethology, activit(y,ies), movement(s), action(s). *Consider also:* aggress(ion,ive), appetitive(ness), attack(ed,ing,s), groom(ed,ing), preen(ed,ing), cannibalism, consummatory behavior(s), nesting, predat(ation, ory), sex behavior(s), copulation, mating, pair bond(s,ing), eliminative behavior(s), escape reaction(s), home range, communication, courtship, display(s), defens(e,ive), defend(ed,ing), protect(ed,ing,ive), distress call(s), division of labor, dominance, explorat(ion,ory), feeding, foraging, hoard(ed,ing), maternal behavior(s), mating, nocturnal behavior(s), open field behavior(s), play(ed,ing,ful,fulness), social behavior(s), vocaliz(e,ed,ing, ation,ations), hibernat(e,ed,ing,ion), imprint(ed,ing), migrat(e,ed,ing,ory, ion,ions), territoriality, threat(s,en, ening,ened). *See also* Alarm responses; Animal aggressive behavior; Animal communication; Animal courtship behavior; Animal defensive behavior; Animal division of labor; Animal dominance; Animal emotionality; Animal exploratory behavior; Animal flight; Animal foraging behavior; Animal grooming behavior; Animal hoarding behavior; Animal locomotion; Animal mate selection; Animal migration; Animal parental behavior; Animal psychology; Animal scent marking; Animal sex behavior; Animal vocalization; Echolocation; Imprinting (psychology); Instinct; Nesting behavior; Stereotyped behavior; Territoriality; Threat postures.

Animal breeding. Animal breeding. *Choose from:* animal(s), livestock, pet(s) or specific animals by name such as: cattle, sheep, horse(s), dog(s), cat(s), rabbit(s), chinchilla(s), hamster(s), rat(s), mice *with:* breeding, bred, crossbreeding, crossbred, inbreeding, inbred, mat(e,ed,ing), cross(ed,ing), propagat(e,ed,ing,ion), whelp(ed,ing), reproduct(ive,ion), sired, pregnan(cy,cies,t), gestation. *See also* Animal courtship behavior; Animal mate selection; Animal sex behavior; Cattle industry; Horse industry; Selective breeding.

Animal coloration. Animal color(s,ation). Body color(s,ation). Secondary sex coloration. Sexual dichromatism. Plumage color. Bill color. Wing patch. Wing spotting. Conspicuous plumage. Blue tails, etc. *Consider also:* animal(s), bird(s) or names of specific animals *with:* color(s,ation), shade(s), marking(s), spot(ted,s), stripe(s,d) or specific colors. *See also* Animal defensive behavior; Pigments.

Animal communication. Animal communication. Zoosemiotics. *Choose from:* animal(s), pet(s), mammal(s,ian), primate(s), nonhuman(s), bird(s), chimpanzee(s), gorilla(s), monkey(s), ape(s), rabbit(s), chipmunk(s), giraffe(s), horse(s), dog(s), cat(s), bat(s), squirrel(s), beaver(s), fox(es), rat(s), mice, mouse, guinea pig(s), bee(s), insect(s) or other animals by name *with:* communicat(e,ed,ing,ion,ions), call(s,ed,ing), language(s), alarm(s), signal(s,led,ling), song(s), semiotic(s), vocal(ize,ized,izing,ization,izations), singing behavior(s), dance(s), ritual(s,ized), visual display(s), echolocation, sex attractant(s), pheromone(s). *See also* Alarm responses; Animal emotionality; Animal intelligence; Animal scent marking; Animal vocalization; Birdsongs; Nature sounds; Pheromones.

Animal courtship behavior. Animal courtship behavior(s). *Choose from:* animal(s), mammal(s,ian), primate(s), instinctive, bird(s), etc. *with:* court(ing, ship), precopulatory, sex appeal, mate choice(s), mate preference(s), mating *with:* behavior(al,s), song(s), call(s), sing(ing), tactic(s), vocaliz(ed,ation), chorus(es,ing), activit(y,ies), movement(s), action(s), danc(e,es,ing), ritual(s). *See also* Animal mate selection; Animal sex behavior.

Animal culture. Animal culture. Animal husbandry. Pastoralism. *Choose from:* animal(s), poultry, cattle, sheep, pig(s), hog(s), meat, livestock *with:* produc(er, ers,tion), stockyard(s), farm(s,ing), rais(e,ed,ing), breed(ing), agricultur(e,al). *See also* Animal domestication; Farming.

Animal culture, environmental enrichment. See *Environmental enrichment (animal culture).*

Animal defensive behavior. Animal defensive behavior(s). *Choose from:* animal(s), mammal(s,ian), primate(s), instinctive, bird(s), insect(s) or specific animals by name *with:* defens(e,ive), defend(ed,ing), defence, anti-predat(or, ion), antipredat(or,ion), escape, protect(ed,ing,ive), guard(ed,ing), hyperdefensive. *Consider also:* distress call(s), alarm response(s), tonic immobility, vigilan(ce,t), avoidance. *See* *also* Alarm responses; Animal coloration; Animal flight; Startle reaction; Tonic immobility; Vigilance; Warnings.

Animal division of labor. Animal division of labor. *Choose from:* animal(s), mammal(s,ian), primate(s), insect(s), ant(s), bee(s), cichlid(s) or specific animals by name *with:* division of labor, task specializ(ed,ing,ation), social organization, caste(s), slave(s,ry), colon(y,ies). *See also* Animal dominance.

Animal domestication. Animal domestication. *Choose from:* animal(s), cattle, wildlife, livestock, dog(s), cat(s), sheep, goat(s), cow(s), rabbit(s), raccoon(s), squirrel(s), etc. *with:* domesticat(e,ed, ing,ion), adapt(ed,ing,ation) to captivity, tam(e,ed,ing), housebreak(ing), housebroken. *Consider also:* pet(s), game farm(s). *See also* Animal breeding; Animal culture; Captivity; Domestic animals; Pets.

Animal dominance. Animal dominance. *Choose from:* animal(s), wolf, wolves, dog(s), mammal(s), primate(s), insect(s), bird(s), pack(s), herd(s) or specific animals by name *with:* dominan(t,ce), pecking order, rank, status, hierarch(y, ies,ical). *Consider also:* territoriality, priority, intraspecies aggression, competitiveness, rivalry. *See also* Animal aggressive behavior; Animal division of labor; Animal scent marking; Dominance.

Animal emotionality. Animal emotion(s,al,ality). *Choose from:* animal(s), mammal(s,ian), primate(s), rat(s), mice, mouse, rabbit(s), cat(s), dog(s), bird(s), chicken(s) or specific animals by name *with:* emotion(s,al, ality), feeling(s), affect, expressiveness, affection, anxiety, anxious(ness), bored(om), enjoyment, fear(ful,fulness), frustrat(ed,ion), grief, irritab(le,ility), jealous(y,ness), loneliness, pleasure, rage. *See also* Alarm responses; Animal psychology: Animal vocalization; Emotional responses; Startle reaction; Vigilance.

Animal environments. Animal environment(s). *Choose from:* animal(s), mammal(s), primate(s), bird(s), insect(s) or specific animals by name *with:* environment(s,al), habitat(s), ecolog(y, ical), spatial, territor(y,ies,ial), setting(s), context(s,ual), condition(s), place(s), area(s), confine(d,ment), cage(s,d), floor covering(s), captiv(e,ity), free-ranging, open field(s), pasture(s), stable(s,d), zoo(s), laborator(y,ies), nest(s), laying site(s), aquarium(s), crowd(ed,ing), isolat(ed,ion), subterranean. *Consider also:* temperature, light exposure. *See also* Bioinvasion; Environmental enrichment (animal culture); Gardening to attract wildlife; Habitat; Home range;

Nesting behavior; Phytogeography; Sanctuary gardens; Territoriality; Wildlife sanctuaries.

Animal ethology. See *Animal behavior.*

Animal experiments. See *Animal studies.*

Animal exploratory behavior. Animal exploratory behavior(s). *Choose from:* animal(s), mammal(s,ian), primate(s), bird(s), insect(s) or specific animals by name *with:* explorat(ory,ion,ions), explor(e,ed,ing), investigat(ory,ive, ion,ions), curiosity, sniff(ed,ing), track(ed,ing), nose poking, search behavior, visual scanning. *See also* Animal foraging behavior; Curiosity; Predatory behavior.

Animal females. See *Females (animal).*

Animal flight. Animal(s) flight(s). *Choose from:* fly(ing), flew, flight(s), flown, airborne, glid(e,ed,ing) *with:* animal(s), bird(s), dragonfl(y,ies), insect(s), drosophila, bat(s), squirrel(s), etc. *See also* Animal defensive behavior; Animal locomotion.

Animal food. Animal food (s). Animal feed(ing,ings). *Choose from:* animal(s), pet(s), cat(s), dog(s), chicken(s), poultry, cattle, sheep, pig(s), hog(s), livestock *with:* food(s), feed(ing,ings), diet(s,ary). *See also* Animal foraging behavior; Farming; Feeding behavior.

Animal foraging behavior. Animal foraging behavior(s). *Choose from:* animal(s), mammal(s,ian), ruminant(s), deer, cattle, sheep, lion(s), wolves, ant(s), llama(s), monkey(s), shrew(s), elephant(s), flock(s), herd(s), etc. *with:* forag(e,ing,ers), graz(e,ed,ing), flocking, ranging. *Choose from:* prey, food, feed, fodder, nourishment, honey *with:* get(ting), gather(ing), find(ing), search(es,ing), wrest(ed,ing), obtain(ed,ing), localiz(ed,ing), select(ed,ing,ion). *See also* Animal exploratory behavior; Animal food; Animal hoarding behavior; Animal navigation; Feeding behavior; Grazing; Habitat; Home range; Predatory behavior; Territoriality.

Animal grooming behavior. Animal grooming behavior. Preen(ed,ing). Whisker trimming. Dustbath(ing). Allogroom(ed,ing). Animal hygiene. *Choose from:* animal(s), cat(s), dog(s), rat(s), rabbit(s), chimpanzee(s), gerbil(s), monkey(s), pigeon(s), guinea pig(s), hamster(s), etc. *with:* groom(ed,ing), autogroom(ed,ing), clean(ed,ing), lick(ed,ing), primp(ed,ing), wash(ed, ing). *Consider also:* groom(ed,ing) *with:* chain(s), network(s), social, self, behavior. *See also* Animal parental behavior; Preening; Social behavior.

Animal hoarding behavior. Animal hoarding behavior. *Choose from:* animal(s), bird(s) or specific animals by

name *with:* hoard(ed,ing), cach(e,es,ed,ing). *See also* Animal foraging behavior; Feeding behavior; Nesting behavior.

Animal-human relationships. See *Human-animal relationships.*

Animal industry. Animal industr(y,ial). Livestock industr(y,ial). Slaughterhouse(s). *Choose from:* animal(s), poultry, chicken(s), turkey(s), duck(s), cattle, sheep, lamb(s), pig(s), hog(s), swine, horse(s), meat, livestock *with:* rais(e,ing), agricultur(e,al), produc(e,er,ers,tion), ranch(es,er,ers, ing), industr(y,ies,ial), assembly-line(s), rear(ed,ing), process(ed,ing), pack(ed, ing), feeding, operation(s), grower(s), market(s,er,ers), price(s), import(s), export(s). *See also* Agribusiness; Cattle industry; Dairying; Horse industry; Meat industry; Slaughterhouses.

Animal infants. See *Animal offspring.*

Animal intelligence. Animal intelligence. *Choose from:* animal(s), dog(s), cat(s), parrot(s), monkey(s), primate(s), chimpanzee(s), orangutan(s) *with:* intelligen(t,ce), cognit(ive,ion), numerical competence, think(ing), thought(s), comprehen(d,ding,sion), us(e,ed,ing) tool(s), self-aware(ness), understand(ing), speech, communicat(e, ed,ing,ion). *See also* Animal communication; Cognition; Intelligence.

Animal locomotion. Animal locomotion. *Choose from:* animal(s), mammal(s,ian), primate(s), insect(s), bird(s), cat(s), rat(s), mice, mouse, rabbit(s), horse(s), dog(s), guinea pig(s), etc. *with:* locomot(ion,or), jump(ed,ing), circl(e, ed,ing), walk(ed,ing), trot(ted,ting), run(ning), ran, gallop(ed,ing), canter(ed,ing), flight, fly(ing), flew, ambulat(e,ed,ing,ion). *See also* Animal flight; Animal migration.

Animal lore. Animal lore. *Choose from:* animal(s), creature(s), monster(s), beast(s), zoological, dolphin(s), dragon(s), gorilla(s), serpent(s), bird(s), lion(s), elephant(s), dog(s), cat(s), horse(s), goat(s), etc. *with:* lore, folklore, folk tale(s), stor(y,ies), anecdote(s), mythology, legend(s), superstition(s), fable(s). *Consider also:* nature lore. *See also* Animals; Bestiaries; Folklore; Mythical animals; Natural history; Naturalists; Nature literature; Snake lore.

Animal magnetism (hypnotic). See *Hypnosis.*

Animal magnetism (navigational). See *Animal navigation.*

Animal mate selection. Animal mate selection. Mating system(s). Pair formation. *Choose from:* animal(s), mammal(s), primate(s), bird(s) or species by name *with:* mat(e,es,ing), spawn(ed,ing), sexual *with:* select(ed,ing,ion,ions), choice(s), preference(s). *See also* Animal courtship behavior; Animal sex behavior.

Animal maternal behavior. See *Animal parental behavior.*

Animal migration. Animal migration(s). Animal navigation. Animal migratory behavior(s). Homing pigeon(s). School(s,ing) of fish. Migratory herd(s). Migrating flock(s). Seasonal migration. *Choose from:* migrat(e,ed,ing, ion,ions,ory), emigrat(e,ed,ing,ion,ions), navigat(e,ed,ion), flock(s,ing), school(s,ing), homing *with:* pigeon(s), bird(s), insect(s), fish(es), sparrow(s), salmon, spider(s), beetle(s), seal(s), bunting(s), warbler(s), whale(s), blackbird(s), duck(s), goose, geese, trout, crane(s), butterfl(y,ies), etc. *See also* Animal environments; Animal navigation; Biogeography; Bioinvasion; Habitat; Home range; Migration patterns; Territoriality; Wildlife sanctuaries.

Animal nature of man. Animal nature of man. Rational animal(s). Biological basis of human behavior. *Consider also:* speciesism, biocartesian(ism). *See also* Anthropocentrism; Evolution; Evolutionary ethics; Human nature; Humanism; Humanity; Mind body problem; Natural law; Philosophical anthropology; Physical anthropology; Sociobiology; Soul.

Animal navigation. Animal(s) navigat(e,ed, ing,ion,or,ors,al). *Choose from:* animal(s), honeybee(s), sea turtle(s), insect(s), bird(s), pigeon(s), fish(es), shark(s), salmon, marine mammal(s), seal(s) *with:* hom(e,ing), navigat(e,ed, ing,ion,or,ors,al), magnetic field(s), magnetic orientation(al), magneto-reception, internal compass(es), internal magnetic compass(es), directional aid(s), spatial memor(y,ies), magnetic map(s), retrac(e,ed,ing) homeward direction(s), celestial cue(s), landmark-based cue(s), landmark memor(y,ies), geomagnet(ic, ism), solar orientation. *Consider also:* animal magnetism, animal orientation. *See also* Animal foraging behavior; Animal migration; Home range; Migration patterns.

Animal offspring. Animal offspring. *Choose from:* animal(s), livestock, pet(s), bird(s), cattle, sheep, goat(s), horse(s), dog(s), cat(s), rabbit(s), hamster(s), rat(s), mice, squirrel(s), fox(es), wolf, wolves, raccoon(s) or other animals by name *with:* offspring, infant(s), neonate(s), newborn(s), juvenile(s), subadult(s), young, orphan(s), nestling(s), fledgling(s), bab(y,ies). *Consider also:* calf, calves, kit(s), kitten(s), pup(s), pupp(y,ies), foal(s), fry, yearling(s), lamb(s),

chick(s), cygnet(s), whelp(s). *See also* Animal parental behavior; Newborn animals.

Animal painting and illustration. Animal(s) paint(ed,ing,ings). Animal(s) illustrat(ed,ing,ion,ions). *Choose from:* animal(s), natural history, wildlife, habitat(s), pet(s), bird(s), cat(s), dog(s), ornitholog(y,ical), horse(s), rabbit(s), zoolog(y,ical) *with:* pictur(e,es,ed,ing), art(s,ist,ists), paint(ed,ing,ings), illustrat(ed,ing,ion,ions), draw(n,ing, ings). *Consider also:* John James Audubon, Rosa Bonheur, Sir Edwin Landseer, Dorothy Lathrop, Louis Agassiz Fuertes, Thomas Bewick, etc. *See also* Arts; Biological illustration; Drawing; Genres (art); Medical illustration.

Animal parental behavior. Animal parental behavior(s). *Choose from:* animal(s), mammal(s,ian), primate(s), instinctive, bird(s), insect(s), etc. *with:* parent(s,al), maternal, paternal, biparental, mother(s), father(s), sire(s), dam(s) *with:* behavior(al,s), activit(y,ies), care, rear(ed,ing), reaction(s), communicat(e, ed,ing,ion,ions), contact(s), defens(e,ive), defend(ed,ing), protect(ed,ing,ive), division of labor, interact(ed,ing,ions). *Consider also:* nesting behavior(s), imprint(ed,ing). *See also* Animal division of labor; Animal grooming behavior; Animal offspring; Maternal behavior; Nesting behavior; Nurturance; Paternal behavior; Stereotyped behavior.

Animal products. Animal product(s). Product(s) from animal(s). Wildlife product(s). Livestock product(s,ion). Animal part(s). Animal resource(s). Dairy product(s,ion). Leather(s). Gelatin. Silk. Wool(en). Meat(s). Bear bile. Ivory. Offal. Pet food. Fur(s). Milk. Egg(s). Cheese(s). Caviar. Lard. *See also* Agribusiness; Anti-fur protests; Food; Fur; Leather industry; Sewage as fertilizer; Slaughterhouses; Wool industry.

Animal psychology. Animal psychology. *Choose from:* animal(s), mammal(s), chimpanzee(s), elephant(s), dolphin(s), rat(s), rabbit(s), cat(s), mice, mouse, dog(s), horse(s), canine(s), feline(s), pig(s) *with:* psycholog(y,ical), sensib(le,ility,ilities), perception(s), behavior(s,al), learn(ed,ing), reinforcement, emotion(s,al), personalit(y,ies), disposition(s), socializ(e,ed,ing,ation), communicat(e,ed,ing,ion), territorial(ity). *See also* Animal behavior; Animal emotionality; Animal intelligence.

Animal remains (archaeology). Animal remain(s). Zooarchaeolog(y,ical). Faunal remain(s). Bone remain(s). *Choose from:* archaeolog(y,ical), antiquit(y,ies), prehistoric, fossil(s,ized), Anglo-Saxon,

early, stone age, bronze age, archaeolog(y,ical), mummif(ied,ication), mumm(y,ies) *with:* skull(s), bone(s), remain(s), skeleton(s), animal(s), fauna, mammal(s). *See also* Age determination by skeleton; Age determination by teeth; Archaeological chemistry; Archaeology; Bone implements; Fossils; Human remains (archaeology); Paleoecology; Paleontology; Physical anthropology; Plant remains (archaeology); Skeleton.

Animal research. See *Animal studies.*

Animal rights movement. Animal rights movement. Animal liberation. *Choose from:* animal rights, rights of animal(s), research animal(s), animals experiment(s,ation), wildlife, zoo(s), wild animal(s), humane treatment, animal torture, animal pain, animal suffering, laboratory animal(s), fur, farm(s), animal trial(s), animal welfare *with:* activist(s), protest(s,or,ors), debate(s), ethic(s,al,ally), moral(ly,ity,s), philosoph(y,ical), question(s), oppos(e,ed,ing,ition), protect(ed,ing, ion). *Consider also:* People for the Ethical Treatment of Animals. PETA, antihunter group(s), anti-hunting, anti-vivisect(ion,ionist,ists,or,ors). *See also* Animal testing alternatives; Animal welfare; Anti-fur protests; Cruelty to animals; Protest movements.

Animal sacrifice. Animal sacrific(e,es,ial). *Choose from:* sacrific(e,es,ial), offering(s), ritual killing(s) *with:* animal(s), lamb(s), firstling(s). *See also* Cruelty to animals; Human sacrifice; Sacrificial rites.

Animal sanctuaries. See *Wildlife sanctuaries.*

Animal scent marking. Animal scent marking. Territorial pheromone(s). *Choose from:* scent(s), olfactory, odor *with:* demarcat(ed,ing,ion,ions), disseminat(e,ed,ing,ion), trail(s). *Consider also:* vaginal, urine *with:* mark(ed,ing,ings). *See also* Animal communication; Animal dominance; Pheromones; Territoriality.

Animal sex behavior. Animal sex behavior(s). *Choose from:* animal(s), mammal(s,ian), primate(s), rat(s), mice, mouse, rabbit(s), cat(s), dog(s), bird(s), chicken(s) or specific animals by name *with:* sex(ual), mating, mate(d), copulat(e,ed,ing,ory), reproductive, breeding *with:* behavior(s), receptivity, function(s). *See also* Animal breeding; Animal mate selection; Pheromones; Sexual reproduction; Stereotyped behavior.

Animal studies. Animal stud(y,ies). *Choose from:* animal(s), mammal(s,ian), primate(s), nonhuman, livestock, rodent(s), ruminant(s), feline, cat(s), canine, dog(s), bovine, cattle, cow(s), swine, pig(s), flock(s), herd(s), wildlife, rat(s), rabbit(s), chimpanzee(s), gerbil(s), kitten(s), mice, mouse, monkey(s), pigeon(s), toad(s), frog(s), rana, guinea pig(s), chick(s,ens), avian, bird(s), hamster(s), fish(es), horse(s), equine, goat(s), goose, geese, duck(s), sheep, lamb(s), bull(s), worm(s), earthworm(s), flatworm(s), clam(s), etc. *with:* stud(y,ies), research, drug trial(s), control group(s), in-vivo, experiment(s, ing,ation), test(ed,ing,s), subject(s). *See also* Agricultural research; Animal testing alternatives; Animal welfare; Animals; Earthworms; Frogs; Experiments; Research subjects.

Animal testing alternatives. Animal testing alternative(s). *Choose from:* alternative(s), simulat(e,ed,ing,ion,ions), substitut(e,ed,ing,ion), tissue culture, mathematical model(s), equivalent model(s), in vitro alternative(s), in vitro method(s), in vitro culture system(s), in vitro assay(s), biomarker assay(s) humane *with:* animal test(s,ed,ing), laboratory animal(s), medical research, biological research diagnostic, laborator(y,ies). *Consider also:* ban(ned,ning) animal test(s,ing). *See also* Animal rights movement; Animal welfare; Animals; Cruelty to animals; Experiments; Scientific models; Simulation.

Animal training. Animal train(ed,er,ers,ing). *Choose from:* school(s,ed,ing), break(ing), broken, teach(ing), housebreak(ing), housebroken, pretrain(ing), instruct(ed,ing,ion), condition(ed,ing) *with:* animal(s), pet(s), dog(s), cat(s), horse(s), goat(s), bird(s), rat(s), rabbit(s). *See also* Domestic animals; Training.

Animal vocalization. Animal vocal(ize,ized,izing,ization). *Choose from:* animal(s), pet(s), mammal(s,ian), primate(s), nonhuman(s), bird(s), chimpanzee(s), gorilla(s), monkey(s), ape(s), dolphin(s), rabbit(s), chipmunk(s), giraffe(s), horse(s), dog(s), cat(s), bat(s), squirrel(s), beaver(s), fox(es), rat(s) mice, mouse, guinea pig(s), whale(s), etc. *with:* vocal(ize,ized,izing,ization), sing(ing), song(s), duet(s), dialect(s), birdcall(s), call(s,ed,ing), language(s), alarm(s), cry(ing), cries, utter(ed,ing), utterance(s), warbl(e,ed,ing), growl(ed,ing,s), whoop(s,ed,ing), squeal(s,ed,ing), bark(s,ed,ing), meow(s,ed,ing), squeak(s,ed,ing), chirp(s,ed,ing). *See also* Alarm responses; Animal communication; Birdsongs.

Animal welfare. Animal welfare. Animalist(s). Anti-vivisection(ism,ists). *Choose from:* animal(s), primate(s), nonhuman(s), mammal(s,ian), cat(s), dog(s), rabbit(s), monkey(s), swine, pig(s), chimpanzee(s), etc. *with:*

bioethic(s,al), bio-ethic(s,al), ethic(s,al), protect(ed,ing,ion), welfare, well-being, prior review, social environment(s), rights, euthanasia, consciousness, immoral(ity), humanitarian, humane(ness). *Consider also animal terms with:* research, experiment(s, ation), stud(y,ies), subject(s) *with:* suffer(ed,ing), pain, distress(ed,ing), depress(ed,ing,ion), anxiety, cruel(ty), stress(ed,ing,ful), tail suspension, tail pinch(es), shock(s,ed,ing). *See also* Animal testing alternatives; Animal studies; Animals; Cruelty to animals; Humanitarianism; Ombudsmen; Research ethics; Shelters; Wildlife conservation; Wildlife sanctuaries.

Animals. Animal(s). Livestock. Pet(s). Mammal(s,ian). Invertebrate(s). Vertebrate(s). Primate(s). Carnivor(a,e,es). Beast(s). Wildlife. Nonhuman(s). Nonhuman(s). Creature(s). Fauna. Predator(s). Ruminant(s). Feline(s). Canine(s). Rodent(ia,s). Muridae. Artiodactyl(s,a). Cetacea. Chiroptera. Edentata. Elephant(s). Hyrax(es). Herbivore(s). Insectivor(a,es). Lagomorph(s,a). Marsupial(s,ia). Monotremata. Perissodactyl(s,a). Pinniped(s,ia). Anthropoid(s,ea). Prosimii. Callithricidae. Cebidae. Cercopithecidae. Pongidae. *Consider also specific animals by name, for example:* rabbit(s), giraffe(s), etc. *See also* Amphibia; Animal studies; Bestiaries; Bison; Cattle; Cats; Chickens; Clams; Coyotes; Dinosaurs: Dogs; Domestic animals; Draft animals; Earthworms; Elephants; Endangered species; Exotic species; Females (animal); Fishes; Flies; Goats; Horses; Onagers; Livestock; Males (animal); Mammals; Mythical animals; Nature sounds; Parasites; Pets; Poultry; Predatory animals; Sheep; Snake lore; Species differences; Vertebrates; Wild animals; Wolves; Zoo animals.

Animals, cruelty to See. *Cruelty to animals.*

Animals, domestic. See *Domestic animals.*

Animals, females. See *Females (animal).*

Animals, juvenile. See *Animal offspring.*

Animals, male. See *Males (animal).*

Animals, mythical. See *Mythical animals.*

Animals, newborn. See *Newborn animals.*

Animals, poisonous. See *Poisonous animals.*

Animals, predatory. See *Predatory animals.*

Animals, sacred. See *Sacred animals.*

Animals, suckling. See *Newborn animals.*

Animals, wild. See *Wild animals.*

Animals, young. See *Animal offspring.*

Animals, zoo. See *Zoo animals.*

Animation (Cinematography). Animat(ed,ion) cinematograph(y,ic). Computer assisted animation. Animated sequence(s). Animated character(s). Classic animation(s). *Choose from:* cartoon(s), toon(s), film(s), program(s), sequence(s), serial(s), television, TV *with:* animat(ed,ing,ion). *See also* Animators; Cartoons.

Animatism. Animatism. Vitalism. *Consider also:* mana. *See also* Animism; Anthropomorphism; Mana; Philosophy; Vitalism.

Animators. Animator(s). Cartoonist(s). Creator of cartoon(s). Animation compan(y,ies). Animation department(s). *Consider also:* Lou Bunin, Walt Disney, Paul Germain, etc. *See also* Animation (Cinematography); Artists.

Animism. Animis(m,tic). Animacy. Animate(s). Aliveness. Life concept. Attribution of life. *Consider also:* totemism, mana, orenda, manitou, alien spirit(s), holy spirit(s), enchant(ed,ment), cult(s) of possession, demonic possession. *See also* Animatism; Anthropomorphism; Mysticism; Mythical animals; Mythology; Personification; Pneuma; Sacred animals; Vitalism; Water spirits.

Animus, racial. See *Racism.*

Annals. Annal(s). Chronicle(s). Annual(s). Historical record(s). Classbook(s). Diar(y,ies). Account(s). Logbook(s). Yearbook(s). Registr(y,ies). *See also* Archives; Diaries.

Annamese-Muong languages. Annamese-Muong languages. Muong. Vietnamese (Annamese). *See also* Language; Languages (as subjects); Southeast Asia; Southeast Asian cultural groups.

Annexation. Annex(ed,es,ing,ation,ations). Incorporat(e,ed,ing,ion,ions). Expansion(ist,ists,ism). Land grab(bing,ber,bers). Add(ed,ing) to tax base. Jurisdiction formation. Intergovernmental pact(s). Expand(ed,ing) tax base. Takeover(s). Unification(s). *Choose from:* addition(s), join(ing), merger(s), unit(e,ing) *with:* referend(a,um). City-county consolidat(e,ed,ing,ion,ions). *Consider also:* local government integration, public service expansion, irredenti(a,sm). *See also* Boundaries; Expansion; International relations; Political geography; Territorial issues; Unification.

Annihilation. Annihilat(e,ed,ing,ion). Demolish(ed,ing). Exterminat(e,ed,ing, ion). Obliterat(e,ed,ing,ion). Extinct(ion). Destroy(ed,ing). Devastat(e,ed,ing,ion). Murder(ed,ing). Slaughter(ed,ing). Butcher(ed,ing). Wholesale killing(s). Blood bath(s).

Decimat(e,ed,ing,ion). Liquidat(e,ed, ing,ion). Genocide. Carnage. *Choose from:* mass, group(s) *with:* murder(s), slaying(s), killing(s), homicide, execut(e,ed,ing,ion,ions), destroy(ed, ing), destruction. *See also* Extinction (species); Genocide; Holocaust; Military capitulations.

Annihilation, self. See *Self destructive behavior; Self hate; Self inflicted wounds; Self mutilation; Suicide.*

Anniversaries and special events. Anniversar(y,ies) and special event(s). Annual observance(s). Yearly observance(s). *Consider also:* holiday(s), birthday(s), ceremon(y,ies), carnival(s), centennial(s), centenar(y,ies), bicentennial(s), dedication(s), commemoration(s), celebration(s), international year(s), world year(s), festival(s), fiesta(s), jubilee(s), fete(s). *See also* Ceremonies; Commemoration; Entertaining; Events; Family reunions; Festivals; Holidays.

Anniversary reactions. Anniversary reaction(s). *Choose from:* anniversar(y, ies) *with:* reaction(s), depress(ion,ions, ive), excitement, agitation, manifest-ation(s), disease. *Consider also:* holiday depress(ive,ion,ions). Holiday reaction(s). *See also* Holiday depression; Reactive depression; Seasonal affective disorder.

Annotations. See *Commentaries.*

Announcements. Announcement(s). Proclamation(s). Statement(s). Press release(s). Decree(s). Broadcast(s). Declar(e,ed,ing,ation,ations). Press leak(s). *See also* Communication (thought transfer); Mass media; Messages; Press conferences; Rumors.

Announcers. See *Broadcasters.*

Annual reports. Annual report(s). Year end report(s). Yearbook(s). Progress report(s). 10-K report(s). Yearly publication(s). Yearly report(s). Annual summar(y,ies). *Consider also:* corporate report(s), financial report(s), financial statement(s), prospectus(es), proxy statement(s). *See also* Accountability; Financial statements; Information.

Annuities. Annuit(y,ies,ant,ants). *Consider also specific types of annuities such as:* certain, contingent, deferred, fixed rate, hybrid, immediate, joint, survivor, no load, perpetuity, refund, single premium, straight life; tax-sheltered, variable payout variable rate *with:* annuit(y,ies, ant,ants). *Consider also:* retirement saving(s), retirement plan(s), individual retirement account(s). *See also* Assets; Retirement income.

Annulment. Annul(ment,ling,led). Nullif(y,ied,ication). Abolish(ed,ing, ment). Abolition. Abjur(e,ed,ing,ation). Void(ed,ance). Invalidat(e,ed,ing,

ion,ions). Disenact(ed,ment). Cancel(led,ling). Recall(ed,ing). Repeal(ed,ing,s). Revok(e,ed,ing). Revocation. Rescind(ed,ing). Abrogat(e,ed,ing,ion). Revers(ed,al,ing). Recant(ed,ing,ation). Retract(ed,ing, ion). Withdraw(n,al). Disclaim(ed,ing). Disavow(ed,ing,al). *See also* Cancella-tion; Disclaim; Divorce; Nullification; Remarriage; Repeal.

Anomalies. Anomal(y,ies,ous). Abnormalit(ies,y). Deviation(s). Aberration(s). Irregular(ity,ities). Deform(ed,ity,ities). Defect(s). Malform(ed,ation,ations). Divergen(t,ce). Variation(s). Variance(s). Asymmetr(y,ies). *Consider also:* eccentric(ity,ities), idiosyncras(y,ies), incongruit(y,ies), peculiarit(y,ies). *See also* Congenitally handicapped; Deviation; Drug induced abnormalities; Exceptions; Human abnormalities; Idiosyncrasies; Physical abnormalities; Variations.

Anomalies, congenital. See *Congenitally handicapped.*

Anomia (inability to remember names). Anom(ia,ic). Dysnom(ia,ic). Autonomas(ia,ic). Inability to name objects. *Choose from:* nominal, amnestic, anomic, amnesic *with:* aphasia. *Consider also:* amnesia, agnosia. *See also* Amnesia; Memory disorders.

Anomie. Anom(ie,ic,y,ia). Social break-down. Normless(ness). *Choose from:* breakdown, loss, disintegrat(e,ed, ing,ion), collapse, lack *with:* belief system(s), social structure, norms, values, standards. Social disorganiza-tion. Social demoralization. Lawless(ness). *See also* Alienation; Decadence; Impersonal; Mass society; Moral conditions; Regression (civiliza-tion); Social disorganization; Social isolation.

Anonymity. Anonym(al,ous,ity,s). Un-named. Nameless(ness). Unknown. Unidentified. Unsigned. Unknown author(ship). Incognit(o,os,a,as). Pseudonym(s,ous). *Consider also:* off record, stranger(s), unattributed. *See also* Disputed authorship; Privileged communications; Self disclosure; Social identity.

Anonyms and pseudonyms. See *Anonym-ity.*

Anorexia nervosa. Anorexia nervosa. Anor(exic,ectic). Pathological loss of appetite. Self starvation. Apepsia hysterica. *Consider also:* aposit(ia,ic), dysorex(ia,ic), phagophob(ia,ic), sitophob(ia,ic), neurotic hunger strike(s), aphagia. *See also* Bulimia; Eating disorders; Fasting; Nutrition; Nutrition disorders; Psychophysiologic disorders.

Anorexic. See *Anorexia nervosa; Thinness.*

Anosmia. Anosm(ia,ic,ization). Anosphres(ia,ic). *Choose from:* smell(ing), olfactory *with:* dysfunction, loss, inability, unable. *See also* Sensory loss; Odor discrimination.

Antagonism. Antagon(ism,istic,ize, ized,izing). Antipath(y,ies). Unfriendl(y,iness). Enmity. Opposition. Counterpressure(s). Hostil(e,ity). Resent(ed,ing,ment). Angry. Anger. Malicious intent. Rage. Animosit(y,ies). Ill will. Grudg(e,ing). Begrudg(e,ing). Spite(ful). Contempt(uous). Enmity. Hatred. Hat(e,ed,ing). Dislik(e,ed,ing). Disaffect(ed,ion). Malevolen(ce,t). Malic(e,ious). Wrath(ful). Rancor(ous). *See also* Anger; Hate; Hostility; Interpersonal conflict; Resentment; Scapegoating.

Antagonism, drug. See *Drug antagonism.*

Antagonists, narcotic. See *Narcotic antagonists.*

Antarctic regions. Antarctic region(s). Antarctica. Antarctic Continent. Antarctic Peninsula. Antarctic Circle. Antarctic Ocean. South Pole. *Consider also:* Weddell Sea, Ross Sea, South Orkney Islands, South Shetland Islands, Graham Land, Palmer Peninsula, British Antarctic Territory, McMurdo Station, Ross Ice Shelf. *See also* South America; Oceania.

Antecedents. See *Ancestors; Causality; Determinism; Predisposition.*

Anthems, national. See *Patriotic music.*

Anthologies. Antholog(y,ies). Collected works. Compilation(s). Selected works. *Consider also:* album(s), compendium(s), literary collection(s), omnibus(es), digest(s), excerpt(s,ed), assemblage(s), accumulation(s), compendi(a,um,ums). *See also* Books; Collections.

Anthropocentrism. Anthropo-centri(c,cally,city,ism). Human centered(ness). Human specialness. Attribut(e,es,ing) self or soul only to humans. *See also* Animal nature of man; Anthropomorphism; Ecology; Environ-mentalism; Philosophical anthropology.

Anthropogeography. Anthropogeo-graph(y,ic). Anthropogeograph(y,ical). Cultural geograph(y,ical). Human geography. Population geography. *Consider also:* urban geography, urban anthropology, human migration pattern(s). *See also* Geographic distribution; Human ecology; Migration patterns; Population distribution; Population genetics.

Anthropoid. Anthropoid(s). New world monkey(s). Old world monkey(s). Platyrrhini. Catarrhini. Hominidae.

Pongidae. Hylobatidae. *See also* Vertebrates.

Anthropologists. Anthropologist(s). Archaeologist(s). Archeologist(s). Ethnologist(s). Anthrobiolog(y,ical). *See also* Anthropology; Folklorists; Social sciences.

Anthropology. Anthropolog(ical,y). Archaeolog(y,ical). Ethnograph(y,ical). Ethnolog(y,ical). Meta-anthropolog(y, ical). Chrono-anthropolog(y,ical). Transcultural. Ethnopsycholog(y,ical). Somatolog(ical,y). Anthropometr(y,ical). Synthetic anthropology. Anthropological linguistics. Educational anthropology. Cultural anthropology. Social anthropology. Physical anthropology. Somatic anthropology. *See also* Anthropologists; Cultural anthropology; Ethnography; Ethnology; Physical anthropology; Social sciences.

Anthropology, cultural. See *Cultural anthropology.*

Anthropology, medical. See *Medical anthropology.*

Anthropology, philosophical. See *Philosophical anthropology.*

Anthropology, physical. See *Physical anthropology.*

Anthropology, psychological. See *Psychological anthropology.*

Anthropology, social. See *Cultural anthropology.*

Anthropometry. Anthropometr(y,ic). Fetometr(y,ic). Caliperometr(y,ic). Cephalometr(y,ic). For animals use "biometr(y,ic)." *Choose from:* bod(y,ies), morphofunctional *with:* assessment(s), indices, index(es), measure(s,ments). *See also* Human remains (archaeology); Physical anthropology.

Anthropomorphism. Anthropomorph(ism,ic,ize,ized,izing). Human attribut(e,es). *Consider also:* animism, animatism, anthropathism, vitalism. *See also* Animism; Animatism; Anthropocentrism.

Anthroposophy. Anthroposoph(y,ic). *Choose from:* theosophy, Steiner schools. *See also* Philosophy; Therapeutic cults.

Anti-alcoholism drugs. See *Alcohol deterrents.*

Anti-Americanism. Anti-American(ism). Anti-west(ern). *Choose from:* enmity, hatred, dislik(e,ed,ing), resent(ment,ful), hostil(e,ity) *with:* American(s), United States, U.S. *Consider also:* ugly American(s), anti-capitalism. *See also* Americans abroad; International conflict; Multinational corporations; Neocolonialism; Prejudice.

Anti-apartheid movement. Anti-apartheid movement(s). Antiapartheid movement(s). *Choose from:* anti-colonial(ism,ist,ists), anticolonial(ism, ist,ists) *with:* Africa(n) *with:* movement(s), group(s), activis(m,t,ts), struggle(s), act(s), demonstrat(ion,ions, or,ors), protest(s,ed,ing,er,ers), coalition(s), polic(y,ies), pressure(s), rall(y,ies), organization(s), fight(s,ing), cause(s). *Consider also:* Free South Africa Movement, African National Congress, ANC, Incatha [Inkatha] Freedom Party, South West African People's Organization, SWAPO, Mass Democratic Movement, United Democratic Front, Inkatha, Congress of South African Trade Unions, COSATU, Under Law Southern Africa Project, TransAfrica, U.N. Center Against Apartheid, Desmond Tutu, Nelson Mandela, Anti-Apartheid Act of 1986. *Consider also:* Amnesty International. *See also* African cultural groups; Apartheid; Civil rights organizations; Resistance movements; Social movements; Sub-Saharan Africa.

Anti-Catholicism. Anti-Catholic(ism). Anti-Popery. *Choose from:* religious ethnocentr(c,ism), prejudice(d,s), discriminat(ed,ing,ion), hat(e,ed, red,ing), hostil(e,ity,ities), intoleran(t,ce), bias(ed), bigot(ed,ry,s), persecut(ed,ion), genocide, stereotype(s), minority status, desecrat(ed,ing,ion), scapegoat(s,ing), killing(s), conspiracy against *with:* Catholic(s,ism), Vatican, Pope(s,ry). *Consider also:* anticlerical(ism). *See also* Anti-Semitism; Bigotry; Exclusivity (Religion); Religious prejudice.

Anti-depressants. See *Antidepressive agents.*

Anti-environmentalism. Anti-environment(al,alism,ist,ists). Brownlash. Anti-green(s). Opponent(s) of environmental movement. Anti-environmental political action committee(s). Intimidat(e,ed,ing) environmentalist(s). Eco-thug(s). Wise Use Movement. Sahara Club. *Choose from:* defunding, rollback, take away power, enem(y,ies), assault(s,ed,ing), cut budget(s), undermin(e,ed,ing), threat(s,en,ened,ening), gut(ted,ting), profit imperative *with:* environmental protection(s), environmental law(s), wilderness, conservation, environmental legislation, Green Party, ecolog(y,ical), environmentalis(m,t,ts), Clean Water Act, Endangered Species Act, Clean Air Act, air-quality standard(s). *Consider also:* ecocide, dump(ed,ing) waste(s). *See also* Anti-science movement; Environmental degradation; Environmental policy; Environmental protection; Environmentalism; Political conservatism; Right wing politics.

Anti-fur protests. Anti-fur protest(s). *Choose from:* animal rights protestor(s), People for the Ethical Treatment of Animals, PETA *with:* endangered species, fur(s), alligator(s). *Consider also:* fake fur(s), *See also* Animal rights movement; Fur; Fur trade.

Anti-government radicals. Anti-government radical(s). Anti-government extremist(s). *Choose from:* anti-government, antigovernment, paramilitary *with:* radical(s), extremist(s), alliance(s), patriot(s), group(s), militia(s). *Consider also:* Ku Klux Klan, Christian Coalition, Neo-Nazi(s), Identity Believer(s), Identity Religion, Christian Reconstructionist(s), Michigan Militia, domestic terroris(m,t,ts), white supremacist(s). *See also* Antiabortion movement; Antifascist movements; Anti-intellectualism; Antisemitism; Civil war; Counterrevolutions; Dissent; Ethnocentrism; Eurocentrism; Fascism; Guerrillas; Hate crimes; Hate groups; Islamic Resistance Movement; Lynching; Militias; National fronts; Paramilitary; Patriotism; Political dissent; Political ideologies; Political violence; Protest movements; Racism; Rebellions; Rebels; Revolution; Secret societies; Separatism; Sexism; Terrorism; White supremacy movements; Xenophobia.

Anti-imperialist movements. See *Decolonization; Liberation movements; National fronts; Nationalist movements; Peasant rebellions; Revolution; Separatism.*

Anti-inflation. Anti-inflation(ary). *Choose from:* strateg(y,ies), fight(ing), slow(ing), combat(ting), attack(ed,ing), control(led,ling), prevent(ed,ing,ion) *with:* inflat(e,ed,ing,ion), rising prices. *Consider also:* control(s,led,ling), restrain(t) *with:* price(s), wage(s), money supply, credit. *See also* Economic stabilization; Inflation (economics); Monetary policy; Price control.

Anti-intellectualism. Anti-intellectual(ism). Antiintellectual(ism). Anti-theoretical. Counter-enlightenment. Obscurant(ism, ist,ists). *Choose from:* expert(s), academ(y,ia,ic,ics), intellectual(s), egghead(s), intelligentsia *with:* gap(s), distrust(ful), erosion of respect, suspicion(s), threaten(ed,ing), attack(s, ed,ing). *Consider also:* neo-Luddite(s). *See also* Absolutism; Anti-government radicals; Anti-science movement; Extremism; Fascism; Intellectual liberty; Intelligentsia; Irrationalism (philosophy); McCarthyism; Political conservatism; Populism; Religious fundamentalism.

Anti-psychiatry. See *Alternative medicine.*

Anti-science movement. Anti-science movement. Anti-scientific. Hostile to science. Critical of science. Antirational(ist,ism). *Choose from:* scien(ce,ces,tific) *with:* hating, misinform(ed,ation), uncritical, irrational(ism), superstitio(n,us), disinformation, distortion(s), misunderstanding(s), exaggeration(s), animus toward, attack on, denounc(e,ed,ing), reject(ed,ing,ion). *Consider also:* anti-evolution, anti-social science, health misinformation, pseudomedicine, paranormal, occult(ism), astrology. *See also* Anti-environmentalism; Anti-intellectual(ism); Extremism; Irrational-ism (philosophy); Postmodernism; Quackery.

Anti-takeover strategies. Anti takeover strateg(y,ies). Anti takeover measure(s). Takeover defense(s). Shark repellent(s). Block(ed,ing,s) takeover(s). *Choose from:* anti-takeover, anti-raider *with:* defense(s), tactic(s), measure(s), by-law change(s), poison pill(s), corporate restructuring, hurdle(s), curb(ed,ing,s), resistance, oppos(e,ed,ing,ition), amendments block(ed,ing,s), device(s), regulation(s), provision(s). *Choose from:* hostile takeover(s), corporate raider(s), merger(s), hostile investor(s), leveraged buyout(s), buyout offer(s), hostile changes of control *with:* defense(s), block(ed,ing,s), by-law change(s), poison pills, corporate restructuring, ward(ing) off, repel(led,ling), prevent(ed,ing), fend(ing) off, resist(ed,ing,ance), oppos(e,ed,ing,ition), killer bee(s). *Consider also:* shareholder rights, stockholder rights. *See also* Buyouts; Corporate acquisitions; Hostile takeovers; Leveraged buyouts; Mergers.

Antiabortion movement. Antiabortion movement(s). *Choose from:* abortion clinic(s) *with:* violence, demonstrator(s), demonstrat(e,ed,ing,ion,ions), picket(s,ed,ing), terroris(m,t,ts). *Choose from:* antiabortion(ist,ists,ism), anti-abortion(ist,ists,ism), fetal right(s), pro-life, right to life *with:* consciousness raising, demonstrator(s), protest(er,ers,s) movement(s), activis(m,ts), resistance, part(y,ies), group(s), campaign(s), mobilization, boycott(s). *Consider also:* Feminists for Life of America, Human Life Foundation, Operation Rescue, etc. *See also* Abortion rights movement; Abortion laws; Anti-government radicals; Civil rights organizations; Feminism; Hate crimes; Hate groups; Political conservatism; Protest move-ments; Radical movements; Suffrage movement; White supremacy move-ments; Women's groups.

Antiaircraft artillery. Antiaircraft artiller(y,ies). Anti-aircraft weapon(s,ry). Air defense unit(s). Non-Cooperative Target Recognition System. Identifica-tion Friend or Foe (IFF) system. Anti-ballistic missile(s). Patriot missile(s). Antiaircraft missile(s). *Choose from:*

antiaircraft, anti-aircraft, air defense *with:* artiller(y,ies), weapon(s,ry), unit(s), missile(s), equipment. *See also* Aerial warfare; Ballistic missiles; Military weapons.

Antianxiety drugs. See *Tranquilizers.*

Antibias curriculum. Antibias curricul(a,um). *Choose from:* antibias, anti-bias, counter(ed,ing) bias, counter(ed,ing) prejudice, social justice, fairness, equity, diversity, cultural sensitiv(ity,e), culturally inclusive *with:* curricul(a,um), classroom(s), discussion(s), pedagogy. *Consider also:* prejudice reduction. *See also* Antiracist education; Cultural sensitivity; Curricu-lum change; Intercultural communica-tion; Multicultural education; World citizenship.

Anticipation. Anticipat(e,ed,ing,ion,ions, ory). Expectation(s). Expect(ed,ing). Expectanc(y,ies). Forecast(ing). Looking forward. Await(ed,ing). Prophec(y,ies). Prophes(y,ying,ied). Predict(ed,ing, ion,ions). Future perspective. Prospect(s). Hop(e,ed,ing). Contemplat(e,ed,ing). *Consider also:* presumption(s), trust, confiden(t,ce), apprehens(ion,ive), anxiet(y,ies). *See also* Apprehension; Attitudes; Emotions; Expectations; Forecasting; Suspense.

Anticlericalism. Anticlerical(ism). Anti-clerical(ism). Critique of cleric(s,alism). *Choose from:* priest(s,hood,craft), the pulpit, cleric(s,alism) *with:* public oppos(e,ed,ing,ition), denunciation, denounc(e,ed,ing), polariz(e,ed,ing, ation), curb(ed,ing) power. *Consider also:* church burning(s), early Protes-tantism, clerical satire. *See also* Clericalism; Church state relationship; Secularism; Secularization.

Antidepressive agents. Antidepressive agent(s). Antidepressant(s). Psychic energizer(s). *Choose from:* anti-depress(ant,ive), antidepress(ant,ive) *with:* drug(s), agent(s). *Consider also:* amitriptyline hydrochloride [Elavil, Endep, Etrafon, Limbitrol, Triavil], amoxapine [Asendin], cocaine [coke, crack, bernies, big C, flake, freebase, free base, happy dust, ice, snow], desipramine hydrochloride [Norpramin], doxepin hydrochloride [Sinequan], imipramine [Tofranil], isocarboxazid [Marplan], maprotiline [Ludiomil], nortriptyline hydrochloride [Pamelor], phenelzine [Nardil], protriptyline [Vivactil], trimipramine [Surmontil], tranylcypromine sulfate [Parnate], trazodone hydrochloride [Desyrel]. *See also* Depression (psychology); Drug therapy.

Antidotes. Antidote(s). Remed(y,ies). Antitoxin(s). Antibod(y,ies). Antivenin(s). Corrective(s). Counteract(er,ers,ant,ants).

Counteractive(s). Counteragent(s). Countermeasure(s). Cure(s). *Consider also:* neutralizer(s), nullifier(s), prevent(ive,ative), vaccin(e,es,ation, ations). *See also* Drug therapy; Drugs; Herbal medicine.

Antifascist movements. Antifascist movement(s). Anti-fascist movement(s). Antifaschismus. Against fascis(m,t,ts). Popular Front. Grand Alliance. *Choose from:* anti-fascis(m,t,), antifascis(m,t), anti-nazi, anti-Franco, anti-Mussolini *with:* movement(s), resistance, under-ground, organization(s), alliance. *Consider also:* World War II, Nazi, Third Reich *with:* partisan(s), resistance, underground, struggle, KPD, SED. *See also* Anti-government radicals; Counter-movements; Fascism; Guerrillas; Nazism; Political movements; Resis-tance; Resistance movements.

Antigens. See *Hypersensitivity.*

Antiheroes. Antihero(es,ic). Anti-hero(es,ic). Non-hero(es,ic). Nonhero(es,ic). Antiheroine(s). Antithesis of hero(es,ic). *Consider also:* tragic hero(e,es,ine,ines), unheroic hero(e,es,ine,ines), hero manque(s), counter-hero(es). *See also* Antinovel; Antithesis; Famous people; Fiction; Heroes; Literature; Nouveau roman; Political fiction; Protagonists.

Antinomianism. Antinomian(ism). *Consider also:* emphasis on grace; pure faith; faith alone, salvation by faith. *See also* Beliefs; Creeds; Faith; Religion; Revealed theology.

Antinovel. Antinovel(s). Anti-roman(s). *Consider also:* avant garde novel(s), non-traditional fiction, experimental fiction. *See also* Antiheroes; Nouveau roman.

Antinuclear movements. Antinuclear movement(s). *Choose from:* antinuclear, anti-nuclear, nuclear freeze, ban the bomb *with:* movement(s), group(s), demonstrat(ion,ions,or,ors), protest(s,er,ers). *See also* Arms control; Nuclear weapons; Nuclear weapons non-proliferation; Peace movements.

Antinuclear programs. See *Nuclear weapons non-proliferation.*

Antipathy. See *Aversion.*

Antiphons. Antiphon(s,y,al,ary,aries). Responsive answering. Responsive reading(s). *See also* Gregorian chants; Liturgy; Prayer; Religious rituals.

Antipoverty programs. Antipoverty program(s). Anti-poverty program(s). War on poverty. Attack(s) on poverty. Poverty program(s). Entitlement program(s). Food assistance program(s). Public assistance. Housing program(s). AFDC. Aid to Families with Dependent children. Income supplement(s).

Negative income tax. Workfare. Wage stop(s). Enterprise zone(s). Dole. *Consider also:* poverty, antipoverty, poor, underclass, disadvantaged *with:* alleviat(e,ed,ing,ion), relief, charit(y,ies), aid, redistribut(ive,ion). *See also* Civic improvement; Government financing; Income maintenance programs; Low income; Microenterprise; Poverty; Public welfare; Social services; Urban renewal.

Antiquarian booksellers. Antiquarian booksell(ing,er,ers). Antiquarian bookshop(s). Antiquarian book fair(s). Antiquarian book trade. Antiquarian book(man,men). *Consider also:* used book(s,store), AB Bookman. *Choose from:* rare, fine, old, antiq(ue,arian), used, o.p. book(s), out-of-print *with:* booksell(ing,er,ers), dealer(s), bookstore(s), book trade. *See also* Antiquarianism; Book collecting; Book imprints; Bookselling; Incunabula; Rare books; Second hand trade.

Antiquarianism. Antiquarianism. Anitquarian spirit. Love of old things. *Choose from:* antique(s), heirloom(s), Americana, artifact(s) *with:* appreciat(e,ed,ing,ation), connoisseur(s), collector(s). *See also* Antiquarian booksellers; Antiques; Collectibles.

Antiques. Antique(s). Heirloom(s). Americana. Artifact(s). *Choose from:* vintage, colonial, Victorian, renaissance, Georgian, 16th century, 17th century, 18th century, 19th century, historic, over 100 years old, Charles X, Ming Dynasty, Qing dynasty, Chippendale *with:* furniture, relic(s), work(s) of art, artwork(s), product(s). *Consider also:* collectible(s), collector's item(s), bibelot(s), objet(s) d'art, old treasure(s). *See also* Antiquarianism; Antiquities (objects); Collectibles; Hobbies; Numismatics; Rare books; Treasure.

Antiquities (objects). Antiquit(y,ies). Ancient relic(s). Archaeological specimen(s). *Consider also time periods such as:* 4th century, 5th century, 6th century, 300 A.D., Stone age, Egyptian, Bronze Age, early Roman, Byzantine, archaeological, Ming dynasty, pre-Columbian, etc. *with:* relic(s), specimen(s), silver, collection(s), treasure(s), artifact(s), art(work,works), vase(s), figurine(s), ornament(s), gold(work), mummified remain(s), pottery. *Consider also:* cultural heritage. *See also* Ancient architecture; Ancient art; Ancient goldwork; Ancient jewelry; Antiques; Antiquity (time); Classical architecture; Classical art; Earthworks; Extinct cities; Figurines; Pottery; Relics.

Antiquity (time). Antiquity. Ancient time(s). Classical period. Pre-classical. Holy Roman empire. Ancient Gree(k,ce). Archaic Gree(k,ce).

Hellen(ic,istic). Earliest time(s). Assyria(n,ns). Babylonia(n,ns). Mesopotamia(n,ns). Cypriot(s). Cret(e,an). Ancient Persia(n). Anatolia(n). Sumer(ian,ians). Hittite(s). Assyria(n,ns). *Consider also:* antediluvian, antiquated, antique(s), archai(c, sm), fossil(s,ize,ized), preglacial, prehistor(y,ic), primeval, primordial, distant past, remote time. *See also* Ancient architecture; Ancient art; Ancient education; Ancient geography; Ancient goldwork; Ancient literature; Antiquities (objects); Archaeology; Classical architecture; Extinct cities, Greek and Roman games; Historical periods; History; Primitive architecture; Roman law; Scholia; Vikings; World history.

Antiracist education. Antiracist education. Anti-racist education. *Choose from:* antiracis(t,m), anti-racis(t,m) *with:* education, train(ing), teach(ing), learn(ing), professional development. *Consider also:* holocaust education, prejudice reduction, prejudice prevention, combat(ing,ting) racism. *See also* Antibias curriculum; Cultural pluralism; Multicultural education.

Antisemitism. Antisemit(ic,ism,e,es). Anti-semit(ic,ism,e,es). Anti-Jewish. *Choose from:* prejudice(d,s), discriminat(ed,ing, ion), hat(e,ed,red,ing), hostil(e,ity,ities), intoleran(t,ce), bias(ed), bigot(ed,ry,s), persecut(ed,ion), genocide, stereotype(s), minority status, desecration, scapegoat(s,ing), concentration camp(s), pogrom(s), holocaust, nazi(s,sm), killing(s) *with:* Jew(s,ish), Judai(c,ism), Semitic, Israel(i). *See also* Anti-Catholicism; Anti-government radicals; Bigotry; Exclusivity (Religion); Hate crimes; Holocaust; Inquisition; Judaism; Nazism; Persecution; Prejudice; Racism; Stereotyping; Tribalism; White supremacy movements.

Antiseptic. Antiseptic(s,ide,ides,ally). Disinfect(ed,ing,ant,ants). Bactericide(s). Decontaminant(s). Cleansing agent(s). Germicide(s). Purifier(s). Sterilizer(s). *Consider also:* scrupulously clean, aseptic, sterile, uncontaminated, germ free, sanit(ary,ize,ized). *See also* Body care; Hygiene.

Antismoking movement. Antismoking movement. Great American Smokeout. National Committee Against Tobacco. Action on Smoking and Health. Campaign to discourage smoking. Tobacco-bashing. Promot(e,ed,ing,ion) nonsmoking. Ban(ned,ning,s) smok(e,ing). Misocapnist(s). *Choose from:* anti-smoking, anti-tobacco, anti-Marlboro, reduc(e,ing) smoking, secondhand smoke, smoking cessation *with:* movement, ad(s), campaign(s), advertis(ement,ements,ing),

regulation(s), ban(s), commercial(s), faction(s), effort(s), lawsuit(s), public service announcement(s). *Choose from:* smoking, smoker(s), tobacco, cigarette(s), cigar(s), snuff, pipe(s), chewing tobacco *with:* ban(ned, ning,s), segrega(te,ted,tes,tion), ostraciz(e,ed,es, ing). *Choose from:* nonsmok(ing,er,ers) *with:* area(s) or section(s) or polic(ies,y) or establishment(s) or segregat(e,ed,es, ion) or isolat(e.ed,es,ion). *See also* Activism; Health education; Protest movements; Smoking; Tobacco habit; Tobacco smoke pollution.

Antisocial behavior. Antisocial behavior(s). Dyssocial behavior(s). Unsociable(ness). Unfriendl(y,iness). Antagonis(tic,m). Hostil(e,ity,ities). Menac(e,ed,ing). Threaten(ed,ing). Misogyn(y,ist,ists). Misanthropic. Misbehavior. Nonconform(ance,ing,ist,ists,ism,ity). Drifter(s). Runaway(s). Truan(cy,t,ts). Rule breaking. Dangerous behavior(s). Eccentric(ity,ities,s). Crime(s). Criminality. *Choose from:* antisocial, dyssocial, deviant *with:* behavior(s), act(s), action(s). *Choose from:* violat(e,ed,ing, ion) *with:* norm(s), taboo(s). *See also* Aggression; Air rage; Antisocial personality disorder; Battered women; Behavior disorders; Belligerency; Cheating; Child abuse; Child neglect; Crime; Cruelty; Cruelty to animals; Deviance; Deviant behavior; Drunk driving; Elder abuse; Fire setting behavior; Harassment; Homicide; Infanticide; Incest; Juvenile delinquency; Misogyny; Persecution; Rape; Rebelliousness; Road rage; Rogues; Runaways; Sex offenders; Sexual abuse; Sexual harassment; Shoplifting; Teasing; Terrorism; Theft; Thieves; Torture; Ugliness; Vandalism; Violence.

Antisocial personality disorder. Antisocial personality disorder. Psychopath(y,s,ic). Sociopath(s,ic). Criminal(ly) mentally abnormal(ity,ities). Unsocialized aggressive(ness). Anethopath(y,ic). Anetopath(y,ic). *Choose from:* antisocial, psychopathic, sociopathic *with:* personalit(y,ies), tendenc(y,ies), trait(s), reaction(s), characteristic(s). *Consider also:* sadis(m,tic), moral insanity, conduct disorder(s,ed), devian(ce,t). *See also* Antisocial behavior; Crime; Deviant behavior; Personality disorders.

Antithesis. Antithes(is,es). Antagonis(m, t,tic). Agonist(ic). Opposite(s). Contradistinct(ion,ive,ively). Contraposit(ion, ive). Contrar(y,iness,iety). Oppos(e,ed, ing,ition). Antipode(s,an). Contra(dictory). Converse(ly). Counter(ed,ing). Revers(e,ed,ing). Inverse(ly). Contrast(ed,ing). *Consider also:* agonis(m,tic), nemesis, Hegelianism. *See also* Antiheroes; Antonyms; Dialectics; Differences; Literary quarrels.

Antitrust law. Antitrust law(s). Monopoly charge(s). *Choose from:* antitrust *with:* law(s), act(s,ion,ions), violation(s), lawsuit(s), case(s), suit(s), charge(s), regulation(s), settlement(s), practice(s). *Choose from:* antitrust, competit(ion,ive) restraint of trade, monopol(y,ies,istic), price fixing, commodity agreement(s), cartel(s), price discrimination, access to market(s) *with:* polic(y,ies), litigat(e,ed, ion). *Consider also:* Sherman Act, Clayton Act, Robinson-Patman Act; Federal Trade Commission Act. *See also* Consumer protection; Economic competition; Market economy; Monopolies; Price fixing; Restraint of trade.

Antitrust regulations. See *Antitrust law.*

Antiwar movement. See *Peace movements.*

Antonyms. Antonym(ic,s,y). Oppositionality. Opposite(s). *Consider also:* reverse. *See also* Antithesis; Polarity; Semantics; Vocabulary; Words.

Anxiety. Anxiet(y,ies), Anxious(ness). Angst. Apprehens(ion,ive,iveness). Fearful(ness). Dread(ed,ing). Stage fright. Uneas(y,iness). Fretful(ness). Nervous(ness). Overanxious(ness). Worr(y,ied,ing). Distress(ed). *Choose from:* anxiet(y,ies) *with:* mathematics, separation, test, communication, neurosis, castration, death, social, separation, speech, writing. *Consider also:* phob(ic,ia,ias), anticipat(e,ed,ing, ion) danger. *See also* Affective disorders; Anger; Angst; Anguish; Anxiety disorders; Apprehension; Castration anxiety; Catharsis; Certainty; Cognitive dissonance; Computer anxiety; Death anxiety; Depression (psychology); Desensitization (psychology); Emotional states; Emotions; Existential anxiety; Fear; Fear of closeness; Fear of crime; Fear of failure; Fear of God; Fear of men; Fear of success; Fear of women; Guilt; Impatience; Inhibition (psychology); Jealousy; Mathematics anxiety; Panic; Panic disorder; Performance anxiety; Personality traits; Phobias; Psychological stress; Relaxation training; Science anxiety; School phobia; Social anxiety; Separation anxiety; Speech anxiety; Stage fright; Stress; Suspense; Tensions; Test anxiety; Threat; Tranquilizers.

Anxiety, castration. See *Castration anxiety.*

Anxiety, computer. See *Computer anxiety.*

Anxiety, death. See *Death anxiety.*

Anxiety, engulfment. See *Fear of closeness.*

Anxiety, existential. See *Existential anxiety.*

Anxiety, mathematics. See *Mathematics anxiety.*

Anxiety, performance. See *Performance anxiety.*

Anxiety, science. See *Science anxiety.*

Anxiety, separation. See *Separation anxiety.*

Anxiety, social. See *Social anxiety.*

Anxiety, speech. See *Speech anxiety.*

Anxiety, test. See *Test anxiety.*

Anxiety disorders. Anxiety disorder(s). *Choose from:* anx(iety,ious,iousness), panic, phob(ic,ia,ias) *with:* neuros(is,es), neurotic, state(s), disturbance(s), depress(ive,ion), syndrome(s), hyster(ia,ical), disorder(s), attack(s). *Consider also:* agoraphobia, castration anxiety, combat disorder(s), daymare(s), death anxiety, mathematics anxiety, neurocirculatory asthenia, nightmare(s), obsessive compulsive disorder(s), panic disorder(s), posttraumatic stress disorder(s), school phobia(s), separation anxiet(y,ies), social anxiet(y,ies), social phobia(s), test anxiet(y,ies). *See also* Affective disorders; Anxiety; Castration anxiety; Computer anxiety; Death anxiety; Fear of closeness; Fear of crime; Fear of failure; Fear of men; Fear of success; Fear of women; Guilt; Hypochondriasis; Mathematics anxiety; Obsessive compulsive personality; Panic disorder; Performance anxiety; Phobias; Post traumatic stress disorders; Science anxiety; Separation anxiety; Social anxiety; Speech anxiety; Test anxiety.

Anxiety reducing drugs. See *Tranquilizers.*

Anxiolytics. See *Tranquilizers.*

Apartheid. Apartheid. *Choose from:* South Africa(n,ns) *with:* Black(s), Negro(es), Asian(s), Coloured(s), separatis(m,t,ts), racis(m,t,ts), pass laws, discriminat(e,ed, ing,ion), prejudic(e,ed), hatred, intoleran(t,ce), inequality, exclud(e,ed, ing), exclus(ion,ive), oppress(ed,ion, ing), segregat(e,ed,ion), backlash, territorial separation, homeland(s), Bantustan(s), Afrikaner Resistance Movement, bigot(s,ed,ry), White supremac(y,ists), White rightist(s). *See also* Anti-apartheid movement; Racism; Racial segregation; Separatism; Sub-Saharan Africa; White supremacy movements.

Apartment houses. Apartment hous(e,es, ing). Apartment building(s). Apartment complex(es). Apartment(s). High rise housing. Multifamily dwelling(s). *See also* Rental housing; Residential facilities.

Apathy. Apath(etic,y). Indifferen(ce,t). Lack of feeling. Lack of interest. Unenthusiastic. Passiv(e,ity,eness). Unambitious. Uninspired. Lack of excitement. Unexcited. Unmoved. Halfhearted. Lukewarm. Uninterested. Deadwood. Diminished interest. Low voter turnout. Lack of feeling. Impassiv(e,ity). Letharg(y,ic). Spiritless(ness).

Listless(ness). Unemotional. Unfeeling. Lack of affect. Hebetude. Stupor(ous). Disengage(d,ment). Detach(ed,ment). Bor(ed,edom,ing). Lassitude. *See also* Alienation; Anhedonia; Boredom; Disengagement; Emotional states; Loss of will; Noninvolvement; Passiveness; Political attitudes; Self neglect; Social attitudes; Voter participation.

Apes. Ape(s). Pongid(ae). *Consider also:* chimpanzee(s) (pan troglodytes), gorilla(s), (gorilla gorilla), orangutan(s) (Pongo pygmaeus), gibbon(s) (hylobates), bonobo(s) (pan paniscus), primate(s), simian(s). *See also* Primates.

Aphasia. Aphas(ia,ic). Logagnos(ia,ic). Speechless(ness). *Consider also:* acalcul(ia,ic), agnos(ia,ic), agrammatism, agraph(ia,ic), alex(ia,ic), amem(ia,ic), amim(ia,ic), amus(ia,ic), anarthr(ia,ic), anom(ia,ic), aprax(ia,ic), aphem(ia,ic), asem(ia,ic), asemas(ia,ic), astereognisis, asyllab(ia,ic), asymbol(ia, ic), atact(ia,ic), dysphas(ia,ic), paragraph(ia,ic), paraphas(ia,ic), strephosymbol(ia,ic), word blind(ness), word deaf(ness). *See also* Acalculia; Agnosia; Alexia; Dysphasia; Language disorders; Learning disabilities; Mutism; Speech disturbances.

Aphorisms. Aphorism(s). Proverb(s,ial). Adage(s). Axiom(s). Maxim(s). Motto(es). Platitude(s). Truism(s). Epigram(s). Byword(s). Slogan(s). Apothegm(s). Precept(s). Sententia(e). *Consider also:* half truth(s), witticism(s). *See also* Adages; Axioms; Catchwords; Dictums; Epigrams; Folklore; Slogans.

Aphrodisiacs. Aphrodisi(a,ac,acs,aca). Sexual stimulant(s). Love potion(s). Pharmacosexology. Love philter(s). *Consider also:* cantharid(in,es), philter, yohimbine, spanish fly. *See also* Anaphrodisiac; Pheromones; Sex attractants; Sexual arousal.

Apnea, sleep. See *Sleep apnea.*

Apocalypse. Apocalyp(tic,se). Judgment Day. Eschatolog(y,ies,ical). Second coming. End of the world. Armageddon. *Consider also:* millenium, millenarian(ism), kingdom of God, resurrection. *See also* Apocalyptic literature; Judgement day; Judgment of God; Millenarianism; Messianic era; Prophets; Religious beliefs.

Apocalyptic literature. Apocalyptic literature. Apocalyptic theme(s). *Consider also:* apocalyptic(ism), cataclysm(ic,s), disaster(s), end of the world, destruction of the world, millennialism, millenarianism, Armageddon, second coming *with:* literature, fiction, myth(s,ology,ological), projection(s), prophe(tic,cy,sy), revelation(s), predict(ed,ing,ion,ions). *Consider also:* Book of Daniel, Revelation to John; 4 Esdras; Ethiopic

Book of Enoch, etc. *See also* Apocalypse; Bible; Jewish literature; Millenarianism; Prophecy; Prophets; Religious literature; Sacred books.

Apologetics. Apologetics. *Choose from:* defend(ing), defense(s), evidence(s), justif(y,ied,ication) *with:* Christian(ity), belief(s), doctrine(s), theolog(y,ical), divin(e,ity), religion, faith. *See also* Apologies; Canons; Defense (verbal); Religious doctrines; Religious literature.

Apologetics (Rhetoric). Apologetic(s). Apologia. Defense(s). Justification(s). *Choose from:* support(ive,ing), endors(e,ed,ing), uphold(ing), sustain(ed,ing), justificatory, vindicat(e,ed,ing,ive), exonerat(e,ed, ing,ive) *with:* argument(s), tactic(s), discourse. *See also* Arguments; Apologetics; Defense (verbal); Persuasion; Rhetoric.

Apologies. Apolog(y,ies). Express(ing,ed, ion) regret(s). Excuse(s). Request for pardon. *Choose from:* acknowledg(e,ed, ing,ment), admit(ted,ting), admission, state(ment) *with:* error(s), remorse, discourtesy. *Consider also:* amends, atone(d,ment), error(s), confess(ed,ing,ion), mea culpa, reparation(s), redress(ed,ing). *See also* Apologetics; Atonement; Etiquette; Forgiveness; Penitents; Regret; Repentence.

Aporia. Apor(ia,iae,etic,ematic). Inherent contradiction(s). *Consider also:* logical dilemma(s), impasse(s), seemingly insoluable difficult(y,ies), insoluable philosophical problem(s), contrary argument(s), puzzle(s), paradox(es). *See also* Deconstruction; Hermeneutics; Irony; Logocentrism; Semiotics; Undecidability.

Apostasy. Apostasy. Apostat(e,ize). Renounc(e,ed,ing) faith. Fall(en,ing) away. Disaffiliat(e,ed,ing,ion). Renunciation of religious faith. Renegade. *See also* Heresy; Irreligion; Political defection; Religious conversion; Schism.

Apostles. Apostle(s,ship). Disciple(s). Crusader(s). Missionar(y,ies). Colporteur(s). Evangelist(s). Missioner(s). Propagandist(s). Proselytizer(s). Supporter(s). Preacher(s). *See also* Advocacy; Christian leadership; Christianity; Disciples; Religious leadership.

Apothegms. See *Aphorisms.*

Apotheosis. Apotheosi(s,ize). Deif(y,ied, ication). Glorif(y,ied,ication). Idealiz(e,ed,ation). Elevat(e,ed,ing,ion) to divine status. Aggrandiz(e,ed,ing, ement). Dignif(y,ied,ication). Exalt(ed,ing,ation). Ennobl(e,ed,ement). Enshrine(d,ment). Idoliz(e,ed,ation). Immortaliz(e,ed,ing,ation). Lioniz(e,ed,ing,ation). *See also* God

concepts; Honored (esteem); Sacredness; Saints; Worship.

Apparatus. See *Equipment; Tools.*

Apparel. See *Clothing.*

Apparitions. Apparition(s). Ghost(s). Doppelgaenger(s). Doubleganger(s). Wraith(s,like). Phantom(s). Specter(s). Spook(s). Banshee(s). *See also* Ghost stories; Ghosts; Haunted houses; Supernatural; Uncanniness.

Appeal, emotional. See *Emotional appeal.*

Appeal, personal. See *Charisma.*

Appeals. Appeal(s). Petition(s). Request(s). Bid(s). Claim(s). Application(s). Solicit(e,ed,ing,ation,ations). Demand(s). Plead(ed,ing). *Consider also:* pray(er,ed,ing), supplicat(e,ed, ing,ion), entreat(y,ies,ment,ing,ingly), implor(e,ed,ing). *See also* Canvassing; Claims; Persuasion; Sympathy.

Appearance, personal. See *Personal appearance.*

Appearance, physical. See *Personal appearance.*

Appeasement. Appeas(e,ed,ing,ement, ements). Conciliat(e,ed,ing,ion). Pacif(y,ied,ication). Assuag(e,ed,ing). Mollif(y,ying,ied). Placat(e,ed,ing,ion). Propitiat(e,ed,ing). *Consider also:* concession(s), compromise(s), palliat(e,ed,ing,ive), whitewash(ed,ing), nonaggression pact(s), land for peace. *See also* Compromises; Negotiation.

Appendices. See *Addendum.*

Apperception. Appercept(ion,ive). Conscious perception. Introspective self-consciousness. Mental perception. Process of understanding. *See also* Comprehension; Perception; Understanding.

Appetite. Appetite(s). Hung(ry,er). Craving(s). Gustatory. Ravenous(ness). Glutton(y,ousness). Insatiab(le,ility). *Choose from:* desir(e,ed,ing), longing, excess(ive), voracious *with:* eat(ing). *Consider also:* acor(ia,ic), bulim(ia,ic), hyperorexia, malacia, parageusia, pica, polyphagia, omnivorous(ness), carnivorous(ness), herbivorous(ness), taste, salivation. *See also* Appetite depressants; Diet; Eating; Hunger, food deprivation; Motivation; Satiation.

Appetite depressants. Appetite depressant(s). *Choose from:* appetite, hunger *with:* regulat(e,ed,ing,ion,or,ors), depressant(s), suppressant(s), depressing drug(s). *Choose from:* anorexigenic, anorectic, anorexic, anti-obesity, anorexiant *with:* drug(s), agent(s). *Consider also:* amphetamine(s) [Biphetamine, Desoxyn Gradumet, Dexedrine, Didrex, dextroamphetamines], diethylpropion hydrochloride [Tenuate], fenfluramine [Pondimin],

mazindol [Sanorex], phendimetrazine tartrate [Bontril, Plegine, Prelu-2], phentermine hydrochloride [Adipex, Fastin, Obe-Nix], phentermine resin [Ionamin]. *See also* Appetite; Drug therapy.

Appetite disorders. See *Eating disorders.*

Appliance repair. Appliance repair(s,ed, ing). *Choose from:* repair(s,ed,ing), maintenance, maintain(ed,ing), fix(ed,ing), salvag(e,ed,ing), patch(ed,ing), overhaul(ed,ing), recover(y,ing,ed), replac(e,ed,ing), mend(ed,ing), rebuild(ing), rebuilt, restor(ed,ing,ation), servic(e,ed,ing) *with:* equipment, apparatus, appliance(s), part(s), tool(s), utensil(s). *See also* Appliances; Customer services; Equipment; Equipment failure; Preventive maintenance; Service contracts.

Appliances. Appliance(s). Device(s). Equipment. Apparatus. Machine(s). Contraption(s). Gadget(s). Furnishing(s). Utensil(s). Implement(s). *Consider also:* refrigerator(s), stove(s), washing machine(s), dryer(s), iron(s), freezer(s), clothes washer(s), microwave oven(s), toaster oven(s), blender(s), food processor(s), garbage disposal(s), vacuum cleaner(s), broiler(s), floor waxer(s), floor polisher(s), hair dryer(s), sewing machine(s), tape recorder(s), radio(s), television set(s), waffle iron(s), CD player(s), stereo(s). *See also* Devices; Equipment; High fidelity sound systems; Housekeeping; Tools.

Applicability. Applicab(le,ility). Relevan(ce,t). Pertinen(t,ce). Bearing. Connect(ed,ion). Pertain(ing). Appurtenan(t,ce). Germane(ness). Apropos. Fitting. Congruous. Opportun(e,ness). Related(ness). Allied. Akin. Appropriate(ness). Suited. Suitab(le,leness,ility). *See also* Appropriate technologies; Relevance.

Applicant interviews, job. See *Employment interviews.*

Applicant screening, job. See *Job applicant screening.*

Applicants. Applicant(s). Petitioner(s). Claimant(s). Appellant(s). Aspirant(s). Entrant(s). Office seeker(s). Postulant(s). *See also* Abortion applicants; Candidates; Claims; Job applicants.

Applicants, abortion. See *Abortion applicants.*

Applicants, job. See *Job applicants.*

Applications, research. See *Research applications.*

Applications for positions. See *Job applicants.*

Applied psychology. Applied psychology. *Choose from:* applied, application(s), practical, use(s), utilization *with:*

psycholog(y,ical). *Consider also:* counseling, pastoral, criminal, educational, child, vocational, industrial, military, clinical, community, consumer, medical, personnel, social, sport *with:* psychology. *Consider also:* human engineering, vocational guidance, psychotechnology. *See also* Educational psychology; Industrial psychology; Social sciences.

Appointments and schedules. Appointment(s). Schedul(e,es,ing). Waiting list(s). Queue(s). Engagement(s). Timetable(s). Docket(s). Agenda(s). Waiting line(s). *Consider also:* time management, programming, work rest cycle(s), shift(s), double session(s), time block(s), rendezvous. *See also* Agenda; Calendar; Extended school year; School schedules; Time utilization.

Apportion (distribution). See *Distribution (apportion).*

Apportionment. Apportion(e,ed,ing,ment, ments). Reapportion(ed,ing,ment,ments). Redistrict(ed,ing). Gerrymander(ing). Voting district boundar(y,ies). School district line(s). Redistribut(e,ed,ing,ion) congressional seats. Lose/gain congressional seat(s). Realign(ed,ing,ment) district(s). Delegate apportionment. Realign(ing) political boundar(y,ies). Overturn(ed,ing) district line(s). Shifting congressional seat(s). Redraw(n,ing) district lines. *See also* Allocation; Political representation.

Appraisal. Apprais(e,ed,ing,als). Estimat(e, ed,ing) value. Valu(ed,ing,ation). Evaluat(e,ed,ing,ion). Assess(ed,ing, ment). Pricing. Review(ed,ing). Critique(s,d). Rate(d). Rating(s). Survey(s,ed,ing). *Consider also:* measur(e,ed,ing), weigh(ed,ing), judg(e,ed,ing), comput(e,ed,ing,ation), calculat(e,ed,ing), determin(e,ed,ing, ation), estimat(e,ed,ing,ion), opinion(s) *with:* value(s), price(s), age(s), worth, weight(s). *See also* Analysis; Art criticism; Assessment; Cost effectiveness; Criticism; Criteria; Needs assessment; Observation methods; Peer review; Performance appraisal; Program evaluation; Qualitative methods; Risk assessment; Self evaluation; Self evaluation (groups); Standards; Teacher evaluation; Technology assessment; Valuation.

Appraisal, employee performance. See *Performance appraisal.*

Appraisal, performance. See *Performance appraisal.*

Appreciation (thanks). See *Gratitude.*

Appreciation, art. See *Art appreciation.*

Appreciation, literature. See *Literature appreciation.*

Appreciation, monetary. See *Gains.*

Apprehension. Apprehens(ion,ive,iveness). Foreboding. Dread(ing). Presentiment(s). Premonition(s). Anxiet(y,ies), Anxious(ness). Angst. Fearful(ness). Expectant dread. Misgiving(s). Trepidation. Stage fright. Uneas(y,iness). Fretful(ness). Nervous(ness). Worr(y,ied,ing). Distress(ed). Anticipat(e,ed,ing,ion) danger. *See also* Anticipation; Anxiety; Fear.

Apprehension, communication. See *Speech anxiety.*

Apprenticeship. Apprentice(d,s,ships). On-the-job training. Mentorship(s). *Consider also:* novice(s), internship(s), probationer(s), beginner(s), neophyte(s), novitiate(s), amateur(s), newcomer(s), rookie(s), trainee(s), student teacher(s). *See also* Experience (background); Field experience programs; Novices; Skill learning; Skilled workers; Training; Vocational education; Work experience; Workfare.

Approach, cross disciplinary. See *Interdisciplinary approach.*

Approach, interdisciplinary. See *Interdisciplinary approach.*

Approach, multidisciplinary. See *Interdisciplinary approach.*

Approach, nonpunitive. See *Nonpunitive approach (discipline).*

Approach, whole language. See *Whole language approach.*

Appropriate technologies. Appropriate technolog(y,ies). Technological equity. Appropriate energy system(s). Technolog(y,ical) option(s). *Choose from:* appropriate, small scale, intermediate, ecolog(y,ical,icaly), village, human perspective, people *with:* technolog(y,ies,ical). *Consider also:* simple living, solar energy, passive energy, heat pump(s), solar greenhouse(s), biomass energy, geothermal energy, windmill(s), woodstove(s), human scale, small is beautiful. *See also* Agricultural ecology; Agricultural mechanization; Alternative energy; Community development; Developing countries; Labor aspects of technology; Sustainable development; Technology and civilization.

Appropriations (set aside). Appropriat(e, es,ed,ing,ion,ions). Allocat(e,es,ed,ing, ion,ions). Line item(s). Budget(ed,ing,s). Entitlement(s). Devot(e,ed,ing) resource(s). Dollars earmarked. Set aside funds. Allot(ed,ing,ments). Reserve(s). *Consider also:* allowance(s), stipend(s), subsid(y,ies). *See also* Allocation; Budgets.

Approval. Approv(al,ed,ing). Admir(e,ed, ing). Esteemed. Highly regarded. Favorable opinion. Prais(e,ed,ing).

Acknowledg(e,ing,ment). Honor(ed,ing). Validat(e,ed,ing,ion). Respect(ed,ing). Approbat(e,ed,ing,ion). Compliment(s, ed,ing). Accept(ed,ing,ance,able). Recog(nized,nition). Endors(ed,ing, ement). Supported. Sanctioned. Upheld. Confirmed. Recommended. Favorably received. Popular(ity). Socially desirable. Fashionable. *See also* Acceptance; Affiliation motivation; Certification; Clearance (authorization); Criticism; Endorsement; Popularity; Social acceptance; Social approval; Social attitudes; Social desirability; Social reinforcement.

Approval, social See *Social approval.*

Approval need. Approval need(s). Approval motiv(e,es,ation). *Choose from:* need(s), desir(e,es,ed,ing), demand(s,ed,ing), want(s,ed,ing), requir(e,es,ed,ing) *with:* approval, admir(e,ed,ing,ation), esteem, prais(e,es), acknowledgement, honor(s), validat(e,ing,ion), respect, compliment(s), acceptance, recognition. *See also* Achievement need; Dependency (personality); Emotional dependence.

Apraxia. Aprax(ia,ic). Akine(sia,tic). Dyspraxia. Inability to carry out purposeful movements. Apractagnos(ia, ic). *Choose from:* akinetic, amnestic, constructional, dressing, dynamic, gait, ideational, idiokinetic, ideomotor, left-sided, sensory *with:* aprax(ia,ic). *See also* Disorders; Ideational apraxia; Speech disorders.

Apraxia, ideational See *Ideational apraxia.*

Aptitude. Aptitude(s). Potential(ity,ities). Intelligen(t,ce). Apt(ness). Astute(ness). Sagacity. Clever(ness). Keen(ness). Capacit(y,ies). Talent(ed,s). Capab(le, ility,ilities). Creativ(e,ity). Gifted. Genius(es). *Consider also:* proficien(t, cy,cies), acuity, ingenu(ity,ous,ousness), proclivit(y,ies), competen(t,cy,cies), expertise. *See also* Ability; Academic ability; Academic aptitude; Aptitude tests; Area of knowledge; Artistic ability; Capacity; Cognitive ability; Gifted; Learning ability; Mathematical ability; Mechanical ability; Musical ability; Nonverbal ability; Spatial ability; Verbal ability.

Aptitude, academic. See *Academic aptitude.*

Aptitude, scholastic. See *Academic aptitude.*

Aptitude tests. Aptitude test(s). *Choose from:* aptitude(s), vocational competenc(y,ies), admissions, creativity, abilit(y,ies), readiness, talent(s), comprehension, capacity, prognostic *with:* test(s), measure(s,ment,ments), scale(s), examination(s), inventor(y,ies), assessment(s), evaluation(s), score(s), checklist(s). *Consider also:* Wisc-R, WRAT, SAT(s), Scholastic aptitude test(s), Strong vocational interest blank,

Iowa test(s) of music literacy, Graduate record examination(s), GRE(s), Stanford Binet test(s), Wechsler scale(s), Army general classification test(s), College entrance examination(s), differential aptitude test(s), General aptitude test battery, Modern language aptitude test(s), school and college ability test(s). *See also* Ability identification; Aptitude; Intelligence tests.

Aquaculture. Aquacultur(e,al). Aquabusiness(es). Fish farm(s,ing). Fisher(y,ies). *Choose from:* salmon, catfish, lobster(s), prawn(s), crayfish, fish, underwater *with:* farm(s,ed,ing), ranch(es,ing), breeding, production. *Consider also:* culture(d) *with:* fish, sturgeon, salmon, mollusc(s). *See also* Mariculture.

Aquatic sports. Aquatic sport(s). Water sport(s). Underwater sport(s). *Consider also:* sailing, stadium sailing, underwater hockey, boat race(s), deep-water running, wakeboarding, waterskiing, swimming, wading, surfing, water training, paddling, canoeing, wind surfing. *See also* Diving; Sports; Swimming.

Aqueducts. Aqueduct(s). Artificial waterway(s). Canal(s). Channel(s). Conduit(s). Water course(s). Watercourse(s). Duct(s). *Consider also:* ditch(es), drain(s), pipeline(s). *See also* Canals; Channels (hydraulic engineering); Water supply.

Arabic medicine. Arabic medicine. *Choose from:* Muslim, Moslem, Islam(ic), Mohammed(an), Arab(ic), Avicenna, or Ibn Sina *with:* health, medical, heal(ed,ing), medicin(e,al), hygien(e,ic), treat(ed,ing,ment), diagnos(is,es), therap(y,ies,eutic), patient(s), disease(s,d), disorder(s), illness(es), cure(s,d), surg(ery,ical). *See also* Traditional medicine.

Arable land. Arable land(s). Farmland(s). Cropland(s). *Choose from:* arable, tillable, agricultural, cultivated, crop *with:* land(s), field(s), soil(s), acreage. *See also* Farming; Farms; Irrigation; Land preservation; Soil conservation; Soil degradation; Soil erosion; Soil fertility.

Arachnidism. See *Spiderbites.*

Arbiters. See *Arbitrators.*

Arbitration. Arbitrat(e,ed,ing,ion,or,ors). Negotiat(e,ed,es,ing,ion,or,ors). Mediat(e,d,ion,ing,or,ors). Bargain(ed, ing). Group problem solving. Adjudicat(e,ed,ing,ion,ions). Conciliat(e, ed,ing,ion,ions). Compromis(e,es,ed, ing). Honest broker(s). Mak(e,ing) concession(s). Conced(e,ed,ing). Reach(ed,ing) agreement(s). Impasse procedure(s). Peacemaking. Referee(s,d, ing). Diplomacy. *Choose from:*

settl(e,ed,ing), resolution(s), management, resolv(e,ed,ing) *with:* impass(es), disagreement(s), dispute(s), conflict(s). *See also* Arbitrators; Collective bargaining; Conflict resolution; Labor disputes; Labor management relations; Litigation; Mediation; Negotiation; Strikes.

Arbitration, industrial. See *Industrial arbitration.*

Arbitration, international. See *International arbitration.*

Arbitrators. Arbitrator(s). Arbiter(s). Adjudicator(s). Mediator(s). Referee(s). Umpire(s). Moderator(s). *Consider also:* ombuds(man,men,person,persons), peacemaker(s), troubleshooter(s). *See also* Arbitration; Conflict resolution; Dispute settlement; Mediation; Negotiation.

Archaeological chemistry. Archaeological chemistry. Prehistoric diet reconstruction. Paleodiet(ary). Bone-chemistry analysis. Paleobotan(y,ical). Archaeological ceramic(s). *See also* Age determination by skeleton; Age determination by teeth; Animal remains (archaeology); Archaeology; Paleoecology; Plant remains (archaeology).

Archaeological museums. Archaeological museum(s). Archaeological exhibit(s,ion,ions). Archaeological collection(s). *Choose from:* archaeolog(y,ical), paleograph(y,ic), antiquit(y,ies), artifact(s), anthropology, extinct culture(s), prehistor(y,ical), ancient societ(y,ies) *with:* museum(s), galler(y,ies), collection(s), exhibit(s,ion, ions), display(s). *See also* Archaeology; Museums.

Archaeological sites, looting of. See *Archaeological thefts.*

Archaeological societies. Archaeological societ(y,ies). Archaeological institute(s). *See also* Archaeology; Associations (organizations); Professional organizations.

Archaeological surveying. Archaeological survey(s,ing). Landscape archaeology. Airborne archaeology. *Consider also:* archaeolog(y,ical), anthropolog(y,ical), antiquity, prehistoric *with:* survey(s,ing), prospecting, site location, close-proximity analysis, seriation, sequential proto-coalition analysis, minimum-spanning-tree method(s), aerial survey(s), geophysical survey(s), aerial photograph(s,y), aerial view(s), satellite view(s), geophysical technique(s), radar imagery. *See also* Archaeology; Data collection; Excavations (Archaeology); Ground penetrating radar; Research; Surveys.

Archaeological thefts. Archaeological theft(s). Loot(ing) antiquities. Loot(ing) archaeological artifact(s). *Choose from:*

paleograph(y,ic), antiquit(y,ies), artifact(s), extinct culture(s), prehistor(y, ical), ancient societ(y,ies), Egypt(ian), Sumer(ian), Byzantine, Ming, pre-Columbian, Maya(n), etc. *with:* loot(s, ed,ing), theft(s), thief, thieve(s,ry), steal(ing), stole(n), burglar(y,s), rob(bed,bing,ber,bers,bery), embezzl(e, ing,ement,er,ers). *See also* Archaeology; Art thefts; Pillage; Thefts.

Archaeology. Archaeolog(y,ical). *Consider also:* paleograph(y,ic), antiquit(y,ies), dating artifact(s), anthropology of extinct culture(s), prehistor(y,ical), study of ancient societ(y,ies). *See also* Age determination by skeleton; Age determination by teeth; Animal remains (archaeology); Antiquity (time); Archaeological chemistry; Archaeological museums; Archaeological societies; Archaeological surveying; Cultural anthropology; Ethnoarchaeology; Excavations (Archaeology); Experimental archaeology; Extinct cities; Fossils; Geographical information systems; Industrial archaeology; Paleoecology; Plant remains (archaeology); Prehistoric people; Prehominids; Primitive architecture; Souterrains; Underwater archaeology.

Archaeology, experimental. See *Experimental archaeology.*

Archaeology, industrial. See *Industrial archaeology.*

Archaeology, landscape. See *Archaeological surveying.*

Archaeology, submarine. See *Underwater archaeology.*

Archaeology, underwater. See *Underwater archaeology.*

Archery. Archer(s,y). Bow(s) and arrow(s). Bow(man,men,woman,women). Longbow(man,men,woman,women). Crossbow(man,men,woman,women). Arbalest(s). Arbalist(s). *See also* Sports.

Arches. Arch(es,way,ways). Arched doorway(s). Arched gateway(s). *Choose from:* drop(ped), flat, horseshoe, elliptical, pointed, semicircular *with:* arch(es,way,ways). *Consider also:* cove(s,d), camber(s). *See also* Architectural styles; Architecture; Interior design.

Arches, triumphal. See *Triumphal arches.*

Archetypes. Archetyp(e,es,ical). Prototyp(e,es,ical). Ideal type(s). *Consider also:* exemplar(s), classic example(s), forerunner(s), paradigm(s,atic), paragon(s), typical example(s), original(s), precursor(s), pattern(s), model(s), collective unconscious, image(s). *See also* Classic (standard); Ideal types.

Architects. Architect(s). Architecture student(s). *Consider also:* designer(s), planner(s), city planner(s), building consultant(s), landscaper(s), drafts(men, man,women,woman). *See also* Architecture; Building codes; Designs; Facility design and construction; Modern architecture.

Architectural accessibility. Architectural accessibility. Accessibility for disabled. Architectural barrier(s). *Choose from:* architectural, facilit(y,ies), housing, environment(s), design(s,ed), building(s), entrance(s), construction *with:* access, accessib(le,ility), barrier(s), barrier-free, ramp(s), elevator(s), curb cut(s), braille sign(s,age). *Choose from:* architectural, facilit(y,ies), housing, environment, design(ed), building(s), entrance(s), construction, access, accessib(le,ility), barrier(s), barrier-free, ramp(s), elevator(s), curb cut(s), braille sign(s,age) *with:* disabled, disabilit(y, ies), handicap(ped,s), blind, hearing impaired, wheelchair(s). *See also* Access; Architecture; Disability; Domestic architecture; Entrances; Facility design and construction; Modern architecture; Physically handicapped; Travel barriers.

Architectural criticism. Architectural critic(s,ism). Critique architecturale. Architectural inquiry. *Choose from:* architectur(e,al), built environment(s), urban design(s), housing design(s), floorplan(s) *with:* critic(s,ism), critique(s), description, analys(is,es), critical deliberation, review(s), overview(s). *See also* Architecture; Chattering class; Criticism; Modern architecture.

Architectural design. See *Architectural drawing; Facility design and construction.*

Architectural drawing. Architectural drawing(s). Architectural rendering(s). Architectural design(s). Blueprint(s). Facility design(s). Floorplan(s). *Consider also:* CAD-CAM system(s). *See also* Facility design and construction; Format: Modern architecture.

Architectural styles. Architectural style(s). *Choose from:* Baroque, Byzantine, Carolingian, Chinese, Classic Revival, Classical, Colonial, Early Christian, Edwardian, Egyptian, Elizabethan, English, Etruscan, European, Gallo-Roman, German, Georgian, Gothic, Gothic Revival, Greco-Roman, Greek, Hellenistic, Industrial, Iranian, Islamic, Italian, Japanese, Latin American, Maori, Medieval, Modern, Norman, Oriental, Ottoman, Persian, Polish, Portuguese, Postmodern, Prehistoric, Primitive, Queen Anne, Renaissance, Rococo, Roman, Romanesque, Russian, Spanish, Victorian *with:* architectur(e,al), building(s), church(es), etc. *See also* Ancient architecture;

Architecture; Arches; Basilicas; Buildings; Classic revival; Classical architecture; Domestic architecture; Entrances; Facility design and construction; Gothic revival; Modern architecture; Primitive architecture.

Architecture. Architectur(e,al). Architectonic(s,ally). *Choose from:* facilit(y,ies), building(s), house(s), housing, spatial, built environment(s), construction *with:* design(s,ed,ing), plan(ned,ning), floorplan(s), engineer(ed,ing). *Consider also:* blueprint(s). *See also* Ancient architecture; Architects; Architectural accessibility; Architectural criticism; Architectural drawing; Architectural styles; Arches; Basilicas; Building codes; Buildings; Civil engineering; Classic revival; Classical architecture; Construction industry; Decoration; Domestic architecture; Entrances; Facility design and construction; Gothic revival; Landscape architecture; Modern architecture; Primitive architecture.

Architecture, ancient. See *Ancient architecture.*

Architecture, classical. See *Classical architecture.*

Architecture, domestic. See *Domestic architecture.*

Architecture, landscape. See *Landscape architecture.*

Architecture, marine. See *Shipbuilding.*

Architecture, modern. See *Modern architecture.*

Architecture, naval. See *Naval architecture.*

Architecture, primitive. See *Primitive architecture.*

Architecture, rural. See *Farmhouses.*

Architecture and handicapped. See *Architectural accessibility.*

Archives. Archiv(al,e,es,ing). Museum(s). Special collection(s). Historical document(s). Presidential librar(y,ies). Presidential papers. Public record(s). Collections of papers. Municipal record(s). Historic record(s). Historic collection(s). Manuscript collection(s). Genealogical collection(s). Official document(s). *Consider also:* athenaeum, atheneum, librar(y,ies), depositor(y,ies), registr(y,ies), register office(s), stack(s), vault(s). *See also* Annals; Archivists; Cultural history; Cultural property; Databases; Depositories; Documentation; History; Information; Knowledge management; Libraries; Library acquisitions; Lost literature; Museums; Oral history; Records management; Social history.

Archivists. Archivist(s). Record(s) historian(s). *Consider also:* curator(s).

See also Archives; Knowledge workers; Librarians; Professional personnel.

Arctic Regions. Arctic Region(s). Greenland. Spitsbergen. *Consider also:* Arctic Circle, Arctic Ocean, Northern Europe(an), North(ern) Siberia(n), North(ern) Alaska(n), North(ern) Canad(a,ian), Bering Straits, Lapland, Hudson Bay, North Pole. *See also* Eastern Europe; Far East; North America; Western Europe.

Area, catchment health. See *Catchment area (health).*

Area of knowledge. Area(s) of knowledge. *Choose from:* area(s), domain(s) *with:* knowledge, expertise, competence, proficienc(y,ies), specialization. *Consider also:* skill(s). *See also* Ability; Aptitude; Capacity; Experts; Job Knowledge; Specialization; Skill.

Area studies. Area studies. Regional studies. Study of national culture(s). American studies. Asian studies. *Choose from:* area, African, Asian, Oriental, Slavic, Russian, Middle East(ern), etc. *with:* studies. *See also* Courses; Cross cultural comparisons; Cultural pluralism; Foreign study; Multicultural education; Social studies; Second language education.

Areal linguistics. Areal linguistic(s). Geographical linguistic(s). *Choose from:* areal diffusion, geographical distribution, geographic spread *with:* language(s), linguistic. *Consider also:* languages in contact, linguistic geography, linguistic minorit(y,ies). *See also* Comparative linguistics; Linguistic geography; Linguistic minorities; Linguistics; Sociolinguistics; Speech communities.

Areas. Area(s). Acre(s,age). Block(s). Catchment(s). Census tract(s). Cit(y,ies). Count(y,ies). District(s). Division(s). Domain(s). Dominion(s). Enclosure(s). Expanse(s). Extent. Field(s). Kingdom(s). Localit(y,ies). Lot(s). MSA(s). Neighborhood(s). Parcel(s). Part(s). Piece(s). Plot(s). Province(s). Precinct(s). Plot(s). Quarter(s). Region(s). Realm(s). Range(s). Space(s). Section(s). Sphere(s). Scope. Site(s). SMSA(s). Territor(y,ies). Township(s). Tract(s). Vicinit(y,ies). Ward(s). Watershed(s). Zip code(s). Zone(s). *See also* Antarctic regions; Arctic Regions; Countries; Districts; Geographic regions; Medically underserved areas; Metropolitan areas; Parishes; Poverty areas; Recreation areas; Rural areas; Zoning.

Areas, low income. See *Poverty areas.*

Areas, medically underserved. See *Medically underserved areas.*

Areas, metropolitan. See *Metropolitan areas.*

Areas, natural. See *Natural areas.*

Areas, poverty. See *Poverty areas.*

Areas, recreation. See *Recreation areas.*

Areas, rural. See *Rural areas.*

Areas, social. See *Public spaces.*

Areas, urban. See *Metropolitan areas; Urban environments.*

Arenas. Arena(s). Amphitheater(s). Auditorium(s). Stadium(s). Coliseum(s). Field house(s). Concert stadium(s). *Consider also:* bowl(s), gridiron(s), skating rink(s), gymnasium(s), outdoor stage(s). *See also* Auditoriums; Halls; Public buildings; Public places.

Arguments. Argument(s,ative,ation). Argue(s,d). Arguing. Disputation(s). Disput(e,ed,ing,es). Conflict(s). Quarrel(s). Contention(s). Altercation(s). Discord. Disagree(d,ing,ment,ments). Counterargu(ed,ing,ment,ments). *Consider also:* battle(s), clash(ed,es,ing), discussion(s), feud(s,ed,ing), protest(s,ed,ing,ation). *See also* Aggression; Apologetics (Rhetoric); Communication (thought transfer); Debate; Feuds; Forensics (public speaking); Interpersonal conflict; Interpersonal relations; Polemics; Refutation; Religious disputations.

Arid lands. Arid land(s). Arid zone(s). Desert(s,ic,ification,ified). Semidesert(s). Arid region(s). Semiarid. Drylands. Badlands. Drought condition(s). Sand dune(s). Dust bowl(s). Dustbowl(s). Barrens. *See also* Arid regions agriculture; Desertification; Deserts; Drought; Geographic regions; Grasslands; Land preservation; Wetlands.

Arid regions. See *Arid lands.*

Arid regions agriculture. Arid regions agriculture. Dry-farm(ed,ing). *Choose from:* agricultur(e,al), farm(s,ed,er, ers,ing), till(ed,ing,age), soil conservation, water conservation, stable yield(s), livestock, crop(s,ping), vegeta(ble, bles,tion), planting, pest control, fertility management, wheat, grain *with:* arid, dry area(s), desert(s), dryland(s), dry-farmed region(s), dry region(s), semiarid, Middle East. *See also* Agriculture; Arid lands; Desertification; Sustainable development.

Aristocracy. Aristocra(cy,t,ts,tic). Hereditary nobility. Patrician. Patriciate. High born. Gentry. Ennoblement. Elite(s). Peerage. Oligarch(y,ies). Ruling class(es). Privileged class(es). Upper class(es). Emir(s). Sultan(s). Her Majesty. Royal house(s). Czar(s). Kaiser(s). Caesar(s). Earl(s). Noble ancestry. Noble(man,men). Pharoah(s). Shah(s). Royal couple(s). Sovereign(s). Dynast(y,ies). Royal line(s). Monarch(s,y). King(s). Queen(s).

Emperor(s). Royal famil(y,ies). Heir(s) to the throne. Royal heir(s). Crown prince(s). Prince(s,ess,esses). Duke(s). Duchess(es). *See also* Elites; Elitism (government); Feudalism; Gentlemen; Heraldry; Monarchy; Oligarchy; Ruling class.

Arithmetic. See *Mathematics.*

Armageddon. See *Apocalypse; Judgment day; Millenarianism.*

Armaments. See *Military weapons; Weaponry.*

Armed forces. Armed force(s). Military force(s). Troop(s). Militia(s). Arm(y,ies). Nav(y,ies). Air Force. Marine(s). Marine corps. Coast Guard. All volunteer force(s). Active duty. U.S. soldier(s). Foreign Legion. Pentagon. G.I.(s). GI(s). West Point Graduate(s). Naval Academy Graduate(s). Soldier(s). Sailor(s). Paratrooper(s). *Choose from:* military, army, nav(y,al) *with:* force(s), base(s), duty, reserve(s), service(s), hierarch(y,ies), officer(s), institution(s). *Choose from:* enlisted, drafted, conscripted, military *with:* man, men, woman, women, person(s), people, personnel. *See also* Army personnel; Air Force personnel; Civil defense; Civil supremacy over the military; Defense spending; Garrisons; Mercenaries; Military bases; Military draft; Military enlistment; Military officers; Military personnel; Military reform; Military service; National security; Navy personnel; Troop strength; War.

Armies. See *Armed forces.*

Armistices. Armistice(s). Truce(s). Cease fire(s). Terminat(e,ed,ing,ion) war(s). Peace treat(y,ies). Cessation of hostilit(y,ies). *See also* Peace; Peace negotiations.

Armor. Armor(ed). Chain mail. Coat(s) of mail. Armor plate. Armature(s). Cuirass(es,ed). *Consider also:* helmet(s), gorget(s), breastplate(s), brassard(s), gauntlet(s), solleret(s), jambeau(x). *See also* Combatant(s); Middle ages; Self defense; Weaponry.

Arms. See *Military weapons; Weaponry.*

Arms control. Arms control. Disarm(ed,ing, ament). Demilitariz(e,ed,ation). Military disengagement. Nuclear freeze. Ban(ned, ning) missile(s). Ban(ned,ning) chemical weapon(s). Peaceful coexistence. Demobiliz(e,ed,ing,ation). Weapons control. Nuclear weapons non-proliferation. Strategic Arms Limitation Talk(s). SALT I. SALT II. Strategic Arms Reduction Talk(s). Denuclearization. Nonaggression pact(s). Cuts in military strength. Dismantle weapons. Troop cuts. *Choose from:* arms, armament(s), weapon(s,ry), troop(s) *with:* demobiliz(ed,ing,ation), ban(s,ned,ning), control, eliminat(e,ion), limit(s,ation,

ations), reduc(e,tion,tions), dismantl(e, ed,ing), cuts, withdraw(n,al). *Consider also:* disarmament *with:* agreement(s), talk(s), accord(s), pact(s), treat(y,ies). *See also* Arms transfers; Balance of power; Disarmament; Military reform; Military weapons; Nuclear weapons nonproliferation; Nuclear proliferation; Peace negotiations; War prevention.

Arms market. Arms market(s,ed,ing). *Choose from:* arms, defense, fighter(s), military supplies, weapon(s,ry) *with:* market(s,ed,ing), trade, supplier(s), business, export(s,ed,ing), import(s,ed, ing), deal(s). *See also* Arms transfers; Defense spending; Firearms industry; Military industrial complex.

Arms race. Arms race(s). Military buildup(s). *Choose from:* militar(y,ily), arm(s,ed) *with:* deterren(,ts,ce), read(y,iness), prepared(ness), power, presence, expansionis(t,m). *Choose from:* arms, weapon(s,ry), missile(s), airpower, seapower *with:* buildup(s), stockpil(e,ed,es,ing). *See also* Arms control; Balance of power; Buildup; Cold war; Detente; Military weapons.

Arms transfers. Arms transfer(s). Transfer(s) of arms. *Choose from:* transfer(s,red,ring), suppl(y,ied,ier,iers), export(ed,er,ers,ing), deliver(ed,ing, y,ies), ship(ped,ping,ment,ments), sell(ing), sold *with:* arm(s,ament, aments), conventional technology, missile(s), hardware, weapon(s,ry), aircraft, defense industry. *Consider also:* nonproliferation polic(y,ies). *See also* Arms control; Arms market; Military weapons; Technical assistance; Technology transfer.

Army life. Army life. Military life. Life in the army. Soldier life. Army career(s). *Choose from:* army, soldier(s), cavalry, Roman officer(s), troop(s), barrack(s), GI(s), Johnny Reb, Billy Yank *with:* life, living, ashore, wife, wives, active duty, career(s), diar(y,ies), letter(s), paper(s), morale, subculture, recollection(s), personal affair(s), famil(y,ies). *See also* Army personnel; Family life; Military families; Military personnel.

Army officers. See *Army personnel; Military officers.*

Army personnel. Army personnel. *Choose from:* Army, US Military Academy, West Point *with:* cadet(s), graduate(s). *Choose from:* Army, military *with:* enlisted, officer(s), soldier(s), enlistee(s), men, man, women, woman, personnel, cadet(s), trainee(s), male(s), female(s), recruit(s), chaplain(s), physician(s), rank(s), sergeant(s), colonel(s), lieutenant(s), private(s), major(s), general(s), sergeant(s). *Consider also:* infantry, cavalry, ground force(s). *See also* Armed forces; Army life; Generals; Infantry; Military personnel.

Aromatherapy. Aromatherap(y,ies,ist,iss). *Choose from:* aroma(s), scent(s,ed), fragrance(s), lavender, essential oil(s) *with:* therap(y,ies,eutic), healing, treatments, stress reduction. *See also* Psychotherapeutic techniques.

Arousal. Arous(al,ed,ing). Readiness. Attention. Wakeful(ness). Vigilan(t,ce). Hyperarousal. Underarousal. Activat(e,ed,ing,ion). Incit(e,ed,ing). Alert(ness). Wak(e,ed,en,ened, ening,ing). Stimulat(e,ed,ing,ion). Anticipatory reaction(s). Autonomic reactivity. Rous(e,ed,ing). Excit(e,ed, ing,ement). Impassioned. *See also* Activation; Altered states of consciousness; Incitement; Sexual arousal; Stimuli; Vigilance.

Arousal, sexual. See *Sexual arousal.*

Arpeggio. Arpeggio(s). Arpa(s). Arpege(s). Arpegio(s). *Consider also:* broken chord(s), arpeggiat(e,ion), arpegement. *See also* Acciaccatura; Music; Ornamentation (music).

Arranged marriages. Arranged marriage(s). *Choose from:* arrang(e,ed, ing), childhood, broker(s,ing) *with:* betrothal(s), engage(d,ment,ments), marriage(s). *See also* Human courtship; Human mate selection; Marriage brokers; Traditional societies.

Arrangement (Music). Arrange(d, ment,ments) music. *Choose from:* music(al), concert(s), organ, band(s), jazz, harpsichord, piano, violin, guitar, orchestra(s), opera, instrument(s) *with:* arrang(e,ed,ment,ments,er,ers,ing), adapt(ed,ing,ation), transcription, transcrib(e,ed), improvis(e,ed,ing,ation), scoring, instrumentation, rendition(s), intabulation(s). *Consider also:* Bach and Vivaldi, etc. *Consider also:* medley(s), pasticcio(s), pastiche(s), variation(s) on theme(s), orchestration, version(s). *See also* Music; Orchestration; Patchwork; Quodlibets; Variations.

Arrears. Arrear(s,age). Mon(ey,ies) due. Indebted(ness). Liabil(ity,ities). *Choose from:* obligation(s), rent(s), installment(s), mortgage(s), debt(s), amount(s), bill(s), payment(s) *with:* unpaid, due, overdue, past due, late, outstanding, owed, balance(s). *See also* Bankruptcy; Credit; Indebtedness; Interest (monetary); Loans.

Arrests. Arrest(s,ed,ing). Rearrest(e,ed,ing). Apprehen(ded,sion) by police. Arrestee(s). Take(n) into police custody. Take(n) prisoner. Take(n) into custody. *Choose from:* detain(ed), seize(d) *with:* police, legal(ly). *Consider also:* Miranda rights, disappearance(s), desaparecid(o, a,os). *See also* Bail; Contempt of Court; Criminal investigations; Criminal proceedings; Detention; Fugitives from justice; Law enforcement; Missing persons; Offenders; Offenses; Plea bargaining; Police brutality; Police questioning; Police records; Political prisoners; Preventive detention; Search and seizure.

Arrests, false. See *False arrests.*

Arrhythmia. Arrhythm(ia,icity). Irregular heartbeat(s). Skipped heartbeat(s). Paroxysmal tachycardia. Heart block. *Choose from:* heart, cardiac, auriculur, ventricular, atrial *with:* flutter, rhythm disorder(s), irregular rhythm, fibrillation, dysrhythmia, premature beat(s). *See also* Heart disorders.

Arson. Arson(ists). Firesett(ing,er,ers). Pyroman(ia,iac,iacs). Pyromanic. Pyrolagnia. Incendiar(ism,ists,ies). Set(ting) fire(s). Start(ing) fire(s). Pyrophilia. Fire setting. Fire raising. Set aflame. Set ablaze. Set afire. Firebomb(ed,ing,ings). Fire convictions. Torch(ed,ing). Malicious burning. *See also* Combustibility; Crime; Fire; Incendiary weapons; Sabotage.

Art. See *Arts.*

Art, abstract. See *Abstract art.*

Art, ancient. See *Ancient art.*

Art, baroque. See *Baroque art.*

Art, body. See *Body art.*

Art, Christian. See *Christian art.*

Art, classical. See *Classical art.*

Art, clip. See *Clip art.*

Art, conceptual. See *Conceptual art.*

Art, concrete. See *Concrete art.*

Art, erotic. See *Erotica.*

Art, feminist. See *Feminist art.*

Art, figurative. See *Figurative art.*

Art, fine. See *Arts.*

Art, folk. See *Folk art.*

Art, futurism. See *Futurism (Art).*

Art, genre. See *Genre art.*

Art, lost works of. See *Lost works of art.*

Art, minimal. See *Minimal art.*

Art, minimalism. See *Minimal art.*

Art, modern. See *Modern art.*

Art, nonobjective. See *Abstract art.*

Art, performance. See *Performance art.*

Art, pop. See *Pop art.*

Art, possible. See *Conceptual art.*

Art, pre-Columbian. See *Pre-Columbian art.*

Art, prehistoric. See *Prehistoric art.*

Art, primitive. See *Primitive art.*

Art, public. See *Public art.*

Art, realism in. See *Realism in art.*

Art, religious. See *Religious art.*

Art, representational. See *Realism in art.*

Art, rock. See *Cave paintings; Carving (decorative arts); Petroglyphs.*

Art, socialist realism in. See *Socialist realism in art.*

Art, street. See *Street art.*

Art appreciation. Art appreciation. Interest in art(s,work,works). Art culture. *Choose from:* art(s,work,works), aesthetic(s), painting(s) *with:* appreciat(e,ed,ing,ion), enjoy(ed,ing,ment), aware(ness), involve(d,ment), support(ed,ing), inspir(e,ed,ation), knowledgeable, admir(e,ed,ing,ation), interest(ed,ing), attitude(s), ideal(s), taste, advocate(s), sponsor(s,ship). *See also* Aesthetic preferences; Aesthetics; Art criticism; Arts; Connoisseurs.

Art criticism. Art criticism *Choose from:* art(s,work,works), aesthetic(s), painting(s), painter(s), engraving(s), woodcut(s), sculpture *with:* critic(s,al, ize,izing,ized,ism), standard(s), classif(y,ied), evaluat(e,ed,ing,ion), valu(e,ed,ing,es), defin(e,ed,ing,ition), assess(ed,ment,ing), review(s,ed,ing), analysis, interpret(ed,ing,ation), comment(s,ed,ing) judg(e,ed,ment, ments). *See also* Art appreciation; Art critics; Arts; Aesthetic preferences; Aesthetics; Appraisal; Chattering class; Connoisseurs; Criticism; Formalism.

Art critics. Art critic(s). Art journalist(s). *Choose from:* art(s,work,works), painting(s), painter(s) *with:* critic(s), journalist(s), viewpoint(s), ally, allies, champion(s,ed), defender(s), commentator(s), interpreter(s). *See also* Art criticism; Arts; Chattering class; Criticism.

Art deco. Art deco. Style Moderne. *Consider also:* Tamara de Lempicka, Paul Manship, Paul Follot, Louis Sue, Andre Mare, Art nouveau. *See also* Art nouveau; Artistic styles; Arts; Decorative arts; Genres (art); Modern art.

Art education. Art education. *Choose from:* art, painting, drawing, aesthetic *with:* education, course(s), appreciation, lesson(s), curriculum, activit(y,ies), program(s), experience(s), achievement(s). *See also* Aesthetic education; Art schools; Artists; Arts.

Art history. Art histor(y,ian,ians). Historical analysis of art. *Choose from:* art(s,work,works), painting(s), painter(s), aesthetic(s), engraving(s), woodcut(s), sculpture *with:* histor(y,icity,ian,ians), historiograph(y, er,ers), historical analysis, historically informed, chronolog(y,ical), modern period, twentieth century, 19th century, nineteenth century, 18th century, eighteenth century, 17th century, 16th century, Roman, Greek, Classical, revisionis(t,m), genealog(y,ical), theor(y,ies), discourse, canon(s,icity). *Consider also:* cultural history. *See also* Ancient art; Ancient architecture; Arts; Humanities.

Art metalwork. Art metalwork. Artistic metalwork(ing). Silverwork. Silversmith(s). Metal-working craft. Bronze-working. Japanese metalwork. African metalwork. *Choose from:* art(s,istic,work,works), statuar(y,ies), flower(s), sword-fittings *with:* metal(lic,s,work), bronze, pewter, copper, alloy(s). *Consider also:* jewelry, ironworking, liturgical metalwork. *See also* Arts; Crafts; Collectibles; Designs; Goldwork; Treasure.

Art movement, Barbizon. See *Barbizon art movement.*

Art museums. Art museum(s). Picture galler(y,ies). *Consider also:* Museum of Fine Arts, Gallery of Modern Art, Museum of Contemporary Art, Museum of Modern Art, Metropolitan Museum, Guggenheim Museum, Tate Gallery, J. Paul Getty Museum, National Gallery of Art, etc. *Consider also:* cultural institution(s). *See also* Arts; Galleries; Museums.

Art nouveau. Art nouveau. Jugendstil. Sezessionstil. Stil Liberty. Modernista. *Consider also:* Aubrey Beardsley, Alphonse Mucha and Louis Comfort Tiffany, Charles Rennie Mackintosh, etc. *Consider also:* art mobilier, Glasgow style, Glasgow School, Modern style, Art Moderne, Style Nouille, Style coup de fouet, Arte joven, Style Metro, Nieuwe kunst, Japonisme. *See also* Art deco; Arts; Artistic styles; Arts and Crafts Movement; Decorative arts; Genres (art); Modern Art.

Art objects. Art object(s). Objet(s) d'art. Art treasure(s). *Consider also:* artifact(s), sculptural work(s), relic(s). *See also* Collectibles; Miniature objects; Relics.

Art patronage. Art(s) patron(s,age). Patron(s) of the arts. *Choose from:* patron(s,age), sponsor(s,ship,ed,ing), underwrit(er,ers,ing,ten), commission(ed,ing), back(ed,ing,er,ers) *with:* artist(s), art(s), painter(s), composer(s), portrait(s), painting(s), art(s,work,works), production(s), composition(s), theater(s), music(ian, ians,al), symphon(y,ies), ballet(s), choral societ(y,ies). *See also* Arts; Benefactors; Corporate social responsibility; Foundations (organizations); Fund raising; Patronage; Philanthropy.

Art publishing. Art publish(ed,er,ers,ing). Art book publishing. *Choose from:* graphic art(s), art(s,ist,ists,istic, work,works), portfolio(s), picture(s), paint(ed,in,ings) *with:* book(s), publish(ed,er,ers,ing), copyright(s,ed). *Consider also:* cultural property. *See also* Artists' books; Arts; Book industry; Publishing; Publishers.

Art schools. Art school(s). University of the Arts. Studio School(s). *Choose from:* school(s), academ(y,ies), college(s), universit(y,ies), workshop(s), institute(s), program(s) *with:* art(s), drawing, painting, sculpture, design, architecture, decorative arts, fine arts. *See also* Arts; Art education; Professional education.

Art societies. Art societ(y,ies). Art league(s). Art(s,ist,ists) club(s). Pastel societ(y,ies). *Consider also:* Salmagundi Club, National Arts Club, etc. *See also* Arts; Societies (organizations).

Art thefts. Art theft(s) Stolen painting(s). *Choose from:* museum(s), galler(y,ies), art(s,work,works), painting(s), antiquit(y,ies), manuscript(s), treasure(s) *with:* stole(n), missing, pilfer(ed,ing), loot(ed,ing), heist(s,ed), smuggle(d), thief, thieves, trafficking, plunder(ed, ing), rob(ber,bers,bery,bed,bing). *Consider also:* Dali, Picasso, Chagall, Louvre, Gardner Museum, etc. *with:* stole(n), missing, pilfer(ed,ing), loot(ed,ing), heist(s,ed), smuggle(d), thie(f,ves), trafficking, plunder(ed,ing), rob(ber,bers,bery,bed,bing). *See also* Archaeological thefts; Arts; Cultural property; Lost works of art; Pillage; Theft.

Art therapy. Art therap(y,ies). Therapeutic art. *Choose from:* art, painting(s), drawing(s), poetry, craft(s), music *with:* therap(y,ies,eutic), psychotherap(y,ies, eutic), rehabilitat(ive,ion), treatment(s), relax(ing,ation). *See also* Dance therapy; Music therapy; Psychopoetry; Psychotherapy; Self expression.

Arthritis. Arthrit(is,ic). *Consider also:* rheumatoid arthritis, osteoarthritis, polyarthritis, arthropathy, chondrocalcinosis, gout, periarthritis, Reiter(s) disease, rheumatic fever, rheumatism. *See also* Disability; Disease.

Articles, journal. See *Journal articles.*

Articles, religious. See *Religious articles.*

Articulation (speech). Articulat(e,ed, ing,ion,ory). Enunciat(e,ed,ing,ion). Consonant production. Coarticulation. Voicing distinction(s). Phonetic(s). Speech sound(s). *Consider also:* pronunciation, elocution, speech production. *See also* Consonants; Phonetics; Pronunciation; Speech characteristics; Speech intelligibility; Verbal communication.

Articulation disorders. Articulation disorder(s). *Choose from:* articulat(e,ed, ing,ion) *with:* impairment(s), disorder(s), inadequate, problem(s), inconsistency, deviation(s), deviant, defect(s), error(s). *Consider also:* dysarthria, misarticulation, anarthria, asyllabia, alalia, aphonia, disordered speech. *See also* Articulation (speech); Dysarthria; Speech disorders; Speech intelligibility; Speech therapy; Stuttering.

Artifacts. Artifact(s). Man-made object(s). Material culture. *Consider also:* tool(s), implement(s), weapon(s,ry), pot(s,tery), amphora(e,s), sculpture, clothing, art object(s). *See also* Bone implements; Crafts; Cultural history; Cultural property; Material culture; Stone implements; Tools.

Artificial body parts. See *Prostheses.*

Artificial disorders. See *Factitious disorders.*

Artificial insemination. Artificial inseminat(ed,ion). Eutelegenesis. Artificial breeding. Artificial reproduction. *Choose from:* artificial, in vitro, intra-uterine, intra-peritoneal, extracorporeal *with:* inseminat(ed,ing,ion), fertiliz(e,ed,ing,ation). Test tube bab(y,ies). *See also* Conception; Fertility enhancement; Fertilization in vitro; Pregnancy; Reproductive technologies; Sexual reproduction; Surrogate mothers.

Artificial intelligence. Artificial intelligence. Machine intelligence. Computer thought. Artificial thinking. *Choose from:* simulat(ed,ing,ion,ions), model(s), synthesiz(e,ed,ing), emulat(e,ed,ing,ion), representation, computer(s) *with:* reasoning, inference, intelligence, knowledge, thinking, thought, cognition, decision(s), problem solving, terminological subsumption, deduction, induction and abduction, analogical reasoning, case-based reasoning, query processing, query optimization, syntactic transformation(s), semantic transformation(s). *Choose from:* knowledge base(s), relational database(s), object-oriented database(s) *with:* architecture(s), validation, verification, acquisition, maintenance. *Consider also:* intelligent system(s), knowledge engineering, knowledge system(s), heuristics, machine learning technique(s), inference technique(s), expert system(s), inferential engine(s), intelligent application(s). *See also* Cognition; Cognitive science; Computers; Cybernetics; Distributed artificial intelligence; Heuristics; Intelligence; Knowledge management; Robotics; User friendly systems.

Artificial intelligence, distributed. See *Distributed artificial intelligence.*

Artificial limbs. See *Prostheses.*

Artificial respiration. Artifical respiration. *Choose from:* artifical(ly), mechanical *with:* respirat(ing,ion,ed,ory,or,ors), ventilat(e,ed,ing,ion), ventilatory support, resuscitat(ed,ing,ion). *Consider also:* cardiopulmonary resuscitation, CPR, iron lung(s), mouth-to-mouth resuscitation, respiratory inhalation therapy, intermittent positive pressure ventilation. *See also* Life support care; Respiratory care units; Respiratory system.

Artificial thinking. See *Artificial intelligence.*

Artificiality. Artificial(ity,ly,ness). Synthetic(ally). Concoct(ed,ion). Factitious(ly). Man-made. Fabricat(e,ed,ion). Dummy. Ersatz. False(ly,ness). Imitat(e,ed,ing,ion). Phon(y,iness). Mock. Sham. Simulat(e,ed,ion). Substitute(s). Fictitious(ly,ness). Spurious(ly,ness). Fak(e,ed,ing). Feign(ed,ing). Put-on(s). *Consider also:* papier-mâché, pretend(ed,ing), unreal(ity), hollow, painted, overdone, quaint, stagy, theatrical, unnatural, cute(sy), goody-goody, mincing, overrefined, simpering, contriv(e,ed,ing). *See also* Deception; Disguise; Factitious disorders; Faking; Literary forgeries and mystifications; Self deception; Simulation.

Artillery. Artiller(y,ies). Large caliber gun(s). Large firearm(s). Gunner(y,ies). Gun system(s). Ordnance(s). Cannon(s). Howitzer(s). Mounted gun(s). Railgun(s). Heavy gun(s). *See also* Military weapons; Weaponry.

Artisans. Artisan(s). Craftworker(s). Crafts(men,man,people,women,woman). Skilled in craft(s). Woodworker(s). Handcraft worker(s). Skilled trade(s). Handicrafts(men,man,people,women,woman). *Consider also:* tie-dying, batik, shoemak(er,ers), weaver(s), blacksmith(s), leatherworker(s), roof(er,ers) metal work(er,er), plumb(er,ers), stonework(er,ers). woodcarving, woodworking, cabinet maker(s), harpsichord maker(s). *See also* Artists; Blacksmithing; Crafts; Guilds; Weaving.

Artistic ability. Artistic abilit(y,ies). *Choose from:* art, artist(s,ic), aesthetic, painter(s), drawing, sculptor(s), musician(s), music, painting, sculpture *with:* abilit(y,ies), creativity, aptitude(s), talent(ed,s), skill(ed,s), sensitivity, potential, development, productivity, craftsmanship, gifted(ness). *See also* Ability; Creativity; Musical ability; Nonverbal ability.

Artistic styles. Art(istic) style(s). Art(istic) trend(s). Art(istic) tradition(s). *Consider also:* abstract expressionism, romanticism, classicism, impressionism, realism, etc. *See also* Abstract art; Abstract expressionism; Aesthetics; Art deco; Art education; Art nouveau; Artists; Arts; Camp (aesthetics);

Conceptual art; Cultural history; Figurative art; Genre art; Genres; Genres (art); Magic realism (art); Modern art; Music; Realism in art; Romanticism; Socialist realism in art.

Artists. Artist(s,e,es). Artistically gifted. Painter(s). Old master(s). *Choose from:* art(istic) *with:* master(s), creator(s), practitioner(s), people, person(s). *Consider also:* dancer(s), composer(s), pianist(s), musician(s), writer(s), virtuos(o,os,i), sculptor(s), crafts(man, men,woman,women,person,persons). *See also* Animators; Artisans; Artistic style(s); Artists' books; Artists' colonies; Arts; Cartoonists; Composers; Creators; Medical illustration; Musicians; Singers.

Artists' books. Artists' book(s). Special edition(s). Book art. Books developed by artist(s). Books combining text and art. *See also* Art publishing; Artists; Drawing books.

Artists' colonies. Artist(s) colon(y,ies). *Choose from:* artist(s) *with:* colon(y,ies), condominium(s) retreat(s), communit(y,ies). *See also* Artists; Vacation houses.

Arts. Art(s). Art form(s). Aesthetics. Acrylic(s). Architecture. Calligraphy. Caricature(s). Cartoon(s). Childrens art. Collage(s). Commercial art. Craft(s). Creative activit(y,ies). Creative work(s). Danc(e,ed,ing). Drafting. Drama(tics). Drawing(s). Engraving(s). Film production. Film(s). Fine art(s). Graphic art(s). Handicraft(s). Illumination(s). Illustration(s). Literature. Motion picture(s). Movie(s). Music. Opera(s). Origami. Painting(s). Pastel(s). Photographic art(s). Photography. Poetry. Poem(s). Pottery. Prose. Sculptur(e,es, ing). Sketch(es). Theatre. Visual art(s). Watercolor(s). Woodcarving(s). *Consider also:* artistic value(s), artwork(s), aesthetic value(s), high culture, art history, masterpiece(s), musical program(s), artist(s), musician(s). *See also* Abstract expressionism; Aesthetics; Ancient art; Animal painting and illustration; Architecture; Art appreciation; Art criticism; Art critics; Art deco; Art education; Art history; Art metalwork; Art museums; Art nouveau; Art patronage; Art publishing; Art schools; Art societies; Art thefts; Art therapy; Artistic styles; Artists; Arts and crafts movement; Assemblage (Art); Barbizon art movement; Baroque art; Biological illustration; Cave paintings; Christian art; Clip art; Collages; Color; Conceptual art; Concrete art; Crafts; Dadaism; Dance; Designs; Drama; Drawing; Earthworks; Expressionism (Art); Engraving; Feminist art; Figurative art; Folk art; Genre art; Genres (art); Glass painting and staining; Graphic arts;

Humanities; Impressionism (art); Influence (literary, artistic, etc.); Ink painting; Literature; Lost works of art; Magic realism (art); Mannerism (art); Medieval sculpture; Minimal art; Modern art; Modern architecture; Monochrome painting; Municipal art; Mural painting and decoration; Museums; Music; Musical instruments; Naturalism; Pop art; Popular culture; Public art; Realism in art; Religious art; Representation (likeness); Sculpture; Socialist realism in art; Theater.

Arts, culinary. See *Cooking.*

Arts, decorative. See *Decorative arts.*

Arts, graphic. See *Graphic arts.*

Arts, martial. See *Martial arts.*

Arts, performing. See *Dance; Drama; Music; Theater.*

Arts and Crafts movement. Arts and Crafts movement. Art Workers Guild. Guild of Handicrafts. *Consider also:* arts and crafts style, aesthetic movement, graffito decoration, John Ruskin, William Morris, Walter Crane, C.R. Ashbee, etc. *See also* Art Nouveau; Arts; Manual training.

Asbestos. Asbestos. Asbestus. *Consider also:* chrysotile, tremolite, actinolite. *See also* Air pollution; Fire prevention; Hazardous materials; Hazardous occupations.

Ascent. Ascen(t,sion). Ascend(ed,ing,ance). Climb(ed,ing). Escalat(e,ed,ing,ion). Scal(e,ed,ing). Mount(ed,ing). Rais(e,ed,ing). Uplift(ed,ing). Elevat(e,ed,ing,ation). Upward movement(s). Mov(e,ed,ing) upward. *See also* Altitude; Altitude effects; Mountaineering.

Asceticism. Ascetic(ism). Strict religious discipline. Self denial. Abstinen(t,ce). Self discipline. Auster(e,ity). Abstention. Renunciation. Self restraint. Stoic(al, ism). Celiba(cy,te). Monastic(ism). Abstemious(ness). Puritanism. Continence. *Consider also:* plain living, spartan, fast(ed,ing), temperance, frugality, self mortification, Manichae(ism,n,nism), Maniche(e, ean,ism,n,nism), askesis, tapas. *See also* Abbeys; Abstinence; Chastity; Fasting; Monasticism; Mysticism; Religious beliefs; Religious life; Religious personnel; Religious practices; Social Isolation; Stoicism.

Ascription. Ascription. *Choose from:* ascribed, inherited *with:* status(es), role(s), occupation(s), title(s), wealth, position(s). *See also* Caste system; Disinheritance; Inheritance; Social status.

Asemia. See *Aphasia.*

Ashamed. See *Body awareness; Embarrassment; Self consciousness; Shame.*

Asia. See *Central Asia; Far East; South Asia; Southeast Asia.*

Asia, central. See *Central Asia.*

Asia, south. See *South Asia.*

Asia, southeast. See *Southeast Asia.*

Asian Americans. Asian American(s). Amerasian(s). *Choose from:* Oriental, Asian, Pacific, Chinese, Japanese, Korean, Filipino, Malaysian, Indochinese, Vietnamese, Cambodian, Thai, Laotian, Samoan, Pakistani *with:* American(s), immigrant(s), refugee(s). *Consider also:* Hawaiian(s), Philippine Islander(s). *See also* Ethnic groups; Japanese Americans; Korean Americans; Minority groups; Pacific Islanders; People of color; Races; Racially mixed.

Asian empires. Asian civilization(s). *Choose from:* Asia(n), India(n), Chin(a,ese), Japan(ese), Korea(n), Vietnam(es), Cambodia(n), Thai(land), etc. *with:* civilization(s), dynast(y,ies), empire(s), kingdom(s), chiefdom(s), culture(s), nation(s), world(s), tribe(s). *China, consider specific periods, for example:* Hsia Dynasty, Shang Dynasty, Chou Dynasty, Ch'in Dynasty, Han Dynasty, Three Kingdoms, Tsin Dynasty, Sui Dynasty, T'ang Dynasty, Period of Five Dynasties, Sung Dynasty, Yuan Dynasty, Ming Dynasty, Ch'ing [Manchu, Qing] Dynasty. *India, consider also, for example:* Indus Valley civilization, Kingdom of Magadha, Kingdom of Kosala, Maurya(n) Empire, Gupta(s) Dynasty, Chalukya(s,n) Dynasty, Vijayanagar, Delhi Sultanate, Mogul Empire. *Japan, consider, for example:* Yamamoto Clan, Fujiwara Family, Minamoto Family, Tokugawa shogunate, Kamakura regime, Meiji period. *Korea, consider, for example:* Kingdom of Koguryo, Paekche Kingdom, Kingdom of Silla, Koryo Dynasty, Yi Dynasty. *Cambodia, consider, for example:* Khmer Empire. *Thailand, consider, for example:* Kingdom of Nanchao, Chakkri [Chakri] Dynasty. *Vietnam consider, for example:* Le Dynasty, Nguyen Dynasty. *See also* African empires; Asian languages; Buddhism; Central Asia; Civilization; Cultural history; Culture contact; Dynasties; Far East; Hinduism; Historical periods; Indian (India) cultural groups; Indigenous populations; Indonesian cultural groups; Islam; Oceania; Oceanic cultural groups; Philippine Islands cultural groups; Pre-Columbian empires; Sino-Thai languages; South Asia; Southeast Asia; Southeast Asian cultural groups; Taoism; Tibeto-Burman languages; Traditional societies; Western civilization; World history.

Asian languages. Asian language(s). Ainu. Japanese. Korean. *See also* Annamese-Muong languages; Asian languages; Dravidian languages; East Altaic languages; Far East; Language; Languages (as subjects); Malayo-Polynesian languages; Mon-Khmer languages; Sino-Thai languages; South Asia; Southeast Asia; Southeast Asian cultural groups; Tibeto-Burman languages; Tokharin languages.

Asociality. See *Social isolation.*

Aspects of technology, labor. See *Labor aspects of technology.*

Asphyxia, sexual syndrome. See *Sexual asphyxia syndrome.*

Aspiration, academic. See *Academic aspiration.*

Aspiration, educational. See *Academic aspiration.*

Aspiration, parent. See *Parent aspiration.*

Aspiration, parental. See *Parent aspiration.*

Aspiration level. Aspiration level(s). *Choose from:* aspiration(s), expectation(s), expectancy, goal(s), striving *with:* level(s), scale(s), setting, high, low. *Consider also:* achievement motivation, success orientation, aspirational group(s). *See also* Academic aspiration; Achievement need; Achievement potential; Aspirations; Expectations; Goal orientation; Occupational aspirations; Parent aspiration.

Aspirations. Aspiration(al,s). Intent(ion,ions). Target(s). Purpose(s). Calling(s). Ambition(s). Ambitious(ness). Achievement orientation(s). Expectation(s) of achievement. Goal(s). Career orientation(s). Achievement motivation(s). Performance motivation(s). Striv(e,ing). Status seeker(s). *Consider also:* academic, occupational, parent(al), education(al), vocation(al), profession(al), status, career *with:* aspiration(s), ambition(s), objective(s), purpose(s), aim(s), goal(s). *See also* Ability; Academic aspiration; Achievement; Aspiration level; Expectations; Goals; Life plans; Motivation; Occupational aspirations; Parent aspiration; Self actualization; Self concept; Self knowledge; Success.

Aspirations, career. See *Occupational aspirations.*

Aspirations, occupational. See *Occupational aspirations.*

Aspirations, vocational. See *Occupational aspirations.*

Assassination. Assassinat(e,ed,ing, ion,ions). Assassin(s). Attempted assassination(s). Presidential assassination(s). Assassin syndrome. Political killing(s). Plot(s) to kill. Shoot(ing) president(s). Homicide with politics. Political murder(s). Attempt(s) on life. Slaying. Slain. Put to death. Execut(e,ed,ing,ion,ions). *Consider specific assassins with their victims, for example:* Sirhan Sirhan *with:* Robert Kennedy, Brutus and Cassius *with:* Gaius Julius Caesar, Lee Harvey Oswald *with:* John F. Kennedy, Gavrilo Princip *with:* Archduke Francis Ferdinand, John Wilkes Booth *with:* Abraham Lincoln, etc. *Consider also:* murder(s,ed,ing), homicide(s), manslaughter, kill(ing), violent death(s), stab(bed,bing,bings), shoot(ing,ings), shot, knif(e,ed,ing,ings), poison(ed,ing,ings). *See also* Homicide; Political violence; Terrorism.

Assassination, character. See *Libel.*

Assassination, political. See *Assassination.*

Assault (battle). Assault(s,ed,ing). Attack(ed,ing). Invad(e,ed,ing). Invasion(s). Bomb(ardment,ed,ing,ings). Offensive(s). Raid(s). Foray(s). Military aggression. Territorial aggression. Onslaught(s). Blitz(ed,ing). Blitzkrieg. Storm(ed,ing). Besiege(d). Strafing(s). Barrage. *See also* Attack (Military science); Battles; Military capitulations; Military operations; Military retreat; Troop movements.

Assault (personal). Assault(ed,ive,iveness, ing). Holdup(s). Victimiz(e,ed,ing,ation). Aggressive act(s). Act(s) of aggression. Violent crime(s). Rape(d). Raping. Mutilat(e,ed,ing,ion). Homicid(e,es,al). Sexual(ly) violen(t,ce). Forced sex. Dat(e,ing) violence. Courtship violence. Harass(ed,ing,ment). Sexual(ly) abus(e,ive). Violen(t,ce). Bit(e,ten,ing). Batter(ed,ing). Beat(en,ing). Club(bed, bing). Bludgeon(ed,ing). Mugg(ed,ing). Kick(ed,ing). Push(ed,ing). Shov(e,ed, ing). Hit(ting). Slaying. Slain. Brawl(ing). Fray. Scuffle. Slash(ing). Rampage. Attack(ed,ing). *See also* Aggression; Confrontation; Crime; Family violence; Homicide; Lynching; Sexual assault; Violence.

Assault, sexual. See *Sexual assault.*

Assay. See *Analysis; Examinations; Tests.*

Assemblage (Art). Assemblage art. Assemblage composition(s). Assemblage sculpture(s). Photomontage(s). Mixed-media construction. Objets trouves. Collage(s). *Consider also:* Merz *with:* art, picture(s), sculpture. Merzbilden. Merzbau. *Consider also:* Joseph Cornell, Marcel Duchamp, Kurt Schwitters, Annette Messager, Melvin Edwards, Ed Kienholz, Robert Rauschenberg, Louise Nevelson, etc. *See also* Arts; Collages; Cubism; Dadaism; Genres (art); Modern art; Surrealism.

Assembly, right of. See *Right of assembly.*

Assembly line methods. See *Assembly lines.*

Assembly lines. Assembly line(s). Assembly system(s). Production line(s). Machine pacing. Assembly method(s). Assembly operation(s). *Choose from:* factor(y,ies), manufacturing, assembly *with:* operation(s), procedure(s), system(s). *Consider also:* interchangeable part(s). *See also* Industry; Factories; Mass production.

Assent. See *Acquiescence; Agreement; Consensus; Consent (law); Informed consent.*

Assertions. Assert(ed,ing,ion,ions). Declar(e,ed,ing,ation,ations). Proclamation(s). Proclaim(ed,ing). Asseveration(s). Affirm(ed,ing,ation, ations). Warrant(ed,ing). Avow(ed,ing, al,als). *Consider also:* acknowledg(e, ed,ing,ement,ements). affidavit(s), attest(ed,ing,ation,ations), confirm(ed, ing,ation), positive statement(s), pronounc(e,ed,ing,ement,ements). *See also* Allegations; Communication (thought transfer); Creeds; Messages; Testimony.

Assertiveness. Assertive(ness). Assertive behavior(s). Self advoca(cy,te). Assertiv(e,ity). Self assert(ive,ion). Assertion(s). Effectiveness skill(s). Self expression. Persist(ence). Aspir(e,ed, ing,ation,ations). Forthright(ness). Straightforward. Direct expression. Express(ed,ing,ion) opinion(s). Defend(ing) interest(s). *Consider also:* social skill(s). *See also* Aggression; Assertiveness training; Empowerment; Inhibition (psychology); Interpersonal relations; Personality traits; Self esteem; Self expression; Social maturity; Social skills; Socialization.

Assertiveness training. Assert(ive, iveness,ion) training. *Choose from:* assert(ive,iveness,ion), effectiveness, personal adjustment, social skills, interpersonal skills *with:* training, therapy. *See also* Assertiveness; Behavior modification; Communication skills; Human relations training; Social skills training.

Assessment. Assess(ed,ing,ment,ments). Analys(is,es). Analyz(e,ed,ing). Apprais(e,ed,ing,al). Diagnos(is,es,tic). Estimat(e,ed,ing,ion,ions). Evaluat(e,ed, ing,ion,ions). Examination(s). Examin(e, ed,ing). Identif(y,ying,ied,ication). Inventor(y,ied,ies). Measur(e,es, ed,ing,ment,ments). Observation(s). Profile(s). Prognos(is,es,tic). Questionnaire(s). Rating(s). Report(s). Screen(ed,ing). Stud(y,ies). Survey(s). Test(ing,s). Valuation(s). *See also* Analysis; Appraisal; Behavioral assessment; Cost effectiveness; Criticism; Criteria; Evaluation; Measurement; Needs assessment; Neuropsychological assessment; Observation methods; Peer review; Performance

appraisal; Personality measures; Program evaluation; Qualitative methods; Risk assessment; Self evaluation; Self evaluation (groups); Standards; Teacher evaluation; Technology assessment; Valuation.

Assessment, behavioral. See *Behavioral assessment.*

Assessment, needs. See *Needs assessment.*

Assessment, neuropsychological. See *Neuropsychological assessment.*

Assessment, performance. See *Performance appraisal.*

Assessment, personality. See *Personality measures.*

Assessment, risk. See *Risk assessment.*

Assessment, self. See *Self assessment.*

Assessment, technology. See *Technology assessment.*

Asset management. Asset management. *Choose from:* asset(s), investment(s), portfolio(s), pension(s), income, property, *with:* manag(e,ed,ement,ing), allocat(e,ed,ing,ion), strateg(y,ies), enhancement. *Consider also:* liabilit(y,ies) manag(e,ed,ing,ement). *See also* Assets; Administration of estates; Capitalization; Debt management; Financial management; Liquidation; Pension fund management; Risk management.

Assets. Asset(s). Savings. Net worth. Capital. Economic status. Financial status. Affluence. Pension(s). Fund(s). Income. Annuit(y,ies). Propert(y,ies). Wealth. Possession(s). Resource(s). Estate(s). Bond(s). Securities. Cash reserve(s). Investment(s). Bank account(s). Checking account(s). Money market account(s). Stock(s). Mutual fund(s). Certificate(s) of deposit. Accounts receivable. Belongings. Chattel. Equity. Real estate. Real property. Securities. *Choose from:* equitable, fixed, frozen, liquid, personal *with:* asset(s). *Consider also:* goodwill. *See also* Annuities; Asset management; Capitalization; Equity (financial); Funds; Intangible property; Investments; Land (property); Liquidation; Liquidity; Personal property; Property values; Resources; Savings; Valuation; Wealth.

Assets, intangible. See *Intangible property.*

Assimilation (cultural). Assimilat(e,ed,ing, ion). Cultural(ly) assimilat(e,ed,ion,ing). Acculturat(e,ed,ion). Accomodat(e,ed, ion). Naturaliz(ed,ation). Culture assimilator(s). Americaniz(ed,ation). Mingl(e,ed,ing). Comingl(e,ed,ing). Cultural fusion. Intermarriage(s). *Choose from:* adaptation, merg(e,ed,ing) *with:* social, society, cultural, sociocultural, change. *Consider also:* disassimilat(e,ed,ing,ion), culture contact, interethnic, detribaliz(e,ed,ing,ation),

irredent(a,ism,ist,ists). *See also* Biculturalism; Cooptation; Culture change; Cultural maintenance; Cultural pluralism; Cultural transformation; Ethnic groups; Ethnic differences; Immigrants; Indigenous populations; Intercultural communication; Interethnic families; Intermarriage; Interracial marriage; Melting pot; Minority groups; Nativism; Newcomers; Racial differences; Racial integration; Racial diversity; Racially mixed; Social cohesion; Social integration; Strangers; Subcultures.

Assimilation (psychology). Assimilat(e,ed, ion). Accomodat(e,ed,ing,ion). *Choose from:* incorporat(e,ed,ing,ion), amalgamat(e,ed,ing,ion), integrat(e,ed, ing,ion) *with:* new situation(s), new information. *See also* Cognitive processes; Learning.

Assistance. Assist(ed,ing,ance). Aid(s,ed,ing). Help(s,ed,ing). Grant(s). Bailout(s). Contribut(e,ed,ing,ion,ions). Benefit(ted,ting,s). Charit(y,ies,able). Sustenance. Support(s,ed,ing). Reinforc(e,es,ed,ing,ement,ements). Rescu(e,ed,ing). Foster(ed,ing). Further(ed,ing,ance). Benevolen(t,ce). Altruis(m,tic). Philanthrop(y,ies,ic). Humanitarian(ism). Kindness(es). Donation(s). *Consider also:* accommodat(e,ed,ing,ation), advice, advis(e,ed,ing), advoca(te,cy), patron(age), collaborat(e,ed,ing,ion). *See also* Agricultural assistance; Antipoverty programs; Bailouts; Charitable behavior; Charities; Contributions; Disaster relief; Economic assistance; Employee assistance programs; Family assistance; Financial support; Food services (programs); Giving; Helping behavior; Human services; Intervention; Medical assistance; Military assistance; Shelters; Social programs; Social services; Technical assistance.

Assistance, agricultural. See *Agricultural assistance.*

Assistance, economic. See *Economic assistance.*

Assistance, family. See *Family assistance.*

Assistance, federal. See *Antipoverty programs; Fiscal federalism; Government financing; Government programs; Government subsidization; Medical assistance; Public welfare.*

Assistance, financial. See *Financial support.*

Assistance, food. See *Food services (programs).*

Assistance, government. See *Antipoverty programs; Enterprise zones; Fiscal federalism; Government aid; Government financing; Government programs; Government subsidization; Medical assistance; National health programs;*

Public welfare; State capitalism; Subsidized housing.

Assistance, medical. See *Medical assistance.*

Assistance, military. See *Military assistance.*

Assistance, public. See *Antipoverty programs; Food services (programs); Medical assistance; Public welfare; Social agencies; Social programs.*

Assistance, technical. See *Technical assistance.*

Assistance, trade adjustment. See *Trade adjustment assistance.*

Assistance in emergencies. Assistance in emergenc(y,ies). *Choose from:* assist(ed,ing,ance), rescue(d,r,rs), CPR , aid(ed,ing), sav(e,ed,ing), ambulance(s), police, EMS, fire department(s), *with:* emergenc(y,ies), disaster(s), disturbance(s), tornado(es), hurricane(s), accident(s), fire(s), flood(s,ing), 911, blue light program(s), danger(s,ous), heart attack(s), choking, life-threatening injury, nuclear meltdowns, earthquakes, oil spill(s). *See also* Ambulances; Crisis intervention; Disasters; Good samaritans; Emergencies; Emergency services; Psychological debriefing.

Assistance programs. See *Antipoverty programs; Employee assistance programs; Food services (programs); Government programs; Medical assistance; Outreach programs; Public welfare; Social programs.*

Assistance programs, employee. See *Employee assistance programs.*

Assistance seeking. See *Help seeking behavior.*

Assistants. Assistant(s). Helper(s). Aid(s,e, es). Ancillar(y,ies). Accessor(y,ies). Accomplice(s). Attendant(s). Auxiliar(y,ies). Aide(s)-de-camp. Coadjut(ant,ants,or,ors). Lieutenant(s). *Consider also:* acolyte(s), co-pilot(s), hench(man,men), minion(s), girl Friday, man Friday, right-hand (man,woman), representative(s), deput(y,ies), co-worker, workfellow, yokemate, colleague(s), subsidiar(y,ies), servant(s). *See also* Agents; Attendants; Associates; Collaborators; Support staff.

Assistants, physicians. See *Physicians assistants.*

Assisted living. Assisted living. *Consider also:* continuing care, retirement communit(y, ies), long term care, homelike environment(s), retirement housing, managed care continuum, care option(s) for older adults, senior living alternative(s), senior housing, extended congregate care. *See also* Consumer directed care; Institutional homes; Nursing homes; Retirement communities; Residential facilities.

Assisted suicide. Assisted suicide. Physician-assisted death. Help patient(s) die. Hasten death. Quicken death. Right to die. Prescribe(d) a deadly dose. End suffering. *Consider also:* terminat(e,ed, ing) life support, Kevorkian, legistrothanatry. *See also* Bioethics; Death; Dying; Euthanasia; Hospices; Physician patient relations; Right to die; Terminal illness.

Assisted suicide, physician. See *Assisted suicide.*

Associate learning, paired. See *Paired associate learning.*

Associates. Associate(s). Accessor(y,ies). Partner(s). Affiliate(s). Assistant(s). Colleague(s). Collaborator(s). Confederate(s). Helper(s). *Consider also:* companion(s), comrade(s), peer(s). *See also* Accomplices; Affiliation (businesses); Assistants; Collaborators; Partners; Peers; Reference groups.

Association (psychology). Associat(ion, ive). *Choose from:* cognitive, internal *with:* contiguity, link(s,ed,ing), connection(s). *Consider also:* connotation(s), free recall, connectionism, conditioning, free association. *See also* Cognitive generalization; Cognitive processes; Context; Word association; Word recognition.

Association, free. See *Free association.*

Association, psychosis of. See *Psychosis of association.*

Association, word. See *Word association.*

Associations (organizations). Association(s). Organization(s). Societ(y,ies). Club(s). Union(s). Federation(s). League(s). Fraternit(y, ies). Sororit(y,ies). Guild(s). Part(y,ies). Co-operative(s). Co-op(s). Fellowship(s). Lodge(s). Brotherhood(s). Affiliation(s). *See also* Agencies; Archaeological societies; Chapters (organizations); Clubs; Law societies; Library associations; Neighborhood associations; Nongovernmental organizations; Nonprofit organizations; Organizations; Professional organizations; Secret societies; Social contact; Societies (organizations); Voluntary associations; Youth organizations.

Associations, campus. See *School clubs.*

Associations, community. See *Community involvement; Neighborhood associations.*

Associations, employers. See *Employers associations.*

Associations, environmental. See *Environmentalism.*

Associations, human rights. See *Abortion rights movement; Activism; Anti-apartheid movement; Antiabortion movement; Black power; Civil disobedi-*

ence; Civil rights organizations; Disability rights movement; Gray power; Homosexual liberation movement; Interest groups; Labor movements; Peace movements; Political movements; Protest movements; Social movements; Suffrage movement; Women's groups; Women's rights; Youth movements.

Associations, library. See *Library associations.*

Associations, neighborhood. See *Neighborhood associations.*

Associations, professional. See *Professional organizations.*

Associations, scientific. See *Scientific societies.*

Associations, trade. See *Trade associations.*

Associations, voluntary. See *Voluntary associations.*

Associations, workingmens. See *Guilds; Labor unions.*

Associations, youth. See *Youth organizations.*

Assumptions. Assumption(s). Presuppos(e, ed,ition,itions). Presum(e,ed,ing,ption, ptions). Surmis(e,ed,ing). Take(n,ing) for granted. Apriorism(s). Posit(ed,ing). Postulat(e,ed,ing,ion). Premise(s). Suppos(e,ed,ing,ition,itions). *Consider also:* thesis, conjectur(e,ed,ing), guess(es,ed,ing), surmis(e,ed,ing), hypothes(is,es), theor(y,ies), axiom(s,atic), fundamental law(s), principle(s), theorem(s), proposition(s). *See also* Beliefs; Constructs; Fundamental; Postulates.

Assurance, quality. See *Quality control.*

Assurances. Assurance(s). Assur(e,ed, edness,ing). Reassurance(s). Reassur(e,ed,ing). Guarantee(s,d,ing). Affirm(ed,ing,ation). Assert(ed,ing,ion, ions). Attest(ed,ing,ation,ations). Commit(ted,ting,ment). Declar(e,ed,ing, ation,ations). Depos(e,ed,ing,ition, itions). Evident(ial). Evidenc(e,ed,ing). Proof(s). Prov(e,en,ing). Promis(e,es,ed, ing). Warrant(s,ed,ing). Sworn statement(s). Under oath. Pledg(e,ed, ing,es). *Consider also:* inspir(e,ed,ing) confidence, convinc(e,ed,ing), self-assur(ance,edness), self-confidence, self-trust(ing), composure, equanimity, sangfroid, temerit(y,ies), audac(ity,ious), brash(ness), brazen(ness). *See also* Certification; Confidence; Credibility; Endorsement; Guarantees; Reliability.

Asthenia. Asthen(ia,ic). Adynam(ia,ic). Weak(ness,ened). Feeble(ness). Debilit(y,ies,ated). Adynam(ia,ic). *Choose from:* lack(ed,ing), loss, losing, lost, diminish(ed,ing), diminution *with:* strength, energy, capacit(y,ies), vitality, abilit(y,ies), concentrat(e,ion). *Consider also:* aphor(ia,ic), amyosthen(ia,ic), amyoton(y,ic). *See also* Debility; Neurasthenia; Neurocirculatory asthenia; Personality disorders.

Asthenia, neurocirculatory. See *Neurocirculatory asthenia.*

Asthma. Asthma(tic,tics). Exercise induced asthma. Wheezing. Preasthma(tic). *See also* Hypersensitivity; Psychophysiologic disorders; Respiratory system.

Astrology. Astrolog(y,ical,er,ers). Horoscope(s). Astromancy. *Choose from:* lunar, full moon, star(s), heavenly bod(y,ies), astral *with:* effect(s), influence(s), divination. *Consider also:* astral projection(s), sign(s) of zodiac. *See also* Alchemy; Divination; Occultism.

Astronautics See *Astronauts; Space exploration; Spacecraft.*

Astronauts. Astronaut(s). Cosmonaut(s). Spacemen. Moon voyager(s). Moon walker(s). *Choose from:* space flight(s), spacecraft(s), space mission(s) *with:* crew(s), pilot(s). Space traveler(s). *See also* Aeronautical museums; Interplanetary voyages; Space exploration; Space suits; Travelers.

Astronomy. Astronom(y,er,ers,ical). Celestial mechanic(s,al). Astrophysic(al,s). Space probe(s). Astrophotograph(y,ic,er,ers). Stargazer(s). Astrograph(y,ic,er,ers). Cosmolog(y,ic,ically,ist,ists). *Consider also:* radio astronomy, radar astronomy, gamma-ray astronomy; x-ray astronomy; gamma-ray telescope(s), x-ray telescope(s), astronomical spectroscopy, astronomical photometry, observatori(y,ies). *See also* Ancient astronomy; Big bang theory; Constellations; Eclipses; Gravitational lenses; Nautical astronomy; Sciences.

Astronomy, ancient. See *Ancient astronomy.*

Astronomy, nautical. See *Nautical astronomy.*

Asylum, political. See *Political asylum.*

Asylum, right of. See *Right of asylum*

Asylums. Asylum(s). Psychiatric hospital(s). *Choose from:* psychiatric, mental, psychotherapeutic *with:* hospital(s), ward(s), institution(s). Sanitorium(s). Hospital(s) for mentally ill. Hospital(s) for the insane. Hospitals for the mentally handicapped. Madhouse(s). Bedlam. State mental hospital(s). *Consider also:* state hospital(s), halfway house(s), hospice(s), sanctuar(y,ies), retreat(s), shelter(s), haven(s), rest home(s). *See also* Halfway houses; Psychiatric hospitals; Shelters.

At risk populations. See *High risk persons.*

Ataractic drugs. See *Tranquilizers.*

Atavism (biology). Atavis(m,tic,tically). Throwback(s). Reversion. Resurrect(ed,ing,ion) ancestral characteristic(s). Carry ancient gene(s). *See also* Family history; Genetics; Hereditary diseases; Inversion; Phenotypes.

Ataxia. Atax(ia,ic). Dystax(ia,ic). Dysmetria. *See also* Hyperkinesis.

Atheism. Atheis(m,t,ts). Nonbeliever(s). Godless(ness). Religious disbelief. Loss of belief. Religious scepticism. *Consider also:* nonreligious, agnostic(s), free thinker(s), unbeliever(s), infidel(s), heretic(s), materialis(m,tic). *See also* Agnosticism; Deities; God concepts; Heresy; Humanism; Infidels; Irreligion; Materialism; Religious beliefs.

Athletes. Athlete(s). Sports(man,men). Sports(woman,women). Sportspeople. Sportsperson(s). *Choose from:* sport(s), athletic(s), game(s), olympic(s), tournament(s), tennis, boxing, swimming, baseball, football, soccer, etc. *with:* competitor(s), performer(s), player(s), competitor(s), amateur(s), professional(s), contender(s), participant(s), team(s). *Consider also:* specific athletes such as: wrestler(s), swimmer(s), ballplayer(s), boxer(s), golfer(s), etc. *Consider also:* sports enthusiast(s). *See also* Adversary; Athletic participation; Drugs in athletics; Sports; Winter sports.

Athletic participation. Athletic participation. *Choose from:* athletic(s), physical activit(y,ies), sport(s), baseball, basketball, ball, boxing, cricket, fencing, football, golf, gymnastic(s), handball, hockey, lacrosse, racing, skating, skiing, soccer, swimming, tennis, volleyball, wrestling, team sport(s) *with:* experience(s), particip(ant,ants,ation), player(s), competit(or,ors,ion), socialization, involvement, activit(y,ies), performance, cooperation, leadership, play(ing), join(ed,ing), team membership. *See also* Athletes; Challenge; Contests; Sports.

Athletics, drugs in. See *Drugs in athletics.*

Atlases (geographic). Atlas(es). Gazetteer(s). Map(s). Chartbook(s). Mapbook(s). Cartography. Roadmap(s). Land survey(s). Street guide(s). *See also* Books; Cartography; Geography; Reference materials.

Atmosphere. Atmosphere. Homosphere. Heterosphere. Ionosphere. Exosphere. Stratosphere. Mesosphere. Thermosphere. Troposphere. Gasses surrounding earth. Ozone layer. Biosphere. Carbon dioxide. Greenhouse gases. *See also* Atmospheric conditions; Atmospheric contamination; Atmospheric temperature; Weather.

Atmosphere (mood). See *Ambience.*

Atmospheric conditions. Atmospher(e,ic) condition(s). Meterological condition(s). *Consider also:* climate, air pollution, atmospheric pressure(s), cosmic radiation, weather, barometric pressure(s), outdoor temperature(s), humidity, meteororolog(y,ical), climatolog(y,ical), rainfall, drought, wind(s). *See also* Air pollution; Atmospheric contamination; Atmospheric temperature; Atmosphere; Climate; Weather.

Atmospheric contamination. Atmospheric contamination. Greenhouse effect. Smog. Concentrat(ed,ion,ions) of carbon monoxide. Automobile exhaust(s). Poor air quality. Acid rain. *Choose from:* air, atmospher(e,ic) *with:* carbon monoxide, dioxin, sulfur dioxide, ozone, lead, crop spraying, automobile exhaust(s), aerosol(s), dust, harmful vapor(s), smoke, nuclear explosion(s), pollut(ed, ing,ion,ant,ants), contaminat(ed,ing,ion, ions), contaminant(s). *See also* Acid rain; Air pollution; Atmospheric conditions; Atmospheric temperature; Atmosphere; Environmental degradation; Environmental pollutants; Greenhouse effect; Sick building syndrome.

Atmospheric temperature. Atmospher(ic, e) temperature(s). Global surface temperature(s). Daily temperature(s). Spring temperature(s). Air temperature(s). Air and soil freeze-thaw frequenc(y,ies). Global warming. Climat(e,ic) warming. *See also* Atmosphere; Atmospheric conditions; Atmospheric contamination; Greenhouse effect; Weather.

Atomic bomb. Atom(ic) bomb(s). Atomic blast(s). A-bomb(s). Mushroom cloud(s). Fission-bomb(s). *See also* Nuclear weapons nonproliferation; Military weapons; Nuclear proliferation; Nuclear warfare; Nuclear winter; Nuclear weapons; Weapons of mass destruction.

Atomic power. See *Nuclear energy; Nuclear power plants.*

Atomism. Atomis(m,t,ts). Hypothesis of atoms. Atomic doctrine of Democritus. *See also* Atoms; Theories.

Atoms. Atom(s). *Consider also:* basic unit(s), minute particle(s), chemical elements. *Consider also:* protons, neutrons, electrons. *See also* Atomism.

Atonality. Atonal(ity). Breakdown of tonality. Absence of tonality. Post-tonal. Serialism. Serial music. *Consider also:* dodecaphony, suspended tonality, Schoenberg, Webern, Berg, paratonal(ity). *See also* Music; Twentieth century Western art music.

Atonement. Aton(e,ed,ing,ement). Mak(e,ing) amends. Repenten(ce,t). Repent(ed,ing). Apolog(y,ies). Apologiz(e,ed,ing). Restitution(s). Reliev(e,ed,ing) guilt. Reparation(s). Penance. *Consider also:* expiat(e,ed, ing,ion), undoing, exemplarism, soteriolog(y,ical), Christus Victor. *See also* Absolution; Apologies; Forgiveness; Guilt; Redemption (theology); Repentence.

Atrocities. Atrocit(y,ies). Brutalit(y,ies). Inhuman(e,ity). Cruel(ty). Barbarity. Savage(ry). Merciless(ness). Bloodthirst(y,iness). Mass killing(s). Mass murder(s). Massacre(s). Encounter killing(s). *Consider also:* Kampuchea, My Lai, genocide, holocaust. *See also* Genocide; Holocaust; Massacres; Terrorism; War atrocities; War crimes.

Atrocities, war. See *War atrocities.*

Attachment, maternal. See *Attachment behavior.*

Attachment behavior. Attachment behavior(s). Bonding. Object relat(ions,ionships,ed,edness). Object loss grief. Symbiotic relation(s,ship, ships). Early attachment(s). Symbiosis. Emotional dependency. Overprotect(ive,ion). Monogam(y,ous). Mating for life. Bonding behavior. *Choose from:* psychological, emotional, human, parent infant, mother infant, father child, maternal, paternal, consort, male female, pair, consort, object *with:* bond(s,ing), attachment(s). *Consider also:* imprinting, separation protest. *See also* Anaclitic depression; Bonding (emotional); Dependency (personality); Emotional dependence; Father child relations; Intimacy; Individuation; Love; Mother child relations; Object relations; Parent child relations; Postpartum depression; Reactive attachment disorder; Separation anxiety; Stranger reactions.

Attachment disorder, reactive. See *Reactive attachment disorder.*

Attachment disorder syndrome. See *Reactive attachment disorder.*

Attack (Military science). Attack(ed,ing). Assault(s,ed,ing). Open fire. Declare war. Begin hostilities. Sniper(s). Invad(e,ed,ing). Invasion(s). Bombard(ment,ments). Bomb(ed, ing,ings). Offensive(s). Raid(s). Foray(s). Military aggression. Territorial aggression. Onslaught(s). Blitz(ed,ing). Blitzkrieg. Storm(ed,ing). Besiege(d). Strafing(s). Barrage. Combat. Assail(ed,ing). Overpower(ed,ing). Invad(e,ed ing). *See also* Aggression; Animal aggressive behavior; Animal defensive behavior; Assault (battle); Assault (personal); Defense (Military science); Military operations; Military strategies; Predatory behavior; War.

Attacks, cyber. See *Cyber attacks.*

Attainder. Attainder. *Consider also:* bill of pains and penalties, den(y,ial) rights. *See also* Civil death; Civil rights.

Attainment. Attain(ed,ing,ment,ments). Accomplish(ed,ing,ment,ments). Achiev(e,ed,ing,ement,ments). Fulfill(ed,ing,ment,ments). Realiz(e, ed,ing,ation,ations). Complet(e,ed,ing, ion). Consummat(e,ed,ing,ion). Actualiz(e,ed,ing,ation). Enact(ed,ing, ment,ments). Success(ful,es). Succeed(ed,ing). *Consider also:* acquisition(s), acquir(e,ed,ing), terminat(e,ed,ing,ation). *See also* Achievement; Competence; Educational attainment; Failure; Occupational success; Performance; Status attainment.

Attainment, educational. See *Educational attainment.*

Attainment, occupational. See *Occupational status; Occupational success.*

Attainment, status. See *Status attainment.*

Attempted suicide. Attempted suicide(s). Parasuicide(s). Deliberate self harm. *Choose from:* suicid(e,es,al,ally, ality) *with:* attempt(s,ed,ing), trie(s,d), try(ing), gesture(s), threat(s,en,ened, ening), reattempt(s,ed,ing), manipulat(e,ed,ing,ion). *See also* Drug overdoses; Manipulation; Self destructive behavior; Self inflicted wounds; Suicidal behavior; Suicide; Suicide prevention; Suicide victims.

Attendance (presence). Attend(ed,ing, ance). Present. Presence. Seats filled. Appear(ed,ing,ance,ances). Tickets sold. Gather(ed,ing) together. *Consider also:* absen(ces,t,teeism), dropout(s), nonattendance, nonappearance, assemblage(s), audience(s). *See also* Absenteeism; Church attendance; School attendance; Student dropouts.

Attendance, church. See *Church attendance.*

Attendance, school. See *School attendance.*

Attendants. Attendant(s). Orderl(y,ies). Cottage parent(s). Institutional staff. Caretaker(s). Personal care attendant(s). *Choose from:* institution(s,al), hospital, residential care, psychiatric, ward *with:* attendant(s), aide(s). *Consider also:* aide(s)-de-camp, helper(s), care provider(s), escort(s), page(s). *See also* Assistants; Entourage; Paraprofessional personnel.

Attendants, birth. See *Midwifery.*

Attendants, flight. See *Aerospace personnel.*

Attention. Attention. Attentive(ness). Concentration. Alert(ness). Vigilan(t,ce). Aware(ness). Mindful(ness). Observant. Focus(ed) consciousness. Watchful(ness). Listen(ed,ing) carefully.

Consider also: monitor(ed,ing), absor(b,bed,bing,ption), heed(ed,ing, ful,fulness). *See also* Attention span; Awareness; Cognition; Conscious (awake); Distraction; Divided attention; Monitoring; Selective attention; Vigilance.

Attention, divided. See *Divided attention.*

Attention, selective. See *Selective attention.*

Attention deficit disorder. Attention deficit disorder(s). Minimal brain dysfunction. *Choose from:* attention(al), concentration *with:* deficit(s), disorder(s), problem(s), difficult(y,ies), span. *Choose from:* minimal(ly), minimum, minor *with:* brain, cerebral *with:* dysfunction(s), disorder(s), pathology, impairment(s). *See also* Distractibility; Hyperkinesis; Impulsiveness; Minimal brain disorders; Sensory defensiveness.

Attention span. Attention span(s). *Choose from:* span(s), duration, sustain(ed,ing), brief(ly), capacit(y,ies), control *with:* attent(ive,ion), vigilan(t,ce). *Consider also:* span(s) of apprehension, perceptual span(s), divided attention, attentional process(es). *See also* Attention deficit disorder; Conceptual tempo; Distraction; Vigilance.

Attest. See *Allegations; Assertions; Deposition; Testimony; Witnesses.*

Attire. See *Clothing; Costume.*

Attitude change. Attitud(e,es,inal) change(d,s). *Choose from:* attitud(e,es, inal), opinion(s), value(s), expectation(s), view(s), idea(s), perception(s), belief(s), bias(es), outlook(s), preference(s), viewpoint(s) *with:* chang(e,ed,ing,es), shift(ed,ing,s), inconsisten(t,cy), adopt(ed,ing,tion), accept(ed,ing,ance). *Consider also:* paradigm shift(s). *See also* Adjustment (to environment); Adoption of ideas; Attitude strength; Attitudes; Behavior modification; Brainwashing; Change agents; Cognitive restructuring; Personality change; Persuasion.

Attitude formation. Attitud(e,es,inal) form(ed,ing,ation). *Choose from:* attitud(e,es,inal), opinion(s), value(s), expectation(s), view(s), idea(s), perception(s), belief(s), bias(es), prejudice(s), outlook(s), preference(s), priorit(y,ies), worldview(s), viewpoint(s) *with:* form(ed,ing,ation), development, learn(ed,ing), condition(ed,ing), induc(e,ed,ing,tion), adopt(ed,ing,tion). *See also* Attitude strength; Attitudes; Socialization; Worldview.

Attitude measurement. Attitude measurement(s). *Choose from:* attitud(e,es,inal), opinion(s), value(s), expectation(s), perception(s), priorit(y,ies), belief(s), bias(es), prejudice(s), outlook(s), preference(s), viewpoint(s), satisfaction, concern(s), agreement, consensus *with:* measur(e,es, ed,ing), measurement(s), inventor(y,ies), test(s), questionnaire(s), survey(s), scale(s), indicator(s), estimate(s), assessment(s), stud(y,ies), profile(s), index(es), indices, analy(sis,ses), instrument(s). *See also* Attitude strength; Attitudes; Beliefs; Library surveys; Measurement; Opinions; Opinion polls; Public opinion; Semantic differential; Sexual behavior surveys; Values.

Attitude of health personnel. Attitude(s) of health personnel. *Choose from:* counselor(s), health personnel, psychotherapist(s), therapist(s), medical personnel, physician(s), doctor(s), nurse(s), dentist(s), medical technician(s), attendant(s), orderl(y,ies), hospital employee(s), hospital staff, general practitioner(s), paramedical personnel, surgeon(s), health practitioner(s), gynecologist(s), obstetrician(s), pediatrician(s), radiologist(s), pathologist(s), medical profession, health provider(s) *with:* attitude(s), belief(s), opinion(s), view(s), reaction(s), orientation, response(s), denial of feeling(s), warmth, cold(ness), sympath(y,ies,etic), preference(s), expectation(s), perception(s), bias(es,ed), prejudice(s,d), outlook(s), priorit(y,ies), defensive(ness), accept(ance,ing). *See also* Allied health personnel; Attitudes; Attitudes toward death; Attitudes toward handicapped; Attitudes toward health; Attitudes toward homosexuality; Attitudes toward mental illness; Attitudes toward mental retardation; Attitudes toward physical handicaps; Attitudes toward physical illness; Attitudes toward the aged; Medical staff; Physicians.

Attitude scale. See *Attitude measurement.*

Attitude similarity. Attitude similarity. Affinity. *Choose from:* attitude(s), preference(s), opinion(s), belief(s), value(s), perception(s), norm(s), goal(s), expectation(s), approach(es), bias(es), prejudice(s), outlook(s), view(s), viewpoint(s), worldview(s), priorit(y,ies), idea(s) *with:* similar(ity), agreement, congruen(t,ce), compatib(le,ility). *See also* Attitudes; Interpersonal compatibility.

Attitude strength. Attitude strength. *Choose from:* attitude(s), opinion(s), intention(s) *with:* strength, embed- dedness, consistency, susceptib(le,ility) to change, moderating effect(s), weak(en,ened,ness), strong(ly), certainty, extreme, persisten(t,ce). *Consider also:* conviction(s). *See also* Attitude change; Attitude formation; Attitude measurement; Attitudes; Opinions.

Attitudes. Attitud(e,es,inal). Accept(ed,ing, ance). Attribut(e,ed,ing,ion). Aversion(s). Belief(s). Bias(ed,es).

Compassion fatigue. Dissatisfaction(s). Disposition toward. Dislike(s). Expectation(s). Feeling(s). Frame of mind. Labeling. Labelling. Like(s). Mind set. Outlook(s). Opinion(s). Orientation. Perception(s). Preference(s). Personal values. Perspective(s). Permissiveness. Predilection(s). Prejudic(e,ed,es). Reaction(s). Reject(ed,ing,ion). Satisf(ied,action). Sportsmanship. Standpoint(s). Stereotype(s). Superstition(s). Value(s). View(s). Viewpoint(s). Worldview(s). *See also* Alcohol drinking attitudes; Anti-Americanism; Antisemitism; Attitude change; Attitude formation; Attitude measurement; Attitude of health personnel; Attitude similarity; Attitude strength; Attitudes toward computers; Attitudes toward death; Attitudes toward handicapped; Attitudes toward health; Attitudes toward homosexuality; Attitudes toward mental illness; Attitudes toward mental retardation; Attitudes toward physical handicaps; Attitudes toward physical illness; Attitudes toward the aged; Attitudes toward work; Beliefs; Bias; Catholic (universality); Client attitudes; Cognitive dissonance; Community attitudes; Consumer behavior; Dogmatism; Dysconscious racism; Economic attitudes; Emotions; Employee attitudes; Employer attitudes; Ethnic attitudes; Expectations; Family planning attitudes; Generation gap; Human dignity; Interests; Judgment; Lower class attitudes; Marriage attitudes; Media portrayal; Moral attitudes; Negativism; Occupational attitudes; Opinions; Parental attitudes; Perceptions; Political attitudes; Predisposition; Preferences; Prejudice; Psychotherapist attitudes; Public opinion; Racial attitudes; Racism; Religious attitudes; Self fulfilling prophecy; Set (psychology); Sex role attitudes; Sexism; Sexual attitudes; Sexual inhibitions; Social attitudes; Social discrimination; Stereotyping; Student attitudes; Superstitions; Teacher attitudes; Therapist attitudes; Upper class attitudes; Worldview.

Attitudes, alcohol drinking. See *Alcohol drinking attitudes.*

Attitudes, client. See *Client attitudes.*

Attitudes, community. See *Community attitudes.*

Attitudes, economic. See *Economic attitudes.*

Attitudes, employee. See *Employee attitudes.*

Attitudes, employer. See *Employer attitudes.*

Attitudes, ethnic. See *Ethnic attitudes.*

Attitudes, family planning. See *Family planning attitudes.*

Attitudes, father. See *Parental attitudes.*

Attitudes, lower class. See *Lower class attitudes.*

Attitudes, marriage. See *Marriage attitudes.*

Attitudes, maternal. See *Parental attitudes.*

Attitudes, middle class. See *Embourgeoisement.*

Attitudes, moral. See *Moral attitudes.*

Attitudes, mother. See *Parental attitudes.*

Attitudes, negative. See *Negativism.*

Attitudes, occupational. See *Occupational attitudes.*

Attitudes, parent. See *Parental attitudes.*

Attitudes, parental. See *Parental attitudes.*

Attitudes, paternal. See *Parental attitudes.*

Attitudes, patient. See *Client attitudes.*

Attitudes, political. See *Political attitudes.*

Attitudes, psychotherapist. See *Psycho- therapist attitudes.*

Attitudes, public. See *Public opinion.*

Attitudes, race attitudes. See *Racial attitudes; Racism.*

Attitudes, racial. See *Racial attitudes.*

Attitudes, religious. See *Religious attitudes.*

Attitudes, sex. See *Sexual attitudes.*

Attitudes, sex role. See *Sex role attitudes.*

Attitudes, sexual. See *Sexual attitudes.*

Attitudes, social. See *Social attitudes.*

Attitudes, stereotyped. See *Stereotyping.*

Attitudes, student. See *Student attitudes.*

Attitudes, teacher. See *Teacher attitudes.*

Attitudes, therapist. See *Therapist attitudes.*

Attitudes, upper class. See *Upper class attitudes.*

Attitudes, war. See *War attitudes.*

Attitudes, work. See *Attitudes toward work; Employee attitudes.*

Attitudes, worker. See *Employee attitudes.*

Attitudes toward aging. See *Age discrimi- nation; Attitudes toward the aged.*

Attitudes toward computers. Attitude(s) to(ward) computer(s). *Choose from:* attitude(s), bias(es), preference(s), reject(ed,ion,ing), resist(ed,ing,ance), accept(ed,ing,ance), opinion(s), belief(s), fear(s), reaction(s), expectation(s) *with:* computer(s,ized, ization), microcomputer(s), automation. *See also* Attitudes; Computer anxiety; Computer addiction; Computer illiteracy; Computer literacy.

Attitudes toward death. Attitude(s)

to(ward) death. *Choose from:* attitude(s), concept(s), fear(s), anxiet(y,ies), belief(s), interpretation(s), wish(es, ing,ed), perception(s), fac(e,ed,ing), view(s), acceptance, accept(ed,ing), psychological aspect(s), emotion(s,al), grief, griev(e,ed,ing), coping, communication, talk(ing), humaniz(e,ed,ing, ation), understanding, reject(ed,ing), response *with:* death, die(d), dead, dying, deceased, terminal patient(s), bereavement, funeral(s). *Consider also:* mourning, grief, thanatopsychology. *See also* Attitudes; Death; Death anxiety.

Attitudes toward disabled. See *Attitudes toward handicapped; Attitudes toward mental retardation; Attitudes toward physical handicaps.*

Attitudes toward handicapped. Attitude(s) to(ward) handicapped. Handicapism. Ableis(m,t). Ablis(m,t). Able-(bodism,bodiedism). Attitude(s) toward mainstreaming. Attitudinal barriers for handicapped. Acceptance of disabled. *Choose from:* accept(ed,ing,ance), ascription, attitude(s), attribution(s,al), belief(s), bias(es), discrimination, empath(y,etic), expectation(s), fear(s), image(s), label(s,ed,ing), labell(ed,ing), marginalize(s,d), misperception(s), misunderstanding(s), misunderstood, perception(s), prejudice(s,d), public opinion, sociometric, stereotyp(es,ed, ing), stigma(s,tized), sympath(y,etic), understanding *with:* handicap(s,ped), amputation(s), amputee(s), disabled, disabilit(y,ies), quadripleg(ia,ic,ics), parapleg(ia,ic,ics), cerebral palsy, blind(ness), etc. *See also* Attitudes; Attitudes toward physical handicaps; Disability; Employment of persons with disabilities; Noninstitutionalized disabled; Public opinion; Stereotyping.

Attitudes toward health. Attitude(s) to(ward) health. *Choose from:* attitude(s), belief(s), activist(s), perception(s), fear(s), response(s), accept(ed,ing,ance), opinion(s), awareness, expectation(s), conception(s), misconception(s), idea(s), prejudice(s), priorit(y,ies) *with:* health, prophylaxis, food, nutrition, smok(e,ed,ing), patient(s), medication(s), vaccination(s), diet(s,ary), hygiene, sanitation, ill(ness,nesses), exercis(e,es,ing), disease(s), aids, cancer, lyme disease, tuberculosis, diabetes, etc. *See also* Attitudes; Attitudes toward physical illness; Holistic health; Preventive medicine; Well being.

Attitudes toward homosexuality. Attitudes to(ward) homosexuality. Homophob(ia, ic). Lesbophob(ia,ic). Antihomosexual. Anti-homosexual. Gay straight split. Heterosexis(m,t,ts). *Choose from:* homosexual(ity,s), lesbian(ism,s), same sex orientation(s), sexual preference(s) *with:* attitude(s), public opinion,

bias(es,ed), prejudice(s), social acceptance, view(s), expectation(s), label(s,ed,ing), labell(ed,ing), stigma(tization), social desirability, discriminat(e,ed,ing,ion), social perception(s), image(s), marginalize(d,s), stereotyp(e,es,ing), ascription(s), social dynamics, dislik(e,ed,ing), estrange(d,ment), persecut(e,ed,ing,ion), attribut(e,ed,ing, ion,ions), reject(ed,ing,ion). *Consider also:* mannerstaat. *See also* Attitudes; Hate crimes; Homosexuality; Homosexual liberation movement; Lesbianism; Male homosexuality; Public opinion; Stereotyping.

Attitudes toward mental illness. Attitudes to(ward) mental illness. *Choose from:* attitude(s), bias(ed,es), expectation(s), label(s), stigma(s,tized), sympath(y,etic), empath(y,etic), public opinion, discriminat(e,ed,ing,ion), cultural perception(s), image(s), stereotype(s), ascription(s), belief(s), marginalize(s,d), misperception(s), misunderstanding(s), misunderstood, attribution(s), prejudice(s,d), reaction(s), portrayal, understanding, toleran(t,ce), accept(ed, ing,ance) *with:* mental disorder(s), psychiatric disorder(s), mental illness(es), mental patient(s), mentally ill, psychiatric patient(s), schizophren(ia, ic,ics), psychos(es,is), psychotic, manic depressi(ve,ves,on), bipolar disorder(s), emotional(ly) disturb(ed,ance,ances), insan(e,ity). *See also* Attitudes; Employment of persons with disabilities; Mental illness; Mentally ill offenders; Noninstitutionalized disabled; Public opinion; Psychiatric patients; Stereotyping.

Attitudes toward mental retardation. Attitudes to(ward) mental(ly) retard(ed, ation). *Choose from:* attitude(s), bias(ed,es), accept(ed,ing,ance), expectation(s), label(s,ed,ing), labell(ed,ing), stigma(s,tized), sympath(y,etic), empath(y,etic), public opinion, social desirability, interpret(ed,ation), discriminat(e,ed,ing, ion), cultural perception(s), image(s), stereotype(s), ascription(s), belief(s), fear(s), marginalize(s,d), misperception(s), perception(s), misunderstanding(s), misunderstood, attribution(s), prejudice(s,d), reaction(s), portrayal, understanding, understood, toleran(t,ce), accept(ed,ing,ance), sociometric *with:* mental(ly) retard(ed,ation), mental(ly) handicap(s,ped), Down's syndrome. *See also* Attitudes; Attitudes toward handicapped; Employment of persons with disabilities; Mental retardation; Noninstitutionalized disabled; Public opinion; Sheltered housing; Sheltered workshops; Stereotyping.

Attitudes toward persons with disabilities. See *Attitudes toward handicapped; Attitudes toward mental retardation; Attitudes toward physical handicaps.*

Attitudes toward physical handicaps. Attitudes to(ward) physical handicap(s). Handicapism. Ableism. Ablism. Disableis(m,t,ts). *Choose from:* attitude(s), bias(ed), prejudice(d), accept(ed,ance), expectation(s), label(s), stigma(s,tized), sympath(y,etic), empath(y,etic), public opinion, social desirability, discriminat(e,ed,ing,ion), perception(s), image(s), stereotype(s), ascription(s), belief(s), fear(s), misperception(s), attribution(s), prejudice(d), reaction(s), portrayal, misunderstanding(s), misunderstood, misconception(s), toleran(t,ce), accept(ed,ing,ance), marginalize(d,s), *with:* handicap(ped,s), disabilit(y,ies), disabled, crippl(ed,ing), physical(ly) impair(ed,ment,ments), cerebral palsy, epilep(sy,tic,tics), parapleg(ia,ic,ics), quadripleg(ia,ic,ics), wheelchair(s), cane(s), crutch(es), brace(s), amputee(s), prosthes(is,es). *See also* Attitudes; Attitudes toward handicapped; Disability; Employment of persons with disabilities; Noninstitutionalized disabled; Public opinion; Stereotyping.

Attitudes toward physical illness. Attitude(s) to(ward) physical illness(es). Stereotype(s) of illness(es). Stigma of illness(es). *Choose from:* attitude(s), bias(ed,es), prejudice(d,s), accept(ed,ing,ance), expectation(s), label(s), label(s,ed,ing), labell(ed,ing), stigma(s,tized), marginalize(d,s), sympath(y,etic), empath(y,etic), public opinion, social desirability, discriminat(e,ed,ing,ion), cultural perception(s), image(s), stereotype(s), ascription(s), belief(s), fear(s), phobi(a,as,ic), misperception(s), misunderstanding(s), misunderstood, attribution(s), reaction(s), expectation(s), portrayal, misconception(s), toleran(t,ce), accept(ed,ing,ance) *with:* patient(s), illness(es), disease(s,d), sick(ness,nesses), contag(ion,ious), AIDS, acquired immunodeficiency syndrome, HIV infection(s), human immunodeficiency virus, leprosy, leper(s), lupus, hypertension, leukemia, cancer(s), Alzheimer's, asthma, emphysema, bronchitis, epilepsy, arthritis, heart attack(s), measle(s), diabetes, etc. *See also* Attitudes; Disease; Epidemics; Public opinion; Stereotyping.

Attitudes toward the aged. Attitudes to(ward) the aged. Age discrimination. Age bias. Ageism. Gerontophilic. Gerontophobic. Double standard of aging. Concept(ion,s) of old age. Age Discrimination in Employment Act. Age consciousness. *Choose from:*

accept(ance,ing), anxiet(y,ies), ascription(s), attitude(s), attribution(s), belief(s), bias(es,ed), celebrat(e,ed, ing,ion,ions), concept(s), depict(ed,ing, ion), discriminat(e,ed,ing,ion), empath(y,etic), expectation(s), fear(s), phobi(a,as,c), image(s), infantilization, interpretation, marginalize(s,d), label(s,ed,ing), labell(ed,ing), toleran(t,ce), misunderstood, misunderstanding, misperception(s), myth(s), perception(s), philosophy, portrayal, prejudice(d,s), public opinion, reaction(s), stereotype(s), support, sympath(y,etic), understanding, stigma(s,tized) *with:* aging, aged, elder(ly), senior citizen(s), old age, older people, older worker(s), old persons, gerontolog(y,ical), geriatric(s). *Consider also:* intergenerational relation(s,ship), ships). *See also* Age discrimination; Aged 80 and over; Attitudes; Elderly; Gray power; Intergenerational relations; Mandatory retirement; Public opinion; Stereotyping.

Attitudes toward work. Attitudes to(ward) work. Workahol(ism,ic). Work satisfaction. *Choose from:* attitude(s), value(s), satisfaction(s), dissatisfaction(s), perception(s), motivation(s), meaning(ful,s), orient(ed,ing), orientation(s), commitment(s), committed, opinion(s), importance, cynicism, alienation, involvement, belief(s), interest(s), expectation(s), enjoyment, morale *with:* work(ing), career(s), job(s), employment, employee(s), staff, worker(s), profession(s,al), occupation(s, al), vocation(s,al). *See also* Attitudes; Employee attitudes; Employee concerns; Employee morale; Work.

Attorneys. Attorney(s). Legal professional(s). Lawyer(s). Barrister(s). Solicitor(s). Member(s) of state bar. Legal counsel. Judge(s). Criminal justice personnel. Magistrate(s). *Choose from:* legal, law *with:* professional(s), consultant(s), practitioner(s), defender(s), student(s), advisor(s), counselor(s), personnel, authorit(y,ies), advocate(s). *See also* Court judges; Judges; Law (practice); Law societies; Legal ethics; Professional personnel.

Attract wildlife, gardening to. See *Gardening to attract wildlife.*

Attractants, sex. See *Sex attractants.*

Attraction, interpersonal. See *Interpersonal attraction.*

Attractiveness. Attractive(ness). Physical attractiveness. Physically attractive. Sexual(ly) attractive(ness). Beauty. Beautiful. Lovel(y,iness). Cute(ness). Neatness. Glamor(ous). Eye appeal. Prett(y,iness). Comel(y,iness). Statel(y,iness). Handsome(ness). Good looking. Gorgeous. Shapely. Graceful. Statuesque. Well proportioned. Well dressed. Elegant. *Choose from:* physical, personal, facial *with:* appearance(s), attractiveness. *Consider also:* unattractive(ness). *See also* Awkwardness; Beauty; Demeanor; Elegance; Facial expressions; Facial features; Interpersonal attraction; Orderliness; Personal beauty; Physical fitness.

Attractiveness, physical. See *Attractiveness.*

Attributes. See *Qualities.*

Attributes of God. Attributes of God. *Choose from:* attribute(s), characteristic(s), definition(s), infinite(ly,ness), eternal(ly), imutab(le,ility), omnipresen(ce,t), omnipoten(t,ce), aseity, simpl(e,icity), merciful(ness), loving, jealous(y), avenging, vengeful(ness), wrathful(ness), righteous(ness), powerful(ly) *with:* god(s), goddess(es), divine being(s), almighty, deit(y,ies), Jehovah, Yahweh, Yahveh, Allah, Ahura Mazda, Loki, Jesus, great spirit. *Consider also:* theodic(y,ies). *See also* Deities; Glory of God; God concepts; Immanence of god; Knowledge of God; Omniscience of God; Oneness of God; Presence of God; Religious beliefs; Revealed theology; Theism; Theophany; Will of God.

Attribution. Attribut(ed,ing,ion,ional). Ascription. Ascrib(e,ed,ing). *Consider also:* perception(s), expectation(s), expectanc(y,ies), stereotype(s). *See also* Attitudes; Impression formation; Inference; Learned helplessness; Locus of control; Reputation; Self fulfilling prophecy; Self knowledge; Social perception.

Attribution of news. Attribut(e,ed,ing,ion) news. News source(s). Press release(s). Spokes(man,men,woman,women,person). Access to classified information. *Choose from:* attribut(e,ed,ing,ion), report(s,ed, ing), source(s), cit(e,ed,ing,ation,ations), credit(s,ed), rumor(s,ed) *with:* news(paper,papers), information, report(s,ed,ing). *See also* Access to information; Bibliographic citations; Information dissemination; Information leaks; Journalism; Journalistic ethics; News policies; Newspapers.

Attrition. Attrition. Reduction(s) in staff. Reduction(s) in workforce. Reduction(s) in force. Decreas(e,ed,ing) size of workforce. Resignation(s). Retirement(s). Dropout(s). *See also* Employee turnover; Patient dropouts; Student dropouts; Workforce planning.

Atypical paranoid disorder. See *Involutional psychosis.*

Au pairs. See *Domestic Service.*

Auctions. Auction(s,ed,ing,eer,eers,eering). Vendue. Bidder(s). Bidding. Gallery sale(s). *Consider also:* estate sale(s), public sale(s), auction house(s), dutch auction(s), silent auction(s), commodity auction(s), Swann Galleries, Sotheby Parke Bernet, Christie's East, Christie Manson and Woods, etc. *See also* Galleries; Sales; Second hand trade.

Audience analysis. Audience analysis. *Choose from:* audience(s), reader(s,ship), viewer(s), listener(s), fan(s), follower(s) *with:* analys(is,es), assess(ed,ing,ment,ments), statistic(s), survey(s), research, profile(s), stud(y,ies). *See also* Audiences; Demographic characteristics (of individuals); Internet traffic; Market research; Market segmentation; Mass media; Opinion polls; Readership; Viewers.

Audiences. Audience(s). Spectator(s). Listener(s). Viewer(s). Attendant(s). Person(s) attend(ing). Observer(s). Witness(es). Onlooker(s). Viewing public. Watcher(s). Hearer(s). Playgoer(s). Filmgoer(s). Reading public. Reader(s,ship). Fan(s). Theatergoer(s). Target group(s). Assemblage. Cable subscriber(s). *Consider also:* crowd(s), galler(y,ies), reach and frequency, Nielsen report(s), Nielsen rating(s), people meter(s). *See also* Audience analysis; Congregations (church); Fans (persons); Internet traffic; Observers; Readership; Spectators; Sports fans; Viewers.

Audiometry. Audiometr(y,ic). *Consider also:* acoustic sensitivity, auditory sensitivity, hearing, auditory threshold, speech discrimination, auditory discrimination *with:* measur(e,ed,ing, ement), screen(ed,ing,ings), test(s), assessment(s), evaluat(e,ed,ing,ion,ions), diagnos(is,es). *Consider also:* audiology. *See also* Hearing; Measurement.

Audiovisual communications. Audiovisual communication(s). *Choose from:* audiovisual, audio-visual, AV, videotape(s,d), video(s), film(ed,s), filmstrip(s), televis(ion,ed), TV, slide tape(s), overhead transparenc(y,ies) *with:* communication(s), technique(s), presentation(s), program(s), material(s), aid(s). *Consider also:* multimedia, audiotape(s), movie(s), motion picture(s). *See also* Cartoons; Communication (thought transfer); Audiovisual instruction; Educational television; Film strips; Films; Mass media; Motion pictures; Photography; Publications; Telecommunications; Television.

Audiovisual education. See *Audiovisual instruction.*

Audiovisual instruction. Audiovisual instruction. *Choose from:* audio-visual, audiovisual, TV, televis(ed,ion), video(s), videotape(s,d), AV, audio-tutorial, audio, visual, multimedia, film(ed,s), media, radio, audiotape(d,s), slide-tape(s), videocassette(s) *with:* instruction(al), education(al), learn(ed,ing), teach(ing), taught, lesson(s), tutorial(s), train(ed,ing), presentation(s), classroom(s). *See also* Audiovisual communications; Audiovisual materials; Educational television; Teaching materials; Teaching methods.

Audiovisual materials. Audiovisual material(s). Audiovisual aid(s). Audio-Visual Aid(s). Audiovisual Resource(s). Audio-Visual Media. Video(s). Videotape(s). Videodisc(s). Instructional Television. Video/audio instruction. Hypermedia. Multimedia. Mixed-Media. Stereograph(s). Stereopticon slide. Motion picture(s). Radio(s). Audiocassette(s). Audiotape(s). Nonprint material(s). CD-ROM(s). Television. Film(s). Visual presentation(s). Instructional film(s). Protocol material(s). Audio disk(s). Audio equipment. *See also* Audiovisual instruction; Educational technology; Educational television; Film strips; Instructional media; Motion pictures; Visual aids.

Audit, financial. See *Financial audit.*

Auditoriums. Auditorium(s). Lecture hall(s). Theater(s). Arena(s). Opera house(s). Assembly room(s). Lecture hall(s). Coliseum(s). Field house(s). Concert stadium(s). Concert hall(s). Assembly hall(s). Amphitheater(s). Movie house(s). Theater(s). *See also* Arenas; Concert halls; Halls: Public buildings; Public places; Religious buildings; Theater.

Auditory fatigue. Auditory fatigue. *Choose from:* auditory, hearing, cochlear *with:* fatigue. *Choose from:* noise induced *with:* threshold shift(s), hearing loss(es). *See also* Hearing disorders.

Auditory hallucinations. Auditory hallucination(s). Hear(ing,d) voice(s). Echo des pensees. Thought echoing. *Choose from:* auditory, musical, vocal, sound(s), noise(s) *with:* hallucination(s), illusion(s), pseudohallucination(s). *See also* Hallucinations; Perceptual disturbances.

Auditory perception. Auditory perception. *Choose from:* auditory, pitch, loudness, speech, sound(s), consonant *with:* perception, discrimination, pattern recognition, sensitivity, identification, threshold(s), fatigue, localization, imperception. *See also* Auditory perceptual disorders; Auditory threshold; Loudness perception; Speech perception.

Auditory perceptual disorders. Auditory perceptual disorder(s). *Choose from:* auditory *with:* perceptual problem(s), learning disabilit(y,ies), perceptual deficit(s), processing disorder(s), perceptual dysfunction(s), figure ground disorder(s). *See also* Auditory percep-

tion; Hearing disorders; Loudness perception; Speech perception.

Auditory threshold. Auditory threshold(s). *Choose from:* auditory, loudness, hearing, speech reception, speech recognition *with:* threshold(s). *See also* Auditory perception; Thresholds.

Aurally handicapped. See *Deafness.*

Austerities. Austerit(y,ies). Ascetic(ism). *Choose from:* religious, sacrificial, tradition(s,al), deit(y,ies), god(s), mourning, magic, ceremon(y,ies,ial) *with:* discipline, abstention, abstinence, abstain(ed,ing), depriv(e,ed,ing, ation,ations), fast(s,ed,ing), flagellat(e, ed,ing,ion), tortur(e,es,ed,ing), suicide(s), sacrific(e,es,ed,ing,ial). *See also* Abstinence; Lifestyle; Monasticism; Poverty; Sacrificial rites.

Australoid race. Australoid race. *Choose from:* Australoid, Australioid aboriginal *with:* tribe(s), race, people. Australian aborigine(s). Australian race. Australasian(s). *Consider also:* Ainus, Autochthonous Dravidian(s), Predravidian(s), Vedda(s,hs), Veddoid(s), Papuan(s), Melanesian(s), Negrito(s). *See also* Aborigines; Pacific Islanders; People of color; Races; Racially mixed.

Austronesian languages. See *Malayo-Polynesian languages.*

Autarky. Autark(y,ic,ical). Autarch(y,ic, ical). Economic(ally) self sufficien(cy,t). Economic(ally) independen(t,ce). *Consider also:* local sustainability, reduc(e,ed,ing) dependence on import(ed,s). *See also* Foreign policy; Import substitution; Isolationism; Noninvolvement; Nontariff trade barriers; Trade protection.

Authenticity. Authentic(ity,ate,ated,ating). Accredited. Authoritative(ness). Believab(le,ility). Credib(le,ility). Creditab(le,ility). Exact(ly,ness). Factual(ity). Reliab(le,ility). Dependab(le,ility). Genuine(ness). Indisputab(le,ility). Truthful(ness). Trusted. Verifiab(le,ility). Verif(y,ied). Confirm(ed,ing). Certifi(ed,able). Guarantee(s,d,ing). Warranted. Approved. Proven. Accept(ed,able). Unquestionab(le,ility). Undisputab(le,ility). *Consider also:* autograph(ed,s), sign(ed,ature,atures), faithful(ness), underwrit(e,ing,ten), insur(e,ed,ing,ance), verac(ity,ious). *See also* Approval; Believability; Certification; Deception; Dependability; Faking; Honesty; Misinformation; Purity; Self deception; Truth.

Authoritarianism (political). Authoritarian(ism). Totalitarian(ism). Absolute monarchy. Fasci(sm,st). Political domination. Caudillismo. Personalismo. Party boss(es). Dictator(s,ial,ships). Despot(s,ic).

Repressive regime. Political repression. Oppression. *See also* Authority (officials); Authority (power); Caciquism; Command (of troops, ships, etc.); Corporate state; Despotism; Dictatorship; Fascism; Military discipline (conduct); Military regimes; Political elites; Political repression; Totalitarianism.

Authoritarianism (psychological). Authoritarian(ism). Rigid(ity). Closed mind(edness). Intoleran(t,ce). Dogmat(ic,ism). Dictatorial. Domineering. Dominat(ing,ion). Command(ed,ing). Despot(ic). Tyrannical. Autocrat(ic). Demand(ing) obedience. Doctrinaire. Imperious(ness). Overbearing. *Choose from:* authoritarian, patriarchal *with:* famil(y,ies), personalit(y,ies). *See also* Dichotomous thinking; Dogmatism; Dominance subordination; Egalitarianism; Obedience; Openmindedness; Patriarchy; Personality traits; Rigid personality; Traditionalism.

Authority (officials). Authorit(y,ies). Official(s). Enforcer(s). Umpire(s). Executive(s). CEO(s). Administrator(s). Supervisor(s). Manager(s). Leader(s). Judge(s). Physician(s). Police(women, woman,man,men). Teacher(s). Coach(es). Commander(s). Commanding officer(s). Admiral(s). General(s). Uniformed figure(s). Ruler(s). President(s). Prime minister(s). Dictator(s). Emperor(s). Empress(es). Monarch(s). King(s). Queen(s). Sovereign(s,ty). *See also* Authority (power); Chiefs; Command (of troops, ships, etc.); Executive branch (government); Generals; Power elite; Power structure; Priests and priestly classes (anthropology); State power.

Authority (power). Authority. Jurisdiction. Domin(ate,ated,ating,ation). Dominion. Administrat(ion,ive). Supervis(ion,ory). Manage(rial,ment). Leader(s,ship). Social influence. Social control. Power. Stature. Respect. Sovereignty. Predominan(t,ce). *Consider also:* legitimate authority, political authority, span of control. *See also* Authoritarianism (political); Authority (officials); Charisma; Dominance subordination; Executive powers; Hierarchy; Influence; Leadership; Legitimacy; Obedience; Political leadership; Power; Power structure; Responsibility (answerability); State power.

Authority, moral. See *Moral authority.*

Authorization, clearance. See *Clearance (authorization).*

Authors. Author(s,ship). Writer(s). Composer(s). Compiler(s). Novelist(s). Narrator(s). Dramatist(s). Screenwriter(s). Poet(s). Essayist(s).

Pamphleteer(s). Biographer(s). Journalist(s). Reporter(s). Playwright(s). Lyricist(s). Chronicler(s). Ghost writer(s). *Consider also:* storyteller(s), narrator(s), newspaper(man,men), publication credit, byline(s), plagiarism, written anonymously, literary scholar(s), literary critic(s,ism). *See also* Authors in exile; Authors' notebooks; Authors' spouses; Autographs; Biographers; Composers; Creators; Disputed authorship; Dramatists; Editors; Ghostwriting; Homosexual authors; Intellectual life; Literary ethics; Literary landmarks; Literary patronage; Literary prizes; Literary quarrels; Literature; Litterateurs; Manuscripts; Minority authors; Prisoners' writings; Publications; Scholars; Scriptwriting; Writers; Writing (composition).

Authors, homosexual. See *Homosexual authors.*

Authors, minority. See *Minority authors.*

Authors' notebooks. Authors' note(s,book,books). Writer's diar(y,ies). *Choose from:* author(s), writer(s), literary figure(s), novelist(s) *with:* note(s,book,books), diar(y,ies), journal(s), manuscript(s), letter(s), memoir(s), chronicle(s,d), scrapbook(s). *See also* Authors; Manuscripts; Travel writing.

Authors' spouses. Authors' spouse(s). *Choose from:* author(s), writer(s), literary figure(s), novelist(s) *with:* spouse(s), wife, wives, husband(s), bride(s), bridegroom(s), married person(s), marital partner(s), better half, significant other(s). *See also* Authors; Spouses.

Authors in exile. Author(s) in exile. *Choose from:* author(s), writer(s), literary figure(s), poet(s), playwright(s)' novelist(s), literature *with:* emigre(s), exile(d), expatriat(e,es,ion), refugee(s), defect(ed), deport(ed,ee,ees,ation). *See also* Authors; Refugees; Political asylum; Political defection; Right of asylum.

Authorship. See *Authors.*

Authorship, disputed. See *Disputed authorship.*

Autism. Autis(m,tic). Endogenous thought. Dereis(m,tic). Kanner's syndrome. Autismus infantum. *Choose from:* child(hood,ren) *with:* introversion, schizophren(ia,ic). *See also* Autistic thinking; Developmental disabilities; Early childhood development; Schizophrenia; Withdrawal (defense mechanism).

Autistic thinking. Autistic thinking. *Choose from:* autistic, dereistic, irrational, idiosyncratic, schizophrenic, endogenous, narcissistic, egocentric *with:* thought(s), thinking, reasoning,

fantas(y,ies). *Consider also:* flight(s) of fancy, daydream(s,ing). *See also* Autism; Thought disturbances.

Autobiography. Autobiograph(y,ies,er,ers). Ego-invented narrative. Diar(y,ies). Personal account(s). Journal writing. Memoir(s). Life histor(y,ies). *Choose from:* personal, self, first hand, eye-witness *with:* narrative(s), account(s), recollection(s), histor(y,ies). *Consider also:* self analysis, reminiscence(s), correspondence, biograph(y,ies,ical), anamnes(is,tic), autohagiography. *See also* Biographical data; Diaries; First person narrative; Letters (correspondence); Life experiences; Life history; Life review; Nonfiction novel; Oral history; Point of view (literature); Travel writing.

Autocracy. Autocra(cy,cies,tic,s). Dictator(s,ship,ships). Despot(s,ic,ism). Absolute monarch(s,y,ies). Absolutism. Autarch(s,y,ies,ic). Tyrann(y,ical,ize). Tyrant(s). Absolute ruler(s). Authoritarian(ism). Totalitarian(ism). Domineer(ing). Fascis(m,t). Oppress(ion,ive). Megalomaniac(al). One man rule. Monocra(tic,cy). Czar(s). Kaiser(s). Caesar(s). Fuhrer(s). Duce. Caudillo(s). Shah(s). Khan.(s) Rajah(s). Sirdar(s). Mogul(s). Sultan(s). Emir(s). Caliph(s). Sheik(s). *See also* Authoritarianism (political); Authority (officials); Authority (power); Dictatorship; Fascism; Totalitarianism.

Autoerotic death. Autoerotic death(s). Autoerotic asphyxiation. Sexual asphyxia syndrome. Dangerous sexual practices. *Choose from:* autoerotic, auto erotic, sexual masochism, sexual arousal, sexual activit(y,ies), eroticism, masturbat(e,ed,ing,ion) *with:* asphyxia(s,ting,tion), death(s), fatalit(y,ies), suicide(s), hanging(s), dangerous(ness). *See also* Death; Masturbation; Sexual deviations.

Autoeroticism. Autoerotic(ism). Autogenital stimulation. Masturbat(e,ed, ing,ion,ory). Autosexual(ity). Autoerotism. Automanipulation. Self pleasur(e,ed,ing). Self gratification. Autofellatio. *Choose from:* manual stimulation, mechanical stimulation, self stimulation, vibrator(s) *with:* genital(ia, s), penis, clitor(is,al), vagina(l). *See also* Masturbation; Orgasm.

Autogenic therapy. Autogenic therap(y,ies). Autogenic training. Relaxation exercises. Suggestibility. Endogenic training. Autogenous training. Progressive relaxation. Self generated therap(y,ies). Autogenic biofeedback. Autogenic repeated behavior therap(y,ies). *See also* Biofeedback training; Psychotherapy; Relaxation training.

Autographs. Autograph(s). Signature(s). Signed by author(s). Inscribe(d).

Inscription(s). John Hancock. Endorse(d,ment,ments). *See also* Authors; Cursive writing; Endorsement; Handwriting; Inscriptions; Letters (correspondence); Manuscripts; Signatures; Writers; Writing.

Autohypnosis. Autohypno(tic,sis). Auto hypno(sis,therapy.) Self hypno(sis, therapy). Self induced hypnosis. Hypno-autohypnosis. Self submersion. *Consider also:* self suggestion, meditation, self relaxation, autosuggest(ion,ive). *See also* Autosuggestion; Catalepsy; Consciousness disorders; Hypnosis; Meditation.

Autokinetic effect. Autokinetic effect(s). Charpentier's illusion. *Choose from:* autokinetic *with:* illusion(s), effect(s), phenomen(a,on), movement. *See also* Motion perception; Space perception; Visual perception.

Automated coding. Automated coding. *Choose from:* automated, electronic, computer(ized), automatic, online, microcomputer(s) *with:* cod(e,ed,ing), data scoring, code assignment, encod(e,ed,ing), data entry. *See also* Automated information storage; Data processing.

Automated information retrieval. Automated information retrieval. Information retrieval system(s). *Choose from:* automat(ed,ion), computer(s,ized), online, microcomputer(s), computer based, offline, database, machine readable, electronic, microcomputer(s), digital, tape, optical, random access, magnetic, compact disc(s), CD-ROM, internet *with:* retriev(e,ed,ing,al), search(ed,es,ing), reference. *Consider also:* search(ed,es,ing), retriev(e,ed,ing,al) *with:* information, record(s), data, document(s), literature, file(s), text(s). *See also* Automated information storage; Image processing; Information networks; Information skills; Library services; Search strategies; User friendly systems.

Automated information storage. Automated information storage. *Choose from:* automat(ed,ion), content addressable, holographic, computer(ized), online, microcomputer(s), computer based, offline, database, machine readable, electronic, digital, tape, optical, random access, magnetic, floppy disk(s), CD-ROM, *with:* stor(e,ed,ing,age), filing, file(s), record(s), data, document(s), literature, information, text(s). *Consider also:* storage media, videodis(c,cs,k,ks). *See also* Automated coding; Automated information retrieval; Bytes; Electronic data processing; Image processing.

Automatic instruments. Automatic instrument(s). Automatophone(s). Automatic violin(s). Violano-Virtuoso(s). Violina(s). Vorsitzer(s). *Choose from:* automatic *with:* zither(s), banjo(s), harp(s), accordion(s), violin(s). *Consider also:* music box(es), player piano(s), player organ(s), barrel organ(s), clockwork organ(s), orchestrelle(s) reproducing piano(s). *See also* Musical instruments; Player pianos.

Automatic (involuntary). See *Involuntary (automatic).*

Automation. Automat(ion,ed). Computeriz(ation,ed). Computing technolog(y,ies). Computer integrated manufacturing. CIM. Computer assisted design. CAD. *Choose from:* computer(s), machine *with:* control(led), based, assisted. *Consider also:* robot(s,ic,ics), golem, automatic pilot(s), personal computing, automat(a,on, ized,ization), post industrial, electronic data processing, deindustrializ(e,ed,ing, ation), man machine systems, smart machine(s), hardware, software, semi-automat(ed,ion), computer(s), online, database(s), microcomputer(s), minicomputer(s), PC(s). *See also* Agricultural mechanization; Artificial intelligence; Computer assisted decision making; Computer assisted diagnosis; Computers; Cybernetics; Data processing; Electronic mail; Electronic publishing; Factory automation; Geographic information systems; Information society; Man machine systems; Management informaton systems; Office automation; Scientific management; Technology transfer.

Automation, factory. See *Factory automation.*

Automation, industrial. See *Automation.*

Automation, office. See *Office automation.*

Automatism. Automatism. *Choose from:* without, lack(ed,ing), impair(ed,ing, ment), deficit, deficient, impoverished *with:* conscious(ness), volitional control, aware(ness). *Consider also:* reflexive, seizure(s,like), epilepsy, somnambulism, psychological blow(s). *See also* Altered states of consciousness; Insanity defense; Psychomotor agitation; Psychomotor disorders.

Automobile driving. Automobile driving. Driving privilege(s). Driver(s). Motorist(s). *Choose from:* driv(e,en, ing,er,ers), operat(e,ed,er,ers,ing), chauffeur(ed,er,ers,ing) *with:* motor vehicle(s), motor transport(s), car(s), automobile(s), taxi(s), bus(es). *Consider also:* driving behavior(s), highway safety, traffic accident(s). *See also* Automobiles; Driving skills; Highway safety; Road rage; Traffic accidents.

Automobile industry. Automobile industry. *Choose from:* automobile(s), auto(s), automotive, car(s), motor vehicle(s) *with:* assembly, manufactur(ing,ers), production, plant(s), firm(s), corporation(s), compan(y,ies),

industr(y,ies,ial), factor(y,ies). *See also* Automobile industry workers; Automobiles; Industry; Metal industry; Motor vehicles.

Automobile industry workers. Automobile industry worker(s). United Auto Worker(s). UAW. *Choose from:* auto(mobile,motive), motor works, General Motors, Ford, Chrysler, Renault, Volkswagen, Volvo, Toyota, Honda, etc. *with:* labor, worker(s), employee(s), assembler(s) striker(s). *See also* Automobile industry; Blue collar workers; Employees; Industrial workers; Iron and steel workers.

Automobiles. Automobile(s). Car(s). Motor vehicle(s). Auto(s). Motor car(s). Limousine(s). Sedan(s). Station wagon(s). Taxicab(s). Jeep(s). Compact car(s). Convertible(s). Automotive. *Consider also:* road traffic, driver(s), bus(es), snowmobile(s), truck(s), vehicular, motoring, lorr(y,ies), hypercar(s). *Consider also:* Buick(s), Cadillac(s), Oldsmobile(s), Pontiac(s), Chrysler(s), Plymouth(s), Lincoln(s), Mercury(s), Ford(s), Rolls-Royce, Bentley(s), Jaguar(s), Mercedes-Benz, Opel(s), Porsche(s), Volkswagen(s), Karmann Ghia(s), Citroen(s), Peugeot(s), Renault(s), Simca(s), Datsun(s), Toyota(s), Honda(s), Fiat(s), Alfa-Romeo(s). *See also* Automobile driving; Motor vehicles; Zero emissions vehicles.

Automutilation. See *Self mutilation.*

Autonomy (government). Autonom(y,ous) government(s). Sovereign nation(s). Independent countr(y,ies). Home rule. *Choose from:* nation(al), government(s), state(s), countr(y,ies), political *with:* autonom(y,ous), independen(t,ce), self-legislating, sovereign(ty), free(dom), self govern(ment,ing), self determination. *Consider also:* autarky, autarchy, autochthon(y,ous). *See also* Decolonization; Freedom; Political self determination; Popular sovereignty; Sovereignty.

Autonomy (personal). See *Inner directed; Freedom; Liberty; Personal independence.*

Autophobia. Autophob(ia,ic). Eremiophob(ia,ic). Eremophob(ia,ic). Monophob(ia,ic). *Consider also:* fear, dread, phob(ia,ic), anxiet(y,ies) *with:* solitude, alone(ness), oneself, self. *See also* Phobias.

Autopsy. Autops(y,ies). Postmortem examination(s). Necrops(y,ies). *Consider also:* forensic, dismemberment, assessment, dissection *with:* postmortem, cadaver(s). *See also* Diagnosis; Dissection; Forensic medicine.

Autosexuality. See *Autoeroticism; Masturbation.*

Autoshaping. Autoshap(ing,ed). Auto-maintained response(s). Auto-maintenance. *See also* Conditioning (psychology); Reinforcement.

Autosuggestion. Autosuggest(ion, ive,ibility). Self-suggestion. Coue method. *Choose from:* sensory imagery conditioning, hypnotherapy, self hypnosis, autohypno(sis,tic). *See also* Autohypnosis; Hypnotherapy.

Avant-garde. Avant-garde. New(est). Progressive. Forerunner(s). Cutting edge. Leading edge. Groundbreaking. Innovative. Forward looking. Vanguard. Ultramodern. Modern(istic). Pioneer(ing,ed). Frontrunner(s). *Consider also:* radical, revolutionary. *See also* Constructivism; Experimental dancing; Experimental literature; Experimental music; Experimental poetry; Experimental theater; Fads; Fashions; Popular culture; Surrealism.

Avarice. See *Greed.*

Avenues. See *Highways; Streets.*

Aversion. Aversion(s). Averse(ness). Aversive(ness,ly). Hat(e,red). Antipath(y,ies). Dislike(s). Avoid(ed,ing, ance). Revulsion. Repugnan(t,ce). Annoy(ed,ing,ance). Distasteful(ness). Disinclined. Resistan(t,ce). Phobia(s). Inhibition(s). *See also* Disgust; Emotions; Hate; Repugnance.

Aversion conditioning. Aversion conditioning. *Choose from:* avers(e,ion,ions,ive), antipath(y,ies), dislike(s), avoidance *with:* condition(ed,ing), stimulus, response(s), learn(ed,ing), develop(ed, ing,ment), acquisition, acquir(e,ed,ing), Pavlovian procedure(s), association(s). *Consider also:* countercondition(ed,ing). *See also* Behavior modification; Conditioning (psychology); Operant conditioning.

Aversive therapy. Aversive therap(y,ies). *Choose from:* avers(ive,ion) *with:* therap(y,ies), treatment(s), technique(s), condition(ed,ing), countercondition(ed,ing), contingent shock(s). *Consider also:* punishment(s), electroaversive therap(y,ies), hypno-aversive technique(s), learned aversion(s). *See also* Behavior modification; Shock therapy.

Aviation accidents. Aviation accident(s). *Choose from:* airplan(e,es), airline(s), airliner(s), aircraft, jet(s), plane(s), mid-air, midair, pilot error(s), air traffic, aviation. aviator(s), airport(s), flight, flying, takeoff, air, aerial *with:* accident(s), collision(s), disaster(s), crash(ed,ing,es), bombing(s). *Consider also:* air traffic violation(s), airline safety, air traffic control(lers). *See also* Air traffic control; Airports; Aviation safety; Safety.

Aviation personnel. See *Aerospace personnel.*

Aviation safety. Aviation safety. *Choose from:* airplan(e,es), airline(s), airliner(s), aircraft, aerial, jet(s), plane(s), mid-air, midair, pilot error, air traffic, air, aviat(ion,or,ors), airport(s), flight *with:* safety, security, safeguard(s), maintenance, fatigue, hazard(s), terroris(m,t,ts), turbulence, seat belt(s), emergenc(y,ies), anti-collision, obstacle avoidance. *Consider also:* airplan(e,es), airline(s), airliner(s), aircraft, aerial, jet(s), plane(s), mid-air, midair, pilot error(s), air traffic, air, aviation, aviator(s), airport(s), flight *with:* prevent(ed,ing, ion), avoid(ed,ing,ance), avert(ed,ing) *with:* accident(s), collision(s), disaster(s), crash(ed,ing,es). *See also* Aircraft; Air traffic control; Airports; Aviation accidents; Safety.

Avitaminosis. See *Vitamin deficiency disorders.*

Avocation. See *Hobbies; Leisure time.*

Avoidance. Avoid(ance,ances,ant,ed,ing). Evad(e,ing). Evasion. Circumvent(ed, ing,ion). Abstinen(t,ce). Abstain(ed,ing). Avert(ed,ing). Avers(ive,iveness, ion,ions). Elud(e,ed,ing). Escap(e,ed, ing). Withdraw(al,n). Procrastinat(ed, ing,ion). Flee(ing). Shun(ned,ning). Dodg(e,ed,ing). Eschew(ed,ing). Forbear(ance). *Choose from:* defense, negative, escape *with:* behavior(s), response(s), reaction(s). *Consider also:* negative stimulus reaction(s), negative tropism, phototaxis, thigmotaxis. *See also* Avoidance learning; Delays; Repression (defense mechanism).

Avoidance, mathematics. See *Mathematics anxiety.*

Avoidance, science. See *Science anxiety.*

Avoidance conditioning. See *Avoidance learning.*

Avoidance learning. Avoidance learning. *Choose from:* avoidance, avers(ion,ive), escape, withdraw(al), inhibit(ory) *with:* learn(ed,ing), condition(ed,ing), respon(d,se,ses), establishment, acquisition, cued, memory, reinforc(e,ed,ing,ement,ements). *See also* Avoidance; Conditioned responses; Operant conditioning.

Avowals. See *Allegations; Assertions.*

Awake (conscious). See *Conscious (awake).*

Awakening, great. See *Great awakening.*

Awakening, religious. See *Enlightenment (state of mind); Religious experience.*

Awards. Award(s). Prize(s). Honor(s). Prizewinner(s). Medal(s). Blue ribbon(s). Medalist(s). Citation(s). Decoration(s). Knighthood. Order of the garter. Honorary degree(s). Certificate(s) of merit. Honorary membership(s). Certificate(s) of recognition. Gold key(s). Nobel prize(s). Pulitzer prize(s). Grand prix. Laureate(s). Accolade(s). Cordon bleu. Highest honor(s). Phi Beta Kappa. *Consider also:* honorari(a,um, ums), scholarship(s), troph(y,ies). *See also* Certificates; Honored (esteem); Incentives; Prestige; Recognition (achievement); Reward; Scholarships (educational).

Awareness. Aware(ness). Notic(e,ed,ing). Attention. Conscious(ness). Attentive(ness). Recogniz(e,ed,ing). Recognition. Sensitivity. Understand(ing). Understood. Watchful(ness). Cognition. Monitor(ed,ing). Realiz(ed,ing,ation). Knowledge(able). Perceptive(ness). Perception(s). Mindful(ness). Comprehen(d,ding,ded,sion). Being cognition. B cognition. Consciousness raising. *Consider also:* feeling(s). *See also* Body awareness; Comprehension; Conscious (awake); Consumer awareness; Deja vu; Divided attention; Freedom (theology); Perception; Personalism.

Awareness, body. See *Body awareness.*

Awareness, consumer. See *Consumer awareness.*

Awareness, race. See *Race awareness.*

Awareness, self. See *Self perception.*

Awareness, social. See *Social consciousness.*

Awkwardness. Awkward(ly,ness). Clums(y,iness). Maladroit(ly,ness). Inept(ly,ness). Gauche(ly,ness). Artless(ness). Gawk(y,iness). Ungainl(y,iness). Blunder(s,ed,ing). Graceless(ness). Ungraceful(ness). Uncoordinated. Bumbl(e,ed,ing). Bungl(e,ed,ing). Flounder(ed,ing). Inelegant(ly). *Consider also:* ill-proportioned, ill-adapted, lubberly, oafish; cumbrous, hulking, ponderous(ly,ness), all thumbs, unpolished, inexpert(ly), halting(ly), heavy-handed(ness), unhand(y,iness), unskillful(ly,ness), ill-chosen, ill-fitting. *See also* Attractiveness; Disability; Motor coordination; Motor skills; Physical agility; Physical characteristics.

Axioms. Axiom(atic,s). Self evident truth(s). Truism(s). Postulate(s). Theorem(s). Assumption(a). Sententia(e). *Consider also:* aphorism(s,atic), proverb(s,ial), adage(s), maxim(s), precept(s), dictum(s), gnom(e,es,ic). *See also* Adages; Aphorisms; Dictums; Postulates; Slogans.

Ayurvedic medicine. Ayurvedic medicine. *Choose from:* ayurved(a,ic), Hindu, India(n) *with:* health, medical, medicine, surg(ery,ical), hygien(e,ic), treat(ed,ing, ment), diagnos(es,is), heal(ed,ing), therap(y,ies,eutic), patient(s), disease(s), disorder(s), illness(es), cure(d,s). *See also* Plant folklore; Traditional medicine.

B

Babies. Bab(y,ies). Infan(t,ts,cy). Newborn(s). Neonat(e,es,al). Toddler(s). *See also* Birth; Infant development; Infant small for gestational age; Premature infants.

Babies, boomerang. See *Post-baby boom generation.*

Babies, crack. See *Drug addicted babies.*

Babies, drug addicted. See *Drug addicted babies.*

Baby boom generation. Baby boom generation. Baby boomer(s). Yuppie(s). New age. Me generation. Pepsi generation. Class of 1968, etc. War bab(y,ies). Post-war bab(y,ies). Spock bab(y,ies). Sputnik generation. Rock generation. Love generation. Now generation. Hippie(s). Generation of the sixties. Protest generation. Woodstock generation. Vietnam generation. Born in the 1940s. Born in the 1950s. Near(ly) elderly. Mature American(s). Mature market. *Consider also:* culture of affluence, born 1946 to 1964. *See also* Birthrate; Generation gap; Population growth; Post-baby boom generation; Young adults.

Baby bust generation. See *Post-baby boom generation.*

Baby busters. See *Post-baby boom generation.*

Baby talk. Baby talk. Pedolalia. Babbl(e,ed,ing). Prespeech development. Infantile speech. *Consider also:* gammacism(s), motherese. *See also* Mother child communication; Mother child relations; Speech development.

Babysitters. See *Child caregivers.*

Bachelors. Bachelor(s,hood). Single person(s). Single(s). Unmarried. Never married. Nonmarried. Unwed. Spouseless. *Choose from:* single, unmarried, bachelor, solo, solitary, divorced *with:* person(s), people, man, men, woman, women, parent(s), male(s), female(s), adult(s), life(style), status, mother(s), father(s). *Consider also:* widow(s), widower(s), divorcee(s), living alone, women alone, woman alone, lone man, lone men. *See also* Living alone; Marital status; Single person.

Back. Back(s). *Consider also:* lumbosacral region, sacrococcygeal region, backbone(s), spin(e,es,al), spinal column(s), vertra(e,l). *See also* Anatomy.

Back to basics. Back to basics. *Choose from:* basic(s), fundamental(s) *with:* education, skill(s), school(s,ing). *Consider also:* traditional school(s), conventional instruction, minimum competency movement. *See also* Academic standards; Basic skills; Competency based education; Traditional schools.

Backache. Backache(s). Lumbago. Back pain(s). Low back syndrome. Back disorder(s). *See also* Back; Chronic pain.

Backbone. See *Fortitude.*

Backers. See *Advocacy.*

Background, educational. See *Educational background.*

Background, family. See *Family background.*

Background, parental. See *Parental background.*

Background, personal. See *Biographical data.*

Background, social. See *Social background.*

Background music. Background music. Muzak. *Consider also:* underscore(s). *See also* Film music; Incidental music; Interludes (music); Music.

Background noise. See *White noise.*

Backlash. See *Countermovements.*

Backlog. Backlog(s,ged). Accumulation(s). Excess inventor(y,ies). Reserve(s). *Choose from:* uncompleted, unfilled, unperformed, unprocessed, accumulated *with:* work, orders, tasks, materials. *Consider also:* reservoir(s), stock, stockpile(s,d), work in process, stored. *See also* Accumulation; Inventories; Work load.

Backup, network. See *Network backup.*

Bacteria. Bacteri(a,um). Bacill(i,us). Germ(s). Microbe(s). Microorganism(s). *See also* Food contamination; Infectious disorders.

Bad debts. Bad debt(s). Uncollectible receivable(s). Bad loan(s). Account failure(s). Failed account(s). Credit delinquency. *Choose from:* uncollectible, unrecoverable, fail(ed,ure,ures), worthless, risky, problem(s), troubled *with:* financial(ly), debt(s), loan(s), obligation(s), overdraft(s), receivable(s). *See also* Bankruptcy; Debt moratoriums; High risk borrowers; Loans.

Bag ladies. See *Homeless.*

Baggage. See *Luggage.*

Bags. Bag(s). Sack(s). Pouch(es). Purse(s). Handbag(s). Pocketbook(s). Knapsack(s). Backpack(s). Carpetbag(s). Briefcase(s). Attache case(s). Tote bag(s). Valise(s). Satchel(s). *See also* Containers; Luggage.

Bahaism. Bahai(sm). *Consider also:* Mirza Husayn Ali, Baha Ullah, Kitab al-Aqdas, Kitab-i Iqan, Haft Wadi, al-Kalimat al-Makninah. *See also* Religion; Religious movements.

Bail. Bail(able,ee,ment). Sct(ting) bail. Released on own recognizance. *Choose from:* pretrial, preadjudicatory, stationhouse, bond *with:* release(d,s). *See also* Arrests; Contempt of Court; Defendants; Imprisonment; Offenders; Preventive detention; Probation; Trial (law).

Bailouts. Bailout(s). Bail(ing,ed,s) out. *Consider also:* emergency aid, emergency loan(s), rescue operation(s). *See also* Assistance; Bank failures; Business failures; Financial support; Rescue.

Bait. See *Decoys.*

Baking. Bak(e,ed,ing). Roast(ed,ing). Toast(ed,ing). Grill(ed,ing). Burn(ed,ing). *See also* Cooking.

Baksheesh. Baksheesh. Bakshish. Bakhshish. *See also* Alms; Begging; Bribery; Service industries; Tipping.

Balance. See *Equilibrium.*

Balance of payments. Balance of payments. Balanced econom(y,ies). *Consider also:* balance(s), imbalance(s) *with:* payment(s), monetary movement(s), reserve transaction(s), convertible currency. *Consider also:* dollar shortage(s), exchange control, capital flight. *See also* Balance of trade; Budget deficits; Debt-for-nature swaps; External debts; International economic integration; International trade; Public debt.

Balance of power. Balance of power. *Choose from:* power(s), domination, superpower(s), great powers, terror, military *with:* balance(d), equilibrium, mutual deterrence, rivalry, bipolar(ity), polycentr(ic,ism). *Consider also:* arms race, nuclear deterrence. *See also* Cold war; Detente; International relations; National security; Spheres of influence; Troop strength; War prevention.

Balance of trade. Balance of trade. Balanced econom(y,ies). *Consider also:* balance(s), imbalance(s), deficit(s), equit(y,ies), inequit(y,ies), gap(s), surplus(es), bilateral *with:* trade, international transaction(s), commerce, export(s), import(s). *Consider also:* American competitiveness, economic independence, trade adjustment. *See also* Balance of payments; Budget deficits;

Emerging markets; External debts; International trade; Nontariff trade barriers; Public debt.

Balance sheets. See *Financial statements; Financial data.*

Balanced budget. Balanced budget(s). *Choose from:* Gramm-Rudman-Hollings, deficit reduction law, creditworth(y,iness). *Choose from:* debt(s), deficit(s), borrow(ed,ing) *with:* limit(s,ed,ing,ation,ations), control(led, ling), reduc(e,ed,ing), restrict(ed,ing, tion,tions), prohibit(ed,ing,ion,ions). *Consider also:* bond rating(s), credit rating(s), credit standing, debt management, spending priorities, steady state economy. *See also* Budget deficits; Fiscal policy; Taxes.

Balancing work and family life. See *Dual career families; Family work relationship; Working women.*

Baldness. See *Alopecia.*

Ball games. Ball game(s). Play(ing) ball. *Consider also:* cricket, volleyball, softball, baseball, handball, hoop ball, basketball, football, soccer, racquetball, lacrosse. *See also* Sports.

Ballads. Ballad(s,eer,eers,ry,ries). Folk song(s). Ditt(y,ies). Carole(s). Chant(ey,eys,ie,es). Popular song(s). *Consider also:* love song(s), blues song(s), boat song(s), traditional song(s), lied(er), balada(s), chanson(s), corrido(s), romanze(n). *See also* Border ballads; Cantatas; Folk songs; Folk literature; Folk poetry; French songs; German songs; Labor songs; Lyrical ballads; Music; Narrative poetry; Popular literature; Popular music; Songs.

Ballads, lyrical. See *Lyrical ballads.*

Ballads, political. See *Political ballads.*

Ballads and songs, revolutionary. See *Revolutionary ballads and songs.*

Ballata. Ballat(a,e). *Consider also:* formes fixes, ripresa, piedi, volta, Niccolo da Perugia, Andreas de Florentia, Bartolino da Padova, Johannes Ciconia, Francesco Landini, caccia. *See also* Formes fixes; Frottola; Lauda; Medieval music; Music; Virelai.

Ballet dancers. Ballet dancer(s). Ballerina(s). Danseu(se,ses,r,rs). Corp(s) de ballet. *See also* Ballet dancing; Ballet shoes; Dance; Dancers; Male dancers.

Ballet dancing. Ballet danc(e,es,ing). Ballet technique. *Consider also:* ballet de cour, courtly dance(s), gavotte(s), passepied(s), bourree(s), rigaudon(s), minuet(s), modern dance. *See also* Ballet dancers; Ballet music; Ballet production; Choreography; Dance; Dance notation.

Ballet music. Ballet music. Ballet suite(s). Ballet score(s). Music(al) for ballet.

Arranged for ballet. *Consider also:* cachucha, bolero. *See also* Ballet dancing; Music.

Ballet production. Ballet production. *Choose from:* ballet(s) *with:* produc(e,ed,ing,tion), stag(e,ed,ing), present(ed,ing,ation), choreograph(ed, ing,er,ers), rework(ed,ing), reviv(e,ed, al,als). *See also* Ballet dancing; Theater.

Ballet shoes. Ballet shoe(s). Toe shoe(s). Ballet slipper(s). Pointe shoe(s). *See also* Ballet dancers; Boots and shoes; Costume.

Ballistic missiles. Ballistic missile(s). BMD system(s). Star Wars. Guided missile(s). Short-range missile(s). Trident missile(s). Ferret missile(s). Patriot missile(s). Rafael Python 4 air-to-air missile(s). AIM-9X . AA-11 Archer. High off-boresight missile(s). *Choose from:* defense(s), anti-ballistic, guided, minuteman, patriot, antisubmarine, antitheater *with:* missile(s). *See also* Aerial warfare; Antiaircraft artillery; Military weapons; Weaponry.

Ballots. Ballot(s). List of candidate(s). Slate(s). Voting ticket(s). Voting paper(s). *See also* Absentee voting; Election law; Local elections; Teledemocracy; Voters; Voting.

Ballroom dancing. Ballroom danc(e,es,ing,er,ers). Partner danc(e,es,ing,er,ers). Waltz(es,ing). Foxtrot(s). Formal social danc(e,es, ing,er,ers). *Consider also:* round danc(e,es,ing,er,ers), popular danc(e,es, ing,er,ers), polka(s), tango(s), swing danc(e,es,ing,er,ers). *See also* Dance; Dance music; Waltz.

Baltic languages. Baltic language(s). Latvian (Lettish). Lithuanian. Old Prussian. *See also* Eastern Europe; Language; Languages (as subjects); Western Europe.

Ban. Ban(ned,ning). Banish(ed,ing,ment). Boycott(ed,ing). Censor(ed,ing,ship). Declar(e,ed,ing) illegal. Disallow(ed,ing, ance). Embargo(s,ed). Exclu(de,ded, ing,sion). *Consider also:* excommunicat(e,ed,ing,ion), forbid(den,ding), injunction(s), interdict(ed,ing,ion), moratorium(s), ostracism(s), prohibit(ed, ing,ion), proscri(be,bed,bing), suppress(ed,ing,ion), veto(s,es). *See also* Blacklisting; Boycotts; Censorship; Forbidden; Negative sanctions; Prohibition.

Band, big. See *Big band.*

Band, stage. See *Big band.*

Bandits. Bandit(s,ry). Bandido(s). Train robber(s). Pirat(e,es). Piracy. Brigand(s,age). Plunderer(s). Robber(s). Outlaw(s). Robber baron(s). Highway(man,men). Armed band(s). Plunderer(s). Pillager(s). Marauder(s).

Rustler(s). Highjacker(s). Skyjacker(s). Looter(s). *Consider also:* Dick Turpin, Hereward the Wake, Robin Hood, Stenka Razin, Fra Diavolo, Jesse James, etc. *See also* Hijacking; Offenders; Robbery; Thugs.

Bands (music). Band(s). Musical group(s). Pop band(s). Music group(s). Pop group(s). String band(s). Big band(s). Brass band(s). Symphonic band(s). Marching band(s). Jug band(s). *Consider also:* instrumental group(s), folk ensemble(s), mariachi band(s). *See also* Instrumental music; Music; Orchestras.

Banging, head. See *Head banging.*

Bank failures. Bank failure(s). FSLIC bailout(s). *Choose from:* bank(s), savings and loan(s), thrift(s), credit union(s), deposit insurance *with:* fail(ed,ing,ure,ures), bankrupt(cy,cies), insolven(t,cy,cies), loss(es), clos(e,ed, ing,ings), cris(is,es). *Consider also:* deposit insurance cris(is,es). *See also* Bad debts; Bailouts; Bankruptcy; Default (negligence); Organizational dissolution; Plant closings.

Banking. Bank(s,ing). Financial institution(s). Loan societ(y,ies). Savings and loan association(s). Credit union(s). Investment firm(s). Banking house(s). Thrift institution(s). Trust compan(y,ies). Commercial house(s). Savings institution(s). S and L. *See also* Assets; Banking law; Capital (financial); Credit; Finance; International banks and banking; Investments; Loans; Money supply; Savings.

Banking, international banks and. See *International banks and banking.*

Banking, water. See *Water banking.*

Banking law. Banking law(s). Banking regulat(ory,ion). Bank deregulation. Usury law(s). *Consider also:* Glass-Steagall Act, Banking Act, Federal Deposit Insurance Corporation, FDIC, Office of the Comptroller and Currency; Federal Reserve, Federal Credit Union Act. Financial Institutions Regulatory Relief Act, Financial Services Competitiveness Act, Truth-in-Savings Act. *See also* Banking; Laws; Regulations.

Bankruptcy. Bankrupt(cy,cies). Insolven(t,cy,cies). Receivership(s). Chapter 11. Out of business. Failed business(es). Foreclos(ed,ure,ures). Deadbeat(s). Liquidation. Debtor(s). Destitute. Insolven(t,cy). *Choose from:* financial(ly), business(es) *with:* deplet(ed,ion), fail(ed,ing,ure,ures), exhausted, ruin(ed), collapse. *Consider also:* default(ed) on mortgage(s). *See also* Arrears; Bad debts; Bank failures; Debt management; Debts; Economic problems; Finance; High risk borrowers; Indebtedness; Plant closings; Organizational dissolution; Organizational survival; Turnaround management.

Banks, blood. See *Blood banks.*

Banks, data. See *Databases.*

Banks, sperm. See *Sperm banks.*

Banks, tissue. See *Tissue banks.*

Banks and banking, international. See *International banks and banking.*

Banned books. See *Censorship; Library censorship.*

Bantu languages. See *Benue-Niger languages.*

Baptism. Baptis(ed,m,ing). Baptiz(ed,m,ing). Baptismal rite(s). Christen(ed,ing). *See also* Infant baptism; Religious rituals; Salvation.

Baptism, infant. See *Infant baptism.*

Bar Mitzvah. See *Rites of Passage.*

Barbizon art movement. Barbizon art movement. *Choose from:* Barbizon *with:* art, artist(s), school. *Consider also:* French landscape paint(er,ers,ing), Francois Millet, Charles-Francois Daubigney, Theodore Rousseau, Narcisse-Virgile Diaz, Jules Dupre, Charles-Emile Jacque, Constant Troyon. *See also* Arts; Naturalism.

Bargaining. Bargain(ed,ing). Bid(s,ding). Offer(s). Concession(s). Haggl(e,ed,ing). Higgl(e,ed,ing). Trad(e,ed,ing). Deal(s,ing). Peddl(e,ed,ing). Dicker(ing). Negotiat(e,ed,ing,ion,ions). Concession strateg(y,ies). Collective bargaining. Barter(ing). Settlement(s). Discuss terms. *See also* Bargaining power; Bartering; Collective bargaining; Deals; Discounts; Firm offers; Negotiation.

Bargaining, collective. See *Collective bargaining.*

Bargaining, plea. See *Plea bargaining.*

Bargaining power. Bargaining power. *Choose from:* bargaining, negotiating *with:* power, strength(s), equilibrium. *Consider also:* bargaining position(s), bargaining surplus(es), balance of power, bargaining strategies, bargaining process(es). *See also* Bargaining; Collective bargaining; Power.

Bark peeling. Bark peel(ing). Dark(ed,ing). *Consider also:* bark, rind, periderm, cork *with:* peel(s,ing), strip(ped,ping). *See also* Plants (botanical); Trees.

Baroque art. Baroque art. *Consider also:* le style jesuite, Gianlorenzo Bernini, Pietro da Cortona, Frans Hals, Sir Peter Paul Rubens. *See also* Arts; Mannerism (art).

Baroque literature. Baroque literature. Barocco. *Consider also:* siglo de oro, euphuism, Hans Jacob Christoph von Grimmelshausen, Andreas Gryphius, Angelus Silesius, Miguel de Cervantes, Lope de Vega, Francisco Gomez de Quevedo, Luis de Gongora. *See also* Literature.

Barren. See *Infertility.*

Barricades. See *Barriers.*

Barrier free environment. See *Architectural accessibility.*

Barriers. Barrier(s). Obstacle(s). Obstruction(s). Hindrance(s). Hurdle(s). Stumbling block(s). Wall(s). Fence(s). Barricade(s). Restriction(s). Impediment(s). Drawback(s). Encumbrance(s). Block(s). Blockade(s). Roadblock(s). Landlocked. Deterrent(s). Ceiling(s). Glass ceiling(s). Sticky floor(s). Restraint(s). Constraint(s). Limit(s,ation,ations). *Consider also:* burden(s,ed,ing), constrain(t,ts,ed,ing), disadvantage(s,d), shortcoming(s), inaccessib(le,ility). *See also* Architectural accessibility; Blockade; Boundaries; Challenge; Constraints; Deadlock; Dysfunctional; Enclosures; Fences; Freedom; Hindrances; Impediments; Impediments to marriage; Inconvenience; Inhibition (psychology); Limitations; Needs; Opportunities; Political repression; Possibilities; Problems; Resources.

Barriers, communication. See *Communication barriers.*

Barriers, nontariff trade. See *Nontariff trade barriers.*

Barriers, trade. See *Nontariff trade barriers; Tariffs; Trade protection.*

Barriers, travel. See *Travel barriers.*

Barriers to employment. See *Employment discrimination.*

Bars. Bar(s,room,rooms). Saloon(s). Taproom(s). Alehouse(s). Cocktail lounge(s). Night club(s). Cafe(s). Tavern(s). Pub(s). Public house(s). Beer parlor(s). Rathskeller(s). Cabaret(s). *See also* Alcohol drinking; Alcoholic beverages; Coffee houses; Cybercafes; Eating establishments; Nightclubs.

Bartering. Barter(ed,ing). Barter econom(y,ies). Swap(s,ped,ping). Trade without money. Trading inventor(y,ies). Reciprocal merchandising. Hidden economy. Cashless transaction(s). Informal economy. Countertrade. Counterpurchas(es,ing). Contratrade. Compensation goods. Gift econom(y,ies). *Choose from:* goods, favors, services, nonmonetary *with:* exchange(e,es,ed,ing), trad(e,es,ed,ing). *See also* Collaboration; Commodities; Deals; Economic exchanges; Economic underdevelopment; Exchange; Money (primitive cultures); Purchasing; Second hand trade; Subsistence economy; Supply and demand.

Baseball clubs. Baseball club(s). Baseball team(s). *Consider also:* Pittsburgh Pirates, Cleveland Indians, New York Mets, Atlanta Braves, etc. *See also* Clubs; Sports.

Bases, air. See *Air bases.*

Bases, military. See *Military bases.*

Basic business education. Basic business education. *Choose from:* basic business *with:* learning, teaching, education, classroom, instruction(al), student(s). *See also* Business students; Consumer education.

Basic education. Basic education. *Choose from:* basic, fundamental, remedial, literacy *with:* education, class(es), curriculum, skill(s), learning. *See also* Adult basic education; Basic skills; Literacy programs; Reading education.

Basic education, adult. See *Adult basic education.*

Basic needs. Basic need(s). Lower level need(s). Necessit(y,ies). Minimum requirement(s). Essential service(s). Subsistence level(s). Essential(s). Minimum facilities. Indispensab(le,ility). Necessar(y,ies). *Consider also:* food, shelter, housing, clothing, sanitation, safe drinking water, good health, steady income, permanent job, permanent home, regular meals, physical survival, well-being, safety, economic security, emotional security, life satisfaction, self acceptance, self esteem, love. *See also* Living standards; Needs; Needs assessment; Quality of life; Subsistence economy; Unmet needs.

Basic skills. Basic skill(s). Litera(cy,te). *Choose from:* reading, writing, mathematic(s,al), communication, computer *with:* skill(s), mastery, competen(t,ce), proficien(t,cy). *See also* Adult basic education; Basic education; Communication skills; Computer literacy; Coping; Language proficiency; Literacy; Mathematics skills; Minimum competencies; Reading skills; Social skills; Spatial ability; Verbal ability; Work skills.

Basics, back to. See *Back to basics.*

Basilicas. Basilica(s,n). *Consider also:* Basilica Porcia, Romanesque church(es), Church of the Nativity at Bethlehem, St. John Lateran, St. Paul's-out-side-the-Walls. *See also* Architectural styles; Architecture; Places of worship; Religious buildings.

Baskets, gift. See *Gift baskets.*

Basse danse. Basse(s) danse(s). Bassadanz(a,e). *Consider also:* quaternari(a.o), quadernari(a,o), saltarello todesco, pas de Brabant, piva, pavana(s). *See also* Music; Renaissance music.

Bastards. See *Illegitimacy (children).*

Bat Mitzvah. See *Rites of Passage.*

Battered children. See *Child abuse.*

Battered women. Battered wom(an,en). Femicide. *Choose from:* battered, violen(t,ce), abus(e,ed,er,ers), assault(s,ed,ing), bash(ed,ing), beat(en,ing), torture(d), kick(ed,ing), punch(ed,ing) *with:* wom(an,en), spous(e,es,al), marital, conjugal, wife, wives, female(s), date(s), courtship. *Consider also:* famil(y,ies,ial), domestic, intrafamily *with:* violen(t,ce), fight(s). *See also* Child abuse; Elder abuse; Family problems; Family violence; Females (human); Marital conflict; Marital rape; Reproductive rights; Sex offenders; Sexual abuse; Sexual oppression; Shelters; Spouse abuse; Stalking; Victimization; Violence.

Battering, wife. See *Battered women; Spouse abuse.*

Battle, assault. See *Assault (battle).*

Battle fatigue. See *Post traumatic stress disorders.*

Battle songs. See *War songs.*

Battles. Battle(s). Military action(s). Assault(s). Barrage(s). Blitzkrieg. Military encounter(s). Military campaign(s). Military engagement(s). Combat. *See also* Assault (battle); Military capitulations.

Bawdy songs. Bawdy song(s). Naughty song(s). *Choose from:* sexually explicit, lewd, licentious, lecherous, obscene, off-color, salacious, suggestive, bawdy, erotic, sultry, burlesque, filthy, saucy, immoral, ribald, backroom, dirty, spicy, porno, tasteless, nasty, unprintable, uncensored, whorehouse, sexy, stag party, risque, unexpurgated, adults only *with:* song(s), ditt(y,ies), sing(ing), music(al,als), ballad(s), tune(s), verse(s), hootenann(y,ies), blues, shant(y,ies), chanson(s), lied(er), cancion(s). *See also* Adult entertainment; Drinking songs; Erotica; Erotic songs; Obscenity; Popular culture; Prurience; Scatology; Songs; Vulgarity.

Beaches. Beach(es). Seashore(s). Shore(s). Waterfront(s). Seaside(s). Oceanfront(s). Seaboard(s). Coast(s,line,lines). *See also* Island ecology; Islands; Recreation areas; Vacations; Shorelines; Shore protection; Tides.

Beads. Bead(s). Bauble(s). Droplet(s). Pearl(s). Necklace(s). Choker(s). String of pearl(s). *Consider also:* rosar(y,ies), chaplet(s). *See also* Crafts; Jewelry; Jewelry making; Treasure.

Beans. Bean(s). Soybean(s). Limas. Stringbean(s). *Consider also:* legume(s), seed(s) *See also* Food; Natural foods; Vegetarianism.

Beat generation. See *Baby boom generation; Hippies.*

Beautification, urban. See *Urban beautification.*

Beauty. Beaut(y,iful,ify,ified). Facial attractiveness. Physical attractiveness. Lovel(y,iness). Comel(y,iness). Prett(y,iness). Esthetic(s). Aesthetic(s). Eye appeal. Glamor(ous,ousness). Allur(e,ing). Attract(ive,iveness,ion). Well proportioned. Fair. Graceful. Ornament(ed,ation). Good taste. Balanc(e,ed). Symmetr(y,ical). *See also* Aesthetics; Attractiveness; Beauty culture; Classic (standard); Human body; Interpersonal attraction; Personal beauty; Physical characteristics; Proportionality; Social desirability.

Beauty culture. Beauty culture. Beauty pageant(s). Beauty contest(s). Beauty industry. Beauty consultant(s). Cosmetolog(y,ist,ists). *Consider also:* medical aesthetics, cosmetic surgery. *See also* Beauty; Beauty operators; Beauty shops; Cosmetics; Hairdressing; Lifestyle; Personal appearance; Personal beauty; Reconstructive surgery.

Beauty operators. Beauty operator(s). Make-up artist(s). *Consider also:* beauty salon(s), barber(s), beautician(s), hair styli(st,sts,ing), hairdress(er,ers,ing). *See also* Beauty culture; Beauty shops; Female intensive occupations; Hairdressing; Personnel; Workers.

Beauty, personal. See *Personal beauty.*

Beauty shops. Beauty shop(s). Beauty salon(s). Hairdressing salon(s). Barber(s). Beauty parlor(s). *Consider also:* beautician(s), cosmetologist(s). *See also* Beauty operators; Cosmetics; Hairdressing; Service industries; Women owned businesses.

Bed occupancy. Bed occupancy. Hospital census(es). Number of inpatients. *Choose from:* bed(s), inpatient facilit(y,ies) *with:* utilization, availab(le,ility), use, occupied. *See also* Hospital environment.

Bed wetting. See *Urinary incontinence.*

Bedding. Bedding. White sale(s). Bed-clothes. *Consider also:* bed linens, sheet(s), blanket(s), mattress(s), pillow(s), electric blanket(s), thermal blanket(s), pillowcase(s). *See also* Coverlets; Furniture; Material culture.

Bedridden. Bedridden. Confined to bed. Housebound. Homebound. *Consider also:* chronic(ally) ill(ness). *See also* Chronic disease; Disability.

Bedwetting. See *Urinary incontinence.*

Bee culture. Bee culture. Beekeep(ing,er,ers). Apicultur(e,al,ist,ists). *Choose from:* bee(s), honeybee(s), honey bee(s) *with:* culture, keep(ing,er,ers), rais(e,ed,ing), breed(ing), agribusiness(es). *See also* Agriculture; Farming.

Begging. Begg(ing,ar,ars,ary). Solicit(ed,ing) money. Panhandl(e,er, ers,ing). Mendicant(s). Pauper(s). Seek(ing) alms. Soliciting contribution(s). *See also* Alms; Almshouses; Baksheesh; Homeless; Poverty; Vagrants.

Beginning. Begin(s,ning). Began. Begun. Start(ed,ing). First part(s). First stage(s). First appearance(s). Initial performance(s). Alpha. Commenc(e,ed, ing,ement). Debut(s). Genesis. Onset(s). Opening(s). Outset. Set(ting) out. Start(ing) out. Inception(s). Origin(s,al, ally,ation). Prologue(s). Introduction(s). *Consider also:* origin(s,al,ate,ating,ated), rudimentary stage(s), early period(s), inaugurat(e,ed,ing,ion), launch(ed,ing), emerg(e,ed,ing,ence,ences), incipien(t,cy), infancy. *See also* Birth; Creativity; Dawn; Initiation; Onset (disorders); Provenance.

Beginnings, openings. See *Beginning; Incipits; Introduction; Onset (disorders); Overtures (music).*

Behavior. Behavior(al,s). Conduct. Performance. Habit(s,ual). Adjustment(s). Assertive(ness). Attach(ed,ing,ment,ments). Autis(m,tic). Cannibalis(m,tic). Ceremonial(s). Communicat(ed,ing,ion). Competitive(ness). Cooperative(ness). Competit(ive,ion). Cooperat(ive,ion). Demeanor(s). Disobedien(t,ce). Drinking. Drug use(r,rs). Displacement. Drinking behavior(s). Escape reaction(s). Explor(e,ed,ing,ation). Exploratory behavior(s). Feeding behavior(s). Fight(ing). Group behavior(s). Hyperactiv(e,ity). Imitat(e,ed,ing,ion). Imitative behavior(s). Inhibit(ed,ion). Leadership. Life style(s). Maternal behavior(s). Misbehavior. Motor activit(y,ies). Obedien(t,ce). Paranoid behavior(s). Paternal behavior(s). Participat(e,ed, ing,ion). Persisten(t,ce). Physical(ly) activ(e,ity). Response(s). Risk taking. Self control. Self mutilation. Smok(e, ed,ing). Sociab(le,ility). Social behavior(s). Spontane(ity,ous). Self stimulat(e,ed,ing,ion). Sex behavior(s). Social conformity. Social dominance. Social facilitation. Spatial behavior(s). Stereotyped behavior(s). Substance abuse(r,rs). Sucking behavior(s). *See also* Action; Adolescent behavior; Affective behavior; Agonistic behavior; Animal aggressive behavior; Animal behavior; Animal courtship behavior; Animal defensive behavior; Animal exploratory behavior; Animal foraging behavior; Animal grooming behavior; Animal hoarding behavior; Animal parental behavior; Animal sex behavior;

Antisocial behavior; Assertiveness; Attachment behavior; Behavior contracting; Behavior development; Behavior disorders; Behavior modification; Behavior patterns; Behavior problems; Behavior theories; Behaviorism; Child behavior; Choice behavior; Collective behavior; Competitive behavior; Competition; Compulsive behavior; Coping; Consumer behavior; Cooperation; Coronary prone behavior; Customs; Dangerous behavior; Demeanor; Deviant behavior; Drinking behavior; Drug use; Exploratory behavior; Feeding behavior; Fire setting behavior; Habits; Harmful behavior; Health behavior; Help seeking behavior; Helping behavior; Human nature; Imitation; Impulsiveness; Individual differences; Instinct; Interaction; Internalization; Learned behavior; Lifestyle; Marital sexual behavior; Mass behavior; Maternal behavior; Nesting behavior; Obsessive behavior; Organizational behavior; Participation; Paternal behavior; Performance; Play; Political behavior; Predatory behavior; Premarital sexual behavior; Prosocial behavior; Public behavior; Religious behavior; Responses; Roles; Self control; Self defeating behavior; Self destructive behavior; Sex behavior; Social behavior; Spatial behavior; Spontaneity; Stereotyped behavior; Student behavior; Sucking behavior; Territoriality; Traditions; Verbal behavior; Violence; Voting behavior; Wandering behavior.

Behavior, acts. See *Act (Philosophy); Action; Behavior; Volition.*

Behavior, adolescent. See *Adolescent behavior.*

Behavior, affective. See *Affective behavior.*

Behavior, agonistic. See *Agonistic behavior.*

Behavior, animal. See *Animal behavior.*

Behavior, animal aggressive. See *Animal aggressive behavior.*

Behavior, animal courtship. See *Animal courtship behavior.*

Behavior, animal defensive. See *Animal defensive behavior.*

Behavior, animal exploratory. See *Animal exploratory behavior.*

Behavior, animal foraging. See *Animal foraging behavior.*

Behavior, animal grooming. See *Animal grooming behavior.*

Behavior, animal hoarding. See *Animal hoarding behavior.*

Behavior, animal maternal. See *Animal parental behavior.*

Behavior, animal parental. See *Animal parental behavior.*

Behavior, animal sex. See *Animal sex behavior.*

Behavior, antisocial. See *Antisocial behavior.*

Behavior, attachment. See *Attachment behavior.*

Behavior, child. See *Child behavior.*

Behavior, choice. See *Choice behavior.*

Behavior, collective. See *Collective behavior.*

Behavior, competitive. See *Competitive behavior.*

Behavior, compulsive. See *Compulsive behavior.*

Behavior, consumer. See *Consumer behavior.*

Behavior, cooperative. See *Cooperation.*

Behavior, coronary prone. See *Coronary prone behavior.*

Behavior, crowd. See *Collective behavior; Mass behavior; Mass hysteria; Riots; Social agitation.*

Behavior, dangerous. See *Dangerous behavior.*

Behavior, deviant. See *Deviant behavior.*

Behavior disorders, child. See *Child behavior disorders.*

Behavior disorders, social. See *Social behavior disorders.*

Behavior, drinking. See *Drinking behavior.*

Behavior, exploratory. See *Exploratory behavior.*

Behavior, feeding. See *Feeding behavior.*

Behavior, fire setting. See *Fire setting behavior.*

Behavior, group. See *Collective behavior.*

Behavior, harmful. See *Harmful behavior.*

Behavior, health. See *Health behavior.*

Behavior, health seeking. See *Health; Health promotion; Holistic health; Mental health; Preventive medicine; Preventive psychiatry; Primary prevention; Quality of life; Well being.*

Behavior, help seeking. See *Help seeking behavior.*

Behavior, helping. See *Helping behavior.*

Behavior, human. See *Behavior.*

Behavior, illness. See *Sick role.*

Behavior, learned. See *Learned behavior.*

Behavior, manipulative. See *Manipulation.*

Behavior, marital sexual. See *Marital sexual behavior.*

Behavior, mass. See *Mass behavior.*

Behavior, maternal. See *Maternal behavior.*

Behavior, nesting. See *Nesting behavior.*

Behavior, obsessive. See *Obsessive behavior.*

Behavior, offensive. See *Aggression; Air rage; Animal aggressive behavior; Antisocial behavior; Arguments; Assault (battle); Assault (personal); Attack (Military science); Belligerency; Disorderly conduct; Dominance; Drivy crimes; Hostility; Interpersonal conflict; Invasion; Juvenile delinquency; Militarism; Rape; Riots; Road rage; Terrorism; Threat; Threat postures; Violence; War.*

Behavior, organizational. See *Organizational behavior.*

Behavior, parental. See *Maternal behavior; Paternal behavior.*

Behavior, passive. See *Passiveness.*

Behavior, paternal. See *Paternal behavior.*

Behavior, political. See *Political behavior.*

Behavior, predatory. See *Predatory behavior.*

Behavior, premarital sexual. See *Premarital sexual behavior.*

Behavior, prosocial. See *Prosocial behavior.*

Behavior, psychosexual. See *Sex behavior.*

Behavior, public. See *Public behavior.*

Behavior, rebellious. See *Rebelliousness.*

Behavior, religious. See *Religious behavior.*

Behavior, self defeating. See *Self defeating behavior.*

Behavior, self destructive. See *Self destructive behavior.*

Behavior, sex. See *Sex behavior.*

Behavior, sexual. See *Sex behavior.*

Behavior, social. See *Social behavior.*

Behavior, socially deviant. See *Deviant behaviors.*

Behavior, spatial. See *Spatial behavior.*

Behavior, stereotyped. See *Stereotyped behavior.*

Behavior, student. See *Student behavior.*

Behavior, submissive. See *Obedience; Submission.*

Behavior, sucking. See *Sucking behavior.*

Behavior, suicidal. See *Suicidal behavior.*

Behavior, traditional. See *Folkways.*

Behavior, verbal. See *Verbal behavior.*

Behavior, voting. See *Voting behavior.*

Behavior, wandering. See *Wandering behavior.*

Behavior change. See *Behavior modification.*

Behavior contracting. Behavior contracting. *Choose from:* performance, behavior(al), contingency, treatment(s), weight loss, behavior modification, therap(y,ies), behavioral management, self reward(s), attendance *with:* contract(ed,ing,s,ual). *See also* Behavior modification; Contingency; Learning contracts.

Behavior development. Behavior(al) development. *Choose from:* behavior(al), social skill(s), psychosocial *with:* development, maturation, matur(ed,ing), learn(ed,ing), acquir(e,ed,ing), habit formation. *Consider also:* socializ(ed,ing,ation). *See also* Animal behavior; Attachment behavior; Behavior; Behavior modification; Behaviorism; Bibliotherapy; Child behavior; Developmental stages; Exploratory behavior; Habits; Nature nurture; Psychological anthropology; Self actualization; Social behavior.

Behavior disorders. Behavior(al,ally) disorder(s,ed). *Choose from:* behavior(al,ally), conduct, habit(s) *with:* disorder(s,ed), disturb(ed,ance,ances), delinquent, problem(s), aggressive, patholog(y,ical), abusive, disruptive, troubled, deviant, pathocharacterological, suicidal, destructive. Berserk. *Consider also:* attention deficit disorder(s). *See also* Acting out; Aggression; Alcoholism; Antisocial behavior; Attention deficit disorder; Attempted suicide; Autism; Behavior; Behavior patterns; Behavior problems; Body rocking; Cheating; Child abuse; Child behavior disorders; Coprophagia; Crime; Deception; Disorders; Drug addiction; Emotionally disturbed; Faking; Fecal incontinence; Fire setting behavior; Head banging; Homicide; Juvenile delinquency; Learning disabilities; Mental illness; Personality disorders; Rape; Recidivism; Self destructive behavior; Self mutilation; Shoplifting; Social behavior disorders; Substance abuse; Suicide; Tantrums; Theft; Truancy; Urinary incontinence; Vandalism; Withdrawal (defense mechanism).

Behavior in systems, chaotic. See *Chaotic behavior in systems.*

Behavior modification. Behavior modification. Operant conditioning. Contingency reinforcement. Behaviorally oriented assertiveness training. Token econom(y, ies). Avers(ive,ion) therap(y,ies). Relaxation technique(s). Biofeedback training. Contingency management. Overcorrection. Omission training. Reciprocal inhibition therap(y,ies). Desensitiz(e,ed,ing,ation). Implosive therap(y,ies). *Choose from:* self *with:* management, monitoring, reinforcement. *Choose from:* behavior(s,al) *with:* modif(y,ying,ied,ication), management,

contract(s,ing), rehearsal, shaping, chang(e,es,ed,ing), control(led,ling), reinforcement, condition(ed,ing), therap(y,ies), treatment(s). *See also* Assertiveness training; Aversive therapy; Behavior contracting; Biofeedback; Classical conditioning; Cognitive restructuring; Cognitive therapy; Contingency; Desensitization (psychology); Fading (conditioning); Implosive therapy; Operant conditioning; Cognitive restructuring; Meditation; Reality therapy; Rehabilitation; Relaxation training; Self help; Self management (individual); Self monitoring; Social reinforcement; Social skills training; Stress management; Token economy.

Behavior patterns. Behavior(al) pattern(s). Habit(s). Recidivism. *Choose from:* behavior, conduct, eating, drinking, smoking, exercise *with:* pattern(s), model(s), cycle(s), recurren(t,ce), rhythm(s), habit(s), characteristic, typical. *See also* Behavior; Behavior disorders; Coping; Deception; Food habits; Habits; Identification (psychology); Imitation; Recidivism; Sociobiology; Study habits.

Behavior problems. Behavior(al) problem(s). Misbehavior. Misconduct. *Choose from:* behavior(al,s), conduct *with:* disorder(s,ed), problem(s), disturbance(s), devian(t,ce), disruptive, unrul(y,iness), assaultive, abnormal, maladaptive. *Consider also:* problem child(ren), poor manner(s), disobedien(t, ce), disorderl(y,iness), rude(ness), naught(y,iness), rowd(y,iness), horseplay, fingersucking, thumbsucking, nail biting, runaway(s), juvenile delinquency, addiction(s), alcoholism, antisocial behavior(s), suicide attempt(s), cheat(ed,ing), child abuse, confabulation, crime(s), deception, drug abuse, drug addiction, head banging, firesetting, malingering, shoplifting, tantrum(s), theft, truancy, vandalism. *See also* Adjustment (to environment); Aggression; Antisocial behavior; Behavior; Behavior disorders; Behavior patterns; Child discipline; Deviant behavior; Emotionally disturbed; Hyperkinesis; Indecent exposure; Mental illness; Minimal brain disorders; Obedience; Personality disorders; Psychopathology; Self control; Self defeating behavior; Self destructive behavior; Withdrawal (defense mechanism).

Behavior surveys, sexual. See *Sexual behavior surveys.*

Behavior theories. Behavior theor(y,ies). Behaviorism. *Choose from:* behavior(al), rational emotive, ego psychology, cognitive behavioral, family systems *with:* theor(y,ies,etical), explanation(s), model(s). *See also* Adaptation level theory; Learning theories; Personality theories; Social theories; Theories.

Behavior therapy. See *Behavior modification.*

Behavioral assessment. Behavioral assessment. *Choose from:* behavior(al,s), social skill(s) *with:* assess(ed,ing), assessment(s), analys(is,es), analyz(ed,ing), rate(d), rating(s), measur(e,es,d,ing,ement), judgment(s). *See also* Analysis; Behavior modification; Empirical methods.

Behavioral genetics. Behavior(al) genetic(s). Psychogenetic(s). *Choose from:* genetic(s), biogenetic(s), evolution, evolv(e,ed,ing), inherit(ed,ing, ance), coevolution, heredit(y,ary, able,ability) *with:* behavior(al), intelligence, cultur(e,al), abilit(y,ies). *Consider also:* nature nurture controversy, sociobiolog(y,ical), psychobiolog(y,ical). *See also* Biological factors; Evolutionary ethics; Genetic psychology; Psychobiology.

Behavioral sciences. See *Social sciences.*

Behaviorism. Behavioris(m,t,ts,tic). Behavioral engineering. Behavioralism. Neobehavioris(m,t,ts). *Consider also:* B. F. Skinner, J. B. Watson, Pavlov(ian, ism), Clark Hull, positive reinforcement, operant behavior, operant conditioning, negative reinforcement, behavior modification. *See also* Behavior; Behavior development; Behavior modification; Classical conditioning; Cognitive psychology; Conditioning (psychology); Empiricism; Learning theories; Operant conditioning; Reinforcement; Stimuli.

Beheading. Behead(ed,ing). Decapitat(e, ed,ing). Decollat(e,ed,ing). Guillotine(d). Execut(e,ed,ing). *See also* Death penalty.

Being, chain of. See *Chain of being.*

Being, well. See *Well being.*

Being alone, fear of. See *Autophobia.*

Beings, extraterrestrial. See *Extraterrestrial life.*

Bel canto. Bel canto. Melodious vocal style. Beautiful singing. *Consider also:* lyric(al) *with:* singing. *See also* Music; Musical ability; Musicians; Opera; Opera singers.

Belief, theological. See *Faith.*

Beliefs. Belief(s). Creed(s). Faith. Social construction(s). Fideism. Interpretation(s). Meaning(s). View(s). Viewpoint(s). Worldview(s). Sentiment(s). Conception(s). Perception(s). Attitude(s). Superstition(s). Conviction(s). Opinion(s). Notion(s). Understanding. Credence. Surmis(e,ed,ing). Presumption(s). Impression(s). Assumption(s). Conjectur(e,ed,ing). Idea(s). *Consider also:* feeling(s). *See* *also* Antinomianism; Assumptions; Attitudes; Attitude measurement; Certainty; Common sense; Concepts; Credibility; Dissent; Dogma; Dogmatism; Fatalism; Hidden curriculum; Ideologies; Irrational beliefs; Magic; Moral attitudes; Mysticism; Norms; Occultism; Opinions; Perceptions; Rationality; Reality; Religion; Religious beliefs; Social attitudes; Social values; Superstitions; Trusting; Truth; Values; Worldview.

Beliefs, irrational. See *Irrational beliefs.*

Beliefs, religious. See *Religious beliefs.*

Believability. Believab(ility,le). Credib(ility,le). Authentic(ity). Plausib(ility,le). Trustworth(y,iness). Dependab(ility,le). Reliab(ility,le). Assurance(s). Reassurance(s). Reassur(e,ed,ing). Sincer(e,ity). Faithful(ness). *See also* Authenticity; Ethics; Deception; Implausibility; Integrity; Public opinion; Reputation.

Bell's mania. Bell's mania. Exhaustion death. Deadly catatonia. Lethal catatonia. *See also* Death; Mental illness.

Belligerency. Belligeren(t,cy). Aggressive(ness). Antagonistic. Battling. Bellicose. Combative(ness). Contentious(ness). Hostil(e,ity). Mean(ness). Hot-tempered. Quarrelsome(ness). *See also* Aggression; Air rage; Road rage; War.

Bells. Bell(s). Handbell(s). Church bell(s). Chime(s). Carillon(s). Tocsin(s). Gong(s). Angelus(es). Cowbell(s). *Consider also:* pellet bell(s), tubular bell(s), orchestral chime(s), tower bell(s), change ringing, campane(lli), glocken(spiel), pavillon, Schallbecher, Schallstuck, schalltrichter, Stahlspiel, Sturze, padiglione, campan(a,elli,ologo), pabellon, cloche(s), cloche(s) tubulaire(s). *See also* Bronze bells; Change ringing; Church music; Medieval music; Musical instruments; Religious music.

Bells, bronze. See *Bronze bells.*

Belly dance. Belly danc(e,es,er,ers,ing). Bellydanc(e,es,er,ers,ing). Danse du ventre. *Consider also:* erotic danc(e,es, er,ers,ing). *See also* Adult entertainment; Dance; Dirty dancing; Entertainment; Nightclubs.

Belongingness. Belongingness. Sense of belonging. Accept(ed,ance). Root(s,ed, edness). Security. Affiliat(ed,ion,ions). Enmesh(ed,ment). Campanilismo. *See also* Acceptance; Affiliation motivation; Brotherliness; Community feeling; Community (social); Comprehensiveness; Group consciousness; Group feeling; Inclusion; Social acceptance; Social cohesion; Social nearness; Social support networks.

Belts, seat. See *Seat belts.*

Benchmarks. Benchmark(s,ed,ing). Bench mark(s,ed,ing). Standard(s). Criterion. Gauge. Guideline(s). Prototype(s). Measure(s). Touchstone(s). Yardstick(s). Point(s) of reference. Basis for evaluation. Exemplar(s). Archetype(s). Standard specimen(s). *See also* Criteria; Performance standards; Standards; Specimens.

Benefactors. Benefactor(s). Altruist(s). Patron(s). Helper(s). Backer(s). Contributor(s). Philanthropist(s). Sponsor(s). Subsidizer(s). Angel(s). Underwriter(s). *See also* Art patronage; Charities; Donations; Philanthropy.

Benefices, ecclesiastical. See *Ecclesiastical benefices.*

Beneficiaries. Beneficiar(y,ies). Devisee(s). Heir(s,ess,esses). Inheritor(s). Successor(s). Legatee(s). *Consider also:* assignee(s), assigns. *See also* Estate planning; Heirs; Inheritance; Legacies; Survivors; Survivors benefits.

Benefit, cost analysis. See *Cost effectiveness.*

Benefits (compensation). Benefit(s, ted,ting). Compensation. Allowance(s). Dole. Entitlement(s). Pension(s). Payment(s). Perquisite(s). Perk(s). Reward(s). Fringe benefit(s). Fringes. Sick leave. Holiday(s). Vacation time. Annual leave(s). *Consider also:* retirement, dependent(s), employee(s), flexible, insurance, maternity, paternity, supplementary, veteran(s) *with:* benefit(s). *See also* Compensation (payment); Compensation management; Employee assistance programs; Employee benefits; Employee incentive plans; Insurance; Pensions; Public welfare; Salaries; Survivors benefits.

Benefits, employee. See *Employee benefits.*

Benefits, fringe. See *Employee benefits.*

Benefits, retirement. See *Pensions; Retirement income.*

Benefits, social. See *Externalities; Social impact.*

Benefits, survivors. See *Survivors benefits.*

Benevolence. Benevolen(t,ce). Altruis(tic,m). Compassion(ate). Friendl(y,iness). Goodwill. Gener(ous, osity). Kindhearted(ness). Kindness(es). *Consider also:* charitable(ness), helpful(ness). *See also* Compassion; Favors; Friendliness; Good; Humanitarianism; Kindness.

Benue-Niger languages. Benue-Niger language(s). Bantu: Bemba, Chinyanja, Chwana, Ganda, Herero, Kikuyu, Kimbundu, Kirundi, Kituba, Lingala, Luba, Luganda, Nyaruanda, Rundi, Shona, Siswati, Sotho, Swahili, Xhosa, Zulu. Non-Bantu: Adamawa group, Ijo,

Ubangi group, Efik, Jukun, Tiv, Kordofanian. *See also* African cultural groups; Language; Languages (as subjects); Sub-Saharan Africa.

Bereavement. Bereave(d,ment). Mourn(ed,ing). Lament(ed,ing, ation,ations). Grief. Heartache(s). *Choose from:* survivor(s), death(s) *with:* loss(es), sorrow(s), sad(ness), distress(ed,es,ing), depriv(e,ed,ation), anguish(ed). *See also* Death; Death counseling; Death rituals; Grief; Laments; Loss (psychology); Sadness.

Bergerette. See *Virelai.*

Best practices. Best practice(s). Award-winning practice(s). *Choose from:* best, award-winning, outstanding, safe(r,st), most effective *with:* practice(s), method(s), procedure(s), system(s). *See also* Excellence; Management methods; Methods; Perfection; Performance; Practices (methods).

Best sellers. Best seller(s). Bestseller(s). Best selling book(s). Best book(s). Notable book(s). Top fiction. Top nonfiction. *See also* Books; Bookselling; Publishing.

Bestiality. Bestiality. *Choose from:* perversion(s), lewd(ness), sexual(ly) *with:* animal(s). *See also* Cruelty to animals; Sexual sadism.

Bestiaries. Bestiar(y,ies). Bestiarum vocabulum. Book of beasts. Mythologised beast(s). Physiologus. Royal collections of animals. Tower Menagerie. *Consider also:* animal(s), bird(s), serpent(s), dragon(s), basilisk(s), siren(s), griffin(s), centaur(s) *with:* symbol(s,ism), fable(s), illuminated manuscript(s), allegor(y,ies,ical). *See also* Animal lore; Animals; Books; Griffins; Literature; Medieval literature; Mythical animals; Mythology; Snake lore.

Beta alcoholism. Beta alcoholism. Alcoholisation. Somatopathic drinking. *See also* Alcoholism.

Betrayal. Betray(ed,ing,al). Disloyal(ty). Treacher(y,ous,ousness). Violat(e,ed,ion) trust. Double cross(ed,ing). Bad faith. Breach of faith. Perfid(y,ious). Duplicit(y,ous). *See also* Deception; Duplicity; Traitors.

Betrothal. Betroth(ed,al,als). Affianc(e,ed, ing). Prenuptial. Engaged to be married. Engagement(s). Fiance(e,es,s). *Choose from:* future, intended *with:* husband(s), wife, wives, bride(s), groom(s). *Consider also:* hope chest(s), trousseau(s,x), bridal shower(s). *See also* Covenant marriage; Human courtship; Human mate selection; Marriage.

Betting. Bet(ting,s,or,ors). Wager(s). Gambl(e,ed,ing,er,ers). Speculat(e,ed, ing,or,ors). Put money. Raffle(s).

Lotter(y,ies). Dice. Sweepstake(s). Game(s) of chance. Shoot craps. *See also* Billiard parlors; Casinos; Compulsive behavior; Gambling; Organized crime.

Beverage industry. Beverage industry. Beverage compan(y,ies). Soft drink account(s). Juice bottler(s). *Choose from:* iced tea, wine, beer, soda, juice(s), microbrews, soft drink(s), fruit drink(s), cocktail(s), cooler(s), *with:* industry, compan(y,ies), account(s), bottler(s), producer(s). *See also* Alcoholic beverages; Beverages; Brewing industry; Coffee industry; Food industry.

Beverages. Beverage(s). Water. Beer(s). Wine(s). Carbonated beverage(s). Coffee(s). Milk. Mineral water(s). Tea(s). Liquor(s). Soda(s). Cocktail(s). Juice(s). Perrier. Coca cola. Pepsi cola. Vichy water. Club soda. Ginger ale. Cocoa. Lemonade. Cider. Herbal tea(s). Soft drink(s). Gin. Vodka. Brandy. Cognac. Whisk(y,ey,ies). Schnapps. Ale(s). Rum. Sherry. Bourbon. Mead. Port. Scotch. Liquer(s). Rye. Slivovitz. Tequila. Coca Cola. Pepsi Cola. Seven Up. *Consider also:* alcoholic beverage(s), nonalcoholic-beverages, thirst quencher(s), cooler(s). *See also* Alcoholic beverages; Beverage industry; Drinking (water, fluids); Drinking water; Fluids; Nutrition.

Beverages, alcoholic. See *Alcoholic beverages.*

Bias. Bias(es,ed,ing). Prejudice(s,d). Distort(ed,ing). Vested interest(s). Selective reporting. Stereotyp(e,es,ed,ing). Partisan. Prejudgment(s). Questionable assumption(s). Aggrandiz(e,ed,ing, ement). Bigot(s,ry). Denigrat(e,ed, ing,ion). Ideological. Subjectiv(e, ity,ism). Loaded dice. Label(ed,ing,s). Labell(ed,ing). Imbalanced. Expectancy effect(s). Ageism. Racism. Sexism. Speciesism. Disparit(y,ies). Preferential. Partial(ity). Predilection. Proclivit(y,ies). Susceptib(le,ility). Skew(ed,ness). Unequal. Inequality. Judgment error(s). Halo effect. Close-minded(ness). *Consider also:* one-sided(ness), intoleran(t,ce), favoritism, narrow-minded(ness), partiality, predispos(ed, ition), warp(ed). *See also* Age discrimination; Antisemitism; Attitudes toward handicapped; Attitudes toward homosexuality; Attitudes toward mental illness; Attitudes toward mental retardation; Attitudes toward physical handicaps; Attitudes toward physical illness; Attitudes toward the aged; Equitability; Ethnocentrism; Favoritism; Halo effect; Hate crimes; Implausibility; Injustice; Male chauvinism; Misinformation; Nativism; Nationalism; Racism; Researcher bias; Rigid personality; Sectarianism; Sex discrimination;

Sexism; Statistical bias; Stereotyping; Xenophobia.

Bias, experimenter. See *Researcher bias.*

Bias, gender. See *Sex discrimination; Sexual inequality; Sexism.*

Bias, race. See *Racial attitudes; Racism.*

Bias, research. See *Research design; Researcher bias; Researcher expectations; Researcher subject relations.*

Bias, researcher. See *Researcher bias.*

Bias, response. See *Response bias.*

Bias, sex. See *Sexism.*

Bias, social. See *Age discrimination; Attitudes toward handicapped; Attitudes toward homosexuality; Attitudes toward mental retardation; Attitudes toward mental illness; Attitudes toward physical handicaps; Attitudes toward physical illness; Attitudes toward the aged; Bias; Bigotry; Ethnocentrism; Male chauvinism; Misanthropy; Nationalism; Prejudice; Racism; Sex discrimination; Sexism; Social discrimination; Xenophobia.*

Bias, statistical. See *Statistical bias.*

Bias, test. See *Test bias.*

Biased sampling. Biased sampling. *Choose from:* bias(ed), selective, censored, nonrandom *with:* sampl(e,es,ed,ing), subject recruitment, subject selection. *See also* Biased selection; Experiment volunteers; Research subjects; Researcher bias; Sampling.

Biased selection. Biased selection. Selection bias(es). Adverse selection. Cherry picking. *Choose from:* bias(es, ed), unrepresentative, disproportionate(ly,ness), favorable, adverse, above average, below average, blended sector *with:* select(ed,ing,ion), case mix. *See also* Allocation; Biased sampling; Demographic characteristics (of individuals); Health maintenance organizations; Insurance pools; Juries; Managed care.

Bible. Bibl(e,ical,icism). Old Testament. New Testament. Gospel(s). Torah. Divine revelation. Hagiographa. Pentateuch. Bibliolatry. Epistles. Scriptur(es,al). Septuagint. Tanak(h). Tanach. Apocrypha. Deuterocanonical scripture. *See also* Apocalyptic literature; Christianity; Devils; Fall of man; God concepts; Jehovah; Jewish law; Jewish literature; Judaism; Millenarianism; Rabbinical literature; Religious beliefs; Religious literature.

Bible, law in the. See *Jewish law.*

Bibliographic citations. Bibliographic(al) citation(s). Bibliographic essay(s). Footnote(s). Cit(e,ed,ing) document(s). Bibliographic record(s). *See also* Attribution of news; Journal articles; Information dissemination.

Bibliographical exhibitions. Bibliographical exhibition(s). Book fair(s). Exhibit(ion) of books. Salon du Livre(s). Literature exhibit(s,ion,ions). Publishers' exhibit(s,ion,ions). Illustrator's Exhibit(s,ion,ions). *See also* Books; Exhibits; Trade shows.

Bibliography. Bibliograph(y,ies,ical). Booklist(s). Literature search(es). Biobibliograph(y,ies,ical). Bibliotheca(l). Publishers list(s). *Choose from:* titles, printed material(s), publications, bibliographic(al), books, holdings, published works, literature *with:* list(s,ing,ings), source(s), catalog(s,ue,ues). *Consider also:* webliograph(y,ies,ical). *See also* Book reviews; Books; Descriptive bibliography; Library catalogs; Literary criticism; Lost literature; National bibliography; Reference materials.

Bibliography, descriptive. See *Descriptive bibliography.*

Bibliography, national. See *National bibliography.*

Bibliomania. Bibliomania(c,cs). Book lover(s). Bibliotaph(e,es,s,ic). Bibliolatr(y,ous). Bibliolater(s). Bibliolatrist(s). *See also* Book collecting; Books; Collecting mania.

Bibliotherapy. Bibliotherap(y,ies,eutic). Bibliocounseling. *Choose from:* poetry, poem(s), literature, reading, book(s) *with:* therap(y,ies,eutic), psychotherap(y, ies,eutic). *See also* Books; Literature; Psychopoetry; Psychotherapy; Reading; Reading materials; Self help; Self help books.

Biculturalism. Bicultural(ism,ity). Cultural mix(ed,ing). Mestizaje. Cultural intersection(s). *Consider also:* biethnic(ity), biracial(ity), bilingual(ism), cultural assimilation, second generation, hyphenated American(s), ethnic group(s), ethnicity, biliteracy, Spanish speaking, Italian American(s), African American(s), French Canadian(s), Mexican American(s), multicultural, multiracial, multilingual, Hispanic American(s), Asian American(s), dual consciousness, irredent(a,ism,ist,ists). *See also* Assimilation (cultural); Acculturation; Bilingual education; Cross cultural competency; Culture contact; Cultural issues; Cultural maintenance; Diversity; Ethnic groups; Intercultural communication; Intercultural relations; Interethnic families; Intermarriage; Language maintenance; Marginality (sociological); Race awareness; Racial integration.

Bicycle helmets. Bicycle helmet(s). Bicycle safety helmet(s). Bike helmet(s). Safety hat(s). Racing helmet(s). *See also* Bicycle racing; Bicycle touring; Clothing; Protection.

Bicycle racing. Bicycle rac(e,es,ing). Cycling race(s). Tour de France. Tour DuPont. Tour de Suisse. Liege-Bastogne-Liege Classic. Bicycle competition(s). Cycling classic(s). Olympic cyclist(s). *See also* Bicycle helmets; Bicycle touring; Sports.

Bicycle touring. Bicycle tour(s,ing). Bike tour(s,ing). Cycle tour(s,ing). *Choose from:* bicycle(s), bicyclist(s), bike(s), cycling, pedaling *with:* tour(s,ing), trip(s), cross-country, destination(s), getaway(s), across the plains, ridc(s). *See also* Bicycle helmets; Bicycle racing; Sports.

Bicycling. Bicycl(e,es,ing,ist,ists). Cycl(ing,ist,ists). Two wheel(er,ers). Tricycl(e,es,ing,ist,ists). Unicycl(e,es, ing,ist,ists). Biking. Bike(s). *Consider also:* bikepath(s), bikeway(s), names of races such as Tour de France, Tour de Trump. *See also* Sports.

Bidialectalism. Bidialectal(ism,ist,ists,s). Second dialect(s). Bidialectial(ism, ist,ists,s). Two dialects. *See also* Biculturalism; Bilingual education; Bilingualism; Dialects; Diglossia; Language; Language maintenance; Language shift; Non-standard English; Sociolinguistics.

Big band. Big band(s). Stage band(s). Large jazz band(s). Large music ensemble(s). *See also* Jazz; Popular music.

Big bang theory. Big bang theory. Big bang. *Consider also:* origin(s) of the universe, formation of the universe, origin(s) of matter, supernova, expanding universe. *See also* Astronomy; Physics.

Big business. Big business(es). Large corporation(s). Forbes 500. Fortune 500. Large firm(s). Largest bank(s). Biggest telecommunications company. Big firm(s). Corporate giant(s). *Consider also:* global economy, corporate concentration, large scale industr(y,ies, ial), billion-dollar industr(y,ies). *See also* Conglomerates; Corporations; Industrial concentration; Mergers; Multinational corporations; Oligopolies; Organization size.

Big churches. Big(gest) church(es). Megachurch(es). Mega church(es). Super church(es). Large(r) church(es). Cathedral(s). *Consider also:* growing churches, large congregation(s), church growth, cathedral(s). *See also* Churches; Organization size.

Bigamy. See *Polygamy.*

Bigotry. Bigot(s,ed,ry). Narrow-minded(ness). Prejudic(e,ed,ial). Intoleran(ce,t). Lack of tolerance. Discriminat(e,ed,ing,ion). Racial(ly) bias(ed). Anti-semit(e,es,ic,ism). Antisemit(e,es,ic,ism). Racis(m,t,ts). Sexis(m,t,ts). Ageis(m,t,ts).

Stereotyp(e,es,ed,ing). Bias(es,ed,ing). Handicapis(m,t,ts). Stigmatiz(e,ed,ing, ation). Inequality. Ethnic attitude(s). Negative attitude(s) toward minorit(y, ies). Ingroup(s). Outgroup(s). Chauvinis(t,ts,tic,m). Ethnocentric(ism). Jingo(ism). Xenophob(ia,ic). *Consider also:* doctrinaire, dogmatis(m,t), narrow-minded(ness), provincial(ism). *See also* Age discrimination; Anti-Catholicism; Antisemitism; Attitudes toward handicapped; Attitudes toward homosexuality; Attitudes toward mental illness; Attitudes toward mental retardation; Attitudes toward physical handicaps; Attitudes toward the aged; Bias; Ethnocentrism; Exclusivity (Religion); Hate crimes; Nativism; Prejudice; Racism; Religious prejudice; Sex discrimination; Sexism; Social discrimination.

Bildungsroman. Bildungsroman(e,s). Kuenstlerroman(e,s). Erziehungs-sroman(e,s). Entwicklungsroman(e,s). *Consider also:* novel(s) *with:* education, awakening, coming-of-age, upbringing, youthful development. *See also* Fiction; Literature; Novels.

Bilingual education. Bilingual education. *Choose from:* bilingual, second language(s), biliterate, two languages, multilingual *with:* education, instruction(al), classroom(s), school(s), learn(ed,ing), curriculum, program(s). *See also* Bilingualism; Language maintenance; Language shift; Language transfer (language learning); Second language education.

Bilingualism. Bilingual(ism,s,ist,ists). *Consider also:* Spanglish, plurilingual(s, ism,ist,ists), trilingual(s,ism,ist,ists), multilingual(s,ism,ist,ists), biliterate, second language(s). *See also* Bidialectalism; Bilingual education; Code switching; Cultural cooperation; Language transfer (language learning); Languages in contact; Linguistic interference; Multicultural education; Native language; Second languages; Translating and translations.

Bill of Rights. Bill of Rights. Constitutional right(s). Civil right(s). Civil libert(y,ies). Freedom of speech. Freedom of the press. Freedom of religion. Freedom of assembly. Right to bear arms. Freedom from unreasonable search and seizure. Freedom from double jeopardy. Privilege against self-incrimination. Right to speedy and public trial. Right to trial by jury. Right to due process. Freedom from excessive bail or cruel and unusual punishment. Writ of habeas corpus. Suffrage. States rights. *See also* Church state relationship; Civil rights; Free thought; Freedom of information; Freedom of religion; Freedom of speech; Freedom of the press; Liberty; Right of assembly; Right of privacy; Separation of powers; Self incrimination.

Billboards. See *Outdoor advertising.*

Billiard parlors. Billiard parlor(s). Pool hall(s). Billiard saloon(s). Eightball game(s). *Consider also:* snooker. *See also* Betting; Casinos; Clubs; Recreation; Recreational facilities.

Billing systems. Billing system(s). *Choose from:* bill(s,ed,ing), invoice(s), account statement(s), list(s) of charges, list(s) of expenditures *with:* system(s), software, package(s), clearinghouse(s), service(s). *Consider also:* collection methods, collection agenc(y,ies). *See also* Accounting; Accounting systems; Accounts payable and receivable; Financial statements; Fees.

Bimetallism. Bimetall(ic,ist,istic,ism). *Choose from:* legal tender, currency, coin(ed,age), monetary, standard, rate of exchange *with:* gold and silver. *Consider also:* demonetisation of silver, Gold Standard Act, Bland Allison Act, Gresham's Law. *See also* Currency; Gold standard; Monetary policy.

Binding theory and government (Linguistics). See *Government binding theory (Linguistics).*

Binge drinking. See *Dipsomania.*

Binge purge syndrome. See *Bulimia.*

Binomial distribution. Binomial distribution(s). *Choose from:* binomial *with:* distribution(s), population(s), model(s). *See also* Statistical data; Statistical norms.

Biochemical markers. Biochemical marker(s). Biologic(al) marker(s). Biomarker(s). Molecular marker(s). Molecular epidemiologic stud(y,ies). *Consider also:* prognostic indices. *See also* Health indices; Health status indicators; Indicators (biology); Screening.

Biodiversity. See *Biological diversity.*

Bioethics. Bioethic(s,al,ist,ists). *Consider also:* ethic(s,al), social(ly) responsib(le,ility), philosoph(y,ical), moral(ity,ly,s) *with:* biolog(y,ical), life science(s), ecolog(y,ical), genetic(s), DNA, eugenic(s), biopolitic(al,s), biocultural(ly), biosocial(ly), biopsychosocial(ly). *See also* Assisted suicide; Bioregionalism; Cloning; Environmentalism; Eugenics; Euthanasia; Gene mapping; Genetic engineering; Genetic research; Medical ethics; Medical philosophy; Morality; Pharmacogenomics; Research ethics; Single nucleotide polymorphisms; Social ethics; War crimes.

Biofeedback. Biofeedback. *Consider also:* psychophysiologic, alpha, EEG, heart rate, EMG, autogenic, GSR, galvanic skin, exteroceptive, body temperature, sensory *with:* feedback. *See also* Feedback; Reinforcement; Relaxation training; Self help; Stimuli; Psycho-physiology.

Biofeedback training. Biofeedback training. *Choose from:* biofeedback *with:* train(ed,ing), regulat(ed,ing,ion), reinforc(e,ed,ement), instruct(ed,ing, ion,ions). *See also* Autogenic therapy; Behavior modification; Biofeedback; Relaxation training.

Biogas. See *Alternative energy.*

Biogeography. Biogeograph(y,ical). Phylogeograph(y,ical). Endem(ic,ism). *Choose from:* population(s) demography, species, speciation *with:* ecolog(y, ical), distribution, geographic range, macrogeograph(y,ic), endemic, diffusion, dispersal, gene flow. *See also* Bioinvasion; Biological diversity; Ecology; Habitat; Natural envirnoment; Phytogeography.

Biographers. Biographer(s). Biography author(s). Chronicler(s). Autobiograph(er,ers,ist). Memoirist(s). Writer of biograph(y,ies). *See also* Authors; Biography; Writers.

Biographical data. Biographical data. Biodata. Life histor(y,ies). Personal histor(y,ies). Biograph(y,ies,ical). Autobiograph(y,ies,ical). *Choose from:* personal, psychosocial, individual(s) *with:* background(s), life, lives, family histor(y,ies), experience(s), histor(y,ies), characteristic(s), variable(s), correlate(s), ethnic background(s), educational background(s), parent(s,al) background(s), socioeconomic background(s). *Consider also:* biobibliograph(y,ies,ical), accomplishment(s), attainment(s), credential(s), training, upbringing, work history. *See also* Autobiography; Demographic characteristics (of individuals); Experience (background); Life experiences; Life history; Police records.

Biographical dictionaries. Biographical dictionar(y,ies). *Choose from:* biograph(y,ies,ical) *with:* dictionar(y,ies), index(es). *See also* Biography.

Biography. Biograph(y,ies,ical). Life stor(y,ies). Hagiograph(y,ies). Autobiograph(y,ies,ical). Memoir(s). Recollection(s). Psychobiograph(y,ies, ical). Biographee(s). Obituar(y,ies). Diar(y,ies). Personal account(s). Personal correspondence. Confession(s). *Consider also:* letters, personal journal(s), reminiscence(s), portrait(s), psychohistor(y,ies,ical), remembrance(s), eulog(y,ies,ize,ized), in memorium, collective portrait(s), life and times. *See also* Autobiography; Biographers; Biographical data; Biographical dictionaries; Hagiography; Historical biography; Historical

research; Nonfiction novel; Psychohistory.

Biography, historical. See *Historical biography.*

Biohazards, containment of. See *Containment of biohazards.*

Bioinvasion. Bioinvasion(s). Biopollut(ed,ing,ion). Biological invasion(s). *Choose from:* introduc(e,ed, es,ing,tion,tions), invasion(s) invasiveness, invader(s) *with:* exotic animal(s), exotic species, exotic plant(s), exotics. *Consider also:* ecological explosion(s), nonindigenous plant(s), nonindigenous animal(s), alien plant(s), alien animal(s), kudzu, zebra mussel(s), Mediterranean fruit fly, etc. *See also* Animal environments; Biogeography; Biological diversity; Environmental degradation; Exotic species; Food chain; Habitat; Imports; Plant introduction; World problems.

Biological clocks. Biological clock(s). Reproductive clock(s). Internal clock(s). Molecular clock(s). Cyanobacteria clock(s). Internal timekeeper(s). *See also* Biological rhythms; Childbearing age; Maternal age; Late childbearing; Senior pregnancies.

Biological determinism. See *Biological factors.*

Biological diversity. Biological(ly) divers(e,ity). Biodiversity. Ecosystem diversity. Species richness. Species diversity. Variety of life forms. Agrobiodivers(e,ity). Gene flow between populations. *Choose from:* divers(e,ity, ification), distribution(s), diffusion, richness, diverge(d,nce,nt), different(ed,ing,iation), heterogene(ity, ous,ousness), variation(s), variability, gene flow *with:* population(s), phylogenetic, genetic(s), species, birds, animal(s), plant(s). *Consider also:* ecological balance, evolution of biotas, pool(s) of genetic resources. *See also* Biogeography; Bioinvasion; Darwinism; Food chain; Habitat; Natural environment; Old growth forests; Phytogeography; Sustainable development; Variations.

Biological drives. Biological drive(s). *Choose from:* physiological, innate, natural, unlearned *with:* drive(s), arousal. *Consider also:* hunger, thirst, sleep. *See also* Instinct; Sex drive.

Biological factors. Biological factor(s). *Choose from:* biolog(y,ical), biobehavioral, biopsychological, biosocial, sociobiological, genetic(s), heredit(y,ary), neurobiologic, biogenic, Darwinian, natural selection *with:* approach(es), aspect(s), bas(is,es), background(s), cause(s), condition(s), constraint(s), characteristic(s), change(s), correlate(s), context(s),

component(s), consideration(s), determinant(s), determinism, determin(ed,ing,ation,ations), difference(s), dimension(s), dynamic(s), effect(s), element(s), explanation(s), factor(s), influence(s), implication(s), indicator(s), impact(s), limit(s), mechanism(s), obstacle(s), pattern(s), precondition(s), predisposition(s), process(es), similarit(y,ies), setting(s), substrate(s), variation(s), variable(s). *Consider also:* biosocial determinism. *See also* Behavioral genetics; Factors; Mind body problem; Organic mental disorders; Organic psychoses; Psychobiology; Physiological psychology; Sex factors.

Biological family. Biological famil(y,ies). *Choose from:* biological, natural, real *with:* famil(y,ies), parent(s), mother(s), father(s). *Consider also:* birth parent(s), birth mother(s), birth father(s). *See also* Family members; Kinship; Nuclear family.

Biological illustration. Biological illustration. *Choose from:* biolog(y,ical), zoolog(y,ical), botan(y,ical), medical, flower(s), butterfl(y,ies), insect(s), animal(s), bird(s), plant(s), ecolog(y, ical) *with:* illustrat(ed,ing,ion), render(ed,ing), pictorial representation, engraving(s), painting(s), art, drawing(s). *See also* Animal painting and illustration; Arts; Drawing; Genres (art); Graphics; Illustrated books; Medical illustration.

Biological invasion. See *Bioinvasion.*

Biological models. Biological model(s). *Choose from:* biolog(y,ical), ecolog(y,ical), Darwinian, botan(y,ical), zoolog(y,ical), ecosystem(s), species, morpholog(y,ical), human tissue *with:* model(s), analogous system(s), fabricat(ed,ing,ion), replica(s,te,ted, tion,tions), representation(s). *See also* Anatomic models; Medical models; Models; Scientific models; Simulation.

Biological rhythms. Biological rhythm(s). Biorhythm(s). Internal temporal program(s). *Choose from:* biologic(al), circadian, infradian, ultradian, diurnal, endogenous, life, internal *with:* rhythm(s,icity), clock(s), cycl(e,es,ic, icity), period(s,ic,icity,icities). *Choose from:* sleep(ing), wak(e,ing), feed(ing), meal, eating, estrous, estral, estrus, oestrus, menstrual, breeding, energy, elimination, sexual desire *with:* cycl(e,es,ic,icity), period(s,ic,icity, icities), pattern(s). *Consider also:* seasonal variation(s), chronobiology, cell cycle(s). jet lag(s), photoperiod(s,ism), sexual cycle(s). *See also* Biological clocks; Jet lag; Lunar cycle; Menstrual cycle; Rhythm; Seasonal affective disorder; Seasonal variations; Seasons; Sleep wake cycle.

Biological warfare. Biological warfare. Biological weapon(s). Germ warfare. *Choose from:* war(fare), warhead(s), weapon(s), bomb(s), shell(s), artillery, arsenal(s) *with:* bacteriological, biochemical, biological, defoliant(s), herbicid(al,es), bacterial, viral, disease(s), germ(s), plague, anthrax, botulism, tularemia, hallucinogen(s,ic), toxin(s). *Consider also:* Marburg virus, Geneva Protocol (1925), Biological Weapons Convention (1972). *See also* Chemical warfare; Epidemics; International offenses; War; Weapons of mass destruction.

Biologists. Biologist(s). Botanist(s). Zoologist(s). Naturalist(s). Conservationist(s). Biology teacher(s). Geneticist(s). Ornithologist(s). Bacteriologist(s). Physiologist(s). Embryologist(s). Biochemist(s). Paleontologist(s). Biophysicist(s). *See also* Naturalists; Research personnel; Scientists.

Biology, experimental. See *Experimental biology.*

Biomass conversion. See *Alternative energy; Energy generating resources.*

Biomass energy. See *Alternative energy.*

Biomedical wastes. See *Medical wastes.*

Biomolecules. Biomolecul(e,es,ar). Macromolecul(e,es,ar). Organic molecule(s). Biological molecule(s). *See also* Blood proteins; Immunity.

Bionics. Bionic(s). Biomedical engineer(ed,ing). Bioengineer(ed,ing). Biomechanic(s,al). Biocybernetic(s,al). *See also* Biotechnology; Man machine systems; Robotics.

Biopiracy. Biopira(cy,te,tes). *Consider also:* bioprospect(ing). *See also* Ecological imperialism; Ethnobotany; Traditional medicine.

Bioregionalism. Bioregionalis(m,t,ts). Ecological integrit(y,ies). Liv(e,ing) in harmony with earth. Self-sufficient communit(y,ies). Sustainability. *Consider also:* local food(s), unity of catchment, protect(ed,ing,ion) ecosystem(s). *See also* Bioethics; Ecology; Environmentalism; Organic farming; Sustainable development.

Bioremediation. See *Decontamination; Rejuvenation; Restoration ecology.*

Biosocial. Biosocial(ly). Interaction of social and biological. Biolog(y,ical) *with:* social behavior. Ecological determinant(s). Evolution(ary) with social behavior(s). Genetic basis of behavior(s). Biopsychosocial. Biocultural. Biopolitical. Nature nurture date. *Choose from:* biolog(y,ical) *with:* social, psycholog(y,ical), personality. *Consider also:* sociobiolog(ic,ical, ically,y). *See also* Sociobiology;

Biological factors; Environmental determinism.

Biosphere. Biospher(e,ic). Earth's ecosystem. Global conservation. Nature on a planetary level. Gaia(n). Spaceship earth. *Consider also:* Biosphere 2, ecological system simulator(s), enclosed ecological laborator(y,ies), mini-planet, mini-Earth. *See also* Atmosphere; Conservation of natural resources; Earth; Environment; Environmental protection.

Biotechnology. Biotechnolog(y,ical,ies). Biotech. Bionic(s). Biological electronic(s). Biocybernetic(s,ally). Bioengineering. Biomedical engineering. Recombinant DNA technolog(y,ies). Biosensor(s). Biocomputer(s). Industrial microbiology. Bioreactor(s). Bioprocess(ing,or,ors). Biorevolution(ary,s). *Choose from:* genetic(s,ally) *with:* engineer(ed,ing), alter(ed,ation,ations), modif(ied,ication,ications). *Consider also:* abzyme(s), ergonomic(s), human factors engineering, test tube bab(y,ies), artificial heart(s), in vitro fertilization. *See also* Agricultural engineering; Bionics; Organ transplantation; Genetic engineering; Plant genetics; Reproductive technologies; Xenotransplantation.

Bipolar disorder. Bipolar disorder(s). Manic depress(ion,ive,ives). Bipolar depression(s). Bipolar affective psychos(is,es). Alternating psychos(is,es). *Consider also:* cyclothym(ia,ic,osis). *See also* Affective disorders; Major depression; Mania.

Bipolarity, international. See *Balance of power.*

Biraciality. See *Racially mixed.*

Bird sanctuaries. See *Wildlife sanctuaries.*

Birds. Bird(s). Aves. Avia(n,ry,ries). Ornitholog(y,ical,ically,ist,ists). Chick(s,en,ens). Duck(s,ling,s). Nestling(s). Eaglet(s). Poultry. Fowl(s). *Consider also:* cuckoo(s), hawk(s), ostrich(es), robin(s), eagle(s), sandpiper(s), etc. *See also* Birdsongs; Birds of prey; Gardening to attract wildlife; Poultry; Preening; Sanctuary gardens; Wildlife Conservation; Wildlife sanctuaries.

Birds, game and game. See *Game and game birds.*

Birds of prey. Bird(s) of prey. Predatory bird(s). Harrier(s). Raptor(s). Eagle(s). Hawk(s). Owl(s). Kestrel(s). Falcon(s, ry). Osprey(s). *See also* Animal aggressive behavior; Birds; Predatory animals.

Birdsongs. Birdsong(s). Bird song(s). *Choose from:* bird(s), songbird(s), aves, sparrow(s), flycatcher(s), finch(es), dove(s), etc. *with:* song(s), sing(s,ing), sang, call(s), syrin(x,xes,ges),

vocalization(s), vocal character(s), loudsong, mimicry. *See also* Animal communication; Animal vocalization; Birds; Nature sounds.

Birth. Birth(ing). Born. Childbirth. Childbearing. Delivery. Parturition. Confinement. Childbed. Accouchement. Giving birth. Whelp(ed,ing). Foaling. Lambing. *See also* Beginning; Date of birth; Infants; Labor (childbirth); Life (biological); Life change events; Life cycle; Midwifery; Natural childbirth; Newborn animals; Newborn infants; Pregnancy; Premature infants; Sex education.

Birth, date of. See *Date of birth.*

Birth, home. See *Home birth.*

Birth, premature. See *Premature infants.*

Birth adjustment. Birth adjustment. *Consider also:* birth experience. *See also* Birth injuries; Birth trauma; Breast feeding.

Birth attendants. See *Midwifery.*

Birth certificates. Birth certificate(s). *Choose from:* birth(s) *with:* certificate(s), registration(s), register(ed,ing), report(ed,ing), record(s). *See also* Death certificates; Documents; Records.

Birth control. Birth control. Contracept(ion,ive,ives). Family planning. *Choose from:* plan(ned,ning), control(ling,led), spacing *with:* parenthood, fertility, population, birth(s), conception, pregnanc(y,ies). *Consider also:* vasectom(y,ies), intrauterine device(s), IUD(s), condom(s), diaphragm(s), spermatocid(e,es,al), tubal ligation, rhythm method, coitus interruptus, antispermatogenic agent(s), steriliz(e,ed,ing,ation). *See also* Abortion; Birth; Contraception; Emergency contraception; Fertility; Population policy; Reproductive rights; Rhythm method; Sex education; Sex information; Sexual abstinence; Sexual ethics; Sterilization (sex).

Birth customs. See *Birth rites.*

Birth defects. See *Congenitally handicapped; Drug induced abnormalities; Physical abnormalities.*

Birth fathers. See *Biological family.*

Birth injuries. Birth injur(y,ies). *Choose from:* birth, perinatal, neonatal, obstetric *with:* injur(y,ies,ed), insult(s), damage(d). *See also* Birth adjustment; Birth trauma; Newborn infants; Severely handicapped infants.

Birth intervals. Birth interval(s). *Choose from:* birth(s), childbirth(s), pregnanc(y,ies) *with:* interval(s), spac(ed,ing), timing. *See also* Birth order; Family planning.

Birth mothers. See *Biological family.*

Birth order. Birth order. Sibling position(s). Ordinal position in family. First born(s). Firstborn(s). Firstling(s). Second born(s). Last born(s). *Choose from:* middle, young(er,est), old(er,est) *with:* child(ren), heir(s), son(s), daughter(s), offspring. *Consider also:* primogeniture, fifth son, third daughter, etc. *See also* Birth intervals; Sibling relations; Siblings.

Birth parents. See *Biological family.*

Birth rate. See *Birthrate.*

Birth rites. Birth rite(s). Traditional birth practice(s). *Choose from:* birth(ing), childbirth, motherhood, pregnancy, breastfeeding, *with:* rite(s), ritual(s), ceremon(y,ies), custom(s), tradition(s, al), practice(s). *Consider also:* christening(s), baptism(s), circumcision(s). *See also* Baptism; Churching of women; Circumcision; Religious rituals.

Birth spacing. See *Birth intervals.*

Birth timing, first. See *First birth timing.*

Birth trauma. Birth trauma. *Choose from:* birth, perinatal, neonatal, gestational, prenatal *with:* trauma(s,atic), stress(es,or, ors), distress(es,ed), adversity, insult(s). *See also* Birth injuries; Birth injuries; Birth adjustment; Early experiences; Early memories; Newborn infants.

Birth weight. Birth weight. Birthweight. *Choose from:* weigh(ed,t,ing), size *with:* birth, born, neonat(e,es,al). *Consider also:* small for gestational age. *See also* Body weight; Infant small for gestational age; Newborn infants; Premature infants.

Birth weight, low. See *Infant small for gestational age; Premature infants.*

Birthing. See *Birth.*

Birthing centers. Birthing center(s). Birthing room(s). Alternate birth site(s). *Consider also:* nonhospital, at-home *with:* birth(s), deliver(y,ies), childbirth(s). *See also* Delivery rooms.

Birthrate. Birthrate(s). Birth rate(s). Natality. Replacement rate(s). *Choose from:* birth(s), fertility, replacement, conception, pregnancy *with:* rate(s), differential(s), ratio(s), expectation(s), trend(s), data, projection(s), pattern(s), incidence. *See also* Birth; Contraception; Family planning; Family size; Fertility; Fertility decline; Health transition; Mortality rates; Overpopulation; Population growth; Population policy; Pregnancy rate.

Births, multiple. See *Multiple births.*

Bisexuality. Bisexual(ity). Ambisexual(ity). *Consider also:* intersex, androgyn(ous, y), amphigenous inversion. *See also* Accidental homosexuality; Androgyny; Homosexuality; Lesbianism; Male

homosexuality; Sex behavior; Sexual preferences; Transsexualism.

Bishops. See *Clergy.*

Bison. Bison(tine). Buffalo(es). Wisent(s). Auroch(s). *See also* Animals; Cattle.

Bites and stings. Bite(s). Bitten. Biting. Sting(s,ing). Stung. Snakebite(s). Dogbite(s). Spiderbite(s). Arachnidism. *Consider also:* nip(ped,ping), envenomizat(e,ed,ing,ion), snakebite(s). *See also* Arachnidism; Insect bites and stings.

Bites and stings, insect. See *Insect bites and stings.*

Biting, nail. See *Nail biting.*

Black Carib literature. Black Carib literature. Black Carib poetry. *Choose from:* Black Carib(s,bean), Karib, Garifuna, negro(s) caribe(s), Hondura(s,n), Afro Carib *with:* litera- ture, poetry, poem(s), writing(s), fiction, novel(s), myth(s,ology). *See also* Caribbean; Folk literature; Literature.

Black community. Black communit(y,ies). *Choose from:* Black(s), Afro- American(s), Afroamerican(s), African- American(s), African American(s), Afro- European(s), African European(s), Negro(es) *with:* communit(y,ies), municipalit(y,ies), neighborhood(s), village(s), town(s), social group(s), parish(es), district(s), suburb(s), housing project(s), fellowship(s), brotherhood(s), solidarity, congregation(s), settlement(s), compan(ies,y), area(s), ties, civic pride, pride, sense of belonging, belongingness. *See also* Black family; Black power; Blacks; Community (social); Ethnic groups; Ethnic neighbor- hoods; Group identity; Social settle- ments.

Black economy. Black econom(y,ies). Informal sector. Black market(s). Gray market(s). *Choose from:* black, illegal, unobserved, second(ary), informal, shadow, submerged, unofficial, under- ground, subterranean, hidden, invisible, twilight *with:* econom(y,ies). *Consider also:* hidden, clandestine, unreported, unrecorded, unregistered *with:* employ- ment, income, wages. *Consider also:* bootleg(ging,ger,gers), tax evasion, secret financing, money laundering. *See also* Bartering; Crime; Gray market; Informal sector; Smuggling; Tax evasion.

Black English. See *Ebonics.*

Black family. Black famil(y,ies). *Choose from:* Black(s), Negro(es), Afro- American(s), Afroamerican(s), African- American(s), African American(s), Afro- European, African European(s) *with:* famil(y,ies,ial), couple(s), parent(s), household(s), kin(ship), sibling(s), intrafamilial, maternal, paternal,

matriarch(y,ies,al), patriarch(y,ies,ial), consanguin(e,ity). *See also* Black community; Blacks; Extended family; Kinship; Womanism.

Black lung disease. Black lung disease. Anthracosis. *See also* Coal miners; Hazardous occupations; Miners; Occupational safety.

Black market. See *Black economy; Gray market; Informal sector.*

Black music. See *Afro-American music.*

Black Muslims. Black Muslim(s). Nation of Islam. *Consider also:* Wali Farad, Elijah Muhammed, Malcolm X, Muhammed Ali. *See also* Black nationalism; Black power; Blacks; Islam.

Black nationalism. Black nationalism. Nation of Islam. Black nationalist movement. *Consider also:* Afro- centric(ism), Black Separat(ism,ion), Louis Farrakhan, Marcus Garvey. *See also* Afrocentrism; Black power; Black Muslims; Nationalism; Tribalism.

Black power. Black power. *Choose from:* Black(s), Afro-American(s), Afroamerican(s), African American(s), African-American(s), Afro-European(s), African European(s) *with:* power, nationalism, militan(t,cy), political activis(m,t,ts), pride, liberation, Black Panther(s). *Consider also:* civil rights movement. *See also* Black Muslims; Black nationalism; Blacks; Civil rights organizations; Ethnic identity; National- ism; Race relations; Racial identity; Pan- Africanism; Political movements; Political power; Social movements.

Black theology. Black theolog(y,ies,ical, ian,ians). *Choose from:* Black, African, Africanadian, Afro-American, African American, AME *with:* eschatolog(y,ies, ical), theolog(y,ies,ical,ian,ians), truth(s), doctrine(s), dogma(s), Chris- tianity. *Consider also:* liberation theology. *See also* Black community; Black power; Blacks; Liberation theology; Religious beliefs; Theology.

Black White relations. See *Race relations.*

Blacklisting. Blacklist(ed,ing). Censor(ed,ing,s,ship). Ban(ned,ning). Proscrib(e,ed,ing). Proscription. Prohibit(ed,ing,ion,ions). Forbid(den). Book burning(s). Suppress(ed,ing,ion). Doctrinal disapproval. Papal index. Index librorum prohibitorum. HUAC. House of Representatives Committee on UnAmerican Activities. McCarthyism. Exclusion(ary). *Consider also:* blackball(ed,ing), boycott(ed,ing). *See also* Academic freedom; Ban; Boycotts; Censorship; Disapproval; Forbidden; Political persecution; Political repres- sion; Prohibition.

Blackouts. See *Unconsciousness.*

Blacks. Black(s). African(s,a). Negroid. Negro(es). Africanadian(s). Afro American(s). Afroamerican(s). African American(s). Aframerican(s). Black American(s). Afro European(s). African European(s). Afro Asiatic(s). Afro Asian(s). Afrasian(s). Afro Cuban(s). Haitian(s). Negritude. Adamanese. African Bushmen. Half Hamite(s). Hottentot(s). Melanesian(s). Negrillo(s). Negrito(s). Papuan(s). Pygm(y,ies). Semang(s). *Consider also names of African tribes or citizens of African countries. See also* African cultural groups; Apartheid; Black community; Black family; Black Muslims; Black power; Black theology; Ebonics; Minority businesses; Minority groups; North Africa; People of color; Race relations; Races; Racial integration; Racial segregation; Racially mixed; Slavery; Sub-Saharan Africa; Womanism.

Blacksmithing. Blacksmith(s,ing). Farrier(s). Ironsmith(s). Iron forg(e,ing). Horseshoe(ing,er,ers). *See also* Agricultural workers; Artisans.

Blame. Blame(d,s). Blaming. Condemn(ed,ing,ation). Disapprov(e,ed, ing,al). Find(ing) fault(s). Rebuk(e,ed, ing). Critic(ism,ize,ized,izing). Censur(e, ed,ing). Recriminat(e,ive,ory,ion,ions). *Consider also:* culpab(le,ility,ilities), complain(ed,ing,t,ts), denounc(e,ed,ing), denunciat(e,ed,ing,ion), incriminat(e,ed, ing,ion), indictment(s), accus(e,ed, ation,ations), admonish(ed,ing, ment,ments). *See also* Allegations; Blameworthy; Censure; Denunciation; Derogation; Disapproval; Guilt; Indictments; Neutralization; Scapegoating; Self accusation.

Blame, self. See *Self accusation.*

Blameworthy. Blameworth(y,iness). Blamab(le,ly). Culpab(le,leness,ility,ly). Censurab(le,ility). Guilt(y,iness). Reprehensib(le,ility). *Consider also:* deserv(e,ed,ing) punishment, deserv(e, ed,ing) reproach, malfeasance, impeachable, indictable, demeritorious, sinful, unholy, uncommendable, unpraiseworthy, delinquent, fault(y,iness,ful), punishab(le,ility), foolish(ly,ness), irresponsib(le,ly,ility), reckless(ly,ness). *See also* Blame; Conviction; Guilt; Indictments; Liability.

Blanche, carte. See *Carte blanche.*

Blasphemy. Blasphem(e,er,y,ous). Profan(e,ity,ness). Curs(e,es,ed,ing). Swear(s,ing). Execrat(e,ed,ing,ion). Damn(ed,ing,s). *See also* Heresy; Obscenity; Offenses against religion; Cursing; Sacrilege; Vulgarity.

Blemishes. See *Imperfection.*

Blended families. See *Remarriage; Stepfamily.*

Blessing. Bless(ed,ing,ings). Prayer(s). Grace. Baptism. Baptiz(e,ed,ing). Beatif(y,ied,ication). Benedict(e,ion). Consecrat(e,ed,ion). Dedicat(e,ed,ion). Make holy. Invocation. Benison. Godspeed. Valediction. Godsend. *See also* Invocation; Prayer; Religious rituals; Worship.

Blindness. Blind(ness). Amblyopia. Amauro(sis,tic). *Choose from:* partial(ly), impair(ed,ment), handicap(ped,s), disabilit(y,ies), disabled, limited, loss, lost, losing *with:* vision, visual(ly), sight(ed). *Consider also:* vision disorder(s). *See also* Vision disorders.

Blindness, color. See *Color blindness.*

Blindness, word. See *Alexia.*

Bloc, African. See *Pan-Africanism.*

Block, writer's. See *Blocking.*

Block books. Block book(s). Blockbook(s). Blockbuch(er). *Consider also:* incunabula , early illustrated book(s), woodcut(s), book(s) of the middle ages. *See also* Block printing; Books; Incunabula.

Block printing. Block print(s,ing). Print(ing) blocks(s). Linoleum print(s,ing). Wood engraving(s). Linoleum cut(s). Linocut(s). Woodcut(s). Relief print(s). *See also* Block books; Book ornamentation; Illustrated books.

Blockade. Blockade(s). Barricade(s). Encircl(e,ed,ing,ement). Obstruct(ed, ing,ion). Obstacle(s). *See also* Barriers; Deadlock; Hindrances; Picketing; Trade protection.

Blockbusting. See *Residential segregation.*

Blocking. Block(ed,ing). Thought deprivation. Thought obstruction. Emotional block(s). Writer's block. *Choose from:* writ(ing,er,ers) *with:* block(ed,s,ing), anxiet(y,ies), inhibit(ed,ing,ion,ions). *See also* Inhibition (psychology).

Blood banks. Blood bank(s). Bloodbank(s). *Consider also:* blood donor(s), blood collection program(s). *See also* Blood donors; Health facilities; Tissue banks.

Blood donors. Blood donor(s). *Consider also:* blood, plasma, primary, universal, platelet *with:* donor(s), donat(e,ed,ing, ion,ions). *See also* Anatomical gifts; Blood banks; Blood proteins; Living donors; Tissue donors.

Blood pressure. Blood pressure. Hypotension. Diastolic pressure. Systolic pressure. *See also* Essential hypertension; High blood pressure; Hypertension.

Blood pressure, high. See *High blood pressure.*

Blood proteins. Blood protein(s). Plasma protein(s). Plasma lipoprotein(s). Alpha fetoprotein(s) . Blood coagulation factor(s). Blood lipoprotein(s). Complement (immunology). Fibronectin(s). Hemoglobin. Immunoglobulin(s). Myoglobin Serum albumin. Taraxein. Thrombin. Transferrin. *See also* Biomolecules; Blood donors.

Blood stains. Blood stain(s). Bloodstain(s). *Consider also:* blood(y) *with:* trace(s), dried, spot(s), shed. *See also* Forensic medicine.

Blooded, cold. See *Cold blooded.*

Blooded, warm. See *Warm blooded.*

Blouses. Blouse(s). Bodice(s). Midd(y,ies). Pullover(s). Shirt(s). T-shirt(s). *See also* Clothing.

Blowing, whistle. See *Whistle blowing.*

Blue collar workers. Blue collar worker(s). Industrial worker(s). Assembly line worker(s). Hardhat(s). Factory worker(s). Manual labor(er,ers). Manual worker(s). Laborer(s). Miner(s). Auto repair(man,men,woman,women). Shift worker(s). Mechanic(s). Railroad worker(s). Machine worker(s). Skilled worker(s). Semi-skilled worker(s). Construction worker(s). Hired help. Laboring class(es). Truck driver(s). Machinist(s). Carpenter(s). Mason(s). Plumber(s). Electrician(s). Journey(men, man,woman,women). Journey worker(s). Roofer(s). Skilled labor. Unskilled worker(s). Working class(es). Animal caretaker(s). Boat operator(s). Grounds keeper(s). Repair(man,men,woman, women). Repairer(s). Stevedore(s). Longshore(men,man,women,woman). Dock worker(s). Craft worker(s). Floor layer(s). Glazier(s). Locomotive engineer(s). Machinist(s). Sign painter(s). Telephone lines(men,man, woman,women). Industrial fore(men, man). *See also* Agricultural workers; Automobile industry workers; Boatmen; Construction workers; Domestic service; Fishermen; Fishery workers; Garbage collectors; Hazardous occupations; Industrial foremen; Industrial personnel; Industrial workers; Iron and steel workers; Labor unions; Longshoremen; Miners; Sailors; Skilled workers; Unskilled workers; White collar workers; Working class.

Bluegrass music. Bluegrass music(ician, icians). Hillbilly music(ician,icians). *Choose from:* old time(y), bluegrass, early country, old southern, western, Kentucky, folk guitar *with:* music, song(s), sing(ing). *Consider also:* Grand Ole Opry, Bill Monroe, Earl Scruggs, Lester Flatt, etc. *See also* Country and western music; Folk culture; Music; Popular culture.

Blueprints. See *Architectural drawing.*

Blues (music). Blues. Blue rhythm(s). Soul music. *Choose from:* blues *with:* music(al,ian,ians), rhythm(s), lyric(s,al), sing(s,ing), song(s), downhome, country, classic, ragtime, Chicago. *Consider also:* jazz , Afro-American music, spiritual(s), boogie woogie. *See also* Afro-American music; Jazz; Music; Popular culture.

Blues, rhythm and. See *Rhythm and blues.*

Blunders, literary errors and. See *Literary errors and blunders.*

Blushing. Blush(ed,ing). Flushed. Red faced. Erythrophobia. Turn(ed,ing) red. Pink faced. Erubescence. Rubedo. *See also* Embarrassment.

Board games. Board game(s). *Consider also:* chess(board,boards), Wei-chi, Monopoly, Scrabble, Trivial pursuit(s), etc. *See also* Adult games; Children's games.

Boarding schools. Boarding school(s). Residential school(s). *See also* Residential facilities.

Boardinghouses. Boardinghouse(s). Boarding house(s). Rooming house(s). Rented room(s). Bed and breakfast. Transient housing. Board and care home(s). *Consider also:* residential, adult care, domicilary, sheltered care, alternative, retirement *with:* facilit(y,ies), home(s), hous(e,es,ing), hotel(s). *See also* Adult foster care; Group homes; Homes for the elderly; Sheltered housing.

Boards, executive. See *Governing boards.*

Boards, governing. See *Governing boards.*

Boards, school. See *School boards.*

Boards of directors. See *Advisory committees; Governing boards.*

Boards of education. See *School boards.*

Boatmen. Boatm(an,en). Boat operator(s). Boater(s). Sailor(s). Riverm(an,en). Yachtsm(an,en). Yachtswom(an,en). *Consider also:* fisherm(an,en). *See also* Blue collar workers; Marine accidents; Seafaring life; Sailors.

Boatmen's songs. See *Sea songs.*

Boats. Boat(s). Banca(s). Brigantine(s). Canoe(s). Carvel(s). Catamaran(s). Chatty raft(s). Clincker(s). Clinker(s). Curragh(s). Dingh(y,i,ies). Ferryboat(s). Fishing smack(s). Float(s). Gharnao(s). Kelek(s). Ketch(es). Lakatoi. Paopao(s). Pelota(s). Piragua. Proa. Raft(s). Sampan(s). Sarnai(s). Sailboat(s). Schooner(s). Sloop(s). Tarappam(s). Tugboat(s). Umiak(s). Wallam(s). Zak(s). *See also* Housoats; Ships.

Bodies, bog. See *Bog bodies.*

Bodies, dead. See *Dead bodies.*

Bodies, legislative. See *Legislative bodies.*

Body, human. See *Human body.*

Body art. Body art. *Choose from:* decorat(e,ed,ing,ion), redecorat(e,ed, ing,ion), tattoo(s,ed,ing), pierc(e,ed,ing), bind(ing), swaddl(e,ed,ing), paint(ed, ing) *with:* bod(y,ies), arm(s), face(s), abdomen(s). *See also* Body ornamentation; Body piercing; Ritual disfigurement.

Body awareness. Body awareness. *Choose from:* bod(y,ies), physical self, heart rate, heartbeat, cardiac, respiratory, somatic, internal state(s), finger temperature *with:* aware(ness), perception, boundar(y,ies), attention, mindful(ness), experienc(e,ed, ing), schema. *Consider also:* body image, self consciousness, interoception. *See also* Body image; Body image disturbances; Self consciousness; Self knowledge; Self perception.

Body care. Body care. Hygien(e,ic). Personal clean(liness,ness,sing). Sanit(ary,ation). Bath(e,ed,ing). Wash(ed,ing). Brush(ed,ing) teeth. Douch(e,ed,ing). Gargl(e,ed,ing). Shampoo(ed,ing). Comb(ed,ing) hair. Shav(e,ed,ing). *Consider also:* preventive medicine, oral hygiene, personal hygiene, disinfect(ed,ion), asep(tic,sis), antiseptic, steriliz(e,ed,ing,ation). *See also* Activities of daily living; Antiseptic; Hand washing; Preventive medicine; Self care.

Body contact. See *Physical contact.*

Body covering (anatomy). Body covering. Hair(s). Plumage. Shell(s). Exoskeleton(s). Skin. Epiderm(is,al). Fur(s,ry). Feather(s). Scale(s). *See also* Anatomy; Fur; Skin.

Body fluids. Body fluid(s). Bodily fluid(s). *Consider also:* blood, cerrospinal fluid, saliva, urine, bile, edema, arterial pressure, peritoneal fluid, interstitial fluid, dehydration, thirst. *See also* Cardiovascular system; Urination.

Body height. Body height. Height. Tall(ness). Short(ness). Stature. Petite. Slight. Long legged. Lanky. Tiny. Medium height. Small boned. Large boned. Towering. Giant(s). Statuesque. *See also* Body weight; Giants; Physique.

Body image. Body image(s). Body schema. Physical self concept. *Choose from:* bod(y,ies,ily) *with:* image(s), schema, ego, feeling(s), concept(s), perception(s), satisfaction. *Consider also:* body image disturbance(s), phantom limb(s). *See also* Body awareness; Body image disturbances; Phantom limb.

Body image disturbances. Body image disturbance(s). Dysmorphophobia(s). Phantom limb(s). *Choose from:* body image(s), somatic, body awareness, body ego, bod(y,ily) transformation(s), bod(y,ily) boundar(y,ies) *with:* disturb(ed,ance,ances), delusion(s), psychopatholog(y,ical), distort(ed, ing,ion,ions), dysfunction(s,al), fragment(ed,ing,ation), aberration(s), anxiet(y,ies), defective, dysperception, hallucination(s), disorder(s). *See also* Body image; Castration anxiety; Cognition disorders; Phantom limb; Somatic delusions.

Body language. Body language. Kinesic(s). Gestur(e,es,ed,ing). Gesticulat(e,ed, ing,ion). Touch(ed,ing). Eye contact. Mime. Postur(ed,ing). Pantomime. Facial expression(s). Hand movement(s). *Consider also:* body, bodily, nonverbal, deictic *with:* language, communicat(e, ed,ing,ion), talk, behavior(s). *See also* Eye contact; Facial expressions; Gestures; Nonverbal communication; Posture; Posture in worship.

Body mind problem. See *Mind body problem.*

Body mind relations (metaphysics). See *Mind-body relations (metaphysics).*

Body ornamentation. Body ornament(s,ation). Ornament(ed,ing) bod(y,ies). Tatoo(s,ed,ing). *Choose from:* face(s), bod(y,ies), ear(s), nose(s), lip(s) *with:* paint(s,ed,ing), ornament(s,ed, ing,ation), scarification. *Consider also:* gummanda, moxa, pelele, earring(s), bracelet(s), anklet(s), hairstyle(s), ear disc(s), lip disc(s). *See also* Body art; Clothing; Cosmetics; Fashions; Material culture.

Body parts, artificial. See *Prostheses.*

Body piercing. Body piercing. *Choose from:* bod(y,ies), nostril(s), lip(s), tongue(s), navel(s), nipple(s) *with:* pierc(e,ed,ing). *Consider also:* ear(s) pierc(e,ed,ing). *See also* Body art; Ritual disfigurement.

Body rocking. Body rocking. *Choose from:* rocking *with:* behavior, compulsive, mannerism(s). *Consider also:* head banging, stereotyped behavior. *See also* Behavior disorders.

Body size. See *Body height; Body weight.*

Body temperature. Body temperature. Hypotherm(ia,ic). Hot flash(es). Heat stress(ed). Hypertherm(ia,ic). Normotherm(ia,ic). *Choose from:* bod(y,ies), rectal, oral, hand, skin, tissue(s), human(s), rat(s) *with:* therm(al,ic), temperature(s), heat, cool(ing). *Consider also:* fever(s), shiver(ed,ing), sweat(ed,ing). *See also* Acclimatization; Temperature effects; Temperature perception; Thermoregulation.

Body types. See *Somatotypes.*

Body weight. Body weight. Non-obese. Height weight ratio. Weight height ratio. Emaciat(ed,ion). Obes(e,ity). Overweight. Underweight. Fat(ness). Thin(ness). Lean(ness). *Choose from:* weigh(t,ed,ing), pounds *with:* body, gain(ed,ing), loss, losing, lost, excess, problem(s), control, birth, reduc(e,ed, ing,tion), normal. *See also* Body height; Obesity; Physique.

Bog bodies. Bog bod(y,ies). Bog People. Peat bod(y,ies). Peat bog remains. Lindow man. Tollund man. *See also* Dead bodies; Prehistoric people.

Bohemianism. Bohemian(ism). Unconventional. Avant garde. Bizarre. Far out. Nonconformist. Unorthodox. Idiosyncratic. *Consider also:* eccentric, radical(s). *See also* Countercultures.

Boilerplate. Boilerplate. Preprinted form(s). Standard(ized) form(s). *Choose from:* preprinted, standard(ized) *with:* form(s), material, language. *Consider also:* template(s). *See also* Documents; Forms.

Bomb threats. Bomb threat(s). *Choose from:* bomb(s,ing,ings), blowup, explosive(s), dynamite *with:* threat(s,en,ened,ening), scare(s), caller(s), attempt(ed,ing,s), hoax(es), warning(s), plant(ed,ing,s). *Consider also:* terrorism, Weathermen, Red Guards, Red Army faction. *See also* Bombings; Guerrillas; Mail bombs; Terrorism; Threat.

Bombing, aerial. See *Aerial warfare.*

Bombings. Bomb(ed,ing,ings,ard,arded). Detonat(e,ed,ing) weapon(s,ry). Blow up. Torpedo(ed,ing). *Consider also:* explosion(s), car bomb(s). *See also* Bomb threats; Bombs; Mail bombs.

Bombs. Bomb(s,ing). Grenade(s). Shell(s). Molotov cocktail(s). Land mine(s). Munition(s). Explosive(s). Dynamite. Warhead(s). Napalm. Bomblet(s). Guided weapon(s). Ammunition. Detonator(s). Torpedo(es). *Choose from:* truck, suicide, letter, homemade *with:* bomb(s,ing). *See also* Bombings; Incendiary weapons; Mail bombs; Military weapons; Weaponry.

Bombs, mail. See *Mail bombs.*

Bond, pair. See *Pair bond.*

Bond, social. See *Social cohesion.*

Bondage. See *Slavery.*

Bonding (emotional). Bond(s,ed,ing). Affiliative bond(s,ed,ing). Object relat(ions,ionships,ed,edness). Object loss grief. Symbiotic relation(s,ship). Early attachment(s). Symbiosis. Emotional dependency. Monogam(y, ous). Mat(e,ed,ing) for life. Bonding behavior(s). *Choose from:* psychological, emotional, human, pet(s), animal(s), parent infant, mother infant, father infant, mother child, father child, parent child, maternal, paternal, consort, male female, pair, consort, object, human pet *with:* bond(s,ing), attachment(s), relation(s,ship,ships), related(ness). *See also* Animal behavior; Attachment behavior; Mother child relations; Father child relations; Human-animal relationships; Pair bond; Emotional dependence.

Bonds, junk. See *Junk bonds.*

Bone implements. Bone implement(s). Bone tool(s). *Choose from:* bone, shell(s), teeth, horn(s), ivory, antler(s) *with:* implement(s), tool(s), awl(s), industr(y,ics), ditage, artifact(s), relic(s), harpoon(s), hairpin(s), needle(s). *See also* Animal remains (archaeology); Artifacts; Ivory; Material culture; Stone implements; Tools.

Bones. Bon(e,es,y). Skelet(al,on,ons). Skull(s). Ossic(le,les,ular). *Consider also:* cartilage, marrow, ossein, femur(s), spine(s), vertebra(e), humer(us,i), tibia, fibula, etc. *See also* Anatomy; Age determination by skeleton.

Bonuses. Bonus(es). Honorar(ia,ium). Reward(s). Award(s). Remuneration. Emolument(s). Tip(s). Additional compensation. Gratuit(y,ies). Bestowal(s). Handout(s). Recompens(e,ed,ation). *See also* Compensation management; Employee benefits; Monetary rewards; Salaries; Tipping.

Book classification. Book classification. *Choose from:* book(s), monograph(s), text(s), volume(s) *with:* classif(y,ied,ication). *Consider also:* Dewey Decimal Classification, Library of Congress Classification, Universal Decimal Classification, Classification Decimale Universelle, Colon Classification. *See also* Books; Classification.

Book collecting. Book collecting. Bibliophil(e,es,ic,ia). Booklover(s). Bibliomania. Bibliolatry. *Choose from:* book(s) *with:* collect(ing,or,ors), hoard(ed,ing), accumulat(e,ed,ing,ion), acquir(e,ed,ing), acquisition(s). *See also* Antiquarian booksellers; Bibliomania; Bookplates; Books; Collectibles; Collecting mania; Hobbies; Rare books.

Book covers. Book cover(s). Paperback cover(s). Cover(s) of book(s). Book jacket(s). Dust jacket(s). Novel cover(s). Mass market cover(s). *See also* Bookbinding; Book design; Book ornamentation; Publishing.

Book design. Book design(s). *Choose from:* book(s), volume(s), edition(s) *with:* design(ed,s,er,ers), layout, decorat(ed,ing,ion), binding(s), graphic(s), typograph(y,ic), typeface, jacket(s), cover(s), illustration(s). *See also* Book covers; Book ornamentation.

Book imprints. Book imprint(s). Printers mark(s). Colophon(s). Biblio. Publisher name(s). *See also* Antiquarian booksellers; Books; Book ornamentation; Colophons; History.

Book industry. Book industry. Publisher(s). Bookseller(s). Bookbinder(s). *Choose from:* publishing, book, textbook *with:* industry, house(s), producer(s), compan(y,ies), press(es), printer(s), jobber(s), seller(s), store(s), approval plan(s). *See also* Art publishing; Bookselling; Editors; Little presses; Publishers.

Book jackets. See *Book covers.*

Book ornamentation. Book ornamentation. Colophon(s). Bibliopeg(y,ic,ist,istic, istical). *Choose from:* book(s), volume(s), manuscript(s), tome(s), Bible(s), publication(s) *with:* graphic art(s), illustrat(ed,ing,ion,ions), layout(s), illuminat(e,ed,ing,ion,ions), ornament(ed,ing,ation), rubric(ation), blind tooling, blind stamping, decorat(e,ive), gauffered edges, gilt edges, gilded edges, deckle edges. *Consider also:* fore edge painting(s), fore edge decoration(s), pictorial binding(s), fine binding(s), fine printing(s), page border(s), extra-illustrat(ed,ion,ions), head piece(s), tail piece(s), printers ornament(s). *See also* Block printing; Book covers; Book design; Book imprints; Bookbinding; Colophons; Decorative arts; Illumination of books and manuscripts; Illustrated books; Printers marks; Rare books.

Book reviews. Book review(s,ing,er,ers). *Choose from:* book(s), litera(ry,ture) *with:* review(s,ing,er,ers), crit(ic,ics, ique), evaluat(ed,ing,ive,ion,ions), recommend(ed,ation,ations). *Consider also:* bullcrit. *See also* Books; Evaluation; Literary criticism; Textbooks.

Book selection. Book selection. Collection development. Bibliographer(s). *Choose from:* book(s), reading material(s), library material(s), textbook(s), picturook(s), periodical(s), serial(s), journal(s), reference work(s) *with:* select(ed,ing,ion,ions), acquisition(s), choice(s), choos(e,ing), collect(ing,ion, ions), preference(s). *See also* Collection development (libraries); Library acquisitions; Library censorship.

Book trade. See *Bookselling; Publishing.*

Bookbinding. Bookbind(ing,er,ers). Bibliopeg(y,ic,ist). Binder(y,ies). Binding operation(s). Bind(ing) book(s). Reliure. *See also* Book covers; Book ornamentation.

Bookkeeping. See *Accounting.*

Bookplates. Bookplate(s). Ex-libris. *See also* Book collecting; Books.

Books. Book(s). Volume(s). Title(s). Text(s). Monograph(s). Tome(s). Publication(s). Writing(s). Collected works. Biblio. Picturook(s). Textbook(s). Prayerbook(s). Storybook(s). Handbook(s). Manual(s). Diar(y,ies). Atlas(es). Almanac(s). Antholog(y,ies). Reference work(s). Library material(s). Paperback(s). Yearbook(s). Annual(s). Incunabul(a,um). Encyclopedia(s). Director(y,ies). Dictionar(y,ies). Thesaur(us,uses,i). Pharmacopoeia(s). Lectionar(y,ies). *Consider also:* bibliotherapy, literature, readings, chapters, proceedings, book imprints, bookplates, incunabula. *See also* Anthologies; Atlases (geographic); Best sellers; Bestiaries; Bibliographical exhibitions; Bibliomania; Block books; Book covers; Book design; Bookbinding; Bookplates; Books of hours; Booksellers; Children's literature; Diaries; Directories; Encyclopedias; Festschriften; Gift books; Illustrated books; Prayerbooks; Printers marks; Publications; Rare books; Reading materials; Reference materials; Self help books; Songbooks; Textbooks.

Books, account. See *Account books.*

Books, artists'. See *Artists' books.*

Books, banned. See *Censorship; Library censorship.*

Books, block. See *Block books.*

Books, comic. See *Comics.*

Books, condemned. See *Censorship.*

Books, drawing. See *Drawing books.*

Books, electronic. See *Electronic books.*

Books, gift. See *Gift books.*

Books, illustrated. See *Illustrated books.*

Books, liturgical. See *Liturgical books.*

Books, lost. See *Lost literature.*

Books, online. See *Electronic books.*

Books, prohibited. See *Blacklisting; Censorship.*

Books, rare. See *Rare books.*

Books, reference. See *Reference materials.*

Books, sacred. See *Sacred books.*

Books, self help. See *Self help books.*

Books and manuscripts, illumination of. See *Illumination of books and manuscripts.*

Books of hours. Book(s) of hours. Livre(s) d'heure(s). Devotional exercise(s). *Consider also:* book(s) of offices, fifteenth century prayerbook(s). *See also* Incunabula; Prayer; Prayerbooks; Rare books; Sacred books.

Booksellers. See *Bookselling.*

Booksellers, antiquarian. See *Antiquarian booksellers.*

Booksellers, secondhand. See *Antiquarian booksellers; Second hand trade.*

Bookselling. Booksell(ing,er,ers). Bookseller(s). Bookshop(s). Book shop(s). Bookstore(s). Book store(s). Book dealer(s). Bibliopol(e,es,ic,y,ist,ists). *Consider also:* book(s), textbook(s), publications *with:* sale(s), dealer(s), merchandising, store(s), market(s,ing), price(s), jobber(s), auction(s), fair(s), vendor(s), club(s), trade, sales(men,man,women,woman), salesperson(s), salespeople. *See also* Antiquarian booksellers; Best sellers; Book industry.

Boom generation, baby. See *Baby boom generation.*

Boom towns. Boom town(s). Boomtown(s). Boom communit(y,ies). *Consider also:* rapid(ly) grow(ing,th) *with:* communit(y, ies), town(s), cit(y,ies). *See also* Community change; Community development; Growth management; Population growth; Real estate development.

Boomerang babies. See *Post-baby boom generation.*

Boomerang children. Boomerang child(ren). Intergenerational coresidence. *Choose from:* adult children, young adult(s) *with:* move home, live with parents, live at home. *Consider also:* boomerang famil(y,ies), stay-at-home offspring. *See also* Adult offspring; Housing; Intergenerational relations.

Boots and shoes. Boot(s) and shoe(s). Footwear. Sandal(s). Slipper(s). Sneaker(s). Galoshes. High heels. Brogan(s). *Consider also:* foot protection, shoemaker(s), leather good(s). *See also* Ballet shoes; Clothing; Leather industry.

Booty (international law). Booty. Spoil(s). Plunder(ed,ing). Loot. Art theft. *See also* Robbery; Property crimes; Theft; Treasure.

Border ballads. Border ballad(s,ry). Ballad(s,ry) of the border. Border music. Border song(s). Song(s) of the [Mexican] border. Corrido(s) de la frontera. Migrant ballad(s). Border poe(m,ms,try). Border legend(s). Border minstrel(s,sy). *Consider also:* musica nortena. *See also* Ballads; Borderlands; Folk culture; Folk music; Folk songs; Mexican American border region; Music.

Border incidents. See *Border wars.*

Border industries. Border industr(y,ies). *Choose from:* border area(s), border region(s), border cit(y,ies), cross-border *with:* agriculture, retailing, industr(y,ies, ial), investment, econom(y,ies,ic), trade, manufactur(e,ed,ing), production, plant(s). *Consider also:* maquiladora(s). *See also* Borderlands; Contracting out;

Factories; Foreign labor; Mexican American border region; Multinational corporations; Offshore production (foreign countries); Subcontracting.

Border region, Mexican American. See *Mexican American border region.*

Border wars. Border war(s). Border conflict(s). *Choose from:* border(s), frontier(s), boundar(y,ies), cross-border *with:* war(s,fare), conflict(s), raid(s), fight(s), command, aggression, problem(s), foray(s), invasion(s), incursion(s), violat(e,ed,ing,ion,ions), combat, adventure(s), massacre(s), captiv(e,es,ity,ities), capture(d), scout(s), patrol(s), skirmish(es), incident(s), surveillance, guard(s), crime(s). *Consider also:* enter(ed,ing) air space(s), territorial violat(e,ed,ing,ion,ions). *See also* Borderlands; Deterritorialization; Territorial issues.

Borderlands. Borderland(s). Borderground(s). Marginal area(s). Fringe area(s). Border cit(y,ies). Border town(s). Outermost bound(s). Marchland(s). Irredent(a,ism,ist,ists). *Choose from:* transition(al), transboundary, transborder, transfrontier, border *with:* area(s), zone(s), region(s). *Consider also:* purlieu(s), environ(s), Baja CA, Tucson, El Paso, frontera norte de Mexico, etc. *See also* Border ballads; Border industries; Border wars; Borders; Boundaries; Circumference; Countries; Deterritorialization; Emigrants; Emigration; Frontiers; Geographic regions; Geopolitics; Immigrants; Immigration; Immigration law; International conflict; International relations; International rivers; Invasion; Languages in contact; Mexican American border region; Political geography; Regional differences; Spheres of influence; Territorial expansion; Territorial issues; Territorial waters; Territoriality; Undocumented immigrants; War.

Borderless world. See *Globalization.*

Borderline mental retardation. Borderline mental retardation. *Choose from:* borderline, mild(ly) *with:* mental(ly) retard(ed,ation,ate,ates). *Consider also:* slow learner(s), borderline intelligence, intellectually sub-average, subnormal intelligence, intellectually disabled. *See also* Mental retardation; Psychosocial mental retardation.

Borderline personality disorder. Borderline personality disorder. *Choose from:* borderline, as if, pre-schizophrenic *with:* disorder(s), state(s), psychos(is,es), personalit(y,ies), syndrome, schizophren(ic,ia). *Consider also:* latent schizophrenia. *See also* Neuroses; Personality disorders.

Borders. Border(s) Border line(s). Ambit(s). Boundar(y,ies). Outer part(s). Edge(s). Brim(s). Brink(s). City limit(s). Dividing line(s). Line(s) of demarcation. Fringe(s). Hem(s). Margin(s). Perimeter(s). Peripher(y,ies). Rim(s). Selvage(s). Verge(s). *Consider also:* butts and bounds, metes and bounds, bound(s), extremity, outer limit(s), frontier(s), beginning(s), outpost(s), outskirt(s), outline(s), verge(s). *See also* Borderlands; Boundaries; Circumference; Demarcation.

Boredom. Boredom. Bore(s). Boring. Monoton(ous,y). Ennui. Cabin fever. Doldrums. Tedious. Malaise. Apath(etic,y). Indifferen(t,ce). Lack of feeling. Letharg(y,ic). Languor. Listless(ness). Uninterested. Jaded. *Consider also:* meaningless work, repetitive tasks, monotonous activities, repetitive work. *See also* Apathy; Emotional states; Monotony.

Boring and drilling. See *Drilling and boring.*

Born, foreign. See *Foreigners.*

Borrowers, high risk. See *High risk borrowers.*

Borstals. See *Correctional institutions.*

Boss rule. See *Political bosses.*

Bosses, political. See *Political bosses.*

Botany, medical. See *Medical botany.*

Bottle feeding. Bottle feed(ing). Infant formula(s). *Choose from:* bottle(s), formula(s) *with:* infant(s), bab(y,ies), fed, feed(ing), nursing, milk. *See also* Breast feeding; Infant care; Infant formula; Infant nutrition; Weaning.

Boundaries. Boundar(y,ies). Line(s) of demarcation. Separating line(s). Perimeter(s). Border(s,land,lands). Cleavage(s). Outline(s). Outermost bound(s). Frontier(s). Margin(s). Fence(s). Frame(s). Bound(s). City limit(s). Outer limit(s). Outer part(s). Edge(s). Transboundary. Lot line(s). Metes and bounds. Plat map(s). *Consider also:* brim(s), brink(s), fringe(s), peripher(y,ies,al), rim(s), selvage(s), butts and bounds, metes and bounds, circumferen(ce,ces,tial), extremit(y,ies), door(s), entrance(s), threshold(s), sideline(s), lip(s). *See also* Annexation; Borderlands; Borders; Boundary maintenance; Boundary spanning; Circumference; Constraints; Demarcation; Enclosures; Expansion; Exteriors; Finite; Frames (physical); Frontier thesis; Geopolitics; Groundwork; Land surveying; Political geography; Shorelines; Social stratification; Social structure; Territorial expansion; Territorial issues; Territorial waters; Territoriality.

Boundaries, territorial. See *Boundaries.*

Boundary maintenance. Boundary maintenance. Maintain(ing)

boundar(y,ies). *Choose from:* boundar(y,ies) *with:* work, issue(s), phenomena, security, retain(ed,ing), maintain(ed,ing), maintenance. *Consider also:* differentiation, dividing mechanism(s), segmentation, cultural cleavage(s), segregation, separation, boundary marker(s). *See also* Boundaries; Social closure; Social processes.

Boundary spanning. Boundary spann(er,ers,ing). *Choose from:* interorganizational, inter-group *with:* relations, dependence, collaboration, cooperation. *Consider also:* corporate interlock(s), organizational ecology, environmental scanning, scout(s), ambassador(s), sentr(y,ies). *See also* Boundaries; Boundaryless organizations; Corporate networks; Interlocking directorates; Interorganizational networks; Strategic alliances.

Boundary spanning social networks. See *Boundary spanning; Interorganizational networks.*

Boundaryless organizations. Boundaryless organization(s). *Choose from:* boundaryless, boundary-less, cross boundar(y,ies), fluid boundar(y,ies) *with:* organization(s), compan(y,ies), structure(s), environment(s). *Consider also:* boundarylessness, quasi-firm(s), network organization(s), modular corporation(s), virtual corporation(s). *See also* Adhocracies; Boundary spanning; Consortia; Contracting out; Human resources; Interorganizational networks; Organizational culture; Organizational structure; Shared services; Virtual organizations.

Bourgeois (adjective). Bourgeois(ie). Mass culture. Populist. Kitsch. Conventional. Uncultured. Unrefined. Ordinary. Unimaginative. Uncultivated. Commonplace. Uninspired. Mundane. Hackneyed. Mediocr(e,ity). *Consider also:* materialistic, acquisitive, money-oriented, middle class. *See also* Embourgeoisement.

Bourgeois societies. Bourgeois societ(y,ies). *Consider also:* capitalist societ(y,ies), bureaucratic societ(y,ies), western societ(y,ies), bourgeoisie, burgher(s). *See also* Capitalist societies; Western society.

Bourgeoisie. Bourgeois(ie). Burgher(s). Embourgeoisement. Petit bourgeois(ie). Petty bourgeois(ie). Bourgeoisification. Capitalist(s). Middle class(es). Owning class(es). Ruling class(es). Business(man,men,woman,women). Financier(s). Landowner(s). Industrialist(s). Shopkeeper(s). Entrepreneur(s). Burgher(s). *See also* Bourgeois societies; Embourgeoisement; Middle class.

Boxing. Box(ed,er,ers,ing). Prizefight(s,ing). Heavyweight

champion(s). Pugilis(m,tic). *See also* Sports.

Boycotts. Boycott(s,ed,ing). Blacklist(ed, ing). Embargo(ed,es,ing). Economic sanction(s). Trade sanction(s). *Consider also:* ban(s,ned,ning), consumer strike(s), walk off job(s), picket(s,ed, ing), strike(s), divest(ed,ing,iture,ment), collective pressure(s), unfair list(s). *See also* Ban; Blacklisting; Disinvestment; Negative sanctions; Prohibition; Protest movements; Social action; Strikes; Student demonstrations.

Boys. See *Males.*

Braceros. See *Agricultural workers; Foreign workers.*

Brahmans. Brahman(s). Brahmin(s,ical,ist). *Consider also:* Hindu priest(s). *See also* Hinduism.

Brain. Brain. Cerrum. Cerral. Cerellum. Medulla oblongata. Brain stem. Cerral ventricles. Diencephalon. Limbic system. Mesencephalon. Telencephalon. *See also* Anatomy; Human body; Nervous system.

Brain, lateralization. See *Laterality.*

Brain damage. Brain damage. *Choose from:* brain, intracranial, cranial, right hemisphere, cerrovascular, temporal lobe, cerral, subarachnoid, craniocerral *with:* damage, injur(ed,y,ies), accident(s), lesion(s), trauma(s,tic), hemorrhage(s), hematoma(s), edema. *Consider also:* concussion(s). *See also* Brain damaged; Head injuries.

Brain damaged. Brain damaged. *Choose from:* brain *with:* damaged, dysfunction(s,al), impair(ed,ment, ments), minimal disorder(s). *Consider also:* aphasia, cerral palsy, epilepsy, perceptually disabled. *See also* Congenitally handicapped; Minimal brain disorders.

Brain death. Brain death. Neocortical death. *Choose from:* brain *with:* dead, death, dying. *Choose from:* cessation, ceas(e,ed,ing), critical deficit *with:* reflex(es), neurological sign(s), cerral blood flow. *See also* Death; Right to die; Vegetative state.

Brain disorders, minimal. See *Minimal brain disorders.*

Brain drain. Brain drain. Flow of skilled manpower. Migration of professionals. Inverse transference of technology. Exported personnel. *Choose from:* migrat(e,ed,ing,ion), migrant(s), outflow(s), inflow(s), influx(es), loss(es), losing, emigrat(e,ed,ing,ion), immigrat(e,ed,ing,ion), expatriate(s), exodus *with:* skill(ed,s), expert(s), intellectual(s), key people, professional(s), scientist(s), engineer(s), physician(s), surgeon(s), dentist(s), nurse(s), personnel, manpower, etc. *See* *also* Emigrants; Emigration; Immigration; Intellectual capital; Professional personnel; Scientists.

Brain injured. See *Brain damaged.*

Brain injuries. See *Brain damage.*

Brainstorming. Brainstorm(ed,ing). Exchang(e,ed,ing) ideas. *Choose from:* group(s), collective *with:* problem solving, creative thinking, task solving, generating alternatives, free association, thinking aloud. *Consider also:* brainwriting, creative thinking, divergent thinking, creative problem solving. *See also* Corporate retreats; Creativity; Divergent thinking; Group discussion; Group dynamics; Group problem solving; Spontaneity.

Brainwashing. Brainwash(ed,ing). Brain wash(ed,ing). Menticide. Coercive persuasion. Indoctrinat(ed,ion). Religious conversion(s). Psychological kidnapping(s). *Choose from:* mind, thought(s) *with:* control(led,ling), manipulat(e,ed,ing,ion,or,ors), reform. *Consider also:* deprogramming. *See also* Attitude change; Coercion; Indoctrination; Persuasion; Political socialization; Propaganda; Psychological warfare; Torture.

Branch, executive government. See *Executive branch (government).*

Branch operations. Branch operation(s). *Choose from:* branch(es), annex(es), subsidiar(y,ies), subdivision(s), wing(s), extension, local office(s), sales office(s), affiliate(s), chapter(s), outpost(s), satellite(s) *with:* operation(s), traffic, business, venture(s), store(s), shop(s), bank(s), librar(y,ies), retailer(s). *Consider also:* supermarket chain(s), chain store(s), franchise(s). *See also* Affiliation (businesses); Chapters (organizations); Corporations; Decentralization; Subsidiaries; Subsidiary management.

Brand identity. Brand identit(y,ies). *Choose from:* brand(s,ing), business name(s), trademark(s) *with:* identit(y,ies), position(s,ed,ing), makeover(s), impact(s), image(s), voice(s), message(s). *Consider also:* personal branding, brandbuilding, cobranding, corporate identit(y,ies), trade name(s). *See also* Advertising campaigns; Brand loyalty; Brand names; Cobranding; Comparative advertising; Corporate image; Marketing; Marketing strategies.

Brand loyalty. Brand loyalt(y,ies). *Choose from:* brand(s), trademark(s), logo(s,type), motto(es), hallmark(s), insignia(s), product(s), customer(s) *with:* loyalt(y,ies), preference(s), commitment(s), repeat purchase(s). *See also* Advertising; Brand identity; Brand names; Consumer behavior; Customer services; Hallmarks; Loyalty cards; Musical ads; Service contracts.

Brand names. Brand name(s). Brand(s,ing). Name brand(s). Trademark(s). Brand advertising. Logo(s). Brand label(s). Logo(s,type). Motto(es). Hallmark(s). Insignia(s). Brand recognition. *See also* Advertising; Brand identity; Brand loyalty; Hallmarks; Market research; Market share; Marketing strategies; Trademarks.

Bravery. See *Courage.*

Breach of the peace. Breach of the peace. Disorderly conduct. Dangerous conduct. *Choose from:* violat(e,ed,ing,ion,ions), disturb(ed,ing,ance,ances), breach(es) *with:* peace, order, public tranquility. *See also* Civil disorders; Disorderly conduct; Public order.

Bread. Bread(s). Bagel(s). Ryebread(s). Panettone(s). Stollen(s). Challah(s). Sandwich(es). Bon Pain. Pita(s). Pizza(s). Donut(s). Tea Loa(f,ves). Muffin(s). Tortilla(s). Pan. *Consider also:* pastri(y,es), baker(y,ies). *See also* Food.

Breakdown. See *Failure.*

Breakdown, social syndrome. See *Social breakdown syndrome.*

Breaks, career. See *Career breaks.*

Breakthrough, psychotherapeutic. See *Psychotherapeutic breakthrough.*

Breakthroughs. See *Discoveries (findings); Innovations; Inventions; Medical innovations; Patents; Product development; Product introduction; Research; Scientific discoveries; Scientific revolutions; Technological change; Technological progress.*

Breast. Breast(s). Nipple(s). Mammary gland(s). *See also* Anatomy.

Breast feeding. Breast feed(ing). Breast fed. Breastfed. Nursing. Breast milk. Mothers milk. Lactation. Breastmilk. Natural feeding. Suckling. *See also* Bottle feeding; Infant care; Lactation; Nutrition; Weaning.

Breeding, animal. See *Animal breeding.*

Breeding, selective. See *Selective breeding.*

Brewing. Brew(s,er,ers,ery,eries,ed,ing). Microbrew(s,er,ers,ery,eries). *Choose from:* beer, ale, malt, hops *with:* mak(e,ing), made, produc(e,ed,ing,tion). *See also* Alcoholic beverages; Brewing industry; Distillation.

Brewing industry. Brewing industry. Brewer(y,ies). Microbrewer(y,ies). Beer market(s). *Choose from:* beer, malt, ale *with:* plant(s), firm(s), corporation(s), compan(y,ies), market(s), market share, industry, maker(s). *Consider also:* Anheuser-Busch, Molson Companies, Coors, Heineken, Kirin Brewery, Miller Brewing, Pabst Brewing, etc. *See also* Alcoholic beverages; Beverage industry; Brewing, Distillation; Liquor industry.

Bribery. Brib(e,ed,es,ing,ery). Payola. Payoff(s). Protection money. Kickback(s). Baksheesh. Cumshaw. Tip(ped,ping,s). Influence peddling. *Choose from:* accept(ed,ing,ance), questionable, illicit, unlawful(ly), corrupt *with:* money, favor(s), gift(s), graft, payment(s), gratuit(y,ies). *Consider also:* corruption, fraud, buy(ing) influence, influence peddling, kickback(s), payoff(s), protection money. *See also* Baksheesh; Corruption in government; Crime; Gratuities; Judicial corruption; Witness tampering; White collar crime.

Bride price. See *Bridewealth.*

Bridewealth. Bridewealth. Bride price. Brideprice. Bridal wealth. Marriage payment(s). Bride payment(s). Marriage by purchase. Lobolo. Dowr(y,ies). *See also* Dowry; Marriage brokers.

Brief psychotherapy. Brief psychotherapy. *Choose from:* brief, short term, time limited, rapid, short contact, short duration, active *with:* psychotherap(y,ies), therap(y,ies), psychiatric treatment(s). *See also* Psychotherapy.

Brigands and robbers. See *Bandits.*

Broadcast journalism. Broadcast journalism. Radio journalism. Television news(writing). Television report(s,age,ing). Broadcast(ing) news. Broadcast(ing) political forum(s). *Choose from:* radio, television, TV *with:* report(s,age,ing), editorial (s,ize,ized,izing). *Consider also:* TV news, CBS reporter(s), etc. *See also* Alternative radio broadcasting; Broadcasters; Broadcasting; Broadcasts; Journalism; Media journalism; Pirate radio broadcasting.

Broadcast journalists. See *Journalists; Broadcast journalism.*

Broadcasters. Broadcaster(s). Newscaster(s). Telecaster(s). Journalist(s). Television personalit(y,ies). Television host(s). Talk show host(s). Broadcast newsroom(s). Radio star(s). News anchor(s). Radio announcer(s). Television announcer(s). Anchor (man,men,woman, women,person). News(man, men,woman,women,person). Radio reporter(s). Sportswriter(s). Broadcast pundit(s). Broadcasting career(s). Commentator(s). *See also* Broadcast Journalism; Broadcasting stations; Commentators; Journalists.

Broadcasting. Broadcast(s,ing). Air(ed,ing). Electronic disseminat(e,ed,ing,ion). Newscast(s,ing). Radio transmission(s). Telecast(s,ing). Reporting on-line. Televis(e,ed,ing). *See also* Alternative radio broadcasting; Broadcast journalism; Broadcasting stations; Bulletins;

Distribution (delivering); Information dissemination.

Broadcasting, alternative radio. See *Alternative radio broadcasting.*

Broadcasting, educational. See *Educational broadcasting.*

Broadcasting, international. See *International broadcasting.*

Broadcasting, offshore radio. See *Pirate radio broadcasting.*

Broadcasting, pirate radio. See *Pirate radio broadcasting.*

Broadcasting, political. See *Political broadcasting.*

Broadcasting censorship. Broadcasting censorship. Communications Decency Act. V-chip amendment. FCC prohibit(ed,ing,ion,ions). Safe harbor hours. *Choose from:* television, TV, radio, programming, program broadcast(s,ing) *with:* censor(ed,ing,s,ship), government interference, regulat(ed,ing,ion,ions), rating system(s), content rating(s), bar(red, ring) indecent material, limit violen(t, ce), limit access. *Consider also:* V-chip(s). *See also* Broadcasting policy; Censorship; Freedom of the press; Indecent communications; Information policy.

Broadcasting policy. Broadcasting polic(y,ies). Equal right to access. Children's Television Act. *Choose from:* radio, television, TV, broadcast, cable network(s), cable station(s), videocassette(s), airwaves *with:* polic(y,ies), rule(s), guideline(s), principle(s), directive(s), manual(s), standard(s), white paper(s), regulatory model(s), regulation(s), regs, public interest, public service, First Amendment. *See also* Broadcasting censorship; Freedom of the press; News policies.

Broadcasting stations. Broadcasting station(s). Radio station(s). TV station(s). Television station(s). *Choose from:* radio, television, TV, broadcast, cable *with:* station(s), affiliate(s), propert(y,ies). *Consider also:* WNJU or WXTV, etc. *See also* Alternative radio broadcasting; Broadcasters; Broadcasting; Pirate radio broadcasting.

Broadcasts. Broadcast(s,ing). Telecast(s). Television program(s,ming). Radio program(s,ming). Cable program(s). Cable news. *Consider also:* air time, newscast(s), radio show(s), sitcoms, situation comed(y,ies), prime time, network news, local news, interviews, television serial(s), television show(s), childrens programs, comedies, drama, soaps, soap opera(s), religious program(s), concert(s), music(al) program(s), documentar(y,ies), docudrama(s), game show(s), cartoon(s).

See also Broadcast journalism; Concerts; Declarations; International broadcasting; Jamming of communications; Mass media; Pirate radio broadcasting; Television.

Broadsides. Broadside(s). Poster(s). Broadsheet(s). Placard(s). Bulletin(s). Flyer(s). Leaflet(s). Pamphlet(s). Handout(s). Handbill(s). Card(s). Tract(s). *See also* Bulletins; Publications.

Brochures. See *Pamphlets.*

Broken homes. Broken home(s). Divorced parent(s). *Choose from:* broken, breakup *with:* famil(y,ies), home(s), marriage(s). *See also* Child custody; Child support; Children's rights; Divorce; Female headed households; Single parent family; Single person.

Brokers. Broker(s). Dealer(s). Distributor(s). Intermediar(y,ies). Negotiator(s). Stock broker(s). Wholesaler(s). *Consider also:* middlem(an,en), vendor(s). *See also* Agents; Dealers; Marriage brokers; Representatives; Stockbrokers.

Brokers, marriage. See *Marriage brokers.*

Brokers, stock. See *Stockbrokers.*

Bronze age. Bronze age. Copper age. 2500-3500 B.C. Early bronze age (3,000 - 2,000B.C.). Late bronze age (1500 - 1200 B.C.). *See also* Prehistoric people.

Bronze bells. Bronze bell(s). *Choose from:* bronze(d) *with:* bell(s), handbell(s), church bell(s), chime(s). *See also* Bells; Church music; Musical instruments.

Brothels. Brothel(s). House(s) of prostitution. Bordello(s). Whorehouse(s). Bawdy house(s). Sporting house(s). House(s) of ill repute. *Consider also:* red light district(s), call girl(s), prostitute(s), pimp(s). *See also* Disorderly houses; Prostitution.

Brotherhoods. Brotherhood(s). *Consider also:* fraternit(y,ies), fraternal societ(y,ies), lodge(s), all male organization(s), male bond(s,ing), male order(s). *See also* Belongingness; Fraternities; Group feeling; Holy men; Holy women; Monasticism; Monks; Religious communities.

Brotherhoods, religious. See *Holy men; Monasticism; Religious communities.*

Brotherliness. Brotherl(y,iness). *Choose from:* unity, fellowship, fraternity, brotherhood *with:* humanity, human race, humankind, mankind, womankind, human beings, people, mortals, races, creeds, men and women. *See also* Enlightenment (state of mind); Altruism; Belongingness; Community feeling; Favors; Humanity; Kindness; Prosocial behavior.

Brothers. Brother(s). *Consider also:* male sibling(s), brethren, brother(s,hood, ly,liness), brother(s) in law, fratriarch(y, ies). *See also* Half siblings; Males (human); Sibling relations; Siblings; Sisters.

Brownfields. Brownfield(s). *Choose from:* contaminated, abandoned, underused, vacant, obsolete, blight(ed), idle, unused, hazardous waste, pollution, dumping *with:* sites, properties, lots, structures, area(s) *with:* cleanup, clean-up, redevelopment, EPA, recycling, remediation, revitalizing, industrial development, environmental protection. *See also* Abandoned properties; Environmental protection; Urban beautification; Urban renewal.

Brush drawing. Brush(work) drawing(s). Brush painting(s). Brush stroke(s). Draw(s,ing,ings) in brush(work). *Consider also:* drawing ink(s). *See also* Drawing.

Brutality, police. See *Police brutality.*

Bruxism. Brux(ism,ist,ists,omania). Stridor dentium. *Choose from:* nocturnal *with:* teeth, tooth *with:* grind(ing), gnash(ed, ing). *Consider also:* toothgrinding, TMJ. *See also* Habits; Sleep disorders.

Buddhism. Buddhis(m,t). Buddha. Zen. Nirvana. Gautama. Tantra. Theravada. Mahayana. Bodhisattva. Buddhist sutra(s). Tipitaka. Tathagata. Buddhadharma. Zen buddhism. Pure land buddhism. Lamais(m,t,tic). Yogacar(a,in,ins). *See also* Asian empires; Meditation; Pantheism (universal divinity); Reincarnation; Religions; Zen Buddhism.

Buddhism, Zen. See *Zen Buddhism.*

Budget, balanced. See *Balanced budget.*

Budget, military. See *Military budget.*

Budget, time. See *Time utilization.*

Budget cuts. Budget(ary,s) cut(s,ting). Across the board cut(s). Downsiz(e,ed,ing). *Choose from:* budget(s,ary), fiscal, appropriation(s) *with:* cut(s,ting), cutback(s), reduc(e,ed, ing,tion,tions), slash(es,ed,ing), crunch(es,ing), constraint(s), containment(s), limit(s,ed,ing,ation, ations), restrict(ed,ing,tion,tions), reconcil(e,es,ed,ing,iation). *Consider also:* retrenchment(s), attrition, Gramm-Rudman-Hollings deficit reduction law, defer(red,ring) raise(s), defer(red,ring) promotion(s), hiring freeze(s). *See also* Balanced budgets; Budget deficits; Business failures; Contracting out; Cost control; Cutbacks; Fiscal policy.

Budget deficits. Budget deficit(s). Indebted(ness). Debt. Government borrowing. Deficit spending. Government bond(s). Gramm-Rudman-Hollings deficit reduction law. Debtor countr(y,ies). Government liabilit(y,ies). Balance of payment(s). Deficit spending. *Choose from:* national, federal, public, U.S., government, external, foreign *with:* debt(s), deficit(s), indebted(ness), arrears, shortfall(s). *Consider also:* credit rating, country creditworthiness, credit standing, red ink. *See also* Balanced budget; Debt; Debt management; External debts; Fiscal policy; Public debt; Wasteful.

Budgets. Budget(ary,ed,s,ing). Appropriat(e,ed,ing,ion,ions). Allocation(s). Allotment(s). Apportionment(s). Expend(ed,ing,iture, itures). *Consider also:* financial, finance(s), fiscal, money, expenditure(s), expense(s), spend(ing), tax(es), revenue(s), income, saving(s) *with:* statement(s), plan(s,ning), list(s), estimat(ed,ing,ion,ions), allocation(s), ration(ing), management, program(s). *See also* Appropriations (set aside); Budget cuts; Budget deficits; Cost control; Cost recovery; Expenditures; Family budgets; Finance; Income; Public debt; Resource allocation.

Budgets, family. See *Family budgets.*

Bug, millennium. See *Millennium bug.*

Bugging. See *Electronic eavesdropping.*

Bugs, computer. See *Computer bugs.*

Building codes. Building code(s). *Choose from:* building(s), facilit(y,ies), housing, apartment(s), real estate, property *with:* code(s), guideline(s), standard(s), regulation(s), inspect(ed,ing,ion,ions, or,ors). *Consider also:* safety code(s), fire code(s). *See also* Construction industry; Facility design and construction; Facility regulation and control; Housing; Housing conditions.

Building, sick syndrome. See *Sick building syndrome.*

Buildings. Building(s). Structure(s). Edifice(s). Hous(e,es,ing). Dwelling(s). Built environment. Tower(s). Superstructure. Skyscraper(s). Facilit(y,ies). High rise(s). *See also* Architectural styles; Architecture; Building codes; Churches; Condemnation of buildings; Dwellings; Facilities; Facility design and construction; High buildings; Historic buildings; Historic houses; Modern architecture; Office buildings; Public buildings; Real estate; Religious buildings; Towers.

Buildings, church. See *Churches; Religious buildings.*

Buildings, condemnation. See *Condemnation of buildings.*

Buildings, high. See *High buildings.*

Buildings, historic. See *Historic buildings.*

Buildings, office. See *Office buildings.*

Buildings, public. See *Public buildings.*

Buildings, religious. See *Religious buildings.*

Buildup. Buildup(s). Accretion(s). Accumulat(e,ed,ing,ion,ions). Amass(ed,ing). Enlarg(e,ed,ing,ement). Escalat(e,ed,ing,ion). Expan(d,ded, ding,sion). Stockpil(e,ed,ing). *See also* Accumulation; Arms race; Business growth; Development; Enlargement.

Bulimia. Bulim(ia,ic,y). Boulim(ia,ic,y). Acor(ia,ic). Bulimarex(ia,ic). Hyperorex(ia,ic). Polyphag(ia,ic). Hyperphag(ia,ic). Glutton(y). *Choose from:* compulsive, morbid, insatiable, excessive, binge *with:* hunger, appetite, eat(ing,ers). *Consider also:* bulmorex(ia,ic), bing(e,ing) purg(e,ing). *See also* Eating disorders; Hyperphagia; Nutrition.

Bullcrit. See *Book reviews; Chattering class.*

Bulletins. Bulletin(s). Announcement(s). Brochure(s). Circular(s). Dispatch(es). Handout(s). Message(s). News report(s). News release(s). Press release(s). *See also* Broadcasting; Broadsides; Catalogs; Pamphlets; Publications.

Bullfights. Bullfight(s,er,ers,ing). Bull fight(s,er,ers,ing). Matador(s,es). Toreador(es). Torero(s). Picador(es). *Consider also:* run(ning) the bull(s), fiesta(s) de toros, fiesta(s) taurinas, tauromachy, corrida(s) de toros. *See also* Cruelty to animals; Sports.

Bungalows. Bungalow(s). *Consider also:* cottage(s), vacation home(s), beach house(s), A-frame house(s). *See also* Dwellings.

Burden, caregiver. See *Caregiver burden.*

Bureaucracies. Bureaucrac(y,ies). Bureaucrat(s,ic). Civil service. Government agenc(y,ies). Government(al) organization(s). Government(al) bureau(s). Large organization(s). Ministr(y,ies). *Choose from:* federal, public sector, government(al), public, state, local, city, county, municipal, regulatory *with:* agenc(y,ies), department(s), bureau(s), organization(s), ministr(y,ies), commission(s), council(s), board(s), administration, official(s). *Consider also:* commissarocrac(y,ies). *See also* Bureaucrats; Civil service; Complex organizations; Hierarchy; Public administration; Public folklore.

Bureaucratization. Bureaucratiz(e,ed,ing,ation). Bureaucrac(y,ies). Bureaucrat(s,ic,ism). Technobureaucrat(ic,ism). *Choose from:* corpocra(cy,cies,t,tic), hierarchical organization, public administration, organizational hierarch(y,ies), rational organization, rational authority, division of labor, rationalized domination, bureaucratic control. *See also* Bureau-

cracies; Hierarchy; Organizational structure; Rationalization (sociology).

Bureaucrats. Bureaucrat(s,ic,). Civil service employee(s). Functionar(y,ies). Apparat(chiki). Apparatchik(s). *See also* Bureaucracies; Government personnel; Local officials and employees; Middle level managers.

Burglary. Burglar(s,y,ized). Robber(y,ies). Theft(s). Thieve(ry,s). Steal(ing). Stolen. Shoplift(ed,ing). Pick pocket(s). Holdup(s). Housebreaking. Break-in(s). Breaking and entering. Forced entry. Loot(ed,ing). Plunder(ed,ing). Mug(ged,ging). Larcen(y,ies). *See also* Crime; Theft; Thieves.

Burials. Burial(s). Interment(s). Funeral(s). Entomb(ed,ing,ment,ments). Reburial(s). *Consider also:* cemeter(y,ies), graveyard(s), sepulcher(s), death, dead *with:* bury(ing), buried, inter(red). *See also* Cemeteries; Death rituals; Funeral rites; Mortuary customs; Religious rituals; Sepulchral monuments.

Burlesque. Burlesque. Bump and grind. Striptease. Ecdysiast(s). Stripping. Adult entertainment. Bubble-queen dancer(s). Show girl(s). Dirty dancing. *See also* Adult entertainment; Theater.

Burn slash agriculture. See *Slash burn agriculture.*

Burnout. Burnout. Burn(ed,t) out. Overstressed. *Consider also:* exhaust(ed,ion), overworked, disillusion(ed,ment), stress(ed), anerg(ia,ic,y). *See also* Coping; Disillusionment; Emotional responses; Industrial fatigue; Info fatigue syndrome; Job satisfaction; Mental fatigue; Morale; Motivation; Negativism; Occupational stress; Organizational climate; Overwork; Persistence; Physiological stress; Psychological stress; Stress reactions.

Business. Business(es). Agribusiness(es). Capitalis(m,tic,t,ts). Cartel(s). Commerc(e,ial). Compan(y,ies). Corporat(e,ions). Enterprise(s). Entrepreneur(s,ship). Export(ed,ing, s,er,ers). Factor(y,ies). Import(ed,ing, s,er,ers). Industr(ial,ies,y). Invest(ing, ment,ments,or,ors). Manufactur(er,ers, ing). Market(ing,s,er,ers). Merchandising. Monopol(y,ies). Private sector. Profit(s,making). Retail(er,ers,ing). Sales. Sell(ing,er,ers). Shop(s). Small business(es). Store(s). Syndicate(s). Trad(e,ed,ing,er,ers). Wholesale(r,rs). *See also* Agribusiness; Business administration; Business cycles; Business diversification; Business ethics; Business failures; Business growth; Business organizations; Business personnel; Businessmen; Capitalism; Commodities; Cooperatives; Corporate acquisitions; Corporate day care; Corporate debt; Corporate image; Corporate networks; Corporate social responsibility; Corporate spouses; Corporations; Corporatism; Economic conditions; Employees; Employer organizations; Employers; Entrepreneurship; Exports; Family businesses; Gains; Home based businesses; Industrial concentration; Industry; Intangible property; International trade; Investments; Labor management relations; Labor unions; Marketing; Markets; Minority businesses; Oligopolies; Oligopsony; Private sector; Products; Profitability; Profits; Purchasing; Retailing; Sales; Self employment; Small businesses; Trade; Women owned businesses.

Business, big. See *Big business.*

Business, foreign. See *Commercial treaties; Exports; Free trade; Imports; International trade; World economy.*

Business, place of. See *Place of business.*

Business, start up. See *Start up business.*

Business administration. Business administration. *Choose from:* business, corporat(e,ion,ions), compan(y,ies), store(s), firm(s), plant(s), bank(s), industr(y,ies,ial) *with:* manage(r,rs, ment), managing, administrat(ion, or,ors), administer(ed,ing), supervis(ion, or,ors), leader(s,ship), plan(ning,ned,ner, ners), personnel manage(ment,r,rs), administrative process(es), financial manage(ment,r,rs), president(s), executive(s), chief executive(s), CEO, middle manage(ment,r,rs). *Consider also:* board(s) of directors. *See also* Administration; Administrative problems; Administrators; Business; Entrepreneurship; Public administration.

Business concentration. See *Industrial concentration; Oligopolies.*

Business conditions. See *Business cycles; Depression (economic); Economic conditions; Inflation (economics); Recession; Socioeconomic factors.*

Business cycles. Business cycle(s). Trade cycle(s). Cyclical business conditions. *Choose from:* business, economic, market(s), price(s), interest rate(s), Wall street, Dow Jones industrial average(s), housing starts, employment, unemployment *with:* cycle(s), cyclical, fluctuation(s), pattern(s), swing(s), surge(s), rall(y,ies), fall(s,ing), fell, downturn(s), depression(s), prosperity, boom(s,ing), downward spiral, plunge,ed,ing), recession(s), bust(s), trend(s), jump start(ed,ing). *Choose from:* Kondratieff(s) *with:* wave(s), cycle(s). *Consider also:* bull(ish), bear(ish) *with:* market(s), economy. *See also* Consumption (economic); Depression (economic); Economic change; Economic conditions; Economic crises; Economic forecasting; Economic stability; Economic stabilization;

Inflation (economics); Price control; Price trends; Production consumption relationship; Productivity; Recession; Stock exchange; Stock options; Supply side economics; Workforce planning.

Business districts. See *Commercial districts.*

Business diversification. Business diversification. *Choose from:* business(es), producer(s), product(s,ion,ions), manufactur(er,ers, ing), export(ed,ing,s,er,ers), firm(s), import(ed,ing,s,er,ers), corporat(e,ion, ions), compan(y,ies) entrepreneur(s, ship), retail(er,ers,ing), wholesale(r,rs) *with:* diversif(y,ied,ication), diversity, vary(ing), varied, variation(s), mix(ed), variegate(d). *Consider also:* add(ed,ing) product line(s), multiproduct(s). *See also* Business growth; Entrepreneurship; Product development.

Business education. Business education. *Choose from:* business, managerial, business administration, MBA *with:* education, course(s), student(s), program(s), curriculum, seminar(s), school(s). *Consider also:* office occupation(s), commercial, accounting, distributive, typing, shorthand, office, secretarial *with:* training, education, course(s), student(s), program(s), curriculum, seminar(s), school(s). *See also* Clerical workers; Vocational education.

Business education, basic. See *Basic business education.*

Business elite. See *Economic elites.*

Business enterprises. See *Business organizations; Enterprises.*

Business enterprises, international. See *Multinational corporations.*

Business ethics. Business ethic(s,al). *Choose from:* business(men,women, people), mercantile, commercial, corporat(e,ion,ions), entrepreneur(s,ial), manager(s), management *with:* ethic(s, al), standard(s) of conduct, bioethic(s, al), moral(ity), integrity, moral values, conscience, conscientious(ness), moral obligation(s), honest(y), common good, upright(ness), code(s) of ethics, code(s) of conduct, altruism, humanism. *See also* Corporate social responsibility; Ethics; Fraudulent advertising; Morality; Organizational culture; Unethical conduct.

Business failures. Business failure(s). Chapter 11. *Choose from:* business(es), firm(s), compan(y,ies), corporat(e,ion, ions), venture(s), store(s), bank(s), savings and loan(s), contractor(s), enterprise(s) *with:* fail(ed,ing,ure,ures), mortalit(y,ies), bailout(s), distress(ed,es), financial trouble(s), bailout(s), liquidation, demise, downsiz(e,ed,ing), insolven(t,cy), bankrupt(cy),

ruin(ed,ation), breakdown. *See also* Bailouts; Bank failures; Bankruptcy; Budget cuts; Default (negligence); Organizational dissolution; Plant closings.

Business growth. Business growth. *Choose from:* business(es), firm(s), compan(y,ies), corporat(e,ion,ions), venture(s), store(s), bank(s), savings and loan(s), contractor(s), enterprise(s) *with:* growth, develop(ed,ing,ment), expansion, expand(ed,ing), fast lane, boom(s, ed,ing), success(ful), advance(ment), buildup(s), enlarge(d,ment), mov(e,ed, ing,ement) forward, progress, prosperity. *See also* Buildup; Business diversification; Community development; Economic development; Entrepreneurship; Growth strategies; Industrial expansion; Product development.

Business incubators. Business incubator(s). *Consider also:* venture capital firm(s), VC firm(s). *Choose from:* fledgling enterprise(s), new business(es), entrepreneur(s), start-up(s), promising project(s), small business(es) *with:* launch(es,ed,ing), incubat(or,ors), research-friendly environment(s), support(ed,ing,s), shelter(s,ed,ing). *See also* Entrepreneurship; Founding; Small businesses; Start up business; Venture capital.

Business orders. See *Orders (business).*

Business organizations. Business organization(s). Compan(y,ies). Corporat(e,ion,ions). Incorporat(e,ed, ion). Sole proprietorship. Partnership(s). Unincorporated business(es). Business associat(es,ion,ions). Private compan(y,ies). Public compan(y,ies). Business firm(s). Shop(s). Store(s). Business establishment(s). Industrial concern(s). Business concern(s). *Consider also:* professional corporation(s). *See also* Advertising agencies; Business; Business personnel; Conglomerates; Corporate retreats; Enterprises; Organizational climate; Organizational culture; Organizations.

Business personnel. Business personnel. Business(women,woman,man,men). Business people. *Choose from:* business(es), industrial, corporat(e,ion), compan(y,ies), firm(s), managerial, management, white collar *with:* worker(s), employee(s), personnel, staff. *Consider also:* merchant(s), sales worker(s), accountant(s), clerical personnel, middle level manager(s). *See also* Businesspersons; Clerical workers; Managers; Middle level managers; Sales personnel; White collar workers.

Business students. Business student(s). *Choose from:* business, MBA, accounting, banking, advertising, marketing, secretarial, office occupation(s) *with:* student(s), major(s,ing), enroll(ed,ment), trainee(s), intern(s). *See also* Business; Business education; Students.

Business travel. Business travel(ers,ling). *Choose from:* business(men,women), executive(s), sales(men,man,woman, women,people), trainer(s) *with:* travel(ers,ling), trip(s), out of town, airfare(s), flight(s), commuter(s), itinerar(y,ies), destination(s). *See also* Air transportation; Businesspersons; Commuting (travel); Destination; Tourism; Travel; Traveling sales personnel.

Businesses, closed. See *Bank failures; Business failures; Deindustrialization; Dislocated workers; Organizational dissolution; Personnel termination; Plant closings.*

Businesses, family. See *Family businesses.*

Businesses, home based. See *Home based businesses.*

Businesses, minority. See *Minority businesses.*

Businesses, sex oriented. See *Sex industry.*

Businesses, small. See *Small businesses.*

Businesses, women owned. See *Women owned businesses.*

Businessmen. See *Businesspersons.*

Businesspersons. Business(man,men, woman,women,person,persons,people). *Choose from:* business, corporate *with:* leader(s), elite, owner(s), establishment, executive(s), magnate(s), tycoon(s). *Consider also:* manager(s), industrialist(s), middle(men,man), capitalist(s), shopowner(s), shopkeeper(s), manufacturer(s), broker(s), stockbroker(s), retailer(s), buyer(s), entrepreneur(s). *See also* Business personnel; Business travel; Capitalists and financiers; Sales personnel; Stockbrokers.

Businesswomen. See *Business personnel; Businessmen.*

Busing. See *School integration.*

Busters, baby. See *Post-baby boom generation.*

Busts. Bust(s,i,o). Portrait(s) sculpt(ure,ures,es). Sculpture(s) of the head. *Consider also:* sepulchral monument(s), memorial sculpture(s), mask(s), cameo(s). *Choose from:* chest, shoulders, head, upper portion of body *with:* sculpture(s), painting(s), drawing(s), engraving(s). *See also* Coin portraits; Portraits.

Butter. Butter(s,y). Ghee. *Consider also:* milk curds, saturated fat(s), margarine, dairy spread(s), dietary fat(s), cholesterol. *See also* Food.

Buyers. Buyer(s). Consumer(s). Customer(s). Client(s). User(s). Student(s). Patient(s). Patron(s). Clientele. Shopper(s). Borrower(s). Depositor(s). Purchaser(s). Passenger(s). Constituenc(y,ies). Prospect(s). Vendee(s). End user(s). *See also* Consumer awareness; Consumer behavior; Consumer organizations; Consumer participation; Consumers.

Buying. Buy(ing). Bought. Purchas(e,es,ed, ing). Procur(e,ed,ing,ment,ments). Acquisition(s). Acquir(e,ed,ing). Shop(ping). Military contract(s). Defense contract(s). Cooperative contract(s,ing). Spend(ing). Spent. *See also* Brand loyalty; Consumer behavior; Consumption (economic); Library acquisitions; Purchasing.

Buying, gold. See *Gold buying.*

Buying, house. See *House buying.*

Buyout packages. Buyout package(s). Early retirement incentive(s). Early buyout(s). *See also* Early retirement; Incentives.

Buyouts. Buyout(s). Buy(ing) out. Bought out. *Choose from:* buy(ing), bought, purchas(e,ed,ing), acquisition(s), acquir(e,ed,ing) *with:* share(s), interest, stock(s), securities, equit(y,ies), business(es), corporat(e,ion,ions), compan(y,ies). *Consider also:* take-over(s), takeover(s), leveraged buyout(s), corporate raider(s). *See also* Anti-takeover strategies; Corporate acquisitions; Employee ownership; Employee stock ownership plans; Hostile take-overs; Leveraged buyouts; Mergers.

Buyouts, leveraged. See *Leveraged buyouts.*

Byte. Byte(s). Binary digit(s). 8 bits. Eight bits. 16 bits. Sixteen bits. *Consider also:* memory unit(s), character storage. *See also* Automated information storage.

C

Cabala. Cabal(a,ism). Cabalist(s,ic). Cabbal(a,ah,ism). Cabbalist(ic,s). Kabal(a,ism). Kabalist(ic,s). Kabbal(a, ah,ism). Kabbalist(ic,s). Qabbala(a,ah, ism). Jewish mysticism. *Consider also:* Zohar, Sefer Bahir. *See also* Jewish literature; Jewish mysticism; Judaism; Mysticism.

Cabinet members. See *Advisory committees.*

Cable television. Cable television. Cable TV. Cable network(s). Cable show(s). Cable system(s). Cable program(s,ing). Cable service(s). *Consider also:* HBO, Home Box Office, public access channel(s), ACE awards, CableAce awards, MTV, leased-access channel(s), CATV, C-SPAN. *See also* Communications media.

Caciquism. Caciqu(e,ism). Political boss(es). *Consider also:* dictator(s), Indian chief(s,tain,tains). *See also* Authoritarianism (political); Dictatorship; Military regimes; Totalitarianism.

Cadence. Caden(ce,ces,tial). Kadenz(en). Cadenza(s). Cadencia(s). *See also* Accents; Inflection; Ornamentation (music); Rhythm.

Cadres. Cadre(s). Work group(s). Core group(s). Nucleus of trained personnel. Staff officers. Inner circle. Key personnel. *See also* Groups; Leadership.

Cafes. See *Bars; Coffee houses; Eating establishments.*

Calculating machines. Calculating machine(s). Calculator(s). Adding machine(s). Pre-computer(s). Computational device(s). *Consider also:* abacus(es), abaci, graphing calculator(s), TI-82, TI-85, etc. *See also* Computers; Equipment.

Calendar. Calendar(s,ic). Calendric. *Consider also:* lunar, solar, annual *with:* cycle(s). *Consider also:* Assyro-Babylonian, Aztec, Constantinian, Egyptian, Gothic, Gregorian, Greek, Islamic, Jewish, Julian, Mayan, permutating, 13-month, world *with:* calendar(s). *Consider also:* time reckoning, liturgical time, Roman feriale, equinox(es), solstice(s), Christian year. *See also* Almanacs; Appointments and schedules; Chronology; Extended school year; Holidays; Time; Time measurement.

Calisthenics. Calisthenics. Exercis(e,es, ing). Physical training. Gymnastic(s). Athletic(s). Slimnastic(s). Aerobic(s). Isometric(s). Warmup(s). Warm up(s). Fitness program(s). *Consider also:* physical fitness. *See also* Gymnastics; Physical fitness.

Calling. See *Careers.*

Calls, house. See *Home visiting programs.*

Calmness. Calm(ness). Peaceful(ness). Tranquil(ity). Atarax(y,ia,ic). Ataractic. Seren(e,ity). Repose. Composed. Collected. Unmoved. Unanxious. Content(ed,ment). Relaxed. Untroubled. Undisturbed. Euthym(ia,ic). *See also* Emotions; Meditation; Orderliness; Public order.

Caloric requirements. Caloric requirement(s). *Choose from:* caloric, nutritional, energy, dietary, carbohydrate(s), protein(s) *with:* need(s), requirement(s), adequa(te,cy). *Consider also:* recommended daily allowance(s), dietary guideline(s). *See also* Calories (food); Diet; Energy expenditure (physical); Weight control.

Calories (food). Calor(ic,ies). Food energy. Nutrient(s). Equicaloric. *Consider also:* high energy diet. *See also* Caloric requirements; Diet; Food; Weight control.

Calvinism. Calvinis(m,t,ts,tic). *Consider also:* predestination, Congregationalism, Puritan(s), Presbyterianism, justification by faith, salvation through work(s), salvational anxiety, Protestant ethic, work ethic, New England theology. *See also* Protestant ethic; Protestantism.

Camels. Camel(s). Dromedar(y,ies). *Consider also:* Bactrian camel(s), camelus. *See also* Mammals; Vertebrates.

Camera, sonata da. See *Sonata da camera.*

Cameras. Camera(s). Photographic equipment. Minicamera(s). Panoramic lens(es). Videotape recorder(s). Videocamera(s). *See also* Photography.

Camp (aesthetics). Camp(y,iness). *Choose from:* camp(y), exaggerated, outrageous, artific(e,ial), affected, self-conscious, theatrical, performative, excess(es,ive), parody, drag, posed, incongru(ous,ity), satiric(al), flamboyant, stylized, unnatural, frivolous, contradictory, preposterous, play(ful,fulness), anti-serious, outlandish(ness), facetious(ness), gay style(s), melodrama(tic), fake glamour, over-blown, overdone *with:* cinema(tic,s), film(s), theater(s), theatrical, aesthetic(s), art(s,work,works), novel(s), ficti(on, tious), poe(try,m,ms), opera(s), musical(s). *See also* Aesthetics; Artistic styles; Genres (art); Subcultures.

Campaign debates. Campaign debate(s). *Choose from:* candidate(s), campaign(s, ed,ing), presidential, vice presidential, gubernatorial *with:* debate(s), face to face, discuss(ed,ing,ion,ions), spar(red, ring). *See also* Debate; Political campaigns; Political platforms; Presentations.

Campaign finance reform. Campaign finance reform. Clean money campaign reform. Clean elections law(s). *Choose from:* campaign(s), election(s), political *with:* finance, fund raising, contribution(s), special interest money, quid pro quo, soft money *with:* limit(s,ed,ing,ation,ations), legal standard(s), reform(s,ed,ing), report(s, ed,ing), disclos(e,ed,ing,ure), combat(ting), ban(ned,ning). *Choose from:* dollar democracy, money based politics, bundling, campaign abuse(s) *with:* report(s,ed,ing), disclos(e,ed,ing, ure), limit(s,ed,ing,ation,ations), legal standard(s), reform(s,ed,ing), combat(ting), ban(ned,ning). *Consider also:* FEC, Federal Election Commission, campaign spending limits. *See also* Advocacy advertising; Campaign funds; Financial disclosure; Election law; Kickbacks; Political campaigns; Political contributions; Political reform.

Campaign funds. Campaign fund(s). *Choose from:* candidate(s), incumbent(s), campaign(s,ed,ing), electioneer(ing), election(s), run(ning) for office, primar(y,ies) *with:* fund(s, raising), contribution(s), contributor(s), PAC(s), Political action committee(s), special interest(s), support(ed,ing,er,ers), brib(e,es,ed,ing), underwrit(er,ers,ten), donat(e,ed,ing,ion,ions), gift(s), honorari(a,um), gratuit(y,ies). *See also* Advocacy advertising; Campaign finance reform; Political broadcasting; Political campaigns; Political candidates; Political contributions; Political patronage.

Campaigning, negative. See *Comparative advertising.*

Campaigns. Campaign(s,ed,ing,er,ers). Crusad(e,es,ed,ing,er,ers). Drive(s). Stump(ed,ing). Hoopla. Mobiliz(e,ed,ing,ation,es). Holy war(s). Barnstorm(ed,ing). *Consider also:* polic(y,ies), reform(ed,ing,er,ers), propagandi(ze,zed,zing,ism), solicitation(s), operation(s), canvass(ed, ing,er,ers). *See also* Activism; Advertising campaigns; Fund raising; Global campaigns; Marketing; Mobilization; Military operations; Political campaigns; Political movements; Protest movements; Social movements.

Campaigns, advertising. See *Advertising campaigns.*

Campaigns, election. See *Political campaigns.*

Campaigns, global. See *Global campaigns.*

Campaigns, military. See *Military operations.*

Campaigns, political. See *Political campaigns.*

Campaigns, presidential. See *Political campaigns; Elections.*

Camping. Camp(ed,er,ers,ing). Encamp(ed). Tenting. Pitch(ed) tent(s). Campfire(s). Scout(s,ing). Sleeping bag(s). Bedroll(s). Sleep(ing) outdoors. *Consider also:* day camp(s), adventure education, summer camp(s), hike(d,s), hiking, backpack(ed,ing), outdoor recreation, Outward Bound. *See also* Outdoor life; Recreation; Sports.

Camps. See *Camping; Concentration camps; Therapeutic camps.*

Camps, concentration. See *Concentration camps.*

Camps, prison. See *Concentration camps.*

Camps, refugee. See *Refugee camps.*

Camps, therapeutic. See *Therapeutic camps.*

Campus associations. See *School clubs.*

Campuses. Campus(es). *Choose from:* college(s) or universit(y,ies) *with:* site(s), setting(s), building(s), ground(s), facilit(y,ies), physical plant(s), quadrangle(s). *See also* Buildings; Colleges; Residential facilities.

Canadians, Japanese. See *Japanese Americans.*

Canals. Canal(s,led,lize,lized). Lift lock(s). *Consider also:* flood control, water transportation, river project(s), aqueduct(s), towpath(s), artificial waterway(s), channel(s), conduit(s). *See also* Channels (hydraulic engineering); Flood control; Stream channelization; Streams; Water transportation.

Cancellation. Cancel(s,led,ling,ation). Abrogat(e,ed,ing,ion). Annul(led,ling, ment). Dissolv(e,ed,ing). Dissolution(s). End(ed,ing,ings). Invalidat(e,ed,ing, ation). Nullif(y,ied,ying,ication). Overrid(ing,den). Overrul(e,ed,ing). Recall(s,ed,ing). Repeal(s,led,ling). Retract(ed,ing,ion). Terminat(e,ed, ing,ation). Suspen(d,ded,ding,sion). Veto(s,ed,ing). *See also* Annulment; Disclaim; Nullification; Repeal.

Cancer. Cancer(s,ous). Carcinoma(s). Malignant neoplasm(s). Sarcoma(s). Tumor(s). Neoplas(m,ms,tic). Malignanc(y,ies). Oncolysis. Medical oncology. Metastas(is,es). *Consider also:* precancerous condition(s),

leukemia(s), carcinogen(ic,s). *See also* Carcinogens; Health status indicators; Occupational diseases; Occupational exposure.

Candid photography. Candid photography. Candids. Candid close-up(s). Candid shot(s). Spontaneous photo(s,graph, graphs,y). Candid picture(s). Spontaneous shot(s). Unposed photo(s,graph, graphs,y). *Choose from:* candid, spontaneous, unposed *with:* photo(s, graph,graphs,y), close-up(s), shot(s). *See also* Photography; Photojournalism.

Candidates. Candidate(s). Candidacy. Office seeker(s). Nominee(s). Stand(ing) for election. Run(ning) for office. Aspirant(s). Front runner(s). Contestant(s). Applicant(s). *Consider also:* prospective employee(s), incumbent(s), bidder(s), contender(s), petitioner(s). *See also* Job applicants; Judicial candidates; Political campaigns; Political candidates; Political parties.

Candidates, judicial. See *Judicial candidates.*

Candidates, political. See *Political candidates.*

Cannabis. See *Street drugs.*

Cannabis abuse. See *Substance abuse.*

Cannibalism. Cannibal(ism,istic,ize,ized,s). Anthropophag(i,y,ite,ous). Thyestean. Endo-cannibalism. Maneat(er,ers,ing). Man-eat(er,ers,ing). Windigo psychosis. Wihtiko psychosis. Pupkilling. Pupkilling. *Choose from:* eat(ing,en), crav(e,ed,ing), devour(ed,ing) *with:* human flesh, offspring. *Consider also:* burial, famine, gastronomic, revenge, ritual *with:* cannibalism. *See also* Depravity; Human sacrifice; Sacrificial rites; Rituals; Shrunken heads; Taboo; Totemism.

Canon (literature). Canon(ical,icity,s,ized). Literary canon(s). Great books. English classics. Sanctioned list(s). *Consider also:* authoritative list(s) of works, core humanities curricul(a,um), classical western literature, great western literary works, classical works, catacaustics, fundamental work(s), recognized literature. *See also* Core; Classic (standard); Educational ideologies.

Canon law. See *Canons.*

Canonization. Canoniz(e,ed,ing,ation). Venerat(e,ed,ing,ion) as a saint. New(ly) saint(ed). Nominat(e,es,ed,ing,ion) for sainthood. Declar(e,ed,ing) a saint. *Consider also:* beatif(y,ied,ication). *See also* Saints; Holy women.

Canons. Canon(s). Holy Writ. Religious laws. Holy Scripture. *Choose from:* ecclesiastical, religious, church *with:* doctrine(s), decree(s), edict(s), dogma(s), rule(s), regulation(s), law(s). *Consider also:* principle(s), rule(s),

standard(s), norm(s), maxim(s). *See also* Apologetics; Codes (rules); Dogma; Eccleciastical courts; Edicts; Generalities; Jewish law; Principles; Religious beliefs; Religious councils and synods; Religious literature; Rules (generalizations).

Cant. Cant. Argot. Jargon. Lingo. Patois. Slang. Vernacular. *Consider also:* swearing, cursing, idiom(s,atic), language of the underworld, colloquialism(s). *See also* Dialects.

Cantatas. Cantat(a,as,e,en). Kantat(e,en, enwerk). Cantade. *Consider also:* sacred concerto(s), vocal chamber music. *See also* Ballads; Choirs (music); Choral music; Church music; Music; Religious music; Songs.

Canticles. Canticle(s). Liturgical song(s). Song of Songs. *See also* Chants; Church music; Music.

Canvassing. Canvass(ed,ing,er,ers). Poll taking. House to house. Door to door. *Consider also:* peddl(e,ed,ing,er,ers), pollster(s), prospecting, telephone sale(s), survey(s,ed,ing), solicit vote(s). *See also* Opinion polls; Surveys.

Capability. See *Ability.*

Capacity. Capacit(y,ies). Magnitude. Amplitude. Ample(ness). Sufficien(t,cy). Bulk(y,iness). Dimension(s). Extent. Range. Volume. Proportion(s). Scope. Size. Quantit(y,ies). *Consider also:* adequa(te,cy), potential, strength. *See also* Ability; Aptitude; Area of knowledge; Competence; Dimensions; Industrial capacity; Proportionality; Size.

Capacity, human channel. See *Human channel capacity.*

Capacity, industrial. See *Industrial capacity.*

Capacity, production. See *Industrial capacity.*

Capgras's syndrome. Capgras's syndrome. *Choose from:* Capgras(s) *with:* syndrome, phenomenon, symptom(s), feature(s). *Consider also:* illusion(s), delusion(al,s) *with:* double(s), false recognition, identit(y,ies), impostor(s). *Consider also:* l'illusion des sosies, misidentification syndrome(s). *See also* Delusions; Mental illness; Thought disturbances.

Capital (financial). Capital. Asset(s). Investment(s). Equity. Accumulated wealth. Net worth. Cash reserve(s). Financial resource(s). Money. Savings. Wealth. *Consider also:* principal, shareholder interest(s), stock, working capital, moneyed wealth. *See also* Assets; Banking; Capital expenditures; Dividends; Economic resources; Economics; Gains; Infrastructure (economics); Profitability; Supply side economics; Venture capital; Wealth.

Capital, cultural. See *Cultural capital.*

Capital, human. See *Human capital.*

Capital, intellectual. See *Intellectual capital.*

Capital, venture. See *Venture capital.*

Capital cities. Capital cit(y,ies). Capital(s). National capital(s). State capital(s). Seat(s) of government. County seat(s). Provincial capital(s). Location of government. Government location. Administrative capital(s). Administrative location(s). Center(s) of government. *See also* Cities; Government agencies.

Capital expenditures. Capital expenditure(s). Capital investment(s). *Choose from:* capital, equipment, construction, building(s), capital asset(s), fixed asset(s), equity, physical plant(s), machinery, land *with:* expenditure(s), cost(s), expense(s), replacement charge(s), investment(s), fund(s,ing), depreciation, spending, bid(s), budget(s). *Consider also:* factor(y,ies), means of production, factor(y,ies). *See also* Amortization; Capital (financial); Expenditures; Investments.

Capital investments. See *Capital expenditures.*

Capital punishment. See *Death penalty.*

Capitalism. Capitalis(m,t,tic). Free enterprise. Private ownership. Corporate ownership. Profit motive. Mercantil(e,ism,ist,istic). Family business(es). Free trade. Free market. Private property. Bourgeois political economy. Private enterprise. Capital accumulation. Profit system. Economic competition. Market economy. Laissez faire government. Entrepreneurial(ism). Private investment. Private ownership. *Consider also:* Protestant ethic, multinational corporation, corporate society, competitive economy, monopoly capitalism, finance capitalism, state capitalism, work ethic. *See also* Capitalist societies; Capitalists and financiers; Communism; Democracy; Economics; Entrepreneurship; Imperialism; Labor unions; Market economy; Marxism; Political ideologies; Private enterprise; Private sector; Privatization; Profit motive; Socialism; State capitalism; Western society; World systems theory.

Capitalism, state. See *State capitalism.*

Capitalist societies. Capitalist societ(y,ies). Enterprise culture. Market econom(y, ies). Western society. Bourgeois societ(y,ies). Capitalism. *Consider also:* capitalist *with:* nation(s), countr(y,ies), state(s), econom(y,ies), societ(y,ies), democrac(y,ies), regime(s). *See also* Bourgeois societies; Capitalism; Industrial societies; Political ideologies; Rationalization (sociology); Welfare state; Western society; Working class.

Capitalists and financiers. Capitalist(s). Financier(s). Rich(est) men. Rich(est) women. Mogul(s) Investor(s). Magnate(s). Billionaire(s). Millionaire(s). Entrepreneur(s). Business people. Forbes Four Hundred list. Corporate raider(s). Tycoon(s). Speculator(s). *Consider also:* banker(s), broker(s), investor(s), moneylender(s), stakeholder(s), landowner(s). *See also* Businesspersons; Capitalism; Speculators; Stockholders.

Capitalization. Capitaliz(e,ed,ing,ation). Recapitaliz(e,ed,ing,ation). Suppl(y,ying,ied) capital. Provid(e,ed,ing) capital. Convert(ed,ing) into capital. *Consider also:* convert(ed,ing) to cash, total(ed,ing) value, total(ed,ing) capital, total(ed,ing) liabilities, bankroll(ed,ing). *See also* Asset management; Assets; Depreciation; Economic value; Investments; Leveraged buyouts; Liquidity; Pension fund management; Valuation.

Capitals. See *Capital cities.*

Capitation fee. Capitation fee(s). *Choose from:* capitation, per capita *with:* charge(s), fee(s), reimbursement. *Consider also:* poll tax(es). *See also* Population; Taxes.

Capitols. Capitol(s). State House(s). Statehouse(s). *Consider also:* Parliament house(s). *See also* Public baths; Public buildings.

Capitulations, military. See *Military capitulations.*

Captions. Caption(s,ed,ing). Banner(s). Headline(s). Subtitle(s,d). Legend(s). Inscription(s). *See also* Cartoons; Magazine illustration; Translating and translations.

Captivity. Captiv(e,es,ity). Capture(d). Cage(d). Behind bars. Take(n) prisoner. Restrain(t,ed). Constrain(t,ed). Bondage. Enslave(d,ment). Imprison(ed,ment). Intern(ed,ment). *Consider also:* hostage(s). *See also* Animal domestication; Environmental enrichment (animal culture); Prisoners of war; Slavery; Zoo animals.

Capture at sea. Capture at sea. Piratically captured. Captured on the high seas. Maritime capture(s). Piratical seizure(s). *Choose from:* capture(d), recapture(d), seize(d) *with:* sea(s), piratical(ly), ship(s), vessel(s), sloop(s). *See also* Piracy (at sea); Privateers; Seizure of ships.

Car pools. Car pool(s,ed,ing). Carpool(s,ed,ing). Car sharing. Ride sharing. Ridesharing. Vanpool(s,ed,ing). Van pool(s,ed,ing). Transportation broker(s,ing). Urban travel reduction. *Choose from:* commut(er,ing), diamond *with:* lane(s). Commuter incentive(s). *Consider also:* high occupancy vehicle(s). *See also* Commuting (travel); Mass transit.

Caravans. Caravan(s). Gypsy wagon(s). Land yacht(s). Trailer(s). Covered wagon(s). Camper(s). House trailer(s). Mobile home(s). Motor home(s). Recreational vehicle(s). RV(s). *Consider also:* camel caravan(s), wagon train(s), touring trailer(s), donkey train(s), compan(y,ies) of travelers, train(s) of pack animals, vehicles traveling together, double-wide(s). *See also* Convoys; Entourage; Ground transportation; Motor vehicles; Tourism; Travelers; Traveling theater.

Carcinogens. Carcinogen(esis,ic,icity,s). Cancer causing. Cancer suspect agent(s). Oncogen(esis,ic,icity,s). Tumorigen(esis, ic,icity,s). Tumor initiating. Tumor initiator(s). Hepatocarcinogen(s). Tumor promoter(s). *Consider also:* aminobiphenyl compound(s), cocarcinogenesis, oncogenic virus(es). *See also* Agricultural chemicals; Air pollution; Cancer; Environmental pollutants; Environmental pollution; Food contamination; Hazards of video display terminals; Hazardous materials; Hazardous wastes; Herbicides; Industrial wastes; Medical wastes; Nuclear waste; Occupational diseases; Occupational exposure; Pesticides; Smoking; Tobacco habit; Tobacco smoke pollution; Water pollution.

Carcinoma. See *Cancer.*

Card fraud, debit. See *Debit card fraud.*

Card systems, punched. See *Punched card systems.*

Cardinal virtues. Cardinal virtue(s). Justice. Fortitude. Temperance. Prudence. *See also* Fortitude; Good works (theology); Justice; Prudence; Temperance; Theological virtues, Virtue.

Cardiovascular system. Cardiovascular system(s). *Consider also:* aorta(s), arteriole(s), capillar(y,ies), myocardium, pericardium, blood vessel(s), arter(y,ies), vein(s), heart(s). *See also* Anatomy; Body fluids; Heart.

Care, adult day. See *Adult day care.*

Care, adult foster. See *Adult foster care.*

Care, ambulatory. See *Ambulatory care.*

Care, body. See *Body care.*

Care, child. See *Child care.*

Care, child day. See *Child day care.*

Care, child self. See *Child self care.*

Care, comprehensive health. See *Comprehensive health care.*

Care, consumer directed. See *Consumer directed care.*

Care, continuity of patient. See *Continuity of patient care.*

Care, corporate day. See *Corporate day care.*

Care, critical. See *Critical care.*

Care, custodial. See *Custodial care.*

Care, day elderly. See *Adult day care.*

Care, dental. See *Dental care.*

Care, domiciliary. See *Boardinghouses; Group homes; Sheltered housing.*

Care, elderly day. See *Adult day care.*

Care, foster day. See *Foster home care; Child day care; Adult day care; Corporate day care.*

Care, foster home. See *Foster home care.*

Care, health. See *Health care.*

Care, health home. See *Home care.*

Care, health rationing. See *Health care rationing.*

Care, health reform. See *Health care reform.*

Care, health surveys. See *Health care surveys.*

Care, health utilization. See *Health care utilization.*

Care, home. See *Home care.*

Care, home services. See *Home care services.*

Care, infant. See *Infant care.*

Care, institutional. See *Hospitalization; Hospitalized children; Institutionalization (persons); Institutionalized children; Institutionalized mentally retarded.*

Care, intensive. See *Intensive care.*

Care, life. See *Life care.*

Care, life support. See *Life support care.*

Care, long term. See *Long term care.*

Care, managed. See *Managed care.*

Care, maternity. See *Maternal health services.*

Care, medical. See *Medical care.*

Care, night. See *Night care.*

Care, nursing. See *Nursing care.*

Care, pastoral. See *Pastoral care.*

Care, patient. See *Health care; Medical care.*

Care, patient acceptance of. See *Patient compliance.*

Care, perinatal. See *Maternal health services.*

Care, personal. See *Hygiene.*

Care planning, patient. See *Patient care planning.*

Care, postnatal. See *Postnatal care.*

Care, postoperative. See *Postoperative care.*

Care, prenatal. See *Prenatal care.*

Care, primary health. See *Primary health care.*

Care, quality of health. See *Quality of health care.*

Care, residential. See *Residential treatment.*

Care, respite. See *Respite care.*

Care, self. See *Self care.*

Care, terminal. See *Terminal care.*

Care facilities, terminal. See *Hospices.*

Care of the sick. Care of the sick. Medical care. *Choose from:* care(d), caring, caregiver(s), caregiving, handfeeding, tube feeding, nursing, monitor(ed,ing), heal(ing,ed) *with:* ill(ness), sick(ness), cancer, patient(s), sickroom(s), convalescen(t,ce), terminal(ly). *Consider also:* healing process(es). *See also* Caregivers; Home care; Illness; Long term care; Medical care; Nursing care; Respite care; Terminal care.

Care rationing, medical. See *Health care rationing.*

Care team, patient. See *Patient care team.*

Care units, respiratory. See *Respiratory care units.*

Career, dual families. See *Dual career families.*

Career aspirations. See *Occupational aspirations.*

Career breaks. Career break(s). Reinstated worker(s). *Choose from:* career, occupational, professional, vocational, job *with:* break(s), sequencing, unpaid leave(s), protracted leave(s), leave(s) of absence, interrupt(ed,ing,ion,ions). *Consider also:* work history, voluntary leave(s). *See also* Career change; Career patterns; Employment history; Displaced homemakers; Family work relationship; Interruption; Life stage transitions; Midcareer change; Reentry women; Work reentry.

Career change. Career change(s). Retooling. Outplacement. Midlife career crisis. Second career(s). Re-careering. Re-entry worker(s). Post-retirement work. *Choose from:* career(s), midcareer, job(s), occupation(s,al), vocation(s,al), profession(s,al), work, calling, employment, livelihood *with:* passage(s), mobility, transition(s), displace(d,ment), chang(e,es,ed,ing), transfer(s,red,ring), re-start(ed,ing). *See also* Career breaks; Career mobility; Displaced homemakers;

Life stage transitions; Midcareer change; Personnel termination.

Career choice. See *Occupational choice.*

Career counseling. See *Vocational guidance.*

Career criminals. Career criminal(s). Habitual offender(s). Repeat offender(s). Chronic offender(s). Criminal career(s). Criminal recidivist(s). Professional criminal(s). *Consider also:* underworld, felon(s), serial killer(s), drug kingpin(s), drug lord(s), Mafia. *See also* Drug lords; Felonies; Offenders; Organized crime; Recidivism; Thugs.

Career development. Career development. *Choose from:* career, professional, vocational, occupational *with:* growth, success(es), strateg(y,ies), develop(ment, ing), plan(ne,ning,s), stage(s), passage(s), identity, advancement, dynamic(s), transition(s), pattern(s), maturity, plateau(s,ing). *See also* Career change; Career education; Career goals; Career ladders; Career mobility; Career patterns; Occupational aspirations; Promotion (occupational); Vocational maturity.

Career education. Career education. *Choose from:* career(s), prevocational, vocation(s,al), occupation(s,al), profession(s,al), job *with:* train(ed,ing), retrain(ed,ing), development, exploration, preparation, planning, course(s), skills development, intern(s,ships), orientation, curriculum, training, awareness, guidance. *Consider also:* career maturity. *See also* Career development; Occupational interests; Vocational education; Vocational guidance.

Career goals. Career goal(s). Occupational aspiration(s). *Choose from:* occupation(s,al), prevocational, vocation(s,al), profession(s,al), career *with:* aspiration(s), goal(s), motivation, plan(s,ned,ning), map(s,ped,ping), choice(s), orientation, decision(s), objective(s), goal(s), ambition(s), expectation(s). *Consider also:* socioeconomic aspirations, career strateg(y,ies). *See also* Career change; Career development; Career ladders; Career mobility; Career patterns; Occupational aspirations; Professional development; Vocational maturity.

Career guidance. See *Vocational guidance.*

Career ladders. Career ladder(s). Career path(s,way,ways). Career lattice(s). Job ladder(s). *Choose from:* profession(s,al), career(s), job(s), work(ing), corporate, employment, occupation(s,al) *with:* ladder(s), track(s), hierarch(y,ies), advance(s,ment,ments), progress(ed,ing, ion,ions), stage(s), passage(s), pattern(s). *Consider also:* mommy track(s), fast track(s,er,ers), job promotion(s), pay steps, pay structure. *See also* Career goals; Career mobility; Career patterns; Continuing education; Employee transfers; Inservice teacher education; Inservice training; Organizational structure; Professional development; Promotion (occupational).

Career mapping. See *Career goals.*

Career maturity. See *Vocational maturity.*

Career mobility. Career mobility. *Choose from:* career(s), profession(al), job(s), occupation(al), vocation(al) *with:* mobil(e,ity), development, structure, paths, ladders, chang(e,ed,es,ing), advanc(e,ed,es,ing,ment), relocat(e,ed, ing,ion), transition(s), transfer(red, ring,s), promot(able,ability,ed,ion). *See also* Career change; Career ladders; Employment opportunities; Labor mobility; Occupational aspirations; Promotion (occupational); Relocation; Socioeconomic status; Yuppies.

Career opportunities. See *Employment opportunities.*

Career patterns. Career patterns. Labor market position(ing). Mid-career change(s). Underemploy(ed,ment). Work experience. *Choose from:* career, occupational, professional, vocational, job(s) *with:* pattern(s), path(s), development, change(s), success(es), accomplish-ment(s), shift(s), break(s), life, interrupt(ed,ing,ion,ions), structure(s), cycle(s), mobility. *Consider also:* work history. *See also* Career breaks; Career mobility; Employment history; Professional development.

Career planning. See *Career change; Career development; Career goals; Career ladders; Occupational choice; Occupational interests; Vocational guidance; Vocational maturity.*

Career satisfaction. See *Job satisfaction.*

Career women. See *Dual career families; Professional women; Working women.*

Careers. Career(s). Profession(s). Occupation(s). Trade. Vocation(s). Job(s). Calling(s). Livelihood(s). Line of business. Lifework. *Consider also:* occupational preference, occupational choice, professional work, professional role, professional orientation, work history, vocational interest(s), job embeddedness. *See also* Blue collar workers; Career breaks; Career change; Career criminals; Career development; Career education; Career goals; Career ladders; Career mobility; Career patterns; Dual career families; Employment; Entrepreneurship; Family work relationship; Female intensive occupations; Job security; Life plans; Male intensive occupations; Nontraditional careers; Occupational adjustment; Occupational aspirations; Occupational attitudes; Occupational choice; Occupa-

tional interests; Occupational qualifications; Occupational roles; Occupational segregation; Occupational status; Occupational structure; Occupational success; Occupational tenure; Occupations; Professional certification; Professional competence; Professional development; Professional education; Professional identity; Professional image; Professional orientations; Professional personnel; Professional socialization; Professional standards; Promotion (occupational); Self actualization; Self employment; Quality of working life; Vocations; White collar workers; Work values.

Careers, nontraditional. See *Nontraditional careers.*

Careers, second. See *Career breaks; Career change; Career mobility; Career patterns; Displaced homemakers; Life stage transitions; Work reentry.*

Caregiver burden. Caregiver burden(s). *Choose from:* caregiver(s), caregiving, caretaker(s), *with:* burden(s), strain(s), responsibilit(y,ies), impact(s), stress(ful), distress, obligat(ed,ion,ions). *See also* Adult offspring; Aging; Burnout; Caregivers; Chronic disease; Coping; Death; Dependent parents; Elder abuse; Filial responsibility; Health problems; Intergenerational-relations; Psychological stress; Role conflict; Widowhood.

Caregivers. Caregiver(s). Care provider(s). Caretaker(s). Caresharing. Carer(s). Support person(s). Sitter(s). Babysitter(s). *Choose from:* respite, home, famil(y,ies,ial), filial, lay, elder(s), parent(s) *with:* car(e,ing), support, foster. *See also* Adult day care; Care of the sick; Caregiver burden; Child caregivers; Child day care; Custodians; Female intensive occupations; Forms of affection; Foster parents; Home care; Long distance caregivers; Mothers; Nurses; Nurses aides; Respite care.

Caregivers, child. See *Child caregivers.*

Caregivers, long distance. See *Long distance caregivers.*

Caretakers. See *Caregivers; Custodians; Janitors.*

Cargo. Cargo(s,es). Freight. Payload(s). Baggage. Lading. Shipment(s). Shipload(s). Truckload(s). Carload(s). *See also* Cargo handling; Carriers (shipping); Freight; Shipping industry.

Cargo cults. Cargo cult(ists,s). *Choose from:* cargo *with:* movement(s), cult(s), religion(s), expectation(s), thinking. *Consider also:* nativ(e,istic), Melanesian, New Guinea, etc. *with:* millenarianism, messianic movement(s). *Consider also:* revitalization phenomena. *See also* Collective suicide; Millenarianism; Nativistic movements; Traditional societies.

Cargo handling. Cargo handl(ing,er,ers). Stevedor(e,es,ing). Longshorem(an,en). Material(s) handling. *Choose from:* shipment(s), cargo(s), freight, material(s) *with:* handl(e,ed,ing), load(ed,ing), unload(ed,ing). *See also* Cargo; Carriers (shipping); Freight; Longshoremen; Shipping industry; Transport workers.

Cargo systems. Cargo system(s). Fiesta system(s). Ladder system(s). Cofradia system(s). *Consider also:* civil religious hierarch(y,ies). *See also* Central American native cultural groups; Community structure; Social order; Social status; Social stratification; Social structure; South American native cultural groups; Traditional societies.

Caribbean. Caribbean. Antigua(n) and Barbuda(n). (Commonwealth of the) Baham(as,ian). Barbad(os,ian). Cayman Islands. Cuba(n). (Commonwealth of) Dominica. Grenad(a,ian). Haiti(an) [Hispaniola]. Jamaica(n). Saint (St.) Lucia(n). Trinidad and Tobago. Saint (St.) Vincent and the Grenadines. *Consider also:* Antille(s,an), Greater Antilles, Lesser Antilles, Caribees, West Indies, Windward Islands, Leeward Islands, Dominican Republic [Santo Domingo, San Domingo], Guadeloupe, Montserrat, Martini(que,can), Netherlands Antilles [Curacao], Aruba, Puerto Ric(o,an), Saba, Saint (St.) Barthelemy, Saint (St.) Eustatius [Statia], Saint (St.) Croix [Santa Cruz], Saint (St.) Kitts-Nevis-Anguilla [Saint (St.) Christopher-Nevis], Saint (St.) Martin [Sint Maarten], Turks and Caicos Islands, Virgin Islands. *See also* Black Carib literature; Central America; Central American native cultural groups; GE-Pano-Carib languages; North America; North American native cultural groups; South America; South American native cultural groups.

Caricatures. Caricature(s). Parod(y,ies). Lampoon(s). Satir(e,ical,ize,ized). Cartoon(s). *See also* Cartoons; Parody; Political humor; Satire.

Carnivals. Carnival(s). Festival(s). Fiesta(s). Fete(s). County fair(s). State fair(s). Worlds fair(s). Mardi Gras. Saturnalia. *Consider also:* religious celebration(s), festivit(y,ies), revelry, masquerade(s), jamboree(s), national day(s), amusement park(s), circus(es), sideshow(s). *See also* Amusement parks; Circus performers; Fools and jesters; Holidays.

Carpentry. Carpentry. Carpenter(s,ing). Woodwork(ing,er,ers). Cabinetmak(er, ers,ing). Cabinet making. Furniture building. Joiner(s). Making furniture. *See also* Manual training; Skilled workers.

Carriages. Carriage(s). Chariot(s). Coach(es). Stagecoach(es). Phaeton(s). Hansom(s). Cab(s). Surrey(s). Brougham(s). Sulk(y,ies). Wagon(s). Cart(s). Cabriolet(s). Four-wheeler(s). *See also* Chariots; Ground transportation.

Carriers (shipping). Carrier(s). Hauler(s). Interstate commerce. Tractor-trailer(s). Truck(er,ers,ing). Transport(ed,ing, ation). Ship(ped,ping). Intermodal carrier(s). Railroad(s). Trucking industry. Truck(load) ship(ping,ment, ments). Truck(load) carrier(s). Shipper(s). Commercial carrier(s). Ocean transport service(s). Shipping line(s). Airline(s). Freight forwarder(s). Integrated carrier(s). *See also* Air cargo; Air transportation; Cargo; Cargo handling; Freight; Shipping industry: Transport workers; Transportation.

Carriers, aircraft. See *Aircraft carriers.*

Carriers, letter. See *Letter carriers.*

Carte blanche. Carte blanche. Free rein. Full power(s). Free license. Unconditional right(s). *Consider also:* power(s) of attorney. *See also* Power; Rights.

Cartels. Cartel(s,ize,ized,izing,ization). Consorti(a,um,ums). Conglomerate(s). Syndicate(s). Trust(s). *See also* Affiliation (businesses); Alliances; Coalitions; Conglomerates; Consortia; Corporate networks; Interorganizational networks; Mergers; Monopolies; Multinational corporations; Oligopolies; Price fixing; Trade associations.

Cartography. Cartograph(y,ic). Mapmaking. Computer map(s,ping,ped). Photogrammetric map(s,ping,ped). Satellite image(s). *Consider also:* aerial photo(s), making atlas(es). *See also* Atlases (geographic); Land surveying; Maps.

Cartons. See *Containers.*

Cartoonists. Cartoonist(s). Reuben award winner(s). *Choose from:* cartoon(s), comic strip(s), comic book(s) *with:* creator(s), drawn by, written by, originator(s), artist(s), writer(s), author(s). *See also* Artists; Cartoons.

Cartoons. Cartoon(ists,s). Toon(s). Comics. Comic strip(s). Caricature(s). Animated cartoon(s). Humorous drawing(s). Humorous sketch(es). Lampoon(ed,ing,s). Funnies. *See also* Animation (Cinematography); Captions; Cartoonists; Caricatures; Humor; Illustrated books; Magazine illustration; Political humor; Satire; Television; Television programs.

Cartoons, political. See *Political humor.*

Cartularies. Cartular(y,ies). Cartulaire(s). Cartulario(s). Cartularium. Chartularium. *Consider also:* account roll(s). *See also* Account books;

Charters; Documents; Legal documents; Records.

Carving (decorative arts). Car(e,ing,ings). Woodcarv(er,ers,ing,ings). Wood carving(s). Whittl(e,ed,er,ers,ing). Scrimshaw. Scrimshander(s). Glyptic(s). Stonecut(ter,ters,ting). *Choose from:* ornament(s,al), decorative, stone, penknife, ivor(y,ies), elephant tusk(s), whalebone(s), baleen, bone(s), tortoiseshell, stone(s), hardstone, chip, soapstone, wood(en), oak, soap *with:* carv(e,ing,ings), chisel(ed,ing), sculpt(ure,ed,ing), statue(s,tte,ttes). *Consider also:* carved figure(s), carved animal(s), totem pole(s), misericord(e,s), kachina doll(s). *See also* Crafts; Glyptics; Ivory; Material culture; Medieval sculpture; Petroglyphs; Prehistoric art; Prehistoric sculpture; Sculpture.

Carving, ivory. See *Carving (decorative arts).*

Carving, stone. See *Carving (decorative arts).*

Carving, wood. See *Carving (decorative arts).*

Carvings, rock. See *Petroglyphs.*

Case mix. Case mix. Casemix(es). Grouping(s) of patients(s). *Consider also:* patient classification system(s), case type classification(s), diagnostic related group(s). DRG(s). *See also* Classification; Diagnosis; Patients.

Case reports. See *Case studies.*

Case studies. Case stud(y,ies). Case report(s). Case record(s). Case histor(y,ies). Casework record(s). Patient histor(y,ies). Individual record(s). *See also* Information; Longitudinal studies; Patient history; Qualitative methods; Research methods.

Cases, court. See *Legal cases.*

Cases, legal. See *Legal cases.*

Casework. See *Social work.*

Casework, social. See *Social work.*

Caseworkers. See *Social workers.*

Cash. Cash. Legal tender. Coin(s). Dollar bill(s). *See also* Coins; Currency; Money.

Cash flow. Cash flow. Liquidity. Reported net income. Ability to pay. *Choose from:* cash, funds, money *with:* flow(s), reserve(s), availab(le,ility). *See also* Accounts payable and receivable; Liquidation; Liquidity.

Cash management. See *Financial management.*

Casinos. Casino(s). Gambling hall(s). Gambling den(s). Gaming house(s). Betting parlor(s). *See also* Betting; Billiard parlors; Gambling.

Caste system. Caste system(s). Caste(s). Brahmin(s). Untouchable(s). Intercaste. Subcaste(s). Jajmani system. Varna. Brahman(a). Rajanya. Kshatriya. Vaishya. Shudra. Sudra. *Choose from:* closed, rigid, birth ascribed *with:* social system(s), social strat(a,um), social stratification. *See also* Ascription; Brahmans; Ethnic groups; Hinduism; Outcastes; Social closure; Social immobility; Social stratification; Social structure; Traditional societies.

Castration. Castrat(e,ed,ion). Steriliz(e,ed,ing,ation). Eunuch(oid,ism). Ovariectom(y,ies). Emasculat(e,ed,ion). Geld(ed,ing). Alter(ed,ing). Desexualiz(e,ed,ation). Asexualiz(e,ed, ation). Vasectom(y,ies). Neuter(ed,ing). Orchidectom(y,ies). Gonadectom(y,ies). Spay(ed,ing). Oophorectom(y,ies). Ovariotom(y,ies). Salpingectom(y,ies). Ovariectom(y,ies). Capon(s). Ankteriasmus. *See also* Desexualization; Eunuchs; Sterilization (sex).

Castration anxiety. Castration anxiety. *Choose from:* castrat(e,ed,ing,ion), genital loss, genital injury *with:* anxiet(y,ies), complex(es), fear(s,ful). *See also* Anxiety disorders; Body image disturbances.

Castration complex. See *Castration anxiety.*

Castration, male. See *Male castration.*

Castratos. See *Eunuchs.*

Casualties. Casualt(y,ies). Accident(s,al, ally). Calamit(y,ies). Catastrophe(s). Debacle(s). Disaster(s). Fatalit(y,ies). Loss(es). Misfortune(s). Misadventure(s). Mischance(s). Mishap(s). Bad luck. Death(s). Missing in action. *See also* Collapse; Fatalities; Victimization; War victims.

Casuistry. Casuist(ry,ries,ical). Fallac(y,ies). Philosophis(m,try). Decept(ion,iveness). Delusion(s). Equivocat(e,ed,ing,ion). Specious(ness). Sophis(m,try). Spurious(ness). *Consider also:* situation(al) ethics, relative morality. *See also* Deception; Ethics; Illogical; Practical theology; Relativism; Scholasticism; Sin.

Cat phobia. Cat phobia(s). Ailurophob(ia,ic). Aelurophob(ia,ic). Galeophob(ia,ic). Gatophob(ia,ic). *See also* Phobias.

Catalepsy. Catalep(sy,tic,tiform,toid). Flexibilitas cerea. Waxlike posture(s). Cataleptic rigidity. *See also* Hysteria; Schizophrenia.

Cataloging. Catalog(ing, uing). Use of MARC subject headings. *Consider also:* index(ing), classif(y,ied,ication), bibliographic utilit(y,ies). *See also* Library catalogs.

Catalogs. Catalog(s,ue,ues). Register(s). List(s,ing,ings). Registr(y,ies). Record(s). Guide(s). Bibliograph(y,ies). Booklist(s). College bulletin(s). Collection description(s). Items offered. Director(y,ies). Index(es). Inventor(y,ies). Mail order list(s). *Consider also:* cataloging, cataloguing, registering, library catalog(s,ue,ues), school catalog(s,ue,ues), repertor(y,ies), repertoire(s). *See also* Bulletins; Library catalogs; Order processing; Orders (business); Publications; Reference materials.

Catalogs, library. See *Library catalogs.*

Catalyst. Catalyst(s). Catalytic agent(s). Activist(s). Agitator(s). Motivator(s). *Consider also:* stimul(i,us), goad(s,ed, ing), impetus, impulse(s), incentive(s), incit(e,ed,ing,ement), motiv(e,es,ation), spur(red,ring), stimula(te,ted,nt,nts). *See also* Change agents.

Catamnesis. See *Posttreatment followup.*

Cataplexy. Cataplex(y,ia). *Consider also:* narcolepsy, cataplectic, temporary paralysis, sleep paroxysm(s). *See also* Narcolepsy.

Catastrophes. Catastrophe(s,ic). Catastrophic event(s). Act(s) of God. Accident(s). Airplane crash(es). Blizzard(s). Bombing(s). Cataclysm(s,ic). Calamit(y,ies). Casualit(y,ies). Collision(s). Crash(es). Cyclone(s). Damag(ed,es,ing). Destruction. Devastat(ed,ion). Disaster(s). Disastrous(ly). Drought(s). Earthquake(s). Emergenc(y,ies). Explosion(s). Famine(s). Fire(s). Flood(s). Gotterdammerung. Hostage(s). Hurricane(s). Landslide(s). Loss of life. Meltdown(s). Natural disaster(s). Nuclear accident(s). Nuclear explosion(s). Oil slick(s). Oil spill(s). Plane wreck(s). Radiation accident(s). Railroad accident(s). Riot(s). Ruin(ed, ing,ation). Ship sunk. Siege(s). Snowstorm(s). Storm(s). Struck by lightning. Tidal wave(s). Tsunami(s). Tornado(es). Twister(s). Typhoon(s). Violent change(s). Volcanic eruption(s). War(s). *See also* Accidents; Adversity; Catastrophic illness; Chaos; Collapse; Defeat; Disaster planning; Disaster relief; Emergency medicine; Emergency services; Explosions; Fire; Hardships; Natural disasters; Nuclear accidents; Nuclear winter; Riots; Storms; Survival; War.

Catastrophic illness. Catastrophic illness(es). *Choose from:* catastrophic *with:* illness(es), disease(s), presentation(s), medicine, infection(s), complication(s). *Consider also:* serious illness(es). Seriously ill. *See also* Acute disease; Catastrophes; Health insurance; Illness; Patients.

Catatonia. Cataton(ia,ic,y). Kataton(ia,ic, y). Rigid involutional depression(s). *Consider also:* cataleptoid. *See also* Catatonic schizophrenia; Symptoms.

Catatonic schizophrenia. Catatonic schizophren(ia,ias,ic,ics). Schizophrenic cataton(ia,ic,y). *Consider also:* catatonia, catalepsy, automatism(s), schnauzkrampf, stereotypy. *See also* Catatonia; Schizophrenia.

Catchment area (health). Catchment area(s). Health service area(s). Area(s) served by hospital(s). Medical care region(s). Service area(s). Region(s) served. *See also* Health care utilization; Health resources; Health services needs and demand; Medical geography; Medically underserved areas.

Catchwords. Catchword(s). Buzzword(s). Byword(s). Catchphrase(s). Cliche(s). Epithet(s). Maxim(s). Motto(s). Refrain(s). Shibboleth(s). Saying(s). Watchword(s). Household word(s). *Consider also:* jargon, battle cry. *See also* Aphorisms; Cliches; Epithets; Jargon; Terminology.

Catechetics. See *Religious education.*

Catechisms. Catechism(s). Creed(s). Catholic doctrine. *See also* Creeds; Religious education.

Categorical aid. See *Fiscal federalism.*

Categorical imperative. Categorical imperative(s). Moral law(s). Kant(ian,s) ethics. Universal law(s). *See also* Absolutism; Moral judgment; Morality.

Categories (philosophy). Categor(y,ies). Highest genera. Genus. Ultimate class. *Consider also:* construct(s), class(es). *See also:* Logic; Predicate (Logic); Social structures.

Categorization. Categoriz(ed,ation,ions,ing). Sort(s,ed,ing). Rank(s,ed,ing). Arrang(e,ed,ing,ement,ements). Classif(y,ies,ied,ication). Pigeonhole(d). Typecast(ing). *See also* Classification; Cognitive generalization; Ideal types; Identification (recognition); Labeling (of persons); Social types; Stereotyping; Types.

Catharsis. Catharsis. Abreact(ion,ive). Psychocathar(sis,tic). Autocathar(sis,tic). *Consider also:* re-experienc(e,ed,ing), reliv(e,ed,ing), express(ed,ing,ion), discharg(e,ed,ing) *with:* trauma(tic,s), tension(s), emotion(s,al), anger, feeling(s). *Consider also:* psychodrama. *See also* Abreaction; Personality processes; Psychoanalysis; Tragedy.

Cathedrals. See *Churches: Places of worship; Religious buildings.*

Cathexis. Cathex(es,is). Cathect(ed,ing,ic,icize,icized). Hypocathex(is,es). Hypercathex(is,es).

Acathex(es,is). *Choose from:* psychic, ego, libidinal, emotional, intellectual *with:* energy, investment(s). *Choose from:* self, auto, object *with:* libido. *Consider also:* phantasy, ego, object *with:* cathexis. *See also* Libido; Personality processes.

Catholic (universality). Catholic(ity,ally, icize). Universal(ity). Cosmopolitan(ism). All-inclusive(ness). All-embracing. All-encompassing. Broad-minded(ness). Ecumenis(m,t,ts). Ecumenical(ism). Global(ly). Planetary. Worldwide. *Consider also:* liberal(ity), broad(ness), comprehensive(ness), inclusive(ness), large-scale, impartial(ity), open-minded(ness), extensive(ness). *See also* Attitudes; Comprehensiveness; Cosmopolitan; Global integration; Globalization; Sophistication; Universalism; Worldview.

Catholicism, Roman. See *Roman Catholicism.*

Cations. Cation(s). Positive ion(s). *Consider also:* electrolyte(s). *See also* Electricity; Physics.

Cats. Cat(s). Feline(s). Felid(s,ae). Felis catus. Kitt(en,ens,y,ies). *Consider also:* lion(s), tiger(s), leopard(s), cheetah(s), jaguar(s), ocelot(s), lynx(es), bobcat(s). *See also* Animals; Domestic animals; Pets.

Cattle. Cattle. Bovidae. Bovine(s). Bull(s). Cow(s). Steer(s). Ox(en). Yak(s). Zebu(s)s. Cal(f,ves). Heifer(s). Buffalo(es). Goat(s). Lamb(s). Ram(s). Sheep. Bison. *Consider also:* ruminant(s). *See also* Animals; Bison; Cattle industry; Draft animals; Farming; Goats; Grazing; Herders; Livestock; Mammals; Sheep.

Cattle industry. Cattle industry. *Choose from:* cattle, livestock, yearling(s), meat, steer(s), heifer(s), cow(s), bovine *with:* industr(y,ies), producer(s), ranch(es,er, ers), packing, feeding, husbandry, operation(s), grower(s), market(s,er,ers), price(s), import(s), export(s). *See also* Agribusiness; Agriculture; Animal industry; Cattle; Dairy products; Dairying; Farming; Meat industry; Ranches; Right of pasture.

Caucasian languages. Caucasian language(s). Abkhazo-Adygheian: Abkhaz-Abazin, Ubykh, Lower Adyghe, Kiakh (Circassian), Kabardian (Upper Circassian). Daghestani: Avaro-Ando Dido, Lezghian, Samurian. Kartvelian: Georgian, Zan (Mingrelian, Laz), Svan. Veinakh: Chechen, Ingush, Bata. *See also* Central Asia; Eastern Europe; Language; Languages (as subjects).

Caucasian race. See *Whites.*

Caucasians. See *Whites.*

Caucuses. See *Conferences; Congresses; Factionalism; Meetings; Political parties; Primaries.*

Caudillo. See *Dictatorship.*

Causal models. Causal model(ing,s). Causal connection(s). Causal hypothe(sis,ses). Model(s) of determinant(s). Model(s) of caus(e,es,ality). Probabilistic model(s). *See also* Causality; Models; Scientific models.

Causality. Causa(l,lity,tion). Cause(s,d). Causing. Causal analys(is,es). Predispos(e,ed,ing,ition,itions). Precipitat(e,ed,ing). Predetermin(e,ed,ing,ation). Agent(s) provocateur. Prime mover(s). *Choose from:* caus(e,es,al) *with:* analy(sis,ses), theor(y,ies), model(s), structure(s), explanation(s), attribut(ed,ing,ion,ions), ascription(s), ascrib(e,ed,ing), inference, relation(s,ship,ships), determin(ed,ing, ation,ations), contribut(e,ed,ing,ory). *Consider also:* motive(s), reason(s), antecedent(s), enabling factor(s), reinforcing factor(s), mind body problem, apriorism, epiphenomenalism, emergent propert(y,ies), historical explanation(s). *See also* Analysis (Philosophy); Attribution; Biological factors; Causal models; Cause of death; Counterfactuals (logic); Determinism; Effects; Environmental determinism; Etiology; Explanation; Geographic determinism; Influence; Interaction; Mind body problem; Nature nurture; Peer influences; Psychophysiology; Random; Social factors; Social influences; Sociocultural factors; Socioeconomic factors; Sources; Time factors.

Causation. See *Causality.*

Cause of death. Cause(s) of death. Death cause(s). Terminal illness(es). Autop(sy, sies). Postmortem indices. Death investigation(s). Preventable death(s). Coroner's inquest(s). Certification of death. Murder investigation(s). Death from natural cause(s). *Choose from:* death(s), fatalit(y,ies), mortalit(y,ies), casualt(y,ies), murder(s), suicide(s) *with:* caus(ing,ed,es,ality), motive(s), antecedent(s), correlat(e,es,ing,ion,ions), analys(es,is), indication(s), explanation(s), ground(s), reason(s), means, manner. *See also* Autopsy; Causality; Disease; Disorders; Forensic medicine; Homicide; Suicide.

Causes. See *Causality.*

Cave paintings. Cave painting(s). Cave art. Painted cave(s). *Consider also:* pintura(s) rupestre(s), arte rupestre, rock painting(s), rock art, petroglyph(s), rock engraving(s). *See also* Arts; Hieroglyphics; Mural painting and decoration; Petroglyphs; Pictography; Prehistoric art; Prehistoric sculpture.

Caves. Cave(s). Cavern(s). Grotto(es,s). *See also* Natural environment.

CD ROMs. CD ROM(s). CD-ROM(s). Compact Disc Read Only Memory. Hybrid CD(s). *See also* Computers; DVDs; Interactive video.

Ceilings, glass. See *Barriers; Employment discrimination; Occupational segregation; Sex discrimination; Sexual division of labor.*

Celebrations. See *Anniversaries and special events; Ceremonies; Entertaining; Festivals; Holidays.*

Celebrities. See *Famous people.*

Celibacy. Celiba(cy,te,tes). Abstention from sexual intercourse. Abstinen(t,ce). Abstain(ing). Monastic(ism). Ascetic(ism). Chast(e,ity). Self-denial. Sexless(ness). *Consider also:* asexual(ity), priesthood. *See also* Abstinence; Alternative lifestyles; Chastity; Monasticism; Self sacrifice; Sex behavior; Sexual abstinence; Virginity.

Celtic languages. Celtic language(s). Brythonic: Breton, Cornish, Middle Welsh, Welsh (Cymric). Continental: Gaulish. Goidelic: Irish, Manx, Middle Irish, Old Irish, Scots Gaelic. *See also* Language; Languages (as subjects); Western Europe.

Cemeteries. Cemeter(y,ies). Graveyard(s). Grave site(s). Burial ground(s). Burial place(s). Burying ground(s). Burying place(s). Potter's field. Tomb(s). Tombstone(s). Entomb(ed,ing). Gravestone(s). Tumul(li,us). Ossuar(y,ies). Sepulcher(s). Sepulchre(s). Churchyard(s). Necropol(is,ises,es,eis,i). *Choose from:* burial, mortuary *with:* pit(s), mound(s), site(s). *Consider also:* boneyard(s), boot hill, God's acre, memorial park(s), polyandrium. *See also* Attitudes toward death; Burials; Cultural property; Death rituals; Grave goods; Sepulchral monuments.

Cenotaphs. See *Monuments.*

Censorship. Censor(ed,ing,s,ship). *Choose from:* ban(ned,ning), proscrib(e,ed,ing), forbid(den), burn(ed,ing,ings), blacklisting, blackout(s), expurgat(e,ed,ing,ion), purg(e,ed,ing), condemn(ed,ation), restrict(ed,ing,ion,ions), block(s,ed,ing) access, restrict(s,ed,ing) access, bowdleriz(e,ed,ing), suppress(ed,ing, ion), doctrinal disapproval, control(led, ling), curb(s,ed,ing) *with:* information, knowledge, book(s), text(s), textbook(s), media, idea(s), press, mail, writing(s), art(s,ist,ists,istic), site(s), server(s), service provider(s). *Consider also:* anti-slamming, blue pencil, Papal index, Index librorum prohibitorum, decency movement(s), citizens for decent literature, gag order(s), biblioclast(s), V

chip(s). *See also* Academic freedom; Ban; Blacklisting; Broadcasting censorship; Censure; Classified information; Desexualization; Forbidden; Freedom of information; Freedom of the press; Government secrecy; Information policy; Library censorship; Lost literature; Malin-formation; Mass media policy; Media portrayal; Moral conditions; Moral education; Morality; Negative sanctions; News policies; Political repression; Pornography; Social values; War news.

Censorship, broadcasting. See *Broadcasting censorship.*

Censorship, library. See *Library censorship.*

Censure. Censur(e,ed,ing). Criticiz(e,ed, ing). Blam(e,ed,ing). Find(ing) fault(s). Fault finding. Condemn(ed,ing). Denounc(e,ed,ing). Denunciat(e,ed, ing,ion). Reprehend(ed,ing). Reprobat(e, ed,ing). *Consider also:* rebuk(e,ed,ing), reprimand(ed,ing), reproach(ed,ing), reprov(e,ed,ing), disdain(ed,ing), scorn(ed,ing), disapprov(e,ed,ing), oppos(e,ed,ing), reject(ed,ing), stigmatiz(e,ed,ing,ation). *See also* Blame; Censorship; Denunciation; Derogation; Disapproval; Negative sanctions; Punishment.

Census. Census(es). Demographic data. Population statistics. Population register(s). Population registr(y,ies, ation). Population count(s). Head count(s). Population survey(s). Demographic indicator(s). Size of population. Demographic characteristic(s). *Consider also:* population enumerat(e,ed,ing,ion), poll(s), number of households. *See also* Community size; Demographic changes; Demographic surveys; Demography; Enumeration; Households; Population (statistics); Statistical data.

Centenarians. See *Aged 80 and over.*

Center and periphery. Center and periphery. *Choose from:* center(s), core(s), central, primary sector(s), developed nation(s), western nation(s) *with:* peripher(y,ies,al,alization), margin(s), marginal(ity,ization), colon(y, ies), latifund(ia,ium,ismo), semi-peripheral, satellite(s), puppet state(s), satrap(s,y), dependen(t,cy). *Consider also:* metropolis(es), inner cit(y,ies) *with:* surrounding(s), suburb(s). *See also* Colonialism; Dependency theory (international); Developing countries; Dual economy; Economic underdevelopment; Global inequality; Imperialism; International division of labor; Labor market segmentation; Majority groups; Marginality (sociological); Metropolitan areas; Minority groups; Social structure; Spheres of influence; Trade; Underdevelopment; World systems theory.

Centeredness, self. See *Egocentrism.*

Centers, birthing. See *Birthing centers.*

Centers, community. See *Community centers.*

Centers, community health. See *Community health centers.*

Centers, day reporting corrections. See *Day reporting centers (corrections).*

Centers, detention. See *Detention centers.*

Centers, information. See *Information centers.*

Centers, learning. See *Learning centers.*

Centers, neighborhood health. See *Community health centers.*

Centers, poison control. See *Poison control centers.*

Centers, rehabilitation. See *Rehabilitation centers.*

Centers, shopping. See *Shopping centers.*

Centers, trauma. See *Trauma centers.*

Centos. Cento(s). Collage(s). Pastiche(s). Literary patchwork(s). Poetic patchwork(s). *See also* Ancient literature; Collage; Intertextuality; Macaronic literature; Patchwork; Quodlibets.

Central America. Central America(n). Belize(an) [British Honduras]. Costa Rica(n). El Salvador. Guatemala(n). Nicaragua(n). Hondura(s,n). Panam(a,anian). *See also* Caribbean; Central American native cultural groups; Latin Americans; Macro-Chibchan languages; North America; Penutian languages; Pre-Columbian empires; South America; Uto-Aztecan languages.

Central American Indians. See *Central American native cultural groups.*

Central American native cultural groups. Central American Indian(s). Central American Amerind(s). Middle American Indian(s). *Choose from:* Indian(s), Mestizo(s), native American(s), indigenismo *with:* Mexico, Belize, Carribean, Nicaragua, El Salvador, Costa Rica, Panama, Honduras, Guatemala. *Consider also:* Chorotega, Chibcha, Olmec, Teotihuacan, Toltec, Mixtec, Zapotec, Aztec, Quiche, Chorotega, Arawak, Carib, San blas, Mosquitia, Lacandones, Huastec, Tarascan, Yaqui, Tarahumara, Cuna, Quekchi, Maya, Mayan, Cakchiquel, Guaymi, etc. *See also* Cargo systems; Central America; Cultural groups; Culture (anthropology); Culture change; Culture contact; Ethnic groups; Hunting and gathering societies; Indigenous populations; Latin Americans; Macro-Chibchan languages; North American native cultural groups; Penutian languages; Pre-Columbian empires; South American native cultural groups; Traditional societies; Uto-Aztecan languages.

Central Asia. Central Asia(n). Kazakh(s,stan) [Kazak, Kazakhi(s,stan, Soviet Union)]. Turkmen(s,istan). Uzbekh(s,istan) [Uzbek]. Tadzhik(s,stan) [Tajik]. Kirghiz(ia,es) [Kirgiz]. *See also* Asian empires; East Altaic languages; Eastern Europe; Luorawetlan languages; Middle East; Samoyedic languages; South Asia; Southeast Asia; West Altaic languages.

Central cities. See *Inner cities.*

Central government. Central(ized) government(s). National government(s). Federal government(s). Federation(s). *See also* Capital cities; Federalism; Local government; Presidents.

Central nervous system. See *Nervous system.*

Central tendency measures. Central tendency measure(s). Measure(s) of central tendency. Centrality index(es). *Consider also:* mean(s), median(s), mode(s). *See also* Statistical significance.

Centrality. Central(ity). Core. *Consider also:* central value system(s), core econom(y,ies). *See also* Core; Group dynamics; Marginality (sociological); Organizational structure; Social structure.

Centralization. Centraliz(ed,ing,ation). Centralized administration(s). Consolidat(ed,ion,ions). Cluster(s,ed, ing). Concentrat(e,ed,ion,ions). Unif(y, ying,ied,ication). *Consider also:* unitary state(s), incorporat(e,ed,ing,ion), integrat(e,ed,ing,ion). *See also* Decentralization; Organizational change; Organizational structure.

Centrally planned economies. Centrally planned econom(y,ies). Command econom(y,ies). Second World. Marxist Leninist state(s). Communist countr(y, ies). *Consider also (through the 1980s):* Albania, Bulgaria, Cambodia, China, Cuba, Czechoslovakia, GDR, Hungary, North Korea, Laos, Mongolia, Poland, Romania, USSR, Vietnam, Yugoslavia. *See also* Countries in transition; Economic planning; Socialism; State planning.

Century, nineteenth. See *Nineteenth century.*

Cephalometry. Cephalometr(y,ic). Craniometr(y,ic). Cephalometr(y,ic). Facial measurement(s). Cephalogram(s). Facial symmetroscope. Craniofacial dimension(s). Dento-facial morphology. *See also* Diagnosis; Physiognomy; Research methods; Somatotypes.

Ceramics. Ceramic(s). Pottery. Earthenware. Porcelain. Brick(s). Vase(s). Tile(s). Clay pot(s). Crock(s). Delftware. Stoneware. Ironstone. Mosaic(s). Transfer ware. *See also* Collectibles; Crafts; Pottery; Sculpture.

Cerebral dominance. Cerebral dominance. *Choose from:* cerebral, hemispheric *with:* specialization, asymmetr(y,ies), lateralization, dominance. *Consider also:* lateral dominance, laterality. *See also* Brain; Laterality.

Cerebral hemorrhage. Cerebral hemorrhage(s). *Choose from:* cerebral, cerebellar, subarachnoid, cerebrum, intracranial, intracerebral, dominant hemisphere, craniocerebral, intracranial, intracerebral, cerebrovascular *with:* hemorrhage(s), hematoma(s), clot(s), hemorrhagic accident(s). *Consider also:* apoplexy, stroke(s), cerebrovascular accident(s), epidural hematoma(s), subdural hematoma(s), subarachnoid hemorrhage(s), brain attack(s). *See also* Cardiovascular system; Hemorrhage.

Cerebral palsy. Cerebral pals(y,ied). Little(s) disease. Spastic paralysis. Cerebral spastic infantile paralysis. *See also* Brain damage; Nervous system.

Cerebrovascular accidents. See *Cerebral hemorrhage.*

Ceremonial exchanges. Ceremonial exchange(s). Ritual(ized) exchange(s). Kula exchange(s). Ritual prestation. Ritual gift exchange(s). Nonutilitarian exchange(s). Ritualized gift-giving. *See also* Ceremonial objects; Folk culture; Money (primitive cultures); Reciprocity; Social exchange; Traditional societies.

Ceremonial objects. Ceremonial object(s). Ritual object(s). Ceremonial piece(s). Ceremonial mask(s). Ceremonial art. Ritualized exchange(s). Magical figure(s). *Choose from:* ceremonial, ritual(s,ized), symbolic, liturgical *with:* object(s), piece(s), mask(s), art, dress, headdress(es), feather(s), shell(s), chalice(s), clothing. Ritualized exchange(s). Magical figure(s). *Consider also:* sanctuary fixture(s), wine, bread, incense, spice(s), paten, cross(es), crucifix(es), rosar(y,ies), prayer shawl(s), kiddush cup(s), menorah(s), mezuzah(s), shofar(s), hanukkiah(s), penjor(s), lamak(s), etc. *See also* Ceremonial exchanges; Chalices; Fetishism; Folk culture; Relics; Religious articles; Religious practices; Totemism.

Ceremonies. Ceremon(y,ies,ials,ious). Rite(s). Ritual(s,istic,ism). Celebrat(ed, ing,ory,ion,ions). *Consider also:* initiation(s), religious service(s), commencement(s), rite(s) of passage, wedding(s), funeral(s), baptism(s), confirmation(s), birth rite(s), death rite(s), initiation rite(s), marriage rite(s). *See also* Anniversaries and special events; Baptism; Confirmation; Festivals; Funeral rites; Holidays; Religious rituals; Rites of passage; Rituals; Weddings.

Ceremonies, religious. See *Religious rituals.*

Certainty. Certain(ty). Certitude. Doubtless(ness). Infallib(le,ility). Confirmed. Unchang(eable,ing). Assur(ed,ance,ances). Reliab(le,ility). Uncertainty reduction. Irrefutab(le,ility). Valid(ated,ity). Verified. *Consider also:* trust, faith, proof, proven, unquestioning, sure(ness), convinced, stability, invariab(le,ility), secur(e,ity). *See also* Anxiety; Beliefs; Infallibility; Morale; Predictability; Risk; Security; Stability; Validity.

Certificates. Certificat(e,es,ion,ions). Acknowledgement(s). Affidavit(s). Affirmation(s). Authentication(s). Authorization(s). Coupon(s). Credential(s). Deposition(s). Diploma(s). Endorsement(s). Guarantee(s). License(s). Permit(s). Record(s). Testament(s). Ticket(s). Voucher(s). Warrant(y,ies). *See also* Accreditation; Awards; Certification; Guarantees; Legal documents; Licenses; Records.

Certificates, birth. See *Birth certificates.*

Certificates, death. See *Death certificates.*

Certification. Certif(y,ying,ied,ication). Credential(s,ing,ism). Accredit(ed,ing, ation). Licens(e,es,ed,ing). Validat(ed, ing,ion,ions). Document(ed,ing). Substantiat(e,ed,ing,ion). Approve(d). Approval(s). Meet(ing) standard(s). Seal of approval. *See also* Accreditation; Assurances; Certificates; Credentialing; Legitimacy; Licenses; Occupational qualifications; Professional certification.

Certification, professional. See *Professional certification.*

Cessation, smoking. See *Smoking cessation.*

Chad languages. Chad language(s). Hausa. Angas. *See also* African cultural groups; Language; Languages (as subjects); Sub-Saharan Africa.

Chain, food. See *Food chain.*

Chain of being. Chain of being. Great chain of being. Arthur Onken Lovejoy. Principle of plenitude. *Consider also:* chain of universal being, tree of life, priorit(y,ies). *See also* Hierarchy; Intellectual history; Philosophy; World history.

Chalices. Chalice(s). Eucharistic cup(s). Communion cup(s). Goblet(s). Holy Grail. Drinking vessel(s). Ceremonial vessel(s). Cibori(a,um). Monstrance(s). Ostensori(a,um). *See also* Ceremonial objects; Religious articles.

Challenge. Challeng(e,es,ed,ing). Attack(ed,ing,s). Confront(ed,ing,ation). Countercharg(e,ed,ing,es). Def(y,ied, ying,iant). Demand(ed,ing). Disput(e,ed, ing). Oppos(e,ed,ing,ition). Protest(ed, ing,ation). Remonstra(te,ted,ing,ance). Threaten(ed,ing). Provocation(s). Question(ed,ing). Doubt(ed,ing). Mistrust(ed,ing). *Consider also:* dar(e,ed,ing), tak(e,en,ing) exception. *See also* Aggression; Athletic participation; Barriers; Competition; Competitive behavior; Quests; Rivalry; Sport psychology; Sports.

Chamber music. Chamber music. Kammermusik. Musique de chambre. Instrumental motet(s). Sonata da camera. Sonata da chiesa. *Consider also:* ensemble(s), quartet(s), sextet(s), septet(s), octet(s), quintet(s), nonet(s), trio sonata(s). *See also* Motets; Music.

Chance. Chance. Fortune. Fate. Luck(y,iness). Gambl(e,er,ers,ing). Odds. Betting. Throw dice. Throw die. Risk(s,y). Tossed coin(s). Lotter(y,ies). Probability. Aleator(y,ic). *See also* Betting; Certainty; Chaos; Contingency; Entropy; Fate; Gambling; Probability; Random; Risk.

Chance composition. Chance composition(s). Aleator(y,ic) music. Chance music. Music of indeterminacy. Musical dice game(s). *Consider also:* dice music, dice composer(s), stochastic music, Fluxus movement, John Cage. *See also* Improvisation (music); Indeterminism; Music; Twentieth century Western art music.

Change. Chang(e,es,ed,ing,over,overs). Adapt(ed,ing,ation,ions). Alter(ed,ing, ation,ations). Awaken(ed,ing). Becoming. Born again. Centration. Convert(ed, ing). Conversion(s). Decentration. Dynamic(s,ally). Emerg(e,ed,ing,ence). Evolution(ary). Evolv(e,ed,ing). Fluctuat(e,ed,ing,ion,ions). Grow(th, ing). Innovat(e,ed,ing,ion,ions). Metamorphos(is,es). Moderniz(e,ed, ing,ation,ations). Modif(y,ying,ied, ication,ications). Movement(s). Mutat(e,ed,ing,ion,ions). Progress(ed, ing). Rebirth. Reborn. Recondition(ed, ing,ion). Reconfigur(e,ed,ing,ation). Reconstruct(ed,ing,ion). Reform(ed, ing,ation,ations). Regenerat(e,ed,ing, ion). Regress(ed,ing,ion). Rehabilitat(e, ed,ing,ion). Remodel(led,ling). Renew(ed,ing,al). Rise and fall. Reorder(ed,ing). Reorganiz(e,ed,ing, ation,ations). Repattern(ed,ing). Restructur(e,ed,ing). Resurgence. Revis(e,ed,ing,ion,ions). Revitaliz(e,ed, ing,ation). Revolution(ary). Shift(ed,ing,s). Transform(ed,ing,ation, ations). Transubstantiat(e,ed,ing,ion). Tweak(ed,ing). Turn(ed,ing). Variation(s). *See also* Adjustment (to environment); Attitude change; Behavior modification; Birth; Career change; Change agents; Community change; Culture change; Death; Demographic changes; Development; Developmental stages; Divorce; Economic change; Editing; Escalation; Evolution; Expansion; Improvement; Innovations; Inventions; Life change events; Life stage transitions; Marriage; Metamorphosis; Midcareer change; Neighborhood change; Organizational change; Peaceful change; Personality change; Progress; Reform; Religious conversion; Relocation; Residential mobility; Revolution; Sex change; Social change; Strategies; Technological change; Trends.

Change, attitude. See *Attitude change.*

Change, behavior. See *Behavior modification.*

Change, career. See *Career change.*

Change, community. See *Community change.*

Change, conversion. See *Change; Metamorphosis.*

Change, cultural. See *Culture change.*

Change, culture. See *Culture change.*

Change, curriculum. See *Curriculum change.*

Change, economic. See *Economic change.*

Change, employment. See *Career change.*

Change, job. See *Career change; Career mobility; Employee turnover; Personnel termination.*

Change, language. See *Language change.*

Change, life events. See *Life change events.*

Change , midcareer. See *Midcareer change.*

Change, neighborhood. See *Neighborhood change.*

Change, opinion. See *Attitude change.*

Change, organizational. See *Organizational change.*

Change, peaceful. See *Peaceful change.*

Change, personality. See *Personality change.*

Change, population. See *Demographic changes.*

Change, residential. See *Residential mobility.*

Change, sex. See *Sex change.*

Change, social. See *Social change.*

Change, societal. See *Social change.*

Change, technological. See *Technological change.*

Change agents. Change agent(s). Agent(s) for change. Reformer(s). *Choose from:* agent(s), leader(ship), organizer(s), catalyst(s), facilitator(s) *with:* change(s), moderniz(e,ed,ing,ation), progress. *Consider also:* young turk(s). *See also* Advocacy; Attitude change; Catalyst;

Community change; Community organizers; Consultants; Dissent; Facilitation; Interest groups; Leadership; Mass media effects; Opinion leaders; Organizational change; Political leadership; Rebels; Social change; Social movements.

Change of life. See *Climacteric.*

Change ringing. Change ringing. *Choose from:* ring(s,ing), rang *with:* bell(s), tower bell(s), change(s), peal(s). *Consider also:* Grandsire triples, Treble bob, Plain hunt, Plain Bob, Cinques, Cambridge Surprise Minor, Stedman Caters, Spliced Major. St Clement's College Bob Caters, Plain Bob Royal, Bristol Surprise. Maximus, Reverse Canterbury Pleasure Place Doubles, Oxford Treble. Bob Minor, Xique-Xique Surprise Maximus, Twelve Spliced Surprise. Minor, Double Norwich Court Bob Major. *See also* Bells; Church music.

Changes, climatic. See *Climatic changes.*

Changes, demographic. See *Demographic changes.*

Changes, role. See *Life stage transitions.*

Channel capacity, human. See *Human channel capacity.*

Channelization, stream. See *Stream channelization.*

Channels (hydraulic engineering). Channel(s). Furrow(s). Groove(s). Ditch(es). Dike(s). Trough(s). Waterway(s). Aqueduct(s). Canal(s). Conduit(s). Duct(s). Watercourse(s). Pipeline(s). Conduit(s). Sluice gate(s). Culvert(s). Stream bed(s). *See also* Aqueducts; Canals; Flood control; Stream channelization; Streams.

Channels, distribution. See *Distribution channels.*

Channels, marketing. See *Distribution channels.*

Chants. Chant(s,ed,ing). *Consider also:* mantra(s), svarita(s), plainsong(s), Gregorian chant(s). *Consider also:* monod(y,ic). *See also* Canticles; Gregorian chants; Music; Plainsong; Religious music.

Chants, Gregorian. See *Gregorian chants.*

Chaos. Chao(s,tic,tically). Anarch(y,ical). Lawless(ness). Mobocra(cy,tic). Ochlocra(t,tic,cy). Misrule. Unrul(y, iness). Utter confusion. Formless(ness). Mad(ness). Disorder(ed,ly). *Consider also:* random(ness), surreal(ism,istic), incongru(ous,ity), chaosthetic(s,ism), bedlam, pandemonium, tumult(uous), turmoil, unrul(y,iness), unpredictab(le, leness,ility), discontin(uity,uous). *See also* Anarchism; Catastrophes; Chance;

Chaotic behavior in systems; Clutter; Confusion (disarray); Disintegration; Entropy; Lawlessness; Random; Social disorganization; Uncertainty.

Chaos management. Chaos management. Business process reengineering. Process innovation. Business process redesign. *See also* Globalization; Organizational change; Organizational development; Strategic management; Virtual organizations.

Chaotic behavior in systems. Chaotic behavior in system(s). Disordered system(s). Chaos theory. *See also* Chaos; Entropy.

Chapels. Chapel(s). Cappella(s). Capella(s). Chapelle(s). Capelle(n). Kappelle(n). Hofkapelle(n). Militarkapelle(n). *See also* Religious buildings; Places of worship; Sacred places.

Chaplains. Chaplain(s,cy). *Consider also:* hospital(s), military, Army, Navy, Air Force, Marines *with:* minister(s), priest(s), clergy(men), rabbi(s), chaplain(s), last rite(s), religious service(s). *See also* Religious personnel.

Chapters (organizations). Chapter(s). Division(s). Subdivision(s). Branch(es). Department(s). Section(s). *See also* Associations (organizations); Branch operations.

Character. Character. Personalit(y,ies). Disposition(s). Individuality. Temperament(s). Ego(s). Idiosyncras(y, ies). Uniqueness. Trait(s). Characteristic(s). *See also* Integrity; Lifestyle; Personal Habits; Personality; Personality traits; Self actualization; Self concept.

Character, national. See *National characteristics.*

Character, oral. See *Oral character.*

Character assassination. See *Libel.*

Character disorders. See *Personality disorders.*

Character sketches. Character sketch(es). Character stud(y,ies). Characterization(s). *Consider also:* character writer(s), vignette(s), literary portrait(s). *See also* Anecdotes; Characterization; Writing (composition).

Characteristics. Characteristic(s). Qualit(y,ies). Aspect(s). Bias(es). Essence(s). Style(s). Caliber(s). Complexion(s). Disposition(s). Propert(y,ies). Attribute(s). Trait(s). Feature(s). Peculiarit(y,ies). Oddit(y,ies). Idiosyncras(y,ies). Singularit(y,ies). Nature. Gift(s). Talent(s). *Consider also:* temperament(s), tendenc(y,ies), abilit(y, ies), capabilit(y,ies), eccentric(ity,ities), virtue(s), propert(y,ies). *See also* Client characteristics; Community characteristics; Cultural characteristics; Demo-

graphic characteristics (of individuals); Employee characteristics; Family characteristics; Idiosyncrasies; National characteristics; Physical characteristics; Population characteristics; Qualities; Residence characteristics; Sex characteristics; Speech characteristics; Student characteristics; Teacher characteristics; Therapist characteristics.

Characteristics, client. See *Client characteristics.*

Characteristics, community. See *Community characteristics.*

Characteristics, cultural. See *Cultural characteristics.*

Characteristics, demographic of individuals. See *Demographic characteristics (of individuals).*

Characteristics, demographic of population. See *Population characteristics.*

Characteristics, employee. See *Employee characteristics.*

Characteristics, family. See *Family characteristics.*

Characteristics, job. See *Job descriptions.*

Characteristics, national. See *National characteristics.*

Characteristics, patient. See *Client characteristics.*

Characteristics, personality. See *Personality traits.*

Characteristics, physical. See *Physical characteristics.*

Characteristics, population. See *Population characteristics.*

Characteristics, residence. See *Residence characteristics.*

Characteristics, sex. See *Sex characteristics.*

Characteristics, speech. See *Speech characteristics.*

Characteristics, student. See *Student characteristics.*

Characteristics, teacher. See *Teacher characteristics.*

Characteristics, therapist. See *Therapist characteristics.*

Characterization. Characteriz(e,ed,ing, ation). Represent(ed,ing,ation) in fiction. Portray(al). Depict(ed,ing,ation). Sketch(ed,es). *Consider also:* stereotyp(e,ed,ing). *See also* Character sketches; Media portrayal; Stereotyping.

Chariots. Chariot(s). Charioteer(s). *Consider also:* horse-drawn vehicle(s), wagon(s), coach(es), phaeton(s). *See also* Carriages; Ground transportation.

Charisma. Charisma(s,tic). Inspirational. Charm(ers,ing). Magnet(ic,izing). Larger than life. Irresistible. Captivating.

Superhuman. Enthralling. Gift of grace. Personal magnetism. *See also* Admiration; Attractiveness; Authority (power); Cults; Leadership style; Messianic movements; Political leadership; Popularity; Social skills.

Charitable behavior. Charitable behavior(s). Donor(s). Donat(e,ed, ation,ations). Aiding. Bequest(s). Volunteer(s,ed,ing). Help(ing). Altruis(m,tic). Prosocial behavior(s). Charit(ability,y,ies). Generous. Generosity. Noblesse oblige. Contribut(e,ed,ing, ion,ions). Share(d). Sharing. Assist(ance, ed,ing). Philanthrop(y,ies,ic). Benefactor(s). Humane(ness). Kind(ness). *Choose from:* charitable, voluntary *with:* giving, donation(s), contribution(s), trust(s), behavior(s). *Choose from:* giving, donating, contributing *with:* aid, help, assistance, deferred, charit(y,ies). *See also* Altruism; Assistance; Charity; Contributions; Favors; Generosity; Gift giving; Giving; Gleaning; Good works (theology); Helping behavior; Humanitarianism; Interpersonal relations; Kindness; Philanthropy; Prosocial behavior; Sharing; Social behavior; Social interaction; Volunteers.

Charitable organizations. See *Charities.*

Charitable trusts. Charitable trust(s). Charitable lead trust(s). Charitable remainder trust(s). Charitable remainder annuity trust(s). Charitable remainder uni-trust(s). *See also* Charities; Philanthropy.

Charities. Charit(y,ies). Philanthrop(y,ies, ic,ists). Humanitarian(s,ism). Goodwill. Donation(s). Contribution(s). Charitable trust(s). Almsgiver(s). Almshouse(s). Benevolence. Donor(s). Gift giving. Voluntary agenc(y,ies). Charitable organization(s). Foundation(s). Eleemosynary organization(s). Welfare work. *Choose from:* philanthropic, humanitarian, charitable, voluntary *with:* agenc(y,ies), organization(s), foundation(s). *Consider also:* American Cancer Society, American Foundation for the Blind, American Heart Association, American Red Cross, Catholic Charities, Easter Seal Society, March of Dimes, Salvation Army, etc. *See also* Agencies; Almshouses; Altruism; Assistance; Benefactors; Civil society; Charitable trusts; Contributions; Financial support; Foundations (organizations); Gift giving; Giving; Human services; Humanitarianism; Nongovernmental organizations; Nonprofit organizations; Philanthropy; Social action; Social agencies; Voluntary associations; Volunteers.

Charity. Charit(y,able). Goodwill. Mercy. Gener(osity,ous). Munificen(t,ce, centness). Unselfish(ness).

Magnan(imity,imous,imousness). Grace. Affection. Attachment. Love. Altruism. Benevolen(t,ce). Humane(ness). Kindl(y,iness). Amity. Friendl(y,iness). *Consider also:* sadaqah. *See also* Alms; Charitable behavior; Goodwill; Mercy; Theological virtues; Virtue.

Charivari. Charivari. Katzenmusik. Scampata. Shivaree. *Consider also:* cacophonous music. *See also* Noise (sounds).

Charters. Charter(s). Written instrument(s). Contract(s). Deed(s). Constitution(s). Conveyance(s). Articles of incorporation. *Consider also:* treat(y,ies), pact(s). *See also* Agreement (document); Cartularies; Constitution (legal); Documents; Legal documents; Manuscripts.

Chassidism. Chassid(im,ism,ic). Chasid(im,ism,ic). Hassid(im,ism,ic). Hasid(im,ism,ic). *Consider also:* Sabbatai Zvi, Baal Shem Tov, Lubavi(tcher,tchers,cher,chers), zaddik(im). *See also* Judaism; Mysticism.

Chastity. Chast(e,ity). Celiba(cy,te,tes). Abstention from sexual intercourse. Abstinen(t,ce). Abstain(ing). Monastic(ism). Continent. Ascetic(ism). Self-denial. *Consider also:* asexual(ity), priesthood. *See also* Celibacy; Monasticism; Sexual ethics; Virginity.

Chattel. See *Personal property.*

Chattering class. Chattering class(es). Pundit(s,ry). Critic(s). *Consider also:* bullcrit. *See also* Architectural criticism; Art criticism; Art critics; Commentators; Criticism; Literary criticism; Media portrayal; Opinion leaders; Social criticism.

Chauvinism. See *Age discrimination; Ethnocentrism; Male chauvinism; Nationalism; Nativism; Racism; Sexism; Social discrimination; Xenophobia.*

Chauvinism, male. See *Male chauvinism.*

Cheap labor. Cheap labor. *Choose from:* cheap, low cost, low wage(s), low pay(ing), low paid, underpaid *with:* labor, worker(s), staff, employee(s). *See also* Contract labor; Exploitation; Forced labor; Income inequality; Labor costs; Labor market segmentation; Living standards; Living conditions; Minimum wage; Prevailing wages; Sweatshops; Unpaid labor; Wage differentials; Wages; Women living in poverty; Workers' rights.

Cheating. Cheat(ed,er,ers,ing,s). Plagiariz(e,ed,ing). Plagiarism. Swindl(e,ed,er,ers). Deceiv(e,ed,ing). Deception(s). Fraud(ulent). Crib(bed,bing). Hoax(es). Ripoff(s). Rip(ped,ping) off. Pretense(s).

Chiseler(s). Phon(y,ies). Bluff(ed,ing,s). Delud(e,ed,ing). False data. Fake(s,ry). Fudg(e,ed,ing). False research. Puffery. Falsif(y,ying,ication). Concoct(ed,ing) data. Bend(ing) rule(s). Dishonest(y). Overvot(e,ed,ing). *Consider also:* termpaper mill(s). *See also* Antisocial behavior; Clandestinity; Codes of ethics; Deception; Deviant behavior; Falsification (scientific); Fraud; Offenses; Plagiarism; Test taking; Unethical conduct.

Checking, fact. See *Fact checking.*

Cheerfulness. Cheerful(ly,ness). Cheery. Optimis(m,t,ts,tic). Good morale. Lighthearted. Blithe. Carefree. Debonair. Jaunty. Buoyant. In good spirits. In high spirits. Of good cheer. Glad(ness). Merry. *Consider also:* playful(ness). *See also* Disposition (personality); Emotions; Frivolity; Happiness; Optimism; Smiling; Youthful.

Chemical contamination. See *Hazardous materials; Hazardous wastes.*

Chemical sensitivities, multiple. See *Multiple chemical sensitivities.*

Chemical warfare. Chemical warfare. Gas warfare. *Choose from:* chemical(s), poison(ous) gas(es), chlorine, phosgene, mustard gas, nitrogen mustard(s), nerve gas(es), tear gas, cyanide, battle gas(es), agent orange, napalm, yellow rain, chloropicrin, toxic agent(s), herbicide(s) *with:* war(fare), bomb(s), weapon(s), arms, munition(s), warhead(s), stockpile(s), artillery, shell(s). *Consider also:* nerve agent(s), VX, sarin, V-gas, precursor chemical(s). *See also* Biological warfare; International offenses; Poisonous gases; War crimes; War; Weapons of mass destruction.

Chemicals, agricultural. See *Agricultural chemicals.*

Chemistry, agricultural. See *Agricultural chemicals.*

Chemistry, archaeological. See *Archaeological chemistry.*

Cherry picking. See *Biased selection.*

Chest. Chest(s). Thorax(es). Thorac(ic,es). *Consider also:* lung(s), breast(s), bosom(s), bust(s), pneumothorax(es), pleura(s,l). *See also* Anatomy; Human body.

Chicanos. See *Mexican American(s).*

Chickens. Chick(en,ens,s). Gallinacea. Poultry. Fowl(s). Pullet(s). Rooster(s). Hen(s). *Consider also:* Leghorn(s), Minorca(s), Aneona(s), Black Spanish, Plymouth Rock, Rhode Island Red, Wyandotte, etc. *See also* Animals; Cocks; Livestock; Poultry.

Chief executive officers. Chief executive officer(s). CEO(s). Chief executive(s). Boss(es). President(s). Top manager(s). Top executive(s). Top post(s). *Consider also:* business leader(s). *See also* Administrators; Managers; Presidents.

Chiefs. Chief(s,tain,tains). Hereditary leader(s,ship,ships). Big men. Big man. Headm(en,an). Sachem(s). Tauvia. Khan(s). Ariki. Aliki. Ingada. *See also* Clans; Monarchy; Priests and priestly classes (anthropology); Primitive government; Traditional societies.

Chiefs, tribal. See *Chiefs.*

Chiesa, sonata da. See *Sonata da chiesa.*

Child. See *Children.*

Child, only. See *Only child.*

Child, unborn. See *Fetus.*

Child abuse. Child abuse. Abused child(ren). Child murder(s). Infanticide. Shaken baby syndrome. *Choose from:* abus(e,ed,ive,ing), cruel(ty), throwaway, harass(ed,ing,ment,ments), threat(s, ened,ening), victimiz(e,ed,ing,ation), tortur(e,es,ed,ing), mistreat(ed,ing, ment), maltreat(ed,ing,ment), shak(e,en), molest(ed,ing,ation,ations), batter(ed, ing), brutal(ity,ities), throwaway *with:* child(ren), boy(s), girl(s), bab(y,ies), infant(s), minor(s), juvenile(s), kid(s). *Consider also:* parent(s,al), famil(y,ies) *with:* brutal(ity), abusive, violen(t,ce). *Consider also:* Child Abuse Prevention and Treatment Act, PL 93-247, emotional abuse, sexual abuse, verbal abuse of children. *See also* Abusive parents; Antisocial behavior; Battered women; Child abuse prevention; Child kidnapping; Child labor; Child neglect; Children; Children's rights; Failure to thrive (psychosocial); Family problems; Family violence; Generational cycle of child abuse; Incest; Molested children; Parent child relations; Punitiveness; Sex offenders; Sexual abuse; Sexual exploitation; Sexual harassment; Spouse abuse; Statutory rape; Victimization; Violence.

Child abuse, generational cycle of. See *Generational cycle of child abuse.*

Child abuse prevention. Child abuse prevention. Child protection. Prevention of child mistreatment. Mentor(s) for abusing parent(s). Parents Anonymous. Child Abuse Prevention and Treatment Act, PL 93-247. *Choose from:* child(ren), student(s), daughter(s), son(s), infant(s), bab(y,ies) *with:* abus(e,ed), mistreat(ed,ment), cruel(ty), harass(ed,ment,ments), threaten(ed,ing), victimiz(ed,ing,ation), tortur(e,ed,ing), maltreat(ed,ment), molest(ed), batter(ed,ing), brutal(ity) *with:* prevent(ing,ed,ion), intervention(s), identification, detect(ed,ing,ion), report(ed,ing), protective service(s),

parent counseling, parent effectiveness training. *See also* Child abuse; Child advocacy; Children's rights; Ombudsmen; Parent help groups; Parent training; Self help groups.

Child adult relations. See *Parent child relations.*

Child advocacy. Child advocacy. *Choose from:* child(ren), juvenile(s), minor(s), youth(s), student(s), pupil(s) *with:* advocat(e,es,ing), ombuds(men,man, woman,women), lobb(y,ies,ying), support(ed,ing), back(ing,crs), defend(ing), protect(ion,ors), guardian(s), surrogate parent(s), in loco parentis, representative(s), behalf. *Consider also:* child(ren), minor(s), juvenile(s), youth, student(s), pupil(s) *with:* rights, justice, best interests. *See also* Advocacy; Child abuse; Child abuse prevention; Child custody; Children's rights; Individual needs; Legal guardians; Ombudsmen.

Child behavior. Child(hood,ren) behavior(s). *Choose from:* child(hood,ren), juvenile(s), student(s), pupil(s), classroom, minor(s) *with:* behavior(s,al), coping, competitive(ness), cooperative(ness), peer relation(s,ships), conduct, misbehavior, play(ed,ing,fulness), habit(s), obedien(t, ce), disobedien(t,ce), conformity, nonconformity, sociability, self-control. *See also* Behavior; Behavior development; Child discipline; Childhood play development.

Child behavior disorders. Child behavior disorder(s). *Choose from:* child(hood,ren,ren) juvenile(s), minor(s), student(s), pupil(s), classroom *with:* antisocial behavior(s), behavior disorder(s), separation anxiet(y,ies), stranger anxiety, nonhunger crying, negativism, reactive disorder(s), hyperkine(sis,tic), delinquen(t,cy), misbehavior, conduct disorder(s), nail biting, thumb sucking, enuresis, masturbat(e,e,ding,ion), tantrum(s), truan(t,cy), fight(ing), quarrel(ed,ing), disobedien(t,ce), lying, steal(ing), set(ting) fire(s), cruelty, vandalism, destructive(ness), sleepwalking, overactivity, devian(t,ce), maladapt(ed,ion). *See also* Behavior disorders; Child behavior; Child development disorders; Child reactive disorders; Childhood adjustment disorders; Childhood neurosis; Childhood psychosis; Childhood schizophrenia.

Child birth. See *Birth.*

Child care. Child care. *Choose from:* child(ren), infant(s), pre-school, preschool, toddler(s) *with:* care, daycare, day care, rearing. *Consider also:* puericulture, babysitt(er,ers,ing), headstart, preschool program(s), nursery

school(s), nurser(y,ies). *See also* Child caregivers; Child day care; Child self care; Child support; Childrearing; Employee benefits; Infant care.

Child care services. See *Child care; Child caregivers; Child day care; Corporate day care.*

Child caregivers. Child caregiver(s). Nann(y,ies). Child's nurse(maid). Nurserymaid(s). *Consider also:* child(ren's), pediatric, nursery school, headstart *with:* worker(s), caregiver(s), housemother(s), houseparent(s), nurse(s), governess(es), *Consider also:* babysitter(s), parent aide(s), amah(s), ayah(s), nana(s). *See also* Caregivers; Child day care; Governesses; Nonprofessional personnel.

Child custody. Child custody. In loco parentis. Joint custody. *Choose from:* child(ren), daughter(s), son(s), juvenile(s), minor(s) *with:* custod(y,ial, ianship), guardian(s,ship,ships), foster placement(s), surrogate parent(s). *See also* Child abuse; Child kidnapping; Child neglect; Child support; Childrearing; Divorce; Legal guardians; Parent child relations; Parental absence; Placement (of a dependent person); Single parent family; Visits.

Child day care. Child day care. Child daycare. *Choose from:* child(ren), infant(s), famil(y,ies) *with:* day(time), after school *with:* care, babysit(ting, ters). *Consider also:* child care *with:* center(s), program(s), services, facilit(y, ies), arrangement(s), setting(s), environment(s), home(s). *Consider also:* preschool institutions, employer supported day care. *See also* Caregivers; Child care; Child caregivers; Corporate day care.

Child development. Child development. *Choose from:* child(ren,hood), juvenile, pediatric, infant(s), bab(y,ies), neonat(e,es,al), adolescen(t,ce), psychosocial, psychosexual, emotional, personality, physical, cognitive, moral, intellectual, social, language, autonomy, motor, physical, sexual, psychophysiological, psychomotor, speech *with:* development(al), develop(ed,ing), growth, matur(ed,ing), maturation, immatur(e,ity), transition(s,al), stage(s). *Consider also:* oral, anal, phallic, genital *with:* stage(s). *See also* Adolescent development; Age differences; Autism; Bonding (emotional); Child development disorders; Child language; Child nutrition; Childrearing; Cognitive development; Delayed development; Developmental disabilities; Developmental stages; Early childhood development; Egocentrism; Emotional development; Euthenics; Failure to thrive (psychosocial); Home environment; Human development; Individual differences; Infant development; Life cycle; Moral development; Motor development; Object relations; Oedipus complex; Perceptual development; Physical development; Psychomotor development; Sensory integration; Socialization.

Child development disorders. Child(ren,hood) development(al) disorder(s). *Choose from:* child(ren, hood), juvenile(s), pediatric, infan(t,ts, cy), neonat(e,es,al) *with:* development(al,ally), growth, maturation(al) *with:* disorder(s), deviation(s), delay(ed, s), disabilit(y,ies), disabled, arrested, retard(ed,ation). *Consider also:* infantilism, autism, dyslexia, dysplasia, minimal brain dysfunction(s), learning disabilit(y,ies), learning disorder(s), hyperact(ive,ivity), hyperkine(sis,tic), delayed speech. *See also* Delayed development; Developmental disabilities; Developmental stages; Failure to thrive (psychosocial); Learning disabilities; Speech disorders.

Child discipline. Child discipline. *Choose from:* child(hood,ren), juvenile(s), student(s), pupil(s), classroom, parental *with:* disciplin(ary,e,ed,ing), punish(ed, ing,ment,ments), enforc(e,ed,ing,ement), obedien(t,ce), rules of conduct, oppositional training, behavior(al) control, management, coercive intervention, sanction(s), spank(ed,ing), regulation(s). *See also* Childrearing; Classroom environment; Corporal punishment; Discipline; Nonpunitive approach (discipline); Parent child communication; Parent child relations; Permissiveness; Punitiveness; School discipline; School expulsion; School suspension.

Child father communication. See *Father child communication.*

Child father relations. See *Father child relations.*

Child guidance. Child guidance. Pupil personnel services. *Choose from:* child(ren), juvenile(s), pediatric, infant(s), school, pupil(s), preschool *with:* guidance, counseling, psychoanalysis, psychiatry, therap(y,ies), casework, social work, psychotherapeutic intervention(s), psychotherap(y,ies), psychiatric treatment(s), play therap(y,ies), art therap(y,ies), role playing, group therap(y,ies). *See also* Family therapy; School counseling.

Child health services. Child health service(s). Pediatrics. *Choose from:* child(ren,hood), pediatric, school, student(s), pupil(s), infant(s) *with:* health, medical, dental, psychiatric, mental health, rehabilitat(ion,ive), nursing, primary, patient, outpatient, clinical, treatment, emergency, dietary *with:* service(s), program(s), outreach,

care, clinic(s), center(s). *See also* Child nutrition; Community health services; Family physicians; Health facilities; Pediatrics; School meals.

Child impersonators. Child impersonat(or,ors,ion,ions). *Choose from:* child(ren), boy(s), girl(s), juvenile(s) *with:* impersonat(or,ors,ion, ions,ing,ed), imitat(or,ors,ion,ions, ing,ed), mimic(s,king,ked), caricature, parod(y,ies). *See also* Acting; Entertainers; Impostor.

Child kidnapping. Child kidnapping. Childsnatch(ed,ing,er,ers). Childsteal(ing,er,ers). Childnapp(ed,ing, er,ers). Childfind(er,ers,ing). *Choose from:* child(ren,hood), adolescen(t,ts,ce), kid(s), youngster(s), daughter(s), son(s), juvenile(s), boy(s), girl(s), infant(s), bab(y,ies) or names of specific victims *with:* stolen, abduct(ed,ing,ion,ions), kidnap(ped,ping), missing, snatch(ed, ing), vanish(ed,ing), seiz(e,ed,ing), captur(e,ed,ing), ransom(ed,ing), hostage(s). *See also* Abduction; Child abuse; Child custody; Hostages; Kidnapping; Missing persons.

Child labor. Child labor(ers). *Choose from:* child(ren), minor(s), juvenile(s), girl(s), adolescent(s), boy(s), student(s), pupil(s), kid(s), 10-year-olds, 14-year-olds, etc. *with:* labor(er,ers,ing), employ(ee,ees,ed,ing,ment), work(er,ers, ed,ing), sweatshop(s), millwork(ers), exploit(ed,ing,ation), payroll, bondage, bonded labor, enslave(d,ment), economic activit(y,ies), forced prostitution, commercial sex. *See also* Child abuse; Employment; Forced labor; Labor economics; Labor force; Labor market; Labor standards; Sexual exploitation; Sweatshops; Trafficking in persons; Workers; Workers' rights.

Child language. Child language. Baby talk. Babytalk. *Choose from:* child(ren,ren's), preschool(er,ers), pre-school(er,ers), early, toddler(s), *with:* speech, sentence(s), language, phonology, vocabular(y,ies), word choice(s), communication. *Consider also:* language acquisition, acquisition of grammar. *See also* Baby talk; Bilingualism; Child development; Children; Egocentrism; Language acquisition; Monolingualism; Pronunciation; Speech development.

Child molestation. See *Incest; Molested children; Sexual abuse; Sexual exploitation; Sexual harassment.*

Child mortality. Child mortalit(y,ies). *Choose from:* child(ren), childhood, juvenile(s), pediatric, minor(s), youth, elementary school student(s) *with:* mortalit(y,ies), death rate, death(s), dead, casualt(y,ies). *See also* Children; Death; Infant mortality; Mortality rates; Survival.

Child mother communication. See *Mother child communication.*

Child mother relations. See *Mother child relations.*

Child neglect. Child neglect. Negligent parent(s). Fail(ed,ing,ure) to care for child(ren). *Choose from:* neglect(ed), abandon(ed,ment), emotional(ly) neglect(ed), deserted, depriv(ed,ation), uncared, underfed, unloved, throwaway, malnourish(ed,ment) *with:* child(ren, hood), infant(s), bab(y,ies), juvenile(s), minor(s). *Consider also:* low weight for age children, starving children, institutional neglect of child(ren), child malnutrition. *See also* Abandoned children; Antisocial behavior; Child abuse; Child advocacy; Child custody; Child nutrition; Childrearing; Children; Deadbeat parents; Failure to thrive (psychosocial); Family problems; Family violence; Foundlings; Homeless children; Parent child relations; Parental absence; Placement (of a dependent person); Psychosocial deprivation; Runaways; Street children; Unwanted children; Victimization.

Child nutrition. Child(ren,hood) nutrition. *Choose from:* nutrition(al), foodservice(s), feeding, food supplement(s), diet(ary,s), body weight, RDA, recommended daily allowance(s), vitamin(s), underfed, malnutrition, malnourish(ed,ment) *with:* child(ren, hood), juvenile(s), infant(s), pupil(s), student(s), minor(s), pediatric. *Consider also:* child(ren,hood) *with:* vitamin deficienc(y,ies), nutritional(ly) depriv(ed,ation). *See also* Child neglect; Food; Food services (programs); Malnutrition; Nutrition; School meals.

Child parent communication. See *Parent child communication.*

Child parent relations. See *Parent child relations.*

Child psychotherapy. See *Child guidance.*

Child reactive disorders. Child reactive disorder(s). *Choose from:* child(hood, ren), juvenile(s), early, preschool(er,ers), pre-school(er,ers), pediatric, pubert(y,al) *with:* reactive episode(s), situational reaction(s), psychiatric sequelae, separation reaction(s), depressive reaction(s), maladapt(ed,ing,ation), psychic trauma(s), reactive psychos(is, es), reactive depression(s), habit(s), fingersucking, thumbsucking, nail biting, runaway reaction(s). *See also* Childhood neurosis; Childhood adjustment disorders; Reactive depression; Reactive psychosis.

Child rearing. See *Childrearing.*

Child self care. Child self care. *Choose from:* self care, latchkey, unsupervised, without supervision, unattended, alone at home, alone after school *with:*

child(ren), juvenile(s), student(s), pupil(s). *See also* After school programs; Child day care.

Child support. Child support. *Choose from:* child(ren), offspring, daughter(s), son(s), famil(y,ies) with support(ed,ing). *Consider also:* child custody, alimony, paternity suit(s). *See also* Child custody; Divorce; Marital separation.

Child welfare. See *Antipoverty programs; Child day care; Child health services; Child support; Family assistence; Public welfare.*

Childbearing, early. See *Teenage mothers.*

Childbearing, late. See *Late childbearing.*

Childbearing age. Childbearing age(s). Sexual maturity. Sexually mature. Reproductive age(s). *Consider also:* young wom(an,en), adolescent girl(s). *See also* Biological clocks; Late childbearing; Maternal age; Senior pregnancies; Sexual maturation; Teenage mothers.

Childbirth. See *Birth; Labor (childbirth).*

Childbirth, home. See *Home birth.*

Childbirth, natural. See *Natural childbirth.*

Childbirth training. Childbirth training. *Choose from:* birth, childbirth, Lamaze, prenatal, expectant mother(s), expectant parent(s) with: train(ed,ing), preparation, education, class(es), discussion group(s). *See also* Birth; Labor (childbirth); Natural childbirth; Pregnancy.

Childfree marriages. See *Childlessness.*

Childhood. See *Children.*

Childhood, early. See *Preschool children.*

Childhood, early education. See *Preschool education; Primary education.*

Childhood adjustment disorders. Childhood adjustment disorder(s). *Choose from:* child(hood,ren), preschool, pre-school, infant(s,ile), juvenile(s), pediatric, pubert(y,al) with: adjustment(s), conduct, habit(s), trait(s), behavior(s), reactive with: disorder(s), disturbance(s), neurotic. *Consider also:* bedwetting, enuresis, nailbiting, thumbsucking, masturbation, tantrum(s), truancy, stealing, destructive(ness), vandalism, running away, tic(s), somnambulism, stutter(ed,ing), overactivity, phobia(s). *See also* Adjustment disorders; Child behavior disorders; Child reactive disorders; Childhood neurosis.

Childhood development. See *Child development.*

Childhood development, early. See *Early childhood development.*

Childhood memories. See *Early memories.*

Childhood neurosis. Childhood

neuros(is,es). *Choose from:* child(hood,ren), preschool, pre-school, infant(s,ile), juvenile(s), pediatric, pubert(y,al) *with:* neuros(is,es), neurotic(ism), psychoneurotic, psychoneuros(is,es), anxious(ness), anxiet(y,ies), bedwetting, depress(ed, ion), obsessive compulsive, nervous(ness), emotional(ly) disturb(ed,ance,ances), character disorder(s), enuresis, personality disorder(s). *See also* Childhood adjustment disorders; Child reactive disorders; Neuroses.

Childhood pervasive development disorders. See *Pervasive development disorders.*

Childhood play development. Childhood play development. *Choose from:* child(ren,hood), early, kindergarten(s,er, ers), preschool(er,ers), pre-school(er, ers), nursery school *with:* development(al), maturation(al), learn(ed,ing), socializ(ed,ing,ation), creativ(e,ity), social function(s), cognit(ive,ion), skill(s), sharing, social skill(s) *with:* play(ed,ing,thing,things), game(s), toy(s). *See also* Child development; Children's games; Play; Playgrounds.

Childhood psychosis. Childhood psychos(is,es). *Choose from:* child(hood,ren), infant(s,ile), juvenile(s), pediatric, pubert(y,al), preschool, pre-school, adolescen(t,ce) *with:* psychos(is,es), psychotic, autis(m,tic), schizophren(ia,ic), borderline state(s), severely disturbed, dementia, echolalia, mental(ly) ill(ness), paranoia(s,d), hallucination(s), depress(ed,ion). *Consider also:* pedophrenia. *See also* Autism; Childhood schizophrenia; Psychoses.

Childhood schizophrenia. Childhood schizophrenia. Schizophrenic child(ren). *Choose from:* child(hood,ren), infant(s, ile), juvenile(s), pediatric, pubert(y,al), preschool, pre-school, adolescen(t,ce) *with:* schizophren(ia,ic). *Consider also:* autis(m,tic), infantile psychos(is,es). *See also* Autism; Childhood psychosis; Schizophrenia; Schizophrenogenic family; Symbiotic infantile psychosis.

Childlessness. Childless(ness). Steril(e,ity). Infertil(e,ity). Optional parenthood. Parenthood option. Childfree. Child free. Reproductive barrier(s). Empty nest. Nullipar(a,ous,ity). *Choose from:* marriage(s), couple(s) *with:* without children. *See also* Delayed parenthood; Family characteristics; Family planning; Family planning attitudes; Family size.

Childrearing. Childrearing. Child rearing. Parent(ing,craft). *Choose from:* child(ren), son(s), daughter(s), offspring, boy(s), girl(s), infan(t,ts,cy), bab(y,ies) *with:* rear(ed,ing), socializ(ed,ing,ation), nurtur(e,ance,ing), toilet training,

discipline, permissive(ness), wean(ed, ing), train(ed,ing), rais(ed,ing), bring(ing) up, brought up, mothering, fathering, care, upbringing. *Consider also:* parent(s,al), maternal, paternal, father(s), mother(s), famil(y,ies,ial) *with:* role(s), permissive(ness), strict(ness), training, effective(ness), democratic, authoritarian(ism), discipline, nurturance, adequa(te,cy), inadequa(te, cy), behavior(s). *See also* Breast feeding; Child care; Child caregivers; Child custody; Child development; Child discipline; Child neglect; Children, Corporal punishment; Cultural transmission; Family relations; Family values; Father child relations; Fathers; Mother child relations; Mothers; Nurturance; Parent adolescent relations; Parent child communication; Parent child relations; Parent role; Parent training; Parental attitudes; Parental permissiveness; Parents; Physical contact; Shared parenting; Socialization; Toilet training; Weaning.

Children. Child(ren,hood). Youth. Youngster(s). Preschooler(s). Toddler(s). Tot(s). Lad(s). Boy(s). Girl(s). Son(s). Daughter(s). Kid(s). Grandchild(ren). Infant(s). Neonate(s). Preadolescen(ts, ce). Latency period. Puberty. Minor(s). Juvenile(s). Preteen(s). Pubescen(t,ce). Young people. Offspring. Kindergarten age. Preschool age. School age. Pediatric. Urchin(s). *Consider also:* adolescen(t,ce). *See also* Abandoned children; Adolescence; Adopted children; Child abuse; Child advocacy; Child behavior; Child behavior disorders; Child custody; Child development; Child development disorders; Child discipline; Child guidance; Child kidnapping; Child labor; Child language; Child mortality; Child neglect; Child nutrition; Child reactive disorders; Child self care; Child support; Childhood adjustment disorders; Childhood neurosis; Childhood play development; Childhood psychosis; Childhood schizophrenia; Daughters; Dependents; Elementary school students; Exceptional children; Family; Family life; Family problems; Foster children; Grandchildren; High school students; Hospitalized children; Human life cycle; Illegitimacy (children); Infants; Institutionalized children; Intermediate school students; Juvenile delinquency; Molested children; Moral development; Nursery school students; Only child; Parent child relations; Predelinquent youth; Preschool children; Play; Schoolchildren; Siblings; Sons; Twins; Unwanted children.

Children, abandoned. See *Abandoned children.*

Children, adopted. See *Adopted children.*

Children, adult. See *Adult offspring.*

Children, battered. See *Child abuse.*

Children, boomerang. See *Boomerang children.*

Children, exceptional. See *Exceptional children.*

Children, foster. See *Foster children.*

Children, grown. See *Adult offspring.*

Children, homeless. See *Homeless children.*

Children, hospitalized. See *Hospitalized children.*

Children, illegitimate. See *Illegitimacy (children).*

Children, institutionalized. See *Institutionalized children.*

Children, latchkey. See *Child self care.*

Children, missing. See *Missing persons.*

Children, molested. See *Molested children.*

Children, neglected. See *Child neglect.*

Children, preschool. See *Preschool children.*

Children, street. See *Street children.*

Children, training of. See *Childrearing.*

Children, unwanted. See *Unwanted children.*

Children's amusements. See *Children's games.*

Children's games. Children(s) game(s). *Choose from:* child(hood,ren,rens), early, youth, juvenile(s), youngster(s), preschool, pre-school, school, student(s), pupil(s) *with:* game(s), recreation(al), play(ed,ing), jump(ing) rope, ball(s), toy(s), checker(s), chess, charades, Parchesi, Boggle, Trivial Pursuits, Monopoly, Scrabble, card(s), sport(s). *See also* Adult games; Board games; Electronic games; Childhood play development; Play; Toy industry.

Children's literature. Children(s) literature. Picture book(s). Newbery Medal(s). Caldecott Medal(s). Nursery rhyme(s). Remedial reader(s). Primer(s). Childrens book(s). Junior reading book(s). Basal reader(s). *Choose from:* book(s), stor(y,ies), literature, novel(s), fiction, poe(try,m,ms), media, fable(s), tale(s), fairy tales, legend(s) *with:* child(ren, hood), juvenile(s), kindergarten, first grade, grade twelve, student(s), pre-K, grade 6, elementary school(s), secondary school(s), high school(s), young people, little one(s), girl(s), boy(s). *Choose from:* basal, McGuffey *with:* reader(s), series. *Consider also:* Jugendliteratur, littérature enfantine, littérature de jeunesse, livre(s) pour enfant(s), literatura infantil. *See also* Books; Children's poetry; Children's songs; Children's theater; Instructional media;

Nursery rhymes; Readability; Reading; Reading materials; Textbooks.

Children's poetry. Children's poe(m,ms,try). Counting-out rhyme(s). Nursery rhyme(s). *Choose from:* child(ren,hood), juvenile(s), kindergarten, first grade, grade twelve, student(s), pre-K, grade 6, elementary school(s), secondary school(s), high school(s), young people, little one(s), girl(s), boy(s) *with:* poe(m,ms,try), rhyme(s), limerick(s), lullab(y,ies), verse(s). *Consider also:* poesía infantil, poésies pour les enfants, Mere l'Oie, Mutter Gans, Mama Gansa, Kinderreime. *See also* Children's literature; Children's songs; Children's theater; Nursery rhymes; Poetry; Rhymes.

Children's rights. Children(s) rights. *Choose from:* child(ren,rens), juvenile(s), minor(s), adolescen(t,ts), youth, student(s), pupil(s) *with:* right(s), consent, law(s), liberat(ed,ing,ion), protect(ed,ing,ion), justice, advoca(cy,te,tes), due process, autonomy, civil libert(y,ies), civil right(s), equal education, equal protection, human right(s). *Consider also:* guardian ad litem, age of consent. *See also* Child abuse prevention; Child advocacy; Civil rights; Coeducation; Ombudsmen; Parent rights; Single sex schools; Student rights.

Children's songs. Children's song(s). Nursery song(s). Cradle song(s). Song(s) for child(ren,hood). *Choose from:* child(ren,hood), juvenile(s), kindergarten, nursery, Mother Goose, first grade, grade twelve, student(s), pre-K, grade 6, elementary school(s), secondary school(s), high school(s), young people, little one(s), girl(s), boy(s) *with:* song(s), sing(ing), music, chant(s), tune(s), lullab(y,ies), hymn(s), ditt(y,ies), melod(y,ies), opera(s). *Consider also:* Kinderlied(er), chanson(s) enfantine(s). *See also* Children's Literature; Children's poetry; Children's theater; Lullabies; Music; Nursery rhymes.

Children's theater. Children's theat(er, ers,re,res). *Choose from:* child(ren, hood), kid(s), juvenile(s), youth(ful), young audience(s), child actor(s), kindergarten, nursery school, first grade, grade twelve, student(s), pre-K, grade 6, elementary school(s), secondary school(s), high school(s), young people, girl(s), boy(s) *with:* theater(s), theatr(e,es,ical), movie(s), drama(s,tize, tized,tizing,tization), thespian(s), dramatic adaptation(s), play(s,house, houses), performance(s), performer(s), on stage, playwriting, Shakespeare, acting, actor(s), actress(es), puppet(s), marionette(s). *See also* Children's literature; Children's poetry; Children's songs; Puppets; Theater.

Chiliasm. See *Millenarianism.*

Chinese languages. See *Sino-Thai languages.*

Chinese medicine. Chinese medicine(s). Acupuncture. Medical treatment in China. Chinese traditional medical practice(s). Barefoot doctor(s). *Choose from:* health, medical, medicin(al,e,es), pharmacolog(y,ical), hygien(e,ic), treat(ed,ing,ment,ments), diagnos(is,es), heal(ed,ing,er,ers), remed(y,ies), acupuncture, herb(s,al), drug(s), therap(y,ies), patient(s), disease(s), disorder(s), illness(es), cure(s), surg(ery,ical), nursing, doctor(s) *with:* China, Chinese, Peking, Beijing, Peiping, Taiwan(ese), Hong Kong, etc. *See also* Far East; Plant folklore; Traditional medicine.

Chivalry. Chivalr(y,ous). Courtl(y,iness). Gallant(ry). Gentleman(ly). Noble(ness). Honorable. Manner(s,ly,iness). Knight(ly). High minded. *See also* Courtly love; Duels; Ethics; Knights and knighthood; Manners.

Choice (psychology). Choice(s). Choos(e,ing). Select(ed,ing,ion). Decid(e,ed,ing). Discriminat(e,ed, ing,ion). *Consider also:* decision making, conflict resolution, prisoner's dilemma, alternative(s), differentiat(e, ed,ing,ion). *See also* Choice behavior; Classification; Decision making; Freedom; Freedom (theology); Human mate selection; Volition.

Choice, career. See *Occupational choice.*

Choice, educational. See *Educational vouchers; School choice.*

Choice, occupational. See *Occupational choice.*

Choice, school. See *School choice.*

Choice, vocational. See *Occupational choice.*

Choice behavior. Choice behavior(s). *Choose from:* choice(s), choos(e,ing), select(ed,ing,ion), decid(e,ed,ing), discriminat(e,ed,ing,ion) *with:* behavior, process(es), strateg(y,ies), task(s), situation(s), alternative(s), preference(s), forced, approach(es), learn(ed,ing). *Consider also:* designat(e,ed,ing,ion), pick(ed,ing), prefer(red,ring). *See also* Choice (psychology); Classification; Decision making; Elective; Freedom; Freedom (theology); Human mate selection; Precedence; Volition.

Choices (alternatives). Choice(s). Choos(e,ing). Option(s). Alternative(s). Possibilit(y,ies). Opportunit(y,ies). *See also* Alternatives; Decision making; Decisions; Dilemmas; Elective; Game theory; Group decision making; Human mate selection; Judgment; Occupational choice; Precedence; Preferences; Rational choices; Selection procedures.

Choices, rational. See *Rational choices.*

Choirs (music). Choir(s). Quire(s). Choral group(s). Choral societ(y,ies). Choral tradition. Church singer(s). Madrigal sing(er,ers,ing). Gospel sing(er,ers,ing). A cappella choir(s). Chorister(s). Choir member(s). Chorale(s). *Consider also:* vocal ensemble(s), choral music, choral singing, chorus(es), Concordia Societ(y, ies), glee club(s), octavo music, les chanteurs, choirmaster(s). *See also* Cantatas; Choral music; Choral singing; Choral societies; Choruses; Church music; Ensembles; Music; Musical societies; Musicians; Singers.

Choral music. Choral music. Choirbook(s). Choral work(s). Chorale(s). *Choose from:* choir(s), chorus(es), choral *with:* music, repertoire, concert(s), workshop(s), mass(es), psalm(s), hymn(s), carol(s), anthem(s), ballad(s), singing, song(s), response(s), work(s), composition(s), canticle(s), oratorio(s), requiem(s). *Consider also:* madrigal(s), glee club(s), antiphonal singing, polychoral, coro battente, cor(o,i) spezzato, Chormusik, Chorliteratur. *See also* Cantatas; Choirs (music); Choral singing; Choral societies; Choruses; Church music; Ensembles; Lyrics; Music; Part songs; Responses (liturgical); Singers; Songs.

Choral singing. Choral sing(s,ing). Choral festival(s). Choral concert(s). Sing(ing) together. Group sing(s,ing). *Choose from:* choir(s), chorus(es), choral *with:* sing(s,ing), sang, sung, song(s), workshop(s), festival(s), jamboree(s), concert(s), eisteddfod(s), hootenann(y,ies). *See also* Choirs (music); Choral music; Choral societies; Choruses; Church music; Ensembles; Part songs; Singers; Singing.

Choral societies. Choral societ(y,ies). Choral club(s). Bel Canto Chorus Singing Societ(y,ies). Community chorus(es). Mendelssohn Glee Club(s). Concordia Societ(y,ies). *Consider also:* federacion coral(s), coro(s), Gesangverein, Sangerbund, Sangerverein(s), Mannergesang(s), Mannergesangverein, Mannerchor(s), Orpheon. *See also* Choral singing; Choral music; Choirs (music); Ensembles; Musicians; Singers.

Chorales. See *Hymns.*

Chords (music). Chord(al,s). *Consider also:* tone cluster(s), pitch aggregate(s), harmonic analysis. *See also* Music.

Choreography. Choreograph(y,ed,er,ers). Set(ting) a dance. Arrang(e,ed,ing, ement) dance movements. *See also* Ballet dancing; Dance notation.

Choreomania. Choreomania. Dancing mania. Tarantism. Tarantulism. Tanzwut. Chorea Germanorum. *See also* Disease; Involuntary (automatic).

Choruses. Chorus(es). Polyphon(y,ic). Antiphon(y,al). Chorale(s). *Consider also:* refrain(s), burden(s), carol(s), part song(s), chant(s), melod(y,ies), aria(s), ariett(e,a,as), cavatina(s), canzonet(ta, tas), counterpoint, contrapuntal composition(s), dithyramb, choral lyric(s). *See also* Choirs (music); Choral music; Choral singing; Ensembles; Music; Opera; Opera singers; Oratorio; Refrain (music); Singers.

Christian art. Christian art. *Choose from:* Christian(ity,s), Christ, Jesus, Mary, saint(s), Catholic, Protestant, crucifixion, devotional, apocalyp(se,tic), New Testament, Bibl(e,ical) *with:* art, fresco(es), carving(s), painting(s), architecture, mosaic(s), monument(s), sculpture. *Consider also:* l'art religieux, Christliche Kunst, der Christlichen Kirchenkunst. *See also* Arts; Christian symbolism; Christianity; Religious art; Religious articles.

Christian leadership. Christian leader(s,ship). Lay leader(s,ship). *Choose from:* Christian, Evangelist, evangelical, Catholic, religious right *with:* leader(s,ship), authorit(y,es). *Consider also:* Cardinal(s), Archbishop(s), Bishop(s), Pope(s). *See also* Apostles; Christianity; Fathers of the church; Lay religious personnel; Leadership; Religious councils and synods; Religious leadership.

Christian symbolism. Christian symbol(s, ism). Crucifix(es). Cross(es). *Choose from:* Christian(ity,s), Christ, Jesus, Mary, saint(s), Catholic, Protestant, crucifixion, New Testament, Bibl(e,ical) *with:* symbol(s,ism), image(s,ry), iconography, icon(s), chalice(s), emblem(s), motif(s), allegor(y,ies). *See also* Christian art; Christianity; Crosses; Crucifixion; Fall of man; Iconography; Images; Religious articles; Religious literature; Sex symbolism; Symbolism.

Christianity. Christian(s,ity). Apostle(s). Baptis(m,t,ts). Born again. Catholic(ism,s). Christianis(e,ed,ing, ation). Christianiz(e,ed,ing,ation). Christian fundamentalis(m,t,ts). Christian Scien(ce,tist,tists). Christendom. Christen(ed,ing,ings). Christmas. Christology. Church of Christ. Church of England. Congregationalis(m,t,ts). Disciple(s) of Christ. Dutch Reformed. Easter. Eastern Orthodox. Episcopalian(s). Evangelical(s). Evangelist(s). Greek Orthodox. Hutterite(s). Jehovahs Witness(es). Jesus. Jesuit(s). Latter Day Saints. Lutheran(s). Mennonite(s). Messiah. Methodis(m,t,ts). Mormon(s). New Testament. Pentecostal(s). Presbyterian(s). Protestant(ism,s). Puritan(s,ism). Quaker(s). Reformation. Roman Catholic(ism,s). Russian Orthodox. Seventh Day Adventist(s).

Shaker(s). Trinit(arian,ians,y). Virgin Mary. *Consider also:* moral majority, gentile(s). *See also* Apostles; Bible; Canons; Christian art; Christian leadership; Christian symbolism; Christians; Crusades; Deities; Devils; Ecumenical movement; God concepts; Intercommunion; Interdenominational cooperation; Judaism; Judgement day; Liturgy; Millenarianism; Paganism; Philosophy; Presence of God; Protestantism; Religion; Religions; Religious affiliation; Religious cultural groups; Religious dialogues; Religious fundamentalism; Religious personnel; Roman Catholicism; Saints; Social gospel; Western civilization.

Christians. Christian(s). Protestant(s). Catholic(s). Roman catholic(s). Baptist(s). Disciples of Christ. Christian Scientist(s). Fundamentalist(s). Jehovah's Witnesses. Methodis(ts). Episcopalian(s). Presbyterian(s). Quaker(s). Lutheran(s). Members of the Dutch Reformed Church. Mormon(s). Seventh Day Adventists. Congregationalist(s). Pentecostal(s). Jesus People. Evangelical(s). Evangelist(s). Missionar(y,ies). Born again. Shaker(s). Mennonite(s). Jesuit(s). Puritan(s). Russian Orthodox. Greek Orthodox. Eastern Orthodox. Reformation. Moral majority. *See also* Christianity; Disciples; Protestantism; Religious affiliation; Roman Catholicism.

Christmas songs. See *Noel.*

Chromosome mapping. See *Gene mapping.*

Chronic disease. Chronic disease(s). Chronicity. *Choose from:* chronic(ally), incurable, persistent, recurrent, long term, lingering, refractory, long standing, long lasting, continual(ly), continuous(ly) *with:* disease(s), sick(ness,nesses), ill(ness,nesses), disorder(s), patient(s), condition(s), ailment(s), backache(s), headache(s). *See also* Caregiver burden; Chronic fatigue syndrome; Chronic pain; Chronic psychosis; Coping; Debility; Disability; Disease; Illness; Invalids; Long term care; Pain; Recurrence; Refractory.

Chronic fatigue syndrome. Chronic fatigue syndrome(s). CFS. Chronic Fatigue and Immune Dysfunction Syndrome. Chronic mononucleosis. Yuppie flu. *Consider also:* myalgic encephalitis, post-viral fatigue syndrome, post-viral syndrome, Iceland disease, Royal Free disease. *Choose from:* chronic, prolonged, persistent, protracted *with:* fatigue, Epstein Barr, post viral. *See also* Chronic disease; Fatigue.

Chronic mental illness. See *Chronic psychosis.*

Chronic pain. Chronic pain. *Choose from:* chronic(ally,icity), long term, longstanding, refractory, persistent, lingering, recurrent, continuing, incurable, protracted, unceasing *with:* lumbago, neuralgia, colic, glossalgia, toothache(s), migraine(s), aphagia, headache(s), ach(es,ing), pain(s,ed,ful), suffering, bellyache(s), cramp(s), discomfort, sore(ness), smarting, throbbing, distress(s), stomachache(s), backache(s), earache(s). *See also* Pain; Psychogenic pain; Refractory.

Chronic psychosis. Chronic psychos(is,es). *Choose from:* chronic(ally), incurable, refractory, persistent, recurrent, long term, continuous(ly), continual(ly) *with:* psychos(es,is), psychotic(ism), insan(e, ity), mental(ly) ill(ness,nesses), psychiatric disorder(s), altered consciousness, pseudopsychos(is,es), schizophren(ia,ic), behavioral breakdown(s), caton(ia,ic), man(ia,ic), delirium tremens, hallucinat(e,ed,ing, ion,ions), hallucinosis, autism, echolalia, Capgras(s) syndrome, organic mental disorders, parano(ia,id), folie-a-deux. *See also* Chronic disease; Psychoses; Refractory.

Chronicity (disorders). See *Chronic disease; Chronic pain.*

Chronicles. Chronicle(s). Historical account(s). Annal(s). Chronolog(y,ies). Epic(s). Log(s). Legend(s). Memoir(s). *Consider also:* narrative report(s), story, version(s), narration(s), recitation(s), recount(ed,ing,al), meeting minutes, saga(s). *See also* Almanacs; Chronology; History; Narratives; Records; Sagas.

Chronology. Chronolog(y,ies,ic,ical). Sequen(ce,ced,tial,tially). Consecutive. *Choose from:* time, calendar, date *with:* order(ed,ing). *Consider also:* chronicle(s), memoir(s), diar(y,ies), ship(s) log(s), horolog(ic,y). *See also* Almanacs; Calendars; Chronicles; Genealogy; History; Records; Time; Time measurement; Time periods.

Chronometry, mental. See *Time perception.*

Chunking. Chunk(ing,ed). Prechunk(ed, ing). *Consider also:* organiz(ed,ing, ation), preorganiz(ed,ing,ation), recod(e, ed,ing) *with:* recall, comprehension. *See also* Learning.

Church, fathers of the. See *Fathers of the church.*

Church and state, separation of. See *Church state relationship.*

Church attendance. Church attendance. Churchgoer(s). *Choose from:* church, religious, sunday school, worship service(s) *with:* attend(ed,ing,ance), member(s,ship), active, participat(e,ed, ing,ion), involve(d,ment). *See also* Church membership; Religious advertising; Religious affiliation; Religious behavior; Religious commitment; Religious practices; Worship.

Church buildings. See *Churches; Religious buildings.*

Church congregations. See *Congregations (church).*

Church membership. Church member(s,ship). Religious identification. *Choose from:* church(es), religious institution(s) *with:* member(s,ship), involvement, belong(s,ed,ing). *See also* Church attendance; Religious affiliation; Religiosity.

Church music. Church music. Hymn(s,al, als,ody,ary,aries). Sung prayer(s). Plainchant. Psalmody. *Choose from:* church, parish, liturgical, gospel, worship, sacred, religious, ecclesiastical, Lutheran, Congregational, Methodist, Protestant, etc. *with:* choir(s), tune(s), music(al,ally,ian,ians), song(s), chant(s), aria(s), anthem(s), antiphon(s), cantata(s), motet(s), bellringing, psalter(s), singing, sung. *Consider also:* Geistliche Lied(er). *See also* A cappella singing; Bells; Bronze bells; Cantatas; Canticles; Change ringing; Chants; Choirs (music); Choral music; Dirges; Funeral music; Hymns; Music; Musical instruments; Musicians; Religious music.

Church schools. See *Private schools.*

Church state relationship. Church state relationship. *Choose from:* church(es), religion(s), religious, theolog(y,ical), ecclesiastical, Christian(s,ity), parochial, Christmas, faith based, Protestant(s,ism), Catholic(s,ism), Jew(s,ish), Judaism, Islam(ic), Moslem(s), Muslim(s), Hindu, holy, sacred, priest(s), bishop(s), archbishop(s), school prayer, moment(s) of silence, nativity scene(s) *with:* government(al), state, nation(s,al), secular(ized,ization), politic(al,s), democrac(y,ies), public school(s), public institution(s), voter(s), election(s), First Amendment, Bill of Rights, Constitutional right(s), public display(s), public property. *Consider also:* theocrac(y,ies), separation of church and state. *See also* Anticlericalism; Churches; Clericalism; Divine right of kings; Freedom of religion; Religions; Religious education; Secularism; Secularization; Sunday legislation; Theocracy.

Churches. Church(es). Chapel(s). Cathedral(s). Minster(s). Place(s) of worship. House(s) of worship. House(s) of God. House(s) of prayer. *Consider also:* temple(s), tabernacle(s), synagogue(s), mosque(s). *See also* Big churches; Church attendance; Church membership; Church music; Church state relationship; Community churches; Congregations (church); Ecumenical movement; Glass painting and staining; Independent churches; Indigenous churches; Nonprofit organizations; Places of worship; Priests; Religious buildings; Religious denominations; Religious institutions; Religious personnel; Sacred places; Sects; Secularization.

Churches, big. See *Big churches.*

Churches, community. See *Community churches.*

Churches, independent. See *Independent churches.*

Churches, indigenous. See *Indigenous churches.*

Churching of women. Churching of women. Churchynge of Women. Thanksgiving of Women after Childbirth. *Consider also:* post-baptismal rite(s), rite(s) for childbearing mother(s). *See also* Birth rites; Religious rituals.

Cicadas. Cicada(s,e). Cicadidae. *Consider also:* homoptera, locust(s), harvest fl(y,ies). *See also* Insects.

Cigarette industry. Cigarette industry. Cigarette firm(s). Cigarette maker(s). Cigarette compan(y,ies). Cigarette brand(s). Tobacco industry. Tobacco marketer(s). Tobacco compan(y,ies). Tobacco corp(oration,orations). *Consider also:* Brown and Williamson, Lorillard Inc., R.J. Reynolds, Philip Morris, Marlboro, etc. *See also* Industry; Smoking Tobacco farms; Tobacco habit; Tobacco industry.

Cigarette smoking. See *Smoking.*

Cigarettes. Cigarette(s). Cigaret(s). Cigarro(s). *See also* Smoking.

Cinema. Cinema(s,tography, tographic, tographically). Movie(s). Film(s). Screenplay(s). Motion picture(s). Cinematography. Talking picture(s). Silent picture(s). Hollywood. Travelogue(s). Documentar(y,ies). Picture show(s). Cine. *See also* Audiovisual communications; Drama; Mass media effects; Mass media violence; Popular culture.

Cinematography. See *Cinema; Motion pictures.*

Circadian rhythms. See *Biological rhythms.*

Circulation. See *Distribution (delivering).*

Circulation (rotation). Circulat(e,ed,ing, ion). Circl(e,es,ed,ing). Rotat(e,ed,ing, ation). Circumrotat(e,ed,ing,ation). Gyrat(e,ed,ing,ion,ions). Orbit(s,ed,ing). Pivot(ted,ting,s). Revolv(e,ed,ing). Revolution(s). Spiral(ling). *Consider also:* roll(ed,ing), spin(ning), spun, swivel(led,ling), whirl(ed,ing). *See also* Equilibrium; Motion; Motion perception.

Circumcision. Circumcis(e,ed,ion,ions,ing). Prepuce surgery. Clitoris surgery. Clitoridectomy. Posthetomy. Prepuce removal. *Consider also:* berit milah, beris (Jewish) or khitan (Islamic). *See also* Birth rites; Female circumcision (ritual).

Circumcision, female ritual. See *Female circumcision (ritual).*

Circumference. Circumferen(ce,tial). Ambit(s). Circuit(s). Girth(s). Perimeter(s). Peripher(y,ies). Bound(s). Confine(s). Limit(s). Border(s). Margin(s). Rim(s). *Consider also:* extremit(y,ies), verge(s). *See also* Borderlands; Borders; Boundaries.

Circumstances, extenuating. See *Extenuating circumstances.*

Circumstantial evidence. Circumstantial evidence. Circumstantial proof. Corpus delicti. Body of the crime. Inference. Indirect evidence. Indirect proof. *Choose from:* evidence, inferen(ce,ces,tial), deduction(s) *with:* fact(s), circumstance(s). *See also* Criminal investigations; Criminal proceedings; Deposition; Evidence; Expert testimony; Fact checking; Legal procedures; Positive evidence; Sufficient evidence; Withholding evidence; Witnesses.

Circus. Circus(es). Ringling Brothers and Barnum and Bailey. Big top. Clown(s). Juggling act(s). High-wire act(s). Walk(ing) a tightrope. *See also* Carnivals; Popular culture; Entertainment.

Circus performers. Circus performer(s). Circus member(s). Circus freak(s). Circus worker(s). Clown(s). Sword swallower(s). Acrobat(s). Sideshow(man,men,woman,women). Ringmaster(s). Fire-eater(s). *See also* Carnivals; Entertainers; Popular culture; Traveling exhibitions; Traveling theater.

Citations, bibliographic. See *Bibliographic citations.*

Cities. Cit(y,ies). Municipal(ity,ities). Urban(ism,ized,ization). Metropolitan. Downtown(s). Megalopolis. Inner cit(y,ies). Urban sprawl. Commercial center(s). Metropolitan area(s). Urban area(s). *See also* Capital cities; Civic improvement; Commercial districts; Community size; Ethnic neighborhoods; Industrial cities and towns; Inner cities; Local government; Local politics; Mayors; Metropolitan areas; Neighborhoods; Public administration; Suburbs; Towns; Urban beautification; Urban environments; Urban planning; Urban politics; Urban population; Urban poverty; Urban renewal; Urban sprawl; Urbanism; Urbanization.

Cities, capital. See *Capital cities.*

Cities, central. See *Inner cities.*

Cities, extinct. See *Extinct cities.*

Cities, inner. See *Inner cities.*

Cities, large. See *Metropolitan areas; Urban environments.*

Cities, ruined. See *Extinct cities.*

Cities and towns, industrial. See *Industrial cities and towns.*

Citizen participation. Citizen participation. Collective action. Mass participation. Community action. Citizen interest group(s). Participatory democracy. Local politics. Grassroots. Role of resident(s). Popular sovereignty. Glasnost. *Choose from:* citizen(s), public, community, taxpayer(s), voter(s), resident(s) *with:* respons(e,iveness), action, appeal(s), movement(s), empowerment, power, involve(d,ment), demand(s,ed,ing), participat(e,ed,ing,ion), voice(s), activism, cooperat(e,ed,ing,ion), action(s), mobiliz(e,ed,ing,ation). *See also* Activism; Advocacy; Citizens; Citizenship; Civic activities; Civil disobedience; Community change; Community development; Community involvement; Community power; Community support; Local politics; Neighborhood associations; Participative decision making; Police community relations; Political campaigns; Political obligation; Political participation; Populism; Representatives; Social action; Social responsibility; Socially responsible investing; Third parties (United States politics); Vigilantes; Voting.

Citizens. Citizen(s,ry). Voter(s). Taxpayer(s). Resident(s). Ratepayer(s). Native(s). Villager(s). Inhabitant(s). John Q Public. General population. Towns(men,man,people,women, woman,people,persons). Civilian(s). National subject(s). Free(men,man, people,women,woman). Man on the street. Country(men,man,people, women,woman). Denizen(s). Individual(s). *Consider also:* city dweller(s), villager(s). *See also* Citizen participation; Civil defense; Civil rights; Civil supremacy over the military; Countries; General public; Inhabitants; Military civilian relations; Political participation; Population; Public opinion; Residents; Voters; Voting.

Citizens, senior. See *Elderly.*

Citizens, surveillance of. See *Surveillance of citizens.*

Citizenship. Citizen(s,ship). National identity. National subject(s). Pledge allegiance. *Consider also:* civic involvement. *See also* Acculturation; Citizen participation; Citizens; Civil rights; Community attitudes; Foreigners; Immigrants; Immigration; Laws; Military service; Naturalization; Patriotism; Political attitudes; Political obligation; National identity; Social responsibility; Statelessness; Voting.

Citizenship, world. See *World citizenship.*

Citizenship education. Citizenship education. *Choose from:* citizenship, civic(s), *with:* education(al), curricul(um,a,ae), learn(ed,ing), course(s), training, class(es,room). *Consider also:* naturalization, political socialization. *See also* Critical thinking; Current events; Political socialization; World citizenship.

Citrus fruits. Citrus(es,y) fruit(s). Rutaceae. *Consider also:* orange(s), lemon(s), grapefruit(s), lime(s), kumquat(s), citrange(s), tangelo(s), ugli fruit(s). *See also* Food; Fruit.

City. See *Cities.*

City government. See *Municipal government.*

City growth. See *Urban development.*

City planning. See *Urban planning.*

Civic activities. Civic activit(y,ies). *Choose from:* civic, community, local, citizen, grassroots, public *with:* activit(y,ies), affair(s), participat(e,ed,ing,ion), dut(y,ies). *See also* Citizen participation; Citizenship; Community involvement.

Civic improvement. Civic improvement(s). Community improvement(s). *Choose from:* improv(e,ed,ing,ement,ements), redevelop(e,ed,ing,ement,ements) *with:* civic, city, town(s), communit(y,ies), stadium(s), public transportation, downtown, blighted area(s). *Consider also:* civic activism, civic leadership, civic hygiene, business improvement district(s). *See also* Antipoverty programs; Cities; Community change; Community development; Housing policy; Improvement; Inner cities; Modernization; Municipal art; Neighborhood preservation; Public housing; Relocation; Urban beautification; Urban development; Urban environments; Urban planning; Urban population; Urban renewal.

Civics. Civics. Civic dut(y,ies). Civic education. Public philosophy. Public-spirited(ness). *Choose from:* civic(s), citizen(s,ship) *with:* dut(y,ies), responsibilit(y,ies), education, lesson(s), awareness, participation, activism, right(s), concern(s), ideal(s). *See also* Social studies.

Civil death. Civil death. Civilly dead. Depriv(e,ed,ing,ation) of civil rights. Los(e,ing,t) civil rights. *Consider also:* civil disabilit(y,ies), revo(ke,cation) driver's license. *See also* Attainder; Civil rights.

Civil defense. Civil(ian) defense. Fallout shelter(s). Air raid shelter(s). Bomb shelter(s). Civilian(s) defense. Civilian(s) preparedness. Surviv(e,al) attack(s). Postattack recover(y,ies).

Plan(s,ned,ning) survival of nuclear attack(s). *See also* Armed forces; Citizens; Coast defenses; Defense (Military science); Disaster planning; Disaster relief; Emergency services; Military civilian relations; National security; Natural disasters; Nuclear warfare; Nuclear weapons; Survival; War.

Civil disobedience. Civil disobedience. Civilian resistance. Grassroots resistance. Ecotage. Ecosabotage. Nonviolent protest(s). Dissent(er,ers). Passive resistance. Nonviolent resist(er,ers,ance). Draft resist(ance,er,ers). Tax resist(er,ers,ance). Nonpayment of tax(es). Refus(e,ed,al) to obey law(s). Burn(ed,ing) draft card(s). Flag burning(s). Burn(ed,ing) flag(s). Disobey(ed,ing) unjust laws. *See also* Activism; Agitators; Boycotts; Civil disorders; Civil rights; Civil rights organizations; Conscientious objectors; Demonstrators; Dissent; Nonresistance to evil; Nonviolence; Peace movements; Political action; Political behavior; Political movements; Political obligation; Political power; Protest movements; Social demonstrations; Suffrage movement; Strikes; Student demonstrations.

Civil disorders. Civil disorder(s). Civilian unrest. Streetfighting. Civil disturbance(s). Urban unrest. Urban disorder(s). Mob violence. Civil outbreak(s). Public demonstration(s). *Choose from:* urban, civil(ian,ians), local, street(s), cit(y,ies) *with:* disorder(s), unrest, fight(s,ing), disturbance(s), outbreak(s), uprising(s), revolt(ed,ing), rebell(ed,ing,ion,ions), loot(ed,ing), pillag(e,ed,ing), protest(s,er,ers), demonstrat(ion, ions,or,ors), violen(t,ce), agitator(s), insurrection(s), turmoil, chaos, terroris(m,t,ts), commotion, riot(s,er, ers,ing). *See also* Activism; Agitators; Breach of the peace; Civil disobedience; Civil rights organizations; Collective behavior; Conflict; Demonstrators; Dissent; Emergencies; Nonviolence; Peasant rebellions; Political repression; Political violence; Protest movements; Riots; Social conflict; Social demonstrations; Social disorganization; Social movements; Social unrest; Student demonstrations.

Civil engineering. Civil engineer(s,ing). Earthquake engineer(s,ing). Highway engineer(s,ing). Transportation engineer(s,ing). Geotechnical engineer(s,ing). *Consider also:* public works, design and construction of road(s), land survey(ing). *Choose from:* construct(ed,ing,ion), design(ed,ing), plan(ned,ning) *with:* highway(s), bridge(s), waterway(s), building(s). *See also* Architecture; Facility design and construction; Urban planning.

Civil procedures. Civil procedure(s). Civil litigation. Civil action(s). Court-ordered arbitration. Civil case(s). Civil settlement(s). Civil appeal(s). *Consider also:* civil justice system. *See also* Legal procedures; Law (practice).

Civil rights. Civil rights. Bill of Rights. Privacy Act. Social justice. Due process. Suffrage. Civil libert(y,ies). Personal libert(y,ies). Equal education. Equal opportunit(y,ies). Equal protection. Freedom of speech. Freedom. Citizenship. Social justice. Universal Declaration of Human Rights. Antidiscrimination law(s). *Choose from:* civil, individual, human, constitutional, natural, equal, legal, voting, privacy, minorit(y,ies), personal, woman(s), women(s), female(s), Negro(es), Black(s), AfroAmerican(s), Afro-American(s), African American(s), student(s), patient(s), citizen(s), institutionalized, disabled, disabilit(y,ies), handicap(s,ped), gay(s), homosexual(s), child(ren,rens), parent(s), worker(s) *with:* right(s). *Consider also:* right to treatment, right to refuse treatment, consent forms, civil libertarians, right to know, access to records, fair employment, work rights. *See also* Attainder; Bill of rights; Black power; Citizenship; Children's rights; Civil death; Civil disobedience; Civil rights organizations; Citizens; Citizenship; Democracy; Democratization; Disability rights movement; Due process; Equal education; Equal job opportunities; Equality before the law; Feminism; Free thought; Freedom of information; Freedom of religion; Freedom of speech; Freedom of the press; Freedmen; Gray power; Homosexual liberation movement; Human rights; Internal security; Legal rights; Liberty; Minority groups; Ombudsmen; Parent rights; Patient rights; Political reform; Prisoners' rights; Privacy; Privacy laws; Property rights; Racial integration; Racial segregation; Search and seizure; Self incrimination; Sex discrimination; Slavery; Social discrimination; Social justice; Suffrage; Voting; Voting rights; Women's rights.

Civil rights movement. See *Civil rights organizations.*

Civil rights movements. See *Abortion rights movement; Activism; Antiapartheid movement; Antiabortion movement; Black power; Civil disobedience; Civil rights organizations; Disability rights movement; Environmentalism; Gray power; Homosexual liberation movement; Protest movements; Social movements; Suffrage movement.*

Civil rights organizations. Civil rights organization(s). Civil rights movement. American Civil Liberties Union. ACLU.

Congress of Racial Equality. CORE. National Association for the Advancement of Colored People. NAACP. Southern Christian Leadership Conference. National Urban League. Black Panthers. Mississippi freedom summer. International League for the Rights of Man. Amnesty International. Civil rights leader(s). *Consider also:* African National Congress, ANC, South West African People's Organization, SWAPO, antiapartheid movement(s). *See also* Abortion rights movement; Activism; Antiapartheid movement; Antiabortion movement; Black power; Civil disobedience; Civil rights; Disability rights movement; Environmentalism; Gray power; Homosexual liberation movement; Interest groups; Political action; Protest movements; Race relations; Social action; Social movements; Suffrage movement.

Civil servants. See *Civil service; Government personnel.*

Civil service. Civil service. Civil servant(s). Public workforce. State job(s). Federal job(s). Public service. *Choose from:* government(al), federal, state, county, city, municipal, local, town, public, civil service, public sector *with:* personnel, employee(s), employed, official(s), executive(s), bureaucra(cy,t,ts), workforce, worker(s), merit system. *See also* Bureaucracies; Government personnel; Local officials and employees; Public administration; Public officers.

Civil society. Civil society. Civil community. *Consider also:* societal well-being, social capital, common good, infrastructure, civic activit(y,ies), nongovernment(al) organization(s), nonprofit organization(s), grass-roots organization(s), church(es), labor union(s), business(es), pressure group(s). *See also* Charities; Community (social); Community involvement; Interorganizational networks; Local politics; Neighborhood associations; Nongovernmental organizations; Nonprofit organizations; Organizations; Social structure; Voluntary associations.

Civil supremacy over the military. Civil supremacy over the military. *Choose from:* civil(ian) *with:* control, limiting, supremacy, superiority, rule, authority, subordinate *with:* military, police force(s), armed forces. *See also* Armed forces; Citizens; Coups d'Etat; Martial law; Military civilian relations; Military personnel; Military reform; Military regimes; Police community relations; Political repression; Surveillance of citizens.

Civil war. Civil war(s). Insurgen(t,ts,cy). Counterinsurgen(t,ts,cy). Rebellion(s). War between the States. War of the

Rebellion. War of Secession. War for Southern Independence. Puritan revolution. Secession cris(is,es). Insurrection(s). Revolution(s,ary). *Consider also:* separatism. *See also* Abolitionists; Antigovernment radicals; Crimes against peace; Guerrillas; Peasant rebellions; Political revolutions; Political violence; Rebellions; Revolution; Revolutionary ballads and songs.

Civilian military relations. See *Military civilian relations.*

Civilians. Civilian(s). Nonmilitary. Noncombatant(s). Private citizen(s). *Consider also:* laic(al,ally), layperson(s), private citizen(s). *See also* Citizens; Noncombatants.

Civilization. Civiliz(ed,ing,ation,ations). *Choose from:* advanced, humane, humaniz(ed,ation), western, eastern, enlighten(ed,ment), ancient *with:* societ(y,ies), civilization(s), nation(s), people(s), culture(s). *See also* African empires; Antiquity (time); Asian empires; Cultural evolution; Cultural history; Cultural values; Cultural universals; Pre-Columbian empires; Traditional societies; Western civilization; World history.

Civilization, modern. See *Modern civilization.*

Civilization, occidental. See *Western civilization.*

Civilization, regression. See *Regression (civilization).*

Civilization, western. See *Western civilization.*

Civilization and technology. See *Technology and civilization.*

Civilizations, non-Western. See *African empires; African cultural groups; Asian empires; Buddhism; Central America; Central American native cultural groups; Central Asia; Civilization; Cultural history; Culture contact; Far East; Indigenous populations; Indonesian cultural groups; Islam; Middle East; North Africa; North American native cultural groups; Oceania; Oceanic cultural groups; Philippine Islands cultural groups; Pre-Columbian empires; South America; South American native cultural groups; South Asia; Southeast Asia; Southeast Asian cultural groups; Sub-Saharan Africa; Taoism; Traditional societies; Western civilization.*

Civilized. Civiliz(e,ed,ing,ation). Culture(d). Civilit(y,ies). Cultivat(e,ed, ing,ion). Edif(y,ied,ication). Good taste. Refine(d,ment). Educated. Enlightened. Decorous(ness,ly). Correct(ness). Suav(e,ity). Urban(e,ity). Sophisticat(e, ed,ion). *See also* Cosmopolitan; Knowledge; Sophistication; Worldview.

Claims. Claim(s,ed,ing). Demand(s,ed,ing). Entitle(d,ment,ments). Expropriat(e,ed, ing,ion). Requisition(ed,ing). Have right(s). Commandeer(ed,ing). Birthright(s). Heritage. Inheritance. Solicit(ed,ing,ation). *Consider also:* claimant(s), applicant(s), petitioner(s), supplicant(s), complainant(s). *See also* Appeals; Applicants; Reparations; Rights; Territorial issues.

Clairvoyance. Clairvoyan(t,ce). Extrasensory perception. ESP. Precognition. Telepath(y,ic). Cardguessing. Nonsensory acquisition of information. Paranormal information transfer. Remote perception. Psychic experience(s). Nonsensory channel(s). Out of body experience(s). *Choose from:* extrasensory, psychic *with:* perception(s), aware(ness), information, phenomena, experience(s), communication(s), stimulation, abilit(y,ies). *See also* Extrasensory perception; Parapsychology.

Clams. Clam(s, shell,shells). Quahog(s). Butter clam(s). Razor clam(s). Littleneck clam(s). Cherrystone clam(s). Soft-shell clam(s). Gaper clam(s). Pismo clam(s). *Consider also:* mussel(s), mollusk(s), bivalve(s). *See also* Animals; Fisheries.

Clandestinity. Clandestin(e,ely,eness,ity). Surreptitious(ly). Covert. Secre(t,cy). Furtive(ly). Stealth(y,ily). Undercover. Under-the-table. Collus(ion,ive). Unethical(ly). Illegal(ity). Unlawful(ly). Unauthorized. *Consider also:* closet(ed), illegitimate(ly), illicit(ly). *See also* Cheating; Covert; Deception; Duplicity; Faking; Fraud; Illegal; Secrecy.

Clans. Clan(ism,ship,s). Kin group(s). Gens. Moiet(y,ies). Phratr(y,ies). Descent group(s). Relative(s). Extended famil(y,ies). Kinship. Common ancestry. Sib. *Consider also:* lineage, tribe(s). *See also* Chiefs; Extended family; Lineage; Traditional societies.

Clarification. Clarif(y,ied,ying,ication). Elucidat(e,ed,ing,ion). Exposition(s). Explanat(ion,ions,atory). Explain(ed, ing). Reason(s). Justification(s). Justif(y,ied,ying). Simplification(s). Elaborat(e,ed,ing,ion). Explicat(e,ed, ing,ion,ions). Comment(s,ary,aries). Annotation(s). Footnote(s). Example(s). Exeges(is,es). Illuminat(e,ed,ing,ion). Interpret(ed,ing,ation,ions). Translation(s). Restatement(s). *See also* Emphasis; Explanation; Interpretation; Definition (words); Meaning.

Class, chattering. See *Chattering class.*

Class, corporate. See *Ruling class.*

Class, economic. See *Economic elites; Lower class; Middle class; Poverty; Socioeconomic status; Upper class; Wealth.*

Class, first. See *Excellence.*

Class, lower. See *Lower class.*

Class, middle. See *Middle class.*

Class, new middle. See *New middle class.*

Class, owning. See *Ruling class.*

Class, ruling. See *Ruling class.*

Class, social. See *Social class.*

Class, upper. See *Upper class.*

Class, working. See *Working class.*

Class action. Class action(s). Representative action(s). *See also* Action; Lawsuits; Legal procedures.

Class analysis. Class analy(sis,tic). *Consider also:* class(es), social stratification, Marxist *with:* theor(y,ies,etical), analy(sis,ses), approach(es). *See also* Analysis; Class differences; Class formation; Class relations; Marxism; Social class; Social stratification; Social structure.

Class attitudes, middle. See *Embourgeoisement.*

Class attitudes, upper. See *Upper class attitudes.*

Class conflict. Class conflict(s). *Choose from:* class(es), underclass(es), elite(s), bourgeois(ie), ruling class(es), owning class(es), working class(es), proletaria(t,n) *with:* conflict(s), struggle(s), warfare, movement(s), polariz(ed,ing,ation), overcom(e,ing), radicalism, politic(s,al), dissent, interest(s), militancy, resistance. *Consider also:* social revolution. *See also* Class consciousness; Class relations; Ideological struggle; Marxism; Proletariat; Social class; Social conflict; Working class.

Class consciousness. Class consciousness. Subjective dimension of class. *Choose from:* conscious(ness), aware(ness), sensitiz(ed,ing,ation), sensitiv(e,ity), common identity *with:* class, class interest, class status, class position, class structure, proletariat. *Consider also:* gender consciousness, false consciousness, class ident(ification,ity), worker consciousness, dual consciousness, class struggle(s). *See also* Class conflict; Class differences; Class identity; Class relations; Lower class attitudes; Marxism; Proletarianization.

Class differences. Class differences. *Choose from:* class(es), social, status, caste, gender, elite(s), underclass(es), middle class(es), bourgeois(ie), lower class(es), upper class(es), caste(s), rank(s), stratification *with:* compar(ison,isons,itive,ability), difference(s), differential(s), inequalit(y,ies), disparit(y,ies), diversity, discrepanc(y,ies), differentiation, distinction(s), variation(s), dissimilarit(y,ies), characteristics, determinant(s), correlat(es,ion,ions), effect(s), dependent, link(s,ed,ing), related, factor(s). *See also* Class analysis; Comparative study; Inequality; Minority groups; Social class; Social stratification; Socioeconomic status.

Class formation. Class formation. *Choose from:* class(es), social stratification, group(s), social segment(s,ation), social strata, elite(s), underclass(es), middle class(es), bourgeois(ie), upper class(es) *with:* form(ed,ing,ation), emerg(e,ed, ing,ence), genesis, transform(ed,ing, ation,ations), develop(ed,ing,ment), differentiat(ed,ing,ion,ions), mak(e,ing), new. *See also* Class analysis; Social class; Social processes.

Class identity. Class identity. *Choose from:* class(es), group(s), social segment(s,ation), social strata, elite(s), underclass(es), middle class(es), bourgeois(ie), upper class(es) *with:* identit(y,ies), identif(y,ied,ication), orientation(s), allegiance(s), conscious(ness). *See also* Class consciousness; Group identity; Social class; Social identity.

Class mobility. Class mobility. Social mobility. Status competition. Cross(ed, ing) class line(s). Achieved status(es). Marr(y,ying,iage) *with:* high(er) status. Loss of status. Change(s) in social status. Intragenerational mobility. Status seeker(s). *Choose from:* social, sociocultural, social class, upward(ly), status, occupational, socioeconomic, downward(ly), intragenerational *with:* mobil(e,ity), immobil(e,ity), destination, aspiration(s), achievement, attainment, improvement(s), opportunit(y,ies), restriction(s). *See also* Career mobility; Educational attainment; Embourgeoisement; Geographic mobility; Intergenerational mobility; Social mobility; Status attainment; Status seekers.

Class politics. Class politics. *Choose from:* politic(al,ally,s), politician(s), voter(s), grass roots, election(s), elect(ed,ing), elector(al,ate), lobby(ing), democra(tic,cy) *with:* class(es), elite(s), bourgeois(ie), underclass(es), working class(es), middle class(es), upper class(es), ruling class(es), owning class(es), social status, social strata, caste(s). *See also* Class relations; Labor movements; Oppression; Working class.

Class relations. Class relation(s,ships). *Choose from:* class(es), group(s), intergroup, social segment(s,ation), social strata, elite(s), underclass(es), middle class(es), bourgeois(ie), upper class(es) *with:* relation(s,ships), politic(s,al), conflict(s), cleavage(s). *See also* Class analysis; Class conflict; Class politics; Ethnic relations; Intergroup relations; Race relations; Social class.

Class society. Class societ(y,ies). Class system(s). Social stratification. Class structure(s). Social structure(s). Class boundar(y,ies). Class crystallization. Class line(s). *See also* Class relations; Social class; Social stratification; Social structure; Society.

Class status. See *Social status.*

Class stratification. Class stratification. Social stratification. Social class structure(s). Horizontal and vertical social structure(s). Social class(es). Social rank(s). Occupational prestige ranking(s). Social strat(a,um). Social hierarch(y,ies). Status differentiation(s). Social inequalit(y,ies). Microstratification. Class division(s). Status division(s). Ranking of statuses. Caste system(s). Caste(s). Dual labor market(s). *Consider also:* sex(ual), gender, school, age, economic, racial *with:* stratification. *See also* Social class; Socioeconomic factors; Socioeconomic status; Social stratification; Stratification.

Class structure. See *Social stratification; Social structure.*

Class struggle. See *Class conflict.*

Classes (logic). Class(es) logic(al). *Consider also:* set(s), aggregate(s). *See also* Logic; Philosophy.

Classes, laboring. See *Working class.*

Classes, priestly and priests anthropology. See *Priests and priestly classes (anthropology).*

Classic (standard). Classic(al). Archetyp(e, es,al). Exemplar(ily,iness,ity). Typical(ly,ity,ness). Model(s). Consummate(ly). Ideal type(s). Paradigm(s,atic). Prototyp(e,es,al,ical). Quintessential(ly). Representative. Standard(s) of excellence. *Consider also:* finest, first class, symmetrical, proportional(ly), well proportioned, elegan(t,ce), tasteful(ly), simpl(e,icity), beau ideal, example(s). *See also* Aesthetics; Archetypes; Beauty; Canon (literature); Classicism; Elegance; Ideal types; Types.

Classic revival. Classic revival. Neoclassic. Greek revival. Neo-Grec. *Choose from:* Neoclassic, Greek revival, Neo-Grec, Doric, Empire, Greek, Greco-Roman, Roman *with:* architecture, home(s), style(s), bedroom(s), cottage(s), mansion(s), form(s), interior(s), building(s), furniture, object(s), house(s), design(s), detail(s). *See also* Architectural styles; Architecture; Classical architecture; Classical art; Classicism; Gothic revival; Hellenism; Historic buildings; Historic houses.

Classical architecture. Classical architecture. Classic style of architecture. Classical building(s). *Choose from:* classic(al,ism), Gree(k,ce), Greco-Roman, Rom(e,an), Cret(e,an), Athen(s,ian) *with:* architectur(e,al). *Choose from:* Doric, Ionic, Corinthian, Tuscan, Composite *with:* column(s,ar). *Consider also:* Parthenon, Temples of Poseidon, Pantheon, etc. *See also* Ancient architecture; Antiquity (time); Architectural styles; Architecture; Classic revival; Classical art; Historic buildings; Historic houses.

Classical art. Classical art. *Choose from:* classic(al,ism), Greek, ancient Greece, ancient Rome, Roman, Italic, archaic, Hellenistic, antiquity, Olympia, Troy, Trojan, Athen(s,ian), Etruscan, Egyptian, Judaea, Greco-Roman *with:* art (s,work, works), painting(s), art treasure(s), aesthetic, iconograph(y,ic), sculpture(s). *Consider also:* classical archeology, antiquities, ancient art(work,works). *See also* Ancient art; Antiquity (time); Classic revival; Classical architecture; Naturalism.

Classical conditioning. Classical conditioning. *Choose from:* Pavlovian, classical, respondent *with:* conditioning. *See also* Conditioning (psychology); Conditioned responses.

Classical literature. See *Ancient literature; Latin literature.*

Classicism. Classicism. Classical standard(s). Classical style(s). Classical period(s). *Choose from:* classic(al), neoclassical, Augustan, Aristotelian, Attic, Doric, Homeric, Ionic, Hellenistic, Grecian, Greek *with:* litera(ture,ry), epic(s), comed(y,ies), traged(y,ies), ode(s), eclogue(s), eleg(y,ies), satire(s), fable(s), poet(ry,ics), art(s), painting(s), music(al), architecture. *Consider also:* classicisme, classicismo, klassisch, classisch, klassizismus, canonical. *See also* Classic (standard); Classic revival; Classical architecture; Classical art; Hellenism; Humanism; Humanists; Idyll; Literary movements; Renaissance; Renaissance literature; Renaissance philosophy.

Classification. Classificat(ion,ions,icatory). Classify(ing). Classified. Categoriz(ed, ation,ions,ing). Sort(ed,ing). Systematics. Taxonom(y,ies). Group(ed,ing). Order(ed,ing). Cod(e,ed,ing). Codif(y, ied,ication). Typolog(y,ies). Grad(e,ed, ing). Cluster(ed,ing). Track(ed,ing). Categorical judgment(s). Label(ed,ing). Labell(ed,ing). Catalog(ed,ing). Index(ed,ing). Nomenclature. Hierarchical relationship(s). DSM-III. Linnaean or Linnean. *Consider also:* apportion(ing,ed,ment), arrang(e,ed,ing, ement), distribut(e,ed,ing,ition), nosolog(y,ic,ical,ically). *See also* Analysis; Book classification; Categorization; Choice (psychology); Choice behavior; Coding; Cognitive processes; Color coding; Content analysis; Data analysis; Documentation; Groups; Hierarchy; Ideal types; Identification (recognition); Labeling (of persons); Language classification; Occupational classification; Social types; Stratification; Structure; Types.

Classification, book. See *Book classification.*

Classification, job. See *Occupational classification.*

Classification, language. See *Language classification.*

Classification, occupational. See *Occupational classification.*

Classified advertising. Classified ad(s,vertising,vertisement,vertisements). Personal ad(s,vertising,vertisement, vertisements). Classifieds. Classified section. *Choose from:* help wanted, employment, real estate, housing, rentals, commercial property, auto sales, merchandise, pets, animals, personals, etc. *with:* ad(s,vertising,vertisement, vertisements). *Consider also:* yellow pages, classified voice mail. *See also* Advertising; Newspapers.

Classified information. Classified information. Official Secrets Act. Confidential government information. Restricted access to information. Sensitive information. Secret data. Top secret. Closed trial(s). *Choose from:* government, military, pentagon, state *with:* censor(ed,ing,ship), secre(t,ts,cy). *Choose from:* classif(y,ied,ication), overclassif(y,ied,ication), secre(t,cy), sensitive *with:* information, report(s), data, evidence, tape(s), diar(y,ies), research, document(s), paper(s), military information, material(s), intelligence. *See also* Access to information; Censorship; Government information; Government secrecy; Information leaks; Information policy; Military intelligence; News policies; Secrecy.

Classism. See *Social discrimination.*

Classless society. Classless societ(y,ies). *Consider also:* utopia(s,n), communism, Marxism, anarchism, syndicalism, egalitarian(ism), blur(red,ring) class line(s). *See also* Egalitarianism; Industrial democracy; Socialism; Utopias.

Classroom environment. Classroom environment(s). *Choose from:* classroom(s) *with:* environment(s), condition(s), setting(s), surrounding(s), milieu, feature(s), atmosphere(s), climate(s), ambience, color(s), tone(s), mood(s), background(s). *See also* Ambience; Educational environment; School discipline; Student attitudes; Student teacher relations; Teacher attitudes.

Classroom method, open. See *Open classroom method.*

Clavichord. Clavichord(s). Clavichorde(s). Klavichord(en). Clavichordo. Clavicordio. *Consider also:* clavier. *See also* Musical instruments.

Clean rooms. Clean room(s). Cleanroom(s). White room(s). Aseptic room(s). *Choose from:* steril(e,ize,ized,izing,ization), aseptic, white, clean, quarantine(d) *with:* room(s), laborator(y,ies), facilit(y,ies), environment(s), area(s). *Consider also:* contamination control. *See also* Research; Laboratories.

Cleansing, ethnic. See *Ethnic cleansing.*

Clearance (authorization). Clear(ed,ing,ancel). Approv(ed,ing,al). Authoriz(e,es,ed,ing,ation). Consent(s, ed,ing). Permission(s). Permit(ted,ting). Sanction(s,ed,ing). *Consider also:* approbat(ion,ory), security clearance, allow(ed,ing,ance), sufferance. *See also* Acceptance; Approval; Consent (law).

Clearing land. See *Deforestation.*

Cleavage, social. See *Social cleavage.*

Cleft palate. Cleft palate. *Choose from:* cleft(s), abnormal, defect(s,ive), fissure(s) *with:* palate(s), palatal, orofacial, lip(s), jaw(s). *Consider also:* cleft lip(s), harelip(s). *See also* Physical abnormalities; Speech disorders.

Clemency. Clemenc(y,ies). Pardon(ed,ing). Amnesty. Lenien(t,cy). Merc(y,iful). Commutation(s). Reprieve(s,d). Sentence(s) lifted. Conviction(s) overturned. Restor(e,ed,ing,ation) of citizenship rights. Restor(e,ed,ing,ation) citizenship. Compassion(ate). *See also* Death penalty; Forgiveness; Life sentence; Pardon; Punishment.

Clergy. Clergy(man,men,woman,women). Rabbi(s,nical). Priest(s,ess,esses). Chaplain(s). Minister(s). Pastor(s). Preacher(s). Deacon(s). Cleric(als,alism, s). Church(man,men,woman,women). Parson(s). Ecclesiastic(s). Prelate(s). Bishop(s). Monsignor(i). Cardinal(s). Vicar(s). Reverend(s). Evangelist(s). Missionar(y,ies). Religious person(s). Mullah(s). Imam(s). *See also* Clericalism; Ecclesiastical benefices; Lay religious personnel; Ministerial ethics (clergy); Ministers; Ordination; Preachers; Preaching; Priests; Rabbis; Religious councils and synods; Religious leadership; Religious personnel; Spiritual direction.

Clerical workers. Clerical worker(s). Clerk(s). Secretar(y,ies). Pink collar worker(s). Stenographer(s). Typist(s). Receptionist(s). Girl Friday(s). Bank teller(s). Bookkeeper(s). Computer equipment operator(s). Data entry operator(s). Mail carrier(s). Telephone operator(s). Desk job(s). *Choose from:* clerical, office, support, data entry, keyboard, mailroom *with:* operator(s), labor, staff, personnel, employee(s),

worker(s), pool(s). *Consider also:* service work(s,er,ers,ing). *See also* Letter carriers; Secretaries; White collar workers.

Clericalism. Clericalis(m,t). Elitist clergy. Power of clerical hierarchy. Ecclesiastical power. Clerical elitism. Cleric-dominated. *See also* Anticlericalism; Church-state relationship; Clergy.

Clerks. See *Clerical workers.*

Cliches. Cliche(s). Platitude(s). Truism(s). Maxim(s). Trite expression(s). Sententia(e). Precept(s). *Consider also:* banalit(y,ies), prosaism(s). *See also* Catchwords; Communication (thought transfer); Jargon; Terminology.

Client attitudes. Client attitude(s). *Choose from:* client(s,ele), patient(s), outpatient(s), consumer(s), customer(s), patron(s), user(s), borrower(s), enduser(s), shopper(s) *with:* attitude(s), preference(s), satisf(ied,action), dissatisf(ied,action), perception(s), expectation(s), attribution(s), judgment(s), mindset. *See also* Attitudes; Clients; Consumer satisfaction; Library surveys; Market research; Patient compliance; Preferences; Promotion (business).

Client centered therapy. Client centered therapy. *Choose from:* nondirective, client centered, Rogerian, person centered, humanistic *with:* therap(y,ies), psychotherap(y,ies), counseling, treatment(s), casework, therapeutic approach(es). *See also* Psychotherapeutic techniques; Psychotherapy.

Client characteristics. Client(s) characteristic(s). *Choose from:* borrower(s), buyer(s), client(s,ele), consumer(s), constituenc(y,ies), customer(s), depositor(s), enduser(s), outpatient(s), patient(s), passenger(s), patron(s), prospect(s), purchaser(s), shopper(s), student(s), user(s) *with:* characteristic(s), personal qualit(y,ies), personality, gender, exceptional, handicapped, gifted, family background, income, place of residence, nationality, religion, health status, marital status, physical characteristics, biodata, biographical data, behavior patterns, traits, socioeconomic status, age, race, religion, educational level, urban, rural. *See also* Characteristics; Client attitudes; Clients; Cultural therapy; Feminist therapy; Health behavior; Individual differences; Market research; Patient history; Patients; Qualities; Student characteristics.

Client education. Client(s) education. *Choose from:* borrower(s), buyer(s), client(s,ele), constituenc(y,ies), consumer(s), customer(s), depositor(s), enduser(s), outpatient(s), passenger(s), patient(s), patron(s), prospect(s), purchaser(s), shopper(s), user(s) *with:*

instruct(ed,ing,ion), educat(e,ed,ing,ion), teach(ing), taught, inform(ed,ing,ation), orientation, train(ed,ing), class(es), tutor(ed,ing,ials). *See also* Consumer awareness; Consumer education; Health education; Patient compliance; Patient education; Therapeutic processes.

Client participation. See *Consumer participation.*

Client professional relations. See *Professional client relations.*

Client relations. Client relations. *Choose from:* borrower(s), buyer(s), client(ele,s), constituenc(y,ies), consumer(s), customer(s), depositor(s), enduser(s), outpatient(s), passenger(s), patient(s), patron(s), purchaser(s), shopper(s), student(s), user(s) *with:* relation(s,ship, ships), expectation(s), trust, acceptance, retention, satisf(y,ied,action), dissatisf(y, ied,action), partner(s,ship,ships), rapport, contract(s). *See also* Client characteristics; Community institutional relations; Confidentiality; Counseling; Customer relations; Dentist patient relations; Helping behavior; Interpersonal relations; Investor relations; Nurse patient relations; Parent school relations; Police community relations; Physician patient relations; Professional client relations; Professional ethics; Professional family relations; Professional malpractice; Psychotherapy; Public relations; Service contracts; Student teacher relations; Therapeutic processes; Therapist role; Vendor relations.

Client rights. Client(s) right(s). *Choose from:* borrower(s), buyer(s), client(s,ele), constituenc(y,ies), consumer(s), customer(s), depositor(s), enduser(s), outpatient(s), patient(s), patron(s), passenger(s), prospect(s), purchaser(s), shopper(s), student(s), user(s) *with:* right(s), privilege(s), obligation(s), ethic(s,al), advoca(te,tes,cy), accountab(le,ility), guarantee(s,d), warrant(y,ies), right to know, privacy, freedom of choice, property right(s), disclosure, information. *See also* Civil rights; Consumer protection; Consumer organizations; Human rights; Informed consent; Ombudsmen; Patient compliance; Patient rights; Product labeling; Product liability; Right of privacy; Right to die; Treatment withholding.

Clients. Client(s,ele). Audience(s). Borrower(s). Buyer(s). Constituenc(y, ies). Consumer(s). Customer(s). Depositor(s). End user(s). Outpatient(s). Passenger(s). Patient(s). Patron(s,age). Prospect(s). Purchaser(s). Seeker(s). Shopper(s). Student(s). Tenant(s). User(s). *Consider also:* market, vendee(s). *See also* Client attitudes; Client characteristics; Client relations; Client rights; Online users; Patients.

Climacteric. Climacter(ic,ium). Change of life. Menopaus(e,al). Cessation of menstruation. Male menopaus(e,al). Andropaus(e,al). *Consider also:* perimenopaus(e,al), postmenopausal, premenopausal, middle age, age critique, viropaus(e,al). *Consider also:* estrogen replacement therapy, ERT. *See also* Aging; Involutional psychosis; Life cycle; Middle age.

Climate. Climat(e,es,ic,ically). Prevailing weather. Characteristic weather. *Consider also:* meteorologic(al) condition(s), atmospheric condition(s), weather condition(s), cold climate(s), desert climate(s), microclimate(s), tropical climate(s). *See also* Air pollution; Climatic changes; Environment; Greenhouse effect; Heat effects; Pollution control; Solar energy; Weather.

Climate, organizational. See *Organizational climate.*

Climate, social. See *Social environment.*

Climatic changes. Climatic change(s). Climate change(s). Climatic evolution. Climate variation(s). Climate variation(s). *Consider also:* global cooling, global warming, ozone depletion, greenhouse effect(s), global average surface temperature(s), temperature variation(s), sea surface temperature(s), increas(e,ed,ing) global temperatures, global tropospheric warming, climatic fluctuation(s) of temperature, arctic warm(ing). *See also* Climate; Glacial epoch; Greenhouse effect; Seasonal variations.

Climatology, medical. See *Medical climatology.*

Climax. Climax(es). Acme(s). Apex(es). Apoge(e,an). Culminat(e,ed,ing,ion). Meridian(s). Fruition. Peak(s). Pinnacle(s). Summit(s). Zenith(s). Highest point. Highest stage. Crest(s,ed, ing). Crown(ed,ing). Fastigium(s). Roof(s). Vertex(es). Vertices. Capsheaf(s). Capstone(s). Crescendo(s). Ne plus ultra. *Consider also:* highlight(s), quintesscen(ce,tial), ultimate(ly), consummation, realization, supreme moment(s), final stage, finish(ed,ing) off, round(ed,ing) off, top(ped,ping) off. *See also* Ecstasy; Enlightenment (state of mind); Fulfillment; Orgasm.

Clinicians, nurse. See *Nurse clinicians.*

Clinics. Clinic(s). Treatment center(s). Outpatient center(s). Dispensar(y,ies). Infirmar(y,ies). Sick bay. *See also* Ambulatory care; Community health centers; Community mental health services; Crisis intervention; Hospitals; Outpatient treatment; Outpatients; Psychiatric clinics; Walk-in clinics.

Clinics, abortion. See *Abortion clinics.*

Clinics, psychiatric. See *Psychiatric clinics.*

Clinics, walk-in. See *Walk-in clinics.*

Clip art. Clip art. *Choose from:* reproducib(le,ility), clip, stencil(s), uncopyrighted, usable *with:* art, drawing(s), illustration(s), image(s). *See also* Arts; Desktop publishing; Electronic publishing; Office automation.

Cliques. Clique(s). Interlocking directorate(s). Interconnected individual(s). Exclusive circle(s). Exclusive group(s). Coterie(s). *See also* Clubs Friendship; Peers; Primary groups; Small groups.

Clitics (grammar). Clitic(s,ize,ization). Proclitic(s). Enclitic(s). Clitic pronoun(s). Clitik(s). *Consider also:* proclisis, enclisis, affix(es,ation). *See also* Affixes; Grammar.

Cloaks. Cloak(s). Cape(s). Mantle(s). *Consider also:* robe(s), overcoat(s), carcoat(s), anorak(s), wind-cheater(s), wind-jacket(s), dolman(s), poncho(s), toga(s), sweater(s), tunic(s), smock(s), sacque(s). *See also* Clothing.

Clocks, biological. See *Biological clocks; Biological rhythms.*

Clocks and watches. Clock(s). Watch(es). Timepiece(s). Stopwatch(es). Wristwatch(es). Horologe(s). Timer(s). Chronometer(s). *Consider also:* speedometer(s). *See also* Horology; Time; Time measurement; Time perception; Tools.

Cloisters. Cloister(s). Monaster(y,ies). Monastic seminar(y,ies). Convent(s). Nunner(y,ies). Abbey(s). Prior(y,ies). Religious communit(y,ies). Lamaser(y, ies). Priorate(s). *See also* Abbeys; Contemplative orders; Monasticism; Religious communities; Religious personnel.

Cloning. Clon(e,ed,ng). Asexual(ly) propagat(e,es,ing,ion). Asexual(ly) reproduc(ed,tion). Duplicate organism reproduc(ed,tion). *Consider also:* replic(a,as,ate,ates,ated,ing,ation), duplicat(e,es,ed,ing,ion), imitator *with:* cell(s,ular), embryo(s), nuclear DNA, gene(s,tic). *See also* Surrogate mother; Bioethics; Reproductive technologies; Pharming.

Close. See *Adjournment; Bankruptcy; Closure; End; Plant closings.*

Closed businesses. See *Bank failures; Business failures; Deindustrialization; Dislocated workers; Organizational dissolution; Personnel termination; Plant closings.*

Closed shop. Closed shop(s). Union shop(s). *Consider also:* modified union shop(s), agency shop(s). *See also* Labor management relations; Labor unions; Open shop.

Closeness. See *Intimacy.*

Closeness, fear of. See *Fear of closeness.*

Closings, factory. See *Plant closings.*

Closings, plant. See *Plant closings.*

Closings, real estate. See *Real estate closings.*

Closure. Closure. Closing(s). Shutdown(s). Close down. Discontinu(e,d,ing). Suspend(ed,ing). Ceas(e,ed,ing). Conclud(e,ed,ing). Conclusion(s). Consummat(e,ed,ing,ation). Denouement. Final(ity). *See also* Adjournment; Bankruptcy; End; Finale; Finite; Plant closings.

Closure (phonetics). Closure. Plosive(s). Africate(s). Nasal(s). Airstream mechanism(s). *Consider also:* roll(s), flap(s), tap(s), lateral(s), fricative(s), stricture(s). *See also* Phonetics.

Closure (Rhetoric). Closure. Sense of an ending. The end. Happy ending(s). Surpris(e,ing) ending(s). Peroration(al). Conclusion(s). Terminat(e,ed,ion). Cessation. Wind up. Wind down. *Consider also:* cloture, complet(e,ed, ing,ion), fulfill(ed,ing,ment). *See also* Literature; Rhetoric.

Closure, perceptual. See *Perceptual closure.*

Closure, social. See *Social closure.*

Clothing. Clothing. Clothes. Apparel. Attire. Bathing suit(s). Bathrobe(s). Belt(s). Bloomer(s). Bodysuit(s). Blouse(s). Bra(s). Brassiere(s). Cape(s). Cassock(s). Coat(s). Costume(s). Dashiki(s). Dress(es). Fashion(s). Garb. Garment(s). Glove(s). Hat(s). Hosiery. Jeans. Jumper(s). Kimono(s). Lingerie. Livery. Mitten(s). Nightgown(s). Overcoat(s). Pajamas. Pant(s,ies). Raincoat(s). Suit(s). Skirt(s). Shirt(s). Slip(s). Sock(s). Stocking(s). Shoe(s). Shorts. Slacks. Slipper(s). Surplice(s). Sweater(s). Undercloth(ing,es). Underwear. Uniform(s). Undershirt(s). Underwear. Veil(s). Vestment(s). Vest(s). Wardrobe(s). *Consider also:* accouter(ed,ment,ments), accoutre(ed, ment,ments), dress codes, protective clothing. *See also* Bicycle helmets; Blouses; Boots and shoes; Cloaks; Clothing workers; Customs; Decorative arts; Demeanor; Fashions; Hats; Headgear; Material culture; Nonverbal communication; Space suits.

Clothing industry. See *Garment industry.*

Clothing workers. Clothing worker(s). Seamstress(es). Tailor(s). Knitting machine operator(s). Sewing machine operator(s). Dressmaker(s). Milliner(s). *Choose from:* garment, apparel, cloth(es,ing), fashion *with:* worker(s). *Consider also:* piecework, sweatshop(s).

See also Fabrics; Garment industry; Knit goods industry; Sewing; Sweatshops; Workers.

Clubs. Club(s). Association(s). Community organization(s). Fraternal societ(y,ies). Voluntary organization(s). Sports team(s). Brotherhood(s). Fellowship(s). Fraternit(y,ies). Sororit(y,ies). Lodge(s). League(s). *Consider also:* sodalit(y,ies), troop(s), Boy Scout(s), Girl Scout(s), Kiwanis, Rotary Club(s), etc. *See also* Alliances; Associations (organizations); Baseball clubs; Billiard parlors; Cliques; Confraternities; Groups; Leisure activities; Organizations; Societies (organizations); Sports; Teams; Voluntary associations; Youth organizations;.

Clubs, baseball. See *Baseball clubs.*

Clubs, school. See *School clubs.*

Clubs, student. See *School clubs.*

Clubs, therapeutic social. See *Therapeutic social clubs.*

Clubs, youth. See *Youth organizations.*

Clues. Clue(s). Hint(s). Cue(s). Indicat(or,ors,ion,ions). Inkling(s). Intimation(s). Notion(s). Suggestion(s). Telltale. Eviden(t,ce,ces). *Consider also:* glimmer(s,ing,ings), pointer(s), trace(s). *See also* Cues; Discovering; Evidence.

Clustering, space time. See *Space time clustering.*

Clusters. Cluster(s,ed,ing,y). Aggregation(s). Agglomerat(e,ed,ing, ion,ions). Group(s,ing,ings). Array(s,ed, ing). Batch(ed,ing,es). Bunch(es,ed,ing). Bundl(e,ed,ing). Clump(ed,ing). Clutch(es,ed,ing). *Consider also:* assembl(y,ies), band(s), bev(y,ies), covey(s), crew(s), herd(s), gaggle(s), swarm(s,ed,ing). *See also* Crowds; Form (aesthetics); Group structure; Groups; Structure.

Clutter. Clutter(ed,ing). Chao(s,tic). Confusing mess(es). Disarray(s). Disorder(ed,ing). Disorganiz(e,ed,ing, ation). Muddle(s,d). Snarl(s,ed). Tangle(s,d). Topsy-turv(y,iness). Jumble(s,d). Muss(es,ed). *Consider also:* litter(ed,ing), mishmash(s), rummage, scramble(s,d), hodgepodge(s), trash(y,iness), untid(y,iness). *See also* Chaos; Confusion (disarray); Disintegration; Entropy; Orderliness; Solid waste; Thought disturbances.

Co-dependency. Co-dependen(t,ce,cy). Codependen(t,ce,cy). Mutual(ly) dependen(t,ce,cy). Enabler(s). Depend(ing,ed,ent) on each other. *Consider also:* symbio(sis,tic), mutual aid, rescuer(s). *See also* Addiction; Dependency (personality); Emotional dependence.

Coal. Coal(s). Coke. Anthracite. Bituminous. Subbituminous. Lignite. Cokeite. *Consider also:* charcoal. *See also* Coal industry; Coal miners; Coal mines and mining; Energy; Energy generating resources; Energy policy; Fuel; Raw materials.

Coal industry. Coal industry. *Choose from:* coal(s), coke, anthracite, bituminous, subbituminous, lignite, cokeite *with:* industr(y,ies,ial), compan(y,ies), mine(s), corp(oration,orations), import(ed,ing,s), export(ed,ing,s), land(s), production, market(s), lobby, process(ed,ing), gasification, futures, enterprise(s), operation(s), company town(s). *See also* Coal; Coal miners; Industry; Mining industry; Oil industry.

Coal miners. Coal miner(s). *Choose from:* coal *with:* miner(s), mineworker(s), union member(s), labor market(s). *See also* Black lung disease; Coal; Coal industry; Coal mines and mining; Industrial personnel; Industrial workers.

Coal mines and mining. Coal mine(s). Coal mining. Collier(y,ies). Coalfield(s). *Choose from:* coal, anthracite, bitumen, coke *with:* mine(d,s), mining, reserve(s), mine shaft(s), pit(s). *Consider also:* mining asset(s), mining compan(y,ies). *See also* Coal; Coal miners; Drilling and boring; Mining industry; Strip mining.

Coalescence. Coalesc(e,ed,ing,ence,ent). Amalgamat(e,ed,ing,ion,ions). Fus(e,ed,ing). Converg(e,ed,ing,ence). Consolidat(e,ed,ing,ing). Intermingl(e, ed,ing). Join(s,ed,ing). Associat(e,ed,ing, ion,ions). Grow(ing,n) together. Unit(e,ed,ing). Bracket(ed,ing). Combin(e,ed,ing,ation). Conjoin(ed, ing). Connect(ed,ing,ion,ions). Link(ed,ing,s). Cleav(e,ing). Cling(ing). Blend(s,ed,ing). Merg(e,ed,ing). Join(ed,ing) forces. *See also* Alliances; Coalition formation; Coalitions; Combinations; Consolidation; Group formation; Pillarization.

Coalition formation. Coalition formation. Coalition(al) politics. *Choose from:* form(ed,ing,ation), emerg(ing,ence), develop(ed,ing,ment) *with:* coalition(s), bloc(s), alliance(s). *Consider also:* coalition politics, coalesc(e,ed,ing), solidarity, block voting. *See also* Coalescence; Coalitions; Group formation; Pillarization; Social movements; Social processes.

Coalitions. Coalition(al,s). Alliance(s). All(y,ies). Cartel(s). Collective action. Cooperative game(s). Bedfellow(s). Bloc(s). Block voting. Solidarity. Popular front(s). Entente(s). Linkage(s). Cooperat(ing,ion). Union(s). League(s). Partnership(s). Bloc(s). Federation(s). Confederation(s). Consort(ia,ium,iums). Clique(s). Junta(s). *Consider also:* coalition politics, coalesc(e,ed,ing, ence,ent), blend(s,ed,ing), confederation(s), syndicate(s), fusion(s). *See also* Alliances; Cartels; Coalescence; Coalition formation; Combinations; Cooperation; Federations; Intergroup relations; International alliances; Mergers; Partners; Pillarization; Political action; Power sharing; Preference voting; Strategic alliances; Teaming; Third parties (United States politics).

Coast defenses. Coast defense(s). *Choose from:* shore(s), port(s), coast(s,al), harbor(s), channel(s), maritime part(s), tidewater(s), seacoast(s), sea-coast(s), waterside *with:* fortress(es), fortification(s), fortify(ing), fortified, fort(s), defense(s), surveillance, armament(s). *Consider also:* Coast Guard. *See also* Civil defense; Harbors; Island ecology; Islands; Military planning; Military operations; Navy yards and naval stations; Ports; Sea power; Shorelines; Territorial waters.

Coastal zone management. See *Shore protection.*

Coasts. See *Shore protection; Shorelines.*

Cobranding. Cobrand(ed,ing). Co-brand(ed,ing). *Choose from:* credit card(s), marketing, advertising campaign(s), brand name(s), logo(s), promotion(s) *with:* alliance(s), link(s), team(s,ing), partner(s,ship,ships). *Consider also:* corporate bank card(s). *See also* Brand identity; Joint ventures; Marketing; Marketing strategies; Strategic alliances; Teaming.

Cocaine. See *Street drugs.*

Cockfighting. Cockfight(s,ing). Cock-fight(s,ing). Rooster(s) fight(s,ing). Fighting cock(s). Fighting rooster(s). Pelea(s) de gallos. Combats de coq(s). *Consider also:* cock pit(s). *See also* Cocks; Cruelty to animals; Sports.

Cocks. Cock(s,es). Gallo(s). Rooster(s). Gamecock(s). Coq(s). Cockerel(s). Game fowl(s). Game bird(s). Game chicken(s). *See also* Chickens; Cock-fighting; Poultry.

Code switching. Code switch(ed,ing,es). Code mixing. Codeswitch(ed,ing,es). *Choose from:* code language(s), interlingual *with:* switch(ed,ing,es), mix(ed,ing), alternat(ing,ion). *See also* Ebonics; Bilingualism; Linguistic interference; Loan words; Socio-linguistics.

Codeine. See *Narcotics.*

Codeperdency. See *Co-dependency.*

Codes (rules). Code(s,x). Codif(y,ied, ying,ication). Compil(e,ed,ing,ation) law(s). Canon(s). Set(s) of law(s). Rule(s). Regulation(s). Maxim(s). *Consider also:* Code Civil, Code Napoleon, Code of Hammurabi, Codex

Gregorianus, Codex Hermogenianus, Codex Justinianeus, Code of Military Justice, etc. *See also* Canons; Codes of ethics; Constitution (legal); Laws; Roman law.

Codes (secret). See *Cryptography.*

Codes, building. See *Building codes.*

Codes, penal. See *Penal codes.*

Codes of ethics. Code(s) of ethics. *Choose from:* code(s), standard(s), legislation, law(s), rule(s), principle(s) *with:* ethic(al,s), honor, conduct, moral(s,ity). *See also* Accountability; Cheating; Codes (rules); Conflict of interest; Deception; Ethics; Financial disclosure; Group norms; Journalistic ethics; Judicial ethics; Loyalty oaths; Literary ethics; Malpractice; Medical ethics; Ministerial ethics (clergy); Misconduct in office; Moral development; Plagia-rism; Professional ethics; Theft; White collar crime.

Codicil. See *Addendum.*

Coding. Cod(e,es,ed,ing). Shorthand. Cryptogram(s). Cryptograph(y). Cryptology. Secret writing. Notation(s). *See also* Automated coding; Classifica-tion; Color coding; Cryptography; Data processing.

Coding, automated. See *Automated coding.*

Coding, color. See *Color coding.*

Coeducation. Coeducation(al). Co-education(al). Coed(s). Mixed sex. Gender balance(d). Integrat(e,ed,ing) men and women. Gender equity polic(y,ies). *See also* Access to educa-tion; Children's rights; Egalitarianism; Equal education; Equal job opportuni-ties; Feminism; Nonsexist education; Sex discrimination; Single sex schools; Social equality; Social equity.

Coercion. Coerc(e,ed,ion,ing,ive). Compel(s,led,ling). Impel(s,led,ling). Persuas(ive,ion). Persuad(e,ed,ing). Obligat(e,ed,ing,ion,ions). Duress. Compulsion. Insist(ed,ing,ence,ent). Induce(d,ment,ments). Inducing. Constraint(s). Arm twisting. Threat(en,ening,ened). Intimidat(e,es,ed, ing,ion,ions). Forc(e,ed,ing). *See also* Brainwashing; Conflict; Control; Dominance; Duress; Hegemony; Obedience; Oppression; Physical restraint; Political violence; Power; Punishment; Sexual coercion; Torture; Violence.

Coercion, sexual. See *Sexual coercion.*

Coexistence, peaceful. See *Peaceful coexistence.*

Coffee houses. Coffee house(s). Coffeehouse(s). Coffee bar(s). Starbucks. Coffee shop(s). Coffee chain(s). Computer cafe(s). Philosophy

cafe(s). Coffee vendor(s). Espresso shop(s). *Choose from:* coffee(s), espresso *with:* house(s), bar(s), shop(s), chain(s), cafe(s), vendor(s). *See also* Bars; Coffee industry; Cybercafes; Eating establishments; Nightclubs; Restaurants.

Coffee industry. Coffee industry. Coffee plantation(s). Coffee field(s). Coffee grower(s). *Choose from:* coffee(s) *with:* industr(y,ies,ial), compan(y,ies), corporation(s), wholesaler(s), retailer(s), supplier(s), price(s), advertis(e,ed,ing, ement,ements), market(s,ing), sell(ing,er,ers), sold, plantation(s), field(s), grower(s). *Consider also:* Nestle, Maxwell House, Chock Full O'Nuts, Folgers, etc. *See also* Agribusiness; Beverage industry; Coffee houses; Industry.

Cognatic descent. Cognatic descent. Bilateral descent. Double descent. Double unilineal descent. *Consider also:* maternal *with:* descent, line(s), lineage. *See also* Kinship; Lineage; Unilineal descent.

Cognition. Cognit(ion,ive). Cognizan(t,ce). Perception. Perceiv(e,ed,ing). Understand(ing). Understood. Comprehen(sion,d,ded,ding). Apprehen(sion,d,ded,ding). Discern(ment,ed,ing). Grasp(ed,ing). Know(n,ing,ledge). Wisdom. Aware(ness). Think(ing). Thought. Conscious(ness). Imagin(e,ed,ing,ation). *Consider also:* cognitive processes, reasoning, convergent thinking, creative thinking, critical thinking, language processing, information processing, learn(ed,ing), logical thinking, memory, mental abilit(y,ies), metacognition, problem solving, serial ordering, social cognition, encoding, intuition, cognitive dissonance. *See also* Abstraction; Animal intelligence; Artificial intelli-gence; Attention; Cognitive ability; Cognitive complexity; Cognitive development; Cognitive discrimination; Cognitive generalization; Cognitive mapping; Cognitive processes; Compre-hension; Concepts; Conscious (awake); Decision making; Epistemology; Human information storage; Imagination; Information processing; Intelligence; Intelligence tests; Intuition; Judgment; Knowledge; Learning; Learning disabilities; Memory; Mind; Phenom-enology; Problem solving; Psychology; Rationality; Synthesis; Theory forma-tion. Thinking; Reasoning.

Cognition disorders. Cognit(ion,ive) disorder(s). Confusion(s,al). Intellectual aging. Diminished competency. *Choose from:* cognit(ion,ive), thought, judgment, memory, perceptual, intellectual, thinking, mental abilit(y,ies) *with:* disorder(s), impair(ed,ment,ments), deficit(s), disturbance(s), incapacity, dysfunction(s,al), deteriorat(ed,ing,ion), loss(es), disabilit(y,ies), deficienc(y,ies), distort(ed,ing,ions), declin(e,ed,ing), slow(ness), failure, problem(s). *Consider also:* learning disab(led,ility,ilities), delirium, delusion(s), overinclusion, amnesia, agnosia, autistic thinking, confabulation, fragmentation, fugue reaction(s), magical thinking, obsession(s), perseveration. *See also* Alzheimer's disease; Body image disturbances; Cognitive enhancers; Legal competency; Memory decay; Memory disorders; Mental confusion; Senile dementia; Thought disturbances; Wandering behavior.

Cognition of time. See *Time perception.*

Cognitions. Cognitions. *Choose from:* thought(s), thinking, idea(s,tion), notion(s), perception(s), concept(s), conceptualization(s), mental representation(s), mental picture(s). *Choose from:* thought(s) *with:* negative, positive, intrusive, dimension(s), content(s). *See also* Attitudes; Beliefs; Concepts; Conceptual imagery; Expectations; Irrational beliefs.

Cognitive ability. Cognitive abilit(y,ies). *Choose from:* cognitive, learning, intellectual, neurocognitive *with:* abilit(y,ies), competence, function(ing), skill(s), performance. *See also* Academic ability; Aptitude; Cognition disorders; Cognitive development; Cognitive enhancers; Cognitive psychology; Cognitive structures; Epistemology; Heuristics; Intelligence; Intuition; Learning ability; Learning disabilities; Mathematical ability; Metacognition; Reading ability; Spatial ability; Verbal ability.

Cognitive complexity. Cognitive complexity. *Choose from:* cognitive, reasoning, thinking, thought process(es), intellectual, conceptual, perceptual, logical *with:* complex(ity), matur(e,ity), level(s), integrat(ion,ive), differentiat(e,ed,ing, ion). *See also* Cognitive development; Cognitive style.

Cognitive development. Cognitive development. Mental development. Cognitive evolution. *Choose from:* cognitive, intellectual, Piagetian, conceptual, logical *with:* stage(s), development, level(s), abilit(y,ies), growth. *Consider also:* concrete operational, formal operational, concept of conservation, concept of compensation, relational concepts, cognitive motor development, development of cognitive mapping, Piagetian theory, perceptual development, verbal development, language development. *See also* Academic aptitude; Adult development; Analogical reasoning; Child development; Cognition; Cognitive ability; Cognitive complexity; Cognitive

dissonance; Cognitive processes; Cognitive psychology; Cognitive structures; Cognitive style; Concept formation; Developmental disabilities; Developmental stages; Egocentrism; Epistemology; Experience (background); Human development; Intellectual development; Judgment; Language acquisition; Language development; Learning theories; Object permanence; Perceptual development; Psychodynamics; Psychogenesis; School readiness; Speech development.

Cognitive discrimination. Cognitive discrimination. *Choose from:* cognitive, comparative, comparison(s), same-different, similarity, appearance-reality *with:* discriminat(e,ed,ing,ion,ions), judgment(s), decision(s), mak(e,ing) distinction(s), differentiat(e,ed,ing,ion, ions). *See also* Cognitive processes; Concept formation.

Cognitive disorders. See *Cognition disorders; Thought disturbances.*

Cognitive dissonance. Cognitive dissonance. Conflicting beliefs. Counterattitudinal. Perceiv(e,ed,ing) discrepan(t,cy,cies). Stimulus incongruity. Perceiv(e,ed,ing) discontinuit(y,ies). Paradox(ical,es). Incongruent information. Dissonance arousal. Cognitive conflict(s). Cognitive distortion(s). Dissonant situation(s). Cognitive inconsistenc(y,ies). Belief discrepan(t,cy, cies). Unfulfilled expectation(s). Insufficient justification(s). Contradictory. Incongruit(y,ies). Ambiguit(y,ies). Unmet expectation(s). Discomforting evidence. Discrepant behavior(s). *See also* Anxiety; Attitudes; Beliefs; Cognition; Cognitive development; Cognitive processes; Cognitive structures; Motivation; Psychological stress; Self concept; Self congruence; Self esteem; Socialization.

Cognitive enhancers. Cognitive enhancer(s). Nootropic(s). Ginko. Ginkoba. Ampakine(s). Alpha-. amino-3-hydroxy-5 -methole-4-isoxasole-propionic-acid(s). *See also* Cognitive ability; Cognition disorders; Memory.

Cognitive generalization. Cognitive generalization. Generaliz(ed,ing,ation, ations). *Consider also:* infer(red,ring), draw(ing,n), form(ed,ing), mak(e,ing), induc(e,ed,ing), deriv(e,ed,ing) *with:* generalit(y,ies), principle(s), inference(s), rule(s), law(s), general conclusion(s), general conception(s), general statement(s). *Consider also:* inferential thinking, syllogistic reasoning, classify(ing), restructur(e,ed,ing), synthesiz(e,ed,ing), categoriz(e,ed,ing, ation,ations). *See also* Analogical reasoning; Association (psychology); Categorization; Cognitive processes; Concept formation; Generalities; Rules (generalizations).

Cognitive hypothesis testing. See *Hypothesis testing.*

Cognitive impairment. See *Cognition disorders.*

Cognitive mapping. Cognitive map(s,ping). Mental map(s,ping). *Choose from:* perceptual, symbolic, internal, mental *with:* representation(s). Spatial memory. Cognitive structure(s). Mental picture(s). *Consider also:* schema. *See also* Cognition; Cognitive structures; Cognitive style; Expectations; Learning; Perception; Spatial ability; Spatial imagery; Spatial memory; Spatial organization.

Cognitive processes. Cognitive process(es). Mental process(es). Thought process(es). Cognition. Learning. Perception. Reasoning. Thinking. Volition. Abstraction. *Choose from:* cognitive, information, mental, thought, thinking, learning, associative *with:* process(es). *Consider also:* abstract reasoning, cognitive discrimination, cognitive generalization, cognitive mediation, concentration, concept formation, conflict resolution, convergent thinking, creative thinking, critical thinking, decision making, decoding, divergent thinking, encoding, fantasizing, generalization, ideation, imagination, inductive deductive reasoning, inference, intellectual performance, intuition, language processing, logical thinking, memory, metacognition, perception, problem solving, serial ordering, social cognition, visualization. *See also* Abstraction; Artificial intelligence; Association (psychology); Choice behavior; Classification; Cognitive development; Cognitive discrimination; Cognitive dissonance; Cognitive generalization; Cognitive mapping; Cognitive psychology; Cognitive structures; Cognitive style; Comprehension; Concentration; Concept formation; Conceptual tempo; Conflict resolution; Creativity; Critical thinking; Decision making; Deduction; Divergent thinking; Epistemology; Field dependence; Group decision making; Group problem solving; Human information storage; Ideation; Imagination; Induction; Inference; Intelligence; Intuition; Learning; Learning disabilities; Logical thinking; Management decision making; Memory; Metacognition; Metalanguage; Naming; Object permanence; Perception; Problem solving; Questioning; Rationality; Reality testing; Reasoning; Role perception; Social consciousness; Spatial ability; Strategies; Thinking; Word association.

Cognitive psychology. Cognitive psychology. Cognitivism. Psychology of thinking. *Choose from:* cognitive, metacognitive *with:* psycholog(y,ical), research, science(s), stud(y,ies), concept(s), theor(y,ies), approach(es), counseling, analys(is,es), investigation(s), structure(s). *See also* Artificial intelligence; Behaviorism; Cognitive ability; Cognitive development; Cognitive processes; Cognitive structures; Cognitive science; Cognitive style; Epistemology; Experimental psychology; Intelligence; Psychophysiology.

Cognitive rehabilitation. Cognitive rehabilitation. Cognitive retraining. Reality orientation. *Choose from:* cognitive, cognition(s), thinking, thought, ideas, representation *with:* rehabilatat(e,ed,ion,ing), retrain(ed,ing), recovery, redevelopment, remediation, remedial, treatment(s). *See also* Cognition disorders; Rehabilitation.

Cognitive restructuring. Cognitive restructuring. Attribution retraining. Rational restructuring. Psychological reconstruction. Anger control therap(y,ies). Anger control treatment(s). *Choose from:* cognitive, cognition(s), thinking, thought, ideas, representation *with:* refram(e,ed,ing), restructur(e,ed, ing), reconstruct(e,ed,ing,ion). *Consider also:* paradigm shift(s). *See also* Attitude change; Behavior modification; Cognitive structures; Cognitive therapy; Counseling; Intervention; Learning disabilities; Learning theories; Psychotherapy; Rational emotive psychotherapy; Rehabilitation; Self control.

Cognitive science. Cognitive science. Cognitive stud(y,ies). Cognitivis(m,t). Computationalis(m,t). Connectionis(m, t). Computer simulation(s) of human cognition. *Choose from:* computational, representational, connectionist *with:* approach(es), metaphor(s), model(s), theor(y,ies) *with:* cognition, cognitive function(s), mind(s), think(ing). *Choose from:* cogniti(ive,on), cognitively oriented *with:* scien(ce,ces,tific), research, model(s), paradigm(s), neuroscien(ce,ces,tific), theor(y,ies, etical), map(s,ped,ping), concept(s), construct(s), assess(ed,ing,ment,ments). *Consider also:* cognitive technique(s), cognitive process(es). *See also* Artificial intelligence; Cognitive psychology.

Cognitive structures. Cognitive structure(s). Personal construct(s). *Choose from:* cognitive, belief(s), concept(s), attitude(s) *with:* organization, schemata, structure(s). *Consider also:* worldviews, world view(s), weltanschauung(en), viewpoint(s). *See also* Attitudes; Cognitive ability; Cognitive development; Cognitive dissonance; Cognitive mapping; Cognitive processes; Cognitive psychology; Cognitive restructuring; Cognitive style; Concept formation; Epistemology; Expectations; Ideologies; Misconceptions; Worldview.

Cognitive style. Cognitive style(s). *Choose from:* cognitive, learning, thinking, attentional, modality *with:* style(s), preference(s), orientation(s), set(s), mode(s). *Consider also:* cognitive complexity, reflection-impulsivity. *See also* Cognitive complexity; Cognitive development; Cognitive mapping; Cognitive processes; Cognitive psychology; Cognitive structures; Conceptual tempo; Field dependence; Impulsiveness; Intuition; Perceptual style; Personality traits.

Cognitive techniques. Cognitive technique(s). Attributional approach(es). Thought stopping. Think aloud technique(s). Cognitively based. Reality orientation. *Choose from:* cognitive, metacognitive, cognition(s), thinking, thought, ideas, attribution(al), representation(s) *with:* treatment(s), enhancement(s), monitor(ed,ing), coping, technique(s), rehabilatat(e,ed, ion,ing), train(ed,ing), retrain(ed,ing), recovery, redevelopment, remediat(ed, ing,ion), remedial, restructur(e,ed,ing), refram(e,ed,ing), resocializ(e,ed,ing, ation), therap(y,ies), reconstruct(ed,ing, ion). *See also* Cognitive restructuring; Cognitive therapy; Rational emotive psychotherapy; Stress management.

Cognitive therapy. Cognitive therap(y,ies). *Choose from:* cognitive, rational *with:* behavior modification, restructur(ed, ing), therap(y,ies), approach(es), treatment(s), intervention(s), skills training. *See also* Behavior modification; Cognitive rehabilitation; Cognitive restructuring; Cognitive techniques; Psychotherapy; Rational emotive psychotherapy; Self management (individual).

Cohabitation. Cohabit(ing,ation,ational). Living together. Trial marriage(s). Spousal equivalent(s). POSSLQ(s). Persons of the opposite sex sharing living quarters. Unmarried relationship. Unmarried couple(s). Domestic partner(s,ship,ships). *Choose from:* common law *with:* marriage(s), wife, wives, husband(s), spouse(s). *Choose from:* live-in *with:* boyfriend(s), girlfriend(s). *Consider also:* significant other(s), palimony, amasiado. *See also* Couples; Family life; Marriage; Premarital sexual behavior; Roommates; Sexual partners; Single person.

Coherence. Coheren(ce,t). Causal cohesion. Continuity. Causal(ly) relat(ed,ion, ionship). Referential relationship. Logical(ly). Rational(ly,ity). Comprehensib(le,ility). Consisten(t,cy). Cohesive(ness). Understandab(le,ility). Intelligib(le,ility). *Consider also:* consonance, harmon(y,ious). *See also* Comprehension; Speech; Verbal communication; Writing (composition); Written communications.

Cohesion, group. See *Social cohesion.*

Cohesion, social. See *Social cohesion.*

Cohort analysis. Cohort analysis. Longitudinal analysis. *See also* Age differences; Age groups; Attrition; Demography; Generation gap; Longitudinal studies; Methods; Panel studies; Research methods.

Cohorts. Cohort(s). Age group(ings,s). Generation(s). Coeval(s). Demographic subgroup(s). *See also* Age groups; Cohort analysis; Colleagues; Generations; Peers.

Cohousing. Cohousing. Co-housing. Collaborative housing. *Consider also:* intentional communit(y,ies), community sustainability, sustainable communit(y, ies), eco-village(s), common house(s). *See also* Collectivism; Communes; Common ownership; Cooperatives; Housing; Sharing.

Coin collecting. See *Numismatics.*

Coin portraits. Coin portrait(s). Susan B. Anthony dollar(s). Lincoln penn(y,ies). *Choose from:* coin(s,age,ages,ing), currenc(y,ies), penn(y,ies), dollar(s), shilling(s) *with:* portrait(s), head(s), bust(s), representation(s,al), king(s), queen(s), president(s,ial). *See also* Busts; Coinage; Currency; Money; Portraits.

Coinage. Coinage. Coin making. Mint(ed,ing) coin(s). Currency production. Creating coin(s). Issue(d) coin(s). *See also* Coin portraits; Coins; Currency; Money; Numismatics.

Coins. Coin(s). Specie. Small change. Peso(s). Penn(y,ies). Nickel(s). Dime(s). Quarter(s). Half dollar(s). Shilling(s). *See also* Cash; Coinage; Currency; Money; Numismatics.

Coitus. Coit(al,us,ion). Sexual intercourse. Copulat(e,ed,ing,ion). Sexual relations. Mate(d). Mating. Fornicat(e,ed,ing,ion). Mak(e,ing) love. Lovemaking. Adulter(y,ous). *Consider also:* coitus interruptus, carezza, karezza, coitus prolongatus, coitus reservatus, onanism, sexual behavior, human sexuality, adultery. *See also* Extramarital relations; Incest; Orgasm; Premarital sexual behavior; Rape; Sex behavior; Sex drive; Sexual arousal; Sexual foreplay; Sexual function disorders; Sexual intercourse; Sexual partners.

Cold, common. See *Common cold.*

Cold blooded. Cold blooded. Poikilotherm(s,ic). Ectotherm(s,ic). Heterotherm(s,ic). Poecilotherm(s,ic). *See also* Animals.

Cold War. Cold war. East west tension(s). Detente. Soviet American relations. Anti-Soviet. Anti-communis(m,t). Coexistence. Iron curtain. Bamboo curtain. Nuclear standoff. *Consider also:* NATO, North Atlantic Treaty Organization, Warsaw Pact, Warsaw Treaty Organization, arms race, Radio Free Europe, Radio Liberty, Berlin wall, Berlin airlift, Cuban missile crisis, superpowers. *See also* Balance of power; Detente; International relations; Peaceful coexistence; War.

Colitis. Colitis. Inflammation of the colon. Gastroenterocolitis. Enterocolitis. Proctocolitis. Inflammatory bowel disease. Ulcerative colitis. Toxic megacolon. *See also* Gastrointestinal disorders.

Collaboration. Collaborat(e,ed,ing,ion,ions,or,ors). Conspir(e,ed,ing). Concur(red,ring). Cooperat(e,ed,ing,ive). Join(ed,ing) force(s). Common cause. Conniv(e,ed,ing). Teamwork. *Choose from:* work(ed,ing), act(ing,ed) *with:* together, cooperatively, in concert. *Consider also:* solidarity. *See also* Accomplices; Alliances; Altruism; Bartering; Coalitions; Collaborators; Intellectual cooperation; Sharing; Teamwork.

Collaborative psychotherapy. See *Multiple psychotherapy.*

Collaborators. Collaborator(s). Collaborationist(s). Accessor(y,ies). Confederate(s). Co-conspirator(s). Cooperator(s). Helper(s). Partner(s) in crime. Teammate(s). Team member(s). Abettor(s). *Consider also:* Quisling(s), fifth column(ist,ists). *See also* Accomplices; Assistants; Associates; Collaboration; Espionage; Ghostwriting; Informers; Partners; Peers; Reference groups; Traitors.

Collage. Collage(s). Papier colle. *Consider also:* montage(s), photomontage(s). *See also* Assemblage (art); Arts; Centos; Combinations; Dadaism; Genres (art); Popular culture.

Collapse. Collaps(e,ed,ing,ible,ibility). Bend(ing). Bent. Break(ing). Broken. Cave in. Crumpl(e,ed,ing). Fold(ed,ing) up. Break(ing) up. Broke(n) up. Break(ing) down. Broke(n) down. Disintegrat(e,ed,ing,ion). Shatter(ed,ing). Succumb(ed,ing). Wilt(s,ed,ing). Droop(y,ed,ing). *Consider also:* weaken(ed,ing), exhaust(ed,ing), tir(e,ed,ing), wear(y,iness), fall(ing,en) helpless, fall(ing,en) unconscious, Gotterdammerung. *See also* Casualties; Catastrophes; Defeat; Failure.

Collateral. Collateral. Security deposit(s). Pledge(s). Surety. *Consider also:* hypothecat(e,ed,ing,ion) account(s), respondentia, asset(s), assurance(s), guarantee(s) of loan(s). *See also* Loans.

Colleagues. Colleague(s). Associate(s). Compatriot(s). Compeer(s). Comrade(s). Confrere(s). Consociate(s). Copartner(s). Coworker(s). Teammate(s). Workfellow(s). Budd(y,ies). Chum(s). Companion(s). Cron(y,ies). Pal(s). *Consider also:* assistant(s), helper(s), cohort(s), collegial(ity,ly), fellow(ship). *See also* Cohorts; Contemporaries; Peers; Reference groups.

Collectibles. Collectible(s). Collectable(s). Keepsake(s). Memorabilia. Collector(s) item(s). Antique(s). Art treasure(s). Objet d' art. Collector car(s). Depression glass. Heirloom(s). Rare book(s). Old doll(s). Model train(s). Oriental rug(s). Oriental ceramic(s). Old jewelry. Old silver. *See also* Antiquarianism; Antiques; Art metalwork; Art objects; Book collecting; Ceramics; Collecting mania; Collections; Folk art; Gems; Glyptics; Goldwork; Hobbies; Investments; Miniature objects; Numismatics; Pottery; Relics; Salvaging; Treasure.

Collecting, book. See *Book collecting.*

Collecting, coin. See *Numismatics.*

Collecting, stamp. See *Philately.*

Collecting mania. Collecting mania. Acquisitive spirit. *Consider also:* hoard(ed,ing), anal *with:* character, personality, orientation. *See also* Accumulation; Acquisition; Bibliomania; Book collecting; Collectibles; Hoarding; Hobbies; Numismatics; Personality disorders; Saving.

Collection, data. See *Data collection.*

Collection development (libraries). Collection development. *Choose from:* recommend(ed,ation,ations), select(ed,ion), chosen, add(ed) *with:* library purchase, library collection(s). *See also* Book selection; Collections; Library acquisitions; Library censorship.

Collections. Collection(s). Accumulation(s). Amass(ed,ing,ment). Stockpile(s). Stock(s). Holding(s). Assemblage(s). Grouping(s). *Consider also:* antholog(y,ies), collected works. *See also* Anthologies; Collectibles; Collection development (libraries); Library materials.

Collective action. Collective action. Solidarity. Social mobilization. Youth movement(s). Collective participation. Political participation. Tax rebellion(s). Citizen activism. Protest movement(s). Cooperative(s). Coalition(s). Common concern(s). Collective movement(s). Collective violence. Group pressure(s). Union(ism). Collective protest(s). Social movement(s). Social action. *Consider also:* collective strateg(y,ies). *See also* Activism; Collective behavior; Collectivism; Peasant rebellions; Political action; Protest movements; Social action.

Collective bargaining. Collective(ly) bargain(ing). Labor negotiation(s). *Choose from:* collective(ly), good faith, pattern, multiunit, multiemployer, public sector *with:* bargain(ing), negotiation(s), labor agreement(s). *Choose from:* bargaining *with:* table, agent(s), practice(s). *Consider also:* negotiated settlement(s), Taft Hartley Act, National Labor Relations Board, NLRB, Public Employee Relations Board, PERB. *See also* Arbitration; Bargaining power; Contracts; Employers; Firm offers; Industrial democracy; Labor force; Labor disputes; Labor management relations; Labor unions; Negotiation; Strikes.

Collective behavior. Collective behavior(s). Fad(s). Panic(s). Craze(s). Hooliganism. Collective suicide(s). Lynch mob(s). Riot(s). Bandwagon effect(s). *Choose from:* collective, group(s), crowd(s), mass(es), mob(s), audience(s) *with:* behavior(s), action, movement(s), protest(s), phenomena, performance(s), violence. *See also* Civil disorders; Collective action; Collective suicide; Copycat crime; Copycat suicide; Crowds; Mass behavior; Mass hysteria; Riots; Social contagion; Social movements.

Collective consciousness. Collective conscious(ness). *Choose from:* collective, shared, group *with:* conscious(ness), representation(s), symbol(s), sentiment(s). *See also* Collective representation; Cultural knowledge; Symbolism.

Collective farms. See *Agricultural collectives.*

Collective memory. See *Collective consciousness; Collective representation; Cultural knowledge; Political myths.*

Collective psychosis. See *Mass hysteria.*

Collective representation. Collective representation(s). Cultural construction(s). Common meaning(s). Collective memor(y,ies). Social representation(s). *See also* Collective consciousness; Concepts; Cultural history; Cultural knowledge; Meaning; Social cohesion; Symbolism.

Collective security. Collective security. *Choose from:* collective, common, general, mutual *with:* security, defense, safety, protection, preservation. *See also* Alliances; Foreign policy; Geopolitics; International alliances; International cooperation; International economic organizations; International organizations; International relations; Military assistance; Power sharing; Treaties.

Collective settlements. See *Agricultural collectives; Communes; Cooperatives.*

Collective suicide. Collective suicide(s). *Choose from:* collective, mass, group *with:* suicide(s). *Consider also:* Jonestown. *See also* Cargo cults; Collective behavior; Copycat crime; Copycat suicide; Mass hysteria; Messianic movements; Social contagion; Suicide victims.

Collectives. See *Agricultural collectives; Communes; Cooperatives.*

Collectives, agricultural. See *Agricultural collectives.*

Collectivism. Collectiv(ism,istic). Collective(s). Collectivit(y,ies). Collectiviz(e,ed,ing,ation). Commons. Communal(ity). Communis(m,tic). Social utopia(n,s). Socialis(m,tic). Commune(s). Kibbutz(im). Common land(s). Unionism. *Choose from:* collective *with:* farms, labor, work. *See also* Agricultural collectives; Cohousing; Common ownership; Communes; Communism; Cooperatives; Corporatism; Employee ownership; Individualism; Industrial democracy; Public good; Public goods; Public lands; Socialism; Universalism.

Collectors. See *Book collecting; Collecting mania; Collectibles; Hobbies; Leisure activities.*

Collectors, garbage. See *Garbage collectors.*

College graduates. College graduate(s). *Choose from:* college(s), higher education, university, postsecondary, bachelor of arts, bachelor of science, liberal arts *with:* graduate(s). Bachelors degree recipient(s). *See also* Academic degrees; College students; Educational attainment; Educational background; Graduate students.

College songs. See *Student songs.*

College students. College student(s). *Choose from:* college, university, higher education *with:* student(s), student body, fresh(man,men), sophomore(s), junior(s), senior(s). College men. College women. *Consider also:* graduate student(s), medical student(s), dental student(s), junior college student(s), law student(s), postgraduate student(s). *See also* Academic degrees; College graduates; Colleges; Fraternities; Graduate students; High school students; High school graduates; Higher education; Married students; Post-baby boom generation; Sororities; Student songs; Universities; Young adults.

College teachers. See *Faculty.*

College teaching. College teaching. College instruction. University teaching. *Choose from:* teach(ing), instruct(ed,ing,ion), pedagog(y,ical) *with:* professor(s), higher education, universit(y,ies), undergraduate, academe. *See also*

Colleges; Faculty; Higher education; Scholars; Teaching.

Colleges. College(s). Universit(y,ies). Institution(s) of higher learning. Technical school(s). Academ(e,ia,ics). Professional school(s). Graduate school(s). *Consider also:* Higher education, alma mater. *See also* Academic libraries; College students; College teaching; Graduate schools; Medical schools; Residential facilities; Undergraduate education; Universities.

Collisions at sea. Collision(s) at sea. *Choose from:* ship(s), marine, offshore, boat(s), warship(s), cruiser(s), aircraft carrier(s), yacht(s), sea *with:* collision(s), collide(d), ram(s,med), bump(s,ed), crash(ed,ing,s). *Consider also:* shipwreck(s), maritime disaster(s), marine accident(s). *See also* Marine accidents; Maritime law; Ships.

Colloquial language. Colloquial language. Colloquialism(s). Vernacular. Idiom(s, atic). Parlance. Everyday speech. Informal speech. Slang. *See also* Slang; Diglossia; Dialects; Idioms.

Colloquies, religious. See *Religious disputations.*

Collusion. Collusion. Collud(e,ed,ing). Complicit(y,ous,ousness). Conniv(e,ed, ing,ance). Secret agreement(s). Secret pact(s). Plot(s,ted,ting). Conspir(e,ed, ing,acy,acies). *See also* Accomplices; Conspiracy; Crime; Fraud; White collar crime.

Colonialism. Colonial(ism). Coloniz(ing,ed,ation). Colonist(s). Colonial conquest(s). Imperial(istic,ism). Spanish rule, British rule, etc. Neocolonial(ism). British empire. Pre-independence. Subjugat(ed,ing,ion). Dependen(t,cy). Economic exploitation. Military occupation. *Choose from:* foreign, imperial *with:* rule, control, domination. *See also* Agricultural colonies; Center and periphery; Colonization; Culture contact; Cultural imperialism; Decolonization; Dependency theory (international); Developing countries; Economic history; Empires; Eurocentrism; Exploitation; Globalization; Imperialism; Indigenous populations; Indirect rule; International division of labor; Liberation theology; Nativism; Neocolonialism; Peasant rebellions; Political self determination; Spheres of influence; Traditional societies; World economy; World history.

Colonialism, internal. See *Exploitation; Inequality.*

Colonies, agricultural. See *Agricultural colonies.*

Colonies, artists'. See *Artists' colonies.*

Colonization. Coloniz(e,ed,ing,ation). Colonist(s). Colonizer(s). Conquests. Colonialization. Early settler(s). Colonial(s). Establishing colon(y,ies). *See also* Colonialism; Decolonization; Frontiers; Human settlements; Immigration; Imperialism; Invasion; Land settlement; Migration; Settlement patterns; Settlers.

Colophons. Colophon(s,y). Printer(s) ornament(s). *See also* Book imprints; Book ornamentation; Printer marks.

Color. Color(s,ed,ing,ation). Hue(s). Tint(s,ed,ing). Dye(s,d). Paint(s,ed,ing). Shade(s). Pigment(s,ed,ation). Stain(ed,ing,s). Chroma(tic). Monochromatic. Complexion(s). Heterochromatic. *Consider also:* blush(es), red, blue, yellow, green, brown, purple, orange, pink, mauve, etc. *See also* Arts; Color perception; Dyes and dyeing; Stimuli; Visual perception.

Color, men of. See *People of color.*

Color, people of. See *People of color.*

Color, women of. See *People of color.*

Color blindness. Color blind(ness). Chromo blind(ness). Achromatopsy. Daltonism. Monochromatism. Deuteranopia. Protanopia. Tritanopia. *Choose from:* green, red, blue, yellow *with:* blind(ness). *See also* Color perception; Vision disorders.

Color coding. Color cod(e,es,ed,ing). Cod(e,es,ed,ing) color image(s). Colormap(ped,ping). Color encod(e,es,ed, ing). *See also* Classification; Coding.

Color perception. Color perception. *Choose from:* color, spectral *with:* perception, vision, discrimination, sense, sensitiv(e,ity), judgment(s), detection, recognition. *See also* Color; Color blindness; Visual perception.

Color vision. See *Color perception; Color blindness.*

Coloration, animal. See *Animal coloration.*

Coma. Coma(tose). Unconscious(ness). Vegetative state(s). Stupor(ous). Stupefied. Insensib(le,ility). Soporose. Coma-vigil. Coma somnolentium. Cataphora. *See also* Consciousness disorders; Injuries; Symptoms; Unconsciousness; Vegetative state.

Combat. Combat(s). Battle(s,fields). War(fare,time,s). Military conflict(s). Struggle(s). Armed attack(s). Bomb(ardment,ing). Bombing raid(s). *See also* Aerial reconnaissance; Aerial warfare; Assault (battle); Combat disorders; Gulf war syndrome; Infantry; Invasion; Military assistance; Military capitulations; Military desertion; Military operations; Military readiness; Military retreat; Military strategies; Missing in action; Theomachy; Violence; War.

Combat disorders. Combat disorder(s). War neuros(is,es). War hysteria. Battle fatigue. War neurasthenia. Da Costa's syndrome. *Choose from:* combat, battle, war *with:* reaction(s), hysteria, stress, exhaustion, fatigue, neuro(tic,sis,ses), psycho(tic,sis,ses). Nuclear allergy. Shell shock(ed). Shellshock(ed). Psychorrhexis. Survivor syndrome. Soldiers heart. Post Vietnam syndrome. War-related stress. Post Vietnam neurosis. *Consider also:* post traumatic stress disorder, traumatic neuros(is,es), posttraumatic neuros(is,es), aftermath neuros(is,es), cardiac neuros(is,es). *See also* Combat; Gulf war syndrome; Post traumatic stress disorders; Psychophysiologic disorders; War.

Combat fatigue. See *Combat disorders; Post traumatic stress disorders.*

Combatants. Combatant(s). Adversar(y, ies). Fighter(s). Battler(s). Warrior(s). Soldier(s). Enem(y,ies). Fencer(s). Jouster(s). Boxer(s). Gladiator(s). Pugilist(s). Wrestler(s). *See also* Armor; Athletes; Combat; Military personnel; Mercenaries.

Combinations. Combin(e,ed,ation,ations). Compound(s,ed). Coalition(s). Composite(s). Synthes(is,ize,ized). Consolidat(e,ed,ing). Incorporat(e,ed, ing). Integrat(e,ed,ing,ion). Merg(e,ed, er,ers,ing). Conglomerat(e,es,ion). *See also* Alliances; Centos; Coalescence; Coalitions; Collage; Complexity; Consolidation; Mergers; Synergy; Teamwork.

Combinatory logic. Combinatory logic. Kombinatorischen Logik. Theory of combinators. *Consider also:* H.B. Curry. *See also* Logic.

Combustibility. Combustib(le,ly,ility). Explosive(ness). Burnab(le,ility). Flammab(le,ility). Ignitab(le,ility). Inflammab(le,ility). *Consider also:* combust(ive,ion), burn(ed,ing), fir(e,ed,ing), ignit(e,ed,ing), kindl(e,ed,ing). *See also* Arson; Fire; Fuel.

Comedians. Comedian(s). Comedienne(s). Comic role(s). Jester(s). Buffoon(s). *Consider also:* humorist(s), clown(s), entertainer(s). *See also* Entertainers; Frivolity; Humor; Humorous songs; Satire; Sense of humor.

Comedy. See *Humor.*

Comfort, human. See *Environment; Ergonomics; Physical comfort.*

Comfort, physical. See *Physical comfort.*

Comfortableness. Comfortab(le,leness,ly). Comfort(s,ed,ing). Acceptab(le,ility). Adequa(te,cy). Agreeable(ness). Decen(t,cy). Gratif(ying,ication). Welcome(e,ed,ing). Pleasant(ly). Pleasing. Restful(ly). Satisf(y,ying,ied).

Satisfactor(y,ily). Suffic(e,ed,ing). Content(ment). *Consider also:* secur(e,ity), comfy, cozy, cushy, snug, soft, serenity, well-being, complacen(t, cy), physical ease, warmth, friendl(y, iness), gemutlich. *See also* Acceptability; Amenities; Contentment; Friendliness; Life satisfaction; Need satisfaction; Physical comfort; Quality of life; Satisfaction; Success; Well being.

Comic books. See *Comics.*

Comic operas. Comic opera(s). Opera bouffe. Opera buffa. Tonadilla(s). Spieloper(n). Komische oper(n). Stegreifkomodien. *Consider also:* opera(s) comique, vaudeville, musical comed(y,ies), operetta(s), zarzuela(s), rescue opera(s). *See also* Commedia dell'arte; Farce; Opera; Opera singers; Parody; Theater; Music; Musicals.

Comics. Comic(s). Comic book(s). Funnies. Comic strip(s). Caricature(s). Cartoon(ist,ists,s). Animated cartoon(s). Fotonovela(s). *Consider also:* Superman, Blondie, etc. *See also* Cartoons; Fiction; Fools and jesters; Humor; Newspapers; Popular culture; Satire.

Command (of troops, ships). Command(ant,ants). Commanding officer(s). Military leader(s,ship). Military bureaucracy. General(s). Admiral(s,ty). Ship's captain. Skipper(s). Officer(s). *Consider also:* rul(e,ed,er,ers), supervis(er,ers,ion), defense minister(s). *See also* Authoritarianism (political); Authority (officials); Dominance; Leadership; Military administration; Military discipline (conduct); Military officers; Political leadership.

Commedia dell'arte. Commedia dell'arte. Italian masked comed(y,ies). Comedie Italienne. *Consider also:* Harlequin(ade), Arlecchino. *See also* Comic operas; Theater.

Commemoration. Commemorat (e,ed, ing,ive,ion,ions). Pay(ing) tribute. Paid tribute. Eulogiz(e,ed,ing,ation). Dedicat(e,ed, ing,ion,ions). Pay respects. Honor(ed, ing). Memorializ(e,ed,ing,ation). *Consider also:* celebrat(e,ed,ing,ion, ions), solemniz(e,ed,ing,ation), enshrin(e,ed,ing,ment). glorif(y,ied, ication), monumentaliz(e,ed,ing,ation), salut(e,ed,ing), consecrat(e,ed,ing,ion), ordination(s), sanctif(y,ied,ication). *See also* Admiration; Anniversaries and special events; Elegies; Epitaphs; Honored (esteem); Monuments; Occasional verse; Tribute; Triumphal arches; War memorials.

Commendation. Commend(ed,ing,ation). Kudo(s). Warm approval. Acclaim(ed, ing). Applaud(ed,ing). Applause. Congratulat(e.ed,ing,ion,ions). Approbat(e,ed,ing,ion). Compliment(ed,

ing). Hail(ed,ing). Prais(e,ed,ing). Recommend(ed,ing,ation). *Consider also:* eulogiz(e,ed,ing), extol(led,ling), approv(e,ed,al,ing), endors(e,ed,ing, ement), laud(ed,ing,ion), testimonial(s), roast(ed,ing). *See also* Admiration; Eulogies; Flattery; Honored (esteem); Praise; Recognition (achievement); Tribute.

Commensalism. See *Symbiotic relations.*

Commentaries. Commentar(y,ies). Comment(s,ed,ing). Annotat(e,ed,ing, ion,ions). Critique(s). Exeges(is,es). Exposition(s). Elucidat(e,ed,ing,ion, ions). Explanation(s). Clarification(s). Footnote(s). Interpretation(s). Expansion(s). Explication(s). *Consider also:* gloss(es), glossar(y,ies), footnote(s), illustrat(e,ed,ing,ion,ions), note(s), remark(s), obiter dictum, observation(s). *See also* Addendum; Analysis; Deciphering; Editorials; Literary criticism; Reviews; Scholia; Travel journalism.

Commentators. Commentator(s). Analyst(s). Annotator(s). Announcer(s). Critic(s). Anchor(s,person,persons,men, man,women,woman). Essayist(s). Interpreter(s). Newscaster(s). Journalist(s). Columnist(s). Reviewer(s). Opinion leader(s). *See also* Broadcasters; Chattering class; Editors; Foreign correspondents; Journalists; Literary criticism; Observers; Opinion leaders; Social criticism.

Commerce. Commerce. Bargain(ed,ing). Barter(ed,ing). Business transaction(s). Buy(ing). Cashless transaction(s). Commercialism. Consumption. Countertrade. Counterpurchas(es,ing). Contratrade. Compensation goods. Economic exchange(s). Economic system(s). Exchange(s) of goods. Export(s,ed,ing). Hidden economy. Import(s,ed,ing). Informal economy. Market(ed,s,ing). Merchandising. Monetary exchange(s). Monetary trade. Nonmonetary exchange(s). Nonmonetary trade. Peddl(e,ing). Purchas(e,es,ed,ing). Relations of exchange. Retail(ing). Sale(s). Sell(ing). Swap(ped,ping,s). Trad(e,ed,ing). Trade without money. Trafficking. Vend(ed,ing). *Consider also:* profit making, mercantil(e,ism), wholesal(e,ing). *See also* Business; Center and periphery; Commodities; Consumption (economic); E-commerce; Economic exchanges; Economics; Emerging markets; Exports; Imports; International economic organizations; Market economy; Marketing; Markets; Products; Retailing; Sales; Supply and demand; Trade protection; Trade shows; V-commerce world economy.

Commerce, electronic. See *E-commerce.*

Commerce, prehistoric. See *Prehistoric commerce.*

Commercial districts. Commercial district(s). *Choose from:* office, commercial, business, mixed use, shopping *with:* district(s), park(s), site(s), complex(es), estate(s), zone(s). *Consider also:* main street(s), convention center(s), downtown(s). *See also* Center and periphery; Industrial districts; Inner cities; Urban development; Urban planning.

Commercial franchises. See *Franchises (commercial).*

Commercial travelers. See *Traveling sales personnel.*

Commercial treaties. Commercial treat(y,ies). Trade agreement(s). Trade Act. *Choose from:* trade, reciprocity, tariff(s), commodity, export(s), import(s), commercial *with:* agreement(s), treat(y,ies). *Consider also:* favored nation clause(s), trade polic(y,ies), trade negotiation(s), commercial regulation(s). *See also* Exports; Foreign trade regulation; Foreign trade zones; Harmonization (trade); Imports; International economic integration; International trade; Nontariff trade barriers; Trade protection.

Commercialization. See *Profit motive; Rationalization (sociology).*

Commercials. See *Advertising.*

Commissions. Commission(s). Delegation(s). Board(s). Council(s). Committee(s). Bureau(s). Department(s). Appointed group(s). Advisory group(s). Panel(s). *See also* Councils; Delegations; Governing boards; Organizations.

Commissions, independent regulatory. See *Independent regulatory commissions.*

Commitment (emotional). Commit(ted, ment,ments). Loyal(ty,ties). Emotional commitment(s). Allegiance. Emotional attachment(s). Affiliation(s). Engage(d). Faith. Faithful(ness). Fidelity. Fealty. Patriot(ic,ism). Steadfast(ness). Unchanging. Constan(t,cy). Unchang(ed,ing). Abiding. Resolute. Solidarity. Dedicat(ed,ing,ion). Pledged. Sworn. Betroth(ed,al,als). Wholehearted(ness). Involve(d,ment, ments). Promised. Vow(s,ed). Covenant(s). Avow(al,ed). *See also* Faithfulness; Intentionality; Involvement; Love; Loyalty; Moral obligation; Motivation; Obligations; Organizational commitment.

Commitment, organizational. See *Organizational commitment.*

Commitment, psychiatric. See *Psychiatric commitment.*

Commitment, religious. See *Religious commitment.*

Committees. Committee(s). Task force(s). Work part(y,ies). Commission(s). Delegation(s). Board(s). Cabinet(s). Chamber(s). Council(s). Bureau(s). Appointed group(s). Advisory group(s). Panel(s). *Consider also:* trustee(s), working group(s). *See also* Advisory committees; Commissions; Delegations; Governing boards; Labor management committees.

Committees, advisory. See *Advisory committees.*

Committees, labor management. See *Labor management committees.*

Committees, political action. See *Interest groups.*

Commodities. Commodit(y,ies). Merchandise. Consumer goods. Goods. Object(s). Stock. Consumer item(s). Wares. Produce. Product(s). Staple(s). *Consider also:* commodit(ize,ized, izing,ization), export(s), import(s), hogs, cattle, grain, etc. *See also* Agribusiness; Agriculture; Bartering; Business; Consumption (economic); Durable goods; Economic exchanges; Farm produce; Production consumption relationship; Products; Raw materials; Scarcity.

Commodity fetishism. Commodity fetishism. Reif(y,ied,ication). *Consider also:* objectif(ied,ication), dereif(y,ied, ication). *See also* Alienation; Marxism.

Commodity market. See *Futures market.*

Common cold. Common cold(s). Coryza. Upper respiratory infection(s). *See also* Disease; Disease susceptibility; Respiratory system.

Common culture. Common culture. *Choose from:* common, shared, unity *with:* culture, values, ritual system(s), goal(s). *Consider also:* dominant culture, all American, civic culture, American culture, national identity, homogeneity. *See also* Acculturation; Cultural identity; Cultural pluralism; Ethnic groups; Hidden curriculum; Melting pot; Multicultural education; Political myths; Social integration.

Common currency. Common currenc(y,ies). *Choose from:* common, unified, single *with:* currenc(y,ies). *Consider also:* Euro, common European currency, European Central Bank, Euroiz(e,ed,ing,ation), Euroland, European Monetary Union [EMU], European Currency Unit, [ECU]. *See also* Common markets; Currency; Economic union; Harmonization (trade); International banks and banking; Monetary unions; World economy.

Common good. See *Public good.*

Common knowledge. Common knowledge. Folk wisdom. Folk knowledge. Common sense. Shared knowledge. Shared explanation(s). Shared view(s). *See also* Beliefs; Everyday life; Folklore; Knowledge; Traditions; Worldview.

Common lands. Common land(s). Communal land(s). Commons. Common pasturage. Public land(s). Public park(s). Communal system of land tenure. Collectively owned land(s). Collectively managed land(s). Propriedad communal. Ejido(s). *See also* Agrarian structures; Agricultural collectives; Common ownership; Communes; Cooperatives; Land (property); Land ownership; Land use; Parks; Recreational facilities; Traditional societies.

Common law. Common law. Unwritten law(s). *Consider also:* case law. *See also* De facto; Laws.

Common law marriage. See *Cohabitation.*

Common man. See *Common people.*

Common markets. Common market(s). International economic integration. Trading bloc(s). *Choose from:* international *with:* market(s). *Consider also:* trade liberalization, interdependent econom(y,ies), European Coal and Steel Community, European Economic Community, European Atomic Energy Community, European community, North American Free Trade Agreement [NAFTA], European Free Trade Association [EFTA], Central European Free Trade Agreement [CEFTA]. *See also* Common currency; Custom unions; Economic relations; Global integration; Harmonization (trade); International banks and banking; International economic integration; International economic organizations; International trade; Trade; World economy.

Common ownership. Common ownership. Copartnership. Joint tenancy. Cooperative(s). Community property. *Choose from:* collective, joint, communal(ly) *with:* ownership, own(ed,ing), possess(ed,ing,ion), tenancy. *See also* Agricultural collectives; Cohousing; Collectivism; Common lands; Communes; Communism; Cooperatives; Employee ownership; Employee stock ownership plans; Industrial democracy; Socialism; Worker control; Worker participation.

Common people. Common people. Citizen(ry,s). Commoner(s). Consumer(s). Folk. General public. Grassroots. Human race. Humankind. Humanity. Laborer(s). Lower class(es). Man in the street. Mankind. Masses. Middle America. Multitude(s). Peasant(ry,s). Bourgeois(ie). Pleb(e,es,s,eian). Populace. Proletaria(n,t). Rank and file. Serf(s). Silent majority. Third estate. Untouchable(s). Voter(s). Voting public. Worker(s). Working class(es). *Choose from:* average, common, ordinary *with:*

man, woman, person, American, Englishman, etc. *See also* General public; Indigenous populations; Masses; Proletariat; Working class.

Common sense. Common sens(e,ical). Everyday thought. Good sense. Practical(ity). Plain sense. Logical. Native intelligence. Practical knowledge. Sound thinking. Sound judgment. Balanced judgment. Level headed. Levelheaded(ness). Reasonable(ness). Resourceful(ness). Sensible. Judicious(ness). Discern(ing,ment). Down to earth. Pruden(t,ce). Sensible(ness). *See also* Beliefs; Everyday life; Feasibility; Folklore; Folkways; Judgment; Knowledge; Prudence; Reason; Resourcefulness; Traditions; Worldview.

Commons. Commons. Common land(s). Public land(s). *Consider also:* park(s), public facilit(y,ies). *See also* Common lands; Common ownership; Common people; General public; Public baths; Public good.

Communal dining. See *Group meals.*

Communal living. See *Communes.*

Communal meals. See *Group meals.*

Communal spirit. See *Community feeling.*

Communes. Commune(s). Kibbutz(im). Utopian communit(y,ies). *Choose from:* communal *with:* living, farm(s), life, group(s). Pueblo(s). Alternative communit(y,ies). Communitas. Communitarian(ism). *Choose from:* collective(ism,s), cooperative(s). *Consider also:* Oneida community, Amana community, Verv, Shakers, Brook Farm, Findhorn, Selene community, etc. *See also* Agricultural collectives; Cohousing; Collectivism; Common lands; Common ownership; Cooperatives; Sharing; Socialism; Utopias.

Communicable diseases. See *Infectious disorders.*

Communication (thought transfer). Communicat(e,ed,ing,ion,ions). Inform(ing). Speak(ing). Tell(ing). Proclaim(ed,ing). Declar(e,ed,ing). Convey(ed,ing). Relat(e,ed,ing). Interchange(s). Exchang(e,ed,ing) views. Explain(ed,ing). Conversation(s). Talk(ing). Voic(e,ed,ing). Intercommunication. Communion. Confabulation. Discourse. Social intercourse. Correspondence. Convey(ed,ing) idea(s). Speech intelligibility. Metacommunication. Message(s). Articulat(e,ed, ing,ion). Gesture(s). Gossip(ed,ing). Interview(ed,ing). Sign language. Verbaliz(e,ed,ing). Rapport. Body language. Eye contact. Express(ion,ing). Call(ed,ing,s). Signal(s). Sign(ed,ing). Discussion(s). Propaganda. Publicity.

Consider also: communication barrier(s), confidentiality, language, truth disclosure, argument(s), bargain(ed,ing), group discussion, negotiat(e,ed,ing,ion,ions). *See also* Animal communication; Announcements; Assertions; Audiences; Cliches; Communication barriers; Communication disorders; Communication skills; Communication styles; Communications research; Content analysis; Credibility; Cybernetics; Deception; Definition (words); Direct discourse; Discussion; Feedback; Inference; Information dissemination; Information exchange; Information seeking; Intercultural communication; Intergroup relations; Interpersonal relations; Interpretation; Language; Language usage; Meaning; Media portrayal; Nonverbal communication; Persuasion; Propaganda; Publicity; Scientific language; Self disclosure; Self expression; Sign language; Speech; Speech acts; Terminology; Verbal communication.

Communication, animal. See *Animal communication.*

Communication, cross cultural. See *Intercultural communication.*

Communication, father child. See *Father child communication.*

Communication, intercultural. See *Intercultural communication.*

Communication, interpersonal. See *Body language; Communication (thought transfer); Communication styles; Confidentiality; Conversation; Discussion; Eye contact; Father child communication; Gossip; Interpersonal relations; Interviews; Intimacy; Laughter; Letters (correspondence); Mother child communication; Negotiation; Nonverbal communication; Persuasion; Rapport; Self disclosure; Self expression.*

Communication, manual. See *Manual communication.*

Communication, mass. See *Mass media.*

Communication, mother child. See *Mother child communication.*

Communication, nonverbal. See *Nonverbal communication.*

Communication, oral. See *Oral communication.*

Communication, parent child. See *Parent child communication.*

Communication, professional. See *Professional literature.*

Communication, scientific. See *Professional literature.*

Communication, verbal. See *Verbal communication.*

Communication, visual. See *Visual communication.*

Communication aids for disabled. See *Communication aids for handicapped.*

Communication aids for handicapped. Communication aids for handicapped. Communication aids for disabled. Gaze controlled communication. Hearing prosthes(is,es). Speech analyzing aid(s) for deaf. Augmentative communication. Alternative communication. *Choose from:* communication aid(s), communication board(s), teletype, computer communication(s), communication device(s), keyboard(s), display board(s), hearing prosthes(is,es), speech analyzing aid(s), speech technology, communications system(s), hearing aid(s), telecommunication(s), signaling system(s), voice synthesizer(s), speech synthesizer(s), closed caption(s,ed,ing), artificial speech, language signs, Morse code *with:* disabilit(y,ies), disabled, hearing impaired, handicapped, deaf(ness), blind(ness), nonverbal, nonvocal, nonfluent, aphasi(a,c), paraplegic(s), quadriplegic(s). *Consider also:* DECTalk, MacinTalk, Provox voice prosthesis, TalksBac, Facilitated communication, Kurzweil reading machine(s), etc. *See also* Communication disorders; Language development disorders; Language disorders; Self help devices; Speech disorders.

Communication apprehension. See *Speech anxiety.*

Communication barriers. Communication barrier(s). *Choose from:* communicat(e, ed,ing,ion,ions), understand(ing), understood, language *with:* barrier(s), problem(s), difficult(y,ies), inability, unable, gap(s). *See also* Barriers; Communication (thought transfer); Communication disorders; Intercultural communication; Jamming of communications; Language development disorders; Language disorders; Speech disorders; Speech intelligibility.

Communication disorders. Communication disorder(s). *Choose from:* communication, communicative(ly), language, speech, articulation, expression, expressiveness *with:* disorder(s,ed), impair(ed,ment,ments), handicap(s,ped), problem(s), delay(s,ed), disab(led,ility, ilities). *Consider also:* aphasia, dyslexia, language development disorder(s), dysarthria, echolalia, mutism, stuttering, nonvocal, hearing impair(ed,ment, ments), aural(ly) handicap(s,ped,ping). *See also* Aphasia; Auditory perceptual disorders; Communication (thought transfer); Communication aids for handicapped; Developmental disabilities; Exceptional persons; Hearing disorders; Language development disorders; Language disorders; Learning disabilities; Mutism; Speech anxiety; Speech disorders; Speech disturbances; Speech intelligibility; Speech therapy.

Communication skills. Communication skill(s). *Choose from:* communicat(ion, ive), conversational, social, verbal, listening, relationship, empathy, language, writing, speaking *with:* skill(s), competence, abilit(y,ies), proficiency, adequacy, effectiveness. *See also* Ability; Communication (thought transfer); Communication disorders; Language proficiency; Verbal ability; Verbal communication; Writing (composition).

Communication styles. Communication style(s). Attentive(ness). Assertive(ness). Responsive(ness). Expressive(ness). *Choose from:* communicat(ion,ive), conflict, conversational, interviewing, verbal, listening, relationship, empathy, language, writing, speaking *with:* style(s), pattern(s). *See also* Conversation; Discussion; Father child communication; Gestures; Mother child communication; Nonverbal communication.

Communications, audiovisual. See *Audiovisual communications.*

Communications, confidential. See *Confidential communications.*

Communications, digital. See *Digital communications.*

Communications, indecent. See *Indecent communications.*

Communications, interception of. See *Electronic eavesdropping.*

Communications, jamming of. See *Jamming of communications.*

Communications, privileged. See *Privileged communications.*

Communications, written. See *Written communications.*

Communications media. Communications media. Mass media. Radio. Television. TV. Press. Fourth estate. Newspaper(s). Magazine(s). Film(s). Video(tapes). Telephone(s). Motion picture(s). Movies. Serial(s). Periodical(s). Broadcasting. Publication(s). Publish(ing,ers). *Choose from:* broadcast, communication(s), news, audiovisual, telecommunication(s) *with:* media, network(s), system(s), industr(y,ies), service(s). *Consider also:* book(s), serial(s), fax, telegraph, broadside(s), catalog(s), government publication(s), manuscript(s), pamphlet(s), audiotape(s), cable television, educational television. *See also* Audiovisual communications; Books; Cable television; Educational television; Films; Mass media; Motion pictures; News media; Newspapers; Photography; Popular culture; Telecommunications; Television.

Communications research. Communication(s) research(er,ers). *Choose from:* communication(s), propaganda, cultural studies, mass media, mass communication *with:* stud(y,ies), scholarship, research(ed,ing,er,ers), experiment(ed, ing,al,ation,s), control groups(s), data collection and analys(is,es), replicat(ed, ing,ion,ions), empiric(al,ism), examin(e,ed,ing,ation,ations). *See also* Communication (thought transfer); Content analysis; Data analysis; Discourse analysis; Evaluation; Information dissemination; Literary criticism; Messages; Propaganda; Research; Technology transfer.

Communicative competence. See *Communication skills.*

Communicative psychotherapy. Communicative psychotherap(y,ist,ists). Communicative psychoanalysis. *Choose from:* communicative approach, communicative intervention(s) *with:* psychotherap(y,ist,ists), therap(y,ist,ists), psychoanalysis. *Consider also:* communicative adaptation. *See also* Countertransference; Humanistic psychology; Psychotherapeutic processes; Psychotherapy.

Communism. Communis(m,t,ts,tic). Eurocommunis(t,m). Marxis(m,t,ts). Bolshevik. Bolshev(ism,ist,ists). Mao(ism,ist,ists). Lenin(ism,ist). Stalin(ism,ist). Soviet(ism). Tito(ism,ist). Trotsky(ism,ite,ites). Castro(ism,ist). Fourier(ism). Comintern. Cominform. Neomarx(ism, ist,ists). Menshev(ism,ist,ists). *Consider also:* revisionism, socialism, communal property, communal organization, dialectical materialism, left wing, class warfare, proletarian revolution, state ownership, Robert Owen, Francois Fourier, Claude Saunt-Simon. *See also* Agricultural collectives; Capitalism; Collectivism; Democracy; Dialectical materialism; Fascism; Government; Imperialism; Marxism; Socialism; Totalitarianism.

Communities. See *Community (geographic locality); Community (social); Neighborhoods; Social support networks.*

Communities, agricultural. See *Rural communities.*

Communities, farming. See *Rural communities.*

Communities, fishing. See *Fishing communities.*

Communities, language. See *Speech communities.*

Communities, planned. See *Planned communities.*

Communities, religious. See *Religious communities.*

Communities, retirement. See *Retirement communities.*

Communities, rural. See *Rural communities.*

Communities, speech. See *Speech communities.*

Community (geographic locality). Communit(y,ies). Municipalit(y,ies). Neighborhood(s). Planned communit(y, ies). Barrio(s). Village(s). Parish(es). Local area(s). Physical communit(y,ies). Borough(s). Town(s,ship,ships). District(s). Ward(s). Settlement(s). Localit(y,ies). Vicinit(y,ies). Environs. Precinct(s). Suburb(s). Hamlet(s). Section(s) of town. *See also* Areas; Cities; Community churches; Community development; Community services; Districts; Fishing communities; Environment; Everyday life; Gemeinschaft and gesellschaft; Human ecology; Land settlement; Living conditions; Local government; Local planning; Local politics; Localism; Neighborhoods; Neighbors; Parishes; Planned communities; Police community relations; Residences; Residential mobility; Retirement communities; Rural communities; Suburbs; Towns.

Community (social). Communit(y,ies). Commun(e,ing,al). Social group(s). Fellowship(s). Brotherhood(s). Solidarity. Congregation(al,s). Local tie(s). Civic pride. Sense of belonging. Sense of community. Gemeinschaft. Interdependen(t,ce). Mutual(ly) dependen(t,ce). Personal tie(s). Friendship(s). Primary relationship(s). Comradeship. Esprit de corps. *Consider also:* interest group(s). *See also* Belongingness; Civil society; Community churches; Community feeling; Community involvement; Community networks; Community support; Cultural diversity; Local government; Local politics; Neighborhood associations; Neighbors; Newcomers; Social cohesion; Social contact; Social support networks.

Community, Black. See *Black Community.*

Community, scientific. See *Scientific community.*

Community, therapeutic. See *Therapeutic community.*

Community action. See *Activism; Citizen participation; Community involvement; Community support; Local politics; Protest movements; Social action.*

Community associations. See *Community involvement; Neighborhood associations.*

Community attitudes. Community attitude(s). *Choose from:* communit(y,ies), grassroot(s), local government, town, village(s), voter(s), neighbor(s,hood,hoods), local(ity,ities), citizen(s), resident(s), tenant(s), popular, peasant(s), homeowner(s), taxpayer(s), urban, suburban, public *with:* attitude(s), opinion(s), mindset, view(s,point, points), perspective(s), values, concern(s), forum(s), consciousness, accept(ance,ed,ing), reject(ed,ing,ion), support(ed,ing), oppos(e,ed,ing,ition), interest, alarm(ed,ing), prejudice(s,d), fear(s). *See also* Community involvement; Community support; Local politics; Moral attitudes; Political attitudes; Public opinion; Social attitudes.

Community based corrections. See *Alternatives to incarceration.*

Community centers. Community center(s). Neighborhood center(s). Settlement house(s). Senior citizen center(s). YMCA(s). YWCA(s). Boys club(s). Girl(s) club(s). Community room(s). *Choose from:* community, neighborhood, district, local, parish *with:* center(s), house(s), meeting place(s). *See also* Community (geographic locality); Community services; Recreational facilities.

Community change. Community change(s). *Choose from:* communit(y,ies), town(s), cit(y,ies), neighborhood(s), area(s), local(ity,ities), region(al) *with:* chang(e,ed,es,ing), alter(ed,ing), evolv(ed,ing), grow(th, ing), expan(d,ding,sion), develop(ing, ment), reconstruct(ed,ing,ion), revitaliz(e,ed,ing,ation), renewal, decay(ed,ing), declin(e,ed,ing), death. *See also* Boom towns; Change agents; Citizen participation; Civic improvement; Community development; Extinct cities; Local planning; Social change; Urban renewal.

Community characteristics. Community characteristics. Local conditions. *Choose from:* communit(y,ies), town(s), area(s), neighborhood(s), local(ity,ities) *with:* characteristic(s), size, attribute(s), trait(s), character, climate, structure(s), need(s), analys(is,es), survey(s), assessment(s), composition, morale, attitude(s), age, history, tradition(s), demographics, condition(s). *Consider also:* social environment(s), social condition(s), anomie, urban environment(s), rural environment(s), suburban environment(s). *See also* Characteristics; Community attitudes; Community development; Community problems; Community size; Community structure; Local government; Neighborhood change; Place of residence; Qualities; Urban environments.

Community churches. Community church(es). *Choose from:* communit(y,ies), neighborhood(s), village(s), parish(es), town(s,ship,ships),

localit(y,ies), suburb(s,an) *with:* church(es), chapel(s). *See also* Churches; Community (geographic locality); Community (social); Neighborhoods; Places of worship; Social support networks.

Community development. Community development. *Choose from:* communit(y,ies), neighborhood(s), area(s), village(s), town(s), local(ity, ities), region(al), urban, suburban, grassroots, enterprise zone(s) *with:* plan(s,ned,ning), building, construction, improvement(s), progress, evolution, evolv(ed,ing), gain(s,ed,ing), grow(th, ing), expan(d,ding,sion), redevelop(ed, ing,ment,ments), develop(ed,ing,ment, ments), reconstruction, regenerat(e,ed, ing,ion), reinvest(ed,ing,ment), invest(ed,ing,ment,ments), revitaliz(e,ed,ing,ation), renewal, zon(ed,ing), rezon(ed,ing). *See also* Boom towns; Citizen participation; Civic improvement; Community (geographic locality); Community change; Community characteristics; Community organizers; Community problems; Community services; Economic development; Growth management; Growth strategies; Industrial promotion; Local planning; Neighborhood change; New towns; Planned communities; Real estate development; Rural development; Urban development; Urban planning; Urban renewal.

Community feeding. See *Group meals.*

Community feeling. Community feeling. Neighborl(y,iness). *Choose from:* communit(y,ies), communal, neighbor(ly,s,hood,hoods), local(ity,ities), citizen(s), resident(s), voluntary, volunteer(s) *with:* feeling, spirit, support, caregiving, caring, mutual interest(s), closeness, shar(e,ed,ing). *See also* Belongingness; Brotherliness; Community (social); Community involvement; Community support.

Community health aides. Community health aide(s). Village health worker(s). Community health worker(s). Community health nurse(s). District nurse(s). Home health aide(s). Public health nurse(s). *See also* Community health nursing; Community health services; Outreach programs.

Community health centers. Community health center(s). *Choose from:* community, neighborhood, district, local *with:* health center(s), health care, clinic(s). *See also* Community health services; Health facilities.

Community health nursing. Community health nursing. Health visitor(s). Visiting nurse(s). Community mental health nurs(e,es,ing). Public health nurse(s). Community nurse(s). Public health

nurs(ing). *See also* Community health services; Nurses.

Community health services. Community health service(s). Outreach clinic(s). Barefoot doctor(s). Public health service(s). *Choose from:* community, rural, village, local, neighborhood, district, outreach *with:* health service(s), medical care, medical service(s), medicine, health council(s), clinic(s), mental health, screening program(s), nutrition program(s), physician(s), primary care, family planning, maternal care, infant care, prevention. *See also* Community health aides; Community health centers; Community health nursing; Community mental health services; Community networks; Community services; Consumer directed care; Health resources; Health services; Walk-in clinics.

Community institutional relations. Community institution(al) relation(s,ship). Town and gown. *Choose from:* communit(y,ies), neighborhood(s), town(s), cit(y,ies), citizen(s) *with:* institution(s,al), school(s), business(es), police, universit(y,ies), college(s), corporation(s), hospital(s) *with:* relation(s,ship,ships), participation, involvement, reaction(s), cooperation, partnership(s), role(s), social responsibility, program(s). *Consider also:* business investment in communit(y,ies), community relations. *See also* Company towns; Corporate social responsibility; Police community relations; Public relations.

Community involvement. Community involvement. Grassroot(s). *Choose from:* communit(y,ies), neighbor(s,hood, hoods), local(ity,ities), citizen(s), resident(s), tenant(s), popular, peasant(s), homeowner(s), taxpayer(s), voter(s), voluntary, volunteer(s) *with:* involve(d,ment), participat(e,ed,ing,ion), activism, response(s), mobiliz(ed,ing, ation), movement(s), network(s,ing), action, group(s), association(s), league(s), cooperat(e,ed,ing,ion), interest(ed), caregiving, opinion(s), support. *Consider also:* caring communit(y,ies), community integration, deliberative democracy. *See also* Citizen participation; Civil society; Community attitudes; Community change; Community feeling; Community power; Community services; Community support; Local politics; Neighborhood associations; Outreach programs; Public services.

Community life. See *Belongingness; Brotherliness; Community (social); Community (geographic locality); Community feeling; Community involvement; Community power; Community problems; Community structure; Community support; Local* *politics; Local news; Localism; Regionalism; Social identity.*

Community medicine. See *Community health services.*

Community mental health. Community mental health. *Choose from:* community, rural, urban, local, households surveyed, local(ity,ities) *with:* mental health, psychology, suicide(s), psychiatric admission(s), personality disorder(s). *See also* Community mental health services; Deinstitutionalization; Rural mental health; Urban mental health.

Community mental health services. Community mental health service(s). PL 88-164. PL 89-105. *Choose from:* community, neighborhood, local, district, rural, village, outreach *with:* mental health service(s), guidance service(s), child guidance, psychiatr(y,ic), psychotherap(y,ies, eutic), service(s) for the mentally ill, mental health visitor(s), mental hospital(s), hotline(s), hot line(s), crisis intervention(s), psychiatrist(s), psychiatric clinic(s), mental health clinic(s). *See also* Community health services; Community mental health; Crisis intervention; Help lines (telephone); Mental health services; Walk-in clinics.

Community networks. Community network(s). *Choose from:* community, neighborhood, local(ity,ities), grassroots, public officials, service providers, health care, primary institutions, citizens, municipal, rural, small town, village(s) *with:* network(s,ing), collaborative partnership(s), team(s), organization(s), information system(s). *Consider also:* telephone hotline(s), buddy services(s), support group(s), bowling league(s), community life, virtual communit(y,ies). *See also* Social Environment; Community Health Services; Community networks (computer); Teledemocracy.

Community networks (computer). Community network(s,ing). Nonprofit Internet service provider(s). Subsidize(d) Internet service. *Consider also:* civic network(s), free-net(s), info-zones, bulletin board(s), tele-villages and smart cit(y,ies), Association For Community Networking, AFCN. *See also* Community networks; Cybercommunities; Information highway; Information networks; Information society; Interactive computer systems; Internet (computer network); Internet service providers; Modern civilization; Postindustrial societies; Social contact; Virtual libraries; Virtual reality.

Community newspapers. Community newspaper(s). *Choose from:* community, local(ity,ities), town(s,ship,ships), village(s), neighborhood(s) *with:* paper(s), newspaper(s), press(es), weekl(y,ies). *See also* House organs;

Local news; Newspapers; Periodicals; Publications.

Community organization. See *Community structure.*

Community organizations. See *Neighborhood associations.*

Community organizers. Community organizer(s). *Choose from:* community, neighborhood, community development, social development *with:* worker(s), organizer(s), officer(s). *See also* Change agents; Community development; Community power; Leadership.

Community participation. See *Community involvement.*

Community planning. See *Local planning.*

Community police relations. See *Police community relations.*

Community politics. See *Local politics.*

Community power. Community power. *Choose from:* communit(y,ies), grassroot(s), local government(s), voter(s), neighbor(s,hood,hoods), local(ity,ities), citizen(s), resident(s), tenant(s), popular, peasant(s), homeowner(s), taxpayer(s), urban, suburban, town(s) *with:* power, representat(ives,ion), empower(ing, ment), politic(al,s), dominat(ed,ion), policy actor(s), leader(s,ship), stakeholder(s), authorit(y,ies), force(s), prestige, influen(ce,ces,ced,tial,ing), involve(d,ment), participat(ed,ing,ion), activism, response(s), mobiliz(ed,ing, ation), movement(s), action. *See also* Citizen participation; Community feeling; Community involvement; Community organizers; Community structure; Community support; Local government; Local politics; Neighborhood associations; Political power.

Community problems. Community problem(s). *Choose from:* communit(y,ies), neighborhood(s), local, municipal(ity,ities), suburban, urban, village(s), town(s,ship,ships) *with:* issue(s), problem(s), risk(s), question(s), dilemma(s), dispute(s). *Consider also:* alcoholism, arson, burglar(y,ies), civil disorders, crime, delinquen(cy,t,ts), desegregat(e,ed,ing,ion), dropout(s), drug abuse, energy, environment, equal rights, homosexual rights, homeless(ness), housing, landfill(s), NIMBY(ism), pollut(e,ed,ing,ion), overpopulation, social problem(s), poverty, prostitution, race relations, racism, riot(s), segregat(e,ed,ing,ion), substance abuse, suicide(s), theft(s), waste disposal, unemployment. *See also* Environmental racism; Local politics; Social problems; Urban crime; Urban mental health; Urban poverty.

Community property. See *Common ownership.*

Community relations. See *Community institutional relations; Public relations.*

Community response. See *Social response.*

Community responsibility. See *Corporate social responsibility.*

Community satisfaction. See *Community support.*

Community service. See *Restorative justice; Volunteers.*

Community services. Community service(s). *Choose from:* communit(y, ies), local government, neighbor(s,hood, hoods), local(ity,ities), urban, suburban, public, town(s) *with:* service(s), clinic(s), outreach, program(s), care, hotline(s), crisis intervention, center(s), dissemination, charit(y,ies), agenc(y,ies), assistance, aid, referral service(s). *See also* Community health aides; Community health nursing; Community health services; Community mental health services; Fire departments; Help lines (telephone); Information services; Local government; Local transit; Mass transit; Referral; Social services.

Community size. Community size. Size of communit(y,ies). *Choose from:* communit(y,ies), municipalit(y,ies), cit(y,ies), neighborhood(s), barrio(s), village(s), parish(es), borough(s), town(s,ship,ships), district(s), ward(s), settlement(s), localit(y,ies), vicinit(y,ies), environs, precinct(s), suburb(s), section(s) *with:* size(s), large, small, density, demographic(s), popul(ous, ation,ations), extent, area(s), boundar(y,ies), limit(s). *See also* Community characteristics; Community structure; Demographic changes; Demographic surveys; Geographic distribution; Overpopulation; Population density; Population distribution; Population growth; Urban population.

Community structure. Community structure. Community organization. Community power structure. Local political system(s). *Choose from:* communit(y,ies), municipal(ity,ities), neighborhood(s), barrio(s), village(s), parish(es), borough(s), town(s,ships), district(s), ward(s) *with:* structure(s), organization(s,al), hierarch(y,ies), network(s), social relations, institution(s), role(s), politics. *See also* Cargo systems; Community size; Community power; Local politics; Poverty areas; Social structure; Suburbs.

Community support. Community support. Community satisfaction. Public opinion. *Choose from:* communit(y,ies), grassroot(s), local government, voter(s), neighbor(s,hood, hoods), local(ity,ities), citizen(s,ry), civic, resident(ial,s), tenant(s), popular, peasant(s), homeowner(s), taxpayer(s), urban, suburban, public *with:* satisf(y,ied, action), accept(ed,ing,ance), support(ed,ing), sentiment(s), involvement, ratif(y,ied,ication), pride, oppos(e,ed,ing,ition), commitment, dissatisf(y,ied,action), reject(ed,ing,ion), response(s), attitude(s), opinion(s), preference(s). *See also* Citizen participation; Community (geographic locality); Community (social); Community attitudes; Community involvement; Community services; Local politics; Public opinion; Public support.

Community theater. See *Little theater.*

Commuter marriages. See *Long distance marriages.*

Commuting (travel). Commut(e,er,ers,ing). Journey(s) to work. Travel to work. Carpool(s,ed,ing). Ride sharing. Ridesharing. Vanpool(s,ed,ing). Home to work trip. High occupancy vehicle(s). Rush hour traffic. Ride to work. Diamond lane(s). *Consider also:* shuttle(s). *See also* Business travel; Car pools; Destination; Mass transit; Proximity of family; Public transportation; Subways.

Comorbidity. Comorbid(ity,ities). *Choose from:* co-occurr(ence,ing), multiple, dual, cluster(s), simultaneous(ly) *with:* diagnos(es,is), disorder(s), syndrome(s), symptom(s). *See also* Diagnosis; Disorders; Symptoms; Physiological correlates.

Compacts (agreements). See *Agreement (document); Contracts; Legal documents; Treaties.*

Compadrazgo. See *Kinship.*

Companies. See *Business organizations.*

Companies, long distance telephone. See *Long distance telephone companies.*

Companionate marriages. Companionate marriage(s). *Choose from:* companionate *with:* marriage(s), marital, couple(s), spouse(s), partner(s,ship,ships). *Consider also:* trial marriage(s). *See also* Alternative family forms; Marriage.

Companions. Companion(s,ship). Friend(s). Comrade(s). Partner(s). Colleague(s). Co-worker(s). Associate(s). Schoolmate(s). Playmate(s). Confidant(s). *Consider also:* share a home, group living. *See also* Friendship; Peers.

Company, holding. See *Holding company.*

Company towns. Company town(s). *Choose from:* single industry, one company, single enterprise *with:* town(s), communit(y,ies), settlement(s), cit(y,ies). *Consider also:* mining town(s), steel towns, mill town(s). *See also* Community institutional relations; Community structure; Industrial towns and cities; Mining towns.

Comparable worth. Comparable worth. *Consider also:* pay, salar(y,ies), wage(s), compensation, earning(s), income, underpaid, underpayment(s) *with:* equity, fair(ness), equal(ity), inequit(y,ies), difference(s), sex bias, gender, women, woman, female(s). *See also* Employment discrimination; Employment of persons with disabilities; Employment opportunities; Equal job opportunities; Equity (payment); Fairness; Female intensive occupations; Justice; Male intensive occupations; Nontraditional careers; Sexual division of labor; Social equity; Social justice; Wage differentials; Working women.

Comparative advertising. Comparative advertising. Product differentiation. Negative advertising. Negative campaign(s,ing). *Choose from:* issue oriented, comparative, negative, attack(s,ed,ing), denigrating, counterattack(s,ed,ing), allegation(s), mean *with:* advertis(ing,ement,ements), ad(s), spot(s), marketing, promotion(al), public relations, publicity, price claim(s), campaign(s,ing). *See also* Advertising; Advertising campaigns; Brand identity; Fraudulent advertising; Marketing plans; Marketing strategies; Political advertising; Promotion (business).

Comparative linguistics. Comparative linguistics. Comparative philology. Contrastive linguistics. Linguistic comparison(s). *See also* Areal linguistics; Diachronic linguistics; Dialects; Grammar; Language varieties; Linguistic geography; Linguistics; Synchronism.

Comparative psychology. Comparative psychology. *Choose from:* comparative, comparison(s), cross cultural, similar(ity,ities), difference(s), dissimilarit(y,ies) *with:* psycholog(y, ical). *See also* Comparison; Psychology; Social sciences.

Comparative study. Comparative stud(y,ies). Differences between subjects. Control groups. *Choose from:* comparative, comparison(s) *with:* stud(y,ies), analys(is,es), evaluation(s), findings, statistics, dimensions. *Consider also:* replication, cross cultural, contrast(s,ed,ing). *See also* Comparison; Cross cultural comparisons; Differences; Norms; Surveys.

Comparison. Comparison(s). Compar(e,ed, ing,ative). Contrast(ed,ing). Apposition(al). Juxtaposition(al). *Consider also:* difference(s), variance(s), commonalit(y,ies), match(ed,ing) up, relative performance(s). *See also* Comparative psychology; Comparative study; Cross cultural comparisons; Social comparison.

Comparison, social. See *Social comparison.*

Comparisons, cross cultural. See *Cross cultural comparisons.*

Comparisons, cultural. See *Cross cultural comparisons.*

Compassion. Compassion(ate). Sympath(y,etic). Concern(ed). Considerat(e,ion). Tender(ness). Loving kindness. Helpful(ness). Humane(ness). Understanding. Solicitude. Benevolence. Merc(y,iful). Clemency. Pity. Gentle(ness). Forgive(ness). Empath(y,etic). *See also* Benevolence; Emotions; Empathy; Humane; Pity.

Compatibility, interpersonal. See *Interpersonal compatibility.*

Compendiums. Compendi(a,um,ums). Brief summar(y,ies). Digest(s). Pandect(s). Précis. Sketch(es). Abstract(s). *Consider also:* survey(s), syllabus(es), abridgment(s), brief(s), conspectus(es), prospectus(es), epitom(e,ize,izes,ized), overview(s). *See also* Abbreviations; Abstracts; Excerpts; Written communications.

Compensation (defense mechanism). Compensat(e,ed,ing,ion,ory). Overcompensat(e,ed,ing,ion). *See also* Achievement need; Defense mechanisms.

Compensation (payment). Compensation. Remuneration. Tip(ping). Pay(ment,ments). Paid. Salar(y,ies). Wage(s). Income(s). Gratuit(y,ies). Bonus(es). Earning(s). Revenue(s). Profit(s). Stipend(s). Honorari(a,um). Repayment(s). Reimburse(d,ment, ments). Economic incentive(s). *Consider also:* payoff(s), indemnit(y,ies), indemnif(y,ied,ication), fine(s), amend(s), redress(ed), restitution, reparation(s). *See also* Benefits (compensation); Bonuses; Compensation management; Employee benefits; Gratuities; Labor costs; Monetary rewards; Prevailing wages; Restitution; Salaries; War damage compensation.

Compensation, benefits. See *Benefits (compensation).*

Compensation, deferred. See *Deferred compensation.*

Compensation, war damage. See *War damage compensation.*

Compensation, workmens. See *Workmens compensation.*

Compensation management. Compensation management. Compensation program(s). Compensation cafeteria(s). Salary management. Compensation structure(s). Pay system(s). Performance-related pay. Wage structure(s). Salary structure(s). Salary administration. Model(s) of pay and performance.

Consider also: wage incentive(s), bonus system(s), incentive compensation, bonus award(s), merit increase(s), salaries, bonus(es), stock option(s), employee incentive(s), job reward(s), wage payment system(s), severance package(s), compensatory time, vacation(s), comp(ensatory) time, overtime pay, performance evaluation system(s). *See also* Benefits (compensation); Compensation (payment); Bonuses; Employee benefits; Employee incentive plans; Monetary rewards; Salaries.

Compensatory education. Compensatory education. Remediation. Bridge program(s). Head Start. *Choose from:* compensatory *with:* education, development, opportunit(y,ies), experience(s), program(s). *See also* After school programs; Rehabilitation; Remedial education; Remedial reading.

Competence. Competen(ce,cy,cies,t). Skill(ed,s,ful,fulness). Abilit(y,ies). Capabilit(y,ies). Capable. Dexterity. Mastery. Savoir faire. Expert(ise,ness). Proficien(cy,t). Qualified. Efficac(y, ious). Experienced. Expert(ness). *See also* Ability; Accountability; Accuracy; Achievement; Capacity; Communication skills; Competency to stand trial; Influence of age on ability; Minimum competencies; Performance standards; Professional competence; Social skills.

Competence, communicative. See *Communication skills.*

Competence, professional. See *Professional competence.*

Competence, social. See *Social skills.*

Competencies, minimum. See *Minimum competencies.*

Competency, cross cultural. See *Cross cultural competency.*

Competency, legal. See *Legal competency.*

Competency based education. Competency based education. *Choose from:* competency, output, consequence, criterion, performance, proficiency *with:* based, oriented, referenced *with:* program(s), instruction, orientation, training, education. *See also* Academic standards; Accountability; Competence; Minimum competencies; Performance.

Competency to stand trial. Competency to stand trial. Compos mentis. Noncompos mentis. Trial fitness. Guilty but mentally ill. Criminal responsibility assessment. *Choose from:* competen(t,cy), incompeten(t,cy), sane, insane, sanity, insanity, fit(ness), unfit(ness), capacity, mental(ly) impair(ed,ment,ments) *with:* stand trial, defendant(s), criminal justice, defense, waiv(e,ed,ing) constitutional rights, plead(ing) guilty. *See also* Insanity defense; Legal competency.

Competition. Competit(ion,ive,iveness). Compet(e,ed,ing). Rival(s,ry). Survival of the fittest. Zero sum game(s). Darwinism. Polemic(s,al). Disputation(s). Contest(s,ed,ant,ants). Drive to win. Killer instinct(s). *Consider also:* battle(s), challenge(s), clash(es), oppos(e,ed,ing,ition). *See also* Achievement need; Aggression; Behavior; Challenge; Competitive behavior; Conflict; Contests; Cooperation; Defeat; Economic competition; Game theory; Goal orientation; Goals; Industrial concentration; Intergroup relations; International conflict; Interpersonal relations; Monopolies; Oligopolies; Performance; Social behavior; Social Darwinism; Social interaction; Sports.

Competition, economic. See *Economic competition.*

Competition, international. See *International conflict; International trade.*

Competitive behavior. Competitive behavior(s). Competitive(ness). Rival(ry). Compet(e,ed,ing,ion,ions). Contest(ed,ing,ant,ants). Challeng(e,ed, ing,er,ers). Competitor(s). Opposing team(s). Vying. Vie(d). Contend(ed,ing, er,ers). *Consider also:* aggressive(ness), sportsmanship. *See also* Adversary; Aggression; Aggressiveness (trait); Athletic participation; Behavior; Challenge; Competition; Sibling relations; Sports.

Competitive intelligence. Competitive intelligence. *Choose from:* competitive, competitor(s), corporate, business, actionable, marketing, analyz(e,ed,ing), monitor(ed,ing) *with:* intelligence, knowledge, information. *Choose from:* analyz(e,ed,ing), monitor(ed,ing) *with:* market(s) customers, suppliers, distributor(s), competitor(s). *Consider also:* potential competitive advantage(s), new business opportunit(y,ies), competitive assessment(s), market information, intelligence source(s), market research, strategic analysis, company knowledge base(s), market scenario(s), recent activit(y,ies), trend(s). *See also* Knowledge management; Industrial espionage; Trade secrets.

Competitors. See *Adversary; Athletes; Competitive behavior; Competitive intelligence.*

Compilations. See *Anthologies.*

Complaints. Complaint(s). Complain(ed, ing). Grievance(s). Gripe(s). Objection(s). Allegation(s). Criticism(s). Indictment(s). Plaint(s). *Consider also:* accus(e,ed,ing,ation,ations), gravamen, cavil(s,ed,ing,led,ling), condemnation(s), denounc(e,ed,ing), denunciation(s), lament(s), whin(e,ed, es,ing), protest(s,ed,ing,ation,ations), imput(e,ed,ing,ation,ations). *See also* Allegations; Client rights; Customer relations; Diatribe; Disputes; Indictments; Jeremiads; Mediation.

Complaints, health. See *Health problems.*

Complementary needs. Complementary needs. Interdependen(t,ce). Symbio(sis, tic). Mutually beneficial. Mutual(ity, ism). *See also* Homogamy; Marital satisfaction; Needs; Personality traits; Symbiotic relations.

Complex, castration. See *Castration complex.*

Complex, electra. See *Electra complex.*

Complex, military industrial. See *Military industrial complex.*

Complex, Oedipus. See *Oedipus complex.*

Complex organizations. Complex organization(s). *Choose from:* differentiat(ed,ing,ion), complex(ity) *with:* firm(s), organization(s). *Consider also:* bureaucrac(y,ies), corporate jungle(s), multi-institutional system(s). *See also* Bureaucracies; Complexity; Organization size; Organizational culture; Organizational structure; Organizations.

Complex societies. Complex societ(y,ies). Division of labor. Differentiat(ed,ion) with societ(ies,y). Complex social formation. *See also* Complexity; Industrial societies; Modern society; Postindustrial societies; Social structure; Society; Specialization.

Complexity. Complex(ity). Complex system(s). Intrica(te,cy). Complicat(e,ed, edness,ing,ion,ions). Elaborat(e,ed,e, ing,ion). *Consider also:* differentiat(e, ed,ion,ing) and integrat(e,ed,ion,ing). *See also* Combinations; Complex organizations; Complex societies; Specialization; Reasoning; Task complexity.

Complexity, cognitive. See *Cognitive complexity.*

Complexity, task. See *Task complexity.*

Compliance. Complian(t,ce). Comply(ing). Obedien(t,ce). Cooperat(ion,ive). Accomodat(e,ed,ing,ion,ions). Acquiescen(ce,t). Yield(ed,ing). Agree(able,ableness). Submit(ted,ting). Submiss(ion,ive,iveness). Oversubmiss(ion,ive,iveness). Dutiful(ness). *Consider also:* conform(ed,ing), abid(e,ing) by, faithful(ly,ness). *See also* Cooperation; Law enforcement; Legislation; Obedience; Patient compliance; Social behavior.

Compliance, medical. See *Patient compliance.*

Compliance, patient. See *Patient compliance.*

Compliance, treatment. See *Patient compliance.*

Complications, postoperative. See *Postoperative complications.*

Complications, postsurgical. See *Postoperative complications.*

Compliments. See *Approval; Commendation; Eulogies; Praise; Tribute.*

Components. Component(s,ial). Ingredient(s). Part(s). Portion(s). Segment(s). Constituent(s). *Consider also:* factor(s), allotment(s), member(s), share(s). *See also* Content; Factor analysis; Factors; Structure.

Composers. Composer(s). Songwriter(s). Songster(s). Melodist(s). *Consider also:* lyricist(s), symphonist(s), arranger(s), author(s), tunesmith(s). *See also* Authors; Artists; Creators; Musical ability; Musicians; Writers.

Composition (writing). See *Writing (composition).*

Composition, chance. See *Chance composition.*

Composition, group. See *Group composition.*

Comprehension.
Comprehen(d,ded,ding,sion). Understand(ing). Understood. Cogni(tion,zance). Wisdom. Insight(s, ful). Aware(ness). Knowledge. Discern(ment,ing). Realiz(e,ed,ing, ation,ations). *See also* Abstraction; Advance organizers; Apperception; Cognition; Cognitive processes; Coherence; Computer literacy; Concept formation; Inference; Intelligence; Intuition; Knowledge; Listening comprehension; Meaning; Metacognition; Misconceptions; Number comprehension; Perception; Reading comprehension; Sentence comprehension; Verbal comprehension; Verstehen.

Comprehension, listening. See *Listening comprehension.*

Comprehension, number. See *Number comprehension.*

Comprehension, reading. See *Reading comprehension.*

Comprehension, sentence. See *Sentence comprehension.*

Comprehension, verbal. See *Verbal comprehension.*

Comprehensive health care. Comprehensive health care. *Choose from:* comprehensive, integrated, coordinat(e,ed,ion) *with:* medical care, health care, health program(s), long term care, service(s), care. *Consider also:* health maintenance organization(s), patient care planning, primary health care, progressive patient care. *See also* Health care; Managed care.

Comprehensiveness. Comprehensive(ness). Complete(ly,ness). Entire(ly). Total(ly,ity). Inclusive(ness). Inclusory. All-inclusive. All-encompassing. Unabridged. Uncut. Encyclopedic. Exhaustive(ness). Thorough(ness). Worldwide. Widespread. Extensive(ly). Expansive(ness). Across-the-board. In-depth. Wide-ranging. Full-scale. *See also* Aggregate economics; Belongingness; Catholic (universality); Ends; Globalization; Inclusion.

Compressed workweek. See *Alternative work patterns.*

Compromises. Compromise(s). Concession(s). Trade-off(s). Accomodation(s). Conciliat(ory,ion, ions). Propitiation. Reconcil(e,ed,ing, iation). Rapprochement. Negotiation(s). Conced(e,ed,ing). Mak(e,ing) deal(s). *Consider also:* middle ground, middle road(s), middle course(s), nonaggression pact(s), land for peace. *See also* Appeasement; Conflict resolution; Mediation; Negotiation.

Compulsive behavior. Compulsive behavior(s). Compulsion(s). Countercompulsion(s). Compulsiv(e, eness,ity). Binge eating. Addiction(s). Pathological gambling. Work addiction. Difficulty controlling impulse(s). Obsessive compulsive behavior(s). Irresistible urge(s). Irresistible impulse(s). *Choose from:* compuls(ive, ion,ions) *with:* urge(s), impulse(s), eat(ing,er,ers), gambl(er,ing), handwashing, firesetting, arson, water drink(ing,er,ers), smok(e,ers,ing), stealing, drink(er,ers,ing), trichotillomania, ritual(s), repetition. *See also* Behavior; Compulsive disorders; Computer addiction; Impulsiveness; Orderliness; Perfectionism; Personality traits; Spontaneity.

Compulsive disorders. Compulsive disorder(s). *Choose from:* compulsive, impulse control, impulsive, problem *with:* disorder(s), drink(ing,er,ers), eat(ing,er,ers), gambl(ing,er,ers), masturbat(e,ing,ion), sexual activit(y, ics), stealing. *See also* Alcoholism; Bulimia; Compulsive behavior; Kleptomania; Obsessions; Obsessive behavior; Obsessive compulsive personality; Pathological gambling; Perfectionism; Problem drinking; Substance abuse.

Compulsive obsessive personality. See *Obsessive compulsive personality.*

Compulsive personality disorder. See *Obsessive compulsive personality.*

Compulsive repetition. See *Compulsive behavior.*

Compulsive sexuality. See *Hypersexuality.*

Compulsivity. See *Compulsive behavior.*

Compulsory. See *Mandate; Requirements.*

Compulsory education. Compulsory education. *Choose from:* compulsory, mandatory, requir(e,ed,ing) *with:* education(al), school(s,ing), school attendance. *See also* Access to education; Educational opportunities; Public schools; Special education.

Compulsory labor. See *Forced labor; Slavery.*

Compulsory military service. See *Military draft.*

Compulsory participation. Compulsory participation. Conscription. *Choose from:* compulsory, mandatory, involuntary, required, coerced, forced, obligatory *with:* participat(e,ing,ion), attendance, treatment, school(ing), service, contribution(s), presence. *See also* Compulsory education; Participation; State power.

Compulsory retirement. See *Involuntary retirement; Mandatory retirement.*

Computer addiction. Computer addict(s,ion,ions,ive). Cyberaddict(s). Cyberholic(s). Internet addict(s,ion, ions). Cyberhooked. Addict(ed,ion) to computer game(s). Webaholic(s). Internet vampire(s). Nethead(s). *Choose from:* addict(s,ion,ions,ive), compuls(ive,ion,ions), devotee(s), hooked, junkie(s), obsess(ed,ion,ions) *with:* computer(s), Internet, E-mail, World Wide Web, channel surfing, online, cyberspace. *Consider also:* Internet related computer addictive behavior,. *See also* Addiction; Attitudes toward computers; Compulsive behavior; Online users; Computers; Man machine systems.

Computer aided instruction. See *Computer assisted instruction.*

Computer anxiety. Computer anxiet(y,ies). Kilobytophob(e,es,ia,ias,ic,ics). Fear of technology. Technophob(e,es,ia,ias, ic,ics). *Choose from:* computer(s), microcomputer(s), technolog(y,ical) *with:* anxiet(y,ies), anxious(ness), fear(s,ful), avoid(ed,ing,ance), phob(ic,ia,ias), stress(es), aversion(s), apprehension(s), apprehensive(ness). *See also* Attitudes toward computers; Mathematics anxiety; Science anxiety; Test anxiety; User friendly systems.

Computer assisted decision making. Computer assisted decision making. Computer based decision(s). Decision support. Expert system(s). Computer aided decision(s). Computer support(ed) decision(s). *Consider also:* management information system(s), knowledge based system(s). *See also* Automation; Computer assisted diagnosis; Computers; Decision making; Knowledge management; Man machine systems; Management information systems.

Computer assisted diagnosis. Computer assisted diagnos(is,es,tic,tics). Automated diagnos(is,es,tic,tics). Computerized diagnos(is,es,tic,tics). *Choose from:* computer(s) *with:* assisted, aided, guided, based *with:* diagnos(is,es,tic, tics), cardiogra(phy,m,ms), electro-cardiogra(phy,m,ms), radiograph(y,ic), tomograph(y,ic), examination(s). *See also* Automation; Computer assisted decision making; Computers; Diagnostic services; Diagnosis; Man machine systems.

Computer assisted instruction. Computer assisted instruction. CAI. Computer assisted learning. CAL. *Choose from:* computerized, programmed, automated, interactive *with:* instruction, teaching, learning, education, curricul(a,um), tutorial(s), training. *Choose from:* computer, machine, microcomputer *with:* based, aided, assisted, managed, mediated, guided *with:* instruction, teaching, learning, education, curricul(a, um), tutorial(s), training. *Consider also:* instructional technology, educational technology. *See also* Computers; Educational laboratories; Educational technology; Feedback; Individualized instruction; Man machine systems; Programmed instruction.

Computer bugs. Computer bug(s). *Choose from:* computer(s), microcomputer(s), software, hardware, disk(s,ette,ettes), PC(s) *with:* bug(s), defect(s,ive), error(s), mistake(s). *See also* Computer crimes; Computer hackers; Computer viruses; Cyber attacks; Debugging; Millennium bug; Network meltdown.

Computer crimes. Computer crime(s). Cyberattack(s). Cybercrook(s). Cybotage. Computer embezzle(r,rs, ment). Computer terror(ism). Computer virus(es). Logic bomb(s). Computer abuse(r,rs). Electronic crime(s,wave, waves). EDP crime(s). Cyberpunk(s). Computer rip-off(s). EFT crime(s). Electronic thieve(s,ry). Electronic embezzle(r,rs,ment). Fake web page(s). Cyberrobber(s). Shoulder surfing. Network pira(cy,te,tes). Stolen voice-mail box(es). Cracker(s). *Choose from:* computer(s,ized), cyber, digital(ly), microcomputer(s), electronic, email, network(s), software, hardware, data processing, high tech(nology), internet, ecommerce *with:* intru(de,ders,sion, sions), steal(ing,th), stolen, perpetrator(s), virus(es), vandal(ism), plague(d,s), destruct(ive,ion), illegal(ity,ities), tamper(ed,ing), damag(e,ed,ing), hack(er,ers,ing), sabot(eur,age,aged), spy(ing), spie(s,d), sell(ing) obscenity, misuse(s,d), unauthorized, attack(ed,ing), rogue(s), fraud(ulent), abus(e,es,ers,ed), counterfeit(ing), money laundering, smuggl(e,ed,er,ers,ing), penetrat(e,ed,

ing), break, extort(ed,ion), crime(s), pirate(s), piracy, terror(ism), thieve(s,ry), thief, theft, espionage. *Consider also:* security, privacy *with:* data, micro-computer(s), computer(s,ized), software. *See also* Computer bugs; Computer hackers; Computer security; Computer viruses; Computers; Crime; Cyber attacks; Cyberlaw; Cyberpunk culture; Electronic eavesdropping; Industrial espionage; Infowar; Network meltdown; Online harassment; Online privacy; Online users; Sabotage; White collar crime.

Computer experts. Computer expert(s). Cyber elite. Internet expert(s). Digerati. *Choose from:* computer(s), hardware, software, digital, online, micro-computer(s), PC(s), internet, LAN(s), Internet, intranet, extranet, network(s), mainframe(s), Windows, MacIntosh, DOS *with:* expert(s), professional(s), specialist(s), mavin(s), master(s), whiz, wiz, wizard(s), genius(es). *Consider also:* computer program(er,ers,mer, mers), computer nerd(s), computer geek(s), computer freak(s). *See also* Computer hackers; Computer personnel; Gold collar workers; Knowledge workers; Labor aspects of technology; Nerds; Professional personnel.

Computer failure. See *Down (computers)*.

Computer firewalls. See *Firewalls (computers)*.

Computer games. Computer game(s). Computer entertainment. Online gambling. *Choose from:* computer(s), Windows, Intel, Microsoft, software, CD-ROM(s), Macintosh, PC, semiconductor(s) *with:* game(s), sport(s), baseball, football, golf, solitaire, card game(s). *See also* Adult games; Electronic games; Entertainment; Interactive computer systems; Leisure activities; Online gambling; Online users.

Computer hackers. Computer hack(er, ers,ing). Superhacker(s). Computer criminal(s). Computer sp(y,ies). Cyberthie(f,ves). Electronic terrorist(s). *Choose from:* computer(s), Internet, cyberspace, online *with:* hacker(s), superhacker(s), criminal(s), sp(y,ies), thie(f,ves). *Consider also:* computer prank(s), hacker cult(s), phone hacker(s), phone phreaker(s), IP spoofing, Internet Protocol spoofing, virus coder(s), password hacker(s), computer cracker(s), computer piracy, computer wizard(s), techno-cracker(s). *See also* Computer bugs; Computer crimes; Computer experts; Computer viruses; Network meltdown; Offenders; Online users.

Computer hardware. See *Hardware (computers)*.

Computer-human interaction. See *Man machine systems*.

Computer illiteracy. Computer illitera(cy, te,tes). *Choose from:* computer(s,ize, ized), microcomputer(s), micro(s), online, CD-ROM(s) *with:* illitera(cy, te,tes), novice(s), naive(te), beginner(s), unsophisticated, unaware, unskilled, uninitiated, newcomer(s), untrained, inability. *Consider also:* scientific, technological *with:* illitera(cy,te). *See also* Computer anxiety; Computer literacy; Computers; Disadvantaged; Information literacy; Technological unemployment; User friendly systems.

Computer industry. Computer industry. *Choose from:* computer(s,ize,izing, ized,ization), microcomputer(s), hardware, mainframe(s), mini-computer(s), microprocessor(s), supercomputer(s), Silicon Valley, microchip(s), software, peripherals *with:* industr(y,ies,ial), factor(y,ies), manufac-turing, produc(t,ts,er,ers,tion). *Consider also:* Datamation, Dell, Hitachi, Microsoft, Packard Bell, IBM, Epson, Intel, Toshiba, etc. *See also* Computers; Hardware (computers); High technology industries; Industry; Millennium bug; Software (computers).

Computer literacy. Computer litera(cy,te, tes). Computerate. Programming skill(s). Computer skill(s). Computer awareness. *Choose from:* computer(s,ized), microcomputer(s), micro(s), online, programming, CD-ROM, software *with:* skill(s), aware(ness), litera(cy,te,tes), familiar(ity), knowledge, competen(t,ce, cy,cies). *See also* Competence; Comprehension; Computer illiteracy; Computers; Information literacy; Information skills; Technocracy.

Computer music. Computer music. Computerized music. Computer songs. *Choose from:* computer(s), internet, web, CD(s), cyberspace, online, digitized *with:* music, recordings, song(s). *Consider also:* computer simulation of music, synthesizer(s). *See also* Electronic music.

Computer networks. Computer network(s,ing). Local area network(s, ing). LAN(s). Wide area network(s,ing). WAN(s). CD-ROM network(s,ing). Communication network(s,ing). Computer based distributed data. Computer conferenc(es,ing). Electronic mail. Computer mediated communication system(s). Value added network(s). Microcomputer network(s,ing). *See also* Automated information retrieval; Automated information storage; Computers; Connectivity; Data transmission systems; Electronic mail; Electronic publishing; Man machine systems; Microcomputers; Network backup; Networks.

Computer networks, community. See *Community networks (computer).*

Computer personnel. Computer personnel. Programmers. Systems analyst(s). Software developer(s). Systems administrator(s). Information systems professional(s). Coder(s). Network administrator(s). Network engineer(s). Applications developer(s). Computer operator(s). *Choose from:* internet, intranet, programming language(s), LAN(s), software, systems, network(s), computer(s), mainframe(s), MacIntosh, DOS, Windows, PC(s) with operator(s), user(s), specialist(s), worker(s), developer(s), professional(s), occupation(s,al), manpower, personnel, staff(er,ers,ing), administrator(s), team(s), engineer(s). *See also* Computer experts; Knowledge workers; Labor aspects of technology; Online users; Personnel.

Computer security. Computer security. Data security. Electronic crime countermeasure(s). *Choose from:* computer(s), mainframe(s), micro(s), microcompu(er,ers,ing), PC(s), personal computer(s), hardware, software, database(s), data, network(s), LAN(s), local area network(s), WAN(s), wide area network(s), EDP, DP, data process(er,ers,ing) *with:* secur(e,ed,ed, ing,ity), protect(s,ed,ing,ion), guard(s,ed,ing), failsafe, safeguard(s,ed, ing), safekeeping, disaster planning, disaster recovery, confidential(ity), control(led) access, disaster prevent(s,ed,ion,ions), contingen(cy, cies), audit(s,ed,ing,or,ors), backup(s), authoriz(e,ed,es,izing,ation,ations), privacy, password(s), verif(y,ied,ies, ying,ication), encrypt(ed,ing,ion,ions). *See also* Computer crimes; Computers; Crime prevention; Cryptography; Firewalls (computers); Infowar; Intangible property; Network backup; Privacy; Privacy laws.

Computer systems, interactive. See *Interactive computer systems.*

Computer thought. See *Artificial intelligence.*

Computer viruses. Computer virus(es). *Choose from:* computer, polymorphic, network, e-mail, macro, diskette(s), disk(s), drive(s), program(s), workstation(s) *with:* virus(es), worm(s), infect(ed,ing,ion,ions), contagio(n,us), attack(s,ed,ing), assault(s,ed,ing). *Consider also:* virus attack(s), boot sector virus(es), program file virus(es), macro virus(es), DOS attack(s), denial-of-service attack(s), computer bug(s). *See also* Computer bugs; Computer crimes; Computer hackers; Cyber attacks; Debugging; Millennium bug; Network meltdown.

Computerization. See *Automation.*

Computers. Computer(s,ize,izing, ized,ization). Laptop computer(s). Laptop(s). Microcomputer(s). Hardware. Mainframe(s). Minicomputer(s). Microprocessor(s). Analog computer(s). Digital computer(s). Computer storage. Computer memory. Input output device(s). Analog digital conversion. Hybrid computer(s). Palm computer(s). Personal computer(s). PC(s). Notebook computer(s). Portable computer(s). Supercomputer(s). *Consider also:* server(s), thin client(s), fat client(s), software, computer language(s), computer program(s), central processing unit(s), CPU(s), data processor(s), cybernetic(s), man machine system(s), timesharing, adding machine(s), calculator(s), Macintosh(es), Mac(s), Pentium(s), iMac(s), I.B.M., Hewlett-Packard, Compaq, etc. *See also* Artificial intelligence; Attitudes toward computers; Automation; Calculating machines; CD ROMs; Computer addiction; Computer anxiety; Computer assisted decision making; Computer assisted diagnosis; Computer assisted instruction; Computer crimes; Computer illiteracy; Computer industry; Computer literacy; Computer networks; Computer security; Cybernetics; Data processing; Data transmission systems; Databases; Debugging; Down (computers); DVDs; Electronic equipment; Electronic mail; Electronic publishing; Expert systems; Fault tolerant computing; Hardware (computers); High technology industries; Man machine systems; Microcomputers; Millennium bug; Mobile computing; Robotics; Software (computers); Telecommunications; User friendly systems.

Computers, attitudes toward. See *Attitudes toward computers.*

Computers, personal. See *Microcomputers.*

Computing, fault tolerant. See *Fault tolerant computing.*

Computing, mobile. See *Mobile computing.*

Conceit. Conceit(ed). Self-importan(t,ce). Self-admir(ing,ation). Vain. Vanity. Narcissis(tic,m). Egotis(m,tical). Boastful(ness). Self-satisf(ied,action). Self-centered. Overbearing. Bragg(ing, art,arts). Arrogan(t,ce). Pompous. *See also* Egotism; Narcissism; Personality traits; Snobs and snobbishness.

Concentration. Concentration. Attent(ion,ional,ive). *Consider also:* engross(ed,ment), scrutin(y,ize,izing), intent(ness), cognitive effort, focussed, vigilance, heed(ing), tak(e,ing) notice. *See also* Cognitive processes; Selective attention.

Concentration, business. See *Industrial concentration; Oligopolies.*

Concentration, industrial. See *Industrial concentration.*

Concentration camp syndrome. Concentration camp syndrome. *Consider also:* emotional anesthesia, surviv(al,or,ors) guilt, surviv(al,or,ors) syndrome. *See also* Guilt; Post traumatic stress disorders; Survivors.

Concentration camps. Concentration camp(s). Prison camp(s). Univers concentrationnaire. Konzentrationslager. Death camp(s). Death factor(y,ies). Anus mundi. Extermination camp(s). Detainment camp(s). Internment center(s). Forced labor camp(s). Relocation camp(s). Nazi detention center(s). Gas chamber(s). Buchenwald. Auschwitz [Oswiecim]. Auschwitz-Birkenau [Brzezinka]. Dachau. Mauthausen. Sachsenhausen. Stutthof. Chelmno. Treblinka. Sobibor. Maidanek [Majdanek]. Belzac. Neuengamme. Vuoht. Natzweiler. Flossenburg. Bergen-Belsen. Ravensbruck. Sachsenhausen. Gross-Rosen. Theresienstadt [Terezin]. *Choose from:* holocaust, shoah, annihilation, genocid(e,al), war crime(s). *Consider also:* camp(s), center(s) *with:* Boer war, Japanese-Americans, political prisoner(s). *Consider also:* Nazi(s), Nuremberg trial(s), Eichmann, Barbie *with:* atrocit(y,ies), victim(s), crime(s), medical experiment(s), Jew(s,ish), gyps(y,ies), Pol(es,ish). *See also* Refugee camps; Forced labor; Holocaust; Penal colonies; Prisons.

Concentration difficulties. Concentration difficult(y,ies). Mental asthenia. *Choose from:* concentrat(e,ing,ion), attention(al) *with:* difficult(y,ies), deficit(s). *Consider also:* dysbulia. *See also* Attention deficit disorder; Attention span; Psychomotor agitation; Restlessness.

Concept, self. See *Self concept.*

Concept formation. Concept formation. Conceptualiz(e,ed,ing,ation). Object conception. Ideation. Abstraction. *Choose from:* utiliz(e,ed,ing,ation) *with:* symbol(s). *Choose from:* concept(s,ual) *with:* form(ed,ing,ation), develop(ed,ing, ment), distinction(s), thinking, framework(s), understanding, attainment, discovery, finding, learning. *Consider also:* cognitive discrimination, cognitive generalization. *See also* Abstraction; Cognitive discrimination; Cognitive development; Cognitive generalization; Cognitive processes; Comprehension; Concepts; Developmental stages; Learning; Logical thinking; Misconceptions; Object permanence.

Concept validity. See *Construct validity.*

Conception. Conception. Conceive(d). Becom(e,ing) pregnant. Fertiliz(e,ed,ing, ation). *Consider also:* reproductive technolog(y,ies). *See also* Artificial insemination; Fertilization; Pregnancy; Sexual reproduction.

Concepts. Concept(ion,s). Idea(s,tional). Notion(s). Abstraction(s). Thinking. Thought(s). Misconception(s). Conceptualization(s). Hypothesis. Inference. Theor(y,ies). Postulate(s). Construct(s). Image(s). Ideal type(s). Paradigm(s). Label(s). Categor(y,ies, ization,izations). Typolog(y,ies). Theme(s). Ideolog(y,ies). Representation(s). *See also* Beliefs; Cognitions; Concept formation; Form (philosophy); God concepts; Hypotheses; Image (philosophy); Mathematical concepts; Themes.

Concepts, God. See *God concepts.*

Concepts, mathematical. See *Mathematical concepts.*

Conceptual art. Concept(ual) art. Con art. Idea art. Conceptual piece(s). Language art. Possible art. Post-object art. Information art. Arte Povera. *See also* Artistic styles; Arts; Earthworks; Genres (art); Performance art.

Conceptual imagery. Conceptual imagery. *Choose from:* image(s,ry), metaphor(s), caricature(s), ideal type(s), representation(s), symbol(s,ization), model(s), concept(s), conceptualization(s) *with:* mental, cultural, social, cognitive, pictorial, visual. *See also* Imagination.

Conceptual tempo. Conceptual tempo. Cognitive tempo. Speed of processing. Speed of mental rotation. Conceptual style(s). Hast(y,iness). Deliberate approach(es). Reflection-impulsivity. *See also* Attention span; Cognitive style; Impulsiveness; Perceptual style; Reaction time.

Conceptualism. Conceptualis(m,t,tic). *Consider also:* nominalis(m,t,tic), conceptual relativism. *See also* Philosophy.

Conceptualization. See *Concept formation.*

Concerns, employee. See *Employee concerns.*

Concert halls. Concert hall(s). Music hall(s). Recital hall(s). Performing arts center(s). Orchestra hall(s). Auditorium(s). Opera hall(s). Symphony hall(s). Concert room(s). Performance hall(s). *Consider also:* Carnegie Hall, Lincoln Center, Opera House, Gewandhaus, Royal Albert Hall, konzerthaus(e,er). *See also* Auditoriums; Halls; Music; Orchestras; Public buildings; Public places; Theater.

Concertmasters. Concertmaster(s). Konzertmeister. Chef(s) d'attaque. Chef(s) de pupitre. Primo violino. Concertino(s). First violinist(s). *See also* Conductors.

Concertos. Concert(o,os,i,ii). Konzert(e,en, es,stuck). Concierto(s). Concertante. Concertino(s). *Consider also:* concerto grosso. *See also* Music.

Concerts. Concert(s). Musical performance(s). Musicale(s). Recital(s). *See also* Broadcasts; Music; Musicians.

Concessions. Concession(s). Conced(e,ed,ing). Surrender(ed,ing). Yield(ed,ing). Admit(ted,ting). Capitulat(e,ed,ion). Abandon(ed,ing, ment). Acquiescen(t,ce). Compliance. Acced(e,ed,ing,ence). Compromise(s,d). *Consider also:* confess(ed,ing,ion,ions), relinquish(ed,ing,ment), grant(ed,ing). *See also* Compromises; Confession; Conflict resolution; Mediation; Military capitulations; Negotiation.

Conciliation. Conciliat(e,ion,ory,ive,or,ors). Reconcil(e,iation). Pacif(y,ication). Appease(ment). Placat(e,ed,ing). Propitiat(e,ed,ing,ion). Settling difference(s). Accomodat(e,ed,ing, ive,ion). *See also* Compromises; Conflict resolution; Negotiation; Mediation; Peace negotiations.

Concord. See *Armistices; Consensus; Peace; Rapport; Peaceful coexistence.*

Concrete art. Concrete art. Art concrete. Concrete painting(s). *Consider also:* non-figurative painting, non-figurative sculpture, Theo Van Doesburg, Max Bill. *See also* Abstract art; Arts; Concrete poetry; Dadaism; Surrealism.

Concrete music. See *Electronic music.*

Concrete poetry. Concrete poetry. Poesia concreta. Konkrete Dichtung. Verbicovisual expression. *Consider also:* Brazilian poetry, Max Bill, Eugen Gomringer, Hans Carl Artmann, Haroldo de Campos, Augusto de Campos. *See also* Concrete art; Dadaism; Poetry; Surrealism.

Concubinage. Concubin(e,es,age). Mistress(es). Paramour(s). Kept woman. *See also* Courtesans; Harems.

Condemnation. See *Blame; Censure; Invective.*

Condemnation of buildings. Condemnation of buildings. *Choose from:* building(s), house(s), firetrap(s), slum(s), tenement(s), apartment(s) *with:* condemn(ing,ation,ed), eminent domain, demolish(ed,ing), demolition, raz(e,ed, ing), torn down, tear down, bulldoz(e,ed, ing). *Consider also:* redevelop(ed,ing, ment), building inspect(ion,or,ors), housing code(s), building code(s). *See also* Abandoned property.

Condemned books. See *Censorship.*

Condensation (fluids). Condens(e,ed,ing, ation). Dew(s). Rainfall. *Consider also:* crystalliz(e,ed,ing,ation), distill(ed,ing, ation), fluidiz(e,ed,ing,ation), precipitat(e,ed,ing,ation). *See also* Distillation.

Condition, physical. See *Disease susceptibility; Health; Health problems; Physical fitness.*

Conditionals. Conditional(s). *Consider also:* hypothetical(ly), contingen(t,cy), provisional(ly), tentative(ly). *See also* Counterfactuals (logic); Grammar; Hypothetical; Phrases; Sentence structure; Sentences.

Conditioned responses. Conditioned response(s). *Choose from:* condition(ed, ing), reinforc(e,ed,ing,ment), stimulus *with:* response(s), behavior, reflex(es). *See also* Classical conditioning; Conditioning (psychology); Operant conditioning; Responses.

Conditioned suppression. Conditioned suppression. *Choose from:* conditioned, reinforce(d,ment) *with:* suppress(ed,ing, ion), inhibit(ed,ing,ion), avoid(ed, ing,ance). *See also* Classical conditioning; Inhibition (psychology); Operant conditioning; Responses.

Conditioning (psychology). Condition(ed, ing). *Choose from:* Pavlov(ian), operant, classical, avers(ive,ion), avoidance, escape, backward, higher order, respondent *with:* condition(ed,ing). *Consider also:* conditioned, learned *with:* response(s), suppression. *Choose from:* conditioned, unconditioned *with:* stimulus. *Consider also:* behavioris(m,t), associative shifting, operant behavior, stimulus generalization, behavior modification, autoshaping, counterconditioning. *See also* Aversion conditioning; Avoidance learning; Behaviorism; Biofeedback; Classical conditioning; Conditioned responses; Conditioned suppression; Extinction (psychology); Fading (conditioning); Instrumental conditioning; Learning theories; Meditation; Operant conditioning; Primary reinforcement; Reinforcement; Stimuli; Unconditioned responses; Unconditioned stimulus.

Conditioning, aversion. See *Aversion conditioning.*

Conditioning, avoidance. See *Avoidance learning.*

Conditioning, classical. See *Classical conditioning.*

Conditioning, fading. See *Fading (conditioning).*

Conditioning, instrumental. See *Instrumental conditioning.*

Conditioning, operant. See *Operant conditioning.*

Conditioning, social. See *Attitude formation; Conditioning (psychology); Learned behavior; Learned helplessness; Social learning; Socialization.*

Conditions, atmospheric. See *Atmospheric conditions.*

Conditions, business. See *Business cycles; Depression (economic); Economic conditions; Inflation (economics); Recession; Socioeconomic factors.*

Conditions, economic. See *Economic conditions.*

Conditions, housing. See *Housing conditions.*

Conditions, labor. See *Working conditions.*

Conditions, living. See *Living conditions.*

Conditions, moral. See *Moral conditions.*

Conditions, rural. See *Rural conditions.*

Conditions, social. See *Social conditions.*

Conditions, working. See *Working conditions.*

Condoms, female. See *Female condoms.*

Conduct. Conduct. Behavior(al,s). Performance. Habit(s). Assertive(ness). Child behavior(s). Classroom behavior(s). Communicat(e,ed,ing,ion). Competitive(ness). Cooperative(ness). Compet(e,ed,ing,ition). Cooperat(e,ed,ing,ion). Demeanor. Disobedien(t,ce). Drinking. Drug use. Displacement. Explor(e,ed,ing,ation). Exploratory behavior(s). Feeding behavior(s). Group behavior(s). Hyperactiv(e,ity). Imitat(e,ed,ing,ion). Imitative behavior(s). Inhibit(ed,ing,ion). Leadership. Life style(s). Maternal behavior(s). Misbehavior. Motor activity. Obedience. Paranoid behavior(s). Paternal behavior(s). Participat(e,ed,ing,ion). Persisten(t,ce). Physical(ly) activ(e,ity). Response(s). Risk taking. Self control. Self mutilation. Smok(e,ed,ing). Sociab(le,ility). Social behavior(s). Spontaneity. Self stimulation. Sex behavior(s). Social conformity. Social(ly) dominan(t,ce). Social facilitation. Spatial behavior(s). Stereotyped behavior(s). Substance abuse(r,rs). Sucking behavior(s). *See also* Behavior; Behavior disorders; Behavior modification; Demeanor; Social behavior; Social behavior disorders; Unethical conduct.

Conduct, disorderly. See *Disorderly conduct.*

Conduct, illegal. See *Unethical conduct.*

Conduct, personal. See *Behavior; Demeanor; Deviant behavior; Habits; Lifestyle; Manners; Social skills.*

Conduct, unethical. See *Unethical conduct.*

Conduct disorders. See *Behavior disorders; Behavior problems.*

Conduct of life. See *Lifestyle.*

Conducting. Conduct(ed,ing,or,ors). *Consider also:* chironomy. *See also* Music.

Conductors. Conductor(s). Chef(s) d'orchestre. Band leader(s). *Consider also:* choir director(s), kapellmeister(s), capellmeister(s), maitre(s) de la musique, Maestro. *See also* Concertmasters; Impresarios; Musicians; Orchestras.

Confederalism. Confederalism. Confederat(e,ed,ing,ion,ions). Association of independent states. States rights. States powers. Weak central government(s). State sovereignty. *Consider also:* local autonomy, decentraliz(ed,ation). *See also* Decentralization; Devolution; Governmental powers; Unification; Unitarism.

Confederation. See *Confederalism.*

Conferences. Conference(s). Meeting(s). Congress(es). Caucus(es). Seminar(s). Staff meeting(s). Sympos(ia,ium). Convention(s). Assembl(y,ies). Annual meeting(s). Council(s). Colloqui(a,m, ms). *See also* Continuing education; Organizations; Professional organizations; Public meetings; Teleconferencing.

Conferences, press. See *Press conferences.*

Confession. Confess(ion,ional,ed,ing, or,ors,s). Admit(ted,ting,s,ance,ances). Admission(s). Self disclosure. Confid(e, ed,ence,ences,ing). Disclos(e,ed,ing, ure). Self incriminat(e,ed,ing,ion). Divulg(e,ed,ing,ence,ences). Acknowledg(e,ed,ing,ement,ements). *Consider also:* Miranda rights, sacrament of penance, penitent(ial), revelation(s). *See also* Concessions; Disclosure; Guilt; Penitents; Religious rituals; Repentence; Roman Catholicism; Self incrimination; Self disclosure; Sin.

Confidants. Confidant(s). Confidante(s). *Choose from:* close, intimate, trusted *with:* friend(s,ship,ships), comrade(s), colleague(s). Comforter(s). Intimate contact(s). *Consider also:* informal, social *with:* support. *See also* Friendship; Significant others.

Confidence. Confidence. Faith. Trust(ed,ing). Assurance. Credence. Fidelity. Loyalty. Sureness. Assured(ness). Positive(ness). *See also* Assurances; Faith; Self esteem; Self concept; Self efficacy; Trusting.

Confidence, public. See *Public support.*

Confidence, self. See *Pride; Self assessment; Self concept; Self efficacy; Self esteem.*

Confidential communications. Confidential communication(s). Privileged communication(s). Confidentiality. Top secret. Classified information. Anonymity of source(s). Confidential source(s). Lawyer client privilege(s). Shield law. Private note(s). Personal information. *Choose from:* client(s), patient(s), therapist(s), psychotherapist(s), psychoanalyst(s), doctor(s), physician(s), attorney(s), lawyer(s), client record(s), news(man,men, woman,women), reporter(s), clergy(men,man,women,woman) *with:* confidential(ity), privacy, privileged relationship(s). Vow(s) of silence. Reporter resource relationship(s). Privacy law(s). Sealed document(s). Prevent(ed,ing,ion) of disclosure. Bar(red,ring) information. Conceal(ed, ing) identit(y,ies). *Choose from:* confidential, secret, private, sealed *with:* information, record(s), source(s), data, document(s), AIDS test(s), confession(s). *Consider also:* trade secret(s), company secret(s), leak(s,ed, ing), proprietary information. *See also* Advisors; Confidential records; Confidentiality; Invasion of privacy; Physician patient relations; Privacy laws; Professional client relations; Secrecy.

Confidential records. Confidential record(s). *Choose from:* confidential(ity), privacy, private, privileged communication(s) *with:* medical record(s), nursing record(s), dental record(s), student record(s), transcript(s), reference(s), file(s), arrest information, patient data. *See also* Confidential communications; Confidentiality; Freedom of information; Medical records; Privacy; Privacy laws; Student records.

Confidentiality. Confidential(ity,ly). Private information. *Choose from:* confidential(ity), private, privacy, privileged, censored, inaccessible, secre(t,cy), sealed, classified *with:* information, communication(s), record(s), source(s), bid(s), verdict(s). *Consider also:* secre(t,cy), confided, right of privacy, strict(est) confidence, records not open to public, entrusted with confidence(s), confidential(ity) of source(s). *See also* Confidants; Confidential communications; Confidential records; Disclosure; Ethics; Interpersonal relations; Invasion of privacy; Investor relations; Online privacy; Physician patient relations; Privacy; Privacy laws; Secrecy.

Confinement. Confine(d,ment). Incarcerat(e,ed,ion). Detention. Detain(ed). Held. Hold(ing). Jail(ed). Imprison(ed,ment). Intern(ed,ment). Custody. Arrest(ed). Commit(ted,ment). Institutionaliz(ed,ation). Hospitaliz(ed, ation). Restricted environment(s). Constrain(ed,ment). Quarantine(d). Caged. Cooped. Homebound. *See also* Bedridden; Housebound; Hospitalization; Institutionalization (persons).

Confinement to home. See *Bedridden; Housebound.*

Confirmation. Confirm(ed,ing,ation). Assur(e,ed,ing,ance,ances). Provid(e,ed, ing) evidence. Acknowledge(ment,

ments). Corroborat(e,ed,ing,ion,ions). Ratification(s). *Consider also:* conversion rite(s), sacrament(s), first Communion, anoint(ed,ing), lay(ing) on of hands. *See also* Acceptance; Approval; Clearance (authorization); Ceremonies; Ratification; Religious rituals; Religious practices; Rites of passage.

Confiscation. Confiscat(e,ed,ing,ion,ory). Eminent domain. Expropriat(e,ed,ing, ation). Tak(e,en,ing) private property. *Consider also:* condemn(ed,ing,ation), seiz(e,ed,ing) *with:* land(s), propert(y, ies), real estate. *See also* Condemnation of buildings; Expropriation; Nationalization; Search and seizure.

Conflict. Conflict(ing,s). Controvers(y,ies, ial). Disagree(d,ing,ment,ments). Oppos(e,ed,ing,ition). Contend(ers,ing). Contest(ed,ing,ant,ants). Argu(e,ed, ing,ment,ments). Argument(ative,s). Quarrel(ed,ing,some). Feud(s,ing). Combat(ive). Disput(e,es,ed,ing). Contentious(ness). Confront(ed,ing, ation,ations). Rival(s,ry). Struggle(s). Dissen(t,sion). *Consider also:* social, cultural, international, ideological, religious *with:* conflict(s). *See also* Aggression; Alliances; Antisocial behavior; Arguments; Civil disorders; Coercion; Competition; Conflict of interest; Conflict resolution; Consensus; Controversial issues; Cultural conflict; Disarmament; Disputes; Dissent; Family conflict; Hostility; Ideological struggle; Industrial conflict; Intergroup relations; Internal conflict; International conflict; Interpersonal conflict; Marital conflict; Political repression; Power; Problems; Religious disputations; Resistance; Revolution; Riots; Role conflict; Sectarian conflict; Social conflict; Threat; Violence; War.

Conflict, class. See *Class conflict.*

Conflict, cultural. See *Cultural conflict.*

Conflict, ethnic. See *Cultural conflict.*

Conflict, family. See *Family conflict.*

Conflict, industrial. See *Industrial conflict.*

Conflict, interethnic. See *Cultural conflict.*

Conflict, intergroup. See *Social conflict.*

Conflict, internal. See *Internal conflict.*

Conflict, international. See *International conflict.*

Conflict, interpersonal. See *Interpersonal conflict.*

Conflict, interrole. See *Role conflict.*

Conflict, marital. See *Marital conflict.*

Conflict, religious. See *Sectarian conflict.*

Conflict, role. See *Role conflict.*

Conflict, sectarian. See *Sectarian conflict.*

Conflict, social. See *Social conflict.*

Conflict management. See *Conflict resolution.*

Conflict of generations. See *Generation gap; Intergenerational relations.*

Conflict of interest. Conflict(ing) interest(s). Ethical conflict(s). Illegal lobbying. Cronyism. Political plum(s). Dual loyalt(y,ies). Double dealing. Dual allegiance(s). Sweetheart deal(s). Collusion. Represent(ed,ing) both sides. Lobbying by former employee(s). Illegal campaign contribution(s). Partisan(ship). Lack of impartiality. Act(ed,ing) questionably. Lack of objectivity. Clubhouse politics. Peddl(e,ed,ing) influence. Improper influence. Insider trading. Violat(e,ed,ing,ion,ions) of confidentiality. *Choose from:* public official(s), government employee(s), Pentagon, Defense Department, HUD, government official(s), senator(s), congress(men,man,women,woman) *with:* favor(s), financial interest(s), stock(s), investment(s), share(s), award(ed,ing) contract(s), close ties, close relation(s,ship,ships), family ties, financial holdings, financial disclosure, honorar(ia,ium,iums), revolving door(s). *See also* Codes of ethics; Corruption in government; Ethics; Financial disclosure; Indecisiveness; Internal conflict; Judicial corruption; Legal ethics; Misconduct in office; Role conflict; Unethical conduct; White collar crime.

Conflict resolution. Conflict resolution(s). Reconcil(e,ed,iation). Mediat(e,ed,ing, ion). Arbitrat(e,ed,ing,ion). Reduc(e,ing) antagonism(s). *Choose from:* conflict(s), dispute(s), grievance(s) *with:* resolv(e, ed,ing), resolution(s), manag(e,ing, ement), reconcil(e,ed,iation), compromise(s), reduc(e,ing,tion), remov(e,ing), negotiat(ed,ing,ion,ions), handl(e,ed,ing), settl(e,ed,ing,ement, ements). *See also* Arbitrators; Arbitration; Cognitive processes; Conflict; Decision making; Dispute settlement; Forgiveness; Internal conflict; Interpersonal conflict; Interpersonal relations; Mediation; Negotiation; Peace; Peaceful change; Persuasion; Problem solving; Revolution; Social interaction.

Conformity (personality). Conform(ing, ity). Compliant personalit(y,ies). Susceptib(le,ility) to peer pressure. Need for approval. Deferen(ce,tial). Conventional(ity). Traditional(ism). *Consider also:* field dependence, external locus of control, suggestibility, comention. *See also* Nonconformity (personality); Other directed; Social behavior; Social conformity; Traditionalism.

Conformity, social. See *Social conformity.*

Confraternities. Confraternit(y,ies). Sodalit(y,ies). Brotherhood(s). Sisterhood(s). Fraternit(y,ies).

Sororit(y,ies). Fellowship(s). *Consider also:* voluntary association(s), cofradia. *See also* Clubs; Secret societies; Societies (organizations); Voluntary associations.

Confrontation. Confront(ation,ed,ing). Showdown(s). Encounter(ed,ing). *Consider also:* conflict(s), battle(s), dispute(s), facing, eye-to-eye, affront(s,ery), oppos(e,ed,ing,ition), resist(ed,ing,ance). *See also* Aggression; Assault (personal); Antisocial behavior; Arguments; Conflict; Controversial issues; Dissent; Polarization; Riots; Violence; War.

Confusion (disarray). Confus(ion,ing). Disarray(ed). Disorder(ed). Out of order. Out of sequence. Anarch(y,istic). Bedlam. Chao(s,tic). Clutter(ed). *Consider also:* havoc, misorder(ed), muddle(d), disarrange(d,ment), snafu, babel, din, hullabaloo, pandemonium, tumult(uous), turbulen(ce,t), untid(y, iness). *See also* Chaos; Lawlessness; Orderliness; Social disorganization; Riots.

Confusion, mental. See *Mental confusion.*

Congenital anomalies. See *Congenitally handicapped.*

Congenitally handicapped. Congenital(ly) handicap(s,ped). Abnormalit(y,ies). Deformit(y,ies). *Choose from:* congenital(ly), birth, neonatal, fetal, amniogenic *with:* disorder(s), defect(s), deformit(y,ies), malform(ed,ation, ations), deform(ed,ation,ations), handicap(s,ped,ping), impair(ed,ment, ments), anomal(y,ies), asymmetr(y,ies). *Consider also:* fetal disease(s), hereditary disease(s), genetic defect(s), teratogen(esis,icity), monster(s). *See also* Birth injuries; Brain damaged; Drug addicted babies; Drug induced abnormalities; Hereditary diseases; Human abnormalities; Physical abnormalities; Severely handicapped infants; Teratology.

Conglomerates. Conglomerat(e,es,ed,ing, ion,ions). Merg(e,er,ers,ing). Multicompany. Multi-industry. Multi-market. Joint concern(s). Trusts. Cartel(s). Corporate mergers. Consort(ia,ium, iums). *Choose from:* organization(s,al), corporat(e,ion,ions), business(es), hospital(s), agenc(y,ies) *with:* merg(e,er,ers,ing), acquisition(s), empire(s), takeover(s), partnership(s), amalgamat(ed,ion,ions), affiliat(e,ed, ing,ion,ions), chain(s), consolidat(e,ed, ing,ion,ions), consort(ia,ium,iums), federat(e,ed,ing,ion,ions). *Consider also:* congloperator(s), conglomerchant(s), big business(es), syndicate(s). *See also* Big business; Business organizations; Cartels; Corporate acquisitions; Corporations; Hostile takeovers; Merger integration; Mergers; Multinational corporations.

Congregate housing. See *Group homes.*

Congregations (church). Congregation(al, s). Church member(s,ship). Church community. Laity. Parishioner(s). Parish(es). *Consider also:* church-goer(s), Quaker meeting(s), assemblage(s). *See also* Audiences; Church attendance; Church membership; Parishes.

Congresses. Congress(es). Conference(s). Meeting(s). Caucus(es). Seminar(s). Staff meeting(s). Sympos(ia,ium). Convention(s). Assembl(y,ies,age,ages). Annual meeting(s). Council(s). Job fair(s). Trade show(s). World(s) fair(s). Exhibition(s). *See also* Information exchange; Legislative bodies; Professional development; Professional organizations.

Congressmen. See *Elected officials.*

Congresswomen. See *Elected officials.*

Congruence, self. See *Self congruence.*

Conjoint counseling. See *Cotherapy; Multiple psychotherapy.*

Conjugal. Conjugal(ly,ity). Marital. Matrimon(y,ial). Nuptial. Married. Wed(lock,ded). Spousal. Bridal. Connubial. Marriage(s). *See also* Marital relationship; Marriage.

Conjugal roles. See *Family roles; Sex roles; Sexual division of labor.*

Conjugal violence. See *Family violence; Battered women; Marital conflict; Spouse abuse.*

Conjuring. Conjur(e,ed,ing). Incantation(s). Bewitch(ed,ing). Cast a spell. *Choose from:* invok(e,ed,ing), summon(ed,ing), call(ed,ing) *with:* devil(s), spirit(s). *See also* Magic; Occultism; Voodooism.

Connectivity. Connectiv(e,ity). Interconnectiv(e,ity). Interconnection(s). Gateway(s). Junction(s). Link(s,ed,ing). *Consider also:* percolation process(es), receptiv(e,ity), connectionis(m,t). combinatorial design(s), seamless(ly, ness), transition(s). *See also* Computer networks; Data transmission systems; Information networks; Internet service providers; Synergy; Telecommunications.

Connoisseurs. Connoisseur(s,ship). Aesthete(s). Aficionado(s). Cognoscente(s). Epicure(s). Gourmet(s). Maven(s). Savant(s). *Consider also:* critic(s), dilettante(s), bon vivant(s). *See also* Aesthetics; Art appreciation; Art criticism; Experts; Gastronomy; Literary criticism; Specialists.

Consanguineous marriage. See *Endogamous marriage.*

Consanguinity. Consanguin(e,eal,eous,ity). Blood relative(s). Blood relation(s,ship,ships).

Geneolog(y,ies,ic,ical). Genealog(y,ies,ic,ical). Kin(ship). Inbreeding. Family tie(s). Common ancest(or,ors,ry). Near kin. Blood tie(s). *See also* Endogamous marriage; Kinship; Marriage; Incest.

Conscience. Conscience. Superego. Moral(ality,s). Ethic(al,s). Scruples. Moral sense. Ethical judgment. Moral development. Sense of right and wrong. Moral behavior(s). Moral standard(s). Guilt(y) feeling(s). *Consider also:* ego-ideal, conscientious objector(s), inner voice, integrity. *See also* Concepts; Examination of conscience; Guilt; Integrity; Moral development; Moral judgment; Moral obligation; Moral reasoning; Morality; Obligations; Shame; Superego; Values.

Conscience, examination of. See *Examination of conscience.*

Conscience, liberty of. See *Liberty of conscience.*

Conscience, unconscious. See *Superego.*

Conscientious objectors. Conscientious object(or,ors,ion). Pacifis(t,ts,m). Draft resister(s). Quaker(s). Draft nonregistrant(s). Object(ed,ing,ion,ions) to military service. War resist(er,ers, ance). War tax resist(er,ers,ance). Peace witness(es). *See also* Civil disobedience; Draft resisters; Liberty of conscience; Military service; Moral authority; Nonresistance to evil; Nonviolence; Pacifism; Peace movements; War attitudes.

Conscious (awake). Conscious(ness). Awake. Alert(ness). Lucid(ity). Aware(ness). Cognizant. Vigilan(t,ce). Wakeful(ness). Attent(ion,ive,iveness). *See also* Awareness; Unconscious.

Consciousness. See *Altered states of consciousness; Awareness; Conscious (awake); Unconscious.*

Consciousness, altered states of. See *Altered states of consciousness.*

Consciousness, class. See *Class consciousness.*

Consciousness, collective. See *Collective consciousness.*

Consciousness, cosmic. See *Enlightenment (state).*

Consciousness, group. See *Group consciousness.*

Consciousness, self. See *Self consciousness.*

Consciousness, social. See *Social consciousness.*

Consciousness, worker. See *Worker consciousness.*

Consciousness disorders. Consciousness disorder(s). Twilight state(s). Fugue(s). Aura(s). Diminished capacit(y,ies).

Choose from: consciousness *with:* disorder(s), disturbance(s), split(ting), level(s), disintegrat(e,ed,ing,ion), cloud(ed,ing), impair(ed,ment,ments). *Consider also:* autohypnosis, automatism, delir(ium,ious), disorient(ed,ation), dream state(s), clouding, confusion, coma(s), fugue state(s), hallucination(s), stupor, trance(s). *See also* Autohypnosis; Coma; Delirium; Disorientation; Hypnosis; Insomnia; Mental confusion; Narcolepsy; Place disorientation; Sleep disorders; Sleep talking; Sleepwalking; Time disorientation; Unconsciousness.

Consciousness raising activities. Consciousness raising activit(y,ies). *Choose from:* growth, consciousness raising, awareness, sensitivity, rap *with:* group(s), activit(y,ies), workshop(s), program(s). *See also* Awareness; Critical thinking; Encounter groups; Group dynamics; Group psychotherapy; Human potential movement; Mobilization; Sensitivity training.

Consensus. Consens(us,ual). General agreement. Solidarity. Accord. Agreement. Cohesion. Common consent. Assent. Unanim(ity,ous). Harmony. Concord. *See also* Agreement; Conflict; Conflict resolution; Consent (law); Disputes; Dissent; General will; Group discussion; Group dynamics; Legitimacy of governments; Political stability; Public opinion; Social cohesion.

Consent (law). Consent(ed,ing). Concurrence of wills. Voluntary yielding. Acquies(ence,ing). Voluntary compliance. Voluntary agreement. Approval. Willing(ness). *Consider also:* assent(ed, ing), age of consent, informed consent, parental consent. *See also* Age of majority; Agreement; Clearance (authorization); Consensus; Informed consent; Justification (law); Parental consent; Sexual consent.

Consent, informed. See *Informed consent.*

Consent, parental. See *Parental consent.*

Consent, sexual. See *Sexual consent.*

Consequences. Consequence(s). Effect(s). Result(s). Outcome(s). Sequel(ae). Repercussion(s). Aftereffect(s). By-product(s). Backlash. Outgrowth. Domino effect(s). Ripple effect(s). Side effect(s). Reaction(s). Aftermath. Response(s). Impact(s). *Consider also:* fallout, reverberation(s), spinoff(s), upshot(s). *See also* Causality; Effectiveness; Effects; Externalities; Failure; Forecasting; Goals; Means ends; Relevance; Results; Sequelae; Social impact; Spinoffs; Success; Treatment outcome.

Conservation, energy. See *Energy conservation.*

Conservation, forest. See *Forest conservation.*

Conservation, soil. See *Soil conservation.*

Conservation, water. See *Water conservation.*

Conservation, wildlife. See *Wildlife conservation.*

Conservation of natural resources.
Conservation of natural resources. Ecological behavior. Energy conservation. Conservation(ist,ists,ism). Ecolog(y,ist,ists). Environmentalis(m,t, ts). Wildlife refuge(s). Forever wild. Nature protection. *Choose from:* sav(e,ed,ing), conserv(e,ed,ing,ation), preserv(e,ed,ing,ation), defense, defend(ing,er,ers), protect(ed,ing,tion), maintain(ed,ing,ance), upkeep, safeguard(s,ed,ing), guard(s,ed,ing), monitor(ed,ing), reclaim(ed,ing), reclamation, reforest(ed,ing,ation), restor(e,ed,ing,ation), replant(ed,ing) *with:* environment(s), ecosystem(s), biosphere, soil, water, air, atmosphere, land, habitat(s), natural resource(s), woodland(s), forest(s), rain forest(s), swamp(s), wetland(s), desert(s), marsh(es), jungle(s), wildlife, animal(s), mammal(s), bird(s), insect(s), species, plant(s), tree(s), fish(es), reptile(s). *See also* Biosphere; Earth; Ecology; Energy conservation; Environment; Environmental pollution; Environmental protection; Environmentalism; Forestry; Forest conservation; Irrigation; Land use; Land preservation; Natural environment; Nonrenewable resources; Organic farming; Plant succession; Pollution control; Quality of life; Recycling; Reforestation; Renewable resources; Resource stress; Restoration ecology; Shore protection; Soil conservation; Submerged lands; Tree planting; Waste to energy; Water conservation; Wildlife conservation; Wildlife sanctuaries.

Conservatism, political. See *Political conservatism.*

Conservative. Conservative(ness). Conservatism. Traditional(ism,ization,ity). Hidebound. Law and order. Old regime(s). Stable societ(y,ies). Old belief(s). Conventional(ity). Conformity. Orthodox(y,ness). Conservative ideolog(y,ies). Moral majority. Reactionar(y,ies). Ultraconservat(ive, ism). Unprogressive. *Choose from:* resist(ed,ing), resistan(t,ce), oppos(e, ed,ing) *with:* change(s), reform(s). *See also* Absolutism; Conformity (personality); Dogmatism; Embourgeoisement; Liberalism; McCarthyism; Natural rights; Personality traits; Political conservatism; Religious fundamentalism; Right wing politics; Social conformity; Traditionalism.

Conservatories. Conservator(y,ies). Conservatoire(s). Konservatori(a,um). Hochschule fur Musik. *Consider also:* Royal Academy of Music, Royal College of Music, Juilliard School, Eastman School of Music, Peabody Conservatory, etc. *See also* Music education; Higher education.

Consistency. Consisten(t,cy). Undeviating. Unswerving. Staunch(ly). Unfailing. Reliab(le,ility). Dependab(le,ility). Unchanging. Stab(le,ility). Constancy. Unfailing. Steadfast(ness). Regular(ity). Fidelity. Safety. Security. Infallib(le, ility). Unquestionable. Indisputable. Incontestable. Uniform(ity). *Consider also:* agree(ing,ment), accord(ing,ant), concordant, congru(ence,ity,), consonant, compatib(le,ility), conform(ing), harmonious. *See also* Reliability.

Consolation. Consol(e,ed,ing,ation). Comfort(ed,ing). Solace. Compassion(ate). Sympath(etic,y,ize). Condol(e,ences). Commiserat(e,ed,ing). Reassur(e,ed,ing,ance,ances). Pacif(y, ying,ied). Assuage. Encourage(ed,ing, ment). Hearten(ed,ing). *See also* Helping behavior; Pity; Sympathy.

Consolidation. Consolidat(e,ed,ing,ion). Amalgamat(e,ed,ing,ion,ions). Blend(ed,ing). Centraliz(e,ed,ing,ation). Coalescen(t,ce). Condens(e,ed,ing, ation). Fus(e,ed,ing,ion,ions). Meld(ed, ing). Solidif(y,ying,ied,ication). Integrat(e,ed,ing,ion). Pool(ed,ing). *See also* Coalescence; Combinations; Industrial concentration; Merger integration; Mergers.

Consonants. Consonant(s,al). *Consider also:* semi-consonant(s,al), contoid(s). *See also* Articulation (speech); Letters (alphabet).

Consortia. Consort(ia,ium). Council(s). Network(s,ed,ing). System(s). Alliance(s). *See also* Affiliation (businesses); Alliances; Boundaryless organizations; Cartels; Cooperative education; Cooperatives; Corporate networks; Interinstitutional relations; Interorganizational networks; Joint ventures; Networks; Organizational affiliation; Organizations; Strategic alliances; Teaming.

Conspecific. Conspecific. Same species. Species specific(ity). Intraspecies. *Consider also:* congeneric. *See also* Animals.

Conspicuous consumption. See *Consumer society; Luxuries.*

Conspiracy. Conspir(e,ed,ing,acy,acies). Espionage. Spy(ing). Spie(s,d). Embezzl(e,ed,ing,ment). Fraud(ulent). Bribe(s,ry). Fix(ed,ing) price(s). Overcharg(e,ed,ing). *Choose from:* plot(ted,ting,s) *with:* overthrow, smuggl(e,ing), murder(s), kill. Illegal scheme(s). Kickback(s). Payoff(s). Defraud(ed,ing). Procurement scandal(s). Collusion. *See also* Collusion; Crime; Fraud; White collar crime.

Constancy. See *Commitment (emotional); Consistency; Dependability; Loyalty; Object permanence; Reliability.*

Constellations. Constellation(s). Asterism(s). Small group(s) of stars. Cluster(s) of stars. Configuration of stars. *Consider also:* galax(y,ies), Pleiades. *See also* Astronomy.

Constipation. Constipat(ed,ing,ion). Obstipat(ed,ing,ion). Defecation disorder(s). Bowel irregularit(y,ies). Fecal impaction(s). Impaction of bowel movement(s). Infrequent bowel movement(s). *See also* Gastrointestinal disorders.

Constituents. Constituen(t,ts,cy,cies). Voter(s). Elector(s,ate). Taxpayer(s). Citizen(s,ry). Resident(s) of district. Home district(s). Supporter(s). *Consider also:* special interest group(s). *See also* Interest groups; Legislators; Lobbying; Public support; Voters.

Constitution (legal). Constitution(s,al). Bylaw(s). Body of laws. Corpus juris. Charter(s). Legal code(s). Governing document(s). Rules. Ordinance(s). Fundamental laws. Rule by law. *See also* Bill of Rights; Charter; Civil rights; Codes (rules); Government publications; Laws; Legal documents; Legal rights; Legislation; Liberty; Provisional government.

Constitutional type. See *Somatotypes.*

Constraints. Constraint(s). Barrier(s). Restrict(ed,ing,ion,ions). Restrain(ed, ing,t,ts). Limit(ed,ing,ation,ations). Control(led,ling). Disciplin(e,ed,ing). Repress(ed,ing). Inhibit(ed,ing,ion,ions). Stifl(e,ed,ing). Suppress(ed,ing). *See also* Access to education; Access to information; Barriers; Boundaries; Demarcation; Encumbrance; Finite; Formal social control; Freedom; Informal social control; Hindrances; Inconvenience; Inhibition (psychology); Limitations; Needs; Opportunities; Political repression; Possibilities; Problems; Resources; Social conformity; Unmet needs.

Constraints, cultural. See *Informal Social control.*

Construct validity. Construct validity. *Choose from:* construct(s), concept(s, ion,ions), paradigm(s), assumption(s), typolog(y,ies), taxonom(y,ies), classificat(ion,ions,ory) *with:* valid(ity, ation), sound(ness). *See also* Constructs; Hypothesis testing; Measurement; Statistical correlation; Test validity; Validity.

Construction, financing. See *Financing construction.*

Construction, test. See *Test construction.*

Construction and design, facility. See *Facility design and construction.*

Construction industry. Construction industry. Home builder(s). Public works. General contractor(s). Building contractor(s). *Choose from:* construction *with:* project(s), firm(s), compan(y,ies). *Choose from:* highway(s), industrial, house(s), home(s), bridge(s), airport(s), warehouse(s), pier(s), rail yard(s), skyscraper(s), etc. *with:* construction, build(ing,er,ers), built. *Consider also:* cement industry, housing industry. *See also* Architecture; Building codes; Construction workers; Contractors; Drilling and boring; Facility design and construction.

Construction of reality, social. See *Social facts; Social meaning; Social reality.*

Construction workers. Construction worker(s). Hardhat(s). *Consider also:* bricklayer(s), cabinetmaker(s), carpenter(s), electrician(s), glazier(s), heavy equipment operator(s), housepainter(s), paperhanger(s), plasterer(s), plumber(s), roofer(s), woodworker(s). *See also* Blue collar workers; Construction industry.

Constructivism. Constructivis(m,t,ts). *Consider also:* Vladimir Tatlin, Alexander Rodchenko, Gustav Klutsis, El Lissitzky, Varvara Stepanova, Liubov Popova, Naum Gabo, Antoine Pevsner, Vsevold Meyerhold. *See also* Abstract art; Avant-garde; Dadaism; Modern architecture; Modern art; Modern literature; Suprematism.

Constructs. Construct(ion,ions,s). Axiom(atic,s). Concept(ion,s). Paradigm(s). Typolog(y,ies). Model(s, ing). Myth(s). Idea(s,tional). Notion(s). Abstraction(s). Conceptualization(s). Generalization(s). Hypothes(es,is). Inference. Theor(ies,y). Postulate(s). Social construct(ion,ions,s). Image(s). Ideal types. Label(s). Categor(y,ies, izations). Theme(s). Ideolog(y,ies). Representation(s). Assumption(s). *See also* Abstraction; Analysis; Assumptions; Concepts; Construct validity; Heuristics; Ideal types; Inference; Models; Paradigms; Research; Research design; Social types; Types.

Consular and diplomatic service. See *Diplomacy (official); Diplomats.*

Consuls. See *Diplomats.*

Consultants. Consultant(s). Consultative service(s). Counselor(s). Advisor(s). Expert(s). Professional advisor(s). *Consider also:* second opinion, confer(ring), expert advice, expert opinion. *See also* Advisors; Advisory committees; Change agents; Consultation; Counselors; Experts; Professional personnel; Technical assistance; Think tanks.

Consultation. Consult(s,ed,ing,ation, ations). Conference(s). Deliberation(s). Discussion(s). Meeting(s). Second opinion(s). Expert advice. Expert testimony. *See also* Advice; Consultants; Expert testimony; Interprofessional relations; Intervention; Referral; Remote consultation; Technical assistance.

Consultation, professional. See *Consultation.*

Consultation, remote. See *Remote consultation.*

Consume (economic). See *Consumption (economic).*

Consume (use). See *Consumption (use).*

Consumer advocates. See *Consumer organizations.*

Consumer awareness. Consumer awareness. *Choose from:* consumer(s), customer(s), client(s,ele), user(s), student(s), patient(s), buyer(s), patron(s), shopper(s), borrower(s), depositor(s), purchaser(s), passenger(s), constituenc(y,ies), prospect(s), tenant(s), end user(s) *with:* aware(ness), knowledge, information, inform(ed,ing), educat(ed,ing,ion), sophisticat(ed,ion), familiar(ity), understanding, experience(d), expertise, proficien(t,cy), adept(ness). *See also* Client education; Consumer education; Loyalty cards; Market development; Marketing strategies; Product labeling; Product liability; Product recall; Product tampering.

Consumer behavior. Consumer behavior(s). Consumerism. Buy(ing). Bought. Purchas(e,ed,ing). Shop(ped, ping). *Choose from:* product(s), brand(s) *with:* choice(s), loyalty, selection, switch(ed,ing), recognition. *Choose from:* consumer(s), customer(s), purchas(er,ers,ing), shopper(s), buyer(s), retail *with:* demand, spending, preference(s), choice(s), boycott(s), fashion(s), taste(s), psychology, style(s), behavior, expenditure(s), expectation(s), research, response(s), satisfaction, decision(s), judgment(s), reaction(s), concern(s), power, attitude(s), opinion(s), influence(s), right(s), advertising effect(s). *See also* Advertising research; Attitudes; Brand loyalty; Brand names; Client attitudes; Consumer satisfaction; Consumer participation; Demand; Loyalty cards; Market research; Purchasing; Test marketing.

Consumer credit. Consumer credit. Credit card(s). Charge account(s). Charge card(s). Layaway(s). *Choose from:* consumer(s), customer(s), shopper(s), personal, household, home equity, automobile(s) *with:* credit(or,ors), loan(s), lend(ing), borrow(ed,ing), debt(s,or,ors), interest rate(s), overdraft(s), past due account(s). *Consider also:* MasterCharge. MasterCard. VISA. Discover. *See also* Agricultural credit; Consumer expenditures; Debit card fraud; Interest (monetary); Loans.

Consumer directed care. Consumer directed care. Self directed care. Client centered care delivery. Autonomy in care. Voluntary care decision(s). *Choose from:* consumer(s), client(s), self, customer(s), patient(s) *with:* direct(ed, ing,ion), supervis(e,ed,ing,ion), plan(s,ned,ning), control(led,ling), hiring, paying, firing, preference(s), input, participation *with:* care, home care, care management, supportive service(s), assisted living service(s), assistance. *Consider also:* cash allowance(s) *with:* (services, assistive devices, home modifications, personal care, long term care). *See also* Alternatives to institutionalization; Assisted living; Community Health Services; Consumers; Home care; Patient rights; Personal independence; Supportive services.

Consumer economy. See *Consumer society.*

Consumer education. Consumer education. *Choose from:* consumer(s), customer(s), client(s,ele), user(s), student(s), patient(s), buyer(s), patron(s), shopper(s), borrower(s), depositor(s), purchaser(s), passenger(s), constituenc(y,ies), prospect(s), enduser(s), tenant(s) *with:* educat(ed,ing, ion), knowledge, information, inform(ed,ing), instruct(ed,ing,ion), teach(ing), taught, learn(ed,ing), handbook(s), manual(s), guide(s). *See also* Basic business education; Consumer awareness; Client education; Consumer protection; Marketing strategies; Patient education; Product labeling; Purchasing.

Consumer expenditures. Consumer expenditure(s). *Choose from:* consumer(s), customer(s), client(s,ele), user(s), student(s), patient(s), buyer(s), patron(s), shopper(s), borrower(s), depositor(s), purchaser(s), passenger(s), constituenc(y,ies), prospect(s), enduser(s), tenant(s) *with:* expenditure(s), expend(ed,ing), spend(ing), income allocation, financial strateg(y,ies), budget(s,ed,ing), credit, payment(s), paid, paying, outlay(ed,s), cost(s). *See also* Consumer credit; Consumer education; Consumer protection; Family budgets; Fares; Health expenditures; Purchasing.

Consumer fraud. Consumer fraud(ulence, ulent). Mail fraud. Questionable marketing practice(s). Lapping. Bait and switch. Hoax(es). Quack(ery,s). Ripoff(s). Scam(s). Sharp practice(s).

Switch selling. Bad faith. *Choose from:* deceit(ful), deceiv(e,ed,ing), decept(ion, ive), dishonest(y), fak(e,ed,ery,ing), false, falsif(y,ied,ication), improper, misrepresent(ed,ing,ation), unsubstantiated, puffery *with:* advertis(e,ed,ing, ements), commercial(s), claim(s), label(s,ed,ing), labell(ed,ing). *Consider also:* pirated *with:* edition(s), paper(s). *See also* Debit card fraud; Fraud; Fraudulent advertising; Product labeling; Product liability; Product recall; Product tampering.

Consumer goods. Consumer goods. *Choose from:* consumer, household, personal *with:* goods, product(s), durable(s), commodit(y,ies), item(s). *Consider also:* merchandise, nondurable goods, soft goods. *See also* Commodities; Consumer satisfaction; Durable goods; Imports; Luxuries; Manufacturers; Patents; Products.

Consumer information. See *Consumer awareness; Consumer education; Consumer protection; Product labeling.*

Consumer organizations. Consumer organization(s). *Choose from:* consumer(s), user(s), student(s), patient(s), buyer(s), patron(s), shopper(s), borrower(s), purchaser(s), tenant(s), neighborhood, enduser(s) *with:* organization(s), union(s), advocate(s), movement(s), association(s), group(s), federation(s), cooperative(s), co-op(s). *See also* Consumer protection; Environmentalism.

Consumer participation. Consumer participation. *Choose from:* consumer(s), citizen(s), customer(s), client(s,ele), user(s), student(s), patient(s), buyer(s), patron(s), shopper(s), patient(s), borrower(s), depositor(s), purchaser(s), constituenc(y,ies), prospect(s), enduser(s) *with:* power, participat(e,ed, ing,ion), involv(e,ed,ing,ement), role(s), activism, board(s), union(s), cooperative(s), co-op(s), pressure group(s), lobb(y,ies). *See also* Consumer awareness; Consumer behavior; Consumer organizations; Consumer protection; Consumer satisfaction; Focus groups.

Consumer protection. Consumer protection. Consumerism. Nader's Raiders. Ralph Nader. Consumer product safety. Better business bureau(s). Underwriters approval. Ombuds(man,men,women, woman). Advertising restrain(t,ts). Federal Trade Commission. *Choose from:* consumer(s), buyer(s), customer(s), client(s,ele), user(s), purchaser(s), enduser(s), tenant(s), passenger(s), depositor(s), patient(s), shopper(s), borrower(s) *with:* protection, rights, affairs, safety, warrant(y,ies), guarantee(s), safeguard(s), standards,

ombuds(men,man,women,woman), interest(s), satisfaction, advocacy. *Choose from:* product(s), service(s), food *with:* malpractice, inspection, evaluation(s), liability, full value, protection, label(s,led,ling), safety, warrant(y,ies), guarantee(s), standards. *See also* Accountability; Advertising; Advertising laws; Antitrust law; Client rights; Consumer education; Consumer fraud; Consumer organizations; Consumer participation; Corporate social responsibility; Deception; Food laws and legislation; Marketing; Product labeling; Product liability; Product recall; Product tampering; Purchasing; Safety.

Consumer research. See *Market research.*

Consumer satisfaction. Consumer satisfaction. *Choose from:* consumer(s), customer(s), client(s), user(s), student(s), patient(s), buyer(s), patron(s), clientele, shopper(s), borrower(s), depositor(s), purchaser(s), passenger(s), constituenc(y,ies), end user(s) *with:* satisfaction, satisf(y,ied), opinion(s), rating(s), attitude(s), content(ed,ment), loyalty, support(ed,ing), enjoy(ed,ing, ment). *See also* Brand loyalty; Client attitudes; Client relations; Consumer behavior; Customer relations; Customer services; Market research; Patient dropouts; Public support; Service contracts; Student dropouts.

Consumer society. Consumer societ(y,ies). Consumer economy. Material(istic,ism). Admass. Affluent societ(y,ies). *Consider also:* conspicuous consumption, status symbol(s). *See also* Consumption (economic); Consumers; Embourgeoisement; Mass society; Shopping centers; Western society.

Consumer spending. See *Consumer expenditures.*

Consumer surveys. See *Market research.*

Consumerism. See *Consumer protection.*

Consumers. Consumer(s). Customer(s). Client(s,ele). Market segment(s). User(s). Student(s). Patient(s). Outpatient(s). Buyer(s). Patron(s). Shopper(s). Borrower(s). Depositor(s). Purchaser(s). Passenger(s). Constituenc(y,ies). Prospect(s). Enduser(s). Seeker(s). Tenant(s). Vendee(s). *Choose from:* affluent, African American, Asian American, baby boom(er), ethnic, gay, Generation X, hispanic, mature, minorit(y,ies), wom(an,en), youth, potential, etc. *with:* client(s), consumer(s), customer(s), buyer(s), purchaser(s), sale(s). *See also* Brand loyalty; Consumer awareness; Consumer behavior; Consumer credit; Consumer directed care; Consumer education; Consumer expenditures; Consumer fraud; Consumer goods; Consumer organizations; Consumer

participation; Consumer protection; Consumer satisfaction; Consumer society; General public; Homosexual consumers; Market research; Market size; Marketing; Markets; Merchants; Products; Purchasing; Retailing; Sales; Shopping centers; Stores.

Consumers, homosexual. See *Homosexual consumers.*

Consumption (economic). Consum(e,ed, ption). Consumer behavior(s). Buy(ing). Bought. Economic behavior(s). Expend(ed,ing,iture,itures). Consumer life style(s). Shop(ped,ping). Purchas(e, es,ed,ing). *See also* Commodities; Consumer credit; Consumer goods; Consumers; Consumption (use); Distributive justice; Economics; Expenditures; Living standards; Luxuries; Markets; Prices; Production; Production consumption relationship; Purchasing; Sales; Saving; Scarcity; Trade; Utilization; Wealth.

Consumption (use). Consum(e,ed,ing, ption). Use(d). Using. Utiliz(e,ed,ing, ation). Deplet(e,ed,ing,ion). Wast(e,ed, ing). Devour(ed,ing). Dissipat(e,ed,ion). Misus(e,ed,ing). Spend(ing). Spent. *See also* Conservation of natural resources; Consumer society; Consumption (economic); Energy conservation; Energy consumption; Lifestyle; Luxuries; Scarcity; Utilization; Wasteful.

Consumption, alcohol. See *Alcohol drinking.*

Consumption, conspicuous. See *Consumer society; Luxuries.*

Consumption, energy. See *Energy consumption.*

Consumption, food. See *Food intake.*

Consumption production relationship. See *Production consumption relationship.*

Contact, body. See *Physical contact.*

Contact, culture. See *Culture contact.*

Contact, eye. See *Eye contact.*

Contact, intergroup. See *Social contact.*

Contact, languages in. See *Languages in contact.*

Contact, physical. See *Physical contact.*

Contact, social. See *Social contact.*

Contagion, social. See *Social contagion.*

Containers. Container(s). Holder(s). Receptacle(s). *Consider also:* bag(s), batch(es), bin(s), bottle(s), bowl(s), box(es), bucket(s), bundle(s), can(s), cannister(s), carton(s), case(s), crate(s), package(s), packaging, packet(s), parcel(s), pot(s), pouch(es), sack(s), storage tank(s), vat(s), wrapper(s). *See also* Bags; Containment of biohazards; Food storage; Litter (waste); Luggage;

Pollution control; Recycling; Shipping industry; Storage.

Containment, cost. See *Cost control.*

Containment of biohazards. Contain(s,ed, ing,ment) of biohazard(s). *Choose from:* contain(s,ed,ing,ment), regulat(e,es,ed, ing,ion,ions), guideline(s), control(s, led,ling) disposal *with:* biohazard(s), pathogen(s), DNA, hospital waste(s), medical waste(s), biological hazard(s). *See also* Containers; Decontamination; Hazardous occupations; Medical wastes; Pollution control; Restoration ecology; Waste spills.

Contamination. Contaminat(e,ed,ion). Impur(e,ity,ities). Dirt(y,ied,iness). Infect(ed). Pollut(e,ed,ion). Soil(ed). Radioactive. Spoil(ed). Spoliation. Taint(ed). Tarnish(ed). Unclean(ness). Filth(y,iness). Miasma(s). Defil(e,ed, ing,ement). *See also* Atmospheric contamination; Environmental pollution; Food contamination; Hazardous materials; Hazardous wastes; Ritual purity;.

Contamination, atmospheric. See *Atmospheric contamination.*

Contamination, food. See *Food contamination.*

Contemplation. Contemplat(e,ed,ing, ion,ive). Reflect(ed,ing,ion,ive). Recollect(ed,ing,ion,ions). Spiritual attention. Spiritual listening. Lectio divina. Centering. Prayer. Spiritual exercise(s). *See also* Meditation.

Contemplative orders. Contemplative order(s). Ordre(s) contemplatif(s). Contemplative discipline(s). Women contemplative. Religious order(s) devoted to prayer and penance *Choose from:* contemplative, cloistered *with:* life, lives, monasticism, nun(s), monk(s), retreat(s), abbey(s), religious women. *Consider also:* Carthusians, Benedictines, Bridgettines, Cistercians, religieuse(s) contemplative(s). *See also* Cloisters; Military religious orders; Monasticism; Monks; Nuns; Religious life; Roman Catholicicism;.

Contemporaries. Contemporar(y,ies). Peer(s). Peer group(s). Friend(s). Neighbor(s). Colleague(s). Reference group(s). Classmate(s). Cohort(s). Co-worker(s). Agemate(s). Playmate(s). Play group(s). Equals. Compeer(s). Companion(s). Fellow. Partner(s). Associate(s). Social group(s). Gang(s). *Consider also:* peer relations, subculture(s), equal status. *See also* Cohorts; Colleagues; Peers; Reference groups.

Contemporary music. See *Twentieth century Western art music.*

Contemporary society. See *Modern society.*

Contempt. Contempt(uous). Disdain(ful). Scorn(ful). Derision. Derid(e,ed,ing). Disapprov(al,e,ed,ing). Disrespect(ful). Hate(d,s). Hatred. Hating. Hostil(e,ity). Abhor(rence). Loath(e,ed,ing). Abominat(e,ed,ing,ion). Despis(e,ed, ing). Detest(ed,ing). Dislik(e,ed,ing). Animosity. Malevolen(t,ce). Aversion. Grudg(e,es,ing). Distaste. Ill will. Enmity. Antipathy. Repugnance. Intoleran(t,ce). *See also* Anger; Contempt of Court; Derision; Disgust; Emotions; Interpersonal conflict; Intolerance; Otherness; Repugnance; Social distance.

Contempt of Court. Contempt of Court. Direct contempt. Constructive contempt. Civil contempt. Criminal contempt. *Choose from:* embarrass(ed,ing,ment), hinder(ed,ing), obstruct(ed,ing), contraven(e,ed,ing,tion), imped(e,ed, ing), frustrat(e,ed,ing,ion), fail(s,ed, ing,ure) to compl(y,ance), *with:* justice, court, injunction(s), decree(s), due process(es). *See also* Arrests; Bail; Contempt; Criminal proceedings; Detention; Due process; Fugitives from justice; Law enforcement; Legal procedures; Obstruction of justice; Plea bargaining; Withholding evidence.

Content. Content(s). Contain(ed,ing). Subject(s). Substance(s). Image(s). Idea(s). Meaning(s). Constitu(te,ted,ent). Component(s). Ingredient(s). Topic(s). Text(s). *See also* Components; Form (aesthetics); Formalism.

Content, emotional. See *Emotional content.*

Content, thought. See *Cognitions.*

Content analysis. Content analy(sis,ses,zing). Subject analy(sis,ses,zing). *Choose from:* content(s), message(s), writing(s), document(s,ary,aries), speech(es) *with:* analy(sis,ses,zing), explicat(e,ed,ion), interpret(ed,ation,ations,ive), clarif(y, ied,ication), concordance(s), content analys(is,es), criticism, critique(s,d), explanation(s), classif(y,ied,ication). *See also* Communication (thought transfer); Communications research; Data analysis; Discourse analysis; Evaluation; Literary criticism; Literary research; Messages; Research methods; Task performance and analysis.

Content integration. See *Multicultural education.*

Contentiousness. Contentious(ness). Argumentative(ness). Quarrelsome(ness). Disputatious(ness). Combative(ness). *Consider also:* belligeren(t,ce), antagonistic, hostile. *See also* Aggressiveness (trait); Arguments.

Contentment. Content(ed,edness,ment). Wellbeing. Well-being. Tranquil(ity).

Happ(y,iness). Seren(e,ity). Peace of mind. Satisf(ying,ied,action). Gratif(ying,ied,ication). *See also* Calmness; Comfortableness; Life satisfaction; Physical comfort; Quality of life.

Contests. Contest(s,ed,ing,ant,ants). Athletic event(s). Card game(s). Competition(s). Duel(s). Game(s). Match(es). Meet(s). Race(s). Regatta(s). Rivalr(y,ies). Spelling bee(s). Tournament(s). Tug-of-war. *Consider also:* contend(ing,er,ers), vie(d), vying. *See also* Athletic participation; Competition; Primaries; Sports.

Context. Context(s,ual,uality,ism). Connection(s). Interconnection(s). Environment(s,al). Setting(s). Condition(s). Climate. Surrounding(s). Proxemic. Proximity. Ecolog(ical,y). Ambience. Milieu. Circumstance(s). Frame(s) of reference. Frame(work, works). *See also* Ambience; Classroom environment; Crowding; Cultural ethos; Extenuating circumstances; Historical perspective; Home environment; Periodization; Social environment; Social isolation; Synchronism; Working conditions; Worldview; Zeitgeist.

Context, social. See *Social environment.*

Contextualization. See *Context.*

Continence. See *Abstinence; Asceticism; Sexual abstinence; Temperance.*

Continental drift. Continent(s,al) drift(ed,ing). *Choose from:* continent(s, al), terrane(s) *with:* drift(ed,ing), exten(sion,d,ded), rift(ed,ing), breakup(s), collid(e,ed,ing). *Consider also:* plate motion(s), plate tectonic(s), megatectonic(s). *See also* Geology.

Contingency. Contingen(cy,cies,t). Juncture(s). Crossroad(s). Cris(is,es) of confidence. Emergenc(y,ies). Exigenc(y,ies). Pinch. Dire strait(s). Turning point(s). Zero hour(s). Opportunit(y,ies). Juncture(s). Exigenc(y,ies). Crucial time(s). Critical state(s). Critical time(s). *See also* Behavior contracting; Behavior modification; Chance; Opportunities; Possibilities; Turning points.

Contingent workers. See *Temporary employees.*

Continuation. Continuation(s). Continu(e,ed,ing). Addition(s). Appendi(x,ces). Epilog(s,ue,ues). Extension(s). Installment(s). Postscript(s). Sequel(s). Supplement(s). Prolongation(s). Protraction(s). *See also* Addendum; Epilogues; Persistence; Periodicals; Sequelae.

Continuing education. Continuing education. *Choose from:* continuing, postdoctoral, refresher, postgraduate, advanced, postemployment, inservice, lifelong, retrain(ed,ing), re-entry *with:* education, fellowship(s), course(s), training, learning. *Consider also:* correspondence course(s), adult education, older learner(s). *Choose from:* continuing, inservice *with:* professional education, dental education, medical education, nursing education, teacher education. *See also* Adult education; Correspondence schools; Lifelong learning; Nontraditional education; Reentry students.

Continuity. Continuit(y,es). Continuation. Continuous(ness). Uninterrupted. Unbroken. Connect(ed,ion). Cohesi(ve,veness,on). Linkage(s). Interrelated(ness). Articulation. Continuum. Contiguity. Perpetu(al,ity). Stable. Stability. *See also* Continuity of patient care; Durability; Permanent; Security; Social equilibrium; Stability.

Continuity of patient care. Continuity of patient care. *Choose from:* continuity, continuum, continuing, follow-up, follow up, post discharge *with:* patient care, health care, medical care, ambulatory care, therap(y,ies), psychotherap(y,ies), treatment. *See also* Patient care planning.

Contraception. Contracept(ion,ive,ives). Birth control. Contraceptive implant(s). Conception control. *Consider also:* vasectom(y,ies), intrauterine device(s), IUD(s), condom(s), diaphragm(s), spermatocid(e,es,al), tubal ligation, rhythm method, coitus interruptus, antispermatogenic agents, steriliz(e,ed, ing,ation). *Choose from:* pregnanc(y,ies), conception *with:* prevent(ed,ing,ion). *See also* Abortion; Birth control; Family planning; Family planning attitudes; Oral contraceptives; Pregnancy; Reproductive rights; Rhythm method; Sex education.

Contraception, emergency. See *Emergency contraception.*

Contraceptive devices, female. See *Female contraceptive devices.*

Contraceptives. See *Oral contraceptives; Contraception.*

Contraceptives, oral. See *Oral contraceptives.*

Contract, social. See *Social contract.*

Contract labor. Contract labor. Contract employee(s). Contract researcher(s). Freelancer(s). Portfolio career(s). Freelance work(er,ers). Portfolio work(er,ers). Portfolio employment. Contract help. *Choose from:* contract, temporary, freelance, contingent *with:* job(s), work, worker(s), employment, labor, employee(s). *Consider also:* labor pool(s), peonage, mercenary soldier(s). *See also* Alternative work patterns; Cheap labor; Contracting out; Independent contractors; Temporary employees.

Contract services. Contract(ed,ing) service(s). Quasi-firm(s). *Choose from:* contract(ed,ing), agreement(s), subscription(s), subscrib(e,ed,ing), prepaid *with:* school(s), service(s), patient provider(s), care, clinic(s), program(s). *Consider also:* management contract(s), group price(s), contract award(s), contract managed, satellite organization(s). *See also* Contractors; Contracts; Independent contractors; Privatization.

Contract workers. See *Independent contractors.*

Contracting, behavior. See *Behavior contracting.*

Contracting out. Contract(ed,ing) out. Contract(ed,ing) in. Outsourc(e,ed,ing). Insourc(e,ed,ing). Farm(ed,ing) out. *Consider also:* subcontract(ed,ing), rightsiz(e,ed,ing), manufactur(e,ed,ing) elsewhere, workforce imbalance correction(s), sublet(ting) operation(s), outside supplier(s). *See also* Adhocracies; Border industries; Boundaryless organizations; Budget cuts; Contract labor; Decentralization; Downsizing; Industrial cooperation; Interorganizational networks; Labor economics; Labor market; Offshore factories (floating); Offshore production (foreign countries). Personnel termination; Privatization; Reengineering; Reorganization; Shared services; Strategic alliances; Subcontracting; Virtual organizations.

Contractors. Contractor(s). Builder(s). *Consider also:* architect(s), constructor(s), planner(s), coordinator(s), jobber(s), middlem(an,en). *See also* Construction industry; Contracting services; Contracts; Employers.

Contractors, independent. See *Independent contractors.*

Contracts. Contract(s,ed,ing,ual). Compact(s). Agreement(s). Written agreement(s). Signed agreement(s). Guarantee(s). Covenant(s). Pact(s). Treat(y,ies). Concordat(s). Deed(s). Lease(s). Subscription(s). Insurance polic(y,ies). *Consider also:* legal protection. *See also* Agreement (document); Behavior contracting; Contract services; Contractors; Discharge of contracts; Earnest money; Guarantees; Learning contracts; Legal documents; Treaties.

Contracts, discharge of. See *Discharge of contracts.*

Contracts, learning. See *Learning contracts.*

Contracts, marriage. See *Marriage contracts.*

Contracts, prenuptial. See *Marriage contracts.*

Contradictions. Contradict(ory,ion,ions). Contralogical. Paradox(es,ical). Incongruit(y,ies). Incongruous(ness). Inherent opposition. Inconsisten(t,cy). Disparit(y,ies). Discrepan(t,cy,cies). Contrar(y,iness). Discordant. Controvers(y,ies,ion). Negat(e,eed, ing,ion). Refut(e,ed,ing). Quandar(y,ies). *See also* Arguments; Conflict; Dialectics; Disputes; Dissent; Oxymoron; Paradoxes; Refutation.

Contredanse. Contredanse(s). Kontertanz(e). Contratanz(es). Contraddanz(a). Contradanz(a). *Consider also:* quadrille(s), cotillon(s), cotillion(s). *See also* Country dance; Dance.

Contributions. Contribut(e,ed,ing,ion,ions). Donor(s), Donat(e,ed,ion,ions). Gift(s). Present(s). Honorar(ia,ium,iums). Endowment(s). Bequest(s). Gratuit(y, ies). Bestowal. Giving aid. Altruis(m, tic). Giv(e,ing) help. Charit(able,y,ies). Generous. Generosity. Gift giving. Assist(ance,ed,ing). Philanthrop(y,ic). Benefactor(s). Voluntary contribution(s). *Choose from:* charitable, political, financial *with:* contribution(s), donation(s). *See also* Assistance; Charitable behavior; Charities; Endowments; Financial support; Gift giving; Giving; Philanthropy; Political contributions; Volunteers.

Contributions, political. See *Political contributions.*

Control. Control(led,ling). Restrain(ed,ing, t). Regulat(e,ed,ing). Curb(ed,ing). Restrict(ed,ing,ion,ions). Constrain(ed, ing). Prohibit(ed,ion,ions). Contain(ed, ment). Direct(ed,ing,ion). Forbid(den). Prevent(ed,ing,ion). Suppress(ed,ing, ion). Maintain(ed,ing) order. Disciplin(e, ed,ing,ary). Regiment(ed,ing,ation). Rul(e,ed,ing). Supervis(e,ed,ing,ory). Law enforcement. Law and order. Sanction(s). Inhibit(ed,ing). Repress(ed, ing,ion). Coerci(ve,on). Oppress(ed,ing, ion). *Consider also:* pacif(y,ied,ication), manipulat(e,ed,ing,ion). *See also* Air traffic control; Arms control; Brainwashing; Coercion; Cost control; Dominance subordination; Drug and narcotic control; Emotional control; Facility regulation and control; Flood control; Formal social control; Gun control; Influence; Informal social control; Locus of control; Management methods; Oppression; Physical restraint; Political repression; Pollution control; Population control; Power; Power sharing; Price control; Quality control; Records management; Regulation Security; Self control; Stability; Weather control; Weight control; Worker control.

Control, air traffic. See *Air traffic control.*

Control, arms. See *Arms control.*

Control, birth. See *Birth control.*

Control, corporate. See *Corporate control.*

Control, cost. See *Cost control.*

Control, drug and narcotic. See *Drug and narcotic control.*

Control, emotional. See *Emotional control.*

Control, flood. See *Flood control.*

Control, formal social. See *Formal social control.*

Control, gun. See *Gun control.*

Control, informal social. See *Informal social control.*

Control, internal external. See *Locus of control.*

Control, locus of. See *Locus of control.*

Control, pollution. See *Pollution control.*

Control, population. See *Population control.*

Control, price. See *Price control.*

Control, production. See *Production control.*

Control, quality. See *Quality control.*

Control, records. See *Records management.*

Control, rent. See *Rent control.*

Control, self. See *Self control.*

Control, social. See *Formal social control; Informal social control.*

Control, thought. See *Brainwashing.*

Control, weather. See *Weather control.*

Control, weight. See *Weight control.*

Control, worker. See *Worker control.*

Control and regulation, facility. See *Facility regulation and control.*

Control centers, poison. See *Poison control centers.*

Control disorders, impulse. See *Impulse control disorders.*

Control groups (research). Control group(s). *Choose from:* control *with:* group(s), population(s), subject(s), condition(s). *Consider also:* experimental control(s), double blind method. *See also* Participants; Research subjects; Research design; Sampling.

Control systems, feedback. See *Cybernetics; Feedback; Robotics.*

Controlled vocabulary. Controlled vocabular(y,ies). *Choose from:* controlled, standard(ized), taxonom(y,ies) *with:* term(s,inology,inologies), language(s), vocabular(y,ies), descriptor(s), heading(s). *Consider also:* thesaur(i,us). *See also* Subject headings; Terminology.

Controlling suburban growth. See *Growth management.*

Controls, experiment. See *Experiment controls.*

Controversial issues. Controversial issue(s). Controvers(y,ies). Dispute(s). Difference(s) of opinion. Contention. Controvertible. Dissen(t,sion). Disagreement(s). *Choose from:* controversial, disputed, disputable, hot, hot button, debat(ed,able) *with:* issue(s), topic(s), subject(s), idea(s). *See also* Conflict; Controversial literature; Dissent; Moral reasoning; Political issues; Religious disputations; Sex education; Social change; Social problems; Values; World problems.

Controversial literature. Controversial literature. *Choose from:* controversial, disputed, disputable, hot, hot button, debat(ed,able), polemical, factious, inflammatory, incendiary, provocative *with:* literature, writing(s), book(s), play(s), work(s), publication(s), tract(s), leaflet(s), handout(s), circular(s), brochure(s). *See also* Controversial issues; Literature; Propaganda.

Controversy. See *Controversial issues.*

Convalescence. Convalescen(t,ce). Recover(y,ies,ed,ing). Recuperat(e,ed, ing,ive,ion). Reviv(e,ed,ing). Rehabilitat(e,ed,ing,ion). *Choose from:* return(ing,ed), restor(e,ed,ing), regain(ed,ing) *with:* health, strength, function(s), normal(ity). *See also* Recovery; Rehabilitation.

Convenience foods. Convenience food(s). Take out food(s). Ready to eat. Home meal replacement(s). Prepared food(s). Food mix(es). *Choose from:* prepared, takeout, pre-cut, pre-cooked, pre-washed, ready to serve, pre-mixed, pre-packaged, bagged, ready to eat, microwaveable, frozen *with:* meal(s), food(s), salad(s), dinner(s), pizza(s). *Consider also:* delicatessen(s), fast food restaurant(s), take out food service, burger(s), junk food. *See also* Diet; Eating; Food; Food additives; Food habits; Junk food; Nutrition; Popular culture.

Conventionalism. See *Authoritarianism (psychological); Conformity (personality); Embourgeoisement.*

Conventions. See *Congresses.*

Convents. Convent(s). Cloister(s). Monaster(y,ies). Monastic seminar(y, ies). Nunner(y,ies). Abbey(s). Prior(y, ies). Religious communit(y,ies). Lamaser(y,ies). Priorate(s). *See also* Holy women; Monasticism; Nuns; Places of worship; Religious communities; Religious institutions; Religious life; Women religious.

Conversation. Convers(e,ed,ing,ation, ational). Dialogue(s). Talk(ed,ing). Discourse. *Choose from:* verbal, interpersonal *with:* exchange(s), communication(s), interaction(s). *Consider also:* monologue(s). *See also* Communication (thought transfer); Conversational analysis; Discussion; Gossip; Imaginary conversations; Rumors; Self expression; Social interaction; Telephone; Verbal communication.

Conversational analysis. Conversational analysis. *Choose from:* convers(e,ed, ing,ation,ational), discourse, dialogue(s), monologue(s), speech(es), laughter, speaker(s), talk(ed,ing), communication(s) *with:* analys(is,es), analyz(e, ed,ing), examin(e,ed,ing,ation,ations), investigat(e,ed,ing,ation,ations). *See also* Content analysis; Conversation; Ethnomethodology; Social interaction; Transactional analysis; Verbal communication.

Conversations, imaginary. See *Imaginary conversations.*

Conversion (change). See *Change; Metamorphosis.*

Conversion, biomass. See *Alternative energy; Energy generating resources.*

Conversion, religious. See *Religious conversion.*

Conversion, year 2000 date. See *Millennium bug.*

Conversion disorder. Conversion disorder(s). Conversion hysteria. Astasia-abasia. Hysterical ataxia. Globus hystericus. Esophageal neuroses. Hysterical conversion neurosis. *Choose from:* conversion, hyster(ia,ical) *with:* disorder(s), neuros(is,es), reaction(s), blindness, paralysis, ataxia, anesthesia, vision disturbance(s), fixation. *Consider also:* functional, nonorganic, psychogenic *with:* disorder(s), symptom(s), ailment(s), disabilit(y,ies), pain(s). *See also* False pregnancy; Functional hearing loss; Hysterical anesthesia; Hysterical paralysis; Hysterical vision disturbances; Hysteria; Mind body problem; Psychogenic pain; Psychophysiologic disorders; Somatoform disorders.

Convict labor. Convict labor(ers). Prison labor. Prison industr(y,ies). Prison workshop(s). Prison shop(s). *Choose from:* prison(er,ers), inmate(s) *with:* work(ed,ing), labor camp(s), roadwork, chain gang(s), employment. *Consider also:* prison made goods, Ashurst-Sumners Act. *See also* Convicts; Ex-offenders; Labor supply; Offenders.

Conviction. Conviction(s). Verdict(s). Decision(s). Judgment(s). Determination(s). Resolution(s). Settlement(s). Finding(s). Opinion(s). Ruling(s). Conclusion(s). Decree(s). Edict(s). Answer(s). Adjudication. *See also* Acquittal; Blameworthy; Court opinions; Guilt; Legal system; Sentencing; Sufficient evidence.

Convicts. Convict(s). Prison inmate(s). *Choose from:* convicted *with:* offender(s), criminal(s), gangster(s), mobster(s), smuggler(s), violator(s), felon(s), racketeer(s), rapist(s), murderer(s), thie(f,ves), drug lord(s), embezzler(s), burglar(s). *See also* Convict labor; Criminal rehabilitation; Ex-offenders; Fugitives from justice; Offenders.

Convoys. Convoy(s). Travel(ing,ling,ed,led) as a pack. *Choose from:* escort(ed,ing), accompan(y,ies,ie) *with:* armed, submarine(s), protect(ion,ive), ship(s), nav(y,al), military, police, truck(s). *Consider also:* patrol(s), safeguard(s,ed), shield(s,ed), usher(ed,s). *See also* Caravans; Entourage; Protection; Transportation; Warships.

Convulsions. Convuls(ive,ion,ions). *Consider also:* eclampsia, epileptic seizure(s), audiogenic seizure(s), fit(s), spasm(s). *See also* Epileptic seizures; Convulsive therapy.

Convulsive therapy. Convulsive therap(y,ies). *Choose from:* convulsive, electroconvulsive, shock, insulin-shock, insulin-coma, Sakels therapy, ECT *with:* therap(y,ies), treatment(s). *See also* Convulsions.

Cookery. See *Cooking; Food preparation.*

Cooking. Cook(ed,ing,ery). Food preparation. Culinary art(s). Food processing. Meal creation. *Choose from:* meal(s), food, dinner(s), lunch(es,eons), breakfast(s), diet(s,ary) *with:* prepar(e, ed,ing,ation), process(e,ed,ing), cook(ed,ing). *Consider also:* broil(ed, ing), brais(e,ed,ing), boil(ed,ing), bak(e,ed,ing), fry(ing), fried, melt(ed, ing), microwav(e,ed,ing). *See also* Baking; Food preparation; Gastronomy; Homemaker services; Nutrition.

Cooperation. Cooperat(e,ed,ing,ive,ion). Co-operat(e,ed,ing,ive,ion). Coalition formation. Compliance. Collaborat(e,ed, ing,ion,ive). Teamwork. Teamplay. Reciprocal. Confederate(s). Combined action. Work(ed,ing) together. Division of labor. Symbio(sis,tic). Synerg(y, istic,ism). Mutuality. Mutual interest(s). Join(ed,ing) forces. Unite(d) effort(s). Joint effort(s). Joint action(s). Collusion. Conspiring. Act(ed,ing) in harmony. Turn taking. Network(s,ed,ing). Partner(s,ship,ships). Workshar(e,ed, ing). Accord(s). Joint research. Consort(ia,ium). Co-produc(e,ed,ing, tion,tions). *Consider also:* quilting bee(s), barn raising(s), cooperative gathering(s). *See also* Alliances; Altruism; Coalitions; Competition; Compliance; Consultation; Cooperative learning; Coordination (interpersonal); Goals; Industrial cooperation; Intellec-

tual cooperation; Intercommunity cooperation; Intergroup relations; Interinstitutional relations; International cooperation; Interpersonal relations; Interstate cooperation; Library cooperation; Networks; Partners; Power sharing; Prosocial behavior; Reciprocity; Sharing; Social behavior; Social exchange; Social interaction; Social reinforcement; Social support networks; Teaming; Teamwork; Trusting; Trustworthy.

Cooperation, cultural. See *Cultural cooperation.*

Cooperation, industrial. See *Industrial cooperation.*

Cooperation, intellectual. See *Intellectual cooperation.*

Cooperation, interagency. See *Interinstitutional relations.*

Cooperation, intercommunity. See *Intercommunity cooperation.*

Cooperation, interdenominational. See *Interdenominational cooperation.*

Cooperation, international. See *International cooperation.*

Cooperation, interstate. See *Interstate cooperation.*

Cooperation, library. See *Library cooperation.*

Cooperative agriculture. See *Agricultural collectives.*

Cooperative behavior. See *Cooperation.*

Cooperative education. Cooperative education. *Choose from:* cooperative *with:* education, training, *Consider also:* work study *with:* experience, program(s). *See also* Practical experience; Vocational education; Work experience.

Cooperative gatherings. See *Cooperation.*

Cooperative learning. Cooperative learning. *Choose from:* Cooperative, teamwork, interdependent, small group(s), subgroup(s), collaborative, shared *with:* learning, classroom, classwork, course(s), assignment(s), homework. *See also* Active learning; Cooperation; Group instruction; Group problem solving; Humanistic education; Peer teaching.

Cooperativeness. See *Cooperation.*

Cooperatives. Cooperative(s). Condominium(s). Co-op(s). Credit union(s). *Choose from:* cooperative(s), co-operative(s) *with:* consumer, agricultural, credit, producer, industrial, hous(ing,holds), food, bank(s,ing), retirement, home(s), care, movement, marketing. *Consider also:* Rochdale Society of Equitable Pioneers, Mondragon. *See also* Agricultural collectives; Cohousing; Collectivism;

Common lands; Common ownership; Communes; Employee ownership; Employee stock ownership plans; Enterprises; Industrial democracy; Marketing; Ownership; Participative decision making; Purchasing; Worker control; Worker participation.

Cooptation. Coopt(ed,ing,ation,ive). Co-opt(ed,ing,ation,ive). Preempt(ion,ive). Appropriat(e,ed,ing,ion). Arrogat(e,ed, ing,ion). Confiscat(e,ed,ing,ion). Usurp(ed,ing). *Consider also:* high handed(ness), peremptory. *See also* Adjustment (to environment); Assimilation (cultural); Change agents; Group dynamics; Group identity; Leadership; Merger integration; Organizational change; Social change; Social cohesion; Stability.

Coordination (interpersonal). Coordinat(e, ed,ing,ion). Cooperat(e,ed,ing,ion). Interrelat(e,ed,ing). Collaborat(e,ed,ing, ion). Organiz(e,ed,ing). Supervis(e, ed,ing). Interfac(e,ed,ing). Unite(d). Uniting. Team leadership. *See also* Cooperation; Leadership; Networks; Supervision; Teamwork.

Coordination, motor. See *Motor coordination.*

Coordination, perceptual motor. See *Perceptual motor coordination.*

Copies. Cop(y,ies). Duplicate(s). Clone(s). Counterfeit(s). Facsimile(s). Forger(y, ies). Imitation(s). Likeness(es). Photocop(y,ies). Photograph(s). Fax(es,ed,ing). Replica(s,ation,ions). Reprint(s). Transcription(s). Xerox(es). *See also* Copying processes; Copyright; Imitation; Microforms; Photography; Representation (likeness).

Coping. Cop(e,ed,ing). Adapt(ion,ive,ing). Contend(ed,ing). Adjust(ing,ment, ments). Makeshift. *Choose from:* survival *with:* strateg(y,ies), skill(s), planning, role(s). *Consider also:* crisis counseling, support system(s), stress reduction, confronting, enduring, support mobilization, networking, problem solving. *See also* Adaptability; Adjustment (to environment); Avoidance; Burnout; Caregiver burden; Crisis management; Decision making; Defense mechanisms; Emotional adjustment; Emotional control; Goal orientation; Improvisation; Life change events; Mental health; Occupational stress; Persistence; Problem solving; Psychological stress; Self care; Sick role; Stigma; Strategies; Stress; Stress management; Well being.

Copper miners. Copper miner(s). *Choose from:* copper *with:* miner(s), mineworker(s), union member(s), labor market(s). *See also* Industrial personnel; Industrial workers.

Coprophagia. Coprophag(ia,y,ic). *Choose from:* ingest(ed,ing,ion), eat(en,ing), ate *with:* fec(es,al), excreta, excrement. *See also* Behavior disorders; Scatology.

Copulation. See *Sexual intercourse.*

Copycat crime. Copycat crime(s). Copycat attack(s). *Choose from:* copycat(s), movie-inspired, mimic(ry,ked,king), contagio(n,us), cop(ied,ies,y), imitat(e,ion,ions,ive) *with:* robber(y,ies), murder(s), fire(s), attack(ed,s), product tampering, terrorism, sabotage, homicide(s), fraud(s), mischief, mayhem, crime(s). *See also* Collective behavior; Collective suicide; Copycat suicide; Crime; Imitation; Mass media effects; Social contagion.

Copycat suicide. Copycat suicide(s). Copycat attack(s). *Choose from:* copycat(s), movie-inspired, mimic(ry, ked,king), contagio(n,us), cop(ied,ies,y), chain reaction, imitat(e,ion,ions,ive) *with:* suicide(s), self-mutilation, self-sacrifice. *See also* Collective behavior; Collective suicide; Copycat crime; Imitation; Mass media effects; Social contagion; Suicide; Suicide victims.

Copying. See *Copying processes; Imitation.*

Copying processes. Copy(ing) process(es). *Choose from:* copy(ing), copied, duplicat(ed,ing,ion), photocopy(ing), photocopied, xerox(ed,ing), photo-reproduc(e,ed,ing,tion), xerograph(y,ic), reproduc(e,tion,tions), multilith(ing), facsimile(s), fax(ed,ing), photo-duplicat(e,ed,ing,ion), reprograph(y,ic), microreproduc(e,ed,ing,tion), microfilm(ed,ing), tape record(ed,ing), videotap(e,ed,ing), videodisc record(ing,ings). *See also* Copies; Copyright; Enlargement; Imitation; Microforms; Photography.

Copyright. Copyright(s,ed). *Choose from:* right(s), ownership *with:* publication(s), published work(s), literary work(s), software, intellectual property. *Consider also:* fair use, protected work(s), literary property, infringement damage(s). *See also* Copies; Copying processes; Government regulation; Information highway; Information policy; Intangible property; Legal rights; License agreements; Patents; Piracy (copyright); Plagiarism; Publications; Trade secrets.

Copyright, piracy. See *Piracy (copyright).*

Core. Core(s). Center(s). Middle(s). Midpoint(s). Marrow(s). *Consider also:* corp(us,ora), germ(s), essence(s), kernel(s), quintessence, essential part(s). *See also* Canon (literature); Centrality; Meaning.

Coronary disease. Coronary disease(s). Angina pectoris. *Choose from:* heart, coronary, cardiovascular, myocardial *with:* disorder(s), disease(s), infarction(s), thrombos(is,es),

vasospasm(s). *Consider also:* arteriosclerosis. *See also* Cardiovascular system.

Coronary prone behavior. Coronary prone behavior(s). *Consider also:* stress(es, ful), tension(s), time urgency, psychological factor(s), life event(s), psychodynamic(s), personalit(y,ies), behavior(s), Type A *with:* coronary, cardiovascular, myocardial, heart, hypertens(ion,ive). *Consider also:* time conscious(ness), hurry sickness. *See also* Coronary disease; Disease susceptibility; Personality traits; Stress management; Stress reactions.

Coronation. Coronation(s). Crowning(s). Accession to the throne. *Consider also:* inauguration(s), regal consecration(s). *See also* Inauguration; Palaces; Royalty.

Corporal punishment. Corporal punishment. Ill-treat(ed,ment). Inflict(ed,ing) pain. Duck(ed,ing). Whip(ped,ping). Spank(ed,ing). Slap(ped,ping). Cane(d). Caning. Beat(en,ing). Atrocit(y,ies). *Choose from:* corporal, physical(ly), bodily, corporeal, harsh, cruel and unusual *with:* punishment(s), abuse(s), cruelt(y,ies), discipline, penalt(y,ies), punitive. *See also* Child discipline; Childrearing; Flagellants and flagellation; Negative reinforcement; Punishment; Torture.

Corporate acquisitions. Corporate acquisition(s). *Choose from:* corporat(e,ion,ions), business(es), compan(y,ies), firm(s) *with:* acquisition(s), acquir(e,ed,ing), buy(ing), bought, buyout(s), takeover(s), amalgamation(s), merger(s), raid(ed, ing,er,ers), tak(e,en,ing) possession. *Consider also:* leveraged buyout(s), LBOs, junk bond(s). *See also* Anti-takeover strategies; Buyouts; Corporate control; Corporate debt; Hostile takeovers; Leveraged buyouts; Merger integration; Mergers.

Corporate class. See *Ruling class.*

Corporate control. Corporate control. Corporate governance. Corporate director(s). *Consider also:* board dismissal(s), takeover(s), leverage, controlling share(s,holder,holders), proxy control, corporate management, blockholder(s). *See also* Corporate acquisitions; Governing boards; Industrial concentration; Interlocking directorates; Mergers; Oligopolies; Organizational power; Power structure.

Corporate culture. See *Organizational culture.*

Corporate day care. Corporate day care. *Choose from:* corporat(e,ion,ions), employer provided, employer supported, employer sponsored, workplace, on-site, worksite, employee benefit(s) *with:* day care, daycare, day nurser(y,ies), child

development center(s), child care, elder care, parent care. *Consider also:* child care benefit(s). *See also* Child day care; Employee assistance programs; Employee benefits.

Corporate debt. Corporate debt(s). Leveraged buyout(s). *Choose from:* corporat(e,ion,ions), business(es), compan(y,ies), firm(s) *with:* debt(s), indebted(ness), borrow(ed,ing), insolven(t,cy), loan(s), lend(ing), megadebt(s), default(ed,ing,ers), bankruptcy, credit(ors), financial obligation(s), arrears, debit(s,ed), liabilit(y,ies). *See also* Bankruptcy; Corporate acquisitions; Debts; Leveraged buyouts; Liability; Loans.

Corporate elites. See *Economic elites.*

Corporate identity. See *Brand identity; Corporate image.*

Corporate image. Corporate image(s). *Choose from:* corporat(e,ion,ions), business(es), compan(y,ies), firm(s), trademark(s), company name(s), logo(s), corporate symbol(s) *with:* image(s), identit(y,ies), stereotype(s), public awareness, visibility, prestige, personalit(y,ies), reputation(s), public confidence, makeover(s), buyer awareness, public perception(s). *See also* Advocacy advertising; Brand identity; Brand names; Corporate social responsibility; Goodwill; Images; Public relations.

Corporate mission. Corporat(e,ion) mission. *Choose from:* corporat(e,ion,ions), firm(s), compan(y,ies), business(es), hospital(s), organization(s,al) *with:* mission(s), strategic plan(s,ning), master plan(s,ning), blueprint(s), goal(s), role(s), objective(s), vision(s). *Consider also:* corporate values, mission statement(s). *See also* Institutional mission; Long range planning; Organizational culture; Organizational objectives; Strategic management; Strategic planning.

Corporate networks. Corporate network(s). Intercorporate network(s,ing). Interlocking directorate(s). Interlocking directorship(s). Common directorship(s). Common corporate directorship(s). Directorship interlock(s). Corporate interlock(s). Intercorporate tie(s). Interlocking board(s). Primary interlock(s). Multiple interlock(s). *Consider also:* cartel(s), oligopol(y,ies). *See also* Boundary spanning; Cartels; Interinstitutional relations; Mergers; Multinational corporations; Networks.

Corporate power. See *Organizational power.*

Corporate retreats. Corporate retreat(s). *Choose from:* corporate leader(s), CEO(s), executive(s), business enterprise(s), compan(y,ies), management *with:* retreat(s), golf resort(s), spa(s), conference center(s), hunting trip(s), outing(s), getaway(s). *See also* Brainstorming; Business organizations; Group problem solving; Rejuvenation; Relaxation.

Corporate social responsibility. Corporate social responsibilit(y,ies). Corporate citizen(s,ship). Socially responsible corporation(s). *Choose from:* corporat(e, ion,ions), business(es), compan(y,ies), firm(s) *with:* philanthrop(y,ies,ic), donat(e,ed,ing,ion,ions), conscience, common good, volunteer(s,ed,ing,ism), cleanup(s), ethic(s,al), social(ly) accountab(le,ility), environmental(ism), social(ly) responsib(le,ility,ilities), community responsibilit(y,ies), divestment(s), social investment(s), ethical investment(s), community reinvestment, civic responsibilit(y,ies), charit(y,ies,able), scholarship(s), foundation(s), contribut(e,ed,ing,ion, ions), giving, social polic(y,ies), community cooperation. *Consider also:* corporat(e,ion,ions), business(es), compan(y,ies), firm(s) *with:* aid, support(s,ed,ing) *with:* education, school(s), art(s), cultural, health care. *See also* Arts patronage; Business ethics; Community institutional relations; Consumer protection; Corporate day care; Corporate image; Disinvestment; Employee assistance programs; Fiduciary responsibility; Industrial wastes; Occupational diseases; Occupational exposure; Occupational health services; Occupational safety; Organizational culture; Product labeling; Public relations; Social responsibility; Socially responsible investing; Working conditions; Waste disposal.

Corporate spouses. Corporate spouse(s). *Choose from:* corporate, compan(y,ies), corporation(s), executive(s), military *with:* wife, wives, spouse(s), domestic partner(s). *See also* Administrators; Business personnel; Family work relationship; Spouses.

Corporate state. Corporate state(s). Corporative state(s). *Consider also:* corporatis(m,t), neo-corporatis(t,m). *See also* Authoritarianism (political); Corporatism; Fascism.

Corporate structure. See *Organizational structure.*

Corporate takeovers. See *Corporate acquisitions; Mergers.*

Corporations. Corporat(e,ion,ions). Incorporat(e,ed). Compan(y,ies). Large industrial organization(s). Corporate world. Corporate bod(y,ies). Corporatiz(e,ed,ing,ation). Intercorporate. Multinational(s). Trusts. Parent compan(y,ies). Holding compan(y,ies). Large business(es). Fortune 500. Big business(es). Chaebol(s). *Consider also:*

artificial person, association of shareholders, conglomerate(s), syndicate(s), firm(s), stockholder(s). *See also* Agribusiness; Big business; Branch operations; Dividends; Family corporations; Going public; Holding company; Home office; Incorporation; Interlocking directorates; Mergers; Multinational corporations; Neocolonialism; Professional corporations; Stockholders.

Corporations, family. See *Family corporations.*

Corporations, farm. See *Agribusiness.*

Corporations, multinational. See *Multinational corporations.*

Corporations, nonprofit. See *Nonprofit organizations.*

Corporations, professional. See *Professional corporations.*

Corporations, transnational. See *Multinational corporations.*

Corporatism. Corporatis(m,t). Neo-corporatism. Liberal corporatism. *Consider also:* corporate state(s). *See also* Collectivism; Corporate state; Interest groups; Labor management relations.

Corpus delicti. See *Circumstantial evidence.*

Correctional institutions. Correctional institution(s). Corrective institution(s). Correctional facilit(y,ies). Penal institution(s). Penal colon(y,ies). Death row. Guardhouse. Brig(s). Penitentiar(y, ies). House(s) of detention. Jail(s). Gaol(s). Prison cell(s). Prison(s). Reformator(y,ies). Correctional school(s). Borstal(s). Correctional rehabilitation. *Consider also:* Sing Sing, Devil's Island, Alcatraz, Dannemora, etc. *See also* Correctional system; Criminal rehabilitation; Delinquents; Institutionalization (persons); Juvenile detention homes; Offenders; Prison culture; Prison violence; Prisoners; Prisonization; Prisons; Reformatories; Sentencing.

Correctional institutions, juvenile. See *Reformatories.*

Correctional law. See *Penal codes.*

Correctional personnel. Correctional personnel. Prison personnel. Parole board member(s). Correctional institution personnel. Correctional institution administrator(s). *Choose from:* prison(s), correction(al,s), penitentiar(y,ies), jail(s), parole *with:* guard(s), officer(s), official(s), staff, employee(s), personnel, psychologist(s), counselor(s), caseworker(s), worker(s), teacher(s), librarian(s). *See also* Attorneys; Correctional institutions; Correctional system; Police personnel; Prison culture; Probation officers; Social workers;.

Correctional rehabilitation. See *Criminal rehabilitation.*

Correctional system. Correctional system(s). Criminal rehabilitation system(s). Penal system(s). Prison system(s). Prison school(s). Penitentiar(y,ies). Jail(s). *See also* Alternatives to incarceration; Correctional institutions; Crime prevention; Criminal justice; Criminal rehabilitation; Imprisonment; Judicial decisions; Legal system; Parole; Penal reform; Penology; Prison culture; Prisoners; Prisons; Probation; Reformatories; Restitution.

Corrections. See *Correctional institutions; Correctional system; Criminal rehabilitation.*

Corrections, community based. See *Alternatives to incarceration.*

Corrections, day reporting centers. See *Day reporting centers (corrections).*

Correctness. Correct(ly,ness). Accura(te, cy). Exact(ness,itude). Proper(ly). Faultless(ness). Infallib(ility,leness). Precis(e,ely,ion). Unerring(ly). *Consider also:* appropriate(ness), propriety, suitab(ility,leness), unfailing(ly). *See also* Accuracy; Errors; Fallacies; Flawless; Infallibility; Validity; Truth.

Correlates, personality. See *Personality correlates.*

Correlates, physiological. See *Physiological correlates.*

Correlation. Correlat(e,es,ed,ion,ional). Correspond(ing,ence). Reciprocal(ity). Mutual relationship. Interdependen(t,ce). Mutuality. Connect(ed,edness,ion). Interrelat(e,ed,ion,ionship). Interconnect(ed,ing,ion,ionship). *See also* Interdependence; Reciprocity; Statistical correlation; Statistical significance; Validity.

Correlation, statistical. See *Statistical correlation.*

Correspondence (letters). See *Letters (correspondence).*

Correspondence, government. See *Government correspondence.*

Correspondence schools. Correspondence school(s). *Choose from:* correspondence, home, televis(ed,ion), long distance *with:* course(s), school(s), study, education. *See also* Adult education; Distance education; Home schooling; Lifelong learning; Nontraditional education; Self education.

Correspondence therapy. See *Postal psychotherapy.*

Correspondents, foreign. See *Foreign correspondents.*

Corrupt practices. See *Bribery; Cheating; Computer crimes; Conflict of interest; Consumer fraud; Corruption in* *government; Covert; Drugs in athletics; Embezzlement; Falsification (scientific); Fraud; Industrial espionage; Judicial corruption; Kickbacks; Political crimes; Price fixing; Product tampering; Professional ethics; Quackery; Racketeering; Scientific misconduct; Unethical conduct; White collar crime.*

Corruption, judicial. See *Judicial corruption.*

Corruption in government. Corruption in government. Government scandal(s). Corrupt politician(s). Pentagon bribery. Political plum(s). Clubhouse politics. Crooked politician(s). Buy(ing) vote(s). Watergate. Iran contra(s). Tammany Hall. *Choose from:* politician(s), elected official(s), government official(s), Federal official(s), State official(s), public officer(s), government employee(s), Congress, Parliament, prime minister(s), governor(s), congress(men,man,women,woman), senator(s), lobbyist(s), president(s,ial), Pentagon, department of, candidate(s), judge(s), political *with:* abuse(s), alter(ed,ing) evidence, alter(ed,ing) record(s), bribe(s,d,ry), collusion, concealment, conflict(s) of interest, conspirac(y,ies), corrupt(ing,ed,ion), criminal behavior(s), crooked, cronyism, deceit(ful), deception, dishonest(ly,y), divert(ed,ing) fund(s), divert(ed,ing) government property, embezzl(e,ed, ing,ement), ethical question(s), forgery, fraud(ulent), graft, illegal(ly,ity,ities), illegal contribution(s), immoral(ity,ities), impropriet(y,ies), improper act(s), kickback(s), launder(ed,ing) money, lax ethics, libel, lining pocket(s), loophole(s), lying, malfeasance, misappropriation(s), misconduct, misdeed(s), misdemeanor(s), nepotism, no-show employee(s), oversight(s), patronage, payoff(s), payola, perjury, pilfer(ed,ing), pork barrel, profiteer(ed, ing), questionable behavior(s), racketeer(ing), revolving door, shred(ded,ding) document(s), skimocrac(y,ies), skirting law(s), sleaze factor, smuggl(e,ed,ing), special tie(s), tainted money, tarnished reputation(s), tax evasion, unethical, unlawful(ly), violation(s), vote buying, withhold(ing) information, wrongdoing(s). *See also* Covert; Crime; Decadence; Deception; Depravity; Financial disclosure; Fraud; Government investigations; Judicial corruption; Judicial ethics; Military patronage; Misconduct in office; Political bosses; Political crimes; Political patronage; Political reform; Professional ethics; Scandals; Unethical conduct; White collar crime; Withholding evidence; Witness tampering.

Cosmeceuticals. See *Cosmetics; Non-prescription drugs.*

Cosmetic surgery. See *Reconstructive surgery.*

Cosmetics. Cosmetic(s,ology). Beauty aid(s). Beauty treat(s,ment,ments). Beauty product(s). Cosmeceutical(s). *Consider also:* herbal cosmetic(s), moisturiser(s), deodorant(s), perfume(s,ry), sunscreen(s), toilet preparation(s), toilet articles), make-up, makeup, skin care, skincare, hair care, shampoo(s), fragrant substance(s), fragrance(s), nail strengthener(s), personal care product(s), hand lotion(s), eye shadow(s), lipstick, face cream(s), eye cream(s), and eye-makeup remover(s), alpha hydroxy acid(s), AHA(s), betahydroxy acid(s), wrinkle cream(s), facelift(s), facial peel(s), cosmetic surgeon(s). *See also* Beauty culture; Beauty shops; Body ornamentation; Fashions; Non-prescription drugs; Reconstructive surgery.

Cosmic consciousness. See *Enlightenment (state).*

Cosmopolitan. Cosmopolitan(ism). Cosmopolite(s). Unprovincial. Broadminded. Sophisticat(ed,ion). Liberal. Cultured. Cultivated. Urbane. Worldly. Internationalism. Global perspective. Catholic(ity). *See also* Attitudes; Catholic (universality); Civilized; Elegance; Globalization; Sophistication; Worldview.

Cost accounting. Cost accounting. Costing. Cost estimat(e,es,ed,ing). Computing cost(s). Cost allocation. *See also* Accounting.

Cost analysis. Cost analys(is,es). *Choose from:* pricing, price(s), charg(ing,e,es), bill(s), amount(s) paid, payment(s), expense(s), expend(ed,iture,itures), fee(s), cost(s) *with:* analys(is,es), analyz(e,ed,ing), distribut(e,ed,ing, ion,ions), budget(s,ed,ing), contain(ed, ing,ment), allocat(e,ed,ing,ion,ions). *Consider also:* break-even analysis, cost-benefit analysis, opportunity cost. *See also* Accountability; Cost effectiveness; Costs; Expenditures; Operations research; Resource allocation; Systems analysis.

Cost benefit analysis. See *Cost effectiveness.*

Cost containment. See *Cost control.*

Cost control. Cost control. Cost containment. *Choose from:* control(ling,led), contain(ed,ing,ment,ments), review(s), cut(ting), reduc(e,ed,ing,tion,tions), holding down, cap(ped,ping), constrain(ed,ing,t,ts), restrain(ed,ing, t,ts), limit(s,ed,ing) *with:* cost(s), cash outlay(s), expenditure(s), expense(s), spending. *Consider also:* downsizing, rightsizing. *See also* Budget cuts; Cost recovery; Cost shifting; Saving; Personnel termination; Wasteful.

Cost effectiveness. Cost effective(ness). Economic efficiency. Cost benefit analys(is,es). Benefit cost analys(is,es).

Cost utility analys(is,es). Operational auditing. Accountability. Rate review(s). *Choose from:* cost(s), price, investment(s), expenditure(s) *with:* benefit(s), worth, value(s,d), justif(y, ied,ication), quality. *Consider also:* risk *with:* reward(s). *See also* Accountability; Cost analysis; Cost recovery; Costs; Effectiveness; Efficiency; Evaluation; Expenditures; Operations research; Organizational effectiveness; Program evaluation; Resource allocation; Risk; Scientific management; Systems analysis.

Cost free. See *Gratis.*

Cost of living. Cost of living. Consumer price index(es). Living cost(s). Inflation rate(s). COLA(s). Purchasing power. Cost index(es). Poverty level(s). Inflation index(es). Consumer price(s). Interest rate(s). *Choose from:* cost(s), price(s), affordab(le,ility) *with:* housing, food, transportation, medical, education, living, family needs, family budget(s). *Choose from:* rent(s), price(s), interest rate(s), cost(s) *with:* guideline(s), escalat(e,ed,ing,ion), increase(s), hike(s), rising, skyrocketing. *See also* Consumer expenditures; Costs; Energy costs; Expenditures; Health expenditures; Housing costs; Income; Inflation (economics); Labor costs; Living standards; Prices; Purchasing power; Utility costs.

Cost recovery. Cost recovery. *Choose from:* cost(s), cash outlay(s), expenditure(s), expense(s), spending, capital *with:* recover(y,ed,ing,able), reimburs(e,ed, ing,able), chargeback(s), charged back, charg(e,ed,es) for service(s). *See also* Amortization; Fares; Fees; Costs; Cost control; Reimbursement mechanisms; Tuition reimbursement.

Cost reduction. See *Budget cuts; Cost control; Saving.*

Cost sharing. Cost sharing. *Choose from:* cost(s), expense(s), financial burden(s), expend(ed,iture,itures), bill(s) *with:* shar(e,ed,ing), split(ting), divid(e,ed, ing). *Consider also:* matching grant(s). *See also* Cost shifting; Costs; Sharing.

Cost shifting. Cost shift(s,ing). *Choose from:* cost(s), entitlement(s), financial burden(s), tax(es) *with:* shift(s,ed,ing), transfer(red,ring,al), offsetting. *Consider also:* recovering uncompensated cost(s). *See also* Cost control; Cost sharing; Costs.

Costs. Cost(ing,s). Expense(s). Expend(ed,iture,itures). Fee(s). Price(s). Charg(es,ed,ing). Bill(ed,ing,s). Financial outlay. Amount(s) paid. Payment(s). Affordability. Affordable. Market price(s). Dollar value. Outlay(s). *Consider also:* entitlement(s), operating expense(s), direct cost(s), fixed cost(s), variable cost(s), construction cost(s), legal cost(s), patient cost(s), program cost(s), student cost(s), unit cost(s). *See also* Compensation (payment); Cost analysis; Cost control; Cost effectiveness; Cost of living; Cost recovery; Cost sharing; Cost shifting; Depreciation; Direct costs; Economic value; Energy costs; Expenditures; Externalities; Face value; Fares; Fees; Financial support; Gratis; Housing costs; Indirect costs; Inflation (economics); Labor costs; Prices; Purchasing power; Salaries; Utility costs.

Costs, direct. See *Direct costs.*

Costs, energy. See *Energy costs.*

Costs, fixed. See *Indirect costs.*

Costs, heating. See *Utility costs.*

Costs, housing. See *Housing costs.*

Costs, indirect. See *Indirect costs.*

Costs, labor. See *Labor costs.*

Costs, social. See *Externalities; Social impact.*

Costs, utility. See *Utility costs.*

Costume. Costume(s). Cloth(es,ing). Apparel. Attire. Bathrobe(s). Belt(s). Blouse(s). Boot(s). Bra(s). Coat(s). Dress(es). Fashion(s). Garb. Garment(s). Glove(s). Hat(s). Jeans. Livery. Mitten(s). Millinery. Nightgown(s). Overcoat(s). Pajama(s). Pantie(s). Pant(s). Raiment(s). Raincoat(s). Scarf. Scarves. Suit(s). Skirt(s). Shirt(s). Slip(s). Sock(s). Stocking(s). Shoe(s). Shorts. Slacks. Slipper(s). Sweater(s). Undercloth(ing,es). Underwear. Uniform(s). Undershirt(s). Vestment(s). Vest(s,ure). Wardrobe(s). *Consider also:* dress code(s), protective clothing, regalia, accouterment(s), doll clothes, theatrical costume(s), stage costume(s), umbrella(s), parasol(s), veil(s), wig(s), masquerade(s), halloween costume(s). *See also* Ballet shoes; Body ornamentation; Clothing; Fashions; Material culture; Nonverbal communication.

Cot death. See *Sudden infant death.*

Cotherapy. Cotherap(eutic,y,ies,ist,ists). Conjoint therap(y,ies). Duotherap(y,ies). Multiple impact therap(y,ies). *Choose from:* multiple, conjoint, cooperative, triad(s,ic), triangular, matrix, collaborative, multiple *with:* psychotherap(y,ies, ist,ists), therap(y,ies,ist,ists), psychoanalytic treatment(s). *Consider also:* auxiliary therapist(s). *See also* Multiple psychotherapy; Psychotherapy.

Cottage industries. See *Home based businesses; Small businesses.*

Cottages, electronic. See *Home based businesses; Small businesses.*

Councils. Council(s). Commission(s). Delegation(s). Board(s). Committee(s). Appointed group(s). Advisory group(s). Panel(s). Panchayat(s). Board(s) of supervisors. Governing board(s). *Consider also:* city council(s), local council(s), regional council(s), national council(s), world council(s), privy council(s). *See also* Advisory committees; Governing boards; Legislative bodies.

Councils, resident. See *Resident councils.*

Councils and synods, religious. See *Religious councils and synods.*

Counseling. Counsel(ed,ing). Casework. Guidance. Microcounsel(ed,ing). Student personnel work. Cocounsel(ed, ing). Co-counsel(ed,ing). Pastoral care. Supportive therap(y,ies). *Consider also:* support group(s), group therap(y,ies), crisis intervention, crisis center(s), crisis line(s), psychotherap(y,ies). *See also* Abortion counseling; Adjustment (to environment); Behavior modification; Cognitive restructuring; Crisis intervention; Death counseling; Divorce counseling; Educational counseling; Employment counseling; Family therapy; Genetic counseling; Group counseling; Helping behavior; Marital therapy; Mental health services; Mentors; Microcounseling; Ombudsmen; Peer counseling; Premarital counseling; Psychological debriefing; Psychotherapy; Rape crisis counseling; Rehabilitation counseling; School counseling; Self expression; Sex therapy; Social work; Vocational guidance.

Counseling, abortion. See *Abortion counseling.*

Counseling, career. See *Vocational guidance.*

Counseling, conjoint. See *Cotherapy; Multiple psychotherapy.*

Counseling, death. See *Death counseling.*

Counseling, divorce. See *Divorce counseling.*

Counseling, educational. See *Educational counseling.*

Counseling, employment. See *Employment counseling.*

Counseling, family. See *Family therapy.*

Counseling, genetic. See *Genetic counseling.*

Counseling, group. See *Group counseling.*

Counseling, guidance. See *School counseling.*

Counseling, job. See *Vocational guidance.*

Counseling, marital. See *Marital therapy.*

Counseling, marriage. See *Family therapy; Marital therapy.*

Counseling, occupational. See *Employment counseling.*

Counseling, pastoral. See *Pastoral care.*

Counseling, peer. See *Peer counseling.*

Counseling, premarital. See *Premarital counseling.*

Counseling, rape crisis. See *Rape crisis counseling.*

Counseling, rehabilitation. See *Rehabilitation counseling.*

Counseling, school. See *School counseling.*

Counseling, sex. See *Sex therapy.*

Counseling, vocational. See *Employment counseling.*

Counselor role. See *Therapist role.*

Counselors. Counselor(s). Caseworker(s). Guidance personnel. Student personnel worker(s). Therap(y,ist,ists). *Consider also:* psychotherapist(s). *See also* Mental health personnel; Parole officers; Rehabilitation counselors; School counselors; Social workers; Vocational counselors.

Counselors, rehabilitation. See *Rehabilitation counselors.*

Counselors, school. See *School counselors.*

Counselors, vocational. See *Vocational counselors.*

Counterconformity. See *Nonconformity (personality).*

Countercultures. Counterculture(s). Counter culture(s). Contraculture(s). Adversary culture(s). New age commune(s). Youth culture(s). Alternative econom(y,ies). Alternative culture(s). New age romanticism. Anarchistic culture(s). Countermovement(s). Hipp(y,ies). Beatnik(s). Beat generation. Flower children. Drug culture. Yipp(y,ies). Rebel(s). Bohemian(ism). Drug subculture. Haight Ashbury. Punk. Sixties generation. *See also* Bohemianism; Countermovements; Cross cultural comparisons; Cults; Cultural conflict; Cultural pluralism; Cultural values; Dissent; Generation gap; Hippies; Lifestyle; Norms; Popular culture; Sects; Social behavior; Subcultures; Youth culture; Youth movements.

Counterfactuals (logic). Counterfactual(s). Contrary-to-fact conditional(s). *Consider also:* subjunctive conditional(s), counteridentical(s), possible world(s). *See also* Causality; Conditionals; Logic.

Counterfeiting. Counterfeit(ing). Credit card fraud(s). Fake(s). Wooden nickel(s). Rubber check(s). Sham(s). *Choose from:* counterfeit, phony, imitation, bogus *with:* stock certificate(s), bond(s), money, currency, goods. *Consider also:* pirated edition(s), pirated goods, piracy, gray market(s). *Choose from:* trade mark(s), copyright(s) *with:* infringement, theft, thievery, abuse. *See also* Copyright; Debit card fraud; Crime; Fraud; Piracy (copyright); Plagiarism; White collar crime.

Counterinsurgency. Counterinsurgen(cy, cies,t,ts). Counter-insurgen(cy,cies,t,ts). Death squad(s). State terroris(m,t,ts). Counterrevolution(s,ary,aries). Counter-revolution(s,ary,aries). Quell(ed,ing) insurgent(t,ts,cy,cies). *Consider also:* Green Beret(s), Rapid Deployment Force, vigilant(e,es,ism), counter(ed,ing) terroris(m,t,ts), counter-terroris(t,ts,m), anti-terroris(t,ts,m). *See also* Counter-revolutions; Coups d'Etat; Guerrillas; Internal security; Military regimes; Political violence; Terrorism.

Countermovements. Countermovement(s). Backlash(es). Brownlash(es). Anti-green(s). Anti-scien(ce,tific). Counter-revolutionar(y,ies). Reactionar(y,ies). Resistance. Counterfeminist(s). Opposition. Counter-insurgen(t,ts,cy, cies). Adversary culture(s). *Consider also:* anarchistic culture(s), youth rebellion(s). *See also* Antifascist movements; Countercultures; Irrational-ism (philosophy); Political movements; Resistance; Social movements.

Counterpoint. Counterpoint. Contrapuntal. Kontrapunkt. Contrepoint. Contrappunto. Contrapunctus. Contrapunto. Punctus contra punctum. *Consider also:* polyphon(y,ic), nota contra notum, contrapunto osservato, Palestrina counterpoint, Bach counter-point, nota cambiata. *See also* Music.

Counterrevolutions. Counterrevolution(s,ary,aries). Counter-revolution(s,ary,aries). *Consider also:* reactionar(y,ies), disestablish(ed,ing, ment). *See also* Alienation; Anti-government radicals; Counterin-surgency; Political dissent.

Countertransference. Countertransfer(ence). *Choose from:* psychotherapist(s), therapist(s), psychoanalyst(s) *with:* counter-identif(y,ied,ication), restimulat(ed,ing,ion). *See also* Communicative psychotherapy; Psychotherapeutic processes.

Countries. Countr(y,ies). Nation(al,alism,ity,s). State(s). Nation state(s). Sovereign state(s). Commonwealth(s). Republic(s). Dominion(s). Empire(s). Kingdom(s). Principalit(y,ies). Union(s). Confederation(s). Confederac(y,ies). Monarch(y,ies). Sovereign entit(y,ies). *See also* Antarctic regions; Arctic Regions; Borderlands; Caribbean; Central America; Central Asia; Devel-oped countries; Developing countries; Eastern Europe; Far East; Homeland;

Least developed countries; Middle East; North Africa; North America; Oceania; South America; South Asia; Southeast Asia; Sub-Saharan Africa; Western Europe.

Countries, advanced. See *Developed countries.*

Countries, advanced developing. See *Newly industrializing economies.*

Countries, allied. See *International alliances.*

Countries, Americans in foreign. See *Americans abroad.*

Countries, developed. See *Developed countries.*

Countries, developing. See *Developing countries.*

Countries, industrial. See *Industrial societies.*

Countries, least developed. See *Least developed countries.*

Countries, less developed. See *Less developed countries.*

Countries, low income. See *Least devel-oped countries; Less developed countries.*

Countries, middle income. See *Less developed countries.*

Countries, newly industrializing. See *Newly industrializing economies.*

Countries, underdeveloped. See *Developing countries.*

Countries, undeveloped. See *Least developed countries.*

Countries by name. See *Antarctic regions; Arctic Regions; Caribbean; Central America; Central Asia; Eastern Europe; Far East; Middle East; North Africa; North America; Oceania; South America; South Asia; Southeast Asia; Sub-Saharan Africa; Western Europe.*

Countries in transition. Countr(y,ies) in transition. Newly Independent State(s). NIS. *Consider also:* former USSR, Eastern Europe, Second World, Commonwealth of Independent States, Albania, Armenia, Azerbaijan, Belarus, Bosnia and Herzegovina, Bulgaria, Croatia, Czech Republic, Estonia, Georgia, Hungary, Kazakhstan, Kyrgyzstan, Latvia, Lithuania, The Former Yugoslav Republic of Macedonia, Moldova, Mongolia, Poland, Romania, Russia, Serbia and Montenegro, Slovakia, Slovenia, Tajikistan, Turkmenistan, Ukraine, Uzbekistan. *Consider also:* European Bank for Reconstruction and Develop-ment. *See also* Centrally planned economies; Decentralization; Decommunization; Democratization;

Developed countries; Developing countries; Eastern Europe; Newly industrializing economies; Post-Communism; Privatization.

Country, father of the. See *Father of the country.*

Country and western music. Country and western music. Country music. Western music. Old time music. Western swing. *Consider also:* hillbilly music, cowboy song(s), Roy Acuff, Texas Ramblers, Bob Wills, Texas Playboys, Ernest Tubb, Hank Williams, Chet Atkins, Merle Haggard, Ricky Skaggs, Eddy Arnold, Glen Campbell, Kenny Rogers, Dolly Parton, Willie Nelson, Barbara Mandrell, etc. *See also* Bluegrass music; Folk music; Folk culture; Music; Popular culture; Western fiction.

Country dance. Country dance(s). English folk danc(e,es,ing). *See also* Contredanse; Folk dancing.

Country homes. Country home(s). Country house(s). Country retreat(s). Country cottage(s). Country estate(s). Rustic cabin(s). Summer villa(s). Rustic retreat(s). Weekend getaway(s). Weekend retreat(s). Lodge-like home(s). Beach house(s). Ski chalet(s). *See also* Vacation houses.

Country life. Country life. Country living. Rural life. Rural America(n). Liv(e,ing) in small town(s). Liv(e,ing) in rural area(s). Back to the land. Farm country. *See also* Lifestyle; Rural conditions; Rural population; Rural communities; Rustic life.

County officials and employees. See *Government personnel; Local govern-ment; Politicians.*

Couples. Couple(d,s). Dyad(ic,s). Court-ship. Intimate relation(s,ship,ships). Partner(s). Cohabit(ing,ation). Love relationship(s). Steady dat(e,ing). Intimate(s). Intimacy. Married. Marital. Marriage(s). Romantic love. Close relationship(s). Twosome. Pair(s). Lover(s). Man and wife. Husband(s) and wife (wives). Mate(s). Deux. Young married(s). Living together. Significant other(s). Conjugal. Premarital relation-ship. *See also* Cohabitation; Dyads; Gay couples; Heterosexual relationships; Marriage; Sexual partners; Social dating; Spouses.

Couples, gay. See *Gay couples.*

Couples, homosexual. See *Gay couples.*

Couples, lesbian. See *Gay couples.*

Couples, married. See *Spouses.*

Couples therapy. Couples therap(y,ies). *Choose from:* couple(s), partner(s), premarital, significant others *with:* therap(y,ies), counseling, conflict resolution, advice, advisory, casework, psychotherap(y,ies), treatment(s), enrichment, communication training. *See also* Family therapy; Feminist therapy; Marital therapy; Premarital counseling; Sex Therapy.

Coups d'Etat. Coup(s) d'Etat. Putsch. Overthr(ew,ow,own). Overturn(ed). Coup attempt(s). Depos(ed,ing,ition, itions). Oust(ed,ing) from office. Seize(d) power. Takeover(s). Revolution(s,ary,ies). Rebel(led,ling, lion,lions). Mutin(ous,y,ies). Insurgen(t,cy,cies). Uprising(s). Assassination plot(s). Junta(s). *See also* Civil supremacy over the military; Counterinsurgency; Martial law; Military regimes; Political violence; Provisional government; Revolution.

Courage. Courag(e,eous). Brave(ry). Fearless(ness). Daring. Valor(ous, ousness). Intrepid(ity,ness). Audacious(ness). Audacity. Temerity. Adventurous(ness). Dauntless(ness). Gallant(ry). Hero(ism). *See also* Personality traits.

Course evaluation. Course evaluation(s). *Choose from:* evaluat(ed,ing,ion,ions), rate(d), rating(s) *with:* course(s), seminar(s), class(es), program(s), activit(y,ies), minicourse(s), instruction, instructor effectiveness. *See also* Courses; Evaluation.

Course load. Course load(s). Academic load(s). Class load(s). Teaching load(s). Credit hour load(s). Credit load(s). *Consider also:* scheduled hours. *See also* Mainstreaming; School enrollment; Work load.

Courses. Course(s). Seminar(s). Class(es). Program(s). Credit(s). Minicourse(s). Curriculum. Workshop(s). Lesson(s). Lecture(s). *See also* Area studies; Course evaluation; Curriculum.

Court, contempt of. See *Contempt of Court.*

Court cases. See *Legal cases.*

Court decisions. See *Judicial decisions; Verdicts.*

Court judges. Court judge(s). *Choose from:* court(s), federal, state, trial, appellate, district *with:* judge(s), judiciary, judgeship(s), magistrate(s). *Consider also:* judicial appointment(s). *See also* Attorneys; Judges; Juries; Judicial candidates; Judicial error; Legal personnel.

Court news. Court(room) news. Trial report(s,ing,er,ers). *Choose from:* judicial, court(s,room,rooms), trial(s), hearing(s), grand jury, sentencing *with:* report(s,ing,er,ers), news, media coverage. *See also* Courts; News coverage; Trial (law).

Court opinions. Court opinion(s). Judicial decision(s). Adjudicat(e,ion,ive,or,ors). Adjudg(e,ment,ments). Decree(ing). Arbitrat(e,ed,ion). Litigation. *Choose from:* court, judicial, judge's *with:* opinion(s), decision(s), determination, decree(ing), ruling(s). *See also* Conviction; Judicial activism; Judicial decisions; Judicial discretion; Judicial error; Verdicts; Sentencing.

Court procedures. See *Legal procedures.*

Courtesans. Courtesan(s). Prostitute(s). Call girl(s). Concubin(e,es,age). Paramour(s). *Consider also:* geisha(s), mistress(es). *See also* Concubinage; Prostitution.

Courtesy. See *Etiquette; Manners.*

Courtly love. Courtly love(r,rs). Courtly romance. Fin amor. Chivalrous love. Court(s) of love. *Consider also:* chivalr(y,ic,ous), gentlemanly conduct, troubadour(s), trouvere(s), refined love. *See also* Chivalry; Idealization of women; Knights and knighthood; Love; Love poetry; Medieval music; Minnesinger; Troubadour; Trouvere; Virtue.

Courts. Court(room,rooms,s). Judge(s). Judiciary. Tribunal(s). Judicial forum(s). Judicial fora. Justice(s) of the peace. Judicial branch(es). Jur(y,ies). Grand jur(y,ies). Petit jur(y,ies). *Choose from:* Supreme, Appeals, District, State, County, Municipal, general trial, appellate, circuit, surrogate, family, juvenile, probate, small claims, traffic, equity, chancery, original jurisdiction *with:* court(s). *Consider also:* adjudication, litigation, sentencing, prosecution, plea bargaining, interpretation of law(s), trial(s), magistrate(s). *See also* Administrative courts; Court judges; Court news; Ecclesiastical courts; Fair trial; Judicial candidates; Juries; Laws; Legal procedures; Legal system; Sentencing; Trial (law).

Courts, administrative. See *Administrative courts.*

Courts, ecclesiastical. See *Ecclesiastical courts.*

Courtship, human. See *Human courtship.*

Courtship behavior, animal. See *Animal courtship behavior.*

Cousin marriage. Cousin marriage(s). *Consider also:* close marriage(s), consanguineous marriage(s), kin marriage(s), endogamous marriage(s), cross-cousin marriage(s), avuncular marriage(s), symmetrical cross-cousin marriage(s), inbreeding. *See also* Consanguinity; Endogamous marriage; Inbreeding.

Couvade. Couvade. Men's childbed. *Consider also:* male pregnanc(y,ies), sympathetic pregnanc(y,ies). *See also* Expectant fathers.

Covenant marriage. Covenant marriage(s). Covenant wedding(s). Covenant vow(s). Tough marriage compact(s). *Choose from:* covenant, stringent, extra commitment, strengthened licensing law(s), sanctity, lifetime, lifelong *with:* marriage(s), vow(s), wedding(s). *Consider also:* marital fidelity, fault-based divorce. *See also* Betrothal; Divorce counseling; Marital therapy; Marriage; Premarital counseling.

Covenants. See *Agreement (document); Promises.*

Cover, plant. See *Vegetation.*

Coverage, insurance. See *Insurance coverage.*

Coverage, media. See *News coverage.*

Coverage, news. See *News coverage.*

Coverage, press. See *News coverage.*

Coverage, television. See *News coverage.*

Covering (anatomy), body. See *Body covering (anatomy).*

Covering laws. Covering law(s). Covering law theory. Covering law model. Deductive nomological theory. Hypothetico-deductive model. Regularity theory. Hempelian model. Positivist theory. *See also* Deduction; Explanation; Scientific method.

Coverlets. Coverlet(s). Bedspread(s). Comforter(s). Bedclothes. Quilt(s). Eiderdown(s). *Consider also:* bed linen(s), bedding. *See also* Bedding.

Covers, book. See *Book covers.*

Covert. Covert(ness). Behind the scenes. Camouflage(d). Clandestine(ness). Conceal(ed,ing,ment). Dissembl(e,ed, ing). Dissimulat(e,ion). Evas(ive, iveness,ion). Furtive(ness). Hid(e,den, ing). Incognito. Insidious(ness). Priva(cy,te). Secre(cy,t,te,ts,tive, tiveness,tness). Stealth(y,iness). Sub rosa. Surreptitious(ness). Sly(ness). Sneak(y,iness). Subterfuge. Suppressed. Undercover. Underground. Undiscovered. Uncommunicated. Unreported. With(hold,held). *See also* Clandestinity; Corruption in government; Secrecy.

Cowardice. See *Fear.*

Cowboys. Cowboy(s). Cowpuncher(s). Cowpoke(s). Cow hand(s). Buckaroo(s). Wrangler(s). Charro(s). Gaucho(s). Vaquero(s). *Consider also:* rodeo(s), cattle drive(s), wild west, ranger(s). *See also* Agricultural workers.

Cows. See *Cattle; Cattle industry.*

Coyotes. Coyote(s). Canis latrans. Prairie wol(f,ves). *See also* Animals; Wild animals; Wildlife conservation; Wolves.

Crack babies. See *Drug addicted babies.*

Cradle songs. See *Lullabies.*

Craft workers. Craft worker(s). Craftworker(s). Crafts(men,women,man,woman). Craftsperson(s). Craft artist(s). Artisan(s). *Choose from:* handicraft(s), handcraft(s), craft(s) *with:* worker(s). Woodworker(s). Handcraft worker(s). Handicrafts(men,women,man,woman). Cabinet maker(s). Harpsichord maker(s). Embroiderer(s). Needleworker(s). Potter(s). Quilter(s). Weaver(s). Woodcarver(s). Woodworker(s). *See also* Crafts; Skilled workers.

Crafts. Craft(s). Folk art(s). Handicraft(s). Craftsman(ship). Handiwork. Manual art(s). *Consider also:* artwork, basket weaving, batik, beadwork, cabinet maker(s), ceramics, china painting, crocheting, doll making, embroidery, flower painting, harpsichord making, knitting, lacework, needlework, pottery, quilting, rug hooking, spinning, textile making, tie-dying, weaving, woodcarving, woodworking. *See also* Art metalwork; Artifacts; Arts; Arts and crafts movement; Beads; Carving (decorative arts); Ceramics; Craft workers; Fancy work; Fibers; Folk art; Folk culture; Glyptics; Jewelry making; Pottery; Weaving.

Craftsmen. See *Craft workers.*

Creation. Creation. Genesis. Origin(s). Beginning(s). Big bang. Creatio ex nihilo. Protobiogenesis. Footprint(s) of God. Cosmogony. First cause(s). *Consider also:* anthropic principle. *See also* Creationism; Creators; Dawn; Founding; Natural theology.

Creation (Literary, artistic etc.). See *Creativity.*

Creation, job. See *Job creation.*

Creationism. Creationis(m,ist,ists). Creation scien(ce,tist,tists). Scientific creationism. Monogenism. Monogenesis. Biblical account of creation. Creation theor(y,ies). Creation controvers(y,ies). Anti-evolution(ary). Monkey trials. Scopes trial. *Consider also:* evolution, Darwin(ism) *with:* fundamentalis(m,ts), bible, biblical, faith, God, Christianity, religion. *Consider also:* anthropic principle. *See also* Creation; Church state relationship; Evolution; Religious beliefs; Religious fundamentalism; Revealed theology; Spontaneous generation.

Creative ability. See *Artistic ability; Concept formation; Creativity; Divergent thinking; Gifted; Imagination; Individuality; Intelligence; Inventions; Inventors; Knowledge; Musical ability; Personality traits; Self expression.*

Creative thinking. Creative thinking. New idea(s). Creativ(ity,eness). Imaginat(ive, ion). Innovative(ness). Originality. Inventive(ness). Gifted. Talented. *Choose from:* creative, imaginative, divergent *with:* thinking, thought(s), process(es), idea(s,tion). *Consider also:* sudden illumination(s), creative solution(s), insight(s), associative fluency. *See also* Creativity; Concept formation; Critical thinking; Divergent thinking; Gifted; Imagination; Individuality; Intelligence; Inventions; Inventors; Knowledge; Personality traits; Resourcefulness; Self expression.

Creativity. Creativ(ity,eness). Imaginat(ive,ion). Innovative(ness). Originality. Inventive. Gifted. Talented. Artist(ic,s). Poet(ic,s). Music(al,ians). Writing ability. *Choose from:* creative, imaginative, divergent *with:* thinking, process(es). *Consider also:* associative fluency. *See also* Artistic ability; Beginning; Concept formation; Creators; Divergent thinking; Gifted; Imagination; Individuality; Intelligence; Inventions; Inventors; Knowledge; Personality traits; Self expression.

Creators. Creator(s). Founder(s). Originator(s). Initiator(s). Inventor(s). Prime mover(s). Organizer(s). Designer(s). Framer(s). Architect(s). Author(s). *Consider also:* father(s), mother(s), crafts(man,men,woman, women,person,persons), producer(s). *See also* Ancestors; Artists; Authors; Creation; Creativity; Composers; Entrepreneurship; Etiology; Founding; Program implementation; Start up business;.

Credentialing. Credential(s,ing). Certif(y, ied,icate,ication). Licens(e,es,ed,ing). Accredit(ed,ing,ation). Legaliz(e,ed,ing). State board examination(s). Licensure. Approv(al,ed). Authorize(d). Endorse(d, ment). Validat(e,ed,ation). Regulated by profession. Approved qualifications. Registration. Registered. Board of examiner(s). *See also* Certification; Credentialism.

Credentialism. Credentialism. Diploma disease. *See also* Credentialing; Professionalism.

Credibility. Credib(ility,le). Believab(ility,le). Authentic(ity). Plausib(ility,le). Trustworth(y,iness). Dependab(ility,le). Reliab(ility,le). Assurance(s). Sincer(e,ity). Faithful(ness). Public expectation(s). Public confidence. Positive image(s). Convincing. Project(ed,ing) competence. *See also* Assurances; Beliefs; Communication (thought transfer); Communication skills; Corporate image; Deception; Ethics; Integrity; Interpersonal relations; Misinformation; Opinions; Persuasion; Political attitudes; Public opinion; Reputation; Social perception; Trusting; Trustworthy; Truth; Truth disclosure; Values.

Credit. Credit(or,ors). Deferred payment(s). Charge account(s). Charge card(s). Layaway(s). Borrowed money. Leveraged. Debt(s). Interest rate(s). Mortgage(s). Insolven(t,cy). Commercial paper. Overdraft(s). Past due account(s). Deficit(s). Usur(y,ious,iousness). Loan(s). Lend(ing). Credit card(s). *Consider also:* commercial paper, loan shark(s,ing), loanshark(s,ing), MasterCharge, MasterCard, VISA, etc. *See also* Arrears; Balance of payments; Banking; Consumer credit; Debts; Economic assistance; Economics; Financial support; Indebtedness; Interest (monetary); Liquidation; Loans; Usury.

Credit, agricultural. See *Agricultural credit.*

Credit, consumer. See *Consumer credit.*

Credulity. Credul(ity,ous,ousness). Gullib(le,leness,ility). Blind faith. Trustful(ness). Unsuspicious(ness). Overtrust(ing). Unquestioning. Uncritical. Unsuspecting. *See also* Trusting; Vulnerability.

Creeds. Creed(al,s). Credo(s). Symbol(a,um). Belief(s). Faith(s). Dogma(s). Doctrine(s). Tenet(s). Principles. Canon(s). Catechism(s). Teachings. Maxim(s). Precept(s). Document(s) of faith. Sententia(e). Credal formula(e). Catechism(s). *Choose from:* profession(s), expression(s), confession(s), statement(s), article(s) *with:* faith. *See also* Antinomianism; Assertions; Dogma; Edicts; Religious beliefs; Religious doctrines; Revealed theology.

Cremation. Cremat(e,ed,ing,ion,ions). Burn(ed,ing) corpse(s). Funeral pyre(s). Funeral pile(s). *Consider also:* suttee(s), cremain(s), cremator(y,ia,ium,iums). *See also* Burials; Death rituals; Funeral rites.

Creoles. Creole(s,ness). Creoliz(e,ed, ization) language(s). Recreoliz(e,ed, ization). Creolistic(s). Trade language(s). Louisiana French. Petit Negre. Sango. Spanglish. *Consider also:* decreoliz(e, ed,ization), lingua(e) franca(s,e), loan word(s), heterogeneous speech, vernacular, dialect(s), hybridized language(s). *See also* Culture contact; Diglossia; Ebonics; Language; Language maintenance; Language shift; Language varieties; Languages in contact; Lingua franca; Linguistic minorities; Loan words; Mobilian trade language; Nonstandard English; Pidgin languages; Speech communities; Trade languages.

Cretinism. Cretin(ism,istic). *Consider also:* deprivative amentia, Kocher-Debre-Semelaigne syndrome, Hoffman(s) syndrome, extreme hypothyroidism. *See also* Mental retardation.

Crews. Crew(s). Aircrew(s). Ship(s) company. Ship(s) complement. Work group(s). *Consider also:* staff(s), personnel, worker(s). *See also* Groups; Teams.

Crib death. See *Sudden infant death.*

Crime. Crime(s). Arson(ist,ists). Assassinat(e,ed,ion,ions). Assassin(s). Assault(s,ed,ing). Batter(ed,ing,ings, er,ers). Bandit(s,ry). Burglar(y,s). Blackmail(ed,ing,er,ers). Bootleg(ging, ged,er,ers). Breach(es) of law. Breach(es) of contract. Break in(s). Bribe(ry). Carjack(er,ers,ed,ing,ings). Cheat(ed,ing,er,ers). Child abuse(r,rs). Conspirac(ies,y). Corrupt(ion). Convict(s). Counterfeit(er,ers). Criminal intent(ion,ions). Criminal(ity). Delinquen(cy,t,ts). Defalcat(e,ed,ion, ions). Dishonest(y). Drug peddl(ing,er, ers). Elder abuse(r,rs). Embezzl(e,ing, ment,er,ers). Extort(ion,ions). Felon(s,y,ies). Filicide(s). Forger(ies,y, er,ers). Hijack(ed,ing,ings). Holdup(s). Homicide(s). Illicit. Illegal(ity,ities). Infanticide(s). Injustice. Kidnap(ped, ping,pings,per,pers). Lawbreaking. Lawless(ness). Fraud(ulent). Larcen(ous, y). Manslaughter(s). Misdemeanor(s). Matricide(s). Malpractice(s). Molest(ed, ing,ation,er,ers). Malfeasance. Mug(ged, ging,gings,ger,gers). Murder(s,er,ers). Neonaticide(s). Offense(s). Offender(s). Outlaw(s,ed). Prostitut(e,es,ion). Parricide(s). Patricide(s). Pornograph(ic, y). Pickpocket(s). Punishable act(s). Rape(s,d). Rapist(s). Riot(ed,s,ing). Robber(ies,y). Scofflaw(s). Sex offense(s). Sex offender(s). Sexual abuse(s). Sexual exploitation(s). Sniper(s). Shoplift(er,ers,ed,ing). Slay(ings). Spouse abuse(r,rs). Theft(s). Thieve(s,ry). Transgression(s). Tort. Trespass(er,ers). Unlawful. Violation(s). Vandal(s,ism). Sabotage. Kickback(s). Ransom. Blackmarket(s). Skyjack(ed, ing,er,ers). Hijack(ed,inger,ers). Flimflam. Mafia. Mafioso. Unione Siciliano. Underworld. Black Hand. Racket(s). Racketeer(ing). War crime(s). White collar crime(s). Organized crime. *See also* Accomplices; Antisocial behavior; Arson; Arrests; Assassination; Assault (personal); Bribery; Burglary; Cheating; Child abuse; Collusion; Computer crimes; Conflict of interest; Copycat crimes; Corruption in government; Crime prevention; Crime rates; Criminal abortion; Criminal act; Criminal intent; Criminal investigations; Driveby Crimes; Drug addiction; Drug and narcotic control; Drug trafficking; Drugs in athletics; Drunk driving; Embezzlement; Falsification (scientific); Fear of crime; Felonies; Follow home crime; Fraud; Hate crimes; Hijacking; Homicide; Illegal; Illicit liquor; Immorality; Industrial espionage; Infanticide; Kickbacks; Kidnapping; Larceny; Law enforcement; Misconduct in office; Money laundering; Offenders;

Offenses; Organized crime; Penal codes; Perjury; Perpetrators; Political crimes; Price fixing; Product tampering; Property crimes; Prostitution; Quackery; Racketeering; Rape; Robbery; Safety; Scientific misconduct; Sex offenders; Sex offenses; Sexual harassment; Shoplifting; Terrorism; Thieves; Thugs; Unreported crimes; Urban crime; Vandalism; Victimization; Victimless crimes; Violence; Violation; War crimes; White collar crime.

Crime, copycat. See *Copycat crime.*

Crime, fear of. See *Fear of crime.*

Crime, follow home. See *Follow home crime.*

Crime, organized. See *Organized crime.*

Crime, urban. See *Urban crime.*

Crime, white collar. See *White collar crime.*

Crime prevention. Crime prevention. Anticrime program(s). Neighborhood watch. Gun control. Self defense. Crimewatch. Crime stopper(s). Crime-fighting. Crimebuster(s). *Choose from:* prevent(ed,ing,ion,ive), deter(red,ring, rent,rents,rence), forestall(ed,ing), protect(ed,ing,ion), reduc(e,ed,ing,tion), combat(ting), fight(ing), control(led, ling), block(ed,ing), antidote(s), halt(ing) *with:* crime(s), delinquency, criminal(s), delinquen(t,ts), vandalism, rape, arson, violence, burglar(y,ies,s), robber(y,ies,s), illegal, unlawful, violation(s). *See also* Correctional system; Crime; Crime rates; Detention; Deterrence; Drug and narcotic control; Drug enforcement; Fear of crime; Gun control; Investigations; Law enforce-ment; Police community relations; Police dogs; Preventive detention; Safety; Security measures; Self defense; Sociological jurisprudence; Substance abuse detection.

Crime rates. Crime rate(s). Uniform crime reporting. Arson rate(s). Burglary rate(s). Homicide rate(s). Crime statistics. Distribution of crime. Delinquency rate(s). *Choose from:* crime(s), delinquency, arrest(s) *with:* survey(s), rate(s), statistics, trend(s), index(es), data. *See also* Crime; Judicial statistics; Mortality rates; Offenses; Rates; Unreported crimes.

Crime victims. See *Victimization.*

Crimes. See *Crime.*

Crimes, computer. See *Computer crimes.*

Crimes, driveby. See *Driveby crimes.*

Crimes, electronic. See *Computer crimes.*

Crimes, hate. See *Hate crimes.*

Crimes, Internet. See *Computer crimes.*

Crimes, nonvictim. See *Victimless crimes.*

Crimes, political. See *Political crimes.*

Crimes, prejudice motivated. See *Hate crimes.*

Crimes, property. See *Property crimes.*

Crimes, sex. See *Sex offenses.*

Crimes, unreported. See *Unreported crimes.*

Crimes, victimless. See *Victimless crimes.*

Crimes, war. See *War crimes.*

Crimes against humanity. See *Ethnic cleansing; Genocide; Holocaust; War crimes.*

Crimes against peace. Crime(s) against peace. Offense(s) against peace. *Choose from:* peace process(es), peacemaking, end civil war(s) *with:* oppos(e,ed,ing,ition), spoiler(s), hinder(ed,ing), obstruct(ed,ing,ion). *See also* Aggression; Civil war; Militarism; Nationalism; Peace negotiations; Peacekeeping forces; War; War preven-tion.

Crimes without victims. See *Victimless crimes.*

Criminal abortion. Criminal abortion(s). *Choose from:* criminal, illegal(ly,ality), unlawful(ly), black market *with:* abortion(s), terminat(e,ed,ing,ion) pregnanc(y,ies). *See also* Abortion; Abortion laws; Crime.

Criminal act. Criminal act(s,ion,ions). Commission of crime(s). Commit(ted, ting) crime(s). Guilty act. Actus reus. Extrajudicial killing(s). *Choose from:* commission, commit(ted,ting), perpetrat(e,ed,ing), act(s,ion,ions), perform(ed,ing,ance) *with:* crime(s), criminal, deed(s), offense(s), illegal(ity, ities), felon(y,ies), murder(s), burglar(y, ies), etc. *See also* Accomplices; Crime; Criminal intent; Felonies; Illegal; Penal codes; Perpetrators.

Criminal intent. Criminal intent(ion,ions). Mens rea. Guilty mind. Felonious intent(ion,ions). *Consider also:* criminal responsibility, knowingly commit(s). *See also* Crime; Criminal act; Insanity defense; Intention; Penal codes.

Criminal investigations. Criminal investigation(s). *Choose from:* criminal, crime(s), arson, assault(s), bombing(s), burglar(y,ies), fraud(s,ulent), homicide(s), larcen(y,ies), murder(s), rape(s), felon(y,ies), etc. *with:* investigat(e,ed,es,ing,ion,ions), detective(s), detect(ed,ing,ion), evidence, undercover operation(s), sting(s), solv(e,ed,ing) case(s), suspect identifica-tion, prob(e,es,ed,ing), track(ed,ing) down, inquir(e,y,ies). *Consider also:* police questioning, crimefighting, criminal DNA database(s), fingerprint(s). *See also* Arrests; Circumstantial evidence; Crime;

Criminal justice; Criminal proceedings; Defendants; Detectives; Evidence; Expert testimony; Extenuating circumstances; Forensic medicine; Law cnforccmcnt; Lie detection; Offenders; Penal codes; Plea bargaining; Police community relations; Police questioning; Search and seizure.

Criminal judgments. See *Judicial decisions; Sentencing.*

Criminal justice. Criminal justice. Criminal court(s). Criminal proceedings. Juvenile justice. *Choose from:* crime(s), misdemeanor(s), felon(y,ies) *with:* sentenc(e,ed,ing). Law enforcement system. Administration of justice. Judicial system. Correctional system. *See also* Arrests; Bail; Civil rights; Correctional system; Criminal investigations; Criminal proceedings; Criminal rehabilitation; Defendants; Evidence; Judicial decisions; Justice; Law enforcement; Litigation; Parole; Penal codes; Restitution; Sentencing; Sociological jurisprudence; Verdicts.

Criminal laws. See *Penal codes.*

Criminal proceedings. Criminal proceedings. Prosecut(e,ed,ing,ion). *Choose from:* criminal(s), offender(s) *with:* prosecut(e,ed,ing,ion), proceeding(s), trial(s), adjudication, appear in court, stand trial, processing, justice, plead(ing), convict(ed,ing,ion), sentencing, punish(ment). *See also* Arrests; Bail; Circumstantial evidence; Contempt of Court; Courts; Crime; Criminal investigations; Criminal justice; Defendants; Defense (verbal); Evidence; Expert testimony; Extenuating circumstances; Instructions to juries; Juries; Law enforcement; Litigation; Offenders; Penal codes; Plea bargaining; Police community relations; Parole; Police questioning; Probation; Prosecution; Sentencing; Trial (law); Verdicts.

Criminal psychology. Criminal psychology. *Choose from:* criminal(s,ity), criminolog(y,ical), convict(s), offender(s), delinquent(s), violator(s) *with:* behavior(s), personalit(y,ies), psychology, motivation, psychodiagnosis, psychodynamics, emotion(s,al), temperament(s), characteristic(s), intent(ion,ions), motiv(e,es,ation), psychiatric, MMPI, trait(s), sociopathic, psychopathic, antisocial, attitude(s). *See also* Competency to stand trial; Criminal intent; Criminal rehabilitation; Expert testimony; Forensic psychiatry; Insanity defense; Legal competency; Mentally ill offenders; Moral development.

Criminal registers. See *Police records.*

Criminal rehabilitation. Criminal rehabilitation. Alternative(s) to prison. College programs in prison(s). *Choose from:* criminal(s), correctional, delinquent(s), prisoner(s), prison(s),

offender(s), inmate(s), convict(s), ex-convict(s), parolee(s) *with:* self-improvement, rehabilitat(e,ed,ion), teach(ing), train(ed,ing), education, counsel(ing), community service, reform, community service, personal goal(s), self-actualization, self-esteem, growth, education, reading, social skill(s), vocational skill(s), work release. *See also* Alternatives to incarceration; Crime prevention; Criminal psychology; Ex-offenders; Offenders; Rehabilitation; Restitution; Restorative justice.

Criminally insane. See *Competency to stand trial; Criminal psychology; Insanity defense; Legal competency; Mentally ill offenders.*

Criminals. See *Offenders.*

Criminals, career. See *Career criminals.*

Criminals, female. See *Female offenders.*

Criminals, insane. See *Competency to stand trial; Insanity defense; Legal competency; Mentally ill offenders.*

Criminals, male. See *Male offenders.*

Criminals, mentally ill. See *Mentally ill offenders.*

Criminals, women. See *Female offenders.*

Crises. Cris(es,is). Crisology. Emergenc(y, ies). Catastroph(e,es,ic). Disaster(s). Trauma(s). Urgen(t,cy). Critical point(s). *Consider also:* juncture(s), decision point(s), turning point(s), survival situation(s). *See also* Crisis intervention; Crisis management; Disasters; Economic crises; Emotional crisis; Events; Experiences (events); Family crises; Identity crisis; Incidents; Maturational crisis; Midlife crisis; Organizational crises; Stress; Turning points.

Crises, economic. See *Economic crises.*

Crises, family. See *Family crises.*

Crises, organizational. See *Organizational crises.*

Crisis, accidental. See *Accidental crisis.*

Crisis counseling, rape. See *Rape crisis counseling.*

Crisis, emotional. See *Emotional crisis.*

Crisis, identity. See *Identity crisis.*

Crisis, maturational. See *Maturational crisis.*

Crisis, midlife. See *Midlife crisis.*

Crisis intervention. Crisis intervention. Hot line(s). Hotline(s). *Choose from:* cris(is,es), suicide(s), violen(t,ce), overdose(s) *with:* intervention, service(s), therap(y,ies), prevention, phone counselor(s), therap(y,ies,eutic), treatment. *Consider also:* emergency medical services, emergency psychiatric services, trauma center(s), poison control center(s), triage. *See also*

Assistance in emergencies; Counseling; Crime prevention; Crisis management; Crises; Disaster relief; Emergency medicine; Emergency services; Help lines (telephone); Psychiatric emergency services; Psychological debriefing; Psychotherapy; Rape crisis counseling; Rescue; Shelters; Suicide prevention; Telephone psychotherapy; Treatment; Walk-in clinics.

Crisis management. Crisis manage(ment, er,ers). *Choose from:* manag(e,ed,ing, ement,er,ers), cop(e,ed,ing) prevent(ed, ing,ion), prepar(e,ed,ing,ion), survival plan(s) *with:* crisis, crises, emergenc(y, ies), disasters, blackout(s), flood(s), power failure(s), etc. *Consider also:* emergency center(s), emergency command center(s). *See also* Coping; Crisis intervention; Crises; Disaster relief; Disaster recovery; Disasters; Economic crises; Problem solving; Stress management.

Crisis reactions. See *Stress reactions.*

Crisis shelters. See *Shelters.*

Criteria. Criter(ia,ion,ions). Multicriteria. Qualities for selection. Standard(s). Benchmark(s). Guideline(s). Model(s). Point(s) of comparison. Standard(s) for judgment. Checklist(s). Measure(s) of quality. *Consider also:* selection procedure(s). *See also* Benchmarks; Decision making; Evaluation; Excellence; Judgment; Perfection; Policy making; Quality; Quotas; School admission criteria; Standards.

Criteria, school admission. See *School admission criteria.*

Criterion referenced tests. Criterion referenced test(s). *Choose from:* criterion referenced, objective, mastery, proficiency *with:* test(s), measure(s, ment,ments). *See also* Achievement tests; Performance tests.

Critical care. Critical care. *Choose from:* critical(ly), intensive, dangerously ill, emergency, life threatening, near death *with:* care, therap(y,ies,eutic), nursing, treatment(s). *See also* Hospital environment; Intensive care; Nursing care.

Critical period (psychology). Critical period(s). *Choose from:* critical, sensitive *with:* period(s), phase(s), age(s). *See also* Development; Imprinting (psychology).

Critical theory. Critical theory. *Consider also:* postmodern critical thinking, poststructuralism, Neo-Marxis(m,t), Frankfurt School, Max Horkheimer, Theodor Adorno, Herbert Marcuse, Leo Lowenthal, Erich Fromm, Jurgen Habermas. *See also* Critical thinking; Hermeneutics; Humanization; Phenomenology; Postmodernism; Social change; Social theories; Social values; Sociology. •

Critical thinking. Critical thinking. Critical thought. Critical reasoning. Analytical thinking. Higher order thinking. Reflective judgment. *Choose from:* critical, analytical, higher order *with:* thinking, thought, reasoning, consciousness. *Choose from:* pedagog(y,ies) *with:* liberat(e,ed,ing,ion), humaniz(e,ed, ing,ion). *Consider also:* critical writing, critical reading, dialogic pedagog(y,ies), Socratic method. *See also* Active learning; Citizenship education; Cognitive processes; Consciousness raising activities; Creative thinking; Critical theory; Dialogic pedagogy; Information literacy; Logical thinking; Reasoning; Thinking.

Criticism. Critic(ize,ized,izing,ism). Critical stud(y,ies). Critique(s,d). Review(s,ed, ing). Comment(s,ed,ing,ary,aries). Analys(is,es). Evaluat(e,ed,ing,ion,ions). Apprais(e,ed,ing,al,als). Judg(e,ed,ing, ment,ments). Assess(ed,ing,ment,ments). Appreciat(e,ed,ing,ion). Interpret(ed,ing, ation,ations). Exposition(s). Comparative stud(y,ies). Literary stud(y,ies). Hermeneutic(s). Exegesis. Poetics. Explication(s). Reader response(s). Muckraker(s). Dissenting opinion(s). Complaint(s). Vet(ted,ting). *See also* Architectural criticism; Art criticism; Art critics; Assessment; Chattering class; Course evaluation; Diatribe; Dramatic criticism; Exegesis; Feminist criticism; Judgment; Literary criticism; Music criticism; Peer review; Personnel evaluation; Policy evaluation; Program evaluation; Self evaluation; Self evaluation (groups); Social approval; Social behavior; Social criticism; Social influences; Teacher evaluation.

Criticism, architectural. See *Architectural criticism.*

Criticism, art. See *Art criticism.*

Criticism, dramatic. See *Dramatic criticism.*

Criticism, feminist. See *Feminist criticism.*

Criticism, literary. See *Literary criticism.*

Criticism, medieval. See *Medieval criticism.*

Criticism, music. See *Music criticism.*

Criticism, social. See *Social criticism.*

Critics. See *Architectural criticism; Art criticism; Art critics; Criticism; Literary criticism; Peer review; Policy evaluation; Program evaluation; Social criticism.*

Critics, art. See *Art critics.*

Crops. Crop(s). Fruit(s,age). Harvest(s). *Consider also:* yield(s), gleaning(s), season(s) growth. *See also* Agriculture; Cultivated Plants; Farming; Plant cultivation; Plant succession; Plants (botanical); Products.

Crops, tree. See *Tree farms; Tree planting.*

Cross addiction. Cross addiction(s). Cross tolerance. Cross dependence. *See also* Drug interactions; Substance abuse; Substance dependence.

Cross-cousin marriage. See *Cousin marriage.*

Cross cultural communication. See *Intercultural communication.*

Cross cultural comparisons. Cross cultural comparison(s). Comparative sociology. Cultural comparison(s). International comparative stud(y,ies). Differences between societies. *Choose from:* cross cultural, cross-cultural, transcultural, international, pancultural, cross national *with:* difference(s), stud(y,ies), research, perspective(s), analys(is,es), appraisal(s), compar(ative,ison,isons), mapping. *See also* Anthropology; Area studies; Biculturalism; Bilingualism; Comparison; Comparative study; Countercultures; Cross cultural competency; Cultural anthropology; Cultural characteristics; Cultural conflict; Cultural issues; Cultural pluralism; Cultural relativism; Cultural universals; Cultural values; Culture (anthropology); Culture change; Culture fair tests; Differences; Ethnic differences; Ethnic groups; Ethnic relations; Ethnicity; Ethnography; Ethnology; Folk culture; Intercultural communication; Intercultural relations; Multilingualism; Racial differences; Social integration; Sociocultural factors; Subcultures.

Cross cultural competency. Cross cultural(ly) competen(t,cy). Transpection. *Choose from:* cross cultural(ly), intercultural(ly), global(ly), interethnic(ally), multicultural *with:* competen(t,cy), perspective(s), empath(y,etic), conscious(ness), worldview. *Consider also:* transpection. *See also* Biculturalism; Cross cultural comparisons; Cultural pluralism; Cultural relativism; Cultural sensitivity; Cultural values; Ethnic differences; Ethnic relations; Ethnic studies; Ethnocentrism; Global integration; Heterogeneity; Humanistic education; Intercultural communication; Internationalism; Multicultural education; Race relations; World citizenship.

Cross cultural psychiatry. Cross cultural psychiatry. *Choose from:* cross cultural, cross-cultural, transcultural, international, pancultural, cross national, comparative *with:* psychiatr(y,ic), psychoanaly(sis,ses,tic). *Consider also:* Ethnopsychiatr(y,ic). *See also* Culture specific syndromes; Ethnopsychology.

Cross disciplinary approach. See *Interdisciplinary approach.*

Cross dressing. See *Transvestism.*

Cross examination. Cross examin(e,ed,ing,ation). Cross-question(ed,ing). Interrogat(e,ed,ing,ion). *Consider also:* deposition(s), direct examin(e,ed,ing,ation), redirect examin(e,ed,ing,ation), interview(s,ing), police question(s,ing). *See also* Legal procedures; Testimony; Witnesses.

Cross eyed. Cross(ed) eye(s). Esotrop(ia,ic). Convergent strabismus. *See also* Eye; Vision disorders.

Crosses. Cross(es). Crucifix(es). Crux(es). Rood(s). Crosslet(s). *Consider also:* religious symbol(s). *See also* Christian symbolism; Religious articles; Religious rituals.

Crossing , racial. See *Racially mixed.*

Crossroads. Crossroad(s). Intersection(s). Junction(s). Interchange(s). Traffic circle(s). *Choose from:* highway(s), road(s), street(s) *with:* rotar(y,ies), roundabout(s), cloverleaf(s), overpass(es), underpass(es). *See also* Highway safety; Highways; Roads; Streets.

Crossroads. Crossroads. Intersection(s). Junction(s). Interchange(s). Traffic circle(s). *See also* Highways.

Crowd behavior. See *Collective behavior; Mass behavior; Mass hysteria; Riots; Social agitation.*

Crowding. Crowd(ed,ing,s). Overpopulat(ed,ing,ion). Social density. Population density. Populous(ness). Overcrowd(ed,ing). Throng(s). Mob(bed,bing). Multitude(s). Full house. Houseful. Congest(ed,ion). Rush hour. Heavy traffic. Standing room only. Horde(s). Crammed. Squeezed. Overflowing. Teeming. Swarming. *Consider also:* food shortage(s), territorial competition, cattle feedlot(s). *See also* Crowds; Overpopulation; Personal space; Population density; Stress.

Crowds. Crowd(s). Mob(s). Swarm(s). Throng(s). Horde(s). Mass(es). Herd(s). High attendance. Large audience(s). Packed stadium(s). Packed theatre(s). Densely populated. Congest(ed,ing,ion). *See also* Clusters; Collective behavior; Crowding; Groups; Mass hysteria; Riots; Social contagion.

Crucifixion. Crucif(y,ied,ies,ixion). Nail(ed,ing) to cross(es). Suffer(ed,ing) on the cross. *Consider also:* passion play(s). *See also* Christian symbolism; Crosses; Religious rituals.

Cruelty. Cruel(ty,ties). Abus(e,es,ed, ive,ing). Harass(ed,ing,ment,ments). Threat(s,ened,ening). Victimiz(e,ed, ing,ation). Tortur(e,es,ed,ing). Mistreat(ed,ing,ment). Maltreat(ed,ing, ment). Molest(ed,ing,ation,ations). Batter(ed,ing,ings). Brutal(ity,ities).

Violen(ce,t). Berat(e,ed,ing). Misus(e,ed,ing). Draconian. *See also* Abusive parents; Antisocial behavior; Battered women; Child abuse; Child abuse prevention; Coercion; Cruelty to animals; Deviant behavior; Elder abuse; Emotional abuse; Family violence; Offenses; Personality traits; Sadism; Sexual abuse; Sexual exploitation; Sexual harassment; Sexual sadism; Sexual violence; Spouse abuse; Threat; Torture; Victimization; Violence.

Cruelty, mental. See *Emotional abuse.*

Cruelty to animals. Cruelty to animal(s). Factory farm(s,ing). Puppy mill(s). Puppy farm(s). Pit bull(s) fight(s,ing). Smuggl(e,ed,ing) endangered species. Cockfight(s,ing). Club(bing) seal(s). Leghold trap(s). Steel jaw trap(s). *Choose from:* animal(s), pet(s), bird(s), waterfowl, dog(s), cat(s), goat(s), sheep, rabbit(s), etc. *with:* abus(e,es,ed,ing), mutilat(e,ed,ing,ion,ions), sacrifice(s), neglect(ed,ing), poison(ed,ing), cruel(ty,ties), inhumane, confin(e,ed, ing,ement), bad(ly) treat(ed,ment), poor(ly) treat(ed,ment), worst treat(ed,ment). *Consider also:* speciesism, animal rights, dolphin(s) *with* tuna(fishing). *See also* Animal rights movement; Animal sacrifice; Animal testing alternatives; Animal welfare; Animals; Bullfights; Cockfighting; Cruelty; Drugs in athletics; Moral development; Sadism; Trapping.

Cruelty to the aged. See *Elder abuse.*

Cruising. Cruis(e,es,ed,ing). Sail(ed,ing). Ocean travel. Travers(e,ed,ing) the sea(s). *Consider also:* journey(s,ing), travel(ed,led,ing,ling), boat(s,ing), cruise ship(s), cruise line(s), voyag(e, es,er,ers,ing), excursion(s), itinerar(y, ies). *See also* Sailing; Ships; Travel; Water transportation.

Crusades. Crusad(e,es,er,ers,ing). Croisades. Knights Hospital(ers,lers). Knights of Jerusalem. Knights Templars. Poor Knights of Christ. Latin Kingdom of Jerusalem. Latin Empire of Constantinople. Destruction of the Holy Sepulch(re,er). *Choose from:* holy war(s), pilgrimage(s), Christendom, Peter the Hermit, Walter the Penniless, Alexius I, Alexius IV, Alexius V, Isaac II, Godfrey of Bouillon, Conrad III, Louis VII, Saladin, Guy of Lusignan, Reginald of Chatillon, Raymond of Tripoli, Richard I, Phillip II, Frederick I, Fulk of Neuilly, Andrew II, Leopold VI, John of Brienne, Pelasius, Frederick II, Thibaut IV, Louis IX, Edward I, Christian(s), Pope Urban, Pope Gregory VIII, St. Bernard of Claivaux, Innocent III, attack(s,ed) *with:* Holy Land(s), Jerusalem, infidel(s), Moslem(s), Muslim(s), Islam(ic), Jerusalem, Palestine, Byzantine(s), Antioch,

Damascus, Adrianople, Jaffa, Ascalon, Cyprus, Tripoli, Constantinople, Damietta, Cairo, Tunis. *See also* Christianity; Expeditions; Feudalism; Infidels; Knights and knighthood; Medieval military history; Medieval theology; Middle ages; Militancy; Pilgrimages; Processions; Quests; Religious conversion.

Crying. Cry(ing). Cried. Cries. Wail(ed, ing). Weep(ing). Wept. Tear(s). Tear drop(s). Sob(s,bed,bing). Lament(ed, ing). Griev(e,ed,ing). *See also* Grief; Infant vocalization; Mourning.

Cryptography. Cryptograph(y,ic,s). Cryptogram(s). Encrypt(ed,ing,ion). *Choose from:* secret, scrambl(ed,ing), code(d), encode(d) *with:* message(s), language(s), data. *Consider also:* permissions-based access, cryptanalysis, coding system(s), data hiding, hidden data, secret code(s), steganograph(y,ic), data embed(ded,ding), public key certificate(s), digital signature(s). *See also* Coding; Computer security; Cyber attacks; Espionage; Firewalls (computers); Government secrecy; Secrecy.

Cubism. Cubis(m,t,e). *Consider also:* Pablo Picasso, Georges Braque, Jean Metzinger, Juan Gris, Marcel Duchamp, Fernand Leger, Roger de La Fresnaye, Robert Delaunay, Albert Gleizes, Frantisek Kupka, Guillaume Apollinaire, Pierre Reverdy, Gertrude Stein. *See also* Assemblage (Art); Futurism (Art); Futurism (Literary movement); Modern art.

Cues. Cue(s,d,ing). Indicator(s). Signal(s). Reminder(s). Prompt(s,ing). Miscue(s,d, ing). Sign(s). *See also* Association (psychology); Clues; Memory; Mnemonic learning.

Culinary arts. See *Cooking.*

Culpability. See *Blameworthy.*

Cultism. See *Cults.*

Cultivated plants. Cultivated plant(s). Plant domestication. *Choose from:* domesticat(e,ed,ing,ion,ions), cultivat(e,ed,ing,ion), cultivars, selective breeding, horticultur(e,al), husbandry *with:* plant(ae,s,ing,ings), crop(s), herb(age,s), flower(s,ing), tree(s), flora, vegetation, vegetable(s), vine(s), berr(y,ies), fruit(s), grass(es), etc. *Consider also:* origin(s) of agriculture. *See also* Agriculture; Crops; Gardening; Plant cultivation; Plant introduction; Plants (botanical); Prehistoric agriculture; Primitive food.

Cultivation, plant. See *Plant cultivation.*

Cults. Cult(s,ism). Therapeutic cult(s). Charismatic sect(s). New religious movement(s). New religion(s). Marginal religious movement(s). Deviant religion. Spiritual communit(y,ies). Christian

commune(s). Religious sect(s). Controversial religion(s). Nativistic movement(s). Ras Tafari. Survivalism. Theosophy. Churchless Christians of Japan. Spiritualist cult(s). Spiritualism. Holy Spirit Movement. Millenialism. Scientology. Jonestown. New religions. Church of the Cosmic Liberty. Jesus Movement. Church of the Sun. Meher Baba. Maharaji Ji. Unification Church. Moonies. Reverend Moon. Sun Myung Moon. Universal Church of the Kingdom of God. Bhagwan Shree Rajneesh. Kirpal Light Satsang. Evangelicals. Santeria Cult. Afro-Cuban Church of Santerian Faith. Movement of Spiritual Inner Awareness. Christian Patriots Defense League. Divine Light Mission. Love Israel's Church of Armageddon. Hare Krishna. Children of God. Jews for Jesus. Pentacostalism. Pentecostal Church Movement. Nation of Islam. Siddha Yoga Movement. Deadhead(s). Skinhead(s). Church of the Subgenius. Voodoo. Religious commune(s). New Mysticism. New Orientalism. Cargo cult(s). Witch cult(s). Satan worship. Satanism. Devil worship. Fundamentalist sect(s). *Consider also:* millenium, deprogramming, millenarian(ism). *See also* Cargo cults; Countercultures; Devils; Independent churches; Mass hysteria; Millenarianism; Mysticism; Occultism; Religious cults; Religious movements; Religious rituals; Secret societies; Sects; Therapeutic cults; Witchcraft.

Cults, cargo. See *Cargo cults.*

Cults, religious. See *Religious cults.*

Cults, therapeutic. See *Therapeutic cults.*

Cultural activities. Cultural activit(y,ies). Cultural event(s). Festival(s). *Choose from:* cultur(e,al), art(s), theatre(s), museum(s) *with:* activit(y,ies), event(s), affair(s), occurrence(s), occasion(s). *Consider also:* cultural consumption, high culture, popular culture, mass culture. *See also* Arts; Cultural events; Cultural literacy; Culture (anthropology); Dance; Festivals; Holidays; Museums; Music; Popular culture; Theater.

Cultural anthropology. Cultural anthropology. Ethnolog(y,ical). Ethnograph(y,ical). Social anthropology. *Choose from:* cultur(e,es,al), civilization(s), preliterate societies *with:* stud(y,ies), comparison(s). *Consider also:* anthropological linguistics, cross cultural studies, folk culture, ethnopsychology, archaeology, sociobiology. *See also* Cross cultural comparisons; Cultural relativism; Culture (anthropology); Customs; Ethnic groups; Ethnoarchaeology; Ethnography; Ethnolinguistics; Ethnology; Medical anthropology; Linguistics; Psychological anthropology; Traditions.

Cultural assimilation. See *Assimilation (cultural).*

Cultural capital. Cultural capital. *Choose from:* cultural *with:* capital, commodification, resource(s), endowment(s), asset(s), heritage, reproduction, transmission. *Consider also:* educational, academic *with:* background, attainment(s), achievement(s), qualification(s). *See also* Cultural property; Cultural transmission; Traditions.

Cultural change. See *Culture change.*

Cultural characteristics. Cultural characteristic(s). *Choose from:* cultur(e,es,al), sociocultural, ethnological, ethnic, subculture(s) *with:* characteristic(s), trait(s), tradition(s), value(s), heritage, custom(s,ary), role(s), difference(s), variation(s), vestige(s). *See also* Characteristics; Cross cultural comparisons; Cultural history; Cultural therapy; Cultural values; Culture (anthropology); Ethnic differences; Ethnic wit and humor; Ethnic values; Ethnicity; Racial identity; Qualities; Traditions.

Cultural comparisons. See *Cross cultural comparisons.*

Cultural comparisons, cross. See *Cross cultural comparisons.*

Cultural conflict. Cultur(e,al) conflict. Kulturkampf. Tribalism. *Choose from:* cultur(e,al), two cultures, ethnic, interethnic, multiethnic, bicultural, multicultural, ethnocultural, immigrant(s), intercultural, bicommunal, foreigner(s), refugee(s) *with:* conflict(s), encounter(s), difference(s), prejudice(d,s), discriminat(e,ed,ing,ion), subjugat(e,ed,ing,ion), resistance, discontent(ed), violen(t,ce), oppress(ed,ing,ion), dominat(e,ed, ing,ion), issue(s), marginaliz(e,ed,ing, ation), antagonism, instability. *Consider also:* marginal man, internal colon(y,ies), cultural imperialism, cultural militant(s), deculturation, ethnocide, chauvinism, nativism, ethnocentr(c,ism), cultural competition, irredent(a,as,ism,ist,ists), culture shock. *See also* Acculturation; Biculturalism; Bilingualism; Conflict; Countercultures; Cross cultural comparisons; Cultural groups; Cultural pluralism; Cultural values; Culture (anthropology); Culture change; Culture contact; Ethnic groups; Ethnic relations; Ethnic slurs; Ethnicity; Ethnocentrism; Eurocentrism; Immigrants; Indigenous populations; Intercultural communication; Intercultural relations; Marginality (sociological); Nativism; Nativistic movements; Political culture; Shock; Social conflict; Tribalism; Xenophobia.

Cultural constraints. See *Informal Social control.*

Cultural cooperation. Cultural cooperation. *Consider also:* cultural integration, cooperation culturelle, integración cultural. *See also* Acculturation; Bilingualism; Cultural relations; Culture contact; Diversity; Ethnic relations; Global integration; Globalization; Intercultural communication; Intercultural relations; International alliances; International cooperation; International educational exchange; International organizations; International relations; Race relations; Social integration.

Cultural deprivation. Cultural(ly) depriv(ed,ation). Cultural(ly) disadvantage(d,ment). *Choose from:* cultural(ly), sociocultural(ly), social(ly) *with:* disadvantage(d,ment), depriv(ed, ation), handicap(ped). Psychosocial(ly) retard(ed,ation). *Consider also:* psychosocial mental retardation, underprivileged, educational(ly) disadvantage(d,ment). *See also* Computer illiteracy; Cultural literacy; Deprivation; Disadvantaged; Illiteracy; Intellectual impoverishment; Pseudoretardation; Psychosocial deprivation; Social environment; Sociocultural factors.

Cultural differences. See *Cross cultural comparisons.*

Cultural diversity. Cultural diversity. Ethnic diversi(ty,ification). Cultural pluralism. Religious diversity. *Choose from:* intercultural, interethnic, multiethnic, bilingual, bicultural, transcultural, pluralistic, multicultural, cross-cultural, ethnically diverse, culturally diverse *with:* societ(y,ies), social unit(s), group(s), team(s), neighborhood(s), organization(s), population(s), workplace(s), countr(y, ies), background(s), student(s), patient(s), client(s,ele). *Consider also:* universalism, culturally sensitive integration, across cultural boundar(y, ies). *See also* Acculturation; Affirmative action; Community (social); Cultural pluralism; Culture (anthropology); Diversity; Ethnic groups; Intercultural communication; Melting pot; Minority groups; Racial diversity.

Cultural ethos. Cultural ethos. World view(s). Worldview(s). Weltanschauung. Belief system(s). World outlook(s). Philosophy of life. Outlook on life. *Consider also:* social realit(y,ies), cultural myth(s), ultimate realit(y,ies), cosmolog(y,ies), weltschmerz. *See also* Mythology; Social reality; Worldview.

Cultural events. Cultural event(s). Cultural activit(y,ies). Festival(s). *Choose from:* cultur(e,al), art(s), theatre(s), museum(s) *with:* activit(y,ies), event(s), affair(s), occurrence(s), occasion(s). *Consider also:* cultural consumption, high culture, popular culture, mass culture. *See also* Arts; Cultural activities; Dance; Festivals; Holidays; Museums; Music; Theater; Traveling theater.

Cultural evolution. Cultural evolution. Social change. Moderniz(e,ed,ing,ation). Societal change. *Choose from:* cultural, culture, values *with:* evolution, evolv(e,ed,ing), develop(ed,ing,ment), chang(e,ed,ing), revolution, adapt(ed,ing,ation). *See also* Culture change; Progress; Social change; Social Darwinism; Social development.

Cultural groups. Cultural group(s). Ethnic group(s). Immigrant group(s). Subculture(s). Cultural subgroup(s). Foreign minorit(y,ies). Cultural minorit(y,ies). *Choose from:* cultural, ethnic, immigrant, foreign, national(ity, ities) *with:* group(s), subgroup(s), minorit(y,ies), subculture(s). *Consider also:* Chinese Americans, etc. *See also* Acculturation; African empires; African cultural groups; Asian empires; Biculturalism; Central American native cultural groups; Cultural conflict; Cultural identity; Cultural pluralism; Cultural values; Culture contact; Ethnic groups; Indonesian cultural groups; Minority groups; North American native cultural groups; Oceanic cultural groups; Pre-Columbian empires; Philippine Islands cultural groups; Religious cultural groups; South American native cultural groups; Southeast Asian cultural groups.

Cultural groups, African. See *African cultural groups.*

Cultural groups, Central American. See *Central American native cultural groups.*

Cultural groups, Indian India. See *Indian (India) cultural groups.*

Cultural groups, Indonesian. See *Indonesian cultural groups.*

Cultural groups, North American. See *North American native cultural groups.*

Cultural groups, Oceanic. See *Oceanic cultural groups.*

Cultural groups, Philippine Islands. See *Philippine Islands cultural groups.*

Cultural groups, religious. See *Religious cultural groups.*

Cultural groups, South American. See *South American native cultural groups.*

Cultural groups, southeast Asian. See *Southeast Asian cultural groups.*

Cultural history. Cultur(e,al) history. Geistesgeschichte. Culturgeschichte. *Consider also:* historism, Volksgeist, spirit of the people. *See also* Ethnohistory; Historic houses; Historic ships; Historic sites; Historical perspective; History; Intellectual history; Literature appreciation; Psychohistory;

Renaissance literature; Renaissance philosophy; World history; Zeitgeist.

Cultural identity. Cultural identit(y,ies). National identit(y,ies). Ethnic identit(y,ies). Racial identit(y,ies). Ethnicity. Immigrant identit(y,ies). *Choose from:* Italian, Jewish, French, German, Japanese, Nigerian, etc *with:* identit(y,ies), identification, ethnicity, pride, heritage, descent, bloodline(s). *See also* Acculturation; Biculturalism; Bilingual education; Common culture; Cultural groups; Cultural knowledge; Cultural maintenance; Cultural pluralism; Cultural transmission; Cultural values; Culture (anthropology); Ethnic identity; Ethnic studies; Ethnicity; Ethnocentrism; Group identity; Immigrants; Language maintenance; Multicultural education; National identity; Nativism; Nativistic movements; Pan-Africanism; Plural societies; Racial identity; Social identity; Speech communities; Subcultures.

Cultural imperialism. Cultural imperialism. Cultural coloniz(e,ed,ing,ation). Cultural Domination. Imperialist Ideolog(y,ies). U.S. domination. American influence(s). Postcolonial(ism). Eurocentric(ism, ismo). Marco Polo syndrome. *Choose from:* postcolonial, United States, U.S., Europe(an), West(ern) *with:* influence(s), legac(y,ies), dominat(e,ed, ing,ion). *See also* Afrocentrism; Colonialism; Ecological imperialism; Imperialism; Intercultural relations; Neocolonialism; Spheres of influence.

Cultural influences. See *Social influences.*

Cultural issues. Cultural issue(s). Cross-cultural issue(s). Cultural contest(s,ed, ing,ation). Sociocultural issue(s). *Consider also:* cultural factor(s), cultural difference(s), cultural(ly) sensitiv(e,ity), culturally based obstacle(s), language barrier(s), cultural perspective(s), cultural oppression. *See also* Acculturation; Biculturalism; Cultural conflict; Cross cultural comparisons; Ethnic differences; Ethnic relations; Ethnocentrism; Nativism; Sociocultural factors; Subcultures; Tribalism.

Cultural knowledge. Cultural knowledge. Collective memory. Culture centered knowledge. *Choose from:* cultural, autochthonous, native, aboriginal, endemic, indigenous *with:* knowledge, wisdom, memor(y,ies). *Consider also:* lieux de memorie, cultural belief(s), enculturat(e,ed,ing,ation), aboriginal worldview, collective conscious(ness), ethnic identity, cultural traditions,. *See also* Collective consciousness; Collective representation; Cultural identity; Cultural literacy; Culture (anthropology); Political myths; Social history; Worldview.

Cultural lag. Cultur(e,al) lag. Cultur(e,al) inertia. *See also* Community change; Culture (anthropology); Culture change; Developing countries; Economic change; Future of society; Industrialization; Modernization; Social change; Technological progress; Urbanization.

Cultural literacy. Cultural(ly) litera(cy,cies,te). Cultural(ly) competen(t,ce,cy,cies). Cultural knowledge. Cultural(ly) aware(ness). Historical(ly) litera(cy,te). *Consider also:* multicultural(ly) competen(t,ce,cy,cies), cultural maturity, social(ly) competen(t,ce,cy,cies), cultural inclusiveness, intercultural literacy, global perspectiv(e,es,ism). *See also* Cultural activities; Cultural deprivation; Cultural knowledge; Cultural transmission; Culture (anthropology); Popular culture.

Cultural maintenance. Cultural maintenance. *Choose from:* cultur(e,es,al,aly), way of life, tradition(s,al,ally), ethnic(ally), sociocultural(ly) *with:* maintain(ed,ing), maintenance, restor(e,ed,ing,ation), retain(ed,ing), preserv(e,ed,ing,ation), revitaliz(e,ed, ing,ation), sustain(ed,ing), keep(ing) alive, reinforc(e,ed,ing,ment), recover(y,ed,ing). *See also* Assimilation (cultural); Acculturation; Biculturalism; Culture contact; Cultural identity; Cultural transmission; Cultural values; Ethnicity; Generativity; Intercultural communication; Intercultural relations; Language maintenance; Preservation.

Cultural pluralism. Cultural plural(ity,ism). Multiculturalism. Pluralistic societ(y,ies). Religious pluralism. Ethnic pluralism. Plural(istic) societ(y,ies). Multicultural societ(y,ies). American diversity. *Choose from:* multicultural, bicultural, pluralis(m,tic), heterogene(eous,ity) *with:* societ(y,ies), accomodat(e,ed,ing,ion,ion), nation(s). *Consider also:* melting pot. *See also* Acculturation; Antiracist education; Area studies; Assimilation (cultural); Biculturalism; Bilingualism; Common culture; Countercultures; Cross cultural comparisons; Cross cultural competency; Cross cultural psychiatry; Cultural conflict; Cultural diversity; Cultural groups; Cultural identity; Cultural relativism; Culture (anthropology); Culture contact; Diversity; Ethnic groups; Ethnic relations; Ethnicity; Intercultural communication; Language policy; Melting pot; Minority groups; Multicultural education; Multilingualism; Pluralism; Plural societies; Political culture; Power sharing; Race relations; Religious accomodation; Subcultures.

Cultural property. Cultural propert(y,ies). Cultural resource(s). National treasure(s). Artwork(s). Work(s) of art. Cultural object(s). Historic building(s). Historic place(s). National monument(s). Archaeological treasure(s). Artifact(s). Item(s) of cultural significance. National heritage. Cultural patrimony. Heritage proper(y,ies). National patrimony. *Consider also:* museum(s), National Historic Preservation Act, Archaeological site reports, UNESCO Cultural Property Convention. *See also* Archives; Art thefts; Art publishing; Artifacts; Arts; Cemeteries; Cultural capital; Cultural history; Earthworks; Historic houses; Historic sites; Literary landmarks; Municipal art; Museums, Natural monuments; Public art; Sanctuaries; Shrines; Underwater archaeology.

Cultural psychiatry, cross. See *Cross cultural psychiatry.*

Cultural relations. Cultural relations. *Choose from:* cultural, artwork(s), work(s) of art, artifact(s) *with:* relations, exchange(s), international flow(s), agreement(s), export(ed,ing), loan(s,ed,ing), diplomacy. *See also* Artifacts; Arts; Cultural cooperation; Diplomacy (official); Exchange of persons.

Cultural relativism. Cultural relativ(ity,ism). Ethical relativ(ity,ism). Moral relativ(ity,ism). Moral diversity. *Consider also:* cultural universals, moral evolution. *See also* Cross cultural competency; Cross cultural psychiatry; Cultural anthropology; Cultural pluralism; Cultural universals; Culture (anthropology); Culture specific syndromes; Determinism; Equitability; Ethnocentrism; Existentialism; Indifferentism (religion); Liberalism (religion); Multicultural education; Objectivity; Relativism; Sociocultural factors; Subjectivity; Value neutral.

Cultural reproduction. See *Cultural capital; Dominant ideologies; Social reproduction.*

Cultural sensitivity. Cultural sensitivity. *Choose from:* cultural(ly), intercultural(ly), diversity, ethnic difference(s) *with:* sensitiv(e,ity), aware(ness), respect(ful,fully), understanding, competen(t,ce,cy). *See also* Antibias curriculum; Cross cultural competency; Culture contact; Ethnic relations; Intercultural communication; Intercultural relations; Multicultural education; Race relations; Racial attitudes.

Cultural therapy. Cultural therapy. Anthropotherapy. Cross cultural therapy. *Choose from:* cultural *with:* therapy, psychotherapy. *Consider also:* conscienceization. *See also* Client characteristics; Cultural characteristics; Feminist therapy; Spiritual healing; Therapist characteristics; Therapy.

Cultural transformation. Cultural transformation. *Choose from:*

cultur(al,e), subculture(s), traditional values, family patterns *with:* transform(ed,ing,ation), adapt(ed,ing, ation), designif(y,ied,ying,ication), revitaliz(e,ed,ing,ation), uproot(ed,ing), transition(s,al), shift(s,ed,ing), obliterat(ed,ing,ion), social adjustment, fragment(ed,ing,ation). *Consider also:* modernization, industrialization, urbanization. *See also* Assimilation (cultural); Culture change; Moderniza- tion; Social change.

Cultural transmission. Cultural transmis- sion. *Choose from:* transmit(ted,ting), transmission, reproduction, socializa- tion, internalization assimilat(e,ed, ing,ion), absor(b,ption) *with:* cultur(e, es,al), values, norm(s), belief(s), custom(s), rite(s), knowledge. (Inter)generational transmission. *See also* Acculturation; Childrearing; Cultural capital; Cultural conflict; Cultural groups; Cultural history; Cultural identity; Cultural literacy; Cultural maintenance; Cultural values; Culture change; Culture contact; Generativity; Hidden curriculum; Information dissemination; Intellectual capital; Intergenerational relations; Oral history; Preservation; Social reproduc- tion; Socialization; Transmission of texts.

Cultural universals. Cultural universal(s). Cultural alternative(s). *See also* Cross cultural comparisons; Cultural relativ- ism; Culture (anthropology); Social norms.

Cultural values. Cultural value(s). *Choose from:* cultur(e,al), social, sociocultural, societ(y,ies), ethnic, immigrant, Protestant, Catholic, Jewish, Muslim, Chinese, Spanish, Mexican, German, gypsy, etc. *with:* value(s), ethic(al,s), belief(s), myth(s,ology,ogies), perspective(s), norm(s), attitude(s), ideolog(y,ies,ical), expectation(s), ideal(s). *See also* Acculturation; Aesthetics; Arts; Biculturalism; Civilization; Counptercultures; Cross cultural comparisons; Cross cultural competency; Cultural conflict; Cultural groups; Cultural identity; Cultural maintenance; Cultural transmission; Culture (anthropology); Ethnic attitudes; Ethnic values; Ideologies; Religious attitudes; Religious cultural groups; Social norms; Social values; Subcul- tures; Traditional societies; Traditions.

Culturally deprived. See *Cultural deprivation.*

Culturally disadvantaged. See *Cultural deprivation.*

Culturally relevant pedagogy. Culturally relevant pedagogy. Culturally congruent pedagogy. Culturally responsive pedagogy. Cultural pedagogy. *Choose*

from: relevan(ce,t), empowering *with:* education(al), instruction(al), curricul(a, ae,um), pedagogy. *Consider also:* pedagogy of the oppressed, culturally appropriate pedagogy. *See also* Educa- tional needs; Multicultural education; Relevance.

Culture (anthropology). Cultur(al,e,es). Social heritage(s). Cultural heritage. *Consider also:* artifact(s), art(s), belief(s), ceremonial(s), civilization(s), custom(s), ethnic(ity), ethnocultural, ethnograph(y,ic), ethnolog(y,ical), ethnopsycholog(y,ies,ical), folklore, folkway(s), humanities, ideolog(y,ies), intercultural, laws, morals, mores, religion(s), ritual(s), social structure(s), sociocultural, sociohistor(y,ical), subculture(s), taboo(s), tradition(al,s), value(s), weltanschauung(en), world view(s). *See also* Acculturation; Arts; Assimilation (cultural); Beliefs; Biculturalism; Civilization; Cross cultural comparisons; Cross cultural psychiatry; Cultural activities; Cultural anthropology; Cultural capital; Cultural characteristics; Cultural conflict; Cultural deprivation; Cultural diversity; Cultural ethos; Cultural events; Cultural evolution; Cultural groups; Cultural history; Cultural identity; Cultural knowledge; Cultural lag; Cultural literacy; Cultural pluralism; Cultural property; Cultural relations; Cultural relativism; Cultural transmission; Cultural universals; Cultural values; Culture change; Culture contact; Culture fair tests; Culture shock; Culture specific syndromes; Customs; Ethnic groups; Ethnography; Ethnology; Folk culture; Folklore; Folkways; Humanities; Intellectual history; Intercultural communication; Linguistics; Material culture; Minority groups; Multicultural education; Organizational culture; Political culture; Popular culture; Prison culture; Psychological anthropology; Public folklore; Races; Religions; Religious cultural groups; Rites of passage; Rituals; Social history; Society; Sociocultural factors; Subcultures; Technology; Traditional societies; Traditions; Worldview; Youth culture;.

Culture, animal. See *Animal culture.*

Culture, beauty. See *Beauty culture.*

Culture, bee. See *Bee culture.*

Culture, common. See *Common culture.*

Culture, corporate. See *Organizational culture.*

Culture, cyberpunk. See *Cyberpunk culture.*

Culture, fish. See *Fisheries; Mariculture.*

Culture, folk. See *Folk culture.*

Culture, intergenerational transmission of. See *Generativity; Cultural transmis- sion.*

Culture, marginal. See *Marginality (sociological).*

Culture, mass. See *Popular culture.*

Culture, material. See *Material culture.*

Culture, organizational. See *Organiza- tional culture.*

Culture, political. See *Political culture.*

Culture, popular. See *Popular culture.*

Culture, prison. See *Prison culture.*

Culture, self. See *Self culture.*

Culture, youth. See *Youth culture.*

Culture change. Culture change. Cultural effects of modernization. *Choose from:* cultur(e,al), sociocultural, value(s), myth(s), norm(s) *with:* change(s), chang(ed,ing), clash(es), moderniz(e, ed,ing,ation), conflict(s), development, evolution, evolv(e,ed,ing), loss(es), shock, unstable, instability, revolution(s), declin(e,ed,ing), drift, convergence, engineering, lag. *Consider also:* acculturation. *Consider also:* social, societal, community *with:* change(s), chang(ed,ing), moderniz(e,ed, ing,ation), conflict(s), development, evolution, evolv(e,ed,ing), loss(es), unstable, instability, revolution(s), declin(e,ed,ing). *See also* Acculturation; Assimilation (cultural); Change; Cross cultural comparisons; Cultural conflict; Cultural evolution; Cultural groups; Cultural transformation; Cultural transmission; Culture (anthropology); Culture contact; History; Indigenous populations; Intercultural communica- tion; Modernization; Social change; Social development; Social integration; Social processes; Sociocultural factors; Technological change; Technological progress; Technology and civilization; Traditional societies; Traditionalism.

Culture contact. Cultur(al,e) contact. Cultural hybrid. Marginal man. Bicultural oscillation. Bicultural(ism). Cultural convergence. Acculturat(ed,ion). Dominant culture. Colonial(ism). Cultur(e,al) borrowing. Creol(es,ization). Expatriate(s). Immigrant(s). *Choose from:* cultural, cross cultural, intercultural, interethnic, interracial, interfaith, inter-religious *with:* contact(s), borrowing, relation(s), communication(s), conflict(s), interac- tion, trust, cross-fertilization, coopera- tion. *See also* Acculturation; Biculturalism; Colonialism; Creoles; Cross cultural comparisons; Cultural conflict; Cultural cooperation; Cultural groups; Cultural maintenance; Cultural pluralism; Cultural sensitivity; Cultural transmission; Culture (anthropology); Culture change; Culture shock; Deterritorialization; Eurocentrism; Indigenous populations; Intercultural communication; Intercultural relations;

Language maintenance; Language shift; Languages in contact; Loan words; Multicultural education; Pidgin languages; Social contact; Traditional societies.

Culture fair tests. Culture fair test(s,ing). Culture free test(s,ing). Unbiased test(s,ing). *See also* Culture (anthropology); Ethnic groups; Multicultural education; Test bias.

Culture shock. Culture shock. Sojourner adjustment. *Choose from:* immigrant(s), immigration, emigration, refugee(s), expatriate(s), foreigner(s), exchange student(s), overseas, migrant(s), peace corps, culture contact, culture conflict, acculturation, cultural transition(s) *with:* stress(es), dysfunction(s,al), mental(ly) ill(ness,nesses), suicide(s), emotional problem(s), mental health, trauma(tic), anxiety, anxious(ness). *See also* Acculturation; Americans abroad; Biculturalism; Cross, cultural comparisons; Cultural conflict; Cultural pluralism; Culture (anthropology); Culture change; Ethnicity; Ethnocentrism; Immigrants; Refugees; Revolution; Social environment; Values.

Culture specific syndromes. Culture specific syndrome(s). Ethnic psychos(is,es). *Consider also:* amok, amuck, amurakh, arctic hysteria, ataque, bangungut, berserk, delahara, echul, espanto, hsieh-ping, imu, jumping Frenchmen of Maine, juramentado, kimilue, koro, latah, mal de pelea, menerik, misala, miryachit, nightmare-death syndrome, piblokto, piloktoq, pseudoamok syndrome, Puerto Rican syndrome, suk-yeong, shook yong, susto, tropenkoller, voodoo death, whitiko, wihtigo, wihtiko, windigo, witigo. *See also* Cross cultural psychiatry; Cultural relativism; Ethnospecific disorders; Psychological anthropology; Psychoses.

Cultures, dominated. See *Dominated cultures.*

Cuneiform. Cuneiform. *Consider also:* Akkad(ian) cuneiform, Sumerian cuneiform, Old Persian syllabary, Ugaritic script(s). *See also* Deciphering; Hieroglyphics; Iconography; Petroglyphs; Pictography; Written communications.

Cunnilingus. See *Oral sex.*

Curiosity. Curio(us,sity). Exploratory behavior(s). Inquisitive(ness). Inquir(y,ing). Asking questions. Questioning. Investigative behavior(s). *See also* Exploratory behavior; Interests; Motivation; Personality traits.

Currency. Currenc(y,ies). Money. Coin(s). Hard currency. Coins of the realm. Cash. Monetary unit(s). U.S. Mint. Foreign exchange rate(s). Legal tender. *Choose from:* currenc(y,ies) *with:* exchange(s), arbitrage, rate(s), devalu(ed,ing,ation), strength, strong, weak(ness). Afghani(s). Baht(s). Balboa(s). Bolivar(s). Cedi(s). Centime(s). Colon(s). Cordoba note(s). Cruzeiro(s). Dalasi(s). Deutsche mark(s). Dinar(s,e). Dobra(s). Dollar(s). Dong(s). Donga(s). Dirham(s). Drachma(s). Ekuwele(s). Escudo(s). Euro(s). Euro(dollars). Finggit(s). Forint(s). Franc(s). Franken(s). Gourde(s). Guarani(s). Guilder(s). Gulf Riyal(s). Kina(s). Kip(s). Koruna(s). Krona(s). Krone(s). Kwacha(s). Kwanza(s). Kyat(s). Lek(s). Lempira(s). Leone(s). Leu(s). Lev(s). Lilangeni(s). Lira(s). Lire(s). Markka(s). Naira(s). Ngultrum(s). Ouguiya(s). Pa'anga(s). Pataca(s). Peseta(s). Peso(s). Pound(s). Pulo(s). Quetzal(s). Rand(s). Rial(s). Riel(s). Ruble(s). Rupee(s). Rupiah(s). Schilling(s). Shekel(s). Shilling(s). Sol(s). Sucre(s). Syli(s). Taka(s). Tala(s). Tughrik(s). Won(s). Yen. Yuan(s). Zaire(s). Zloty(s). *See also* Bimetallism; Cash; Coin portraits; Coinage; Coins; Devaluation (of currency); Emergency currency; Gold buying; Gold standard; Monetary policy; Monetary unions; Money supply.

Currency, common. See *Common currency.*

Currency, devaluation of. See *Devaluation (of currency).*

Currency, emergency. See *Emergency currency.*

Currency speculation. Currency speculation. Currency trader(s). *Consider also:* currency option(s). *See also* Devaluation (of currency); Gold buying; Purchasing power; Speculation.

Current events. Current event(s). News of the day. *Choose from:* current, contemporary *with:* affair(s), topic(s), news, event(s), history. *See also* Citizenship education; Controversial issues; Politics; Social problems; World problems.

Currents, electric. See *Electric currents.*

Curriculum. Curricul(um,a,ae,ar). *Consider also:* core course(s), qualifying course(s), course outline(s), recommended course(s). *See also* Courses; Curriculum change; Curriculum development; Hidden curriculum.

Curriculum, antibias. See *Antibias curriculum.*

Curriculum, hidden. See *Hidden curriculum.*

Curriculum change. Curriculum change. *Choose from:* curriculum, curricula(r), core. course(s), educational program(s) *with:* chang(e,ed,ing), transform(ed,ing), reform(ed,ing), reorient(ed,ing). *See also* Antibias curriculum; Curriculum;

Curriculum development; Multicultural education.

Curriculum development. Curriculum development. *Choose from:* curricul(a,um), core course(s), educational program(s) *with:* plan(ned,ning), develop(ed,ing,ment), adapt(ed,ing, ation), improv(e,ed,ing,ement,ements), modification(s), organiz(e,ed,ing,ation), reorganiz(e,ed,ing,ation), revis(e,ed, ing,ions), design(ed,ing), construct(ed, ing,ion). *See also* Curriculum; Curriculum change; Instructional media; Teaching materials.

Cursing. Curs(e,es,ed,ing). Swear(ing). Damn(ed,ing,ation). Blasphem(y,ing, ous) Tak(e,ing) the name of God in vain. Cuss(es,ed,ing). Execrat(e,ed,ing,ion). Profan(e,ity,ities). Oath(s). Expletive(s). Four letter word(s). Malediction. *Consider also:* accursed, bedeviled, damned, hell fire. *See also* Blasphemy; Sin; Voodooism.

Cursive writing. Cursive writing. *Choose from:* handwriting, signature(s), italics, script writing, penmanship. *See also* Autographs; Signatures; Writing.

Curtain tunes. See *Interludes (music).*

Custodial care. Custodial care. *Choose from:* custodial, residential, domiciliary *with:* care, treatment(s), facilit(y,ies), unit(s). *Consider also:* personal care *with:* attendant(s), service(s), home(s). *See also* Adult day care; Adult foster care; Boardinghouses; Group homes; Institutional homes; Institutionalization (persons); Institutionalized mentally retarded; Sheltered housing.

Custodians. Custodian(s). Guardian(s,ship, ships). Guard(s). Caretaker(s). Curator(s). Overseer(s). Warden(s). Bodyguard(s). *Consider also:* concierge(s), conservator(s), janitor(s), steward(s). *See also* Caregivers; Custodial care; Janitors.

Custody, child. See *Child custody.*

Custom unions. Custom union(s). Common external tariff(s). *Consider also:* free trade area(s), free trade zone(s), regional market(s), partial economic integration, trade creation, wasteful production, trade diversion, Zollverein, European Economic Community. *See also* Common markets; Economic union; Exports; Foreign trade zones; Free trade; Harmonization (trade); Imports; International economic integration; International trade; Trade preferences.

Customer relations. Customer(s) relation(s,ship,ships). Complaint department(s). Consumer(s) advoca(cy, te,tes). *Choose from:* customer(s), consumer(s), user(s) *with:* relation(s, ship,ships), satisf(ied,action,ying), information, request(s), complaint(s), affair(s), support, service. *See also*

Brand loyalty; Client relations; Consumer participation; Consumer satisfaction; Complaints; Corporate image; Customer services; Merchants; Promotion (business); Public relations; Service contracts; Vendor relations.

Customer satisfaction. See *Consumer satisfaction.*

Customer services. Customer service(s). *Choose from:* customer(s), user(s), request(s), consumer(s) *with:* service(s), deliver(y,ies), handling, treat(ed,ing, ment), shipment(s), respect. *Consider also:* customer focus, put(ting) customer first, user-friendl(y,iness), quality assurance. *See also* Appliance repair; Brand loyalty; Client relations; Consumer satisfaction; Customer relations; Maintenance; Service contracts.

Customers. Customer(s). Client(s). User(s). Student(s). Patient(s). Buyer(s). Patron(s). Clientele. Shopper(s). Consumer(s). Borrower(s). Plaintiff(s). Depositor(s). Purchaser(s). Passenger(s). Constituenc(y,ies). Prospect(s). Enduser(s). Seeker(s). *See also* Client characteristics; Client relations; Consumers; Online users.

Customs. Custom(ary,s). Ritual observance(s). Ritual(s). Tradition(al,s). Convention(al,ality,s). Folkway(s). Norm(s). Manners. Etiquette. Holiday(s). Ceremon(y,ies). Observance(s). Fashion(s). Socially prescribed. Unwritten law(s). *See also* Behavior; Body ornamentation; Clothing; Culture (anthropology); Ethnicity; Ethnography; Ethnology; Etiquette; Fashions; Festivals; Folk culture; Folklore; Folkways; Heritage; Holidays; Laws; Marriage customs; Mortuary customs; Rites of passage; Rituals; Social norms; Taboo; Traditional societies; Traditions; Wife lending.

Customs, birth. See *Birth rites.*

Customs, drinking. See *Drinking customs.*

Customs, marriage. See *Marriage customs.*

Customs, mortuary. See *Mortuary customs.*

Customs, sex. See *Sex customs.*

Customs administration. Customs administrat(ion,ions,ing,or,ors). Customs service(s). Customs inspect(ion,ions, or,ors). Border search(es). Border restriction(s). *Consider also:* smuggl(ed,ing), gray market(s,eer,eers, eering), black market(s,eer,eers,eering). *See also* Drug trafficking; Law enforcement; Smuggling.

Cutbacks. Cutback(s). Cut(ting) back(s). Cut(ting)down. Curtail(ed,ing,ment). Decreas(e,es,ed,ing). Reduc(e,ed,ing, tion,tions). Retrench(ed,ing,ment, ments). *Consider also:* economiz(e,ed,

ing), trim(med,ming). *See also* Budget cuts; Dismissal of staff; Personnel termination.

Cuts, budget. See *Budget cuts.*

Cutting scores. Cutting score(s). *Choose from:* cut(ting), critical, cutoff, minimum passing *with:* score(s), point(s). *See also* Criterion referenced tests.

Cyber attacks. Cyber attack(s). Computer attack(s). Hack attack(s). Spam attack(s). System break-ins. *Choose from:* cyber, computer, spam(ming), internet, e-mail, web site(s), home page(s), web page(s), hackers *with:* attack(sed,ing), warfare, intruder(s), intrusion(s), security threat(s), security penetration(s), vandal(s,ism), espionage, infring(e,ed, ing) trademark(s), violat(e ,ed,ing) copyright(s), steal(ing) data, virus attack(s). *See also* Computer bugs; Computer crime; Computer viruses; Cryptography; Electronic eavesdropping; Weapons of mass destruction.

Cybercafes. Cybercafe(s). Internet café(s). Web café(s). *Choose from:* Internet, net, cyberspace, cyber, web, www *with:* café(s), coffee bar(s), coffee house(s), restaurant(s). *See also* Bars; Coffee houses; Eating establishments; Internet (computer network); Online users; Popular culture; Restaurants.

Cybercommunities. Cybercommunit(y,ies). Electronic communit(y,ies). *Choose from:* Internet, virtual, net, web(s), cyberspace *with:* communit(y,ies), social aggregation(s), public discussion(s), public sphere(s), social system(s). *Consider also:* listserv(s), electronic democrac(y,ies), global village(s), Usenet, MUD(s), MultiUser Dungeon(s), MOO(s), MUD Object Oriented, newsgroup(s), Cybersociet(y, ies). *See also* Community networks (computer); Information highway; Information society; Internet (computer network); Popular culture; Social support; Virtual organizations; Virtual reality.

Cybercrooks. See *Computer crimes.*

Cyberlaw. Cyberlaw(s). Cyber-rule(s). *Choose from:* Internet, information superhighway, information highway, infohighway, I-way, infobahn, cyberspace, information infrastructure, electronic superhighway, National Spatial Data Infrastructure, geospatial data, digital data, digital information, electronic copying, online services, communications, telephone, cable television, satellite industry *with:* law(s), legislation, bill(s), copyright, public polic(y,ies), regulat(e,ed,es,ing,ion,ions), deregulat(e,ed,es,ing,ion,ions), public good(s), guaranteed access, First Amendment, freedom(s), intellectual property right(s), censorship, licens(e,ed, ing), doctrine(s), restriction(s). *See also*

Computer crimes; Digital signatures; Electronic eavesdropping; Electronic publishing; Information highway; Internet (computer network); Laws; Privacy laws; Surveillance of citizens; Telecommunications.

Cybernetics. Cybernetic(s). *Consider also:* feedback, cyborg, psychocybernetic(s), neurocybernetic(s), biocybernetic(s), general systems theory. *See also* Artificial intelligence; Automation; Communication (thought transfer); Computers; Feedback; Game theory; Information processing; Man machine systems; Robotics; Technological progress.

Cyberpunk culture. Cyberpunk culture. Hacker culture. Cyberpunk aesthetic(s). *Consider also:* rave/techno subculture, protogeek(s). *See also* Computer crimes; Popular culture.

Cybersex. Cybersex. Net sex. Virtual sex. Online sex. Sex chat line(s). *Choose from:* chat room(s), internet, email, cyberculture, cyberchat, cyberspace *with:* porn(ography), sex(ual,ually), sexual fantas(y,ies), kinky, sadomasochistic, sexual harassment, adult entertainment, erotica, aphrodisiacs, sex toy(s), pickup(s), set up assignation(s). *Consider also:* cyberfleshpot(s), long distance sex, telephone sex, electronic bordello(s), cyberdello(s), cyberbrothel(s). *See also* Adult entertainment; Indecent communications; Obscenity; Online harassment;. Pornography; Scatology; Sex industry; Sexual exploitation; Sexual harassment; Vulgarity.

Cycle, generational of child abuse. See *Generational cycle of child abuse.*

Cycle, human life. See *Human life cycle.*

Cycle, life. See *Life cycle.*

Cycle, lunar. See *Lunar cycle.*

Cycle, menstrual. See *Menstrual cycle.*

Cycle, product life. See *Product life cycle.*

Cycle, sleep wake. See *Sleep wake cycle.*

Cycle, song. See *Song cycle.*

Cycles, business. See *Business cycles.*

Cycles, economic. See *Business cycles.*

Cycles, trade. See *Business cycles.*

Cycles, work rest. See *Work rest cycles.*

Cycling. See *Bicycling.*

Cyclothymic disorder. Cyclothymic disorder. Cyclothymic personality. Cycloth(emia,thymia). Cyclophren(ia, ic). *Choose from:* periodic, fluctuat(e,ed,ing,ion,ions) *with:* excitement(s), high(s), low(s), depression(s), mood(s). Phasic affective disorder(s). Bipolar affective disorders. *See also* Bipolar disorder; Hypomania;

Manic disorder; Seasonal affective disorder.

Cynicism. Cynic(al,ism,s). Satirical. Sardonic. Sarcas(m,tic). Misanthrop(ic, y). Pessimis(m,tic). Misogyn(ic,ism). Distrust(ful). Defeat(ist,ism). Suspicious(ness). Skeptic(al,ism). Scornful. Disparag(ing,ement). Disdain(ful). Negativ(ity,ism). Derisive(ness). *Consider also:* jaundiced view(s). *See also* Negativism; Personality traits; Pessimism; Social perception; Worldview.

Cynics. See *Cynicism.*

D

Dadaism. Dada(ism,ist). Nonsense poem(s). Ready-made. Merz. *Consider also:* anti-art, Neo-Dada, Neue Sachlichkeit, Tristan Tzara, George Grosz, Aragon, Jean (or Hans) Arp, Marcel Duchamp, Francis Picabia, Man Ray, Kurt Schwitters, Max Ernst. *See also* Abstract art; Absurd; Assemblage (Art); Collage; Concrete art; Concrete poetry; Constructivism; Futurism (Art); Modern art; Nihilism; Performance art; Pop art; Surrealism.

Daily. Daily. Circadian. Per diem. Quotidian. Diurnal(ly). Once every day. *Consider also:* everyday, habitual(ly), customar(y,ily). *See also* Activities of daily living; Everyday life; Frequently.

Daily activities. See *Activities of daily living; Everyday life.*

Daily life. See *Activities of daily living; Everyday life.*

Daily living, activities of. See *Activities of daily living.*

Dairy products. Dairy product(s). Dairy spread(s). *Consider also:* milk, butter, cheese(s), yogurt, cream, sour cream, whey, infant formula(s), milkshake(s). *See also* Animal industry; Cattle industry; Food; Food industry; Food inspection; Milk industry.

Dairying. Dair(y,ies,ing). Dairy farm(s,ing). Dairy development. Dairy cooperative(s). Milk cooperative(s). *See also* Agribusiness; Agriculture; Animal industry; Farming; Meat industry; Milk industry.

Damage. Damag(e,ed,ing,s). Harm(ed,ing). Hurt(ing,s). Wound(ed,ing,s). Casualt(y, ies). Mutilat(ed,ing,ion). Wreck(ed,ing). Vandal(ism,ize,ized,izing). Ruin(ed,ing). Break(ing). Broken. Spoil(ed,ing). Defac(e,ed,ing,ement). Wreak(ed,ing) havoc. *See also* Brain damage; Defacement; Disasters; Imperfection; Strike damage.

Damage, brain. See *Brain damage.*

Damage, liability for toxic substances. See *Toxic torts.*

Damage, strike. See *Strike damage.*

Damage compensation, war. See *War damage compensation.*

Damaged, brain. See *Brain damaged.*

Damages. Damages. Punitive punishment(s). *Choose from:* injur(y,ies,ious), defam(e,ed,es,ation, ing), victim(s,ization), liabilit(y,ies), hazard(s,ous), harm(ed,ing) *with:* compensation, settle(d,ment,ments), award(s). *Consider also:* malpractice suit(s), mass tort(s) litigation (as in Bhopal disaster), crime victim(s) compensation, class action suit(s), caus(e,ed,ing) loss(es). *See also* Exemplary damages; Lawsuits; Liability; Malpractice; Reparations; Toxic torts.

Damages, exemplary. See *Exemplary damages.*

Damages, hedonic. See *Hedonic damages* .

Dams. Dam(s,ming,med). *Consider also:* hydroelectric power, hydropower. *See also* Drainage; Earthwork; Flood control; Irrigation.

Dance. Danc(e,es,er,ers,ing). Danse(s). Tanz(e). Choreography. Disco. *Consider also:* aerobic danc(e,ing), ballroom dancing, ballet, body popping, bolero, boogie, breakdancing, break-danc(e, ing), bunny hop, capoeira, cha cha, charleston, clog, conga, contredanse, cotillion, cumbia, danse macabre, dancercis(e,ing), folk dancing, fox trot, galliard, gavotte, habanera, highland fling, hoe down, hora, hornpipe, hula, Irish jig, jazz danc(e,ing), jazzercis(e, ing), jitterbug(ging), lambada, mazurka, merengue, minuet, modern dance, moonwalk(s,ed,ing), pas de deux, pavane, polka, quadrille, rhumba, rhythmic exercise(s), salsa, samba, saraband(e), schottische, soft shoe, square dance, tango, tap danc(e,ing), tarantella, twist, Virginia reel, waltz(es,ing). *See also* Ballet dancers; Ballet dancing; Ballroom dancing; Belly dance; Choreography; Contredanse; Cultural activities; Dance education; Dance music; Dance notation; Dance therapy; Dancers; Dirty dancing; Experimental dance; Folk culture; Folk dancing; Improvisation (dancing); Jazz; Jazz dance; Male dancers; Music; Rhythm; Theater; Waltz.

Dance, belly. See *Belly dance.*

Dance, country. See *Country dance.*

Dance, jazz. See *Jazz dance.*

Dance education. Dance education. *Choose from:* danc(e,ing), ballet *with:* lesson(s), class(es), instruction, school. *See also* Aesthetic education; Dance; Dance music; Dance therapy.

Dance music. Dance music. Dance repertor(y,ies). Dance composition(s). *Consider also:* pavane(s), galliard(a), allemande(s), saraband(e,es,s), courante(s), jig(s), gigue(s), gavotte(s), minuet(s), waltz(es), ballet(s), etc. *See also* Ballroom dancing; Dance; Dance education; Dance notation; Folk dancing.

Dance notation. Dance notation. Labanotation. Benesh Movement Notation. Eugene Loring's system of dance notation. *Consider also:* dance transcription, record(ing) a dance, video recording(s) of a dance. *See also* Ballet dancing; Choreography; Dance.

Dance therapy. Dance therap(y,ies). Choose from: danc(e,ing), terpsichortrance, movement with: therap(y,ies,eutic). *Consider also:* rhythmic exercises, authentic movement. *See also* Dance; Movement therapy; Music therapy; Play therapy; Self expression.

Dancers. Dancer(s). Dance team(s). Ballerina(s). Dance career(s). Member(s) of dance compan(y,ies). *See also* Ballet dancers; Dance; Male dancers.

Dancers, ballet. See *Ballet dancers.*

Dancers, male. See *Male dancers.*

Dancing, ballet. See *Ballet dancing.*

Dancing, ballroom. See *Ballroom dancing.*

Dancing, dirty. See *Dirty dancing.*

Dancing, experimental. See *Experimental dancing.*

Dancing, folk. See *Folk dancing.*

Dancing mania. See *Choreomania.*

Danger. Danger(s,ous,ousness). Unsafe. Unsound. Precarious(ness). Threat(s,en, ened,ening). Counterthreat(s). Intimidat(e,ed,ing,ion). Menac(e,ed,ing). Peril(s,ous). Risk(s,y). Hazard(s,ous). Jeopard(y,ize,ized,izing). Frighten(ing). Imperil(ed,ing). *Consider also:* warning(s), omen(s), caution(s). *See also* Dangerous behavior; Dangerousness; Hazardous materials; Hazards; Threat; Violence; Vulnerability; Warnings.

Dangerous behavior. Dangerous behavior(s). *Choose from:* dangerous(ness), violen(t,ce), endanger(ed,ing), assault(ed,ing,ive) *with:* behavior, act(s,ions), conduct, habit(s). *Consider also:* dangerousness standard(s), considered dangerous. *See also* Aggression; Criminal intent; Danger; Dangerousness; Maximum security facilities; Threat postures; Violence.

Dangerousness. Dangerous(ness,ly). *Choose from:* danger(ous), peril(ous), frightening, unsafe, hazard(s,ous), risky, precarious, lethal, deadly, alarming, menac(e,ed,ing), peril(ous,ousness), threaten(ed,ing), treacherous(ness), unsound, vulnerab(le,ility) *with:*

situation(s), condition(s), dut(y,ies), patient(s), offender(s), task(s), driving, behavior(s), signal(s). *Consider also:* war zone(s), combat zone(s). *See also* Aggressiveness (trait); Danger; Dangerous behavior; Harmful behavior; Hazardous occupations; Threat; Violence.

Danse, basse. See *Basse danse.*

Darwinism. Darwin(ian,ism). Evolution(ary) theor(y,ies). Survival of the fittest. Origin of Species. Natural selection. Speciat(e,ion,ional). Neo-Darwinism. *Consider also:* Lysenkoism, evolutionary genetics, sexual selection, rise of species, adapt(ed,ing,ation) to environment, genetic variability, polygenism, anthropic principle. *See also* Biological diversity; Creationism; Evolution; Evolutionism; Evolutionary ethics; Genetics; Natural history; Social Darwinism; Sociobiology.

Darwinism, social. See *Social Darwinism.*

Data. Data. Information. Fact(s). Factual information. Statistic(s). Profile(s). Score(s). Statistical material(s). Document(s,ation). Note(s). Statistical table(s). Abstract(s). Database(s). Record(s). Report(s). Transcript(s). Statistical summar(y,ies). Questionnaire result(s). Test result(s). Rate(s). Compilation(s). Dossier(s). *Consider also:* evidence, note(s), memo(s), text(s). *See also* Data analysis; Data collection; Data interpretation; Data processing; Databases; Facts; Information; Statistical data; Trivia.

Data, biographical. See *Biographical data.*

Data, financial. See *Financial data.*

Data, statistical. See *Statistical data.*

Data analysis. Data analy(sis,ses,zing). Analy(sis,ses,zing) of data. Statistic(s,al) analy(sis,ses,zing). Microanalysis of data. Contingency analysis. Analysis of variance. Correlation. Linear analysis. Multivariate analysis. Regression analysis. *Consider also:* data interpretation. *See also* Classification; Data; Data collection; Data interpretation; Communications research; Content analysis; Data processing; Statistical data; Statistical inference; Statistical significance.

Data banks. See *Databases.*

Data collection. Data collection. *Choose from:* data, information, fact(s), statistic(s), profile(s), score(s), statistical material(s), document(s,ation), note(s), statistical table(s), rate(s), abstract(s), record(s), report(s), transcript(s), summar(y,ies), result(s), input, feedback *with:* collect(ed,ing,ion), gather(ed,ing), accumulat(e,ed,ing,ion,ions), assembl(e,ed,ing), generat(e,ed,ing), acquir(e,ed,ing), acquisition(s).

Consider also: polling, interview(s,ing), case stud(y,ies), census(es), content analys(is,es), experiment(ation,s), fieldwork, life histor(y,ies), longitudinal stud(y,ies), observation, participant observation. *See also* Archaeological surveying; Data analysis; Data entry; Data interpretation; Data processing; Health care surveys; Information processing; Push-polling; Questionnaires; Research; Sampling; Sexual behavior surveys; Statistical data; Surveys.

Data entry. Data entry. Text entry. Text encoding. Data input. Data captur(e,ed,ing). Key(ing,er,ers). Keyboard(ing,er,ers). *Consider also:* voice recognition software, scanner(s), pen-based computer(s), note taking, hand-writing recognition software. *See also* Data collection; Data processing.

Data interchange, electronic. See *Electronic data interchange.*

Data interpretation. Data interpretation. *Choose from:* data, information, fact(s), statistic(s,al), profile(s), score(s), document(s,ation), note(s), table(s), rate(s), abstract(s), record(s), report(s), transcript(s), summar(y,ies), result(s), input, feedback *with:* assess(ed,ing, ment,ments), interpret(ed,ing,ation, ations), massag(e,ed,ing), explanation(s), explain(ed,ing), analys(es,is). *See also* Data analysis; Hypothesis testing; Interpretation; Statistical inference; Test interpretation.

Data processing. Data processing. *Choose from:* data *with:* process(ed,ing), entry, manage(d,ment), tabulat(ed,ing,ion), handl(e,ed,ing), manipulat(ed,ing,ion), massag(e,ed,es,ing). *See also* Automated coding; Automated information storage; Automation; Data collection; Data entry; Databases; Electronic data processing; Information processing; Punched card systems.

Data processing, electronic. See *Electronic data processing.*

Data scrambling. See *Cryptography.*

Data structures. Data structure(s). Information structure. *Consider also:* flat file database(s), relational database(s), data independence. *See also* Databases.

Data transmission systems. Data transmission system(s). *Choose from:* data, information, signal(s) *with:* transmission(s), transmit(ted,ting, tal,tals), download(ing), send(ing), sent, rout(e,ed,ing), forward(ed,ing), convey(ed,ing), dispatch(ed,ing), ship(ped,ping), telephone lines, network(s), communicat(e,ed,ing), channel(s). *See also* Computer networks; Computers; Connectivity; Telecommunications.

Database management. Database management. Data management. *Choose from:* data(base,bases), file(s), record(s) *with:* management, managing, warehousing. *Consider also:* data compression, data dictionar(y,ies), data warehousing file organization, text processing. *See also* Databases.

Database marketing. Database marketing. Relationship marketing. Contact management program(s). Prospect database(s). Telemarketing list(s). *Choose from:* mailing lists, customer database(s), customer(s) record(s), customer relations(hip,hips), customer service(s), customer account(s) *with:* marketing. *See also* Advertising; Direct mail marketing; Management information systems; Order processing; Telemarketing.

Databases. Database(s). Databank(s). *Choose from:* data *with:* base(s), bank(s), file(s), collection(s), librar(y,ies), set(s), storage, online, machine readable, offline. *Consider also:* computer(ized) data. *See also* Automated information retrieval; Automated information storage; Computer networks; Computers; Data; Database management; Electronic publishing; Full-text databases; Information dissemination; Information services.

Databases, full-text. See *Full-text databases.*

Date conversion, year 2000. See *Millennium bug.*

Date of birth. Date(s) of birth. Birthdate(s). Birthday(s). *See also* Birth.

Date rape. See *Acquaintance rape.*

Dating, social. See *Social dating.*

Datum, sense. See *Sense datum.*

Daughters. Daughter(s). *Choose from:* female(s), girl(s) *with:* offspring, child(ren), descendent(s). *Consider also:* granddaughter(s). *See also* Children; Females (human); Parent child relations; Sibling relations; Siblings.

Dawn. Dawn(ing). Sunrise(s). Early light. Break of day. Daybreak. First light. Sunup. Auror(a,al,ean). Cockcrow(ing). *See also* Beginning; Creation; Daytime; Time.

Day, judgement. See *Judgement day.*

Day, working. See *Alternative work patterns; Personnel scheduling; Work load; Work schedules; Workday shifts; Working conditions; Worktime.*

Day care, adult. See *Adult day care.*

Day care, child. See *Child day care.*

Day care, corporate. See *Corporate day care.*

Day care, elderly. See *Adult day care.*

Day care, foster. See *Foster home care; Child day care; Adult day care; Corporate day care.*

Day of Rest. See *Sabbath.*

Day reporting centers (corrections). Day reporting center(s). Correction(s,al) day program(s). Daily probation. *Choose from:* correction(s,al), justice, sanction(s), decarcerat(e,ed,ing,ion), detention, supervised liberty, probation, parol(e,ee,ees), sentenc(e,ed,ing) *with:* day center(s), day report(ing) facilit(y,ies), day reporting program(s). *See also* Alternatives to incarceration.

Daydreaming. Daydream(s,ing). Fantasy life. Reverie(s). Day dream(s,ing). Fantasiz(e,ed,ing,ings). Wishing. Pipe dream(s). Castles in the air. Imagin(e,ed, ing,ings,ary,ation). Figment(s) of imagination. Preoccup(ied,ation,ations). *See also* Absentmindedness; Fantasies (thought disturbances); Imagery; Imaginary conversations; Imagination; Sexual fantasies.

Days hospitalized. See *Length of stay.*

Daytime. Daytime. Daylight hour(s). Full sun. Working day(s). *See also* Dawn; Time; Workday shifts.

De facto. De facto. In reality. In actuality. Actual(ly). Genuine(ly). Tangibl(e,y). Veritabl(e,y). *Consider also:* exist(ing, ent), extant, not formally recognized, factum probandum, outside the law, inadvertent(ly). *See also* Act (Philosophy); Action; Common law; De jure; Racial segregation; Squatters.

De jure. De jure. By right. Of right. Legitimat(e,cy). Lawful(ly). By just title. Compl(y,ying,ied,iance) with law. Rightful(ly). *See also* De facto; Justification (law); Legal rights; Legitimacy; Validity.

De-skilling. See *Labor process; Mass production; Proletarianization; Scientific management.*

Dead. See *Ancestor worship; Death; Thanatology.*

Dead bodies. Dead bod(,ies). Corpse(s). Cadaver(s). Carcass(es). Human remains. *See also* Bog bodies; Anatomical gifts; Organ transplantation; Tissue banks; Tissue donors.

Deadbeat parents. Deadbeat parent(s). *Choose from:* deadbeat(s), nonsupport, obligor(s) *with:* parent(s), dad(s), father(s), mom(s), mother(s), paternity. *Choose from:* skip(ped,ping), neglect(ed, ing), fail(ed,ing,ure), owe(d), owing, neglect(ed,ing), negligent, delinquent *with:* child support. *Consider also:* Child Support Recovery Act, Personal Responsibility and Work Opportunity Act. *See also* Abandoned children; Child

neglect; Debts; Desertion; Parental absence.

Deadlock. Deadlock(s,ed). Block(ed,ing, age). Checkmate(s,d). Dead end(ed,s). Gridlock(ed,ing). Impasse(s). Stalemate(s,d). Standoff(s). Tie(s,d). *Consider also:* demosclero(sis,tic), analysis paralysis, standstill. *See also* Barriers; Blockade; Dilemmas; Hindrances; Limitations.

Deafness. Deaf(ness,ened). Anacus(is,ia,ic). Anacous(is,ia,ic). Hearing loss(es). Hearing impair(ed,ment,ments). Hard of hearing. Partial(ly) hearing. Dysmelodia. Tune deafness. Hearing disorder(s). Aural(ly) handicap(s,ped). *Consider also:* deaf(ness) *with:* sensorineural, partial(ly). *Consider also:* hearing aid(s), lipreading, presbycusis, tinnitus. *See also* Disability; Hearing disorders; Partial hearing; Tone deafness; Word deafness.

Deafness, tone. See *Tone deafness.*

Deafness, word. See *Word deafness.*

Deal, new. See *New Deal.*

Dealers. Dealer(s). Business(woman, women,man,menperson,persons). Merchandiser(s). Trader(s). Trades(man, men,people). Trafficker(s). Merchant(s). Retailer(s). Marketer(s). Vendor(s). Shopkeeper(s). Dealer(s). Jobber(s). Middle(man,men). Huckster(s). Higgler(s). Peddler(s). Wholesaler(s). *Consider also:* banker(s), business owner(s). *See also* Agents; Brokers; Merchants; Stock brokers.

Dealers, securities. See *Stock brokers.*

Deals. Deal(s,ing). Bargain(s,ing). Good buy(s). Discount(s). Giveaway(s). *Consider also:* kickback(s). *See also* Bargaining; Bartering; Discounts; Economic exchanges; Exchange; Firm offers; Kickbacks; Negotiation; Purchasing; Sales.

Deals, sweetheart. See *Conflict of interest.*

Deans. See *Educational administrators.*

Death. Death(s). Dying. Died. Dead. Mortal(ly) wound(s,ed). Deceased. Lethal(ly). Expire(d). Fatal(ity,ties). Mortalit(y,ies). Terminal(ly). Still(birth, born). Euthanasia. Drown(ed,ing). Post mortem. Kill(ed,ing). Mercykilling. Neomort. Terminal(ly) ill(ness,nesses). Thanatology. Asphyxia(ted). Brain dea(th,d). Cadaver(s,ous). Postmortem change(s). Rigor mortis. Succumb(ed, ing). Murder(s,ed). Homicide(s). Passed away. Suicide(s). Genocide(s). Infanticide(s). Fratricide(s). Patricide(s). *Consider also:* funeral(s), burial(s), memorial service(s), last rite(s), tomb(s,stone,stones), grave(s), cemeter(y,ies), obituar(y,ies), autops(y, ies), extinct(ion), afterlife, necrolog(y, ies), hospice(s), widow(ed,er), loss of

loved one, mourn(ed,ing), bereave(d,ment). *See also* Assisted suicide; Attitudes toward death; Autoerotic death; Brain death; Burials; Caregiver burden; Cause of death; Cemeteries; Child mortality; Cremation; Dead bodies; Death anxiety; Death certificates; Death education; Death instinct; Death penalty; Death rituals; Drowning; Dying; Euthanasia; Fatalities; Fetal death; Funeral rites; Homicide; Hospices; Infant mortality; Life (biological); Life change events; Life cycle; Life expectancy; Loss (psychology); Mass murders; Mortality rates; Near death experiences; Obituaries; Sudden infant death; Suicide; Suicide victims; Terminal care; Terminal illness; Thanatology; Widowhood.

Death, attitudes toward. See *Attitudes toward death.*

Death, autoerotic. See *Autoerotic death.*

Death, brain. See *Brain death.*

Death, cause of. See *Cause of death.*

Death, civil. See *Civil death.*

Death, cot. See *Sudden infant death.*

Death, crib. See *Sudden infant death.*

Death, fetal. See *Fetal death.*

Death, language. See *Extinct languages; Language obsolescence.*

Death, late fetal. See *Fetal death; Infant mortality.*

Death, presumption of and absence. See *Absence and presumption of death.*

Death, sudden infant. See *Sudden infant death.*

Death anxiety. Death anxiet(y,ies). *Choose from:* death(s), dying, mortal(ity,ities) *with:* concern(s), anxiet(y,ies), anxious(ness), apprehens(ive,iveness, ion,ions), dread(ed,ing), frighten(ed, ing), fantas(y,ies), worr(y,ies,ied), fear(s,ful,fulness). *See also* Attitudes toward death; Anxiety disorders; Death; Dying.

Death certificates. Death certificat(e,es, ion). *Choose from:* certificat(e,es,ion), certif(y,ied), document(ed,ing,ation), determin(e,ed,ing,ation) *with:* suicide(s), death(s), murder(s), fatalit(y,ies). *See also* Autopsy; Death; Documents.

Death counseling. Death counseling. *Choose from:* death, dying, terminal(ly), euthanasia, funeral(s), burial(s), memorial service(s), last rite(s), griev(e,ed,ing), hospice(s), widow(ed, er), loss of loved one, mourning, bereave(d,ment) *with:* pastoral, counsel(ed,ing), psychotherap(y,ies), psychosocial care, therap(y,ies), support(ive). *See also* Bereavement; Counseling; Death; Death education; Hospices; Loss (psychology); Loss adjustment; Pastoral care; Widowhood.

Death education. Death education. *Choose from:* death, dying, thanatology, terminal illness(es) *with:* course(s), curriculum, education, program(s), training, teaching, preparation, workshop(s). *See also* Aging education; Death; Death counseling; Humanistic education; Patient education; Professional education.

Death experiences, near. See *Near death experiences.*

Death instinct. Death instinct. Thanatos. *Choose from:* death, die *with:* drive(s), instinct(s), impulse(s), wish(es). *Consider also:* destrudo, mortido. *See also* Death; Self destructive behavior; Suicide; Suicide victims; Unconscious (psychology).

Death of God (theology). Death of God. God is dead. *Consider also:* nihilis(m,tic), Nietzsche(an). *See also* Alienation; Existentialism; Presence of God; Religious beliefs; Secularization.

Death of spouse.. See *Widowhood.*

Death penalty. Death penalt(y,ies). Capital punishment. Death row. Execut(e,ed,ion,ions). Electric chair. Capital defendant(s). Capital offense(s). Hang(ed,ing,ings). Behead(ed,ing,ings). Gibbet(s). Guillotine(s). *Choose from:* death, capital *with:* sentenc(e,ed,es,ing), penalt(y,ies). *Consider also:* burn(ed, ing) at the stake, crucifixion(s). *See also* Beheading; Clemency; Death; Deterrence; Life sentence; Punishment.

Death rates. See *Mortality rates.*

Death rituals. Death ritual(s). Death rite(s). Death custom(s). Funeral custom(s). Funeral practice(s). Mourn(ed,ing). Death observance(s). Feast(s) for the dead. Prayer(s) for the dead. Prayer(s) for the deceased. Burial(s). Cremat(ing, ed,ion,ions). Funeral(s). Ghost dance(s). Wake(s). Suttee. Mortuary practice(s). Celebration(s) of death. Kaddish. *See also* Burials; Cemeteries; Cremation; Death; Fetal propitiatory rites; Funeral rites; Loss adjustment; Loss (psychology); Mummies; Obituaries; Religious rituals; Rites of passage.

Death squads. Death squad(s). Hit squad(s). *Consider also:* lynch mob(s), terrorist group(s), secret police, terrorist state(s). *See also* Missing persons; Paramilitary; Vigilantes.

Debacle. *See Defeat; Collapse.*

Debasement, self. See *Self debasement.*

Debate. Debat(e,ed,er,ers,ing). Discuss(ed, ion,ions). Deliberat(e,ed,ing,ion,ions). Argu(e,ed,ing,ment,ments,mentation). Exchange views. For(a,um,ums). Dispute(d,s). Disputation. Polemic(s). *Consider also:* dissent(ed,ing). *See also* Campaign debates; Discourse; Discussion; Disputes; Forensics (public speaking); Literary quarrels; Oratory; Persuasion; Political campaigns; Presentations; Public meetings; Public speaking; Religious disputations.

Debates, campaign. See *Campaign debates.*

Debates, religious. See *Religious disputations.*

Debility. Debilit(y,ies). Weakness(es). Infirm(ity,ities). Feeble(ness). Enfeeble(ment). Enervat(e,ed,ing). Asthenia. Exhaust(ed,ion). Lassitude. Decrepit(ude). Listless(ness). Frail(ty,ties). Faint(ness). Degeneration. *See also* Asthenia; Chronic disease; Decline; Disability.

Debit card fraud. Debit card(s) fraud(ulence,ulent). Debit card counterfeit(s,ed,ing). *Choose from:* debit card(s), bank card(s) *with:* fraud(ulence, ulent), counterfeit(s,ed,ing), stolen, steal(ing), unauthorized transaction(s). *See also* Consumer credit; Consumer expenditures; Consumer fraud; Counterfeiting; Fraud; Impostor; Victimization.

Debriefing, psychological. See *Psychological debriefing.*

Debris. Debris. Detritus. Dregs. Dross. Flotsam. Garbage. Junk. Offal. Rubbish. Trash. Waste. Rubble. Rubbish. *Consider also:* fragment(s), ruins, wreck(s,age), remains. *See also* Fragments; Litter (waste); Ruins; Solid waste; Wrecks.

Debt, corporate. See *Corporate debt.*

Debt, foreign. See *Public debt.*

Debt, national. See *Public debt.*

Debt, public. See *Public debt.*

Debt-for-nature swaps. Debt-for-nature swap(s). Debt-for-nature exchange(s). Trad(e,ing) debt(s) for conservation. Nature for debt trade off(s). *Choose from:* debt(s) *with:* environment(al,ally), ecolog(y,ical), nature, conservation, park(s), reforest(ed,ing,ation) *with:* swap(s), exchange(s), trad(e,ing), trade off(s), forgive(ness), exchange(s,d), convert(ed,ing). *See also* Balance of payments; Debt moratoriums; Developing countries; Economic development; External debts; Financial support; Forest conservation; International relations; Public debt; Sustainable development.

Debt management. Debt management. *Choose from:* debt(s), credit card(s), *with:* manag(e,ed,ing,ement), handl(e,ed,ing), adjust(ed,ing,ment), recoup(ed,ing), reduc(e,ed,ing,tion), buyback(s), eliminat(e,ed,ing,ion), negotiat(e,ed,ing,ion), relief, refinanc(e,ed,ing). *Consider also:* bankruptcy. *See also* Asset management; Bankruptcy; Budget deficits; Debt moratoriums; Debts; Liquidation; Turnaround management.

Debt moratoriums. Debt moratori(a,um, ums). *Choose from:* debt(s) *with:* moratori(a,um,ums), renegotiat(e,ed, ing,ation), restructur(e,ed,ing), repric(e,ed,ing), repackag(e,ed,ing), delay(s,ed,ing) repayment(s), breather on repayment(s). *See also* Bad debts; Debt-for-nature swaps; Debt management; Debts; External debts; Public debt; Refinancing.

Debts. Debt(s). Indebted(ness). Megadebt(s). Deferred payment(s). Borrowed money. Leveraged buyout(s). Interest rate(s). Mortgage(s). Insolven(t,cy,cies). Commercial paper. Overdraft(s). Past due account(s). Deficit(s). Usury. Loan(s). Lend(ing). Deadbeat(s). Default(ing,er,ers). Bankruptc(y,ies). Owe(d). Owing. Arrears. Debit(s,ed). *Consider also:* collection agenc(y,ies), credit(or,ors), charge account(s), layaway, financial obligation(s), balance sheet(s), defeasance, collateral(ize,ized,izing), liabilit(y,ies), red ink. *See also* Bankruptcy; Bad debts; Corporate debt; Credit; Deadbeat parents; Debt management; Debt moratoriums; Default (negligence); Encumbrance; External debts; Interest (monetary); Leveraged buyouts; Loans; Money; Public debt; Refinancing.

Debts, bad. See *Bad debts.*

Debts, external. See *External debts.*

Debugging. Debug(ged,ging). *Choose from:* correct(ed,ing,ion), detect(ed,ing,ion), eliminat(e,ed,ing,ion), remov(e,ed, ing,al), scan(ned,ning) *with:* error(s), fault(s), bug(s), virus(es), problem(s), malfunction(s). *See also* Computer bugs; Computer viruses; Computers; Electronic eavesdropping; Fault tolerant computing; Millennium bug; Quality control; Software (computers).

Debut. See *Beginning.*

Decadence. Decaden(t,ce). Decadentism. Self-destruct(ion,ive). Decline and Fall. Dissipat(e,ed,ing,ion). Decay(ed,ing). Corrupt(ed,ing,ion). Perver(t,ted,sion). Debase(d,ment). Degenerat(e,ed,ing, ion). Downfall. Breakdown of moral(s,ity). *Choose from:* social(ly), cultural(ly), moral(ly) *with:* deteriorat(e, ed,ing,ion), dissolution, decay(ed,ing), degenerat(e,ed,ing,ion), regress(ed,ing, ion), pessimism, disintegrat(e,ed,ing, ion), decompos(e,ed,ing,ition), subjectivism. *See also* Anomie; Corruption in government; Decline; Deterioration; Moral conditions; Regression (civilization); Social disorganization.

Decadence (Literary movement). Decaden(ce,t) movement. *Consider also:* Jules La Forgue, Arthur Symons, Oscar Wilde, Ernest Dowson, Lionel Johnson. *See also* Literary movements; Symbolist movement.

Decapitation. See *Beheading.*

Decay, memory. See *Memory decay.*

Deceit. See *Deception.*

Deceiving. See *Artificiality; Cheating; Deception; Disguise; Faking; Falsification (scientific); Fraud; Fraudulent advertising.*

Decency. Decen(t,cy). Appropriate(ness). Befit(ting). Correct(ness). Respectab(le, ility). Propriety. Seeml(y,iness). Decor(um,ous,ousness). Gentility. Good form. Appropriate(ness). Fitting(ness). Suitab(le,ility). Ceremonious(ness). Conventional(ity). Formalit(y,ies). Social(ly) acceptab(le,ility). *Consider also:* etiquette, correct(itude,ness), orderl(y,iness), proper(ness), propriety. *See also* Acceptability; Etiquette; Humility; Modesty; Norms; Public order.

Decentralization. Decentraliz(ed,ing,ation). Distribut(e,ed,ing,ion) power. Downsiz(ed,ing). Delegat(e,ed,ing,ion) authority. Dispers(e,ed,ing,al). Confederation(s). States rights. Subcontract(ing). Diversif(y,ied,ication). Polycentr(ic,ism). Network(ed,ing). New federalism. Deregulat(e,ed,ing,ion). Deglomerat(e,ed,ing,ion). Branch office(s). Distributed data. Dual sovereignty. Collegial style. Laissez-faire. Regionalis(t,m). Cultural particularism. Privatiz(e,ed,ing,ation). Local control. Local power. Local authority. Grassroots. Secondary centers. Subcenters. Suburbanization. Outwork. Farm(ed,ing) out. Multi-plant. Urban to rural migration. Multicore. Disaggregat(e,ed,ion). Counterurbanization. Deconcentrat(e,ed,ing,ion). Cottage plan. *See also* Adhocracies; Branch operations; Centralization; Confederalism; Contracting out; Countries in transition; Devolution; Downsizing; Networks; Organizational change; Organizational development; Organizational structure; Reengineering.

Deception. Deception. Deceiv(e,ed,ing). Deceit(ful,fulness). Double-dealing(s). Alter(ed,ing) statistic(s,al). Bad faith. Breach(ed,ing) truth. Camouflag(e,ed, ing). Cheat(ed,ing,er,ers) . Clandestine. Conceal(ed,ing) fact(s). Confabulat(e,ed, ing,ion). Contragate. Cover(ed,ing) up. Coverup(s). Defraud(ing). Dishonest(y). Disinformation. Dissembl(e,ed,ing). Dissimulat(e,ed,ing,ion). Disguis(e,ed, ing). Duplicity. Entrapment. Evasion. Evasive(ness). Exaggerat(e,ed,ing,ion). Fabricat(e,ed,ing). Fak(e,ed,ing). False feedback. False testimony. Falsehood(s). Falsif(y,ied,ication). Feign(ed,ing). Forge(d,ry,er,ers). Fraud(ulent). Fudg(e,ed,ing) data. Half truth(s). Hid(e,den,ing). Hoax(es). Insincer(e,ity). Lack of candor. Liar(s). Lie(s,d). Lying. Machiavellian(ism). Malinger(ed,ing).

Manipulative. Mislead(ing). Misled. Obfuscat(e,ed,ing,ion). Perjur(e,ed,ing, y). Phon(y,iness). Plagiar(ize,ized,ism). Secre(t,ts,cy). Sham(s). Shell game(s). Skulduggery. Sophis(m,try). Spurio(sity, us). Sting(s). Suppress(ion) of truth. Surreptitious(ness). Underhanded. Untruthful(ness). Watergate. Whitewash(ed,ing). *Consider also:* unfounded allegation(s), crimen falsi. *See also* Artificiality; Authenticity; Casuistry; Cheating; Clandestinity; Credibility; Decoys; Disguise; Duplicity; Faking; Falsification (scientific); Fraud; Fraudulent advertising; Hyperbole; Hypocrisy; Implausibility; Lie detection; Malingering; Perjury; Secrecy; Self deception; Traitors; Tricksters; Unethical conduct; White collar crime.

Deception, self. See *Self deception.*

Deciding. See *Decisions.*

Deciphering. Decipher(ed,ing,s,ment). Decod(e,ed,ing). Disentangl(e,ed,ing). Decrypt(ed,ing,ion). Interpret(ed,ing, ation). Translat(e,ed,ing,ion). Explain(ed,ing). Explanation(s). *Consider also:* Rosetta Stone, Decree of Canopus. *See also* Analysis; Commentaries; Cuneiform; Hieroglyphics; Iconography; Interpretation.

Decision making. Decision making. Mak(e,ing) choice(s). Decid(e,ed,ing). Determination(s). Making judg(e) ment(s). *Choose from:* decision(s), choice(s), *with:* mak(e,ing,er,ers), made, analysis, strateg(y,ies), theory, support, model(s), approach(es). *Consider also:* adjudicat(e,ed,ing,ion), indecision, vacillat(e,ed,ing,ion), waver(ed,ing), choice behavior(s), game theory. *See also* Ambivalence; Choice (psychology); Choice behavior; Choices (alternatives); Cognitive processes; Computer assisted decision making; Conflict resolution; Coping; Criteria; Decisions; Dilemmas; Discretion; Discretionary powers; Discussion; Evaluation; Forecasting; Freedom (theology); Game theory; Group decision making; Hesitancy; Heuristics; Holism; Judgment; Management decision making; Management information systems; Occupational choice; Participative decision making; Policy making; Precedence; Priorities; Problem solving; Rational choices; Risk; Selection procedures; Systems analysis; Vocational maturity; Volition.

Decision making, computer assisted. See *Computer assisted decision making.*

Decision making, group. See *Group decision making.*

Decision making, management. See *Management decision making.*

Decision making, participative. See *Participative decision making.*

Decision support systems. Decision support system(s). DSS. Decision support data(base). *Choose from:* decision(s), choice(s) *with:* theory, model(s), information, support system(s), software, computeraided. *See also* Accounting systems; Inventory management; Knowledge management; Management decision making; Management information systems; Strategic management.

Decisions. Decision(s). Decid(e,ed,ing). Choice(s). Judgment(s). Verdict(s). Resolution(s). Determination(s). Conclusion(s). Finding(s). *Consider also:* adjudg(e,ed,ing), adjudicat(e,ed, ing,ion). *See also* Choice behavior; Choices (alternatives); Decision making; Discretion; Discretionary powers; Elective; Judicial decisions; Judgment; Rational choices.

Decisions, court. See *Judicial decisions; Verdicts.*

Decisions, judicial. See *Judicial decisions.*

Declarations. Declar(e,ed,ing,ation,ations). Affidavit(s). Announcement(s). Credo(s). Creed(s). Edict(s). Formal notice(s). Formal statement(s). Manifesto(s). Proclamation(s). Proclaim(ed,ing). Advertisement(s). Pronounc(e,ed,ing,ment,ments). *Consider also:* avow(ed,ing,al,als), acknowledg(e,ed,ing,ement,ements), affirm(ed,ing,ation,ations), assert(ed,ing, ion,ions), protest(ed,ing,ation,ations), statement(s), testimon(y,ies,ial), notif(y,ied,ication,ications). *See also* Advertising; Broadcasts; Edicts; Manifesto; Messages; Propaganda.

Decline. Declin(e,ed,ing). Wan(e,ed,ing). Decreas(e,ed,ing). Diminish(ed,ing). Abate(d). Subside(d). Ebb(ed,ing). Fade(d). Obsolescen(t,ce). Obsolete. Fail(ed,ing). Worsen(ed,ing). Deteriorat(e,ed,ing). Degenerat(e,ed, ing,ion). Decay(ed,ing). Atroph(y,ied). Downturn(s). Lessen(ed,ing). Downward shift(s). Meltdown(s). *See also* Aging; Debility; Decadence; Depression (economic); Deterioration; Fertility decline; Obsolescence; Population decline; Recession; Regression (civilization).

Decline, fertility. See *Fertility decline.*

Decline, population. See *Population decline.*

Decoding. See *Deciphering.*

Decolonization. Decoloniz(e,ing,ation). Postcolonial. National independence. Former(ly) colon(y,ies,ized). Liberation. National(ist,istic,ism). Nation building. Colonial nationalism. End of colonial era. War of independence. Indigenization. Self determination. Organization of African Unity. Pan-African Freedom Movement. *Choose* *from:* nation(al,alism) *with:* building, identity, unity, pride, sentiments, struggle, solidarity. *See also* Colonialism; Colonization; Democratization; National fronts; Pan-Africanism; Peasant rebellions; Political self determination.

Decommunization. Decommuniz(e,ed, ing,ation). Debrezhneviz(e,ed,ing,ation). Formerly communist. Dissassociat(e,ed, ing) from communism. Glasnost. Perestroika. *Consider also:* debolsheviz(e,ed,es,ing,ation), debrezhneveviz(e,ed,es,ing,ation), lustrat(e,cd,cs,ing,ion), dcmocratiz(e,cd, ing,ation), introduc(e,ed,ing) free market, post-communis(m,t), restor(e, ed,ing,ation) private property. *See also* Countries in transition; Democratization; Market economy; Nationalism; Postcommunism; Privatization.

Deconstruction. Deconstruction(ism, ist,ists). Deconstruct(ive,ively). Deconstruire. Decenter(ed,ing). Apor(ia,etic). *Choose from:* dislocat(e, ed,ing,ion), destabiliz(e,ed,ing,ation), undermin(e,ed,ing) *with:* authority, foundation(s), construct(s), truth(s), *Consider also:* Jacques Derrida, depropriation, defamiliariz(e,ed,ing), denaturaliz(e,ed,ing), undecidab(le,ility), logocentric(ism), wordplay(s), poststructural(ism,ist,ists), poststructuralist text(s), attack(s,ed,ing) culture. *See also* Aporia; Feminist criticism; Iconoclasm; Irony; Logocentrism; Metaphysics; Postmodernism; Undecidability.

Decontamination. Decontaminat(e,ed,ing, ion,ions). Purif(y,ied,ication). Bioremediat(e,ed,ing,ion). Phytoremediat(e,ed,ing,ion). Disinfect(ed,ing, ion,ions). *Choose from:* remov(e,ed, ing,al), destroy(ed,ing,s), neutraliz(e, ed,ing,ion,ions) *with:* radioactiv(e,ity), chemical(s), biological, toxic(ity), poison(s,ous), industrial waste(s), etc. *See also* Containment of biohazards; Ecosysytem management; Environmental protection; Pollution control; Restoration ecology; Sanitation.

Decoration. Decorat(e,ed,ion). Ornament(s, ation). Adorn(ed,ment,ments). Garnish(ed,ment,ments). Beautif(y,ied, ication). Embellish(ed,ing,ment,ments). *Consider also:* enrich(ed,ing,ment), elaborat(e,ion), garnsh(ed,ing,ment), trim(med,ming,mings), frill(s,ed), embroider(ed,ing). *See also* Architecture; Designs; Interior design.

Decoration, interior. See *Interior design.*

Decoration, mural painting and. See *Mural painting and decoration.*

Decorative arts. Decorative art(s). Applied art(s). Home art(s). *Consider also:* castplaster relief(s), panel painting(s), photograph(y,s), painted mural(s), craft(s), type design(s), weav(e,ing), dyeing, jewelry, artifact(s), ceramics,

folk art, ethnic art, memorabilia, art object(s). *See also* Aesthetics; Art deco; Decorative arts; Arts; Book ornamentation; Clothing; Decoration; Furniture; Interior design; Material culture; Popular culture.

Decorum. See *Decency.*

Decoys. Decoy(s). Lure(s). *Consider also:* bait(s,ed,ing), entrap(ped,ping,ment), allur(e,ed,ing,ement). *See also* Deception; Duck hunting; Hunting.

Decriminalization. Decriminaliz(e,ed, ing,ation). Depenaliz(e,ed,ing,ation). Legitimiz(e,ed,ing,ation). Legaliz(ed, ing,ation). *Choose from:* liberaliz(e,cd, ing,ation), weaken(ed,ing) *with:* law(s), penalt(y,ies). Reduc(ed,ing) penalt(y, ies). Reduce to misdemeanor(s). *See also* Crime; Criminal justice; Deregulation; Legalization of drugs; Marijuana laws; Offenses; Victimless crimes.

Dedication. See *Commitment (emotional).*

Dedications (speeches). See *Commemoration.*

Deduction. Deduc(e,ed,tion). Inferen(ce, ces,tial). Inductive deductive reasoning. Deductive reasoning. Deductive process(es). Syllogis(m,ms,tic). *Consider also:* causal reasoning, logical reasoning, formal reasoning, derivation(al), ratiocinat(e,ed,ion). *See also* Abstraction; Covering laws; Induction; Inference; Judgment (logic); Logic; Logical thinking; Principles; Reasoning; Scientific method; Statistical inference.

Deductions, tax. See *Tax deductions.*

Deeds (action). See *Action.*

Deeds (contracts). See *Agreement (document); Contracts.*

Deep ecology. Deep ecology. Transpersonal ecology. Related(ness) of all things. Ecocentr(ic,ism). Gaia. Radical environmentalis(m,t,ts). *See also* Ecology; Human ecology; Pantheism (universal divinity); World citizenship.

Deer. Deer. Cervidae. Venison. *Consider also:* caribou, elk, moose, reindeer, wapiti. *See also* Game and game birds; Game protection; Hunting; Mammals; Poaching; Vertebrates; Wild animals.

Defacement. Defac(e,ed,ing,ement). Mar(red,ring). Blemish(ed,ing,s). Disfeatur(e,ed,ing). Disfigur(e,ed, ing,ement). Mutilat(e,ed,ing,ion). Break(ing). Broken. Spoil(ed,ing). Desecrat(e,ed,ing,ion). Wreak(ed,ing) havoc. Scar(red,ring). Scratch(ed,ing). Dent(ed,ing). Torn. Damag(e,ed,ing,s). Obliterat(e,ed,ing,ion). Render(ed,ing) illegible. Batter(ed,ing). Mangl(e,ed, ing). Ruin(ed,ing,s). *Consider also:* flaw(ed,s), imperfection(s), wreck(ed, ing). *See also* Damage; Destruction of

property; Graffiti; Imperfection; Sabotage; Vandalism.

Defamation. Defam(e,ed,ing,ation,atory). Denigrat(e,ed,ing,ion). Vilif(y,ied, ication). Denounc(e,ed,ing). Denunciation. Revil(e,ed,ing). Deprecat(e,ed, ing,ion). Calumn(y,iate,iated,iating). Slander(ed,ing). Libel(led,ling). *Consider also:* aspersion(s), character assassination, disparag(e,ed,ing,ement), calumn(y,ious), false(ly) accus(e,ed,ing, ation,ions), innuendo(s), insinuat(e,ed, ing,ion,ions), malicious(ness), misrepresent(ed,ing,ation), slur(s), smear(ed,ing), vituperat(e,ed,ing, ive,ion). *See also* Denunciation; Derogation; Gossip; Gossip sites; Labeling (of persons); Libel; McCarthyism; Negativism; Political campaigns; Public opinion; Pushpolling; Reputation; Rumors; Scandals; Scapegoating; Witch hunting.

Default (negligence). Default(ed,ing). Negligen(t,ce). Fail(ed,ing,ure,ures). Deficien(t,cy). Inadequa(te,cy). Neglectful(ly). Delinquen(t,cy). Derelict(ion). Oversight(s). Fault(y,s). Laps(e,ed,ing). Disregard(ed,ing). Omission(s). Omit(ted). Nonfeasan(t,ce). Nonfulfillment(s). Nonpayment(s). Nonperformance(s). Nonremittance(s). *Consider also:* inadvertent(ly), slopp(y,iness), late(ness). *See also* Bank failures; Business failures; Debts; Errors; Failure; Inadequacy; Indebtedness; Insolvency.

Defeat. Defeat(ed,ing,s). Annihilat(e,ed, ing,ion). Conquer(ed,ing). Beat(ed,ing). Crush(ed,ing). Overpower(ed,ing). Overcom(e,ing). Overthrow(ing,n). Subdu(e,ed,ing). Subjugat(e,ed,ing). Vanquish(ed,ing). *Consider also:* demolish(ed,ing), hinder(ed,ing), imped(e,ed,ing), entrap(ped,ing,ment), outsmart(ed,ing), outmaneuver(ed,ing), obstruct(ed,ing,ion), debacle(s), rout(ed,ing), smash(ed,ing). *See also* Catastrophes; Collapse; Competition; Destruction; Hopelessness; Success.

Defecation. Defecat(e,ed,ing,ion). Hypochoresis. *Consider also:* fecal, feces *with:* discharge, incontinen(t,ce). *Consider also:* diarrhea, bowel habit(s), bowel movement(s), encopresis. *See also* Diarrhea; Fecal incontinence; Urination.

Defection, political. See *Political defection.*

Defects. See *Imperfection.*

Defects, birth. See *Congenitally handicapped; Drug induced abnormalities; Physical abnormalities.*

Defendants. Defendant(s). Accused. Respondent(s). Offender(s). Appellant(s). Litigant(s). Miranda warning(s). Criminal defense(s). Stand(ing) trial. Plea bargaining. Plead(ing) guilty. Plead(ing) innocent.

Acquittee(s). *See also* Arrests; Bail; Competency to stand trial; Criminal investigations; Criminal proceedings; Defense (verbal); Evidence; Juries; Litigation; Offenders; Plea bargaining; Preventive detention; Prosecution; Sentencing; Trial (law); Verdicts; Witnesses.

Defense (military science). Defense (Military science). Fortress warfare. Defense strateg(y,ies). Siege warfare. Aerospace defense. Strategic air power. Fortification(s). Trench fighting. Military deterrence. Counterblitz. Camouflage. Land mine(s). Defensive tactic(s). Armament(s). Guard(ed,ing). Protect(ed,ing,ion). Weapon(s,ry). Fort(s,ress,resses). Stronghold(s). *See also* Attack (Military science); Civil defense; Fortification; Military operations; Military strategies; Siege warfare; War.

Defense (verbal). Defense(s). Defend(ed, ing,ant,ants,able,ability). Apologetic(s). Apolog(y,ia,ies). Justif(y,ying,ied, ication). Answer(ed,ing,s). Rejoinder(s). Repl(y,ies,ied). Response(s). Retort(s). *Consider also:* exculpat(e,ed,ing,ion), excus(e,ed,ing,es), explanation(s), explain(ed,ing), rationaliz(e,ed,ing, ation), denial(s), plea(s), argument(s) in support, maintain(ed,ing), assertion(s), claim(s), contend(ed,ing), contention(s), vindicat(e,ed,ing,ion), champion(ed,ing), support(ed,ing), uphold(ing), upheld, speak on behalf, stand up for, stick up for, contest(ed,ing), clarif(y,ying, ied,ication), elucidat(e,ed,ing,ion), interpret(ed,ing,ation). *See also* Advocacy; Apologetics (Rhetoric); Criminal proceedings; Defendants; Judicial decisions; Litigation; Plea bargaining; Prosecution.

Defense, civil. See *Civil defense.*

Defense, insanity. See *Insanity defense.*

Defense, perceptual. See *Perceptual defense.*

Defense, personal. See *Self defense.*

Defense, self. See *Self defense.*

Defense, takeover. See *Anti-takeover strategies.*

Defense industry. See *Defense spending; Military industrial complex.*

Defense mechanisms. Defense mechanism(s). Defense reaction(s). Defensiveness. Fear adaptation(s). *Choose from:* defense(s), defensive(ness), fear, anxiet(y,ies), survival *with:* mechanism(s), reaction(s), adaptation(s), ego, function(s), style(s), drive(s). *Consider also:* acting out, affect equivalents, cathexis, compensation, compartmentalization, conversion, denial, depersonalization, displacement, dissociation, dissociative disorders,

fantasy, idealization, identification, incorporation, intellectualization, introjection, isolation, negativism, phantasy, perceptual defense, projection, postponement of affects, rationalization, reaction formation, regression, repression, reversal, sublimation, substitution, suppression, symbolization, transference, transposition, turning against self, undoing, scapegoating, withdrawal. *Consider also:* character defense. *See also* Coping; Compensation (defense mechanism); Denial (psychology); Displacement (psychology); Fantasies (thought disturbances); Identification (psychology); Intellectualization (defense mechanism); Introjection; Isolation (defense mechanism); Mental illness; Projection (psychological); Rationalization (defense mechanism); Reaction formation; Regression (defense mechanism); Repression (defense mechanism); Self debasement; Sublimation; Suppression (defense mechanism); Withdrawal (defense mechanism).

Defense spending. Defense spending. *Choose from:* defense, military, Pentagon, weapons *with:* spend(ing), spent, expenditure(s), expenses, procurement(s), contract(s), cost(s), cost overrun(s), profit(s). *See also* Armed forces; Arms market; Firearms industry; Government procurement; Military budget; Military industrial complex; Military market; Military patronage; Military reform; Militarism; Mobilization; National security; War.

Defenses, actions and. See *Lawsuits.*

Defenses, air. See *Air defenses.*

Defenses, coast. See *Coast defenses.*

Defensive. Defensive(ness,ly). Protect(ive, ing). Overprotect(ive,ing). Shield(ing). Guard(ed,ing). Safeguard(ed,ing). *Consider also:* suspicious(ness). *See also* Fear; Personality traits; Sensory defensiveness.

Defensive behavior, animal. See *Animal defensive behavior.*

Defensiveness. See *Defensive.*

Defensiveness, sensory. See *Sensory defensiveness.*

Defensiveness, tactile. See *Sensory defensiveness.*

Deference. Deferen(ce,tial). Submiss(ive, iveness,ion). Complian(ce,t). Docil(e, ity). Obeisan(ce,t). Respectful. Complaisant. Obedien(ce,t). Acquiescen(ce,t). Subordination. Resign(ed,ation). Yield(ed,ing). Nonresistan(t,ce). Obsequious(ness). Unassertive(ness). Servil(e,ity). *See also* Dependency (personality); Passiveness; Superior subordinate relationship.

Deferred compensation. Deferred compensation. Deferred pay(ment,

ments). Delayed benefit(s). *Choose from:* postpon(e,ed,ing), defer(red,ring), delay(ed,ing) *with:* compensat(ed,ion), reward(s), pay(ment,ments), benefit(s). *See also* Achievement need; Delay of gratification; Monetary rewards; Retirement income; Retirement planning; Reward.

Deficiencies, nutritional. See *Malnutrition; Nutrition disorders.*

Deficiency, mental. See *Mental retardation.*

Deficiency diseases. Deficiency disease(s). Deficiency disorder(s) *Choose from:* anaem(ia,ic), anem(ia,ic), poor condition, avitaminosis, malnutrition, maknourish(ed,ment) *with:* disease(s), disorder(s). *Choose from:* nutrition(al), dietary, metabolic, protein, amino acid(s), vitamin(s), mineral(s), calor(ic, ies), nutrient(s), magnesium, copper, zinc, calcium, potassium, ascorbic acid, vitamin A, vitamin B, vitamin D, vitamin E *with:* disease(s), disorder(s). *See also* Disease susceptibility; Hereditary diseases; Malnutrition; Nutrition disorders.

Deficiency disorders, vitamin. See *Vitamin deficiency disorders.*

Deficit, attention disorder. See *Attention deficit disorder.*

Deficit, federal. See *Public debt.*

Deficits, budget. See *Budget deficits; Debt.*

Definition (words). Defin(e,ed,ing,ition, itions). Demarcat(e,ed,ing,ion,ions). Delineat(e,ed,ing,ion). Delimit(ed,ing). Explain(ed,ing). Explanation(s). Elucidat(e,ed,ing,ion). Mak(e,ing) definite. Describe meaning(s). Denot(e,ed,ing,ing,ation). *See also* Ambiguity; Clarification; Communication (thought transfer); Demarcation; Description; Explanation; Meaning; Terminology; Translating and translations; Verbal meaning; Word meaning.

Deforestation. Deforest(ed,ation). Slash and burn. Clearcut(ting). Clear(ing,ed) rainforest(s). Forest depletion. Logging. Waldsterben. Forest death. Close cut(ting). *Choose from:* forest(s), woodland(s), timber, timberland(s), habitat(s), wilderness, tree(s) *with:* deplet(e,ed,ing,ion), clear(ed,ing,ance), cut(ting), destruction, destroy(ed,ing), conversion, convert(ed,ing), disappear(ed,ing,ance), desertif(ied, ication), desertiz(ed,ation), threat(s,en, ening), extract(ed,ing,ion). *Consider also:* swidden. *See also* Conservation of natural resources; Desertification; Ecological imperialism; Environmental degradation; Forest conservation; Fire ecology; Forest ecology; Forest fires; Forest reserves; Forestry; Land preservation; Lumber industry; Natural resources; Old growth forests; Plant succession; Reforestation; Resource stress; Timber; Tree farms; Tree planting; Trees; Wildlife conservation; Wildlife sanctuaries.

Deformity. See *Physical disfigurement.*

Defraud. See *Fraud.*

Defunct. Defunct(ion). Dead. Decease(d). Discontinu(e,ed,ing). Expire(d). Extinct(ion). Inoperative. Lapse(d). Nonexistent. Obsole(te,scent). Outmoded. *Consider also:* asleep, broken, departed, exanimate, inanimate, lifeless(ness), inactiv(e,ity), inert(ness), sluggish(ness), bygone, gone, lost, vanished, sunset(ted,ting), passe. *See also* Anachronisms; Inactivity; Obsolescence; Product discontinued; Product recall; Skills obsolescence.

Degeneration. See *Deterioration.*

Degradation, environmental. See *Environmental degradation.*

Degrees, academic. See *Academic degrees.*

Degrees, advanced. See *Academic degrees.*

Degrees, educational. See *Academic degrees.*

Dehumanization. Dehumaniz(e,ed,ation). Depersonaliz(e,ed,ing,ation). Depersonal(ism). Mechanical. Impersonal(ity). Meaningless(ness). Robotic. Automaton. Insensitiv(e,ity, eness). Cold-blooded. Inhuman(e). Technocrat(ic,ism). Taylorism. Deskilling. Alienat(ing,ion). Affectless. Antihuman(istic). Anti-human(istic). Self alienation. *See also* Alienation; Depravity; Impersonal; Meaninglessness; Rationalization (sociology); Scientific management; Technocracy; Technology and civilization.

Deindustrialization. Deindustrializ(e,ed, ing,ation). *Consider also:* declin(e,ed, ing), disinvest(ed,ing,ment) *with:* industr(y,ies,ial,ialization), manufactur(e,ed,er,ers,ing), factor(y,ies). *See also* Disinvestment; Economic change; Employment trends; Plant closings; Postindustrial societies; Service industries; Technology and civilization.

Deinstitutionalization. Deinstitutionaliz(e, ed,ing,ation). Decarcerat(e,ed,ing,ion). Alternative(s) to institutionalization. Halfway house(s). Day treatment. Adult day care. Noninstitutionalized. *Choose from:* group, independent, congregate, communal *with:* home(s), house(s), residence(s), living. *Choose from:* community *with:* plac(ed,ing,ment, ments). *Consider also:* resettl(e,ed, ing,ement), hostel(s), aging out. *See also* Alternatives to incarceration; Alternatives to institutionalization; Community mental health services; Homeless; Institutional release; Mental retardation; Noninstitutionalized disabled; Personal independence; Psychiatric patients;

Psychosocial readjustment; Psychosocial rehabilitation; Restorative justice; Social adjustment.

Deism. Deis(t,ts,m). Supernatural rationalism. *Consider also:* freethinker(s). *See also* Deities; God concepts; Presence of God; Rationalism; Religious beliefs; Theism.

Deities. Deit(y,ies). God(s). Goddess(es). Divinit(y,ies). Divine Being(s). Divine personage(s). Creator. Supreme Being(s). Supernatural being(s). Almighty. Godhead. Holy One. Infinite spirit. Jehovah. Yahweh. Yahveh. Adonai. Elohim. Allah. Shaddai. Zurishaddai. Khuda. Atahocan. Brahma. Buddha. Vishnu. Shiva. Mazda. Ormazd. Ahura Mazda. Loki. Jupiter. Zeus. Apollo. Imana. Jok. Mawu. *Consider also:* Olympian(s), Hermes, Poseidon, Neptune, Hephaestus, Vulcan, Dionysius, Bacchus, Hades, Pluto, Kronos, Saturn, Eros, Cupid, Aesir, Vanir, Balder, Frey, Heimdall, Hoder, Hoenir, Odin, Woden, Wotan, Thor, Donar, Tyr, Tiu, Ull, Ullr, Vali, Vidar, Ymir, Agni, Dyaus, Ganesa, Ganpati, Hanuman, Indra, Marut, Savitar, Soma, Surya, Varuna, Vidar, Ymir, Chac. *See also* Atheism; Attributes of God; Deism; Glory of God; Goddesses; God concepts; Immanence of god; Jehovah; Mother goddesses; Mythology; Omniscience of God; Paganism; Prayer; Religions; Religious beliefs; Religious doctrines; Sacrificial rites; Worship.

Deja vu. Deja vu. *Consider also:* deja fait, deja voulu. *See also* Awareness.

Delay of gratification. Delay of gratification. *Choose from:* delay(ed,ing), defer(red,ment), postpone(d,ment) *with:* reward, reinforce(ment,ers), gratification, fulfillment. *Consider also:* restraint, self control. *See also* Deferred compensation; Impulsiveness; Locus of control; Motivation; Needs; Reinforcement; Reward; Self concept; Unmet needs.

Delayed, language. See *Language delayed.*

Delayed development. Delayed development. *Choose from:* development(al,ally) *with:* delay(s,ed), retard(ed), lag(ging, ged), slow(ly), deficit(s). *Consider also:* delay(s,ed) *with:* articulation, language development, growth, motor development, psychosocial development, cognitive development, mental development, onset of walking, social maturation. *Consider also:* late talker(s), failure to thrive. *See also* Delayed puberty; Developmental disabilities; Failure to thrive (psychosocial); Language delayed; Physical development; Retarded speech development.

Delayed parenthood. Delayed parenthood. Older first-time mothers. Older primipara. *Choose from:* postponed, midlife,

waited, delayed, deferred, late *with:* parenthood, motherhood, childbearing, having a baby, have a baby, birthtiming. *See also* Childlessness; Family planning; Family planning attitudes; Parent role.

Delayed puberty. Delayed puberty. *Choose from:* delay(ed) *with:* adolescence, puberty, menarche, pubescence, sexual development. *Consider also:* sexual infantilism, pubertal failure, impaired sexual maturation. *See also* Delayed development; Physical development; Puberty.

Delays. Delay(ed,ing,s). Defer(red,ral, ment). Detain(ed,ing). Detention. Dilator(y,iness). Decelerat(e,ed,ing,ion). Filibuster(ed,ing). Hesitat(e,ed,ing,ion). Interrupt(ed,ing,ion,ions). Interval(s). Intermission(s). Lag(ged,ging,s). Linger(ed,ing). Moratorium(s). Postpon(e,ed,ing,ement). Suspen(d,ded, ding,sion). Recess(ed,es,ing). Procrastinat(e,ed,ing,ion). *Consider also:* hang up, mire, slow(ed,ing) up, slow(ed,ing) down, block(ed,ing), hinder(ed,ing), imped(e,ed,ing,ement, ements), obstruct(ed,ing), put(ting) off, stay(ed,ing), suspend(ed,ing), dawdl(e, ed,ing), loiter(ed,ing), mull(ed,ing), wait(ed,ingz), falter(ed,ing), vacillat(e, ed,ing), waver(ed,ing), hold(ing) off, hold(ing) over, hold(ing) up, slacken(ed,ing). *See also* Adjournment; Avoidance; Procrastination; Time factors.

Delegates. Delegate(s). Representative(s). Deput(y,ies). Spokesperson(s). Prox(y,ies). Surrogate(s). *Consider also:* agent(s), alternate(s), replacement(s), stand-in(s), substitute(s), emissar(y,ies), spokes(man,men,woman,women, person,persons), envoy(s). *See also* Agents; Delegations; Democracy; Representatives.

Delegation of powers. Delegat(e,es,ed, ing,ion) power(s). Express power(s). Implied power(s). Enumerated power(s). *Choose from:* delegat(e,es,ed,ing,ion), grant(ed,ing), distribut(e,ed,ing) *with:* power(s), authority, decision(s), executive(s), management, control, implement(ing,ation). *Consider also:* emergency power(s), agency autonomy, quasi-independen(t,ce), oversight, dual sovereignty, separation of powers. *See also* Democracy; Discretionary powers; Executive powers; Federalism; Legislators; Legislative powers; Separation of powers.

Delegations. Delegation(s). Embass(y,ies). Envoy(s). Legation(s). Commission(s). Committee(s). Contingent(s). Delegate(s). Mission(s). *See also* Commissions; Committees; Delegates; Embassies.

Delinquency, juvenile. See *Juvenile delinquency.*

Delinquency, sexual. See *Promiscuity; Sexual offenses.*

Delinquents. Delinquent(s). Predelinquent(s). Criminal(s). Offender(s). Street gang(s). Gangster(s). Gun(men,man). Mobster(s). Scofflaw(s). Smuggler(s). Violator(s). Culprit(s). Perpetrator(s). Felon(s). Racketeer(s). Abuser(s). Rapist(s). Murderer(s). Thie(f,ves). Deviant(s). Ex-offender(s). Crime suspect(s). Probationer(s). Embezzler(s). Parolee(s). Hoodlum(s). Burglar(s). *Consider also:* juvenile delinquent(s), geriatric delinquent(s). *See also* Crime prevention; Juvenile delinquency; Offenders; Recidivism; Thugs.

Delirium. Delir(ium,ia). Hallucinat(e,ed, ory,ion,ions). Delirious(ness). Illusional falsification(s). Insan(e,ity). Disorient(ed,ation). Deranged. Cloud(ed,ing) consciousness. *See also* Consciousness disorders.

Delirium, alcohol withdrawal. See *Alcohol withdrawal delirium.*

Delivering (distribution). See *Distribution (delivering).*

Delivery of services. Delivery of service(s). Delivery system(s). Outreach program(s). Home care. Health care delivery. Public law 91-515. Delivery of primary care. *Choose from:* delivery, referral system(s), deploy(ment), provision, provid(e,er,ers,ing), distribut(e,ing,ion,er,ers), access(ible, ibility), vend(ing,or,ors,orship), diffusion, meeting needs, utilization *with:* service(s), care, relief, treatment, program(s), system(s), mechanism(s), medical care, health care, dental care, mental health care. *See also* Catchment area (health); Health care utilization; Outreach programs; Referral; Telemedicine.

Delivery rooms. Delivery room(s). *Choose from:* birth(ing), delivery *with:* center(s), room(s). *Consider also:* labor room(s). *See also* Birthing centers.

Delta alcoholism. Delta alcoholism. Inveterate drink(ing,er,ers). *See also* Alcoholism.

Delusion of doubles. See *Capgras's syndrome.*

Delusions. Delusion(s,al). Delire. Derang(ed,ement). Parano(id,ia). False belief(s). Exaggerated idea(s). Apperson(ation,ification). *Choose from:* feeling(s), illusion(s), delusion(s) *with:* persecution, control(led,ling), grandeur. *Consider also:* Capgras(s) syndrome, cacodemonomania. *See also* Capgras's syndrome; Delusions of grandeur; Groundless; Implausibility; Irrational beliefs; Somatic delusions; Thought disturbances.

Delusions, somatic. See *Somatic delusions.*

Delusions of grandeur. Delusion(s) of grandeur. *Choose from:* grandiose, grandeur, expansive, extravagant, exalted *with:* delusion(s,al), idea(s), paranoi(d, ia). *Consider also:* megalomania(c,cs). *See also* Delusions; Irrational beliefs; Thought disturbances.

Demagogues. Demagogue(s,ry). Demagog(y,ic,ism). Agitator(s). Rabble rouser(s). Soapbox orator(s). Malcontent(s,ed). Fanatic(s). *See also* Extremism; Fanaticism; Social agitation.

Demand. Demand(s,ed,ing). Claim(ed,ing). Order(s,ed,ing). Requisition(s,ed,ing). Request(s,ed,ing). Urgent(ly) need(ed). Willing(ness) to purchase. *Consider also:* purchasing power, appl(y,ied, ication), bid(ding), insisten(t,ce), mandate(s,de), petition(s), stipulat(e,ed, ing,ion), ultimatum(s). *See also* Consumer behavior; Economic competition; Market share; Production consumption relationship; Supply and demand.

Demand, health services. See *Health services needs and demand.*

Demand, supply and. See *Supply and demand.*

Demarcation. Demarcat(e,ed,ing,ion). Delimit(ed,ing,ate,ation). Mark limit(s). *Choose from:* determin(e,ed,ing,ation), limit(ed,ing,ation,s), mark(ed,ing), measur(e,ed,ing), establish(ed,ing) fix(ed,ing), set(ting), assign(ed,ing), defin(e,ed,ing,ition), prescrib(e,ed,ing) *with:* bound(s,ary,aries), border(s), edge(s), line(s), frontier(s). *Consider also:* differentiat(e,ed,ing,ion), discriminat(e,ed,ing,ion), separat(e,ed, ing,ion), set(ting) apart, set(ting) off. *See also* Borders; Boundaries; Constraints; Definition (words); Finite.

Demeanor. Demeanor. Bearing. Comport(ed,ing,ment). Deportment. Mien. *Consider also:* facade, presence, attitude, carriage, posture, visage, facial expression(s), manner(ism,is,s). *See also* Attractiveness; Behavior; Clothing; Conduct; Facial expressions; Personal appearance; Personal beauty; Physical characteristics.

Dementia. Dementia(s). *Choose from:* memory, intellect(ual), mental, judgment(s,al), *with:* deteriorat(ed,ing, ion,ive), impair(ed,ment,ments), reduced, reduction(s), inability, deficit(s), loss(es), losing, declin(e,ed,ing), disintegrat(e,ed,ing, ive,ion,ions). *Consider also:* apoplectica, abiotrophic, atrophic, boxer's, circular, dialytica, driveling, epileptic, higher, infantilis, paralytica, paranoides gravis, parlor, post-traumatic, praecocissima, praecox, praesenilis, presenile, pugilistic, relative, schizo-phrenic, simple, semantic, senile,

thalamic, traumatic *with:* dementia(s). *Consider also:* pseudodementia. *See also* Organic mental disorders; Presenile dementia; Senile dementia.

Dementia, alcoholic. See *Alcoholic dementia.*

Dementia, presenile. See *Presenile dementia.*

Dementia, senile. See *Senile dementia.*

Demilitarization. See *Demobilization; Disarmament; Peace negotiations.*

Demobilization. Demobiliz(e,es,ed, ing,ation). Decommission(ed,s,ing). Deactivat(e,ed,es,ing,ion). Disarm(s,ed, ing,ament). Troop reduction(s). Swords into ploughshares. *Choose from:* military, defense industr(y,ies) *with:* convert(ed,ing), conversion, reconvert(ed,ing), reconversion, shift(s,ed,ing) *with:* civilian, peacetime. *Consider also:* peace time *with:* force(s), Army, Navy, military. *See also* Arms control; Disarmament; Military pensions; Troop strength; Peace.

Democracy. Democrac(y,ies). Democrat(ic,ization). Republic(s). *Choose from:* representative, constitutional, popular, self *with:* government(s). Home rule. Government by the people. Commonwealth(s). *Consider also:* individual freedom, equality, human dignity, rule of law, popular sovereignty, constitutionalism, referendum and recall, majority rule, accountab(le,ility) to the people, civil liberties, Bill of Rights, Declaration of Independence. *Consider also:* democratic, western, open *with:* societ(y,ies), government(s), nation(s), countr(y,ies). *See also* Capitalism; Civil rights; Elections; Freedom; Freedom of information; Freedom of religion; Freedom of speech; Freedom of the press; Industrial democracy; Legislative bodies; Liberalism; Majorities (political); Personal independence; Political campaigns; Political self determination; Progressivism; Separation of powers; Social democracy; Totalitarianism; Voting.

Democracy, economic. See *Industrial democracy.*

Democracy, industrial. See *Industrial democracy.*

Democracy, social. See *Social democracy.*

Democratization. Democratiz(ed,ing,ation). Democratic reform(s). Demokratizatsiya. Perestroika. *Choose from:* becom(e,ing), became, transition(s,ing,al), implement(ed,ing), consolidat(e,ed ing,ion), achiev(e,ed,ing), adopt(ed,ing, ion) *with:* democratic, free election(s), political reform(s), constitution(al), human rights, freedom of expression. *Consider also:* political liberaliz(ed,ing, ation), glasnost, de-nazifi(ed,cation). *See* *also* Civil rights; Decolonization; Decommunization; Industrial democracy; Liberation movements; Political reform; Political self determination; Post-communism; Social change.

Demographic changes. Demographic changes. Historical demography. Population change(s). Depopulat(ed, ion). Aging population. Geographic mobility. Population growth. *Choose from:* demograph(y,ic), population, fertility, mortality, mobility, migration(s), sociodemograph(ic,y) *with:* chang(e,es,ed,ing), growth, declin(e,es,ing), trend(s), development, projection(s), pattern(s), transition(s,al), process(es), turnaround(s), shift(s,ing), variation(s). *See also* Community change; Fertility decline; Geographic mobility; Migration; Migration patterns; Population decline; Population distribution; Population dynamics; Population growth; Workforce planning.

Demographic characteristics (of individuals). Demographic characteristics. *Choose from:* birthplace, national origin(s), income, education, sex, age, race, place of residence. *See also* Age groups; Audience analysis; Biased selection; Biographical data; Characteristics; Client characteristics; Economic statistics; Educational background; Income; Internet traffic; Place of residence; Qualities; Races; Socioeconomic status; Student characteristics; Teacher characteristics; Therapist characteristics.

Demographic characteristics (of population). See *Population characteristics.*

Demographic policy. See *Population policy.*

Demographic surveys. Demographic survey(s). Population survey(s). *Choose from:* demographic, population, households, household data, community, sociodemographic, consumers, residents, citizens *with:* survey(s,ed,ing), profile(s), characteristics, track(ed,ing), count(s,ed,ing). *Consider also:* census(es), demographic profile(s), sociodemographic characteristic(s), consumer research, demographic variable(s), demographic analys(is,es). *See also* Census; Community size; Demographic changes; Demography; Enumeration; Social surveys.

Demography. Demograph(y,ic,cal,s). Vital statistics. Macrodemograph(ic,y). Microdemograph(ic,y). Sociodemograph(y,ic). Birth rate(s). Employment pattern(s). Geographic distribution. Racial composition. Residential pattern(s). Social distribution. Urban rural distribution. Age distribution. Size of ethnic group(s). Number of handicapped. Size of minority group(s). Population density.

Sex distribution. Sex ratio(s). Morbidity. Infant mortality. Maternal mortality. Overpopulation. Residential pattern(s). Life table(s). Nuptiality. Divorce rate(s). Employment figure(s). Unemployment rate(s). Catchment area(s). *Choose from:* population, fertility, mortality, migration, census(es), life expectancy, epidemiological, depopulat(ed,ion), mobility *with:* characteristics, stud(y,ies), distribution, research, pattern(s), growth, model(s), data, table(s), statistic(s,al), variable(s), rate(s), predict(ion,ions,or,ors). *See also* Census; Community size; Demographic changes; Demographic characteristics (of individuals); Demographic surveys; Employment trends; Fertility; Fertility decline; Geographic mobility; Land settlement; Migration; Migration patterns; Mortality rates; Overpopulation; Place of residence; Population (statistics); Population characteristics; Population decline; Population density; Population distribution; Population growth; Racial diversity; Unemployment rates; World population.

Demolition. Demolition. Demolish(ed,ing). Raz(ed,ing). Torn down. Tear(ing) down. Flattened. Removed structure(s). Destroy(ed,ing) building(s). Topple(d). Levell(ed,ing). Wrecking ball(s). Implosion of building(s). Pull(ed) down. Gutt(ed,ing). Wreck(ed,ing). Dismantl(e, ed,ing). *See also* Destruction; Destruction of property; Urban renewal; Wrecks.

Demonic possession. See *Spirit possession.*

Demons. Demon(ic,ology,s). Daemon(s). Daimon(s). Devil(s). Evil spirit(s). Afreet. Afrit. Cacodemon(ic,s). Lucifer. Mammon. Asmodeus. Asmodei. Satan. Beelzebub. Leviathan. Belphegor. Mephistopheles. Moloch. Diabolus. Genie(s). Ghoul(s). Incubus(es). Imp(s). Vampire(s). Werewol(f,ves). Ogre(s). Troll(s). Sprite(s). Elf. Elves. Pixy. Pixies. Leprechaun(s). Goblin(s). Banshee(s). Hobgoblin(s). Dybbuk(s). Pan. *See also* Devils; Elves; Evil; Evil eye; Fairies; Folk literature; Folklore; Ghosts; Spirit possession; Witchcraft.

Demonstrations, political. See *Social demonstrations.*

Demonstrations, social. See *Social demonstrations.*

Demonstrations, student. See *Student demonstrations.*

Demonstrators. Demonstrator(s). Sit-in(s). Rall(y,ies). March(es). Parade(s). Peace march(es). Protest movement(s). Social protest(s). Political protest(s). *Consider also:* activ(ism,ist,ists), protest(s,er,ers), movement(s), insurgen(cy,ts), revolt(s), picket(ed,s,ing), uprising(s), militan(cy, ce,t,ts), organized against, strik(ing,er, ers,es), general strike(s), dissen(t,ting,

ter,ters,sion), petition(s,ed,ing), riot(ed, ing,s), struggle(s), sympathizer(s), opposition, mobiliz(ed,ing,ation), resist(ance), collective action. *See also* Activism; Activists; Boycotts; Civil disobedience; Civil disorders; Political movements; Protest movements; Protest songs; Social demonstrations; Social unrest; Student demonstrations.

Demoralization. Demoraliz(e,ed,ing,ation). Dispirited. Dishearten(ed,ment). Hopeless(ness). *Choose from:* low, destruction, destroy(ed,ing) *with:* morale. *Consider also:* personal disorganization, confus(ed,ion), bewilder(ed,ment). *See also* Hopelessness; Learned helplessness; Pessimism.

Demotion (occupational). Demot(e,ed, ing,ion). Demotee(s). *Choose from:* occupation(al), labor, work, job(s), career(s), employment, vocational, employee(s), staff, faculty, teacher(s), personnel, worker(s) *with:* downgrad(e, ed,ing), demot(e,ed,ing,ion,ional), de-escalat(e,ed,ing,ion), step(ped,ping) down, status deprivation, reclassif(y,ied, ication) to lower rank. *Consider also:* outplacement, declassif(y,ied,ication), reduce in rank. *See also* Budget cuts; Career breaks; Career change; Career goals; Career mobility; Career patterns; Job performance; Probation; Promotion (occupational); Salaries.

Demythologization. Demythologiz(e,es,ed, ing,ation). Without myth(s,ology, ological). *Consider also:* demystif(y,ied, ication), exeges(is,es), exegetical, critical interpretation, existential interpretation. *See also* Existentialism; Reality; Reality therapy; Social reality; Truth.

Denial (psychology). Den(y,ied,ying,ial). Anosognos(ia,ic). Wish fulfilling fantas(y,ies). Negation. Disavow(al,ing, ed). Resistance. Defensive(ness). Intellectualiz(e,ed,ing,ation). *Consider also:* inability to accept, neutraliz(e,ed, ing,ation), refus(e,ed,ing) to admit, perceptual defense, Anton(s) syndrome, Anton-Babinski(s) syndrome, hemiasomatognosia. *See also* Blame; Defense mechanisms; Dysconscious racism; Ego dystonic homosexuality; Justification; Neutralization; Rationalization (defense mechanism); Scapegoating; Shame.

Denial, self. See *Self denial.*

Denominations, religious. See *Religious denominations.*

Density, population. See *Population density.*

Density, social. See *Social density.*

Dental care. Dental care. Dentistry. *Choose from:* dental, oral, teeth, periodontal, gingival *with:* evaluation, care, treatment(s), hygiene, therap(y,ies), management, procedure(s). *See also*

Dental surgery; Dentist patient relations; Oral health.

Dental facilities. Dental facilit(y,ies). *Choose from:* dental, dentistry *with:* center(s), office(s), facilit(y,ies), laborator(y,ies), unit(s), clinic(s). *See also* Health facilities.

Dental health. See *Oral health.*

Dental surgery. Dental surgery. *Choose from:* dental, dentistry, oral, gum(s), teeth, tooth *with:* surg(ery,ical), operat(ive,ing,ion,ions), excision(s), extraction(s), replantation(s). *Consider also:* apicoectomy, gingivectomy, gingivoplasty, glossectomy, mandibular prosthesis, maxillofacial prosthesis. *See also* Dental care; Dentist patient relations; Surgery.

Dentist patient relations. Dentist patient relation(s,ship,ships). *Choose from:* dental specialist(s), dentist(s), orthodontist(s) *with:* client(s), patient(s) *with:* relation(s,ship,ships), interaction(s), rapport, covenant(s), role(s), trust, agreement(s), distrust, attitude(s), perception(s), communication(s), influence(s). *See also* Interpersonal relations; Physician patient relations; Professional client relations.

Dentists. Dentist(s). Dental surgeon(s). Dental graduate(s). DDS. Doctor of dental surgery. Orthodontist(s). Dental practitioner(s). Periondontist(s). Endodontist(s). *See also* Dentist patient relations; Medical personnel supply; Medical staff.

Denunciation. Denunciat(e,ed,ing,ion). Denounc(e,ed,ing). Admonish(ed,ing, ment). Belittl(e,ed,ing). Critic(ize,ized, izing,ism,isms). Deprecat(e,ed,ing,ion). Blam(e,ed,ing). Condemn(ed,ing,ation). Derogat(e,ed,ing,ion). *Consider also:* attack(ed,ing,s), castigat(e,ed,ing,ion), censur(e,ed,ing), reprehend(s,ed,ing), accus(e,ed,ing,ation), incriminat(e,ed, ing,ion), indict(ed,ing,ment), slander(ed, ing), revil(e,ed,ing). *See also* Allegations; Blame; Censure; Defamation; Derogation; Scapegoating; Self accusation.

Deontic logic. Deontic logic. Deontic reasoning. Deontolog(ical,y). *Consider also:* moral obligation(s), formalism, intuitionism. *See also* Ethics; Logic.

Deontology. Deontolog(y,ical). *Choose from:* theor(y,ies,etical), principle(s) *with:* moral duty, moral obligation, obligation(s), rightness of action. *Consider also:* ethics, ethical theor(y,ies). *See also* Codes of ethics; Conduct; Ethics; Philosophy.

Department stores. Department store(s). Empori(a,um). Grandes almacenes. *Consider also:* Macy's, Harrods, Penney's, Sears, etc. *See also* Discount stores; Discounts; Retailing; Shopping centers; Stores.

Departmentalization. Departmentaliz(e,ed, ing,ation). Compartmentaliz(e,ed,ing, ation). Group(ed,ing,ings). Segment(ed, ing). Subdivid(e,ed,ing). *See also* Division of labor; Labor market segmentation; Organizational structure.

Departments. Department(al,s). Division(s). Bureau(s). Office(s). Subdivision(s). Branch(es). Section(s). Unit(s). Agenc(y,ies). *See also* Administration; Bureaucracies; Bureaucrats; Decentralization; Organizational structure.

Departments, fire. See *Fire departments.*

Dependability. Dependab(le,ility). Reliab(le,ility). Responsib(le,ility). Stab(le,ility). Honorable. Trustworth(y, iness). Constan(t,cy). Loyal(ty). Upright(ness). Faithful(ness). Unfailing. Sincer(e,ity). Devot(ed,ion). Honest(y). Authentic(ity). Steadfast(ness). Fidelity. Safe(ty). Secur(e,ity). Truthful(ness). Conscientious(ness). Careful. Infallib(le, ility). Believab(le,ility). Credib(le,ility). Assur(ed,ance,ances). Guaranteed. Unquestionable. Indisputable. Incontestable. *See also* Credibility; Fault tolerant computing; Personality traits; Reliability; Trustworthy.

Dependence, economic. See *Economic dependence.*

Dependence, emotional. See *Emotional dependence.*

Dependence, field. See *Field dependence.*

Dependence , heroin. See *Substance dependence.*

Dependence, narcotic. See *Substance dependence.*

Dependence, substance. See *Substance dependence.*

Dependency (personality). Dependency. Dependent personalit(y,ies). Inability to make decisions. Helpless(ness). Learned helplessness. Hyperdependen(t,ce). Overdependen(t,ce). Need for approval. Addictogenesis. *Choose from:* psychological(ly), emotional(ly), neurotic(ally), passive, pathological(ly), psychosocial, interpersonal, morbid(ly) *with:* dependen(t,ce). *Consider also:* regression, childish(ness), maternal attachment, anaclitic, anaclisis, anaclinic, emotional beggar(s). *See also* Alcoholism; Attachment behavior; Economic dependence; Emotional dependence; Field dependence; Personal independence; Personality traits; Social parasites; Substance dependence.

Dependency, alcohol. See *Alcoholism; Problem drinking.*

Dependency, drug. See *Substance dependence.*

Dependency theory (international). Dependency theory. Underdevelopment. Imperial colonial relationship. Neoimperialism. Neocolonialism. *Choose from:* third world, developing countr(y,ies) *with:* exploit(ed,ing,ation), dependen(t,ce,cy), unequal exchange(s). *Consider also:* imperialism, colonialism, maldevelopment. *See also* Center and periphery; Colonialism; Developing countries; Dual economy; Economic assistance; Economic dependence; Economic development; Economic underdevelopment; Imperialism; Income inequality; International division of labor; Multinational corporations; Neocolonialism; Spheres of influence; Subsistence economy; World economy; World systems theory.

Dependent parents. Dependent parent(s). Intergenerational support. Filial responsibilit(y,ies). *Choose from:* dependen(t,cy), care, caring, support, responsibilit(y,ies) *with:* elder(s,ly), aged, aging *with:* parent(s,al), father(s), mother(s), famil(y,ies,ial), filial. *Consider also:* sandwich generation. *See also* Caregiver burden; Dependents; Family assistance; Filial responsibility; Financial support; Intergenerational relations.

Dependent personality. See *Dependency (personality).*

Dependent variables. Dependent variable(s). Y variable(s). *See also* Independent variables; Statistical correlation; Statistical data.

Dependents. Dependent(s). Financial dependen(ce,cy,t,ts). Pensioner(s). Grantee(s). Welfare recipient(s). Receiving support. *Consider also:* minor(s). *See also* Child support; Dependent parents; Financial support; Welfare recipients.

Dependents, military. See *Military families.*

Depersonalization (social). See *Dehumanization.*

Depersonalization disorder. Depersonalization disorder. Depersonaliz(ed,ation). Estrang(ed,ement). Loss of sense of reality. Derealiz(ed,ation). *Choose from:* feeling(s), emotion(s,al), sense *with:* unreal(ity), empt(y,iness), loss of identity, impersonalization. *Consider also:* as-if personality, alienation, acenesthes(ia,ic), disaffect(ed). *See also* Affective symptoms; Alexithymia; Alienation; Anhedonia; Dissociative disorders.

Deportation. Deport(ed,ing,ation,ations). Denaturaliz(e,ed,ing,ation). Expulsion(s). Expel(led,ling). Extradit(e, ed,ing,tion,tions). Oust(ed,ing). Exil(e, ed,ing). Banish(ed,ing). *Consider also:* forc(e,ed,ing), order(ed,ing) *with:*

return(ed,ing), flee(ing), fled. *See also* Expatriates; Population transfer; Purges; Refugees; Right of asylum; Statelessness.

Deportment. *See Demeanor.*

Deposition. Depos(e,ed,ing,ition,itions). Deponent(s). Transcript(s) of testimony. *Consider also:* affidavit(s), attest(ed,in, ation,ations), sworn statement(s), under oath, state's evidence. *See also* Affidavit; Circumstantial evidence; Evidence; Expert testimony; Testimony; Withholding evidence; Witness tampering; Witnesses.

Depositories. Depositor(y,ies). Repositor(y, ies). Reservoir(s). Safe keeping. Safe-deposit box(es). Vault(s). Storehouse(s). Museum(s). *See also* Archives; Libraries; Museums; Storage.

Depravity. Depravit(y,ies). Moral(ly) degrad(e,ed,ing,ation). Moral turpitude. Ethical turpitude. Corrupt(ed,ing,ion, ions). Immoral(ity). Wicked(ness). Moral(ly) lax(ness). Sleaz(y,iness). Decaden(t,ce). Heinous(ly,ness). Scandal(ous). Brutal(ity). Kink(y,iness). Vice. Base act(s). Sin(ful,fulness). *See also* Cannibalism; Corruption in government; Dehumanization; Evil; Immorality; Malinformation; Moral attitudes; Moral conditions; Paraphilias; Popular culture; Pornography; Scandals; Sin; Violence; War crimes.

Depreciation. Depreciat(e,ed,ing,ion). Life cycle costing. Life cost(s). Capital consumption allowance(s). *See also* Amortization; Capitalization; Costs; Economic value; Face value.

Depressants, appetite. *See Appetite depressants.*

Depression (economic). Depression. Economic(ally) depress(ed,ion,ions). Recession(s). Stock market crash(es,ed). Financial panic(s). Deflation. Stagflation. Hard times. Bank failure(s). Black Monday. Great depression. *Choose from:* economic, Wall St., financial *with:* cris(is,es), slump(s), contraction(s), turndown(s), downward spiral(s), fall(en,ing), plung(e,es,ed,ing), meltdown(s), crash(ed,es,ing), downturn(s). *Consider also:* rust belt, bread line(s), soup kitchen(s), Works Projects Administration, WPA, Civilian Conservation Corps, CCC. *See also* Bank failures; Bankruptcy; Business cycles; Business failures; Decline; Economic conditions; Economic crises; Economic problems; Plant closings; Recession; Unemployment rates.

Depression (psychology). Depress(ed,ion, ive). Mental depression. Desponden(t, cy). Deject(ed,ion). Gloom(y,iness). Sad(ness). Despair(ed,ing). Discourage(d,ment). Low(er,ered) mood. Defeatis(t,m). Hopeless(ness). Feeling worthless(ness). Learned helplessness. Lonel(y,iness). Lack of affect. Listless(ness). Intropunitive(ness). Unhapp(y,iness). Hypochondria(c,cal). Stupor. Weltschmerz. Dysthym(ia,ic,ics). Athym(ia,ic). Melanchol(y,ia). *Consider also:* self *with:* denial, abnegation, neglect, abuse, deprecation, depreciation, accusation, destructive. *Consider also:* suicid(e,es,al). *See also* Agitated depression; Anaclitic depression; Anhedonia; Antidepressive agents; Anxiety; Bereavement; Bipolar disorder; Depressive disorder; Dysphoria; Emotionally disturbed; Emotions; Grief; Holiday depression; Hopelessness; Involutional psychosis; Learned helplessness; Loneliness; Major depression; Neurotic depressive reaction; Nothingness; Pessimism; Postpartum depression; Psychopathology; Reactive depression; Sadness; Seasonal affective disorder; Self accusation; Self neglect.

Depression, agitated. See *Agitated depression.*

Depression, anaclitic. See *Anaclitic depression.*

Depression, emotional. See *Depression (psychology).*

Depression, holiday. See *Holiday depression.*

Depression, involutional. See *Involutional psychosis.*

Depression, major. See *Major depression.*

Depression, manic. See *Bipolar disorder.*

Depression, mental. See *Depression (psychology)*

Depression, postnatal. See *Postpartum depression.*

Depression, postpartum. See *Postpartum depression.*

Depression, reactive. See *Reactive depression.*

Depression, winter. See *Seasonal affective disorder.*

Depressive disorder. Depressive disorder. *Choose from:* severe, prominent, persistent, psychotic, endogen(ous,ic,etic), delusion(s,al), hallucination(s) *with:* depression(s), depressive, dysthym(ia,ic). *See also* Agitated depression; Anaclitic depression; Bipolar disorder; Depression (psychology); Involutional psychosis; Major depression; Neurotic depressive reaction; Postpartum depression; Reactive depression; Seasonal affective disorder.

Depressive reaction, neurotic. See *Neurotic depressive reaction.*

Depressive reactions, psychotic. See *Major depression.*

Deprivation. Depriv(ed,ation). Dispossessed. Denied privilege(s). Destitut(e, ion). Scarcit(y,ies). Isolat(ed,ion). Lonel(y,iness). Friendless. Homeless(ness). Disadvantage(d,ment). Socially handicapped. Underprivileged. Unemploy(ed,ables). Health impaired. Lower income. Low socioeconomic status. Welfare. Lower class. Delayed development. Poverty. Retarded. Malnourished. Malnutrition. Illiter(ate,acy). Disenfranchise(d,ment). Disfranchise(d,ment). Impoverish(ed, ment). Indigent. Poor. Neglected. Cultural deprivation. Powerless(ness). Downtrodden. Underclass(es). *Consider also:* handicapped, disabled, disabil(ity, ities), migrant worker(s), immigrant(s), minorit(y,ies), disadvantaged youth, economically disadvantaged, educationally disadvantaged, socially disadvantaged, inequality of access, multiple deprivation, transmitted deprivation, inadequa(te,cy), poverty trap, relative deprivation. *See also* Adversity; Child neglect; Cultural deprivation; Disadvantaged; Disinheritance; Destitution; Failure to thrive (psychosocial); Hardships; Homeless; Hunger, food deprivation; Inadequacy; Low income; Malnutrition; Maternal deprivation; Needs; Paternal deprivation; Poverty; Psychosocial deprivation; Relative deprivation; Scarcity; Sensory deprivation; Sleep deprivation; Social isolation; Underprivileged; Unmet needs; Water deprivation.

Deprivation, cultural. See *Cultural deprivation.*

Deprivation, emotional. See *Psychosocial deprivation.*

Deprivation, maternal. See *Maternal deprivation.*

Deprivation, paternal. See *Paternal deprivation.*

Deprivation, psychosocial. See *Psychosocial deprivation.*

Deprivation, relative. See *Relative deprivation.*

Deprivation, REM dream. See *REM dream deprivation.*

Deprivation, sensory. See *Sensory deprivation.*

Deprivation, sleep. See *Sleep deprivation.*

Deprivation, social. See *Cultural deprivation; Psychosocial deprivation.*

Deprivation, water. See *Water deprivation.*

Deprived, culturally. See *Cultural deprivation.*

Deprived, emotionally. See *Psychosocial deprivation.*

Depth perception. Depth perception. *Consider also:* distance, stereoscopic, three dimensional *with:* perception, vision, visual. *Consider also:* stereopsis. *See also* Space perception.

Deregulation. Deregulat(e,ed,ion). Decontrol(led,ling). Repeal of law(s). Repeal of regulation(s). Easing restriction(s). *See also* Decriminalization; Legalization of drugs.

Derision. Derision. Derid(e,ed,ing). Mock(ed,ing). Ridicul(e,ed,ing). Scoff(s,ed,ing). Jeer(s,ed,ing). Teas(e,es,ed,ing). Taunt(s,ed,ing). Sneer(s,ed,ing). Flout(s,ed,ing). *See also* Contempt; Satire; Teasing; Verbal abuse.

Dermatoglyphics. Dermatoglyphic(s). Fingerprint(s). Plantar print(s). Footprint(s). Palmar print(s). Palmprint(s). Sole print(s). Finger ridge pattern(s). Hallucal pattern(s). *See also* Crime prevention; Detectives; Identification (recognition); Patient identification systems.

Derogation. Derogat(e,ed,ing,ion). Belittl(e, ed,ing). Critic(ize,ized,izing,ism,isms). Deprecat(e,ed,ing,ion). Blam(e,es,ed, ing). Condemn(ed,ing,ation). Defam(e, ed,ing,ation). Disapprov(e,ed,ing,al). Find(ing) fault(s). Rebuk(e,ed,ing). Censur(e,ed,ing). Censor(ious). Disparag(e,ed,ing,ment). Demean(ed, ing). Degrad(e,ed,ing,ation). Disdain(ed, ing,ful). Libel(ous). Slander(ous). Uncomplimentar(y,iness). Vilif(y,ying, ied). *Consider also:* complain(ed,ing, t,ts), denounc(e,ed,ing), denunciat(e,ed, ing,ion), slur(s), incriminat(e,ed,ing, ion), indict(ed,ing,ment,ments), accus(e, ed,ation,ations), admonish(ed,ing,ment, ments). *See also* Allegations; Blame; Censure; Defamation; Denunciation; Disapproval; Libel; Scapegoating; Self debasement.

Desaparecido. See *Missing persons.*

Descent. Descen(t,ded,dant,dants,dent, dents). Genealog(y,ies,ological). Heir(s). Progen(y,iture). Offspring. Pedigree(s). Unilineal(ity). Unilateral descent. Double descent. Bilateral descent. Indirect descent. *Consider also:* lineage, matrilineal(ity), patrilineal(ity), inherit(ed,ance), paternity, maternity, begats, posterity, scion(s), dynast(y,ies), ancestry, ancestor(s). *See also* Cognatic descent; Genealogy; Heirs; Kinship; Matrilineality; Patrilineality; Unilineal descent.

Descent, cognatic. See *Cognatic descent.*

Descent, unilineal. See *Unilineal descent.*

Descent groups. See *Clans; Extended family.*

Description. Description(s). Describ(e,ed, ing). Descriptive statement(s). Descriptive passage(s). Descriptive adjective(s). Notational device(s). Notation(s). Representation(s). Likeness(es).

Delineat(e,ed,ing,ion). Depict(ed,ing, ion,ions). Picture(s). Portrait(s,ure). Portray(ed,ing,al). Imagery. *See also* Definition (words); Figurative language; Job descriptions; Media portrayal; Metaphors; Representation (likeness).

Descriptions, job. See *Job descriptions.*

Descriptive bibliography. Descriptive bibliography. *Choose from:* descriptive, analytical, annotat(ed,ion,ions), historical, critical *with:* bibliograph(y, ies). *Consider also:* bibliographic essay(s). *See also* Bibliography; National bibliography.

Desegregation. Desegregat(e,ed,ion). Integrat(e,ed,ion). *Choose from:* biracial(ly), multiracial(ly), interracial(ly), multiethnic *with:* transition(s), enrollment(s), balance(d), cooperation, tolerance. *Choose from:* racial(ly), ethnic(ally), culturally *with:* mix(ed,ing), balance(d). *Consider also:* magnet school(s), controlled choice, racial diversity, school busing, end(ed, ing) discrimination, equal rights, open housing. *See also* Anti-apartheid movement; Civil rights; Diversity; Equal education; Inclusion; Mainstreaming; Melting pot; Racial diversity; Racial integration; Racially mixed; School integration; Social integration; Tokenism.

Desegregation, school. See *School integration.*

Desensitization (psychology). Desensitiz(e,ed,ing,ation). *Choose from:* desensitiz(e,ed,ing,ation) *with:* systematic, therap(y,ies), psychotherap(y,ies). *Consider also:* implosion, implosive therapy, flooding, imagin(ary,ed) exposure, counterconditioning, counterphobia, decondition(ed,ing). *See also* Behavior modification; Progressive relaxation therapy; Relaxation training.

Desensitization, systematic. See *Desensitization (psychology).*

Desertification. Desertif(ied,ication). Desertiz(ed,ation). Dust bowl(s). Encroaching sand. *Choose from:* soil(s), land, environment(s,al), landscape(s), ecological *with:* degrad(ing,ed,ation), weather(ed,ing). *Choose from:* desert(s), sand dune(s), wasteland(s) *with:* spread(ing), encroach(ed,ing,ment). *Consider also:* deforestation, overgrazing, arid land(s), dry farming. *See also* Arid lands; Arid regions agriculture; Deforestation; Deserts; Ecological imperialism; Environmental degradation; Forest conservation; Irrigation; Land preservation; Resource stress; Slash burn agriculture; Soil conservation; Soil degradation; Soil erosion.

Desertion. Desert(ed,ion,ions,ing,er,ers). Abandon(ed,ing,ment). Forsake(n). Disavow(ed,al,ing). Defect(ed,ing,ion).

Dereliction. Withdrawal. Relinquish(ment). Repudiat(e,ed,ion). Betray(al). Apostasy. *Choose from:* runaway *with:* father(s), parent(s), mother(s), husband(s), wife, wives, spouse(s). *Consider also:* neglect(ed, ing,ful), nonsupport, AWOL. *See also* Abandoned children; Abandonment; Apostasy; Deadbeat parents; Military desertion; Runaways.

Desertion, military. See *Military desertion.*

Deserts. Desert(s,ic,ification,ified). Semidesert(s). Arid zones. Arid regions. Arid land(s). Semiarid. Drylands. Badlands. Drought condition(s). Drought prone area(s). Sand dune(s). Dustbowl(s). Barren(s). *Consider also:* Gobi, Shamo, Kara Kum, Kizil Kum, Kalahari, Atakama, Arabian, Great Sandy, Dahna, Persian, Samnan, Tarim, Sinkiang, Great Victoria, Gidi, Libyan, Mojave, Mohave, Death Valley, Negev, Sahara, Sonora, Nullarbor Plain, Chihuahuan, Great Basin, etc. *See also* Arid lands; Desertification.

Desexualization. Desexualiz(e,ed,ing, ation). Desex(ed,ing). Sanitiz(e,ed,ing, ation). Expurgat(e,ed,ing). Neutraliz(e, ed,ing,ation). Clean(ed,ing) up. Water(ed,ing) down. *Consider also:* prudish(ness). *See also* Castration; Censorship; Morality; Sexual inhibitions; Sterilization (sex).

Design, architectural. See *Architectural drawing; Facility design and construction.*

Design, book. See *Book design.*

Design, environmental. See *Environmental design.*

Design, experimental. See *Research design.*

Design, industrial. See *Industrial design.*

Design, interior. See *Interior design.*

Design, job. See *Job design.*

Design, research. See *Research design.*

Design, stage. See *Stage design.*

Design, work. See *Job design.*

Design and construction, facility. See *Facility design and construction.*

Designer drugs. Designer drug(s). Underground chemist(s). Bucket chemist(s). Biker lab(s). *Choose from:* analog(s,ue,ues), reverse ester(s), synthe(sis,tic,sized) *with:* heroin, narcotic(s), drug(s), meperidine, fentanyl, mescaline, opi(oid,oids,um). *Choose from:* illegal, illicit, clandestine *with:* synthesi(s,ze,zed,zing) *with:* drug(s), narcotic(s). *Consider also:* MPPP, MPTP, 3-methyl fentanyl [Sublimaze], ecstasy, anilerdine, alphaprodine, MDMA, methylenedioxymethamphetamine,

MDMA, Adam, etryptamine, methamphetamine [Methedrine, bombit, crank, crystal, meth, speed], china white, new heroin, pethidine, arylhexylamines, phencyclidine [PCP, Sernyl, peace pills, angel dust]. *See also* Drug addiction; Drug trafficking; Hallucinogens; Narcotics; Pharmacogenomics; Street drugs; Substance abuse.

Designs. Design(s). Plan(s). Plot(s). Blueprint(s). Map(s). Pattern(s). Draft(s). Outline(s). Sketch(es). Layout(s). Chart(s). Diagram(s). Prototype(s). Archetype(s). *See also* Architecture; Art metalwork; Arts; Decoration; Diagrams; Environmental design; Facility design and construction; Form (aesthetics); Format; Frames (physical); Guidelines; Groundwork; Industrial design; Interior design; Job design; Planning; Research design.

Desirability, social. See *Social desirability.*

Desire, inhibited sexual. See *Sexual inhibitions.*

Desire, sexual. See *Sexual arousal.*

Desires. See *Motivation.*

Deskilling. See *Labor process; Mass production; Proletarianization; Scientific management.*

Desktop publishing. Desktop publish(ing,er,ers). *Choose from:* desktop *with:* publishing, system(s), application(s), software, digital document management. *Consider also:* Adobe PageMaker, QuarkXPress, I Publish 2.0., PrintMaster Gold Deluxe 4.0, The Print Shop Signature Greetings, Publisher 97, Windows Draw. *See also* Clip art; Electronic publishing; Office automation.

Despair. Despair(ed,ing). Dishearten(ed,ing, ment). Dismay(ed,ing). Discourag(e,ed, ing,ment). Deject(ed). Depressed. Desponden(t,cy). Pessimis(m,tic). *See also* Depression (psychology); Hopelessness; Learned helplessness; Pessimism.

Despotism. Despot(s,ic,ism). Autocrat(ic,s). Dictator(s,ship,ship). Absolute monarch(y,ies). Absolutism. Tyrann(y, ical,ize). Tyrant(s). Absolute ruler(s). Authoritarian(ism). Totalitarian(ism). Domineer(ing). Fascis(m,t,ts). Oppress(ion,ive). Megalomaniac(al). One-man rule. Monocra(tic,cy). *See also* Absolutism; Abuse of power; Authoritarianism (political); Dictatorship; Fascism; Imperialism; Oppression; Political ideologies; Political repression; Totalitarianism.

Destination. Destination(s). Terminus(es). Target(s). Port(s) of call. Journey(s) end(s). Point(s) of debarkation. End of the road. Last stop. Stopping place(s). *See also* Air transportation; Business travel; Commuting (travel); Ends; Goals; Tourism; Travel.

Destiny. Destin(y,ed). Fate(d,ful). Ordained. Predestin(y,ed,ation). Karma. Inescap(able,ability,ableness). Inevit(able,ability,ableness). Predetermin(ed,ation). Necessity. Fortune. Foreordained. Doomed. Unavoid(able,ableness,ability). *See also* Determinism.

Destiny, manifest. See *Territorial expansion.*

Destitution. Destitut(e,ion). Poverty. Poor. Indigent. Low income(s). Impoverish(ed,ment). Welfare. Disadvantage(d,ment). Homeless(ness). Vagran(t,ts,cy). Lower class. Low status. Low socioeconomic status. Needy. Economic disadvantagement. Economic(ally) insecur(e,ity). Economic plight. Economically depressed. Slum(s). Ghetto(es). Privation. Penniless. Pauper. Penury. Indigen(t,cy). Impecunious. Economic hardship. Poverty area(s). Underprivileged. Beggar(s). *See also* Deprivation; Hardships; Homeless; Poverty; Starvation; Subsistence economy.

Destruction. Destruct(ion,ive). Destroy(ed,ing). Demolition. Demolish(ed,ing). Wreck(ed,ing). Mutilat(e,ed,ion). Pulveriz(e,ed,ing, ation). Raz(e,ed,ing). Gut(ted,ting). Pull(ing) down. Tear(ing) down. Break(ing) down. Knock(ing) down. Shatter(ed,ing). Ravag(e,ed,ing). Devastat(e,ed,ing). Havoc. Ruin(ed,ing,ation). Despoil(ed,ing, ment). Plunder(ed,ing). Pillag(e,ed,ing). Ransack(ed,ing). Injur(e,ed,ing,ious). Vandaliz(e,ed,ing). Catastroph(e,es,ic). Annihilat(e,ed,ing,ion). *See also* Arson; Defeat; Demolition; Destruction of property; Disasters; Natural disasters; Vandalism.

Destruction, weapons of mass. See *Weapons of mass destruction.*

Destruction of property. Destruct(ion,ive) of property. Destroy(ed,ing) property. Property crime(s). Demolish(ed,ing). Demolition. Raz(e,ed,ing). Pillag(e,ed, ing). Ransack(ed,ing). Wrecking crew(s). Arson. Loot(ed,ing). Plunder(ed,ing). Spoils of war. Vandaliz(e,ed,ing). Sabotag(e,ed,ing). Bomb(ed,ing). Letter bomb(s). Pilfer(ed,ing,age). Graffiti. *See also* Arson; Computer crimes; Defacement; Demolition; Destruction; Graffiti; Pillage; Terrorism; Vandalism.

Destructive behavior, self. See *Self destructive behavior.*

Detachment. Detach(ed,ment). Aloof(ness). Unworldliness. Separat(e,ion,eness). Disengag(ed,ement). Alienat(e,ed, ing,ion). Estrange(d,ment). Dissociat(ed, ion). Outsider(s). Disaffected. Dispossessed. Instrumentalism. Disaffiliat(ed, ion). Dehumaniz(ed,ation). Social detachment. Kafkaesque. *Consider also:* powerless(ness), anomic, rootless(ness), helplessness, psychological deprivation, depersonalization, unrelatedness. *See also* Alienation; Anomie; Dehumanization; Disengagement; Fragmentation (experience); Loneliness; Social isolation.

Detection, lie. See *Lie detection.*

Detection, substance abuse. See *Substance abuse detection.*

Detective and mystery television programs. Detective and mystery television program(s). *Choose from:* detective(s), myster(y,ies), crime, police drama(s), murder drama(s), murder myster(y,ies), police and gangster(s), private eye *with:* televis(ed,ing,ion), TV, telly(s), show(s), program(s). *Consider also:* NYPD Blue, Murder She Wrote, Perry Mason, etc. *See also* Mass media; Popular culture; Suspense; Television; Television plays; Television programs.

Detectives. Detective(s). Private investigator(s). Private eye. Sleuth. FBI agent(s). Police(man,men,woman, women). Sheriff(s). Guard(s). *See also* Crime prevention; Criminal investigations; Law enforcement; Police personnel.

Detente. Detente. Peaceful coexistence. Balance of power. Peaceful cohabitation. *Consider also:* perestroika, new world order, end of the arms race, global community, nonalignment, U.S. Soviet cooperation. *See also* Balance of power; Cold war; Disarmament; International relations; Foreign policy.

Detention. Detention. Detain(ed,ing). *Choose from:* legal(ly), pretrial, court ordered, preadjudicatory, judicial *with:* detention, detain(ed,ee,ees), incarcerat(e, ed,ion). Denied bail. Held under warrant. *Consider also:* restrain(t,ed, ing), held, hold(ing), remand(ed), custody, intern(ed,ment), incarcerat(e,ed, ing,ion), confin(e,ed,ing,ement), jail(ed,ing), imprison(ed,ing,ment), quarantin(e,ed). *See also* Arrests; Bail; Contempt of Court; Imprisonment; Legal rights; Martial law; Missing persons; Preventive detention; Psychiatric commitment; Punishment; Punitiveness.

Detention centers. Detention center(s). Detention system(s). Detention facilit(y,ies). Jail(s). Prison(s). Internment camp(s). House(s) of detention. Concentration center(s). Holding facilit(y,ies). *See also* Concentration camps; Correctional institutions; Prisons.

Detention homes, juvenile. See *Juvenile detention homes.*

Detention, preventive. See *Preventive detention.*

Deterioration. Deteriorat(e,ed,ing,ion). Degenerat(e,ed,ing,ion). Declin(e,ed, ing). Decelerat(e,ed,ing,ion). Dissolution. Corrod(e,ed,ing). Corrosion. Decaden(t,ce). Decompos(e,ed,ing, ition). Dilapidat(e,ed,ing,ation). Disintegrat(e,ed,ing,ation). Disrepair. Fail(ed,ing). *Consider also:* disease progression, progressive disease(s), loss of function(s), aging process, biological aging, memory loss(es), senescen(t,ce), abiotroph(y,ic), atroph(y,ic,ied). *See also* Aging; Decline; Decadence; Loss of function; Physiological aging; Regression (civilization).

Deterioration, alcoholic. See *Alcoholic deterioration.*

Determination, age by skeleton. See *Age determination by skeleton.*

Determination, age by teeth. See *Age determination by teeth.*

Determination, eligibility. See *Eligibility determination*

Determination, self individual. See *Inner directed; Personal independence.*

Determination, self national. See *Autonomy (government); Freedom; Political self determination; Popular sovereignty.*

Determination, threshold. See *Threshold determination.*

Determinism. Determinis(m,tic). Determinan(cy,t,ts). Determination. Predestin(y,ed,ation,arianism). Predetermin(ed,ation). Codetermin(ed, ation). Predispos(ed,ing,ition). Precipit(ed,ing). Caus(al,ation,ing). Necessary consequence(s). Pre-arranged. Inevitab(ility,le). *Consider also:* foreknowledge, historism, historicism, absolute idealism, foregone, ordained, destin(y,ed), preordained, foreordained, antecedent(s), reductionism, emergent propert(y,ies), providential(ly). *See also* Absolutism; Causality; Cultural relativism; Destiny; Dialectics; Economic determinism; Environmental determinism; Epistemology; Explanation; Factors; Fatalism; Freedom (theology); Geographic determinism; Indeterminism; Mind body problem; Nature nurture; Reductionism; Sociocultural factors; Socioeconomic factors.

Determinism, biological. See *Biological factors.*

Determinism, economic. See *Economic determinism.*

Determinism, environmental. See *Environmental determinism.*

Determinism, geographical. See *Geographical determinism.*

Determinism, social. See *Determinism; Social factors; Socioeconomic factors.*

Deterrence. Deter(red,rent,rents,rence,ring). Constrain(s,ed,ing,t,ts). Dissua(de,sion). Inhibit(s,ed,ing,ion,ions). Discourag(e, es,ed,ing,ement,ements). Block(s,ed,ing, age). Impediment(s). Preclud(e,es,ed, ing). Inaccess(ible,ibility). Hinder(s,ed, ing). Barrier(s). Hamper(s,ed,ing). Prevent(s,ed,ing,ion). Crime control. Thwart(s,ed,ing). Obstruct(s,ed,ing,ion, ions). Strategic balance. Reciprocated disarmament. Defensive shield(s). Disarm(ed,ing) first strike(s). *See also* Alcohol deterrents; Balance of power; Crime prevention; Death penalty; Hindrances; Impediments; Impediments to marriage; Life sentence; Punishment.

Deterrents, alcohol. See *Alcohol deterrents.*

Deterritorialization. Deterritorializ(e,ed, ing,ation). Deterritorialized nation state(s). Border cultural life. Transnational social movement(s). Supraterritorial(ity). Reterritorializ(e,ed, ing,ation). *Choose from:* transnational(ism), postnational(ism), global(ism), transborder *with:* communit(y,ies), identit(y,ies), arena(s), solidarit(y,ies), cultur(e,al), connectedness, integration. *Consider also:* postcolonial(ism), dissolv(e,ed,ing) traditional frontier(s), blur(red,ring) territorial boundaries, transnational mass culture, internationaliz(e,ed,ing,ation). *See also* Border wars; Borderlands; Culture contact; Globalization; Mexican American border region; Multicultural education; Refugees; Regionalism; Territorial expansion; Territorial issues; World citizenship.

Detoxification. Detoxif(y,ication). Detoxi(cate,cation). *Consider also:* drug rehabilitation, alcohol rehabilitation. Alcohol(ic,ism) treatment(s). Disulfiram. Antabuse. Hospitalized alcoholic(s). Anti-alcoholic agent(s). *See also* Alcohol deterrents; Alcohol withdrawal delirium; Alcohol rehabilitation; Drug rehabilitation; Drug withdrawal; Narcotic antagonists; Self-help groups; Substance withdrawal syndrome.

Detoxification, alcohol. See *Detoxification.*

Deux, folie a. See *Psychosis of association.*

Devaluation (of currency). Devaluation of currency. Shrinking value of dollar. *Choose from:* devalu(e,ed,ation,ing), fluctuat(ion,ing), fall(en,ing), drop(ped,ping), revalu(e,ed,ing,ation) *with:* money, currenc(y,ies), dollar(s), shekel(s), ruble(s), mark(s), peso(s), dong(s), etc. *Consider also:* exchange depreciation, dollarization. *See also* Currency; Currency speculation; Emergency currency; Monetary policy;

Monetary unions; Money supply; Purchasing power.

Devaluation, money. See *Devaluation (of currency).*

Developed countries. Developed countr(y,ies). DC(s). Advanced econom(y,ies). First world. Industrial(ized) countr(y,ies). Developed nation(s). Industrial(ized) world. Western societ(y,ies). Western nation(s). Industrial power(s). Industrial(ized) democrac(y,ies). Industrial societ(y,ies). Modern civilization(s). Advanced countr(y,ies). High-income countr(y,ies). *Choose from:* western, developed, industrial(ized), advanced, urbanized *with:* countr(y,ies), nation(s), state(s), societ(y,ies), world, communit(y,ies). *Consider also:* Andorra, Australia, Austria, Belgium, Bermuda, Canada, Denmark, Faroe Islands, Finland, France, Germany, Greece, Holy See, Iceland, Ireland, Israel, Italy, Japan, Liechtenstein, Luxembourg, Malta, Mexico, Monaco, Netherlands, New Zealand, Norway, Portugal, San Marino, South Africa, Spain, Sweden, Switzerland, Turkey, UK, US, Hong Kong, South Korea, Singapore, Taiwan. *See also* Countries in transition; Industrial societies; Mass society; Modern society; North America; Western civilization; Western Europe; Western society.

Developed nations. See *Developed countries.*

Developing countries. Developing countr(y,ies). Third world. Fourth world. LDC(s). UDC(s). Group of seventy-seven. G-77. *Choose from:* developing, less developed, least developed, threshold, emerging, underdeveloped, non-aligned *with:* countr(y,ies), nation(s), area(s), world. *Consider also:* Afghanistan, Algeria, Angola, Antigua and Barbuda, Argentina, Aruba, the Bahamas, Bahrain, Bangladesh, Barbados, Belize, Benin, Bhutan, Bolivia, Botswana, Brazil, Burkina Faso, Burma, Burundi, Cambodia, Cameroon, Cape Verde, Central African Republic, Chad, Chile, China, Colombia, Comoros, Democratic Republic of the Congo, Costa Rica, Cote d'Ivoire, Cyprus, Djibouti, Dominica, Dominican Republic, Ecuador, Egypt, El Salvador, Equatorial Guinea, Ethiopia, Fiji, Gabon, the Gambia, Ghana, Grenada, Guatemala, Guinea, GuineaBissau, Guyana, Haiti, Honduras, India, Indonesia, Iran, Iraq, Jamaica, Jordan, Kenya, Kiribati, Kuwait, Laos, Lebanon, Lesotho, Liberia, Libya, Madagascar, Malawi, Malaysia, Maldives, Mali, Malta, Marshall Islands, Mauritania, Mauritius, Mexico, Federated States of Micronesia, Morocco, Mozambique, Namibia, Nepal, Netherlands Antilles, Nicaragua, Niger, Nigeria, Oman,

Pakistan, Panama, Papua New Guinea, Paraguay, Peru, Philippines, Qatar, Republic of the Congo, Rwanda, Saint Kitts and Nevis, Saint Lucia, Saint Vincent and the Grenadines, Samoa, Sao Tome and Principe, Saudi Arabia, Senegal, Seychelles, Sierra Leone, Solomon Islands, Somalia, South Africa, Sri Lanka, Sudan, Suriname, Swaziland, Syria, Tanzania, Thailand, Togo, Trinidad and Tobago, Tunisia, Turkey, UAE, Uganda, Uruguay, Vanuatu, Venezuela, Vietnam, Yemen, Zambia, Zimbabwe. American Samoa, Anguilla, British Virgin Islands, Brunei, Cayman Islands, Christmas Island, Cocos Islands, Cook Islands, Cuba, Eritrea, Falkland Islands, French Guiana, French Polynesia, Gaza Strip, Gibraltar, Greenland, Grenada, Guadeloupe, Guam, Guernsey, Jersey, North Korea, Macau, Isle of Man, Martinique, Mayotte, Montserrat, Nauru, New Caledonia, Niue, Norfolk Island, Northern Mariana Islands, Palau, Pitcairn Islands, Puerto Rico, Reunion, Saint Helena, Saint Pierre and Miquelon, Tokelau, Tonga, Turks and Caicos Islands, Tuvalu, Virgin Islands, Wallis and Futuna, West Bank, Western Sahara. *See also* Caribbean; Central America; Central Asia; Colonialism; Countries in transition; Debt-for-nature swap(s); Eastern Europe; Far East; Foreign aid; Imperialism; Import substitution; Least developed countries; Less developed countries; Middle East; Newly industrializing economies; North Africa; Oceania; South America; South Asia; Southeast Asia; Sub-Saharan Africa; Subsistence economy; Technology transfer; Traditional societies; Tropical medicine; World systems theory.

Developing countries, advanced. See *Newly industrializing economies.*

Developing nations. See *Developing countries.*

Development. Develop(ed,ing,ment,ments, mental). Grow(ing,n,th). Evol(ve,ved, ving,ution). Matur(e,ed,ing,ity). Expan(d,ded,ding,sion). Improv(e,ed, ing,ment,ments). Exten(d,ded,sion). Progress(ed,ing,ion,ions). Strengthen(ed, ing). Further(ing,ance). Spread(ing). Perfect(ed,ing). Accelerat(e,ed,ing). Advanc(es,ed,ing,ement,ements). Enrich(ed,ment). Moderniz(ed,ing, ation). Promot(e,ed,ing,ion). Transform(ed,ing,ation). Ontogen(y,etic, etically). Phylogen(y,etic,etically). *See also* Adolescent development; Adult development; Buildup; Change; Career development; Childhood play development; Child development; Cognitive development; Critical period (psychology); Developing countries; Developmental stages; Enlargement; Expansion; Future orientation; Future of society;

Human development; Implementation; Improvement; Industrialization; Modernization; Organizational development; Physical development; Planning; Population growth; Progress; Psychosexual development; Professional development; Psychogenesis; Reform; Reorganization; Social change; Social development; Sustainable development.

Development, adolescent. See *Adolescent development.*

Development, adult. See *Adult development.*

Development, behavior. See *Behavior development.*

Development, career. See *Career development.*

Development, child. See *Child development.*

Development, childhood. See *Child development.*

Development, childhood play. See *Childhood play development.*

Development, cognitive. See *Cognitive development.*

Development, collection libraries. See *Collection development (libraries).*

Development, community. See *Community development.*

Development, curriculum. See *Curriculum development.*

Development, delayed. See *Delayed development.*

Development disorders, child. See *Child development disorders.*

Development disorders, language. See *Language development disorders.*

Development disorders, pervasive. See *Pervasive development disorders.*

Development, early childhood. See *Early childhood development.*

Development, economic. See *Economic development.*

Development, emotional. See *Emotional development.*

Development, employee. See *Staff development.*

Development, faculty. See *Faculty development.*

Development, human. See *Human development.*

Development, individual. See *Adolescent development; Adult development; Behavior development; Career development; Child development; Cognitive development; Emotional development; Enlightenment (state of mind); Human development; Human potential movement; Infant development; Intellectual development; Language development;*

Moral development; Motor development; Personality development; Physical development; Psychomotor development; Psychosexual development; Psychosocial development; Self actualization; Skill learning; Socialization; Speech development.

Development, industrial. See *Industrialization.*

Development, infant. See *Infant development.*

Development, intellectual. See *Intellectual development.*

Development, land. See *Real estate development.*

Development, language. See *Language development.*

Development, market. See *Market development.*

Development, mental. See *Cognitive development.*

Development, moral. See *Moral development.*

Development, motor. See *Motor development.*

Development, neonatal. See *Infant development.*

Development, organizational. See *Organizational development.*

Development, perceptual. See *Perceptual development.*

Development, personal. See *Adolescent development; Adult development; Behavior development; Career development; Child development; Cognitive development; Emotional development; Enlightenment (state of mind); Human development; Human potential movement; Infant development; Intellectual development; Language development; Moral development; Motor development; Personality development; Physical development; Psychomotor development; Psychosexual development; Psychosocial development; Self actualization; Skill learning; Socialization; Speech development.*

Development, personality. See *Personality development.*

Development, physical. See *Physical development.*

Development, precocious. See *Precocious development.*

Development, prenatal. See *Prenatal development.*

Development, product. See *Product development.*

Development, professional. See *Professional development.*

Development, program. See *Program development.*

Development, psychological. See *Behavior development; Cognitive development; Emotional development; Enlightenment (state of mind); Human development; Human potential movement; Intellectual development; Language development; Moral development; Personality development; Psychomotor development; Psychosexual development; Psychosocial development; Self actualization; Socialization.*

Development, psychomotor. See *Psychomotor development.*

Development, psychosexual. See *Psychosexual development.*

Development, psychosocial. See *Psychosocial development.*

Development, real estate. See *Real estate development.*

Development, regional. See *Regional development.*

Development, residential. See *Planned communities.*

Development, retarded speech. See *Retarded speech development.*

Development, rural. See *Rural development.*

Development, scientific. See *Scientific development.*

Development, sensory. See *Perceptual development.*

Development, sexual. See *Psychosexual development; Sexual maturation.*

Development, skill. See *Skill learning.*

Development, social. See *Social development.*

Development, social individual. See *Emotional maturity; Psychosocial development; Social maturity; Social skills; Socialization.*

Development, speech. See *Speech development.*

Development, staff. See *Staff development.*

Development, suburban. See *Suburban development.*

Development, sustainable. See *Sustainable development.*

Development, technology. See *Product development; Scientific development; Scientific discoveries; Scientific revolutions; Technological change; Technological innovations; Technological progress.*

Development, urban. See *Urban development.*

Development, verbal. See *Language development; Speech development; Verbal learning.*

Development, water resources. See *Water resources development.*

Developmental age groups. See *Age groups.*

Developmental disabilities. Developmental disabilit(y,ies). *Choose from:* developmental(ly), maturational(ly) *with:* disabilit(y,ies), disabled, handicap(s,ped), lag(s,ging,ged), defect(s,ive,ives), disorder(s,ed), delay(s,ed), deficien(t,cy,cies), aprax(ic,ia,ias), problem(s). *Consider also:* cerebral pals(y,ied), epilep(sy,tic), autis(m,tic), blind(ness), deaf(ness), mut(e,ism), muscular dystrophy, osteogenesis imperfecta, familial dysautonomia, mental(ly) retard(ed, ation), spina bifida, special needs, handicap(ped,ping), disabled disabilit(y, ies) *with:* child(ren,hood), juvenile, infan(t,ts,cy), babies. *See also* Congenitally handicapped; Delayed development; Disability; Drug addicted babies; Drug induced abnormalities; Learning disabilities; Mental retardation; Physical abnormalities.

Developmental stages. Developmental stage(s). Stage(s) of development. Developmental process(es). Cognitive stage(s). Life stage(s). Career stage(s). Stage(s) of learning. Stage(s) of emotional development. Stage theor(y,ies). Erikson(ian) stage(s). Piaget(ian) stage(s). Kohlberg stage(s). Kubler Ross stage theory. Transition(s). Passage(s). Level(s) of development. Rite(s) of passage. Aging. Unfold(ed, ing). Life change event(s). Growing up. *Consider also:* infant development, autarchy, midlife change(s), menopause, embryo(s), fetus(es), zygote(s), developmental psychology, individual development. *See also* Adolescent development; Adult development; Age (Psychology); Age differences; Ages of man; Aging; Behavior development; Child development; Climacteric; Cognitive development; Development; Embryology; Economic development; Emotional development; Human development; Human life cycle; Influence of age on ability; Object permanence; Oral stage; Organizational development; Perceptual development; Physical development; Prenatal development; Psychogenesis; Psychological aging; Puberty.

Deviance. Devian(ce,cy,t,ts). Deviate(s). Divergent behavior(s). Deviation amplification. Social(ly) unacceptable. Atypical. Antisocial. Nonconform(ing,ist,ists,ity). Eccentric(ity,ities,s). Peripheral member(s). Marginal(ity). Marginal state(s). Drifter(s). Runaway(s). Sinner(s). Liminal state(s). Abnormal. Cacogenic. Sexual deviation(s). Sexual perver(t,ts,sion,sions). Undefined state(s). Crime(s). *Consider also:* label(led,ling), label(ed,ing), norm(s,

ative), stigma(tize,tized,tization), stereotyp(e,es,ing), abnormal behavior(s), prostitut(e,es,ion), delinquen(t,ts,cy). *See also* Anomie; Deviant behavior; Exceptions; Juvenile delinquency; Labeling (of persons); Marginality (sociological); Nonconformity (personality); Sexual deviations; Social disorganization; Stigma.

Deviant behavior. Deviant behavior(s). Devian(ce,cy,t,ts). Misbehav(e,ed,ing, ior). Nonconform(ance,ing,ist,ists,ity). Drifter(s). Runaway(s). Truan(t,ts,cy). Dropout(s). Dangerous behavior(s). Eccentric(ity,ities,s). Deviant sexual behavior(s). Antisocial behavior(s). Crime(s). *Choose from:* deviant, unconventional, divergent, abnormal, unauthorized *with:* behavior(s), conduct, action(s). *Choose from:* violat(e,ed,ing, ion,ions) *with:* taboo(s), norm(s), rule(s). *See also* Alcoholism; Antisocial behavior; Behavior problems; Career criminals; Cheating; Crime; Cruelty; Deviance; Drug addiction; Impulsiveness; Indecent exposure; Juvenile delinquency; Predelinquent youth; Promiscuity; Recidivism; Rogues; Runaways; Self destructive behavior; Sex offenders; Sexual deviations; Substance abuse; Truancy.

Deviant behavior, socially. See *Deviant behavior.*

Deviation. Deviation(s,ism,ist,ists). Aberration(s). Abnormalit(y,ies). Anomal(y,ies). Difference(s). Discrepanc(y,ies). Divergence(s). Inconsisten(cy,cies,t). Irregularit(y,ies). Variation(s). Departure from course. *Consider also:* bend(s,ing), bent, curv(e,es,ed,ing), declination(s), variance(s), veer(ed,ing), shift(ed,ing), alter(ed,ing,ation), modif(y,ied,ication). *See also* Anomalies; Exceptions; Individual differences; Variations.

Deviations, sexual. See *Sexual deviations.*

Devices. Device(s). Appliance(s). Instrument(s). Apparatus. Mechanism(s). Contrivance(s). Invention(s). Implement(s). Gadget(s). Utensil(s). *See also* Appliances; Equipment; Prostheses; Safety devices; Self help devices; Tools.

Devices, female contraceptive. See *Female contraceptive devices.*

Devices, safety. See *Safety devices.*

Devices, self help. See *Self help devices.*

Devils. Devil(s). Evil spirit(s). Satan(ic,ism). Beelzebub. Baalzebub. Belial. Evil One. Prince of Darkness. Demon(ic,ism, ology,s). Fallen angel(s). Abaddon. Afrit. Angra Mainyu. Apollyon. Asmodeus. Asmodei. Badimo(s). Banshee(s). Belphegor. Cacodemon(ic,s). Chindi. Diabolus. Dybbuk(s). Elf. Elves. Genie(s). Ghoul(s). Goblin(s). Hobgoblin(s). Imp(s). Incub(i,us,uses).

Leprechaun(s). Leviathan. Lucifer. Mammon. Mephistopheles. Moloch. Ogre(s). Pan. Pix(y,ies). Sprite(s). Troll(s). Succub(i,us,uses). Vampire(s). Werewol(f,ves). *See also* Demons; Elves; Evil; Evil eye; Fairies; Folk literature; Folklore; Ghosts; Good spirits; Spirit possession; Succubus; Witchcraft.

Devolution. Devolution(sry,ist,ists). Deteriorat(e,ed,ing,ion). *Choose from:* delegat(e,ed,ing,ion), deregulat(e,ed,ing, ion), declin(e,ing), fragment(ed,ing,ion), regress(ed,ing,ion), regressive(ness), retrogress(ed,ion,ive,iveness), reced(e, ed,ing), retrograd(e,ing,ation), *with:* power(s), property, responsibilit(y,ies). *Consider also:* federal shrinkage, New Federalism, local autonomy, Contract with America. *See also* Confederalism; Decentralization; Downsizing; Reengineering; Regionalism; Regression (civilization); Reorganization.

Devotion. Devot(e,ed,ing,ion,ional). Ardent love. Fidelity. Strong affection. Attachment. Ardor. Fervor. Passion(ate). Piety. Fanatic(ism). Zeal(ous). Enthusias(m,tic). Eager(ness). Earnest(ness). Perseverance. *See also* Enthusiasm; Fanaticism; Religiosity.

Devotional poetry. Devotional poe(try,m, ms). *Choose from:* inspirational, sacred, religious, holy, devotional, spiritual(ity, ism), liturgical, faith, prayer(s) *with:* poe(try,tical,m,ms), verse(s), lament(s), lyric(s), sonnet(s). *Consider also:* hymn(s). *See also* Prayer; Religious literature; Sacred songs.

Dexterity, physical. See *Physical dexterity.*

Diabetes. Diabet(es,tic). Diabetes mellitus. Prediabetic. Diabetes insipidus. *Consider also:* diabetic acidosis, diabetic ketosis, diabetic angiopath(y, ies), diabetic retinopath(y,ies), diabetic coma, hyperglycemic hyperosmolar nonketotic coma, diabetic nephropath(y, ies), diabetic neuropath(y,ies). *See also* Disorders.

Diachronic linguistics. Diachronic linguistics. Glottochronolog(y,ical). Historical linguistics. *Choose from:* histor(y,ical), diachronic *with:* linguistic(s), language(s). *See also* Comparative linguistics; Historical linguistics; Language change; Lingusitics.

Diagnosis. Diagnos(e,ed,tic,is,es). Electrodiagnos(is,tic). Medical history taking. Pathognom(y,ic,onic). *Choose from:* medical, problem(s), handicap(s), abnormalit(y,ies), risk(s), disease(s), disabilit(y,ies), condition(s), symptom(s) *with:* assess(ed,ing,ment,ments), evaluat(ed,ing,ion,ions), identif(y,ied, ying,ication,ications), detect(ed,ing,ion), predict(ed,ing,ion,ions), classif(y,ied,

ying,ication,ications), label(s,ed,ing), label(led,ling), misdiagnos(is,es,ed,ing), recogni(ze,zed,zing,tion). *Consider also:* screening program(s), mass screening, telemedicine . *See also* Behavioral assessment; Comorbidity; Computer assisted diagnosis; Diagnostic imaging; Diagnostic services; Diagnostic tests; Neuropsychological assessment; Patient history; Personality measures; Psychodiagnosis.

Diagnosis, computer assisted. See *Computer assisted diagnosis.*

Diagnosis, dual. See *Comorbidity.*

Diagnosis, educational. See *Educational diagnosis.*

Diagnosis of alcohol intoxication. Diagnosis of alcohol intoxication. *Choose from:* alcohol *with:* breath instrument(s), breath analy(sis,zer), gas chromatography, intoximeter(s), breathalyzer(s), alcolmeter(s), blood alcohol level(s), screen(ed,ing). *See also* Alcohol drinking; Diagnosis; Drunk driving; Drunkenness.

Diagnostic imaging. Diagnostic imaging Neuroimag(e,ed,es,ing). *Choose from:* diagnos(is,tic) *with:* imaging, radiology, image guided, roentgen, ultramicroscop(y,ic), image interpretation, computer assisted, magnetic resonance, electron microscop(y,ic), photograph(y, ic), radiograph(y,ic), radionuclide, nearinfrared spectroscopy, subtraction technique, thermograph(y,ic), tomograph(y,ic), transillumination, ultrasonograph(y,ic), ultrasonic. *See also* Diagnosis; Diagnostic services; Diagnostic tests.

Diagnostic services. Diagnostic service(s). Diagnostic center(s). Radioassay service(s). Endoscopy service(s). Facilities for prenatal diagnos(is,tic). Cytology screening service(s). *Consider also:* screening test(s), diagnostic test(s), mass screening(s), genetic screening(s), mass chest x-ray(s), multiphasic screening(s), mobile health unit(s), psychological screening(s). *See also* Diagnosis; Diagnostic imaging; Health services; Screening.

Diagnostic tests. Diagnostic test(s). *Choose from:* diagnostic, screening, routine, preadmission, prehospitalization, hospital admission *with:* test(ing,s), assessment(s), assay(s), examination(s), lab(oratory) work, evaluation(s). *Consider also:* urinalys(is,es), biops(y,ies), blood sample(s), cytology screening, chest x-ray(s), electroencephalogra(m,ms,phy), electrocardiogra(m, ms,phy), etc. *See also* Diagnostic imaging; Diagnosis; Screening.

Diagrams. Diagram(s). Graphic design(s). Blueprint(s). Chart(s). Graph(s). Schematic representation(s). *Consider*

also: draft(s), drawing(s), outline(s), illustration(s), schematic(s), sketch(es). *See also* Designs; Graphics; Guidelines; Planning; Plans.

Dialectical materialism. Dialectical materialism. Materialist dialectic(s). Dialectical interaction of world and consciousness. *Consider also:* Marxist economics, historical materialism, thesis and antithesis. *See also* Communism; Dialectics; Marxism; Social theories.

Dialectics. Dialectic(al,icism,icizing,s). Thesis, antithesis, synthesis. Hegelian theory. Countermovement(s). *See also* Antithesis; Contradictions; Determinism; Dialectical materialism; Logic; Materialism; Marxism; Philosophy; Polarization; Refutation; Synthesis.

Dialects. Dialect(al,ally,ology,s). Vernacular. Lingo. Jargon. Cant. Argot. Slang. Accent(s). Patois. Idiomatic language. Regional language(s). Nonstandard language(s). Bidialectical(ism). Common speech. Colloquial speech. Colloquialism(s). Bidialectal. Local language(s). Linguistic variation(s). Diglossia. Sociolinguistic dispersion. *Consider also:* ghetto speech, Black English, Ebonics, vestigial Spanish, Lingua(e) Franca(e,s), La Platica, El Consejo, La Castigada, el Chiste, el Cuento, la Historia, el Verso, el Dicho, Pachuquismos, Calo, Swiss German, high German, low German, Plattdeutsch, Castilian Spanish, Catalan Spanish, Valencian Spanish. *See also* Accents; Bidialectalism; Cant; Colloquial language; Comparative linguistics; Diglossia; Ebonics; Idioms; Language shift; Language maintenance; Linguistic geography; Nonstandard English; Sociolinguistics; Speech communities.

Dialects, regional. See *Dialects.*

Dialogic pedagogy. Dialogic pedagogy. Dialogic(al) education. Dialogic(al) teaching. Talk write pedagogy. *Choose from:* dialogic(al,ized) *with:* learning, teaching, education, pedagogy. *Consider also:* Socratic method, democratic education, democratic teaching. *See also* Active learning; Equal education; Perspective taking; Critical thinking.

Dialogue. Dialogue(s). Discuss(ed,ing,ion,ions). Duologue(s). Interlocution. Convers(e,ed,ing,ation, ations,ational). Talk(s,ed,ing). Discourse. Verbal exchange(s). *See also* Debate; Direct discourse; Discussion; Group decision making; Negotiation; Persuasion; Rhetoric.

Dialogues, religious. See *Religious dialogues.*

Diaries. Diar(y,ies). Journal(s). Daily record(s). Log(s). Logbook(s). Chronicle(s). Annal(s). Memoir(s). Chronolog(y,ies). Account(s). *See also*

Annals; Autobiography; First person narrative; Oral history; Reminiscence; Travel writing.

Diarrhea. Diarrhea. Dysentery. Watery stool(s). Watery bowel movement(s). *Consider also:* fecal incontinence. *See also* Defecation.

Diaspora. Diaspora. Disband(ed,ing,ment). Dispers(e,ed,ing,al,ion). Mass exodus. *Consider also:* Babylonian exile, outside Palestine, exile(s), refugee(s). *See also* Forced migration; Geographic distribution; Migration; Refugees; Relocation.

Diatribe. Diatribe(s). Castigat(e,ed,ing,ion). Abusive speech(es), Denounc(e,ed,ing). Denunciation(s). Jeremiad(s). Philippic(s). Tirade(s). *See also* Complaints; Criticism; Jeremiads; Militancy.

Dichotomous thinking. Dichotomous thinking. *Choose from:* either-or, black-white *with:* thinking. *See also* Authoritarianism (psychological); Dogma; Dogmatism; Rigid personality; Thinking.

Dictators. See *Dictatorship.*

Dictatorship. Dictator(s,ship,ships). Despot(s,ic,ism). Autocrat(ic,s). Absolute monarch(s,y). Absolute ruler(s). Absolutism. Autarch(ic,y,ies). Tyrann(y,ical,ize). Tyrant(s). Authoritarian(ism). Totalitarian(ism). Domineer(ing). Fascis(m,t). Oppress(ion,ive). Megalomaniac(s,al). One-man rule. Monocra(tic,cy). Czar(s). Kaiser(s). Caesar(s). Fuhrer(s). Duce(s). Caudillo(s). Shah(s). Khan(s). Rajah(s). Sirdar(s). Mogul(s). Sultan(s). Emir(s). Caliph(s). Sheik(s). *Consider also:* strongman. *See also* Authoritarianism (political); Caciquism; Despotism; Fascism; Nazism; Oppression; Totalitarianism.

Dictionaries. Dictionar(y,ies). Wordbook(s). Lexicon(s). Glossar(y,ies). Wordlist(s). *Consider also:* vocabular(y,ies). *See also* Glossaries; Lexicography; Reference materials.

Dictums. Dict(a,um,ums). Adage(s). Maxim(s). Aphorism(s). Apothegm(s). Axiom(s). Caveat(s). Proverb(s). Brocard(s). Saying(s). Truism(s). Gnome(s). Sententia(e). Precept(s). *Consider also:* sententious(ness). *See also* Adages; Aphorisms; Axioms; Postulates.

Didactic analysis. Didactic analys(es,is). Tuitional analys(is,es). Training analys(is,es). *See also* Analysis; Teaching methods.

Die, right to. See *Right to die.*

Diet. Diet(s,ary,etic,etics). Meal(s). Nutrition(al). Eating habits. *Choose from:* food, meal(s), nutrient(s), calor(ie,ies,ic), diet(s,ary) *with:* intake, consumption, limit(s,ed,ation,ations), habit(s), deficien(t,cy,cies), allowance(s), pattern(s), requirement(s), choice(s), restrict(ed,ion,ions). *See also* Calories (food); Convenience Foods; Diet fads; Eating; Feeding practices; Food; Food additives; Food preferences; Food services (programs); Fish as food; Gastronomy; Junk food; Malnutrition; Natural foods; Nutrition; Nutrition disorders; Seafood; Vegetarianism.

Diet fads. Diet(ary) fad(s). *Choose from:* eating, diet(s,ary), food(s), nutrition(al) *with:* fad(s,dism), craze(s), mania, quack(ery,s), cult(s), fallac(y,ies), bizarre. *Consider also:* appetite suppressant(s), macrobiotic, liquid diet(s), lite food(s), light food(s), starch blocker(s), liquid protein, fast food(s). *See also* Diet; Fasting; Junk food; Malnutrition; Natural foods; Nutrition; Popular culture; Vegetarianism.

Dietary likes and dislikes. *See Food habits.*

Differences. Differen(t,ce,ces,tials,tiation). Antithesis. Contrast(ed,ing,s). Contrary. Compar(itive,ison,isons,ability). Deviation(s). Diverg(e,ed,ing,ence). Discrepan(t,cy,cies). Dissimilar(ity,ities). Divers(e,ity). Disparit(y,ies). Distinct(ion,ions,iveness). Heterogene(ity,ous). Inequal(ity,ities). Nonconform(ing,ity). Opposit(e,ion). Variance. Variable(s). Variabilit(y,ies). Variation(s). Variet(y,ies). Unequal. Unlike(ness). *See also* Age differences; Antithesis; Class differences; Comparative study; Cross cultural comparisons; Deviance; Distinction; Diversity; Gender differences; Generation gap; Heterogeneity; Individual differences; Language varieties; Racial differences; Regional differences; Resemblance; Rural urban differences; Similarity; Specialization; Status.

Differences, age. See *Age differences.*

Differences, class. See *Class differences.*

Differences, cultural. See *Cross cultural comparisons.*

Differences, ethnic. See *Ethnic differences.*

Differences, ethnocultural. See *Ethnic differences.*

Differences, gender. See *Gender differences.*

Differences, human sex. See *Gender differences.*

Differences, individual. See *Individual differences.*

Differences, racial. See *Racial differences.*

Differences, regional. See *Regional differences.*

Differences, rural urban. See *Rural urban differences.*

Differences, sex. See *Gender differences.*

Differences, species. See *Species differences.*

Differential, semantic. See *Semantic differential.*

Differentials, wage. See *Wage differentials.*

Differentiation. See *Discrimination (psychology).*

Differentiation, sex embryogenetic. See *Sex differentiation (embryogenetic).*

Difficulties. Difficult(y,ies). Burden(s). Problem(atic,s). Annoyance(s). Puzzle(s). Riddle(s). Conundrum(s). Enigma(tic). Tribulation(s). Gordian knot(s). Question(s). Quandar(y,ies). Dilemma(s). Predicament(s). Impasse(s). Bone of contention. Subject of dispute. Mind boggl(ing,ers). Labyrinth(s). Hidden meaning(s). Plight(s). Perplex(ed,ing,ity,ities). Issue(s). Obstacle(s). Cris(is,es). Disorder(s). Challenge(s). Multi-problem(s). Barrier(s). Trouble(s). Constraint(s). Limitation(s). Bothersome. *See also* Adjustment (to environment); Barriers; Conflict; Constraints; Crises; Disorders; Hindrances; Limitations; Problems.

Difficulties, concentration. See *Concentration difficulties.*

Diffusion. Diffus(e,ed,eness,ing,ion,ional, ionism). Scatter(ed,ing). Distribut(e,ed, ing,ion,ions). Spread(ing). Social contagion. Dispers(e,ed,ing,al). Disseminat(e,ed,ing,ion). Propagat(e,ed, ing,ion). Transmission of culture. *Consider also:* borrow(ed,ing), adoption of new ideas, adoption of innovations, circumfus(e,ed,ing,ion), dissipat(e,ed, ing,ion). *See also* Adoption of ideas; Distribution channels; Epidemics; Fashions; Information dissemination; Networks; Technology transfer.

Diffusion, language. See *Language spread.*

Diffusion of innovation. Diffusion of innovation. *Choose from:* technolog(y,ies), innovation(s), new technology, new idea(s), novel approach(es), technological development(s) *with:* diffusion, transfer(ring,red,s), adopt(ed,ing,ion), spread, borrow(ed,ing), accept(ed,ing,ance), disseminat(e,ed, ing,ion). *See also* Adoption of ideas; Educational innovations; Information dissemination; Modernization; Technology transfer.

Digerati. See *Computer experts.*

Digestion. Digest(ed,ing,ion,ive). Digestive function(s). *Choose from:* breakdown, absorb(ed,ing), absorption, assimilat(e, ed,ing,ion) *with:* nutrient(s), food, starch(es), protein(s), fat(s), etc. *Consider also:* uptake by the small and large intestine, ingest(ion,ive,ible). *See also* Digestive system; Eating.

Digestive system. Digestive system(s). Biliary tract(s). Bile duct(s). Gallbladder(s). Esophagus(es). Esophagogastric junction(s). Gastrointestinal system(s). GI system(s). Intestine(s,al). Stomach(s). Liver(s). Pancreas(es). Islands of Langerhans. Pancreatic duct(s). *See also* Anatomy; Digestion.

Digital communications. Digital communication(s). *Choose from:* digital(ize,ized,ization), compressed data, wideband data *with:* interface(s), communication(s), channel(s), signal(s), multiplex(ing), modulat(e,ed,ing,ion), demodulat(e,ed,ing,ion), modem(s), network(s,ed,ing), transmission(s), transmit(ted), teletransmission(s), receiv(e,ed,ing), rout(ed,ing), message(s). *Consider also:* communications network(s), Internet, electronic publishing, information superhighway. *See also* Digital money; Digital signatures; E-commerce; Electronic mail; Electronic eavesdropping; Electronic publishing; Information dissemination.

Digital education. *See Distance education.*

Digital money. Digital money. Digital wallet(s). Electronic money. E-wallet(s). Electronic cash. *Consider also:* CyberCash, electronic funds transfer(s), digital signature(s). *See also* Digital communications; Digital signatures; E-commerce; Electronic data interchange; Information society; Internet (computer network); Small businesses; V-commerce.

Digital signatures. Digital signature(s). *Choose from:* digital, Internet, electronic mail, fax(ed,ing), World Wide Web, WWW, Web-based, on-line *with:* signature(s), identification card(s), authenticat(e,ed,ing,ion) identit(y,ies). *Consider also:* digital certificate(s). *See also* Cyberlaw; Digital communications; Digital money; E-commerce; Electronic data interchange; Electronic mail; Global integration; Identification cards; Information society; Online privacy; Signatures; Small businesses; V-commerce.

Diglossia. Digloss(ia,ic). Trigloss(ia,ic). Polygloss(ia,ic). Bilingual dialect(s). *Consider also:* vernacular, colloquial, formal, literary *with:* language(s), speech. *Consider also:* spanglish. *See also* Bilingualism; Colloquial language; Creoles; Culture contact; Dialects; Language maintenance; Language shift; Language varieties; Linguistic minorities; Multilingualism.

Dignity, human. See *Human dignity.*

Dignity, individual. See *Human dignity.*

Dikes (engineering). Dike(s). Levee(s). Flood wall(s). *Consider also:* flood control, dam(s), breakwater(s), embankment(s). *See also* Flood control; Floods; Irrigation; Shore protection.

Dilemmas. Dilemma(s). Predicament(s). Quandar(y,ies). Difficult choice(s). Mixed motive(s). Ambivalen(t,ce). Muddle(s). Conflict(s). Uncertainty. Risk taking. Risky shift(s). Perplex(ed,ity). *See also* Ambivalence; Barriers; Choices (alternatives); Conflict; Deadlock; Decision making; Problems; Risk.

Diligence. Diligen(t,tly,ce). Assidu(ity,ous, ousness). Industrious(ness). Sedulous(ly, ness). *Consider also:* persever(e,ed,ing, ance), persist(ed,ing,ent), unflagging, intent(ness), steady, earnest, painstaking(ly). *See also* Academic persistence; Persistence; Personality traits; Work.

Dimensions. Dimension(s,al,al,ally,ality). Size(s). *Consider also:* height, weight, length, breadth, circumference(s), extent, magnitude, measure(s), proportion(s), perimeter(s). *See also* Capacity; Proportionality; Size.

Diminished responsibility. See *Insanity defense.*

Dining, communal. See *Group meals.*

Dining and dinners. See *Dinners and dining.*

Dinners and dining. Dinners and dining. Banquet(s). Main meal(s). Potluck(s). Supper(s). Feast(s). Repast(s). Refection(s). Table d'hote(s). Buffet(s). A la carte. *See also* Eating; Entertaining; Entertainment; Gastronomy; Grace at meals; Hospitality; Meals; Sacred meals; Social activities; Tableware.

Dinosaurs. Dinosaur(s,ia). Ornithischia. Stegosaurus(es). Triceratop(s). Iguanodon(s). Saurischia. Tyrannosaurus(es). Apatosaurus(es). Brontosaurus(es). Diplodicus(es). *Consider also:* camarasaurus(es), neoceratopsian(s), ornithomimosaur(s), oviraptoridae, protoceratop(s), majungasaurus, araripesuchus, titanosaur sauropod(s). *See also* Animals; Extinction (species).

Dioceses. Dioces(e,es,an). Bishopric(s). *See also* Districts; Localism; Parishes.

Dioxin. Dioxin(s). TCDD. *Consider also:* polychlorinated biphenyl(s), polychlorinated dibenzo-p-dioxin(s), PCDD(s), tetrachlorodibenzo-p-dioxin, agent orange. *See also* Agricultural chemicals; Environmental pollutants; Pesticides.

Diplomacy. Diploma(cy,t,ts,tic). Tact(ful,fulness). Savoir faire. Finesse. Adroit(ness). Suave. Urbane. Politic. Gracious(ness). Polished. Refined. Sagac(ity,iousness). Polite. Discretion. *Consider also:* artful(ness),

judicious(ness). *See also* Discretion; Etiquette; Tact.

Diplomacy (official). Diploma(cy,t,ts,tic). Statecraft. Summit(s,ry). Summit meeting(s). Statesmanship. Machiavellian(ism). *Choose from:* diplomatic, ambassador(s,ial) *with:* activit(y,ies), channel(s), conference(s), exchange(s), meeting(s), negotiat(e,ed, ing,ion,ions), polic(y,ies), relations. *Choose from:* quiet, conference, summit, parliamentary, behind the scene *with:* diplomacy. *See also* Diplomatic documents; Diplomatic etiquette; Diplomatic privileges and immunities; Diplomats; Embassies; Foreign policy; Foreign policy making; International alliances; International cooperation; International relations; Negotiation; Treaties.

Diplomatic and consular service. See *Diplomacy (official); Diplomats.*

Diplomatic documents. Diplomatic document(s). Diplomatic paper(s). *Choose from:* diplomat(s,ic), embass(y,ies), consulate(s), foreign policy, envoy(s) *with:* letter(s), document(s,ation), correspondence, dispatch(es), protocol(s), pouch(es), record(s), archiv(e,es,al). *See also* Diplomacy (official); Diplomats.

Diplomatic etiquette. Diplomatic etiquette. *Choose from:* diplomat(s,ic), foreign policy, State department, embass(y,ies), ambassador(s), consulate(s), envoy(s) *with:* etiquette, courtesy, protocol(s). *Consider also:* state dinner(s), White House dinner(s), diplomatic mission(s). *See also* Diplomacy (official); Diplomats; Etiquette; Protocols.

Diplomatic privileges and immunities. Diplomatic privilege(s). Diplomatic immunit(y,ies). Diplomatic protection. Diplomatic convention(s). *Choose from:* diplomat(s,ic), consular, embass(y,ies), ambassador(s), consulate(s), envoy(s) *with:* privilege(s), immunit(y,ies), civil process(es), criminal process(es), law(s) enforcement, criminal law(s), scofflaw(s), unpaid parking ticket(s), illegal(ity,ities), violation(s), waive immunity, persona non grata. *See also* Diplomacy (official); Diplomats; Embassies; Immunity.

Diplomats. Diplomat(ist,s). Diplomatic agent(s). Ambassador(ial,s). Envoy(s). Emissar(y,ies). Consul(s). Consulate(s). Consular officer(s). Attache. Charge d'affaires. Ambassador extraordinary and plenipotentiary. Envoy extraordinary. Minister plenipotentiary. Representative. Diplomatic corps. Agent(s). Legate(s). Diplomatic mission(s). Papal legate and nuncio. Papal internuncio. Minister resident. Foreign minister(s). *Consider also:* agent(s), arbitrator(s), peacemaker(s), negotiator(s). *See also* Diplomacy (official); Diplomatic documents; Diplomatic etiquette; Diplomatic privileges and immunities; Messengers.

Dipsomania. Dipsomania. Dypsomania. Epsilon alcoholism. *Choose from:* paroxysmal, binge, periodic *with:* drinking. Drinking bout(s). *See also* Alcoholism.

Direct costs. Direct cost(s). Variable cost(s). Material cost(s). *Consider also:* real cost(s). *See also* Cost analysis; Costs; Labor costs.

Direct discourse. Direct discourse. Oratio recta. Direct address(es). Direct speech. Direct exchange(s). *See also* Communication (thought transfer); Discourse; Dialogue; Indirect discourse; Speech.

Direct legislation. See *Referendum.*

Direct mail advertising. Direct mail advertis(e,ed,ing,ement,ements). Direct mail order(s,ed,ing). Direct response advertis(e,ed,ing,ement,ements). Direct mail campaign(s). *Choose from:* retail(er,ers,ing), advertis(e,ed,ing, ement,ements), market(ed,ing), promotion(s), solicit(ed,ing,ation), unsolicited, sell(ing), sale(s), gift certificate(s) *with:* direct mail, mail-order, credit-card(s), junk mail, catalog(s), mailing list(s), E-mail. *Consider also:* spam(med,ming), print advertising campaign(s). *See also* Advertising; Database marketing; Direct marketing; Marketing; Marketing strategies; Order processing; Orders (business); Telemarketing.

Direct marketing. Direct marketing. Target marketing. *Choose from:* real time, direct, personalized *with:* marketing, sales *Consider also:* direct response advertising, shopping online. *See also* Advertising; Database marketing; Marketing; Marketing strategies; Target marketing; Telemarketing.

Direct sales. See *Direct marketing.*

Directed, inner. See *Inner directed.*

Directed, other. See *Other directed.*

Directed, tradition. See *Traditionalism.*

Directed discussion. Directed discussion(s). *Choose from:* discussion(s), seminar(s) *with:* directed, leader(s,ship), led, structured, controlled, guided. *See also* Discussion; Group discussion.

Directed learning, self. See *Individualized instruction.*

Directed reverie therapy. Directed reverie therap(y,ies). *Choose from:* guided, directed, therap(y,ies), psychotherap(y, ies) *with:* daydream(s,ing), fantas(y,ies), reverie, imagery. *See also* Psychotherapeutic techniques.

Direction, self psychology. See *Inner directed; Personal independence.*

Direction, spiritual. See *Spiritual direction.*

Directives, advance. See *Advance directives.*

Directorates, interlocking. See *Interlocking directorates.*

Directories. Director(y,ies). Address list(s). Registr(y,ies). Membership list(s). Roster(s). Telephone book(s). Address book(s). *See also* Reference materials.

Directors. See *Administrators.*

Directors, boards of. See *Advisory committees; Governing boards.*

Dirges. Dirge(s). Song(s) of lamentation. *Choose from:* song(s), hymn(s), march(es) *with:* grief, lament(ing,ed, ation), mourn(ed,ing,ful), burial(s), wake(s), funeral(s), memorial(s). *See also* Church music; Laments; Music; Religious music.

Dirty dancing. Dirty danc(ing,e,er,ers). Lap danc(ing,e,er,ers). Lap-danc(ing,e,er, ers). *Choose from:* sex(ual,ually,uality), erotic(ism), striptease, stripper(s), homosexual(ly,uality), exotic, burlesque, kinky, table *with:* danc(ing,e,er,ers), entertain(er,ers,ment). *Consider also:* lambada. *See also* Adult entertainment; Belly dance; Dance; Entertainment; Nightclubs.

Disabilities, attitudes toward persons with. See *Attitudes toward handicapped; Attitudes toward mental retardation; Attitudes toward physical handicaps.*

Disabilities, developmental. See *Developmental disabilities.*

Disabilities, employment of persons with. See *Employment of persons with disabilities.*

Disabilities, learning. See *Learning disabilities.*

Disabilities, mental. See *Cognition disorders; Learning disabilities; Mental illness; Mental retardation.*

Disabilities, physical. See *Disability; Physically handicapped.*

Disabilities, reading. See *Reading disabilities.*

Disabilities, visual. See *Blindness; Partially sighted; Vision disorders.*

Disability. Disabilit(y,ies). Disabled. Handicap(ped,pism,s). Handicapping condition(s). Afflict(ed,ion,ions). Crippl(e,ed,ing). Infirm(ity,ities). Physically challenged. Differently able(d). Physical(ly) weak(ness). Health impair(ed,ment,ments). Exceptional child(ren). Exceptional person(s). Special child(ren). Exceptional student(s). Special education student(s). Special population(s). Rehabilitation

client(s). Subnormal child(ren). Special health problem(s). Physical(ly) defect(s,ive). Blind(ness). Partial(ly) sight(ed). Limited sight. Visual impairment(s). Deaf(ness). Hearing loss(es). Lame(ness). Defective hearing. Hard of hearing. Stutter(er,ers,ing). Stammer(ing,er,ers). Mut(e,ism). Amput(ation,ee,ees). Parapleg(ia,ics). Quadripleg(ia,ics). Hemipleg(ia,ic). Multi-disabled. Birth defect(s). Thalidomide bab(y,ies). Defective child(ren). Defective infant(s). Abnormalit(y,ies). Monster(s). Facial cleft. Cleft palate. Down(s) syndrome. Myelomeningocele. Retard(ation,ed). Gigantism. Dwarfism. Neurological(ly) damage(d). Epilep(tic,sy). Brain damaged. Brain dysfunction. Hyperactiv(e,ity). Attention deficit disorder(s). Cerebral palsy. Spastic(ity). Pals(y,ied). Mental disorder(s). *Choose from:* perceptual, sight(ed), vision, visual, hearing, speech, language, orthopedic, mobility, ambulat(ory,ion), motor, physical(ly), congenital(ly), multipl(e,y), birth, neurological(ly), learning, emotional(ly), mental(ly), aural(ly), adventitious(ly) *with:* impair(ed,ment,ments), handicap(s,ped), dysfunction(s), loss(es), disabilit(y,ies), disorder(s), deficit(s), retard(ed,ation), limit(ed, ation,ations), abnormalit(y,ies). *Consider also:* sheltered workshop(s), PL 94-142. *See also* Adventitious impairments; Architectural accessibility; Attitudes toward handicapped; Attitudes toward mental retardation; Attitudes toward physical handicaps; Awkwardness; Birth injuries; Communication aids for handicapped; Communication disorders; Blindness; Congenitally handicapped; Deafness; Debility; Developmental disabilities; Disability rights movement; Disabled workers; Drug induced abnormalities; Employment of persons with disabilities; Human abnormalities; Language development disorders; Language disorders; Loss of function; Mental retardation; Multiply handicapped; Noninstitutionalized disabled; Physical disfigurement; Physical mobility; Physically handicapped; Severely handicapped infants; Sheltered housing; Sheltered workshops; Self help devices; Speech disorders; Travel barriers; War victims.

Disability evaluation. Disability evaluation(s). *Choose from:* disabilit(y, ies), work capacity, handicap(ped,s), workmens compensation *with:* evaluat(e,ed,ing,ion,ions), rat(e,ed,ings), eligib(le,ility), certificat(e,ion), assess(ed,ing,ment,ments). *See also* Disability; Eligibility determination; Insurance; Screening.

Disability rights movement. Disability rights movement. *Choose from:* disabled, disabilit(y,ies), handicapped, blind, mobility impaired, wheelchair(s), deaf *with:* power, empower(ed,ing, ment), activis(m,t,ts), militan(t,cy), lobb(y,ies,ying), protest(ed,er,ers,s), community action, demonstrat(ed, ing,ion,ions), demonstrator(s), social action, rights group(s), radical(s,ism), political participation, citizen participation, political activit(y,ies), vot(e,es, ed,ing), consumerism, rebellion(s), liberation, assertive(ness), crusade(s), march(es), rall(y,ies). *Consider also:* Disabled American Veterans; Coalition of Citizens with Disabilities; National Federation of the Blind; National Coordinating Council on Spinal Cord Injury. *See also* Activism; Activists; Advocacy; Architectural accessibility; Attitudes toward Handicapped; Attitudes toward mental illness; Attitudes toward physical handicaps; Attitudes toward physical illness; Civil rights organizations; Employment of persons with disabilities; Militancy; Protest movements; Social action; Social movements.

Disabled. See *Disability.*

Disabled, accessibility for. See *Architectural accessibility.*

Disabled, attitudes toward. See *Attitudes toward handicapped; Attitudes toward mental retardation; Attitudes toward physical handicaps.*

Disabled, communication aids for. See *Communication aids for handicapped.*

Disabled, noninstitutionalized. See *Noninstitutionalized disabled.*

Disabled, perceptually. See *Brain damaged.*

Disabled personnel. See *Disabled workers.*

Disabled workers. Disabled worker(s). *Choose from:* worker(s), labor(er,ers), workforce, crew(s), employee(s), hiree(s), hir(e,ed,ing), laborer(s), manpower, womanpower, nonprofessional(s), career(s), employment, job(s), office force, operator(s), personnel, paraprofessional(s), professional(s), staff, wage earner(s), work(men,man,women,woman), crafts(men,man,women,woman) *with:* disabilit(y,ies), disabled, handicap(ped, s), impair(ed,ment,ments), rehabilitat(ed, ion), blind, deaf, sightless, parapleg(ia, ic), quadripleg(ia,ic), retard(ed,ation). *See also* Disability; Disability evaluation; Employment of persons with disabilities; Sheltered workshops.

Disadvantaged. Disadvantage(d,ment). Depriv(ed,ation). Socially handicapped. Underprivileged. Unemploy(ed,ables). Depressed area(s). Appalachia. Ghetto. Health impaired. Low(er) income. Low(er) socioeconomic status. Welfare. Inner city. Lower class(es). Delayed development. Skid row. Poverty. Slum(s). Shantytown(s). Retard(ed, ation). Malnourished. Malnutrition. Illiter(ate,acy). Disenfranchise(d,ment). Disfranchise(d,ment). Disprivileged. Impoverished. Indigen(t,ts,cy). Poor. Neglected. Cultural deprivation. Powerless(ness). Downtrodden. Underclass. *Consider also:* handicapped, disabled, disabil(ity,ities), migrant worker(s), immigrant(s), minorit(y,ies), disadvantaged youth, economically disadvantaged, educationally disadvantaged, socially disadvantaged. *See also* Computer illiteracy; Cultural deprivation; Deprivation; Homeless; Illiteracy; Intellectual impoverishment; Lower class; Oppression; Poverty; Pseudoretardation; Psychosocial deprivation; Socially handicapped.

Disadvantaged, culturally. See *Cultural deprivation.*

Disadvantaged, economically. See *Deprivation; Disadvantaged; Poverty.*

Disadvantaged, socially. See *Cultural deprivation; Disadvantaged; Psychosocial deprivation.*

Disadvantagement, social. See *Cultural deprivation; Disadvantaged; Psychosocial deprivation.*

Disagreements. Disagreement(s). Disput(e,es,ed,ation). Controvers(y,ies, ial). Debate(s). Discussion(s). Quarrel(s). Argument(s). Antagonism(s). Altercation(s). Clash(es). *Consider also:* conflict(s), contradict(ed,ing,ion,ions), altercation(s). *See also* Arguments; Disputes; Misunderstanding.

Disappeared persons. See *Missing persons.*

Disappointment. Disappoint(ed,ing,ment, ments). Dishearten(ed,ing). Chagrin(ed). Discourag(e,ed,ing,ement,ements). Discontent(ed,ment,ments). Frustrat(ed, ing,ion,ions). Disillusion(ed,ing,ment, ments). Letdown. Comedown. Dissatisf(ied,ying,action,actions). Deject(ed,ion). Disgruntle(d,ment). *See also* Disillusionment; Dissatisfaction; Frustration; Emotions.

Disapproval. Disapprov(e,ed,ing,al,als). Berat(e,ed,ing). Castigat(e,ed,ing,ion). Deprecat(e,ed,ing,ion). Frown upon. Discommend(ed,ing,ation). Discountenanc(e,ed,ing). Criticiz(e,ed, ing). Criticism(s). Denounc(e,ed,ing). Denunciation(s). Reprehend(ed,ing). Decr(y,ying,ied). Disparag(e,ed,ing, ement). *Consider also:* condemn(ed,ing, ation), displeasure, dissatisf(y,ied, action), disfavor, blam(e,ed,ing), censur(e,ed,ing), remonstrat(e,ed,ing), repudiat(ed,ing,ation). *See also* Blacklisting; Blame; Censure; Denunciation; Derogation; Negative sanctions; Opinions; Punishment.

Disarmament. Disarm(ed,ing,ament). Demilitariz(e,ed,ation). Military disengagement. Decommission(ed,ing). Surrender weapon(s). Nuclear freeze. Ban missile(s). Ban chemical weapon(s). Peaceful coexistence. Demobiliz(e,ed, ing,ation). Weapons control. Nuclear weapons non-proliferation. Strategic Arms Limitation Talks. SALT I. SALT II. Strategic Arms Reduction Talks. Denuclearization. Nonaggression pact(s). Cut(s) military strength. Dismantle weapons. Troop cut(s). *Choose from:* arms, armament(s), weapon(s,ry), troop(s) *with:* demobiliz(ed,ing,ation), ban(s,ned,ning), control, eliminat(e,ion), limit(s,ation, ations), reduc(e,tion,tions), surrender, dismantl(e,ed,ing), cuts, withdraw(n,al). *Consider also:* disarmament *with:* agreement(s), talk(s), accord(s), pact(s), treat(y,ies). *See also* Antinuclear movements; Arms control; Demobilization; Nuclear weapons non-proliferation; Peace; Peaceful coexistence; War prevention.

Disarmament, nuclear. See *Arms control; Disarmament; Nuclear weapons non-proliferation.*

Disarray. See *Clutter; Confusion (disarray).*

Disaster planning. Disaster plan(s,ning). Disaster readiness. Emergency preparedness. Catastrophe plan(s,ning). Bomb shelter(s). Disaster program(s). Disaster preparedness. Air raid drill(s). Fire drill(s). Disaster readiness. Disaster alert system(s). Evacuation plan(s). Early warning alert. Emergency alarm system(s). Civil defense. Fallout shelter(s). *Choose from:* disaster(s), catastrophe(s), emergenc(y,ies), evacuation or specific types of disaster such as flood(s), earthquake(s), etc. *with:* plan(s,ning), readiness, preparation(s), prepare(d,dness), alert(s), alarm(s), shelter(s), mitigat(e,ed,ing, ion), reduc(e,ed,es,ing) risk(s), warning system(s), safeguard(s), protection, food reserve(s), stockpil(e,es,ing), checklist(s). *See also* Disaster relief; Disaster recovery; Disasters; Emergency services; Planning; State planning.

Disaster preparedness. See *Disaster planning.*

Disaster recovery. Disaster recovery. *Choose from:* disaster(s), serious disruption(s), system-wide disruption(s), systems failure(s), catastrophe(s), emergenc(y,ies) *with:* recover(y,ies,ed, ing), restor(e,ed,ing,ation), lifeline(s), clean-up, clean(ed,ing) up, reclaim(ed, ing), reconstruct(ed,ing,ion). *See also* Crisis management; Disaster relief; Disaster planning; Down (computers); Psychological debriefing; Recovery.

Disaster relief. Disaster relief. Search and rescue operation(s). *Choose from:* disaster(s), catastrophe(s), emergenc(y, ies), evacuation or specific types of disaster such as fire(s), flood(s), blizzard(s), earthquake(s) or famine(s) *with:* relief, rescu(e,ed,ing), aid(ed,ing), reconstruct(ed,ing,ion), sav(e,ed,ing), assist(ed,ing,ance), help(ed,ing), contribution(s), releas(e,ed,ing), extricat(e,ed,ing), recover(ed,ing,y), response(s), rehabilitat(e,ed,ing,ion), salvag(e,ed,ing), retriev(e,ed,ing). *See also* Crisis management; Disaster planning; Disaster recovery; Emergency services; Food relief; International organizations; Psychological debriefing; Relief services; Rescue.

Disasters. Disaster(s). Disastrous(ly). Catastrophe(s). Catastrophic event(s). Cataclysm(s,ic). Calamit(y,ies). Casualit(y,ies). Emergenc(y,ies). Violent change(s). Ruin(ed,ing,ation). Devastat(ed,ion). Fire(s). Famine(s). Bombing(s). War(s). Flood(s). Drought(s). Natural disaster(s). Blizzard(s). Snowstorm(s). Landslide(s). Explosion(s). Earthquake(s). Tidal wave(s). Tornado(es). Hurricane(s). Typhoon(s). Cyclone(s). Accident(s). Act(s) of God. Meltdown(s). Radiation accident(s). Nuclear accident(s). Nuclear explosion(s). Railroad accident(s). Airplane crash(es). Plane wreck(s). Ship sunk. Collision(s). Crash(es). Oil slick(s). Oil spill(s). Volcanic eruption(s). Struck by lightning. Storm(s). Riot(s). Bombing(s). War(s). Siege(s). Hostage(s). Damag(ed,es,ing). Destruction. Loss of life. Natural disaster(s). System crash(es). *See also* Accidents; Assistance in emergencies; Catastrophes; Crisis management; Crises; Damage; Disaster recovery; Disaster relief; Fire; Good samaritans; Natural disasters; Nuclear accidents; Nuclear winter; Stress; Survival.

Disasters, natural. See *Natural disasters.*

Disbursement. Disburs(e,ed,ing,ement,ements). Dispens(e,ed,ing). Dol(e,ed,ing) out. Distribut(e,ed,ing,ion,ions). Pay(ing) out. Paid out. Payment(s). *See also* Allocation; Distribution (apportion); Expenditures; Financial management.

Discharge. See *Deinstitutionalization; Institutional release.*

Discharge, patient. See *Patient discharge.*

Discharge of contracts. Discharge of contract(s). Releas(e,ed,ing) from contract(s). Cancel(led,ling) contract(s). Fulfill(ed,ing,ment) of contract(s). Releas(e,ed,ing) from legal obligation(s). *See also* Contracts; Earnest money.

Discharge of feelings. See *Abreaction; Catharsis; Psychodrama.*

Disciples. Disciple(s). Follower(s). Adherent(s). Believer(s). Proselyte(s). Apostle(s). Convert(s). Devotee(s).

Supporter(s). Votar(y,ies). *Consider also:* worship(er,ers), admirer(s). *See also* Apostles; Christians; Followers; Novices.

Disciplinary, cross approach. See *Interdisciplinary approach.*

Discipline. Disciplin(e,ed,ing). Behavioral control(s). Supervis(e,ed,ing,ion). Direct(ed,ing). Govern(ed,ing). *Choose from:* train(ed,ing), correct(ed,ing,s), mold(ed,ing,s), perfect(ed,ing,s) *with:* faculties, moral(s), character, behavior. *Consider also:* self-command, self-control, self-discipline, self-government, self-mastery, self-restraint, willpower. *See also* Child discipline; Employee discipline; Military discipline (punishment); Prison discipline; School discipline.

Discipline, child. See *Child discipline.*

Discipline, employee. See *Employee discipline.*

Discipline, mental. See *Mental discipline.*

Discipline, military conduct. See *Military discipline (conduct).*

Discipline, military punishment. See *Military discipline (punishment).*

Discipline, prison. See *Prison discipline.*

Discipline, school. See *School discipline.*

Discipline, self. See *Self control.*

Disciplines, academic. See *Academic disciplines.*

Disclaim. Disclaim(ed,ing,s,er,ers). Disaffirm(ed,ing,ation). Renounc(e,ed, ing). Renunciation(s). Den(y,ying,ied). Disacknowledg(e,ed,ing,ement). Disallow(ed,ing). Disavow(ed,ing). Disown(ed,ing). Repudiat(e,ed,ing,ion). Contradict(ed,ing,ion). *Consider also:* deprecat(e,ed,ing,ion), belittl(e,ed,ing, ement), disparag(e,ed,ing,ement), minimiz(e;ed,ing,ation), abjur(e,ed, ing,ation), forswear(ing), recant(ed,ing), retract(ed,ing,ion,ions), criticiz(e,ed, ing). *See also* Annulment; Cancellation; Nullification; Repeal.

Disclosure. Disclos(e,ed,ing,ure). Divulg(e, ed,ing,ence,ement). Revelation(s). Reveal(ed,ing). Expos(e,es,ed,ing,ure, ures). Exposition(s). Confess(ed,ing,ion, ions). Leak(s,ed,ing). Unveil(ed,ing). Admit(ted,ting). Admission(s). Uncover(ed,ing). Broadcast(ed,ing). *Consider also:* expose(s), display(sed, ing), proclamation(s), declaration(s). *See also* Confidentiality; Confession; Freedom of information; Revealed theology; Self disclosure; Truth disclosure.

Disclosure, financial. See *Financial disclosure.*

Disclosure, medical. See *Informed consent.*

Disclosure, self. See *Self disclosure.*

Disclosure, truth. See *Truth disclosure.*

Disco music. Disco music. *Choose from:* disco(theque,theques), nightclub(s), night club(s), nite club(s), cabaret(s), bar(s), Latino *with:* music, song(s), dance(s). *See also* Heavy metal (music); Jazz; Popular culture; Nightclubs; Popular music; Rhythm and blues; Rock and roll; Rock music.

Discontent. See *Dissatisfaction; Dissent.*

Discontinued, product. See *Product discontinued.*

Discount stores. Discount store(s). *Choose from:* discount, off-price, low-price(s) *with:* store(s), retailer(s), supplier(s), house(s), merchandiser(s), market(s), vendor(s), outlet(s). *Consider also:* warehouse club(s), discount club(s), discount chain(s), discounted brand name products, supermarket(s), drugstore chain(s), Wal-Mart, Kmart, etc. *See also* Department stores; Discounts; Retailing; Stores.

Discounts. Discount(ed,ing,s). Rebate(s). Deduction(s). Cut rate(s). Markdown(s). Rollback(s). *Consider also:* bulk discount(s), bulk price(s), reduced price(s), price reduction(s), decreasing price(s), money-off coupon(s), price cut(s), bargain price(s), lower price(s), package deal(s). *See also* Bargaining; Deals; Department stores; Discount stores; Kickbacks; Purchasing; Retailing; Sales; Stores.

Discouraged workers. Discouraged worker(s). Hidden unemploy(ed,ment). Drop(ped,ping) out of labor market. *See also* Disguised unemployment; Unemployment.

Discourse. Discourse. Discursive(ness). Discuss(ed,ing,ion,ions). Verbal interchange(s). Convers(e,ed,ing,ation, ations,ational). Dialog(s,ue,ues). Talk(s,ed,ing). Verbal exchange(s). Negotiation(s). *Consider also:* rhetoric(al), debate(s), Socratic method(s), argument(s,ation), critique(s), narrative(s), text(s). *See also* Conversation; Dialogue; Direct discourse; Discourse analysis; Discussion; Indirect discourse.

Discourse analysis. Discourse analy(sis,ses, zing). Disambiguat(e,ed,ing). *Choose from:* discourse, conversation, rhetoric, dialogue(s), speech(es), lecture(s), sermon(s), address(es) *with:* analy(sis, ses,zing), study, review(s), explicat(e,ed, ion), interpret(ed,ation,ations,ive), clarif(y,ied,ication), concordance(s), content analys(is,es), criticism, critique(s,d), explanation(s). *See also* Coherence; Communication (thought transfer); Communications research; Content analysis; Discourse; Speech acts.

Discourse, direct. See *Direct discourse.*

Discourse, indirect. See *Indirect discourse.*

Discoveries (findings). Discover(y,ies). Idea(s). Breakthrough(s). Serendipity. Result(s). Find(ing,ings). Invention(s). *See also* Scientific discoveries; Scientific revolutions.

Discoveries (geography). Discover(y,ies,ed,ing). *Choose from:* discover(y,ies,ed,ing), find(ing), found, explor(e,ed,ing,ation,ations), recogniz(e, ed,ing), recognition, identif(y,ied, ication) *with:* travel(s), expedition(s), explorer(s), satellite photography, place(s), world(s), forest(s), ocean(s), mountain(s), region(s), cave(s), continent(s). *See also* Discovering; Explorers; Pioneers; Spanish explorers.

Discoveries, scientific. See *Scientific discoveries.*

Discovering. Discover(ed,ing). Find(ing). Found. Detect(ed,ing,ion). Explor(e,ed, ing,ation,ations). Recogniz(e,ed,ing). Recognition. Identif(y,ied,ication, ications). Uncover(ed,ing). Reveal(ed, ing). Observ(e,ed,ing,ation,ations). Empirical evidence. Discern(ed,ing). Determin(ed,ing,ation,ations). *See also* Clues; Discoveries (findings); Discoveries (geography); Scientific method.

Discovery learning. Discovery learning. Guided discovery. Independent discovery. Unguided discovery. *Choose from:* discovery, inquiry, experien(ce,tial), exploratory *with:* learning, teaching, instruction, guided, training, tutoring, directed. *Consider also:* indirect, insight, inductive, trial and error, errorful *with:* learning. *See also* Active learning; Activity units; Heuristics; Observational learning.

Discrepancies. Discrepan(t,cy,cies). Differ(ing,ence,ences). Disagree(ing, ment,ments). Inconsisten(t,cy,cies). Error(s). Variance(s). Disparit(y,ies). Deviation(s). Incongruit(y,ies). Incongruen(t,ce). Divergence(s). Conflict(ing). Credibility gap(s). Discordan(t,ce). Miscalculation(s). Mistake(s). *See also* Differences; Errors.

Discrepant, age marriages. See *Age discrepant marriages.*

Discretion. Discretion. Discreet. Careful(ness). Pruden(ce,t). Judicious(ness). Responsible. Maturity. Sagac(ity,ious). Cautious(ness). Circumspect. Reasonable. Reasoned judgment(s). Diplomatic. Tactful(ness). Wise. Wisdom. *See also* Diplomacy; Elective; Judgment; Judicial discretion.

Discretion, judicial. See *Judicial discretion.*

Discretionary powers. Discretionary power(s). Discretionary decision making. Administrative discretion. Judicial discretion. Discretionary justice.

Consider also: delegat(e,ed,ing,ion) authority, arbitrar(y,iness). *See also* Delegation of powers; Discretion; Judicial activism; Judicial discretion; Separation of powers.

Discrimination (psychology). Discriminat(e,ed,ing,ion). Differentiat(e, ed,ion). Distinguish(ing). Same different decision. Discern(ment). Recogni(tion, zing). Assess(ing,ment) difference(s). Sensitivity. Detect(ing,ion) of difference(s). Mak(e,ing) distinction(s). Judgment. Judgement. *See also* Cognitive discrimination; Distinction; Figure ground discrimination; Odor discrimination; Perceptual discrimination; Pitch discrimination; Space perception; Tactual perception; Taste perception; Visual discrimination.

Discrimination, age. See *Age discrimination.*

Discrimination, cognitive. See *Cognitive discrimination.*

Discrimination, employment. See *Employment discrimination.*

Discrimination, figure ground. See *Figure ground discrimination.*

Discrimination, gender. See *Labor market segmentation; Sex discrimination; Sexism; Sexual division of labor; Sexual inequality.*

Discrimination, handicap. See *Attitudes toward handicapped.*

Discrimination, housing. See *Residential segregation.*

Discrimination, job. See *Employment discrimination.*

Discrimination, odor. See *Odor discrimination.*

Discrimination, perceptual. See *Perceptual discrimination.*

Discrimination, pitch. See *Pitch discrimination.*

Discrimination, race. See *Racial attitudes; Racial segregation; Racism.*

Discrimination, racial. See *Racial attitudes; Racial segregation; Racism.*

Discrimination, religious. See *Religious prejudice.*

Discrimination, reverse. See *Reverse discrimination.*

Discrimination, sex. See *Sex discrimination.*

Discrimination, sexual. See *Labor market segmentation; Male chauvinism; Sex discrimination; Sexism; Sexual division of labor; Sexual inequality.*

Discrimination, social. See *Social discrimination.*

Discrimination, visual. See *Visual discrimination.*

Discussion. Discuss(ed,ing,ion,ions). Exchange ideas. Consultation. Dialogue(s). Debat(ed,es,ing). Argu(e,ed,ing,ment,ments). Disput(ation,e,ed,es,ing). Conversation(s). Discourse(s). Talk(ed,ing). Confer(red,ring). Conference(s). *See also* Conversation; Debate; Dialogue; Discourse; Directed discussion; Group discussion; Negotiation; Nondirected discussion method; Verbal communication.

Discussion, directed. See *Directed discussion.*

Discussion, group. See *Group discussion.*

Discussion method, nondirected. See *Nondirected discussion method.*

Disease. Disease(s,ed). Ill(ness,nesses). Physical illness(es). Disorder(s). Ail(ing,ment,ments). Sick(ly,ness, nesses). Infect(ed,ion,ions). Affect(ed). Poor health. Unhealthy. Unwell. Malad(y,ies). Afflict(ed,ion,ions). Morbidity. Syndrome(s). Malaise. Contag(ion,ious). Epidemic(s). Patholog(y,ies,ical). Catastrophic illness(es). *Consider also:* specific conditions or diseases such as: AIDS, alcoholism, allerg(y,ies), anemia, arthritis, asthma, cancer, diabetes, drug addiction, epilepsy, heart attack(s), hypertension, influenza, leprosy, meningitis, obesity, plague(s), poliomyelitis, seizures, stroke(s), syphilis, tuberculosis, etc. *Choose from:* communicable, occupational, acute, chronic, iatrogenic *with:* disease(s). *See also* Acute disease; Agricultural workers disease; AIDS; Alzheimer's disease; Black lung disease; Cancer; Chronic disease; Coronary disease; Disease susceptibility; Disorders; Epidemics; Etiology; Health problems; Hereditary diseases; Hypertension; Illness; Infectious disorders; Laryngeal diseases; Morbidity; Occupational diseases; Onset (disorders); Pick's disease; Premorbidity; Prognosis; Psychophysiologic disorders; Public health; Recovery; Relapse; Remission; Sanitation; Severity of disorders; Sexually transmitted diseases; Symptoms; Tay Sachs disease; World health.

Disease, acute. See *Acute disease.*

Disease, agricultural workers. See *Agricultural workers disease.*

Disease, Alzheimer's. See *Alzheimer's disease.*

Disease, black lung. See *Black lung disease.*

Disease, chronic. See *Chronic disease.*

Disease, coronary. See *Coronary disease.*

Disease, Pick's. See *Pick's disease.*

Disease, resistance to. See *Immunity.*

Disease, Tay Sachs. See *Tay Sachs disease.*

Disease prevention. See *Health; Holistic health; Mental health; Preventive medicine; Prevention; Quality of life; Sanitation; Well being.*

Disease susceptibility. Disease susceptibility. Morbidity differential(s). Immune deficien(t,cy). Immunodeficien(t,cy). *Choose from:* disease(s), illness(es), disorder(s), infection(s), AIDS, alcoholism, allerg(y,ies), anemia, arthritis, asthma, cancer, diabetes, drug addiction, epilepsy, heart attack(s), hypertension, influenza, leprosy, meningitis, obesity, plague(s), stroke(s), syphilis, tuberculosis, etc. *with:* susceptib(le,ility), risk(s), vulnerab(le, ility), prone(ness), link(s,ed), probability, predispos(e,ed,ing,ition), determinant(s), antecedent(s), abnormal sensitivity, resistance, unprotected, immunity. *See also* Accident proneness; AIDS; Deficiency diseases; Disease; Environmental determinism; Epidemics; Hereditary diseases; High risk persons; Immunity; Occupational diseases; Occupational exposure; Onset (disorders); Predisposition; Premorbidity; Psychoneuroimmunology; Vulnerability.

Diseases, communicable. See *Infectious disorders.*

Diseases, deficiency. See *Deficiency diseases.*

Diseases, familial. See *Hereditary diseases.*

Diseases, hereditary. See *Hereditary diseases.*

Diseases, laryngeal. See *Laryngeal diseases.*

Diseases, occupational. See *Occupational diseases.*

Diseases, prehistoric. See *Paleopathology.*

Diseases, sexually transmitted. See *Sexually transmitted diseases.*

Diseases, social. See *Sexually transmitted diseases.*

Diseases, venereal. See *Sexually transmitted diseases.*

Disemployment. Disemployment. Jobless(ness). Dislocated worker(s). Unemploy(ed,ment). *Choose from:* worker(s), laborer(s), workmen, employee(s), personnel, staff *with:* dismiss(ed,al), layoff(s), laid off, terminat(ed,ion,ions), displace(d,ment), turnover, disemploy(ed,ment), fired, firing(s), retrench(ed,ment), cutback(s), eliminat(ed,ion). *See also* Personnel termination; Unemployment.

Disengagement. Disengage(d,ment). Detach(ed,ment). Alienat(ed,ion). Estrange(d,ment). Disconnected(ness). Disaffiliat(e,ed,ing,ion). Abdicat(e,ed, ing,ion). Abandon(ed,ing,ment).

Consider also: mourn(ed,ing), apath(etic,y), indifferen(ce,t), unenthusiastic, unambitious, uninspired, halfhearted, uninterested, diminished interest, low voter turnout, lack(ed,ing) interest, lack(ed,ing) feeling, impassiv(e,ity). *See also* Abdication; Alienation; Anomie; Apathy; Ceding; Detachment; Fragmentation (experience); Noninvolvement; Social isolation; Solitude.

Disequilibrium. Disequilibrium. Disequilibrat(e,ing,ation). Out of balance. Imbalance. Unbalanced. Lack of equilibrium. *Consider also:* economic imbalance, incentive(s) to change, need(ing) adjustment, out of phase, dysfunctional. *See also* Social equilibrium.

Disfigurement, physical. See *Physical disfigurement.*

Disfigurement, ritual. See *Ritual disfigurement.*

Disguise. Disguise(s,d). Camouflage(d). Costumes(s). Mask(s,ed,ing). Veil(ed,ing). Conceal(ed,ing) identity. Hidden. Hid(e,ing). Masquerad(e,ed, es,ing). Change color(s,ing). Facade(s). False front(s). *Consider also:* veneer(s, ed), deception, delusion, specious(ness), charade(s), make-believe, pretension(s), pretentious(ness), counterfeit(ed,ing), mumming, masque(s). *See also* Artificiality; Deception; Faking; Impostor; Masking; Mistaken identity.

Disguised unemployment. Disguised unemployment. *Choose from:* unemploy(ed,ment) *with:* disguised, hidden, underestimated. *Consider also:* underutiliz(e,ed,ation) of labor, discouraged worker(s). *See also* Discouraged workers; Employment trends; Seasonal unemployment; Unemployment; Unemployment rates.

Disgust. Disgust(ed,ing). Disagreeable(ness). Objectionable(ness). Distaste(ful). Abominab(le,ly). Abhorren(t,ce). Loathsome. Odious(ness). Repulsive(ness). Detestab(le,ility). Sicken(ing). Offensive. Offend(ed,ing). Revolting(ly). Unpleasant(ness). *See also* Aversion; Contempt; Reaction formation; Repugnance.

Dishonesty. See *Deception.*

Disillusionment. Disillusion(ed,ing,ment). Disenchant(ed,ing,ment). Disappoint(ed, ing,ment,ments). Discontent(ed,ment). Existential despair. Discourage(d,ment). Heartache(s). Disentrance(d). *Consider also:* shatter(ed,ing) illusion(s). *See also* Alienation; Burnout; Disappointment; Political defection.

Disinflation. Disinflat(e,ed,es,ing,ion, ionary). Inflation slowdown. Lower(ed,ing) inflation. *Consider also:*

increas(ed,ing) purchasing power, interest rate increase(s). *See also* Business cycles; Inflation (economics).

Disinformation. See *Deception.*

Disinheritance. Disinherit(ed,ance). Dispossess(ed). Deprive(d) of inheritance. Cut off. Disown(ed). Repudiate(d). *Consider also:* bereave(d,ment). *See also* Ascription; Deprivation; Heirs; Inheritance; Legacies.

Disintegration. Disintegrat(e,ed,ing, ion,ive). Disorganiz(e,ed,ing,ation). Disrupt(ed,ing,ion). Decompos(e,ed, ition). Breakdown. Break up. Fall apart. Dissolution. Dissolv(e,ed,ing). Chao(s, tic). Anom(ic,ie). Demoraliz(e,ed,ing, ation). Severe tie(s). Destroy(ed,ing). Destruction. Crumbl(e,ed,ing). Disband(ed,ing). *See also* Chaos; Clutter; Decline; Deterioration; Entropy.

Disinvestment. Disinvest(ed,ing,ment). Withdraw investment(s). Reduc(e,ed, ing) capital stock. Divest(ed,ing,iture, itures,ment,ments). Negative invest(ed, ing,ment). *Choose from:* reduc(e,ed,ing), withdraw(al), halt(ed,ing), discontinu(e, ed,ing) scrap(ped,ping), nonreplacement, liquidat(e,ed,ing,ion), sale(s), dispos(e, ed,ing), unload(ed,ing) *with:* capital goods, fund(s,ing), invest(ed,ing,ment, ments), stock(s). *Consider also:* disencumber(ed,ing), disinherit(ed,ing). *See also* Boycotts; Corporate Social Responsibility; Deindustrialization; Investment policy; Investments; Negative sanctions.

Dislike. See *Aversion.*

Dislikes, dietary likes and. See *Food habits.*

Dislikes, likes and. See *Preferences.*

Dislocated workers. Dislocated worker(s). Jobless(ness). *Choose from:* worker(s), laborer(s), workmen, employee(s), personnel, staff *with:* dismiss(ed,al), layoff(s), laid off, terminat(ed,ion,ions), displace(d,ment), turnover, disemploy(ed,ment), fired, firing(s), retrench(ed,ment), cutback(s), eliminat(ed,ion). *See also* Discouraged workers; Dismissal of staff; Labor economics; Labor market; Plant closings; Personnel termination; Seasonal unemployment; Skills obsolescence; Technological unemployment; Unemployment.

Dismissal of staff. Dismiss(al) of staff. Outplac(e,ed,ing,ement). Downsiz(e,ed, ing). Involuntary separation. Laid off. Lay-off. Laying off. Layoff(s). Terminat(e,ed,ing,ion) employment. Nonrenewal of contract. *Choose from:* dismiss(ed,al,als), terminat(e,ed,ion, ions), fired, firing(s), layoff(s), laid off, discharge(d), discharging, etrench(ed, ing,ment,ments), reduc(e,ed,tion,tions), trim, cut(s), cutback(s) *with:* job(s), employee(s), staff, personnel, worker(s), workforce, position(s), laborforce, faculty, teacher(s). *Choose from:* involuntary, mandatory, obligatory, forced *with:* career change(s), job change(s), retire(ment,ments), relocation(s). *Choose from:* job(s), employment, position(s) *with:* loss, lose, lost, insecurity, suspension(s), suspended, eliminat(e,ed,ing,ion). *See also* Cutbacks; Involuntary retirement; Labor aspects of technology; Labor market; Labor mobility; Mandatory retirement; Outplacement services; Plant closings; Personnel termination; Seasonal unemployment; Severance pay; Technological unemployment; Unemployment.

Disobedience. Disobedien(t,ce). Disobey(ed,ing). Insubordinat(e,ed, ation). Noncomplian(t,ce). Defian(t,ce). Naught(y,iness). Derelict. Remiss. Delinquen(t,ts,cy). Unrul(y,iness). Wayward(ness). Unmanageable. Uncontrollable. Undisciplined. Intransigen(t,ce). Recalcitran(t,ce). Fail(ure,ing) to obey. Refus(e,ed,ing,al) to obey. Rebellious(ness). *See also* Behavior problems; Obedience; Passiveness; Truancy.

Disobedience, civil. See *Civil disobedience.*

Disorder, alcohol amnestic. See *Alcohol amnestic disorder.*

Disorder, antisocial personality. See *Antisocial personality disorder.*

Disorder, attachment syndrome. See *Reactive attachment disorder.*

Disorder, attention deficit. See *Attention deficit disorder.*

Disorder, atypical paranoid. See *Involutional psychosis.*

Disorder, bipolar. See *Bipolar disorder.*

Disorder, borderline personality. See *Borderline personality disorder.*

Disorder, compulsive personality. See *Obsessive compulsive personality.*

Disorder, conversion. See *Conversion disorder.*

Disorder, cyclothymic. See *Cyclothymic disorder.*

Disorder, depersonalization. See *Depersonalization disorder.*

Disorder, depressive. See *Depressive disorder.*

Disorder, dysthymic. See *Dysthymic disorder.*

Disorder, explosive. See *Explosive disorder.*

Disorder, histrionic personality. See *Histrionic personality disorder.*

Disorder, hysterical personality. See *Histrionic personality disorder.*

Disorder, manic. See *Manic disorder.*

Disorder, panic. See *Panic disorder.*

Disorder, passive aggressive personality. See *Passive aggressive personality disorder.*

Disorder, reactive attachment. See *Reactive attachment disorder.*

Disorder, schizotypal personality. See *Schizotypal personality disorder.*

Disorder, seasonal affective. See *Seasonal affective disorder.*

Disorder, shared paranoid. See *Psychosis of association.*

Disorderly conduct. Disorderly conduct. *Choose from:* disorderly, scandal(ize,ized,izing,ous), shocking, obscene, coarse, threatening, abusive, offensive, noisy, reckless(ly), violent *with:* conduct, behavior, utterance(s), gesture(s). *See also* Breach of the peace; Ugliness; Violence.

Disorderly houses. Disorderly house(s). *Choose from:* bawdy, disorderly, gambling, prostitut(e,es,ion), bawdy, nuisance(s), crime(s), drug(s), crack, cocaine *with:* house(s), residence(s). *See also* Brothels; Drug trafficking; Prostitution

Disorders. Disorder(ed,s). Disease(s,ed). Disturb(ed,ance,ances). Dysfunction(s, al). Abnormalit(y,ies). Aberration(s). Aberrant(s). Deviation(s). Instabilit(y, ies). Unstable. Complaint(s). Irregularit(y,ies). Patholog(y,ies,ical). Physiopatholog(y,ies,ical). Psychopatholog(y,ies,ical). Complication(s). Ill(ness,nesses). Ail(ing,ment,ments). Problem(s). Sick(ly,ness,nesses). Infect(ed,ion,ions). Affect(ed,ion,ions). Poor health. Unhealthy. Unwell. Malad(y,ies). Afflict(ed,ion,ions). Morbidity. Psycho(tic,sis). Neuro(sis,tic). *Consider also:* syndrome(s), malaise, contag(ion, ious), epidemic(s), patholog(y,ies,ical), susceptibility. *See also* Adjustment disorders; Affective disorders; Anxiety disorders; Articulation disorders; Auditory perceptual disorders; Backache; Behavior disorders; Cancer; Child behavior disorders; Child development disorders; Child reactive disorders; Childhood adjustment disorders; Cognition disorders; Combat disorders; Comorbidity; Compulsive disorders; Consciousness disorders; Disease; Disease susceptibility; Dissociative disorders; Eating disorders; Ethnospecific disorders; Etiology; Factitious disorders; Female genital disorders; Gastrointestinal disorders; Growth disorders; Hearing disorders; Hereditary diseases; Illness; Impulse control disorders; Infectious disorders; Injuries; Labyrinth disorders; Language development disorders; Language disorders; Liver disorders; Lung disorders; Male genital disorders; Memory disorders; Menstrual disorders; Mental illness; Minimal brain disorders; Morbidity; Neuroses; Nutrition disorders; Organic mental disorders; Organic psychoses; Onset (disorders); Paranoid disorders; Personality disorders; Pervasive development disorders; Physical abnormalities; Physical disfigurement; Post traumatic stress disorders; Premorbidity; Prognosis; Psychophysiologic disorders; Psychomotor disorders; Psychoses; Recovery; Relapse; Remission; Repetitive motion disorders; Sexual deviations; Sexual function disorders; Severity of disorders; Sleep disorders; Social behavior disorders; Somatoform disorders; Speech disorders; Substance induced organic mental disorders; Substance induced psychoses; Substance use disorders; Symptoms; Thought disturbances; Vision disorders; Vitamin deficiency disorders; Voice disorders

Disorders, adjustment. See *Adjustment disorders.*

Disorders, affective. See *Affective disorders.*

Disorders, anxiety. See *Anxiety disorders.*

Disorders, appetite. See *Eating disorders.*

Disorders, articulation. See *Articulation disorders.*

Disorders, artificial. See *Factitious disorders.*

Disorders, auditory perceptual. See *Auditory perceptual disorders.*

Disorders, behavior. See *Behavior disorders.*

Disorders, character. See *Personality disorders.*

Disorders, child behavior. See *Child behavior disorders.*

Disorders, child development. See *Child development disorders.*

Disorders, child reactive. See *Child reactive disorders.*

Disorders, childhood adjustment. See *Childhood adjustment disorders.*

Disorders, civil. See *Civil disorders.*

Disorders, cognition. See *Cognition disorders.*

Disorders, cognitive. See *Cognition disorders; Thought disturbances.*

Disorders, combat. See *Combat disorders.*

Disorders, communication. See *Communication disorders.*

Disorders, compulsive. See *Compulsive disorders.*

Disorders, conduct. See *Behavior disorders; Behavior problems.*

Disorders, consciousness. See *Consciousness disorders.*

Disorders, dissociative. See *Dissociative disorders.*

Disorders, eating. See *Eating disorders.*

Disorders, ethnic. See *Culture specific syndromes; Ethnospecific disorders.*

Disorders, ethnospecific. See *Ethnospecific disorders.*

Disorders, factitious. See *Factitious disorders.*

Disorders, female genital. See *Female genital disorders.*

Disorders, gastrointestinal. See *Gastrointestinal disorders.*

Disorders, genetic. See *Hereditary diseases.*

Disorders, growth. See *Growth disorders.*

Disorders, gynecological. See *Female genital disorders.*

Disorders, hearing. See *Hearing disorders.*

Disorders, heart. See *Heart disorders.*

Disorders, impulse control. See *Impulse control disorders.*

Disorders, infectious. See *Infectious disorders.*

Disorders, labyrinth. See *Labyrinth disorders.*

Disorders, language. See *Language disorders.*

Disorders, language development. See *Language development disorders.*

Disorders, liver. See *Liver disorders.*

Disorders, lung. See *Lung disorders.*

Disorders, male genital. See *Male genital disorders.*

Disorders, memory. See *Memory disorders.*

Disorders, menstrual. See *Menstrual disorders.*

Disorders, mental. See *Cognition disorders; Mental illness.*

Disorders, minimal brain. See *Minimal brain disorders.*

Disorders, neurotic. See *Neuroses.*

Disorders, nutrition. See *Nutrition disorders.*

Disorders, organic mental. See *Organic mental disorders.*

Disorders, paranoid. See *Paranoid disorders.*

Disorders, personality. See *Personality disorders.*

Disorders, pervasive development. See *Pervasive development disorders.*

Disorders, physiological mental. See *Organic mental disorders.*

Disorders, post traumatic stress. See *Post traumatic stress disorders.*

Disorders, posttraumatic stress. See *Post traumatic stress disorders.*

Disorders, psychiatric. See *Cognition disorders; Mental illness.*

Disorders, psychomotor. See *Psychomotor disorders.*

Disorders, psychophysiologic. See *Psychophysiologic disorders.*

Disorders, psychosexual. See *Sexual deviations; Sexual function disorders.*

Disorders, psychosomatic. See *Psychophysiologic disorders.*

Disorders, psychotic. See *Psychoses.*

Disorders, repetitive motion. See *Repetitive motion disorders.*

Disorders, severity of. See *Severity of disorders.*

Disorders, sex. See *Sexual deviations; Sexual function disorders.*

Disorders, sexual function. See *Sexual function disorders.*

Disorders, sham. See *Factitious disorders.*

Disorders, sleep. See *Sleep disorders.*

Disorders, social behavior. See *Social behavior disorders.*

Disorders, somatoform. See *Somatoform disorders.*

Disorders, somatopsychic. See *Psychophysiologic disorders.*

Disorders, speech. See *Speech disorders.*

Disorders, substance induced organic mental. See *Substance induced organic mental disorders.*

Disorders, substance use. See *Substance use disorders.*

Disorders, vision. See *Vision disorders.*

Disorders, visual. See *Vision disorders.*

Disorders, vitamin deficiency. See *Vitamin deficiency disorders.*

Disorders, voice. See *Voice disorders.*

Disorganization, social. See *Social disorganization.*

Disorganized schizophrenia. Disorganized schizophrenia. Hebephrenic schizophrenia. Hebephren(ia,ias,ic,ics). *Consider also:* nuclear, process *with:* schizophrenia(s). *See also* Schizophrenia.

Disorientation. Disorient(ed,ation). Bewildered. Dazed. Confus(ed,ion). *Consider also:* disturbance(s) *with:* orientation. *See also* Consciousness disorders.

Disorientation, place. See *Place disorientation.*

Disorientation, time. See *Time disorientation.*

Displaced homemakers. Displaced homemaker(s). *Choose from:* aging, displaced *with:* homemaker(s). *Choose from:* reentry, reentering, retraining *with:* women, woman, homemaker(s), housewives, housewife. *Consider also:* empty nest syndrome. *See also* Midlife crisis; Reentry students; Reentry women; Work reentry; Women living in poverty.

Displaced persons. Displaced person(s). Refugee(s). Deport(ed,ation). Wetback(s). Defect(ed,or,ors,ion). Territorial asylum. Political asylum. Escapee(s). Escap(e,ed,ing) persecution. Emigre(s). Exile(s,d). Seek(ing) refuge. Seek(ing) asylum. Resettle(d,ment). Fugitive(s). Boat people. Boat person(s). Expatriate(s). Stateless(ness). Expelled from country. *Consider also:* repatriation, relocation. *See also* Emigrants; Ethnic cleansing; Expatriates; Homeland; Homeless; Immigrants; Land reform; Political asylum; Refugee camps; Refugees; Residential mobility; Statelessness; Urban renewal; War victims.

Displaced workers. See *Dislocated workers.*

Displacement (psychology). Displacement. *Choose from:* displac(e,ed,ing,ement), transpos(e,ed,ing,ition), project(ed,ing,ion) *with:* feeling(s), affect, aggression, hostility. *Consider also:* dream(s,ing), scapegoat(ing), blam(e,ed,ing). *See also* Defense mechanisms; Projection (psychological); Scapegoating.

Displacement, job. See *Personnel termination.*

Displacement, residential. See *Relocation.*

Displays, tactual. See *Tactual displays.*

Displays, visual. See *Visual aids.*

Disposable income. Disposable income. Disposable personal income. *Choose from:* disposable, discretionary, after tax(es) *with:* income, spending power, purchasing power, assets, financial capacity. *Consider also:* consumption expenditures. *See also* Income; Luxuries.

Disposal. Dispos(al,ition). Arrangement(s). Placement(s). Ordering. Grouping(s). Provision(s). Conclusion(s). Allocation(s). Distribut(e,ed,ing,ion). Dispens(e,ed,ing). Assign(ed,ment, ments). Settlement(s). Determination(s). Decision(s). Process(ed,ing). *See also* Judicial decisions; Placement (of a dependent person).

Disposal, refuse. See *Waste disposal.*

Disposal, rubbish. See *Waste disposal.*

Disposal, sewage. See *Sewage disposal.*

Disposal, waste. See *Waste disposal.*

Disposition (personality). Disposition(s). Nature. Outlook(s). Frame of mind. Personalit(y,ies). Character(s). Temperament(s). Persona. Behavior pattern(s). Aptitude(s). Attitude(s). Social identit(y,ies). Self perception(s). Idiosyncras(y,ies). Ego(s). Type A. Type B. Coronary prone behavior(s). Emotional makeup. Id. Gender identit(y,ies). Superego(s). Emotional maturity. Individuality. Optimism. Sexuality. *Choose from:* personality, character(ological), behavior, psychological, patient, MMPI *with:* trait(s), characteristic(s), profile(s), structure(s), type(s). *Consider also:* aggressiveness, assertiveness, courage, defensiveness, emotionality, expressiveness, extroversion, introversion, self actualization, passivity, independence, dependence, timidity, sociability, locus of control, self concept, self esteem. *See also* Cheerfulness; Individual differences; Individuality; Lifestyle; Personality traits; Self concept.

Disposition (Philosophy). Disposition(s,al). Propensit(y,ies). Tendenc(y,ies) to act. Tendenc(y,ies) to react. *See also* Philosophy; Predisposition; Tendencies.

Disputations, religious. See *Religious disputations.*

Disputations, theological. See *Religious disputations.*

Dispute resolution. See *Dispute settlement.*

Dispute settlement. Dispute settlement. *Choose from:* dispute(s), disagreement(s), quarrel(s), argument(s), conflict(s), impasse(s) *with:* settl(e,ed, ing,ement,ements), resolv(e,ed,ing), resolution(s), negotiat(e,ed,ing,ion,ions), mediat(e,ed,ing,ion,ions), conciliat(e, ed,ing,ion,ions), common ground, compromis(e,ed,es,ing), de-escalat(e,ed, ing,ion), defus(e,ed,ing), adjudicat(e,ed, ing,ion). *See also* Arbitrators; Arbitration; Conflict resolution; Mediation; Negotiation; Peace negotiations.

Disputed authorship. Dispute(d) author(s,ship). Question(able) author(s,ship). Actually written by. Anonymous work(s). *Choose from:* authentic(ity), attribut(e,ed,ion,ing), misattribut(e,ed,ion) ascription, ascribed, dispute(d), dubious, unproven, spurio(sity,us) *with:* author(s,ship), compos(er,ers,ed). *See also* Anonymity; Authenticity; Authors; Literary quarrels; Pseudonyms.

Disputes. Disput(e,es,ed,ation). Disagreement(s). Controvers(y,ies,ial). Debate(s). Discussion(s). Quarrel(s). Argument(s). Antagonism(s). Altercation(s). Clash(es). Conflict(s). *See also* Arguments; Conflict; Controversial issues; Debate; Dispute settle-

ment; Literary quarrels; Religious disputations.

Disputes, labor. See *Labor disputes.*

Disruption. Disrupt(ed,ing,ion,ions). Disorder(ly,ed). Disintegrat(e,ed,ing,ion, ive). Disorganiz(e,ed,ing,ation). Disarray. Dissarrange(d,ment). Interrupt(ed,ing,ion,ions). Detach(ed,ing, ment). Dishevel(ed,ment). Breakup. Dissolution. Dissolv(e,ed,ing). Chao(s,tic). Disunit(y,e). Disengag(e,ed, ing,ement). Anom(ic,ie). Sever tie(s). Severance. Rupture(s,d). Disconnect(ed, ing). Destroy(ed,ing). Destruction. *See also* Destruction; Disintegration; Interruption; Marital disruption.

Disruption, marital. See *Marital disruption.*

Dissatisfaction. Dissatisf(action,ied). Discontent(ed,ment). Annoy(ance,ed). Unsatisf(ied,ying). Unfulfilled. Unhapp(y,iness). Dysphor(ic,ia). Displeas(ed,ure). Resent(ful,ment). Lack of satisfaction. Disappoint(ed,ment). Dissent(ed,ing). Frustrat(ed,ing,ion). Malcontent. Disaffected. Uneas(y,iness). Alienat(ed,ion). Discordant. *See also* Attitudes; Dissent; Frustration; Resentment; Resistance; Social unrest.

Dissection. Dissect(ed,ing,ion). Vivisect(s,ed,ing,ion). Anatomiz(e,es,ed,ing,ation). *Consider also:* dismember(ed,ing,ment), carv(e,ed,ing), cleav(e,ed,ing), cut(ting) apart, cut(ting) up, dissever(ed,ing), sever(ed,ing), slic(e,ed,ing), split(ting). *Choose from:* separat(e,ed,ing,ion), expos(e,es,ed,ing), *with:* piece(s), part(s). *See also* Anatomy; Autopsy.

Dissemination, information. See *Information dissemination.*

Dissent. Dissen(t,ter,ters,tient,sion,sus). Disagree(d,ing,ment,ments). Difference(s) of opinion. Nonconcurrence. Nonconform(ity,ist,ists,ing). Prisoner(s) of conscience. Refusenik(s). Contradict(ing,ion,ions). Contrary opinion(s). Dissiden(ce,t,ts). Disput(e,ed,ing). Oppos(e,ed,ing,ition). Rebel(s,led,ling,lion). Protest(s,ed,ing, er,ers). Conscientious objector(s). Oppos(e,ed,ing,ition). Contest(ed,ing, ation). Heterodox(y,ies). Heres(y,ies). Heretic(s,al). *Consider also:* skeptic(ism), sceptic(ism), disunity, resistan(t,ce), antithetical, discontent(ment), antagonis(m,tic), antinomian(ism), political prisoner(s). *See also* Anti-government radicals; Apostasy; Change agents; Civil disobedience; Conflict; Countercultures; Countermovements; Dissatisfaction; Dissidents; Family conflict; Nonconformity (personality); Partisan; Protest movements; Protestors; Peasant rebellions; Political defection; Political

dissent; Rebels; Religious dissenters; Social conflict; Social unrest.

Dissent, political. See *Political dissent.*

Dissenters, religious. See *Religious dissenters.*

Dissertations. Dissertation(s). Thesis. Theses. *Consider also:* practicum paper(s), treatise(s), essay(s), disquisition(s). *See also* Graduate students; Information; Scholarship.

Dissidents. Dissident(s). Dissenter(s). Nonconformist(s). Protester(s). Refusenik(s). Nonconformist(s). Heretic(s). Rebel(s). Radical(s). Agitator(s). Freethinker(s). Extremist(s). *See also* Agitators; Dissent; Heresy; Nonconformity (personality); Political defection; Political dissent; Protest movements; Radical history; Rebellions; Rebels; Schism; Social demonstrations.

Dissipation, energy. See *Energy dissipation.*

Dissociative disorders. Dissociative disorder(s). Dissociat(ed,ion). Fugue(s). Hypochondria(c,sis). Hysterical neuros(is,es). Somnambulism. Psychogenic amnesia. Divided consciousness. Personality dissociation(s). Identity splitting. Multiple personalit(y,ies). Dissociative identity disorder. Fragmentation of experience. Fugue reaction. Amnesia. Depersonalization. *Choose from:* dissociative *with:* hysteria, reaction(s), neurosis, disorder(s), patterns, tendenc(y,ies), process(s), state(s), periods. *Choose from:* conversion *with:* hysteria, reaction(s), neurosis, disorder(s). *See also* Conversion disorder; Neuroses; Hysteria; Hysterical anesthesia; Hysterical paralysis; Hysterical vision disturbances.

Dissolute persons. See *Skid row alcoholics*

Dissolution, marital. See *Divorce; Marital separation.*

Dissolution, organizational. See *Organizational dissolution.*

Dissonance, cognitive. See *Cognitive dissonance.*

Distance, interpersonal. See *Personal space; Proxemics.*

Distance, social. See *Social distance.*

Distance education. Distance education. Distance learning. Distance teaching. *Choose from:* educator(s), teach(ing,er, ers), classroom(s), instruct(ed,ing,ion), learn(ed,ing), education(al) *with:* distance, online, on-line, teleconferenc(e,es,ing), digital, virtual, e-mail, web(site,sites), net, Internet. *Consider also:* virtual universit(y,ies), extended campus(es), telementor(ed,ing), correspondence course(s), diploma mill(s). *See also* Access to education; Correspondence schools; Educational technology; Home schooling; Nontraditional education; Remote consultation; Telemedicine.

Distance perception. Distance perception. *Choose from:* spatial, distance *with:* perception, discrimination, judgment, estimation. *See also* Space perception.

Distillation. Distill(ed,ing,ation). Extract(ed,ing,ation) essence(s). Brew(ed,ing). Condens(e,ed,ing,ation). Vaporiz(e,ed,ing,ation). *Consider also:* distiller(y,ies), bootleg(ged,ging,ger, gers), moonshine. *See also* Alcoholic beverages; Brewing; Brewing industry; Condensation (fluids); Illicit liquor; Liquor industry.

Distinction. Distinct(ion,ions,ness). Discrimination(s). Different(e,ed,ion). Distinguish(ed,ing,ment). Unlike. Rare. Unique(ness). Unusual. Uncommon. Notable. Exceptional. *See also* Differences; Discrimination (psychology); Individuality.

Distortion. Distort(ed,ion,ions,ing). Deform(ed,ing,ation,ations). Contort(ed,ion,ions). Misshapen. Twisted. Bias(ed). Slant(ed). Misrepresent(ed,ing,ation,ations). Falsif(y,ying,ied,ication,ications). Tamper(ed,ing). Embellish(ed,ing, ment,ments). Exaggerat(e,ed,ing,ion, ions). Misinterpret(ed,ing,ation,ions). Misstate(d,ment,ments). Misconstru(e, ed,ing). Misinform(ed,ing,ation). Overemphasiz(e,ed,ing). Overemphasis. Card stacking. Manipulat(e,ed,ing) statistics. Rig(ged) research. *Consider also:* factoid(s). *See also* Bias; Errors; Falsification (scientific); Fraud; Hyperbole; Illusion (philosophy); Illusions (perception); Misconceptions; Misinformation; Perceptual distortion.

Distortion, perceptual. See *Perceptual distortion.*

Distractibility. Distractib(le,ility). Attentional dysfunction. Inattentive(ness). Attentional deficit(s). Mindwandering. Daydreaming. *Consider also:* lack(s,ed,ing), shift(s,ed,ing), wander(ed,ing), span *with:* attention. Inability to concentrate, inability to focus attention. *See also* Attention deficit disorder; Distraction.

Distraction. Distract(ed,ing,ion,ions). Interference learning. Diversion(s). Divert(ed,ing). Selective attention. Extraneous task(s). Disruption(s). Interruption(s). Intervention(s). Diversion(s). Sidetrack(ed,s). *Consider also:* confus(ed,ion), bewilder(ment), perplexed, preoccup(ation,ied), amusement(s), entertainment(s), recreation, commotion(s), disturbance(s), preoccup(ied,ation, ations). *See also* Attention span; Distractibility; Divided attention; Selective attention.

Distress. Distress(ed,ing,ful). Afflict(ed,ing, ion). Anguish(ed). Anxiet(y,ies). Ache(s). Aggravat(e,ed,ing). Agitat(e, ing,ed,ion). Agon(y,ies,ized,izing). Deject(ed,ion). Desolat(ed,ion). Discomfort(ed,ing). Discontent(ment). Disturb(ed,ing). Disquiet(ening). Emotional trauma(s). Fearful(ness). Grief. Griev(e,ed,ing). Heartache(s). Malaise. Miser(able,y,ies). Ordeal(s). Painful(ness). Perturb(ed,ing). Restless(ness). Suffer(ed,ing). Torment(s,ed,ing). Uneas(y,iness). Woe(s). Worr(y,ies,ied). Vex(ed,ing, ation). Wretched(ness). *See also* Dissatisfaction; Emotional states; Emotional trauma; Restlessness; Stress; Suffering.

Distress, psychological. See *Psychological distress.*

Distributed artificial intelligence. Distributed artificial intelligence. Distributed intelligent system(s). *See also* Artificial intelligence; Information dissemination.

Distribution (apportion). Distribut(e,ed, ive,ion,ing). Divid(e,ed,ing). Deal(t,ing). Dol(e,ed,ing). Apportion(ed,ing,ment). Shar(e,ed,ing). Allot(ed,ing,ment, ments). Ration(ed,ing). Partition(ed,ing). Appropriat(e,ed,ing,ion,ions). Prorat(e, ed,ing). Allocat(e,ed,ing,ion,ions). Maldistribut(e,ed,ive,ion,ions,ing). Disburs(e,ed,ing,ment,ments). *See also* Allocation; Disbursement; Frequency distribution; Geographic distribution; Income distribution; Income redistribution; Population distribution; Waiting lists.

Distribution (delivering). Distribut(e,ive, ion,ing). Dispens(e,ed,ing). Dispatch(ed, ing). Deal(t,ing). Dol(e,ed,ing). Scatter(ed,ing). Deliver(ed,ing). Disburs(e,ed,ing). Dispers(al,e,ed,ing, ion). Diffus(ed,ing,ion). Disseminat(e, ed,ing). Circulat(e,ed,ion). Broadcast(ing). *Consider also:* propagat(e,ed,ing,ion), spread(ing), transmit(ted,ting), transmission(s), promulgat(e,ed,ing,ion), advertis(e,ed, ing,ement,ements), make public, put forth. *See also* Broadcasting; Delivery of services; Distribution channels; Distributors; Information dissemination; Logistics; Technology transfer; Transmission of texts.

Distribution, binomial. See *Binomial distribution.*

Distribution, frequency. See *Frequency distribution.*

Distribution, geographic. See *Geographic distribution.*

Distribution, income. See *Income distribution.*

Distribution, normal. See *Normal distribution.*

Distribution, population. See *Population distribution.*

Distribution, spatial. See *Spatial organization.*

Distribution channels. Distribution channel(s). Marketing channel(s). *Choose from:* business, marketing, distribution *with:* channel(s), logistics, bridgehead(s), chain(s). *Consider also:* distribution center(s), distribution operation(s), distribution system(s). *See also* Diffusion; Distribution (delivering); Distributors; Drug trafficking; Economic development; Internet service providers; Networks; Technology transfer.

Distribution programs, food. See *Food services (programs).*

Distributive justice. Distributive justice. Material justice. Wage justice. *Choose from:* fair(ness), equit(y,able), just(ice) *with:* distribut(e,ed,ing,ive,ion), redistribut(e,ed,ing,ive,ion), divid(e,ed,ing), deal(t,ing), dol(e,ed,ing), apportion(ed,ing,ment), shar(e,ed,ing), allot(ed,ing,ment), ration(ed,ing), partition(ed,ing), appropriat(e,ed,ing, ion), prorat(e,ed,ing), allocat(e,ed,ing, ion), disburs(e,ed,ing,ment). *See also* Allocation; Equity (payment); Income maintenance programs; Income redistribution; Justice.

Distributors. Distributor(s). Supplier(s). Wholesaler(s). Transporter(s). Shipper(s). Dealer(s). Trader(s). Merchandiser(s). Delivery service(s). Marketer(s). Reseller(s). *Consider also:* retailer(s). *See also* Distribution (delivering); Distribution channels; Warehouse.

Districts. District(s). Localit(y,ies). Zone(s). Region(s). Parish(es). Diocese(s). Area(s). Precinct(s). Ward(s). Division(s). Province(s). Communit(y, ies). Neighborhood(s). Domain(s). Ghetto(es,s). Tract(s). Prefecture(s). *Consider also:* geographical area(s), realm(s). *See also* Areas; Commercial districts; Community (geographic locality); Dioceses; Election districts; Geographic regions; Industrial districts; Local government; Parishes; Zoning.

Districts, business. See *Commercial districts.*

Districts, commercial. See *Commercial districts.*

Districts, election. See *Election districts.*

Districts, industrial. See *Industrial districts.*

Distrust. Distrust(ful,fulness). Mistrust(ful, fulness). Suspicious(ness). Suspecting. War(y,iness). Misgivings. Disbelief. Doubt(ful,fulness). Dubious(ness). Incredul(ity,ousness). Uncertainty. Qualm(s). Uneas(y,iness). Skeptic(al, ism). *See also* Doubt; Suspicion; Uncertainty.

Disturbances. See *Civil disorders; Emotionally disturbed; Violence.*

Disturbances, body image. See *Body image disturbances.*

Disturbances, hysterical vision. See *Hysterical vision disturbances.*

Disturbances, judgment. See *Judgment disturbances.*

Disturbances, perceptual. See *Perceptual disturbances.*

Disturbances, speech. See *Speech disturbances.*

Disturbances, thought. See *Thought disturbances.*

Disturbed, emotionally. See *Emotionally disturbed.*

Divergent thinking. Divergent thinking. *Choose from:* divergent, creative, productive, critical, original *with:* thinking, problem solving, cognit(ive, ion), thought(s). *Consider also:* creativity, originality, associative fluency. *See also* Abstraction; Cognitive processes; Creativity; Intelligence.

Diversification. Diversif(y,ied,ying,ication). Vary(ing). Varied. Variation(s). Variability. *Consider also:* crop rotation(s), crop introduction, multiproduct(s), redeploy(ed,ing,ment), restructur(e,ed, ing), expand(ed,ing), reorganiz(e,ed, ing). *See also* Agricultural diversification; Business diversification; Diversity.

Diversification, agricultural. See *Agricultural diversification.*

Diversification, business. See *Business diversification.*

Diversified farming. See *Agricultural diversification.*

Diversity. Diversity. Heterogene(ity,ous, ousness). Nonuniform(ity). Unlike(ness). Irregular(ity). Diversif(y,ied,ying,ication). Dissimilar(ity,ities). Variation(s). Variability. *Consider also:* disparate(ness), variegated. *See also* Cultural cooperation; Cultural diversity; Cultural pluralism; Melting pot; Multicultural education; Multilingualism; Racial diversity; Variations.

Diversity, biological. See *Biological diversity.*

Diversity, cultural. See *Cultural diversity.*

Diversity, ecological. See *Biological diversity.*

Diversity, racial. See *Racial diversity.*

Divestiture. See *Disinvestment.*

Divided attention. Divided attention. *Choose from:* divided, split, selective, distribution, shifting, asymmetry *with:* attention(al). *Consider also:* dual, concurrent, simultaneous *with:* stimuli, task(s). *See also* Attention; Awareness; Distractibility; Distraction; Selective attention.

Dividends. Dividend(s). *Choose from:* stock(s,holder,holders), share(s,holder, holders), investment(s), securit(y,ies) *with:* distribution(s), earning(s), profit(s), income(s), return(s). *Consider also:* nonwage income. *See also* Capital (financial); Corporations; Investments; Investor relations; Profitability; Profits; Stock exchange; Stock options; Stockholders.

Divination. Divin(e,ed,er,ers,ing,ation, atory). Astrolog(y,ical,er,ers). Augur(y,ed,ing). Interpret(ed,ing,ation) dream(s). Interpret(ed,ing,ation) omen(s). Fortune tell(ing,ers). Fortune cookie(s). Oracle(s). Palmistry. Clairvoyan(t,ce). Prophec(y,ies). Prophes(y,ied). Extrasensory perception. ESP. Horoscope(s). Forebod(e,ing). Forecast(ing). Soothsay(ing,er,ers). *Consider also:* aeromancy, alectryomancy, alectoromancy, aleuromancy, alomancy, alphitomancy, amniomancy, angang, anthropomancy, apantomancy, ariolist, astragolomancy, astromancy, aruspicy, austromancy, axinomancy, belomancy, beltonism, benge, botanomancy, capnomancy, cartomancy, catoptromancy, ceromancy, chaomancy, chiromancy, cleromancy, crithomancy, crystallomancy, dactyliomancy, daphneomancy, estispicy, geloscopy, genethliacs, glyphomancy, haruspic(es,ation), hepatoscopy, hieromancy, hippomancy, hydromancy, icthyomancy, lampadomancy, lecanomancy, lithomancy, mantic science, margaritomancy, molybdomancy, myomancy, necromancy, nephelomancy, oneiromancy, onychomancy, orniscopy, ornithomancy, psephomancy, pyromancy, rhabdomancy, scapulomancy, scrying, sideromancy, sortition, spirit rapping, tephramancy, theomancy, xylomancy. *See also* Divining rods; Extrasensory perception; Omen; Oracles; Prediction; Prophets.

Divine right of kings. Divine right of king(s). *Choose from:* divine right(s), suprem(e,acy) *with:* sovereign(s), king(s), monarch(s,y), emperor(s), royalty, ruler(s). *Consider also:* appointed by God. *See also* Absolutism; Church state relationship; Emperor worship; Monarchy; Political power; Royal supremacy; Sovereignty; Theocracy.

Diving. Diving. Dive. Dove. Diver(s). Bell div(e,ing,er,ers). Skindiv(e,ing,er,ers). Scuba div(e,ing,er,ers). Underwater swimming. Barotrauma. Hyperbaric exposure. Hyperbaric pressure. Caisson workers. Plunge(d) into water. Submerge(d). *See also* Aquatic sports; Sports; Swimming.

Divining rods. Divining rod(s). Water witching. Dows(e,ed,ing,er,ers). Dous(e,ed,ing,er,ers). Waterwitcher(s). Water divin(e,ed,ing,er,ers). Rhabdoman(cy,tic). *See also* Divination; Water supply.

Divinity, pantheism universal. See *Pantheism (universal divinity).*

Division of labor. Division of labor. Relations of production. Division of work. Subdividing work. *Consider also:* task allocation, specialization, work role(s), dual labor market(s), labor process, de-skill(ing), scientific management, labor aristocracy, horizontal organization, departmentalization. *See also* Animal division of labor; Center and periphery; Departmentalization; International division of labor; Labor market segmentation; Mass production; Scientific management; Sexual division of labor.

Division of labor, animal. See *Animal division of labor.*

Division of labor, domestic. See *Sexual division of labor.*

Division of labor, family. See *Sexual division of labor.*

Division of labor, household. See *Sexual division of labor.*

Division of labor, international. See *International division of labor.*

Division of labor, sexual. See *Sexual division of labor.*

Divorce. Divorce(d,s,ing). Divorcee(s). Sever marriage tie(s). Sever marital bond(s). Broken home(s). Formerly married. *Choose from:* terminat(e,ed,ing, ion), dissol(ve,ved,ution), breakup *with:* marriage(s). *Consider also:* legal(ly) separat(ed,ing,ion,ions), post divorce adjustment. *See also* Alimony; Child custody; Female headed households; Former spouses; Life change events; Parental absence; Remarriage; Single parent family; Stepfamily.

Divorce counseling. Divorce counseling. *Choose from:* counseling, therapy, workshop(s), prevention, casework *with:* divorc(e,ed,es,ing), pre-divorce, post-divorce, displaced homemaker(s), marriage dissolution. *See also* Covenant marriage; Family therapy; Marital therapy.

Divorced people. Divorced people. Divorcee(s). Former spouse(s). *Choose from:* divorced *with:* person(s), people, man, men, woman, women, parent(s), male(s), female(s), adult(s), life(style), status, mother(s), father(s). *See also* Divorce; Marital separation; Marital status; Single mothers; Single parent family; Single person.

Dizziness. Dizz(y,iness). Vertigo. Lightheaded(ness). Light headed. Unstead(y,iness). Vertiginous. *See also* Symptoms.

Do not resuscitate orders. Do not resuscitate order(s). Comfort measures only. Forego(ing) life sustaining measure(s). No heroic measure(s). *See also* Advance directives; Euthanasia; Termination of treatment; Treatment withholding.

Dock workers. See *Longshoremen*.

Dockets. See *Appointments and schedules*.

Docks. See *Piers*.

Docks, dry. See *Dry docks*.

Doctor patient relationships. See *Physician patient relations*.

Doctors. See *Physicians*.

Doctors, spin. See *Spin doctors*.

Doctrine, just war. See *Just war doctrine*.

Doctrines. Doctrin(e,es,al). Precept(s). Maxim(s). Tenet(s). Creed(s). Canon(s). Gospel(s). Ideolog(y,ies,ical). Philosoph(y,ies,ical). Dogma(s). Sententia(e). Belief system(s). *Consider also:* myth(s), theolog(y,ies,ical), worldview(s), social thought, political belief(s). *See also* Creeds; Ideologies; Laws; Philosophy; Religious doctrines.

Doctrines, religious. See *Religious doctrines*.

Document, agreement. See *Agreement (document)*.

Documentary films. See *Documentary theater*.

Documentary theater. Documentary theater(s). *Choose from:* factual, objective, nonfiction *with:* theatre(s), film(s), movie(s), motion picture(s), television, TV. *See also* Films; Motion pictures; Nonfiction novel; Photojournalism; Television; Television programs.

Documentation. Document(s,ation,ary). Documentary evidence. Authentication. Report(s). Record(s). Published data. Footnote(s). Credit(ing) source(s). Credential(s). *Consider also:* proof(s), background information, corroborating evidence, instruction manual(s). *See also* Archives; Documents; Information; Publications; Research methods.

Documents. Document(s). Publication(s). Recorded knowledge. *Choose from:* printed, published *with:* material(s), matter, data. Record(ed,s,keeping). Chronicle(s). Official paper(s). Checklist(s). Credential(s). Account(s). Will(s). Worksheet(s). Diploma(s). Birth certificate(s). Death certificate(s). Registr(y,ies). Chart(s). Charter(s). Report(s). Voucher(s). Log(s). Chartbook(s). Signed agreement(s). Data report(s). Form(s). Certificate(s). Register(s). Ships log(s). Diar(y,ies). Logbook(s). Deed(s). Catalog(s). Catalogue(s). Minute(s). Transcript(s). Transaction(s). Contract(s). Receipt(s). *See also* Boilerplate; Cartularies; Charters; Documentation; Legal documents; Letters (correspondence); Government publications; Publications; Records.

Documents, diplomatic. See *Diplomatic documents*.

Documents, government. See *Government publications*.

Documents, identification. See *Identification cards*.

Documents, legal. See *Legal documents*.

Dogma. Dogma(s,ta). Doctrine(s). Decree(s). Tenet(s). Article(s) of faith. *Consider also:* axiom(s), belief(s), precept(s). *See also* Absolutism; Creeds; Doctrines; Edicts; Revealed theology.

Dogmatism. Dogmat(ic,ism). Doctrinaire. Opinionated. Authoritarian(ism). Inflexib(le,ility). Autocratic. Closeminded(ness). Closed mind(ed, edness). Close minded(ness). *Consider also:* ethnocentric, fanatic(al,ism). *See also* Authoritarianism (psychology); Conservative; Dogma; Ideologies; Irrationalism (Philosophy); Moral attitudes; Openmindedness; Opinions; Personality traits; Rigid personality.

Dogs. Dog(s). Canine(s). Canis familiaris. Hound(s). Bitch(es). Pooch(es). Pup(s,py,pies). Mongrel(s). Mutt(s). *Consider also:* Beagle(s), German shepherd(s), Labrador retriever(s), Poodle(s), Spaniel(s), Weimaraner(s), etc. *Consider also:* canid(s). *See also* Animals; Hunting dogs; Mammals; Pets; Police dogs.

Dogs, hunting. See *Hunting dogs*.

Dogs, police. See *Police dogs*.

Doll play. Doll play. *Choose from:* doll(s), puppet(s), stuffed animal(s), teddy bear(s) *with:* play(ed,ing), house(s), preference(s), choice(s), interest. *See also* Childhood play development; Dolls; Puppets.

Dolls. Doll(s,y,ies). Barbie(s). Raggedy Ann(s). Raggedy Andy(s). Baby doll(s). Paper doll(s). Cornhusk doll(s). Rag doll(s). *Consider also:* figurine(s), toy soldier(s), teddy bear(s), puppet(s), marionette(s). *See also* Doll play; Puppets; Toy industry; Toys.

Dolmen. Dolmen. Cromlech(s). Druidic altar(s). Stone table(s). *Consider also:* megalith(s). *See also* Cults; Death rituals; Monuments; Religious rituals.

Domain, public. See *Public goods; Public lands*.

Domestic animals. Domestic(ated) animal(s). Tame(d) animal(s). Pet(s). Trained animal(s). *Choose from:* housebroken, home raised, home reared, housetrained, house trained *with:* animal(s). *Consider also:* livestock, cattle, cat(s), dog(s), goat(s), horse(s), pig(s), sheep, etc. *See also* Animal training; Cats; Livestock; Pets.

Domestic architecture. Domestic architecture. *Choose from:* dwelling(s), home(s), domestic, house(s) *with:* design(ed,ing), architecture, blueprint(s). *See also* Architectural styles; Architecture; Architectural accessibility; Facility design and construction; Modern architecture.

Domestic division of labor. See *Sexual division of labor*.

Domestic labor. See *Domestic service; Housekeeping; Sexual division of labor*.

Domestic rape. See *Marital rape*.

Domestic relations. See *Family relations*.

Domestic service. Domestic service. Au pair(s). Household help. Homemaker service(s). Home care service(s). Housekeeper(s). Home aide(s). Domestic(s). Domestic labor. Domestic help(er,ers). Maid service(s). Janitor(s). Cleaning service(s). Domestic worker(s). Nann(y,ies). Butler(s). Charwom(en,an). Chauffeur(s). Houseboy(s). Household servant(s). Maid(s). *Choose from:* domestic, household, maid, homemaker, home, cleaning *with:* service(s), help, labor, worker(s), servant(s). *See also* Housekeeping; Janitors.

Domestic support. See *Alimony; Dependent parents; Family assistance; Family budgets; Filial responsibility; Food services (programs); Public welfare*.

Domestic violence. See *Family violence*.

Domestication, animal. See *Animal domestication*.

Domestication, plant. See *Cultivated plants*.

Domicile. See *Dwellings*.

Domiciliary care. See *Boardinghouses; Group homes; Sheltered housing*.

Dominance. Dominan(ce,t). Leader(s,ship). Dominat(e,ed,ing,ation). Commanding. Rul(e,ed,ing). Predominant. Autocratic. Subjugat(e,ed,ing). Despot(ic,ism). Domineering. Authority figure(s). Controlling influence(s). Power(ful). Authoritarian(ism). Patriarch(al). Superordination. Superior(ity). *See also* Animal dominance; Authoritarianism (political); Authoritarianism (psychological); Coercion; Command (of troops, ships, etc.); Dominance subordination; Hegemony; Hierarchy; Imperialism; Majority groups; Power; Power elite; Power structure; Spheres of influence;

Social dominance; Superior subordinate relationship.

Dominance, animal. See *Animal dominance.*

Dominance, lateral. See *Laterality.*

Dominance, social. See *Social dominance.*

Dominance subordination. Dominan(ce,t) subordinat(e,ion). Dominance relation(s,ship,ships). Dominat(e,ed, ing,ation). Pecking order. Class status. Social rank. Social position(s). Superordination. Ascendance submission. Deference submission. Superior subordinat(e,es,ion). Social inequalit(y, ies). Unequal. *Choose from:* power, dominan(t,ce), dominat(e,ed,ing,ion), deference *with:* hierarch(y,ies), relationship(s), struggle(s), subordin(ance,ation), submission. *Consider also:* sex stereotype(s), family structure(s), governmental structure(s), social status, social stratification, social ranking, social hierarch(y,ies), apartheid. *See also* Authoritarianism (political); Coercion; Dominance; Hegemony; Hierarchy; Oppression; Political power; Power structure; Slavery; Social dominance; Superior subordinate relationship.

Dominant genes. Dominant gene(s). *Choose from:* gene(s,tic,tically), trait(s), inheritance, characteristic(s), mutation(s), transmission *with:* dominan(t,ce). *See also* Genetics.

Dominant groups. See *Majority groups.*

Dominant ideologies. Dominant ideolog(y,ies). Dominant class ideolog(y,ies). Ideolog(y,ies) of ruling group(s). Ideological hegemon(y,ies). *Consider also:* false consciousness. *See also* Hegemony; Ideologies; Mass media effects; Mass society; Popular culture; Political ideologies.

Dominated cultures. Dominated culture(s). Enslavement. *Choose from:* dominat(e, ed,ing,ion), oppress(ed,ing), subjugat(e, ed,ing,ion), subordinat(e,ed,ing,ion) *with:* culture(s), group(s), subculture(s). *Consider also:* social degradation, gender oppress(ive,ion), submerged voice(s), marginaliz(e,ed,ing,ation), occupied countr(y,ies). *See also* Intercultural communication; Minority groups; Oppression; Social discrimination; Social dominance.

Domination. See *Authoritarianism (political); Authoritarianism (psychological); Colonialism; Imperialism.*

Donation, organ. See *Anatomical gifts.*

Donations. Donat(e,ed,ion,ions). Donor(s). Contribut(e,ed,ing,ion,ions,er,ers). Gift(s). Present(s). Honorar(ia,ium). Endowment(s). Bequest(s). Gratuit(y, ies). Bestowal. Giving aid. Altruis(m, tic). Giving help. Charit(able,y).

Genero(us,sity). Gift giving. Assist(ance,ed,ing). Philanthrop(y,ic). Benefactor(s). Voluntary contribution(s). *Choose from:* charitable, political, financial *with:* contribution(s), donation(s). *See also* Assistance; Benefactors; Blood donors; Charitable behavior; Charities; Contributions; Endowments; Financial support; Gift giving; Philanthropy; Tissue donors; Volunteers.

Donors. *See Art patronage; Benefactors; Charities; Donations; Generosity; Philanthropy; Volunteers.*

Donors, blood. See *Blood donors.*

Donors, living. See *Living donors.*

Donors, tissue. See *Tissue donors.*

Doping in sports. See *Drugs in athletics.*

Dormancy. Dorman(t,cy). Immobil(e,ity). Inactiv(e,ity). Inert(ness). Inoperative. Laten(t,cy). Letharg(y,ic). Motionless(ness). Passiv(e,ity). Sluggish(ness). Quiescen(t,ce,cy). Stagna(nt,ting,te,ted,tion). Torpid(ity). Couch potato(es). Sedentar(y,iness). *See also* Hibernation; Immobility; Inactivity; Rest; Sleep.

Dosage. Dosage(s). Dose(s). Quantit(y,ies). Portion(s). *Consider also:* overdos(e,ed,ing,s). *See also* Drug therapy.

Double bind interaction. Double bind interaction. Double message(s). Double bind(ing). Schizophrenogenic. Paradoxical communication(s). Contradictory message(s). Catch 22. *See also* Ambiguity; Communication (thought transfer); Interpersonal relations; Manipulation; Schizophrenogenic family.

Double employment. Double employment. Moonlight(ing). Multiple job(s,holding). Second job. Two jobs. Extra job. Secondary employment. *See also* Part time employment; Part time farming; Underemployment; Unemployment.

Double entendre. See *Double meanings.*

Double insanity. See *Psychosis of association.*

Double meanings. Double meaning(s). Double entendre(s). Doublespeak. Double-talk. Ambiguit(y,ies). Ambiguous(ness). Equivocat(ing,ion). Pun(s). Wordplay. Word play(s). Anagram(s). *See also* Ambiguity; Communication (thought transfer); Puns.

Double-talk. See *Ambiguity; Double bind interaction; Double meanings.*

Doubles, delusion of. See *Capgras's syndrome.*

Doubt. Doubt(s,ful,fulness,ing). Uncertaint(y,ies). Lack(ed,ing) confidence. Apprehens(ion,ions,ive).

Brood(ed,ing). Waver(ed,ing). Indecis(ion,ive,iveness). Distrust(ful, fulness). Mistrust(ful,fulness). Suspicious(ness). Suspecting. War(y,iness). Misgiving(s). Disbelief. Dubious(ness). Incredul(ity,ousness). Qualm(s). Uneas(y,iness). Skeptic(al, ism). *See also* Confusion; Distrust; Suspicion; Mental confusion; Uncertainty.

Doubt, religious. See *Agnosticism; Uncertainty.*

Doubting mania. Doubting mania. Folie du doute. Doubting madness. Maladie du doute. *See also* Doubt; Mental illness.

Down (computers). Down (computers). *Choose from:* computer(s), microcomputer(s), PC(s), network(s) *with:* down, crash(ed,ing,es), frozen, freez(e,ing), inoperative, malfunction(s,ed,ing), out of order, fail(ed,ure), fatal error(s), nonfunction(ed,ing). *Consider also:* offline. *See also* Computers; Disaster recovery; Up (computers).

Downs syndrome. Down(s) syndrome. Mongolism. Down(s) anomaly. Trisomy 21. 21-trisomy. *Consider also:* congenital mental retardation, Kalmuk idiocy. *See also* Genetics; Mental retardation.

Downgrade. See *Censure; Defamation; Demotion (occupational); Derogation; Devaluation (of currency); Disapproval; Negativism; Self-debasement; Soil degradation; Verbal abuse.*

Downsizing. Downsiz(e,ed,ing). Reduc(e, ed,ing) workforce. Workforce imbalance correction(s). Rightsiz(e,ed,ing). *Consider also:* restructur(e,ed,ing), re-engineer(s,ed,ing), layoff(s), lay(ing) off, laid off, attrition, outplac(e,ed,ing, ement), outsourc(e,ed,ing). *See also* Contracting out; Decentralization; Devolution; Industrial efficiency; Labor economics; Merger integration; Offshore production (foreign countries); Outplacement services; Personnel termination; Privatization; Reengineering; Reorganization; Turnaround management.

Downturns. See *Decline.*

Dowry. Dowr(y,ies). Marriage payment(s). Marriage gift(s). Marriage portion(s). *Consider also:* brideprice, bridewealth, groomwealth, dower. *See also* Bridewealth; Marriage.

Dowsing. See *Divining rods.*

Draft, military. See *Military draft.*

Draft animals. Draft animal(s). Beast(s) of burden. Draft horse(s). Farm horse(s). *Consider also:* ox(en), mule(s), water buffalo(es). *See also* Animals; Cattle; Farming; Livestock.

Draft resisters. Draft resister(s). *Choose from:* draft, military service, conscription *with:* resister(s), evader(s), dodger(s), violator(s), nonregistrant(s), object(ed,ing,ion,ions). *Consider also:* conscientious object(or,ors,ion). *See also* Civil disobedience; Conscientious objectors; Military draft; Nonviolence; Peace movements.

Dragons, four. See *Newly industrializing economies.*

Drain, brain. See *Brain drain.*

Drainage. Drain(s,ed,ing,age). Gutter(s,ing) system(s). Seepage. *Consider also:* culvert(s), irrigat(e,ed,es,ing,ion), water management, sewer system(s), ditch(es), runoff, drainwater, aqueduct(s), funnel(s), downspout(s). *See also* Dams; Earthwork; Flood control; Irrigation; Public health; Sanitation; Sewage; Sewage disposal; Water pollution; Wetlands.

Drama. Drama(tic,tics,turgy,turgical). Theatre(s). Theater(s). Theatrical play(s). Playwrit(e,es,ing). Dramatic production(s). Dramatic presentation(s). Dramatic reading(s). Dramatic activit(y,ies). Creative dramatics. Stage play(s). Stagecraft. Theatrical(s). Comed(y,ies). Script(s). Traged(y,ies). Performing arts. Burlesque. Thespian(s). Melodrama(s). *See also* Acting; Actors and actresses; Cinema; Drama festivals; Dramatic criticism; Dramatists; Folk culture; Folk drama; Folk literature; Historical drama; Japanese drama; Jewish drama; Latin drama; Literature; Medieval drama; Method (acting); Miracle plays; Morality plays; Poetry; Religious drama; Theater; Theatrum mundi; Tragedy.

Drama, folk. See *Folk drama.*

Drama, historical. See *Historical drama.*

Drama, Japanese. See *Japanese drama.*

Drama, Jewish. See *Jewish drama.*

Drama, Latin. See *Latin drama.*

Drama, liturgical. See *Liturgical drama.*

Drama, lyric. See *Opera.*

Drama, medieval. See *Medieval drama.*

Drama, religious. See *Religious drama.*

Drama, television. See *Television plays.*

Drama festivals. Drama festival(s). Theatre festival(s) Plays festival(s). *Choose from:* festival(s), fest(s) *with:* playwright(s), drama(s), theater(s), play(s), Shakespeare(an), Stratford. *See also* Drama; Festivals; Pageants; Theatre.

Dramatic criticism. Drama(tic) critic(ism). Critique of drama. *Choose from:* drama(tic), play(s), movie(s), theatre(s), theater(s), theatrical, radio, television *with:* critic(ize,ized,izing,ism), critical stud(y,ies), critique(s,d), review(s,ed, ing,er,ers), comment(s,ed,ing,ary,aries), analys(is,es), evaluat(e,ed,ing,ion,ions), apprais(e,ed,ing,al,als). *See also* Acting; Actors and actresses; Cinema; Criticism; Drama; Theater.

Dramatic music. Dramatic music. Incidental music. Entr'act(es). Act tune(s). Curtain tune(s). Intermezzo(s). Zwischenspiel musik. Stage music. Off-stage music. Music for a play. Music for the stage. Theatrical music. Theater music. *Consider also:* melodrama(s,tic), monodrama(s), duodrama(s), movie music. *See also* Music.

Dramatic poetry. Dramatic poe(try,m,ms). *Choose from:* dramat(ic,ize,ized, ization, izations) *with:* poe(try,m,ms), poesy, verse(s), stanza(s), couplet(s). *See also* Lyric poetry; Poetry.

Dramatists. Dramatist(s). Playwright(s). Dramatizer(s). Dramaturg(e,s,es). *See also* Authors; Drama; Scriptwriting; Theater; Writers.

Dravidian languages. Dravidian language(s). Brahui. Gondi. Telegu. Tulu. Kanarese. Kurukh. Malayalam. Tamil. *See also* Indian (India) cultural groups; Language; Languages (as subjects); South Asia.

Drawing. Draw(n,ing). Sketch(es,ed,ing). Tracing(s). Design(ed,ing). Illustrat(e,ed, ing). Etch(ed,ing). Chiaroscuro. Pen and ink. Freehand. *See also* Animal painting and illustration; Arts; Biological illustration; Brush drawing; Drawing books; Etching; Ink painting; Mono-chrome painting.

Drawing, architectural. See *Architectural drawing*

Drawing, brush. See *Brush drawing.*

Drawing books. Drawing book(s). Sketchbook(s). Tracing book(s). Drawing handbook(s). *Consider also:* coloring book(s). *See also* Artists' books; Drawing.

Drawings, rock. See *Cave paintings; Petroglyphs.*

Dream deprivation, REM. See *REM dream deprivation.*

Dream interpretation. Dream interpretation(s). Dream analysis. Dream work. *Choose from:* dream(s,ing) *with:* interpret(ed,ing,ation,ations), analy(sis, ze,zed), symbol(s,ize,ized,izing,izes), psychoanaly(sis,ze,zed), unconscious, mean(ing,ings). *See also* Dreams; Psychoanalysis; Psychoanalytic interpretation; Sex symbolism; Symbolism; Unconscious (psychology).

Dreams. Dream(s,ing). Nightmare(s). Night terror(s). Pavor nocturnus. *Consider also:* daydream(s,ing), talking in sleep, somnambulism, sleepwalking, bruxism, sleep disorder(s), REM dream(s). *See also* Dream interpretation; Night terror; Nightmares; REM dream deprivation; REM dreams; REM sleep.

Dreams, REM. See *REM dreams.*

Dressing, cross. See *Transvestism.*

Drift, continental. See *Continental drift*

Drill and minor tactics. Drill(s,ed,ing). Minor tactic(s). March(ed,ing). Military drill(s). Precision marching. Cavalry drill(s,ed,ing). Parade drill(s,ed,ing). *See also* Military discipline (conduct); Military schools; Military training.

Drilling and boring. Drill(ed,ing). Bor(e,ed,ing). Sink mine(s). Hole drilling. Make hole(s). Excavat(e,ed, ing,ion,ions). Drilling operation(s). Hydraulic drilling. Jig-borer(s). Groundwater exploration. Cor(e,ed,ing). *Consider also:* blast(ed,ing), countersink(ing). *See also* Coal mines and mining; Construction industry.

Drinking (water, fluids). Drink(ing). Polydips(ia,ic). Hyperdips(ia,ic). Dipsogenic. Suckling. *Choose from:* water, liquid(s), fluid(s), juice(s), milk *with:* drink(ing), drank, consum(e,ed, ing,ption), intake, ingest(ed,ing,ion). *See also* Beverages; Drinking water; Eating; Fluids; Sucking behavior; Thirst; Water deprivation

Drinking, alcohol. See *Alcohol drinking.*

Drinking, binge. See *Dipsomania.*

Drinking, problem. See *Problem drinking.*

Drinking, social. See *Social drinking.*

Drinking alcohol, attitudes. See *Alcohol drinking attitudes.*

Drinking behavior. Drinking behavior(s). Drinking on the job. Tavern going. Pub regular(s). *Choose from:* hard, casual, social, problem *with:* drink(er,ers,ing). *Choose from:* drinking, alcohol(ic) consumption, alcohol use, drunk(en, enness) *with:* compulsive, casual, habit(s), pattern(s), trend(s), practice(s), indices, context(s), setting(s), style(s), correlate(s). *Consider also:* water drinking behavior, meal pattern(s), water intake, polydipsia, hyperdipsia. *See also* Alcohol drinking; Alcoholic beverages; Alcoholism; Alpha alcoholism; Delta alcoholism; Dipsomania; Drinking customs; Drinking vessels; Drunk driving; Gamma alcoholism; Illicit liquor; Problem drinking.

Drinking customs. Drinking custom(s). Wine culture. Toast(s,ing). Cultural drinking pattern(s). *Choose from:* drink(ing,er,ers), saloon(s), cocktail(s), tavern(s), pub(s), Bacchus, alcohol(ic) *with:* custom(s), ritual(s), etiquette, polite(ness). *See also* Alcohol drinking; Alcohol drinking attitudes; Drinking behavior; Drinking songs; Drinking vessels; Social drinking.

Drinking songs. Drinking song(s). Brindisi. Trinklied(er). Chanson(s) a boire. *Choose from:* drinking, conviviality, beer garden(s), beergarden(s), pub(s), bacchanalian, booze, wine, tavern(s), bar room(s), cabaret(s), happy hour(s) *with:* song(s), ditt(y,ies), sing(ing), music(al,als), ballad(s), tune(s), verse(s), hootenann(y,ies), blues, shant(y,ies), chanson(s), lied(er), cancion(es). *See also* Bawdy songs; Drinking customs; Social drinking; Songs; Student songs.

Drinking vessels. Drinking vessel(s). Drinking horn(s). Chalice(s). *Consider also:* cup(s), glass(es), goblet(s), mug(s), teacup(s), tumbler(s), stein(s). *See also* Collectibles; Drinking behavior; Drinking customs.

Drinking water. Drinking water. Potable water. Pure water. Safe water. Bottled water. *Consider also:* tap water, community water system(s), drinking fountain(s). *See also* Beverages; Drinking (water, fluids); Environmental protection; Fluids; Health; Pollution control; Water purification; Water supply.

Drive. Drive(s). Tension(s). Excitation. Sexual drive. Libido. Aggressive energy. Destructive energy. Preferences. Ambition. Intent(ion,ionality,ions). Ambitious(ness). Aggressive(ness). Initiative. Arous(e,ed,al). Motivat(e,ed,ing,ion,ions,ional). Motive(s). Goal orientation. Incentive(s). Desire(s). Urge(s). Wish(es). Personal causation framework. Interest(ed,s). Self generated outcome(s). Approach-avoidance. Aspir(e,ed,ing,ation,ations). Hope(s). Impulse(s). Inducement(s). *Consider also:* instinct(s,ual), cognitive dissonance, goal(s), aspiration(s), initiative(s), hunger, thirst, achievement need(s), exploratory behavior(s), food deprivation, water deprivation, achievement motivation, affiliation motivation, extrinsic motivation, intrinsic motivation, fear of success, fear of failure, temptation(s). *See also* Achievement need; Affiliation motivation; Ambitiousness; Approval need; Aspirations; Biological drives; Commitment (emotional); Curiosity; Delay of gratification; Educational incentives; Employee motivation; Extrinsic motivation; Fear of failure; Fear of success; Hunger, food deprivation; Incentives; Instinct; Intrinsic motivation; Monetary incentives; Motivation; Profit motive; Procrastination; Sex drive; Temptation; Thirst.

Drive, sex. See *Sex drive.*

Driveby crimes. Driveby Crime(s). *Choose from:* drive-by, driveby *with:* crime(s), shooting(s), gunshot(s), gunfire, gun

spree(s), hat(e,red). *Consider also:* harangu(e,ed,es,ing,ings), gunfire from car(s). *See also* Crime; Follow home crime; Hate crimes; Juvenile gangs; Road rage; Urban crime.

Drivers. See *Automobile driving.*

Drives, biological. See *Biological drives.*

Driving, aggressive. See *Road rage.*

Driving, automobile. See *Automobile driving.*

Driving, drunk. See *Drunk driving.*

Driving skills. Driving skill(s). *Choose from:* driving, chaffeur(s,ing) *with:* skill(s), abilit(y,ies), competenc(y,ies), performance. *See also* Automobile driving.

Driving under the influence. See *Drunk driving.*

Dropouts, patient. See *Patient dropouts.*

Dropouts, potential. See *Potential dropouts.*

Dropouts, school. See *Student dropouts.*

Dropouts, student. See *Student dropouts.*

Dropouts, treatment. See *Patient dropouts.*

Drought. Drought. Parched earth. Barren land. Desert(s). Lack of rain(fall). Dryness. Torrid. Arid. Dry weather. Rain shortage. Dry spell(s). *Choose from:* low(er,ering,ered) *with:* river(s), lake level(s), water supply. *Choose from:* water *with:* shortage(s), lack(ed,ing), ration(ed,ing), ban(s), restriction(s). *See also* Arid lands; Desertification; Deserts; Disaster relief; Natural disasters; Water levels.

Drowning. Drown(ed,ing,ings). *Consider also:* perish(ed), lost, dead, death(s), died *with:* sea, ocean, underwater, swimming. *See also* Accidents; Death; Fatalities; Marine accidents; Swimming.

Drowsiness. Drows(y,iness). Sleep(y,iness). Hypnagogic. Half asleep. Doz(e,ed,ing). Yawn(ed,ing). *Consider also:* somnolen(t,ce), twilight sleep, nap(ped,ping), snooz(e,ed,ing). *See also* Sleep; Sleep onset.

Drug abuse. See *Drug addiction; Substance abuse.*

Drug addicted babies. Drug addicted bab(y,ies). Crack bab(y,ies). Drug bab(y,ies). *Choose from:* narcotic(s), crack, cocaine, drug addict(s,ed,ion), heroin, alcohol *with:* bab(y,ies), infan(t,ts,cy), fetal, fetus(es), newborn(s), neonat(e,es,al), gestation(al), intrauterine, in utero, prenatal(ly), perinatal(ly), pregnan(t,cy,cies), teratogen(ic,icity), congenital, birth defect(s), embryo(nic), embryogenesis, maternal-fetal exchange. *Consider also:* drug abus(e,er,ers,ing), drug addict(ed,ion,ions), substance

dependen(t,ce), substance abus(e,er, ers,ing) *with:* maternal, mother(s). *See also* Congenitally handicapped; Developmental disabilities; Drug addiction; Drug induced abnormalities; Fetal alcohol syndrome; Fetus; Gateway drugs; Physical abnormalities; Substance abuse.

Drug addiction. Drug addiction. Cocainis(m,t,ts). Opiumis(m,t,ts). Heroinis(m,t,ts). Heroinomania. Crackhead(s). *Choose from:* drug(s), narcotic(s), polydrug(s), opiate(s), tranquilizer(s), sedative(s), medicine(s), medication(s), depressant(s), barbiturate(s), quaalude(s), amphetamine(s), heroin, crack, freebase, basuco, basuko, bazuco, bazuko, cocaine, cannabis, marijuana, marihuana, PCP, phencyclidine, morphine or other drugs by name *with:* addict(s,ed,ion,ions,ive), dependen(t,ce), crav(e,ing,ings), overdependen(t,ce), habit(ual,s), habituation. *Consider also:* basehead(s), base head(s). *See also* Addiction; Alcoholism; Drug addicted babies; Drug effects; Drug induced abnormalities; Drug interactions; Drug overdoses; Drug rehabilitation; Drug tolerance; Drug use; Drug withdrawal; Drugs; Gateway drugs; Hallucinogens; Narcotics; Needle sharing; Street drugs; Substance abuse; Substance dependence; Substance use disorders; Tranquilizers.

Drug adverse reactions. See *Drug effects.*

Drug and narcotic control. Drug and narcotic control. *Choose from:* drug(s), narcotic(s), marihuana, marijuana, cannabis, opium, heroin, cocaine, tranquilizer(s), controlled substance(s) *with:* control, legislation, law(s), legal(ization), Pl 91-513, polic(y,ies), Comprehensive Drug Abuse Prevention and Control Act of 1970, Uniform Controlled Substances Act. *See also* Crime prevention; Drug enforcement; Drug trafficking; Law enforcement; Medical marijuana; Police dogs; Street drugs; Substance-abuse detection.

Drug antagonism. Drug antagonism. *Choose from:* drug(s), narcotic(s) *with:* antagonis(m,t,ts,tic), inhibitor(s), incompatib(le,ility), hazard(s,ous) mixing, undesirable interaction(s), adverse interaction(s). *See also* Drug interactions; Hypersensitivity; Narcotic antagonists.

Drug dependency. See *Substance dependence.*

Drug education. Drug education. *Choose from:* drug(s), narcotic(s), heroin, cocaine, marijuana, marihuana *with:* education(al), instruction(al), communication, mass media, information(al), campaign(s), awareness. *See also* Alcohol education; Drugs; Gateway drugs; Patient education.

Drug effects. Drug effect(s). *Choose from:* effect(s), side effect(s), iatrogenic, related problem(s), induced, toxic(ity), exacerbat(ed,ion,ions), react(ed,ing, ion,ions), adverse, interaction(s), hazard(s), sensitiv(e,ity), allerg(y,ies), hypersensitiv(e,ity,ities), addiction(s), dependen(t,cy), poison(ed,ing) or specific effects such as tardive dyskinesia *with:* drug(s), medication(s), medicine(s), prescription(s), chemotherap(y,ies) or specific drugs or classes of drug such as neuroleptics, analgesics, tranquilizers or drugs by name. *See also* Altered states of consciousness; Drug interactions; Drug tolerance; Hypersensitivity; Iatrogenesis; Medication errors.

Drug enforcement. Drug enforcement. Drug czar(s). Drug Enforcement Administration. Anti-drug. War on drug(s). *Choose from:* drug(s), narcotic(s), cocaine, heroin, marijuana, marihuana, hashish, crack *with:* undercover operation(s), sting(s), charge(s), arrest(s), agent(s), law enforcement, police, patrol(s), bust(s,ed), squad(s). *See also* Crime prevention; Drug and narcotic control; Drug trafficking; Law enforcement; Police community relations; Street drugs.

Drug induced abnormalities. Drug induced abnormalit(y,ies). Embryotoxic effect(s). Fetal alcohol syndrome. *Choose from:* drug(s), narcotic(s), crack, cocaine, heroin, marijuana, sedative(s), lysergic acid diethylamide, LSD, alcohol, smoking, tobacco, DES, anticoagul(ants,ation), poison(s,ed,ing), herbicide(s), pesticide(s), thalidomide, toxic insult(s), specific drugs by name *with:* teratogen(ic,icity), congenital, impairment(s), birth defect(s), abnormalit(y,ies), malformation(s), fetal sequelae, embryo development, embryogenesis, prenatal, fetus, maternal-fetal exchange. *See also* Congenitally handicapped; Drug addicted babies; Fetal alcohol syndrome; Human abnormalities; Physical abnormalities; Teratology.

Drug induced psychoses. See *Substance induced psychoses.*

Drug information services. Drug information service(s). *Choose from:* drug(s), narcotic(s), cocaine, heroin, marijuana, marihuana or other drugs by name *with:* information service(s), education, film(s), warning(s), prevention, information program(s), public(ity, izing). *See also* Drug education; Health promotion; Information services.

Drug interactions. Drug interaction(s). *Choose from:* drug(s), medication(s), prescription(s), medicine(s), sedative(s), tranquilizer(s) or names of specific drugs *with:* interaction(s), potentiat(ed,ion, ions), synerg(ism,istic), enhanc(e,ed, ing,ement,ements), inhibit(ed,ing,ion), cross tolerance, combined effect(s), antagon(ism,istic), agon(ism,istic), block(ers,ing). *See also* Cross addiction; Drug effects.

Drug lords. Drug lord(s). Drug dealer(s). Drug kingpin(s). *See also* Career criminals; Drug trafficking; Street drugs.

Drug overdoses. Drug overdose(s). Exceed(ed,ing) maximum therapeutic level(s). *Consider also:* drug(s), medication(s), medicine(s), sedative(s), tranquilizer(s), aspirin(s), cough medicine(s) or other drugs by name *with:* overdos(e,ed,ing,s), lethal dose(s), toxic dose(s), poison(ed,ing), heav(y,ily) dose(s,d), intoxication, overdosage(s). *See also* Attempted suicide; Dosage; Drug therapy; Drug tolerance; Drug use; Poisoning; Rape drugs; Suicidal behavior; Suicide; Suicide victims.

Drug potentiation. See *Drug interactions.*

Drug rehabilitation. Drug rehabilit(ed,ing, ation). *Choose from:* cocaine, crack, heroin, narcotic(s), opiate(s), barbiturate(s), drug(s) dependen(t,ce), drug addict(s,ed,ion,ions), drug abus(e,er,ers), chemical(ly) dependen(t, ce), substance abuse, substance dependen(t,ce), inhalant abuse *with:* rehab, rehabilitat(e,ed,ing,ation), treat(ment,ed,ing), social skills training, assertiveness training, acupuncture, avers(ive,ion), biofeedback, detox(ify, ified,ification), halfway house(s), behavior therapy, counsel(ed,ing), casework, hospitaliz(e,ed,ation), psychotherap(y,ies,eutic), residential program(s), residential care, day treatment(s), employee assistance, withdraw(al), psychosocial(ly) readjust(ed,ment,ments). *Consider also:* methadone *with:* program(s), maintain(ed,ing), maintenance, clinic(s). *See also* Alcohol rehabilitation; Detoxification; Drug addiction; Drug withdrawal; Employee assistance programs; Methadone maintenance; Psychosocial readjustment; Psychosocial rehabilitation; Rehabilitation; Rehabilitation counseling; Self help groups; Social skills training; Smoking cessation; Substance abuse.

Drug side effects. See *Drug effects.*

Drug synergism. See *Drug interactions.*

Drug testing. See *Substance abuse detection.*

Drug therapy. Drug therap(y,ies). Chemotherap(y,ies). Pharmacotherap(y, ies). Psychopharmacotherap(y,ies). Medicat(e,ed,ing,ion,ions). *Choose from:* drug(s), chemical, medication(s) *with:* therap(y,ies), treatment(s), maintenance, course(s). *Consider also:* photochemotherap(y,ies), premedication,

prescription(s). *See also* Antidotes; Dosage; Drug effects; Drug interactions; Drug overdoses: Drug tolerance; Drugs; Herbal medicine; Non-prescription drugs; Prescription drugs; Traditional medicine.

Drug tolerance. Drug toleran(ce,t). *Consider also:* drug(s) or specific drugs by name *with:* toleran(ce,t), fad(e,ed, ing), attenuat(e,ed,ing,ion). *See also* Drug addiction; Drug effects: Drug overdoses; Drug use; Drugs; Gateway drugs; Habituation (psychophysiology).

Drug trade. See *Drug trafficking.*

Drug trafficking. Drug trafficking. *Choose from:* drug(s), narcotic(s), heroin, cocaine, marijuana, marihuana, crack *with:* trade, traffic(king), deal(er,ers,ing), sell(ing), sold, ring(s), smuggl(e,ed,ing, er,ers), peddl(e,ed,ing,er,ers), ship(ped, ping), shipment(s), push(ed,ing,er,ers), distribut(ed,ing,or,ors), network(s), gang(s), import(ed,ing,er,ers), export(ed, ing,er,ers), supplier(s). *Consider also:* narcoterroris(m,t,ts). *See also* Crime; Designer drugs; Disorderly houses; Distribution channels; Drug and narcotic control; Drug enforcement; Drug lords; Money laundering; Racketeering; Smuggling; Street drugs.

Drug use. Drug use(r,rs). *Choose from:* drug(s), narcotic(s), polydrug(s), opiate(s), tranquilizer(s), sedative(s), medicine(s), medication(s), depressant(s), barbiturate(s), quaalude(s), amphetamine(s), heroin, crack, cocaine, cannabis, marijuana, marihuana, PCP, phencyclidine, morphine or other drugs by name *with:* use(d), use(r,rs), usage, utiliz(e,ed,ing,ation), smok(e,ed,er, ers,ing), tak(e,en,ing), abus(e,ed,er, ers,ing), consum(e,ed,er,ers,ing,ption), administer(ed,ing), administration, dosage, involvement, toleran(t,ce), addict(s,ed,ion,ions,ing,ive), dependen(t, ce), crav(e,ing,ings), overdependen(t,ce), habit(ual,s), habituation. *See also* Drug addiction; Drug tolerance; Drugs in athletics; Gateway drugs; Needle sharing; Substance abuse; Substance dependence; Substance use disorders.

Drug withdrawal. Drug withdraw(al). *Choose from:* drug(s), narcotic(s), opiate(s), opioid(s), sleeping pill(s), tranquilizer(s), sedative(s), caffeine, stimulant(s), medicine(s), medication(s), depressant(s), barbiturate(s), amphetamine(s), heroin, crack, cocaine, cannabis, marijuana, marihuana, PCP, phencyclidine, morphine or other drugs by name *with:* withdraw(al), dose reduction, depriv(e,ed,ing,ation), abstinen(ce,t), quit(ting), discontinu(e, ed,ing,ation), cold turkey. *See also* Alcohol rehabilitation; Alcohol withdrawal delirium; Detoxification; Drug addiction; Drug rehabilitation; Substance withdrawal syndrome.

Drugs. Drug(s). Medicinal plant(s). Herb(s). Medicine(s). Hormone(s). Vitamins(s). Sedative(s). Marihuana. Non-prescription drug(s). Nostrum(s). Placebo(s). Psychoactive drug(s). Psychotropic drug(s). Pill(s). Pharmaco(logy,logical, poeia). Prescription(s). Prescription drug(s). Pharmaceutical(s). Medication(s). Remed(y,ies). Vitamin(s). Ergot(s). Barbiturate(s). Diuretic(s). Steroid(s). Antidote(s). Aphrodisiac(s). Capsule(s). Colloid(s). Tablet(s). Liniment(s). Ointment(s). Powder(s). Suppositor(y,ies). Salicylate(s). Antigen(s). Antitoxin(s). Emetic(s). Antiemetic(s). Antihistamine(s). Immunosuppressive agent(s). Antimalarial(s). Antiprotozoal agent(s). Antiplatyhelmintic agent(s). Antihelmintic(s). Antibiotic(s). Antifungal agent(s). Anti-infective agent(s). Antitreponemal agent(s). Antitubercular agent(s). Antiviral agent(s). Leprostatic agent(s). Sulfonamide(s). Contraceptive(s). Fertility agent(s). Enzyme inhibitor(s). Coenzyme(s). Hypoglycemic agent(s). Depressant(s). Analgesic(s). Anesthetic(s). Anticonvulsant(s). Hypnotic(s). Narcotic(s). Analeptic(s). Tranquilizer(s). Bronchodilator agent(s). Miotic(s). Parasympatholytic(s). Parasympathomimetic(s). Sympatholytic(s). Sympathomimetic(s). Adrenergic beta receptor agonist(s). Adrenomimetic(s). Relaxant(s). Neuromuscular blocking agent(s). Neuromuscular depolarizing agent(s). Cardiovascular agent(s). Antiarrhythmia agent(s). Cardiotonic agent(s). Vasoconstrictor agent(s). Vasodilator agent(s). Antacid(s). Cathartic(s). Anticoagulant(s). Fibrinolytic agent(s). Anti-infective agent(s). *See also* Abortifacients; Analgesia; Antidepressive agents; Antidotes; Appetite depressants; Designer drugs; Drug addiction; Drug antagonism; Drug effects; Drug interactions; Drug overdoses; Drug therapy; Drug tolerance; Drugs in athletics; Hallucinogens; Herbal medicine; Narcoanalytic drugs; Narcotic antagonists; Narcotics; Non-prescription drugs; Prescription drugs; Quackery; Rape drugs; Street drugs; Tranquilizers; Vitamins.

Drugs, anti-alcoholism. See *Alcohol deterrents.*

Drugs, antianxiety. See *Tranquilizers.*

Drugs, anxiety reducing. See *Tranquilizers*

Drugs, ataractic. See *Tranquilizers.*

Drugs, designer. See *Designer drugs.*

Drugs, gateway. See *Gateway drugs.*

Drugs, hallucinogenic. See *Hallucinogens.*

Drugs, legalization of. See *Legalization of drugs.*

Drugs, narcoanalytic. See *Narcoanalytic drugs.*

Drugs, non-prescription. See *Non-prescription drugs.*

Drugs, nonprescription. See *Non-prescription drugs.*

Drugs, plant. See *Herbal medicine; Medical botany.*

Drugs, prescription. See *Prescription drugs.*

Drugs, psychedelic drugs. See *Hallucinogens; Narcotics; Street drugs.*

Drugs, psychotomimetic. See *Hallucinogens.*

Drugs, psychotropic. See *Antidepressant agents; Designer drugs; Hallucinogens; Narcoanalytic drugs; Narcotics; Street drugs; Tranquilizers.*

Drugs, rape. See *Rape drugs.*

Drugs, street. See *Street drugs.*

Drugs, synthetic. See *Designer drugs.*

Drugs in athletics. Drugs in athletic(s). Doping in sport(s). *Choose from:* athlete(s), athletic(s), wrestl(er,ers,ing), box(er,ers,ing), baseball, blood doping, carboload(ed,ing), runn(er,ers,ing), football, track and field, weightlift(er, ers,ing), greyhound(s), horse(s), racehorse(s), olympic(s), extramural, sport(s,ing), NFL, sports(men,man, women,woman), jockey(s), player(s), team(s) *with:* dop(e,ed,ing), drug abuse, drug(s,ged,ging), steroid(s), analgesic(s), amphetamine(s), stimulant(s), narcotic(s), coffee, caffeine, marijuana, marihuana. *Choose from:* racehorse(s), horse(s) *with:* drug(s), lasix, phenylbutazone, morphine, methadone, bute. *See also* Athletes; Cruelty to animals; Drug addiction; Drug effects; Drug overdoses; Drug tolerance; Drug use; Drugs; Horse sports; Sports; Stimulants.

Drugs of abuse. See *Designer drugs; Hallucinogens; Narcotics; Street drugs; Tranquilizers.*

Drunk driving. Drunk(en) driv(er,ers,ing). Drinking driv(er,ers,ing). DWIs. *Choose from:* drunk(en), drinking, under the influence, alcohol(ic,ism), intoxicat(ed, ing,ion), inebriat(ed,ion), liquor, breath tests, impaired, drug(s,ged) *with:* driv(er, ers,ing), motorist(s), operating a motor vehicle, traffic safety, traffic problems, motor vehicle accident(s), automobile(s). *Consider also:* alcohol breath tests, driving while drugged, DWD, impaired driving. *See also* Alcohol drinking; Alcoholism; Automobile driving; Drinking behavior; Drunkenness; Problem drinking; Social drinking.

Drunkenness. Drunk(en,enness). *Choose from:* alcohol(ic), ethanol, beer, wine(s), liquor(s) *with:* intoxicat(ed,ion), coma(s, tose), breathalyzer(s), misuse(d), inebriat(ed,ion), twilight state(s), impaired judgment, unstead(y,iness), blackout(s), blood level(s). *Consider also:* alcoholism, DWI, driving while intoxicated. *See also* Alcoholism; Drunk driving; Problem drinking.

Dry docks. Dry dock(s,ing). Drydock(s). Graving dock(s). *Consider also:* shipyard(s), shipbuild(ing,er,ers), ship repair(s,ing). *See also* Harbors; Marine accidents; Ports; Shipping industry; Ships.

Dual career families. Dual career famil(y, ies). *Choose from:* dual career(s), two career(s), two paycheck(s), dual occupation(s), two income(s), dual worker(s), dual earner(s) *with:* famil(y, ies), couple(s), marriage(s), household(s). Dual career(s). Working wife. Working wives. *Consider also:* work, job(s), career(s), profession(s,al) *with:* famil(y,ies) *with:* conflict(s), balanc(e,ed,ing). *Consider also:* commuter marriage(s), long-distance marriage(s), career break(s), working parent(s). *See also* Egalitarian families; Family roles; Family-work relationship; Long-distance marriages; Proximity of family; Sex roles; Sexual division of labor; Shared parenting; Working women.

Dual diagnosis. See *Comorbidity.*

Dual earner families. See *Dual career families.*

Dual economy. Dual econom(y,ies). Second econom(y,ies). Segmented econom(y, ies). Shadow econom(y,ies). Dual labor market. Economic dualism. Internal colonialism. Core sector(s). Peripheral sector(s). Economic segment(s,ation). Informal econom(y,ies). Enclave econom(y,ies). *See also* Agrarian societies; Center and periphery; Colonialism; Dependency theory (international); Developing countries; Economic development; Imperialism; Labor market segmentation; Sexual division of labor; Underclass.

Dual labor markets. See *Labor market segmentation.*

Dual personality. See *Multiple personality.*

Dualism. Dualis(m,t,tic). Binary thinking. Two-value(s,d). *Consider also:* mind body dualism, good versus evil, noumenal phenomenal, Manichae(ism,n, nism), Maniche(e,ean,ism,n,nism). *See also* Mind body problem; Monism; Philosophy.

Dualism, economic. See *Economic dualism.*

Duck hunting. Duck hunting. *Choose from:* duck(s), mallard(s), waterfowl, goose, geese, brant(s), coot(s), game bird(s) *with:* shoot(ing), shot, call(ed,ing), bag(ged,ging). *See also* Decoys; Fowling; Game and game birds; Hunting; Poaching; Sports.

Due process. Due process. Fair trial. Day in court. Constitutional criminal procedure(s). Right to counsel. Right to a fair hearing. Fifth amendment. Procedural due process. Administrative due process. *See also* Civil rights; Contempt of Court; Equality before the law; Equity pleading and procedure; Instructions to juries; Justice; Law (practice); Legal procedures; Obstruction of justice; Penal codes; Rule of law; Self incrimination; Trial (law).

Dueling. Duel(s,ed,ing). Affair(s) of honor. Affaire(s) d'honneur. Monomachy. *See also* Chivalry; Fights.

Dullness. Dull(ness). Boring. Colorless(ness). Dismal(ness). Drear(y,iness). Hackneyed. Monoton(y,ous,ousness). Tedious(ness). Tiresome(ness). Unexciting. Unimaginative(ness). Uninspiring. Uninteresting. Wear(y,isome). *See also* Fatuity; Hackneyed; Monotony.

Dump. See *Landfill.*

Dumping, ocean. See *Water pollution.*

Duplicate. *See Cloning; Copies; Copying processes; Experimental replication; Imitation.*

Duplicity. Duplicit(y,ous,ousness). Betray(ed,al). Breach(es) of trust. Chicaner(y,ies). Deceit(ful,fulness). Deceptive(ness). Deceiv(e,ed,ing). Deception(s). Dishonest(y). Disloyal(ty). Faithless(ness). Falsehood(s). Fraud(ulent,ulence). Hypocri(sy,te, tes,tical,tically). Infidelit(y,ies). Insincer(e,ity,ities). Mendacious(ly, ness). Mendacit(y,ies). Perfid(y,ious, iousness). Treacher(y,ous,ousness). *See also* Betrayal; Clandestinity; Deception; Falsification (scientific); Machiavellianism; Traitors.

Durability. Durab(le,leness,ly,ility). Immutab(le,leness,ly,ility). Long lasting. Long standing. Imperishab(le,leness, ly,ility). Sturd(y,iness). Substantial(ness). Resistan(t,ce). Longevity. Steadfast(ness). Unchangeab(le,leness, ly,ility). Unswerving. Unending(ly). Unbreakab(le,ility). Tenac(ity,ious, iousness). *Consider also:* endur(ing, ance), perdurab(le,ing), permanent(ly), stab(le,ility), stout(ness), strong, strength, tough(ness). *See also* Continuity; Endlessness; Permanent; Security; Stability.

Durable goods. Durable good(s). Big ticket item(s). *Choose from:* durable, longlasting *with:* good(s), merchandise, product(s), equipment, commodit(y,ies). Houseware(s). Furniture. Appliance(s). *Consider also:* semidurable good(s), consumer good(s). *See also* Commodities; Consumer goods; Exports; Imports; Product discontinued; Products.

Duration, response. See *Response duration.*

Duration, treatment. See *Length of stay.*

Duration of institutionalization. See *Length of stay.*

Duress. Duress. Coerc(e,ed,ing,ion). Unlawful threat(s,en,ened,ening). Constrain(ed,ing,t). Forcible restrain(ed,ing,t). Forc(e,ed,ing). *See also* Coercion; Involuntary (unwilling); Physical restraint.

Dustbowls. See *Arid lands.*

Duties. Dut(y,ies). Function(s). Task(s). Chore(s). Job(s). Assignment(s). Lesson(s). Exercise(s). Burden(s). Mission(s). Errand(s). Homework. Responsibilit(y,ies). Routine(s). Obligation(s). Commitment(s). Devoir. *Choose from:* ethical, moral, religious *with:* imperative(s), obligation(s). *See also* Accountability; Fiduciary responsibility; Integrity; Moral obligation; Obligations; Responsibility (answerability); Supererogation; Tasks.

Duty. See *Duties; Obligations.*

DVDs. DVD(s). Digital Versatile Disc(s). Digital Video Disc(s). DVD Audio. DVD Video. DVDROM. DVDRAM. DVDR. Hybrid DVD(s). *Consider also:* multimedia, laserdisc(s), optical storage disc(s). *See also* CD ROMs; Computers; Interactive video.

Dwarfism. Dwarf(ed,s,ish,ism). Hypopituitarism. Achondroplas(ia,tic). Chondrodystrophia foetalis. Fetal rickets. *Consider also:* midget(s), Cockayne(s) syndrome, cretin(ism), nanism, undersized adult(s). *See also* Congenitally handicapped.

Dwellings. Dwelling(s). Housing. Abode(s). Domicile(s). Lodging(s). Residence(s). Apartment(s). Single family dwelling(s). Home(s). House(s). Living quarters. Flat(s). Living arrangement(s). Public housing. Private residence(s). Living conditions. Shelter(s). Government housing. Council house(s). Residential hotel(s). Lodge(s). Living environment. Farmhouse(s). Townhouse(s). Habitat(s). Lodging(s). Dig(s,gings). Domicile. Billet. Homestead(s). Cottage(s). Mansion(s). Tenement(s). Barrack(s). Penthouse(s). Boarding home(s). College housing. Dormitor(y,ies). Hotel(s). Low rent housing. Middle income housing. Migrant housing. Suburban housing. Group home(s). *See also* Buildings; Bungalows; Home ownership; Occupancy; Public housing; Residence characteristics; Residence requirements; Residences; Residential facilities; Residential preferences; Urban planning.

Dyads. Dyad(s,ic). Pair(s). Couple(s). Two-person group(s). Partner(s). Mate(s). *See also* Couples; Pair bond; Small groups; Triads.

Dyeing and dyes. See *Dyes and dyeing.*

Dyes and dyeing. Dye(s,d,ing,stuff). Pigment(s). Color(ed,ing,s,ant,ants). Tint(ed,ing,s). Stain(ed,ing,s). Tincture(s). Coloring matter. *Consider also:* paint(ed,ing), bleach(ed,ing). *See also* Color; Pigments.

Dying. Dying. Terminal(ly) ill(ness,nesses). End stage(s). Near death. Moribund. Deathbed. Declining. Expir(e,ed,ing). Drown(ed,ing). Chok(e,ed,ing) to death. Asphyxiat(ed,ing). Freez(e,ing) to death. Dying of: overexposure, hypothermia, thirst, starvation, etc. *Choose from:* terminal(ly), dying, last, final, advanced, fatal, mortal(ly) *with:* ill(ness,nesses), patient(s), condition(s), sick(ness, nesses), wound(s,ed). *Consider also:* life threatening illness(es), life prolongation, prolong(ed,ing) life, hospice(s), terminal care, last rite(s), last breath, euthanasia. *See also* Assisted suicide; Death; Death anxiety; Death counseling; Death rituals; End; Hospices; Last words; Terminal care; Terminal illness.

Dynamics. Dynamics. Interact(ive,ing,ion, ional,ionism). Interplay. Reciproc(al,ity). Interdependen(ce,t). Mutual influence. Transaction(s,al). Joint determination. Symbio(sis,tic). Interchange(s). Exchange(s). Interweav(e,ing). Interwoven. Feedback. Rebut(tal). *See also* Conflict; Family relations; Feedback; Group dynamics; Intergroup relations; Manipulation; Negotiation; Population dynamics; Reciprocity; Social facilitation; Symbiotic relations.

Dynamics, family. See *Family relations.*

Dynamics, group. See *Group dynamics.*

Dynamics, intergroup. See *Intergroup relations.*

Dynamics, political. See *Political stability.*

Dynamics, population. See *Population dynamics.*

Dynamics, social. See *Dynamics; Group dynamics; Intergroup relations; Population dynamics; Social change; Social interaction; Social processes.*

Dynasties. Dynast(y,ies,ic). Hereditary nobility. Peerage. Hereditary oligarch(y,ies). Ruling class(es). Royal descent. Royal line(s). Royal famil(y,ies). Heir(s) to the throne. Royal heir(s). Crown prince(s). Suzerain(ty). Royal house(s). Noble ancestry. *Consider also:* privileged class(es), emir(s), sultan(s), czar(s), kaiser(s), caesar(s), earl(s), noble(men,man), noblewom(en,an), pharoah(s), shah(s), monarch(s,y), king(s), queen(s), emperor(s), prince(s,ess,esses), duke(s), duchess(es). *See also* African empires; Asian empires; Heirs; Lineage; Pre-Columbian empires; Royalty; Ruling class.

Dysarthria. Dysarthr(ia,ic). *Choose from:* articulat(e,ing,ory,ion) *with:* disorder(s), impair(ed,ment,ments), disturbance(s), difficult(y,ies), handicap(ped,s). *Consider also:* stutter(ing), stammer(ing), anarthr(ia,ic), oral dyskinesia. *See also* Articulation disorders; Speech disorders.

Dysconscious racism. Dysconscious racism. *Choose from:* dysconscious(ness), unacknowledged, unconscious(ly), uncritical, unaware(ness), underlying *with:* racis(m,t,ts). *See also* Attitudes; Denial (psychology); Racial attitudes; Racism.

Dysfunction, erectile. See *Impotence.*

Dysfunction, orgasmic. See *Orgasmic dysfunction.*

Dysfunction, psychosexual. See *Sexual function disorders.*

Dysfunction, sexual. See *Sexual function disorders.*

Dysfunctional. Dysfunction(al,ality,s). Impaired function(ing). Abnormal function(ing). *Choose from:* interfer(e,es,ing,ence), block(ed,ing), imped(e,ing,iment,iments), disturbance, hindrance *with:* function(s,ing,ality), interests, needs, aims, purpose(s), integration, adjustment, stability. *See also* Barriers; Contradictions; Dysfunctional families; Impotence; Orgasmic

dysfunction; Paradoxes; Sexual function disorders.

Dysfunctional families. Dysfunctional famil(y,ies). *Choose from:* famil(y,ies, ial), home, domestic, marital, parent(s, al), mother child(ren), father child(ren) *with:* dysfunction(s,al), scapegoat(s,ed, ing), triangulat(e,ed,ing,ion), reject(ed, ing,ion), overprotect(ed,ing,ion), inadequate, chaotic, rigid(ity), enmesh(ed,ment), disorganiz(ed,ation), abuse(s,d), abusive, stress(es,ful), cris(is,es), conflict(s), disrupt(ed,ing, ion,ions), troubled, feud(ing,ed,s), fight(s,ing), distress(ed), disturbed, multiproblem(s), unhappy. *See also* Family conflict; Family crises; Family influence; Family life; Family problems; Family relations; Family violence; Home environment; Schizophrenogenic family.

Dyslexia. Dyslex(ia,ic). *Consider also:* word blind(ness), reading difficult(y,ies), reading disabilit(y,ies). *See also* Learning disabilities; Reading disabilities.

Dysmenorrhea. Dysmenorrhe(a,ic). *Choose from:* menstrua(l,tion) *with:* pain(s,ful), cramp(s,ing), symptom(s), distress, discomfort. *See also* Menstrual disorders.

Dysmorphophobia. Dysmorphophob(ia,ic). *Choose from:* disturbed, disturbance(s), delusion(s,al), psychopatholog(y,ical) *with:* body, bodily, somatic *with:*

image(s), perception(s). Atypical somatoform disorder(s). *Consider also:* hypochondr(ia,iac,iacal) *with:* paranoi(a,d). *See also* Somatoform disorders.

Dyspareunia. Dyspareunia. *Consider also:* pain(ful), discomfort *with:* coitus, intercourse, sexual relations. *See also* Frigidity; Sexual intercourse; Vaginismus.

Dysphasia. Dysphas(ia,ic). Developmental language disorder(s). Abnormal language development. *Choose from:* language *with:* impair(ed,ment,ments), disorder(s,ed). *Consider also:* alexia, anomia. *See also* Alexia; Aphasia; Language disorders.

Dysphoria. Dysphor(ia,ic). Discontent(ed). *Choose from:* bad, unpleasant *with:* mood(s). *See also* Depression (psychology); Major depression.

Dysphoria, gender. See *Transsexualism.*

Dyssocial reaction. Dyssocial reaction(s). Adaptive delinquency. *See also* Adjustment (to environment); Adjustment disorders; Maladaptation; Social factors.

Dysthymic disorder. Dysthymic disorder(s). Dysthym(ia,ic). Depressive neuros(is,es). Neurotic depression(s). *See also* Asthenia; Neurasthenia.

Dystopias. Dystop(ic,ian). Anti-utopia(s,n). *See also* Nihilism; Negativism.

E

E-commerce. E-commerc(e,ial). E-business. Ecommerce. Electronic commerce. Electronic business(es). Microcommerce. Digital marketplace. Electronic shopping. Electronic transaction(s). Banknet. Marketnet. Cybermall(s). *Choose from:* e, electronic, Internet, electronic mail, fax(ed,ing), World Wide Web, WWW, Web-based, on-line, intranet(s) *with:* shopping, purchas(e,ed, es,ing), doing business, transaction(s), bank(s,ing), sale(s), marketplace(s), marketing, check(s), cash, deal(s), price quotation(s), purchase order(s), confirmation(s). *Consider also:* electronic funds transfer(s), unsolicited commercial e-mail, e-trade, spam(med,ming), digital signature(s), internet tax(es,ing), online gambling. *See also* Commerce; Digital communications; Digital signatures; Digital money; Electronic data interchange; Electronic mail; Electronic trading (securities); Global integration; Information society; Internet (computer network); Online users; Small businesses; V-commerce.

E-Mail. See *Electronic mail.*

Eagerness. See *Enthusiasm.*

Ear. Ear(s). *Consider also:* external ear(s), middle ear(s), inner ear(s), labyrinth(s), cochlea(r), semicircular canal(s), vestibular apparatus, ear canal(s), otolog(ic,y), earlobe(s), auricular, eustachian tube(s). *See also* Anatomy; Labyrinth disorders.

Early childbearing. See *Teenage mothers.*

Early childhood. See *Preschool children.*

Early childhood development. Early childhood development. *Choose from:* early childhood, young child(ren), preschool(er,ers), toddler(s), nursery school, first six years, kindergarten(er, ers) *with:* development(al), grow(th,ing), matur(e,ed,ing,ation). *See also* Childhood play development; Early experiences; Early memories; Infant development; Nursery schools; Preschool children; Preschool education.

Early childhood education. See *Preschool education; Primary education.*

Early experiences. Early experience(s). *Choose from:* earl(y,iest), early childhood, preschool, preverbal, preweaning, young child(ren), infant(s), infancy, bab(y,ies), nursery school, toddler(s) *with:* experience(s), education, memor(y, ies), recollection(s), trauma(s,tic). *See also* Age regression (hypnotic); Early childhood development; Early memories.

Early intervention. Early intervention. *Choose from:* early childhood, young child(ren), preschool, nursery school *with:* intervention, prevent(ive,ion), screen(ed,ing), early treatment(s), early modification(s), stimulation. *Consider also:* early identification(s), handicap identification. *See also* Primary prevention; Preventive medicine; Screening.

Early man. See *Prehistoric people.*

Early memories. Early memor(y,ies). Life review(s). Autobiographical memor(y, ies). *Choose from:* earl(y,iest), childhood, past, perinatal, infant(s), infancy, young child(ren), preweaning, bab(y, ies), birth, prenatal *with:* recollection(s), memor(y,ies), remembrance(s), remember(ing). *See also* Age regression (hypnotic); Early childhood development; Early experiences; Reminiscence.

Early people. See *Prehistoric people.*

Early retirement. Early retirement(s). *Choose from:* earl(y,ier), partial, phased, before 65, premature, flexible, non-mandatory *with:* retir(e,ed,ing), retirement(s), retiree(s), withdrawal from workforce, disengagement, discontinue(d) work(ing). *See also* Buyout packages; Flexible retirement; Part time employment; Retirement.

Earners, wage. See *Wage earners.*

Earnest money. Earnest money. Down payment(s). Downpayment(s). Binder(s). Deposit(s). Retainer(s). *Consider also:* surety bond(s). *See also* Agreement (document); Contracts; Discharge of contracts; Economic exchanges; Purchasing.

Earnings. Earning(s). Earned income(s). Salar(y,ies). Wage(s). Revenue(s). Rate of return. Asset accumulation. Remunerat(ion,ive). Compensation. Payment(s) received. Interest earned. Earned money. Receipt(s). Profit(s). Proceeds. Gains. Payment received. Honorar(ia,ium). Annuit(y,ies). Pension(s). Subsid(y,ies). Stipend(s). Recompense. Pay(check). Net worth. Financial status. Economic status. Monetary reward(s). *Choose from:* income, return(s) *with:* generat(e,ed, ing,ion), earn(ed,ing). *See also* Gains; Income; Income distribution; Income inequality; Income redistribution; Interest (monetary); Profits; Salaries; Wage differentials; Wages.

Earth. Earth. The world. Globe. Gaia(n,ist,ists). Terra firma. Great goddess. Our planet. *See also* Arctic Regions; Arid lands; Biosphere; Conservation of natural resources; Ecology; Environment; Environmental pollution; Environmental protection; Environmentalism; Geographic determinism; Geographic regions; Geopolitics; Globes; Mother goddesses; Natural environment; Natural resources; Oceans; Shore protection; Soil conservation; Topography; Universe; Weather.

Earthquakes. Earthquake(s). Quake(s). Temblor(s). Epicentre(s). Richter scale. Earth tremor(s). Aftershock(s). *Choose from:* seismic *with:* wave(s), shock(s), disturbance(s). *Consider also:* earth fault(s), San Andreas fault, etc. *See also* Natural disasters.

Earthwork. Earthwork. Earthmoving. Excavat(e,ed,ing,ion). *Consider also:* embankment(s), mound(s), landfill(s), backfill(s), reinforced soil(s), land-forming, retaining wall(s), tunnel(s, led,ling), earthen liner(s), heavy construction, earth wall(s), landscap(e,ed,ing). *See also* Agricultural engineering; Dams; Drainage; Earthworks; Garden structures; Topography; Tunnels.

Earthworks. Earthworks. Earth work(s). Embankment(s). Mound(s). Land art. Earth art. Earth(work) sculpture(s). Moat(s,ed). Crop art. Tumul(li,us). *Consider also:* rock(s) in art, hillfort(s). *See also* Ancient art; Antiquities (objects); Arts; Conceptual art; Cultural property; Earthwork.

Earthworms. Earthworm(s). Terrestrial annelid(a,s). Lumbric(us,idae). Lumbricus rubellus. Aporrectodea caliginosa. *Consider also:* worm(s). *See also* Animal studies; Animals.

East Altaic languages. East Altaic language(s). Mongolian: Oirat, Kalmuck, Afghanistan Mongol, literary Mongolian, Khalkha Mongolian, Urga, South Mongolian, Harachin, Chahar, Ordos, Buryat, Selenga. Tungusic: Evenki (Tungus), Even (Lamut), Negidal, Manchurian, Udekhe. *See also* Central Asia; Far East; Japanese language; Language; Languages (as subjects).

East, Middle See *Middle East.*

East, Near. See *Middle East.*

Eastern Europe. East(ern) Europe(an). Republic of Albania [Albania(n), Republika e Shqiperise, Shqiperia, People's Socialist Republic of Albania]. Republic of Armenia [Armenia(n), Hayastani Hanrapetut'yun, Hayastan, Armenian Soviet Socialist Republic; Armenian Republic]. Azerbaijani

Republic [Azerbaidzhan(i,ians), Azerbaijanian(s)], Azerbaijan, Azarbaycan Respublikasi, Azerbaijan Soviet Socialist Republic]. Republic of Belarus [Belarus(ia,ian), Respublika Byelarus', Belorussian (Byelorussian) Soviet Socialist Republic, B(y)elorussia(n) Belorus(sia)]. Bosnia and Herzegovina [Republic of Bosnia and Herzegovina, Republika Bosna i Hercegovina, Republika Srpska]. Republic of Bulgaria [Bulgaria(n)]. Commonwealth of Independent States [Union of Soviet Socialist Republics USSR, Soviet Union]. Republic of Croatia [Croatia(n), Republika Hrvatska]. Czech Republic [Ceska Republika, Cechy, Czechoslovakia(n), Czech and Slovak Federative Republic, Czechoslovak Socialist Republic]. Republic of Estonia [Estonia(n), Eesti Vabariik, Eesti, Estonian Soviet Socialist Republic]. Republic of Georgia [Georgia(n), Sak'art'velos Respublika, Sak'art'velo, Georgian Soviet Socialist Republic]. Republic of Hungary [Hungar(y,ian), Magyar Koztarsasag, Magyarorszag]. Republic of Latvia [Latvia(n), Latvijas Republika, Latvian Soviet Socialist Republic]. Republic of Lithuania [Lithuania(n), Lietuvos Respublika, Lietuva, Lithuanian Soviet Socialist Republic]. The Former Yugoslav Republic of Macedonia [Republika Makedonija, Makedonija, FYROM]. Republic of Moldova [Moldova, Moldava, Republica Moldova, Soviet Socialist Republic of Moldova, Moldavia(n)]. Republic of Poland [Poland, Rzeczpospolita Polska, Polska]. Romania(n) [Rumania(n), Roumania(n)]. Serbia and Montenegro [Srbija-Crna Gora, Federal Republic of Yugoslavia, Socialist Federal Republic of Yugoslavia (SFRY), Yugoslavia(n), Jugoslavia(n), Kingdom of the Serbs, Croats and Slovenes]. Slovak Republic [Slovakia, Slovenska Republika, Slovensko, Czech and Slovak Federative Republic, Czechoslovak Socialist Republic]. Republic of Slovenia [Slovenia(n), Republika Slovenije, Slovenija]. Ukraine [Ukrayina, Ukrain(e,ian), Ukraina, Ukrainian Soviet Socialist Republic]. *Consider also:* Eastern bloc, Warsaw Pact nation(s), Germany [German Democratic Republic, East German(y)], Russia(n) [Russian Empire, Rossiya]. *See also* Baltic languages; Caucasian languages; Central Asia; Countries in transition; Finno-Ugric languages; Former Yugoslav republics; Samoyedic languages; Slavic languages; Thraco-Illyrian languages; Thraco-Phrygian languages; West Altaic languages; Western Europe.

Eating. Eat(ing,en). Feed(ing). Food intake. Ingest(ed,ing,ion). Snack(s,ed,ing). Digest(ed,ing,ion). Consum(e,ed,ing) food. Overeat(ing). Food consumption. Lunch(es). Breakfast(s). Dinner(s). Dine(d). Dining. Feast(ed,ing). Tak(e,ing) nourishment. Meal(s,time). Diet(s,ing). Gorg(e,ed,ing). *Consider also:* eating habits, feeding behavior(s), feeding practice(s), eating pattern(s), table manner(s). *See also* Appetite; Convenience Foods; Diet; Dinners and Dining; Digestion; Drinking (water, fluids); Food; Food intake; Gastronomy; Junk food; Natural foods; Nutrition; Vegetarianism; Weaning.

Eating disorders. Eating disorder(s). Eating disorder(s). Overeat(ing). Bulim(ia,ic). Boulim(ia,ic). Anorex(ia,ic). Hyperphag(ia,ic). Dysorex(ia,ic). Bulimarex(ia,ic). Pica. Obes(e,ity). Vomit(ed,ing). Rumination disorder(s). *Consider also:* laxative abuse. *See also* Anorexia nervosa; Bulimia; Hyperphagia; Malnutrition; Nausea; Nutrition disorders; Obesity; Pica.

Eating establishments. Eating establishment(s). Restaurant(s). Cafeteria(s). Cafe(s). Coffee shop(s). Coffeehouse(s). Coffee house(s). Diner(s). Tavern(s). Pub(s). Lunchroom(s). Luncheonette(s). Eating place(s). Eating house(s). Delicatessen(s). Lunch counter(s). Lunchroom(s). Buffet(s). Pizzeria(s). Grill(s). Steakhouse(s). Tearoom(s). Snack bar(s). Fast food outlet(s). *See also* Alcoholic beverages; Beverages; Coffee houses; Cybercafes; Food; Small businesses; Tableware; Waitperson.

Eating habits. See *Food habits.*

Eavesdropping. Eavesdrop(ped,ping). Overhear(d,ing). Listening in. Unauthorized interception. *Choose from:* intercept(ed,ing,ion), taping, surveillance, listen(s,ed,ing) *with:* unauthorized, information, call(s), conversation(s), mobile phone(s). *Consider also:* intelligence gathering. *See also* Electronic eavesdropping; Industrial espionage; Intelligence service; Invasion of privacy; Right of privacy; Secret police; Surveillance of citizens; Trivia.

Eavesdropping, electronic. See *Electronic eavesdropping.*

Ebonics. Ebonic(s). Black English vernacular. African American English. African American language. African American vernacular. Spoken Black English. Spoken African American English. Ghetto English. *Choose from:* black, African American, ghetto *with:* English, dialect(al,ally,ology, ologies,s), vernacular, lingo, jargon, cant, argot, slang, patois. *Consider also:* hip hop culture. *See also* Blacks; Code switching; Creoles; Dialects; Nonstandard English.

Ecclesiastical benefices. Ecclesiastical benefice(s). Ecclesiastical propert(y,ies). Temporalit(y,ies). Ecclesiastical preferment(s). *Consider also:* benefit of clergy, simon(y,ies), rector(y,ies), vicarag(e,es), perpetual curac(y,ies). *See also* Clergy; Ordination; Patronage.

Ecclesiastical courts. Ecclesiastical court(s). Courts Christian. Church court(s). Spiritual court(s). *Consider also:* Archdeacon's Court, Consistory Court, Court of Arches of Canterbury, Chancery Court of York, Court of Faculties, Court of Final Appeal, Judicial Committee of the Privy Council, Papal judge(s). *See also* Canons; Courts; Religious councils and synods.

Echo baby boom generation. See *Echo boom generation.*

Echo boom generation. Echo boom generation. Generation Y. X-tronic generation. Net generation. Born 1977 to 1997. *See also* Post-baby boom generation.

Echolalia. Echolal(ia,ic). Echophasia. Parrot(ed,ing) speech. *See also* Language disorders.

Echolocation. Echolocat(e,ed,ing,ion). Echo locat(e,ed,ing,ion). Echorang(e, ed,ing). *Choose from:* echo(s) *with:* information, detect(ed,ing,ion), target ranging. *Consider also:* sound localization, bat sonar. *See also* Animal vocalization.

Eclecticism. Eclectic(ally,ism). Select(ive, ity). Divers(e,ity). Nondoctrinaire. Nondogmatic. Synthesiz(e,ed,ing). Synthesis. Heterogeneous. *See also* Interdisciplinary approach; Philosophy.

Eclipses. Eclip(se,ses,tic). Obscur(e,ed, ing,ation). *Choose from:* partial, total, lunar, solar *with:* eclipse(s). *Consider also:* earth's shadow, moon's shadow. *See also* Ancient astronomy; Astronomy.

Ecological agriculture. See *Organic farming.*

Ecological diversity. See *Biological diversity.*

Ecological imperialism. Ecological imperialism. Imperialismo ecologico. Biological expansion. *Choose from:* ecolog(y,ical), biodiversity, biolog(y,ical), nature, environment(al), rainforest(s), wetlands *with:* imperialism, migration(s), injustice, militariz(e, ed,ing,ation), politic(s,al), exploit(ed, ing,ation), poison(ed,ing). *Consider also:* ecological history, aboriginal depopulation, environmental racism, clearing of forests land(s), chemical dumping, garbage imperialism. *See also* Agribusiness; Biopiracy; Cultural imperialism; Deforestation; Desertification; Ecotourism; Environmental racism; Land settlement; Neocolonialism; Rainforests; Slash burn agriculture.

Ecological movement. See *Environmentalism.*

Ecology. Ecolog(y,ies,ical). Binomic(s). Ecosystem(s). Habitat(s). Natural surrounding(s). Climate(s). Condition(s). *Consider also:* tundra(s), coniferous forest(s), temperate grassland(s), desert(s), tropical forest(s), rainforest(s), high altitude(s), deciduous forest(s), subtropical, tropical grassland(s), temperate climate(s), arctic condition(s), natural resource(s), pollution, topography, competitive interaction, temperature(s), seasonal variation(s), natural competition, food availability, thermal conditions, host availability, predator-prey interaction, prey distribution, resource availability, wildlife, indigenous plant(s), natural condition(s), food superabundance, food competition. *See also* Adjustment (to environment); Alternative energy; Air pollution; Anthropocentrism; Biogeography; Bioregionalism; Climate; Conservation of natural resources; Deep ecology; Ecosysytem management; Edible plants; Energy conservation; Environment; Environmental impacts; Environmental pollution; Environmental protection; Environmental stress; Evolution; Fire ecology; Food chain; Forest ecology; Habitat; Human ecology; Island ecology; Marine ecology; Natural environment; Noise (sounds); Noise levels (work areas); Occupational exposure; Paleoecology; Quality of life; Quality of working life; Recycling; Shore protection; Shorelines; Soil conservation; Waste disposal; Waste to energy; Wastes; Water pollution; Water purification; Water safety; Water supply; Weather; Working conditions.

Ecology, agricultural. See *Agricultural ecology.*

Ecology, deep. See *Deep ecology.*

Ecology, fire. See *Fire ecology.*

Ecology, forest. See *Forest ecology.*

Ecology, human. See *Human ecology.*

Ecology, island. See *Island ecology.*

Ecology, marine. See *Marine ecology.*

Ecology, medical. See *Medical geography.*

Ecology, prehistoric. See *Paleoecology.*

Ecology, restoration. See *Restoration ecology.*

Ecology, social. See *Human ecology.*

Economic assistance. Economic assistance. Resource sharing. *Choose from:* economic(ally), financial(ly), monetar(y, ily), food, World Bank, humanitarian *with:* assist(ed,ing,ance), aid(s,ed,ing), help(s,ed,ing), grant(s), contribut(e,ed, ing,ion,ions), support(s,ed,ing), donation(s). *See also* Donations; Economic dependence; Economic

stabilization; Economic underdevelopment; Foreign aid; Income redistribution; International banks and banking; International trade; Welfare policy.

Economic attitudes. Economic attitude(s). *Choose from:* economic, market, commercial, capitalis(m,t,tic), socialis(m,t,tic) *with:* opinion(s), discontent, attitude(s). *Consider also:* work ethic, profit ethic, economic socialization, economic understanding. *See also* Attitudes; Profit motive.

Economic change. Economic change(s). Chang(e,ing) economic order. Economic reform(s). Socioeconomic change(s). Economic contraction(s). Economic growth. Chang(e,ing) economic structure. *Consider also:* business cycle(s), economic cycle(s), depression(s), inflation(s). *See also* Business cycles; Deindustrialization; Economic development; Economic forecasting; Economic planning; Industrialization; Labor market; Social change; Supply side economics; Technological change.

Economic class. See *Economic elites; Lower class; Middle class; Poverty; Socioeconomic status; Upper class; Wealth.*

Economic competition. Economic competition. Free market(s). Price competition. Economic competitiveness. Antitrust. Competitive system. Demand elasticity. Marketplace. Free trade. Competitive market(s). Deregulat(ed, ing,ion). Pro-competit(ive,ion). Price war(s). Capitalis(tic,m). Free enterprise. *Choose from:* compet(ion,itive), market(s) *with:* model(s), demand, forces, bidding. *See also* Antitrust law; Capitalism; Demand; Economic resources; Entrepreneurship; Labor market; Market economy; Private enterprise; Private sector.

Economic conditions. Economic condition(s). Economic indicator(s). Business condition(s). Climate for investment. Capital market(s). Flow of capital. Gross national product. GNP. Gross domestic product. GDP. National income. National earnings. Living condition(s). Cost of living. Standard(s) of living. *Choose from:* business, econom(y,ic), market, fiscal, monetary, macroeconomic, microeconomic, socioeconomic, industrial *with:* condition(s), fluctuation(s), cycle(s), climate, progress, decline, inflation, depression, survey(s), health, slump(s), situation, outlook, problems, prospect(s), recovery, revival, indicator(s), statistics, recession(s), adversity, prosperity, profile(s), opportunit(y,ies), development, ills, ailing, status, activit(y,ies), forecast(s), rating(s), expansion, cris(is,es).

Consider also: leading indicator(s), stagflation, prosperity, sluggish economy, reflation, affluence, poverty. *See also* Adversity; Business cycles; Depression (economic); Economic change; Economic crises; Economic development; Economic indicators; Economic well being; Industrial capacity; Inflation (economics); Labor market; Living conditions; Living standards; Migration of industry; National income; Production; Production consumption relationship; Productivity; Scarcity; Social conditions; Recession; Socioeconomic factors; Subsistence economy; Wealth; World economy; Zero economic growth.

Economic consumption. See *Consumption (economic).*

Economic crises. Economic cris(is,es). Stock market crash. Debt crisis. Food production crisis. Depression(s). Runaway inflation. *Choose from:* econom(y,ic), business, market, fiscal, financial, monetary, inflation(ary) *with:* cris(is,es), stress(es), crash(es), panic(s), demise, disaster(s), emergenc(y,ies), meltdown(s), free fall. *See also* Budget deficits; Business cycles; Crisis management; Depression (economic); External debts; Economic conditions; Inflation (economics); Public debt.

Economic cycles. See *Business cycles.*

Economic democracy. See *Employee ownership; Industrial democracy.*

Economic dependence. Economic(ally) depende(n,t,ce). Financial(ly) depende(n,t,ce). Dependency theory. Underdevelopment. Imperial colonial relationship. Neoimperialism. Neocolonialism. Third world exploitation. Third world dependency. *Consider also:* imperialism, colonialism. *See also* Center and periphery; Dependency theory (international); Developing countries; Dual economy; Economic development; Economic underdevelopment; Income inequality; Income-maintenance programs; Income redistribution; Indigence; Industrial capacity; Multinational corporations; Production; Productivity; Subsidized housing; Subsistence economy; Welfare recipients; Welfare state; World economy.

Economic depression. See *Depression (economic).*

Economic determinism. Economic determinism. Economic factor(s). Econom(ism,istic). *Choose from:* income, earnings, poverty, indigen(t,cy), disadvantage(d,ment), wealth, employment, unemployment, occupation, socioeconomic status, SES, socioeconomic, economic(ally), production, base and superstructure *with:* bas(is,es), background(s), causal, cause(s), constraint(s), correlate(s), correlation, context(s), component(s), consideration(s), determinant(s), determin(ed,ing,ation), difference(s), dimension(s), dynamic(s), effect(s), element(s), explanation(s), factor(s), influence(s), implication(s), indicator(s), impact(s), limit(s), obstacle(s), pattern(s), precondition(s), predis-position(s), process(es), reductionism, variable(s). *See also* Causality; Deter-minism; Economic conditions; Eco-nomic geography; Socioeconomic factors; Social conditions.

Economic development. Economic development. Economic progress. Economic growth. Socioeconomic development. Industrialization. Miracle econom(y,ies). Transfer of technology. Economic transformation. Capitalist development. Socialist development. Agricultural development. Industrial development. Industrializ(e,ed,ing, ation). Improved balance of trade. *Choose from:* econom(ic,y,ies), socioeconomic, industr(ial,y,ies), agricultural, GNP, Gross National Product, GDP, Gross Domestic Product, national income *with:* develop(ed,ing, ment,mental), grow(ing,n,th), evol(ve, ved,ving,ution), restructur(e,ed,ing), accelerat(e,ed,ing,ion), transition(s), matur(e,ed,ing,ity), expan(d,ded,ding, sion), improv(e,ed,ing,ment,ments), exten(d,ded,sion), progress(ed,ing,ion), strengthen(ed,ing), further(ing,ance), spread(ing), advanc(es,ed,ing,ement, ements), enrich(ed,ment), revolution(s), moderniz(e,ed,ing,ation), retool(ed,ing), promot(e,ed,ing,ion), increas(e,es,ed, ing). *See also* Agricultural diversifica-tion; Agricultural mechanization; Business growth; Community develop-ment; Debt-for-nature swap(s); Depen-dency theory (international); Developing countries; Distribution channels; Economic change; Economic depen-dence; Economic history; Economic planning; Growth strategies; Industrial promotion; Industrialization; Job creation; Modernization; Progress; Production; Productivity; Regional development; Rural development; Rural industries; Scientific development; Sustainable development; Technical assistance; Technology transfer; Workforce planning; Zero economic growth.

Economic dualism. Economic dualism. Dual econom(y,ies). Second econom(y, ies). Segmented econom(y,ies). Shadow econom(y,ies). Dual labor market. Internal colonialism. Core sector(s). Peripheral sector(s). Economic segment(s,ation). Informal econom(y, ies). Enclave econom(y,ies). *See also* Agrarian societies; Center and periph-ery; Colonialism; Dependency theory (international); Developing countries;

Economic development; Imperialism; Labor market segmentation; Sexual division of labor; Underclass.

Economic elites. Economic elite(s,ist,ists, ism). Managerial class(es). Economic hegemon(y,ies). Oligopol(y,ies). Wealth(y). Upper class(es). Interlocking directorate(s). High economic status. Economic royalist(s). Captains of industry. *Choose from:* economic, business, corporate, managerial, financial *with:* elite(s), leader(s), hegemon(y,ies), oligarch(y,ies), privileged, high rank(ing), opinion maker(s), opinion leader(s), influential people, power structure, hierarch(y,ies). *See also* Interlocking directorates; Industrial concentration; Oligopolies; Political elites; Power elite; Ruling class; Upper class.

Economic exchanges. Economic exchange(s). Barter(ed,ing). Exchange(s). Swap. Non-monetary trade. Non-monetary exchange(s). Trade without money. Trading inventory. Trade services. Reciprocal merchandising. Exchange of goods. Hidden economy. Cashless transaction(s). Informal economy. Yard sales. Garage sales. Countertrade. Counterpurchas(es,ing). Contratrade. Compensation goods. *See also* Bartering; Black economy; Deals; Earnest money; Exchange; Gray market; Informal sector; Money (primitive cultures); Real estate closings; Sales; Second hand trade.

Economic factors. See *Economic determin-ism; Socioeconomic factors.*

Economic fluctuations. See *Business cycles.*

Economic forecasting. Economic forecast(s,ing). *Choose from:* economic, econometric, macroeconomic, micro-economic, budget(s,ary), econom(y,ies), inflation(s), depression(s), recession(s), business cycle(s), consumer demand, money supply, exchange rate(s), monetary, fiscal, market, investment(s) *with:* forecast(s,ing), outlook(s), predict(ed,ing,ion,ions), trend(s), projection(s), futur(e,es,ist,ists,ism), year 2000, prognosticat(e,ed,ing,ion,ions), 21st century, prospect(s); scenario(s). *See also* Business cycles; Economic indicators; Economic planning; Economic statistics; Future; Monetary policy.

Economic geography. Economic geograph(y,ies). Economic atlas(es). *Choose from:* spatial, regional, geo-graphic, macro-region(s), rural, urban *with:* econom(ic,y,ies), profit(s), capital, labor, jobs, industr(y,ial), poverty. *See also* Economic determinism; Economics; Geography; Geographical determinism; Geopolitics; Historic geography; Political geography.

Economic growth. See *Business growth; Economic development.*

Economic growth, zero. See *Zero economic growth.*

Economic history. Economic history. *Choose from:* econom(ic,y,ies), profit(s), capital, labor, jobs, industr(y,ial), poverty *with:* change(s), development, trend(s), nineteenth century. *See also* Colonialism; Economic development; Geopolitics; Industrialization; World economy; World history.

Economic indicators. Economic indicator(s). Gross National Product. GNP. Gross Domestic Product. GDP. Consumer Price Index. CPI. Interest rate(s). Prime rate(s). Cyclical indicator(s). Lagging indicator(s). Leading indicator(s). Coincident indicator(s). *Choose from:* industrial production, business inventories, money supply, new construction, employment, unemployment, productivity levels, farm income, international transactions *with:* rate(s), statistic(al,s), data, indicator(s). *Consider also:* stock market(s), Dow Jones average(s), Nikkei index, composite index, Europe Australia Far East Index, EAFE. *See also* Business cycles; Business failures; Business growth; Economic conditions; Economic forecasting; Economic planning; Economic statistics; Economic well being; Employment trends; Gross National Product; Interest (monetary); Living standards; National income; Production; Productivity; Unemploy-ment rates.

Economic inequality. See *Center and periphery; Dependency theory (interna-tional); Dual economy; Economic underdevelopment; Global inequality; Imperialism; Income inequality; International division of labor; Labor market segmentation; Occupational segregation; Sexual division of labor; Women living in poverty; World systems theory.*

Economic integration, international. See *International economic integration.*

Economic man. Economic man. Economic self-interest. *Consider also:* rational egotist(s), self-interested behavior, rational man, human nature. *See also* Individualism; Monetary incentives; Profit motive; Self interest.

Economic organizations, international. See *International economic organiza-tions.*

Economic panics. See *Economic crises.*

Economic patterns. See *Business cycles.*

Economic planning. Economic plan(s,ning). Development plan(s,ning). Socialist plan(s,ning). Socioeconomic plan(s,ning). Industrial plan(s,ning).

Five year plan(s). Economic strateg(y, ies). Economic overhaul(s). *Choose from:* central planning *with:* econom(ic, y,ies), socialis(t,m). *Consider also:* planned econom(y,ies), economic development, economic intensification, economic restructuring, economic reorganization, economic reform, development strateg(y,ies). *See also* Centrally planned economies; Economic statistics; Economics; Government; Growth strategies; Local planning; Planning; Price control; Social planning; State planning; World economy; Zero economic growth.

Economic policy. See *Balanced budget; Budget deficits; Capitalism; Collectivism; Economic planning; Fiscal policy; Market economy; Monetary policy; Nationalization; Private enterprise; Privatization; Public debt; Socialism; World systems theory.*

Economic problems. Economic problem(s). Indebted(ness). National debt. Recession(s). Depression(s). Income uncertainty. Ailing economy. Economics of decline. Hard times. Stagflation. Economic ills. Sluggish economy. Poverty. Scarcity. Runaway inflation. Bankrupt(cy). *Choose from:* business, econom(y,ic), market, fiscal, monetary, income, cash flow, macroeconomic, microeconomic, socioeconomic *with:* problem(s), decline, inflation, depression, slump(s), instability, unstable, recession(s), adversity, ills, stress(es), cris(is,es), uncertain(ty), vulnerability, underdevelopment, strain(s,ed), stagnat(e,ed,ing,ion). *See also* Adversity; Bankruptcy; Depression (economic); Economic crises; Inflation (economic); Poverty; Scarcity; Unemployment.

Economic recovery. See *Economic stabilization; Economic well being.*

Economic relations. Economic relations. *Choose from:* economic, business, financial, trade, trading, macroeconomic *with:* relations(hip,hips), interdependen(t,ce), cooperation, reciprocity, reciprocal, agreement(s), deficit(s), dominance, sanction(s), partner(s), link(s,age,ages). *Consider also:* Marshall plan, technolgy transfer(s). *See also* Economic assistance; Economic dependence; Economic underdevelopment; Foreign aid; Harmonization (trade); Monetary unions; Trade preferences; Trade protection.

Economic relations, international. See *Balance of payments; Colonialism; Dependency theory (international); Embargo; Exports; Foreign aid; Foreign investment; Foreign trade regulation; Foreign exchange; Imports; International division of labor; International economic integration; International economic organizations; International relations; Multinational corporations; Trade protection; World economy.*

Economic research. Economic research. Socio-economic research. *Choose from:* econom(ic,y,ies), economist(s), econometric, monetar(y,ist,ism), income *with:* research, positivism, normativism, pragmatism, methodological approach(es), quantitative method(s), qualitative method(s), analy(sis,ses, yze,yzed,yzing), linear relation(s), nonlinear relation(s). *See also* Actuarial analysis; Economics; Market research; Research.

Economic resources. Economic resource(s). Resource(s). Asset(s). Reserve(s). Income. Cash. Propert(y,ies). Possession(s). Holdings. Wealth. Profit(s). Real estate. Savings. Worth. Suppl(y,ies). *Consider also:* land, labor, capital, manpower, mineral(s), raw material(s). *See also* Energy generating resources; Marine resources; Natural resources; Nonrenewable resources; Raw materials; Renewable resources; Resource management; Resources.

Economic security. Economic security. *Choose from:* economic(ally), financial(ly), income *with:* secur(e,ity), guarantee(s,d), assured, assurance(s), maintenance. *Consider also:* safety net(s), financial freedom, liquidity, economic well-being. *See also* Economic stability; Social stability; Wealth.

Economic self sufficiency. See *Autarky.*

Economic stability. Economic stability. Flation. Stable money. Stabilization polic(y,ies). *Consider also:* creeping inflation. *See also* Business cycles; Economic conditions; Economic stabilization; Political stability.

Economic stabilization. Economic stabilization. *Choose from:* business cycle(s), unemployment, inflation, hyperinflation, recession(s), depression(s), market(s), price(s), interest rate(s), Dow Jones industrial average(s) *with:* recover(y,ing,ed), stabiliz(e,ed,ing,ation), adjustment polic(y,ies), smooth(ed,ing), regulat(e,ed,ing,ion), jump start(ed,ing). *Consider also:* control(led,ling) inflation(ary), economic polic(y,ies). *See also* Business cycles; Depression (economic); Economic forecasting; Economic stability; Economic well being; Inflation (economics); Price trends; Recession; Zero population growth.

Economic statistics. Economic statistic(s). Economic index(es). Economic data. Econometric(s). *Choose from:* econom(ic,y,ies), microeconomic, macroeconomic, socio-economic, business, price(s), labor, market(s), population, trade, investment, financial institution(s), money, monetary, capital, interest rate(s), banking, securities, savings *with:* time series, statistic(s,al). *See also* Demographic characteristics (of individuals); Economic conditions; Economic indicators; Economic forecasting; Economic planning; Economic statistics; Economics; Employment trends; Financial data; Gross national product; Living standards; Market statistics; National income; Population (statistics); Production; Productivity; Statistical data; Unemployment rates.

Economic trends. See *Business cycles; Depression (economic); Inflation (economics); Recession.*

Economic underdevelopment. Economic underdevelopment. *Choose from:* economic(ally), productivity, manufacturing, socio-economic(ally), trade, import(s), export(s) *with:* underdevelop(ed,ment), backward(ness), dependen(t,ce,cy,cies), pauperiz(e,ed, ing,ation), powerless(ness). *Consider also:* unequal development, deindustrialization, international economic dependen(cy,cies). *See also* Agrarian societies; Bartering; Center and periphery; Colonialism; Dependency theory (international); Developing countries; Dual economy; Economic development; Imperialism; International division of labor; Least developed countries; Subsistence economy; Sustainable development.

Economic union. Economic union(s). Economic unity. European Union. European Economic Community. European Community. Common market(s). Preferential trade agreement(s). Economic communit(y, ies). European Free Trade Association. EFTA. North American Free Trade Association. NAFTA. *Choose from:* regional economic *with:* group(s), cooperation. *Consider also:* customs union(s), Benelux Economic Union, Treaty of Rome, European Atomic Energy Community [EURATOM]. *See also* Common currency; Common markets; Custom unions; Free trade; Harmonization (trade); International banks and banking; International economic integration; International economic organizations; Monetary unions; Tariffs.

Economic value. Economic value(s). Monetary worth. Book value(s). Depreciated cost(s). Valuation. Appraised value(s). *Consider also:* appreciat(e,ed,ing,ion), cost(s), price(s), fair return, net worth. *See also* Appraisal; Assessment; Capitalization; Costs; Depreciation; Face value; Valuation.

Economic well being. Economic well being. Net worth. Gross domestic product. American Demographics Index of Well-Being. Money supply. *Choose from:* financial, business, econom(y,ic), market, fiscal, monetary, macroeconomic, microeconomic, socioeconomic, industrial *with:* progress, health, recovery, revival, prosperity, opportunit(y,ies), expansion. *See also* Economic conditions; Economic indicators; Economic stabilization; National income.

Economic well being (individuals). See *Austerities; Basic needs; Consumption (use); Deprivation; Disadvantaged; Everyday life; Living conditions; Living standards; Quality of life; Socioeconomic status; Wealth.*

Economically disadvantaged. See *Deprivation; Disadvantaged; Poverty.*

Economics. Economics. Economic science. Econometric(s). Microeconomics. Macroeconomics. Socioeconomics. Supply and demand. Economic system(s). Price theor(y,ies). Economic maximization. Keynesian theory. Fiscal polic(y,ies). *Consider also:* economic, socioeconomic *with:* factor(s), analy(ses,sis). *See also* Business; Economic geography; Economic research; Economic statistics; Supply side economics.

Economics, aggregate. See *Aggregate economics.*

Economics, home. See *Home economics.*

Economics, labor. See *Labor economics.*

Economics, medical. See *Medical economics.*

Economics, neoclassical. See *Supply side economics.*

Economics, supply side. See *Supply side economics.*

Economies, advanced. See *Developed countries.*

Economies, centrally planned. See *Centrally planned economies.*

Economies, newly industrializing. See *Newly industrializing economies.*

Economies of scale. Econom(y,ies) of scale. Econom(y,ies) of size. Size efficienc(y,ies). Optimum size(s). Optimum scale. Minimum efficient scale. Diseconom(y,ies) of scale. *See also* Prices; Purchasing.

Economy (The Economy). See *Economic conditions.*

Economy, black. See *Black economy.*

Economy, consumer. See *Consumer society.*

Economy, dual. See *Dual economy.*

Economy, international. See *World economy.*

Economy, market. See *Market economy.*

Economy, parallel. See *Informal sector.*

Economy, subsistence. See *Subsistence economy.*

Economy, subterranean. See *Informal sector.*

Economy, token. See *Token economy.*

Economy, underground. See *Black economy; Informal sector.*

Economy, world. See *World economy.*

Economy principle. See *Occam's razor.*

Ecosystem management. Ecosystem management. Ecosystem maintenance. *Choose from:* ecosystem(s), ecological system(s), food chain(s), food web(s), biodiversity, habitat(s), biogeocoenosis *with:* manag(e,ed,ing,ement), maintenance, maintain(ed,ing), oversight, conservation. *Consider also:* land management. *See also* Decontamination; Ecology; Environmental impacts; Environmental protection; Food chain; Forest conservation; Habitat; Land preservation; Natural resourses; Restoration ecology; Wildlife conservation.

Ecosystems. See *Ecology.*

Ecotourism. Ecotouris(m,t,ts). Ecotouris(m,t,ts). Sustainable touris(m,t,ts). Responsible touris(m,t,ts). Nature touris(m,t,ts). Tourist(s) interested in ecology. *Choose from:* ecolog(y,ical), environmental protection, conservation, environmentalis(m,t,ts), bird-watching, wilderness *with:* tour(ism,ist,ists), travel(er,ers), vacation(s). *Consider also:* environmental education. *See also* Ecological imperialism; Ecology; Environmental impacts; Environmental protection; Forest conservation; Land preservation; Natural resources; Wildlife conservation.

Ecstasy. Ecsta(sy,tic). Exult(ant,ation). Exhilarat(e,ed,ion). Raptur(e,ous). Elat(ed,ion). Bliss(ful). Thrill(ed,ing). Orgas(m,tic). Peak experience(s). Rapture. Exuberan(t,ce). *See also* Climax; Emotions; Happiness; Trance.

Ecumenical movement. Ecumenical movement. Ecumenic(al,ity,ism). Christian unity. Open pulpit(s). Intercommunion. *Choose from:* interchurch, interreligious, interfaith, interdenominational *with:* movement(s), dialogue(s), cooperation, unification. Church merger(s). Church union(s). Pan-evangelicalism. *See also* Christianity; Intercommunion; Interdenominational cooperation; Religious dialogues; Religious institutions; Social movements.

Ecumenism. See *Catholic (universality); Ecumenical movement.*

Edible plants. Edible plant(s). Edible green(s). *Choose from:* edible, digestible, nourishing, nutritious, medicinal *with:* weed(s), plant(s), green(s), fruit(s), berr(y,ies), herb(s), flower(s), mushroom(s), nut(s). *Consider also:* fiddlehead(s), vegetable(s), forage plant(s). *See also* Ecology; Food; Natural foods; Plants (botanical); Poisonous plants.

Edicts. Edict(s). Command(s). Commandment(s). Declaration(s). Decree(s). Proclamation(s). Pronouncement(s). *Consider also:* directive(s), ruling(s), ukase(s), manifesto(s), fiat(s), injunction(s), mandate(s), pronunciamento(s), canon(s), decret(a,al,als,um), ordinance(s), precept(s), prescript(s), regulation(s), rule(s), statute(s). *See also* Canons; Creeds; Declarations; Dogma; Principles; Regulations.

Edifices. See *Buildings.*

Editing. Edit(ed,ing). Revis(e,ed,ing,ion). Rewrit(e,ten,ing). *Consider also:* correct(ed,ing,ion), annotat(e,ed,ing, ion), blue pencil, rephras(e,ed,ing), tweak(ed,ing). *See also* Editors; Journalism; Writing (composition).

Editorials. Editorial(s,ize,ized,ization). Opinion piece(s). Op-ed(s). *Choose from:* editorial *with:* page(s), article(s), space(s). *Consider also:* press endorsement(s), media condemnation, news analysis. *See also* Commentaries; Editors; Journalism; Media portrayal; News agencies; Opinion leaders; War news.

Editors. Editor(s,ship,ships). Reviser(s). Compiler(s). Editor-in-Chief. *Consider also:* newspaper(man,men, woman,women). *See also* Authors; Book industry; Commentators; Editing; Editorials; Journalism; Journalists; Lexicography; Literary ethics; Opinion leaders; Publishers; Writers.

Educable mentally retarded. Educable mental(ly) retard(ed,ation). Mild(ly) mental(ly) retard(ed,ation). Moron(s). IQ 50-70. Mild(ly) retard(ed,ation). Educable retarded. *Choose from:* mild(ly), educable *with:* mental(ly), intellectual(ly) *with:* retard(ed,ation), impair(ed,ment,ments), handicap(s,ped), subnormal(ality,alities). *Consider also:* special education student(s), educationally subnormal. *See also* Education of mentally retarded; Employment of persons with disabilities; Sheltered workshops.

Education. Educat(e,ed,ing,ion,ional). Train(ing,ed,ee,ees). Apprentice(s,ship, ships). Academic. Class(es,room,rooms). Coach(ed,ing). Course(s). Correspondence course(s). Curricul(a,um). Development. Didactic(s,ism). Directed learning. Drill(ed,ing). Educational process(es). Enrichment. Indoctrinat(e, ed,ing,ion). Initiat(e,ed,ing,ion). Instruct(ed,ing,ion,ional). Intern(ed,ing, s,ship,ships). Learn(ed,ing). Lesson(s). Orient(ed,ing,ation). Pedagog(y,ic,ical). Preceptor(ship). Prepar(e,ed,ing,ation). Pupil(s). Renewal. Retrain(ed,ing). School(ed,ing). Scholar(ly,ship). Scholastic. Seminar(s). Student(s). Stud(y,ies). Study(ing). Teach(ing). Taught. Tutor(ed,s,ing,ials). *See also* Ability grouping; Academic achievement; Academic education; Acceleration (education); Access to education; Adapted physical education; Adult basic education; Adult education; Aesthetic education; Aging education; Alcohol education; Ancient education; Art education; Audiovisual instruction; Basic education; Basic business education; Bilingual education; Business education; Career education; Classroom environment; Client education; Compensatory education; Competency based education; Compulsory education; Consumer education; Continuing education; Cooperative education; Curriculum; Curriculum development; Dance education; Death education; Drug education; Education of mentally retarded; Elementary education; Equal education; Extracurricular activities; Graduate education; Health education; Higher education; Humanistic education; Inservice teacher education; Inservice training; Knowledge; Learning; Literacy programs; Mathematics education; Mainstreaming; Medical education; Moral education; Multicultural education; Music education; Nonprofessional education; Nontraditional education; Nursing education; Nutrition education; Patient education; Parent training; Preschool education; Primary education; Professional education; Psychiatric training; Reading education; Religious education; Remedial education; Rural education; Schools; Secondary education; Second language education; Self education; Sex education; Socialization; Special education; Students; Study habits; Teachers; Teaching; Training; Undergraduate education; Urban education; Vocational education.

Education, academic. See *Academic education.*

Education, acceleration. See *Acceleration (education).*

Education, access to. See *Access to education.*

Education, adapted physical. See *Adapted physical education.*

Education, adult. See *Adult education.*

Education, adult basic. See *Adult basic education.*

Education, aesthetic. See *Aesthetic education.*

Education, affective. See *Humanistic education.*

Education, aging. See *Aging education.*

Education, alcohol. See *Alcohol education.*

Education, ancient. See *Ancient education.*

Education, antiracist. See *Antiracist education.*

Education, art. See *Art education.*

Education, audiovisual. See *Audiovisual education.*

Education, basic. See *Basic education.*

Education, basic business. See *Basic business education.*

Education, bilingual. See *Bilingual education.*

Education, boards of. See *School boards.*

Education, business. See *Business education.*

Education, career. See *Career education.*

Education, citizenship. See *Citizenship education.*

Education, client. See *Client education.*

Education, compensatory. See *Compensatory education.*

Education, competency-based. See *Competency-based education.*

Education, compulsory. See *Compulsory education.*

Education, consumer. See *Consumer education.*

Education, continuing. See *Continuing education.*

Education, cooperative. See *Cooperative education.*

Education, dance. See *Dance education.*

Education, death. See *Death education.*

Education, digital. See *Distance education.*

Education, distance. See *Distance education.*

Education, drug. See *Drug education.*

Education, early childhood. See *Preschool education; Primary education.*

Education, elementary. See *Elementary education.*

Education, equal. See *Equal education.*

Education, ethical. See *Moral education.*

Education, family. See *Parent training.*

Education, family life. See *Parent training.*

Education, gender fair. See *Nonsexist education.*

Education, global. See *International education.*

Education, graduate. See *Graduate education.*

Education, health. See *Health education.*

Education, higher. See *Higher education.*

Education, humanistic. See *Humanistic education.*

Education, inclusive. See *Inclusive education.*

Education, inservice teacher. See *Inservice teacher education.*

Education, international. See *International education.*

Education, liberal. See *Academic education.*

Education, liberal arts. See *Humanistic education.*

Education, literacy. See *Literacy programs.*

Education, mathematics. See *Mathematics education.*

Education, medical. See *Medical education.*

Education, medieval. See *Medieval education.*

Education, mentally retarded. See *Education of mentally retarded.*

Education, moral. See *Moral education.*

Education, multicultural. See *Multicultural education.*

Education, music. See *Music education.*

Education, nonprofessional. See *Nonprofessional education.*

Education, nonsexist. See *Nonsexist education.*

Education, nontraditional. See *Nontraditional education.*

Education, nursing. See *Nursing education.*

Education, nutrition. See *Nutrition education.*

Education, patient. See *Patient education.*

Education, physical. See *Physical education.*

Education, preschool. See *Preschool education.*

Education, primary. See *Primary education.*

Education, professional. See *Professional education.*

Education, psychiatric. See *Psychiatric training.*

Education, reading. See *Reading education.*

Education, religious. See *Religious education.*

Education, remedial. See *Remedial education.*

Education, rural. See *Rural education.*

Education, second language. See *Second language education.*

Education, secondary. See *Secondary education.*

Education, self. See *Self education.*

Education, sex. See *Sex education.*

Education, special. See *Special education.*

Education, theological. See *Religious education.*

Education, undergraduate. See *Undergraduate education.*

Education, urban. See *Urban education.*

Education, vocational. See *Vocational education.*

Education of mentally retarded. Education of mentally retarded. *Choose from:* mental(ly) retard(ed,ation), mentally handicapped, retarded student(s) *with:* special education, tutor(ed,ing), train(ed,ing), feedback, condition(ed, ing), mainstream(ed,ing), remediation. *See also* Educable mentally retarded; Mainstreaming.

Education students. Education student(s). Education major(s). Student teacher(s). *Consider also:* teacher trainee(s), prospective teacher(s). *See also* College students.

Educational administration. Educational administration. School administration. Educational management. *Choose from:* education(al), school(s), school district(s), college(s), universit(y,ies), educational institution(s), higher education *with:* administrat(ive,ion), organization, management, planning, polic(y,ies), organizational pattern(s), principal(s), dean(s), supervis(ion,ing), leadership, department head(s), management, governance, regulation(s), administrator(s), authority, board(s). *See also* Administration; Educational administrators.

Educational administrators. Educational administrator(s). *Choose from:* educational, school(s), college(s), universit(y,ies) *with:* administrator(s), admissions officer(s), assistant principal(s), dean(s), principal(s), registrar(s), official(s), financial aid officer(s), coordinator(s), personnel director(s), president(s), superintendent(s), supervisor(s), director(s), department head(s), department(al). *See also* Administrators; Educational administration. chair(men,man, person,persons), headmaster(s), administrative personnel.

Educational aspiration. See *Academic aspiration.*

Educational attainment. Educational attainment. Highest grade completed. Formal education. Degree(s) earned.

Educational background. *Choose from:* educational, academic, schooling *with:* attainment, complet(ed,ion), development, status, level. *See also* Academic achievement; Academic degrees; Educational background; Socioeconomic status.

Educational background. Educational background. Educated. Uneducated. Poorly educated. Level of preparation. Schooled. Formal schooling. Trained. Untrained. Unschooled. Educational correlates. *Choose from:* education(al), academic, training, schooling *with:* experience, background, attainment, level(s), status, completed, degrees earned, preparation, years spent. *See also* Educational attainment; Experience (background); Expertise.

Educational broadcasting. Educational broadcast(s,ing). Telecourse(s). *Consider also:* childrens program(s), documentar(y,ies), docudrama(s). *See also* Educational television.

Educational choice. See *Educational vouchers; School choice.*

Educational counseling. Educational counseling. *Choose from:* education(al), academic *with:* counsel(ing,or,ors), advis(ing,ement,or,ors), advice, guidance, mentor(s,ing). *See also* Academic aspiration; Counseling; School counseling; Vocational guidance.

Educational degrees. See *Academic degrees.*

Educational diagnosis. Educational diagnos(is,es,tic,tics). *Choose from:* education(al), reading, *with:* diagnos(is,es,tic,tics), assessment(s), screening. *See also* Diagnostic tests; Learning disabilities; Reading disabilities.

Educational environment. Educational environment(s). School organizational climate. *Choose from:* educational, academic, school(s), classroom(s), teaching, learning, college(s), universit(y,ies) *with:* environment(s), climate(s), condition(s), setting(s). *See also* Classroom environment; Educational facilities; Hidden curriculum; Organizational climate; Student teacher relations.

Educational equality. See *Equal education.*

Educational equalization. See *Equal education.*

Educational equity. See *Equal education.*

Educational exchange, international. See *International educational exchange.*

Educational facilities. Educational facilit(y,ies). *Choose from:* education(al), school, teaching, instruction(al), college, study, learning *with:* facilit(y,ies), center(s), plant(s), complex(es), room(s), building(s), office(s), space(s). *Consider also:* crafts room(s), classroom(s), carrel(s), audiovisual center(s), study center(s), demonstration center(s), learning laborator(y,ies), learning resource(s) center(s), reading center(s), school shop(s), skill center(s), campus(es), educational laborator(y,ies), language laborator(y,ies), school librar(y,ies). *See also* Colleges; Educational laboratories; Flight schools; Language laboratories; Libraries; Learning centers; Museums; Parks; Schools.

Educational field trips. Educational field trip(s). *Choose from:* educational, school, instructional, class *with:* field, farm, museum, park, zoo *with:* trip(s), visit(s). *See also* Teaching methods.

Educational grading. See *Grading (educational).*

Educational guidance. See *Educational counseling.*

Educational ideologies. Education(al) ideolog(y,ies). Foundations of education. *Choose from:* education(al), pedagog(y, ical), instruction(al), teaching, school, pupil control *with:* ideolog(y,ies,ical), philosoph(y,ies,ical), doctrine(s), tenet(s), canon(s). *See also* Canon (literature); Educational administration; Educational reform.

Educational incentives. Educational incentive(s). *Choose from:* education(al), academic, learning, student(s), pupil(s), classroom *with:* incentive(s), inducement(s), inspir(e,ing,ation), motivat(e, ed,ing,ion,ors), reward(s), stimul(ate,us), encouragement. *Consider also:* educational goals. *See also* Educational motivation; Incentives; Learning contracts; Motivation; Student motivation.

Educational innovations. Educational innovation(s). Reinvent(ing) education. Education reform(s). *Choose from:* education(al), curriculum, school(s), teaching, training *with:* innovation(s), restructur(e,ed,ing), reform(s,ing), alternative(s), new technolog(y,ies), improv(e,ed,ing,ement,ements). *See also* Adoption of ideas; Diffusion of innovation; Extended school year; Home schooling; Innovations; Nontraditional education; Organizational innovation; School schedules.

Educational laboratories. Educational laborator(y,ies). *Choose from:* educational, learning, language, writing, reading, mathematics *with:* laborator(y,ies), lab(s), learning center(s). *See also* Educational facilities; Educational technology; Language laboratories.

Educational malpractice. Educational malpractice. *Choose from:* education(al), instruction(al), academic, pedagog(y, ical), educator(s), faculty, teacher(s), professor(s) *with:* malpractice, negligence suit(s), misguidance, misfeasance. *See also* Accountability; Professional ethics; Student teacher relations.

Educational management. See *Educational administration.*

Educational measurement. Educational measurement. *Choose from:* educational, achievement, equivalency, mastery, competenc(e,y,ies), admission, entrance, student(s), proficiency, academic, scholastic *with:* measur(e,es,ement, ements,ing), test(s,ing), criteria, examination(s), evaluation(s), assess(ed,ing,ment,ments). *See also* Educational diagnosis; Entrance examinations; Grading (educational); Minimum competencies; Screening.

Educational media. See *Instructional media.*

Educational methods. See *Teaching methods.*

Educational motivation. Educational motivation. *Choose from:* education(al), student, academic achievement, learning, classroom, study, scholastic *with:* motivat(ed,ing,ion,ional), aspiration(s), persistence, incentive(s). *See also* Educational incentives; Motivation; Student motivation.

Educational needs. Educational need(s). *Choose from:* education(al), student(s), instruction(al), training, literacy, curriculum, skill(s), information *with:* need(s,ed,ing), basic(s), necessary, necessit(y,ies), requirement(s), requisite(s), prerequisite(s), essential(s), core course(s), insufficien(t,cy,cies), lack(s,ing), deprivation, deficien(cy, cies), demand(s). *See also* Culturally relevant pedagogy; Educational objectives; Nontraditional education; Relevance; Special education.

Educational objectives. Educational objective(s). *Choose from:* education(al), course, instructional, teacher(s), school(s), training, academic *with:* objective(s), goal(s), purpose(s). *See also* Academic aspirations; Educational environment; Educational needs; Educational plans; Lesson plans; Objectives.

Educational opportunities. Educational opportunit(y,ies). *Choose from:* education(al), academic, learning, student(s), pupil(s), training, college, school *with:* opportunit(y,ies), alternative(s), possibilit(y,ies), choice(s). *See also* Access to education; Affirmative action; Compulsory education; Equal education; Nontraditional education.

Educational personnel. See *Educational administrators; Faculty; School counselors; Teachers.*

Educational placement. Educational placement. *Choose from:* educational, student(s), school(s), class(es), grade(s) *with:* placement(s), eligibility decision(s). *See also* Ability grouping; Educational diagnosis; Inclusive education; Mainstreaming; Remedial reading; Screening; Special education.

Educational plans. Educational plan(s). *Choose from:* education(al), academic, learning, student(s), pupil(s), training, college, school *with:* plan(s), intent(ions), aspiration(s), goal(s), ambition(s). *See also* Academic aspirations; Academic degrees; Educational objectives; Life plans.

Educational programs. Educational program(s). *Choose from:* education(al), academic, scholastic, school, learning, training, teaching, instruction(al), study *with:* program(s), activit(y,ies), schedule(s). *See also* Courses; Curriculum; Internships; Literacy programs; Tracking (education).

Educational psychology. Educational psychology. *Choose from:* education(al), learning, teaching, pedagog(y,ical), classroom, instruction(al) *with:* psycholog(y,ical). *See also* Applied psychology; Social psychology.

Educational reform. Educational reform(s). *Choose from:* education(al), academic, school, pedagog(y,ical), instruction(al), university, college, classroom *with:* reform(s), change(s), restructur(e,ed, ing), revis(e,ed,ing,ion,ions), improv(e, ed,ing,ment,ments), reorganiz(e,ed, ing,ation,ations). *See also* Change agents; Educational ideologies; Extended school year; Policy; School schedules.

Educational segregation. See *School segregation.*

Educational status. See *Educational attainment.*

Educational technology. Educational technology. Instructional technology. *Choose from:* educator(s), teach(ing,er, ers), classroom(s), instruct(ed,ing,ion), learn(ed,ing), education(al) *with:* technolog(y,ical), high-tech, computer(s, ized), software, Internet, World Wide Web, digital librar(y,ies), media, multimedia. *See also* Audiovisual materials; Computer assisted instruction; Distance education; Educational laboratories; Educational television; Instructional media; Programed instruction; Teaching materials.

Educational television. Educational television. *Choose from:* educational, instructional, informational, public service, course(s) *with:* televis(ed,ion),

video, videocassette(s), TV. *See also* Audiovisual materials; Educational broadcasting; Educational technology; Television; Television programs.

Educational toys. Educational toy(s). *Choose from:* educational, instructional, enrichment, learning *with:* toy(s), game(s), play material(s). *See also* Toy industry; Toys.

Educational vouchers. Educational voucher(s). Voucher plan(s). Voucher program(s). *Choose from:* school(s), education(al) *with:* voucher(s). *See also* Private schools; Privatization; Reimbursement mechanisms; Scholarships (educational); School choice; Student financial aid; Tuition reimbursement.

Educators. See *Elementary school teachers; Faculty; High school teachers; Junior high school teachers; Teachers.*

Effect, autokinetic. See *Autokinetic effect.*

Effect, greenhouse. See *Greenhouse effect.*

Effect, halo. See *Halo effect.*

Effect, primacy. See *Primacy effect.*

Effectiveness. Effective(ness). Efficac(y,ious,iousness). Effectivity. Competenc(e,y). Adequa(cy,te). Capabilit(y,ies). Efficien(t,cy). Useful(ness). Practical. Productiv(e, eness,ity). Positive impact. Successful(ness). Proficien(t,cy). Sufficien(t,cy). *See also* Accountability; Achievement; Effects; Efficiency; Evaluation; Failure; Feasibility; Organizational effectiveness; Productivity; Program evaluation; Redundancy; Relevance; Self efficacy; Success; Treatment efficacy; Treatment outcome.

Effectiveness, cost. See *Cost effectiveness.*

Effectiveness, organizational. See *Organizational effectiveness.*

Effectiveness training, parent. See *Parent training.*

Effects. Effect(s). Consequence(s). Result(s). Outcome(s). Sequel(a,ae). Repercussion(s). Aftereffect(s). Byproduct(s). Backlash. Outgrowth. Ripple effect(s). Domino effect(s). Side effect(s). Reaction(s). Aftermath. Response(s). Impact(s). *Consider also:* imping(e,ed,ing) upon, affected, influenced. *See also* Acceleration effects; Altitude effects; Causality; Drug effects; Effectiveness; Environmental effects; Followup studies; Forecasting; Gravitational effects; Heat effects; Mass media effects; Means ends; Noise effects; Relevance; Sequelae; Temperature effects; Treatment outcome; Underwater effects.

Effects, acceleration. See *Acceleration effects.*

Effects, altitude. See *Altitude effects.*

Effects, drug. See *Drug effects.*

Effects, elevation. See *Altitude effects.*

Effects, environmental. See *Environmental effects.*

Effects, gravitational. See *Gravitational effects.*

Effects, heat. See *Heat effects.*

Effects, mass media. See *Mass media effects.*

Effects, noise. See *Noise effects.*

Effects, side drugs. See *Drug effects.*

Effects, television. See *Mass media effects.*

Effects, temperature. See *Temperature effects.*

Effects, underwater. See *Underwater effects.*

Effects of technology, workplace. See *Labor aspects of technology.*

Effeminacy. Effemina(cy,te). Unmanly. Overrefine(d,ment). Feminine qualit(y,ies). Epicen(e,ism). Miss-Nancyish. Pans(yish,ified). Prissy. Siss(y,ified). *See also* Feminization; Transvestism.

Efficacy. See *Effectiveness; Self efficacy.*

Efficacy, self. See *Self efficacy.*

Efficacy, treatment. See *Treatment efficacy.*

Efficacy expectations. See *Self efficacy.*

Efficiency. Efficien(t,cy,cies). Effective(ness). Efficac(y,ious,iousness). Adept(ness). Competen(t,ce). Expert(ise). Proficien(t,cy). Capab(le, ility). Resourceful(ness). Productiv(e, ity). *Consider also:* mastery, prowess, skill(ed,s,ful,fulness). *See also* Cost effectiveness; Effectiveness; Operations research; Resource management.

Efficiency, employee. See *Employee efficiency.*

Efficiency, industrial. See *Industrial efficiency.*

Efficiency, managerial. See *Organizational effectiveness.*

Effigies. Effig(y,ies). Efigie(s). *Consider also:* voodoo doll(s),scarecrow(s), likeness(es), magia imitativa, idol(s), la quema de Judas, la quema del diablo. *See also* Emblems; Folk culture.

Effluents. See *Sewage.*

Effort. See *Energy expenditure (physical).*

Egalitarian families. Egalitarian famil(y,ies). *Choose from:* famil(y,ies ,ial), marriage(s), marital, spous(e,es,al), conjugal, husband wife, sex role(s), parenting, *with:* egalitarian(ism), role sharing, equity, equal(ity), division of labor, balanc(e,ed,ing) power. *Consider also:* marital symmetry. *See also* Dual career families; Power sharing; Sex roles; Sexual Division of Labor; Shared parenting.

Egalitarianism. Egalitarian(ism). Equalitarian(ism). Equal(ity). Coequal(ity). Parity. Impartial(ity). Nondiscriminat(ion,ory). Equity. Equal pay. Equal worth. Equal(ity) before the law. *Consider also:* democracy, reciprocity, fair(ness), justice, social justice, communal, socialism, industrial democracy, classless. *See also* Classless society; Coeducation; Democracy; Equal education; Equal job opportunities; Equity (payment); Industrial Democracy; Justice; Single sex schools; Socialism; Social equality; Social equity; Social justice.

Ego. Ego. Self. Identit(y,ies). Superego. Alter-ego. *Consider also:* self concept, egoism, body image, self congruence, self esteem, self awareness, self efficacy. *See also* Egoism; Pride; Self esteem; Self concept; Self psychology.

Ego dystonic homosexuality. Ego dystonic homosexuality. *Choose from:* homosexual(ity), lesbian(ism) *with:* ego-alien, conflict(s), denial, unwanted feeling(s), distressful impulse(s). *See also* Denial (psychology); Homosexuality.

Ego state, adult. See *Emotional maturity.*

Egocentrism. Egocentri(c,city,sm). Self bias. Self centered(ness). Preoccup(ied, ation) with self. Self focus(ed). *Consider also:* solipsis(m,tic), self concern(ed), selfish(ness), self reference, self interest, self gratification, self serving. *See also* Cognitive development; Egotism; Narcissism; Personality traits; Self consciousness; Self psychology; Selfishness (egocentric); Solipsism.

Egoism. Egois(m,t,tic). Self importan(t,ce). Self assur(ed,ance). Self confiden(t,ce). Self possess(ed,ion). *Consider also:* conceit(ed), egotis(m,tical), self pride, self glory, self importan(t,ce). *See also* Ego; Narcissism; Pride; Self esteem; Self concept; Snobs and snobbishness.

Egotism. Egotis(m,tic,tical). Egocentri(c, city,sm). Egois(m,tic,tical). *Consider also:* self importan(t,ce), egomania, egopathy, conceit(ed), self admiration, vain, vanity, self satisf(ied,ication), boastful(ness). *See also* Egocentrism; Narcissism; Self consciousness; Self interest; Snobs and snobbishness.

Egress. Egress(ion). Depart(ing,ure). Exit(s,ing,ed). Outlet(s). Escape(s,ed, ing). Way out. *Consider also:* door(s), gateway(s), vent(s). *See also* Exits; Halls; Openings.

Eidetic imagery. Eidetic image(ry,s). Primary memory image(s,ry). Photographic memor(y,ies). *See also* Ekphrasis; Episodic memory; Spatial memory.

Eighteenth century. Eighteenth century. 18th century. 1700's. American revolution. French revolution. Enlightenment period. *See also* Historical periods; Nineteenth century.

Ejaculation. Ejaculat(e,ed,ing,ory,ion,ions). *Consider also:* male orgasm(s), nocturnal emission(s). *See also* Ejaculatory incompetence; Orgasm; Premature ejaculation.

Ejaculation, premature. See *Premature ejaculation.*

Ejaculatory incompetence. Ejaculatory incompetence. Coitus sine ejaculatione. Ejaculatio deficiens. Dry orgasm(s). *See also* Ejaculation.

Ekphrasis. Ekphras(is,tic). Ecphras(is,tic). Transference between visual and verbal art. *Consider also:* literary response(s), verbal representation(s), poetry, poes(y,ies) *with:* visual art(s), visual experience(s). *See also* Eidetic imagery; Figurative language; Imagery; Imagination; Metaphors.

Elder abuse. Elder abuse. Crime(s) against the elderly. Granny bashing. Granny dumping. King Lear syndrome. *Choose from:* abus(e,es,ed,ive,ing), cruel(ty), harass(ed,es,ing,ment,ments), threat(s, en,ened,ens,ening), victim(s,ize,izes, ized,izing,ization), tortur(e,es,ed,ing), mistreat(ed,s,ing,ment,ments), maltreat(ed,s,ing,ment), molest(ed,s, ing), batter(s,ed,ing), brutal(ity,ities), violen(ce,t), mugging(s), neglect(ed, ing), assault(s,ed,ing) *with:* elderly, aged, senior citizen(s), nursing home patients, old(er) people, grandparent(s), parent(s), grandmother(s), grandfather(s). *See also* Age discrimination; Aged 80 and over; Attitudes toward the aged; Caregiver burden; Cruelty; Elderly; Family violence; Self neglect; Torture.

Elderly. Elder(s,ly). Geriatric. Gerontology. Older adult(s). Advanced age. Older American(s). Old(er) people. Old age. Senium. Senescen(ce,t). Seniors. Senior citizen(s). Older persons. Grandparent(s, hood). Age related deficits. Gray power. Grey power. Gray Panthers. Ageful. Advanced in years. Pensioner(s). Retire(d,ment,e,es). Postretirement. Grandmother(s). Grandfather(s). Old(er) men. Old(er) women. Old(er) man. Old(er) woman. Later years. Later adulthood. Matur(e,ity). Sexagenarian(s). Septuagenarian(s). Octogenarian(s). Nonagenarian(s). Centenarian(s). Over 70. Aged. *Consider also:* geezer(s), young old (65–75), old old (75–85), grann(y,ies), crone(s), hag(s), gramp(s), golden years, sunset years, old folks, oldest old, almost old (62–64), longevity. *See also* Age discrimination; Aged 80 and over; Aging; Attitudes toward the aged;

Dependent parents; Elder abuse; Elderly offenders; Filial responsibility; Frail elderly; Generation gap; Geriatric patients; Geriatric psychotherapy; Gerontocracy; Grandparents; Gray power; Human life cycle; Intergenerational relations; Middle age; Pensions; Retirement; Widowhood.

Elderly, frail. See *Frail Elderly.*

Elderly, homes for. See *Homes for the elderly.*

Elderly day care. See *Adult day care.*

Elderly liberation movement. See *Gray power.*

Elderly offenders. Elderly offender(s). Aged offender(s). *Choose from:* elderly, aged, older *with:* offender(s), offense(s), crime(s), criminal(s), shoplift(ers,ing). *See also* Elderly; Offenders.

Elected officials. Elected official(s). Public office holders. Elected city official(s). Politician(s). Legislator(s). Judge(s). Congress(man,men,woman,women). Senator(s). Elected representative(s). Lawmaker(s). Member(s) of Congress. Mayor(s). Town supervisor(s). Governor(s). Lieutenant governor(s). President(s). Vice president(s). Premier(s). Prime minister(s). Member(s) of Parliament. Member(s) of boards of education. County supervisor(s). County executive(s). County legislator(s). City manager(s). Member(s) of the House of Commons. City council(man,men,woman,women). Assembly(man,men,woman,women). Select(man,men,woman,women). County coroner(s). County executive(s). *Consider also:* government official(s). *See also* Elections; Governors; Government personnel; Judicial candidates; Legislative bodies; Legislators; Local officials and employees; Political candidates; Politicians; Public officers; Tenure of office.

Election campaigns. See *Political campaigns.*

Election districts. Election district(s). Ward(s). Precinct(s). *Choose from:* election, legislative, Congressional, electoral *with:* district(s). *Consider also:* gerrymander(ed,ing). *See also* Areas; Districts; Elections; Parishes; Political geography.

Election forecasting. See *Political forecasting.*

Election law. Election law(s). *Choose from:* election(s), voting right(s), vote, electoral, ballot(s) *with:* law(s), constitution(ality), statute(s). *Consider also:* Elections Act. Voting Rights Act. *See also* Ballots; Campaign finance reform; Elections; Laws; Voting.

Elections. Elect(ed,ing,ion,ions,orate). Vot(e,ed,ing,er,ers). Voter registration. Political poll(s). Primar(y,ies). Ballot(ing,s). Voting machine(s). Choos(e,ing) president(s), senator(s), congress(men,man, woman,women, person,persons), etc. Plebiscite(s). *Choose from:* primary, nonpartisan, at-large, district, presidential, state(wide), congressional, general *with:* election(s), race(s), campaign(s). *Consider also:* suffrage, poll tax(es), voting behavior, voting rights, voting precinct(s), polling place(s), campaign issue(s), referendum, constituenc(y,ies), franchise, disenfranchise(ment), psepholog(y,ical,ist). *See also* Absentee voting; Ballots; Election law; Legislators; Local elections; Political candidates; Political parties; Political reform; Preference voting; Primaries; Recall of government officials; Voters; Voting.

Elections, local. See *Local elections.*

Elections, political. See *Elections.*

Elective. Elective(ly,ness). Appointive. Chosen. Choos(e,ing). Discretionar(y,iness). Option(s,al). Nonobligator(y,ily). Non- obligator(y,ily). Voluntar(y,ily,iness). *Consider also:* facultative(ly). *See also* Choice behavior; Choices (alternatives); Decisions; Discretion.

Elective mutism. Elective(ly) mut(e,eness, ist,ists,ism). Reluctant speech. *Consider also:* selective(ly), psychogenic, situation specific mut(e,ism). *See also* Mutism.

Electorate. Electorate. Voter(s). Taxpayer(s). Constituen(t,ts,cy,cies). Citizen(s). Balloter(s). *See also* Citizens; Voters; Voting.

Electra complex. Electra complex(es). *Choose from:* electra *with:* conflict(s), complex(es). *Consider also:* oedip(al,us) *with:* women, woman, girl(s). *See also* Oedipus complex; Psychoanalytic interpretation.

Electric currents. Electric current(s). Amper(e,es,age). *Consider also:* constant current(s), volt(s,age), flow of electricity, alternating current(s), direct current(s). *See also* Electricity.

Electric power plants. Electric power plant(s). Generator(s). Generating plant(s). *Consider also:* utility plant(s). *See also* Electricity; Energy generating resources; Fuel.

Electric shock. See *Electroschock.*

Electric utilities. Electric utilit(y,ies). Power utilit(y,ies). Light compan(y,ies). *See also* Electricity; Public utilities.

Electricity. Electric current(s). Electric power. *See also* Cations; Electric currents; Electric power plants; Electric utilities; Electrification.

Electrification. Electrif(y,ied,ication). *Choose from:* provid(e,ed,ing) *with:* electric(ity), power, sustainable energy. *Consider also:* Rural Utilities Service. *See also* Electricity; Industrialization; Modernization; Rural development; Rural industries.

Electrification, rural. See *Rural development.*

Electro-acoustic music. See *Electronic music.*

Electroconvulsive therapy. See *Shock therapy.*

Electrocutions. Electrocut(e,ed,ing,ion, ions). Electric chair(s). Fatal electrical shock(s). *Choose from:* live wire(s), electrified, downed power line(s), electric(ity) *with:* fatal,(ity,ities), mortalit(y,ities), dead, death, execut(e,ed,ing,ion,ions). *See also* Accidents; Death penalty.

Electroencephalography. Electroencephalograph(y,ic). EEG. Brain wave analys(is,es). Record(ed,ing) brain waves. Electroencephalogram(s). *See also* Alpha rhythm; Diagnostic tests.

Electronic books. Electronic book(s). Online book(s). Cybertext(s). *Choose from:* online, digital, digitize(d), hypertext, CDROM, electronic, full text, computerized, interactive, multimedia *with:* book(s), librar(y,ies), fiction, literary work(s), prose, Bible(s), encyclopedia(s), edition(s), atlas(es), monograph(s), dictionar(y,ies), text(s). *Consider also:* electronic source(s), online material(s). *See also* Electronic publishing; Electronic journals; Full-text databases.

Electronic commerce. See *E-commerce.*

Electronic cottages. See *Home-based businesses.*

Electronic crimes. See *Computer crimes.*

Electronic data interchange. Electronic data interchange. EDI. *Consider also:* filing electronically, electronic funds transfer, electronic tax form(s), paperless exchange of business document(s), digital signature(s). *See also* Digital money; Digital signatures; E-commerce; Interactive computer systems; Internet (computer network); Information highway; Information society; Performance standards; Quality control; Regulation; V-commerce.

Electronic data processing. Electronic data processing. Automatic data processing. *See also* Automated information storage; Data processing; Office automation.

Electronic eavesdropping. Electronic eavesdropping. Bug(s,ging,ged). Wiretap(ping,ped,s). Tap(ping,ped) phone(s). Tap(ping,ped) telephone(s). Listening device(s). Electronic bug(s).

Electronic surveillance. *Choose from:* monitor(ed,ing), intercept(ed,ing,ion) *with:* conversation(s), communication(s), message(s), wire, radio, voice, data, computer, verbal. *Choose from:* eavesdropping *with:* electronic, satellite(s), telephone(s), phone(s), device(s). Signals intelligence. SIGINT. *See also* Computer crimes; Cyber attacks; Cyberlaw; Debugging; Digital communications; Eavesdropping; Industrial espionage; Intelligence service; Invasion of privacy; Jamming of communications; Military intelligence; Online privacy; Right of privacy; Surveillance of citizens.

Electronic equipment. Electronic equipment. Electronic instrument(s). *Choose from:* electronic, electric, batter(y,ies) *with:* device(s), equipment, instrument(s), component(s), chassis. *See also* Computers; Equipment; Mobile computing; Scientific equipment.

Electronic games. Electronic game(s). Video game(s). Atari. Nintendo. *Choose from:* electronic, video *with:* football, baseball, golf, game(s), entertainment. *Consider also:* computer game(s), learning game(s). *See also* Adult games; Children's games; Computer games; Computers; Entertainment; Leisure activities.

Electronic instruments. Electronic instrument(s). Electric instrument(s). Electric guitar(s). Hypercello(s). Hyperinstrument(s). Electronic keyboard(s). Ondes Martenot(s). Ondes musicale(s). Hammond organ(s). Novachord(s). Theremin(s). Trautonium(s). Electrophone(s). *Choose from:* electric, electronic, electro-acoustic, electrostatic, electromagnetic *with:* guitar(s), keyboard(s), flute(s), saxophone(s), violin(s), viola(s), cello(s), bass(es), carillon(s), piano(s), kettledrum(s), organ(s). *Consider also:* telharmonium(s), synthesizer(s). *See also* Electronic music; Musical instruments; Popular culture.

Electronic journals. Electronic journal(s). Zine(s). E-zine(s). E-journal(s). Cyberzine(s). Electronic fanzine(s). Webzine(s). *Choose from:* online, electronic *with:* journal(s), magazine(s), periodical(s). *Consider also:* full-text database(s). *See also* Electronic books; Electronic publishing; Fanzines; Full-text databases; Internet (computer network); Magazine advertising; Periodicals; Push technology; Virtual libraries.

Electronic mail. Electronic mail. Computer mail. E-mail. Email. Instant message(s). *Consider also:* electronic banking, electronic tax filing(s). *See also* Direct mail advertising; Digital communications; Digital signatures; E-commerce;

Information dissemination; Junk email; Letters (correspondence); Office automation; Push technology; Telecommunications; V-commerce.

Electronic money. See *Digital money.*

Electronic music. Electronic music. Electroacoustic music. Electro-acoustic music. Concrete music. Musique concrete. Techno music. Electronic ambient music. Computer-aided music. Electronic dance music. *Consider also:* rave music, chill out, tape music, sound synthesizer(s). *See also* Computer music; Electronic instruments; Electronic organs; Experimental music; Music; Popular culture; Serial music; Twentieth century Western art music.

Electronic organs. Electronic organ(s). Hammond organ(s). Wurlitzer organ(s). *See also* Electronic music; Musical instruments; Organs (music).

Electronic publishing. Electronic publishing. Electronic text(s). Electronic journal(s). *Choose from:* electronic, online, optical, machine readable, microcomputer, CD-ROM, Internet, network, disk(s), disc(s) *with:* publish(ed,ing), publication(s), information dissemination, document(s), news service(s), journal(s), serial(s), book(s), director(y,ies), media, newsletter(s), bulletin board(s). *Consider also:* paperless book(s). *See also* Clip art; Computers; Copyright; Cyberlaw; Databases; Desktop publishing; Digital communications; Electronic books; Electronic journals; Full-text databases; Information dissemination; Internet (computer network); Office automation; Publishing; Push technology.

Electronic surveillance. See *Electronic eavesdropping.*

Electronic trading (securities). Electronic trading. Online trading. Online securities trading. Online stock trading. Online broker(s,age). *Choose from:* electronic, E, online, Internet *with:* broker(s,age), trading, track(ing), buy(ing), sell(ing), list(ing) *with:* securities, investments, mutual funds, stocks. *See also* E-commerce; Investments; Stock brokers; Stock exchange; Stockholders.

Electronics industry. See *High technology industries.*

Electronics industry workers. Electronics industry worker(s). High tech worker(s). *Choose from:* electronic(s), high technology, high tech, advanced technolog(y,ies), mechatronic(s), semiconductor(s), microelectronic(s), computer(s), microcomputer(s), telecommunication(s), General Electric, Sony, Texas Instruments, etc. *with:* engineer(s), technician(s), manager(s), executive(s), staff, worker(s),

employee(s), personnel, official(s). *See also* High technology industries; Workers.

Electroshock. Electroshock(s,ed). Electroconvulsive shock(s,ed). Electric shock(s). Shock(ed,ing) by electricity. Electric foot shock(s). Footshock(s). *See also* Negative reinforcement; Punishment; Shock therapy.

Electrosleep treatment. Electrosleep treatment(s). Electrosleep therap(y,ies). Electrotherap(y,ies). *Consider also:* electronarcosis, electroanesthesia, electric anesthesia, electroanalgesia, electroacupuncture. *See also* Shock therapy; Sleep treatment.

Elegance. Elegan(ce,t,tly). Beaut(y,iful). Daint(y,iness). Delicate(ness). Digni(ty,fied). Exquisite(ness). Good taste. Gorgeous(ness). Grace(ful, fulness). Handsome(ness). Tasteful(ness). Lovel(y,iness). Lush(ness). Luxurious(ness). Magnificen(t,ce). Majestic. Opulen(t,ce). Ornate(ness). Rich(ness). Splend(or,id). Statel(y,iness). Superior(ity). Stylish(ness). Sumptuous(ness). *Consider also:* charm(ing), cultivat(ed,ion), culture(d), polish(ed), refine(d,ment), sophisticat(ed,ion), propriety, urban(e,ity), ornament(ed, ation), precision, restraint, neat(ness), simpl(e,icity), well made. *See also* Aesthetics; Attractiveness; Classic (standard); Cosmopolitan; Sophistication; Styles.

Elegiac poetry. Elegiac poe(try,m,ms). *Choose from:* elegiac(al) *with:* poe(try,m,ms), couplet(s), stanza(s), distich(s), quatrain(s). *Consider also:* eleg(y,ies). *See also* Elegies; Narrative poetry; Poetry.

Elegies. Eleg(y,ie,ies). *Consider also:* lament(s,ation,ations), nostalgi(a,c), epitaph(s). *See also* Commemoration; Elegiac poetry; Epitaphs; Laments; Poetry.

Elementarism. See *Reductionism.*

Elementary education. Elementary education. *Choose from:* primary, elementary *with:* school(s), education, grade(s). Grade school(s). Middle school(s). *See also* Elementary school students; Elementary schools; Intermediate school students; Primary education.

Elementary school students. Elementary school student(s). First grader(s), 2d grader(s), etc. Grade school student(s). *Choose from:* elementary, primary, middle, intermediate, grammar *with:* school(s), grade(s) *with:* student(s), pupil(s), child(ren). *See also* Elementary schools; Intermediate school students; Primary school students.

Elementary school teachers. Elementary school teacher(s). Grade school teacher(s). *Choose from:* grammar, elementary, primary, middle, intermediate *with:* school *with:* teacher(s). *See also* Elementary schools.

Elementary schools. Elementary school(s). Grade school(s). *Choose from:* grammar, primary, elementary, intermediate, middle *with:* school(s), grade(s). *Consider also:* grade one, grade two, grade three, grade four, grade five, grade six, first grade, second grade, third grade, fourth grade, fifth grade, sixth grade. *See also* Elementary education; Elementary school teachers.

Elephants. Elephant(s,idae). Loxodonta Africana. Elephas maximus. *See also* Animals; Vertebrates.

Elevation effects. See *Altitude effects.*

Eligibility determination. Eligibility determination *Choose from:* eligib(le,ility), disabilit(y,ies), work capacity, handicap(ped,s), age *with:* evaluat(e,ed,ing,ion,ions), review(s), screen(ed,ing), determin(e,ed,ing, ation,ations), requirement(s), rat(e,ed,ings), criter(ia,ion), certificat(e,ion), assess(ed,ing, ment,ments). *See also* Disability evaluation; Needs assessment.

Elite, business. See *Economic elites.*

Elite, power. See *Power elite.*

Elites. Elite(s,ist,ists,ism). Privileged class(es). Celebrit(ies,y). High rank(ing). Peerage. Advantaged. Intelligentsia. Intellectual(s). Leadership group(s). Oligarch(y,ies). Ruler(s). Aristocra(cy, t,ts). Leisure class. New class. Priviligentsia. Jet set. Inner circle(s). Inner group(s). Mandarin(ate,s). Important people. Gentry. Nobility. Ruling class(es). Upper class(es). Upper echelon. Opinion maker(s). Opinion leader(s). Influential(s). Authorities. Power broker(s). Kingmaker(s). Power behind the throne. Influential(s). Power elite(s). Power structure. Political elite(s). Social elite(s). Privileged class(es). Prestig(e,ious). First famil(y,ies). Social register. Dominant class. Rentier(s). Insider(s). Big wig(s). Top brass. Snob(s). Highbrow(s). Chattering class(es). Mover(s) and shaker(s). Ivy league. *Choose from:* television, TV, entertainment, film, sports, media *with:* star(s), personalit(y, ies). *Choose from:* economic, business, military, government(al), religious, church *with:* elite(s), leader(s,ship). *See also* Aristocracy; Brahmans; Economic elites; Elitism (government); Gentry; Intelligentsia; Political elites; Power elite; Power structure; Preferential treatment; Privilege; Ruling class; Scientific community; Social structure; Status attainment; Upper class; Wealth.

Elites, corporate. See *Economic elites.*

Elites, economic. See *Economic elites.*

Elites, political. See *Political elites.*

Elites, social. See *Elites.*

Elitism (government). Elitis(m,t,ts). Elite(s). Dominance by powerful. Governance by powerful minority. Ruling elite(s). Party elite(s). Ruling group(s). *Choose from:* weighted voting, veto power, power elite(s), oligarch(y, ies). *See also* Hegemony; Political elites; Political power.

Eloquence. Eloquen(t,ce). Persuasive discourse. Fluen(cy,t). Articulate(ness). Expressive(ness). Expressiv(e,ity). Persuasiv(e,eness). Forceful(ness). *See also* Fluency; Oratory; Rhetoric; Self expression.

Elves. Elves. Elf. Leprechaun(s). Cluricaune(s). *Consider also:* dwarf, dwarves, dvergar(s). *See also* Demons; Devils; Fairies.

Email. See *Electronic mail.*

Email, junk. See *Junk email.*

Emancipation. Emancipat(e,ed,ing,ion). Free(ing). Gain(ed,ing) freedom. Liberat(e,ed,ing,ion). Enfranchis(e,ed, ement,ing). Manumit(ting). Manumission. Releas(e,ed,ing) from slavery. Releas(e,ed,ing) from bondage. *See also* Abolitionists; Civil war; Freedom; Freedmen; Fugitive slaves; Liberty; Personal independence; Salvation.

Embargo. Embargo(ed,es). Economic blockade(s). *Choose from:* curtail(ed, ing), prohibit(ed,ing,ion), stop(ped, ping,page), ban(ned,ning), restrict(ed, ing,ion,ions), bar(red,ring), curb(ed, ing,s), restrain(t,ed,ing), suspend(ed, ing), suspension, cutoff(s) *with:* trade, import(s,ing), sale(s), export(s), goods, commerce, purchase(s), shipment(s). *Consider also:* boycott(s), economic leverage, economic sanction(s). *See also* Boycotts; Exports; Imports; Maritime war; Prohibition; Tariffs; Trade; Trade protection.

Embarrassment. Embarrass(ed,ing,ment). Self conscious(ness). Sham(e,ed,ing). Ashamed. Stage fright. Humiliat(e,ed,ion). Losing face. Social inhibition(s). Chagrined. Abash(ed,ment,ing). Bashful(ness). Blush(ed,ing). *Consider also:* discomfit(ure), discompos(e,ed,ure), disconcert(ed,ing,ion,ment), chagrin(ed). *See also* Blushing; Emotions; Guilt; Humiliation; Self consciousness; Shame.

Embassies. Embass(y,ies). Consulate(s). Consular office(s). Legation(s). Diplomatic office(s). *Consider also:* ministr(y,ies), embassade(s). *See also* Commissions; Delegations; Diplomacy (official); Diplomatic privileges and immunities.

Embellishment. See *Decoration.*

Embellishment (music). Embellishment(s). Ornament(s,ation). Agrement(s). Fioritur(a,e). Verzierung(en). Manier(en). Appoggiatura(s). Acciaccatur(a,e). Trill(s). *Consider also:* grace note(s), diminution, augmentation, mordent(e,s). *See also* Acciaccatura; Music; Ornamentation (music).

Embezzlement. Embezzl(e,ed,ing, ement,er,ers). *Choose from:* financial *with:* scandal(s), impropriet(y,ies). *Choose from:* misappropriat(e,ed,ing, ion,ions), steal(th,ing), stole(n), loot(ed,ing), abscond(ed,ing), defraud(ed,ing), bilk(ed,ing), theft, thievery, larceny, pilfer(ed,ing), siphon(ed,ing), misus(e,ed,ing), divert(ed,ing), plunder(ed,ing) *with:* fund(s), money, profit(s). *See also* Crime; Computer crimes; Drug trafficking; Fraud; Smuggling; Theft; White collar crime.

Emblems. Emblem(s,atic). Flag(s). Seal(s). State flower(s). Insignia. Heraldic device(s). Great seal(s). Token(s). Memento(s). *See also* Effigies; Flags; Insignia; National emblems; Political symbolism; Printers marks; Symbolism; Totemism.

Emblems, national. See *National emblems.*

Embourgeoisement. Embourgeoisement. Middle class attitude(s). Middle class value(s). Middle class standard(s). Middle class perception(s). Values of the middle class. *Choose from:* middle class, bourgeois(ie) *with:* standard(s), culture, attitude(s), value(s), belief(s), ideolog(y, ical,ies), stereotype(s), interest(s), characteristic(s), tolerance, morality, bias(es), norm(s), mores, preference(s), cultur(e,al), notion(s), social code(s), ethic(al,s), prejudice(s,d), view(s), lifestyle(s), orientation(s), acceptance, perception(s), mindset, liberalism, conservatism. *Consider also:* consumer society, admass, organization man. *See also* Bourgeoisie; Consumer society; Lifestyle; Popular culture; Shopping centers; Social conformity; Social mobility; Social values; Traditionalism; Working class.

Embryology. Embryo(nic,s,ology,ologies). Embryogenesis. *Consider also:* fetus(es), zygote(s). *See also* Developmental stages; Fetus; Prenatal development; Sex differentiation (embryogenetic).

Emergencies. Emergenc(y,ies). *Consider also:* cris(is,es), exigen(t,cy), urgen(t,cy), critical situation(s), desperate(ly), acute situation(s), call(s) for action, zero hour. *See also* Accidents; Assistance in emergencies; Crises; Disasters; Family crises; Fire; Good samaritans; Natural disasters; Victimization.

Emergencies, assistance in. See *Assistance in emergencies.*

Emergency contraception. Emergency contracept(ion,ive,ives). Morning after birth control. Morning after pill(s). *Consider also:* overdose(s,d) *with:* Ovral, Lo-Ovral, Triphasil, Nordette, RU-486. *See also* Abortifacients; Birth control; Oral contraceptives.

Emergency currency. Emergency currenc(y,ies). Emergency monetary measure(s). *Choose from:* emergency *with:* coin(s), bank note(s), loan(s), scrip. *Consider also:* currency stabilization, emergency aid, paper currency. *See also* Currency; Devaluation of currency; Money supply.

Emergency medical technicians. Emergency medical technician(s). *Choose from:* emergency, ambulance, rescue *with:* personnel, staff(s), technician(s), paramedic(s), attendant(s), worker(s), team(s). *See also* Allied health personnel.

Emergency medicine. Emergency medicine. Traumatology. Emergency room(s). *Consider also:* emergenc(y,ies), disaster(s), catastrophe(s), accident(s) *with:* medicine, medical, care, physician(s), surg(ical,ery). *See also* Disaster planning; Disaster relief; Emergency services.

Emergency preparedness. See *Disaster planning.*

Emergency services. Emergency service(s). *Choose from:* emergenc(y,ies), rescue, crisis, casualt(y,ies), disaster(s), trauma, burn(s), poison control *with:* service(s), squad(s), center(s), ward(s), department(s), room(s), unit(s), program(s), readiness. *Consider also:* ambulance(s), shelter(s), first aid, resuscitation, hotline(s), suicide prevention, triage. *See also* Assistance in emergencies; Crisis intervention; Disaster relief; Emergency medicine; Help lines (telephone); Psychiatric emergency services; Rape crisis counseling; Rescue; Shelters; Suicide prevention; Trauma centers; Walk-in clinics.

Emergency services, psychiatric. See *Psychiatric emergency services.*

Emerging markets. Emerging market(s). *Choose from:* emerging, developing countr(y,ies), developing econom(y,ies), 21st century, tomorrow, future, potential, expansion, expand(s,ed,ing), fast growing *with:* market(s), import(s,ed, ing), export(s,ed,ing), trading partner(s). *Consider also:* commercial opportunit(y,ies), emerging econom(y,ies), regional economic driver(s). *See also* Balance of trade; Commerce; Exports; Foreign trade regulation; Imports; International trade; Small businesses.

Emigrants. Emigrant(s). Emigre(s). Refugee(s). Defector(s). Displaced person(s). Transient(s). Defector(s). Nomad(s). Migrant(s). Migrator(s). Migratory worker(s). Exile(s,d). Expatriate(s). Wetback(s). Brain drain. Nansen passport(s). *Consider also:* alien(s), colonist(s), evacuee(s), fugitive(s), immigrant(s), foreign born, foreign worker(s), foreign labor, guest worker(s), resettl(e,ed,ing,ment), foreigner(s), Chicano(s). *See also* Brain drain; Borderlands; Displaced persons; Emigration; Expatriates; Illegal aliens; Immigration; Political asylum; Refugees; Relocation.

Emigration. Emigrat(e,ed,ing,ion,ions). Flee(ing). Fled. Seek(ing) sanctuary. Deport(ed,ing,ation). Wetback(s). Defect(ed,ing,ion). Displaced person(s). Brain drain. Nomad(s). Transient child(ren). Migrat(e,ed,ing,ion,ions,ory). Migrant(s). Exile(s,d). Move(d,ment) in search of work. Exodus. Expatriate(s). Nansen passport(s). Relocat(e,ed,ing, ion). Expelled from countr(y,ies). Expelled from homeland(s). Emigre(s). Emigrant(s). Refugee(s). Defector(s). *Consider also:* immigrat(e,ed,ing,ion), immigrant(s), alien(s), foreign born, foreign worker(s), foreign labor, guest worker(s), resettl(e,ed,ing,ment), foreigner(s), Chicano(s). *See also* Brain drain; Borderlands; Displaced persons; Emigrants; Homeland; Illegal aliens; Immigration; Overpopulation; Political asylum; Population decline; Population transfer; Refugees; Relocation.

Eminence. Eminen(ce,t). Celebrated. Celebrit(y,ies). Distinguished. Esteemed. Exalted. Illustrious(ness). Preeminen(ce, t). Prestig(e,ious). Prominen(ce,cy,t). Renown(ed). Notable(s). Fam(e,ous, ousness). *Consider also:* great(ness), loft(y,iness), importan(ce,t), influential, honored, foremost, highest repute. *See also* Famous people; Heroes; Idolatry; Royalty.

Eminent domain. See *Confiscation; Expropriation; Nationalization.*

Emissaries. See *Agents; Messengers.*

Emissions, zero vehicles. See *Zero emissions vehicles.*

Emotion, expressed. See *Emotionality; Self expression.*

Emotional abuse. Emotional(ly) abuse(s, ed). Scapegoat(ed,ing). Threaten(ed,ing) withdraw(al) of love. Belittl(e,ed,ing). Humiliat(e,ed,ing,ion). *Choose from:* emotional(ly), mental(ly), verbal(ly), psychological(ly), psychosocial *with:* abuse(s,ed), abusive(ness), exploit(ed, ing,ation), cruel(ty), injur(y,ies,ed), maltreat(ed,ing,ment), damag(e,ed, es,ing), harm(ed,ing,ful), trauma(tic), depriv(e,ed,ing,ation). *See also* Insensitivity; Invective; Molested children; Online harassment; Psychologically abused men; Psychosocial deprivation; Scapegoating; Self neglect; Sexual abuse; Sexual harassment; Verbal abuse.

Emotional adjustment. Emotional(ly) adjust(ed,ment). *Choose from:* emotional(ly), psychological(ly), personal(ly), behavioral, self, psychosocial(ly), mental(ly), sexual(ly), identity, illness(es) *with:* adjust(ed,ing, ment,ments), adapt(ed,ing,ation,ations), habituat(ed,ion), accept(ed,ing,ance), accomodat(ed,ing,ion,ions). *Consider also:* tolerance, coping, self realization, adaptive behavior(s), psychological survival, grieving, stress management. *Consider also:* well-being, life satisfaction, emotional(ly) maladjust(ed,ment). *See also* Adjustment to environment; Alienation; Coping; Emotional control; Identity crisis; Interpersonal relations; Morale; Social adjustment.

Emotional agitation. See *Restlessness.*

Emotional appeal. Emotional(ly) appeal(s,ling). Ad hominem. Ad feminam. Emotional ad(s,vertisement, vertisements). *Choose from:* appeal(s,ed, ing) *with:* emotion(s,al,ality), loyalt(y, ies), fear(s), prejudice(s), feeling(s). *See also* Advertising; Persuasion; Propaganda.

Emotional aspects of abortion. Emotional aspects of abortion. *Choose from:* abort(ed,ing,ion,ions), postabort(ion, ive), pregnancy terminat(e,ed,ing,ion, ions) *with:* emotion(s,al), response(s), personal problem(s), adjustment, depress(ion,ive), relief, reaction(s), coping, neuro(sis,tic), impact(s), psycholog(y,ical), psychiatric, sequelae, effect(s), subjective, consequence(s), guilt(y,iness), accept(ed,ing,ance). *See also* Abortion applicants; Abortion counseling; Fetal propitiatory rites.

Emotional, bonding. See *Bonding (emotional).*

Emotional commitment. See *Commitment (emotional).*

Emotional content. Emotional content. *Choose from:* emotional(ly), affect(ive), feeling(s), arousing, charged, arousal eliciting, anxiety arousing *with:* content(s), word(s), message(s), load(s,ed), theme(s), laden, association(s), expression(s), meaning(ful,s), qualit(y,ies), topic(s), information. *See also* Content analysis; Emotional appeal; Emotional responses; Messages.

Emotional control. Emotional control. *Choose from:* control(led,ling), restrain(ed,ing,t), regulat(ed,ing,ion), overcontrol(led,ling), manag(e,ed, ing,ement), inhibit(ed,ing,ion,ions), disciplin(ed,ing), suppress(ed,ing,ion) *with:* emotion(s,al,ally), anger, angry, hostil(e,ity), affect(ive,ion), rage, feeling(s), warmth, lov(e,ing). *See also* Coping; Emotional adjustment; Inhibition (psychology).

Emotional crisis. Emotional cris(es,is). *Choose from:* emotional, personal, personality, identity, psychosocial, creative, behavioral, post traumatic, life, mid-life, dysthymic *with:* cris(es,is), upset(s), trauma(s,tic), juncture(s), decision point(s), turning point(s). *Consider also:* personal disruption(s), post traumatic states. *See also* Crises; Crisis intervention; Family crises; Identity crisis; Life change events; Life stage transitions; Maturational crisis; Midlife crisis; Psychological debriefing; Stress reactions.

Emotional dependence. Emotional dependence. *Choose from:* psychological, emotional, support, security, affection, shelter, love, mothering, protection *with:* dependen(t,ce), need(s), motivation(s). *Consider also:* lonel(y, iness), anaclisis, anaclitic, anaclinic. *See also* Co-dependency; Dependency (personality); Emotional development; Emotional immaturity; Substance dependence.

Emotional deprivation. See *Psychosocial deprivation.*

Emotional development. Emotional development. Affective education. Emotional(ly) liberat(ed,ing,ion). *Choose from:* emotion(s,al), psychological, psychosocial, affect(ive), ego, psychic, socio-emotional, socio-emotional, personality, character, social, behavioral, identity *with:* development, maturation, growth. *Consider also:* self actualization, autonomy, personal growth, socialization. *Consider also:* self confidence, trust, self esteem, empathy *with:* develop(ed,ing,ment). *See also* Attachment behavior; Childhood play development; Developmental stages; Object relations; Personality development; Psychogenesis; Psychosexual development; Psychosocial development.

Emotional expressiveness. See *Emotionality.*

Emotional health. See *Mental health; Morale; Psychological well being.*

Emotional illness. See *Mental illness.*

Emotional immaturity. Emotional(ly) immatur(e,ity). Childish(ness). *Consider also:* emotional(ly), psychological(ly), personalit(y,ies), ego, affect(ive), psychosocial(ly), behavior, character, social(ly) *with:* immatur(e,ity), delayed development, dependent, inadequate, late maturing, arrested development. *Consider also:* unresolved emotional conflict(s), emotional(ly) block(s,ed),

social imperception. *See also* Emotional maturity; Personality traits.

Emotional inferiority. Emotional inferiority. Ugly duckling complex. *Choose from:* emotion(s,al,ally), feeling(s), self concept, self perception *with:* inferior(ity), inadequa(cy,te), insignifican(t,ce), unimportan(t,ce), unworth(y,iness), helpless(ness). *See also* Personality traits.

Emotional instability. Emotional instability. Mood(y,iness). *Choose from:* emotion(s,al,ally), affect(ive), mood(s), psychological(ly), mental(ly), psychosocial(ly) *with:* instability, unstable, labil(e,ity), change(s), swing(s), cycle(s), variab(le,ility), variation(s), unpredictab(le,ility). *Consider also:* immatur(e,ity), sulk(y,iness), low tolerance for frustration. *See also* Emotional stability; Moodiness; Personality traits.

Emotional investment. See *Cathexis.*

Emotional maturity. Emotional(ly) matur(e,ity). *Choose from:* emotional(ly), ego, affective, psychological(ly), affect(ive), personality, character *with:* matur(e,ity), development, strength, integration. *Consider also:* adult ego state(s), neopsychic, age-appropriate. *See also* Emotional development; Self actualization; Social maturity; Personality traits.

Emotional needs. See *Psychological needs.*

Emotional problems. See *Emotionally disturbed.*

Emotional responses. Emotional response(s). *Choose from:* emotion(s,al, ally), psychophysiological, fear(ful), affective, psychological, defensive, subjective, angry, hostile, loving, warm, gut *with:* response(s), react(ed,ing, ion,ions), feedback. *Consider also:* defense mechanism(s). *See also* Animal emotionality; Emotional appeal; Emotions; Laughter; Stranger reactions.

Emotional restraint. See *Emotional control.*

Emotional security. Emotional(ly) secur(e,ity). Spiritual growth. Coping skills. Feeling competent. Invulnerab(le, ility). Self efficacy. Resilien(t,ce). Security blanket(s). Unanxious. Undistressed. Unconcerned. Calm(ness). Unperturbed. Untroubled. *Choose from:* inner, emotional(ly), psychological(ly), mental(ly), spiritual(ly,ity), interpersonal *with:* secur(e,ity), strength(s), support, stability, stable, resources, feelings, growth, matur(e,ity). *Consider also:* religious beliefs, self confidence, self-assurance, self esteem, emotional(ly) insecur(e,ity). *See also* Contentment; Emotional stability; Personality traits.

Emotional stability. Emotional(ly) stab(le,ility). Even temper(ed,ament). Emotional(ly) health(y). *Choose from:* invulnerab(le,ility) *with:* stress(es), tension(s), distract(ed,ing,ion,ions). Self possessed. Inner strength. Impassiv(e, ity). Easygoing. Unmoved. Unexcitable. Unflappable. Unperturbed. Untroubled. Undistressed. Equanimity. Steadfast(ness). *Choose from:* emotional(ly), mood(s), personalit(y,ies), mental(ly), affective, feeling(s), ego *with:* stab(ility, le), matur(e,ity), balance, invulnerab(le, ility), resilien(t,ce), unvarying, unswerving, calm(ness). *See also* Emotional instability; Emotional security.

Emotional states. Emotional state(s). Mood(s). Emotional arousal. Feeling(s). Temperament(s). *Choose from:* emotional, affective, feeling, happiness, fear, anger, sadness, internal, unhappiness, depressive, manic, consciousness *with:* state(s), status, predisposition(s). *Consider also:* anger, rage, anxiety, boredom, compassion, euphoria, fear, panic, frustration, grief, guilt, shame, happiness, hate, hostility, jealousy, laughter, love, alienation, ambivalence, depression, distress, doubt, emotional trauma, loneliness, mental confusion, optimism, pessimism, pleasure, restlessness, suffering. *See also* Alienation; Ambivalence; Anxiety; Boredom; Compassion; Depression (psychology); Distress; Doubt; Emotional trauma; Euphoria; Fear; Happiness; Hopefulness; Hopelessness; Irritability; Learned helplessness; Loneliness; Optimism; Panic; Pessimism; Pleasure; Restlessness; Suffering.

Emotional superiority. Emotional(ly) superior(ity). Grandiosity. Self love. Smug(ness). *Choose from:* emotional(ly), feeling(s), self attribution(s), self concept, self perception, belief(s) *with:* superior(ity). *Consider also:* self importan(t,ce), conceit(ed), proud, vanity, vain(ness). *See also* Personality traits; Self concept.

Emotional trauma. Emotional(ly) trauma(tic,ta). Traumatiz(e,ed,ing). *Choose from:* traumatic *with:* event(s), experience(s), loss(es). Stress disorder(s). Post traumatic stress. Posttraumatic stress. Survivor syndrome. *Choose from:* emotional(ly), psychic, personal, mental(ly), psychological(ly), childhood, memor(y,ies), psychodynamic(s), survivor(s) *with:* trauma(tic, ta), traumatiz(e,ed,ing), hurt(s), post traumatic, post traumatic, shock. *See also* Emotional crisis; Post traumatic stress disorders; Psychological debriefing.

Emotionality. Emotional(ity,ism). Emotional reaction(s). Emotional lability. Overexcitab(le,ility). Sentimental(ity). *Choose from:* emotional(ly), affect, affectiv(e,ity) *with:* react(ion,ions,ivity), labil(e,ity), excitab(le,ility), expressiv(ity,ive,iveness), level(s), style(s), range, tendenc(y,ies), arousal, responsiv(e,eness,ity), restraint. *Consider also:* affective behavior. *See also* Animal emotionality; Personality traits; Self expression.

Emotionality, animal. See *Animal emotionality.*

Emotionally deprived. See *Psychosocial deprivation.*

Emotionally disturbed. Emotional(ly) disturb(ed,ance,ances). Adjustment disorder(s). *Choose from:* emotional(ly), affective(ly), behavior(ally), conduct, mental(ly) *with:* disturbed, disturbance(s), handicapped, disabled, problem(s), disorder(s,ed), upset(s), symptom(s), maladjust(ed,ment), conflict(s,ed), withdrawn, dysfunction(s, al), deviant, impaired, ill(ness,nesses). *Choose from:* disturbed, maladjust(ed, ment) *with:* child(ren), adolescent(s), famil(y,ies). *Consider also:* neurotic, neuros(is,es), inappropriate behavior. *See also* Adjustment disorders; Affective symptoms; Acting out; Autism; Behavior disorders; Childhood neurosis; Childhood psychosis; Emotional instability; Emotional states; Neuroses.

Emotions. Emotion(s,al,ality). Feeling(s). Subjective experience(s). Emotional pattern(s). Affect(ivity). Affective domain. Mood(y,iness). Passion(s). Emotional response(s). Sentiment(s, ality). Expressive(ness). Affection(ate). Alienation. Ambivalence. Anger. Anxiety. Apathy. Boredom. Compassion(ate). Depression. Distress(ed). Doubt(ful). Egocentrism. Embarrass(ed,ment). Empathy. Euphoria. Fear. Frustrat(ed,ion). Grief. Guilt. Happiness. Hate. Hostil(e,ity). Irritab(le,ility). Jealousy. Laughter. Loneliness. Love. Morale. Motivation. Optimism. Panic. Pessimism. Pleasure. Rage. Resentment. Restlessness. Shame. Suffering. Warmth. *See also* Affect; Affection; Alienation; Ambivalence; Anger; Angst; Animal emotionality; Anxiety; Apathy; Aversion; Boredom; Cheerfulness; Compassion; Depression (psychology); Distress; Doubt; Egocentrism; Embarrassment; Emotional responses; Emotional states; Empathy; Euphoria; Fear; Frustration; Grief; Guilt; Happiness; Hate; Hopefulness; Hopelessness; Hostility; Humiliation; Irritability; Jealousy; Laughter; Loneliness; Love; Nostalgia; Optimism; Panic; Pessimism; Pity; Pleasure; Rage; Resentment; Restlessness; Sadness; Shame; Suffering; Sympathy.

Emotive psychotherapy, rational. See *Rational emotive psychotherapy.*

Empathy. Empath(y,ic,etic,ize,ized,izing). Understanding. Perceptual congruence. Vicarious. *Choose from:* affective, emotional, intellectual *with:* identification. *Consider also:* role taking, verstehen, affinit(y,ies), compassion(ate), rapport, sympath(y,etic,ize, ized,izing). *See also* Communication (thought transfer); Compassion; Interpersonal relations; Role taking; Verstehen.

Emperor worship. Emperor worship. *Choose from:* emperor(s), king(s), monarch(s), imperial, ruler(s) *with:* worship(ped,ping,s), cult(s), divin(e,ity, ities), sacred. *See also* Divine right of kings; Royal supremacy; Royalty; Traditional societies.

Emperors. Emperor(s). Khan(s). Sovereign(s). Ruler(s). Rex. Czar(s). Kaiser(s). King(s). Great Mogul(s). Imperator(s). *Consider also:* dynast(y,ies), imperial robe(s). *See also* Empires; Monarchy; Royalty.

Emphasis. Emphasi(s,ze,zed,zing). Accentuat(e,ed,ing). Dramatiz(e,ed,ing, ation). Headline(s). Underlin(e,ed,ing). Underscor(e,ed,ing). Italiciz(e,ed,ing, ation). High priority. Stress(ed,ing). Spotlight(ed,ing). Emphatic(ally). Limelight. *See also* Clarification; Explanation; Meaning; Recognition (achievement).

Empires. Empire(s). Domain(s). Realm(s). Kingdom(s). Dominion(s). Colon(y,ies). Colonial(ism). Commonwealth(s). Imperial(ism,istic). *Consider also:* emperor(s). *See also* Colonialism; Imperialism; Monarchy.

Empires, African. See *African empires.*

Empires, Asian. See *Asian empires.*

Empires, Pre-Columbian. See *Pre-Columbian empires.*

Empirical methods. Empirical method(s,ology,ologies). *Choose from:* measurable, countable, empirical(ly), verifiable, objective, operational *with:* method(s,ology,ologies), inquir(y,ies), research, investigation(s), analy(sis,ses), stud(y,ies), data, basis, assessment, validat(ed,ing,ion,ions), analy(sis,ses), finding(s), evidence, definition(s). *Consider also:* experiment(s,al), content analysis, discourse analysis, field work, fieldwork, observation(s,al), questionnaire(s), longitudinal stud(y,ies), panel stud(y,ies), random sample(s), survey(s). *See also* Empiricism; Experimental replication; Data analysis; Data collection; Data interpretation; Objectivity; Observation methods; Qualitative methods; Quantitative methods; Research methods; Scientific method; Value neutral.

Empiricism. Empiric(al,ism,ist,ists). Positivis(m,t,ts). Principle of verification. *Consider also:* observable fact(s), empirical science. *See also* A posteriori; Behaviorism; Epistemology; Empirical methods; Experiments; Holism; Logical positivism; Materialism; Observation; Validity.

Employability. Employab(le,ility). Marketable skill(s). *Choose from:* employment, job, work, vocational, occupational *with:* potential, readiness, asset(s), likelihood, competenc(y,ies), preparation, skill(s). *Consider also:* occupational handicap(s), unemployab(ility,le,les). *See also* Educational background; Employee characteristics; Employment history; Employment preparation; Occupational qualifications; Professional education; Work experience; Work skills.

Employed mothers. See *Dual career families; Family work relationship; Female headed households; Professional women; Working women.*

Employed women. See *Dual career families; Professional women; Working women.*

Employee absenteeism. See *Absenteeism.*

Employee assistance programs. Employee assistance program(s). EAP(s). *Choose from:* employee(s), staff, personnel, worksite, workplace *with:* assistance program(s), counseling, stress management, weight loss, physical fitness, exercise, drug rehabilitation, outplacement service(s), safety program(s), health program(s), wellness program(s). *See also* Alcohol rehabilitation; Corporate social responsibility; Counseling; Drug rehabilitation; Employee benefits; Mental health programs; Personnel management; Quality of working life.

Employee attitudes. Employee attitude(s). *Choose from:* personnel, work(ing), job(s), employment, employee(s), staff, worker(s), manpower, workforce, office force, laborforce, crew(s) *with:* alienat(ed,ion), apathy, attitude(s), belief(s), value(s), satisfaction(s), dissatisfaction(s), perception(s), motivation(s), meaning(ful,s), orient(ed,ation,ations), commitment(s), opinion(s), importance, cynicism, involvement, view(s,point,points), mindset, interest, expectation(s), enjoyment, morale, loyalty. *Consider also:* workahol(ism,ic). *See also* Attitudes toward work; Employee concerns; Employee morale; Employee motivation; Job involvement; Job satisfaction; Vocational maturity.

Employee benefits. Employee benefit(s). Nonwage payment(s). Nonwage compensation. Fringe benefit(s). *Choose from:* employee(s), personnel, staff, job, employment *with:* benefit(s), bonus(es), assistance program(s), medical insurance, health insurance, dental insurance, discount(s), day care, child care, expense account(s), annual leave, holiday(s), parental leave(s), maternity leave(s), paternity leave(s), pension(s), fringe benefit(s), stock option(s), compensation, perquisite(s), perk(s), sick pay, sick leave, remuneration, insurance plan(s), retirement plan(s), ESOP(s), employee stock ownership plan(s), profit-sharing plan(s), postretirement increase(s), merit increase(s), merit system(s), fringes, vacation(s), recreation program(s), qualified parking. *See also* Child care; Compensation (payment); Compensation management; Employee assistance programs; Employee concerns; Employee incentive plans; Employee stock ownership plans; Insurance; Job enrichment; Personnel training; Pensions; Salaries.

Employee characteristics. Employee(s) characteristic(s). *Choose from:* employee(s), staff, personnel, crew(s), worker(s) *with:* characteristic(s), intelligence, skill(s), employment history, personal qualit(y,ies), personality, gender, exceptional, handicapped, disabilit(y,ies), marital status, biodata, biographical data, physical characteristics, gifted, family background, income, place of residence, nationality, religion, health status, behavior patterns, traits, socioeconomic status, age, race, religion, educational level, urban, rural. *See also* Academic degrees; Characteristics; Educational background; Employee attitudes; Employee efficiency; Employee motivation; Employees; Employment history; Job Knowledge; Personnel loyalty; Personnel specifications; Qualities; Skill; Work skills.

Employee concerns. Employee concern(s). *Choose from:* employee(s), personnel, workforce, staff, worker(s), crew(s), troop(s) *with:* concern(s), interest(s), right(s). *See also* Attitudes toward work; Employee attitudes; Employee morale; Employee benefits; Personnel management; Quality of working life.

Employee development. See *Staff development.*

Employee discipline. Employee discipline. *Choose from:* employee(s), team(s), worker(s), staff(s), manager(s), personnel *with:* disciplin(e,ary), penalt(y,ies), penaliz(e,ed,ing), control(led,ling), dismissal(s), regulat(e,ed,ing,ion,ions), correct(ed,ing). *Consider also:* performance appraisal. *See also* Discipline; Nonpunitive approach (discipline); Performance appraisal; Personnel evaluation; Personnel termination; Punitiveness.

Employee efficiency. Employee efficiency. *Choose from:* employee(s), worker(s), staff, personnel, crew(s), team(s) *with:* efficien(t,cy), effective(ness), output, efficac(y,ious,iousness), competenc(e,y), capabilit(y,ies), productiv(e,eness,ity), successful(ness), proficien(t,cy). *See also* Employee attitudes; Employee motivation; Employee productivity; Job performance; Performance standards; Personnel loyalty; Staff development.

Employee evaluation. See *Personnel evaluation.*

Employee grievances. Employee grievance(s). Grievance procedure(s). *Choose from:* employee(s), staff, faculty, worker(s), labor, union(s) *with:* griev(ance,ances,ants,e,ing), complain(t,ts,ing), dispute(s), demand(s), conflict(s), protest(s), negotiat(e,ed,ing,ion,ions), arbitration, right(s), lawsuit(s). *Consider also:* Fair Labor Standards Act. *See also* Employee grievances; Employee turnover; Employment discrimination; Job satisfaction; Personnel loyalty.

Employee health insurance. See *Health insurance.*

Employee incentive plans. Employee incentive plan(s). *Choose from:* employee(s), worker(s), personnel, staff, work, productivity, efficiency, performance *with:* incentive(s), motivation technique(s), merit pay, reward(s,ing), recognition, promotion plan(s). *See also* Compensation management; Employee motivation; Employee ownership; Employee productivity; Job involvement; Participative management; Personnel loyalty; Profit sharing.

Employee morale. Employee morale. *Choose from:* occupation(s,al), job(s), staff, work(er,ers), executive(s), manager(s), profession(s,al), employee(s), employment, career(s), teacher(s), nurse(s), driver(s), secretar(y,ies), clerk(s), administrative assistant(s) *with:* cooperat(e,ed,ing, ive,ion), motivat(e,ed,ion), empower(ed, ing,ment), absentee(ism), turnover, productiv(e,ity), trust(ing,ful), cynic(ism), insecur(e,ity,ities), demoraliz(ed,ation), loyal(ty), satisf(ied,action), positive attitude(s), commit(ted,ment), self-esteem, team builder(s), good feeling(s), optimis(m, tic), pessimis(m,tic), dedicat(ed,ion), esprit de corps, aimless(ness), purposeless(ness), enthusias(m,tic), sense of common purpose. *See also* Attitudes toward work; Employee attitudes; Employee concerns; Employee motivation; Job involvement; Job satisfaction; Participative management.

Employee motivation. Employee motivation. *Choose from:* employee(s), personnel, staff(s), worker(s), work, job(s), employment, subordinate(s), professional(s) *with:* incentive(s), motivat(ed,ing,ion,ional), interest, commitment(s), satisfaction, aspiration(s). *See also* Employee attitudes; Employee efficiency; Employee incentive plans; Employee morale; Employee ownership; Employee productivity; Employer attitudes; Job design; Job enrichment; Job involvement; Job performance; Job satisfaction; Job security; Participative management; Personnel loyalty; Profit sharing; Work humanization.

Employee ownership. Employee own(ed,ership). Worker own(ed,ership). Employee stock ownership. ESOPs. Employee buyout(s). Worker capitalis(m,t,ts). *Choose from:* employee(s), worker(s) *with:* cooperative(s), ownership, profit sharing, gainsharing, sharehold(er,ers, ing), participative ownership, buyout(s), takeover(s). *Consider also:* self employ(ed,ment). *See also* Agricultural collectives; Buyouts; Collectivism; Common ownership; Cooperatives; Employee stock ownership plans; Industrial democracy; Participative management; Power sharing; Worker control; Worker participation.

Employee participation. See *Employee ownership; Industrial democracy; Participative management; Worker control; Worker participation.*

Employee performance appraisal. See *Performance appraisal.*

Employee productivity. Employee productiv(ity,eness). Work quality. Work quantity. *Choose from:* productiv(e,ity, eness), production, output, yield(s), counterproductiv(e,ity), efficien(t,cy), effective(ness), achievement(s), accomplishment(s), performance *with:* employee(s), labor, labor force, manpower, collective, work(er,ers), job(s), staff, crew(s), personnel, operator(s), team(s). *See also* Employee efficiency; Employee motivation; Job performance.

Employee promotion. See *Promotion (occupational).*

Employee recognition. Employee(s) recogni(ze,zed,zing,tion). *Choose from:* employee(s), staff, worker(s), personnel, productivity, secretar(y,ies), sales(men,man,women,woman, people,person), teacher(s), etc. *with:* recogni(ze,zed,zing,tion), reward(s, ed,ing), award(s,ed,ing), bonus(es), honor(ed,ing,s). *Consider also:* performance award(s), incentive award(s), merit pay, pay-for-performance. *See also* Employee incentive plans; Employees; Monetary rewards.

Employee relations. See *Labor management relations; Superior subordinate relationship.*

Employee representation in management.
See *Employee ownership; Industrial democracy; Participative management; Worker control; Worker participation.*

Employee selection. See *Personnel selection.*

Employee skills. See *Work skills.*

Employee stock ownership plans.
Employee stock ownership plan(s). ESOP(s). Employee owned. Employee buyout(s). Nonqualified stock plan(s). *Choose from:* employee(s), union(s) *with:* stock appreciation right(s), phantom stock(s), stock transfer plan(s), restricted stock grant(s), stock option grant(s), shareholder(s). *See also* Buyouts; Common ownership; Cooperatives; Employee benefits; Employee ownership; Industrial democracy; Participative management; Power sharing; Worker control; Worker participation.

Employee supervisor interaction. See *Superior subordinate relationship.*

Employee termination. See *Personnel termination.*

Employee transfers. Employee transfer(s). *Choose from:* employee(s), staff, personnel, workforce, labor, worker(s) *with:* transfer(s,red,ring), relocat(e,ed, ing,ion), shift(ed,ing,s), mobility. *See also* Career ladders; Career mobility; Employment opportunities; Occupational tenure; Personnel placement; Relocation.

Employee turnover. Employee turnover. Organizational turnover. *Choose from:* labor, employee(s), employment, worker(s), staff, personnel, enlistee(s) *with:* turnover, switching, reenlist(ment), job change, leav(e,ing), terminat(e,ed, ing,ion,ions), resign(ed,ing,ation,ations), mobility, attrition, quit(ting). *Consider also:* exit interview(s). *See also* Attrition; Career breaks; Career change; Career goals; Career mobility; Employment history; Human resources; Job security; Labor economics; Labor supply; Occupational tenure; Organizational dissolution; Personnel termination; Resignations; Retirement.

Employees. Employee(s). Personnel. Workforce. Operator(s). Staff. Manpower. Worker(s). Work force. Office force. Sales force. Subordinates. Labor force. Labor supply. Functionar(y,ies). Crew(s). Troop(s). Hired help. Coworker(s). Occupational group(s). Laborer(s). Practitioner(s). Paraprofessional(s). Professional(s). Nonprofessional(s). Air traffic controller(s). Attorney(s). Administrator(s). Agricultural personnel. Blue collar worker(s). Caseworker(s). Church worker(s). Civil servant(s). Caregiver(s). Clerk(s). Clergy. Consultant(s). Computer programmer(s). Crafts(man,men, person,people). Designer(s). Driver(s). Director(s). Domestic servant(s). Editor(s). Faculty. Firefighter(s). Guard(s). Government employee(s). Health personnel. Hairdresser(s). Home economist(s). Librarian(s). Machine operator(s). Military personnel. Nurse(s). Police officer(s). Pilot(s). Programmer(s). Sales(men,man,women, woman,people,person). Secretar(y,ies). Stevedore(s). Teacher(s). Technician(s). Trainer(s). Typist(s). White collar worker(s). *Choose from:* employed, civil service, working, hired *with:* woman, women, men, man, people, group(s), male(s), female(s), person(s), civilian(s). *Consider also:* apprentice(s), intern(s), assistant(s), working person(s), working people, wage earner(s), jobholder(s). *See also* Automobile industry workers; Blue collar workers; Civil service; Clerical workers; Dislocated workers; Employee recognition; Employers; Foreign workers; Government personnel; Iron and steel workers; Knowledge workers; Labor management relations; Migrant workers; Occupational roles; Personnel evaluation; Professional personnel; Professional women; Quality of working life; Superior subordinate relationship; Temporary employees; White collar workers; Working women.

Employees, federal. See *Civil service; Government personnel.*

Employees, government. See *Civil service; Government personnel.*

Employees, local officials and. See *Local officials and employees.*

Employees, municipal. See *Civil service; Government personnel.*

Employees, office. See *Clerical workers; White collar workers.*

Employees, professional. See *Professional personnel.*

Employees, public. See *Elected officials; Government personnel.*

Employees, relocation of. See *Employee transfers.*

Employees, state. See *Civil service; Government personnel.*

Employees, temporary. See *Temporary employees.*

Employees and officials, county. See *Government personnel; Local government; Politicians.*

Employer attitudes. Employer attitude(s). *Choose from:* employer(s), manager(s), owner(s), boss(es), proprietor(s), superintendent(s), supervisor(s) *with:* attitude(s), belief(s), opinion(s), expectation(s), preference(s), prejudice(s), bias(es), perception(s), mindset, reaction(s). *See also* Attitudes; Attitudes toward work; Employers.

Employers. Employer(s). Boss(es). Contractor(s). Manager(s). Owner(s). Proprietor(s). Director(s). Superintendent(s). Supervisor(s). Administrator(s). Captain(s). Executive(s). Principal(s). Headmaster(s). President(s). *Consider also:* business(men,man,women, woman,person,persons), capitalist(s), compan(y,ies), overseer(s). *See also* Administrators; Contractors; Labor management relations; Managers; Personnel management.

Employers associations. Employer(s) organization(s). *Choose from:* employer(s), industrialist(s), multiemployer, multi-employer, business interest(s) *with:* organization(s), forum(s), group(s), association(s). *See also* Business; Labor management relations; Labor unions; Trade associations.

Employment. Employ(ed,ee,ees,ment). Overemployed. Underemployed. Full time work. Part time work. Hir(e,ed,ing). Career pattern(s). Work(er,ers,ing). Career development. Return to work. Occupational mobility. Job(s). Reemployment. Pre-employment. Job placement. Paycheck. Job creation. Labor force participation. Vocation. Moonlighting. *Choose from:* multiple, overseas, part-time, seasonal *with:* work, job(s), employment, position(s), post(s). *Consider also:* assignment(s), dut(y,ies), profession(s). *See also* Careers; Child labor; Dual career families; Employability; Employment agencies; Employment history; Employment of persons with disabilities; Employment opportunities; Employment status; Employment trends; Job applicants; Job creation; Job descriptions; Job requirements; Job search; Job security; Moonlighting; Occupational choice; Occupational roles; Part time employment; Personnel recruitment; Quality of working life; Self employment; Underemployment; Unemployment; Work reentry; Work sharing; Working women.

Employment, barriers to. See *Employment discrimination.*

Employment, double. See *Double employment.*

Employment, extra. See *Moonlighting.*

Employment, household. See *Domestic service.*

Employment, maternal. See *Dual career families; Family work relationship; Female headed households; Professional women; Working women.*

Employment, part time. See *Part time employment.*

Employment, self. See *Self employment.*

Employment agencies. Employment agenc(y,ies). *Choose from:* employment, professional placement, job, temporary help, outplacement, out-placement *with:* agenc(y,ies), service(s), firm(s), source(s), office(s), resource(s), clearinghouse(s), program(s). Headhunter(s). Head hunter(s). Recruiting service(s). *See also* Job applicant screening; Personnel recruitment; Temporary help services.

Employment change. See *Career change.*

Employment counseling. Employment counseling. *Choose from:* employment, career(s), outplacement, guidance, vocation(al), job(s), relocation, placement, occupation(s,al), vocational rehabilitation, work adjustment *with:* counsel(ing,ed). *See also* Employment agencies; Occupational adjustment; Outplacement services; Personnel placement; Personnel termination; Vocational guidance.

Employment discrimination. Employment discrimination. Job discrimination. Wage gap(s). Wage differen(ces,tials). Labor market segmentation. Feminized occupation(s). Business set asides. Mandatory retirement. Job ghetto(s). Glass ceiling(s). Sticky floor(s). *Choose from:* job(s), employ(ee,ees,ed,ing, er,ers,ment), work(er,ers), workplace, personnel, labor force, union(s), wage(s), underemploy(ed,ment), occupational, vocational *with:* unequal, discriminat(ed,ing,ion,ory), prejudice(d), exclus(ivity,ion), bias(ed), inequalit(y, ies), tokenism, segregat(ed,ion), intolerance, bigot(ry), chauvinis(m,tic), apartheid, handicapis(m,t), racis(m,t), sexis(m,t), ageis(m,t). *See also* Affirmative action; Age discrimination; Attitudes toward homosexuality; Attitudes toward handicapped; Attitudes toward physical handicaps; Attitudes toward the aged; Equal job opportunities; Equity (payment); Hindrances; Labor market segmentation; Nontraditional careers; Occupational segregation; Oligopsony; Oppression; Personnel selection; Racism; Sexism; Sexual division of labor; Wage differentials.

Employment forecasting. Employment forecasting. *Choose from:* employment, laborforce, labor force, workforce, occupation(al), job(s) *with:* forecast(s, ing), outlook(s), predict(ed,ing,ion,ions), trend(s), projection(s), futur(e,es,ist, ists,ism), year 2000, prognosticat(e, ed,ing,ion,ions), 21st century, prospect(s), scenario(s). *See also* Business cycles; Economic forecasting; Employment opportunities; Employment trends; Future; Future of society; Plant closings; Unemployment; Workforce planning.

Employment history. Employment histor(y,ies). Years of service. Years of teaching. Length of employment. Career development. Resume(s). Vita(s). Vocational histor(y,ies). *Choose from:* employ(ed,ment), work(ed), job(s), vocational, career(s), occupation(s,al) *with:* experience(s), history, background, previous(ly), longevity, duration. *See also* Career change; Career development; Career patterns; Employment status; Expertise; Occupational success; Occupational tenure; Professional development; Work experience.

Employment interviews. Employment interview(s,ed,ing). *Choose from:* job candidate(s), job applicant(s), employee selection, hiring, job placement, employment, personnel selection *with:* interview(s,ed,ing). *See also* Employability; Employment agencies; Employment counseling; Job search; Personnel selection;

Employment of persons with disabilities. Employment of person(s) with disabilit(y,ies). Sheltered workshop(s). *Choose from:* disabilit(y,ies), handicap(ped,pism,s), disabled, blind(ness), health impaired, deaf(ness), impair(ed,ment,ments), developmental disabilit(y,ies), mut(e,ism), parapleg(ia,ics), quadripleg(ia,ics), retard(ation,ed), epilep(tic,sy), speech disorder(s), hearing disorder(s), visual disorder(s), learning disorder(s), hemipleg(ia,ic), multiple handicap(s, ped), multiply handicapped, brain damage(d), hyperactiv(e,ity), mobility impair(ed,ment,ments), mental(ly) handicap(s,ped), learning disabilit(y,ies), cerebral palsy *with:* job(s), employ(ed, ing,ment), labor market, hir(e,ed,es,ing), affirmative action, work(ed,ing), workplace(s), worksite(s), occupational advancement, career(s), profession(s). *See also* Disability; Disability evaluation; Disabled workers; Employer attitudes; Employment discrimination; Equal job opportunities; Rehabilitation centers; Rehabilitation counseling; Sheltered workshops; Vocational rehabilitation.

Employment opportunities. Employment opportunit(y,ies). Job opportunit(y,ies). Job vacanc(y,ies). Promotion ladder(s). Labor market. *Choose from:* job(s), career(s), employ(ee,ees,ed,ing,er, ers,ment), work(er,ers), workplace, personnel, labor force, union(s), occupational, vocational, professional *with:* opportunit(y,ies), possibilit(y,ies), choice(s), alternative(s), option(s), barrier(s), access, prospect(s). *Consider also:* job fair(s), labor market segmentation, feminized occupation(s), underemployment. *See also* Career ladders; Career mobility; Employment discrimination; Employment trends; Equal job

opportunities; Job requirements; Job search; Labor economics; Labor market; Labor market segmentation; Occupational qualifications; Personnel recruitment; Promotion (occupational); Self employment; Work reentry; Workforce planning.

Employment potential. See *Employability.*

Employment preparation. Employment preparation. Job training. *Choose from:* vocational, prevocational, occupational, job skill(s), career development, trade *with:* education, training, school(s), student(s), orientation, instruction, preparation, curriculum, program(s), apprenticeship(s). *See also* Educational background; Employment history.

Employment qualifications. See *Employability; Occupational qualifications.*

Employment satisfaction. See *Job satisfaction.*

Employment status. Employment status. *Choose from:* employ(ed,ment), unemploy(ed,ment). Part time work. Full time work. Retire(d,ment). Nonemploy(ed,ment). Working. Nonworking. *See also* Academic rank; Career ladders; Employment; Employment history; Part time employment; Promotion (occupational); Retirement; Seniority; Underemployment; Unemployment.

Employment termination. See *Personnel termination.*

Employment tests. See *Occupational tests.*

Employment trends. Employment trend(s). *Choose from:* labor, job(s), employment, hiring *with:* trend(s), growth, declin(e,ed,ing), demand, outlook(s), forecast(s,ed,ing), opportunit(y,ies), market(s), shortage(s), indicator(s). *See also* Economic statistics; Employment forecasting; Employment opportunities; Disguised unemployment; Labor economics; Labor market; Unemployment rates; Workforce planning.

Empowerment. Empower(ed,ing,ment). Self efficacy. Devictimiz(e,ed,ing,ation). *Choose from:* shared, socialized *with:* power. *Consider also:* transformational leadership, participat(ive,ory) management, participat(ory,ive) decision making, enabl(e,ed,ing,ement), self-advocacy. *Consider also:* regenerat(e,ed, ing,ion), intrinsic motivation, internal power, autonomy, authenticity, self confidence, accredit(ing,ation), entitle(d), validat(e,ed,ing,ation). *See also* Assertiveness; Leadership; Personal independence; Power; Power sharing; Self efficacy.

Enactment. Enact(ed,ing,ment). Decree(d, ing,s). Establish(ed,ing) law(s). Ratif(y,ied,ication). Make law(s). Pass(ed,ing) law(s). *Consider also:*

authoriz(e,ed,ing,ation), institut(e,ed, ing,ion), legislat(e,ed,ing,ion), proclamation(s), proclaim(ed,ing). *See also* Action; Government regulation; Laws; Legislation; Legislative processes; Policy making; Presentations; Referendum; Statutes.

Enclosures. Enclosure(s). Enclos(e,ed,ing). Inclosure(s). Fenc(e,ed,es,ing). Street gate(s). Packag(e,ed,es,ing). Courtyard(s). Curtilage(s). Quadrangle(s). Yard(s). Pen(s,ned,ning). Corral(s). Paddock(s). Stockade(s). *See also* Barriers; Boundaries; Limitations.

Encomiendas. See *Forced labor; Slavery.*

Encopresis. See *Fecal incontinence.*

Encounter groups. Encounter group(s). *Choose from:* sensitivity, encounter, human relations, marathon, Esalen, T *with:* group(s). *Consider also:* human relations, sensitivity *with:* training. *See also* Consciousness raising activities; Humanistic psychology; Sensitivity training.

Encounters. See *Social interaction.*

Encouragement. Encourag(e,ed,ing,ement). Support(ed,ing,ive). Positive comment(s). Reassur(e,ed,ing,ance). Social support. Cheer(ed,ing). Enhearten(ed,ing). Hope(ful). Hoping. Urg(e,ed,ing). Boost(ed,ing). Embolden(ed,ing). Rally(ing). Exhort(ed,ing,ation). Rous(e,ed,ing). *Consider also:* advoca(cy,te,ted,ting), assur(e,ed,ing,ance,ances), assist(ed, ing,ance), back(ed,ing), comfort(ed,ing), inspir(e,ed,ing,ation), invigorat(e,ed, ing,ation), motivat(e,ed,ing,ation), reassur(e,ed,ing,ance,ances), stimulat(e, ed,ing,ation). *See also* Exhortation; Feedback; Positive reinforcement; Recognition (achievement); Social support; Social reinforcement.

Encryption. See *Cryptography.*

Enculturation. See *Socialization.*

Encumbrance. Encumbrance(s). Encumber(ed,ing). Incumbrance(s). Claim(s) against property. Promise(s) to pay. Hindrance(s). Impedance(s). Impediment(s). *Consider also:* disadvantage(s), handicap(s), load(s), difficult(y,ies), hardship(s), inconvenien(t,ce,ces), mortgage(s), burden(s,ed,ing). *See also* Barriers; Constraints; Debts; Impediments; Inconvenience; Limitations.

Encyclopedias. Encyclopedia(s). Cyclopedia(s). Book(s) of knowledge. *Consider also:* annual(s), almanac(s). *See also* Books; Reference materials.

End. End(s,ing,ings). Fin(is). Finale(s). Finish(ed,ing). Amen(s). Terminat(e,ed, ing,ion,ions). Conclusion(s). Conclud(e,ed,ing). Expir(e,ed,ing,ation). Cessation(s). Ceas(e,ed,ing).

Stop(ped,ping,page). Clos(e,ed,ing,ure). Discontinu(e,ed,ing,ance). Epilog(s,ue, ues). Complet(e,ed,ing,ion). Consummat(e,ed,ing,ion). *Consider also:* bring down the curtain, run the course, attain(ed,ing,ment), denouement, final outcome(s), fulfill(ed,ing,ment), result(s), retire(d,ment), wind(ing) up. *See also* Adjournment; Closure; Dying; Epilogues; Fatalism; Finale; Finite; Goals; Judgement day; Means ends; Sequelae; Teleology.

Endangered species. Endangered species. Species loss. Biotic impoverishment. *Choose from:* endanger(ed,ing,ment), threaten(ed,ing), imperiled, extinct(ion), dwindling, dying out, poach(ed,ing), devastat(ed,ion), diminish(ed,ing), disappearing, die-off(s), slaughter(ed, ing), deforestation, illegal hunting, illegal trapping, protect(ed,ion), rarity, vanish(ed,ing), sensitive *with:* species, breed(s), habitat(s), fauna, ecosystem(s), nesting area(s), wildlife, mammal(s), bird(s), waterfowl, insect(s), plant(s), animal(s), whale(s,ing), reptile(s), snake(s), fish(es). *Consider also:* tiger salamander(s), timber wolves, red wolves, black footed ferret(s), manatee(s), monarch butterfl(y,ies), Canada geese, caribou, Guam rail(s), ferret(s), bald eagle(s), condor(s), falcon(s), whooping crane(s), songbird(s), kestrel(s), elephant(s), gorilla(s), chimpanzee(s), osprey(s), otter(s), cougar(s), lynx(es), lion(s), golden monkey(s), sea turtle(s), panda(s), coelacanth(s), seal(s), rhinoceros(es), trumpeter swan(s), marten(s), etc. *See also* Animals; Habitat; Reptiles; Turtles; Wildlife conservation; Wildlife sanctuaries.

Endless punishment. See *Future punishment.*

Endlessness. Endless(ly,ness). Ad infinitum. Unending(ly). Everlasting. Ceaseless(ly). Continual(ly). Continuous(ly). Forever. Perpetual(ly). Limitless(ness). Boundless(ly,ness). Etern(al,ity). Immortal(ity). Never-ending. Unending(ly). World-without-end. Deathless(ness). Undying. Without end. *Consider also:* immeasurabl(e,y), indefinite(ly), infinite(ly), measureless(ness), unbounded, unlimited, unmeasured, limitless(ness), unbounded, unceasing, uninterrupted. *See also* Durability; Eternity; Immeasurability; Immortality; Indefiniteness; Infinity; Permanent.

Endocrine system. Endocrine system(s). *Consider also:* chromaffin system(s), endocrine gland(s), adrenal gland(s), gonad(s), ovar(y,ies), testis, islands of langerhans, parathyroid gland(s), pineal bod(y,ies), pituitary adrenal system(s), pituitary gland(s), thyroid gland(s), neurosecretory system(s), hypothalamo-

hypophyseal system(s). *See also* Anatomy.

Endogamous marriage. Endogamous marriage(s). *Choose from:* consanguinity, consanguineous, endogam(y,ous) *with:* marriage(s), mating(s). *Consider also:* inbreeding, inbred. *See also* Consanguinity; Marriage.

Endorphins. Endorphin(s). Enkephalin(s). Lipotropin fragment c. Endopioid(s). Enkephalinamide. Enkephalinergic. Preproenkephalin. Metenkephalin. *Consider also:* endogenous *with:* opiate(s), opioid(s), neuropeptide(s), neural peptide(s). *See also* Analgesia.

Endorsement. Endors(e,ed,ing,ement, ements). Approv(e,ed,ing,al). Accept(ed, ing,ance). Authoriz(e,ed,ing,ation). Sanction(ed,ing). Stamp of approval. Seal of approval. Warrant(y,ies,ed). Assurance(s). Guarantee(s,d). Authenticat(e,ed,ing,ation). Cosign(ed, ing). Countersign(ed,ing). Recommend(ed,ing,ation,ations). Commend(ed, ing,ation,ations). Underwrit(e,ing,ten). Vouch(ed,ing). Ratif(y,ied,ication). Notariz(e,ed,ing,ation). *See also* Assurances; Autographs; Certification; Signatures.

Endowment of research. Endow(ed,ing, ment,ments) research. Sponsor(ed,ing,s) research. Support(ed,ing,s) research. *Choose from:* endow(ed,ing,ment, ments), fund(ed,ing), federal aid, state aid , grant(s), support(ed,ing), public money, corporat(e,ion,ions) fund(s,ed, ing), foundation(s) fund(s,ed,ing) *with:* research, R&D. *See also* Foundations (organizations); Grants; Research; Research support.

Endowments. Endow(ed,ing,ment,ments). Bestow(ed,ing,al). Gift(s). Subsidiz(e,ed, ing,ation). Donat(e,ed,ing,ion,ions). Scholarship fund(s). *Consider also:* philanthrop(y,ist,ists), patron(s,age), alumni contribution(s), endowed chair(s), restricted donation(s), fellowship(s), bequest(s) conferral(s), stipend(s), trust fund(s). *See also* Contributions; Donations; Foundations (organizations); Giving; Organized financing.

Ends. End(s). Purpose(s). Goal(s). Aim(s). Objective(s). Destin(y,ies). Destination(s). Result(s). Target(s). Target date(s). Outcome(s). Effect(s). Consequence(s). Completion. Terminat(e,ed, ing,ion,ions). Expir(e,ed,ing,ation). Conclusion(s). Finale. Adjourn(ed,ing, ment). Fulfillment. Realiz(e,ed,ing, ation). Consummat(e,ed,ing,ion). Culminat(e,ed,ing,ation). Closing(s). *See also* Adjournment; Comprehensiveness; Destination; Means ends; Teleology.

Ends, means. See *Means ends.*

Endurance. Endur(e,ed,ing,ance). *Consider also:* last(ed,ing), work capacit(y,ies), energy level(s), physical performance, surviv(e,ed,ing,al), strength(s), hard(y, iness), maximum workload, staying power, treadmill performance, exercise tolerance, work(ing) capacity, perseverance, fortitude, patience, withstand(ing), withstood, stoic(ism), sufferance, sustain(ed,ing,ment), stamina, immutab(le, ility), immovab(le,ility). *See also* Fortitude; Patience; Physical fitness; Psychological endurance; Stoicism; Stress; Well being.

Endurance, physical. See *Endurance.*

Endurance, psychological. See *Psychological endurance.*

Enemies. Enem(y,ies). Foe(s). Military adversar(y,ies). Opponent(s). Combatant(s). Invader(s). Antagonist(s). Hostile nation(s). Axis. *See also* Adversaries; Enemy property.

Enemy property. Enemy propert(y,ies). Alien propert(y,ies). *Choose from:* enem(y,ies), war *with:* claim(s), loot(ed,ing), steal(ing), stolen. *See also* Abandoned property; Enemies; Property crimes.

Energy. Energy. Power. Fuel(s). Heat. Calor(ie,ies,ic). Electricity. Electron(s). *Choose from:* kinetic, potential, nuclear, solar, chemical, electrical, tidal, thermal, geothermal, non-nuclear, coal generated, oil, gas *with:* energy, power. *Consider also:* radiation, methane fermentation, energy from waste, solar heating, solar hot water, photovoltaic power, wave power, hydropower, solar sea power, fuel cells, windpower. *See also* Alternative energy; Coal; Energy conservation; Energy consumption; Energy costs; Fuel; Energy dissipation; Energy generating resources; Energy policy; Nuclear energy; Recycling; Solar energy; Waste to energy; Water power; Wind power.

Energy, alternative. See *Alternative energy.*

Energy, biomass. See *Alternative energy.*

Energy, nuclear. See *Nuclear energy.*

Energy, solar. See *Solar energy.*

Energy, waste to. See *Waste to energy.*

Energy conservation. Energy conservation. *Choose from:* energy, power, heat(ing), electricity, fuel(s), gas, coal *with:* conserv(e,ed,ing,ation), recovery, audit(s), sav(e,ed,ing), management, efficien(t,cy). *Consider also:* solar, passive, wind *with:* energy, power, heat(ing). Heat pump(s). Passive solar. Insulation. Wind power. *See also* Alternative energy; Renewable resources; Recycling; Solar energy; Waste to energy.

Energy consumption. Energy consumption. Energy use. *Choose from:* energy, fuel(s), heat(ing), power, electric(ity), gas, oil, coal, utilit(y,ies), solar, nuclear *with:* consum(e,ed,ing,ption), use(d,s), using, burn(ed,ing). *See also* Alternative energy; Energy policy; Lifestyle; Nonrenewable resources; Renewable resources.

Energy costs. Energy cost(s). *Choose from:* energy, calor(ic,ies), heat, power, electricity *with:* expend(ed,iture,itures), budget(s), efficien(t,cy), cost(s), bill(s), charge(s,d), saving(s). *See also* Energy; Energy consumption; Family budgets; Utility costs.

Energy dissipation. Energy dissipation. Energy loss(es). *Choose from:* energy, power, AC, transformer(s) *with:* dissipat(e,ed,ion,ive), release, lost, loss(es). *See also* Energy.

Energy expenditure (physical). Energy expenditure. Exert(ed,ion). Metabolic rate. Metabolic cost. Exercis(e,ed,ing). Heat production. Work load. Workload. Bioenerg(y,etic). Thermogenesis. Energetics. Force required. Physical activity. Physical work. Metabolic expenditure. Strenuous activity. Oxidation. Oxidative phosphorylation. Photosynthesis. Effort. *Choose from:* energy, calor(ic,ies), heat *with:* expend(ed,iture,itures), metabol(ism, ized), requirement(s), required, mobilization, balance, output, consum(e,ed, ing,ption). *See also* Caloric requirements; Exercise; Exertion.

Energy generating resources. Energy generating resource(s). Energy resource(s). Cogeneration. Energy source(s). Power plant(s). Fossil fuel(s). Biomass conversion. Biofuel(s) Bioconversion of agricultural waste(s). Energy crop(s). *Choose from:* energy, heat, calor(ie,ies,ic), power, electricity, fuel(s) *with:* generat(e,ed,ing,ion), source(s), produc(e,ed,ing,tion), suppl(y,ying,ier,iers), extract(ed,ing,ion). *Consider also:* alcohol, ethanol, methanol, coal, coke, petroleum, oil(s), gas(oline,ohol), kerosene, nuclear fusion, nuclear fission, nuclear energy, solar energy, methane fermentation, energy from waste, peat fuels, photovoltaic power suppl(y,ies), wave power, tidal power, tidal energy, hydropower, thermal power, solar sea power, geothermal energy, nuclear energy, non-nuclear energy resource(s), fuel cell(s), windpower. *See also* Alternative energy; Coal; Electric power plants; Fuel; Gas industry; Light sources; Natural resources; Nonrenewable resources; Nuclear energy; Nuclear power plants; Offshore oil; Oil spills; Recycling; Renewable resources; Solar energy; Waste to energy; Water power; Wind power.

Energy policy. Energy polic(y,ies). *Choose from:* energy, fuel(s), heat(ing), power, electric(ity), gas, oil, coal, utilit(y,ies), solar *with:* polic(y,ies), regulation(s), guideline(s), rule(s), plan(s), manual(s). *See also* Alternative energy; Coal; Economic development; Energy conservation; Energy consumption; Environmental law; Nuclear energy; Public policy; Solar energy; Transportation policy.

Energy use. See *Energy consumption; Energy costs.*

Enforcement, drug. See *Drug enforcement.*

Enforcement, law. See *Law enforcement.*

Enfranchisement. See *Voting rights.*

Engagement (philosophy). See *Involvement.*

Engenderment. Engenderment. *Choose from:* gender *with:* socializ(e,ed,ing, ation), reinforc(e,ed,ing,ement). Gender-biased education(al). *See also* Gender identity; Psychosocial development; Socialization.

Engineering, agricultural. See *Agricultural engineering.*

Engineering, civil. See *Civil engineering.*

Engineering, environmental. See *Environmental engineering.*

Engineering, genetic. See *Genetic engineering.*

Engineering, human. See *Biotechnology; Ergonomics.*

Engineering, human factors. See *Biotechnology; Ergonomics.*

Engineering, industrial. See *Industrial engineering.*

Engineering, social. See *Social engineering.*

Engineering psychology. Engineering psychology. *Choose from:* human factor(s), man machine, psycholog(y, ical), psychophysical, psychophysiolog(y,ical) *with:* design(ed,ing,s), keyboard(s), engineer(ed,ing), architecture, workspace, workstation(s), computer(s), microcomputer(s), task performance. *Consider also:* human engineering, industrial psychology, man-machine system(s), robotic(s), ergonomic(s). *See also* Ergonomics.

Engineers. Engineer(s). *Consider also:* engineering *with:* staff, personnel, major(s,ing), student(s), trainee(s), researcher(s), lecturer(s), professor(s), faculty, graduate(s), professional(s). *See also* Professional personnel.

English, Black. See *Ebonics.*

English, nonstandard. See *Nonstandard English.*

Engraving. Engrav(e,ed,ing,ings). Etch(ed,ing,ings). Photoengrav(e,ed, ing,ings). *See also* Arts; Etching; Graphic arts; Illustrated books; Printing.

Engravings, rock. See *Petroglyphs.*

Engulfment anxiety. See *Fear of closeness.*

Enhancement, fertility. See *Fertility enhancement.*

Enhancers, cognitive. See *Cognitive enhancers.*

Enjoyment. Enjoy(ed,ing,ment). Pleasure(ful). Delight(ed,ing,ful). Hedon(ic,ism). Gratif(y,ied,ication, ications). Joy(ful,fully,ance). Delect(able,ation). Glad(ness). Diversion(s). Relish(ed,ing). Amusement(s). Entertainment(s). Indulgence(s). Savor(ed,ing). Content(ment). *Consider also:* creature comfort(s), treat(s), bliss(ful,fully), ecstas(y,tic). *See also* Anhedonia; Euphoria; Happiness; Hedonism; Pleasure; Recreation; Relaxation; Satisfaction.

Enlargement. Enlarg(e,ed,ing,ement). Amplif(y,ied,ying,ication). Magnif(y,ied, ying,ication). Augment(ed,ing,ation, ations). Doubl(e,ed,ing). Tripl(e,ed,ing). Quadrupl(e,ed,ing). *Consider also:* inflat(ed,ing,ion), expand(ed,ing), swell(ed,ing), swollen, grow(th,ing), wax(ed,ing), sprout(ed,ing), matur(e,ed, ing,ity,ation). *See also* Accumulation; Buildup; Copying processes; Development.

Enlightenment (state of mind). Enlighten(ed,ment). Nirvana. Mystic(al) union(s). Unio mystica. Transcendent experience(s). Cosmic consciousness. Cosmic sensitivity. Samadhi. Satori. Buddha mind. Buddhahood. Sunyata. Samatha. *Choose from:* spiritual, intellectual, religious *with:* awakening, revelation(s), liberation. *Consider also:* peak experience(s), expanded consciousness, bodhisattva, emptiness of mind, unconditioned mind, revelation(s), intuitive understanding, egoless(ness), anatman, authentic identity. *See also* Altruism; Brotherliness; Climax; Grace (theology); Guru; Healing; Meditation; Religious experience; Rejuvenation; Self actualization; Salvation; Spiritual exercises; Spiritual formation.

Enlisted military personnel. Enlisted military personnel. Enlistee(s). Draftee(s). *Choose from:* military *with:* conscript(s), inductee(s), recruit(s). *Choose from:* enlisted, drafted, noncommissioned, petty *with:* personnel, men, man, women, woman, service(men,man, women,woman), male(s), female(s), officer(s), recruit(s), crewmember(s), submariner(s), soldier(s), sailor(s), marine(s). *Consider also:* sergeant(s),

seamen. *See also* Military draft; Sailors; Volunteer military personnel.

Enlistment, military. See *Military enlistment.*

Enrichment, environmental. See *Environmental enrichment.*

Enrichment, environmental animal culture. See *Environmental enrichment (animal culture).*

Enrichment, job. See *Job enrichment.*

Enrichment, marital. See *Marital enrichment.*

Enrollment, school. See *School enrollment.*

Ensembles. Ensemble(s). Musical group(s). Trio(s). Quartet(s). Troupe(s). Musical compan(y,ies). Choir(s). Chamber group(s). *Consider also:* corps de ballet. *See also* Choral music; Choral singing; Choral societies; Choruses; Musical societies; Musicians; Singers.

Enslavement. See *Slavery.*

Entendre, double. See *Double meanings.*

Enterprise, free. See *Market economy.*

Enterprise, private. See *Private enterprise.*

Enterprise zones. Enterprise zone(s). Empowerment zone(s). Zone(s) with business incentive(s). Job-creation zone(s). *Consider also:* local economic development, reindustrializ(e,ed,ing, ation), urban development corporation(s), ghetto factor(y,ies). *See also* Government subsidization; Industrial promotion; Urban renewal; Zoning.

Enterprises. Enterprise(s). Partnership(s). Venture(s). Business(es,man,men, woman,women). Undertaking(s). Industr(ies,y). Small business(es). Commerc(e,ial). Manufactur(er,ers,ing). Export(ed,ing,s). Import(ed,ing,s). Sales. Trad(e,ed,ing). Market(ing,s). Corporat(e,ions). Compan(y,ies). Merchandising. Selling. Promoting. Entrepreneur(s,ship). Invest(ing,ment, ments). Private sector. Profit(s,making). Retail. Wholesale. Capitalis(m,tic). Monopol(y,ies). *See also* Agribusiness; Business organizations; Cooperatives; Corporations; Entrepreneurship; Factories; Family businesses; Going public; Industrial enterprises; Minority businesses; Private enterprise; Public sector; Small businesses; Women owned businesses.

Enterprises, business. See *Enterprises.*

Enterprises, industrial. See *Industrial enterprises.*

Enterprises, international business. See *Multinational corporations.*

Enterprises, public. See *Public sector.*

Entertainers. Entertainer(s). Actor(s). Actress(es). Circus clown(s). Comedian(s). Concert pianist(s).

Dancer(s). Hollywood. Impersonator(s). Leading man. Leading lady. Member(s) of the cast. Movie star(s). Movie idol(s). Showmen. Television star(s). Theatrical performer(s). *Consider also:* supernumerar(y,ies). *See also* Circus performers; Comedians; Entertainment; Entertainment industry; Famous people; Popular culture.

Entertaining. Entertain(ed,ing). Host(ed, ing). Partygiving. Invit(e,ed,ing) guest(s). Dinner part(y,ies). Hospitality. Provide entertainment. *Choose from:* bachelor, lavish, extravagant, stag, birthday, anniversar(y,ies) *with:* dinner(s), part(y,ies). Celebrat(e,ed,ing, ion,ions). Feast(s,ing). Bat mitzvah(s). Bar mitzvah(s). Reunion(s). Wedding(s). Shower(s). Debutante ball(s). *See also* Anniversaries and special events; Dinners and Dining; Entertainment; Hospitality.

Entertainment. Entertainment. Amusement(s). Banquet(s). Carnival(s). Circus(es). Comed(y,ies). Concert(s). Danc(e,es,ing). Diversion(s). Entertainer(s). Feast(s). Game(s). Hollywood. Movie(s). Parade(s). Part(y,ies). Pastime(s). Picnic(s). Play(s,ed,ing). Radio(s). Recreation(al). Show(s). Sport(s). Television. Theatrical performance(s). Theatrical production(s). Vacation(s). *Consider also:* fun, pleasure, merriment, revelry. *See also* Adult entertainment; Audiences; Belly dance; Circus; Computer games; Dinners and Dining; Dirty dancing; Electronic games; Entertaining; Mass media; Motion pictures; Popular culture; Word games; Word play.

Entertainment, adult. See *Adult entertainment.*

Entertainment industry. Entertainment industry. Show business. Box office(s). *Consider also:* amusement park(s), Disneyland, circus(es), theme park(s), television industry, Tony Award(s), Emmy Award(s), Grammy Award(s), MTV Video Music Award(s), theatre music industry. *See also* Adult entertainment; Entertainment; Entertainers; Impresarios; Industry.

Enthusiasm. Enthusias(m,tic). Eager(ness). Avid. Excit(e,ed,ment). Earnest(ness). Keen(ness). Intent(ness). Intens(e,ity, eness). Fervor. Ardor. Fervent. Devot(ed, ion). Zeal(ous,ousness). Passion(ate). Fanatic(ism). Exuberan(ce,t). Intens(e,ity). Spirited. Ebullient. Energetic. Determin(ed,ation). Vehemen(t,ce). *See also* Emotions; Morale; Motivation.

Enthusiasts. Enthusiast(s). Aficionado(s). Devotee(s). Fan(s). Zealot(s). Fanatic(s). Supporter(s). Follower(s). Disciple(s). Extremist(s). Partisan(s). *See also*

Audiences; Fans (persons); Followers; Nerds; Zealots.

Entitlements. See *Antipoverty programs; Government programs; Income distribution; Income maintenance programs; Medical assistance; Public welfare; Social programs; Social services; Transfer payments; Unemployment relief; Workfare.*

Entourage. Entourage(s). Attendant(s). Retinue(s). Cortege(s). Escort(s). Bodyguard(s). *Consider also:* subordinate(s), convoy(s), courtier(s), follower(s), retainer(s), sycophant(s). *See also* Attendants; Caravans; Convoys; Support staff.

Entr'acte. See *Interludes (music).*

Entrance examinations. Entrance examination(s). *Choose from:* entrance, admission, qualifying, matriculation *with:* examination(s), screening, test(s), batter(y,ies). *See also* Admissions; Educational diagnosis.

Entrances. Entrance(s,way,ways). Door(s). Doorway(s). Driveway(s). Entryway(s). Portal(s). Place(s) of entry. *Consider also:* ingress(ion), passageway(s), gangway(s), lobb(y,ies), corridor(s), anteroom(s), waiting room(s), aperture(s), opening(s), threshold(s). *See also* Architectural accessibility; Architectural styles; Architecture; Exits; Facility design and construction; Gatekeepers; Halls; Openings; Travel barriers;

Entrapment. See *Electronic eavesdropping; Espionage; Undercover operations.*

Entrapment games. Entrapment game(s). *Choose from:* entrap(ment,ped,ping), trap(s,ped,ping) *with:* conflict(s), situation(s), psychological, game(s). *Consider also:* confidence, dilemma *with:* game(s). *See also* Game theory; Trapping.

Entrepreneurship. Entrepreneur(s,ship, ial,ing). Threshold compan(y,ies). Enterpris(er,ers,ing). Startup(s). Start-up(s). *Consider also:* intrapreneur(s, ship), infopreneur(s,ship), promoter(s), producer(s), small business(es,man, woman,men,women). *See also* Business Incubators; Creators; Family businesses; Founding; Intrapreneurship; Micro-enterprise; Minority businesses; Private enterprise; Risk; Small businesses; Self employment; Start up business; Women owned businesses.

Entropy. Entrop(y,ic,ically). State of disorder. Degrad(e,ing,ation). Decay(ed,ing). *Consider also:* chao(s, tic) random(ness), disorganiz(ed,ation), run(ning) down. *See also* Chaos; Chaotic behavior in systems; Clutter; Disintegration; Orderliness.

Entry. See *Admissions; Entrances; Gatekeepers; Intake (agency); Patient admission.*

Entry, data. See *Data entry.*

Enumeration. Enumerat(e,ed,ing,ion). Quantif(y,ied,ication). Count(ed,ing,s). Tall(y,ies). Poll(ed,ing,s). Census(es). Nosecount(s). Roster(s). *Consider also:* itemiz(e,ed,ing,ation), naming, listing, detailing, comput(e,ed,ing), calculat(e, ed,ing). *See also* Census; Inventories; Measurement; Demographic surveys; Sampling; Surveys.

Enuresis. See *Urinary incontinence.*

Environment. Environment(s,al). Milieu. Setting(s). Surrounding(s). Context(s, ual). Living condition(s). Home condition(s). Furnishing(s). Climat(e,ic). Quality of life. Eco-aesthetic(s). Proxemic. Proximity. Ecolog(ical,y). Nature vs. nurture. Design of dwelling(s). Decor. Ambien(ce,t). Ambian(ce,t). Habitat(s). Physical condition(s). Social condition(s). Air quality. Water. Water quality. Soil(s). Soil quality. Green space(s). Over-crowd(ed,ing). Crowd(ed,ing). Workspace(s). Work space(s). Workplace(s). Working condition(s). Job site(s). Life space(s). Human factors engineering. Pollution. Organizational climate(s). Isolat(ed,ion). Neighborhood(s). Communit(y,ies). Radiation. Light. Humidity. Noise(s). Sound(s). Odor. Thermal condition(s). Altitude(s). Season(s). Environmental design(s). *Consider also:* atmospher(e, es,ic), aura(s), background(s), backdrop(s). *See also* Academic environment; Ambience; Animal environments; Architectural accessibility; Classroom environment; Communes; Community (geographic locality); Context; Economic conditions; Environmentalism; Environmental enrichment; Environmental impacts; Environmental pollutants; Environmental protection; Extenuating circumstances; Extraterrestrial environment; Home environment; Hospital environment; Living conditions; Neighborhoods; Noise (sounds); Organizational climate; Place of residence; Poverty areas; Restoration ecology; Rural communities; Social environment; Suburbs; Therapeutic community; Urban environments; Working conditions.

Environment, academic. See *Academic environment.*

Environment, adaptation to. See *Adjustment (to environment).*

Environment, adjustment to. See *Adjustment (to environment).*

Environment, barrier free. See *Architectural accessibility.*

Environment, classroom. See *Classroom environment.*

Environment, educational. See *Educational environment.*

Environment, extraterrestrial. See *Extraterrestrial environment.*

Environment, family. See *Family life; Home environment.*

Environment, health facility. See *Health facility environment.*

Environment, home. See *Home environment.*

Environment, hospital. See *Hospital environment.*

Environment, impoverished. See *Cultural deprivation; Maternal deprivation; Psychosocial deprivation; Social isolation.*

Environment, natural. See *Natural environment.*

Environment, school. See *Educational environment.*

Environment, social. See *Social environment.*

Environment, spacecraft. See *Extraterrestrial environment.*

Environment, work. See *Organizational culture; Organizational climate; Working conditions.*

Environmental adjustment. See *Adjustment (to environment).*

Environmental associations. See *Environmentalism.*

Environmental degradation. Environmental degradation. Biodegradation. *Choose from:* environmental(ly), groundwater, reef(s), soil(s), forest(s), air, water *with:* deteriorat(e,ed,ing,ion), destruct(ing,ive, ion), contaminant(s), erosion, erod(e,ed, ing), declin(e,ed,ing), displac(e,ed,ing, ement,ements). *Consider also:* deforestation, rise in sea level, desertification, drought(s). *See also* Anti-environmentalism; Atmospheric contamination; Bioinvasion; Deforestation; Desertification; Environmental impacts; Environmental pollution; Regression (civilization); Resource stress.

Environmental design. Environmental design. *Choose from:* environment(al), building(s), classroom(s), facilit(y,ies), interior(s), exterior(s), lighting, furniture, park(s), communit(y,ies), urban, habitat(s,ion), workspace, work setting(s), living space(s), housing, space utilization, living quarter(s), dormitor(y,ies), house(s), residence(s), home(s) *with:* design(ed,ing), architectur(e,al), plan(ned,ning), engineering. *Consider also:* landscap(e, ed,ing), architectural design. *See also*

Architectural accessibility; Architecture; Environment; Environmental engineering; Exteriors.

Environmental determinism.
Environmental(ly) determin(ed,ism). Environmentalism. *Choose from:* environmental(ly), geographical(ly), climat(e,es,ic), habitat(s), ecolog(y,ical, ically) *with:* determin(ed,ism). *See also* Determinism; Economic determinism; Environmental effects; Euthenics; Nature nurture; Geographic determinism; Human ecology; Sociocultural factors; Socioeconomic factors.

Environmental effects. Environmental effect(s). *Choose from:* ambience, environment(al), surrounding(s), condition(s), ecolog(y,ical), radiation, altitude, atmospheric condition(s), cold, heat, gravit(y,ational), noise, seasonal variation(s), temperature, climate, weather condition(s), underwater condition(s), weightlessness, crowding, economic condition(s), home condition(s), living condition(s), classroom condition(s), setting(s), barrier(s) *with:* effect(s), factor(s), response(s), consequen(t,ces), affected, result(s), sequel(ae), repercussion(s), aftereffect(s), byproduct(s), reaction(s), impact(s), influence(s), cause(s,d), interaction(s), stress(ors), determinant(s). *See also* Altitude effects; Ambience; Biological factors; Crowding; Economic determinism; Environment; Environmental determinism; Environmental impacts; Environmental pollutants; Environmental pollution; Environmental psychology; Environmental stress; Heat; Heat effects; Home environment; Human ecology; Interior design; Gravitational effects; Greenhouse effect; Lunar cycle; Noise effects; Sick building syndrome; Temperature effects; Tropical medicine; Underwater effects; Weather.

Environmental engineering. Environmental engineering. *Choose from:* environment(al,ally), solid waste, hazardous waste *with:* design(s,ed,ing), technolog(y,ies), management, remediation, construction. *See also* Environmental design; Environmental planning; Environmentalism.

Environmental enrichment. Environmental(ly) enrich(ed,ment). *Choose from:* environment(s,al,ally), housing, conditions, milieu(s), setting(s) *with:* enrich(ed,ment), stimulat(e,ed,ing,ion), attention. *Consider also:* environmental complexity. *See also* Environment.

Environmental enrichment (animal culture). Environmental enrichment. *Choose from:* zoo(s), confined animal(s), captiv(e,ity), rehabilitating animal(s) or baboon(s), chimpanzee(s), etc. *with:* enclosure design(s), sensory stimulation,

quality of life, wellbeing, enrichment, enclosure furnishing(s), floor space, captive maintenance. *See also* Animal environments; Captivity; Zoo animals.

Environmental impacts. Environmental impact(s). *Choose from:* environment(al), ecolog(y,ical), ecosystem(s), wildlife, climat(e,es,ic,ological), habitat(s), plant(s), animal(s), species, air, water, atmosphere, biosphere, soil, land, landscape, natural resources, groundwater, river(s), lake(s), ocean(s), bay(s), stream(s), cloud(s), rain, wetland(s), sensitive land(s), desert(s), woodland(s), forest(s), prairie(s) *with:* impact(s), effect(s), affect(ed,ing), degrad(e,ed,ing,ation), extinct(ion), buffer(s), fragment(ed,ing,ation), build(ing), reshap(e,ed,ing), tam(e,ed, ing), pollut(e,ed,ing,ant,ants,ion), hazard(s,ous), expos(e,ed,ing,ure), contaminat(e,ed,ing,ion), noise(s), residue(s), stress(es), spill(s), acid rain, blight(ed). *See also* Air pollution; Atmospheric contamination; Conservation of natural resources; Deforestation; Desertification; Ecosystem management; Environmental degradation; Environmental effects; Environmental law; Environmental policy; Environmental pollutants; Environmental pollution; Environmental protection; Food chain; Greenhouse effect; Hazardous wastes; Industrial wastes; Land preservation; Pollution control; Recycling; Sick building syndrome; Sewage as fertilizer; Sewage disposal; Slash burn agriculture; Soil conservation; Tobacco smoke pollution; Tree planting; Waste disposal; Waste to energy; Waste transport; Water conservation; Water pollution.

Environmental law. Environmental law(s). *Choose from:* environment(al), natural resource(s), waste disposal, pollution, hazardous substance(s), habitat protection, wetland(s), wildlife, biodiversity *with:* law(s,suit,suits), treat(y,ies), regulation(s), requirement(s), standard(s), rule(s), court decision(s). *Consider also:* Clean Air Act, Endangered Species Act, Clean Water Act, Environmental Protection Act, Environmental Protection Agency, EPA, green law(s). *See also* Energy policy; Environmental impacts; Environmental policy; Environmental pollution; Environmentalism; Laws; Natural resources; Policy; Regulations.

Environmental movement. See *Environmentalism.*

Environmental planning. See *Environmental design.*

Environmental policy. Environmental polic(y,ies). *Choose from:* environment(al), natural resource(s), forest(s), smog, waste disposal, pollution, global warming, ozone, park(s), hazardous

substance(s), habitat protection, wetland(s), green *with:* polic(y,ies), approach(es), norm(s), custom(s), regulation(s), plan(s), requirement(s), standard(s), rule(s). *See also* Anti-environmentalism; Environmental impacts; Environmental law; Environmental pollution; Environmentalism; Policy; Regulations; Transportation policy.

Environmental pollutants. Environmental pollutant(s). Noxious cloud(s). Tobacco smoke. Litter(ed,ing). Noise pollution. Smog. Thermal pollution. Fallout. Ecological imbalance. Automobile exhaust(s). Automobile emission(s). Acid rain. Lead contamination. *Choose from:* environment(al), ecolog(y,ical), air, water, soil(s) *with:* risk(s), carcinogen(ic,s), chemical(s), toxin(s), neurotoxin(s), toxicant(s), hydrocarbon(s), hazard(s,ous), toxic(ity), contaminant(s), contaminat(ed,ion), danger(ous,ousness), threaten(ing), infectious, pollut(ed,ing,ant,ants), atomic, nuclear, radioactive. *Consider also:* PCBs, polychlorinated biphenyls, asbestos, poisonous gas(es), radon, alar, DDT, chlordane, dioxin, agent orange, defoliant(s), volatile hydrocarbons, chlorine gas, benzene, mercury, cadmium, lead, heavy metal(s), pesticide(s), herbicide(s), hydrogen cyanide *with:* environment(al,s), air, water, soil, atmosphere, groundwater, river(s), ocean(s), lake(s), waterway(s), biosphere, level(s), refuse, garbage, sewage, slurry, waste(s), incinerat(or,ors, ion), trash, ash(es), residue(s), dump(s, ing), cloud(s), rain, effluent(s), rubbish, debris, dust, emission(s), sweeping(s), tailing(s), oil spill(s,age), petroleum spill(s,age), food chain. *Choose from:* hazardous *with:* substance(s), dump(s), waste(s). *Choose from:* chemical(s) *with:* contaminat(e,ed,ing,ion), pollut(e,ed,ing, ion), toxic(ity), emission(s). *Choose from:* toxic(ity) *with:* contaminat(e,ed, ing,ion), emission(s), dump(s), level(s), ash(es). *Choose from:* radioactive, nuclear, atomic *with:* waste(s), emission(s), contaminat(ed,ing,ion). *See also* Acid rain; Agricultural chemicals; Air pollution; Carcinogens; Containment of biohazards; Dioxin; Environmental effects; Environmental impacts; Environmental pollution; Environmental protection; Food contamination; Greenhouse effect; Hazardous materials; Hazardous wastes; Herbicides; Industrial wastes; Medical geography; Medical wastes; Nuclear accidents; Nuclear waste; Oil spills; Pesticides; Pollution control; Sewage; Sick building syndrome; Smoking; Solid waste; Tobacco smoke pollution; Toxic substances; Waste disposal; Waste to energy; Waste transport; Water pollution.

Environmental pollution. Environmental pollut(e,ed,ant,ants,ing,ion). Thermal pollution. Environmental exposure. Food contamination. Noise pollution. Noise intensity. Traffic noise. Pesticide residue(s). Waste product(s). Global distillation. Litter(ed,ing). Contaminat(e, ed,ing,ant,ants). Waste problem(s). Dirt(y,iness). Unclean. Soot(y). Smok(e, ing,y). Unhealthy condition(s). Unhygienic. Exhaust(s). Dust(y,iness). Concentrations of ozone, heavy metals, etc. Poor air quality. Nuclear waste(s). Toxic metal(s). Tobacco smoke. Smoke exposure. Passive smoking. Secondary cigarette smoke. Exposure to chemical(s). Concentration of carbon monoxide. Automobile exhaust(s). Automobile emission(s). Smog. Pesticide(s). Herbicide(s). Environmental stress(es). Oil spill(s). Acid rain. Decayed physical setting. Environmental quality. Blight(ed). Nonreturnable beverage container(s). *Choose from:* environment(al), ecolog(y,ical), air, water, atmosphere, biosphere, soil, groundwater, river(s), lake(s), ocean(s), bay(s), stream(s), cloud(s), rain, effluent(s), dust, food chain, waste(s), incinerat(ors,ion), trash, spill(s) *with:* pollut(e,ed,ing,ant,ants,ion), toxic(ity), carcinogen(s,ic), contaminat(ed,ion), hazard(ous), radioactive. *See also* Acid rain; Agricultural chemicals; Air pollution; Atmospheric contamination; Bioinvasion; Carcinogens; Containment of biohazards; Contamination; Environmental degradation; Environmental effects; Environmental impacts; Environmental law; Environmental policy; Environmental pollutants; Environmental protection; Environmental stress; Food contamination; Greenhouse effect; Hazardous occupations; Hazardous wastes; Herbicides; Industrial wastes; Medical geography; Medical wastes; Noise (sounds); Nuclear accidents; Nuclear waste; Oil spills; Organic farming; Pesticides; Pollution control; Sick building syndrome; Smoking; Solid waste; Tobacco smoke pollution; Urban health; Waste disposal; Waste to energy; Waste transport; Water pollution.

Environmental protection. Environment(al,ally) protect(ed,ing,ion). Environmental impact statement(s). EPA. Environmental Protection Agency. Ecolog(y,ist,ists). Anti-pollution. Environmentalis(m,t,ts). Conservation(ism,ist,ists). Wildlife refuge(s). Forever wild. Environmental defense. Recycl(e,ed,ing). *Choose from:* sav(e,ed,ing), conserv(e,ing,ation), preserv(e,ed,ing,ation), defend(ing,er, ers), protect(ed,ing,tion), maintain(ance), safeguard(ing), monitor(ing), reclaim(ed,ing), reclamation, reforest(ed, ing,ation), restor(e,ed,ing,ation),

replant(ed,ing) *with:* environment(al, ally), ecolog(y,ical), natural resource(s), wilderness(es), soil, water, air, atmosphere, biosphere, ecosystem(s), habitat(s), ocean(s), river(s), lake(s), land, woodland(s), forest(s), rain forest(s), swamp(s), wetland(s), desert(s), marsh(es), jungle(s), park(s), wildlife, animal(s), mammal(s), bird(s), species, plant(s), tree(s), fish(es), reptile(s). *Choose from:* environmental, conservation, waste(s), toxic material(s), ocean dumping *with:* planning, polic(y,ies), regulat(ion,ions,ory), movement(s). *Consider also:* Earth day. *See also* Alternative energy; Anti-environmentalism; Biosphere; Brownfields; Conservation of natural resources; Containment of biohazards; Decontamination; Drinking water; Earth; Ecology; Ecosysytem management; Environment; Environmental pollution; Environmental stress; Environmentalism; Food chain; Forest conservation; Forestry; Irrigation; Land preservation; Land use; Medical wastes; Natural environment; Natural foods; Natural resources; Neighborhood preservation; Oil spills; Organic farming; Plant succession; Pollution control; Quality of life; Reclamation of land; Reforestation; Renewable resources; Resource stress; Restoration ecology; Shore protection; Soil conservation; Solid waste; Submerged lands; Tree planting; Waste disposal; Waste to energy; Waste transport; Water conservation; Water purification; Wildlife conservation; Wildlife sanctuaries; Zero emissions vehicles.

Environmental psychology. Environmental psychology. *Choose from:* environment(al), surroundings, ambience, working conditions, color, milieu, setting(s), facility design *with:* psycholog(y,ical), behavior(al), mental state(s), mood(s), emotional impact(s). *See also* Ambience; Environmental effects.

Environmental racism. Environmental racism. Environmental discrimination. *Choose from:* environmental(ly), siting, landfill(s), hazardous waste(s), waste facilit(y,ies), *with:* racis(m,t,ts), discriminatory practice(s), discriminat(e, ed,ing,ion), racial minorities, nonwhite, people of color. *Consider also:* environmental injustice(s). *See also* Community problems; Ecological imperialism; Hazardous wastes; Industrial wastes; Poverty areas; Racism; Urban poverty; Waste disposal.

Environmental regulations. See *Environmental law; Environmental policy.*

Environmental sciences. Environmental science(s). Environmental biology. *Choose from:* ecolog(y,ical),

environment(al) *with:* scien(tific,ce,ces), research. *See also* Sciences.

Environmental stress. Environment(al,ally) stress(es,ed,or,ors). Stressful environment(s). Bad weather. Exposure to noise. Nois(y,iness). Crowd(ed,ing). Overcrowd(ed,ing). Natural disaster(s). Catastrophe(s). Cold exposure. Food stress. Aversive setting(s). Traffic condition(s). Excessive heat. Poor housing. Poor condition(s). Unsanitary condition(s). Deprivation. Pollut(ed,ing,ant,ants). Dangerous condition(s). Lack of privacy. Smoke exposure. Anxiety producing situation(s). Confine(d,ment). Relocation stress. Unfamiliar environment(s). *Choose from:* environment(al,ally,s), ambient, travel, transit, condition(s), exposure, housing, setting(s), temperature(s), socioenvironmental, situations, heat, cold, altitude, working condition(s), relocation *with:* stress(es,ed,or,ors,ful). *See also* Altitude sickness; Crowding; Deprivation; Drought; Environment; Environmental effects; Natural disasters; Noise effects; Organic farming; Overpopulation; Physiological stress; Resource stress; Sick building syndrome; Sustainable development; Tropical medicine.

Environmental therapy. See *Milieu therapy; Socioenvironmental therapy; Therapeutic communities.*

Environmental tobacco smoke. See *Tobacco smoke pollution.*

Environmentalism. Environmentalis(m,t,ts). Conservation(ism,ist,ists). Environmental movement(s). Conservation movement(s). Eco-aware(ness). Gaiais(m,t,ts). Ecoconscious(ness). Ecofeminis(m,t,ts). Ecolog(y,ical) movement(s). Naturalist(s). Green(s) party. Green politics. Pro-environment(al). Ecolog(y,ical,ist,ists,ism). *Choose from:* environment(al,ally), ecolog(y,ically), conservation *with:* conscious(ness), concern(ed), awareness, activis(t,ts,m), ethic(s,al,ally), debate(s). Environmental Protection Agency. Ecological behavior(s). Ecolog(y,ist, ists). Anti-pollution activist(s). Environmental ethic(s). Environmental issue(s). Conservation planning. Environment(al) protection. Forever wild. Environmental defense. Recycling. *Consider also:* Back to the Land movement, Greenpeace, Natural Resources Defense Council, Sierra Club, Nature Conservancy, Cousteau Society, National Wildlife Federation, Environmental Defense Fund, Earth First, etc. *See also* Anthropocentrism; Anti-environmentalism; Bioregionalism; Conservation of natural resources; Consumer organizations; Energy conservation; Environmental engineering; Environmental law; Environmental policy; Environmental protection; Forest conservation; Land preservation; Naturalists; Recycling; Restoration ecology; Shore protection; Social movements; Soil conservation; Sustainable development; Tree planting.

Environmentalism, radical. See *Deep ecology.*

Environments, animal. See *Animal environments.*

Environments, factory. See *Working conditions.*

Environments, rural. See *Rural areas.*

Environments, urban. See *Urban environments.*

Envoys. See *Agents; Delegates; Diplomats; Messengers.*

Envy. See *Jealousy.*

Envy, penis. See *Penis envy.*

Epic literature. Epic literature. Epic novel(s). Primary epic(s). Secondary epic(s). Chanson(s) de geste. Charlemagne legend(s). *Choose from:* epic, heroic *with:* litera(ry,ture), poe(try,m,ms), theater, drama, simile(s), Homeric, Arthurian, Greek. *Consider also:* Iliad, Odyssey, Aeneid, Cantar de mio Cid, La Chanson de Roland, Divine Comedy, Nibelungenlied, Mahabharata, Ramayana, Paradise Lost, Beowulf, Gerusaleme Liberta, Faerie Queene, Lusiads, Kalevala, etc. *See also* Folk literature; Historical poetry; Legends; Narrative poetry; War poetry.

Epic poetry. See *Epic literature.*

Epidemics. Epidemic(s). High morbidity. Outbreak(s) of disease. Spread of disease. Plague(s). High incidence. Prevalence of disease. Pandem(ia,ic,ics). Endemoepidemic. *Consider also:* contag(ious,ion), hyperendemic, incidence of disease, disease reservoir(s), pestilence(s). *See also* Disease; Medical geography; Plague; Public health; Sanitation; Tropical medicine; Urban health; World health

Epigrams. Epigram(s,matic,matically, matize,matism,matist,matists). Epigramm(s,ata). Sinngedicht(en). *Consider also:* concise poe(m,ms,try), witty paradoxical saying(s). *See also* Aphorisms; Latin epigrams; Poetry; Slogans.

Epigrams, Latin. See *Latin epigrams.*

Epigraphs. Epigraph(s,ical,y). Engraved inscription(s). Quotation(s). *See also* Epitaphs; Inscriptions; Latin inscriptions; Monuments; Obituaries; Quotations.

Epilepsy. Epilep(sy,tic,tica,toid,tology, togenic,tosis). Aura. Absentia. Analepsis. Cataptosis. Furor epilepticus. Status epilepticus. Haut mal. Petit mal. Grand mal. *Consider also:* convulsion(s),

seizure(s). *See also* Developmental disabilities; Epileptic seizures; Experimental epilepsy; Minimal brain disorders; Petit mal epilepsy.

Epilepsy, experimental. See *Experimental epilepsy.*

Epilepsy, petit mal. See *Petit mal epilepsy.*

Epileptic seizures. Epileptic seizure(s). Myoclonic jerk(s). Kindled amygdaloid seizure(s). Jacksonian seizure(s). Ictus. *Choose from:* epilep(sy,tic,tics), epileptiform, grand mal, petit mal *with:* activity, attack(s), fit(s), convulsion(s), status, symptom(s), episode(s), seizure(s), spasm(s). *See also* Epilepsy.

Epilogues. Epilog(s,ue,ues). Afterword(s). Conclusion(s). Finale(s). Postlude(s). Ending(s). Summation(s). Peroration(s,al). Coda(s). Codicil(s). Final word(s). *Consider also:* follow-up(s), postscript(s), sequel(s). *See also* Addendum; Adjournment; Continuation; End; Sequelae.

Epinosic gains. See *Secondary gains.*

Episodic memory. Episodic memor(y,ies). *Choose from:* episodic, flashbulb *with:* memor(y,ies), recognition, retrieval, encoding(s), remember(ed,ing), forget(ting), amnesia. *See also* Eidetic imagery.

Epistemology. Epistemolog(y,ical). *Choose from:* theor(y,ies), philosoph(y,ies), model(s), valid(ity), limit(s) *with:* knowledge, understanding. *See also* Determinism; Dialectics; Empiricism; Existentialism; Holism; Indeterminism; Individuation (philosophy); Inquiry (theory of knowledge); Nihilism; Philosophy; Pragmatism; Realism; Reductionism; Relativism; Social epistemology; Teleology.

Epistemology, social. See *Social epistemology.*

Epitaphs. Epitaph(s,ic,ial). Commemorative inscription(s). Hic jacet. Here lies. Funeral oration(s). Tribute(s) to deceased. *See also* Commemoration; Elegies; Epigraphs; Monuments; Obituaries; War poetry.

Epithalamia. Epithalam(ia,ium,iums,ion,ic). Marriage song(s). Wedding Poem(s). Wedding Poetry. Nuptial song(s). Wedding song(s). *Choose from:* marriage, wedding, nuptial *with:* song(s), poem(s), poetry, song(s), cento(s). *See also* Latin laudatory poetry; Laudatory poetry; Love poetry; Lyric poetry; Occasional verse; Weddings.

Epithets. Epithet(s,ical). Appellat(ive,ives, ion). Nickname(s). By-word(s). Nickname(s). Pet name(s). *Consider also:* curse(s), expletive(s), oath(s). *See also* Catchwords; Names; Obscenity; Language usage; Slang; Vulgarity.

Epoch, glacial. See *Glacial epoch.*

Epsilon alcoholism. See *Dipsomania.*

Equal education. Equal education. *Choose from:* equal(ize,ized,izing,ization), egalitarian, equity, democratic, open access, desegregat(e,ed,ing,ion) *with:* education(al), school(s,ing). *Consider also:* universal public education, Education of all Handicapped Children Act, PL 94-142. *See also* Access to education; Affirmative action; Coeducation; Civil rights; Dialogic pedagogy; Education of mentally retarded; Mainstreaming; Multicultural education; Nonsexist education; School integration; Single sex schools; Student rights; Universalism.

Equal job opportunities. Equal job opportunit(y,ies). Equal employment. Affirmative action. Comparable worth. Equal Employment Opportunity Commission. EEOC. Title VII of the Civil Rights Act of 1964. Equal Employment Act of 1972. Equal Pay Act of 1963. Age discrimination in employment act of 1967. Title IX Education Amendments Act of 1972. Rehabilitation Act of 1973, Sections 503 and 504. Americans with Disabilities Act of 1990. Vietnam Era Veterans Readjustment Assistance Act of 1974. *Choose from:* job(s), employ(ee,ees,ed,ing,er, ers,ment), work(er,ers), workplace, personnel, labor force, union(s), wage(s), earning(s), pay, promotion(s), occupation(s,al), vocation(s,al) *with:* opportunit(y,ies), equal(ity), equity, parity. *See also* Affirmative action; Civil rights; Coeducation; Comparable worth; Employment opportunities; Equal education; Single sex schools.

Equal opportunities. See *Equal education; Equal job opportunities.*

Equal rights for women. See *Women's rights.*

Equalitarianism. See *Egalitarianism.*

Equality. See *Comparable worth; Egalitarianism; Equity (payment); Fairness; Nonsexist language; Social equality; Social equity; Social justice.*

Equality, educational. See *Equal education.*

Equality, gender. See *Affirmative action; Comparable worth; Equity (payment); Fairness; Nonsexist language; Sex discrimination; Sexual division of labor; Sexual inequality; Social equality; Social equity.*

Equality, racial. See *Affirmative action; Social equality; Social equity; Social justice.*

Equality, sexual. See *Affirmative action; Comparable worth; Equity (payment); Fairness; Nonsexist language; Sex discrimination; Sexual division of labor;*

Sexual inequality; Social equality; Social equity.

Equality, social. See *Social equality.*

Equality before the law. Equality before the law. Constitutional right(s). Fourteenth amendment. *Choose from:* equal(ity), equal protection, level playing field(s), inequalit(y,ies), bias(ed,es) *with:* Supreme Court, Warren Court, high court, constitutionality. *Consider also:* civil rights. *See also* Civil rights; Due process; Equity pleading and procedure; Fairness; Social equality; Social equity; Social justice.

Equalization, educational. See *Equal education.*

Equilibrium. Equilibrium. Balanc(e,ed, ing). Stab(le,ility). Homeostasis. Stabiliz(ed,ing,ation). Postural adaptation(s). Counterbalance(s,d). Centered. Roll tilt reflex(es). Righting reflex(es). Body righting. Gravity center(s). Postural readjustment. Adjustment to body sway. Postural sway. *Consider also:* disequilibrium, disequilibrator, stabilometer, acid base status, PH regulation, symmetry, unbalanced, imbalance(s), vertigo, symmetry. *See also* Circulation (rotation); Perceptual motor processes; Social equilibrium.

Equilibrium, social. See *Social equilibrium.*

Equipment. Equipment. Apparatus. Tool(s). Utensil(s). Device(s). Appliance(s). Machine(ry,s). Fixture(s). Gadget(s). Contrivance(s). Instrument(s). Meter(s). Recorder(s). Engine(s). Furniture. Prosthes(is,es). Calculator(s). Electromechanical aid(s). Vehicle(s). Office machine(s). Camera(s). Amplifier(s). Computer(s). *See also* Appliances; Calculating machines; Devices; Electronic equipment; Equipment failure; Equipment safety; Furniture; Military weapons; Safety devices; Scientific equipment; Self help devices; Tools; Weaponry.

Equipment, electronic. See *Electronic equipment.*

Equipment, military. See *Military weapons.*

Equipment safety. Equipment safety. *Choose from:* equipment, device(s), prosthes(is,es), apparatus, instrument(s), machine(s,ry), appliance(s), applicator(s), tool(s), engine(s), meter(s), tool(s) or equipment by name *with:* safe(ty), unsafe, accident(s,al), harm(ed,ing,ful), hazard(s,ous), risk(s,ed,ing,y), danger(s,ous), endanger(ed,ing), injur(e,ed,ing,y,ies), protect(ion,ive). *See also* Equipment; Equipment failure; Safety; Safety devices.

Equipment, scientific. See *Scientific equipment.*

Equipment failure. Equipment fail(ed,ing, ure,ures). *Choose from:* equipment, device(s), prosthes(is,es), apparatus, instrument(s), machine(s,ry), appliance(s), applicator(s), tool(s), engine(s), meter(s), tool(s) or equipment by name *with:* fail(ed,ing,ure,ures), defect(s,ive), malfunction(ed,ing), fault(y,s), unreliab(le,ility), breakdown. *See also* Equipment; Equipment safety; Preventive maintenance.

Equitability. Equitab(le,ility). Even handed(ness). Fair minded(ness). Impartial(ity). Unbiased. Disinterested. Dispassionate(ly). Unprejudiced. Neutral(ity). Nondiscriminatory. Openminded(ness). Reasonable(ness). Toleran(t,ce). *See also* Bias; Cultural relativism; Impartiality; Objectivity; Rationality; Value neutral.

Equity (financial). Equit(y,ies). Ownership interest. Property ownership. Residual ownership. Net worth. *Consider also:* venture capital, equity capital, equity securit(y,ies), common equity, equity partnership(s). *See also* Assets; Capitalization; Investments; Stockholders.

Equity (payment). Equity. Comparable worth. *Choose from:* pay(ed,ing,ment, ments), reward(s), income, compensation, salar(y,ies), wage(s) *with:* equit(y,able), parity, equal(ity), fair(ness). *Consider also:* equal pay for equal work. *See also* Comparable worth; Egalitarianism; Fairness; Justice; Prevailing wages; Sexual division of labor; Social equity; Wage differentials.

Equity, educational. See *Equal education.*

Equity, gender. See *Affirmative action; Social equality; Social equity; Social justice.*

Equity, racial. See *Affirmative action; Social equality; Social equity; Social justice.*

Equity, sex. See *Affirmative action; Social equality; Social equity; Social justice.*

Equity, sexual. See *Affirmative action; Social equality; Social equity; Social justice.*

Equity, social. See *Social equity.*

Equity pedagogy. See *Multicultural education.*

Equity pleading and procedure. Equity pleading and procedure. Chancery. Court(s) of equity. Equity jurisprudence. *See also* Due process; Equality before the law.

ERA. See *Women's rights.*

Era, messianic. See *Messianic era.*

Eras. Era(s). Epoch(s). Time period(s). Generation(s). Eon(s). Time span(s). *See also* Historical periods.

Erectile dysfunction. See *Impotence.*

Erections, penile. See *Penile erections.*

Ergonomics. Ergonomic(s). Man machine system(s). *Choose from:* man, worker(s), human, physiolog(,ical), psycho-physiolog(y,ical) *with:* machine(s), computer(s), technology, automat(ed, ion) *with:* system(s), partnership(s), dialog(s), interface(s), interact(ive,ion, ions), assist(ed,ance), function(s), integration, natural language, operation, psycholog(y,ical). *Consider also:* human engineering, work physiology, engineering physiology, engineering psychology, human factors engineering. *See also* Cybernetics; Industrial engineering; Man machine systems; Workstations; Working conditions.

Ergot alkaloids. Ergot alkaloid(s). *Consider also:* ergotamine, ergonovine, LSD, lysergic acid diethylamide. *See also* Ergotism; Hallucinogens.

Ergotism. Ergotism. St. Anthony's fire. Saint Anthony's fire. *See also* Drugs; Ergot alkaloids.

Erosion, soil. See *Soil erosion.*

Erotic art. See *Erotica.*

Erotic films. See *Erotica.*

Erotic literature. See *Erotica.*

Erotic poetry. Erotic poe(try,m,ms). *Choose from:* erotic, sexual(ly), love, lover(s), amor(e,es,ous), romance(s), libertin(e, ism), cuckold(ing), libid(o,inous) *with:* poe(tic,try,m,ms), lyric(s,al), quatrain(s), ghazal(s), verse(s), fabliau(x). *See also* Erotica; Poetry.

Erotic songs. Erotic song(s). *Choose from:* erotic, sexual(ly), love, lover(s), amor(e,es,ous), romance(s), libertin(e, ism), cuckold(ing), libid(o,inous) *with:* song(s), chanson(s), ballad(s), lyric(s), ditt(y,ies), sing(ing), music(al,als). *See also* Bawdy songs; Erotica; Love songs; Music; Obscenity; Songs; Vulgarity.

Erotica. Erotica. Erotic art. Porn(o, ographic,ography). Centerfold(s). Sexually explicit. Explicit sexual stimuli. X-rated. Sin strip(s). Sexually oriented advertising. Indecen(t,cy). Bawdy. Lewd(ness). Obscen(e,ity). Hustler magazine. Pos(ed,ing) nude. Sex shop(s). Dial-a-porn. Playboy. Penthouse. Child pornography. *Choose from:* obscen(e,ity), indecen(t,cy), licentious, adult, X-rated, erotic, suggestive, nude, porn(o,ographic,ography), salacious, explicit sex, sensual(ly), bawdy, pedophilic, sexually provocative, hard core *with:* art, picture(s), movie(s), film(s), video(s), literature, poetry, poem(s), riddle(s), joke(s), doggerel, stor(y,ies), verse(s), book(s), bookstore(s), show(s), magazine(s), material(s), radio, club(s), advertis(ment, ments,ing), theater(s). *Consider also:* strip joint(s), erotic club(s), massage parlor(s), topless bar(s), libidream(s). *See also* Bawdy songs; Erotic poetry; Erotic songs; Pornography; Sex offenses; Sexual arousal; Sexual deviations.

Eroticism. Eroticism. Erotism. Seductive. *Choose from:* sexual(ly), erotic *with:* excit(e,ed,ing,ement), arous(e,ed,ing,al), stimulat(e,ed,ing,ion), fantas(y,ies), pleasure, stimuli. *See also* Erotica; Femmes fatales; Seduction; Sexual arousal; Sex behavior; Sexual fantasies.

Erotized hanging. See *Sexual asphyxia syndrome.*

Erotomania. Erotoman(ia,ic). Aidoioman(ia,ic). Don Juanism. Don Juan syndrome. *Consider also:* preoccup(ied,ation,ations), obsession(s), obsessive *with:* sex(ual,ually), sexuality, psychosexual(ly), erotic(ism). *Consider also:* nymphomania(c,cs), satyriasis, sex(ual) addict(s,ion), stalker(s). *See also* Hypersexuality; Obsessive Love; Stalking.

Errata. See *Errors.*

Error, judicial. See *Judicial error.*

Error analysis. Error analys(is,es). *Choose from:* error(s), mistake(s), wrong response(s), inaccurac(y,ies) *with:* analys(is,es), classif(y,ied,ication), measure(s), typolog(y,ies), rate(s), pattern(s). *See also* Errors.

Errors. Error(s). Errata. Mistake(s,n). Inaccura(cy,cies,te). Incorrect. Erroneous. Discrepan(cy,cies). Miscue(d,s). Misconception(s). Deficit(s). Misdiagnos(ed,is,es). Fallac(y,ies, iousness). Misbelief(s). Misapprehension. Misjudg(ed,ment). Misspelling(s). Solecis(m,tic). Misprint(ed,s). Mislocat(ed,ion). Misread. Misspoke(n). Misunderstood. Misunderstand(ing). Wrong answer(s). Wrong feedback. Slip(s) of tongue. Freudian slip(s). Anomal(y,ies). Miscalculat(e,ed,ion, ions). Omission(s). Omit(ted). Irregularit(y,ies). Misdeal(t). Misdirect(ed). Misfile(d). Misjudge(d). Mispronounce(d). Misquote(d). Blunder(s,ed). Misremember(ed). Misstep(ped). Misstate(d). Mistook. Misvalued. Miswrite. Flaw(ed). Oversight. Incorrectness. Uncorrect. Misplay. Misperception(s). Misidentif(ied,ication). False negative reaction(s). False positive reaction(s). Bogus. Illogic(al). Glitch(es). *See also* Accuracy; Anachronisms; Correctness; Default (negligence); Error analysis; Fallacies; Fallibility; Fault tolerant computing; Faux pas; Halo effect;

Illogical; Illusion (philosophy); Improprieties; Inappropriateness; Incorrect; Journalistic errors; Judgment errors; Judicial error; Literary errors and blunders; Medication errors; Misinformation; Mistaken identity; Reliability; Scientific errors; Speech errors; Truth.

Errors, journalistic. See *Journalistic errors.*

Errors, judgment. See *Judgment errors.*

Errors, medication. See *Medication errors.*

Errors, scientific. See *Scientific errors.*

Errors, speech. See *Speech errors.*

Errors and blunders, literary. See *Literary errors and blunders.*

Escalation. Escalat(e,ed,ing,ion). Intensif(y,ied,ication). Increas(e,ed,ing). Heighten(ed,ing). Grow(ing,n,th). Spread(ing). Broaden(ed,ing). Accelerat(e,ed,ing,ation). Expand(ed, ing). Expansion. Advanc(e,ed,ing). Deepen(ed,ing). Widen(ed,ing). Amplif(y,ied,ication). Magnif(y,ied, ication). Step(ped,ping) up. *See also* Change; Expansion.

Escape. Escap(e,es,ed,ing). Run(ning) away. Runaway(s). AWOL. Abscond(ed,ing). Elud(e,ed,ing). Flee(ing). Fled. Elope(d,ment). Desert(ed,ing,ion). Jailbreak. *See also* Avoidance; Defense mechanisms; Imprisonment.

Escape reaction. Escape reaction. *Choose from:* escape, avoidance, flight *with:* reaction(s), response(s), respond(ed,ing), condition(ed,ing). *See also* Avoidance learning.

Escenica, tonadilla. See *Interludes (music); Opera.*

Eschatology. See *Apocalypse.*

Eskimo-Aleut languages. Eskimo-Aleut language(s). Aleut. Eskimo. Inupiac. Yupik. Inuktitut. Inupiat. Inupik. Netsilik. Numamiut. Taremiut. *See also* Arctic Regions; Eskimos; Language; Languages (as subjects); North America; North American native cultural groups.

Eskimos. Eskimo(an,s). Alaska native(s). Canada native(s). Greenland native(s). Aleut(s). Arctic people(s). Igloolik. Yuk. Inuit. Athabascan(s). Athapascan(s). *See also* Arctic Regions; Ethnic groups; Eskimo-Aleut languages; Indigenous populations; Minority groups.

ESOP. See *Employee stock ownership plans.*

ESP. See *Extrasensory perception.*

Espionage. Espionage. Counterespionage. Spy(ing). Spie(s,d). Foreign agent(s). Electronic intruder(s). Wiretap(ping). Bugging. Penetrate agency. KGB agent(s). Foreign intelligence. Counterintelligence. Infiltrat(e,ed,ing). Double

agent(s). Triple agent(s). Piracy of patent(s). Informant(s). Subvers(ion,ive). Agent(s) provocateur. Exporting sensitive information. Destabilization. Covert politics. Counterinsurgen(cy,t). Covert action. Underground resistance. Sedition. Undercover agent(s). *Choose from:* security *with:* leak(s,ed,ing), laps(e,es,ed,ing), breach(es,ed,ing). *Choose from:* communicat(e,ed,ing,ion), leak(ed,ing), unauthorized, intercept(ed, ing), deliver, divulg(e,ed,ing), sell(ing), sold, steal(ing), stolen, pass(ed,ing) *with:* secret(s), classified information, classified document(s), sensitive information, plan(s). *Consider also:* back-channel informant(s), mole(s). *See also* Collaborators; Cryptography; Electronic eavesdropping; Government secrecy; Intelligence service; Industrial espionage; Informers; Infowar; International relations; Military intelligence; National security; Sabotage; Secrecy; Secret police; Treason; Undercover operations.

Espionage, industrial. See *Industrial espionage.*

Essay tests. Essay test(s). *Choose from:* essay(s), written *with:* test(ing,s), scor(e,es,ings), response(s), exam(s, ination,inations), question(s), quiz(zes), answer(s), item(s). *See also* Essays; Tests; Writing (composition).

Essays. Essay(s,es,ist,ists). Essais. Editorial(s). Photo-essay(s). Treatise(s). Tract(s). Brief discourse(s). Think piece(s). Literary sketch(es). *See also* Essay tests; Literature; Literary criticism; Nature literature; Prose.

Essence. Essence. Essential part(s). Core. Chief constituent(s). Crux. Essential(ity, ities,ness). Gist. Main idea(s). Heart. Quintessen(ce,tial). Vital part(s). Fundamental(s). Principle(s). *See also* Essence (philosophy); Fundamental; Meaning; Pneuma; Soul.

Essence (philosophy). Essence. Essentialis(m,t). *Consider also:* primary substance(s), haeccit(y,ism), quiddit(y, ative), basic nature, true nature. *See also* Essence; Fundamental; Identity; Ontology; Philosophy; Soul.

Essential hypertension. Essential hypertension. Hyperpies(ia,is). *Choose from:* hypertens(ion,ive), high blood pressure, elevated blood pressure *with:* essential, functional, stress. *Consider also:* essential hypertonia. *See also* Cardiovascular system; Hypertension.

Establishment. Establishment(s). Ruling class(es). Dominant class(es). Ruling clique(s). Mandarin(s,ate). Hegemon(y, ies). Political elite(s). Power elite(s). Intelligentsia. Oligarch(y,ies). Owning class(es). Upper class(es). *See also* Authority (officials); Authority (power); Oligarchy; Political elites; Power elite;

Ruling class; Traditionalism; Upper class.

Establishments, eating. See *Eating establishments.*

Estampie. Estampie(s). Estampida(s). Istanpit(a,e). Stantipe(s). *See also* Medieval music.

Estate planning. Estate planning. *Choose from:* estate(s), will(s), heir(s), inherit(ed,ing,ance), surviving spouse(s), beneficiar(y,ies) *with:* plan(ning,ned), management, tax exemption(s). *Consider also:* guardianship(s), trust fund(s), revocable trust(s), irrevocable trust(s), estate tax(es), charitable remainder trust(s), pre-death gifting. *See also* Administration of estates; Beneficiaries; Estates (law); Heirs; Inheritance; Legacies; Survivors benefits.

Estates (law). Estate(s). Real propert(y,ies). Personal propert(y,ies). Personalt(y,ies). Asset(s). *Consider also:* inheritance(s), landed wealth, asset(s), propert(y,ies), holding(s), belonging(s), chattel(s). *See also* Administration of Estates; Heirs; Inheritance; Land ownership; Legacies.

Estates (social orders). See *Social class.*

Estates, administration of. See *Administration of estates*

Esteem, self. See *Self esteem.*

Esthetics. See *Aesthetics.*

Estimation. Estimat(e,ed,ing,ion,ions). *Consider also:* predict(ed,ing,ion,ions), extrapolat(ed,ing,ion,ions), guess(es, ed,ing), calculat(e,ed,ing,ion,ions), infer(red,ring), inference(s), evaluat(e, ed,ing,ion,ions), judg(e,ed,ement, ements), overestimat(e,ed,ing,ion,ions), underestimat(e,ed,ing,ion,ions), assess(ed,ing,ment,ments), approx-imation(s), interpolat(e,ed,ing,ion,ions), conjectur(e,ed,ing), surmis(e,ed,ing). *See also* Forecasting; Measurement; Prediction; Probability; Statistical inference.

Estimation, time. See *Time perception.*

Estrangement. Estrange(d,ment). Alienat(ed,ion). Dissociat(e,ed,ion). Misanthrop(e,ic). Detach(ed,ment). Outsider(s). Hopeless(ness). Meaning-less(ness). Absurd(ity,ness). False consciousness. Objectification. Reification. *Consider also:* power-less(ness), anomie, rootless(ness), helpless(ness), psychological depriva-tion, depersonalization, negativism, impersonal(ity), insensitiv(e,ity), demoraliz(e,ed,ation), impotence, disillusion(ed,ment), disenchant(ed, ment), dispossess(ed,ion), boredom. *See also* Alienation; Anomie; Apathy; Depersonalization disorder; Disengage-ment; Impersonal; Loneliness; Marginal-ity (sociological); Pessimism;

Reification; Role conflict; Social isolation.

Etching. Etch(ed,ing,ings). Engrav(e,ed, ing,ings). Imprint(ed,ing). *Consider also:* inscrib(e,ed,ing). *See also* Drawing; Engraving; Graphic arts; Inscriptions; Printing.

Eternity. Eternity. Eternal. Endless(ness). Forever. Time without end. Infinit(e,ity). Timeless(ness). World without end. Time everlasting. Immeasurable time. Sempitern(al,ally,ity). Never ending. *See also* Endlessness; Heaven; Hell; Immeasurability; Immortality; Infinity.

Ethanol. See *Ethyl alcohol.*

Ethic, Protestant. See *Protestant ethic.*

Ethic, Puritan. See *Protestant ethic.*

Ethic, work. See *Protestant ethic.*

Ethical education. See *Moral education.*

Ethical neutrality. See *Value neutral.*

Ethical practices. Ethical practices. *Choose from:* ethic(s,al), honest(y), philosoph(y, ical), fair(ness), conscientious, honor-able, bioethic(s,al), moral(s,ity), relig(ion,ious), theolog(y,ical), humani-tarian, metaethic(s,al), welfare, social good, common good, individual right(s), self determination, free choice, freedom, value(s), human dignity, free will *with:* practice(s), guideline(s), action(s), decision(s), behavior,responsibilit(y,ies), imperative, obligation(s). *See also* Ethics; Medical ethics; Moral authority; Morality; Unethical conduct.

Ethical relativism. See *Relativism.*

Ethics. Ethic(s,al). Moral philosophy. Moral principle(s). Moral values. Righteous(ness). Bioethic(s,al). Metaethic(s,al). Moral(ity). Integrity. Conscience. Conscientious(ness). Good(ness). Just(ice,ness). Rectitude. Moral obligation(s). Deontolog(y,ical). Honest(y). Upright(ness). Virtuous(ness). Honor(able). *Consider also:* codes of ethics, moral values, altruism, humanism, standard(s) of conduct. *See also* Bioethics; Business ethics; Casuistry; Codes of ethics; Corporate social responsibility; Deontic logic; Feminist ethics; Fiduciary responsibility; Interest (ethics); Legal ethics; Literary ethics; Medical ethics; Military ethics; Moral attitudes; Moral authority; Moral conditions; Morality; Nursing ethics; Political ethics; Professional ethics; Practical theology; Relativism; Research ethics; Sex education; Sexual ethics; Social ethics; Socially responsible investing; Unethical conduct.

Ethics, business. See *Business ethics.*

Ethics, codes. See *Codes of ethics.*

Ethics, evolutionary. See *Evolutionary ethics.*

Ethics, experimental. See *Research ethics.*

Ethics, feminist. See *Feminist ethics.*

Ethics, journalistic. See *Journalistic ethics.*

Ethics, judicial. See *Judicial ethics.*

Ethics, legal. See *Legal ethics.*

Ethics, life sciences. See *Bioethics.*

Ethics, literary. See *Literary ethics.*

Ethics, medical. See *Medical ethics.*

Ethics, military. See *Military ethics.*

Ethics, ministerial clergy. See *Ministerial ethics (clergy).*

Ethics, naturalistic. See *Evolutionary ethics.*

Ethics, newspaper. See *Journalistic ethics.*

Ethics, nursing. See *Nursing ethics.*

Ethics, political. See *Political ethics.*

Ethics, professional. See *Professional ethics.*

Ethics, research. See *Research ethics.*

Ethics, sexual. See *Sexual ethics.*

Ethics, situation. See *Relativism.*

Ethics, social. See *Social ethics.*

Ethnic attitudes. Ethnic attitude(s). Cultural pride. Nationalis(m,tic). *Choose from:* ethnic group(s), Korean American(s), Mexican American(s), African American(s), Navajo(s), etc. *with:* attitude(s), way(s) of thinking, value(s), perspective(s), belief(s), concept(s). *Consider also:* cultural difference(s). *See also* Attitudes; Cultural values; Ethnic values; Ethnicity.

Ethnic cleansing. Ethnic(ally) cleans(ed,ing). Ethnic(ally) murder(s,ed,ing). Genocid(e,al). Pogrom(s). *Consider also:* war crime(s), concentration camp(s), refugee camp(s), forced expulsion(s), war victim(s), killing field(s), driven from home-land(s), virulent nationalism. *See also* Cultural conflict; Displaced persons; Genocide; Hate crimes; Holocaust; Massacres; Offenses against religion; Racism; War atrocities; War crimes; Xenophobia.

Ethnic conflict. See *Cultural conflict; Ethnic cleansing; Ethnic slurs; Xeno-phobia.*

Ethnic differences. Ethnic difference(s). Ethnocultural difference(s). *Choose from:* ethnic(ity), cultur(e,al), minority, ethnosocial, ethnocultural, ethnospecific, Hispanic, Chinese, Japanese, Chicano, Italian(s), Jew(s,ish), Pol(ish,e,es), German(s), Spanish, etc. *with:* characteristic(s), profile(s), variation(s), variance, pattern(s), difference(s), factor(s), unique(ness), variabilit(y,ies), style(s), contrast(s), comparison(s), deviation(s), divergen(ce), discrepan(cy, cies), disparit(y,ies), distinction(s), inequalit(y,ies). *See also* Assimilation (cultural); Biculturalism; Cultural conflict; Cultural issues; Cross cultural comparisons; Cross cultural competency; Ethnic identity; Ethnicity; Intercultural communication; Interethnic families; Intermarriage; Racial differences; Racial identity.

Ethnic disorders. See *Culture specific syndromes; Ethnospecific disorders.*

Ethnic groups. Ethnic group(s). Ethnic minorit(y,ies). Ethnos. Ethnic communit(ies,y). Bicultural. Tricultural. Tribe(s). Cultural group(s). Ethnic culture(s). Racial cultural group(s). Cultural minorit(y,ies). Tribal population(s). Immigrant(s). Ethnic identit(y,ies). Ethnomedical. Ethnocultural. Ethnopsycholog(y,ical). Ethnobehavioral. Hyphenated American(s). Allophone(s). Aboriginal(s). African American(s). Alaska native(s). American Indian(s). Anglo American(s). Arab American(s). Arab Canadian(s). Asian American(s). Basque(s). Bulgarian American(s). Cajun(s). Canada native(s). Chinese American(s). Croatian American(s). Cuban American(s). Dukhobor(s). Eskimo(s). Filipino American(s). French Canadian(s). German American(s). Greek American(s). Gyps(y,ies). Haitian American(s). Hispanic American(s). Hungarian American(s). Irish American(s). Italian American(s). Japanese American(s). Jew(s). Korean American(s). Maori(s). Mexican American(s). Native American(s). Naga(s). Pacific American(s). Polish American(s). Polish Canadian(s). Portuguese American(s). Rumanian American(s). Russian American(s). Samoan American(s). Scandinavian American(s). Slovak(s). Sorb(s,ian). Spanish American(s). White(s). Wend(s,ish). *See also* African cultural groups; Asian Americans; Blacks; Central American native cultural groups; Culture specific syndromes; Ethnic groups; Ethnic wit and humor; Ethnohistory; Ethnolinguistics; Ethnopsychology; Ethnospecific disorders; Hispanic Americans; Indigenous populations; Italian Americans; Japanese Americans; Korean Americans; Linguistic minorities; Mexican Americans; North American native cultural groups; Minority groups; Oceanic cultural groups; Religious cultural groups; South American native cultural groups; Speech communities; Traditional societies.

Ethnic identity. Ethnic identit(y,ies). Ethnicity. First generation. Second generation. Third generation. Hyphenated American(s). Maintenance of ancestral language. *Choose from:* ethnic,

ethnocultural, cultural, Italian(s), German(s), Chinese, etc. *with:* identit(y,ies), consciousness, identification, upbringing, background, solidarity, affirmation, involvement, homophily, descent, bloodline(s). *Consider also:* biculturalism, ethnocentrism, racial identification, Blackness, Africanity, Black consciousness, Afrocentrism. *See also* Cultural identity; Ethnicity; Ethnocentrism; Group identity; Identity; Race awareness; Racial identity; Social identity; Speech communities.

Ethnic minorities. See *Ethnic groups; Minority groups.*

Ethnic neighborhoods. Ethnic neighborhood(s). Ethnic communit(y, ies). Ethnic enclaves. Black neighborhood(s). Jewish neighborhood(s). Italian neighborhood(s). Polish communit(y, ies). Ghetto(s,es). Barrio(s). Chinatown. Ghettoiz(ation,ed). Minority neighborhood(s). Segregated neighborhood(s). Segregated area(s). *Choose from:* minority, ethnic, poor, Black, Greek, Italian, Jewish, German, Polish, Chinese, Mexican, Hispanic, Spanish, Chicano, Cajun, etc. *with:* communit(y,ies), neighborhood(s), settlement(s), enclave(s), area(s), ghetto(es,s). *Consider also:* Harlem, slums, poverty area(s), low income urban areas, redlining, tenement(s), shantytown(s). *See also* Black community; Ethnic groups; Neighborhoods; Poverty areas; Social settlements; Residential segregation.

Ethnic relations. Ethnic relations. Multiculturalism. Ethnic plurality. Melting pot. Racism. Apartheid. Internal colonialism. Assimilation of ethnic groups. *Choose from:* interethnic, cross cultural, intercultural, bicultural, tricultural, interracial, biracial, minority, interreligious, multicultural, ethnocultural, bicommunal, polyethnic, intergroup *with:* relations, tension(s), conflict(s), interaction, antagonism(s), segregation, communication, integration, rivalry, intermarriage(s), discrimination, acceptance, violence, hostility, contact(s), assimilation. *See also* Biculturalism; Cross cultural competency; Cultural cooperation; Cultural conflict; Cultural issues; Cultural pluralism; Cultural sensitivity; Desegregation; Ethnocentrism; Intercultural communication; Intercultural relations; Melting pot; Race relations; Social discrimination; Social integration.

Ethnic slurs. Ethnic slur(s). Ethnophaulism(s). *Choose from:* ethnic, national, religious, cultural, ethnocultural, ethnosocial or names of specific groups *with:* slur(s), derogatory name(s), negative image(s), stereo-type(s), nickname(s), derogatory term(s). *Consider also:* ethnocentrism, xenopho-

bia. *See also* Cultural conflict; Ethnic cleansing; Ethnocentrism; Invective; Nativism; Verbal abuse; Stereotyping; Xenophobia.

Ethnic studies. Ethnic studies. *Choose from:* ethnic, cultural oriented, Puerto Rican, Chicano, Mexican, Jewish, Polish, Asian American, etc. *with:* studies, course(s), history, curriculum material(s), book(s), periodical(s), heritage. *Consider also:* multicultural education. *See also* Cross cultural competency; Cultural identity; Ethnic groups; Multicultural education.

Ethnic values. Ethnic value(s). *Choose from:* ethnic, cultural, culture(s), ethnoaesthetic, societal, social, traditional, tribal, national, subcultural or names of specific ethnic groups *with:* value(s), belief system(s), ties, norm(s), moral(s), preference(s), belief(s), mores, affiliation, worldview(s), tradition(s), orientation(s), attitude(s). *See also* Cultural values; Ethnic attitudes; Ethnicity; Social values.

Ethnic wit and humor. Ethnic wit(ty, ticism,ticisms). Ethnic humor(ous). *Choose from:* Ethnic, Black, Dutch, Polish, Jewish, Italian, minority group(s), etc. *with:* joke(s), comed(y,ies, ic,ian,ians), fun(ny), cartoon(s), comic, parod(y,ies), vaudeville, laugh(ter), caricature(s,d). *Consider also:* ethnic stereotype(s). *See also* Cultural characteristics; Ethnic groups; Humor; Jokes; Sense of humor.

Ethnicity. Ethnicity. *Choose from:* ethnic, national, religious, cultural, ethnocultural, ethnosocial, Italian(s), Greek(s), Chinese, Japanese, German(s), Jew(ish,s), Russian(s), Polish, Spanish, Hispanic, Mexican(s), Chicano, Puerto Rican(s), Black(s), Anglo(s), etc. *with:* identification, identit(y,ies), upbringing, background, self identity, affirmation, involvement, group identification, group identity, homophily, pride, awareness, allegiance, loyalt(y,ies), unity, consciousness, tradition(s), custom(s). *Consider also:* ethnocentrism, racial identification, Blackness, Africanity, Black consciousness, maintenance of ancestral language, second generation, third generation, hyphenated American(s). *See also* Black power; Cultural characteristics; Cultural groups; Cultural identity; Cultural maintenance; Ethnic attitudes; Ethnic groups; Ethnic values; Ethnic differences; Racial identity; Religious cultural groups; Socialization.

Ethnoarchaeology. Ethnoarchaeolog(y, ical). *Choose from:* archaeolog(y,ical) *with:* anthropolog(y,ical), ethnic(ity), cultur(e,al), social, societ(y,ies), agricultur(e,al). *Consider also:* Biblical archaeolog(y,ical). *See also* Archaeology; Cultural anthropology; Experimental archaeology; Prehistoric people; Prehistoric agriculture.

Ethnobotany. Ethnobotan(y,ical). Etnobotánica. *Choose from:* indigenous, native, folk, primitive, traditional *with:* classification(s), rule(s), taxonom(y,ies, ic), terminolog(y,ies), catalog(s,os) *with:* flora, botan(y,ical), vegeta(tion,ble,bles), plant(s,as), flower(s), herb(s,al,als). *Consider also:* ethnoscien(ce,tific), ethnopharmacolog(y,ical), ethnomedicine(s), biomedicine(s), folk medicine(s), medicinal plant(s). *See also* Biopiracy; Herbal medicine; Medical botany; Plant folklore; Psychotropic plants; Traditional medicine.

Ethnocentrism. Ethnocentr(ic,icity,ism). Sociocentr(ic,icity,ism). Chauvin(ism, ist,ists,istic). Jingoism. Attitudes toward foreign(ers). Xenophob(ic,ia). Eurocentric(ism). Euro-centric(ism). Afrocentric(ism). Afro-centric(ism). Religiocentric(ism). Religio-centric(ism). Anglophile(s). Nativis(m,tic). Prejudice(d) toward. *Choose from:* ethnic, cultural, outgroup(s) *with:* attitude(s), stereotyp(e,es,ed,ing), label(s,ed,ing), labell(ed,ing), bias(es), prejudice(s), identification, intolerance, discrimination. *Consider also:* nationalis(m,tic). *See also* Afrocentrism; Anti-government radicals; Cross cultural competency; Cultural conflict; Cultural issues; Ethnic differences; Eurocentrism; Jingoism; National characteristics; Nationalism; Nativism; Racism; Sectarianism; Stereotyping; Tribalism; White supremacy movements; Xenophobia.

Ethnocultural differences. See *Ethnic differences.*

Ethnography. Ethnograph(y,ies,ic,ical, ically,er,ers). Descriptive anthropology. Microethnograph(y,ic,ical,ically,er,ers). *Choose from:* holocultural, cultural, ethnological *with:* stud(y,ies). Video-ethnograph(y,ies). *Consider also:* participant observation, anthropological fieldwork, ethnomethodology. *See also* Anthropology; Cross cultural comparisons; Culture (anthropology); Folk culture; Folklore; Folklorists; Oral history; Traditional societies.

Ethnohistory. Ethnohistor(y,ical,ian,ians). *Choose from:* culture, non-literate *with:* histor(y,ies,ical). *See also* Cultural history.

Ethnolinguistics. Ethnolinguistic(s). Sociolinguistic(s). Anthropological linguistic(s). Ethnography of communication. *Consider also:* dialectology, dialect geography, class dialect(s), occupational dialect(s). *See also* Bilingualism; Creoles; Diglossia; Ethnic groups; Ethnography; Ethnology; Intercultural communication; Language; Linguistic minorities; Psychological anthropology; Sociolinguistics; Speech communities.

Ethnology. Ethnolog(y,ical). Social anthropology. Cultural anthropology. Comparative study of culture(s). Theor(y,ies) of culture. *Consider also:* historiograph(y,ic), ethnograph(y,ic), ethnomedical, ethnohistor(y,ical), ethnopsychoanalytic, ethnobehavioral. *See also* Anthropology; Comparative study; Cross cultural comparisons; Culture (anthropology); Cultural anthropology; Ethnic groups; Ethnography; Ethnolinguistics; Ethnomusicology; Folk culture; Folklore; Kinship; Mythology; Traditional societies.

Ethnomethodology. Ethnomethodolog(y,ical). Structure(s) of everyday life. Social order of everyday life. Sociology of everyday activities. Conversational analys(is,es). *Consider also:* phenomenolog(y,ical), practical reasoning, routine behavior(s). *See also* Conversational analysis; Everyday life; Fieldwork; Participant observation; Social interaction.

Ethnomusicology. Ethnomusicolog(y,ical, ist). Comparative musicolog(y,ical,ist). Vergleichende Musikwissenschaft. Etnomusicolog(ía,os). *Choose from:* ethnic, primitive, indigenous, tribal, native, folk, traditional, anthropolog(y, ical), non-Western, Indian, African, Latin American, Inter-American, Oriental, Japan(ese), Haiti(an), Java(nese), etc. *with:* music(al), musicolog(y,ical,ist), rhythm(s,ic), melod(y,ies,ic), harmon(y,ies,ic), tone(s). *See also* Ethnology; Folk culture; Folk music; Folk songs; Music; Musicology.

Ethnopsychiatry. See *Cross cultural psychiatry; Culture specific syndromes.*

Ethnopsychology. Ethnopsycholog(y,ical). *Choose from:* ethnic(ity), culture, cultural, race, racial, Black, Japanese, Italian(s), Norwegian(s), German(s), etc. *with:* personality trait(s), personality type(s), psycholog(y,ical). *See also* Cross cultural psychiatry; Culture specific syndromes; Ethnospecific disorders; Mental illness; Psychological anthropology.

Ethnos. See *Ethnic groups.*

Ethnospecific disorders. Ethnospecific disorder(s). *Choose from:* ethnic(ity), ethnospecific, culture(e,al) *with:* disorder(s), neuros(is,es), psychos(is,es), mental illness(es). *Consider also:* ethnopsychiatry. *See also* Cross cultural psychiatry; Culture specific syndromes; Mental illness; Psychological anthropology; Psychoses.

Ethology, animal. See *Animal behavior.*

Ethos, cultural. See *Cultural ethos.*

Ethyl alcohol. Ethyl alcohol. *Consider also:* alcoholic beverage(s), ethanol, ethamoxytriphetol, ethanolamines, ethylene chlorohydrin, mercaptoethanol, alcohol phenethyl, tribrumoethanol, trifluoroethanol. *See also* Alcoholic beverages.

Etiology. Etiolog(y,ies,ic,ical). Aetiolog(y, ies,ic,ical). Early symptom(s). Course of the disease(s). Caus(e,es,ing,ation,ality). Origin(s). Predisposing factor(s). Precipitating factor(s). Predispos(ed,ing, ition). Disease development. Pathogenesis. Psychogenesis. Psychodevelopment(al). Illness onset. History of disorder(s). Development of disorder(s). Carcinogenesis. Genesis of disorder(s). Developmental model(s). Contributing factor(s). Antecedent(s). Inducement(s). Creation. Determinant(s). Fundamental(s). Primary stimulus. Beginning(s). Provocation(s). Provok(e,ed,ing). Reason(s). Underlying. Underlie. Generat(e,ed,ion,ing). Explanation(s). Anamnes(is,tic). *See also* Causality; Creators; Disease; Disease susceptibility; Disorders; Founding; Mental illness; Mind body problem; Onset (disorders); Patient history; Premorbidity; Psychogenesis; Psychoneuroimmunology.

Etiquette. Etiquette. Good manners. Proper. Propriet(y,ies). Well behaved. Courtesy. Courteous(ness). Polite(ness). Gentlemanly. Ladylike. Decorum. *Consider also:* protocol, netiquette, social usage. *See also* Amenities; Apologies; Customs; Decency; Diplomatic etiquette; Faux pas; Manners; Protocols; Tact.

Etiquette, diplomatic. See *Diplomatic etiquette.*

Etymology. Etymolog(y,ies,ical). Word history. *Choose from:* word(s), language(s) *with:* origin(s), root(s), deriv(e,ed,ing,ation,ations), history. *Consider also:* linguistic history, onomastic(s,on). *See also* Language; Language change; Languages (as subjects); Linguistics.

Eufunction. Eufunction(al). Positive function(s,ing,al). Helpful function(s, ing,al). *Choose from:* satisfying, positive, contribut(e,ion), benefit(s,ting), helpful, promot(e,ing) *with:* function(s, ing,al,ality), stability, survival, integration, needs. *See also* Functionalism; Survival.

Eugenics. Eugenic(s,ally). *Consider also:* genetic selection, aristogenic(s), applied genetics, eugenism. *See also* Bioethics; Euthenics; Family planning; Genetic counseling; Genetic screening; Involuntary sterilization; Nazism; Selective breeding; Social Darwinism; Sterilization (sex).

Eulogies. Eulog(y,ies). Encomium(s). Panegyr(ize,ized,ic,ical,ically). Tribute(s). Salutation(s). Funeral oration(s). Homage(s). Extol(led,ling). Prais(e,es,ed,ing). *See also* Admiration; Commemoration; Commendation; Flattery; Honored (esteem); Laudatory poetry; Speeches (formal discourse); Praise; Tribute.

Eunuchs. Eunuch(s,ism). Castrato(s). Castrated m(an,en). *Consider also:* intersex(ual), male soprano(s), male contralto(s). *See also* Castration.

Euphoria. Euphor(ia,ic,iant,igenic). *Consider also:* manic, elat(ed,ion), ecsta(sy,tic). *See also* Emotions; Enjoyment; Happiness; Pleasure.

Eurocentrism. Eurocentri(c,sm). Europeaniz(e,ed,ing). European focus. Westerniz(e,ed,ing). *Choose from:* Christian(ity), Europe(an), western, US, America(n), Canad(a,ian) *with:* colonial(ism), expansion, domination, theor(y,ies,etical), notion(s) of order, tradition(s), paradigm(s), value(s), viewpoint(s), music(al), technolog(y, ical), racis(m,t,ts), oppress(ed,ion), philosoph(y,ies), religion(s), art(s), literature(s), language(s). *See also* Afrocentrism; Anti-government radicals; Colonialism; Cultural conflict; Culture contact; Ethnocentrism; Racism; Tribalism; Western civilization; White supremacy movements.

Europe, eastern. See *Eastern Europe.*

Europe, western. See *Western Europe.*

Eurythmy. Eurythm(y,ic,ics). Eurhythm(y, ic,ics). *Consider also:* Dalcroze system, musical game(s), musical gymnastic(s). *Choose from:* rhythmic movement(s) *with:* music education, gymnastic(s). *See also* Music education.

Euthanasia. Euthan(asia,ized). Physician assisted suicide. Living will(s). Nontreatment. Hemlock Society. *Choose from:* mercy *with:* kill(ed,ing,ings), death(s). *Choose from:* death(s) *with:* dignity, natural(ly). *Choose from:* disconnect(ed,ing), withdraw(n,ing,al), discontinu(e,ed,ing,ation), forego(ing) *with:* respirator(s), life support(s), nutrition(al), life sustaining, treatment(s). *Choose from:* permit(ted,ting), allow(ed,ing), enabl(e,ed,ing) right(s) *with:* die, death(s). *Choose from:* withhold(ing), terminat(e,ed,ing), refus(e,ed,ing) *with:* treatment(s), resuscitat(e,ed,ing,ion), medication(s), surgery, hospitaliz(e,ed,ing,ation). *See also* Assisted suicide; Bioethics; Death; Do not resuscitate orders; Dying; Medical ethics; Physician patient relations; Professional ethics; Terminal illness; Thanatology.

Euthenics. Euthenic(s,ist,ists). *Choose from:* child development, human being(s), human development *with:* environment(al), family life, living condition(s), standard of living,

parent(al) support *with:* design(ed), effect(s), influence(s), enhanc(e,ed,ing, ement,ements). *See also* Environmental determinism; Eugenics; Nature nurture; Child development; Parent help groups; Psychogenesis.

Evacuation. Evacuat(e,ed,ing,ion). Relocat(e,ed,ing,ion). Flee(ing). Fled. Vacat(e,ed,ing). Empty cit(y,ies). Depart(ed,ing). Abandon(ed,ing,ment). Withdraw(n,ing). *See also* Disasters; Displaced persons; Refugees.

Evaluation. Evaluat(e,ed,ing,ion,ions,ive). *Consider also:* assess(ed,ing,ment, ments), apprais(e,ed,ing,al,als), review(s,ed,ing), interpret(ed,ing,ation, ations), surveillance, reevaluat(e,ed,ing, ion,ions), judgment(s), judgement(s), criticism(s), analys(is,es), determin(e,ed, ing,ation) worth, determin(e,ed,ing, ation) effectiveness, vet(ted,ting). *See also* Communications research; Course evaluation; Criticism; Disability evaluation; Excellence; Literary criticism; Needs assessment; Peer review; Perfection; Personnel evaluation; Policy evaluation; Program evaluation; Reviews; Risk assessment; Self evaluation; Self evaluation (groups); Standards; Teacher evaluation; Technology assessment.

Evaluation, course. See *Course evaluation.*

Evaluation, disability. See *Disability evaluation.*

Evaluation, employee. See *Personnel evaluation*

Evaluation, faculty. See *Teacher evaluation.*

Evaluation, job. See *Job evaluation.*

Evaluation, peer. See *Peer review.*

Evaluation, performance. See *Performance appraisal; Personnel evaluation.*

Evaluation, personnel. See *Personnel evaluation.*

Evaluation, policy. See *Policy evaluation.*

Evaluation, program. See *Program evaluation.*

Evaluation, self. See *Self evaluation.*

Evaluation, self groups. See *Self evaluation (groups).*

Evaluation, teacher. See *Teacher evaluation.*

Evangelical revival. Evangelical revival(s). *Choose from:* fundamentalis(m,t,ts), evangeli(sm,st,cal), pentecostal, religious, Christian(ity), spiritual *with:* revival(s), reaffirm(ed,ing,ation), renew(al,als,ed), rall(y,ies), prayer meeting(s), regenerat(e,ed,ing,ion), awaken(ed,ing). *Consider also:* born again, pietis(m,t,ts,tic). *See also* Evangelists; Rejuvenation; Regeneration

(theology); Religious conversion; Religious gatherings; Religious revivals.

Evangelistic work. Evangelistic work. Convert making. Evangeliz(e,ed,ing, ation). *Choose from:* evangelis(m,tic), evangelical(s), religious, Christian(ity), pentecostal(ism), gospel(s), church(es), Gideon(s), Bib(le,les,ical) *with:* work(er,ers), mission(s,ary,aries), proselyti(ze,zes,zing,zed,sm), rock music, radio station(s), novel(s). *See also* Evangelists; Missionaries; Proselytism; Religious conversion.

Evangelists. Evangelis(m,t,ts,tic). Evangeliz(e,ed,ing). Evangelical(ism). United Church of Christ. Muscular Christianity. Fundamental(ism,ist,ists). New Christian right. Televangelis(m,ts). Conservative Church(es). Methodism. Personal conversion. Born again Christian(s). *Choose from:* evangelical *with:* Christian(s), alliance, United Brethren Church. *Consider also:* religious revival(s,ism), pietism, Billy Sunday, Billy Graham, Oral Roberts. *See also* Evangelical revival; Evangelistic work; Protestantism; Religious fundamentalism; Religious revivals.

Evasion, tax. See *Tax evasion.*

Events. Event(s). Occurrence(s). Happening(s). Incident(s). Occasion(s). Affair(s). Episode(s). Historical fact(s). *See also* Anniversaries and special events; Crises; Everyday life; Experiences (events); Incidents; Periodization.

Events, anniversaries and special. See *Anniversaries and special events.*

Events, cultural. See *Cultural events.*

Events, current. See *Current events.*

Events, life change. See *Life change events.*

Events, speech. See *Speech acts.*

Everyday life. Everyday life. Habits. Life world. Lebenswelt. Lifeworld. *Choose from:* everyday, daily, normal, customary, common(place), ordinary, mundane, profane *with:* activit(y,ies), event(s), experience(s), routine(s), world, life, living, schedule(s). *See also* Common knowledge; Common people; Common sense; Daily; Events; Life history; Lifestyle; Oral history; Public order; Quality of life; Social life.

Eviction. Eviction(s). Evict(ed,ing). Forced to leave. Forced to vacate. Terminate(d) lease. Displac(e,ed,ing,ement). Condo conversion(s). Expell(ed,ing). Oust(ed,ing). Eject(ed,ing). *See also* Homeless; Housing; Landlord tenant relations; Landlords; Leasing; Occupancy; Refugees; Tenant relocation; Tenants.

Evidence. Eviden(ce,tiary). Corpus delicti. Testimon(y,ial,ials). Self incriminat(ing, ion). Incriminat(e,ed,ing,ion). Proof.

Admissib(le,ility). Prov(e,ing,en). Confession(s). Substantiation. Out-of-court statement(s). Expert witness(es). Eyewitness(es). Corroborat(e,ed,ing, ion). Grounds for suspicion. Authenticat(e,ed,ing,ion). Confirm(e,ed,ing, ation). Validat(e,ed,ing,ion). Verif(y,ied, ication). Documentation. Attest(ing, ation). Deposition. Affidavit(s). Sworn statement(s). Fact(s). Certification. Demonstrated. *Consider also:* fingerprint(s); DNA typ(e,ed,es,ing), DNA profil(e,ed,es,ing), hearsay, firsthand document(s), primary reference work(s), informant(s). *See also* Affidavit; Circumstantial evidence; Clues; Criminal investigations; Criminal proceedings; Deposition; Expert testimony; Extenuating circumstances; Fact checking; Inadmissible; Legal procedures; Positive evidence; Sources; Sufficient evidence; Withholding evidence; Witnesses.

Evidence, circumstantial. See *Circumstantial evidence.*

Evidence, legal. See *Evidence.*

Evidence, positive. See *Positive evidence.*

Evidence, sufficient. See *Sufficient evidence.*

Evidence, withholding. See *Withholding evidence.*

Evil. Evil(doer,doers). Sin(ful,fulness). Immoral(ity). Corrupt(ion). Wicked(ness). Iniquit(y,ies,ous). Heinous. Sinister. Contemptible. Despicable. Atroc(ious,ity,ities). Unholy. Ungodly. Devil(s,try). Vicious(ness). Bad(ness). Baseness. Foul(ness). Mean(ness). Malevolen(t,ce). Opprobrium. Ignomin(y,ious). Disgrace(ful). Infam(y,ous). Perfid(y,ious). Treacher(y, ous). Vile(ness). Deprav(ed,ity). Villain(y,ous). Damnable. Diabolic(al). *Consider also:* satanic, demon(s,ic), witchcraft, voodoo(ism). *See also* Demons; Depravity; Devils; Good; Sin; Spirit possession; Voodooism; Witchcraft.

Evil, nonresistance to. See *Nonresistance to evil.*

Evil eye. Evil eye(s). Jettat(ura,ore). *See also* Evil; Superstitions; Witchcraft.

Evil spirits. See *Devils.*

Evolution. Evolution(ary,ism). Evolv(e,ed,ment,ing). Origin of species. Origins of man. Darwin(ism,ian,s). Survival of the fittest. Adaptive genetics. Progressive diversification. Neoten(y, ous). Phylogen(y,etic,etically,esis). Polygenism. *Consider also:* gradual change(s), progress. *See also* Animal nature of man; Biological factors; Change; Cultural evolution; Creationism; Darwinism; Evolutionary ethics; Evolutionism; Prehistoric people; Sociobiology; Spontaneous generation.

Evolution, cultural. See *Cultural evolution.*

Evolution, human. See *Evolution.*

Evolution, social. See *Culture change; Social change; Social Darwinism; Social development; Progress.*

Evolutionary ethics. Evolutionary ethics. Naturalistic ethics. *Choose from:* evolution(ary), naturalistic, *with:* ethics, morality, selflessness, altruism. *Consider also:* philosophical anthropology, social evolution. *See also* Animal nature of man; Behavioral genetics; Darwinism; Evolution; Moral development; Moral reasoning; Physiological psychology; Psychobiology; Social Darwinism; Sociobiology;

Evolutionism. Evolutionism. Evolutionist sociology. Evolutionary theor(y,ies) of societ(y,ies). Evolutionary model(s) of societ(y,ies). Social progress. Social evolution. Social development. Neo-evolutionism. Sociological functionalism. *Choose from:* Spencer, Marx, Durkheim, Comte, Saint-Simon *with:* evolution(ary). *Consider also:* law of succession, Durkheim's Division of Labor, teleolog(y,ical). *See also* Darwinism; Evolution; Social Darwinism.

Ex-offenders. Ex-offender(s). Ex-convict(s). Ex-felon(s). Former prisoner(s). Released offender(s). Parolee(s). Former delinquent(s). Ex-inmate(s). Discharged prisoner(s). Post-prison. Postprison. *See also* Convict labor. *See also* Criminal rehabilitation; Parole.

Examination, cross. See *Cross examination*

Examination, self. See *Examination of conscience.*

Examination of conscience. Examination of conscience. Self examination. Self scrutin(y,ize,ized,izing). *Choose from:* follow (ed,ing,s), scrutin(y,ize,ized, izing), pay attention to, listen to, awaken(ed,ing), examin(e,ed,ing,ation), develop(ed,ing,ment), aware(ness) of *with:* conscience, inner voice(s), spiritual(ity), moral sense, ethical sense, ethics. *Consider also:* examine motiv(e,es,ation), personal ethic(s). *See also* Conscience; Guilt; Integrity; Moral development; Moral judgment; Moral reasoning; Morality; Obligations; Shame; Superego; Values.

Examinations. Exam(s,ination,inations). Test(s). Assay(s). Assessment(s). Audit(s). Batter(y,ies). Checklist(s). Checkup(s). Diagnostic(s). Essay question(s). Evaluation(s). Instrument(s). Inventor(y,ies). Measure(s,ment,ments). Midterm(s). Questionnaire(s). Quiz(zes). Rating(s). Scale(s). Schedule(s). Screening(s). Score(s). Trial(s). *Consider also:* medical test(s), autops(y,ies), biop(sy,sies), urinalysis, etc. *See also* Achievement tests; Entrance examinations; Health examinations; Measurement; Performance tests; Screening.

Examinations, entrance. See *Entrance examinations.*

Examinations, health. See *Health examinations.*

Examinations, physical. See *Health examinations.*

Examples. Example(s). Exemplif(y,ied, ying,ication). Exempl(a,um). Model(s). Instance(s). Precedent(s). Case(s). *Consider also:* benchmark case(s), exempla(r), specimen(s), paragon(s), archetyp(e,es,ical), illustration(s), prototyp(e,es,ical), typical(ly). *See also* Ideals; Models; Role models; Scientific models; Simulation; Specimens.

Excavations (archaeology). Excavat(e,ed, ion,ions). Archaeolog(y,ical,ically) dig(s,ging,gings). *Choose from:* excavat(e,ed,ion,ions), stratigraphic, unearth(ed,ing), dig(s,ging,gings), dug, site(s) *with:* archaeolog(y,ical,ically), antiquit(y,ies), artifact(s), fossil(s), remains, ancient. *See also* Archaeology; Archaeological surveying; Extinct cities; Fieldwork; Kitchen middens; Primitive architecture.

Excellence. Excellen(t,ce,cy). Superior(ity). Eminen(t,ce). Outstanding. Merit(orious). Perfect(ion). Quality. Virtu(e,ous,ousness). Valu(e,able). Worth(y,iness). Distinct(ive,ion). Fine(ness). Good(ness). Superb(ness). Preeminen(t,ce). Great(ness). Nobility. Noble. Suprem(e,acy). First class. First rate. Grade A. Premium. Choice. Superlative(s). Supreme. Unparalleled. Unsurpassed. *See also* Accuracy; Achievement; Best practices; Criteria; Evaluation; Failure; Perfection; Performance; Quality; Standards; Success; Supererogation; Virtue.

Exceptional children. Exceptional child(ren). *Choose from:* child(ren), juvenile(s), student(s), pupil(s) *with:* exceptional, disabilit(y,ies), impair(ed, ment,ments), handicap(s,ped), retard(ed,ation), disturbed, gifted, genius, atypical, deaf, superior, blind. *Consider also:* special education student(s). *See also* Gifted; Disability; Exceptional persons; Mental retardation.

Exceptional persons. Exceptional person(s). *Consider also:* gifted handicapped, gifted, handicap(ped,s), disabilit(y,ies), disabled, exceptional child(ren), retard(ed,ation), genius(es), gifted, amputee(s), blind, brain damaged, deaf, emotionally disturbed, health impaired, idiot savant(s), partially hearing impaired, partially sighted, slow learner(s), atypical, talented, special student(s). *See also* Disability; Exceptional children; Gifted; Mental retardation.

Exceptions. Exception(s,al). Anomal(y,ies). Inconsisten(t,cy,cies). Irregular(ity,ies). Nonconform(ing,ity,ities). Odd(ity,ities). Peculiar(ity,ities). Unusual case(s). *Consider also:* extraordinary, phenomenal(ly), rar(e,ity,ities), remarkab(le,ly), singular(ly), uncommon(ly), uncustomar(y,ily), unique(ly), unordinar(y,ily), unusual(ly), infrequent(ly). *See also* Anomalies; Deviance; Deviation; Variations.

Excerpts. Excerpt(s,ed). Abridgement(s). Abridgment(s). Condensation(s). Abstract(s). Abbreviated form(s). Passage(s). Quotation(s). *See also* Abbreviations; Abstracts; Compendiums; Quotations.

Excess. Excess(es). Exceed(s,ed,ing) limit(s). Redundan(t,cy,cies). Surplus(es). Oversuppl(y,ied). Overproduction. *Consider also:* overabundan(t, ce), overflow(ed,ing), overkill, superflu(ity,ous), surfeit(s,ed,ing), profusion(s), superabundan(t,ce), overstock(s,ed,ing), overrun(s), byproduct(s). *See also* Fatness; Redundancy; Surplus.

Exchange. Exchang(e,es,ing). Barter(ed, ing). Trad(e,es,ed,ing). Swap(ped,ping). Reciprocity. Reciprocat(e,ed,ing,ion). Trade off(s). *See also* Bartering; Deals; Economic exchanges; Supply and demand.

Exchange, foreign. See *Foreign exchange.*

Exchange, information. See *Information exchange.*

Exchange, international educational. See *International educational exchange.*

Exchange, social. See *Social exchange.*

Exchange, stock. See *Stock exchange*

Exchange of persons. Exchange(s) of persons. *Choose from:* exchange(s,d), Fulbright *with:* people, person(s), student(s), scholar(s), teacher(s), professional(s). *Consider also:* cultural, educational, academic *with:* exchange(s). *Consider also:* sister cities, pen pal(s). *See also* Foreign study; International educational exchange.

Exchange theory. Exchange theor(y,ies). Exchange model(s). *Consider also:* exchange relations, generalized exchanges, utilitarianism. *See also* Patronage; Reciprocity; Social exchange; Social interaction; Utilitarianism.

Exchanges, ceremonial. See *Ceremonial exchanges*

Exchanges, economic. See *Economic exchanges.*

Excise. See *Taxes.*

Excitation. See *Sexual arousal.*

Excitement, sexual. See *Sexual arousal.*

Exclusive neighborhoods. Exclusive neighborhood(s). Exclusionary enclave(s). *Choose from:* exclusive, exclusionary, gated, insular homogeneous, affluent, exclusively white *with:* neighborhood(s), communit(y,ies), enclave(s), real estate. *Consider also:* exclusionary zoning, upper-class residence(s), residential segregation, segregated neighborhood(s), lifestyle communit(y,ies), retirement community(y,ies), leisure communit(y,ies), prestige communit(y,ies), security-zone communit(y,ies), new town(s), discriminatory real estate practice(s). *See also* Neighborhood associations; Residential patterns; Residential preferences; Residential segregation; Upper class.

Exclusivity (religion). Religio(n,us,usly) exclusiv(e,ity,ism). Absolute truth(s). Absolute claim on the truth. Religious intolerance. *Choose from:* religio(n,us, usly) *with:* exclusiv(e,ity,ism), intoleran(t,ce), fundamentalis(m,t,ts), absolutis(m,t,ts), hat(e,ed,red), conflict(s), violen(ce,t), fanatic(ism), extrem(e,ism). *Consider also:* anti-Semitism, jihad(s), holy war(s). *See also* Absolutism; Anti-Catholicism; Antisemitism; Bigotry; Practical theology; Prejudice; Relativism; Religious beliefs; Religious fundamentalism; Religious prejudice; Social discrimination.

Excommunication. Excommunicat(e,ed, ing,ion). *Choose from:* expel(led,ling), expulsion(s), oust(ed,ing), dismiss(ed, al), ban(ned,ning) *with:* communit(y,ies), church(es), organization(s), fellowship(s), Eucharist. *Consider also:* anathema. *See also* Heresy; Roman Catholicism; Social isolation.

Excretion. Excret(e,ed,a,ion,ing). Excretory behavior. Urinary output. Discharge of bodily fluids. *Consider also:* scent marking, enuresis, feces, urination, defecation, excrement, expectoration, respiration, incontinence, sputum, sweat, urine, semen, expel(ling) waste products, micturition. *See also* Defecation; Fecal incontinence; Urinary incontinence; Urination.

Excursions. See *Cruising; Expeditions; Tourism.*

Excuses. See *Apologies; Explanation; Justification; Rationalization (defense mechanism).*

Executions. See *Death penalty.*

Executive ability. Executive abilit(y,ies). Administrative abilit(y,ies). *Choose from:* executive(s), administrator(s), manager(ial,s), corporate leader(s), CEO(s), gubernatorial, president(ial) *with:* abilit(y,ies), performance, success(ful), productiv(e,ity), leadership skill(s), people skill(s), charisma(tic). *Consider also:* leadership. *See also* Administrators; Leadership; Leadership style; Managerial skills; Managers; Work skills.

Executive boards. See *Governing boards.*

Executive branch (government). Executive branch. Presiden(t,ts,cy,tial). *Choose from:* executive, administrative, presiden(t,ts,cy,tial) *with:* branch(es), department(s), power(s), function(s), discretion, dut(y,ies), veto(es). *Choose from:* president(s), White House, vice president(s), governor(s), lieutenant governor(s), county commissioner(s), mayor(s), town supervisor(s), cabinet post(s). *See also* Presidents; Provisional government; Separation of powers.

Executive officers, chief. See *Chief executive officers.*

Executive powers. Executive power(s). *Choose from:* executive(s), executive branch, presiden(t,ts,cy,cies,tial), Commander-in-chief, minister(s,ial), administrator(s), manager(ial,s), corporate leader(s), CEO(s), gubernatorial, governor(s) *with:* power(s,ful), authorit(y,ies), dut(y,ies), responsibilit(y,ies), prerogative(s), empowerment, privilege(s), leadership. *Consider also:* imperial presidency. *See also* Executive branch (government); Presidents; Separation of powers.

Executive search firms. Executive search firm(s). Executive recruit(er,ers,ing, ment). Executive search consultant(s). Executive recruiting firm(s). Headhunt(ing,er,ers). Managerial CEO search firm(s). *Consider also:* executive job bank(s), executive database(s), Internet executive recruiter(s). *See also* Executive ability; Managerial skills; Personnel recruitment; Personnel placement.

Executives. See *Administrators; Managers; Presidents.*

Executives' wives. See *Corporate spouses.*

Exegesis. Exege(sis,ses,tical). Explicat(e,ed, ing,ion). Explanat(ion,ions,ory). Explain(ed,ing). Exposition(s). Interpret(ed,ing,ation,ations). Elucidat(e, ed,ing,ion,ions). Clarif(y,ied,ying, ication,ications). Criticism(s). Critique(s). Gloss(es). Comment(s,ary, aries). Annotat(e,ed,ing,ion,ions). Marginalia. Schol(ia,um,ums). *Consider also:* biblical exegesis, critical interpretation(s), hermeneutic(s,al). *See also* Analysis; Criticism; Hermeneutics; Interpretation; Scholia; Theoretical interpretations.

Exempla. See *Example.*

Exemplary damages. Exemplary damage(s). *Choose from:* exemplary, punitive, vindictive, triple, treble, multiple *with:* damage(s), award(s). *See also* Damages; Lawsuits; Liability; Malpractice.

Exemption (law). Exempt(ed,ing,ion,ions). Immun(e,ity). Impunity. *Choose from:* relieve(d), waiv(e,ed,ing), discharg(e,ed, ing), excus(e,ed,ing), releas(e,ed,ing), set free *with:* liabilit(y,ies), dut(y,ies), obligation(s), service(s), tax(es,ation), bankrupt(cy), attachment(s). *See also* Amnesty; Law enforcement; Laws; Pardon; Privileges and immunities; Tax exemption.

Exemption, tax. See *Tax exemption.*

Exercise. Exercis(e,es,ed,ing). Calisthenic(s). Physical education. Workout(s). Work(ed,ing) out. Physical training. Gym(nastics). Athletic(s). Slimnastic(s). Aerobic(s). Isometric(s). Warmup(s). Warm(ing,ed) up. Fitness program(s). Physical fitness. Nautilus machine(s). Jog(ging,ger,gers). Body building. Lifting weight(s). Health club(s). Endurance training. Movement therapy. Creative movement. Dancercise. Jazzercise. Aquarobics. *Consider also:* walking, jogging, running, dancing, hiking, athletics. *See also* Athletic participation; Heart rate; Motion; Physical fitness; Physical strength; Walking; Weight control; Weight lifting; Yoga.

Exercise, physical. See *Exercise.*

Exercise therapy. Exercise therap(y,ies). Prescribed exercise(s). Isometric muscle training. Stretching exercise(s). Kinesitherapy. Kinesiotherapy. Kinetotherapy. Medical gymnastics. Cardiac exercise program(s). *Choose from:* exercise, gymnastic(s), physical, isometric, movement, sport *with:* therap(y,ies,eutic). *Consider also:* aerobics, dance therapy, calisthenics, adapted physical education, breathing exercises. *See also* Exercise; Physical therapy.

Exercises, spiritual. See *Spiritual exercises.*

Exertion. Exert(ed,ing,ion). Physical effort. Physical load. Struggl(e,ed,es,ing). Exercis(e,ed,es,ing). Physical activit(y,ies). Physical work. Physical performance. Athletic(s). Physical maneuvers. Walk(ed,ing). Isometric(s). Aerobic(s). Jog(ged,ging). Bicycling. Treadmill running. *Consider also:* fatigue, endurance. *See also* Athletic participation; Energy expenditure (physical); Exercise.

Exhaustion. See *Fatigue.*

Exhibitionism. Exhibition(ism,ist,ists). Indecent exposure. Flasher(s). Streaker(s). Exposed him(self), her(self). Exposer(s). Expos(e,ed,ing) genitals.

Consider also: ecdysias(m,t,ts). *See also* Indecent exposure; Sexual deviations; Voyeurism.

Exhibitions. See *Exhibits.*

Exhibitions, bibliographical. See *Bibliographical exhibitions.*

Exhibitions, traveling. See *Traveling exhibitions.*

Exhibits. Exhibit(s,ion,ions). Science fair(s). Exposition(s). Fair(s). Thematic display(s). Showing(s). Viewing(s). Demonstration(s). Museum(s). Book fair(s). Sideshow(s). Presentation(s). Public showing(s). *See also* Aeronautical museums; Bibliographical exhibitions; Museums; Trade shows; Traveling exhibitions.

Exhortation. Exhort(ed,ing,ation). Admon(ish,ished,ishing,ition,itions). Advice. Encourag(e,ed,ing,ement). Incit(e,ed,ing,ement). Urg(e,ed,ing,ings). Warn(ed,ing,ings). *See also* Advice; Encouragement; Incitement.

Exile. See *Deportation; Forced migration; Political asylum; Purges; Refugees; Religious refugees.*

Exile, authors in. See *Authors in exile.*

Existence. See *Everyday life.*

Existence of God. See *God concepts; Immanence of God; Knowledge of God; Presence of God.*

Existential anxiety. Existential anxiet(y,ies). Existential anguish. Angst. *Consider also:* weltschmerz. *See also* Alienation; Anxiety; Existential psychology.

Existential neurosis. Existential neuros(is,es). Existential vacuum. *See also* Existential psychology; Meaninglessness.

Existential psychology. Existential psycholog(y,ical). Humanist(ic) psycholog(y,ical). Existential therap(y,ies). Existential psychoanaly(sis,tical). Existential-phenomenological psycholog(y,ical). Existential counseling. *Consider also:* existential phenomenology, search(es,ed,ing) for meaning(s), existential ontolog(y,ical), existential metaphysics, psychophenomenolog(y,ical). *See also* Existential anxiety; Existential neurosis; Existential psychology; Existential therapy; Phenomenological psychology; Phenomenology.

Existential therapy. Existential therap(y, ies). Logotherapy. *Choose from:* existential, humanistic, experiential, daseins, reality *with:* therap(y,ies), psychotherap(y,ies), counseling, analysis, treatment(s), psychoanalytic approach(es), psychoanalysis. Reality therapy. *Consider also:* phenomenology, ontoanalytic programming. *See also*

Existential psychology; Existentialism; Psychotherapy.

Existentialism. Existential(ism,ist,ists). Existential approach(es). Existential philosoph(y,ies). Existential-phenomenological. *Consider also:* Sartre, Jaspers, Heidegger, Kierkegaard, Kafka, Camus. *See also* Absurd; Anomie; Death of God (theology); Demythologization; Existential therapy; Existential psychology; Freedom (theology); Meaningfulness; Meaninglessness; Personalism; Philosophy.

Exits. Exit(s,ed,ing). Door(s,way,ways). Gate(s). Outlet(s). Way(s) out. Egress(ion). Porthole(s). Hatch(es). *See also* Egress; Entrances; Halls; Openings.

Exogamy. See *Intermarriage.*

Exorcism. Exorcis(e,m,t,ts,ing). Ritual(istic) expulsion. *Choose from:* banish(ed,ing), driv(e,ing) out, cast(ing) out, deliverance *with:* evil, devil(s), demon(s), spirit possession. *See also* Evil; Evil eye; Faith; Incantations; Religious mysteries; Traditional medicine; Witchcraft; Witchcraft trials.

Exotic psychosis. See *Culture specific syndromes; Ethnospecific disorders.*

Exotic species. Exotic species. Exotics. *Choose from:* exotic, imported, foreign, unnative, non-native, alien, novel *with:* species, animal(s), mammal(s), plant(s), vegetation, herb(s), fauna, flora, weed(s), fish(es), bird(s), etc. *See also* Animals; Bioinvasion; Exoticism; Imports; Zoo animals.

Exoticism. Exotic(ally,ness,ism,ist). Exotism. Mysteriously different. *Consider also:* foreign, imported, alien, strangely different, unusual, romantic, alluring, enticing, fascinating, glamorous, mysterious. *See also* Exotic species; Imports; Rare books.

Expanding universe. Expanding universe. Emerging universe. *Choose from:* expand(ed,ing), evolv(e,ed,ing) *with:* universe or solar system(s). *See also* Extraterrestrial space.

Expansion. Expansion(s). Expand(ed,ing). Aggrandiz(e,ed,ing,ement). Amplifi(y, ied,ication). Augment(ed,ing,ation). Broaden(ed,ing). Widen(ed,ing). Deepen(ed,ing). Enlarg(e,ed,ing,ement). Inflat(e,ed,ing,ation). Lengthen(ed,ing). Magnif(y,ied,ication). Grow(th,n,ing). *Consider also:* thicken(ed,ing), prolong(ed,ing,ation), protract(ed,ing). *See also* Annexation; Boundaries; Change; Development; Escalation.

Expansion, industrial. See *Industrial expansion.*

Expansion, territorial. See *Territorial expansion.*

Expansiveness (personality).
Expansive(ness). Effusive(ness).
Cordial. Demonstrative(ness).
Loquacious(ness). Overfriendl(y,iness).
Lack(ing) reserve. Lack(ing) restraint.
See also Extraversion (psychology);
Personality.

Expatriates. Expatriat(e,es,ion).
Denaturaliz(e,ed,ing,ation). Loss of
citizenship. Abandon(ed,ing,ment)
allegiance. Relinquish(ed,ing) citizenship. Exile(d,s). Emigre(s). Living
abroad. Defect(ed,or,ors). Renounc(e,
ed,ing) citizenship. Seek(ing) asylum.
Political asylum. Expel(led,ling)
national(s). Expel(led,ling) from
country. Banish(ing,ed) from country.
Refusenik(s). Deport(ed,ing). Displaced
person(s). Emigrant(s). *See also*
Deportation; Displaced persons;
Emigrants; Homeland; Immigrants;
Political asylum; Refugees.

Expectancy, life. See *Life expectancy.*

Expectant fathers. Expectant father(s).
Choose from: expectant, prenatal,
pregnan(t,cy), birth, trimester *with:*
father(s,hood), paternal, spouse(s),
husband(s). *See also* Couvade; Pregnancy.

Expectant mothers. Expectant mother(s).
Pregnan(t,cy,cies). Gravid(a,ism,ity).
Obstetrical patient(s). Primigravid(a,as).
Gravida I. *Consider also:* parturient(s).
See also Maternal age; Maternal health
services; Maternity leave; Pregnancy;
Prenatal care; Teenage mothers.

Expectations. Expectation(s). Expect(ed,
ing). Expectanc(y,ies). Await(ed,ing).
Anticipat(ed,ing,ion,ions,ory).
Prophec(y,ies). Prophes(y,ied).
Predict(ed,ing,ion,ions). Future
perspective. Prospect(s). Hop(e,ed,ing).
Contemplat(e,ed,ing). *Consider also:*
presumption(s), trust, confidence,
apprehension, anxiet(y,ies) *with:* future.
See also Aspirations; Attitudes;
Cognitive mapping; Halo effect; Learned
helplessness; Life expectancy; Life
plans; Prediction; Researcher expectations; Role expectations; Self efficacy;
Self fulfilling prophecy; Set (psychology); Stereotyping; Teacher expectations.

Expectations, efficacy. See *Self efficacy.*

Expectations, experimenter. See *Researcher expectations.*

Expectations, researcher. See *Researcher
expectations.*

Expectations, role. See *Role expectations.*

Expectations, teacher. See *Teacher
expectations.*

Expeditions. Expedition(s). Pioneering
venture(s). Journey(s). Travel(s).
Quest(s). Explorer(s). Exploration(s).
Voyage(s). Excursion(s). Trip(s).

Tour(s). Cruise(s). Safari(s). *See also*
Crusades; Pilgrimages; Pioneers; Quests;
Scientific expeditions; Tourism; Travel.

Expeditions, scientific. See *Scientific
expeditions.*

Expelled. See *Deportation; Expatriates;
Extradition; Purges; School expulsion.*

Expenditure, energy. See *Energy expenditure (physical).*

Expenditures. Expenditure(s).
Disbursement(s). Expense(s). Cost(s).
Price(s). Charge(s). Outlay(s). Fee(s).
Payment(s). *See also* Amortization;
Budgets; Capital expenditures; Con-
sumer expenditures; Cost effectiveness;
Cost of living; Costs; Disbursement;
Gratis; Health expenditures; Luxuries;
Prices; Resource allocation; Wasteful.

Expenditures, capital. See *Capital
expenditures.*

Expenditures, consumer. See *Consumer
expenditures.*

Expenditures, government. See *Government expenditures.*

Expenditures, health. See *Health expenditures.*

Expenditures, public. See *Government
expenditures; Public finance.*

Expenses. See *Costs; Expenditures.*

Experience (background). Experience(d).
Experiential. History. Senior(ity).
Background. Lifework. Life
experience(s). Life event(s).
Matur(e,ity). Sophisticat(ed,ion).
Worldl(y,iness). Knowledgeable.
Skillful(ness). Qualified. Expert(ness).
Expertise. *See also* Biographical data;
Early experiences; Educational back-
ground; Employment history; Expertise;
Family background; Occupational
qualifications; Life experiences; Life
history; Practical experience; Sophistica-
tion; Work experience.

Experience, field programs. See *Field
experience programs.*

Experience, job. See *Work experience.*

Experience, practical. See *Practical
experience.*

Experience, religious. See *Religious
experience.*

Experience, work. See *Work experience.*

Experience pleasure, inability to. See
Anhedonia.

Experiences (events). Experien(ce,ces,tial).
Event(s). Occurrence(s). Happening(s).
Adventure(s). Transaction(s). Back-
ground. Lifework. Episod(e,es,ic).
Affair(s). Encounter(s). Vicissitude(s).
Life stor(y,ies). Employment
histor(y,ies). Life change(s). Life
stress(es). Action(s). Past record(s).
Previous event(s). *See also* Crises; Early

experiences; Everyday life; Events;
Happening (art); Incidents; Life
experiences; Near death experiences;
Psychedelic experiences; Turning points;
Vicarious experiences.

Experiences, early. See *Early experiences.*

Experiences, life. See *Life experiences.*

Experiences, near death. See *Near death
experiences.*

Experiences, out of body. See *Near death
experiences.*

Experiences, psychedelic. See *Psychedelic
experiences.*

Experiences, vicarious. See *Vicarious
experiences.*

Experiment controls. Experiment
control(s). *Choose from:* control(led,
ling) *with:* experiment(s,al), group(s),
research. *Consider also:* randomiz(ed,
ing,ation). *See also* Research design;
Research methods; Research subjects.

Experiment volunteers. Experiment
volunteer(s). *Choose from:*
volunteer(s,ed,ing), voluntary *with:*
experiment(s), research, subject(s),
stud(y,ies). *See also* Informed consent;
Research design; Research ethics;
Research subjects; Researcher subject
relations.

Experimental archaeology. Experimental
archaeolog(y,ical). Experimental kiln
firing(s). Experimental tool(s). Simulated primitive agriculture. Reproduc(e,
ed,ing) artifact(s). *Choose from:*
archaeolog(y,ical) *with:* experiment(s,al,
ation), simulat(e,ed,ing,ion,ions),
replication(s), practical test(s,ed,ing,
ings). *See also* Archaeology;
Ethnoarchaeology.

Experimental biology. Experimental
biology. *Choose from:* experiment(s,
ation,al), test(s), trial(s), trial run(s),
prob(e,es,ed), research(ed,ing,er,ers),
investigat(e,ed,ing,ion), analy(sis,ize,
ized), stud(y,ies) *with:* biolog(y,ical),
botan(y,ical), zoolog(y,ical), in-vitro, in-
vivo. *See also* Experiments; Life
sciences; Sciences.

Experimental dancing. Experimental
danc(e,ing,er,ers). Avant-garde
danc(e,ing,er,ers). *Choose from:*
experimental, avant-garde, computer
program(s), artificial intelligence *with:*
danc(e,ing,er,ers), ballet(s). *Consider
also:* experimental film(s), experimental
video(s), underground danc(e,ing,er,ers),
innovative danc(e,ing,er,ers). *See also*
Avant-garde; Dance; Experimental
music.

Experimental design. See *Research design.*

Experimental epilepsy. Experimental
epilepsy. *Choose from:* experimental,
induced, kindl(ed,ing) *with:* seizure(s),
epilepsy, amygdaloid, convulsion(s),

epileptiform activity. *See also* Epilepsy; Research.

Experimental ethics. See *Research ethics.*

Experimental games. Experimental game(s). *Choose from:* simulat(e,ed, ing,ion,ions), management, educational, experimental, experiential, dilemma, sex role, multiple reality, mixed motive, prisoners dilemma *with:* game(s). *Consider also:* computer game(s). *See also* Research design; Research methods.

Experimental instructions. Experiment(s, al) instruction(s). *Choose from:* instruction(s,al), direction(s), task(s) assign(ed,ment,ments), subject orientation, subject preparation, forewarn(ed, ing,ings) *with:* experiment(s,al). *See also* Research design; Research methods.

Experimental literature. Experimental literature. Experimental fiction. *Choose from:* experimental, avante garde, postmodern(ism), creative, interactive *with:* novel(s), literature, fiction. *Consider also:* experimental writing. *See also* Avant-garde; Experimental poetry; Experimental theater; Literature; Postmodernism.

Experimental methods. See *Empirical methods; Research methods.*

Experimental music. Experimental music. Avant-garde music. *Consider also:* experiment(al,ation) composer(s), rap music, computer music, cult band(s), recombinant rock, experimental dance music, new wave music. *See also* Avant-garde; Electronic music; Experimental dance; Music.

Experimental neurosis. Experimental neuros(is,es). *Choose from:* condition(ed,ing), experimental(ly), artificial, experimentally induced *with:* neurotic, neuros(is,es). *Consider also:* learned helplessness. *See also* Experimental psychosis; Learned helplessness.

Experimental poetry. Experimental poe(m,ms,try,tics). *Choose from:* experiment(s,al), avante-garde, postmodern(ism), visual *with:* poe(m,ms,try,tics), lyric(s,al,ist,ists). *Consider also:* pattern poe(m,ms,try), language poe(m,ms,try), "Third Generation Poets," street poetry. *See also* Avant-garde; Experimental literature; Poetry; Postmodernism.

Experimental psychology. Experimental psychology. *Choose from:* experiment(s,al,ation), trial(s), investigation(s) *with:* psycholog(y,ical), behavior(al), neuropsycholog(y,ical). *See also* Psychology; Social sciences.

Experimental psychosis. Experimental psychos(is,es). *Choose from:* drug induced, experimental(ly), artificial, experimentally induced *with:* psychotic,

psychos(is,es). *See also* Experimental neurosis; Hallucinogens.

Experimental replication. Experiment(al) replication. Retest(ed,ing) theor(y,ies). Re-test(ed,ing) theor(y,ies). *Choose from:* replicat(e,ed,ing,ion,ions), comparison(s), compar(e,ed,ing), extension, retest(ed,ing), re-test(ed,ing), reevaluat(e,ed,ing,ion,ions), re-evaluat(e, ed,ing,ion,ions), duplicat(e,ed,ing,ion), reassess(ed,ing,ment,ments), test(ed,ing) validity, repetition *with:* experiment(al, s), stud(y,ies), finding(s), result(s), previous work, sample(s), procedure(s). *See also* Experiments; Reliability; Repetition; Research methods; Verification.

Experimental subjects. See *Research subjects.*

Experimental theater. Experimental theater(s). Teatr(o,i) experimental. Experimental drama(s). Avant-garde theater(s). *Consider also:* radical theatre(s), laboratory theatre(s), alternative theatre(s), underground theatrical group(s), "poor theatre," "Living Theatre," "Cafe La Mama," "Open Theatre," "Bread and Puppet Theatre," "New York Shakespeare Festival Public Theatre." *See also* Avant-garde; Experimental literature; Performance art; Theater.

Experimentation. See *Experiments; Research.*

Experimentation, human. See *Human experimentation.*

Experimenter bias. See *Researcher bias.*

Experimenter expectations. See *Researcher expectations.*

Experimenters. See *Research personnel.*

Experiments. Experiment(s,ing,ation). *Choose from:* tryout(s), trial(s), test(s,ing) *with:* principle(s), theor(y,ies). *Consider also:* investigation(s), research, inquir(y,ies), pilot stud(y,ies), demonstration(s). *See also* Animal testing alternatives; Data collection; Empirical methods; Experiment controls; Experiment volunteers; Experimental biology; Experimental instructions; Experimental replication; Hypotheses; Laboratories; Measurement; Observation; Observation methods; Research design; Research methods; Research subjects; Sampling; Scientific method; Verification.

Experiments, animal. See *Animal studies.*

Expert systems. Expert system(s). Knowledge based system(s). Knowledge base(s). Knowledge engineering. Knowledge system(s). *Consider also:* intelligent system(s). *See also* Artificial intelligence; Computer assisted decision making; Computer assisted diagnosis;

Computer assisted instruction; Man machine systems.

Expert testimony. Expert testimony. *Choose from:* expert(s,ise), medical, psychiatric, medicolegal *with:* testimony, witness(es), evidence. *Consider also:* expert opinion(s). *See also* Circumstantial evidence; Criminal investigations; Deposition; Experts; Forensic medicine; Forensic psychiatry; Legal procedures; Witnesses.

Expertise. Expertise. Skill(ful,fulness). Adept(ness). Expert(ness). Proficien(t, cy). Adroit(ness). Experienced. *Consider also:* accomplished, well informed, knowledgeable, well-versed, masterful. *See also* Educational background; Employment history; Experience (background); Occupational qualifications; Practical experience; Skill; Work skills.

Experts. Expert(ness,s). Specialist(s). Authorit(y,ies). Scientific community. Master(s). Scholar(s). Professional(s). Connoisseur(s). Skilled practitioner(s). Technocra(t,ts,cy). *Consider also:* expertise, specialized knowledge, advisor(s), consultant(s). *See also* Advisors; Area of knowledge; Connoisseurs; Consultants; Expert testimony; Intelligentsia; Scientists; Think tanks.

Experts, computer. See *Computer experts.*

Explanation. Explanat(ion,ions,atory). Explain(ed,ing). Reason(s). Justification(s). Justif(y,ied,ying). Elaborat(e,ed,ing,ion). Explication(s). Comment(s,ary,aries). Annotation(s). Footnote(s). Example(s). Exegesis. Illumination. Clarif(y,ied,ying,ication). Interpretation(s). Translation(s). Restatement(s). *Consider also:* historical reason(s,ing). *See also* Causal models; Causality; Covering laws; Deduction; Emphasis; Clarification; Definition (words); Determinism; Dialectics; Function; Goals; Hypotheses; Inquiry (theory of knowledge); Intentionality; Interpretation; Meaning; Periodization; Probability; Scientific method; Teleology; Verstehen.

Exploitation. Exploit(ed,ing,ive,iveness, ation). Misus(e,ed,ing). Usur(y,ious, iousness). Overcharg(e,ed,ing). Exorbitant interest rate(s). Improper use. Take advantage. Overexploit(ed,ing, ation). Misemploy(ed,ment). Overwork(ed,ing). Overburden(ed,ing). Violat(e,ed,ing,ion). Impose upon. Deceiv(e,ed,ing). *Consider also:* dominance, unfree, imperialism, slavery, sweatshop(s), press gang(s), domestic servitude, begging industr(y,ies), colonialism, internal colonialism, oppression, dependen(ce,cy). *See also* Abuse of power; Agricultural colonies; Cheap labor; Child labor; Colonialism; Machiavellianism; Oppression; Peonage;

Political repression; Powerlessness; Sex industry; Sexual exploitation; Sexual harassment; Slavery; Social parasites; Sweatshops; Trafficking in persons; Usury; Workers' rights; World systems theory.

Exploitation, sexual. See *Sexual exploitation.*

Exploration. See *Expeditions; Exploratory behavior; Explorers.*

Exploration, space. See *Space exploration.*

Exploratory behavior. Exploratory behavior(s). Explor(e,ed,ing,ation, ations). *Consider also:* prob(e,ed,ing), investigat(e,ed,ing), scrutiniz(e,ed,ing, ation), curiosity, observ(e,ed,ing,ation, ations). *See also* Animal exploratory behavior; Curiosity; Information seeking.

Exploratory behavior, animal. See *Animal exploratory behavior.*

Explorers. Explorer(s). Astronaut(s). Discoverer(s). Pioneer(s). Adventurer(s). Space traveler(s). *Consider also:* Marco Polo, Christopher Columbus, Amerigo Vespucci, Magellan, Henry Hudson, Capt. James Cook, Hernando De Soto, Meriwether Lewis and William Clark, Ponce De Leon, Balboa, Vasco Da Gama, Sir Francis Drake, Eric the Red, Lief Eric Ericson, Roald Amundsen, Robert Peary, Matthew Henson, Neil Armstrong, Yuri Gagarin, Alan Shepard, John Glenn, Virgil Grissom, Scott Carpenter, Edward White, Valery Bykovsky, Valentina Tereshkova, Alexei Leonov, Maurice Herzog, Thor Heyerdahl, Vilhjalmur Stefansson, etc. *See also* Discoveries (geography); Frontier and pioneer life; History; Pioneers; Spanish explorers; Travelers.

Explorers, Spanish. See *Spanish explorers.*

Explosion, population. See *Population growth.*

Explosions. Explosion(s). Explo(de,ded, ding,sions). Bomb(s,ing,ings). Detonat(e,ed,ing,ion). Blowup(s). Blowout(s). Blow(n) up. Blew up. Erupt(ed,ing). Outburst(s). Flare-up(s). Blast(s,ed,ing). *Consider also:* explosive(s). *See also* Catastrophes; Explosives.

Explosive disorder. Explosive disorder. *Consider also:* episodic dyscontrol, explosive personalit(y,ies). *See also* Personality disorders.

Explosives. Explosive(s). Bomb(s). Mine(s). Explosive device(s). Dynamite. Firebomb(s). Firework(s). Hand grenade(s). Molotov cocktail(s). TNT. Gunpowder. Nitroglycerin. Ammonium nitrate. *Consider also:* volatile substance(s), black powder. *See also* Explosions; Incendiary weapons; Military weapons.

Exports. Export(ed,ing,ation,s). Export subsid(y,ies). Free trade. *Choose from:* international, foreign, global, European, Asian *with:* trad(e,ing), market(s), business treat(y,ies). *Consider also:* trade *with:* agreement(s), war(s), accord(s), pact(s), relations, gap(s), tie(s), deal(s), surplus, sanctions, embargo(es). *Consider also:* most favored nation clause, European Economic Community, EEC, GATT, General Agreement on Tariffs and Trade, NAFTA, North American Free Trade Agreement. *See also* Commercial treaties; Custom unions; Emerging markets; International economic integration; Imports; International trade; Trade protection.

Exposure, indecent. See *Indecent exposure.*

Exposure, occupational. See *Occupational exposure.*

Expressed emotion. See *Emotionality; Self expression.*

Expression, self. See *Self expression.*

Expressionism (art). Expressionis(m,t,ts,tic). New objectivity. Neue Sachlichkeit. Fauv(es,ism). Blaue Reiter Group. "Degenerate art." *Consider also:* Post-Impressionism, Vincent van Gogh, Georges Seurat, Edvard Munch, James Ensor, Henri Matisse, Andre Derain, Georges Roualt, Georg Baselitz, Marc Chagall, Chaim Soutine, Emil Nolde, Ernst Ludwig Kirchner. *See also* Abstract expressionism; Arts; Folk art; Genres (art); Impressionism (art); Symbolism; Modern art; Post-Impressionism; Primitive art; Sex symbolism.

Expressionism, abstract. See *Abstract expressionism.*

Expressions, facial. See *Facial expressions.*

Expressiveness, emotional. See *Emotionality.*

Expressivity. See *Self expression.*

Expressways. See *Highways.*

Expropriation. Expropriat(e,ed,ing,ion). Confiscat(e,ed,ing,ion). Seiz(e,ed,ing). Commandeer(ed,ing). Impound(ed,ing, ment). Take custody. Take possession. Misappropriat(e,ed,ing,ion). Dispossess(ion). Depriv(e,ed,ing) of property. Takeover(s). *Consider also:* forfeit(ed,ing,ure), redistribut(e,ed, ing,ion), eminent domain. *See also* Collectivism; Forfeiture; Nationalization; Ownership; Property rights.

Expulsion, school. See *School expulsion.*

Extemporization. See *Improvisation (acting); Improvisation (dancing); Improvisation (music).*

Extended family. Extended famil(ies,y). Kin(ship). Clan(s). Phratr(y,ies).

Agnate(s). Consanguinity. Consanguineal famil(y,ies). Ahl(s). Joint famil(y,ies). Extended familism. Family tie(s). Intergenerational famil(y,ies). Three generation famil(y,ies). Intergenerational exchange(s). Family network(s). Multigenerational famil(y,ies). Joint famil(y,ies). Extended kinship tie(s). Related famil(y,ies). Expanded famil(y,ies). Consanguine famil(y,ies). *Consider also:* descent group(s), affine(s), cross aunt(s), parallel aunt(s), avunculate(s), aunt(s), incle(s), avuncular, materteral, stem famil(y,ies). *See also* Alternative family forms; Intergenerational relations; Kinship; Stem family.

Extended school year. Extended school year(s). Year-round school(s). Year-round education. YRE. *Choose from:* school(s), academic, education *with:* year round, extended year, extended calendar(s). *Choose from:* restructur(e, ed,ing), redesign(ed,ing), adapt(ed,ing), alternative(s) *with:* school calendar(s), quarter system(s), semester system(s), trimester system(s), academic year(s). *See also* Academic environment; Acceleration (education); Calendar; Educational innovations; Educational reform; Leadership; Organizational change; Organizational innovation; School schedules.

Extension, agricultural. See *Agricultural extension.*

Extension, life. See *Life extension.*

Extenuating circumstances. Extenuating circumstance(s). *Choose from:* extenuat(e,ed,ing), mitigat(e,ed,ing), palliat(e,ed,ing), temper(ed,ing), lessen(ed,ing), moderat(e,ed,ing) *with:* circumstance(s). *Consider also:* extraordinary circumstance(s). *See also* Circumstantial evidence; Context; Criminal investigations; Criminal proceedings; Environment; Evidence; Fact checking; Justification (law); Justifiable homicide; Necessity (law); Positive evidence; Self defense.

Exteriors. Exterior(s). Coating(s). Facade(s). Cover(s). Covering(s). Rind(s). Peel(s). Shell(s). Skin(s). Surface(s). Frontage(s). *See also* Environmental design; Boundaries.

External debts. External debt(s). External public debt(s). Debtor countr(y,ies). *Choose from:* external, foreign, doomsday, overseas, world market(s) *with:* debt(s), deficit(s), indebted(ness), creditor(s). *See also* Balance of payments; Balance of trade; Budget deficits; Debt-for-nature swap(s); Debt moratoriums; Debts; Economic crises; Government expenditures; Government finances; Public debt; World economy.

External internal control. See *Locus of control.*

External rewards. External reward(s). Extrinsic reward(s). Tangible reward(s). *Choose from:* external, extrinsic, tangible, material, food, physical, monetary, concrete, token, financial, secondary *with:* reward(s), reinforcement, incentive(s), feedback. *Consider also:* token econom(y,ies), payoff(s), compensation, remuneration, recognition. *See also* Extrinsic motivation; Locus of control; Reinforcement.

External world (philosophy). External world. Cartesian picture of the mind. *Consider also:* everyday world, objective impression(s), real world, realism. *See also* Philosophy; Solipsism.

Externalities. Externalit(y,ies). External benefit(s). Spillover(s). External economies. External diseconomies. *Choose from:* social, economic, societal *with:* benefit(s), cost(s), consequence(s), effect(s), repercussion(s). *See also* Consequences; Social impact; Sequelae.

Externalization. Externaliz(e,ed,ing,ation). *Choose from:* projection, acting out, antisocial behavior(s). *Consider also:* outerdirected(ness), external goal(s), external focus, external stimulation. *See also* Other directed; Personality processes.

Extinct cities. Extinct cit(y,ies). Ghost town(s). Ghost cit(y,ies). Lost cit(y,ies). *Choose from:* extinct, deserted, lost, dead, buried, abandoned, sunken, ruin(s,ed) *with:* cit(y,es), town(s), village(s), communit(y,ies). *Consider also:* lost civilization(s), lost empire(s). *Consider also specific examples such as:* Gerasa (Jerash, Gerash), Summus Poeninus, Pompeii, Chichen Itza, Copan, Palenque, etc. *See also* Ancient architecture; Antiquities (objects); Antiquity (time); Archaeology; Community change; Excavations (Archaeology); Mining towns; Primitive architecture; Ruins.

Extinct languages. Extinct language(s). Dead language(s). Ancient language(s). *See also* Language; Language maintenance; Language obsolescence.

Extinction (psychology). Extinction. Disappearance of excitability. Inattent(ion,ive). Dishabituat(ed,ing, ion). Weaken(ed,ing) of habit(s). *Choose from:* extinct(ion) *with:* response(s), sensory, learning, reinforcement, condition(ed,ing), reward(s), nonreward(s), rate(s), resistance. *See also* Learning; Reinforcement.

Extinction (species). Extinct(ion). Died out. Disappeared. Annihilat(e,ed,ing,ion). Vanish(ed,ing) species. Exterminat(e,ed, ion). Eradicat(e,ed,ion). Obliterat(e,ed, ion). Abolish(ed,ing). Nonsurvival. *See also* Dinosaurs; Endangered species; Wildlife conservation; Wildlife sanctuaries.

Extortion. Extortion(ist,ists). Extort(ed,ing). Bribe(s,ry). Racketeer(s,ing). Shakedown(s). Threatening letter(s). Death threat(s). Chantage. Blackmail(ed,er,ers,ing). Ransom. Protection money. Payment(s) for protection. Vote buying. Sting operation(s). Payoff(s). *See also* Crime.

Extra employment. See *Moonlighting.*

Extracurricular activities. Extracurricular activit(y,ies). *Choose from:* leisure, extracurricular, cocurricular, after school, extraclass *with:* activit(y,ies), participat(e,ed,ing,ion), affiliat(e,ed, ing,ion), involv(e,ed,ing,ement), group(s), athletic(s). *Consider also:* boys club(s), Boy Scouts, Girl Scouts, glee club(s), varsity, intervarsity, school club(s), sororit(y,ies), fraternit(y,ies), youth organization(s), sports participation. *See also* After school programs; Recreation; School clubs; School newspapers; School sports; Sports; Student activities.

Extradition. Extradit(e,ed,ing,ion,able). Return(ed,ing) to face charges. *Choose from:* rendition, surrender(ed,ing), return(ed,ing), deport(ed,ing,ation) *with:* fugitive(s). *See also* Criminal proceedings.

Extramarital relations. Extramarital relation(s,ship,ships). Fornicat(e,ed,ing, ion). Open marriage(s). Open relationship(s). Errant spouse(s). Nonmonogam(y,ous). Nonmonogamous marriage(s). Swinging marriage(s). Wife swapping. Mate swapping. Intimate network(s). Adulter(y,er,ers,eress, eresses,ous). Cuckold(ed,ing,ry). Gigolo(s). Mistress(es). *Choose from:* extramarital, exnuptial, comarital, co-marital, nonmarital *with:* relation(s,ship, ships), sex(ual,uality), intercourse, affair(s). *Choose from:* marital *with:* infidelity, unfaithful(ness), promiscuity, promiscuous(ness). *See also* Polyamory; Premarital sexual behavior; Promiscuity; Sexual behavior surveys; Sexual ethics; Sexual misconduct; Sexual partners; Sexual permissiveness.

Extranets. Extranet(s). Intercompany groupware. *Choose from:* limited access, external, selected customer(s), authorized outsider(s), intercompany, business partner(s) *with:* intranet(s), private network(s,ing). *Consider also:* Automotive Network Exchange, Virtual Private Network(s), granular communication(s). *See also* Information exchange; Intranets.

Extrasensory perception. Extrasensory perception. ESP. Clairvoyan(t,ts,ce). Precognition. Telepath(y,ic). Remote perception. Psychic experience(s). Nonsensory channel(s). Out of body experience(s). Clairaudience. *Choose from:* extrasensory, psychic, paranormal *with:* perception, aware(ness), information, phenomena, experience(s), communicat(e,ed,ing,ion,ions), stimulat(e,ed,ing,ion,ions), abilit(y,ies). *See also* Divination; Omen; Parapsychology; Telepathy.

Extraterrestrial beings. See *Extraterrestrial life.*

Extraterrestrial environment. Extraterrestrial environment(s). Exobiolog(y,ical). Weightless(ness). *Choose from:* extraterrestrial, spaceflight, spacecraft, spaceship(s), outer space, outerspace, planet(s,ary), lunar, mar(s,tian), sealed cabin, geostationary *with:* ecology, environment(s,al), life, conditions, atmosphere(s), temperature(s). *Consider also:* space exploration, space colonization, space travel, space flight, lunar research, closed ecological system(s). *See also* Extraterrestrial life; Extraterrestrial space; Plurality of worlds; Space exploration; Space law; Space stations; Weightlessness.

Extraterrestrial life. Extraterrestrial life. Extraterrestrial being(s). Extraterrestrial alien(s). Space invader(s). Alien spacecraft. Alien visit(or,ors,s). UFO(s). Unidentified flying object(s). Martian(s). War of the worlds. Life in space. Life on other planet(s). Space alien(s). Life in the galaxy. Life beyond earth. Extraterrestrial intelligence. *See also* Extraterrestrial environment; Extraterrestrial space; Plurality of worlds; Space stations; Spacecraft.

Extraterrestrial space. Extraterrestrial space. Cos(mos,ic,mological). Outer space. Gala(xy,xies,ctic). Universe. Big bang. Extraterrestrial. Black hole(s). Solar system(s). Extragalactic. Milky way. Star(s). Starburst(s). Planet(s,ary). Nova(s). *See also* Expanding universe; Extraterrestrial environment; Extraterrestrial life; Plurality of worlds; Space exploration; Space law; Space stations; Spacecraft.

Extraversion (psychology). Extraver(sion, t,ted). Extrover(sion,t,ted). Exteriorization. Outgoing. Outward(ly) directed(ness). Sociab(ility,le). Congenial(ity). Unselfish(ness). People oriented. Friendly. Agreeable(ness). *Consider also:* extraverted feeling type, extraverted intuition type, extraverted sensation type, extraverted thinking type. *See also* Expansiveness; Introversion; Other directed; Personality traits; Sociability.

Extreme aged. See *Aged 80 and over.*

Extreme sports. Extreme sport(s). Bungee jump(s,er,ers,ing). Canyon(ing). Gorgewalk(ing). Black water raft(ing). *Consider adding "extreme" to any sports name such as:* extreme skiing, extreme fighting. *See also* Aeronautical sports; Risk taking; Sensation seeking;

Sport psychology; Sports; Sports violence.

Extremism. Extremis(m,t,ts). Radical(ness). Zealot(s). Zealous(ness). Fanatic(al, ism,s). Extreme left wing. Extreme right wing. Revolutionar(y,ies). Insurrectionist(s). Anarchist(s). Passionate follower(s). True believer(s). Ultraconservative. Diehard(s). *Choose from:* self-immolation, kamikaze, hunger strike(s,r, rs), vigilant(e,es,ism), terroris(ts,m). *See also* Absolutism; Anti-intellectualism; Anti-science movement; Factionalism; Left wing; Partisan; Polarization; Radical movements; Religious fundamentalism; Right wing politics; Schism; Vigilantes; Zealots.

Extremism, political. See *Extremism.*

Extrinsic motivation. Extrinsic motivation. *Choose from:* extrinsic(ally), external *with:* motivat(ed,ing,ion,ional), motive(s), locus of control, value(s), pressure(s), incentive(s), reward(s), satisfaction(s), constraint(s), orientation, influence(s). *See also* External rewards; Locus of control; Motivation; Needs.

Extroversion. See *Extraversion.*

Eye. Eye(s). Ocular. Optic(al). Opthalmic. Eyelid(s). Eyeball(s). Intraocular. Opthalmolog(y,ical). Oculus. Anterior eye segment. Aqueous humor. Conjunctiva. Cornea. Lacrimal apparatus. Crystalline lens. Oculomotor muscles. Pigment epithelium of the eye. Retina. Sclera. Trabecular meshwork. Uvea. Vitreous body. Eye rods. Eye cones. Iris. Eye lens. Pupil of the eye. Fovea. Choroid. *See also* Sense organs; Vision.

Eye, cross. See *Cross eye.*

Eye contact. Eye contact. Gaze reciprocation. Mutual glances. Eyes meet(ing). Eyes met. Face to face. Eyeball to eyeball. Exchang(e,ed,ing) looks. *Choose from:* eye(s), gaz(e,ing) visual, glanc(e,es,ing), star(e,ing), looks, smile(s), wink(s) *with:* contact(s,ing), exchang(e,es,ing), dyad(s,ic), interaction(s), communicat(e,ed,ing,ion), reciprocat(e,ed,ing,ion), mutual(ity). *See also* Gaze; Nonverbal communication; Social interaction.

Eye witnesses. See *Witnesses.*

F

Fables. *See Anecdotes; Fabliaux; Folklore; Mythology.*

Fabliaux. Fabliau(x). Fableau(x). *Consider also:* conte(s), fable(s). *See also* Folk literature; Folklore; Legends.

Fabrics. Fabric(s). Yard goods. Cotton material(s). Synthetic material(s). Textile(s). Cloth. Woolen(s). Piece Goods. *Consider also:* burlap, broadcloth, sackcloth, towelling, velvet(een), worsted, homespun, linsey-woolsey, canvas, tweed, serge, corduroy, flannel, cotton, muslim, calico, gingham, poplin, seersucker, chintz, silk, cretonne, brocade, taffeta. *See also* Clothing workers; Fibers; Sewing; Wool industry.

Face. Face(s). Facies. Facial. Visage(s). Craniofacial. Midfacial. Maxillofacial. Dentofacial. Gustofacial. *Consider also:* cheek(s), chin(s), brow(s), eye(s), forehead(s), mouth(s), nose(s), mask(s). *See also* Attractiveness; Facial expressions; Facial features.

Face value. Face value. Par value. Face amount. Maturity value. Stated value. Undiscounted value. Nominal value. *See also* Costs; Depreciation; Economic value; Prices; Valuation.

Facial expressions. Facial expression(s). Smile(s,ing). Lack of expression. Expressionless. Countenance(s). Grimace(s). Frown(ed,ing). Sneer(s,ing). Mien. Grin(ned,ning). Expressive eyes. Raised eyebrow(s). Questioning look(s). Pleasant expression(s). Mak(e,ing) face(s). *Choose from:* facial(ly) *with:* expression(s), expressive(ness), affect, animat(ed,ing,ion), display(s), cue(s). *Choose from:* face(s) *with:* expressive(ness), happy, angry, sad. *See also* Demeanor; Face; Nonverbal communication; Smiling.

Facial features. Facial feature(s). *Choose from:* facial(ly), face(s) *with:* feature(s), characteristic(s), resemblance(s), disfigur(ed,ement,ements), structure, attractive(ness), appearance, unsightly, deformit(y,ies), deformed, prett(y,iness), plain(ness). *Consider also:* prominent nose(s), high cheekbones, full lips, thin lips, weak chin(s), sunken face(s). *See also* Attractiveness; Face; Facial expressions.

Facilitation. Facilitat(e,ed,ing,ion). Forward(ed,ing). Further(ed,ing). Advanc(e,ed,ing). Promot(e,ed,ing, ion,ional). Aid(ed,ing). Expedit(e,ed, ing). *Consider also:* foster(ed,ing), simplif(y,ied,ication), support(ed,ing). *See also* Change agents; Foster (promote); Leadership; Social behavior; Social facilitation; Social influences; Social reinforcement.

Facilitation, social. See *Social facilitation.*

Facilities. Facilit(y,ies). Building(s). Structure(s). Plant(s). Edifice(s). Complex(es). Office(s). *Consider also:* center(s), clinic(s), factor(y,ies), hospital(s), hotel(s), laborator(y,ies), museum(s), school(s), store(s). *See also* Buildings; Clinics; Dental facilities; Educational facilities; Facility design and construction; Facility regulation and control; Factories; Health facilities; Hospices; Hospitals; Hotels; Laboratories; Libraries; Maximum security facilities; Mental hospitals; Museums; Nuclear power plants; Parks; Places of worship; Prisons; Public baths; Recreational facilities; Residential facilities; Schools; Shelters; Skilled nursing facilities; Stores.

Facilities, dental. See *Dental facilities.*

Facilities, educational. See *Educational facilities.*

Facilities, health. See *Health facilities.*

Facilities, maximum security. See *Maximum security facilities.*

Facilities, recreational. See *Recreational facilities.*

Facilities, religious. See *Religious buildings.*

Facilities, residential. See *Residential facilities.*

Facilities, school. See *Educational facilities.*

Facilities, skilled nursing. See *Skilled nursing facilities.*

Facilities, terminal care. See *Hospices.*

Facility, health environment. See *Health facility environment.*

Facility, health size. See *Health facility size.*

Facility design and construction. Facility design. Facility construction. *Choose from:* architectural, facilit(y,ies), building(s), house(s), hospital(s), office(s), structure(s) *with:* design, construction, specifications, layout, blueprints, building standards, building code(s), redesign, adaptation, conversion, retrofitting, plan(s,ned,ning), guideline(s), accessibility. *Consider also:* architectural barriers. *See also* Architectural styles; Architecture; Architectural accessibility; Architectural drawing; Building codes; Civil engineering; Construction industry; Domestic architecture; Entrances; Facilities; Industrial design; Modern architecture; Site selection.

Facility regulation and control. Facility regulation and control. *Choose from:* facilit(y,ies), building(s), structure(s), plant(s), clinic(s), factor(y,ies), hospital(s), hotel(s), laborator(y,ies), museum(s), school(s), store(s) *with:* regulat(e,ed,ing,ion,ions), standard(s), control(ling,led), licens(e,ed,ing), approv(e,ed,ing,al), requir(e,ed,ing, ement,ements), review(s,ed,ing), guideline(s). *See also* Building codes; Facilities; Licenses; Standards.

Facsimiles. See *Copies; Copying processes; Imitation; Microforms; Photography; Representation (likeness).*

Fact checking. Fact checking. Check(ed,ing) factual information. Verif(y,ied,ication). Substantiat(e,ed,ing, ion). Corroborat(e,ed,ing,ion). Establish(ed,ing) proof. Validat(e,ed, ing,ion). *See also* Circumstantial evidence; Evidence; Extenuating circumstances; Financial audit; Verification.

Factionalism. Faction(s,al,alism). Divisive(ness). Dissension. Factious(ness). Schism(s). Disunity. Breach. Rift(s). Fractious(ness). Social cleavage(s). Party system. Partisanship. Denomination(s). Coalition(s). Pillarization. Segmentation. Segregation. Stratification. Splinter part(y,ies). Contingent(s). Sector(s). Caucus(es). Bloc(s). Sectarian(ism). *See also* Cults; Partisan; Polarization; Schism; Sectarianism; Sects; Social cleavage; Social segmentation; Social stratification.

Factitious disorders. Factitious disorder(s). Pathomimicry. Hysterical pseudodementia. Pseudopsychos(is,es). Hospital addiction. Hospital hobo(es). Affective eudemonia. Faxen psychos(is,es). Buffoonery psychos(is,es). *Choose from:* Ganser(s), Munchausen(s), nonsense *with:* syndrome. *Choose from:* factitious, factitial, artificial, sham *with:* disorder(s), fever(s), illness(es), psychos(is,es). *See also* Artificiality; Ganser syndrome; Malingering; Mental illness.

Factor analysis. Factor analy(sis,ses,tic). Factor structure. Eigen analysis. Factor score estimates. Analysis of factors. Principal components analysis. *Consider also:* oblique rotation, orthogonal rotation, cluster analysis, equimax rotation, interaction analysis, item analysis, quartimax rotation, statistical rotation, varimax rotation. *See also*

Components; Factors; Statistical correlation; Statistical significance.

Factories. Factor(y,ies). Manufacturing plant(s). Industrial plant(s). Industrial facilit(y,ies). Mill(s). Assembly line(s). Assembly plant(s). Foundr(y,ies). Sweatshop(s). Workshop(s). Machine shop(s). *See also* Border industries; Facilities; Factory automation; Industrial enterprises; Offshore factories (floating); Offshore production (foreign countries); Plant relocation; Production control.

Factories, offshore floating. See *Offshore factories (floating).*

Factors. Factor(s). Determinant(s). Element(s). Explanation(s). *Consider also:* aspect(s), basis, background(s), cause(s), condition(s), constraint(s), characteristic(s), change(s), correlate(s), consideration(s), context(s), component(s), consideration(s), determin(ed,ing,ation), difference(s), dimension(s), dynamic(s), effect(s), facet(s), force(s), influence(s), ingredient(s), implication(s), indicator(s), impact(s), mechanism(s), obstacle(s), pattern(s), precondition(s), process(es), similarit(y,ies), setting(s), variation(s). *See also* Biological factors; Components; Determinism; Factor analysis; Sex factors; Social factors; Sociocultural factors; Socioeconomic factors.

Factors, biological. See *Biological factors.*

Factors, economic. See *Socioeconomic factors.*

Factors, sex. See *Sex factors.*

Factors, social. See *Social factors.*

Factors, sociocultural. See *Sociocultural factors.*

Factors, socioeconomic. See *Socioeconomic factors.*

Factors, sociological. See *Social factors; Sociocultural factors; Socioeconomic factors.*

Factors, time. See *Time factors.*

Factory and trade waste. See *Industrial wastes*

Factory automation. Factory automation. *Choose from:* factor(y,ies), plant(s), mill(s), assembly line(s), manufactur(e, ed,ing,er,ers) *with:* automat(e,ed,ing, ion), robot(s,ic), computeriz(ation,ed). *Consider also:* computer integrated manufacturing, CIM, automatic factor(y,ies). *See also* Automation; Factories; Factory system; High technology industries; Labor aspects of technology; Production control; Robotics.

Factory closings. See *Plant closings.*

Factory environments. See *Working conditions.*

Factory shutdowns. See *Plant closings.*

Factory system. Factory system. Factory movement. *Consider also:* assembly line(s), production line(s), factory automation system(s). *See also* Factory automation; Industrialization.

Factory workers. See *Industrial workers.*

Facts. Fact(s,ual,ually). Actual(ly,ity). Authentic(ity). Certain(ty,titude). Verit(y,ies). Real(ity,ities). Eviden(ce,tial). *See also* Data; Truth; Social facts; Trivia.

Facts, social. See *Social facts.*

Faculty. Facult(y,ies). Academ(e,ia,ic,ics). Academician(s). Academic status. Academic staff. Teaching staff. Academic personnel. School master(s). Schoolmaster(s). University teacher(s). University teaching staff. Professoriate. Professor(s). Instructor(s). Dean(s). Teacher(s). Don(s). Academician(s). Educational personnel. College teacher(s). *Consider also:* docent(s), tutor(s), lecturer(s). *See also* Academic rank; College teaching; Colleges; Professional personnel; Scholars; Teaching.

Faculty development. Faculty development. *Choose from:* facult(y,ies), teacher(s), academic staff *with:* professional development, inservice education, continuing education, study leave(s), renewal, retrain(ed,ing), revitaliz(e,ed,ing,ation), updat(ed,ing). *See also* Continuing education; Faculty; Inservice teacher education; Professional development; Professional isolation; Teachers.

Faculty evaluation. See *Teacher evaluation.*

Faculty tenure. See *Academic tenure.*

Fading (conditioning). Fad(ed,ing). Fading procedure. Vanishing. Gradual removal of prompts. *See also* Behavior modification; Discrimination (psychology).

Fads. Fad(s). Faddis(t,ts,m,h,hness). Fashion(able,s). Vogue. Trendy. Stylish. Newest thing. Latest thing. Dandy. Latest style(s). Craze(s). Modish. Popular standard(s). Bestseller(s). Hit parade(s). Top ten. Happening(s). Flavor of the week. *See also* Diet fads; Fashions; Mass behavior; Popular culture.

Fads, diet. See *Diet fads.*

Failure. Fail(ed,ing,ure,ures). Defeat(ed). Downfall. Loser(s). Error(s). Falter(ed, ing). Deficien(t,cy,cies). Defective. Breakdown(s). Down time(s). Computer disaster(s). Meltdown(s). Critical stress(es). Stoppage. Collapse(d). Unsuccessful. Fiasco. Founder(ed,ing). Ruptur(e,ed,ing). Disrupt(ed,ing,ion). Insufficien(t,cy,cies). Flunk(ed,ing). Inadequa(te,cy,cies). Bankrupt(cy,cies).

Out of business. Default(ed,ing). Vain attempt(s). Ruin(ed,ing,ation). Insolven(t,cy,cies). Financial disaster(s). Collaps(e,ed,ing). *Consider also:* poor(ly), deficit(s), low, disappointing, incomplete, unattained goal(s), performance(s), outcome(s), achievement(s), result(s). *See also* Academic achievement; Academic failure; Achievement; Aspirations; Bank failures; Business failures; Collapse; Default (negligence); Effectiveness; Errors; Equipment failure; Excellence; Evaluation; Fear of failure; Fear of success; Goals; Motivation; Perfection; Performance; Quality; Success; Treatment outcome; Underachievement.

Failure, academic. See *Academic failure.*

Failure, computer. See *Down (computers).*

Failure, equipment. See *Equipment failure.*

Failure, fear of. See *Fear of failure.*

Failure to thrive (psychosocial). Fail(ure,ed,ing) to thrive. Reactive attachment disorder. *Choose from:* failure, insufficient *with:* growth, development, weight gain, thrive. *Consider also:* anaclitic depression, hospitalism *with:* infant(s), bab(y,ies). *See also* Abandoned children; Anaclitic depression; Child abuse; Child neglect; Delayed development; Hunger, food deprivation; Infant development; Nutrition; Nutrition disorders.

Failures, bank. See *Bank failures.*

Failures, business. See *Business failures.*

Fainting. See *Syncope.*

Fair education, gender. See *Nonsexist education.*

Fair trial. Fair trial(s). *Choose from:* fair, unbiased, impartial *with:* trial(s). *Consider also:* fair, impartial jur(y,ies), fair, impartial tribunal(s). *See also* Courts; Fairness; Impartiality; Justice; Trial (law); Withholding evidence.

Fair trial, free press and. See *Freedom of the press; Fair trial; Trial (law).*

Fairies. Fair(y,ies). Little people. Elf. Elves. Faer(y,ies). Pix(y,ies). Sprite(s). Nymph(s). *See also* Devils; Folklore; Ghosts; Mermaids.

Fairness. Fair(ness). Equit(y,able). Unbiased. Unprejudiced. Objectiv(e,ity). Impartial(ity). Disinterested(ness). Dispassionate(ness). Even-handed(ness). Just(ice). Candor. Detach(ed,ment). Nonpartisan(ship). Neutral(ity). Fair treatment. Fair play. Scrupulous(ness). Scrupulosity. Sportsmanship. *See also* Comparable worth; Due process; Equity (payment); Fair trial; Fairness and accuracy in reporting; Impartiality; Justice; Social justice.

Fairness and accuracy in reporting.
Fairness and accuracy in reporting.
Fair(ness) report(s,ing). Accura(te,cy)
report(s,ing). Unbiased report(s,ing).
Fair coverage. *Choose from:* fair(ness),
accura(te,cy), inaccurac(y,ies), lies,
mislead(ing), misinform(ed,ation) *with:*
report(ing,er,ers), journalis(m,t,ts),
media, talk radio press, news coverage,
newspaper(s), television. *Consider also:*
editorial integrity. *See also* Fairness;
Impartiality; Media portrayal; Misinformation; News coverage; War news.

Fairy tales. Fairy tale(s). Maerchen. Tale(s)
of wonder. Chimerat(s). *See also* Folk
literature; Folklore; Mythical animals;
Mythology.

Faith. Faith(ful). Belief(s). Trust(ing,ful).
Credence. Certitude. Believ(e,ed,ing).
Theological belief(s). Unsuspecting.
Unquestioning. Confiden(ce,t).
Sure(ness). Convinced. Credulous.
Hav(e,ing) faith. Rely(ing) upon.
Depend(ing) upon. *Consider also:*
fideism, grace, gift(s) of the spirit. *See
also* Antinomianism; Beliefs; Ideologies;
Knowledge of god; Presence of God;
Redemption (theology); Regeneration
(theology); Religions; Revealed
theology; Spiritual healing; Theological
virtues.

Faith healing. See *Spiritual healing.*

Faithfulness. Faithful(ly,ness).
Conscientious(ly,ness). Allegian(t,ce).
Loyal(ty). Resolute(ly,ness).
Staunch(ly,ness). Steadfast(ly,ness).
Dependab(le,ility). Reliab(le,ility).
Trustworth(y;iness). Firm adherence.
Unswerving(ly). Firm(ly)
commit(ted,ment). Strict(ly)
obedien(t,ce). Impervious(ness).
Unwavering(ly). *See also* Commitment
(emotional); Loyalty; Honor (integrity);
Patriotism; Personnel loyalty; Personal-
ity traits.

Faiths. See *Religions.*

Faking. Fak(e,ed,es,er,ers,ing). Act(ed,ing).
Bogus. Charlatan(s). Contrived.
Counterfeit. Decept(ive,ion,ions).
Deceit(ful). Deceive(d,r). Disguise(d).
Dissembl(e,ed,ing). Dissimulat(ed,ing,
ion). Ersatz. Exaggerat(e,ed,ing,ion).
Fabricat(ed,ing,ion). Factitious. False.
Falsehood(s). Falsif(y,ication).
Feign(ed,ing). Fictitious. Forge(d,r,
rs,ry). Fraud(ulent,ulently). Hoax(es).
Imitat(e,ed,ing,ion). Imposter(s).
Insincer(e,ity). Lie(s). Lying.
Malinger(ing). Meretricious(ness).
Mock. Phon(y,iness). Plagiar(ize,ism).
Pretend(ed,ing). Pretense(s). Pseudo.
Quack(s,ery,eries). Sham(s). Simulat(e,
ed,ing,ion,ions). Specious(ness).
Spurio(sity,us). Unreal(ity,ness).
Whitewash(ed). *See also* Artificiality;
Authenticity; Clandestinity; Deception;
Disguise; Fraud; Fraudulent advertising;
Quackery; Self deception; Tricksters.

Fall of man. Fall of man. Original sin. Sin
of Adam and Eve. *Consider also:*
"Paradise Lost," forbidden fruit, Garden
of Eden. *See also* Bible; Christian
symbolism; Guilt; Religious literature;
Sin.

Fallacies. Fallac(y,ies,iousness). Error(s).
Mistake(s,n). Inaccura(cy,cies,te).
Incorrect. Erroneous(ness). Discrep-
an(cy,cies). False belief(s). Miscue(d,s).
Misconception(s). Mistaken notion(s).
Misdiagnos(ed,is,es). Misbelief(s).
Misapprehension. Misjudg(ed,ment).
Mislocat(ed,ion). Misread. Misunder-
stood. Misunder-stand(ing). Wrong
answers. Wrong feedback.
Miscalculat(e,ed,ion). Misdirect(ed).
Misjudge(d). Mispronounce(d).
Misquote(d). Misremember(ed).
Misstate(d). Mistook. Misvalued.
Incorrect(ness). Misidentif(ied,ication).
Illogic(al). Sophis(m,try). *See also*
Accuracy; Correctness; Error analysis;
Errors; Fallibility; Halo effect; Illogical;
Illusion (philosophy); Incorrect;
Judgment (logic); Judgment errors;
Reliability; Truth.

Fallibility. Fallib(le,ility). Imperfect(ion).
Erra(ble,nt). Liab(le,ility) to error.
Human error(s). Mistake(s,n). Wrong
action(s). *Consider also:* absurd(ity,
ities), careless(ness), fault(s,y). *See also*
Errors; Fallacies; Inappropriateness;
Journalistic errors; Judgment errors;
Literary errors and blunders; Medication
errors; Philosophical anthropology;
Scientific errors.

Falls, accidental. See *Accidental falls.*

False advertising. See *Fraudulent advertising.*

False arrests. False arrest(s). Framed.
Choose from: false(ly), wrongful(ly),
improper, unlawful, illegal, mistaken(ly),
erroneous(ly) *with:* arrest(s,ed,ing),
convict(ed,ing,ion,ions), imprison(ed,
ment,ments), jailed, accus(e,ed,ation,
ations). *See also* Arrests.

False memory. See *Paramnesia.*

False pregnancy. False pregnanc(y,ies).
Hysterical pregnanc(y,ies). Pseudocyesis. *See also* Conversion disorder.

False pretenses. See *Fraud.*

Falsehoods. See *Deception.*

Falsification (scientific). Falsif(y,ying,ied,
ication). *Choose from:* falsif(y,ying,
ied,ication), counterfactual, counterfeit,
falsehood(s), false, decept(ive,ion,ions),
deceiv(e,ed,ing), deceitful, duplicity,
plagiar(ize,ized,ism), cheat(ed,ing),
fraud(ulent), exaggerat(e,ed,ing,ion),
forge(d,ry,ries), fake(d,ry,ries), faking,
dishonest(y), suppress(ed,ing,ion),
hoax(es), mislead(ing), misled,
misrepresent(ed,ing,ation), mis-
stat(e,ed,ing,ement,ements),

tamper(ed,ing), untruth-ful(ness),
adulterat(e,ed,ing,ion), fudg(ed,ing),
sham(s), fabricat(e,ed,ing),
whitewash(ed,ing), phon(y,iness) *with:*
data, result(s), scientific, science,
experiment(s,al,ed,ing), case stud(y,ies),
replicat(e,ed,ing,ion,ions), finding(s),
empirical, observation(s), test(s,ed,ing),
survey(s). *See also* Cheating; Deception;
Duplicity; Misinformation; Professional
ethics; Research; Research ethics;
Research methods; Researcher bias;
Scientific errors; Scientific misconduct;
Statistical bias; Test bias; Unethical
conduct.

Fame. See *Famous people.*

Familial diseases. See *Hereditary diseases.*

Familiarity. Familiar(ity,ize,ized,ization).
Choose from: personal, previous,
frequen(t,cy,cies), prior *with:* knowledge, contact(s), encounter(s), experience, exposure, background. Preexposure. Preexposure. Initiated.
Habituated. Inured. *Consider also:*
accustom(ed), commonplace, everyday,
habitual(ly), traditional(ly), hackneyed,
mundane. *See also* Experience (background); Frequently; Hackneyed;
Practice (repetition); Stranger reactions.

Families. See *Family.*

Families, blended. See *Remarriage;
Stepfamily.*

Families, dual career. See *Dual career
families.*

Families, dual earner. See *Dual career
families.*

Families, dysfunctional. See *Dysfunctional
families.*

Families, egalitarian. See *Egalitarian
families.*

Families, interethnic. See *Interethnic
families.*

Families, military. See *Military families.*

Families, reconstituted. See *Remarriage;
Stepfamily.*

Families, two career. See *Dual career
families.*

Families, two income. See *Dual career
families.*

Familism. Familis(tic,m). Familialism.
Strong sense of family. Famil(y,ial)
value(s). Family ideology. Family
orientation. Family tradition(s). Family
loyalty. *See also* Family; Family
relations.

Family. Famil(y,ies,ial). Kin(folk,ship).
Relative(s). Stepfamil(y,ies,ial).
Intrafamilial. Intergenerational.
Sib(ling,lings,ship,ships).
Consanguin(e,eous,ity). Descendant(s).
Geneolog(y,ical). Parent(s,age).
Child(ren). Offspring. Progeny.

Ancestor(s). Pedigree(s). *Consider also:* marriage(s), spouse(s), husband(s), wives, wife, sister(s), brother(s), mother(s), father(s), cohabitee(s), agnate(s), patrilineal(ity), matrilineal(ity), descent, exogamy, endogamy, patrilocal, filial, phratr(y,ies), clan(s), birth order. *See also* Biological family; Birth order; Black family; Dual career families; Dysfunctional families; Egalitarian families; Extended family; Familism; Family background; Family budgets; Family businesses; Family characteristics; Family conflict; Family corporations; Family crises; Family farms; Family history; Family influence; Family life; Family members; Family power; Family problems; Family relations; Family roles; Family size; Family socioeconomic status; Family stability; Family traditions; Family values; Family violence; Family work relationship; Genealogy; Grandparents; Heads of households; History of the family; Homemakers; Interethnic families; Kinship; Marriage; Military families; Nuclear family; Parents; Proximity of family; Remarriage; Schizophrenogenic family; Siblings; Single parent family; Spouses; Stem family; Stepfamily.

Family, biological. See *Biological family*.

Family, Black. See *Black family*.

Family, extended. See *Extended family*.

Family, history of. See *History of the family*.

Family, natural. See *Biological family*.

Family, nuclear. See *Nuclear family*.

Family, one parent. See *Single parent family*.

Family, proximity of. See *Proximity of family*.

Family, schizophrenogenic. See *Schizophrenogenic family*.

Family, single parent. See *Single parent family*.

Family, stem. See *Stem family*.

Family assistance. Family assistance. *Choose from:* famil(y,ies,ial), relative(s), parent(s,al), filial, child(ren), intergenerational, sibling(s) *with:* support, care(giving), caring, responsibilit(y,ies), obligation(s), help(ed,ing). *See also* Child support; Dependent parents; Filial responsibility; Financial support; Public welfare.

Family background. Famil(y,ies,ial) background. Parental birthplace. Famil(y,ies) of origin. Family of procreation. Family variable(s). Childhood role model(s). Family life. Family relationship(s). Birth order. Family socialization. *Choose from:* famil(y,ies,ial), parent(s,al), home,

relative(s), grandparent(s), mother(s), father(s) *with:* background(s), environment, history, birthplace, characteristic(s), cohes(ion,iveness), politics, factor(s), egalitarianism, authoritarianism, strictness, permissiveness, antecedent(s), structure(s), variable(s), role model(s), violence, pressure(s), foreign born, second generation, origin(s), socioeconomic status, social status, educational background, relation(s,ship,ships), deprivation, socialization, social experience(s). *See also* Biographical data; Early experiences; Family characteristics; Family traditions; Heritage; Parental background.

Family budgets. Family budget(ary,ed, s,ing). *Choose from:* famil(y,ies), household(s), couple(s) *with:* budget(ary,s,ed,ing), allocation(s), financial, finances, fiscal, money, expenditure(s), expense(s), spend(ing), food stamp(s), income(s). *See also* Budgets; Energy costs; Health expenditures; Housing costs; Income; Savings; Wasteful; Utility costs

Family businesses. Family business(es). *Choose from:* family run, family owned, family, mom and pop *with:* business(es), enterprise(s), store(s), operation(s). *Consider also:* family farm(s), boardinghouse operator(s). *See also* Small businesses; Family corporations; Family farms; Minority businesses; Women owned businesses.

Family characteristics. Family characteristics. Family structure(s). Family composition. Family constellation. Family type(s). *Choose from:* famil(y,ies,ial), home(s), parent(s,al) *with:* characteristic(s), structure(s), organization, background(s), size(s), environment(s), composition, constellation(s), type(s), military, small, large, problem(s), traditional, patriarchal, matriarchal, authoritarian, style(s), profile(s), variable(s), socioeconomic level(s), educational background, schizophrenogenic, single parent(s), pattern(s), role(s), disrupted, disorganized, female dominant, equalitarian, egalitarian, form(s), extended, nuclear, position(s), role(s) of women, variant(s). *See also* Birth order; Characteristics; Childlessness; Dual career families; Extended family; Family background; Family history; Family life; Family relations; Family size; Family socioeconomic status; Family stability; Family traditions; Matriarchy; Military families; Nuclear family; Parental absence; Parental attitudes; Parental background; Parental permissiveness; Patriarchy; Polygamy; Qualities; Siblings; Single parent family; Stem family; Stepfamily.

Family conflict. Family conflict(s). *Choose from:* domestic, home(s), famil(y,ies),

parent(s,al), parent child, mother child, father child, sibling(s) *with:* trouble(s,d), stress(es), distress(ed,es), dissension, problem(s), conflict(s), role strain(s), argument(s), competetive(ness), competition, frustration(s), aggression, dissatisf(ied,action,actions), unhapp(y,iness), discord, resent(ful, ment,ments), hostil(e,ity,ities), disintegrat(e,ed,ing,ion), impasse(s), misunderstanding(s), fight(s,ing), clash(es), incompatib(le,ility), dysfunctional, instability, unstable. *See also* Family relations; Family stability; Family violence; Home environment; Intergenerational relations; Marital conflict; Misunderstanding; Parent child relations.

Family corporations. Family corporat(e, ion,ions). *Choose from:* famil(y,ies), dynast(y,ies), matriarch(y,ies), patriarch(y,ies) *with:* firm(s), incorporat(e,ed,ion), compan(y,ies), large industrial organization(s), shareholder(s), corporation(s), controll(ed,ing) interest, conglomerate(s), big business(es), chaol(s). *See also* Corporations; Family businesses; Stockholders.

Family counseling. *See Family therapy*.

Family crises. Famil(y,ies,ial) cris(is,es). *Choose from:* famil(y,ies,ial), domestic, home, parent(s,al), marital *with:* cris(is,es), stress(es), dispute(s), disrupt(ed,ing,ion,ions), conflict(s), breakdown(s), distress(ed,es), dispute(s), catastrophe(s), death(s), divorce(s), hospitalization(s), illness(es), life change(s). *See also* Family conflict; Family violence; Life change events; Stress.

Family division of labor. See *Sexual division of labor*.

Family dynamics. See *Family relations*.

Family education. See *Parent training*.

Family environment. See *Family life; Home environment*.

Family farms. Family farm(er,ers,s). Small farm(er,ers,s). Farming famil(y,ies). Individual farm(s,er,ers). Part time farm(er,ers,ing). *Choose from:* farm(s, ing) *with:* famil(y,ies), household(s), peasant(s). *See also* Family businesses; Farming; Part time farming; Size of farms.

Family finances. See *Family budgets; Family socioeconomic status; Income*.

Family forms, alternative. See *Alternative family forms*.

Family history. Famil(y,ies,ial) histor(y,ies). *Choose from:* famil(y,ies,ial), genetic, inherited, hereditary, parent(s,al), relative(s), grandparent(s), mother(s), father(s), ethnic *with:* background(s), histor(y,ies), factor(s). *Consider also:*

inherited predisposition(s). *See also* Atavism (biology); Family background; Family characteristics; Hereditary diseases; Local history; Parental background; Predisposition.

Family income. See *Family socioeconomic status; Income; Retirement income.*

Family influence. Family influence(s). *Choose from:* famil(y,ies,ial), parent(s, al), home, relative(s), grandparent(s), mother(s), father(s) *with:* influence(s), impact(s), effect(s), affect(ed,ing), pressure(s), support(ed,ing,ive), back(ed,ing), approv(e,ed,ing,al), disapprov(e,ed,ing,al), persuad(e,ed, ing), role model(s), inspir(e,ed,ing, ation), determinant(s), constraint(s). *See also* Family background; Family characteristics; Family roles; Parental attitudes; Parental background.

Family life. Family life. Family living. Home life. Family stability. Intergenerational conflict(s). Family culture. Home conditions. *Choose from:* home(s), famil(ial,y,ies), domestic, household(s) *with:* life, lifestyle(s), living, violence, style(s), ritual(s), division of labor, interaction, stress(es), influence(s), cohesion, conflict(s), context, ethics, relation(s,ship,ships), environment(al), support(ed,ive,ing), stability, atmosphere, conditions, culture, circumstances, situation(s), background. *Consider also:* cocoon(ed, ing). *See also* Army life; Family background; Family characteristics; Home economics; Home environment; Military families; Sexual division of labor; Private sphere.

Family life and work, balancing. See *Dual career families; Working women.*

Family life education. See *Parent training.*

Family members. Family member(s). Familial. Relative(s). Consanguin(ity, eal). Clan(s). *Choose from:* blood, near, first degree *with:* relat(ed,ion,ions,ives). Intergenerational. Forbear(s). Ancestor(s). Progenitor(s). Offspring. Cousin(s). Second cousin(s). Kin(sman, smen,ship,folk). Sibling(s). Parent(s). Child(ren). Grandparent(s). Sister(s). Brother(s). Aunt(s). Uncle(s). Wi(fe, ves). Husband(s). Intrafamil(y,ial). Mother-in-law. Father-in-law. Sister-in-law. Brother-in-law. Hereditary. Patern(al,ity). Matern(al,ity). Generation gap. Affin(e,es,al,ity). Agnat(e,es,ion). Spouse(s). Daughter(s). Mother(s). Son(s). Father(s). Grandchildren. Mother(s). Son(s). Stepchild(ren). Stepparent(s). Extended famil(y,ies). Nuclear famil(y,ies). *Consider also:* foster, adopted, surrogate *with:* daughter(s), mother(s), son(s), child(ren), parent(s), father(s), parent(s), grandchild(ren), mother(s), son(s). *See also* Adopted children; Adoptive parents;

Adult offspring; Ancestors; Biological family; Brothers; Daughters; Fathers; Foster children; Foster parents; Grandchildren; Grandparents; Husbands; Mothers; Siblings; Sisters; Sons; Spouses; Stem family; Stepfamily; Wives.

Family physicians. Family physician(s). *Choose from:* family, primary care *with:* physician(s), practitioner(s), doctor(s). *Consider also:* general practitioner(s), family practice, family medicine. *See also* Physicians.

Family planning. Family planning. Birth spacing. Pregnancy interval(s). *Consider also:* birth, fertility, population, conception, pregnanc(y,ies) *with:* control. *Consider also:* contracept(ion, ive,ives), planned parenthood. *See also* Birth control; Birth intervals; Contraception; Delayed parenthood; Family planning attitudes; Family size; First birth timing; Late childbearing; Oral contraceptives; Reproductive rights; Sex education; Zero population growth.

Family planning attitudes. Family planning attitude(s). Abortion attitude(s). Family size preference(s). *Choose from:* family planning, birth control, contracept(ive,ion), family size, pregnancy interval(s), voluntar(y,ily) childless(ness), fertility *with:* attitude(s), preference(s), knowledge, awareness, ideal, desire(s,d), intention(s), decision(s), choice(s), norms. *See also* Attitudes; Family planning; Sex education.

Family policy. Family polic(y,ies). *Choose from:* famil(y,ies,ial), parent(al,hood,s), marriage(s), marital, matrimonial, domestic, juvenile(s), child(ren), divorc(e,es,ed,ing), fertility *with:* polic(y,ies), legal, legislation, law(s). *See also* Population policy; Social legislation.

Family power. Family power. *Choose from:* famil(y,ies,ial), marital, conjugal, spousal, marriage(s), husband(s), wife, wives, parent(s,al) *with:* power, dominan(ce,t), decision making, equity, egalitarian, authority, head(ship). *Consider also:* family ideolog(y,ies), breadwinner role(s), family dynamics. *See also* Family relations; Family roles; Parent child relations; Sexual division of labor.

Family practitioners. See *Family physicians.*

Family problems. Family problem(s). *Choose from:* famil(y,ies,ial), home, domestic, marital, parent(s,al), mother child(ren), father child(ren) *with:* problems(s), disorganiz(ed,ation), violence, abuse(s,d), stress(es,ful), cris(is,es), disaster(s), death(s), bereavement, conflict(s), disrupt(ed,ing,ion, ions), troubled, feud(ing,ed,s),

fight(s,ing), distress(ed), dysfunctional, disturbed, multiproblem(s). *Consider also:* child abuse, spouse abuse, incest(uous,uousness), runaway(s), divorce(s). *See also* Child abuse; Dysfunctional families; Elder abuse; Family conflict; Family crises; Family therapy; Family violence; Marital conflict; Runaways; Schizophrenogenic family.

Family professional relations. See *Professional family relations.*

Family relations. Family relation(s,ship, ships). Family life. Kinship network(s). Family mental health. Family atmosphere. Family process(es). Family network(s). Sibling relation(s,ship, ships). Childrearing practices. *Choose from:* famil(y,ial), home, domestic, parent(al), intrafamil(y,ial) *with:* relation(s,ship,ships), life, living, lifestyle, interaction(s), support, disciplin(e,ary), communication, participation, reject(ed,ing,ion), accept(ed,ing,ance), expectation(s), dynamics, pattern(s), socialization, integration, involvement, attitude(s), permissive(ness), strict(ness). *Choose from:* maternal, paternal, mother child, father child *with:* behavior, deprivation, relationship(s). *See also* Family conflict; Family life; Family problems; Home environment; Marital relationship; Parent child relations; Sibling relations; Schizophrenogenic family.

Family reunions. Family reunion(s). *Choose from:* famil(y,ies), clan(s) *with:* annual meeting(s), reunion(s), celebrat(e,ed,ions). *Consider also:* wedding(s), funeral(s), anniversar(y,ies), birthday part(y,ies). *See also* Anniversaries and special events; Family traditions; Holidays.

Family roles. Family role(s). Concept of motherhood. Family responsibilit(y,ies). Breadwinner(s). Household head(s). Patriarch(al). Matriarch(al). Filial responsibilit(y,ies). Work family conflict. Position in family. Household division of labor. Caregiver role. *Choose from:* famil(y,ial), parent(al), mother, child, father, maternal, paternal, husband, wife, marital, conjugal, housewife, provider *with:* role(s), concept, expectation(s). *See also* Egalitarian families; Family relationships; Parent adolescent relations; Parent child relations; Parent role; Shared parenting; Sex roles; Sexual division of labor.

Family size. Family size. Size of famil(y,ies). Number of offspring. Number of siblings. Number of family members. Small famil(y,ies). Fertility decisions. Large famil(y,ies). Number of children. Spacing of children. Interbirth interval(s). Childbearing plan(s).

Childbirth expectation(s). Spacing of children. Household size. *See also* Extended family; Family planning; Nuclear family.

Family socioeconomic status. Family socioeconomic status. Status of family of origin. Family income. *Choose from:* famil(y,ies), parent(s,al), father(s), mother(s) *with:* socioeconomic status, SES, social status, economic status, socioeconomic level, poor, poverty, wealth, well-to-do, upper class, middle class, lower class, disadvantaged, income, social class, socioeconomic classification, working class, socioeconomic background, social background, family resources. *See also* Socioeconomic factors; Socioeconomic status; Social class.

Family stability. Family stability. *Choose from:* famil(y,ies), home(s), domestic, parent(s,al) *with:* stab(ility,le), continuity, resilien(t,ce), strength(s), intact(ness), stress resistan(t,ce), well-being, dependab(le,ility), durab(le,ility), endur(ing,ance), cohesion, cohesive(ness), invulnerab(ility,le), permanen(t,ce), preserv(e,ed,ation), reliab(le,ility), secur(e,ed,ity), solidarity, steadfast. *See also* Family conflict; Family relations; Family traditions; Social stability.

Family structure. See *Family characteristics.*

Family therapy. Family therap(y,ies). Family life counseling. Family crisis treatment. Family intervention. Family centered approach. Parent effectiveness training. Family process therapy. Bowen's family systems therapy. *Choose from:* famil(y,ies,ial), parent(s,al), marriage(s), marital, couple(s), relative(s), concurrent *with:* therap(y,ies), social work, counseling, casework, crisis intervention, treatment(s), problem solving, psychiatry, psychotherap(y,ies). *See also* Couples therapy; Divorce counseling; Marital therapy.

Family traditions. Family tradition(s). *Choose from:* famil(y,ies), kin(ship), clan(s) *with:* tradition(s,al,alism), custom(s), belief(s), festival(s), reunion(s), ritual(s), legend(s), rite(s), practice(s), holiday(s), heritage. *See also* Customs; Family background; Family reunions; Family stability; Family values; Heritage; Traditions.

Family values. Family values. Conservative parental value(s). Importance of the family. *Choose from:* famil(y,ies,ial), parent(s,al,hood,ing), mother(ing,hood), father(ing,hood) *with:* polic(y,ies), value(s), closeness, responsibilities, commitment(s), ethic(s,al), moral(s,ity), norm(s), mores, relig(ion,ions,ious). *Consider also:* spiritual, Christian,

traditional *with:* values. *Consider also:* family friendly. *See also* Childrearing; Family; Family traditions; Moral conditions; Morality; Value orientations; Values.

Family violence. Family violence. Domestic violence. Family fight(s). Violent famil(y,ies). *Choose from:* famil(y,ies, ial), domestic, spousal, marital, parental, conjugal, intrafamil(y,ial) *with:* violen(t,ce). *Choose from:* battered, abuse(d), mistreat(ed,ing,ment), beat(en,ing), bash(ed,ing) *with:* child(ren), wives, wife, husband(s), spouse(s), parent(s), grandparent(s), relationship(s), elderly parent(s), sibling(s). *See also* Abusive parents; Assault (personal); Battered women; Child abuse; Elder abuse; Family conflict; Family stability; Home environment; Incest; Infanticide; Marital rape; Sexual abuse; Social problems; Spouse abuse; Stalking; Torture; Victimization; Violence.

Family work relationship. Family work relationship(s). *Choose from:* famil(y,ies,ial), domestic, household, housework, homemaker(s), parent(s,al), child care, childcare, caregiver(s) *with:* profession(s,al), career(s), work(life), employment, occupation(s,al) *with:* role conflict(s), balanc(e,ed,ing), commitment(s), expectation(s), gender role(s), sharing work, work role(s), relationship(s). *See also* Career breaks; Corporate spouses; Dual career families; Egalitarian families; Family life; Family power; Family roles; Female headed households; Home environment; House husbands; Military families; Private sphere; Public sphere; Sex roles; Sexual division of labor; Shared parenting; Working women.

Famine. Famine(s). Food shortage(s). Food poverty. Lack of food. Scarce food. Food scarcity. Dearth of food. Bare subsistence. Semistarv(ed,ing,ation). Starv(e,ed,ing,ation). *Choose from:* food(stuffs), nourishment, rations *with:* scarc(e,ity,ities), shortage(s), shortfall(s), lack(s,ed,ing), dearth, paucity, meager(ness). *See also* Economic conditions; Economic problems; Food supply; Hunger, food deprivation; Poverty; Scarcity; Starvation; World health.

Famous people. Famous people. Famous person(s). *Choose from:* prominent, well known, high profile(s), eminent, preeminent, esteemed, foremost, respected, renown(ed), celebrated, noted, notable, famous, distinguished, venerable, acclaimed, immortal(ized), influential, prestigious, highly regarded, popular(ity), august *with:* people, person(s), star(s), personage(s), public official(s), figure(s), men, women, winner(s), player(s), pianist(s),

violinist(s), conductor(s), artist(s), writer(s), painter(s). *Consider also:* pop star(s), public life, celebrit(y,ies), glitterati, hero(es), heroine(s), big name(s), limelight, luminar(y,ies), protagonist(s), superhero(es), superstar(s), movie idol(s), movie star(s), sports figure(s), cult of personality, first lad(y,ies), Oscar award(s), Emm(y,ies), Nobel prize winner(s), rock star(s), rock group(s). *See also* Antiheroes; Eminence; Entertainers; Heroes; Idolatry; Politicians; Presidents; Prestige; Royalty.

Fanaticism. Fanatic(al,ism,s). Extremis(m, t,ts). Partisan(s,ship). Disciple(s). Enthusiast(s). Chauvinis(m,t,ts). Devotee(s). Radical(s,ness). Zealot(s). Zealous(ness). Fan(s). Extreme left wing. Extreme right wing. Revolutionar(y,ies). Insurrectionist(s). Anarchist(s). Passionate follower(s). True believer(s). Ultraconservative. Diehard(s). *Choose from:* self immolation, kamikaze, hunger strike(s,r,rs), vigilant(e,es,ism), terroris(ts,m). *See also* Extremism; Fans (persons); Left wing; Malinformation; Nerds; Prejudice; Radical movements; Right wing politics; Vigilantes; Zealots.

Fancy work. Fancy work. Needlework. Embroider(y,ies,ing,ed). Needlepoint. Quilt(ed,ing,s). Ribbon work. Beadwork. Cross stitch. Canvas work. Crewel embroidery. *Consider also:* tapestr(y,ies), crochet(ed,ing), knit(ted,ting). *See also* Crafts; Fibers; Sewing.

Fans (persons). Fan(s). Devotee(s). Afficionado(s). Buff(s). Habitué(s). Trainspotter(s). *Consider also:* enthusiast(s), junkie(s), freak(s), addict(s), buff(s), devotee(s), hound(s), fanatic(s). *See also* Audiences; Enthusiasts; Fanaticism; Fanzines; Followers; Mass behavior; Motion picture fans; Nerds; Readership; Sports fans.

Fans, motion picture. See *Motion picture fans.*

Fans, sports . See *Sports fans.*

Fantasia (music). Fantasia(s). Phantas(ia,ias,ie,ies,iestucke). Fantasio(s). Fantasie(s). *See also* Fantasy (literary); Improvisation (music).

Fantasies (imagination). See *Daydreaming.*

Fantasies (thought disturbances). Fantas(y,ies,ize,izing,ized). Phantas(y,ies,ize,izing,ized). Poor reality testing. *Choose from:* thinking, thought(s), idea(s), fantas(y,ies,ize, izing,ized) *with:* disturb(ed,ance,ances), patholog(y,ical), violent, aggressive, sadistic, masochistic, unrealistic, distort(ed,ing,ion,ions). *Choose from:* anal, rape, beating, cannibalistic, fellatio, hetaeral, incest(uous), king slave, pompadour, pregnancy, primal, procreative, rebirth, rescue, spider, womb *with:* fantas(y,ies), phantas(y,ies). *Consider also:* delusion(s,al), hallucination(s). *See also* Thought disturbances.

Fantasies, sexual. See *Sexual fantasies.*

Fantasy (literary). Fantas(y,ies). Fairy tale(s). Fairy stor(y,ies). Ghost stor(y,ies). Tales of imagination. Folktale(s). Whims(y,ical). Nonsense tale(s). Unicorn(s). Fair(y,ies). Magic(al). Dragon(s). Ghost(s). Folklore. Goblin(s). Imaginary creature(s). Fairyland. Elves. Elf. Brown(ies). Leprechaun(s). Oz. Pixie(s). *See also* Fantasia; Folk literature; Imaginary places; Literature; Mythology; Nonsense literature.

Fanzines. Fanzine(s). Fan magazine(s). *Consider also:* zine(s), tabloid(s). *See also* Fans (persons); Electronic journals; Magazine advertising; Motion picture fans; Periodicals.

Far East. Far East. People's Republic of China. Hong Kong(er,ers,ite). Japan(ese). South Korea(n). Republic of Korea. North Korea(n). Democratic People's Republic of Korea. Mongolia(n) People's Republic [Outer Mongolia]. Taiwan(ese) [Formosa(n)]. Republic of China. *Consider also:* Pacific Rim, Macao(n) [Macau(n)], Mongol Empire, Nihon, Nippon, Chinese. *See also* Asian empires; Asian languages; Chinese medicine; East Altaic languages; Oceania; Pacific region; Sino-Thai languages; South Asia; Southeast Asia; Tibeto-Burman languages; Tokharin languages.

Farce. Farc(e,es,ical). Mock(ery). Sham. Satirical comed(y,ies). Burlesque(s). Spoof(s). *Consider also:* slapstick, satir(e,ical), travest(y,ies), caricature(s, d), parod(y,ies), mimic(ry), ridicul(e,ed, ing). *See also* Comic opera; Humor; Jokes.

Fares. Fare(s). Charge(s). Cost(s). Fee(s). Ticket price(s). Toll(s). Carfare. *Consider also:* rate(s). *See also* Consumer expenditures; Cost recovery; Costs; Fees.

Farm corporations. See *Agribusiness.*

Farm laborers. See *Agricultural workers.*

Farm life. Farm life. Rural life. Farm society. Living on the land. Rural culture. Family farm(s). Farm famil(y,ies). Farm household(s). Farm(ing) communit(y,ies). *Consider also:* barnyard(s), farmer(s). *See also* Agricultural workers; Agrarian societies; Farmhouses; Rural communities; Rural housing; Rustic life.

Farm management. Farm management. Dairy management. Precision farming.

Site-specific farming. Farm forestry. Niche farm(ing,er,ers). *Choose from:* efficient management, land-diversion, sustainable, new technology, financial incentive(s), alternative use(s), production of renewable-energy, environmental quality, environment-friendly, safe practice(s) *with:* farm(s,ing), dair(y,ies), agricultur(e,al), grazing, crop(s), cultivation. *See also* Agribusiness; Agricultural mechanization.

Farm mechanization. See *Agricultural mechanization.*

Farm population. See *Agricultural workers; Rural population.*

Farm produce. Farm produce. Agricultural commodit(y,ies). Agricultural product(s,ion). Farm good(s). Organic produce. *Choose from:* farm(ing,er,ers), agricultur(e,al), organic *with:* produce, commodit(y,ies), product(s,ion), good(s). *Consider also:* corn, wheat, soybean(s), fruit(s), etc. *See also* Agricultural diversification; Commodities; Farming; Food supply; Grain trade; Grocery trade.

Farm tenancy. See *Tenant farmers.*

Farm women. See *Rural women.*

Farm workers. See *Agricultural workers.*

Farmers. See *Agricultural workers.*

Farmers, tenant. See *Tenant farmers.*

Farmers' wives. See *Rural women.*

Farmhouses. Farmhouse(s). Farm house(s). Homestead(s). Farmstead(s). *Choose from:* farm(s), country, plantation(s), rural, grange, peasant(s), rural *with:* house(s), housing, home(s), cottage(s), dwelling(s), cabin(s), hut(s), residence(s), architecture. *Consider also:* country retreat(s), vacation home(s). *See also* Farm life; Housing; Rural housing.

Farming. Farm(ing,er,ers,s). Agricultur(e,al, ist,ists). Agronom(y,ics,ist,ists). Agrarian. Agribusiness. Animal husbandry. Cattle breeding. Crop raising. Cropping. Dairying. Farm management. Harvest(ed,ing). Horticultur(e,al). Hydroponics. Market gardening. Pasturage. Raising livestock. Ranching. Sharecropper(s). Soil culture. Stock raising. Tillage. Truck farm(ing,ers). Viticulture. *See also* Agribusiness; Agriculture; Animal culture; Animal food; Arable land; Bee culture; Cattle; Cattle industry; Crops; Dairying; Draft animals; Farm produce; Farms; Fertility (farming); Gardening; Gleaning; Harvesting; Herbicides; Horse industry; Livestock; Mariculture; Nut industry; Organic farming; Part time farming; Pesticides; Tobacco farms.

Farming, diversified. See *Agricultural diversification.*

Farming, fertility . See *Fertility (farming).*

Farming, organic. See *Organic farming.*

Farming, part time. See *Part time farming.*

Farming communities. See *Rural communities.*

Farming out (work). See *Contracting out.*

Farms. Farm(s). Ranch(es,o). Plantation(s). Hacienda(s). Farmstead(s). Grange(s). *Consider also:* orchard(s), cropland(s), vineyard(s), pasture(s), dair(y,ies), granar(y,ies). *See also* Agricultural collectives; Arable land; Family farms; Farming; Grazing lands; Ranches; Rural areas; Size of farms.

Farms, collective. See *Agricultural collectives.*

Farms, family. See *Family farms.*

Farms, livestock . See *Farms; Ranches*

Farms, size of. See *Size of farms*

Farms, small. See *Small farms.*

Farms, state. See *Agricultural collectives.*

Farms, tobacco . See *Tobacco farms.*

Farms, tree . See *Tree farms.*

Fascism. Fascis(m,mo,t,ts). Neo-fascis(m,t,ts). Nazi(s,sm). Neo-nazi(s,m). National Socialis(m,t,ts). Mussolini government. Black Shirt(s). Franco government. Falangis(t,ts). Ku-Klux-Klan. Klansmen. KKK. Falang(e,ist,ists). Extreme nationalism. Racis(m,t,ts). Peronism. Integralismo. Skinhead(s). Aryan nation(s). Nazi sympathiser(s). Bigot(s,ry,ed). White supremac(y,ist,ists). White liberation movement. Posse Comitatus. White Aryan Resistance. The Covenant, the Sword and the Arm of the Lord. Order of the Silent Brotherhood. Afrikaner resistance movement. White power group(s). White freedom movement. White patriot party. Bruder Schweigen strike force II. Schweigen order II. Christian Identity cult. Aryan Republican Army. Invisible Empire. National Association for the Advancement of White People. *Consider also:* cross burning(s), dictatorship(s), regimentation, authoritarianism, far right, ultra right, hatemonger(s), anti-semit(ic,ism), antisemit(ic,ism), apartheid. *See also* Anti-intellectualism; Antifascist movements; Anti-government radicals; Authoritarianism (political); Corporate state; Dictatorship; Futurism (Art); Militarism; Militias; Nationalism; Racism; Social Darwinism; Totalitarianism; Xenophobia.

Fashion industry. See *Garment industry.*

Fashions. Fashion(able,s). Clothing style(s). Haute couture. Fad(s). Chic. Faddis(t,ts, h,hness). Vogue. Popular(ity). Trendy. Dapper. Stylish(ness). Dandy. Latest style(s). Craze. Modish. Good taste. Tasteful(ly). Popular standards.

Trendsett(ing,er,ers). *Choose from:* peer influence, reference group influence *with:* clothing, taste(s), choice(s). *See also* Body ornamentation; Clothing; Cosmetics; Customs; Fads; Hats; Headgear; Mannequins (Figures); Models (persons); Popular culture.

Fasting. Fast(s,ed,ing). Sawm. *Choose from:* forego, abstain(ed,ing), abstinence *with:* food, eating, meal(s). *Consider also:* dietary restriction(s), meatless day(s), bread and water, Lent(en), quadragesima(l), Yom Kippur. *See also* Anorexia nervosa; Asceticism; Diet fads; Hunger, food deprivation; Hunger strikes; Sacred meals.

Fatalism. Fatalis(m,ist,ists,istic). Predestin(ed,ation). Despair(ed,ing). Desponden(t,cy). *Choose from:* sense of control, lack of control *with:* destin(y, ies), fate(s). Doomed. Foreordained. End time thinking. *Consider also:* determinis(m,tic), predetermin(ed, ing,ation), ordained, preordained, Armageddon. *See also* Determinism; End; Fate; Freedom (theology); Philosophy.

Fatalities. Fatalit(y,ies). Death(s). Mortality. Fatal. Violent death(s). Casualt(y,ies). Lethal. Execution(s). Murder(s). Dying. Deceased. Expir(e,ed,ation). Body count(s). *Choose from:* loss(es) los(e,t,ing) *with:* life, lives. *See also* Accidents; Casualties; Death; Missing in action; Mortality rates; Suicide.

Fatality rates. See *Mortality rates.*

Fate. Fate(d,ful). Destin(y,ed). Predestin(y,ed,ation). Karma. Inescap(able,ability,ableness). Inevit(able,ability,ableness). Predetermin(ed,ation). Necessity. Fortune. Foreordained. Ordained. Unavoid(able,ableness,ability). *See also* Chance; Fatalism; Religious beliefs.

Father absence. See *Paternal deprivation.*

Father, age of. See *Paternal age.*

Father attitudes. See *Parental attitudes.*

Father child communication. Father child communication. *Choose from:* father(s), paternal, male parent(al,s), *with:* infant(s), child(ren), toddler(s), preschooler(s), newborn(s), daughter(s), son(s) *with:* child directed language, communicat(e,ed,ing,ion), conversation(s,al), talk(ed,ing), speech, relationship, emotional exchange(s), affective exchange(s), emotional expression(s), sharing, verbal directive(s), interaction(s), interactive, language, discourse, interchange(s), message(s), dialogue, utterances, play(ed,ing). *See also* Father child relations.

Father child relations. Father child relation(ship,s). Paternal attitudes. Fathering. *Choose from:* father(s),

paternal, male parent(s,al) *with:* infant(s), child(ren), son(s), daughter(s) *with:* relation(s,ship,ships), dyad(s,ic), attachment(s), love, care, feeling(s), bond(ing), play, interaction(s), comfort(ed,ing), abus(e,ed,ing,ive), overprotect(ion,ive), nurturance, deprivation, communication, incest, role(s), dependenc(e,y), independence, conflict(s), support, dynamics, understanding, acceptance, rejection, expectation(s), rell(ious,iousness,ion), inadequate, absence, presence. *Consider also:* electra conflict(s), electra complex, paternal power, patria potestas, menism. *See also* Attachment behavior; Childrearing; Family relations; Father child communication; Incest; Nurturance; Overprotection; Parent role; Parental attitudes; Parental permissiveness; Parent role; Paternal behavior; Paternal deprivation; Paternalism; Possessiveness; Schizophrenogenic family.

Father of the country. Father of the country. Pater patriae. Founding father(s). *See also* History; Revolution.

Father role. See *Father child communication; Father child relations; Parent role; Paternal behavior.*

Fatherhood. See *Fathers.*

Fatherlessness. See *Paternal deprivation.*

Fathers. Father(s,hood,ing). Paternal. Paternity. Patriarch(s,al). Male parent(s). Dad(s,dy,dies). *Consider also:* father child relations, adolescent fathers. *See also* Family members.

Fathers, absentee. See *Paternal deprivation.*

Fathers, adolescent. See *Teenage fathers.*

Fathers, birth. See *Biological family.*

Fathers, expectant. See *Expectant fathers.*

Fathers, single. See *Single parent family.*

Fathers, teenage. See *Teenage fathers.*

Fathers of the church. Fathers of the church. Church father(s). Church hierarch(y,ies). Patristic(s). *See also* Christian leadership; Priests; Religious councils and synods; Religious leadership; Religious personnel.

Fatigue. Fatigue(d). Exhaust(ed,ion). Tired(ness). Lassitude. Wear(y,iness). Drows(y,iness). Sleep(y,iness). Letharg(y,ic). Ennervat(ed,ion). Ennui. Languor(ous,ousness). Listless(ness). Burnout. Burned out. Burnt out. *See also* Burnout; Info fatigue syndrome; Sleep.

Fatigue, auditory. See *Auditory fatigue.*

Fatigue, battle. See *Post traumatic stress disorders.*

Fatigue, combat. See *Combat disorders; Post traumatic stress disorders.*

Fatigue, industrial. See *Industrial fatigue.*

Fatigue, mental. See *Mental fatigue.*

Fatigue syndrome, chronic. See *Chronic fatigue syndrome.*

Fatigue syndrome, info. See *Info fatigue syndrome.*

Fatigue syndrome, information. See *Info fatigue syndrome.*

Fatigue syndrome, post-viral. See *Chronic fatigue syndrome.*

Fatness. Fat(ness,ten). Gain(ed,ing) weight. Overweight. Obes(e,ity). Corpulen(ce,t). Plump(ness). Heav(y,iness). Stout(ness). Excess weight. Weight problem. Weight increase(s). Grow(ing) fat. Putting on weight. *See also* Body weight; Excess; Personal appearance.

Fatuity. Fatu(ity,ous,ousness). Complacent(ly) stupid(ity). Dull(ness). Foolish(ness). *See also* Dullness; Personality.

Fault. See *Blame; Default (negligence); Errors; Guilt; Offenses.*

Fault tolerant computing. Fault tolerant computing. Fault-tolerant architecture. Fault-tolerant software. *Choose from:* fault(s), disturbance(s), error(s), malfunction(ed,ing,s), contaminat(e,ed, ing,ion), failure(s), *with:* toleran(t,ce), protect(ed,ing,ion), tolerat(e,ed,ing,es), avoid(ed,ing,ance), correct(ed,ing,ive), recover(ed,ing,y,ies) *with:* comput(er,ers, ing), system(s), software, architecture, microprocessor(s), minicomputer(s), structure(s), mechanism(s). *Consider also:* redundancy, backup(s), error correction. *See also* Artificial intelligence; Computers; Dugging; Dependability; Errors; Reliability.

Faute de mieux. See *Accidental homosexuality.*

Faux pas. Faux pas. Gaffe(s). Blunder(s,ed, ing). Breach(es) of etiquette. Blooper(s). Impropriet(y,ies). Indiscretion(s). Misstep(s). Slipup(s). Transgression(s). Wrong move(s). *See also* Etiquette; Errors; Manners; Speech errors.

Favelas. See *Slums.*

Favorites, royal. See *Royal favorites.*

Favoritism. Favoritism. Nepotism. Partisan(ship). Preferential treatment. Partiality. Bias(ed,es). *Consider also:* patronage, unfair(ness), inequit(y,ies)*See also* Bias; Nepotism; Inequality; Injustice; Preferences; Preferential treatment; Royal favorites.

Favors. Favor(s). Gift(s). Good deed(s). Good turn(s). Boon(s). Benevolence(s). Blessing(s). Kindness(es). Dispensation(s). Indulgence(s). Courtes(y,ies). *Consider also:* charitable act(s), mitzvah(s). *See also* Altruism; Benevolence; Brotherliness; Charitable behavior; Generosity; Gift giving; Good samaritans; Helping behavior; Kindness; Prosocial behavior; Sharing; Social behavior.

Fear. Fear(s,ful,fulness). Phobic disorder(s). Fear of success. Phob(ia,ias,ic). Anxiety. Anxious(ness). War(y,iness). Panic(s, ky). Fright(ened). Stagefright. Dread(ed, ing). Scared. Shy(ness). Terror. Trepidation. Apprehens(ion,ive). Angst. Coward(ly,ice). Timid(ity). Afraid. *See also* Anxicty; Fear of closeness; Fear of crime; Fear of failure; Fear of God; Fear of men; Fear of success; Fear of women; Horror; Intimidation; Panic disorder; Phobias; Psychological warfare; Shyness; Stranger reactions; Timidity.

Fear, morbid. See *Phobias.*

Fear of being alone. See *Autophobia.*

Fear of closeness. Fear of closeness. *Choose from:* closeness, intimacy, enmeshment, commitment(s), self disclosure *with:* fear(s,ed,ing), anxiet(y, ies), ambivalen(ce,t), barrier(s), avoid(s,ed,ing,ant,ance), resistance, inhibit(ed,ing,ion,ions). *Consider also:* agroman(ia,ic), engulfment anxiet(y,ies), pseudointimacy, social anxiet(y,ies), shyness, distancing. *See also* Fear; Fear of men; Fear of women; Interpersonal relations.

Fear of crime. Fear of crime. Defensive weapon ownership. Crime fear. *Choose from:* fear(ful,fulness), insecur(e,ity, ities), protective(ness), apprehens(ive, ion), afraid, feel(ing) threatened, dread(ed,ing), fright(en,ened,ening), terror, terrified, worr(y,ied), concern(ed) *with:* crime(s), criminal(s), violen(t,ce), assault(ed,ing,s), holdup(s), robber(y, ies), abus(e,ive,iveness), murder(s), homicid(al,e,es), break in, rape(s), molest(ing,ation), pickpocket(s), theft(s), thiev(es,ery), mugging(s), attack(s,ing), beat(ing,en), victimization. *See also* Crime; Crime prevention; Crime rates; Fear.

Fear of failure. Fear of failure. Test anxiety. Perfection(ism,ist,ists). Self handicapping. Coercive achievement motivation. Pressure to achieve. Pressure to succeed. *Choose from:* fail(ure,ing), test(s) *with:* anxiety, fear(ed,ing,ful), motiv(e,es, ation), dread(ed,ing), expect(ed,ing, ation,ations), threat(en,ened,ening). *See also* Achievement need; Failure; Fear of success.

Fear of God. Fear(ful) of God. Theophob(ia,ic). *Choose from:* fear(s,ed,ing,ful), dread(ed,ing), frighten(ed,ing), trepidation(s), afraid, trembling, awe *with:* God, divin(e,ity), Yahweh, Lord, almighty. *See also* Fear; Glory of God; God concepts.

Fear of men. Fear of men. Androphob(ia,ic). *Consider also:*

apandria, misandry. *See also* Fear of women; Fear of closeness.

Fear of success. Fear of succ(ess,eeding). Success avoidance. Achievement anxiety. Avoid(ing) success. Fear of career success. Success fear. *See also* Fear of failure; Self defeating behavior.

Fear of women. Fear of women. Gynophob(ia,ic). Gynephob(ia,ic). Horror feminae. *See also* Fear of closeness; Fear of men.

Feasibility. Feasib(ility,le,leness). Workab(ility,le,leness). Practicab(ility, le,leness). Usab(ility,le,leness). Achievab(ility,le,leness). Attainab(ility, le,leness). Realizab(ility,le,leness). Reachab(ility,le,leness). Within reach. Obtainab(ility,le,leness). *Consider also:* expedien(t,ce,cy), viab(ility,le,leness). *See also* Common sense; Effectiveness; Feasibility studies; Idealism; Reality.

Feasibility studies. Feasibility stud(y,ies). *Consider also:* pilot stud(y,ies), cost benefit analys(is,es). *See also* Feasibility; Research.

Feasts. See *Dinners and dining; Entertaining; Festivals; Holidays.*

Features, facial. See *Facial features.*

Fecal incontinence. Fecal incontinence. Encopresis. *Consider also:* fecal, bowel(s), defecat(e,ed,ing,ion) *with:* incontinen(t,ce), involuntary, loss of control. *See also* Behavior disorders; Defecation; Diarrhea; Gastrointestinal disorders; Symptoms; Urinary incontinence.

Fecundity. Fecund(ity,ability). Fertil(e,ity). Multiparous. *Consider also:* birthrate(s), childbearing, fruitful, prolific, superfecundation, induced ovulation. *See also* Birth intervals; Population growth.

Federal agencies. See *Government agencies.*

Federal assistance. See *Antipoverty programs; Fiscal federalism; Government financing; Government programs; Government subsidization; Medical assistance; Public welfare.*

Federal deficit. See *Public debt.*

Federal employees. See *Civil service; Government personnel.*

Federal funding. See *Government financing.*

Federal regulations. See *Government regulation.*

Federalism. Federalis(m). Federal system(s). Federal state relations. Federation(s). Government(al) with division of powers. States rights. States prerogative(s). Powers of states. Federal powers. Shared powers. Powers reserved to the states. *Consider also:* cooperative federalism, creative federalism,

enumerated powers, dual federalism, horizontal federalism, vertical federalism, marble cake federalism, new federalism, new partnership federalism, picket-fence federalism, regulatory federalism. *Consider also:* federal provincial government, federal preemption. *See also* Confederalism; Fiscal federalism; Intergovernmental relations; Unitarism.

Federalism, fiscal. See *Fiscal federalism.*

Federations. Federation(s). Confederation(s). Alliance(s). Union(s) of organization(s). Confederac(y,ies). League(s). Coalition(s). *Consider also:* amalgamation(s), syndicate(s). *See also* Coalitions; Confederalism; Networks; Power sharing; Unitarism.

Fee, capitation. See *Capitation fee.*

Feed additives. See *Food additives.*

Feedback. Feedback. *Consider also:* biofeedback, myofeedback, knowledge of result(s), closed loop(s), cybernetic(s), comment(s,ary,aries), reaction(s). *See also* Artificial intelligence; Biofeedback; Cybernetics; Expert systems; Knowledge of results; Man machine systems; Reinforcement.

Feedback, sensory. See *Sensory feedback.*

Feedback, visual. See *Visual feedback.*

Feedbackcontrol systems. See *Cybernetics; Feedback; Robotics.*

Feeding, bottle. See *Bottle feeding.*

Feeding, breast. See *Breast feeding.*

Feeding, community . See *Group meals.*

Feeding behavior. Feeding behavior(s). Table manners. *Choose from:* eating, dietary, feeding, food, mealtime, table *with:* behavior(s), pattern(s), habit(s), manners, ritual(s), rate(s), intake. *See also* Animal food; Animal foraging behavior; Eating.

Feeding practices. Feeding practice(s). *Choose from:* feeding(s) *with:* practice(s), technique(s), schedule(s), method(s), pattern(s), interaction, timing, bottle, breast, enteral, parenteral. *Consider also:* mealtime(s). *See also* Diet; Eating; Food habits.

Feeds. See *Foods.*

Feeling, community. See *Community feeling.*

Feeling, group. See *Group feeling.*

Feelings. See *Awareness; Beliefs; Emotions.*

Feelings, discharge of. See *Abreaction; Catharsis; Psychodrama.*

Fees. Fee(s). *Consider also:* cost(s), charge(s), rate(s), fine(s), penalt(y,ies), tuition, dues, payment(s), price(s), pricing, bill(s,ing), compensation, charging polic(y,ies), gratuit(y,ies), honorarium(s), tip(s), toll(s), commission(s), recompense, remuneration. *See also* Billing systems; Cost recovery; Costs; Fares; Fines.

Fees, prescription. See *Prescription fees.*

Fellatio. See *Oral sex.*

Fellowship. Fellowship. Comrade(s,ship). Camaraderie. Companion(s,ship). Brotherhood(s). *Consider also:* affab(le,ility), club(s), fraternit(y,ies), guild(s), league(s), sodalit(y,ies), union(s). *See also* Belongingness; Brotherhoods; Brotherlinesss; Community (social); Friendship.

Fellowships (educational). Fellowship(s). Scholarship(s). Assistantship(s). Training support. Stipend(s). Student loan(s). Educational award(s). Tuition grant(s). Scholarship loan(s). Educational financial assistance. *Consider also:* tuition voucher(s), school federal aid, school financial assistance. *See also* Financial support; Scholarships (educational); Tuition reimbursement.

Felonies. Felon(y,ies,ious). *Choose from:* heinous, grave(r), aggravated *with:* crime(s), offense(s) *Consider also:* punishable by death, treason, murder, aggravated assault, etc. *See also* Career criminals; Crime; Criminal act; Penal codes.

Female animals. See *Females (animal).*

Female circumcision (ritual). Female circumcision(s). Clitorectom(y,ies). Clitoridectom(y,ies). Female genital mutilation. Vaginal mutilation. Female infibulation. *Choose from:* female(s), wom(an,en) girl(s) *with:* ritual genital operation(s), ritual disfigurement, vulvectom(y,ies), excision of external genitalia, pharaonic circumcision. *See also* Circumcision; Ritual disfigurement; Sexual abuse.

Female condoms. Female condom(s). *Consider also:* female-controlled barrier method(s), sexual barrier device(s). *See also* Female contraceptive devices.

Female contraceptive devices. Female contraceptive device(s). *Choose from:* female(s), woman, women *with:* contraceptive device(s), birth control, contraception. *Choose from:* intrauterine, vaginal *with:* contraceptive device(s), diaphragm(s), sponge(s), ring(s). *Consider also:* IUD(s), Femcap, contraceptive diaphragm(s), contraceptive barrier(s). *See also* Female condoms; Oral contraceptives;

Female criminals. See *Female offenders.*

Female dominated occupations. See *Female intensive occupations.*

Female dominated occupations, men in. See *Nontraditional careers.*

Female genital disorders. Female genital disorder(s). *Choose from:* female(s), woman, women *with:* genital disorder(s), genital disease(s), herpes genitalis, sterility. *Choose from:* vagina(l), ovar(y,ies,ian), uter(i,us,ine), endometrial, cervi(x,ical), menstrua(l,tion), premenstrual, vulva(r,e), vulvovaginal, rectovaginal, vesicovaginal, gynecological *with:* disease(s), disorder(s), neoplasm(s), tumor(s), infect(ed,ion,ions,ious), acute, cyst(ic,s), polycystic, inflam(ed, mation,mations,matory), wound(ed,s), swell(ing), swollen, hyperplasia, dysplasia, erosion, hypertrophy, incompetence, prolapse, rupture(s), perforation, fistula(s), defect(s), affect(ed,ion,ions), syndrome(s), tuberculosis. *Consider also:* oophoritis, parametritis, salpingitis, anovulation, gynatresia, hematocolpos, hematometria, amenorrhea, dysmenorrhea, menorrhagia, oligomenorrhea, pseudopregnanc(y,ies), dyspareunia, cervicitis, vulvitis, vulvovaginitis, endrometritis, metrorrhagia, candidiasis, kraurosis vulvae, pruritis vulvae. *See also* Female genitalia; Menstrual disorders; Premenstrual syndrome.

Female genitalia. Female genital(ia,s). *Choose from:* female(s) *with:* sex(ual), perineal, reproductive, genital, pelvic *with:* organ(s), region(s), area(s). *Consider also:* adnexa uteri, broad ligament(s), fallopian tube(s), ovar(y,ies), round ligament(s), uterus(es), cervix uteri, endometrium, myometrium, vagina(s,l), hymen, vulva, Bartholins glands, clitor(is,al), cervix(es), labia(l). *See also* Female genital disorders.

Female headed households. Female headed household(s). *Choose from:* female(s), women, woman, mother(s) *with:* head(s,ed) *with:* household(s), famil(y,ies). *Consider also:* matriarch(s). *See also* Family work relationship; Single parent family; Working women.

Female homosexuality. See *Lesbianism.*

Female impersonators. See *Transvestism.*

Female intensive occupations. Female intensive occupation(s). Female job(s). Velvet ghetto(s). Glass ceiling(s). Woman(s) work. Women(s) work. *Choose from:* female dominated, female intensive, traditionally female *with:* job(s), career(s), occupation(s,al), profession(s,al), business(es), industr(y,ies), work, work group(s), field(s), organization(s). *Consider also:* babysitt(ing,er,ers), beautician(s), clerical work, data entry, dental hygienist(s), hair styli(st,sts,ing), hairdress(er,ers,ing), housekeeper(s), librarian(s,ship), nurs(e,es,ing), schoolteach(er,ers,ing), secretar(y,ies,

ial), service occupation(s), stenograph(ic,er,ers), word processing. *See also* Beauty operators; Caregivers; Clerical workers; Comparable worth; Corporate spouses; Domestic service; Home care; Male nurses; Nontraditional careers; Nurses; Nurses aides; Sexual division of labor; Teachers.

Female male relations. *See Heterosexual relationships.*

Female offenders. Female offender(s). Female criminal(s,ity). Crime(s) committed by females. *Choose from:* woman, women, female(s) *with:* criminal(s,ity), crime(s), prison inmate(s), offender(s), incarcerated, correctional institution(s), convict(s), felon(s,y,ies), prisoner(s), offense(s), drug abuser(s), shoplifter(s), prostitute(s), arrest(s,ed), crime rate(s), defendant(s), embezzler(s). *See also* Females (human); Offenders; Sex offenders.

Female orgasm. Female orgasm(s). *Choose from:* female(s), woman, women, vaginal, clitoral *with:* orgasm(s,ic), sexual response peak(s), sexual satisfaction. *Consider also:* female(s) *with:* ejaculation, anorgas(tic,mia), orgasmic dysfunction, preorgasmic, nonorgasmic. *See also* Masturbation; Sexual intercourse.

Female role. See *Gender identity; Images of women; Sex roles.*

Female spirituality. Female spirituality. *Choose from:* female(s), women, woman, feminine, feminiz(e,ed,ing, ation) *with:* spiritual(ity), mystic(al,ism), divin(e,ity), monastic(ism), pious(ness), saint(s,ly,liness), visionar(y,ies), hol(y,iness), devout(ness), prayerful, mindful(ness), religiosity, Godl(y,iness), religious(ness), contemplative. *Consider also:* ecofeminism, goddess worship, spiritual feminism. *See also* Feminist theology; Goddesses; Nuns; Religiosity; Religious commitment; Spiritual gifts; Spirituality.

Females (animal). Female(s). Cow(s). Doe(s). Hen(s). Dam(s). Mare(s). Queen bee(s). Bitch(es). Ewe(s). Heifer(s). Fill(y,ies). Vixen(s). Sow(s). Lioness(es). Tigress(es). Bidd(y,ies). *See also* Animals.

Females (human). Human female(s). Wom(an,en,yn). Wimmin. Girl(s). Actress(es). Amazon(s). Aunt(s). Baroness(es). Beauty queen(s). Bride(s). Businesswom(an,en). Coed(s). Concubine(s). Congresswom(an,en). Countess(es). Courtesan(s). Crone(s). Daughter(s). Dame(s). Dowager(s). Distaff. Duchess(es). Fair sex. First lad(y,ies). Geisha(s). Goddess(es). Governess(es). Granddaughter(s). Grandmother(s). Heroine(s). Housewi(fe,ves). Hostess(es). Lad(y,ies).

Lass(es,ie,ies). Laywom(en,an). Lesbian(s). Madam(s). Madame. Maid(s, en,ens). Maternal. Matriarch(y,al). Matron(s). Midwi(fe,ves). Mistress(es). Mrs. Ms. Miss. Mother(s). Nymph(s). Nun(s). Ombudswom(an,en). Peeress(es). Princess(es). Queen(s). Seamstress(es). Sister(s). Sororit(y,ies). Spinster(s). Squaw(s). Vahine. Widow(s). Wi(fe,ves,fely). Witch(es). *Consider also:* femin(ine,ism,inity), wom(an,en) faculty, wom(an,en) athlete(s), battered wom(en,an), club wom(an,en), displaced homemaker(s), employed wom(an,en), holy wom(an, en), homeless wom(an,en), medicine wom(an,en), older wom(en,an), younger wom(an,en), pregnant student(s), wom(en,an) dentist(s), women physician(s), working wom(an,en), adolescent mother(s), female criminal(s), female delinquent(s), fallen wom(an,en), unwed mother(s), reentry wom(an,en), rural wom(en,an), single wom(an,en), wom(an,en) of color, wom(an,en) religious, herstor(y,ies), materteral. *See also* Fear of men; Fear of women; Female circumcision (ritual); Female genital disorders; Female genitalia; Female headed households; Female offenders; Female orgasm; Female spirituality; Females (animal); Feminin- ity; Feminism; Feminist theology; Gender differences; Harems; House- wives; Images of women; Mothers; Private sphere; Professional women; Sex roles; Sex stereotypes; Sexism; Sexual division of labor; Sexual revolution; Single mothers; Single sex schools; Wives; Women living in poverty; Women owned businesses; Women religious; Women's groups; Women's rights; Working women.

Females, battered. See *Battered women.*

Femininity. Femininity. *Choose from:* feminine, female, women(s), woman(s) *with:* identit(y,ies), identif(y,ied,ication), orientation. Ladylike. *Consider also:* anima, ankh, herstor(y,ies). *See also* Androgyny; Feminization; Females (human); Masculinity; Sex roles.

Feminism. Feminis(m,t,ts). Suffragette(s). Maternal right(s). Neofeminis(m,t,ts). Profeminis(m,t,ts). Ecofeminis(m,t,ts). Protofeminis(m,t,ts). Female chauvinis(m,t,ts). *Choose from:* women(s), woman(s), female(s), girl(s), lesbian(s), feminis(m,t,ts), feminine, reproductive, sex(ual), gender *with:* rights, suffrage, movement(s), liberation, equality, power, equal protection, consciousness raising, affirmative action, status, politics, equity, comparable worth, fair(ness), equal pay, equal employment, equal opportunit(y,ies), equal education. *Choose from:* anarcha, Black, French, German, etc., career, cultural, first wave, global, lesbian,

liberal, mainstream, male, Marxist, nonaligned, third world, psychoanalytic, radical, socialist, spiritual *with:* feminis(m,t,ts). *Consider also:* womanis(t,ts,m), feminine spirituality, feminist theory, sisterhood. *See also* Coeducation; Females (human); Feminist art; Feminist criticism; Feminist theology; Feminist therapy; Lesbianism; Men's movement; Mother goddesses; Sexism; Single sex schools; Social movements; Suffrage movement; Womanism; Women's groups; Women's rights.

Feminist art. Feminist art(ist,ists). Womanist art(ist,ists). Feminist painting(s). *Choose from:* feminis(m,t, ts), feminin(e,ity), women, woman(ist), lesbian *with:* art(ist,ists), painting(s), sculpture(s). *Consider also:* women artist(s), feminist art historian(s). *See also* Arts; Feminism; Genres (art).

Feminist criticism. Feminist critic(s,ism). Feminist critique(s). Feminist interpretation(s). *Choose from:* feminis(m,t,ts), feminin(e,ity), women, woman, lesbian *with:* critic(s,ism), critique(s), interpret(ed,ing,ation,ations), review(er,ers,ing), judge(s,ment,ments), epistemolog(,ical,ically,ist). *Consider also:* women critic(s,ism), feminist art critic(s). *See also* Criticism; Deconstruction; Feminism; Feminist therapy; Social epistemology.

Feminist ethics. Feminist ethic(s,al). *Choose from:* feminis(m,t,ts), feminin(e,ity), women, woman(ist), lesbian, maternal(ist), wife, wives, gender, sexual orientation *with:* ethic(s,al), value(s), moral(s,ity), personal guideline(s). *Consider also:* sexual ethic(s,al,ally). *See also* Ethics; Feminism; Feminist therapy; Sexual ethics.

Feminist movement. See *Feminism; Suffrage movement; Women's groups; Women's rights.*

Feminist organizations. See *Feminism; Suffrage movement; Women's groups.*

Feminist theology. Feminist theolog(y,ies,ical,ians). *Choose from:* feminis(m,t,ts) *with:* theolog(y,ies,ical, ians), hermeneutic(s), Gospel(s), religious, divin(e,ity), Christian, Jewish, Islam, Muslim, Buddhis(m,t,ts) *with:* thought, opinion(s), principle(s), truth(s), doctrine(s), dogma(s). *Consider also:* goddess(es) *with:* worship(ped, ing). *See also* Female spirituality; Goddess religion; Goddesses; Mother goddesses.

Feminist therapy. Feminist therap(y,ies). *Choose from:* feminis(t,m), feminist principle(s), neofeminis(m,t,ts) *with:* therap(y,ies), psychotherap(y,ies), social work, casework, healing, mental health. *See also* Abortion counseling; Couples

therapy; Cultural therapy; Females (human); Feminism; Feminist criticism; Feminist ethics; Marital therapy; Psychotherapy; Spiritual healing; Therapy.

Feminization. Feminiz(e,ed,ing,ation). Feminine values. Feminine institution(s). Gynecocentrism. Effemina(te,cy). *Consider also:* feminism, feminine qualit(y,ies). *See also* Effeminacy; Female intensive occupations; Feminin- ity; Women living in poverty.

Feminization of poverty. See *Women living in poverty.*

Feminized occupations. See *Female intensive occupations.*

Femmes fatales. Femmes fatale(s). Adventuress(es). Evil heroine(s). Dark lad(y,ies). Sinister vamp(s). Demonic wom(en,an), Siren(s). She-devil(s). Vampire(s). Gold digger(s). Dangerous wom(en,an). Manipulative wom(en,an). Sexual predator(s). *See also* Eroticism; Images of women; Sexual fantasies.

Fences. Fence(s). Stockade(s). Barricade(s). Guardrail(s). Balustrade(s,d). Palisad(e,es,ed,ing). *Consider also:* hurdle(s), chainlink, post and rail, barrier(s), blockade(s), hedgerow(s), hedge(s,ed), wall(ed,s).*See also* Barriers; Hindrances; Security measures.

Fermentation. Ferment(ed,ing,ation,able). Anaerobic respiration Leaven(ing). Pickl(e,ed,ing). Mother of vinegar. *Consider also:* methanogenesis, yeast, sourdough(s). *See also* Alcoholic beverages; Food preservation.

Fertility. Fertil(e,ity). Fecund(ity,ability). Multiparous. *Consider also:* birthrate(s), natality, childbearing, fruitful, superfe- cundation, induced ovulation, prolific. *See also* Birthrate; Demography; Family size; Fecundity; Fertility (farming); Fertility decline; Fertility enhancement; Population growth; Pregnancy rate.

Fertility (farming). Fertil(e,ity). Fruitful(ness). Fruit-bearing. *Choose from:* fertil(e,ity), abundan(t,ce), bountiful, fecund(ity), prolific, lush(ness), luxurious(ness), plenteous(ness), profus(e,eness,ion), copious *with:* crop(s), yield(s), growth, harvest(s), product(s,ion). *See also* Farming; Fertility; Fertilization; Gardening; Soil fertility.

Fertility decline. Fertility decline. *Choose from:* birth(s), birthrate(s), birth rate(s), fertility, replacement rate, childbearing *with:* declin(e,ed,es,ing), limit(s,ed,ing), slowing down, decreas(e,ed,es,ing). *See also* Birthrate; Demographic changes; Family planning; Health transition; Population decline.

Fertility enhancement. Fertility enhancement. *Choose from:* fertility *with:* agent(s), drug(s),enhancement(s). *Consider also:* artificial insemination, conception technique(s), induced ovulation, spermhormone, in-vitro fertilization, invitro fertilization, reproductive technolog(y,ies). *See also* Fertilization in vitro; Oral contraceptives; Pregnancy; Reproductive technologies; Sexual reproduction.

Fertility, soil. See *Soil fertility.*

Fertilization. Fertiliz(e,ed,ing,ation). Fecundat(e,ed,ing,ion). *Consider also:* inseminat(e,ed,ing,ion), impregnat(e,ed, ing,ion), pollinat(e,ed,ing,ion), enrich(ed,ing,ment). *See also* Artificial insemination; Conception; Fertility (farming); Fertility enhancement; Fertilization in vitro; Pregnancy; Reproductive technologies; Sexual reproduction; Surrogate mothers.

Fertilization in vitro. Fertilization in vitro. Fertiliz(e,ed,ing,ation) *with:* in vitro. *Consider also:* embryo transfer(s), ectogene(tic,sis), test tube bab(y,ies), external fertilization. *See also* Artificial insemination; Fertility enhancement; Fertilization; Pregnancy; Reproductive technologies; Sexual reproduction; Sperm banks; Surrogate mothers.

Fertilizer, sewage as. See *Sewage as fertilizer.*

Festivals. Festival(s). Fiesta(s). Celebration(s). Ceremonie(s). Holy day(s). Feast(s). Feast day(s). Festivit(y, ies). Holiday(s). Saints day(s). Mardi gras. Holiday(s). Merrymaking. Revelry. Field day(s). Jubilee(s). Anniversar(y, ies). Carnival(s). Reunion(s). *Consider also:* festspiel(en). *See also* Ceremonies; Drama festivals; Fiestas; Folk festivals; Holidays; Rituals; Sacred meals.

Festivals, drama. See *Drama festivals*

Festivals, folk. See *Folk festivals*

Festivals, religious. See *Festivals; Holidays.*

Festivities. See *Festivals.*

Festschriften. Festschrift(en). Commemorative volume(s). Anniversary volume(s). *Consider also:* collected works. *See also* Books; Recognition (achievement).

Fetal alcohol syndrome. Fetal alcohol syndrome. *Consider also:* alcohol(ic,ics,ism), ethanol *with:* offspring, prenatal, embryo(s,pathy), fetal, fetus, newborn(s), neonat(e,es,al), perinatal, infan(t,ts,cy), pregnan(t,cy, cies), congenital(ly). *See also* Alcoholism; Drug addicted babies; Drug induced abnormalities; Fetus; Mental retardation; Prenatal development.

Fetal death. Fetal death(s). Stillborn(s). Stillbirth(s). *Consider also:* spontaneous abortion(s), embryo resorption, fetal resorption. *Choose from:* embryo(s,nic), fetal, fetus(es), prenatal, perinatal, intrauterine, utero *with:* death(s), dying, mortalit(y,ies). *See also* Death; Fetal propitiatory rites; Fetal surgery; Fetus; Pregnancy.

Fetal death, late. See *Fetal death; Infant mortality.*

Fetal propitiatory rites. Fetal propitiatory rite(s). Mizuko kuyo. Mizuko jizo. *Choose from:* memorial service(s), ritual(s), prayer(s), statuette(s), jizo statue(s) *with:* miscarriage(s), stillbirth(s), infan(t,cy) death(s), abort(ed,in,ions). *See also* Death rituals; Emotional aspects of abortion; Fetal death; Funeral rites; Mourning.

Fetal surgery. Fetal surgery. *Choose from:* fetal, fetus(es), intrauterine, unborn, utero, prenatal *with:* surger(y,ical), neurosurg(ery,ical), thyroidectom(y,ies), encephalectom(y,ies), hypophysectom(y,ies), nephrostom(y,ies), thymectom(y,ies). *See also* Fetal death; Fetus; Surgery.

Fetishism. Fetish(ism,ist,ists,istic). Retifis(m,t,ts). *Consider also:* genitaliz(e,ed,ing,ation), partialism. *See also* Ceremonial objects; Idolatry; Magic; Reification; Supernatural; Talisman.

Fetishism, commodity. See *Commodity fetishism.*

Fetus. Fetus(es). *Consider also:* fetal, unborn, prenatal, embryo(s,nic), intrauterine, in utero. *See also* Drug addicted babies; Embryology; Fetal alcohol syndrome; Fetal death; Fetal surgery; Infants; Newborn infants; Pregnancy.

Feudal law. Feudal law(s). Feodarum Consuetudines. *Choose from:* feudal(ism), fiefdom, lord(s), vassal(s) *with:* law(s), legal. *See also* Feudalism; Homage (feudal law); Laws.

Feudalism. Feudal(ism,istic,ity). *Choose from:* lord(s), overlord(s), suzerain(ty) *with:* vassal(s,age), knight(s), serf(s), fief(s), peasant(s). Medieval societ(ies, y). Prccapitalist societ(y,ies). Serf(s,dom). Precolonial. Fief(s,dom). Shogun(ate) [shoen]. *Consider also:* slave(s,ry), indentured, enslave(d,ment), hacienda(s), plantation(s), squire(s), subinfeudat(e,ed,ing,ion), tenant farm(er,ers,ing), sharecropp(ers,er,ing), latifund(ia,ismo), junker(s), pronoia(rios), votchin(a,nik), hereditary overlord(s), seigneurial rule, seignioral right(s), manorial right(s). *See also* Agrarian societies; Aristocracy; Crusades; Feudal law; Homage (feudal law); Medieval education; Medieval military history; Medieval technology; Medieval theology; Middle ages; Manors; Peasants; Sharecropping.

Feuds. Feud(ing,s). Hostilities. Enmit(y,ies). Vendetta(s). Blood feud(s). Animosit(y, ies). Quarrel(s). *Consider also:* foe(s), enem(y,ies). *See also* Arguments; Homicide; Literary quarrels; Reprisals; Revenge; Shrunken heads; War.

Feuds, literary. See *Literary quarrels.*

Fever. Fever(s,ish). Hypertherm(ia,ic). Pyrex(ia,ic). Pyretic. Hyperpyrex(ia,ic). Frile. *Choose from:* high, elevated *with:* bod(y,ily) *with:* temperature(s). *Consider also:* inflammat(ory,ion). *See also* Symptoms.

Fever, hay. See *Hay fever.*

Fiats. See *Edicts; Mandate.*

Fibers. Fiber(s). Fibr(e,es,ous). Filament(s). Thread(s). Spider silk. Tendril(s). Fibril(s). Root hair(s). Gossamer. *See also* Crafts; Fabrics; Fancy work; Sewing.

Fiction. Fiction(al). Novel(ette,ettes,s). Tale(s). Stor(y,ies). Romance(s). Fable(s). Myth(s,ical). Short stor(y,ies). Legend(s). Fairy tale(s). Allegor(y,ies). Parable(s). Saga(s). Photonovel(s). Penny-dreadful(s). *Consider also:* creative writing, fictitious(ly), imaginary, make-believe, spurious(ness), airport fiction. *See also* Adventure stories; Antiheroes; Bildungsroman; Gothic romances; Heroes; Historical fiction; Legends; Literature; Love stories; Nature literature; Nonfiction novel; Novels; Political fiction; Popular culture; Protagonist; Western fiction.

Fiction, historical. See *Historical fiction*

Fiction, political. See *Political fiction.*

Fiction, western. See *Western fiction.*

Fiduciary responsibility. Fiduciary responsibilit(y,ies). Fiduciary dut(y,ies). Fiduciary obligation(s). Fiduciary trust(s). *Choose from:* fiduciary, ERISA, Employee Retirement Income Security Act , employee benefit plan(s) *with:* manager(s), executor(s), fiduciar(y,ies), administrat(or,ors,ion), trustee(s), *with:* responsibilit(y,ies), dut(y,ies), obligation(s). *Consider also:* money manager(s), fund manager(s), pension manager(s), hold(ing) in trust, held in trust. *See also* Accountability; Corporate social responsibility; Duties; Ethics; Pensions; Responsibility (answerability); Obligations.

Field, track and. See *Track and field.*

Field dependence. Field dependen(t,ce,cy). *Consider also:* figure ground perception, field independen(t,ce,cy), disembedding performance, field theory, gestalt. *See also* Cognitive style; Personality traits.

Field experience programs. Field experience program(s). Field experience(s). Field exposure. Fieldwork. Field work. Supervised farm practice. *Choose from:*

field *with:* experience(s), instruction, work, course(s), investigation(s), stud(y,ies), training, trip(s), placement. *Consider also:* internships, practicums. *See also* Educational field trips; Field work.

Field independence. See *Field dependence.*

Field trips, educational. See *Educational field trips.*

Fieldwork. Fieldwork. *Choose from:* field *with:* work, research, experience, investigation(s), stud(y,ies), experiment(s). *Consider also:* participant observ(ation,er,ers), ethnograph(y, ic). *See also* Excavations (Archaeology); Field experience programs; Practical experience.

Fiestas. Fiesta(s). Holy day(s). Feast day(s). Festivit(y,ies). Holiday(s). Saints day(s). Mardi gras. Festival(s). Celebration(s). Ceremon(y,ies). Holiday(s). Merrymaking. Revelry. Field day(s). Jubilee(s). Anniversar(y,ies). Carnival(s). Reunion(s). *See also* Festivals; Folk festivals; Holidays; Rituals.

Fifth world. See *Labor market segmentation; Sex discrimination; Sexual division of labor; Sexual inequality.*

Fighting. See *Assault (personal); Disagreements; Duels; Fights.*

Fights. Fight(s,ing). Assault(ed,ing,s). Attack(ed,ing,s). Battle(s). Besiege(d,ment). Bout(s). Boxing. Brawl(ing,s). Combat. Conflict(s). Duel(s). Feud(s,ing). Hostilities. Offensive. Siege(s). Skirmish(es). Struggle(s). War(fare). Wrestl(e,ed,ing). *See also* Assault (personal); Disagreements; Duels; Violence.

Figural aftereffect. Figural aftereffect(s). *Choose from:* figural, perceptual, color, motion, form, kinesthetic *with:* aftereffect(s). *Consider also:* after-effect test, McCollough Effect, afterimage(s). *See also* Perceptual distortion.

Figurative art. Figurative art(ist,ists). Representational art(ist,ists). Realist(ic) art(ist,ists). Figurative paint(er,ers, ing,ings). *Consider also:* life drawing, figurative sculpture, naturalistic art, realism. *See also* Artistic styles; Arts; Genres (art); Magic realism (art); Realism in art; Socialist realism in art.

Figurative language. Figurative language. Figure(s) of speech. Metaphor(s). Simile(s). Trope(s). Allegor(ical,ies,y). Idiom(s,atic). Verbal imagery. Pun(s,ning,ned). *Choose from:* figurative, nonliteral, allegorical, imagistic, metaphoric *with:* sense(s), language(s), speech. *See also* Adages; Allegory; Allusions; Description; Ekphrasis; Gothicism; Idioms; Language; Metaphors; Personification; Satire; Sex symbolism; Symbolism.

Figure ground discrimination. Figure ground discrimination. Pattern discrimination. Visual contrast. Display contrast. Detection with background. Contrast sensitivity. Figure vs ground. Disembed(ded,ding). *Consider also:* visual noise, background noise, density. *See also* Pattern recognition; Perceptual discrimination.

Figure-ground perception. *See Figure ground discrimination.*

Figure, human. See *Human figure*

Figures (mannequins). *See Mannequins (figures).*

Figures, public. See *Public figures.*

Figures of speech. See *Figurative language.*

Figurines. Figurine(s). Statuette(s). *Consider also:* doll(s), china figure(s). *See also* Ancient art; Antiquities (objects); Images; Religious articles.

Files and filing. File(s). Filing. *Consider also:* information storage, organiz(ed,ing), paperwork, office management, alphabetiz(e,ed,ing,ation). *Consider also:* fil(e,es,ing), collection(s), material(s) *with:* organiz(e,ed,ing,ation). *See also* Records management.

Filial piety. Filial piety. Fourth commandment. *Choose from:* aged, elder(s,ly), older, parent(s), mother(s), father(s), grandmother(s), grandfather(s), grandparent(s), ancestor(s) *with:* respect, rever(e,ed,ence), honor(ed,ing), piety, dutiful. *See also* Adult offspring; Filial responsibility; Intergenerational relations; Parent child relations; Piety.

Filial responsibility. Filial responsibilit(y,ies). Intergenerational support. Filial support. *Choose from:* aged, elder(ly), older, aging *with:* adult child(ren), adult daughter(s), adult son(s), filial, caregiv(er,ers,ing), relative(s). *See also* Adult offspring; Caregiver burden; Family assistance; Filial piety; Intergenerational relations.

Filing and files. See *Files and filing.*

Filing systems. See *Files and filing; Records management.*

Film adaptations. Film adaptation(s). Filmed book(s). Adapted to screen. *Choose from:* adapt(ed,ing,ation, ations,ability), based, tie-in, version *with:* book(s), novel(s,la,las) *with:* cinema(s), film(s), movie(s). *See also* Films; Mass media; Religious films.

Film genres. Film genre(s). Motion picture genre(s). Film categor(y,ies). *Choose from:* midcult, science fiction, martial arts, horror, gangster, comedy, melodrama, action, special effect, disaster, gross out, chiller, shocker, patriotic, war, flag waver *with:* film(s), cinema, movie(s), motion picture(s), pic(s).

Consider also: message movie(s), A Western(s), B Western(s), non-fiction film(s), film noir, B movie(s), biopic(s), oater(s), horse opera(s), spaghetti western(s), docudrama(s), shockumentar(y,ies), gorefest(s), slasher flick(s), actioner(s), bodice ripper(s). *See also* Films; Form (aesthetics); Genres; Horror films; Motion picture fans; Motion pictures; Types.

Film music. Film music. *Choose from:* film(s), movie(s), cinema(s,atic), screenplay(s), motion picture(s), cinematograph(y,ic,ically), talking picture(s), silent picture(s) *with:* accompan(iment,ied), music(al,als, ally,ian,ians), score(s), underscore(s), tune(s), theme song(s). *Consider also:* movie musical(s). *See also* Background music; Films; Motion pictures; Music.

Film strips. Film strip(s). Filmstrip(s). Film clip(s). Film loop(s). *Consider also:* film(s), short film(s). *See also* Audiovisual communications; Audiovisual materials.

Films. Film(s). Movie(s). Cinema(s). Screenplay(s). Motion picture(s). Cinematograph(y,ic,ically). Talking picture(s). Silent picture(s). Hollywood. Travelogue(s). Documentar(y,ies). Picture show(s). Cine. *See also* Audiovisual communications; Documentary theater; Erotica; Film adaptations; Film genres; Film music; Lost motion pictures; Religious films.

Films, documentary. See *Documentary theater.*

Films, erotic. See *Erotica.*

Films, horror. See *Horror films.*

Films, religious. See *Religious films.*

Filtered noise. Filter(ed,ing) noise(s). *Choose from:* reject(ed,ing), speech discrimination, detect(ed,ing,ion) tone(s), selective frequenc(y,ies) *with:* noise(s). *Consider also:* filter(ed,ing) *with:* audiovisual, bandwidth(s). *See also* Noise (sounds); Perceptual stimulation.

Finale. Finale. Clos(e,ed,ing). Conclusion(s). Swan song(s). Terminat(e,ed,ing,ion). *See also* Adjournment; Closure; End; Last words.

Finance. Financ(e,es,ial,ially). *Consider also:* bank(s,ing), budget(s,ary,ing), investment(s), fiscal, pecuniary, economic(s), money, monetary, capital, revenue(s), fund(s), cash, currency, dollar(s), Euromoney, purse strings, credit, debt(s), expenditure(s), pay(ed, ment,ments), savings, asset(s), stock(s), holdings, cost(s), loan(s), tax(es,ed, ation), wealth. *See also* Assets; Bankruptcy; Budgets; Costs; Credit; Debts; Economic assistance; Economics; Entrepreneurship; Expenditures;

Financial support; Loans; Prices; Savings; Taxes; Trade; Wealth.

Finance, local. See *Local finance.*

Finance, municipal. See *Municipal finance.*

Finance, public. See *Public finance.*

Finance reform, campaign. See *Campaign finance reform.*

Financed, publicly. See *Government financing.*

Finances, family. See *Family budgets; Family socioeconomic status; Income.*

Finances, government. See *Government finances.*

Finances, state. See *Government finances.*

Financial aid, student. See *Student financial aid.*

Financial assistance. See *Financial support.*

Financial audit. Financial audit(s). *Choose from:* financ(e,es,ial), tax(es), account(s,ing), IRS, Internal revenue *with:* audit(ed,ing,s), evaluat(e,ed,ing, ion,ions), examin(e,ed,ing,ation,ations), review(s,ed,ing), inspect(ed,ing, ion,ions). *See also* Accountants; Accounting; Accounting standards; Accuracy; Fact checking; Financial management; Financial statements; Verification.

Financial capital. See *Capital (financial).*

Financial data. Financial data. *Choose from:* financial, banking, cash flow(s), income, expense(s), economic, fiscal, monetary, asset(s), liabilit(y,ies), debit(s), credit(s) *with:* data, book(s), sheet(s), report(s), datafile(s), figure(s), information, statistic(s,al). *Consider also:* balance sheet(s), account book(s), cashbook(s). *See also* Economic statistics; Financial statements; Statistical data.

Financial disclosure. Financial disclosure. *Choose from:* financ(e,es,ial), campaign finance, campaign fund(s), financial interest(s), donation(s), contribution(s), gift(s), honoraria, income, transaction(s), account(s,ing), asset(s), investment(s), holdings *with:* report(ed,ing,s), disclos(e,ed,ing,ure), determin(e,ed, ing,ation), investigat(e,ed,ing,ion). *See also* Advocacy advertising; Campaign finance reform; Codes of ethics; Conflict of interest; Corruption in government; Judicial corruption; Misconduct in office; Political ethics; Unethical conduct; White collar crime.

Financial equity. See *Equity (financial).*

Financial growth. See *Earnings; Gains; Income; Profits.*

Financial institutions. See *Banking.*

Financial management. Financial management. Budget(s,ed,ing). *Choose from:* fiscal, financial, income, money, cash, financ(e,es,ial), capital, expenditure(s), fund(s), account(s), dollar(s), asset(s), disbursement(s) *with:* plan(s,ned,ning), statement(s), manag(e,ed,ing,ement), control(led, ling), accountab(le,ility). *See also* Accountability; Accounting standards; Asset management; Budget cuts; Budget deficits; Budgets; Credit; Disbursement; Finance; Financial planning; Financial statements; Fiscal policy; Investments; Savings.

Financial planning. Financial plan(s,ning). *Choose from:* financial, finance(s), invest(ing,ment,ments), money, wealth, income, saving(s) *with:* plan(s,ning), manag(e,ed,ing,ement), decision(s), forecast(s,ed,ing). *See also* Budgets; Financial management; Investments; Personal financing; Planning; Retirement income; Retirement planning; Savings.

Financial problems. See *Economic problems; Poverty.*

Financial reports. See *Financial statements.*

Financial statements. Financial statement(s). Balance sheet(s). Bank statement(s). Company report(s). Annual report(s). Auditor's report(s). Financial rating(s). Reported corporate earnings. Reported return on asset(s). Financial report(s,ing). Statement(s) of cash flow. Income statement(s). 10-K report(s). 10-Q report(s). *Consider also:* net worth, balance sheet(s), account book(s), cashbook(s), ledger(s), running account(s), prospectus(es). *See also* Accountability; Accounting; Accounting standards; Annual reports; Billing systems; Financial audit; Financial data; Financial management.

Financial support. Financial(ly) support(ed). Assistantship(s). Bailout(s). Bail-out(s). Endowment(s). Fee(s). Federal aid. Entitlement(s). Financed. Fund(ed). Grant(s). Loan(s). Rais(ed, ing) funds. Scholarship(s). State aid. Sources of funds. Stipend(s). Subsid(y, ies,ization). Trusts. Alimony. *Choose from:* financial, economic *with:* aid, assistance, award(s), contribution(s), support. *See also* Alimony; Antipoverty programs; Bailouts; Charities; Child support; Contributions; Economic assistance; Fellowships (educational); Financing; Fiscal federalism; Food relief; Food services (programs); Foreign aid; Giving; Government financing; Grants; Income maintenance programs; Organized financing; Public welfare; Subsidies; Unemployment relief; Workfare.

Financiers, capitalists. See *Capitalists and financiers.*

Financing. Financ(e,ed,ing). Fund(ed,ing). Capitaliz(e,ed,ing). Endow(ed,ing,ment). Subsidiz(e,ed,ing). Underwrit(e,ing,ten). *Choose from:* financial, money, monetar(y,ily), funds, capital, leverage *with:* back(ed,ing), borrow(ed,ing), furnish(ed,ing), offer(ed,ing), provid(e, ed,ing), rais(e,ed,ing), suppl(y,ied,ying). *See also* Financial support; Government financing; Organized financing; Personal financing.

Financing, government. See *Government financing.*

Financing, organized. See *Organized financing.*

Financing, personal. See *Personal financing.*

Financing construction. Financing construction. *Choose from:* financ(e,ed,ing), bond issue(s), fund(ed,ing), capital outlay, loan(s), borrow(ed,ing) *with:* construction, building(s), public work(s), new facilit(y,ies), new school(s), new dormitor(y,ies), new librar(y,ies). *See also* Facility design and construction; Financial support.

Findings (discoveries). See *Discoveries (findings).*

Fine arts. See *Arts.*

Fine motor skills. Fine motor skill(s). *Choose from:* fine motor, sensorimotor, complex motor, perceptual motor, drawing *with:* skill(s), abilit(y,ies), control, behavior(s), performance, development. *See also* Perceptual motor learning.

Fines (penalties). Fine(s). Penalt(y,ies). Damage(s). Mulct(s). Amerce(ment, ments). *Consider also:* sanction(s), restitution, punitive damage award(s), lev(y,ies), pecuniary punishment(s), mulct(s), forfeit(s,ure). *See also* Fees; Penalties.

Finger tapping. Finger tapping. Fingertapping. *Choose from:* tap(ping,ped), drum(med,ming) *with:* finger(s), hand(s,ed), key(s). *See also* Motor coordination.

Fingerprints. See *Dermatoglyphics.*

Fingers (anatomy). Finger(s). Thumb(s). Digit(s). Fingertip(s). *Consider also:* fingerprint(s), hand extremities, phalanx, phalanges. *See also* Anatomy.

Fingerspelling. Fingerspell(ed,ing). Finger spell(ed,ing). Dactylology. *Consider also:* spel(led,ling), alphabet(s,ic) *with:* finger(s), manual(ly). *Consider also:* sign language. *See also* Manual communication; Sign language.

Fingersucking. Fingersucking. Thumbsucking. *Choose from:* suck(ed,ing) *with:* finger(s), thumb(s). *See also* Child behavior disorders.

Finite. Finite(ness). Finitude. Circumscrib(e,ed,ing). Bounded. Limit(s,ed,ing). Confined. Restrict(ed,ing). Terminable(ness). Demarcat(e,ed,ing,ion). Measurab(le,ility). Delimited. *See also* Boundaries; Closure; Constraints; Demarcation; End; Nonrenewable resources.

Finno-Ugric languages. Finno-Ugric language(s). Finnic: Cheremiss, Estonian, Finnish (Suomi), Karelian, Lapp, Livonian, Loparian, Mordvinian, Vepse, Vote. Permian: Komi Permian, Komi Zyrian, Votyak. Ugric: Hungarian (Magyar), Obi, Ugrian, Ostyak (Khanty), Vogul (Mansi). *See also* Eastern Europe; Language; Languages (as subjects); Western Europe.

Fire. Fire(s). Arson. Combustion. Ignit(e,ed,ing,ion). Spark(s). Flame(s). Blaz(e,ing). Campfire(s). Bonfire(s). Forest fire(s). Wildfire(s). Pyre(s). Conflagration. Burn(ed,ing). Ablaze. Ember(s). *Consider also:* flammable. *See also* Arson; Combustibility; Fire prevention; Fire setting behavior; Forest fires; Safety.

Fire departments. Fire department(s). Fire dept. Fire compan(y,ies). Volunteer fire department(s). *Consider also:* firefighting equipment, fire truck(s), fire alarm(s), department of emergency service(s). *See also* Community services; Fire prevention; Local government; Municipal government; Volunteers.

Fire ecology. Fire ecology. *Choose from:* fire(s), burned woods, wildfire, post-fire, controlled burning with: ecolog(y,ical), ecosystem(s), managing land(s), regreening, seedling(s), vegetation, grassland(s), plant(s), food web(s), food chain(s), parkland(s), biomass, forest(s), wildlife, forest maintenance, forest management, pine(s). *Consider also:* fire regime(s), forest fire(s). *See also* Deforestation; Ecology; Forest fires; Grassland fires; Rainforests.

Fire prevention. Fire prevention. *Choose from:* fire(s), arson, flame(s), smoke *with:* protect(ed,ing,ion), prevent(ed,ing,ion), retardant(s), control(led,ling), resist(ed,ing,ant), safe(ty), reduc(ed,ing) risk(s), detector(s). *Consider also:* nonflammable, non-inflammable, heat sensor(s), fire fighter(s), firemen. *See also* Crime prevention; Fire; Fire departments; Safety; Security measures.

Fire setting behavior. Fire setting behavior. Arson(ist,ists). Firesett(ing,er,ers). Pyroman(ia,ic,iac,iacs). Pyrolagn(ia, iac,iacs). Pyrophil(ia,iac,iacs). *Choose*

from: fire(s), aflame, ablaze, afire *with:* set(ting), start(ed,ing), rais(e,ed,ing). Firebomb(ing,ings,ed). Torch(ed,ing). Malicious burning(s). Incendiar(ism,ists, ist,ies). *See also* Antisocial behavior; Behavior disorders; Incendiary weapons.

Firearms. See *Weaponry.*

Firearms industry. Firearms industry. Weapons industry. Gun shop(s). *Choose from:* arms, gun(s), weapon(s,ry), revolver(s), handgun(s), rifle(s), assault weapon(s), pistol(s) *with:* maker(s), manufactur(e,ed,er,ing), industr(y,ies, ial), distributor(s), store(s), dealer(s), shop(s), black market(s), seller(s). *Consider also:* gun market(s), Colt Manufacturing, Remington Arms Co., Navegar Inc. *See also* Arms market; Defense spending; Gun control; Military industrial complex; Weaponry.

Fires, forest. See *Forest fires.*

Fires, grassland. See *Grassland fires.*

Firewalls (computers). Firewall(s). *Consider also:* internal network security, protected network(s), private network(s), packet filter(s,ing), proxy server(s), stateful inspection(s). *See also* Computer security; Cryptography; Extranets; Information exchange.

Firing (personnel). Firing(s). Fire(d). Personnel terminat(ed,ion,ions). Outplacement. Lay-off. Laying off. Layoff(s). Laid off. *Choose from:* dismiss(ed,al), terminat(e,ed,ion,ions), dismiss(ed,al,als), fired, firing(s), layoff(s), laid off, discharge(d), terminat(e,ed,ion,ions), retrench(ed,ing,ment,ments) *with:* job(s), employee(s), staff, personnel, worker(s). *Choose from:* reduc(e,ed,tion,tions), trim, cut(back) *with:* staff, force, workforce, position(s), laborforce. *See also* Dismissal of staff; Involuntary retirement; Mandatory retirement; Personnel termination; Plant closings; Unemployment.

Firm offers. Firm offer(s). *Choose from:* firm, binding, enforceable, established, irreversible, irrevocable, secure, serious, set, unchangeable, written *with:* offer(s), bid(s). *See also* Bargaining; Collective bargaining; Deals; Negotiation.

Firms. See *Corporations; Industrial enterprises.*

Firms, executive search. See *Executive search firms.*

First birth timing. First birth timing. Tim(e,ing) of first birth. Age at first birth. Birth timing. Late parenthood. Delayed childbearing. Delayed parenthood. Early childbearing. Early parenthood. *Choose from:* early, late, tim(e,ing), delayed, young(er), old(er), postpone(d,ment), age of mother *with:* first birth, first child, primigravida,

gravida I, childbearing, parenthood. *See also* Family planning.

First class. See *Excellence.*

First person narrative. First person narrat(ive,ives,or,ors,ion). Monologue(s). Monodrama(s). One-man show(s). One-woman show(s). Soliloqu(y,ies). Personal narrative(s). *Consider also:* narrator(s), speak(ing) for themselves, personal writing, writ(e,ten) in the first-person, autobiograph(y,ical), first-person voice(s), self-portrait(s), personal element(s). *See also* Autobiography; Diaries; Life history; Narratives; Point of view (literature); Self report.

First World. See *Developed countries.*

Fiscal federalism. Fiscal federalism. *Choose from:* direct federalism, categorical aid, categorical funding, categorical grant(s), block grant(s), grants-in-aid, revenue sharing, formula grants, application grants, project grants. *Consider also:* State and Local Fiscal Assistance Act. Fiscal policy. *See also* Federalism; Financial support; Government financing.

Fiscal policy. Fiscal polic(y,ies). Federal budget(s). Reagonomics. Keynesian(ism). Thatcherism. Supply side economics. Trickle down theor(y,ies). Free market economics. Monetarism. Deficit spending. Deficit economics. Balanced budget(s). Tax polic(y,ies). Budgetary polic(y,ies). Economic polic(y,ies). *Consider also:* monetary polic(y,ies), withholding tax(es), excise tax(es), corporate tax(es), depletion allowance(s), amortization rule(s), government subsid(y,ies,ization), economic stabilization, price stability, military expenditures, government spending, exchange rate polic(y,ies). *See also* Budget deficits; Balanced budget; Cost control; Cost recovery; Expenditures; Fiscal federalism; Government financing; Monetary policy; Public debt.

Fish as food. Fish as food. Edible fish(es). *Choose from:* edible, food, eat(ing,en), diet(s,ary), consum(e,ed,ing) *with:* seafood, fish(es,y), sashimi, carp(s), salmon, scrod, trout, etc. *See also* Diet; Fishes; Food; Mariculture; Seafood.

Fish culture. See *Fisheries; Mariculture.*

Fisheries. Fisher(y,ies). Fish canner(y,ies). Fish industry. Fish hatcher(y,ies). Fish processing plant(s). Fish farm(s,ing). Fishing banks. Fishing place(s). Weir(s). *See also* Clams; Fishing; Fishery workers; Food supply; Mariculture; Marine resources; Natural resources; Territorial waters

Fishermen. Fisher(men,man,s). Fishing crew(s). Fisherfolk. Shrimper(s). Angler(s). Whaler(s). Piscator(y).

Trawler(s). *See also* Blue collar workers; Fishermen; Fishing.

Fishery workers. Fishery worker(s). *Choose from:* fisher(y,ies), fish canner(y,ies), fish industry, fish hatcher(y,ies), fish processing plant(s), fish farm(s,ing) *with:* worker(s), personnel, staff, operator(s), employee(s). *See also* Blue collar workers; Fishermen; Fisheries; Fishing.

Fishes. Fish(es). Ichthyology. Pisces. *Consider also:* Abramis, Agnatha, Angelfish, Albacore, Anchovy, Anguilla, Bass, Brcam, Carassius, Carp, Catfish, Chinook, Cichlidae, Coho, Cyprinus, Cyprinidae, Cyclostomes, Chondrichthyes, Dogfish, Elasmobranch, Electrophorous, Eel, Esox, Flounder, Fundulus, Gadus, Gasterosteus, Goldfish, Guppy, Haddock, Halibut, Hagfish, Herring, Killifish, Lamprey, Listes, Lepomia, Loach, Mackeral, Medaka, Menhaden, Minnow, Mullet, Oncorhynchus, Oryzias, Osteichthyes, Perch, Pike, Plaice, Ray, Roach, Salmo, Salmon(idae), Salvelinus, Sardine, Shad, Shark, Skipjack, Smelt, Snapper, Sockeye, Sole, Squalus, Steelhead, Sticklack, Sturgeon, Swordfish, Teleost, Tilapia, Trout, Tuna, Whitefish, Zader. *See also* Animals; Fish as food; Marine ecology; Marine mammals; Marine resources; Seafood.

Fishing. Fish(ery,eries,ing). Catch(ing) fish. Fish catching. Fish(ing) industr(y,ies). Angling. Sportfishing. Trawling. Seining. Netting. Trolling. Piscator(y, ial). *Consider also:* fish farming. *See also* Fisheries; Fishery workers; Mariculture; Primitive fishing; Oceans; Sports; Tides.

Fishing, prehistoric. See *Primitive fishing.*

Fishing, primitive. See *Primitive fishing.*

Fishing communities. Fishing communit(y,ies). Fishing village(s). Fisherfolk. *See also* Community (geographic locality).

Fitness, physical. See *Physical fitness.*

Fixed costs. *See Indirect costs.*

Fixed interval reinforcement. Fixed interval reinforcement. *Choose from:* fixed interval(s), FI, fixed time(s), schedule(s,d) *with:* reinforc(e,ed,ing, ement,ements), food, feeding. *See also* Reinforcement schedule.

Fixes, formes. See *Formes fixes.*

Fixing, price. See *Price fixing.*

Fixtures. *See Equipment.*

Flagellants and flagellation. Flagellant(s) and flagellat(e,ed,ing,ion). Flog(s,ged,ging). Cane(r,rs,d). Caning. Whip(s,ped,ping). Lash(es,ed,ing). Horsewhip(s,ped,ping). Beat(en,ing,

ings). *See also* Corporal punishment; Masochism; Sadism; Sexual deviations; Sexual masochism; Sexual sadism; Punishment; Torture; Violence.

Flagellation, flagellants and. See *Flagellants and flagellation.*

Flags. Flag(s). Banner(s). Pennant(s). Union Jack. Stars and stripes. Old Glory. Ensign(s). Star spangled banner. *See also* Insignia; Loyalty oaths; National emblems; Nationalism; Patriotism; Political symbolism.

Flashbacks. See *Hallucinations.*

Flattery. Flatter(y,ed,ing). Adulat(e,ed,ing, ion). Exalt(ed,ing,ation). Extol(led,ling). Prais(e,es,ed,ing), Salut(e,ed,ing,ation). Glorif(y,ied,ication). Laud(ed,ing,ation). *Consider also:* eulogiz(e,ed,ing,ation), eulog(y,ies), puffery, overprais(e,ed,ing). *See also* Admiration; Commendation; Eulogies; Honored (esteem); Machiavellianism; Manipulation; Positive reinforcement; Praise; Tribute.

Flawless. Flawless(ness). Unflawed. Defectless(ness). Faultless(ness). Immaculate. Impeccab(le,ility). Spotless(ness). Stainless(ness). Taintless(ness). Unblemished. Unmarred. Unimpaired. Undamaged. Unsullied. Untarnished. Virgin. Chaste. Clean(liness). Unbroken. Complete. Whole. Intact. *See also* Accuracy; Correctness; Imperfection; Infallibility; Quality control; Validity.

Flaws. See *Imperfection.*

Flexibility. See *Adaptability.*

Flexible retirement. Flexible retirement. Semi-retire(d,ment). *Choose from:* phased, partial, transition(al), gradual(ly), part-time, deferred, restructur(ed,ing) *with:* retirement, withdraw(al) from workforce. *Consider also:* part-time work(ers), part-time job(s) *with:* retiree(s), pensioner(s), annuitant(s), postretirement, over 65, over sixty five, senior citizen(s), elderly, older worker(s). *See also* Flexible workplace practices; Part time employment; Retirement; Retirement income.

Flexible work schedules. See *Alternative work patterns; Personnel scheduling; Work load; Work schedules; Workday shifts; Worktime.*

Flexible workplace practices. Flexible workplace practice(s). *Choose from:* flexible, flex(ibility,ing), innovative *with:* workplace(s), office(s), job(s), work environment(s) *with:* practice(s), polic(y,ies), program(s), option(s), model(s), *Consider also:* telecommuting, casual dress(ing) polic(y,ies), non-monetary benefit(s), job shar(e,es,ing), flextime, flexiplace, compressed workweek(s), innovative pay system(s), flexible work organiza-

tion. *See also* Alternative work patterns; Flexible retirement; Job sharing; Moonlighting; Part time employment.

Flies. Fly. Flies. Housefl(y,ies). Fruit fl(y,ies). Drosophila melanogaster. Musca domestica. *Choose from:* fruit, sand, black, house *with:* fl(y,ies). *Consider also:* diptera(n), gnat(s), midge(s), maggot(s), mosquito(es). *See also* Agricultural workers disease; Animals; Insect bites and stings; Insects.

Flight, animal. See *Animal flight.*

Flight, space. See *Space exploration.*

Flight attendants. See *Aerospace personnel.*

Flight instrumentation. Flight instrument(s,ation). *Choose from:* flight, aircraft, cockpit, pilot(s), plane(s), airplane(s), jetliner(s), landing(s), takeoff *with:* instrument(s,ation), simulator(s), display(s), cathode ray tube(s), CRTs, radar system(s). *Consider also:* visual approach slope indicator(s). *See also* Aviation safety; Flight simulation.

Flight schools. Flight school(s). Air pilot school(s). Airline pilot school(s). Flight training. Pilot training. Aviation education. *See also* Educational facilities; Flight simulation.

Flight simulation. Flight simulat(ion,ions, or,ors). Simulated flight(s). *Choose from:* simulat(e,ed,ing,ion,ions,ors) *with:* flight(s), landing(s), pilot(s), helicopter(s), training, runway(s), aircraft. *See also* Acceleration effects; Flight schools; Gravitational effects.

Flood control. Flood control. *Choose from:* flood(s,ed,ing), floodplain(s), swollen river(s), rising water, high tide(s), overflow(ing) river(s) *with:* control(led, ling,s), dam(s,med,ming), levee(s), canal(s), drain(ed,ing,age), divert(ed, ing), diversion(s), prevent(ed,ing,ion), manag(e,ement,ing), mitigat(e,ed,ing, ion), regulat(e,ed,ing,ion), watch(es). *See also* Canals; Channels (hydraulic engineering); Dams; Dikes (engineering); Disaster planning; Disaster relief; Drainage; Irrigation; Natural disasters; Water resources development.

Flooding. See *Implosive therapy.*

Floods. Flood(s,ed,ing). Deluge(d). Inundat(ed,ion). Downpour. Overflow(ing). Tidal wave(s). Tsunami(s). Submerge(d). Torrent(s). Torrential rain(s). Swollen river(s). Water soaked. Rising water. High tide(s). Cloudburst(s). Highwater. Underwater. Rivers overflowing. *Choose from:* rising, crest(ed,ing), swollen, overflow(ing) *with:* river(s), stream(s), tide(s), bay(s). *Consider also specific floods by date and location, for example:* Miami river in 1913; Mississippi river in 1927; Connecticut river in 1935-36; Red river in 1950; Johnstown, Pa. flood of 1889; Galveston, Texas flood of 1900. *See also* Dikes (engineering); Flood control; Natural disasters; Rivers; Streams; Tides; Water levels.

Floods, prevention of. See *Flood control*.

Floriculture. See *Flowers*.

Flow, cash. See *Cash flow*.

Flowers. Flower(s,ing). Flor(a,al,et,ets). Floricultur(e,al,ist,ists). Blossom(s). Bloom(s). Bouquet(s). Bud(s). Angiosperm(s,ophyta). Monocotyledon(s,ae). Dicotyledon(s,ae). *Consider also:* ornamental plant(s), florist(s), petal(s), camellia(s), azalea(s), gardenia(s), rose(s), violet(s), tulip(s), pans(y,ies), chrysanthemum(s), impatiens, geranium(s), dahlia(s), dais(y,ies), sunflower(s), etc. *See also* Formal gardens; Fruit; Gardening to attract wildlife; Gardens; Natural gardens; Plants (botanical); Sanctuary gardens.

Fluctuations. Fluctuat(e,ed,ing,ion,ions). Flux. Vacillat(e,ed,ing,ion,ions). Waver(ed,ing). Unstable(ness). Instability. Unstead(y,iness). Hesitat(e,ed,ing, ion). Indecis(ion,ive,iveness). Irresolut(e,ion). Capricious(ness). Uncertain(ty). Changeable(ness). Vary(ing). Variation(s). Swing(ing). Variab(le,ility). *Consider also:* oscillat(e,ed,ing,ion,ions), shift(ed,ing). *See also* Hesitation; Seasonal variations; Stability; Transience; Variations.

Fluctuations, economic. See *Business cycles*.

Fluency. Fluen(cy,t). *Choose from:* language, communicative, linguistic, verbal *with:* proficien(t,cy), performance, abilit(y,ies), skill(s). *Consider also:* articulate, eloquen(t,ce), expressive(ness), word knowledge. *See also* Eloquence; Language acquisition; Language proficiency; Second language education.

Fluids. Fluid(s,ity). Liquid(s,ity). Geofluid(s). Aqueous(ness). Water(s,y). Gas(es). *Consider also:* hydraulic(s), hydrodynamic(s), hydroelectric, hydrograph(y,ic), hydrolog(y,ical), hydrogeolog(y,ical), soak(ed,ing). *See also* Beverages; Drinking water; Drinking (water, fluids); Gas.

Fluids, body. See *Body fluids*.

Fluids, condensation. See *Condensation (fluids)*.

Flute. Flute(s). Flote(s). Flaut(o,i). Flauta(s). Flageolet(s). Fife(s). Pan pipe(s). Alto recorder(s). Bass recorder(s). Piccolo(s). Shakuhachi(s). *Consider also:* alto flute(s), C flute(s), bass flute(s), transverse flute(s), ottavino(s), pickelflote(n), whistle(s). *See also* Musical instruments.

Flux. See *Fluctuations*.

Flying machines. Flying machine(s). Flying robot(s). Aircraft(s). Flight vehicle(s). Airplane(s). Aeroplane(s). *Consider also:* glider(s). *See also* Aircraft; Aeronautical museums.

Focus groups. Focus(ed) group(s). Group interview(s). Focused interview(s). Focused evaluation(s). *See also* Advertising research; Consumer participation; Market research; Research methods.

Folie a deux. See *Psychosis of association*.

Folk art. Folk art(s,ist,ists,isan,isans). Folk painting(s). Popular art. *Choose from:* folk, peasant, traditional, Native American, Indian, African American, Norwegian, Mexican, etc. *with:* art(s,ist,ists,isan,isans), decoration(s), object(s), woodcarving(s), embroider(y,ies), lace(s), basket(s,ware), earthenware(s). *See also* Arts; Collectibles; Crafts; Expressionism (art); Genres (art); Primitive art.

Folk culture. Folk culture(s). Folk custom(s). Folkways. Folklore. Oral tradition(s). Shamanism. *Choose from:* folk, traditional, native, non-literate, indigenous, gemeinschaft, village *with:* way of life, mores, norm(s), experience(s), belief(s), world view(s), religion(s), weltanschauung, value(s), art(s,istic), music(al), moral(s), law(s), ritual(s), sociohistory, tradition(s), ceremon(y,ies,ial), cannibalism, superstition(s), magic(al), taboo(s), craft(s), custom(s), dance(s), drama, literature, myth(s), poe(m,ms,try), tale(s). *See also* Bluegrass music; Border ballads; Ceremonial exchanges; Ceremonial objects; Country and western music; Crafts; Cultural values; Customs; Effigies; Ethnography; Ethnomusicology; Folk dancing; Folk drama; Folk music; Folkways; Ghost stories; Haunted houses; Mescal (cactus); Music; Mythology; Plant folklore; Psychotropic plants; Popular culture; Shamanism; Superstitions; Traditional medicine; Traditional societies; Traditions.

Folk dancing. Folk danc(e,es,er,ers,ing). *Choose from:* folk, native, tribal, primitive, national(istic), country, ethnic *with:* danc(e,es,er,ers,ing). *Consider also:* bailecito(s), baile de palos, ballo(s), ballo de Mantova, bambuco barn danc(e,es,er,ers,ing), batuque(s), bergamasca, bharata-natyam, bomba(s), bossa-nova, cachua(s), calypso, cachucha(s), chacarera(s), chachacha(s), charanga(s), congada(s), contradanza(s), cramignon, cueca(s), cumbia(s), csardas(es), czardas(es), fandango(s), farando(le,ulo), flamenco(s), forlan(a,o), gato(s), gavotte(s), gigue, habanera, halling, highland fling(s), hoedown(s),

hornpipe(s), huapango(s), huayno(s), Irish jig(s), jenkka(s), joropo(s), jota(s), kalimatianos, kashua(s), kathak(ali), koleda(s), maclote, mambo(s), mangulina(s), marinera(s), mazurka(s), merengue(s), monferrina(s), Morris dance(r,rs), passepied, pasillo(s), pidichtos, polka(s), polska(s), polskdans, purpuri(s), quashwa(s), reel(s), reisado(s), rejdovak(s), rumba(s), sacred danc(e,es,er,ers,ing), samba(s), sardana(s), schottisch(es), sousedska(s), sousta, square danc(e,es,er,ers,ing), strathspey(s), sword danc(e,es,er,ers, ing), syrtos, tamborito(s), tarantella(s), tsamikos, tospring, valse(s) criollos, Virginia reel(s), zeibekikos, zevensprong, etc. *See also* Afro-Cuban music; Afro-American music; Contredanse; Country dance; Dance; Dance music; Folk culture; Folk drama; Folk music; Traditional societies.

Folk drama. Folk drama(s,tic,tics,tization, tizations). Folk theatre(s). *Consider also:* folk opera(s). *See also* Drama; Folk culture; Folk dancing: Japanese drama.

Folk festivals. Folk festival(s). Pageant(s). *Choose from:* folk, ethnic, primitive, Mayan, Mexican, Indonesian, etc. *with:* festival(s), carnival(s), fair(s), festivit(y,ies), feast day(s). *Consider also:* Mardi Gras. *See also* Festivals; Fiestas; Pageants.

Folk healers. See *Shamanism; Traditional medicine*.

Folk literature. Folk literature. Oral tradition(s,al). Fable(s). Fairy tale(s). Legend(s). Myth(s,ology). Parable(s). Proverb(s). Epic(s). *Choose from:* folk *with:* ballad(s), song(s), poem(s), poetry, tale(s), riddle(s), proverb(s), play(s), drama. *See also* Ballads; Black Carib literature; Epic literature; Fabliaux; Folklore; Folk culture; Folk poetry; Folk songs; Jewish literature; Mermaids; Mythology; Oral history.

Folk medicine. See *Shamanism; Traditional medicine*.

Folk music. Folk music. Traditional music. Volksmusik. *Choose from:* folk, native, tribal, primitive, national(istic), country, ethnic, oldtime, carnival, soul, oral tradition, rural, epic(s) *with:* music(al, ian,ians), fiddle(s,r,rs), singer(s), song(s), ballad(s), melod(y,ies), tune(s), harmony, string band(s), banjo(s), mandolin(s), guitar(s), accordion(s), recording(s). *Consider also:* aguinaldo(s), baile de palos, baile de tambor, baile(s) pastoris, folk rock; galeron, modinha, p'ansori, posada(s), sanjo, sprechgesang, street music, street cries, reisado(s), villancico(s), tonada(s), tonos de velorio, yodel(s). *See also* Afro-American music; Afro-Cuban music; Border ballads; Country and western music; Ethnomusicology; Folk dancing; Folk songs; Gypsy music; Melody; Music; Musical instruments; Popular music.

Folk poetry. Folk poe(try,m,ms). *Choose from:* folk, oral, indigenous *with:* poem(s), poetry, rhyme(s), tongue twister(s), riddle(s) *Consider also:* oral poetic tradition, skipping rhyme(s), counting rhyme(s), Finnish Kalevala meter poetry, street poetry. *See also* Ballads; Folk literature; Folk songs; Folklore; Jazz; War poetry.

Folk psychiatry. Scc *Shamanism; Traditional medicine.*

Folk societies. See *Traditional societies.*

Folk songs. Folk song(s) Corrido(s). Volkslied(er). Folkevise(n). *Choose from:* folk, native, tribal, primitive, national(istic), patriotic, epic, cradle, mourning, gypsy, country, ethnic, gospel, coffee-house(s), oldtime, cowboy, drinking, love, sledge, herding, sea, Kleftic *with:* song(s), singer(s), songwriter(s), lyric(s), ballad(s), melod(y,ies), milonga(s), tune(s), chant(s), ditt(y,ies), refrain(s), dance(s). *Consider also:* work song(s), folk lyric(s), sea shant(y,ies), traditional ballad(s), religious song(s), lullab(y,ies), carol(s), dance song(s), round(s), nursery song(s), political ditt(y,ies), spiritual(s), revival song(s), alabado(s), alabanza(s), alala(s), baguala(s), bushi, cancion(es), cifra(s), corrido(s), desafio(s), embolada(s), estilo(s), fado, fadinho, golpe(s), hootenann(y,ies), joiku(s), juoigos, milonga(s), miroloyi, patinada, syrtos, toada(s), tonada(s), triste(s), vidal(a,alita). *See also* Ballads; Border ballads; Ethnomusicology; Folk literature; Folk music; Folk poetry; Folklore; French songs; Geisslerlieder; German songs; Labor songs; Lyrical ballads; Lullabies; Nonsense literature; Protest songs; Refrain (music); Revolutionary ballads and songs; Sea songs; Singing; Work songs.

Folklore. Folklor(e,ism). Folklife. Folktale(s). Folkway(s). Folk wisdom. Legend(s). Lore. Folksong(s). Fable(s). Myth(s,ology). Fairy tale(s). Maerchen. Tale(s) of wonder. Proverb(s). Proverbial tale(s). Voodoo. Hex(es,ed). Magical belief(s). Shaman(s,istic). Medicine (men,man). Oral history. *Choose from:* folk, traditional, ethnic, native, tribal, indigenous *with:* tale(s), myth(s), fable(s), legend(s), artifact(s), superstition(s), tradition(s), riddle(s), proverb(s), stor(y,ies), life, music, song(s), art, dance(s), movement, remed(y,ies), medicine, psychiatry, healer(s), belief(s), custom(s). *See also* Adages; Allegory; Animal lore; Culture; Customs; Ethnography; Fairies; Fabliaux; Folk culture; Folk literature;

Folk music; Folk poetry; Folk songs; Folklorists; Local history; Mermaids; Mescal (cactus); Mythical animals; Mythology; Nature literature; Occupational folklorc; Oral history; Oral tradition; Plant folklore; Psychotropic plants; Sagas; Slogans; Snake lore; Superstitions; Traditional medicine.

Folklore, medical. See *Traditional medicine.*

Folklore, occupational. See *Occupational folklore.*

Folklore, plant. See *Plant folklore.*

Folklore, public. See *Public folklore.*

Folklorists. Folklorist(s). Folk expert(s). *Choose from:* folk(lore,ways,life) *with:* scholar(s,ship), researcher(s), expert(s), fieldworker(s). *See also* Anthropologists; Ethnography; Folklore.

Folkways. Folkways. *Choose from:* traditional *with:* behavior, custom(s), norm(s), value(s), norm(s), rite(s), ritual(s). *Consider also:* mores. *See also* Culture (anthropological); Social norms.

Follow home crime. Follow home crime(s). Driveway robber(y,ies). *Choose from:* follow home, driveway(s), garage(s) *with:* robber(y,ies), invasion(s), crime(s). *See also* Crime; Driveby crimes.

Followers. Follower(s). Disciple(s). Supporter(s). Adherent(s). Admirer(s). Devotee(s). Protege(s). Fan(s). Sycophant(s). Following. Advocate(s). True believer(s). Worshiper(s). Worshipper(s). *See also* Audiences; Disciples; Entertainers; Famous people; Fans (persons).

Followup, posttreatment. See *Posttreatment followup.*

Followup studies. Followup stud(y,ies). Follow up stud(y,ies). Subsequent stud(y,ies). Later stud(y,ies). Followup(s). Follow up(s). *Consider also:* case report(s), outcome(s), process assessment, posttreatment followup, catamnesis, graduate surveys. *See also* Aftercare; Effects; Posttreatment followup; Psychotherapeutic outcomes; Research design; Results; Treatment outcome.

Food. Food(s). Feed. Meal(s). Edible(s). Nutrition. Fat(s). Carbohydrate(s). Protein(s). Diet. Egg(s). Grain(s). Meat(s). Seafood(s). Milk. Snack(s). Cereal(s). Beverage(s). Fruit(s). Peanut(s). Bread(s). Dessert(s). Cake(s). Pie(s). Sweet(s). Ice cream. Appetizer(s). Rice. Potato(es). Vegetable(s). Pellet(s). Cand(y,ies). Cocoa. Chocolate(s). Cheese(s). Bean(s). Honey. Butter. Margarine. Sugar. Corn. Maize. Wheat. Rice. Flour. Sauce(s). Spice(s). Apple(s). Orange(s). Pear(s). Banana(s). Pineapple(s). Apricot(s). Berr(y,ies).

Lettuce, Carrot(s). Pea(s). Beet(s). Broccoli. Cabbage. Celery. Onion(s). Eggplant. Tomato(es). Mushroom(s). Bean sprout(s). Avocado(es). Artichoke(s). Poultry. Veal. Beef. Pork. Lamb. Bluefish. Catfish. Flounder. Haddock. Salmon. Scrod. Shellfish. Shrimp(s). Sole. Swordfish. Trout. *See also* Agriculture; Animal products; Beans; Bread; Butter; Citrus fruits; Caloric requirements; Calories (food); Convenience Foods; Dairy products; Diet; Edible plants; Fish as food; Food additives; Food industry; Food inspection; Food preparation; Food preservation; Food storage; Fruit; Gardens; Grain; Hunger, food deprivation; Junk food; Locally produced food; Meat industry; Natural foods; Nutrition; Pasta; Seafood.

Food, animal. See *Animal food*

Food, calories. See *Calories (food).*

Food, fish as. See *Fish as food.*

Food, junk. See *Junk food.*

Food, locally produced. See *Locally produced food.*

Food, primitive. See *Primitive food.*

Food additives. Food additive(s). *Choose from:* food(s), feed(s), diet(s,ary), cereal(s), grain(s), meat(s), soft drink(s), beverage(s), bread(s), baked good(s), bakery product(s), cheese(s), frozen dinner(s), frozen vegetable(s), dessert(s) *with:* added ingredient(s), preservative(s), additive(s), medicat(e,ed,ing, ion,ions), foreign substance(s), flavor(ed,ing,ings), coloring agent(s), sugar added, salt added, supplement(s), nitrite(s), artificial sweetener(s), artificial(ly) flavor(ed,ing,ings), enriched, added vitamin(s), added mineral(s). *Consider also:* nutriceutical(s), medical food(s). *See also* Carcinogens; Food; Food contamination; Junk food; Medical foods; Natural foods; Nutrition.

Food adulteration. See *Food additives; Food contamination; Food inspection; Herbicides; Pesticides; Product tampering.*

Food allergies. See *Food hypersensitivity.*

Food assistance. See *Food services (programs).*

Food chain. Food chain(s). Trophic level(s). Detrital pathway(s). Grazing pathway(s). Food web(s). *Consider also:* pyramid of numbers. *See also* Bioinvasion; Biological diversity; Ecology; Ecosystem management; Environmental impacts; Environmental protection; Forest conservation; Habitat; Land preservation; Marine ecology; Natural resourses; Wildlife conservation.

Food consumption. See *Food intake.*

Food contamination. Food contamination. Tainted food. *Choose from:* taint(ed), contaminated, adulterated, salmonella, mold(y), spoiled, bacteria, pesticide(s), fungus, aflatoxin(s), additive(s), tamper(ed,ing), residue(s), fungicide(s), rodenticide(s), chemical(s), hormon(e,es, al), PCB(s), polychlorinated biphenyl(s), PBB, polybrominated biphenyl(s) *with:* food(s), cheese(s), milk, bread, grape(s), vegetable(s), fruit(s). *Consider also:* food containing toxic substances, irradiated food(s), radioactive milk, adulterated fruit juice(s), food-borne illness(es), red tide, cyanimide laced tea. *Consider also:* strontium *with:* milk; dioxin *with:* carton(s); lead *with:* china; listeria *with:* beef; alar *with:* apple(s); parasite(s) *with:* sushi; restaurant(s) *with:* violation(s). *See also* Agricultural chemicals; Bacteria; Carcinogens; Food additives; Food inspection; Food poisoning; Herbicides; Nuclear accidents; Nuclear waste; Parasites; Pesticides.

Food deprivation. See *Hunger, food deprivation.*

Food distribution programs. See *Food services (programs).*

Food habits. Food habits. *Choose from:* food, diet(s,ary), eating, nutritional *with:* habit(s), daily ration(s), consumption, preference(s), pattern(s), usual, intake, consume, ingest(ed,ing). *Consider also:* specific food items *with:* consumption, intake, eat(en,ing), consum(e,ed,ing, ption), ingest(ed,ing,ion). *See also* Convenience Foods; Diet; Eating; Junk food; Nutrition.

Food hypersensitivity. Food hypersensitivity. *Choose from:* food(s), diet(s,ary), shellfish, milk, tomato(es), squash(es), peanut(s) or other foods by name *with:* allerg(y,ies,ic), hypersensitiv(e,ity,ities), intoleran(t,ce), sensitiv(e,ity,ities). *See also* Food; Hypersensitivity; Intolerance.

Food industry. Food industry. Food technolog(y,ies). *Choose from:* food(s,stuff,stuffs), nutrition(ist,ists), diet(s,ary), bread(s), dair(y,ies), meat(s), cheese(s), cereal(s), etc. *with:* industr(y,ies,ial), production, manufactur(e,ed,ing), marketing, compan(y,ies), supplier(s), retailer(s), wholesaler(s). *See also* Agribusiness; Beverage industry; Dairy products; Food; Grocery trade; Meat industry; Milk industry; Nut industry.

Food inspection. Food inspect(ed,ing,ion). *Choose from:* food(s,stuff,stuffs), feed, meat(s), poultry, grain(s), rice, flour, dairy, milk, egg(s), seafood(s), juice(s) *with:* screen(ed,ing,ings), inspect(ed,ing,ion), microbiological testing, capillary electrophoresis, analy(sis,zed), monitor(s,ed,ing),

sampl(e,es,ed,ing), identif(y,ied,ication) bacteri(a,um), detect(ed,ing,ion) microorganism(s). *Consider also:* Food and Drug Administration. *See also* Dairy products; Food; Food contamination; Food laws and legislation; Food poisoning; Meat industry; Sanitation; Slaughterhouses.

Food intake. Food intake. Eat(s,ing,en). Ate. *Choose from:* food(stuff,stuffs), feeding(s), diet(s,ary), nutrient(s), nutrition(al), calor(ic,ies), meal(s), protein(s), carbohydrate(s), fat(s), vitamin(s), mineral(s), saline, salt, milk, grain(s), meat, fish, poultry, rice, fruit(s), beverage(s), egg(s), vegetable(s), dairy product(s), sugar, sweetener(s), pellet(s), calcium, fluid(s), junk food *with:* intake, consum(e,ed,ing,ption), overfeeding, uptake, ingest(ed,ion). *Consider also:* satiety, eating behavior, nutritional pattern(s). *See also* Eating.

Food laws and legislation. Food laws and legislation. FDA regulation(s). Food labelling regulation(s). *Choose from:* food(s,stuff,stuffs), cheese(s), milk, meat(s), poultry, bread(s), etc. *with:* law(s), legal, polic(y,ies), regulat(e,ed, ing,ion,ions), ban(s,ned,ning), liability, enforc(e,ed,ing,ement), Food and Drug Act, safety standard(s), Food and Drug Administration, FDA, General Agreement on Tariffs and Trade, GATT. *See also* Consumer protection; Food inspection; Laws; Quality control.

Food poisoning. Food poison(ing,ings, ed,ous). Aflatoxin(s). Botulism. Ergotism. Enterotoxin(s). Foodborne illness(es). Lathryism. Lupinosis. Salmonella. *Consider also:* cheese, fish, forage, food, meat, milk, mushroom(s), sausage, seafood, shellfish *with:* poison(ing,ings,ed,ous), toxin(s), toxicos(is,es), toxic(ity), bacteria, contaminat(ed,ion). *See also* Food; Food contamination; Food inspection; Poisoning.

Food preferences. Food preference(s). *Choose from:* food, snack(s), dinner(s), menu(s), eating, dietary *with:* preference(s), prefer(red), choice(s), rating(s). *Consider also:* plate waste. *See also* Diet; Diet fads; Food habits.

Food preparation. Food preparation. Cook(ed,ing,ery). Culinary art(s). Food processing. Meal creation. *Choose from:* meal(s), food, dinner(s), lunch(es,eon, eons), breakfast(s), diet(s,ary) *with:* prepar(e,ed,ing,ation), process(e,ed,ing), cook(ed,ing). *See also* Calories (food); Cooking; Food preservation.

Food preservation. Food preservation. *Choose from:* food(s), edible(s), fats, fish, grain(s), meat(s), beef, lamb, pork, ham(s), veal, sausage(s), seafood(s), milk, cereal(s), fruit(s), vegetable(s), cucumber(s), cheese, butter, margarine,

poultry, shellfish, sauce(s), wheat, rice, flour, egg(s) *with:* preserv(e,ed,ation), preservative(s), pasteuriz(e,ed,ing), radiat(e,ed,ing,ion), irradiat(e,ed,ing, ion), salt(ed,ing), kipper(ed,ing), smok(e,ed,ing), dry(ing), dried, pickl(e,ed,ing), ferment(ed,ing), process(ed,ing), antimicrobial(s), heat treat(ed,ing), radiopasteuriz(e,ed, ing,ation), extend(ed,ing) shelf life. *Consider also:* can(ned,ning), bottl(e,ed, ing), vacuum pack(ed,ing), packag(e,ed, ing). *See also* Fermentation; Food contamination; Food storage.

Food relief. Food relief. Food stamp(s). Soup kitchen(s). Food bank(s). Breadline(s). Bread line(s). Women, Infants and Children Nutrition Program. WIC. Food distribution program(s). *Choose from:* food, meal(s), breakfast(s), lunch(es), nutrition(al), hunger, anti-hunger, famine(s), malnutrition *with:* aid, assistance, entitlement(s), service(s), program(s). *See also* Disaster relief; Food services (programs); International organizations; Relief services.

Food services (programs). Food service(s). Food distribution program(s). *Choose from:* school(s) *with:* lunch(es), breakfast(s), nutrition. *Choose from:* food, meal(s), breakfast(s), lunch(es), nutrition(al) *with:* aid, service(s), program(s). Child feeding program(s). Foodservice(s). Meals on wheels. Cafeteria(s). Lunch room(s). Public catering system(s). Meal deliver(y,ies). Meal ticket(s). Meal service(s). Food stamp(s). Cafeteria service(s). Canteen(s). Restaurant(s). Soup kitchen(s). Women, Infants and Children Nutrition Program. WIC. *See also* Nutrition; Public welfare; Social programs.

Food storage. Food storage. *Choose from:* food(s), edible(s), fats, fish, grain(s), meat(s), seafood(s), milk, cereal(s), fruit(s), vegetable(s), cheese, butter, margarine, sugar, poultry, shellfish, wheat, rice, flour, egg(s) *with:* store(d), storage, shelflife, hydrochilling, preserv(e,ed,ation), refrigerat(e,ed,ing, ion), can(ned,ning), bottle(d), vacuum packed, packag(e,ed,ing). *See also* Containers; Food preservation.

Food supply. Food supply. *Choose from:* food(s), commodit(y,ies), agricultural product(s), grain(s), legume(s), sorghum, soybean(s), meat(s), beef, lamb, pork, fish, seafood(s), milk, cereal(s), fruit(s), vegetable(s), cheese, poultry, corn, wheat, rice, pasta, potato(es), flour, egg(s) *with:* suppl(y,ies), availab(le,ility), shortfall(s), shortage(s), surplus(es), glut(s). *Consider also:* subsistence agriculture, food cris(is,es), food security, food polic(y,ies), food output, world hunger.

See also Farm produce; Food; Famine; Gardens; Hunger, food deprivation; Locally produced food.

Foods, convenience. See *Convenience foods.*

Foods, health. See *Natural foods.*

Foods, medical. See *Medical foods.*

Foods, natural. See *Natural foods.*

Foods, organic. See *Natural foods.*

Fools and jesters. Fool(s). Jester(s). Dunce(s). Motley(s). Buffoon(s). Clown(s). Comedi(an,ans,ienne,iennes). *See also* Carnivals; Comics; Humor; Humorous songs; Frivolity; Sense of humor.

Foot. Foot. Feet. *Consider also:* heel(s), toe(s), hallux, metatarsal, instep, sole(s), tarsal, paw(s), hoof, hooves. *See also* Anatomy.

Foraging behavior, animal. See *Animal foraging behavior.*

Forbidden. Forbid(den,ding). Forbad(e). Ban(ned,ning). Prohibit(ed,ing,ion). Proscri(be,bed,bing). Proscription. Outlaw(ed,ing). Interdict(ed,ing,ion). Censor(ed,ing,ship). Declar(e,ed,ing) illegal. Disallow(ed,ing,ance). Embargo(s,ed). Exclu(de,ded,ing,sion). *Consider also:* taboo(s,ed), injunction(s), moratorium(s), ostracism(s), suppress(ed,ing,ion), veto(s,es), preclud(e,ed,ing), turn(ed,ing) down. *See also* Ban; Blacklisting; Censorship; Illegal; Inadmissible; Prohibition; Taboo.

Force, all volunteer military. See *Volunteer military personnel.*

Force, labor. See *Labor force.*

Force, life. See *Vitalism.*

Force, reduction in. See *Involuntary retirement; Mandatory retirement; Personnel termination; Plant closings.*

Force, work. See *Labor force.*

Forced choice tests. Forced choice test(s). Forced choice technique(s). *Choose from:* forced choice, true false, binary choice, two alternative(s), multiple choice, multiple option *with:* test(s), technique(s), situations, trial(s), question(s), item(s), questionnaire(s), instrument(s), schedule(s), exam(s,ination,inations), answer(s). *See also* Measurement; Tests.

Forced labor. Forced labor. Slave labor. Chain gang(s). Encomienda(s). *Choose from:* compulsory, forced, involuntary, convict(s), prisoner(s), prison(s), prisoner(s) of war, inmate(s), concentration camp(s) *with:* labor, employment, work, fieldwork, servitude. *Consider also:* labor camp(s), Gulag, death camp(s), road camp(s), labor colon(y,ies), blackbird(ed,ing), kanaka,

Laogai inmate(s), prison labor, slave-made goods, child labor, forced prostitution. *See also* Child labor; Concentration camps; Penal colonies; Peonage; Slavery; Trafficking in persons; Workers' rights.

Forced migration. Forced migration(s). Exile(s,d). Flee(ing). Fled. Seek(ing) sanctuary. Deport(ed,ation). Diaspora. Displaced person(s). Expelled. Expulsion(s). *Choose from:* forced, involuntary *with:* migrat(e,ed,ing, ion,ions), migrant(s), resettl(e,ed,ing, ement,ements), relocat(c,cd,ing,ion), emigrat(e,ed,ing,ion), removal(s). *See also* Deportation; Diaspora; Purges; Refugees; Right of asylum.

Forced retirement. See *Involuntary retirement; Mandatory retirement.*

Forced sterilization. See *Involuntary sterilization.*

Forces, armed. See *Armed forces.*

Forces, military. See *Armed forces.*

Forces, peacekeeping. See *Peacekeeping forces.*

Forces, social. See *Social factors.*

Fordism. See *Scientific management.*

Forecasting. Forecast(s,ing). Predict(ing,ion,ions). Postdiction(s). Futurology. Conjectur(e,ed,ing). Future trend(s). Probabilit(y,ies). Prognos(is,es, tics). Futur(e,es,ist,ists,ism). Five year outlook. Prognosticat(e,ed,ing,ion,ions). Crystal ball(s). 21st century. Prophe(cy, cies,sy,tic). Forewarn. Foretell. Augur(y). Soothsayer(s). Prophet(s). Prospect(s). Scenario(s). Anticipat(e,ed, ing,ion,ions). *Consider also:* third wave, post industrial society, technetronic era, technetronic age, 2010, 2050, tomorrow, America's third century, 21st century, twenty first century, space age, information age, outlook(s), projection(s). *See also* Economic forecasting; Employment forecasting; Future; Future of society; Hopefulness; Imminent; Impending; Political forecasting; Prediction; Prophets; Technological change; Technological innovations; Technological progress; Trends; Weather forecasting.

Forecasting, economic. See *Economic forecasting.*

Forecasting, election. See *Political forecasting.*

Forecasting, employment. See *Employment forecasting.*

Forecasting, political. See *Political forecasting.*

Forecasting, technological. See *Technological forecasting.*

Forecasting, weather. See *Weather forecasting.*

Foreign affairs. See *Detente; Foreign policy; International relations.*

Foreign aid. Foreign aid. Famine relief. Foreign assistance. Aid to developing countries. International aid. Marshall Plan. U.N. Disaster Relief. International relief effort(s). International relief organization(s). International relief agenc(y,ies). *Choose from:* foreign, overseas, abroad, U.N., United Nations, United Nations Development Program, International Red Cross, World Bank, International Monetary Fund, U.S. Agency for International Development, U.S. International Development Agency, Alliance for Progress, Colombo Plan, European Development Fund, EEC, European Economic Community, Organization for Economic Cooperation and Development, African Development Bank, Asian Develoment Bank, Inter-American Development Bank *with:* shipment(s), food, medicine(s), airlift(s), airdrop(s), medical assistance, military aid, humanitarian assistance, medical supplies, arms shipments, disaster relief, funds, economic assistance, credit, financial assistance, loan(s), cash assistance, payment(s), capital grant(s), help, relief, technical assistance, advisory group(s). *See also* Developing countries; Economic development; Financial support; Foreign policy; International relations; Military assistance; World economy.

Foreign born. See *Foreigners.*

Foreign business. See *Commercial treaties; Exports; Free trade; Imports; International trade; World economy.*

Foreign correspondents. Foreign correspondent(s). Foreign reporter(s). *Choose from:* foreign, overseas, abroad, international *with:* journalist(s), correspondent(s), reporter(s), press corps, editorial writer(s), news agenc(y,ies), editor(s), broadcaster(s), foreign bureau(s), news gathering community, wire service(s). *See also* Commentators; Foreign news; Journalists; News coverage.

Foreign countries, Americans in. See *Americans abroad.*

Foreign debt. See *Public debt.*

Foreign exchange. Foreign exchange rate(s). FX. European monetary system. International monetary system. Real exchange rate(s). Mobile capital. International financial market(s). Flight of international capital. Dollar-yen parity. Dollar index(es). Foreign currency transaction(s). Purchasing power of the dollar. Capital flight. Eurodollar(s). Euromoney. ECU dollar. Cheap imports. Foreign investment(s). *Consider also:* exchange rate(s), substitution, convertib(le,ility), inconvertib(le,ility), hedging, strength, weak(ness), declin(e,ed,ing), rise(n), rising, stabiliz(e,ed,ing) *with:* currenc(y,ies), money, coin(s), cash, monetary unit(s), afghani(s), baht(s), balboa(s), bolivar(s), cedi(s), centime(s), colon(s), cordoba note(s), cruzeiro(s), dalasi(s), Deutsche mark(s), dinar(e,s), dobra(s), dollar(s), dong(s), donga(s), dirham(s), drachma(s), ekuwele(s), escudo(s), finggit(s), forint(s), franc(s), franken(s), gourde(s), guarani(s), guilder(s), gulf riyal(s), kina(s), kip(s), koruna(s), krona(s), krone(s), kwacha(s), kwanza(s), kyat(s), lek(s), lempira(s), leone(s), leu(s), lev(s), lilangeni(s), lira(s), lire(s), markka(s), naira(s), ngultrum(s), ouguiya(s), pa'anga(s), pataca(s), peseta(s), peso(s), pound(s), pulo(s), quetzal(s), rand(s), rial(s), riel(s), ruble(s), rupee(s), rupiah(s), schilling(s), shekel(s), shilling(s), sol(s), sucre(s), syli(s), taka(s), tala(s), tughrik(s), won(s), yen, yuan, zaire(s), zloty(s). *See also* Currency; Devaluation (of currency); Economic union.

Foreign investment. Foreign investment(s). *Choose from:* foreign, international, transnational, global, overseas, abroad, multinational, host country, third world *with:* invest(ed,ing,ment,ments), equity, portfolio(s). *Consider also:* foreign investments in the United States, British owned real estate in the United States, debt equity swap(s), U.S. Soviet joint venture(s), Japanese investments in U.S. real estate, foreign ownership, Asian investors, etc. *See also* Colonialism; Corporations; Dependency theory (international); Developing countries; Economic development; Economic underdevelopment; Investment policy; Investments; Junk bonds; Multinational corporations; Oligopolies; World economy.

Foreign labor. Foreign labor. Guest-worker(s). Bracero(s). *Choose from:* foreign, guest, imported, immigrant(s), international, migrant(s), migratory, alien(s), interstate *with:* worker(s), labor(er,ers), fruit picker(s), farmworker(s), farm hand(s), ranch hand(s). *Consider also:* Padrone system, Padron(e,i,es). *See also* Alien labor; Border industries; Brain drain; Foreign professional personnel; Foreign workers; Foreigners; Migrant workers; Offshore production (foreign countries); Sweatshops.

Foreign language learning. See *Second language education.*

Foreign language translation. See *Translating and translations.*

Foreign languages. See *Second languages.*

Foreign ministers. See *Diplomats.*

Foreign nationals. See *Foreigners.*

Foreign news. Foreign news. International news(paper,papers). Foreign press. *Choose from:* foreign, overseas, abroad, international, global, transborder, worldwide, third world, Middle East(ern), Africa(n), Europe(an), Asia(n), Latin America(n), France, French, German(y), Chin(a,ese), Brazil(ian), Egypt(ian), etc. *with:* news(paper,papers), press, stor(y,ies), news service(s), news agenc(y,ies), wire service(s), information, media coverage, television news, broadcast journalism, data flow, *Consider also:* Le Monde, El Mundo, Die Welt, etc. *See also* Foreign correspondents; International broadcasting; News coverage.

Foreign origin. See *Foreigners.*

Foreign policy. Foreign polic(y,ies). International polic(y,ies). Justification(s) for war. Decision(s) for war. Militarism. Imperialism. Accord(s). Treat(y,ies). Free Trade Zone(s). Economic sanctions. Arms race. Counterterrorism. Peace Accord(s). Peace treat(y,ies). *Choose from:* foreign, isolationism, arms, war, international, diplomatic, balance of power, militaristic, international cooperation, imperialistic, big stick, free Trade, detente, nonalignment, neutralism, anti-communis(m,t), peace, State Department *with:* polic(y,ies), treat(y,ies), accord(s), charter(s). *Consider policies of specific nations toward areas or countries or specific treaties, charters or accords, for example:* Monroe doctrine, Atlantic Charter, Treaty of Versailles, Helsinki Accords, Geneva Accords, Realpolitik. *Consider also:* trade polic(y,ies), defense polic(y,ies), national security polic(y,ies), United States policy toward, U.S. policies, America's policy. *See also* Alliances; Autarky; Balance of power; Collective security; Diplomacy (official); Foreign aid; Imperialism; International alliances; International relations; Isolationism; Neutrality; Nonalignment; Trade protection; Treaties.

Foreign policy making. Foreign policy making. *Choose from:* foreign, international, isolationism, war, diplomatic, balance of power, militarism, balance of power, international cooperation, imperial(ism,istic), trade, arms *with:* polic(y,ies) *with:* form(ed,ing,ation), evolution, evolv(e,ed,ing), making, made, design(ed,ing), plan(s,ned,ning), decision(s), source(s), justif(y,ied,ication,ications). *See also* Foreign policy; Policy making.

Foreign professional personnel. Foreign professional personnel. *Choose from:* foreign(er,ers), immigrant(s), alien(s), exile(s,d), expatriate(s) *with:* professional(s), medical graduate(s), physician(s), scientific personnel, nurse(s), veterinarian(s), intellectual(s),

faculty, professor(s). *Consider also:* brain drain. *See also* Alien labor; Foreign labor; Foreign workers; Foreigners; Professional personnel.

Foreign relations. See *International relations.*

Foreign students. Foreign student(s). *Choose from:* foreign, international, expatriate *with:* student(s). *Consider also:* Japanese, Iranian, German, Chinese, etc. *with:* student(s). *See also* International education; International educational exchange.

Foreign study. Foreign study. International education. Scholarship exchange. *Choose from:* stud(y,ied,ing), train(ed,ing), junior year, student(s), scholarship(s) *with:* France, Germany, Spain, Italy, England, etc., overseas, abroad, exchange(s), foreign countr(y,ies), host countr(y,ies). *Consider also:* Fulbright scholar(s, ship,ships). *See also* Area studies; International education; International educational exchange.

Foreign trade regulation. Foreign trade regulation(s). International export control. Export-import regulation(s). Trade negotiation(s). Import quota(s). Import dut(y,ies). Import reduction. Trade barrier(s). Restrict(ing,ion, ions,ed) import(s). Customs dut(y,ies). Tariff(s). Hawley Smoot Tariff Act. *Choose from:* import(ed,ing,ation,s), trade, foreign exchange, export(s) *with:* regulation(s), deregulation, regulatory law(s), sanction(s), market policy, quota(s), dut(y,ies), restrain(t,ed,ing), restrict(ing,ions,ed), tariff(s,ication,y), *Consider also:* foreign trade polic(y,ies), GATT, General Agreement on Tariffs and Trade, European Community, European Union, Common Market, NAFTA, North American Free Trade Agreement, Uruguay Round. *See also* Commercial treaties; Emerging markets; Foreign trade zones; International economic integration; International trade; Nontariff trade barriers; Trade protection.

Foreign trade zones. Foreign trade zone(s). FTZ. Free zone(s). Free port(s). Duty free enclave(s). Free trade zone(s). Free economic zone(s). Special economic zone(s). *Consider also:* bonded storage, bonded warehouse(s). *See also* Commercial treaties; Custom unions; Free trade; Foreign trade regulation; Offshore production (foreign countries).

Foreign workers. Foreign worker(s). Bracero(s). Guestworker(s). Employed refugee(s). Foreign laborforce. *Choose from:* guest, foreign, imported, undocumented, alien *with:* worker(s), labor(er,ers), employee(s), picker(s), farmhand(s). *Consider also:* migrant worker(s), migratory worker(s). *See also*

Alien labor; Foreign labor; Foreign professional personnel; Foreigners; Immigration law; Labor economics; Labor mobility; Sweatshops; Undocumented immigrants.

Foreigners. Foreigner(s). Alien(s). Immigrant(s). Guestworker(s). Outlander(s). Overseas Chinese. Non-native. Refugee(s). Expatriate(s). Exile(s). Displaced person(s). Boat people. Emigre(s). Political asylum. Emigrant(s). International student(s). Temporarily residing abroad. Living overseas. Citizen(s) of other countries. *Choose from:* foreign *with:* born, national(s), newcomer(s), migrant(s). *Choose from:* foreign, international, alien or country name, such as Chinese or French, etc. *with:* worker(s), origin(s), resident(s), student(s), professional(s), physicians, women, men, population, employee(s), personnel. *See also* Alien labor; Citizenship; Displaced persons; Foreign labor; Foreign professional personnel; Foreign students; Foreign workers; Naturalization; Refugees; Strangers.

Foremen. See *Industrial foremen; Managers.*

Foremen, industrial. See *Industrial foremen.*

Forensic medicine. Forensic medicine. Paternity test(s,ing). Medicolegal autops(y,ies). Medical evidence. Forensic evidence. *Choose from:* forensic(ally), expert witness(es), *with:* medicine, medical, patholog(y,ical), bloodstain(s), autops(y,ies), dentist(s,ry). *See also* Criminal investigations; Criminal proceedings; Forensic psychiatry.

Forensic psychiatry. Forensic psychiatr(y, ic,ist,ists). *Choose from:* forensic, criminal justice, court(s,room,rooms), trial(s), expert witness(es) *with:* psychiatr(y,ic,ist,ists), mental health service(s), psycholog(y,ical,ist,ists). *See also* Criminal proceedings; Forensic medicine.

Forensics (public speaking). Forensic(s). Argumentat(ion,ive). Oral argument(s). Closing argument(s). Main argument(s). Dat(e,ed,ing). Disputation(s). Disput(e,ed,ing). Moot(ing). Trial lawyer(s) statement(s). Legal argument(s). *Choose from:* forensic, legal, courtroom *with:* contest(s), orator(y,s), argument(s). *See also* Arguments; Date; Public speaking.

Foreplay, sexual. See *Sexual foreplay.*

Forest conservation. Forest conservation. Forest management. Arrest(ed,ing) deforestation. Reforest(ing,ation). Sav(e,ed,ing) redwoods. *Choose from:* sav(e,ed,ing), conserv(e,ed,ing,ation), preserv(e,ed,ing), protect(ed,ing,tion),

maintain(ed,ing), maintenance, safeguard(ing), monitor(ed,ing), reclaim(ed,ing), reclamation, restor(e,ed,ing,ation), replant(ed,ing), replenish(ed,ing), re-establish(ed,ing), return(ed,ing) *with:* woodland(s), forest(s), jungle(s), wilderness, wood(s), rainforest(s), ecosystem(s), habitat(s). *Consider also:* debt *with:* nature, biosphere, forest(s), rainforest(s) *with:* swap(s). *See also* Biological diversity; Conservation of natural resources; Debt-for-nature swaps; Deforestation; Ecosytem management; Environmental protection; Food chain; Lumber industry; Old growth forests; Rainforests; Reclamation of land; Reforestation; Restoration ecology; Soil conservation; Timber; Tree farms; Tree planting.

Forest ecology. Forest(s,ry) ecolog(y,ical). Forest ecosystem(s). Forest rotation. Forest habitat(s). *Choose from:* ecolog(y,ical), ecosystem(s), environment(s,al,ally) *with:* forest(s,ry), tree(s), log(ged,ging). *See also* Deforestation; Ecology; Forest fires; Forestry; Habitat; Timber; Tree farms.

Forest fires. Forest fire(s). Wildfire(s). *Choose from:* woodland(s), forest(s), national park(s), wilderness, wood(s), timberland(s), wooded area(s) *with:* fire(s), wildfire(s), burn(ed,ing). *See also* Fire; Fire ecology; Forest ecology; Fire prevention; Forestry; Grassland fires; Rainforests; Timber.

Forest management. See *Forestry.*

Forest reserves. Forest reserve(s). Land reserve(s). National forest(s). *Choose from:* forest(s), land(s), nature, jungle(s), rainforest(s), wilderness, swamp(s) *with:* reserve(s), preserve(s). *Consider also:* national park(s), U.S. Forest Service, grazing land(s), rangeland(s), forever wild, public lands, state preserve(s). *See also* Deforestation; Forestry; Natural resources; Old growth forests; Parks; Sanctuaries; Timber; Tree farms; Wildlife sanctuaries

Forestry. Forestry. Silvicultur(e,al,ally). *Choose from:* forest(s), timber(lands), wood(s,lands), wooded area(s) *with:* care, cultivat(e,ed,ing,ion), manag(e,ed,ing,ement), control, develop(ed,ing,ment), protect(ed,ing, ion), preservation. *See also* Conservation of natural resources; Deforestation; Environmental protection; Forest conservation; Forest fires; Forest ecology; Forest reserves; Land use; Old growth forests; Plant cultivation; Reclamation of land; Soil conservation; Timber; Tree farms; Tree planting.

Forests, old growth. See *Old growth forests.*

Forfeiture. Forfeit(ed,ing,ure). Fine(s). Penalt(y,ies). Seiz(e,ed,ing). Confiscat(e,

ed,ing,ion). Impound(ed,ing,ment). Amerc(e,ed,ement,iable). *See also* Expropriation; Punishment; Search and seizure.

Forgeries and mystifications, literary. See *Literary forgeries and mystifications.*

Forgery. Forge(d,r,rs,ry). Forging. Fraudulent document(s). *Choose from:* forge(d,r,rs,ry), forging, fraud(ulent), falsif(y,ying,ication), fak(e,ed), counterfeit(ed,ing), alter(ed,ing) *with:* document(s), passport(s), signature(s), cop(y,ies), art print(s), record(s), check(s). *See also* Fraud; Manuscripts; Plagiarism; Signatures.

Forgetting. Forget(ting,ful,fulness). Forgot(ten). *Choose from:* memory, recognition, recall, remember(ed,ing), retention *with:* fail(ed,ing,ure,ures), loss(es), losing, lost, delay(ed,ing), inability, inaccessib(le,ility), inhibit(ed,ing,ion). *Consider also:* repress(ed,ing,ion), amnes(ia,ic). *See also* Memory; Memory disorders; Retention (psychology); Suppression (defense mechanism).

Forging. See *Forgery*

Forgiveness. Forgive(ness). Forgiv(en,ing). Redemption. Redeem(ed,ing). Absolution. Absolv(e,ed,ing). Pardon(ed,ing). Repriev(e,ed,ing,al), Amnesty. Exonerat(e,ed,ing,ion). Reconcil(e,ed, ing,iation). Remission of sin(s). *See also* Absolution; Clemency; Guilt; Indulgences; Salvation; Shame; Sin.

Form (aesthetics). Form (aesthetics). Shape(s). Structur(e,es,al). Contour(s). Spatial feature(s). Configuration(s). Conformation(s). Figure(s). Outline(d,s). Profile(s,d). Silhouette(s). Symmetr(y,ical). Asymmetr(y,ical). Unity. *Consider also:* arrang(e,ed,ement), style(s), artistic mean(s), meter (poetry), pattern(s), eidos, idealized form(s), general feature(s). *See also* Aesthetics; Clusters; Content; Designs; Film genres; Formalism; Genres (art); Morphology; Structure; Unity (Literature).

Form (philosophy). Form (philosophy). Essential character. Plato(nic,s) form(s). Universals. Ideal type(s). *Consider also:* concept(s,ualization,ualizations). *See also* Concepts; Philosophy; Reality.

Form, literary. See *Literary form.*

Form perception. Form perception. *Choose from:* form(s), shape(s), contour(s), spatial feature(s) *with:* perception, perceiv(e,ed,ing), recognition, recogniz(e,ed,ing), identif(y,ied,ication). *See also* Figure ground discrimination; Perception.

Formal gardens. Formal garden(s). Parterre(s). Controlled garden(s). *Choose from:* formal, 18th century, baroque, colonial *with:* garden(s), flower bed(s). *See also* Flowers; Garden structures; Gardens; Landscape architecture; Natural gardens.

Formal social control. Formal social control. *Choose from:* social, societal, community, local, town, city, municipal, state, federal, official, government *with:* control(led,ling), rule(s), regulat(e,ed,ing,ion,ions), licens(e,es,ed,ing,ure), auspices, ordinance(s), inspect(ed,ing,ion,ions), certif(y,ied,ying,ication), sanction(s,ed,ing). *Consider also:* law and order, police, law(s), law enforcement, jurisprudence, public polic(y,ies), legislation. *See also* Government regulation; Identification cards; Law enforcement; Negative sanctions; Public order; Punishment; Reward; Social pressure.

Formalism. Formalism. Cult of form. *Consider also:* structuralism, Anglo-American New Criticism, Conrad Fiedler, Adolf von Hildrand, Alois Riegl, Erwin Panofsky. *See also* Aesthetics; Art criticism; Content; Form (aesthetics); Literary criticism.

Format. Format(s). Arrangement(s). Blueprint(s). Layout(s). Dimension(s). Framework. Specification(s). *Consider also:* appearance(s), setup. *See also* Architectural drawing; Designs; Frames (physical); Groundwork; Structure.

Formation, attitude. See *Attitude formation.*

Formation, class. See *Class formation.*

Formation, coalition. See *Coalition formation.*

Formation, concept. See *Concept formation.*

Formation, group. See *Group formation.*

Formation, impression. See *Impression formation.*

Formation, policy. See *Policy Making.*

Formation, reaction. See *Reaction formation.*

Formation, spiritual. See *Spiritual formation.*

Formation, theory. See *Theory formation.*

Former spouses. Former spouse(s). Formerly married. Exhusband(s). Exwife. Exwives. *Choose from:* former, first, second *with:* wife, wives, husband(s), spouse(s). *See also* Divorce; Remarriage; Stepfamily.

Former Yugoslav republics. Former Yugoslav republic(s). *Consider also:* Federal Republic of Yugoslavia, Ex-Yugoslav republic(s), Ex-Yugoslavia(n), Slovenia(n), Croatia(n), Bosnia Herzegovina, Macedonia(n), Serbia(n), Montenegr(o,an). *See also* Eastern Europe.

Formes fixes. Formes fixes. *Consider also:* ballade(s,n), rondeau(x), virelai, bergerette(s). *See also* Ballata; Medieval music; Music; Virelai.

Forms. Form(s). Form letter(s). Tax form(s). Application form(s). Data sheet(s). Questionnaire(s). Boilerplate. Entry blank(s). *See also* Boilerplate; Documents.

Forms, alternative family. See *Alternative family forms.*

Forms of affection. Form(s) of affection. Affectionate(ly). *Choose from:* form(s), demonstration(s), show(s,ed,ing), gesture(s) *with:* affection, endearment, love, warmth. *Consider also:* hug(s,ged,ging), kiss(ed,ing), air kiss(ed,ing), lovemaking, touch(ed,ing), listen(ed,ing). *See also* Affection; Caregivers; Human courtship; Love; Touch.

Formula, infant. See *Infant formula.*

Formulas. Formula(s). Formular(y,ies). Recipe(s). Prescription(s). *Consider also:* antidotar(y,ies), direction(s), specification(s). *See also* Methods.

Fornication. See *Extramarital relationships; Premarital sexual behavior.*

Fortification. Fortif(y,ied,ication,ions). Buttress(ed,ing). Reinforce(d,ment). Walled cit(y,ies). Fort(s). Fortress(es). Augment(ed,ing,ation). Brac(e,ed,ing). Buoy(ed,ing). Enhanc(e,ed,ing,ement, ements). Intensif(y,ied,ication). Enrich(ed,ing,ment). Invigorat(e,ed, ing,ion). *Consider also:* siege warfare, fortified cit(y,ies), garrison(s). *See also* Defense (Military science); Intensification; Protection; Security; Siege warfare.

Fortitude. Fortitude. Sufferance. Patien(t,ce). Endur(e,ed,ing,ance). Long suffering. Forbearance. Strength. Courage(ous). Staying power. Backbone. Grit(ty,tiness). Guts. Spunk(y,iness). Mettle(some). Resolute(ness). Tenacity. Brave(ry). Dauntless(ness). Fearless(ness). Intrepid(ity). Valorous(ness). Stamina. Determin(e,ed,ation). Perseverance. Strength of mind. *Consider also:* intestinal fortitude. *See also* Cardinal virtues; Endurance; Patience; Physical fitness; Psychological endurance; Well being.

Fortune. See *Chance; Destiny; Fate; Wealth.*

Fortune telling. See *Divination.*

Forums. See *Courts; Date; Public meetings.*

Fossils. Fossil(s,ized,ization). *Consider also:* paleontolog(y,ical), petrified remains, petrified wood, petrification. Caution: fossil may appear as "fossil fuels." *See also* Animal remains (Archaeology); Archaeology; Paleo-

botany; Paleodontology; Paleography; Paleopathology; Plant remains (archaeology); Prehistoric people.

Foster (promote). Foster(ed,ing). Promot(e,ed,ing,ion,ional). Advoca(te, cy). Cultivat(e,ed,ing,ion). Sustain(ed, ing). Encourag(e,ed,ing,ement). *Consider also:* cherish(ed,ing), nourish(e,ed,ing,ment), nurtur(ed,ing), support(ed,ing), uphold(ed,ing), shelter(ed,ing), accommodat(ed,ing), patroniz(e,ed,ing), assist(ed,ing).*See also* Advocacy; Facilitation; Leadership; Protection; Social facilitation; Social reinforcement.

Foster care, adult. See *Adult foster care.*

Foster children. Foster child(ren). *Choose from:* child(ren), juvenile(s), minor(s), boy(s), girl(s) *with:* foster, temporary placement. *Consider also:* foster parent(s). *See also* Adopted children; Foster home care; Foster parents.

Foster day care. See *Foster home care; Child day care; Adult day care; Corporate day care.*

Foster home care. Foster home care. *Choose from:* foster *with:* home(s), placement, parent(s), famil(y,ies), mother(s), grandparent(s), care. Custodianship. *See also* Adult foster care; Child day care.

Foster parents. Foster parent(s). *Choose from:* foster *with:* parent(s,hood), famil(y,ies), mother(s), father(s). *Consider also:* foster care, foster home(s), informal(ly) adopt(ed,ion), surrogate parent(s), foster grandparent(s), substitute famil(y,ies), foster placement(s). *See also* Caregivers; Foster children; Foster home care; Parents.

Foundations (organizations). Foundation(s). Philanthropic organization(s). Charitable trust(s). Fellowship program(s). *Choose from:* philanthropic, charitable, benevolent, humane, arts, humanities, educational *with:* association(s), institute(s), organization(s), societ(y,ies). *Consider also:* endowment(s), nonprofit organization(s), trusteeship(s). *Consider names of specific foundations such as:* Ford Foundation, National Science Foundation, etc. *See also* Art patronage; Endowment of research; Endowments; Grants; Nongovernmental organizations; Nonprofit organizations; Philanthropy.

Founders. See *Creators.*

Founding. Found(ed,ing). Establish(ed,ing, ment). Start(ed,ing). Creat(e,ed,ing). Originat(e,ed,ing). Organiz(e,ed,ing). Incorporat(e,ed,ing,ion). Construct(ed, ing,ion). Lay(ing) foundation. Laid foundation. *See also* Business incubators; Creation; Creators; Entrepreneurship; Etiology; Incorporation; Program implementation; Start up business; Venture capital.

Foundlings. Foundling(s). Abandoned infant(s). *Choose from:* infant(s), newborn(s), bab(y,ies) *with:* abandon(ed,ing,ment), desert(ed,ing). *Consider also:* orphan(s). *See also* Abandoned children; Child neglect; Unwanted children.

Four Dragons. See *Newly industrializing economies.*

Fourth world. See *Least developed countries.*

Fowling. Fowl(ing,er,ers). Hunt(ing,ed) wildfowl. Bird hunting. *Choose from:* hunt(ing,ed,er,ers), kill(ed,ing) *with:* wildfowl, waterfowl, wild bird(s), wildlife, water bird(s). *See also* Duck hunting; Game and game birds; Hunting; Poaching; Sports.

Fragmentation (experience). Fragment(ed,ing,ation,ary). Fractured. Scattered. Piecemeal. Disconnected(ness). Detach(ed,ment). Discontinu(ous,ity,ities). *See also* Absurd; Alienation; Detachment; Disengagement; Impersonal; Info fatigue syndrome; Modern society; Postmodernism; Social disorganization.

Fragmentation (schizophrenia). Fragmentation schizophren(ia,ic). *Choose from:* fragment(ed,ation), bizarre, disordered schizophrenic *with:* thinking, thought(s). *See also* Schizophrenia; Thought disturbances.

Fragmentation (social). See *Social disorganization.*

Fragments. Fragment(s). Bit(s). Chip(s). Chunk(s). Piece(s). Particle(s). Shard(s). Smithereen(s). Splinter(s). Sliver(s). Scrap(s). Remnant(s). Remainder(s). Crumb(s). Snippet(s). Shred(s). *Consider also:* morsel(s), section(s). *See also* Debris; Ruins; Scrap materials.

Frail elderly. Frail elder(s,ly). *Choose from:* elder(s,ly), geriatric, advanced age, older people, old age, senior citizen(s), older person(s), old(er) men, old(er) women, old(cr) man, old(cr) woman *with:* frail(ty), vulnerab(le,ility), weak(ness), infirmit(y,ies), susceptib(le,ility), brittle, fragile, dependen(t,cy), dilit(y,ies), at risk. *See also* Aged 80 and over; Elderly.

Frame of reference. Frame(s) of reference. Presupposition(s). Viewpoint(s). *See also* Context; Worldview.

Frames (physical). Frame(s,work,works). Casing(s). Chass(is,es). Groundwork(s). Hull(s). Rafter(s). Girder(s). Beam(s). Underpinning(s). Scaffold(s,ing). Shell(s). Skeleton(s). Shape(s). *Consider also:* structure(s), substructure(s), groundwork, curtain stretcher(s), loom(s), rack(s), outline(s). *See also* Boundaries; Designs; Format; Ground-

work; Morphology; Skeleton; Structure.

Framework. See *Paradigms.*

Franchises (commercial). Franchis(e,es,ed, ee,ees,or,ors,ing). Multifranchise(s). Refranchise(s). *Consider also:* chain store(s), restaurant chain(s), fast food chain(s). *See also* Business organizations; Small businesses.

Frankness. See *Honesty.*

Fraternities. Fraternit(y,ies). Greek letter societ(y,ies). Greek organization(s). Greek membership. Fraternal organization(s). Grcck systcm. *Consider also:* sororit(y,ies), brotherhood(s). *See also* Associations (organizations); Clubs; School clubs; Societies (organizations); Sororities.

Fraud. Fraud(ulence,ulent). Bad faith. Bait and switch. Bilk(ed,ing). Charlatan(s). Cheat(ed,er,ers,ing). Chicanery. Collusion. Con man. Confidence game(s). Counterfeit. Deceit(ful). Deceiv(e,ed,ing). Decept(ion,ions,ive). Defraud(ed,ing). Dishonest(y). Double-dealing. Embezzl(e,ed,ing,ement). Fak(e,ed,ery,eries,ing). False account(s). False advertising. False claim(s). False data. False pretense(s). Falsif(y,ied, ication). Graft. Grifter(s). Factifudging. Flim-flam. Flimflam. Forger(ies,y). Fudg(e,ing) data. Hoax(es). Imposter(s). Improper(ly) label(s,ed,ing). Improper(ly) labell(ed,ing). Insider trading. Inveigl(e,ed,ing). Kickback(s). Kiting. Lapping. Mislead(ing). Misled, Misrepresent(ed,ing,ation). Payola. Phony. Pirated edition(s). Puffery. Ripoff(s). Scam(s). Sharp practice(s). Shell game(s). Skimocrac(y,ies). Subterfuge(s). Swindl(e,ed,ing,er,ers). Switch selling. Tax evasion. Unsubstantiated claim(s). Wooden nickel(s). *See also* Cheating; Clandestinity; Collusion; Consumer fraud; Corruption in government; Debit card fraud; Deception; Falsification (scientific); Fraudulent advertising; Misinformation; Quackery; Unethical conduct; Victimization.

Fraud, consumer. See *Consumer fraud.*

Fraud, debit card. See *Debit card fraud.*

Fraud, literary. See *Literary forgeries and mystifications.*

Fraud, scientific. See *Falsification (scientific).*

Fraudulent advertising. Fraudulent advertis(ing,ement,ements). Fraud(ulence,ulent). *Choose from:* misrepresent(ed,ing,ation), misleading, phon(y,iness), decept(ive,ion), deceiv(e,ed,ing), deceit(ful), false, quackery *with:* media, ad(s), advertis(ing,ment,ments), commercial(s), promotion(s,al), solicitation(s). False claim(s). Improper(ly) label(s,ed,ing). Improper(ly)

labell(ed,ing). *See also* Advertising; Business ethics; Comparative advertising; Consumer fraud; Product labeling; Unethical conduct.

Free, cost. See *Gratis.*

Free, nuclear. See *Nuclear weapons nonproliferation.*

Free association. Free association. Spontaneous thought(s). *Consider also:* associative process(es), Freudian analy(sis,ses). *See also* Imagination; Psychoanalysis.

Free enterprise. See *Market economy; Private enterprise.*

Free love. See *Sexual permissiveness.*

Free press and fair trial. See *Freedom of the press; Fair trial; Trial (law).*

Free recall. Free recall. Associative retrieval. *Choose from:* recall(ed,ing), response(s), respond(s,ing), retrieval *with:* free(ly), associat(ive,ion,ions). *See also* Learning; Recall.

Free schools. See *Nontraditional education.*

Free speech. See *Freedom of speech.*

Free thought. Free thought. Freethought. Free-thought. Freethink(er,ers,ing). Skeptic(al,ism). Open-minded(ness). *Consider also:* secular human(ism,ist), rationalis(t,m), church-state separation, secular thought. *See also* Academic freedom; Bill of rights; Civil rights; Freedom of information; Freedom of speech; Intellectual liberty.

Free time. See *Leisure time.*

Free trade. Free trade. Open trade. *Choose from:* trade, market(s,place), import(s), export(s), commerce *with:* liberaliz(e,ed, ing,ation), expan(sion,d,ded,ding), free, open, unrestricted, unhampered, competitive(ness), agreement(s). *Consider also:* trade war(s). *See also* Custom unions; Economic union; Exports; Foreign trade zones; Harmonization (trade); Imports; International economic integration; International economic organizations; International trade; Minimal government; Nontariff trade barriers; Trade preferences.

Free trade zones. See *Foreign trade zones.*

Free universities. See *Nontraditional education.*

Free will. See *Volition.*

Freed slaves. See *Freedmen.*

Freedmen. Freed(men,man). Freed slave(s). Ex-slave(s). Freedom of slave(s). Former slave(s). Free people of color. *Consider also:* emancipation, born into slavery, fugitive slave(s), found(ed,ing) Liberia, reconstruction, postbellum South, sui juris. *See also* Abolitionists; Civil rights; Emancipation; Fugitive slaves; Slavery.

Freedom. Free(dom). Emancipat(ed,ion). Right(s). Libert(y,ies). Autonom(y,ous). Sovereign state. Sovereignty. Liberat(ed,ion). Independen(t,ce). Self govern(ing,ment). Self determinat(ing, ion). Self rule. Liberat(ed,ion,ing). Free will. Democra(cy,tic). Bill of Rights. Civil rights. Suffrage. Enfranchise(d, ment). Glasnost. *See also* Autonomy (government); Bill of Rights; Choice (psychology); Civil Rights; Democracy; Emancipation; Freedom (theology); Human rights; Liberty; Personal independence; Political self determination.

Freedom (theology). Divine freedom. God's freedom. Freedom to love. De servo arbitrio. Act(ing,ion) in accord(ance) with reason(s). Act(ing, ion) in accord(ance) with God. *Consider also:* freedom of the will, liberum arbitrium, scholastic(ism). *See also* Action; Awareness; Choice (psychology); Choice behavior; Decision making; Existentialism; Freedom; Intentionality; Personalism; Theology; Volition; Voluntarism (philosophy).

Freedom, academic. See *Academic freedom.*

Freedom, intellectual. See *Academic freedom; Civil rights; Freedom of information; Freedom of speech; Intellectual liberty.*

Freedom, religious. See *Freedom of religion.*

Freedom, sexual. See *Sexual permissiveness.*

Freedom of information. Freedom of information. Freedom of Information Act. Sunshine laws. Open government. Open records. Unclassified information. Public disclosure. Government accountability. Glasnost. Independent press. *Choose from:* free flow, access, right(s) *with:* information, files, data, document(s), know(ledge). *See also* Academic freedom; Access to information; Censorship; Civil rights; Classified information; Disclosure; Free thought; Freedom of speech; Government correspondence; Government secrecy; Information policy; News policies; Truth disclosure; Whistle blowing.

Freedom of religion. Freedom of religion. First amendment. Separation of church and state. *Choose from:* free(dom), liberty, tolerance, free exercise, neutral(ity), nondiscrimination, right(s), constitutional guarantee(s), equal protection *with:* religious, religion(s), conscience, worship, faith(s), creed(s), prayer. *See also* Church state relationship; Civil rights; Liberty of conscience; Religious prejudice; Religious refugees.

Freedom of speech. Freedom of speech. Free speech. First Amendment right(s).

Freedom of expression. Right to communicate. Equal time rule. Protected speech. *Consider also:* ban(s,ned,ning), censor(s,ed,ing,ship), regulat(e,ed,ing), limit(ed,ing,ation,ations), prohibit(ed, ing), control(led,ling), restrict(ed,ing), restrain(t,ts,ed,ing) *with:* speech, expression, communication, broadcast(s, ing), advertising, disclosure(s). *Consider also:* academic freedom, intellectual freedom, freedom to read, freedom to know, Library Bill of Rights, flag burning(s), libel, slander, gag order(s), doctrine of prior restraint, prepublication review(s), chilling effect(s), Meese Commission Report on Pornography. *See also* Academic freedom; Access to information; Bill of Rights; Censorship; Civil rights; Free thought; Freedom of information; Government secrecy; Information leaks; News policies; Right of assembly; Whistle blowing.

Freedom of the press. Freedom of the press. Independent newsroom(s). *Choose from:* press, journalis(t,ts,m), media, broadcast(s,er,ers,ing), reporter(s), newspaper(s), news agenc(y, ies), wire service(s), newsroom(s), publisher(s), news(men,man,women, woman), newsgather(ing,er,ers) *with:* free(dom) of speech, First Amendment right(s), freedom of expression, equal time rule, protected speech, ban(s,ned, ning), register(ed,ing), censor(s,ed,ing, ship), regulat(e,ed,ing), limit(ed,ing, ation,ations), prohibit(ed,ing), control(led,ling), restrict(ed,ing), fairness doctrine, muzzl(e,ed,ing), prior restrain(t,ts). *Consider also:* freedom to read, freedom to know, libel, slander, glasnost, gag order(s), prepublication review(s), chilling effect(s). *See also* Broadcasting censorship; Broadcasting policy; Censorship; Civil rights; Freedom of information; Freedom of speech; Government secrecy; Indecent communications; Information policy; Journalistic ethics; Libel; News policies.

Freedom of the seas. Freedom of the sea(s). *Choose from:* ship(s), shipowner(s), seafarer(s), sealane(s). international strait(s), shipping route(s), fishing water(s), seafaring, sailor(s), maritime, merchant marine(s), nav(y,ies), coast guard, ocean(s), sea(s), coastal water(s), international water(s), navigational *with:* freedom, access, right(s), neutral(ity). *See also* Maritime law; Maritime war.

Freedom of worship. See *Freedom of religion.*

Freelance. See *Contract labor.*

Freight. Freight(age). Cargo(s). Shipment(s). Lading(s). Payload(s). Load(s). Ship(ped,ping) goods. Carload(s). Boatload(s). *Consider also:* shipping cost(s), parcel service(s), air freight, forwarder(s), deferred delivery, third day delivery. *See also* Air freight; Cargo; Cargo handling; Carriers (shipping); Shipping industry.

Freight, air. See *Air freight.*

French songs. French song(s). Chanson(s). *Choose from:* French, Franc(e,aise,o), Paris(ian) *with:* song(s), folk music, melod(y,ies), tune(s), chanson(s), chant(s), cantique(s), hymne(s). *Consider also:* chanteur(s), trouvere song(s), chanteuse(s). *See also* Ballads; Folk songs; Songs.

Frequencies. See *Rates.*

Frequency, response. See *Response frequency.*

Frequency, word. See *Word frequency.*

Frequency distribution. Frequency distribution(s). *Choose from:* statistical, normal, skew(ed), sampling, chi square(d), binomial, beta, gamma, F shaped, T shaped, L shaped, J shaped, symmetric, asymmetric, population *with:* distribution(s). *Consider also:* distribution *with:* frequenc(y,ies). *See also* Statistical norms.

Frequently. Frequent(ly,ness). Often(times). Oft. Many times. Repeatedly. Constant(ly). Commonly. Continual(ly). Customar(y,ily). Habitual(ly). Daily. Persistent(ly). Usual(ly). Recurrently. *See also* Daily; Familiarity; Habits; Incidence; Prevalence; Rates; Transience.

Friars. Friar(s). Mendicant(s). Monk(s). *See also* Holy men; Monasticism; Monks; Religious life.

Friendliness. Friendl(y,iness). Affab(le, ility). Amicab(le,ility). Amiab(le,ility). Congenial(ity). Neighborl(y,iness). Sociab(le,ility). Companionab(le,ility). Easygoing(ness). Good-natured(ness). Comrade(ly,liness). *Consider also:* sympathetic, gemutlichkeit, approachable(ness), warmhearted(ness), gracious(ness), cordial(ity), courteous(ness), polite(ness), considerate(ness). *See also* Affection; Affiliation motivation; Benevolence; Comfortableness; Friendship; Goodwill; Gregariousness; Kindness; Likability; Personality traits.

Friendship. Friend(s,ship,ships). Companion(s,ship,ships). Confidant(s). Pal(s). Budd(y,ies). Social bond(s). Social tie(s). Social relationship(s). Comrade(s,ship). Peer acceptance. Friendly relationship(s). *Consider also:* interpersonal attraction, affinity, neighborly, social network(s), popularity, sociometric status, brotherhood. *See also* Friendliness; Interpersonal relations; Peer relations; Popularity; Significant others; Social dating; Social life; Social support.

Fright, stage. See *Stage fright.*

Frigidity. Frigid(ity). Anorgasm(y). Anorgastic. Sexual(ly) unresponsive(ness). Orgasmic dysfunction. Nonorgasmic. *Consider also:* anhedonia, coldness. *See also* Dyspareunia; Female orgasm; Imperviousness; Sexual function disorders; Vaginismus.

Fringe, urban. See *Urban fringe.*

Fringe benefits. See *Employee benefits.*

Frivolity. Frivol(ity,ous,ousness,ously). Light hearted(ness). Gaiety. Foolish(ness). Gidd(y,iness). Levity. Shallow(ness). Playful(ness). Flight(y,iness). Sill(y,iness). *See also* Cheerfulness; Comedians; Fools and jesters; Humor; Humorous songs; Laughter

Frogs. Frog(s). Ran(a,id,idae). Xenopus. Rana pipiens. *Consider also:* diplasiocoela, spring peeper(s), leopard frog(s). *See also* Amphibia; Animal studies; Reptiles.

Frontier and pioneer life. Frontier life. Pioneer life. Border life. *Choose from:* pioneer(s), early settler(s), homesteader(s), cattleman, frontier(s), American west, borderland(s), *with:* spirit, life, famil(y,ies), myth(s), culture, American character, personal stor(y,ies), local recipe(s), experience(s), small town(s), societ(y,ies), dwelling(s), women, hardship(s), *Consider also:* bushrat(s), homesteading, wagon train(s), homespun, westward movement. *See also* Explorers; Frontier thesis; Pioneers; Pioneering; Settlers.

Frontier thesis. Frontier thesis. Frontier hypothesis. Frontier theory. Turner thesis. *Consider also:* Frederick Jackson Turner. *See also* Boundaries; Frontier and pioneering life; Frontiers; Geopolitics; Land settlement; Pioneering; Pioneers.

Frontiers. Frontier(s). Border(s). Borderland(s). Perimeter(s). Boundar(y,ies). Edge(s). Outline(s). Verge(s). Rim(s). Outer limit(s). Outpost(s). Peripher(y,ies). Far(ther) reaches. Fringe(s). Unexplored. Unsettled. *Consider also:* free land(s), edge of settlement(s). *See also* Areas; Borderlands; Colonization; Frontier thesis; Historic geography; Land settlement.

Fronts, national. See *National fronts.*

Frottola. Frottol(a,e). *Consider also:* barzellett(a,e), oda, capitolo, strambotto, rispett(i,o). *See also* Ballata; Medieval music; Music; Renaissance music.

Frugality. Frugal(ity,ness). Careful management. Economiz(e,ed,ing). Parsimon(y,ious,iousness). Penurious(ness). Sparing(ness). Sting(y,iness). Temperance. Thrift(y,iness). Scrimping. Miserl(y,iness). *Consider also:* self-

den(ying,ial), self-restraint, penny-pinching. *See also* Abstinence; Misers; Prudence; Saving; Thriftiness.

Fruit. Fruit(s,ed). *Consider also:* apple(s), orange(s), pear(s), banana(s), melon(s), peach(es), nectarine(s), blackberr(y,ies), raspberr(y,ies), pineapple(s), etc. *Consider also:* pea pod(s), nut(s), tomato(es). *See also* Citrus fruits; Flowers; Food; Grapes.

Fruits, citrus. See *Citrus fruits*

Frustration. Frustrat(e,ed,ing,ion,ions). Denial of gratification. Thwarted. Disappoint(ed,ment). Defeated. Foiled. Nonreward(ing). Non-reward(ing). Nonreinforcement. Counterconditioning. *See also* Boredom; Confusion; Coping; Dissatisfaction.

Fuel. Fuel(s). Combustible matter. Wood. Coal. Gas(oline). Natural gas. Oil. Petrol(eum). Kerosene. Peat. Buffalo chip(s). Kindling. Tinder. *Consider also:* fuel cell(s), power, diesel fuel. *See also* Alternative energy; Coal; Combustibility; Electric power plants; Energy; Energy generating resources; Nonrenewable resources; Nuclear energy; Nuclear power plants; Offshore oil; Renewable resources; Waste to energy.

Fuels, alcohol. See *Alternative energy.*

Fugitive slaves. Fugitive slave(s). Runaway slave(s). *Choose from:* slave(s), African(s), enslaved people *with:* fugitive(s), runaway, ran away, fled, escape(es,d), route to freedom, led to freedom. *Consider also:* Harriet Tubman, Underground Railroad. *See also* Abolitionists; Emancipation; Freedmen, Maroons; Slavery.

Fugitives. Fugitive(s). Runaway(s). Deserter(s). Escapee(s). AWOL. Absconder(s). Wanderer(s). Vagabond(s). Truant(s). *See also* Missing persons; Runaways.

Fugitives from justice. Fugitive(s) from justice. Escaped criminal(s). Most wanted. Jumped bail. *Choose from:* fugitive(s), aggravated escape, flight, fled, manhunt, elude(s) police detection, hiding *with:* justice, sentenc(e,ed,ing), arrest(s,ed,ing), apprehend(ed), charged, extradition, arraignment, arrest warrant(s), anti-government. *See also* Arrests; Contempt of Court; Convicts; Fugitives.

Fugue reaction. Fugue reaction. Fugue(s). *Consider also:* long-term amnesia, multiple personalit(y,ies), dissociative disorder(s). *See also* Amnesia; Dissociative disorders; Memory disorders; Thought disturbances; Epilepsy; Forgetting.

Fulfilling prophecy, self. See *Self fulfilling prophecy.*

Fulfillment. Fulfill(ing,ed,ment). Satisf(y,ying,ied,action). Bliss(ful). Comfort(able). Content(ed,ment). Delight(ed). Enjoyment. Gratif(y,ied, ication). Glad(ness). Happ(y,iness). Morale. Meaningful(ness). Opinion(s). Orgasm(s,ic). Peace of mind. Peak experience(s). Pleasure. Pride. Rating(s). Relief. Self-efficacy. Values. Well-being. *See also* Climax; Happiness; Satiation; Self actualization; Self esteem.

Full-scale. See *Comprehensiveness.*

Full-text databases. Full-text database(s). Full text data base(s). Electronic text(s). *Choose from:* full-text, electronic *with:* journal(s), database(s), data base(s), newsletter(s), magazine(s), record(s), book(s), newspaper(s), title(s), article(s), *Consider also:* full-text retrieval. *See also* Databases; Electronic books; Electronic publishing; Electronic journals; Transmission of texts.

Function. Function(al,s). Eufunction(al,s). Dysfunction(al,s). Role(s). Activit(y,ies). Purpose(s). Process(es). Perform(ed,ing, ance). Use(s). Dut(y,ies). Assignment(s). Mission(s). Operation(s,al). Operat(ive, ing). Service(able,ability). Utilit(y,ies, arian). *See also* Activities of daily living; Behavior; Functionalism; Roles.

Function, loss of. See *Loss of function.*

Function, social. See *Function; Functionalism.*

Function disorders, sexual. See *Sexual function disorders.*

Functional hearing loss. Functional hearing loss. *Choose from:* functional(ly), psychogenic, nonorganic *with:* deaf(ness), hearing loss(es), hearing disorder(s), hearing disabilit(y,ies), hearing impairment(s), deaf(ness). *See also* Conversion disorder; Somatoform disorders.

Functional imperatives. Functional imperative(s). Functional prerequisite(s). Functional requisite(s). *See also* Needs; Structural imperatives.

Functionalism. Functionalis(m,t,ts,tic). Functional theor(y,ies). Functional approach. Structur(e,al) function(al). Macrofunctional(ism). Holis(m,tic). Microfunctional(ism). *Consider also:* dysfunction(al), eufunction(al), interelated(ness), interact(ion,ing), interdependen(t,ce), system theory, organic model(s). *See also* Evolution; Function; Holism; Social theories; Teleology.

Functioning, intellectual. See *Cognitive ability.*

Functions, management. See *Management functions.*

Fund. See *Financing.*

Fund management, pension. See *Pension fund management.*

Fund raising. Fund raising. Fundraising. Financ(e,ial) campaign(s). Financ(e,ial) drive(s). Church canvas(es). Bond drive(s). Philanthropic fund(s). Grantsmanship. *Choose from:* fund(s), financial, money, contribution(s), soft money, hard money *with:* rais(e,ed,er, ers,ing), campaign(s,ed,ing), gift(s), pledge(s), donat(ed,ing,ion,ions), bequest(s), solicit(ing,ed), giving, philanthrop(y,ic). *See also* Art patronage; Charities; Donations; Financial support; Political campaigns; Scholarships (educational).

Fundamental. Fundamental(s). Basic(s). Underlying. Foundation(al). Vital. Essential(ly). Essence(s). Intrinsic(ally). *Consider also:* groundwork, quintessence, elixir, sine qua non, pith(y,iness), crux, principle(s). *See also* Assumptions; Essence; Essence (philosophy); Principles.

Fundamentalism, Islamic. See *Islamic fundamentalism*

Fundamentalism, religious. See *Religious fundamentalism.*

Funding. See *Financial support; Government financing; Organized financing; Personal financing.*

Funding, federal. See *Government financing.*

Fundraising. See *Fund raising.*

Funds. Funds. *Choose from:* available, ready, pocket *with:* money, cash. *Consider also:* asset(s), bank account(s), capital, endowment(s), grant(s), treasury, coffer(s), savings, nest egg(s). *See also* Assets; Liquidity; Money; Money supply.

Funds, campaign. See *Campaign funds.*

Funeral hymns. *See Funeral music.*

Funeral music. Funeral hymn(s). Dirge(s). *Consider also:* requiem mass(es), funeral march(es), tonos de velorio. *See also* Church music; Funeral rites; Hymns; Religious music.

Funeral rites. Funeral rite(s). Requiem(s). Obsequ(y,ies). Eulog(y,ies). *Choose from:* funeral, dead, death, burial, memorial *with:* rite(s), service(s), ceremon(y,ies), mass(es). *Choose from:* Kaddish *with:* yahrzeit, jahrzeit. *Consider also:* averil(s), Missa pro defunctis, Dies irae, wake(s), velorio, vela. *See also* Death; Death rituals; Fetal propitiatory rites; Funeral music; Obituaries.

Funk (music). Funk(y). *Choose from:* earthy, sexual, danceable, gospel influence *with:* music, recording(s), jazz. *Consider also:* soul jazz, hard bop, rhythm and blues. *See also* Afro-American music; Jazz.

Fur. Fur(s,ry,riness). Fur coat(s). Animal skin(s). Pelt(s). Mink coat(s). Sheepskin. *Consider also:* furrier(s), leather(s). *See also* Animal products; Anti-fur protests; Body covering (Anatomy); Hair; Fur trade; Leather industry.

Fur trade. Fur trade(r,rs). Fur trapper(s). Fur(s). *Choose from:* trapper(s), trade(r,rs), market(s,ing,place), provide(d,ing,er,ers), economic(s) *with:* fur(s), beaver(s), marten(s), mink(s). *Consider also:* Hudson's Bay Company. *See also* Anti-fur protests; Fur; Trapping.

Furnishings, house. See *House furnishings.*

Furniture. Furniture. Furnishing(s). Household goods. *Consider also:* chair(s), table(s), bed(s), dresser(s), sofa(s), couch(es), bureau(s), bookcase(s), desk(s). *See also* Bedding; Decorative arts; Designs; Environment; Fashions; Housing; Material culture.

Future. Future(s). Prospect(s,ive). Outlook(s). Prognosis. Coming. Forthcoming. Impending. Pending. Predict(ed,ion,ions). Approaching. Imminent. Tomorrow. Futuristic. Year 2010, 2020, etc. 21st Century. Scenario(s). Coming decade(s). Third millenium. Next century. *See also* Forecasting; Future of society; Historical periods; Imminent; Impending; Prediction; Technological change; Technological progress; Trends; Workforce planning.

Future interests. Future interest(s). Future estate(s). Interest(s) of future generation(s). *Consider also:* probate(s,d), will(s). *See also* Wills.

Future life. See *Immortality.*

Future of society. Future(s) of society. Futuristic(s). *Choose from:* future(s), prospect(s,ive), outlook(s), prognosis, coming, forthcoming, impending, pending, predict(ed,ions), approaching, imminent, tomorrow, futuristic, Year 2000, 21st Century, progress, scenario(s), coming decade(s), third millenium, next century *with:* society, human race, civilization, mankind, humankind, humanity, world, earth, human community. *See also* Appropriate technologies; Cultural lag; Developing countries; Future orientation; Imminent; Planning; Political forecasting; Regression (civilization); Relevance; Social change; Social indicators; Sustainable development; Technological change; Technological forecasting; Technological progress; Trends; Workforce planning.

Future orientation. Future orientation(s). Scenario(s). Delphi technique(s). Anticipat(e,ing,ion,ions). Expectation(s). Threat(s). Hop(e,es,ing). Worr(y,ies). Optimis(m,tic). Pessimis(m,tic). Prospect(s,ive). Outlook(s). Prognosis. Predict(ed,ion,ions). Plan(s,ning). Utopian. *Choose from:* future, coming, forthcoming, impending, pending, approaching, imminent, tomorrow, futuristic, year 2000, 2010, etc., 21st Century, coming decade(s), third millenium, next century, progress *with:* concept(s,ion,ions), intent(ion,ions), implication(s), perspective(s), view(s), direction(s), trend(s), possibilit(y,ies), orientation(s), opinion(s), apprehens(ion,ive), postulate(s), conjecture. *See also* Development; Future of society; Generativity; Imminent; Optimism; Perceptions; Pessimism; Time.

Future punishment. Future punishment. Endless punishment. Everlasting punishment. Eternal punishment. Damn(ed,ation). Fear of death. Underworld. Hell. *See also* Afterworld; Hell; Punishment.

Futures market. Futures market(s). Commodities market(s). Forward market(s). Futures contract(s). *Consider also:* contingent pricing, Chicago Board of Trade, Chicago Mercantile Exchange, Chicago Rice and Cotton Exchange, Coffee Sugar and Cocoa Exchange, Commodity Exchange, International Monetary Market, Kansas City Board of Trade, MidAmerica Commodity Exchange, Minneapolis Grain Exchange, New York Futures Exchange, New York Mercantile Exchange, Philadelphia Board of Trade. *See also* Grain trade; Investments; Markets; Stock Exchange.

Futurism (Art). Futuris(m,t,tic) art. *Consider also:* futurism(o,i), cubo-futurism, futuris(m,t,tic) fashion(s), Filippo Tommaso Marinetti, Gino Severini, Umberto Boccioni, Carlo Carra, Antonio Sant' Elia, Luigi Russolo, Giacomo Balla, Mikhail Larionov, Natalia Goncharova, Kasimir Malevich. *See also* Cubism; Dadaism; Fascism; Futurism (Literary movement); Futurism (music); Modern art.

Futurism (Literary movement). Futuris(m,tic) litera(ture,ry). Futuris(m,tic) work(s). Futuristic poe(try,m,ms). *Consider also:* Filippo Tommaso Marinetti, Mina Loy, Guillaume Apollinaire, Ezra Pound, Gerardo Diego, Antonio Espina, Velimir Khlnikov, Vladimir Mayakovsky. *See also* Cubism; Futurism (Art); Futurism (music); Literary movements.

Futurism (music). Futurism. Futurismo. Musica futuristica. *Consider also:* Francesco Pratella, Luigi Russolo. *See also* Futurism (art); Futurism (Literary movement); Twentieth century Western art music.

Futurology. See *Forecasting.*

G

Gadgets. See *Appliances; Devices; Equipment; Tools.*

Gain, weight. See *Weight gain.*

Gains. Gain(s). Capital gain(s). Achievement(s). Acquistion(s). Appreciat(e,ed,ing,ion). Attainment(s). Benefit(s). Dividend(s). Earning(s). Growth. Harvest(s). Income. Increase(s) Increment(s). Proceeds. Profit(s). Receipts. Returns. Winning(s). Yield(s). *See also* Business; Capital (financial); Dividends; Earnings; Income; Investments; Monetary incentives; Profitability; Profits.

Gains, achievement. See *Achievement gains.*

Gains, epinosic. See *Secondary gains.*

Gains, secondary. See *Secondary gains.*

Galleries. Galler(y,ies). Art galler(y,ies). Exhibition hall(s). Exhibition room(s). Museum(s). Showroom(s). Salon(s). Consider also: auction galler(y,ies), Swann Galleries, Sotheby Parke Bernet, Christie's East, Christie Manson and Woods, etc. *See also* Art museums; Auctions; Museums.

Galvanic skin response. Galvanic skin response. GSR. *Choose from:* psychogalvanic, electrodermal, skin conductance *with:* respons(e,es,ivity), reflex(es), activity. *Consider also:* Fere phenomenon, Fere method. *See also* Diagnosis; Lie detection.

Gamblers. See *Gambling; Pathological gambling.*

Gambling. Gambl(e,ed,er,ers,ing). Bet(s,tor,tors,ting). Game(s) of chance. Wager(s,ing). Poker. Casino(s). Blackjack. Lotter(y,ies). Risk taking. Risking. Pari mutuel. Monte carlo. Gaming house(s). Dice. Numbers racket. Playing the horses. *Consider also:* compulsive gambling, gamblers anonymous, sports betting, bookmaking. *See also* Casinos; Lotteries; Online gambling; Pathological gambling.

Gambling, online. See *Online gambling.*

Gambling, pathological. See *Pathological gambling.*

Game and game birds. Game. Game bird(s). Gamebird(s). Wild animal(s). Hunted bird(s). Pheasant(s). Quail(s). Goose. Geese. Wildfowl. Wildlife. Duck(s). Grouse. Free-range animal(s). Antelope(s). Wild boar(s). Deer. Bear(s). *Consider also:* big game. *See also* Deer; Duck hunting; Fowling; Game laws; Game protection; Hunting; Poaching; Wildlife sanctuaries.

Game laws. Game law(s). Hunting law(s). Fishing law(s). *Choose from:* hunt(s,ing), fish(ing), game, deer, moose, beaver(s), wildlife, cougar(s), bear, geese, duck(s), bison, seal(s), endangered species, big game, small game *with:* law(s), illegal, restriction(s), prohibit(ed,ing,ion), post(ed,ing) propert(y,ies), limit(s,cd,ing,ation), ban(s,ned,ning), regulation(s). *Consider also:* hunting season(s), game taboo(s), poach(ed,ing,er,ers), hunting license(s). *See also* Hunting; Game and game birds; Game protection; Poaching.

Game protection. Game protection. Bird protection. Gamekeep(ing,er,ers). Game reserve(s). Game preserve(s). *Choose from:* wildlife, waterfowl(s), wild animal(s), wild mammal(s), habitat(s), wetland(s), desert(s), whale(s), turtle(s), elephant(s), endangered species, deer, moose, beaver(s), cougar(s), lion(s), fox(es), stag(s), hare(s), bear, geese, duck(s), bison, buffalo(es), seal(s), eagle(s), pigeon(s), big game, small game *with:* protect(ed,ing,ion), predator management, preserv(e,ed,ing,ation), conservation, maintenance, maintain(ed,ing). *See also* Deer; Game and game birds; Game laws; Habitat; Hunting; Poaching; Wildlife sanctuaries.

Game theory. Game theor(y,ies,etic). *Choose from:* game(s), metagame(s) *with:* approach(es), theor(y,ies,etic), analys(is,es). *See also* Entrapment games; Simulation; Simulation games; Theories.

Games, adult. See *Adult games.*

Games, board. See *Board games.*

Games, children's. See *Children's games.*

Games, computer. See *Computer games.*

Games, electronic. See *Electronic games.*

Games, entrapment. See *Entrapment games.*

Games, experimental. See *Experimental games.*

Games, Greek and Roman. See *Greek and Roman games.*

Games, language. See *Word games.*

Games, linguistic. See *Word games.*

Games, non zero sum. See *Non zero sum games.*

Games, simulation. See *Simulation games.*

Games, word. See *Word games.*

Gamma alcoholism. Gamma alcoholism. *Choose from:* addictive, malignant, essential, regressive, idiopathic *with:* alcoholism. *See also* Alcoholism.

Gangs, juvenile. See *Juvenile gangs.*

Ganser syndrome. Ganser syndrome. Syndrome of approximate answers. Nonsense syndrome. *See also* Factitious disorders.

Gap, gender. See *Gender differences.*

Gap, generation. See *Generation gap.*

Garage sales. See *Secondhand trade*

Garbage. See *Solid waste.*

Garbage collectors. Garbage collector(s). Garbologist(s). Garbage(man,men,woman,women). Dust(man,men,woman,women). *Choose from:* sanitation, garbage *with:* crew(s), man, men, woman, women, personnel, staff(s), department(s), hauler(s), carter(s). *See also* Blue collar workers; Hazardous occupations; Sanitation; Waste disposal.

Garden structures. Garden structure(s). Garden architecture. Trellis(es). Garden(s) pagoda(s). *Consider also:* landscape architecture, garden design(s). *See also* Earthwork; Formal gardens; Landscape architecture.

Gardening. Garden(ing,er,ers). Horticultur(e,ist,ists). Landscap(e,er,ers,ing). *Choose from:* cultivat(e,ed,ing), caretaker(s) *with:* garden(s), plant(s), flower(s), tree(s). *Consider also:* yardwork, weed(ing), hoe(ing), prun(e,ed,ing), plant(ed,ing), rototill(ed,ing), till(ed,ing), seed(ed,ing), water(ed,ing), mulch(ed,ing), fertiliz(e,ed,ing), rak(e,ed,ing). *See also* Cultivated Plants; Farming; Gardening to attract wildlife; Gardens; Plant cultivation; Sanctuary gardens.

Gardening to attract wildlife. Gardening to attract wildlife. Wildlife friendly garden(s,ing). *Choose from:* garden(s,ing), backyard(s), back yard(s), plant(s,ing,ings), natural area(s), landscap(e,ed,ing), vegetation, flower(s), lawn(s), wildflower(s), native plant(s), horticulture *with:* wildlife, habitat(s), bird(s), butterfl(y,ies), animal(s), hummingbird(s) *Consider also:* bird feeder(s), attracting butterfl(y,ies), nectar from flower(s), food plant(s), host plant(s), bat house(s), bird house(s), chemical free lawn(s), perching branch(es), nesting material(s), seed producing flower(s), hummingbird feeder(s). *See also* Animal environments; Birds; Flowers; Gardens; Habitat; Human-animal relationships; Landscape architecture; Natural environment; Natural gardens; Sanctuary gardens; Wildlife conservation; Wildlife sanctuaries.

Gardens. Garden(s). Cultivated area(s). *Choose from:* vegetable, melon, potato, berry, tomato, taro *with:* patch(es), plot(s). *Consider also:* herb(s), rock, rose(s), victory, formal, kitchen, cactus, flower(s), vegetable(s) *with:* garden(s). *Consider also:* greenhouse(s), cold frame(s). *See also* Flowers; Food; Food supply; Formal gardens; Gardening to attract wildlife; Home grounds; Landscape architecture; Locally produced food; Natural gardens; Sanctuary gardens.

Gardens, formal. See *Formal gardens.*

Gardens, natural. See *Natural gardens.*

Gardens, sanctuary. See *Sanctuary gardens.*

Garment industry. Garment industr(y,ies). *Choose from:* garment, apparel, cloth(es,ing), fashion *with:* industr(y, ies), factor(y,ies), worker(s), production, manufactur(ers,ing). *Consider also:* piecework, sweatshop(s), seamstress(es), tailor(s), dressmak(ing,er,ers), needle trade(s). *See also* Clothing; Clothing workers; Fashions; Industry; Knit goods industry; Mannequins (Figures); Models (persons); Sweatshops.

Garrisons. Garrison(s). Military post(s). Military installation(s). Military stronghold(s). Fort(s). *Consider also:* military, army, marine *with:* base(s), station(s,ed). *See also* Armed forces; Military bases.

Gas. Gas(es,eous). Ether. Vapor(s). Exhaust(s). Air. *Consider also:* carbon monoxide, methane, etc. *See also* Fluids; Gas industry; Gas pipelines; Poisonous gases.

Gas, nerve. See *Chemical warfare.*

Gas industry. Gas industry. Gas utilit(y,ies). Gas producer(s). Natural gas market(s). Gas well(s). Gas plant(s). *Choose from:* gas *with:* industry, utilit(y,ies), producer(s), production, consumption, deliver(y,ies), stock(s), reservoir(s), import(s,ed,ing), export(s,ed,ing), distribut(ed,ing,ion), compan(y,ies), cooperative(s), pipeline(s), manufac-turer(s), process(ing,or,ors). *See also* Energy generating resources; Gas pipelines; Industry; Oil industry.

Gas manufacture. See *Gas industry.*

Gas pipelines. Gas pipeline(s). Methane pipeline(s). Alaska Pipeline(s). Gas trunk line(s). *Consider also:* gas grid(s), gas infrastructure, gas transport route(s), gas pipe(s), gas network(s), *See also* Gas; Gas industry

Gas warfare. See *Chemical warfare.*

Gases, poisonous. See *Poisonous gases.*

Gastrointestinal disorders. Gastrointestinal disorder(s). Gastrointestinal disease(s). *Choose from:* gastrointestinal, postgastrectomy, stomach, colon, GI, gastric, bowel(s), colorectal *with:* disease(s), disorder(s), symptom(s,atic, atology), ulcer(s), patholog(y,ical), disturbance(s), pain, hyperactivity, fistula(s), polyp(s), neoplasm(s), cancer(s), tumor(s), hemorrhage(s), syndrome(s), tuberculosis, bleeding, stress, distress, illness(es). *Consider also:* gastroenteritis, inguinal hernia(s), peptic ulcer(s), visceroptosis, vomiting, colitis, constipation, diarrhea, fecal incontinence, irritable bowel syndrome, milk intolerance, lactose intolerance, enteritis, rectocolitis, hiatus hernia(s), flatulen(t,ce), ulcerative colitis, Crohn(s) disease, dysentery, diverticulitis, ileitis, celiac disease. *See also* Colitis; Diges-tive system; Vomiting; Psychophysi-ologic disorders.

Gastrointestinal system. See *Digestive system.*

Gastronomy. Gastronom(y,e,er,ic,ical,ist). Culinary custom(s). Culinary art. Cook(ing,ery). Gourmet(s). Art of good eating. Epicure(an,anism). Bonne cuisine. Bon vivant(s). *See also* Connoisseurs; Cooking; Diet; Dinners and Dining; Eating.

Gatekeepers. Gatekeeper(s). Sentr(y,ies). Doorkeeper(s). *Consider also:* watch(man,men), guard(s), border security, border patrol(s), admission officer(s), ticket collector(s). *See also* Crime prevention; Entrances; Security guards.

Gateway drugs. Gateway drug(s). Gateway substance(s). *Choose from:* early experiment(s,ed,ing,ation), first use(s,d), used first, precondition, progress(ed,ing,ion), lead(ing) to abuse *with:* alcohol, wine, liquor, tobacco, cigarettes, marijuana, cannabis. *See also* Addiction; Alcoholism; Drug addicted babies; Drug addiction; Drug education; Drug tolerance; Drug use; Habituation (psychophysiology); Narcotics; Street drugs; Substance abuse; Substance dependence; Substance use disorders; Teenage suicide.

Gathering and hunting societies. See *Hunting and gathering societies.*

Gatherings, cooperative. See *Cooperation.*

Gatherings, religious. See *Religious gatherings.*

Gauchos. See *Cowboys.*

Gay. See *Homosexuality; Lesbianism; Male homosexuality.*

Gay couples. Gay couple(s). *Choose from:* gay, homosexual, lesbian *with:* couple(s), dyad(ic,s), commitment(s), committed relationship(s), courtship, intimate relation(s,ships), partner(s), cohabit(ing,ation), love relationship(s), steady dating, intimate(s), intimacy, marriage(s), married(s), close relationship(s), twosome(s), pair(s), lover(s), living together, significant other(s). *See also* Alternative family forms; Alternative lifestyles; Bisexuality; Homosexuality; Lesbianism; Sexual partners.

Gay liberation movement. See *Homo-sexual liberation movement.*

Gay men. See *Male homosexuality.*

Gay rights. See *Homosexual liberation movement.*

Gay women. See *Lesbianism.*

Gaze. Gaz(e,ed,ing). Stare(d). Gape(d). Look(ed) intent(ly). *See also* Eye contact; Observers.

GE-Pano-Carib languages. GE-Pano-Carib languages. Bororo. Carib. Caxibo. GE. Puelche. *See also* Caribbean; Language; Languages (as subjects); South America; South American native cultural groups.

Geisslerlieder. Geisslerlied(er). Flagellant song(s). *Consider also:* penitential flagellation *with:* song(s). *See also* German songs; Folk songs; Lauda.

Gemeinschaft and gesellschaft. Gemeinschaft and [und] gesellschaft. *Choose from:* folk, traditional, rural, agricultural *with* secular, urban, modern, industrial, post-industrial. *See also* Developed countries; Developing countries; Mass society; Modern society; Subsistence economy; Traditional societies; Western society.

Gems. Gem(s). Jewel(s,ry). Precious stone(s). Semiprecious stone(s). Semi-precious stone(s). *Consider also:* pearl(s), diamond(s), rub(y,ies), emerald(s), sapphire(s), etc. *See also* Collectibles; Glyptics; Jewelry; Treasure.

Gender bias. See *Sex discrimination; Sexual inequality; Sexism.*

Gender differences. Gender difference(s). Gender gap. Sex difference(s). Male(s) vs female(s). Female(s) vs male(s). Male female difference(s). Women vs men. Girls vs boys. Daughters vs sons. Mothers vs fathers. Male female comparison(s). *Choose from:* sex, gender, male(s) female(s), men women, boys(s) girl(s) *with:* differen(t,ce,ces, tials,tiation), contrast(ed,ing,s), compar(itive,isons,ability), discrepan(t,cy,cies), dissimilar(ity,ities), divers(e,ity), disparit(y,ies), distinct(iveness,ion,ions), inequal(ity, ities), variabilit(y,ies), variation(s), unequal, stereotype(s), correlate(d,s), dependent, link(ed,s,age), factor(s). *Consider also:* gendered speech, genderlect, gender conflict(s). *See also* Age differences; Androgyny; Females (animal); Females (human); Gender identity; Individual differences; Males (animal); Males (human); Physical characteristics; Sex discrimination; Sex roles; Sex stereotypes; Sexism; Sexual division of labor; Sexual inequality; Women's rights.

Gender discrimination. See *Labor market segmentation; Sex discrimination; Sexism; Sexual division of labor; Sexual inequality.*

Gender dysphoria. See *Transsexualism.*

Gender equality. See *Affirmative action; Comparable worth; Equity (payment); Fairness; Nonsexist language; Sex discrimination; Sexual division of labor; Sexual inequality; Social equality; Social equity.*

Gender equity. See *Affirmative action; Social equality; Social equity; Social justice.*

Gender fair education. See *Nonsexist education.*

Gender gap. See *Gender differences.*

Gender identity. Gender identity. Masculinity. Femininity. *Choose from:* sex(ual), gender, masculin(e,ity), feminin(e,ity), male, female, man(s), woman(s), men(s), women(s) *with:* role(s), identit(y,ies), orientation, identification, traits, behavior, stereotype(s), appearance. *Consider also:* androgyn(y,ous), machismo, macho, effemina(te,cy), tomboy(s), siss(y,ies). *See also* Engenderment; Gender differences; Images of women; Psychosexual development; Same sex; Self knowledge; Sex roles; Sexual orientation; Sexual preferences; Transsexualism.

Gender inequality. See *Sexual inequality.*

Gender roles. See *Sex roles.*

Gender stereotypes. See *Sex stereotypes.*

Gene mapping. Gene map(s,ping). Genome map(s,ping). Genetic map(s,ping). *Consider also:* chromosome map(s, ping), linkage map(s,ping), genom(e,ic) organization. *See also* Bioethics; Genetic engineering; Genetic research; Genetics; Pharmacogenomics; Single nucleotide polymorphisms.

Gene mapping, human. See *Gene mapping.*

Genealogy. Genealog(y,ies,ical). Pedigree(s). Family tree(s). Peerage. Nobility. Ancestral line(s). Lineage. Dynast(y,ies). Direct descen(t,dant,dants, dent,dents). Blood line(s). *Consider also:* heraldry, coat(s) of arms, heraldic register(s), family crest(s), family reconstitution. *See also* Ancestors; Descent; Family history; Heraldry; Kinship; Lineage; Local history.

General adaptation syndrome. General adaptation syndrome. Adaptation syndrome. *Consider also:* alarm reaction, stage of resistance, exhaustion stage. *See also* Defensive; Fear; Stress reactions.

General public. General public. Average man. Bourgeoisie. Citizens. Consumers. Common man. Commoner(s). Common people. Community. Folk. Grass roots. Humankind. Human race. Mankind. Man in the street. Masses. Middle America. Middle class(es). Multitudes. Peasant(ry,s). Populace. Population. Proletariat. Society. Third estate. Voters. Voting public. Working class(es). Ordinary people. *See also* Common people; Proletariat; Voters.

General welfare. See *Public good.*

General will. General will. Popular acquiescence. *Consider also:* direct democracy. *See also* Consensus; Legitimacy of governments.

Generalities. Generalit(y,ies). Abstraction(s). Abstract principle(s). Generalization(s). General law(s). General observation(s). General rule(s). Vague statement(s). Loose statement(s). Sweeping statement(s). *See also* Codes (rules); Cognitive generalization; Hypotheses; Laws; Norms; Principles; Rules (generalizations); Theories.

Generalization (psychology). See *Cognitive generalization; Concept formation; Reasoning; Response generalization.*

Generalization, cognitive. See *Cognitive generalization.*

Generalization, response. See *Response generalization.*

Generalizations, rules. See *Rules (generalizations).*

Generals. General(s,issimo). Military commander(s). Brigadier general(s). Lieutenant general(s). Major general(s). *See also* Army personnel; Authority (officials); Marine personnel; Military personnel.

Generating energy, resources. See *Energy generating resources.*

Generation, baby boom. See *Baby boom generation.*

Generation, baby bust. See *Post-baby boom generation.*

Generation, beat. See *Hippies.*

Generation, echo baby boom. See *Echo boom generation.*

Generation, echo boom. See *Echo boom generation.*

Generation, income. See *Earnings.*

Generation, net. See *Echo boom generation.*

Generation, post-baby boom. See *Post-baby boom generation.*

Generation, spontaneous. See *Spontaneous generation.*

Generation gap. Generation gap. Intergenerational conflict. Differences between generations. Cross generational changes. Adolescents vs their parents. Intergenerational reconciliation. *Choose from:* generation(al), transgenerational, multigenerational, intergeneration(al) *with:* gap, conflict, relation(s,ship,ships), differences, values, communication, discrepancies, changes, politics, war, disagreements, understanding, reconciliation. *See also* Age differences; Age discrepant marriages; Age groups; Attitudes; Baby boom generation; Countercultures; Family conflict; Intergenerational relations; Moral attitudes; Opinions; Parent child relations; Post-baby boom generation; Social change; Social mobility.

Generation X. See *Post-baby boom generation.*

Generation Y. See *Echo boom generation.*

Generational cycle of child abuse. Generational cycle of child abuse. *Choose from:* generation(s,al), family correlate(s), parent background, predispos(ed,ing,ition), family histor(y,ies) *with:* abus(e,ed,er,ers,ive), maltreat(ed,ment,ing), mistreat(ed,ment, ing), batter(ed,ing,er,ers) *with:* child(ren), infant(s), bab(y,ies), son(s), daughter(s). *Consider also:* abusing famil(y,ies), parents who were abused. *See also* Child abuse; Family background; Family history; Family violence; Parent child relations; Predisposition.

Generations. Generation(s). Age group(s). Cohort(s). *Consider also:* epoch(s), era(s), lifetime(s), lifespan(s). *See also* Age groups; Cohorts; Time periods.

Generations, conflict of. See *Generation gap; Intergenerational relations.*

Generative grammar. Generative grammar(s). Realistic grammar(s). Network grammar(s). *Consider also:* finite-state grammar(s), phrase-structure grammar(s), transformational grammar(s), arc-pair grammar(s), lexical functional grammar(s), generalized phrase-structure grammar(s), case grammar(s), Montague grammar(s), relational grammar(s). *See also* Grammar; Lexical phonology; Psycholinguistics.

Generativity. Generativ(e,ity). Intergenerational transfer(s). Pass(ed,ing) on tradition(s). *Choose from:* pass(ed,ing), transmit(ted,ting), perpetuat(e,ed,ing), maintain(ed,ing, ance) *with:* tradition(s), culture, cultural identity, knowledge, skills, inspiration, guidance, legacy, wisdom, values, memories, history. *Consider also:* keepers of community, cultural inheritance. *See also* Cultural maintenance; Cultural transmission; Future orientation; Intergenerational relations; Oral history.

Generosity. Generosity. Generous(ly,ness). Bounteous(ness). Munificence. Good will. Unselfish(ness). Public spirited. Big-hearted(ness). Benevolen(t,ce). Chivalr(ous,y). Considerate(ness). Magnani(mous,mousness,ity). Altruis(tic,m). Charitable(ness). Kindhearted(ness). Thoughtful(ness). Ungrudging(ly). Unselfish(ness). *See also* Altruism; Charitable behavior; Favors; Gift giving; Kindness; Magnanimity; Philanthropy; Sharing; Unselfishness.

Genes, dominant. See *Dominant genes.*

Genes, recessive. See *Recessive genes.*

Genetic counseling. Genetic counseling. *Choose from:* genetic(s), prenatal, amniocentesis, eugenic(s), heredit(y, ary), inherit(ed,ing) *with:* counsel(ed, ing), advice, advis(ed,ing,or,ors), guidance. *See also* Congenitally handicapped; Genetic screening; Genetics; Hereditary diseases; Involuntary sterilization.

Genetic disorders. See *Hereditary diseases.*

Genetic engineering. Genetic(ally) engineer(s,ing,ed). Genetic(ally) alter(ed,ing,ation,ations). Transgenic animal(s). Transgenic mice. Gene therap(y,ies). Protein engineer(ed,ing). *Choose from:* gene(s,tic,tically), DNA *with:* engineer(s,ing,ed), alter(ed,ing, ation,ations), intervention(s), transformation(s), manipulat(e,ed,ing, ion), modif(y,ying,ied,ication,ications), technolog(y,ies), biotechnolog(y,ies). *Consider also:* reverse transcriptase, clon(e,es,ed,ing), sex preselection, recombinant DNA, DNA amplification, recombinant organism(s), engineered mutation(s), transgenic bacteria, transgenic virus(es), transgenic plant(s), transgenic animal(s), genetic pollution. *See also* Bioethics; Gene mapping; Genetic research; Hereditary diseases; Medical ethics; Medical innovations; Pharming; Single nucleotide polymorphisms; Plant genetics; Reproductive technologies.

Genetic psychology. Genetic psychology. Evolutionary psychology. *Choose from:* natural selection, evolution(ary), heredit(y,ary), inherit(ed,ing), gene(s,tic,tically), *with:* mental disorder(s), intelligence, crav(e,ed,ing, ings), behavior(al), psycholog(y,ical), moral(s,ity), inclination(s), sex difference(s), violen(ce,t). *Consider also:* social Darwinism, neurobiolog(y,ical). *See also* Behavioral

genetics; Psychobiology; Sociobiology.

Genetic research. Genetic research. *Choose from:* genetic(s,ally), genome(s), clon(e,es,ed,ing), congenital(ly), familial, chromosome(s), DNA, heredit(y,ary), reverse transcriptase *with:* research(ed,ing,er,ers), experiment(s,ed, er,ers,ation), control groups(s), data collection, data analys(is,es), replicat(ed,ing,ion,ions). *See also* Bioethics; Gene mapping; Genetic engineering; Genetics; Pharmacogenomics; Pharming; Research; Single nucleotide polymorphisms.

Genetic screening. Genetic screening. Genetic test(s,ed,ing). *Choose from:* gene(s,tic), chromosome abnormalit(y,ies), genotype(s), karyotype(s), phenotypic expression, genome(s), mutation(s), DNA, heredit(ary,y), congenital(ly), heterozygote(s), prenatal(ly), hereditary disorder(s), sickle cell, Tay Sachs, diabetes, etc. *with:* test(s,ed,ing), diagnosis, screen(ed, ing), detect(ed,ing,ion), register(s). *Consider also:* heterozygote detection, genetic assay(s), genotyping. *See also* Genetic counseling; Hereditary diseases.

Genetic testing. See *Genetic screening.*

Geneticists. Geneticist(s). Genetic scientist(s). Genetic researcher(s). Authority on gene(s,tic,tics). *See also* Scientists.

Genetics. Genetic(s,ally). Congenital(ly). Heredit(y,ary,ability). Inborn. Innate. Atavis(m,tic). Connate(ly). Familial. Chromosome(s). DNA. Inbreed(ing). Inbred. Consanguin(e,eous,ity). Dominant trait(s). Recessive trait(s). Inherited characteristic(s). Genotype(s). Genome(s). Hybrid(s). Mendelian. Gene(s). Clon(e,es,ed,ing). Mutation(s). Throwback(s). *Choose from:* genetic *with:* link(s,age), model(s), recombination, transformation. *Consider also:* cytogenetic(s), extrachromosomal inheritance, biogenetics, immunogenetic(s), pharmacogenetic(s), phenotype(s), sex determination. *See also* Animal mate selection; Atavism (biology); Behavioral genetics; Bioethics; Eugenics; Gene mapping; Genetic counseling; Genetic engineering; Genetic research; Genetic screening; Hybrids (biology); Plant genetics; Population genetics; Recessive genes; Species differences.

Genetics, behavioral. See *Behavioral genetics.*

Genetics, plant. See *Plant genetics.*

Genetics, population. See *Population genetics.*

Genie. See *Demons; Spirits.*

Genital disorders, female. See *Female genital disorders.*

Genital disorders, male. See *Male genital disorders.*

Genital mutilation. See *Female circumcision (ritual).*

Genitalia, female. See *Female genitalia.*

Genitalia, male. See *Male genitalia.*

Genitalis, herpes. See *Herpes genitalis.*

Genitals. See *Female genitalia; Male genitalia.*

Genius. See *Gifted; Intelligentsia.*

Genocide. Genocid(e,al). Ethnocid(e,al). Systematic destruction. Holocaust. Shoah. Crimes against humanity. Exterminat(e,ed,ion). Threatened extinction. Ethnocide. Death camp(s). Extermination camp(s). Gas chamber(s). Death factor(y,ies). Final solution. Die Endlosung. Mass murder(s). *Choose from:* Armenia(n,ns), Turk(ish,s), Pol Pot, Khmer Rouge, Kampuchea, Nazi(s), Bosnia(n), Serb(s,ian), Rwanda(n) *with:* genocid(e,al), exterminat(e,ed,ion,ions), atrocit(y,ies), war crime(s), ethnocide. *Choose from:* war *with:* crime(s), atrocit(y,ies), victim(s), crime trial(s). *Consider also:* killing field(s), international crime(s), Nuremberg tribunal, Genocide Convention, Tokyo Tribunal, Principles of Nuremberg, Nuremberg judgment, international military tribunal(s), UN War Crimes Commission. *See also* Antisemitism; Colonialism; Ethnic cleansing; Holocaust; Indigenous populations; International offenses; Massacres; Nazism; War atrocities; War crimes; Weapons of mass destruction.

Genotypes. See *Phenotypes.*

Genre art. Genre art. Genre painting(s). Genre scene(s). *Consider also:* Dutch 17th century artists, scene(s) from daily life, Pieter Brueghel, Ter Borch, Terborch, Gabriel Metsu, Pieter de Hooch, Jan Vermeer. *See also* Artistic styles; Arts; Genres (art).

Genres. Genre(s). Brand(s). Categor(y,ies). Class(es). Classification(s). Fashion(s). Genus(es). Species. Type(s). Variet(y,ies). *See also* Artistic styles; Film genres; Genres (art); Literary form; Types.

Genres (art). Art genre(s). *Choose from:* art, painting(s) *with:* genre(s), categor(y,ies), style(s), school(s), type(s), branch(es). *Consider also:* landscape(s), portrait(s,ure), still life(s), drawing(s), etching(s), etc. *See also* Abstract art; Abstract expressionism; Animal painting and illustration; Art deco; Art nouveau; Artistic styles; Arts; Assemblage (art); Biological illustration; Camp (aesthetics); Collages; Conceptual art; Expressionism (art); Feminist art; Figurative art; Folk art; Form (aesthetic); Genre art; Genres; Graphic arts; Magic realism (art); Modern art; Realism in art; Socialist realism in art; Types.

Genres, film. See *Film genres*

Gentlemen. Gentle(men,man,manly, manliness). Man of noble birth. Aristocrat(s). Squire(s). Esquire. Man of substance. Hidalgo(s). Patrician(s). Gent(s). Sahib(s). Prince(s). Noble(s,men,man). Duke(s). Lord(s). Earl(s). Viscount(s). Marquis. Monseigneur(s). Baron(s). Knight(s). *See also* Aristocracy.

Gentrification. See *Urban renewal.*

Gentry. Gentry. Gentlefolk. Lad(y,ies). Gentle(man,men). Aristocracy. Upper class(es). Landowner(s). Elite(s). *See also* Elites.

Genuineness. See *Sincerity.*

Geographic determinism. Geographical(ly) determin(ed,ism). Anthropogeograph(y,ic). *Choose from:* geography, geographical(ly), climat(e,es,ic), topograph(y,ical,ically), altitude(s), rainfall, location, access, ingress, egress, port(s) *with:* determin(e,ed,ing,ism), factor(s). *See also* Environmental determinism; Economic geography; Geopolitics; Human ecology; Political geography.

Geographic distribution. Geographic distribution. Diaspora. Nationwide. Statewide. Worldwide. Transcontinental. Global. *Choose from:* geographic(al), territorial, regional, spatial *with:* spread, distribut(e,ed,ing,ion,ions), pattern(s), dispers(e,ed,al,ion,ions), diffusion(s), disseminat(e,ed,ing,ion,ions). *See also* Diaspora; Geographic mobility; Geographic regions; Internal migration; Migration patterns; Phytogeography; Population distribution; Settlement patterns.

Geographic information systems. Geographic information system(s). GIS. Land information system(s). Computerized map(s,ped,ping). Spatially referenced database(s). *Choose from:* spatial data, geographic record(s), geographic data *with:* automat(ed, ing,ion), digital map(s,ped,ping), *Consider also:* aerial photograph(s), satellite image(s), Theissen polygon(s), geocod(er,ers,ing), global positioning system(s), Geographic Coordinate Data Base Measurement Management. *See also* Archaeology; Aerial reconnaissance; Automation; Geography; Human geography; Information; Land surveying; Management informaton systems.

Geographic locality, community. See *Community (geographic locality).*

Geographic mobility. Geographic(al) mobil(e,ity). Migrat(e,ed,ing,ion,ions). Relocat(ed,ing,ion,ions). Residential(ly) mobil(e,ity). Family move(s). Residen-

tial move(s). Transient(s). Itinerant(s). *See also* Demographic changes; Geographic distribution; Geographic regions; Internal migration; Migration; Military families; Military personnel; Relocation; Social mobility; Travel.

Geographic regions. Geographic region(s). Region(al,s). Nation(s). State(s). Continental. Territor(y,ial,ies). Provinc(e,es,ial). Count(y,ies). *Choose from:* geographic(al) *with:* context(s), subdivision(s), section(s), area(s), district(s), zone(s). *See also* Antarctic regions; Arctic Regions; Areas; Arid lands; Borderlands; Frontiers; Geographic distribution; Grasslands; Metropolitan areas; Phytogeography; Regional development; Regional differences; Regional government; Regional movements; Regionalism; Rural areas; Suburbs; Wetlands

Geographical atlases. See *Atlases (geographical).*

Geographical perception. Geographical perception. Environmental perception. Perception(s) of location(s). Perceptual cartography. Perceptual map(s). *Consider also:* spatial abilit(y,ies), sense of direction, cognitive map(s,ping), place navigation, spatial orientation. *See also* Orientation; Perceptual localization.

Geography. Geograph(y,ic). *Consider also:* geopolitic(s,al), oceanograph(y,ic), cosmograph(y,ic), physiograph(y,ic), geode(sy,tic). *See also* Ancient geography; Countries; Economic geography; Environment; Geographic information systems; Human geography; Land surveying; Maps; Medical geography; Social sciences.

Geography, ancient. See *Ancient geography.*

Geography, Economic. See *Economic geography.*

Geography, historical. See *Historical geography.*

Geography, human. See *Human ecology.*

Geography, language. See *Linguistic geography.*

Geography, linguistic. See *Linguistic geography.*

Geography, medical. See *Medical geography.*

Geography, medieval. See *Medieval geography.*

Geography, plant. See *Phytogeography.*

Geography, political. See *Political geography.*

Geography, social. See *Human ecology; Human geography.*

Geological time. Geologic(al) time. *Choose from:* geologic(al) *with:* time, era(s),

period(s), epoch(s), age(s), chron(s). *Consider also:* absolute age, geochronology. *See also* Geological time scales.

Geological time scale. Geological time scale. *Choose from:* cenozoic, mesozoic, palaeozoic, precambrian *with:* era(s). *Choose from:* tertiary, cretaceous, jurassic, triassic, permian, carboniferous, devonian, silurian, ordovician, cambrian, precambrian *with:* period(s). *Choose from:* holocene, pleistocene, pliocene, miocene, oligocene, eocene, palaeocene *with:* epoch(s). *See also* Geological time.

Geology. Geolog(y,ical). *Consider also:* mineralogy, petrology, plate tectonics, sedimentology, geochemistry, geophysics, hydrogeology, geotechnical engineering, hydrometallurgy, structural geology, stratigraphic geology. *See also* Continental drift; Ground penetrating radar; Historic geology; Paleobotany; Paleontology.

Geology, historical. See *Historical geology.*

Geopolitics. Geopolitic(al,s). Geopolitik. Heartland theory. Lebensraum. Rimland theory. Geostrategic. Strategic geography. *Consider also:* geographical causation, geographic determinism, climatic determinism, political geography, electoral geography, global political economy, frontier in American history, buffer state(s), global strateg(y,ies). *See also* Borderlands; Boundaries; Collective security; Economic geography; Economic history; Frontier thesis; Frontiers; Geographic determinism; Historical geography; International alliances; International rivers; Marine resources; Natural resources; Pan-Africanism; Political geography; Regionalism; Rivers; Spheres of influence; Territorial expansion; Territorial issues; Territorial waters; Territoriality.

Geriatric patients. Geriatric patient(s). *Choose from:* geriatric(s), older adult(s), gerontology, old age, aging, aged, elderly, psychogeriatric, senior citizen(s), retire(d,ment) *with:* patient(s), inpatient(s), outpatient(s), hospital population(s). *Consider also:* nursing home(s) *with:* patient(s), resident(s). *See also* Aged 80 and over; Elderly; Patients.

Geriatric psychotherapy. Geriatric psychotherapy. Psychogeriatric(s). *Choose from:* geriatric(s), gerontology, older adult(s), aging, aged, old age, elderly, senior citizen(s) *with:* psychotherap(y,ies,eutic), group therap(y,ies), psychiatric service(s), mental health clinic(s), milieu therap(y,ies), rational emotive therap(y,ies), relaxation training, art therap(y,ies), music therap(y,ies), dance therap(y,ies), counseling, casework. *See also* Geriatric patients; Psychotherapy.

Geriatrics. Geriatric(s). Geriatric patient(s). Gerontolog(y,ic,ical,ist,ists). *Choose from:* geriatric, elderly, old age, gerontolog(y,ical) *with:* medicine, medical care, surgery, care, medical service(s), hospital(s). *See also* Medical sciences.

Germ warfare. See *Biological warfare.*

German songs. German song(s). Lied(er,es,chen). Gesang(e,en). Volkslied(er,es). Hoflied(er,es). Gesellschaftslied(er,es). Gesellen-lied(er,es). Wanderlied(er). Jugenlied(er,es). *Consider also:* German ballad(s), Deutsche Musik, Deutsche Lied, Ode(n). *See also* Ballads; Folk songs; Geisslerlieder; Hymns; Songs.

Germanic languages. Germanic language(s). East Germanic: Gothic, Vandalic, Burgundian. North Germanic: Old Norse, Old Icelandic, Icelandic, Norwegian, Dano-Norwegian, Landsmaal, Old Swedish, Swedish, Old Danish, Danish, Faeroese. West Germanic. High German: Swiss German, Pennsylvania Dutch, Alsatian, Swabian, Franconian, Old High German, Middle High German, Yiddish. Low German: Old Saxon, Plattdeutsch [Modern Low German], Old Low Franconian, Flemish. Dutch, Afrikaans, Anglo-Frisian, Old Frisian, Old English, Middle English, Middle Scots, English. *See also* Language; Languages (as subjects); Western Europe.

Gerontocracy. Gerontocra(cy,tic). Old men as rulers. *Choose from:* old, older, elderly *with:* rul(e,ed,er,ers,ing), dominance, respect, revered. *See also* Elderly; Political systems.

Gesellschaft and gemeinschaft. See *Gemeinschaft and gesellschaft.*

Gestalt psychology. See *Gestalt theory; Gestalt therapy.*

Gestalt theory. Gestalt theor(y,ies). *Choose from:* gestalt *with:* psychology, theor(y,ies), framework(s), concept(s). *See also* Gestalt therapy; Theories.

Gestalt therapy. Gestalt therap(y,ies). *Choose from:* gestalt *with:* therap(y,ies), treatment(s), marathon(s), personal growth, technique(s), psychotherap(y,ies). *See also* Gestalt theory; Psychotherapy.

Gestation. See *Pregnancy.*

Gestational age, small for infant. See *Infant small for gestational age.*

Gestures. Gestur(e,es,ing,al). Pantomime. Gesticulat(e,ed,ing,ion). Mime. Bodily communication. Posturing. *Choose from:* nonverbal, deictic *with:* behavior(s), communication. *Choose from:* hand, arm *with:* movement(s), signal(s). *Choose from:* manual, sign, body *with:* language. *See also* Body language; Nonverbal communication; Oratory.

Ghettos. See *Ethnic neighborhoods; Poverty areas.*

Ghettos, urban. See *Ethnic neighborhoods; Poverty areas.*

Ghost stories. Ghost stor(y,ies). Spooky stor(y,ies). Stor(y,ies) of hobgoblin(s), goblin(s). *Choose from:* ghost(s,ly), apparition(s), hobgoblin(s), specter(s) of dead, haunt(ed,ing), ghoul(s), kobold(s), grave(s) *with:* stor(y,ies), tale(s), folktale(s), superstitio(us,n,ns). *See also* Anecdotes; Apparitions; Folk culture; Ghosts; Haunted houses; Horror films; Horror tales; Superstitions; Suspense.

Ghost towns. See *Extinct cities.*

Ghosts. Ghost(s). Hobgoblin(s). Goblin(s). Ghoul(s). Manes. Spirit(s). Spook(s). Lemure(s). Revenant(s). Banshee(s). Evil spirit(s). Revenant(s). Tzitzimitl. Baloma. *Consider also:* haunt(ed,ing), bereaved spirit(s), specter(s). *See also* Ancestor worship; Apparitions; Death; Devils; Fairies; Ghost stories; Haunted houses; Horror tales; Supernatural; Superstitions; Uncanniness.

Ghostwriting. Ghostwrit(ing,er,ers,en). Ghost writ(ing,er,ers,en). Ghost wrote. *Consider also:* collaborat(e,ed,ing,ion), dictated autobiograph(y,ies). *See also* Authors; Collaborators.

Giants. Giant(s,ess,esses). Strongman. Colossus. Titan(s). Goliath. Samson. Hercule(s,an). Tarzan. Paul Bunyan, King Kong. Superman. *See also* Body height.

Gift baskets. Gift basket(s). *Choose from:* gift, holiday, goodwill, gourmet, greetings, Christmas, preserves, jelly, cheddar cheese, smoked salmon, fruitcake, roasted nuts, fruit(s) *with:* basket(s), package(s). *See also* Gifts; Salutations.

Gift books. Gift book(s). *Consider also:* donate(d) book(s), literary annual(s), Christmas book(s). *See also* Books.

Gift giving. Gift giving. Ritual giving. Gift relationship. Potlatch. Voluntary offering(s). *Choose from:* gift(s), present(s), favor(s) *with:* giv(e,ing), gave, exchang(e,ed,ing), offer(ing). *See also* Altruism; Charities; Contributions; Favors; Generosity; Giving; Kindness; Philanthropy; Reciprocity; Rituals; Unselfishness.

Gifted. Gifted(ness). Genius(es). Intellectually gifted. Talented. Bright child(ren). Precocious(ness). Accelerated classes. Clever(ness). Artistic. Adept. Dexterous(ness). Adroit(ness). Astute(ness). Smart(ness). Ingenious(ness). Scholarship winner(s). Superior student(s). *Choose from:* exceptional(ly), outstanding, super(ior), high(ly) *with:* intelligen(t,ce), IQ, abilit(y,ies), intellectual, talent(s,ed), bright, gifted. *Consider also:* academically gifted, gifted disabled, gifted disadvantaged, gifted child(ren), quick witted. *See also* Ability; Academic ability; Academically gifted; Aptitude; Artistic ability; Creativity; Exceptional children; Exceptional persons; Intelligence; Mathematical ability.

Gifted, academically. See *Academically gifted.*

Gifts. Gift(s). Present(s). Favor(s). Offering(s). Handout(s). Alm(s). Bequest(s). Benefaction(s). Donation(s). Endowment(s). Largesse. Gratuit(y,ies). Contribution(s). *Consider also:* organ donation(s). *See also* Alms; Anatomical gifts; Awards; Donations; Gift baskets; Gift giving; Gratis; Gratuities.

Gifts, anatomical. See *Anatomical gifts.*

Gifts, spiritual. See *Spiritual gifts.*

Gilds, neighborhood. See *Social Settlements.*

Girls. See *Women.*

Giving. Giving. Give(n). Gave. Allocat(e,ed,ing,ation). Apportion(ed,ing,ment). Award(ed,ing,s). Bestow(ed,ing). Confer(red,ring). Consign(ed,ing). Contribut(e,ed,ing,ion). Convey(ed,ing). Deliver(ed,ing). Dispens(e,ed,ing). Distribut(e,ed,ing,ion). Dol(e,ed,ing). Donat(e,ed,ing,ation). Endow(ed,ing,ment,ments). Grant(ed,ing). Handout(s). Lend(ing). Proffer(ed,ing). Subsidiz(e,ed,ing,ation). *See also* Altruism; Assistance; Charitable behavior; Charities; Contributions; Endowments; Financial support; Gift giving; Philanthropy; Political contributions.

Giving, gift. See *Gift giving.*

Glacial epoch. Glacial epoch(s). Glacial period(s). Glaciation(s). Ice age(s). *Consider also:* megaberg(s), glacial maximum(s). *See also* Climatic changes; Glaciers.

Glaciers. Glacier(s). Glaci(al,ology). Ice cap(s). Ice sheet(s). Greenland. Antarctica. *Choose from:* valley, mountain, piedmont, continental *with:* glacier(s). *See also* Glacial epoch.

Glass ceilings. See *Barriers; Employment discrimination; Occupational segregation; Sex discrimination; Sexual division of labor.*

Glass harmonica. Glass harmonica(s). Musical glass(es). Armonica(s). *See also* Musical instruments.

Glass painting and staining. Glass painting and staining. *Choose from:* stain(ed,ing), paint(ed,ing), luminous art, Tiffany *with:* glass, window(s). *See also* Arts; Churches.

Gleaning. Glean(ed,ing). *Choose from:* gather(ed,ing), cull(ed,ing), collect(ed,ing) *with:* leaving(s), remain(s,der,ders). *Consider also:* giv(e,ing) unused food to needy. *See also* Charitable behavior; Farming.

Global campaigns. Global campaign(s). *Choose from:* global(ly), worldwide, international(ly), universal(ly) *with:* campaign(s), publicity, advertis(e,ed,ing), advertisement(s), marketing, promotion(s) propagand(a,ize,izing). *See also* Advertising; Campaigns; Catholic (universality); Global integration; Globalization; Internationalism; Multinational corporations.

Global education. See *International education.*

Global inequality. Global inequality. *Choose from:* global(ization), worldwide, nation(s,al), industrial world, developing world *with:* income inequality, injustice, gap in per capita income, gap between rich and poor, polariz(e,ed,ing) economically, economic disparit(y,ies), economic inequality. *See also* Center and periphery; Income inequality; Inequality; World economy; World systems theory.

Global integration. Global(ly) integrat(e, ed,ing,ion). Global economic integration. *Choose from:* global(ly,ize, ized,izing,ization), world-wide, universal(ly,ity), international(ly), supranational(ly) *with:* integrat(e,ed,ing, ion), interoperab(le,ility), infrastructure(s), deploy(ed,ing,ment), implement(ed,ing,ation), operation(s), standard(s), system(s), service(s), econom(ic,y,ies), law(s). *Consider also:* global economy, international(ly), invest(ed,ing,ment,ments), international commerc(e,ial,ially), Multilateral Agreement on Investment (MAI), supermarket to the world, international free trade agreement(s), International Monetary Fund. *See also* Catholic (universality); Cross cultural competency; Cultural cooperation; Digital signatures; E-commerce; Global campaigns; Globalization; Harmonization (trade); Intercultural communication; Intergovernmental relations; International broadcasting; International cooperation; International division of labor; International economic organizations; International education; International educational exchange; International languages; International law; International organizations; International police; International relations; International trade; Internationalism; Multicultural education; Multinational corporations; Neocolonialism; Universalism; World economy; World health; World population; World problems.

Global perspective. See *Globalization.*

Global relationships, strategic. See *Strategic global relationships.*

Global village. See *Globalization.*

Global warming. See *Atmospheric contamination; Greenhouse effect.*

Globalization. Globaliz(e,ed,ing,ation). Global village. Global society. Global living room. Global economy. Global perspective. One world. Borderless world. Universaliz(e,ed,ing,ation). International(ism,ize,ized,izing,ization). Anti-statism. International community. International basis. Community of nations. Transcend(ing) national boundar(y,ies). United Nations. League of Nations. Commission of the European Community. Commonwealth of Nations. Concert of Europe. Council of Europe. Organization of American States. Organization of African Unity. Organization of Central American States. *Consider also:* global reach, global network(s), supranational(ism), international(ism,ization), multinational(ism), transnational, global(ization), worldwide, universal(ism,ization), cross-national(ism), all inclusive, all encompassing. *See also* Catholic (universality); Chaos management; Colonialism; Comprehensiveness; Cultural cooperation; Deterritorialization; Global campaigns; Global integration; Holism; Imperialism; Inclusive education; Intercultural communication; Intergovernmental relations; International broadcasting; International cooperation; International economic organizations; International educational exchange; International languages; International law; International organizations; International police; International relations; International trade; Internationalism; Modern civilization; Modernization; Multicultural education; Multinational corporations; Neocolonialism; Universalism; World citizenship; World economy; World health; World population; World problems; World systems theory.

Globes. Globe(s). Sphere(s). Ball(s). Orb(s). Spherical. *Consider also:* planet earth, map of the world. *See also* Earth; Maps.

Glockenspiel. See *Bells.*

Glory. Glor(y,ies). Honor(s,ed). Fam(e,ous). Acclaim(ed). Magnificen(ce,t). Kudo(s). Accolade(s). Tribute(s). Praised. Distinction. Renown(ed). *See also* Admiration; Heroes; Honored (esteem); Prestige; Social approval; Reward.

Glory of God. Glory of God. *Choose from:* God, the Lord *with:* glor(y,ification), majesty, omnipoten(t,ce), eternal, sacred, grace, power(ful), hol(y,iness), divin(e,ity), timeless(ness),

ineffab(le,ility), transcendental, love, justice, mercy, everlasting, universal(ism), spacious(ness), omniscien(t,ce), all-knowing. *See also* Attributes of God; Deities; God concepts; Immanence of god; Knowledge of god; Omnipotence; Omniscience of God.

Glossaries. Glossar(y,ies). Word list(s). Nomenclature(s). Terms with meaning(s). *Consider also:* gloss(es,ing), gloz(e,ed,ing). *See also* Dictionaries; Vocabulary.

Glosses. See *Exegesis; Glossaries.*

Glossolalia. Glossolalia. Speaking in tongue(s). Gift of tongues. Tongues-speaking. Glossolalic jargon. *Consider also:* crazy talk, nonsense speech. *See also* Mental illness; Religious Practices.

Glue sniffing. See *Inhalant abuse.*

Glyptics. Glyptic(s). Carv(e,ed,ing) gem(s,stone,stones). Engrav(e,ed,ing) gem(s,stone,stones). *Consider also:* scarab(s). *See also* Carving (decorative arts); Collectibles; Crafts; Gems.

Goal orientation. Goal orient(ed,ation). *Choose from:* goal(s), objective(s), grade(s), achievement *with:* orient(ed,ation), focus(sed,sing), aspir(e,ed,ing,ation,ations), set(ting), monitor(ed,ing), conscious(ness). *Consider also:* teleolog(y,ical), intentional(ity). *See also* Aspirations; Goals; Teleology.

Goal setting. See *Goal orientation.*

Goals. Goal(s). Objective(s). Aim(s). Intent(ion,ions). Aspiration(s). Target(s). Purpose(s). Ambition(s). Destination(s). *Consider also:* conat(ive,ion). *See also* Aspirations; Career goals; Commitment (emotional); Destination; End; Incentives; Intentionality; Life plans; Long range planning; Means ends; Motivation; Needs; Objectives; Organizational objectives; Planning; Precedence; Short term planning; Social goals; Teleology.

Goals, career. See *Career goals.*

Goals, organizational. See *Organizational objectives.*

Goals, social. See *Social goals.*

Goats. Goat(s). Capra. *Consider also:* ibex(es), markhor(s), antelope(s). *See also* Animals; Cattle; Livestock; Mammals.

God. See *Deities.*

God, attributes of. See *Attributes of God.*

God, death of theology. See *Death of God (theology).*

God, existence of. See *God concepts; Immanence of God; Knowledge of God; Presence of God.*

God, fear of. See *Fear of God.*

God, glory of. See *Glory of God.*

God, hidden. See *Presence of God.*

God, image of. See *God concepts.*

God, immanence of. See *Immanence of God.*

God, judgment of. See *Judgment of God.*

God, kingdom of. See *Apocalypse; Apocalyptic literature; Heaven; Judgement day; Millenarianism.*

God, knowledge of. See *Knowledge of God.*

God, oneness of. See *Oneness of God.*

God, prescience of. See *Omniscience of God.*

God, presence of. See *Presence of God.*

God, trust in. See *Faith.*

God, unicity of. See *Oneness of God.*

God, unity of. See *Oneness of God.*

God, will of. See *Will of God.*

God concepts. God concept(s). Concept of god. Imago dei. Idea(s) about god. Female concept of god. Divine other. Almighty. *Choose from:* interpretation(s), belief(s), perception(s), view(s), imagery, image(s), fear(s,ful), concept(s), idea(s), perspective(s), relationship, definition(s) *with:* god(s), goddess(es), divine being(s), almighty, deit(y,ies), Jehovah, Allah, Yahweh, Yahveh, Ahura Mazda, Loki, Jesus, Christ, Great Spirit. *Consider also:* theodic(y,ies). *See also* Atheism; Attributes of God; Apotheosis; Deities; Existentialism; Glory of God; Goddesses; Good; Humanism; Immanence of God; Jehovah; Knowledge of God; Mother goddesses; Omniscience of God; Oneness of God; Pantheism (polytheism); Pantheism (universal divinity); Presence of God; Religious beliefs; Revealed theology; Theism; Theology; Theophany.

Goddess religion. Goddess religion. Goddess worship. Goddess feminism. Goddess of the garden. Goddess cult(s). Goddess movement. *Choose from:* goddess(es), feminist *with:* religion(s), worship(s,ed,ing), ritual(s), movement, spirit, spirituality, tradition(s). *Consider also:* Marija Gimbutas, feminine face of God, Wicca movement. *See also* Feminist theology; Goddesses; Mother goddesses.

Goddesses. Goddess(es). She-God(s). Queen of heaven. *Choose from:* female, women, woman *with:* deit(y,ies), divinit(y,ies), god(s), deif(y,ied,ying), ication). *Consider also:* female archetype(s), Gaia, mother earth, great mother, Isis, Astarte, Demeter, Hera, Juno, Ceres, Demeter, Proserpina, Persephone, Artemis, Diana, Minerva, Athena, Aphrodite, Venus, Vesta, Hestia, Cybele, Rhea, Ge, Gaea, Nike, Freya, Freyja, Frigg, Frigga, Hel, Nanna, Ithunn, Idun, Sif, Sigyn, Chandi, Devi, Durga, Gauri, Kali, Lakshmi, Parvati, Sarasvati, Uma, Ushas, Cihuacoatl. *See also* Deities; Feminist theology; God concepts; Goddess religion; Images of women; Matriarchy; Mother goddesses; Religious beliefs.

Goddesses, mother. See *Mother goddesses.*

Gods. See *Deities.*

Going private. See *Privatization.*

Going public. Go(ing) public. Went public. Sell(ing) shares publicly. Public offering(s). Initial public offering(s). IPO. *Consider also:* capitaliz(e,ed,ing, ation), public financing, trad(e,ed,ing) publicly. *See also* Corporations; Enterprises; Incorporation; Investments; Stock exchange; Stockholders.

Gold buying. Gold buying. *Choose from:* gold(en), ore(s) *with:* buy(ing), bought, purchas(e,ed,ing), acquir(e,ed,ing), mint price, exchange rate, redeem currency, price(s), trading, movement(s), market(s), selloff, *Consider also:* jewelry buying. *See also* Currency; Currency speculation; Gold standard.

Gold collar workers. Gold collar work(er,ers,ing). Gold collar manag(er,ers,ement). Knowledge work(er,ers,ing). New economy work(er,ers,ing). Professional eclectic(s). *See also* Computer experts; Knowledge workers; Managers; New middle class; Occupational classification; Occupations; Paraprofessional personnel; Professional personnel; Specialists.

Gold standard. Gold standard. Gold bullion standard. Gold monetary standard. Gold exchange standard. *Choose from:* gold *with:* monetary system(s), standard, convert(ed,ing,tible,tibility). *Consider also:* gold certificate(s), limping standard. *See also* Bimetallism; Currency; Gold buying; Monetary policy.

Goldwork. Goldwork. Gold work. Gold article(s). Goldweight(s). *Choose from:* gold(en), gold alloy *with:* work, article(s), cup(s), goblet(s), ornament(s), treasure(s), relic(s), jewelry, object(s), artifact(s), shield(s). *Consider also:* goldsmith(ing). *See also* Ancient goldwork; Art metalwork; Collectibles; Jewelry; Treasure.

Goldwork, ancient. See *Ancient goldwork.*

Gonorrhea. Gonorrhea(l). Neisseria gonorrhoeae. Gonorrhoea. Gonococc(al, i,us). Gonococcal ophthalmia neonatorum. *See also* Sexually transmitted diseases.

Good. Good(ness). Virtuous(ness). Moral(ity). Righteous(ness). Honorable. Honest(y). High minded(ness). Noble. Loft(y,iness). Wholesome(ness). Pur(e,ity). Chast(e,ity). Innocen(t,ce). Unsullied. Untainted. Pious(ness). Saintl(y,iness). Angelic. Godl(y,iness). God fearing. Devout(ly,ness). Religious(ly,ness). *See also* Benevolence; Evil; God concepts; Good works (theology); Honor (integrity); Humanitarianism; Mercy; Validity; Virtue.

Good, common. See *Public good.*

Good, public. See *Public good.*

Good samaritans. Good samaritan(s). Brother's keeper(s). Emergency helping behavior. *Choose from:* bystander(s), ordinary citizen(s), stranger(s), insurance agent(s), white helmet(s) *with:* assist(ed,ing,ance), intervention, volunteer(s), rescue(d,r,rs), humanitarian, CPR, responsive(ness), help(ed,ing), initiative. *See also* Altruism; Assistance in emergencies; Disasters; Emergencies; Favors; Helping behavior; Kindness.

Good spirits. Good spirit(s). Protector(s). Angel(s). Aornarssuk. Apsara(s). *See also* Demons; Devils; Elves; Evil; Evil eye; Fairies; Folk literature; Folklore; Ghosts; Religious beliefs; Spirit possession; Witchcraft.

Good works (theology). Good works (theology). Good deed(s). *Choose from:* charit(y,able), good work(s) *with:* salvation, justification. *Consider also:* oper(a,um)bon(a,orum), bonis operibus, gute(n) wercke(n). *See also* Cardinal virtues; Charitable behavior; Good; Humanitarianism; Practical theology; Redemption (theology); Virtue.

Goods, consumer. See *Consumer goods.*

Goods, durable. See *Durable goods.*

Goods, grave. See *Grave goods.*

Goods, public. See *Public goods.*

Goodwill. Goodwill. Good will. Friendl(y,iness). Kind(ly,liness,ness). Benevolen(t,ce). Beneficen(t,ce). Amiab(le,leness,ility). Amicab(le,leness, ility). Cheerful(ly) willing(ness). *Consider also:* intangible asset(s), good reputation, gracious(ness). *See also* Charity; Humanitarianism; Friendliness; Public relations; Prestige.

Gospel, social. See *Social gospel.*

Gospel music. Gospel music. Gospel song(s). Gospel hymn(s). *Consider also:* Mahalia Jackson, Marion Williams, Blind Willie Johnson, Rev. Gary Davis, Rosetta Tharpe, Dixie Hummingbirds, Soul Stirrers, etc. *See also* Afro-American music; Hymns; Soul music.

Gossip. Gossip(ing). Rumor(s). Hearsay. Idle personal talk. Small talk. Grapevine(s). Whispering campaign(s). Mud slinging. Idle chatter. *Consider* *also:* schadenfreude. *See also* Conversation; Defamation; Gossip sites; Grapevine; Information exchange; Messages; Rumors; Scandals; Sensationalism; Tabloids; Trivia.

Gossip sites. Gossip site(s). Cybersleaze. *Choose from:* online, cyber(space), internet, web, site(s), website(s), home page(s) *with:* gossip, insider information, renegade, buzz, rumor(s), hearsay, scandal(s), scandalmonger(er,ers,ing). *Consider also:* Drudge Report. Velvet Rope, Ain't It Cool News, Cybersleaze, Coming Attractions, Dark Horizons, Zentertainment. *See also* Defamation; Gossip; Grapevine; Information exchange; Online harassment; Online privacy; Rumors; Scandals; Sensationalism; Tabloids; Trivia.

Gothic revival. Gothic revival(s). Revival of gothic architecture. Neo-gothic. *Choose from:* gothic revival, gothick, medievalized *with:* architecture, home(s), style(s), bedroom(s), cottage(s), mansion(s), form(s), interior(s), building(s), furniture, object(s), house(s), design(s), detail(s). *Consider also:* Rococo, Augustus Welby Northmore Pugin, Sir George Gilbert Scott, Viollet Le Duc. *See also* Architectural styles; Architecture; Classic revival; Gothicism; Historic buildings; Historic houses.

Gothic romances. Gothic romance(s). *Choose from:* gothic, pseudomedieval *with:* fiction, novel(s), literature, romance(s), tale(s), stor(y,ies). *See also* Fiction; Gothicism; Grotesque; Horror tales; Literature; Novels; Suspense.

Gothicism. Gothicism. Gothic tradition. *Choose from:* gothic *with:* mode(s), tradition(s), poetic(s), image(s), theme(s), motif(s), convention(s), formula(s). *Consider also:* vampir(e,es, ism), fear, doom, graveyard(s), murky, horror(s), terror, gloom(y), ghost(s,ly), macabre, mysterious, dark, gaunt, haunt(ed,ing), castle(s), live burial(s), medieval *with:* image(s), theme(s), motif(s), convention(s), setting(s), atmosphere(s), formula(s). *Consider also:* southern gothic, postmodern gothic, urban gothic, American gothic. *See also* Allusions; Figurative language; Gothic romances; Grotesque; Literature; Literary movements; Metaphors; Modern literature; Uncanniness; Vampires.

Governesses. Governess(es). Au pair(s). Nann(y,ies). Baby sitter(s). Babysitter(s). Nursemaid(s). *Consider also:* wet nurse(s), duenna(s), chaperone(s), child care provider(s). *See also* Child caregivers.

Governing. Govern(ed,ing). Administer(ed, ing). Assum(e,ed,ing) command. Tak(e,en,ing) charge. Exercis(e,ed,ing)

authority. Manag(e,ed,ing). Reign(ed, ing). Presid(e,ed,ing). Oversee(ing). Supervis(e,ed,ing,ion). Tak(e,en,ing) control. Superintend(ed,ing). Wield(ed, ing) power. Rul(e,ed,ing). Tak(e,en,ing) the helm. *See also* Administration; Leadership; Power sharing.

Governing boards. Governing board(s). Trustees. Board(s) of governors. Regents. Board(s) of supervisors. Citizens board(s). Community board(s). Governing bod(y,ies). Board(s) of directors. Common council(s). City council(s). Executive board(s). Board(s) of education. *Consider also:* board members. *See also* Advisory committees; Corporate control; Councils; Interlocking directorates; Legislative bodies; Policy making; Power structure.

Government. Government. Governing bod(y,ies). Administrative bod(y,ies). Congress(es). Parliament(s). Senate(s). House of Representatives. House of Commons. House of Lords. Presiden(t,cy). White House. Knesset. Duma. *Consider also:* government, federal, state *with:* bureaucrac(y,ies), agenc(y,ies). *See also* Autonomy (government); Central government; Constitution (legal); Corruption in government; Democracy; Executive branch (government); Foreign policy making; Government agencies; Government personnel; Government programs; Law enforcement; Laws; Legislative bodies; Legislators; Legitimacy; Local government; Military regimes; Municipal government; Political ideologies; Political systems; Primitive government; Provisional government; Public policy; Public sector; Regional government; Ruling class; State government.

Government, central. See *Central government.*

Government, city. See *Municipal government.*

Government, corruption in. See *Corruption in government.*

Government, executive branch. See *Executive branch (government).*

Government, local. See *Local government.*

Government, metropolitan. See *Municipal government.*

Government, military. See *Military regimes.*

Government, minimal. See *Minimal government.*

Government, municipal. See *Municipal government.*

Government, national. See *Central government.*

Government, primitive. See *Primitive government.*

Government, provisional. See *Provisional government.*

Government, regional. See *Regional government.*

Government, representative. See *Democracy.*

Government, resistance to. See *Civil disobedience; Civil disorders; Conscientious objectors; Decolonization; Demonstrators; Guerrillas; National fronts; Nonviolence; Peasant rebellions; Political action; Protest movements; Resistance; Revolution; Social demonstrations; Separatism.*

Government, self. See *Autonomy (government); Freedom; Political self determination; Popular sovereignty.*

Government, state. See *State government.*

Government, tribal. See *Chiefs; Priests and priestly classes (anthropology); Primitive government.*

Government agencies. Government agenc(y,ies). *Choose from:* federal, government(al), state, local, public, municipal, city, county, town(ship), district *with:* agenc(y,ies), department(s), commission(s), authorit(y,ies), council(s), board(s). *Consider specific agencies by name. See also* Bureaucracies; Capital cities; Government regulation; Independent regulatory commissions; Legislative bodies; Public administration; Public policy; Public sector; Public services.

Government aid. Government aid. Parochaid. *Choose from:* government, federal, state, public, welfare *with:* aid, assistance, support(s,ed,ing), subsid(y, ies,ization). *See also* Antipoverty programs; Fiscal federalism; Government financing; Government programs; Government subsidization; Medical assistance; Public welfare.

Government assistance. See *Antipoverty programs; Enterprise zones; Fiscal federalism; Government aid; Government financing; Government programs; Government subsidization;Medical assistance; National health programs; Public welfare; State capitalism; Subsidized housing.*

Government autonomy. See *Autonomy (government).*

Government binding theory (Linguistics). Government binding theory. Government and binding theory. Government-binding analysis. Principles and parameters approach. *Consider also:* d-structure, s-structure, logical form(s), phonetic form, x-bar theory, theta theory, binding theory, bounding theory, government theory. *See also* Grammar; Linguistics.

Government correspondence. Government correspondence. *Choose from:* public official(s), government(s), federal agenc(y,ies), government agenc(y,ies), FDA, Food and Drug Administration, OSHA, Occupational Safety and Health Administration, etc. *with:* correspondence, letter(s), memo(s), written comment(s), proposal(s), petition(s), electronic mail, e-mail, *Consider also:* presidential records, federal records, freedom of information. *See also* Access to information; Freedom of information; Government information.

Government documents. See *Government publications.*

Government employees. See *Civil service; Government personnel.*

Government expenditures. Government expenditure(s). *Choose from:* government(al), public, federal, state, county, city, municipal, taxpayer(s), Pentagon, human services, entitlement(s), defense *with:* expenditure(s), disbursement(s), expense(s), cost(s), spending, price(s), charge(s,), outlay(s), fee(s), payment(s). *See also* Budget deficits; External debts; Fiscal federalism; Fiscal policy; Government finances; Public debt; Public finance.

Government finances. Government finance(s). *Choose from:* federal, state, provinc(e,es,ial), government(al), public, county, city, municipal, local or unit by name such as California, etc. *with:* appropriat(e,ed,ing,ion,ions), bond(s), borrow(ed,ing), budget(ed,ing,s), cash flow, credit rating(s), deficit(s), debt(s), expenditure(s), expense(s), finance(s), fiscal, fund(s,ing), indebtedness, liabilit(y,ies), loan(s), lotter(y,ies), paid, pay(ing), payment(s), payroll(s), revenue(s), shortfall(s), spend(s,ing), spent, tax(es,ed,ing). *Consider also:* government borrowing, deficit spending, Gramm-Rudman-Hollings Deficit Reduction law, Proposition 13. *See also* External debts; Fiscal policy; Government expenditures; Public finance; Public debt; Taxes.

Government financing. Government financ(ed,ing). Financial support from government. Block grant(s). Bailout(s). Bail-out(s). *Choose from:* government, public, state, federal, taxpayer(s) *with:* financ(ed,ing,ial), support(ed), aid, assistance, expense, grant(s), subsid(y, ies,ization), aid, fund(ed,ing,s). *Consider also:* Hill Burton Act, Social Security, Aid to Families with Dependent Children, public education, public welfare, disability insurance, Old Age Assistance, unemployment insurance, medicare, medicaid, workmens compensation, veterans programs, etc. *See also* Antipoverty programs; Financing; Fiscal federalism; Government aid; Government programs; Government subsidization; Medical assistance; Public welfare.

Government information. Government information. *Choose from:* government, state, federal, classified, official, military, Pentagon, Department of State, Defense Department, OMB, Office of Management and Budget, President(s), Cabinet member(s), Congress(ional), Supreme Court, Washington, White House, government agenc(y,ies) *with:* information, misinformation, disinformation, announcement(s), spokes(man,men,woman,women,person), secrecy, coverup(s), censor(ed,ship), report(s), data, evidence, tape(s), diar(y,ies), research, document(s), paper(s), record(s), material(s), intelligence. *Consider also:* government openness, glasnost, Freedom of Information Act, FOIA, Paperwork Reduction Act. *See also* Classified information; Freedom of information; Government correspondence; Government publications; Government publicity; Government records; Government secrecy; Military intelligence.

Government intervention. See *State intervention.*

Government investigations. Government(al) investigat(e,ed,ing,ion,ions). Government inquir(y,ies). Commission(s) of inquiry. Independent counsel(s). U.S. prosecutor (s). *Choose from:* government(al), public, congress(ional), Department of Justice, Small Business Administration, Federal Bureau of Investigation, National Science Foundation, Department of Health and Human Services, etc. *with:* inquir(y,ies), investigation(s), subpoena(s), probe(s), special prosecutor(s), evidence against, search warrant(s). *See also* Corruption in government; Political crimes.

Government officials. See *Elected officials; Government personnel.*

Government officials, recall of. See *Recall of government officials.*

Government ownership. See *Government property; Nationalization; Socialism.*

Government personnel. Government personnel. *Choose from:* government(al), federal, state, county, city, municipal, local, town, public, civil service *with:* personnel, employee(s), official(s), executive(s), bureaucra(cy, t,ts), administrator(s), workforce, worker(s). *Choose from:* civil, public *with:* servant(s). *Consider also:* elected officials, public service, employed in public sector, public payroll, public office, state employment, county agent(s), customs inspector(s), extension agent(s), food and drug inspector(s), foreign diplomat(s), immigration inspector(s), military personnel, public school teacher(s), military personnel, public health service nurse(s). *See also* Bureaucrats; Civil service; Elected officials; Government travel; Legislators; Local officials and employees; Public folklore; Public officers; State government.

Government planning. See *State planning.*

Government policy. See *Public policy.*

Government procurement. Government procurement. *Choose from:* government, public, federal, state, county, city, pentagon, defense department *with:* purchas(e,es,ed,ing), procurement, contract(s,ed,or,ors), cost overrun(s), buy(ing), bought, acquire(d,s), order(s,ed,ing), pricing, overcharg(e,ed, ing), sell(ing), sold, supply, supplie(d,r, rs,s), hire(d), hiring, rent(ed,ing), leas(e,ed,ing). *See also* Conflict of interest; Corruption in government; Defense spending; Government expenditures; Government property; Military budget; Military industrial complex; Military market; Public debt.

Government programs. Government program(s). Comprehensive Employment and Training Act [CETA]. Servicemans Readjustment Act. Manpower Development and Training Act. Elementary and Secondary Education Act [ESEA]. Job Corps. Neighborhood Youth Corps. Peace Corps. Aid to Families with Dependent Children [AFDC]. Veterans administration. War on poverty. Civil defense. Postal service. Project Head Start. Upward bound. Volunteers in service to America [VISTA]. Government sponsored program(s). Federal program(s). State program(s). National program(s). Food stamp(s). Basic educational opportunity grant(s). Welfare service(s). Teacher corps. Federally supported program(s). Regional medical library network(s). Medicare. Medicaid. Social security. Child support enforcement. Community food and nutrition program(s). *See also* Government subsidization; National health programs; Public welfare; Social programs; Social services.

Government property. Government property. *Choose from:* government, public(ly), federal(ly), state, county, city, U.S., United States *with:* propert(y,ies), own(ed,ership), possession(s), claim(s), hold(ing) title(s). *See also* Government procurement; Nationalization; Public sector; Public works.

Government publications. Government publication(s). *Choose from:* government, Federal, public, Government Printing Office, GPO, state, city, municipal, official *with:* publication(s), document(s), report(s). *See also*

Freedom of information; Government information; Government publicity; Government records; Publications.

Government publicity. Government publicity. Government propaganda. Official propaganda. Public information. *Choose from:* government, federal, state, *with:* publicity, propaganda, press office(s), announcement(s), credibility, advertising, journalism, mass communication, press-release(s), news management, spokes(man,men,woman, women,person,persons). *Consider also:* United States Information Agency, Congressional Record, Bill Digest, THOMAS, congressional on-line service, federal government BBS(s), federal bulletin board system(s), national statistics. *See also* Government information; Government publications; Government secrecy; Government records; Information policy.

Government records. Government record(s). *Choose from:* government, public, federal, state, county, city, municipal, town, diplomatic *with:* record(s), archive(s), file(s), document(s), register(s), registr(y,ies), dossier(s), account(s), paper(s), meeting minute(s), recordkeeping, paperwork. *Consider also:* taxpayer, criminal, traffic *with:* record(s). *See also* Access to information; Classified information; Documents; Government publications; Government publicity; Police records; Surveillance of citizens.

Government regulation. Government regulation(s). Government intervention. *Choose from:* regulatory *with:* commission(s), agenc(y,ies), program(s), *Choose from:* government(al), federal(ly), state, local, FDA, EPA, FAA, FCC, etc., county, city, Congressional, police, fire department, health department, Port Authority, legal, public *with:* regulat(e,ed,ing,ion,ions,ory), registration, register(ed,ing), curb(s,ed,ing), control(s,led,ling), standard(s), oversight, certif(y,ied,ication), inspect(ed, ion), requirement(s), rule(s), guideline(s), review, polic(y,ies), ordinance(s), directive(s), law(s), ban(ned,ning), tax(ed,es,ing), monitor(ed,ing), quota(s), minimum(s), mandat(e,ed,es,ing,atory), instruction(s), ruling(s), licens(e,ed,ing), sanction(s,ed, ing). *See also* Agricultural laws and legislation; Enactment; Formal social control; Government; International travel regulations; Land use; Legislation; Patents; Pollution control; Regulation; State capitalism; State intervention.

Government secrecy. Government secre(t,ts,cy). Classified information. Official secret(s). Official Secrets Act. State secret(s). Secrecy pledge(s). Administrative secre(t,ts,cy). Executive privilege. *Choose from:* government(al, s), official, federal, national, state *with:* censor(ed,ing,ship), classified information, disinformation, covert operation(s), top secret, sensitive information. *Choose from:* government(al,s), official, federal, national, state *with:* refus(e,ed,al) to disclose, restrict(ed,ing) access, limit(ed,ing) access, clampdown, suppress(ed,ing,ion), withhold(ing), control(led,ling), coverup(s), leak(s,ed) *with:* data, information, press, media, report(s), paper(s). *See also* Access to information; Censorship; Classified information; Cryptography; Freedom of information; Government information; Government publicity; Information leaks; Information policy; News policies; Withholding evidence.

Government spending. See *Government expenditures.*

Government sponsored housing. See *Public housing.*

Government subsidization. Government subsidiz(ed,ing,ation). Government subsid(y,ies). Pork barrel(ing,ling). Porkbarrel(ing,ling). Income based rent(s). *Choose from:* government, federal, public, congressional, state, county, city, local, taxpayer(s), etc. *with:* subsid(y,ies,ized,ization), underwrit(e, ing,ten), financ(ed,ing), support(ed,ing), tax break, tax writeoff, bailout, bailing out, sponsor(ed,ing,ship), aid, investment, fund(ed,ing,s), price support(s), loan(s), pay(ing) the bill, picking up the tab, scholarship(s), assistance. *Consider also:* housing, farm(s), export(s), employment, agriculture, railroad(s) *with:* subsid(y,ies). *See also* Agricultural laws and legislation; Antipoverty programs; Enterprise zones; Fiscal federalism; Government aid; Government financing; Government programs; Medical assistance; National health programs; Public welfare; State capitalism; Subsidized housing.

Government travel. Government travel(er,ers,ing). *Choose from:* federal employee(s), official(s), government employee(s), civil service, White House personnel, government business *with:* travel(er,ers,ing), travel(ing) abroad. *Consider also:* government travel allowance(s), government transportation request(s). *See also* Government personnel; Travel.

Government workers. See *Civil service; Government personnel.*

Governmental powers. Government(al) powers. *Choose from:* government(al), executive, legislative, judicial, state, police, tax(ing), eminent domain, treaty-making, constitutional, delegat(ed,ion), enumerated, implied, exclusive *with:* power(s), authority, jurisdiction. *Consider also:* constitution(al,s), checks and balances. *See also* Confederalism;

Executive branch (government); Executive powers; Intergovernmental relations; Legislative bodies; Legislative powers; Separation of powers.

Governments, legitimacy of. See *Legitimacy of governments.*

Governors. Governor(s). Gouverneur(s). Chief executive(s). *See also* Elected officials; Political elites; State government.

Grace (theology). Grace (theology). Gift of God. God's goodwill. Prevenient grace. Sanctifying grace. Supernatural grace. *Consider also:* salvation, born again. *See also* Enlightenment (state of mind); Redemption (theology); Religious beliefs; Salvation.

Grace at meals. Grace at meals. Table blessing(s). *Consider also:* ask(ing) a blessing, giv(e,ing) thanks, benediction, thanksgiving *with:* meal(s), dinner(s), eating. *See also* Dinners and dining; Prayer; Religious rituals; Sacred meals.

Grade repetition. Grade repetition. *Choose from:* ingrade, in-grade, grade *with:* retention. Nonpromotion. Non-promotion. *Choose from:* also: repeat(ed), failed *with:* grade(s), course(s). *Consider also:* academic failure. *See also* Academic failure; Repetition; Student motivation; Underachievement.

Grading (educational). Grad(e,es,ed,ing). *Choose from:* credit-no-credit, pass-fail, scholastic, educational *with:* grad(e,es,ed,ing), mark(ed,s,ing). *See also* Academic achievement; Educational measurement; Student records.

Graduate education. Graduate education. *Consider also:* graduate, doctoral, PhD, masters, postdoctoral, postgraduate *with:* education, training, stud(y,ies), program(s), school(s). *See also* Higher education.

Graduate schools. Graduate school(s). *Choose from:* graduate, professional *with:* school(s). *Consider also:* law school(s), library school(s), medical school(s), dental school(s), veterinary school(s), etc. *See also* Higher education.

Graduate students. Graduate student(s). *Choose from:* graduate, doctoral, masters, PhD, *with:* candidate(s), student(s). *Consider also:* medical student(s), law student(s), etc. *See also* College students.

Graduates, college. See *College graduates.*

Graduates, high school. See *High school graduates.*

Graffiti. Graffit(i,o,ist,ists). *Choose from:* subway(s), train(s), railway building(s), train station(s), restroom(s) *with:* paint(ed,s,ing,ings), spraypaint(ed,ing, ings), defac(e,ed,ing), vandal(s,ism,ize, ized,izing). *Consider also:* satanic symbol(s). *See also* Defacement; Destruction of property; Nonverbal communication; Outdoor advertising; Street art; Vandalism.

Grain. Grain(s). Seed(s). Kernel(s). Grit(s). Cereal(s). *Consider also:* buckwheat, wheat, rice, corn, oats, barley, rye, groat(s). *See also* Agriculture; Food; Natural foods.

Grain trade. Grain trade. *Choose from:* grain(s), corn(s), wheat, cereal(s), flour, feed, agricultural *with:* trad(e,ing), market(s,ing), demand, handling, sector(s), import(s), export(s), agreement(s), procurement. *See also* Agribusiness; Agricultural prices; Agricultural price supports; Farm produce; Futures market.

Grammar. Grammar. Grammatical rule(s). Language rule(s). Language structure. Lexicogrammatical. *Consider also:* accidence, sentence structure, parts of speech, morphology of language, syntax. *See also* Comparative linguistics; Conditionals; Dialects; Generative grammar; Government binding theory (Linguistics); Imperative mood; Language; Language usage; Phrases; Sentence structure; Sentences.

Grammar, generative. See *Generative grammar.*

Grammar schools. See *Elementary schools.*

Grandchildren. Grandchild(ren). Grandson(s). Granddaughter(s). *Consider also:* descendant(s). *See also* Extended family; Grandparents.

Grandeur, delusions of. See *Delusions of grandeur.*

Grandparents. Grandparent(s). Grandmother(s). Grandfather(s). Grandpa(s). Grandma(s). Granddad(s). Grandmom(s). *Consider also:* forefather(s), progenitor(s). *See also* Extended family; Grandchildren.

Grandparents, great. See *Ancestors.*

Grants. Grant(s). Honorari(a,um,ums). *Consider also:* endowment(s), award(s), donation(s), bequest(s), subsid(y,ies), allotment(s), underwriting, financing, financial support, contribution(s), gift(s), fellowship(s), scholarship(s), stipend(s), allowance(s), gratuit(y,ies). *See also* Contributions; Donations; Endowment of research; Financial support; Foundations (organizations); Philanthropy; Scholarships (educational).

Grapes. Grape(s). Vitaceae. Vitis. *Consider also:* V. vinifera, V. rotundifolia, V. labrusca, grapevine(s), vineyard(s). *See also* Alcoholic beverages; Fruit.

Grapevine. Grapevine(s). Informal communication network(s). Old boy network(s). Old girl network(s). *See also* Gossip; Gossip sites; Informal social control; Information dissemination; Information exchange; Trivia.

Graphic arts. Graphic art(s). Graphics. Graphic design(s). Drawing(s). Print(s). *Consider also:* illustration(s). *See also* Arts; Engraving; Etching; Genres (art); Graphics; Illlustrated books; Printing; Visual communication.

Graphics. Graphics. Computer generated image(s). Drawing(s). Illustration(s). Chart(s). *Choose from:* pictorial, visual *with:* material(s), representation(s), likeness(es), image(s). *See also* Biological illustration; Diagrams; Graphic arts; Illustrated books; Medical illustration.

Graphology. Grapholog(y,ical,ist,ists). Handwriting assessment(s). Graphoanalysis. Handwrit(ten,ing) analysis. *Consider also:* handwriting *with:* character analysis. *See also* Handwriting.

Grass roots. See *Citizen participation; Community involvement; Community power; Community support; Local government; Local politics; Neighborhood associations; Populism.*

Grasses. Grass(es). Pastur(e,es,age). Vegetation. Hay. Fodder. Lawn(s). Grazing herbage. Gramineae. Cyperaceae. Juncaceae. *Consider also:* ground cover(s,age), wildrye, fescue(s), switchgrass(es), prairie flora. *See also* Grassland fires; Grasslands; Grazing lands; Land preservation; Plants (botanical); Vegetation; Wetlands.

Grassland fires. Grassland fire(s). Prairie fire(s). *Choose from:* fire(s) *with:* grassland(s), prairie(s), brush. *See also* Fire ecology; Forest fires; Grasses; Grasslands.

Grasslands. Grassland(s). Pasture(s). Savanna(s). Plain(s). Prairie(s). Meadow(s,land,lands). Down(s). Moor(s,land,lands). Veld(s). Veldt(s). Steppe(s). Pampa(s). Wold(s). *Consider also:* tundra(s), salt marsh(es). *See also* Arid lands; Geographic regions; Grasses; Grassland fires; Grazing lands; Land preservation; Rural areas; Vegetation; Wetlands.

Grassroots. See *Citizen participation; Community involvement; Community power; Community support; Local government; Local politics; Neighborhood associations; Populism.*

Gratification, delay of. See *Delay of gratification.*

Gratification, need. See *Need satisfaction.*

Gratis. Gratis. Complimentary. Free of charge. Cost free. Chargeless. No cost. Expense free. Gratuitous. Without charge. Costless. Expenseless. *See also* Costs; Expenditures; Gifts; Prices.

Gratitude. Gratitude. Grateful(ness). Thankful(ness). Giving thanks. Thanksgiving. Appreciat(ive,ion). Acknowledge(ment). Testimonial(s). Tribute(s). *See also* Emotions.

Gratuities. Gratuit(y,ies). Bonus(es). Contribution(s). Fringe benefit(s). Gift(s). Honorari(a,um,ums). Reward(s). Tip(s,ped,ping). Perk(s). Perquisite(s). Douceur(s). Lagniappe(s). Cumshaw(s). Baksheesh. *See also* Bribery; Compensation (payment); Monetary rewards; Tipping.

Grave goods. Grave goods. *Choose from:* grave(s), tomb(s), vault(s) *with:* content(s), treasure(s), object(s), goods. *See also* Cemeteries; Grave robbing; Sepulchral monuments.

Grave robbing. Grave robbing. *Choose from:* grave(s), churchyard(s), cemeter(y,ies), tomb(s), corpse(s), bod(y,ies), cadaver(s) *with:* rob(bed, bing,ber,bers), violat(ed,ing,ion,ions), stealing, stolen. *Consider also:* body snatching, resurrectionist(s), William Burke and William Hare, burking, burkers, bodysnatcher(s). *See also* Cemeteries; Grave goods; Robbery.

Graveyards. See *Cemeteries.*

Gravitation and gravity. See *Gravity and gravitation.*

Gravitational effects. Gravitational effect(s). *Choose from:* Gz, G, gravitational *with:* stress(es), strain(s), disorientation. *Choose from:* tilt *with:* effect(s), aftereffect(s). *Consider also:* force(s) of gravity, G forces, gravitoinertial force, centrifug(e,al), hypergravitation(al), gravity, microgravity. *Choose from:* gravitation(al) *with:* effect(s), response(s), influence(s), aftereffect(s), affect(ed,ing). *See also* Acceleration effects; Altitude effects; Flight simulation; Space exploration; Weightlessness.

Gravitational lenses. Gravitational lens(es,ing). Gravity lens(es). *Consider also:* celestial reflector(s), cosmic lens(es), occultation astronomy, curved space as lens, Einstein cross. *See also* Astronomy.

Gravity and gravitation. See *Gravitational effects.*

Gray market. Gray market(s). Unauthorized source(s). Informal source(s). *Consider also:* illegal source(s), black market(s). *See also* Bartering; Black economy; Economic exchanges; Informal sector.

Gray power. Gray power. Grey power. Gray Panthers. *Choose from:* elderly, senior citizen(s), old age, older person(s), aging population(s), older citizen(s), older people, retiree(s), older American(s) *with:* power, empower(ed,ing,ment), activis(m,t,ts), militan(t,cy), lobb(y,ies,ying), protest(ed,er,ers,s), community action, demonstrat(ed,ing, ion,ions), demonstrator(s), social action, rights group(s), radical(s,ism), political participation, citizen participation, political activit(y,ies), vot(e,es,ed,ing), consumerism, rebellion(s), liberation, assertive(ness), crusade(s), march(es), rall(y,ies). *Consider also:* American Association of Retired Persons, AARP, Maggie Kuhn, gerontocrac(y,ies). *See also* Activism; Activists; Age discrimination; Aged 80 and over; Attitudes toward the aged; Elderly; Militancy; Social action; Protest movements; Social movements.

Grazing. Graz(e,ed,ing). Brows(e,ed,ing). Forag(e,ed,ing). Nibbl(e,ed,ing). Chew(ing). *See also* Animal foraging behavior; Cattle; Grazing lands.

Grazing lands. Grazing land(s). Grassland(s). Prairie(s). Meadow(s). Pasture(s). Rangeland(s). Range land(s). *See also* Farms; Grasslands; Grasses; Grazing; Rural areas; Transhumance; Vegetation; Right of pasture; Rangelands.

Great awakening. Great awakening. Spiritual regeneration. *Consider also:* Christolog(y,ical), pietism, Jonathan Edwards, Gilbert Tennent, George Whitefield, New Lights, Old Lights. *See also* Regeneration (theology); Religious movements; Religious revivals.

Great grandparents. See *Ancestors.*

Great men. See *Famous people; Heroes; Martyrs; Role models; Saints.*

Greed. Greed(y,iness). Aplest(ia,ic). Avaricious(ness). Grasping. Possessive(ness). Hoard(ed,ing). Rapacious(ness). *See also* Hoarding; Possessiveness.

Greek and Roman games. Greek and Roman game(s). *Choose from:* Gree(k,ce), Rom(e,an), Pan-Hellenic, Etruscan *with:* game(s), festival(s). *See also* Antiquity (time); Sports.

Greek languages. Greek language(s). Achean. Aeolic. Attic. Byzantine Greek. Classical Greek. Corinthian. Cyprian. Doric. Ionian [Homeric Greek]. Koine. Modern Greek. *See also* Language; Languages (as subjects); Western Europe.

Greek music, ancient. See *Ancient Greek music.*

Greenhouse effect. Greenhouse effect. Warm world scenario(s). Greenhouse gas(es). Rising sea level(s). Global distillation. *Choose from:* global, atmospheric *with:* warm(er,ed,ing). *Choose from:* climate, climatic, polar

environment, global environment *with:* change(s), modification(s). *Choose from:* destruction, destroy(ed,ing), deplet(e,ed,ing,ion) *with:* ozone layer. *Choose from:* carbon dioxide, methane and nitrous oxide, chlorofluorocarbon(s) *with:* global, increas(e,es,ed,ing), buildup(s). *See also* Acid rain; Air pollution; Atmospheric contamination; Atmospheric temperature; Climatic changes; Environmental impacts; Environmental pollutants; Environmental pollution; Environmental protection; Environmentalism; Sustainable development.

Greetings. See *Salutations.*

Gregariousness. Gregarious(ness). *Choose from:* interpersonal competence, sociab(le,ility), affab(le,ility), friend(ly,liness), neighbor(ly,liness), companionable, amicab(le,ility), genial(ity), cordial(ity), warm hearted, kind(ly,liness), friend(ly,liness), warmth, charming, likeab(le,ility), loveab(le,ility). *See also* Affiliation motivation; Friendliness; Personality traits; Sociability.

Gregorian chants. Gregorian chant(s). Roman chant(s). Plainsong, Plainchant. Ordinary chant(s), Proper chant(s). Cantus gregorianus. *Consider also:* responsorial singing, responsor(y,ies, ium), melisma(tic). *See also* Antiphons; Chants; Liturgy; Plainsong.

Gridlock. See *Deadlock.*

Grief. Grief. Griev(e,ed,ing). Mourn(ed,ing,er,er,ers). Melancholy. Bereave(d,ment). Sad(ness). Feeling of loss. Sense of loss. Despair. Anguish(ed). Miser(y,able). Sorrow(ful). Lament(ation). Morose. Depress(ed,ion). *See also* Bereavement; Crying; Death rituals; Emotions; Laments; Loss (psychology); Mourning; Suffering.

Grievance procedures. See *Employee grievances.*

Grievances. See *Complaints.*

Grievances, employee. See *Employee grievances.*

Griffins. Griffin(s). Gryphon(s). Griffon(s). *See also* Mythical animals.

Grimaces. Grimac(e,es,ing). *Choose from:* mak(e,ing), made, contort(ed,ing,ion, ions), distort(ed,ion,ions), wry *with:* face(s), facial. *Consider also:* facial expression(s), frown(s,ed), scowl(s,ed, ing), glar(e,es,ed,ing), sneer(s,ed,ing), glower(ed,ing), pout(ed,ing). *See also* Facial expressions; Nonverbal communication.

Grinding teeth, nocturnal. See *Bruxism.*

Grocery trade. Grocery trade. Grocer(s). Grocery store(s). Supermarket(s). Super market(s). Superstore(s). Grocery industry. Grocery chain(s). Food

emporium(s). Macrobiotic co-op(s). *Consider also:* Food Lion, Safeway, Star Market, Great Atlantic and Pacific Tea Co, Giant Food Inc, Bread and Circus Inc., Albertson's, Grand Union. *See also* Farm produce; Food industry.

Grooming. See *Hygiene.*

Grooming behavior, animal. See *Animal grooming behavior.*

Gross motor skills. Gross motor skill(s). *Choose from:* gross motor *with:* skill(s), abilit(y,ies), control, behavior(s), development, performance. *Consider also:* balance *with:* task(s), performance. *See also* Perceptual motor learning; Skill learning.

Gross national product. Gross national product. GNP. Gross national income. *Consider also:* Gross domestic product, GDP. *See also* Economic conditions; Economic development; Economic indicators; Economic statistics; Living standards; National income; Production consumption relationship.

Grotesque. Grotesque(ness). Grotesquerie. Gruesome(ness). Strange(ness). Freak(s,ish). Bizarre(ness). Misshapen. Twisted. Gnarled. Deformed. Unnatural. Ugl(y,iness). Distorted. Incongru(ous, ity). *Consider also:* gargoyle(s), black humor. *See also* Absurd; Gothic romances; Gothicism; Literature; Ugliness.

Ground effect machines. Ground effect machine(s). Ground-effect craft(s). Ground-effect flight machine(s). Low-flying aircraft. Ground-effect hybrid-craft. Hovercraft. Hydrofoil(s). Ekranoplane(s). *Consider also:* helicopter(s), vertically rising aircraft, planing boat(s), surface skimmer system(s), Air Cushion Transport System (ACTS), pneumatically suspended transit vehicle(s), aerodynamic ground effect. *See also* Air transportation; Aircraft; Transportation; Water transportation.

Ground figure discrimination. See *Figure ground discrimination.*

Ground penetrating radar. Ground penetrating radar. Ground Penetrating Imaging Radar. (GPIR). Georadar(gram, grams). *See also* Archaeological surveying; Hydrogeology; Geology.

Ground transportation. Ground transport(ation). *Choose from:* bus(ses,sing,sed), auto(s), automobile(s), truck(s), train(s), motor vehicle(s), rail, railroad(s), railway(s), motorcycl(e,es, ing), bicycl(e,es,ing), car(s) *with:* travel(led,ling), transport(ed,ing,ation). *See also* Caravans; Carriages; Chariots; Commuting (travel); Highways; Mass transit; Motor vehicles; Railroads; Transport workers.

Groundless. Groundless. Baseless. Conjectur(e,ed,ing,al). Imagin(e,ed,ing, ary). Speculat(e,ed,ive). Unfounded. Ungrounded. Unjustifi(ed,able). Unprovoked. Unsubstantia(l,ted). Unsupported. Unwarranted. Supposition(s,al). Senseless. *See also* Delusions; Illogical; Implausibility; Irrational beliefs; Superstitions.

Grounds, home. See *Home grounds.*

Grounds, proving. See *Proving grounds.*

Groundwork. Groundwork. Base(s). Basis. Foundation(s). Fundamental(s). Infrastructure(s). Substrat(a,um). Underpinning(s). Understructure(s). *Consider also:* essential(s), preliminar(y, ies), core(s), preliminar(y,ies). *See also* Boundaries; Designs; Format; Frames (physical); Morphology; Structure.

Group behavior. See *Collective behavior.*

Group cohesion. See *Social cohesion.*

Group composition. Group composition. *Choose from:* group(s), team(s), communit(y,ies), congregation(s), tribe(s), gang(s), squad(s), troop(s), troupe(s), crew(s), guild(s), league(s), faction(s), famil(y,ies), clan(s), club(s), jur(y,ies), panel(s), organization(s,al), association(s) *with:* composition, member(s,ship,ship), population, distribution, heterogene(ity,ous), homogene(ity,ous), makeup, demographics. *See also* Community (social); Demographic characteristics (of individuals); Ethnicity; Group dynamics; Group formation; Group identity; Group size; Group structure; Heterogeneity; Homogeneity; Races; Sex ratio.

Group consciousness. Group consciousness. Group mind. Syntality. *Consider also:* groupthink, group harmony, consensus. *See also* Belongingness; Ethnic identity.

Group counseling. Group counseling. Group work. Counseling group(s). Group therap(y,ies). Self help group(s). Treatment group(s). *Choose from:* group(s), workshop(s) *with:* counseling, therap(y,ies), self help, treatment, guidance, support, assert(iveness,ion) training, marital enrichment, personal growth, employment counseling, career counseling, vocational counseling, session(s). *Consider also:* leaderless groups. *See also* Family therapy; Group discussion; Group dynamics; Group psychotherapy.

Group decision making. Group decision making. *Choose from:* group(s), cooperative, jur(y,ies), team(s), unanimous, staff(s), famil(y,ies) panel(s), triad(s), coalition(s) *with:* decision making, choice(s), decision(s), verdict(s). *Consider also:* participative decision making, cooperative choice(s), consensus, majority rule, delphi

technique. *See also* Choice behavior; Choices (alternatives); Consensus; Group discussion; Group dynamics; Participative decision making; Problem solving; Teamwork.

Group discussion. Group discussion. *Choose from:* group(s), class(es,room), open, panel(s), seminar(s), team(s) *with:* discussion(s), decision making, process(es), program(s), confrontation(s), interaction(s), session(s), argument(s), consensus, experience(s), problem solving. *See also* Brainstorming; Discussion; Group counseling; Group dynamics.

Group dynamics. Group dynamic(s). *Choose from:* group(s), team(s), social, committee(s), communit(y,ies), organization(s,al) *with:* dynamic(s), interaction, pressure(s), process(es), relation(s,ship,ships), interdependence, behavior(s), influence, leadership, reward structure(s), disrupt(ive,ion), performance, change(s), cooperat(ion, ive), competit(ion,ive), participation, cohesion, climate, flexibility, environment, role(s), reference point(s). *Consider also:* role differentiation, common basis for action, intergroup dynamics. *See also* Brainstorming; Collective behavior; Consciousness raising activities; Group decision making; Group formation; Group norms; Group participation; Group processes; Organizational politics; Peer influences; Role playing; Social cohesion; Social dominance; Social loafing; Social support; Transactional analysis.

Group feeling. Group feeling. Herd instinct. Social bond(s). *Choose from:* group(s), club(s), association(s) *with:* awareness, feeling(s), conscious(ness). *Consider also:* gregarious(ness), togetherness. *See also* Affiliation motivation; Belongingness; Class consciousness; Community feeling; Ethnic identity; Group consciousness; Group identity; Gregariousness; Racial identity; Social cohesion; Social identity.

Group formation. Group formation. *Choose from:* group(s), team(s), congregation(s), tribe(s), gang(s), squad(s), troop(s), troupe(s), crew(s), guild(s), league(s), faction(s), band(s), club(s), association(s), coalition(s), collectivit(y,ies), committee(s), famil(y,ies), communit(y,ies) *with:* form(ation,ed,ing), organiz(e,ed,ing), establish(ed,ing), rise, construction, reconstruction, solidif(y,ied,ication). *See also* Class formation; Coalescence; Coalition formation; Group composition; Social segmentation.

Group homes. Group home(s). *Choose from:* group, communal, congregate, shared, sheltered, supportive, assisted, senior(s), developmentally disabled

with: home(s), residence(s), residential care home(s), residential setting(s), living. *Consider also:* dormitor(y,ies), halfway house(s), board and care home(s). *See also* Adult foster care; Boardinghouses; Deinstitutionalization; Homes for the elderly; Noninstitutionalized disabled; Residential facilities; Sheltered housing.

Group identity. Group identity. Group identification. Collective identity. Political identification. Shared identity. *Choose from:* group(s), team(s), subgroup(s), subcultur(al,e,es), congregation(al,s), trib(al,e,es), gang(s), troop(s), troupe(s), crew(s), guild(s), league(s), faction(s), band(s), ingroup(s), in-group(s), famil(y,ies), clan(s), club(s), sororit(y,ies), fraternit(y,ies), class(es), association(s), collectivit(y,ies), collective, ethnic, or name of specific group *with:* identity, identification, pride, involvement, awareness, consciousness, tradition(al,s). *See also* Black community; Class consciousness; Cooptation; Cultural identity; Ethnic identity; Group consciousness; Group feeling; Group norms; Organizational commitment; Racial identity; Social identity.

Group instruction. Group instruction. Instruction(al) group(s). Group lesson(s). *Choose from:* group(s), cooperative, collective, team *with:* instruction(al), lesson(s), tutorial(s), training, teaching, presentation(s), study. *Consider also:* classroom instruction. *See also* Cooperative learning; Group dynamics; Teaching methods.

Group marriage. Group marriage(s). Cenogamy. Common marital arrangement. Common marriage. *Consider also:* polygam(y,ous), polyandr(y,ous), polygyn(y,ous), plural marriage(s), stirpiculture, group concubinage, expanded marriage(s). *See also* Alternative family forms; Polyamory.

Group meals. Group meal(s). *Choose from:* group(s), congregat(e,ion), communal, community, public *with:* meal(s,time, times), dinner(s), lunch(es,eon,eons), breakfast(s), dining, feeding. *See also* Eating; Group homes.

Group norms. Group norm(s). Social norm(s). Socially (un)acceptable. Interactional norm(s). Cultural standard(s). Moral system(s). Shared normative framework. Group reference points. Organizational rules. Conform(ity,ing). Common bas(is,es) for action. Codes of conduct. *Choose from:* shared, social, group(s), member(s), team(s), congregation(al,s), trib(al,e,es), gang(s), troop(s), troupe(s), crew(s), guild(s), league(s), faction(s), band(s), famil(y,ies), clan(s), club(s), sororit(y, ies), fraternit(y,ies), class(es), association(s), organization(al,s), division(al,s) section(s), branch(es), collectiv(e,ity,ities), committee(s) *with:* norm(s), normative, standard(s), rule(s), code(s), expectation(s), obligation(s), values. *See also* Acceptability; Codes of ethics; Group dynamics; Norms; Peer influences; Social approval; Social behavior; Social cohesion; Social norms.

Group participation. Group participation. Group participant(s). *Choose from:* group(s), social, meeting(s), committee(s), social activit(y,ies), conference(s), classroom(s), communit(y,ies), organization(al,s) *with:* participat(e,ed,ing,ion), participant(s), involvement, interaction, attendance, leadership, member(s,ship,ships), affiliat(e,ed,ing,ion). *See also* Collective behavior; Group dynamics; Involvement; Participation; Social loafing.

Group performance. Group performance. Group effectiveness. *Choose from:* group(s), team(s), workgroup(s), staff, player(s) *with:* performance, effectiveness, success, failure, productivity, achievement(s), outcome(s), attainment, satisfaction, results, creativity. *See also* Collective behavior; Group dynamics; Group processes; Social loafing.

Group problem solving. Group problem solving. Brainstorm(ing). Cooperative problem solving. Problem solving group(s). *Choose from:* group(s), committee(s), panel(s), triad(s,ic), famil(y,ies), staff, collective, congregation(s), communit(y,ies) *with:* problem solving, solving problems, resolving problems, thinking task(s), task performance. *Consider also:* think tank(s), group decision making, collective thinking. *See also* Brainstorming; Cooperative learning; Corporate retreats; Group decision making; Problem solving.

Group processes. Group process(es). Group behavior(s). Teamwork. Team work. Collective creativity. Collective opinion(s). Consensus(es). Pecking order(s). Gang behavior(s). Collective exchange process(es). *Choose from:* group(s), team(s), workgroup(s), collectiv(e,ity,ities), communit(y,ies), committee(s), congregation(s,al), crowd(s), crew(s), neighbor(s), neighborhood(s), organization(s,al), association(s), triad(s,ic), intergroup *with:* behavior, decision making, decision(s), problem solving, relations, solidarity, distance, dominance, cohesion, discussion(s), participation, performance, dynamic(s), brainstorming, process(es), interaction(s), polarization, approach(es), meeting(s), experience(s), confrontation(s), development, pressure(s), conflict(s), effectiveness, conformity, activit(y,ies). *See also* Brainstorming; Group decision making;

Group discussion; Group dynamics; Group formation; Group norms; Group participation; Group performance; Group problem solving; Group structure; Groups; Humanistic education; Informal social control; Interaction; Interpersonal relations; Organizational culture; Peer influences; Role playing; Sensitivity training; Social loafing; Transactional analysis.

Group psychotherapy. Group psychotherap(y,ies). *Choose from:* psychotherap(y,ies,eutic), treatment(s), therapeutic, remotivation therap(y,ies), fantasy therap(y,ies), self control training, social work, self help, counseling, behavior modification, rehabilitation, desensitization, relaxation therap(y,ies), therap(y,ies), family therap(y,ies), sensitivity training, encounter, psychoanalytic, marathon *with:* group(s). *Consider also:* conjoint therapy, therapeutic communit(y,ies), psychodrama, role playing. *See also* Consciousness raising activities; Encounter groups; Group counseling; Group dynamics; Marathon group therapy; Milieu therapy; Psychodrama; Self help groups; Sensitivity training; Therapeutic community; Transactional analysis.

Group research. Group research. Sociometr(y,ic). *Choose from:* group(s), crowd(s), collectiv(e,es,ity,ities) *with:* research, experiment(al,s), stud(y,ies). *See also* Groups; Research.

Group size. Group size(s). *Choose from:* size(s), small(er,est), larg(e,er,est), magnitude *with:* group(s), class(es), audience(s), flock(s), crowd(s), subunit(s), unit(s), population, subgroup(s), workshop(s). *Consider also:* critical mass, number of witnesses, mini-groups. *See also* Group dynamics; Groups; Size.

Group structure. Group structure. Group organization. Organizational chart(s). Egalitarian group(s). Shared power. *Choose from:* group(s), team(s), famil(y,ies), troop(s), club(s), association(s), congregation(s) *with:* structure(s), monolithic, polariz(ed, ing,ation), leader(s,ship), leaderless, hierarch(y,ies), dominance, submission. *Consider also:* social structure, organization(al,s) structure, governmental structure. *See also* Agrarian structures; Clusters; Family characteristics; Group dynamics; Organizational structure; Power structure; Social structure; Sociometric technics.

Group testing. Group test(s,ing). Group intelligence test(s,ing). *Choose from:* group(s), population(s), subgroup(s), class(es) *with:* test(s,ing), evaluation(s), examination(s), instrument(s), questionnaire(s), screening, measure(s,

ment,ments), assess(ed,ing,ment,ments), rating(s), score(s). *See also* Groups; Educational measurement; Tests.

Group therapy. See *Group counseling; Group psychotherapy.*

Group therapy, marathon. See *Marathon group therapy.*

Group unity. See *Social cohesion.*

Group work. Group work. Groupwork. *Choose from:* group(s) *with:* social work, treatment, self help, counseling, therap(y,ies). *Consider also:* family therap(y,ies), psychodrama, role playing, therapeutic communit(y,ies), youth work. *See also* Group counseling; Group psychotherapy; Self help groups.

Grouping, ability. See *Ability grouping.*

Groups. Group(s). Association(s). Assembl(y,ies). Band(s). Branch(es). Brotherhood(s). Cadre(s). Clan(s). Class(es). Clique(s). Club(s). Cluster(s). Collectivit(y,ies). Collective(s). Committee(s). Coalition(s). Congregation(s). Communit(y,ies). Crew(s). Crowd(s). Division(s). Dyad(s). Faction(s). Famil(y,ies). Fraternit(y,ies). Gang(s). Group(s). Guild(s). Inner circle(s). League(s). Lodge(s). Minorit(y,ies). Majorit(y,ies). Neighbor(s,hood,hoods). Network(s). Organization(s). Part(y,ies). Section(s). Sisterhood(s). Societ(y,ies). Sororit(y, ies). Squad(s). Subgroup(s). Subunit(s). Subculture(s). Team(s). Triad(s). Tribe(s). Troop(s). Troupe(s). Unit(s). Workgroup(s). *Choose from:* primary, interest, women's, men's, small, community, voluntary, reference, constituent, social, secret, support, youth *with:* group(s), association(s), societ(y,ies), club(s), network(s), organization(s). *Consider also:* ingroup(s), in-group(s), outgroup(s), intergroup, semi-group(s), communal, connectivity, belonging, affiliation, member(s,ship), heterogeneity, homogeneity. *See also* Age groups; Audiences; Cadres; Clusters; Coalitions; Community (social); Crowds; Cultural groups; Group composition; Group consciousness; Group dynamics; Group formation; Group participation; Group performance; Group processes; Group size; Group structure; Group testing; Group work; Interest groups; Majorities (political); Majority groups; Minority groups; Neighbors; Organizational politics; Organizations; Parent help groups; Reference groups; Self help groups; Small groups; Social support networks; Stratification; Teams; Women's groups; Work groups.

Groups, advisory. See *Advisory committees.*

Groups, advocacy. See *Advocacy; Change agents; Interest groups; Lobbying; Social movements.*

Groups, African cultural. See *African cultural groups.*

Groups, age. See *Age groups.*

Groups, Central American cultural. See *Central American native cultural groups.*

Groups, control research. See *Control groups (research).*

Groups, cultural. See *Cultural groups.*

Groups , descent. See *Clans; Extended family.*

Groups, developmental age. See *Age groups.*

Groups, dominant. See *Majority groups.*

Groups, encounter. See *Encounter groups.*

Groups, ethnic. See *Ethnic groups.*

Groups, focus. See *Focus groups.*

Groups, hate. See *Hate groups.*

Groups, interest. See *Interest groups.*

Groups, majority. See *Majority groups.*

Groups, minority. See *Minority groups.*

Groups, national minority. See *Ethnic groups; Linguistic minorities; Minority groups; National identity; Nationalism.*

Groups, North American cultural. See *North American native cultural groups.*

Groups, Oceanic cultural. See *Oceanic cultural groups.*

Groups, parent help. See *Parent help groups.*

Groups, peer. See *Peers.*

Groups, pressure. See *Interest groups; Lobbying.*

Groups, primary. See *Primary groups.*

Groups, racial. See *Races.*

Groups, reference. See *Reference groups.*

Groups, religious. See *Monasticism; Religions; Religious cults; Religious cultural groups.*

Groups, religious cultural. See *Religious cultural groups.*

Groups, self help. See *Self help groups.*

Groups, small. See *Small groups.*

Groups, social. See *Groups.*

Groups, South American cultural. See *South American native cultural groups.*

Groups, special interest. See *Interest groups; Lobbying; Political movements; Women's groups.*

Groups, T. See *Sensitivity training.*

Groups, white supremacy. See *White supremacy movements.*

Groups, women's. See *Women's groups.*

Groups, work. See *Work groups.*

Grown children. See *Adult offspring.*

Growth. See *Development.*

Growth, city. See *Urban development.*

Growth, controlling suburban. See *Growth management.*

Growth, economic. See *Business growth; Economic development.*

Growth, financial. See *Earnings; Gains; Income; Profits.*

Growth, personal. See *Enlightenment (state of mind); Human potential movement; Moral development; Psychosocial development; Self actualization.*

Growth, physical. See *Physical development.*

Growth, population. See *Population growth.*

Growth, spiritual. See *Spiritual formation.*

Growth, zero economic. See *Zero economic growth.*

Growth, zero population. See *Zero population growth.*

Growth disorders. Growth disorder(s). Gigantism. Human growth hormone disorder(s). HGH disorder(s). GH disorder(s). Dwarfism. Skeletal retardation. Fetal growth retardation. Failure to thrive. Psychosocial dwarfism. Acromegaly. Constitutional delay. Hyposomatropic dwarfism. *Choose from:* growth *with:* disorder(s), retard(ed,ation), delay(ed), impair(ed, ment,ments), disturb(ed,ance,ances), failure, falter(ed,ing), accelerat(ed,ion). *Consider also:* Cushing(s) syndrome, Bartter(s) syndrome, Kugel Welander(s) syndrome, Schwartz Jampel(s) syndrome, hypogonadism, pituitary disorders, Klinefelter(s) syndrome, Turner(s) syndrome, hypopituitarism. *See also* Congenitally handicapped; Delayed development; Developmental disabilities; Failure to thrive (psychosocial); Physical development; Psychosexual development; Psychosocial deprivation; Psychosocial development; Psychosocial mental retardation.

Growth management. Growth management. Anti-growth polic(y,ies). *Choose from:* grow(th,ing), sprawl, development, expansion, expand(ed,ing), supercit(y,ies), megacit(y,ies), boomtown(s), boom(s) *with:* manag(e, ed,ing,ement), control(s,led,ling), regulat(e,ed,ing,ion,ions), restrict(s,ed, ing), constrain(t,ts,ed,ing), oppos(e, ed,ing,ition), halt(s,ed,ing), curb(s,ed, ing), slow(s,ed,ing). *Consider also:* zon(e,ed,ing), smart growth, green spaces, livable communities. *See also* Boom towns; Community development; Real estate development; Rural development; Rural land; Sustainable develop-

ment; Urban development; Urban planning; Zoning.

Growth motivation. See *Metamotivation.*

Growth strategies. Growth strateg(y,ies). *Choose from:* growth, development, progrowth, productivity, expan(d,ded, ding,sion), industrialization, export(s), redevelop(ed,ing,ment,ments), improv(e, ed,ing,ment,ments), advanc(es,ed,ing, ement,ements), moderniz(ed,ing,ation) *with:* strateg(y,ies), boost(s,ing,ed,er,ers, erism), polic(y,ies), intervention(s), incentive(s), scenario(s), plan(s,ned, ning), promot(e,ed,ing,ion). *See also* Business growth; Community development; Economic development; Economic planning; Local planning; Planning; Social planning; Strategic management.

Grunge music. See *Rock music.*

Guaranteed income. See *Income maintenance programs.*

Guarantees. Guarantee(s,d,ing). Guarant(y, ies). Assurance(s). Warrant(y,ies,ed). Bond(ed). Certif(y,ied). Endorse(d, ment). Insur(e,ed,ing). Secur(e,ed,ing). Indemnif(y,ied). Underwrit(e,ten). *See also* Agreement (document); Assurances; Certificates; Contracts; Product safety; Promises; Service contracts.

Guardians, legal. See *Legal guardians.*

Guards. See *Correctional personnel; Security guards.*

Guards, prison. See *Correctional personnel.*

Guerilla warfare. Guerilla warfare. Guerilla tactic(s). Maquis. *Choose from:* guerilla(s), partisan(s), underground, unconventional *with:* war(s,fare), tactic(s), fight(s,ing), operation(s), battle(s), action(s). *Consider also:* industrial sabotage, espionage, resistance force(s). *See also* Guerrillas; National fronts; Paramilitary; Political violence; Rebellions; Revolution; Separatism; Terrorism; War.

Guerrillas. Guerrilla(s). Guerilla(s). Guerrillerismo. Irregular warfare. Vietcong. Rebel(s). Insurgen(t,ts,cy). New Peoples' Army. Contra(s). Sandinista(s). *Consider also:* brigand(s), bandit(s,ry), saboteur(s), bushfighter(s), partisan(s), resistance fighter(s), underground fighter(s), terroris(m,t,ts), hijacking(s), rebel(s), Mau Mau, Maoism, Castroism, war(s) of national liberation, Basque separatist(s), ETA, Che Guevara, Regis Debray, Carlos Marighela, Palestine Liberation Organization [PLO], Irish Republican Army [IRA], Hamas, intifada, Mujahid(een,in) [Mujahed(een,din)], Tupac Amaru Revolutionary Movement [MRTA], Sendero Luminoso [Shining Path, Senderista(s)], Guatemalan

National Revolutionary Unity [Unidad Revolucionaria Nacional Guatamalteca, URNG], Farabundo Marti National Liberation Front [FMLN], Sandinista National Liberation Front [FSLN], Popular Unified Action Movement - Lautaro [Movimento de Popular Unida, MAPU-Lautaro], Honduran Popular Movement for the Liberation of Cinchoneras, Ejercito de Liberacion Nacional [ELN], Colombian National Liberation Army [Fuerzas Armadas Revolucionarios de Colombia, FARC], Nestor Paz Zamora Commission. Zapatista(s). Ejercito Zapatista de Liberacion Nacional. [EZLN]. *See also* Antifascist movements; Anti-government radicals; Civil war; Guerilla warfare; Internal security; Islamic Resistance Movement; National fronts; Paramilitary; Peasant rebellions; Political violence; Rebellions; Rebels; Resistance movements; Revolution; Revolutionary ballads and songs; Separatism; Terrorism.

Guessing. Guess(ed,es,ing,work,timate, timates). *Consider also:* conjectur(e,ed, ing), surmis(e,ed,ing), estimat(e,ed,ing), hypothesiz(e,ed,ing), postulat(e,ed,ing), reckon(ed,ing), suppos(e,ed,ing,ition, itions). *See also* Intuition; Questioning; Strategies; Test taking.

Guest workers. See *Foreign workers.*

Guests. Guest(s). Boarder(s). Lodger(s). Vacationer(s). Roomer(s). Caller(s). Visitor(s). *Consider also:* freeloader(s), habitue(s), frequenter(s). *See also* Hospitality; Visitors.

Guidance, career. See *Vocational guidance.*

Guidance, child. See *Child guidance.*

Guidance, educational. See *Educational counseling.*

Guidance, occupational. See *Vocational guidance.*

Guidance, vocational. See *Vocational guidance.*

Guidancecounseling. See *School counseling.*

Guidebooks. Guidebook(s). Guide(s). *Consider also:* manual(s), handbook(s), travelogue literature, travel guide(s), travel guidebook(s), information source(s), reference source(s). *See also* Texts; Travel literature.

Guided missiles. See *Ballistic missiles.*

Guidelines. Guideline(s). *Consider also:* checklist(s), principle(s), rule(s), formula(s), guide(s), regulation(s),

instruction(s), model(s), pattern(s), indicator(s), form(s), standard(s), outline(s), prescription(s), recommendation(s), directions, prototype(s), sample(s), specimen(s). *See also* Designs; Diagrams; Goals; Planning; Regulations.

Guides. See *Texts.*

Guides, personal. See *Self help books.*

Guild socialism. Guild socialism. National Guilds League. *Consider also:* Arthur J. Penty, syndicalis(m,t). *See also* Guilds; Labor unions; Socialism.

Guilds. Guild(s,ship,sman). Craft guild(s). Trade union(s). Craft union(s). Hanseatic league. Occupational association(s). *Consider also:* workingmen's association(s), or journeymen's societies. *See also* Artisans; Crafts; Guild socialism; Labor unions; Trade associations; Weaving.

Guilt. Guilt(y,iness). Ashamed. Shame. Remorse(ful). Need for punishment. Self blame. Confession(s). Repentan(t,ce). Self punishing. Self punitive(ness). Self chastising. Culpab(le,ility). Mea culpa. Blameworthy. Censurable. Contrit(e, eness,ion). Peniten(t,ce). Penance. Compunction(s). Self condemnation. Self reproach. Self accusation. *Consider also:* culprit(s). *See also* Anxiety; Anxiety disorders; Blame; Blameworthy; Conscience; Conviction; Denial (psychology); Embarrassment; Emotions; Examination of conscience; Fall of man; Humiliation; Liability; Neutralization; Penitents; Rationalization (defense mechanism); Repentence; Self accusation; Self debasement; Shame; Sin.

Guitars. Guitar(s). Kithara(s). Guitare(s). Gitarre(n). Chitarra(s). Guitarra(s). Violao(s). *Consider also:* electric guitar(s), gittern(s), gyterne(s), guitarron(s). *See also* Musical instruments.

Gulf war syndrome. Gulf war syndrome. Desert fever. Desert storm syndrome. Persian war syndrome. *Choose from:* Gulf war, Desert storm *with:* syndrome(s), illness(es), disorder(s), disabilit(y, ies), chemical exposure, chemical poisoning, chemical war(fare), fatigue, fever, PTSD, posttraumatic stress disorder(s), memory loss. *See also* Combat; Combat disorders; War; Weapons of mass destruction.

Gun control. Gun control(s). Gun regulation(s). *Choose from:* prohibit(ed, ing,ion), forbid(den,ding) *with:* sale, import(ed,ing,ation), possess(ed,ing, ion), carry(ing) *with:* gun(s),

handgun(s). *Choose from:* gun(s), firearm(s), handgun(s), weapon(s), pistol(s), rifle(s), musket(s), machinegun(s), assault rifle(s), automatic rifle(s), *with:* control(s,led,ling), ban(ned,ning), registration, register(ed,ing), waiting period(s), restrict(ed,ing,ion,ions), regulat(e,ed,ing,ion,ions), prohibit(ed, ing,ion), law(s), curb(s,ed,ing). *Consider also:* Second Amendment. *See also* Crime prevention; Firearms industry; School violence; Weaponry.

Guns. See *Weaponry.*

Guru. Guru(s). Swami. *Choose from:* spiritual, religious *with:* leader(s), mentor(s), guide(s), counselor(s), teacher(s). *Consider also:* Buddha(s). *See also* Enlightenment (state of mind); Mentors; Religious leadership; Spiritual direction.

Gymnastics. Gymnastic(s). *Consider also:* exercis(e,es,ing), tumbling, calisthenics, yoga, dance therapy, acrobatic(s), trampoline(s), weight lifting, pole vault(ing), somersault(s,ing), lift(ing) weight(s). *See also* Acrobats; Aerialists; Athletic participation; Calisthenics; Exercise.

Gynecological disorders. See *Female genital disorders.*

Gynocide. Gynocid(e,es,al). Matricid(e,es, al). Dowry death(s). Suttee. Sati. Female infanticide(s). *Choose from:* kill(ed,ing), murder(s,ed,ing) *with:* female *with:* bab(y,ies), infant(s), newborn(s). *Choose from:* bride(s), bridal, witch(es), sorceress(es), goddess(es) *with:* burn(s,ed,ing), drown(ed,s,ing,ings), sacrific(e,es,ial), murder(s,ed,ing). *Consider also:* serial kill(ing,ings,er,ers), serial murder(s,er,ers) *with:* woman, women, female(s), girl(s). *Consider also:* Boston Strangler, Ted Bundy, Arthur Shawcross, Jack the Ripper, etc. *See also* Genocide; Homicide; Infanticide.

Gypsies. Gyps(y,ies). Gips(y,ies). Roman(i,y). Tzigane(s). Gitan(s,o,os,a). Zigeuner. Sinti. Roma. *See also* Gypsy music; Migrants; Nomads; Traditional societies.

Gypsy music. Gypsy music. Csardas. *Choose from:* gyps(y,ies), gips(y,ies), roman(i,y), tzigane, tsigane, gitan(o,a), Zigeuner(in) *with:.* music(ian,ians), repertor(y,ies), dance(s), song(s), rhapsod(y,ies). *Consider also:* Verbunkos, Hungarian music, Zigeunerkapelle(n). *See also* Folk music; Gypsies.

H

Habit, tobacco. See *Tobacco habit.*

Habitat. Habitat(s,ation). Homeground(s). Natural home(s). Natural abode(s). *Choose from:* native, natural, home *with:* environment(s), territor(y,ies). *See also* Animal environments; Biogeography; Bioinvasion; Biological diversity; Food chain; Game protection; Gardening to attract wildlife; Home range; Housing; Natural environment; Phytogeography; Territoriality; Wildlife sanctuaries.

Habits. Habit(s,ual). Addiction(s). Custom(ary,arily,s). Usage. Routine(s). Usual practice(s). Dependen(t,ce). Prone(ness). Indulgen(t,ce). *Consider also:* habit form(ation,ing), habit disorder(s), fingersucking, thumb-sucking, nail biting, smoking, chain smoker(s), hair pulling. *See also* Alcoholism; Drinking behavior; Drug use; Fingersucking; Food habits; Frequently; Hair pulling; Interests; Lifestyle; Nail biting; Saving; Scratching; Smoking; Study habits; Substance abuse.

Habits, eating. See *Food habits.*

Habits, food. See *Food habits.*

Habits, study. See *Study habits.*

Habituation (psychophysiology). Habituat(e,ed,ing,ion). Becoming accustomed. Gradual adaptation. Negative adaptation. Acquired tolerance. Overhabituat(e,ed,ing,ion). Accustom(ed,ing). Familiariz(e,ed,ing, ation). Acclimat(e,ize,ization). Attenuation of response. *Consider also:* habit formation, craving(s), psychological dependence, addict(ed,ing,ion), dishabituation. *See also* Attention; Drug tolerance; Sensory adaptation.

Haciendas. See *Plantations.*

Hackers, computer. See *Computer hackers.*

Hackneyed. Hackneyed. Banal(ity). Commonplace. Cliche(d,s). Overused. Dull(ness). Ordinar(y,iness). Familiar(ity). Insipid(ity,ly). Outdated. Outmoded. Tedious(ness). Trite(ness). Uninspired. Unoriginal. Overworked. Unimaginative. Stale(ness). Quotidian. *See also* Dullness; Familiarity; Jargon.

Hagiography. Hagiograph(y,ic,ical). *Choose from:* saint(s), venerated person(s) *with:* life, lives, biograph(y, ical), legend(s). *See also* Biography; Saints.

Haiku. Haiku. Haikai. Haikkai. Hokku. *Consider also:* tanka, haiga, Japanese poetry. *See also* Imagery; Japanese drama; Poetry.

Hair. Hair(s,y,ed). Hirsute. Vibrissae. Whiskers. Eyelash(es). Eyebrow(s). Fur(ry,riness). Wool(y,iness). Beard(ed). Moustache(s). Bristle(s). Pilar(y). Fleece. Lanugo. *Consider also:* hairless(ness), bald(ness). *See also* Alopecia; Human body.

Hair loss. See *Alopecia.*

Hair pulling. Hair pulling. Hairpulling. Trichotillomania. *See also* Behavior disorders; Habits; Self destructive behavior.

Hairdressing. Hairdress(ing,er,ers). Coiffure(s). Haircut(ting,s). Hairstyle(s). Hair-style(s). Hair-do(s). Barber(s). Hair salon(s). *Choose from:* hair, wig(s) *with:* fashion(s), straighten(ed,ing), dye(ing, d), bleach(ed,ing), preparation(s), styl(ist,ing), comb(ed,ing), color(ing,ed, ist,ists), glamor(ous), upswept, accessor(y,ies), afro(s), cornrow(s), long, close-cropped, short, bushy, shaved, plaited, frizzy, braid(s,ed,ing), blond texture(s), limp, thin, flat, dreadlock(s). *Consider also:* head gear(s), *See also* Beauty culture; Beauty operators; Beauty shops; Head-gear.

Hajj. See *Pilgrimages.*

Half siblings. Half sibling(s). Half sib(s). Half brother(s). Half sister(s). *Consider also:* stepsister(s), stepbrother(s). *See also* Brothers; Siblings; Sisters; Stepfamily.

Halfway houses. Halfway house(s). Half-way houses. Sheltered care home(s). *Choose from:* transitional *with:* hostel(s), home(s), housing. *Consider also:* deinstitutionalization, therapeutic communit(y,ies), furlough center(s), board and care home(s), hostel(s), borstal(s), group home(s), residential placement, after-care. *See also* Aftercare; Correctional institutions; Deinstitutionalization; Group homes; Psychiatric hospitals; Rehabilitation centers; Shelters.

Hallmarks. Hallmark(s). Trademark(s). Earmark(s). Emblematic(al,ally). Emblem(s). Authenticat(e,ed,ing,ation). Mark of authenticity. Official mark(s). Official stamp(s). Official seal(s). *Consider also:* distinguishing characteristic(s). *See also* Brand loyalty; Brand names; Trademarks.

Halls. Hall(s). Hallway(s). Corridor(s). Foyer(s). Couloir(s). Passageway(s). Breezeway(s). Lobb(y,ies). *Consider also:* common dining room(s), entrance room(s), lobb(y,ies), large room(s), assembly room(s), assembly hall(s), auditorium(s), amphitheater(s), ballroom(s), lecture room(s), lyceum(s), meetinghouse(s). *See also* Arenas; Auditoriums; Concert halls; Egress; Entrances; Exits.

Halls, concert. See *Concert halls.*

Hallucinations. Hallucinat(e,ed,ing, ion,ions,ory). Hallucinosis. Delirium. See(ing) vision(s). Hear(ing) voice(s). Drug flashback(s). Doppelganger. Psychomimetic effect(s). Psychotomi-metic effect(s). Trip(s,ping). Audible thought(s). *Choose from:* auditory, drug induced, hypnagogic, visual *with:* hallucination(s). *Consider also:* hallucinogens. *See also* Auditory hallucinations; Hallucinogens; Hallucinosis; Hypnagogic hallucinations; Near death experiences; Psychedelic experiences; Visual hallucinations.

Hallucinations, auditory. See *Auditory hallucinations.*

Hallucinations, hypnagogic. See *Hypnagogic hallucinations.*

Hallucinations, visual. See *Visual hallucinations.*

Hallucinogenic drugs. See *Hallucinogens.*

Hallucinogens. Hallucinogen(s). Hallucinogenic drug(s). Opiate(s). Psychedelic(s). Psychodysleptic(s). Dimethyltryptamine [DMT, DET, DPT]. Harmine [ayahuasca]. Lysergic acid diethylamide [LSD, ergot fungus, acid, pink wedges, sandos, sugar cube(s)]. Mescal(ine) [peyote, barf tea, big chief, buttons, cactus, mesc]. Methyldimethoxy-amphetamine [DOM, STP]. Morning glory seeds [bind weed, bindweed, rivea corymbosa, flower power, heavenly blue, pearly gates]. Muscarine [amanita muscaria, fly]. Myristicin [nutmeg, MMDA]. Phencyclidine [sernyl, angel dust, PCP, peace pills]. Psilocin [psilocyb(e,in), psilocybe mexicana, business man's acid, magic, mushroom]. *Choose from:* psychotomimetic *with:* agent(s), compound(s), plant(s). *Consider also:* adrenochrome, anadenanthera, bufotenin(e), caapi, cocaine [coke, crack, bernies, big C, flake, freebase, free base, happy dust, ice, snow], dimethyltryptophan, ditran, fly-agaric mushroom(s), heroin [diacetylmorphine, Diamorphine, Acetomorphine, H, hard stuff, horse, junk, skag, smack], ibogaine, ibotenic acid, jimson weed, P-methoxyamphet-amine, methylenedioxyamphetamine, methoxydimethyltryptamine(s), yage, p-funk, synthetic heroin. *See also* Drugs; Ergot alkaloids; Hallucinations; Mescal (cactus); Narcotics; Psychotropic plants; Stimulants; Street drugs.

Hallucinosis. Hallucino(sis,tic). Hallucinatory psychosis. Recurrent hallucination(s). Persistent hallucinations. Alcoholic hallucinosis. *Consider also:* alcoholic psychoses, alcohol amnestic disorder, alcohol withdrawal delirium, delirium tremens, Korsakoffs psychosis. *See also* Alcoholic hallucinosis; Hallucinations; Psychoses.

Hallucinosis, alcohol. See *Alcoholic hallucinosis: Alcohol withdrawal delirium.*

Halo effect. Halo effect(s). Cultural halo(s). Radiating effect(s). Reflecting effect(s). *Choose from:* halo(s,es) *with:* rating(s), error(s), effect(s). *Choose from:* aura(s), attribut(e,ed,ing,ion,ions), expectancy *with:* attractive(ness), glory, sentiment. *Consider also:* venerat(e,ed,ing,ion), idealiz(e,ed,ing,ation). *See also* Errors; Expectations; Researcher bias; Social perception.

Hamitic languages. Hamitic language(s). Egyptian: Ancient Egyptian, Coptic. Berber: Old Libyan, Guanche, Numidian, Modern Berber, Tuareg, Kabyle, Siwa, Rif. Cushitic: Somali, Galla. *See also* African cultural groups; Language; Languages (as subjects); North Africa; Semitic languages.

Hand. Hand(s). *Consider also:* finger(s), thumb(s), wrist(s), interdigital, handshake(s), fingerprint(s), digital. *See also* Anatomy.

Hand washing. Hand washing. Handwashing. Wash(es,ed,ing) hand(s). *Choose from:* hand(s), finger(s) *with:* wash(ed,es,ing), scrub(bed,bing), keep(ing) clean, hygiene, disinfect(ed,ing,ion), soap(ed,ing), clean(ed,ing), steril(e,ize,ized,izing). *Consider also:* clean hand(s) *See also* Body care; Compulsive behavior; Hygiene; Sanitation.

Handbooks. Handbook(s). Guidebook(s). Instruction book(s). Reference manual(s). Director(y,ies). Instruction manual(s). How-to-do-it book(s). Pocket guide(s). *See also* Texts.

Handedness. See *Laterality.*

Handguns. See *Weaponry.*

Handicap discrimination. See *Attitudes toward handicapped.*

Handicapped. See *Disability.*

Handicapped, architecture and. See *Architectural accessibility.*

Handicapped, attitudes toward. See *Attitudes toward handicapped.*

Handicapped, aurally. See *Deafness.*

Handicapped, communication aids for. See *Communication aids for handicapped.*

Handicapped, congenitally. See *Congeni-* tally handicapped.

Handicapped, infants severely. See *Severely handicapped infants.*

Handicapped, mentally. See *Mental retardation.*

Handicapped, multiply. See *Multiply handicapped.*

Handicapped, orthopedically. See *Physically handicapped.*

Handicapped, physically. See *Physically handicapped.*

Handicapped, socially. See *Socially handicapped.*

Handicapped, speech. See *Speech disorders.*

Handicapped, visually. See *Blindness; Partially sighted; Vision disorders.*

Handicaps, attitudes toward physical. See *Attitudes toward physical handicaps.*

Handicaps (impediments). See *Barriers; Blockade; Constraints; Deadlock; Deterrence; Employment discrimination; Fences; Impediments; Limitations.*

Handicaps, physical. See *Physically handicapped.*

Handicrafts. See *Crafts.*

Handling (touching). Handling. *Choose from:* handl(e,ed,ing), tactual stimulation, tactile stimulation, fondl(e,ed,ing), pet(ted,ting), pat(ted,ting), strok(e,ed,ing,es), hold(ing), held, cuddl(e,ed,ing), hug(ging,ged), caress(ed,ing), rub(bed,bing), touch(ed,ing), embrac(e,ed,ing), snuggl(e,ed,ing). *See also* Personal space; Sexual foreplay; Touch.

Handling, cargo. See *Cargo handling.*

Handling, snake. See *Snake handling.*

Handwriting. Handwrit(ing,ten). *Consider also:* cursive writing, handletter(ed,ing), inscription(s), paleography, penmanship, longhand, script writing, forge(ry,ries), signature(s), calligraphy, graphology. *See also* Autographs; Graphology; Inscriptions; Signatures; Verbal communication; Writing (composition); Written communications.

Hanging, erotized. See *Sexual asphyxia syndrome.*

Happening (art). Happening(s). Spontaneous entertainment. Spontaneous plotless theatrical event(s). *Consider also:* spectator participation. *See also* Experiences (events); Performance art; Popular culture.

Happiness. Happ(y,iness). Joy(ful,fulness,ous,ousness). Glad(ness). Exuberan(t,ce). Gaiety. Cheer(ful,fulness). Delight(ful). Bliss(ful). Felicit(y,ous). Jubil(ant,ation). Exhilarat(ed,ion). Good spirits. Content(ed,ment). Elat(ed,ion). Pleasure. Life satisfaction. Satisfactions.

Satisfied. Fulfill(ed,ment). High spirits. Lighthearted. Enjoy(ed,ment). *See also* Cheerfulness; Emotions; Enjoyment; Euphoria; Life satisfaction; Love; Optimism; Pleasure; Satisfaction; Self esteem; Well being.

Harassment. Harass(ed,ing,ment). Annoy(ed,ing,ance,ances). Beleagur(e,ed,ing). Racial profiling. Pester(ed,ing). Molest(ed,ing). Afflict(ed,ing). Teas(e,ed,ing). Taunt(ed,ing). Heckl(e,ed,ing). Torment(ed,ing). Provok(e,ed,ing). Hassl(e,ed,ing). Pick(ed,ing) on. *Consider also:* victimiz(e,ed,ing,ation). *See also* Antisocial behavior; Hazing; Intimidation; Online harassment; School violence; Sexual harassment; Street harassment; Teasing; Verbal abuse.

Harassment, online. See *Online harassment.*

Harassment, sexual. See *Sexual harassment.*

Harassment, street. See *Street harassment.*

Harbors. Harbor(s,age). Haven(s). Port(s). Anchorage. Port facilit(y,ies). *See also* Coast defenses; Dry docks; Piers; Ports; Ships.

Hard-core unemployed. Hard-core unemploy(ed,ment). Unemployable. Hard-to-employ. *Choose from:* hardcore, hardcore, long term, chronic(ally) *with:* jobless(ness), out of work, unemploy(ed,ment), unwaged. *See also* Discouraged workers; Employability; Homeless; Personnel termination; Plant closings; Poverty; Underemployment; Unemployment; Unemployment rates; Unemployment relief.

Hardships. Hardship(s). Affliction(s). Adversit(y,ies). Hurt(s). Harm(ed). Ruin(ed,ation). Desolat(e,ion). Destitut(e,ion). Auster(e,ity). Privation(s). Want(s,ed,ing). Need(s,ed,ing). Difficult(y,ies). Plight(s). Predicament(s). Tough times. Deprivation(s). Misfortune(s). Mishap(s). Mischance(s). Misadventure(s). Setback(s). Burden(s,some). Travail(s). Tribulation(s). Trouble(s). Distress(es). *See also* Accidents; Adversity; Catastrophes; Deprivation; Destitution; Indigence; Poverty; Unmet needs; Women living in poverty.

Hardware. Hardware. Appliance(s). Equipment. Durable(s). Big ticket item(s). Fixture(s). Furnishing(s). Gear. Implement(s). Machine(s,ry). Tool(s). Utensil(s). Implement(s). Accouterment(s). Metalware. *See also* Hardware (computers); Industrial property; Machinery; Tableware; Tools; Weaponry.

Hardware (computers). Hardware (computers). Motherboard(s). Chip(s). Memory. Keyboard(s). Monitor(s). Read only memory. ROM. Random access memory. RAM. Central processing unit. CPU(s). Hard drive(s). HDD(s). Disk drive(s). CDROM drive(s). DVD drive(s). *Choose from:* computer(s), microcomputer(s), Pentium(s), Macintosh, *with:* processor(s), memory, cache(s), controller(s), BIOS, adapter(s). *Consider also:* computer(s), micro-computer(s), Pentium(s) *with:* installa-tion, configuration. *See also* Computer industry; Computers; Hardware; Software (computers).

Harems. Harem(s). Seraglio(s). Concubinage(s). Zenana(s). *Consider also:* odalisque(s), gynaeceum(s), female slave(s,ry). *See also* Concubinage; Private sphere; Purdah; Sex roles; Sexism; Sexual division of labor; Sexual oppression; Slavery; Veiling of women.

Harlots. See *Prostitution.*

Harmful behavior. Harmful behavior(s). *Choose from:* harmful, abusive, dangerous, violent, assaultive, battering, aggressive *with:* behavior(s), act(s), action(s), conduct. *See also* Aggression; Antisocial behavior; Child abuse; Dangerousness; Elder abuse; Family violence; Spouse abuse.

Harmfulness. See *Dangerousness; Harmful behavior.*

Harmlessness. Harmless(ness). Benign(ity,ly). Innocuous(ness). Innoffensive(ness). Innoxious(ness). Unoffending. Unhurtful(ness). Innocen(t,ce). Blameless(ness). Non-irritating. Unobjectionable. Nontoxic. Nonpoisonous. *Consider also:* gentle(ness), bland(ness), insipid(ity), pallid(ness), painless(ness), safe. *See also* Innocence; Purity; Safety; Simplic-ity.

Harmonica, glass. See *Glass harmonica.*

Harmonization. Harmoniz(e,ed,ing,ation). Agree(d,ing,ment). Coincid(e,ed,ing). In balance. Balanc(ed,ing). Concur(red, ring,rence). In accord(ance). Conform(ed,ing). Correspond(ed,ing). Dovetail(ed,ing). Bring(ing) into consonance. Attune(d). Coordinat(e,ed, ing). Integrat(e,ed,ing,ion). In propor-tion. Reconcil(e,ed,iate,iation). In tune. Blend(ed,ing). Orchestrat(e,ed,ing,ion). Synthesiz(e,ed,ing). Unif(y,ied,ication). *Consider also:* reciprocal, intermutual, generic, parallel, cooperat(e,ed,ing,ion), confidence-building. *See also* Agree-ment; Orchestration; Proportionality; Synchronism; Uniformity.

Harmonization (trade). Harmoniz(e,ed, ing,ation). *Choose from:* harmoniz(e,ed, ing,ation), unif(y,ied,ication) *with:* system(s), commodity description(s), regulation(s), law(s), standard(s), customs, currenc(y,ies), monetary polic(y,ies), exchange-rate(s), interest-rate polic(y,ies), fiscal polic(y,ies).

Consider also: Euroiz(e,ed,ing,ation). *See also* Commercial treaties; Common currency; Common markets; Customs unions; Economic relations; Economic union; Free trade; Global integration; International banks and banking; International economic integration; International economic organizations; International trade; Nontariff trade barriers; Trade; World economy.

Harmony. Harmon(y,ies,ic,ious). Chord(al) structure(s). Vertical structure(s). *Consider also:* pre-tertian harmony, tertian harmony, quartal harmony, post-tertian harmony, tonality. *See also* Music.

Harvesting. Harvest(ed,ing). Glean(ed,ing). Log(ged,ging). Clearcut(ting). Haying. Crop(ped,ping). Reap(ed,ing). Pick(ed,ing). Pluck(ed,ing). *See also* Agriculture; Farming.

Hassidism. See *Chassidism.*

Hate. Hate(d,s). Hatred. Hating. Hostil(e, ity). Abhor(rence). Loath(e,ing). Abominat(e,ion). Despise(d). Detest(ed). Dislike(d). Animosity. Execrate. Malevolen(t,ce). Aversion. Grudg(e,ing). Contempt. Distaste. Ill will. Enmity. Antipathy. Repugnance. Intoleran(t,ce). *See also* Anger; Aversion; Hostility; Interpersonal conflict; Repugnance.

Hate crimes. Hate crime(s). Bias related crime(s). Racially motivated crime(s). Incite(d,ment) to racial hatred. Racist rape(s). Racist killing(s). Racial violence. Swastika(s). Crossburning(s). Burn(ed,ing) cross(es). *Choose from:* hate(s), hatred, racial(ly), race, racist, anti-Black, anti-Asian, gay(s), homosexual(ity), lesbian(s), transsexual(s,ity), homophob(ia,ic), AIDS, minorit(y,ies), ethnic, religious, white power, skinhead(s) *with:* attack(s,ed,ing,ive), abus(e,ed,ing,ive), bashing, crime(s), violen(t,ce), harass(ed,ing,ment), victim(s,ize,ized, izing), torment(s,ed,ing), assault(s,ed), killing(s), murder(s,ed,ing,er,ers). *See also* Antiabortion movement; Anti-government radicals; Antisemitism; Attitudes toward homosexuality; Driveby Crimes; Ethnic cleansing; Ethnocentrism; Fascism; Holocaust; Lynching; Malinformation; Militias; Nazism; Offenses against religion; Racism; Religious prejudice; Reprisals; Sacrilege; Sexism; War crimes; White supremacy movements; Xenophobia.

Hate groups. Hate group(s). Hate-monger(s). Hate monger(s). *Choose from:* hate, anti-Black, anti-Semitic, White supremacist, racist *with:* group(s), movement(s) *Consider also:* Ku Klux Klan, Church of the Creator, skinheads, White Aryan Resistance, Nation of Islam, etc. *See also* Antiabortion movement; Anti-government radicals;

Malinformation; Nazism; Racism; Social discrimination; White supremacy movements.

Hate, self. See *Self hate.*

Hats. Hat(s). Millinery. Headwear. Bonnet(s). Cap(s). Headpiece(s). Headgear. Crown(s). Helmet(s). Beret(s). Mortarboard(s). Skullcap(s). Chapeau(s). Headdress(es). Busb(y,ies). Beanie(s). Nightcap(s). Fedora(s). Top-hat(s). Yarmulke(s). Tam(s). *See also* Clothing; Fashions; Head-gear.

Haunted houses. Haunted house(s). *Choose from:* haunted, spook(y), ghost(ly), apparition(s), sinister *with:* house(s), mansion(s), place(s), castle(s), site(s). *See also* Anecdotes; Apparitions; Folk culture; Ghost stories; Ghosts; Horror tales; Superstitions; Suspense.

Hawkers. See *Street vendors.*

Hay fever. Hay fever. Hayfever. Pollinosis. Allergic rhinitis. *Consider also:* allerg(y,ies,ic) *with:* rhinitis, pollen(s), ragweed, nasal. *See also* Hypersensitiv-ity.

Hazardous materials. Hazardous material(s). Hazmat(s). Haz mat(s). Chemical(ly) contaminat(e,ed,ing,ion). Chemical contaminant(s). Toxic contamina(nt,nts,tion). Dangerous level(s). Toxic algae. Radioactive waste(s). Chemical emission(s). Acid rain. Spoiled food. Tainted fish. Noxious cloud(s). Atomic waste(s). Nuclear waste(s). Poisonous gas(es). Agent orange. Pollut(ed,ant,ants,ion,ing). Chemical pollut(ant,ants,ion). *Choose from:* contaminat(e,ed,ing,ion) *with:* mercury, heavy metals, cadmium, lead, pesticide(s), etc. *Choose from:* hazard(s,ous), toxic(ity), contaminat(e, ed,ing,ion), contaminant(s), poison(ous), noxious, danger(ous,ousness), threaten(ing), infectious, carcinogenic, pollut(ed,ing,ant,ants), atomic, nuclear, radioactive *with:* level(s), refuse, substance(s), garbage, material(s), matter, stock, suppl(y,ies), sewage, slurry, waste(s), water, incinerat(or,ors, ion), trash, ash(es), residue(s), dump(s, ing), cloud(s), rain, chemical(s), agent(s), gas(es), effluent(s), rubbish, debris, dust, emission(s), sweeping(s), tailing(s), product(s), by-product(s), groundwater, oil spill(s), food chain, soil(s). *Consider specific substances, for example:* PCBs, polychlorinated biphenyls, asbestos, poisonous gas(es), radon, alar, DDT, chlordane, dioxin, agent orange, defoliant(s), volatile hydrocarbons, chlorine, benzene, hydrogen cyanide. *See also* Carcino-gens; Environmental pollutants; Environmental pollution; Environmental protection; Poisonous plants; Hazardous occupations; Hazardous wastes; Poisonous gases; Poisons; Toxic substances.

Hazardous occupations. Hazardous occupation(s). Dangerous work. Workplace risk(s). *Choose from:* hazard(s,ous), danger(s,ous), risk(s,y, iness), hazmat, exposure *with:* job(s), worker(s), labor(er,ers), profession(al, als), occupation(s,al,ally), industrial, worker(s), employee(s), work(place, places), worksite(s), workstation(s), office(s), working conditions, factor(y, ies), compan(y,ies), operator(s), VDT(s), CRT(s). *Consider also:* electrical work(er,ers), construction work(er,ers), bridge work(er,ers), etc. *See also* Agricultural workers disease; Asbestos; Black lung disease; Blue collar workers; Containment of biohazards; Dangerousness; Environmental pollution; Garbage collectors; Hazardous materials; Hazardous wastes; Hazards of video display terminals; Industrial accidents; Industrial workers; Military personnel; Mine accidents; Noise levels (work areas); Occupational diseases; Occupational exposure; Occupational neuroses; Occupational safety; Repetitive motion disorders; Sick building syndrome; Transport workers; Working conditions.

Hazardous wastes. Hazardous waste(s). *Choose from:* contaminat(e,ed,ing,ion), contaminant(s), taint(ed,ing), poison(ed, ous), hazard(s,ous), pollut(ant,ants,ed, ing,ion), threaten(ed,ing), threat(s), danger(s,ous,ousness), unsafe, vulnerab(le,ility), risk(s,y), endanger(ed, ing,ment), imperil(ed,ing), jeopard(y,ize, ized,izing), liab(le,ility), peril(ous), radioact(ive,ivity), explosive, red bag, menac(e,ing), infect(ed,ious), noxious, toxic(ity), toxin(s), poison(ous), nuclear, PCBs, polychlorinated biphenyls, mercury, lead, heavy metals, pesticide(s) etc. *with:* garbage, waste(s), effluent(s), slurry, trash, refuse, rubbish, offal, discard(ed,ing,s), junk, emission(s), litter(ing), sludge, landfill(s), compost(ed,ing), dust, ash(es), incinerat(or,ors,ion), residue(s), mill tailing(s), dump(s,ing), debris, oil spill(s), wastewater. *Consider also:* Superfund. *See also* Carcinogens; Environmental pollutants; Environmental pollution; Environmental protection; Environmental racism; Hazardous materials; Hazardous occupations; Industrial wastes; Medical geography; Medical wastes; Nuclear waste; Poisonous gases; Poisons; Solid waste; Toxic substances; Waste disposal; Waste spills; Waste transport.

Hazards. Hazard(s,ous). Contaminat(ed,ing, ion). Taint(ed). Poison(s,ous). Pollut(ant, ants,ed,ing,ion). Threat(s,en,ened,ening). Danger(s,ous,ousness). Unsafe. Vulnerab(le,ility). Risk(s,y). Endanger(ing,ed,ment). Imperil(ed,ing). Jeopard(y,ized,izing). Liab(le,ility, ilities). Peril(ous). Radioactiv(e,ity). Infect(ed,ing,ious). Contag(ion,ious).

Explosive(s). Menac(e,ed,ing). *See also* Accidents; Carcinogens; Danger; Dangerous behavior; Dangerousness; Disease; Disasters; Hazardous materials; Hazardous wastes; Hazards of video display terminals; Natural disasters; Poisoning; Risk; Safety; Survival; Threat; Toxic substances.

Hazards, industrial. See *Hazardous wastes; Industrial accidents; Occupational disease; Occupational exposure; Occupational safety; Occupational stress.*

Hazards, occupational. See *Agricultural workers disease; Black lung disease; Hazardous materials; Hazards of video display terminals; Industrial accidents; Multiple chemical sensitivities; Occupational diseases; Occupational exposure; Occupational neuroses; Occupational safety; Occupational stress; Repetitive motion disorders; Sick building syndrome.*

Hazards, work. See *Agricultural workers disease; Black lung disease; Hazardous materials; Hazards of video display terminals; Industrial accidents; Multiple chemical sensitivities; Occupational diseases; Occupational exposure; Occupational neuroses; Occupational safety; Occupational stress; Repetitive motion disorders; Sick building syndrome.*

Hazards of video display terminals. Hazard(s) of video display terminal(s). *Choose from:* vdt, crt, vdv, cathode ray, video display, display screen(s) *with:* hazard(s,ous), danger(s,ous,ousness), eyestrain, eye strain, headache(s), backache(s), fatigue, eye problem(s), cataract(s), miscarriage(s), birth defect(s), abnormalit(y,ies), stress(es), health, cancer, risk(s). *See also* Backache; Cancer; Carcinogens; Congenitally handicapped; Disorders; Hazardous occupations; Hazards; Physical abnormalities.

Hazing. Haz(e,ed,ing). *Choose from:* fraternit(y,ies), sororit(y,ies), cadet(s), midshipm(en,an), Greek letter societ(y,ies) *with:* induction ritual(s), induction rite(s), harassment, victimiz(e,ed,ation), ridicul(e,ed,ing), bully(ing). *See also* Harassment; Initiation rites.

Head banging. Head banging. Head-banging. *Choose from:* head(s) *with:* hit(ting), knock(ing). *Consider also:* self injurious behavior, self destructive behavior(s), temper tantrum(s). *See also* Self destructive behavior.

Head-gear. Head-gear. Headgear. Helmet(s). Head wear. Headwear. Head covering(s). Head ornament(s). Head wrap(s). Crown(s). Tiara(s). Turban(s). Bandana(s). Babushka(s). *See also* Clothing; Fashions; Hairdressing; Hats.

Head injuries. Head injur(y,ies). *Choose from:* head(s), brain(s), maxillofacial, skull(s), cranial, intracerebral, forehead(s), cranio-cerebral, craniocerebral, intracranial *with:* injur(y,ies), fracture(s), concussion(s), trauma(s,tic), wound(s,ed). *See also* Brain damage.

Headache. Headache(s). Cephal(gia,algia). Cerebralgia. Migraine. *Choose from:* head *with:* ache(s), pain(s). *See also* Psychophysiologic disorders.

Headache, muscle contraction. See *Muscle contraction headache.*

Headaches, migraine. See *Migraine headaches.*

Headed, female households. See *Female headed households.*

Headhunters (Personnel). See *Personnel recruitment.*

Headings, subject. See *Subject headings.*

Headmasters. See *Educational administrators.*

Headquarters. See *Home office.*

Headquarters relocation. Headquarters relocation. *Choose from:* headquarters, main office(s), central office(s), parent company, administrative office(s), home office(s) *with:* relocat(e,ed,ing,ion), new location(s), change(d) address, move(d), moving. *See also* Home office; Office buildings; Place of business; Plant closings; Plant relocation; Relocation.

Heads of households. Head(s) of household(s). *Choose from:* head(s,ed) *with:* household(s), famil(y,ies). *Consider also:* patriarch(s), matriarch(s). *See also* Female headed households; Households; Single parent family.

Heads of state. Head(s) of state. Chief(s) of state. Constitutional head(s). Prime minister(s). Premier(s). Chancellor(s). General Secretar(y,ies). President(s). *See also* Monarchy; Political elite; Power elite; Presidents; Ruling class; Upper class.

Heads, shrunken. See *Shrunken heads.*

Healers, folk. See *Shamanism; Traditional medicine.*

Healers, native. See *Shamanism; Traditional medicine.*

Healers, traditional. See *Shamanism; Traditional medicine.*

Healing. Heal(ed,ing,ers). Cur(e,ed,es,ing). Restor(e,ed,ing). Treat(ed,ing). Treatment(s). Dress wound(s). Sooth(e,ed, ing). Return(ed,ing) to health. Remed(y,ies). Reinvigorat(e,ed,ing). Artificial respiration. Lifesaving. Resuscitat(e,ed,ing,ion). Rehabilitat(e, ed,ing,ion). Reviv(e,ed,ing). *See also* Herbal medicine; Home care; Nostrums; Rejuvenation; Religious experience; Spiritual healing; Traditional medicine.

Healing, faith. See *Spiritual healing.*

Healing, mental. See *Spiritual healing.*

Healing, religious. See *Spiritual healing.*

Healing, spiritual. See *Spiritual healing.*

Health. Health(y). Well being. Well(ness). Hygiene. Health effects. Health(ful). Good health. Poor health. Physical condition. Physical(ly) fit(ness). Hard(y,iness). Sound(ness). Robust(ness). Vigor(ous,ousness). Good condition. Good shape. Good life. *Consider also:* family health, mental health, occupational safety, public health, oral health, physical fitness, rural health, urban health, world health, community health, holistic health. *See also* Accidents; Blood pressure; Community mental health; Dental care; Diagnosis; Diet; Disability; Disease susceptibility; Disease; Drinking water; Epidemics; Fatigue; Holistic health; Hygiene; Injuries; Life expectancy; Medical care; Mental health; Nutrition; Occupational health services; Occupational safety; Patients; Preventive medicine; Public health; Safety; Sanitation; Sleep; Stress; Water safety; Well being; World health.

Health, attitudes toward. See *Attitudes toward health.*

Health, dental. See *Oral health.*

Health, emotional. See *Mental health; Morale; Psychological well being.*

Health, holistic. See *Holistic health.*

Health, mental. See *Mental health.*

Health, oral. See *Oral health.*

Health, physical. See *Health.*

Health, public. See *Public health.*

Health, rural. See *Rural health.*

Health, rural mental. See *Rural mental health.*

Health, urban. See *Urban health.*

Health, wholistic. See *Holistic health.*

Health, world. See *World health.*

Health agencies, voluntary. See *Voluntary health agencies.*

Health aides, community. See *Community health aides.*

Health behavior. Health behavior(s). Prophylaxis. *Choose from:* health(y), wellness, preventive, nutrition *with:* behavior(s), promot(e,ed,ing,ion), lifestyle(s), maintain(ed,ing), maintenance, enhanc(e,ed,ing,ement,ements). *Consider also:* preventive medicine, prevent(ed,ing,ion) disease. *See also* Health; Holistic health; Hygiene; Natural foods; Primary prevention; Preventive medicine; Quality of life; Sanitation; Well being.

Health care. Health care. *Choose from:* preventive, health, wellness, patient(s) *with:* care, medicine, service(s), treatment(s), therap(y,ies). *Consider also:* eye care, preventive care, dental care, nursing care, preoperative care, postoperative care, home care, ambulatory care, patient care, etc. *See also* Ambulatory care; Dental care; Holistic health; Health care reform; Health care surveys; Health promotion; Health services; Medical care; Mental health; Postnatal care; Postoperative care; Prenatal care; Preventive medicine; Preventive psychiatry; Primary health care; Primary prevention; Psychotherapy; Well being.

Health care, comprehensive. See *Comprehensive health care.*

Health care, home. See *Home care.*

Health care occupations. See *Health occupations.*

Health care, patient acceptance of. See *Patient compliance.*

Health care, primary. See *Primary health care.*

Health care, quality of. See *Quality of health care.*

Health care rationing. Health care rationing. Triage. *Choose from:* allocat(e,ed,ing), ration(ed,ing), distribut(e,ed,ing,ion) *with:* medical resources, health care. *See also* Health care reform; Health care utilization; Health expenditures; Health resources; Health services needs and demand; Managed care; Medical economics; Triage.

Health care reform. Health care reform(s). *Choose from:* health care, health insurance, *with:* reform(s,ed), change(s), call(s,ed) for action, press(ed,ing) for passage, pending legislation. *See also* Health care; Health care rationing; Health policy; Health services needs and demand; Managed care; National health programs.

Health care regulations. See *Health policy.*

Health care services. See *Health services.*

Health care surveys. Health care survey(s). *Choose from:* health care, primary care, medicare, managed care, general practitioner(s), hospitalization(s), hospital stay(s), hospital discharge(s), health outcome(s), patient satisfaction, epidemiolog(ic,y), care provider(s), treatment(s), eye care, preventive care, dental care, nursing care, preoperative care, postoperative care, home care, ambulatory care, patient care, etc. *with:* survey(s,ed,ing), data(set, sets), questionnaire(s), regression analy(sis,ses), scale(s), interview(s), self-assessment, followup stud(y,ies), demograph(ic,y), national profile(s),

representative sample(s). *Consider also:* healthcare utilization survey(s). *See also* Data Collection; Health care; Health surveys; Surveys.

Health care utilization. Health care utilization. *Choose from:* physician(s) service(s), doctor(s) service(s), HMO, health care, health service(s), primary care, medical care, medical service(s), treatment, prenatal care, dental care, dental service(s), mental health service(s), hospital(s) *with:* visit(s), demand, use(rs), consumer(s), consumption, utiliz(e,ed,ing,ation), seeking, compliance, broken appointment(s), consult(ed,ing,ation,ations). *See also* Catchment area (health); Delivery of services; Health care rationing; Health services needs and demand; Medically underserved areas.

Health care workers. See *Health manpower.*

Health centers, community. See *Community health centers.*

Health centers, neighborhood. See *Community health centers.*

Health complaints. See *Health problems.*

Health education. Health education. *Choose from:* health, wellness, hygiene, patient(s), anti-smoking, drug(s), antidrug(s), alcohol(ism), anti-alcohol, nutrition, lamaze *with:* educat(e,ed,ing, ion), train(ed,ing), teach(ing), information, class(es), instruct(ed,ing,ion), promot(e,ed,ing,ion), propaganda, campaign(s), course(s). *Consider also:* class(es) for expectant parents. *See also* Alcohol education; Antismoking movement; Childbirth training; Drug education; Nutrition education; Patient education.

Health examinations. Health examination(s). *Choose from:* health, physical, patient, medical *with:* examination(s), test(s), assay(s), assessment(s), audit(s), batter(y,ies), scan(s), checkup(s), diagnostic(s), evaluation(s), inventor(y,ies), measure(s,ment,ments), questionnaire(s), rating(s), scale(s), schedule(s), screen(ed,ing,ings), score(s), trial(s), detection. *Consider also:* mammograph(y,ies), chest x-ray(s), dental x-ray(s), pap smear(s), blood test(s), urine test(s), prostate screening, electrocardiogram(s), glaucoma test(s), sigmoidoscop(y,ies), etc. *See also* Diagnosis; Diagnostic services; Diagnostic tests; Screening.

Health expenditures. Health expenditure(s). *Choose from:* health, medical, surgical, dental, ill, illness(es), injur(y,ies), disease(s), hospitalization(s) *with:* expenditure(s), expense(s), spending, spent, cost(s), price(s), charge(s), payment(s). *See also* Cost of living; Costs; Expenditures; Family budgets; Health care rationing; Health care utilization; Health insurance; Health resources; Medical assistance; Medical economics.

Health facilities. Health facilit(y,ies). *Choose from:* health, treatment(s), psychiatric, dental, mental health, psychoeducational, nursing, medical, ambulatory care, poison control, rehabilitation, perinatal, fertility, hygiene, total care, primary care *with:* facilit(y,ies), center(s), building(s), office(s), institution(s), institute(s), station(s), unit(s), complex(es), establishment(s). *Consider also:* hospital(s), clinic(s), nursing home(s), laborator(y,ies), leper colon(y,ies), nurser(y,ies), pharmac(y,ies), physicians office(s), tissue bank(s), sanatorium(s). *See also* Blood banks; Clinics; Community health centers; Community mental health services; Health facility environment; Health facility size; Health resorts; Hospices; Hospitals; Mental hospitals; Nursing homes.

Health facility environment. Health facilit(y,ies) environment(s). *Choose from:* hospital(s), clinic(s), nursing home(s), nurser(y,ies), sanatorium(s), patient(s) room(s), ward(s), health facilit(y,ies), health center(s), treatment facilit(y,ies), psychiatric facilit(y,ies), mental health facilit(y,ies), medical facilit(y,ies), rehabilitation center(s), total care facilit(y,ies), primary care facilit(y,ies) *with:* setting(s), design, environment(s,al), milieu(s), personal space, homelike, surrounding(s), decor, ambience, crowd(ed,ing). *See also* Environmental design; Environmental psychology; Health facilities; Health facility size; Hospital environment; Milieu therapy; Therapeutic community.

Health facility size. Health facilit(y,ies) size. *Choose from:* hospital(s), clinic(s), nursing home(s), nurser(y,ies), sanatorium(s), ward(s), health facilit(y,ies), health center(s), treatment facilit(y,ies), psychiatric facilit(y,ies), mental health facilit(y,ies), medical facilit(y,ies), rehabilitation center(s), total care facilit(y,ies), primary care facilit(y,ies) *with:* size(s), capacit(y,ies), overbedding, number of beds, number of rooms. *See also* Health facilities; Health facility environment.

Health foods. See *Natural foods.*

Health impaired. See *Health problems.*

Health indices. Health indices. *Choose from:* health(y,iness), wellness, well-being, fitness *with:* index(es), parameter(s), indicator(s), measure(s,ment,ments), inventor(y,ies), indices, scale(s), ratio(s), correlate(s), sign(s), indicant(s). *See also* Biochemi-cal markers; Child mortality; Health status; Health status indicators; Health surveys; Indexes (indicators); Indicators (biology); Infant mortality; Medical geography; Morbidity; Mortality rates; World health.

Health insurance. Health insurance. *Choose from:* health, medical, disability, dental, hospitalization, surgical, accident, pharmaceutical service(s), prescription(s), physician service(s), psychiatric *with:* insurance, benefits. Blue cross. Blue shield. *Consider also:* workmen's compensation, medigap. *See also* Health expenditures; Health maintenance organizations; Insurance coverage; Medical assistance; National health programs.

Health insurance, employee. See *Health insurance.*

Health maintenance organizations. Health maintenance organization(s). HMO(s). *Choose from:* prepaid *with:* group health organization(s), group practice(s). Individual practice association(s). *Consider also:* preferred provider organization(s), managed care, group health plan(s). *See also* Biased selection; Health expenditures; Health insurance.

Health manpower. Health manpower. Health service(s) personnel. Human resources in health care. Medical social worker(s). Medical support staff. Community health worker(s). Nurses aide(s). Practical nurse(s). *Choose from:* health, healthcare, hospital, paramedical, medical, clinic(s) *with:* manpower, personnel, staff, human resources, social worker(s), professional(s), paraprofessional(s), worker(s), occupation(s). *Consider also:* allied health personnel, dentist(s), medical consultant(s), nurse(s), pharmacist(s), physician(s), psychologist(s), veterinarian(s), coroner(s), medical examiner(s), attendant(s), general practitioner(s), gynecologist(s), internist(s), medic(s), neurologist(s), obstetrician(s), optometrist(s), paramedic(s), pathologist(s), pediatrician(s), physical therapist(s), psychiatrist(s), surgeon(s). *See also* Allied health personnel; Dentists; Health occupations; Health resources; Hospital volunteers; Human resources; Labor supply; Manpower; Medical personnel supply; Medical staff; Nursing staff; Nurses; Paraprofessional personnel; Physicians.

Health occupations. Health occupation(s). Health care provider(s). Medical profession(s). *Choose from:* health, medical, medicine, therapeutic, nutrition, biomedical *with:* occupation(s), worker(s), personnel, provider(s), manpower, profession(s), practitioner(s), career(s), vocation(s). *Consider also:* allied health occupation(s), audiologist(s), biomedical engineer(s), chiropractor(s), dentist(s), dietitian(s), hospital administrator(s), hospitalist(s), nurse(s), practical nurs(es), nutritionist(s), occupational therapist(s), optometrist(s), pharmacologist(s), pharmacist(s), physician(s), physical therapist(s), podiatrist(s), speech pathologist(s), dental technician(s), medical technician(s), veterinarian(s). *See also* Allied health personnel; Health manpower; Medical education; Social medicine.

Health personnel. See *Allied health personnel; Health manpower; Health occupations; Physicians.*

Health personnel, allied. See *Allied health personnel.*

Health personnel, attitude of. See *Attitude of health personnel.*

Health planning. Health planning. *Choose from:* medical care, medical service(s), nursing care, nursing service(s), health care, health resource(s), health service(s), health program(s), health insurance, health facilit(y,ies), health system(s) *with:* plan(ned,ning), estimat(e,ed,ing), priorit(y,ies), polic(y,ies). *See also* Catchment area (health); Delivery of services; Health care; Health care rationing; Health care utilization; Health facilities; Health manpower; Health policy; Health services needs and demand; Health resources; Local planning; Medically underserved areas; National health programs.

Health policy. Health polic(y,ies). *Choose from:* health(care), medical, nursing, patient care, surgical, physician(s), primary care, dental, hospital(s), clinic(s) *with:* polic(y,ies), regulation(s), guideline(s), rule(s), law(s). *See also* Birth control; Child mortality; Disease; Environmental protection; Epidemics; Eugenics; Family policy; Health care; Health care reform; Health planning; Health promotion; Health resources; Health services; Health services needs and demand; Infant mortality; Morbidity; Pollution control; Public health; Social legislation; Waste disposal.

Health problems. Health problem(s). Malaise. Ail(ing,ment,ments). Poor health. Health complaint(s). Afflict(ed, ion,ions). Infirm(ity,ities). Physical illness(es). Unhealthy. Unwell. Disabilit(y,ies). Sick(ly,liness). Dysphoria. Depressive symptom(s). Disabling condition(s). Minor illness(es). Frequent absence(s). Run down. Chronic(ally) ill(ness). Chronic condition(s). *Choose from:* medical, health *with:* complaint(s), complication(s), impair(ed,ment,ments), chronic. *See also* Caregiver burden; Chronic disease; Chronic pain; Disability; Disease; Eating disorders; Illness; Injuries; Lead poisoning; Malnutrition; Morbidity; Obesity; Occupational diseases; Stress.

Health professions. See *Allied health personnel; Health occupations; Nurses; Physicians.*

Health programs, national. See *National health programs.*

Health programs, universal. See *National health programs.*

Health promotion. Health promot(e,ed, ing,ion). Preventive medicine. Health education. Prophylaxis. *Consider also:* health, breakfast, immunization, lunch, mental health, family health *with:* program(s). *Choose from:* health, wellness, mental health *with:* promot(e, ed,ing,ion), program(s), campaign(s), public relations, workshop(s), advertis(e,ed,ing), publiciz(e,ed,ing), promulgat(e,ed,ing), public education. *See also* Holistic health; Medical advertising; Preventive medicine; Preventive psychiatry; Primary prevention; Quality of life; Safety; Well being.

Health resorts. Health resort(s). Sanitor(ia, ium,iums). Sanitar(ia,ium,iums). Spa rehabilitation. Natural health resource(s). Health resort facilit(y,ies). *Choose from:* health, rehabilitat(ive,ion), diet *with:* resort(s), spa(s). *Consider also:* balneology. *See also* Health facilities; Health promotion.

Health resources. Health resource(s). *Choose from:* health, medical, surgical, psychiatric, dental *with:* resource(s), service(s), facilit(y,ies), program(s), suppl(y,ies), reserve(s). *See also* Health care rationing; Health expenditures; Health facilities; Health manpower; Health planning; Health policy; Health services needs and demand; Triage; Voluntary health agencies.

Health screening. See *Mass screening.*

Health seeking behavior. See *Health; Health promotion; Holistic health; Mental health; Preventive medicine; Preventive psychiatry; Primary prevention; Quality of life; Well being.*

Health services. Health service(s). Health care. Health care service(s). Medical care. Medical service(s). *Choose from:* health, medical, dental, psychiatric, mental health, rehabilitat(ion,ive), nursing, pediatric, obstetrical, primary, patient, prenatal, outpatient, clinical, treatment, emergency, dietary *with:* service(s), program(s), outreach, care, clinic(s), center(s). *See also* Community health services; Community mental health services; Emergency medicine; Health care utilization; Hospices; Hospitals; Medical care; Mental health services.

Health services, child. See *Child health services.*

Health services, community. See *Community health services.*

Health services, indigenous. See *Traditional medicine.*

Health services, industrial. See *Occupational health services.*

Health services, maternal. See *Maternal health services.*

Health services misuse. Health service(s) misuse. *Choose from:* health, medical, dental, psychiatric, mental health, rehabilitat(ion,ive), nursing, pediatric, obstetrical, primary, patient, outpatient, clinical, treatment, emergency, dietary *with:* service(s), program(s), care, clinic(s), center(s) *with:* abuse(s), decept(ion,ive), fraud(ulent), misuse(d,s), overutiliz(e,ed,ing,ation). *Consider also:* unnecessary surgery, iatrogenic disease(s), malinger(ed,ing). *See also* Fraud; Iatrogenesis; Malingering; Malpractice.

Health services needs and demand. Health services needs and demand. *Choose from:* health care, health service(s), primary care, medical care, medical service(s), treatment(s), dental care, dental service(s), mental health service(s) *with:* need(s), demand(s), potential use(rs), consumer(s), utiliz(e,ed,ing,ation), consumption. *See also* Catchment area (health); Health care rationing; Health care reform; Health care utilization; Health planning; Health resources; Managed care; Medical personnel supply; Medically underserved areas; Triage.

Health services, occupational. See *Occupational health services.*

Health services, personal. See *Personal health services.*

Health services, preventive. See *Preventive medicine; Preventive psychiatry; Primary prevention.*

Health services, school. See *Student health services.*

Health services, student. See *Student health services.*

Health status. Health status. Level of health. Well being. Health problems. Ill health. Fit(ness). Well(ness). Ill(ness). Health(y). Sick(ness). *Consider also:* fair, good, excellent, poor, failing, assessment *with:* health, medical condition(s). *See also* Health; Health surveys; Illness; Quality of life; Well being.

Health status indicators. Health status indicator(s). *Choose from:* health, disease(s), medical status, epidemiolog(y,ical) *with:* indicator(s), index(es), indices. *See also* Biochemical

markers; Health indices; Health surveys; Indicators (biology); Indexes (indicators); Infant mortality; Medical geography; Morbidity; Mortality rates; Quality of life; Well being; World health

Health surveys. Health survey(s). *Choose from:* health, medical, mental health, dental health, periodontal, genetic, nutrition, diet, sanitary, child growth, morbidity, epidemiolog(y,ical) *with:* survey(s), questionnaire(s), screening, statistics, surveillance. *Consider also:* mass chest x-ray(s). *See also* Health care surveys; Health indices; Health status indicators; Infant mortality; Medical geography; Morbidity; Mortality rates; Screening; World health.

Health transition. Health transition. *Choose from:* demographic, epidemiologic, population, socio-economic distribution *with:* chang(e,es,ing), transition(s,al), ageing, momentum transformation, trend(s) *with:* health status, quality of life, illness(es), morbid(ity), disabilit(y,ies), health condition(s), fertility, birth(s), mortality, cause(s) of death, coronary heart disease, infectious disease(s), non-infectious disease(s), cancer, health care need(s). *See also* Birthrate; Fertility decline; Infant mortality; Life expectancy; Mortality rates; Population characteristics; Population dynamics.

Hearing. Hearing. Auditory perception. Acoustic reception. Aural(ly). Audition. Listen(ing). Auscultation. *Consider also:* acoustic stimulation, psychoacoustics, auditory discrimination, auditory localization, loudness discrimination, loudness perception, pitch discrimination, pitch perception, speech perception. *See also* Auditory fatigue; Auditory perception; Auditory perceptual disorders; Auditory threshold; Deafness; Hearing disorders; Noise (sounds); Partial hearing.

Hearing aids. Hearing aid(s). *Choose from:* hearing, auditory, binaural *with:* prosthes(is,es), aid(s,ing). *Consider also:* binaural amplification. *See also* Hearing disorders; Prostheses.

Hearing disorders. Hearing disorder(s). *Choose from:* hearing, aural, auditory *with:* loss(es), disorder(s), disease(s), problem(s), disturbance(s), defect(s). *Consider also:* ear problem(s). *See also* Auditory fatigue; Auditory perceptual disorders; Deafness; Hearing aids; Partial hearing; Tone deafness.

Hearing loss. See *Deafness.*

Hearing loss, functional. See *Functional hearing loss.*

Hearing, partial. See *Partial hearing.*

Heart. Heart(s). Myocard(ium,ial,iac). Cardiac. Endocardium. Pericardium. Intracardiac. Coronary. Perimyocardial.

Cardiovascular. Cardiogenic. Epicardial. Aortocoronary. *See also* Anatomy; Cardiovascular system.

Heart disorders. Heart disorder(s). *Choose from:* heart, cardiac, coronary, myocard(ial,ium) *with:* disorder(s), attack(s), failure(s), patient(s), disease(s), aneurysm(s), problem(s), palpitation(s), fibrillation, disturbance(s), occlusion(s), defect(s), arrest(s,ed). *Consider also:* angina pectoris, arrhythmia(s), bradycardia, myocardial infarction(s), heart aneurysm(s), coronary thrombosis, tachycardia, mitral valve prolapse. *See also* Arrhythmia; Heart surgery.

Heart rate. Heart rate(s). Heartbeat(s). *Choose from:* cardiac, heart, pulse *with:* rate(s), rhythm(s), beat(s), response(s). *See also* Arrhythmia; Exercise; Heart.

Heart surgery. Heart surgery. *Choose from:* heart, cardiac, myocard(ial,ium), coronary, aortocoronary *with:* induced arrest, massage, valve prosthesis, revascularization, bypass, artery implantation, artery anastomosis, surg(ery,ical), pacemaker implant(ation). *See also* Heart disorders; Surgery.

Heartbeat. See *Heart rate.*

Heat. Heat. Heat(ed,ing). Elevated temperature(s). Thermal. Warm(th,ness). Hot(ness). Calor(ic,ie,ies). Tepid(ity, ness). Lukewarm(ness,th). Summer(y). Roast(ed,ing). Broil(ed,ing). Scorch(ed, ing). Boil(ed,ing). Toast(ed,ing). Sear(ed,ing). Fier(y,iness). *See also* Environmental effects; Heat effects; Temperature effects; Thermal acclimatization.

Heat effects. Heat effect(s). *Choose from:* heat(ed,ing), elevated temperature(s), thermal, warm(th), hot(ness) *with:* effect(s), tolerance, stroke, stress(ed,ing, or,ors), discomfort, uncomfortab(le,ly), stimulat(ed,ing,ion), hyperpyrexia, fever(s), asthenia, response(s), performance, acclimatiz(e,ed,ation), reaction(s). *Consider also:* hyperthermia, thermotolerance, heatstroke, heat induced illness. *See also* Environmental effects; Heat; Temperature effects; Thermal acclimatization.

Heathen. See *Infidels.*

Heathenism. See *Paganism.*

Heating costs. See *Utility costs.*

Heaven. Heaven(ly). Janna. Kingdom of God. Olympus. Life everlasting. Elysian field(s). Valhalla. Holy City. Avalon. New Jerusalem. Happy hunting ground(s). Idavoll. Valaskjolf. Gladsheim. Alfheim. Asgard. Gimle. Vingolf. Indraloka. Devaloka. Pitriloka. Glitnir. Bilskirnir. *Consider also:* rebirth, karma, Nirvana, afterlife, purgatory, celestial. *See also* Hell; Immortality; Paradise; Reincarnation.

Heavy metal (music). Heavy metal music. Metal band(s). Heavy metal singer(s). Death metal rock. *Choose from:* heavy metal, neometal *with:* song(s), album(s), rocker(s), band(s), rock group(s). *Consider also:* grunge-rock, hard rock, hard core rock. *See also* Disco music; Music; Popular culture; Popular music; Rhythm and blues; Rock and roll; Rock music; Rock musicians.

Hebephrenic schizophrenia. See *Disorganized schizophrenia.*

Hebrew songs. See *Jewish music.*

Hedonic damages. Hedonic damage(s). Anhedonia damages(s). *Choose from:* enjoyment of life, quality of life, pleasur(e,es,able) *with:* loss(es), lost, inability *with:* damage(s), suit(s), lawsuit(s). *See also* Anhedonia; Lawsuits; Pleasure.

Hedonism. Hedonis(m,tic,t,ts). Hedonic. Self gratification. Pleasure seeking. Sensual. Self satisfaction. Indulgences. Enjoy(ment,ing). Epicurean(ism). High living. Pursuit of pleasure. Overindulgence. Immoderation. *Consider also:* utilitarianism, la dolce vita. *See also* Attitudes; Enjoyment; Interest (ethics); Pleasure; Philosophy; Self interest; Utilitarianism.

Hegemony. Hegemon(y,ies,ic,ical,ial,ism). Dominan(t,ce). Dominat(e,ed,ing,ion). Power relation(s). Power elite. Superpower(s). Great power(s). Imperialis(m,tic). Preponderant influence. *See also* Coercion; Dominance; Dominant ideologies; Political elites; Political power; Ruling class; Spheres of influence.

Height, body. See *Body height.*

Heirs. Heir(s,ship,ess,esses). Heritor(s). Inheritor(s). Legatee(s). *Consider also:* hereditary, beneficiar(y,ies), descendant(s), posterity, successor(s), progeny, posterity. *See also* Beneficiaries; Descent; Disinheritance; Dynasties; Estate planning; Estates (law); Inheritance; Legacies.

Hell. Hell. Hades. Inferno. Jahannam. Lower world. Hellfire. Bottomless pit. Eternal fire(s). Gehenna. Tarturus. Naraka. Niflheim. Tophet. Avichi. Abaddon. Erebus. Sheol. Orcus. Dis. Avernus. Nether region(s). *See also* Future punishment; Heaven; Immortality; Reincarnation; Voyages to the otherworld.

Hellenism. Hellenism. Grecism. Imitat(e,ed,ing,ion) ancient Greek(s). *See also* Classic revival; Classicism.

Helmets. See *Hats; Headgear.*

Helmets, bicycle. See *Bicycle helmets.*

Help. See *Assistance; Helping behavior; Helping, kind behavior.*

Help, self. See *Self help.*

Help, self books. See *Self help books.*

Help, self devices. See *Self help devices.*

Help, self groups. See *Self help groups.*

Help groups, parent. See *Parent help groups.*

Help lines (telephone). Help line(s). Hotline(s). Infoline(s). Crisis line(s). *Choose from:* crisis, information, referral, counseling, poison, emergency, suicide prevention *with:* line(s), dial access, telephone(s), hotline(s), phone(s), emergency number(s). *See also* Crime prevention; Crisis intervention; Disaster relief; Emergencies; Emergency services; Information services; Psychiatric emergency services; Rape crisis counseling; Referral; Remote consultation; Shelters; Suicide prevention; Telephone psychotherapy.

Help programs, mutual. See *Self help groups.*

Help seeking behavior. Help seeking behavior(s). Assistance seeking. *Choose from:* assistance, help, advice, care, psychotherapy, counseling, aid, treatment, consultation *with:* seeking, sought, request(ed,ing), demand(ed,ing). *See also* Abortion applicants; Assistance; Health care utilization; Health services needs and demand; Information seeking; Search; Self help; Self help groups.

Helpers. See *Assistants; Collaborators; Colleagues.*

Helping behavior. Helping behavior(s). Donat(e,ed,ing,ion,ions). Donor(s). Aid(ed,ing). Assist(ed,ing,ance). Altruis(m,tic). Bystander intervention. Help giving. Helping process(es). Helping relationship(s). Helpful(ness). Nurtur(e,ed,ing,ance). Benefactor(s). Support(ed,ing). Rescue(d,r,rs). Sav(e,ed,ing) lives. Willingness to help. Cooperative problem solving. Helping hand(s). Helper(s). Shar(e,ed,ing). Gift giving. Good samaritan(s). Helping response(s). Generosity. Humanitarian(ism). Supportive(ness). Charit(able,y,ies). Render(ing) aid. *Consider also:* prosocial behavior. *See also* Altruism; Assistance; Charitable behavior; Client relations; Consolation; Counseling; Favors; Good samaritans; Help seeking behavior; Intervention; Kindness; Prosocial behavior; Self help; Self help groups; Social responsibility; Social support networks; Sympathy.

Helplessness, learned. See *Learned helplessness.*

Hemorrhage. Hemorrhag(e,es,ed,ing,ic). Acute blood loss. Hemorrhagenic. Hematorrhea. Uncontrolled blood flow. Profuse bleeding. *Consider also:* bleeding, blood loss, rhinorrhagia, nosebleed(s), postoperative bleeding, postsurgery bleeding, ecchymosis, epistaxis, hemarthrosis, hematocele, hematoma, hematuria, hemopericardium, hemoperitoneum, hemoptysis, hemothorax, hyphema. *See also* Cardiovascular system; Cerebral hemorrhage.

Hemorrhage, cerebral. See *Cerebral hemorrhage.*

Hemp, sisal. See *Sisal hemp*

Heraldry. Herald(s,ry,ic). Coat(s) of arms. Armorial bearing(s). Armorial ensign(s). Personal insignia. Family insignia. Family emblem(s). City seal(s). Heraldic register(s). Family crest(s). *Consider also:* blazonry, escutcheon(s), Heralds' College. *See also* Aristocracy; Genealogy; Insignia; National emblems.

Herbal medicine. Herbal medicine. Herbalis(m,t,ts). Herbal(s). Ethnopharmacology. *Choose from:* herb(s,al), plant(s) *with:* medicin(e,es,al), pharmacopoeia, tea(s), drug(s), remed(y,ies), enema(s), cure(s). *Consider also:* nutriceutical(s), allheal, healall, chamomile, peppermint, juniper, barberry, fennel, catnip, ginseng, myrrh, anise, cedar, mullein, witch hazel, comfrey, penny royal, valerian, lobelia, mugwort, rosemary, gentian, fenugreek, garlic, hops, poke root, echinacea, elderberry, etc. *See also* Alternative medicine; Antidotes; Ethnobotany; Medical botany; Medical foods; Naturopathy; Nostrums; Plant folklore; Psychotropic plants; Quackery; Self medication; Traditional medicine.

Herbicides. Herbicid(e,es,al). Defoliant(s). Weed control. *Consider also:* agent orange, paraquat. *See also* Agricultural chemicals; Agricultural workers disease; Carcinogens; Environmental pollutants; Organic farming; Pesticides; Poisons.

Herbs. See *Herbal medicine.*

Herd instinct. See *Affiliation motivation; Gregariousness; Group feeling.*

Herders. Herder(s). Herds(man,men). Shepherd(s). Cowherder(s). Drover(s). Grazier(s). *Consider also:* cowboy(s), cow hand(s), cowpoke(s). *See also* Agricultural workers; Cattle; Livestock; Pastoral societies; Sheep; Transhumance.

Herding societies. See *Pastoral societies.*

Hereditary diseases. Hereditary disease(s). *Choose from:* hereditar(y,ily), heredity, heritability, inherit(ed,able), familial, genetic(ally), mutation(s), genetic damage *with:* disorder(s), disease(s), caus(ed,ation), factor(s), defect(s,ive), predisposition(s), abnormalit(y,ies), monster(s), handicap(s,ped), psychos(is, es), neuros(is,es). *Consider also specific disorders such as:* Tay Sachs, sickle cell anemia, hemophilia, Down(s) syndrome, albinism, amaurotic familial idiocy,

autosome disorders, chromosome disorders, crying cat syndrome, chromosome deletion, dysautonomi(a,c), Klinefelter(s) syndrome, phenylketonuria, porphyria, testicular feminization syndrome, trisomy, Turner(s) syndrome, xeroderma pigmentosum, hereditary nonpolyposis colon cancer, Lynch syndrome, hereditary breast cancer. *Consider also:* congenital, inherit(ed, able) *with:* disease(s), disorder(s), cancer(s). *See also* Albinism; Atavism (biology); Bioethics; Congenitally handicapped; Deficiency diseases; Developmental disabilities; Down's syndrome; Genetic counseling; Genetic screening; Pharmacogenomics; Medical ethics; Mutation; Prenatal development; Single nucleotide polymorphisms; Tay Sachs disease.

Heredity. See *Genetics; Hereditary diseases.*

Heresy. Heres(y,ies). Heretic(s,al). Dissent(er,ers,ing). Heterodox(y,ical). Apostasy. Ecclesiastical controvers(y,ies). Anti-sacerdotalism. Agnostic(s,ism). Blasphem(y,ous). Irreveren(t,ce). *Consider also:* unorthodox, free thought, nonconformity, iconoclasm, renegade(s), recusancy, infidel(s), Arianism, Apollinarianism, Basilides, Catharism, Docetism, Donatism, Gnosticism, Jansenism, Manich(aeism,eism), Monarchianism, Montanism, Valentinians, Waldensian(s,ism). *See also* Agnosticism; Apostasy; Atheism; Blasphemy; Dissent; Iconoclasm; Infidels; Inquisition; Irreligion; Offenses against religion; Rebels; Religion; Religious beliefs; Religious dissenters; Sacrilege.

Heritage. Heritage. Ancestr(y,al). Bequest(s). Birthright. Bloodline(s). Family histor(y,ies). Filia(l,tion). Inherit(ed,ance). Legac(y,ies). Lineage(s). Tradition(s,al,ally). *See also* Customs; Family background; Family traditions; Historic sites; Inheritance; Traditions.

Heritage, racial. See *Races.*

Hermaphroditism. Hermaphrodit(e,es, ism,ic). *Choose from:* pseudo-hermaphrodit(e,es,ism,ic), genital(ia) ambiguit(y,ies), sexual(ly) dimorph(ic, ism), androgyn(e,eity,ism), androgenital syndrome, hermaphroditismus ambiglandularis, pseudohemaphroditismus femininus, intersex(ual,uality, es), virilism, hermaphroditic genitalia, sexual ambiguit(y,ies), gynand(er,rism, ria,roid), gynandromorph(ism), monoecism. *See also* Female genital disorders; Female genitalia; Male genital disorders; Male genitalia.

Hermeneutics. Hermeneutic(al,ian,ians,s). Interpret(ive,ation). Hermeneutic circles. *Choose from:* theor(y,ies,etical),

principle(s), method(s), context(ual), worldview, meaning(s) *with:* interpret(ing,ive,ation), exegesis. *Consider also:* understanding, empathy, verstehen, phenomenology, geisteswissenschften. *See also* Analysis; Aporia; Critical theory; Empiricism; Exegesis; Interpretation; Phenomenology; Semiotics; Sociolinguistics; Verstehen; Worldview.

Hermits. See *Social isolation.*

Heroes. Hero(ic,es). Heroine(s). Champion(s). Protagonist(s). Superhero(es). Movie idol(s). Sports figure(s). Star(s). Great man. Great woman. Lead(ing) part(s). Matinee idol(s). Famous people. Famous person(s). Notable(s). Personage(s). Dignitar(y,ies). Prominent people. Celebrit(y,ies). Well known people. Eminent. Preeminent. Esteemed. Respected. Renowned. Celebrated. Big name(s). Noted. Fame. Distinguished. Venerable. Acclaimed. Immortalized. Luminar(y,ies). Prestigious. Warrior(s). *See also* Antiheroes; Adventure stories; Athletes; Eminence; Famous people; Fiction; Glory; Idolatry; Literature; Political fiction; Protagonist; War poetry; Western fiction.

Heroin dependence. See *Substance dependence.*

Heroines. See *Heroes.*

Herpes genitalis. Herpes genitalis. Hsv-2 infection. Herpesvirus-2. *Choose from:* herpes(virus) *with:* venereal, genital(is), progenitalis, sexual(ly) transmit(ted, ting), sexual transmission. *See also* Sexually transmitted diseases.

Hesitancy. Hesitan(t,cy). Indecision(s). Indecisive(ness). Irresolut(e,eness,ion). Indeterminat(e,ion). Uncertain(ty,ties). Doubt(ing,ful,fulness). Dubious(ness). Misgiving(s). Qualm(s). Misgiving(s). Unsettle(d). Ambivalen(t,ce). Waiver(ed, ing). Equivocat(e,ed,ing,ion). *Consider also:* avoid(ed,ing,ance), evad(e,ed,ing), evasion(s), misgiving(s). *See also* Ambivalence; Decision making; Hesitation; Indecisiveness; Internal conflict; Timidity.

Hesitation. Hesitat(e,ed,ing,ion). Pause(s). Inaction(s). Inactiv(e,ity). Break(s). Stop(ped,ping,s). Halt(ed,ing). Cessation(s). Ceas(e,ed,ing). Discontinu(e,ed,ing,ance). Interrupt(ed,ing,ion). Postpon(e,ed,ing,ement). Procrastinat(e, ed,ing,ation). Holding pattern(s). Abeyance. *See also* Fluctuations; Hesitancy; Inactivity; Procrastination.

Heterogamy. See *Intermarriage.*

Heterogeneity. Heterogene(ity,ous, ousness,ously). Heterogen(y,ous). Mixed composition. *Consider also:* difference(s), dissimilarit(y,ies). *See also* Cross cultural competency; Differences;

Group composition; Homogeneity; Mainstreaming; Melting pot; Population genetics; Racial diversity.

Heterosexism. See *Attitudes toward homosexuality.*

Heterosexual relationships. Heterosexual relation(s,ship,ships). *Choose from:* opposite sex, male female, female male, cross-sex, heteroerotic *with:* dyad(s), relation(s,ship,ships). *Choose from:* wom(an,en), female(s), girl(s) *with:* man, men, male(s), boy(s) *with:* relation(s,ship,ships), romance(s), friendship(s), attraction, interaction, intimacy, bond(s), companion(s,ship, ships). *Consider also:* courtship(s), intimate relationship(s), mate(s), dat(es,ing), boyfriend(s), girlfriend(s), sweetheart(s), lover(s), spouse(s), heterosocial relationship(s). *See also* Friendship; Human courtship; Interpersonal attraction; Interpersonal compatibility; Marital relationship; Sexual foreplay; Sexual intercourse; Sexual partners; Social dating.

Heterosexuality. Heterosexual(ity,s,ly). Heteroerotic(ism). *Choose from:* preference, attract(ed,ing,ion) *with:* opposite sex. *See also* Heterosexual relationships; Sexual preferences.

Heterozygotic twins. Heterozygotic twin(s). Heterozygous twin(s). Dizygotic twin(s). *See also* Twins.

Heuristics. Heuristic(s). *Choose from:* heuristic(s) *with:* device(s), model(ing, s), assumption(s), data analys(is,es), approximation(s), algorithm(s), approach(es), problem solving, stud(yies), strateg(y,ies), mathematical model(s). *Consider also:* conceptual device(s), conceptual scheme(s), ideal type(s), model(s), sensitizing concept(s), simulation(s), assumption(s). *See also* Constructs; Hypotheses; Ideal types; Models; Postulates; Simulation; Theories.

Hibernation. Hibernat(e,ed,ing,ion). Diapause. *Consider also:* brown fat, shallow torpor, deep sleep, dorman(t,cy), estivat(e,ion), estival, aestivat(e,ion), aestival, prehibernation. *See also* Biological rhythms; Dormancy; Seasonal variations; Seasons; Temperature effects.

Hidden curriculum. Hidden curriculum. *Choose from:* curricul(um,a,ae,ar), pedagog(y,ical), education(al) *with:* unstated, unacknowledged, hidden, unexamined, conventionalized, unintended *with:* agenda(s), assumption(s), attitude(s), belief(s), bias(ed,es), worldview, values. *Consider also:* hidden agenda(s), structural discrimination, social construction of knowledge. *See also* Beliefs; Common culture; Cultural transmission; Curriculum; Educational environment; Social

attitudes; Socialization; Sociology of knowledge; Values.

Hidden God. See *Presence of God.*

Hierarchy. Hierarch(al,ical,y,ies,ization). Rank(ing,ed). Hierocrac(y,ies). Caste(s). Seniority system(s). Social taxonom(y, ies). Leader follower. Social ranking. Social hierarch(y,ies). Social categor(y, ies,ize,ized,ization). Division of labor. Dominat(e,ed,ing,ation). Dominan(ce,t). Dominance relationship(s). Dominance hierarch(y,ies). Pecking order(s). Class status. Patriarch(al,y). Authority figure(s). Controlling influence(s). Social status. Social stratification. Social position. Patriarch(al). Superordination. Pyramid(s). Vertical organization(s). *Consider also:* chain of being, unity of command. *See also* Authority (power); Bureaucracies; Bureaucratization; Chain of being; Dominance subordination; Power structure; Ranking; Social status; Social stratification; Stratification.

Hierarchy, social. See *Dominance subordination; Hierarchy; Social dominance; Superior subordinate relationship.*

Hieroglyphics. Hieroglyphic(s). Hieroglyphika grammata. *Consider also:* sacred carved letters, sacred carving(s), hieratic script(s), demotic script(s). *See also* Cave paintings; Cuneiform; Deciphering; Iconography; Petroglyphs; Pictography; Written communications.

Higglers. See *Street vendors.*

Higgling. See *Bargaining.*

High blood pressure. High(er) blood pressure. Hypertens(ion,ive,ives). Elevated blood pressure. Above normal blood pressure. Increased blood pressure. *Consider also:* high tension, hyperexcitability, hyperirritability, high tonus, hypertonus, high systolic pressure, high diastolic pressure, hyperpies(ia,is). *See also* Hypertension; Stress reactions.

High buildings. High building(s). Office tower(s). Skyscraper(s). Tower(s). *Choose from:* high, highrise, high rise, tall *with:* building(s), structure(s), edifice(s), apartment(s). *See also* Buildings; Towers; Urban environments.

High fidelity sound systems. High fidelity sound system(s). Hi-Fi system(s). *Consider also:* stereo system(s). *See also* Appliances.

High risk borrowers. High risk borrower(s). Bad risk borrower(s). *Choose from:* high risk(s), bad risk(s), poor risk(s), former bankrupt(s), financial problem(s), subprime, substandard, impaired credit, nonconforming *with:* borrower(s), loan applicant(s). *Consider also:* credit rating(s), credit risk(s), loan default(s).

See also Bad debts; Bankruptcy; Poverty.

High risk persons. High risk person(s). *Choose from:* high risk, prone, predispos(ed,ition), at risk, susceptib(le, ility), tendenc(y,ies), tend(ed,ing) toward, vulnerab(le,ility), lack(ed,ing) resistance, without protection, unprotected *with:* person(s), population(s), student(s), patient(s), neonate(s), infant(s), child(ren), woman, women, man, men, adolescent(s), group(s). *Consider also:* preterm infant(s), high risk pregnanc(y,ics), premature infant(s), potential dropout(s), life threatening condition(s). *See also* Disease susceptibility; Potential dropouts; Predelinquent youth; Predisposition; Premature infants; Vulnerability.

High school graduates. High school graduate(s). *Choose from:* high school(s), secondary school(s) *with:* graduat(e,es,ed,ing,ion,ions), diploma(s). *See also* High schools; Young adults.

High school students. High school student(s). Secondary school student(s). College bound student(s). *Choose from:* high school, secondary school *with:* fresh(men,man), sophomore(s), junior(s), senior(s), team(s), varsity, athlete(s). *Consider also:* 9th grade, 10th grade, 11th grade, 12th grade, ninth grade, tenth grade, eleventh grade, twelfth grade *with:* student(s). *See also* Adolescence; College students; High schools; Student songs.

High school teachers. High school teacher(s). Secondary school teacher(s). *Choose from:* high school, secondary school *with:* teacher(s), facult(y,ies), coach(es). *See also* High schools; Teachers.

High schools. High school(s). Secondary school(s). 9th grade. 10th grade. 11th grade. 12th grade. Grade(s) 9-12. Grade(s) nine through twelve. Pre-college. College preparatory. Prep(aratory) school(s). Upper level school(s). Upper grade(s). Senior class. Junior class. Sophomore class. Freshman class. Upper school. *Consider also:* British grammar schools, comprehensive schools, A levels, O levels, vocational high schools. *See also* High school graduates; High school students; High school teachers.

High schools, junior. See *Junior high schools.*

High technology industries. High technology industr(y,ies). *Choose from:* high technology, high tech, advanced technolog(y,ies), mechatronic(s), semiconductor(s), leading-edge, electronic(s), microelectronic(s), Silicon Valley, micro-chip(s), computer(s), microcomputer(s), telecommunication(s) *with:* industr(y,ies,ial), factor(y,ies), manufacturing, production. *Consider also:* research and development, IBM, DEC, etc. *See also* Appropriate technologies; Automation; Computer industry; Computers; Electronics industry workers; Factory automation; Future of society; Industry; Inventions; Metal industry; Modernization; Obsolescence; Postindustrial societies; Production control; Technocracy; Technological innovations; Technological progress; Technological unemployment; Technology transfer.

Higher education. Higher education. Higher learning. *Choose from:* graduate, continuing, undergraduate, doctoral, masters, college, baccalaureate, university, professional, postsecondary *with:* education, stud(y,ies), training, course(s), class(es), degree(s), program(s), school(s). *Consider also:* ivy league college(s). *See also* Academic education; College teaching; Colleges; Conservatories; Graduate education; Postgraduate training.

Highway, information. See *Information highway.*

Highway safety. Highway safety. *Choose from:* automobile(s), car(s), driv(er,ers, ing), traffic, highway(s), seat belt(s), mass transportation, vehicle(s), speed(ing,s), road(s), pedestrian(s), motorcycle(s), *with:* safe(ty), precaution(s), accident(s), victim(s), risk(s), prevent(ed,ing,ion), sav(e,ing) lives. *Consider also:* seat belt(s), 55 mph, speed limit(s), road sign(s), highway sign(s), driver training, driver education, driving law(s), highway fatalit(y,ies), automobile collision(s), drunk driving, DWI. *See also* Accidents; Crossroads; Drunk driving; Motor vehicles; Pedestrian accidents; Pedestrians; Road rage; Safety; Street traffic; Transportation policy.

Highways. Highway(s). Turnpike(s). Thruway(s). Freeway(s). Parkway(s). Road(s,way,ways). Expressway(s). Toll road(s). Route(s). Interstate highway(s). Superhighway(s). Thoroughfare(s). Causeway(s). Access road(s). Arterial(s). Traffic route(s). Boulevard(s). Motorway(s). Autobahn. Beltway(s). *See also* Crossroads; Highway safety; Streets; Transportation.

Hijacking. Hijack(ed,er,ers,ing,ings). Highjacked. Air piracy. Hold up airliner. Skyjacking(s). Seize aircraft. Demand to be flown. Storm cockpit. Threaten pilots. Kidnap(ped,ping). Bus hostage(s). Jet hostage(s). Hold pilot captive. *Choose from:* seiz(e,ed,ing), hold up, hostage(s) *with:* ship(s), barge(s), boat(s), yacht(s), liner(s), freighter(s), bus(ses), plane(s), airplane(s), aircraft, jetliner(s), jet(s),

747(s), etc. *Consider also:* carjack(er,ers,ed,ing,ings), Achille Lauro, airline security. *See also* Bandits; Crime; Hostages; Kidnapping; Piracy (at sea); Privateers; Terrorism.

Hindrances. Hindrance(s). Hinder(ed,ing). Impediment(s). Obstacle(s). Obstruction(s). Barrier(s). Interference(s). Stumbling block(s). Barricade(s). Encumbrance(s). Snag(s). Hitch(es). Inhibition(s). Constraint(s). Handicap(s). *See also* Barriers; Blockade; Constraints; Deadlock; Deterrence; Difficulties; Employment discrimination; Fences; Impediments; Limitations.

Hinduism. Hindu(ism,s). *Consider also:* Vishnu, Shiva, Upanishads, Ayurvedic, Bhagavad Gita, Ramakrishna, Veda(s), Vedanta, Atman Brahman, Brahman(s, ic), Brahmin, Harijan(s), Dharma(pada), Dhammapada, Karma, Maya, Ramakrishna, Patanjali yoga, Raja yoga, Ramayana, Mahabharata. *See also* Caste system; Reincarnation; Religion.

Hinterland. Hinterland(s). Back country. Inland territor(y,ies). Outlying area(s). Remote region(s). Australian bush. Outback. Unexplored territor(y,ies). *See also* Rural areas; Rural land.

Hippies. Hipp(y,ies). Beatnik(s). Beat generation. Flower children. Alienated youth. Angry young (man,men). Drug culture. Yippie(s). Rebel(s). Bohemian lifestyle(s). Counterculture. Drug subculture. Haight Ashbury. Counter culture. Punk. *Consider also:* amotivational syndrome. *See also* Alternative lifestyles; Countercultures; Cults; Dissent; Generation gap; Lifestyle; Subcultures; Youth culture.

Hiring. See *Personnel selection.*

Hispanic Americans. Hispanic American(s). Hispanic(s). Puerto Rican(s). Chicano(s). Chicana(s). Latino(s). Spanish surname(s). Spanish speaking. *Choose from:* Hispanic, Mexican, Latin, Spanish, Cuban, Dominican, Colombian, Venezuelan, Puerto Rican, Costa Rican, Nicaraguan, Portuguese, South, Central *with:* American(s). *See also* Bilingual education; Bilingualism; Ethnic groups; Latin Americans; Migrant workers; Minority groups.

Historians. Historian(s). Historiographer(s). Antiquarian(s). Archaeologist(s). Medievalist(s). Compiler(s) of chronicle(s). *Consider also:* archivist(s), biographer(s), memorialist(s), paleologist(s). *See also* Historiography; History; Radical history; Scholars.

Historic buildings. Historic building(s). Historic house(s). Historic neighborhood(s). Old neighborhood(s). Historic town(s). *Choose from:* historic, 16th century, 17th century, 18th century,

19th century *with:* building(s), town hall(s), fort(s,ress,resses), guildhall(s), estate(s), manor(s), castle(s), propert(y, ies), place(s), district(s), house(s), home(s), farmhouse(s), structure(s), homestead(s), town(s), building(s), barn(s). *See also* Buildings; Classic revival; Classical architecture; Gothic revival; Historic houses; Historic ships; Historic sites; History; Land preservation; Manors; Preservation.

Historic houses. Historic house(s). Historic site(s). Victorian house(s). Classic revival house(s). Gothic revival house(s). Colonial home(s). Period house(s). Vintage home(s). 16th century mansion(s). Original homestead(s). *Choose from:* historic, 16th century, sixteenth century, 17th century, seventeenth century, 18th century, eighteenth century, 19th century, nineteenth century *with:* estate(s), mansion(s), house(s), home(s), farmhouse(s), homestead(s). *See also* Buildings; Classic revival; Classical architecture; Cultural history; Cultural property; Gothic revival; Historic buildings; Historic sites; History; Local history; Palaces.

Historic ships. Historic ship(s). *Choose from:* historic, civil war, World War I, World War II, 16th century, sixteenth century, 17th century, seventeenth century, 18th century, eighteenth century, 19th century, nineteenth century, etc. *with:* naval, nav(y,ies), fleet(s), armada(s), ship(s), shipwreck(s), seagoing vessel(s), warship(s), sailboat(s), boat(s), yacht(s), whaler(s), gunboat(s), sidewheeler(s), riverboat(s), ferr(y,ies), steam ship(s), steamer(s), ironclad(s), schooner(s). *Consider also:* trireme(s), galley(s), galleon(s), nao(s), carrack(s), caravel(s), shallop(s), dreadnought(s), U-boat(s), liberty ship(s). *See also* Historic buildings; Historic houses; Historic sites; History; Naval architecture; Sailing ships; Ships.

Historic sites. Historic site(s). Memorial(s). *Choose from:* historic, heritage, ancient, medieval, Civil War, ante-bellum, Revolutionary War, Elizabethan, Victorian, Edwardian, preservation, 17th century, 18th century, nineteenth century, etc. *with:* site(s), landmark(s), trail(s), tour(s), town(s), district(s), village(s), cit(y,ies), house(s), home(s), birthplace(s), inn(s), fort(s,ress,resses), ruin(s), monument(s), battlefield(s). *See also* Cultural history; Cultural property; Historic buildings; Historic ships; Historical libraries; History; Literary landmarks; Local history; Natural monuments; Ruins; Triumphal arches; War memorials.

Historical biography. Historical biograph(y,ies). *Choose from:* histor(y,ies,ical), psychohistor(y,ies,ical)

with: biograph(y,ies), diar(y,ies), memoir(s), autobiograph(y,ies), letter(s), correspondence. *See also* Biographical data; Biography; Historical research; History; Psychohistory.

Historical drama. Historical drama. Historical play(s). *Choose from:* historical, period, 3rd century, twelfth century, 19th century, Samurai, Elizabethan, Tudor, Stuart, Shakespeare(an), medieval, etc. *with:* drama(s,tic), reenact(ed,ing,ment,ments), movie portrayal(s), onstage, movie(s), theatr(e,es,ical), docudrama(s), pagcant(s), puppet(s,ry), stag(e,ed,ing). *See also* Drama; Historical fiction; Latin drama; Literature; Miracle plays; Pageants.

Historical fiction. Historical fiction. Historical novel(s). La novela historica. Der historische Roman. Le roman historique. *Choose from:* histor(y,ical), period, revolution(ary), antebellum, baroque, Biblical, byzantine, Civil war, colonial, counter reformation, Edwardian, Elizabethan, medieval, Napoleonic, Post-war, romantic(ism), Victorian, Korean War, Vietnam War, World War I, World War II *with:* fiction, novel(ette,ettes,s), tale(s), stor(y,ies), fable(s), myth(s), short stor(y,ies), legend(s), fairy tale(s), saga(s), photonovel(s). *See also* Fiction; Historical drama; Nonfiction novel; Political fiction.

Historical geography. Historical geography. Atlas(es) of history. *Choose from:* histor(y,ical), military history, world affairs, civilization(s), empire(s), conquest(s), war(s) *with:* geograph(y, ical), atlas(es), cartograph(y,ic), map(s). *See also* Ancient geography; Economic geography; Frontiers; Geopolitics; Political geography; Territorial issues; World history.

Historical geology. Historical geology. Earth history. *Choose from:* histor(y, ical), evol(ution,ving,ved) *with:* earth, geolog(y,ic,ical). *Consider also:* geologic(al) time. *See also* Geology.

Historical libraries. Historical librar(y,ies). Historical collection(s). Archive(s). *Consider also:* historical societ(y,ies), historical museum(s), family papers, presidential librar(y,ies). *See also* Historical museums; History; Libraries.

Historical linguistics. Historical linguistics. Diachronic linguistics. *Choose from:* historical, diachronic *with:* linguistics, phonology, morphology, syntax, language *Consider also:* comparative philology, glottochronolog(y,ical), lexicostatistics, evolution of language(s). *See also* Diachronic linguistics; Language obsolescence; Linguistics.

Historical materialism. See *Dialectical materialism.*

Historical museums. Historical museum(s). *Choose from:* histor(y,ical) *with:* museum(s), organization(s), societ(y,ies), exhibit(s), display(s), curator(s,ship,ships). *See also* Historic sites; Historical libraries; Historical societies; History; Museums.

Historical periods. Historical period(s). Roman empire. *Choose from:* dark, middle *with* ages. *Choose from:* American revolution, Ancien regime, antebellum, ante-bellum, baroque, Biblical, byzantine, Civil war, classical, colonial, counter reformation, depression, Edwardian, Elizabethan, enlightenment, French revolution, future, Grcat Awakening, Hellenic, industrial revolution, Korean War, medieval, Napoleonic, new deal, pre-colonial, pre-histor(y,ical), progressive, prohibition, post-war, reconstruction, reformation, renaissance, revolutionary America, revolutionary France, revolutionary Russia, revolutionary war, romantic, Russian revolution, Victorian, Vietnam War, World War I, World War II *with:* period(s), age(s), era(s). *Consider also:* 1st, 2nd, 15th, 16th, 17th, seventeenth, eighteenth, nineteenth, etc. *with:* centur(y,ies). *Consider also:* Chou, Ch'in, Han, Hsia, Ming, Shang, Sui, Sung, T'ang, Tsin *with:* dynast(y,ies). *Consider also:* three kingdoms, five dynasties, ten independent states *with:* period(s). *Consider also:* Mogul empire, Byzantium, Enlightenment, blue period, Weimar Germany, Augustan Rome, modernism, Cold War, New Deal, late capitalism, postmodern historiography, late Renaissance, etc. *See also* African empires; Antiquity (time); Archaeology; Asian empires; Bronze age; Civilization; Cultural history; Eighteenth century; Eras; Historical perspective; History; Medieval military history; Middle ages; New Deal; Nineteenth century; Periodization; Pre-Columbian empires; Prehistoric people; Renaissance; War; World history.

Historical perspective. Historical perspective(s). Historical sensibility. Temporal propriet(y,ies). Historical continuit(y,ies). *Choose from:* chronological(ly), historical(ly), temporal, past *with:* frame(work), plac(e,ed,ing,ement), context, continuit(y,ies), perspective(s), sensibility, propriet(y,ies), paradigm(s). *Consider also:* historicism. *See also* Anachronisms; Context; Cultural history; Historiography; Periodization; Psychohistory; Synchronism; Zeitgeist.

Historical poetry. Historical poetry. Epic poe(try,m,ms). Poetic myth(s,ology). Narrative poe(try,m,ms). *Consider also:* classical epic(s), romantic epic(s), chanson(s) de geste, ballad(s), medieval rhyming chronicle(s), euhemeris(m,

t,tic). *See also* Epic literature; Poetry; War poetry.

Historical realism. Historical realis(m,t,t,s). Representationalis(m,t,ts). Perspectival realism. Reconstructionis(m,t,ts). *See also* Historiography; Naturalism; Realism; Realism in art; Relativism.

Historical research. Historical research. *Choose from:* research, qualitative method(s), quantitative method(s), data collection, data analys(is,es), case stud(y,ies) *See also* Historical biography; Historical realism; Historiography; Psychohistory; Research methods.

Historical societies. Historical societ(y,ies). Historical Association(s). Institute(s) of History. *Consider also:* athenæum(s). *See also* Historical museums.

Historiography. Historiograph(y,ic). *Choose from:* histor(y,ies,ical) *with:* record(ed,ing), compil(e,ed,ing), writ(e,ing,ten). *Consider also:* historian(s) *with:* work(s), view(s). *See also* Historians; Historical biography; Historical perspective; Historical realism; History; Intellectual history; Oral history; Periodization; Radical history; Scholarship; Social history; Synchronism; Zeitgeist.

History. Histor(y,ies,ical,ically). Chronolog(y,ies,ical). Ancient. Psychohistor(y,ies,ical). Protohistor(y, ies,ical). Historic(ity,ism). Herstor(y,ies). Historical article(s). Historical biograph(y,ies). Historiography. Historical period(s). Prosopograph(y, ic,ical). Genealog(y,ies,ical). Archiv(al,e, es). Antiquit(y,ies). *See also* Antiquity (time); Archaeology; Chronicles; Chronology; Civilization; Cultural history; Cultural evolution; Folklore; Founding fathers; Genealogy; Historians; Historic houses; Historical libraries; Historical museums; Historical periods; Historiography; Intellectual history; Life history; Local history; Military history; Oral history; Political movements; Prehistoric people; Progress; Psychohistory; Revolution; Social history; Social movements; War.

History, art. See *Art history.*

History, cultural. See *Cultural history.*

History, economic. See *Economic history.*

History, employment. See *Employment history.*

History, family. See *Family history.*

History, intellectual. See *Intellectual history.*

History, life. See *Life history.*

History, local. See *Local history.*

History, medical. See *Patient history.*

History, medieval military. See *Medieval military history.*

History, military. See *Military history.*

History, natural. See *Natural history.*

History, naval. See *Military history.*

History, oral. See *Oral history.*

History, patient. See *Patient history.*

History, radical. See *Radical history.*

History, social. See *Social history.*

History, word. See *Etymology.*

History, work. See *Work experience.*

History, world. See *World history.*

History of ideas. See *Intellectual history.*

History of psychology. History of psychology. *Choose from:* psychology, social psychology, clinical psychology, associationism, behaviorism, Freudian psychoanalytic school, functionalism, gestalt psychology, Jungian psychology, Adlerian psychology, neopsychoanalytic school, structuralism, psychoanalysis, psychotherapy *with:* early concepts, history, 19th century, 20th century, historical overview(s), early psychologists, historical development, contribution(s) to thought. *Consider also:* Sigmund Freud, J. B. Watson, C. Jung, Pavlov, William James, etc. *See also* Psychology; Theories.

History of the family. History of the family. *Choose from:* parent child relationship(s), mother child relationship(s), father child relationship(s), family life, marriage(s), family relations, famil(y, ies), child care, childrearing, childhood, mother(s), father(s), parent(s,al,hood, ing), child discipline, kinship, primogeniture *with:* histor(y,ical), nineteenth century, eighteenth century, 17th century, 16th century, 1820, 1830, 1840, 1850, 1860, 1870, etc., early settler(s), colonial America, ancient Greece, ancient Rome, antiquity, turn of the century, medieval, slave(s,ry), prehistoric, feudal, Victorian. *See also* Family; Historical periods; History.

History taking, medical. See *Medical history taking.*

History taking, patient. See *Medical history taking.*

Histrionic personality disorder. Histrionic personality disorder. *Choose from:* histrionic, hysterical, repressive *with:* personalit(y,ies), syndrome(s), trait(s), psychopathy. *See also* Personality disorders.

HMOs. See *Health maintenance organizations.*

Hoarding. Hoard(ed,ing). Stockpil(e,ed, ing). Accumulat(e,ed,ing,ion). Amass(ed,ing). Collect(ed,ing,ion,ions). Backlog(s,ged,ging). *Consider also:* nest egg, reservoir(s), garner(ed,ing). *See also* Accumulation; Collecting mania; Greed; Saving.

Hoarding behavior, animal. See *Animal hoarding behavior.*

Hoaxes. Hoax(es). Inauthentic. Fake(s,ry). False report(s). False evidence. Practical joke(s). Prank(s). Con game. Fabricat(e,ed,ing,ion). Ruse(s). Scam(s). Imposter(s). Swindl(e,ed,er,ers,ing). Phony. Counterfeit. Flim flam. Cheat(ed,ing). Shell game(s). *See also* Deception; Fraud; Tricksters.

Hoaxes, literary. See *Literary forgeries and mystifications.*

Hobbies. Hobb(y,ies). Leisure pursuit(s). Leisure time interests. Collect(or,ors, ing). Avocation(s). Pastime(s). Diversion(s). Recreation(s,al). Amusement(s). Play. Entertainment. Divertissement. Side interest(s). Distraction(s). *Consider also:* book collecting, numismatics, philately, athletic participation, baseball, basketball, camping, game(s), danc(e,ing), football, gambling, judo, sports, swimming, television, tennis, traveling, vacationing. *See also* Antiques; Book collecting; Collectibles; Collecting mania; Leisure activities; Numismatics; Recreation; Sports; Word games; Word play.

Hobos, yuppie. See *Yuppie hobos.*

Hodgepodge. See *Patchwork.*

Hokan-Siouan languages. Hokan-Siouan language(s). Caddoan: Pawnee. Coahuiltecan: Comecrudo. Hokan: Barbareno Chumash, Shasta, Yana, Yuma. Iroquoian: Cherokee, Mohawk, Oneida, Seneca, Tuscarora, Wyandot [Huron]. Jicaque. Keresan: Western Keresan, Acoma. Muskogean: Chickasaw, Choctaw, Creek, Seminole. Siousan: Assiniboin, Catawba, Crow, Hidatsa, Mandan, Osage, Ponca, Sioux, Winn.ago. *See also* Language; Languages (as subjects); North America; North American native cultural groups.

Holding company. Holding compan(y,ies). Parent compan(y,ies). *Consider also:* investment compan(y,ies). *See also* Corporations; Home office; Subsidiaries.

Holiday depression. Holiday depression. *Choose from:* anniversar(y,ies), season(s,al,ality), winter, holiday(s), Christmas, New Year(s), birthday(s), Sunday(s), weekend(s) *with:* affect(ive), depress(ive,ion), suicid(es,al), mood(s,y, iness), psycho(sis,tic), malaise, blahs, blues, melanchol(y,ia), dejection, schizoaffective, neuros(is,es), syndrome. *Consider also:* seasonal affective disorder, winter depression, seasonal depression. *See also* Anniversary reactions; Holidays; Seasonal affective disorder; Seasonal variations; Seasons.

Holidays. Holiday(s). Festival(s). Holy day(s). Saints day(s). Feast day(s). Fiesta(s). Observance(s). Christmas. Hannukah. Chanukah. Kwansaa. Easter. Thanksgiving. Boxing day. Fourth of July. Memorial day. Labor day. Washington's birthday. Lincoln's birthday. Veterans Day. Columbus Day. Martin Luther King's birthday. Mardi Gras. Yom Kippur. Passover. Vacation day. Day(s) off. Liturgical celebration(s). Seasonal ritual(s). Seasonal rite(s). Commemorat(ive,ion,ions). Sacred meal(s). Seder(s). *Consider also:* graduation(s), anniversar(y,ies), Ramadan. *See also* Celebrations; Customs; Family reunions; Festivals; Holiday depression; Religious rituals; Rituals; Sabbath; Sacred meals.

Holidays, religious. See *Holidays.*

Holiness. See *Sacredness.*

Holism. Holis(m,tic). Wholis(tic,m). Globally interconnected world. *Consider also:* functionalism, integrative interaction, organicism, gestalt psychology, frame of reference, ultimate reality. *See also* Epistemology; Gestalt theory; Globalization; Holistic health; Interdisciplinary approach; Philosophy; Social theories; Systems theory.

Holistic health. Holistic health. Total wellness. Positive wellness. Total well being. Holism. Health giving. Salubrious. Salutary. Promoting healthfulness. Positive health. Positive well being. *Choose from:* holistic, wholistic, total, positive *with:* health, medicin(e,al), fitness, healing, wellness, well being, nursing, veterinary practice. *See also* Health behavior; Holism; Lifestyle; Meditation; Mind-body relations (metaphysics); Natural foods; Preventive medicine; Preventive psychiatry; Psychological well being; Quality of life; Well being.

Holocaust. Holocaust. Shoah. Final solution. Die entlosung. Concentration camp(s). Death camp(s). Death factor(y,ies). Kristallnacht. Univers concentrationnaire. Anus mundi. Extermination camp(s). Detainment camp(s). Internment Center(s). Forced labor camp(s). Relocation camp(s). Nazi detention center(s). Konzentrationslager. Gas chamber(s). Buchenwald. Auschwitz [Oswiecim]. Auschwitz-Birkenau. Dachau. Mauthausen. Sachsenhausen. Stutthof. Chelmno. Treblinka. Sobibor. Maidanek [Majdanek]. Belzac. Neuengamme. Vuoht. Natzweiler. Flossenburg. Bergen-Belsen. Ravensbruck. Sachsenhausen. Gross-Rosen. Theresienstadt [Terezin]. Mauthausen. *Consider also:* Nazi, Nuremberg trial(s), Eichmann, Barbie *with:* atrocit(y,ies), victim(s), crime(s), medical experiment(s), Jew(s,ish), gyps(y,ies), Pol(es,ish), annihilation, genocid(e,al), war crime(s). *See also* Antisemitism; Concentration camp syndrome; Concentration camps; Ethnic cleansing; Genocide; Hate crimes; International offenses; Martyrs; Nazism; Nuclear winter; Prisoners; Prisoners of war; War; War crimes.

Holy men. Holy men. Sadhu(s). Fakir(s). Swami(s). Mendicant(s). Friar(s). Monk(s). Abbot(s,cy,ship). Saint(s). Monastic(s,ism). Ascetic(s,ism). Contemplative life. Vows of celibacy, poverty, obedience. *See also* Abstinence; Asceticism; Friars; Martyrs; Monasticism; Monks; Priests; Religious life; Religious personnel; Sacredness; Saints.

Holy women. Holy women. Nun(s). Women religious. *Choose from:* female(s), women, woman *with:* saint(s), canoniz(e,ed,ing,ation), martyr(s,ed,ing), religious order(s), convent(s), abbey(s), ascetic(s,ism), contemplative life, vows of celibacy, poverty, obedience. *Consider also:* Virgin Mary, Madonna, priestess(es), witch(es). *See also* Abstinence; Asceticism; Canonization; Female spirituality; Goddesses; Martyrs; Nuns; Religious life; Religious personnel; Sacredness; Saints; Women religious.

Homage (feudal law). Homage (feudal law). *Choose from:* feudal(ism), vassal(s,age), lord(s), sovereign, tenant(s) *with:* homage, deference, obeisance, reverence, honor. *Consider also:* liege homage, simple homage, ancestral homage. *See also* Feudal law; Feudalism.

Home, confinement to. See *Housebound.*

Home, foster care. See *Foster home care.*

Home, work at. See *Home based businesses.*

Home accidents. Home accident(s). *Choose from:* home, household, domestic, bathtub, lawn mower(s), space heater(s), baby walker(s), swimming pool(s), stove(s), snowblower(s), appliance(s) *with:* accident(s), injur(y,ies), safety, mishap(s), fall(s), fire(s), burn(s). *See also* Accident prevention; Accident proneness; Accidental falls; Accidents; Households; Safety.

Home based businesses. Home based business(es). Home based work(er,ers). Home labor. Electronic cottage(s). Cottage industr(y,ies). Telecottag(e,es, ing). Telecommut(e,ed,ing,er,ers). Telework(ed,ing). Telestaff(ed,ing). Outwork(er,ers). Homeworker(s). Piece work. Putting out system(s). Home office(s). Home worksite(s). Remote working. Flexiplace. *Choose from:* work(ed,ing), office(s) *with:* home(s). *Choose from:* home(s), home based *with:* business(es), enterprise(s), labor, industr(y,ies), production, retail(er,ers), workplace(s). *Consider also:* independent contractor(s). *See also* Alternative

work patterns; Crafts; Independent contractors; Manufacturers; Microenterprise; Minority businesses; Self employment; Small businesses; Women owned businesses; Working women.

Home birth. Home birth(s,ing). Homebirth(s). *Choose from:* home(s), out-of-hospital, midwife, midwives *with:* birth(s,ing), childbirth, deliver(y,ies), parturition. *See also* Birth; Birthing centers; Midwifery.

Home care. Home care. Home nursing. *Choose from:* home(s), famil(y,ies), parent(s), domiciliary, spousal *with:* care, nurs(ed,ing), caretaker(s), caregiver(s), therap(y,ies), treatment(s), remed(y,ies), dialysis, management. *Consider also:* self administ(ered, ration), informal care. *See also* Care of the sick; Caregivers; Consumer directed care; Home care services; Respite care; Self medication.

Home care services. Home care service(s). Homebirth. Home health agenc(y,ies). Friendly visitor program(s). Home health aide(s). *Choose from:* home, family, personal care *with:* aide(s), attendant(s). Visiting nurse(s). Visiting homemaker(s). *Consider also:* home(s) *with:* patient management, visit(s,ing, ation), care, support(ive), birth(s), therap(y,ies), respiratory care, dialysis, hemodialysis, medical care, deliver(y,ies), counseling, aide(s), midwi(ves,fery), attendant(s). *Consider also:* household worker(s), domestic service(s), home health aide(s). *See also* Domiciliary care; Home care; Home visiting programs; Homemaker services; Visitors to patients.

Home childbirth. See *Home birth.*

Home economics. Home economics. *Choose from:* home(s), domestic, house(s,hold,holds) *with:* economics, management. *Consider also:* cook(ing, ery), cost(s) of living, standard(s) of living, food preparation, house furnishing(s), interior decoration. *See also* Family life; Housekeeping; Women living in poverty.

Home environment. Home environment(s). Familial support. Home life. Family life. Family stability. Family living. Atmosphere of family. Family climate. Home conditions. Family environment. Living space. Personal space. Home setting. Living conditions. Family atmosphere. Home atmosphere. Family characteristics. Family culture. *Choose from:* home(s), famil(ial,y,ies) *with:* environment(s), life, support, stability, stable, atmosphere, setting(s), conditions, culture, circumstance(s), situation(s), background(s). *See also* Family background; Family influence; Family life; Family relations; Family

traditions; Family violence; Interior design; Living conditions; Marital relationship; Parent adolescent relations; Parent child relations; Parental absence; Parental permissiveness.

Home grounds. Home ground(s). Nesting ground(s). Backyard(s). Courtyard(s). Flower garden(s). Landscaped home(s). Home landscape(s). *See also* Gardens.

Home health care. See *Home care.*

Home labor. See *Home based businesses.*

Home life. See *Family life.*

Home nursing. See *Home care.*

Home office. Home office(s). Headquarters. Main office(s). Central office(s). Administrative office(s). Corporate office(s). *Consider also:* parent compan(y,ies) *See also* Corporations; Headquarters relocation; Holding company; Office buildings; Place of business.

Home ownership. Home owner(s,ship). Homeowner(s,ship). House purchase(r,rs). Owner occupied. Landowner(s). Landlord(s). *Choose from:* home(s), house(s), residence(s), dwelling(s), real estate, homestead(s) *with:* own(er,ers,ership), purchas(e,ed, ing,ers), possess(ion,ed). *See also* House buying; Housing; Housing costs; Land ownership; Provenance; Real estate; Refinancing.

Home range. Home range(s). *Choose from:* home *with:* base(s), orientation, range(s). *Consider also:* homing behavior, homeward orientation, place preference(s), habitat(s). *See also* Animal migration; Animal navigation; Animal foraging behavior; Habitat; Territoriality; Rangelands; Right of pasture.

Home reared mentally retarded. Home reared mentally retarded. *Choose from:* home reared, noninstitutionalized, home care, home environment, living at home *with:* mental(ly) retard(ed,ation), developmentally disabled, retarded child(ren), retardate(s), Down(s) syndrome, mentally handicapped. *See also* Mental retardation; Institutionalized mentally retarded.

Home remedies. See *Herbal medicine; Non-prescription drugs; Nostrums; Quackery; Traditional medicine; Vitamin therapy.*

Home rule. Home rule. Self government. *See also* Autonomy (government); Freedom; Delegation of powers; States' rights.

Home schooling. Home school(ed,ing). Homeschool(ed,ing). Homeschooler(s). Home education. Home learning. Learning at home. *Consider also:* non-formal education, flexi-schooling, homework, deschooling, family-centered education, home-based education. *See also* Access to education; Correspondence schools; Distance education; Educational innovations; Individualized instruction; Nontraditional education; Teaching.

Home visiting programs. Home visiting program(s). House call(s). *Choose from:* home, homemaker(s) *with:* visit(s,ing), instruction, care, service(s), based training, intervention program(s), tutoring, respite care, educational program(s). *Consider also:* visiting nurse(s), health visitor(s), friendly visit(ing,or,ors) program(s). *See also* Home care; Home care services; Visitors; Visitors to patients.

Home workplaces. See *Home based businesses.*

Homebound. See *Housebound.*

Homeland. Homeland(s). Homeland(s). Mother countr(y,ies). Fatherland(s). Native land(s). *Choose from:* home, mother, father, native, birthplace *with:* countr(y,ies), land(s), nation(s), soil. *See also* Countries; Displaced persons; Emigration; Expatriates; Illegal aliens; Immigration; Nationalism; Refugees; Relocation.

Homeless. Homeless(ness). Streetpeople. Indigen(t,cy). Wanderer(s). Park people. Cardboard cit(y,ies). Residential instability. Without home(s). Transient(s). Migrant(s). Vagran(t,ts,cy). Rootless(ness). Tent dweller(s). Houseless(ness). Runaway(s). Panhandler(s). Beggar(s). Mendican(t,ts, cy). Squatter(s). Streetnik(s). Skid row. Tramp(s). Itinerant(s). Vagabond(s). Uproot(ed,ing). Hobo(s). Urban nomad(s). *Choose from:* bag, shoppingbag *with:* lad(y,ies), women, woman. *Choose from:* street, pavement, transient, shelter(s) *with:* dweller(s), people, person(s), child(ren), kid(s), population, resident(s). *See also* Deinstitutionalization; Displaced persons; Homeless children; Homeless shelters; Homesteading; Housing; Housing costs; Housing policy; Indigence; Population transfer; Poverty; Refugees; Shelters; Skid row; Squatters; Underclass; Vagrants.

Homeless children. Homeless child(ren). Homeless youth. *Choose from:* homeless(ness), shelter(s), unaccompanied, abandoned, missing, runaway(s) *with:* child(ren), infant(s), bab(y,ies), son(s), daughter(s), offspring, juvenile(s), minor(s), famil(y,ies). *Consider also:* homeless famil(y,ies), *See also* Abandoned children; Child neglect; Homeless; Homeless shelters; Street children.

Homeless shelters. Homeless shelter(s). Shelter(s) for homeless. *Choose from:* homeless(ness), streetpeople, street

people, indigen(t,ts,cy), transient(s), migrant(s), vagrant(s), runaway(s), itinerant(s), bag lad(y,ies), street dweller(s) *with:* shelter(s), refuge(s), asylum(s), haven(s), sanctuar(y,ies), transitional living center(s), group home(s), temporary housing, residence(s), residential setting(s), commune(s), living center(s), accomodation(s), living facilit(y,ies), dormitor(y,ies), halfway house(s), board and care home(s), mission(s), poorhouse(s). *See also* Homeless; Homeless children; Homesteading; Housing; Sanctuaries; Sheltered housing; Shelters; Squatters; Underclass; Vagrants.

Homemaker services. Homemaker service(s). Domestic service personnel. Domestic helper(s). Home aide(s). Home health aide(s). Household help. Home helper(s). Maid(s). Home assistant(s). Domiciliary worker(s). Visiting homemaker(s). *See also* Home care services; Housekeeping.

Homemakers. Homemaker(s). House husband(s). Housewives. Housewife. *Consider also:* housekeeper(s), family manager(s), lady of the house. *See also* Family life; House husbands; Housewives; Sexual division of labor.

Homemakers, displaced. See *Displaced homemakers.*

Homemaking. See *Housekeeping.*

Homeopathy. Homeopath(y,ic,ics). Homoeopathic medicine(s). Homoeopathic science. Homoeopathic philosophy. Homeopathic care. Homeopathic product(s). Healing with microdose(s). Diluted remed(y,ies). *Choose from:* homeopathic, natural substance(s), herbal *with:* treatment(s), remed(y,ies). *Consider also:* bioenergetic medicines, materia medica. *See also* Alternative medicine; Nostrums.

Homeostasis. Homeosta(sis,tic). Social equilibrium. Water balance. Stable state. Balanced. Thermoregulation. Equilibrium. Stability. Tendency to return to normal. Water electrolyte balance. Autoregulation. Acid base equilibrium. Body temperature regulation. *Consider also:* feedback. *See also* Instinct; Physiological stress.

Homepages. Homepage(s). Home page(s). Personal page(s). Portal site(s). Main page(s). Main screen(s). Landing page(s). *Consider also:* internet gateway(s), web site(s), web portal(s). *See also* Hypertext; Information networks; Internet service providers; Virtual libraries; Virtual reality.

Homes. See *Housing.*

Homes, broken. See *Broken homes.*

Homes, country. See *Country homes.*

Homes, group. See *Group homes.*

Homes, institutional. See *Institutional homes.*

Homes, juvenile detention. See *Juvenile detention homes.*

Homes, nursing. See *Nursing homes.*

Homes for the elderly. Home(s) for the elderly. Home(s) for the aged. *Choose from:* aged, old age, rest, retirement, elderly, geriatric, senior citizen(s), older adults, retired *with:* home(s), institution(s), center(s), complex(es), communit(y,ies). *See also* Adult foster care; Adult day care; Adult day care; Boardinghouses; Group homes; Sheltered housing.

Homesickness. See *Nostalgia.*

Homesteading. Homestead(er,ers,ing). Sweat equity. Squatter(s). *See also* Agrarian structures; Home ownership; Homeless; Homeless shelters; Land settlement; Settlers; Squatters.

Homicide. Homicid(e,es,al). Murder(s,ed, ing). Slay(ing,ings). Slain. Kill(ed,ing, ings). Violent death(s). Manslaughter. Lynch(ed,ing,ings). Strangl(e,ed,ing). Slaughter(ed,ing). Assassinat(e,ed,ing, ion,ions). Execut(e,ed,ing,ion,ions). Bride burning(s). Slash(er,ers). Driveby(s). Snuff film(s). Snuff video(s). Gerontocide(s). Gynocide(s). Invalidicide(s). Matricide(s). Patricide(s). Fratricide(s). Infanticide(s). Genocid(e,al). Regicide(s). Parricide(s). Sororicide(s). Uxoricide(s). Vaticide(s). Wrongful death(s). Filicide(s). Behead(ed,ing,ings). Massacre(s). Euthanasia. Shootout(s). Bullet ridden bod(y,ies). *Choose from:* fatal(ly), dead(ly), death(s) *with:* hit and run, force, wrong(ful), liab(le,ility), shot, shooting(s), stab(bed,bing,bings), child abuse, serial, mass, product tampering, beat(en,ing,ings). *See also* Antisocial behavior; Assassination; Drunk driving; Euthanasia; Feuds; Genocide; Gynocide; Infanticide; Justifiable homicide; Lynching; Serial murderers.

Homicide, justifiable. See *Justifiable homicide.*

Homilies. See *Sermons.*

Homo sapiens. Homo sapiens. Human race. Mankind. Humankind. Humanity. Hominidae. Hominid(s). Human(s). Hominoid(s). Human being(s). Human species. Earthling(s). People. Person(s). Populace. Mortal(s). Primitive man. *Consider also:* women, woman, men, man, child(ren), infant(s). *See also* Humanity; Prehistoric people.

Homogamy. Homogam(y,ous). Assortive mating. Assortative mating. *See also* Complementary needs; Endogamous marriage; Human mate selection; Marriage; Marital satisfaction.

Homogeneity. Homogen(eity,eous, eously,ization). Uniform(ity). Similar(ity). Common characteristics. Same kind. *Consider also:* homophily, homogamy. *See also* Group composition; Groups; Heterogeneity; Population characteristics.

Homographs. See *Homonyms.*

Homonyms. Homonym(ic,ous,ously,y). Homograph(s,ic). Homophon(y,e,es,ic). Namesake. *Consider also:* homogram(s), orthographically identical, lexical ambigu(ity,ous), semantic(ally) ambigu(ity,ous), spelled alike, identical spelling, similar sound(s). *See also* Language; Semantics; Vocabulary.

Homophobia. See *Attitudes toward homosexuality.*

Homophones. See *Homonyms.*

Homosexual authors. Homosexual author(s). *Choose from:* homosexual, gay, lesbian, bisexual *with:* author(s), writer(s), composer(s), compiler(s), novelist(s), narrator(s), dramatist(s), screenwriter(s), poet(s), essayist(s), pamphleteer(s), biographer(s), journalist(s), reporter(s), playwright(s), lyricist(s), chronicler(s), narrator(s), newspaper(man,men), scholar(s), literary critic(s,ism). *See also* Authors; Homosexuality.

Homosexual consumers. Homosexual consumer(s). *Choose from:* homosexual, gay, lesbian, bisexual *with:* consumer(s), customer(s), client(s,ele), market(s), user(s), student(s), patient(s), outpatient(s), buyer(s), patron(s), shopper(s), borrower(s), depositor(s), purchaser(s), passenger(s), constituenc(y,ies), enduser(s), seeker(s), tenant(s). *See also* Consumers; Homosexuality; Markets.

Homosexual couples. See *Gay couples.*

Homosexual liberation movement. Homosexual liberation movement. Gay liberation movement. Gay rights. *Choose from:* homosexual, gay, lesbian, homophile *with:* liberation(ist), power, activis(m,t,ts), civil rights, advocacy, equal rights, movement(s), demonstrat(ion,ions,or,ors), politics, protest(er,ers,s), militan(cy,ts), radical(s), social action. *Consider also:* Daughters of Bilitis, Mattachine, Gay and Lesbian Pride, ACT UP, Aids Coalition to Unleash Power, Human Rights Campaign Fund. *See also* Attitudes toward homosexuality; Gay couples; Homosexuality; Lesbianism.

Homosexual marriages. See *Gay couples.*

Homosexual relationships. See *Gay couples.*

Homosexuality. Homosexual(ity,ism). Lesbian(ism). Homoerotic(ism). Homoerotism. Homogenitality.

Gay(ness). Tribade. *Choose from:* same sex *with:* orientation(s), preference, relationship. *Choose from:* sexual, absolute, amphigenous *with:* inversion. *Consider also:* pseudohomosexual(ity), bisexual(ity), Greek love, sexual minorit(y,ies), sexual variations, out of the closet, closet queen(s), gym bunn(y,ies). *See also* Attitudes toward homosexuality; Bisexuality; Gay couples; Homosexual consumers; Homosexual liberation movement; Lesbianism; Male homosexuality; Sexual preferences; Sodomy; Transsexualism.

Homosexuality, accidental. See *Accidental homosexuality.*

Homosexuality, attitudes toward. See *Attitudes toward homosexuality.*

Homosexuality, ego dystonic. See *Ego dystonic homosexuality.*

Homosexuality, female. See *Lesbianism.*

Homosexuality, male. See *Male homosexuality.*

Honesty. Honest(y). Truth(ful). Frank(ness). Open(ness). Guileless. True statements. Veracity. Under oath. Integrity. Outspoken. Trustworth(y,iness). Ingenuous. Genuine(ness). Truth telling. Undeceiving. Upright. Incorruptible. Uncorrupted. Honorable. Sincer(e,ity). Candid. *Consider also:* moral(ity), ethic(s,al). *See also* Morality; Personality traits; Sincerity; Trustworthy; Truth.

Honor (integrity). Honor(able). Honest(y). Integrity. Moral(ity). Rectitude. Human dignity. Good name. Sincer(e,ity). Upright. Faithful. Truthful. Trustworthy. Virtuous. Fidelity. Self respect. Loyal(ty). Incorruptible. *See also* Ethics; Faithfulness; Good; Honesty; Moral development; Morality; Self respect.

Honored (esteem). Honor(ed). Respected. Reverence. Revered. Adulation. Esteemed. Worshipped. Adored. Venerat(ed,ion). High(ly) regard(ed). Lauded. Deference. Homage. Tribute. Testimonial(s). Reputable. Popular(ity). Laurel(s). Eulogized. Exalted. Lionized. Immortalized. Deified. Glorified. Renowned. Obeisance. *See also* Admiration; Apotheosis; Charisma; Commemoration; Commendation; Eulogies; Flattery; Glory; Prestige; Recognition (achievement); Reputation; Respect; Social desirability; Tribute.

Hopefulness. Hope(ful,fully,fulness). Expectant. Anticipat(e,ed,ing,ory). Promising. Inspiriting. Optimis(m,t,ts, tic). Hop(e,ed,ing). High hopes. Positiveness. Positive attitudes. Positive approach. Healthy outlook. Happy outlook. Positive mental attitude. Belief in just world. Faith. Bright outlook. Great expectations. Encouraging. Bullish. *See also* Forecasting; Happi-

ness; Inspiration; Optimism; Personality traits; Psychological endurance; Psychological well being; Theological virtues; Trusting; Worldview.

Hopelessness. Hopeless(ly,ness). Pessimis(m,tic,t,ts). Demoraliz(ed,ation). Dejected. Inconsolable. Disconsolate. Defeatis(m,t). Negativ(ism,ity). Discourage(d,ment). Despair(ed,ing). Gloom(y). Desponden(cy,t). Melancholy. Cynical. Morose. Unhapp(iness, y). Worr(y,ied). Depressed. Dismal. Distrustful. Morbid. Dispirited. Brokenhearted. Heartbroken. Suicidal. *Choose from:* negative *with:* attitude(s), expectation(s). *See also* Abjection; Alienation; Cynicism; Defeat; Distress; Nihilism; Negativism; Personality traits; Pessimism; Powerlessness; Social attitudes; Worldview.

Horizon, time. See *Time utilization.*

Horizontal organization. See *Departmentalization; Division of labor; Labor market segmentation.*

Horology. Horolog(y,ical). *Choose from:* time, hour(s), minute(s), day(s) *with:* measur(e,ed,ing,ment), record(ed,ing). *Consider also:* clock(s), watch(es), sundial(s), sun-dial(s), pendulum(s), clockwork(s), hourglass(es), clepsydra, horologiography, shadow clock(s), water clock(s). *See also* Clocks and watches; Time; Time measurement.

Horoscope. See *Astrology.*

Horror. Horror(s). Fear(ful,fulness). Alarm(ed,ing). Dismay(ed). Dread(ed,ful,ing). Fright(en,ene,ening). Panic. Terror. Terrif(y,ying,ied). Trepid(ation,ity). *Consider also:* aversion, repugnance, repulsive, horrible. *See also* Fear; Repugnance.

Horror films. Horror film(s). Splatter film(s). Horror noir film(s). Shockumentar(y,ies). Gorefest(s). Slasher flick(s). *Choose from:* horror, splatter, gore, monster(s), grotesque, violen(ce,t), evil, grave(s), graveyard(s), vampire(s), terror(s), slasher(s), death, Frankenstein, Dracula, Alfred Hitchcock *with:* film(s), movie(s), cinema(tic), flick(s), video(s), motion picture(s), television, TV, laserdisc(s) *See also* Film genres; Ghost stories; Horror tales; Mass media; Mass media effects; Mass media violence; Motion picture fans; Motion pictures; Postmodernism; Suspense; Vampires.

Horror tales. Horror tale(s). *Choose from:* gothic, ghost(s,ly), supernatural, creepy, intrigue, suspense, uncanny, apparition(s), murder(s), vampire(s), nightmare(s), terror(s), witch(es,craft), strange, spook(s,y), haunt(ed,ing) *with:* tale(s); stor(y,ies), thriller(s), fiction, novel(s), oral tradition. *See also* Ghost stories; Ghosts; Gothic romances;

Haunted houses; Horror films; Popular culture; Popular literature; Suspense; Uncanniness; Vampires.

Horse industry. Horse industry. *Choose from:* horse(s), equine, thoroughbred(s), racehorse(s) *with:* breed(ing), rac(e,ed, ing), farm(s), price(s), rid(ing,er,ers), stable(s), ranch(es), farrier(s), feed(ing), jockey(s), saddle(s), bridle(s), tack, trainer(s), auction(s). *Consider also:* horse-drawn vehicle(s), horse drawn carriage(s), horse and wagon team(s), equestrian(s), cavalr(y,ies). *See also* Agribusiness; Animal breeding; Animal industry; Farming; Horse sports; Horsemanship; Horses; Industry.

Horse sports. Horse sport(s). Equestrian competition(s). Rodeo(s). Equestrian sport(s). Show riding. Horse racing. Harness racing. Horse trotting. *Choose from:* horse(s), pon(y,ies), equestrian, equine *with:* rid(e,er,ers,ing), rac(e,er, ers,ing), show(s), competion(s), sport(s), *Consider also:* dressage, steeplechase, Olympic equestrian team(s), chuckwagon race(s), polo, racehorse(s), fox hunting. *See also* Drugs in athletics; Horse industry; Horsemanship; Sports.

Horsemanship. Horseman(ship). Equestrian(s,ism). Horseback-rid(ing,er,ers). horseback rid(ing,er,ers). Horse riding. Horse train(ing,er,ers). *Consider also:* riding stable(s), horse show(s), dressage, riding school(s), riding academ(y,ies). *See also* Horse industry; Horse sports.

Horses. Horse(s). Equus caballus. Equine(s). Equidae. Racehorse(s). Thoroughbred(s). Mount(s). Steed(s). Stallion(s). Mare(s). Gelding(s). Foal(s). Colt(s). Fill(y,ies). Hunter(s). Trotter(s). Pacer(s). *Choose from:* American saddle, Arab(ian), Barb, Belgian, Cleveland Bay, Clydesdale, Coach, draft, hackney, Morgan, Mustang, Percheron, Quarter, Shire, Suffolk, Turk, *with:* horse(s). *Consider also:* tarpan(s), Przhevalsky's horse(s), ass(es), onager(s), zebra(s). *See also* Animals; Horse industry; Onagers.

Horseshoers. See *Blacksmithing.*

Horticulture. See *Gardening; Gardens.*

Hospices. Hospice(s). Palliative care. Hospitals for the dying. Terminal care hospital(s). Supportive care for the dying. Care of terminally ill. End-of-life care. *See also* Assisted suicide; Death; Dying; Home care; Terminal care; Terminal illness; Thanatology.

Hospital addiction. See *Factitious disorders.*

Hospital environment. Hospital environment(s). *Choose from:* hospital(s), medical center(s), hospice(s), ward(s), health facilit(y,ies) *with:* environment(s), setting(s), physical feature(s), climate(s), atmosphere(s),

milieu(s). *See also* Adjustment (to environment); Health facility environment; Hospitals; Environment; Environmental design; Environmental effects.

Hospital staff. See *Allied health personnel; Health occupations; Medical staff; Nursing staff; Physicians.*

Hospital volunteers. Hospital volunteer(s). Hospital auxiliar(y,ies). Patient escort service(s). *Choose from:* hospital(s), medical center(s) *with:* volunteer(s), auxiliar(y,ies), voluntary worker(s), friendly visitor(s), candystriper(s). *See also* Visitors to patients; Volunteers.

Hospitalism. See *Anaclitic depression.*

Hospitality. Hospitalit(y,ies). Hospitabl(e,y). Welcom(e,ed,ing). Friendl(y,iness). Neighborl(y,iness). Amicab(le,ility). Congenial(ity). Gemutlichkeit. Sociab(le,ility). Receptive(ness). Gracious(ness). Cordial(ity). Genero(us,sity). *Consider also:* honor(ed,ing) guest(s). *See also* Dinners and Dining; Entertaining; Friendliness; Guests; Hotels.

Hospitality industry. Hospitality industr(y,ies). Hotel business(es). Lodging industr(y,ies). Travel and tourism industr(y,ies). *See also* Hotels; Service industries.

Hospitalization. Hospitaliz(ed,ation). Residential treatment. *Choose from:* hospital(s), ward(s) *with:* admission, readmission, admit(ted,ting), readmit(ted,ting), transfer(red,ring), stay, commit(ted,ment). *See also* Admissions; Deinstitutionalization; Institutional release; Institutionalization (persons); Medical care; Patient admission; Patient discharge; Patient readmission; Residential treatment.

Hospitalization, partial. See *Adult day care.*

Hospitalization, psychiatric. See *Psychiatric hospitalization.*

Hospitalized, days. See *Length of stay.*

Hospitalized children. Hospitalized child(ren). *Choose from:* child(ren,hood), pediatric, juvenile(s), minor(s), student(s), pupil(s), neonat(e,es,al), infant(t,ts,cy), bab(y,ies), adolescen(t,ts,ce), girl(s), boy(s) *with:* hospitaliz(ed,ation), inpatient(s). *See also* Children; Hospitalization.

Hospitals. Hospital(s). Therapeutic institution(s). Sanitarium(s). Sanitorium(s). Medical center(s). Infirmar(y,ies). Sickbay(s). Health facilit(y,ies). Ward(s). Mental institution(s). Psychiatric facilit(y,ies). Asylum(s). *Choose from:* inpatient *with:* facilit(y,ies), setting(s), care. *Consider also:* intermediate care facilit(y,ies), hospice(s), surgicenter(s). *See also* Clinics; Hospices; Hospital environ-

ment; Hospitalization; Intensive care; Maximum security facilities; Nursing homes; Operating rooms; Psychiatric clinics; Psychiatric hospitals; Respiratory care units; Sanatoriums.

Hospitals, mental. See *Psychiatric hospitals.*

Hospitals, psychiatric. See *Psychiatric hospitals.*

Hospitals, state mental. See *Psychiatric hospitals.*

Hostages. Hostage(s). Stockholm syndrome. Guestage(s). *Choose from:* hold(ing), held, kidnap(ped,ping), hijack(ed,ing), terroris(m,t,ts) *with:* captive(s), ransom, extortion, prisoner(s), victim(s). *See also* Child kidnapping; Kidnapping; Missing persons; Terrorism; Victimization.

Hostile takeovers. Hostile takeover(s). *Choose from:* hostile, unfriendly *with:* takeover(s), acquisition(s), buyout(s), tender offer(s). *Consider also:* corporate raider(s). *See also* Antitakeover strategies; Buyouts; Conglomerates; Corporate acquisitions; Leveraged buyouts; Mergers.

Hostility. Hostil(e,ity). Resent(ed,ing, ment,ments). Ang(ry,er). Malicious intent. Rage. Animosit(y,ies). Antagon(ism,istic). Ill will. Grudg(e,ing). Begrudg(e,ing). Spite(ful). Contempt(uous). Enmity. Hatred. Hat(e,ed,ing). Dislik(e,ed,ing). Disaffect(ed,ion). Malevolen(ce,t). Malic(e,ious). Wrath(ful). Rancor(ous). *See also* Aggression; Aggressiveness (trait); Air rage; Anger; Alienation; Conflict; Hate; Paranoid disorders; Prejudice; Resentment; Road rage; Scapegoating; Social behavior; Tensions; Threat; Threat postures; Ugliness.

Hot lines. See *Help lines (telephone).*

Hotels. Hotel(s). Inn(s). Motel(s). Hostel(s). Motor inn(s). Boardinghouse(s). Lodge(s). Lodging house(s). Single room occupancy. Bed and breakfast. Tourist home(s). Tourist house(s). Roadhouse(s). Tavern(s). Hospitality industry. *See also* Buildings; Hospitality; Hospitality industry; Tourism; Vacations.

Hotels, single room occupancy. See *Single room occupancy hotels.*

Hotlines. See *Help lines (telephone).*

Hours, books of. See *Books of hours.*

Hours, work. See *Alternative work patterns; Personnel scheduling; Work load; Work schedules; Workday shifts; Worktime.*

Hours, working. See *Alternative work patterns; Personnel scheduling; Work load; Work schedules; Workday shifts; Worktime.*

Hours of labor. See *Alternative work patterns; Personnel scheduling; Work load; Work schedules; Workday shifts; Worktime.*

House buying. House buying *Choose from:* house(s), home(s), housing, dwelling(s), real estate *with:* buy(ing), bought, price(s), purchas(e,ed,ing), mortgage(s), market(s,ing), *Consider also:* homebuyer(s). *See also* Affordable housing; Home ownership; Housing costs; Housing market; Real estate.

House calls. See *Home visiting programs.*

House furnishings. See *Appliances; Bedding; Furniture; Interior design.*

House husbands. House husband(s). Househusband(s). *See also* Homemaker(s); Housewives; Sexual division of labor.

House organs. House organ(s). *Choose from:* house, company, internal, employee, staff, industrial *with:* organ(s), newsletter(s), publication(s), magazine(s). *See also* Community newspapers; Employee attitudes; Information dissemination; Newspapers.

Houseboats. Houseboat(s). Badjara(s). Budgerow(s). *Consider also:* Sampan(s). *See also* Boats; Housing; Living conditions.

Housebound. Housebound. Homebound. Bedridden. *Choose from:* confine(d, ment) *with:* home(s), house(s), bed(s). *Consider also:* chronic(ally) ill(ness), house arrest(s). *See also* Chronic disease; Disease; Disability; Home based businesses; Home care; Home care services; Home visiting programs; Homemaker services.

Housecleaning. See *Housekeeping.*

Household division of labor. See *Sexual division of labor.*

Household employment. See *Domestic service.*

Household labor. See *Domestic service.*

Household management. See *Housekeeping.*

Household tasks. See *Housekeeping.*

Households. Household(s). Domestic establishment(s). Menage(s). Family unit(s). *See also* Family life; Female headed households; Heads of households; Housing.

Households, female headed. See *Female headed households.*

Households, heads of. See *Heads of households.*

Househusbands. See *House husbands.*

Housekeepers. See *Domestic service.*

Housekeeping. Housekeep(er,ers,ing). Housecleaning. Maid service(s).

Housework. Cleaning service(s). Homemak(er,ers,ing). Janitor(s). Dishwash(er,ers,ing). Household work. Cook(ed,ing). Wash(ed,ing) clothes. Vacuum(ed,ing). Dust(ed,ing). Wax(ed,ing) floor(s). Scrub(bed,bing) floor(s). Wash(ed,ing) window(s). Launder(ed,ing). Wash(ed,ing) dishes. *Choose from:* house(s,hold), home(s) *with:* keeping, cleaning, econom(y,ics), management, task(s), chore(s), responsibilit(y,ies). *See also* Domestic service; Family life; Home economics; Homemaker services; Sexual division of labor.

Houses, apartment. See *Apartment houses.*

Houses, coffee. See *Coffee houses.*

Houses, disorderly. See *Disorderly houses.*

Houses, halfway. See *Halfway houses.*

Houses, haunted. See *Haunted houses.*

Houses, historic. See *Historic houses.*

Houses, vacation. See *Vacation houses.*

Houses of prayer. See *Places of worship.*

Housewife's syndrome. Housewife(s) syndrome. Housewife(s) neuros(is,es). Craig(s) wife syndrome. *Choose from:* housewives, housewife, homemaker(s), nonworking wives, nonworking mother(s) *with:* syndrome(s), neuros(is,es), neurotic. *See also* Housewives; Neuroses.

Housewives. Housewives. Housewife. Homemaker(s). Family manager(s). *Choose from:* traditional role(s), home oriented, homemaking, domestic *with:* women, woman, wife, wives. *Consider also:* housework, housekeeper(s), home economist(s), househusband(s). *See also* Family life; Homemakers; Housekeeping; Sexual division of labor.

Housework. See *Housekeeping.*

Housing. Housing. Dwelling(s). Abode(s). Domicile(s). Lodging. Residence(s). Apartment(s). Single family dwelling(s). Home(s). House(s). Living quarters. Flat(s). Living arrangement(s). Public housing. Private residence(s). Living conditions. Shelter(s). Government housing. Council house(s). Residential hotel(s). Lodge(s). Living environment. Farmhouse(s). Townhouse(s). Habitat(s). Lodging(s). Digs. Domicile. Billet(s). Homestead(s). Cottage(s). Mansion(s). Tenement(s). Barrack(s). Penthouse(s). Boarding home(s). College housing. Dormitor(y,ies). Hotel(s). Low rent housing. Middle income housing. Migrant housing. Suburban housing. Group home(s). *See also* Boardinghouses; Boomerang children; Buildings; Cohousing; Farmhouses; Home environment; Home ownership; Homeless; Homeless shelters; Hotels;

Hous.oats; Households; Housing conditions; Housing costs; Housing market; Housing policy; Landlord tenant relations; Landlords; Living conditions; Neighborhoods; Occupancy; Place of residence; Public housing; Real estate; Relocation; Residence characteristics; Residence requirements; Residences; Residential facilities; Residential mobility; Residential patterns; Residential preferences; Rural housing; Squatters; Urban planning; Vacation houses.

Housing, affordable. See *Affordable housing.*

Housing, congregate. See *Group homes.*

Housing, government sponsored. See *Public housing.*

Housing, low income. See *Affordable housing; Public housing.*

Housing, public. See *Public housing.*

Housing, rental. See *Rental housing.*

Housing, retirement. See *Retirement communities.*

Housing, rural. See *Rural housing.*

Housing, segregated. See *Residential segregation.*

Housing, shared. See *Group homes.*

Housing, sheltered. See *Sheltered housing.*

Housing, subsidized. See *Subsidized housing.*

Housing conditions. Housing conditions. *Choose from:* housing, dwelling(s), residence(s), apartment(s), home(s), house(s), living quarters, living arrangement(s) *with:* condition(s), quality, adequacy, safety, repair(ed,s), standard(s), characteristics, suitab(le, ility), evaluation(s). *See also* Housing; Interior design; Living conditions; Living standards; Residence requirements; Residential preferences.

Housing costs. Housing cost(s). *Choose from:* housing, dwelling(s), residence(s), shelter(s), residential, apartment(s), home(s), house(s), living quarters, living arrangement(s) *with:* cost(s), economic(s), affordable, affordability, inexpensive, low cost, moderate(ly) price(d,s), expensive, rent(s), mortgage rate(s). *See also* Affordable housing; Home ownership; House buying; Housing; Housing market; Property values; Rent control; Subsidized housing.

Housing discrimination. See *Residential segregation.*

Housing market. Housing market(s). Property value(s). Real estate speculation. *Choose from:* housing, home(s), house(s), property, real estate, condominium(s), residen(tial,ce,ces) inventory, affordability, sales, activity, slump, speculation. *Consider also:* mortgage rate(s), housing starts. *See also* Affordable housing; House buying; Housing; Housing costs; Real estate; Residential patterns; Residential segregation; Property values.

Housing patterns. See *Residential patterns.*

Housing policy. Housing polic(y,ies). Housing legislation. *Choose from:* housing *with:* polic(y,ies), legislation, regulation(s), allowance(s), subsid(y,ies), assistance, privatization, voucher(s), deregulation. Government role in housing. United States Housing Act of 1937. Housing and Urban Development Act of 1965. Housing and Community Development Act of 1974. *Consider also:* public housing, building code(s), rent control, housing reform, zoning, land use polic(y,ies), commission on housing, no-growth polic(y,ies), Federal Housing Authority (FHA), Government National Mortgage Association (GNMA), Public Housing Administration, Department of Housing and Urban Development (HUD). *See also* Civic improvement; Housing; Public policy; Social legislation; Urban renewal.

Housing preferences. See *Residential preferences.*

Housing projects. See *Public housing.*

Housing segregation. See *Residential segregation.*

Human. See *Females (human); Humanity; Humans; Individuals; Inhabitants; Males (human); Masses; Personnel; Population.*

Human abnormalities. Human abnormalit(y,ies). *Choose from:* human, infant(s), bab(y,ies), child(ren), girl(s), boy(s), person(s), people, men, man, women, woman *with:* anomal(y,ies), abnormalit(y,ies), monster(s), birth defect(s), deformit(y,ies), deform(ed, ation), dwarf(s), malformation(s), developmental defect(s). *Consider also:* freak(s), elephant man, Siamese twin(s), terato(logy,genesis). *See also* Anomalies; Congenitally handicapped; Disability; Drug induced abnormalities; Physical abnormalities; Physical disfigurement; Teratology.

Human-animal relationships. Human-animal relationship(s). *Choose from:* human(s), people, scientist(s), experimenter(s), owner(s), master(s), mistress(es), man(kind) *with:* animal(s), pet(s), wildlife, waterfowl, bird(s) *with:* relationship(s), bond(s,ed,ing). *Consider also:* sacred cow(s), respect for life, hunting, animal rights, domestic animal(s). *See also* Bonding (emotional); Gardening to attract wildlife; Pet therapy; Pets; Sacred animals.

Human behavior. See *Behavior.*

Human body. Human bod(y,ies). Human anatomy. Male bod(y,ies). Female bod(y,ies). Corpse(s). Human carcass(es). Cadaver(s). *Choose from:* human *with:* anatomy, bod(ies,y), physique, organism(s), build, shape(s), physiognom(y,ies), soma, physiology, figure(s), corporeal(ity). *See also* Abdomen; Anatomy; Back; Biofeedback; Biological factors; Blood pressure; Body awareness; Body height; Body temperature; Body weight; Brain; Breast; Cardiovascular system; Chest; Digestive system; Ear; Endocrine system; Eye; Face; Female genitalia; Fingers; Foot; Male genitalia; Hand; Hair; Heart; Human development; Human figure; Hygiene; Nervous system; Physique; Respiratory system; Sense organs.

Human capital. Human capital. Social capital. Educational investment. Employee education. *Choose from:* invest(ed,ing,ment,ments) *with:* training, education. *See also* Economic development; Human resources; Inservice training; Labor supply; Manpower; Productivity.

Human channel capacity. Human channel capacity. *Choose from:* channel, mental, information processing, psychological, perceptual, cognitive *with:* workload, capacit(y,ies), overload, load, strain. *Consider also:* competing task(s), cognitive interference. *See also* Attention; Human information storage.

Human comfort. See *Environment; Ergonomics; Physical comfort.*

Human-computer interaction. See *Man machine systems.*

Human courtship. Human court(ing,ship). Betroth(ed,al). Marriage proposal(s). Dating. Wooing. Sexually inviting behavior. Mate selection. Love affair(s). Lovemaking. Fall(en,ing) in love. Lover(s). Sweetheart(s). Fiance(s,e,es). Boyfriend(s). Girlfriend(s). Roman(ce, tic). Bundling. *Choose from:* premarital, romantic *with:* dyad(s), couple(s), relationship(s), affair(s). *See also* Arranged marriages; Forms of affection; Human mate selection; Love letters; Love poetry; Marriage brokers; Premarital sexual behavior; Romantic love; Sex behavior; Sexual behavior surveys; Sexual foreplay; Social dating.

Human development. Human development. *Choose from:* human, personal, self, individual, personality, psychosexual, social, vocational, adolescent, adult, behavior, career, child, cognitive, creative, emotional, moral, physical, skill, talent, midlife *with:* develop(ed, ing,ment,mental), growth, life cycle(s), matur(e,ed,ing,ation), aging, growing up. *See also* Adolescent development; Adult development; Age differences;

Ages of man; Aging; Child development; Developmental stages; Emotional development; Life cycle; Midlife crisis; Physical development; Psychological aging; Psychogenesis; Social development.

Human dignity. Human dignity. Individual dignity. Human worth. Worthiness. *Choose from:* human, individual *with:* dignity, integrity, worth(iness), honor, honesty, morality, courage, goodness. *Consider also:* human rights, human conscience, transcendence, humanism, self esteem, humanitarianism, personhood. *See also* Attitudes; Civil rights; Honor (integrity); Honored (esteem); Humanism; Humanitarianism; Moral attitudes; Respect; Self esteem; Social values; Student rights.

Human ecology. Human ecolog(y,ies). Social ecolog(y,ies). Urban ecolog(y,ies). *Choose from:* human, social, people, population, socio-ecological *with:* environmental(ly), ecolog(y,ies,ical), sustenance, natural area(s), sub-environment(s), context(s), conservation, competit(ion,ive), cooperat(ion,ive), seasonal variation(s), habitat(ion), land use(s), global change(s), infrastructure(s), lifespace(s), territor(y,ies,ial), natural phenomena, food availability, resource(s), space, coexistence, coevolution, distribution, shelter, natural conditions, energy, food superabundance, food competition, wildlife. *Consider also:* social geography, community structure, anthropo-geography. *See also* Air pollution; Anthropogeography; Community (geographic locality); Community (social); Community development; Community size; Deep ecology; Energy conservation; Environment; Environmental determinism; Environmental effects; Environmental racism; Environmental stress; Geographic determinism; Human geography; Infrastructure (economics); Medical geography; Natural resources; Pollution control; Soil conservation; Water conservation; Waste disposal.

Human engineering. See *Biotechnology; Ergonomics.*

Human evolution. See *Evolution.*

Human experimentation. Human experiment(s,ation). *Choose from:* experiment(s,ation), research, drug trial(s) *with:* human(s), man, men, woman, women, child(ren), human rights, human subject(s), volunteer(s), patient(s). *Consider also:* medical ethics, research ethics, informed consent, Helsinki declaration, experiment volunteer(s). *See also* Human subjects (research); Informed consent; Patient rights; Research ethics; Research subjects; Researcher subject relations.

Human factors engineering. See *Biotechnology; Ergonomics.*

Human females. See *Females (human).*

Human figure. Human figure(s). Human bod(y,ies). Nude figure(s). Human anatomy. *Choose from:* human, female, male, woman(s), women(s), man(s), men(s), nude *with:* figure(s), bod(y,ies). *Consider also:* body beautiful, human image(s), figure drawing(s), figure painting(s). *See also* Human body.

Human gene mapping. See *Gene mapping.*

Human geography. Human geography. *Choose from:* human, economic, political, historical, urban, medical, social *with:* geograph(y,ical), geographic information system(s), map(s,ped,ping). *See also* Geographic information systems; Geography; Human ecology, Medical geography.

Human information processing. See *Human information storage.*

Human information storage. Human information storage. Encod(e,ed,ing). Decod(e,ed,ing). *Choose from:* human information, memory *with:* process(ed, ing), retrieval, recall, acquisition, reactivat(ed,ion), consolidat(e,ed,ing, ion), recogni(tion,ize,ized), storage. *See also* Cognitive processes; Human channel capacity; Info fatigue syndrome; Memory; Word recognition.

Human life cycle. Human life cycle(s). Life stage(s). Life span(s). Lifespan(s). Cradle to grave. *Consider also:* adult development, human development, child development, maturation, midlife crisis, midlife change(s). *See also* Adult; Age groups; Aging; Children; Developmental stages; Elderly; Life expectancy; Maturation; Middle age; Young adults.

Human machine systems. See *Man machine systems.*

Human mate selection. Human mate selection. Matchmaking. Partner selection. *Choose from:* spouse(s), mate(s), wife, wives, husband(s), partner(s), marriage, marital *with:* choice(s), preference(s), choos(e,ing), select(ed,ing,ion), desirability. *Consider also:* court(ing,ship), engage(d,ment), dating, premarital, love affair(s), romantic affair(s), fall(en,ing) in love, lover(s), sweetheart(s), fiancee(s), boyfriend(s), girlfriend(s), romance. *See also* Arranged marriages; Choice (psychology); Human courtship; Interpersonal attraction; Marriage brokers; Premarital sexual behavior; Social dating.

Human migration. See *Migration.*

Human nature. Human nature. Characteristic(s) of man. Innate human qualit(y,ies). Universal human qualit(y,ies). Human characteristic(s). Nature of human beings. Human character trait(s). *Consider also:* original sin, perfectability of man, transcendence, human potential, human condition, condition of man, human soul, human consciousness, capacity for good and evil, theor(y,ies) of human behavior, sociobiolog(y,ical), selfish gene, nature vs nurture, culture *with:* behavior. *See also* Animal nature of man; Behavior; Emotions; Mind; Mind body problem; Nature nurture; Needs; Personality theories; Philosophical anthropology.

Human needs. See *Achievement need; Affiliation motivation; Approval need; Basic needs; Educational needs; Health services needs and demand; Individual needs; Psychological needs.*

Human potential movement. Human potential movement. *Consider also:* gestalt therapy, consciousness raising, sensitivity training, growth center(s), transactional analysis, personal growth technique(s), Esalen, Erhard seminar training, encounter group(s), humanistic psychology, T group(s), self actualization, sensory awareness, meditation, learned optimism, assertiveness training, human relations training. *See also* Assertiveness training; Consciousness raising groups; Encounter groups; Gestalt therapy; Human relations training; Humanistic psychology; Meditation; Self actualization; Sensitivity training; Third-force therapy; Transactional analysis.

Human race. See *Humanity.*

Human relations. See *Interpersonal relations.*

Human relations training. Human relations training. *Choose from:* human relations, marriage enrichment, small group, awareness, empathy, interpersonal, social development, group relations, personal growth, social skills, race relations, encounter, assertiveness, human potential, problem solving *with:* training, program(s), group(s), unit(s), seminar(s). *See also* Assertiveness training; Communication skills; Encounter groups; Marathon group therapy; Marital enrichment; Parent training; Personnel training; Sensitivity training; Social skills training.

Human remains (archaeology). Human remains. Fossil hominid(s). *Choose from:* human(s), hominid(s), early man, prehistoric people(s), neanderthal(s), neandertal(s) *with:* remains, fossil(s), bone(s), skelet(al,on,ons). *Consider also:* mumm(y,ies), paleoanthropology. *See also* Age determination by skeleton; Age determination by teeth; Animal remains (Archaeology); Anthropometry; Kitchen middens; Ossuaries; Physical anthropology; Skeleton.

Human reproduction. See *Sexual reproduction; Artificial insemination; Birth; Conception; Fertility enhancement; Fertilization; Fertilization in vitro; Genetics; Pregnancy; Reproductive technologies; Sex behavior; Sexual intercourse; Surrogate mothers.*

Human resources. Human resources. Personnel supply. Labor market. Undermanned. Understaffed. Overstaffed. Staffing level(s). Manning level(s). Reserve army of the unemployed. *Choose from:* personnel, manpower, labor, workforce *with:* supply, shortage(s), scarcit(y,ies), needs, surplus, availab(ility,le). *See also* Boundaryless organizations; Human capital; Intelligentsia; Labor force; Labor supply; Manpower; Medical personnel supply; Personnel; Technical assistance.

Human rights. Human right(s). Natural right(s). Liberty. Freedom. Informed consent. *Choose from:* human, civil, women(s), woman(s), inalienable, citizen(s), individual(s), child(ren), patient(s), consumer(s), student(s), teacher(s), man(s), men(s), legal, parental, minor(s), minority, political, social, criminal(s) *with:* right(s). *Choose from:* right(s) *with:* die, death, dignity, health care, abortion, life, live, privacy, accused, treatment. *Consider also:* civil liberties, due process, freedom of speech, patient advocacy, social justice, equal education, natural law. *See also* Bill of rights; Children's rights; Client rights; Civil rights; Equal education; Human dignity; Legal rights; Natural law; Ombudsmen; Parent rights; Patient rights; Reproductive rights; Right of privacy; Right to die; Right to work; Social contract; Social equality; Student rights; Voting rights; Women's rights.

Human rights associations. See *Abortion rights movement; Activism; Antiapartheid movement; Antiabortion movement; Black power; Civil disobedience; Civil rights organizations; Disability rights movement; Gray power; Homosexual liberation movement; Interest groups; Labor movements; Peace movements; Political movements; Protest movements; Social movements; Suffrage movement; Women's groups; Women's rights; Youth movements.*

Human rights violations. See *Medical ethics; Oppression; Political prisoners; Political repression; War crimes.*

Human sacrifice. Human sacrifice(s). Ritual murder(s). Blood sacrifice(s). *Choose from:* human being(s), first born, human blood, living bod(y,ies), victim(s), limb(s), arm(s), finger(s) *with:* sacrific(e,es,ial), ritual(s,istic), ritualistic burning(s), offering(s). *Consider also:*

ritual autocremation, ritual self-immolat(ion,or,ors), ritual suicide(s). *See also* Animal sacrifice; Cannibalism; Sacrificial rites; Shrunken heads; Rituals.

Human sciences. See *Social sciences.*

Human services. Human service(s). *Choose from:* human, social, child care, welfare, social work, social, sociopsychological, community, charitable, helping, health, medical, day care, mental health, foster care, homemaker, information, referral, library, nursing, legal, outreach, protective, supportive *with:* service(s), service organization(s), institution(s), agenc(y,ies). *See also* Assistance; Child day care; Child health services; Community services; Counseling; Disaster relief; Employee assistance programs; Employment counseling; Government programs; Health services; Law enforcement; Mental health services; Needs; Public services; Social services.

Human settlements. Human settlement(s). Cit(y,ies). Town(s). Village(s). Hamlet(s). Camp(s). *Consider also:* resettlement, community development, squatter(s), urbanization. *See also* Settlement patterns; Colonization; Land settlement.

Human sex differences. See *Gender differences.*

Human sexuality. See *Sexuality.*

Human subjects (research). Human subject(s). Human research subject(s). *Choose from:* human(s), people, person(s), men, man, women, woman, child(ren), infant(s), retarded, handicapped, elderly, patient(s), client(s) *with:* research, experiment(al,s), drug trial(s), control group(s), subject(s), respondent(s), informant(s), interviewee(s). *Consider also:* informed consent. *See also* Human experimentation; Informed consent; Patient rights; Research ethics; Research subjects; Researcher subject relations.

Humane. Humane(ly,ness). Kindhearted(ness). Compassion(ate). Warmhearted(ness). Benevolen(t,ce). Gentle(ness). Kind(ly). Sympathetic. Considerate(ness). Forgiving. Merciful(ness). Good natured. *Consider also:* charitable, altruistic, eleemosynary, good, humanitarian, philanthropic. *See also* Altruism; Compassion; Humanitarianism; Kindness.

Humane societies. See *Shelters.*

Humanism. Humanis(m,tic,tically). Humanist(s). *Consider also:* humane, humaniz(e,ed,ing,ation), human values, human concerns, humanitarian(ism). *See also* Agnosticism; Animal nature of man; Atheism; Classicism; God concepts; Human dignity; Human

potential movement; Humanistic education; Humanistic psychology; Humanists; Individualism; Liberalism (Religion); Philosophical anthropology; Religious beliefs; Renaissance; Renaissance literature; Renaissance philosophy.

Humanistic education. Humanistic education. *Choose from:* humanis(m,tic), affective, humane, holistic, liberal, humanities, multicultural *with:* education, learning, teaching(s). *Consider also:* humanism, popular psychology. *See also* Active learning; Cooperative learning; Cross cultural competency; Humanism; Humanistic psychology; Humanization; Individualized instruction; Liberalism; Multicultural education; Progressivism; Self actualization; Sensitivity training; Values.

Humanistic psychology. Humanistic psychology. *Choose from:* humanistic, transpersonal, wholistic, holistic, transcenden(t,ce), higher states of consciousness, spiritual(ity), visionary, mystical *with:* psycholog(y,ical), growth, development. *See also* Human potential movement; Self actualization; Third-force therapy.

Humanistic therapy. See *Human potential movement; Humanistic psychology; Third-force therapy.*

Humanists. Humanist(s). Humanist tradition(s). *Consider also:* classical scholar(s,ship), Renaissance man, neohumanist scholar(s), Medieval scholar(s), Renaissance scholar(s). *See also* Classicism; Humanism; Renaissance; Renaissance literature.

Humanitarianism. Humanitarian(s,ism). Philanthrop(ic,y,ist,ists). Altruis(m,t,ts,tic). Public spirited. Benevolen(ce,t). Charit(y,able,ies). Compassion(ate). Unselfish. Genero(sity,us). Merciful. Humane(ness). Beneficent. Respect for life. Moral progress. Moral development. *See also* Altruism; Benevolence; Citizen participation; Community involvement; Good works (theology); Good; Goodwill; Human dignity; Humane; Kindness; Mercy; Political attitudes; Progressivism; Social action; Social attitudes; Social responsibility; Social services; Social values.

Humanities. Humanities. Classics. High culture. Literary culture. *Choose from:* classical, liberal, ancient Greek, Roman, Mesopotamian, ancient Egyptian *with:* studies, literature, arts, education. *Consider also:* philosphy, literature, art, fine arts, languages, history, music, religion. *See also* Ancient Art; Art history; Arts; Cultural anthropology; History; Literature; Music; Poetry; Philosophy; Religion.

Humanity. Human(ity,ness). Mankind. Human race. Humankind. Hominid(s,ae). Hominoid(s). Homo sapiens. Humans. Human being(s). Human species. Earthlings. People. Person(s). Populace. Mortals. Primitive man. People(s) of the world. Race(s) of man. Brotherhood of man. *See also* Animal nature of man; Brotherliness; Common people; Homo Sapiens; Philosophical anthropology.

Humanity, crimes against. See *Ethnic cleansing; Genocide; Holocaust; War crimes.*

Humanization. Humaniz(e,ed,ing,ation). Meaningful(ness). Purposeful(ness). Human dimension. De-alienation. Rehumaniz(e,ed,ing,ation). Patient centered. Client centered. Student centered. People oriented. Theory Y. Theory Z. Self actualiz(e,ed,ing,ation). Humanis(m,tic). Human factor(s). Mak(e,ing) humane. *Consider also:* character building, sympath(y,ize, izing,ized), empath(y,ize,izing,ized), compassion(ate), self realization, moral development. *See also* Attitudes; Critical theory; Environmental enrichment; Ergonomics; Holism; Human dignity; Humanism; Humanistic education; Humanistic psychology; Liberalism; Life satisfaction; Lifestyle; Milieu therapy; Progressivism; Quality of life; Quality of working life; Self actualization; Work humanization.

Humanization, work. See *Work humanization.*

Humans. Human(s). Human race. Mankind. Humankind. Humanity. Hominidae. Homo sapiens. Hominid(s). Hominoid(s). Human being(s). Human species. Earthling(s). People. Person(s). Populace. Mortal(s). Primitive man. *Consider also:* women, woman, men, man, child(ren), infant(s). *See also* Common people; Humanity; Homo Sapiens; Prehistoric people.

Humans, female. See *Females (human).*

Humans, male. See *Males (human).*

Humiliation. Humiliat(e,ed,ion). Shame(d,ful). Mortif(y,ied,ying,ication). Humble(d). Disgrace(d,ful). Dishonor(ed). Discredited. Disrepute. Downfall(en). *Consider also:* loss of face, cast down, debase(d,ment), degrad(e,ed,adation), demean(ed), abject(ness), self-abase(d,ment). *See also* Embarrassment; Emotions; Guilt; Self consciousness; Shame; Stigma.

Humility. Humility. Meek(ness). Humble(ness). Submissive(ness). Servil(e,ity). Subservien(t,ce). Obsequious(ness). Modest(y). Unpretentious(ness). *Consider also:* humiliation. *See also* Decency; Modesty; Passiveness.

Humor. Humor(ous,ousness). Wit(ty,tiness). Comed(y,ies). Satir(e,ical). Caricature(s). Laugh(ed,ing,ter,able). Cartoon(s). Jok(e,ed,es,ing). Amus(e,ed, ing,ment,ments). Comical. Mirth. Riddle(s). Comedi(an,ans). Clown(s, ing). Absurdit(y,ies). Whims(y,ical). Droll. Facetious(ness). Jocularity. Witticism(s). Jest(ing). Funn(y,iness). Slapstick. Levity. Kidding. Ludi-crous(ness,ly). *Consider also:* farc(e,es,ical), parod(y,ies), one-liner(s). *See also* Cartoons; Comedians; Comics; Ethnic wit and humor; Farce; Fiction; Fools and jesters; Frivolity; Humorous poetry; Humorous songs; Laughter; Literature; Political humor; Satire; Sense of humor.

Humor, ethnic and wit. See *Ethnic wit and humor.*

Humor, political. See *Political humor.*

Humor, sense of. See *Sense of humor.*

Humoralism. Humoralism. Bodily humor(s). *Choose from:* humor(s,al), humour(s,al) *with:* physiolog(y,ical), melanchol(y,ia), bod(y,ies), health(y,iness), disease(s,d), illness(es), complexion(s), fluid(s), blood, phlegm, yellow bile, black bile, medicine(s), Empedocles. *See also* Traditional medicine.

Humorists. See *Comedians.*

Humorous poetry. Humorous poe(try,m, ms). Limerick(s). Light verse(s). Fabliau(x). *Choose from:* humor(ous), light(hearted), light hearted, funny, jok(e,es,ing), amusing, pok(e,ed,ing) fun, comic, comed(y,ies) *with:* poe(try,m,ms), verse(s), ballad(s). *See also* Humor; Humorous songs; Macaronic literature; Nonsense literature; Poetry; Political humor.

Humorous songs. Humorous song(s). *Choose from:* humor(ous), comic, comed(y,ies), hilarious, lighthearted, funny, amusing, satirical, ridiculous, parod(y,ies) *with:* song(s), glee(s), catch(es), round(s), folksong(s), ballad(s). *See also* Comedians; Fools and jesters; Frivolity; Humor; Humorous poetry; Satirical songs; Songs.

Hunger, affect. See *Psychosocial deprivation.*

Hunger, food deprivation. Hung(er,ering,ry,riness). Appetite(s). Malnourish(ed,ment). Malnutrition. Starv(e,ed,ing,ation). Famine(s). Semistarv(ed,ing,ation). Hunger strike(s). Diet(ing). Nutritional abuse. Reduced food intake. Undernourish(ed, ment). Undernutrition. Famish(ed,ment). *Choose from:* food, feed, diet(s,ary), calor(ic,ies), protein(s), vitamin(s), carbohydrate(s) *with:* depriv(ed,ation), restrict(ed,ion), scarc(e,ity), lack(ed,ing),

shortage(s), deficien(cy,t), inadequate. *Choose from:* anticipat(e,ed,ing), crav(e,ed,ing) *with:* food, feeding, meal(s). *See also* Asceticism; Eating disorders; Famine; Fasting; Food; Malnutrition; Nutrition; Nutrition disorders; Poverty; Satiation; Starvation.

Hunger strikes. Hunger strik(e,es,er, ers,ing). Fast unto death. Jail fast(s). Fasting to protest. *Choose from:* hunger, fast(s,ed,ing) *with:* protest(ed,ing,er,ers), jail(ed,s), strike(s,r,rs). *See also* Fasting; Nonviolence; Protest movements; Protesters; Social demonstrations; Starvation.

Hunting. Hunt(ed,s,ing). Track(ed,ing). Pursu(e,ed,ing,it) game. Venery. Hawking. Stalk(ed,ing). Falconry. Trailing. *Consider also:* slaughter(ing) game, sports(man,men), decoy(s), bird dog(s). *See also* Decoys; Deer; Duck hunting; Fowling; Game and game birds; Game laws; Hunting dogs; Hunting trophies; Poaching; Sports; Subsistence hunting.

Hunting, duck. See *Duck hunting.*

Hunting, job. See *Job search.*

Hunting, primitive. See *Primitive hunting.*

Hunting, subsistence. See *Subsistence hunting.*

Hunting, witch. See *Witch hunting.*

Hunting and gathering societies. Hunt(ing,er) and gather(er,ing) societ(y,ies). *Choose from:* hunt(ing,er), gather(er,ing), forag(e,ed,ing) *with:* societ(y,ies), communit(y,ies). *See also* Nomads; Prehistoric commerce; Prehistoric people; Prehistoric transpor-tation; Primitive fishing; Primitive warfare; Subsistence hunting; Tradi-tional societies.

Hunting dogs. Hunting dog(s). Bird dog(s). *Consider also:* pointer(s), retriever(s), English setters, hound(s), fox hunting. *See also* Dogs; Hunting.

Hunting trophies. Hunting troph(y,ies). *Choose from:* hunt(ing), bowhunting, sportsm(an,en), Polar bear, big game, deer, whitetail, wildlife, buck(s), antler(s), *with:* record(s), world record(s), troph(y,ies). *See also* Hunting; Reward.

Hurdles. See *Barriers.*

Hurry (speed). Hurr(y,ying,ied). Accelerat(e,ed,ing,ion). Act(ed,ing) quickly. Dash(ed,ing). Expedit(e,ed,ing). Facilitat(e,ed,ing). Hasten(ed,ing). Mak(e,ing) haste. Mov(e,ed,ing) quickly. Mov(e,ed,ing) speedily. Speed(ing). Racing. Rush(ed,ing). *See also* Acceleration (speed); Motion; Velocity.

Husbands. Husband(s). Male spouse(s). Househusband(s). *Choose from:* male(s),

men, man *with:* married, wives. Married father(s). Married sailor(s), etc. Wife abuser(s). Bridegroom(s). Consort(s). *See also* Males (human); Spouses.

Husbands, house. See *House husbands.*

Hybrid organizations. See *Joint ventures.*

Hybrids (biology). Hybrid(s,ization, ism,ity). *Choose from:* genetic(ally), strain(s), species, line(s) *with:* cross(es,ed,ing). *Choose from:* heterozyg(ote,otes,ous), heterosis, cross(bred,breed,breeding), hybridogenetic, interspecies mating(s), introgression, mongrel(s). *See also* Genetics.

Hygiene. Hygien(e,ic). Clean(liness,ness, sing). Sanit(ary,ation). Body care. Bath(ing). Wash(ed,ing). Brush(ed,ing) teeth. Douch(e,ed,ing). Gargl(e,ed,ing). Shampoo(ed,ing). Groom(ed,ing). Personal care. *Consider also:* preventive medicine, oral hygiene, personal hygiene, disinfect(ed,ion), asep(tic,sis), antiseptic, sterilizing. *See also* Activities of daily living; Antiseptic; Dental care; Hand washing; Health education; Preventive medicine; Public health; Sanitation; Self care; Self neglect; World health.

Hygiene, industrial. See *Agricultural workers disease; Black lung disease; Industrial accidents; Multiple chemical sensitivities; Noise levels (work areas); Occupational diseases; Occupational exposure; Occupational health services; Occupational neuroses; Occupational safety; Occupational stress; Repetitive motion disorders; Sick building syndrome; Working conditions.*

Hygiene, social. See *Public health*

Hygienic. See *Antisepetic; Hygiene.*

Hymnals. See *Songbooks.*

Hymns. Hymn(s,al,als,ody, odies,ary,aries,ica,en). Chorale(s). Geistliche Lied(er). Kirchenlied(er). Sacred ballad(s). Carol(s). Psalter(s). Metrical psalm(s). Methodist tune(s). Psalm tune(s). Anthem(s). *Consider also:* psalm(s,ody), song(s) of praise, lyric poetry, ode(s), liturg(y,ies,ical), motet(s), Gregorian chant(s), plainsong(s), sacred folk songs, spiritual(s). *See also* Church music; Funeral music; German songs; Gospel music; Lauda; Oratorio; Plainsong; Religious music.

Hymns, funeral. See *Funeral music.*

Hyperactivity. See *Hyperkinesis.*

Hyperbole. Hyperbol(e,ic,ical,ically). Exaggerat(e,ed,ing,ion). Overstat(e,ed, ing,ement). Embellish(ed,ing,ment). *See also* Deception; Distortion; Misinforma-tion; Personification.

Hyperkinesis. Hyperkine(sis,tic). Hyperactiv(e,ity). *Consider also:* attention deficit disorder(s), minimal brain dysfunction, minimal cerebral dysfunction, attentional deficit(s), inability to concentrate, inattentive(ness). *See also* Attention deficit disorder; Attention span; Minimal brain disorders; Restlessness.

Hypermnesia. Hypermnes(ia,ic,tic). *Choose from:* enhanced, exaggerated *with:* recall, memory, ability to remember. *See also* Memory.

Hyperphagia. Hyperphag(ia,ic). Hyperbulim(ia,ic). Bulim(ia,ic). Overeat(ing,en). Insatiable hunger. *Choose from:* eating, appetite(s) *with:* excess(ive), inordinate, binge(s). Bulimarexia. Bulimirexia. *Choose from:* gorg(e,ed,ing), bing(e,ed,ing) *with:* purg(e,ed,ing). *See also* Bulimia; Eating disorders; Obesity; Psychophysiologic disorders.

Hypersensitivity. Hypersensitiv(e,ity, eness). Allerg(y,ies,ic). Urticaria. Eczema. Hives. Asthma(tic). Hay fever. Atop(y,ic). Anaphylaxis. *Consider also:* irritab(le,ility), photosensitivity, Wissler(s) syndrome, angioneurotic edema. *Consider also:* antigen(s,ic), autoantigen(s), hapten(s,e,es), immunongen(s). *See also* Asthma; Food hypersensitivity; Hay fever; Multiple chemical sensitivities; Psychophysiologic disorders; Sick building syndrome.

Hypersensitivity, food. See *Food hypersensitivity.*

Hypersexuality. Hypersexual(ity). Nymphoman(ia,iac). Don Juan(ism,s). Androman(ia,ic). Erotoman(ia,iac,ic). Oversexed. Pseudohypersexual(ity). Satyriasis. Erotocrat(s,ic). Casanova(s). Compulsive sexuality. *See also* Erotomania; Promiscuity.

Hypersomnia. Hypersomn(ia,ic). *Choose from:* sleep, drows(y,iness), letharg(y,ic) *with:* excess(ive), uncontrollable, pathological. *Consider also:* coma vigil, parasomnia, lethargic encephalitis, akinetic mutism, Kleine Levin(s) syndrome, Cairn(s) stupor. *See also* Sleep; Sleep disorders.

Hypertension. Hypertens(ion,ive,ives). High(er) blood pressure. Elevated blood pressure. Above normal blood pressure. Increased blood pressure. *Consider also:* high tension, hyperexcitability, hyperirritability, high tonus, hypertonus, high systolic pressure, high diastolic pressure, hyperpies(ia,is). *See also* Cardiovascular system; Disease; Essential hypertension; Relaxation training.

Hypertension, essential. See *Essential hypertension.*

Hypertext. Hypertext(ual). Hypermedia. Hyperlink(s). Hypertext Markup Language. HTML. *Consider also:* Hypertext transfer protocol, HTTP, associative link(s), extensible markup language, XML. *See also* Home pages; Interactive computer systems; Internet (computer network); Man machine systems.

Hyperthermia. See *Fever.*

Hyperventilation. Hyperventilat(e,ed, ing,ion,ory). Ventilatory hyperoxia. Hyperpnea. Overbreathing. *Consider also:* hypocapnia, spasmophilia, respiratory alkalosis. *See also* Respiratory system.

Hyphenated Americans. See *Biculturalism.*

Hypnagogic hallucinations. Hypnagogic hallucination(s). *Choose from:* hypnogogic, falling asleep *with:* hallucination(s), experience(s), state(s), imagery, dream(s). *Consider also:* hypnopompic, semiconscious, waking *with:* hallucination(s), imagery, dream(s). *See also* Hallucinations; Perceptual disturbances; Sleep disorders.

Hypnosis. Hypnosis. Hypnot(ic,ism, ize,ized). Braidism. Induced somnambulism. *Consider also:* hypnotherap(y,ies, eutic), animal magnetism, autosuggestion, autohypno(sis,tism), mesmer(ism, ize,ized), hypnoanalysis, posthypno(tic, tically,sis), hypnotizab(le,ility), hypnoanalgesia, hypnoanesthesia, hynosuggestion(s), prehypno(tic,sis). *See also* Age regression (hypnotic); Autohypnosis; Hypnotherapy; Hypnotic susceptibility; Psychotherapeutic imagery.

Hypnosis, self. See *Autohypnosis.*

Hypnotherapy. Hypnotherap(y,eutic). Hypnoanaly(sis,tical). Hypnocatharsis. Electrohypnotherapy. Hypnotic approach. Hypnobehavioral therapy. *Choose from:* treat(ed,ing,ment,ments), therap(y,ies,eutic), intervention(s), pain, clinical, phobia(s), psychotherap(y,ies, eutic), healing, desensitization, cathar(sis,tic) *with:* hypno(sis,tic). *See also* Age regression (hypnotic); Autosuggestion; Hypnosis; Progressive relaxation therapy; Relaxation training.

Hypnotic age regression. See *Age regression (hypnotic).*

Hypnotic susceptibility. Hypnotic susceptibility. Hypnotiz(able,ability). *Choose from:* hypno(tic,sis), trance(s), posthypno(tic,sis) *with:* susceptib(le, ility), responsiv(ity,eness), suggestib(le, ility). *See also* Hypnosis; Personality traits; Trance.

Hypnotism. See *Hypnosis.*

Hypochondriasis. Hypochondria(sis, c,cs,cal). Nosoman(ia,ic). Somatic

overconcern. Invalidism. *Choose from:* imagined, imaginary, delusion(s,al) *with:* ill(ness,nesses), disease(s), disorder(s). *Consider also:* morbid anxiety, overconcern(ed), phob(ia,ias,ic), delusion(s,al), preocccupation(s), fear(s) *with:* health, body, bodily, somatic, symptom(s), infestation(s), disease(s). *See also* Anxiety disorders; Conversion disorder; Invalids; Psychogenic pain; Psychophysiology; Somatoform disorders.

Hypocrisy. Hypocri(sy,te,tical,ticalness). Sanctimon(y,ious,ousness). Tartuff(ery, ism). Sham. Glib(ness). Insincer(e,ity). Lip-service. Dissembl(e,ed,ing). *See also* Deception; Machiavellianism; Self deception; Tokenism.

Hypomania. Hypoman(ia,ic). Hyporesponsive(ness). Mild mania. *See also* Cyclothymic disorder; Mental illness.

Hypothermia. Hypotherm(ia,ic). Abnormally low body temperature. *Consider also:* hibernation. *See also* Body temperature; Endocrine system; Hibernation.

Hypotheses. Hypoth(es,is,eses,etical,esize). *Consider also:* postulate(s), explanation(s), inference(s), proposition(s), theor(y,ies,em,ems), model(s), construct(s), generalit(y,ies), generaliz(ation,ations,izability), paradigm(s), assumption(s), presumption(s), thesis(es), conclusion(s), deduction(s), interpretation(s), premise(s), principle(s). *See also* Concepts; Experiments; Explanation; Falsification (scientific); Generalities; Heuristics; Hypothesis testing; Predictive validity; Research design; Research methods; Rules (generalizations); Statistical inference; Statistical significance; Verification.

Hypothesis testing. Hypothes(is,es) test(ing). *Choose from:* hypothes(is,es), hypothetical, postulate(s), explanation(s), inference(s), proposition(s), theor(y,ies), model(s), construct(s), generalit(y,ies), generaliz(ation,ations, ability), paradigm(s), assumption(s) *with:* test(s,ing), evaluat(e,ed,ing,ion), significan(t,ce), assess(ed,ing,ment, ments), confirm(ing,ed,ation), disconfirm(ing,ation), corroborat(ed,ing, ion), support(ed,ing), proof, prov(e,en, ing), disprov(e,en,ing), clarif(y,ying, ied,ication), evidence, examination. *See also* Construct validity; Evaluation; Experimental replication; Experiments; Falsification (scientific); Null hypothesis testing; Prediction; Predictive validity; Probability; Research design; Research methods; Statistical inference; Statistical significance; Theory verification.

Hypothesis testing, null. See *Null hypothesis testing.*

Hypothetical. Hypothetical(ly). Postulat(e, ed,ing). Conjectural(ly). Debatab(le, ility). Doubtful(ly). Guess(ed,ing). Imagine(d). Infer(red). Presum(e,ed,ing, ptive). Speculat(e,ed,ing,ive). Suppos(e,ed,ing). Surmis(e,ed,ing). Theoretical(ly). Presuppos(e,ed,ing, ition,ions). Uncertain(ty,ties). *See also* Conditionals; Postulates; Theories.

Hysteria. Hyster(ia,ical,ics). Briquet(s) syndrome. *Choose from:* anxiety, combat, degenerative, epidemic, fixation, major, masked, reflex, retention, traumatic *with:* hysteria. *Consider also:* conversion hysteria, dissociative hysteria, mass hysteria. *See also* Catalepsy; Conversion disorder; Dissociative disorders; Hysterical anesthesia; Hysterical paralysis; Hysterical vision disturbances; Mass hysteria;

Hysteria, mass. See *Mass hysteria.*

Hysterical anesthesia. Hysterical anesthesia. *Choose from:* hysterical *with:* anesthe(sia,tic), hemianesthesia, paresthesia, hemihypesthesia, hemihypoesthesia. *See also* Conversion disorder; Neuroses.

Hysterical paralysis. Hysterical paralysis. *Choose from:* hysteric(al), conversion, psychogenic *with:* paraly(sis,zed), pleg(ia,ias,ic), quadripleg(ia,ias,ic), parapleg(ia,ias,ic), hemipleg(ia,ias,ic). *Consider also:* hysterical ataxia, astasia-abasia. *See also* Conversion disorder; Neuroses; Somatoform disorders.

Hysterical personality disorder. See *Histrionic personality disorder.*

Hysterical vision disturbances. Hysterical vision disturbance(s). *Choose from:* conversion, hyster(ia,ical), psychogenic, functional *with:* vision disturbance(s), blind(ness), color blind(ness), visual(ly), neuro-ophthalmologic, vision disorder(s). *See also* Conversion disorder; Neuroses; Vision.

I

Iatrogenesis. Iatrogen(esis,ic,y). *Choose from:* physician induced, physician aggravated, doctor induced, iatrogenic *with:* illness(es), disorder(s). *Consider also:* nosocomial. *See also* Drug effects; Health services misuse; Malpractice; Medication errors; Physician patient relations; Treatment outcome.

Ice age. See *Glacial epoch.*

Iconic memory. Iconic memor(y,ies). *Choose from:* visual, sensory *with:* memor(y,ies), impression(s), image(s), retention, persistence. *See also* Short term memory.

Iconoclasm. Iconoclas(m,tic,tically). Image breaker(s). Irreveren(t,ce). Skeptic(al, ism). Condemn(ed,ing,ation). Denounc(e,ed,ing). *Consider also:* desacraliz(e,ed,ing,ation), antichristian, antireligious, impious, irreligious, atheistic, heretic(al), nonbeliev(er,ers, ing), unconventional attitude(s). *See also* Deconstruction: Heresy; Nonconformity (personality); Political radicalism.

Iconography. Iconograph(y,ies). Pictorial. Pictur(e,es,ed). Illustrat(e,ed,ing,ion, ions). Image(s,ry). Symbol(s,ism,ic). *See also* Christian symbolism; Cuneiform; Deciphering; Hieroglyphics; Illustrated books; Images; Petroglyphs; Representation (likeness); Sex symbolism; Symbolism; Visual communication; Written communications.

Id. Id. *Consider also:* unconscious, instinct(s,ual,ive), biological drive(s), psychic drive(s). *Consider also:* libido. *See also* Unconscious (psychology).

Ideal types. Ideal(ized) typ(e,es,ical). Constructed type(s). Typolog(y,ies). Pure type(s). Polar type(s). Mental construct(s). Hypothetical representation(s). *Consider also:* conceptualization(s), stereotype(s), model(s), paradigm(s), ideal picture(s). *See also* Analysis; Categorization; Classic (standard); Constructs; Heuristics; Models; Social types; Stereotyping; Theories; Verstehen.

Ideal woman. See *Idealization of women.*

Idealism. Idealis(m,t,ts). Perfectionis(m,t, ts). Devot(e,ed,ing,ion) to ideal(s). High minded(ness). Forward looking. Visionar(y,ies). Conscientious(ness). Utopian(ism). *Consider also:* neo-idealis(m,t,ts), leading idea(s), dominant idea(s), Ideenlehre, universal mind. *See also* Determinism; Feasibility; Idealists; Idealization of women; Images of women; Intellectual history; Materialism; Monism; Pantheism (universal divinity); Perfectionism; Personalism;

Phenomenology; Realism; Symbolism; Utopias.

Idealists. Idealist(s). Visionar(y,ies). Dreamer(s). Perfectionist(s). Philosopher(s). Spiritualist(s). Ideologist(s). Romanticist(s). *See also* Idealism; Utopias

Idealization of women. Idealiz(e,ed,ing, ation) wom(en,an). Ideal wom(en,an). *Choose from:* ideal(ized), pedestal(s), perfection(ism,ist), overidealiz(e,ed,ing, ation), overestimat(e,ed,ing,ion), stereotyp(e,ed,es,ing) wom(en,an), female(s), virgin(s), womanhood, mother(s), daughter(s), sister(s). *Consider also:* chivalry, courtly love. *See also* Beauty culture; Courtly love; Idealism; Images of women; Mother goddesses; Personal beauty; Sex stereotypes.

Idealized self. Ideal(ized) self. Ideal(ized) image. *Choose from:* ideal(ized), grandiose, perfection(ism,ist,ists), overestimat(e,ed,ing,ion) *with:* self image(s), self concept(s), self perception. *See also* Perfectionism; Pride; Self concept; Self congruence; Self debasement; Self esteem; Self perception; Snobs and snobbishness.

Ideals. Ideal(s). Standard(s). Value(s). Model(s). Purpose(s). Meaning(s,ful). Ideolog(y,ical). Priorit(y,ies). Goal(s). Intention(s). Objective(s). Prototype(s). Archetype(s). Example(s). *See also* Examples; Goals; Heroes; Life plans; Priorities; Social values; Standards; Values.

Ideas. See *Ideation.*

Ideas, adoption of. See *Adoption of ideas.*

Ideas, history of. See *Intellectual history.*

Ideation. Ideation(al). *Choose from:* idea(s), image(s), concept(s), conceptualization(s) *with:* form(ed,ing,ation), generat(e,ed,ing,ion). Cognit(ive,ion). Think(ing). Thought. Conceptual(ization). Imagin(e,ed,ing,al,ation, ing). *See also* Cognitive processes; Image (philosophy); Imagination.

Ideational apraxia. Ideational apraxia. Ideomotor apraxia. Sensory apraxia. *Consider also:* dressing, motor, akinetic *with:* apraxia. *See also* Apraxia.

Identical twins. See *Monozygotic twins.*

Identification (psychology). Identification. Introjection. Self identification. *Choose from:* identif(y,ied,ication), *with:* psycholog(y,ical), defense mechanism(s), emotional, aggressor(s), parent(s), teacher(s), authority, object.

Consider also: incorporation, primary identification, secondary identification, projective identification. *See also* Defense mechanisms; Introjection.

Identification (recognition). Identif(y,ying, ied,ication). Recogni(tion,ze,zed,zing). Detect(ed,ing,ion). Discover(ed,ing,ies). Case finding. Uncover(ed,ing). Distinguish(ed,ing). Report(ed,ing). Differentiat(e,ed,ing). Diagnos(is,es). Psychodiagnos(is,es). Indicat(e,ed,ing). Verif(y,ying,ied,ication). Corroborat(e, ed,ing,ion). Authenticat(e,ed,ing,ion). Substantiat(e,ed,ing,ion). Reveal(ed,ing). Recall(ed,ing). Remember(ed,ing). Name(e,ed,ing). Apprehend(ed,ing). *See also* Categorization; Diagnosis; Identification cards; Identity; Scientific discoveries; Research; Symptoms; Verification.

Identification, ability. See *Ability identification.*

Identification, news source. See *Attribution of news.*

Identification, self. See *Identification (psychology).*

Identification cards. Identification card(s). Passport(s). Drivers license(s). Credit card(s). Identity card(s). Green card(s). *Choose from:* identification, ID *with:* card(s), document(s). *Consider also:* barcod(e,es,ed,ing), bar-cod(e,es,ed,ing). *See also* Digital signatures; Formal social control; Identity; Immigrants; Social identity; Surveillance of citizens.

Identification documents. See *Identification cards.*

Identification systems, patient. See *Patient identification systems.*

Identity. Identit(y,ies). Identification. Social role(s). Role conception(s). Self concept. Presentation of self. Reconstruction of self. Essential character. *Choose from:* cultural, ethnic, gender, racial, sexual, social, professional *with:* identit(y,ies), identification. *Consider also:* body image, reference group. *See also* Cultural identity; Essence (philosophy); Ethnic identity; Gender identity; Group identity; Mistaken identity; National identity; Professional identity; Racial identity; Reference groups; Self concept; Sex stereotypes; Social identity; Stereotyping.

Identity, brand. See *Brand identity.*

Identity, class. See *Class identity.*

Identity, corporate. See *Brand identity; Corporate image.*

Identity, cultural. See *Cultural identity.*

Identity, ethnic. See *Ethnic identity.*

Identity, gender. See *Gender identity.*

Identity, group. See *Group identity.*

Identity, mistaken. See *Mistaken identity.*

Identity, national. See *National identity.*

Identity, professional. See *Professional identity.*

Identity, racial. See *Racial identity.*

Identity, sex. See *Gender identity.*

Identity, sex role. See *Gender identity.*

Identity, sexual. See *Gender identity.*

Identity, social. See *Social identity.*

Identity crisis. Identity crisis. *Choose from:* identity, role(s), self-image *with:* conflict(s), cris(is,es), confus(ed,ion), threaten(ed,ing), disrupt(ed,ing,ion, ions), damag(e,ed,ing), destroy(ed,ing). *Consider also:* loss of self. *See also* Emotional adjustment; Personality development; Social identity; Stress.

Ideological struggle. Ideological struggle(s). *Choose from:* ideolog(y, ies,ical), philosophical, dogma(s), belief(s), worldview(s) *with:* struggle(s), conflict(s), dispute(s), issue(s), disagreement(s), clash(es), divergence(s), dissension, incompatibility. *See also* Class conflict; Conflict; Geopolitics; Ideologies; Political ideologies; Worldview.

Ideologies. Ideolog(y,ies,ical). Doctrine(s). Philosoph(y,ies,ical). Dogma(s). Belief system(s). *Consider also:* myth(s), theolog(y,ies,ical), worldview(s), conservatism, liberalism, egalitarianism, fundamentalism, social thought, utopianism, nationalism, Marxism, political belief(s), ideal vision(s), political creed(s), belief system(s), philosoph(y,ies) of life. *See also* Absolutism; Beliefs; Cognitive structures; Dogmatism; Dominant ideologies; Educational ideologies; Egalitarianism; Elitism (government); Irrationalism (Philosophy); Philosophy; Political attitudes; Political ideologies; Political systems; Religious doctrines; Social theories; Social values; Values; Worldview; Zeitgeist.

Ideologies, dominant. See *Dominant ideologies.*

Ideologies, educational. See *Educational ideologies.*

Ideologies, political. See *Political ideologies.*

Idiocy. See *Mental retardation.*

Idioms. Idiom(s,atic,atically). *Consider also:* home-spun expression(s), folk saying(s), figurative language, ready-made utterance(s), habitual collocation(s). *See also* Colloquial language; Dialects; Figurative language. Nonstandard English; Slang.

Idiosyncrasies. Idiosyncras(y,ies). Mannerism(s). Affectation(s). Quirk(s). Eccentricit(y,ies). Peculiar(ity,ities). Oddit(y,ies). Singularit(y,ies). *See also* Anomalies; Characteristics; Individuality.

Idleness. See *Laziness; Leisure time.*

Idolatry. Idolatr(y,ies). Ador(e,ed,ing,ation). Idoliz(e,ed,ing,ation). Idolatrism. Worship. *Consider also:* materialistic ideology, paganism, heathenism, worship(ping) false god(s), worship(ping) image(s), worship(ping) idol(s), hero worship. *See also* Eminence; Famous people; Fetishism; Heroes.

Idyll. Idyll(s,es). Idyl(s). Eclogue(s). *Choose from:* rustic, pastoral, rural, tranquil(lity) *with:* poem(s), poetry, verse(s), prose, music(al). *See also* Classicism; Pastorale; Poetry; Rustic life.

Ignorance. Ignoran(ce,t). Uneducated. Unenlightened. Illiterate. Uninformed. Unschooled. Unlearned. Uninitiated. Unaware(ness). Misinformed. Unlettered. Unread. Unfamiliar(ity). *See also* Illiteracy; Knowledge; Literacy.

Ill, mentally. See *Mental illness; Psychiatric patients.*

Ill-advised. See *Inappropriateness.*

Illegal. Illegal(ly,ity,ities). Illegitima(te, tely,cy). Illicit(ly). Prohibited. Proscribed. Unauthorized. Unlawful(ly). Unlicensed. Unsanctioned. Wrongful(ly). Lawless(ness). Contraband. *Consider also:* forbidden, improper(ly). *See also* Clandestinity; Crime; Criminal act; Forbidden; Inadmissible; Violation.

Illegal aliens. Illegal alien(s). Hidden workforce. Wetback(s). Mexicano(s) no documentados. *Choose from:* illegal, undocumented, clandestine, smuggled *with:* alien(s), immigrant(s), worker(s), border crossing(s), entry, migrant(s), migration, immigration, population, refugee(s), status, expatriate(s), Central American(s), Mexican(s). *Consider also:* permanent tourist(s), non-citizen(s), wartime relocation, Immigration Reform and Control Act, United States Border Patrol, Bracero Program, Sanctuary movement, immigration amnesty. *See also* Borderlands; Emigrants; Foreign workers; Homeland; Immigrants; Immigration law; Labor migration; Mexican American border region; Migrant workers; Political asylum; Refugees; Right of asylum; Undocumented immigrants; Underclass; Vagrants.

Illegal conduct. See *Criminal act; Unethical conduct.*

Illegal immigrants. See *Illegal aliens.*

Illegality. See *Arson; Arrests; Assassination; Assault (personal); Bribery; Burglary; Cheating; Child abuse; Collusion; Computer crimes; Conflict of interest; Copycat crimes; Corruption in government; Crime prevention; Crime rates; Criminal abortion; Criminal act; Criminal intent; Criminal investigations; Drug trafficking; Drugs in athletics; Drunk driving; Driveby Crimes; Embezzlement; Falsification (scientific); Felonies; Fraud; Hate crimes; Hijacking; Homicide; Illegal; Industrial espionage; Infanticide; Kickbacks; Kidnapping; Larceny; Law enforcement; Misconduct in office; Money laundering; Offenders; Offenses; Organized crime; Penal codes; Perjury; Perpetrators; Poaching; Political crimes; Price fixing; Product tampering; Property crimes; Prostitution; Quackery; Racketeering; Rape; Robbery; Safety; Scientific misconduct; Sex offenders; Sex offenses; Sexual harassment; Shoplifting; Terrorism; Unreported crimes; Urban crime; Vandalism; Victimization; Victimless crimes; Violation; War crimes; White collar crime.*

Illegitimacy (children). Illegitimacy. *Choose from:* illegitmate *with:* child(ren), birth(s). *Consider also:* born out of wedlock, bastard(s,y), unmarried mother(s). *See also* Birth; Children; Family members; Parental absence; Paternal deprivation; Single mothers; Single parent family; Unwanted pregnancy.

Illicit. See *Clandestinity; Crime; Criminal act; Forbidden; Illegal; Violation.*

Illicit liquor. Illicit liquor. Illicit distill(ing,er,ers,ery,eries). Moonshin(er,ers,ing). *Choose from:* illicit, illegal, smuggled, bootleg(ged), contraband, homemade, bathtub, corn *with:* liquor, alcohol, whiskey, gin. *Consider also:* drinking, alcohol *with:* minor(s), under age. *See also* Alcoholic beverages; Crime; Distillation; Drinking behavior; Liquor industry.

Illiteracy. Illitera(cy,te,tes). Nonliterate. Uneducated. Unschooled. Unlettered. Unable to read. Inability to read. Prelitera(te,cy). *See also* Adult literacy; Ignorance; Literacy; Literacy programs

Illiteracy, computer. See *Computer illiteracy.*

Illness. Ill(ness,nesses). Disease(s). Sick(ness,nesses). Disorder(s). Pain. Headache(s). Ailment(s). Health problem(s). Morbidity. Malad(y,ies). Infection(s). Poor health. Failing health. Infirm(ity,ities). *See also* Acute disease; Care of the sick; Catastrophic illness; Chronic disease; Disease; Epidemics; Health care; Health problems; Invalids;

Morbidity; Patients; Self care; Sick role; Symptoms; Terminal illness.

Illness, attitudes toward mental. See *Attitudes toward mental illness.*

Illness, attitudes toward physical. See *Attitudes toward physical illness.*

Illness, behavior. See *Sick role.*

Illness, catastrophic. See *Catastrophic illness.*

Illness, chronic mental. See *Chronic psychosis.*

Illness, emotional. See *Mental illness.*

Illness, mental. See *Mental illness.*

Illness, physical. See *Illness.*

Illness, terminal. See *Terminal illness.*

Illogical. Illogical(ly,ity,ness). Senseless(ness). Contrary to logic. Unreasonable(ness). Absurd(ity,ities). Preposterous(ly,ness). Fallac(y,ies,ious). Irrational(ity). Nonrational. Unscientific(ly). Unsound(ness). Meaningless(ness). Senseless(ness). *See also* Casuistry; Errors; Fallacies; Groundless; Implausibility; Irrational beliefs; Scientific errors.

Illumination (light). See *Light; Light sources.*

Illumination of books and manuscripts. Illuminat(e,ed,ing,ion) book(s), manuscript(s). *Choose from:* illuminat(e,ed,ing,ion), ornament(ed, ation), ornamental design(s), emblazon(ed,ing), decorat(e,ed,ing, ation,ive), gild(ed,ing), color(ed,ing), drawing(s), foliated border(s), droller(y,ies) *with:* book(s), manuscript(s), cod(ex,ices), psalter(s). *Consider also:* Gothic miniature(s), book(s) of hour(s). *See also* Book ornamentation; Illustrated books; Incunabula; Manuscripts; Rare books.

Illusion (philosophy). Illusion(s). Fallac(y,ies). Misconception(s). Misinterpret(ed,ing,ation). Erroneous perception(s). Mistaken notion(s). Miscalculat(e,ed,ion,ions). False premise(s). False notion(s). *See also* Errors; Fallacies; Distortion; Misinformation.

Illusions (perception). Illusion(s). Afterimage(s). Mirage(s). McCollough effect. *Choose from:* optical, percept(ion,ual) *with:* illusion(s), aftereffect(s), distort(ed,ion,ions). *See also* Afterimage; Perceptual distortion; Perceptual disturbances; Synesthesia.

Illusions, optical. See *Optical illusions.*

Illustrated books. Illustrated book(s). *Choose from:* illustrat(ed,ion,ions), picture, illuminat(ed,ion), decorated, pictorial, coffee table, photograph(s,y), engrav(ed,ing,ings), drawing(s),

painting(s), water color(s) *with:* book(s), volume(s), text(s), textbook(s). *Consider also:* childrens book(s), picturebook(s). *See also* Biological illustration; Block printing; Book ornamentation; Books; Cartoons; Engraving; Graphic arts; Graphics; Iconography; Illumination of books and manuscripts; Magazine illustration; Medical illustration; Photography.

Illustration, biological. See *Biological illustration.*

Illustration, magazine. See *Magazine illustration.*

Illustration, medical. See *Medical illustration.*

Illustration and painting, animal. See *Animal painting and illustration.*

Image (philosophy). Image(s). Imagin(e,ed,ary,ing). Remember(ed,ing). Imago. Phantasm(s,al,ic). Figment(s) of the imagination. Mental representation(s). Mental picture(s). *See also* Concepts; Ideation; Imagery.

Image, body. See *Body image.*

Image, corporate. See *Corporate image.*

Image, professional. See *Professional image.*

Image, self. See *Self concept.*

Image disturbances, body. See *Body image disturbances.*

Image of God. See *God concepts.*

Image processing. Image processing. Coherent image formation. *Choose from:* image(s), photo(s,graph,graphs) *with:* process(ed,ing), alter(ed,ing), reconstruct(ed,ing,ion,ions), restor(e,ed, ing,ation), compress(ed,ing,ion), contrast, sharpness, manipulat(e,ed,ing, ion), improv(e,ed,ing) picture quality. *See also* Automated information retrieval; Automated information storage; Information processing.

Imagery. Imag(e,es,ed,ery,ing). Imagin(al, ation,ary,ed,ing). Idol(s). Metaphor(s). Conception(s). Phantasm(s). Specter(s). Visualiz(ation,ations,ing). Mental representation(s). Icon(s). Mental rehearsal(s). Fantas(y,ies). Daydream(s, ing). Vision(ary,s). Mental preparation. Dream(s,ed,t,ing). Mental transformation(s). Pictur(ed,ing). Envision(ed, ing). *Consider also:* conceptual imagery, spatial imagery. *See also* Conceptual imagery; Eidetic imagery; Ekphrasis; Haiku; Image (philosophy); Imagination; Metaphors; Poetics; Similes; Spatial imagery.

Imagery, conceptual. See *Conceptual imagery.*

Imagery, eidetic. See *Eidetic imagery.*

Imagery, psychotherapeutic. See *Psychotherapeutic imagery.*

Imagery, spatial. See *Spatial imagery.*

Images. Image(s). Mental representation(s). Stereotype(s). Concept(ion,ions). Perception(s). Attribut(e,ed,ing,ion, ions). Impression(s). Mental picture(s). Imago. Recept(s). *Consider also:* appearance(s), likeness(es), cop(y,ies), facsimile(s), resemblance(s), replica(s). *See also* Arts; Christian symbolism; Concepts; Figurines; Iconography; Imagery; Metaphors; Perceptions; Sex symbolism; Stereotyping; Symbolism.

Images of women. Image(s) of wom(an,en). *Choose from:* image(s), stereotype(s), pedestal(s), idealiz(e,ed,ing,ation), overidealiz(e,ed,ing,ation), prejudice(s,d), denigrat(e,ed,ing,ion), perception(s), attribut(e,ed,ing,ion,ions), bias(ed,es) *with:* wom(en,an), female(s), virgin(s), mother(s), sister(s), daughter(s), feminin(e,ity). *Consider also:* amazon(s), angel(s) in the house, angel(s), baroness(es), beauty queen(s), bimbo(s), bitch(es), bluestocking(s), bride(s), broad(s), castrating female(s), cheerleader(s), cheesecake, concubine(s), countess(es), courtesan(s), crone(s), cunt(s), dame(s), debutante(s), den mother(s), duchess(es), earth mother(s), Eve(s), fallen wom(en,an), femme(s) fatale(s), flirt(s), geisha(s), goddess(es), harlot(s), ideal(ized) wom(an,en), lad(y,ies), Lolita(s), madam(s), madonna(s), mamm(y,ies), Marianismo, mermaid(s), Mona Lisa(s), nag(s), nun(s), nurturer(s), odalisque(s), old maid(s), pinup(s), princess(es), prostitute(s), queen(s) for a day, queen(s), scold(s), seductress(es), siren(s), sister(s), slut(s), Snow White(s), sphinx(es), spinster(s), stepmother(s), strumpet(s), succub(i,us), supermom(s), superwom(an,en), tease(s), temptress(es), vagina dentata, vampire(s), vamp(s), virago(s), Virgin Mary, virgin(s), waif(s), widow(s), witch(es), wom(an,en) the gatherer(s), wonder wom(an,en). *See also* Females (human); Femmes fatales; Gender identity; Idealization of women; Mermaids; Pornography; Sex discrimination; Sex roles; Sex stereotypes; Sexism; Sexual oppression; Stereotyping; Succubus.

Imaginary conversations. Imaginary conversation(s). *Choose from:* imagin(ary,ed) *with:* conversation(s), confrontation(s), audience(s), dialogue(s), argument(s). *Consider also:* conversation(s) with God, self-talk, monologue(s). *See also* Conversation; Daydreaming; Imagination.

Imaginary places. Imaginary place(s). *Choose from:* imaginary, imagin(ed,ation), fantastic, mythical, legendary, fiction(al), science fiction, fantasy *with:* place(s), land(s), cit(y,ies), kingdom(s), societ(y,ies), voyage(s), world(s), realm(s). *Consider also:* promised land(s), Gulliver's travels, lost world(s), Shangri La, Oz, Atlantis, etc. *See also* Fantasy (literary); Literature; Utopias; Voyages to the otherworld.

Imagination. Imagin(e,ed,ings,ation,ative, ativeness,ary). Fantas(y,ies). Imagery. Imaging ability. Creativ(e,ity). Creative power. Vision(s,ary). Daydream(s,ing). Reverie(s). Inventive(ness). *Consider also:* intuitive(ness), sixth sense. *See also* Cognitive processes; Conceptual imagery; Creativity; Ekphrasis; Fantasy (literary); Ideation; Imagery; Imaginary conversations; Intuition; Magical thinking; Psychotherapeutic imagery; Vicarious experiences.

Imagination, fantasies. See *Daydreaming.*

Imaging, diagnostic. See *Diagnostic imaging.*

Imitation. Imitat(e,ed,ion). Imitative behavior(s). Emulat(e,ed,ion,ions). Modeling behavior(s). Mimic(ry). Mimick(ed,ing). Copy(ing). Copie(d,s). Fak(e,es,ed,ing). Forger(y,ies). Impersonat(e,ed,ing,ion,ions). Facsimile(s). Reproduction(s). Simulat(e,ed,ing,ion,ions). Clon(e,ed, ing). Counterfeit(ed,ing). Duplicat(e,ed, ing,ion). Follow(ed,ing) example(s). Mirror(ed,ing,s). *See also* Copies; Copycat crime(s); Copying processes; Identification (psychology); Observational learning; Role models; Social learning; Socialization.

Immanence of God. Immanence of God. *Consider also:* Advaita, presence of God, union with Lord, union with God, espousal to Christ, communion. *See also* Attributes of God; Deities; Glory of God; God concepts; Knowledge of God; Natural theology; Oneness of God; Pantheism (universal divinity); Presence of God; Redemption (theology); Religious beliefs; Revealed theology; Theophany.

Immaturity. Immatur(e,ity). Youthful(ness). Undeveloped. Unformed. Incomplete. Half-grown. Inexperienced. Childish(ness). Unsophisticated. Juvenile. Unripe(ned). Naive(te). Innocen(t,ce). Untrained. Infantile. *See also* Emotional immaturity; Infantilism; Innocence; Maturation; Self control.

Immaturity, emotional. See *Emotional immaturity.*

Immeasurability. Immeasurab(ility,le,ly, leness). Boundless(ly,ness). Endless(ly, ness). Inestimab(le,ly,ility). Measureless(ly,ness). Incalculab(le,ly,ility). Beyond calculation. *Consider also:* countless(ly), innumerabl(e,y), unnumbered, uncountab(le,ly,ility), unmeasurab(le,ly,ility), unmeasured, unreckonab(le,ility), immens(e,ity),

inexhaustib(le,ility), unfathomab(le, ility). *See also* Endlessness; Eternity; Infinity.

Immigrants. Immigrant(s). Naturalized citizen(s). Alien(s). Illegal alien(s). Emigre(s). Emigrant(s). Refugee(s). Defector(s). Foreigner(s). Chicano(s). Wetback(s). Displaced person(s). Nomad(s). Transient(s). Foreign born. Foreign origin(s). Foreign labor. Foreign worker(s). Guest worker(s). Exile(s). Migrant(s). Settler(s). Expatriate(s). Foreign invasion. Foreign origin(s). Second generation. First generation. Hyphenated American(s). Dual citizenship. War bride(s). Newcomer(s). Denizen(s). Yellow peril. *Consider also:* melting pot, heterophobia, xenophobia, host society, Greeks in Canada, Italian-Americans, etc. *See also* Asian Americans; Assimilation (cultural); Biculturalism; Borderlands; Citizenship; Cultural conflict; Cultural identity; Displaced persons; Emigrants; Ethnicity; Expatriates; Foreigners; Hispanic Americans; Illegal aliens; Immigration; Immigration law; Italian Americans; Japanese Americans; Korean Americans; Mexican Americans; Naturalization; Nativism; Newcomers; Refugees; Social settlements; Undocumented immigrants.

Immigrants, illegal. See *Illegal aliens.*

Immigrants, undocumented. See *Undocumented immigrants.*

Immigration. Immigrat(e,ed,ing,ion). Cross(ed,ing) border. Emigrat(e,ed,ing, ion). Seek(ing) sanctuary. Deport(ed, ation). Defect(ed,ion). Brain drain. Relocat(e,ed,ing,ion). Resettlement. Foreign invasion. Political asylum. Left native country. Nansen passport(s). *Choose from:* movement, chang(e,ed, ing) *with:* residence. *Choose from:* international, transnational *with:* migrat(e,ed,ing,ion,ory). *See also* Borderlands; Citizenship; Colonization; Emigrants; Emigration; Foreigners; Homeland; Immigrants; Immigration law; Land settlement; Migration; Naturalization; Political asylum; Population transfer; Refugees; Right of asylum.

Immigration law. Immigration law(s). Deportation law(s). *Choose from:* immigrat(e,ed,ing,ion), deport(ed,ing, ation), emigration, refugee(s), alien(s), naturaliz(e,ed,ing,ation), passport(s), foreign labor, migrant(s), foreigner(s) *with:* law(s), legal text(s), polic(y,ies), illegal, rule(s). *Consider also:* Immigration and Nationality Act, McCarran Walter Act, Illegal Immigration Reform and Immigrant Responsibility Act. *See also* Borderlands; Foreign workers; Illegal aliens; Immigrants; Immigration; Migration; Public policy; Refugees; Undocumented immigrants.

Imminent. Imminent(ly). Fast approaching. Impending. Pending. Loom(ed,ing). Forthcoming. Proximate(ly). Upcoming. *See also* Forecasting; Future; Future of society; Future orientation; Impending.

Immobility. Immobil(e,ity,ize,ized,izing). Fixed. Motionless. Anchored. Grounded. Moored. Immovab(le,ility). Unmovab(le,ility). Stationary. *Consider also:* inflexib(le,ility), immotile, immotive, irremovable, steadfast(ly), stagna(nt,ting,te,ted,tion), frozen, stiff(ly,ness), rigid(ity). *See also* Dormancy; Motor activity; Physical restraint; Social immobility; Tonic immobility.

Immobility, social. See *Social immobility.*

Immobility, tonic. See *Tonic immobility.*

Immorality. Immoral(ly,ity). Amoral. Sinful(ly,ness). Sin(s,ned,ner,ners,ning). Cardinal sin(s). Erosion of value(s). Cheating. Indiscretion(s). Deprav(ed, ity). Wicked(ness). Corrupt(ed,ing,ion). Err(ed,ing). Evil. Original sin. Mortal sin(s). Misdeed(s). Wrongdoing. Guilt. Crime. Debt. Shame(less,lessness). Transgression(s). Trespass(es). Unethical. Mea culpa. Dishonor(able,ed). Degenerate. Error of ways. Vice(s). Unprincipled. Unrepentant. *See also* Crime; Depravity; Forgiveness; Guilt; Religious beliefs; Scandals; Sexual misconduct; Shame; Sin.

Immortality. Immortal(ity). Eternal life. Future life. Afterlife. Afterworld. Life after death. Life everlasting. Hereafter. Deathless(ness). Endless(ness). Timeless(ness). Unending life. Perepetuity. Perpetuat(e,ed,ing,ion). Resurrection. Beatitude. Eternal bliss. *Consider also:* reincarnat(e,ed,ing,ion). *See also* Endlessness; Eternity; Heaven; Hell; Reincarnation; Soul.

Immovability. See *Immobility.*

Immunities and diplomatic privileges. See *Diplomatic privileges and immunities.*

Immunities and privileges. See *Privileges and immunities.*

Immunity. Immun(e,ity,ized,ation). Natural resistance to infection(s). Resistan(t,ce) to disease(s). Unsusceptib(le,ility). Resistan(t,ce) to disease(s). *Consider also:* antigen(s), antibod(y,ies), autoimmun(e,ity), auto-immun(e,ity), cellular immunity, hemagglutinin, hemolys(is,ins), immunobiolog(y,ical), immunoche(mical,mistry), maternally acquired immunity, phagocyt(es,ic). *See also* Biomolecules; Diplomatic privileges and immunities; Disease susceptibility; Preventive medicine; Vaccinations.

Immunizations. See *Vaccinations*

Immunodeficiency syndrome, acquired. See *AIDS.*

Impact. See *Effects.*

Impact, social. See *Social impact.*

Impacts, environmental. See *Environmental impacts.*

Impaired, health. See *Health problems.*

Impaired professionals. Impaired professional(s). *Choose from:* troubled, distressed, impaired, alcoholic, chemically dependent, mentally ill, exploitive, abusive, problem drinking, substance abuse, suicidal, addicted *with:* professional(s), practitioner(s), psychologist(s), psychiatrist(s), social worker(s), nurse(s), counselor(s), therapist(s), psychoanalyst(s), dentist(s), physician(s), doctor(s), surgeon(s). *See also* Alcoholism; Malpractice; Physician impairment; Professional client relations; Professional ethics; Professional liability; Professional malpractice; Professional personnel; Professional standards; Substance abuse; Unethical conduct.

Impairment, cognitive. See *Cognition disorders.*

Impairment, physician. See *Physician impairment.*

Impairments. See *Disability.*

Impairments, adventitious. See *Adventitious impairments.*

Impairments, visual. See *Blindness; Partially sighted; Vision disorders.*

Impartiality. Impartial(ity). Detach(ed, ment). Disinterest(ed). Dispassionate(ly). Evenhanded(ness). Fair(ness). Neutral(ity). Nondiscriminatory. Unbiased. Unprejudiced. Unbigoted. Just(ness). Objectiv(e,ity). *See also* Equitability; Fair trial; Fairness; Fairness and accuracy in reporting; Objectivity; Impersonal; Justice; Social justice.

Impasse. See *Deadlock.*

Impatience. Impatien(ce,t,tly). Short temper(s,ed). Abrupt(ness). Brusque(ness). Fretful(ness). Hast(y,iness). Restless(ness). Uneas(y,ily,iness). Irascib(le,ility). Seeth(ing). Test(y,iness). *Consider also:* eager(ly,ness), avid(ly), clamor(ing,ed,ous), intoleran(t,ce), demanding, rude(ness). *See also* Anxiety; Intolerance; Irritability; Nervousness; Road rage; Tensions.

Impediments. Impediment(s). Barricad(e,ed,ing,s). Barrier(s). Hindrance(s). Hinder(ed,ing). Encumbrance(s). Encumber(ed,ing). Obstacle(s). Obstruct(ed,ing,ion,ions). Stumbling block(s). Road block(s). Restraint(s). Restrain(ed,ing). Burden(s,ed,ing). Restrict(ed,ing, ion,ions). Oppos(e,ed,ing,ition). Deter(red,ring,ment,ments). Delay(s). Bottleneck(s). Red tape. Snag(s).

Hurdle(s). *See also* Barriers; Deterrence; Encumbrance; Hindrances; Impediments to marriage; Nontariff trade barriers.

Impediments to marriage. Impediments to marriage. Bar(red,ring) marriage. *Choose from:* impediment(s), bar(ring, red), hindrance(s), obstacle(s), barrier(s), stumbling block(s), oppos(e,ed,ing, ition), censure(d), unlawful(ness), object(ed,ing,ion), block(ed,ing) *with:* engagement, marry(ing), marri(ed,age, ages), wedding(s), matrimon(y,ial). *See also* Barriers; Deterrence; Impediments; Marriage.

Impending. Impending. Imminent. Upcoming. Forthcoming. Approaching. Looming. Portending. Brewing. Lurking. Hovering. Nearing. *See also* Forecasting; Future; Imminent; Prediction.

Imperative. Imperative. Binding. Compelling. Compulsory. Inescapab(le,ility). Mandatory. Necessar(y,ily). Obligatory. Unavoidab(le,ly). Indispensable. High priority. Essential. Required. *Consider also:* dire necessity, urgen(t,cy), exigenc(y,ies). *See also* Moral judgment; Necessity (law); Needs.

Imperative, categorical. See *Categorical imperative.*

Imperative mood. Imperative mood. *Choose from:* command, imperative *with:* mood, mod(e,al,ality). *See also* Grammar; Sentences.

Imperatives, functional. See *Functional imperatives.*

Imperatives, structural. See *Structural imperatives.*

Imperfection. Imperfect(ion,ions). Imperfect(ness). Defect(s,ive,iveness). Fault(s,ed,y). Inadequa(cy,cies,te). Flaw(s,ed). Blemish(es,ed). Deficien(t, cy,cies). *Consider also:* vice(s), drawback(s), scar(red,s), blister(ed,s), blotch(ed,es), disfigure(d,ment), pockmark(s,ed), wart(s), snag(ged,s), torn, birthmark(s), blot(s), spot(ted,s), crack(s,ed), scratch(es,ed), discolor(ed, ation), foible(s), frailt(y,ies), irregular(ity,ities), kink(s), bug(s), omission(s), unsound(ness), weakness(es). *See also* Damage; Defacement; Flawless; Inadequacy; Product liability; Quality control.

Imperialism. Imperial(ism,istic). Expansion(ism). Conquest. Domination. Empire(s). Hegemon(y,ies,ism). Manifest destiny. Neo-colonialism. Colonialism. Coloniz(e,ed,ing,ation). Subordination. Exploitation. Pacification. Dollar diplomacy. Monopolistic capitalism. *Consider also:* trading compan(y,ies), mercantilism, industrialized core, peripheral econom(y,ies), economic imperialism, cultural imperialism, United Fruit company,

protectorate(s). *See also* Capitalism; Center and periphery; Colonialism; Cultural imperialism; Despotism; Dominance; Economic underdevelopment; Empires; Foreign policy; Geopolitics; Invasion; International division of labor; Militarism; Multinational corporations; Neocolonialism; Political ideologies; Social Darwinism; Spheres of influence; State power; Territorial expansion; War.

Imperialism, cultural. See *Cultural imperialism*

Imperialism, ecological. See *Ecological imperialism.*

Impersonal. Impersonal(ly). Businesslike. Cold(ly). Detached. Emotionless(ly). Unfriendl(y,iness). Cold-blooded. Unimpassioned. Matter-of-fact. Colorless(ly). Poker-faced. *Consider also:* neutral(ity), remote(ness), disinterested, dispassionate(ly), impartial(ly), nondiscriminatory, objective(ly), unbiased, uncolored, unprejudiced. *See also* Absurd; Alienation; Anomie; Dehumanization; Estrangement; Fragmentation (experience); Impartiality; Meaninglessness; Modern society; Neutrality; Objectivity; Value neutral.

Impersonation. See *Acting; Disguise; Impostor; Transvestism.*

Impersonators, child. See *Child impersonators.*

Impersonators, female. See *Transvestism.*

Imperviousness. Impervious(ness). Imperviab(le,ility). Impenetrab(le,ility). Impassab(le,ility). Impermeab(le,ility). Indestructib(le,ility). Teflon coated. Airtight. Watertight. Waterproof. Vacuum packed. Imperishab(le,ility). Sealed tight. Inert(ness). Unreactive. Indissolub(le,ility). Unbreakab(le,ility). *Consider also:* unsympathetic, insensitiv(e,ity), unfeeling, callous(ly,ness), unresponsive(ness), unfeeling, hard-hearted(ness), unswayab(le,ility), unmovab(le,ility), inflexib(le,ility), immovab(le,ility), unmovab(le,ility), unamenab(le,ility), unyielding. *See also* Frigidity; Insensitivity; Passiveness; Refractory; Stubbornness.

Impetuous. Impetuous(ness,ly). Impetuosity. Hast(y,iness). Abrupt(ness,ly). Precipitate(ness,ly). Precipitant(ly,ness). Rash(ness,ly). Temerity. Reckless(ness,ly). Brash(ness,ly). Foolhard(y,iness). Impulsiv(e,ity,eness). Thoughtless(ness,ly). *Consider also:* headlong, hurried(ly), sudden(ly,ness), spontaneous(ly). *See also* Impulsiveness; Personality traits; Spontaneity; Surprise.

Implausibility. Implausib(le,ly,ility). Doubtful(ness). Dubious(ly). Improbab(le,ly,ility). Inconceivab(le,ly, ility). Unconceivab(le,ly,ility). Questionab(le,ility). Unbelievab(le,ility). Incredib(le,ly,ility). Unimaginab(le,ly). Unconvincing(ly). Unlikel(y,iness). Conjectural(ly). Unfounded. *Consider also:* flims(y,iness), unbelievab(le,ly, ility), unsubstantial, weak argument(s), tenous(ly), problematic. *See also* Believability; Bias; Deception; Delusions; Groundless; Illogical; Irrational beliefs.

Implementation. Implement(ed,ing,ation). Enforc(e,ed,ing,ment). Put in place. Put into effect. Execut(e,ed,ing,ion). Enabl(e,ed,ing). Make possible. Administer(ed,ing). Praxis. Perform(ed, ing,ance). *See also* Development; Management methods; Performance; Planning; Policy implementation; Practices (methods); Program implementation; Short term planning.

Implementation, policy. See *Policy implementation.*

Implementation, program. See *Program implementation.*

Implements. See *Artifacts; Bone implements; Devices; Stone implements; Tools.*

Implements, agricultural. See *Agricultural implements.*

Implements, bone. See *Bone implements.*

Implements, lithic. See *Stone implements.*

Implements, stone. See *Stone implements.*

Implications. Implication(s). Impl(y,ying, ied). Connot(e,ed,ing). Denot(e,ed,ing). Suggest(ed,ing). Indicat(e,ed,ing). Insinuat(e,ed,ing). Implicat(e,ed,ing). Tacit(ly). Unspoken. Unexpressed. *Consider also:* infer(red,ring,ential), hint(ed,ing), between the lines, unwritten, betoken(ed,ing). *See also* Inference; Meaning

Implosive therapy. Implosive therapy. *Consider also:* flooding, implos(ion,ive) *with:* therap(y,ies), psychodrama, paradoxical intention(s). *See also* Behavior modification.

Import quotas. See *Trade protection.*

Import substitution. Import substitut(ion, ing). Import substitution industrialization. ISI. Produc(e,ed,ing) substitute(s) for import(s). *Choose from:* import(s), foreign goods *with:* substitut(ion,ing). *Choose from:* domestic market(s), domestic product(s), domestic industr(y,ies), locally owned industr(y, ies), local entrepreneur(s,ship) *with:* promot(e,ed,ing,ion), increas(e,ed,ing) demand, protect(ed,ion), *Consider also:* infant industry protection, limit(ing) import(s). *See also* Autarky; Developing countries; Industrialization; Nontariff trade barriers; Trade protection.

Imports. Import(ed,ing,ation,s). Import dut(y,ies). Tariff(s). Customs dut(y,ies). Most favored nation clause. Import quota(s). Tariff war(s). Retaliatory dut(y,ies). Free trade. European Economic Community. GATT. General Agreement on Tariffs and Trade. NAFTA. North American Free Trade Agreement. *Choose from:* international, foreign, global, European, Asian *with:* trad(e,ing), market(s), business treat(y,ies). *Consider also:* trade *with:* agreement(s), war(s), accord(s), pact(s), gap(s), tie(s), deal(s), surplus, sanctions, embargo(es). *Consider also:* foreign, imported, international, nondomestic *with:* commodit(y,ies), product(s), article(s). *See also* Bioinvasion; Commercial treaties; Custom unions; Emerging markets; Exotic species; Exoticism; Exports; International division of labor; International economic integration; International trade; Nontariff trade barriers; Shipping industry; Tariffs; Trade; Trade protection; World economy.

Impostor. Impostor(s). Imposter(s). Pretender(s). Phon(y,iness). Fraud(ulent). Sham. Fak(e,ed,ery,ing). Counterfeit. Imposture. Impersonat(er, ers,ion,ions). Imitat(e,ed,ing,ion). Hoax(es). Disguise(d). Pose(d). Posing. Swindler(s). Practicing medicine without a license. Masquerad(e,ing). Charlatan(s). Quack(ery). *See also* Debit card fraud; Deception; Disguise; Fraud.

Impotence. Impoten(ce,cy,t). Male sexual inadequacy. Male sexual dysfunction. *Choose from:* erect(ion,ile) *with:* difficult(y,ies), failure, dysfunction(s). *See also* Male genital disorders; Sexual function disorders.

Impoverished environment. See *Cultural deprivation; Maternal deprivation; Psychosocial deprivation; Social isolation.*

Impoverishment, intellectual. See *Intellectual impoverishment.*

Impresarios. Impresari(o,os). Record producer(s). *Choose from:* manager(s), producer(s), conductor(s), promoter(s), sponsor(s), director(s) *with:* theatr(e,ical), opera(s), concert(s), sport(s), show(s), ballet(s). *See also* Conductors; Entertainment industry; Leadership; Managers.

Impression formation. Impression formation. *Choose from:* impression(s), judgment(s), perception(s), opinion(s) *with:* form(ed,ing,ation). *Consider also:* first, initial, early *with:* impression(s). *Consider also:* attribut(e,ed,ing,ion), stereotyp(e,ed,ing), assessment(s), person perception. *See also* Attitudes; Attribution; Impression management; Social interaction; Social perception.

Impression management. Impression management. Ingratiat(e,ed,ion,ory). Suave(ness). Self present(ed,ing,ation). *Choose from:* impression(s), image(s), appearance(s) *with:* manag(e,ed,ing, ement), creat(e,ed,ing,ion), control(led, ling), build(ing). *See also* ploy(s), pretension(s), pretentious(ness), boast(ing,ful), deference, self disclosure. *See also* Impression formation; Manipulation; Self monitoring; Self presentation; Social behavior; Social interaction; Social perception.

Impressionism (art). Impressionis(m,t,ts). *Consider also:* Claude Monet, Alfred Sisley, Camille Pisarro, Frederic Bazille, Pierre-Auguste Renoir, Edgar Degas. *See also* Expressionism (art); Impressionism (music); Modern art; Post-Impressionism.

Impressionism (music). Impressionism(m,t,ts). *Consider also:* Claude Debussy, Maurice Ravel, Bela Bartok, Olivier Messiaen, Gyorgy Ligeti, George Crumb. *See also* Impressionism (art); Music.

Imprinting (psychology). Imprint(ed,ing). Praegung; *See also* Critical period (psychology); Animal offspring; Critical period (psychology); Social learning.

Imprints, book. See *Book imprints.*

Imprisonment. Imprison(ed,ment). Incarcerat(ed,ion). Inmate(s). Captiv(e,ity). Captured. Confine(d, ment). House arrest(s). Jailed. Remand(ed) to penal institution. Penitentiar(y,ies). Maximum security institution(s). Federal correctional institution(s). Detention center(s). Concentration camp(s). Prison(er,ers). Hostage(s). Solitary confinement. Correctional institution(s). Institutionalized person(s). Prisoner(s) of war. Borstal(s). *See also* Alternatives to incarceration; Correctional system; Detention; Institutionalization (persons); Offenders; Parole; Penal reform; Preventive detention; Prison culture; Prison psychosis; Prisonization; Prisoners; Prisons; Probation; Recidivism; Sentencing.

Impromptu. See *Ad lib; Improvisation; Improvisation (acting); Improvisation (music).*

Impromptu (music). See *Improvisation (music).*

Improprieties. Impropriet(y,ies). Improper(ly). Incorrect(ness,nesses). Nonconform(ing,ance). Indecor(um,ous, ousness). Bad taste. Blunder(s,ed,ing). Immodest(y,ly). Unseeml(y,iness). Impruden(t,ce). Unsuitab(le,ility). Gauch(erie). Mistake(s). *See also* Errors; Misconduct in office; Scandals; Unethical conduct.

Improvement. Improv(e,ed,ement,ing). Benefit(ted,ting). Better(ing,ment). Make better. Upgrad(e,ed,ing). Ameliorat(e,ed,ing,ion). Enrich(ed,ing, ment). Advancement(s). Promot(ed, ing,ion). Renew(al,ed,ing). Revis(e,ed, ing,ion). Reliev(e,ed,ing). Correct(ed, ing,ion). Refin(e,ed,ing). Rectif(y,ied). Repair(ed,ing). Reclaim(ed,ing). Reclamation. Restor(e,ed,ing,ation). Mend(ed). *Consider also:* tweak(ed,ing), amend(ed,ing,ment,ments), progress(ed, ing,ion), achiev(e,ed,ing,ement), meliorat(e,ed,ing,ion,ism). *See also* Achievement; Achievement gains; Antipoverty programs; Civic improvement; Innovations; Progress; Reform; Rehabilitation; Satisfaction; Success; Urban renewal.

Improvement, civic. See *Civic improvement.*

Improvisation. Improvis(e,ed,ing,ation). Extemporiz(e,ed,ing,ation). Ad-lib(bed, bing). Impromptu. Extempore remark(s). Makeshift. *See also* Coping; Improvisation (acting); Improvisation (dancing); Improvisation (music); Problem solving.

Improvisation (acting). Improvisation (acting). Improvisator(s). *Choose from:* improvisation(s,al), improvis(e,ed,ing), ad-libb(er,ers,ing), extempor(aneous, aneously,ization); impromptu, extempor(e,ize,ized), unrehearsed *with:* act(ing,or,ors), performer(s), theatr(e,es, ical), drama(s,tic), play(s). *See also* Acting; Actors and actresses; Ad lib; Method (acting); Theater.

Improvisation (dancing). Improvis(e,ed, ation,ational) danc(e,er,ers,ing). Improv. *Choose from:* improvis(e,ed,ation, ational), spontaneous(ly), innovat(ive,or, ors), creative, extempor(aneous, aneously,ization) *with:* danc(e,er,ers, ing), ballet, tap. *See also* Dance; Improvisation (music).

Improvisation (music). Improvis(e,ed, ation,ational,atory) music(al,ally,ian, ians). *Choose from:* improvis(e,ed,ation, ational), extemporiz(e,ed,ing,ation), spontaneous(ly) *with:* organ virtuoso(s), music(al,ally,ian,ians), fug(al,ue,ues), prelude(s), jazz , passage(s), variation(s). *Consider also:* variations on theme(s), jam session(s), cadenza(s), impromptu(s), riff(s). *See also* Chance composition; Fantasia (music); Improvisation (acting); Improvisation (dancing); Jazz; Music; Preludes.

Impulse, irresistible. See *Insanity defense.*

Impulse control disorders. Impulse control disorder(s). *Choose from:* impuls(e,ive) *with:* disorder(s), steal(ing), perversion(s), neuros(is,es). *Consider also:* kleptomania, pyromania, intermittent explosive disorder(s), catathymic cris(is,es), isolated explosive disorder(s), addict(ed,ion,ions), fireset(ting,er,ers), shoplift(ing,er,ers), episodic dyscontrol, pathologic gambling, paraphilia(s), compulsion(s), impulsiveness, pica, pathological stealing, obsessive stealing. *See also* Compulsive disorders; Impulsiveness; Kleptomania; Pathological gambling; Psychokinesis; Pyromania.

Impulsiveness. Impulsiv(e,eness,ity). Impulsive behavior. *Consider also:* compulsive behavior, obsessive behavior, poor impulse control, low self control, extemporaneous, impetuous(ity), reckless(ness), spontane(ity,ous), instinctive(ness). *See also* Compulsive behavior; Delay of gratification; Deviant behavior; Impetuous; Impulse control disorders; Need satisfaction; Personality traits; Reflectiveness; Self indulgence; Spontaneity.

In loco parentis. See *Legal guardians.*

In vitro fertilization. See *Fertilization in vitro.*

Inability to experience pleasure. See *Anhedonia.*

Inability to remember names. See *Anomia (inability to remember names).*

Inability to smell. See *Anosmia.*

Inability to speak. See *Aphasia: Speech disorders; Speech disturbances.*

Inaccuracy. See *Errors; Fallibility; Fallacies.*

Inactivity. Inactiv(e,ity). Dorman(t,cy). Idle(ness). Immovab(le,ility). Inanimate. Indolen(t,ce). Inert(ness). Inoperative(ness). Languid(ly,ness). Laten(t,cy). Letharg(y,ic). Lifeless(ness). Motionless(ness). Nonfunctioning. Nonperforming. Paus(e,ed,ing). Quiescen(t,ce). Sedentary. Sluggish(ness). Somnolen(t,ce). Stagnan(t,ce). Stationary. Stop(ped, ping). Torpid. Unemployed. Unmoving. *See also* Defunct; Dormancy; Hesitation; Laziness; Rest.

Inadequacy. Inadequa(te,cy). Insufficien(t, cy). Deficien(t,cy). Incomplete(ness). Medioc(re,rity). Inferior(ity). Unsatisfactor(y,iness). Scant(y,iness). Meager(ness). Deficit(s). Dearth(s). Scarc(e,ity). Paucit(y,ies). Unsatisfactor(y,iness). Spars(e,ely,ity,eness). *Consider also:* defective(ness), flaw(s,ed), incapab(le,ility), incompeten(t,ce), unsuitab(le,ility). *See also* Default (negligence); Deprivation; Imperfection; Scarcity.

Inadequate personality. Inadequate personalit(y,ies). Immature personalit(y, ies). *Choose from:* emotional(ly), psychological(ly), personalit(y,ies) *with:* inadequa(cy,te). *Consider also:* passiv(e,eness,ity), inept(ness), unadaptable, inadaptability, ineffectual(ity), poor judgment, social incompatibility, lack of stamina. *See also* Personality disorders.

Inadmissible. Inadmissib(le,ly,ility). Unallow(ed,able). Preclu(ded,sive). Objectionab(le,ly,ness). Improper(ly). Immaterial(ity,ities). Inappropriate(ly, ness). Unacceptab(le,ility). Untenab(le, ility). *Consider also:* unsuitab(le,ility), inapplicab(le,ility), irrelevan(t,ce), unfeasib(le,ility), inept(ly,ness), unbecoming, unseasonable, unseemly ill-favored, undesirable, unwanted, unwelcome. *See also* Evidence; Forbidden; Illegal; Judicial ethics.

Inanimate objects. Inanimate object(s). Thing(s). Physical object(s). Art objects. Objet(s) d'art. Artifact(s). Artefact(s). *See also* Equipment; Material culture; Tools; Weaponry.

Inappropriateness. Inappropriate(ly,ness). Ill advised. Discordant(ly). Improper(ly). Ill-adapted. Ill-suited. Unfitted. Unmeet. Unsuitab(le,leness). Unsuited. Indecorous(ly). Unseeml(y, iness). Inconsonant. Ill-timed. Inept(ly,ness). Unbecoming. Unbefitting. Undu(e,ly). Unseasonab(le,ly). Unsuitab(le,ly). Untimel(y,iness). *See also* Errors; Fallibility; Negligence.

Inauguration. Inaugurat(e,ed,ing,ion). Initiat(e,ed,ing,ion). Commenc(e,ed,ing, ement). Induct(ed,ing,ion). Install(ed, ing,ation). Launch(ed,ing). Ord(ain, ained,aining,ination). Establish(ed,ing, ment). *See also* Beginning; Coronation; Product introduction.

Inbreeding. Inbreed(ing). Inbred. Consanguineous marriage(s). Consanguinity with marriage. Incestuous marriage(s). *Consider also:* endogamy, endogamous marriage(s). *See also* Consanguinity; Endogamous marriage; Incest.

Incantations. Incantation(s,al). Incantatory. Magical text(s). Magical invocation(s) Adjuration. *Consider also:* mantra(s), spell(s), bless(ed,ing,ings), curs(e,ed,es, ing), imprecat(e,ed,ing,ion). *See also* Exorcism; Prayer; Voodooism.

Incapacitation. Incapacitat(e,ed,ing,ion). Damag(e,ed,ing). Deactivat(e,ed,ing, ion). Disarm(ed,ing). Disqualif(y,ied, ing). Immobiliz(e,ed,ing). Impair(ed, ing,ment,ments). Inactivat(e,ed,ing,ion). Invalidat(e,ed,ing,ion). Weaken(ed,ing). Neutraliz(e,ed,ing,ation). *See also* Legal competency; Loss of function; Sensory loss.

Incarceration. See *Imprisonment.*

Incarceration, alternatives to. See *Alternatives to incarceration.*

Incendiarism. See *Fire setting behavior.*

Incendiary weapons. Incendiary weapon(s,ry). Fire bomb(s,ing,ings). Flame thrower(s). *Choose from:*

incendiary, fire, inflammatory *with:* weapon(s,ry), canister(s), bomb(s,ing,ings). *Consider also:* napalm, incendiaries, incendiary device(s), smokeless powder(s), mail bomb(s), fireworks. *See also* Arson; Bombs; Explosives; Fire setting behavior; Military weapons; Weaponry.

Incentive plans, employee. See *Employee incentive plans.*

Incentives. Incentive(s). Inducement(s). *Consider also:* reward(s), motive(s), motivation(al), expected benefit(s), token(s), reinforcement(s), reinforcer(s), payoff(s), gratification, prize(s), impetus, desired consequence(s), merit pay, production bonus(es), lure(s,d), enticement(s), knowledge of results. *See also* Awards; Buyout packages; Educational incentives; Encouragement; Goals; Meritocracy; Monetary incentives; Motivation; Needs; Penalties; Positive reinforcement; Profit motive; Recognition (achievement); Reward; Token economy.

Incentives, educational. See *Educational incentives.*

Incentives, monetary. See *Monetary incentives.*

Incest. Incest(uous,uousness). *Choose from:* seduct(ive,ion), sexual relation(s), rape(d), sexual(ly) abuse(s,d), pedophilia(c,cs) *with:* parent(s), mother(s), father(s), son(s), daughter(s), sibling(s), brother(s), sister(s). *See also* Abusive parents; Child abuse; Consanguinity; Inbreeding; Molested children; Oedipus complex; Pedophilia; Perpetrators; Rape; Sex offenders; Sex offenses; Sexual abuse; Sexual exploitation; Taboo; Unwanted pregnancy; Victimization.

Incidence. Incidence. Number of new cases. Extent. Epidemiolog(y,ic,ical). Occurrence. Spread. Widespread. Distribution. Pattern(s) of use. Trend(s). Epidemic(s). Ubiquitous. Seasonal fluctuation(s). Seroprevalence. Disease outbreak(s). Space time clustering. Attendance. Birth rate(s). Dropout rate(s). Enrollment rate(s). Morbidity rate(s). Mortality rate(s). Accident rate(s). *Consider also:* prevalen(t,ce), frequency, rate(s). *See also* Attendance (presence); Birthrate; Census; Demography; Frequently; Geographic distribution; High risk persons; Infant mortality; Longitudinal studies; Morbidity; Mortality rates; Population distribution; Probability.

Incidental learning. Incidental learning. Passive learning. *Choose from:* incidental, unintentional *with:* learning, recall, memory, cue(s), recognition. *Consider also:* latent learning. *See also* Hidden curriculum; Learning.

Incidental music. Incidental music.

Buehnenmusik. *Consider also:* overture(s), entr'acte(s), interlude(s), intrad(a,en). *See also* Background music; Film music; Interludes (music); Music; Overtures (music).

Incidents. Incident(s). Adventure(s). Affair(s). Circumstance(s). Encounter(s). Episode(s). Event(s). Experience(s). Happening(s). Occasion(s). Occurrence(s), *See also* Crises; Events; Experiences (events).

Incidents, border. See *Border wars.*

Incipits. Incipit(s). Opening word(s). Introduction(s). Introductory word(s). *See also* Incunabula; Introduction; Rare books.

Incitement. Incit(e,ed,ing,ement). Incitant(s). Inciter(s). Activat(e,ed,ing, ion). Actuat(e,ed,ing,ion). Exhort(ed,ing, ation). Instigat(e,ed,ing,ion). Abet(ted, ting). Foment(ed,ing). Spur(red,ring) to action. Goad(ed,ing). Inflam(e,ed,ing). Influenc(e,ed,ing). Inspir(e,ed,ing,ation). Motivat(e,ed,ing,ion). Provok(e,ed,ing). Rous(e,ed,ing). *See also* Agitators; Arousal; Influence.

Inclusion. Inclusi(on,ive,iveness). Comprehensive(ness). All-embracing. All-encompassing. Enclos(e,ed,ing). Incorporat(e,ed,ing). *See also* Belongingness; Comprehensiveness; Desegregation; Inclusive education; Social acceptance.

Inclusive education. Inclusive education. Inclusive school(s). *Choose from:* inclus(ive,ion,ionary), includ(e,ed,ing), integrat(e,ed,ing,ion), reintegrat(e,ed, ing,ion) *with:* classroom(s), student(s), education, curricul(um,ae), setting(s), environment(s). *See also* Educational placement; Globalization; Inclusion; Mainstreaming; Multicultural education.

Inclusive schools. See *Inclusive education.*

Income. Income(s). Earning(s). Salar(y,ies). Revenue(s). Rate(s) of return. Asset accumulation. Remunerat(ion,ive). Compensation. Payment(s) received. Wage(s). Interest earned. Family allowance(s). Earned money. Receipts. Profit(s). Proceeds. Honorar(ia,ium). Annuit(y,ies). Pension(s). Subsid(y,ies). Stipend(s). Recompense. Paycheck(s). Monetary reward(s). Gains. Recompense. *Consider also:* capital gain(s), yield. *See also* Budgets; Capital (financial); Compensation (payment); Cost of living; Expenditures; Financial support; Gains; Gross national product; Income distribution; Income inequality; Income maintenance programs; Income redistribution; Informal sector; Living standards; Minimum wage; Pensions; Poverty; Privatized pension systems; Profitability; Profits; Purchasing power; Retirement income; Salaries; Savings; Socioeconomic status; Tax deductions;

Wages; Wealth.

Income, disposable. See *Disposable income.*

Income, family. See *Family socioeconomic status; Income; Retirement income.*

Income, guaranteed. See *Income maintenance programs.*

Income, low. See *Low income.*

Income, national. See *National income*

Income, retirement. See *Retirement income.*

Income distribution. Income distribution. Pareto's law. *Choose from:* income(s), earning(s), reward(s), wealth, salar(y,ies), compensation, wage(s), profit(s), proceeds, gains *with:* distribut(e,ed,ing,ion), redistribut(e,ed, ing,ion), determination, apportionment, transfer, mobility, elasticity, shift(s), equaliz(e,ed,ing,ation), differential(s), level(s). *See also* Distributive justice; Income; Income inequality; Income redistribution; Living standards; Salaries; Wage differentials; Wages; Wealth.

Income generation. See *Earnings.*

Income inequality. Income inequality. Concentration(s) of wealth or poverty. *Choose from:* pay, income(s), earning(s), reward(s), wealth, salar(y,ies), economic, compensation, wage(s), profit(s), proceeds, gains *with:* inequalit(y,ies), inequit(y,ies), disparit(y,ies), gap(s), difference(s), variation(s), unequal, differential(s). *Consider also:* comparable worth, comparable wages. *See also* Cheap labor; Dependency theory (international); Distributive justice; Global inequality; Income; Income distribution; Income redistribution; Labor economics; Labor market segmentation; Occupational segregation; Prevailing wages; Regressive taxes; Sexual division of labor; Social class; Social stratification; Socioeconomic status; Wage differentials; Wages; Wealth.

Income level. See *Low income; Middle income level; Minimum wage; Poverty; Socioeconomic status; Upper income level.*

Income level, lower. See *Poverty.*

Income level, middle. See *Middle income level.*

Income level, upper. See *Upper income level.*

Income maintenance programs. Income maintenance program(s). Guaranteed income. Income support(s). Unemployment compensation. Guaranteed minimum income. Family allowance(s). Income assistance. *Choose from:* income *with:* support, maintenance, assistance, minimum, security, guarantee(s,d), supplement(s,al). *Consider also:* public assistance, welfare program(s), social insurance program(s), unemployment benefit(s), food stamp(s), entitlement(s), antipoverty program(s), negative income tax(es). *See also* Antipoverty programs; Elderly; Family assistance; Food relief; Low income; Medical assistance; Public housing; Public welfare.

Income redistribution. Income redistribution. Redistribut(e,ed,ing,ion) income. *Consider also:* progressive tax(es), progressive income tax(es), tax progressivity, windfall recapture, equitable tax(es), welfare, public assistance, guaranteed income, negative income tax(es), welfare state(s), socialis(m,t,tic). *See also* Income maintenance programs; Taxes; Welfare state.

Incompetence. See *Insanity defense; Legal competency.*

Incompetence, ejaculatory. See *Ejaculatory incompetence.*

Inconsistency, status. See *Status inconsistency.*

Incontinence, fecal. See *Fecal incontinence.*

Incontinence, urinary. See *Urinary incontinence.*

Inconvenience. Inconvenien(ce,ces,t). Annoyance(s). Awkward(ness,ly). Bothersome(ness). Cumbersome(ness). Troublesome(ness). Nuisance(s). Unhand(y,iness). Untimel(y,iness). Inappropriate(ness). *See also* Barriers; Constraints; Encumbrance.

Incorporation. Incorporat(e,ed,ing,ion). Affiliat(e,ed,ing,ion). Amalgamat(e,ed, ing,ion). Consolidat(e,ed,ing,ion). Integrat(e,ed,ing,ion). Federat(e,ed, ing,ion). *See also* Corporations; Founding; Going public; Mergers.

Incorrect. Incorrect(ly,ness). Inaccurate(ly, ness). Inexact(ly,ness). Imprecise(ly, ness). Mistaken(ly). Erroneous(ly). Wrong(ly). False(ly,ness). Untru(e, thful). Defective(ly,ness). Fault(y,iness). Flaw(ed,s). Imperfect(ly,ness). *See also* Errors; Fallacies; Journalistic errors; Medication errors; Scientific errors.

Incrimination, self. See *Self incrimination.*

Incubators, business. See *Business incubators.*

Incunabula. Incunabul(um,a). Early printed book(s). 15th century book(s). Fifteenth century book(s). Gutenberg bibles. *Choose from:* book(s) *with:* Gutenberg, Jenson, Caxton, Aldus Manutius. *Consider also:* early typography. *See also* Antiquarian booksellers; Block books; Books of hours; Illumination of books and manuscripts; Incipits; Rare

books; Scholia.

Indebtedness. Indebted(ness). Debt(s). Liabilit(y,ies). Financial obligation(s). Arrears. Debit(s). Deferred payment(s). Borrowed money. Leveraged buyout(s). Interest rate(s). Mortgage(s). Insolven(t,cy). Commercial paper. Overdraft(s). Past due account(s). Deficit(s). Usury. Loan(s). Lend(ing). Default(ed,ing,er,ers). Bankruptcy. Collection agenc(y,ies). Insolven(t,cy). Credit(or,ors). Charge account(s). Layaway. *See also* Arrears; Bankruptcy; Credit; Finance; Interest (monetary); Loans; Money; Public debt.

Indecency. See *Adult entertainment; Bawdy songs; Belly dance; Burlesque; Depravity; Dirty dancing; Obscenity; Pornography; Scatology; Vulgarity.*

Indecent communications. Indecent communication(s). Cybersex. *Choose from:* indecent, obscen(e,ity), harmful to minors, pornograph(y,ic), dirty talk, dirty picture(s) *with:* communication(s), online, disseminat(e,ed,ing,ion), World Wide Web, broadcast(ing), network(s), email, chat room(s), chat line(s), download(ed,ing). *See also* Adult entertainment; Broadcasting censorship; Cybersex; Freedom of the press; Information policy; Malinformation; Obscenity; Online harassment;. Pornography; Scatology; Sexual exploitation; Sexual harassment; Verbal abuse; Vulgarity.

Indecent exposure. Indecent exposure. Public nudity. Flasher(s). Masturbat(e, ed,ing,ion) in public. Bare(d) breast(s). *Choose from:* indecent, lewd, nud(e,ity), *with:* public(ly), expos(e,ed,ure), act(s), display(s,ed,ing). *Consider also:* topless bar(s), exhibitionis(m,t,ts). *See also* Behavior problems; Deviant behavior; Exhibitionism; Sex offenders; Sex offenses; Sexual deviations.

Indecisiveness. Indecisive(ness). Ambivalen(t,ce). Changeable(ness). Diffiden(t,ce). Doubtful(ness). Falter(ed,ing). Fluctuat(e,ed,ing). Hesitan(t,ce). Indefinite(ness). Irresolute(ness). Uncertain(ness). Undecided. Unresolved. waver(ed,ing). *See also* Ambivalence; Conflict of interest; Hesitancy; Internal conflict.

Indefiniteness. Indefinite(ly,ness). Ambiguous(ly,ness). Boundless(ly,ness). Ill-defined. Immeasurab(le,ly). Incalculab(le,ly). Inconclusive(ly). Indeterminab(le,ly). Limitless(ness). Indistinguishab(le,ly). Inexact(ly,ness). Inexplicit(ly,ness). Obscur(e,ely,ity). Uncertain(ty,ties). Unclear(ly,ness). Undecided. Undefined. Undetermined. Unfixed. Unknown. Vague(ness). *See also* Endlessness; Uncertainty.

Independence. See *Autonomy (govern-*

ment); Freedom; Personal independence; Political self determination.

Independence, field. See *Field dependence.*

Independence, personal. See *Personal independence.*

Independent churches. Independent church(es). *Choose from:* non-denominational, independent, leav(e,es,ing) denomination, charismatic *with:* church(es), Christian organization(s). *See also* Churches; Cults; Religious denominations.

Independent contractors. Independent contractor(s). *Choose from:* independent *with:* contractor(s), worker(s). *Choose from:* contract(ual) *with:* work, job(s), worker(s), employee(s), employment, personnel, operator(s), staff, manpower, professional(s), sales(man,men,woman, women,people,person,persons), work force, office force, labor force, labor(er,ers), crew(s), help, secretar(y, ies). *Consider also:* quasi-firm(s), satellite organization(s). *See also* Contract labor; Contract services; Self employment; Temporary employees; Temporary help services.

Independent living. See *Deinstitutionalization; Group homes; Institutional release; Living alone; Noninstitutionalized disabled; Personal independence; Retirement communities.*

Independent regulatory commissions. Independent regulatory commission(s). Regulatory agenc(y,ies). Regulatory bod(y,ies). Government regulation. *Consider also:* Federal Banking Commission, Federal Reserve Board, Federal Trade Commission, etc. *See also* Government agencies.

Independent states, newly. See *Countries in transition.*

Independent variables. Independent variable(s). Experimental variable(s). X variable(s). Predictor(s). Regressor(s). *Choose from:* independent, predict(ive, or), stimulus, explanatory *with:* variable(s). *Consider also:* cause(s). *See also* Correlation; Dependent variables; Research design.

Indeterminism. Indetermin(ism,istic, acy,ate). Uncertain(ty,ties). Acausal. Unpredictab(le,leness,ility). *Consider also:* imprecision, random(ness). *See also* Chance; Chance composition; Determinism; Epistemology; Postmodernism; Uncertainty; Voluntarism (philosophy).

Indexes (indicators). Index(es). Indicator(s). Measure(s,ment,ments). Inventor(y,ies). Indices. *Consider also:* scale(s), ratio(s), correlate(s), sign(s), indicant(s). *See also* Economic indicators; Health indices; Health status indicators; Inventories; Living standards;

Measurement; Social indicators; Tests; Trends; Vital statistics.

Indian (India) cultural groups. Indian cultural group(s). *Choose from:* India(n) *with:* indigenous, native, *with:* population(s), people(s), group(s), populace, tribe(s), resident(s), inhabitant(s). *Consider also:* Agris, Aryans, Asurs, Badagas, Baigas, Balahis, Baltis, Bargundas, Basors, Bathuria, Bengali, Bhantus, Bhils, Bhiriguids, Bhuiyas, Bhumiyas, Birhors, Bondos, Brahuis, Bumij, Burushos, Chaks, Changs, Chenchoos, Dards, Dharnas, Doms, Dravidians, Gadabas, Gaddis, Garhwali, Garos, Gonds, Hindus, Hos, Irulas, Juangs, Kacharis, Kadars, Kandhs, Kanets, Kanikars, Kasubas, Katkaris, Kaws, Khasis, Kherias, Kinnar, Kijahs, Kilarians, Kolis, Kondhs, Konkani, Konyaks, Korwas, Kotas, Kukis, Kunnuvans, Kurmi-Mahtos, Kurmis, Kurumbas, Ladakhi, Lepchas, Luchai, Maitais, Malabars, Malaiali, Malas, Malers, Malpaharias, Malsers, Mannans, Marias, Maroongs, Marvars, Meenas, Meithis, Mikirs, Moghias, Mookwas, Moduvans, Mundas, Muria, Musurs, Nagas, Nahals, Nairs, Noatia, Oraons, Paharia, Paliyans, Pandarams, Paniyans, Parsis, Pondans, Porojas, Prabhus, Rajbansis, Rajis, Rajputs, Rawalttas, Reddis, Riang, Sabakhias, Samuls, Sangtams, Santals, Sathiyas, Savaras, Shokas, Sikhs, Sindhis, Sugalis, Swalgiri, Tamarias, Tamils, Telegu, Todas, Urali, Varlis, Weddid, Yenadis, etc. *See also* Asian empires; Cultural groups; Culture (anthropology); Culture change; Culture contact; Dravidian languages; Indo-Iranian languages; South Asia.

Indian medicine. See *Ayurvedic medicine.*

Indian reservations. See *American Indian territories.*

Indian territories, American. See *American Indian territories.*

Indians, American. See *Central American native cultural groups; Indigenous populations; North American native cultural groups; South American native cultural groups.*

Indians, Central American. See *Central American native cultural groups.*

Indians, North American. See *North American native cultural groups.*

Indians, South American. See *South American native cultural groups.*

Indicators. See *Indexes (indicators).*

Indicators (biology). Indicator(s) biolog(y,ical). Bioindicator(s). Bio-indicator(s). Biomarker(s). *Choose from:* biolog(y,ical), vir(us,al), bacteria(l), species, bird(s), animal(s), etc. *with:* marker(s), indices, index(es), indicator(s), key(s). *See also* Biochemical markers; Health indices; Health status indicators; Screening.

Indicators, economic. See *Economic indicators.*

Indicators, health status. See *Health status indicators.*

Indicators, social. See *Social indicators.*

Indices, health. See *Health indices.*

Indictments. Indictment(s). Indict(ed,ing,able). True bill(s). *Consider also:* grand jur(y,ies), presentment(s). *See also* Allegations; Blame; Blameworthy; Complaints; Offenses; Prosecution; Sufficient evidence; Trial (law).

Indies, West. See *Caribbean.*

Indifference. Indifferen(ce,t). Disinterested(ness). Apath(etic,y). Lack of feeling. Unconcerned. Unenthusiastic. Passiv(e,ity). Unambitious. Uninspired. Lack of excitement. Unexcited. Unmoved. Half hearted. Lukewarm. Uninterested. Deadwood. Diminished interest. Lack of interest. Lack of feeling. Impassiv(e,ity). Letharg(y,ic). Spiritless(ness). Listless(ness). Unemotional. Unfeeling. Lack of affect. Hebetude. Stupor(ous). Disengage(d, ment). Detach(ed,ment). Bor(ed,edom, ing). Lassitude. Acathexis. Ameleia. *See also* Alienation; Anhedonia; Boredom; Disengagement; Noninvolvement; Nothingness; Passiveness; Political attitudes; Social attitudes;

Indifferentism (religion). Indifferent(ism) religi(on,ous). Adiaphoris(t,tic,m). *Consider also:* polydoxy, *See also* Cultural relativism; Liberalism (Religion); Objectivity.

Indigence. Indigen(t,ce,cy). Poverty. Poor. Penury. Impoverish(ed,ment). Welfare. Disadvantage(d,ment). Homeless(ness). Vagran(t,ts,cy). Need(y,iness). Economic disadvantagement. Economic(ally) insecur(e,ity). Economic plight. Privation. Destitut(e,ion). Penniless. Pauper(ism). Impecunious. Economic hardship. Underprivileged. Beggar(s). *See also* Economic dependence; Hardships; Homeless; Poverty.

Indigenismo. See *Central American native cultural groups; Indigenous populations; Traditional societies.*

Indigenous churches. Indigenous church(es). *Choose from:* indigenous, native, ethnic *with:* church(es), religious institution(s), Christian(ity). *Consider also:* enculturation. *See also* Churches; Missionaries.

Indigenous health services. See *Traditional medicine.*

Indigenous people. See *Indigenous populations.*

Indigenous populations. Indigenous population(s). Indigenismo(s). *Choose from:* indigenous, native, aboriginal, autochthon(ous,ic) *with:* population(s), people(s), group(s), populace, tribe(s). *Consider also:* resident(s), inhabitant(s). *See also* Aborigines; Acculturation; African empires; African cultural groups; Alaska natives; Asian empires; Assimilation (cultural); Australoid race; Central American native cultural groups; Colonialism; Cultural conflict; Culture change; Culture contact; Eskimos; Ethnic groups; Ethnic relations; Hunting and gathering societies; Indian (India) cultural groups; Indonesian cultural groups; Intercultural communication; Natives; Nativism; Nativistic movements; North American native cultural groups; Oceanic cultural groups; Pacific Islanders; Philippine Islands cultural groups; Pre-Columbian empires; South American native cultural groups; Traditional societies.

Indirect costs. Indirect cost(s). Fixed cost(s). *Choose from:* indirect, fixed, constant, nonvariable, stable, undeviating *with:* cost(s), expense(s). *Consider also:* absorption costing, indirect expense(s), manufacturing cost(s), overhead, running cost(s). *See also* Cost analysis; Costs; Direct costs.

Indirect discourse. Indirect discourse. Oratio obliqua. Reported speech. Indirect quotation(s). Indirect speech. *Choose from:* indirect, reported *with:* discourse, speech, quotation(s) style. *See also* Direct discourse; Discourse; Quotations; Speech.

Indirect rule (government). Indirect rule. *Choose from:* colon(y,ies,ial), imperial(istic,ism) *with:* co-opt(ation), indigenous political system(s), native political system(s), native ruler(s), precolonial authority structure(s), native authorities, indigenous leadership. *See also* Colonialism.

Individual and the state. Individual and the state. Social contract(s). *Choose from:* human right(s), individual(s,ism), self-determination, individual liberty, John Doe, Jane Doe, personal freedom, personal autonomy, patient autonomy, private property, minorit(y,ies) *with:* state(s), government(s,al), collective right(s), democrac(y,ies), democratic, totalitarian(ism), authoritarian(ism), constitution(al), authorit(y,ies). *See also* Citizenship; Civil rights; Personal independence; Social responsibility; Voting rights.

Individual development. See *Adolescent development; Adult development; Behavior development; Career development; Child development; Cognitive development; Emotional development; Enlightenment (state of mind); Human* *development; Human potential movement;Infant development; Intellectual development; Language development; Moral development; Motor development; Personality development; Physical development; Psychomotor development; Psychosexual development; Psychosocial development; Self actualization; Skill learning; Socialization; Speech development.*

Individual differences. Individual difference(s). Heterogene(ity,ous). Individuality. Background difference(s). Differences between individuals. Individual profile(s). Individual reaction(s). Individual variability. *Choose from:* individual(s), interindividual, intraindidvidual, respondent(s), subject(s), member(s) *with:* characteristic(s), profile(s), variation(s), variance, pattern(s), difference(s), unique(ness), variabilit(y,ies), style(s), contrast(s), comparison(s), deviation(s), divergen(ce), discrepan(cy,cies), disparit(y,ies), distinction(s), inequalit(y,ies), nonconformit(y,ies), trait(s). *Consider also:* age difference(s), intelligence difference(s), sex difference(s). *See also* Age differences; Cultural characteristics; Deviation; Gender differences; Individual needs; Individual psychology; Individuality; Nature nurture; Physical characteristics; Racial differences; Social background; Variations.

Individual dignity. See *Human dignity.*

Individual needs. Individual need(s). *Choose from:* individual(s), human, client(s), student(s), learner(s), hierarch(y,ies), basic, higher, personal, social, psychological, emotional, status, recognition, security, gratification, self actualization, esteem, achievement, affiliation, belonging, physiological, biological *with:* need(s), motiv(e,es, ation). *Consider also:* deficiency motivation. *See also* Affiliation motivation; Human dignity; Individual differences; Individual psychology; Individualized instruction; Need satisfaction; Needs; Needs assessment; Psychological needs; Sex drive; Well being.

Individual psychology. Individual psychology. *Choose from:* individual development, holistic, ego, Adlerian, personality *with:* theor(y,ies), perspective(s). *See also* Human development; Individual differences; Individual needs; Lifestyle; Personal independence; Personality traits; Psychological needs; Self actualization.

Individual psychotherapy. Individual psychotherap(y,ies). Individual counseling. *Choose from:* individual, one-to-one, client-centered, dyadic *with:* psychotherap(y,ies), counseling, therap(y,ies), pastoral care, casework. *See also* Psychotherapy.

Individual rights. See *Bill of rights; Civil rights; Human rights.*

Individual self determination. See *Personal independence.*

Individual testing. Individual(ized) test(s,ing). *Choose from:* individual(ly,s, ized), self scoring *with:* test(s,ing), measure(s,ment,ments), assessment(s), checklist(s), diagnostic(s), question(s), questionnaire(s), examination(s), evaluation(s), rating(s), scale(s), schedule(s), screening(s), score(s), trial(s). *See also* Group testing; Test taking.

Individualism. Individualis(m,istic). Individual interest(s). Self interest(s). Individual right(s). *Consider also:* Protestantism, subjectivity, egoism, self reliance, self direction, autonomy, self development, dignity of man, privacy. *See also* Creativity; Economic man; Existentialism; Human dignity; Humanism; Individuals; Intellectual liberty; Libertarianism; Minimal government; Particularism; Personal independence; Personalism; Phenomenology; Philosophy; Political ideologies; Progressivism; Self actualization; Social development; Self expression; Self interest; Social values.

Individuality. Individuality. Sense of self. Idiosyncra(sy,sies,tic). Uniqueness. Distinctive features. Singular(ity). Original(ity). Nonconformity. Unconforming. *Choose from:* individual *with:* differences, characteristics, features. *Consider also:* idiocentrism, differentiat(ion,ing), separateness, autonomy, ego(centric,centrism), self interest. *See also* Distinction; Idiosyncrasies; Nonconformity (personality); Personality traits; Subjectivity.

Individualized instruction. Individualized instruction. *Choose from:* individualiz(ed,ing), personalized, student directed, self paced, self directed, independent *with:* instruction, education, curriculum, learning, course(s), remediation, tutoring, teaching method(s), class(es), presentation(s). *See also* Active learning; Adapted physical education; Computer assisted instruction; Continuing education; Home schooling; Open classroom method; Programed instruction; Self education; Teaching methods.

Individuals. Individual(s). Person(ae,s,age, ages). Human being(s). Mortal(s). Actor(s). Character(s). John Doe. Jane Doe. Self. Some(one,body). Child. Woman. Man. *See also* Adult development; Age groups; Child development; Conscience; Disability; Experience (background); Gifted; Human rights; Individuality; Inhabitants; Life satisfaction; Masses; Moral development; Personality; Population; Roles; Self actualization; Self concept; Self disclosure; Self esteem; Self help; Socialization; Subjectivity.

Individuals, unrelated. See *Unrelated individuals.*

Individuation. Individuation. Leav(e,ing) home. Disengag(e,ed,ing,ement). Disaffiliat(e,ed,ing,ion). *Choose from:* mother, psychological, emotional *with:* separat(e,ed,ing,ion), separat(eness,ion), differentiat(ing,ion). *Choose from:* develop(ed,ing), form(ed,ing,ation) *with:* autonomy, identity, individuality. *See also* Adolescent development; Child development; Infant development; Object relations; Separation anxiety;

Individuation (philosophy). Individuation. Principle of individuation. Criterion of identity. Principium individuationis. *See also* Epistemology.

Individuation, separation. See *Individuation.*

Indo-Iranian languages. Indo-Iranian language(s). Dardic or Pisacha: Kafiri, Kashmiri, Khowar, Khohistani, Romany [Gypsy], Shina. Indic or Indo-Aryan: Pali, Pakrits, Sanskrit, Vedic, Eastern Hindi, Awadhi, Bagheli, Chattisgarhi [Laria], Western Hindi, Khari Boli [Hindustani], literary Hindi, Urdu, East Indic, Assamese, Bengali, Bihari [Bhojpuri, Magahi, Maithili], Oriya. Northwest Indic: Punjabi, Sindhi. Pahari: Central Pahari [Kumaoni, Gahrwali], Eastern Pahari [Khas-kura, Gorkhali, Nepali], Western Pahari. Sinhalese: Sinhalese, Mahl. South Indic: Marathi, Konkani. West Indic: Bhili, Gujarati, Khandesi, Rajastani. Iranian: Avestan, Old Persian. East Iranian: Khwarazmian, Ossetic, Pamir dialects, Pushtu [Afghan], Saka [Khotanese], Sogdian, Yaghnobi. West Iranian: Baluchi, Kurdish, Middle Persian [Pahlavi], Parthian, Persian [Farsi], Tajiki. *See also* Indian (India) cultural groups; Language; Languages (as subjects); Middle East; South Asia.

Indoctrination. Indoctrinat(ed,ion). Manufactured consent. Shap(e,ed,ing) attitude(s). Instill(ed,ing). Inculcat(e,ed, ing). Implant(ed,ing) idea(s). Propagandiz(e,ed,ing). Instruct(ed,ing). Brainwash(ed,ing). Brain wash(ed,ing). Menticide. Coercive persuasion. Mind control. Mind manipulation. Mind manipulator(s). Thought control. Thought reform. Coercion. Persuasive communication. Religious conversion. Psychological kidnapping. *See also* Attitude change; Political socialization; Propaganda.

Indonesian cultural groups. Indonesian cultural group(s). *Choose from:*

Indonesia(n), Netherlands East Indies, Dutch East Indies, Borneo, Brunei (Darussalam), Java, Lesser Sundas, Moluccas, Celebes, Sabah, Sarawak, Sumatra *with:* indigenous, native(s), population(s), people, ethnic group(s), minority group(s), populace, tribe(s), resident(s), inhabitant(s). *Consider also:* Alor, Ambon, Aru, Atjehnese, Babar, Badui, Bahau, Bajau, Bali, Banda, Batak, Batjan, Buru, Ceram, Ceramlaut, Damar, Enggano, Flores, Gayo-Alas, Goram, Gorontalo, Halmahera, Iban, Javanese, Kayan, Kei, Kenya, Kisar, Klamantan, Kubu, Land Dyak, Leti, Loinang, Lombok, Madura, Makassar, Mentawei, Minangkabau, Mori-Laki, Ngadju, Nias, Nila, Obi, Orang Laut, Punan, Redjang-Lampong, Roti, Sadang, Salon, Sangirese, Savu, Sea Gypsies, Sermata, Sula, Sumba, Sumbawa, Sundanese, Tanimbar, Tenggerese, Ternate, Timor, Toala, Toradja, Watubela, Wetar, etc. *See also* Far East; Indian (India) cultural groups; Malayo-Polynesian languages.; Oceania; Oceanic cultural groups; Philippine Islands cultural groups; South Asia; Southeast Asia; Southeast Asian cultural groups.

Induced abnormalities, drug. See *Drug induced abnormalities.*

Induced abortion. Induced abort(ion,ions). *Choose from:* induced, artificial, therapeutic, eugenic, legal, discretionary, elective, induction *with:* abortion(s), forced deliver(y,ies), interrupt(ed,ing, ion) pregnanc(y,ies), terminat(e,ed,ing, ion) pregnanc(y,ies). *See also* Abortifacients; Abortion.

Induced organic mental disorders, substance. See *Substance induced organic mental disorders.*

Induced psychoses, drug. See *Substance induced psychoses.*

Induced psychoses, substance. See *Substance induced psychoses.*

Induction. Induct(ion,ive). Inferen(ce,ces, tial). *Consider also:* causal reasoning, logical reasoning, formal reasoning, propositional reasoning, formal logic. *See also* Analogical reasoning; Cognitive generalization; Deduction; Learning; Research methods; Scientific method; Transfer (learning).

Indulgence, self. See *Self indulgence.*

Indulgences. Indulgence(s). Forbearance. Clemency. Lenienc(e,y). Merciful(ness). Tolera(ance,tion). Remission of purgatorial punishment. *Consider also:* pardon(ed,ing) guilt, reconciliation. *See also* Absolution; Forgiveness; Pardon.

Industrial accidents. Industrial accident(s). *Choose from:* industr(y,ies,ial), occupational, work(er,ers,ing), workplace(s), factor(y,ies), job, employee(s), mine(s), mining, machine(s,ry) *with:* risk(s), death(s), hazard(ous,s), injur(y,ies,ed), accident(s), unsafe, safety, danger(s), fatalit(y,ies). *See also* Injuries; Mine accidents; Hazardous occupations; Occupational exposure; Occupational safety; Personal injuries.

Industrial arbitration. Industrial arbitration. Arbitration decision(s). *Choose from:* industrial, factor(y,ies), manufacturer, plant labor, National Labor Relations Board, NLRB, *with:* arbitrat(e,ed,ing,ion), dispute resolution(s), resolv(e,ed,ing) dispute(s), dispute settlement(s), settl(e,es,ing) dispute(s), independent third party. *Consider also:* labor court(s), industrial tribunal(s), labor commissioner(s). *See also* Labor management relations.

Industrial archaeology. Industrial archaeology. Industrial history. Industrial monument(s). *Choose from:* antiquit(y,ies), histor(y,ical), industrial revolution, 18th century, 19th century, archaeolog(y,ist,ists) *with:* industrial art(s), industrial building(s), manufactur(e,ed,ing), min(e,es,ing), mill(s), factor(y,ies), engine(s), locomotive(s), aqueduct(s), bridge(s), railway(s), train(s), canal(s), working structure(s). *See also* Archaeology; Industrialization.

Industrial automation. See *Automation.*

Industrial capacity. Industrial capacit(y, ies). Product(ion,ive) capacit(y,ies). *Choose from:* technological, plant(s), manufacturing, industr(y,ial), factor(y, ies), product(ion,ive), mill(s), transportation, railroad(s) *with:* capacit(y,ies), overcapacit(y,ies), glut(s,ted), limit(s), size, potential. *Consider also:* peak capacity, scheduled production. *See also* Capacity; Industrial efficiency; Production; Production control; Productivity.

Industrial cities and towns. Industrial cit(y,ies). Industrial town(s). Mill town(s). *Choose from:* industrial, factory, mill, manufactur(ing), compan(y,ies), corporat(e,ion,ions) *with:* cit(y,ies), town(s), communit(y,ies). *See also* Cities; Company towns; Industry; Migration of industry; Mining towns.

Industrial concentration. Industr(y,ial) concentration. *Choose from:* industr(y, ies,ial), economic, manufacturing, market(s,place), capital, business, conglomerate(s) *with:* concentrat(e,ed, ing,ion), centraliz(e,ed,ing,ation), dominat(e,ed,ing,ation), consolidat(e,ed, ing,ion). *Consider also:* industrial structure, megamerger(s), corporate concentration, interlocking directorship(s), conglomerate merger(s), marketplace market-dominating enterprise(s). *See also* Big business; Business; Competition; Consolidation; Corporate control; Corporations;

Economic elites; Industry; Monopolies; Multinational corporations; Oligopolies.

Industrial conflict. Industrial conflict(s). *Choose from:* industr(y,ies,ial), union(s), management, labor, shoproom, workplace, worker(s) *with:* absenteeism, conflict(s), struggle(s), coercion, control, dispute(s), opposition, argument(s), disagree(d,ing,ment,ments), tension(s), controvers(y,ies), unrest, militancy, noncooperation, polariz(e,ed,ing,ation), resistance, sabotage. *See also* Collective bargaining; Labor management relations; Strikes.

Industrial cooperation. Industrial cooperation. *Choose from:* industr(y,ies,ial), industrywide, compan(y,ies), corporat(e,ion,ions), manufacturer(s), R&D, technolog(y,ies,ical), producer(s) *with:* cooperat(e,ed,ing,ive,ion), co-operat(e,ed,ing,ive,ion), coalition(s), collaborat(e,ed,ing,ion), network(s,ed, ing), joint venture(s), partnership(s), voluntary standardization, work(ing) together, join(ed,ing) forces. *See also* Consortia; Contracting out; Cooperation; Industrial production; Interorganizational networks; Strategic alliances; Virtual organizations.

Industrial countries. See *Industrial societies.*

Industrial democracy. Industrial democrac(y,ies). Worker participation. Worker owned firm(s). Works council(s). Worker control. Co-determination. Self management. Labor managed. Producer cooperative(s). Economic democracy. Work cooperative(s). Participative management. Workplace democracy. Worker managed. Democratic firm(s). Syndicalism. *Consider also:* trade unionism, collective bargaining. *See also* Collective bargaining; Cooperatives; Democratization; Employee ownership; Employee stock ownership plans; Labor management relations; Labor unions; Power sharing; Worker control; Worker participation.

Industrial design. Industrial design(s). *Choose from:* design(ing,ed), modeling *with:* industr(y,ics,ial), manufactur(e,ed, ing), product(s), furniture, equipment, packaging, graphic(s), transportation, fashion, architectural, camera(s). *Consider also:* virtual manufacturing, CAD/CAM software, computer assisted design. *See also* Designs; Facility design and construction; Industrial production.

Industrial development. See *Industrialization.*

Industrial districts. Industrial district(s). *Choose from:* research, biotechnology, industrial, manufacturing, technology, factory, mixed use *with:* district(s), park(s), site(s), complex(es), estate(s), zone(s). *See also* Commercial districts; Land use.

Industrial efficiency. Industrial efficiency. *Choose from:* industr(y,ial), business(es), factor(y,ies), assembly line(s) *with:* efficien(cy,t), productiv(e,ity), profitab(le,ility), cut(ting) cost(s), reduc(e,ed,ing) cost(s), downsiz(e,ed, ing), rightsizing. *Consider also:* scientific management, motion stud(y,ies). *See also* Downsizing; Industrial capacity; Industrial production; Industry; Production; Production control; Productivity; Reengineering; Turnaround management.

Industrial engineering. Industrial engineering. Industrial systems engineering. Man-machine engineering. *Consider also:* computer integrated manufacturing system(s), industrial ergonomic(s), human engineering, ergonomics of manufacturing. *See also* Ergonomics; Industrial psychology; Man machine systems; Working conditions.

Industrial enterprises. Industrial enterprise(s). Industrial establishment(s). Industrial firm(s). Industrial organization(s). Industrial collective(s). Factor(y,ies). Industrial corporation(s). Industrial cooperative(s). Industrial complex(es). Industrial plant(s). *See also* Industrial management; Industrial production; Industrial workers; Industry; Nationalization; Privatization.

Industrial espionage. Industrial espionage. Industrial piracy. Steal(ing) technology. *Choose from:* piracy, pirat(e,ed,es,ing), conspir(e,ed,ing,acy), espionage, steal(ing,th), stolen, theft, divulg(e,ed, ing), leak(s,ing), illegal exchange(s), trafficking, fraud, brib(e,ed,es,ery), pass(ed,ing), intercept(ed), divulg(e,ed, ing) *with:* information, secret(s), patent(s), intellectual propert(y,ies), copyright(s), trade secret(s), blueprint(s), plan(s), document(s). *Choose from:* business(es), corporat(e,ion,ions), compan(y,ies), trade, multinational, industrial, manufacturing, production, design, research *with:* spy(ing), spie(s,d), electronic intruder(s), wiretap(ping), bugging, steal(ing) secret(s), stolen secret(s), passing secret(s), breach(es) of security, piracy, informant(s). *Choose from:* defense contracts *with:* fraud, brib(e,ed,es,ery), kickback(s), leak(s). *Consider also:* competitive intelligence. *See also* Competitive intelligence; Computer crimes; Crime; Eavesdropping; Electronic eavesdropping; Trade secrets.

Industrial expansion. Industrial expansion. *Choose from:* technological, plant(s), industr(y,ial), factor(y,ies), mill(s), mine(s) *with:* expand(ed,ing), expansion, capital invest(ed,ing,ment,ments), moderniz(e,ed,ing,ation), grow(th,ing,n), retool(ed,ing), develop(ed,ing,ment). *See also* Business growth; Economic

development; Industrialization; Plant closings.

Industrial fatigue. Industrial fatigue. *Choose from:* night shift(s), truck driver(s), air traffic controller(s), air traffic control officer(s), overtime, pilot(s), aircrew(s), crew(s), technician(s), machine operator(s), worker(s), employee(s), personnel, staff *with:* fatigue(d), overtired, burnout, burn(ed,t) out, sleep deprivation, deprive(d) of sleep, stress(ed,or,ors), strain(ed,ing), heavy workload(s). *See also* Burnout; Ergonomics; Occupational stress; Overwork; Working conditions.

Industrial foremen. Industrial fore(man,men). Industr(y,ial) *with:* supervisor(s). Industr(y,al) group leader(s). Shop steward(s). Plant steward(s). Union steward(s). Industrial line manager(s). Industrial manager(s). Supervisor(s) in plant. Crew leader(s). Overseer(s). Head(man,men,woman, women). *See also* Blue collar workers; Business personnel; Industrial personnel; Managers.

Industrial hazards. See *Hazardous wastes; Industrial accidents; Occupational disease; Occupational exposure; Occupational safety; Occupational stress.*

Industrial health services. See *Occupational health services.*

Industrial hygiene. See *Agricultural workers disease; Black lung disease; Industrial accidents; Multiple chemical sensitivities; Noise levels (work areas); Occupational diseases; Occupational exposure; Occupational health services; Occupational neuroses; Occupational safety; Occupational stress; Repetitive motion disorders; Sick building syndrome; Working conditions.*

Industrial laborers. See *Blue collar workers; Skilled workers; Unskilled workers.*

Industrial management. Industrial management. Industrial organization. Industrial supervision. Corporate management. Middle manage(er,ers, ment). Top level manage(ers,ment). Industrial hierarch(y,ies). Management of production. Industrial democrac(y, ies). Worker participation. Worker owned firm(s). Works council(s). Worker control. Co-determination. Self management. Producer cooperative(s). Economic democracy. Work cooperative(s). Participative management. Workplace democracy. Worker managed. *See also* Cooperatives; Employee ownership; Employee productivity; Industrial democracy; Industrial enterprises; Industrial foremen; Industrial personnel; Labor management relations; Personnel

management; Worker control; Worker participation;

Industrial management (self). See *Industrial democracy; Worker control; Worker participation.*

Industrial medicine. See *Occupational health services.*

Industrial military complex. See *Military industrial complex.*

Industrial museums. Industrial museum(s). *Choose from:* industr(y,ial), technolog(y, ical), min(e,es,ing), windmill(s), needle(s), automo(tive,bile,biles), etc. *with:* museum(s), galler(y,ies) *Consider also:* science museum(s). *See also* Industry; Medieval technology; Museums.

Industrial parks. See *Industrial districts.*

Industrial personnel. Industrial personnel. *Choose from:* compan(y,ies), plant(s), manufacturing, industr(y,ial), shift, trade(s), factor(y,ies), production, steel, mill(s), transportation, railroad(s) *with:* worker(s), employee(s), personnel, staff, associates. *Consider also:* blue collar worker(s), industrial fore(men,man), skilled worker(s). *See also* Blue collar workers; Coal miners; Copper miners; Employees; Human resources; Industrial workers.

Industrial plants. See *Factories.*

Industrial production. Industrial production. Mass production. Factory output. *Choose from:* industrial, mass, factory, manufacturing *with:* production, output, productivity. *See also* Automation; Industrial design; Industrial enterprises; Industrial efficiency; Industrial expansion; Industrialization; Labor process; Manufacturers; Production control.

Industrial promotion. Industrial promotion. Growth machine. *Choose from:* industr(y,ies,ial), compan(y,ies), corporat(e,ion,ions), manufactur(ing, er,ers), technolog(y,ies,ical), producer(s), factor(y,ies), mill(s), plant(s), business(es) *with:* promot(e,ed,ing,ion), incentive(s), nurtur(e,ed,ing), lur(e,ed, ing), enterprise zone(s), foster(ed,ing). *Consider also:* local development, tax incentive(s), economic development, enterprise zone(s), redevelopment. *See also* Business growth; Economic development; Enterprise zones; Industry; Progress; Sustainable development.

Industrial property. Industrial propert(y,ies). Proprietary right(s). Patent(s). Copyright(s). Know how. Trade secret(s). Goodwill. Software. Trademark(s). *Choose from:* industrial, corporat(e,ion,ions), compan(y,ies) *with:* equipment, software, hardware, asset(s), technology, real estate. *Consider also:* intellectual property. *See also* Assets; Copyright; Hardware; Industrial

Industrial psychologists. Industrial psychologist(s). *Choose from:* industr(y,ies,ial), business organization(s,al), workplace(s) *with:* psychologist(s). *See also* Industrial personnel; Psychologists.

Industrial psychology. Industrial psychology. *Choose from:* industrial, organizational, engineering, employee(s), job(s), workplace, working condition(s), vocational *with:* psycholog(y,ical). *Consider also:* human engineering, absenteeism, efficiency, job satisfaction, task performance and analysis, time and motion studies. *See also* Applied psychology; Industrial engineering; Job satisfaction; Organizational climate; Organizational development; Personnel management; Quality of working life; Work humanization.

Industrial relations. See *Labor management relations.*

Industrial revolution. See *Industrialization.*

Industrial safety. See *Industrial accidents; Occupational health services; Occupational safety.*

Industrial sector. See *Industry.*

Industrial self management. See *Industrial democracy; Worker control; Worker participation.*

Industrial societies. Industrial societ(y,ies). Developed countr(y,ies). First world. Modern civilization. Service econom(y,ies). Mass societ(y,ies). Industrial capitalism. Industrial(ized) world. Industrial power(s). Industrial(ized) democrac(y,ies). Modern civilization(s). *Choose from:* western, developed, advanced, urban(ized), industrial(ized) *with:* countr(y,ies), nation(s), state(s), societ(y,ies), world, communit(y,ies). *Consider also:* postindustrial societ(y,ies), information society. *See also* Capitalist societies; Civilization; Complex societies; Developed countries; Gemeinschaft and gesellschaft; Industrialization; International division of labor; Mass society; Modern society; Modernization; Postindustrial societies; Rationalization (sociology); Urbanization; Western society.

Industrial therapy. See *Occupational therapy.*

Industrial wastes. Industrial waste(s). *Choose from:* industr(y,ies,ial), commercial, manufactur(ing,er,ers), factor(y,ies), plant(s), mill(s), plant(s), foundr(y,ies), tanner(y,ies) *with:* waste(s), refuse, wastewater(s), groundwater(s), sewerage, sewage, garbage, trash, rubbish, ash(es), flyash, sweeping(s), dregs,

runoff, sludge, dioxin, PCBs, debris, pollut(e,ed,ing,ion), dump(s,ed,ing), incinerator(s), effluent(s). *Consider also:* Superfund, Love canal, Hooker Chemical. *See also* Acid rain; Air pollution; Carcinogens; Corporate social responsibility; Environmental impacts; Environmental pollutants; Environmental pollution; Environmental protection; Environmental racism; Greenhouse effect; Hazardous wastes; Manufacturers; Occupational diseases; Occupational exposure; Sewage; Toxic substances; Waste disposal; Waste to energy; Waste transport; Water pollution.

Industrial workers. Industrial worker(s). Factory worker(s). *Choose from:* industr(y,ial), assembly line, mine(s), production line, plant, factory, blue collar, sweatshop *with:* worker(s), personnel, staff, operator(s), employee(s). *See also* Automobile industry workers; Blue collar workers; Coal miners; Copper miners; Hazardous occupations; Industrial personnel; Iron and steel workers; Labor management relations; Labor supply; Labor unions; Workers.

Industrialization. Industrializ(e,ed,ing, ation). Industrial revolution. Great Leap Forward. Reindustrializ(ed,ing,ation). *Choose from:* commercializ(e,ed,ing, ation), machine, de-skill(ed,ing), moderniz(e,ed,ing), industrial *with:* production, manufacturing. *Choose from:* growth, development, rise *with:* technocra(cy,tic), industrial societ(y,ies), factor(y,ies), assembly line(s). *Choose from:* industrial, technological, technical, manufacturing *with:* organization, societ(y,ies), progress, development, advance(s), change(s), growth, transformation, restructuring, formation, projection, diffusion, decentralization. *Consider also:* postindustrial, factory system. *See also* Cultural lag; Developed countries; Developing countries; Economic assistance; Economic development; Economic history; Electrification; Employment opportunities; Factory system; Gemeinschaft and gesellschaft; Import substitution; Industrial archaeology; Industrial production; Industrial societies; Labor process; Modernization; Social change; Technology and civilization; Technology transfer; Urbanization; World history.

Industrialized nations. See *Industrial societies.*

Industrializing countries, newly. See *Newly industrializing economies.*

Industrializing economies, newly. See *Newly industrializing economies.*

Industries, aerospace. See *Aerospace industries.*

Industries, border. See *Border industries.*

Industries, cottage. See *Home based businesses; Small businesses.*

Industries, high technology. See *High technology industries.*

Industries, primitive. See *Primitive industries.*

Industries, rural. See *Rural industries.*

Industries, service. See *Service industries.*

Industry. Industr(y,ies,ial). *Choose from:* industr(y,ies,ial), factor(y,ies), manufactur(ing), mill(s), plant(s) *with:* light, heavy, chemical, construction, electronics, garment, machine tool, manufacturing, metal, mining, petroleum, publishing, retail, service, shipping, textile(s). *Consider also:* manufactur(ing,er,ers), production, factor(y,ies), industrial organization(s), plant(s), enterprise(s), firm(s), corporation(s), compan(y,ies). *See also* Aerospace industries; Agribusiness; Automobile industry; Book industry; Cattle industry; Cigarette industry; Coffee industry; Commodities; Computer industry; Entertainment industry; Fisheries; Forestry; Garment industry; Gas industry; High technology industries; Home based businesses; Horse industry; Industrial capacity; Industrial concentration; Industrial efficiency; Industrial enterprises; Industrial management; Industrial museums; Industrial promotion; Industrial societies; Industrial cities and towns; Industrial workers; Iron industry; Labor management relations; Lumber industry; Machine tool industry; Maritime industry; Marketing; Metal industry; Migration of industry; Military industrial complex; Nut industry; Oil industry; Plant closings; Postindustrial societies; Production; Productivity; Private sector; Raw materials; Rubber industry; Service industries; Shipping industry; Textile industry; Technology; Tobacco industry; Toy industry; Transportation.

Industry, aircraft. See *Aircraft industry.*

Industry, airplane. See *Aircraft industry.*

Industry, animal. See *Animal industry.*

Industry, automobile. See *Automobile industry.*

Industry, beverage. See *Beverage industry.*

Industry, book. See *Book industry.*

Industry, brewing. See *Brewing industry.*

Industry, cattle. See *Cattle industry.*

Industry, cigarette. See *Cigarette industry.*

Industry, clothing. See *Clothing industry.*

Industry, coal. See *Coal industry.*

Industry, coffee. See *Coffee industry.*

Industry, computer. See *Computer industry.*

espionage; Intangible property; Land (property); Patents; White collar crime.

Industry, construction. See *Construction industry.*

Industry, defense. See *Defense spending; Military industrial complex.*

Industry, electronics. See *High technology industries.*

Industry, entertainment. See *Entertainment industry.*

Industry, fashion. See *Garment industry.*

Industry, firearms. See *Firearms industry.*

Industry, food. See *Food industry.*

Industry, garment. See *Garment industry.*

Industry, gas. See *Gas industry.*

Industry, horse. See *Horse industry.*

Industry, hospitality. See *Hospitality industry.*

Industry, iron. See *Iron industry.*

Industry, knit goods. See *Knit goods industry.*

Industry, leather. See *Leather industry.*

Industry, liquor. See *Liquor industry.*

Industry, logging. See *Lumber industry.*

Industry, lumber. See *Lumber industry.*

Industry, machine tool. See *Machine tool industry.*

Industry, maritime. See *Maritime industry.*

Industry, meat. See *Meat industry*

Industry, metal. See *Metal industry.*

Industry, migration of. See *Migration of industry.*

Industry, milk. See *Milk industry.*

Industry, mining. See *Mining industry.*

Industry, nut. See *Nut industry.*

Industry, oil. See *Oil industry.*

Industry, relocation of. See *Migration of industry.*

Industry, rubber. See *Rubber industry.*

Industry, sex. See *Sex industry.*

Industry, shipping. See *Shipping industry.*

Industry, textile. See *Textile industry.*

Industry, tobacco. See *Tobacco industry.*

Industry, toy. See *Toy industry.*

Industry, travel. See *Tourism.*

Industry, whiskey. See *Liquor industry.*

Industry, wood. See *Lumber industry.*

Industry workers, electronics. See *Electronics industry workers.*

Ineffable, The. See *Deities; God concepts; Religious beliefs.*

Inequality. Inequality. Inequit(y,ies). Unequal. Uneven development. Disparit(y,ies). Unfair(ness). Injustice(s).
Difference(s). Differential(s). Disproportionate. Discrimination. Favoritism. Unequal opportunit(y,ies). Inegalitarian(ism). Servitude. Racial exclusion. Stigma. Minority status. Sexism. Racism. Ageism. Caste(s). Discrimination. Oppression. Privilege(d). Underprivileged. Segregation. Stratification. School tracking. Social difference(s). Internal colonialism. *See also* Favoritism; Global inequality; Income inequality; Injustice; Occupational segregation; Oppression; Political repression; Prejudice; Racial segregation; Sexual division of labor; Sexual inequality; Social discrimination; Social justice; Stratification; Tracking (education); Wage differentials.

Inequality, economic. See *Center and periphery; Dependency theory (international); Dual economy; Economic underdevelopment; Global inequality; Imperialism; Income inequality; International division of labor; Labor market segmentation; Occupational segregation; Sexual division of labor; Women living in poverty; World systems theory.*

Inequality, gender. See *Sexual inequality.*

Inequality, global. See *Global inequality.*

Inequality, income. See *Income inequality.*

Inequality, sexual. See *Sexual inequality.*

Inequality, social. See *Inequality.*

Infallibility. Infallib(le,ly,ility). Inerran(t, cy). Unerring(ly). Inerrab(le,ly,ility). *Consider also:* unfailing(ly), flawless(ness), impeccab(le,ly,ility), faultless(ness), believab(le,ly,ility), incontestab(le,ly,ility), incontrovertab(le, ly,ility), indisputab(le,ly,ility), irrefutab(le,ly,ility), unquestionab(le,ly, ility), accurate(ly), correct(ly,ness), dependab(le,ly,ility), reliab(le,ly,ility), trustworth(y,iness). *See also* Beliefs; Certainty; Correctness; Flawless; Religious fundamentalism.

Infancy. See *Infants.*

Infant baptism. Infant baptism. *Choose from:* infant(s), bab(y,ies) *with:* baptis(ed,m,ing), baptiz(ed,m,ing), baptismal rite(s), christen(ed,ing), immersion. *See also* Baptism; Infant salvation; Infants.

Infant care. Infant care. *Choose from:* infant(s), neonate(s), neonatal, newborn(s), bab(y,ies), postnatal *with:* care, caring, incubator(s), feed(ing), fed, nurs(ed,ing), diaper(ed,ing), intensive care, hold(ing), held, rock(ed,ing), comfort(ed,ing). *See also* Bottle feeding; Breast feeding; Infant nutrition; Nurseries; Postnatal care.

Infant death, sudden. See *Sudden infant death.*

Infant development. Infant development. *Choose from:* infant(s), neonate(s), neonatal, newborn(s), bab(y,ies), postnatal, perinatal *with:* development(al,ally), maturation(al), weight gain(s), grow(ing,th), transition(s), neurodevelopment(al,ally). *See also* Early childhood development; Failure to thrive (psychosocial); Physical development; Psychogenesis.

Infant formula. Infant formula(s). Baby formula(s). Breastmilk substitute(s). *See also* Bottle feeding; Infant care; Infant nutrition.

Infant mortality. Infant mortalit(y,ies). Stillbirth(s). Stillborn(s). *Choose from:* infant(s), perinatal, fetal, neonatal, birth(s), newborn(s), bab(y,ies), postneonatal *with:* mortalit(y,ies), death rate, death(s), dead. *See also* Abortion; Fetal death; Health transition; Infanticide; Medical geography; Miscarriages; Mortality rates; World health.

Infant nutrition. Infant nutrition. *Choose from:* infant(s), neonate(s), neonatal, newborn(s), bab(y,ies) *with:* feed(ing), dietetic(s), nutrition(al), nutrient(s), nourish(ed,ing,ment), human milk, breast milk, suckling, wean(ed,ing), breast feed(ing), diet(s,ary), food, vitamin(s), vitamin deficienc(y,ies), malnutrition, formula(s), bottle feed(ing). *See also* Breast feeding; Bottle feeding; Infant care; Infant formula.

Infant salvation. Infant salvation. *Choose from:* little child(ren), infant(s), bab(y,ies) *with:* salvation, save(d), faith, spiritual condition(s), regeneration, religious status. *Consider also:* infant damnation. *See also* Infant baptism; Infants; Salvation.

Infant small for gestational age. Infant small for gestational age. *Consider also:* small for date(s), SGA, low birthweight, growth retard(ed,ation), light for date, immature, *with:* infant(s), newborn(s), neonate(s), bab(y,ies). *Consider also:* growth retard(ed,ation) *with:* fetus(es), fetal. *See also* Birth weight; Newborn infants; Premature infants; Very low birth weight infants.

Infant vocalization. Infant vocalization. Prelinguistic. Preverbal communication. Prespeech. Early speech. *Choose from:* infant(s), neonate(s), neonatal, newborn(s), bab(y,ies), early *with:* utterance(s), vocaliz(e,ed,ing,ation, ations), babbl(e,ed,es,ing), vocal interaction(s), conversation(s,al), vocal response(s), vocal behavior(s). *See also* Crying; Vocalization.

Infanticide. Infanticide. Neonaticide. *Choose from:* sacrific(e,ed,ing), kill(ed,ing), murder(ed,ing), euthanasia *with:* girl(s), baby, babies, first born(s), infant(s), young child(ren), newborn(s).

Consider also: prolicide. *See also* Abortion; Antisocial behavior; Family violence; Homicide; Infant mortality; Neonaticide.

Infantile neurosis. See *Childhood neurosis.*

Infantile psychosis, symbiotic. See *Symbiotic infantile psychosis.*

Infantilism. Infantil(e,ism,istic). Hypoevolut(e,ism). Psychoinfantil(e, ism). Underdevelop(ed,ment). *Consider also:* late maturing, retarded development, childish(ness), arrested development, infantile characteristic(s), microsomia, dwarf(ism,ish,ishness), hypogenitalism, juvenil(e,ism), persistent pubert(y,ism), ateliosis, puerilism, hypopituitarism, immatur(e,ity). *See also* Immaturity.

Infantry. Infantr(y,ies,yman). Foot soldier(s). Groundtroop(s). Men-at-arms. *See also* Army personnel; Combat.

Infants. Infan(t,ts,cy). Bab(y,ies). Newborn(s). Neonat(e,es,al). Toddler(s). *See also* Birth injuries; Birth weight; Children; Developmental stages; Fetus; Infant baptism; Infant development; Infant salvation; Infant small for gestational age; Newborn infants; Premature infants; Severely handicapped infants.

Infants, animal. See *Animal offspring.*

Infants, low birth weight. See *Infant small for gestational age; Premature infants.*

Infants, newborn. See *Newborn infants.*

Infants, premature. See *Premature infants.*

Infants, severely handicapped. See *Severely handicapped infants.*

Infants, very low birth weight. See *Very low birth weight infants.*

Infectious disorders. Infectious disorder(s). Infection(s). *Choose from:* infect(ive, ious), contagious, communicable, transmissable, bacteria(l), protozoa(n) *with:* disease(s), disorder(s). *Consider also:* epidemic(s), virus(es), viral, germ(s). *See also* Acute disease; AIDS; Bacteria; Chronic disease; Disease; Disease susceptibility; Epidemics; Etiology; Morbidity; Premorbidity; Sexually transmitted diseases; Vaccinations.

Inference. Inferenc(e,es,ed,ing). Infer(red, ring,ential,entially). *Consider also:* extrapolat(ed,ing,ion), implicat(e,ed,ing, ion), surmis(e,ed,ing), deduc(e,ed,ing, tion), discern(ed,ing,ment), deductive thinking, inductive reasoning, corollar(y,ies), suppos(e,ed,ing,ition), constru(e,ed,ing). *See also* Abduction (logic); Cognitive processes; Communication skills; Deduction; Implications; Induction; Logical thinking; Reasoning; Thinking.

Inference, statistical. See *Statistical inference.*

Inferiority, emotional. See *Emotional inferiority.*

Infertility. Infertil(e,ity). Infecundity. Steril(e,ity). Inability to conceive. Reproductive barrier(s). Unable to conceive. *Consider also:* barren(ness), childless(ness), oligospermia. *See also* Childlessness; Female genital disorders; Fertility; Fertility enhancement; Male genital disorders; Sexually transmitted diseases.

Infidelity. See *Extramarital relations.*

Infidelity, marital. See *Extramarital relations.*

Infidels. Infidel(s,ic). Heathen(s,ism,dom, ize,ized). Unbeliever(s). Outside the faith. Heretic(s,al,ally). Disbeliever(s). Irreligionist(s). Pagan(s). Gentile(s). Giaour. *Consider also:* agnostic(s), free thinker(s). *See also* Atheism; Crusades; Heresy; Irreligion; Otherness; Paganism.

Infinitum, ad. See *Endlessness.*

Infinity. Infinit(e,y,ude,eness). Unlimited(ness). Limitless(ness). Illimitab(ility,leness). Unbounded(ness). Boundless(ness). Bottomless(ness). Measureless(ness). Inexhaustib(le,leness, ility). Endless(ness). *See also* Endlessness; Eternity; Immeasurability.

Inflation (economics). Inflation(ary). Inflated currency. Hyperinflation. Decreased purchasing power. Bull market(s). *Choose from:* high, rising, spiral(s,ling), runaway, inflated *with:* price(s), cost(s). *Consider also:* stagflation, hesiflation, overheat(ed,ing) econom(y,ies). *See also* Business cycles; Cost control; Disinflation; Economic change; Economic conditions; Economic crises; Economic indicators; Economic problems; Economic stabilization; Price control; Price trends; Prices; Purchasing power; Supply side economics.

Inflection. Inflect(ed,ion,ional,ions). Intonation(al). Intoned. Prosod(y,ic,ical). Phonological stress. *Choose from:* stress(ed,ing), accent(ed,ing), duration, emphasis *with:* syllable(s), word(s), vowel(s), pattern(s). *Consider also:* modulation, pitch pattern(s), lilt(ing), cadence *with:* vocal, speech, utterance(s). *See also* Cadence; Intonation (phonetics); Lexical phonology; Speech characteristics; Suprasegmentals; Voice.

Influence. Influenc(e,es,ing). Influential(ity). Impact(ing,ed,s). Persua(de, ding,sion). Sway(ed,ing). Affect(ed,ing). Bring pressure(s). Determin(e,ed,ing,ant, ants). Urge(d). Compel(led,ling). Modif(y,ication). Rule(d). Incite(d). Deter(red,ring,rent). Facilitat(e,ed,ing). Prevail(ing). Constrain(t,ts,ing).

Mediat(e,ed,ing). Leadership. Power. Authority. Ascendan(cy,t). Inspir(e,ed,ing). Inspiration(al). Predispos(e,ed,ing,ition). Predominat(e,ing). Predominant(ly). Counterbalance. Manipulat(e,ed,ing, ion). Win(ning) support. *See also* Family influence; Influence (literary, artistic, etc.); Informal Social Control; Incitement; Interpersonal influences; Inspiration; Machiavellianism; Peer influences; Political power; Social influences.

Influence (literary, artistic etc). Influence(s). Intertextuality. Intertext(s). Literary tradition(s). *Choose from:* litera(ry,ture), poet(s,ic,ry), art(s,ist, ists,istic), music(al,ally), musician(s), work(s) *with:* influence(s,d), philosophical framework, draw(s,n) from theme(s), quotation(s), use(s,d) established literature, borrow(ed,ing) from, source(s), assimilate(s,d) idea(s), rest(ed,ing,s), on writings, similar plot structure(s), imitat(e,ed,ion), structural influence(s), thematic influence(s), literary convention(s), parallel(s), tradition(s,al). *See also* Arts; Influence; Intertextuality; Literature; Music; Quotations.

Influence, family. See *Family influence.*

Influence, parent. See *Family influence.*

Influence, spheres of. See *Spheres of influence.*

Influence of age on ability. Influence of age on ability. *Choose from:* age change(s), developmental change(s), age difference(s), school age, younger, old age, older, middle age(d), role of aging, longitudinal survey(s) *with:* learning abilit(y,ies), performance, memory, cognitive skill(s), competence, problem solving, symbolic abilit(y,ies), wisdom, expertise. *See also* Ability level; Aging; Competence; Developmental stages.

Influence on nature. See *Environmental impacts.*

Influences. See *Acceleration effects; Altitude effects; Behavioral genetics; Biological factors; Causality; Determinism; Drug effects; Environmental determinism; Environmental effects; Environmental impacts; Geographic determinism; Gravitational effects; Heat effects; Influence; Interpersonal influences; Mass media effects; Mind body problem; Nature nurture; Noise effects; Peer influences; Psychobiology; Sex factors; Social factors; Social influences; Sociobiology; Sociocultural factors; Socioeconomic factors; Temperature effects; Time factors; Underwater effects.*

Influences, cultural. See *Social influences.*

Influences, interpersonal. See *Interpersonal influences.*

Influences, peer. See *Peer influences.*

Influences, social. See *Social influences.*

Info fatigue syndrome. Info fatigue syndrome. Stress caused by information overload. *Choose from:* information, info, communication(s), message(s), junk mail, image(s), electronic media, sound(s), sensory *with:* overload(ed, ing), flood(ing), overabundance, bombard(ed,ing), huge amount(s) *with:* stress(ed,ing,or,ors), overwhelm(ed,ing), cop(e,ing), hazard(s,ous). *Consider also:* analysis paralysis, technostress(es,or, ors). *See also* Burnout; Fatigue; Fragmentation (experience); Human information storage; Information society; Mental fatigue; Stress.

Infobahn. See *Information highway.*

Infomercials. Infomercial(s). Advertorial(s). *Choose from:* commercial(s), advertisement(s) promotion(al,s), ad(s) *with:* disclosure(s) information(al), education(al), informative. *See also* Advertising; Newspaper advertising; Television programs.

Informal sector. Informal sector. Informal econom(y,ies). Underground econom(y, ies). Subterranean econom(y,ies). Black market(s). Gray market(s). Hidden econom(y,ies). Parallel econom(y,ies). *See also* Bartering; Black economy; Economic exchanges; Gray market; Self employment.

Informal social control. Informal social control. *Choose from:* social, informal, peer(s), public *with:* influence(s), norm(s), label(s,ed,ing), label(led,ling), pressure(s), sanction(s), censur(e,ed, ing), punishment(s), conformity, reinforcement, approval, coercion, opinion(s). *Consider also:* cultural constraint(s). *See also* Cultural values; Influence; Interpersonal influences; Negative sanctions; Norms; Peer influences; Public opinion; Public opposition; Public support; Social influences; Social pressure; Social support; Social values; Stereotyping.

Informants. See *Espionage; Informers; Respondents; Whistle blowing.*

Information. Information(al). Message(s). Data. Fact(s). Briefing(s). Report(s). News. Record(s). Text(s). Communique(s). Notice(s). Grey literature. Technical literature. Technical publication(s). Technical publish(er,ers,ing). Report(s). Brochure(s). Guide(s). Product information. Product description(s). *Consider also:* document(s), blueprint(s), book(s), letter(s), manuscript(s), source(s), knowledge. *See also* Annual reports; Automated information retrieval; Automated information storage; Case studies; Communication (thought transfer); Data; Data analysis; Data collection; Data interpretation; Data processing; Diffusion; Diffusion of innovation; Dissertations; Documentation; Geographic information systems; Information dissemination; Information exchange; Information leaks; Information processing; Information services; Information theories; Knowledge level; Messages; Research; Technological change; Technical information; Trivia.

Information, access to. See *Access to information.*

Information, classified. See *Classified information.*

Information, consumer. See *Consumer awareness; Consumer education; Consumer protection; Product labeling.*

Information, freedom of. See *Freedom of information.*

Information, sex. See *Sex information.*

Information, technical. See *Technical information.*

Information age. See *Information society.*

Information centers. Information center(s). Information clearinghouse(s). Learning resource center(s). Information office(s). Information service(s). Information provider(s). *See also* Archives; Information services; Libraries.

Information dissemination. Information dissemination. *Choose from:* information, data, knowledge, document(s), intellectual property, innovation(s), research result(s), message(s) *with:* transfer(s), exchange, feedback, fax(ed,ing), facsimile transmission, diffusion, shar(e,ed,ing), reporting, delivery, disclos(e,ed,ure), suppl(y,ying, ied), popularization, conduit(s), disseminat(e,ed,ing,ion), transmi(t,ted, ting,ssion), switching, flow, communicat(e,ed,ing,ion), circulat(e,ed,ing,ion), network(s,ing), grapevine(s). *Consider also:* media coverage, newspaper coverage, propaganda, citation pattern(s), technology transfer(s). *See also* Adoption of ideas; Attribution of news; Automated information retrieval; Bibliographic citations; Broadcasting; Communication (thought transfer); Communications research; Delivery of services; Diffusion; Diffusion of innovation; Digital communications; Distributed artificial intelligence; Documentation; Electronic mail; Electronic publishing; Freedom of information; House organs; Information centers; Information exchange; Information leaks; Information processing; Information services; Libraries; Mass media; News agencies; News coverage; News media; Newspapers; Press conferences; Propaganda; Publishing; Reference materials; Referral; Technology transfer.

Information exchange. Information(al) exchange(s). Upward communication(s). Downward communication(s). Briefing(s). Report(s). Communique(s). Feedback. *Choose from:* information(al), message(s), data, fact(s), news, record(s), text(s), account(s) *with:* exchange(s), transfer(red,ring,s,rence), diffusion, communicat(e,ed,ing,ion), share(d), sharing, flow, supply(ing), supplied, disclos(e,ed,ing,ure), report(ed,ing,s), disseminat(e,ed,ing, ion). *Consider also:* newsgroup(s), groupware, common work project(s), shared product catalog(s). *See also* Communication (thought transfer); Extranets; Firewalls (computers); Gossip; Gossip sites; Grapevine; Information dissemination; Intranets; Press conferences.

Information fatigue syndrome. See *Info fatigue syndrome.*

Information highway. Information highway(s). Information superhighway(s). Internet. Open computer network(s). Global information. Infobahn. *Consider also:* network(s) of network(s), infohighway, I-way, cyberspace, information infrastructure, electronic superhighway(s), digital data, electronic copying, online services, telephone network(s), communication(s) satellite(s). *See also* Community networks (computer); Copyright; Cybercommunities; Cyberlaw; Electronic data interchange; Information networks; Information society; Information skills; Interactive computer systems; Internationalism; Internet (computer network); Internet service providers; Internet traffic; Online privacy; Privacy laws; Teledemocracy; World citizenship.

Information leaks. Information leak(s). Unauthorized disclosure. *Choose from:* leak(ed,s), disclos(e,ed,ing,ure), divulg(e,ed,ing), reveal(ed,ing), publish(ed,ing), broadcast(ed,ing), releas(e,ed,ing) *with:* confidential, classified, secret, private *with:* information, sources, data, message(s), document(s), note(s), record(s). *See also* Access to information; Attribution of news; Censorship; Classified information; Gossip; Government secrecy; Grapevine; Journalistic ethics; News coverage; News policies; Press conferences; Whistle blowing.

Information literacy. Information literacy. *Choose from:* information, search(ing), data, digital, media, problem solving, critical thinking, library *with:* litera(cy, te), competen(ce,cy,t), skill(s), knowledge, abilit(y,ies). *See also* Computer illiteracy; Computer literacy; Critical thinking; Information skills; Information society; Intellectual capital; Knowledge workers; Literacy; Skills obsolescence.

Information management. See *Archives; Automated information retrieval; Automated information storage; Competitive intelligence; Computer assisted decision making; Data collection; Data processing; Decision support systems; Image processing; Information dissemination; Information processing; Information services; Knowledge management; Management information systems; Records management.*

Information networks. Information network(s,ing). Computer network(s). WAN(s). LAN(s). Telecommunications network(s). Internet service provider(s). Supercomputing network(s). Internet gateway(s). *Consider also:* Internet, network(s) of network(s), electronic gateway(s), online service(s), networking environment, internetworked computer(s), intranet(s), extranet(s), CompuServe, America Online, Prodigy, AT&T, Delphi, GEnie, etc. *See also* Automated information retrieval; Community networks (computer); Connectivity; Electronic data interchange; Home pages; Information highway; Internet (computer network); Internet service providers; Network backup.

Information overload. See *Info fatigue syndrome.*

Information policy. Information polic(y, ies). *Choose from:* information, online, information superhighway(s), supercomputing network(s), librar(y,ies), data, website(s), World Wide Web, Internet, record(s), archive(s), secre(cy,t,ts) *with:* polic(y,ies), regulat(e,ed,ing,ion,ions), deregulat(e, ed,ing,ion), prohibit(ed,ing,ion), restrict(ed,ing,ion,ions), classified, standard(s), guideline(s). *Consider also:* Freedom of Information Act, First Amendment, Communications Decency Act, Joint Committee on Printing, Government Printing Office, Access to Information and Privacy Act [Canada], National Archives of Canada Act. *See also* Access to information; Broadcasting censorship; Censorship; Copyright; Classified information; Cyberlaw; Freedom of information; Freedom of the press; Government publicity; Government secrecy; Indecent communications; Information highway; Malinformation; Mass media policy; News policies; Political repression; Pornography; Social values.

Information processing. Information processing. *Choose from:* information, data, knowledge, message(s) *with:* collect(ed,ing,ion), storage, retrieval, process(ed,ing), massag(e,ed,es,ing), coding, code(s,d), assess(ed,ing,ment). *See also* Automated information retrieval; Automated information storage; Cognition; Communication (thought transfer); Cybernetics; Data collection; Data processing; Documentation; Image processing; Information dissemination; Information services; Knowledge management; Records management.

Information processing, human. See *Human information storage.*

Information retrieval, automated. See *Automated information retrieval.*

Information retrieval, online. See *Automated information retrieval*

Information retrieval systems. See *Automated information retrieval.*

Information seeking. Information seeking. *Choose from:* seek(ing), sought, desir(e,ed,ing), need(ed,ing), search(ed, ing), request(ed,ing,s), collect(ed,ing) *with:* information, data. *Consider also:* inquir(y,ies), question(ed,ing), ask(ed, ing), search strateg(y,ies). *See also* Access to information; Communication (thought transfer); Information exchange; Information services; Library users; Problem solving; Questioning; Search, Search strategies.

Information services. Information service(s). *Choose from:* information *with:* center(s), dissemination, service(s), system(s), source(s), provider(s), network(s), retrieval. *Consider also:* librar(y,ies), reference service(s). *See also* Automated information retrieval; Automated information storage; Information centers; Information dissemination; Information processing; Information seeking; Libraries; Library instruction; Referral.

Information skills. Information skill(s). Information litera(te,cy). *Choose from:* information, media *with:* literacy, skill(s), proficien(t,cy), competen(ce,cy, cies,t), abilit(y,ies). *See also* Automated information retrieval; Computer literacy; Information highway; Information literacy; Information society; Library instruction; Library services; Minimum competencies.

Information society. Information society. Information age. Post-information society. Digital age. *Consider also:* cyberspace, virtual reality, information driven society, global information revolution, technological future(s). *See also* Automation; Community networks (computer); Cybercommunities; Digital money; Digital signatures; Information literacy; E-commerce; Electronic data interchange; Info fatigue syndrome; Information highway; Information skills; Interactive computer systems; Internationalism; Internet (computer network); Millennium bug; Modern civilization; Online users; Postindustrial societies; Technology and civilization;

Teledemocracy; V-commerce; Virtual libraries; Virtual reality; World citizenship.

Information storage, automated. See *Automated information storage.*

Information storage, human. See *Human information storage.*

Information superhighway. See *Information highway.*

Information systems, geographic. See *Geographic information systems.*

Information systems, management. See *Management information systems.*

Information theory. Information theor(y,ies). *Choose from:* information, message(s), encoding, decoding, recoding, communication *with:* theor(y,ies), axiom(s,atic), construct(s), generalization(s), hypothes(is,es,ize,ized,izing), model(s), paradigm(s). *See also* Information; Theories.

Informed consent. Informed consent. *Choose from:* consent, signed permission *with:* treatment(s), patient(s), operat(e,ed,ion,ions), therap(y,ies,eutic), immunization(s), medical, surg(ery,ical), physician(s). *Choose from:* consent, permission *with:* valid, form(s), prox(y,ies), sign(ed,ature), written, right to know. *Consider also:* Helsinki declaration, right to refuse, voluntary admission form. *See also* Civil rights; Consent (law); Experiment volunteers; Human experimentation; Involuntary sterilization; Legal competency; Parental consent; Patient compliance; Patient rights; Research ethics; Research subjects; Treatment withholding; Truth disclosure.

Informers. Informer(s). Informant(s). Anonymous caller(s). Reverse sting(s). *Consider also:* press leak(s), intelligence work, mole(s), gossip(s,ed,ing), intelligence team(s), leak(ed,ing) to the press. *See also* Accomplices; Collaborators; Espionage; Whistle blowing.

Infowar. Infowar(s,fare). Information war(s,farc). Cyberwar(s,fare). Netwar(s,fare). Infowarrior(s). Cyberwarrior(s). Net warrior(s). *Consider also:* computer espionage, computer counterintelligence, computer terror(ism,ist,ists). *See also* Computer crimes; Computer security; Espionage.

Infrastructure (economics). Infrastructure. Social overhead capital. *Consider also:* public utilit(y,ies), public service(s), public work(s), transport(ation) system(s), gas, electricity, water system(s), road(s), highway(s), bridge(s), airport(s), sewage, railway(s), railroad(s), telephone system(s), communication system(s). *See also* Airports; Capital (financial); Human ecology; Local finance; Municipal government; Regional development; Sustainable development; Public administration; Public works.

Ingratiation. See *Impression management.*

Inhabitants. Inhabitant(s). Habitant(s). Dweller(s). Occupant(s). Addresee(s). Resident(s). Householder(s). Tenant(s). Renter(s). Boarder(s). Roomer(s). Settler(s). Native(s). Villager(s). Towns(men,man,people,woman, women). Civilian(s). Denizen(s). *Consider also:* citizen(s), voter(s), taxpayer(s), ratepayer(s). *See also* Citizens; Occupancy; Population.

Inhalant abuse. Inhalant abuse(r,rs). Glue sniffing. *Choose from:* sniff(ed,ing), inhal(e,ed,ing) inhalation, abus(e,ed,ing) *with:* solvent(s), glue(s), toluene, benzine, toluol, carbon tetrachloride, naptha, amyl nitrite, nitrous oxide, gasoline, vapor, cleaning fluid(s), laughing gas, correction fluid, thinner(s). *See also* Solvent abuse; Substance abuse; Toxic inhalation.

Inhalation, toxic. See *Toxic inhalation.*

Inheritance. Inherit(ed,ing,ance). Patrimon(y,ial). Heritage. Legac(y,ies). Birthright. Intergenerational transfer(s). Neopatrimonialism. *Consider also:* will(s), testament(s,ary), succession. *See also* Administration of estates; Ascription; Beneficiaries; Birth order; Descent; Disinheritance; Estate planning; Estates (law); Heirs; Heritage; Kinship; Land (property); Legacies; Personal property.

Inherited status. See *Ascription.*

Inhibited sexual desire. See *Sexual inhibitions.*

Inhibition (psychology). Inhibit(ed,ion, ions). Block(s,ing,ed). Mental block(s). Hangup(s). Hang up(s). Interference in learning. Learning interference. Restrain(t,ed). Repressed. Held back. Self denying. Reserve(d). Self control. Reticen(t,ce). Constrained. Abstinen(t,ce). Self censor(ing,ship). *Consider also:* superego. *See also* Anxiety; Fear of closeness; Fear of failure; Fear of God; Fear of men; Fear of success; Fear of women; Learned helplessness; Personality traits; Self control; Sexual inhibitions.

Inhibition, proactive. See *Proactive inhibition.*

Inhibition, reactive. See *Reactive inhibition.*

Inhibition, retroactive. See *Retroactive inhibition.*

Inhibitions, sexual. See *Sexual inhibitions.*

Initiation rites. Initiation rite(s). *Consider also:* initiation(s), pubertal, passage(s), entry, induction *with:* rite(s), ritual(s), ceremon(y,ies). *Consider also:* hazing.

See also Hazing; Life stage transitions; Religious rituals; Rites of passage; Ritual disfigurement.

Initiative (personal). Initiative(s). Enterprising. Energetic. Bold(ness). Forceful(ness). Adventurous(ness). Will power. Taking the lead. Self determination. Independent behavior(s). Independen(t,ce). Autonom(y,ous). Enthusias(m,tic). Ambitious(ness). Aggressive(ness). Aspiring. *See also* Ambitions; Ambitiousness; Enthusiasm; Personal independence; Personalism; Personality traits.

Injured, brain. See *Brain damaged.*

Injuries. Injur(y,ies). Wound(s,ed). Trauma(s,tic). Abrasion(s). Burn(ed,s). Fracture(d,s). Lacerat(ed,ing,ion,ions). Scald(ed,s). Contusion(s). Dislocat(ed, ion,ions). Cut(s). Bruise(d,s). Black eye(s). Fall(s). Sprain(s). Strain(s). Gunshot wound(s). Knocked out. Blow(s). Rupture(d,s). Concussion(s). Lesion(s). Puncture(d,s). Stab(bed, bings). Insect bite(s). Sting(s). Drowning(s). Frostbite. *See also* Abdominal injuries; Accident prevention; Accidental falls; Accidents; Birth injuries; Brain damage; Coma; Disability; Disorders; Head injuries; Hemorrhage; Industrial accidents; Lesions; Paraplegia; Personal injuries; Physical disfigurement; Quadriplegia; Safety; Self inflicted wounds; Spinal cord injuries.

Injuries, abdominal. See *Abdominal injuries.*

Injuries, birth. See *Birth injuries.*

Injuries, brain. See *Brain damage.*

Injuries, head. See *Head injuries.*

Injuries, occupational. See *Agricultural workers disease; Black lung disease; Hazardous materials; Hazards of video display terminals; Industrial accidents; Injuries; Multiple chemical sensitivities; Occupational diseases; Occupational exposure; Occupational neuroses; Occupational safety; Occupational stress; Repetitive motion disorders; Sick building syndrome.*

Injuries, personal. See *Personal injuries.*

Injuries, spinal cord. See *Spinal cord injuries.*

Injustice. Injustice. Unfair(ness). Unjust(ness). Inequit(y,ies,able). Inequality. Iniquit(y,ies). Wrong(s,ed,ful, fulness). Wrongdoing(s). Partial(ity). Discriminat(e,ed,ing,ory). Bigot(s,ed, ry). Abuse(s). Favoritism. Grievance(s). Infring(e,ed,ing,ement,ements). Encroach(ed,ing,ment,ments). Oppression. *See also* Age discrimination; Bias; Favoritism; Inequality; Restraint of trade; Sex discrimination; Social discrimination.

Ink blot tests. Ink blot test(s). Inkblot test(s). Inkblot technique(s). Rorschach inkblot(s). Holtzman inkblot test(s,ing). Rorschach test(s,ing). *See also* Projective techniques.

Ink painting. Ink painting. Chinese brush painting. Chinese painting. Japanese ink painting. *Choose from:* Chinese ink, India(n) ink, Japanese ink *with:* paint(ing,ings), draw(ing,ings). *See also* Arts; Drawing.

Inland water transportation. Inland water transportation. Inland navigation. Inland waterway(s). Canal route(s). Navigable river(s). *Consider also:* St. Lawrence seaway, Inland waterway system, etc. *See also* Rivers; Water transportation.

Inmates. See *Inpatients; Institutionalization (persons); Institutionalized children; Institutionalized mentally retarded; Prisoners.*

Inmates, prison. See *Prisoners.*

Inner cities. Inner cit(y,ies). Central cit(y,ies). City center(s). Downtown(s). Urban neighborhood(s). Midtown. Ghetto(s,es). Slum(s). Business district(s). Shopping district(s). Business area(s). Commercial district(s). Industrial district(s). *See also* Cities; Civic improvement; Commercial districts; Ethnic neighborhoods; Poverty areas; Slums.

Inner directed. Inner direct(ed,edness,ion). Intrinsic motivation. Internal locus of control. Internalized goal(s). Internal(ized) value system. Self direct(ed,ion). *Consider also:* self efficacy, introver(t,ted,sion). *See also* Locus of control; Other directed.

Inner speech. Inner speech. Inner language. Subvocal. *See also* Self talk.

Innocence. Innocen(ce,t). Blameless(ness). Chast(e,ity). Naive. Inexperienced. Unsullied. Free(dom) from guilt. Free(dom) from sin. Unsophisticated. Unaware(ness). Unfamiliar(ity). Unknowing(ness). *See also* Harmlessness; Immaturity; Morality; Purity; Simplicity; Virginity.

Inoculation. See *Prevention; Vaccinations.*

Innovation, diffusion of. See *Diffusion of innovation.*

Innovation, organizational. See *Organizational innovation.*

Innovation, social. See *Social change.*

Innovations. Innovat(ion,ions,ive,iveness). New technolog(y,ies). New ideas. New approach(es). New synthes(is,es). Invention(s). Improvement(s). Reconceptualiz(e,ed,ing,ation). New practice(s). Reshaping. Reforming. *Consider also:* fostering change(s), change agent(s), adoption of practice(s), experimental, creativ(e,ity). *See also*

Adoption of ideas; Agricultural innovations; Agricultural mechanization; Alternatives; Change; Discoveries (findings); Educational innovations; Experiments; Improvement; Intrapreneurship; Inventions; Medical innovations; Modernization; Research applications; Technological innovations; Technology transfer.

Innovations, agricultural. See *Agricultural innovations.*

Innovations, educational. See *Educational innovations.*

Innovations, medical. See *Medical innovations.*

Innovations, technical. See *Technological innovations.*

Innovations, technological. See *Technological innovations.*

Innovativeness. See *Creativity.*

Inpatients. Inpatient(s). Hospital(ized) patient(s). Hospital(ized) child(ren). Ward patient(s). Admitted to hospital. *Choose from:* hospital(ized), ward, institution(al,alized) *with:* resident(s), patient(s), inmate(s), person(s). *Consider also:* clinical populations. *See also* Hospitalization; Patients.

Inquiries. See *Investigations; Questioning.*

Inquiries, public. See *Government investigations.*

Inquiry (theory of knowledge). Inquiry (theory of knowledge). Prov(e,ed,en,ing) assumption(s). Examin(e,ed,ing) assumption(s). In-depth look(s). Pursu(e,ed,it) of knowledge. Search for truth. Scientific method. Scientific inquir(y,ies). Historical inquir(y,ies). Ask(ed,ing) question(s). Pose(d) question(s). *See also* Epistemology; Explanation; Investigations; Knowledge; Questioning; Scientific knowledge; Scientific method; Social epistemology.

Inquisition. Inquisition. *Choose from:* suppress(ed,ing), persecut(e,ed,ing,ion), repress(ed,ing,ion), punish(ed,ing), burn(ed,ing) at the stake, inquisitor(s,ial) *with:* idol(s,atry), religious syncretism, heresy, heretic(s), blasphemy. *Consider also:* mihna, expulsion of Jews, Marrano(s), Marano(s). *See also* Antisemitism; Heresy; Persecution; Witch hunting.

Inquisitiveness. See *Curiosity.*

Insane. See *Insanity; Mental illness; Mentally ill offenders; Psychoses.*

Insane, criminally. See *Competency to stand trial; Criminal psychology; Insanity defense; Legal competency; Mentally ill offenders.*

Insane criminals. See *Competency to stand trial; Insanity defense; Legal competency; Mentally ill offenders.*

Insanity. Insan(e,ity). Alienatio mentis. *See also* Mental illness; Mentally ill offenders; Psychoses.

Insanity, double. See *Psychosis of association.*

Insanity, pleading. See *Insanity defense.*

Insanity defense. Insanity defense. *Choose from:* insan(e,ity), irresistible impulse, diminished responsibility, incompeten(t, cy) *with:* defense, guilt(y), stand trial, plea(s,d,ding). *Consider also:* McNaughton rule(s), M'Naghten rule(s), knowledge test, Durham rule(s), non compos mentis, mens rea, guilty mind, criminal intent, irresistible impulse(s), fit(ness) *with:* trial, diminished responsibility. *See also* Automatism; Competency to stand trial; Criminal intent; Forensic psychiatry; Legal competency; Mentally ill offenders.

Inscriptions. Inscription(s,al). Inscrib(e,ed, ing). Superscription(s,al). Superscrib(e, ed,ing). Epigraph(s,y). *See also* Autographs; Epigraphs; Epitaphs; Handwriting; Latin inscriptions; Paleography; Signatures.

Inscriptions, Latin. See *Latin inscriptions.*

Insect bites and stings. Insect bite(s). Insect sting(s). *Choose from:* insect(s), bee(s), wasp(s), fly, flies, yellow jacket(s), fire ant(s), honeybee(s), flea(s), tick(s), chigger(s), mosquito(es), bug(s) *with:* bite(s), bitten, sting(s), stung. *See also* Arachnidism; Flies; Insects.

Insect phobia. Insect phobia(s). Acarophob(ia,ic). *Consider also:* parasitophob(ia,ic), entomophob(ia,ic), arachneophob(ia,ic). *See also* Insect bites and stings; Phobias; Spider phobia.

Insecticides. See *Pesticides.*

Insects. Insect(a,s). Bug(s). Spider(s). Centipede(s). *Consider also:* fl(y,ies), bee(s), hornet(s), wasp(s), moth(s), cicada(s), termite(s), etc. *See also* Agricultural pests; Cicadas; Flies; Insect bites and stings.

Insecurity. Insecurit(y,ies). Timid(ity). Self-doubt(ing). Shy(ness). Apprehensive(ness). Lack(ing) confidence. Hesitan(t,cy). Self-conscious(ness). Diffiden(t,ce). Irresolute. Rootless(ness). Unsure. Wavering. Unstable. Instability. *See also* Certainty; Control; Crime prevention; Emotional security; Fear; Fear of closeness; Fear of crime; Fear of failure; Fear of God; Fear of men; Fear of success; Fear of women; National security; Phobias; Threat; Vulnerability.

Insemination, artificial. See *Artificial insemination.*

Insensitivity. Insensitiv(e,ity). Callous(ness). Unfeeling. Cold(ness). Unempathetic. Unkind(ness). Uncaring. Pitiless(ness). Unthinking.

Thoughtless(ness). Merciless(ness). Unsympathetic. Heartless(ness). Hard hearted. *See also* Emotional abuse; Cruelty; Cynicism; Egocentrism; Imperviousness; Personality traits; Psychologically abused men.

Inservice teacher education. Inservice teacher education. *Choose from:* inservice training, staff development, continuing education, retraining, workshop(s) *with:* teacher(s), teaching staff, faculty, educator(s). *See also* Continuing education; Faculty development; Inservice training; Teachers.

Inservice training. Inservice training. On the job training. *Choose from:* inservice, in-house, personnel, company offered, staff, work related, employee(s) *with:* training, education, development, enrichment, renewal, orientation, workshop(s), course(s), retraining. *See also* Continuing education; Inservice teacher education; Staff development; Upskilling.

Insight. Insight(ful,s). Enlighten(ed,ing, ment). Peak experience(s). Understand(ing). Knowledge. Aware(ness). Comprehension. Self awareness. Self understanding. Self knowledge. Intuit(ive,ion). Realization. Perception. Apperception. Abyssing. Discern(ed,ing,ment). Sensitivity. Perceptive(ness). Aha experience(s). *Consider also:* synthesiz(e,ed,ing) apparent opposites. *See also* Cognition; Comprehension; Imagination; Intuition; Perceptiveness (personality); Reasoning; Self knowledge.

Insight therapy. Insight therapy. *Choose from:* insight, self awareness, self understanding, self comprehension, self knowledge, self realization *with:* therap(y,ies), process(s), psychotherap(y,ies), counseling. *See also* Psychotherapy.

Insignia. Insign(ia,e,ias). Badge(s). Emblem(s), Decoration(s). Regalia. Distinguishing mark(s). Medallion(s). *Consider also:* school pin(s), school ring(s), chevron(s). *See also* Emblems; Flags; Heraldry; National emblems.

Insolvency. Insolven(t,cy). Indebted(ness). Default(ing) payments. Bankrupt(cy). Receivership. Chapter 11. Out of business. Failed business(es). Foreclos(ed,ure). *See also* Bad debts; Bank failures; Bankruptcy; Default (negligence); Organizational dissolution; Plant closings.

Insomnia. Insomn(ia,iac). Hyposomn(ia, iac). Insomnolence. Agrypn(ia,ic). Ahypn(ia,ic,osia,osic). Aypn(ia,ic). Alector(s). *Consider also:* wakeful(ness), sleep(ing) badly, poor sleeper(s), pseudoinsomnia, sleep disorder(s), sleep disturbance(s), sleep apnea, nocturnal myoclonus, restless legs syndrome. *See also* Consciousness disorders; Sleep disorders; Symptoms.

Inspection, food. See *Food inspection*

Inspiration. Inspir(e,ed,ing,ation,ationally). Invigorat(e,ed,ing,ion). Energiz(e,ed, ing). Vitaliz(e,ed,ing,ation). Reviv(e,ed, ing,ify). Revitaliz(e,ed,ing,ation). Inspirit(ed,ing). Hearten(ed,ing). Uplift(ed,ing). Encourag(e,ed,ing, ement). Boost spirit(s). Afflat(us,ion). *See also* Hopefulness; Influence; Religious life; Spiritual formation; Spirituality.

Instability. Instability. Unstable. Unstead(y,iness). Shak(y,iness). Unsubstantial(ity). Changeab(le,ility). Inconsisten(t,cy). Vulnerab(le,ility). Restless(ness). Fluctuat(e,ed,ing,ion, ions). Fickle(ness). Vacillat(e,ed,ing, ion,ions). Irresolute(ness). Waver(ed, ing). Uncertain(ty). Risk(y,iness). Unsound(ness). Precarious(ness). Flight(y,iness). Indecisive(ness). Equivocat(e,ed,ing,ion,ions). *See also* Continuity; Economic crises; Emotional instability; Fluctuations; Stability.

Instability, emotional. See *Emotional instability.*

Instinct. Instinct(s,ive,ual). Drive(s). *Choose from:* instinct(s,ive,ual), innate, species specific, congenital, unlearned, inheritable, species type, primal, basic *with:* drive(s), impulse(s), defense(s), reaction(s), nature, response(s), behavior(s). *Consider also:* homing behavior, herd instinct, life instinct, death instinct, eros, thanatos, inherited disposition, inborn drive(s). *See also* Animal behavior; Animal courtship behavior; Animal foraging behavior; Animal parental behavior; Animal sex behavior; Hunger, food deprivation; Motivation; Sex drive; Stereotyped behavior.

Instinct, death. See *Death instinct.*

Instinct, herd. See *Affiliation motivation; Group feeling; Gregariousness.*

Institutional care. See *Hospitalization; Hospitalized children; Institutionalization (persons); Institutionalized children; Institutionalized mentally retarded.*

Institutional community relations. See *Community institutional relations.*

Institutional homes. Institutional home(s). Residential center(s). Live-in institution(s). Congregate care. Community home(s). *See also* Assisted living; Boardinghouses; Custodial care; Group homes; Halfway houses; Homes for the elderly; Institutionalization (persons); Life care; Nursing homes; Psychiatric hospitals; Residential facilities; Retirement communities; Sheltered housing.

Institutional mission. Institutional mission. *Choose from:* institution(s,al), organization(s,al), college(s), universit(y, ies), agenc(y,ies), foundation(s), hospital(s) *with:* mission(s), strategic plan(s,ning), master plan(s,ning), blueprint(s), goal(s), role(s), vision(s). *Consider also:* positioning statement(s). *See also* Corporate mission; Objectives; Organizational climate; Organizational objectives; Organizational survival; Public policy; Strategic management; Strategic planning.

Institutional release. Institutional release. Deinstitutionaliz(ed,ation). Postinstitutionalization. Former inmate(s). Formerly institutionalized. *Choose from:* institution(al,s), prison(s,er,ers), inmate(s), offender(s), incarceration, correctional facilit(y,ies), state school(s), hospital(s) *with:* releas(e,ed,ing), discharg(e,ed,ing), furlough(s), parole, postrelease, halfway house(s). *See also* Deinstitutionalization; Halfway houses; Patient discharge; Psychosocial readjustment; Psychosocial rehabilitation.

Institutional schools. Institutional school(s). *Choose from:* institution(s,al, alized), hospital(s), patient(s), incarcerat(ed,ion), inmate(s), correctional facilit(y,ies), prison(s) *with:* school(s), academic, instruction(al), education(al). *Consider also:* residential school(s). *See also* Boarding schools; Correctional institutions; Criminal rehabilitation; Residential facilities;

Institutionalization (persons). Institutionaliz(e,ed,ation). Incarcerat(e,ed,ing,ion). Imprison(ed,ing). *Choose from:* institution(al), involuntary, prison *with:* commit(ted,ing,ment), consign(ed,ing, ment), incarcerat(e,ed,ing,ion), residential placement. *Consider also:* institutionalized *with:* person(s), child(ren), adolescent(s), adult(s), men, man, women, woman. *Consider also:* psychiatric commitment, hospitalization. *See also* Alternatives to incarceration; Alternatives to institutionalization; Hospitalization; Hospitalized children; Imprisonment; Institutional homes; Institutionalized children; Institutionalized mentally retarded; Intake (agency); Length of stay; Orphanages; Patient admission; Psychiatric commitment; Psychiatric hospitalization; Residential facilities; Sentencing.

Institutionalization (social). Institutionaliz(e,ed,ing,ation). Institutional embodiment. Codif(y,ied,ication). Bureaucratization. Institutionalism. Development of stable patterns. Formaliz(e,ed,ing,ation). Crystallization. Regularization. *Consider also:* culture complex(es), interrelated roles, societal institutions, ritual conformity, social control, state control. *See also* Bureaucratization; Formal social control; Rituals; Social behavior; Social institutions; Social processes.

Institutionalization, alternatives to. See *Alternatives to institutionalization.*

Institutionalization, duration of. See *Length of stay.*

Institutionalized children. Institutionalized child(ren). *Choose from:* child(ren, hood), juvenile(s), minor(s), adolescen(t,ts,ce), girl(s), boy(s), delinquent(s) *with:* institution(s,al, alized,alizing), commit(ted,ment,), borstal(s), residential care, prison(s). *See also* Children; Hospitalized children; Institutional schools; Institutionalized mentally retarded; Residential treatment.

Institutionalized mentally retarded. Institutionalized mentally retarded. *Choose from:* custod(y,ial), hospitaliz(e, ed,ing,ation), institutionaliz(e,ed,ation), state school(s), commit(ted,ment), consign(ed), institutional placement *with:* mental(ly) retard(ed,ation), mentally handicapped, mentally deficient, Down(s) syndrome. *See also* Home reared mentally retarded; Institutionalized children; Mental retardation; Residential facilities.

Institutions (organizations). See *Agencies; Alliances; Associations (organizations); Consortia; Corporations; Federations; Groups; Labor unions; Organizations; Political parties; Professional organizations; Teams.*

Institutions, correctional. See *Correctional institutions.*

Institutions, financial. See *Banking.*

Institutions, juvenile correctional. See *Reformatories.*

Institutions, religious. See *Religious institutions.*

Institutions, scientific. See *Scientific societies.*

Institutions, social. See *Social institutions.*

Instruction. See *Education; Teaching.*

Instruction, audiovisual. See *Audiovisual instruction.*

Instruction, computer aided. See *Computer assisted instruction.*

Instruction, computer assisted. See *Computer assisted instruction.*

Instruction, group. See *Group instruction.*

Instruction, individualized. See *Individualized instruction.*

Instruction, library. See *Library instruction.*

Instruction, programed. See *Programed instruction.*

Instruction, self. See *Individualized instruction.*

Instruction, sex. See *Sex education.*

Instructional media. Instructional media. Educational media. *Choose from:* teaching, school, instruction(al), education(al), curriculum, classroom, autoinstructional, course(s) *with:* media, material(s), audiovisual aid(s), computer assisted, televis(ed,ion), textbook(s), motion picture(s), programed textbook(s), machine(s), technolog(y, ies), multimedia, film(s). *See also* Audiovisual materials; Children's literature; Educational technology; Educational television; Motion pictures; Teaching; Teaching materials; Visual aids.

Instructional methods. See *Teaching methods.*

Instructional objectives. See *Educational objectives.*

Instructions, experimental. See *Experimental instructions.*

Instructions to juries. Instruction(s) to jur(y,ies,or,ors). Jury instruction. *Choose from:* instruct(ed,ing,ion,ions), preinstruct(ed,ing,ion,ions), pre-instruct(ed,ing,ion,ions), fully informed *with:* jur(y,ies,or,ors). *Consider also:* judges' instruction(s), trial instruction(s), argumentative instruction(s), cautionary instruction(s), mandatory instruction(s), peremptory instruction(s), Allen charge(s), dynamite charge(s), shotgun instruction(s), third degree instruction(s), Golden rule argument(s). *See also* Criminal proceedings; Due process; Judicial decisions; Juries; Trial (law).

Instructors. See *Teachers.*

Instrumental conditioning. Instrumental conditioning. *Choose from:* instrumental, Type II, Type R *with:* condition(ed, ing), learn(ed,ing). *See also* Operant conditioning.

Instrumental music. Instrumental music. Ensemble music. Chamber music. Orchestral music. Solo music. *Choose from:* instrumental, keyboard, chamber, orchestral, organ *with:* music, piece(s), suite(s), ensemble(s), score(s). *See also* Bands (music); Music; Musical instruments.

Instrumentalism (philosophy). Instrumentalis(m,t). Instrumentality. *Consider also:* heuristic(ally), operationalis(m,t), pragmatis(m,t), pragmatic, instrumental value, instrumental rationality, instrumental pluralism, theory of intentionality. *See also* Pragmatism; Philosophy; Rationalization (sociology); Speech act theory.

Instrumentation, flight. See *Flight instrumentation.*

Instruments. See *Inventories; Tests; Tools.*

Instruments, automatic. See *Automatic instruments.*

Instruments, electronic. See *Electronic instruments.*

Instruments, legal. See *Legal documents.*

Instruments, musical. See *Musical instruments.*

Instruments, scientific. See *Scientific equipment.*

Insults. See *Invective; Verbal abuse.*

Insurance. Insurance. Insur(e,ed,er,ers, ing,able). Underwrit(ten,er,ers). Surety. Indemnity. Indemnif(y,ication). Assurance(s). Guarantee(s,d). Warrant(y,ies). *Consider also:* workers compensation, social security. *See also* Financial support; Health insurance; Insurance coverage; Insurance pools; Life insurance; Retirement income; Retirement planning; Workmens compensation.

Insurance, employee health. See *Health insurance.*

Insurance, health. See *Health insurance.*

Insurance, health employee. See *Health insurance.*

Insurance, life. See *Life insurance.*

Insurance, medical. See *Health insurance.*

Insurance coverage. Insurance coverage. Insurance protection. Insurance benefit(s). *Choose from:* health care plan(s), insurance, health maintenance organization(s), managed care, indemnity plan(s), liabilit(y,ies) *with:* cover(age,ed,ing), protection, benefit(s), scope. *Consider also:* universal coverage. *See also* Health insurance; Insurance; Insurance pools.

Insurance pools. Insurance pool(s). *Choose from:* insur(e,ed,ance), risk, reinsurance, care, public entity, health *with:* pool(s). *See also* Biased selection; Driving skills; Insurance; Insurance coverage; Traffic accidents.

Insurgency. See *Rebellions.*

Insurrections. See *Rebellions.*

Intake (agency). Intake(s). Initial contact(s). Enroll(ed,ing,ment). *Choose from:* initial, applicant(s), admission *with:* assessment(s), interview(s), screen(ed,ing). *See also* Abortion applicants; Admissions; Hospitalization; Institutionalization (persons); Patient admission; Patient readmission; School admission criteria.

Intake, food. See *Food intake.*

Intangible assets. See *Intangible property.*

Intangible property. Intangible propert(y,ies). Intangible asset(s). Intangible(s). Intellectual propert(y,ies). Intellectual work(s). Literary propert(y,ies). Patent(s). Copyright(s). Know how. Trade secret(s). Goodwill. Software. Computer program(s). Information. Data. *Choose from:* intangible *with:* asset(s), right(s), property. *Choose from:* technolog(y,ies, ical), information, data *with:* transfer(red,ring,s,ence), transport. *Consider also:* warrant(s), insurance polic(y,ies), negotiable instrument(s), chose(s) in action, data flow(s). *See also* Assets; Computer security; Copyright; Customer relations; Discoveries (findings); Intellectual capital; Knowledge management; License agreements; Patents; Piracy (copyright); Plagiarism; Property rights; Technological innovations; Trade secrets; Valuation.

Integration, content. See *Multicultural education.*

Integration, global. See *Global integration*

Integration, international economic. See *International economic integration.*

Integration, merger. See *Merger integration.*

Integration, racial. See *Racial integration.*

Integration, school. See *School integration.*

Integration, sensory. See *Sensory integration.*

Integration, social. See *Social integration.*

Integrity. Integrity. Upright(ness). Guiltless(ness). Blameless(ness). Innocen(ce,t). Righteous(ness). Honest(y). Honor(able). Faithful(ness). Loyal(ty). Conscientious(ness). Moral(s,ly,ity). Ethic(al,ally,s). Conscience. Social(ly) responsib(le,ility). Virtue. Virtuous(ness). Fair(ness). Just(ness). Ethical behavior. Moral maturity. Truthful(ness). Sincer(e,ity). Forthright(ness). Trustworth(y,iness). Moral consistency. *See also* Bioethics; Conscience; Corruption in government; Credibility; Deception; Duties; Ethics; Examination of conscience; Guilt; Honor (integrity); Moral development; Moral education; Moral judgment; Moral reasoning; Morality; Personal values; Purity; Religious beliefs; Reputation; Responsibility (answerability); Shame; Truth.

Intellect. See *Intelligence; Academic aptitude; Cognitive ability; Cognitive development; Creativity; Divergent thinking; Gifted; Intellectual development; Intelligence quotient; Mental age.*

Intellectual capital. Intellectual capital. Knowledge base(s). Knowledge asset(s). Knowledge capital. *Choose from:* knowledge, skills, experience, expertise, intuition, attitudes, learning, collective wisdom *with:* workforce, researcher(s), scientist(s), engineer(s). *Consider also:* brain trust, brain power, megabrain(s), human capital, tacit knowledge, learning organization(s), knowledge organization(s), net generation. *See also* Brain drain; Cultural transmission; Information literacy; Intelligentsia; Intangible property; Job Knowledge; Knowledge management; Knowledge workers; Lifelong learning.

Intellectual cooperation. Intellectual cooperation. *Choose from:* collaborat(ion,ive), cooperat(ion,ive), shar(e,ed,ing), partnership(s), exchange(s) *with:* invention(s), inventor(s), research(er,ers), research and development, R & D, scientific, science(s), technolog(y,ies,ical), academi(a,c), laborator(y,ies), teacher(s), intellectual, writing, theater, forum(s), data. *See also* Collaboration; Cooperation; Interdisciplinary approach; Interprofessional relations.

Intellectual development. Intellectual development. Cognitive development. Concept learning. *Choose from:* intellect(ual), cognitive, intelligence, understanding, mental, creativ(e,eness, ity) *with:* develop(ed,ing,ment), grow(th,ing), matur(e,ing,ity), improv(e,ed,ing,ement), achiev(e,ed, ing,ement). *See also* Cognitive development; Creativity; Intellectual liberty; Intelligence; Mental age.

Intellectual freedom. See *Academic freedom; Civil rights; Freedom of information; Freedom of speech; Intellectual liberty.*

Intellectual functioning. See *Cognitive ability.*

Intellectual history. Intellectual history. History of ideas. History of mentalities. Intellectual heritage. *Choose from:* histor(y,ies,iography) *with:* intellectual, idea(s), thought, consciousness, belief(s), presumption(s), mind, mental life, sensibilit(y,ies), mentalit(y,ies,es), assumption(s), opinion(s), social dimension(s). *Consider also:* Annales school, enlightenment, Wilhem Dilthey, Geistesgeschichte, Weltanschauung(en), Zeitgeist, Weltbild(er), l'histoire social des idees, Ideengeschicte. *See also* Chain of being; Cultural history; Historiography; History; Idealism; Literary movements; Social history; Social thought; Sociology of knowledge; Worldview.

Intellectual impoverishment. Intellectual(ly) impoverish(ed,ment). Poverty of ideas. *See also* Cultural deprivation; Deterioration; Pseudoretardation; Psychosocial deprivation; Rigid personality.

Intellectual liberty. Intellectual liberty. *Choose from:* free(dom), liberty *with:* intellectual, academic, thought, think(ing), idea(s). *See also* Academic freedom; Anti-intellectualism; Civil rights; Free thought; Freedom of information; Freedom of speech; Right of privacy.

Intellectual life. Intellectual life. Academic life. Community of thinkers. Intellectual circle(s). *Choose from:* intelligentsia, intellectual(s), scholar(s), academic(s), academia, professor(s), ivory tower(s), sage(s), thinker(s), well-read, well-educated, author(s), artist(s), renaissance man, literati *with:* life(style), tradition(s), cultur(e,al), value system(s), communit(y,ies), identit(y,ies), activit(y,ies), commitment to ideas. *Consider also:* academic freedom, intellectual history. *See also* Academic freedom; Authors; Elites; Gifted; Intelligentsia; Lifestyle; Litterateurs; Professional personnel; Scholars; Scientific community; Scientists; Writers.

Intellectual property. See *Intangible property.*

Intellectualization (defense mechanism). Intellectualiz(e,ed,ing,ation). Brood(ed, ing). *Consider also:* denial of affect, repress(ed,ing,ion), displacement, lack of emotional tone, objectif(y,ied,ying, ication), thinking compulsion. *See also* Defense mechanisms.

Intellectually gifted. See *Gifted.*

Intellectuals. See *Intelligentsia.*

Intelligence. Intelligen(t,ce). Comprehension. Mental-age. IQ. Intelligence quotient. *Choose from:* intellectual, academic, mental, creative, cognitive *with:* abilit(y,ies). *Consider also:* keen, shrewd(ness), perspicacious(ness), discerning, perceptive(ness), gifted, wise, intellectual(ity), knowledgeable, clever(ness), intelligentsia, savant(s), bright student(s), sagacity, common sense, ingenuity, genius, adroit(ness). *See also* Ability; Academic aptitude; Academic ability; Animal intelligence; Artificial intelligence; Cognitive ability; Cognitive development; Cognitive processes; Creativity; Divergent thinking; Gifted; Intellectual development; Intelligence quotient; Mental age; Nature nurture.

Intelligence, animal. See *Animal intelligence.*

Intelligence, artificial. See *Artificial intelligence.*

Intelligence, competitive. See *Competitive intelligence.*

Intelligence, distributed artificial. See *Distributed artificial intelligence.*

Intelligence, military. See *Military intelligence.*

Intelligence, social. See *Social maturity; Social skills.*

Intelligence levels. See *Intelligence quotient.*

Intelligence measures. See *Intelligence tests.*

Intelligence quotient. Intelligence quotient(s). IQ(s). *Choose from:* intelligence *with:* quotient(s), level(s), test score(s), score(s), rating(s). *Consider also:* academic abilit(y,ies). *See also* Intelligence; Intelligence tests; Mental age.

Intelligence service. Intelligence service(s). Counterintelligence. Espionage. Spies. Spy(ing). *Choose from:* strategic, national, international, civilian, military *with:* intelligence. *Choose from:* intelligence, back-channel *with:* work, agent(s), agenc(y,ies), office(s,r,rs), official(s), operation(s), organization(s), system(s), oversight, polic(e,ing), unit(s), team(s), communit(y,ies), corp(s), activit(y,ies). *Consider also:* Central Intelligence Agency, CIA, Federal Bureau of Investigation, FBI, KGB, secret service(s), cointelpro. *See also* Eavesdropping; Electronic eavesdropping; Espionage; Military intelligence; secret police; Subversion; Surveillance of citizens; Traitors; Treason; Undercover operations.

Intelligence tests. Intelligence test(s). *Choose from:* intelligence, intellect(ual), mental development, mental function(s, ing), IQ, problem solving, cognitive *with:* test(ing,s), measure(s,ment,ments), assessment(s), scale(s), score(s), profile(s), inventor(y,ies). *Consider also:* Wechsler Adult Intelligence Scale, the Wechsler Intelligence Scale for Children, etc. *See also* Ability identification; Academic aptitude; Aptitude tests; Intellectual development; Intelligence quotient; Mental age; Psychological tests.

Intelligentsia. Intelligentsia(s). Intellectual(ity,s,ism). Intellectual hierarchy. Intellectual class(es). Scholar(s,ly). Intellectualist. Academic world. Academ(ia,e). Knowledge elite(s). Literati. Philosophe(s). Savant(s). Genius(es). Mental giant(s). Think tank(s). Brain trust(s). Enlightened. Egghead(s). Mastermind(s). Pundit(s). Learned person(s). Educated stratum. *Choose from:* intellectual, academic, artistic, musical, social, political, cultural *with:* elite(s), vanguard, leader(s). *Consider also:* intellectual orientation, intellectual style, intellectual craftsmanship, intellectual discourse. *See also* Academic aptitude; Anti-intellectualism; Authors; Educational attainment; Elites; Experts; Gifted; Intellectual capital; Intellectual life; Intelligence; Professional personnel; Scholars; Scholarship; Scientific community; Scientists; Upper class; Writers.

Intelligibility, speech. See *Speech intelligibility.*

Intensification. Intensif(y,ied,ication). Concentrat(e,ed,ing,ation). Worsen(ed, ing). Reinforc(e,ed,ing,ment). Enrich(ed, ing,ment). Enhanc(e,ed,ing,ement, ements). Magnif(y,ied,ication). Sharpen(ed,ing). Aggravat(e,ed,ing,ion). Exacerbat(e,ed,ing,ion). Accelerat(e,ed, ing,ation). Heighten(ed,ing). Deepen(ed, ing). Widen(ed,ing). Strengthen(ed,ing). Thicken(ed,ing). *See also* Acceleration (speed); Fortification; Reinforcement.

Intensive care. Intensive care. *Choose from:* intensive, special, coronary, respiratory, critical, burn *with:* care, therapy. *Consider also:* recovery room(s). *See also* Critical care; Hospital environment; Hospitals; Nursing care.

Intent, criminal. See *Criminal intent.*

Intention. Intention(s,al,ality). Intent. Intend(ed,ing). Purpose(s). Goal(s). Aim(s). Aspiration(s). Ambition(s). Resolve(d). *See also* Action; Commitment (emotional); Intentionality; Motivation.

Intentional learning. Intentional learning. *Choose from:* intention(al), purposive, active, motivated *with:* learn(ed,ing), memoriz(e,ed,ing), recall, attention, retention. *See also* Advance organizers; Educational motivation; Educational objectives; Incidental learning; Observational learning; Testwiseness.

Intentionalism. See *Intentionality.*

Intentionality. Intent(ion,ions,ionality). Purpos(e,ive,iveness). Resolv(e,ed,ing). Determin(e,ed,ation). Intend(ed,ing). *Consider also:* commitment, goals, will, volition, aspiration, ambition, meaning(s,ful,fulness), teleolog(y,ical), conat(ive,ion). *See also* Action; Commitment (emotional); Consciousness raising activities; Freedom (theology); Goals; Judgment (logic); Motivation; Phenomenology; Rationality; Speech act theory; Volition.

Interaction. Interact(ive,ing,ion,ional, ionism). Dynamics. Interplay. Reciproc(al,ity). Interdependen(ce,t). Mutual influence. Transaction(s,al). Joint determination. Symbio(sis,tic). Interchange(s). Exchange(s). Interweav(e,ing). Interwoven. Feedback. Rebut(tal). *Consider also:* emergent propert(y,ies). *See also* Alliances; Behavior; Causality; Communication (thought transfer); Conflict; Feedback; Human nature; Manipulation; Negotiation; Participation; Reciprocity; Responses; Social interaction; Spatial behavior; Symbiotic relations; Violence.

Interaction, double bind. See *Double bind interaction.*

Interaction, human-computer. See *Man machine systems*

Interaction, interpersonal. See *Social interaction.*

Interaction, social. See *Social interaction.*

Interaction, supervisor employee. See *Superior subordinate relationship.*

Interaction, teacher student. See *Student teacher relations.*

Interaction, therapist patient. See *Psychotherapeutic processes; Therapeutic processes.*

Interactions, drug. See *Drug interactions.*

Interactive computer systems. Interactive computer system(s). *Choose from:* interact(ive), feedback *with:* computer system(s), computer graphic(s), media, multimedia, service(s), educational project(s), entertainment, forum(s), marketing. *Consider also:* computer game(s), information superhighway(s). *See also* Community networks (computer); Computer games; Electronic data interchange; Hypertext; Information highway; Information society; Internet (computer network); Interactive video; Teledemocracy.

Interactive video. Interactive video(s). *Choose from:* interactive, two-way *with:* video(s), television, TV, cable TV, CD-ROM(s), compact disk(s), banking, application(s), videodisk(s), kiosk(s). *Consider also:* interactive *with:* media, multimedia, World Wide Web, www, web site(s). *See also* CD ROMs; DVDs; Interactive computer systems; Teleconferencing,

Interagency cooperation. See *Interinstitutional relations.*

Interception of communications. See *Electronic eavesdropping.*

Interchange, electronic data. See *Electronic data interchange.*

Intercommunion. Intercommunion. Interdenominational participation in communion. Communion between churches. *Consider also:* Catholic-Evangelical joint action. *See also* Christianity; Ecumenical movement; Interdenominational cooperation; Religious dialogues.

Intercommunity cooperation. Intercommunity cooperation. Sister cit(y,ies). *Choose from:* intercommunity, interlocal, intercity, municipal(ities) *with:* cooperat(e,ed,ing,ion), cosponsor(ed,ing,ship), teamwork, exchange(s), collaborat(e,ed,ing,ion), interaction, joint action(s), mutual aid, mutual assistance, resource sharing, shar(e,ed,ing) service(s). *See also* Cooperation; Exchange of persons; Intergroup relations; International cooperation; Sharing.

Intercorporate networks. See *Corporate networks; Interorganizational networks.*

Intercourse, anal. See *Sodomy.*

Intercourse, oral. See *Oral sex.*

Intercourse, premarital. See *Premarital sexual behavior.*

Intercourse, sexual. See *Sexual intercourse.*

Intercultural communication. Intercultural communication. Global approach. *Choose from:* intercultural, multicultural, cross-cultural *with:* communication(s), encounter(s), contact(s), sensitivity, understanding, misunderstanding, conflict(s), relation(s). *Consider also:* cosmopolitanism, creole(s), pidgin(s), bilingualism. *See also* Antibias curriculum; Assimilation (cultural); Acculturation; Biculturalism; Bidialectalism; Bilingualism; Communication (thought transfer); Cross cultural competency; Cultural conflict; Cultural cooperation; Cultural diversity; Cultural groups; Cultural maintenance; Cultural pluralism; Cultural sensitivity; Culture change; Culture contact; Dominated cultures; Ethnic differences; Ethnic relations; Ethnocentrism; Ethnolinguistics; Global integration; Globalization; Indigenous populations; Intercultural relations; Interethnic families; International cooperation; Melting pot; Misunderstanding; Multicultural education; Race relations; Racial attitudes; Racial differences; Social integration; Subcultures.

Intercultural relations. Intercultural relations. *Choose from:* intercultural, multicultural, cross-cultural, ethnocultural *with:* conflict(s), relation(s,ship,ships), survival, resist(ed,ing,ance), assimilation, imperialism, propaganda, relativism, cooperation, encounter(s), tie(s), dialogue(s), exchange(s), borrow(ed, ing), contact(s), understanding, confrontation(s), clash(es), toleran(ce,t), peace(ful), understanding. *See also* Acculturation; Bilingualism; Cultural cooperation; Cultural conflict; Cultural imperialism; Cultural maintenance; Cultural relations; Cultural sensitivity; Culture contact; Diversity; Ethnic relations; Ethnocentrism; Global integration; Globalization; Indigenous populations; Intercultural communication; International alliances; International conflict; International cooperation; International educational exchange; International organizations; International relations; Race relations; Social integration; Traditional societies.

Interdenominational cooperation. Interdenominational cooperation. Unit(ed,ing) churches. Ecumenical movement(s). Ecumenical student movement(s). Ecumenism. Simultaneum. *Consider also:* World Student Christian Federation, WSCF, National Ecumenical Student Christian

Council, NESCC, theology of dialogue. *See also* Christianity; Ecumenical movement; Intercommunion; Religious dialogues.

Interdepartmental relations. Interdepartmental relations. *Choose from:* interdepartmental *with:* interaction(s), communication(s), conflict(s), cooperat(e,ed,ing,ion). Communication between departments. Integrated management. Interdepartmental interdependency. *See also* Bureaucracies; Communication (thought transfer); Interdependence; Interpersonal relations.

Interdependence. Interdependen(t,ce,cy). Mutual(ly) dependen(t,ce,cy). Mutual(ly) relian(t,ce). Symbio(sis,tic). Depend(ing,ent) on each other. Global village. *Consider also:* mutual aid, codependen(t,ce,cy), codependen(t,ce,cy). *See also* Co-dependency; Globalization; Interdepartmental relations; Symbiotic relations; Trade; World citizenship.

Interdisciplinary approach. Interdisciplinary approach. *Choose from:* interdisciplinary, cross disciplinary, multidisciplinary *with:* approach(es), team(s), cooperation, stud(y,ies), research, experiment(s,al), course(s). *See also* Eclecticism; Globalization; Holism; Intellectual cooperation; Interdisciplinary treatment; Interprofessional relations; Multicultural education; Teamwork.

Interdisciplinary treatment. Interdisciplinary treatment. Multi-therapy. Therapeutic communit(y,ies). Patient care team(s). *Choose from:* interdisciplinary, multidisciplinary, collaborat(ive,ion), holistic, team(s), integrat(ed,ion), coordinated, eclectic, multimodal, team work, teamwork, multiprofessional team(s), multispecialty, joint, transdisciplinary *with:* treatment(s), therap(y,ies,eutic), diagnos(is,es), medical care, health care, hospital(s), consultation(s), clinic(s,al), medical, psychiatric, pediatric, surgical, medicine, assessment, rehabilitation, patient service(s), mental health, approach(es), clinical team(s). *See also* Interdisciplinary approach; Interprofessional relations; Multiple psychotherapy.

Interest (ethics). Interest. Eudaimoni(a,sm). Happiness. Well-being. Success. Living well. Doing well. Felicity. *Consider also:* summum bonum. *See also* Ethics; Hedonism; Philosophy; Utilitarianism.

Interest (monetary). Interest. Rate of return on capital. Yield from investment. *Consider also:* interest rate(s), rate(s) of interest, compound interest, simple interest, interest bearing, usur(y,ious, iously,iousness). *See also* Arrears; Consumer credit; Consumption (economic); Credit; Debt; Earnings; Economic indicators; Indebtedness;

Inflation (economics); Monetary policy; Money supply.

Interest (psychology). See *Activism; Attitudes; Attitudes toward work; Citizen participation; Commitment (emotional); Community involvement; Interests; Involvement; Job involvement; Political participation; Social cohesion; Worker participation.*

Interest, conflict of. See *Conflict of interest.*

Interest, public. See *Public good.*

Interest, self. See *Self interest.*

Interest, social. See *Community feeling; Group feeling; Prosocial behavior.*

Interest groups. Interest group(s). Political action committee(s). PACS. Political action group(s). Citizen group(s). Collective action organization(s). Interest organization(s). Social movement(s). Pressure group(s). Lobb(y,ies). Special interest group(s). Aggregation of interests. Single issue coalition(s). Advocacy group(s). Gadfl(y,ies). *Consider also:* campaign contributions. *See also* Activism; Change agents; Civil rights organizations; Corporatism; Influence; Legislation; Lobbying; Political action; Political behavior; Political contributions; Political power; Public policy; Social movements; Trade associations; Voting behavior.

Interest inventories. Interest inventor(y, ies). *Choose from:* interest(s), preference(s), hobb(y,ies) *with:* inventor(y,ies), scale(s), survey(s), score(s), measure(s), assessment(s), test(s), scale(s), index(es), check list(s), checklist(s). *See also* Interest patterns; Interests; Inventories.

Interest patterns. Interest pattern(s). *Choose from:* interest(s), hobb(y,ies), preference(s) *with:* pattern(s), structure(s), correlation(s), score(s), congruence, continuity, profile(s). *Consider also:* interest inventor(y,ies), interest cluster(s). *See also* Interest inventories; Interests.

Interests. Interest(s,ed). Preference(s). *Consider also:* enthusias(tic,m), values, choice(s), inclination(s), enjoyment, responsiveness, appreciat(ion,ive), satisf(y,ied,ying,action), fond(ness), favor(ed,ing,ites), attitude(s), intrigued, curious, attracted, find interesting, involvement, liking, hobb(y,ies). *See also* Affective behavior; Curiosity; Hobbies; Interest inventories; Interest patterns; Occupational interests; Participation.

Interests, future. See *Future interests.*

Interests, occupational. See *Occupational interests.*

Interests, reading. See *Reading interests.*

Interethnic conflict. See *Cultural conflict.*

Interethnic families. Interethnic famil(y,ies). *Choose from:* interethnic, trans-ethnic, interracial, trans-racial, biracial, mixed race, mestizo(s) *with:* famil(y,ies), child(ren), offspring, adoption(s). *See also* Assimilation (cultural); Biculturalism; Ethnic differences; Intercultural communication; Interracial marriage; Intermarriage; Melting pot; Racial differences; Racial integration; Racially mixed.

Interethnic marriage. See *Intermarriage.*

Interethnic relations. See *Ethnic relations.*

Interfaith marriage. See *Intermarriage.*

Interference (learning). Interference in learning. Latent inhibition. Block(ed, ing) response(s). Response competition. Conditioned inhibition. Kamin blocking effect. Color word interference. *Choose from:* learning, conditioning, recall *with:* interference, block(s,ed,ing), problem(s), inhibit(ed,ing,ion,ions) intervention, intrusion(s). *Choose from:* stroop *with:* phenomena, effect(s), interference. *Consider also:* proactive inhibition, retroactive inhibition. *See also* Forgetting; Learning; Linguistic interference; Proactive inhibition; Retention (psychology); Retroactive inhibition.

Interference (noise). See *Noise (interference).*

Interference, linguistic. See *Linguistic interference.*

Interference, response. See *Response interference.*

Intergenerational mobility. Intergenerational mobility. Intergenerational occupational mobility. Intergenerational class mobility. Father to son mobility. *Choose from:* intergenerational, second generation, cross-generational *with:* mobil(e,ity), attainment, fluidity. *Consider also:* upward mobility, downward mobility, status inheritance, status transmission, status ascription, silver spoon. *See also* Career mobility; Family work relationship; Generation gap; Social mobility.

Intergenerational relations. Intergenerational relations. Generation gap. Differences between generations. Cross generational change(s). Adolescent(s) vs parent(s). Intergenerational reconciliation. Sandwich generation. *Choose from:* generation(al,s), cross-generational, transgenerational, multigenerational, intergeneration(al), mother daughter, father daughter, mother son, father son, grandparent(s) grandchild(ren) *with:* interaction(s), bond(s,ing), tension(s), help(ed,ing), gap(s), conflict(s), relation(s,ship,ships), distanc(e,es,ing), exchange(s), awareness, difference(s), dissension, dynamics, support, contact(s), values, communication, changes, politics, war, intimacy, closeness, disagreement(s), understanding, reconciliation. *See also* Adult offspring; Age differences; Age groups; Boomerang children; Caregiver burden; Cultural transmission; Elderly; Extended family; Family conflict; Family relations; Filial responsibility; Generation gap; Generativity; Grandparents; Parent child relations.

Intergenerational transmission of culture. See *Generativity; Cultural transmission.*

Intergovernmental organizations. See *International organizations.*

Intergovernmental relations. Intergovernmental relations. Interstate relations. *Choose from:* local, county, school district(s), special district(s), town(s, ship,ships), village(s), municipal(ity, ities), cit(y,ies), metropolitan, community, regional *with:* state, federal, national, provincial, central or other local governments *with:* relations, mandate(s), aid, planning, fiscal, consolidation, grant(s)-in-aid, block grant(s), matching fund(s), transfer(s), contract(s), compact(s), service(s), property tax equalization, limitation(s). *Consider also:* federalism, revenue sharing, states rights, Lakewood plan, regional planning, home rule. *See also* Federalism; Government aid; Government finances; Governmental powers; Interstate cooperation; Legislative bodies; Local government; Separation of powers; State government; Taxes.

Intergroup conflict. See *Social conflict.*

Intergroup contact. See *Social contact.*

Intergroup dynamics. See *Intergroup relations.*

Intergroup relations. Intergroup relations. *Choose from:* intergroup, subgroup, between groups, ingroup(s) outgroup(s), intercorporate, interfamilial, interfaith, interracial, interethnic *with:* dynamics, conflict(s), process(es), competition, activities, development, contact(s), perception(s), gap(s), attraction, relations, alienation, cooperation, differentiation. discrimination, interaction(s), bias(es), favoritism, differences, prejudice(s), fairness, negotiations, tension(s). *Consider also:* ethnic relations, interfaith relations, racial relations. *See also* Alliances; Center and periphery; Class relations; Coalitions; Communication (thought transfer); Competition; Conflict; Conflict resolution; Cooperation; Cross cultural comparisons; Ethnic relations; Ethnocentrism; Human relations training; Individual and the state; Intercultural relations; Interinstitutional relations; Intermarriage; Interorganizational networks; Labor management relations; Majority groups; Multicultural

education; Nativism; Prejudice; Race relations; Social contact; Social discrimination; Social integration; Social mobility; Social unrest.

Interinstitutional relations. Interinstitutional relations. *Choose from:* interinstitutional, institution(s,al), intercollegiate, interlibrary, interagency, interorganizational *with:* cooperation, collaboration, cosponsorship, articulation, planning, teamwork, consort(ia,ium), relations. *See also* Associations (organizations); Boundary spanning; Consortia; Corporate networks; Federations; Intergroup relations; Interlocking directorates; Interorganizational networks; Organizations.

Interior decoration. See *Interior design.*

Interior design. Interior design. *Choose from:* interior, indoor environment(s), room(s), furnishing(s), office(s), bedroom(s), kitchen(s), lounge(s), work space(s), apartment(s), home(s), classroom(s) *with:* design(ed,ing), decorat(e,ed,ing), redecorat(e,ed,ing), use of color. *Consider also:* furniture, furnishing(s) *with:* arrangement(s), placement. *See also* Architecture; Arches; Color; Decoration; Designs; Environmental design; Environmental effects; Furniture; Home environment; Housing conditions; Living conditions; Spatial organization.

Interlibrary loans. Interlibrary loan(s). Inter-library loan(s). Interlibrary borrowing. Interloan(s). Interlending. *Consider also:* librar(y,ies) *with:* telefacsimile, fax. *See also* Consortia; Cooperation; Library cooperation; Library services.

Interlocking directorates. Interlocking directorate(s). Corporate interlock(s). Intercorporate tie(s). Interlocking board(s). Primary interlock(s). Multiple interlock(s). Intercorporate network(s). Corporate network(s). *Choose from:* interlock(s,ed,ing), common *with:* directorate(s), directorship(s). *Consider also:* conglomerate(s). *See also* Associations (organizations); Boundary spanning; Consortia; Corporate control; Corporate networks; Corporations; Governing boards; Interorganizational networks; Organizations; Power structure.

Interludes (music). Interlude(s). Entr'acte(s). Entre-acte(s). Intermezz(o,i). Intermedi(o). Zwischenspiel. *Consider also:* intermed(i,e,es), act tune(s), incidental music, curtain tune(s), jacara(s), tonadilla(s) escenica(s). *See also* Background music; Incidental music; Morality plays; Music.

Intermarriage. Intermarriage(s). Intermarry(ing). Exogam(y,ous).

Outmarr(y,iage). Heterogam(y,ous). *Choose from:* interfaith, interracial(ly), mixed, interethnic, exogamous, intercultural, outside religion, outside faith, Jewish Gentile, Protestant Catholic, intertribal, Black White *with:* marriage(s), famil(y,ies), marr(y,ying, ied), mating(s), matrimony, courtship(s). *See also* Assimilation (cultural); Biculturalism; Clans; Ethnic differences; Interethnic families; Intergroup relations; Interracial marriage; Marriage; Melting pot; Racial differences; Racially mixed; Social integration.

Intermarriage, religious. See *Intermarriage.*

Intermediate school students. Intermediate school student(s). *Choose from:* intermediate school, 4th grade, 5th grade, fourth grade, fifth grade, intermediate grade(s) *with:* student(s), pupil(s), child(ren). *Consider also:* middle school student(s). *See also* Children; Elementary school students; Elementary schools.

Interments. See *Burials.*

Intern programs. See *Internships.*

Internal colonialism. See *Inequality; Exploitation.*

Internal conflict. Internal conflict(s). Contradict(ed,ing,ion,ions,ory). Paradox(es,ical). Ambivalen(t,ce). Inconsisten(t,cy,cies). Incompatib(le,ility,ilities). Inner conflict(s). Self contradictory. Against one's nature. Ego dystonic. Divided self. Divided opinion(s). *Consider also:* social, cultural, international, ideological, religious, role(s) *with:* conflict(s). *See also* Ambivalence; Conflict; Ego dystonic homosexuality; Hesitancy; Indecisiveness; Role conflict.

Internal external control. See *Locus of control.*

Internal labor market. See *Labor market segmentation.*

Internal migration. Internal migration. *Choose from:* internal, interregional, interstate, interprovincial, urban to rural, rural to urban *with:* migrat(e,ed,ing,ion, ional), migrant(s), relocat(e,ed,ing,ion), transient(s), resettlement, movement, mobility, redistribution, dispersal. *See also* Geographic mobility; Migrants; Migration; Migration patterns; Population distribution; Residential mobility; Rural population; Rural to urban migration; Urban population; Urban to rural migration.

Internal rewards. Internal reward(s). Intrinsic reward(s). *Choose from:* intrinsic, self, internal, personal(ly) *with:* reward(s,ed,ing), satisf(y,ying,ied, action), reinforc(e,ed,ing,ement,er,ers), incentive(s). *Consider also:* internal locus of control. *See also* Intrinsic motivation; Locus of control; Motivation; Reward.

Internal security. Internal security. Prevent(ed,ing) terrorism. Security intelligence. National Guard(s,smen, sman). Loyalty oath(s). Law and order. *Choose from:* internal, environmental, political, social, domestic, regional *with:* stability, security. *Consider also:* national security, internal challenge(s), insurgenc(e,y,ies), anti-terrorist activit(y,ies), policing, government surveillance, police surveillance, rule of law, House UnAmerican Activities Committee, HUAC. *See also* Civil rights; Counterinsurgency; Guerrillas; Intimidation; Martial law; Military regimes; Political revolutions; R.ellions; Surveillance of citizens; Terrorism.

Internalization. Internaliz(e,ed,ing,ation). *Consider also:* introjection, identification, socialization. *Choose from:* superego *with:* form(ed,ing,ation), develop(ed,ing,ment). *Choose from:* incorporat(e,ed,ing,ation), assimilat(e, ed,ing) *with:* idea(s), standard(s), value(s), opinion(s), norm(s). *See also* Assimilation (psychology); Conscience; Introjection; Identification (psychology); Superego.

International affairs. See *International relations.*

International agencies. See *International organizations.*

International aid. See *Foreign aid.*

International alliances. International alliance(s). *Choose from:* international, intergovernmental, military *with:* alliance(s), collaboration, pact(s), bloc(s), entente(s). *Consider also:* Act of Chapultepec, Baghdad Pact, Dunkirk Treaty, Western European Union, Japanese American Security Treaty, Rio Treaty, North Atlantic Treaty Organization (NATO), Warsaw Treaty Organization (WTO), Arab League, Organization of African Unity (OAU), Southeast Asia Collective Defense Treaty (SEATO), Anzus Pact, Central Treaty Organization (CENTO). *See also* Alliances; Collective security; Countries; Cultural cooperation; Diplomacy (official); Foreign policy; Geopolitics; International cooperation; International economic organizations; International organizations; International relations; Military assistance; Power sharing; Spheres of influence; Treaties.

International arbitration. International arbitration. *Choose from:* international, multinational, intergovernmental, United Nations *with:* arbitrat(e,ed,ing,ion, ional,or,ors), broker(ed,ing), deliberat(e, ed,ing,ion,ions), conciliat(e,ed,ing,ion) go-between, mediat(e,ed,ing,ion), third-party settlement(s), dispute resolution,

conflict resolution, third-party intervention(s), peaceful resolution, tribunal(s), talks, arbiter(s). *Consider also:* International Court of Justice. *See also* International intervention; International law.

International banks and banking. International bank(s,ing). Universal banking. *Choose from:* international, transnational, multinational, cross-border, foreign, overseas *with:* bank(s,ing), World Bank. *Consider also:* Bank of Credit and Commerce International, Citibank, European Bank for Reconstruction and Development, RD, European Monetary Union, International Bank for Reconstruction and Development, IBRD, International Finance Corporation, International Development Association, International Monetary Fund. *See also* Banking; Common currency; Economic assistance; Economic union; Harmonization (trade); International economic integration; International economic organizations.

International bipolarity. See *Balance of power.*

International broadcasting. International broadcasting. World news service(s). BBC World Service. Radio Free Europe. Radio Liberty Inc. Radio Free Asia. *Choose from:* international, global, overseas *with:* broadcast service(s), radio program(s), radio station(s). *Consider also:* shortwave radio, Central Europe Today, Voice of America. *See also* Broadcasts; Foreign news; Global integration; Globalization; Internationalism.

International business enterprises. See *Multinational corporations.*

International competition. See *International conflict; International trade.*

International conflict. International conflict(s). *Choose from:* international, foreign, global, United Nations, world, east west, north south, great powers, developing countries *with:* confrontation, hostility,ies), escalation, invasion(s), threat(s,en,ening), aggression, rivalr(y,ies), military action(s), dispute(s), conflict(s), cris(is,es), tension(s), intervention, issue(s). *Consider also:* war(s), limited war(s), cold war, middle east conflict, international terrorism, border dispute(s), arms race, mutually assured destruction, imperialism, colonialism. *See also* Borderlands; Conflict; Countries; Geopolitics; International relations; Invasion; Military operations; War.

International cooperation. International cooperation. *Choose from:* international, overseas, east west, intercontinental, world wide, universal, global, pan-African, Soviet American, inter-American *with:* cooperation,

exchange(s), collaboration, interaction, joint action, aid, support, mutual assistance, congress(es), commission(s), resource sharing. *See also* Collective security; Cooperation; Countries; Cultural cooperation; Intercultural communication; International alliances; International relations; Military assistance; Technical assistance; Technology transfer.

International dependency theory. See *Dependency theory (international).*

International division of labor. International division of labor. *Choose from:* core *with:* peripheral econom(y,ies), periphery. *Consider also:* neoimperialism, neocolonialism, uneven development, world system theory, imperialism, fifth world. *See also* Center and periphery; Colonialism; Dependency theory (international); Developing countries; Division of labor; Economic underdevelopment; Exports; Global integration; Imperialism; Imports; Industrial societies; International economic integration; Labor migration; World economy.

International economic integration. International economic integration. Trade bloc(s). Trading group(s). Trade agreement(s). Customs union(s). Global market(s). Global investment(s). Global capital market(s). Global(ize,ized, ization) economy. *Consider also:* Andean Common Market, Asia-Pacific Economic Cooperation [APEC], Caribbean Community, Caribbean Free Trade Association, Central American Common Market, Council for Mutual Economic Assistance, Economic and Monetary Union [EMU], European Union[EU], European Community [EC], European Economic Community [EEC], General Agreement on Tariffs and Trade [GATT], World Trade Organization [WTO], Organization for Economic Cooperation and Development [OECD], International Monetary Fund [IMF], Treaty of Asuncion, Southern Cone Common Market Treaty [MERCOSUR], Mercado Comun del Sur [MERCOSUL], North American Free Trade Agreement [NAFTA]. *See also* Balance of payments; Commercial treaties; Common markets; Custom unions; Economic union; Exports; Foreign trade regulation; Free trade; Harmonization (trade); Imports; International banks and banking; International division of labor; International economic organizations; International relations; Nontariff trade barriers; Regionalism; Trade protection.

International economic organizations. International economic organization(s). *Consider also:* World Trade Organization [WTO]. International Monetary Fund [IMF], World Bank, International

Bank for Reconstruction and Development [IBRD], International Finance Corporation [IFC], International Development Association [IDA], European Investment Bank, European Economic Community [EEC], European Community Free Trade Association [EFTA], Inter-American Development Bank, African Development Bank, Asian Development Bank, United Nations Conference on Trade and development [UNCTAD], United Nations Industrial Development Agency [UNIDO], United Nations Institute for Training and Research [UNITAR], Colombo Plan, General Agreement on Trade and Tariffs [GATT], Export-Import Bank, Generalized System of Preferences [GSP], Organization of Petroleum Exporting Countries [OPEC], Central American Common Market, Latin American Free Trade Association[LAFTA], Latin American Integration Association [LAIA], Asociación LatinoAmericana de Integración, Andean Group, Caribbean Community and Common Market, [CARICOM]. *See also* Banking; Collective security; Common currency; Common markets; Countries; Economic development; Economic relations; Economic underdevelopment; Economic union; Economics; Free trade; Global integration; Harmonization (trade); International alliances; International banks and banking; International economic integration; International organizations; International trade; Trade; World economy.

International economic relations. See *Balance of payments; Colonialism; Dependency theory (international); Embargo; Exports; Foreign aid; Foreign investment; Foreign trade regulation; Foreign exchange; Imports; International division of labor; International economic integration; International economic organizations; International relations; Multinational corporations; Trade protection; World economy.*

International economy. See *World economy.*

International education. International education. Global education. *Choose from:* international, abroad, overseas, foreign countr(y,ies), foreign language(s), United Nations, world affairs, global, cross-cultural *with:* education(al), school(s), academic program(s), studies, learning, college(s), universit(y,ies), academ(y,ies). *See also* Foreign students; Foreign study; Global integration; International educational exchange; World citizenship.

International educational exchange. International educational exchange(s). Student exchange(s). Exchange student(s). Student exchange program(s). Junior year abroad. Study abroad. Study overseas. Fulbright scholarship(s). *See also* Americans abroad; Cultural cooperation; Culture contact; Exchange of persons; Foreign students; Global integration; International education; Technical assistance.

International intervention. International intervention(s). U.S. intervention. Interventionism. *Choose from:* international, foreign, military, World Court, humanitarian *with:* interven(e,ed,ing, tion), mediation, intercession, interced(e,ed,ing), interfer(e,ed,ing, ence), destabiliz(e,ed,ing,ation), arbitrat(e,ed,ing,ion), peacemaking, assist(ed,ing,ance). *Consider also:* support(ed,ing), aid(ed,ing) *with:* insurgen(t,ts,cy,cies,ce), rebel(s,lion, lions), resistance, dictator(s,ship,ships), regime(s). *See also* Arbitration; Countries; International Arbitration; International conflict; International organizations; International police; Mediation; Military assistance; Peacekeeping forces; War prevention.

International languages. International language(s). Lingua(e) franca(e,s). Esperanto. Universal(ized) language(s). *Consider also:* creol(e,es,ized), pidgin(s), common language(s), commercial language(s). *See also* Bidialectalism; Creoles; Dialects; Global integration; Language; Language maintenance; Language policy; Language shift; Language spread; Languages (as subjects); Lingua franca; Trade languages.

International law. International law. *Choose from:* international, transnational *with:* treat(y,ies), legislation, legal, judicial, criminal court, arbitration, arbitral. International Court of Justice. Permanent court of international justice. World court. International Law Commission. Law of the Sea. *Consider also:* Law of nations. *See also* Conflict resolution; Countries; Foreign policy; Global integration; International Arbitration; International conflict; International cooperation; International organizations; International relations; Marine resources; Maritime law; Natural law; Treaties; War; World citizenship.

International offenses. International offense(s). International crim(e,es,inal, inals). Transnational crime(s). *Consider also:* terroris(m,t,ts), war crimes, crimes against humanity, genocide, ethnic cleansing, violat(e,ed,ing,ion,ions) sovereignty. *See also* Biological warfare; Chemical warfare; Ethnic cleansing; Holocaust; Genocide; Nazism; Prisoners of war; War crimes; Weapons of mass destruction.

International organizations. International organization(s). International agenc(y, ies). *Choose from:* international, multinational, intergovernmental *with:* union(s), organization(s), commission(s), agenc(y,ies). *Consider also:* Red Cross, Red Crescent, United Nations [UN], Commission on Human Rights, Commission on Science and Technology for Development, Commission on the Status of Women, Commission on Sustainable Development, World Health Organization [WHO], Pan American Health Organization, League of Nations, Council of Europe, Organization for Economic Cooperation and Development [OECD], Council of Europe, North Atlantic Treaty Organization [NATO], North Atlantic Cooperation Council, European Community [EC], European Economic Community [EEC], European Coal and Steel Community [ECSC], European Atomic Energy Community [EURATOM], European Free Trade Association [EFTA], Southeast Asian Treaty Organization [SEATO], Atlantic Community, Organization of American States [OAS], Warsaw Treaty Organization [WTO], Benelux, Latin American Integration Association [LAIA], Central American Common Market [CACM], Council of Mutual Economic Assistance [COMECON], Arab League, Organization of African Unity [OAU], Amazon Pact, Andean Common Market, Asian and Pacific Council [ASPAC], Association of Southeast Asian Nations [ASEAN], Caribbean Community and Common Market [CARICOM], Central Treaty Organization [CENTO], Western European Union [WEU],World Customs Organization, Commonwealth of Nations, Nordic Council, Organization of Central American States [ODECA], etc. *See also* Associations (organizations); Collective security; Cultural cooperation; Disaster relief; Food relief; Global integration; International alliances; International cooperation; International economic organizations; International intervention; International law; International police; International relations; Nongovernmental organizations; Peacekeeping forces; Regionalism.

International police. International police. International Criminal Police Organization [INTERPOL]. *Choose from:* international, multinational *with:* police, drug force(s). *See also* Crime; Crime prevention; Global integration; International organizations; Peacekeeping forces; Smuggling.

International problems. See *World problems.*

International relations. International relations. Balance of power. Cold war. Foreign polic(y,ies). Summit(ry). *Choose from:* international, foreign, diplomatic, global, United Nations, world, east west, north south, great powers *with:* relations, affair(s), dispute(s), conflict(s), cooperation, cris(is,es), alignment(s), non-alignment, diplomacy, tension(s), negotiation(s), interaction(s), intervention, communication(s), understanding, politics, statesmanship, rival(s,ry), institution(s), issue(s). *Consider also:* wars, peace, detente, disarmament, cold war, relations between developed and developing nations, geopolitics, middle east conflict, international terrorism, border dispute(s), arms race, internationalism, imperialism, colonialism, neoimperialism, neocolonialism, relations between specific countries. *See also* Alliances; Balance of power; Borderlands; Cold war; Collective security; Colonialism; Countries; Cultural cooperation; Debt-for-nature swap(s); Detente; Developed countries; Developing countries; Diplomacy (official); Disarmament; Espionage; Foreign aid; Foreign policy; Global integration; International cooperation; International economic integration; International law; International organizations; Internationalism; National security; Peace; Political defection; Technical assistance; Treaties; War prevention; World economy.

International relief. See *Disaster relief; Emergency services; Food relief; International organizations; Relief services; Rescue.*

International rivers. International river(s). *Choose from:* international, transboundary, transfrontier, border(s) *with:* river(s), riparian, water(s), watercourse(s), waterway(s), stream(s), creek(s), tributar(y,ies), estuar(y,ies). *See also* Borderlands; Geopolitics; Rivers.

International trade. International trade. Export(s,ed,ing). Import(s,ed,ing). International market(s,place). Global market(s). Foreign market(s). European market. International business treaties. Selling abroad. Foreign trade. Free trade. Customs union(s). Common market. Most favored nation. GATT. General Agreement on Tariffs and Trade. Protectionis(m,t). North American Free Trade Agreement. NAFTA. *Choose from:* trade, import(s) *with:* agreement(s), war(s), accord(s), pact(s), ties, reciprocity, gap(s), surplus(es), deficit(s), balance(s), imbalance(s), retaliat(e,ed,ing,ion), negotiation(s), deal(s), sanction(s), barrier(s), embargo(es), dumping, price war(s). *See also* Balance of payments; Commercial treaties; Custom unions; Emerging markets; Exports; Foreign trade regulation; Global integration; Harmonization (trade); Imports; International division of labor; International economic integration; International economic organizations; International relations; Nontariff trade barriers; Trade protec-

tion.

International travel regulations. International travel regulation(s). *Choose from:* international, abroad, overseas, foreign countr(y,ies), European, Asian, Latin America(n), Africa(n), America(n), Australian, global *with:* travel(ler,lers), touris(t,ts,m), passport(s), visitor(s) *with:* restrict(ed,ing,ion,ions), ban(ned, ning), regulation(s), prohibit(ed,ing,ion, ions), tax(es). *Consider also:* border control(s), customs administration, emigration and immigration law, alien(s). *See also* Government regulation; Travel; Tourism.

Internationalism. International(ism, ization). Anti-statism. Globalization. Global village. Global society. International solidarity. International basis. Community of nations. Transcend(ing) national boundaries. United Nations (UN). League of Nations. *Consider also:* supranationalism, international(ism, ization), multinational, transnational, global(ization), worldwide, universal(ism,ization), regionalism. *See also* Common markets; Cross cultural competency; Global campaigns; Global integration; Globalization; Information highway; Information society; International broadcasting; International relations; Multicultural education; Nationalism; Political ideologies; World citizenship; World health; World history; World problems.

Internet (computer network). Internet(ed, ing,ted,ting). The Net. Information highway. Information superhighway. National Information Initiative (NII). Extranet(s). Intranet(s). *Consider also:* World Wide Web, the Web, WWW, Gopher(s), electronic mail, e-mail, web site(s), ARPANET, BITNET, CSNET, NSFNET, Internet 2, Internet II, next generation Internet, internetwork(ed, ing), web site(s), open computer network(s), global information, network of networks, infohighway, I-way, Inet, infobahn, cyberspace, electronic superhighway, information service provider(s), *See also* Community networks (computer); Cybercommunities; Cybercafes; Cyberlaw; Digital money; E-commerce; Electronic data interchange; Electronic journals; Electronic publishing; Hypertext; Information highway; Information networks; Information society; Interactive computer systems; Internet service providers; Internet traffic; Online harassment; Online users; Push technology; V-commerce; Virtual libraries; Virtual reality.

Internet addiction. See *Computer addiction.*

Internet crimes. See *Computer crimes.*

Internet service providers. Internet service

provider(s). ISP(s). Internet access compan(y,ies). Backbone provider(s). *See also* Community networks (computer); Connectivity; Distribution channels; Electronic data interchange; Home pages; Information highway; Information networks; Internet (computer network); Long distance telephone companies; Network backup.

Internet sex. See *Cybersex.*

Internet traffic. Internet traffic *Choose from:* Internet, web site(s), net, homepage(s), server log(s) *with:* traffic, unique visitor(s), visit(s), monitor(ed, ing), audience measur(e,ed,ing,ement), audience(s) count(s,ed,ing), representative sampl(e,ed,ing), track(s,ed,ing) use. *Consider also:* net audience(s), page impression(s), page view(s), surfing habit(s), page hit(s). *See also* Audience analysis; Audiences; Demographic characteristics (of individuals); Information highway; Internet (computer network); Market research; Online users; Opinion polls; Readership; Viewers.

Internships. Internship(s). Intern(s). *Consider also:* externship(s), assistantship(s), apprenticeship(s), practicum(s), practice teaching, residenc(y,ies), field experience. *See also* Field experience programs; Inservice teacher education; Inservice training; Practicum supervision; Professional education.

Interobserver reliability. See *Interrater reliability.*

Interorganizational networks. Interorganizational network(s). Power network(s). *Choose from:* interagency, intercorporate, interorganizational *with:* network(s,ing), connection(s), interdependence, exchange(s), relationships, coordination, cooperation, conflicts. *Consider also:* consort(ia,ium), boundary spanning social network(s), interdependent organization(s), virtual organization(s). *See also* Adhocracies; Affiliation (businesses); Associations (organizations); Boundary spanning; Boundaryless organizations; Cartels; Consortia; Contracting out; Corporate networks; Interlocking directorates; Multi-institutional systems; Networks; Organizational affiliation; Organizations; Regionalism; Trade associations; Virtual organizations.

Interpersonal attraction. Interpersonal attraction(s). Rapport. Attractive(ness). Love at first sight. Likeab(le,ility). Choice of friends. Charisma(tic). Desirability. Impression formation. Popularity. Sociometric(s). *Choose from:* attract(ed,ive,ion,ions), charismatic, likeable, well-liked, well-loved, admired, preferred, preference(s), sought, desir(ed,able), popular(ity) *with:* person(s), people, male(s), female(s), women, woman, men, man, interpersonal, figures, friend(s,ships), stranger(s), partner(s), mate(s). *See also* Affection; Attractiveness; Attachment behavior; Body image; Emotional responses; Friendship; Human mate selection; Interpersonal compatibility; Interpersonal relations; Likability; Personal beauty; Physical characteristics; Rapport; Self congruence; Social dating; Social life.

Interpersonal communication. See *Body language; Communication (thought transfer); Communication styles; Confidentiality; Conversation; Discussion; Eye contact; Father child communication; Gossip; Interpersonal relations; Interviews; Intimacy; Laughter; Letters (correspondence); Mother child communication; Negotiation; Nonverbal communication; Persuasion; Rapport; Self disclosure; Self expression.*

Interpersonal compatibility. Interpersonal compatibility. Similarit(y,ies). Complementarity. Compatib(le,ility). Complementary need(s). Congruence of cognitive style(s). Team cohesiveness. Congruent role expectations. Interpersonal affinities. Best friend(s). Similar likes and dislikes. Similarities between partners. Interpersonal congruence. Symbiotic relationship. Symbiosis. Interpersonal attraction. Congruency between personalities. Similar opinions. Match of personal styles. Cognitive style matching. Mutuality. Consensus in dyads. Closeness. Agreement. Like mindedness. Rapport. Unison. Amicab(le,ility). Harmon(y,ious). *See also* Attitude similarity; Family life; Friendship; Heterosexual relationships; Homosexual relationships; Interpersonal attraction; Interpersonal relations; Intimacy; Marital relationship; Marital satisfaction; Primary relationships; Rapport; Social life; Teamwork.

Interpersonal conflict. Interpersonal conflict(s). *Choose from:* interpersonal, father son, mother daughter, sibling(s), husband wife, peer(s), friend(s), colleague(s), neighbor(s), classmate(s), playmate(s), companion(s), partner(s) *with:* conflict(s), aggression, discord, dispute(s), distance, distrust, fighting, jealousy, rejection, rival(s,ry), tension(s). *See also* Aggression; Conflict resolution; Family conflict; Hate; Hostility; Interpersonal relations; Jealousy; Marital conflict; Social conflict.

Interpersonal coordination. See *Coordination (interpersonal).*

Interpersonal distance. See *Personal space; Proxemics.*

Interpersonal influences. Interpersonal influence(s). *Choose from:* interpersonal, group, peer, social, crowd, reference group(s), interactional, other(s), mentor(s), family, friend(s), significant others, spouse(s), husband(s), wife(s), parent(s,al), colleague(s), etc. *with:* influence(s), power, pressure(s), dynamics, compliance, reinforcement, norm(s), determinant(s). *Consider also:* mentor relationship, clout, leadership, manipulation, persuasion, give and take process, school influences, peer orientation, external locus of control, advice. *See also* Group dynamics; Interpersonal relations; Peer influences; Seduction; Social behavior; Social influences; Social interaction.

Interpersonal interaction. See *Social interaction.*

Interpersonal perception. See *Social perception.*

Interpersonal relations. Interpersonal relation(ship,s). Personal relation(ship, ships,s). Social relation(s,ship,ships). Face to face. Intimacy. Significant other(s). Confidante(s). Friend(s). Neighbor(s). Colleague(s). Eye contact. Argument(s). Group relation(s,ship, ships). Group process(es). Dyad(ic,s). Triad(ic,s). Couple(s). Social interaction(s). Related(ness). Interrelation(ship,s). Interrelated(ness). Personal connect(ed,ing,ion,ions). *Choose from:* personal, interpersonal, social, sexual, famil(y,ies) *with:* abuse, absence, acceptance, affair(s), affiliation(s), affinity, aggression, alliance(s), association(s), attachment(s), attraction, bond(s,ing), care, closeness, cohesiveness, collaborat(ed,ing,ion), comfort(ed,ing), communicat(ed,ing, ion), compatibility, conflict(s), cooperat(ed,ing,ion), dependenc(e,y), depriv(e,ed,ing,ation), disciplin(e,ed, ing), discord, dispute(s), distance, distrust, dynamics, empathy, expectation(s), feedback, feeling(s), fight(s,ing), friendship, guilt, helping, incest(uous), independen(t,ce), influence(s), interaction(s), interconnect(ed,ions), interdependen(t,ce), intervention(s), intimacy, involve(ment), jealous(y), kinship, lov(e,ing), liaison(s), link(s,ages), mutual(ity), negotiation(s), nurtur(ing,ed,ance), overprotect(ion,ive), partner(s,ship,ships), participat(ed,ing, ion), permissive(ness), play(ed,ing), presence, prosocial, rapport, reject(ed, ing,ion), rebell(ious,iousness,ion), reciproc(al,ity), reference, response(s), rival(s,ry), role(s), solidarity, social(ity), support(ed,ing), symbio(tic,sis), sympath(y,etic), teamwork, tension(s), trust(ed,ing), understanding, understood, unity. *Consider also:* oedip(al,us), oedip(al,us), electra *with:* conflict(s), complex(es), fathering, mothering, parenting. *See also* Brotherliness; Co-dependency; Dentist patient relations; Family life; Family relations; Father child relations; Friendship; Gay couples; Group formation; Heterosexual relationships; Homosexual relationships; Intergenerational relations; Interpersonal attraction; Interpersonal compatibility; Interpersonal conflict; Interpersonal influences; Interprofessional relations; Intimacy; Landlord tenant relations; Love; Manipulation; Marital relationship; Mother child relations; Nurse patient relations; Parent adolescent relations; Parent child relations; Physician patient relations; Primary relationships; Professional client relations; Professional family relations; Secondary relationships; Sexual partners; Sibling relations; Significant others; Social dating; Social life; Social nearness; Social support; Social support networks; Spouses; Symbiotic relations.

Interpersonal skills. See *Social skills.*

Interplanetary voyages. Interplanetary voyage(s). Space travel(ler,lers). Space mission(s). Space tourism. Star flight(s). Astronaut(s). Voyage(s) in outer space. Travel to Mars. Time-travel(ler,lers). Space probe(s). *Choose from:* space, solar system, extraterrestrial, planetary, interplanetary, interstellar *with:* explor(e,ed,ation), flight(s), travel, mission(s), expedition(s), probe(s), shuttle(s), satellite(s), touris(t,ts,m). *Consider also:* space flight, space vehicle(s), moon flight(s). *See also* Astronauts; Plurality of worlds; Space exploration; Terraforming.

Interpretation. Interpret(ed,ing,ation, ations). Explain(ed,ing). Explanation(s). Explicat(e,ed,ing,ation,ations). Clarif(y,ied,ying,ication,ications). Illuminat(e,ed,ing,ation). Commentar(y, ies). Concordance(s). Annotat(e,ed,ing, ation,ations). Demonstrat(e,ed,ing,ation, ations). Illustrat(e,ed,ing,ation,ations). Defin(e,ed,ing,ition,itions). Criticism(s). Exposition(s). Rendition(s). Hermeneutic(s). *Consider also:* biblical exegesis, translat(e,ed,ing,ion,ions). *See also* Analysis; Clarification; Comprehension; Deciphering; Exegesis; Hermeneutics; Meaning; Translating and translations; Verstehen.

Interpretation, data. See *Data interpretation.*

Interpretation, dream. See *Dream interpretation.*

Interpretation, psychoanalytic. See *Psychoanalytic interpretation.*

Interpretation, test. See *Test interpretation.*

Interpretations, theoretical. See *Theoretical interpretations.*

Interpretive method. See *Verstehen.*

Interprofessional relations. Interprofessional relation(s,ship,ships). Professional interrelationship(s). *Choose from:* physician nurse, professional(s), interprofessional, interdisciplinary, professional bureaucratic, faculty staff *with:* relation(s,ship,ships), collaborat(e, ed,ing,ion,ions), consult(ed,ing,ation, ations), cooperat(e,ed,ing,ion), conflict(s), communicat(e,ed,ing,ion), teamwork, negotiat(e,ed,ing,ion,ions), rival(s,ry), dispute(s), interaction(s), team(s). *See also* Allied health personnel; Intellectual cooperation; Interdisciplinary treatment; Interpersonal relations; Mentors; Peer review; Professional client relations; Professional family relations; Professional isolation; Professional personnel; Teamwork.

Interracial adoption. See *Interethnic families.*

Interracial marriage. Interracial marriage(s). Outmarriage(s). Miscegenous marriage(s). Mixed marriage(s). Intermarriage. Miscegenation. *Choose from:* interethnic, intercultural, Black White, interracial(ly), mixed race, Korean American, European Oriental, Japanese American *with:* marriage(s), married, couple(s), mate(s), mating(s). *See also* Assimilation (cultural); Biculturalism; Ethnic differences; Intercultural relations; Interethnic families; Intermarriage; Melting pot; Racial differences; Racial integration; Racially mixed.

Interracial offspring. See *Interracial marriage; Racially mixed.*

Interracial relations. See *Race relations.*

Interrater reliability. Interrater reliability. *Choose from:* interobserver, interrater, interjudge, interjudgmental, multirater, interscorer, experts *with:* reliability, agreement, consistency, analysis. *See also* Observation methods.

Interresponse time. Interresponse time(s). *Choose from:* interresponse, response(s), respond(ed,ing), leverpressing, keypeck(s,ed,ing), barpressing *with:* interval(s), temporal pattern(s), timing, pause(s), delay(s,ed,ing). *See also* Response frequency; Response parameters.

Interrogation. See *Questioning.*

Interrole conflict. See *Role conflict.*

Interruption. Interrupt(ed,ing,ion). Suspen(d,ded,ding). Suspension. Discontinu(e,ed,ing,ance). Abeyanc(e, y). Halt(ed,ing). Cessation. Ceas(e,ed, ing). Disrupt(ed,ing,ion). *Consider also:* intermission, dorman(t,cy), laten(t,cy), quiescen(t,ce,cy), hiatus, interim. *See also* Career breaks; Disruption; Termination of treatment.

Intersections. See *Crossroads.*

Intersensory processes. Intersensory

process(es). *Choose from:* intersensory, across sensory, supramodal, cross modal(ity,ities) *with:* process(es), perception, cue(s), organization, information. *See also* Perceptual motor processes.

Interstate cooperation. Interstate cooperation. *Choose from:* interstate, multistate, regional *with:* cooperat(e,ed,ing,ive,ion), compact(s), project(s), shar(e,ed,ing), pollution control, waste disposal, acid rain. *Consider also:* New York Port Authority, Columbia Basin, etc. *See also* Intergovernmental relations; Local government; Regional development; Regional government; Regionalism; State government; State role.

Interstimulus interval. Interstimulus interval(s). *Choose from:* interstimulus, interfood, stimul(i,us) *with:* interval(s), separation(s), gap(s), delay(ed,ing,s), pause(s), frequenc(y,ies), spac(e,ed,ing). *See also* Reinforcement schedule; Stimuli.

Intertextuality. Intertextualit(y,e). Literary influence(s). *Choose from:* parod(y,ies), pastiche(s), allusion(s), imitation(s), anxiety of influence, misprison, misreading, derivative(s), interdependen(ce,t) *with:* author(s), writer(s), poet(s), literary, literature, book(s), writing(s), prose, poetry, fiction, novel(s). *See also* Influence (literary, artistic, etc.); Literature; Modern literature; Patchwork; Postmodernism; Semantics; Semiotics.

Intertrial interval. Intertrial interval(s). *Choose from:* intertrial, inter-trial, inter-test, intertest, test(ing) phase(s) *with:* interval(s), timeout(s), spac(e,es,ed,ing), detention, delay(s,ed,ing), frequenc(y, ies). *Consider also:* distributed practice, spaced exposure, intertrial nonreinforcement. *See also* Reinforcement; Stimuli.

Interval, interstimulus. See *Interstimulus interval.*

Interval, intertrial. See *Intertrial interval.*

Interval reinforcement, fixed. See *Fixed interval reinforcement.*

Interval reinforcement, variable. See *Variable interval reinforcement.*

Intervals and scales, musical. See *Musical intervals and scales.*

Intervals, birth. See *Birth intervals.*

Intervention. Intervention(s). Crisis treatment. Mediation. Intercession. Interced(e,ed,ing). Arbitrat(e,ed,ing,ion). Peacemaking. Therap(y,ies). Interven(e, ed,ing). Care. Facilitat(e,ed,ing,ion). Assist(ed,ing,ance). Support(ed,ing). Aid(ed,ing). *Consider also:* crisis intervention, treatment, suicide prevention, remediation, special education, interfer(e,ed,ing,ence). *See also*

Assistance; Behavior modification; Child abuse prevention; Counseling; Crime prevention; Crisis intervention; Drug and narcotic control; Early intervention; Employee assistance programs; Helping behavior; International intervention; Mediation; Protection; Psychotherapy; Rehabilitation; Social action; Social legislation; Social work; State intervention; War prevention.

Intervention, crisis. See *Crisis intervention.*

Intervention, early. See *Early intervention.*

Intervention, government. See *State intervention.*

Intervention, international. See *International intervention.*

Intervention, military. See *International intervention.*

Intervention, state. See *State intervention.*

Interview, psychological. See *Psychological interview.*

Interviews. Interview(ed,ing,s). Elicit(ed, ing,ation) information. Question(ed,ing). Microcounsel(ed,ing). Counsel(ed,ing). Casework. Debrief(ing,ed). Interrogat(e, ed,ing,ion). Reinterview(ed,ing,s). Discussion(s). Question and answer session. Press conference(s). Probe(s). Cross examin(e,ed,ing,ation,ations). *See also* Employment interviews; Intake (agency); Medical history taking; Oral history; Psychological d.riefing; Qualitative methods; Questioning; Surveys.

Interviews, employment. See *Employment interviews.*

Interviews, job applicant. See *Employment interviews.*

Intimacy. Intimacy. Intimate relationship(s). Close(ness) relationship(s). Interpersonal closeness. Love. Psychological merger(s). Bonding. Tenderness. Caress(ed,es,ing). Close contact(s). Endearment. Intens(e,ity) relationship(s). Affective attachment. Familiarity. Committed relationship(s). Close association(s). *Choose from:* intimate, close, love, loving, romantic, intense, personal *with:* relationship(s), relations, friendship(s), dyad(s), involvement, couples, contact(s), attachment(s), association(s). *See also* Attachment behavior; Friendship; Interpersonal compatibility; Interpersonal relations; Love; Marital enrichment; Marital satisfaction; Marital sexual behavior; Physical contact; Rapport; Self disclosure; Sexual partners; Sexual satisfaction; Social nearness.

Intimidation. Intimidat(e,ed,ing,ion). Scare(d). Frighten(ed,ing). Overawed. Cowed. Daunt(ed,ing). Bully(ing).

Bullied. Coerc(e,ed,ing,ion). Terroriz(e,ed,ing). *See also* Fear; Fear of crime; Harassment; Internal security; Online harassment; Psychological warfare; Sexual coercion; Sexual harassment; Teasing; Terrorism; Threat; Threat postures.

Intolerance. Intoleran(t,tness,tly,ce). Zero tolerance. Unsympathetic(ally). Unforbearing. Unwilling to endure. Inhospitable(ness). Unindulgent. Impatient(ly). *Consider also:* cynical(ly), contemptuous(ly), disdainful(ly), fractious(ly), inflexib(le, ility), obdurate(ly,ness). *See also* Contempt; Food hypersensitivity; Impatience; Prejudice.

Intonation (phonetics). Intonation(al). Inflection. *Consider also:* accent, tone, intonology, pitch pattern(s), ris(e,ing) pitch, fall(ing) pitch, tone of voice. *See also* Inflection; Speech characteristics; Suprasegmentals; Voice.

Intoxication, alcohol. See *Drunkenness.*

Intoxication, diagnosis of alcohol. See *Diagnosis of alcohol intoxication.*

Intranets. Intranet(s). Internal network(s, ing). Internal TCP/IP network(s,ing). *Consider also:* private network(s), corporate web(s). interlinked local area network(s). *See also* Extranets; Firewalls (computers); Information exchange.

Intrapreneurship. Intrapreneur(s,ship, ing,ial,ialism). *Choose from:* internal, corporate *with:* entrepreneur(s,ship, ing,ial,ialism). Corporate innovater(s). *Choose from:* risk taking, innovative, creative *with:* manager(s). Innovation team(s). *Consider also:* enterprise culture. *See also* Entrepreneurship; Innovations; Leadership; Organizational culture.

Intrinsic motivation. Intrinsic motivation. *Choose from:* intrinsic(ally), internal(ly), self, personal(ly) *with:* motiv(e,es,ating, ated,ation), interest(s,ed,ing), rewarding, satisf(ying,action). *Consider also:* intentionality, purpose(s) in life, inner direct(ion,ed,edness), personal goal(s), internal locus of control. *See also* Goal orientation; Internal rewards; Locus of control; Needs.

Introduction. Introduc(e,ed,ing,tion,tions). Present(ed,ing,ation,ations). Announc(e, ed,ing,ement,ements). *Consider also:* foreward(s), preface(s), prefatory writing(s), prefatory note(s), preamble(s), prologue(s), lead paragraph(s), einleitung(en), eingang, introduzione(s), introduccion(s), introit(us). *See also* Incipits; Overtures (music); Preludes.

Introduction, plant. See *Plant introduction.*

Introduction, product. See *Product*

introduction.

Introjection. Introject(s,ed,ing,ion,ive). *Choose from:* assimilat(e,ed,ing), incorporat(e,ed,ing,ion) *with:* love object(s). *Consider also:* secondary identification, secondary narcissism. *See also* Defense mechanisms; Identification (psychology); Internalization.

Introspection. Introspect(ion,ive,iveness). Internal awareness. Private thought(s). Narcissis(m,tic). Soul searching. Intrapersonal exploration. Inner life. *Choose from:* self, inner *with:* consciousness, aware(ness), analysis, preoccup(ied,ation,ations), reflection(s), reflective(ness), examination(s), observation(s), contemplation. *See also* Enlightenment (state of mind); Personality processes; Self disclosure; Self understanding.

Introversion. Introver(t,ted,ts,sion). Phantasy cathexis. Internality. Withdrawn. Seclusive(ness). Shy(ness). Inner directed. Preoccup(ation,ied) with oneself. Self centered. *Consider also:* narcissism, hypochondria(c), seclusion, subjective(ness). *See also* Narcissism; Personality traits; Shyness; Social phobia; Withdrawal (defense mechanism).

Introversion, social. See *Introversion.*

Intuition. Intuit(ive,iveness,ion,ions). Direct apprehension. Immediate understanding. Direct knowledge. Sensing. Sensitivity. Empath(y,etic). Precognit(ive,ion). Prerecognition. Subconsciously. Subconscious awareness. Discern(ing,ment). Sixth sense. Foreboding. Presentiment. Foreknowledge. Hunch(es). Premonition(s). *See also* Cognition; Comprehension; Guessing; Imagination; Insight; Reasoning; Verstehen.

Invalids. Invalid(s). *Choose from:* sick(ly), infirm, unwell, ill(ness), weak(ly), feeble, unhealthy, diseased, bedridden, indisposed, convalescent, home-bound, shut-in, dying, hospitalized *with:* person(s), patient(s), people, men, man, women, woman, child(ren). *Consider also:* inpatient(s), valetudinarian(s). *See also* Chronic disease; Hypochondriasis; Illness.

Invasion. Invasion. Invad(e,ed,er,ers,ing). Territorial intrusion. Violate(d) personal space. Intrud(e,ed,ers,ing). Intrusion(s). Occupation of land. Penetration. Maraud(e,ed,er,ers,ing). Make inroads. Police action. Infringement. Irruption. *See also* Aerial reconnaissance; Aggression; Assault (battle); Borderlands; Colonization; Combat; Imperialism; International conflict; Military operations; Military retreat; War.

Invasion, biological. See *Bioinvasion.*

Invasion of privacy. Invasion of privacy.

Invad(e,es,ed,ing) priva(cy,te). *Choose from:* invad(e,es,ed,ing), invasion(s), deceptive(ly) collect(ed,ing,ion), misus(e,ed,es,ing), abus(e,ed,es,ing), threat(en,encd,cning,s), compromis(e,ed, es,ing), monitor(ed,es,ing), track(ed,s, ing), spy(ing), videotap(e,ed,ing), wiretap(s,ped,ping), tape-record(s,ed, ing), sell(ing), sold *with:* priva(cy,te), personal information, identifiable information, information on citizens, sensitive information, financial data, personal data, health-care record(s), medical record(s), telephone conversation(s), Social Security number(s), credit report(s), confidential(ity), *Consider also:* right(s) to privacy, phone security, protect(ed,ing,ion) of privacy. Snoop(ed,ing). Strip search(ed,ing). Disclos(e,ed,ure) of medical history. Hidden video camera(s). Eavesdrop(ped, ping). Random drug test(s,ing). Spy(ing). Spied upon. Violat(e,ed,ing) confiden(ce,ces,tial,tiality). Big brother. Citizen surveillance. Warrantless search(es). Unauthorized release of record(s). Disclos(e,ed,ure) of personal information. Fourth amendment. *See also* Confidentiality; Eavesdropping; Electronic eavesdropping; Online privacy; Personal space; Privacy laws; Right of privacy; Surveillance of citizens; Voyeurism.

Invective. Invective(ly,ness). Abusive language. Put-down(s). Rude comment(s,ary). Insult(s). Insulting remark(s). Verbal abuse. Vile word(s). Bad word(s). Foul language. Vituperat(ive,ory,ous). *Consider also:* opprobrious(ness), scurril(e,ous, ousness), truculent(ly), censorious(ness), condemnat(ion,ory), damn(ed,ing,atory), denunciat(ion,ory), reproach(ed,ing,ful). *See also* Emotional abuse; Ethnic slurs; Obscenity; Sexual harassment; Street harassment; Verbal abuse; Vulgarity.

Inventions. Invent(ed,or,ors,ing,ive). Patent(ed,s,ing). New applications. New technology. Discover(y,ed,ies,ing). Innovation(s). New device(s). Better mousetrap. Prototyp(e,es,ical). Laboratory breakthrough(s). Improvisation(s). Original product(s). Creation(s). Breakthrough(s). *See also* Change; Creativity; Discoveries (findings); Experiments; High technology industries; Innovations; Intangible property; Inventors; Patents; Problem solving; Product introduction; Research applications; Technological forecasting; Technological innovations; Technological progress; Technology transfer.

Inventories. Inventor(y,ies,ied,ying). Backlog(s). Roster(s). Census(es). Register(s). List(s) of assets. Merchandise on hand. Stockpile(s). Item(,ized, ization). Index(es). Schedule(s). Checklist(s). Rating scale(s). Classification instrument(s). Tall(y,ies). Rating form(s). Scale(s). Poll(s,ed,ing). Check list(s). Listing(s). Questionnaire(s). Registr(y,ies). Enumeration(s). Survey(s). Screening program(s). Indicator(s). Statistic(s). Director(y,ies). Statistical information. *See also* Backlog; Enumeration; Indexes (indicators); Interest inventories; Measurement; Personality measures; Tests.

Inventories, interest. See *Interest inventories.*

Inventories, personality. See *Personality measures.*

Inventors. Inventor(s). Creator(s). Crafts(man,men,woman,women,person). Innovator(s). Originator(s). Architect(s). Author(s). Founder(s). Developer(s). Pioneer(s). Father(s) of invention. Designer(s). *See also* Creativity; Inventions.

Inventory management. Inventory management. *Choose from:* inventor(y,ies), stock(pile,piles), suppl(y,ies), backlog(s), asset(s) *with:* manag(ement,ing), handl(e,ed,ing), decision(s), logistic(s,al), control(led, ling), data, optimiz(e,ed,ing,ation), reduc(e,ed,ing,tion), deplet(e,ed,ing,ion). *Consider also:* warehousing, distribution center(s). *See also* Decision support systems; Management information systems; Storage.

Inversion. Inversion(s). Invert(ed,ing,ible). Transpos(e,ed,ing,ition,itions,al). Revers(al,ed,ing,ion,ions). Retroflex(ion), Retroversion(s). *Consider also:* per motu contrario, per arsin et thesin, palindrom(e,ic), overturn(ed,ing). *See also* Atavism (biology).

Invertebrates. Invertebrate(s). Nonchordate animal(s). *Consider also:* tunicata, cephalochordata, protozoa, porifera, coelenterata, echinodermata, platyhelminthes, nemathelminthes, annelida, mollusca, arthropoda, insect(s), plankton, arachnida, sea squirt(s), lancelet(s), brachiopoda, crustacea, mollusk(s), sponge(s), worm(s), etc. *See also* Animals; vertebrates.

Investigations. Investigat(e,ed,ing,ion,ions). Research(ed,ing). Explor(e,ed,ing,ation, ations). Home evaluation(s). Police report(s). Frisk(ed,ing). Search(ed,ing). Search and seizure. Sting(s). Fact finding. Prob(e,es,ed,ing). Scrutin(y,ize, ized,izing). Inquir(e,ed,ing,y,ies). Enquir(e,ed,ing,y,ies). Audit(s,ed,ing). Question(ed,ing). Interrogat(e,ed,ing, ion,ions). Inspect(ed,ing,ion,ions). Examin(e,ed,ing,ation,ations). *Consider also:* autops(y,ies), interview(s), questionnaire(s), forensic medicine, analys(is,es), diagnos(is,es),

experiment(s,ed,ing,ation), oversight, surveillance, monitor(ed,ing), pinpoint(ed,ing), finding(s), detect(ed, ing,ion). *See also* Assessment; Detectives; Drug enforcement; Experiments; Gun control; Inquiry (theory of knowledge); Invasion of privacy; Law enforcement; Observation; Questioning; Quests; Research.

Investigations, criminal. See *Criminal investigations.*

Investigations, government. See *Government investigations.*

Investing, socially responsible. See *Socially responsible investing.*

Investment, emotional. See *Cathexis.*

Investment, foreign. See *Foreign investment.*

Investment policy. Investment polic(y,ies). *Choose from:* investment(s), portfolio(s), investor(s), capital gain(s) *with:* polic(y, ies), code(s), law(s), objective(s), priorit(y,ies), incentive(s), agreement(s), guarantee(s,d). *See also* Disinvestment; Foreign investment; Investments; Public policy.

Investments. Invest(ed,ing,ment,ments). Human capital. Equity. Portfolio. Stock(s). Securities. Bond(s). Annuit(y, ies). Mutual fund(s). Individual retirement account(s). IRAs. Certificate(s) of deposit. All savers certificate(s). Money market account(s). *Consider also:* trust fund(s), pension plan(s), ethical investment(s), disinvest(ed,ing,ment,ments). *See also* Banking; Capital (financial); Capitalization; Collectibles; Credit; Disinvestment; Dividends; Electronic trading (securities); Equity (financial); Finance; Financial planning; Futures market; Gains; Investment policy; Junk bonds; Land (property); Ownership; Personal property; Profitability; Profits; Savings; Stock exchange; Stock options; Stockholders; Wealth.

Investments, capital. See *Capital expenditures.*

Investor relations. Investor relations. *Choose from:* investor(s), stockholder(s), shareholder(s), bondholder(s) *with:* relation(s,ship,ships), expectation(s), trust, acceptance, retention, satisf(y,ied, action), dissatisf(y,ied,action), partner(s, ship,ships), rapport, contract(s). *See also* Client relations; Confidentiality; Dividends; Professional client relations; Professional ethics; Public relations; Stockholders.

Investors. See *Capitalists and financiers; Stockholders.*

Invocations. Invocat(ion,ions,ional,ory). Beseech(ed,ing,ment). Petition(ed,ing). Entreat(y,ies). Plea(s). Plead(ed,ing). Implor(e,ed,ing). Pray(ed,ing).

Prayer(s). Incantation(s). Evocation(s). *See also* Blessing; Liturgy; Prayer; Religious rituals; Worship.

Involuntary (automatic). Involuntar(y,ily). Automatic(ally). Reflex. Unconscious(ly). Instinctive(ly). Spontaneous(ly). Uncontrolled. *See also* Reflex.

Involuntary (unwilling). Involuntar(y,ily). Unwilling(ness). Reluctan(ce,t,tly). Forced. Under duress. Against one's will. Compelled. Compulsory. Oblig(atory,ed). *See also* Compulsory participation; Duress; Involuntary retirement; Involuntary sterilization.

Involuntary retirement. Involuntary retirement. *Choose from:* involuntar(y, ily), health reasons, plant closing(s), unwilling(ness), reluctan(ce,t,tly), forced, under duress, compelled, compulsory, oblig(atory,ed) *with:* retir(e,ed,ing,ment). *See also* Mandatory retirement; Personnel termination; Plant closings; Retirement; Severance pay.

Involuntary sterilization. Involuntary steriliz(e,ed,ing,ation). *Choose from:* involuntary, compulsory, mandatory, eugenic, forced, genetic defect(s) *with:* steriliz(e,es,ed,ing,ation), castrat(e,ed, es,ing,ion). *Choose from:* forbid(den, ding), prohibit(ed,ing) *with:* marr(y, ying,iage,iages). *Consider also:* eugenics law(s). *See also* Eugenics; Genetic counseling; Informed consent; Involuntary (unwilling); Reproductive rights; Sterilization (sex).

Involutional depression. See *Involutional psychosis.*

Involutional psychosis. Involutional psychos(is,es). Atypical paranoid disorder(s). *Choose from:* involutional, climacteric, middle age, mid-life, midlife *with:* depression(s), depressive, melancholia, paraphrenia, parano(ia,id), delusion(s), agitation, psychos(is,es). *See also* Climacteric; Paranoid disorders; Paranoid schizophrenia.

Involvement. Involv(e,ed,ement,ing). Engag(ed,ing,ement). Commit(ted, ment). Participat(e,ed,ing,ion). Activ(e,ism,ist,ists). Participant(s). Vested interest(s). Interested. Concern(ed). Interaction. Leadership. Interdependen(t,ce). Absorb(ed). Absorption. Attract(ed,ing,ion). Concentrat(e,ed,ing,ion). Affiliation(s). Binding. Cooperat(e,ed,ing,ion). Bond(ed,ing). Input. Helping relationship(s). Care(d). Caring. Contribut(e,ed, ing). Support(ed,ing). Emotional investment(s). Accept(ed,ing) responsibility. Helping behavior. Attachment(s). Relationship(s). Engross(ed,ing). Preoccup(ation,ied). Hold(ing) attention. Pledged. Entangle(d,ment). Dedicat(ed, ing,ion). *See also* Activism; Citizen participation; Commitment (emotional);

Community involvement; Compulsory participation; Job involvement; Participative decision making; Participative management; Political participation; Social cohesion; Worker participation.

Involvement, community. See *Community involvement.*

Involvement, job. See *Job involvement.*

Involvement, parental. See *Involvement; Parent adolescent relations; Parent aspiration; Parent child relations; Parent school relations; Parental attitudes.*

Iron and steel workers. Iron worker(s). Steel worker(s). Steelworker(s). Ironworker(s). Steelwork(s) grinder(s). *Consider also:* auto worker(s), iron puddler(s), machinist(s). *See also* Automobile industry workers; Blue collar workers; Employees; Iron industry; Industrial workers.

Iron industry. Iron industry. Iron manufacturing. Steel industry. Foundr(y,ies). Iron production. Steel production. Iron Compan(y,ies). Iron Works. *See also* Iron and steel workers; Industry; Metal industry.

Irony. Iron(y,ies,ic). Sardonic(ally). Skeptically humorous. Metairony. *Consider also:* understat(e,ed,ing, ement), meio(sis,tic,tically), dissimulat(e,ed,ing,ion), sarcas(m,tic), hyperbole, overstat(e,ed,ing,ement), mock(ed,ing,ery), sneer(ed,ing), pun(s), parod(y,ies,ic,istic), contradict(ory,ion, ions), wordplay. *See also* Absurd; Allegory; Aporia; Deconstruction; Metaphors; Oxymoron; Paradoxes; Postmodernism; Satire; Scatology.

Irrational beliefs. Irrational belief(s). Cognitive distortion(s). Unreasoning belief(s). *Choose from:* irrational, illogical, erroneous, distorted, maladaptive, unreasonable, inconceivable, groundless, implausible, untenable, superstitious, magical *with:* belief(s), idea(s), conviction(s), cognition(s), thought(s), thinking, attitude(s), opinion(s). *See also* Beliefs; Delusions; Groundless; Illogical; Implausibility; Irrationalism (Philosophy); Magical thinking; Thought disturbances; Superstitions.

Irrationalism (philosophy). Irrationalism. False rationality. *Consider also:* anti-rationalism, nonsense language, beyond logic, irrational use of language, play on language, irrational form(s) of expression, inconsistenc(y,ies), ideological apologia, anti-scien(ce,tific), distrust of science, neo-rationalists, reactionary. *See also* Anti-intellectualism; Anti-science movement; Countermovements; Dogmatism; Ideologies; Irrational beliefs; Philosophy; Rationalism.

Irreducibility. Irreducib(le,ility). *Consider*

also: sui generis, emergent propert(y, ies), idiosyncratic, inexplicab(le,ly,ility), idiosyncratic, immanent, autonomous, phenomenological. *See also* Causality; Phenomenological psychology; Phenomenology.

Irreligion. Irreligio(n,us,usly). Religious nonaffiliation. Impiet(y,ies). Irreveren(t,ce). Non church-affiliated. Unchurched. Infidel(s). Unbelief. Unbelieving. Neglect(ful) of religion. Lack of religion. Godless. Nonreligious. Unreligious. *See also* Agnosticism; Apostasy; Atheism; Heresy; Infidels; Religious beliefs; Secularization; Uncertainty.

Irresistible impulse. See *Insanity defense.*

Irreversibility. Irreversibility. Irreversibl(e, y). Irrevocabl(e,y). Irreparabl(e,y). Unreversible. Irremediable. Unregainable. Irrecoverable. Irretrievabl(e,y). Irredeemabl(e,y). Unredeemable. Irreclaimable. Unsalvageable. Beyond saving. Beyond salvaging. Forever lost. Extinct(ion). *Consider also:* irreversible process(es), entropy, nonequilibrium thermodynamics, open systems. *See also* Extinction (species).

Irrigation. Irrigat(e,ed,ing,ion). Watering system(s). Microirrigation. *Consider also:* runoff recycling, ditch(es), canal(s), flume(s), weir(s). *See also* Arable land; Conservation of natural resources; Dams; Desertification; Dikes (engineering); Drainage; Environmental protection; Land preservation; Reclamation of land; Restoration ecology; Rural development; Soil conservation; Soil erosion; Water resources development.

Irritability. Irritab(le,ility). Impatien(t,ce). Petulan(t,ce). Test(y,iness). Excitab(le, ility). Hypersensitiv(e,ity). Hot temper(ed). High strung. Noise sensitiv(e,ity). Ill tempered. Resentful(ness). Annoy(ed,ance). Contentious(ness). Quarrelsome. Mood(y,iness). Easily provoked. *See also* Emotional states; Hypersensitivity; Impatience; Moodiness; Personality traits.

Islam. Islam(ic,ite,ist,ists,icist,icists). Moslem(s). Muslim(s). Muhammad. Mahdi(s). Mohammed(an,ans,anism). *Consider also:* Koran, Quran, Qur'an, Mecca, Imam(s), Jihad, Kalif, Sharia, Muslim, Mussulman, Mussalman, Shahada, Salah, Ramadan, Zakat, Haj, Sunni(s), Shi'ite(s), Taliban. *See also* African cultural groups; African empires; Asian empires; Black Muslims; Indian (India) cultural groups; Indonesian cultural groups; Islamic fundamentalism; Islamic Resistance Movement; Jewish-Arab relations; Middle East; Moslem prayer; North Africa; Philippine Islands cultural groups; Religion; Religious affiliation; Religious funda-

mentalism; Religious revivals; South Asia; Southeast Asia; Southeast Asian cultural groups.

Islamic fundamentalism. Islamic fundamentalis(m,t,ts). *Choose from:* Islam(ic,ite,ist,ists,icist,icists), Moslem(s), Muslim(s), Mahdi(s). Mohammed(an,ans,anism) *with:* militant(s), conservative(s), fundamentalis(m,t,ts), extremis(m,t,ts), movement, radical(s). *Consider also:* Islamic Salvation Front, Gamaa al-Islamiya, Islamist(s), Moslem Brotherhood, Muslim Brotherhood, shari'a. *See also* Islam; Islamic Resistance Movement; Moslem prayer; Religious fundamentalism.

Islamic Resistance Movement. Islamic Resistance Movement. Hamas. Islamic Jihad. Extremist Palestinian group(s). Islamic Salvation Front. Armed Islamic Group. *Choose from:* Islam(ic,ist,ists), Palestinian(s), Algeria(n,ns), Egypt(ian, ians), Hamas *with:* suicide bomber(s), bombing(s), extremist(s), guerrilla(s), resistance, terrorist(s), radical group(s), militant(s). *See also* Anti-government radicals; Guerrillas; Islam; Islamic fundamentalism; Jewish-Arab relations; National fronts.

Island ecology. Island ecology. *Choose from:* island(s), isle(s), islet(s), atoll(s), ait(s), key(s) *with:* sea level(s), shoreline(s), ecological imbalance(s), ecological balance(s), ecolog(y,ical), biogeograph(y,ical), conservation, species, habitat(s), plant(s), animal(s), bird(s), insect(s), flora, fauna. *See also* Beaches; Coast defenses; Ecology; Islands; Shorelines; Shore protection; Submerged lands; Territorial waters.

Islanders, Pacific. See *Pacific Islanders*

Islands. Island(s). Isle(s). Islet(s). Atoll(s). Ait(s). Key(s). *Consider also:* archipelago(s,es), coral reef(s), barrier isle(s). *See also* Beaches; Coast defenses; Island ecology; Shorelines; Shore protection; Submerged lands; Territorial waters.

Isolation. Isolat(e,ed,ing,ion). Sequestrat(e, ed,ing,ion). Separat(e,ed,ing,ion). Dissociat(e,ed,ing,ion). Detach(ed,ing ment). Disconnect(ed,ing). Estrange(d, s,ment). Segregat(e,ed,ing,ion). Quarantin(e,ed). Solitary confinement. *Consider also:* sensory deprivation, withdrawal, loneliness. *See also* Alienation; Anomie; Deprivation; Disengagement; Isolation (defense mechanism); Loneliness; Marginality (sociological); Otherness; Professional isolation; Sensory deprivation; Social distance; Social isolation; Solitude.

Isolation (defense mechanism). Isolat(ed, ion). Intrapsychic isolation. *Consider also:* avoidance, alienation, detach(ed, ment) from self, intellectualiz(e,ed,es, ing,ion), repress(es,ed,ing,ion), stoic(ism). *See also* Defense mechanisms; Intellectualization (defense mechanism); Solitude; Stoicism; Withdrawal (defense mechanism).

Isolation, patient. See *Patient isolation.*

Isolation, professional. See *Professional isolation.*

Isolation, social. See *Social isolation.*

Isolationism. Isolation(ism,ist,ists). Noninvolvement. Autarky. Autarchy. *Consider also:* neutrality, continentalism, hemispheric isolationism, economic self-sufficiency, Monroe doctrine, Fortress America. *See also* Autarky; Foreign policy; Neutrality; Noninvolvement; Trade protection.

Issues. See *Problems.*

Issues, controversial. See *Controversial issues.*

Issues, cultural. See *Cultural issues.*

Issues, political. See *Political issues.*

Issues, social. See *Controversial issues; Political issues; Social movements; Social problems.*

Issues, territorial. See *Territorial issues.*

Italian Americans. Italian American(s). American Italian(s). American(s) of Italian descent. Little Italy. *Choose from:* Italian, Sicilian, Roman *with:* background(s), ancest(ry,ors), famil(y,ies), forefather(s), descent, descend(ent,ents, ant,ants). *See also* Ethnic groups; Minority groups.

Italic non-romance languages. Italic non-romance languages. Classical Latin. Faliscan. Medieval Latin. Old Latin. Oscan. Umbrian. Vulgar Latin. *See also* Language; Languages (as subjects); Romance languages; Western Europe.

Itinerant workforce. See *Migrant workers.*

Ivory. Ivory. *Choose from:* elephant, walrus, narwhal, rhino(s,ceros,ceroses), mammoth(s), mastodon(s), pachyderm(s) *with:* tusk(s), horn(s), *Consider also:* piano key(s) *See also* Bone implements; Carving (decorative arts).

Ivory carving. See *Carving (decorative arts).*

J

Jails. See *Prisons*.

Jainism. Jain(a,as,ism). *Consider also:* Jina, Mahavira, kaivalya, Digambaras, Svetambaras, nayavada, tirthankaras, ahimsa. *See also* Religion; Religious affiliation; Karma.

Jamming of communications. Jamming of communications. *Choose from:* interfer(e,ed,ing,ence), jam(med,mer, mers,ming) *with:* communication(s), airwave(s), multitone, radar, radio, signal(s), telecommunication(s), tone(s). *See also* Broadcasts; Communication barriers; Electronic eavesdropping.

Janissary music. Janissary music. *Choose from:* Janissar(y,ies), Ottoman Turk(s,ish,ey) *with:* music, march(es), fanfare(s), ensemble(s). *Consider also:* Turkish music, alla turca. *See also* Military music; War songs.

Janitors. Janitor(s,ial). Housing maintenance worker(s). Custodian(s). Subway cleaning person(s). *Consider also:* building cleaning compan(y,ies), janitorial service(s), cleaning service(s), building superintendent(s). *See also* Custodians; Domestic service.

Japanese Americans. Japanese American(s). Nisei. Issei. Sansei. American Japanese. Kibei. *Choose from:* Japanese descent, Japanese background, Japanese ancestry *with:* America(n,ns), United States. *Consider also:* Japanese Canadian(s), Canadian-Japanese. *See also* Asian Americans; Ethnic groups; Minority groups.

Japanese Canadians. See *Japanese Americans*.

Japanese drama. Japanese drama. *Choose from:* Japan(ese), No(h), Kabuki *with:* drama(s,tic), play(s), theat(re,er). *See also* Drama; Folk drama; Haiku.

Japanese language. Japanese language. *Choose from:* Japan(ese) *with:* language, word(s), term(s), speech, parlance, grammar, grammatical(ly), linguistic(s, ally), syntax, semantic(s,ally), *Consider also:* Altaic language(s). *See also* East Altaic languages; Languages (as subjects).

Jargon. Jargon. Neologism(s). Argot. Hackneyed speech. Cliche(s). Buzz word(s). Buzzword(s). Legalese. Bureaucratese. Journalese. Overused word(s). Trite language. Newspeak. Gobbledygook. Officialese. Geek(icon, speak). *Consider also:* technobabble, eurobabble, ecobabble, psychobabble. *See also* Catchwords; Cliches; Communication (thought transfer); Hackneyed;

Language; Language shift; Language usage; Language varieties.

Jazz. Jazz. Progressive jazz. Cool jazz. Dixieland. The blues. Bop. Bebop. Rebop. Ragtime. Swing music. Scat singing. *Consider also:* third stream, modern jazz, West Coast jazz, barrelhouse, boogie woogie, bossa-nova, samba(s). *See also* Afro-American music; Blues (music); Dance; Disco music; Folk poetry; Funk (music); Improvisation; Jazz dance; Jazz musicians; Music; Popular culture; Popular music.

Jazz dance. Jazz danc(e,ed,ing). Boogie. Jitterbug. Charleston. *Choose from:* jazz, Dixieland, the blues, bop, bebop, rebop, ragtime, swing music *with:* danc(e,ed, ing), tap, choreograph(y,ies,ic,ed,ing), *Consider also:* jazzercise. *See also* Blues (music); Dance; Jazz (music); Jazz musicians; Popular culture.

Jazz musicians. Jazz musician(s). Scat singer(s). Stride pianist(s). *Choose from:* jazz, Dixieland, the blues, bop, bebop, rebop, ragtime, swing music *with:* ensemble(s), singer(s), artist(s), drummer(s), saxophonist(s), clarinetist(s), band(s), bandleader(s), pianist(s), group(s), quartet(s), sextet(s), vocalist(s), instrumentalist(s). *Consider also:* W.C. Handy, Scott Joplin, Blind Lemon Jefferson, Huddie Ledbetter (Leadbelly), Big Bill Broonzy, Duke Ellington, Louis Armstrong, Jelly Roll Morton, Eubie Blake, Bix Beiderbecke, Benny Goodman, Artie Shaw, Tommy Dorsey, Harry James, Charlie "Bird" Parker, Lester Young, Thelonius Monk, Dizzy Gillespie, Miles Davis, Lennie Tristano, Dave Brubeck, Mahalia Jackson, Gertrude "Ma" Rainey, Ethel Waters, Bessie Smith, Billie Holiday, Fats Waller, etc. *See also* Blues (music); Jazz dance; Jazz (music); Musicians.

Jealousy. Jealous(y,ness). Env(y,ious, iousness). Covet(ous,ousness). Rival(s,ry). Resent(ful,ment). Distrust(ing,ful). Doubt(ing). Mistrust(ful,ing). Possessive(ness). Suspicious(ness). Spiteful(ness). Grudging. Begrudging. Backbiting. *See also* Anger; Anxiety; Emotions; Interpersonal conflict; Literary quarrels; Negativism; Personality traits; Possessiveness; Sexual violence; Spouse abuse; Resentment.

Jehovah. Jehovah. Yahweh. Yahveh. YHVH. YHWH. *Consider also:* adonai, elohim. *See also* Bible; Deities; God concepts; Omniscience of God; Oneness of God; Presence of God.

Jehovah's Witnesses. Jehovah's Witness(es). Russellite(s). International Bible Students Association. *Consider also:* Charles Taze Russell, Kingdom Hall, The Watchtower, Awake, West Virginia State Board of Education v. Barnette. *See also* Millenarianism; Protestantism; Religious fundamentalism.

Jeremiads. Jeremiad(s). Harangue(s). Complaint(s). Diatribe(s). Tirade(s). Prolonged lament(ation). *See also* Complaints; Diatribe.

Jesters, fools and. See *Fools and jesters*.

Jet lag. Jet lag. *Consider also:* air travel, travel(er,ers,ler,lers), flight(s), flying *with:* biological clock(s), circadian. *See also* Air transportation; Biological rhythms.

Jewelry. Jewel(s,ry). *Consider also:* buckle(s), comb(s), ring(s), earring(s), bracelet(s), brooch(es), pin(s), necklace(s), locket(s), pendant(s), rosar(y,ies), tiara(s), crown(s), diadem(s), nosering(s). *See also* Beads; Gems; Goldwork.

Jewelry, ancient See *Ancient jewelry*.

Jewelry making. Jewelry making. *Choose from:* jewelry, necklace(s), bracelet(s), earring(s), ring(s), pin(s), brooch(es) *with:* design(er,ers,ed,ing), fashion(ed, ing), construct(ed,ing,ion), making, made. *See also* Beads; Crafts; Jewelry.

Jewish-Arab relations. Jewish-Arab relations. *Choose from:* Jew(ish), Israel(i,is), Netanyahu, Yitzhak Rabin, Shimon Peres *with:* Arab(s), Palestinian(s), P.L.O. , Hamas, Yasir Arafat, Anwar Sadat, Syria(n,ns), Leban(on,ese), Egypt(ian,ians), Jordan(ian,ians), Kuwait(i,is), West Bank, Gaza *with:* relations(hip), tension(s), olive branch, peace agreement(s), peace process, terrorism, deadlock(ed), polic(y,ies), negotiation(s), mediation, arbitration, violence, talks, conflict. *Consider also:* Camp David accords. *See also* Islam; Islamic Resistance Movement; Judaism; Middle East.

Jewish drama. Jewish drama. *Choose from:* Jewish, Judeo, Jewish-American(s), Yiddish, Hebrew, Ladino *with:* drama (tic,tics,turgical), dramatist(s), theatre(s), theater(s), theatrical(s), play(s), music hall(s), playwrit(e,es,ing), comed(y,ies), script(s), traged(y,ies), *Consider also:* Judischer Kulturbund, Jewish Art Theatre, Jewish Repertory Theatre. *See* *also* Drama; Jewish literature; Jewish music; Judaism; Theater.

Jewish law. Jewish law(s). Mosaic law. Torah. Five books of Moses. Pentateuch. Halak(ah,ic). Halach(a,ic). Talmud(ic). Mishna(h). Gemara(h). *Choose from:* Jew(s,ish), Israel, Judaism, Leviticus, Mosaic, kosher, kashrut(h), rabbinic(al), Hebrew(s), Hebraic *with:* law(s), legal, code(s), tradition(s,al), practice(s), custom(s), restriction(s), rule(s), prohibition(s). *Consider also:* Ten Commandments, Rabbinical court(s), Targum, Sanhedrin, Law in the Bible, Biblical law(s). *See also* Bible; Canons; Judaism; Laws; Rabbinical literature; Religious councils and synods; Religious fundamentalism; Religious practices.

Jewish literature. Jewish literature. *Choose from:* Jew(s,ish,ry), Judeo, Judai(sm,c,ca), Jewish-American(s), Yiddish, Hebrew, Aramaic, Hebraic, Zionis(t,m), Ladino, Judeo-Spanish, Ashkenazi(c,m), Sephardi(c,m), holocaust *with:* literature, literary, short stor(y,ies), fiction, novel(s), book(s), poe(try,m,ms), prose, play(s), biograph(y,ies), text(s,ual), historio-graph(y,ies), autobiograph(y,ies), memoir(s), essay(s), satir(e,ical), humor, legend(s,ary), anecdote(s), proverb(s), myth(s,ology), tale(s), oral tradition(s), letter(s), newspaper(s), monograph(s,ic), scholarly work(s). *Consider also:* Judaica, Golem, Haskalah, Jewish author(s), Midrash(im), Forverts, Jewish Daily Forward, Jewish Forward, Der Tag, Apocrypha. *See also* Apocalyptic literature; Bible; Cabala; Folk literature; Jewish drama; Jewish music; Jewish mysticism; Literature; Rabbinical literature.

Jewish music. Jewish music. *Choose from:* Jewish, Judeo, Jewish-American(s), Yiddish, Hebrew, Ladino, Sephardic, Ashkenazic, Israel(i), synagogue(s), Hassidic, klezm(er,orim) *with:* music(al), psalm(s,ody), hymn(s), song(s), tune(s), repertor(y,ies), *Consider also:* cantor(s), cantillation, chazzan(im), piyyut(im), Missinai tune(s), Barekhu, Kedushah, Kaddish, Kol Nidre, romancero(s), niggun(im). *See also* Jewish drama; Jewish literature; Music; Religious music.

Jewish mysticism. Jewish mystic(s,ism,al). Zohar. Kabbalah. *Choose from:* Judaism, Jewish *with:* mystic(s,ism,al), talisman(s,ic), magic(al). *See also* Cabala; Jewish literature; Mysticism; Talisman.

Jewish sects. Jewish sect(s). *Consider also:* Pharisee(s), Essene(s), ultra-Orthodox Jew(s,ish), Lubavitch(er), Hasidim, Chabad-Lubavitch sect, early Christian(s), Qumran sect, 'Fourth

Philosophy,' Karaite(s). *See also* Judaism; Sects.

Jewish songs. See *Jewish music*

Jews. See *Judaism.*

Jingoism. Jingo(ism,ist,ists). Militaris(m, tic,t,ts). Warmonger(ing,s). Hawk(s,ish, ishness). Patriot(s,ism,ic). Nationalist(s). Flag waver(s). Chauvinis(m,t,ts, tic). *See also* Ethnocentrism; Nationalism; Nativism; Patriotism; Tribalism; War attitudes; Xenophobia.

Jinni. See *Spirits.*

Job analysis. See *Job descriptions.*

Job applicant interviews. See *Employment interviews.*

Job applicant screening. Job applicant screening. *Choose from:* applicant(s), job candidate(s), entry level, resume(s) *with:* test(ed,ing), screen(ed,ing), evaluat(ed,ing,ion), rate(d), rating(s), selection instrument(s). *See also* Employment agencies; Job applicants; Job search; Occupational tests; Personnel evaluation; Personnel management; Personnel selection.

Job applicants. Job applicant(s). Applicant(s). Applicant pool(s). Seeking employment. *Choose from:* job(s), position(s) *with:* applicant(s), candidate(s), seek(ing,er,ers), application(s), hunt(er,ers,ing). *Consider also:* employment interview(s), employability, employment potential, employee selection, hiring decision(s). *See also* Dislocated workers; Displaced homemakers; Employability; Employment interviews; Employment opportunities; Employment preparation; Job applicant screening; Job requirements; Job search; Occupational aspirations; Occupational qualifications; Work reentry.

Job change. See *Career change; Career mobility; Employee turnover; Personnel termination.*

Job characteristics. See *Job descriptions.*

Job classification. See *Occupational classification.*

Job counseling. See *Vocational guidance.*

Job creation. Job creation. Employment generation. Employment creation. Develop(ed,ing) local employment *Choose from:* creat(e,ed,ing,ion), develop(ed,ing,ment), generat(e,ed,ing, ion), add(ed,ing) *with:* job(s), employment. *Consider also:* job growth, lower(ed,ing) unemployment, reduc(e,ed,ing) unemployment. *See also* Economic development; Employment; Unemployment;

Job descriptions. Job description(s). *Choose from:* job(s), position(s), occupation(s,al), work *with:* description(s), responsibilit(y,ies),

typ(e,es,ology), dimension(s), characteristic(s), complexity, structure, functions, analysis, audit, specifications, duties, content, data, requirements, dimensions, components, activities, objectives, patterns, task(s), classification, competencies, attributes, assignments. *Consider also:* work load. *See also* Description; Job design; Job evaluation; Job requirements; Nontraditional careers; Occupational classification; Occupational qualifications; Occupational roles; Occupational stress; Personnel specifications; Tasks; Work skills.

Job design. Job design. Task delineation. *Choose from:* job(s), position(s), work, task(s) *with:* design(s,ed,ing), redesign(s,ed,ing), restructur(e,ed,ing), defin(e,ed,ing,ition,itions), simplif(y, ying,ication), reform(ed,ing), organiz(e, ed,ing,ation), reorganiz(e,ed,ing,ation), modif(y,ied,ying,ication), enlarg(e,ed, ing,ement), enrich(ed,ing,ment). *Consider also:* Fordism, Taylorism, deskill(ed,ing). *See also* Job descriptions; Job enrichment; Job satisfaction; Scientific management; Work simplification.

Job discrimination. See *Employment discrimination.*

Job displacement. See *Personnel termination.*

Job enrichment. Job enrichment. *Choose from:* job(s), task(s), work, working life, work role(s), career(s), worker(s) *with:* enrich(ed,ing,ment), expand(ed,ing), enlarg(e,ed,ing,ement), improv(e,ed,ing) quality, improv(e,ed,ing) content, satisfaction, upgrad(ed,ing), reclassif(y, ied,ication), redesign(ed,ing), restructur(e,ed,ing). *See also* Employee attitudes; Employee motivation; Job design; Job evaluation; Job involvement; Job rotation; Job satisfaction; Occupational adjustment; Organizational development; Quality of working life; Work humanization; Working conditions.

Job evaluation. Job evaluation. *Choose from:* job(s), task(s), work, employment *with:* evaluat(e,ed,ing,ion), apprais(e,ed, ing,al,als). *Consider also:* performance appraisal(s). *See also* Job descriptions; Job enrichment; Job satisfaction; Scientific management; Work simplification.

Job experience. See *Work experience.*

Job hunting. See *Job search.*

Job involvement. Job involvement. Workahol(ic,ism). *Choose from:* job(s), work, career(s), profession(s,al), occupation(s,al), vocation(s,al), organizational *with:* involv(e,ed, ement,ing), commit(ted,ment), identit(y,ies), identification, socialization, leadership, participat(e,ed,ing,ion), activ(e,ism,ist), interest(ed,s), concern(s, ed), absorb(ed,ing), concentrat(e,ed, ing,ion), contribut(e,ed,ing), emotional investment(s), responsibilit(y,ies), engross(ed,ing), dedicat(ed,ing,ion). *See also* Attitudes toward work; Employee attitudes; Employee incentive plans; Employee morale; Employee motivation; Employee ownership; Job performance; Job satisfaction; Participative management; Personnel loyalty; Worker control; Worker participation.

Job knowledge. Job knowledge. Professional knowledge. Expert knowledge. Occupational knowledge. *Choose from:* job, professional, expert, occupation(al) *with:* knowledge, expertise, aware(ness). *See also* Area of knowledge; Employee Characteristics; Intellectual capital; Knowledge Level; Job Performance; Work skills.

Job market. See *Labor market.*

Job mobility. See *Career mobility.*

Job opportunities. See *Employment opportunities.*

Job opportunities, equal. See *Equal job opportunities.*

Job performance. Job performance. Employee performance appraisal. Performance contingent pay. Work rate. *Choose from:* worker(s), work, job, operator(s), task, staff, workplace, supervisor(s), employee(s), teacher(s), faculty, personnel *with:* performance, productivity, rate, effectiveness, output, quality, efficiency. *See also* Employee attitudes; Employee efficiency; Employee productivity; Job involvement; Job knowledge; Personnel evaluation; Work load.

Job placement. See *Personnel placement.*

Job promotion. See *Promotion (occupational).*

Job qualifications. See *Occupational qualifications.*

Job recruitment. See *Personnel recruitment.*

Job redesign. See *Job design.*

Job requirements. Job requirement(s). Occupational qualification(s). *Choose from:* job, vocation(al), occupation(al), profession(al), career(s), work, employment, employee(s), hiree(s), labor market *with:* abilit(y,ies), qualif(y,ied, ication,ications), credential(s), skill(s), background, experience, education, over-educat(ed,ion), underqualif(y,ied), overqualif(y,ied), certification, prerequisite(s), licens(e,es,ing,ure), requirement(s), congruence. *Consider also:* worker job match, employability. *See also* Job descriptions; Occupational classification; Occupational qualifica-

tions; Personnel specifications.

Job retraining. See *Retraining.*

Job rewards. See *Employee benefits; Compensation (payment).*

Job rotation. Job(s) rotat(e,ed,ing,ion). *Choose from:* job(s), employee(s), department(s), executive(s), assignment(s), location(s) *with:* rotat(e,ed, ing,ion), interchange(able,ability), exchange(able,ability). *Consider also:* cross training. *See also* Job enrichment; Management training; Professional development.

Job safety. See *Occupational safety.*

Job satisfaction. Job satisfaction. Quality of working life. Professional pride. *Choose from:* job(s), employee(s), professional(s), work, career, staff, worker(s), subordinate(s), occupational *with:* reward(s,ing), pride, satisfaction(s), satisfying, dissatisfaction(s), adjustment, morale, attitude(s). *See also* Attitudes toward work; Burnout; Career change; Employee assistance programs; Employee attitudes; Employee morale; Job enrichment; Job evaluation; Job involvement; Life satisfaction; Morale; Occupational adjustment; Occupational attitudes; Occupational roles; Occupational status; Organizational climate; Organizational development; Quality of working life; Satisfaction; Self actualization; Workplaces; Work humanization; Work values.

Job search. Job search. *Choose from:* job(s), work, employment *with:* search(ing), seek(ing), hunting. *Consider also:* job fair(s), hiring fair(s), headhunter(s), send(ing) resume(s). *See also* Career change; Dislocated workers; Displaced homemakers; Employment agencies; Employment interviews; Employment opportunities; Job applicant screening; Job applicants; Job requirements; Labor market; Occupational qualifications; Search; Severance pay; Unemployment; Work reentry.

Job security. Job security. Tenur(e,ed). Permanent(ly) employ(ed,ment). Permanent appointment(s). Continuing appointment(s). *Choose from:* job(s), employ(ed,ee,ees,ment), position(s), work, career(s), vocation(s,al), occupation(s,al), labor market *with:* secur(e,ity), stability, stable, certainty, guarantee(s,d), permanen(t,tly,ce). *Consider also:* job insecurity, threat(s) of layoff. *See also* Business failures; Employee transfers; Employee turnover; Occupational tenure; Personnel termination; Plant closings; Retirement; Unemployment.

Job segregation. See *Labor market segmentation; Occupational segregation.*

Job selection. See *Occupational choice.*

Job sharing. Job sharing. *Choose from:* job(s), post(s), position(s), workload *with:* shar(e,ed,ing), rotat(e,ed,ing,ion). *Consider also:* flex-time, part-time, shorter workweek(s), alternative work schedule(s). *See also* Alternative lifestyles; Alternative work patterns; Flexible workplace practices; Part time employment; Work sharing.

Job skills. See *Work skills.*

Job specifications. See *Job requirements; Personnel specifications.*

Job status. See *Occupational status.*

Job stress. See *Occupational stress.*

Job tenure. See *Occupational tenure.*

Job training. See *Personnel training.*

Job vacancies. See *Employment opportunities.*

Jobholding, multiple. See *Moonlighting.*

Jobs. Job(s). Position(s). Appointment(s). Employment. Gainful(ly) employ(ed, ment). Occupation(s). Livelihood. Work. Pursuit(s). Calling(s). Profession(s,al). Trade(s). Craft(s). Vocation(s,al). Career(s). *See also* Blue collar workers; Careers; Craft personnel; Occupations; Professional personnel; Vocations; White collar workers.

Joint ventures. Joint venture(s). *Consider also:* hybrid organization(s), shared risk(s), satellite organization(s), common platform(s), seamless service(s), alliance partner(s). *See also* Affiliation (businesses); Cobranding; Consortia; Strategic alliances.

Jokes. Jok(e,es,ed,ing). Riddle(s). Pun(s). Amusing stor(y,ies). Verbal humor. Quip(s). Stand up comics. Punch line(s). Witticism(s). Wisecrack(s). One liner(s). Wordplay. Play on words. Prank(s). Gag(s). Caper(s). Farce(s). Lampoon(s). Parod(y,ies). Cartoon(s). Comic strip(s). *See also* Ethnic wit and humor; Farce; Humor; Puns; Stereotyping; Tricksters.

Journal articles. Journal article(s). *Choose from:* journal(s), magazine(s), periodical(s), bulletin(s), serial(s) *with:* article(s), contribution(s), feature(s), citation(s), review(s), source(s), piece(s), column(s), commentar(y,ies), stor(y,ies), literature. *See also* Addendum; Bibliographic citations; Periodicals; Professional literature.

Journalism. Journalism. Newspaper writing. Newspaper publishing. News report(ing,age). Fourth estate. Newspaper columnist(s). Newsroom(s). Press. Photojournalism. Edit(ed,ing,orial, orials). *See also* Attribution of news; Broadcast journalism; Editing; Editorials; Editors; Freedom of information; Freedom of speech; Freedom of the press; Information dissemination; Information leaks; Journalistic errors;

Journalists; Literature; Mass media; Media journalism; News agencies; News coverage; News media; News policies; Newspapers; Periodicals; Photojournalism; Publications; Television; Television programs; Travel journalism; Writing (composition); Written communications.

Journalism, broadcast. See *Broadcast journalism.*

Journalism, media. See *Media journalism.*

Journalism, travel. See *Travel journalism.*

Journalistic errors. Journalistic error(s). *Choose from:* journalis(m,t,ts,tic), press, news, media, newspaper(s), edit(ed,ing, orial,orials) *with:* err(ed,or,ors,oneous), errata, mistake(s), misuse(s,d), wrong(ly), inaccura(cy,cies,te), incorrect(ly), discrepan(cy,cies), fallac(y,ies,iousness), misspell(ed, ing,ings), misprint(ed,s). omission(s), omit(ted). *Consider also:* factoid(s). *See also* Errors; Fallibility; Incorrect; Journalism.

Journalistic ethics. Journalistic ethics. *Choose from:* journalis(t,ts,m), the press, editor(s,ial), the media, paparazz(i,o), newspaper(s), tabloid(s), magazine(s), documentar(y,ies), columnist(s) *with:* ethic(s,al), moral(ity), confidential(ity), confidential source(s), privacy, fair(ness), accuracy, responsibility, honest(y), propaganda, standard(s), guideline(s), news-worthiness, attack(s,ed,ing), perspective(s), nonpartisan, impartial(ity), objectivity, ethical conflict(s), full disclosure, bias(ed), opposing views, conflict(s) of interest(s), credibility, quest for profit(s), market orientation, sentiment(al,ality), sensational(ism), titillat(e,ed,ing,ion), mendac(ity,iousness), off-the-record, partiality, irresponsib(le,ility), plagiari(ze,zed,sm), lying, libel(lous, ous). *See also* Attribution of news; Codes of ethics; Freedom of the press; Information leaks; Journalists; Libel; Literary ethics; Media portrayal; News coverage; Plagiarism; Professional ethics; Professional malpractice; Sensationalism; Tabloids; Unethical conduct.

Journalists. Journalist(s). Journalism personnel. Writer(s). Foreign correspondent(s). War correspondent(s). Press(man,men). Newspaper reporter(s). News(woman,women,man,men). Newspaper(woman,women,man,men). Newsmonger(s). Newspaper editor(s). Photojournalis(m,t,ts). Journalism graduate(s). Newscaster(s). Radio station reporter(s). Anchor(man,men). TV reporter(s). Correspondent(s). Columnist(s). Critic(s). Commentator(s). Copywriter(s). *Consider also:* paparazz(o,i). *See also* Broadcasters; Commentators; Editors; Foreign correspondents; Journalism; Journalistic

ethics; Literary ethics; Photographers; War news; Writing (composition); Workers.

Journalists, broadcast. See *Broadcast journalists.*

Journals. See *Periodicals; Professional literature.*

Journals, electronic. See *Electronic journals.*

Journals, professional. See *Professional literature.*

Journals, scholarly. See *Scholarly periodicals.*

Journey to work. See *Commuting (travel).*

Journeymen's societies. See *Guilds.*

Journeys. See *Cruising; Expeditions; Pilgrimages; Travel.*

Joy. See *Happiness.*

Judaism. Judai(c,sm). Jew(ish,s). Judeo. Hebrew(s). Talmud(ic). Torah. Haggadah. Old Testament. *Consider also:* rabbi(s,nical), synagogue(s), Rosh ha-Shanah, Yom Kippur, Shavuot, Purim, Hannukah, Passover, kosher, Hasid(ic,im), Chassid(ic,im), Israel(i), Ashkenaz(i,is,ic,im), Sephard(im,ic), Mizrachi(m), Yiddish, Ladino, Zion(ism,ist,ists). *See also* Antisemitism; Bible; Devils; God concepts; Jewish-Arab relations; Jewish drama; Jewish law; Jewish sects; Presence of God; Rabbinical literature; Religions; Religious attitudes; Religious behavior; Religious beliefs; Religious cultural groups; Religious fundamentalism; Religious literature; Religious practices; Religious prejudice; Western civilization.

Judgement day. Judgement day. Doomsday. Last day. *Consider also:* second advent, second coming, millenium, last judgment, end of the world, apocalyp(tic,se), armageddon, eschatolog(y, ical). *See also* Apocalypse; Christianity; End; Judgment of God; Messianic movements; Millenarianism.

Judges. Judge(s). Magistrate(s). Justice(s) of the court. *Consider also:* judicator(s), adjudicator(s), mullah(s), justice(s) of the peace. *See also* Attorneys; Court judges; Legal professionals.

Judges, court. See *Court judges.*

Judgment. Judgment(s,al). Judg(ed,ing). Subjective estimate(s). Evaluat(e,ed, ing,ion,ions). Jur(or,ors,y,ies) decision(s). Discern(ed,ing,ment). Judicious(ness). *See also* Accuracy; Attitudes; Choice behavior; Criteria; Criticism; Decision making; Decisions; Errors; Evaluation; Judgment (logic); Judgment disturbances; Judgment errors; Judgment of God; Moral judgment; Probability judgment; Rational choices; Reasoning; Values.

Judgment (ethics). See *Moral judgment.*

Judgment (logic). Judgment(s). Affirm(ed, ing,ation). Negat(e,ed,ing,ion). *Choose from:* assert(ing,ion), deny(ing), denial *with:* predicat(e,es,ion), relation(s,ship). *Choose from:* problematic, assertoric, apodeictic, probable, improbable, possible, true, false, necessary, impossible, correct, erroneous *with:* judgment(s), judgement(s). *Consider also:* akra(sia,tic), acra(sia,tic), enkrateia. *See also* Deduction; Fallacies; Intentionality; Judgment; Logic; Reasoning;

Judgment, moral. See *Moral judgment.*

Judgment, probability. See *Probability judgment.*

Judgment disturbances. Judgment disturbance(s). *Choose from:* judgment, judgement *with:* disturbance(s), maladapt(ation,ive), impair(ed,ment, ments). *Consider also:* irrational, disturbed, dysfunction(al), confused, impaired *with:* cognit(ive,ion), thinking, thought(s). *See also* Judgment; Thought disturbances.

Judgment errors. Judgment error(s). *Choose from:* judgment, judgement, discrimination, estimat(ing,ion), rating *with:* error(s), inaccura(te,cy,cies), incorrect. *Consider also:* misjudg(ed, ment) restrictive error(s), expansive error(s), halo effect, erroneous inference(s). *See also* Errors; Fallibility; Judgment.

Judgment of God. Judgment of God. God's judgment. Divine judgment. Divine action. *Consider also:* fury of the Lord, final judgment. *See also* Apocalypse; Judgement day; Will of God.

Judgments, criminal. See *Judicial decisions; Sentencing.*

Judicial activism. Judicial activism. Activist judiciary. Judge-made law. Judicial lawmaking. *Choose from:* judicial, judiciary, court(s) *with:* activis(m,t,ts), increased authority, lawmaking, expansion of power(s), expan(ed,ing) power(s), imperial role, social engineering, depart(ed,ing,ure) from original intent. *See also* Court opinions; Discretionary powers; Judicial decisions; Judicial power; Separation of powers.

Judicial candidates. Judicial candidates. Court nominee(s). *Choose from:* judicial, bench, judgeship(s), court *with:* candidate(s), running for, campaign(s, ing), nominee(s). *See also* Candidates; Court judges; Courts; Elected officials.

Judicial corruption. Judicial corruption. *Choose from:* judicia(l,ry), judge(s), magistrate(s), chief justice(s), prosecutor(s) *with:* corrupt(ed,ing,ion), taint(ed,ing), political(ly) influence(s,d), misconduct. *See also* Bribery; Conflict of interest; Corruption in government; Financial disclosure; Judicial ethics; Kickbacks; Misconduct in office; Obstruction of justice; Professional ethics; Unethical conduct; White collar crime.

Judicial decisions. Judicial decision(s). Adjudicat(e,ion,ive,or,ors). Adjudg(e,ment). Decree(ing). Arbitrat(e,ed,ion). Litigation. Fatwa(h). *Choose from:* court, judicial, judge's *with:* opinion(s), decision(s), determination, decree(ing), ruling(s). *See also* Criminal justice; Criminal proceedings; Defendants; Defense (verbal); Evidence; Instructions to juries; Judicial activism; Judicial discretion; Judicial error; Judicial power; Juries; Law enforcement; Litigation; Offenders; Plea bargaining; Sentencing; Sociological jurisprudence; Trial (law); Verdicts.

Judicial discretion. Judicial discretion. *Choose from:* judicial, judge(s), court(s), magistrate(s), *with:* discretion(ary), option(s), variability, disparate treatment, judicial philosophy, inconsistenc(y,ies). *Consider also:* sentencing *with:* discretion, disparit(y,ies), guideline(s). *See also* Court opinions; Discretion; Discretionary powers; Judicial decisions; Sentencing.

Judicial error. Judicial error(s). Poor legal judgment. Miscarriage(s) of justice. Wrongful death penalty. *Choose from:* prosecutor(s), court(s), judge(s) *with:* error(s), erroneous(ly), questionable ruling(s), wrongful(ly) convict(ed, ion,ions), bad decision(s), ineptitude, incompeten(t,ce). *See also* Court judges; Court opinions; Errors; Judicial decisions.

Judicial ethics. Judicial ethics. *Choose from:* judicial, judicia(l,ry), judge(s), magistrate(s), chief justice(s), court(s), prosecutor(s) *with:* ethic(s,al,ally), unethical(ly), fair(ness), prejudg(e,ed, ing), predispos(ed,ing,ition,itions); propriety; impropriet(y,ies), humane, moral(s,ity), immoral(ity), deception, obligation(s), integrity, accountability, honest(y), principle(s), code(s), openness, fidelity, conscience, conscientious(ness), incorruptib(le,ility), improper, misdeed(s), misconduct, conflict(s) of interest, malpractice, bribe(s,ry), corrupt(ion), alcoholi(c,sm), politicized, political(ly) influence(s,d), campaign fund(s), illegal(ity,ities), collusion, scandal(s), breach of confidence, fraud(ulent), unprofessional, breach of decorum, withholding information, accept(ance) of gift(s), wrongdoing(s), unscrupulous(ness), trust violation(s), inappropriate conduct, tax evasion, financial irregularit(y,ies), kickback(s), illegal contribution(s), mishandling funds, defraud(ed,ing). *See*

also Codes of ethics; Corruption in government; Inadmissible; Judicial corruption; Judicial restraint; Unethical conduct.

Judicial opinions. See *Court opinions; Judicial decisions.*

Judicial power. Judicial power(s). *Choose from:* judicia(l,ry), court(s), judge(s) *with:* power(s), authority, discretion(ary), dut(y,ies), role(s). *See also* Judicial activism; Judicial decisions; Judicial restraint; Separation of powers.

Judicial process. See *Adjudication; Due process; Legal procedures.*

Judicial restraint. Judicial restraint. Judicial self restraint. *Choose from:* judicia(l,ry), judge(s), magistrate(s), chief justice(s), court(s), juridical *with:* restraint, strict construction(ism), originalis(m,t,ts), strict adherence to the Constitution, conventionalist approach, moderation, conservative. *See also* Judicial activism; Judicial ethics; Judicial power.

Judicial statistics. Judicial statistics. *Choose from:* judicia(l,ry), court(s), litigation *with:* annual report(s), statistic(s,al). *See also* Crime rates; Mandatory reporting; Rates.

Judicial system. See *Legal system.*

Judo. Judo. *Consider also:* martial arts, karate, self defense training, tai kwan do, jujitsu, judogi. *See also* Martial arts; Recreation; Sports.

Jumping. Jump(ed,ing,s). Leap(ed,ing). Hop(ped,ping). Hurdle(s). Spring(ing). Bounc(e,ed,ing). Vault(ed,ing). Skip(ped,ping). *See also* Motor coordination; Motor skills; Sports.

Junior college students. Junior college student(s). *Choose from:* junior college(s), two year college(s), associates degree(s), community college(s) *with:* student(s), female(s), male(s), freshmen, sophomore(s). *See also* Colleges; Students.

Junior high school students. Junior high school student(s). *Choose from:* junior high, seventh grade, eighth grade, ninth grade *with:* student(s), pupil(s). *Consider also:* 7th, seventh, 8th, eighth, 9th, ninth *with:* grader(s). *See also* Junior high schools; Students.

Junior high school teachers. Junior high school teacher(s). *Choose from:* junior high, seventh grade, eighth grade, ninth grade *with:* teacher(s), teaching staff, faculty, educator(s). *See also* Junior high schools; Teachers.

Junior high schools. Junior high school(s). Intermediate school(s). *Choose from:* 7, 8, 9, 7th, 8th, 9th, seventh, eighth, ninth, 7th - 9th *with:* grade(s). *See also* High schools.

Junk bonds. Junk bond(s). High-yield bond(s). High-risk, high yield securit(y,ies). *Choose from:* high-risk, high yield, unsecured *with:* bond(s), securit(y,ies), debenture(s), issue(s), fund(s), investment(s). *See also* Foreign investment; Investments; Speculation; Stock exchange.

Junk email. Junk email. *Choose from:* junk, unsolicited, advertis(e,ed,ing, ements), ad(s), promotion(al,s) *with:* e-mail, email, electronic mail, instant message(s) *Consider also:* spam(ming,mer,mers). *See also* Advertising; Electronic mail; Online harassment; Push technology.

Junk food. Junk food(s). Snack food(s). Hostess Twinkies. Fast food(s). *Consider also:* unhealthy food(s), fattening food(s), potato chip(s), cand(y,ies), hot dog(s), french fries. *See also* Convenience Foods; Diet; Diet fads; Eating; Food; Food additives; Food habits; Nutrition; Obesity; Popular culture.

Junk mail. See *Direct mail advertising.*

Juries. Jur(y,ies). Juridic. Juryman. Juror(s). Panels of judges. Tribunal(s). Veniremen. *Consider also:* mock jur(y,ies), grand jur(y,ies), petit jur(y,ies), straw poll(s), voir dire examination(s), judgment of peer(s). *See also* Adjudication; Biased selection; Criminal proceedings; Defendants; Due process; Instructions to juries; Judicial decisions; Litigation; Trial (law); Verdicts.

Juries, instructions to. See *Instructions to juries*

Jurisdiction. Jurisdiction. Power. Authority. Control. Dominion. Sovereignty. Rule. Reign. Prerogative. Purview. *See also* Authority (power); Courts; Territoriality.

Jurisprudence. Jurispruden(ce,tial,tially). *Choose from:* legal, justice *with:* system(s), trial(s), proceeding(s). Court(s,room,rooms). Jurist(s). Juror(s). Judge(s). *Choose from:* court(s), legal *with:* decision(s), jurisdiction, litigation, adjudication, process(es), issue(s), testimony, defense(s), prosecution. *Consider also:* law(s), tort(s). *See also* Criminal justice; Criminal proceedings; Judicial decisions; Law (legal philosophy and theory); Law (practice).

Jurisprudence, sociological. See *Sociological jurisprudence.*

Just-in-time manufacturing. Just-in-time manufacturing. Kanban. *See also* Adhocracies.

Just war doctrine. Just war doctrine. Just-war principle. Just cause for going to war. *Choose from:* warranted, just(ified, iable,ification), morally permissible, just cause(s) *with:* war(s), warfare, use of force, fighting, killing(s), military conflict, armed violence, armed resistance, military operation(s). *Consider also:* holy war(s), crusade(s). *See also* Justification (law); Noncombatants; Pacifism; Peacekeeping forces; War; War attitudes; War prevention.

Justice. Justice. Just due. Equit(y,able, ableness). Even handed(ness). Fair(ness). Impartial(ity,ness). Unprejudiced. Objectiv(e,ity). Disinterested(ness). Neutral(ity). Dispassionate(ness). Open-minded(ness). *See also* Cardinal virtues; Comparable worth; Criminal justice; Distributive justice; Due process; Egalitarianism; Equity (payment); Fair trial; Fairness; Impartiality; Rule of law; Social equity; Social justice; Withholding evidence.

Justice, criminal. See *Criminal justice.*

Justice, distributive. See *Distributive justice.*

Justice, fugitives from. See *Fugitives from justice.*

Justice, obstruction of. See *Obstruction of justice.*

Justice, restorative See *Restorative justice.*

Justice, social See *Social justice.*

Justifiable homicide. Justifiable homicide. *Choose from:* justif(iable,ied), defen-

sible, warranted, self-defense *with:* homicide(s), kill(ed,ing,ings), fatal shooting(s). *See also* Extenuating circumstances; Homicide; Justification (law).

Justification. Justif(y,ied,ying,ication,ications). Reason(s). Basis. Explanation(s). Ground(s). Account(s). Defense(s). Rationaliz(e,ed,ing,ation). Excuse(s). Just cause(s). *See also* Causality; Explanation; Meaning; Rationalization (defense mechanism).

Justification (law). Justification. Justifiable cause. *Choose from:* just(ified,iable, ification), lawful, defensible, permissible, warranted, just cause(s), sufficient reason, provocation, sanctioned by law, extenuating circumstance(s), extenuating grounds *with:* act(s), fail(ure,ing) to act, homicide(s), assault(s), libel, self defense. *Consider also:* demonstrated ability, supporting data. *See also* Consent (law); De jure; Extenuating circumstances; Just war doctrine; Justifiable homicide; Necessity (law); Self defense; Sufficient evidence.

Justification of war. See *Just war doctrine.*

Juvenile animals. See *Animal offspring.*

Juvenile correctional institutions. See *Reformatories.*

Juvenile delinquency. Juvenile delinquen(cy,t,ts). Predelinquen(t,ts,cy). *Choose from:* juvenile(s), youth(ful),

adolescen(t,ts,ce), child(ren), teen(s), teenage(r,rs), minor(s) *with:* crim(e,es, inal,inals), murderer(s), offender(s), antisocial behavior(s), vandalism, violence, steal(ing), deviant behavior(s), larceny, gang(s), misdemeanor(s), lawbreaking, theft(s), robber(y,ies), mugging(s), prostitut(e,es,ion). *Consider also:* delinquent subculture(s), delinquent drift. *See also* Adolescence; Antisocial behavior; Crime; Delinquents; Deviance; Juvenile gangs; Moral development; Offenders; Police community relations; Predelinquent youth; Recidivism; Runaways; Shoplifting; Theft; Vandalism; Violence; Young adults.

Juvenile detention homes. Juvenile detention home(s). *Choose from:* juvenile(s), youth, child(ren), young criminal(s), *with:* detention home(s), detention facilit(y,ies), detention center(s), correctional institution(s). *See also* Correctional institutions; Prisons; Reformatories; Residential facilities.

Juvenile gangs. Juvenile gang(s). Street gang(s). *Choose from:* juvenile, teenage, street, adolescent, youth, student, delinquent, urban *with:* gang(s), subculture. *See also* Delinquents; Driveby crimes; Juvenile delinquency; Peer influences; Youth culture.

Juvenile offenders. See *Juvenile delinquency.*

K

Kapellmeister. See *Conductors.*

Karate. See *Martial arts.*

Karma. Karm(a,ic). *Consider also:* ahimsa, rebirths, reincarnation, just reward(s), kismet, fate. *See also* Buddhism; Fate; Hinduism; Jainism; Reincarnation; Religious beliefs.

Kibbutz. See *Communes.*

Kickbacks. Kickback(s). Payoff(s). Brib(e,es,ery). Corrupt(ed,ing,ion). Fraud(ulent). Payola. Illegal campaign contribution(s). Illegal gift(s). Graft. Protection money. Quid pro quo. Pothole politics. *See also* Campaign finance reform; Deals; Discounts; Fraud; Judicial corruption; White collar crime.

Kidnapping. Kidnap(ped,ping). Abduct(ed, ing,ion). Shanghai(ed). *Choose from:* hold(ing), held, detain(ed,ing) *with:* ransom, hostage(s). *Consider also:* snatch(ed,ing), seiz(e,ed,ing), steal(ing) *with:* pet(s), infant(s), bab(y,ies), child(ren). *Consider also:* Lindbergh law. *See also* Abduction; Child kidnapping; Hostages; Missing persons.

Kidnapping, child. See *Child kidnapping.*

Killers, serial. See *Serial murderers.*

Killing, mercy. See *Euthanasia.*

Kindergarten students. See *Preschool children.*

Kindness. Kindness(es). Kind(ly,liness). Kind deed(s). Kindhearted(ness,ly). Neighborl(y,iness). Charitable(ness). Good(ness). Benevolen(t,ce). Gentle(ness). Compassion(ate). Courte(sy,ous). Humane(ness). Helpful(ness). Altruis(m,tic). *Consider also:* favor(s), dispensation(s), willing to help, genero(us,sity), hospita(lity,ble), merc(y,iful,ifulness). *See also* Altruism; Benevolence; Brotherliness; Charitable behavior; Favors; Friendliness; Generosity; Gift giving; Good samaritans; Helping behavior; Humane; Humanitarianism; Prosocial behavior; Sharing; Social behavior.

Kindness, loving. See *Compassion.*

Kinesics. Kinesic(s). Body language. Gestur(e,es,ing). Gesticulat(e,ed,ing, ion). Touching. Eye contact. Mime. Posturing. Pantomime. Facial expression(s). Hand movement(s). *Consider also:* body, bodily, nonverbal, deictic *with:* language, communication, talk, behavior(s). *See also* Body language; Eye contact; Facial expressions; Gestures; Motion; Nonverbal communication; Posture.

Kinesthesia. See *Muscular sense.*

Kinetics. See *motion.*

King, supremacy of the See *Royal supremacy; Divine right of kings; Sovereignty.*

Kingdom of God. See *Apocalypse; Apocalyptic literature; Heaven; Judgement day; Millenarianism.*

Kings and rulers. See *Aristocracy; Emperors; Monarchy; Oligarchy; Ruling class.*

Kings, divine right of. See *Divine right of kings.*

Kinship. Kin(ship). Kins(man,men,folk). Relative(s). Consanguineous(ness). Common ancestry. Clan(s). Gens. Phratry. Affinal relative(s). Agnat(e,es, ion). Cognation. Common lineage. Consanguin(ity,eous). Intergenerational exchange. Distant relative(s). Compadrazgo. Home circle. Amitate(s). Marriage alliance(s). Matrimonial alliance(s). *Choose from:* famil(y,ies) *with:* tie(s), intergenerational, extended, three generation(s), network(s), multigenerational, joint, expanded, consanguine. *Choose from:* blood *with:* relative(s), relation(s), tie(s). *See also* Adoption; Affinal; Black family; Clans; Cognatic descent; Consanguinity; Daughters; Descent; Ethnography; Ethnology; Extended family; Family; Family characteristics; Family history; Family relations; Family traditions; Genealogy; Inheritance; Lineage; Marriage; Matriarchy; Nuclear family; Parents; Patriarchy; Remarriage; Siblings; Sons; Spouses; Stem family; Stepfamily; Traditional societies; Unilineal descent.

Kitchen middens. Kitchen midden(s). Refuse heap(s). Dunghill(s). *Consider also:* refuse remanence. *See also* Excavations (Archaeology); Human remains (archaeology); Prehistoric people.

Kleptomania. Kleptomania(s,c,cs). *Choose from:* compuls(ive,ion,ions), impulsive, impulse control disorder(s) *with:* steal(ing), theft. *See also* Impulse control disorders; Impulsiveness; Personality disorders.

Knighthood, knights and. See *Knights and knighthood.*

Knights and knighthood. Knight(s,ed, hood). *Consider also:* Knights Templar, Teutonic knight(s). honorary title(s), errant knight(s), knight(s) errant, Sir Lancelot, Sir Galahad, etc. *See also* Chivalry; Courtly love; Crusades.

Knit goods industry. Knit goods industry. Knitting industry. *Choose from:* knit(ting,ted,s), knitwear, sweater(s), stocking(s) *with:* industr(y,ies,ial), design(ed,ing,er,ers), manufactur(e,ed, ing), loom(s), mill(s), dye(s,d), process(es,ed,ing), putting-out, produc(e,ed,ing,tion), compan(y,ies), firm(s). *See also* Clothing workers; Garment industry; Textile industry; Textile workers; Wool industry.

Know, right to. See *Freedom of information.*

Knowledge. Knowledge. Epistemolog(y, ical). Know(n). Know-how. Well-informed. Expert(ise,ness). Common sense. Scientific knowledge. Answer(s). Finding(s). Cognizance. Wisdom. Erudit(e,ion). Aware(ness). Sophisticat(ed,ion). Experience(d). Insight(ful). Comprehend(ed,ing). Comprehension. Understood. Understand(ing). *See also* Academic achievement; Civilized; Common sense; Comprehension; Discovery learning; Epistemology; Experts; Ignorance; Information; Inquiry (theory of knowledge); Intellectual development; Intellectual history; Knowledge level; Learning; Scholarship; Scientific knowledge; Social epistemology; Sociology of knowledge; Theories; Wisdom.

Knowledge, area of. See *Area of knowledge.*

Knowledge, common. See *Common knowledge.*

Knowledge, cultural. See *Cultural knowledge.*

Knowledge, job. See *Job knowledge.*

Knowledge, scientific. See *Scientific knowledge.*

Knowledge, self. See *Self knowledge.*

Knowledge, sociology of. See *Sociology of knowledge.*

Knowledge, subjective. See *Subjectivity.*

Knowledge level. Knowledge level(s). *Choose from:* knowledge, awareness, information, understanding, comprehension *with:* level(s), extent, degree. *See also* Academic achievement; Achievement; Comprehension; Educational attainment; Educational background; Job Knowledge; Knowledge; Learning; Performance standards; Scholarship.

Knowledge management. Knowledge management. KM. Learning evaluation. Evaluat(e,ed,ing,ion) intangible assets. *Choose from:* knowledge, skill(s), expertise *with:* control(led,ling), manag(e,ed,ing,ement), generat(e,ed, ing,ion), identif(y,ied,ying,ication), capitaliz(e,ed,ing,ation), acquir(e,ed, ing), acquisition, fus(e,ed,ing,ion), adapt(ed,ing,ation), network(ed,ing), add(ed,ing,ition), shar(e,ed,ing), disseminat(e,es,ed,ing,ation). *Consider also:* knowledge-based system(s), building corporate memory, knowledge engineering. *See also* Archives; Artificial intelligence; Competitive intelligence; Computer assisted decision making; Decision support systems; Information processing; Intangible property; Intellectual capital; Management information systems.

Knowledge of God. Knowledge of God. *Choose from:* hidden(ness), substan-tiat(e,ed,ing,ion), incomprehensib(le, ility), comprehen(d,ded,ding,sion), revelation, reveal(ed,ing), experienc(e,ed,ing), unknowable(ness), knowable(ness), know(n,ing), cognition, self-manifest(ed,ing,ation), perception(s), eclipse *with:* God,
almighty, Jehovah, etc. *See also* Attributes of God; Faith; Glory of God; God concepts; Immanence of God; Presence of God; Religious beliefs; Theophany.

Knowledge of results. Knowledge of result(s). *Choose from:* knowledge, awareness *with:* result(s), performance, outcome(s). *Consider also:* feedback, biofeedback. *See also* Feedback.

Knowledge workers. Knowledge worker(s). Information workers(s). Information professional(s). Information analyst(s). Online searcher(s). Online professional(s). Database searcher(s). Document retrievalist(s). Literature searcher(s). Documentation specialist(s). Documentation manager(s). Information entrepreneur(s,ship). Infopreneur(s,ial). Information manager(s). Technical writer(s). *Consider also:* cybrarian(s,ship), cyber-librarian(s,ship), information specialist(s), information scientist(s), Internet trainer(s), online searcher(s), database searcher(s),
literature searcher(s), bibliographer(s), web site coordinator(s), web designer(s), web site developer(s), webmaster(s), webmistress(es), web designer(s), web site developer(s). *See also* Computer experts; Librarians; Archivists; Information literacy; Intellectual capital; Professional personnel; Computer personnel; Gold collar workers.

Korean Americans. Korean American(s). American Korean(s). American(s) of Korean descent. *Choose from:* Korean *with:* background(s), ancest(ry,ors), famil(y,ies), forefather(s), descent, descend(ant,ants,ent,ents) *with:* America(n,ns), United States. *See also* Asian Americans; Ethnic groups; Minority groups.

Korsakoff's syndrome. See *Alcohol amnestic disorder.*

Kwa languages. Kwa language(s). Akan. Bini. Fanti. Twi. Ewe. Ga. Ibo. Igbo. Yoruba. Kru group. *See also* African cultural groups; Language; Languages (as subjects); Sub-Saharan Africa.

L

Labeling (of persons). Label(ed,s,ing). Labell(ed,ing). Classif(y,ying,ied, ication,ications). Stigma(tize,tized, tizing,tization). Typ(ed,ing). Typecast. Image(s). Designat(ed,ion). Stereotyp(ing,ic,ical,ed,e,es). Identif(ication, ied). Defin(ed,ition,itions). Categor(y,ies,ized). Brand(ed,ing). *Consider also:* attribution, deviancy amplification, misdiagnos(is,es), diagnos(is,es). *See also* Attitudes; Categorization; Defamation; Deviance; Deviant behavior; Diagnosis; Gossip; Identification (psychology); Libel; McCarthyism; Marginality (sociological); Names; Political campaigns; Psychodiagnostic typologies; Reputation; Rumors; Scandals; Scapegoating; Self fulfilling prophecy; Social perception; Social response; Social types; Stereotyping; Stigma; Witch hunting.

Labeling, product. See *Product labeling*.

Labor. See *Collective bargaining; Division of labor; Employees; Employment; Human resources; Industrial democracy; Labor disputes; Labor force; Labor management relations; Labor market; Labor market segmentation; Labor movements; Labor process; Labor supply; Labor unions; Personnel; Union members; Work humanization; Workers; Working conditions.*

Labor (childbirth). Labor. Active birth. *Consider also:* birth(ing), accouchement, childbearing, childbirth, delivery, parturition, confinement, travail. *See also* Birth; Childbirth training; Midwifery; Pregnancy.

Labor, agricultural. See *Agricultural workers.*

Labor, alien. See *Alien labor.*

Labor, animal division of. See *Animal division of labor.*

Labor, cheap. See *Cheap labor.*

Labor, child. See *Child labor.*

Labor, compulsory. See *Forced labor; Slavery.*

Labor, contract. See *Contract labor*

Labor, convict. See *Convict labor.*

Labor, division of. See *Division of labor.*

Labor, domestic. See *Domestic service; Housekeeping; Sexual division of labor.*

Labor, domestic division of. See *Sexual division of labor.*

Labor, family division of. See *Sexual division of labor.*

Labor, forced. See *Forced labor.*

Labor, foreign. See *Foreign labor.*

Labor, home. See *Home based businesses.*

Labor, hours of. See *Alternative work patterns; Personnel scheduling; Work load; Work schedules; Workday shifts; Worktime.*

Labor, household. See *Domestic service.*

Labor, household division of. See *Sexual division of labor.*

Labor, international division of. See *International division of labor.*

Labor, manual. See *Blue collar workers.*

Labor, migrant. See *Migrant workers.*

Labor, organized. See *Labor unions.*

Labor, regional workers. See *Migrant workers.*

Labor, seasonal. See *Migrant workers; Temporary employees.*

Labor, sexual division of. See *Sexual division of labor.*

Labor, skilled. See *Skilled workers.*

Labor, surplus. See *Labor supply; Unemployment.*

Labor, unpaid. See *Unpaid labor.*

Labor aspects of technology. Labor aspects of technology. *Choose from:* technolog(y,ies,ical), high technolog(y, ies), high tech, advanced technolog(y, ies), new technolog(y,ies), biotechnolog(y,ies,ical), smart machine(s), laptop(s), fax machine(s), semiconductor(s), robot(s,ic,ics), supersonic transport(ation), technocra(cy,cies,t,ts, tic,tization), electronic(s), microelectronic(s), Silicon Valley, microchip(s), computer(s), microcomputer(s), telecommunication(s), laser(s), satellite(s), optic fiber(s), automat(e,ed, ing,ion) *with:* work(er,ers), human resource(s), workforce, job(s), labor, labor force, division of labor, manpower, workplace, union(s), shopfloor, staff, personnel, employee(s), employer(s), executive(s), middle manager(s), morale, underemploy(ed,ment), unemploy(ed, ing,ment), employ(ed,ing,ment), organizational control, social adaptation, telecommut(e,ed,ing,er,ers), homeworker(s), women, people, human being(s), occupational hazard(s), training. *See also* Appropriate technologies; Computer experts; Computer personnel; Factory automation; Hazards of video display terminals; Industrial accidents; Occupational exposure; Occupational safety; Occupational stress; Production control; Quality of working life; Technological unemployment.

Labor conditions. See *Working conditions.*

Labor costs. Labor cost(s). *Choose from:* labor, employee(s), worker(s), employment *with:* cost(s), wage(s), salar(y,ies), benefit(s), compensation. *Consider also:* payroll(s), minimum-wage(s), labor economics. *See also* Cheap labor; Compensation (payment); Cost of living; Costs; Direct costs; Labor economics; Labor market; Prevailing wages; Salaries; Wages.

Labor disputes. Labor dispute(s). Industrial conflict(s). Labor conflict(s). Strike(s). Wildcat strike(s). Walkout(s). Lockout(s). Labor insurgency. Shopfloor resistance. Labor militancy. *Choose from:* worker(s), labor, union(s), workplace, workforce, industrial, shopfloor *with:* dispute(s), conflict(s), strike(s), insurgency, resistance. *See also* Collective bargaining; Disputes; Labor management relations; Labor unions; Lockouts; Strikes; Workers; Working conditions.

Labor economics. Labor economics. Labor market(s). *Choose from:* labor, employment, unemployment, working class, jobless(ness), workforce *with:* economics, supply and demand. *Consider also:* minimum wage, labor force participation, capital-labor ratio, wage subsid(y, ies), labour theory of value. *See also* Child labor; Contracting out; Dislocated workers; Downsizing; Employee turnover; Employment opportunities; Employment trends; Foreign workers; Income inequality; Labor costs; Labor force; Labor market; Labor market segmentation; Labor migration; Labor mobility; Labor supply; Occupational segregation; Offshore production (foreign countries); Oligopsony; Prevailing wages; Privatization; Sexual division of labor; Subcontracting; Underemployment; Unemployment; Workforce planning.

Labor force. Labor force. Work force. Workforce. Human resources. Reserve army of unemployed. Laborer(s). Worker(s). Laboring class(es). Working class(es). Wage earner(s). *Choose from:* labor *with:* force, power, market, supply, sector. *Consider also:* proletaria(n,t), employee(s), staff, personnel, peonage, indentured servant(s). *See also* Child labor; Dislocated workers; Employee turnover; Employees; Human capital; Human resources; Labor economics; Labor market; Labor supply; Manpower; Occupational classification; Peonage;

Personnel; Personnel training; Work reentry; Working class; Working women.

Labor laws. Labor law(s). Employment law(s). *Choose from:* labor, union(s, ized), sweatshop(s), child labor, slavery, compensatory time, overtime, minimum wage(s), compensation, layoff(s), family leave, whistle blow(ing,er,ers), strik(e,er,ers,es,ing), strikebreak(ing,er, ers), workplace(s), worker(s), employee(s), workforce, employer(s), salaried professional(s), American Federation of Labor, Congress of Industrial Organization(s), AFL-CIO *with:* law(s), statute(s), legislation, federal contract(s), amendment(s), suit(s), court ruling(s). *Consider also:* National Labor Relations Board, NLRB, Fair Labor Standards Act, Civil Rights Act, Occupational Safety and Health Act, Americans with Disabilities Act (ADA), Federal Employers' Liability Act, Railway Labor Act, Family and Medical Leave Act, work(er,ers) compensation, collective bargaining agreement(s), right to work law(s). *See also* Labor policy; Labor standards; Prevailing wages; Social legislation; Working conditions.

Labor management committees. Labor management committee(s). *Choose from:* labor management, management labor, union management *with:* committee(s), partnership(s), task force(s), advisory group(s), panel(s), collaboration, cooperation. *See also* Committees; Labor management relations; Participative management; Worker participation.

Labor management relations. Labor management relations. Labor relations. Industrial relations. *Choose from:* labor, union(s) *with:* management, compan(y, ies), corporat(e,ion,ions), employer(s). *Consider also:* labor management committee(s), labor arbitration, labor negotiation(s), collective bargaining, trade unions, employers associations, industrial democracy, codetermination, labor movement(s), joint labor management. *See also* Arbitration; Collective bargaining; Corporations; Corporatism; Employer organizations; Employers; Guilds; Industrial arbitration; Industrial democracy; Industrial management; Industry; Labor disputes; Labor management committees; Labor process; Labor unions; Managers; Mediation; Paternalism; Personnel management; Personnel policy; Quality of working life; Scientific management; Strikes; Superior subordinate relationship; Union shop; Worker participation; Workers; Working conditions.

Labor market. Labor market. Job market. Labor submarket(s). Labor force trend(s). Employment competition. *Consider also:* jobless rate(s), unem- ployment rate(s), joblessness, underem- ployment, tertiary labor sector. *See also* Child labor; Contracting out; Dislocated workers; Displaced homemakers; Economic crises; Employee turnover; Employment opportunities; Foreign workers; Employment trends; Job applicants; Job requirements; Job search; Jobs; Labor costs; Labor economics; Labor force; Labor market segmentation; Labor migration; Labor mobility; Labor process; Labor supply; Offshore production (foreign countries); Oligop- sony; Prevailing wages; Sweatshops; Subcontracting; Underemployment; Unemployment; Work skills; Workers.

Labor market, internal. See *Labor market segmentation.*

Labor market segmentation. Labor market segmentation. Dual labor market(s). Occupational ghetto(s,ization). Sexual division of labor. Marginalized labor force. Occupational segmentation. Feminized occupation(s). Fifth world. Underclass. Workplace inequality. Maquiladora. *Choose from:* dual, internal, split, segmented, segregated, ethnic, primary, secondary, tertiary *with:* labor market(s). *Consider also:* horizontal organization. *See also* Center and periphery; Cheap labor; Departmen- talization; Dual economy; Employment discrimination; Income inequality; Labor economics; Labor market; Occupational segregation; Oligopsony; Oppression; Sex roles; Sexism; Sexual division of labor; Sexual oppression; Social closure; Social segmentation; Underclass; Working women.

Labor markets, dual. See *Labor market segmentation.*

Labor migration. Labor migration. Expatriate worker(s). Undocumented worker(s). Foreign worker(s). Bracero(s). Guest worker(s). Guestworker(s). Imported labor. Imported worker(s). *Choose from:* emigrat(e,ed,ing,ion), immigrant(s), immigrat(e,ed,ing,ion), migrat(e,ed, ing,ory), migrant(s), interstate, transient(s), seasonal *with:* labor, worker(s), farm worker(s), agricultural worker(s), fruit picker(s), farmworker(s), farm hand(s). *See also* Brain drain; Foreign workers; International division of labor; Labor economics; Labor mobility; Migrant workers; Oligopsony; Undocumented immigrants.

Labor mobility. Labor mobility. *Choose from:* labor, worker(s), manpower, laborforce, workforce, human resources, unemployed, job seeker(s), executive(s), professor(s), professional(s) *with:* mobil(e,ity), relocat(e,ed,ing,ion,ions), transfer(red,ring,s), export(ed,ing), migrat(e,ed,ing,ion,ions), willing(ness) to move. *Consider also:* brain drain. *See* *also* Brain drain; Career breaks; Career change; Career patterns; Employment opportunities; Labor economics; Labor migration; Migrant workers; Migrants; Migration; Occupational tenure; Oligopsony; Promotion (occupational); Relocation; Social mobility.

Labor movements. Labor movement(s). Trade unionism. Labor organization(s). *Choose from:* labor, worker(s), farmworker(s), union, working class *with:* movement(s), solidarity, militancy, struggle(s), protest(s), radicalism. *See also* Class politics; Labor songs; Labor unions; Political movements; Political power; Protest songs; Worker conscious- ness; Workers; Workers' rights; Working class.

Labor organizations. See *Guilds, Labor unions.*

Labor output. See *Productivity.*

Labor policy. Labor polic(y,ies). Labor legislation. State protection of workers. *Choose from:* employment, labor, union(s), collective bargaining *with:* polic(y,ies), law(s), legislation(s), regulation(s). *See also* Economic planning; Labor laws; Labor standards; Public policy; Social legislation; Unemployment; Workers' rights.

Labor process. Labor process. Work process. Scientific management. *Choose from:* assembly line(s), mass production, rationalization of work, restructuring work, quality circle(s), works council(s), labor intensification, Fordism, Taylorism, deskilling, de-skilling, work humanization, corporate paternalism, bureaucratic regulation(s). *See also* Capitalism; Division of labor; Economic value; Exploitation; Industrial produc- tion; Industrialization; Labor aspects of technology; Labor management relations; Labor market; Mass produc- tion; Production; Productivity; Proletari- anization; Rationalization (sociology); Raw materials; Scientific management; Technology; Tools; Work; Work humanization.

Labor productivity. See *Productivity.*

Labor recruiting. See *Personnel recruit- ment.*

Labor relations. See *Labor management relations.*

Labor songs. Labor song(s). *Choose from:* labor, union(s), solidarity, factor(y,ies), mill(s), socialis(m,t), working class, UAW, AFL, CIO *with:* anthem(s), music, song(s), singing, chorus(es), folksong(s), chant(s), melod(y,ies). *Consider also:* Solidarity Forever, etc. *See also* : Ballads; Folk songs; Labor movements; Protest songs; Revolutionary ballads and songs; Social cohesion.

Labor standards. Labor standard(s). Fair employment practices. Worker(s) rights. *Choose from:* ILO, International Labor Organization, working condition(s), *with:* standard(s), convention(s). *Consider also:* labor legislation. *See also* Child labor; Labor disputes; Labor laws; Labor policy; Legislation; Social legislation; Working conditions.

Labor supply. Labor supply. Personnel supply. Human resources. Labor market(s). *Choose from:* personnel, manpower, labor, human resources *with:* supply, shortage(s), scarcit(y,ies), needs, surplus(es), availab(ility,le). Undermanned. Understaffed. Overstaffed. Staffing level(s). Manning level(s). Reserve army of the unemployed. *See also* Economic change; Economic conditions; Employee turnover; Employment forecasting; Employment trends; Human capital; Labor economics; Labor force; Labor market; Manpower; Medical personnel supply; Migration of industry; Occupational qualifications; Oligopsony; Supply and demand; Underemployment; Unemployment; Unemployment rates; Workforce planning.

Labor turnover. See *Employee turnover.*

Labor union organizing. See *Organizing activities.*

Labor unions. Labor union(s). Trade union(s). Union(ization,ism,s). Labor movement(s). Organiz(ed,ing) labor. Organiz(ed,ing) union(s). Trade unionist(s). Collective bargaining. Closed shop. Open shop. Labor arbitration. Union management relations. Labor leader(s). Employee negotiations. Labor relations. Teachers union(s). Local union(s). Public employee union(s). Employee representation. Worker representation. Workingmen's association(s). *Consider also:* United Farm Workers [UFW], American Federation of Labor, Congress of Industrial Organizations, AFL-CIO, United Mineworkers [UMW], Teamsters Union, United Auto Workers [UAW], International Ladies Garment Workers Union [ILGWU], Fair Labor Standards Act, featherbedding, Taft Hartley Act, strike(s), journeymen's societ(y,ies). *See also* Arbitration; Collective bargaining; Employer organizations; Employers; Guild socialism; Guilds; Industrial democracy; Labor disputes; Labor force; Labor management relations; Labor movements; Negotiation; Oligopsony; Quality of working life; Strikes; Trade associations; Union members; Union shop; Workers; Workers' rights; Working conditions.

Laboratories. Laborator(y,ies). Lab(s). Proving ground(s). Testing ground(s). Darkroom(s). *See also* Clean rooms; Educational laboratories; Experiments; Facilities; Language laboratories; Research.

Laboratories, educational. See *Educational laboratories.*

Laboratories, language. See *Language laboratories.*

Laboratories, learning. See *Educational laboratories.*

Laborers (farm). See *Agricultural workers.*

Laborers (industrial). See *Blue collar workers; Skilled workers; Unskilled workers.*

Laborers, agricultural. See *Agricultural laborers.*

Laboring classes. See *Working class.*

Labyrinth disorders. Labyrinth disorder(s). Labyrinthitis. Otitis interna. Meniere(s) disease. *Choose from:* labyrinth(ine), vestibular, inner ear, internal ear *with:* disease(s), disorder(s), fistula, infection(s), syndrome(s), hydrops, deafness, defect(s). *Consider also:* motion sickness, vertigo. *See also* Ear; Motion sickness.

Lactation. Lactat(e,ing,ion,ions). Breastfeed(ing). Lactogen(ic,esis). Suckling period. *Choose from:* mammary gland *with:* function(s), secretion(s). *Choose from:* milk *with:* eject(ion), produc(e,ed,ing,tion), secret(e,ed,ing,ion). *See also* Breast feeding; Postnatal period.

Ladders, career. See *Career ladders.*

Ladies, bag. See *Homeless.*

Ladino literature. See *Jewish literature.*

Lag, cultural. See *Cultural lag.*

Lag, jet. See *Jet lag.*

Laissez faire. See *Market economy; Privatization.*

Laity. See *Laymen.*

Laity, religious. See *Lay religious personnel.*

Laments. Lament(s,ed,ing,ation,ations, o,os). Mourn(ed,ing) aloud. Sob(bed, bing). Wail(ed,ing). Bemoan(ed,ing). Bewail(ed,ing). Griev(e,ed,ing). Moan(ed,ing). Weep(ing). Wept. *Consider also:* plaint(s), planh(s), deploration(s), tombeau(x). *See also* Bereavement; Dirges; Elegies; Grief; Loss (psychology); Mourning.

Land (property). Land(s). Property. Real estate. Acre(s,age). Tract(s). Plat(s). Plot(s). Tillage. Rural area(s). Pastoral area(s). Agricultural holding(s). Upland(s). Landholding(s). Rangeland(s). Farmland(s). Woodland(s). Grassland(s). Pasture(s). Countryside. Coastland(s). Beach(es). Swamp(s). Wetland(s). Wilderness. Open area(s).

Grounds. Territor(y,ies). Smallholdings. Hectares. Parcel(s). *See also* Common lands; Farms; Land ownership; Land preservation; Land reform; Land settlement; Land speculation; Land surveying; Land tenure; Land use; Land values; Landlords; Natural resources; Parks; Place of residence; Production; Property rights; Rangelands; Right of pasture; Real estate; Reclamation of land; Site selection; Soil conservation; Soil degradation; Soil erosion; Soil fertility; Valuation; Zoning.

Land, arable. See *Arable land.*

Land, clearing. See *Clearing land.*

Land, reclamation of. See *Reclamation of land.*

Land, rural. See *Rural land.*

Land development. See *Real estate development.*

Land mines. Land mine(s). Landmine(s). Anti-personnel mine(s). Antipersonnel mine(s). APM(s). Smart mine(s). Self-destructing mine(s). *Consider also:* military mine(s), minefield(s), mine field(s), de-mining, demining, mine-blowing, mine clearing, mine detector(s), Ottawa Process. *See also* Military weapons; Weaponry.

Land ownership. Land ownership. Agricultural holdings. Landowner(s, ship). Legal title to land. Land tenure. Landlord(s). Landholding(s). Small-holding(s). Alod(ial) land(s). Fee simple estate. Land warrant(s). *Choose from:* land(s), propert(yies), real estate, acre(s,age), tract(s), plat(s), plot(s), farm(s,land,lands), woodland(s), territor(y,ies), hectares, parcel(s) *with:* own(ed,ers,ership,ing), title, tenure, holding(s), acquisition, oligopol(y,ies), transfer(s), purchase(d,s), possess(ed, ing,ion,ions), claim(s), deed(s), sell(ing), sold, bought, buy, squatter(s), takeover, grant(s,ed). *See also* Common lands; Estates (law); Home ownership; Land (property); Land speculation; Land tenure; Landlords; Provenance; Tenant farmers; Tenants.

Land preservation. Land preservation. *Choose from:* sav(e,ed,ing), conserv(e, ing,ation), preserv(e,ing), protect(ed, ing,tion), mainten(ance), safeguard(ing), monitor, reclaim(ed,ing), reclamation, restor(e,ed,ing,ation), replant(ed,ing), replenish(ed,ing), re-establish(ed,ing), return(ed,ing) *with:* land(s), wood-land(s), forest(s), swamp(s,land), pasture(s), desert(s), field(s), wood(s), marsh(es), jungle(s), rain forest(s), propert(y,ies), acreage, ecosystem(s). Arrest(ed,ing) deforestation. Reforest(ing,ation). Contour plowing. Erosion control. Flood control. Preserv(e,ing) ecosystem(s). Conserv(e,ed,ing) rain forest(s).

Sav(e,ing) redwoods. Soil conservation. Park(s). Greenway(s). Greenbelt(s). Forest management. *Choose from:* nature, fish, wildlife *with:* preserve(s). *See also* Arable land; Arid lands; Conservation of natural resources; Deforestation; Desertification; Ecology; Ecosystem management; Environment; Environmental protection; Food chain; Forest conservation; Forestry; Grasslands; Grasses; Irrigation; Land (property); Land use; Natural environment; Natural resources; Reclamation of land; Restoration ecology; Shore protection; Slash burn agriculture; Soil conservation; Soil degradation; Soil erosion; Soil fertility; Submerged lands; Tree planting; Vegetation; Wetlands; Wildlife conservation; Wildlife sanctuaries.

Land reform. Land reform. Agrarian reform. Redistribut(e,ed,ing,ion) land. Appropriat(e,ed,ing,ion) land. Breakup large estate(s). *See also* Agrarian societies; Agrarian structures; Land ownership; Land tenure; Liberation theology; Peasant rebellions; Peasants; Plantations; Political reform; Relocation; Rural development; Rural land; Social legislation; Social reform; Sharecropping; Tenant farmers.

Land settlement. Land settlement *Choose from:* land(s), territor(y,ies), frontier(s), rainforest(s), woodland(s), prairie(s), hinterland(s) *with:* settl(e,ed,ing,ement), resettl(e,ed,ing,ement), occup(y,ied, ation), migrat(e,ed,ing,ion), coloniz(e, ed,ing,ation). *See also* Colonization; Community (geographic locality); Demography; Ecological imperialism; Frontier thesis; Frontiers; Homesteading; Human settlements; Land (property); Land tenure; Land use; Migration; Nomads; Place of residence; Population density; Population distribution; Refugees; Relocation; Residential patterns; Rural to urban migration; Settlement patterns; Settlers; Squatters; Urban to rural migration.

Land settlement patterns. See *Settlement patterns.*

Land speculation. Land speculation. *Choose from:* land(s), propert(y,ies), real estate, tract(s), farm(s) *with:* invest(ed,ing,or,ors), speculat(ive,ion), investment(s), gain(s), loss(es). *Consider also:* land value(s), land price(s). *See also* Land (property); Land ownership; Land use; Land values; Neighborhood preservation; Property values; Real estate; Speculation.

Land subdivisions. Land subdivision(s). *Choose from:* plot(s), parcel(s), plat(s), tract(s) *with:* land(s), propert(y,ies). *Consider also:* ranchette(s), farm subdivision(s), farmland development. *See also* Land use; Local planning;

Residential patterns; Urban planning.

Land surveying. Land survey(s,ing,or,ors). Map drawing. *Choose from:* land(s), territor(y,ies) *with:* survey(s,ing,or,ors), map(ped,ping), chart(ed,ing), measur(e, ed,ing), plot(ting,ted). *Consider also:* geographic information system(s), GIS, global positioning system(s). *See also* Boundaries; Cartography; Geographic information systems; Geography; Land (property); Maps.

Land tenure. Land tenure. Land holdings. Agricultural holdings. Primogeniture. Gavelkind. Borough-English. Escheat. Socage tenure. Landholdings. Smallholdings. *Choose from:* land(s), propert(y,ies), real estate, acre(s,age), tract(s), plat(s), plot(s), lot(s), farm(s,land,lands), woodland(s), territor(y,ies), hectares, parcel(s) *with:* tenure, occupancy, rights, access, holding(s). *Consider also:* tenant farm(ers,er,ing), groundrent, ground rent, sharecropping, croft(ing), chung-jun system. *See also* Agrarian societies; Agrarian structures; Farms; Homesteading; Land ownership; Land reform; Land settlement; Sharecropping; Tenant farmers.

Land titles. See *Land ownership.*

Land use. Land use(s). *Choose from:* land(s,scape,scapes), desert(s), floodplain(s), wetland(s), open space, farmland(s), habitat(s), wilderness(es), coastal zone(s), tundra(s), rain forest(s), forest(s), countryside, soil, real estate *with:* manag(ement,ing), administration, retention, zon(e,ed,ing), consolidation, preserv(e,es,ing,ation), utiliz(e,ed,ing, ation), regulat(e,ed,ing,ion,ions), protect(ed,ing,ion), conservation, expropriat(e,ed,ing,ion), taking(s), condemn(ed,ing,ation), eminent domain, development, use(s), planning, polic(y,ies), reserv(e,es,ation,ations), subdivision(s), valu(e,es,ation), assessment. *Choose from:* urban, community, city, rural *with:* planning, development, containment. *Consider also:* residential, industrial, commercial, business, public, recreational *with:* use(s). *Consider also:* agricultural development, aforestation, environmental planning, environmental impact statement(s), vanishing land(s), building permit(s), siting, riparian right(s), land economics, highest and best use(s), excess condemnation, land market(s), growth management, conservation polic(y,ies), nonresidential use(s), deed restriction(s). *See also* Agrarian structures; Agribusiness; Agricultural collectives; Agricultural diversification; Agriculture; Common lands; Community development; Conservation of natural resources; Deforestation; Desertification; Environmental pollution; Environmental protection; Forest

conservation; Forestry; Land preservation; Land speculation; Land subdivisions; Land values; Parks; Real estate development; Reclamation of land; Recreational facilities; Resource management; Resource stress; Rural development; Rural land; Site selection; Slash burn agriculture; Soil conservation; Soil degradation; Soil erosion; Sustainable development; Transportation policy; Urban development; Wildlife sanctuaries; Zoning.

Land values. Land value(s). *Choose from:* land(s), property, real estate, acre(s,age), tract(s), plat(s), plot(s), tillage, agricultural holding(s), landholding(s), rangeland(s), farmland(s), woodland(s), coastland(s), beach(es), territor(y,ies) *with:* value(s), price(s), valuation(s), valuable, market(s), assessment(s), apprais(al,ed,ing). *See also* Housing costs; Housing market; Land (property); Land speculation; Land use; Property values; Real estate; Site selection; Valuation.

Landfill. Landfill(s,ed,ing). Dump(s,ing). Toxic dump(s). Dump site(s). Waste disposal facilit(y,ies). Sludge site(s). Junkyard(s). Illegal dumping. Fly-tipping. Fly tipping. Trash incinerator(s). Sanitary landfill(s). Landfill conversion. Love canal. *Choose from:* solid waste(s), garbage *with:* dump(s), disposal, conversion, facilit(y,ies). *See also* Reclamation of land; Solid waste; Waste disposal; Waste to energy; Waste transport.

Landlord tenant relations. Landlord tenant relation(s,ship,ships). *Choose from:* landlord(s), property owner(s) *with:* tenant(s), renter(s), relation(s,ship, ships), conflict(s), disagreement(s), dispute(s), conflict(s), impasse(s), negotiat(e,ed,es,ing,ion,ions), mediat(ed,ion,ing), bargain(ed,ing), compromise(d,s), concession(s), agreement(s), evict(ed,ing,ion,ions). *See also* Eviction; Home ownership; Landlords; Rent strikes; Rental housing; Resident councils; Tenant farmers; Tenant relocation; Tenants.

Landlords. Landlord(s). Landlad(y,ies). Innkeeper(s). Proprietor(s). Lessor(s). Slumlord(s). *Consider also:* let(ting) room(s), rentier(s), rental housing, leas(ing,es,ed), sublet(ting), property owner(s), landowner(s), leaseholder(s). *See also* Absentee ownership; Home ownership; Land ownership; Landlord tenant relations; Real estate; Rental housing; Tenants.

Landmarks, literary. See *Literary landmarks.*

Lands, arid. See *Arid lands.*

Lands, common. See *Common lands.*

Lands, grazing. See *Grazing lands.*

Lands, public. See *Public lands.*

Lands, semi arid. See *Arid zones.*

Lands, submerged. See *Submerged lands.*

Landscape. Landscape(s). Natural scene(s,ry). Country scene(s,ry). Landform(s). Scenic view(s). *Consider also:* vista(s), panorama(s). *See also* Landscape architecture; Topography.

Landscape archaeology. See *Archaeological surveying.*

Landscape architecture. Landscape architectur(e,al). Landscape planning. Landscape design. *Consider also:* landscape gardening, style of gardening, topiar(y,ies). *See also* Formal gardens; Gardens; Garden structures; Gardening to attract wildlife; Landscape; Natural gardens; Urban planning.

Language. Language(s). Tongue(s). Slang. Jargon. Bilingual(ism). Multilingual(ism). Second language(s). Foreign language(s). Terminology. Medspeak. Translat(e,ed,ing,ion,ions). Dialect(s). Vernacular. Native speaker(s). Mother tongue. Lingua(e) franca(e,s). Semiotic(s). Esperanto. Pidgin(s). Creole(s). Artificial language(s). Child language. Baby talk. Figurative language. Interlanguage. Nonstandard English. Official language(s). Polyglot. Programing language(s). Sign language(s). Symbolic language(s). Tone language(s). Unwritten language(s). Street language. Written language(s). *Consider also:* adjective(s), adverb(s), alphabet(s), anagram(s), antonym(s), conversation, ethnolinguistic(s), etymolog(y,ical), grammar, homograph(s), homonym(s), inflection, language universal(s), linguistic(s), metaphor(s), monolingual(ism), morpheme(s), name(s), neologism(s), nomenclature, noun(s), onomastic(s), philology, phoneme(s), phonetic(s), phonology, phrase(s), pronoun(s), psycholinguistic(s), semantic(s), sentence structure, speech, syllable(s), synonym(s), syntax, transformational generative grammar, verb(s), vocabular(y,ies). *See also* Bidialectalism; Child language; Creoles; Dialects; Diglossia; Ethnolinguistics; Etymology; Extinct languages; Figurative language; Grammar; Homonyms; Jargon; Language acquisition; Language classification; Language delayed; Language development; Language development disorders; Language disorders; Language laboratories; Language maintenance; Language obsolescence; Language planning; Language policy; Language proficiency; Language shift; Language tests; Language usage; Language varieties; Languages (as subjects); Linguistics; Literacy; Metalanguage; Metaphors; Monolingualism; Multilingualism; Neologisms; Nonsexist language; Nonstandard English; Numbers; Phonemes; Phonetics; Phrases; Rhetoric; Psycholinguistics; Schizophrenic language; Second languages; Semiotics; Sentence structure; Sentences; Sexist language; Sign language; Slang; Sociolinguistics; Speech; Symbolism; Verbal communication; Vocabulary; Word frequency; Word meaning; Words; Writing (composition); Written communications.

Language, abusive. See *Invective; Verbal abuse.*

Language, African American. See *Ebonics.*

Language, body. See *Body language.*

Language, child. See *Child language.*

Language, colloquial. See *Colloquial language.*

Language, figurative. See *Figurative language.*

Language, Japanese. See *Japanese language.*

Language, Mexican. See *Nahuatl language.*

Language, Mobilian trade. See *Mobilian trade language.*

Language, Nahuatl. See *Nahuatl language.*

Language, nonsexist. See *Nonsexist language.*

Language, patriarchal. See *Sexist language.*

Language, philosophy of. See *Philosophy of language.*

Language, psychology of. See *Psycholinguistics.*

Language, schizophrenic. See *Schizophrenic language.*

Language, scientific. See *Scientific language.*

Language, second order. See *Metalanguage.*

Language, sexist. See *Sexist language.*

Language, sign. See *Sign language.*

Language ability. See *Verbal ability.*

Language acquisition. Language acquisition. *Choose from:* language(s), verbal, linguistic, lexical *with:* acquisition, acquir(e,ed,ing), development, learn(ed, ing). *See also* Child language; Language; Language delayed; Language development; Psycholinguistics; Second language education; Verbal learning; Vocabulary.

Language approach, whole. See *Whole language approach.*

Language art (fine arts). See *Conceptual art.*

Language change. Language change. Linguistic change. *Choose from:* language(s), linguistic *with:* chang(e,es,ing), evol(ve,ved,ving,ution). *See also* Diachronic linguistics; Etymology; Linguistics;.

Language classification. Language classification. Linguistic classification. *Choose from:* language(s), linguistic, tongue(s) *with:* typolog(y,ies), taxonom(y,ies). *Consider also:* nostratic hypothesis. *See also* Classification; Language.

Language communities. See *Speech communities.*

Language death. See *Extinct languages; Language obsolescence.*

Language delayed. Language delayed. *Choose from:* language, speech, verbal(ly) *with:* delay(s,ed), backward. *See also* Delayed development; Language; Language development; Language development disorders.

Language development. Language development. *Choose from:* language(s), verbal, linguistic, vocabulary, phonetic(s), speech, syntax, psycholinguistic *with:* development(al), acquisition, readiness, growth, attainment. *See also* Cognitive development; Intellectual development; Language acquisition; Language delayed; Psychogenesis; Second language education; Verbal learning.

Language development disorders. Language development disorder(s). *Choose from:* language, speech, articulation *with:* handicap(ped,s), developmental disabilit(y,ies), retarded development, learning disorder(s,ed), delay(s,ed), impair(ed,ment,ments), impediment(s). *See also* Developmental disabilities; Language delayed; Speech development; Speech disorders.

Language diffusion. See *Language spread.*

Language disorders. Language disorder(s). *Choose from:* language, speech, verbal *with:* handicap(s,ped), disorder(ed,s), disabilit(y,ies), deficit(s), retarded development, delay(s,ed), deficienc(y, ies). *Consider also:* dyslexia, agraphia, anomia. *See also* Aphasia; Communication disorders; Dysphasia; Echolalia; Learning disabilities; Mutism; Psycholinguistics; Schizophrenic language; Speech disorders.

Language education, second. See *Second language education.*

Language games. See *Word games.*

Language geography. See *Linguistic geography.*

Language laboratories. Language laborator(y,ies). Language learning laborator(y,ies). Language lab(s). *Choose from:* audio active, audio active compare, audio passive, language, language media *with:* laborator(y,ies). *See also* Languages (as subjects); Programed instruction; Second language education; Self education.

Language learning, foreign. See *Second language education.*

Language learning, second. See *Second language education.*

Language maintenance. Language maintenance. *Choose from:* language(s), mother tongue, linguistic *with:* maintenance, retention, revitalization, loyalty, continuity. *Consider also:* marginalized languages, cultural maintenance. *See also* Biculturalism; Bilingualism; Creoles; Cultural identity; Cultural maintenance; Diglossia; Extinct languages; Language; Language obsolescence; Language planning; Language policy; Language shift; Language spread; Language usage; Languages (as subjects); Linguistic minorities; Loan words; Multilingualism; Pidgin languages; Sociolinguistics; Speech communities.

Language obsolescence. Language obsolescence. *Choose from:* language(s), linguistic, word(s), lexical, vocabular(y, ies), dialect(s) *with:* obsolescen(ce,t), obsolete, death, dead, dying, die off, died, extinct(ion), threatened, moribund, endanger(ed,ing,ment). *See also* Extinct languages; Historical linguistics; Language; Language maintenance.

Language planning. Language planning. *Choose from:* language, linguistic, vocabular(y,ies), spelling, grammar *with:* planning, reform(s), engineeering, construct(ed,ion), regulat(e,ed,ing,ion, ions), standardization, simplification, modernization, phoneticization. *Consider also:* Chinese character simplification, Pinyin Chinese. *See also* Bilingual education; Bilingualism; Language; Language maintenance; Language policy; Language usage; Languages (as subjects); Multilingualism.

Language policy. Language polic(y,ies). Linguistic polic(y,ies). *Choose from:* language(s), linguistic(s) *with:* polic(y,ies), official, national, state. *Consider also:* specific countries with language policies, for example, Welsh Language Act. *See also* Biculturalism; Bilingual education; Bilingualism; Language; Language maintenance; Language planning; Language usage; Languages (as subjects); Plural societies; Political culture; Social legislation; Sociolinguistics.

Language proficiency. Language proficiency. *Choose from:* language(s), linguistic, bilingual, English, French, Spanish, Japanese, Tagalog, etc. *with:* proficien(t,cy), fluen(t,tly,cy),

competen(t,ce,cy,cies), performance, comprehension, abilit(y,ies), skill(s). *See also* Bilingualism; Communication skills; Fluency; Language tests; Second language education; Verbal ability.

Language shift. Language shift(s). *Choose from:* language(s), linguistic, dialect(s) *with:* shift(s). *Consider also:* language contact, codeswitching. *See also* Acculturation; Creoles; Culture contact; Diglossia; Language; Language maintenance; Linguistics; Loan words; Minority groups; Pidgin languages; Sociolinguistics.

Language skills. See *Language proficiency.*

Language spread. Language spread. Language diffusion. *Choose from:* language(s), lexical, word(s) *with:* spread(ing), diffusion, expansion. *Consider also:* lexical influence(s), loan word(s). *See also* International languages; Language maintenance; Language varieties; Linguistic geography; Speech communities.

Language tests. Language test(s). *Choose from:* language, language proficiency, vocabulary, language comprehension, language disabilit(y,ies), aphas(ia,ic), language disorder(s), language difficult(y,ies), language skill(s) *with:* test(s), assessment(s), diagnos(is,tic, tics), evaluation(s), examination(s), inventor(y,ies), measure(s,ment,ments), questionnaire(s), rating(s), scale(s), score(s). *See also* Achievement tests; Language proficiency; Languages (as subjects); Listening comprehension; Reading tests; Verbal tests.

Language transfer (Language learning). Cross language transfer(red,ring,s). Native language transfer(red,ring,s). First-to-second-language transfer(red, ring,s). Lexical transfer(red,ring,s). *Choose from:* transfer(red,ring,s) *with:* language, spirantiz(e,ed,ation), spirant(s), syllable structure(s). *See also* Bilingual education; Bilingualism; Linguistic interference; Second language education.

Language translation, foreign. See *Translating and translations.*

Language usage. Language usage. *Choose from:* language(s), dialect(s), vocabulary *with:* use(s), usage, patterns, variations, traits, spoken, conversation(al). *Consider also:* code switching, daily language, everyday speech, officialese, idiom(s, atic), epithets, jargon, discourse. *See also* Dialects; Diglossia; Epithets; Ethnolinguistics; Grammar; Jargon; Language; Language maintenance; Language planning; Language policy; Language varieties; Languages (as subjects); Linguistic minorities; Linguistics; Obscenity; Slang; Sociolinguistics; Speech.

Language varieties. Language varieties. Dialect(s). Ethnolinguistics. Sociolinguistics. Loan word(s). Creol(e,es,ization). Pidgin(s,ization). Slang. Vernacular. Patois. Jargon. Black English. *Choose from:* language(s), linguistic, vocabular(y,ies), dialect(s) *with:* variet(y,ies), regional, provincial, idiomatic, variant(s). *See also* Comparative linguistics; Creoles; Dialects; Diglossia; Jargon; Language; Language spread; Language usage; Linguistics; Loan words; Pidgin languages; Slang; Sociolinguistics.

Languages (as subjects). Language(s). Lingual. Lingua(e) franca(e,s). Tongue(s). Lingo. Vernacular. Dialect(s). Creole(s). Common speech. *Consider also:* specific languages by name. *See also* Bilingualism; Etymology; Language; Language maintenance; Language planning; Language policy; Language usage; Language varieties; Linguistics; Monolingualism; Multilingualism; Translating and translations; Algonquian languages; Anatolian languages; Annamese-Muong languages; Asian languages; Baltic languages; Benue-Niger languages; Caucasian languages; Celtic languages; Chad languages; Dravidian languages; East Altaic languages; Eskimo-Aleut languages; Finno-Ugric languages; Germanic languages; Greek languages; Hamitic languages; Hokan Siouan languages; Indo-Iranian languages; International languages; Italic non-romance languages; Japanese language; Kwa languages; Luorawetlan languages; Macro-Chibchan languages; Macro-Khoisan languages; Macro-Otomanguean languages; Malayo-Polynesian languages; Mandingo (Mande) languages; Mon-Khmer languages; Nadene languages; Niger-Congo languages, Atlantic (western); Nilo-Saharan languages; Penutian languages; Romance languages; Samoyedic languages; Semitic languages; Sino-Thai languages; Slavic languages; Sudanic languages; Thraco-Illyrian languages; Thraco-Phrygian languages; Tibeto-Burman languages; Tokharin languages; Translating and translations; Uto-Aztecan languages; Voltaic (Gur) languages; West Altaic languages.

Languages, African. See *Benue-Niger languages; Chad languages; Hamitic languages; Kwa languages; Macro-Khoisan languages; Mandingo (Mande) languages; Niger-Congo languages, Atlantic (Western); Nilo-Saharan languages; Semitic languages; Sudanic languages; Voltaic (Gur) languages.*

Languages, Algonquian. See *Algonquian languages.*

Languages, Anatolian. See *Anatolian languages.*

Languages, Andean-Equatorial. See *Andean-Equatorial languages.*

Languages, Annamese-Muong. See *Annamese-Muong languages.*

Languages, Asian. See *Asian languages.*

Languages, Austronesian. See *Malayo-Polynesian languages.*

Languages, Baltic. See *Baltic languages.*

Languages, Benue-Niger. See *Benue-Niger languages.*

Languages, Caucasian. See *Caucasian languages.*

Languages, Celtic. See *Celtic languages.*

Languages, Chinese. See *Sino-Thai languages.*

Languages, Dravidian. See *Dravidian languages.*

Languages, East Altaic. See *East Altaic languages.*

Languages, Eskimo-Aleut. See *Eskimo-Aleut languages.*

Languages, extinct. See *Extinct languages.*

Languages, Finno-Ugric. See *Finno-Ugric languages.*

Languages, foreign. See *Second languages.*

Languages, GE-Pano-Carib. See *GE-Pano-Carib languages.*

Languages, Germanic. See *Germanic languages.*

Languages, Greek. See *Greek languages.*

Languages, Hamitic. See *Hamitic languages.*

Languages, Hokan-Siouan. See *Hokan-Siouan languages.*

Languages, Indo-Iranian. See *Indo-Iranian languages.*

Languages, international. See *International languages.*

Languages, Italic non-romance languages. See *Italic non-romance languages.*

Languages, Kwa. See *Kwa languages.*

Languages, Luorawetlan. See *Luorawetlan languages.*

Languages, Macro-Chibchan. See *Macro-Chibchan languages.*

Languages, Macro-Khoisan. See *Macro-Khoisan languages.*

Languages, Macro-Khoisan. See *Macro-Khoisan languages.*

Languages, Macro-Otomanguean. See *Macro-Otomanguean languages.*

Languages, Malayo-Polynesian. See *Malayo-Polynesian languages.*

Languages, Mandingo Mande. See *Mandingo (Mande) languages.*

Languages, mixed. See *Creoles.*

Languages, Mon-Khmer. See *Mon-Khmer languages.*

Languages, Nadene. See *Nadene languages.*

Languages, native. See *Native languages.*

Languages, Niger-Congo Atlantic Western. See *Niger-Congo languages, Atlantic (Western).*

Languages, Nilo-Saharan. See *Nilo-Saharan languages.*

Languages, official. See *Language policy.*

Languages, Penutian. See *Penutian languages.*

Languages, pidgin. See *Pidgin languages.*

Languages, private. See *Secret languages.*

Languages, Romance. See *Romance languages.*

Languages, Samoyedic. See *Samoyedic languages.*

Languages, second. See *Second languages.*

Languages, secret. See *Secret languages.*

Languages, Semitic. See *Semitic languages.*

Languages, Sino-Thai. See *Sino-Thai languages.*

Languages, Slavic. See *Slavic languages.*

Languages, Sudanic. See *Sudanic languages.*

Languages, Thraco-Illyrian. See *Thraco-Illyrian languages.*

Languages, Thraco-Phrygian. See *Thraco-Phrygian languages.*

Languages, Tibeto-Burman. See *Tibeto-Burman languages.*

Languages, Tokharin. See *Tokharin languages.*

Languages, trade. See *Trade languages.*

Languages, Uto-Aztecan. See *Uto-Aztecan languages.*

Languages, Voltaic Gur. See *Voltaic (Gur) languages.*

Languages, West Altaic. See *West Altaic languages.*

Languages in contact. Language contact. Languages come into contact. *Consider also:* language mixing, lexical borrowing, Spanglish, hybrid language(s), borrow(ed,ing) lexical item(s), borrow(ed,ing) words. *See also* Bilingualism; Borderlands; Creoles; Culture contact; Linguistic minorities; Loan words; Pidgin languages; Speech communities.

Larceny. Larceny. Theft. Thieve(ry,s). Steal(ing,th). Shoplift(er,ers,ing). Pickpocket(s). Illegal(ly) expropriat(e, ed,ing,ion,ions). Property offender(s). Property crime(s). Embezzle(r,rs,ment). Insider trading. Rob(bed,bing,bery, ber,bers). Burglar(s,y,ize,izing,ized). *See also* Burglary; Crime; Offenses; Robbery; Shoplifting; Thieves.

Large cities. See *Urban environments; Metropolitan areas.*

Laryngeal diseases. Laryngeal disease(s). *Choose from:* laryngeal, larynx(es), larynges, vocal cord(s) *with:* disease(s), disorder(s), granuloma, edema, neoplasm(s), perichondritis, tuberculosis, paralysis, cancer, cyst(s), coccidoidomycosis, complications, pathology, obstruction(s), lesion(s). *Consider also:* laryngismus, laryngitis, laryngostenosis. *See also* Respiratory system.

Lassitude. See *Fatigue.*

Last words. Last words. Last testament. Death-song(s). *Choose from:* last, deathbed, near death, dying, final *with:* word(s), testament, confession(s), request(s), wish(es), statement(s). *See also* Dying; End; Finale; Speeches (formal discourse).

Latchkey children. See *Child self care.*

Late childbearing. Late childbearing. Middle age(d) mother(s,ing,hood). *Choose from:* older, over 30, over 35, over 40 *with:* primipara(s), primigravida(s), mother(s). *Choose from:* delay(s,ed,ing), last chance, late, postpon(e,ed,ing,ement,ements,able) *with:* motherhood, pregnan(t,cy,cies), reproduc(ing,tion,tive), conception, conceiv(e,ed,ing). *Consider also:* timing, spacing *with:* child(ren), baby, babies, family. *See also* Biological clocks; Childbearing age; Family planning; First birth timing; Maternal age; Senior pregnancies.

Late fetal death. See *Fetal death; Infant mortality.*

Latency, response. See *Response latency.*

Latency period. Latency period. Prepubert(y,al). Prepubescen(ce,t). *Choose from:* latency *with:* age, stage, period, child(ren), boy(s), girl(s), development. *Consider also:* prelatency, postlatency. *See also* Child development; Children; Developmental stages; Life stage transitions; Puberty.

Latent schizophrenia. Latent schizophren(ia,ias,ic,ics). *Choose from:* incipient, prepsychotic, pseudoneurotic, pseudopsychopathic, borderline *with:* schizophren(ia,ias,ic,ics). *See also* Schizophrenia.

Lateral dominance. See *Laterality.*

Laterality. Laterality. Handed(ness). Ambidext(erity,rous). Lefthanded(ness). Righthanded(ness). Sinistral(s,ity). Dextral(s,ity). *Choose from:* prefer(red, ence,ences), dominan(ce,t) *with:* hand(s), lateral(ity), left, right. *See also* Cerebral dominance; Motor development; Physical characteristics.

Lateralization (brain). See *Laterality.*

Latifundio. See *Feudalism; Plantations.*

Latin America. See *Central America; South America.*

Latin American literature. Latin American literature. *Choose from:* Spanish America(n), Hispanic, Latin America(n), Argentin(a,ian), Bolivia(n), Brazil(ian), Brasil(ian), Chile(an), Colombia(n), Costa Rica(n), Cuba(n), Dominican, Ecuador(ean), Salvador(an), Guatemala(n), Haiti(an), Hondura(s,n), Mexic(o,an), Nicaragua(n), Panama(nian), Paraguay(an), Peru(vian), Uruguay(an), Venezuela(n), Puerto Ric(o,an) *with:* litera(ture,ry), poetry, poem(s), ballad(s,ry), heroic verse, prose, writing(s), narrative(s), novel(la,las,s,ist,ists), little magazine(s), essay(s), sketch(es), letter(s), play(s), short stor(y,ies), theatre, fiction, lyric(s), epic(s), melodrama, comed(y,ies), satire(s), drama(s), sonnet(s), Neoclassicism, Romantic generation, Romanticism, Naturalism, Realism, Parnassianism, Ultraísmo, Postmodernism. *Consider also:* Modernis(m,mo,tas), Gongorism, gaucho literature, cuadro de costumbres, Indianista literature. *Consider also Latin American authors, for example:* Rubén Darío, José Martí, Gabriela Mistral, Alfonsina Storni, Pablo Neruda, Manuel Bandeira, Jorge Amado, Octavio Paz, Jorge Luis Borges, Miguel Angel Asturias, Gabriel García Márquez, Carlos Fuentes, Mario Vargas Llosa, Luis Rafael Sánchez, Elena Poniatowska, Clarice Lispector. *See also* Latin Americans; Literature.

Latin Americans. Latin American(s). Spanish American(s). Portuguese American(s). *Choose from:* Cuban(s), Central America(n,ns), Belize(an,ans), Costa Rica(n,ns), El Salvador, Salvadoran(s), Guatemala(n,ns), Nicaragua(n,ns), Hondura(s,n,ns), Panam(a,anian,anians), Mexic(o,an,ans), South America(n,ns), Argentin(a,ian, ians), Bolivia(n,ns), Brazil(ian,ians), Chile(an,ans), Colombia(n,ns), Ecuador(ian,ians), Guyan(a,ese), Paraguay(an,ans), Peru(vian,vians), Surinam(e,ese), Uruguay(an,ans), Venezuela(n,ns), French Guian(a,ese), South Georgia(n,ns), Falkland Islands [Islas Malvinas] *with:* resident(s), citizen(s,ry), voter(s), taxpayer(s), resident(s), native(s), inhabitant(s), population, civilian(s), national subject(s). *Consider also:* Latino(s). *See also* Central America; Central American native cultural groups; Hispanic Americans; Latin American literature; South America; South American native cultural groups.

Latin drama. Latin drama(s). Latin traged(y,ies). *Choose from:* Latin, Roman, Seneca(s), Plautus, Terence, Livius Andronicus, etc. *with:* drama(s), traged(y,ies), play(s), playwright(s). *See also* Ancient literature; Drama; Historical drama; Latin literature.

Latin epigrams. Latin epigram(s). *Choose from:* Latin(e,o), lateinische *with:* epigram(m,mata,matum,maton,s), epigrammatis(m,tic,tic,ts). *See also* Ancient literature; Epigrams; Epigraphs; Latin literature.

Latin inscriptions. Latin inscription(s). *Choose from:* Latin, Roman *with:* inscription(s), epigraphy. *Consider also:* inscriptiones Latinae, Lateinische Inschriften, fasti consulares. *See also* Ancient literature; Epigraphs; Inscriptions; Latin literature.

Latin laudatory poetry. Latin laudatory poetry. *Choose from:* Latin, Roman *with:* laudatory, panegyric(al,ally), encomium, eulog(y,ies,istic) epideictic *with:* poe(m,ms,try). *Consider also:* Latin ode(s). *See also* Ancient literature; Epithalamia; Latin literature; Laudatory poetry; Poetry.

Latin literature. Latin literature. Roman literature. *Choose from:* Latin, Roman *with:* literature, literary work(s), prose, poetry, lyric(s), eleg(y,ies), satire, *Consider also:* classical literature; lateinischer Literatur, Cicero, Julius Caesar, Sallust, Varro, Vergil, Horace, Tibullus, Propertius, Ovid, Livy, Seneca, Lucan, Persius, Statius, Martial, Juvenal, Petronius, Frontinus, Pliny the Elder, Pliny the Younger, Tacitus, Quintilian, Claudian, Fronto, Marcus Aurelius, etc. *See also* Ancient literature; Latin drama; Latin epigrams; Latin inscriptions; Latin laudatory poetry; Roman law.

Latinos. See *Hispanic Americans.*

Lauda. Laud(a,e,i,ario). *Consider also:* Geisserlied(er), frottola. *See also* Ballata; Geisserlieder; Hymns; Medieval music; Music; Renaissance music.

Laudatory poetry. Laudatory poe(try,m,ms). Praise poe(m,ms,try). Tribute poe(m,ms,try). Eulog(y,ies,ize, izing) poe(m,ms,try). *Consider also:* panegyric(s,al,ally), encomi(a,um,ums), epithalami(a,c,on,um,ums). *See also* Epithalamia; Latin laudatory poetry; Love poetry; Occasional verse; Poetry.

Laudatory poetry, Latin. See *Latin laudatory poetry.*

Laughter. Laugh(ed,ing,ter). Giggl(e,ing). Chuckl(e,ing). Snicker(ed,ing). Humor(ous,ousness). Risibility. Smil(e,ed,es,ing). Gelasmus. *Consider also:* gelastic *with:* seizure(s), epilepsy. *See also* Emotional responses; Frivolity; Humor; Nonverbal communication; Sense of humor; Smiling; Vocalization.

Laundering, money. See *Money laundering.*

Law (legal philosophy and theory). Law(s). *Choose from:* law(s), legal, court(s,room), jurisprudence, judicial, justice, criminal justice, constitution(s, al,ality), statut(e,es,ory), ordinance(s) *with:* theor(y,ies), philosoph(y,ical,ies), doctrine(s), code(s), concept(s), definition(s). *Consider also:* Magna Carta, Bill of Rights. *See also* Abortion laws; Civil rights; Constitution (legal); Contracts; Due process; International law; Jurisprudence; Law (practice); Laws; Legal rights; Legal system; Legislation; Marijuana laws; Maritime law; Martial law; Military law; Space law; Theories.

Law (practice). Law(s). *Choose from:* law(s), statut(e,es,ory), ordinance(s), legal, court(s,room,rooms), jurisprudence, judicial, justice, criminal justice, constitution(s,al,ality), litigation *with:* system(s), institution(s), psychology, attitude(s), sanction(s), social order, implication(s), warrant(s), arrest(s), injunction(s), plea bargain(ed,ing), equity, penalt(y,ies), punishment(s), remed(y,ies), resolution(s), right(s), suit(s), due process. *Consider also:* civil, criminal, common, constitutional, international *with:* law(s). *See also* Accident law; Attorneys; Civil procedures; Court opinions; Due process; Law (legal philosophy and theory); Law enforcement; Laws; Lawsuits; Legal cases; Legal procedures; Legal system; Rights.

Law, administrative. See *Administrative law.*

Law, antitrust. See *Antitrust law.*

Law, banking. See *Banking law.*

Law, common. See *Common law.*

Law, correctional. See *Penal codes.*

Law, election. See *Election law.*

Law, environmental. See *Environmental law.*

Law, equality before. See *Equality before the law.*

Law, feudal. See *Feudal law.*

Law, immigration. See *Immigration law.*

Law, international. See *International law.*

Law, Jewish. See *Jewish law.*

Law, maritime. See *Maritime law.*

Law, martial. See *Martial law.*

Law, military. See *Military law.*

Law, Mosaic. See *Jewish law.*

Law, natural. See *Natural law.*

Law, rule of. See *Rule of law.*

Law, space. See *Space law.*

Law, supremacy of. See *Rule of law.*

Law enforcement. Law enforcement. Criminal sanctions. Criminal justice system. Crime prevention. Correction(s). Punish(ed,ing,ment,ments). Crime deterrent(s). Incarcerat(ed,ing,ion). Legal arrest(s). Legal detention. *Choose from:* law(s), legal, rule(s), sanction(s), police *with:* enforc(e,ed,ing,ement), execut(e,ed,ing,ion), discharg(e,ed,ing), implement(ed,ing,ation), prosecut(e,ed, ing,ion), crackdown(s). *Choose from:* report(ed,ing), patrol(led,ling,s), apprehend(ed,ing), arrest(ed,ing), detain(ed,ing), action, intervention *with:* police(man,men,woman,women), guard(s), sheriff(s). *Consider also:* prosecut(e,ed,ing,ion). *See also* Arrests; Bail; Compliance; Contempt of Court; Crime prevention; Criminal investigations; Criminal justice; Criminal proceedings; Defendants; Drug and narcotic control; Evidence; Exemption (law); Formal social control; Investigations; Judicial decisions; Law (legal philosophy and theory); Law (practice); Law enforcement personnel; Offenders; Offenses; Penalties; Police brutality; Police community relations; Police dogs; Police personnel; Police questioning; Police records; Prosecution; Search and seizure; Sentencing; Social order; Substance abuse detection; Verdicts; Vigilantes.

Law enforcement personnel. Law enforcement personnel. Law enforcement officer(s). Sheriff(s). Correctional officer(s). Police. Members of juvenile justice panel(s). Sheriff's department. Criminal court judge(s). Probation officer(s). Parole officer(s). Correctional social worker(s). State investigator(s). District attorney(s). *Choose from:* criminal justice, law enforcement, police, correction(al,s), prison *with:* personnel, officer(s), functionar(y,ies), department(s), social worker(s), career(s), guard(s), investigator(s). *See also* Correctional personnel; Crime prevention; Criminal proceedings; Government personnel; Law enforcement; Paramilitary; Police brutality; Police community relations; Police dogs; Police personnel; Police questioning; Police records.

Law in the Bible. See *Jewish law.*

Law makers. See *Legislative bodies; Legislators.*

Law of nations. See *International law.*

Law of nature. See *Natural law.*

Law reform. Law reform. *Choose from:* reform(s,ed,ing), overhaul, revision, restructur(e,ed,ing), improv(e,ed,ing,ement,ements), amend(ed,ing,ment,ments), rewrite, rewritten, chang(e,es,ed,ing) *with:* law(s), legal system(s), legal structure, civil rights polic(y,ies), judicial, code(s), constitution(al), statut(e,es,ory). *See also* Laws; Legislative processes; Social reform.

Law societies. Law societ(y,ies). *Choose from:* law, legal, bar, lawyers' *with:* societ(y,ies), association(s), foundation(s), institute(s) *Consider also:* American Bar Association. *See also* Associations (organizations); Attorneys; Professional certification; Professional development; Professional education; Professional organizations; Societies (organizations).

Lawlessness. Lawless(ness). Anarch(y,ic, ism). Chaos. Terrorism. Rebellion(s). Nihilis(m,tic). Reign of terror. Mutin(y,ies). Riot(s,ing). Uprising(s). Mob rule. Insurrection(s). *Consider also:* disobedien(ce,t), corrupt(ed,ion). *See also* Anarchism; Anomie; Chaos; Confusion (disarray); Corruption in government; Crime; Military offenses; Rebellions; Terrorism.

Lawmakers. See *Legislative bodies; Legislators.*

Laws. Law(s). Rule(s). Regulation(s). Legal requirement(s). Statute(s). Legislation. Code(s). Legal polic(y,ies). Act(s). Legal prohibition(s). Supreme court decision(s). State restriction(s). Constitutional right(s). Outlaw(ed,ing). Court order(s). Constitutional amendment(s). Legal code(s). Case law. Common law. *Consider also:* legal *with:* aspect(s), issues, context(s), decision(s), sanction(s), position(s). *See also* Abortion laws; Banking law; Censorship; Citizenship; Civil rights; Codes (rules); Common law; Constitution (legal); Consumer protection; Cyberlaw; Election law; Enactment; Environmental law; Exemption (law); Feudal law; Food laws and legislation; Generalities; International law; Jewish law; Law (legal philosophy and theory); Law (practice); Law enforcement; Law reform; Legislation; Martial law; Marijuana laws; Maritime law; Military law; Privacy laws; Roman law; Rules (generalizations); Space law; Statutes.

Laws, abortion. See *Abortion laws.*

Laws, advertising. See *Advertising laws.*

Laws, agricultural and legislation. See *Agricultural laws and legislation.*

Laws, covering. See *Covering laws.*

Laws, criminal. See *Penal codes.*

Laws, game. See *Game laws.*

Laws, labor. See *Labor laws.*

Laws, marijuana. See *Marijuana laws.*

Laws, privacy. See *Privacy laws*

Laws and legislation, food. See *Food laws and legislation.*

Lawsuits. Lawsuit(s). Litigation. Injunction(s). Arbitration. Court hearing(s). Prosecut(e,ed,ing,ion). Class action(s). Liability case(s). *Choose from:* judge(s), jur(y,ies), court(s) *with:* award(s), finding(s), rul(e,ed,ing,ings), decision(s), verdict(s), settlement(s), reconsider(ed,ing,s), argument(s), reject(ed,ing,ion), uphold, upheld, sue(d), suit(s). *See also* Arbitration; Attorneys; Civil rights; Class action; Court judges; Court opinions; Defendants; Evidence; Hedonic damages; Litigation; Juries; Legal cases; Legal procedures; Legal rights; Legal system; Liability; Libel; Negligence; Property rights; Trial (law); Verdicts.

Lawyers. See *Attorneys.*

Lay ministry. See *Lay religious personnel.*

Lay religious personnel. Lay religious personnel. Lay ministry. Religious laity. Laicism. *Choose from:* lay(men,man), laity, volunteer(s) *with:* religious, religion(s), ministry, minister(s), church(s), Catholic(s), sunday school teacher(s), evangelism, preacher(s). *Consider also:* imam(s). *See also* Christian leadership; Clergy; Evangelists; Laymen; Missionaries; Preaching; Religious leadership; Religious personnel.

Lay therapists. Lay therapist(s). *Choose from:* lay, lay(man,men), nonprofessional, blue collar, indigenous *with:* counselor(s), psychotherapist(s), therapist(s). *See also* Counselors; Laymen; Peer counseling; Therapist characteristics; Therapists.

Laymen. Laym(en,an). Laywom(en,an). Layperson(s). Laypeople. Laity. *Choose from:* lay, untrained, nonprofessional *with:* personnel, ministry, minister(s), leader(s), counselor(s), teacher(s), reader(s), people, advisor(s), midwife, midwives, worker(s). *Consider also:* citizen(s), amateur(s), man in the street, nonprofessional(s), peer counselor(s). *See also* Amateurs; Lay religious personnel; Lay therapists; Nonprofessional personnel.

Layoffs. See *Personnel termination.*

Laywomen. See *Laymen.*

Laziness. Laz(y,iness). Idle(ness). Indolen(t,ce). Shiftless(ness). Sloth(ful,fulness). Sluggish(ness). Unenterprising(ness). Unambitious(ness). Unindustrious. Worthless(ness). Listless(ness).

Lack(ed,ing) ambition. *Consider also:* inert(ness), languor(ous,ousness), lassitude, indolen(t,ce), inactiv(e,ity), inert(ia), passiv(e,eness,ity), apath(y, etic), sluggish(ness). *See also* Inactivity; Passiveness; Personality traits; Social loafing; Social parasites.

Lead poisoning. Lead poisoning. Saturnism. Saturnine. Plumbism. Blood lead level(s). *Choose from:* lead *with:* poison(ed,ing), expos(ed,ure), induced, absorption, absorb(ed,ing), deposits in the body, intoxication, toxicity, nervous system, dos(e,ed,es), in bone(s), in tissue(s), hazard(s), level(s), neurological effects, neurotoxicology. *See also* Health problems; Living conditions; Pica; Toxic substances.

Leader, loss. See *Loss leader*

Leaders, opinion. See *Opinion leaders.*

Leadership. Leader(s,ship). Set(ting) trend(s). Set(ting) an example. Managerial skill(s). Direct(ed,ing,ion). Conduct(ed,ing). Guid(e,ed,ing,ance). Adminis(ter,tered,tering,tration). Supervis(e,ed,ing,ion). Govern(ed,ing, ance). Manag(e,ed,ing,ement). Inspir(e,ed,ing,ation). Authority. Control(led,ling). Command(ed,ing). *Consider also:* trendsetter(s), trend setter(s), bellwether(s), pacesetter(s), change agent(s), chief(tain,s), captain(s), directorship(s), superordinate(s), manager(s), administrator(s), executive(s), conductor(s), charisma, charismatic leader(s), president(s,ial), innovator(s), organizer(s), informal leader(s,ship), mover(s) and shaker(s). *See also* Administration; Administrators; Authority (power); Change agents; Charisma; Christian leadership; Command (of troops, ships, etc.); Cooptation; Empowerment; Executive ability; Facilitation; Foster (promote); Governing; Impresarios; Intrapreneurship; Leadership style; Legislative bodies; Managerial skills; Middle level managers; Moral authority; Opinion leaders; Organizational culture; Organizational innovation; Organizational politics; Political leadership; Politicians; Power; Power elite; Religious leadership; Responsibility (answerability); Social facilitation; Superior subordinate relationship; Supervision.

Leadership, Christian. See *Christian leadership.*

Leadership, political. See *Political leadership.*

Leadership, religious. See *Religious leadership.*

Leadership style. Leadership style(s). *Choose from:* leader(s,ship), managerial, management, manager(s), administrator(s), administrative, supervisor(y,s) *with:* style(s), behavior(s), cooptation, threats, democratic, authoritarian, method(s), respons(e,iveness), effective(ness), ineffective(ness), qualit(y,ies), authenticity, initiat(ive,ion), abilit(y,ies), practice(s), skill(s), technique(s), strateg(y,ies), competence. *See also* Charisma; Executive ability; Leadership; Management methods; Organizational culture; Superior subordinate relationship; Supervision.

Leaflets. See *Pamphlets.*

Leagues. See *Federations.*

Leaks, information. See *Information leaks.*

Learned behavior. Learned behavior(s). *Choose from:* learn(ed,ing), acquir(ed, ing), induc(e,ed,ing,ement,ements), train(ed,ing), condition(ed,ing), pattern(ed,ing), imitat(ed,ing,ion) *with:* behavior(s,al), conduct, performance, habit(s), assertive(ness), competitive(ness), cooperative(ness), compet(e,ed,ing), cooperat(e,ed,ing,ion), leadership, obedien(t,ce), response(s), self control, social behavior, conformity. *See also* Behavior; Behavior contracting; Behavior modification; Imitation; Learned helplessness; Role models.

Learned helplessness. Learned helplessness. *Choose from:* learn(ed,ing), induced, train(ed,ing), condition(ed,ing) *with:* helpless(ness), inactivity, powerless(ness). *Consider also:* attributional models of depression, causality attribution(s), locus of control, failure attribution(s), perceived inability. *See also* Attribution; Emotional states; Learned behavior; Locus of control; Obedience; Oppression; Passiveness.

Learned periodicals. See *Scholarly periodicals.*

Learned writing. See *Scholarship.*

Learners, slow. See *Slow learners.*

Learning. Learn(ed,ing). Acquir(e,ed,ing) knowledge. Skill acquisition. Self instruction. Comprehend(ed,ing). Memoriz(e,ed,ing). Stud(y,ying,ied). Edif(y,ied,ying,ication). Educat(e,ed, ing,ion). Condition(ed,ing). Imprint(ed,ing). Instruct(ed,ing,ion). Pattern(ed,ing). Intellectual attainment. Pursu(e,ed,ing) education. Lesson(s). Apprentice(ship). Train(ed,ing). Scholarship. Studious(ness). Transfer of training. Gain(ed,ing) information. Precondition(ed,ing). Orient(ed,ing, ation). *Consider also:* cognitive process(es), discovery, mastery, generalization, habituation, imprinting, overlearning, practice, problem solving, reinforcement, socialization. *See also* Academic achievement; Active learning; Avoidance learning; Classical conditioning; Cognitive processes; Concept formation; Conditioning (psychology); Discovery learning; Education; Extinction (psychology); Feedback; Forgetting; Habits; Incidental learning; Intentional learning; Interference (learning); Learning ability; Learning rate; Learning schedules; Learning theories; Lifelong learning; Mastery learning; Maze learning; Memory; Mnemonic learning; Nonverbal learning; Observational learning; Operant conditioning; Overlearning; Paired associate learning; Perceptual motor learning; Primacy effect; Probability learning; Reinforcement; Relearning; Retention (psychology); Reversal learning; Rote learning; Second language education; Sequential learning; Serial learning; Skill learning; Social learning; State dependent learning; Strategies; Transfer (learning); Verbal learning.

Learning, active. See *Active learning.*

Learning, adult. See *Adult development; Lifelong learning.*

Learning, avoidance. See *Avoidance learning.*

Learning, cooperative. See *Cooperative learning.*

Learning, discovery. See *Discovery learning.*

Learning, foreign language. See *Second language education.*

Learning, incidental. See *Incidental learning.*

Learning, intentional. See *Intentional learning.*

Learning, lifelong. See *Lifelong learning.*

Learning, mastery. See *Mastery learning.*

Learning, maze. See *Maze learning.*

Learning, mnemonic. See *Mnemonic learning.*

Learning, nonverbal. See *Nonverbal learning.*

Learning, observational. See *Observational learning.*

Learning, paired associate. See *Paired associate learning.*

Learning, perceptual motor. See *Perceptual motor learning.*

Learning, probability. See *Probability learning.*

Learning, reversal. See *Reversal learning.*

Learning, rote. See *Rote learning.*

Learning, second language. See *Second language education.*

Learning, self directed. See *Individualized instruction.*

Learning, sequential. See *Sequential learning.*

Learning, serial. See *Serial learning.*

Learning, skill. See *Skill learning.*

Learning, social. See *Social learning.*

Learning, state dependent. See *State dependent learning.*

Learning, transfer of. See *Transfer (learning).*

Learning, verbal. See *Verbal learning.*

Learning ability. Learning abilit(y,ies). *Choose from:* capacity, abilit(y,ies), aptitude(s), potential *with:* learning, cognitive, intellectual, numerical, verbal. *Consider also:* self organizing system(s). *See also* Academic ability; Academic aptitude.

Learning centers. Learning center(s). *Choose from:* learning, education(al) resource(s), interest, tutoring, writing *with:* center(s), station(s). *See also* Discovery learning; Educational facilities; Individualized instruction.

Learning contracts. Learning contract(s). Contract(s) for learning. Contract grading. Contract Education. *Consider also:* performance contract(s), goal setting, contingency contracting. *See also* Behavior contracting; Contracts; Educational incentives.

Learning disabilities. Learning disabilit(y,ies). Learning disorder(s). School difficult(y,ies). School immaturity. Maturational lag. Language difficult(y,ies). Dyslex(ia,ic). *Choose from:* learning, studying, comprehen(ding,sion), reading *with:* disabilit(y,ies), disorder(s), difficult(y,ies), deficit(s), disabled, problem(s), impair(ed,ment,ments). *See also* Acalculia; Agraphia; Aphasia; Attention deficit disorder; Dyslexia; Hyperkinesis; Minimal brain disorders; Perceptual disturbances; Slow learners.

Learning laboratories. See *Educational laboratories.*

Learning motivation. See *Educational motivation.*

Learning rate. Learning rate(s). *Choose from:* time factor(s), rate(s), time(s), speed(s), slow, fast, average time, accelerated *with:* learn(ed,ing), acquir(e,ed,ing) skill(s), practic(e,ed,ing), information processing, acquisition, extinction. *See also* Learning.

Learning schedules. Learning schedule(s). *Choose from:* learning, training, practice, repeated acquisition, extinction *with:* schedule(s), sequence(s), procedure(s), spaced, spacing, paced, pacing. *Consider also:* distributed, massed *with:* practice. *See also* Learning.

Learning style. See *Cognitive style.*

Learning theories. Learning theor(y,ies). *Choose from:* learn(ing,er,ers), transfer of training, overlearning, recall, acquisition, concept formation, cognitive *with:* theor(y,ies,etical), model(s). *Consider also:* instruction(al), education(al) *with:* theor(y,ies,etical), model(s). *See also* Behavior theories; Behaviorism; Cognitive processes; Conditioning (psychology); Learning; Theories.

Leases. See *Leasing.*

Leasing. Leas(e,es,ed,ing). Leaseback(s). Leasehold. Rental agreement(s). Rental contract(s). Rent(ed,al,ing,s). Tenan(t,ts,cy). Sublet(ting). Subleas(e,ed,ing). Landlord(s). Hir(e,ed,ing) car(s). Auto rental(s). Let(ting) room(s). Room(s) to let. Leasehold(er). *Consider also:* subinfeudation. *See also* Eviction; Landlord tenant relations; Landlords; Rental housing; Sharecropping; Tenant farmers; Tenants.

Least developed countries. Least developed countr(y,ies). LLDC(s). Fourth world. Undeveloped countr(y,ies). *Choose from:* poorest, least developed, nonindustrialized *with:* nation(s), countr(y,ies). *Consider also:* Afghanistan, Bangladesh, Benin, Bhutan, Botswana, Burkina Faso, Burma, Burundi, Cape Verde, Central African Republic, Chad, Comoros, Djibouti, Equatorial Guinea, Eritrea, Ethiopia, The Gambia, Guinea, GuineaBissau, Haiti, Kiribati, Laos, Lesotho, Malawi, Maldives, Mali, Mauritania, Mozambique, Nepal, Niger, Rwanda, Samoa, Sao Tome and Principe, Sierra Leone, Somalia, Sudan, Tanzania, Togo, Tuvalu, Uganda, Vanuatu, Yemen. *See also* Caribbean; Central America; Central Asia; Developing countries; Eastern Europe; Far East; Less developed countries; Middle East; North Africa; Oceania; South America; South Asia; Southeast Asia; Sub-Saharan Africa.

Leather industry. Leather industry. Fellmonger(s,ed,ing,y). *Choose from:* leather, footwear, shoc(s), hide(s) *with:* product(s,ion), industr(y,ies,ial), market(s), tanning, preserving, processing. *Consider also:* saddlery, harness making. *See also* Animal products; Boots and shoes; Fur.

Leave, absent without. See *Military desertion.*

Leave, maternity. See *Maternity leave.*

Leave, parental. See *Maternity leave; Paternity leave.*

Leave, paternity. See *Paternity leave.*

Leave, sick. See *Sick leave.*

Leavers, school. See *Student dropouts.*

Leaves of absence. Leave(s) of absence. Leave(s) with pay. Leave(s) without pay. Sabbatical(s). Authorized absence(s). *Choose from:* annual, sick, vacation, employee(s), paid, personal, compensatory, maternity, paternity *with:* leave(s), time. *See also* Attendance (presence); Employee benefits; Holidays; Vacations.

Lebenswelt. See *Everyday life.*

Lecture method. Lecture method. Formal lecture(s). Expository teaching. Formal presentation(s). Traditional teaching. *Choose from:* lecture *with:* format, classroom(s), course(s), student(s). *See also* Discussion; Lectures and lecturing; Teaching methods.

Lectures and lecturing. Lectur(e,es,ed,ing). Speaking at workshop(s). Speaking at seminar(s). Speech(es). Address(es). Speaking invitation(s). Discourse(s). Sermon(s). Homil(y,ies). Oration(s). *Choose from:* deliver(ed,ing), present(ed,ing), mak(e,ing), made, giv(e,en,ing) *with:* speech(es), sermon(s), eulog(y,ies), talk(s), lecture(s). *See also* Lecture method; Oratory; Presentations; Public speaking; Rhetoric; Speeches (formal discourse); Teaching.

Lecturing, lectures and. See *Lectures and lecturing.*

Left, new. See *Left wing; Protest movements; Social movements; Youth movements.*

Left wing. Left wing. Left(ist,ists). Socialis(m,t,ts,tic). Liberal(s,ism,ity, ization). Neoliberal(ism,s). New left. Left liberal(s). Communis(m,t,ts,tic). Labor part(y,ies). Progressivism. Progressive force(s). Political left. Sociopolitically liberal. *Consider also:* radical(s,ism), fellow traveller(s), anarchism, syndicalism, Trotskyism, Maoism, Castroism, Marxism, neo-Marxism, Greens, trade union movement, Students for a Democratic Society, SDS, Student Non-violent Coordinating Committee, SNCC, Weathermen, Baader-Meinhof, Zengakuren, Red Army Faction, Black Panthers, Yippies, Symbionese Liberation Army. *See also* Communism; Extremism; Politics; Progressivism; Protest movements; Radical movements; Right wing politics; Socialism.

Legacies. Legac(y,ies). Bequest(s). Inheritance(s). Bequeath(ed,ing,al,als). Fidei-commissum. *Consider also:* legatee(s), dowr(y,ies). *See also* Administration of estates; Beneficiaries; Disinheritance; Estate planning; Estates (law); Heirs; Inheritance.

Legal abortion. Legal abortion(s). *Choose from:* abortion(s), pregnancy terminat(e,ed,ion) *with:* legal(ized, ization), liberal(ized,ization), right to choose, lawful, decriminal(ized,izing, ization). *See also* Abortion; Abortion counseling; Abortion laws; Abortion rights movement; Antiabortion movement.

Legal arrests. See *Arrests.*

Legal cases. Legal case(s). *Choose from:* court(room,rooms), law, legal, judicial, criminal, civil *with:* case(load,s), hearing(s), proceeding(s), settlement(s), arbitration. *Consider also:* litigation, trial(s), plea bargaining, prosecution(s). *See also* Criminal proceedings; Judicial decisions; Legal procedures; Legal system; Litigation.

Legal competency. Legal(ly) competen(t,ce, cy). Compos mentis. *Choose from:* legal(ly), power(s) of attorney, guardian(s,ship), civil commitment *with:* incompeten(t,ce,cy), competen(t,ce,cy), decisional incapacity, cognitive decline, mental incapacit(y,ated), dement(ed, ing,ias), mental(ly) impair(ed,ment, ments), non compos mentis. *See also* Cognition disorders; Competency to stand trial; Incapacitation; Insanity defense; Legal guardians; Psychiatric commitment.

Legal documents. Legal document(s). Legal instrument(s). Documentary evidence. Legal form(s). Receipt(s). Writ(s). Patent(s). Ancient document(s). Document(s) of title. Deed(s). Will(s). Judicial document(s). Decree(s). Warrant(s). Public document(s). *See also* Agreement (document); Cartularies; Certificates; Charters; Constitution (legal); Contracts; Documents.

Legal ethics. Legal ethic(s). Judicial ethic(s). *Choose from:* legal profession, judicial, judiciary, attorney(s), lawyer(s), American Bar Association *with:* ethic(s, al,ally), canon(s), professional conduct, professional responsibility, unethical, moral dut(y,ies), conflict of interest(s). *See also* Attorneys; Conflict of interest; Ethics; Legal professionals; Professional ethics; Unethical conduct.

Legal evidence. See *Evidence.*

Legal guardians. Legal guardian(s,ship). Legal surrogate(s). Wardship. Legal custody. Surrogate parent(s). In loco parentis. Proxy. Guardian(s) ad litem. Attorney ad litem. Court appointed child advocate. Court appointed special advocate. *Consider also:* power(s) of attorney, parens patriae, legal paternalism. *See also* Child custody; Foster home care; Foster parents; Legal competency.

Legal instruments. See *Legal documents.*

Legal liability (professional). See *Professional liability.*

Legal personnel. Legal personnel. Paralegal personnel. *Choose from:* legal, law

office(s), court(s) *with:* staff, paraprofessional(s), personnel, employee(s). *See also* Attorneys; Court judges; Juries; Legal professionals; Prosecution.

Legal procedures. Legal procedure(s). *Choose from:* civil, criminal, legal, justice, judicial, court(s,room,rooms), due *with:* procedure(s), process(es), proceeding(s), decision(s), determination, injunction(s), inquir(y,ies), remed(y,ies), review, bring action(s), judgment(s), suit(s), trial(s). Adjudicat(e, ion,ive,or,ors). Litigat(e,ed,ing,ation). Adjudg(e,ment). Court decision(s). Decree(s,d,ing). Arbitrat(e,ed,ion). Court ruling(s). Litigat(e,ed,ing,ion). Trial(s). Interpret(ed,ing,ation) law(s). Judicial selection. Stare decisis. Preliminary hearing(s). Dissenting opinion(s). Habeas corpus. Plaintiff(s). Defendant(s). Plea(s,ding). Cross examination of witness(es). Testimony. Rules of evidence. Certiorari. Common law. *See also* Acquittal; Adjournment; Adjudication; Arbitration; Amnesty; Circumstantial evidence; Civil procedures; Class action; Contempt of Court; Court opinions; Cross examination; Due process; Evidence; Law (practice); Lawsuits; Litigation; Obstruction of justice; Plea bargaining; Roman law; Rule of law; Self incrimination; Trial (law); Verdicts; Withholding evidence.

Legal professionals. Legal professional(s). Lawyer(s). Attorney(s). Barrister(s). Solicitor(s). Member(s) of state bar. Legal counsel. Judge(s). Criminal justice personnel. Magistrate(s). *Choose from:* legal, law *with:* professional(s), consultant(s), practitioner(s), defender(s), student(s), advisor(s), counselor(s), personnel, authorit(y,ies), advocate(s). *Consider also:* praetor(s,ial,ship). *See also* Attorneys; Court judges; Judges; Law (practice); Legal ethics; Legal personnel.

Legal responsibility. See *Liability.*

Legal rights. Legal right(s). *Choose from:* legal, constitutional, civil, legitimate *with:* right(s), libert(y,ies), freedom(s), independence, entitle(d,ment), autonomy. *Consider also:* Bill of Rights, due process, citizenship, self-determination. *See also* Bill of Rights; Children's rights; Civil rights; Client rights; De jure; Due process; Freedom; Freedom of information; Freedom of religion; Freedom of speech; Freedom of the press; Human rights; Intellectual liberty; Liberty; Legal procedures; Ombudsmen; Parent rights; Patient rights; Personal independence; Political self determination; Property rights; Student rights; Voting rights; Women's rights.

Legal system. Legal system. *Choose from:* legal, judicial, judiciary, correctional, penal, criminal justice, justice, court

with: system(s), structure(s), institution(s). *Consider also:* rule of law, legal philosophy, law enforcing agencies, courts. *See also* Correctional system; Criminal justice; Due process; Law enforcement; Legal cases; Legal personnel; Litigation; Penal codes; Rule of law; Separation of powers.

Legal tender. See *Money.*

Legal testimony. See *Testimony.*

Legalization, marijuana. See *Legalization of drugs; Marijuana laws.*

Legalization of drugs. Legalization of drug(s). Marihuana legalization. *Choose from:* drug(s), narcotic(s), marijuana, marihuana, cannabis, cocaine, heroin, amphetamine(s) *with:* legaliz(ed,ing, ation), decriminaliz(ed,ing,ation), reform of law(s), weaken(ed,ing), reduc(ed,ing) penalt(y,ies). *See also* Decriminalization; Deregulation; Marijuana laws; Medical marijuana; Victimless crimes.

Legends. Legend(s,ary). Myth(s). Tale(s). Folklore. Saga(s). Epic(s). Fairy tale(s). Fable(s). Allegor(y,ies). Parable(s). Ballad(s). Folktale(s). Stor(y,ies). Lore. *See also* Adventure stories; Epic literature; Fabliaux; Fiction; Folk culture; Folk literature; Folklore; Literature; Metaphors; Mythology; Sagas.

Legislation. Legislat(e,ed,ion). Legislative process(es). Lawmaking. Introduc(e,ed, ing) bill(s). Legislative act(s,ion,ions). Laws passed. *Choose from:* Congress(al), Senate, House of Representatives, Parliament(ary), Knesset, etc. *with:* act(ed,ing,ion,ions,s). Sign(ed,ing) into law. Enact(ed,ing, ment) of law(s). *Consider also:* public law(s), statute(s), bill(s). *See also* Compliance; Constitution (legal); Enactment; Government regulation; Interest groups; Laws; Legislative bodies; Legislative processes; Lobbying; Policy implementation; Policy making; Politics; Public policy; Referendum; Social legislation; Statutes; Veto.

Legislation, direct. See *Referendum*

Legislation, social. See *Social legislation.*

Legislation, Sunday. See *Sunday legislation.*

Legislation and laws, agricultural. See *Agricultural laws and legislation.*

Legislation and laws, food. See *Food laws and legislation.*

Legislative apportionment. See *Apportionment.*

Legislative bodies. Legislative bod(y,ies). Legislature(s). Legislative branch. Bicameral system. Unicameral system. Parliament(s). House of Representatives. Congress(es). Senate(s). Lower house.

Upper house. Assembl(y,ies). National Assembly. Landsgemeinden. Diet(s). Althing. National Diet. Bundesversammlung. Cortes. Knesset. Majlis. Oireachtas. Bundestag. Folketing. Riksdag. States-General. Storting. Supreme Soviet. Supreme Council. Estates-General. Congresso Nacional. State Council. Eduskunta. Nationalrat. Assemblee Nationale Constituante. *Consider also:* Congressional committees (standing, select, special, rules, ad hoc, joint legislative, etc.), legislative caucus(es), Congressional budget office, General Accounting Office of Congress, etc. *See also* Councils; Democracy; Governing boards; Legislation; Legislative powers; Legislative processes; Legislators; Political power; Political representation; Political systems; Provisional government; Separation of powers.

Legislative powers. Legislative power(s). *Choose from:* legislat(ive,ure,ures), congress(es,ional), parliament(s,ary), senat(e,es,orial), house of representative(s), assembl(y,ies), house of commons, burgesses, lawmak(er,ers,ing) *with:* power(s), authority, control, regulation, budget(s,ary), privilege(s), immunit(y,ies), responsibilit(y,ies). *Consider also:* filibuster(s,ed,ing). *See also* Delegation of powers; Governmental powers; Legislative bodies; Political power; Political representation; Separation of powers.

Legislative processes. Legislative process(es). Legislat(ed,ion). *Choose from:* legislat(ive,or,ors,ure,ures), senate(s), lawmaker(s), assembl(y,ies), house(s), council(s), congress(es,ional), parliament(s,ary) *with:* history, opposition, vot(e,es,ing), roll call voting, issue(s), activit(y,ies), measure(s), act(s,ion,ions), passage, procedure(s), process(es), veto(ed), bill(s), proposal(s), hearing(s), policymaking, approval, ratif(y,ied,ication). *Choose from:* pass(ing,age,ed), approv(e,ed,ing), draft(ing), report(ed,ing) out, kill(ed), reading, tabl(e,ing), veto(ed) *with:* legislation, law(s), statute(s), ordinance(s), appropriation(s), amendment(s), act(s), resolution(s), rider(s). *Consider also:* before congress, legislative calendar, legislative session(s), Congressional research service, Senate bill(s), House bill(s), HR bill(s), filibuster(ing). *See also* Appropriations (set aside); Enactment; Interest groups; Law reform; Laws; Legislation; Legislative bodies; Legislators; Lobbying; Policy making; Political patronage; Political power; Political representation; Ratification; Referendum; Repeal; Separation of powers; Veto.

Legislators. Legislator(s). Legislatress(es). Senator(s). Representative(s). Assembly(man,men,woman,women). Congress(men,man,woman,women). Congressperson(s). Member(s) of Parliament. M.P. Lawmaker(s). Lawgiver(s). Council(man,men,woman, women). County commissioner(s). Alder(man,men,woman,women). Party whip. Floor leader. Speaker of the House. Minority leader. Majority leader. President of the Senate. *Consider also:* specific legislators by name. *Consider also:* legislative aids, legislative staff, precinct warden(s), precinct captain(s), lawmaker(s), law maker(s). *See also* Corruption in government; Legislative bodies; Legislative processes; Political representation; Politicians.

Legislatures. See *Legislative bodies.*

Legitimacy. Legitima(cy,te,tion). Legitimiz(e,ed,ation). Legitimatiz(e,ed, ation). Lawful. Legal. Authoriz(ed, ation). Ratif(y,ied,ication). Sanctioned. Accredited. Accepted. Authentic. Recognized. Verified. Valid(ate,ated, ation). Licit. *Consider also:* official recognition, legitimate authority. *See also* Accreditation; Authority (power); Certification; De jure; Legitimacy of governments; Provisional government; Validity; Verification.

Legitimacy, political. See *Legitimacy of governments.*

Legitimacy of governments. Legitimacy of government(s). *Choose from:* legitimacy, legitimat(e,ion), consent theory, justification(s) of authority, accountability *with:* government(s), politic(s,al), state, democra(cy,cies,tic), regime(s). *Consider also:* political legitimacy, legitimate authority. *See also* General will; Consensus; Legitimacy; Moral authority; Political ethics; Political obligation; Political stability; Social contract; Social stability.

Legs. Leg(s). Ankle(s). Knee(s). Lower limb(s). Lower extremit(y,ies). Femur. Tibia. Fibula. Patella. *Consider also:* foot, feet, hip(s), thigh(s). *See also* Anatomy.

Leisure activities. Leisure activit(y,ies). Leisure time activit(y,ies). Pastime(s). *Consider also:* work leisure relationship, entertainment, sports, walking, jogging, bicycling, bowling, gardening, card games, skating, amusements, hobb(y,ies), game(s), vacation(s), dancing, homo ludens, recreational reading, athletic participation, baseball, basketball, camping, social activit(y,ies), football, gambling, summer camps, swimming, television viewing, tennis, traveling, festivities, festival(s), celebrations. *Choose from:* recreational, leisure, cultural, spare time, holiday(s), playground(s), relaxation *with:* activit(y,ies), event(s). *See also* Adult games; Computer games; Electronic games; Entertainment; Hobbies; Leisure time; Play; Recreation; Relaxation; Sports; Vacations.

Leisure time. Leisure time. Free time. Idle hours. *Choose from:* leisure, spare, free, recreational, discretionary *with:* time, hour(s), moment(s). *Consider also:* leisure activities, inactiv(e,ity), retirement, idleness, nonwork, recreation, avocation(s,al), vacation(s). *See also* Holidays; Leisure activities; Retirement; Sabbath; Vacations.

Leitmotiv. Leitmotiv(s). Leitmotif(s). Leitmotif(s). Recurr(ent,ing) theme(s). *Consider also:* grundthem(a,en), motif(s), hauptmotiv. *See also* Music; Opera; Refrain (music); Symphonic poems; Themes.

Length of stay. Length of stay. Days hospitalized. Long term care. Early discharge(s). *Choose from:* length, duration, short, long, protracted, prolonged, extended, time limited *with:* stay, hospitaliz(ed,ation), institutionaliz(ed,ation). *Consider also:* treatment duration. *See also* Patient admission; Patient discharge; Termination of treatment.

Length of working life. Length of working life. Productive life span. *Choose from:* worklife, productive life *with:* span(s), year(s), length, longer, estimate(s), table(s). *See also* Early retirement; Involuntary retirement; Life expectancy; Mandatory retirement; Retirement.

Lenses, gravitational. See *Gravitational lenses.*

Lesbian couples. See *Gay couples.*

Lesbianism. Lesbian(s,ism). Female homosexual(s,ity). *Choose from:* homosexual(s,ity), gay, same sex(ual) preference(s), bisexual(ity) *with:* women, woman, female(s). *Consider also:* sapph(o,ic,ist), amor lesbicus, tribad(e,ism), gym bunn(y,ies). *See also* Attitudes toward homosexuality; Bisexuality; Females (human); Gay couples; Homosexual liberation movement; Homosexuality; Same sex; Women's groups; Women's rights.

Lesions. Lesion(s). Incision(s). Ablation(s). Abscess(es,ed). Bleb(s). Blister(s). Boil(s). Bulla(e). Carbuncle(s). Chancre(s). Crust(s). Cyst(s). Excoriation(s). Felon(s). Papule(s). Pimple(s). Pustule(s). Rash(es). Scale(s). Scar(s). Sore(s). Tubercle(s). Tumefaction(s). Tumor(s). Ulcer(s). Wheal(s). Wound(s). *See also* Injuries.

Less developed countries. Less developed countr(y,ies). LDC(s). Low income countr(y,ies). *Consider also:* advanced developing countr(y,ies), developing countr(y,ies), Four Dragons, Four

Tigers, least developed countr(y,ies), LLDC(s), middle income countr(y,ies), newly industrializing econom(y,ies), NIE(s), Third World, underdeveloped countr(y,ies), undeveloped countr(y,ies), Afghanistan, Algeria, American Samoa, Angola, Anguilla, Antigua and Barbuda, Argentina, Aruba, The Bahamas, Bahrain, Bangladesh, Barbados, Belize, Benin, Bhutan, Bolivia, Botswana, Brazil, British Virgin Islands, Brunei, Burkina Faso, Burma, Burundi, Cambodia, Cameroon, Cape Verde, Cayman Islands, Central African Republic, Chad, Chile, China, Christmas Island, Cocos Islands, Colombia, Comoros, Democratic Republic of the Congo, Republic of the Congo, Cook Islands, Costa Rica, Cote d'Ivoire, Cuba, Cyprus, Djibouti, Dominica, Dominican Republic, Ecuador, Egypt, El Salvador, Equatorial Guinea, Eritrea, Ethiopia, Falkland Islands, Fiji, French Guiana, French Polynesia, Gabon, The Gambia, Gaza Strip, Ghana, Gibraltar, Greenland, Grenada, Guadeloupe, Guam, Guatemala, Guernsey, Guinea, GuineaBissau, Guyana, Haiti, Honduras, Hong Kong, India, Indonesia, Iran, Iraq, Jamaica, Jersey, Jordan, Kenya, Kiribati, North Korea, South Korea, Kuwait, Laos, Lebanon, Lesotho, Liberia, Libya, Macau, Madagascar, Malawi, Malaysia, Maldives, Mali, Isle of Man, Marshall Islands, Martinique, Mauritania, Mauritius, Mayotte, Federated States of Micronesia, Mongolia, Montserrat, Morocco, Mozambique, Namibia, Nauru, Nepal, Netherlands Antilles, New Caledonia, Nicaragua, Niger, Nigeria, Niue, Norfolk Island, Northern Mariana Islands, Oman, Palau, Pakistan, Panama, Papua New Guinea, Paraguay, Peru, Philippines, Pitcairn Islands, Puerto Rico, Qatar, Reunion, Rwanda, Saint Helena, Saint Kitts and Nevis, Saint Lucia, Saint Pierre and Miquelon, Saint Vincent and the Grenadines, Samoa, Sao Tome and Principe, Saudi Arabia, Senegal, Seychelles, Sierra Leone, Singapore, Solomon Islands, Somalia, Sri Lanka, Sudan, Suriname, Swaziland, Syria, Taiwan, Tanzania, Thailand, Togo, Tokelau, Tonga, Trinidad and Tobago, Tunisia, Turks and Caicos Islands, Tuvalu, UAE, Uganda, Uruguay, Vanuatu, Venezuela, Vietnam, Virgin Islands, Wallis and Futuna, West Bank, Western Sahara, Yemen, Zambia, Zimbabwe; note similar to the new International Monetary Fund (IMF) term "developing countries" which adds Malta, Mexico, South Africa, and Turkey but omits in its recently published statistics American Samoa, Anguilla, British Virgin Islands, Brunei, Cayman Islands, Christmas Island, Cocos Islands, Cook Islands, Cuba, Eritrea, Falkland Islands, French Guiana, French Polynesia, Gaza Strip, Gibraltar, Greenland, Grenada, Guadeloupe, Guam, Guernsey, Jersey, North Korea, Macau, Isle of Man, Martinique, Mayotte, Montserrat, Nauru, New Caledonia, Niue, Norfolk Island, Northern Mariana Islands, Palau, Pitcairn Islands, Puerto Rico, Reunion, Saint Helena, Saint Pierre and Miquelon, Tokelau, Tonga, Turks and Caicos Islands, Tuvalu, Virgin Islands, Wallis and Futuna, West Bank, Western Sahara. *See also* Developing countries; Least developed countries; Newly industrializing economies.

Lesson plans. Lesson plan(s). *Choose from:* lesson(s), class(es), instruction(al), learning, curriculum, teaching, classroom activities *with:* plan(s,ned,ning), outline(s), package(s), sequenc(e,es,ing), structure, objective(s), guide(s), module(s), design, manual(s). *See also* Curriculum; Curriculum development; Planning; School schedules; Teaching; Teaching methods.

Letter carriers. Letter carrier(s). Postal carrier(s). Mail carrier(s). *Consider also:* mail handler(s), postal worker(s), postal service, mail service, RFD. *See also* Clerical workers; Mail room; Messengers; Postal service.

Letters (alphabet). Letter(s). Alphabet(s, ic). *Consider also:* consonant(s), vowel(s), character(s), alpha numeric, alphanumeric, graphem(e,es,ic,ics, ically), phonem(e,es,ic,ics,ically), orthograph(y,ic,ical,ically), spell(ed,ing). *See also* Alphabets; Consonants; Literacy; Phonemes; Written communications.

Letters (correspondence). Letter(s). Correspondence. Mail. Epistle(s). Epistolar(y,ies). Epistolograph(y,ies). Billet doux. Postcard(s). *Consider also:* personal document(s), birthday card(s), greeting card(s), note(s), missive(s), interoffice communication(s), paperwork, inbox(es), outbox(es), written communication(s). *Consider also:* business, form, circular, chain, open, personal, electronic *with:* letter(s), mail. *See also* Autobiography; Autographs; Documents; Electronic mail; Love letters; Manuscripts; Postal psychotherapy; Postal service; Salutations; Travel writing; Verbal communication; Writing (composition); Written communications.

Letters, love. See *Love letters*.

Level, ability. See *Ability level*.

Level, activity. See *Activity level*.

Level, adaptation theory. See *Adaptation level theory*.

Level, aspiration. See *Aspiration level*.

Level, income. See *Low income; Middle income level; Minimum wage; Poverty; Socioeconomic status; Upper income level*.

Level, knowledge. See *Knowledge level*.

Level, middle income. See *Middle income level*.

Level, upper income. See *Upper income level*.

Levels, intelligence. See *Intelligence quotient*.

Levels, noise work areas. See *Noise levels (work areas)*.

Levels, water. See *Water levels*.

Leveraged buyouts. Leveraged buyout(s). Leveraged buy out(s). LBO(s). Leveraged takeover(s). *Consider also:* strategic leverage, leveraged firm(s), leveraged transaction(s). *See also* Antitakeover strategies; Buyouts; Capitalization; Corporate acquisitions; Corporate debt; Hostile takeovers; Mergers.

Lexical phonology. Lexical phonolog(y, ical). *Consider also:* phrasal phonology, postlexical phonology. *See also* Generative grammar; Inflection.

Lexicography. Lexicograph(y,er,ers,ical). *Choose from:* dictionar(y,ies), thesaur(i,us), encyclopedia(s) *with:* editor(s,ial), compiler(s), maker(s). *Consider also:* toponym(y,ist,ists). *See also* Dictionaries; Editors.

Liability. Liabilit(y,ies). Liable. Tort. *Consider also:* obligat(ed,ion,ions), legal(ly) responsib(le,ity,ities), indemn(ity,ification), accountab(le,ility), answerab(le,ility), blame, culpab(le, ility), malpractice, insolven(t,cy), debt(s). *See also* Accountability; Blameworthy; Guilt; Libel; Litigation; Malpractice; Negligence; Personal injuries; Product liability; Professional liability; Responsibility (answerability).

Liability, legal professional. See *Professional liability*.

Liability, manufacturer. See *Product liability*.

Liability, product. See *Product liability*.

Liability, professional. See *Professional liability*.

Liability for toxic substances damage. See *Toxic torts*.

Liar paradox. Liar paradox(es). Strengthened paradox(es). *Consider also:* insolubilia. *See also* Paradoxes; Semantics.

Libel. Libel(ous). Malicious statement(s). Malicious publication(s). Mudslinging. Lies. Lying. Personal attack(s). Actionable words. Defam(e,ed,ing). Defamat(ion,ory). Smear tactic(s). Smear campaign(s). Smear list(s). Slur(s). Slander(ed,ing). Reputation damaged. Trash(ed,ing). Character assassination(s). Negative campaign(s, ing). Third person effect. Moral assassination(s). *See also* Corruption in government; Defamation; Gossip; Journalistic ethics; Labeling (of persons); Lawsuits; Liability; Political campaigns; Reputation; Right of privacy; Rumors; Scandals; Sensationalism; Tabloids.

Liberal arts education. See *Humanistic education.*

Liberal education. See *Academic education.*

Liberal theology. See *Liberalism (Religion).*

Liberalism. Liberal(s,ism,ity). *Choose from:* liberal(s,ism,ity) *with:* ideolog(y, ies), idea(s), perspective(s), orientation, attitude(s), agenda, value(s), influence(s), view(s), rhetoric, politic(s,al), reaction(s), part(y,ies). *Consider also:* accepting change, change oriented, favor(ed,ing) social change, neo-liberal(s,ism,ist,ists), new left, middle of the road, centrist(s), liberal Democrat(s,ic), left wing, freedom of choice, noninterference, social(ly) permissive(ness). *See also* Civil rights; Conservative; Democracy; Humanistic education; Humanistic psychology; Humanitarianism; Humanization; Individualism; Left wing; Liberty; New Deal; Political ideologies; Political liberalism; Political socialization; Progressivism; Social thought; Social values; Utilitarianism; Welfare state.

Liberalism (Religion). Liberal(s,ism). Religious liberal(s). Liberal theolog(y, ian,ians). *Choose from:* liberal(s,ism), reform(ed,ing), modern(ize,ized,ity), *with:* Protestant(s,ism), Catholic(s,ism), Jew(s,ish), Judaism, Islam(ic). *Consider also:* Friedrich Schleiermacher, Albrecht Ritschl, Henry N. Wieman, Haskalah, Unitarian(ism), Universalism. *See also* Cultural relativism; Humanism; Indifferentism (religion); Multicultural education; Relativism; Secularization.

Liberalism, political. See *Political liberalism.*

Liberation. See *Autonomy (government); Emancipation; Freedom; Liberty; Personal independence; Political self determination.*

Liberation, national. See *Decolonization; National fronts; Nationalist movements; Peasant rebellions; Revolution; Separatism.*

Liberation, sexual. See *Sexual permissiveness.*

Liberation, wars of. See *Peasant rebellions.*

Liberation, women's. See *Women's rights.*

Liberation movement, African. See *Anti-apartheid movement.*

Liberation movement, elderly. See *Gray power.*

Liberation movement, gay. See *Homosexual liberation movement.*

Liberation movement, homosexual. See *Homosexual liberation movement.*

Liberation movements. Liberation movement(s). *Choose from:* liberation, anti-imperialist, devolution, revolutionary, self determination, self governance, nationalist, protonationalist(s), anticolonial, freedom, opposition *with:* group(s), campaign(s), movement(s), rebellion(s), struggle(s), collective action(s), solidarity, organization(s), societ(y,ies), consciousness, front(s), uprising(s), *Consider also:* equal sharing of power, freedom fighter(s), liberator(s), breakaway republic(s), breakaway enclave(s), indigenous activist(s), secession(ist,ists), Moro Islamic Liberation Front, Intifada, Irish Revolution, IRA, National League for Democracy, Popular Movement for the Liberation of Angola, Eritrean People's Liberation Front, Zapatista National Liberation Army, EZLN, Anti-Imperialist Cell, AIZ, Boxer Rebellion, etc. *See also* Decolonization; Democratization; Guerrillas; Liberation theology; National fronts; Peasant rebellions; Resistance movements; Separatism.

Liberation theology. Liberation theolog(y, ian,ians). Teologia de la liberacion. Indigenous theolog(y,ian,ians). *Consider also:* Gustavo Gutierrez, Leonardo Boff, Juan Luis Segundo, liberationist priest(s), popular church, progressive church. *See also* Black theology; Feminist theology; Land reform; Liberation movements; Peasant rebellions; Political movements; Practical theology; Religious beliefs; Social action.

Libertarianism. Libertarian(s,ism). Minarchis(m,t,ts). *Consider also:* Robert Nozick, Samuel Brittan. *See also* Anarchism; Individualism; Liberty; Minimal government.

Liberty. Libert(y,ies). Freedom(s). Emancipat(ed,ion). Enfranchise(d,ment). Independen(t,ce). Democra(tic,cy). Self-govern(ing,ment). Sovereignty. Privacy act. Individual rights. Social justice. Constitutional rights. Equal rights. Right of self defense. Personal liberty. Right of habeas corpus. Right to vote. Freedom of conscience. Religious freedom. Right to treatment. Student rights. Citizen advocacy. Civil liberties. Civil libertarian(s). Rights of institutionalized. Access to records. Right to privacy. Minority rights. Personal liberty. Equal education. Equal opportunit(y,ies). Equal protection. Freedom of speech.

Social justice. *Consider also:* natural right(s), sui juris. *See also* Bill of Rights; Children's rights; Civil Rights; Client rights; Constitution (legal); Due process; Emancipation; Freedom; Freedom of information; Freedom of religion; Freedom of speech; Freedom of the press; Freedom of the seas; Human rights; Intellectual liberty; Liberalism; Libertarianism; Natural law; Parent rights; Patient rights; Personal independence; Political self determination; Property rights; Voting rights; Women's rights.

Liberty (theology). See *Freedom (theology).*

Liberty, intellectual. See *Intellectual liberty.*

Liberty, religious. See *Freedom of religion.*

Liberty of conscience. Liberty of conscience. Libertie of conscience. Private conscience. *Consider also:* tolera(nce, tion), conscientious self. *See also* Conscientious objectors; Public opinion; Religious dissenters; Freedom of religion; Tolerance.

Liberty of the will. See *Freedom (theology); Volition.*

Libido. Libid(o,inous,inal,inousness). Libidiniz(e,ed,ing,ation). Eros. Sexual appetite. Sexual urge. Sexual hunger. Elan vital. Love. Lust(ful). Sexual(ly) arous(al,ed). Sexual energy. Life instinct. Sex drive. Emotional investment(s). *See also* Sex drive; Vitalism.

Librarians. Librarian(s,ship). Library profession(al,als). Library director(s). Cataloger(s). Library faculty. Library administrator(s). Bibliographer(s). *Choose from:* special, acquisitions, school, reference, research, media, multimedia, network services, technical services, database, CD-ROM, online services, Internet, digital, electronic, serials, documents, collection development *with:* librarian(s,ship) *Consider also:* cybrarian(s,ship), cyber-librarian(s,ship), information specialist(s), information scientist(s), Internet trainer(s), online searcher(s), database searcher(s), literature searcher(s), bibliographer(s), web site coordinator(s), web designer(s), web site developer(s), webmaster(s), webmistress(es), web builder(s), web designer(s), web site developer(s). *See also* Archivists; Knowledge workers; Professional personnel.

Libraries. Librar(y,ies). Learning resource(s) center(s). Archive(s). Media center(s). Information center(s). Information service(s). Information resource(s). Reference service(s). Book collection(s). *Consider also:* academic librar(y,ies), college librar(y,ies), university librar(y,ies), branch librar(y, ies), depository librar(y,ies), public librar(y,ies), research librar(y,ies), school librar(y,ies), special librar(y,ies), hospital librar(y,ies), medical librar(y,ies), business-librar(y,ies). *See also* Academic libraries; Archives; Depositories; Historical libraries; Information centers; Information dissemination; Information processing; Information services; Library acquisitions; Library administration; Library associations; Library catalogs; Library cooperation; Library instruction; Library services; Library surveys; Library users; Resources.

Libraries, academic. See *Academic libraries.*

Libraries, historical. See *Historical libraries.*

Libraries, virtual. See *Virtual libraries.*

Library acquisitions. Library acquisition(s). Collection development. *Choose from:* librar(y,ies), bibliographer(s) *with:* acquisition(s), acquir(e,ed,ing), purchas(e,es,ed,ing), approval plan(s), approval program(s). *Consider also:* book(s), reference material(s), media, serial(s), periodical(s), journal(s), monograph(s), scientific literature, government document(s), rare book(s), children's book(s), non-print, audio-cassette(s), video-cassette(s), CD-ROM(s), microfiche, microfilm(s), microform(s), film(s), newspaper(s) *with:* acquisition(s), acquir(e,ed,ing), subscrib(e,ed,ing), subscription(s), purchas(e,es,ed,ing), buy(ing), bought, order(s,ed,ing), choos(e,ing), chosen, select(ed,ing,ion). *See also* Book selection; Books; Collection development (libraries); Libraries; Library catalogs; Library materials; Information; Publications; Purchasing.

Library administration. Library administration. *Choose from:* librar(y,ies) *with:* manag(e,ed,ing,ement), budget(ed,ing,s), leader(s,ship), polic(y,ies), governance. *Consider also:* librar(y,ies,ian,ians) *with:* director(s), administrator(s), head(s), chief(s), supervisor(s,y), official(s). *See also* Libraries; Library services.

Library associations. Library association(s). *Choose from:* librar(y,ies, ian,ians), information science *with:* organization(s), association(s), societ(y,ies), federation(s), council(s). *See also* Associations (organizations); Libraries; Professional organizations.

Library catalogs. Library catalog(s). Card catalog(s). Book catalog(s). Online catalog(s). Shelflist(s). Library holding list(s). Author catalog(s). Title catalog(s). Subject catalog(s). Union catalog(s). Dictionary catalog(s). Divided catalog(s). *See also* Bibliography; Cataloging; Libraries; Library

cooperation; National bibliography; Reference materials.

Library censorship. Library censorship *Choose from:* librar(y,ies,ian,ians), multi-media center(s), *with:* censor(ed, ing,s,ship), ban(ned,ning), proscrib(e,ed, ing), forbid(den), political control(led, ling), censure screen(ed,ing), watchdogs, political control. *Consider also:* blocking software, filtering software, Communications Decency Act. *See also* Access to information; Book selection; Censorship; Collection development (libraries).

Library cooperation. Library cooperation. *Choose from:* librar(y,ies), archive(s) *with:* cooperat(e,ed,ing,ion), co-operat(e,ed,ing,ion), cooperatives, resource sharing, cooperative acquisition(s), consorti(a,um), joint-use, network(s,ed,ing), centralized processing, union catalogue(s) *Consider also:* interlibrary lending, interlibrary loan(s), regional library resource center(s), library system(s), Farmington plan. *See also* Cooperation; Interlibrary loans; Libraries; Library catalogs; National bibliography; Virtual organizations.

Library instruction. Library instruction. Bibliographic instruction. *Choose from:* librar(y,ies,ian,ians), bibliographic *with:* orientation, instruction, user education. *Consider also:* library skill(s), information skill(s), teaching the internet. *See also* Information skills; Libraries; Library services.

Library materials. Library material(s). *Choose from:* librar(y,ies,ian,ians) *with:* material(s), book(s), source(s), collection(s), media, serial(s), periodical(s), journal(s), monograph(s), scientific literature, government document(s), rare book(s), children's book(s), non-print, audio-cassette(s), video-cassette(s), CD-ROM(s), microfiche, microfilm(s), microform(s), film(s), newspaper(s), abstract(s), almanac(s), atlas(es), bibliograph(y,ies), catalog(s), dictionar(y,ies), director(y,ies), discograph(y,ies), encyclopedia(s), filmograph(y,ies), glossar(y,ies), handbook(s), guide(s), index(es), thesaur(i,us), yearbook(s). *See also* Collections; Library acquisitions; Reference materials; Teaching materials.

Library services. Library service(s). *Choose from:* library, readers, reference, information, online search, bibliographic, research *with:* service(s). *Consider also:* information retrieval, document delivery, information and referral service(s), storytelling, interlibrary loan(s), bookmobile(s). *See also* Automated information retrieval; Information dissemination; Information services; Information skills; Libraries; Library catalogs; Library instruction; Library surveys.

Library surveys. Library survey(s). *Choose from:* librar(y,ies,ian,ians,ianship), library user(s), library holding(s), bibliographic holding(s), library collection(s), library service(s), library activities, library budget(s) *with:* survey(s), questionnaire(s), stud(y,ies), poll(s,ed,ing), measur(e,ed,ing,ement, ements). *See also* Attitude measurement; Client attitudes; Libraries; Library services; Library users; Opinion polls; Questionnaires; Surveys.

Library users. Library user(s). *Choose from:* librar(y,ies) *with:* user(s), borrower(s), cardholder(s), client(s,ele), patron(s), reader(s), customer(s), supporter(s). *See also* Access to information; Clients; Information seeking; Information services; Libraries; Library services; Library surveys; Reading interests; User friendly systems.

Librettos. Librett(o,os,i,ist,ists). Livret(s). Opernlibretto(s). *Choose from:* text(s) *with:* opera(s), operetta(s), oratorio(s). *Consider also:* argument(o,i), versi virgolati. *See also* Lyrics; Opera; Oratorio; Recitative.

License agreements. License agreement(s). *Choose from:* licens(e,es,ing) *with:* agreement(s), pact(s), renewal(s). *Consider also:* permit(s), technology licens(e,es,ing), program licens(e,es, ing), software licens(e,es,ing). *See also* Copyright; Intangible property; Licenses; Patents; Rights; Strategic alliances.

Licenses. Licens(e,es,ed,ing,ure). Permit(s). Warrant(s). Certif(icate,ication). Credential(s). Approved. Authoriz(ation, ed). Validat(e,ed,ation). Approved qualifications. Registration. Registered. *See also* Certificates; Certification; License agreements; Occupational qualifications; Professional certification.

Licensing. See *Certification; License agreements; Licenses; Professional certification.*

Licensing, professional. See *Professional certification.*

Licensing agreements. See *License agreements.*

Lie detection. Lie detect(ion,or,ors). Polygraph(s,ic). Stress detect(ed,ing,ion, or,ors). *Choose from:* lie(s), lying, deception, deceit(ful) *with:* detect(ed, ing,ion,or,ors), electrodermal response(s), electrodermal lability, GSR, galvanic skin response, voice stress analyzer(s). *See also* Criminal investigations; Deception; Galvanic skin response.

Lieder. See *German songs; Songs.*

Lies. See *Deception.*

Life (biological). Life. Living. Alive(ness). In-vivo. Breathing. Vital signs. Surviv(e,ed,ing,or,ors). Viab(le,ility). Subsist(ing,ed). *Consider also:* growth, animation, exist(ence), vitality, endurance, plant life, animal life, etc. *See also* Birth; Death; Life cycle; Life expectancy; Life extension; Living conditions; Quality of life; Spontaneous generation; Survival.

Life, army. See *Army life.*

Life, community. See *Belongingness; Brotherliness; Community (social); Community (geographic locality); Community feeling; Community involvement; Community power; Community problems; Community structure; Community support; Local politics; Localism; Regionalism; Social identity.*

Life, conduct of. See *Lifestyle.*

Life, country. See *Country life.*

Life, daily. See *Everyday life.*

Life, everyday. See *Everyday life.*

Life, extraterrestrial. See *Extraterrestrial life.*

Life, family. See *Family life.*

Life, farm life. See *Farm life.*

Life, frontier and pioneer. See *Frontier and pioneer life.*

Life, future. See *Immortality.*

Life, home. See *Family life.*

Life, intellectual. See *Intellectual life.*

Life, length of working. See *Length of working life.*

Life, literary. See *Litterateurs.*

Life, monastic. See *Abstinence; Asceticism; Contemplative orders; Convents; Friars; Holy men; Holy women; Middle ages; Monasticism; Monks; Nuns; Religious communities; Religious personnel; Women religious.*

Life, necessities of. See *Basic needs.*

Life, philosophy of. See *Worldview.*

Life, quality of. See *Quality of life.*

Life, quality of working. See *Quality of working life.*

Life, religious. See *Religious life.*

Life, right to. See *Antiabortion movement.*

Life, rural. See *Country life.*

Life, rustic. See *Rustic life.*

Life, seafaring. See *Seafaring life.*

Life, social. See *Social life.*

Life, spiritual. See *Spirituality.*

Life, stage of. See *Theatrum mundi.*

Life, way of. See *Lifestyle.*

Life care. Life care. Lifecare. Lifetime retirement communit(y,ies). *Choose from:* life, lifetime, continuing, long term *with:* care, living arrangement(s), residen(ce,ces,ts). *See also* Retirement communities; Sheltered housing.

Life change events. Life chang(ing,e) event(s). *Choose from:* life(style), psychosocial, career, personal, role(s) *with:* transition(s), chang(e,ed,es,ing), readjustment(s), disruption(s), relocation(s), cris(is,es), stress(es), trauma(tic), turning point(s). Life threatening experience(s). Social readjustment. Life experience(s). Stressful event(s). Life event(s). Loss of loved one(s). Family dissolution. Divorce. Relocation syndrome. Situational cris(is,es). *See also* Birth; Career change; Death; Displaced homemakers; Divorce; Life cycle; Life stage transitions; Midcareer change; Midlife crisis; Rites of passage; Stress; Turning points.

Life cycle. Life cycle(s). Lifecourse(s). Ontogen(y,etic). Maturation(al) course. *Choose from:* life(long,time), adult(hood), maturation(al) *with:* cycle(s), course(s), stage(s), span(s), histor(y,ies), transition(s). *Consider also:* status passage, rite(s) of passage, Eriksonian stage(s). *See also* Aging; Birth; Child development; Climacteric; Death; Human development; Life (biological); Life change events; Life history; Life stage transitions; Menarche; Puberty.

Life cycle, human. See *Human life cycle.*

Life cycle, product. See *Product life cycle.*

Life expectancy. Life expectancy. Lifespan. Longevity. Lifetime(s). *Choose from:* life, survival, death, mortality *with:* expectancy, span(s), shorten(ed,ing), extend(ed,ing), pattern(s), rate(s), table(s), duration of life. *See also* Aging; Death; Health; Health indices; Health transition; Human life cycle; Mortality rates; Survival; World health.

Life experiences. Life experience(s). *Choose from:* life(time,span), lives, personal *with:* review(s), experience(s), event(s), change(s), stor(y,ies), stress(es), histor(y,ies), satisfaction, development, transition(s), situation(s), path(s), course. Everyday life. Everyday experience(s). Daily life. Daily lives. Turning point(s) in life. Experience of living. Own past. Personal background. Individual experience(s). Stressful life. Reminisc(ences,ent,ing). Biograph(y,ies,ical). Autobiograph(y,ies,ical). Anamnes(is,tic). *See also* Age regression (hypnotic); Biographical data; Early experiences; Educational background; Employment history; Everyday life; Experience (background); Life change events; Life history; Life review; Life stage transitions; Lifestyle.

Life extension. Life extension. Emortality. *Choose from:* life, youth(ful,fulness), vitality *with:* extend(ed,ing), extension, prolong(ed,ing,ation). *Choose from:* aging *with:* control(led,ling), retard(ed,ing,ation), inhibit(ed,ing). *Choose from:* death, dying *with:* conquest, conquer(ed, ing), postpon(e,ed,ing,ement). *Consider also:* cryonic suspension, fountain of youth, immortal(ity). *See also* Aging; Death; Life (biological); Life support care; Right to die.

Life force. See *Vitalism.*

Life history. Life histor(y,ies). Memoir(s). Life experience(s). Biograph(y,ies,ical). Autobiograph(y,ies,cal). *Choose from:* life(time,span), lives, personal *with:* memories, course, remember(ing), remembrance(s), review, experience(s), events, change(s), stor(y,ies), stress(es), histor(y,ies), development, transition(s), path(s), reminisc(ences,ent,ing). Everyday life. Everyday experience(s). Daily life. Daily lives. Turning points in life. Experience of living. Own past. Personal background. Individual experience(s). Anamnes(is,tic). *See also* Biographical data; Early experiences; Educational background; Employment history; Experience (background); First person narrative; Genealogy; Life cycle; Life experiences; Life review; Oral history; Psychohistory.

Life insurance. Life insurance. Flight insurance. Term insurance. Life assurance. Life insurer(s). Insure(d) life. *See also* Insurance.

Life on other planets. See *Extraterrestrial life.*

Life plans. Life plan(s,ning). *Choose from:* life, career, college, retirement *with:* plan(s,ning), decision(s), expectation(s), aspiration(s). *See also* Aspirations; Career goals; Career mobility; Careers; Educational plans; Expectations; Goals; Life satisfaction; Long range planning; Occupational success; Planning.

Life review. Life review(s). Guided autobiograph(y,ies). Reminiscence group(s). Personal inventor(y,ies). Personal account(s). Memoir(s). Life histor(y,ies). *Consider also:* family history. *See also* Autobiography; Life experiences; Life history; Oral history.

Life satisfaction. Life satisfaction(s). Mental(ly) health(y). Meaningful(ness). Psychological well-being. Wellbeing. Work satisfaction. Perceived self efficacy. World view. Role satisf(ied, action). Subjective well-being. Hope(ful,fulness). Fulfill(ed,ing,ment). Happ(y,iness). Exhilarat(ed,ing,ion). Good spirit(s). Content(ed). Creativ(e,ity). Morale. Affective state(s). *Choose from:* life *with:* satisfaction(s), positive regard, quality, purpose, meaning(s,ful,fulness), outlook. *See also*

Attitudes; Comfortableness; Experience (background); Happiness; Humanization; Job satisfaction; Life experiences; Life plans; Lifestyle; Living standards; Marital satisfaction; Mental health; Need satisfaction; Quality of life; Quality of working life; Self actualization; Social conditions; Social indicators; Social life; Social status; Well being.

Life sciences. Life science(s). Biological science(s). Health science(s). Bioscience(s). *Consider also:* agricultur(e, al), biolog(y,ical), medical science(s). *See also* Agriculture; Experimental biology; Medical sciences; Sciences.

Life sciences ethics. See *Bioethics*

Life sentence. Life sentence(d). Sentenced for life. *Consider also:* lifer(s), long-term imprisonment. *See also* Clemency; Death penalty; Deterrence; Punishment; Sentencing.

Life skills. See *Basic skills; Communication skills; Coping; Social skills; Work skills.*

Life space. Life space(s). *Choose from:* life, personal, shared, private *with:* space(s), context(s), environment(s), arena(s). *Consider also:* body boundar(y,ies), social ecology, locational context(s), territorial behavior. *See also* Crowding; Nonverbal communication; Privacy; Proxemics; Social interaction; Spatial behavior; Territoriality.

Life span. See *Life expectancy.*

Life stage transitions. Life stage transition(s). Life change event(s). Loss of loved one(s). Family dissolution. Divorc(e,es,ed,ing). Relocation syndrome. Situational cris(is,es). Transition(s) in the life cycle. Retir(e,ed,ing,ement). Chang(e,ed,ing) role(s). Rite(s) of passage. Remarriage. *Choose from:* lifecourse, lifecycle, lifetime, midlife, role(s), psychosocial, mid-career, career(s), personal, status *with:* transition(s), change(s), juncture(s), adjust(ed,ing,ment,ments), readjust(ed,ing,ment,ments), disrupt(ed,ing,ion,ions), shift(s,ed,ing), relocation(s), cris(is,es), turning point(s), choice(s). *Choose from:* passage(s), transition(s) *with:* school, work, parenthood, death(s), adulthood. *Consider also:* liminal(ity) *with:* phase(s), period(s), entit(y,ies), state(s). *See also* Adjustment (to environment); Adult development; Aging; Career change; Developmental stages; Displaced homemakers; Divorce; Initiation rites; Life change events; Life cycle; Life experiences; Life cycle; Marital disruption; Marriage; Midcareer change; Middle age; Parenthood; Puberty; Rites of passage; Role changes; Turning points; Widowhood.

Life stages. See *Ages of man; Human life cycle; Life cycle; Life stage transitions.*

Life style. See *Lifestyle.*

Life support care. Life support care. Intensive care. Trauma care. Prolong(ed, ing) life. Therapeutic perseverance. Care of incompetent terminally ill. *Choose from:* life support, extraordinary, life maintaining, life prolonging, *with:* care, treatment(s), measure(s). *Consider also:* Quinlan case, Saikewicz case. *See also* Artificial respiration; Life extension; Right to die.

Life world. See *Everyday life.*

Life course transition. See *Life stage transitions.*

Lifelong learning. Lifelong learning. *Choose from:* lifelong, life-long, life span, adult(s,hood), continuing, preretirement, retirement *with:* learning, personal development, personal growth, education(al), class(es), instruction(al). *Consider also:* upskilling, elderhostel(s), andragog(y,ical), androgog(y,ical). *See also* Adult education; Adult students; Continuing education; Correspondence schools; Intellectual capital; Self help books; Self education; Self help.

Lifesaving. Lifesav(ing,er,ers). Saving life. Rescu(e,ed,ing). Heimlich maneuver. *See also* Artificial respiration.

Lifestyle. Lifestyle(s). Life style(s). Life-style(s). Way of life. Conduct of life. *Choose from:* life, living *with:* style(s), characteristic(s), mode(s), satisfactions, way(s). *Consider also:* couch potato(es), independent living, homosexuality, living together, cohabitation, childfree life, child free living, embourgeoisement, proletarianization, spending patterns, manner of dress, way of speaking, personal appearance, domestic habits, downshift(er,s,ing), simple life, yupp(y,ies), personal conduct. *See also* Alternative family forms; Alternative lifestyles; Behavior; Beauty culture; Character; Cohabitation; Consumption (economic); Countercultures; Country living; Cultural values; Disposition (personality); Embourgeoisement; Energy consumption; Everyday life; Exercise; Feminism; Habits; Hippies; Holistic health; Humanization; Human life cycle; Intellectual life; Life experiences; Life satisfaction; Living alone; Living conditions; Living standards; Natural foods; Personal independence; Personality; Quality of life; Rural urban differences; Saving; Sexual orientation; Simplicity; Social history; Social life; Sociocultural factors; Worldview; Youth culture.

Lifestyles, alternative. See *Alternative lifestyles.*

Lifting, weight. See *Weight lifting.*

Light. Light(ed,ing,s). Illuminat(ed,ing,ion). Radian(t,ce). Shin(e,ed,ing). Lumin(ance,osity,escence,escent).

Daylight. Skylight. Flash(es). Bright(ness). Bioluminescen(t,ce). Glare. Houselight(s). Candlepower. Candle(s). Headlight(s). Sunlight. Sunshine. Sunbeam(s). Gleam(ed,ing). Incandescen(t,ce). Sparkl(e,ed,ing). Twinkl(e,ed,ing). Lamplight. Firelight. Beacon(s). Alight. Floodlight. *Consider also:* photopic, photic, photoperiod, visibility, phosphorescen(t,ce). *See also* Color; Light adaptation; Light refraction; Light sources; Solar access; Solar energy; Visual stimulation.

Light, illumination. See *Light; Light sources.*

Light adaptation. Light adaptation. Photosensitiv(e,ity). *Choose from:* adapt(ed,ing,ation), adjust(ed,ing,ment), sensitiv(e,ity) *with:* light(s,ed,ing), bright(ness), photopic, flash, illumination. *See also* Light.

Light refraction. Light refraction. Photorefract(ed,ing,ive,ion). *Choose from:* ocular, light, corneal *with:* refract(ed,ing,ion,ive), refringen(t,ce), birefringen(t,ce). *See also* Light.

Light sources. Light source(s). *Choose from:* light(ed,ing,s), illuminat(ed,ing, ion) *with:* source(s), *Consider also:* window(s), skylight(s). *See also* Energy generating resources; Light; Solar access.

Likability. Likab(le,ility). Pleasing. Amiab(le,ility). Social(ly) validat(ed, ion). Attractive(ness). Friendl(y,iness). Lovable. Winning. Congenial(ity). *Consider also:* charisma(tic). *See also* Friendliness; Interpersonal attraction; Personality traits; Social approval; Social perception.

Likeness (representation). See *Representation (likeness).*

Likes and dislikes. See *Preferences.*

Liking. See *Affection.*

Limb, phantom. See *Phantom limb.*

Limbs, artificial. See *Prostheses.*

Limerence. See *Obsessive love.*

Liminality. See *Life stage transitions; Rites of passage.*

Limitations. Limit(ed,ing,ation,ations). Boundar(y,ies). Regulat(e,ed,ing, ion,ions). Ration(ed,ing). Secured. Cutback(s). Minimum(s). Maximim(s). Deadline(s). Constraint(s). Barrier(s). Restrict(ed,ing,ion,ions). Restrain(ed, ing,t,ts). Muzzl(e,ed,ing). Enclos(e,ed, ing). Bounded. Set bounds. Confin(e,ed, ing). Hamper(ed,ing). Control(led,ling). Repress(ed,ing). Inhibit(ed,ing). Stifl(e,ed,ing). Suppress(ed,ing). *See also* Barriers; Boundaries; Budget cuts; Enclosures; Encumbrance; Constraints; Hindrances; Problems; Time.

Limited psychotherapy, time. See *Brief psychotherapy.*

Lineage. Lineage. Sublineage(s). Descent group(s). Common ancestor(s). Genealog(y,ies,ical). Pedigree. Family tree(s). Ancestral line. Dynast(y,ies). Direct descent. Descendant(s). Descendent(s). Blood line(s). Family link(s,age). Kin(ship) group(s). Clan(s). Matrilineal. Patrilineal. Parentage. *See also* Clans; Descent; Genealogy; Kinship.

Lines, assembly. See *Assembly lines.*

Lines, help telephone. See *Help lines (telephone).*

Lines, hot. See *Help lines (telephone).*

Lingua franca. Lingua franca(s). Linguae francae. Langue franque. Lingue franche. Commercial tongue(s). Common language(s). *Consider also:* Pidgin English, Swahili, Chinook jargon. *See also* Creoles; International languages; Loan words; Mobilian trade language; Pidgin languages; Trade languages.

Linguistic games. See *Word games.*

Linguistic geography. Linguistic geography. Language geography. *Choose from:* language(s), linguistic *with:* border(s), boundar(y,ies), geograph(y,ical), distribution. *Consider also:* geolinguistic(s), areal linguistics. *See also* Areal linguistics; Comparative linguistics; Dialects; Language spread; Linguistics; Speech communities.

Linguistic interference. Linguistic interference. Communicative interference. *Consider also:* negative transfer(s). *See also* Bilingualism; Code switching; Interference (learning); Language transfer (language learning); Psycholinguistics; Second language education; Speech errors.

Linguistic minorities. Linguistic minorit(y, ies). *Choose from:* language, linguistic *with:* minorit(y,ies). Marginalized language(s). Sidestream language(s). *Choose from:* Finlandssvensk, Gaelic, Welsh, Franco-Ontarians, French-speaking Swiss, French-speaking Canadians, Spanish-speaking Americans, etc. *Consider also:* hyphenated Americans, bilingual(ism). *See also* Areal linguistics; Creoles; Ethnic groups; Ethnolinguistics; Language maintenance; Language usage; Languages in contact; Minority groups; Plural societies; Speech communities.

Linguistic policy. See *Language policy.*

Linguistic shift. See *Language shift.*

Linguistics. Linguistic(s). Language theor(y,ies). *Consider also:* psycholinguistic(s), sociolinguistic(s), philology, generative grammar, syntax, phonology, etymology, lexicology, semiotics, semantics, biolinguistics, ethnolinguistics, neurolinguistics, comparative linguistics, computational linguistics, deep structure, surface structure, diachronic linguistics, synchronic linguistics, anthropological linguistics, applied linguistics, contrastive linguistics, descriptive linguistics, mathematical linguistics, paralinguistics, structural linguistics, nomenclature, philolog(y,ical), phonetics, etymology, inflection, language morphology, transformational grammar, transformational generative grammar. *See also* Areal linguistics; Communication (thought transfer); Comparative linguistics; Diachronic linguistics; Dialects; Ethnolinguistics; Etymology; Government binding theory (Linguistics); Grammar; Historical linguistics; Language; Language change; Language shift; Language usage; Language varieties; Languages (as subjects); Linguistic geography; Logocentrism; Metalanguage; Philosophy of language; Phonetics; Psycholinguistics; Semantics; Semiotics; Sociolinguistics; Speech; Stylistics; Synchronism; Translating and translations; Verbal communication.

Linguistics, areal. See *Areal linguistics.*

Linguistics, comparative. See *Comparative linguistics.*

Linguistics, diachronic. See *Diachronic linguistics.*

Linguistics, historical. See *Historical linguistics.*

Linguostylistics. See *Stylistics.*

Lipreading. Lipread(ing). Lip read(ing). Read(ing) lips. Speechread(ing). Speech read(ing). *See also* Deafness; Speech perception; Visual perception.

Liquidation. Liquidat(e,ed,ing,ion). Cash(ed,ing) out. Cash(ed,ing) in. Clos(e,ed,ing) out. Convert(ed,ing) to cash. Sell(ing) stock. Sold stock. *Choose from:* discharg(e,ed,ing), settl(e,ed,ing, ement), clear(ed,ing), pay, paid, satisf(y, ying,ied) *with:* debt(s), indebtedness. *See also* Accounts payable and receivable; Asset management; Assets; Cash flow; Credit; Liquidity; Pension fund management.

Liquidity. Liquidity. Liquid assets. Available cash. Special drawing rights. Reserve currency. Cash reserve(s). Paper gold. Solvency. *Consider also:* cash, funds *with:* flow. *See also* Accounts payable and receivable; Assets; Capitalization; Cash flow; Credit; Funds; Liquidation.

Liquor. See *Alcoholic beverages.*

Liquor industry. Liquor industry. Whiskey Industry. Distiller(y,ies,s). Brewer(y,ies, s). Winer(y,ies). *Choose from:* liquor, whisk(ey,ies), alcoholic beverage(s), spirits, wine(s) *with:* industry, store(s), superstore(s), business(es), product(s, ion), retail(er,ers), sale(s), selling, outlet(s), making, maker(s). *Consider also:* vintner(s), viticulture. *See also* Alcoholic beverages; Brewing industry; Distillation; Illicit liquor; Wine.

Listeners. See *Audiences.*

Listening comprehension. Listening comprehension. *Choose from:* listening, auditory, aural *with:* comprehension, abilit(y,ies), understand(ing), understood, competenc(y,ies), skill(s). *Choose from:* verbal, speech *with:* comprehension, understand(ing), understood. *See also* Auditory fatigue; Auditory perception; Oral reading.

Lists, waiting. See *Waiting lists.*

Literacy. Litera(cy,te,tes). Print awareness. Neo-literate(s). Post-litera(cy,te,tes). *Choose from:* read(ing), writ(e,ing) *with:* ability, able, skill(s), learn(ing). *Consider also:* bilitera(te,cy), schooled, educated, well read, adult litera(cy,te, tes), functional(ly) litera(cy,te), scientific litera(cy,te), computer litera(cy,te), numeracy. *See also* Adult literacy; Basic skills; Computer literacy; Ignorance; Illiteracy; Information literacy; Language; Letters (alphabet); Literacy programs; Minimum competencies; Reading; Reading skills; Vocabulary; Writing (composition).

Literacy, adult. See *Adult literacy.*

Literacy, computer. See *Computer literacy.*

Literacy, cultural. See *Cultural literacy*

Literacy, information. See *Information literacy.*

Literacy education. See *Literacy programs.*

Literacy programs. Literacy program(s). *Choose from:* literacy, illiteracy, primary education, basic education, read(ing), writ(e,ing) *with:* program(s), campaign(s), plan(s), *Consider also:* adult education, compensatory education, moonlight schools, each one teach one. *See also* Adult basic education; Adult literacy; Educational programs; Literacy; Minimum competencies; Reading education; Reading interests; Reading skills.

Literary criticism. Literary critic(ism,s). *Choose from:* literary, literature, essay(s), book(s), writing(s), prose, poet(s,ry), fiction, novel(s) *with:* critical stud(y,ies), critique, review(s,ed,ing), comment(s,ed,ing,ary,aries), analys(is, es), evaluat(e,ed,ing,ion), apprais(e,ed, ing,al), judg(e,ed,ing,ment), assess(ed, ing,ment), appreciat(e,ed,ing,ion), interpret(ed,ing,ation), exposition(s). *See also* Book reviews; Chattering class; Commentators; Communications research; Connoisseurs; Content analysis; Essays; Evaluation; Formalism; Literary ethics; Literary research; Literary societies; Literary style; Literary terms; Literary theory; Literature; Literature appreciation; Readership.

Literary errors and blunders. Literary error(s). *Choose from:* liter(ary,ature), book(s), writing(s), article(s), fiction, novel(s), poetry, prose *with:* error(s), errata, blunder(s), mistake(s), misconception(s), misuse(s,d), wrong. *Consider also:* corrigend(um,a), anachronism(s). *See also* Addendum; Anachronisms; Errors; Fallibility; Literary forgeries and mystifications; Literature.

Literary ethics. Literary ethic(s). *Choose from:* author(s), writer(s), literary *with:* ethic(s,al), unethical, plagiari(sm,ze,zed, zing), borrow(ed,ing), sensationalis(m, t,ts), bias, invective(s), half truth(s), acknowledg(e,ed,ing) source(s), credit(ed,ing) source(s), fair(ness), unlawful, forger(y,ies). *See also* Authors; Codes of Ethics; Editors; Ethics; Journalistic ethics; Journalists; Literary criticism; Literary forgeries and mystifications; Plagiarism; Sensationalism.

Literary feuds. See *Literary quarrels*

Literary forgeries and mystifications. Literary forger(y,ies). Literary mystification(s). *Choose from:* literary, literature, book(s), scholarship *with:* forger(y,ies), mystification(s), pira(cy, te,ted), hoax(es), fake(d), false(ly) attribut(ed,ing,ion), fraud(ulent), imposter(s). *See also* Artificiality; Literary errors and blunders; Literary ethics; Plagiarism; Pseudonyms.

Literary form. Literary form(s). Literary genre(s). *Choose from:* literary, literature *with:* form(s), genre(s), categor(y,ies). *Consider also:* epic(s), comed(y,ies), traged(y,ies), short stor(y,ies), novel(la, las,s), tragicomed(y,ies), letter(s). *See also* Genres; Literature.

Literary fraud. See *Literary forgeries and mystifications.*

Literary hoaxes. See *Literary forgeries and mystifications.*

Literary landmarks. Literary landmark(s). *Choose from:* literary, literature, author(s) *with:* landmark(s), birthplace(s), haunt(s), gazetteer(s), atlas(es). *See also* Authors; Cultural property; Historic sites; Natural monuments.

Literary life. See *Litterateurs.*

Literary movement, decadence. See *Decadence (Literary movement).*

Literary movement, futurism. See *Futurism (Literary movement).*

Literary movements. Literary movement(s). Poetic movement(s). *Consider also:* intellectual tradition(s), literary history; literary generation(s), literary lineage(s), literary heritage. *See also* Acmeism; Aestheticism; Classicism; Decadence (Literary movement); Futurism (Literary movement); Gothicism; Intellectual history; Literary styles; Literary theory; Modern literature; Postmodernism; Romanticism; Symbolist movement.

Literary parallels. Literary parallel(s). Parallelism. Parallel clause(s). Parallelismus membrorum. *Consider also:* chiasmus. *See also* Alliteration; Literature; Poetry.

Literary patronage. Literary patronage. *Choose from:* patron(s,age), sponsor(s, ship,ed,ing), underwrit(er,ers,ing,ten), commission(ed,ing), benefactor(s), back(ed,ing,er,ers) *with:* writer(s), author(s), composer(s), playwright(s), poet(s), fiction, novel(s), biograph(y,ies), essayist(s), literary. *See also* Authors; Patronage.

Literary prizes. Literary prize(s). Literary honor(s). Literary award(s). *Consider also:* National Book Award(s), Nobel Prize for Literature, Pulitzer Prize(s). *See also* Authors; Prizes; Recognition (achievement); Writers.

Literary property. See *Copyright.*

Literary quarrels. Literary quarrel(s). *Choose from:* literary, author(s), writer(s) *with:* quarrel(s), dispute(s), debate(s), antithesis, enem(y,ies), rivalr(y,ies). *See also* Antithesis; Authors; Debate; Disputed authorship; Feuds; Disputes; Rivalry; Writers.

Literary recreations. Literary recreation(s). *Choose from:* literary, literature *with:* game(s), conundrum(s), quiz(zes), pun(s). *See also* Anagrams; Word games.

Literary research. Literary research. *Choose from:* literary, literature, poet(s,ry), essay(s), book(s), writing(s), prose, fiction, novel(s), text(s,ual), bibliograph(y,ies,ical) *with:* research, analys(is,es), investigat(e,ed,ing,ion, ions). *See also* Content analysis; Literary criticism; Literary theory; Literature; Research; Texts.

Literary sketches. See *Essays.*

Literary societies. Literary societ(y,ies). Literary group(s). *Choose from:* literary, literature, poetry *with:* societ(y,ies), group(s), circle(s), club(s). *Consider also:* Association of Literary Scholars and Critics, Modern Language Association, Manuscript Club, Goethean Literary Society, Diagnothian Literary Society, Literarische Gesellschaft(en). *See also* Literary criticism; Literature; Readership; Societies (organizations).

Literary style. Literary style(s). *Choose from:* literary, literature, poet(s,ry), essay(s), book(s), writing(s), prose, fiction, novel(s), writing, dramatic, author(s) *with:* style(s), approach(es), stylistic(s), device(s). *See also* Aesthetics; Literary criticism; Literary movements; Literary theory; Literature.

Literary taste. See *Literature appreciation.*

Literary terms. Literary term(s,inology). *Choose from:* literary, literature *with:* term(s,inology,inologies), glossar(y,ies), dictionar(y,ies), jargon, language, lexicon, nomenclature. *See also* Literary criticism; Literature; Terminology.

Literary theory. Literary theor(y,ies). *Choose from:* literature, literary, novel(s), essay(s), poe(m,ms,try), play(s) *with:* theor(y,ies,etical), philosoph(y,ies, ical), axiom(s,atic), construct(s), interpretation(s), metatheor(y,ies,etical), model(s), thes(es,is), principle(s), symbol(s,ic), typolog(y,ies). *Consider also:* gender theory, feminist theory, critical theory. *See also* Literature; Literary criticism; Literary research; Literary style; Literary movements; Theories.

Literary tradition. See *Influence (literary, artistic, etc.).*

Literary transmission. See *transmission of texts.*

Literature. Literature. Drama. Literary work(s). Writings. Fiction. Novel(s). Poetry. Prose. Play(s). Biograph(y,ies). Autobiograph(y,ies). Belles lettre(s). Literary description(s). Memoir(s). Essay(s). Literary criticism. Classic(s). Creative writing. Theater. Theatre. Satire. Versification. Journalism. Collected works. Legend(s). Anecdote(s). Aphorism(s). Proverb(s). Bible(s). Myth(s,ology). Philology. Short stor(y,ies). *Consider also:* author names, titles of works. *See also* Absurd; Addendum; Allegory; Allusions; Ancient literature; Antiheroes; Authors; Autobiography; Baroque literature; Bildungsroman; Biography; Black Carib literature; Books; Closure (Rhetoric); Controversial literature; Diaries; Epic literature; Essays; Experimental literature; Fiction; Figurative language; Folk culture; Folk literature; Gothic romances; Gothicism; Grotesque; History; Historical drama; Heroes; Humanism; Humanities; Humor; Imaginary places; Influence (literary, artistic, etc.); Intertextuality; Jewish literature; Journalism; Language; Latin American literature; Letters (correspondence); Literary criticism; Literary errors and blunders; Literary forms; Literary parallels; Literary research; Literary societies; Literary style; Literary terms; Literary theory; Literature appreciation; Lost literature; Medieval literature;

Metaphors; Minimalism (literature); Modern literature; Mythology; Nature literature; Nonfiction novel; Philosophy; Poetry; Point of view (literature); Popular culture; Professional literature; Prose; Protest literature; Rabbinical literature; Religious literature; Renaissance literature; Rhetoric; Satire; Scatology; Selected readings; Symbolism; Transmission of texts; Unity (Literature).

Literature, ancient. See *Ancient literature.*

Literature, apocalyptic. See *Apocalyptic literature.*

Literature, baroque. See *Baroque literature.*

Literature, Black Carib. See *Black Carib literature.*

Literature, children's. See *Children's literature.*

Literature, classical. See *Ancient iterature; Latin literature.*

Literature, controversial. See *Controversial literature.*

Literature, epic. See *Epic literature.*

Literature, erotic. See *Erotica.*

Literature, experimental. See *Experimental literature.*

Literature, folk. See *Folk literature.*

Literature, Jewish. See *Jewish literature.*

Literature, Ladino. See *Jewish literature.*

Literature, Latin. See *Latin literature.*

Literature, Latin American. See *Latin American literature.*

Literature, lost. See *Lost literature.*

Literature, macaronic. See *Macaronic literature.*

Literature, medieval. See *Medieval literature.*

Literature, Mexican. See *Latin American literature.*

Literature, minimalism. See *Minimalism (literature).*

Literature, modern. See *Modern literature.*

Literature, modernism. See *Modern literature.*

Literature, nature. See *Nature literature.*

Literature, nonsense. See *Nonsense literature.*

Literature, popular. See *Popular literature.*

Literature, professional. See *Professional literature.*

Literature, protest. See *Protest literature.*

Literature, rabbinical. See *Rabbinical literature.*

Literature, religious. See *Religious literature.*

Literature, renaissance. See *Renaissance literature.*

Literature, scientific. See *Professional literature.*

Literature, self improvement. See *Self help books.*

Literature, Spanish American. See *Latin American literature.*

Literature, travel. See *Travel literature.*

Literature, unity. See *Unity (Literature).*

Literature appreciation. Literature appreciation. *Choose from:* literary, literature, essay(s), book(s), writing(s), prose, poet(s,ry), fiction, novel(s), printed word *with:* appreciat(e,ed,ing, ion), interpret(ed,ing,ation), award(s), valu(e,ed,ing), of aesthetic(s), awareness, understanding, heritage, enrichment. *Consider also:* literary taste(s), literary evening(s), literary stud(y,ies), great literature, literature instruction. *See also* Cultural history; Literary criticism; Literature; Litterateurs.

Literature reviews. See *Book reviews; Literary criticism; Reviews.*

Lithic implements. See *Stone implements.*

Litigation. Litigat(e,ed,ing,ion). Litigant(s). Litigiousness. Lawsuit(s). Suit(s). Judicial process(es). Legal procedure(s). *Choose from:* civil, criminal, legal, justice, judicial, court(s,room,rooms), due *with:* procedure(s), process(es), decision(s), determination, battle(s), case(s). Adjudicat(e,ion,ive,or,ors). Adjudg(e,ment). Court decision(s). Decree(s,d,ing). Arbitrat(e,ed,ion). Court ruling(s). *See also* Arbitration; Attorneys; Court judges; Defendants; Defense (verbal); Evidence; Juries; Legal cases; Legal procedures; Legal system; Liability; Trial (law); Verdicts.

Litter (waste). Litter(ed,ing). Garbage. Waste. Waste material(s). Refuse. Trash. Debris. Broken bottle(s). Empty beer can(s). Empty bottle(s). Empty beverage container(s). Rubbish. Junk. Sweepings. Dust. Leaving(s). Picnic remains. Discarded wrapper(s). Cigarette butt(s). Pigeon droppings. Dog droppings. Waste paper. Litterbug(s). Litterpig(s). Plastic pollution. *Choose from:* dirty, slovenly, trash covered, littered, unkempt *with:* sidewalk(s), street(s), roadside(s), highway(s), walkway(s), lawn(s), park(s). *Consider also:* throwaway society, disposable society. *See also* Containers; Debris; Environmental protection; Scrap materials; Solid waste; Waste disposal.

Litterateurs. Litterateur(s). Literary life. (Man,woman) of letters. Learned (man,men,woman,women,person,persons). *Consider also:* intellectual life. *Consider also:* literary agent(s). *See also* Authors; Intellectual life; Literary criticism; Literature appreciation.

Little presses. Little press(es). Small(er) press(es). *Choose from:* little, small(er), private, independent, literary *with:* press(es), publisher(s). *See also* Alternative press; Book industry; Publishing; Publishers.

Little theater. Little theater(s). Community theater(s). Community play(s,er,ers). Amateur theater. Neighborhood playhouse(s). Theater workshop(s). Summer theater(s). *Consider also:* thespian societ(y,ies), parlor theatrical(s). *See also* Amateur theatricals; Amateurs; Theater; Traveling theater.

Liturgical books. Liturgical book(s). Cantatorium. Sacramentarium. Book of Common Prayer. *Consider also:* missale, graduale, breviarium, antiphon(er,ale, arium), Kyriale, vesperale, Liber Usualis, tonar(y,ies). *See also* Liturgical drama; Liturgy; Prayerbooks; Religious literature; Sacred books.

Liturgical drama. Liturgical drama(s). Medieval church drama(s). *Choose from:* liturg(y,ical), medieval church *with:* drama(s,tic), play(s). *Consider also:* mystery play(s). *See also* Liturgical books; Liturgy; Medieval drama; Medieval music; Miracle plays; Morality plays; Opera; Religious drama; Religious mysteries; Religious rituals.

Liturgical posture. See *Posture in worship.*

Liturgical responses. See *Responses (liturgical).*

Liturgy. Liturg(y,ies,ical). Religious rite(s). Eucharistic sacrifice. Religious service(s). *Consider also:* form of public worship, mass, sermon(s), homil(y,ies), Lord's supper, vesper(s), liturgical movement, litan(y,ies), lectionar(y,ies), sacrament(s,aries), offertor(y,ies), trisagion, religious ritual(s). *See also* Antiphons; Christianity; Gregorian chants; Invocation; Liturgical books; Liturgical drama; Masses (music); Religious rituals; Responses (liturgical); Worship.

Liver. Liver. Hepatic. Hepato-. *Consider also:* bile, intrahepatic bile duct(s), bile canaliculi. *See also* Liver disorders.

Liver disorders. Liver disorder(s). Liver disease(s). Anhepatia. Hepatectomy. Hepatotoxicity. *Choose from:* liver, hepatic, hepatobiliary, hepatocellular *with:* disease(s), disorder(s), patholog(y,ical), failure, toxic injur(y,ies) damage(d), reduced function, insufficiency, granulomatosis, defect(s), dysfunction, hematoma, necrosis, fibrosis, function disorder(s), deranged function. *Consider also:* acute yellow atrophy, intrahepatic cholestasis, fatty liver, hepatic encephalopathy, hepatic vein thrombosis, hepatitis, hepatolenticular degeneration, hepatomegaly, portal hypertension, liver abscess, liver cirrhosis, alcoholic liver disease(s), parasitic liver disease(s), liver neoplasm(s), peliosis hepatitis, hepatic tuberculosis, liver cirrhosis, hepatitis, jaundice. *See also* Liver; Parasites.

Livestock. Livestock. Farm animal(s). *Consider also:* cattle, cow(s), calves, calf, goat(s), horse(s), pig(s), swine, poultry, chicken(s), sheep, lamb(s), turkey(s), duck(s). *See also* Animals; Cattle; Chickens; Draft animals; Goats; Herders; Pets; Sheep; Vertebrates.

Livestock farms. See *Farms; Ranches.*

Living, activities of daily. See *Activities of daily living.*

Living, assisted. See *Assisted living.*

Living, communal. See *Communes.*

Living, cost of. See *Cost of living.*

Living, independent. See *Deinstitutionalization; Group homes; Institutional release; Living alone; Noninstitutionalized disabled; Personal independence; Retirement communities.*

Living, standard of. See *Living standards.*

Living accomodations. See *Housing.*

Living alone. Living alone. Live(s,d) alone. Seclusion. Solitary life. Solitary living. Hermit(s). Recluse(s). *See also* Living conditions; Single person; Social isolation; Solitude.

Living conditions. Living conditions. Habitability. Standard of living. Quality of life. Material well being. *Choose from:* living, housing, residen(ce,tial), home(s), famil(y,ies) *with:* condition(s), environment(s), assessment(s), characteristics, satisfaction, arrangement(s), space, setting, circumstance(s), situation(s). *Consider also:* per capita income, homeless(ness). *See also* Cheap labor; Community (geographic locality); Community characteristics; Disadvantaged; Economic conditions; Hazards; Home environment; Houseboats; Housing; Housing conditions; Interior design; Lifestyle; Living standards; Social conditions; Quality of life; Quality of working life; Wealth.

Living donors. Living donor(s). Live donor(s). *Choose from:* liv(e,ing), unrelated, related, sibling(s), twin(s) *with:* donor(s), donation(s), *Consider also:* marrow donor(s), kidney donor(s), renal donor(s), organ donor(s). *See also* Anatomical gifts; Blood donors; Organ transplantation; Tissue banks; Tissue donors.

Living standards. Living standard(s). Household subsistence level(s). Material well being. Consumption pattern(s). Living conditions. Habitability. Standard(s) of living. *Choose from:* better, simple(r), good, easy, easier,

hard(er) *with:* life. *Consider also:* living decently, nutritional status, socioeconomic profile(s), basic health service(s), sanitation, per capita income, minimum income, infant mortality, economic indicator(s), social indicator(s), deprivation, shortage(s) of food, per capita income, longevity, mortality rate(s), morbidity rate(s), cost(s) of living, spending habit(s), lifestyle(s), employment rate(s), unemployment rate(s). *See also* Amenities; Cheap labor; Community development; Consumption (economic); Developed countries; Developing countries; Disadvantaged; Economic conditions; Economic security; Economic statistics; Economics; Environmental protection; Gross national product; Income; Income distribution; Life satisfaction; Lifestyle; Living conditions; Luxuries; Poverty; Prevailing wages; Prices; Purchasing power; Quality of life; Social indicators; Socioeconomic factors; Wages; Wealth.

Living together. See *Cohabitation.*

Living wills. See *Advance directives; Do not resuscitate orders; Right to die; Termination of treatment; Wills.*

Load, course. See *Course load.*

Load, mental. See *Human channel capacity.*

Load, work. See *Work load.*

Loafing, social. See *Social loafing.*

Loan words. Loan word(s). Loanword(s). Borrow(ed,ing) word(s). Lexical borrowing. *Choose from:* foreign word(s), foreign expression(s), foreign phrase(s) *with:* invasion(s), invading, everyday speech, borrow(ed,ing), loan(s,ed,ing). *Consider also:* calquing, lexical contamination (lexical), pidgin(s), Americaniz(e,ed,ing,ation), Neudeutsche. *See also* Code switching; Creoles; Culture contact; Language maintenance; Language shift; Language varieties; Languages in contact; Lingua franca; Nonstandard English; Pidgin languages; Trade languages.

Loans. Loan(s). Lend(ing). Advance money. Debt(s). Indebted(ness). Deferred payment(s). Borrowed money. Leveraged buyout(s). Mortgage(s). Commercial paper. Overdraft(s). Past due account(s). Deficit. Usury. Default(ed, ing,er,ers). Charge account(s). Time payment(s). Layaway. Financial obligation. Arrears. Debit(s). *Consider also:* moneylend(ing,er,ers), interest rate(s), collection agenc(y,ies), credit(or,ors). *See also* Arrears; Balance of payments; Balanced budget; Bankruptcy; Consumer credit; Credit; Debts; Money; Public debt; Refinancing; Subsidies.

Loans, interlibrary. See *Interlibrary loans.*

Loansharking. See *Usury.*

Lobbying. Lobby(ing). Lobb(y,ies). Lobbyist(s). Political advoca(cy,te,tes). Influencing legislator(s). Political influence(s). Political force(s). Political action committee(s). PAC(s). Voice in Washington. Interest group(s). Special interest group(s). *Consider also:* political clout. *See also* Activism; Interest groups; Legislation; Legislative bodies; Legislative processes; Legislators; Political action; Political power; Representatives; Spheres of influence.

Local elections. Local election(s). *Choose from:* local, municipal, city, city hall, county, mayoral *with:* election(s), race(s), campaign(s), ballot(s). *See also* Elections; Local politics.

Local finance. Local finance. *Choose from:* local, county, district(s), special district(s), town(ship), village(s), municipal(ity,ities), cit(y,ies), metropolitan, community, regional *with:* financ(e,es,ial), budget(s), fiscal(ly), investment(s), loss(es), bankrupt(cy), bond(s), borrow(ed,ing) money, resource allocation(s), tax(es), taxpayer(s), federal aid, revenue(s), spend(ing), spent, grant(s), accounts receivable, fund(s,ing,ed), cost(s), payment(s). *See also* Infrastructure (economics); Local government; Municipal government.

Local government. Local government. Local authorities. *Choose from:* local, county, district(s), special district(s), town(ship), village(s), municipal(ity, ities), cit(y,ies), metropolitan, community, regional *with:* government(s), council(s), mayor(s), community control, manager(s), management, elected official(s), commission(s), charter(s), authorit(y,ies), service(s), infrastructure, welfare, public facilit(y,ies), law(s), ordinance(s), regulation(s), planning, personnel, budget(s,ed,ing), bureaucrac(y,ies), jurisdiction(s). *Consider also:* mayor-council, city manager(s). *See also* Cities; Community services; Fire departments; Infrastructure (economics); Local officials and employees; Local finance; Local planning; Local politics; Mayors; Municipal government; Public meetings; School boards; Urban planning; Urban politics.

Local history. Local history. *Choose from:* town(s), township(s), count(y,ies), local, localit(y,ies), neighborhood(s), communit(y,ies), district(s), parish(es), region(s,al), municipal(ity,ities), cit(y,ies) *with:* histor(y,ies,ic,ical), historian(s), genealog(y,ical), chronolog(y,ies,ical), ancient, medieval, renaissance, 17th century, 18th century, 19th century, seventeenth century, eighteenth century, nineteenth century, archiv(al,e,es), antiquit(y,ies). *See also*

Family history; Folklore; Genealogy; Historic houses; Historic sites; History; Oral history; Social history.

Local news. Local news *Choose from:* local, small town, town(ship), village, community, hometown, regional, city, neighborhood *with:* news(paper,papers), stor(y,ies), media, press, journalism, weekl(y,ies), column(s,ist,ists), web page(s), webpage(s), web site(s), website(s), home page(s), homepage(s), television news, broadcast(s). *See also* Community newspapers; Localism; Newspapers.

Local officials and employees. Local official(s). Local employee(s). *Choose from:* county, city, municipal, local, town, village, *with:* personnel, employee(s), official(s), executive(s), bureaucra(cy,t,ts), civil serv(ice,ant, ants), administrator(s), workforce, worker(s), agent(s), public school teacher(s). *See also* Bureaucrats; Civil service; Elected officials; Government personnel; Local government; Politicians; Public officers; State government.

Local planning. Local planning. *Choose from:* town(s), township(s), count(y,ies), local, localit(y,ies), neighborhood(s), communit(y,ies), district(s), region(s,al), municipal(ity,ities), cit(y,ies) *with:* plan(s,ned,ning), zon(e,ed,ing), building permit(s), historic preservation, conservation, design(ed,ing), develop(ed,ing,ment), redevelop(ed,ing, ment), polic(y,ies), redevelopment, revitaliz(e,ed,ing,ation), decision making, studies, capital improvement, strategic planning, subdivision regulations, growth management. *See also* Community (geographic locality); Community development; Economic planning; Growth strategies; Health planning; Land subdivisions; Local government; Local politics; New towns; Planned communities; Real estate development; Social planning; State planning; Urban planning.

Local politics. Local politics. Machine politics. Localism. *Choose from:* local, town(ship), village, city, municipal, metropolitan, county, regional, district, grass roots *with:* election(s), coalition(s), alliance(s), politician(s), part(y,ies,isan), voter(s), electorate, lobb(y,ies,ying), or political *with:* campaign(s), candidate(s), issue(s), interest group(s), influence(s), process(es), activit(y,ies), power, strateg(y,ies), pressure(s), activis(t,ts), behavior, leader(s). *See also* Cities; Citizen participation; Civil society; Community involvement; Community power; Community support; Local elections; Local government; Mayors; Neighborhood associations; Political participation; Politics; Urban politics.

Local transit. Local transit. Jitney(s). Streetcar(s). Trolley car(s). Subway(s). Commuter train(s). *Choose from:* local *with:* mass transit, public transportation, bus(ses). *See also* Community services; Mass transit.

Localism. Localism. Provincial(ism,ity). Regionalism. *Choose from:* local, provincial, locale(s), county, district(s), special district(s), town(s,ship,ships), village(s), municipal(ity,ities), cit(y,ies), metropolitan, communit(y,ies), regional, parish(es), school district(s) *with:* attitude(s), public opinion, involvement, concern(s), constituenc(y,ies), action, life. *See also* Community (geographic locality); Cosmopolitan; Dioceses; Local news; Locally produced food; Regionalism; Social attitudes; Social identity.

Locality, geographic community. See *Community (geographic locality).*

Localization, perceptual. See *Perceptual localization.*

Localization, sound. See *Sound localization.*

Locally produced food. Locally produced food. Local produce. Home grown. *Choose from:* local(ly), region(al,ally) *with:* grow(n,er,ers), produce(d), harvest(ed,ing) *with:* vegetable(s), fruit(s), food(s), crop(s), potato(es), corn, tomato(es), apple(s), etc. *Consider also:* farm(ers) market(s), greenmarket(s). *See also* Food; Food supply; Gardens; Localism; Natural foods.

Location, address. See *Place of business; Place of residence.*

Lockouts. Lockout(s). Lock out(s). *Consider also:* work stoppage(s), withhold(ing) employment. *See also* Labor disputes; Strikes.

Locomotion, animal. See *Animal locomotion.*

Locus of control. Locus of control. Internal external locus of control. Locus of drinking problem. Sense of control. Perception of personal control. Internal control orientation. Sense of power. Sense of powerlessness. *Choose from:* internal, external, locus, sense, perception, expectanc(y,ies) *with:* control. *Consider also:* inner directed, other directed, tradition directed, learned helplessness, self efficacy. *See also* Attribution; Delay of gratification; External rewards; Extrinsic motivation; Field dependence; Inner directed; Internal rewards; Intrinsic motivation; Other directed; Personal independence; Personality traits; Self concept.

Logging industry. See *Lumber industry.*

Logic. Logic(al). *Consider also:* inference, syllogis(m,tic), boolean logic, symbolic logic, mathematical logic, compound

propositions, propositional calculus, truth function theory, predicate calculus, set theory, boolean algebra, reasoning, pure reason, induct(ion,ive), deduct(ion, ive), hypothetico deductive, rationale, ratiocinat(ion,ive). *See also* A priori; A posteriori; Abduction (logic); Analysis (Philosophy); Categories (philosophy); Classes (logic); Combinatory logic; Counterfactuals (logic); Deduction; Deontic logic; Dialectics; Induction; Inference; Judgment (logic); Logical thinking; Medieval logic; Paradoxes; Philosophy; Predicate (Logic); Rationality; Reasoning; Validity.

Logic, abduction. See *Abduction (logic)*

Logic, combinatory. See *Combinatory logic.*

Logic, deontic. See *Deontic logic.*

Logic, medieval. See *Medieval logic.*

Logical positivism. Logical positivis(m,t, ts). Logical empiricis(m,t,ts). Scientific empiricis(m,t,ts). *See also* Analysis (Philosophy); Empiricism; Philosophy.

Logical thinking. Logical thinking. *Choose from:* logical, rational, reasonable, formal operational, critical, syllogistic *with:* thinking, thought(s), reasoning, argument(s). *Consider also:* deduction, induction, ratiocination, propositional logic, rule learning, hypothesis testing, conditional reasoning, common sense, rationality, thinking skill(s). *See also* Critical thinking; Deduction; Induction; Inference; Logic.

Logistics. Logistic(s,al). *Choose from:* coordinat(e,ed,ing,ion), direct(ed,ing, ion), execut(ed,ing,ion), handl(e,ed,ing), manag(e,ed,ing,ement), oversee(ing), strateg(y,ies), supervis(e,ed,ion), procur(e,ed,ing,ement), maintenance, transport(ed,ing,ation) *with:* detail(s), operation(s), facilit(y,ies), personnel, suppl(y,ies), etc. *See also* Distribution (delivering); Management functions; Military planning; Planning; Program implementation.

Logocentrism. Logocentr(ism,ic,ist,istic). Phallogocentr(ism,ic,ist,istic). Phallocentr(ism,ic,ist,istic). Theologocentr(ism,ic,ism,istic). Phonocentr(ism,ic,ist,istic). Grammatolog(y,ic,ical). *Choose from:* authorit(y,ative,arian), dominan(t,ce), sovereign(ty), central(ity) *with:* word(s), text, signifier(s), sign(s), logos, writing, idea(s), system(s) of thought, ideolog(y,ies). *Consider also:* textuality, ontotheolog(y,ic,ical). *See also* Aporia; Deconstruction; Linguistics; Metaphysics; Postmodernism.

Logotherapy. See *Existential therapy.*

Lone parents. See *Single parent family.*

Loneliness. Lonel(y,iness). Aloneness. Homesick(ness). Social(ly) isolat(ed,ion). Lonesome. Left out. Disaffiliat(ed,ion). Socially withdrawn. Estrange(d,ment). Friendless. Forlorn. Outsider(s). *See also* Abandonment; Alienation; Anger; Depression (psychology); Emotional states; Social contact; Social isolation; Solitude.

Long distance caregivers. Long distance caregiver(s). *Choose from:* long distance, afar, remote, out-of-state, distan(t,ce), geographically separated, geographic(ally) distan(t,ce) *with:* caretak(er,ers,ing), caregiv(er,ers,ing), care provider(s), eldercare. *See also* Caregivers; Proximity of family; Supportive services.

Long distance marriages. Long distance marriage(s). *Choose from:* long distance, commut(er,ing), geographically separated, separate residence(s), separate home(s), geographic(ally) distan(t,ce) *with:* marriage(s), couple(s), wedlock, marital, relationship(s). *See also* Alternative family forms; Marital relationship; Marital satisfaction; Marriage; Proximity of family.

Long distance telephone companies. Long distance telephone compan(y,ies). *Choose from:* long distance, global phone *with:* compan(y,ies), service(s), provider(s), carrier(s), network(s). Telco(s). *Consider also:* high-speed data service(s), wireless compan(y,ies), Internet service(s), Wide area telephone service(s), WATS, Internet services, AT&T, AT and T, American Telephone and Telegraph, MCI, Sprint, Internet backbone, '800' service(s), baby bell(s), Regional Bell Operating Companies, RBOC(s), Ameritech, Network Long Distance, British Telecommunications PLC, BT PLC, US One Communications, Total-Tel USA Communications, Working Assets Long Distance, LDDS Communications, IDB Communications Group, WorldCom, MFS Communications, SBC Communications, Bell Atlantic, long distance common carrier(s), long distance call(s,ing), tolls call(s,ing), Wide Area Telephone Service(s), WATS, Dime Line. WorldCom. 10321. America Online. *See also* Internet service providers; Telecommunications; Telephone.

Long range planning. Long range plan(s,ning). Long range vision(s). Master plan(s). *Choose from:* long range, long term, overall, future *with:* plan(s,ning), chart(s,ing) course(s), goal(s), objective(s), forecast(s,ed,ing), vision(s). *See also* Corporate mission; Life plans; Management planning; Organizational objectives; Planning; Short term planning; Strategic management; Strategic planning.

Long term care. Long term care. *Choose from:* long term, long stay, continuing, life support, chronic(ally) *with:* care,

treatment(s), patient(s), medical followup, resident(s). *See also* Care of the sick; Chronic disease; Medical care.

Long term memory. Long term memor(y,ies). *Choose from:* long term, remote, early, earliest, autobiograph(y, ical), past, childhood event(s), reactivat(e,ed,ing) *with:* memor(y,ies), retention, recall, recollection(s), recognition, storage. *Consider also:* reminiscence(s). *See also* Memory.

Long term planning. See *Long range planning.*

Longevity. Longevity. Life span. Lifespan. Duration of life. Lifetime. *Choose from:* long(er), exten(d,ded,ding,sion), length *with:* life, liv(e,ed,es,ing), old age. *Consider also:* survival pattern(s), mortality rate(s), life table(s), life expectancy, centenarian(s). *See also* Aging; Life expectancy; Mortality rates; Survival.

Longitudinal studies. Longitudinal stud(y,ies). *Choose from:* followup, semilongitudinal, longitudinal, panel, long term *with:* stud(y,ies), test(s), research, data, assessment(s), method(s), analy(sis,ses), survey(s), comparison(s), observation(s), factor(s), model(s), evaluation(s), experiment(s), investigation(s), case stud(y,ies). *Consider also:* case histor(y,ies), stud(y,ies) over time, time series, followups, sequential stud(y,ies), time structured data, life span research, aging stud(y,ies), measurement over time, developmental histor(y,ies), retrospective stud(y,ies). *Consider also: specific time periods, for example:* five month study, five year study or 1950 to 1980, etc. *See also* Attrition; Case studies; Cohort analysis; Incidence; Panel studies; Research methods; Sampling; Trends.

Longshoremen. Longshore(men,man). Dock worker(s). Docker(s). Stevedore(s). Waterside worker(s). *See also* Blue collar workers; Shipping industry; Transport workers.

Looting. See *Pillage.*

Looting of archaeological sites. See *Archaeological thefts.*

Lords, drug. See *Drug lords.*

Lore. See *Folklore.*

Lore, animal. See *Animal lore*

Lore, plant. See *Plant folklore.*

Lore, snake. See *Snake lore.*

Loss (psychology). Loss(es). *Choose from:* loss(es), lost, parted, betrayal, farewell(s) *with:* emotional, spiritual, psychological, sad(ness), traumatic, loved one(s), close friend(s), family member(s), valued possession(s), death(s). *Consider also:* grieving, grief, traumatic life event(s). *See also*

Bereavement; Death; Death counseling; Death rituals; Grief; Laments; Loss adjustment; Sadness.

Loss, functional hearing. See *Functional hearing loss.*

Loss, hair. See *Alopecia.*

Loss, hearing. See *Deafness.*

Loss, sensory. See *Sensory loss.*

Loss, weight. See *Weight loss.*

Loss adjustment. Loss adjustment. Mourn(ed,ing). *Choose from:* loss(es), bereavement, grief, widowhood, sorrow, sadness *with:* adjust(ed,ing,ment), cope(d), coping, impact(s), resolution, adapt(ed,ing,ation), accept(ed,ing,ance), accomodat(e,ed,ing,ion), reconcil(e,ed, ing,iation). *Consider also:* abandonment reaction(s). *See also* Adjustment (to environment); Bereavement; Death counseling; Emotional adjustment; Loss (psychology); Mourning; Widowhood.

Loss leader. Loss leader(s). Merchandising leader(s). *Consider also:* price lining. *See also* Marketing; Marketing strategies.

Loss of function. Loss of function(s). Incapacitat(e,ed,ion). Impair(ed,ment, ments). Disab(ility,ilities,led). Physiological aging. Degenerat(e,ed,ion). *Choose from:* loss, los(e,ing), deteriorat(e,ed,ing), declin(e,ed,ing), weaken(ing), limit(ed,ing) *with:* function(s,ing), abilit(y,ies), mobility, sensory, hearing, vision, sight. *See also* Aging; Deterioration; Disability; Incapacitation; Physiological aging.

Loss of sense of smell. See *Anosmia.*

Loss of sight. See *Blindness.*

Loss of speech. See *Aphasia: Speech disorders; Speech disturbances.*

Loss of will. Loss of will. Lack of will. Apath(y,etic). Platonization. Lack of interest. Abuli(a,c). Abouli(a,c). Hypobuli(a,c). Hypobouli(a,c). *See also* Apathy; Passiveness.

Lost books. See *Lost literature.*

Lost literature. Lost literature. Lost book(s). *Choose from:* lost, forgotten, buried, hidden *with:* literature, book(s), novel(s), novella(s), fiction, manuscript(s). *See also* Archives; Bibliography; Censorship; Literature.

Lost motion pictures. Lost motion picture(s). Lost movie(s). *Choose from:* lost, undiscovered, found, disappeared, discover(ed,y,ies), recover(y,ed), rediscover(ed,y,ies), missing, hidden, cache, stolen, forgotten, unreleased *with:* motion picture(s), movie(s), footage, film(s). *See also* Films; Motion pictures.

Lost works of art. Lost work(s) of art. *Choose from:* lost, undiscovered, found, disappeared, discover(y,ies,ed), recover(y,ed), rediscovered, missing, hidden, cache, stolen, theft(s), forgotten, excavat(e,ed,ing), buried, stored away, stolen, theft(s) *with:* painting(s), masterpiece(s), art, artwork(s), sculpture(s), statuette(s), figurine(s), Da Vinci(s), Rembrandt(s), Picasso(s), Matisse(s), Van Gogh(s), Michelangelo(s). *Consider also:* Art Loss Register. *See also* Art thefts; Arts; Lost works of music.

Lost works of music. Lost work(s) of music. *Choose from:* lost, undiscovered, found, disappeared, discover(y,ies,ed), recover(y,ed), rediscovered, missing, hidden, cache, stolen, theft(s), forgotten, excavat(e,ed,ing), buried, stored away, stolen, theft(s) *with:* music(al), chamber work(s), song(s), dance(s), opera(s), ballad(s), hymn(s), symphon(y,ies), libretto(s), lyric(s). *See also* Lost works of art; Music.

Lotteries. Lotter(y,ies). Lotto. Sweep(s, stakes). Pari-mutuel(s). Raffle(s). Drawing(s). Buy(ing) chance(s). Bingo. *Consider also:* gambl(e,ed,er,ers,ing), giveaway(s), numbers game(s). Bet(ting). *See also* Gambling; Online gambling; Pathological gambling.

Loudness. Loud(ness,ly). Nois(e,es,y,iness). Deafening. Sonorous. Forte. Big voiced. Full throated. Tumultuous(ness). Raucous(ness). *Choose from:* sound(s), noise(s), vocal, voice(s), music, acoustic(s,al), tone(s), monaural, stereo(s) *with:* ampli(tude,fication), intensity, level(s), volume(s). *See also* Auditory threshold; Loudness perception; Noise (sounds); Noise levels (work areas); Perceptual stimulation.

Loudness perception. Loudness perception. *Choose from:* loud(ness), nois(e,es,y, iness), sound volume, sound intensity, auditory intensity, loudness variation(s) *with:* perception, perceiv(e,ed,ing), discriminat(e,ed,ing,ion), coding, distinguish(ed,ing), judgment(s), estimat(e,ed,ing,ion), threshold(s), quantif(y,ied,ication), annoyance response, discomfort level(s), aversion level(s), audib(le,ility). *See also* Auditory perception: Auditory perceptual disorders; Auditory threshold; Loudness.

Love. Lov(e,ed,ing). Eros. Agape. Affection. Attachment. Unselfish concern. Roman(ce,tic). Amorous(ness). Sentiment. Tenderness. Ador(e,ing, ation). Lover(s). Fond(ness). Cherish(ed, ing). Devot(ed,ion). Intima(cy,te). Infatuat(ed,ion). Car(e,ed,ing). *Consider also:* self love, narcissism, object love, lik(e,ed,ing). *See also* Affection; Attachment behavior; Courtly love; Emotions; Family relations; Forms of affection; Happiness; Interpersonal attraction; Interpersonal relations;

Intimacy; Love letters; Love poetry; Marital relationship; Maternal love; Narcissism; Needs; Nurturance; Romantic love; Sexual satisfaction.

Love, courtly. See *Courtly love*

Love, free. See *Sexual permissiveness.*

Love, maternal. See *Maternal love.*

Love, obsessive. See *Obsessive love.*

Love, romantic. See *Romantic love.*

Love, self. See *Egotism; Narcissism.*

Love letters. Love letter(s). *Choose from:* love(r,rs), passionate, romance, romantic, courtship, sentiment(al), flirtatious *with:* letter(s), e-mail, correspondence, note(s). *Consider also:* valentine(s), romantic verse(s). *See also* Human courtship; Letters (correspondence); Love; Love poetry; Love stories; Romantic love.

Love philters. See *Aphrodisiacs.*

Love poetry. Love poe(try,m,ms). *Choose from:* love(s,er,ers), sentiment(al), erotic, amor(ous), amour, valentine(s), homoerotic, passionate, romance, romantic, courtship, flirtatious *with:* poe(try,m,ms), lyric(al,s), sonnet(s), ode(s). *See also* Courtly love; Epithalamia; Human courtship; Laudatory poetry; Love; Love letters; Love songs; Love stories; Lyric poetry; Minnesinger; Romantic love.

Love potions. See *Aphrodisiacs.*

Love songs. Love song(s). Canzo(s). Canso(s). Chanso(s). *Choose from:* love(s,r,rs), sentiment(al), erotic, amor(ous), amour, valentine(s), homoerotic, passionate, romance, romantic, courtship, flirtatious *with:* song(s), chanson(s), ballad(s), lyric(s), ditt(y,ies), sing(ing), music(al,als). *See also* Erotic songs; Love poetry; Love stories; Romantic love.

Love stories. Love stor(y,ies). *Choose from:* love(s,er,ers), romantic, romance, sexy, passionate, sentiment(al), erotic, amor(ous), intima(cy,te) *with:* novel(ette,ettes,s) fiction, stor(y,ies). *Consider also:* historical romance(s), romantic melodrama(s), tearjerker(s). *See also* Fiction; Love letters; Love songs; Love poetry; Novels; Romantic love.

Lovemaking. See *Affection; Forms of affection; Human courtship; Sexual behavior; Sexual foreplay; Sexual intercourse.*

Lovers. See *Couples; Gay couples; Sexual partners.*

Loving kindness. See *Compassion.*

Low birth weight infants. See *Infant small for gestational age; Premature infants.*

Low birth weight infants, very. See *Very low birth weight infants.*

Low income. Low(er,est) income. Reduced income. Reduced means. Low(er,est) level of earnings. Low SES. *Choose from:* low(er,est) socioeconomic *with:* strata, status, level(s), background. Poor. Near poor. Poverty level. Welfare. Indigen(t,cy,ce). Economically disadvantaged. Lower class. Low(er,est) salar(y,ies). Poorly paid. Meager income(s). Minimum wage(s). Underpaid. Subsistence level earning(s). Subsistence wage(s). *See also* Deprivation; Disadvantaged; Income inequality; Income maintenance programs; Lower class; Minority groups; Peasants; Poverty; Slums; Socioeconomic status; Underemployment; Welfare recipients; Working class.

Low income areas. See *Poverty areas.*

Low income countries. See *Least developed countries; Less developed countries.*

Low income housing. See *Affordable housing; Public housing.*

Lower class. Lower class(es). Low(er,est) socioeconomic class. Impoverished. Inner city neighborhood(s). Rural family life style. Poor(est). Low(er,est) socioeconomic status. Low(er,est) SES. Low income. Working class. Poverty. Low status. Disadvantaged. Underclass. Peasant(s). Working man. Low(er,est) social status. Low(er,est) status. Blue collar worker(s). Plebe(s,ian). Common people. Common man. Proletar(iat,ian). Untouchable(s). Manual labor(er,ers). Wage earner(s). *See also* Blue collar workers; Disadvantaged; Low income; Lower class attitudes; Peasants; Proletariat; Socioeconomic status; Underclass; Underprivileged; Welfare recipients; Working class.

Lower class attitudes. Lower class attitude(s). *Choose from:* lower class(es), underclass(es), working poor, working class(es), low income famil(y,ies) *with:* attitude(s), goal(s), orientation(s), expectation(s), interest(s), reaction(s), belief(s), opinion(s), norm(s), mindset, satisfaction(s), concept(s) held, cultural values. *See also* Attitudes; Class consciousness; Class identity; Class politics; Lower class; Socioeconomic status; Upper class attitudes; Working class.

Lower income level. See *Poverty.*

Loyalty. Loyal(ty,ties,ness). Commitment(s). Emotional(ly) commit(ted,ment). Allegiance. Emotional attachment. Affiliation. Psychological identification. Faithful(ness). Fidelity. Fealty. Patriot(ic,ism). Steadfast. Unchanging. Constancy. Unchanging. Abiding. Resolute.

Solidarity. Dedication. Devotion. *See also* Brand loyalty; Commitment (emotional); Faithfulness; Loyalty oaths; Patriotism; Personnel loyalty; Personality traits.

Loyalty, brand. See *Brand loyalty.*

Loyalty, personnel. See *Personnel loyalty.*

Loyalty, political. See *Loyalty; Loyalty oaths; Patriotism.*

Loyalty cards. Loyalty card(s). Affinity card(s). *See also* Brand loyalty; Consumer awareness; Consumer behavior; Market research; Marketing; Retailing.

Loyalty oaths. Loyalty oath(s). Daily pledge. Pledge of allegiance. Secrecy pledge(s). *See also* Flags; Loyalty; Oaths; Patriotism.

LSD. See *Hallucinogens.*

Luck. See *Chance.*

Luggage. Luggage. Baggage. Suitcase(s). Trunk(s). Portmanteau(s,x). Duffel bag(s). Valise(s). Case(s). Bag(s). Carry-on(s). Garment bag(s). Flight bag(s). Satchel(s). Knapsack(s). Backpack(s). Briefcase(s). Attache case(s). *See also* Bags; Containers; Travel.

Lullabies. Lullab(y,ies). Berceuse(s). Weigenlied(er). Schlummerlied(er). Ninna nanna(s). Cancion(es) de cuna. Cradle song(s). *See also* Children's songs; Folk songs; Music; Nursery rhymes.

Lumber industry. Lumber industry. Logging industry. Wood industry. *Choose from:* logging, lumber, hardwood, timber, plywood, fiberboard, board, wood, hardboard, softwood *with:* industry, plant(s), mill(s), compan(y,ies), *Consider also:* sawmill(s). *See also* Deforestation; Forest conservation; Industry; Lumbermen; Timber; Tree farms; Trees.

Lumbermen. Lumberm(en,an). Lumber worker(s). Lumberjack(s). Logger(s). Woodcutter(s). *Choose from:* logging, forestry, lumber *with:* worker(s). *Consider also:* woodworker(s), Paul Bunyan, woodsm(en,an). *See also* Lumber industry; Workers.

Lunar cycle. Lunar cycle(s). *Choose from:* lunar, moon *with:* cycle(s), phase(s). *Consider also:* lunar effect(s), lunar activity, new moon, full moon, half moon. *See also* Biological rhythms; Environmental effects.

Lung disease, black. See *Black lung disease.*

Lung disorders. Lung disorder(s). Broncho-pneumonia. Pneumonia. Bronchopneumopath(y,ies). Asbestosis. Cystic fibrosis. *Choose from:* lung, pulmonary, bronchopulmonary *with:* disease(s), disorder(s), infection(s), lesion(s), inflammation(s), complication(s), pathology, hemorrhage(s), fibrosis, abscess(es), neoplasm(s). *Consider also:* respiratory disorder(s). *See also* Lungs; Respiratory system.

Lungs. Lung(s). *Consider also:* bronchi, pulmonary alveoli, pulmonary, bronchopulmonary, pulmo-, pneumo-. *See also* Lung disorders; Respiratory system.

Luorawetlan languages. Luorawetlan language(s). Chukchi. Kamchadal. Koryak. *See also* Central Asia; Language; Languages (as subjects).

Luxuries. Luxur(y,ies,ious,iousness). Excess(es). Extravagan(t,ce,ces). Nonessential(s). Status symbol(s). *Consider also:* conspicuous consumption. *See also* Amenities; Consumer goods; Consumption (economic); Expenditures; Living standards; Production consumption relationship; Wealth.

Lying. See *Deception.*

Lying under oath. See *Perjury.*

Lynching. Lynch(ed,ing,ings). *Choose from:* mob, collective, vigilante(s) *with:* hanging(s), murder(s), execution(s). *See also* Anti-government radicals; Assault (personal); Hate crimes; Homicide; Vigilantes; White supremacy movements.

Lyric drama. See *Opera.*

Lyric poetry. Lyric(al) poe(try,m,ms). Poetic lyricism. Melic poe(try,m,ms). Lyrical verse(s). *Consider also:* song poe(m,ms,try), psalm(s), lyrical hymn(s), patristic song(s), ode(s) Mozarabic lyric(s). *See also* Dramatic poetry; Epithalamia; Haiku; Love poetry; Lyrical ballads; Poetry.

Lyrical ballads. Lyrical ballad(s). Ballade(s) lyrique(s). Lyrical song(s). *Consider also:* legendary ballad(s), minstrel ballad(s), lyrical piece(s), dramatic lied(er), dramatic ballad(s), dramatic song(s). *See also* Ballads; Folk songs; Lyrical poetry.

Lyrics. Lyric(s). Song text(s). Words of song(s). Wordbook(s). *Consider also:* verse(s), stanza(s). *See also* Choral music; Librettos; Songs.

Lysergic acid diethylamide. See *Hallucinogens.*

M

M'Naghten rule. See *Insanity defense.*

Macaroni products. See *Pasta.*

Macaronic literature. Macaronic literature Macaronic song(s). Macaronic verse(s). Nudelverse. Maccaronischen Poesie. Maccaronische Gedichte. Maccheronico. *Consider also:* Carmen maccaronicum, Maccaroneae, Polemo-Middinia. *See also* Centos; Humorous poetry; Nonsense literature.

Machiavellianism. Machiavellian(ism). Manipulat(ive,iveness,ing,ion). Hidden agenda(s). *Consider also:* power play(s), power struggle(s), use power, lying, lie(s,d), deception, duplicity, deceit(ful), unethical, cunning, bad faith, engineering consent, unscrupulous(ness), calculating. *See also* Deception; Duplicity; Exploitation; Flattery; Hypocrisy; Influence; Manipulation; Personality traits; Social parasites; Value orientations.

Machine politics. See *Political bosses.*

Machine tool industry. Machine tool industry. Machine tool compan(y,ies). Tool maker(s). *Consider also:* metalworking industry, woodworking industry, tool and die industry, machine shop(s), machinery industry. *See also* Industry; Machinery; Metal industry; Tools.

Machinery. Machine(s,ry). Mechan(ized, ical) equipment. Engine(s). Hardware. *Consider also:* appliance(s), implement(s), tool(s), welder(s), press(es), lathe(s), technology, technics, automobile(s), tractor(s), vehicle(s). *See also* Agricultural mechanization; Automation; Hardware; Industry; Maintenance; Machine tool industry; Material culture; Tools.

Machinery, agricultural. See *Agricultural mechanization.*

Machines, calculating. See *Calculating machines.*

Machines, flying. See *Flying machines.*

Machines, ground effect. See *Ground effect machines.*

Machines, political. See *Political bosses.*

Machismo. Machismo. Cult of virility. Masculine aggressive(ness). Macho. *Consider also:* Rambo, intransigen(t,ce), indifferen(t,ce). *See also* Aggressiveness (trait); Androcentrism; Male chauvinism; Personality traits.

Macro-Chibchan languages. Macro-Chibchan languages. Chibcha. Paez. San Blas. *See also* Central America; Central American native cultural groups; Language; Languages (as subjects); Pre-Columbian empires; South America; South American native cultural groups.

Macro-Khoisan languages. Macro-Khoisan languages. Hatsa. Sandawe. Khoisan: Bushman, Hottentot. *See also* African cultural groups; African empires; Language; Languages (as subjects); Sub-Saharan Africa.

Macro-Otomanguean languages. Macro-Otomanguean languages. Chorotega. Mixtec. Otomi. Trique. Zapotec. *See also* Central America; Central American native cultural groups; Language; Languages (as subjects); North America; North American native cultural groups.

Macroeconomics. See *Aggregate economics.*

Madness. See *Deviance; Mental illness; Psychoses.*

Magazine advertising. Magazine advertis(ement,ements,ing). *Choose from:* magazine(s), periodical(s), serial(s), journal(s), mass publication(s), print media *with:* ad(s), advertis(ement, ements,ing), promotion(s,al,als). *See also* Advertising; Electronic journals; Fanzines; Periodicals.

Magazine illustration. Magazine illustration(s). Illustrat(e,ed,ing) magazine(s). *Choose from:* magazine(s), periodical(s), journal(s), serial(s) *with:* illustrat(ed,ion,ions), picture(s), pictorial, photograph(s,y), engrav(ed, ing,ings), drawing(s), painting(s), water color(s) *Consider also:* pictorial journalism. *See also* Captions; Cartoons; Illustrated books; Periodicals.

Magazines. See *Periodicals.*

Magic. Magic(al). Amulet(s). Astral projection. Astral travel. Astrolog(y,ical). Apparition(s). Arungquilta. Black magic. Cabal(a,ism). Chakra(s). Cosmolog(y, ical). Clairvoyan(t,ce). Deathbed vision(s). Demon(ic,ology). Demon possession. Devil(s). Divination. Divining rod(s). Dows(e,ed,ing). Duende(s). Dybbuk(s). Earth ray(s). Extrasensible. Exorcis(m,t). Fortune telling. Firewalking. Flying saucer(s). Ghost(s). Hobgoblin(s). Haunted house(s). Haunting. Horoscop(e,y). Human aura. Hex(es). Incantation(s). Jinx(es). Kirlian photography. Levitation(s). Medium(s). Mental healing. Mystic(al,ism,s). Near death experience(s). Necroman(cy,tic,cer,cers). Out of body. Obe. Obeah. Occult(ism). Orgone energy. PSI. Parapsycholog(y, ical). Paranormal. Pseudoscientific. Parapsychosomatics. Phantom(s). Possession trance(s). Precognition. Psychic(al,s). Psychic healing. Psychokine(sis,tic). Psychophotography. Poltergeist(s). Radiesthesia. Reincarnat(ed,ion). Seance(s). Shamanis(m,tic). Spell(s). Spirit possession. Spiritualis(m,tic). Supernatural(ism). Survival after death. Telekine(sis,tic). Telepath(y,ic). Thaumaturgy. Voodoo(ism). Witchcraft. *Consider also:* muti. *See also* Alchemy; Beliefs; Conjuring; Evil eye; Fetishism; Spiritual healing; Occultism; Shamanism; Supernatural; Superstitions; Talisman; Voodooism; Witchcraft.

Magic realism (art). Magic(al) realism. *Consider also:* Neue Sachlichkeit, sharp-focus detail painting(s), Rene Magritte. *See also* Artistic styles; Arts; Genres (art); Figurative art; Magic realism (Literature); Naturalism; Realism; Realism in art; Socialist Realism in Art; Surrealism.

Magic realism (Literature). Magic realism. *Consider also:* Alejo Carpentier, Jorge Amado, Jorge Luis Borges, Julio Cortazar, Gabriel Garcia Marquez, Isabel Allende, Gunter Grass, John Fowles. *See also* Magic realism (art); Modern literature.

Magical thinking. Magical thinking. Incantation(s). Superstit(ious,iousness, ion,ions). *Choose from:* magic(al), archaic, prelogical, primitive, mystic(al), supernatural, extrasensible, animistic, superstitious, pseudoscientific, parapsychological *with:* thinking, thought, belief(s), explanation(s), consciousness, convictions, orientation. *See also* Fantasies (thought disturbances); Imagination; Superstitions; Thinking; Thought disturbances.

Magistrates. See *Judges.*

Magnanimity. Magnanimit(y,ies). Magnanimous(ly,ness). Generous(ly,ity). Benevolen(t,ce). Chivalr(y,ous). Greathearted(ness). *Consider also:* altruis(m,tic), unselfish(ness), highminded(ness), nobility of feeling. *See also* Altruism; Generosity; Philanthropy; Prosocial behavior; Unselfishness.

Magnetism, animal hypnotic. See *Hypnosis.*

Magnetism, animal navigational. See *Animal navigation.*

Magnetism, personal. See *Charisma.*

Maids. See *Domestic Service.*

Maids, old. See *Unmarried women.*

Mail. See *Letter carriers; Postal service.*

Mail, electronic. See *Electronic mail.*

Mail, junk. See *Direct mail advertising.*

Mail advertising, direct. See *Direct mail advertising.*

Mailbombs. Mail bomb(s,ing,ings). Letter bomb(s,ing,ings). Postal bomb(s,ing, ings). *Consider also:* suspicious package(s). Unabomber. *See also* Bomb threats; Bombings; Bombs; Terrorism.

Mailroom. Mail room(s). Mailroom(s). *Choose from:* mail(ing), post(al), shipping, receiving *with:* room(s), office(s), outlet(s). *Consider also:* mailbox(es). *See also* Letter carriers; Postal service.

Mainstreaming. Mainstream(ed,ing). Deinstitutionalization of disabled. Regular class placement. Normalization of handicapped. Least restrictive environment. Pl 94-142. Public law 94 142. Education of all handicapped children act. *Choose from:* handicap(s, ped), disabled, disabilit(y,ies), retard(ed, ation), impair(ed,ment,ments), special needs, exceptional child(ren) *with:* regular class(es), integrat(e,ed,ing,ion), assimilat(e,ed,ing,ion), least restrictive educational environment. *See also* Academically gifted; Architectural accessibility; Course load; Disability; Education of mentally retarded; Educational placement; Equal education; Heterogeneity; Inclusive education; Individualized instruction; Multicultural education; Special education.

Maintenance. Maintenance. Maintain(ed, ing). Repair(s). Care. Upkeep. Preserv(e,ed,ing,ation). Control depreciation. *Consider also:* management. *See also* Buildings; Customer services; Equipment; Facilities; Machinery; Obsolescence; Preservation; Preventive maintenance; Service contracts.

Maintenance, boundary. See *Boundary maintenance.*

Maintenance, cultural. See *Cultural maintenance.*

Maintenance, language. See *Language maintenance.*

Maintenance, methadone. See *Methadone maintenance.*

Maintenance, preventive. See *Preventive maintenance.*

Maintenance programs, income. See *Income maintenance programs.*

Major depression. Major depression(s). *Choose from:* depress(ed,ion,ions), melancholia *with:* major, psycho(ses, sis,tic), agitat(ed,ion), severe(ly), self destructive, gross impairment(s). Dysphoria. Unipolar depression. Melancholia. *See also* Affective

disorders; Anhedonia; Depression (psychology); Dysthymic disorder; Dysphoria; Manic disorder; Neurotic depressive reaction; Postpartum depression; Reactive depression.

Majorities (political). Majorit(y,ies). Party in power. Majority party. Majority leader(s). Majority rule. *See also* Democracy; Dominant ideologies; Majority groups; Political elites; Political parties; Political power; Politics; Preference voting; Third parties (United States politics); Voters.

Majority, age of. See *Age of majority.*

Majority, moral. See *Religious fundamentalism; Right wing politics; Social conformity; Traditionalism.*

Majority groups. Majority group(s). Ethnic majorit(y,ies). Dominant group(s). Dominant culture(s). *Choose from:* White Anglo-Saxon Protestants, WASPs, English-speaking Canadians, White South Africans, etc. *See also* Center and periphery; Dominance; Dominant ideologies; Ethnocentrism; Intergroup relations; Majorities (political); Minority groups; Race relations; Social structure.

Makers, law. See *Legislative bodies; Legislators.*

Making, jewelry. See *Jewelry making.*

Making, policy. See *Policy making.*

Making decisions. See *Decision making.*

Making foreign policy. See *Foreign policy making.*

Maladaptation. Maladapt(ed,ation). Maladjust(ed,ment). Poor(ly) adapt(ed, ation). Inadequate(ly) adapt(ed,ation). Adult situational disorder(s). Transient situational disorder(s). *Consider also:* crisis reaction, social inadequacy. *See also* Adjustment (to environment); Adjustment disorders; Dyssocial reaction; Maladjustment.

Maladaptation, social. See *Adjustment disorders; Dyssocial reaction; Maladaptation; Maladjustment.*

Maladjustment. Maladjust(ed,ment). Adjustment problem(s). Mismatch(ed). Unsuit(ed,able). Ill-suited. Poor(ly) adjust(ed,ment). Unadjusted. *Consider also:* maladapt(ed,ation), nonconform(ity,ing). *See also* Adjustment (to environment); Adjustment disorders; Maladaptation.

Malayo-Polynesian languages. Malayo-Polynesian languages. Austronesian languages. Indonesian (Malayan): Malagasy, Malay (Bahasa Indonesia), Javanese, Kawi, Sundanese, Balinese, Dyak, Tagalog, Ilocano, Bisaya, Igorot. Melanesian: Fijian, Malo, Marovo, Mono. Micronesian: Marianas, Caroline, Marshallese, Gilbertese. Polynesian: Maori, Tongan, Samoan, Rarotongan,

Hawaiian, Tahitian, Marquesan, Rapa Nui. *See also* Indonesian cultural groups; Language; Languages (as subjects); Oceania; Oceanic cultural groups; Philippine Islands cultural groups.

Male animals. See *Males (animal).*

Male castration. Male castration. *Choose from:* castrat(e,ed,ing,ion), geld(ed,ing), neuter(ed,ing), gonadectom(y,ies,ized), orchidectom(y,ies,ized), autocastrat(e,ed, ing,ion), surgical removal of testis, orchiectom(y,ies,ized), orchotom(y,ies, ized), desex(ed,ing) *with:* male(s). *Consider also:* capon(s), gelding(s), steer(s), eunuch(s,ism), emasculat(ed, ing,ion). *See also* Sterilization (sex); Vasectomy.

Male chauvinism. Male chauvin(ist,ists, ism). Sex discrimination. Sex(ism,ist, ists). Sex bias(es,ed). Discriminat(e,ed, ing,ion) against women. Treat(ed,ing) as sex object(s). Misogyn(y,ist,ists). Patriarch(y,ies,al). Phallocentri(c,sm). *Choose from:* female(s), women, woman, sex(ual), gender, girl(s), feminin(e,ity) *with:* inequality, inequit(y,ies), discrepanc(y,ies), unfair, discriminat(e,ed,ing,ion), prejudic(e,ed, ial), bias(ed,es), stereotype(s), stratification, segregat(ed,ion), chauvinism, intolerance, harassment. *Consider also:* phallic criticism, phallagocentrism, androcentris(m,t,ts). *See also* Androcentrism; Harems; Images of women; Labor market segmentation; Machismo; Men's movement; Misogyny; Patriarchy; Sex discrimination; Sexism; Sexual harassment; Sexual inequality; Sexual oppression.

Male criminals. See *Male offenders.*

Male dancers. Male dancer(s). Men dancer(s). Danseur(s). *See also* Ballet dancers; Dance; Dancers.

Male dominated occupations. See *Male intensive occupations.*

Male dominated occupations, women in. See *Nontraditional careers.*

Male female relations. See *Heterosexual relationships.*

Male genital disorders. Male genital disorder(s). *Choose from:* male(s), men, man *with:* herpes genitalis, urethritis, sterility. *Choose from:* male genital, male genito-urinary, male urogenital, penile, penis, prostat(e,ic), scrotal, scrotum, testis, testes, testicular, vas deferens, epididymis, intrascrotal *with:* disorder(s), infect(ed,ion,ions,ious), acute, neoplasm(s), induration(s), inflam(ed,mation,mations,matory), disease(d,s), calculi, wound(ed,s), swelling(s), swollen, defect(s), affect(ed,ion,ions), syndrome(s), tuberculosis, hematocele(s), hydrocele(s), varicocele(s). *Consider* *also:* epididymitis, balanitis, kraurosis penis, phimosis, paraphimosis, priapism, prostatic hypertrophy, prostatitis, impoten(t,ce), spermatic cord torsion, spermatocele, infertility, oligospermia, orchitis, Klinefelter(s) syndrome, testicular feminization syndrome, cryptorch(ism,ids), retarded ejaculation, erectile disorder(s), eunuch(s,oid). *See also* Infertility; Male genitalia; Sexually transmitted diseases.

Male genitalia. Male genital(s,ia). *Choose from:* male(s) *with:* genital, reproductive, sex(ual) *with:* organ(s), tract(s), system(s), gland(s). *Consider also:* bulbourethral gland(s), ejaculatory duct(s), penis(es), prostate(s), scrotum(s), seminal vesicle(s), spermatic cord(s), test(is,es), epididymis, leydig cell(s), rete testis, seminiferous tubule(s), sertoli cell(s), vas deferens. *See also* Male genital disorders; Penis.

Male homosexuality. Male homosexual(s,ity). *Choose from:* homosexual(ly,s,ity), gay, homoerotic, bisexual(ly,s,ity), sodomy, fellatio *with:* male(s), men, man, bachelor(s), father(s), son(s), relationship(s), couple(s), rape(s,d), prostitute(s). *Consider also:* sexual minorit(y,ies), sexual variation(s), asexual preference(s). *See also* Attitudes toward homosexuality; Bisexuality; Gay couples; Homosexuality; Homosexual liberation movement; Sexual preferences.

Male intensive occupations. Male intensive occupation(s). *Choose from:* male dominated, male intensive, masculine *with:* career(s), occupation(s), profession(s), business(es), industr(y, ies), work group(s), field(s), organization(s). *Consider also:* manufacturing, lumbering, mining, construction, high technology, scientist(s), accountant(s), management, firemen, policemen, hardhat(s). *See also* Comparable worth; Female intensive occupations; Labor market segmentation; Nontraditional careers; Sex discrimination; Sexual division of labor.

Male menopause. See *Climacteric.*

Male nurses. Male nurse(s). *Choose from:* male(s), men, masculine(e,ization) *with:* nurse(s), nursing, midwifery, LPNs, practical nurse(s), RNs, registered nurses. *See also* Female intensive occupations; Nontraditional careers.

Male offenders. Male offender(s). Male criminal(s). *Choose from:* criminal(s, ity), offender(s), felon(s), delinquent(s), criminal behavior, defendant(s), molester(s), homicidal, arsonist(s), murderer(s), gangster(s), smuggler(s), perpetrator(s), embezzler(s), burglar(s), thie(f,ves), criminally insane, rapist(s), penitentiary inmate(s), probation(er,ers), arrest(s,ed), convict(s,ed,ing,ion,ions),

incarcerat(ed,ion) *with:* male(s), men, man, boy(s). *See also* Males (human); Offenders; Sex offenders.

Male role. See *Gender identity; Sex roles.*

Malediction. See *Cursing.*

Males (animal). Male(s). Sire(s,d). Stallion(s). Buck(s). Bull(s). Boar(s). Ram(s). Cock(s). Rooster(s). Gander(s). Stag(s). Tomcat(s). Drake(s). Billy goat(s). *See also* Animals.

Males (human). Male(s). Men. Man(hood,ly,liness,like). Husband(s). Beau(x,s). Mister. Bachelor(s). Boy(s). Son(s). Father(s). Nephew(s). Grandfather(s). Grandson(s). Uncle(s). Brother(s). Widower(s). Masculin(e,ity, ize,ized,ization). Patern(al,ity). Patriarch(al). Machismo. Macho. Gentle(man,men). Fellow(s). Groom(s). Brave(s). Lad(s). Priest(s). Monk(s). Guy(s). Clergy(men,man). Duke(s). Prince(s). King(s). Congress(men,man). Police(man,men). Businessm(an,en). *See also* Gender differences; Gender identity; Machismo; Masculinity; Patriarchy; Sex role attitudes; Sex roles; Sex stereotypes.

Malevolence. See *Hate.*

Malinformation. Malinformation. Bad information. *Choose from:* dangerous, damaging, inflammatory, inciting, hate(ful), demagogic, seditious, sensational(istic), salacious, obscene, indecent, offensive *with:* information, content, message(s), webpage(s), discussion group(s), chat room(s), publication(s), material, document(s). *See also* Agitators; Censorship; Depravity; Fanaticism; Hate crimes; Hate groups; Indecent communications; Information policy; Obscenity; Pornography; Propaganda; Publications; Sexual exploitation; Vulgarity.

Malingering. Malinger(ed,ing,er,ers). *Choose from:* feign(ed,ing), simulat(ed,ing,ion), self induced, sham, fak(e,ed,ing) *with:* sickness(es), ill(ness,nesses), symptom(s), disorder(s), disease(s). *See also* Deception; Factitious disorders; Health services misuse; Psychophysiologic disorders; Self deception.

Malls. See *Shopping centers.*

Malls, medical. See *Walk-in clinics.*

Malnutrition. Malnutrition. Malnourish(ed,ment). Nutritional deficienc(y,ies). Starv(e,ed,ing,ation). Protein deficien(cy,t). Vitamin deficien(cy,t). Calorie deficien(t,cy). Inadequate diet. Lack of food. Poor diet. Semistarv(ed,ing,ation). Reduced food intake. Undernourish(ed,ment). Undernutrition. Food deprivation. Food deprived. Restricted food. Restricted calories. *Consider also:* kwashiorkor,

pellagra, Wernicke's syndrome. *See also* Alcoholism; Anorexia nervosa; Deficiency diseases; Eating disorders; Diet fads; Failure to thrive (psychosocial); Food intake; Hunger, food deprivation; Nutrition disorders; Starvation; Undernourishment; Unmet needs; Vitamin deficiency disorders.

Malpractice. Malpractice(s). Malfeasance. Misconduct. Careless(ness). Neglect. Medical(ly) negligen(t,ce). Iatrogenic disorder(s). Litigation against doctor(s). Medical liabilit(y,ies). Physician(s) liability. Unethical medical practice(s). *Consider also:* liability insurance, academic malpractice, teacher malpractice, professional malpractice, educational malpractice, defensive medicine, physician impairment. *See also* Accountability; Educational malpractice; Iatrogenesis; Impaired professionals; Liability; Medical ethics; Medication errors; Negligence; Physician patient relations; Professional ethics; Professional malpractice; Quackery.

Malpractice, educational. See *Educational malpractice.*

Malpractice, medical. See *Malpractice.*

Malpractice, professional. See *Professional malpractice.*

Malthusian theory. Malthusian theory. Neo-Malthusianism. *Choose from:* malthus(ian) *with:* population, demograph(y,ic), food production, food supply. *Consider also:* Malthusianism. *See also* Population growth; Population policy.

Mammals. Mammal(s,ian). Marsupial(s). Animal(s). Primate(s). Artiodactyla. Carnivora. Cetacea. Chiroptera. Edentata. Elephants. Hyraxes. Insectivora. Lagomorpha. Marsupialia. Monotremata. Perissodactyla. Pinnipedia. Rodentia. Anthropoidea. Prosimii. Pongidae. Antelope(s). Armadillo(s). Baboon(s). Bat(s). Beaver(s). Bear(s). Buffalo(es). Camel(s). Cat(s). Cattle. Cheetah(s). Chimpanzee(s). Chinchilla(s). Deer. Dog(s). Dolphin(s). Echidna. Elephant(s). Ferret(s). Fox(es). Gerbil(s). Goat(s). Gorilla(s). Guinea pig(s). Hamster(s). Hedgehog(s). Horse(s). Kangaroo(s). Lemur(s). Lion(s). Mole(s). Mouse. Mice. Mink(s). Mongoose(s). Monkey(s). Opossum(s). Otter(s). Pig(s). Porpoise(s). Platypus. Raccoon(s). Rabbit(s). Rat(s). Rodent(s). Seals. Sheep. Shrew(s). Skunk(s). Sloth(s). Squirrel(s). Swine. Walrus(es). Whale(s). Wolf. Wolves. *See also* Animals; Camels; Cattle; Cats; Deer; Dogs; Goats; Marine mammals; Sheep; Vertebrates.

Mammals, marine. See *Marine mammals.*

Man, ages of. See *Ages of man.*

Man, animal nature of. See *Animal nature of man.*

Man, common. See *Common people.*

Man, early. See *Prehistoric people.*

Man, economic. See *Economic man.*

Man, fall of. See *Fall of man.*

Man, organization. See *Conformity (personality); Embourgeoisement; Organizational commitment; Other directed.*

Man, prehistoric. See *Prehistoric people.*

Man, primitive. See *Prehistoric people; Prehominids.*

Man machine systems. Man machine systems. *Choose from:* human(s), man, woman, men, women, worker(s), people, person(s), operator(s) *with:* machine(s), computer(s), technology, automat(ed, ion), keyboard(s), *with:* system(s), partnership(s), dialog(s), interface(s), interact(ive,ion,ions), assist(ed,ing,ance), function(s), integration, natural language, operation, psycholog(y,ical). *Consider also:* expert system(s), virtual reality, human engineering, ergonomic(s), hypertext, intelligent interface(s), engineering psychology. *See also* Automation; Bionics; Computer addiction; Computer assisted decision making; Computer assisted diagnosis; Computer assisted instruction; Computer networks; Cybernetics; Data processing; Electronic mail; Electronic publishing; Ergonomics; Expert systems; Feedback; Hypertext; Industrial engineering; Management information systems; Mobile computing; Office automation; Robotics; User friendly systems.

Man nature relationship. See *Human ecology.*

Mana. Mana. Supernatural force(s). Supernatural power(s). Imunu. Manitou. Wakan. Hasina. Baraka. Manngur. *Consider also:* dynamism. *See also* Power; Sacredness; Supernatural; Traditional societies.

Managed care. Managed care. Managed care organization(s). MCO(s). Managed care program(s). Managed care plan(s). Health maintenance organization(s). HMO(s). Preferred provider organization(s). PPO(s). *Consider also:* medical care, health care *with:* control(led,ling), reduc(e,ed,ing), cut(ting) *with:* cost(s), premium(s). *See also* Biased selection; Comprehensive health care; Health care rationing; Health care reform; Health services needs and demand; National health programs.

Management. See *Administration; Industrial management; Management methods; Organizational effectiveness; Leadership style; Superior subordinate relationship; Supervision.*

Management, asset. See *Asset management.*

Management, cash. See *Financial management.*

Management, chaos. See *Chaos management.*

Management, coastal zone. See *Shore protection.*

Management, compensation. See *Compensation management.*

Management, conflict. See *Conflict resolution.*

Management, crisis. See *Crisis management.*

Management, database. See *Database management.*

Management, debt. See *Debt management.*

Management, ecosystem. See *Ecosystem management.*

Management, educational. See *Educational administration.*

Management, employee representation in. See *Employee ownership; Industrial democracy; Participative management; Worker control; Worker participation.*

Management, farm. See *Farm management.*

Management, financial. See *Financial management.*

Management, forest. See *Forestry.*

Management, growth. See *Growth management.*

Management, household. See *Housekeeping.*

Management, impression. See *Impression management.*

Management, industrial. See *Industrial management.*

Management, industrial self. See *Industrial democracy; Worker control; Worker participation.*

Management, information. See *Archives; Automated information retrieval; Automated information storage; Competitive intelligence; Computer assisted decision making; Data collection; Data processing; Decision support systems; Image processing; Information dissemination; Information processing; Information services; Knowledge management; Management information systems; Records management.*

Management, inventory. See *Inventory management.*

Management, knowledge. See *Knowledge management.*

Management, labor committees. See *Labor management committees.*

Management, labor relations. See *Labor management relations.*

Management, money. See *Financial management.*

Management, participative. See *Participative management.*

Management, pension fund. See *Pension fund management.*

Management, personnel. See *Personnel management.*

Management, records. See *Records management.*

Management, resource. See *Resource management.*

Management, risk. See *Risk management.*

Management, school. See *Educational administration; School boards.*

Management, scientific. See *Scientific management.*

Management, self individual. See *Self management (individual).*

Management, self industrial. See *Industrial democracy; Worker control; Worker participation.*

Management, strategic. See *Strategic management.*

Management, stress. See *Stress management.*

Management, subsidiary. See *Subsidiary management.*

Management, time. See *Time utilization.*

Management, turnaround. See *Turnaround management.*

Management decision making. Management decision making. *Choose from:* administrat(ive,or,ors), manage(r,rs, ment), director(s), leader(s), president(s), executive(s), supervisor(s), officer(s), chairperson(s), coordinator(s), principal(s) *with:* decision(s), decid(e,ed, ing), risk taking, choice(s), judgment(s). *See also* Cognitive processes; Decision making; Decision support systems; Group decision making; Management methods; Management planning; Participative decision making.

Management functions. Management function(s). *Consider also:* supervis(e, ed,ing,ion), plan(ned,ning), coordinat(e, ed,ing), direct(ed,ing), liaison, decision making, accounting, budget(ed,ing), command(ed,ing), control, administration, regulat(ing,ion), oversight, guidance, stewardship, organiz(ing, ation), staffing, reporting. *See also* Accountability; Accounting; Budgets; Coordination (interpersonal); Decision making; Logistics; Management decision making; Management information systems; Management methods; Management planning; Organizational politics; Personnel management;

Planning; Staff development; Supervision.

Management information systems.
Management information system(s).
MIS. Management information base.
Choose from: expert system(s),
information system(s), knowledge-based
support system(s) *with:* management,
accounting, executive, corporat(e,ion,
ions), organization(s,al), strategic,
manufacturing, decision(s), planning,
performance, inventor(y,ies) sales,
operations, marketing, financial, human
resources. *Consider also:* office
information system(s), management
accounting and control system(s). *See
also* Accounting sytems; Administration;
Database marketing; Decision making;
Decision support systems; Geographic
information systems; Inventory
management; Knowledge management;
Man machine systems; Management
structures; Office automation; Strategic
management.

Management methods. Management
method(s). *Choose from:* manage(rial,
ment), managing, administrative,
leadership, supervisory *with:* method(s),
practice(s), principle(s), doctrine(s),
style(s), model(s), skill(s), technique(s),
system(s), philosoph(y,ies), strateg(y,
ies). *Consider also:* management by
objectives, participat(ive,ory) management, quality circle(s), theory X, theory
Y, theory Z, Fordism, Taylorism, de-
skilling, scientific management,
humanistic management, authoritarian
management, statistical process control,
statistical quality control. *Consider also:*
theories of W. Edwards Deming, Joseph
M. Juran, Phillip B. Crosby, Genichi
Taguchi, Kaoru Ishikawa, Peter Drucker,
Frederick W. Taylor, etc. *Consider also:*
management theor(y,ies), management
science, executive development, span of
control, task force(s), managerial grid,
personnel management, decision tree(s),
decision theory, delegat(e,ed,ing,ion)
authority, delegat(e,ed,ing,ion) responsibility, satisficing, accountability, task
organization, code(s) of ethics, merit
system(s), theory of constraints, TOC,
organizational dynamics, human
relations program(s), mission
statement(s). *See also* Adhocracies;
Administration; Best practices; Industrial management; Labor management
relations; Leadership styles; Management decision making; Management
planning; Management structures;
Participative management; Practices
(methods); Scientific management;
Subsidiary management; Superior
subordinate relationship; Supervision;
Teams; Turnaround management; Work
humanization; Work schedules; Worker
control; Worker participation.

Management personnel. See *Managers.*

Management planning. Management
planning. *Choose from:* management,
manager(s,ial), administrat(ive,ion),
organization(s,al) *with:* plan(s,ned,ning),
objective(s), goal setting. *Consider also:*
managment by objectives. *See also* Long
range planning; Management decision
making; Management functions;
Marketing; Organizational objectives;
Short term planning; Strategic management; Strategies.

Management practices. See *Management
methods.*

Management retreats. See *Corporate
retreats.*

Management skills. See *Managerial skills.*

Management strategies. See *Management
methods.*

Management structures. Management
structure(s). *Choose from:* manage(ment,
rial), governance, decision making,
bureaucra(cy,tic) *with:* structur(e,ed,es,
ing), architecture, restructur(ed,ing),
hierarch(ical,y,ies), team(s,ing,work),
downsiz(ed,ing), role(s), system(s),
chart(s), reorganiz(ed,ing,ation),
layer(s), linkage(s), level(s),
decentraliz(ed,ing,ation), centraliz(ed,
ing,ation), disaggregat(e,ed,ing,ation),
pyramid(s). *Consider also:* executive
team(s), flow of information, personal
communication network(s), macro-
structure(s), strategic structure(s), work
process structure(s). *See also* Leadership
styles; Management information
systems; Management methods;
Organizational structure; Participative
management; Power structure; Strategic
management.

Management style. See *Leadership style;
Management methods.*

Management techniques. See *Management
methods.*

Management training. Management
training. *Choose from:* manager(s,ial),
management, administrator(s),
administrat(ive,ion), executive(s),
supervisor(s,y), officer(s), leader(s,ship),
director(s), official(s) *with:* trainee(s),
train(ed,ing), development, seminar(s),
course(s), continuing education. *See also*
Inservice training; Leadership; Job
rotation; Professional development; Staff
development.

Management union relations. See *Labor
management relations.*

Managerial efficiency. See *Organizational
effectiveness.*

Managerial skills. Managerial skill(s).
Choose from: managerial, management,
executive(s), administrat(ive,or,ors)
with: skill(s), talent(s,ed), abilit(y,ies).
Consider also: people skills. *See also*
Executive ability; Executive search

firms; Leadership; Superior subordinate
relationship; Work skills.

Managers. Manager(s). Manage(ment,rial)
personnel. Administrator(s). *Choose
from:* administrative, executive,
management, supervisory *with:*
personnel, staff, hierarch(y,ies).
Executive(s). Executive officer(s).
Supervisor(s). Boss(es). Superin-
tendent(s). Leader(s). Authorit(y,ies).
Director(ate,ship,s). Employer(s).
Overseer(s). Fore(man,men). Captain(s).
Commander(s). President(s). Chief(s).
Governor(s). Dean(s). Chair(man,men,
women,woman). Chairperson(s).
Coordinator(s). Department head(s).
Development officer(s). Officer(s) of the
company. Administration. Official(s).
Top official(s). Officer(s). Admissions
officer(s). Assistant principal(s).
Personnel director(s). Principal(s).
Trustee(s). Middle level management.
Top level management. *See also*
Administrators; Administration; Chief
executive officers; Employers; Executive
ability; Gold collar workers; Impresarios; Leadership style; Management
functions; Middle level managers;
Organizational effectiveness; Power
structure; Superior subordinate relationship.

Managers, middle level. See *Middle level
managers.*

Managers, top level. See *Administrators.*

Mandate. Mandate(s). Mandatory.
Commanded. Obligatory. Fiat(s).
Decree(d,ing,s). Ordered. Dictated.
Require(d). Compel(led,ling). Compul-
sory. *Consider also:* binding, enforced,
requisite. *See also* Compulsory educa-
tion; Compulsory participation;
Mandatory retirement; Military draft;
Requirements.

Mandatory reporting. Mandatory
reporting. *Choose from:* mandat(e,es,ed,
ory), requir(e,ed,ing,ements), state
law(s) *with:* report(s,ed,ing), disclos(e,
ed,ure), inform(ed,ing,ation), notification, document(ed,ation) *with:* abuse,
neglect, violence, finding(s), disease,
suspected incident(s), suspected case(s),
suspicions, animal cruelty, etc. *Consider
also:* voluntary reporting. *See also*
Medical records; Judicial statistics;
Unreported crimes.

Mandatory retirement. Mandatory
retirement. *Choose from:* mandatory,
compulsory, forced, age limit(s), ageism,
age discrimination *with:* retire(d,ing,
ment). *Consider also:* Age Discrimination in Employment Act, ADEA,
involuntary retirement. *See also* Age
discrimination; Attitudes toward the
Aged; Involuntary retirement; Length of
working life; Personnel termination;
Retirement.

Mandingo (Mande) languages. Mandingo (Mande) languages. North Mandingo: Bambara, Dyula, Malinke, Soninke. South Mandingo: Kpele, Mende. *See also* African cultural groups; Language; Languages (as subjects); Sub-Saharan Africa.

Manhood. See *Masculinity.*

Mania. Mania(s). Manic. Hyperman(ia,ias, ic). Hypoman(ia,ias,ic). Bell's mania. Exhaustion death. Lethal catatonia. Deadly catatonia. Delirious mania(s). Delirium grave. Typhomania(s). Collapse delirium. *See also* Affective disorders; Bipolar disorder; Manic disorder.

Mania, Bell's. See *Bell's mania.*

Mania, collecting. See *Collecting mania.*

Mania, dancing. See *Choreomania.*

Mania, doubting. See *Doubting mania.*

Manic depression. See *Bipolar disorder.*

Manic disorder. Manic disorder. Mani(a,c). Hypomani(a,c). Hypermani(a,c). Flight of ideas. Psychomotor overactiv(e,ity). *Consider also:* agitat(ed,ion), distractib(le,ility), typhomani(a,c), delirium grave, unipolar disorder, ecstatic symptom(s). *See also* Affective disorders; Agitation; Cyclothymic disorder; Mania.

Manifest destiny. See *Territorial expansion.*

Manifesto. Manifesto(es,s). Public declaration(s). Proclamation(s). Pronouncement(s). Announcement(s). *See also* Declarations; Public relations.

Manipulation. Manipulat(e,ed,ing,ion,ive). Ingratiat(e,ing). Machiavellian(ism). Exploit(ive,ation). Triangulat(e,ed,ing, ion). Extort(ing) sympathy. Hidden agenda(s). Brinksmanship. Double-talk. Doublethink. Con(ned,ning). Main(s) syndrome. Manipulative behavior. *Consider also:* impression management, propagand(a,ize), cunning, schem(e,ed, ing), conniv(e,ed,ing), spin doctor(s). *See also* Attempted suicide; Exploitation; Flattery; Interpersonal relations; Machiavellianism; Social behavior; Social parasites; Spin doctors.

Manipulative behavior. See *Manipulation.*

Mankind. See *Humanity.*

Manliness. See *Masculinity.*

Mannequins (Figures). Mannequin(s). Manikin(s). Mannikin(s). Dumm(y,ies). *Consider also:* store model(s), dress form(s), lay figure(s). *See also* Fashions; Garment industry; Models; Models (persons).

Mannequins (Persons). See *Models (persons).*

Mannerism (Art). Mannerism. Mannerist. Maniera. Italian art and architecture from 1520-1600. *Consider also:* mannered, manieriste, manierismo, Giorgio Vasari, Parmigianino (Girolamo Francesco Mazzola), Pontormo (Jacopo Carucci), Agnolo Bronzino (Agnolo di Cosimo), Giovanni Battista Rosso, Domenico Beccafumi, Giovanni da Bologna, etc. *See also* Arts; Baroque art.

Manners. Manners. Courtes(y,ies). Nicet(y,ies). Well mannered. Rules of conduct. Custom(ary,s). Tradition(al,s). Mores. Social code(s). Formalities. Polite(ness). Civilit(y,ies). Propriet(y, ies). Decorum. Social convention(s). Protocol. Folkway(s). Norm(s). Etiquette. Socially prescribed. Unwritten law(s). *Consider also:* netiquette. *See also* Amenities; Etiquette; Faux pas; Norms; Protocols; Social skills.

Manors. Manor(s,ial,ialism). Landed estate(s). *Consider also:* copyhold(s), landed elite(s), mansion(s), castle(s), chateau(x,s), quinta(s), country villa(s). *See also* Agrarian structures; Feudalism; Historic buildings; Palaces.

Manpower. Manpower. Womanpower. Personpower. Personnel. Workforce. Operator(s). Employee(s). Staff. Worker(s). Supervisor(s). Work force. Office force. Sales force. Subordinate(s). Labor force. Labor supply. Functionar(y, ies). Crew(s). Troop(s). Hired help. Manager(s). Coworker(s). Occupational group(s). Laborer(s). Practitioner(s). Paraprofessional(s). Professional(s). Nonprofessional(s). Air traffic controller(s). Attorney(s). Administrator(s). Agricultural personnel. Blue collar worker(s). Caseworker(s). Church worker(s). Civil servant(s). Caregiver(s). Clerk(s). Consultant(s). Computer programmer(s). Crafts(man,men,women, woman). Craftsperson(s). Craftspeople. Designer(s). Driver(s). Director(s). Domestic servant(s). Editor(s). Faculty. Firefighter(s). Guard(s). Government employee(s). Health personnel. Hairdresser(s). Home economist(s). Librarian(s). Machine operator(s). Military personnel. Nurse(s). Police officer(s). Pilot(s). Programmer(s). Sales(men,man,women,woman,people, person,persons). Secretar(y,ies). Stevedore(s). Teacher(s). Technician(s). Trainer(s). Typist(s). White collar worker(s). *Choose from:* employed, civil service, working, hired *with:* woman, women, men, man, people, group(s), SS, males, female(s), person(s), civilian(s). *See also* Allied health personnel; Ancillaries; Dislocated workers; Employee turnover; Health manpower; Human resources; Labor market; Labor supply; Nonprofessional personnel; Personnel termination; Professional personnel; Troop strength; Workers.

Manpower, health. See *Health manpower.*

Manslaughter. See *Homicide.*

Manual communication. Manual communication. Sign language. Signed English. ASL. American sign language. Signing. Finger spelling. *Choose from:* manual, sign(ed,ing) nonverbal, gestur(al,e,es, ed), nonvocal *with:* communication, language, alphabet. *Consider also:* cued speech. *See also* Communication (thought transfer); Communication skills; Deafness; Oral communication; Sign language.

Manual labor. See *Blue collar workers.*

Manual training. Manual training. Industrial arts. Technology education. *Consider also:* bench work, manual arts, woodwork(ing). *See also* Arts and Crafts movement; Carpentry; Vocational education.

Manual workers. See *Blue collar workers.*

Manuals, sex. See *Sex information.*

Manufacture, gas. See *Gas industry.*

Manufacturer liability. See *Product liability.*

Manufacturers. Manufacturer(s). Producer(s). Industrialist(s). Creator(s). Factory owner(s). *See also* Consumer goods; Home based businesses; Industrial production; Industrial wastes; Mass production; Textile industry.

Manufacturing. See *Factories; Industry; Industrial production.*

Manumission. See *Emancipation.*

Manumission of slaves. See *Emancipation.*

Manuscripts. Manuscript(s). Letter(s). Text(s). Diar(y,ies). Typescript(s). Pre-print paper(s). Handwritten text(s). Draft(s). Correspondence. Notebook(s). Literary draft(s). Memoranda. Handwritten script(s). Author's copy. Rough draft. *Consider also:* codex, codices, manoscritt(i,a). *See also* Autographs; Authors; Authors' notebooks; Charters; Forgery; Illumination of books and manuscripts; Letters (correspondence); Medieval manuscripts; Publications; Scribes; Written communications.

Manuscripts, medieval. See *Medieval manuscripts.*

Manuscripts and books, illumination of. See *Illumination of books and manuscripts.*

Mapping, career. See *Career goals.*

Mapping, chromosome. See *Gene mapping.*

Mapping, cognitive. See *Cognitive mapping.*

Mapping, gene. See *Gene mapping.*

Mapping, human gene. See *Gene mapping.*

Maps. Map(s). Mapp(ed,ing). Cartogram(s). Cartography. World globe(s).

Projection(s) of the world. Chartbook(s). Chart(s). Navigational log(s). Navigational chart(s). Atlas(es). Street guide(s). Gazetteer(s). Plat(s). Grid(s). Guide(s). *See also* Cartography; Geographic information systems; Geography; Globes; Land surveying.

Maquiladoras. See *Border industries; Offshore production (foreign countries).*

Marathon group therapy. Marathon group therap(y,ies). Marathon group(s). *Choose from:* marathon *with:* encounter(s), group(s), experience(s), therap(y,ies), workshop(s), growth group(s). *Consider also:* accelerated interaction, time extended therap(y,ies). *See also* Group psychotherapy; Human relations training; Psychotherapy; Sensitivity training.

Marches. March(es). Marche(s). Marsch(e,es,en). Marcia(s). Marcha(s). Processional(s). *Consider also:* military music, marching band(s), parade(s), John Philip Sousa, Parademarsch, pas ordinaire, Geschwindmarsch, pas redouble, paso doble, Sturmmarsch, pas de charge, funeral march(es). *See also* Military music; Music; Patriotic music; Processions; Rhythm; War songs.

Marginal culture. See *Marginality (sociological).*

Marginality (sociological). Marginal(s,ism, ity,ize,ized,izing,ization). Marginal man. Outsider(s). Cultural hybrid. Marginal culture. Social marginality. Marginal group(s). *Consider also:* bicultural(ism), bilingual(ism), peripheral, emargination, underclass, deviance, eccentric(ity), underrepresented, ghetto(ize,ized,izing, ization), exclud(e,ed,ing), pauper(ize, ized,izing,ization). *See also* Alienation; Center and periphery; Centrality; Deviance; Labeling (of persons); Minority groups; Ostracism; Otherness; Social distance; Social isolation; Social status; Social structure; Socially handicapped; Underclass; Vagrants.

Marginality, social. See *Marginality (sociological).*

Marginalization. See *Age discrimination; Antisemitism; Apartheid; Attitudes toward handicapped; Attitudes toward homosexuality; Attitudes toward mental retardation; Attitudes toward mental illness; Attitudes toward physical handicaps; Attitudes toward physical illness; Attitudes toward the aged; Biculturalism; Bidialectism; Bilingualism; Bigotry; Caste system; Center and periphery; Class differences; Cultural groups; Disadvantaged; Employment discrimination; Ethnic groups; Ethnic identity; Ethnic relations; Ethnicity; Ethnocentrism; Exclusivity (Religion); Labor market segmentation; Linguistic minorities; Male chauvinism; Marginality (sociological); Nativism; Oppression;*

People of color; Persecution; Prejudice; Racial attitudes; Racial segregation; Racism; Religious prejudice; Residential segregation; Reverse discrimination; Separatism; Sex discrimination; Sexual division of labor; Sexual inequality; Sexual oppression; Sexism; Social discrimination; Stigma; Subcultures; Subjugation.

Mariculture. Mariculture. Marine aquaculture. Fish culture. Fish farm(s,ing). Sea farm(s,ing). Ocean kelp farm(s). *See also* Agriculture; Farming; Fish as food; Fisheries; Seafood.

Marihuana. See *Street drugs.*

Marijuana. See *Street drugs.*

Marijuana, medical. See *Medical marijuana.*

Marijuana abuse. See *Substance abuse.*

Marijuana laws. Marijuana law(s). *Choose from:* cannabis, marihuana, marijuana, hashish *with:* law(s), legaliz(e,ed,ing, ation), legal status, Uniform Controlled Substances Act, decriminaliz(e,ed,ing). *See also* Drug and narcotic control; Drug enforcement; Legalization of drugs; Medical marijuana; Street drugs.

Marijuana legalization. See *Legalization of drugs; Marijuana laws; Medical marijuana.*

Marine, merchant. See *Shipping industry.*

Marine accidents. Marine accident(s). Shipwreck(s). *Choose from:* marine(r,rs), sea, underwater, ship(s), swimmer(s), boat(s), yacht(s), schooner(s), submarine(s,r,rs), ocean(s), sailor(s), ferr(y,ies), cutter(s), oceanliner(s), sloop(s), barge(s) *with:* run aground, ran aground, sank, sunk(en), capsiz(e,ed,ing), overturn(ed, ing), keel(ed) over, swamp(ed), founder(ed,ing), scuttl(e,ed,ing), crash(ed,ing,es), accident(s,al,ally), wreck(s), disaster(s), fire(s), mishap(s), collaps(e,ed,es,ing). *See also* Accidents; Boatmen; Drowning; Dry docks; Collisions at sea; Sailing; Seafaring life; Ships; Wrecks.

Marine architecture. See *Shipbuilding.*

Marine ecology. Marine ecolog(y,ical, ist,ists). Marine ecosystem(s). *Choose from:* fish(es,ery,eries), seabed(s), seagrass(es), seaforest(s), ocean(s), sea(s), underwater, marine life, phytoplankton, zooplankton, krill, whale(s), shark(s), *with:* overfish(ed,ing), sport fishing, whaling, nutrient(s), habitat(s), ecosystem(s), ecolog(y,ical,ically), food chain(s). *See also* Ecology; Fishes; Food chain; Marine resources; Natural resources; Oceans; Tides.

Marine mammals. Marine mammal(s). Seal(s). Sea lion(s). Whale(s). Narwhal(s). Rorqual(s). Porpoise(s).

Dolphin(s). Cetacea. Manatee(s). Dugong(s). Sea cow(s). Sirenia. *Choose from:* aquatic, pelagic, coastal, marine, ocean(ic,s), offshore, sea(s) *with:* mammal(s). *See also* Animals; Mammals; Marine resources.

Marine personnel. Marine personnel. *Choose from:* marine(s) *with:* corps, personnel, enlistee(s), recruit(s), officer(s), enlisted, non-commissioned officer(s), force(s), trainee(s), general(s), colonel(s), lieutenant(s), sergeant(s). *See also* Armed forces; Generals; Military personnel.

Marine resources. Marine resource(s). Fisher(y,ies). *Choose from:* aquatic, archipelagic water(s), coastal water(s), continental shel(f,ves), fishing water(s), international strait(s), international water(s), marine, maritime, nautical, ocean(s), offshore, sea(s), seabed(s), seafloor, underwater, Atlantic Ocean, Pacific Ocean, Mediterranean Sea, Caribbean Sea, Red Sea, South China Sea, Indian Ocean, Arctic Ocean, Antarctic Ocean, Baltic Sea, North Sea, Irish Sea, Adriatic Sea, Ionian Sea, Aegean Sea, Black Sea, etc. *with:* resource(s), reserve(s), conservation, mineral(s), mining, deposit(s), petroleum, oil, gas, geolog(y,ical), living resource(s), ecosystem(s), vegetation, plant(s), fish(es), mammal(s), peaceful use(s), exploit(ed,ing,ation). *See also* Fisheries; Fishes; Geopolitics; International law; Mariculture; Marine ecology; Marine mammals; Maritime industry; Maritime law; Natural resources; Oceans; Offshore oil; Shipping industry; Territorial waters.

Marionettes. See *Puppets.*

Marital adjustment. See *Marital conflict; Marital relationship.*

Marital conflict. Marital conflict(s). *Choose from:* marital, marriage(s), married, husband wife, spous(e,es,al), conjugal, domestic, couple(s) *with:* trouble(s,d), stress(es), distress(ed,es), dissension, problem(s), conflict(s), role strain(s), sex conflict(s), pathology, difficult(y,ies), argument(s), competetive(ness), competition, frustration(s), aggression, breakup(s), fail(ed,ure,ures), dissatisf(ied,action, actions), unhapp(y,iness), discord, resent(ful,ment,ments), hostil(e,ity,ities), impasse(s), misunderstanding(s), fight(s,ing), clash(es), incompatib(le, ility), dysfunctional, instability, unstable. *See also* Arguments; Battered women; Family conflict; Family crises; Family relations; Family stability; Family violence; Marital disruption; Marital relationship; Spouse abuse.

Marital counseling. See *Marital therapy.*

Marital disruption. Marital disruption. *Choose from:* marriage(s), marital, married, conjugal, couple(s), spous(e,es, al), family, parent(s,al), wife, wives, husband(s) *with:* disrupt(ed,ion), breakdown, problem(s), conflict(s), dissatisfaction, violence, dysfunction(s, al), unhapp(y,iness), burnout, instability, separat(e,ed,ing,ion), leaving, uncoupling, breakdown, dissolv(e,ed,ing), dissolution, estrange(d,ment), sever(ed, ing), break-up, desert(ed,ing,ion). *Consider also:* pre-divorce, broken homes, non-cohabitation, divorce(s,d), annulment. *See also* Divorce; Divorce counseling; Family conflict; Family crises; Family problems; Family relations; Family stability; Family violence; Marital conflict; Marital relationship; Marital separation; Parental absence; Widowhood.

Marital dissolution. See *Divorce; Marital separation.*

Marital enrichment. Marital enrichment. *Choose from:* marital, marriage(s), famil(y,ies), couple(s), intimate relationship(s) *with:* enrich(ed,ing, ment), enhanc(e,ed,ing,ement), happ(y,ier,iness), creative(ness), encounter(s), growth, strengthen(ed,ing), human relations training, centering, empower(ed,ing). *See also* Human relations training; Intimacy; Marital satisfaction; Sensitivity training; Sex therapy.

Marital infidelity. See *Extramarital relations.*

Marital rape. Marital rape. *Choose from:* marital, marriage(s), conjugal, wife, wives, spouse(s), husband(s), domestic *with:* rape(s,d), forc(e,ed,ible) intercourse, forc(e,ed,ible) sex(ual,ually), sexual(ly) assault(ed,ing), sexual coercion, sexual(ly) violat(e,ed,ion, ions). *See also* Battered women; Marital sexual behavior; Rape; Reproductive rights; Sex offenders; Sexual exploitation; Spouse abuse.

Marital relations. See *Marital sexual behavior.*

Marital relationship. Marital relation(s, ship,ships). *Choose from:* marriage, marital, married, husband wife, spous(al,es), conjugal, couple, domestic *with:* adjustment, problem(s), instability, unstable, relation(s,ship,ships), happiness, intimacy, conflict, jealousy, functioning, dependency, satisfaction, stress(es), distress(es), discord, interaction(s), problem solving, communicaton, cohesion, role(s), structure, quality, compatibility, lifestyle(s), cohesiveness, contentment, adjustment, satisfaction, mutual influence. *See also* Dual career families; Extramarital relations; Family planning; Family power; Family relations; Family

roles; Family stability; Family violence; Home environment; Husbands; Interpersonal relations; Love; Marital conflict; Marital satisfaction; Marital sexual behavior; Spouse abuse; Spouses; Wives.

Marital roles. See *Family roles; Parent role; Sex roles; Sexual division of labor.*

Marital satisfaction. Marital satisfaction. *Choose from:* marriage(s), marital, married, remarriage(s), remarital, remarried, husband wife, spous(al,es), conjugal, couple(s), domestic *with:* adjustment, bond(s,ing), cohesion, cohesiveness, commitment, compatib(le, ility), contentment, enrichment, functioning, happ(y,iness), integration, interaction(s), intimacy, lifestyle(s), love, mutual influence, problem solving, communicaton, quality, relation(s,ship, ships), role(s), satisf(ied,action), satisfy(ing), commitment, stability, structure, success, support, understanding, well-being. *See also* Annulment; Complementary needs; Divorce; Family life; Homogamy; Life satisfaction; Marital disruption; Marital enrichment; Marital sexual behavior; Marital relationship; Marriage attitudes; Need satisfaction; Self actualization; Sexual satisfaction.

Marital separation. Marital separation. Broken home(s). Non-cohabitation. Divorce(s,d). Annulment. *Choose from:* marriage(s), marital, married, conjugal, couple(s), spous(e,es,al), family, parent(s,al), wife, wives, husband(s) *with:* separat(e,ed,ing,ion,ions), leaving, uncoupling, breakdown, disrupt(ed,ion), dissolved, dissolution, estrange(d,ment), sever(ed,ing), break-up, desert(ed,ing, ion). *See also* Child custody; Child support; Divorce; Divorce counseling; Divorced people; Marital disruption; Marital status; Parental absence; Single parent family; Single person.

Marital sexual behavior. Marital sexual behavior. Sexuality in marriage. Marital relations. Marital intimacy. *Choose from:* spouse(s), marriage(s), marital, married, husband(s), wife, wives, conjugal, honeymoon, bride(s) *with:* sex(ual,uality), orgasm(s,ic), intercourse, intimacy, sex behavior, sex disorder(s), coitus, sexual abstinen(t,ce), libid(o, inal), intimate relations, sexual relations, psychosexual, sexual deviation(s), sex drive. *See also* Extramarital relations; Intimacy; Marital rape; Marital relationship; Marital satisfaction; Sex therapy; Sexual foreplay; Sexual intercourse; Sexual satisfaction.

Marital status. Marital status. Marr(ied, iage,iages). Single(s). Unmarried. Widow(s,ed,er,ers,hood). Divorc(ed, ee,ees). Marital history. Separated. Remarr(ied,iage,iages). Marital state. Unwed. Wed(ded). Wives. Wife.

Husband(s). Spinster(s,hood). Bachelor(s,hood). *See also* Bachelors; Divorced people; Husbands; Marriage; Single person; Unmarried women; Widowhood; Wives.

Marital therapy. Marital therap(y,ies). *Choose from:* marital, marriage(s), couple(s), premarital, paramarital *with:* therap(y,ies), counseling, conflict resolution, advice, advisory, casework, psychotherap(y,ies), treatment(s), enrichment, communication training. *Consider also:* divorce counseling. *See also* Counseling; Couples therapy; Covenant marriage; Divorce counseling; Family problems; Family therapy; Feminist therapy; Marital conflict; Marital disruption; Marital separation; Psychotherapy; Sex therapy.

Marital violence. See *Family violence; Marital rape; Spouse abuse.*

Maritime industry. Maritime industr(y,ies). Shipping industr(y,ies). Shipbuild(ing, er,ers). Shipyard(s). Merchant marine(s). Merchant fleet(s). Fishing fleet(s). Seatrade. *See also* Fisheries; Fishermen; Maritime law; Marine resources; Sea power.

Maritime law. Maritime law(s). Admiralty. *Choose from:* aquatic, archipelagic water(s), coast guard, coastal water(s), continental shel(f,ves), fishing water(s), international strait(s), international water(s), marine, maritime, merchant marine(s), navigational, nav(y,ies), nautical, ocean(s), offshore, sailor(s), sea(s), seabed(s), seafar(ing,er,ers), seafloor, ship(s), shipowner(s), shipping route(s), Atlantic Ocean, Pacific Ocean, Mediterranean Sea, Caribbean Sea, Red Sea, South China Sea, Indian Ocean, Arctic Ocean, Antarctic Ocean, Baltic Sea, North Sea, Irish Sea, Adriatic Sea, Ionian Sea, Aegean Sea, Black Sea, etc. *with:* boundary claim(s), convention(s), court decision(s), exclusive economic zone(s), EEZ, jurisdiction(s,al), legal(ity, ities), illegal(ly,ity,ities), licens(e,ed,ing), neutral(ity), warrant(s), treat(y,ies), agreement(s), law(s), accord(s), pact(s), regulation(s), right(s), rule(s), act(s). *See also* Boundaries; Collisions at sea; Freedom of the Seas; International law; Marine resources; Maritime war; Naval offenses; Oceans; Offshore factories (floating); Offshore oil; Piracy (at sea); Sea power; Shipping industry; Ships; Slave trade; Territorial waters; Underwater archaeology.

Maritime war. Maritime war(s). *Choose from:* naval, maritime, marine, nav(y,ies), ship(s), vessel(s), submarine(s), sea(s) *with:* war(s,fare), battle(s), WWII, World War I, World War II, *Consider also:* sea power. *See also* Embargo; Freedom of the Seas; Maritime law; Territorial waters.

Markers, biochemical. See *Biochemical markers.*

Market, arms. See *Arms market.*

Market, black. See *Gray market; Informal sector.*

Market, commodity. See *Commodity market.*

Market, futures. See *Futures market.*

Market, gray. See *Gray market.*

Market, housing. See *Housing market.*

Market, internal labor. See *Labor market segmentation.*

Market, job. See *Labor market.*

Market, labor. See *Labor market.*

Market, military. See *Military market.*

Market, open. See *Free trade; Private enterprise; Privatization.*

Market, stock. See *Stock exchange.*

Market development. Market development. Category development. Market growth. *Consider also:* market size, annual sales growth, U.S. market, European market, Japanese market, etc. *See also* Advertising; Consumer awareness; Market research; Market segmentation; Marketing; Marketing plans; Marketing strategies; Markets; Target marketing.

Market economy. Market economy. Laissez faire. Entrepreneurial(ism). Competitive econom(y,ies). Capitalis(m,t,tic). Corporate ownership. Profit motive. Market forces. Bourgeois political economy. Capital accumulation. Profit system. Economic competition. *Choose from:* free, private, corporate *with:* enterprise, ownership, trade, market, property, investment(s). *Consider also:* Adam Smith, Protestant ethic, multinational corporation, corporate society, Wall Street, commodification. *See also* Antitrust law; Business cycles; Capitalism; Consumer society; Decommunization; Economic competition; Markets; Post-communism; Private sector; Production consumption relationship; Supply and demand; Supply side economics; Trade; Trade protection.

Market research. Market(s,ing) research. *Choose from:* market(s,ing), consumer(s), retail, merchandis(e,ing), advertising, buying power, demand, customer(s) *with:* research, survey(s), stud(y,ies), poll(s), analys(is,es), forecast(s,ed,ing), predict(ed,ing,ion, ions). *Choose from:* consumer(s), shopper(s), buyer(s), purchaser(s), customer(s) *with:* measur(e,ing,ment, ments), panel(s). *Consider also:* product planning, test market(s), Nielsen rating(s), focus group(s). *See also* Advertising research; Consumer behavior; Consumers; Economic research; Focus groups; Internet traffic;

Loyalty cards; Market development; Market segmentation; Market share; Market size; Market statistics; Marketing; Marketing plans; Marketing strategies; Markets; Online privacy; Retailing; Surveys; Target marketing; Test marketing.

Market segmentation. Market segmentation. Segment(ed,ing,ation) market(s). Splitting market(s). *Choose from:* segment(ed,ing,ation), target(s,ed,ing) *with:* customer(s), consumer(s), market(s), audience(s), niche(s), cluster(s). *Consider also:* niche market(s,ing), preferred demographics, strategic marketing decision(s). *See also* Audience analysis; Market development; Market research; Marketing; Marketing plans; Marketing strategies; Target marketing.

Market segmentation, labor. See *Labor market segmentation.*

Market share. Market share(s). Percent(age) of market(s). Share of market(s). Relative market position(s). *Consider also:* level(s) of consumption, oligopsonistic market(s), atomistic market(s). *See also* Demand; Market research; Market size; Market statistics; Marketing; Markets; Retailing; Sales; Supply and demand.

Market size. Market size. *Choose from:* market(s), demand, customer(s), consumer(s), potential buyer(s) *with:* size, number(s), statistic(s,al), demographic(s), growth, data, declin(e,ed,ing). *See also* Consumers; Market research; Market share; Market statistics.

Market statistics. Market statistic(s). *Choose from:* market(s,ing), consumer(s), retail, merchandis(e,ing), advertising, buying power, demand, customer(s), sales, market size, market share(s), household(s) *with:* statistic(s, al), data(bank,banks), demographic(s), profile(s), survey(s), zip code(s), fact sheet(s), basebook(s), trend(s). *See also* Demographic characteristics (of individuals); Economic statistics; Market research; Market share; Market size; Marketing; Markets.

Market surveys. See *Market research.*

Market value. Market value(s). Current value(s). Open market price(s). Sale price(s). Fair value(s). Replacement cost(s). *See also* Prices; Supply and demand.

Market women. See *Street vendors; Women merchants.*

Marketing. Market(ed,ing). Merchandis(ed, ing). Retailing. Salesmanship. Wholesaling. Develop(ed,ing) market(s). Selling. Market segmentation. Market research. Influencing consumers. Market strateg(y, ies). Advertis(e,ed,ing,ments).

Promotion(al). Promot(e,ed,ing). Creating image(s). Packaging. Target(ing) audience(s). Trade shows. Telemarket(ed,ing). Cold call(s,ing). Marketer(s). *See also* Advertising; Brand identity; Cobranding; Consumer awareness; Consumer education; Consumer organizations; Consumer participation; Consumer satisfaction; Direct mail advertising; Direct marketing; Loss leader; Loyalty cards; Market development; Market research; Market segmentation; Marketing plans; Marketing strategies; Markets; Order processing; Orders (business); Products; Purchasing; Sales; Target marketing; Telemarketing; Trade.

Marketing, direct. See *Direct marketing.*

Marketing, niche. See *Market segmentation.*

Marketing, target. See *Target marketing.*

Marketing, test. See *Test marketing.*

Marketing channels. See *Distribution channels.*

Marketing plans. Marketing plan(s). *Choose from:* market(ed,s,ing), merchandising, sales, advertis(e,ed,ing, ement,ements), promot(e,ed,ing,ion, ional), distribution, *with:* plan(s,ned, ning), objective(s), goal(s), launch(ed, ing), campaign(s), target(s,ed,ing). *Consider also:* consumer research. *See also* Advertising; Advertising campaigns; Comparative advertising; Market development; Market research; Market segmentation; Marketing; Marketing strategies; Target marketing.

Marketing strategies. Marketing strateg(y, ies). *Choose from:* market(ing), salesman(ship), sale(s), advertis(e,ed, ing,ement,ements), merchandis(e,ed,ing) *with:* strateg(y,ies), plan(s,ning), scheme(s), tactic(s), campaign(s). *See also* Advertising; Advertising campaigns; Brand identity; Cobranding; Comparative advertising; Consumer awareness; Consumer education; Direct mail advertising; Direct marketing; Loss leader; Market development; Market research; Market segmentation; Marketing; Marketing plans; Target marketing; Telemarketing.

Marketplaces. See *Stores.*

Markets. Market(s). Demand. Market capability. Marketplace(s). Buying power. *Choose from:* labor, housing, real estate, commodity *with:* market(s). *Choose from:* affluent, African American, Asian American, baby boom(er), ethnic, gay, generation x, green, hispanic, mature, minorit(y,ies), wom(an,en), youth, potential, European, U.S., etc. *with:* consumer(s), customer(s), buyer(s), purchaser(s), sale(s). *Consider also:* fair(s). *See also* Business; Consumers; Consumption (economic); Economic competition; Futures market; Homosexual consumers; Housing market; Labor market; Market development; Market economy; Market research; Market share; Marketing; Military market; Stock exchange; Supply and demand; Target marketing; Trade; Trade protection.

Markets, common. See *Common markets.*

Markets, dual labor. See *Labor market segmentation.*

Markets, emerging. See *Emerging markets.*

Marking, animal scent. See *Animal scent marking.*

Marks, printers. See *Printers marks.*

Maroons. Maroon(s). Cimarron(es). Fugitive slave(s). *Consider also:* les marrons, negros cimarrones. *See also* Fugitive slaves.

Marriage. Marriage(s). Marital relationship(s). Marr(y,ied). Marital union(s). Conjugal. Spouse(s). Wife. Wives. Husband(s). Couple(s). Bride(s). Bridal. Wed(ded,ding,dings,lock). Remarr(y,iage,iages). Monogam(y,ous). Endogam(y,ous). Exogam(y,ous). Polygam(y,ous). Hypergam(y,ies). Hypogam(y,ies). Mate selection. Intermarr(y,iage). Matrimon(y,ial). Nuptial(s). *Consider also:* mate(s), betroth(al,ed), coupling, honeymoon, newlywed(s), bridewealth. *See also* Affinal; Age discrepant marriages; Alternative family forms; Arranged marriages; Bridewealth; Cohabitation; Companionate marriages; Consanguinity; Couples; Cousin marriage; Covenant marriage; Dowry; Endogamous marriage; Family; Gay couples; Group marriage; Homogamy; Human courtship; Human mate selection; Impediments to marriage; Intermarriage; Interracial marriage; Kinship; Life stage transitions; Long distance marriages; Marital conflict; Marital disruption; Marital enrichment; Marital relationship; Marital satisfaction; Marital sexual behavior; Marital status; Marriage attitudes; Marriage customs; Marriage patterns; Marriage rates; Marriage timing; Married students; Monogamy; Polygamy; Remarriage; Serial polygamy; Single mothers; Single person; Spouse abuse; Spouses; Stepfamily; Virginity; Weddings; Widowhood.

Marriage, common law. See *Cohabitation.*

Marriage, consanguineous. See *Endogamous marriage.*

Marriage, cousin. See *Cousin marriage.*

Marriage, covenant. See *Covenant marriage.*

Marriage, cross-cousin. See *Cousin marriage.*

Marriage, endogamous. See *Endogamous marriage.*

Marriage, group. See *Group marriage.*

Marriage, impediments to. See *Impediments to marriage.*

Marriage, interethnic. See *Intermarriage.*

Marriage, interfaith. See *Intermarriage.*

Marriage, interracial. See *Interracial marriage.*

Marriage age. Marriage age. Age at marriage. Marital age. *Consider also:* age of consent, delayed marriage(s), early marriage(s). *See also* Marriage timing; Maternal age; Teenage fathers; Teenage mothers.

Marriage attitudes. Marriage attitude(s). Decision(s) to marry. Attitude(s) toward marrying. *Choose from:* marriage(s), marital, married, marry(ing), conjugal, husband(s), wife, wives, spous(e,es,al), couple(s), *with:* attitude(s), satisf(ied, action), dissatisf(ied,action), value(s), perception(s), expectation(s), preference(s), concept(s), role expectation(s), happiness, unhappiness. *Choose from:* predispos(ed,ition) *with:* marry, marriage(s). Predisposed to remain single. Love attitude(s). *See also* Attitudes; Divorce; Marital satisfaction; Marriage.

Marriage brokers. Marriage broker(s). Marriage market(s). Matchmak(ing,er, ers). Match-mak(ing,er,ers). Matrimonial agenc(y,ies). *Consider also:* bride price(s), go-between(s). *See also* Arranged marriages; Bridewealth; Brokers; Human courtship; Human mate selection; Traditional societies.

Marriage contracts. Marriage(s) contract(s, ed). Antenuptial contract(s). Prenuptial contract(s). Premarital agreement(s). *Consider also:* domestic contract(s), cohabitation agreement(s), separation agreement(s). *See also* Alternative family forms; Marriage settlements; Sexual division of labor.

Marriage counseling. See *Family therapy; Marital therapy.*

Marriage customs. Marriage custom(s). *Choose from:* wedding(s), marriage(s), matrimon(y,ial), nuptial(s), brid(e,es,al), honeymoon(s), conjugal *with:* custom(s), mores, practice(s), tradition(s, al), convention(s), ceremon(y,ies), rite(s), ritual(s), observ(e,ed,ing,ance, ances). *Consider also:* wedding ring(s), dowr(y,ies), polygamy, bridewealth, groom fee(s), gifta, beweddung, lobolo. *See also* Bridewealth; Customs; Dowry; Marriage; Marriage patterns; Weddings.

Marriage partners. See *Spouses.*

Marriage patterns. Marriage pattern(s). *Choose from:* marriage, nuptial(ity), matrimonial, family *with:* pattern(s),

model(s). *Consider also:* matrilocal, matri-patrilocal, patrilocal, agamy, endogam(y,ous), exogam(y,ous), monogam(y,ous), polyandr(y,ous), polygam(y,ous), polygyn(y,ous), bigam(y,ous), intermarriage, mixed marriage(s), affinal marriage(s), avuncular marriage(s), beena marriage(s), common law marriage(s), companionate marriage(s), morganatic marriage(s), cross-cousin marriage(s), matrilateral marriage(s), patrilateral marriage(s), cenogamy, extended affinal marriage(s), group marriage(s), interfamilial exchange marriage(s), primary marriage(s), secondary marriage(s), serial polygamy, sequential marriage(s), symmetrical cross-cousin marriage(s), tandem polygamy, term marriage(s). *See also* Companionate marriages; Endogamous marriage; Marriage; Polygamy.

Marriage rates. Marriage rate(s). Marriage frequenc(y,ies). Nuptiality. *Choose from:* marriage(s) *with:* rate(s), frequenc(y,ies), table(s). *Consider also:* nuptiality table(s). *See also* Demography; Fertility; Marriage.

Marriage rites. See *Weddings.*

Marriage settlements. Marriage settlement(s). *Choose from:* marriage, prenuptial, postnuptial *with:* settlement(s), agreement(s). *See also* Alimony; Marriage contracts.

Marriage songs. See *Epithalamia.*

Marriage therapy. See *Marital therapy.*

Marriage timing. Marriage timing. Tim(e,ing) of marriage(s). Age at marriage. Late marriage(s). Marital readiness. Age discrepant marriage(s). *Choose from:* early, late, tim(e,ing), delayed, postpone(d,ment), age(s), young(er), old(er) *with:* wedding(s), marriage(s), nuptial(s), marital, bride(s), groom(s). *See also* Biological clocks; Divorce; First birth timing; Marriage; Marriage age; Maternal age; Remarriage; Young adults.

Marriage vows. See *Weddings.*

Marriages, age discrepant. See *Age discrepant marriages.*

Marriages, arranged. See *Arranged marriages.*

Marriages, childfree. See *Childlessness.*

Marriages, commuter. See *Long distance marriages.*

Marriages, companionate. See *Companionate marriages.*

Marriages, homosexual. See *Gay couples.*

Marriages, long distance. See *Long distance marriages.*

Marriages, mixed. See *Intermarriage.*

Marriages, open. See *Extramarital relations.*

Marriages, plural. See *Polygamy.*

Marriages, second. See *Remarriage.*

Married couples. See *Spouses.*

Married men. See *Husbands.*

Married people. See *Spouses.*

Married students. Married student(s). *Choose from:* student(s), college women, college woman, college men, college man *with:* marriage(s), marital, marr(y, ied), spouse(s), wife, wives, husband(s). *See also* Adult students; College students; High school students; Marital status; Marriage.

Married women. See *Wives.*

Marshes and swamps. See *Wetlands.*

Martial arts. Martial arts. *Choose from:* martial, self defense *with:* arts. *Consider also:* judo, karate, tai kwan do, tae kwon do, tae kwondo, taekwon-do, kung fu, black belt(s), jujitsu, judogi, savate, aikido, kung fu, wu-su. *See also* Meditation; Self defense.

Martial law. Martial law. Military rule. Military control. Curfew(s). Military crackdown. State of emergency. State of siege. Military junta. Military government. Detention without trial. *See also* Civil supremacy over the military; Coups d'Etat; Detention; Internal security; Military civilian relations; Military law; Military regimes; Provisional government.

Martyrs. Martyr(s,ed,ing,dom,hood). Self sacrificing. Sacrificial. *Choose from:* die(d), dying, death(s), victim(s), sufferer(s), self-immolat(e,ed,ing,ion), crucifi(y,ied,ixion,ixions), scapegoat(s), persecut(ed,ion) *with:* faith, God, Christian, Islamic, Jewish, Buddhist, religion(s), patrioti(c,sm), country, political. *Consider also:* saint(s), mashhad, shahid, ziyara, kiddush hashem, yad vashem. *See also* Holocaust; Holy men; Holy women; Patience; Persecution; Saints; Self sacrifice.

Marxism. Marxis(m,t). Marxian. Communist theor(y,ies). Communist doctrine(s). Dialectical materialism. Dictatorship of the proletariat. Classless society. Communist Manifesto. Das Kapital. *Consider also:* historical materialism, class struggle, class warfare, dictatorship of the proletariat, neo-Marxism, communism, Lenin(ism,ist), Castro(ism, ist), Marxism-Leninism, Marxist-Leninist, bolshevi(c,sm), Mao(ism,ist), Tito(ism,ist), Stalin(ism, ist), Trotsky(ism,ist), revisionis(t,m). *Consider also:* Karl Marx, Friedrich Engels, Vladimir Ilyich Lenin, Mao Zedong [Mao Tse-tung], Leon Trotsky, Josef Stalin, Josip Broz Tito. *See also*

Bourgeois societies; Capitalism; Class analysis; Class consciousness; Class formation; Class society; Collectivism; Classless society; Communism; Determinism; Dialectical materialism; Dialectics; Economics; Guerrillas; Ideologies; Materialism; Peasant rebellions; Political ideologies; Political power; Proletariat; Realism; Reification; Revolution; Social criticism; Socialism; Utopias.

Masculinity. Masculin(e,ity,ization). Man(ly,liness). Maleness. Machismo. Macho. Phallic. Viril(e,ity). Manful(ness). Manhood. *Choose from:* male, men, man, masculine *with:* sex role(s), identification, attitudes, identity, spirituality, orientation(s), gender role(s), body image. *Consider also:* androcentri(c,sm), homosocial(ity), unfeminine, animus. *See also* Androcentrism; Androgyny; Femininity; Gender identity; Males (human); Personality traits; Sex role attitudes; Sex roles.

Masking. Mask(ed,ing). Disguis(e,ed,ing). Obscur(e,ed,ing,ation). Veil(ed,ing). Camouflag(e,ed,ing). *Consider also:* background noise, visual noise, white noise, filter(s,ed,ing). *See also* Disguise; Perceptual masking; Perceptual stimulation; Visual masking.

Masking, perceptual. See *Perceptual masking.*

Masking, visual. See *Visual masking.*

Masochism. Masochis(m,t,tic). Sadomasochis(m,t,tic). Pseudomasochis(m,t,tic). Sacher-Masoch. *Choose from:* self *with:* punish(ing,ment), punitive, abuse, abasement, abasing, demean(ed,ing), humiliat(e,ed,ing,ion). *See also* Flagellants and flagellation; Masochistic personality; Sadism; Self destructive behavior; Sexual masochism.

Masochism, sexual. See *Sexual masochism.*

Masochistic personality. Masochistic personality. *Choose from:* masochis(m, tic), sadomasochis(m,tic) *with:* personalit(y,ies), tendenc(y,ies), character(s,istic,istics), trait(s). *Consider also:* self destructive(ness), prone(ness) to accident(s), submissive(ness), passivity, death instinct. *See also* Masochism; Personality disorders; Self destructive behavior; Sexual masochism.

Masquerade. See *Disguise.*

Mass behavior. Mass behavior(s). Collective behavior(s). Mob(s). Jonestown. Epidemic. Group violence. Lynching(s). Fan violence. Mass psychogenic illness(es). Team spirit. Gang behavior(s). Fashion(s). Collective behavior(s). Fad(s). Epidemic hysteria. Teamwork. Riot(s). Political movement(s). Craze(s). Massification. Civil disorder(s). *Choose from:* group,

mass, collective, crowd, mob, group, team, gang, cult *with:* behavior(s), hysteria, suicide(s), stress(es), illness(es), violence, response(s), spirit, psychos(is,cs), reaction(s), demonstration(s), action(s), movement(s), migration(s). *See also* Collective behavior; Fads; Fans (persons); Fashions; Mass hysteria; Mass media; Mass psychology; Mass society; Popular culture; Social contagion.

Mass communication. See *Mass media.*

Mass culture. See *Popular culture.*

Mass destruction, weapons of. See *Weapons of mass destruction.*

Mass hysteria. Mass hysteria. Social contagion. Craze(s). Hysterical contagion. Mass reaction(s). Mass psychogenic illness(es). Dancing mania. Biting mania. *Choose from:* epidemic, crowd(s), mass(es), collective, group(s) *with:* hysteri(a,cal), faintness, panic(s), violence. *Consider also:* collective psycho(sis,ses). *See also* Cargo cults; Collective suicide; Hysteria; Mass behavior; Mass psychology; Messianic movements; Social contagion.

Mass media. Mass media. Broadcast(s,ing). Documentar(y,ies). Docudrama(s). Film(s). Magazine(s). Mass communication(s). Movie(s). News coverage. News media. News(paper,papers). Popular media. Press. Primetime. Public service announcement(s). Radio. Sitcom(s). Soap opera(s). Tabloid(s). Television. TV. *Consider also:* sound bite(s), infobit(s), infomercial(s), infotainment. *See also* Advertising; Announcements; Audiences; Audiovisual communications; Communications media; Content analysis; Detective and mystery television programs; Entertainment; Film adaptations; Films; Horror films; Information dissemination; Information services; Journalism; Mass behavior; Mass media effects; Mass media policy; Mass media violence; Mass psychology; Mass society; Media portrayal; Messages; News agencies; News coverage; News media; Newspapers; Political campaigns; Popular culture; Popular literature; Propaganda; Public relations; Publications; Sensationalism; Soap operas; Tabloids; Telecommunications; Television; Television programs; War news.

Mass media effects. Mass media effects. *Choose from:* media, radio, television, TV, prime time, sitcom(s), soap opera(s), childrens program(s), broadcast(s,ing), film(s), movie(s), magazine(s), comic(s), pulp magazine(s) *with:* effect(s), affect(ed,ing), consequence(s), stereotype(s), shap(e,ed,ing) opinion(s), myth(s,making), impact(s), depict(ed, ing,ion,ions), image(s), reinforc(e,ed, ement,ing), propagand(a,ize,ized,izing), imitat(ive,ion,ions), aggress(ion, iveness), behavior(s), social development, role model(s), identification, attitude(s), influence(s), violence, public opinion, response(s), social perception(s), socialization, motivation, escape reaction(s), learning, perception, arousal, interpersonal relations, emotional development, cognitive development, comprehension, psychosocial development, peer relations, selfishness, preference(s), personality, attitude change, persuas(ion,ive), distract(ed, ion), fantasy. *See also* Advertising; Audiences; Cartoons; Change agents; Copycat crimes; Copycat suicide; Dominant ideologies; Films; Horror films; Learning; Mass media; Mass media violence; Media portrayal; News coverage; News media; Newspapers; Opinion leaders; Popular culture; Propaganda; Public opinion; Social change; Television; Television programs.

Mass media policy. Mass media polic(y, ies). *Choose from:* mass media, broadcasting, radio, commercial television, cable television, educational television, film(s), movie(s), mass communication, telecommunication(s), information technology, press, newspaper(s) *with:* polic(y,ies), regulat(e,ed,ing,ion,ions), control(led,ling), licens(e,ed,ing), resolution(s), act(s), law(s). *See also* Censorship; Information policy; Mass media; News policies.

Mass media violence. Mass media violence. *Choose from:* media, radio, television, TV, prime time, sitcom(s), soap opera(s), childrens program(s), broadcast(s,ing), film(s), movie(s), magazine(s), comic(s), pulp magazine(s) *with:* criminogenic, antisocial, violen(ce, t), negative stereotype(s), imitat(ive,ion) aggression, aggress(ion,iveness), selfishness, murder(s), robber(y,ies), vandal(ism,ize), atrocit(y,ies), rape(s), frighten(ing), terror(ist,ists,ism,ize, ized,izing), loot(ed,ing), assault(ed, iveness,ing), riot(s,ed,ing), batter(ed, ing), beat(en,ing). *See also* Cartoons; Films; Horror films; Mass media; Mass media effects; News coverage; News media; School violence; Sports violence; Television; Television plays; Television programs; Violence.

Mass murders. Mass murder(s,ers). Shooting spree(s). Murder spree(s). Killing spree(s). Shooting rampage. Serial kill(er,ers,ings). Serial murder(er, ers). Massacre(s,d). Mass slaying(s). Fired on crowd. *Choose from:* mass *with:* murder(s), killing(s), shooting(s), homicide(s), execution(s), slaying(s). *See also* Atrocities; Genocide; Homicide; Massacres.

Mass production. Mass production. Large scale production. Assembly line(s). Taylorism. De-skilling. Work simplifica-

tion. Fordism. Scientific management. Automation of production. *See also* Assembly lines; Manufacturers; Proletarianization; Scientific management; Work simplification.

Mass psychology. Mass psychology *Choose from:* mass, crowd(s), group(s), mob(s) *with:* dynamic(s), psycholog(y,ical), process(es), behavior(s,al), *See also* Mass behavior; Mass Hysteria; Mass media; Social psychology.

Mass screening. Mass screening(s). Health screening(s). *Choose from:* mass, school admission(s), preschool, genetic, early periodic, newborn(s) *with:* screening(s), routine test(s), handicap identification, chest x-ray(s), preventive examination(s), survey(s), checkup(s). *See also* Diagnostic services; Diagnostic tests; Screening.

Mass society. Mass societ(y,ies). Modern societ(y,ies). Gesellschaft. Large scale societ(y,ies). Secondary relations. Atomized societ(y,ies). Urban society. Secular societ(y,ies). *Consider also:* impersonal(ity), mass behavior, mass culture, admass, consumer societ(y,ies), alienation, anomie. *See also* Alienation; Anomie; Consumer society; Dominant ideologies; Elites; Industrial societies; Mass behavior; Mass media; Masses; Modern society; Popular culture; Shopping centers; Society; Urbanization.

Mass transit. Mass transit. Public transportation. Public transit. Rapid transit. Bus route. Subway(s). Commuter train(s). Bus(ses). Bus system(s). Urban transportation system(s). Trolley car(s). Local transit. Light rail transit. LRT. METRO. BART. Passenger transport. Regional transit. RTA. Rail transit. Streetcar(s). Transit system(s). Passenger bus(ses). Cable car(s). *See also* Car pools; Community services; Public transportation; Subways; Transport workers; Transportation; Transportation policy; Urban planning.

Mass transportation. See *Mass transit.*

Massacres. Massacre(s,d). Mass murder(s,er,ers). Carnage. Shooting spree(s). Murder spree(s). Killing spree(s). Blood bath(s). Bloodbath(s). Shooting rampage. Killing rampage. Mass slayings. Pogrom(s). Holocaust. *Choose from:* mass *with:* slaughter, slaying(s), execution(s), assassination(s), murder(s), homicide(s), extermination. *Consider also:* annihilation, liquidation, genocide, serial killer(s). *See also* Atrocities; Ethnic cleansing; Genocide; Homicide; Mass murders; War atrocities.

Massage. Massage(s,d). Rubdown. Rubb(ed,ing). Knead(ed,ing). Strok(ed, ing). Manipulat(ed,ing,ion). Masseu(se, ses,r,rs). Rolf(ed,ing). Massotherapy. *Consider also:* fondl(e,ed,ing),

handl(ed,ing), pet(ted,ting), chiropractic. *See also* Massage; Physical contact; Touch.

Massage parlors. Massage parlor(s). Massage practitioner(s). Massage therapist(s). Sex oriented business(es). *Consider also:* prostitut(e,es,ion), masseu(se,ses,r,rs). *See also* Massage; Prostitution.

Massed practice. Massed practice. *Choose from:* closely spaced, massed *with:* practice(s), presentation(s), repetition(s), trial(s), training. *See also* Learning; Practice (repetition).

Masses. Mass(es). General public. Proletariat. Citizen(ry,s). Consumer(s). Worker(s). Working class(es). Peasant(ry,s). Voter(s). Voting public. Populace. Population. Community. Society. Nation. Common man. Common people. Bourgeoisie. Middle America. Multitude(s). Mankind. Humankind. Human race. Man in the street. Grass roots. Folk(s). Average man. Untouchable(s). Pleb(es,eian). Third estate. Lower class(es). Ordinary people. *See also* Common people; Elites; General public; Mass society; Middle class; Peasants; Proletariat; Working class.

Masses (music). Mass(es). Messe. Missa. Misa. *Consider also:* eucharistia. *See also* Liturgy; Religious rituals; Worship.

Mastery, self. See *Self control.*

Mastery learning. Mastery learning. *Choose from:* mastery *with:* learning, achievement, model, instruction(al). *Consider also:* Blooms taxonomy of educational objectives. *See also* Academic achievement; Academic standards; Achievement; Learning; Minimum competencies; Performance; Skill learning.

Masturbation. Masturbat(e,ing,ion,ory). Autoerotic activit(y,ies). Automanipulation. Autosexual(ity). Self pleasuring. *Choose from:* manual stimulation, mechanical stimulation, self stimulation, vibrator(s) *with:* genital(ia,s), penis, clitor(is,al), vagina(l). *Consider also:* onanism. *See also* Autoeroticism; Orgasm; Self indulgence; Self stimulation; Sex behavior; Sexual arousal; Sexual fantasies.

Mate selection, animal. See *Animal mate selection.*

Mate selection, human. See *Human mate selection.*

Mate swapping. See *Extramarital relations.*

Materia medica, vegetable. See *Medical botany.*

Material culture. Material culture. Physical object(s). Artifact(s). Relic(s). Traditional article(s). Utensil(s). Tool(s).

Ornament(s). Product(s). Souvenir(s). Memento(s). Material(s). Inanimate object(s). Craft(s). Cloth(es,ing). Art. Monument(s). Historical remains. Historical site(s). Material condition(s). Religious object(s). Sacred object(s). *See also* Artifacts; Arts; Bedding; Body ornamentation; Bone implements; Carving (decorative arts); Clothing; Crafts; Culture (anthropology); Decorative arts; Fashions; Inanimate objects; Machinery; Monuments; Religious articles; Tools; Traditional societies.

Materialism. Materialis(m,t,ts,tic). Economism. Economic basis. Postmaterialis(m,t,tic). Material basis. Material argument(s). Materialistic determinism. *Consider also:* epiphenom-enalism, values of affluence, desire for wealth, interest in acquiring material goods, accumulat(e,ed,ing,ion) wealth, bourgeois values. *See also* Atheism; Embourgeoisement; Dialectics; Empiricism; Idealism; Marxism; Monism; Ontology; Popular culture; Realism; Social theories.

Materialism, dialectical. See *Dialectical materialism.*

Materialism, historical. See *Dialectical materialism.*

Materials, audiovisual. See *Audiovisual materials.*

Materials, hazardous. See *Hazardous materials.*

Materials, library. See *Library materials.*

Materials, raw. See *Raw materials.*

Materials, reading. See *Reading materials.*

Materials, reference. See *Reference materials.*

Materials, scrap. See *Scrap materials.*

Materials, teaching. See *Teaching materials.*

Materials, waste. See *Litter (waste); Scrap materials; Solid waste.*

Maternal age. Maternal age. *Choose from:* maternal, mother(s), pregnancy, child-bearing, reproduct(ive,ion), primipara(s), primigravida(s) *with:* age(s,d), adolescen(t,ce), middle age(d), early, late, older, young(er), teen(age), after 40, 35, over 35. *See also* Biological clocks; Childbearing age; Late child-bearing; Marriage timing; Mothers; Senior pregnancies.

Maternal attachment. See *Attachment behavior.*

Maternal attitudes. See *Parental attitudes.*

Maternal behavior. Maternal behavior(s). Mother(ing,ly,liness). *Choose from:* mother(s), maternal, postpartum *with:* behavior, deprivation, schizophren-ogenic, nurtur(e,ed,ing,ance), role(s),

comfort(ed,ing), care, affection, aggression, cannibalism, responsive(ness), response(s), contact, communicat(ed,ing,ion), competence, relation(s,ship). *See also* Breast feeding; Infant nutrition; Maternal deprivation; Maternal love; Mother child relations; Mother child communication; Mothers; Nurturance.

Maternal behavior, animal. See *Animal parental behavior.*

Maternal deprivation. Maternal(ly) depriv(ed,ation). Motherless(ness). Loss of mother(s). *Choose from:* mother(s, ing), maternal *with:* absen(t,cc), desert(ed,ing,ion), separat(ed,ing,ion), missing, inadequate, abandon(ed,ing, ment), neglect(ed,ing,ful). Death of mother. Lack of mothering. Depriv(ed, ation) of maternal care. *Consider also:* abandoned children. *See also* Abandoned children; Absence; Anaclitic depression; Maternal behavior; Mothers; Parental absence.

Maternal employment. See *Dual career families; Family work relationship; Female headed households; Professional women; Working women.*

Maternal health services. Maternal health service(s). *Choose from:* maternal, maternity, postnatal, prenatal, childbear-ing, perinatal, mother(s) *with:* infant(s), birthing, midwif(e,ery), obstetrical *with:* care, service(s), center(s), health service(s), protection, clinic(s). *See also* Health services; Infant mortality; Maternal mortality; Maternal welfare; Mothers.

Maternal love. Maternal love. *Choose from:* maternal, mother child(ren), mother infant, mother son(s), mother daughter(s) *with:* affection(ate,ately), warmth, attachment(s), closeness, love(d), loving, care, feeling(s), bond(s, ed,ing), cuddl(e,ed,ing), cradl(e,ed,ing), sing(ing), play(ing), interaction(s), comfort(ed,ing), nurturance, support(ed, ing), understanding, accept(ed,ing,ance). *Consider also:* mothering. *See also* Bonding (emotional); Love; Maternal behavior; Mother child communication; Mothers; Nurturance.

Maternal mortality. Maternal mortality. *Choose from:* maternal, mother(s), childbirth *with:* mortalit(y,ies), death(s), dying. *See also* Infant mortality; Maternal health services; Maternal welfare; Mortality rates; Mothers.

Maternal rights. See *Parent rights.*

Maternal welfare. Maternal welfare. *Choose from:* maternal, mother(s), maternity, pregnan(t,cy,cies) *with:* health(y), welfare, protection, care, leave(s). *See also* Child abuse preven-tion; Child health services; Child nutrition; Maternal health services; Maternal mortality; Mothers.

Maternity. See *Birth; Mothers.*

Maternity care. See *Maternal health services.*

Maternity leave. Maternity leave(s). Parental leave(s). Leave for mother(s). Time off for birth. Time off for new parent(s). *Choose from:* mother(s), maternal, maternity, birth, childbirth, childbearing, adoption, infant care *with:* leave(s) of absence, time off, release(d) time, leave without pay, sick leave. *Consider also:* maternity benefit(s), maternity polic(y,ies), pregnancy polic(y,ies), parental leave(s), paternal leave(s). *See also* Employee benefits; Paternity leave; Pregnancy.

Mates. See *Spouses.*

Math ability. See *Mathematical ability.*

Math anxiety. See *Mathematics anxiety.*

Math avoidance. See *Mathematics anxiety.*

Mathematical ability. Mathematical abilit(y,ies). Numera(cy,te). *Choose from:* mathematic(s,al), numerical, arithmetic(al), quantitative, algebr(a,ic), geometr(y,ic), trigonometr(y,ic), calculus, computational *with:* abilit(y,ies), aptitude(s), skill(s), talent(s,ed), facility, genius(es), gifted, knowledge. *See also* Ability; Academic aptitude; Mathematics; Mathematics achievement; Mathematics skills; Number comprehension; Scientific knowledge.

Mathematical concepts. Mathematic(s,al) concept(s). *Choose from:* mathematic(s, al), arithmetic(al), geometr(y,ic), numer(ical,ation), number(s), algebra(ic), trigonometr(y,ic), calculus, binary *with:* concept(s,ual), construct(s), rule(s), principle(s), law(s). *Consider also:* conservation concept, algorithm(s). *See also* Concepts; Mathematical models; Mathematics; Mean; Median.

Mathematical models. Mathematical model(s,ing). Computer simulation(s). Probabil(ity,istic) model(s,ing). Weighted model(s). Incidence model(s). Bayesian model(s). Probability distribu-tion model(s). *Choose from:* maximiza-tion, optimalization, optimization *with:* model(s), theor(y,ies). *Choose from:* mathematical *with:* model(s,ing), simulation(s), analys(is,es), statement(s), formulation(s), reformulation(s). *See also* Game theory; Heuristics; Math-ematics; Models; Operations research; Scientific models; Statistical tables; Stochastic processes.

Mathematics. Mathematic(al,s). Arithmetic(al). Probabilit(y,ies). Trigonometry. Fourier analysis. Cardinality. Equation(s). Number(s). Algebr(a,aic). Calculus. Geometr(y,ic). Statistics. *Consider also:* add(ed,ing, ition), subtract(ed,ing,ion). *See also*

Logic; Mathematical concepts; Mathematical models; Number systems; Numbers; Probability; Statistical data.

Mathematics ability. See *Mathematical ability.*

Mathematics achievement. Mathematic(s, al) achievement. *Choose from:* mathematic(s,al), numerical, arithmetic(al), algebr(a,aic), geometr(y,ic), trigonometr(y,ic), calculus, computational *with:* achievement(s), achiev(e,ed,ing), performance, score(s), comprehension, placement, mastery, skill(s), knowledge. *See also* Academic achievement; Academic skills; Mathematical ability; Mathematics education; Mathematics skills; Reading achievement.

Mathematics anxiety. Mathematics anxiety. Mathophob(e,es,ia,ias,ic). Symbol inhibition. *Choose from:* math, mathematic(s,al), algebra, geometry, trigonometry, calculus *with:* anxiet(y, ies), anxious(ness), avoid(ed,ing,ance), aversive(ness), aversion(s), phob(ic,ia, ias), disabilit(y,ies), stress(es). *See also* Anxiety; Computer anxiety; School phobia; Science anxiety; Test anxiety.

Mathematics education. Mathematics education. *Choose from:* mathematic(s,al), numerical, arithmetic(al), algebr(a,aic), geometr(y,ic), trigonometr(y,ic), calculus, computational, addition, subtraction, multiplication, long division *with:* education(al), educat(e,ed,ing), learn(ed,ing), teach(ing), taught, remedia(l,tion), tutor(ed,ing,ial), instruct(ed,ing,ion), homework, course(s), class(es), skill development. *See also* Mathematics.

Mathematics skills. Mathematic(s,al) skill(s). Numera(cy,te). *Choose from:* mathematic(s,al), numerical, arithmetic(al), quantitative, algebr(a,aic), geometr(y,ic), trigonometr(y,ic), calculus, computational *with:* skill(s), knowledge, competenc(y,ies), proficien(t,cy,cies), expertise, mastery. *See also* Mathematical ability; Mathematics; Mathematics achievement.

Matriarchy. Matriarch(al,ate,y,ies,s). Female head of household. Maternal domination. Dominant mother. Maternal authority. Materfamilias. Female head of family. Mother as head of family. Matricentric. *Choose from:* female(s), women, woman, mother(s), grandmother(s) *with:* dominan(t,ce), authorit(y,ies), leadership, head of household(s). *Consider also:* matrifocal, matrilineal(ity), matrilocal(ity), matricentric, matripotestal, matrilateral, matriliny, gynarch(y,ies). *See also* Family characteristics; Females (human); Femininity; Kinship; Matrilineality; Matrilocal residence; Mother goddesses; Patriarchy.

Matricide. See *Gynocide.*

Matriculation. See *School enrollment.*

Matrilineality. Matrilineal(ity). Matrilinear. Matrilineage(s). Matriliny. Matriclans. Matrilineal inheritance. Matrilineal clans. Uterine descent. *Consider also:* matripotestal, matrilocal, avunculate, matrifocal, matriarch(y,ies), patrilineality. *See also* Descent; Kinship; Lineage; Matriarchy; Patrilineality.

Matrilocal residence. Matrilocal residence. Matrilocality. Uxorilocal residence. *Consider also:* amitalocal. *See also* Family characteristics; Kinship; Matriarchy; Patrilocal residence; Residences.

Matrimony. See *Marriage.*

Maturation. Matur(e,ed,ing,ation). Grow(th,ing,n). Full(y) develop(ed, ment). Full(y) grown. *Choose from:* reach(ed,ing), attain(ed,ing) *with:* maturity, adulthood, manhood, womanhood, voting age. *See also* Adolescent development; Adult development; Age of majority; Aging; Behavior development; Career development; Child development; Cognitive development; Emotional development; Human life cycle; Life stage transitions; Maturational crisis; Moral development; Personality development; Physical development; Self actualization; Self help; Sexual maturation.

Maturation, sexual. See *Sexual maturation.*

Maturational crisis. Maturational cris(is,es). *Consider also:* developmental, normative *with:* cris(is,es). *See also* Identity crisis; Maturation; Turning points.

Maturity, career. See *Vocational maturity.*

Maturity, emotional. See *Emotional maturity.*

Maturity, physical. See *Physical maturity.*

Maturity, social. See *Social maturity.*

Maturity, vocational. See *Vocational maturity.*

Maxims. See *Aphorisms; Axioms; Cliches; Creeds; Doctrines.*

Maximum security facilities. Maximum security facilit(y,ies). *Choose from:* maximum security, high security, secure care *with:* prison(s), penitentiar(y,ies), setting(s), facilit(y,ies), psychiatric hospital(s), treatment, unit(s). High security unit(s). Tight security. Death row. *See also* Dangerous behavior; Prisons; Psychiatric hospitals.

Mayors. Mayor(al,s). Burgomaster(s). Town supervisor(s). *Consider also:* elected city officials. *See also* Cities; Elected officials; Local government; Local politics; Politicians.

Mazdaism. See *Zoroastrianism.*

Maze learning. Maze learning. *Choose from:* maze(s) *with:* learn(ed,ing), performance(s), behavior(s), navigat(e,ed,ing,ion), memory, solving, running, trial(s), recollection. *See also* Learning; Mazes.

Maze pathways. Maze pathway(s). *Choose from:* maze(s), labyrinth(s) *with:* runway(s), pathway(s), tunnel(s), structure(s), layout(s), alleyway(s), arm(s), alley(s), geometry. *See also* Mazes; Tunnels.

Mazes. Maze(s). Labyrinth(s). *See also* Maze learning; Maze pathways.

McCarthyism. McCarthy(ism,ite). Red baiting. Anti-communism. Blacklisting. HUAC. House Un-American Activities. *Consider also:* witch hunt(ing,s). *See also* Anti-intellectualism; Conservative; Defamation; Labeling (of persons); Persecution; Political attitudes; Political conservatism; Political persecution; Political repression; Right wing politics; Scapegoating; Witch hunting.

McNaughton rule. See *Insanity defense.*

Meals. Meal(s). Breakfast(s). Lunch(eon, es). Dinner(s). Supper(s). Banquet(s). Brunch(es). *Consider also:* barbecue(s), cookout(s), picnic(s), clambake(s), feast(s). *See also* Diet; Dinners and dining; Food; Food intake; Food preparation; Food services (programs); Group meals; Malnutrition; Nutrition; School meals.

Meals, communal. See *Group meals.*

Meals, grace at. See *Grace at meals.*

Meals, group. See *Group meals.*

Meals, public. See *Group meals.*

Meals, sacred. See *Sacred meals.*

Meals, school. See *School meals.*

Mean. Mean. Arithmetic mean. Arithmetic average. *See also* Mathematical concepts; Statistical data.

Meaning. Meaning(s). Significan(t,ce). Impl(y,ying,ied). Implication(s). Connot(e,ed,ing,ation,ations). Interpretation(s). Purpose(s). Inferen(ce,ces,tial). Self referent. Definition(s). Information. Them(e,es, atic). Associative. Concept(s,ual). Clarification(s). Intent(ion,ions). Purport. Import. Denot(e,ed,ing,ation). Gist. *Consider also:* understanding, recognition, intrinisic value, perception, subjective response(s), expectation(s), symbol(s,ized,izing,ization), analog(y, ies), metaphor(s), imagery, essence, core, message(s). *See also* Ambiguity; Analogy; Clarification; Collective representation; Communication (thought transfer); Comprehension; Core; Definition (words); Emphasis; Essence;

Existentialism; Explanation; Implications; Meaningfulness; Messages; Nonverbal meaning; Pragmatism; Sex symbolism; Social meaning; Speech acts; Symbolism; Translating and translations; Verbal meaning; Verstehen; Word meaning.

Meaning, nonverbal. See *Nonverbal meaning.*

Meaning, social. See *Social meaning.*

Meaning, verbal. See *Verbal meaning.*

Meaning, word. See *Word meaning.*

Meaningfulness. Meaningful(ness). Significan(t,ce). Meaning(s). Social construction of reality. Purpose(s,ful). Import(ance). Aim(s). Goal(s). Emotional(ly) charge(d). Consequential. Empha(tic,sized). Relevan(ce,cy,t). Substantive. Momentous. *Consider also:* logotherapy, logoanalysis, existentialism, worldview. *See also* Existential therapy; Existentialism; Intentionality; Meaning; Meaninglessness; Optimism.

Meaninglessness. Meaningless(ness). Alienat(e,ed,ing,ion). Social drift. Existential(ism). Depersonalization. Disenchantment. Estrange(d,ment). Empty etiquette. Dissociat(ed,ion). Detached. Outsider(s). Hopeless(ness). Absurd(ity). Death of God. Disaffected. Dispossessed. Emasculat(ed,ion). Disaffiliat(ed,ion). Dehumaniz(ed,ation). Social detachment. Kafkaesque. *Consider also:* powerless(ness), anomie, rootless(ness), helplessness, psychological deprivation, senseless(ness), inan(e,ity), futil(e,ity), normlessness, unrelatedness. *See also* Alienation; Anomie; Apathy; Dehumanization; Depersonalization disorder; Disengagement; Existentialism; Hopelessness; Hostility; Impersonal; Loneliness; Marginality (sociological); Meaningfulness; Pessimism; Presence of God; Reification; Role conflict; Social attitudes; Social isolation.

Meanings, double. See *Double meanings.*

Meanness. Mean(ness). Pett(y,iness). Selfish(ness), Malic(e,ious,iousness). Vexatious(ness). Ignoble. Abject. Sordid. Sting(y,iness). Small-minded(ness). Ill temper(ed). Degrad(ed,ation). Debase(d, ment). Abject(ness). *See also* Belligerency; Misers; Personality traits; Selfishness (stingy).

Means ends. Means end(s). *Choose from:* purposeful behavior, purposive action, means goals, rational model of action, acts *with:* consequences. *Consider also:* unintended consequence(s). *See also* Change; Effects; End; Ethics; Goals; Justification; Methods; Sequelae.

Measurement.
Measur(e,ed,es,ing,ement,ements). Mensurat(e,ed,ing,ion). Metrolog(y,ical). Commensurat(e,ed,ing,ion). Metric(s). Rating. Rate(s,d). Scoring. Score(s,d). Assess(ed,ing,ment,ments). Test(ed,ing, s). Scaling. Scale(s,d). Discriminant validity. Index(ed,es,ing). Checklist(s). Indicator(s). Inventor(y,ies,ied). Gaug(e, ed,ing). Gag(e,ed,ing). Apprais(e,ed, ing,al). Survey(s). Screening(s). Valuat(ed,ing,ion). Evaluat(e,ed,ing,ion, ions). Quantif(y,ied,ying,ication). *Consider also:* sociometr(y,ic), psychometr(y,ic), biometr(y,ic), bibliometr(y, ic), volume, cubic content, weight(s) colorimctr(y,ic), geodesy, measuring instrument(s), computation of length(s), magnitude, numerical(ly) comparab(le, ility). *See also* Achievement tests; Accuracy; Aptitude tests; Behavioral assessment; Construct validity; Content analysis; Criterion referenced tests; Culture fair tests; Dependent variables; Diagnostic tests; Economic indicators; Empirical methods; Enumeration; Essay tests; Evaluation; Experiments; Forced choice tests; Health indices; Health status indicators; Independent variables; Ink blot tests; Intelligence tests; Inventories; Language tests; Living standards; Market statistics; Mathematical models; Methods; Multidimensional scaling; Needs assessment; Neuropsychological assessment; Norms; Nonprojective personality measures; Observation; Occupational tests; Perceptual measures; Performance tests; Personality measures; Population (statistics); Predictive validity; Preference measures; Profiles (measurement); Projective techniques; Psychological tests; Quantitative methods; Quantity; Questionnaires; Ranking; Reading tests; Reliability; Research; Response bias; Retention measures; Risk assessment; Scaling; Screening; Selection tests; Self assessment; Semantic differential; Social indicators; Sociometric technics; Standards; Statistical bias; Statistical correlation; Statistical data; Statistical significance; Statistical tables; Surveys; Technology assessment; Test bias; Test construction; Test interpretation; Test reliability; Test validity; Tests; Testwiseness; Trends; Verbal tests; Vital statistics.

Measurement, attitude. See *Attitude measurement.*

Measurement, educational. See *Educational measurement.*

Measurement, opinion. See *Attitude measurement.*

Measurement, time. See *Time measurement.*

Measurement, work. See *Work measurement.*

Measures. See *Measurement.*

Measures, achievement. See *Achievement tests.*

Measures, intelligence. See *Intelligence tests.*

Measures, nonprojective personality. See *Nonprojective personality measures.*

Measures, perceptual. See *Perceptual measures.*

Measures, personality. See *Personality measures.*

Measures, preference. See *Preference measures.*

Measures, retention. See *Retention measures.*

Measures, security. See *Security measures.*

Meat industry. Meat industry. Butcher(s). *Choose from:* meat, beef, steak(s), hamburger(s), veal, lamb, pork, sausage(s), ham(s), bacon, poultry, chicken, turkey *with:* packinghouse(s), packing plant(s), processor(s), slaughterhouse(s), abbatoir(s), business(es), compan(y,ies), food service(s), rais(e, ing), produc(e,er,ers,tion), ranch(es,er, ers,ing), industr(y,ies,ial), assembly-line(s), market(s,er,ers), price(s), import(s), export(s). *Consider also:* Smithfield Foods, John Morrell & Company, Hillshire Farm, Kahn's Co., Parks Sausage Co., Fair Oaks Farms Inc., Greater Omaha Packing Co., etc. *See also* Agribusiness; Animal industry; Animal products; Cattle industry; Food; Food industry; Food inspection; Slaughterhouses.

Mechanical ability. Mechanical abilit(y, ies). *Choose from:* mechanic(s,al), machin(ery,ist,ists), hand tool(s), technical, engineer(s,ing) *with:* abilit(y, ies), aptitude(s), skill(s), talent(s,ed), comprehension, reasoning, knowledge. *See also* Aptitude; Nonverbal ability.

Mechanisms, defense. See *Defense mechanisms.*

Mechanisms, reimbursement. See *Reimbursement mechanisms.*

Mechanization, agricultural. See *Agricultural mechanization.*

Mechanization, farm. See *Agricultural mechanization.*

Media, communications. See *Communications media.*

Media, educational. See *Instructional media.*

Media, instructional. See *Instructional media.*

Media, mass. See *Mass media.*

Media, news. See *News media.*

Media, violence in. See *Mass media violence.*

Media coverage. See *News coverage.*

Media effects, mass. See *Mass media effects.*

Media journalism. Media journalis(m,t,ts). *Choose from:* television, media, radio, newspaper(s), free press *with:* journalis(m,t,ts,tic), editorial(s), commentator(s), opinion piece(s), journalistic practice(s). *Consider also:* media bias(es), press coverage, ethical issues in journalism, media credibility: *See also* Broadcast journalism; Journalism; Journalistic ethics.

Media policy, mass. See *Mass media policy.*

Media portrayal. Media portrayal. Media attention. Media influence(s). Hype. Factoid(s). Yellow journalism. *Choose from:* media, journalis(m,t,ts,tic), newspaper(s), radio, television, TV, broadcast(s,ing,er,ers), news agenc(y,ies), wire service(s), press, periodical(s), magazine(s), reporting, reporter(s), anchor(ing,person,persons, man,men,woman,women,people), newspeople, news, newsroom(s), newsweekl(y,ies), columnist(s), NBC, ABC, CBS, New York Times, scandal(s), election(s), etc. *with:* portray(ed,ing,al, als), slant(ed,ing,s), depict(ed,ing,ion, ions), bias(es,ed), characteriz(e,ed,ing, ation,ations), caricatur(e,es), stereotyp(e, ed,es,ing,ical,ically), coverage, lack of coverage, attitude(s), propagand(a,ize, ized,izing,ist,ists), objectiv(e,ity,eness), unbiased, selectiv(e,ity,eness), account(s), description(s), interpretation(s), opinion(s,ated), censor(ed,s,ing), invad(e,ed,ing) privacy, gatekeep(ing,er, ers), accura(cy,te), inaccura(cy,te), distort(ed,ing,ion,ions). *See also* Accuracy; Attitudes; Censorship; Characterization; Chattering class; Communication (thought transfer); Description; Editorials; Fairness and accuracy in reporting; Journalistic ethics; Mass media; Mass media effects; News coverage; Opinion leaders; Propaganda; Public opinion; Representation (likeness); Journalists.

Media violence, mass. See *Mass media violence.*

Median. Median(s). Midpoint. Second quartile. 50th percentile. Fifth decile. *Consider also:* quantiles. *See also* Mathematical concepts; Statistical data.

Mediated responses. Mediated response(s). *Choose from:* mediat(e,ed,ing), preparatory *with:* response(s), respond(ed,ing), performance. *See also* Responses.

Mediation. Mediat(e,ed,ing,or,ors,ion,ions). Arbitrat(e,ed,ing,or,ors,ion,ions). Arbiter(s). Honest broker(s). Shuttle diplomacy. Alternative(s) to courtroom. Private judge(s). Render(ed,ing,s) judgment. Referee(s). Moderat(e,ed,ing, or,ors). Interceding. Go-between(s). Tribunal(s). Fact finding. Third part(y, ies). *Consider also:* conciliat(e,ed,ing, ion), conflict management, reconcil(ed,

ing,iation). *See also* Arbitrators; Arbitration; Complaints; Conflict resolution; Dispute settlement; Disputes; Intervention; Labor management relations; Negotiation; Peace negotiations.

Medical abortion. Medical abortion(s). Non-surgical abortion(s). Abortion pill(s). RU-486. Mifepristone. *Consider also:* methotrexate *with:* misoprostol. *See also* Abortifacients; Abortion.

Medical advertising. Medical advertis(ing, ement,ements). *Choose from:* medical profession, medical practitioner(s), physician(s), physical therapist(s), dentist(s), doctor(s), veterinarian(s), prescription drug(s), pharmaceutical(s), *with:* marketing, advertis(ing,ement, ements), promotional item(s), paid announcement(s). *See also* Advertising; Health promotion; Professional ethics.

Medical anthropology. Medical anthropolog(y,ist,ists). *Choose from:* medical, health, medicine, sickness, healing, healer(s), physician(s), doctor(s), pain, illness *with:* anthropolog(y,ist,ists), cross-cultural, indigenous. *See also* Cultural anthropology; Mescal (cactus); Paleopathology; Physical anthropology; Psychotropic plants; Traditional medicine.

Medical assistance. Medical assistance. Medicare. Limited eligibility health care system. Governmental health service. Public assistance patient(s). National health service. Health care voucher(s). Federal financing of long term care. Medical development assistance. Medicaid. Health insurance for aged and disabled title 18. Medical assistance title 19. *See also* Antipoverty programs; Assistance; Community health services; Community mental health services; Government aid; Government financing; Government programs; Government subsidization; Health expenditures; Health insurance; Health policy; Health services needs and demand; Income maintenance programs; Medical care; National health programs; Public welfare; Social programs; Unemployment relief.

Medical botany. Medical botany. *Choose from:* medical, medicin(e,al), health, remed(y,ies), healing, psychotropic, drug(s) *with:* plant(s), herb(s), botan(y,ical), vegetable(s). *Consider also:* vegetable materia medica. *See also* Ethnobotany; Herbal medicine; Medical foods; Mescal (cactus); Psychotropic plants; Traditional medicine.

Medical care. Medical care. *Choose from:* medical, health, patient(s) *with:* care, treatment(s), therap(y,ies). *See also* Ambulatory care; Care of the sick; Critical care; Dental care; Healing; Health care; Health services; Home care;

Hospitalization; Intensive care; Long term care; Night care; Nursing care; Postnatal care; Postoperative care; Prenatal care; Primary health care; Psychotherapy; Residential treatment; Terminal care; Trauma centers; Treatment.

Medical care rationing. See *Health care rationing.*

Medical climatology. Medical climatology *Choose from:* medical, disease(s), epidemiolog(y,ical), health, mortality, morbidity, pandemic(s), epidemic(s), patient(s) *with:* climate(s), climatic change(s), climatolog(y,ical,ist,ists), tropic(s,al), subtropic(s,al), arctic, high altitude(s), cold weather. *See also* Medical geography; Tropical medicine.

Medical compliance. See *Patient compliance.*

Medical diagnosis. See *Diagnosis.*

Medical disclosure. See *Informed consent.*

Medical ecology. See *Medical geography.*

Medical economics. Medical economics. *Choose from:* medical care, health care, hospital(s,ization) *with:* cost(s), economic(s), financing, cost-effectiveness. *See also* Health care rationing; Health expenditures.

Medical education. Medical education. *Consider also:* medical, medicine, physician(s), nursing, pharmaceutical, veterinary, psychiatric, biomedical, pediatric, surgery, obstetrics, gynecology, urology, neurology, dentistry, immunology, dermatology, cardiology, endocrinology, gastroenterology, hematology, oncology, nephrology, rheumatology, neonatology, perinatology, venereology, anesthisology, pathology, public health, radiology, neurosurgery, opthalmology, orthopedics, plastic surgery, thoracic surgery *with:* education, training, curriculum, school(s), college(s), intern(s,ship, ships), resident(s), residen(cy,cies). *See also* Allied health personnel; Health education; Health occupations; Nursing education; Patient education; Physicians; Professional education.

Medical ethics. Medical ethics. Informed consent. Patient confidentiality. Helsinki declaration. Hippocratic oath. *Choose from:* medical, clinical, doctor(s), physician(s), medicine, surg(ery,ical), genetic(s), treatment(s), euthanasia, death(s), dying, nontreatment, abortion(s), eugenics, wrongful life, wrongful death, transplant(ed,ing,ation), treatment refusal, withhold(ing) treatment, in vitro fertilization, right to life, right to die, right to treatment, DNA research, prolong(ing,ed,ation) of life, organ donor(s), extraordinary treatment, host mother(s), life extension, justifiable killing, living will(s), sterilization, birth defect(s), malpractice, iatrogenic disease(s), cloning, embryo transfer(s), involuntary commitment(s), contraception, pain, suffering, illness, prenatal surgery *with:* ethic(s,al), philosoph(y, ical), bioethic(s,al), moral(s,ity), relig(ion,ious), theolog(y,ical), humanitarian, metaethic(s,al), welfare, social good, common good, individual right(s), self determination, free choice, freedom, value(s), human dignity, free will, responsibilit(y,ies), obligation(s). *See also* Bioethics; Ethical practices; Ethics; Malpractice; Nursing ethics; Pharmacogenomics; Physician patient relations; Professional ethics; Quackery; Research ethics; Single nucleotide polymorphisms; Unethical conduct.

Medical folklore. See *Traditional medicine.*

Medical foods. Medical food(s). Nutriceutical(s). Medicinal herb(s). *Consider also:* yogurt, fiber, phytochemical(s), phytoestrogen(s), isoflavone(s), plant polyphenol(s), flavonoid(s), capsaicin, carotenoid(s), beta-carotene, glucosinolate(s), terpene(s). *See also* Food additives; Herbal medicine; Medical botany; Natural foods; Vitamin therapy.

Medical geography. Medical geograph(y, ical). *Choose from:* medical, disease(s), health, mortality, morbidity, pandemic(s), epidemic(s), patient(s), epidemiolog(y,ical) *with:* geograph(y, ical), geographic information system(s), atlas(es), map(s,ping,ped), location(s), ecolog(y,ical), neighborhood(s), spatial distribution(s), global variation(s), socio-geographical pattern(s). *Consider also:* disease ecologist(s), medical geographer(s), medical geopolitic(s), epidemiology. *See also* Catchment area (health); Environmental pollutants; Environmental pollution; Epidemics; Geography; Hazardous wastes; Health surveys; Health indices; Health status indicators; Human ecology; Human geography; Infant mortality; Medical climatology; Medically underserved areas; Morbidity; Mortality rates; World health.

Medical history. See *Patient history.*

Medical history taking. Medical history taking. *Choose from:* medical history, medical background *with:* tak(e,en,ing). *Choose from:* patient(s), medical, preanesthesia, intake *with:* interview(s), obtain(ing) history, interrogation. *See also* Medical records; Patient history; Psychodiagnosis.

Medical illustration. Medical illustration(s). *Choose from:* medical, anatom(y,ical), biological *with:* illustration(s), drawing(s), sketch(es), photograph(s,y), photo(s). *Consider also:* moulage(s). *See also* Animal painting and illustration; Artists;

Biological illustration; Graphics; Illustrated books.

Medical innovations. Medical innovation(s). New medical device(s). *Choose from:* medical, health care, treatment(s), biomedical, biotechnolog(y,ical) *with:* innovation(s), new technolog(y,ies), 21st century, progress, new development(s). *See also* Genetic engineering; Innovations; Scientific discoveries; Technological innovations.

Medical insurance. See *Health insurance.*

Medical malls. See *Walk-in clinics.*

Medical malpractice. See *Malpractice.*

Medical marijuana. Medical marijuana. *Choose from:* marijuana, marihuana, cannibis, cannabinoid(s), hash, hashish, hemp, pot, sinsemilla, tetrahydrocannab(inol,oid,oids) *with:* prescrib(e,es, ing), prescription(s), therapeutic, therap(y,ies), doctor recommended, physician recommended, medic(al,ation, ations,icinal,ine), pallia(tion,tive), cancer, neoplasm(s), chemotherapy, pain, clinical trial(s), oncology, vomit(ing,s), nause(a,ating,ate,ated), glaucoma, cache(ctic,cexia), AIDS wasting syndrome, muscle spasms. *See also* Drug and narcotic control; Legalization of drugs; Marijuana laws; Street drugs.

Medical missions. Medical mission(s,ary, aries). *Choose from:* medical, doctor(s), surgeon(s) *with:* mission(s,ary,aries) *See also* Missionaries; Traditional medicine.

Medical model. Medical model(s). *Choose from:* medical, biopsychosocial, disease, biomedical, pharmacotherapeutic, illness, sickness, faulty mechanism *with:* model(s), framework(s), approach(es), ideolog(y,ies), perspective(s). *See also* Biological models; Disease; Etiology; Health care; Medical philosophy; Medical sociology; Models; Social medicine.

Medical personnel. See *Allied health personnel; Health manpower; Health occupations; Mental health personnel; Military medical personnel; Physicians.*

Medical personnel, military. See *Military medical personnel.*

Medical personnel supply. Medical personnel supply. *Choose from:* health, healthcare, hospital, paramedical, medical, clinic *with:* manpower, personnel, staff, human resources, social worker(s), professional(s), paraprofessional(s), allied health personnel, dentist(s), medical consultant(s), nurse(s), pharmacist(s), physician(s), psychologist(s), veterinarian(s), coroner(s), medical examiner(s), general practitioner(s), gynecologist(s), internist(s), neurologist(s), obstetrician(s), optometrist(s),

paramedic(s), pathologist(s), pediatrician(s), physical therapist(s), psychiatrist(s), surgeon(s) *with:* supply, demand, allocat(e,ed,ing,ion,ions), utilization, shortage(s), surplus(es), distribution, needs, overutiliz(e,ed,ing, ation), underutiliz(e,ed,ing,ation). *See also* Allied health personnel; Catchment area (health); Health manpower; Health services needs and demand; Human resources; Labor supply; Medically underserved areas; Mental health personnel; Military medical personnel; Physicians.

Medical philosophy. Medical philosophy. *Choose from:* medical, medicine, health care, physician(s), ill(ness,nesses), disease(s), disorder(s) *with:* philosoph(y, ies,ical,er,ers), ideolog(y,ies), ethic(s,al), model(s). *Consider also:* Helsinki declaration, Hippocratic oath. *See also* Euthanasia; Medical ethics; Medical model; Philosophy; Physician patient relations; Research ethics.

Medical privacy. Medical privacy. *Choose from:* abortion, vital, medical, health, patient(s), genetic, hospital, blood bank(s), HIV, AIDS, prescription(s), treatment, DNA , doctor-patient relations(hip), cancer, disabilit(y,ies), diabet(es,ic), epilep(sy,tic), Alzheimer's, psychiatric *with:* record(s), data, database(s), information, file(s) *with:* privacy, private, access, control, disclosure, confidential(ity), privileged information, security. *Consider also:* Fair Health Information Practices Act. *See also* Patient rights; Privacy laws.

Medical professions. See *Allied health personnel; Health occupations; Nurses; Physicians.*

Medical records. Medical record(s). *Choose from:* medical, psychiatric, physician(s), patient(s), health, pediatric, clinical, hospital, nursing *with:* record(s), histor(y,ies), chart(s), data, document(s), account(s). *See also* Mandatory reporting; Medical history taking; Nursing records; Patient history; Records; Scientific records.

Medical regimen compliance. See *Patient compliance.*

Medical schools. Medical school(s). *Choose from:* medical, medicine, *with:* school(s), college(s), academic. *Consider also:* teaching hospitals. *See also* Colleges; Medical education; Medical sciences; Medical students; Professional education.

Medical sciences. Medical science(s). Medicine. Medical specialt(y,ies). Medical specialization(s). Health science(s). Biomedical science(s). Medical profession. *Consider also:* aerospace medicine, adolescent medicine, adolescent psychiatry, allergy and immunology, anesthesiology, audiology, behavioral medicine, biological psychiatry, biomedicine, cardiology, child psychiatry, colon and rectal surgery, community epidemiology, community psychiatry, dentistry, dermatology, dietetics, electroencephalography, emergency medicine, endocrinology, epidemiology, family practice, forensic medicine, forensic psychiatry, gastroenterology, geriatric psychiatry, geriatrics, gynecology, hematology, internal medicine, medical genetics, medical sociology, military medicine, military psychiatry, naval medicine, neonatology, nephrology, neurology, neuropathology, neuropsychiatry, neurosurgery, nuclear medicine, nursing, obstetrics, occupational medicine, oncology, ophthalmology, orthopedics, orthopsychiatry, osteopathy, otolaryngology, pathology, pediatrics, perinatology, pharmacology, pharmacy, physical medicine, plastic surgery, podiatry, preventive medicine, preventive psychiatry, primary health care, public health, psychosomatic medicine, psychiatry, radiology, rehabilitation, rheumatology, social medicine, social psychiatry, sports medicine, submarine medicine, surgery, thoracic surgery, toxicology, transcultural psychiatry, tropical medicine, urology, venereology, veterinary medicine. *See also* Academic disciplines; Bioethics; Biotechnology; Dental care; Genetics; Geriatrics; Health; Health care; Holistic health; Human body; Illness; Life sciences; Medical model; Medical schools; Medical sociology; Pediatrics; Physician patient relations; Primary health care; Psychiatrists; Traditional medicine; Treatment; Tropical medicine.

Medical sociology. Medical sociology. Sociology of medicine. Sociomedical. Sociomedicine. *Choose from:* medical(ly), medicine, health, disease(s), ill(ness,nesses), disorder(s), disab(ility, ilities,led), handicap(ped), epidemi(ology), epidemic(s), therap(y,ies,eutic), cure(s) *with:* sociolog(y,ical), social science(s), social condition(s). *See also* Medical model; Medical sciences; Social medicine.

Medical staff. Medical staff. *Choose from:* medical, hospital, resident medical *with:* staff, physician(s), officer(s), doctor(s), personnel, surgeon(s). *Consider also:* house staff physician(s). *See also* Allied health personnel; Health manpower; Health occupations; Medical personnel supply; Nursing staff; Nursing team; Physicians.

Medical students. Medical student(s). *Choose from:* medical college, medical school(s), medicine *with:* student(s), trainee(s), intern(s,ship,ships). *Consider also:* premed student(s), medical intern(s). *See also* Graduate students; Medical education.

Medical technicians, emergency. See *Emergency medical technicians.*

Medical treatment. See *Drug therapy; Treatment.*

Medical wastes. Medical waste(s). Biomedical waste(s). Red bag(s). Biohazard(s, ous). *Choose from:* waste(s), trash, rubbish, refuse, discard(ed), dispos(e,es, ing,able,ables), sewage, dumping, debris, sludge, garbage, pollution, incinerat(ed,or,ors), emmission(s) *with:* hospital(s), medical, infectious, biomedical, oncolog(y,ical), clinical, sloproom, antineoplastic, neoplastic, laborator(y,ies), blood(y), pathogen(s, ic). *See also* Air pollution; Carcinogens; Containment of biohazards; Environmental pollutants; Environmental pollution; Environmental protection; Hazardous wastes; Nuclear waste; Pollution control; Toxic substances; Solid waste; Waste disposal; Water pollution.

Medically underserved areas. Medically underserved area(s). Physician shortage(s). Medically underserved communit(y,ies). *Consider also:* health services accessibility, national health service corps. *See also* Catchment area (health); Health manpower; Health services needs and demand; Medical geography; Medical personnel supply; Triage; Tropical medicine.

Medication errors. Medication error(s). Mistaken ingestion. Inadvertent ingestion. Illegibility of prescription(s). *Choose from:* medication(s), medicine(s), prescription(s), treatment(s), drug(s), injection(s), physician(s), pharmacist(s), dosage(s), therapy *with:* error(s), mistake(s,n), inadvertent, erroneous(ly), incorrect, careless(ness). *Consider also:* iatrogenic disorders. *See also* Errors; Drug effects; Fallibility; Iatrogenesis; Incorrect; Malpractice.

Medication, self. See *Self medication.*

Medications. See *Drugs.*

Medicinal plants. See *Herbal medicine; Medical botany.*

Medicine, aerospace. See *Aerospace medicine.*

Medicine, alternative. See *Alternative medicine.*

Medicine, Arabic. See *Arabic medicine.*

Medicine, Ayurvedic. See *Ayurvedic medicine.*

Medicine, Chinese. See *Chinese medicine.*

Medicine, community. See *Community health services.*

Medicine, emergency. See *Emergency medicine.*

Medicine, folk. See *Shamanism; Traditional medicine.*

Medicine, forensic. See *Forensic medicine.*

Medicine, herbal. See *Herbal medicine.*

Medicine, Indian. See *Ayurvedic medicine.*

Medicine, industrial. See *Occupational health services.*

Medicine, oriental. See *Oriental medicine.*

Medicine, preventive. See *Preventive medicine.*

Medicine, primitive. See *Traditional medicine.*

Medicine, social. See *Social medicine.*

Medicine, socialized. See *National health programs; State medicine.*

Medicine, sports. See *Sports medicine.*

Medicine, state. See *State medicine.*

Medicine, traditional. See *Traditional medicine.*

Medicine, tropical. See *Tropical medicine.*

Medicinemen. See *Shamanism.*

Medicines. See *Drugs; Herbal medicine; Non-prescription drugs; Nostrums; Prescription drugs; Traditional medicine.*

Medicines, over the counter. See *Non-prescription drugs.*

Medicines, proprietary. See *Non-prescription drugs.*

Medieval criticism. Medieval critic(s,ism). *Choose from:* medieval, middle ages, courtly literature, 500-1500 A.D., Carolingian, Anglo Saxon *with:* critic(s,ism), commentar(ies,y), literary theory, interpretation. *See also* Medieval literature.

Medieval drama. Medieval drama(tic,tics, turgical). *Choose from:* medieval, mediaeval, Middle Ages, medieval, middle ages, 500-1500 A.D., Carolingian, Anglo Saxon, Anglo-Norman, Moyen Age, Mittelalters, médiévaux *with:* play(s), drama(tic,tics,turgical), stage, theatre(s), theater(s), pageant(s), comed(y,ies). *See also* Drama; Liturgical drama; Medieval literature; Miracle plays; Morality plays; Religious drama.

Medieval education. Medieval education. *Choose from:* education(al), illitera(te, cy), litera(te,cy), learning, universit(y, ies), school(s), schoolmaster(s) *with:* medieval, middle ages, Anglo-Saxon(s), Carolingian, tenth century, twelfth century, fourteenth century, fifteenth century, etc. *See also* Feudalism; Medieval technology; Medieval theology; Middle ages; Religious education.

Medieval geography. Medieval geography. *Choose from:* medieval, middle ages, tenth century, twelfth-century, fourteenth century, fifteenth century, etc. *with:* atlas(es), cartograph(y,ical), geograph(y, ical), geolog(y,ical), map(s,ped,ping). *Consider also:* flat error, time-slice map(s). *See also* Geography; Medieval technology; Middle ages.

Medieval literature. Medieval literature. *Choose from:* medieval, mediaeval, middle ages, 500-1500 A.D., Carolingian, Anglo Saxon, courtly, Anglo-Norman, Moyen Age, Mittelalters, medievaux, Gothic, Romanesque, Arthurian, Goliardic *with:* literature, romance(s), drama, play(s), poem(s), poet(ry,ics), song(s), bestiar(y,ies), lyric(s), manuscript(s), romance(s) *Consider also:* Canterbury Tales, Chaucer, scholasticism, Goliard(s), minnesang, minnesinger(s), Le Morte D'Arthur, Abelard, St. Bernard of Clairvaux, St. Anselm, Bede, Geoffrey of Monmouth, Matthew Paris, Walter Map, Suger, William of Tyre, St. Bonaventure, St. Albert Magnus, St. Thomas Aquinas, Duns Scotus, William of Occam, Vincent of Beauvais, Jacobus de Voragine, etc. *See also* Bestiaries; Literature; Medieval criticism; Medieval drama, Medieval logic; Medieval manuscripts; Medieval poetry; Medieval theology; Middle ages; Minnesinger; Miracle plays; Modern literature; Morality plays; Renaissance literature; Scholasticism; Scribes.

Medieval logic. Medieval logic(ian,ians). Insolub(ilia,les). *Choose from:* medieval, middle ages *with:* logic(ian,ians), syllogism(s). *See also* Logic; Medieval literature; Medieval philosophers; Renaissance philosophy.

Medieval manuscripts. Medieval manuscript(s). *Choose from:* medieval, middle ages, 500-1500 A.D., Carolingian, Anglo Saxon, courtly, Anglo-Norman, Moyen Age, Mittelalter(s, lichen) médiévaux *with:* manuscript(s), manoscritt(i,a), manuscrit(o,s), letter(s), handschrift(en). *See also* Manuscripts; Medieval literature; Scribes.

Medieval military history. Medieval military history. *Choose from:* medieval, middle ages, 500-1500 A.D., Carolingian, Anglo Saxon, Anglo-Norman *with:* military art, military history, archer(s), battle(s), invasion(s), war(s,fare), combat, soldier(s), arm(y,ies), *Consider also:* Hundred Years' War, Crusades. *See also* Crusades; Feudalism; Historical periods; Medieval technology; Middle ages; Military history; Triumphal arches; War memorials.

Medieval music. Medieval music(ian,ians). *Choose from:* medieval, mediaeval, middle ages, 500-1500 A.D., Carolingian, Anglo Saxon, Anglo-

Norman, Gothic, Romanesque *with:* music(al,ally,ian,ians), ballad(es), rondeaux, virelais, madrigal(s), chanson(s). *Consider also:* Gregorian chant(s), ars antiqua, ars nova, ars subtilior, minnesinger(s), early music, troubadour(s), trouvere(s), Geisserlied(er). *See also* Ballata; Bells; Courtly love; Estampie; Formes fixes; Frottola; Laude; Liturgical drama; Middle ages; Music; Renaissance music; Troubadour; Trouvere; Virelai.

Medieval philosophers. Medieval philosopher(s). *Choose from:* medieval, middle ages, Anglo-Saxon(s), Carolingian, tenth century, twelfth century, fourteenth century, fifteenth century, etc. *with:* philosopher(s), theologian(s), logician(s). *Consider also:* Saint Thomas Aquinas, Saint Albertus Magnus, Saint Anselm, Boethius, Saint Bonaventure, John Duns Scotus, Roger Bacon, Moses Maimonides, William of Ockam, etc. *Consider also:* scholasticism. *See also* Medieval logic; Philosophy; Renaissance philosophy; Scholasticism.

Medieval plays. See *Medieval drama*.

Medieval poetry. Medieval poe(t,ts,try,m, ms,tics). *Choose from:* medieval, mediaeval, middle ages, 500-1500 A.D., Carolingian, Anglo Saxon, courtly, Anglo-Norman, Moyen Age, Mittelalters, medievaux *with:* poe(t,ts,try,m, ms,tics), epic(s), lyric(s,al), lyrique(s), lyrik, ballad(s,en), poesia, verse(s), rhym(e,es,ing), song(s), hymn(s,ody), couplet(s). *See also* Medieval literature; Poetry; Skaldic poetry.

Medieval sculpture. Medieval sculpture. *Choose from:* medieval, mediaeval, Middle Ages, medieval, middle ages, 500-1500 A.D., Carolingian, Gothic, Norman, Romanesque, Anglo Saxon, Anglo-Norman, Moyen Age, Mittelalters, medievaux *with:* sculpture(s), skulptur(en), carving(s), *See also* Arts; Carving (decorative arts); Middle ages; Sculpture.

Medieval technology. Medieval technology. *Choose from:* medieval, middle ages, Crusades, Renaissance, dark ages, Anglo-Saxon(s), Carolingian, tenth century, twelfth century, fourteenth century, fifteenth century, etc. *with:* technolog(y,ical), invention(s), tool(s), implement(s), innovation(s), machine(s), mechanical(ly), harrow(s), plow(s), scythe(s), pitchfork(s), cannon(s), compass(es), dam(s), grindstone(s), harness(es), horseshoe(s), loom(s), paper-making, spectacle(s), saddle(s), stirrup(s), whippletree(s), windmill(s), cast iron, wrought iron. *Consider also:* alchem(y,cal), medieval scien(ce,tific). *See also* Agricultural mechanization; Alchemy; Feudalism; Industrial

museums; Medieval education; Medieval geography; Medieval military history; Middle ages; Technological innovations; Technological progress; Technology; Technology and civilization; Tools.

Medieval theater. See *Medieval drama*.

Medieval theology. Medieval theolog(y,ical). *Choose from:* medieval(ism), mediaeval(ism), twelfth century, 12th century, thirteenth century, 13th century, etc., dark ages, feudal(ism), Holy Roman Empire, crusade(r,rs,s) *with:* theolog(y,ical), doctrin(e,es,al), creed, dogma(s), Trinity, Fall of man, transubstantiation, consubstantiation, ascension, spirituality, asceticism, Christianity, mysticism, Biblical text, scripture, analogia entis, analogia fidei, atonement salvation, divine grace, sacraments atonement, perichoresis Apostles' creed, Nicene creed, Vulgate, prayer(s). *See also* Crusades; Feudalism; Medieval education; Medieval literature; Middle ages; Monasticism; Papacy; Renaissance; Renaissance philosophy; Scholasticism; Theology; Transubstantiation.

Medieval warfare. See *Medieval military history*.

Meditation. Meditat(e,ed,ing,ive,ion,ional). Yoga. Mantra repetition. *Consider also:* prayer, relaxation training, mind expansion, centering, relaxation response, chant(ed,ing), contemplat(e, ed,ing,ion), higher consciousness, transcendental states of consciousness, absolute bliss. *See also* Altered states of consciousness; Attention; Calmness; Contemplation; Enlightenment (state of mind); Holistic health; Human potential movement; Hypnosis; Martial arts; Metacognition; Prayer; Psychoneuro-immunology; Psychophysiologic disorders; Psychophysiology; Relaxation; Relaxation training; Religion; Religious experience; Religious life; Religious practices; Self congruence; Spiritual exercises.

Meekness. See *Humility*.

Meetings. Meeting(s). Conference(s). Congress(es). Caucus(es). Seminar(s). Staff meeting(s). Sympos(ia,ium). Convention(s). Assembl(y,ies). Annual meeting(s). Council(s). Gathering(s). Session(s). Hearing(s). *See also* Agenda; Negotiation; Professional development; Public meetings.

Meetings, open. See *Public meetings*.

Meetings, public. See *Public meetings*.

Melancholia. See *Depression (psychology)*.

Melancholy. See *Sadness*.

Melodrama (music). Melodrama(s). Monodrama(s). Duodrama(s). *See also* Opera.

Melody. Melod(y,ies,ic). Melodia. Meloidia. Melos. *Consider also:* ragas, maqams, tune(s), tonada(s), toada(s). *See also* Folk music; Music.

Meltdown, network. See *Network meltdown.*

Melting pot. Melting pot. Cultural plural(ity,ism). Cultural heterogeneity. Multicultural(ism). Bicultural(ism). Pluricultural(ism). Cultural accomodation. Religious pluralism. Plural(istic) societ(y,ies). Multicultural societ(y,ies). American diversity. *Choose from:* ethnic(ally), cultural(ly), religious(ly), racial(ly) *with:* heterogeneity, heterogeneous, integrat(ed,ion), divers(e,ity), assimilat(ed,ion), plural(ism,istic), intermarriage. *See also* Acculturation; Assimilation (cultural); Biculturalism; Common culture; Cultural diversity; Interethnic families; Intermarriage; Interracial marriage; Racial diversity; Racially mixed; Religious accommodation; Plural societies; Social integration.

Members, cabinet members. See *Advisory committees.*

Members, family. See *Family members.*

Members, union. See *Union members.*

Membership. See *Organization membership; Organizational affiliation; Religious affiliation.*

Membership, church. See *Church membership.*

Membership, organization. See *Organization membership.*

Memoirs. See *Autobiography; Biography.*

Memoria technica. See *Mnemonic learning.*

Memorials, war. See *War memorials.*

Memories, childhood. See *Early memories.*

Memories, early. See *Early memories.*

Memory. Memor(y,ies). Recall. Recollect(ion,ions). Remember(ed,ing). Memoriz(e,ed,ing,ation). Mnemonic. Reminiscence(s). Retention. Encod(e,ed, ing). Human information storage. Recognition. Recogniz(e,ed,ing). Decod(e,ed,ing). *Consider also:* chunking, learning, eidetic imagery. *See also* Chunking; Cognitive enhancers; Cognitive processes; Cues; Early memories; Eidetic imagery; Episodic memory; Forgetting; Human information storage; Hypermnesia; Iconic memory; Long term memory; Memory decay; Memory disorders; Memory trace; Metacognition; Mnemonic learning; Recall; Relearning; Reminiscence; Retention (psychology); Rote learning; Serial learning; Short term memory; Spatial memory; Verbal learning; Verbal memory; Visual memory.

Memory, collective. See *Collective consciousness; Collective representation; Cultural knowledge; Political myths.*

Memory, episodic. See *Episodic memory.*

Memory, false. See *Paramnesia.*

Memory, iconic. See *Iconic memory.*

Memory, long term. See *Long term memory.*

Memory, short term. See *Short term memory.*

Memory, spatial. See *Spatial memory.*

Memory, verbal. See *Verbal memory.*

Memory, visual. See *Visual memory.*

Memory decay. Memory decay. Forget(ful,ting). *Choose from:* memory, learned response(s) *with:* decay(ed,ing), loss(es), losing, decline, impair(ed,ment, ments), fade(d), fading, deteriorat(e,ed, ing,ion), decreas(e,ed,ing), aging. *See also* Cognition disorders; Forgetting; Memory disorders.

Memory disorders. Memory disorder(s). Dysmnes(ia,ic). Amnes(ia,ic). Amnest(ia,ic). *Choose from:* anterograde, retrograde, circumscribed, selective, generalized, continuous, psychogenic *with:* amnesia. Deja-vu. Fugue reaction. *Choose from:* memory *with:* disorder(s,ed), impair(ed,ment, ments), deficit(s), alteration(s), loss(es), disturbance(s), dysfunction(s), deficien(t,cy,cies), deficit(s), forget(ful), defect(s), distort(ed,ion,ions). *See also* Alzheimer's disease; Amnesia; Cognition disorders; Fugue reaction; Memory; Memory decay; Senile dementia.

Memory trace. Memory trace(s). Mnemonic trace(s). Mneme(s). Engram(s). *See also* Memory.

Memory training. See *Mnemonic learning.*

Men. See *Males (human).*

Men, fear of. See *Fear of men.*

Men, gay. See *Male homosexuality.*

Men, great. See *Famous people; Heroes; Martyrs; Role models; Saints.*

Men, holy. See *Holy men.*

Men, married. See *Husbands.*

Men, medicine. See *Shamanism.*

Men, psychologically abused. See *Psychologically abused men.*

Men, single. See *Bachelors; Single person.*

Men in female dominated occupations. See *Nontraditional careers.*

Men of color. See *People of color.*

Men's movement. Men's movement. *Choose from:* men, man, male(s), husband(s), father(s), son(s) *with:* support group(s), movement, liberation, right(s). *Consider also:* fathers' rights, misogyn(y,ist,ists). Promise Keepers, Padare, Men's Forum on Gender. *See also* Feminism; Male chauvinism; Misogyny; Political movements; Sex role attitudes; Social movements; Women's rights.

Men's role. See *Gender identity; Sex roles.*

Menarche. Menarch(e,eal,al). First menstrual period. Begin menstruation. First menses. Sex maturation in girls. Perimenarch(al,ial). *Choose from:* pubert(y,al) *with:* girl(s), female(s). Menstrual cycle onset. *See also* Adolescent development; Life cycle; Menstrual cycle; Menstruation; Puberty; Sex education; Sexual maturation.

Mendicant orders. See *Friars.*

Mennonites. Mennonite(s). Swiss Brethren. Dordrecht Confession of Faith. Mennonite Church. Old Mennonites. Amish. *Consider also:* Anabaptist(s), Pennsylvania Dutch. *Consider also:* Hutterite(s). *See also* Protestantism.

Menopause. See *Climacteric.*

Menopause, male. See *Climacteric.*

Menstrual cycle. Menstrual cycle. *Choose from:* menstrual, ovarian, sexual hormonal, intermenstrual, feminine *with:* cycle(s). *Choose from:* premenstrual, menstrual, hormonal, intermenstrual phase, follicular, luteal *with:* phase(s), stage(s), follicular phase(s). Luteal phase(s). Luteal stage(s). Reproductive cycle(s). *Consider also:* premenstrual tension, ovulation. *See also* Menarche; Menstrual disorders; Menstruation; Premenstrual syndrome.

Menstrual disorders. Menstrual disorder(s). Amenorrhea. Dysmenorrhea. Hypomenorrhea. Menorrhagia. Retrograde menstruation. Oligomenorrhea. Polymenorrhea. Pseudocyesis. *Choose from:* menstruation, menstrual, premenstrual, perimenstrual, menses *with:* disorder(s), distress, symptom(s), problem(s), irregular(ity,ities), stress, dysfunction, disturbance(s), discomfort. *See also* Female genital disorders; Menstruation; Premenstrual syndrome.

Menstruation. Menstruat(e,ed,ing,ion). Menstrual. Menses. Monthly period(s). Feminine cycle(s). *Consider also:* amenorrhea, catamenia, hypomenstrual, premenstrual, menarche, follicular phase(s), luteal phase(s). *See also* Menarche; Menstrual cycle; Menstrual disorders; Premenstrual syndrome.

Mensuration. See *Measurement; Quantitative methods.*

Mental abilities. Mental abilit(y,ies). Gift(ed,s). *Choose from:* mental, cognit(ive,ion), problem solving, intellectual, spatial, artistic, verbal, piaget(ian), linguistic, thinking, mathematical, memory *with:* abilit(y, ies), acuity, keen(ness), talent(ed,s), capacit(y,ies), capabilit(y,ies), competen(t,ce,cy,cies), skill(s), aptitude(s), strength(s), proficien(t,cy), expertise. *See also* Ability; Academic ability; Cognitive development; Cognitive structures; Intelligence; Intuition; Metacognition; Spatial ability.

Mental age. Mental age(s). Mental ability level. Intelligence age. *See also* Developmental stages; Intelligence; Intelligence quotient.

Mental chronometry. See *Time perception.*

Mental confusion. Confus(ion,ional,ed). Mental(ly) confus(ed,ion). Disordered orientation. Disturb(ed,ance) of consciousness. Disorient(ed,ation). Doubt(s,ing). Disorganiz(ed,ing,ation). Derange(d,ment). Perplexed. Deliriant. Bewildered. Sundowner(s). Perplex(ed, ity). Anamnestic confusion. Wander(ed, ing,er,ers). Memory loss(es). *Consider also:* confabulat(e,ed,ing,ion), turmoil, tumult, pandemonium, commotion, turbulence. *See also* Cognition disorders; Doubt; Frustration; Thought disturbances; Wandering behavior.

Mental cruelty. See *Emotional abuse.*

Mental deficiency. See *Mental retardation.*

Mental depression. See *Depression (psychology).*

Mental development. See *Cognitive development.*

Mental disabilities. See *Cognition disorders; Learning disabilities; Mental illness; Mental retardation.*

Mental discipline. Mental discipline. Disciplined mind(s). *Choose from:* discipline(d), well organized, peak performance(s), power, control(led) *with:* mental(ly), mind(s), intellect(ual, ually), learning abilit(y,ies). *See also* Self control; Self management (individual); Self culture.

Mental disorders. See *Cognition disorders; Mental illness.*

Mental disorders, organic. See *Organic mental disorders.*

Mental disorders, physiological. See *Organic mental disorders.*

Mental disorders, substance induced organic. See *Substance induced organic mental disorders.*

Mental fatigue. Mental(ly) fatigue(d). *Choose from:* mental(ly), cognitive(ly), intellectual(ly), psychic, psychosomatic *with:* fatigue(d), overwork(ed), exhaust(ed,ing,ion), overload(ed). *Consider also:* burnout, burn(t,ed) out, burn-out, mental load(s), mental asthenia. *See also* Burnout; Industrial fatigue; Info fatigue syndrome; Occupational stress; Overwork.

Mental healing. See *Spiritual healing.*

Mental health. Mental health. Mental hygiene. Psychohygienic. *Choose from:* mental(ly), psychologic(al,ally), emotional(ly), psychosocial(ly) *with:* health, hygien(e,ic), health(y), well being, matur(e,ity), sound(ness), stab(le,ility). *See also* Adjustment (to environment); Community mental health; Coping; Emotional adjustment; Hygiene; Life satisfaction; Mental illness; Morale; Neuroses; Psychoses; Psychological well being; Rural mental health; Self actualization; Suburban mental health; Urban mental health; Well being.

Mental health, community. See *Community mental health.*

Mental health personnel. Mental health personnel. *Choose from:* mental health, psychiatric, mental hospital(s), psychiatric institution(s) *with:* personnel, practitioner(s), professional(s), staff, paraprofessional(s), employee(s), attendant(s), worker(s), clinician(s), counselor(s), specialist(s). *Consider also:* psychiatrist(s), psychotherapist(s), psychiatric social worker(s), psychiatric nurse(s), school psychologist(s), clinical psychologist(s), hypnotherapist(s), psychiatric aide(s), psychoanalyst(s). *See also* Allied health personnel; Counselors; Human resources; Paraprofessional personnel; Psychiatrists; Psychologists; Social workers.

Mental health prevention, primary. See *Preventive psychiatry.*

Mental health programs. Mental health program(s). *Choose from:* mental health, stress control, psychiatric, drug abuse, alcoholism, psychological, child guidance, crisis intervention, detoxification, methadone maintenance, suicide prevention *with:* program(s), partial hospitalization, treatment, intervention(s), counseling, hot line, outreach, project(s), prevention, service(s), center(s). *See also* Child guidance; Community mental health services; Crisis intervention; Deinstitutionalization; Drug rehabilitation; Health care; Home visiting programs; Help lines (telephone); Mental health; Mental health services; Primary prevention; Psychiatric clinics; Public health; Suicide prevention.

Mental health, rural. See *Rural mental health.*

Mental health services. Mental health service(s). *Choose from:* mental health, psychiatric, counseling, guidance, psychiatric social work, psychothcrap(y, eutic), psychogeriatric *with:* service(s), clinic(s), care, program(s), treatment. *See also* Child guidance; Community mental health services; Community services; Counseling; Delivery of services; Health care; Mental health; Mental health programs; Prevention; Psychiatric emergency services; School counseling; Social services; Social work; Student personnel services.

Mental health services, community. See *Community mental health services.*

Mental health, suburban. See *Suburban mental health.*

Mental health, urban. See *Urban mental health.*

Mental hospitals. See *Psychiatric hospitals.*

Mental hospitals, state. See *Psychiatric hospitals.*

Mental illness. Mental illness(es). Mental disorder(s). Madness. Insan(e,ity). Dement(ed,ia,ias). Psycho(tic,ses). *Choose from:* mental(ly), psychiatric, neuropsychological, neuropsychiatric, psychological, nervous, emotional, affective *with:* disorder(s), disease(s), ill(ness,nesses), manifestations, patients, symptoms, inpatients, disabilit(y,ies), disturb(ances,ed), breakdown. *Consider also:* autis(m,tic), schizophren(ia,ic), borderline state(s), depress(ion,ives), neuros(is,es), adjustment disorder(s), personality disorder(s), dysthymic disorder(s), panic disorder(s), seasonal affective disorder(s), addiction(s). *See also* Affective disorders; Alcoholism; Anorexia nervosa; Anxiety disorders; Autism; Behavior disorders; Bipolar disorder; Bulimia; Culture specific syndromes; Cyclothymic disorder; Defense mechanisms; Depression (psychology); Disorders; Eating disorders; Emotionally disturbed; Ethnospecific disorders; Etiology; Glossolalia; Hypomania; Insanity defense; Irrational beliefs; Mental health; Mentally ill offenders; Neuroses; Onset (disorders); Paranoid disorders; Phobias; Psychiatric patients; Psychopathology; Psychoses; Seasonal affective disorder; Schizophrenia; Senile dementia.

Mental illness, attitudes toward. See *Attitudes toward mental illness.*

Mental illness, chronic. See *Chronic psychosis.*

Mental load. See *Human channel capacity.*

Mental patients. See *Psychiatric patients.*

Mental processes. See *Cognitive processes.*

Mental retardation. Mental(ly) retard(ed,ation). Amentia. Cretin(ism). Mongol(ism,oid). Mongolian idiocy. Borderline intelligence. Idiocy. Trisomy 21. Subnormal intelligence. Idiot(s) savant. Imbecile(s). Feebleminded(ness). Oligophren(ia,ic). *Choose from:* mental(ly), intellectual(ly) *with:* retard(ed,ation), handicap(s,ped), deficient, defective, disabled, inadequa(te,cy), impair(ed,ment,ments), deficien(t,cy,cies). *Choose from:* severe(ly), mild(ly), moderate(ly), profound(ly) *with:* retard(ed,ation). *Consider also:* amaurotic familial idiocy, anencephaly, Cockayne's syndrome, cri du chat syndrome, Delange's syndrome, fragile x syndrome, Gangliosidosis, Gaucher(s) disease, Hallervorden Spatz syndrome, Hartnup disease, hydrocephalus, homocystinuria, kernicterus, kinky hair syndrome, Laurence Moon Biedl syndrome, Lesch Nyhan syndrome, lipochondrodystrophy, maple syrup urine disease, microcephaly, mucolipidosis, Niemann Pick disease, neurofibromatosis, oculocer. rorenal syndrome, phenylketonuria, Prader Willi syndrome, Rubinstein Taybi syndrome, Sandhoff disease, Tay Sachs disease, tuberous sclerosis. *See also* Attitudes toward mental retardation; Borderline mental retardation; Custodial care; Deinstitutionalization; Developmental disabilities; Down's syndrome; Educable mentally retarded; Education of mentally retarded; Exceptional persons; Home reared mentally retarded; Institutionalized mentally retarded; Intelligence; Learning disabilities; Profoundly mentally retarded; Psychosocial mental retardation; Severely handicapped infants; Severely mentally retarded; Tay Sachs disease; Trainable mentally retarded.

Mental retardation, attitudes toward. See *Attitudes toward mental retardation.*

Mental retardation, borderline. See *Borderline mental retardation.*

Mental retardation, mild. See *Educable mentally retarded.*

Mental retardation, psychosocial. See *Psychosocial mental retardation.*

Mentally handicapped. See *Mental retardation.*

Mentally ill. See *Mental illness; Psychiatric patients; Psychoses.*

Mentally ill offenders. Mentally ill offender(s). Insanity defense. Criminal psychopath(s). Maximum security psychiatric patient(s). Competen(t,cy) to stand trial. Not guilty by reason of insanity. *Choose from:* mental(ly) ill(ness), mental(ly) disorder(ed), mental(ly) handicap(s,ped), mentally abnormal, mental disease, mental impairment(s), mentally impaired, mental patient(s), personality disordered, disturbed, schizophren(ia,ic), borderline, psychopath(s,ic), sociopath(s,ic), antisocial, insan(e,ity), psychiatric, paranoi(a,d), neuropsychologically impaired, manic depressive, bipolar disorder, psychotic, psychos(is,es), hallucin(ating,ation,ations), organic brain syndrome(s) *with:* correction(al,s), prison inmate(s), prison(s,er,ers),

offender(s), arrest(s,ed), criminal(ly,s, ization), jail(ed,s), felon(s), defendant(s), defense, acquittee(s), acquitted, incarcerat(ed,ion). *See also* Competency to stand trial; Insanity defense; Mental illness; Offenders; Sex offenders.

Mentally retarded. See *Mental retardation.*

Mentally retarded, educable. See *Educable mentally retarded.*

Mentally retarded, education of. See *Education of mentally retarded.*

Mentally retarded, home reared. See *Home reared mentally retarded.*

Mentally retarded, institutionalized. See *Institutionalized mentally retarded.*

Mentally retarded, profoundly. See *Profoundly mentally retarded.*

Mentally retarded, severely. See *Severely mentally retarded.*

Mentally retarded, trainable. See *Trainable mentally retarded.*

Menticide. See *Brainwashing.*

Mentors. Mentor(s,ing,ship). Peer counselor(s). *Consider also:* advisor(s), guide(s), confidant(s), guru(s), coach(es), preceptor(s,ship), support relationship(s), master(s) *with:* apprentice(s), old boy(s) network(s), role model(s). *See also* Adult development; Apprenticeship; Counseling; Development; Guru; Interpersonal relations; Interprofessional relations; Occupational aspirations; Peer counseling; Peer influences; Professional development; Role models; Significant others; Social influences; Spiritual direction; Vocational counselors.

Mentors, spiritual. See *Clergy; Guru; Mentors; Wise person.*

Mercenaries. Mercenar(y,ies). Hired troop(s). Hired gun(s). Gun(s) for hire. *Consider also:* Foreign Legion, dogs of war. *See also* Armed forces; Military assistance; Military personnel.

Merchandise. See *Consumer goods.*

Merchandising. See *Marketing.*

Merchant marine. See *Shipping industry.*

Merchants. Merchant(s). Retailer(s). Trades(people,men,man). Marketer(s). Vendor(s). Shopkeeper(s). Dealer(s). Trader(s). Jobber(s). Middle(man,men). Huckster(s). Higgler(s). Peddler(s). Trafficker(s). Butcher(s). Florist(s). Grocer(s). Baker(s). Store owner(s). Salesclerk(s). Salespeople. Salesperson(s). Sales(woman,women, man,men). *See also* Business personnel; Businessmen; Consumers; Customer relations; Dealers; Entrepreneurship; Marketing; Retailing; Sales; Sales personnel; Stores; Vendor relations; Women merchants.

Merchants, women. See *Women merchants.*

Mercy. Merc(y,iful,ifulness). Forgive(ness). Clemency. Pardon(ed,ing). Humanitarian(ism). Charit(y,able). Magnanim(ity,ous). *Consider also:* compassion(ate), pity, sympath(y,etic), generous(ness), generosity, forbearance, toleran(t,ce), kindhearted(ness). *See also* Amnesty; Charity; Good; Humanitarianism; Pity.

Mercy killing. See *Euthanasia.*

Merger integration. Merger integration. *Choose from:* merger(s), merged operations, merged entities, merg(e,ed, ing), megacompan(y,ies), megamerger(s) *with:* integrat(ed,ing,ion), combin(e,ed, ing,ation), shared vision, cross-selling, consolidat(e,ed,ing,ion), reconcil(e,ed, ing,iation), synerg(y,ies), transition(s,al). *See also* Conglomerates; Consolidation; Cooptation; Corporate acquisitions; Downsizing; Mergers; Organizational change; Organizational development; Organizational structure; Reengineering; Reorganization; Unification.

Mergers. Merg(e,ed,er,ers,ing). Megamerger(s). Organizational merger(s). Corporate merger(s). Business takeover(s). Coalescence. Conurbation. Corporate marriage(s). *Consider also:* acquisition(s), takeover(s), partnership(s), amalgamat(e,ed,ing,ion,ions), affiliat(e,ed,ing,ion,ions), conglomerat(e, ed,ing,ion,ions), consolidat(e,ed,ing, ion,ions), consort(ia,ium), federat(e,ed, ing,ion,ions), LBO(s), leveraged buyout(s), earn-out(s). *See also* Anti takeover strategies; Big business; Business; Buyouts; Cartels; Centralization; Coalitions; Combinations; Conglomerates; Consolidation; Corporate acquisitions; Corporate control; Corporations; Hostile takeovers; Incorporation; Leveraged buyouts; Merger integration; Organizational structure; Power sharing; Teaming; Unification.

Meritocracy. Meritocrac(y,ies). Meritocrat(ic,ization). *Consider also:* credentialism, tracking, reward(s) with merit. *See also* Elitism (government); Incentives; Political ideologies; Technocracy.

Mermaids. Mermaid(s). Merm(an,en). Siren(s). *Consider also:* Lorelei, Melusin(e,a), sea nymph(s), nix(ie,y,es), undine, water spirit(s), sea maid(s). *See also* Fairies; Folk literature; Folklore; Images of women; Mythical animals; Superstitions; Water spirits.

Mescal (cactus). Mescal. Mezcal. Peyot(e,l). Payote. Mescal button(s). *Consider also:* Lophophora williamsii, pulque, maguey. *See also* Folk culture; Folklore; Hallucinogens; Medical anthropology; Medical botany; Plant folklore; Plants (botanical); Psychotropic plants.

Mesolithic period. Mesolithic period. Middle stone age. *Consider also:* Azilian, Tardenoisian, Maglemosian, Ertebolle, kitchen-midden, Campignian, Asturian, Natufian, Badarian, Gerzean, Capsian, etc. *with:* culture(s). *See also* Ancient architecture; Paleolithic period; Prehistoric people.

Messages. Message(s). Information(al). Verbal expression(s). Multimessage(s). Information form(s). Announcement(s). Proclamation(s). Memo(s). Letter(s). Statement(s). News. Command(s). Decree(s). Note(s). Meaning(s). Intent. Rumor(s). Sign(s). Communication(s). Prose. Content(s) of communication(s). Content analy(sis,tic). Communique(s). *See also* Announcements; Assertions; Audiences; Communication (thought transfer); Communications research; Content analysis; Declarations; Gossip; Information; Mass media; Meaning; Rumors.

Messengers. Messenger(s). Courier(s). Carrier(s). Bearer(s). Envoy(s). Emissar(y,ies). Go-between(s). Intermediar(y,ies). Mediator(s), Dispatcher(s). Deput(y,ies). Prox(y,ies). Delegate(s). Ambassador(s). Diplomat(s). Envoy(s). *Consider also:* advocate(s), attorney(s), legat(e,or,ors), plenipotentiar(y,ies), internuncio(s), representative(s). *See also* Agents; Diplomats; Letter carriers; Representatives.

Messiahs. Messiah(s). Messianic figure(s). Savior(s). Saviour(s). Mahdi(s). Jesus Christ. Meshiach. Mashiach. Moshiach. Vishnu. Wovoka. Imam. Muhtadun. Hudat al muhtadun. Holy one(s). *Consider also:* prophet(s), deliverer(s), redeemer(s), emancipator(s), liberator(s). *See also* Charisma; Messianic era; Messianic movements; Mysticism; Prophecy; Prophets; Redemption (theology); Salvation.

Messianic era. Messianic era. *Choose from:* messianic *with:* era(s), age(s), coming. *Consider also:* Eretz Israel, Jewish eschatology. *See also* Apocalypse; Messiahs.

Messianic movements. Messianic movement(s). Messianism. Messianic expectation(s). Second coming. Messianismo. *Consider also:* millenialism, millenarianism, apocalyp(se,tic), revitalization movement(s), judgement day, resurrection, cargo cult(s), eschatolog(y,ical), religious revivalism. *See also* Cargo cults; Collective suicide; Judgement day; Mass hysteria; Messiahs; Millenarianism; Nativistic movements; Religious cults; Religious gatherings; Religious movements; Religious revivals; Salvation; Social contagion.

Mestizos. See *Racially mixed.*

Metacognition. Metacognit(ion,ive). Metacognit(ion,ive). Metamemory. Meta memory. Metaknowledge. Meta knowledge. Mnemonic mediator(s). Mediated memory. Metamnemonic. Meta-attention. Mediator production. Memorization strateg(y,ies). Metapragmatic knowledge. *Choose from:* awareness, self perceived, self monitored, auto-control, mediated, understand(ing) *with:* retrieval cue(s), recall strateg(y,ies), memory process(es), cognitive function(s), retrieval cue(s). *See also* Cognitive processes; Cognitive ability; Communication skills; Comprehension; Meditation; Memory; Phenomenological psychology; Self control; Self evaluation.

Metal, heavy music. See *Heavy metal (music).*

Metal industry. Metal industry. *Choose from:* metal(s), iron, steel, copper, aluminum, scrap metal, sheet metal *with:* forge(s), foundr(y,ies), industr(y,ies,ial), production, factor(y,ies), manufactur(ing), mill(s,ing), plant(s), broker(ed, ing), trade, process(ed,ing). *Consider also:* metalwork(ing), smelt(ing), can recycling, metallurgy. *See also* Automobile industry; High technology industries; Iron industry; Machine tool industry.

Metalanguage. Metalanguage. Second order language. Higher level language. *Consider also:* metalinguistic(s), metagrammar, metarule(s), language awareness. *See also* Cognitive processes; Language; Linguistics; Psycholinguistics; Terminology.

Metals, transmutation of. See *Alchemy.*

Metalwork, art. See *Art metalwork.*

Metamemory. See *Metacognition.*

Metamorphosis. Metamorphos(e,is,es). Transform(ed,ing,ation). Transmutat(e, ed,ing,ion). *Consider also:* chang(e,ed, ing), commut(e,ed,ing), convert(ed,ing), conversion(s), transfigur(e,ed,ing), translat(e,ed,ing), transmogrif(y,ied, ication), transpos(e,ed,ing), transubstantiat(e,ed,ing,ion). *See also* Change; Sex change; Transubstantiation.

Metamotivation. Metamotivation. Growth motivation. Being motivation. B motivation. *See also* Motivation.

Metaphors. Metaphor(s,ical,ically). Simil(e,itude). *Choose from:* figur(e,es, ative) *with:* speech, language, sentence(s). *Consider also:* metonym(y,ies,ic,ical), syndecdoch(e,es, ic,ical,ically), analog(y,ies), trope, nonliteral, literary imagery. *See also* Adages; Allegory; Allusions; Analogy; Description; Ekphrasis; Figurative language; Gothicism; Imagery; Irony;

Language; Legends; Literature; Personification; Poetics; Semantics; Sex symbolism; Similes; Symbolism.

Metaphysics. Metaphysic(s,al,ians). Transcendent. Immanent. Supersensible. Supernatural. *Consider also:* ontolog(y, ical), cosmolog(y,ical), epistemolog(y, ical), speculative philosophy. *See also* Deconstruction; Logocentrism; Nihilism; Ontology; Philosophy; Reality; Teleology; Theology.

Metayer system. See *Sharecropping.*

Meter (poetry). Meter. Versif(y,ied,ication). Poetic rhythm(s). *Choose from:* syllabic, accentual, accentual-syllabic, quantitative *with:* prosody, construction, system(s). *Consider also:* syllabism, pentameter. *See also* Poetics; Poetry; Prosody; Rhythm; Stanzas.

Methadone. See *Narcotics.*

Methadone maintenance. Methadone maintenance. *Choose from:* methadone *with:* maintenance, maintain(ed), treatment, narcotic withdrawal, program(s). *See also* Detoxification; Drug addiction; Drug rehabilitation; Drug withdrawal; Narcotics; Substance dependence; Substance withdrawal syndrome.

Method (acting). Method acting. Stanislavsky Method. Stanilavsky's Method. Stanislavski's Method. Stanislavski's effective memory technique. *See also* Acting; Actors and actresses; Drama; Improvisation (acting); Theater.

Method, interpretive. See *Verstehen.*

Method, lecture. See *Lecture method.*

Method, nondirected discussion. See *Nondirected discussion method.*

Method, open classroom. See *Open classroom method.*

Method, rhythm. See *Rhythm method.*

Method, scientific. See *Scientific method.*

Methodology. See *Data analysis; Data collection; Methods; Research methods.*

Methods. Method(s,ology,ological). Research method(s). Technique(s). Application(s). Approach(es). Strateg(y,ies). Guideline(s). Model(s). Procedure(s). Mode(s). Process(es). Principle(s). Modus operandi. Means. Formula(e,s). Practice(s). Function(s). Plan(s). Tactic(s). Design(ed,ing,s). Routine(s). Program(s). Code(s). Guide(s). *Consider also:* analys(is,es), survey(s), stud(y,ies), testing, algorithm(s), branching, correlation(s), critical incidents method, critical path method, inference, delphi technique, fixed sequence, heuristics, holistic approach, home visit(s), inquir(y,ies), interdisciplinary approach, network analysis(is,es), pacing, sequential approach(es), simulation(s). *See also* Best practices; Change agents; Cognitive techniques; Empirical methods; Feeding practices; Heuristics; Interdisciplinary approach; Lecture method; Legal procedures; Management methods; Means ends; Mutual storytelling technique; Nondirected discussion method; Nonpunitive approach (discipline); Observation methods; Open classroom method; Paradoxical techniques; Practices (methods); Projective techniques; Psychotherapeutic techniques; Qualitative methods; Quantitative methods; Research methods; Rhythm method; Scientific method; Selection procedures; Simulation; Teaching methods; Verstehen.

Methods, assembly-line. See *Assembly lines.*

Methods, educational. See *Teaching methods.*

Methods, empirical. See *Empirical methods.*

Methods, experimental. See *Empirical methods; Research methods.*

Methods, instructional. See *Teaching methods.*

Methods, management. See *Management methods.*

Methods, observation. See *Observation methods.*

Methods, practices. See *Practices (methods).*

Methods, qualitative. See *Qualitative methods.*

Methods, quantitative. See *Quantitative methods.*

Methods, research. See *Research methods.*

Methods, teaching. See *Teaching methods.*

Metrics. See *Meter (poetry).*

Metrology. See *Measurement.*

Metropolitan areas. Metropolitan area(s). Cit(y,ies). Urbaniz(ed,ation). Urban. Standard metropolitan statistical area(s). SMSA(s). Megalopolis. Greater city. Suburban environment(s). Suburban area(s). Conurbation. *Choose from:* metropolitan, urbaniz(ed,ation), urban *with:* area(s), region(s), environment(s). *Consider also:* area(s) of dominant influence, ADI(s), designated market area(s). *Consider also:* Berlin, Boston, Chicago, London, Moscow, New York, Paris, Rome, Tokyo, etc. *See also* Areas; Center and periphery; Cities; Geographic regions; Municipalities; Neighborhoods; Suburbs; Urban environments; Urban fringe; Urban sprawl; Urbanization.

Metropolitan government. See *Municipal government.*

Mexican American border region. Mexican American border region. *Choose from:* Mexic(an,o) *with:* America(n), U.S., United States *with:* border(s,land,lands), border region(s), frontier(s), frontera, boundar(y,ies), transborder, deterritorializ(e,ed,ing, ation). *Consider also:* Rio Grande, northeastern Sonora, Baja CA, Tucson, El Paso, frontera norte de Mexico. *See also* Border ballads; Border industries; Borderlands; Deterritorialization; Illegal aliens; Mexican Americans;.

Mexican Americans. Mexican American(s). Chicano(s). Chicana(s). Texmex. Mexicano(s). *Choose from:* Mexic(o,an) *with:* immigrant(s), migrant worker(s). *Consider also:* Hispanic American(s). *See also* Ethnic groups; Hispanic Americans; Mexican American border region; Minority groups.

Mexican language. See *Nahuatl language.*

Mexican literature. See *Latin American literature.*

Microcomputers. Microcomputer(s). Microprocessor(s). Personal computer(s). PC(s). Micro(s). Word processor(s). Laptop computer(s). Laptop(s). Notebook computer(s). Desktop computer(s). Desk-top(s). Luggable computer(s). Home computer(s). Portable computer(s). Desktop computer(s). *Consider also:* pentium(s), etc. *See also* Computer networks; Computers; Debugging; Mobile computing.

Microcounseling. Microcounsel(ed,ing). Micro-counsel(ed,ing). *Consider also:* microtrain(ed,ing), microvideoanalysis, micro-interview(ed,ing), microteaching, micro-skills training. *See also* Counseling; Education; Interviews; Paraprofessional personnel.

Microenterprise. Microenterprise(s). Microloan(s). Mini-entrepreneur(s). Microbusiness(es). Microfunding. *Consider also:* informal economic sector, peer lending, Grameen Bank, Self-Employed Women's Association, Accion International, etc. *See also* Antipoverty programs; Entrepreneurship; Home based businesses; Minority businesses; Self employment; Small businesses; Women owned businesses.

Microfilming. Microfilm(s,ed,ing). *Consider also:* microreproduc(e,ed,tion), microphotograph(y,ed,ing), micropublish(ed,ing), microform reproduction(s), microfiche, computer output microfilm. *See also* Automated information storage; Information; Microforms.

Microforms. Microform(s). Microformat(s). Microfiche. Microfilm(ed,ing). Micropublication(s). *Consider also:* micropublish(ing), microreproduc(e,ed, ing,tion), microfilm master(s), micro-

form reproduction(s). *See also* Copies; Copying processes; Microfilming.

Micropublications. See *Microforms.*

Midcareer change. Midcareer change. Second career(s). *Choose from:* middle age(d), midlife, mid-life, middle life, midcareer, mid-career, middle years, matur(e,ity), menopaus(e,al), climacteric, empty nest, displaced homemaker(s), post-menopaus(e,al), postmenopausal, over 40, age(d,s) 50 to 64, age(d,s) 40 to 59 *with:* career(s), job(s), employment, occupation(s,al), work(ing) *with:* retrain(ed,ing), chang(e,es,ed,ing), transition(s,al), turning point(s), juncture(s), cris(is,es), choice(s), disrupt(ed,ing,ion,ions), passage(s), adjust(s,ed,ment,ments), re-entry, re-enter(ed,ing), readjust(s,ed, ment,ments), shift(ing,s,ed), promot(ed, ion,ions). *See also* Career change; Life stage transitions; Middle age; Midlife crisis.

Middens, kitchen. See *Kitchen middens.*

Middle age. Middle age(d). Midlife. Mid-life. Middle life. Midcareer. Mid-career. Middle years. Matur(e,ity). Menopaus(e, al). Climacteric. Age critique. Age(d,s) 40 to 59. Age(d,s) 40 to 60. Age(d,s) 45 to 64. Over 40. Over 45. 50 years old. Over 50. Over 55. *Consider also:* empty nest, sandwich generation, displaced homemaker(s), post-menopaus(e,al), postmenopausal. *See also* Adult; Adult development; Age discrimination; Aging; Attitudes toward the aged; Climacteric; Developmental stages; Early retirement; Elderly; Human life cycle; Life stage transitions; Midcareer change; Retirement planning.

Middle ages. Middle ages. Medieval(ism). Mediaeval(ism). 8th - 15th centuries. Dark ages. Feudal period. Moyen age. Mittelalter(s,lich). *Consider also:* Holy Roman Empire, crusade(r,rs,s), serf(s,dom), Anglo-Saxon(s). Carolingian, tenth century, twelfth century, fourteenth century, fifteenth century, etc. *See also* Armor; Crusades; Feudalism; Historical periods; Medieval education; Medieval geography; Medieval literature; Medieval military history; Medieval music; Medieval sculpture; Medieval technology; Medieval theology; Monasticism; Papacy; Peasants; Renaissance; Renaissance music.

Middle class. Middle class(es). Middle income. Middle socioeconomic status. Middle socioeconomic class(es). Middle socioeconomic group(s). Bourgeois(ie). Burgher(s). Embourgeoisement. Moderate income. Middle status. Average person. Middle America. Silent majority. *Consider also:* owning class(es), business(man,men,woman, women), working class(es), working man, working woman, common man. *See also* Bourgeoisie; Embourgeoisement; General public; Masses; New middle class; Proletarianization; Social class; Socioeconomic status.

Middle class attitudes. See *Embourgeoisement.*

Middle class, new. See *New middle class.*

Middle East. Middle East(ern). Afghanistan. Bahrain(i) [Bahrein(i)]. (Arab Republic of) Egypt(ian) [United Arab Republic]. Iran(ian) [Persia(n)]. Iraq(i). Israel(i). (Hashemite Kingdom of) Jordan(ian). Kuwait(i). Leban(on,ese). (Sultanate of) Oman [Muscat and Oman]. Qatar(i). Saudi Arabia(n). Syria(n) (Arab Republic). Turk(ey,ish) [Ottoman Empire]. United Arab Emirates [Trucial coast, Trucial Oman, Trucial States]. (Republic of) Yemen(i) [North Yemen, Yemen Arab Republic, People's Democratic Republic of Yemen, South Yemen]. *Consider also:* Near East, Arabian Peninsula, Arabian Desert, Mesopotamia(n), Gulf of Oman, Palestin(e,ian), Holy Land(s), Canaan, Mecca(n). *See also* African empires; Anatolian languages; Asian empires; Central Asia; Eastern Europe; Hamitic languages; Jewish-Arab relations; North Africa; Semitic languages; South Asia; Western Europe.

Middle income countries. See *Less developed countries.*

Middle income level. Middle income level(s). Middle class. *Choose from:* middle, average, moderate, median, mean *with:* income(s), earning(s). *Consider also:* middle *with:* class(es), socioeconomic level(s), socioeconomic status, SES. *Consider also:* working class, middle America, bourgeoisie. *See also* Low income; Middle class; Socioeconomic status; Upper income level.

Middle level managers. Middle level manager(s). Middle manager(s). Mid-management. *Choose from:* middle, mid-level, midlevel, intermediate level, second line *with:* manage(r,rs,ment), executive(s), administrator(s), supervisor(s). *Consider also:* supervisory personnel, personnel manager(s), department head(s), unit chair(s), department manager(s), program director(s), coordinator(s), junior manager(s). *See also* Administration; Administrators; Leadership; Organizational structure; Power structure.

Middle range theories. Middle range theor(y,ies). Miniature theor(y,ies). Partial theor(y,ies). Intermediate theor(y,ies). *Consider also:* minor working hypothe(sis,ses). *See also* Social theories.

Middle school students. Middle school student(s). *Choose from:* middle school, 6th grade, 7th grade, 8th grade, sixth grade, seventh grade, eighth grade *with:* student(s), pupil(s), children. *Consider also:* intermediate school student(s). *See also* Elementary school students.

Middle Stone Age. See *Mesolithic period.*

Midlife crisis. Midlife cris(is,es). Mid-life cris(is,es). *Choose from:* middle age(d), midlife, mid-life, middle life, midcareer, mid-career, middle years, matur(e,ity), menopaus(e,al), climacteric, postmenopaus(e,al), postmenopausal, over 40, age(d,s) 50 to 64, age(d,s) 40 to 59 *with:* life change event(s), loss(es), death(s), dissolution(s), divorce(s), relocation(s), illness(es), chang(e,ed,ing) role(s), upset(s), trauma(s), chang(e,es, ed,ing), transition(s,al), decision point(s), turning point(s), juncture(s), cris(is,es), choice(s), remarriage(s), disrupt(ed,ing,ion,ions), passage(s), adjust(s,ed,ment,ments), readjust(s,ed, ment,ments), shift(ing,s,ed). *Consider also:* empty nest(s), displaced homemaker(s). *See also* Aging; Career breaks; Career change; Displaced homemakers; Early retirement; Life stage transitions; Middle age; Retirement planning; Self actualization; Social development; Turning points.

Midlife transition. See *Career change; Displaced homemakers; Life stage transitions; Midlife crisis.*

Midwifery. Midwife(ry). Midwives. Traditional birth attendant(s). Accoucheu(r,se,ses). *Consider also:* nurse midwives. *See also* Birth; Birthing centers; Labor (childbirth); Paramedical sciences; Paraprofessional personnel.

Migraine headaches. Migraine headache(s). Migrain(e,es,ous). *Consider also:* sick, bilious, essential, tension, pseudomigraine *with:* headache(s), hemicrania. *See also* Pain; Psychophysiologic disorders; Symptoms.

Migrant labor. See *Migrant workers.*

Migrant workers. Migrant worker(s). Bracero(s). Guestworker(s). *Choose from:* migratory, interstate, migrant, transient, imported, guest, illegal immigrant(s), foreign, seasonal, itinerant *with:* farm worker(s), agricultural worker(s), labor, fruit picker(s), grape picker(s), farmworker(s), farm hand(s), workforce. *See also* Agricultural workers; Foreign workers; Illegal aliens; Labor migration; Migrants; Seasonal unemployment; Temporary employees.

Migrants. Migrant(s). Migrat(ion,ions, ing,ory). Internal immigrant(s). Emigre(s). Emigrat(e,ed,ion). Immigrant(s). Immigrat(e,ion). Imported labor. Transient(s). Vagran(cy,t,ts). Homeless(ness). Rootless(ness).

Nomad(s,ic). Gyps(y,ies). Itinerant(s). Refugee(s). Forced relocation(s). Relocat(ed,ion). Resettle(d,ment). Transmigrat(ion,ory). Foreign worker(s). Foreign national(s). Vagabond(s). Uproot(ed,ing). Guest worker(s). World traveler(s). Geographic mobility. Residential mobility. Population dispersal. Geographic(al,ally) mobil(e,ity). Population mobility. Sojourner(s). *Consider also:* human migration, migrant farm worker(s), emigrant(s), transnational group(s), wetback(s), bedouin, brain drain, deport(ed,ing,ation). *See also* Brain drain; Foreign labor; Foreign professional personnel; Geographic mobility; Immigrants; Immigration; Migrant workers; Migration; Migration of industry; Migration patterns; Newcomers; Refugees; Travelers.

Migrateurs. See *Vagrants.*

Migration. Migrat(e,ed,ing,ion,ions,ional, ory). Migrant(s). Relocat(e,ed,ing,ion). Resettl(e,ed,ing,ement). Cross(ed,ing) border(s). Emigrat(e,ed,ing,ion,ions). Defect(ed,or,ors,ion,ions,ing). Flee(ing). Fled. Seek(ing) sanctuary. Deport(ed, ing,ation). Brain drain. Nomad(s,ic). Transient(s). Immigrat(e,ed,ing,ion, ions,ory). Exile(d). Move(ment) of residence. Chang(e,ed,ing) residence. Foreign invasion(s). Move in search of work. Import(ed) labor. Export(ed) labor. Diaspora. *Choose from:* population(s) *with:* movement(s), mobility, import(ed), export(ed), redistribution, dispersal. *Consider also:* pilgrimage(s), wander(ed,ing). *See also* Forced migration; Geographic mobility; Immigration law; Internal migration; Labor migration; Migrants; Migration of industry; Migration patterns; Population transfer; Refugees; Relocation; Repatriation; Return migration; Rural to urban migration; Urban to rural migration.

Migration, animal. See *Animal migration.*

Migration, forced. See *Forced migration.*

Migration, human. See *Migration.*

Migration, internal. See *Internal migration.*

Migration, labor. See *Labor migration.*

Migration, return. See *Return migration.*

Migration, rural to urban. See *Rural to urban migration.*

Migration, urban to rural. See *Urban to rural migration.*

Migration of industry. Migration of industr(y,ies). *Choose from:* factor(y, ies), plant(s), industr(ial,y,ies), mill(s), foundr(y,ies), compan(y,ies), corporat(e, ion,ions), firm(s), business(es), production *with:* migrat(e,ed,ing,ion), relocat(e, ed,ing,ion), dislocat(e,ed,ing,ion), runaway, mobility, move(s,d,ment, ments), moving, flight, remov(e,ed,ing, al,als), re-establish(ed,ing,ment), resituat(e,ed,ing), displac(e,ed,ing, ement), transfer(red,ring), translocat(e, ed,ing,ion), lur(e,ed,ing), attract(ed,ing), leav(e,ing), left, pull(ed) up roots, evict(ed,ing,ion,ions). *Consider also:* plant closing(s). *See also* Economic conditions; Industrial cities and towns; Labor supply; Migration; Plant relocation; Supply and demand.

Migration patterns. Migration pattern(s). *Choose from:* migrat(ion,ions,ing,ory), immigrant(s), emigrat(e,ed,ing,ion,ions), immigrat(e,ed,ion,ions), imported labor, transient(s), vagran(cy,ts), moving, relocation, resettle(d,ment), transmigrat(ion,ions,ory), residential mobility, population dispersal, geographic(al,ally) mobil(e,ity), population mobility, human migration, migrant farm worker(s), emigrant(s), transnational group(s), wetback(s), brain drain, nomad(s,ic), deport(ed,ation) *with:* pattern(s), trend(s), rate(s), distribution, flow(s), dynamics, declin(e, es,ing), increas(e,ed,es,ing). *See also* Animal migration; Animal navigation; Demography; Geographic distribution; Internal migration; Migrants; Migration; Population distribution; Relocation; Residential patterns; Settlement patterns.

Migratory workers. See *Migrant workers.*

Mild mental retardation. See *Educable mentally retarded.*

Milieu. See *Environment.*

Milieu therapy. Milieu therapy. Therapeutic communit(y,ies). Total-push therap(y, ies). *Choose from:* milieu, communit(y, ies), socioenvironmental, environmental, situational *with:* therap(y,ies,eutic). *See also* Family therapy; Group psychotherapy; Humanization; Psychiatric hospitals; Rehabilitation centers; Socioenvironmental therapy; Therapeutic communities.

Militancy. Militanc(y,e). Militant(s,ism). Combative(ness). Aggressive(ness,ly). Outspoken. Demand(s,ing). *Consider also:* revolutionar(y,ies), crusader(s), protest movement(s), activis(t,ts,m), contentious(ness), militarism, martialism, hawkish, warmongering. *See also* Activism; Aggressiveness (trait); Citizen participation; Civil disobedience; Civil rights organizations; Crusades; Diatribe; Dissent; Dissidents; Interest groups; Lobbying; Peasant rebellions; Political movements; Political radicalism; Protest movements; Social agitation; Social criticism; Social demonstrations; Social movements; Social unrest.

Militarism. Militarism. Militarist(ic,ically, s). Militari(zation,sation). Paramilitarism. Military orientation. Military values. Hawkish. Warmongering. Martialism. Praetorianism. Military

spirit. Military esprit de corps. *Consider also:* military regime(s), warmonger(s, ing), imperial militarism, defense establishment, war econom(y,ies), Samurai, warmaker(s), warmonger(s), martial law, Pentagon. *See also* Armed forces; Crimes against peace; Elitism (government); Fascism; Imperialism; Invasion; Military industrial complex; Military music; Military regimes; Military weapons; Nationalism; Pacifism; Patriotic music; War; War attitudes; War songs.

Military, civil supremacy over. See *Civil supremacy over the military.*

Military administration. Military administrat(ion,or,ors). Pentagon. *Choose from:* military, Army, National Guard, Navy, naval, Air Force, Marine Corps *with:* commandant, general(s), admiral(s), command(ed,ing,er,ers), hegemony, leader(s,ship), headquarter(s). *Consider also:* admiralty. *See also* Administration; Armed forces; Command (of troops, ships, etc.); Military budget; Military discipline (conduct); Military industrial complex; Military planning.

Military airplanes. Military airplane(s). War plane(s). *Choose from:* war(fare), military, fighter, antisubmarine, reconnaissance, combat, transport, Air Force, Army, Navy *with:* plane(s), aircraft, airplane(s), air tanker(s), jet(s), *Consider also:* bomber(s), military helicopter(s), stealth aircraft, stealth bomber(s), F16(s), KC10A(s), F22(s), MIG(S), etc. *See also* Aerial reconnaissance; Aerial warfare; Air bases; Air defenses; Air power; Aircraft carriers.

Military assistance. Military assistance. Arms shipment(s). Military aid. *Choose from:* militar(y,ily), arms, armed forces, troops, militia, Army, Navy, Air Force, Marines, Marine Corps, Coast Guard, soldiers, weapon(s) *with:* assist(ed,ing, ance), aid, invit(e,ed,ation). *See also* Collective security; Foreign aid; International alliances; Mercenaries; Military weapons.

Military bases. Military base(s). Airbase(s). Fort(s). Arsenal(s). Ammunition depot(s). Munitions depot(s). *Choose from:* military, army, national guard, airforce, marine *with:* installation(s), headquarter(s), post(s), site(s), camp(s), fortification(s), fort(s), station(s), base(s), facilit(y,ies), district(s), yard(s), field(s), outpost(s). *See also* Armed forces; Garrisons; Military readiness; Proving grounds; Navy yards and naval stations.

Military budget. Military budget(s). *Choose from:* military, defense, Pentagon, armament(s), arms, weapon(s,ry), missile(s), aircraft, bomber(s), ship(s) *with:* budget(s,ed,

ing), appropriat(e,ed,ing,ion,ions), economic(s), expenditure(s), spending. *See also* Defense spending; Military administration; Military industrial complex; Military market.

Military campaigns. See *Military operations.*

Military capitulations. Military capitulation(s). Surrender(ed,ing). *Choose from:* military, arm(y,ies), regiment(s), platoon(s), troop(s), fort(s), nav(y,ies), fleet(s), ship(s), general(s), admiral(s) *with:* capitulat(e,ed,ing, ion,ions), defeat(ed,ing), surrender(ed, ing), lay(ing) down arms, ced(e,ed,ing), fall(en), fell, relinquish(ed,ing), yield(ed,ing), white flag(s), acced(e,ed, ing), renounc(e,ed,ing), transfer(red, ring) control, collaps(e,ed,ing), abandon(ed,ing), give(n) up, hand(ed) over, resign(ed,ing). *Consider also:* armistice treat(y,ies), conclud(e,ed,ing) hostilities, ceasefire(s), *See also* Abdication; Annihilation; Assault (battle); Battles; Combat; Concessions; Disengagement; Military operations; Military retreat; Prisoners of war; Renunciation; Resignations.

Military civilian relations. Military civilian relation(s,ship,ships). *Choose from:* armed force(s), military force(s), troop(s), militia, military base(s), Army, Navy, Air Force, Marines, soldier(s), G.I.s., GIs., enlisted, sailor(s) *with:* general public, citizen(s,ry), populace, inhabitant(s), resident(s), voter(s), communit(y,ies), townspeople, native(s), civilian(s), local population(s), city official(s). *See also* Armed forces; Americans abroad; Citizens; Civil defense; Civil supremacy over the military; Coups d'Etat; Interpersonal relations; Martial law; Military industrial complex; Military personnel; Military regimes; Police community relations; Political repression; Surveillance of citizens.

Military combat. See *Combat.*

Military dependents. See *Military families.*

Military desertion. Military desertion. Absent without leave. AWOL. *Choose from:* military, Army, Navy, National Guard, Air Force, Marines, armed forces *with:* desert(ed,ing,er,ers), disloyal(ty), abandon(ed,ing,ment), defect(ed,ion, ions), absen(t,ce,ces) without leave. *Consider also:* draft *with:* violator(s), evader(s), dodger(s). *See also* Absence; Combat; Desertion; Draft resisters; Military discipline (punishment); Military law; Military offenses; Military personnel; Naval offenses.

Military discipline (conduct). Military discipline. Military conduct. *Choose from:* military, armed forces, arm(y,ies), nav(y,ies), soldier(s), sailor(s), airm(en, an), airwom(en,an), Marine(s), officer(s), enlisted personnel, cadet(s), midshipm(en,an) *with:* conduct, bearing, manner(s), deportment, behavior, indoctrinat(e,ed,ing,ation), rule(s), honor code, obedience to life-threatening orders, perform(ed,ing,ance) dut(y,ies), moral standard(s), chain of command, obey(ed,ing) order(s). *Consider also:* drill(s,ed,ing), basic training, routine(s), boot camp. *See also* Authoritarianism (political); Command (of troops, ships, etc.); Drill and minor tactics; Military administration; Military ethics; Military officers; Military schools; Military training.

Military discipline (punishment). Military discipline. *Choose from:* military, armed forces, arm(y,ies), nav(y,ies), soldier(s), sailor(s), airm(en,an), airwom(en,an), Marine(s), officer(s), enlisted personnel, cadet(s), midshipm(en,an) *with:* disciplin(e,ary), courts-martial, punish(ed,ing,ment), reprimand(ed,ing), penalt(y,ies), penaliz(e,ed,ing), strip(ped, ping) ranks, brig, dishonorable discharge, less than honorable discharge, pass(ed,ing) over for promotion, loss of privilege(s), cancel(led,ling,lation) liberty, fine(s). *See also* Discipline; Military law; Military desertion; Military offenses; Military personnel; Naval offenses.

Military draft. Military draft(s). Military conscription. Selective service. Compulsory military service. Universal military service. Universal Military Training and Service Act. Peacetime conscription. Draft board(s). *Choose from:* military, Army, Navy, National Guard, Air Force, Marines, armed forces *with:* draft(ed,ee, ees), conscription. *See also* Compulsory participation; Draft resisters; Military enlistment.

Military enlistment. Military enlistment. *Choose from:* military, Army, Navy, National Guard, Air Force, Marines, armed forces *with:* enlist(ed,ee,ees, ing,ment), reenlist(ed,ing,ment), draft(ed,ee,ees), induct(ed,ion), signup(s), recruit(s,ed,ing), conscription, application(s). *See also* Military draft; Military recruitment; Volunteer military personnel.

Military equipment. See *Military weapons.*

Military ethics. Military ethic(s,al). *Choose from:* military, prisoner(s) of war, armed forces, nuclear war(fare), chemical war(fare), biological war(fare), terroris(m,t,ts), weapon(s), missile(s), troops, Army, Navy, Air Force, Marines, Marine Corps, Coast Guard, soldier(s) *with:* ethic(s,al), moral(ity), philosoph(y, ies,ical). *Consider also:* war crime(s), dirty war(s,fare). *See also* Ethics; International law; Military discipline (conduct); Military offenses; Naval offenses; Professional ethics; Unethical conduct; War crimes.

Military families. Military famil(y,ies). *Choose from:* military, Navy, Army, Marine Corps, Air Force, Coast Guard, service(man,men,woman,women), armed force(s), armed service(s), Vietnam returnee(s), veteran(s), GI(s), MIA(s), POW(s), submariner(s), soldier(s), sailor(s), prisoner(s) of war, enlisted personnel, noncommissioned officer(s), petty officer(s), sergeant(s), captain(s), lieutenant(s), commander(s), colonel(s), major(s) *with:* spouse(s), famil(y,ies), child(ren), marriage(s), marital, wife, wives, husband(s), father(s), mother(s), sister(s), brother(s), widow(s), orphan(s), dependent(s). *Consider also:* war widow(s), Army brat(s), Navy junior(s). *See also* Americans abroad; Army life; Family; Family life; Family stability; Family work relationship; Geographic mobility.

Military force, all volunteer. See *Volunteer military personnel.*

Military forces. See *Armed forces.*

Military government. See *Military regimes.*

Military history. Military histor(y,ies). Military literature. War corresponden(t, ts,ce). Military operations. *Choose from:* military, war(fare,s), weapon(s,ry), veteran(s), service(men,women), army, naval, navy, marine corps, air force, combat, soldier(s), troop(s), specific division, e.g. artillery *with:* histor(y,ies), oral histor(y,ies), personal narrative(s), film(s), documentar(y,ies), correspondence, librar(y,ies), archive(s), museum(s), 18th century, eighteenth century, 19th century, nineteenth century, etc. *Consider also:* First Dutch War, French Revolution, Revolutionary War, Civil War, World War I, World War II, Korean War, Vietnam War, Spanish American War, Texas War of Independence, etc. *Consider also:* battles by name such as the battles of Manila Bay, Gettysburg, Normandy, Dienbienphu, Waterloo, etc. *See also* History; Medieval military history; Triumphal arches; War memorials; Wars; Warships; World history.

Military history, medieval. See *Medieval military history.*

Military industrial complex. Military industrial complex. Military complex. Armaments complex. *Choose from:* military, defense, Pentagon, armament(s), arms, weapon(s,ry) *with:* corporat(e,ion,ions), business(es), supplier(s), market(s), industrialist(s) *with:* wealth, investment(s), interest(s), profit(s). *Consider also:* military, defense, Pentagon, armament(s), arms, space, aerospace, weapon(s,ry), DOD *with:* contract(s,ed,ing,or,ors), supplier(s), producer(s), vendor(s), manufactur(e,ed,ing,er,ers), establishment. *See also* Arms market; Corpora-

tions; Defense spending; Firearms industry; Military administration; Military budget; Military civilian relations; Military patronage; Militarism.

Military intelligence. Military intelligence. Counterintelligence. Intelligence community. *Choose from:* military, defense, Pentagon, strategic, armament(s), arms, weapon(s,ry), missile(s), troop(s) *with:* intelligence, information, document(s), blueprint(s), surveillance, satellite photo(s,graph, graphs), monitor(s,ed,ing), covert, secret(s), classified, reconnaissance, spy(ing), spie(d,s). *See also* Aerial reconnaissance; Classified information; Espionage; Electronic eavesdropping; Government information; Intelligence service; Military readiness; Secret police; Surveillance of citizens.

Military intervention. See *International intervention.*

Military law. Military law(s). Court(s) martial. *Choose from:* military, armed forces, arm(y,ies), nav(y,ies), soldier(s), sailor(s), airm(en,an), airwom(en,an), Marine(s), officer(s), enlisted personnel, cadet(s), midshipm(en,an) *with:* court(s), judge(s), justice, magistrate(s), trial(s), appeal(s), panel(s), court(s), judicial hearing(s), prosecut(e,ed,ing,ion), justice, adjudicatory process(es), tribunal(s) military magistrate(s). *See also* International law; Laws; Martial law; Military desertion; Military discipline (punishment); Naval offenses; War crimes.

Military market. Military market(s). *Choose from:* military, defense, Pentagon, armament(s), arms, weapon(s,ry), missile(s), aircraft, bomber(s), ship(s) *with:* market(s), sale(s), economic(s), procurement, contract(s,ed,ing), trade, expenditure(s), supplier(s), spending, profit(s,eer,eers, eering). *See also* Defense spending; Government procurement; Military budget; Military industrial complex; Military supplies; Military weapons.

Military medical personnel. Military medical personnel. *Choose from:* military, Army, Navy, Marine Corps, Air Force *with:* medical personnel, physician(s), corpsmen, psychiatrist(s), nurse(s), paramedical personnel, physician(s) assistant(s), medical administrator(s), surgeon(s), dentist(s). *See also* Allied health personnel; Health manpower; Health occupations; Medical personnel supply; Military personnel.

Military music. Military music. Musique militaire. Militaermusik. Military March(es). Military band(s). Fanfare(s). *Choose from:* military, martial, war, Civil War, Army, Navy, Air Force, Marines, battle, parade, march(ing,es) *with:* music, song(s), tune(s), ditt(y,ies), piece(s), fanfare(s), band(s). *Consider also:* band muster rolls, United States Marine Band, Marine Drum and Bugle Corps, Dutch Royal Military Band, Edinburgh Military Tattoo, John Philip Sousa, Edwin Franko Goldman. *See also* Janissary music; Marches; Militarism; Morale; Patriotic music; Political ballads; War songs.

Military offenses. Military offense(s). Mutin(y,ies). Military crim(e,es,inal, inals). *Choose from:* military, armed forces, arm(y,ies), nav(y,ies), soldier(s), sailor(s), airm(en,an), airwom(en,an), Marine(s), officer(s), enlisted personnel, cadet(s), midshipm(en,an) *with:* offense(s), crim(e,es,inal,inals), absence without leave, AWOL, desert(ed,ing, ion), misconduct, insubordinat(e,ion), malinger(ing), mutin(y,ies,ous,ied), violat(e,ed,ing,ion,ions), conduct unbecoming an officer. *Consider also:* military tribunal(s), court(s) martial, dishonorable discharge(s). *See also* Lawlessness; Military desertion; Military discipline (punishment); Military ethics; Naval offenses; War; War crimes; War victims.

Military officers. Military officer(s). Commissioned officer(s). Non-Commissioned officer(s). *Choose from:* military, Army, Navy, National Guard, Air Force, Marines, armed forces *with:* officer(s), professional(s), academy graduate(s). *Consider also:* Admiral(s), General(s), Captain(s), Colonel(s), Commander(s), Lieutenant Colonel(s), Lieutenant(s), Major(s), Ensign(s). *See also* Command (of troops, ships, etc.); Military discipline (conduct); Military personnel; Military regimes; Veterans.

Military operations. Military operation(s). *Choose from:* militar(y,ily), armed force(s), troops, militia, Army, Navy, Air Force, Marines, Marine Corps, Coast Guard, soldiers *with:* operation(s), exercise(s), maneuver(s), venture(s), clash(es), conflict(s), skirmish(es), role(s), mission(s), tactic(s), campaign(s), strateg(y,ies), battle(s), combat, bomb(ed,ing,ings), sortie(s), attack(s,ed,ing), action(s), movement(s), engagement(s), undertaking(s), deployment(s), mobiliz(e,ed,ing,ation), raid(s,ed,ing), interven(e,ed,ing,tion, tions), mount(ed,ing) offensive(s), secur(e,ed,ing) base(s). *See also* Aerial warfare; Assault (battle); Attack (Military science); Coast defenses; Combat; Defense (Military science); Invasion; Military capitulations; Military retreat; Military strategies; National fronts; Naval strategy; Nuclear warfare; Political violence; Sea power; Terrorism; Troop movements.

Military patronage. Military patronage. *Choose from:* patronage, pork(barrel), politics as usual, scratch(ed,ing) back(s),

roll(ed,ing) log(s), bargain(ed,ing), broker(ed,ing), corrupt practice(s), corruption, political economy *with:* military expenditure(s), officer(s), national defense, defense procurement, military hardware, military technology, weapon(s), missile(s), defense contract(s). *See also* Corruption in government; Defense spending; Military industrial complex; Patronage.; Political patronage.

Military pensions. Military pension(s). War pension(s). *Choose from:* military, war, veteran(s), ex-service(men,man,women, woman), Civil War, Union Army, World War I, World War II, Korean War, Vietnam War, Desert Storm *with:* pension(s), retirement pay, benefits, retirement income, economic support. *Consider also:* disability pension(s). *See also* Demobilization; Military personnel; Pensions; Retirement income; Veterans.

Military personnel. Military personnel. Enlistee(s). Draftee(s). Marines. National guards(men,man,women, woman). Commissioned officer(s). Noncommissioned officer(s). ROTC. Veteran(s). Military troop(s). Soldier(s). Military pilot(s). Armed force(s). Sailor(s). West Point graduate(s). Naval Academy graduate(s). Green Beret(s). Submariner(s). G.I.s. GI(s). Paratrooper(s). Active duty reservist(s). Service(men,man,women,woman). Militia(men,man,women,woman). warrior(s). *Consider also:* enlisted, Army, Navy, Marine, Air Force, military, *with:* men, man, women, woman, personnel, officer(s), cadet(s), recruit(s), volunteer(s), reservist(s). *Consider also:* militia(s), troop(s), cavalr(y,ies), infantr(y,ies), foot soldier(s), warrior(s), mercenar(y,ies), combat personnel. *See also* Air Force personnel; Armed forces; Army life; Army personnel; Astronauts; Chaplains; Civil supremacy over the military; Enlisted military personnel; Generals; Hazardous occupations; Marine personnel; Mercenaries; Military discipline (punishment); Military draft; Military enlistment; Military medical personnel; Military officers; Military pensions; Navy personnel; Troop strength; Noncommissioned officers; Volunteer military personnel; Veterans.

Military personnel, enlisted. See *Enlisted military personnel.*

Military personnel, volunteer. See *Volunteer military personnel.*

Military planning. Military plan(s,ned, ning). *Choose from:* militar(y,ily), defense, national security, armed forces, Army, Navy, naval, Air Force, Marines, Marine Corps, Coast Guard, war(fare), Pentagon *with:* plan(s,ned,ning), coordinat(e,ed,ing), prepar(e,ed,ing, ation,ations), initiative(s), contingenc(y, ies), objective(s). *See also* Coast

defenses; Logistics; Military administration; Military budget; Military readiness; Military strategies; Mobilization; Naval strategy.

Military policy. Military polic(y,ies). Detente. *Choose from:* militar(y,ily), defense, national security, armed forces, Army, Navy, naval, Air Force, Marines, Marine Corps, Coast Guard, war(fare), Pentagon, chemical weapon(s), biological weapon(s), nuclear weapon(s), retaliat(ory,ion), first-strike, deterrence, antiproliferation *with:* polic(y,ies), principle(s), objective(s), treat(y,ies), agreement(s), accord(s), doctrine(s). *See also* Military planning; Policy; Treaties.

Military posts. See *Military bases; Garrisons.*

Military power. Military power. Armament(s). Military force(s). Militariz(ed,ation). Military production. Defense industrial base. *Choose from:* military, weapon(s,ry), conventional weapons, arms, armament(s), munitions, aircraft, offensive, defensive, nuclear weapon(s,ry), missile(s), helicopter(s), tank(s), defense technology, *with:* power(s,ful), control(led,ling), strength, presence, show force(s), security, strateg(y,ies,ic), supremacy, manpower, deterrence, capabilities, production. *See also* Military readiness; Military strategies; Naval strategy; Sea power; Troop strength.

Military psychology. Military psychology. *Choose from:* military, combat, war(time) *with:* psycholog(y,ical), psychiatr(y,ic). *See also* Psychology.

Military readiness. Military readiness. *Choose from:* militar(y,ily) *with:* read(y,iness), alert(s), prepared(ness), power, presence, expansion(ism). *Choose from:* arms, weapon(s,ry), missile(s), military, tank(s) *with:* buildup(s), stockpil(e,ed,es,ing), robust(ing). Beef(ing) up Army. Airpower. Seapower. *See also* Military intelligence; Military planning; Military power; Military weapons; National security; Naval strategy; Sea power; Troop strength; Warships.

Military recruitment. Military recruit(ment,ing). *Choose from:* military, Army, Navy, Air Force, Marine Corps, ROTC, armed force(s), armed service(s), war office *with:* recruit(ment,ing), join(ed,ing), selection of personnel, voluntary, volunteer(ed,ing), procurement, enlist(ed,ing,ment), application(s), conscription, induction, draft. *Consider also:* universal military service. *See also* Military enlistment; Military draft; Volunteer military personnel.

Military reform. Military reform(s). *Choose from:* military, armed forces, military-industrial complex, Pentagon

Department of Defense, armed services, army, navy, marine(s), air force *with:* reorganiz(e,ed,ing,ation), chang(es,ed, ing), reform(s,ed,ing), accountab(le, ility), downsiz(e,ed,ing), civilian control, curtail(ed,ing,ment), moderniz(e,ed,ing, ation), transform(s,ed,ing), reduc(e,ed, ing) size, revitaliz(e,ed,ing,ation). *See also* Armed forces; Arms control; Civil supremacy over the military; Defense spending; Reform.

Military regimes. Military regime(s). Garrison state(s). *Choose from:* militar(y,istic) *with:* dictatorship(s), societ(y,ies), authority, junta(s), coup(s), oligarch(y,ies), rule(d,rs), clique(s). *See also* Authoritarianism (political); Caciquism; Civil supremacy over the military; Coups d'Etat; Despotism; Dictatorship; Fascism; Internal security; Martial law; Military civilian relations; Military officers; Political repression; Provisional government; Totalitarianism.

Military religious orders. Military religious order(s). Templar(s). Teutonic knight(s). Hospitaller(s). Hospitaller Order of St. John of Jerusalem. Order of the Hospital of St. John of Jerusalem. Order of the Temple. *Consider also:* religious order(s) *with:* military tradition(s), Crusade(s). *See also* Contemplative orders; Monks.

Military retreat. Military retreat(s). Strategic withdrawal(s). Counter-march(es). *Choose from:* troop(s), military, armed forces, platoon(s), division(s), infantr(y,ies) *with:* withdraw(n,ing,al,als), volte-face, about-face, pullout(s), evacuat(e,ed,ing,ion), retreat(ed,ing). *Consider also:* surrender(ed,ing). *See also* Assault (battle); Combat; Invasion; Military capitulations; Military operations; Military strategies; Troop movements; War.

Military schools. Military school(s). *Choose from:* military, Army, Navy, Air force, Marines, Coast Guard, officer candidate, armed service(s) *with:* academ(y,ies), school(s), college(s). *Consider also:* West Point, Annapolis, Colorado Springs. *See also* Colleges; Drill and minor tactics; High schools; Military discipline (conduct); Military training.

Military service. Military service. *Choose from:* military, Army, Navy, Marine Corps, Air Force *with:* serv(ed,ice), experience, participation. *See also* Armed forces; Military personnel; Veterans.

Military service, compulsory. See *Military draft.*

Military services. See *Armed forces.*

Military spouses. See *Military families.*

Military strategies. Military strateg(y,ies). *Choose from:* militar(y,ily), defense, armed force(s), arm(y,ies), nav(y,ies), naval, air force(s), marine(s), war(fare), Pentagon, chemical weapon(s), biological weapon(s), nuclear weapon(s), strike force(s), retaliat(ory, ion), maritime, missile(s), bomber(s), troop(s) *with:* strateg(y,ies,ic), tactic(s, al), contingenc(y,ies), plan(ned,ning,s), countermeasure(s). *See also* Aerial reconnaissance; Aerial warfare; Assault (battle); Attack (Military science); Combat; Defense (Military science); Invasion; Military operations; Military planning; Military power; Military readiness; Military retreat; Naval strategy; Sea power; Siege warfare; Strategic management; Strategies; Troop movements; War.

Military supplies. Military suppl(y,ies). *Choose from:* military, battle, army, navy *with:* suppl(y,ies), provision(s), equipment, furnishing(s), outfit(s), camouflage, screen(s), kit(s), netting, bag(s), hose(s), oil tank(s), uniform(s), radio(s), generator(s), truck(s), etc. *See also* Military market; Miitary technology; Military weapons.

Military technology. Military technology. Weapons technology. Military techno-logical innovation(s). Military application(s). *Choose from:* military, Army, Navy, naval, Air Force, offensive, defensive, defense *with:* technolog(y, ical) hardware, innovation(s), application(s). *See also* Military supplies; Military weapons.

Military trade. See *Arms trade; Defense spending; Government procurement; Military budget; Military market; Military industrial complex.*

Military training. Military training. *Choose from:* military, Army, Navy, naval, Air Force, Marines, Coast Guard, armed services, ROTC, enlisted, enlistee(s), soldier(s), sailor(s), reserve(s), officer candidate(s) *with:* educat(e,ed,ing,ion), train(ed,ing), school(s), instruct(ed,ing, ion), basic skill(s), boot camp(s), basic training, course(s), cadet(s), midship(man,men), retrain(ed,ing). *See also* Colleges; Drill and minor tactics; High schools; Military discipline (conduct); Military schools; Training.

Military veterans. See *Veterans.*

Military weapons. Military weapon(s,ry). Military arsenal. Military hardware. Anti-aircraft missile(s). Arms. Artiller(y,ies). Bayonet(s). Beretta. Binary weapon(s). Biological weapon(s). Bomber(s). Bullet(s). Chemical warfare. Chemical weapon(s). Colt rifle(s). Conventional weapon(s). Cruise missile(s). Exocet(s). Gun(s, nery). M16 rifle(s). Military aid. Military explosive(s). Military force(s).

Military power. Military robot(s). Minefield(s). Missile(s). Munition(s). MX system(s). Nerve gas. Nuclear missile(s). Ordnance. Patriot missile(s). Pistol(s). Robotic weapon(s). Robot(s). Rocket(s). Scud missile(s). SDI. Silkworm(s). Star war(s). Stealth bomber(s). Stinger missile(s). Strategic weapon(s). Strike force(s). Submachine gun(s). Tank(s). Torpedo(es). UZI(s). Warhead(s). *Choose from:* military, Army, Navy, naval, Air Force, offensive, defensive, defense, battle *with:* weapon(s,ry), arms, armaments, arsenal(s), gun(s), bomber(s), etc. *See also* Antiaircraft artillery; Arms control; Arms transfers; Arms race; Artillery; Atomic bomb; Ballistic missiles; Bombs; Incendiary weapons; Land mines; Military assistance; Military market; Military readiness; Military supplies; Military technology; Nuclear proliferation; Nuclear weapons; Proving grounds; Weaponry; Weapons of mass destruction.

Militias. Militia(s). Patriot movement. *Consider also:* Randy Weaver, Ruby Ridge, Waco disaster, conspiracy theor(y,ies), white separatist(s), xenophobi(a,c), redneck(s), radical right, Viper Militia movement, Christian Identity cult, Aryan Republican Army, Invisible Empire, National Association for the Advancement of White People, Timothy McVeigh. *See also* Anti-government radicals; Fascism; Hate crimes; Paramilitary; White supremacy movements; Xenophobia.

Milk industry. Milk industry. Cream(ery, ies). *Choose from:* milk, dairy product(s), butter, cheese, cream, yogurt, sour cream, buttermilk *with:* industr(y, ies,ial), production, manufactur(e,ed, ing), marketing, compan(y,ies), supplier(s), retailer(s), wholesaler(s). *See also* Dairy products; Dairying; Food industry.

Mill towns. See *Industrial cities and towns.*

Millenarian movements. See *Millenarianism.*

Millenarianism. Millenarian(ism). Millenarian movement(s). Millenium. Millenial(ism,istic). Millenarist. Chilias(m,ts,tic). Apocalypse. Apocalyptic(ism). Messian(ic,ism). *Consider also:* judgment day, doomsday, second coming, parousia, armageddon, revitalization movement(s), resurrection, cargo cult(s), ghost dance(s), eschatolog(y,ical), religious revival(ism), messianism, kingdom of God. *Consider also:* Anabaptists, Adventists, Montanis(m,t,ts), Islamic Mahdi movements, Jehovah's Witnesses, Rastifari(an), T'ai-p'ing movement, Watch Tower movement(s), One thousand A.D., Second Advent. *See also*

Anabaptists; Apocalypse; Apocalyptic literature; Bible; Cargo cults; Christianity; Jehovah's Witnesses; Judgement day; Nativistic movements; Prophecy; Prophets; Religious beliefs; Religious fundamentalism; Religious cults; Social movements; Utopias.

Millenialism. See *Millenarianism.*

Millennium bug. Millennium bug(s). Y2K Bug. Year 2000 Bug. Year 2000 Problem. Y2K Problem. Millennium virus. Millennium time bomb. Millennium glitch(es). *Choose from:* year 2000, Y2K, millennium *with:* problem(s), glitch(es), bug(s), crisis, virus(es). *Consider also:* millennium fix(es), millennium compliant, year 2000 date conversion, TEOTWAWKI, The End Of The World As We Know It. *See also* Computer bugs; Computer industry; Computer viruses; Computers; Debugging; Information society.

Millionaires. See *Capitalists and financiers; Wealth.*

Mind. Mind. Mental facult(y,ies). Intellect(uality,s). Mentalit(y,ies). Psyche(s). Mental image(s,ry). Imagination. Reflective process(es). Human nature. Cognitive process(es). Rationality. Consciousness. Subconscious. Unconscious. Ego. Id. Superego. Conscience. Brains. Intelligence. Wit(s). Mental abilit(y,ies). Mental agility. *See also* Awareness; Cognition; Concept formation; Concepts; Conscience; Human nature; Images; Mind body problem; Soul; Thinking; Unconscious (psychology); Volition.

Mind, enlightenment state of. See *Enlightenment (state of mind).*

Mind body problem. Mind body problem. Mind body split. *Consider also:* physical monism, neutral monism, mental monism, interactionism, psychophysical parallelism, psychosomatic. *See also* Animal nature of man; Behavioral genetics; Biological factors; Causality; Conversion disorder; Determinism; Dualism; Environmental determinism; Etiology; Mind; Mind-body relations (metaphysics); Monism; Nature nurture; Philosophical anthropology; Psychobiology; Psychoneuroimmunology; Psychophysiologic disorders; Psychophysiology.

Mind-body relations (metaphysics). Mind-body relation(s,ship). *Choose from:* body, physical fitness, pain, illness, health(y,iness), neurolog(y,ical), biolog(y,ical), physical exercise *with:* psyche(s), locus of control, emotions, yoga, mental, conscious(ness), mindful(ness), meditat(e,ed,ing,ion), spiritual(ly), soul, stress *with:* relation(s,ship) treatment(s), problem(s), therap(y,ies), dual(ity,ism), program(s), process(es), technique(s). *Consider also:*

mind-body duality. *See also* Holistic health; Mind body problem; Psychophysiology; Somatoform disorders; Well being.

Mind set. See *Attitudes; Predisposition; Set (psychology).*

Minded, narrow. See *Rigid personality.*

Mine accidents. Mine accident(s). Mine explosion(s). *Choose from:* mine(s), mining, pit(s), quarr(y,ies) *with:* risk(s), death(s), hazard(ous,s), injur(y,ies,ed), accident(s), unsafe, safety, danger(s), fatalit(y,ies). *See also* Hazardous occupations; Industrial accidents; Miners; Mining industry; Occupational exposure; Occupational safety.

Miners. Miner(s). Mineworker(s). Mine worker(s). *Consider also:* black lung disease. *See also* Black lung disease; Blue collar workers; Coal miners; Mine accidents.

Miners, coal. See *Coal miners.*

Miners, copper. See *Copper miners.*

Mines and mining, coal. See *Coal mines and mining.*

Mines, land. See *Land mines.*

Miniature objects. Miniature object(s). *Choose from:* miniature, tiny, mini, small scale *with:* object(s), monument(s), souvenir(s), replica(s), cop(y,ies). *Consider also:* miniature painting(s), miniature portrait(s). *See also* Art objects; Collectibles; Relics; Toys.

Minimal art. Minimal art. *Choose from:* minimal(ism,ist) *with:* art(ist,ists), piece(s), aesthetic(s). *Consider also:* Carl Andre, Don Judd, Tony Smith. *See also* Arts; Minimalism (literature); Monochrome painting.

Minimal brain disorders. Minimal brain disorder(s). Minimal brain dysfunction. Attention deficit disorder(s) with hyperactivity. *Choose from:* minimal(ly), minimum, minor *with:* brain, cerebral *with:* dysfunction(s), disorder(s), pathology, impairment(s). *Choose from:* attention deficit(s), neuropsychological deficit(s) *with:* motor perception dysfunction(s), hyperactivity, disorder(s). *See also* Attention deficit disorder; Brain damaged; Hyperkinesis.

Minimal government. Minimal government(s). Minimal monarch(y,ies). Minimal regulation(s). Minimal direct government involvement. Minimal government regulation(s). Least government(s,al). *See also* Free trade; Individualism; Libertarianism; Privatization.

Minimalism (art). See *Minimal art.*

Minimalism (literature). Minimalism (literature). Literary minimalism(e). *Choose from:* minimalism(e,o,a,ist,ists)

with: litera(ry,ture), narrative(s), prose, l'Ecriture, proza. *Consider also:* Zen koan(s). *See also* Literature; Minimal art.

Minimum competencies. Minimum competenc(y,ies). *Choose from:* minimum, minimal, basic, essential *with:* competenc(y,ies), skill(s). *See also* Back to basics; Basic skills; Competency based education; Information skills; Literacy; Mathematics skills; Performance; Reading skills; Writing (composition).

Minimum wage. Minimum wage(s). Minimum salar(y,ies). Basic wage(s). Wage floor. Living wage(s). *Consider also:* poverty line. *See also* Cheap labor; Income; Income maintenance programs; Poverty; Prevailing wages; Wages; Labor movements; Labor policy; Labor unions.

Mining, strip. See *Strip mining.*

Mining and mines, coal. See *Coal mines and mining.*

Mining industry. Mining industry. *Choose from:* mining, mine(s), extractive, mineral(s), ore(s) *with:* industr(y,ies,ial), compan(y,ies), mine(s), corp(oration, orations), import(ed,ing,s), export(ed, ing,s), land(s), production, market(s), lobb(y,ies), process(ed,ing), futures, enterprise(s), operation(s), company town(s), strike(s), lockout(s). collective bargaining. *Consider also:* United Mine Workers, Western Federation of Miners, mine worker(s), mining research. *See also* Coal industry; Coal mines and mining; Mine accidents; Mining towns.

Mining towns. Mining town(s). Mine company town(s). Mining camp(s). Mining communit(y,ies). Mining village(s). *Choose from:* mine(s), mining, camp(s), Gold Rush *with:* town(s), camp(s), communit(y,ies), village(s). *Consider also:* Dawson NM, Elko Nev, Tombstone NM, Leadville CO, etc. *See also* Company towns; Extinct cities; Industrial cities and towns; Mining industry.

Ministerial ethics (clergy). Ministerial ethic(s). *Choose from:* clergy(men,man, person,woman,women), pastor(s), priest(s), rabbi(s), preacher(s), deacon(s), parson(s), missionar(y,ies), parish minister(s) *with:* humane, ethic(s,al), ideal(s), integrity, moral(s,ity), immoral(ity), deception, obligation(s), integrity, accountability, honest(y), principle(s), code(s), openness, fidelity, conscience, conscientious(ness), conflict of interest, trust(worthy,worthiness), truth(ful, fulness), incorruptib(le,ility), unethical(ly), improper, misdeed(s), misconduct, conflict(s) of interest, malpractice, bribe(s,ry), sex(ual,ually) abuse(s,d), corrupt(ion), alcoholi(c,sm), drug abuse(rs), violat(e,ed,ing,ions), illegal(ity,ities), impropriet(y,ies), collusion, scandal(s), breach of confidence, fraud(ulent), unlawful(ly), slcaz(e,y), unprofessional, breach of decorum, wrongdoing(s), nepotism, unscrupulous(ness), trust violation(s), inappropriate conduct, falsif(y,ying,ied, ication), sexual misconduct, scandal(s), financial irregularit(y,ies), illegal contribution(s), mishandling funds, defraud(ed,ing). *See also* Clergy; Codes of ethics; Misconduct in office; Professional ethics; Scandals; Unethical conduct.

Ministerial responsibility (government). Ministerial responsibilit(y,ies). *Choose from:* minister(s,ial), legislator(s), elected official(s), congress(men,man, woman,women), public service, assembly(men,man,woman,women), senator(s) *with:* responsibilit(y,ies), accountab(le,ility), answerable, liab(le,ility,ilities), dut(y,ies), obligat(ed, ing,ion,ions), performance measure(s), performance assessment(s). *See also* Accountability; Administrative responsibility.

Ministers. Minister(s,ial,ing). Ministry. Clergy. Pastor(s). Parson(s). Reverend. Ministerial student(s). Clergy(men,man, women,woman). Preacher(s). Seminarian(s). Seminary student(s). Divinity student(s). Chaplain(s). Cleric(als,s). Ecclesiastic(s). Televangelist(s). *See also* Clergy; Ordination; Priests; Religious personnel.

Ministers, foreign. See *Diplomats.*

Ministry, lay. See *Lay religious personnel.*

Minnesinger. Minnesinger(s). *Consider also:* Minnesang(s,er), Meistersinger(s), Meistergesang(s,en), Heinrich von Morungen, Walther von der Vogelweide, Oswald von Wolkenstein, Gottfried von Strassburg, Wolfram von Eschenbach. *See also* Courtly love; Love poetry; Medieval literature; Poets; Singers; Troubadour; Trouvere.

Minor tactics, drill and. See *Drill and minor tactics.*

Minorities, ethnic. See *Ethnic groups; Minority groups.*

Minorities, linguistic. See *Linguistic minorities.*

Minority authors. Minority author(s). *Choose from:* ethnic(ity), minorit(y,ies), African American(s), Black(s), ex-slave(s), Alaska native(s), Aleut(s), Eskimo(s), Native American(s), American Indian(s), immigrant(s), Asian American(s), Korean American(s), Chinese American(s), Japanese American(s), Hispanic(s), Chicano(s), Latino(s), Mexican American(s), Mexican(o), Puerto Rican *with:* author(s,ship), writer(s), composer(s),

compiler(s), novelist(s), narrator(s), dramatist(s), screenwriter(s), poet(s), essayist(s), biographer(s), journalist(s), reporter(s), playwright(s), lyricist(s), chronicler(s), ghost writer(s). *Consider also:* black literature, ex-slave narrative(s). *See also* Authors; Minority groups.

Minority businesses. Minority business(es). *Choose from:* minorit(y,ies), minority owned, Black(s), Alaska native, Aleut(s), Eskimo(s), Native American(s), American Indian(s), immigrant(s), Asian American(s), Korean American(s), Chinese American(s), Japanese American(s), Hispanic(s), Mexican American(s) *with:* business(es), entrepreneur(s,ship), enterprise(s), firm(s), compan(y,ies), corporation(s), factor(y,ies), industr(y,ies), retail(er,ers), production, operation(s), store(s), shop(s). *See also* Business; Enterprises; Entrepreneurship; Family businesses; Home based businesses; Microenterprise; Minority groups; Self employment; Small businesses; Stores.

Minority groups. Minority group(s). Minorit(y,ies). Out-group(s). *Choose from:* racial, religious, cultural, ethnic, stigmatized, stereotyped *with:* minorit(y,ies), identit(y,ies), background(s). *Choose from:* minority *with:* population(s), worker(s), student(s), child(ren). Socially inferior. Guest people. Outsider(s). *Consider also:* specific groups by name such as African American(s), Afro-American(s), Basque American(s), Black(s), Bulgarian American(s), Chicano(s), Latino(s), Ladino(s), Nonwhite(s), Non-white(s), Puerto Rican(s), Spanish American(s), Latin American(s), French Canadian(s), Jew(s,ish), Polish American(s), Italian American(s), Irish American(s), Asian American(s), Chinese American(s), Japanese American(s), Eurasian(s), Oriental American(s), Korean American(s), Native American(s), Negro(es), Eskimo(s), Inuit(s), Aleut(s), Alaska Native(s), Canadian Native(s), Greek American(s), Mexican American(s), Portuguese American(s), Samoan American(s), Slavic American(s), Gyps(y,ies), Spanish surname(s), Cuban(s), Haitian(s), Dominican(s), Filipinos, American Indian(s), etc. *Consider also:* elderly, senior citizen(s), homosexual(s), gay(s), female(s), woman, women, sexual minorit(y,ies), handicapped, disabled, people with disabilities. *See also* Affirmative action; Alaska natives; Asian Americans; Assimilation (cultural); Biculturalism; Bidialectalism; Bilingualism; Blacks; Center and periphery; Central American native cultural groups; Civil rights; Class differences; Cultural diversity; Cultural groups; Cultural pluralism; Disadvantaged; Dominated

cultures; Eskimos; Ethnic groups; Ethnic identity; Ethnic relations; Ethnicity; Gypsies; Hispanic Americans; Indigenous populations; Judaism; Language shift; Linguistic minorities; Majority groups; Marginality (sociological); Minority authors; Minority businesses; Multicultural education; North American native cultural groups; Oppression; People of color; Plural societies; Prejudice; Races; Race relations; Religious cultural groups; Social discrimination; Social structure; South American native cultural groups; Subcultures.

Minority groups, national. See *Ethnic groups; Linguistic minorities; Minority groups; National identity; Nationalism.*

Minority owned. See *Minority businesses.*

Minors. See *Adolescence; Children.*

Minstrels. Minstrel(s,sy). Menetrier(s). Menestrel(s). Spielmann(er). Menestrello(s). Ministril(es). Ministerali(s). Jongleur(s). Wandering singer(s) of ballads. *Consider also:* jestour(s), jester(s), minstrel show(s), troubadour(s), trouvere(s), corridista(s), trovador(es), payador(es), menestraudie, menestrandise, bard(s). *See also* Poets; Singers; Troubadour; Trouvere.

Miracle plays. Miracle play(s). Mystery play(s). Passion play(s). York play(s). Towneley play(s). Wakefield play(s). Coventry play(s). Chester play(s). *Consider also:* medieval drama, Passion Play at Oberammergau, Passionsspiele. *See also* Drama; Historical drama; Liturgical drama; Medieval drama, Medieval literature; Morality plays; Pageants; Religious drama; Religious mysteries; Theater.

Miracles. Miracle(s). Miraculous(ness). Extraordinary event(s). Divine intervention(s). *Consider also:* marvel(ous), phenomenon, portent(s), prodig(y,ies), sensation(al), apparition(s), spiritual healing. *See also* Mysticism; Omen; Religious experience; Spiritual gifts; Spiritual healing; Supernatural.

Misanthropy. Misanthrop(e,y,ic,os). Misogyn(y,ist,ists). Malevolen(t,ce). Man hating. Man hater(s). Woman hating. Woman hater(s). Misogamist(s). Cynic(s,al,ism). Inhuman(e,ity). Antisocial. *Consider also:* negativ(e,ism,ity), schadenfreude. *See also* Cynicism; Misogyny; Negativism; Personality traits; Pessimism; Social perception.

Misbehavior. See *Behavior problems.*

Miscarriages. Miscarriage(s). Miscarr(y, ied). Spontaneous abortion(s). Abortus. *Choose from:* pregnanc(y,ies), bab(y,ies) *with:* loss(es), lost. *See also* Abortion.

Miscegenation. See *Interethnic families; Intermarriage; Interracial marriage; Racially mixed.*

Misconceptions. Misconception(s). Misconceive(d). Misinterpret(ed,ing, ation,ations). Misunderstanding(s). Misunderstood. Misconstrue(d). Misconstruction. Misread(ing). Fallac(y,ies). Mistaken conception(s). Factoid(s). *Choose from:* dysfunctional, distorted, false *with:* idea(s), belief(s), impression(s). *See also* Cognitive structures; Comprehension; Concept formation; Concepts; Mathematical concepts; Misinformation; Mistaken identity; Misunderstanding.

Misconduct. See *Behavior problems.*

Misconduct, scientific. See *Scientific misconduct.*

Misconduct, sexual. See *Sexual misconduct.*

Misconduct in office. Misconduct in office. *Choose from:* misconduct, allegation(s), disciplinary matter(s), malpractice, corrupt(ion), criminal act(s), impropriet(y,ies), misappropriat(e,ed, ing,ion), offense(s), bribery, high crimes, misdemeanor(s), fraud(ulent), perjur(e, ed,ing,y) *with:* office(r,rs), police, official(s), executive(s), president(s), legislator(s), representative(s), manager(s), clergy(man,men,woman, women), corporat(e,ion,ions), employee(s), teacher(s), *Consider also:* special prosecutor(s), impeach(ed,ing, ment), Watergate, Iran Contra. *See also* Codes of ethics; Conflict of interest; Corruption in government; Crime; Financial disclosure; Improprieties; Judicial corruption; Ministerial ethics (clergy); Political ethics; Unethical conduct, Whistle blowing.

Misdemeanors. See *Corruption in government; Crime; Immorality; Misconduct in office; Offenses; Unethical conduct.*

Misers. Miser(s,ly,liness). Cheapskate(s). Penny pinch(er,ers,ing). Sting(y,iness). Churl(ish,ishness). Tightwad(s). Begrudg(e,ed,ing). Skinflint(s,y,iness). *Consider also:* thrift(y,iness), frugal(ity). *See also* Frugality; Meanness; Possessiveness; Selfishness (stingy).

Misfortune. See *Adversity.*

Misinformation. Misinform(ed,ing,ation). *Choose from:* false, out of date, incomplete, misleading, unreliable, inaccurate, malicious, distort(ed,ing), misrepresenting *with:* information, content, message(s), web page(s), discussion group(s), chat room(s), publication(s), material, document(s). *Consider also:* rumor(s), gossip, conspiracy theor(y,ies), libel, disinformation, unsigned, unknown authorship, anonymous source(s),

factoid(s). *See also* Authenticity; Bias; Credibility; Distortion; Errors; Fairness and accuracy in reporting; Falsification (scientific); Fraud; Hyperbole; Illusion (philosophy); Misconceptions.

Misogyny. Misogyn(ic,ist,ists,istic). Woman hater(s). Misogam(y,ist,ists,ic). *Consider also:* male chauvinis(m,t,ts), confirmed bachelor(s), sexis(m,t,ts). *See also* Androcentrism; Antisocial behavior; Male chauvinism; Men's movement; Misanthropy; Sexism; Sexual attitudes; Witchcraft trials.

Misprints. See *Errors.*

Missiles, ballistic. See *Ballistic missiles.*

Missiles, guided. See *Ballistic missiles.*

Missing children. See *Missing persons.*

Missing in action. Missing in action. MIA(s). Missing in Vietnam, Indochina, etc. Prisoner remains. Listed as missing. *Choose from:* missing, captive(s), lost, held prisoner, captured *with:* servicem(an,en), servicewom(an,en), soldier(s), infantrym(an,en), sailor(s), military, officer(s), troop(s). *See also* Absence and presumption of death; Combat; Fatalities; Missing persons; Prisoners of war.

Missing persons. Missing person(s). Desaparecid(o,a,os). *Choose from:* missing, disappear(ed,ance), lost, found, stray(ed), wandered off, vanish(ed), last seen, failed to show, failed to appear, never returned, whereabouts, kidnap(ped,ping), abducted, runaway *with:* child(ren), girl(s), boy(s), teenager(s), student(s), woman, women, man, men, person(s), people, daughter(s), son(s), mother(s), father(s), grandfather(s), grandmother(s), camper(s), hiker(s), explorer(s). *Consider also:* seek(ing) identit(y,ies), found, discovered, unidentified *with:* bod(y,ies), person(s). *Consider also:* runaway(s), street kid(s), homeless youth, jump(ed,ing) bail, found wandering. *See also* Abduction; Absence and presumption of death; Arrests; Child kidnapping; Death squads; Fugitives; Homeless; Kidnapping; Missing in action; Political crimes; Prisoners of war; Runaways; Wandering behavior.

Mission, corporate. See *Corporate mission.*

Mission, institutional. See *Institutional mission.*

Missionaries. Mission(ary,aries). Mission health service(s). Mission hospital(s). Medical missionar(y,ies). Evangelist(s, ic). Evangelical. Church revival(s). Evangeliz(e,ed,ing). Convert(ing) heathen. Propagat(e,ed,ing) faith. Missioner(s). *Consider also:* muscular Christianity, missiology, catechist(s). *See also* Clergy; Evangelistic work; Indigenous churches; Medical missions;

Proselytism; Religious conversion; Religious personnel.

Missions, medical. See *Medical missions.*

Mistaken identity. Mistaken identit(y,ies). Misidentified. Erroneously identified. *Choose from:* mistaken, fictional, phony, disguise(d), conceal(ed), hide, hidden *with:* name(s), identit(y,ies), life, origin(s), identification. *Consider also:* look-alike(s), disguise(s,d), mistakenly attributed. *See also* Disguise; Errors; Identity; Misconceptions.

Mistakes. See *Errors.*

Mistresses. See *Extramarital relations.*

Misunderstanding. Misunderstanding(s). Misunderstood. Disagreement(s). Controvers(y,ies). Discord(ant). *Consider also:* fail to understand, interpret(ed) incorrectly, misapprehend(ed,ing), miscomprehend(ed,ing), misconceive(d), misconstrue(d), misinterpret(ed), misread, mistake(s,n). *See also* Disagreements; Family conflict; Intercultural communication; Misconceptions.

Misuse, health services. See *Health services misuse.*

Mix, case. See *Case mix.*

Mixed languages. See *Creoles.*

Mixed marriages. See *Intermarriage.*

Mixed race adoption. See *Interethnic families.*

Mixed races. See *Interethnic families; Intermarriage; Interracial marriage; Racially mixed.*

Mixed, racially. See *Racially mixed.*

Mnemonic learning. Mnemonic learning. Mnemonic(s). Mnemotechnic(s). *Choose from:* mnemonic *with:* image(s,ry), encoding, training, method(s), strateg(y, ies), code(s), device(s). *Consider also:* memory, learning, recall, remember(ed, ing) *with:* aid(s), scheme(s), strateg(y, ies), peg(s), train(ing), technique(s). *Consider also:* metamemory, keyword method, Memoria technica. *See also* Cues; Learning; Memory; Recall; Retention (psychology); Self culture.

Mob rule. See *Riots.*

Mob violence. See *Riots.*

Mobile computing. Mobile computing *Choose from:* mobile, wireless, ubiquitous, portable, cellular, wearable, hand-held *with:* computer(s), computing device(s), internetworking, network(s), workstation(s), digital equipment. *Consider also:* laptop computer(s), hand-held computer(s). *See also* Computers; Electronic equipment; Man machine systems; Microcomputers.

Mobilian trade language. Mobilian trade language. Mobilian Jargon. Mobilian tongue. *Consider also:* native American pidgin, Indian lingua franca *See also* Creoles; Lingua franca; Pidgin languages; Trade languages.

Mobility, career. See *Career mobility.*

Mobility, class. See *Class mobility.*

Mobility, geographic. See *Geographic mobility.*

Mobility, intergenerational. See *Intergenerational mobility.*

Mobility, job. See *Career mobility.*

Mobility, labor. See *Labor mobility.*

Mobility, occupational. See *Career mobility.*

Mobility, physical. See *Physical mobility.*

Mobility, population. See *Migration.*

Mobility, residential. See *Residential mobility.*

Mobility, social. See *Social mobility.*

Mobility, upward. See *Class mobility; Social mobility; Status seekers.*

Mobility, vocational. See *Career mobility.*

Mobility aids. Mobility aid(s). Ambulatory aid(s). *Consider also:* seeing eye dog(s), guide dog(s), wheelchair(s), artificial sensing aid(s), cane(s), laser cane(s), crutch(es), sonic guide(s), path sounder(s), driving aid(s), tactual map(s), tactile map(s), obstacle detector(s), tactile route configuration(s), auditory map(s), sonic glasses, walking stick(s), walker(s). *Consider also:* mobility training. *See also* Disability; Prostheses; Self help devices.

Mobilization. Mobiliz(e,ed,ing,ation). Energiz(e,ed,ing,ation). Engender(ed, ing). Vitaliz(e,ed,ing,ation). Revitaliz(e,ed,ing,ation). Enlist support(ers). Incit(e,cd,ing,cmcnt). Activat(e,ed,ing,ation). Rous(e,ed,ing). Arous(e,ed,ing). Instigat(e,ed,ing,ion). Agitat(e,ed,ing,ation,or,ors). Accelerat(e,ed,ing) production. *Consider also:* rise of social movements, formation of new political parties, consciousness raising, rearm(ed,ing), business boom(s), convert(cd,ing) to wartime use(s). *See also* Activism; Activation; Consciousness raising activities; Military planning; Political action; Social agitation.

Mobilization, social. See *Consciousness raising activities; Mobilization; Social agitation.*

Mobs. See *Crowds.*

Model, medical. See *Medical model.*

Models. Model(s). Prototyp(e,es,ical). Archetyp(e,es,ical). Example(s). Exemplification. Sample(s). Standard(s). Pattern(s). Design(s). Paradigm(s). Simulat(ion,ions,or,ors). Replica(s).

Dumm(y,ies). *See also* Anatomic models; Biological models; Causal models; Examples; Mannequins (Figures); Mathematical models; Models (persons); Operations research; Research design; Research methods; Role models; Scientific models; Simulation; Structural models; Systems analysis; Theories.

Models (persons). Models (persons). Supermodel(s). Fashion model(s). Cover girl(s). *Choose from:* model(s), mannequin(s) *with:* person(s), girl(s), female(s), women, woman, male(s), men, boy(s), child(ren), black, African American, Asian, cheesecake, couturier(s), artist(s), photographer(s). *Consider also:* modeling agenc(y,ies), beauty queen(s), fashion celebrit(y,ies), beautiful girl(s), clotheshorse(s). *See also* Fashions; Garment industry; Mannequins (Figures); Models.

Models, anatomic. See *Anatomic models.*

Models, biological. See *Biological models.*

Models, causal. See *Causal models.*

Models, mathematical. See *Mathematical models.*

Models, role. See *Role models.*

Models, scientific. See *Scientific models.*

Models, structural. See *Structural models.*

Moderation. Moderat(e,ed,ing,ion,eness). Temperance. Restrain(t,ed). *Consider also:* happy medium, golden mean, middle way, middle road, middle ground. *See also* Reasonableness; Temperance; Tolerance.

Modern architecture. Modern architecture. *Choose from:* modern(ist), 20th century, current, postmodern, international style, functionalism, avant-garde, art nouveau, de Stijl *with:* architectur(e,al), architect(s), building(s). *Consider also:* skyscraper(s), The Santa Monica school of architecture, Louis H. Sullivan, Frank Lloyd Wright, J.J. P. Oud, Walter Gropius, Raymond Hood, Albert Kahn, Louis Kahn, Le Corbusier, Eero Saarinen, Felix Candela, I.M. Pei. *See also* Architects; Architectural styles; Architectural accessibility; Architectural criticism; Architectural drawing; Architecture; Arts; Buildings; Constructivism; Domestic architecture; Facility design and construction; Modern art; Postmodernism; Suprematism; Towers.

Modern art. Modern art(ist,ists). Modern painter(s). Nonfigurative art. Contemporary work(s) of art. *Consider modern art movements such as:* Impressionis(m, t,ts), Surrealism, Cubism, Fauvism, Constructivism, Supremism, Dada(ism), Abstract Expressionism, Bauhaus, New Objectivity. *Consider also:* Theo van Doesburg, Paul Klee, Lyonel Feininger, Jean Arp, Marcel Duchamp, Kurt

Schwitters, Pablo Picasso, Salvador Dali, Yves Tanguay, Max Ernst, Andre Derain, Joan Miro, Amedeo Modigliani, George Grosz, Otto Dix, Max Beckmann, Peter Blume, Jack Levine, William Gropper, Ben Shahn, Arshile Gorky, Jackson Pollock, Willem de Kooning, Julio Gonzalez, Alexander Calder, Henry Moore, Barbara Hepworth, etc. *See also* Art deco; Art Nouveau; Artistic styles; Arts; Assemblage (Art); Futurism (Art); Constructivism; Cubism; Dadaism; Genres (art); Expressionism (art); Impressionism (art); Modern architecture; Post-Impressionism; Pop art; Suprematism.

Modern civilization. Modern civilization. Modern society. 20th century civilization. Postmodern civilization. Modern world. Modern culture. *Choose from:* modern, 20th century, twentieth-century, postmodern, information, western, industrial, contemporary *with:* civilization(s), societ(y,ies), culture(s), age(s). *Consider also:* modern science, scientific revolution, twentieth-century capitalism, Western society, consumer societ(y,ies), postmodern condition, post-Western civilization(s), American society, machine age, computer age, industrial civilization, secular age, modernity, contemporary world. *See also* Community networks (computer); Globalization; Information society; Internationalism; Modern society; Modernization; Multicultural education; Multinational corporations; Neocolonialism; Postindustrial societies; Postmodernism; Teledemocracy.

Modern literature. Modern literature. *Choose from:* twentieth-century, nineteenth-century, modern(ist,ism), 20th century, 19th century, recent, contemporary, postwar, romantic(ism), realism, socialist realism, Victorian, naturalism, avant garde, existential(ism), expressionism, impressionism, surrealistic, stream of consciousness *with:* literature, writer(s), literary criticism, novel(s), literary work(s), fiction, poetry, drama. *Consider also:* little magazine(s), angry young men, lost generation, beat generation, palaeo-modernism, neomodernism, vers libre. *See also* Constructivism; Intertextuality; Gothicism; Literary movements; Literature; Magic realism (Literature); Medieval literature; Modern society; Naturalism; Realism.

Modern music. See *Twentieth century Western art music.*

Modern painters. See *Modern art.*

Modern philosophy. See *Deconstruction; Egalitarianism; Empiricism; Ethics; Existentialism; Humanism; Logocentrism; Phenomenology;*

Political philosophy; Postmodernism; Pragmatism; Realism; Reductionism; Semiotics; Social philosophy; Voluntarism (philosophy).

Modern society. Modern societ(y,ies). Mass societ(y,ies). Gesellschaft. Large scale society. Secondary relations. Atomized society. Urban society. *Choose from:* modern, contemporary, twentieth century, western, mass, postindustrial, industrial, urban, secular *with:* societ(y,ies), life, world, culture, civilization. *Consider also:* impersonal(ity), mass behavior, mass culture, admass, consumer society, alienation, anomie. *See also* Complex societies; Community networks (computer); Developed countries; Fragmentation (experience); Gemeinschaft and gesellschaft; Impersonal; Industrial societies; Mass society; Modern civilization; Modernization; Popular culture; Postindustrial societies; Urbanization; Western society.

Modernism (literature). See *Modern literature.*

Modernization. Moderniz(e,ing,ation). Modern(ity,ism,ists). *Consider also:* streamlin(e,ed,ing). prioritiz(e,ed,ing). Urbaniz(e,ed,ing,ation). Globaliz(e,ed, ing,ation). Develop(ing,ed,ment). Democratiz(e,ed,ing,ation). Industrializ(e,ed,ing,ation). Postindustrial(ization). Post-industrial(ization). Reform(s). Social goals. Historical development. Evolution. Evolv(e,ed,ing). Update(d). Renovat(e,ed,ing). Streamlin(e,ed,ing). Refurbish(ed,ing). Rejuvenat(e,ed,ing). Refresh(ed,ing). *See also* Civic improvement; Cultural transformation; Culture change; Economic development; Electrification; Globalization; Industrialization; Modern civilization; Modern society; Preservation; Progress; Rationalization (sociology); Rejuvenation; Rural industries; Scientific revolutions; Secularization; Social change; Technological progress; Technology transfer; Traditional societies; Urban renewal; Urbanization.

Modes, musical. See *Musical intervals and scales.*

Modesty. Modest(y). Self effac(ing,ement). Unpretentious(ness). Unobtrusive(ness). Unostentatious(ness). Constrain(t,ed). Humble(ness). Humility. Reticen(t,ce). Unassuming(ness). Subdued. Meek(ness). *See also* Decency; Humility; Personality traits.

Modification, behavior. See *Behavior modification.*

Mohammedanism. See *Islam.*

Moieties. See *Clans.*

Molestation, child. See *Incest; Molested children; Sexual abuse; Sexual exploitation; Sexual harassment.*

Molested children. Molest(ed,ing) child(ren). Child molest(ation,er,ers). Sexual(ly) abuse(d) child(ren). Child(hood) sexual abuse. Incest(uous). Famil(ial,y) sexual abuse. *Choose from:* child(ren,hood), juvenile(s), prepubescent, pubescent *with:* sexual(ly) abuse(d), sexual(ly) exploit(ed,ation), rape(d), incest(uous), prostitut(e,es,ion), moral offense(s), molest(ed,ation), pornograph(y,ic), sex offense(s), sexual(ly) exploit(ed,ing,ation), pedophil(e,es,ia,iacs), exhibitionis(m,t, ts). *See also* Child abuse; Incest; Online harassment; Rape; Sexual abuse; Sexual exploitation; Sexual harassment.

Mon-Khmer languages. Mon-Khmer language(s). Mon (Talaing). Cham. Khmer (Cambodian). *See also* Language; Languages (as subjects); Southeast Asia; Southeast Asian cultural groups.

Monadology. Monad(ology,ism). Monad(s). *Consider also:* Gottfried Wilhelm Leibniz, pre-established harmony. *See also* Pluralism.

Monarchy. Monarch(s,y,ies,ial). King(s,ships,dom,doms). Queen(s). Emperor(s). Royal famil(y,ies). Heir(s) to throne. Royal heir(s). Crown prince(s). Emir(s). Sultan(s). Majesty. Royal house(s). Czar(s). Tsar(s). Tzar(s). Kaiser(s). Caesar(s). Mikado. Tenno. Pharoah(s). Shah(s). Royal couple. Sovereign(s). Crowned head(s). Royal line. *See also* Chiefs; Divine right of kings; Emperor worship; Palaces; Royal favorites; Royal supremacy; Ruling class; Sovereignty.

Monarchy, absolute. See *Despotism.*

Monasteries. See *Cloisters.*

Monastic life. See *Abstinence; Asceticism; Contemplative orders; Convents; Friars; Holy men; Holy women; Middle ages; Monasticism; Monks; Nuns; Religious communities; Religious personnel; Women religious.*

Monasticism. Monastic(ism). Monaster(y, ies). Ascetic(s,ism). Contemplative life. *Choose from:* vow(s) *with:* celibacy, poverty, obedience, silence. Evangelical counsel(s). Cenobitic monasticism. Eremitic monasticism. Religious brotherhood(s). Mendicant(s). Mendicant order(s). Friar(s). Monk(s). Nun(s). Vihara. Vinaya pitaka. *Consider also:* St. Anthony, St. Pachomius, Benedictine(s), Cistercian(s), Capuchins; Confraternities, Misercordia sisters, Ursulines, Scalabrinians, Dominican(s), Franciscan(s), Beghard(s), Beguine(s), Trappist(s), Jesuit(s), Paulist(s), Sisters of Charity of Mother Seton,

Carthusian(s), Augustinian(s), Carmelite(s), Zoe, Sotir, Basilian, Maronite, Hindu, Jaina, Theravada, Zen, Buddhist, Taoist, etc. *with:* order(s), brotherhood(s), monaster(y,ies), mendicant(s), monastic(ism), monk(s), nun(s), abbey(s), prior(y,ies). *Consider also:* simple vow(s), solemn vow(s). *See also* Abstinence; Alternative lifestyles; Asceticism; Contemplative orders; Convents; Friars; Holy men; Holy women; Medieval theology; Middle ages; Monks; Nuns; Religious communities; Religious life; Religious personnel; Women religious.

Monetary incentives. Monetary incentive(s). *Choose from:* monetar(y, ily), pay(ment), wage(s), income, salar(y,ies), financial, cash, money *with:* incentive(s), motivation, reinforcement, reward(s), payoff(s), bonus(es), remuneration, inducement(s). *Consider also:* merit pay, fine(s), tax incentive(s), bribe(s,ry). *See also* Economic man; Employee incentive plans; Gains; Incentives; Monetary rewards; Motivation; Profit motive; Profit sharing; Profitability; Profits; Self interest.

Monetary policy. Monetary polic(y,ies). *Choose from:* Federal Reserve Board, central bank(s), discretionary, interest rate(s) *with:* polic(y,ies). *See also* Bimetallism; Devaluation (of currency); Fiscal policy; Gold standard; Interest (monetary); Money supply.

Monetary rewards. Monetary reward(s). Wage(s). Income. Salar(y,ies). Performance contingent pay. *Choose from:* monetar(y,ily), pay(ment), financial, cash, money *with:* reward(s), award(s), prize(s), incentive(s), reward(s), payoff(s), bonus(es), remuneration, inducement(s). *Consider also:* merit pay, tax incentive(s), refundable deposit(s), bribe(s,ry), tip(s,ped,ping), baksheesh. *See also* Baksheesh; Bonuses; Compensation (payment); Compensation management; Deferred compensation; Employee recognition; Monetary incentives; Profits; Reinforcement; Tipping.

Monetary unions. Monetary union(s). *Choose from:* monetary, currenc(y,ies) *with:* union(s), integration, unification, collective. *Consider also:* European Monetary System, Eurocurrency, Eurodollar(s), Euromoney, European Currency Unit(s), ECU(s), European Monetary System, EMS, Maastricht Treaty. *See also* Common currency; Currency; Economic union.

Monetary worth. See *Economic value.*

Money. Mon(ey,ies). Medium of exchange. Cash. Legal tender. Specie. Monetar(y, ily). Currenc(y,ies). Dollar(s). Cent(s). Payment(s). Coin(s,age). Gold standard. Silver standard. Savings. Liquid assets.

Income. Liquidity. Fund(s,ing). Penn(y,ies). Nickel(s). Dime(s). Pound(s). Franc(s). Ruble(s). Mark(s). *See also* Capital (financial); Cash; Credit; Coin portraits; Coinage; Coins; Currency; Debts; Devaluation (of currency); Economic exchanges; Expenditures; Finance; Funds; Income; Investments; Loans; Monetary policy; Monetary unions; Money supply; Payments; Profits; Savings; Wealth.

Money (primitive cultures). Money. *Choose from:* shell(s), cowries, pearlshell(s), wampum, bead(s), whales' teeth, dog tooth, feather(s), stone disk(s), cattle, seed(s), iron bar(s), knives, salt, cocoa, bean(s), ivory *with:* money, medium of exchange, wealth object(s), valu(e,able) symbol(s,ism). *Consider also:* moon money, sounding coin, pig money. *See also* Bartering; Ceremonial exchanges; Economic exchanges; Traditional societies; Wealth.

Money, digital. See *Digital money.*

Money, earnest. See *Earnest money.*

Money, electronic. See *Digital money.*

Money, velocity of. See *Velocity of money.*

Money devaluation. See *Devaluation (of currency).*

Money laundering. Money laundering. *Choose from:* launder(ed,ing), hid(e,ing), hidden *with:* money. *Choose from:* secret, dummy, hid(e,ing), hidden, Swiss, offshore *with:* bank account(s), monetary transaction(s), cash flow. *Consider also:* narcodollar(s), hot money. *See also* Crime; Drug trafficking; Smuggling.

Money management. See *Financial management.*

Money raising. See *Fund raising.*

Money supply. Money supply. Liquidity. Sum of circulating currency. *Choose from:* money, currency, monetary, funds, cash *with:* supply, reserve(s), growth, control(s), creation. *Consider also:* private sector liquidity. *See also* Devaluation (of currency); Emergency currency; Funds; Interest (monetary); Monetary policy; Money; Velocity of money.

Mongolism. See *Down's syndrome.*

Mongoloid race. Mongoloid race. Asian(s). Asiatic people(s). Oriental(s). Amerindian(s). Amer-Indian(s). American Indian(s). *Consider also:* Alaska native(s), Canada native(s), Asian American(s), Chinese American(s), Eskimo(s), Inuit(s), Filipino American(s), Hawaiian(s), Japanese American(s), Korean American(s), Indochinese, Cambodian(s), Laotian(s), Samoan American(s), Vietnamese American(s), Athabascan Indian(s),

Evenki, Indonesian(s), Japanese, Korean(s), Malayan(s), Mongolian(s), Samoyedes, Tibetan(s), Tungus, Thais. *See also* Asian Americans; Central American native cultural groups; North American native cultural groups; Oceanic cultural groups; Pacific Islanders; People of color; Races; Racially mixed; South American native cultural groups;.

Monism. Monis(m,t,ts,tic). Monismus. Singularism. Monistische Weltanschauung. *Consider also:* physicalism, neutral monism. *See also* Dualism; God concepts; Idealism; Materialism; Mind body problem; Oneness of God; Pantheism (universal divinity); Pluralism.

Monitoring. Monitor(s,ed,ing). Observ(e,ed,er,ers,ing,ation). Record(ed,ing). Regulat(ed,ing,ion). Diary keeping. Keep(ing) record(s). Log(s). Vigilan(t,ce). Keep(ing) track. Proctor(ed,ing). Track(ed,ing). Check(ed,ing). Scan(ned,ner,ners,ning). Counter(s). *See also* Attention; Awareness; Perception; Selective attention; Self monitoring; Vigilance.

Monitoring, self. See *Self monitoring.*

Monks. Monk(hood,s). Cenobite(s). Monastic order(s). Monastic(ism). Cenobitic monasticism. Eremitic monasticism. Mendicant order(s). Friar(s). *Consider also:* St. Anthony, St. Pachomius, Benedictine(s), Cistercian(s), Dominican(s), Franciscan(s), Trappist(s), Jesuit(s), Paulist(s), Carthusian(s), Augustinian(s), Carmelite(s). *See also* Abstinence; Contemplative orders; Friars; Holy men; Military religious orders; Monasticism; Religious life; Religious personnel.

Monochrome painting. Monochrome painting(s). La peinture monochrome. Monochromes. *Choose from:* monochrom(e,atic) *with:* painting(s), lithograph(s), sketch(es), canvas(es), print(s), reproduction(s). *Consider also:* Yves Klein, minimal art. *See also* Arts; Drawing; Minimal art.

Monogamy. Monogam(y,ous). One spouse. Single marriage. Mate for lifetime. *Consider also:* fidelity, nuclear famil(y,ies), serial polygamy. *See also* Marriage; Polygamy.

Monogenism. See *Creationism.*

Monolingualism. Monolingual(ism). Unilingual. *Consider also:* first language(s), mother tongue. *See also* Bilingualism; Child language; Language; Language proficiency; Multilingualism; Native language; Sociolinguistics.

Monologue. See *First person narrative.*

Monopolies. Monopol(y,ies,istic,ize, izing,ization). Cartel(s). Control market. Exclusive control. Exclusive possession. Exclusive rights. Corner the market. *Consider also:* eliminating competition, unfair competition, market closure, dominat(e,ed,ing) the market, oligopol(y,ies). *See also* Antitrust law; Cartels; Economic competition; Industrial concentration; Market share; Oligopolies; Price fixing; Restraint of trade.

Monotheism. See *Oneness of God.*

Monotony. Monoton(y,ous). Unvar(ied, ying). Unchang(ed,ing). Repetitious(ness). Uneventful. Humdrum. Routine(s). Dull(ness). Tedious(ness). Tiresome. Wearisome. Prosaic. Uninteresting. Unexciting. Bore(d,dom). Boring. Uninspiring. Dreary. Commonplace. Bland(ness). Vapid. Flat(ness). Fatuous(ness). *See also* Boredom; Dullness.

Monozygotic twins. Monozygotic twins. Monozygoticity. *Choose from:* monozygotic, monozygous, identical *with:* twins. *See also* Multiple births; Siblings.

Monuments. Monument(s). Memorial(s). Tomb(s). Tombstone(s). Gravestone(s). Cenotaph(s). Commemorative(s). Cairn(s). Shrine(s). Reliquar(y,ies). Headstone(s). Sepulch(er,ers,re,res). Mausoleum(s). Megalith(s,ic). *Consider also:* sculpture. *See also* Arts; Commemoration; Dolmen; Epigraphs; Epitaphs; Material culture; Natural monuments; Sculpture; Sepulchral monuments; Statues; Triumphal arches; War memorials.

Monuments, natural. See *Natural monuments.*

Monuments, sepulchral. See *Sepulchral monuments.*

Mood, atmosphere. See *Ambience.*

Mood, imperative. See *Imperative mood.*

Moodiness. Mood(y,iness). Negative mood state(s). *Choose from:* mood, emotion(s,al), affect *with:* change(s), variability, swing(s), variation(s), labil(e,ity), instability, unstable. Moody blues. *Consider also:* gloomy, unhapp(y,iness), downcast, discouraged, miserable, glum, dour, grim, sullen, sulk(y,iness), morose, dismal, melancholy, sad, dispirited, depress(ed,ion), disheartened, disconsolate, ill humored, temperamental, irritab(le,ility), impatient, petulan(t,ce), irascible, ill tempered, grouchy, capricious, fickle, inconstant, flighty, volatile, erratic, dysphor(ia,ic), euphor(ia,ic), man(ia,ic). *See also* Emotional states; Emotions; Personality traits; Sadness.

Moods. See *Emotions; Moodiness.*

Moonlighting. Moonlight(ing). Multiple job(s,holding). Second job(s). Two job(s). Extra job(s). Double employment. Secondary employment. Extra employment. *Consider also:* double dip(ping,per,pers). *See also* Alternative work patterns; Employment; Flexible workplace practices; Overtime work; Part time employment; Underemployment.

Moonshine. See *Illicit liquor.*

Moral attitudes. Moral attitude(s). Moral outlook. *Choose from:* moral(s,ity), ethic(s,al) *with:* attitude(s), outlook(s), judgment, confusion, skeptic(s,al), conservationism, relativism, conservativ(e,ism), values, perception(s), reasoning, sense of obligation, toleran(ce,t). *Consider also:* conventional morality, sexual revolution, culture war(s), decency, chastity, taboo(s), altruis(m,tic), prudish(ness). *See also* Altruism; Attitudes; Beliefs; Community attitudes; Depravity; Dogmatism; Ethics; Generation gap; Human dignity; Moral development; Moral education; Moral obligation; Moral reasoning; Morality; Public opinion; Puritanism; Racial attitudes; Religious attitudes; Sexual attitudes; Sexual revolution; Social attitudes.

Moral authority. Moral authority. *Choose from:* moral(s,ity), ethic(s,al,ally), spiritual *with:* authority, leader(s,ship), influen(ce,ces,ced,cing,tial), power(s), crusader(s). *See also* Civil disobedience; Conscientious objectors; Draft resisters; Ethical practices; Ethics; Leadership; Legitimacy of governments; Liberty of conscience; Moral obligation; Moral reasoning; Morality; Nonresistance to evil; Nonviolence; Pacifism; Peace movements; Responsibility (answerability); Role models; Social values; Spiritual direction.

Moral conditions. Moral condition(s). *Choose from:* moral(s,ly,ity), spiritual(ity), ethic(al,ally,s) with condition(s), culture, standard(s), decline, turpitude, sense. *Consider also:* personal(ly) responsib(le,ility), con-science, social(ly) responsib(le,ility), integrity, fairness, just(ice,ness), honest(y), traditional values, family values. *See also* Anomie; Decadence; Depravity; Ethics; Family values; Morality; Regression (civilization); Social conditions; Social disorganization; Social reality; Social values; Values.

Moral development. Moral development. *Choose from:* moral, ethical, sociomoral, character, conscience *with:* reasoning, judgment(s), development, stages, education, consciousness, comprehension, values, thought, matur(ity,ation), decay. *Choose from:* conventional,

preconventional, postconventional, guru *with:* level(s), stage(s). *Consider also:* values clarification, moral cognitive development, moral reasoning development, moral thought, generalization of moral principles, Kohlberg(ian). *See also* Adult development; Child development; Children; Codes of ethics; Cruelty to animals; Criminal psychology; Ethics; Evolutionary ethics; Examination of conscience; Integrity; Juvenile delinquency; Moral attitudes; Moral education; Moral judgment; Moral reasoning; Morality; Personality development; Psychosocial development; Spiritual formation; Values.

Moral education. Moral education. Character education. Transmission of values. *Choose from:* ethic(s,al), moral, religious, character, values *with:* instruct(ed,ing,ion), form(ed,ing,ation), train(ed,ing), educat(e,ed,ing,ion), develop(ed,ing,ment), indoctrinat(ed,ing, ion). *See also* Ethics; Moral attitudes; Moral development; Morality; Religious education.

Moral judgment. Moral judgment. *Choose from:* moral, ethical, right and wrong, sociomoral, values *with:* conviction(s), rationale(s), attitude(s), reasoning, judgment(s), consensus, comprehension, thought, thinking, orientation. *Consider also:* conscientious objector(s), civil disobedience, legitimacy judgment(s), superego, conscience, morality, values clarification, generalization of moral principles, Kohlberg(ian). *See also* Categorical imperative; Conscience; Ethics; Examination of conscience; Imperative; Integrity; Judgment; Moral development; Moral reasoning; Morality.

Moral majority. See *Religious fundamentalism; Right wing politics; Social conformity; Traditionalism.*

Moral obligation. Moral obligation(s). *Choose from:* moral(s,ity), ethic(al,ally), integrity, honest(y), principle(s,d), conscience, conscientious(ness), trustworth(y,iness), truth(ful,fulness), openness, fidelity, incorruptib(le,ility) *with:* obligation(s), oblig(e,ed), obligat(e,ed,ory), dut(y,ies), responsibilit(y,ies). *Consider also:* pledged, committed. *See also* Commitment (emotional); Conscience; Duties; Moral attitudes; Moral authority; Morality; Obligations; Personal values; Political ethics; Political obligation; Responsibility (answerability); Rights; Social contract; Social ethics; Supererogation.

Moral philosophy. See *Ethics.*

Moral reasoning. Moral reasoning. *Choose from:* moral(s,ity), ethic(s,al,ally), sociomoral, justice, conscience *with:* reason(ed,ing), rational(ity,ize,

ized,ization,izations), judgment(s), logic(al), conscious(ness), comprehen(d, ded,ding,sion), thought, think(ing). *Consider also:* values clarification, moral thought, moral generalization(s), Kohlberg(ian). *See also* Conscience; Evolutionary ethics; Examination of conscience; Moral attitudes; Moral authority; Moral development; Moral judgment; Reasoning; Values.

Moral relativism. See *Relativism.*

Moral responsibility. See *Moral obligation.*

Moral turpitude. See *Depravity.*

Moral values. See *Ethics; Moral attitudes.*

Morale. Morale. Esprit de corps. Courage. Satisf(ied,action). Discourage(d,ment). Fighting spirit. Psychological well being. Confidence. Hopeful(ness). Zeal. Zest. Subjective well being. Job satisfaction. *Consider also:* motivation, involvement, commitment, team spirit. Well being. *See also* Attitudes toward work; Burnout; Effectiveness; Emotional adjustment; Emotional states; Emotions; Enthusiasm; Honored (esteem); Job performance; Job satisfaction; Mental health; Military music; Motivation; Need satisfaction; Occupational stress; Organizational climate; Organizational culture; Peer relations; Psychological well being; Self actualization; Self concept; Self esteem; Teamwork: Well being.

Morale, employee. See *Employee morale.*

Morality. Moral(s,ly,ity). Ethic(al,ally,s). Conscience. Social(ly) responsib(le, ility). Integrity. Chastity. Virtue. Virtuous(ness). Fairness. Justness. Ten commandments. Morally relevant behavior. Conscientious(ness). Upright(ness). Guiltless(ness). Blameless(ness). Innocen(t,ce). Righteous(ness). Moralistic. Sense of right and wrong. Honest(y). Honor(able). Traditional values. Good deed(s). Good intention(s). Purity. Faithful(ness). Loyal(ty). Family values. *Choose from:* moral, ethical *with:* values, development, reasoning, behavior, commitment, education, maturity, action(s), adjustment. *Consider also:* sin, immoral(ly,ity), amoral(ity), shame, misdeeds, erosion of values, guilt, values clarification, civility. *See also* Bioethics; Categorical imperative; Censorship; Conscience; Corruption in government; Desexualization; Ethics; Examination of conscience; Family values; Guilt; Honor (integrity); Innocence; Integrity; Machiavellianism; Moral attitudes; Moral authority; Moral conditions; Moral development; Moral education; Moral judgment; Moral obligation; Obligations; Personal values; Purity; Religious beliefs; Reputation; Sexual ethics; Shame; Sin; Social equity;

Social ethics; Social justice; Social values; Truth; Utilitarianism; Values.

Morality, offenses against public. See *Victimless crimes.*

Morality plays. Morality play(s). Paternoster play(s). *Consider also:* medieval drama, Everyman, Elckerlijk. *See also* Drama; Interludes (music); Liturgical drama; Medieval drama, Medieval literature; Miracle plays; Religious drama; Theater.

Morals. See *Ethics; Moral development; Morality; Values.*

Morals offenses. See *Victimless crimes.*

Moratoriums, debt. See *Debt moratoriums.*

Morbid fear. See *Phobias.*

Morbidity. Morbidity. Ill(ness). Sick(ness). Disease(s). Symptom prevalence. Ill health. Health risk(s). Epidem(ics, iology). *Choose from:* disease(s), illness(es), disability *with:* incidence, pattern(s), trend(s), prevalence, probability, rate(s), extent, risk(s), data. *See also* Disease; Epidemics; Health problems; Illness; Medical geography; Mortality rates; Public health; World health.

Mores. See *Folkways; Social norms; Social values.*

Mormons. Mormon(s). Latter Day Saints. Joseph Smith. Book of Mormon. Brigham Young. *See also* Protestantism.

Morning after pill. See *Emergency contraception.*

Morphology. Morpholog(y,ical). Structure(s). Form(s). Topographic feature(s). Landscape(s). *Consider also:* morpheme(s), anatom(y,ical), morphometric. *See also* Form (aesthetics); Frames (physical); Grammar; Groundwork; Social structure; Structure.

Morphology, social. See *Social structure.*

Mortality. See *Death; Fatalities; Mortality rates.*

Mortality, child. See *Child mortality.*

Mortality, infant. See *Infant mortality.*

Mortality, maternal. See *Maternal mortality.*

Mortality rates. Mortality rate(s). Survival rate(s). Life table(s). Longevity followup. Mortuary statistics. *Choose from:* mortality, survival, longevity, life, death, fatality, life expectancy, infant mortality, suicide, fetal death(s), maternal mortality *with:* rate(s), data, table(s), risk(s), number(s), frequenc(y, ies), incidence, expectanc(y,ies), expectation(s), time series, odds, longitudinal stud(y,ies), pattern(s), trend(s), differential(s), figures, statistics, per thousand, project(ed,ing, ion,ions). *See also* Child mortality;

Crime rates; Death; Demography; Fatalities; Health; Health transition; Infant mortality; Life expectancy; Longevity; Maternal mortality; Medical geography; Morbidity; Population (statistics); Rates; Suicide; Suicide victims; World health.

Mortuary customs. Mortuary custom(s). Funeral(s). *Choose from:* mortuary, funera(l,ry) *with:* custom(s), science, rite(s), practice(s). *Consider also:* mummies, burial(s), cremat(e,ed,ing, ion), wake(s), mourning, embalming, coffin(s), undertaker(s), mortician(s), funeral home(s), interment, mausoleum(s), tomb(s,stones), cemeter(y,ies), grave goods. *See also* Attitudes toward death; Burials; Cemeteries; Cremation; Death; Death rituals; Funeral rites; Religious rituals.

Mosaic law. See *Jewish law.*

Moslem prayer. Moslem prayer(s). *Choose from:* prayer(s), devotion(s), supplication(s), devotional practice(s) *with:* Islam(ic,ite,ist,ists,icist,icists), Moslem(s), Muslim(s), Mohammed(an, ans,anism), Shi'i(te), Sunni(te), Sufi(sm). *Consider also:* salla, salat, calverly, du'a, sura. *See also* Islam; Islamic fundamentalism; Prayer; Religious rituals; Worship.

Moslems. See *Islam.*

Mosques. Mosque(s). House(s) of prayer. *Consider also:* musalla, namazgah. *See also* Islam; Places of worship; Religious institutions; Sacred places.

Motels. See *Hotels.*

Motets. Motet(s,us). Mott(ectus,etto). Stilus moteticus. *Consider also:* grand motet(s), petit motet(s), polyphony, organum triplum. *See also* Chamber music; Music; Religious music; Renaissance music.

Mother, age of. See *Maternal age.*

Mother absence. See *Maternal deprivation.*

Mother attitudes. See *Parental attitudes.*

Mother child communication. Mother child communication. Maternal speech. Maternal language. Maternal talk. Motherese. Mother(s) with babytalk. Mother child sharing. *Choose from:* mother(s), maternal *with:* infant(s), child(ren), toddler(s), preschooler(s), newborn(s), daughter(s), son(s) *with:* communicat(e,ed,ing,ion), conversation(s,al), talk(ed,ing), speech, relationship(s), emotional exchange(s), affective exchange(s), emotional expression(s), sharing, verbal directive(s), interaction(s), interactive, language, discourse, interchange(s), message(s), dialogue, utterance(s), play(ed,ing). *Consider also:* motherese. *See also* Mother child relations;

Maternal behavior; Parent child communication.

Mother child relations. Mother child relation(ship,s). Maternal attitude(s). Mothering. *Choose from:* mother(s), maternal *with:* infant(s), child(ren), son(s), daughter(s) *with:* relation(s, ships), dyad(s,ic), attachment(s), love, care, feeling(s), bond(s,ing), cuddl(e,ed, ing), cradl(e,ed,ing), sing(ing), play(ed,ing), interact(ed,ing,ion,ions), comfort(ed,ing), abuse, overprotect(ed, ing,ion,ive), nurtur(ed,ing,ance), depriv(e,ed,ing,ation), communicat(ed, ing,ion), incest(uous), role(s), dependen(t,ce,cy), independen(t,ce), conflict(s), support, dynamics, understand(ing), accept(ed,ing,ance), reject(ed,ing,ion), expectation(s), rebell(ious,iousness,ion), absence, presence. *Consider also:* oedip(al,us) conflict(s), oedip(al,us) complex(es). *See also* Attachment behavior; Childrearing; Incest; Individuation; Maternal behavior; Maternal deprivation; Maternal love; Mother child communication; Nurturance; Oedipus complex; Overprotection; Parent role; Parental attitudes; Parental permissiveness; Possessiveness; Postpartum depression; Schizophrenogenic family; Symbiotic infantile psychosis.

Mother goddesses. Mother goddess(es). *Choose from:* mother(s,hood), maternal, matriarch(y,ies,al), fertility *with:* goddess(es), deit(y,ies), divin(e,ity), cosmic, archetype(s). *Consider also:* Isis, Astarte, Cybele, Demeter, Gaia, Great Mother, woman deit(y,ies), archetypal woman, Mother of Heaven, Mother Earth, Prajnaparamita, Mother of All Buddhas. *See also* Deities; Earth; Feminism; Feminist theology; Goddess religion; Goddesses; God concepts; Idealization of women; Matriarchy; Mothers; Oracles; Religious mysteries.

Mother role. See *Maternal behavior; Maternal love; Mother child communication; Mother child relations; Parent role.*

Mother tongue. See *Native language.*

Motherhood. See *Maternal behavior; Maternal love; Mother child communication; Mother child relations; Mothers; Parent role.*

Mothering. See *Maternal behavior; Maternal love; Mother child communication; Mother child relations.*

Motherlessness. See *Maternal deprivation.*

Mothers. Mother(hood,ing,ly,liness,s). Mother child relation(s,ship,ships). Maternal(ly). Maternity. Multipara. Primipara. Matriarch(s,al,y). Stepmother(s). Female parent(s). Supermom(s). Breastfeeding. *Consider also:* unwed mother(s), schizophrenogenic mother(s), adolescent mother(s). *See also* Biological family; Caregivers; Dual career families; Expectant mothers; Family work relationship; Female headed households; Maternal deprivation; Maternal behavior; Matriarchy; Matrilineality; Matrilocal residence; Mother goddesses; Nurturance; Single mothers; Stepfamily; Single mothers; Surrogate mothers; Teenage mothers; Wives.

Mothers, absentee. See *Maternal deprivation.*

Mothers, adolescent. See *Teenage mothers.*

Mothers, birth. See *Biological family.*

Mothers, employed. See *Dual career families; Family work relationship; Female headed households; Professional women; Working women.*

Mothers, expectant. See *Expectant mothers.*

Mothers, single. See *Female headed households; Single mothers; Single parent family.*

Mothers, surrogate. See *Surrogate mothers.*

Mothers, teenage. See *Teenage mothers.*

Mothers, unwed. See *Single mothers.*

Mothers, working. See *Dual career families; Family work relationship; Female headed households; Professional women; Working women.*

Motion. Motion. Kinetic(s). Kinesis. Kinematic(al,ally,s). Chang(e,ed,ing) position(s). Chang(e,ed,ing) place(s). Movement(s). Mov(e,ed,ing). Drift(ed,ing,age). Propel(led,ling). Travel(ed,ing,led,ling). Trajector(y,ies). Path(s). Orbit(s). Oscillat(e,ed,ing,ion, ions). Action(s). Activit(y,ies). Flow(s, ed,ing). Roam(s,ed,ing). Sway(s,ed,ing). Swing(s,ing). Wander(ed,ing). Mobil(e, ity). Stir(red,ring). *Consider also:* momentum, push(ed,ing), pull(ed,ing). *See also* Acceleration effects; Acceleration (speed); Circulation (rotation); Hurry (speed); Kinesics; Motion perception.

Motion and time studies. See *Time and motion studies.*

Motion disorders, repetitive. See *Repetitive motion disorders.*

Motion perception. Motion perception. *Choose from:* movement(s), motion(s), moving target(s), moving sound(s) *with:* perception, perceiv(e,ed,ing), detect(ed, ing,ion), estimat(e,es,ed,ing,ion), judg(e,ed,ing,ement), aware(ness). *See also* Circulation (rotation); Motion; Perception.

Motion picture fans. Motion picture fan(s). *Choose from:* movie(s), motion picture(s), Hollywood, screen star(s),

flick(s) *with:* fan(s), aficionado(s), enthusiast(s), junkie(s), freak(s), addict(s), buff(s), devotee(s), habitué(s), hound(s), fanatic(s). *See also* Fans (persons); Fanzines; Film genres; Horror films; Motion pictures.

Motion picture music. See *Film music.*

Motion pictures. Motion picture(s). Movie(s). Film(s). Filmstrip(s). Cinema(s,tic). Cinematograph(y,ic, ically). Cine. Documentar(y,ies). Travelogue(s). Hollywood. Screenplay(s). Picture show(s). Talking picture(s). Silent picture(s). Pic(s). *Consider also:* kinescope, audiovisual material(s), cineangiography, cineradiography. *See also* Arts; Audiovisual materials; Communications media; Documentary theater; Entertainment; Film genres; Film music; Horror films; Instructional media; Lost motion pictures; Mass media; Motion picture fans.

Motion pictures, lost. See *Lost motion pictures.*

Motion sickness. Motion sick(ness). Airsick(ness). Carsick(ness). Seasick(ness). Mal de mer. *Choose from:* travel, train, car, sea, air, swing *with:* sick(ness). *Consider also:* motion disturbance, reactivity to motion. *See also* Labyrinth disorders.

Motivation. Motivat(ed,ing,ion,ions,ional). Motive(s). Drive(s). Tension(s). Excitation. Sexual drive. Libido. Aggressive energy. Destructive energy. Preference(s). Ambition. Intent(ion, ionality,ions). Ambitious(ness). Aggressive(ness). Initiative. Arous(e,ed, al). Goal orientation. Incentive(s). Desire(s). Urge(s). Wish(es). Personal causation framework. Interest(ed,s). Self generated outcome(s). Approach-avoidance. Aspir(e,ed,ing,ation,ations). Hope(s). Impulse(s). Inducement(s). Provocation. *Consider also:* instinct(s, ual), cognitive dissonance, goal(s), aspiration(s), initiative(s), hunger, thirst, achievement need(s), exploratory behavior, food deprivation, water deprivation, achievement motivation, affiliation motivation, extrinsic motivation, intrinsic motivation, fear of success, fear of failure, temptation(s). *See also* Ability; Academic failure; Achievement need; Affiliation motivation; Appetite; Approval need; Aspirations; Attention span; Attitudes toward work; Burnout; Cognitive dissonance; Commitment (emotional); Curiosity; Delay of gratification; Dependency (personality); Educational incentives; Educational motivation; Employee motivation; Encouragement; Extrinsic motivation; Failure; Fear of failure; Fear of success; Feedback; Goal orientation; Goals; Hunger, food deprivation;

Incentives; Initiative (personal); Instinct; Intentionality; Intrinsic motivation; Job performance; Metamotivation; Monetary incentives; Morale; Needs; Nurturance; Performance; Positive reinforcement; Procrastination; Profit motive; Promotion (occupational); Psychodynamics; Reinforcement; Reward; Satiation; Self actualization; Self fulfilling prophecy; Sex drive; Stimuli; Student motivation; Success; Temptation; Thirst; Wants.

Motivation, academic achievement. See *Educational motivation.*

Motivation, achievement. See *Achievement need.*

Motivation, affiliation. See *Affiliation motivation.*

Motivation, educational. See *Educational motivation.*

Motivation, employee. See *Employee motivation.*

Motivation, extrinsic. See *Extrinsic motivation.*

Motivation, growth. See *Metamotivation.*

Motivation, intrinsic. See *Intrinsic motivation.*

Motivation, learning. See *Educational motivation.*

Motivation, student. See *Student motivation.*

Motive, profit. See *Profit motive.*

Motor activity. Motor activity. *Choose from:* motor, body, locomotor, physical *with:* activity, behavior, reflex(es), movement(s), response(s). *Consider also:* hyperkine(tic,sia), hypokine(tic, sia), hyperactiv(e,ity), turning behavior, circling. *See also* Activity level; Agitation; Animal locomotion; Exercise; Finger tapping; Immobility; Jumping; Motor coordination; Motor development; Motor skills; Muscle tone; Perceptual motor processes; Physical agility; Physical dexterity; Physical restraint; Posture; Psychomotor agitation; Restlessness; Running; Sucking behavior; Swimming; Tonic immobility; Walking.

Motor coordination. Motor coordination. *Choose from:* motor, psychomotor, eye hand, visuomotor, locomotor *with:* coordination, skill(s), abilit(y,ies), process(es), performance, control. *Consider also:* marksmanship, object manipulation. *See also* Akwardness; Motor development; Motor skills; Perceptual motor coordination; Physical agility.

Motor coordination, perceptual. See *Perceptual motor coordination.*

Motor development. Motor development. *Choose from:* motor, psychomotor, sensorimotor, locomotor, neuromotor, coordination, prehensile, manual *with:* develop(ed,ing,ment). *See also* Child development; Developmental stages; Motor coordination; Physical agility; Physical development; Psychomotor development; Prehension; Speech development.

Motor learning, perceptual. See *Perceptual motor learning.*

Motor processes, perceptual. See *Perceptual motor processes.*

Motor skills. Motor skill(s). *Choose from:* motor, manual, mechanical, sensorimotor, locomotor, psychomotor *with:* skill(s), abilit(y,ies), dexterity, performance, coordination. *See also* Ability; Awkwardness; Fine motor skills; Gross motor skills; Motor activity; Motor coordination; Nonverbal ability.

Motor skills, fine. See *Fine motor skills.*

Motor skills, gross. See *Gross motor skills.*

Motor vehicle accidents. See *Traffic accidents.*

Motor vehicles. Motor vehicle(s). Automotive vehicle(s). Bus(es,ses). Motorcycle(s). Truck(s). Lorr(y,ies). Taxi(s). Taxicab(s). Motor bicycle(s). Motorbike(s). Auto(s). Automobile(s). Car(s). Van(s). Service vehicle(s). *See also* Automobile driving; Automobile industry; Automobiles; Caravans; Driving skills; Transportation; Transportation accidents; Zero emissions vehicles.

Mountaineering. Mountaineer(ing). *Consider also:* mountain(s), alp(s,ine), high altitude(s), peak(s) *with:* climb(ed,ing), ascend(ed,ing). *See also* Altitude effects; Ascent; Sports.

Mourning. Mourn(ing,ed,er,ers). Griev(e, ed,ing). Lament(ed,ing). Bereave(d, ment). Grief stricken. *Consider also:* abandonment reaction. *See also* Bereavement; Death counseling; Death rituals; Fetal propitiatory rites; Grief; Laments; Loss adjustment.

Mouse. See *Mice.*

Movement, abortion rights. See *Abortion rights movement.*

Movement, African liberation. See *Anti-apartheid movement.*

Movement, anti-apartheid. See *Anti-apartheid movement.*

Movement, antiabortion. See *Antiabortion movement.*

Movement, antismoking. See *Antismoking movement.*

Movement, antiwar. See *Peace movements.*

Movement, Arts and Crafts. See *Arts and Crafts movement.*

Movement, Barbizon art. See *Barbizon art movement.*

Movement, civil rights. See *Civil rights organizations.*

Movement, disability rights. See *Disability rights movement.*

Movement, ecological. See *Environmentalism.*

Movement, ecumenical. See *Ecumenical movement.*

Movement, elderly liberation. See *Gray power.*

Movement, environmental. See *Environmentalism.*

Movement, feminist. See *Feminism; Suffrage movement; Women's groups; Women's rights.*

Movement, gay liberation. See *Homosexual liberation movement.*

Movement, homosexual liberation. See *Homosexual liberation movement.*

Movement, human potential. See *Human potential movement.*

Movement, Islamic Resistance. See *Islamic Resistance Movement.*

Movement, men's. See *Men's movement.*

Movement, symbolist. See *Symbolist movement.*

Movement, women's. See *Feminism; Political movements; Social movements; Suffrage movement; Women's groups; Women's rights.*

Movement therapy. Movement therapy. *Choose from:* movement, exercise, danc(e,ing) *with:* therap(y,ies,eutic). *See also* Dance therapy; Recreation therapy.

Movements, anti imperialist. See *Decolonization; Liberation movements; National fronts; Nationalist movements; Peasant rebellions; Revolution; Separatism.*

Movements, antinuclear. See *Antinuclear movements.*

Movements, civil rights. See *Abortion rights movement; Activism; Anti-apartheid movement; Antiabortion movement; Black power; Civil disobedience; Civil rights organizations; Disability rights movement; Environmentalism; Gray power; Homosexual liberation movement; Protest movements; Social movements; Suffrage movement.*

Movements, labor. See *Labor movements.*

Movements, liberation. See *Decolonization; Guerrillas; Liberation movements; Liberation theology; National fronts; Peasant rebellions; Separatism.*

Movements, literary. See *Literary movements.*

Movements, messianic. See *Messianic movements.*

Movements, millenarian. See *Millenarianism.*

Movements, nationalist. See *Nationalist movements.*

Movements, nativistic. See *Nativistic movements.*

Movements, peace. See *Peace movements.*

Movements, political. See *Political movements.*

Movements, protest. See *Protest movements.*

Movements, radical. See *Radical movements.*

Movements, regional. See *Regional movements.*

Movements, religious. See *Religious movements.*

Movements, revolutionary. See *Decolonization; Guerrillas; National fronts; Nationalism; Nativism; Patriotism; Peasant rebellions; Political self determination; Protest movements; Radical movements; Separatism; Social movements.*

Movements, separatist. See *Anti-government radicals; Decolonization; Guerrillas; Liberation movements; National fronts.*

Movements, social. See *Social movements.*

Movements, student. See *Social movements; Youth movements.*

Movements, suffrage. See *Suffrage movements.*

Movements, temperance. See *Temperance movements.*

Movements, troop. See *Troop movements.*

Movements, war protest. See *Peace movements.*

Movements, white supremacy. See *White supremacy movements.*

Movements, youth. See *Youth movements.*

Movies. See *Motion pictures.*

Moving. See *Residential mobility.*

Mugging. See *Robbery.*

Mulattos. See *Racially mixed.*

Multi-institutional systems. Multi-institutional system(s). Network(s). Consort(ia,ium). School district(s). *Consider also:* interinstitutional, multiunit, inter-institutional, multi-campus, college-school, intercollegiate, multi-institutional, multihospital *with:* coordination, cooperation, collaboration, system(s), arrangement(s), network(s). *See also* Associations (organizations); Boundary spanning; Interinstitutional relations; Interlocking directorates; Interorganizational networks; Networks.

Multi-national states. See *Plural societies.*

Multicultural education. Multicultural education. Multi-ethnic education. *Choose from:* multicultural, multi-ethnic, multireligious, intercultural, bicultural, cross-cultural, universalization, global approach, multiculturalism, interethnic, interracial, cultur(e,al,ally) divers(e,ity), cultur(al,ally) plural(ism,istic), cultur(e,al,ally) differen(ces,t) *with:* education, class(es), school(s), curriculum, literacy, orientation. *Consider also:* antiracist education, equity pedagogy, multicultural literacy, rainbow curriculum. *See also* Antibias curriculum; Antiracist education; Area studies; Biculturalism; Bilingual education; Bilingualism; Cross cultural comparisons; Cross cultural competency; Cultural activities; Cultural pluralism; Cultural relations; Cultural relativism; Cultural sensitivity; Cultural values; Culture contact; Culturally relevant pedagogy; Curriculum change; Deterritorialization; Equal education; Ethnic differences; Ethnic groups; Ethnic relations; Ethnic studies; Ethnicity; Ethnocentrism; Global integration; Heterogeneity; Humanistic education; Intercultural communication; Interdisciplinary approach; Intergroup relations; Internationalism; Liberalism (Religion); Mainstreaming; Minority groups; Modern civilization; Multilingualism; Relativism; Social integration; Social equality; Social equity; Social justice; Social nearness; World citizenship.

Multiculturalism. See *Cultural pluralism.*

Multidimensional scaling. Multidimensional scal(e,es,ing). *Choose from:* multidimensional, multivariate, multidimensionable, interactive conjoint, multitrait multimethod *with:* scal(e,es, ing), assessment(s), measurement(s), rating(s), matrix, matrices, analys(is,es), instrument(s), approach(es). *Consider also:* intransitivity, nonmetric data reduction, hierarchical clustering. *See also* Analysis; Measurement; Scaling.

Multidisciplinary approach. See *Interdisciplinary approach.*

Multilingualism. Multilingual(ity,ism). Pluralingual(ity,ism). *Consider also:* bilingual(ism), trilingual(ism), polyglot(s), multi-speak, multi-lingual, multi-linguistic. *See also* Bilingual education; Bilingualism; Cultural pluralism; Diglossia; Intercultural communication; Language; Language maintenance; Language planning; Language policy; Monolingualism; Multicultural education; Psycholinguistics; Second language education; Second languages; Sociolinguistics.

Multinational corporations. Multinational corporation(s). Multinationals.

Transnationals. *Choose from:* multinational, transnational, global, worldwide, international *with:* enterprise(s), corporation(s), organization(s), compan(y,ies), business(es), firm(s), monopol(y,ies), operation(s), bank(s). *Consider also:* virtual corporation(s), business abroad, overseas business(es). *See also* Americans abroad; Anti-Americanism; Big business; Border industries; Cartels; Corporations; Dependency theory (international); Global campaigns; Global integration; Globalization; Industrial concentration; Modern civilization; Neocolonialism; Offshore production (foreign countries); Oligopolies; Subsidiaries; Subsidiary management; World economy.

Multinational states. See *Plural societies.*

Multiple births. Multiple birth(s). *Consider also:* quadruplet(s)s, quintuplet(s), sextuplet(s), triplet(s). *See also* Family members; Heterozygotic twins; Monozygotic twins; Siblings; Twins.

Multiple chemical sensitivities. Multiple chemical sensitivities. Chemical hypersensitivit(y,ies). Total allergy syndrome. MCS. Environmental illness(es). *See also* Hypersensitivity; Occupational exposure; Occupational safety; Sick building syndrome.

Multiple choice tests. See *Forced choice tests.*

Multiple jobholding. See *Moonlighting.*

Multiple personality. Multiple personalit(y, ies). *Choose from:* dual, multiple, split, primary, secondary, tertiary, alternating, co-conscious *with:* personalit(y,ies), identit(y,ies), subpersonalit(y,ies). *Consider also:* dissociative disorder(s), Dr. Jekyl and Mr. Hyde, double consciousness. *See also* Dissociative disorders.

Multiple psychotherapy. Multiple psychotherap(ies,ists,y). *Choose from:* multiple, conjoint, collaborative, role divided, cooperative *with:* psychotherap(y,ists), therap(y,ists), counsel(ing,or,ors). *See also* Cotherapy.

Multiply handicapped. Multipl(y,e) handicap(s,ped). Multi-handicapped. Deaf blind. Deaf mute. *Choose from:* multipl(e,y), multisensory *with:* handicap(s,ped), disabilit(y,ies), disabled, impair(ed,ment,ments). *Consider also:* severe(ly), profound(ly) *with:* handicap(s,ped), impair(ed,ment, ments), disabilit(y,ies), disabled. *See also* Disability; Severely handicapped infants; Severity of disorders.

Mummies. Mumm(y,ies,ified,ification). *Consider also:* embalm(ed,ing), preserv(e,ed,ing,ation) *with:* bod(y,ies), corpse(s). *See also* Death rituals.

Munchausen syndrome. See *Factitious disorders.*

Municipal Art. Municipal Art. Public art. Art in public place(s). Civic art. *Choose from:* art(s), painting(s), mural(s), decoration(s) *with:* municipal, city, public, outdoor(s). *Consider also:* outdoor sculpture, urban beautification, landmark(s), graffiti art. *See also* Arts; Civic improvement; Cultural property; Mural painting and decoration; Public art; Sculpture; Street art; Urban environments; Urban planning.

Municipal employees. See *Civil service; Government personnel.*

Municipal finance. Municipal finance(s). *Choose from:* cit(y,ies), municipal(ity, ities), urban, local government(s), or city by name *with:* appropriat(e,ed,ing, ion,ions), bankrupt(cy,cies), bond(s), budget(ed,ing,s), cash flow, credit rating(s), debt(s), deficit(s), expenditure(s), expense(s), finance(s), financial problem(s), fiscal, fund(s,ing), indedtedness, liabilit(y,ies), loan(s), paid, pay(ing), payment(s), payroll(s), revenue(s), spend(s,ing), spent, tax(es). *Consider also:* cit(y,ies), municipal(ity, ities), urban, local government(s), or city by name *with:* federal aid, state aid, impact fee(s), user fee(s), privatiz(e,ed, ing,ation), pricing. *See also* Cities; Community services; Government finances; Municipal government; Municipalities; Public finance; Public debt.

Municipal government. Municipal government. Municipal corporation(s). *Choose from:* municipal(ity,ities), cit(y,ies), town(s,ship,ships), borough(s), village(s), metropol(is,itan), urban *with:* government(s), council(s), mayor(s), community control, consolidation, politic(s,al), machine(s), manager(s), management, elected official(s), commission(s), charter(s), authorit(y,ies), service(s), infrastructure, welfare, public facilit(y,ies), law(s), ordinance(s), regulation(s), planning, personnel, budgeting. *See also* Cities; Community services; Fire departments; Infrastructure (economics); Local finance; Local government; Local politics; Metropolitan areas; Municipal finance; Municipalities; Regional government; Urban development; Urban planning; Urban politics; Urban population; Urban renewal.

Municipal politics. See *Local politics.*

Municipalities. Municipal(ity,ities). Cit(y,ies). Urban(ism,ized,ization). Metropolitan. Downtown(s). Megalopolis. Inner cit(y,ies). Urban sprawl. *See also* Cities; Metropolitan areas; Municipal governments; Urban development; Urban environments; Urban fringe; Urban planning; Urban population; Urban renewal; Urban sprawl.

Mural painting and decoration. Mural painting. Mural decoration. *Choose from:* mural(s), fresco(es), wall(s) *with:* decorat(e,ed,ing,ion,ions), paint(ed,ing, ings), draw(n,ing,ings). *Consider also:* cave painting(s), Encaustic painting, Graffito decoration, La peinture murale, Die Wandmalerei(n). *See also* Arts; Cave paintings; Municipal Art; Public art; Street art.

Murder. See *Homicide.*

Murder, political. See *Assassination.*

Murder, ritual. See *Human sacrifice.*

Murderers, serial. See *Serial murderers.*

Murders, mass. See *Mass murders.*

Muscle contraction headache. Muscle contraction headache(s). *Choose from:* muscle contraction, tension *with:* headache(s), cephalalgia. *See also* Headache; Pain; Symptoms.

Muscle relaxation. Muscle relaxation. *Choose from:* muscle(s), neuromuscular *with:* relax(ed,ing,ation). *Consider also:* progressive relaxation. *See also* Progressive relaxation therapy; Relaxation; Relaxation training.

Muscle tone. Muscle tone. *Choose from:* muscle(s), muscular *with:* tone, tonus, tonicity, aton(ia,ic), tension. *See also* Motor activity; Reflex.

Muscular sense. Muscular sense. Kinesthes(ia,ias,is). Kinesthe(ses,tic, tically). Propriocept(ion,ive). *Consider also:* musc(le,les,ular) coordination. *See also* Proprioception; Sensory feedback.

Museums. Museum(s). Art galler(y,ies). Art collection(s). Exhibition(s). Exhibit(ion) hall(s). *Choose from:* historical, artifact(s), painting(s), memorabilia, art(work) *with:* museum(s), collection(s), display(s). *Consider also:* archive(s). *See also* Aeronautical museums; Archaeological museums; Archives; Anthropology; Art museums; Arts; Depositories; Educational field trips; Exhibits; Galleries; Historical museums; History; Industrial museums; Material culture; Recreational facilities; Traveling exhibitions.

Museums, aeronautical. See *Aeronautical museums.*

Museums, archaeological. See *Archaeological museums.*

Museums, art. See *Art museums.*

Museums, historical. See *Historical museums.*

Museums, industrial. See *Industrial museums.*

Music. Music(al,ally,ians). Song(s). Concert(s). Tune(s). Melod(y,ies,ic). Chorus(es). Play(ed,ing) instrument(s). Harmon(y,ies). Aria(s). Anthem(s). Antiphon(s). Bhangra. Cantata(s). Motet(s). Hymn(s). Lullab(y,ies). Fugue(s). Rondo(s). Ballad(s). Sonata(s). Waltz(es). Opera(s). Concerto(s). Symphon(y,ies). Polka(s). Mazurka(s). Blue(s). Folk music. Spiritual(s). Dixieland. Calypso. Soca [sokah]. Rock and roll. Reggae. Vocal music. Jazz. A capella. A cappella. March(es). House music. Disco music. Rap music. *See also* A cappella singing; Absolute music; Acciaccatura; Afro-American music; Afro-Cuban music; Ancient Greek music; Arrangement (music); Arpeggio; Arts; Atonality; Background music; Ballads; Ballata; Ballet music; Bands (music); Basse danse; Bel canto; Bluegrass music; Blues (music); Border ballads; Cantatas; Canticles; Chamber music; Chance composition; Chants; Children's songs; Choirs (music); Choral music; Choruses; Church music; Comic operas; Concert halls; Concertos; Concerts; Conducting; Counterpoint; Country and western music; Dance; Dirges; Dramatic music; Electronic music; Embellishment (music); Ethnomusicology; Erotic songs; Experimental music; Film music; Folk culture; Folk music; Formes fixes; Frottola; Harmony; Heavy metal (music); Impressionism (music); Improvisation (music); Incidental music; Instrumental music; Influence (literary, artistic, etc.); Interludes (music); Jazz; Jewish music; Lauda; Leitmotiv; Lost works of music; Lullabies; Marches; Medieval music; Melody; Motets; Music criticism; Music education; Music therapy; Musical instruments; Musicians; Musicology; Opera; Orchestration; Ornamentation (music); Overtures (music); Pastorales; Political ballads; Popular culture; Program music; Program symphony; Religious music; Renaissance music; Romanticism; Rondo; Songs; Symphonic poems; Tabulature; Textless vocal works; Virelai.

Music, absolute. See *Absolute music.*

Music, Afro-American. See *Afro-American music.*

Music, Afro-Cuban. See *Afro-Cuban music.*

Music, aleatory. See *Chance composition.*

Music, ancient Greek. See *Ancient Greek music.*

Music, background. See *Background music.*

Music, ballet. See *Ballet music.*

Music, Black. See *Afro-American music.*

Music, bluegrass. See *Bluegrass music.*

Music, chamber. See *Chamber music.*

Music, choral. See *Choral music.*

Music, church. See *Church music.*

Music, computer. See *Computer music.*

Music, concrete. See *Electronic music.*

Music, contemporary. See *Twentieth century Western art music.*

Music, country and western. See *Country and western music.*

Music, dance. See *Dance music.*

Music, disco. See *Disco music.*

Music, dramatic. See *Dramatic music.*

Music, electro-acoustic. See *Electronic music.*

Music, electronic. See *Electronic music.*

Music, experimental. See *Experimental music.*

Music, film. See *Film music.*

Music, folk. See *Folk music.*

Music, funeral. See *Funeral music.*

Music, funk. See *Funk (music).*

Music, futurism. See *Futurism (music).*

Music, gospel. See *Gospel music.*

Music, grunge. See *Rock music.*

Music, gypsy. See *Gypsy music.*

Music, impressionism. See *Impressionism (music).*

Music, impromptu. See *Improvisation (music).*

Music, incidental. See *Incidental music.*

Music, instrumental. See *Instrumental music.*

Music, janissary. See *Janissary music.*

Music, jewish. See *Jewish music.*

Music, lost works of. See *Lost works of music.*

Music, masses. See *Masses (music).*

Music, medieval. See *Medieval music.*

Music, military. See *Military music.*

Music, modern. See *Twentieth century Western art music.*

Music, motion picture. See *Film music.*

Music, negro. See *Afro-American music.*

Music, ornamentation. See *Ornamentation (music).*

Music, overtures. See *Overtures (music).*

Music, patriotic. See *Patriotic music.*

Music, popular. See *Popular music.*

Music, program. See *Program music.*

Music, religious. See *Religious music.*

Music, renaissance. See *Renaissance music.*

Music, rock. See *Rock music.*

Music, serial. See *Serial music.*

Music, soul. See *Soul music.*

Music, twentieth century western art. See *Twentieth century Western art music.*

Music criticism. Music critic(s,al,icize, icizing,icized,ism). *Choose from:* music(al), opera(s,tic), operetta(s), dance, concert(s) *with:* critic(s,al,icize, icizing,icized,ism), review(s,ed,ing), comment(s,ed,ing), judg(e,ed,ment, ments). *See also* Aesthetic preferences; Criticism; Musicology; Music.

Music education. Music education. *Choose from:* music(al,ian,ians), piano, singing, voice, choral, violin, band, musical instrument(s) *with:* education(al), instruction(s,al), student(s), train(ed, ing), skill(s) development, learn(ed,ing), conservator(y,ies), curriculum. *Consider also:* ear training, Suzuki method. *See also* Aesthetic education; Conservatories; Education; Eurythmy; Music; Musicians.

Music therapy. Music therapy. *Choose from:* music(al), melod(y,ies,ic) *with:* therap(y,ies,eutic), psychotherap(y,ies, eutic), rehabilitat(ed,ing,ion). *Consider also:* psycho-opera. *See also* Art therapy; Dance therapy; Play therapy; Psychotherapy; Recreation therapy; Self expression.

Musical ability. Musical abilit(y,ies). *Choose from:* music(al,ally,ian,ians), singing, operatic, songwriter(s), composer(s), instrumentalist(s), *with:* creativ(e,ity), abilit(y,ies), talent(s,ed), gifted, aptitude(s), prodig(y,ies). *See also* Ability; Artistic ability; Bel canto; Composers; Creativity; Musicians.

Musical ads. Musical ad(s). *Choose from:* musical(ly), underscore(s), soundtrack(s), score(s), aural icon(s), tune(s), jingle(s), ditt(y,ies), musical theme(s), musical signature(s) *with:* ad(s), advertis(e,ed,ing), advertisement(s), commercial(s), promotion(s,al). *See also* Advertising; Advertising campaigns; Brand loyalty; Political advertising; Popular culture.

Musical instruments. Musical instrument(s). *Choose from:* music(al), percussion, wind, valve, string(ed), brass, reed, woodwind, baroque, medieval, band, orchestra(l) *with:* instrument(s). *Consider also:* accordion(s), aeotana(s), aerophone(s), algoja(s), alphorn(s), alto horn(s), anklung(s), antara(s), Apache fiddle(s), arghool(s), arghul(s), armonica(s), arpa(s), arpeggione(s), arpicordo(s), atabal(e), atabaque(s), aulo(s), autoharp(s), automatic instrument(s), automatophone(s), bagana(s), bagpipe(s), bajo sexto(s), bajon(s,illo,illos), balalaika(s), bandola(s), bandoneon(s),

bandor(a,as,e), bandura(s), bandoura(s), bandurria(s), banjo(s), baroque lute(s), barrel organ(s), barrel piano(s), bassoon(s), bata(s), bathyphone(s), beganna(s), bersag horn(s), biniou(s), biwa(s), bladder pipe(s), bodhran(s), bombo(s), bonang(s), bongo(s), bouzouki(s), bugle(s), buisine(s), bullroarer(s), cabaca(s), caisse(s), caja(s), calliope(s), caramba(s), carimba(s), carillon(s), cassa(s), castanet(s), cavaco(s), caval(s), cavaquinho(s), celesta(s), cello(s), cellone(s), cembalo(s), cencerro(s), ceterone(s), chabbabeh, chalumeau(x), charango(s), chatzozerah, chekker(s), chelys, chilwa, chime(s), ch'in, Chinese block(s), chirimia(s), chittarra(s), chittarone(s), chordophone(s), cimbalom(s), cimbasso(s), cithara(s), citole(s), cittern(s), clairseach, claquebois, clappers, clarinet(s), clavichord(s), clavier(s), claviorgan(s), clempung(s), cog rattle(s), colascione(s), concertina(s), contra-violon(s), contraviolon(s), cornemuse(s), cornet(t,ts,a,as,s), cornetto(s), corno(s), cow horn(s), crembal(a,um), cromhorn(s), cross flute(s), crumhorn(s), crwth(s), cuica(s), curtal(s), cymbal(e,es,s,um), daluka(s), darabukkah(s), darabuka(s), darbouka(s), daouli(s), davul(s), deff(s), derbouka(s), dhola(s), dobro(s), dohol(s), dolzaina(s), dombra(s), double reed(s), drum(s), duct flute(s), dudy, dulcimer(s), dulcitone(s), dumbalak(s), echeia, epigoni(a,um), epinette(s), erbeb(s), erh-hu, euphonium(s), fagott(s,o), fiscorno(s), flageolet(s), flicorno(s), flugelhorn(s), flute(s), fortepiano(s), frame drum(s), french horn(s), friction drum(s), gadulka(s), gaida(s), gaita(s), gajdy, gambang(s), garamut(s), ghutru(s), glass harmonica(s), gong(s), goura(s), gourd rattle(s), gubo(s), guimbarde(s), guitar(s), gusla(s), halam(s), halil(s), halmpipe(s), hammered dulcimer(s), hammerklavier(en), handbell(s), handchime(s), handja(s), happu(s), harmonica(s), harp(s), harpsichord(s), hatzotzerot(s), heem(s), hichiriki, highland pipe(s), horn(s), huehuetl(s), hurdy-gurd(y,ies), hydraulis(es), idiophone(s), Irish harp(s), Jew's harp(s), jouhikantele(s), kakko(s), kalamo(s), kalimba(s), kamanjah(s), kantele(s), kasso(s), kazoo(s), kemence(s), kempyang(s), kendang(s), kenong(s), kesselpauke(n), kethuk(s), kettledrum(s), khene(s), khunchir, khuur, kielflugel, kinandi(s), kinnor(s), komabue(s), kortholt(s), koto(s), kynnor(s), kithara(s), klong khek(s), kouitara(s), koundyeh(s), kundu(s), kurtar(s), kussir(s), lamellophone(s), lap organ(s), launedda(s). lauto(s), limbe, lira(s), lissoir(s), lute(s), lyra(s), lyre(s), magadis(es), mandolin(s), maraca(s), marimba(s), marimbula(s),

marouvane(s), mbira(s), mejoranera(s), mellophone(s), melophon(s), membranophone(s), metziltayim(s), midwinterhoorn, minagnghinim(s), mrdangam(s), mridang(s), mouth organ(s), mrdangam(s), mukkuri, musette(s), nagasvaram(s), nai(s), naqqarah(s), nebel(s), ngoma(s), nose flute(s), nyckelharpa(n), oboe(s), ocarina(s), omerti(s), ophicleide(s), organ(s), orpharion(s), pan pipe(s), panpipe(s), pandor(a,as,e,en), pandura(s), penny whistle(s), phunga(s), piano(s), pianola(s), pibgorn(s), pibroch(s), piccolo(s), pierementen, piffero(s), pincullus, p'i-p'a, pitchpipe(s), platillo(s), psalmodikon, psalter(y,ies), quena(s), quijonga(s), rabab(s), rattle(s), rebec(s), recorder(s), reedpipe(s), ryuteki, sackbut(s), sahnai(s), sansa(s), santouri(s), sarangi(s), sarod(s), saron(s), saunggauk(s), schwegel(en), schwegelpfeife(n), seljefloyte fipple flute(s) shakuhachi(s), shaman's fiddle(s), shamisen(s), shandze, shawm(s), sho, shofar(s), sistrum(s), sitar(s), sleigh bell(s), snare drum(s), sousaphone(s), spike fiddle(s), spindle flute(s), spinet(s), spitzharfe(s), steel drum(s), steel guitar(s), stierhorn(s), suling(s), syrinx(es), tabbalat(s), tabl(s), tabla(s), tambora(s), tambourin(e,es), tambura(s), tam-tam(s), tanbur(s), tavil(s), teponaztli(s), tibia(s), timbal(e,s), timpan(i,um), tobshuur, tof(s), tom tom(s), tong-a-tong(s), tonkori, triangle(s), tromba marina(s), trombone(s), trumpet(s), tuba(s), tupan(s), udakea(s), uilleann(s), ukulele(s), union pipe(s), vibraharp(s), vibraphone(s), vina(s), viola(s), viola(s) da gamba. violin(s), violoncello(s), woodwind(s), xylophone(s), zambumbia(s), zither(s), zummarah(s), zurna(s). *See also* Arts; Automatic instruments; Bands (music); Bells; Bronze bells; Clavichord; Electronic instruments; Electronic organs; Folk music; Flutes; Glass harmonica; Guitars; Instrumental music; Music; Organs (music); Player pianos.

Musical intervals and scales. Musical interval(s). Musical scale(s). Chromatic scale. Pitch class(es). Diatonic scale. Octave(s). Major scale(s). Minor scale(s). Semitone(s). Tone(s). Pentatonic scale(s). Scale degree(s). Raga(s). *Consider also:* music(al) *with:* modal(ity), mode(s). *Consider also:* church tone(s), tala. *See also* Musical theory; Musicology; Solmization; Tuning.

Musical modes. See *Musical intervals and scales.*

Musical scoring. See *Orchestration.*

Musical societies. Musical societ(y,ies). *Consider also:* collegi(a,um) music(a,um), kantorei, convivium musicum, university ensemble(s), puy, pui. *See also* Choral societies; Ensembles.

Musical theory. Musical theor(y,ies). Musiktheorie. La teoria musical. *Choose from:* music(al,ianship), pitch, timbre, acoustic(s), tuning, scales, modes, melody, harmony, counterpoint, rhythm, meter, tonality *with:* theor(y,ies,etical, ems), fundamental(s), axiom(s,atic), explanation(s), hypothes(is,es,ize,ized, izing), paradigm(s), concept(s), thes(es,is), principle(s), symbol(s,ic), typolog(y,ies), form-and-analysis. *Consider also:* musica theorica. *See also* Musical intervals and scales; Musicology; Solmization; Tuning.

Musicals. Musical(s). Musical play(s). Broadway musical(s). Musical theater. Broadway show(s). Traditional musical(s). *Choose from:* broadway, off Broadway, theater(s), play(s), theatrical, prime time, show(s), comed(y,ies) *with:* musical(s), song and dance, singing and dancing. *Consider also:* dance compan(y,ies), Victor Herbert, Richard Rodgers, Cole Porter, Stephen Sondheim, Oscar Hammerstein, Lorenz Hart, Frank Loesser, Frederick Loewe, Alan Jay Lerner, 'Annie Get Your Gun,' 'Cabaret,' 'Fiddler on the Roof,' 'Guys and Dolls,' 'The King and I,' 'My Fair Lady,' etc. *See also* Comic operas; Popular music; Theater; Traveling exhibitions.

Musicians. Musician(s). Organist(s). Pianist(s). Accompanist(s). Soloist(s). Violinist(s). Fiddler(s). Flutist(s). Flautist(s). Harpist(s). Lutist(s). Lutanist(s). Lyrist(s). Fifer(s). Trumpeter(s). Cornettist(s). Cellist(s). Bugler(s). Piper(s). Drummer(s). Percussionist(s). Saxophonist(s). Clarinetist(s). Horn player(s). Band leader(s). Concertmaster(s). Vocalist(s). Singer(s). Folksinger(s). Songwriter(s). Virtuoso(s). *Choose from:* music(al) *with:* performer(s), player(s), composer(s), artist(s), conductor(s), ensemble(s), singer(s), artist(s), band(s), pianist(s), group(s), quartet(s), sextet(s). *See also* Artists; Choirs (music); Choral societies; Composers; Concerts; Conductors; Ensembles; Jazz musicians; Music; Musical ability; Rock musicians; Singers.

Musicians, jazz. See *Jazz musicians.*

Musicians, rock. See *Rock musicians.*

Musicology. Musicolog(ist,ists,y). Musicologie. Musikologie. Musikwissenschaft. Musikforschung. Musicologia. *Choose from:* music(al) *with:* scholar(ly,s,ship), theor(y,ies, etical), criticism, histor(y,ical) *See also* Ethnomusicology; Music; Music criticism; Musical intervals and scales; Musical theory.

Muslims. See *Islam.*

Muslims, Black. See *Black Muslims.*

Mutation. Mutat(e,ed,ing,ion,ions). Alter(ed,ing,ation) *with:* gene(s,tic), chromosome(s), hereditary material. Mutant(s). *See also* Genetic engineering; Genetics.

Mutilation, genital. See *Female circumcision (ritual).*

Mutilation, self. See *Self mutilation.*

Mutism. Mut(e,eness,ism). *Consider also:* aphon(ia,y,ic), voiceless(ness), loss of speech, dysphonia. *Choose from:* unable, inability *with:* communicate verbally, speak, speech. *See also* Aphasia; Elective mutism; Language disorders; Speech disorders; Speech disturbances.

Mutism, elective. See *Elective mutism.*

Mutual help programs. See *Self help groups.*

Mutual storytelling technique. Mutual storytelling technique. Therapeutic storytelling. *Choose from:* storytelling, story telling, story making, telling stor(y,ies) *with:* mutual, technique(s), therap(y,ies,eutic), psychotherap(y,ies, eutic), rehabilitation. *See also* Psychotherapeutic techniques.

Mysteries, religious. See *Religious mysteries.*

Mystery and detective television programs. See *Detective and mystery television programs.*

Mystery plays. See *Liturgical drama.*

Mystical union. See *Enlightenment (state).*

Mysticism. Mystic(ism,al,s). Vision(s). Sorcery. Psychic(s). Numinous. Religious vision(s). Miracle(s). Spirit possession. Mystical state(s). Mystical revelation(s). Tarot. Parapsycholog(y, ical). Visionary madness. Mystic tradition(s). Divine light. Mystic(al) consciousness. Mystical belief(s). Mystical phenomen(a,on). Bewitch(ed). Golem legend. Magic(al). Mystical event(s). Magic(al) belief(s). Visionary experience(s). Occult belief(s). Trance(s). Hearing voice(s). Mystic(al) power. Intense religious experience(s). *See also* Asceticism; Animism; Beliefs; Cabala; Chassidism; Cults; Enlightenment (state of mind); Jewish mysticism; Literature; Messiahs; Miracles; Occultism; Omen; Philosophy; Prayer; Religion; Religious beliefs; Religious experience; Religious practices.

Mysticism, Jewish. See *Jewish mysticism.*

Mystifications, literary forgeries and. See *Literary forgeries and mystifications.*

Mythical animals. Mythical animal(s) Phoenix(es,like). Unicorn(s). Loch Ness monster. Griffin(s). Dragon(s). *Choose from:* myth(ical,ological,s), legendary, fiction(al), fantastic *with:* animal(s), creature(s), beast(s), snake(s), monster(s). *Consider also:* gargoyle(s). *See also* Animal lore; Animals; Bestiaries; Fairy tales; Folklore; Griffins; Mermaids; Mythology; Snake lore.

Mythology. Mytholog(y,ies,ize,ized). Mythical(ly). Myth(s,os,ification). Legend(s,ary). Psychomytholog(y,ies, ize,ized). Psychomythical(ly). Psychomyth(s,os,ification). Mythmaking. Folklore. Saga(s). Tale(s). Fairy tale(s). Fable(s). Apologue. Symbolic account(s). Folk culture. *Consider also:* hero(es), collective conscience, metaphor(s), symbolism, shaman(s), evil eye(s), fantas(y,ies), genie(s), demythif(y,ied,ication), demytholog(ize,ized,ization), cultural image(s). *See also* Allegory; Ancient literature; Animism; Bestiaries; Cross cultural psychiatry; Cults; Deities; Ethnology; Folk culture; Folklore; Legends; Literature; Medieval literature; Mythical animals; Political myths; Rituals; Sex symbolism; Snake lore; Symbolism; Theomachy; Water spirits.

Myths. See *Anecdotes; Folk culture; Mythology.*

Myths, political. See *Political myths.*

N

Nadene languages. Nadene language(s). Athabascan: Apache, Carrier, Chasta Costa, Chipewyan, Hoopa (Hupa), Kutchin (Loucheux), Navaro, Sarsi, Upper Umpqua. Haida. Tlingit. *See also* Language; Languages (as subjects); North America; North American native cultural groups.

Nahuatl language. Nahuatl language. Nahua language. Mexicano. Mexican language. *Consider also:* Hidalgo, Mecayapan, Pajapan, Santa Catarina, Texcoco, Tetelcingo, Vera Cruz, etc. *with:* dialect(s). *See also* Uto-Aztecan languages.

Nail biting. Nail biting. Onychophagi(a,c). Nailbiting. *Choose from:* bit(e,ing), bitten, chew(ed,ing) *with:* nail(s), fingernail(s). *See also* Behavior disorders; Habits.

Names. Name(s,d). Naming. Anonym(s, ous). Pseudonym(s,ous). Eponym(s,ous). Surname(s). Nominative. Forename(s). Nickname(s). Nom(s) de plume. Nom(s) de guerre. Onomastic(s). *Consider also:* nomenclature, title(s). *Choose from:* proper, family, given, middle, first, last, assumed, maiden, married, pen *with:* name(s). *See also* Brand names; Epithets; Labeling (of persons); Naming.

Names, brand. See *Brand names.*

Names, inability to remember. See *Anomia (inability to remember names).*

Names of countries. See *Caribbean; Central America; Central Asia; Eastern Europe; Far East; Middle East; North Africa; North America; Oceania; South America; South Asia; Southeast Asia; Sub-Saharan Africa; Western Europe.*

Naming. Naming. *Choose from:* nam(e,es, ing) *with:* pattern(s), practice(s), repetition, trend(s), generat(ing,ion), change(s). *Consider also:* nickname(s), given name(s), maiden name(s), surname(s), first name(s), given name(s), personal name(s). *See also* Identity; Kinship; Lineage; Meaning; Names; Nonsexist language; Rituals; Sexist language; Sociolinguistics.

Naming (identification). See *Identification (recognition).*

Nannies. See *Child caregivers.*

Narcissism. Narciss(ism,istic,istically). Self love. Egotis(m,t,tic). Self centered. Egocen(tric,trism). Egomaniacal. Egois(m,t,tic). *Choose from:* narcissus *with:* myth(s), model(s), image(s). *Consider also:* solipsis(m,t,tic), self orient(ed,ation), auto-erotic(ism). *See also* Egocentrism; Egoism; Egotism;

Neuroses; Personality traits; Self consciousness; Self esteem; Self psychology; Selfishness (egocentric); Snobs and snobbishness; Solipsism.

Narcoanalysis. See *Narcotherapy.*

Narcoanalytic drugs. Narcoanalytic drug(s). Truth serum(s). *Choose from:* amobarbital [Amytal], droperidol [Inapsine, Innovar], ketamine [Ketalar], pentothal. *See also* Drugs; Narcotherapy.

Narcolepsy. Narcolep(sy,tic). Friedmann(s) disease. Paroxysm(s) of sleep. Cataplexy. Sleep attack(s). Morbus Gelineau. Gelineau(s) syndrome. *See also* Cataplexy; Consciousness disorders; Sleep disorders.

Narcotherapy. Narcotherap(y,ies). Narcoanaly(sis,tic). Narcosuggestion. Narcocatharsis. Narcosynthesis. Amytal interview(s). Truth serum. Pentothal interview(s). Sleep treatment(s). Sleep therap(y,ies). Narcopsychotherap(y,ies). *Consider also:* therap(y,ies) *with:* subnarcosis. *See also* Drug therapy; Narcoanalytic drugs; Sleep treatment.

Narcotic and drug control. See *Drug and narcotic control.*

Narcotic antagonists. Narcotic antagonist(s). *Choose from:* narcotic(s), opiate(s), opioid(s) *with:* antagonist(s), antagonism, block(er,ers,ade), inhibit(or,ors), suppress(ed,ing,or,ors). *Consider also:* naloxone [Narcan], naltrexone [Trexan]. *See also* Detoxification; Drugs; Drug antagonism; Narcotics.

Narcotic dependence. See *Substance dependence.*

Narcotics. Narcotic(s). Opiate(s). Opioid(s). Opium. Morphi(ne,a). Heroin [diacetyl-morphine, diamorphine, acetomorphine, H, hard stuff, horse, junk, skag, smack]. Cocaine [methyl benzoyl ecgonine, bernies, big C, coke, crack(head,heads), flake, happy dust]. Codeine [hydro-codone, oxycodone]. *Consider also:* addictive analgesic(s), alfentanyl hydrochloride [Alfenta], butalbital [Esgic, Fioricet, Fiorinal, Medigesic, Pacaps, Phrenilin Forte, Repan, Sedapap, Tencet, Tencon], butorphanol tartrate [Stadol], dezocine [Dalgan], fentanyl citrate [Innovar, Sublimaze], morphine sulfate [Astramorph, Duramorph, MS Contin, MSIR, Oramorph, Roxanol], hydromorphone hydrochloride [Dilaudid], levorphanol tartrate [Levo-Dromoran], meperidine hydrochloride [Demerol, Mepergan], methadone hydrochloride [Dolophine, Amidone, Phenadone, methadyl acetate],

oxymorphone [Numorphan], pentazo-cine [Talacen, Talwin], propoxyphene napsylate [Darvocet, Darvon], sufentanil citrate [Sufenta]. *See also* Analgesia; Drug addiction; Drug and narcotic control; Drug education; Drug effects; Drug enforcement; Drug induced abnormalities; Drug information services; Drug interactions; Drug overdoses; Drug rehabilitation; Drug tolerance; Drug trafficking; Drug use; Drug withdrawal; Drugs; Drugs in athletics; Gateway drugs; Methadone maintenance; Narcotic antagonists; Street drugs; Tranquilizers.

Narcotics trafficking. See *Drug trafficking.*

Narrative, first person. See *First person narrative.*

Narrative poetry. Narrative poe(try,m,ms). Epic poe(try,m,ms). *Consider also:* metrical romance, recitativ(e,i,o,os), historical poe(try,m,ms), metrical tale(s). *See also* Ballads; Elegiac poetry; Epic literature; Poetry; Recitative.

Narratives. Narrat(e,ed,ing,ion,ions, ive,ives). Narratolog(y,ical). Personal account(s). Storytelling. Recount(ed, ing). Recapitulat(e,ed,ing). Retell(ing). Retold. Recit(e,ation,ations). *Consider also:* message(s), hearing(s), monologue(s), dialogue(s), memoir(s), diar(y,ies), chronolog(y,ies), testimon(y,ial,ials), ethnographic text(s), oral histor(y,ies), third person narrative(s), autobiograph(y,ies,ical). *See also* Autobiography; Biography; Chronicles; Diaries; First person narrative; Interviews; Oral history; Point of view (literature); Sagas; Storytellers; Storytelling; Verbal communication.

Narratives, personal. See *First person narrative.*

Narrow minded. See *Rigid personality.*

Natality. See *Birthrate.*

Nation. See *Antarctic Regions; Arctic Regions; Caribbean; Central America; Central Asia; Countries; Eastern Europe; Far East; North Africa; North America; Middle East; Oceania; South America; South Asia; Southeast Asia; Sub-Saharan Africa; Western Europe.*

National anthems. See *Patriotic music.*

National bibliography. National bibliograph(y,ies). National biblio-graphic record(s). National book record(s). Copyright catalog(s). *Consider also:* National Union Catalog, British National Bibliography, Bibliographie de la France, Deutsche Bibliographie, etc. *See also* Bibliography; Descriptive bibliography; Library catalogs; Library cooperation; Reference materials.

National character. See *National characteristics.*

National characteristics. National characteristic(s). *Choose from:* national(ity,ities), ethnic(ity), cultur(e,al), ethnosocial, ethnocultural, Swiss, Japanese, Italian(s), Finns, Dutch, Swede(s), Irish, etc. *with:* character(s), characteristic(s), personalit(y,ies), profile(s), value(s), spirit, mind, patterns, trait(s), unique(ness), style(s), westernized, individualis(tic,m), collectivism, stereotype(s), identity, aggressive(ness), assertive(ness), typical, type(s), practical(ity), attitude(s), caricature(s). *Consider also:* esprit des nation(s), volksgeist, spirit of the people, national myth(s). *See also* Characteristics; Cultural characteristics; Ethnic differences; Ethnic identity; Ethnicity; Ethnocentrism; National identity; Personality traits; Psychohistory; Qualities; Stereotyping; Traditions.

National debt. See *Public debt.*

National emblems. National emblem(s). National symbol(s). Patriotic emblem(s). Patriotic symbol(s). *Consider also:* national flower(s), emblemas patrios, Great Seal, Privy Seal, Exchequer Seal, Signet(s), political symbol(s), National song(s). *See also* Emblems; Flags; Heraldry; Insignia; Nationalism; Patriotism; Political symbolism..

National fronts. National front(s). Independence movement(s). *Choose from:* liberation, national, popular, people(s), democratic *with:* front(s), movement(s), organization(s), rebellion(s). *See also* Anti-government radicals; Decolonization; Guerrilla warfare; Guerrillas; Islamic Resistance Movement; Nationalism; Peasant rebellions; Resistance movements; Revolution; Separatism.

National government. See *Central government.*

National health programs. National health program(s). National health insurance. National health service. *Choose from:* universal, national, state, social(ized) *with:* medical, medicine, health. *Consider also:* Medicaid, Medicare, national health insurance. *See also* Biased selection; Government programs; Government subsidization; Health care reform; Health insurance; Health planning; Managed care; Medical assistance; Social programs; Socialism.

National identity. National identity. Ethnonationalism. National(ism,ity). *Choose from:* national, ethnic, ethnonational, religious, cultural, ethnocultural, ethnosocial, Italian(s), Greek(s), Chinese, Japanese, German(s), Russian(s), Polish, Spanish, Irish, etc. *with:* identification, identit(y,ies), upbringing, background, affirmation, involvement, group identification, homophily, pride, awareness, orientation, allegiance, loyalt(y,ies), unity, consciousness, tradition(s). *Consider also:* chauvinism, xenophobia, ethnocentrism, national stereotype(s), national character, etc., ancestral language, second generation, third generation, hyphenated American(s), national minority group(s). *See also* Citizenship; Cultural identity; Cultural groups; Countries; Ethnic identity; National characteristics; Nationalism; Racial identity.

National income. National income. Net national product at factor cost. *Consider also:* gross national product, gross domestic product. *See also* Economic conditions; Economic indicators; Economic statistics; Economic well being; Gross national product.

National liberation. See *Decolonization; National fronts; Nationalist movements; Peasant rebellions; Revolution; Separatism.*

National minority groups. See *Ethnic groups; Linguistic minorities; Minority groups; National identity; Nationalism.*

National planning. See *State planning.*

National product, gross. See *Gross national product.*

National security. National security. State security. Defense policy. Security strateg(y,ies). Global security. Security pact(s). *Consider also:* deterrence, strategic defense initiative, arms race, star wars, military expenditure(s). *See also* Arms control; Balance of power; Classified information; Defense spending; Espionage; Government secrecy; International relations; Military readiness; Military weapons; Nuclear weapons non-proliferation; Secrecy; War; War prevention.

National self determination. See *Political self determination.*

National songs. See *Patriotic music.*

Nationalism. National(ist,istic,ism). Patriot(ic,ism). Superpatriot(ism,ic). Pledge of allegiance. Nationality preference(s). Irredentism. Partisan(s). Indigenisation. Indigenization. National liberation. Decolonization. Self determination. Liberation front(s). War of independence. National spirit. Chauvin(ism,istic). Jingoism. Xenophobia. *Choose from:* national(ist), patriotic *with:* allegiance, identit(y,ies), unity, front(s), independence, attachment, pride, sentiment(s), heritage, ideolog(y, ies), preference(s), struggle(s), loyalt(y,ies), unification, revitaliz(e,ed, ing,ation), solidarity, hero(es), liberation. *Consider also:* decommuniz(e,es, ing,ation), Scottish independence, Zionism, independence for Puerto Rico, Quebec separatis(m,ts), integral nationalism, totalitarian nationalism, fascism. *See also* Black nationalism; Black power; Colonialism; Countries; Crimes against peace; Decommunization; Developing countries; Ethnic groups; Ethnicity; Ethnocentrism; Fascism; Flags; Foreign policy; Homeland; Imperialism; International relations; Internationalism; Jingoism; Militarism; Nativism; National emblems; National identity; National fronts; Nazism; Particularism; Patriotic music; Patriotism; Peasant rebellions; Political self determination; Post-communism; Regionalism; Separatism; Speech communities; Tribalism; World history; Xenophobia.

Nationalism, black. See *Black nationalism.*

Nationalist movements. Nationalist movement(s). Liberation movement(s). Independence movement(s). *Consider also:* irredentism, South-West Africa Peoples Organization, Zionis(m,t,ts), Palestine Liberation Organization, African National Congress, Movimento Popular de Libertacao, Zimbabwe African People's Union. *See also* Decolonization; National fronts; Nationalism; Pan-Africanism; Peasant rebellions; Political self determination; Separatism; Social movements; Revolution.

Nationality. See *Cultural groups.*

Nationalization. Nationaliz(e,ed,ation). Nationalis(e,ed,ation). *Choose from:* national, government, state, public sector *with:* confiscate(s,d), takeover(s), control(led), own(ed,ership), operated, seized, expropriat(e,ed), manage(d), run *with:* industr(y,ies), manufacturing, firm(s), compan(y,ies), factor(y,ies), plant(s), mine(s), railroad(s), shipyard(s), shop(s), mill(s), foundr(y, ies), bank(s). *Consider also:* socialism, public enterprise, eminent domain. *See also* Expropriation; Government property; Industrial enterprises; Ownership; Privatization; Public sector; State capitalism; State power; Welfare state.

Nationals, foreign. See *Foreigners.*

Nations. See *Countries.*

Nations, developed. See *Developed countries.*

Nations, developing. See *Developing countries.*

Nations, industrialized. See *Industrial societies.*

Nations, law of. See *International law.*

Nations by name. See *Antarctic Regions; Arctic Regions; Caribbean; Central America; Central Asia; Eastern Europe; Far East; North Africa; North America; Middle East; Oceania; South America; South Asia; Southeast Asia; Sub-Saharan Africa; Western Europe.*

Native Americans. See *Central American native cultural groups; Indigenous populations; North American native cultural groups; South American native cultural groups.*

Native cultural groups, Central American. See *Central American native cultural groups.*

Native cultural groups, North American. See *North American native cultural groups.*

Native cultural groups, South American. See *South American native cultural groups.*

Native healers. See *Shamanism; Traditional medicine.*

Native language. Native language(s). First language(s). Primary language(s). Mother tongue. *Consider also:* native speaker(s), vernacular(ly). *See also* Bilingualism; Language; Language proficiency; Monolingualism; Sociolinguistics.

Native peoples. See *Aborigines; African cultural groups; Australoid race; Central American native cultural groups; Indigenous populations; Mongoloid race; North American native cultural groups; Oceanic cultural groups; South American native cultural groups; Traditional societies.*

Native races. See *Aborigines; African cultural groups; Australoid race; Central American native cultural groups; Indigenous populations; Mongoloid race; North American native cultural groups; Oceanic cultural groups; South American native cultural groups; Traditional societies.*

Natives. Native(s). Aborigine(s). Aboriginal population(s). Original resident(s). Inhabitant(s). Indigenous people(s). Autochthon(s,es). *Consider also:* mother country, fatherland, birthplace(s). *See also* Aborigines; African cultural groups; Alaska natives; Australoid race; Central American native cultural groups; Indigenous populations; Mongoloid race; North American native cultural groups; Oceanic cultural groups; Pacific Islanders; South American native cultural groups; Traditional societies.

Natives, Alaska. See *Alaska natives.*

Nativism. Nativis(m,tic). Anti-immigration polic(y,ies). Chauvin(ism,istic). Jingois(m,tic). Negative attitudes toward foreigners. Xenophob(ic,ia). *Choose from:* distrust, prejudice(s), suspicious(ness), negative attitude(s), dislik(e,ed,ing), hostil(e,ity), hatred, discriminat(e,ed,ing,ion), intolerance, restrictive law(s), protect labor market *with:* foreign(er,ers), outgroup, ethnic(ity), minorit(y,ies), Nonwhite(s), Asian(s), Black(s), Latino(s), Spanish speaking. *Consider also:* anti-Latino, nationalis(m,tic), eurocentric(ism), ethnocentr(ic,icity,ism), Boxer rebellion, Proposition 187. *See also* Assimilation (cultural); Cultural conflict; Cultural issues; Ethnic relations; Ethnicity; Ethnocentrism; Folk culture; Foreigners; Immigrants; Indigenous populations; Intergroup relations; Jingoism; Nationalism; Nativistic movements; Social attitudes; Social discrimination; Social integration; Tribalism; Xenophobia.

Nativistic movements. Nativistic movement(s). Retraditionalization. Retribalization. Cultural nationalism. *Choose from:* ethnic, indigenous, native, native culture *with:* reestablish(ed,ing, ment), pride, resurgence, power, consciousness, revitaliz(e,ed,ing,ation), self-determination, activis(m,t,ts), charismatic movement(s). *Consider also:* renewal movement(s), revitalization movement(s), Indigenous Women's Movement, American Indian Movement, Red Power, Spirit Camp(s), Language Revitalization, Third World Strike, Holy Spirit Movement, Ghost dance(s), spirit movement(s), Black Muslim(s). *See also* Cargo cults; Cultural conflict; Cultural identity; Indigenous populations; Messianic movements; Millenarianism; Nativism; Resistance movements; Tribalism.

Natural areas. Natural area(s). *Choose from:* natural, forest, nature, conservation, wilderness, unspoiled, unspoilt *with:* site(s), reserve(s), habitat(s), area(s), region(s), park(s), land(s), refuge(s), environment(s), beach(es). *Consider also:* game reserve(s), wildland(s), open land, wildlife refuge(s), rural environment(s), nesting site(s), marine reserve(s). *See also* Natural environment; Natural monuments; Wilderness; Wildlife sanctuaries.

Natural childbirth. Natural childbirth. *Choose from:* natural, prepared, home, gentle, Leboyer, Lamaze, alternative *with:* birth(ing,s), childbirth(s), deliver(y,ies), childbearing. *Consider also:* alternative birth(ing,s), homebirth(s), childbirth without violence, birth without violence. *See also* Birth; Birth adjustment; Birthing centers; Childbirth training; Labor (childbirth); Midwifery.

Natural disasters. Natural disaster(s). Natural hazard(s). Mine explosion(s). Landslide(s). Mudslide(s). Typhoon(s). Tidal wave(s). Tsunami(s). Avalanch(es). Tornado(es). Cyclone(s). Blizzard(s). Catastrophe(s). Earthquake(s). Hurricane(s). Tornado(es). Twister(s). Flood(s,ing). Natural calamit(y,ies). Acts of God. Storm(s). Lightning. Forest fire(s). Volcanic explosion(s). Volcanic eruption(s). Sand storm(s). Sandstorm(s). Wind storm(s). Brushfire(s). Snowstorm(s). Snow storm(s). Drought(s). *Consider also:* specific disasters such as Mount St. Helen's, Johnstown flood, Buffalo creek disaster, etc. *Consider also:* disaster area(s), disaster warning(s). *See also* Civil defense; Disaster planning; Disaster relief; Disasters; Drought; Earthquakes; Emergency services; Environmental stress; Famine; Fire; Flood control; Floods; Hazards; Reconstruction; Safety; Scarcity; Storms; Stress; Survival; Weather.

Natural environment. Natural environment(s). Eco-aesthetic(s). Nature vs nurture. Air quality. Water quality. Water supply. Wildlife. Physical environment. Soil quality. Crowd(s,ed, ing). Ecosystem(s). *Choose from:* natural, environmental, ecological, outdoors, wilderness, terrestrial, underwater *with:* setting(s), condition(s), climate(s), surrounding(s), milieu, site(s), crowding, overcrowd(ing), space. *See also* Biogeography; Biological diversity; Caves; Conservation of natural resources; Deforestation; Earth; Ecology; Environment; Environmental pollution; Environmental protection; Environmentalism; Gardening to attract wildlife; Habitat; Natural areas; Natural gardens; Natural resources; Nature literature; Nature worship; Open spaces; Parks; Phytogeography; Sanctuary gardens; Shore protection; Shorelines; Wilderness.

Natural family. See *Biological family.*

Natural foods. Natural food(s). *Choose from:* natural, organic(ally), unsprayed, health, pesticide-free, low salt, without additive(s), additive-free, without preservative(s), pure, unadulterated *with:* food(s), edible(s), bread(s), fish, grain(s), meat(s), seafood(s), milk, cereal(s), apple(s), fruit(s), juice(s), vegetable(s), cheese(s), poultry, shellfish, wheat, bean(s), rice, flour, pasta, egg(s). *Consider also:* cholesterol-free, fat-free, vegeburger(s), Aqua Libra, Perrier water. *See also* Beans; Diet; Eating; Edible plants; Food; Food additives; Grain; Health behavior; Herbicides; Holistic health; Lifestyle; Locally produced food; Medical foods; Nutrition; Organic farming; Pasta; Pesticides; Preventive medicine; Well being; Quality of life; Vegetarianism.

Natural gardens. Natural garden(s). Naturalistic garden(s). Informal garden(s). *Consider also:* natural(ized) landscaping, wildflowers. *See also*

Flowers; Formal gardens; Gardening to attract wildlife; Gardens; Landscape architecture; Natural environment.

Natural history. Natural histor(y,ian,ians). *Consider also:* naturalist(s), nature lover(s), natural science, natural lore. *See also* Animal lore; Evolution; Darwinism; Naturalists; Nature literature.

Natural law. Natural law(s). Law(s) of nature. Law(s) of human nature. Fundamental moral principle(s). *Consider also:* common morality, inalienable right(s), individual right(s), personal sovereignty, natural right(s), cultural universal(s). *See also* Animal nature of man; Conservative; Human rights; International law; Liberty; Naturalism; Philosophical anthropology; Political ethics; Principles.

Natural monuments. Natural monument(s). Sacred mountain(s). Natural heritage site(s). World Heritage List. World Heritage Site(s). National Park(s). Commemorative site(s). Commemorative place(s). Sacred place(s). National landmark(s). Sanctuar(y,ies). *Consider also:* Native American petroglyph(s), wildlife refuge(s), Egypt(ian) pyramid(s), national battlefield(s), etc. *See also* Cultural property; Sanctuary gardens; Historic sites; Literary landmarks; Monuments; Natural areas; Parks; Wilderness.

Natural religion. See *Natural theology.*

Natural remedies. See *Naturopathy.*

Natural resources. Natural resource(s). Nonrenewable resource(s). *Consider also:* mineral deposit(s), oil reserve(s), coal, land, soil, subsoil, water, forest(s), timber, woodland(s), fish, marine resource(s), pineland(s), tree(s), plant(s), plant resource(s), ocean resource(s), agricultural land(s), food, raw material(s), air, atmosphere, biosphere, ecosystem(s), rainforest(s), wilderness(es), swamp(s), wetland(s), desert(s), marsh(es), jungle(s), wildlife, animal(s), mammal(s). *See also* Agricultural diversification; Alternative energy; Animals; Conservation of natural resources; Earth; Ecology; Ecosystem management; Energy conservation; Energy generating resources; Environment; Environmental impacts; Environmental law; Environmental pollution; Environmental protection; Environmental stress; Environmentalism; Fisheries; Food; Food chain; Forest conservation; Forest reserves; Geopolitics; Human ecology; Land preservation; Land use; Marine ecology; Marine resources; Natural environment; Natural foods; Nonrenewable resources; Oceans; Organic farming; Parks; Raw materials; Renewable resources; Shore protection;

Shorelines; Soil conservation; Trees; Water supply; Wildlife conservation; Wildlife sanctuaries.

Natural resources, conservation of. See *Conservation of natural resources.*

Natural rights. See *Human rights; Natural law.*

Natural scenery. See *Landscape.*

Natural selection. See *Darwinism.*

Natural theology. Natural theology. Theologia naturalis. *Consider also:* theological naturalis(m,t,ts,tic), natural religion. *See also* Creation; God concepts; Immanence of God; Pantheism (universal divinity); Rationalism; Reason; Revealed theology; Teleology; Theology.

Natural therapy. See *Naturopathy.*

Naturalism. Naturalis(m,tic). Natural law(s). Natural propert(y,ies). Natural School. *Choose from:* naturalism, naturalist(s,ic) *with:* philosoph(y,ical,er,ers), aesthetic(s), ethic(s,al), theolog(y,ical), paint(ing,ings,er,ers), novel(s), play(s). For philosophy, *Consider also:* Herbert Spencer, Thomas Henry Huxley, Ernst Heinrich Haeckel, George Santayana, etc. For literature, *Consider also:* Emile Zola, Stephen Crane, Frank Norris, Theodore Dreiser, Guy de Maupassant, Giovanni Verga, etc. For music, *Consider also:* verismo, veristic, Cavalleria rusticana, Pietro Mascagni, Pagliacci, Il tabarro, Puccini, etc. *See also* Arts; Barbizon art movement; Classical art; Historical realism; Modern literature; Natural law; Realism; Realism in art.

Naturalistic ethics. See *Evolutionary ethics.*

Naturalists. Naturalist(s). Environmentalist(s). Conservationist(s). Nature lover(s). Natural scientist(s). Biologist(s). Bird watcher(s). Ecologist(s). Entomologist(s). Ornithologist(s). Plant collector(s). *Consider also:* naturalists by name such as Charles Darwin, Alexander Freiherr von Humboldt, Thomas Henry Huxley, Sir Charles Lyell, John Muir, etc. *See also* Animal lore; Biologists; Environmentalism; Natural history.

Naturalization. Naturaliz(ation,ed). *Choose from:* becom(e,ing), grant(ed,ing), acquir(e,ed,ing), acquisition *with:* citizen(s,ship). *See also* Acculturation; Citizenship; Foreigners; Immigrants; Immigration.

Nature. See *Natural environment.*

Nature, human. See *Human nature.*

Nature, influence on. See *Environmental impacts.*

Nature, law of. See *Natural law.*

Nature literature. Nature literature. Nature novel(s). Nature writing(s). *Choose from:* natural history, nature, habitat(s), ecology, environmental tradition, seasons, weather, pastoral, animal(s), bird(s), country life, insect(s), landscape(s), river(s), ocean(s), sea(s), season(s), tree(s), vine(s), wilderness *with:* literature, writing(s), novel(s), poetry, poem(s). *See also* Animal lore; Essays; Fiction; Folklore; Literature; Natural environment; Natural history; Nature sounds; Poetry.

Nature nurture. Nature nurture. Nature versus nurture. *Choose from:* genetic(s), gene(s), heredit(y,ary), inherit(ed,ance), nativism *with:* nurture, environment(al, alism). *See also* Behavioral genetics; Biological factors; Determinism; Educational background; Environmental determinism; Euthenics; Family background; Genetics; Nurturance; Parental background; Psychobiology; Social background; Sociobiology.

Nature of man, animal. See *Animal nature of man.*

Nature protection. See *Conservation of natural resources.*

Nature sounds. Nature sound(s). Birdsong(s). *Choose from:* nature, bird(s), animal(s), water, rain, thunder, thunderstorm(s), earth, wildlife, wind, ocean, surf, waves, whale(s), dolphin(s), thrush(es), meadowlark(s), bobolink(s), frog(s), loon(s), lion(s), jungle(s) *with:* sound(s), song(s), music, call(s), noise(s). *Consider also:* sonic geography, environmental soundscape. *See also* Animal communication; Animals; Birdsongs; Nature literature; Noise (sounds); Wild animals; Wilderness.

Nature trails. Nature trail(s). Guided trail(s). Marked trail(s). Blazed trail(s). Interpretive trail(s). *Choose from:* trail(s), path(s) *with:* nature, hiking, scenic, woods, outdoor education, ecology, environmental education. *See also* Recreational facilities.

Nature worship. Nature worship. Naturis(m,t,ts). *Choose from:* nature, Earth, mountains, wilderness, living things, life, universe, Garden of Paradise *with:* worship(ping,ped), spiritual(ity), reverenc(e,ed,ing). *Consider also:* Sun worship. *See also* Natural environment; Paradise; Sanctuary gardens; Worship.

Nature writing. See *Nature literature.*

Naturopathy. Naturopath(y,ies,ic). *Choose from:* natural, drugless *with:* remed(y, ies), therap(y,ies). *Consider also:* light therapy, heat therapy, air therapy, water therapy, massage therapy. *See also* Alternative medicine; Exercise therapy; Herbal medicine; Nostrums; Quackery;

Therapeutic cults; Traditional medicine; Vitamin therapy.

Nausea. Nausea(te,ted,ting). Nauseous(ness). *Consider also:* seasick(ness), morning sickness, mal de mer, naupathia, motion sick(ness), upset stomach, queas(y,iness), air sick(ness), car sick(ness). *See also* Eating disorders; Migraine headaches; Vomiting.

Nautical astronomy. Nautical astronomy. *Choose from:* navigat(e,ed,ing,ion), longitude, latitude *with:* astronomy, star(s), stellar method(s), Pole Star, celestial. *Consider also:* guidestar(s), celestial navigation, mariner's compass. *See also* Ancient astronomy; Astronomy; Time.

Naval architecture. Naval architecture. *Choose from:* architectur(e,al), architect(s), design(s,ed,ing), model(s,ing), specification(s), blueprint(s), drawing board(s) *with:* naval, navy, nautical, ship(s), ship hull(s), seaworth(y,iness), vessel(s), warship(s), catamaran(s), sailboat(s), boat(s), yacht(s), tugboat(s), whaler(s), gunboat(s), sloop(s), destroyer(s), aircraft carrier(s), battleship(s), submarine(s), destroyer tender(s), tanker(s), sidewheeler(s), riverboat(s), ferr(y,ies), troopship(s), steamship(s), steamship(s), shallow draft steamer(s), ironclad(s), schooner(s), dreadnought(s), nuclear submarine(s). *Consider also:* shipbuilding, boatbuilding *See also* Historic ships; Sailing ships; Ships; Shipbuilding; Warships.

Naval history. See *Military history*.

Naval offenses. Naval offense(s). *Choose from:* nav(y,ies), naval, ship(s,board), sailor(s), petty officer(s) *with:* offense(s), insubordinat(e,ion), mutin(y,ies,ous), pira(cy,te,tes), trial(s), court martial(s), unauthorized sailing, sabotage, crime(s), scandal(s), profiteer(ed,ing), bribe(s,ry), theft(s), illegal(ity,ities). *See also* Maritime law; Military desertion; Military discipline (punishment); Military ethics; Military law; Military offenses; Unethical conduct; War crimes.

Naval policy. See *Military policy; Sea power.*

Naval power. See *Sea power.*

Naval stations, navy yards and. See *Navy yards and naval stations.*

Naval strategy. Naval strateg(y,ies). *Choose from:* naval, nav(y,ies), U.S. fleet, Royal Navy, maritime, shipbuilding, seapower, sea power, nautical, armada(s), flotilla(s), fleet(s), aircraft carrier(s), sea lane(s), surface ship(s), surface vessel(s), submarine(s), battleship(s), U boat(s), torpedo boat(s), destroyer(s), armored cruiser(s), gunboat(s), frigate(s), sloop(s), warship(s), harbor

installation(s) *with:* strateg(y,ies,ist,ists), buildup(s), goal(s), objective(s), tactic(s,al), mission(s), decision(s), strategic role, offensive capability, plan(ned,ning,ner,ners), preparations, forward deployment, crisis response, convoy(s), surprise attack(s), confrontation(s). *Consider also:* naval intelligence, amphibious landing(s), antisubmarine warfare, coastal warfare, naval campaign(s), naval supremacy, naval presence, naval campaign(s), naval operations, naval parity, ocean warfare, naval superpower(s). *See also* Military operations; Military planning; Military power; Military readiness; Military strategies; Sea power; Warships.

Navigation, animal. See *Animal navigation*

Navy personnel. Nav(y,al) personnel. Submariner(s). Mariner(s). Sea(men,man). Lieutenant(s). Ensign(s). Commander(s). Captain(s). Admiral(s). Midship(men,man). Petty officer(s). CPO. Chief petty officer(s). Seabee(s). *Choose from:* nav(y,al), submarine, marine(s) *with:* personnel, trainee(s), student(s), diver(s), officer(s), pilot(s), cadet(s), crew(s), apprentice(s), technician(s), recruit(s), aviator(s), enlisted, enlistee(s), reserve personnel, engineer(s), male(s), female(s), men, man, women, woman. *See also* Armed forces; Enlisted military personnel; Military personnel; Military officers.

Navy yards and naval stations. Navy yard(s). Naval station(s). *Choose from:* navy, naval, submarine, destroyer, amphibious *with:* installation(s), headquarter(s), station(s), base(s), facilit(y,ies), district(s), dockyard(s), fortification(s), port(s), yard(s). *Consider also:* shipyard(s), harbor(s), dry dock(s), torpedo station(s), anchorage, home port(s). *See also* Coast defenses; Military bases; Ports; Sea power.

Nazism. Nazi(s,m). National Socialistische Deutsche Arbeiterpartei. *Consider also:* fascis(m,mo,t,ts), racis(m,t,ts), Ku-Klux-Klan, klans(men,man), neonazi(s,sm), Falang(e,ist,ists), Mussolini, Franco, neofascis(m,t,ts), Peronis(m,t,ts), skinhead(s), Hitler, Eichmann, Aryan nation(s), anti-semit(ic,ism), antisemit(ic,ism), bigot(s,ry), White supremac(y,ists), apartheid, White liberation movement(s), Posse Comitatus, White Aryan Resistance, the Covenant Sword and the Arm of the Lord, Order of the Silent Brotherhood, Afrikaner resistance movement, White power group(s), White freedom movement, White Patriot party, Bruder Schweigen strike force, Schweigen order II, cross burning(s), hatemonger(s), hate group(s). *See also* Antifascist movements; Antisemitism; Dictatorship; Eugenics; Fascism; Genocide; Hate

crimes; Hate groups; Holocaust; International offenses; Nationalism; Political movements; Social movements; Racism; Totalitarianism; War crimes; White supremacy movements.

Near death experiences. Near death experience(s). *Choose from:* parapsycholog(y,ical), religious, miraculous, supernatural *with:* death, dying, died, dead. *Consider also:* out of body, near death, survival after death, borderline survival, temporarily dead, temporary death, reviv(e,ed,ing), close to death, come back after death, brought back to life, reincarnat(e,ed,ion). *See also* Death; Experiences (events); Hallucinations.

Near East. See *Middle East*.

Near poor. See *Low income*.

Nearness, social. See *Social nearness*.

Necessities. See *Needs*.

Necessities of life. See *Basic needs*

Necessity (law). Necessity. Controlling force(s). Irresistible compulsion. Under duress. No acceptable choice. Reasonably necessary. *Consider also:* indispensable, reasonably needed, inevitab(le,ility), reasonably requisite. *See also* Extenuating circumstances; Imperative; Justification (law).

Necromancy. See *Magic*.

Necropolises. See *Cemeteries*.

Need, achievement. See *Achievement need*.

Need, approval. See *Approval need*.

Need for affiliation. See *Affiliation motivation*.

Need gratification. See *Need satisfaction*.

Need satisfaction. Need satisfaction. *Choose from:* need(s) *with:* satisf(y,ied, action,actions), gratif(y,ied,ication, ications), fulfill(ed,ing,ment), meet(ing), met, responsive(ness). *Consider also:* need reduction. *See also* Community support; Consumer satisfaction; Delay of gratification; Goal orientation; Individual needs; Job satisfaction; Life satisfaction; Marital satisfaction; Morale; Needs; Personal satisfaction; Psychological needs; Self actualization; Sexual satisfaction; Unmet needs.

Needle sharing. Needle sharing. *Choose from:* needle(s), syringe(s), injecting equipment, injecting paraphernalia *with:* shar(e,ed,ing), borrow(ed,ing), contaminated. *See also* AIDS; Drug addiction; Drug use; Risk taking; Street drugs; Subcultures; Substance abuse.

Needle trades. See *Garment industry*.

Needs. Need(s,ing,ed). Necessit(y,ies). Requirement(s). Requisite(s). Prerequisite(s). Essential(s). Indispensab(le,ility). Necessar(y,ies).

Consider also: wish(es), want(s,ing), insufficien(t,cy,cies), lack(s,ed,ing), deprivation, desire(s), desideratum, deficien(cy,cies), demand(s), paucity, request(s), satisfaction(s), drive(s), need(y,iness), dependen(t,cy), motive(s). *Consider also:* basic, economic, educational, emotional, financial, health, housing, individual, information, intellectual, labor, medical, personal, personnel, research, space, transportation, student *with:* need(s). *See also* Achievement need; Advocacy; Affiliation motivation; Appropriate technologies; Approval need; Assistance; Basic needs; Complementary needs; Constraints; Delay of gratification; Deprivation; Educational needs; Extrinsic motivation; Functional imperatives; Goals; Health services needs and demand; Human nature; Human services; Humanization; Imperative; Incentives; Individual needs; Intrinsic motivation; Love; Monetary incentives; Motivation; Need satisfaction; Needs assessment; Nurturance; Priorities; Psychological needs; Relevance; Resources; Satisfaction; Security; Social acceptance; Unmet needs; Wants; Well being.

Needs, basic. See *Basic needs.*

Needs, complementary. See *Complementary needs.*

Needs, educational. See *Educational needs.*

Needs, emotional. See *Psychological needs.*

Needs, health services. See *Health services needs and demand.*

Needs, human. See *Achievement need; Affiliation motivation; Approval need; Basic needs; Educational needs; Health services needs and demand; Individual needs; Psychological needs.*

Needs, individual. See *Individual needs.*

Needs, psychological. See *Psychological needs.*

Needs, psychosocial. See *Psychological needs.*

Needs, social. See *Affiliation motivation; Individual needs; Psychological needs.*

Needs, unmet. See *Unmet needs.*

Needs assessment. Needs assessment. Assess(ing) need(s). *Choose from:* needs *with:* assess(ment,ed,ing), questionnaire(s), mentor(ed,ing), measur(e,ed, ing,ment), calculat(e,ing), determin(e, ing), identif(y,ied,ying), identification, evaluat(ed,ing,ion), survey(s), stud(y,ies, ied), analys(is,es), estimat(e,ed,es,ing). *Consider also:* demand, market *with:* assess(ed,ing,ment), survey(s). *See also* Advisory committees; Delivery of services; Evaluation; Needs; Planning; Policy making; Priorities; Resource allocation; Self evaluation (groups);

Surveys; Systems analysis; Tests; Unmet needs.

Negative advertising. See *Comparative advertising.*

Negative attitudes. See *Negativism.*

Negative campaigning. See *Comparative advertising.*

Negative reinforcement. Negative reinforcement. *Choose from:* negative, aversive *with:* reinforc(e,ed,ement), feedback, consequence(s), treatment(s), contingenc(y,ies). *Consider also:* disapproval, punish(ed,ing,ment), electric shock(s), nonreward(s), escape learning, avoidance conditioning. *See also* Corporal punishment; Extinction (psychology); Positive reinforcement; Punishment; Reinforcement; Social reinforcement.

Negative sanctions. Negative sanctions. Enforcement rule(s). Social control. Coercive measure(s). Coercive intervention. Punish(ed,ing,ment). Restrict(ed, ing,ion,ions). Retaliat(ion,ory). Condemn(ed,ing,ation). Censur(e,ed, ing). Ban(ned,ning). Embargo(es,ed). Pressure tactic(s). Economic pressure(s). Boycott(s). Penalt(y,ies). Tariff(s). Cut(ting) diplomatic relations. Cut(ting) diplomatic ties. Diplomatic pressure(s). International pressure(s). Pressure of world opinion. Curb(ed,ing) sale(s). Cut(ting) trade. Suspend(ing) sales. Suspend(ing) shipment(s). Halt(ing) import(s). Loss of reward(s). Blacklist(ed,ing). Disinvest(ed,ing,ment, ments). Divest(iture,ed,ing,ment,ments). *Consider also:* economic leverage. *See also* Ban; Boycotts; Censorship; Censure; Disapproval; Disinvestment; Formal social control; Informal social control; Nontariff trade barriers; Penalties; Punishment; Social pressure; Strikes; Trade protection.

Negative transfer. Negative transfer. *Consider also:* mixed transfer, mediation transfer, overtraining, overlearning. *See also* Transfer (learning).

Negativism. Negativ(ism,istic,ity). Contrar(y,iness,iety). Resistan(t,ce). Cynic(al,ism). Negative(ly) distort(ed, ion,ions). Contrasuggestibility. Oppos(e,ed,ing,ition). Pervers(e,ity). Recalcitran(t,ce). Noncooperation. Defeatis(t,m). Alienat(ed,ion). Self defeating. *Choose from:* negative *with:* attitude(s), thought(s), self evaluation, self concept, behavior(s), view(s). *Consider also:* schadenfreude, passiv(e,ity) aggressive(ness). *See also* Alienation; Attitudes; Anti-Americanism; Antisemitism; Burnout; Cynicism; Defamation; Dystopias; Gossip; Guilt; Hate; Hopelessness; Jealousy; Labeling (of persons); Misanthropy; Nihilism; Pessimism; Personality traits; Political campaigns; Racism; Resentment;

Rumors; Scandals; Scapegoating; Self debasement; Sexism; Witch hunting.

Neglect, child. See *Child neglect.*

Neglect, self. See *Self neglect.*

Neglected children. See *Child neglect.*

Negligence. Negligen(ce,t,tly). Neglectful(ness). Careless(ness). Delinquent(cy). Derelict. Disregard(ing,ed,ful). Lax(ness). Remiss(ly,ness). Slack(ness). Heedless(ness). Inadvertent(ly). Inattentive(ness). Inconsiderate(ness). Thoughtless(ness). Unheedful. Unthinking. *Consider also:* unconcerned; slipshod, slovenly, lack of care act(s) of omission. *See also* Accountability; Inappropriateness; Law suits; Liability; Malpractice; Product liability; Professional malpractice; Social responsibility.

Negligence, default. See *Default (negligence).*

Negotiation. Negotiat(e,ed,es,ing,ion, or,ors). Mediat(ed,ion,ing,or,ors). Bargain(ed,ing). Group problem solving. Adjudicat(ed,ing,ion). Conciliation. Arbitrat(e,ed,ing,ion,or,ors). Compromise(d,s). Making concession(s). Conced(e,ed,ing). Reach(ing) agreement(s). Impasse procedure(s). Peacemaking. Referee(s,d,ing). Diplomacy. *Choose from:* settl(e,ed,ing), resolv(e,ed,ing), resolution, manag(e,ed, ing,ment) *with:* disagreement(s), dispute(s), conflict(s). *See also* Arbitrators; Arbitration; Bargaining; Collective bargaining; Conflict resolution; Diplomacy (official); Discussion; Firm offers; Mediation; Ombudsmen; Peace negotiations; Persuasion; Plea bargaining; Social behavior.

Negotiations, peace. See *Peace negotiations.*

Negro music. See *Afro-American music.*

Negro race. See *Blacks.*

Neighborhood associations. Neighborhood association(s). *Choose from:* neighborhood(s), communit(y,ies), community-based, local, block, grassroots, citizen(s), barrio(s), resident(s) *with:* improvement association(s), organization(s), club(s), group(s), collective(s), council(s), self-help. *Consider also:* tenant(s) association(s). *See also* Associations (organizations); Citizen participation; Civil society; Community (geographic locality); Community involvement; Community services; Exclusive neighborhoods; Local politics.

Neighborhood change. Neighborhood change. Gentrification. Zone(s) in transition. *Choose from:* neighborhood(s), block(s), communit(ies,y), environ(s), residential area(s), precinct(s), housing project(s), school district(s), parish(es), vicinit(y,ies), localit(y,ies), suburb(s), village(s), area(s), outskirt(s), ward(s), borough(s), quarter(s) *with:* chang(e,es,ed,ing), shift(s,ing), transition(al,s), deterioration, blight(ed), speculation, transform(ed,ation), declin(e,ed,ing), develop(ed,ing,ment), displacement, renewal, revitaliz(ed,ing,ation). *See also* Community change; Community development; Neighborhood preservation; Neighborhoods; Urban planning.

Neighborhood gilds. See *Social Settlements.*

Neighborhood health centers. See *Community health centers.*

Neighborhood newspapers. See *Community newspapers; Local news.*

Neighborhood preservation. Neighborhood preservation. *Choose from:* neighborhood(s), historic building(s), historic house(s), block(s), communit(ies,y), residential area(s), housing project(s), school district(s), parish(es), vicinit(y,ies), localit(y,ies), suburb(s), village(s), area(s), ward(s), borough(s), quarter(s) *with:* preserv(e, ed,ing,ation), repair(ed,ing), protect(ed, ing,ation), conserv(e,ed,ing,ation), sustainab(le,ility), revitaliz(e,ed,ing, ation), renew(ed,ing,al), reconstruct(ed, ing,ion). *See also* Civic improvement; Environmental protection; Land speculation; Neighborhood change; Neighborhoods; Restoration ecology; Urban beautification; Urban planning; Urban renewal.

Neighborhood segregation. See *Residential segregation.*

Neighborhoods. Neighborhood(s). Block(s). Neighbor(s). Communit(ies,y). Environ(s). Residential area(s). Residential environment(s). Precinct(s). Housing project(s). School district(s). Vicinit(y, ies). Localit(y,ies). Residential suburb(s). Village(s). District(s). Residential setting(s). Area(s). Region(s). Parish(es). Residential communit(y,ies). Ward(s). Borough(s). Quarter(s). Ghetto(es,s). Bedroom communit(y,ies). *See also* Cities; Community (geographic locality); Community (social); Community characteristics; Community churches; Ethnic neighborhoods; Housing; Inner cities; Metropolitan areas; Neighborhood associations; Neighborhood change; Neighborhood preservation; Neighbors; Parishes; Place of residence; Poverty areas; Residential mobility; Residential patterns; Social environment; Suburbs; Urban fringe; Zoning.

Neighborhoods, ethnic. See *Ethnic neighborhoods.*

Neighborhoods, exclusive. See *Exclusive neighborhoods.*

Neighbors. Neighbor(s,ly,liness). Nearby resident(s). Next door. Adjoining property owner(s). *Consider also:* informal social ties, community resident(s). *See also* Community (geographic locality); Community (social); Groups; Neighborhoods; Newcomers; Residents; Social contact.

Neo-Impressionism. See *Post-Impressionism.*

Neo-liberalism. See *Progressivism.*

Neoclassical economics. See *Supply side economics.*

Neocolonialism. Neocolonial(ism). Neocolonial(ism). Neoimperial(ism,istic). Neo-imperial(ism,istic). Foreign exploitation. Dollar diplomacy. *Consider also:* industrialized core, peripheral econom(y,ies), economic imperialism, monopolistic capitalism, United Fruit Company, etc. *See also* Americans abroad; Anti-Americanism; Center and periphery; Colonialism; Corporations; Cultural imperialism; Dependency theory (international); Ecological imperialism; Economic development; Economic underdevelopment; Foreign investment; Global integration; Globalization; Imperialism; Modern civilization; Multinational corporations; Offshore production (foreign countries); Oligopolies; World economy.

Neologisms. Neolog(ism,isms,y,istic,ical). Meaningless word(s). New word(s). *See also* Language; Vocabulary; Words.

Neonatal development. See *Infant development.*

Neonates. See *Infants; Newborn animals; Newborn infants.*

Neonaticide. Neonaticide(s). *Choose from:* murder(ed,ing,s), abandon(ed,ing,ment), kill(ed,s,ing,ings), dispos(e,ed,es,ing,al), hid(e,es,den) dump(s,ing,ed,ster,sters), throwaway(s) *with:* bab(ies,y), infant(s, icide,icides), newborn(s), neonat(e,es, al), kid(s). *See also* Abortion; Antisocial behavior; Family violence; Homicide; Infant mortality; Infanticide.

Neophobia. Neophobia. *Choose from:* fear(s,ful), anxiety, phob(ia,ias,ic), anxious(ness), apprehension, apprehensiveness *with:* new, novel, novelty. *See also* Animal exploratory behavior; Avoidance; Fear; Instinct; Phobias.

Neoplasms. See *Cancer.*

Nepotism. Nepotism. *Choose from:* hir(e, ed,ing), benefit(s,ting,ted), payroll, employ(ed,ees,ment,ing), salar(y,ies) *with:* famil(y,ies), kin, friend(s), wife, wives, brother(s), sister(s), father(s), mother(s), son(s), daughter(s). *Consider also:* favoritism, old boy(s) network(s), patronage. *See also* Family businesses; Favoritism; Occupational structure; Personnel selection; Royal favorites.

Nerds. Nerd(s). Anorak(s). Trivia freak(s). Propeller head(s). Propellor head(s). Tech(y,ies). Geek(s). Trainspotter(s). Otaku. Technology fanatic(s). Technology fan(s). *Consider also:* obsessive interest(s). *See also* Computer experts; Enthusiasts; Fanaticism; Fans (persons).

Nerve gas. See *Chemical warfare.*

Nervosa, anorexia. See *Anorexia nervosa.*

Nervous system. Nervous system(s). Central nervous system(s). CNS. Autonomic nervous system(s). Neural system(s). Neural network(s). *Consider also:* abducens nerve, acoustic nerve, adrenergic nerves, amygdaloid body, auditory cortex, auditory neurons, autonomic ganglia, autonomic nervous system, axons, baroreceptors, basal ganglia, brain, brain stem, caudate nucleus, cerebellum, cerebral cortex, cerebral ventricles, chemoreceptors, cholinergic nerves, corpus callosum, cranial nerves, cranial spinal cord, dendrites, diencephalon, dorsal roots, eye cones, eye rods, extrapyramidal tracts, facial nerve, frontal lobe, ganglia, geniculate bodies, thalamus, globus pallidus, gyrus cinguli, hippocampus, hypothalamo-hypophyseal system, hypothalamus, inferior colliculus, limbic system, lumbar spinal cord, mechanoreceptors, medulla oblongata, meninges, mesencephalon, motor cortex, motor neurons, myelin sheath, nerve endings, nerve net, nerve tissues, neural analyzers, neural pathways, neural receptors, neurons, neurosecretory systems, occipital lobe, olfactory nerve, optic chiasm, optic lobe, optic nerve, parasympathetic nervous system, parietal lobe, peripheral nerves, photoreceptors, pons, proprioceptors, pyramidal tracts, receptive fields, reticular formation, sensory neurons, somatosensory cortex, spinal cord, spinal ganglia, spinal nerves, spinothalamic tracts, superior colliculus, sympathetic nervous system, synapse, telencephalon, temporal lobe, thalamic nuclei, thalamus, thermoreceptors, trigeminal nerve, vagus nerve, ventral roots, visual cortex. *See also* Anatomy; Instinct.

Nervousness. Nervous(ness). Tense(ness). Tension. Uneas(y,iness). Stage fright. Neurotic. High strung. Ill at ease. Agitat(ed,ion). Anxiety. Anxious(ness). Excit(able,ed). Fearful. Impatient. Jumpy. Fretful. Timid(ity). Perturb(ed,able). Flustered. *See also* Agitation; Impatience; Neuroses; Personality traits.

Nesting behavior. Nesting behavior. Brood(ing). Burrow(ed,ing). *Choose from:* nest(s,ed,ing), burrow(s), web(s), den(s) *with:* behavior, build(ing), communal, dig(ging), dug, choosing site(s), density, spacing, rebuild(ing), care, construction, structure. *See also*

Animal behavior; Animal environments; Animal parental behavior.

Net generation. See *Echo boom generation.*

Network backup. Network backup(s). *Choose from:* network(s), LAN(s), WAN(s), netware server(s) *with:* backup(s), back(ed,ing) up, protect(ed, ing,ion), restor(e,ed,ing,ation). *See also* Computer networks; Computer security; Information networks; Internet service providers; Security measures

Network meltdown. Network meltdown(s). System meltdown(s). *Choose from:* network(s), system(s) *with:* meltdown(s), failure(s), crash(es,ed,ing). *Consider also:* broadcast storm(s), system overload(s,ed,ing). *See also* Computer bugs; Computer crimes; Computer hackers; Computer viruses.

Networks. Network(s,ed,ing). Tie(s). Affiliation(s). Link(s,age,ages). Social orbit(s). Friendship(s). Interlock(s,ing). Pattern(s) of association. Interconnected(ness). Kinship system(s). Clique(s). Support group(s). Support(ive) system(s). Supportive relationship(s). Alliance(s). Informal social organization(s). Consort(ia,ium). Council(s). *See also* Alliances; Computer networks; Cooperation; Coordination (interpersonal); Corporate networks; Decentralization; Diffusion; Distribution channels; Information dissemination; Interorganizational networks; Interinstitutional relations; Mentors; Multiinstitutional systems; Organizational structure; Political power; Social contact; Social support networks.

Networks, community. See *Community networks.*

Networks, community computer. See *Community networks (computer).*

Networks, computer. See *Computer networks.*

Networks, corporate. See *Corporate networks.*

Networks, information. See *Information networks.*

Networks, intercorporate. See *Corporate networks; Interorganizational networks.*

Networks, interorganizational. See *Interorganizational networks.*

Networks, social. See *Networks; Social support networks.*

Networks, social boundary spanning. See *Boundary spanning; Interorganizational networks.*

Networks, social support. See *Social support networks.*

Networks, strategic. See *Strategic alliances*

Networks, support. See *Social support networks.*

Neurasthenia. Neurasthen(ia,ic,oid). Neurasthenic neuros(is,es). Nervous debilit(y,ies). Asthenic reaction(s). *Consider also:* asthenic personalit(y,ies), aviator's neurasthenia. *See also* Dysthymic disorder; Hypochondriasis; Neurocirculatory asthenia; Neuroses; Stress reactions; Seasonal affective disorder.

Neuro-linguistic programming. Neuro-linguistic programming. Neurolinguistic programming. NLP. Design human engineering. DHE. *See also* Psychotherapy.

Neurocirculatory asthenia. Neurocirculatory asthenia. War neurasthenia. Effort syndrome. *Choose from:* cardiac, heart, cardiovascular *with:* neuros(is,es). Irritable heart. Soldiers heart. *See also* Asthenia; Neurasthenia; Stress reactions.

Neuropsychological assessment. Neuropsychological assessment(s). *Choose from:* neuropsychological, neurobehavioral, toxicopsychological *with:* test(ed,ing,s), assess(ed,ing,ment,ments), screen(ed,ing), examination(s). *Consider also:* names of specific neuropsychological tests. *See also* Brain damage; Diagnosis; Diagnostic tests; Measurement; Psychophysiologic disorders; Physiological psychology; Tests.

Neuroses. Neuros(is,es). Neurotic(s,ism). Neurotic disorder(s). Psychoneuros(is, es). Psychoneurotic(s). Emotional disorder(s). Emotional(ly) disturb(ed, ances). Personality problem(s). Depress(ed,ion,ions). Phobia(s). Nervous(ness). *Consider also:* affective disorder(s), cyclothymic disorder(s), depressive disorder(s), neurasthenia, anxiety disorder(s), castration anxiet(y, ies), separation anxiet(y,ies), neurocirculatory asthenia, obsession(s), obsessive compulsive disorder(s), trichotillomania, phobic disorder(s), agoraphob(ia,ic), post traumatic stress disorder(s), combat disorder(s), dissociative disorder(s), depersonalization disorder(s), multiple personality disorder(s), factitious disorder(s), Munchausen syndrome, somatoform disorder(s), conversion disorder(s), hypochondria(c,cs,sis), hysteria(s), hysterical anesthesia, hysterical paralys(is,es), hysterical vision disturbance(s), neurotic depressive reaction(s), occupational neuros(is, es), phobic neuros(is,es), traumatic neuros(is,es). *See also* Affective disorders; Affective symptoms; Anhedonia; Anxiety disorders; Childhood neurosis; Depression (psychology); Emotional dependence; Emotionally disturbed; Emotional immaturity; Emotional instability; Existential neurosis; Experimental neurosis; Mental illness; Narcissism; Neurotic depressive reaction; Obsessive behavior; Obsessive compulsive personality; Occupational

neuroses; Personality disorders; Phobias; Post traumatic stress disorders; Psychophysiologic disorders.

Neuroses, occupational. See *Occupational neuroses.*

Neuroses, war. See *Combat disorders.*

Neurosis, childhood. See *Childhood neurosis.*

Neurosis, existential. See *Existential neurosis.*

Neurosis, experimental. See *Experimental neurosis.*

Neurosis, infantile. See *Childhood neurosis.*

Neurosis, traumatic. See *Post traumatic stress disorders.*

Neurotic depressive reaction. Neurotic depressive reaction. Depressive episode(s). *Consider also:* neuro(tic, tically,sis) *with:* depress(ed,ion,ive,ives). *See also* Depression (psychology); Neuroses.

Neurotic disorders. See *Neuroses.*

Neutral, value. See *Value neutral.*

Neutrality. Neutral(ism,ist,ity). Neutral(s, ity). Impartial(ity). Uninvolved. Pacifist(ic). Nonbelligerent. Nonalign(ed,ment). Non-align(ed,ment). Zone(s) of peace. Nonpartisan(ship). Isolationis(t,m,ism). Noninvolvement. Middle of the road. Noncombat(ive,ant, ants,ance). Impartial. Disinterested. Uncommitted. Noncommit(ed,ment). Peaceful nation(s). Peacekeeping force(s). *Consider also:* semialign(ed, ment), semi-align(ed,ment), nuclear free zone(s), uninvolved. *See also* Foreign policy; Impersonal; Noncombatants; Noninvolvement; Nonviolence; Pacifism; Political ideologies; War attitudes; War prevention.

Neutrality, ethical. See *Value neutral.*

Neutralization. Neutraliz(e,ed,ing,ation). Desexualiz(e,ed,ing,ation). Deaggressiviz(e,ed,ing,ation). *Consider also:* blam(e,ed,ing) the victim, trivializ(e,ed,ing,ation), accomodation pattern(s), rationaliz(e,ed,ing,ation), justification(s), excuse(s), denial(s) of responsibility, condemn the condemner(s), dissonance reduction. *See also* Blame; Denial (psychology); Guilt; Rationalization (defense mechanism); Shame.

New Deal. New Deal. *Consider also:* social reconstruction, economic nationalism, interwar years, great depression, National Recovery Administration, Social Security Act of 1935, Civilian Conservation Corps, Public Works Administration, Works (Progress, Projects) Administration, Agricultural Adjustment (Administration,Act),

National Industrial Recovery Act, National Youth Administration, Wages and Hours Act, National Labor Relations Act. *See also* Historical periods; Liberalism; Progressivism; Social reform.

New left. See *Left wing; Protest movements; Social movements; Youth movements.*

New middle class. New middle class(es). New middle strata. Intermediate social categor(y,ies). *Choose from:* educated labor, salaried worker(s), white collar worker(s), pink collar worker(s), clerical worker(s), sales(men,man,women, woman,people), new working class(es). *See also* Gold collar workers; Middle class; White collar workers.

New religions. See *Cults.*

New right. See *Right wing politics.*

New towns. New town(s). New communit(y,ies). Planned communit(y,ies). *Consider also:* satellite communit(y,ies), greenbelt communit(y,ies), garden cit(y,ies). *See also* Community development; Local planning; Planned communities; Real estate development; Retirement communities; Suburbs; Urban fringe.

Newborn animals. Newborn animal(s). *Choose from:* animal(s) *with:* newborn, neonat(al,e,es), infant(s), baby, babies, suckling, postnatal, preweanling(s), day old, birth weight, newly hatched. *Consider also:* calf, calves, piglet(s), pupp(y,ies), pup(s), kitten(s), chick(s), fledgling(s), weanling(s), foal(s), lamb(s), ratling(s). *See also* Animal offspring.

Newborn infants. Newborn infant(s). Neonate(s). Newborn child(ren). Newborn(s). Early infancy. *Choose from:* very young, newborn, new, tiny, premature, postmature *with:* infant(s), bab(y,ies). *Consider also:* neonat(al, ology), birth weight. *See also* Birth injuries; Birth trauma; Birth weight; Fetus; Infant mortality; Infant small for gestational age; Infants; Premature infants.

Newcomers. Newcomer(s). New employee(s). New resident(s). Recent arrival(s). Immigrant(s). Migrant(s). *See also* Assimilation (cultural); Community (social); Employees; Immigrants; Migrants; Neighbors; Strangers.

Newly independent states. See *Countries in transition.*

Newly industrializing countries. See *Newly industrializing economies.*

Newly industrializing economies. Newly industrializing econom(y,ies). NIE(s). Newly industrializing countr(y,ies). NIC(s). Advanced developing countr(y,ies). Four Dragons. Four Tigers. *Consider also:* Hong Kong,

South Korea, Singapore, Taiwan, Brazil. *See also* Countries in transition; Developing countries; Less developed countries.

News, attribution of. See *Attribution of news.*

News, court. See *Court news.*

News, foreign. See *Foreign news.*

News, local. See *Local news.*

News, slanted. See *Media portrayal*

News, war. See *War news.*

News agencies. News agenc(y,ies). Wire service(s). *Choose from:* news, press *with:* agenc(y,ies), service(s), association(s). *Consider also:* Washington bureau(s), Associated Press, United Press International, Reuters, Inter Press Service, Agence France-Presse, Pan African News Agency, International Press Institute. *See also* Editorials; Information dissemination; Mass media; News coverage; News media; Newspapers; Opinion leaders.

News coverage. News coverage. Newsworth(y,iness). Fair press. *Choose from:* news(paper), journalistic, editorial, press, media, television, TV, radio, broadcast, print, network, newsmonger(s) *with:* cover(age,ed,ing), report(s,ed,ing), portray(al,als), construction, analy(sis,ses), stor(y,ies), disclosure, account(s), treatment, scrutin(y,ize,ized,izing), visibility, rais(e,ed,ing) issue(s), target(s,ed,ing), distort(ed,ing,ion), bias(ed,es), represent(ed,ing,ation), misrepresent(ed, ing,ation). *Consider also:* media event(s), photo op(s), photo oportunit(y, ies). *See also* Court news; Fairness and accuracy in reporting; Foreign correspondents; Foreign news; Information dissemination; Information leaks; Journalism; Journalistic ethics; Mass media; Mass media effects; Mass media violence; Media portrayal; News agencies; News media; News policies; Newspapers; Opinion leaders; Television programs; War news.

News media. News media. News(paper, papers). Radio. Television network(s). TV. Television. News broadcast(s,ing). News service(s). News agenc(y,ies). Public service announcement(s). Documentar(y,ies). News coverage. Press. Daily paper(s). Fourth estate. Periodical(s). Magazine(s). Mass media. *See also* Freedom of information; Freedom of speech; Information dissemination; Information leaks; Information services; Journalism; Journalists; Mass media; Mass media effects; Mass media violence; News agencies; News coverage; News policies; Newspapers; Opinion leaders; Press conferences; Television; Television programs.

News policies. News polic(y,ies). Freedom of the press. Open meeting law(s). Censor(ed,ship). Sunshine law(s). Classif(y,ied) government information. Gag the press. *Choose from:* press, media, information, journalist(s), reporter(s), radio, television, newspaper(s), news, communications, government information, journalist source(s) *with:* polic(y,ies), free(dom), barrier(s), bar(red), censor(ed,ship), government control, limit(s,ed,ing), ban(s,ned,ning), gag order(s), restrict(ed, ing,ion,ions), stricture(s), control(led, ling), curb(s,ed,ing), blackout(s), classif(y,ying,ied), protect(ed,ing,ion). *See also* Access to information; Attribution of news; Broadcasting policy; Censorship; Classified information; Freedom of information; Freedom of speech; Government secrecy; Information leaks; Information policy; Mass media policy; Policy.

News source identification. See *Attribution of news.*

Newspaper advertising. Newspaper advertis(ing,ement,ements). *Choose from:* newspaper(s), tabloid(s), press, daily paper(s), gazette(s), classified *with:* ad(s), advertis(ing,ement,ements), blurb(s). *Consider also:* media marketing, infomercial(s), ad(s,vertising) web(site,sites), advertorial(s), personals. *See also* Advertising; Classified advertising; Infomercials; Newspapers;

Newspaper ethics. See *Journalistic ethics*

Newspapers. Newspaper(s). Newsletter(s). School newspaper(s). Tabloid(s). Gazette(s). Press. Daily paper(s). Hometown paper(s). Big city paper(s). Weekly paper(s). Weekl(y,ies). Dailies. Yellow sheet. *Consider also:* advertorial(s). *Consider also:* newspapers by name, for example New York Times, Wall Street Journal, Washington Post, Christian Science Monitor, Los Angeles Times, etc. *See also* Attribution of news; Classified advertising; Comics; Community newspapers; Journalism; Local news; Mass media; Mass media effects; News agencies; News coverage; News media; News policies; Newspaper advertising; Obituaries; Periodicals; Popular culture; Readership; Sensationalism; Student newspapers and periodicals; Tabloids.

Newspapers, community. See *Community newspapers.*

Newspapers, neighborhood. See *Community newspapers; Local news.*

Newspapers, school. See *School newspapers.*

Newspapers, tabloid. See *Tabloids.*

Newspapers and periodicals, student. See *Student newspapers and periodicals.*

Niche marketing. See *Market segmentation.*

Niger-Congo languages, Atlantic Western. Niger-Congo language(s). Gur language(s). Senufo. More. Mossi. Dogon. Mande. Mandingo. Mende. Atlantic (Western): Fulani, Gola, Kissi, Limba, Serer, Temne, Wolof. *See also* African cultural groups; Language; Languages (as subjects); Sub-Saharan Africa.

Night care. Night care. Third shift nurs(e,es,ing). *Choose from:* night(time), evening *with:* care, ward(s), nurse(s), service(s), nursing. *See also* Nursing care.

Night terror. Night terror(s). Sleep terror(s). Pavor nocturnus. *See also* Dreams; Nightmares.

Nightclubs. Nightclub(s). Night club(s). Cabaret(s). Bar(s). Playboy club(s). Discotheque(s). Disco(s). Strip joint(s). Strip club(s). Dance club(s). Jazz club(s). Cafe(s). Supper club(s). Dance hall(s). Comedy club(s). Folk music club(s). Nightspot(s). Rock club(s). Music spot(s). *See also* Adult entertainment; Alcohol drinking; Bars; Coffee houses; Dirty dancing; Disco music; Eating establishments; Entertainment.

Nightmares. Nightmare(s). Incubus. Ephialtes. Bangungut. *Choose from:* bad, anxiety, frightening, traumatic, terrifying, catastrophic, helpless(ness), suffocat(e,ed,ing,ion) *with:* dream(s,ed, ing,t). *See also* Dreams; Night terror; Succubus.

Nihilism. Nihilis(m,tic,ts). Delusion of nonexistence. Renunciation. Renounc(e, ed,ing). Abnegat(e,ed,ing,ion). Negativis(m,tic). Pessimis(m,tic). Cynic(al,ism). *Consider also:* radical(s, ism), anarchis(m,tic), new left, alienat(ed,ion), destructive(ness). *See also* Anarchism; Dadaism; Dystopias; Epistemology; Metaphysics; Negativism; Nothingness; Pessimism; Philosophy; Political ideologies; Terrorism.

Nilo-Saharan languages. Nilo-Saharan languages *Choose from:* Nilo-Saharan, Coman, Koman, Maban, Saharan, Chari Nile *with:* language(s), word(s). *Consider also:* Fur (language), Songhai. *See also* African cultural groups; African empires; Languages (as subjects).

Nineteenth century. Nineteenth century. 19th century. 1800's. *Choose from:* antebellum, ante-bellum, Civil War, industrial revolution, reconstruction, Victorian *with:* period(s), age(s), era(s). *Consider also:* gilded age, gay nineties. *See also* Eighteenth century; Historical periods.

Nirvana. See *Enlightenment (state of mind).*

Nobility. See *Aristocracy.*

Nocturnal teeth grinding. See *Bruxism.*

Noel. Noel(s). *Choose from:* Christmas, nativity, yule, yuletide, Xmas, birth of Jesus Christ *with:* carol(s,er,ers,ling), song(s), singing, folksong(s), round(s), ballad(s), melod(y,ies), chorale(s), hymn(s), chant(s), chorus(es), wassailer(s), folksong(s), ballad(s), popular tune(s). *Consider also:* Jingle Bells, Silent Night, etc. *See also* Songs.

Noise (interference). Noise. Interference. Static. Jam(ming). Block(ing). Interception. *See also* Noise effects.

Noise (sounds). Nois(e,y,iness). Sound(s). Din. Loud(ness). Pandemonium. Clamor. Tumult. Fracas. *Consider also:* bang(s), boom(s), crash(es), thud(s), roar(s), shout(s), cry, cries, squawk(s), yelp(s), whimper(s), whine(s), whistle(s), squeak(s), rumble(s), sigh(s), purr(ing), hum(ming), screech(ing), whir(ring), scream(ing). *See also* Charivari; Ecology; Environment; Environmental pollution; Filtered noise; Hearing; Loudness; Nature sounds; Noise effects; Noise levels (work areas); Silence; Sound localization; White noise.

Noise, background. See *White noise.*

Noise, filtered. See *Filtered noise.*

Noise, white. See *White noise.*

Noise effects. Noise effect(s). Effect(s) of noise(s). Noise induced hearing loss(es). *Choose from:* noise(s), audiogenic, loud(ness), sound(s) *with:* effect(s), response(s), stress, oppressive(ness), risk(s), induced, significance, influenc(e, ed,ing), produced, damage(d), action, exposure, pollution, hearing loss, hazard(s), anxiety, annoyance, sensitiv(e, ity), memory, disturbance(s), adaptation, impact(s). *Consider also:* acoustic trauma, boiler maker(s) deafness. *See also* Environmental effects; Environmental pollution; Noise (interference); Noise (sounds); Noise levels (work areas).

Noise levels (work areas). Noise level(s) in work area(s). *Choose from:* occupation(s,al,ally), job(s), industrial, worker(s), employee(s), work, workplace(s), worksite(s), workstation(s), office(s), working conditions, factor(y,ies), compan(y,ies), labor, operator(s), machine(s,ry), typewriter(s), drill(s,ed,ing), hammer(ed, ing) *with:* noise(s), nois(y,iness), sound(s), loud(ness). *Consider also:* occupational hearing loss. *See also* Hazardous occupations; Loudness; Noise (sounds); Noise effects; Occupational exposure; Occupational stress; Perceptual stimulation; Working conditions.

Nomads. Nomad(ic,s,ism). Bedouin(s). *Consider also:* gyps(y,ies), migratory population(s), hunter-gatherer societ(y,ies), semi-nomad(ic,s,ism), wanderer(s), wandering life, Lapp(s), Kirghiz, horde(s), nomad(o,a,as). *See also* Hunting and gathering societies; Gypsies; Land settlement; Migrants; Migration; Pastoral societies; Prehistoric people; Transhumance.

Nomenclature. Nomenclature. Terminolog(y,ies,ical). Taxonom(y,ies). Classification(s). Designation(s). Name(s). Term(s). Descriptor(s). Definition(s). Vocabular(y,ies). Noun(s). Categor(y,ies). Jargon. Label(s). Acronym(s). Eponym(s). Index term(s). Abbreviation(s). Antonym(s). Pseudonym(s). *See also* Language; Terminology; Vocabulary; Words.

Non-objective art. See *Abstract art.*

Non-prescription drugs. Non-prescription drug(s). *Choose from:* over the counter, OTC, non-prescription, folk, traditional, old fashioned, patent, proprietary *with:* drug(s), medicin(e,es,al), medication(s), painkiller(s), sedative(s), stimulant(s), sleep aid(s), pill(s), tranquilizer(s), remed(y,ies). *Consider also:* tonic(s), elixir(s), cosmeceutical(s), nutriceutical(s). *See also* Cosmetics; Herbal medicine; Prescription drugs; Quackery; Self medication; Stimulants; Vitamin therapy.

Non-proliferation, nuclear weapons. See *Nuclear weapons non-proliferation.*

Non-victim crimes. See *Victimless crimes.*

Non-Western civilizations. See *African empires; African cultural groups; Asian empires; Buddhism; Central America; Central American native cultural groups; Central Asia; Civilization; Cultural history; Culture contact; Far East; Indian (India) cultural groups; Indigenous populations; Indonesian cultural groups; Islam; Middle East; North Africa; North American native cultural groups; Oceania; Oceanic cultural groups; Philippine Islands cultural groups; Pre-Columbian empires; South America; South American native cultural groups; South Asia; Southeast Asia; Southeast Asian cultural groups; Sub-Saharan Africa; Taoism; Traditional societies; Western civilization.*

Non zero sum games. Non zero sum game(s). Nonzero sum game(s). *Consider also:* competitive, nonconstant sum, nonempty core *with:* game(s). *Consider also:* prisoner's dilemma game, Shapley value. *See also* Entrapment games; Game theory.

Nonalignment. See *Neutrality.*

Noncombatants. Noncombatant(s). Not engaged in combat. Innocent(s). Innocent person(s). *Consider also:* chaplain(s), women and children. *See* *also* Civilians; Just war doctrine; Neutrality; Nonviolence; Pacifism; War attitudes.

Noncommissioned officers. Noncommissioned officer(s). NCOs. Petty officer(s). Chief petty officer(s). Sergeant(s). *See also* Enlisted military personnel; Military personnel.

Nonconformists, religious. See *Religious dissenters*

Nonconformity (personality). Nonconform(ity,ing,ist,ists,ism). Non-conformity. Rebellious(ness). Counterconform(ity,ing,ist,ists,ism). Inability to conform. Dissident(s). Unique(ness). Devian(t,ts,ce). Sensation seek(er,ers,ing). Pervers(e,ity). Unconventional(ity). Noncomplian(t,ce). Bohemian. Dissent(ing,er,ers). Disagree(d,ing,ment). Malcontent. Heretic(s). Secessionist(s). Separatist(s). Renegade(s). Original(ity). Unorthodox. Uncommon. Iconoclast(s,ic). *See also* Conformity (personality); Deviance; Dissent; Iconoclasm; Individuality; Religious dissenters.

Nonconsensual sex. See *Sexual coercion.*

Nondirected discussion method. Nondirected discussion method. *Choose from:* class(room), small group, self directed, nondirected, unstructured, open ended *with:* discussion(s). *Consider also:* nondirected teaching method(s), open ended interchange(s). *See also* Teaching methods.

Nondirective therapy. See *Client centered therapy.*

Nonfiction novel. Nonfiction novel(s). Non-fiction novel(s). Journalistic novel(s). Documentary prose. Creative nonfiction. *Consider also:* autobiograph(y,ical), biograph(y,ical), memoir(s), non-fiction, journalistic, factual *with:* fiction(al, alize,alized), novel(s). *Consider also:* docudrama(s). *See also* Autobiography; Biography; Documentary theater; Fiction; Historical fiction; Literature; Political fiction.

Nongovernmental organizations. Nongovernmental organization(s). NGO(s). Non-governmental organization(s). Non-governmental agenci(y,ies). Non-government group(s). *Choose from:* non-governmental, civic, international, nonprofit, not-for-profit *with:* institution(s), organization(s), association(s). *Consider also:* quasi-autonomous non-governmental organization(s), quango(s), citizen group(s). *See also* Agencies; Associations (organizations); Charities; Civil society; Foundations (organizations); International organizations; Nonprofit organizations; Organizations; Social agencies; Voluntary associations.

Nongraded schools. Nongraded school(s). *Choose from:* nongraded, ungraded *with:* instructional group(s,ing), school(s), class(es), curriculum, elementary program(s), primary program(s), instructional system(s). *Consider also:* one room school(s), multiple progress plan(s). *See also* Schools.

Nonindustrial societies. See *Traditional societies.*

Noninstitutionalized disabled. Noninstitutionalized disabled. *Choose from:* homebound, home care, deinstitutionaliz(e,ed,ing,ation), alternative(s) to institutionalization, halfway house(s), day treatment, day care, noninstitutionalized, independent living, group home(s), communal hous(ing,es) *with:* disabilit(y,ies), disabled, handicap(ped, s), retard(ed,ation), mental(ly) ill(ness), psychiatric patient(s), emotional(ly) disturb(ed,ance,ances). *See also* Attitudes toward handicapped; Attitudes toward mental illness; Attitudes toward mental retardation; Attitudes toward physical handicaps; Coping; Deinstitutionalization; Disability; Employment of persons with disabilities; Group homes; Halfway houses; Institutional release; Mental illness; Mental retardation; Sheltered housing; Sheltered workshops; Social adjustment.

Nonintervention. See *Isolationism; Neutrality; Permissiveness.*

Noninvolvement. Noninvolve(d,ment). Non-involve(d,ment). Uninvolve(d,ment). Detach(ed,ment). Lack of involvement. Absence of involvement. *Consider also:* nonparticipation, laissez-faire, neutral(ity), noninterference, uncaring, unentangled. *See also* Apathy; Autarky; Disengagement; Indifference; Isolationism; Neutrality; Passiveness; Powerlessness.

Nonorgasmic. See *Orgasmic dysfunction.*

Nonprescription drugs. See *Non-prescription drugs.*

Nonprofessional education. Nonprofessional education. *Choose from:* job(s), vocational, industrial, inplant, nonprofessional, paraprofessional, clerical, skilled, unskilled, blue collar, custodian, on-the-job, off-the-job, cooperative, distributive, occupational, prevocational, technical, trade, paramedical *with:* education, training, staff development, apprenticeship(s), school(s), student(s), preparation, learning. *See also* Education; Inservice training; Job requirements; Nonprofessional personnel; Personnel training; Professional education; Technological unemployment; Training; Vocational education.

Nonprofessional personnel. Nonprofessional personnel. *Choose from:*

nonprofessional, clerical, sales, semiskilled, service, skilled, unskilled, support, non-certified *with:* personnel, worker(s), staff, employee(s), womanpower, manpower, women, woman, men, man, attendant(s), aide(s), occupation(s), assistant(s). *Consider also:* paraprofessional(s). *See also* Agricultural workers; Business personnel; Child caregivers; Clerical workers; Industrial workers; Paraprofessional personnel; Professional personnel; Sales personnel; Skilled workers; Technical personnel; Unskilled workers; Waitperson

Nonprofit corporations. See *Nonprofit organizations.*

Nonprofit organizations. Nonprofit organization(s). Charit(y,ies). Not-for-profit organization(s). *Choose from:* organization(s), institution(s), agenc(y, ies), association(s), foundation(s), corporation(s), group(s), compan(y,ies), hospital(s), school(s), universit(y,ies), college(s) *with:* nonprofit, non-profit, not for profit, volunteer, voluntary, tax-exempt, public service, community service, eleemosynary, charitable. *See also* Agencies; Charities; Churches; Civil society; Colleges; Foundations (organizations); Government; Hospitals; Nongovernmental organizations; Organizations; Philanthropy; Religious institutions; Schools; Universities; Voluntary associations; Voluntary health agencies.

Nonprojective personality measures. Nonprojective personality measure(s). *Choose from:* nonprojective *with:* technique(s), test(s), personality measure(s), verbal measure(s), scale(s), inventor(y,ies), schedule(s), questionnaire(s), checklist(s), survey(s). *Consider also specific tests or measures by name. See also* Measurement; Personality measures; Projective techniques.

Nonproliferation. See *Arms control; Nuclear weapons non-proliferation.*

Nonpunitive approach (discipline). Nonpunitive approach(es). Gentle rod. Redirect(ed,ing,ion). *Choose from:* nonpunitive, positive, permissive(ness), alternative(s), constructive *with:* disciplin(e,ing,ary), contingenc(y,ies). *Consider also:* differential reinforcement. *See also* Child discipline; Employee discipline; Parent child relations; Punitiveness; School discipline.

Nonrelatives. See *Unrelated individuals.*

Nonrenewable resources. Nonrenewable resource(s). *Choose from:* nonrenewable, non-renewable, deplet(e,ed,ing,ion), finite, shortage(s), exhaustible *with:* resource(s), material(s), fuel(s), asset(s), reserve(s), mineral(s). *Consider also:* limit(s,ed,ing) growth, sustainable development, conservation. *See also* Alternative energy; Conservation of natural resources; Energy conservation; Energy consumption; Energy generating resources; Finite; Fuel; Natural resources; Renewable resources; Sustainable development.

Nonresistance to evil. Nonresistance to evil. Passive resistance. *Choose from:* nonresist(ance), nonretaliation, passive submission *with:* evil, violen(t,ce), force(s), oppress(ed,ing,ion,ive). *Consider also:* pacifis(m,tic), Biblical nonresistance, peace witness(es). *See also* Civil disobedience; Conscientious objectors; Moral authority; Nonviolence; Pacifism; Peace movements.

Nonsense literature. Nonsense literature Nonsense verse(s). *Choose from:* nonsens(e,ical), absurd(ity,ities), ridiculous(ly,ness) *with:* literature, verse(s), song(s), poetry, poem(s), book(s). *Consider also:* limerick(s), Edward Lear. *See also* Fantasy (literary); Folk songs; Humorous poetry; Macaronic literature; Nonsense syllables.

Nonsense syllables. Nonsense syllable(s). Nonword(s). Pseudoword(s). *Choose from:* nonsense, meaningless *with:* syllable(s), trigram(s), word(s). *See also* Nonsense literature; Verbal learning.

Nonsexist education. Nonsexist education. *Choose from:* nonsexist, gender fair(ness), sex neutral, gender neutral, unbias(es,ed), bias-free, sex equitable, egalitarian, democratic *with:* education(al), school(s,ing), curricul(a,um), textbook(s), career counseling, sport(s), scholarship(s), college(s), universit(y,ies). *Consider also:* Title IX, Women's Educational Equity Act. *See also* Access to education; Affirmative action; Coeducation; Equal education; Single sex schools.

Nonsexist language. Nonsexist language. *Choose from:* nonsexist, sex neutral, gender neutral, unbias(es,ed), bias-free, sex fair(ness), gender indefinite, sex equitable, desexed *with:* language, speech, speaking, pronoun(s), noun(s), verb(s), title(s), name(s), pronominal, label(s,ling), rhetoric, word(s), definition(s), symbol(s), metaphor(s). *Consider also:* genderlect, womanspeak. *See also* Language; Naming; Sexism; Sexist language; Social equity; Social meaning; Stereotyping.

Nonstandard English. Nonstandard English. *Choose from:* nonstandard, dialect(s), Black, ghetto, regional, urban, vernacular, bidialect(ism,al,ical), pidgin, Hawaiian, accent(s), street *with:* English. *See also* Accents; Creoles; Dialects; Ebonics; Idioms; Jargon; Language; Loan words; Pidgin languages; Slang; Sociolinguistics.

Nontariff trade barriers. Nontariff trade barrier(s). *Choose from:* trade, trading, economic relations, import(s,ed,ing), export(s,ed,ing), international market(s), transborder business(es), commerc(e,ial) *with:* barrier(s), distortion(s), impediment(s) *with:* nontariff, tax incentive(s), subsid(y,ies), technical barrier(s), quota(s), polic(y,ies), control(s), restriction(s). *Consider also:* buy national policy, import quota(s), price support(s). *See also* Autarky; Balance of trade; Commercial treaties; Foreign trade regulation; Free trade; Harmonization (trade); Impediments; Import substitution; Imports; International economic integration; International trade; Negative sanctions; Tariffs; Trade; Trade protection.

Nontheistic religion. Nontheistic religion(s). Non-theis(m,t,ts,tic). *Consider also:* Buddhis(m,t,ts), Confucian(ism,s), Taois(m,t,ts), Pantheis(m,t,ts,tic), Death of God theology, humanis(m,t,ts). *See also* Agnosticism; Buddhism; Humanism; Pantheism (universal divinity); Religion; Taoism.

Nontraditional careers. Nontraditional career(s). Sex atypical aspiration(s). *Choose from:* nontraditional, atypical, *with:* occupation(s,al), profession(s,al), career(s), vocation(s,al), role(s), setting(s), field(s), job(s), employment. Househusband(s). Housespouse(s). *Choose from:* woman, women, female(s) *with:* male dominated occupation(s), male intensive occupation(s), blue collar job(s), police officer(s), firefighter(s), sanitation worker(s), corrections officer(s), electrician(s), plumber(s), carpenter(s), mathematician(s), engineer(s), hard hat(s), construction worker(s), bricklayer(s), mason(s), etc. *Choose from:* men, man, male(s) *with:* female dominated occupation(s), female intensive occupation(s), feminized occupation(s), nurse(s), schoolteacher(s), beautician(s), librarian(s), secretar(y,ies), clerical work, social worker(s). *See also* Affirmative action; Alternative lifestyles; Alternative work patterns; Comparable worth; Employment opportunities; Equal job opportunities; Female intensive occupations; Male intensive occupations; Occupational aspirations; Occupational choice; Occupational segregation; Professional women; Sex roles; Sex stereotypes; Sexual division of labor; Working women.

Nontraditional education. Nontraditional education. *Choose from:* nontraditional, alternative, magnet, open, flexible, innovative, Montessori, noncampus *with:* education, school(s), college(s), universit(y,ies), degree requirements, teaching, grading, instruction(al), curriculum, training. *Consider also:*

free(dom) school(s), open universit(y, ies), folk school(s), distance education, deschooling. *See also* Access to education; Continuing education; Correspondence schools; Distance education; Educational innovations; Educational needs; Educational opportunities; Field experience programs; Home schooling; Individualized instruction; Innovations; Reentry students; Traditional schools.

Nonverbal ability. Nonverbal abilit(y,ies). *Choose from:* nonverbal, perceptual, psychomotor, symbolic, artistic, musical, numerical, manual, motor, kinesthetic, tactile *with:* abilit(y,ies), skill(s), development, understand(ing), cognit(ion,ive). *See also* Ability; Artistic ability; Mathematical ability; Mechanical ability; Motor skills; Nonverbal communication; Nonverbal learning; Spatial ability; Verbal ability.

Nonverbal communication. Nonverbal communication. Touch interaction. Manual communication. Nonspeech. Kinesic(s). Expressive movement(s). Gesture(s). Gesticulat(e,ed,ing,ion). Posture(s). Tactile presentation. Facial expression(s). Facial cue(s). Signal(s). Yawning. Gaze aversion. Touching behavior. Total communication. Eye contact. Body expression. Blush(ed,ing). Smil(e,es,ing). Frown(s,ed,ing). Grimac(e,es,ing). Raised eyebrow(s). Sour expression(s). Hand movement(s). *Choose from:* nonverbal, nonvocal, body, bodily, manual, extra-verbal *with:* communication, assertiveness, interaction(s), behavior, language, indicator(s), intervention(s), stimuli, message(s), meaning, sign(s,als), expression(s), cue(s). *Consider also:* nonverbal language(s). *See also* Body language; Clothing; Communication (thought transfer); Communication barriers; Communication skills; Eye contact; Facial expressions; Gestures; Laughter; Manual communication; Nonverbal ability; Nonverbal learning; Personal space; Self expression; Silence; Smiling; Speech; Symbolism; Verbal communication.

Nonverbal learning. Nonverbal learning. *Choose from:* nonverbal, perceptual, motor, kinesthetic, tactile *with:* learn(ed, ing), memor(y,ies), recall(ed,ing), train(ed,ing), recogni(ze,zed,tion), understand(ing), cognit(ion,ive), acquisition, reason(ed,ing), retention. *See also* Learning; Nonverbal ability; Nonverbal communication; Perceptual motor learning; Skill learning; Social learning.

Nonverbal meaning. Nonverbal meaning(s). *Choose from:* nonverbal, kinesthetic, nonlinguistic, figural, gestur(e,es,ed,al) *with:* representation(s), cue(s), comprehension, understanding, information, stimuli, intelligence, feedback, memory, encoding, recall, message(s), response(s), communication, learning, explanation(s), decoding, meaning(s). *Consider also:* iconicity, sign language(s). *See also* Meaning; Nonverbal ability; Nonverbal communication.

Nonverbal reinforcement. Nonverbal reinforcement. *Choose from:* nonverbal, gestur(e,ed,es,ing,al), signal(s,ed,ing), tangible *with:* reinforc(e,ed,ing,ement), praise, feedback, approval. *See also* Reinforcement; Social behavior; Social reinforcement.

Nonviolence. Nonviolen(ce,t). Pacif(ism,ist, ists,istic). Peaceful protest(s). Ahimsa. Noninjury. Alternative(s) to violence. Passive resistance. Nonaggress(ive,ion). Nonconflict. Oppos(ed,ition) to violence. Peace(ful,fulness,able, making). Peace keeping. Peace loving. Quaker(s). Dov(es,ish). Noncombative. War resister(s). Irenic. Conciliatory. Conscientious objector(s). *Consider also:* Mahatma Gandhi, Satyagraha, Martin Luther King, civil disobedience, noncooperation. *See also* Activism; Civil disobedience; Civil rights organizations; Conscientious objectors; Hunger strikes; Noncombatants; Nonresistance to evil; Pacifism; Peace movements; Social movements; Violence.

Nonviolent resistance. See *Nonviolence.*

Nonwage payments. See *Employee benefits.*

Nonwhite. See *Alaska natives; Asian Americans; Australoid race; Blacks; Mongoloid race; Pacific Islanders; People of color; Races; Racially mixed.*

Normal distribution. Normal distribution. *Choose from:* normal, bell shaped, Gaussian *with:* curve(s), distribution. *See also* Frequency distribution; Statistical data.

Normlessness. See *Anomie.*

Norms. Norm(ative,s). Common expectation(s). Manner(s). More(s). Folkway(s). Taboo(s). Moral system(s). Socially acceptable. Counternorm(s). Social expectation(s). Institutionalized role(s). Institutionalized rule(s). Rule(s) of social life. Etiquette. Behavior standard(s). Shared morality. *See also* Action; Behavior; Beliefs; Countercultures; Cultural universals; Cultural values; Customs; Decency; Fashions; Formal social control; Generalities; Group norms; Ideologies; Informal social control; Laws; Manners; Reference values; Roles; Rules (generalizations); Sex customs; Sex roles; Social behavior; Social conformity; Social disorganization; Social influences; Social institutions; Social values; Standards; Taboo; Traditions; Uniformity; Utilitarianism.

Norms, group. See *Group norms.*

Norms, social. See *Social norms.*

Norms, statistical. See *Statistical norms.*

North Africa. North Africa(n). Algeria(n). (Arab Republic of) Egypt(ian) [United Arab Republic]. Libya(n). Morocc(o,an) [French Morocc(o,an), Spanish Morocc(o,an), Maroc]. (Republic of the) Sudan(ese). Tunisia(n). *Consider also:* Barbary State(s), Tangier Zone, Sahara(n) [Saharian]. *See also* African empires; Hamitic languages; Middle East; Semitic languages; Sub-Saharan Africa; Sudanic languages.

North America. North America(n). Bermuda(n). Canad(a,ian). Greenland. Mexic(o,an). (United States of) America(n). *See also* Algonquian languages; Arctic regions; Caribbean; Central America; Eskimo-Aleut languages; Hokan-Siouan languages; Macro-Otomanguean languages; Nadene languages; North American native cultural groups; Penutian languages; Uto-Aztecan languages; Western civilization.

North American Indians. See *North American native cultural groups.*

North American native cultural groups. North America(n,s) Indian(s). North American Amerind(s). Indians of North America. Canadian Indian(s). Amerindian(s). Native American(s). Canad(a,ian) native(s). Alaska(n) native(s). Reservation Indian(s). *Consider also specific groups by name, for example:* Kwakiutl, Haida, Tsimshian, Nootka, Arikara, Hidatsa, Mandan, Spokan, Paiute, Nez Perce, Shoshone, Cherokee, Creek, Pomo, Plains Indian(s), Natchez, Choctaw, Navajo, Navaho, Pima, Tlaxcaltecan, Zuni, Apache, Salish, Mohawk, Iroquois, Hopi, Aztec, Papago, Seminoles, Chippewa, Arapaho, Cheyennes, Mohave, Ojibwa, Multnomah, Algonquin, Sioux, Comanche, Kiowa, Algonquan, Abenaki, Abnaki, Manitou, Manibozho, Manabaus, Mandan, Muskogean, Nadene, Chipewyan, Spokane, Blackfoot, Cree. *Consider also:* Eskimo(s), Aleut(s), Athapascan, Athabascan, Inuit(s), Mestizos, indigenous American(s). *See also* Algonquian languages; American Indian territories; Caribbean; Central American native cultural groups; Cultural groups; Culture (anthropology); Culture change; Culture contact; Eskimo-Aleut languages; Ethnic groups; Hokan-Siouan languages; Indigenous populations; Macro-Otomanguean languages; Nadene languages; North America; Penutian languages; Pre-Columbian empires; South American native cultural groups; Storytellers; Traditional societies; Uto-Aztecan languages.

Nostalgia. Nostalg(ia,ic,ically). Homesick(ness). Wistful(ness). Yearn(ed,ing). Longing(s). Reminisc(e,ed,ing). Pining. Languish(ed,ing). *See also* Emotions; Reminiscence.

Nostrums. Nostrum(s). Fraudulent remed(y, ies). Quack(ery). Medicine show(s). Medical folklore. *Choose from:* secret, unprov(ed,en), unsubstantiated, homeopathic *with:* remed(y,ies), cure(s), medicine(s). *See also* Alternative medicine; Homeopathy; Quackery; Traditional medicine.

Not-for-profit organizations. See *Nonprofit organizations.*

Notation, dance. See *Dance notation.*

Notebooks, authors'. See *Authors' notebooks.*

Nothingness. Nothing(ness). Nihility. Null(ity). Nada. Nonexisten(t,ce). Vacu(ity,ous). Existence(less). Nonreal(ity). *Consider also:* unreal(ity), unactual(ity), incorporeal(ity), insubstantial(ity), nonsubsisten(t,ce), inexisten(t,ce), nonbeing, nonentit(y,ies), impalpability, imperceptib(le,ility), oblivion, blank, vacuum, empt(y,iness), vacuum, void, ungrund, empty space, nonpresence, nowhere(ness). *See also* Depression (psychology); Indifference; Nihilism; Unconsciousness.

Nouveau roman. Nouveau roman. New novel(s). *Consider also:* antinovel(s), Alain Robbe-Grillet, Claude Simon, Nathalie Sarraute, Michel Butor, Marguerite Duras. *See also* Antiheroes; Antinovel.

Novel, nonfiction. See *Nonfiction novel.*

Novels. Novel(s). Fiction(alized). Novella(s). Nouveau roman. Literature. Literary work(s). Writings. Prose. Belles lettres. Literary description(s). Literary classic(s). Creative writing. Spy thriller(s). Myster(y,ies). Love stor(y,ies). Penny-dreadful(s). Aga saga(s). *Consider also:* author names, titles of works. *See also* Bildungsroman; Books; Fiction; Gothic romances; Literature; Love stories; Political fiction; Western fiction.

Novelty seeking. See *Sensation seeking.*

Novices. Novice(s). Beginner(s). Learner(s). Neophyte(s). Student(s). Pupil(s). Disciple(s). Trainee(s). Apprentice(s). Amateur(s). Tyro(s). Nonprofessional(s). *See also* Amateurs; Apprenticeship; Disciples; Students.

NREM sleep. NREM sleep. Nonrapid eye movement sleep. Neosleep. *Choose from:* NREM, nonREM non-REM, slow wave, quiet, delta, telencephalic, orthodox, synchronized *with:* sleep. *See also* Sleep.

Nuclear accidents. Nuclear accident(s). Nuclear meltdown(s). *Choose from:* nuclear safety, plutonium processing, nuclear weapon(s), atomic energy, nuclear energy, nuclear reactor(s), nuclear waste(s) *with:* meltdown(s), melted down, fallout, spill(s), radiation level(s), taint(ed,ing), negligen(ce,t), human error(s), unsafe, leukemia(s), deadly waste(s), hazardous waste(s), radioactive waste(s), dump(ing), security, trag(ic,edy,edies), explosion(s), disaster(s), leak(y,s,ing,ed), emission(s), mismanagement, death(s), illness(es), debris, emergenc(y,ies), accident(s,al), contaminat(e,ed,ing,ion), environmental concern(s), pollut(e,ed,ing,ion), cleanup, clean up. *Consider also:* Chernobyl, Three-Mile Island, etc. *See also* Accidents; Air pollution; Carcinogens; Catastrophes; Disasters; Environmental pollutants; Environmental pollution; Nuclear energy; Nuclear power plants; Nuclear waste; Nuclear weapons; Nuclear weapons non-proliferation; Occupational exposure; Waste disposal; Waste transport; Water pollution.

Nuclear disarmament. See *Arms control; Disarmament; Nuclear weapons non-proliferation.*

Nuclear energy. Nuclear energy. *Choose from:* nuclear, atomic, fusion, fission *with:* energy, power, technology, reactor(s). *See also* Antinuclear movements; Energy; Energy generating resources; Energy policy; Fuel; Nuclear accidents; Nuclear power plants; Nuclear safety; Nuclear waste.

Nuclear family. Nuclear famil(y,ies). Small famil(y,ies). Modern famil(y,ies). One child famil(y,ies). Isolated conjugal unit(s). Conjugal famil(y,ies). Conjugal household(s). Elementary famil(y,ies). *See also* Alternative family forms; Biological family; Extended family; Family characteristics; Family life; Family relations; Family size; Kinship; Parent child relations; Single parent family; Stem family; Stepfamily.

Nuclear free. See *Nuclear weapons non-proliferation.*

Nuclear power. See *Nuclear energy.*

Nuclear power plants. Nuclear power plant(s). *Choose from:* nuclear, atomic *with:* power, energy, electricity *with:* plant(s), produc(e,ed,ing,tion), industry, generat(e,ed,ing,ion), station(s). *See also* Antinuclear movements; Energy; Energy generating resources; Energy policy; Fuel; Nuclear accidents; Nuclear energy; Nuclear safety; Nuclear waste.

Nuclear proliferation. Nuclear proliferation. *Choose from:* atomic bomb(s), nuclear weapon(s), nuclear arms, war games, strategic arms, atomic weapon(s) *with:* proliferat(e,ed,ing,ion), spread(ing), buildup(s),

stockpil(e,es,ed,ing). *See also* Arms control; Atomic bomb; Military weapons; Nuclear warfare; Nuclear winter; Nuclear weapons; Nuclear weapons non-proliferation.

Nuclear safety. Nuclear safety. *Choose from:* nuclear, atomic, radioactive, uranium, plutonium, radiation, fallout *with:* safe(r,st,ty,ness), safeguard(s), security, health(y), risk(s), hazard(s), disaster(s), fire(s), accident(s), shelter(s), precaution(s,ary), alarm(s), protect(ed,ing,ion), emergenc(y,ies). *See also* Accident prevention; Nuclear accidents; Nuclear energy; Nuclear power plants; Nuclear waste; Occupational exposure; Occupational safety; Safety.

Nuclear warfare. Nuclear war(fare). Doomsday. Mutual(ly) assured destruction. Nuclear epidemic. A-bomb(s). Last epidemic. Manhattan project. Hiroshima. Nagasaki. Nuke(s,d). Hydrogen bomb(s). *Choose from:* nuclear, atom(ic) *with:* war(fare), bomb(s,ing), arms, survivor(s), warhead(s), weapon(s,ry), missile(s), battlefield(s). *See also* Antinuclear movements; Atomic bomb; Civil defense; Disarmament; Military weapons; Nuclear accidents; Nuclear weapons; Nuclear weapons non-proliferation; Nuclear proliferation; Nuclear winter; War; Weapons of mass destruction.

Nuclear waste. Nuclear waste(s). *Choose from:* nuclear, atomic, radioactiv(e,ity), fallout, uranium, radon *with:* dump(s,ed, ing), emission(s), burial(s), waste(s), tailing(s), garbage, refuse, landfill(s), effluent(s), sludge, trash, litter, rubbish, junk, debris, sweeping(s), runoff, spill(s), dregs, dust, leaving(s), discard(s,ed), ash(es). *Consider also:* below regulatory concern, low level radioactive waste(s). *See also* Air pollution; Carcinogens; Environmental effects; Environmental impacts; Environmental pollutants; Environmental pollution; Environmental protection; Food contamination; Hazardous wastes; Industrial wastes; Medical wastes; Nuclear accidents; Nuclear energy; Nuclear power plants; Nuclear safety; Nuclear warfare; Nuclear weapons non-proliferation; Nuclear winter; Occupational exposure; Toxic substances; Solid waste; Waste disposal; Waste transport; Water pollution.

Nuclear weapons. Nuclear weapon(s,ry). *Choose from:* nuclear, atom(ic), hydrogen *with:* weapon(s,ry), arms, arsenal(s), bomb(s), *Consider also:* arms race, nuclear deterrence, balance of terror, nuclear power, nuclear proliferation, nuclear forces. *See also* Antinuclear movements; Atomic bomb; Civil defense; Military weapons; Nuclear accidents; Nuclear warfare; Nuclear

weapons non-proliferation; Nuclear proliferation; Nuclear winter; War; Weapons of mass destruction.

Nuclear weapons non-proliferation. Nuclear weapons non-proliferation. Disarmament talk(s). SALT talk(s). Strategic arms limitation treaty. Strategic arms reduction treaty. *Choose from:* nuclear weapon(s), nuclear arms, antinuclear, anti-nuclear, strategic arms, atomic weapon(s), atomic bomb(s) *with:* non-proliferation, nonproliferation, control(s), freeze(s), test ban(s), ban(s,ned,ning), halt(ed,ing), limit(s,ed, ing,ation,ations), reduction, security guarantee(s), export control, free zone(s). *Consider also:* Rarotonga treaty. *See also* Antinuclear movements; Arms control; Atomic bomb; Deterrence; Disarmament; Military weapons; Nuclear proliferation; Nuclear warfare; Nuclear winter; Nuclear weapons; War prevention.

Nuclear winter. Nuclear winter. Nuclear devastation. Protracted nuclear war(s). *Consider also:* nuclear epidemic(s), ground zero, doomsday. *See also* Antinuclear movements; Atomic bomb; Catastrophes; Disasters; Nuclear accidents; Nuclear warfare; Nuclear weapons; Nuclear weapons non-proliferation; Nuclear proliferation; War.

Nudity. Nud(e,ity). Naked(ness). Indecent exposure. Nudis(m,t,ts). Topless. Strip joint(s). Striptease. Birthday suit. Bare. Unclothed. Undress(ed,ing). Disrob(e, ed,ing). Unclad. Strip(per,pers,ped). Streaker(s). *See also* Body image; Clothing; Cultural values; Human body; Lifestyle.

Null hypothesis testing. Null hypothes(is, es) test(ing). *Choose from:* null hypothes(is,es), *with:* test(s,ing), assert(ing,ion), significance, assessment, confirm(ing,ation), corroborat(e,ed,ing, ion), support(ed,ing), proof, prov(e,en, ing), evidence. *See also* Experiments; Hypothesis testing; Research design.

Nullification. Nullif(y,ied,ying,ication). Abolish(ed,ing,ment). Abrogat(e,ed, ing,ion). Annul(led,ling,ment). Invalidat(e,ed,ing,ion). Cancel(ed,ing, ation). Cancel(led,ling,lation). Negat(e,ed,ing,ion). Null and void. Void(ed,ing). Rescind(ed,ing). Revok(e,ed,ing). Revocation(s). Veto(ed,es,ing). Undo(ne,ing). Terminat(e,ed,ing,ation). *Consider also:* counteract(ed,ing), neutraliz(e,ed,ing, ation), compensat(e,ed,ing,ation), counterbalanc(e,ed,ing), countervail(ed, ing), suspen(d,ded,ding,sion). *See also* Annulment; Cancellation; Disclaim; Repeal.

Number comprehension. Number comprehension. Numeracy. *Choose from:* number(s), numeral(s), integer(s), counting, seriation, quantitative *with:* comprehension, comprehend(ed,ing), understand(ing), understood, literacy, conceptualiz(e,ed,ing,ation), learn(ed, ing). *See also* Comprehension; Mathematical ability.

Number systems. Number(ing) system(s). *Choose from:* arithmetic, counting, numeration, number(ing), numerical *with:* system(s). *Consider also:* number concept(s), number base(s), perfect number(s), prime number(s), natural number(s), decimal system(s), real number(s), binary scale(s), Fibonacci sequence(s). *See also* Mathematics; Numbers.

Numbers. Number(s). Numeral(s). Digit(s). Numerical unit(s). Cipher(s). Figure(s). Integer(s). *Consider also:* rational, real, imaginary, whole, cardinal, ordinal, roman, arabic *with:* number(s), numeral(s). *See also* Language; Mathematics; Number systems.

Numeracy. See *Mathematical ability.*

Numismatics. Numismatic(s). *Choose from:* collect(ed,ing,or,ors,ion,ions), study *with:* coin(s), medal(s), medallion(s). *See also* Antiques; Coinage; Coins; Collecting mania; Collectibles; Hobbies.

Nuns. Nun(s). Roman Catholic sister(hood, s). Sisters of Mercy. Catholic sister(s). Catholic female religious. Catholic teaching sister(s). Women religious. Convent(s). Feminine monasticism. Religious orders of women. Reverend Mother. Abbess. Mother Superior. Sisters of Good Shepherd. Sisters of Charity. Little Sisters of the Poor. *See also* Clergy; Contemplative orders; Female spirituality; Monasticism; Religious life; Religious personnel.

Nuptiality. See *Marriage rates.*

Nurse administrators. Nurs(e,ing) administrator(s). *Choose from:* nurs(e,es, ing) *with* director(s), manager(s,ial), administrat(or,ors,ion), dean(s), officer(s), head(s), chief(s), supervis(or, ors,ory,e,ed,ing,ion). *Consider also:* headnurse(s), head nurse(s). *See also* Administrators; Nurses.

Nurse clinicians. Nurse clinician(s). Clinical nurse specialist(s). *Choose from:* nurse(s) *with:* clinician(s), clinical role(s), therapist(s), specialt(y,ies). *See also* Nurses.

Nurse patient relations. Nurse patient relation(s,ship). *Choose from:* nurse(s) *with:* client(s), patient(s) *with:* relation(s, ship), interaction(s), rapport, cooperation, teamwork, compliance, helping, support, covenant(s), role(s), trust, agreement(s), distrust, collaboration, attitude(s), perception(s), communication(s), influence(s). *See also* Interpersonal relations; Nurses; Patients.

Nurse practitioners. Nurse practitioner(s). *Choose from:* nurse(s) *with:* practitioner(s), private practice, joint practice, family practice. *See also* Nurses; Patient education; Physicians assistants.

Nurseries. Nurser(y,ies). *Consider also:* infant(s), neonat(e,es,al), bab(y,ies) *with:* intensive care, care unit(s), special care. *See also* Infant care.

Nursery rhymes. Nursery rhyme(s). Nursery song(s). Lullab(y,ye,ies). Mother Goose. *Consider also:* pat-a-cake," nonsense word(s), nonsense rhyme(s), nursery riddle(s), Jack and Jill, Humpty Dumpty. *See also* Children's literature; Children's poetry; Children's songs; Lullabies; Rhymes.

Nursery school students. Nursery school student(s). *Choose from:* nursery school(s), preschool, head start, prekindergarten *with:* student(s), child(ren), pupil(s), boy(s), girl(s). *Consider also:* preschooler(s), prekindergartener(s). *See also* Nursery schools; Preschool children.

Nursery schools. Nursery school(s). Nurser(y,ies). Kindergarten(s). Early childhood education. Day care center(s). Preschool education. Preschool class(es). Preschool(s). Play school(s). Child care center(s). Infant school(s) Head start. Headstart. *See also* Child day care; Corporate day care; Early childhood development; Preschool education.

Nurses. Nurse(s). Nursing graduate(s). RN(s). LPN(s). Nursing student(s). *Choose from:* nursing *with:* staff, personnel. Nursing sister(s). Practical nurse(s). Registered nurse(s). School nurse(s). Nurse anesthetist(s). Nurse administrator(s). Nurse clinician(s). Nurse midwife. Nurse midwives. Nurse practitioner(s). Psychiatric nurse(s). Public health nurse(s). *See also* Allied health personnel; Caregivers; Health occupations; Male nurses; Medical staff; Nurse administrators; Nurse patient relations; Nurse practitioners; Nurses aides; Nursing care; Nursing education; Nursing ethics; Nursing staff; Nursing students; Nursing team.

Nurses, male. See *Male nurses.*

Nursesaides. Nurs(es,ing) aide(s). Nursing assistant(s). Rest home aide(s). Hospital attendant(s). Practical nurse(s). *See also* Allied health personnel; Caregivers; Community health aides; Health occupations; Medical staff; Nurses; Paraprofessional personnel; Psychiatric aides.

Nursing, community health. See *Community health nursing.*

Nursing, home. See *Home care.*

Nursing care. Nursing care. *Choose from:* nurs(e,es,ed,ing) *with:* care, practice(s), responsibilit(y,ies), process(es), function(s), skill(s), dut(y,ies), role(s), support(ive). *Consider also:* emergency room, geriatric, obstetrical, occupational health, operating room, pediatric, psychiatric, surgical *with:* nursing. *See also* Care of the sick; Caregivers; Community health nursing; Medical care; Nurses; Nurses aides; Nursing homes; Skilled nursing facilities.

Nursing education. Nursing education. *Choose from:* nurse(s), nursing, nurse practitioner(s), nurse midwife, nurse midwives *with:* education, training, curriculum, school(s), college(s), diploma program(s), baccalaureate program(s), graduate program(s), doctoral program(s). *See also* Medical education; Nurses.

Nursing ethics. Nursing ethics. *Choose from:* nursing, nurse(s), RN(s), LPN(s) *with:* ethic(s,al), values, moral(ity), humane, compassion(ate), confidential(ity), principle(s,d), standard(s) of conduct, integrity, conscience, conscientious(ness), moral obligation(s), honest(y), philosoph(y,ical), bioethic(al). *See also* Ethics; Nursing; Medical ethics; Professional ethics.

Nursing facilities, skilled. See *Skilled nursing facilities.*

Nursing homes. Nursing home(s). Skilled nursing facilit(y,ies). Long term care facilit(y,ies). Chronic care home(s). Intermediate care facilit(y,ies). *Consider also:* residential home(s), geriatric facilit(y,ies), convalescent home(s), home(s) for aged, home(s) for elderly. *See also* Assisted living; Hospices; Hospitals; Medical care; Residential treatment; Skilled nursing facilities.

Nursing records. Nursing record(s). *Choose from:* nurs(ing,e,es) *with:* record(s), note(s), chart(s). *See also* Medical records; Records; Scientific records.

Nursing staff. Nursing staff. *Choose from:* nurs(e,es,ing) *with:* staff, personnel, employee(s). *See also* Medical staff; Nurses; Nursing team.

Nursing students. Nursing student(s). *Choose from:* student(s), undergraduate(s), training *with:* nursing, nurse(s). *See also* College students; Nurses.

Nursing team. Nursing team(s). Nursing group(s). Teamwork in nursing. *Choose from:* team(work) *with:* nurs(es,ing), care. *See also* Medical staff; Nurses; Nursing staff.

Nurturance. Nurtur(e,ed,er,ers,ing, ant,ance). Nourish(ed,ing,ment). *Consider also:* foster(ed,ing), mother(ed,ing), father(ed,ing), parent(ed,ing), further(ed,ing), strengthen(ed,ing), encourag(e,ed,ing), promot(e,ed,ing), support(ed,ing), supportive(ness), helpful(ness), sustain(ed,ing), provid(e,ed,ing) for, tak(e,ing) care of, caring, care(d), caregiving, need gratification, comfort(ed,ing), caretaking, sustenance, menism. *See also* Animal parental behavior; Father child relations; Love; Mother child relations; Motivation; Needs; Parent child relations; Personality traits.

Nurture nature. See *Nature nurture.*

Nut industry. Nut industry. Nut production. *Choose from:* nut(s), peanut(s), walnut(s), cashew(s), pecan(s), macadamia nut(s), pistachio(s), hazelnut(s), Brazil nut(s), chestnut(s) *with:* produc(tion,er,ers), industry, processing, sale(s), selling, factor(y,ies), grow(er,ers), crop(s), import(s,ed,ing), export(s,ed,ing), economic(s), demand, market(s,ed,ing). *Consider also:* Sun-Diamond Growers, Planters' peanuts, etc. *See also* Agribusiness; Farming; Food industry; Industry.

Nutriceuticals. See *Food additives; Medical foods; Vitamin therapy.*

Nutrition. Nutrition(al). Nutritious(ness). Nutritive value. Nutritional requirement(s). Nourish(ment,ing). Protein(s). Nutrient(s). Carbohydrate(s). Calorie(s). Diet(s,ary). Fat(s). Eating habit(s). Foodstuff(s). Menu(s). Vitamin(s). Meal(s). Nutriment(s). Daily bread. Grocer(y,ies). Edible(s). Feed. Fodder. Sustenance. *Choose from:* food(s) *with:* intake, habit(s), preference(s), supplement(s), consumption. *Consider also:* malnutrition, malnourish(ed,ment), undernourish(ed, ment). *See also* Anemia; Anorexia nervosa; Beverages; Bulimia; Breast feeding; Convenience Foods; Diet; Diet fads; Eating; Failure to thrive (psychosocial); Food; Food additives; Food habits; Food services (programs); Health; Hunger, food deprivation; Junk food; Malnutrition; Natural foods; Nutrition disorders; Nutrition education; Nutrition surveys; Obesity; Vegetarianism.

Nutrition, child. See *Child nutrition.*

Nutrition, infant. See *Infant nutrition.*

Nutrition disorders. Nutrition disorder(s). *Choose from:* nutrition(al), diet(s,ary) *with:* disorder(s), deficien(t,cy,cies), deficit(s), stress(es), abuse, unbalanced, problem(s). *Consider also:* malnourish(ed,ment), starv(e,ed,ing, ation), dehydration, hunger, deficiency disease(s), anorexia, failure to thrive syndrome, vitamin deficienc(y,ies), undernourish(ed,ment), obesity, undernutrition, pellagra, beriberi, scurvy, kwashiorkor, steatitis, rickets, avitaminosis, Wernicke(s) encephalopathy, pernicious osteomalacia, anemia. *Consider also:* ascorbic acid, vitamin A, vitamin B, choline, folic acid, pyridoxine, riboflavin, thiamine, vitamin B12, vitamin D, vitamin E, vitamin K, magnesium, potassium, protein, calorie(s), carbohydrate(s) *with:* deficien(t,cy,cies). *See also* Alcoholism; Anorexia nervosa; Deficiency diseases; Eating disorders; Diet; Failure to thrive (psychosocial); Hunger, food deprivation; Malnutrition; Nutrition; Starvation; Thinness; Undernourishment; Vitamin deficiency disorders.

Nutrition education. Nutrition education. *Choose from:* nutrition(al), nutritious(ness), nutritive value(s), nourish(ment,ing), diet(s,ary), eating, menu(s), vitamin(s), meal(s) *with:* educat(e,ed,ing,ion), knowledge, instruct(ed,ing,ion), teach(ing), train(ed,ing), taught, handbook(s), guideline(s), class(es). *See also* Health education; Nutrition; Patient education.

Nutrition surveys. Nutrition survey(s). *Choose from:* nutrition(al), diet(s,ary), food intake, food consumption, nourishment, undernourish(ed,ment) *with:* survey(s), assess(ing,ment), measurement, questionnaire(s), classification, surveillance. *See also* Diet; Nutrition; Surveys; World health.

Nutritional deficiencies. See *Malnutrition; Nutrition disorders.*

Nymphomania. See *Hypersexuality.*

O

Oath, lying under. See *Perjury.*

Oaths. Oath(s). Sworn statement(s). Swearing in. Sworn in. Solemn promise(s). Pledge(s). *Choose from:* assertory oath(s), promissory oath(s), *Consider also:* compurgation. *See also* Loyalty oaths; Promises.

Oaths, loyalty. See *Loyalty oaths.*

Obedience. Obedien(t,ce). Obey(ed,ing). Amenable. Submissive(ness). Submit(ting,ted). Submission. Subordinat(e,ed,ing,ion). Follow(ed,ing, er,ers). Complian(t,ce). Conform(ed,ing, ity). Adherence to rule(s). Acquiescen(t, ce). Docil(e,ity). Subjection. Tractab(le, ility). Dutiful(ness). Meek(ness). Deferential. Subservien(t,ce). Obsequious(ness). Servil(e,ity). Obeisance. Law abiding. *See also* Authoritarianism (psychological); Authority (power); Behavior problems; Child discipline; Coercion; Compliance; Learned helplessness; Parent child relations; Passiveness; Personality traits; Power; Social behavior; Submission; Superior subordinate relationship.

Obesity. Obes(e,ity,eness). Hyperobes(e, ity,eness). Fat(ness). Weight gain. Gain(ed,ing) weight. Excess weight. Superobes(e,ity,eness). Fleshy. Corpulen(t,ce). Adipos(is,ity). Polysarcia. Excessive body fat. Overweight. *See also* Body weight; Diet; Eating disorders; Hyperphagia; Junk food; Nutrition; Psychophysiologic disorders.

Obituaries. Obituar(y,ies). Obit(s). Death notice(s). Memorial biograph(y,ies). Necrolog(y,ies). *Consider also:* eulog(y,ies,istic). *See also* Death; Death rituals; Epigraphs; Epitaphs; Funeral rites; Newspapers.

Object permanence. Object permanence. Object constancy. *Consider also:* object relatedness. *See also* Cognitive processes; Concept formation; Developmental stages.

Object relations. Object relations. *Choose from:* object *with:* love, libido, internaliz(ed,ation), cathexis. *Consider also:* symbiotic relation(s,ship,ships). *See also* Anaclitic depression; Attachment behavior; Child development; Emotional development; Individuation; Psychoanalytic theory; Psychosocial development; Transitional objects.

Objectives. Objective(s). Aim(s). Destination(s). Goal(s). Purpose(s). *Consider also:* target(s), ambition(s), mark(s), meet(ing) quota(s). *See also* Educational objectives; Goals; Institu-tional mission; Organizational objectives.

Objectives, educational. See *Educational objectives.*

Objectives, instructional. See *Educational objectives.*

Objectives, organizational. See *Organizational objectives.*

Objectivity. Objectiv(e,ely,ity). Fair(ness). Impartial(ity). Unbiased. Dispassion(ate). Disinterested. Detach(ed,ment). Nonsubjective. Equitab(le,ility). Evenhanded(ness). Impartial(ity). Neutral(ity). Value neutral(ity). Value free. Open minded. Unprejudiced. *Choose from:* objective *with:* measure(s), judgment(s), criteria, description(s), method(s), test(s,ing), science. *Consider also:* balance(d), nonpartisan, reasonab(le,ility). *See also* Bias; Biased sampling; Cultural relativism; Dogmatism; Empirical methods; Equitability; Falsification (scientific); Impartiality; Impersonal; Indifferentism (religion); Media portrayal; News coverage; Norms; Personality traits; Rational choices; Rationality; Relativism; Research ethics; Research methods; Researcher bias; Response bias; Scholarship; Scientific method; Scientific misconduct; Statistical bias; Subjectivity; Test validity; Truth; Uncertainty; Value neutral; Values.

Objectors, conscientious. See *Conscientious objectors.*

Objects, art. See *Art objects.*

Objects, ceremonial. See *Ceremonial objects.*

Objects, inanimate. See *Inanimate objects.*

Objects, miniature. See *Miniature objects.*

Objects, religious. See *Religious articles.*

Objects, ritual. See *Ceremonial objects.*

Objects, transitional. See *Transitional objects.*

Obligation, moral. See *Moral obligation.*

Obligation, political. See *Political obligation.*

Obligation, social. See *Social ethics.*

Obligations. Obligation(s). Obligat(e,ed, ory). Obliged. Dut(y,ies). Responsibilit(y,ies). Assignment(s). Commission(s). Chore(s). Task(s). *Consider also:* pledged, committed, compelled, constrained, require(d, ments), mandat(ed,ory), compulsory. *See also* Commitment (emotional); Con-science; Duties; Examination of conscience; Fiduciary responsibility; Morality; Moral obligation; Responsibility (answerability); Rights; Supererogation.

Obscenity. Obscen(e,ity). Profan(e,ity). Blasphem(y,ous). Swear(ing). Dirty word(s). Four letter word(s). Taboo word(s). Indecen(t,cy). Smut. Bawd(y, iness). Lewd(ness). Lascivious(ness). Wanton(ness). Vulgar(ity,ities). Improp(er,riety,rieties). Objectionable content(s). Pornograph(ic,y). Indelica(cy,te). Suggestive remark(s). Licentious(ness). Double entendre(s). Erotolalia. Fecal speech. Coprola(lia, phasia). Cacolalia. Koprolalia. Coprophemia. Koprophemia. Scatolog(y,ia). *See also* Adult entertainment; Antisocial behavior; Bawdy songs; Blasphemy; Cybersex; Epithets; Erotic songs; Indecent communications; Invective; Language usage; Malinformation; Morality; Pornography; Prurience; Scatology; Verbal abuse; Vulgarity.

Observation. Observation(al,s). Examin(e, ed,ing,ation,ations). Inspect(ed,ing, ion,ions). Surveillance. Monitor(ed,ing). Notic(e,ed,ing). Recogniz(e,ed,ing). View(ed,ing). Oversee(ing). Scrutin(y, ize,ized,izing). Witness(ed,ing). Eyewitness(es). Watch(ing). Field research. Fieldwork. *See also* Data collection; Empiricism; Evaluation; Experiments; Fieldwork; Interrater reliability; Measurement; Observation methods; Observational learning; Observers; Participant observation; Research methods; Self monitoring.

Observation methods. Observation(al,s) method(s). *Choose from:* observation(al, s), monitor(ed,ing), examin(e,ed,ing, ation), inspect(ed,ing,ion), surveillance, field research, fieldwork, participant observation *with:* method(s), technique(s), procedure(s), measure(s), criteria. *See also* Interrater reliability; Observation; Participant observation; Research methods; Self monitoring.

Observation, participant. See *Participant observation.*

Observational learning. Observational learning. Modeling. *Choose from:* imitat(ive,ion), observ(e,ed,ing,ation, ational), demonstration(s) *with:* learn(ed,ing,er,ers), acquisition, training, memory. *See also* Discovery learning; Identification (psychology); Imitation; Incidental learning; Intentional learning; Observation; Role models.

Observers. Observer(s). Viewer(s). Eyewitness(es). Bystander(s). Witness(es). Interobserver. *Consider also:* observ(ed,ation,ational), surveillance, rater(s), coder(s), informant(s), monitor(s,ing), viewer(s), participant observ(er,ers,ation,ations), spectator(s), onlooker(s), auditor(s), lookout, watcher(s), audience(s), sightseer(s), beholder(s), commentator(s). *See also* Audiences; Commentators; Gaze; Observation.

Obsessions. Obsession(s,al). Obsess(ed, ing). Ruminat(e,ed,ing,ion,ions). Ruminative thinking. Preoccup(y,ying, ied,ation,ations). Brooding. Persistent doubt(s). *See also* Compulsive behavior; Compulsive disorders; Obsessive behavior; Obsessive compulsive personality; Obsessive love.

Obsessive behavior. Obsessive behavior. Ritualistic behavior. *Consider also:* compulsiv(ity,iveness), re-checking, ritual(s), recurrent compulsion(s), repetition compulsion, repetitive act(s), handwashing, ceremonial(s), counting, ablutoman(ia,ic), arithmal mania, arithmoman(ia,ic). *See also* Compulsive behavior; Obsessions; Obsessive compulsive personality.

Obsessive compulsive personality. Obsessive compulsive personality. Anancas(tia,tic,m). Anankas(tia,tic,m). *Choose from:* compuls(ive,ion,ions), overinhibited, overconscientious, rigid(ity), obssess(ive,ion,ions) *with:* personalit(y,ies), neuros(is,es), character(s), disorder(s). *Consider also:* perfectionis(m,t,ts), brooding compulsion(s), obsessional brooding. *See also* Compulsive behavior; Compulsive disorders; Obsessions; Obsessive behavior; Personality disorders.

Obsessive love. Obsessive Love. Limerence. *Consider also:* obsessional jealousy, unreciprocated love, stalk(ed,ing,er,ers). *See also* Erotomania; Obsessions; Stalking.

Obsolescence. Obsolescen(ce,t). Obsolete. Outdated. Outmoded. Passe. Archaic. Antiquated. Out of date. Superannuated. Old fashioned. Antique. Anachronis(m, ms,tic). Out of print. *Consider also:* discontinued. *See also* Anachronisms; Automation; Defunct; Maintenance; Preservation; Product life cycle; Skills obsolescence; Technological progress; Time.

Obsolescence, language. See *Language obsolescence.*

Obsolescence, skills. See *Skills obsolescence.*

Obstacles. See *Barriers.*

Obstruction of justice. Obstruction of justice. *Choose from:* obstruct(ed,ing, ion), imped(e,ed,ing,ance), hinder(ed, ing) *with:* justice, lawful process(es), court order(s), court proceeding(s). *Consider also:* influenc(e,ed,ing) juror(s). *See also* Contempt of Court; Due process; Judicial corruption; Legal procedures; Withholding evidence; Witness tampering.

Occam's razor. Occam(s) razor. Principle of economy. Law of parsimony. Economy principle. *See also* Principles.

Occasional verse. Occasional verse(s). *Choose from:* occasional, commemorative, inaugura(l,ation,ations), birthday(s), funeral(s), public *with:* verse(s), poem(s), poetry, sonnet(s), ode(s), epigram(s). *See also* Commemoration; Epithalamia; Laudatory poetry; Poetry

Occidental civilization. See *Western civilization.*

Occultism. Occult(ism). Astral projection(s). Astral travel. Astrolog(y,ic). Amulet(s). Black magic. Apparition(s). Cabal(a,ism). Chakra(s). Cosmolog(y, ical). Clairvoyan(t,ce). Deathbed vision(s). Demon(ic,ology). Demon possession. Devil(s). Divination. Divining rod(s). Dowsing. Dracula cult. Duende(s). Dybbuk(s). Earth ray(s). ESP. Extrasensory perception. Extrasensible. Exorcis(m,t). Fortune telling. Firewalking. Flying saucer(s). Ghost(s). Hobgoblin(s). Haunted house(s). Haunting. Horoscop(e,y). Human aura(s). Hex(es). Jinx(es). Incantation(s). Kirlian photography. Levitation(s). Magic(al). Medium(s). Mental healing. Mystic(al,ism,s). Near death experience(s). Necromancy. Out of body. Obe. Obeah. Orgone energy. PSI. Palm reading. Parapsycholog(y,ical). Paranormal. Pseudoscientific. Parapsychosomatics. Phantom(s). Possession trance(s). Precognition. Psychic(al,s). Psychic healing. Psychokine(sis,tic). Psychophotography. Poltergeist(s). Radiesthesia. Reincarnation. Seance(s). Seer(s). Shamanis(m, tic). Spirit possession. Spiritualis(m,tic). Supernatural(ism). Survival after death. Telekine(sis,tic). Telepath(y,ic). Thaumaturgy. Voodoo. Werewol(f,ves). Witchcraft. *See also* Alchemy; Astrology; Beliefs; Conjuring; Cults; Divination; Magic; Mysticism; Parapsychology; Spiritualism; Superstitions; Voodooism; Witchcraft.

Occupancy. Occupan(t,ts,cy). Occup(y,ied). Possess(ed,ing,ion). Tak(e,en,ing) possession. Ownership. *Consider also:* tenan(t,ts,cy), residen(cy,ce), resid(e,ed, ing), dwell(s,ed,ing), inhabit(ed,ing, ancy). *See also* Acquisition of territory; Dwellings; Eviction; Housing; Inhabitants; Squatters.

Occupancy, bed. See *Bed occupancy.*

Occupation. See *Blue collar workers; Careers; Nonprofessional personnel; Occupations; Professional personnel; Vocations.*

Occupation, parental. See *Parental occupation.*

Occupational accidents. See *Industrial accidents.*

Occupational achievement. See *Occupational success.*

Occupational adjustment. Occupational adjustment. *Choose from:* career(s), work, occupation(s,al), vocation(s,al), job(s), profession(s,al), employ(ee,ees, ment), work(ing) life *with:* adapt(ed,ing, ation,ations), adjust(ed,ing,ment,ments), cop(e,ed,ing), orientation. *Consider also:* occupational deviance, job satisfaction, employee turnover, occupational behavior, job changer(s), job performance problem(s), first job(s), job relocation, occupational congruence, occupational socialization, occupational readjustment. *See also* Adjustment (to environment); Career change; Job satisfaction; Occupational neuroses; Occupations; Quality of working life.

Occupational aspirations. Occupational aspiration(s). *Choose from:* occupation(s,al), prevocational, vocation(s,al), profession(s,al), career *with:* aspiration(s), goal(s), motivation(s), plan(s), choice(s), orientation, decision(s), objective(s), goal(s), ambition(s), expectation(s). *Consider also:* socioeconomic aspiration(s). *See also* Aspirations; Attitudes toward work; Career change; Career development; Career goals; Career ladders; Career mobility; Careers; Mentors; Nontraditional careers; Occupational choice; Occupational interests; Occupational qualifications; Occupations; Professional development; Promotion (occupational); Vocational maturity; Work values.

Occupational attainment. See *Occupational status; Occupational success.*

Occupational attitudes. Occupational attitude(s). *Choose from:* career, job, occupation(s,al), vocation(s,al), work, profession(s,al), *with:* perception(s), attitude(s), preference(s), commitment(s), rating(s), stereotype(s), expectation(s). *See also* Attitudes toward work; Vocational maturity; Work values.

Occupational choice. Occupational choice. Career choice. Calling. *Choose from:* job(s), vocation(s,al), occupation(s,al), profession(s,al), career(s), work *with:* choice(s), choos(e,ing), chosen, preference(s), objective(s), plan(s,ned, ning), select(ed,ing,ion), decision(s), commitment(s), preference(s). *Consider also:* life choice(s). *See also* Career change; Career development; Career education; Career goals; Decision making; Employment opportunities; Interest inventories; Job applicants; Nontraditional careers; Occupational aspirations; Occupational interests; Occupations; Vocational guidance; Vocational maturity; Work reentry.

Occupational classification. Occupational classification. *Choose from:* work, occupation(s,al), job(s), profession(al,s), employment, vocation(s,al), career(s) *with:* classif(y,ied,ication,ications), rank(s,ing,ings), categor(y,ies,ized, ization,izations), taxonom(y,ies), group(s,ed,ing,ings), typolog(y,ies), grad(es,ed,ing), index(es). *See also* Blue collar workers; Classification; Job descriptions; Job requirements; Labor force; Occupational qualifications; Occupational segregation; Occupational structure; Occupations; Professional personnel; White collar workers; Work skills.

Occupational counseling. See *Employment counseling.*

Occupational diseases. Occupational disease(s). *Choose from:* occupational, vocational, workplace, industrial, job-related, worker(s), employee(s), on-the-job *with:* disease(s), neuros(is,es), carcinogen(s,esis), dust induced bronchitis, asthma, cancer(s), hearing impairment(s), health, sclerosis, respiratory tract infection(s), expos(ed, ure), poison(s,ing), lung infection(s), tuberculosis, dermatitis, burnout, burn(ed,t) out, stress, ulcer(s). *Consider also:* farmer(s) lung, silo filler(s) disease, bird fancier(s) lung, inert gas narcosis, pneumoconiosis, bagassosis, berylliosis, byssinosis, Caplan(s) syndrome, siderosis, anthracosilicosis, silicotuberculosis, mushroom worker(s) lung, brown lung disease, black lung disease, asbestosis, hazardous occupation(s), chronic painter(s) syndrome. *See also* Absenteeism; Agricultural workers disease; Cancer; Carcinogens; Corporate social responsibility; Hazardous occupations; Industrial accidents; Industrial fatigue; Lead poisoning; Noise levels (work areas); Occupational exposure; Occupational neuroses; Occupational safety; Occupational stress; Overwork; Quality of working life; Repetitive motion disorders; Sanitation; Sick building syndrome; Workers; Working conditions; Workplaces.

Occupational exposure. Occupational exposure. Sick building syndrome. Chronic painter(s) syndrome. *Choose from:* occupation(s,al,ally), job(s), industrial, worker(s), employee(s), work, workplace(s), worksite(s), workstation(s), office(s), working conditions, factor(y,ies), compan(y,ies), labor, operator(s), VDT(s), CRT(s) *with:* glare, noise, dust, fume(s), vapor(s), health

effects, expos(ed,ure), risk(s), toxic(ity), neurotoxic(ity), radiation, poison(ed,ing, s), contaminat(e,ed,ing,ion), hazard(s), reproductive hazard(s), solvent(s), chemical(s), paint(s), pesticide(s), herbicide(s), heavy metal(s), lead, mercury, carbon monoxide, hydrocarbon(s), PCBs, carcinogen(s), asbestos, toluene. *Consider also:* occupational disease(s). *See also* Agricultural workers disease; Air pollution; Carcinogens; Corporate social responsibility; Environmental pollutants; Environmental pollution; Hazardous occupations; Hazards of video display terminals; Herbicides; Industrial accidents; Industrial wastes; Medical wastes; Mine accidents; Multiple chemical sensitivities; Noise levels (work areas); Nuclear accidents; Nuclear safety; Nuclear waste; Occupational diseases; Occupational safety; Pesticides; Quality of working life; Safety; Sick building syndrome; Tobacco smoke pollution; Water pollution; Working conditions.

Occupational folklore. Occupational folklore. Occupational lore. Work-song(s). Work song(s). *Choose from:* occupation(s,al), work(place,places), union(s,ism), miner(s), farm worker(s), factor(y,ies), farmer(s) *with:* myth(s), folklore, lore, song(s), culture, art, stereotyp(e,es,ing), belief(s), folklife. *See also* Folklore; Organizational culture; Public folklore.

Occupational guidance. See *Vocational guidance.*

Occupational hazards. See *Agricultural workers disease; Black lung disease; Hazardous materials; Hazards of video display terminals; Industrial accidents; Multiple chemical sensitivities; Occupational diseases; Occupational exposure; Occupational neuroses; Occupational safety; Occupational stress; Repetitive motion disorders; Sick building syndrome.*

Occupational health services. Occupational health services. *Choose from:* occupation(s,al,ally), job(s), industrial, worker(s), employee(s), work, workplace(s), worksite(s), workstation(s), office(s), work(ing) condition(s), factor(y,ies), compan(y,ies) *with:* health, wellness, fitness, exercise, nutrition *with:* service(s), promot(e,ed,ing,ion), screening, program(s), education, clinic(s). *Choose from:* industrial, corporate, compan(y,ies) *with:* medicine, physician(s), medical director(s), doctor(s), nurs(e,es,ing). *See also* Corporate social responsibility; Employee assistance programs; Health services.

Occupational injuries. See *Agricultural workers disease; Black lung disease; Hazardous materials; Hazards of video*

display terminals; Industrial accidents; Injuries; Multiple chemical sensitivities; Occupational diseases; Occupational exposure; Occupational neuroses; Occupational safety; Occupational stress; Repetitive motion disorders; Sick building syndrome.

Occupational interests. Occupational interest(s). *Choose from:* occupational, vocational, professional, career, job, work *with:* interest(s), preference(s), attitude(s), decision making, exploration, information seeking, aspiration(s). *See also* Career development; Interests; Occupational aspirations; Occupational choice; Occupations; Vocational education; Vocational guidance; Vocational maturity.

Occupational mobility. See *Career mobility.*

Occupational neuroses. Occupational neuros(is,es). *Choose from:* occupation(s,al), job-related, work-related, vocation(s,al), profession(s,al) *with:* neurotic(s,ism), neurotic disorder(s), psychoneuros(is,es), emotional disorder(s), emotional(ly) disturb(ed,ances), depress(ed,ion,ions), phobia(s), nervous(ness), anxiet(y,ies), fear(s,ful), emotional distress. *See also* Hazardous occupations; Neuroses; Occupational adjustment; Occupational diseases; Occupational stress; Quality of working life.

Occupational preference. See *Occupational choice.*

Occupational promotion. See *Promotion (occupational).*

Occupational qualifications. Occupational qualification(s). *Choose from:* job, vocation(al), occupation(s,al), profession(s,al), career(s), work, employment, labor market *with:* qualif(y,ied), qualification(s), credential(s), skill(s), background, experience, education, over-educat(ed,ion), underqualif(y,ied, ications), overqualif(y,ied), overqualification(s), certification, licens(e,es,ed, ing,ure), requirement(s), congruence. *Consider also:* worker job match, employability, employer employee match. *See also* Academic degrees; Certification; Employability; Employment opportunities; Experience (background); Expertise; Job applicant screening; Job descriptions; Job requirements; Occupational aspirations; Occupational classification; Occupational status; Occupations; Qualifications; Unemployment; Vocational education; Work experience; Work skills.

Occupational roles. Occupational role(s). *Choose from:* career(s), occupation(s,al), vocation(s,al), profession(s,al), job(s), work, employ(ment,ee,ees) *with:* role(s), position(s), expected behavior(s), function(s), status, identit(y,ies), purpose(s), profile(s), dut(y,ies), image(s), stereotype(s), socialization. *See also* Employment; Job descriptions; Job requirements; Job satisfaction; Nontraditional careers; Occupational status; Occupations; Quality of working life; Role ambiguity; Role models; Roles; Sexual division of labor; Tasks; Workers; Working women.

Occupational safety. Occupational safety. *Choose from:* occupation(s,al,ally), job(s), industrial, worker(s), employee(s), work, workplace(s), worksite(s), workstation(s), office(s), working conditions, factor(y,ies), compan(y,ies), labor, operator(s), VDT(s), CRT(s) *with:* safe(ty), hazard(s,ous), health effect(s), expos(ed,ure), risk(s), toxic(ity), accident(s,al), danger(s,ous), mortalit(y, ies), fatalit(y,ies), neurotoxic(ity), radiation, poison(ed,ing,s), contaminat(e,ed,ing,ion). *Consider also:* specific occupations such as miners or police officers *with:* specific hazards or safe practices. *See also* Agricultural workers disease; Black lung disease; Corporate social responsibility; Hazards; Hazardous occupations; Hazards of video display terminals; Hazardous materials; Health; Industrial accidents; Mine accidents; Multiple chemical sensitivities; Nuclear accidents; Nuclear safety; Occupational diseases; Occupational exposure; Occupational health services; Occupational neuroses; Occupational stress; Public health; Quality of working life; Repetitive motion disorders; Safety; Sanitation; Sick building syndrome; Working conditions; Workplaces.

Occupational satisfaction. See *Job satisfaction.*

Occupational segregation. Occupational segregation. Sexual division of labor. Dual labor market(s). Internal labor market(s). Split labor market(s). Primary labor market(s). Secondary labor market(s). Tertiary labor market(s). Underclass. Glass ceiling(s). Sticky floor(s). *Choose from:* occupation(s,al), labor market(s), labor force, job market(s), workplace, earnings *with:* segregat(e,ed,ing,ation), segment(ed, ation), stratif(ied,ication), ghettoization, feminiz(ed,ation), racial division(s), Black White differen(ces,tials), marginalized, inequalit(y,ies), male female differen(ces,tials), sex(ual) differen(ces,tials), gender differen(ces, tials), rac(e,ial) differen(ces,tials), ethnic differen(ces,tials), gender specific, women(s) role(s), woman(s) role(s). *See also* Comparable worth; Dual economy; Employment discrimination; Equal job opportunities; Female intensive occupations; Job requirements; Labor economics; Labor market segmentation;

Male intensive occupations; Nontraditional careers; Sex roles; Sexism; Sexual division of labor; Sexual oppression; Tipping; Wage differentials.

Occupational status. Occupational status. *Choose from:* occupation(s,al), profession(s,al), career(s), employment, position(s), vocation(s,al), job(s) *with:* status, prestig(e,ious), menial(ity), marginal(ity), ranking(s), grade level(s), categor(y,ies), hierarchical position, earnings, attainment(s), achievement(s), social perception(s). *See also* Career mobility; Careers; Occupational qualifications; Occupational success; Occupational roles; Occupational tenure; Occupations; Prestige; Privilege; Professional image; Professional personnel; Promotion (occupational); Status; Status attainment; Work experience; Work skills; Working women.

Occupational stress. Occupational stress(es). Professional stress syndrome. *Choose from:* occupation(s,al), job(s), work(er,ers), organization(s,al), role(s), executive(s), manager(s), profession(s, al), employee(s), employment, career(s), teacher(s), nurse(s), social worker(s), child care worker(s), labor conditions, vocation(s,al) *with:* mental fatigue, exhaust(ed,ion), stress(es,ful,fulness), role conflict(s), mental health, mental load, work demands, burned out, burnt out, burnout, psychogenic illness(es), strain(s). *See also* Burnout; Coping; Employee morale; Employee turnover; Family work relationship; Industrial fatigue; Job descriptions; Morale; Occupational diseases; Occupational neuroses; Occupational safety; Overwork; Psychological stress; Quality of working life; Sick building syndrome; Working conditions.

Occupational structure. Occupational structure. *Choose from:* career, managerial, occupation(al), vocation(al), profession(al), job, work, industry, firm, company, corporate *with:* structur(e,es, al), stratification, distribution of positions, pyramid(s), hierarch(y,ies), division of labor, ladder(s), hiring pattern(s). *Consider also:* occupational labor market(s), internal labor market(s), occupational prestige. *See also* Employment; Industrialization; Labor market segmentation; Occupational classification; Occupational segregation; Occupational status; Occupations; Stratification; Tasks; Work; Workers.

Occupational success. Occupational success. Upward mobility. *Choose from:* career, managerial, calling, occupation(al), vocation(al), profession(al), job, work, business, trade *with:* success(es, ful,fully), succeed(ed,ing), advanc(e,ed, ing,ement), achiev(e,ed,ing,ement), promotion(s), attainment(s),

accomplishment(s), fulfillment, maturity. *See also* Achievement; Career mobility; Career patterns; Careers; Employment history; Job performance; Life plans; Occupational status; Occupations; Promotion (occupational).

Occupational tenure. Occupational tenure. Permanent appointment. Permanent status. *Choose from:* occupational, position, teacher, job, employment *with:* tenure(d), length, years, permanence, duration, long term, longevity, seniority, reenlistment, retention. *See also* Academic tenure; Career mobility; Employee turnover; Employment history; Job security; Occupational status; Occupations; Personnel termination; Tenure of office.

Occupational tests. Occupational test(s). *Choose from:* occupational, employment, personnel, vocational, job, career, promotion(al), employee selection, clerical, civil service, federal service, pre-employment *with:* test(s,ing), exam(s,ination,inations), measure(s, ment), assessment(s), evaluation(s), questionnaire(s), score(s). *Consider also:* aptitude(s), skill(s) *with:* test(s), measure(s,ment). *See also* Aptitude tests; Interest inventories; Job applicant screening; Job requirements; Occupational interests; Occupational qualifications; Prediction; Vocational guidance; Work skills.

Occupational therapy. Occupational therapy. Work therapy. Ergotherapy. *Consider also:* horticultural, craft(s), diversion(s,al), work, industrial, occupational training, cultural, movement, gardening, art(s), dance, creative activit(y,ies) *with:* therap(y,ies,eutic), rehabilitat(ive,ion). *See also* Physical therapy; Psychotherapy; Rehabilitation; Recreation therapy; Therapeutic camps.

Occupational training. See *Vocational education.*

Occupations. Occupation(s,al). Career(s). Employment. Job(s). Vocation(s). Work. Calling. Livelihood. Work(er) role(s). Profession(al,s). Trade(s). Business(es). Work activit(y,ies). *Consider also:* occupational status, vocational interest(s), work history, self employ(ed,ment). *Consider specific occupations or groups of occupations such as:* architect(s), artist(s), automotive worker(s), aviation personnel, beautician(s), bricklayer(s), carpenter(s), civil service employee(s), clergy, clerical personnel, construction worker(s), craftsmen, diver(s), driver(s), electrician(s), engineer(s), farm worker(s), firefighter(s), government employee(s), health personnel, laborer(s), lawyer(s), librarian(s), management personnel, mason(s), military personnel, miner(s), musician(s), nurse(s), plumber(s), police, professional athlete(s), professional personnel, physician(s), railroad worker(s), sales personnel, scientist(s), seamstress(es), secretar(y,ies), service worker(s), skilled worker(s), social worker(s), teacher(s), technical personnel, white collar worker(s), writer(s). *See also* Allied health personnel; Blue collar workers; Career change; Career development; Career education; Careers; Division of labor; Employment history; Employment opportunities; Entrepreneurship; Female intensive occupations; Gold collar workers; Health occupations; Human resources; Industrial psychology; Job descriptions; Labor market; Male intensive occupations; Nonprofessional personnel; Nontraditional careers; Occupational adjustment; Occupational aspirations; Occupational choice; Occupational classification; Occupational interests; Occupational safety; Occupational stress; Occupational structure; Occupational tenure; Professional personnel; Quality of working life; Sales personnel; Sexual division of labor; Traveling sales personnel; Vocational guidance; Vocations; Working conditions; Working women.

Occupations, female dominated. See *Female intensive occupations.*

Occupations, female intensive. See *Female intensive occupations.*

Occupations, feminized. See *Female intensive occupations.*

Occupations, hazardous. See *Hazardous occupations.*

Occupations, health. See *Health occupations.*

Occupations, health care. See *Health occupations.*

Occupations, male dominated. See *Male intensive occupations.*

Occupations, male intensive. See *Male intensive occupations.*

Occupations, men in female dominated. See *Nontraditional careers.*

Occupations, women in male dominated. See *Nontraditional careers.*

Occurrences. See *Rates.*

Ocean dumping. See *Water pollution.*

Oceania. Oceania(n). Oceanica(n). Melanesia(n). (Federated States of) Micronesia(n). Polynesia(n). Fiji(an). Vanuatu(an) [New Hebrides]. Pitcairn Island. (Republic of) Nauru [Pleasant Island]. Solomon Islands. Tonga(n) [Friendly Islands]. Tuvalu(an) [Ellice Islands]. Western Samoa(n). Papua New Guinea(n). (Republic of) Palau. Marshall(ese) Islands [Trust Territory of the Pacific Islands]. *Consider also:*

Australasia(n), Australia(n), New Zealand, Guam(anian), New Caledonia(n), Mariana Islands, Northern Marianas, Caroline Islands, Hawaii(an) [Sandwich Islands], Austronesia(n), Tuamoto Archipelago, Cook Islands, Niue. *See also* Asian empires; Indonesian cultural groups; Malayo-Polynesian languages.; Oceanic cultural groups; Pacific region; Philippine Islands cultural groups; South Asia; Southeast Asia.

Oceanic cultural groups. Oceanic cultural group(s). Pacific Islander(s). *Choose from:* Oceanic, Australia(n), Australasian, New Guinea(n), Melanesia(n), Micronesia(n), Polynesia(n) *with:* indigenous, native, *with:* population(s), people(s), group(s), populace, tribe(s), resident(s), inhabitant(s). *Consider groups by name, for example:* Abelam, Ambulas, Ambae, Anuta, Aranda, Asmat, Banaro, Bau, Belau, Bikini, Boazi, Chambri, Chamorros, Chimbu, Choiseul Island, Cook Islands, Dani, Daribi, Dieri, Dobu, Easter Island, Eipo, Foi, Fore, Futuna, Gahuku-Gama, Gainj, Garia, Gebusi, Gnau, Gogodala, Goodenough Island, Guadalcanal, Gururumba, Hawaiians, Iatmul, Kaluli, Kamilaroi, Kapauku, Kapingamarangi, Karadjeri, Kariera, Keraki, Kewa, Kilenge, Kiribati, Kiwai, Koiari, Kosrae, Kurtatchi, Kwoma, Lak, Lakalai, Lau, Lesu, Loyalty Islands, Mae, Enga, Mafulu, Mailu, Maisin, Malaita, Malekula, Manam, Mandak, Mangareva, Manihiki, Manus, Maori, Mardudjara, Marind-anim, Maring, Marquesas Islands, Marshall Islands, Mejbrat, Mekeo, Melpa, Mendi, Mimika, Miyanim, Motu, Mountain Arapesh, Mundugumor, Murik, Murngin, Muyu, Namau, Nasioi, Nauru, New Georgia, Ngatatjara, Nguna, Ningerum, Nissan, Niue, Nomoi, Ontong Java, Orokaiva, Orokolo, Pentecost, Pintupi, Pohnpei, Pukapuka, Rapa, Raroia, Rennell Island, Rossel Island, Rotuma, Sambia, Samoa, San Cristobal, Santa Cruz, Selepet, Sengseng, Siane, Sio, Siwai, Tahiti, Tairora, Tangu, Tanna, Tasmanians, Tauade, Telefolmin, Tikopia, Tiwi, Tokelau, Tolai, Tonga, Tongareva, Tor, Torres Strait Islanders, Trobriand Islands, Truk, Tuvalu, Ulithi, Usino, Uvea, Wamira, Wantoat, Wape, Warlpiri, Waropen, Wik Mungkan, Wogeo, Woleai, Wongaibon, Wovan, Yangoru Boiken, Yap, Yir Yoront, Yungar. *See also* Aborigines; Cultural groups; Culture (anthropology); Culture change; Hunting and gathering societies; Indigenous populations; Oceania; Traditional societies.

Oceans. Ocean(ic,ography,s). Sea(s). High seas. Pacific Ocean. Atlantic Ocean. Indian Ocean. Arctic Ocean. Antarctic

Ocean. *Consider also:* Caribbean Sea, Mediterranean Ocean, Tyrrhenian Sea, Ligurian Sea, Caspian Sea, Black Sea, Dead Sea, Gulf of Mexico, Baltic Sea, Gulf of Bothnia, North Sea, Adriatic Sea, Ionian Sea, Persian Gulf, Red Sea, Arabian Sea, Gulf of Aden, Gulf of Guinea, Bay of Bengal, Andaman Sea, Yellow Sea, Sea of Japan, Sea of Okhotsk, South China Sea, Gulf of Carpentaria, Timor Sea, Tasman Sea, Great Australian Bight, Coral Sea. *See also* Earth; Fishing; Marine ecology; Natural resources; Offshore oil; Shipping industry; Territorial waters; Tides.

Octogenarians. See *Aged 80 and over.*

Ocular accommodation. Ocular accommodation. *Choose from:* ocular, visual, lens, eye(s) *with:* focus(ed,ing), accommodat(ed,ing,ion). *See also* Depth perception; Reflex.

Odes. See *Lyric poetry; Poetry.*

Odor discrimination. Odor discrimination. *Choose from:* odor(s,ant,ants), olfactory, scent(s), chemosensory *with:* discriminat(e,ed,ing,ion), match(ed,ing), detect(ed,ing,ion), perception, recogniz(e,ed,ing), recognition, differentiat(e,ed,ing,ion), classif(y,ied, ication), assess(ed,ing,ment), threshold(s), sensitiv(e,ity, preference(s), responsive(ness), stimulat(e,ed,ing,ion), recognition, recogniz(e,ed,ing). *Consider also:* olfaction, olfactory receptor(s), smell, sense of smell, nasal chemosensitiv(e,ity). *See also* Odors; Perceptual discrimination; Taste perception.

Odors. Odor(s,ant,ants). Scent(s,ed). Aroma(s,tic). Smell(s). Fragran(t,ce,ces). Perfume(s,d). Redolen(t,ce). *Consider also:* olfactory *with:* stimulation, cue(s), stimul(i,us), threshold(s). *See also* Odor discrimination.

Oedipus complex. Oedip(al,us) complex. *Choose from:* oedip(al,us) *with:* complex(es), phase(s), period(s), fantas(y,ies), influence(s), resolution, fixation(s), theme(s), myth(s). *Consider also:* mother complex(es), father conflict(s), Little Nell complex(es), electra complex(es), dyadic phallic development problem(s). *See also* Child development; Incest; Mother child relations; Psychoanalytic interpretation; Sexual deviations.

Offenders. Offender(s). Criminal(s). Convict(s). Criminal class(es). Outlaw(s). Gangster(s). Grifter(s). Gun(men,man). Hacker(s). Mobster(s). Scofflaw(s). Smuggler(s). Underworld. Violator(s). Culprit(s). Perpetrator(s). Felon(s). Batterer(s). Racketeer(s). Abuser(s). Abductor(s). Kidnapper(s). Rapist(s). Murderer(s). Killer(s). Pickpocket(s). Shoplifter(s). Thie(f,ves).

Ex-offender(s). Drug kingpin(s). Drug lord(s). Crime suspect(s). Probationer(s). Embezzler(s). Burglar(s). Delinquent(s). Criminally insane. Prison inmate(s). *Consider also:* crime suspect(s), ex-offender(s), parolee(s). *See also* Alternatives to incarceration; Arrests; Bandits; Career criminals; Computer hackers; Crime; Criminal investigations; Criminal justice; Defendants; Delinquents; Deterrence; Deviant behavior; Elderly offenders; Female offenders; Imprisonment; Insanity defense; Juvenile delinquency; Juvenile gangs; Male offenders; Mentally ill offenders; Offenses; Parole; Perpetrators; Preventive detention; Prisoners; Recidivism; Restitution; Rogues; Serial murderers; Sentencing; Sex offenders; Thugs; Victimization.

Offenders, elderly. See *Elderly offenders.*

Offenders, female. See *Female offenders.*

Offenders, juvenile. See *Juvenile delinquency.*

Offenders, male. See *Male offenders.*

Offenders, mentally ill. See *Mentally ill offenders.*

Offenders, sex. See *Sex offenders.*

Offenses. Offense(s). Misdemeanor(s). Crime(s). Wrongdoing(s). Malfeasance. Misconduct. Infraction(s). Misdeed(s). Sin(s). Felon(y,ies). Illegalit(y,ies). *Choose from:* criminal, illegal, punishable, indictable *with:* act(s), behavior, inciden(t,ts,ce). *Consider also:* banditry, blackmail, illegal gambling, littering. *See also* Antisocial behavior; Arson; Arrests; Assassination; Assault (personal); Bribery; Burglary; Cheating; Child abuse; Computer crimes; Conflict of interest; Corruption in government; Crime; Crime prevention; Crime rates; Criminal abortion; Criminal intent; Drug addiction; Drug trafficking; Drugs in athletics; Drunk driving; Embezzlement; Falsification (scientific); Fraud; Hate crimes; Homicide; Indictments; Industrial espionage; Infanticide; Kickbacks; Kidnapping; Larceny; Law enforcement; Money laundering; Offenders; Organized crime; Penal codes; Perpetrators; Political crimes; Price fixing; Product tampering; Property crimes; Prostitution; Quackery; Racketeering; Rape; Robbery; Scientific misconduct; Sex offenses; Sexual harassment; Shoplifting; Terrorism; Unreported crimes; Urban crime; Vandalism; Victimization; Victimless crimes; Violation; White collar crime.

Offenses, international. See *International offenses.*

Offenses, military. See *Military offenses.*

Offenses, morals. See *Victimless crimes.*

Offenses, naval. See *Naval offenses.*

Offenses, sex. See *Sex offenses.*

Offenses against persons. See *Abusive parents; Antisocial behavior; Acquaintance rape; Assault (personal); Atrocities; Battered women; Child abuse; Coercion; Concentration camps; Corporal punishment; Cruelty; Driveby crimes; Elder abuse; Emotional abuse; Ethnic cleansing; Family violence; Flagellants and flagellation; Forced labor; Genocide; Gynocide; Hate crimes; Holocaust; Homicide; Infanticide; Lynching; Marital rape; Massacres; Molested children; Police brutality; Rape; Sadism; Sexual abuse; Sexual exploitation; Sexual harassment; Sexual sadism; Sexual violence; Spouse abuse; Terrorism; Threat; Torture; Victimization; Violence; War crimes.*

Offenses against property. See *Property crimes.*

Offenses against public morality. See *Victimless crimes.*

Offenses against religion. Offense(s) against religion. Religious persecution. Faith based persecution. *Choose from:* church(es), mosque(s), synagogue(s), religious symbol(s), religious book(s), sacred, sacrament(s), cemeter(y,ies) *with:* burn(ed,ing,ings), destroy(ed), destruction, terror(ized), atrocit(y,ies), torment(ed,ing), victim(s,ize,ized,izing), violence, persecut(e,ed,ing,ion). *Consider also:* blasphemy, apostasy, sacrileg(e,ious,iously), simony. *See also* Apostasy; Blasphemy; Ethnic cleansing; Hate crimes; Heresy; Religious prejudice; Sacrilege.

Offensive behavior. See *Aggression; Air rage; Animal aggressive behavior; Antisocial behavior; Arguments; Assault (battle); Assault (personal); Attack (Military science); Belligerency; Disorderly conduct; Dominance; Driveby crimes; Hostility; Interpersonal conflict; Invasion; Juvenile delinquency; Militarism; Rape; Riots; Road rage; Terrorism; Threat; Threat postures; Violence; War.*

Offerings. See *Sacrificial rites.*

Offers, firm. See *Firm offers.*

Office, home. See *Home office.*

Office, misconduct in. See *Misconduct in office.*

Office, tenure of. See *Tenure of office.*

Office, term of. See *Tenure of office.*

Office automation. Office automation. *Choose from:* office(s), workplace(s), workstation(s) *with:* automat(ed,ing,ion), electronic, digital, paperless, word processor(s), PC(s), software, spreadsheet(s), web, internet, computer(s,ized,izing,ization). *Consider also:* document-management system(s), forms software, desktop publishing. *See also* Automated information storage; Automation; Clip art; Data processing; Desktop publishing; Electronic data processing; Electronic mail; Electronic publishing; Man machine systems.

Office buildings. Office building(s). City spire(s). Headquarters. Executive suite(s). *Choose from:* office, commercial *with:* space, tower(s), mall(s), center(s), complex(es), park(s). *See also* Buildings; Headquarters relocation; Home office; Place of business.

Office employees. See *Clerical workers; White collar workers.*

Office visits. Office visit(s). *Choose from:* office *with:* consultation(s), visit(s), call(s). *See also* Ambulatory care; Walk-in clinics.

Office workers. See *Clerical workers; White collar workers.*

Officers, army. See *Army personnel; Military officers.*

Officers, chief executive. See *Chief executive officers.*

Officers, military. See *Military officers.*

Officers, noncommissioned. See *Noncommissioned officers.*

Officers, parole. See *Parole officers.*

Officers, probation. See *Probation officers.*

Officers, public. See *Public officers.*

Official diplomacy. See *Diplomacy (official).*

Official languages. See *Language policy.*

Official secrets. See *Censorship; Classified information; Government secrecy; News policies.*

Officials (authority). See *Authority (officials).*

Officials, elected. See *Elected officials.*

Officials , government. See *Elected officials; Government personnel.*

Officials, public. See *Elected officials; Government personnel.*

Officials, recall of government. See *Recall of government officials.*

Officials, state. See *Elected officials; Government personnel.*

Officials and employees, county. See *Government personnel; Local government; Politicians.*

Officials and employees, local. See *Local officials and employees.*

Offshore factories (floating). Offshore factor(y,ies). *Choose from:* offshore, floating, ocean sited *with:* factor(y,ies), production. *See also* Contracting out; Factories; Offshore oil; Territorial waters.

Offshore oil. Offshore oil. *Choose from:* offshore or coastal *with:* oil(field(s), oil rig(s), installation(s), drill(ing), petroleum, gas, right(s), platform(s), leas(e,es,ing). *See also* Energy generating resources; Fuel; Marine resources; Oceans; Oil industry; Oil spills; Territorial waters.

Offshore production (foreign countries). Offshore produc(er,ers,tion). Maquiladora(s). Border industrialization. *Choose from:* maquila *with:* industr(y, ies), operation(s), manufacturing, plant(s). *Choose from:* maquila(dora, doras), offshore, U.S. Mexico border, overseas, Singapore *with:* produc(e,ed, ing,tion), industr(y,ies,ial), plant(s), subcontract(ed,ing,er,ers), assembl(y, ies), parts. *Consider also:* foreign subsidiar(y,ies), United States parent company, job migration. *See also* Border industries; Contracting out; Downsizing; Factories; Foreign labor; Labor economics; Labor market; Multinational corporations; Neocolonialism; Production; Subsidiary management; World economy.

Offshore radio broadcasting. See *Pirate radio broadcasting.*

Offspring. Offspring. *Consider also:* progen(y,iture), child(ren), son(s), daughter(s), descendant(s), begats, brood, posterity, scions. *See also* Adult offspring; Animal offspring; Children; Descent; Filial responsibility; Heirs; Only child; Parent child relations.

Offspring, adult. See *Adult offspring.*

Offspring, animal. See *Animal offspring.*

Offspring, interracial. See *Interracial marriage; Racially mixed.*

Oil, offshore. See *Offshore oil.*

Oil industry. Oil industr(y,ies). *Choose from:* oil *with:* industr(y,ial,ies), sector, trade, price(s), invest(ed,ing,ment), privatiz(ed,ing,ation), refiner(y,ies), market(s,ed,ing), econom(y,ic,ics), supply, demand, produc(tion,er,ers), processing, sale(s), selling, import(s,ed,ing), export(s,ed,ing). *See also* Coal industry; Gas industry; Industry; Offshore oil; Oil spills.

Oil spills. Oil spill(s). *Choose from:* oil(y), tanker(s), diesel fuel, gasoline, gas, pipeline, petroleum, refiner(y,ies) *with:* spill(s,ed,ing,age), leak(s,ed,ing,y,age), ruptur(e,ed,ing), break(ing), broken, overflow(ed), pollut(ed,ing,ion), beach(es), slick, water surface(s), foul(ing), befoul(ed,ing), dump(ed,ing), dirty. *Choose from:* oil(y), tanker(s), diesel fuel, gasoline, gas, pipeline, petroleum, refiner(y,ies) *with:* kill(ing) *with:* bird(s), animal(s), fish(es), wildlife. *See also* Energy generating resources; Environmental pollutants; Environmental pollution; Environmental

protection; Offshore oil; Oil industry; Waste spills; Water pollution.

Old, oldest. See *Aged 80 and over.*

Old, very. See *Aged 80 and over.*

Old age. See *Aged 80 and over; Elderly.*

Old growth forests. Old growth forest(s). *Choose from:* old growth, original, virgin, primeval, ancient *with:* forest(s), tree(s), wood(s,land,lands). *Consider also:* rain forest(s), cloud forest(s), variable-retention logging. *See also* Biological diversity; Deforestation; Forest conservation; Forest reserves; Forestry; Rainforests; Timber; Trees; Wildlife sanctuaries.

Old maids. See *Unmarried women.*

Older adults. See *Elderly; Aged 80 and over.*

Oldest old. See *Aged 80 and over.*

Olfactory perception. See *Odor discrimination.*

Olfactory stimulation. See *Odors.*

Oligarchy. Oligarch(ic,ical,y,ies,ization). Monopoly of political power. Elitis(m,t). Power elite. Control by special interests. Dominance by powerful. Governance by powerful minority. Ruling elite(s). Party elite(s). Fascist elite(s). Ruling group(s). Ruling class(es). Plutocrac(y,ies). *Consider also:* weighted voting, veto power, despoti(c,sm), concentrat(ed,ion, ions) power, bureaucratic elite(s), junta(s). *See also* Aristocracy; Elitism (government); Gerontocracy; Political elites; Power elite; Ruling class; Technocracy.

Oligopolies. Oligopol(y,ies). Duopol(y,ies). Cartel(s). Conscious parallel action. Cooperative equilibrium. Control market. Corner the market. *Consider also:* business concentration, market concentration, eliminating competition, unfair competition, market closure, monopol(y,ies,istic,ize,izing), price fixing. *See also* Big business; Business; Cartels; Competition; Corporate control; Corporations; Economic elites; Industrial concentration; Industry; Monopolies; Multinational corporations; Neocolonialism; Price fixing; Prices; Trade associations.

Oligopsony. Oligopson(y,ies,istic). *Consider also:* duopson(y,ies,istic), monopson(y,ies,istic), hiring hall(s), buyers market. *See also* Employment discrimination; Labor economics; Labor market; Labor market segmentation; Labor migration; Labor mobility; Labor supply; Labor unions.

Ombudsmen. Ombuds(man,men,woman, women). People's watchdog. Defend(er) of citizen rights. *Choose from:* citizen(s), disabled, inmate(s), retarded, patient(s), prisoner(s) *with:* advoca(te,tes,cy),

representative(s), observer(s). *See also* Animal welfare; Bureaucrats; Child abuse prevention; Children's rights; Civil rights; Client rights; Counseling; Elected officials; Government personnel; Human rights; Legal rights; Negotiation; Parent rights; Patient rights; Voting rights; Women's rights.

Omen. Omen(s). Portent(s). Portend(ed, ing). Foretoken(s). Augur(y,ies). Bod(e,ed,ing,ement). Harbinger(s). Forewarn(ed,ing). Presentiment(s). Warning sign(s). *See also* Divination; Extrasensory perception; Miracles; Mysticism; Oracles; Precognition; Prediction; Threat.

Omission, acts of. See *Negligence.*

Omnipotence. Omnipoten(t,ce). Almight(y,iness). All-powerful(ness). Unlimited power(s). *Consider also:* omniscien(t,ce), all-knowing. *See also* Glory of God, Omniscience of God; Oneness of God; Power; Will of God.

Omniscience of God. Omniscience of God. *Choose from:* prescien(t,tly,ce), omniscien(t,tly,ce), infinite awareness, infinite understanding, foreknowledge, all-knowing, all-seeing *with:* God, divine, almighty, supreme being. *Consider also:* divine intelligence, God's plan, God's will, theodic(y,ies). *See also* Attributes of God; Deities; Glory of God; God concepts; Immanence of god; Jehovah; Omnipotence; Oneness of God; Prophecy.

On the job training. See *Inservice training.*

Onagers. Onager(s). Kiang(s). Kulang(s). Kulan(s). Chigetai(s). *Consider also:* wild horse(s). *See also* Animals; Horses.

Onanism. See *Masturbation; Self indulgence.*

One parent family. See *Single parent family.*

One world. See *Globalization.*

Oneness of God. Oneness of God. One God. *Choose from:* God, creator, divin(e,ity) *with:* one(ness), simplicity, unity, unicity, all inclusive. *Consider also:* monotheis(m,t,ts,tic,tical,tically), the Shema, Shahada. *See also* Attributes of God; God concepts; Immanence of God; Jehovah; Monism; Omniscience of God; Omnipotence; Presence of God; Religious beliefs; Theism.

Online books. See *Electronic books.*

Online gambling. Online gambl(ing,er,ers). Internet casino(s). *Choose from:* online, Internet, Internet service provider(s), cyberspace, electronic, computer, web, net, www, virtual *with:* gambling site(s), bet(s,ting), roulette, wager(s,ing), sports betting, lotter(y,ies). *See also* Computer games; Gambling; Lotteries; Pathological gambling.

Online harassment. Online harass(ing, ment,ments,er,ers). Computer stalk(er, ers,ing). Unsolicited pornograph(y,ic) email(s). *Choose from:* online, internet, cyberspace, email, e-mail, Usenet, bulletin board(s) *with:* harass(ing,ment, ments,er,ers), personal attack(s), threat(s,en,ened,ening), disturbing message(s), inappropriate content, objectionable, misogynist, sexist, unwarranted, unwanted, unsolicited, intimidat(e,ed,ing,ion). *Consider also:* unsafe site(s), spam(med,ming), unwanted online advertisement(s), online sales pitch(es), unsolicited product email(s), unsolicited online invitation(s), banner ad(s), banner advertisement(s). *See also* Acquaintance rape; Computer crimes; Cybersex; Emotional abuse; Gossip sites; Harassment; Indecent communications; Internet (computer network); Intimidation; Junk email; Molested children; Online privacy; Online users; Push Technology; Sex offenses; Sexual coercion; Sexual harassment; Stalking; Victimization.

Online information retrieval. See *Automated information retrieval.*

Online periodicals. See *Electronic journals.*

Online privacy. Online privacy. *Choose from:* online, cyber(space), electronic mail, email, e-mail, electronic fund transfer(s) , internet, computerized data, computerized medical record(s), digital, e-commerce, credit file(s), web, site(s), website(s), home page(s), track(ed,ing) user(s), virtual communit(y,ies) *with:* privacy, encrypt(ed,ing,ion), cryptograph(y,ic), confidential(ity), security. *Consider also:* disabl(e,ed,ing) cookie(s). *See also* Computer crimes; Confidentiality; Digital signatures; Electronic eavesdropping; Gossip sites; Invasion of privacy; Market research; Online harassment; Online users; Privacy; Privacy laws; Right of privacy; Surveillance of citizens; Virtual reality.

Online publishing. See *Electronic Publishing.*

Online services. See *Information networks.*

Online sex. See *Cybersex.*

Online users. Online user(s). *Choose from:* online, Internet, Net, Web, WWW, email, e-mail, cyber(space), e-commerce, virtual, digital, AOL, Compuserve, Prodigy, etc. *with:* user(s), subscriber(s), addict(s), enthusiast(s), customers(s), consumer(s), enduser(s), shopper(s), buff(s), fanatic(s), freak(s). *Consider also:* cyberwonk(s), nethead(s). *See also* Clients; Computer addiction; Computer crimes; Computer games; Computer hackers; Computer personnel; Customers; Cybercafes; E-commerce; Information society; Internet (computer network); Internet traffic;

Online harassment; Online privacy; User friendly systems; Virtual reality.

Only child. Only child(ren). Without siblings. *Choose from:* one child, single child *with:* famil(y,ies). *See also* Birth order; Family characteristics; Family members; Family size; Offspring.

Onomatopoeia. Onomatopoe(ia,ic,ically). Onomatopoetic(ally). Echoic. Sound symbolism. Mimetic expression(s). Sound symbolic word(s). *See also* Poetry; Synesthesia.

Onset (disorders). Onset. Premorbid(ity). Trigger(ed,ing). Symptom manifestation(s). Initial period(s). First episode(s). First occurrence(s). Inception. Develop(ed,ing,ment) of illness. Became ill. Becoming ill. First admission. 1st admission. *Consider also:* etiolog(y,ical), precipit(ation,ant,ants), beginning(s), start(ed,ing), origin(s), commencement, first appearance(s), genesis, psychogenesis, early symptom(s), anamnes(is,tic) *with:* disease(s), disorder(s), illness(es), ill, psychos(is,es). *See also* Beginning; Disease; Disease susceptibility; Disorders; Etiology; Mental illness; Premorbidity.

Onset, sleep. See *Sleep onset.*

Ontogeny. See *Development.*

Ontology. Ontolog(y,ical). *Consider also:* existence, reality, deontolog(y,ical), noumen(a,on), entit(y,ies), being, metaphysics. *See also* Dialectics; Essence (philosophy); Holism; Metaphysics; Materialism; Reality.

Open classroom method. Open classroom method. *Choose from:* open, discovery, humanistic, nongraded, nontraditional, open plan, student centered, individualized *with:* classroom(s), class(es), education(al), instruction(al), school(s), learning, teaching, approach(es), curriculum, program(s), method(s). *See also* Discovery learning; Individualized instruction; Teaching; Teaching methods.

Open market. See *Free trade; Private enterprise; Privatization.*

Open marriages. See *Extramarital relations.*

Open meetings. See *Public meetings.*

Open prisons. See *Alternatives to incarceration.*

Open shop. Open shop(s). *Consider also:* right to work. *See also* Closed shop; Labor management relations; Labor unions.

Open society. See *Democracy.*

Open spaces. Open space(s). Open place(s). Park(s). Prairie(s). Outdoor area(s). Yard(s). School field(s). Land

preserve(s). *Choose from:* open, uninhabited, unsettled, unused, undeveloped, preserved *with:* space(s), country, territor(y,ies), expanse(s), area(s), land(s), forest(s), place(s), wood(lands,s). *Consider also:* national park(s). *See also* Environmental protection; Habitat; Natural environment; Parks; Rangelands; Right of pasture; Wilderness.

Open universities. See *Nontraditional education.*

Openings. Opening(s). Hiatus(es). Aperature(s). Hole(s). Orifice(s). Outlet(s). Vent(s). Peephole(s). Pore(s). *Consider also:* break(s), notch(es), slot(s), slit(s), split(s), crack(s), crevice(s), fissure(s), interstices. *See also* Entrances; Egress; Exits; Halls.

Openings (beginnings). See *Beginning; Incipits; Introduction; Onset (disorders); Overtures (music).*

Openmindedness. Openminded(ness). Open mind(ed,edness). *Choose from:* openness, toleran(t,ce), open belief system(s), receptive to new ideas, broad mind(ed,edness), unbiased, dispassionate, disinterested, impartial, unprejudiced. *See also* Authoritarianism (psychological); Dogmatism; Tolerance; Permissiveness; Personality traits.

Opera. Oper(a,as,atic,n). Lyric drama(s). Music(al) drama(s). Drame lyrique. Dramma lirico. Dramma giocoso. *Consider also:* operett(a,as,e), singspiel(e), dramma per musica, ballad opera(s), opera seria, opera semiseria, verismo, number opera, madrigal comed(y,ies), pasticcio, lyrical dialogue(s), tonadilla escenica, zarzuela(s). *See also* Bel canto; Choruses; Comic operas; Leitmotiv; Librettos; Liturgical drama; Theater; Melodrama (music); Music; Opera singers; Overtures (music).

Opera singers. Opera singer(s). *Choose from:* opera(s), Wagnerian *with:* singer(s), soloist(s), voice(s), virtuos(o,i), soprano(s), mezzo-soprano(s), contralto(s), alto(s), tenor(s), bass(es), baritone(s), bel canto. *Consider also singers by name, for example:* Placido Domingo, Luciano Pavarotti, Leontyne Price, Elisabeth Schwarzkopf, Lawrence Tibbett, etc. *See also* Bel canto; Choruses; Comic operas; Opera; Singers.

Operant conditioning. Operant conditioning. Instrumental conditioning. *Consider also:* Skinner box(es), Skinnerian, operant behaviorism. *See also* Aversion conditioning; Avoidance learning; Behavior modification; Classical conditioning; Conditioning (psychology); Conditioned responses; Conditioned suppression; Fading (conditioning); Instrumental conditioning;

Learning; Polydipsia; Reinforcement; Self stimulation; Unconditioned stimulus.

Operas, comic. See *Comic operas.*

Operas, soap. See *Soap operas.*

Operating rooms. Operating room(s). Operating theatre(s). Surgical suite(s). Operating suite(s). *Consider also:* delivery room(s). *See also* Hospitals.

Operations, branch. See *Branch operations.*

Operations, search and rescue. See *Disaster relief; Relief services.*

Operations, undercover. See *Undercover operations.*

Operations research. Operation(s,al) research. *Consider also:* monte carlo method, probability theory, flow chart(s), operational assessment(s), optimization theory, dynamic programming, control theory, simulation(s), critical path analysis, linear programming. *See also* Action research; Cost effectiveness; Efficiency; Mathematical models; Models; Planning; Quality control; Scientific models.

Operators, beauty. See *Beauty operators.*

Ophidiophobia. See *Snake phobia.*

Opinion, public. See *Public opinion.*

Opinion, second. See *Referral.*

Opinion, student. See *Student attitude(s).*

Opinion advertising. See *Advocacy advertising.*

Opinion change. See *Attitude change.*

Opinion leaders. Opinion leader(s,ship). Trendsetter(s). Consumer elite(s). Opinion elite(s). Opinion maker(s). *Consider also:* charismatic leader(s,ship), informal leader(s,ship), political elite(s), power elite(s), mover(s) and shaker(s), bellwether(s), cutting edge, ahead of the curve, ahead of the mainstream, forward thinking. *See also* Change agents; Chattering class; Commentators; Editorials; Editors; Leadership; Mass media effects; Media portrayal; News agencies; News coverage; News media; Opinions; Political leadership; Power elite; Press conferences; Social influences.

Opinion measurement. See *Attitude measurement.*

Opinion polls. Opinion poll(s). Opinion ind(ex,exes,ices). Straw poll(s). Exit poll(s). Opinionnaire(s). *Choose from:* Gallup, Roper, Harris, Yankelovitch, ICPSR, opinion, election, voter(s), attitude(s) *with:* poll(s), survey(s), data, sampl(e,es,ing), index(es), indicator(s), measur(e,es,ing,ment), stud(y,ies), assess(ed,ing,ment), predict(ed,ing,ions). *Consider also:* survey data, public

opinion research, mail survey(s), phone survey(s). *See also* Biased sampling; Canvassing; Fieldwork; Internet traffic; Library surveys; Opinions; Political attitudes; Public opinion; Push-polling; Questionnaires; Surveys; Voting behavior.

Opinion research, public. See *Opinion polls.*

Opinions. Opinion(ated,s). Sentiment(s). Attitude(s). Belief(s). Perception(s). Judgment(s). Judgement(s). Stereotype(s). Supposition(s). Expectation(s). Premise(s). Notion(s). Assumption(s). Slant(s). Prejudice(s). Perspective(s). Preconception(s). Conception(s). Misconception(s). Preference(s). Tolerance. Group support. Public opinion. Approval. Disapproval. Surmise. Impression(s). Conjecture. Point of view. Presumption. Presupposition. Viewpoint. Outlook. *See also* Attitude strength; Attitudes: Attitude measurement; Beliefs; Court opinions; Credibility; Dissent; Disapproval; Dogmatism; Expectations; Generation gap; Interest inventories; Opinion leaders; Opinion polls; Public opinion; Questionnaires; Reputation; Surveys.

Opinions, court. See *Court opinions.*

Opinions, judicial. See *Court opinions; Judicial decisions.*

Opinions, political. See *Political attitudes.*

Opium. See *Narcotics.*

Opportunities. Opportunit(y,ies). Possibilit(y,ies). Favorable circumstance(s). Suitable circumstance(s). Favorable time. Good moment. Prospect(s). Contingenc(y,ies). Probabilit(y,ies). Choice(s). Fortuit(y,ous). Occasion. *Consider also:* access, equality, openings. *See also* Access to education; Affirmative action; Architectural accessibility; Barriers; Constraints; Contingency; Cultural deprivation; Educational opportunities; Employment discrimination; Employment opportunities; Entrepreneurship; Equal education; Equal job opportunities; Family background; Possibilities; Social closure; Social discrimination.

Opportunities, career. See *Employment opportunities.*

Opportunities, educational. See *Educational opportunities.*

Opportunities, employment. See *Employment opportunities.*

Opportunities, equal. See *Equal education; Equal job opportunities.*

Opportunities, equal job. See *Equal job opportunities.*

Opportunities, job. See *Employment opportunities.*

Opportunities, tax. See *Tax opportunities.*

Opposite sex relations. See *Heterosexual relationships.*

Opposition. See *Resistance.*

Opposition, public. See *Public opposition.*

Oppression. Oppress(ion,ive,iveness, or,ors,ed). Persecut(e,ed,ing,ion). Suppress(ed,ing,ion). Subjugat(e,ed, ing,ion). Misuse(d). Exploit(ed,ing, ation). Repress(ive,ed,ing,ion). Slave(s,ry). Racis(m,t). Sexis(m,t). Ageis(m,t). *Choose from:* human rights *with:* abuse(s), violation(s). *Consider also:* tyrann(y,ize), despot(ic,ism), subordination, victimiz(ed,ation), cruel(ty), mistreat(ed,ment), maltreat(ed,ment). *See also* Abuse of power; Age discrimination; Class politics; Coercion; Despotism; Dictatorship; Disadvantaged; Dominated cultures; Employment discrimination; Exploitation; Human rights; Inequality; Labor market segmentation; Learned helplessness; Peonage; Persecution; Political prisoners; Political repression; Powerlessness; Racism; Servitude; Sexism; Sexual oppression; Slavery; Social discrimination; Sweatshops; Subjugation; Totalitarianism; Trafficking in persons; Tyranny; White supremacy movements.

Oppression, sexual. See *Sexual oppression.*

Optical illusions. Optical illusion(s). *Choose from:* optical, visual, perception, perceptual, geometric *with:* illusion(s), distortion(s), aftereffect(s). *Consider also:* afterimage(s), spatial distortion(s), mirage(s), illusory color(s), apparent motion(s), tilt illusion(s), subjective brightness. *Consider also specifically named types of illusions such as:* Hering, horizontal-vertical, Jastrow, Mueller-Lyer, oculogyral, Ponzo, staircase, Zoellner *with:* illusion(s). *See also* Afterimage; Illusions (perception); Perceptual distortion; Perceptual disturbances.

Optimism. Optimis(m,t,ts,tic). Hopeful(ness). Hop(e,ed,ing). High hopes. Positiveness. Cheerful(ness). Positive attitudes. Positive approach. Life satisfaction. Healthy outlook. Happy outlook. Positive mental attitude. Belief in just world. Faith. Radiance. Bright outlook. Buoyancy. Enthusiasm. Upbeat. Assured. Lighthearted. Carefree. *Consider also:* pollyanna(s,ism), great expectations, encourag(e,ed,ing,ement), melioris(m,t,tic), bullish(ly,ness). *See also* Cheerfulness; Emotional states; Future orientation; Happiness; Hopefulness; Personality traits; Pessimism; Psychological endurance; Psychological well being; Social attitudes; Trusting; Worldview.

Options, stock. See *Stock options.*

Opulence. See *Wealth*.

Oracles. Oracle(s). Oracular shrine(s). Oracle at Dodona. Delphic oracle. *Consider also:* sibyl(ic,lic,line), prophet(s,ess,esses), augur(s), soothsayer(s), diviner(s), forecaster(s), astrologer(s). *See also* Divination; Mother goddesses; Omen; Prediction; Prophets; Religious mysteries.

Oral character. Oral character. Orality. *Choose from:* oral *with:* drive, aggression, erot(ism,icism). *Consider also:* oral, sucking, biting *with:* phase(s), period(s), gratification. *See also* Oral stage; Personality traits.

Oral communication. Oral communication. Speech. Speak(ing). Spoken word(s). Expressive language. Discuss(ed,ing,ion, ions). Conversation(al,s). Convers(e,ed, ing). Verbaliz(e,ed,ation). Stating. Restat(e,ing). Discourse. Utterance(s). Whisper(ed,ing). Talk(ed,ing). Dialogue(s). Public speaking. Reading aloud. *Choose from:* oral, verbal, spoken, language *with:* communication(s), express(ion,ions,ive,iveness), processing, comprehension, message(s), feedback. *See also* Oral reading; Public speaking; Self talk; Speech characteristics; Verbal ability; Verbal communication; Vocalization.

Oral contraceptives. Oral contraceptive(s). *Choose from:* oral, pill(s) *with:* contraceptive(s), contraception, birth control. *Consider also:* oral combined, oral hormonal, oral sequential, oral synthetic *with:* contracept(ion,ive,ives). *See also* Birth control; Contraception; Emergency contraception; Female contraceptive devices; First birth timing; Family planning; Fertility enhancement.

Oral health. Oral health. *Choose from:* oral, mouth, dental, periodontal, teeth, gingival *with:* health, status, condition(s), diagnos(is,es), disease(s), rehabilitat(ed,ing,ion). *See also* Dental care.

Oral history. Oral history. Oral literature. Oral narrative(s). Storyteller(s). Reminisc(ence,ences,ing). Folk narrative(s). Folk histor(y,ies). *Consider also:* word of mouth, transmitted verbally, eyewitness account(s), bystander account(s), ethnohistory. *See also* Autobiography; Cultural transmission; Ethnography; Family history; Folklore; Generativity; History; Interviews; Legends; Life history; Local history; Narratives; Oral tradition; Sagas; Social history; Storytellers; Storytelling.

Oral intercourse. See *Oral sex*.

Oral reading. Oral reading. *Consider also:* read(ing) aloud, poetry reading(s). *See also* Oral communication; Poetry; Reading; Silent reading.

Oral sex. Oral sex. Oral intercourse. Orogenital activity. Oral genital contact. Fellatio(n). Fellat(ic,or,ors,rice,rices). Cunnilin(gus,ctio,ction,gam). Autofellatio. Self irrumation. Anilingus. Aniliction. *Choose from:* buccal *with:* onanism, intercourse. *See also* Sex behavior.

Oral stage. Oral stage. *Choose from:* oral *with:* need(s), erot(ic,icism,ism), stage(s), sadis(m,tic). *Consider also:* orality, oral erogeneity. *See also* Developmental stages; Oral character.

Oral tradition. Oral tradition(s). Bardic performance(s). Narrative performance(s). Oral transmission. Oral work(s). Epic(s). Sharing stories. *Choose from:* voiced performance(s), spoken word(s), aloud, living text(s), oral, oralization *with:* family history, family pride, folklore, stor(y,ies). *See also* Folklore; Oral history.

Oral transmission. See *Oral tradition*.

Oratorio. Oratorio(s). Oratorium(s). Oratoriani. Oratoir(es). *Consider also:* actus musicus, historia, sepolcri, cantata(s). *See also* Choruses; Hymns; Librettos.

Oratory. Orator(y,ical,ically,s). Rhetoric(al,ally). Art of public speaking. Eloquen(t,ce). Declamat(ion,ory). *Consider also:* euphuistic, flowery, grandiloquent, magniloquent, overblown, sonorous *with:* speech(es), spoke(n), lectur(e,es,ed,ing), delivery. *See also* Debate; Eloquence; Gestures; Lectures and lecturing; Persuasion; Political rhetoric; Rhetoric; Speeches (formal discourse).

Oratory, political. See *Political rhetoric*.

Orchestras. Orchestra(s). Orchestre(s). Orchester. Orquesta(s). *See also* Bands (music); Concert halls; Conductors.

Orchestration. Orchestrat(e,ed,ing,ion). Musical scoring. *Consider also:* instrumentation. *See also* Arrangement (Music); Harmonization; Music; Variations.

Order, birth. See *Birth order*.

Order, pecking. See *Animal dominance*.

Order, public. See *Public order*.

Order, social. See *Social order*.

Order, world. See *Globalization; International cooperation; International economic integration; International law; International organizations; International relations; World economy; World problems*.

Order processing. Order processing. *Choose from:* order(s), request(s), requisition(s), application(s), reservation(s) *with:* process(es,ing), handl(e,ed,ing), expedit(e,ed,ing), fill(ed,ing), ship(ped,ping). *See also* Catalogs; Database marketing; Direct mail advertising; Orders (business); Sales.

Orderliness. Orderl(y,iness). Neat(ness). Tid(y,iness). Uncluttered. Well balanced. Well groomed. methodical(ly). Systematic(ally). Symmetrical(ly). *Consider also:* correct(ness), decorous(ness), decorum, proper(ness), propriet(y,ies), seeml(y,iness), clean(ed,ing,liness). *See also* Anal personality; Attractiveness; Calmness; Clutter; Compulsive behavior; Confusion (disarray); Entropy; Personality traits; Thriftiness.

Orders (business). Order(s). Purchas(e,ing) agreement(s). Requisition(s). Reservation(s). Booking(s). *Choose from:* material(s), goods, suppl(y,ies), etc. *with:* order(s), request(s), application(s), reservation(s). *See also* Advertising; Catalogs; Direct mail advertising; Marketing; Order processing; Sales; Telemarketing.

Orders, contemplative. See *Contemplative orders*.

Orders, do not resuscitate orders. See *Do not resuscitate orders*.

Orders, mendicant. See *Friars*.

Orders, military religious. See *Military religious orders*.

Orders, religious. See *Contemplative religious orders; Military religious orders; Monasticism; Monks; Nuns*.

Ordination. Ordination. Ordain(ed,ing, ment). Consecrat(e,ed,ing,ion). Appoint(ed,ing,ment) to office. *Choose from:* invest(ed,ing,ment), appoint(ed, ing,ment) *with:* ministerial, sacerdotal. *Consider also:* laying on of hands, tonsur(e,ed). *See also* Clergy; Ecclesiastical benefices; Ministers; Priests; Rabbis; Religious councils and synods; Religious rituals.

Ordnance. See *Artillery; Military weapons*.

Organ donation. See *Anatomical gifts*.

Organ transplantation. Organ transplant(s, ation). *Choose from:* organ(s), heart(s), kidney(s), tissue(s), cardiac, bone marrow *with:* transplant(ed,ing,s, ion,able), don(or,ors,ated,ation), source(s), procure(ment). *Consider also:* anatomical gift(s), cadaver source(s). *See also* Anatomical gifts; Dead bodies; Living donors; Tissue banks; Tissue donors; Xenotransplantation.

Organic farming. Organic farm(s,ing,er, ers). *Choose from:* organic, natural, ecological, alternative, low-input, sustainable, without pesticide(s), without chemical(s) *with:* farm(s,ing,er,ers), crop(s), agricultur(e,al). *See also* Agricultural chemicals: Agricultural diversification; Agricultural ecology;

Bioregionalism; Environmental pollution; Environmental protection; Environmental stress; Environmentalism; Farming; Herbicides; Natural foods; Natural resources; Pesticides; Restoration ecology; Sewage as fertilizer; Sustainable development.

Organic foods. See *Natural foods.*

Organic mental disorders. Organic mental disorder(s). Psycho-organic syndrome(s). Brain damage(d). Neuropsychological impairment(s). Organic amnesia. Cerebral atrophy. *Choose from:* brain, cerebral *with:* disorder(s), syndrome(s), impairment(s), disturbance(s), disease(s), tumor(s). *Consider also:* senile psychos(is,es), toxic psychos(is,es), arteriosclerotic dementia, multi-infarct dementia, degenerative dementia. *See also* Alzheimer's disease; Dementia; Organic psychoses; Pick's disease; Presenile dementia; Psychosurgery; Senile dementia; Substance induced organic mental disorders.

Organic mental disorders, substance induced. See *Substance induced organic mental disorders.*

Organic psychoses. Organic psychose(s). Psychotic organic mental disorder(s). *Choose from:* organic, alcohol(ic,ism), presenile, senile, exhaustion, nutritional, Alzheimer(s), Jakob-Creutzfeldt, substance-induced, opium, Korsakoff(s), Pick(s), traumatic, arterioscler(tic,sis), toxic, febrile *with:* psychos(is,es), psychotic, amnestic, amnesia(s), delusion(s,al), hallucin(osis,ation, ations,atory), dementia(s), deliri(a,um). *Consider also:* delirium tremens. *See also* Organic mental disorders; Substance induced psychoses.

Organic therapies. See *Somatic therapies.*

Organicism. Organicism. Organistic. Biologism. *Choose from:* biological, organic *with:* analog(y,ies), theor(y,ies). *See also* Holism; Social theories.

Organization. See *Organizational structure.*

Organization, community. See *Community structure.*

Organization, horizontal. See *Departmentalization; Division of labor; Labor market segmentation.*

Organization, social. See *Caste system; Occupational segregation; Oppression; Organizational structure; Political elites; Political repression; Power elite; Power structure; Racial segregation; Residential segregation; Social cleavage; Social reality; Social stratification; Social structure.*

Organization, spatial. See *Spatial organization.*

Organization man. See *Conformity (personality); Embourgeoisement; Organizational commitment; Other directed.*

Organization membership. Organization member(s,ship). *Choose from:* organization(s), club(s), group(s), voluntary association(s), cult(s), political part(y,ies), sororit(y,ies), fraternit(y,ies), league(s), brotherhood(s), alliance(s), federation(s), societ(y,ies), team(s), lodge(s) *with:* member(s,ship), participat(e,ed,ing,ion), belong(ed,ing), dues paying, affiliat(ed,ing,ion,ions). *See also* Affiliation motivation; Church membership; Clubs; Organizational commitment; Organizations; Fraternities; Sororities; Voluntary associations.

Organization size. Organization(al,s) size. *Choose from:* organization(s), agenc(y,ies), association(s), group(s), compan(y,ies), corporation(s), societ(y,ies), group(s), team(s), club(s), church(es), firm(s), institution(s), establishment(s), plant(s), firm(s) *with:* size, growth, large(r,st), big(ger,gest), small(er,est), giant(s). *See also* Big business; Big churches; Complex organizations; Group size; Industry; Mergers; Organizations; Small businesses.

Organizational affiliation. Organization(s, al) affiliat(ed,ion). Member organization(s). *Consider also:* organization(s), institution(s), agenc(y,ies), hospital(s), school(s), universit(y,ies), college(s) *with:* network(s,ing), cooperative program(s), coalition(s), cooperation, multihospital system(s), multi-institutional system(s), shared service(s), link(ed,s), membership(s). *See also* Affiliation (businesses); Alliances; Consortia; Corporate networks; Interorganizational networks; Organizations.

Organizational behavior. Organizational behavior. *Choose from:* organization(al), institution(al), work group, corporate *with:* behavior, decision making, support, communication, effectiveness, politics, productivity, retaliation, mores, culture, socialization, leadership, motivation, climate, loyalty, psychology, role(s), social process(es), dynamics, regulation(s), commitment, power, relations, influences. *See also* Group dynamics; Leadership style; Management functions; Organizational change; Organizational climate; Organizational culture; Organizational effectiveness; Organizational objectives; Organizational politics; Organizational power; Organizational survival; Organizational politics; Organizations; Social behavior.

Organizational change. Organizational change(s). *Choose from:* organization(al, s), institution(al,s), department(s,al), agenc(y,ies), work, job, bureaucra(tic,

cy,cies), firm(s) *with:* chang(e,es,ed,ing), develop(ment,ed,ing), innovation(s), reorganiz(ed,ing,ation), redesign(ed,ing), reform(ed,ing,s), reformulat(e,ed,ing, ion), retrench(ed,ment), restructur(ed, ing) transform(ed,ing,ation), grow(th,n,ing), democratiz(ed,ation), merg(ed,ing,er,ers), reconstruct(ed,ion), remodel(led,ling), transition(s), centraliz(e,ed,ing,ation), decentraliz(e, ed,ing,ation), evolv(e,ed,ing), evolution, revolutioniz(e,ed,ing). *Consider also:* reconfigurable organization(s), self designing organization(s), learning organization(s), organizational learning, self organizing system(s). *See also* Change agents; Chaos management; Centralization; Change; Change agents; Cooptation; Decentralization; Merger integration; Mergers; Organizational crises; Organizational development; Organizational dissolution; Organizational innovation; Organizational politics; Organizational structure; Organizational survival; Organizations; Strategic management.

Organizational climate. Organizational climate(s). Quality of work life. Work settings. Bureaucratization. *Choose from:* organization(al), corporate, institution(al), work *with:* climate(s), culture(s), atmosphere(s), context(s), setting(s), environment(s), morale, composition, ecology, humanization. *See also* Burnout; Educational environment; Industrial psychology; Job satisfaction; Morale; Organizational crises; Organizational culture; Organizational development; Organizational politics; Organizations; Power structure; Quality of working life; Working conditions.

Organizational commitment. Organizational commitment. *Choose from:* organization(al,s), agenc(y,ies), association(s), group(s), compan(y,ies), corporation(s), societ(y,ies), group(s), team(s), club(s), firm(s), institution(s), establishment(s), plant(s), firm(s), worker(s), employee(s), staff, personnel *with:* commit(ted,ment), allegiance, loyal(ty,tiness), devot(ed,edness,ion), dedicat(ed,ion), involve(d,ment), solidarity, support. *See also* Attitudes toward work; Commitment (emotional); Group identity; Organization membership; Organizations.

Organizational crises. Organizational cris(is,es). *Choose from:* organization(s, al), intraorganization(al), interdepartmental, agenc(y,ies), association(s), compan(y,ies), corporat(e,ion,ions), institution(s), establishment(s) *with:* cris(is,es), conflict(s), stress(es,ed,ing), dispute(s), problem(s), breakdown(s), disorganization. *See also* Bankruptcy; Organizational change; Organizational climate; Organizational dissolution; Organizational survival; Organizations; Plant closings; Stress.

Organizational culture. Organization(al) culture(s). Corporat(e,ion) culture(s). Organizational values. Work culture. Company culture. Corporate style. Ethical management. Organizational environment(s). Work climate. Professional culture. Corporate jungle(s). Corporate tribe(s). Customer centered culture(s). *Choose from:* management, corporation(s), compan(y,ies), business(es), agenc(y,ies), firm(s), organization(s,al), worksite, agenc(y, ies), workplace *with:* culture(s), climate(s), values, myth(s,making), legend(s), ideolog(y,ies), slogan(s), creed(s), codes, ethics, esprit de corps. *Consider also:* ethical management, organizational environment(s), work climate, professional culture. *See also* Boundaryless organizations; Business ethics; Complex organizations; Corporate social responsibility; Corruption in government; Intrapreneurship; Leadership style; Morale; Occupational folklore; Organizational behavior; Organizational climate; Organizational politics; Organizations; Public folklore; Quality of working life; Social values; White collar crime; Working conditions.

Organizational development. Organizational development. *Choose from:* organization(al,s), agenc(y,ies), association(s), group(s), compan(y,ies), corporation(s), societ(y,ies), group(s), team(s), club(s), firm(s), institution(s), establishment(s), plant(s), firm(s), managerial, management, worker(s), employee(s), staff, personnel *with:* develop(ed,ing,ment), grow(n,ing,th), improv(e,ed,ing,ement), build(ing), built, strengthen(ed,ing), expand(ed,ing), expansion. *See also* Administration; Alliances; Chaos management; Developmental stages; Faculty development; Job enrichment; Job satisfaction; Management methods; Merger integration; Morale; Organizational change; Organizational climate; Organizational dissolution; Organizational objectives; Organizations; Participative decision making; Power structure; Quality of working life; Social processes; Staff development; Strategic alliances; Teaming; Teamwork; Working conditions.

Organizational dissolution. Organizational dissolution. *Choose from:* organization(al,s), enterprise(s), factor(y,ies), brewer(y,ies), mill(s), church(es), plant(s), firm(s), corporation(s), compan(y,ies), institution(al,s), department(s,al), agenc(y,ies), bureaucra(tic,cy,cies) *with:* retrench(ed, ment), dissolution(s), dissolv(e,ed,es, ing), dysfunction(s,al,ality,alities), failure(s), mortality, declin(e,ed,es,ing), closure(s), ceas(e,ed,ing), breakdown(s), disintegration, insolven(t,cy), bankrupt. *See also* Bankruptcy; Deindustrial-

ization; Organizational change; Organizational development; Organizational power; Organizational survival; Organizations; Plant closings; Social cohesion; Social conflict; Social disorganization; Turnaround management.

Organizational effectiveness. Organizational effectiveness. *Choose from:* organization(al,s), institution(al,s), group(s), work unit(s), agenc(y,ies), firm(s), business(es), compan(y,ies), corporat(e,ion,ions), hospital(s), store(s), school(s), librar(y,ies), etc. *with:* effective(ness), performance, output, profit(s), bottom line, success(ful), succeed(ing), product(ive,ivity,ion), excellen(t,ce), capabilit(y,ies), outcome(s), efficien(t,cy), failure, inefficien(t,cy), ineffective(ness), unsuccessful. *See also* Administration; Cost effectiveness; Effectiveness; Industrial management; Management methods; Managers; Organizational behavior; Organizational objectives; Organizational politics; Organizational survival; Organizations; Productivity; Quality control; Self evaluation (groups); Subsidiary management; Success.

Organizational goals. See *Organizational objectives.*

Organizational innovation. Organizational innovation(s). *Choose from:* organization(s,al), corporat(e,ion,ions), compan(y,ies), institution(s,al), agenc(y,ies), establishment(s), association(s), managerial, management, administrative, administration, leadership, workplace *with:* innovation(s), innovative(ness), innovat(e,ed,ing), change(s), creativ(e,ity), restructur(e,ed, ing), reform(ed,ing,s), improvis(e,ed,ing, ation), reorganiz(e,ed,ing), improv(e,ed, ing,ement,ements), problem solving. *Consider also:* cutback management. *See also* Change agents; Educational innovations; Extended school year; Leadership; Organizational change; School schedules.

Organizational mergers. See *Mergers.*

Organizational objectives. Organizational objective(s). *Choose from:* organization(s,al), management, manager(s,ial), institution(s,al), compan(y,ies), corporat(e,ion), agenc(y,ies) *with:* goal(s), objective(s), priorit(y,ies). *See also* Accountability; Corporate mission; Institutional mission; Long range planning; Management methods; Objectives; Organizational development; Organizational effectiveness; Organizational politics; Organizations; Planning; Quality control; Strategic management; Strategic planning.

Organizational performance. See *Organizational effectiveness.*

Organizational politics. Organizational politics. *Choose from:* organization(s,al), institution(s,al), group(s), compan(y,ies), corporat(e,ion,ions), workplace, work environment *with:* politics, political behavior, power, decision making, authority, control, influence, leader(s,ship). *Consider also:* office politics. *See also* Group dynamics; Groups; Leadership; Management functions; Organizational behavior; Organizational change; Organizational climate; Organizational culture; Organizational effectiveness; Organizational objectives; Organizational power; Organizational survival; Organizing activities; Organizations; Power structure.

Organizational power. Organizational power. *Choose from:* organization(al,s), agenc(y,ies), association(s), group(s), compan(y,ies), corporat(e,ions), societ(y,ies), group(s), team(s), club(s), firm(s), institution(s), establishment(s), plant(s) *with:* power(ful), influen(ce, tial), control(led,ling), resource(s), domina(nt,nce,tion), strength, strong, weak(ness), clout, coerc(ion,ive). *See also* Corporate control; Organizational dissolution; Organizational politics; Organizations; Power; Power structure.

Organizational research. Organizational research. *Choose from:* organization(al, s), agenc(y,ies), association(s), group(s), compan(y,ies), corporat(e,ion,ions), societ(y,ies), group(s), team(s), club(s), firm(s), institution(s), establishment(s), plant(s) *with:* research, analy(sis,ses, zing), stud(y,ies), survey(s), investigation(s), data collection, inquir(y,ies), theor(y,ies), evaluat(e,ed, ing,ion), assess(ed,ing,ment). *See also* Organizations; Research.

Organizational structure. Organization(al) structure(s). Work organization. Self managed work group(s). Channel(s) of authority. *Choose from:* organization(s, al), power, control, bureaucra(tic,cy, cies), authority, firm(s), corporat(e,ion, ions) *with:* hierarch(y,ies), structure(s), model(s), complexity, differentiation, centralization, decentralization, typolog(y,ies), design, form(s), pyramid(s), matrix(es), circle(s), ladder(s), tier(s,ed), salary grade(s), restructur(e,ed,ing). *Consider also:* organization chart(s), broadbanding, directorate(s). *See also* Adhocracies; Boundaryless organizations; Bureaucratization; Career ladders; Centrality; Centralization; Decentralization; Departmentalization; Departments; Management structures; Merger integration; Mergers; Middle level managers; Networks; Organizational change; Organizational survival; Organizations; Power structure; Reengineering; Social structure;

Superior subordinate relationship; Virtual organizations.

Organizational survival. Organizational survival. *Choose from:* organization(al, s), enterprise(s), factor(y,ies), brewer(y, ies), mill(s), church(es), plant(s), firm(s), corporation(s), compan(y,ies), institution(al,s), department(s,al), agenc(y,ies), bureaucra(tic,cy,cies) *with:* stable, stability, viable, viability, surviv(al,e,ed,es,ing), resilien(t,ce), continuity, intact(ness), stress resistance, cohesion, preserv(e,ed,ing,ation), reliable, reliability, strength(s), solidarity, last(ed,ing), endur(e,ed,ing). *See also* Bankruptcy; Organizational behavior; Organizational change; Organizational crises; Organizational dissolution; Organizational effectiveness; Organizational politics; Organizational structure; Organizations; Plant closings; Survival; Turnaround management.

Organizations. Organization(s). Agenc(y,ies). Association(s). Group(s). Consort(ia,ium). Union(s). League(s). Coalition(s). Alliance(s). Federation(s). Confederation(s). Compan(y,ies). Corporation(s). Societ(y,ies). Conglomerate(s). Political part(y,ies). Political faction(s). Group(s). Team(s). Club(s). Brotherhood(s). Fraternit(y,ies). Lodge(s). Sororit(y,ies). Academ(y,ies). Congress(es). Establishment(s). Firm(s). Commission(s). Institution(s). Organized bod(y,ies). Aggregation(s). Guild(s). Formally organized. Professional groups. *Consider also:* specific organizations, affiliation(s), formal organization, incorporated. *See also* Agencies; Associations (organizations); Bureaucracies; Business organizations; Charities; Churches; Civil rights organizations; Civil society; Clubs; Collective behavior; Commissions; Committees; Complex organizations; Consortia; Cooperatives; Consumer organizations; Councils; Departments; Enterprises; Federations; Foundations (organizations); Fraternities; Governing boards; Government agencies; Guilds; Health maintenance organizations; International organizations; International economic organizations; Interorganizational networks; Labor unions; Mergers; Neighborhood associations; Nonprofit organizations; Organization membership; Organization size; Organizational affiliation; Organizational behavior; Organizational change; Organizational climate; Organizational commitment; Organizational crises; Organizational culture; Organizational development; Organizational dissolution; Organizational effectiveness; Organizational innovation; Organizational objectives; Organizational politics; Organizational power; Organizational research; Organizational structure;

Organizational survival; Political parties; Professional organizations; Religious communities; Sororities; Social institutions; Social structure; Work groups; Women's groups; Youth organizations.

Organizations (associations). See *Associations (organizations).*

Organizations, boundaryless. See *Boundaryless organizations.*

Organizations, business. See *Business organizations.*

Organizations, charitable. See *Charities.*

Organizations, civil rights. See *Civil rights organizations.*

Organizations, community. See *Neighborhood associations.*

Organizations, complex. See *Complex organizations.*

Organizations, consumer. See *Consumer organizations.*

Organizations, feminist. See *Feminism; Suffrage movement; Women's groups.*

Organizations, health maintenance. See *Health maintenance organizations.*

Organizations, hybrid. See *Joint ventures.*

Organizations, intergovernmental. See *International organizations.*

Organizations, international. See *International organizations.*

Organizations, international economic. See *International economic organizations.*

Organizations, labor. See *Guilds, Labor unions.*

Organizations, nongovernmental. See *Nongovernmental organizations.*

Organizations, nonprofit. See *Nonprofit organizations.*

Organizations, not-for-profit. See *Nonprofit organizations.*

Organizations, professional. See *Professional organizations.*

Organizations, self designing. See *Organizational change.*

Organizations, vertical. See *Hierarchy.*

Organizations, virtual. See *Virtual organizations.*

Organizations, youth. See *Youth organizations.*

Organized crime. Organized crime. Mafia. Mafioso. Racketeer(s,ing). Yakuza. Cosa Nostra. Black hand. Dacoit(y). Underworld. Mob infiltration. Career criminal(s). Professional criminal(s). Crime syndicate(s). Genovese crime family. Criminal gang(s). Criminal organization(s). *See also* Accomplices; Black economy; Career criminals;

Corruption in government; Family businesses; Gambling; Gray market; Prostitution; Racketeering; White collar crime.

Organized financing. Organized financing. *Choose from:* organized, corporate, foundation, state, federal *with:* aid, grant(s), financ(e,ed,ing), fund(ed,ing,s). Trust(s). Endowment(s). Insurance. *Consider also:* financial support, endowment(s), health insurance reimbursement, foreign aid. *See also* Charities; Endowments; Financing; Foundations (organizations); Government financing.

Organized labor. See *Labor unions.*

Organizers, advance. See *Advance organizers.*

Organizers, community. See *Community organizers.*

Organizing activities. Organizing activit(y,ies). Union organiz(ing,er,ers). Union representation campaign(s). *Choose from:* organiz(e,ed,ing) *with:* drive(s), technique(s), tactic(s), campaign(s). *Consider also:* mobiliz(e,ed,ing,ation), recruit(ed,ing, ment), unionization, salting. *See also* Activism; Change agents; Coordination (interpersonal); Labor unions; Local politics; Networks; Organizational politics; Organizations; Social movements.

Organizing, labor union. See *Organizing activities.*

Organs (music). Organ(s). Orgue(s). Orgel(en). Organo(s). Organett(o,i). *Consider also:* barrel organ(s), portative organ(s), blockwerk, harmonium(s), reed organ(s). *See also* Electronic organs; Musical instruments.

Organs, electronic. See *Electronic organs.*

Organs, house. See *House organs.*

Organs, sense. See *Sense organs.*

Orgasm. Orgasm(ic). Sexual climax. Orgastic. Preorgasmic. Ejaculat(ed, ing,ion). *Consider also:* climax *with:* intercourse, sex(ual), foreplay, masturbat(ed,ing,ion). *Consider also:* nocturnal emission(s), premature ejaculation(s). *See also* Aphrodisiacs; Climax; Ejaculation; Female orgasm; Frigidity; Impotence; Orgasmic dysfunction; Sex therapy; Sexual arousal; Sexual function disorders; Sexual intercourse; Sexual satisfaction.

Orgasm, female. See *Female orgasm.*

Orgasmic dysfunction. Orgasmic dysfunction(s). Orgasmus deficiens. Anorgasm(ia,ic,y). Anorgastic. Nonorgasmic. Nonorgasmic. Inorgasm(ia,ic). Inorgastic. *Choose from:* orgasm(s,ic, ically), orgastic, psychosexual, sexual function, sexual response(s), sexual climax(es) *with:* dysfunction(s,al), fail(ed,ing,ure), difficult(y,ies), inability, inhibit(ed,ing,ion). *See also* Frigidity; Orgasm; Sex therapy; Sexual function disorders; Sexual inhibitions; Sexual intercourse.

Oriental medicine. Oriental medicine. Acupuncture. Barefoot doctor(s). *Choose from:* Japan(ese), Chin(a,ese), Korea(n), Asia(n), Oriental, Indochin(a, ese), Thai(land), Burm(a,ese), Vietnam(ese), Cambodia(n), Tibet(an) *with:* drug(s), herb(s,al,alism), health, medical, heal(ed,ing), medicin(e,al), hygien(e,ic), treat(ed,ing,ment), diagnos(is,es), therap(y,ies,eutic), cure(s,d), surg(ery,ical), doctor(s). *See also* Ayurvedic medicine; Chinese medicine; Plant folklore; Traditional medicine.

Orientation. Orient(ed,ing,ation,ating) to physical, personal, social environment. Kinesis. Spatial location. Spatial localization. Get bearings. Echolocat(ing,ion). Self referen(t,ce). Spatial self reference system(s). Co-orientation. *Choose from:* orient(ed,ing,ation,ating) *with:* space, perceptual, spatial, time, values, home, sounds. *Consider also:* adaptation, orienting behavior. *See also* Adjustment (to environment); Echolocation; Geographical perception; Orienting reflex; Orienting responses; Perceptual localization; Spatial memory.

Orientation, goal. See *Goal orientation.*

Orientation, school. See *School orientation.*

Orientation, sexual. See *Sexual orientation.*

Orientation, theoretical. See *Theoretical orientation.*

Orientations, future. See *Future orientation.*

Orientations, professional. See *Professional orientations.*

Orientations, sex role. See *Gender identity; Sex role attitudes; Sexual orientation.*

Orientations, value. See *Value orientations.*

Orientations, work. See *Attitudes toward work; Occupational adjustment; Professional orientations.*

Orienting reflex. Orienting reflex(es). *Choose from:* orient(ed,ing,ation), righting *with:* reflex(es), reaction(s), adapt(ed,ing,ation). *Consider also:* coriolis vestibular response(s), pupil dilation(s), galvanic skin response(s). *See also* Orientation; Reflex; Sensory adaptation.

Orienting responses. Orienting respons(es, iveness). Head righting response(s). Orienting reaction(s). *Consider also:* orientation, tropism, habituat(ed,ing, ion), taxis. *See also* Responses; Sensory adaptation.

Origin, foreign. See *Foreigners.*

Originality. See *Creativity.*

Origins. See *Causality; Etiology; Provenance.*

Ornamentation, body. See *Body ornamentation.*

Ornamentation, book. See *Book ornamentation.*

Ornamentation (music). Ornamentation. Grace(s). Grace note(s). *Consider also:* acciaccatura(e,s), anschlag(en), appoggiatura(e,s), cadent(s,en), coule, grace note(s), mordent(s,en), nachschlag(en), port(s) de voix, pralltriller, relish, ribattuta di gola, schneller, slide(s), tirade(s), tremolo(s), trill(s,o), turn(s), arpeggio(s), rubato(s), suspension(s), balancement(s), bebung(en), messa di voce, portamento(s), sanglot(s), vibrato, diminution(s), cadenza(s). accent(s), aspiration(s), battement(s), chute(s), flatte, gruppetto(s), martellement, plainte, quiebro, redoble, tour de gosier. *See also* Acciaccatura; Arpeggio; Cadence; Embellishment (music); Music; Trills.

Orphanages. Orphanage(s). *Choose from:* orphan(s), foundling(s), abandoned child(ren), homeless child(ren), runaway child(ren) *with:* residen(ce,ces,tial), nurser(y,ies), home(s), institution(s). *See also* Institutionalized children; Orphans; Shelters.

Orphans. Orphan(s,ed). Parentless. Loss of parents. Fatherless. Motherless. Parental loss. Foundling(s). *See also* Adopted children; Family members; Foster children; Orphanages.

Orthodoxy. See *Religious fundamentalism; Traditionalism.*

Orthodoxy, religious. See *Religious fundamentalism.*

Orthomolecular therapy. Orthomolecular therap(y,ies). *Consider also:* megavitamin, vitamin(s), nonstandard *with:* therap(y,ies), psychiatry, prophylaxis, treatment(s). *See also* Alternative medicine.

Orthopedically handicapped. See *Physically handicapped.*

Ossuaries. Ossuar(y,ies). *Consider also:* reliquar(y,ies), skeletal remains, depositor(y,ies) for bone(s), fossil(s), cemeter(y,ies). *See also* Cemeteries; Death rituals; Human remains (archaeology).

Ostracism. Ostracis(m,ed). Ostraciz(e,ed, ing). Banish(ed,ing,ment). Exile(d). Oust(ed,ing). Reject(ed,ion,ing). Refus(e,ed,ing) admit(tance). Abandon(ed,ing,ment). Rebuff(ed,ing). Blackball(ed,ing). Shun(ned,ning). Ignor(e,ed,ing). Spurn(ed,ing).

Renounc(e,ed,ing). Disown(ed,ing). Exclu(de,ding,sion). Eject(ed,ing,ion). Avoid(ed,ing,ance). *Consider also:* segregation, apartheid, outcaste(s), pariah(s), ban(ned,ning). *See also* Alienation; Marginality (sociological); Otherness; Outcasts; Rejection (psychology); Social attitudes; Social behavior; Social contact; Social distance; Social isolation; Stigma.

Other directed. Other direct(ed,edness,ion). Extrinsic motivation. External locus of control. Fluid identity. Need for approval. Superficial relationship(s). Other directed man. Organization man. Heteronomous superego. *Consider also:* social ethic. *See also* Externalization; Locus of control; Inner directed.

Other planets, life on. See *Extraterrestrial life.*

Otherness. Otherness. Differentness. Unfamiliar(ity). The other. Alterity. *Consider also:* minority status, marginaliz(e,ed,ing,ation), nondominan(t,ce), objectif(y,ied,ication), outcast(s), isolat(e,es,ed,ing,ion), exclud(e,es,ed,ing), exclusion, subaltern group(s). *See also* Contempt; Infidels; Isolation; Marginality (sociological); Ostracism; Outcasts; Prejudice; Social attitudes; Social class; Social distance; Social isolation; Social status; Stereotyping; Stigma.

Others, significant. See *Significant others.*

Otherworld, voyages to the. See *Voyages to the otherworld.*

Out of body experiences. See *Near death experiences.*

Outcastes. Outcaste(s). Untouchable(s). *See also* Caste system; Outcasts.

Outcasts. Outcast(s). Pariah(s). Despised. Fugitive(s). Ostracized. Vagabond(s). Nonperson(s). Friendless. Unwanted. Discarded. *Consider also:* out-group(s), scapegoat(s). *See also* Deportation; Forced migration; Ostracism; Otherness; Outcastes; Purges; Refugees; Social isolation.

Outcome, therapeutic. See *Treatment outcomes.*

Outcome, treatment. See *Treatment outcome.*

Outcomes. See *Effects; Results.*

Outcomes, psychotherapeutic. See *Psychotherapeutic outcomes.*

Outdoor activities. See *Camping; Recreation; Sports; Vacations.*

Outdoor advertising. Outdoor advertis(ing, ement,ements). Billboard(s). Open air advertising. Outdoor boards. Outdoor ad(s). Roadside advertis(ing,ement, ements). Highway sign(s). *Choose from:* outdoor, open air, roadside, highway *with:* advertis(ing,ement,ements), board(s), ad(s), sign(s,age). *Consider also:* poster advertising, advertising sign(s), Burma-Shave sign(s), poster(s) in public place(s), ambient advertising. *See also* Advertising; Graffiti.

Outdoor life. Outdoor life. *Choose from:* outdoor(s), alfresco, fresh air *with:* life, lifestyle, living, activit(y,ies). *Consider also:* outdoor recreation, mountain climbing, mountain sport(s), hiking, camping, skiing, hunting, fishing, boating. *See also* Camping; Recreation; Sports; Survival; Vacations.

Outer space. See *Extraterrestrial space.*

Outlaws. See *Bandits; Career criminals; Computer hackers; Delinquents; Deviant behavior; Elderly offenders; Female offenders; Juvenile gangs; Male offenders; Mentally ill offenders; Offenders; Perpetrators; Serial murderers.*

Outlook (attitude). See *Attitudes; Worldview.*

Outlook (future). See *Economic forecasting; Employment forecasting; Forecasting; Future; Future of society; Political forecasting; Prediction; Trends; Weather forecasting.*

Outpatient treatment. Outpatient treatment. *Choose from:* outpatient(s), ambulatory, walk-in, clinic(s), dispensar(y,ies) *with:* treat(ed,ing, ment,ments), therap(y,ies), surger(y,ies), psychotherap(y,ies), service(s). *Consider also:* aftercare. *See also* Aftercare; Ambulatory care; Ambulatory surgery; Clinics; Drug therapy; Home care; Outpatients; Psychiatric clinics; Walk-in clinics.

Outpatients. Outpatient(s). *Choose from:* ambulatory, clinic, aftercare, polyclinic, ambulatory center(s), walk-in *with:* patient(s), client(s), population(s). *See also* Aftercare; Ambulatory care; Clinics; Patient discharge; Patients; Walk-in clinics.

Outplacement services. Outplacement service(s). Career transition tool(s). *Choose from:* outplacement, reemployment *with:* service(s), firm(s), program(s), counseling, agenc(y,ies). *Choose from:* unemploy(ed,ment), downsized, dismiss(ed,al), fired, firing(s), layoff(s), laid off, discharge(d), terminat(e,ed,ion,ions), retrench(ed,ing, ment,ments), displace(d,ment,ments) *with:* job(s), employee(s), staff, personnel, worker(s), *with:* opportunit(y, ies), vocational guidance, counseling, job placement, benefit(s), support program(s), transition program(s). *Consider also:* dislocated worker program(s), transition management process. *See also* Dismissal of staff; Downsizing; Employment counseling; Personnel termination; Severance pay.

Output. See *Productivity.*

Output, labor. See *Productivity*

Outreach programs. Outreach program(s). Outreaching. *Choose from:* outreach, community, extended, extension, branch, village, neighborhood, store front, local(ity,ities) *with:* program(s), service(s), worker(s), campus(es), librar(y,ies), health care, nurse(s), recruitment, operation(s). *Consider also:* community *with:* health, relations, medicine, mental health, psychiatry. *See also* After school programs; Antipoverty programs; Community health centers; Community health services; Community institutional relations; Community mental health services; Community services; Delivery of services; Food services (programs); Health promotion; Health services; Help lines (telephone); Home visiting programs; Intervention; Mental health programs; Social programs.

Outsiders. See *Alienation; Ostracism; Social isolation.*

Outsourcing. See *Contracting out; Downsizing; Privatization; Subcontracting; Temporary help services.*

Over 80. See *Aged 80 and over.*

Over the counter medicines. See *Nonprescription drugs.*

Overachievement. Overachiev(ement,ers, ed,ing). Superwom(an,en). Supermom(s). Achievement beyond expectation(s). Type A personalit(y,ies). Excel(led,ling). Achievement oriented. Perfection(ism,ist,ists). *Consider also:* high, superior, outstanding *with:* achiev(ement,ers,ed,ing), performance(s). *See also* Academic overachievement; Achievement; Perfectionism; Success; Underachievement.

Overachievement, academic. See *Academic overachievement.*

Overdoses, drug. See *Drug overdoses.*

Overeating. See *Bulimia; Hyperphagia.*

Overinclusion. Overinclus(ion,ive,iveness). *Consider also:* schizophrenic speech, disturbance(s) *with:* association, thought, thinking. *See also* Thought disturbances.

Overlearning. Overlearn(ed,ing). *Consider also:* too much practice, overtrain(ed, ing), overcorrect(ed,ing,ion), overpractic(e,ed,ing), overextinction, excess(ive) practice. *See also* Learning.

Overload, information. See *Info fatigue syndrome.*

Overpopulation. Overpopulat(ion,ed). Population explosion. Rapid population growth. Grow(th,ing) population. Ris(e,ing) population(s). Dense(ly) populat(ed,ion). Overcrowd(ed,ing).

Crowd(ed,ing). Social density. Urban density. *Choose from:* population *with:* boom, explosion, bomb, problem(s), density, capacity. *Consider also:* fertility rate(s), population trend(s). *See also* Birthrate; Community size; Crowding; Demography; Emigration; Environmental stress; Family planning; Fertility; Population density; Population distribution; Population growth; Population policy; Social problems; Survival; Urban population; World population; World problems.

Overprotection. Overprotect(ed,ing,ive, iveness,ion). Excessive(ly) protect(ed, ion,ive). Sheltered childhood. *Consider also:* enmesh(ed,ment), parental fear(s), overcontrol(led,ling), overinvolv(ed, ement), affectionless control, overindulgen(t,ce), shield(ed,ing). *See also* Father child relations; Mother child relations; Parent child relations; Possessiveness;

Overtime work. Overtime work. Work(ing) overtime. Work(ing) off the clock. Off the clock work. Long workday(s). Work(ing) extra hour(s). 60 hour week(s). *Consider also:* overwork(ed, ing), working night(s). *See also* Alternative work patterns; Moonlighting; Part time employment; Personnel scheduling; Work load; Work schedules; Workday shifts; Working conditions; Worktime.

Overtures (music). Overture(s). Ouverture(s), Prelude(s). *Consider also:* baroque suite(s), vorspiel(en), sinfonia, introduzione(s). *See also* Incidental music; Introduction; Music; Opera; Preludes; Symphonic poems.

Overweight. See *Obesity.*

Overwork. Overwork(ed,ing). Work(ed,ing) overtime. Overtax(ed,ing). Overburden(ed,ing). Overexert(ed,ing). Overstrain(ed,ing). Overload(ed,ing). Overladen. Overextend(ed,ing). Overdo(ne,ing). Overemploy(ed,ing). Overstress(ed,ing). Overlabor(ed,ing). *See also* Burnout; Industrial fatigue; Occupational stress; Sweatshops; Working conditions.

Owned, minority. See *Minority businesses.*

Owned, privately. See *Private enterprise.*

Ownership. Own(ed,ing,er,ers,ership). Possess(ed,ing,or,ors,ion). Proprietor(s, ship). Hold(ing) title. Proprietary. Landowner(s). Landlord(s). Belonging(s). Usufruct. *See also* Abandoned property; Absentee ownership; Acquisition; Common ownership; Cultural property; Employee ownership; Expropriation; Government property; Home ownership; Industrial property; Intangible property; Land ownership; Nationalization; Personal property; Privatization; Property rights; Provenance; Public property; Real estate; Slavery; Wealth.

Ownership, absentee. See *Absentee ownership.*

Ownership, common. See *Common ownership.*

Ownership, employee. See *Employee ownership.*

Ownership, government. See *Government property; Nationalization; Socialism.*

Ownership, home. See *Home ownership.*

Ownership, land. See *Land ownership.*

Ownership, stock. See *Employee stock ownership plans; Investments; Stockholders.*

Ownership, worker. See *Employee ownership; Syndicalism.*

Owning class. See *Ruling class.*

Oxymoron. Oxymoron(s,ic). Self contradict(ion,ory). Incongruous combination(s). Contradictory opposition(s). Marriage of opposites. Juxtaposition of contra(ry,dictions). *Consider also:* paradox(es,ical,ically). *See also* Contradictions; Irony; Paradoxes.

P

Pacific Islanders. Pacific Islander(s). *Choose from:* Pacific Island(s), Guam, Samoa(n), Saipan, Tinian, Caroline Islands, Marshall Islands, Marianas Islands, Marianne Islands *with:* population(s), people(s), group(s), populace, tribe(s), resident(s), inhabitant(s). *Consider also:* Polynesian(s), Micronesian(s), Hawaiian(s). *See also* Asian Americans; Australoid race; Indigenous populations; Mongoloid race; People of color; Races; Racially mixed.

Pacific region. Pacific region. Pacific countr(y,ies). Pacific rim. *See also* Far East; Oceania; South Asia; Southeast Asia.

Pacifism. Pacif(ism,ist,ists,istic). Oppos(e,ed,ing,ition) to violence. Oppos(e,ed,ing,ition) to war. Peace(ful,fulness,able,making). Peace loving. Nonviolen(ce,t). Dovish. Dove(s). Noncombat(ant,ants,ive). War resister(s). Irenic. Conscientious objector(s). *See also* Conscientious objectors; Just war doctrine; Moral authority; Neutrality; Noncombatants; Nonresistance to evil; Nonviolence; Peace movements; War attitudes; War prevention.

Packages, buyout. See *Buyout packages.*

Packaging. See *Containers.*

Packinghouses. See *Meat industry.*

Paganism. Pagan(ism,ize,ization). Heathen(s,ism). Polythe(ism,istic). Idol(s,atry). Astral cult(s). Deistic plurality. Witchcraft. Infidel(s). Irreligious. Panthe(ism,istic). Demon(ism). *Consider also:* heres(y, ies), heretic(s), Druid(s), witch(es), pre-Christian. *See also* Animism; Deities; Infidels; Sacrificial rites; Traditional societies.

Pageants. Pageant(s,ry). Spectacle(s). Show(s). Exhibition(s). Pomp. Ceremon(y,ies). Parade(s). Procession *with:* float(s). Tableau(x) vivant. *Consider also:* miracle play(s). *See also* Drama festivals; Historical drama; Folk festivals; Miracle plays.

Pagodas. See *Temples.*

Pain. Pain(s,ed,ful). Ach(es,ing). Aphagia. Back pain. Backache(s). Bellyache(s). Colic. Cramp(s). Discomfort(s). Distress. Dysphoria. Earache(s). Glossalgia. Hurt(ing). Lumbago. Malaise. Migraine. Neuralgia. Nociperception. Nocicept(ion,ive,ors). Pang(s). Prickl(e,ed,ing). Smarting. Sore(ness). Sting(ing). Stung. Stomachache(s).

Suffer(ed,ing). Temporomandibular joint syndrome. Throb(s,bing). Twinge(s). Toothache(s). *Consider also:* intractable, postoperative, chronic, intermittent, constant, psychogenic *with:* pain(s), ache(s), discomfort, sore(ness). *Choose from:* migraine, muscle contraction, cluster, vascular *with:* headache(s). *Consider also:* algesia, algesthesia. *See also* Backache; Chronic disease; Chronic pain; Headache; Psychogenic pain; Pain perception.

Pain, chronic. See *Chronic pain.*

Pain, psychogenic. See *Psychogenic pain.*

Pain perception. Pain perception. *Choose from:* pain(s,ful), ache(s), discomfort, shock(s), footshock(s), noxious stimuli *with:* perception, perceived, awareness, threshold(s), assess(ed,ment), judgment(s), report(ed,ing,s), responsivity, rating(s), estimate(d,s), tolerance, measurement, recall, description, sensation(s), sensitivity. *Consider also:* noci-perception, nocicept(ive,ors). *See also* Analgesia; Chronic pain; Pain; Pain phobia.

Pain phobia. Pain phobia(s). Algophob(ia, ic). Odynophob(ia,ic). *Consider also:* pain, discomfort *with:* phob(ia,ias,ic), fear(ful). *See also* Pain; Pain perception; Phobias.

Pain relief. See *Analgesia.*

Pain thresholds. See *Pain perception.*

Painters, modern. See *Modern art.*

Painting, ink. See *Ink painting.*

Painting, monochrome. See *Monochrome painting.*

Painting and decoration, mural. See *Mural painting and decoration.*

Painting and illustration, animal. See *Animal painting and illustration.*

Painting and staining, glass. See *Glass painting and staining.*

Paintings, cave. See *Cave paintings.*

Pair bond. Pair bond(s). Coupling. Couple(s). Mated pair(s). *Choose from:* mate(s,d) *with:* life(long,time). Human bond(s,ing). *See also* Bonding (emotional); Dyads.

Paired associate learning. Paired associate learning. *Choose from:* paired associat(e, ion,ions) *with:* learn(ed,ing), recall, task(s). *See also* Verbal learning; Word association.

Pairs. See *Dyads.*

Palaces. Palace(s). Royal residence(s). Royal house(s). Royal mansion(s).

Choose from: royal(ty), king(ly), palatial, monarch(al,ical), sovereign(s) *with:* residence(s), house(s), mansion(s), estate(s), home(s), chateau(x,s). *Consider also:* Windsor Castle, etc. *See also* Coronation; Historic houses; Manors; Monarchy; Royalty.

Palate, cleft. See *Cleft palate.*

Paleobotany. Paleobotan(y,ical). *Choose from:* ancient, Carboniferous, Cretaceous, Cambrian, Devonian, Jurassic, Triassic, Permian, Silurian, Ordovician, fossil(s,ized) *with:* fern(s), fung(us,i), mushroom(s), cupule(s), flower(s), fruit(s), pollen(s), spore(s), plant(s), sporophyte(s), gametophyte(s), forest(s), tree(s), seed(s), botan(y,ical). *Consider also:* palynology. *See also* Fossils; Geology; Paleontology.

Paleodontology. Paleodontolog(y,ical). *Choose from:* pre-Columbian, prehistoric, paleobiophysical, early man, bronze age, ancient *with:* dental, teeth, tooth, caries, orthodontic. *See also* Paleontology; Paleopathology; Prehistoric people.

Paleoecology. Paleoecolog(y,ical). Prehistoric ecology. Paleoenvironment(s,al). Paleoclimat(e,es,ology,ological). *Choose from:* fossil(s,ized), ancient, antiquity, prehistoric, primitive culture(s), bronze age, iron age, stone age, ice age, neolithic, paleolithic, Quaternary Period, Jurassic, Holocene, Pleistocene, dinosaur(s) *with:* ecolog(y,ies,ical), plant(s), animal(s), physical environment(s), geolog(y,ical), climate, organism(s), biologic(al) relationship(s), vegetation, land cover, fire effect(s). *Consider also:* palynolog(y,ical). *See also* Animal remains (archaeology); Archaeological chemistry; Archaeology; Ecology; Plant remains (archaeology).

Paleography. Paleograph(y,ic). *Consider also:* archaeolog(y,ical), ancient, early, rustic, Carolingian, Roman *with:* inscription(s), writing, handwriting, majuscule(s), minuscule(s). *See also* Inscriptions; Writing.

Paleolithic period. Paleolithic period. Palaeolithic period. Old stone age. *Choose from:* Choukoutienian, Clactonian, Chellean-Abbevillian, Acheulian, Levalloisian, Mousterian, Aurignacian, Perigordian, Solutrean, Magdalenian *with:* period(s), culture(s). *Consider also:* earliest human ancestors, Chopper chopping-tool industry, Neanderthal man. *See also* Mesolithic period; Prehistoric people.

Paleontology. Paleontolog(y,ic,ical,ist,ists). Palaeontolog(y,ical). Fossil(s,ized, ization). Micropaleontolog(y,ical). Paleoanthropolog(y,ical). Paleoecolog(y, ical). Paleodontolog(y,ical). Paleopatholog(y,ical). *See also* Animal remains (archaeology); Evolution; Fossils; Geology; Human remains (archaeology); Paleobotany; Paleodontology; Paleography; Paleopathology; Physical anthropology; Plant remains (archaeology).

Paleopathology. Paleopatholog(y,ies,ical). Prehistoric disease(s). *Choose from:* pre-Columbian Indian(s), pre-Hispanic, prehuman, fossil(s), paleobiophysical, early man, ice age, antiquity, prehistoric, primitive culture(s), bronze age, iron age, stone age, neolithic, paleolithic *with:* patholog(y,ies,ical), osteopatholog(y,ies,ical), paleodiet(s,ary), parasite(s), morbidity, health, disease(s), diagnos(is,es), disorder(s), disabilit(y ,ies), cause(s) of death, wound(s), injur(y,ies), infect(ed,ing,ion,ions), nutrition, trauma(tic), degenerative, arthritis, dental wear, tooth loss, inflammat(ion,ions,ory), tumor(s), malignan(t,cy,cies), cancer. *See also* Medical anthropology; Paleodontology; Physical anthropology; Prehistoric people; Traditional medicine.

Palliative treatment. Palliative treatment(s). Palliat(e,ed,ing,ion,ions). *Choose from:* palliat(e,ed,ing,ive), alleviat(e,ed,ing, ion,ions), analgesic *with:* therap(y,ies), measure(s), treatment(s), management, care, intervention(s), procedure(s). *Consider also:* reliev(e,ed,ing,er,ers), relief, manag(e,ed,ing,ement), control(led,ling), treatment *with:* pain(ful), suffering, distress. *See also* Analgesia; Placebos.

Palsy, cerebral. See *Cerebral palsy.*

Pamphlets. Pamphlet(s). Brochure(s). Leaflet(s). Booklet(s). Flyer(s). Broadside(s). *Consider also:* handout(s), bulletin(s), circular(s), tract(s), prospectus(es). *See also* Bulletins; Publications.

Pan-Africanism. Pan-African(ism). African bloc. African unity. *Consider also:* Organization of African Unity, African National Congress, Pan African Congress, Polisario, SWAPO, South-West African Peoples Organization. *See also* Black power; Cultural identity; Decolonization; Geopolitics; Nationalist movements; Political self determination; Regional movements.

Panegyrics. See *Commemoration; Laudatory poetry; Tribute.*

Panel studies. Panel stud(y,ies). *Choose from:* followup, semilongitudinal, longitudinal, panel, long term *with:* stud(y,ies), test(s), research, data, assessment(s), method(s), analy(sis,ses), survey(s), comparison(s), observation(s),

factor(s), model(s), evaluation(s), experiment(s), investigation(s), case stud(y,ies). *Consider also:* case histor(y,ies), stud(y,ies) over time, time series, followups, sequential stud(y,ies), time structured data, life span research, aging stud(y,ies), measurement over time, developmental histor(y,ies), retrospective stud(y,ies). *Consider specific time periods, for example:* five month study, five year study or 1950 to 1980, etc. *See also* Longitudinal studies.

Panhandling. See *Begging.*

Panic. Panic(s,ky). Overwhelming anxiet(y,ies). Terror(s,ized). Extreme anxious(ness). Very afraid. Highly fearful. Unreasoning terror. Sudden fear. *Choose from:* panic(s), anxiet(y,ies), fright(ened) *with:* overpowering, struck, stricken, state(s), attack(s). *Consider also:* stage fright. *See also* Anxiety; Fear; Panic disorder.

Panic disorder. Panic disorder(s). *Consider also:* panic attack(s), agoraphob(ia,ic, ics), free floating anxiet(y,ies). *See also* Anxiety disorders; Panic.

Panics, economic. See *Economic crises.*

Pantheism (polytheism). Pantheis(t,tic, tical,tically). Polytheis(t,tic,tical,tically). Polydemonis(t,tic,tical,tically). Polydaemonis(t,tic,tical,tically). Plural(ity) of gods. *See also* God concepts; Religious beliefs; Sacred animals.

Pantheism (universal divinity). Pantheis(t, tic,tical,tically). God is all. *Choose from:* divin(e,ity), sacred(ness), God *with:* univers(e,al,ality), indwelling, inherent, ever present, infinity, unlimited(ness), all inclusive(ness), reality, unity, creativity, all pervasive(ness), immanen(ce,t), essence. *Consider also:* acosmi(c,sm,t, ts), akosmi(c,sm,t,ts), emanation, ecospiritual(ity), creation theology, Gaia, divine mind, divine whole, divine principle. *See also* Buddhism; Deep ecology; God concepts; Immanence of god; Monism; Natural theology; Nontheistic religion; Personalism; Presence of God; Religion; Religious beliefs; Sacred animals; Taoism.

Papacy. Papa(l,cy). Pope(s). Bishop of Rome. Pontiff. Pontifical. *Choose from:* Julius I, Innocent I, Leo I, Gregory I, Martin I, Leo III, Gregory VII, Alexander III, Innocent III, Clement V, Gregory XI, Alexander VI, Clement XIV, Pius VII, Leo XIII, Pius X, Benedict XV, Pius IX, Pius XII, John XXIII, etc. *Consider also:* Pontifex, Roman Curia, Vatican, petrine, Holy See, Great Schism, Council of Trent, Lateran treaty. *See also* Clergy; Medieval theology; Religious councils and synods; Religious leadership; Roman Catholicism.

Paparazzi. See *Journalistic ethics; Journalists; Photographers; Tabloids.*

Parables. Parable(s). Allegor(y,ies,ical). Fable(s). Moral(ity) stor(y,ies). Moral(ity) play(s). *See also* Folk literature; Folklore; Personification.

Paradigms. Paradigm(s). Microparadigm(s). Framework(s). *Consider also:* schema, major concept(s), conceptual framework(s), theor(y,ies), codification of categor(y, ies), construct(s), archetype(s), scientific revolution(s), normal science. *See also* Constructs; Qualitative methods; Research; Theories.

Paradise. Paradise. Garden of Eden. Shangri-la. Xanadu. Kingdom come. Beulah Land. Nirvana. Land of the Lotus Eaters. Fairyland. Happy hunting ground(s). *See also* Heaven; Nature worship; Utopias.

Paradoxes. Paradox(es,ical). Contradict(ory,ion,ions). Conflict(ing). Incongru(ity,ities,ous). Discrepan(t,cy, cies). Inconsisten(t,cy,cies). Oxymoron(ic,s). Self-contradict(ory,ion, ions). Antinom(y,ies,ic). *Consider also:* equivocat(e,ed,ing,ion), puzzl(e,ed,ing), baffl(e,ed,ing), dilemma(s), enigma(s, tic), perplex(ed,ing), ambiguit(y,ies). *See also* Contradictions; Dialectics; Dissent; Irony; Liar paradox; Oxymoron.

Paradoxical techniques. Paradoxical technique(s). Paradigmatic technique(s). Reframing. *Choose from:* paradox(ical), contralogical *with:* treatment(s), technique(s), psychotherap(y,ies), therap(y,ies), procedure(s), instruction(s), method(s), therapeutic, prescription(s). *See also* Behavior modification; Psychotherapeutic techniques.

Parallel economy. See *Informal sector.*

Parallelism. See *Literary parallels.*

Parallels, literary. See *Literary parallels.*

Paralysis, hysterical. See *Hysterical paralysis.*

Paramedical personnel. See *Allied health personnel.*

Paramedical sciences. Paramedical science(s). Health science(s). *Choose from:* paramedical, allied health *with:* science(s), field(s), subject(s). *Consider also:* physical therapy, physiotherapy, pharmacy, pharmacology, psychopharmacology, audiology, nursing, optometry, nurse practitioner(s), physician assistant(s), paramedic(s), paramedical personnel, health care worker(s). *See also* Medical sciences; Nurses; Physical therapy; Psychopharmacology.

Parameters, response. See *Response parameters.*

Paramilitary. Paramilitar(ism,y). Minute(men,man,women,woman). Political gang(s). *Consider also:* guerrilla(s), vigilant(e,es,ism), vigilance committee(s), Freikorps, Fasci di Combattimenti, People's Militia. *See also* Anti-government radicals; Armed forces; Death squads; Guerrilla warfare; Guerrillas; Vigilantes; White supremacy movements.

Paramnesia. Paramnesia. *Choose from:* false *with:* memor(y,ies), recognition. *Consider also:* deja entendu, deja pense, deja raconte, deja vecu. *See also* Memory disorders.

Paranoid disorder, atypical. See *Involutional psychosis.*

Paranoid disorder, shared. See *Psychosis of association.*

Paranoid disorders. Paranoi(a,d,dal,c,ac). Delusion(s) of persecution. Persecution complex(es). Paranoid psychos(is,es). Suspicious(ness). Jealous(y,ness). Distrust(ful). Mistrust(ful). *Choose from:* paranoid *with:* behavior(s), disorder(s), personality, symptom(s), trait(s), syndrome(s), dementia, delusion(s), obsession(s). *See also* Mental illness; Paranoid schizophrenia; Psychosis of association.

Paranoid schizophrenia. Paranoid schizophreni(a,as,c,cs). *Choose from:* schizophreni(a,as,c,cs) *with:* paranoi(d, a). *Consider also:* litigious, depressed, persecutory, grandiose, erotomaniacal *with:* schizophreni(a,as,c,cs). *See also* Paranoid disorders; Schizophrenia.

Paranormal. See *Extrasensory perception; Occultism; Parapsychology.*

Paraphilias. Paraphilia(s). *Consider also:* sex offense(s), impulse control disorder(s), sexual deviation(s), bestiality, exhibitionis(m,t,ts), fetishis(m,t,ts), frottage, frotteur(s,ism,ist,ists), masochis(m,t,ts), pedophil(e,es,ia), sadis(m,t,ts), transvest(ite,ites,ism), voyeur(s,ism), incest(uous), transsexualism, perversion(s), pervert(ed), zoophil(e,es,ia), zooerasty, coprophil(ia, iac,iacs), klismaphil(e,es,ia), mysophil(e,es,ia), necrophil(e,es,ia), telephone scatalogia, urophil(e,es,ia), scopophil(e,es,ia), algamatophil(e,es,ia), erotomania, sexual aberration(s). *See also* Depravity; Exhibitionism; Fetishism; Incest; Pedophilia; Sexual deviations; Sexual masochism; Sexual sadism; Transsexualism; Transvestism; Voyeurism.

Paraplegia. Parapleg(ia,ias,ic,ics). *Consider also:* quadripleg(ia,ias,ic,ics). *Consider also:* paralysis, spinal cord injur(y,ies) *with:* leg(s), lower extremit(y,ies). *See also* Disability; Injuries; Spinal cord injuries.

Paraprofessional personnel. Paraprofessional personnel. Paraprofessional(s). Paralegal(s). Paramedic(s). Physicians assistant(s). Teacher aide(s). *Choose from:* nonprofessional, subprofessional, paraprofessional *with:* personnel, worker(s), counselor(s). *Choose from:* agricultural, casework, chemical, child, community, community health, dental, electronic, emergency medical, engineering, environmental, family, forestry, health care, housing management, laboratory, library, marine, mechanical design, medical, medical records, metallurgical, nuclear power plant, nursing, operating room, paramedical, pharmacist(s), physician(s), production, radiography, school, social work, teacher(s), veterinary *with:* paraprofessional(s), nonprofessional(s), subprofessional(s), assistant(s), technician(s), aide(s), caregiver(s), trained volunteer(s), auxiliar(y,ies), attendant(s). *See also* Allied health personnel; Attendants; Gold collar workers; Nonprofessional personnel; Professional personnel.

Parapsychology. Parapsycholog(y,ical). Amulet(s). Apport. Astral projection. Astral travel. Astrology. Apparition(s). Black magic. Cabal(a,ism). Chakra(s). Cosmology. Clairvoyan(t,ce). Deathbed vision(s). Demon(ic,ology). Demon possession. Devil(s). Divination. Divining rods. Dowsing. Duende(s). Dybbuk(s). Earth ray(s). ESP. Extrasensory perception. Extrasensible. Exorcis(m,t). Fortune telling. Firewalking. Flying saucer(s). Ghost(s). Hobgoblin(s). Haunted house(s). Haunting. Horoscop(e,y). Human aura. Hex(es). Jinx(es). Incantation(s). Kirlian photography. Levitation(s). Magic(al). Medium(s). Mental healing. Mystic(al, ism,s). Near death experience(s). Necromancy. Nostradamus. Out of body. Obe. Obeah. Occult(ism). Orgone energy. PSI. Paranormal. Pseudoscientific. Parapsychosomatic(s). Phantom(s). Possession trance(s). Precognition. Psychic(al,s). Psychic healing. Psychokine(sis,tic). Psychophotography. Poltergeist(s). Radiesthesia. Reincarnation. Seance(s). Shamanis(m,tic). Spirit possession. Spiritualis(m,tic). Supernatural(ism). Survival after death. Telekine(sis,tic). Telepath(y,ic). Thaumaturgy. Verver(s). Voodoo. Werewol(f,ves). Witchcraft. *See also* Clairvoyance; Extrasensory perception; Near death experiences; Occultism; Telepathy; Witchcraft.

Parasites. Parasit(e,es,ic,ism,oid,oids, ology). Ectoparasit(e,es,ic,ism). Endoparasit(e,es,ic,ism). Obligate parasite(s). Facultative parasite(s). Helminth(s,ic,iases). Trematod(e,es,a). Cestod(e,es,a). *Consider also:* bloodsucking animal(s), flea(s), lice, louse, tapeworm(s), liver fluke(s), ascarid(s), leech(s), mite(s), parasitic worm(s), parasitic copepod(s,a), parasitic nematod(e,es,a), parasitic disease(s). *See also* Animals; Food contamination; Liver disorders; Predatory animals.

Parasites, social. See *Social parasites.*

Pardon. Pardon(ed,ing,s). Forgive(n,ness). Forgave. Amnesty. Repriev(al,e). Absolve(d). Early release. Stay execution. Shortened prison term. Free(ing) prisoner(s). Allow exile(s) to return. Term commuted. Release(d) prisoner(s). Merc(y,iful). Clemenc(y,ies). Exonerat(ed,ion). Commute(d) sentence(s). *See also* Amnesty; Clemency; Courts; Exemption (law); Forgiveness; Indulgences.

Parent, single family. See *Single parent family.*

Parent adolescent relations. Parent adolescent relation(ship,s). *Choose from:* adolescen(ts,ce), teen(s,age,aged,ager, agers), high school student(s), junior high school student(s), youth *with:* parent(al,s), mother(s), father(s) *with:* relation(s,ships), lov(e,ing), influence(s), attachment(s), support, feeling(s), bond(s,ing), play(ed,ing), interact(ed, ing,ion,ions), comfort(ed,ing), abuse, discipline, permissiveness, overprotect(ion,ive), nurtur(ed,ing,ance), depriv(e,ed,ing,ation), communicat(e,ed, ing,ion), incest(uous), role(s), dependenc(e,y), independen(t,ce), conflict(s), dynamics, understand(ing), understood, accept(ed,ing,ance), reject(ed,ing,ion), expectation(s). *Consider also:* oedip(al,us) *with:* conflict(s), complex(es). *See also* Family background; Father child relations; Generation gap; Home environment; Mother child relations; Parent child relations; Shared parenting.

Parent aspiration. Parent aspiration(s). *Choose from:* parent(s,al), mother(s), father(s), paternal, maternal *with:* expectation(s), aspiration(s), goal(s), hope(s), prediction(s), encouragement. *See also* Aspirations; Parent child relations; Parent adolescent relations; Parent role.

Parent attitudes. See *Parental attitudes.*

Parent child communication. Parent child communication(s). *Choose from:* parent(s,al), mother(s), father(s), maternal, paternal *with:* child(ren), infant(s), offspring, student(s), adolescent(s), daughter(s), son(s) *with:* rapport, disclosure, discussion, self expression, interaction, communication(s), communicat(e,ed,ing), verbaliz(e,ed,ing,ation), conversation(s), conflict resolution, dialog(s), message(s), closeness. *See also* Father child communication; Mother child communication; Parent child relations.

Parent child relations. Parent child relation(ship,s). Parenting. Mothering. Fathering. *Choose from:* infant(s), child(ren), youngster(s), toddler(s), boy(s), girl(s), son(s), daughter(s), preadolescen(ts,ce), juvenile(s), adolescen(ts,ce), teen(s,age,aged,ager, agers), high school student(s), junior high school student(s), youth *with:* parent(al,s), mother(s), father(s) *with:* relation(s,ships), lov(e,ing), influence(s), attachment(s), support, feeling(s), bond(s,ing), play(ed,ing), interaction(s), comfort(ed,ing), abuse, discipline, permissive(ness), overprotect(ion,ive), nurtur(ed,ing,ance), depriv(e,ed,ing, ation), communicat(e,ed,ing,ion), incest(uous), role(s), dependenc(e,y), independen(t,ce), conflict(s), dynamics, understand(ing), understood, accept(ed,ing,ance), reject(ed,ing,ion), expectation(s), rebell(ious,iousness,ion), absence, presence. *Consider also:* oedip(al,us), electra *with:* conflict(s), complex(es). *See also* Child discipline; Childrearing; Father child relations; Mother child relations; Nurturance; Overprotection; Parent adolescent relations; Parent child communication; Parent role; Parent training; Parental attitudes; Possessiveness.

Parent effectiveness training. See *Parent training.*

Parent help groups. Parent help group(s). *Choose from:* parent(s), mother(s), father(s), famil(y,ies) *with:* association(s), self help, support group(s), group psychotherapy, aide(s), anonymous, helper(s), lay therapy, mutual aid, mutual support. *See also* Child abuse prevention; Euthenics; Parent training; Self help groups.

Parent influence. See *Family influence.*

Parent rights. Parent(s,al) right(s). *Choose from:* parent(s,al), maternal, paternal, father(s), mother(s) *with:* right(s), due process, advoca(tes,cy). *Consider also:* custody rights, right to maternity leave, parental access. *See also* Child advocacy; Children's rights; Civil rights; Human rights; Ombudsmen; Student rights.

Parent role. Parent(s,al) role(s). Parenting. Mothering. Fathering. *Choose from:* parent(s,al,ing), mother(s), father(s), maternal, paternal, childrearing child care *with:* role(s), influence(s), behavior(s), function(s), involvement, authority. *See also* Family roles; Parent child relations; Parent adolescent relations; Parental attitudes; Parental permissiveness.

Parent school relations. Parent school relation(s,ship). PTA. Parent teacher association. *Choose from:* parent(s,al), father(s), mother(s), home *with:* school(s), teacher(s) *with:* relation(s,ship), involvement, interaction(s), conference(s), cooperation, conflict(s), communication(s). *See also* Parent aspiration; Parental attitudes; School adjustment; Student teacher relations.

Parent teacher relationship. See *Parent school relations.*

Parent training. Parent training. Parent effectiveness training. *Choose from:* parent(ing,hood), child management, family life, marriage *with:* effectiveness training, training, education, moral education, program(s), group(s), learning skill(s), class(es). *See also* Child abuse prevention; Parent help groups; Parent role; Parenthood.

Parental absence. Parental absence. Broken home(s). Fatherless(ness). Motherless(ness). *Choose from:* maternal, paternal, parent(s,al,hood), mother(s), father(s) *with:* deprivation, absen(t,ce), death, separation, loss, desert(ed,ing,ion), lone, single, neglect(ful,ing). *Consider also:* one parent, motherless, fatherless *with:* famil(y,ies). *Consider also:* latchkey kid(s), working mother(s). *See also* Abandoned children; Anaclitic depression; Child custody; Deadbeat parents; Failure to thrive (psychosocial); Maternal deprivation; Single parent family.

Parental aspiration. See *Parent aspiration.*

Parental attitudes. Parent(al) attitude(s). *Choose from:* parent(al,s), mother(s), father(s), paternal, maternal *with:* attitude(s), opinion(s), expectation(s), feeling(s), perception(s), concern(s), acceptance, rejection, fear(s), aspiration(s), hope(s), mindset. *See also* Childrearing; Parent child relations; Parent role; Parental consent; Parental permissiveness.

Parental background. Parent(s,al) background. Family size. Maternal employment. Parent(s,al) residence. Home resource(s). *Choose from:* famil(y,ies,ial), parent(s,al), mother(s), father(s), maternal, paternal *with:* background, educational background, level of education, literacy, schooling, status, socioeconomic status, income, background, occupation(s,al), values, marital status, employment, profile(s), residen(ces,tial), aspiration(s), rac(e,ial), religion, ethnic(ity), expectation(s), resource(s). *See also* Family background; Family characteristics; Family history; Family influence.

Parental behavior. See *Maternal behavior; Paternal behavior.*

Parental behavior, animal. See *Animal parental behavior.*

Parental consent. Parent(al,s) consent(ed, ing). *Choose from:* parent(al,s), mother(s), father(s) *with:* consent(ed, ing), approv(e,ed,ing,al), permit(ted, ting), permission(s), assent(ed,ing), sanction(s,ed,ing). *Consider also:* parental notification. *See also* Age of majority; Consent (law); Informed consent; Parental attitudes; Parental permissiveness.

Parental involvement. See *Involvement; Parent adolescent relations; Parent aspiration; Parent child relations; Parent school relations; Parental attitudes.*

Parental leave. See *Maternity leave; Paternity leave.*

Parental occupation. Parental occupation(s). *Choose from:* parent(s,al), mother(s), father(s), paternal, maternal, famil(y,ies) *with:* occupation(s,al), work(ed,ing), job(s), employ(ed,ing, ment), dual career(s), profession(s,al). *See also* Family socioeconomic status; Family work relationship; Parental background.

Parental permissiveness. Parental permissiveness. *Choose from:* parent(s,al,ally), mother(s), father(s), maternal, paternal *with:* permissive(ness), indulgent, lenien(t,cy), unrestrictive, lax(ity,ness), unrestrained, overindulgent, toleran(t,ce), easygoing, unstructured, appeas(e,ed,er,ers,ment). *See also* Child discipline; Childrearing; Family relations; Parental attitudes; Parental consent.

Parental power. See *Family power.*

Parental rights. See *Parent rights.*

Parenthood. Parent(s,ing,hood). Parental relationship(s). Parent role(s). Mother(s,ing,hood). Father(s,ing,hood). Matern(al,ity). Patern(al,ity). *See also* Childlessness; Childrearing; Delayed parenthood; Family size; Life stage transitions; Single parent family.

Parenthood, delayed. See *Delayed parenthood.*

Parenthood, planned. See *Birth control; Family planning.*

Parenting. See *Childrearing.*

Parenting, shared. See *Shared parenting.*

Parentis, in loco. See *Legal guardians.*

Parents. Parent(s,al,ing,hood). Mother(s, ing,hood). Maternal. Father(s,ing,hood). Paternal. *Consider also:* stepparent(s), biological parent(s), adoptive parent(s), surrogate parent(s), foster parent(s). *See also* Adoptive parents; Fathers; Mothers; Schizophrenogenic family; Single mothers; Single parent family; Stepfamily; Surrogate mothers.

Parents, abusive. See *Abusive parents.*

Parents, adoptive. See *Adoptive parents.*

Parents, birth. See *Biological family.*

Parents, deadbeat. See *Deadbeat parents.*

Parents, dependent. See *Dependent parents.*

Parents, foster. See *Foster parents.*

Parents, lone. See *Single parent family.*

Parents, runaway. See *Desertion.*

Pariahs. See *Outcasts.*

Parishes. Parish(es). Ecclesiastical district(s). Vicariate(s). Bishopric(s). Precinct(s). Prefecture(s). Arrondisement(s). Ward(s). Province(s). Borough(s). Canton(s). Domain(s). Demesne(s). Glebe(s). Quarter(s). *See also* Areas; Community (geographic locality); Congregations (church); Dioceses; Districts; Election districts; Neighborhoods.

Parishioners. Parishioner(s). *Choose from:* parish *with:* inhabitant(s), member(s), registr(y,ies), register(s), faithful. *Consider also:* church member(s), congregation(s). *See also* Church membership.

Parks. Park(s,land,lands). Playground(s). Nature preserve(s). Game preserve(s). Minipark(s). Open space. Green space. Wildland(s). Recreational area(s). Commons. Village green(s). Sanctuar(y, ies). Preserved area(s). Forever wild. Bird sanctuar(y,ies). Historic site(s). Forest preserve(s). *See also* Common lands; Forest reserves; Natural monuments; Recreation areas; Wildlife sanctuaries.

Parks, amusement. See *Amusement parks.*

Parks, industrial. See *Industrial districts.*

Parliaments. See *Legislative bodies.*

Parlors, billiard. See *Billiard parlors.*

Parlors, massage. See *Massage parlors.*

Parochial schools. See *Private schools.*

Parody. Parod(y,ying,ie,ies,ied). Travest(y, ies,ied,ying). *Consider also:* comic relief, contrafact(a,um), burlesque(d). *See also* Caricatures; Comic operas; Satire.

Parole. Parol(e,ee,ees,ed). *Choose from:* offender(s), prisoner(s), delinquent(s), inmate(s), exoffender(s), ex-offender(s) *with:* halfway houses, post release, postrelease, release program(s), work release, work training release, provisional release, conditional release, probation, restorative justice. *See also* Alternatives to incarceration; Correctional system; Prisoners; Probation; Psychosocial readjustment; Psychosocial rehabilitation; Restorative justice; Vocational rehabilitation.

Parole officers. Parole officer(s). *Choose from:* parole, community corrections *with:* agent(s), worker(s), personnel,

board(s), aide(s), officer(s), supervisor(s), counselor(s). *Consider also:* probation officer(s), correctional counselor(s). *See also* Counselors; Criminal rehabilitation; Parole; Probation; Social workers.

Part songs. Part song(s). Madrigal(s). Fala(s). Canzonette(s). Catch(es). Round(s). Glee(s). *See also* Choral music; Choral singing; Songs; Singing; Song cycle; Work songs.

Part time employment. Part time employ(ed,ee,ees,ment). Part time, half time, part week *with:* work(er,ers,ing), job(s), employment, labor, staff, employee(s), personnel, teacher(s), position(s), post(s), operator(s), farming. *Consider also:* substitute teach(ing,er, ers), partial retirement, moonlight(ing), shorter hour(s), side job(s). *See also* Alternative work patterns; Flexible retirement; Flexible workplace practices; Job sharing; Moonlighting; Overtime work; Part time farming; Unemployment; Work sharing; Workday shifts.

Part time farming. Part time farm(er,ers, ing). Off farm work. Off farm employment. *Choose from:* farmer(s), farm worker(s) *with:* side job(s), part time. Part time agriculture. Sundown farmer(s). Gentle(man,men) farmer(s). *See also* Family farms; Part time employment; Small farms.

Part time work. See *Part time employment.*

Parthenogenesis. Parthenogenesis. Unisexual reproduction. Clon(e,ed,ing). Nonsexual reproduction. *See also* Sexual reproduction.

Partial hearing. Partial(ly) hearing. Hearing impair(ed,ment,ments). Hearing loss(es). Hard of hearing. Cochlear impaired. Auditory handicap(s). Hearing disabilit(y,ies). Hearing disabled. *Consider also:* hearing aid user(s). *See also* Deafness.

Partial hospitalization. See *Adult day care.*

Partially sighted. Partial(ly) sight(ed). Partial(ly) blind(ness). *Choose from:* low, partial, residual *with:* vision. *Choose from:* visual(ly), sight, seeing *with:* impair(ed,ment,ments), difficult(y,ies), handicap(s,ped), disabilit(y,ies). *Consider also:* monocular blinding. *See also* Vision disorders.

Participant observation. Participant observ(ers,ation). Participatory research. *Consider also:* ethnography, ethnomethodology. *See also* Ethnomethodology; Fieldwork; Observation methods; Research methods.

Participants. Participant(s). Participator(s). Partaker(s). Team member(s). Contributor(s). Partner(s). Shareholder(s). Abettor(s). Accomplice(s). *See also* Athletic participation; Audiences; Participation; Research subjects; Teams.

Participation. Participat(e,ed,ing,ion,ive, or,ors,ory). Participant(s). Shar(e,ed, ing). Partner(s,ship). Profitsharing. Member(s,ship,ships). Affiliat(e,ed,ion). Active role. Active(ly) involv(ed,ement). Involve(d,ment). Fair share. Partner(s). Copartner(s). Attend(ed,ance). Activis(m,ts). Engag(e,ed,ing) in activit(y,ies). Volunteer(ed,ing). Join(er,ers,ed,ing). Commit(ted,ment). Cooperat(e,ed,ing,ion). Collaborat(e, ion,or,ors). Teamwork. Tak(e,ing) part. *Consider also:* consumer(s), patient(s), audience(s), citizen(s), communit(y,ies), famil(y,ies), parent(s), school(s), student(s), teacher(s), group(s) *with:* participation, involvement. *See also* Activism; Athletic participation; Attendance (presence); Church membership; Citizen participation; Community involvement; Discussion; Group participation; Organizational affiliation; Participative decision making; Participative management; Performance; Political participation; Social behavior; Volunteers; Worker participation.

Participation, athletic. See *Athletic participation.*

Participation, citizen. See *Citizen participation.*

Participation, client. See *Consumer participation.*

Participation, community. See *Community involvement.*

Participation, compulsory. See *Compulsory participation.*

Participation, consumer. See *Consumer participation.*

Participation, employee. See *Worker participation.*

Participation, group. See *Group participation.*

Participation, patient. See *Patient participation.*

Participation, political. See *Political participation.*

Participation, public. See *Citizen participation.*

Participation, social. See *Group participation; Involvement; Prosocial behavior.*

Participation, sports. See *Athletic participation.*

Participation, voter. See *Voter participation.*

Participation, worker. See *Worker participation.*

Participative decision making. Participative decision making. *Choose from:* cooperat(e,ed,ion), collaborat(e,ion,ive, or,ors), team, group, shar(e,ed,ing), participat(e,ed,ing,ion,ive,or,ors,ory), involve(d,ment), consultat(ion,ive) *with:* decision(s), problem solving, choice(s), planning. *Consider also:* deliberative democracy. *See also* Decision making; Group problem solving; Power sharing; Worker participation.

Participative management. Participat(ive, ory) management. Participative decision making. Team management. *Choose from:* employee(s), worker(s), labor, worksite, shopfloor, workplace *with:* involvement, participat(ory,ive,ion), cooperative(s), consultat(ive,ion,ions), ownership, self management, represent(ed,ing,ation), democra(tic,cy), egalitarian(ism). *Consider also:* quality circle(s), profit sharing, gainsharing, industrial democra(cy,tization), participatory decision making, democratic workplace(s), participation team(s), power sharing, managing cooperatively, codetermination, worker managed, humanistic management, workplace participation, participative team(s), theory Z, participative ownership, economic democracy, Scanlon plan. *See also* Employee morale; Employee ownership; Employee stock ownership plans; Industrial democracy; Labor management committees; Management structures; Participative decision making; Power sharing; Worker control; Worker participation.

Particularism. Particularis(m,t,tic). Particularit(y,ies). Exclusivity. Separatis(t,m). *Consider also:* single caus(e,ative,ation), partial truth(s), partial insight(s), partisan(ship), denominationalis(m,t,tic), narrow minded(ness), specialis(m,t), ethno specific(ity). *See also* Individualism; Nationalism; Partisan; Personalism; Specialization.

Parties, political. See *Political parties.*

Parties, third United States politics. See *Third parties (United States politics).*

Partisan. Partisan(s,ship). Supporter(s). Follower(s). *Choose from:* partisan, party, political *with:* loyal(ty,ties), allegiance(s), identification, identit(y,ies), supporter(s), adherent(s), backer(s), sympathizer(s). *Consider also:* factional(ism), polariz(e,ed,ation), sectarian, fanatic(ism), zealous(ness), bipartisan, nonpartisan. *See also* Dissent; Factionalism; Particularism; Polarization; Political dissent; Political parties; Schism; Sectarianism.

Partisan politics. See *Political parties.*

Partisan warfare. See *Guerrilla warfare.*

Partners. Partner(s,ships). Team(s). Duo. Dyad(s). Co-partner(s). Copartner(s). Mate(s). Comrade(s). Co-worker(s). Co-owner(s,ship,ships). Associate(s). Budd(y,ies). Helpmate. Spouse(s). Collaborative agreement(s). *See also* Accomplices; Affiliation (businesses); Alliances; Associates; Coalitions;

Collaborators; Cooperation; Power sharing; Significant others; Spouses.

Partners, marriage. See *Spouses.*

Partners, sexual. See *Sexual partners.*

Partnership. See *Partners.*

Partnerships. See *Partners.*

Parts, artificial body. See *Prostheses.*

Parturition. See *Birth.*

Passage, rites of. See *Rites of passage.*

Passages. See *Life stage transitions.*

Passion plays. Passion play(s). *Choose from:* Holy Week, Eucharist, Last Supper, Easter story, crucifixion, Christ *with:* play(s), drama. *Consider also:* Oberammergau. *See also* Miracle plays.

Passive aggressive personality disorder. Passive aggressive personality disorder. *Choose from:* passive(ness), passivity *with:* aggressive(ness), aggression, dependen(t,ce,cy). *Consider also:* resist(ant,ance) to authority, defian(t,ce) of authority, dawdl(e,ed,ing), procrastinat(e,ed,ing,ion), stubborn(ness). *See also* Personality disorders; Stubbornness.

Passive behavior. See *Passiveness.*

Passive resistance. See *Nonviolence.*

Passive smoking. See *Tobacco smoke pollution.*

Passiveness. Passive(ness). Passivity. Indifferen(t,ce). Resign(ed,ation). Acquiescen(t,ce). Apath(y,etic). Unresponsive(ness). Impassive. Undemonstrative. Nonparticipat(ing, ion). Uninterested. Inaction. Submiss(ion,ive). Long suffering. Meek(ness). Unassertive. Apologetic. Humility. Humble. Servile. Obsequious(ness). Tractable. Obliging. Listless(ness). Indolen(t,ce). Insipid(ness). Laissez faire. Forbear(ing, ance). Deference. Unassuming. Subdued. *See also* Humility; Imperviousness; Laziness; Learned helplessness; Loss of will; Noninvolvement; Obedience; Personality traits.

Pasta. Pasta. Macaroni(s). Spaghetti(s). Linguin(e,i,is). Cappelletti(s). Noodle(s). Ravioli(s). Capellini(s). Tubetti(s). Orecchiette(s). Farfalle(s). Penne(s). Fetticcine(s). Gemelli(s). Vermicelli(s). Manicotti(s). Orzo(s). Ziti(s). Rotini(s). Ditalini(s). *See also* Food; Natural foods.

Pasticcio. See *Arrangement (Music); Centos; Intertextuality; Patchwork.*

Pastiche. See *Arrangement (Music); Centos; Intertextuality; Patchwork.*

Pastimes. See *Leisure activities.*

Pastoral care. Pastoral care. *Choose from:* pastor(al), priest(s), ministry,

minister(s,ial), chaplain(s), clergy(men,man,women), cleric(al), religious, Christian, Jewish, rabbi(s), Protestant, Catholic *with:* psychology, counsel(ing), support group(s), treatment, psychotherapy, consultation, referral(s), therapy, marriage preparation, penitent relationship(s), confession(s), comforting, interview(s,ing). *See also* Counseling; Psychotherapy.

Pastoral counseling. See *Pastoral care.*

Pastoral poetry. See *Pastorales.*

Pastoral societies. Pastoral societ(y,ies). Herding societ(y,ies). Shepherd(s). Agropastoralis(m,t,ts). Monopastoralis(m,t,ts). Pastoralis(m,t,ts). *Consider also:* sheepherd(ing,er,ers), goatherd(ing,er,ers), herder(s) of camel(s), cattle herder(s). *See also* Herders; Livestock; Nomads; Peasants; Primitive agriculture; Traditional societies; Transhumance.

Pastorales. Pastorale(s). *Choose from:* pastoral, countryside, shepherd(s,ess, esses), rural *with:* literature, poetry, poem(s), eleg(y,ies), drama(s), romance(s), prose, music, madrigal(s), play(s), opera(s). *Consider also:* eclogue(s), pastourelle(s), pastorela(s). *See also* Idyll; Music; Poetry.

Pastors. See *Clergy.*

Pasture, right of. See *Right of pasture.*

Pastures. See *Grazing lands.*

Patchwork. Patchwork. Hodgepodge. Hotchpotch. Mishmash. Jumble(s,d). Crazy quilt(s). Pastiche(s). Pasticcio(s). Farrago(es). Potpourri(s). Medley(s). Melange(s). Gallimaufr(y,ies). Olio(s). Salmagundi(s). Assortment(s). Mixed bag(s). *Consider also:* pentiment(o,i). *See also* Arrangement (Music); Centos; Intertextuality; Postmodernism; Quodlibets.

Patents. Patent(s,ed,ing,able). Protect(ed, ing,ion) of invention(s). Statutory invention registration. Certificate(s) of inventorship. Trademark assignment. *Consider also:* copyright(s,ed,ing), licens(e,ed,ing). *See also* Copyright; License agreements; Property rights; Intangible property; Technological innovations; Technology transfer; Trade secrets.

Paternal age. Paternal age. Age of father. Father's age. *See also* Childbearing age; Maternal age.

Paternal attitudes. See *Parental attitudes.*

Paternal behavior. Paternal behavior. Father(ing,ly,liness). Paternalis(m,tic). Delilah syndrome. *Choose from:* father(s), paternal *with:* behavior(s), depriv(e,ed,ation), incest(uous), nurtur(e,ed,ing,ance), role(s), comfort(ed,ing), care, affection, interaction(s), disciplin(e,ary), aggression, responsive(ness), response(s), contact, adequacy, love, communicat(ed, ing,ion), competence, relation(s,ship). *Consider also:* menism. *See also* Father child communication; Father child relations; Parent role.

Paternal deprivation. Paternal deprivation. Fatherless(ness). *Choose from:* father(s), paternal *with:* absen(t,ce,ces), loss(es), los(t,e), neglect(ed,ing,ful), death(s), inadequa(te,cy,cies), killed, missing, abscond(ed,ing), desert(ed,ion,ing). *See also* Absence; Child neglect; Parental absence; Paternal behavior.

Paternal rights. See *Parent rights.*

Paternalism. Paternalis(m,t,tic). Paternal boss(es). *Consider also:* benevolent despot(ism), benevolent(ly) overbearing, authoritarian(ism). *See also* Authoritarianism (political); Authoritarianism (psychological); Patronage; Superior subordinate relationship.

Paternity. Paternity. *Consider also:* father(ed,ing,hood), sired, putative father(s), parentage, male parent(s). *See also* Accountability; Fathers; Hereditary diseases; Lineage.

Paternity leave. Paternity leave(s). Parental leave(s). Leave for father(s). Time off for birth. *Choose from:* father(s), paternal, paternity *with:* leave(s) of absence, time off, release time. *See also* Employee benefits; Fathers.

Pathogenesis. See *Etiology.*

Pathological gambling. Pathological gambl(ing,er,ers). *Choose from:* pathological, compulsive, addict(ed,ive) *with:* gambl(ing,er,ers), speculat(e,ed, ing,ion), poker, horse race(s), betting, bettor(s), risk taking, lotter(y,ies). *Consider also:* Gamblers Anonymous. *See also* Behavior disorders; Gambling; Impulsiveness; Online gambling.

Pathways, maze. See *Maze pathways.*

Patience. Patien(t,ce). Forbear(ing,ance). Toleran(t,ce). Tolerat(e,ed,ing,ation). Endur(e,ed,es,ing,ance). Restrain(t,ed, ing). Long suffering. Stoic(ism). *Consider also:* persisten(t,ce), persever(e,ed,ing,ance), uncomplaining(ness), compos(ed,ure), equanim(ity, ities), imperturbab(le,ility), self-control. *See also* Endurance; Fortitude; Martyrs; Persistence; Psychological endurance; Stoicism; Suffering; Tolerance.

Patient acceptance of health care. See *Patient compliance.*

Patient admission. Patient admission. *Choose from:* patient(s), emergenc(y,ies) *with:* admission(s), admit(ted,ting, tance), intake, hospitaliz(e,ed,ing,ation), preadmission, receiv(e,ed,ing), enter(ed,ing) hospital. *See also* Admis-

sions; Hospitalization; Intake (agency); Length of stay; Patient readmission.

Patient advocacy. Patient advoca(te,tes,cy). Patient ombuds(man,men,women, woman). *Choose from:* patient(s), aged, elderly, disabled, handicapped, disabilit(y,ies), ill(ness), mental(ly) ill(ness), dying *with:* advoca(te,tes,cy), ombuds(man,men,women,woman). *Consider also:* patient right(s) *with:* treatment, refuse treatment, refuse medication, privacy, health care, confidentiality, right to know. *See also* Informed consent; Patient rights; Protective services.

Patient attitudes. See *Client attitudes.*

Patient care. See *Health care; Medical care.*

Patient care, continuity of. See *Continuity of patient care.*

Patient care planning. Patient care plan(s,ned,ning). *Choose from:* patient(s), outpatient(s), medication(s), drug(s), diet(s,ary), care, treatment(s), aftercare, health care, nursing care, surgery, therap(y,ies,eutic), medical care, regimen *with:* plan(s,ned,ning), propos(e,ed,al), goal(s), recommendation(s), objective(s). *See also* Continuity of patient care; Medical care.

Patient care team. Patient care team(s). *Choose from:* patient care, nursing, health care, interdisciplinary health, medical care, physician nurse, primary care, integrated rehabilitation, multispecialty *with:* team(s). *See also* Allied health personnel; Medical care; Patient care planning.

Patient characteristics. See *Client characteristics.*

Patient compliance. Patient compliance. *Choose from:* patient(s), outpatient(s), medication(s), drug(s), diet(s,ary), care, treatment(s), aftercare, medical advice, health care, physician recommendation(s), therap(y,ies,eutic), medical recommendation(s), regimen *with:* compliance, comply(ing), complied, noncompliance, refus(e,ed,ing,al), uncooperative, adher(e,ed,ing,ence), cooperat(e,ed,ing,ion), motivation, follow(ed,ing), accept(ed,ing,ance), maintenance, defaulting, dropout(s). *Consider also:* against medical advice. *See also* Patient dropouts; Patient education; Patient participation; Patients; Self administration.

Patient dentist relations. See *Dentist patient relations.*

Patient discharge. Patient discharge(s,d). *Choose from:* patient(s), hospital(s), medical, therapy, treatment, institution(s,al) *with:* discharg(e,ed,ing), releas(e,ed,ing), dismiss(ed,al), transfer(red,s), drop(ped,ping),

terminat(e,ed,ing,ion), sent home, send home. *See also* Length of stay; Patient dropouts; Physician patient relations; Prognosis; Psychosocial readjustment; Psychosocial rehabilitation; Remission; Termination of treatment.

Patient doctor relations. See *Physician patient relations.*

Patient dropouts. Patient dropout(s). *Choose from:* patient(s), treatment(s), therap(y,ies) *with:* dropout(s), noncompliance, refusal(s), no show(s), drop(ped,ping) out, discontinu(e,ed,ing, ance), fail(ed,ing) to complete, broken appointment(s), cancel(led,ling) appointment(s), attrition, premature termination, elopement. *Consider also:* leav(e,ing), left *with:* against medical advice. *See also* Patient discharge; Physician patient relations; Psychotherapeutic outcomes; Psychotherapeutic resistance; Recovery; Recidivism; Relapse; Remission; Termination of treatment.

Patient education. Patient education. *Choose from:* patient(s), inpatient(s), outpatient(s) *with:* educat(e,ed,ing,ion), inform(ed,ing,ation), instruct(ed,ing, ion), teach(ing). *Consider also:* client(s), consumer(s) *with:* health, medical, self examination, inhospital, diabet(ic,es), home care, sexual(ity), sex, birth control, family planning, disease(s), drug(s), medication(s) *with:* educat(e,ed,ing,ion), inform(ed,ing,ation), instruct(ed,ing, ion), teach(ing). *Consider also:* health promotion. *See also* Health education; Nutrition education; Patient compliance; Patient participation; Patient rights; Physician patient relations; Preventive medicine; Self administration.

Patient history. Patient histor(y,ies). *Choose from:* medical, patient(s), treatment, case, psychiatric *with:* histor(y,ies), background(s). *See also* Biographical data; Client characteristics; Diagnosis; Etiology; Medical history taking; Medical records; Premorbidity; Psychodiagnosis.

Patient history taking. See *Medical history taking.*

Patient identification systems. Patient identification system(s). *Choose from:* patient(s), newborn(s), personal, victim(s) *with:* identification, IDs, fingerprint(s), footprint(s), finger print(s), foot print(s). *Consider also:* denture identification. *See also* Dermatoglyphics.

Patient isolation. Patient(s) isolat(e,ed, ing,ion). *Consider also:* quarantine, protected environment(s), germ free isolation, isolation unit(s), solitary room(s), isolation ward(s), sterile room(s), seclusion. *See also* Clean rooms; Social isolation.

Patient nurse relations. See *Nurse patient relations.*

Patient participation. Patient participation. *Choose from:* patient(s), client(s) *with:* participat(e,ed,ing,ion), right(s), decision making, collaborat(e,ed,ing,ion), role(s), goal setting, choice(s), preference(s), self determination, involv(e,ed,ing, ement), negotiat(e,ed,ing,ion). *See also* Patient care planning; Patient education; Patient compliance; Patient rights; Self administration.

Patient physician relations. See *Physician patient relations.*

Patient practitioner relations. See *Physician patient relations; Professional client relations.*

Patient professional relations. See *Professional client relations.*

Patient readmission. Patient readmission. *Choose from:* patient(s), hospital(s), institution(s) *with:* readmission, readmit(ted,ting), recidivism, rehospitaliz(e,ed,ing,ation), return(ed, ing). *See also* Patient admission; Recidivism.

Patient rights. Patient(s) right(s). Patient(s) bill of right(s). *Choose from:* patient(s), nursing home resident(s), client(s), retarded, elderly, minor(s), institutionalized, mentally retarded, impaired, disab(led,ility,ilities) *with:* right(s), right to know, right to refuse treatment, right to medical care, autonomy, ethic(s,al), freedom of choice, privacy, ombuds(man,men,woman,women), self determination, property rights, least restrictive alternative, least restrictive environment, informed consent, humane treatment, due process, living will(s), right to die, abortion right(s), access to medical record(s), advoca(te,tes,cy), religious freedom, voting rights, freedom to marry, right to employment, right to appeal, right to sue health plans. *Consider also:* PL 94-142. *See also* Advance directives; Civil rights; Consumer directed care; Education of mentally retarded; Human experimentation; Human rights; Human subjects (research); Informed consent; Mainstreaming; Medical privacy; Ombudsmen; Patient advocacy; Privacy laws; Research ethics; Truth disclosure.

Patient self determination. See *Advance directives; Consumer directed care; Human rights; Informed consent; Patient rights; Right to die; Termination of treatment.*

Patient therapist interaction. See *Psychotherapeutic processes; Therapeutic processes.*

Patients. Patient(s). Inpatient(s). Outpatient(s). Analysand(s). *Choose from:* hospital(ized) *with:* adult(s), child(ren), client(s), population(s). *Choose from:* medical *with:* user(s), client(s). Clinical population(s). Under treatment. Ill person(s). *See also* Geriatric patients; Hospitalization; Hospitalized children; Inpatients; Outpatients; Psychiatric patients.

Patients, AIDS. See *AIDS; Patients.*

Patients, geriatric. See *Geriatric patients.*

Patients, mental. See *Psychiatric patients.*

Patients, psychiatric. See *Psychiatric patients.*

Patients, transportation of. See *Transportation of patients.*

Patients, visitors to. See *Visitors to patients.*

Patriarchal language. See *Sexist language.*

Patriarchy. Patriarch(al,alism,ate,ies,y). Male head of household. Male social dominance. Male head of family. Father dominated. Paterfamilias. Patria potestas. Male supremacy. Male authority figure(s). *Consider also:* patripotestal, male dominance, sex hierarchy, patrilocal(ity), patrilineal(ity), androcrac(y,ies), androcentric. *See also* Androcentrism; Family power; Family roles; Kinship; Matriarchy; Paternalism; Sexual oppression.

Patrilineality. Patriline(al,ality,age). Agnat(e,ion). Patronym(ic,y). *Consider also:* patriliny, patriarch(y,ies). *See also* Lineage; Matrilineality; Unilineal descent.

Patrilocal residence. Patrilocal residence. Virilocal residence. *See also* Kinship; Residences.

Patriotic music. Patriotic music. National anthem(s). Les hymnes nationaux. Nationalhymnen. *Choose from:* national(ist,istic,ism), patriotic(ic,ism), jingoistic, chauvinistic *with:* music, song(s), anthem(s), lyric(s), march(es). *Consider also:* God save the Queen, O Canada, Star Spangled Banner, America the Beautiful, La Marseillaise, Advance Australia Fair, La Brabanconne, Hatiqvah, God defend New Zealand, Istiklal Marsi, etc. *See also* Marches; Militarism; Military music; Nationalism; Political ballads; War songs.

Patriotism. Patriot(ic,ism,s). Pledge allegiance. National pride. National feeling(s). Allegiance. Flag waving. Nationalis(m,t,ts,tic). Chauvinis(m,t,ts, tic). Jingo(ism,istic). National loyalty. *See also* Anti-government radicals; Citizenship; Faithfulness; Flags; Jingoism; Loyalty oaths; McCarthyism; National emblems; Nationalism; Political ideologies; Political myths; War attitudes; War poetry; Xenophobia.

Patristics. See *Fathers of the Church.*

Patronage. Patron(s,age). Sponsor(ed,s,ing, ship). Support(ed,ing,er,ers). Back(ed, ing,er,ers). Help(ed,ing,er,ers). Aid(ed,ing). Encourag(ed,ing,ement). Boost(ed,ing,er,ers). Promot(e,ed,ing, er,ers). Foster(ed,ing). *Consider also:* spoils, pork barrel. *See also* Art patronage; Ecclesiastical benefices; Exchange theory; Literary patronage; Military patronage; Paternalism; Political patronage; Sponsorship; Superior subordinate relationship.

Patronage, art. See *Art patronage.*

Patronage, literary. See *Literary patronage.*

Patronage, military. See *Military patronage.*

Patronage, political. See *Political patronage.*

Patronage, royal. See *Royal favorites.*

Patronizing. Patron(ize,ized,izing). Condescen(ding,sion). Scorn(ful). Disdain(ful). Supercilious(ness). Contempt(uous). Imperious. Overbearing. High-handed. Presumptious(ness). Arrogant. Haughty. Uncharitable. *See also* Personality traits.

Patrons. See *Clients.*

Pattern recognition. Pattern recognition. *Choose from:* pattern(s), character(s), form(s) *with:* recogni(ze,zed,zing,tion), discriminat(e,ed,ing,ion), perception, classif(y,ied,ication), perceiv(e,ed,ing), detect(ed,ing,ion), identif(y,ied,ication). *See also* Classification; Perceptual discrimination; Visual memory.

Patterns, alternative work. See *Alternative work patterns.*

Patterns, behavior. See *Behavior patterns.*

Patterns, career. See *Career patterns.*

Patterns, economic. See *Business cycles.*

Patterns, housing. See *Residential patterns.*

Patterns, interest. See *Interest patterns.*

Patterns, land settlement. See *Settlement patterns.*

Patterns, marriage. See *Marriage patterns.*

Patterns, migration. See *Migration patterns.*

Patterns, residential. See *Residential patterns.*

Patterns, settlement. See *Settlement patterns.*

Pauperization of women. See *Women living in poverty.*

Pay. See *Salaries.*

Pay, severance. See *Severance pay.*

Pay equity. See *Equity (payment).*

Payable and receivable accounts. See *Accounts payable and receivable.*

Payment, compensation. See *Compensation.*

Payment, equity. See *Equity (payment).*

Payments. Pay(ing,ment,ments). Paid. Remittance(s). Overpay(ing,ment, ments). Underpay(ing,ment,ments). Prepay(ing,ment,ments). Repay(ing, ment,ments). Overpaid. Underpaid. Prepaid. Repaid. *Consider also:* compensation, recompense, restitution, remuneration, alimony, allowance(s), annuit(y,ies), bonus(es), salar(y,ies), earning(s), stipend(s), wage(s), income, receipt(s), revenue(s), royalt(y,ies), earning(s), fee(s), charge(s), tip(s), gratuit(y,ies), refund(s), rebate(s), reimburse(d,ment), tax(es), tariff(s), toll(s). *See also* Alimony; Child support; Compensation (payment); Costs; Expenditures; Fees; Prices; Reimbursement mechanisms.

Payments, balance of. See *Balance of payments.*

Payments, nonwage. See *Employee benefits.*

Payments, third party. See *Reimbursement mechanisms.*

Payments, transfer. See *Transfer payments.*

Payments, vendor. See *Reimbursement mechanisms.*

Peace. Peace. Peace(able,ful,fulness, maker,makers). Pacifis(m,t,ts,tic). Dov(e,es,ish). Nonviolen(ce,t). Ceasefire. Cease-fire. Reconciliation. Pacification. Appease(d,ment). Truce. Armistice. Suspen(d,sion) hostilit(y,ies). Absence of conflict. Guns are silen(t,ced). Goodwill. Brotherhood. Swords into plowshares. Concord. Harmon(y,ious). Bloodless. Unmilitant. Unmilitaristic. Halcyon. Irenic. Warless(ness). Nonwar. Lack of warfare. *Consider also:* Ahimsa. *See also* Armistices; Arms control; Balance of power; Conflict resolution; Disarmament; National security; Nuclear weapons non-proliferation; Pacifism; Peace movements; Peace negotiations; Peaceful change; Peaceful coexistence; Peacekeeping forces; Public order; War prevention.

Peace, breach of. See *Breach of the peace.*

Peace, crimes against. See *Crimes against peace.*

Peace movements. Peace movement(s). Peacenik(s). War protest movement(s). *Choose from:* peace, pacifist, non-aligned, nonviolent, anti-war, antiwar, anti-nuclear, antinuclear, nuclear freeze, disarmament(s), green(s), demilitarization, arms control, war protest *with:* movement(s), demonstrat(ions,or,ors), activis(m,t,ts), protest(s,or,ors), advoca(cy,te,tes), camp(s), project(s), march(es,er,ers), action(s), group(s), alignment(s), council(s), center(s), initiative(s), league(s), organization(s), part(y,ies), campaign(s). *Consider also:* dove(s), American Friends Service Committee, Fellowship of Reconciliation, War Resisters League, Women's International League for Peace and Freedom, Committee for a Just world Peace, International Trade Union Committee for Peace and Disarmament, Campaign for Nuclear Disarmament. *See also* Antinuclear movements; Civil disobedience; Conscientious objectors; Moral authority; Neutrality; Nonresistance to evil; Nonviolence; Pacifism; War attitudes; War prevention.

Peace negotiations. Peace negotiation(s). Peace talk(s). Olive branch(es). Peace process(es). *Choose from:* talk(s), proposal(s), negotiat(ing,ed,ion,ions), settlement(s), agree(d,ing,ment,ments), dialog(s), conference(s), mediat(ed,ing, ion,ions), reconciliation, discuss(ed, ion,ions), acknowledgment(s), meeting(s), pact(s), solution(s), initiative(s), declaration(s), accord(s) *with:* ceasefire, cease fire, war(s,ring), fight(ing), violence, terroris(t,ts,m), withdraw(al) of troops, POW exchange(s), truce(s), peace(keeping, ful), end hostilit(y,ies), demobiliz(ed, ing,ation), disengag(e,ed,ing,ement), disarm(ed,ing,ament). *Consider also:* peacemak(ing,er,ers), summitry, resum(e,ed,ing) diplomatic relations, preventive diplomacy, pacific settlement(s), armistice. *See also* Armistices; Crimes against peace; Disarmament; Dispute settlement; Mediation; Negotiation; Peacekeeping forces; War prevention.

Peace talks. See *Peace negotiations.*

Peaceful change. Peaceful change(s). *Choose from:* peaceful(ly), nonviolen(t, ce), bloodless *with:* transition(s), change(s), election(s), reform(s,ed,ing, ation), dismantl(e,ed,ing), reorganiz(e, ed,ing,ation), restructur(e,ed,ing), reorder(ed,ing), transform(ed,ing,ation), coups d'etat. *Consider also:* constitutional change(s), peace talk(s), political transformation. *See also* Change; Conflict resolution; Peace; Social change; Social integration; War prevention.

Peaceful coexistence. Peaceful(ly) coexist(ence,ing). Balance of power. Detente. Peaceful cohabitation. *Consider also:* perestroika, new world order, end of the arms race, global community, nonalignment, international cooperation. *See also* Arms control; Balance of power; Detente; Disarmament; Nuclear weapons non-proliferation; Peace; War prevention.

Peaceful transformation. See *Peaceful change.*

Peacefulness. See *Calmness.*

Peacekeeping forces. Peacekeeping force(s). Peace-keeping force(s). Peacekeeping mission(s). Peace-keeper(s). Peacekeeping troops. Blue helmet(s). International police force(s). United Nations International Police Force. United Nations Truce Supervisory Organization. Truce observer(s). Peace monitor(s). Peace supervising force(s). Peace supervising bod(y,ies). Military observer(s). *Consider also:* stand-by force(s), hemispher(e,ic) police force(s), United Nations Emergency Force (UNEF), United Nations Disengagement Observer Force (UNDOF), United Nations Operation in the Congo (ONUC), United Nations Interim Force in Lebanon (UNIFIL), United Nations Observer Group in India and Pakistan (UNMOGIP), United Nations Force in Cyprus (UNFICYP), United Nations presence, United Nations Protection Forces (UNPROFOR). *See also* Crimes against peace; Just war doctrine; Peace negotiations; War prevention.

Peasant rebellions. Peasant rebellion(s). Peasant revolt(s). Peasant revolution(s). Anti-colonialism. War(s) of liberation. War(s) of national liberation. Freedom fighter(s). Guerrilla movement(s). National liberation movement(s). Overthrow colonialism. Class struggle(s). Agrarian socialist movement(s). Landless movement(s). Social banditry. Putsch(es). Maois(m,t, ts). Mujahed(een,din). Mujahid(een,in). *Choose from:* peasant(s,ry), common people, folk, agrarian, farmer(s), labor, campesino(s), villager(s), proletaria(n,t) *with:* revolutionar(y,ies), liberation, movements, militant(s), revolt(s), protest(s,er,ers), insurgen(t,ts,cy), riot(s), strife, revolution(s), uprising(s), rebel(s), rebellion(s), rebellious(ness), overthrow(n,ing), coalitions, change(s), strike(s), insurrection(s), resistance, radical(s,ization), mobilization, struggle(s). *Consider also:* intifada, holy war(s), jihad, mutin(y,ies), sedition. *See also* Decolonization; Guerrillas; Land reform; Liberation movements; Liberation theology; National fronts; Peasants; Political self determination; Political violence; Rebellions; Resistance; Revolutionary ballads and songs; Separatism.

Peasants. Peasant(ry,s). Serf(dom,s). Tenant farmer(s). Campesino(s). Sharecropper(s). Villager(s). Rural laborer(s). Landless. Small landowner(s). Farmer(s). Fellah(in,een). *Choose from:* farm, rural, agrarian, agricultural, folk, peasant, verv, village *with:* societ(y,ies), laborer(s), poor, class(es), communit(y, ies), worker(s), population, *Consider also:* proletaria(n,t), populace, rural population, common people, folk, untouchables, common man, masses, pleb(e,es,s,eian), third estate, lower class(es). *See also* Agricultural workers; Common people; Farming; Feudalism; Lower class; Masses; Peasant rebellions; Plantations; Rural population; Servitude; Sharecropping; Working class.

Pecking order. See *Animal dominance.*

Pedagogy. See *Teaching.*

Pedagogy, culturally relevant. See *Culturally relevant pedagogy.*

Pedagogy, dialogic. See *Dialogic pedagogy.*

Pedagogy, equity. See *Multicultural education.*

Peddlers. See *Street vendors.*

Pederasty. See *Pedophilia.*

Pedestrian accidents. Pedestrian accident(s). *Choose from:* pedestrian(s), walker(s), foot traffic, jaywalker(s), road crossing(s) *with:* accident(s,al), safe(ty), injur(y,ies,e,ed,ing), danger(s,ous), fatalit(y,ies). *See also* Highway safety; Pedestrians; Personal injuries; Street traffic; Traffic accidents.

Pedestrians. Pedestrian(s). Walker(s). Jaywalk(ing,ers). Foot traffic. *Consider also:* hiker(s), stroller(s), ambulat(ion,ory), jogger(s). *See also* Pedestrian accidents; Street traffic.

Pediatrics. Pediatric(s,ians). Neonatalogy. Perinatology. *Choose from:* neonatal, perinatal, childrens, pediatric *with:* medicine, medical care, surgery, care, medical service(s), hospital(s). *See also* Medical sciences.

Pedology. See *Soil science.*

Pedophilia. Pedophilia(c,cs,ia). Pederast(y,s,ic,ically). Pederosis. Pedophil(e,es,ic). Paedophilia erotica. *Consider also:* child(ren,hood), girl(s), boy(s), minor(s), juvenile(s) *with:* sexual abuse(r,rs), molest(er,ers), rapist(s). *See also* Bisexuality; Incest; Homosexuality; Molested children; Rape; Sex behavior; Sexual abuse; Sexual deviations; Sexual exploitation; Sexual harassment.

Peeling, bark. See *Bark peeling.*

Peer counseling. Peer counsel(ing,or,ors). Peer therap(y,ies). Peer group counseling. Lay counsel(ing,or,ors). Peer career counseling. Partnership counsel(ing,or, ors). Peer facilitation program(s). Self help group(s). Volunteer counsel(ing,or, ors). Peer group work. Co-counseling. Mutual aid. Re-evaluation counseling. *See also* Counseling; Peers; Self help groups.

Peer evaluation. See *Peer review.*

Peer groups. See *Peers.*

Peer influences. Peer influence(s). *Choose from:* peer(s), interpersonal, group(s), social, crowd, reference group(s),

interactional, neighbor(s), classmate(s), playmate(s), co-worker(s), partner(s), companion(s), associate(s), other(s), friend(s), colleague(s) *with:* influence(s), power, pressure(s), dynamics, compliance, reinforcement, norm(s), determinant(s). *Consider also:* leadership, manipulation, persuasion, give and take process, peer orientation, external locus of control, advice, social compliance. *See also* Conformity (personality); Group dynamics; Peer relations; Peers; Social influences; Social conformity; Social values.

Peer rating. See *Peer review.*

Peer relations. Peer relation(ship,s). *Choose from:* peer(s), friend(s), colleague(s), neighbor(s), classmate(s), playmate(s), agemate(s), equals, compeer(s), reference group(s), contemporar(y,ies), companion(s), *with:* related(ness), interrelation(ship,s), interrelated(ness), acceptance, affinity, aggression, alliance(s), association(s), attachment(s), attraction, bond(s,ing), care, closeness, cohesiveness, collaboration, comfort(ing), communication, compatibility, conflict(s), connection(s), cooperation, dependenc(e,y), discord, dispute(s), distance, distrust, dynamics, empathy, expectation(s), feedback, feeling(s), fighting, friendship, guilt, helping, independence, influence(s), interactions, interconnect(ed,ion,ions), interdependence, involve(ment), jealousy, lov(e,ing), mutuality, participation, play, rapport, rejection, reciprocity, response(s), rival(s,ry), role(s), solidarity, social(ity), support, symbiosis, sympathy, teamwork, tension(s), trust, understanding, unity. *See also* Brotherliness; Friendship; Peer counseling; Peer influences; Peer teaching; Peers; Popularity; Social acceptance; Teamwork.

Peer review. Peer review. Peer evaluation(s). *Choose from:* peer, collegial, colleague(s) *with:* review(s), judgment(s), appraisal(s), evaluat(ed,ing,ion,ions), ranking(s), rating(s), report(s). *See also* Performance appraisal; Personnel evaluation.

Peer teaching. Peer teaching. *Choose from:* peer(s), cross-age *with:* tutor(s,ed,ing), teach(ing,er,ers), tutee(s), coach(ed,ing), train(ed,ing,er,ers). *Consider also:* student learning team(s). *See also* Cooperative learning; Peer relations; Peers; Teaching methods.

Peers. Peer(s). Peer group(s). Contemporar(y,ies). Friend(s). Neighbor(s). Colleague(s). Reference group(s). Classmate(s). Cohort(s). Co-worker(s). Agemate(s). Playmate(s). Play group(s). Equals. Compeer(s). Companion(s). Fellow. Partner(s). Associate(s). Social group(s). Gang(s). *Consider also:* peer

relations, subculture(s), equal status, same generation. *See also* Age groups; Associates; Cohorts; Collaborators; Colleagues; Companions; Contemporaries; Reference groups; Significant others; Social status.

Pen names. See *Pseudonyms.*

Penal codes. Penal code(s). Criminal law(s). Criminal code(s). Penal law(s). *Choose from:* penal, criminal *with:* law(s), code(s), statute(s), sanction(s). *Consider also:* Mens rea, actus reus, punishable offense(s), indictable offense(s), criminal judgment(s), criminal adjudication, guilty verdict(s). *See also* Crime; Criminal act; Criminal investigations; Criminal intent; Criminal justice; Criminal proceedings; Due process; Felonies; Legal system; Offenses; Penology.

Penal colonies. Penal colon(y,ies). Gulag. *Choose from:* penal, prison *with:* colon(y,ies), camp(s). *Consider also:* death camp(s), labor camp(s), prison labor, prison manpower. *See also* Concentration camps; Forced labor; Prisons.

Penal reform. Penal reform. *Choose from:* prison(s), penal, criminal justice, jail(s), correction(s,al), police, imprisonment *with:* reform(s), alternative(s), change(s), reorganiz(e,ed,ing,ation), revis(e,ed,ing, ion,ions), improv(e,ed,ing,ement, ements), rebuil(t,d,ding), renovat(e,ed, ing,ion,ions). *See also* Alternatives to incarceration; Correctional system; Imprisonment; Parole; Prisons; Social legislation.

Penal system. See *Correctional system.*

Penalties. Penalt(y,ies). Fine(s). Sentence(s). Punishment(s). Penance(s). *See also* Crime prevention; Death penalty; Deterrence; Fines; Negative sanctions; Punishment; Punitiveness; Sentencing; War prevention.

Penalty, death. See *Death penalty.*

Penile erections. Penile erection(s). *Choose from:* penile, penis *with:* erect(ion,ions, ile), reflex(es), response(s), tumescen(t, ce). *See also* Sexual arousal.

Penis. Penis(es). Penile. Phall(us,ic). Male genitalia. Male sexual organ(s). Male reproductive organ(s). *See also* Male genitalia.

Penis envy. Penis envy. Female castration complex. *See also* Psychoanalytic theory.

Penitentiaries. See *Prisons.*

Penitents. Penitent(s,ial). Repentan(t,ts,ce). Contrit(e,ion). Confessional. Mary Magdalenes. Prodigal son(s). Hair shirt(s). Sack cloth(es). *Consider also:* sinner(s), reconciliation, forgive(ness) of sin(s), penance, absolution, remorseful, apologetic, attrition(al), compunc-tious(ness), regretful. *See also* Apologies; Confession; Guilt; Regret; Repentence; Sin.

Penology. Penology. Prison(s). Prison system(s). Prison management. Punishment(s). Crime deterren(t,ts,ce). Minatory deterren(t,ts,ce). Incarcerat(e, ed,ing,ion). Correctional treatment. Detention. Imprison(ed,ing,ment). *Choose from:* criminal justice, correctional, criminolog(y,ical), penal *with:* rehabilitation, system(s), theor(y,ies), code(s), practice(s), philosophy, institution(s), measure(s). *See also* Alternatives to incarceration; Correctional institutions; Correctional system; Criminal rehabilitation; Imprisonment; Parole; Penal codes; Prisons.

Pension fund management. Pension fund management. *Choose from:* pension(s), employee benefit(s), retirement *with:* fund(s), trust(s), plan(s) *with:* manag(e, ed,ing,ement), administration, investment polic(y,ies). *See also* Asset management; Capitalization; Liquidation; Pensions; Risk management.

Pension systems , privatized. See *Privatized pension systems*.

Pensions. Pension(s,ers). Pension plan(s). Post retirement increase plan(s). Annuit(y,ies,ants). Retired worker benefit(s). Social security. Superannuation. Keogh plan(s). 401(k). IRA(s). Individual retirement account(s). *Choose from:* retirement *with:* plan(s), benefit(s), system(s), savings, account(s), pay. *See also* Fiduciary responsibility; Income; Military pensions; Pension fund management; Privatized pension systems; Retirement; Retirement planning.

Pensions, military. See *Military pensions*.

Pensions, war. See *Military pensions*.

Penutian languages. Penutian language(s). Costanoan. Kalapuya. Lower Umpqua. Copehan: Wintun. Huave. Mariposan: Yokuts. Mayan: Huastec, Itza, Quiche, Yucatec. Mixe-Zoque: Zoque. Sahaptin-Chinook: Cayuse, Klamath, Modoc, Sahaptin. Totonacan: Totonac. Tsimshian. *See also* Language; Languages (as subjects); North America; North American native cultural groups.

Peonage. Peon(s,age). Bondage. Serf(s,dom). Servitude. Thrall(dom). *Consider also:* enslav(e,ed,ement), indentured servant(s), convict labor. *See also* Exploitation; Forced labor; Labor force; Oppression; Plantations; Sharecropping; Slavery.

People. See *Civilians; Females (human); Humanity; Individuals; Inhabitants; Males (human); Masses; People of color; Personnel; Population*.

People, aboriginal. See *Aborigines; Indigenous populations*.

People, common. See *Common people*.

People, divorced. See *Divorced people*.

People, early. See *Prehistoric people*.

People, famous. See *Famous people*.

People, indigenous. See *Indigenous populations*.

People, married. See *Spouses*.

People, primitive. See *Prehistoric people; Prehominids*.

People, street. See *Homeless*.

People, white. See *Whites*.

People, young. See *Adolescence; Young Adults*.

People of color. People of color. Wom(en, an) of color. Men of color. Man of color. Nonwhite(s). *Consider also:* African American(s), Afro American(s), Afro Caribbean(s), Afro European(s), Alaskan Indian(s), Alaskan Native(s), Aleut(s), Amerasian(s), American Indian(s), Asian American(s), Black(s), Cambodian American(s), Chinese American(s), Filipino American(s), Haitian American(s), Indochinese American(s), Korean American(s), Native American(s), Thai American(s), Vietnamese American(s). *See also* Asian Americans; Australoid race; Blacks; Mongoloid race; Pacific Islanders; Races; Racially mixed.

Peoples, native. See *Aborigines; African cultural groups; Australoid race; Central American native cultural groups; Indigenous populations; Mongoloid race; North American native cultural groups; Oceanic cultural groups; South American native cultural groups; Traditional societies*.

Perception. Percept(ion,ive). Perceiv(e,ed, ing). Apperception. Sens(es,ation). Taste. Sensory evaluation. Subjective representation. Sensory awareness. Differential threshold(s). *Choose from:* auditory, speech, kinesthetic, tactual, visual, depth, form, motion, size, social, space, speech, time, weight *with:* perception. *See also* Apperception; Attention; Auditory perception; Discrimination (psychology); Extrasensory perception; Form perception; Illusions (perception); Intersensory processes; Odor discrimination; Perceptual closure: Perceptual defense; Perceptual development; Perceptual discrimination; Perceptual distortion; Perceptual disturbances; Perceptual localization; Perceptual masking; Perceptual measures; Perceptual motor coordination; Perceptual motor learning; Perceptual motor processes; Perceptual skills; Perceptual stimulation; Perceptual style; Role perception; Social percep-tion; Space perception; Synesthesia; Tactual perception; Taste perception; Time perception; Visual perception.

Perception, auditory. See *Auditory perception*.

Perception, color. See *Color perception*.

Perception, depth. See *Depth perception*.

Perception, distance. See *Distance perception*.

Perception, extrasensory. See *Extrasensory perception*.

Perception, figure-ground. See *Figure ground discrimination*.

Perception, form. See *Form perception*.

Perception, geographical. See *Geographical perception*.

Perception, illusions. See *Illusions (perception)*.

Perception, interpersonal. See *Social perception*.

Perception, loudness. See *Loudness perception*.

Perception, motion. See *Motion perception*.

Perception, olfactory. See *Odor discrimination*.

Perception, pain. See *Pain perception*.

Perception, person. See *Social perception*.

Perception, pitch. See *Pitch perception*.

Perception, role. See *Role perception*.

Perception, self. See *Self perception*.

Perception, size. See *Size perception*.

Perception, social. See *Social perception*.

Perception, sound. See *Auditory perception*.

Perception, space. See *Space perception*.

Perception, spatial. See *Space perception*.

Perception, speech. See *Speech perception*.

Perception, tactual. See *Tactual perception*.

Perception, taste. See *Taste perception*.

Perception, temperature. See *Temperature perception*.

Perception, texture. See *Texture perception*.

Perception, time. See *Time perception*.

Perception, visual. See *Visual perception*.

Perception, weight. See *Weight perception*.

Perceptions. Perception(s). Observation(s). Standpoint. Opinion(s). View(s). Frame of mind. Mind set. Outlook. Reaction(s). Prejudic(ed,es). Orientation(s). Label(s,ed,ing). Labell(ed,ing). Viewpoint(s). Attitud(e,es,inal). Public opinion. Preconception(s). Preference(s). Bias(ed,es). Perspective(s). Anti-intellectualism. Belief(s). Stereotyp(e,es, ed,ing). Expectation(s). Attribut(e,ed, ing,ion,ions). Dissatisfaction. Satisfaction. Worldview(s). Weltanschauung(en). Disposition toward. *See also* Attitudes; Beliefs; Consciousness raising activities; Expectations; Future orientation; Images; Images of women; Opinions; Orientation; Relative deprivation; Sensory defensiveness; Social perception.

Perceptions, public. See *Public opinion.*

Perceptiveness (personality). Perceptive(ness). Personal understanding. Empath(y,etic,ize,ized,izing). Verstehen. Intuit(ive,ion). Sensitiv(e,ity). Aware(ness). Discern(ing,ment). Insight(ful). Alert(ness). Sagacious. Astute(ness). Shrewd. Percipien(t,ce). Observant. *See also* Insight; Personality traits.

Perceptual closure. Perceptual closure. Perceptual fill. *Choose from:* gestalt, auditory, perceptual *with:* closure, completion phenomena. *See also* Perception.

Perceptual defense. Perceptual defense. Perceptive protection. *Choose from:* linguistic, taboo words, anxiety provoking words *with:* defense, threshold(s). *Consider also:* perceptual vigilance, perceptual sensitization, denial, selective perception. *See also* Defensive; Perceptions; Sensory defensiveness.

Perceptual development. Perceptual development. *Choose from:* percept(ion, ual), visual, vision, auditory, sensory, sensorimotor *with:* development(al), maturation. *See also* Child development; Perceptual motor coordination; Perceptual motor learning; Sensory integration; Spatial ability.

Perceptual discrimination. Perceptual discrimination. *Choose from:* perceptual, sensory, somatosensory, auditory, olfactory, hearing, visual, vision, pattern, odor, figure-ground, tactile, temperature *with:* discrimination, acuity, judgment(s), differentiat(e,ed,ing,ion), detect(ed,ing,ion), sensitiv(e,ity). *See also* Auditory perception; Figure ground discrimination; Odor discrimination; Pattern recognition; Perception; Visual discrimination.

Perceptual disorders, auditory. See *Auditory perceptual disorders.*

Perceptual distortion. Perceptual distortion(s). *Choose from:* perceptual, sensory, somatosensory, auditory, olfactory, hearing, visual, vision *with:* aberration(s), distort(ed,ing,ion,ions), illusion(s), illusory, alter(ed,ation,ions), hallucinat(e,ed,ing,ion,ions), differ(ing, ed,ent,ence,ences). *See also* Illusions (perception); Perception; Perceptual disturbances.

Perceptual disturbances. Perceptual

disturbance(s). *Choose from:* perceptual(ly), perception, sensory, auditory, visual, vision *with:* disturbance(s), disorder(s), deficit(s), dysfunction(s), impairment(s), illusion(s). *Consider also:* agnosia, aphasia, hallucination(s), phantom limb(s), hypnotic blindness. *See also* Agnosia; Auditory hallucinations; Hallucinations; Illusions (perception); Learning disabilities; Mental illness; Perception.

Perceptual localization. Perceptual localization. *Choose from:* perceptual, auditory, audiovisual, visual, stimulus, spatial *with:* localization, location cue(s), location judgment(s). *See also* Auditory perception; Geographical perception; Orientation.

Perceptual masking. Perceptual masking. *Choose from:* perceptual(ly), auditory, visual(ly), noise, tone(s), dichotic, monotic, backward, forward *with:* mask(ed,ing). *Consider also:* white noise. *See also* Perception; White noise.

Perceptual measures. Perceptual measure(s). *Choose from:* percept(ion, ual), sensory, tactual, visual, vision, auditory, hearing, spatial ability, olfactory, *with:* test(s), measure(s,ment), assessment. *See also* Auditory threshold; Measurement; Perception; Taste threshold; Threshold determination; Thresholds.

Perceptual motor coordination. Perceptual motor coordination. *Choose from:* perceptual motor, psychomotor, eye-hand, hand-eye, visual motor, sensory motor, sensorimotor *with:* coordination, performance. *Consider also:* physical dexterity. *See also* Motor coordination; Perceptual motor processes; Physical dexterity; Sensory integration.

Perceptual motor learning. Perceptual motor learning. *Choose from:* perceptual motor, psychomotor, gross motor, fine motor, kinesthetic, eye-hand, hand-eye, visual motor, sensorimotor, sensory motor, drawing *with:* skill(s), learning, education, development. *See also* Fine motor skills; Gross motor skills; Sensory integration; Skill learning; Visual tracking.

Perceptual motor processes. Perceptual motor process(es). *Choose from:* perceptual motor, psychomotor, sensorimotor, sensory motor, kinesthetic, visual motor, eye-hand *with:* process(es), coordination, performance, skill(s), function(s,ing), abilit(y,ies), integration. *Consider also:* marksmanship, object manipulation, motor skill(s), physical dexterity, rotary pursuit, tracking. *See also* Equilibrium; Motor coordination; Perceptual motor coordination; Perceptual motor learning; Physical agility; Physical dexterity; Visual tracking.

Perceptual skills. Perceptual skill(s).

Choose from: perceptual, spatial, sensory, visual, auditory *with:* skill(s), competence, capabilit(y,ies), sensitivity, integration, memory, discrimination. *See also* Fine motor skills; Gross motor skills; Perception; Skill; Skill learning.

Perceptual stimulation. Perceptual stimulation. *Choose from:* perceptual, sensory, visual, auditory, noise, illumination, loud(ness), olfactory, pitch, prismatic, somesthetic, stereoscopic, tachistoscopic, tactual, taste, somatosensory, multisensory *with:* stimul(i,us, ation). *See also* Loudness; Masking; Noise levels (work areas); Odors; Photopic stimulation; Subliminal stimulation; Tactual stimulation; Taste stimulation; Visual stimulation; Stimuli.

Perceptual style. Perceptual style(s). *Choose from:* primary, preferred, preference(s) *with:* modalit(y,ies), representational system(s). *Consider also:* perceptual preference(s). *See also* Cognitive style; Conceptual tempo; Perception.

Perceptually disabled. See *Brain damaged.*

Perfection. Perfect(ed,ing,ion,ibility). Ideal(ity). Inimitab(le,leness,ility). Incomparab(le,leness,ility). Paragon(s). Excellen(t,ce). Preeminen(t,ce). Flawless(ness). Complete(ness). Entire(ness). Whole(ness). Integrity. Crown jewel(s). Epitom(e,ize,ized, izing). Quintessen(ce,tial). Archetype(s). Exemplar(y). *See also* Accuracy; Achievement; Best practices; Criteria; Evaluation; Excellence; Failure; Performance; Quality; Standards; Success; Virtue.

Perfectionism. Perfection(ism,ist,ists). Hypercritical(ness). Overdemanding(ness). Fastidious(ness). Critical(ness). Fuss(y,iness). Purist(s). Scrupulous(ness). Meticulous(ness). Exacting. Conscientious(ness). Painstaking. *Consider also:* high expectations, ideal(ism,ist,ists). *See also* Compulsive behavior; Idealism.

Performance. Perform(ance,ances,ing). Accomplishment(s). Product(ion,ions, ivity). Function(ed,ing). Complet(e,ed, ing,ion). Execut(e,ed,ing,ion). Attain(ed,ing,ment). Conclusion(s). Finish(ed,ing). Fulfill(ed,ment). Realiz(e,ed,ing,ation). Achievement(s). Feat(s). Deed(s). *Consider also:* efficiency, effectiveness, behavior, success(es), failure(s), losing, winning. *See also* Ability; Academic achievement; Accountability; Achievement; Aptitude; Aspirations; Awards; Best practices; Competence; Competency based education; Effectiveness; Errors; Evaluation; Expectations; Excellence; Feedback; Goals; Group performance; Implementation; Job performance; Knowledge level; Mastery learning;

Minimum competencies; Motivation; Observation; Organizational effectiveness; Participation; Peer review; Performance anxiety; Performance appraisal; Performance standards; Performance tests; Practices (methods); Qualifications; Quality; Quality control; Recognition (achievement); Relevance; Reliability; Standards; Success; Task performance and analysis; Time and motion studies.

Performance, academic. See *Academic achievement.*

Performance, group. See *Group performance.*

Performance, job. See *Job performance.*

Performance, organizational. See *Organizational effectiveness.*

Performance, school. See *Academic achievement.*

Performance and analysis, task. See *Task performance and analysis.*

Performance anxiety. Performance anxiety. *Choose from:* performance, writing, communication, test, speech, task, situation *with:* anxiety, anxious(ness), apprehens(ion,ive,iveness). *Consider also:* stage fright, writer(s) block, task avoidance. *See also* Anxiety; Anxiety disorders; Performance; Speech anxiety; Stage fright.

Performance appraisal. Performance appraisal. *Choose from:* performance, effectiveness, product(ion,ivity), accomplishment(s), achievement(s), merit(s), employee(s), personnel, staff, peer *with:* evaluat(ed,ing,ion,ions), rate(d), rating(s), appraisal(s), benchmarking, assess(ed,ing,ment), review(ed,ing,s). *See also* Peer review; Performance; Personnel evaluation.

Performance art. Performance art. Fluxus. *Consider also:* Joseph Beuys. *See also* Conceptual art; Dadaism; Experimental theater; Happening (art).

Performance assessment. See *Performance appraisal.*

Performance evaluation. See *Performance appraisal; Personnel evaluation.*

Performance standards. Performance standard(s). Benchmark(s). *Choose from:* performance, professional, care, medicare, service(s), product(s) *with:* criteria, measure(s), standard(s), specification(s), requirement(s), quality control, quality assurance, appraisal(s), assessment(s), guideline(s). *See also* Benchmarks; Electronic data interchange; Performance; Performance tests; Standards.

Performance tests. Performance test(s). *Choose from:* performance, skill(s), achievement, proficiency, competenc(y,ies), progress *with:*

measure(s,ment), task(s), sample(s), evaluation(s), scale(s), rating(s), test(s,ing), batter(y,ies), score(s), assessment(s), evaluat(ion,ing), checklist(s), inventor(y,ies). *See also* Achievement tests; Aptitude tests; Criterion referenced tests; Occupational tests; Performance.

Performers, circus. See *Circus performers.*

Performers, tightrope. See *Aerialists.*

Performing arts. See *Dance; Drama; Music; Theater.*

Perinatal care. See *Maternal health services.*

Period, critical psychology. See *Critical period (psychology).*

Period, latency. See *Latency period.*

Period, mesolithic. See *Mesolithic period.*

Period, paleolithic. See *Paleolithic period.*

Period, postnatal. See *Postnatal period.*

Periodic phenomena. See *Periodicity.*

Periodicals. Periodical(s). Scholarly journal(s). Journal(s). Serial(s). Magazine(s). Newsletter(s). Newspaper(s). Dail(y,ies). Weekl(y,ies). Quarterl(y,ies). Bimonthl(y,ies). Annual(s). Published periodically. Loose leaf service(s). *Consider also:* advertorial(s), magalog(s), ragazine(s), zine(s). *See also* Community newspapers; Electronic journals; Fanzines; Journal articles; Journalism; Library acquisitions; Magazine advertising; Magazine illustration; News media; Reading materials; Scholarly journals; Student newspapers and periodicals.

Periodicals, learned. See *Scholarly periodicals.*

Periodicals, online. See *Electronic journals.*

Periodicals, scholarly. See *Scholarly periodicals.*

Periodicals, sex oriented. See *Pornography.*

Periodicals, student. See *Student newspapers and periodicals.*

Periodicals and newspapers, student. See *Student newspapers and periodicals.*

Periodicity. Periodicity. Periodic phenomena. *Consider also:* biological, seasonal, circadian, activity, diurnal, sleep wake, circahoral, hibernation, annual, circannual, hourly, weekly, monthly, yearly, reproductive, menstrual, ultradian *with:* period(s,ic), cycle(s), cyclic, rhythm(s), seasonal variation(s), clock(s), fluctuation(s), oscillation(s). *Consider also:* photoperiod(s,ic), internal clock(s), biorhythm(s), chronobiolog(y,ical). *See also* Time factors; Time periods.

Periodization. Periodiz(e,ed,ing,ation). Colligat(e,ed,ing,ation,ory). Contextualiz(e,ed,ing,ation,ism). Period dating. *Consider also:* period terminology, period marker(s), survey courses, macrohistor(y,ical), chronological frame(work). *See also* Context; Events; Explanation; Historical periods; Historical perspective; Historiography; Zeitgeist.

Periods, historical. See *Historical periods.*

Periods, time. See *Time periods.*

Peripatetics. Peripatetic(s). Aristotelian(ism). *Consider also:* Hylomorphism, Theophrastus, Eudemus, Strato. *See also* Philosophy; Scholasticism.

Periphery (economics). See *Center and periphery.*

Periphery, and center. See *Center and periphery.*

Perjury. Perjur(e,ed,y,ious). False swearing. Falsely sworn. Mak(e,ing) false statement(s). *Choose from:* lying, lie(d,s), perjur(e,ed,y,ious), false(ly), dishonest(ly,y) *with:* testimony, testif(y,ying,ied), under oath, grand jury, witness stand, statement(s), court(s). *Consider also:* crimen falsi, subornation of perjury. *See also* Deception; Legal procedures.

Permanence, object. See *Object permanence.*

Permanent. Permanen(t,ce,cy). Unchang(ing,able). Continu(e,ed,ing). Changeless(ness). Last(ed,ing). Durable. Stab(le,ility). Endur(e,ed,ing). Uninterrupted. Surviving. Unremittent. Perpetual(ly). Perpetuity. Immutab(le, ility). Irrevocab(le,ility). Indelib(le,ility). Indestructib(le,ility). Imperishab(le, ility). Inextinguishab(le,ility). Indissolub(le,ility). *See also* Continuity; Durability; Endlessness; Job security; Security.

Permissiveness. Permissive(ness). Nonauthoritarian. Indulgent. Lenien(t,cy). Unrestrictive. Liberalism. Lax(ness). Unrestrained. Overindulgent. Toleran(t,ce). Permitting. Accomodating. Unstrict. Less strict. Lack of strictness. Forbear(ing,ance). Open minded. Easygoing. Unstructured. *See also* Childrearing; Father child relations; Mother child relations; Openmindedness; Parental attitudes; Parental permissiveness; Sexual permissiveness; Tolerance.

Permissiveness, parental. See *Parental permissiveness.*

Permissiveness, sexual. See *Sexual permissiveness.*

Perpetrators. Perpetrator(s). Offender(s). Molester(s). Batterer(s). Assaulter(s).

Obscene phone caller(s). Victimizer(s). Criminal(s). Violent husband(s). Violent men. Assaulter(s). Assailant(s). Child abuse(r,rs). Maltreating parent(s). Incestuous (step)father(s). Violator(s). Culprit(s). Felon(s). Abuser(s). Rapist(s). Murderer(s). Thie(f,ves). *Choose from:* abusive, abusing *with:* men, man, women, woman, parent(s). *See also* Crime; Criminal act; Offenders; Sex offenders; Thugs; Victimization.

Perquisites. See *Benefits (compensation); Employee benefits.*

Persecution. Persecut(ed,ion,ory). Tortur(e,ed,ing). Discriminat(e,ed,ing, ion). Stigma(tized). Inferiorized. Concentration camp(s). Scapegoat(ing). Pogrom(s). Holocaust. Martyr(ed,dom). Castigat(e,ed,ing,ion). Punish(ed,ing, ment). Mistreat(ed,ing,ment). Ill treated. Maltreat(ed,ing,ment). Torment(ed,ing). Atrocit(y,ies). Wrong(ed,ing). *See also* Holocaust; Inquisition; Martyrs; McCarthyism; Oppression; Racism; Sexism; Social discrimination; Political persecution; Political prisoners; Victimization; Witch hunting; Witchcraft trials.

Persecution, political. See *Political persecution.*

Persecution, religious. See *Anti-Catholicism; Antisemitism; Hate crimes; Offenses against religion; Religious prejudice; Religious refugees.*

Perseverance. See *Persistence.*

Perseveration. Perseverat(ion,ions,ive). *Choose from:* persistent, pathological, continu(ed,ous) *with:* repetition. *Consider also:* palilexia, paliphrasia, palilalia, verbigeration, cataphasia, stereotypy. *See also* Thought disturbances.

Persistence. Persisten(ce,t). Persever(e,ed, ing,ance). Persist(ed,ing). Steadfast(ness). Endur(e,ed,ing,ance). Indefatigable. Continu(e,ed,ing,ance). Stamina. Diligen(ce,t). Tenac(ious,ity). *See also* Continuation; Diligence; Motivation; Patience; Personality traits.

Persistence, academic. See *Academic persistence.*

Person, single. See *Single person.*

Person, wise. See *Wise person.*

Person perception. See *Social perception.*

Persona. See *Point of view (literature).*

Personal accounts. See *Autobiography.*

Personal adjustment. Personal adjustment. *Choose from:* personal, emotional, social, interpersonal, individual(s) *with:* adjust(ed,ment), toleran(t,ce), adapt(ed,ing,ation,ive), accomodat(e,ed, ing,ion), cop(e,ed,ing), accept(ed,ing, ance). *See also* Adjustment (to environ-

ment); Coping; Emotional control; Emotional responses; Identity crisis; Social adjustment; Occupational adjustment.

Personal appeal. See *Charisma.*

Personal appearance. Personal appearance. Physical(ly) attractive(ness). Physical characteristic(s). Healthy looking. Suntan(ned). Pleasant appearance. Sexual(ly) attractive(ness). Physical appearance. Beaut(y,iful). Cute(ness). Comel(y,iness). Lovel(y,iness). Neat(ness). Facial appearance. Visage. Facial attractive(ness). Glamor(ous, ousness). Eye appeal. Prett(y,iness). Statel(y,iness). Handsome(ness). Good look(s,ing). Shapel(y,iness). Well groomed. Gorgeous. Demeanor. Mien. Visage. *Consider also:* makeup, haircare, grooming, stylish(ness), complexion, physique, haircut(s), dress code(s), body type(s), attire(d), unattractive(ness), ungainl(y,iness), ugl(y,iness). *See also* Attractiveness; Beauty culture; Body ornamentation; Clothing; Demeanor; Face; Facial expressions; Facial features; Personal beauty; Physical characteristics.

Personal assault. See *Assault (personal).*

Personal autonomy. See *Personal independence.*

Personal background. See *Biographical data.*

Personal beauty. Personal beauty. Glamor(ous,ousness). Lovel(y,iness). Comel(y,iness). Prett(y,iness). Pulchritud(e,inous). Beauty title(s). Beauty contestant(s). Facial beauty. Younger-looking skin. Beauty secret(s). Pinup girl(s). Sex appeal. Hairstyle(s). Personal appearance. Physical(ly) attractive(ness). *Consider also:* inner beauty, inner glow, cosmetic(s), eye makeup, skin care, hair care, wardrobe, grooming, cosmetic surgery. *See also* Attractiveness; Beauty; Beauty culture; Demeanor; Idealization of women; Interpersonal attraction; Personal appearance; Physical characteristics; Social desirability.

Personal care. See *Hygiene.*

Personal computers. See *Microcomputers.*

Personal conduct. See *Behavior; Demeanor; Deviant behavior; Habits; Lifestyle; Manners; Social skills.*

Personal defense. See *Self defense.*

Personal development. See *Adolescent development; Adult development; Behavior development; Career development; Child development; Cognitive development; Emotional development; Enlightenment (state of mind); Human development; Human potential movement;Infant development; Intellec-

tual development; Language development; Moral development; Motor development; Personality development; Physical development; Psychomotor development; Psychosexual development; Psychosocial development; Self actualization; Skill learning; Socialization; Speech development.*

Personal financing. Personal financing. *Choose from:* family, personal, individual(s) *with:* financial planning, financ(e,es,ed,ing,ial), credit, expenditure(s), bank account(s), financial management, loan(s), expense(s), income. *Consider also:* privately financed, private capital, private loans. *See also* Family budgets; Financial planning; Financing; Loans.

Personal growth. See *Enlightenment (state of mind); Human potential movement; Moral development; Psychosocial development; Self actualization.*

Personal guides. See *Self help books.*

Personal health services. Personal health service(s). *Choose from:* personal, private, family *with:* health service(s), medical service(s), physician(s), medical care. *Consider also:* primary care. *See also* Health care.

Personal hygiene. See *Hygiene.*

Personal independence. Personal independen(ce,t). Autonom(y,ous). Freedom from parental control. Social freedom. Sui juris. Function(ed,ing) independently. Independent living. Liberty. Emancipat(ed,ion). Individuation. Human rights. Self relian(t,ce). Self direct(ed,ion). *Choose from:* self, personal, individual *with:* independen(ce,t), autonom(y,ous), empower(ed, ing,ment), direct(ed,ing,ion), freedom, liberty, liberation, relian(ce,t), responsibility, advocacy, supporting, control, actualiz(ation,ing), sufficien(cy,t), determination, direction. *See also* Consumer directed care; Freedom; Inner directed; Personalism; Responsibility (answerability); Salvation; Self education; Voting rights.

Personal injuries. Personal injur(y,ies). Injured part(y,ies). *Choose from:* person(s,al), client(s), victim(s), individual(s), part(y,ies), patient(s) *with:* injur(y,ies,ed,ing), accident(s,al), wound(s,ed), harm(ed), lesion(s), abrasion(s), concussion(s), trauma(s), laceration(s), contusion(s), stab(bed). *See also* Accidents; Industrial accidents; Injuries; Liability; Pedestrian accidents; Safety; Traffic accidents; Victimization.

Personal magnetism. See *Charisma.*

Personal narratives. See *First person narrative.*

Personal property. Personal property. Personalty. Possession(s). Belonging(s).

Personal effects. Private propert(y,ies). Estate(s). Chattel(s). Appurtenance(s). Asset(s). Paraphernalia. Baggage. Goods. Stock. Inheritance. Movables. Holding(s). Private paper(s). *See also* Acquisition; Ownership; Provenance; Real estate; Valuation.

Personal relationships. See *Family life; Friendship; Gay couples; Heterosexual relationships; Homosexual relationships; Interpersonal compatibility; Interpersonal relations; Intimacy; Marital relationship; Parent child relationship; Primary relationships; Social life.*

Personal satisfaction. Personal satisfaction. Fulfill(ed,ing,ment). Satisf(y,ied,action). Content(ed,ment). Sense of well being. Happ(y,iness). Peak experience(s). Meaningful(ness). Gratif(ying,ied, ication). Enjoy(ing,ment). Pleasure(s). *Consider also:* job satisfaction, need gratification. *See also* Happiness; Quality of life; Self actualization.

Personal space. Personal space. Privacy. Body boundar(y,ies). Body buffer zone(s). Crowd(ed,ing). Living area(s). Breathing room. Space bubble(s). Proxemics. Conversational distance(s). Seating arrangement(s). Sociospatial. Face-to-face. *Choose from:* personal, private, extrapersonal, interpersonal, intimate, living *with:* spac(e,es,ing), zone(s), distanc(e,es,ing), territor(y,ies), boundar(y,ies). *Choose from:* proxemic, spatial *with:* behavior, violation(s), intrusion(s), density. *See also* Crowding; Invasion of privacy; Physical contact; Proxemics; Social density.

Personal values. Personal values. *Choose from:* personal, interpersonal, religious, moral *with:* value(s), preference(s), priorit(y,ies), belief(s), principle(s), norm(s), criteria, standard(s), construct system(s), ideal(s). *Consider also:* morals, mores, aesthetic values, work ethic, value choices, Protestant ethic, value orientation(s), belief system(s), moral judgment(s). *See also* Altruism; Beliefs; Dissent; Egocentrism; Ethnocentrism; Ideologies; Life satisfaction; Moral development; Moral obligation; Political attitudes; Standards; Traditionalism; Values.

Personal welfare. See *Well being.*

Personalism. Personalis(m,t,ts). Transpersonalis(m,t,ts). Personalist(ic) approach(es). Personalist(ic) thought. Transpersonal approach(es). *Consider also:* spiritualism, Borden Parker Bowne. *See also* Awareness; Existentialism; Freedom (theology); Idealism; Individualism; Initiative (personal); Pantheism (universal divinity); Particularism; Personal independence; Phenomenology; Spirituality.

Personality. Personality. Personality trait(s). Character. Disposition. Temperament. Persona. Pattern(s) of behavior. Attitude(s). Social identit(y,ies). Self perception. Ego. Type A. Type B. Coronary prone behavior. Id. Gender identity. Superego. Emotional maturity. Individuality. *Choose from:* personality character(ological), emotional, behavior(al), psychological, MMPI *with:* trait(s), characteristic(s), profile(s), structure(s), type(s). *Consider also:* aggressive(ness), assertive(ness), courag(e,eous), creativ(e,ity), defense mechanism(s), defensive(ness), emotional(ity), expressive(ness), extrover(t,ted,sion), introver(t,ted,sion), self actualiz(ing,ation), passiv(e,ity), independen(t,ce), dependen(t,ce), timid(ity), sociab(le,ility), optimis(m, tic), pessimis(m,tic), rigid(ity), sexuality, locus of control, self concept, self esteem. *See also* Anal personality; Antisocial personality disorder; Attribution; Behavior; Client characteristics; Coronary prone behavior; Dependency (personality); Disposition (personality); Emotional adjustment; Emotions; Habits; Human nature; Inadequate personality; Individual differences; Individuals; Lifestyle; Masochistic personality; Multiple personality; Obsessive compulsive personality; Personal independence; Personality change; Personality correlates; Personality development; Personality disorders; Personality measures; Personality processes; Personality theories; Personality traits; Psychodynamics; Psychological well being; Rigid personality; Self actualization; Self concept; Socialization; Soul; Subjectivity; Teacher personality; Temperament; Therapist characteristics.

Personality, alternating. See *Multiple personality.*

Personality, anal. See *Anal personality.*

Personality, dependent. See *Dependency (personality).*

Personality, dual. See *Multiple personality.*

Personality, inadequate. See *Inadequate personality.*

Personality, masochistic. See *Masochistic personality.*

Personality, multiple. See *Multiple personality.*

Personality, obsessive compulsive. See *Obsessive compulsive personality.*

Personality, psychopathic. See *Antisocial personality disorder.*

Personality, rigid. See *Rigid personality.*

Personality, sociopathic. See *Antisocial personality disorder.*

Personality, split. See *Multiple personality.*

Personality, teacher. See *Teacher personality.*

Personality, therapist. See *Therapist characteristics.*

Personality, type A. See *Coronary prone behavior.*

Personality assessment. See *Personality measures.*

Personality change. Personality change(s). *Choose from:* personalit(y,ies), character, self concept, self esteem, locus of control, self, ego, emotional state(s), disposition(s), temperament(s), identit(y,ies), habit(s) *with:* change(s,d), transform(ed,ing,ation,ations), matur(ed,ing,ation), alter(ed,ing,ation, ations), develop(ed,ing,ment), growth, transcend(ed,ing,ence). *Consider also:* behavior change. *See also* Attitude change; Behavior modification; Change; Emotional development; Life stage transitions; Personality; Personality development.

Personality characteristics. See *Personality traits.*

Personality correlates. Personality correlate(s). *Choose from:* personality, psychological, MMPI, *with:* correlate(s, d), factor(s), characteristic(s), score(s), trait(s), variable(s), cluster(s). *See also* Personality; Personality traits; Physiological correlates; Sex factors; Social factors; Sociocultural factors; Socioeconomic factors.

Personality development. Personality development. *Choose from:* personality, ego, identity, superego, personal integrity, self acceptance, self knowledge, self awareness, character, moral, self concept, sexual identification, ego ideal, psychosocial, emotional *with:* develop(ed,ing,ment), form(ed, ing,ation), grow(th,ing), matur(ed,ing, ation). *Consider also:* Erikson(ian) stages, child development, socialization, individuation. *See also* Emotional development; Identity crisis; Individuation; Moral development; Personality change; Personality measures; Personality processes; Psychogenesis; Psychosocial development; Self actualization; Social maturity.

Personality disorder, antisocial. See *Antisocial personality disorder.*

Personality disorder, borderline. See *Borderline personality disorder.*

Personality disorder, compulsive. See *Obsessive compulsive personality.*

Personality disorder, histrionic. See *Histrionic personality disorder.*

Personality disorder, hysterical. See *Histrionic personality disorder.*

Personality disorder, passive aggressive.
See *Passive aggressive personality disorder.*

Personality disorder, schizotypal. See
Schizotypal personality disorder.

Personality disorders. Personality
disorder(s). *Choose from:* personality,
character(ological), emotional(ly),
psychological, psychosexual(ly) *with:*
disorder(s,ed), problem(s),
abnormal(ity,ities), maladjust(ed,ment),
instability, unstable, disturbance(s),
inadequa(te,cy,cies), disorganiz(ed,
ation). *Consider also:* antisocial,
borderline, compulsive, dependent,
depressive, histrionic, impulse-control,
impulse-ridden, paranoid, passive-
aggressive, schizoid, schizotypal,
asthenic, cyclothymic, explosive,
hysterical, inadequate, masochistic,
narcissistic, obsessive, as if, sadomasochistic *with:* personalit(y,ies),
character(s). *See also* Antisocial
personality disorder; Borderline
personality disorder; Dissociative
disorders; Ethnospecific disorders;
Explosive disorder; Histrionic personality disorder; Inadequate personality;
Kleptomania; Masochistic personality;
Narcissism; Obsessive compulsive
personality; Paranoid disorders; Passive
aggressive personality disorder;
Personality traits; Pyromania;
Schizotypal personality disorder;
Stubbornness.

Personality measures. Personality
measure(s). Personality inventor(y,ies).
Personality assessment(s). *Choose from:*
personality, temperament, motivation,
behavioral, psychological, emotional,
assertiveness, trait(s), self esteem, self
concept, anxiety, ego identity, needs,
projective *with:* measure(s), inventor(y,
ies), assessment(s), questionnaire(s),
scale(s), rating(s), survey(s), test(s),
research, form(s), profile(s), diagnosis,
screening, schedule(s). *Consider specific
tests or measures by name. See also*
Attitude measurement; Measurement;
Nonprojective personality measures;
Personality; Projective techniques;
Psychometrics; Semantic differential.

Personality measures, nonprojective. See
Nonprojective personality measures.

Personality processes. Personality
process(es). Primary process(es).
Psychodynamics. *Choose from:*
personality, ego, superego, id, emotional, self, inner *with:* process(es),
mechanism(s), function(s,ed,ing),
dynamics, organization, regression,
differentiation, investment, individuation, involvement, reevaluation,
development, formation, alteration,
wholeness, conflict(s), integration,
reintegration, deintegration, transference, catharsis, cathexis, defense

mechanism(s), externalization, inhibition, introspection, ideation, depersonalization, personalization, object relations,
autonomy. *See also* Catharsis; Cathexis;
Defense mechanisms; Externalization;
Inhibition (psychology); Introspection;
Personality; Reality testing.

Personality tests. See *Personality measures.*

Personality theories. Personality
theor(y,ies). *Choose from:* personality,
personal construct, ego, self,
character(ological), human nature,
psyche(s) *with:* theor(y,ies), model(s),
concept(s), typolog(y,ies). *Consider
also:* factorial, Cattell's, biological,
constitutional, Sheldon's, holistic,
Goldstein's, Maslow's *with:* theory of
personality. *See also* Behavior theories;
Personality; Theories.

Personality traits. Personality trait(s).
Disposition. Temperament. Persona.
Patterns of behavior. Locus of control.
Ego. Type A. Type B. Coronary prone
behavior. Emotional makeup. *Choose
from:* personality, character(ological),
behavior, psychological *with:* trait(s),
feature(s), characteristic(s), profile(s),
structure(s), type(s). *Consider also:*
adaptab(le,ility), conservat(ism,ive),
dishonest(y), ego strength,
expressive(ness), gender identity,
intelligen(t,ce), leadership ability,
psychosexual development. *See also*
Adaptability; Androgyny; Anxiety;
Assertiveness; Authoritarianism
(psychological); Charisma; Cognitive
style; Complementary needs; Compliance; Compulsive disorders; Conformity
(personality); Courage; Creativity;
Cruelty; Curiosity; Cynicism; Coronary
prone behavior; Defensive; Dependency
(personality); Diligence; Dogmatism;
Egalitarianism; Egocentrism; Egotism;
Emotional immaturity; Emotional
instability; Emotional maturity;
Emotional security; Emotional stability;
Emotional superiority; Emotionality;
Emotions; Empathy; Extraversion
(psychology); Faithfulness; Femininity;
Field dependence; Friendliness;
Gregariousness; Honesty; Humor;
Hypnotic susceptibility; Idealism;
Impetuous; Impulsiveness; Individuality;
Initiative (personal); Insensitivity;
Insight; Introversion; Irritability;
Jealousy; Laziness; Liberalism;
Likability; Locus of control; Loyalty;
Machiavellianism; Machismo; Masculin-
ity; Misanthropy; Moodiness; Narcis-
sism; Negativism; Nervousness;
Nonconformity (personality);
Nurturance; Obedience; Openmind-
edness; Optimism; Oral character;
Orderliness; Passiveness; Perceptiveness
(personality); Perfectionism; Persis-
tence; Personality; Personality disorders;
Personality measures; Pessimism;
Reasonableness; Rebelliousness;

Repression sensitization; Rigid personality; Self control; Self esteem; Self
monitoring; Selfishness (stingy);
Selfishness (egocentric); Sensation
seeking; Sensitivity (personality);
Seriousness; Sexuality; Sincerity; Snobs
and snobbishness; Sociability; Social
maturity; Spirituality; Timidity;
Tolerance; Trustworthy.

Personification. Personif(y,ied,ication).
Embod(y,ied,iment). Incarnat(e,ion).
Human attribute(s). Personiz(e,es,ed,ing,
ation). *See also* Allegory; Animism;
Figurative language; Hyperbole;
Metaphors; Parables; Sacred animals.

Personnel. Personnel. Workforce.
Operator(s). Employee(s). Staff.
Manpower. Womanpower. Personpower.
Worker(s). Supervisor(s). Work force.
Office force. Sales force. Subordinate(s).
Labor force. Labor supply. Functionar(y,
ies). Crew(s). Troop(s). Hired help.
Manager(s). Coworker(s). Occupational
group(s). Laborer(s). Practitioner(s).
Paraprofessional(s). Professional(s).
Nonprofessional(s). Air traffic
controller(s). Attorney(s). Administ-
trator(s). Agricultural personnel. Blue
collar worker(s). Caseworker(s). Church
worker(s). Civil servant(s). Caregiver(s).
Clerk(s). Clergy(women,woman,
man,men). Consultant(s). Computer
programmer(s). Crafts(woman,women,
man,men). Craftsperson(s).
Craftspeople. Designer(s). Driver(s).
Director(s). Domestic servant(s).
Editor(s). Faculty. Firefighter(s).
Guard(s). Government employee(s).
Health personnel. Hairdresser(s). Home
economist(s). Librarian(s). Machine
operator(s). Military personnel.
Nurse(s). Police officer(s). Pilot(s).
Programmer(s). Sales(men,man,women,
woman). Salespeople. Salesperson(s).
Secretar(y,ies). Stevedore(s). Teacher(s).
Technician(s). Trainer(s). Typist(s).
White collar worker(s). *Consider also:*
employed, civil service, working, hired
with: woman, women, men, man,
people, group(s), SS, males, female(s),
person(s), civilian(s). *See also* Aerospace personnel; Air Force personnel;
Allied health personnel; Army personnel; Beauty operators; Blue collar
workers; Business personnel; Careers;
Computer personnel; Correctional
personnel; Educational administrators;
Employment; Enlisted military personnel; Faculty; Foreign professional
personnel; Government personnel;
Health manpower; Health occupations;
Human resources; Industrial personnel;
Industrial psychology; Labor management relations; Law enforcement
personnel; Lay religious personnel;
Legal personnel; Managers; Marine
personnel; Mental health personnel;
Middle level managers; Military medical
personnel; Military personnel; Navy

personnel; Nonprofessional personnel; Nontraditional careers; Nurses; Occupations; Paraprofessional personnel; Personnel evaluation; Personnel loyalty; Personnel management; Personnel placement; Personnel policy; Personnel recruitment; Personnel scheduling; Personnel selection; Personnel specifications; Personnel termination; Personnel training; Physicians; Police personnel; Professional personnel; Religious personnel; Research personnel; Sales personnel; Staff development; Teachers; Technical personnel; Volunteer military personnel; White collar workers; Workers; Working women.

Personnel, aerospace. See *Aerospace personnel.*

Personnel, Air force. See *Air Force personnel.*

Personnel, allied health. See *Allied health personnel.*

Personnel, army. See *Army personnel.*

Personnel, attitude of health. See *Attitude of health personnel.*

Personnel, aviation. See *Aerospace personnel.*

Personnel, business. See *Business personnel.*

Personnel, computer. See *Computer personnel.*

Personnel, correctional. See *Correctional personnel.*

Personnel, disabled. See *Disabled workers.*

Personnel, educational. See *Educational administrators; Faculty; School counselors; Teachers.*

Personnel, enlisted military. See *Enlisted military personnel.*

Personnel, foreign professional. See *Foreign professional personnel.*

Personnel, government. See *Government personnel.*

Personnel, health. See *Allied health personnel; Health manpower; Health occupations; Physicians.*

Personnel, industrial. See *Industrial personnel.*

Personnel, law enforcement. See *Law enforcement personnel.*

Personnel, lay religious. See *Lay religious personnel.*

Personnel, legal. See *Legal personnel.*

Personnel, management. See *Managers.*

Personnel, marine. See *Marine personnel.*

Personnel, medical. See *Allied health personnel; Health manpower; Health occupations; Mental health programs; Military medical personnel; Physicians.*

Personnel, mental health. See *Mental health personnel.*

Personnel, military. See *Military personnel.*

Personnel, military medical. See *Military medical personnel.*

Personnel, navy. See *Navy personnel.*

Personnel, nonprofessional. See *Nonprofessional personnel.*

Personnel, paramedical. See *Allied health personnel.*

Personnel, paraprofessional. See *Paraprofessional personnel.*

Personnel, police. See *Police personnel.*

Personnel, prison. See *Correctional personnel.*

Personnel, professional. See *Professional personnel.*

Personnel, religious. See *Religious personnel.*

Personnel, research. See *Research personnel.*

Personnel, sales. See *Sales personnel.*

Personnel, technical. See *Technical personnel.*

Personnel, traveling sales. See *Traveling sales personnel.*

Personnel, volunteer military. See *Volunteer military personnel.*

Personnel evaluation. Personnel evaluation. *Choose from:* personnel, staff, employee(s), worker(s) *with:* evaluat(e, ed,ing,ion), assess(ed,ing,ment), rating(s), review(s,ed,ing). *Consider also:* 360 degree feedback. *See also* Competence; Employees; Evaluation; Job performance; Occupational qualifications; Peer review; Performance appraisal; Personnel; Personnel management; Personnel selection; Personnel termination; Promotion (occupational); Self evaluation (groups); Teacher evaluation.

Personnel loyalty. Personnel loyalty. *Choose from:* personnel, staff, employee(s), worker(s) *with:* loyal(ty, ties), commit(ted,ment), devot(ed,ion), dedicat(ed,ion), allegiance. *See also* Commitment (emotional); Faithfulness; Job involvement; Organizational commitment; Personnel; Loyalty.

Personnel management. Personnel management. Personnel administration. Supervis(ion,ory). Manpower planning. *Choose from:* personnel, staff, employee(s), manpower, worker(s) *with:* management, administration, supervision. *Consider also:* personnel, staff, employee(s), manpower, worker(s) *with:* selection, rating, training, placement, evaluat(e,ing,ion), schedul(e,ed,ing), apprais(al,ing), recruitment, termination.

Consider also: collective bargaining, employee discipline, employee grievance(s), employee incentive(s), quality circle(s), personnel staffing, job analysis, job interview(s), job applicant screening, labor management relations, personnel placement. *See also* Administration; Employee concerns; Industrial psychology; Labor management relations; Management methods; Performance appraisal; Personnel; Personnel evaluation; Personnel placement; Personnel policy; Personnel recruitment; Personnel scheduling; Staff development; Superior subordinate relationship; Supervision; Workforce planning.

Personnel placement. Personnel placement. Outplacement. *Choose from:* personnel, job, worker(s), employee(s), staff, position(s), employment, manpower, occupational, executive(s), vocational *with:* placement(s), assign(ed,ment, ments), reassign(ed,ment,ments), appoint(ed,ment,ments). *See also* Career development; Executive search firms; Personnel management.

Personnel policy. Personnel polic(y,ies). *Choose from:* personnel, employment, hiring, staff, employee(s), worker(s), office *with:* polic(y,ies), regulation(s), guideline(s), rule(s), manual(s). *See also* Administration; Administrative policy; Affirmative action; Job requirements; Labor management relations; Management methods; Occupational qualifications; Peer review; Personnel; Personnel placement; Personnel recruitment; Superior subordinate relationship; Supervision; Working conditions; Workers.

Personnel promotion. See *Promotion (occupational).*

Personnel recruitment. Personnel recruitment. *Choose from:* recruit(ed,ing,ment), hir(e,ed,es,ing), select(ed,ing,ion) *with:* personnel, staff, employee(s), worker(s), executive(s), teacher(s), faculty, manpower. Employment recruiter(s). Headhunter(s). *Consider also:* job applicant(s), hiring practice(s), hiring decision(s), publicizing job opening(s), advertising position(s), job placement, induct(ed,ing,ion), conscript(ed,ing,ion), draft(ed), employment process(es), executive search firm(s), college campus recruitment. *See also* Affirmative action; Executive search firms; Military recruitment; Teacher recruitment; Personnel management; Personnel selection.

Personnel scheduling. Personnel scheduling. *Choose from:* personnel, staff, employee(s), worker(s), workforce, crew(s), work unit(s), faculty, teacher(s) *with:* schedul(e,es,ed,ing), workload, utilization, staffing, teaching load, work(ing) hours, allocat(e,ed,ing,ion) of time, assigned hour(s), flextime, assignment(s), work pattern(s), shift(s). *See also* Alternative work patterns; Overtime work; Work load; Work schedules; Workday shifts; Worktime.

Personnel selection. Personnel selection. Hiring decision(s). Employment decision(s). Evaluat(e,ed,ing) candidate(s). Decision(s) to hire. *Choose from:* personnel, employee(s), employment, staff, worker(s), workforce, job applicant(s), job candidate(s), hiring *with:* select(ed,ing,ion), interview(s), recruitment, choice, choos(e,ing), screen(ed,ing). *See also* Affirmative action; Eligibility determination; Employability; Employment agencies; Employment interviews; Job applicant screening; Job requirements; Labor market; Personnel evaluation; Personnel policy; Personnel recruitment; Personnel specifications; Selection procedures.

Personnel services, student. See *Student personnel services.*

Personnel specifications. Personnel specification(s). Job specification(s). *Choose from:* personnel, employee(s), employment, staff, worker(s), workforce, job applicant(s), job candidate(s), hiring *with:* specification(s), predictor(s), abilit(y,ies), skill(s), education, training, work experience, physical characteristic(s). *See also* Job requirements; Occupational qualifications; Personnel; Personnel selection.

Personnel supply. See *Human resources; Labor supply; Manpower.*

Personnel supply, medical. See *Medical personnel supply.*

Personnel termination. Personnel terminat(ed,ion,ions). Job turnover. Involuntary separation. Outplacement. Involuntary career change(s). Mandatory retirement(s). Laid off. Lay(ing) off. Layoff(s). Forced job change(s). Golden parachute(s). Tin parachute(s). Downsiz(e,ed,ing). Out of work. Jobless(ness). Forced relocation(s). Nonrenewal of contract(s). Job suspension(s). Personnel cutback(s). Quit(ting) job(s). Leave employment. Career loss. Attrition in workforce. Severance. Plant closing(s). Workforce reduction(s). Pink slip(s). *Choose from:* dismiss(ed,al), fired, firing(s), layoff(s), laid off, discharge(d), terminat(e,ed,ion, ions), retrench(ed,ing,ment,ments), displace(d,ment,ments) *with:* job(s), employee(s), staff, personnel, worker(s), faculty, teacher(s). *Choose from:* reduc(e,ed,ing,tion), trim, cut(s,back), eliminat(e,ed,ing,ion) *with:* staff, force, workforce, personnel, line item(s), position(s), laborforce. *Choose from:* compulsory, mandatory, forc(ed,ing), obligatory *with:* retire(ment). *See also* Contracting out; Cutbacks; Dismissal of

staff; Downsizing; Employment history; Involuntary retirement; Job security; Mandatory retirement; Occupational tenure; Outplacement services; Personnel management; Plant closings; Retirement; Severance pay; Technological unemployment; Unemployment.

Personnel training. Personnel training. Staff training. Job training. Personnel development. *Choose from:* personnel, staff, job, employee(s), operator(s), inservice, worker(s), employment, occupational, vocational *with:* training, development, orientation, education, retraining, instruction, preparation. *Consider also:* apprenticeship(s), management development. *See also* Apprenticeship; Human relations training; Inservice training; Management training; Military training; Sensitivity training.

Persons. See *Civilians; Females (human); Humanity; Individuals; Inhabitants; Males (human); Masses; People of color; Personnel; Population.*

Persons, abuse of. See *Abusive parents; Battered women; Child abuse; Corporal punishment; Cruelty; Elder abuse; Emotional abuse; Family violence; Marital rape; Police brutality; Rape; Sadism; Sexual abuse; Sexual sadism; Sexual violence; Spouse abuse; Terrorism; Torture; Violence.*

Persons, disappeared. See *Missing persons.*

Persons, displaced. See *Displaced persons.*

Persons, dissolute. See *Skid row alcoholics.*

Persons, exceptional. See *Exceptional persons.*

Persons, exchange of. See *Exchange of persons.*

Persons, high risk. See *High risk persons.*

Persons, missing. See *Missing persons.*

Persons, offenses against. See *Abusive parents; Antisocial behavior; Acquaintance rape; Assault (personal); Atrocities; Battered women; Child abuse; Coercion; Concentration camps; Corporal punishment; Cruelty; Driveby crimes; Elder abuse; Emotional abuse; Ethnic cleansing; Family violence; Flagellants and flagellation; Forced labor; Genocide; Gynocide; Hate crimes; Holocaust; Homicide; Infanticide; Lynching; Marital rape; Massacres; Molested children; Police brutality; Rape; Sadism; Sexual abuse; Sexual exploitation; Sexual harassment; Sexual sadism; Sexual violence; Spouse abuse; Terrorism; Threat; Torture; Victimization; Violence; War crimes.*

Persons, titled. See *Royalty.*

Persons, trafficking in. See *Trafficking in persons.*

Persons of color. See *People of color.*

Persons *with*: disabilities, attitudes toward. See *Attitudes toward handicapped; Attitudes toward mental retardation; Attitudes toward physical handicaps.*

Perspective, global. See *Globalization.*

Perspective, historical. See *Historical perspective.*

Perspective, time. See *Time perspective.*

Perspective taking. Perspective taking. *Choose from:* perspective(s), role(s), viewpoint(s), view(s) *with:* tak(e,en,ing), perception, perceiv(e,ed,ing), understanding. *Consider also:* empath(y,ic, etic), social intelligence. *See also* Consciousness raising activities; Dialogic pedagogy; Egocentrism; Emotional development; Empathy; Identification (psychology); Insensitivity; Point of view (literature); Role perception; Role playing; Self concept; Sensitivity (personality); Social development.

Perspectives. See *Attitudes; Orientation; Perception.*

Persuasion. Persuas(ion,ive,iveness). Persuad(e,ed,ing). Proselytiz(e,ed,ing). Induce(ment,ments). Cajol(e,ed,ing). Coax(ed,ing). Convinc(e,ed,ing). Coerc(e,ed,ing,ive,ion). Urg(e,ed,ing). Seduc(e,ed,ing,tion). Brainwash(ed,ing). Hard sell. Soft sell. Induced attitude change(s). Induced belief change(s). Rhetoric(al,ally). Argument(ation,s). Debate. Propagand(a,ize,ism). Advertisement(s). Dissuas(ion,ive, iveness). Dissuad(e,ed,ing). Influenc(e, ed,ing). Espous(e,ed,ing). Commercial(s). High pressure communication(s). Sway(ing) opinion(s). Threat(ening,s). Conver(t,ting,sion,sions). Psychological warfare. Suggest(ed,ing,ion,ions). *See also* Advertising; Apologetics (Rhetoric); Brainwashing; Conflict resolution; Communication (thought transfer); Credibility; Debate; Interpersonal influences; Negotiation; Oratory; Political campaigns; Political rhetoric; Propaganda; Public speaking; Seduction; Social agitation.

Pervasive development disorders. Pervasive development(al) disorder(s). Autis(m,tic). *Consider also:* child(ren, hood) *with:* atypical, symbiotic *with:* psychos(is,es), schizophren(ia,ic). *See also* Developmental disabilities.

Perversions, sexual. See *Paraphilias; Sexual deviations.*

Pessimism. Pessimis(m,tic,t,ts). Hopeless(ness). Negative attitude(s). Attitude negativity. Discontent(ed, edness). Defeatis(m,t). Negativis(m,tic). Discourage(d,ment). Despair(ed,ing). Gloom(y,iness). Gloom and doom.

Desponden(cy,t). Melancholy. Doubt(ed,ing). Cynical. Morose. Unhapp(y,iness). Worr(y,ied). Depressed. Dismal. Distrustful(ness). Morbid(ity). Dispirited. *See also* Abjection; Alienation; Cynicism; Future orientation; Guilt; Hopelessness; Negativism; Optimism; Personality traits; Psychological distress; Self accusation; Self debasement; Self defeating behavior; Social attitudes; Worldview.

Pesticides. Pesticide(s). Pest management. Insecticide(s). Fungicide(s). Miticide(s). Fleapowder. Bug bomb(s). Termiticide(s). Malathion. Chlordane. Dieldrin. Sevin. Captan. Ethylene dibromide. *Consider also:* pest(s), insect(s), flea(s), termite(s), flies, fly, mosquito(es), bug(s), worm(s), moth(s), beetle(s), mite(s), bedbug(s), tick(s), locust(s), medfl(y,ies), botfl(y,ies), aphid(s), leaf hopper(s), borer(s), boll weevil(s), scale(s), wireworm(s), cutworm(s), caterpillar(s), slug(s) *with:* management, spray(s), control, chemical(s). *See also* Agricultural chemicals; Agricultural pests; Agricultural workers disease; Carcinogens; Dioxin; Farming; Herbicides; Organic farming; Poisons.

Pestilences. See *Epidemics; Plague.*

Pests, agricultural. See *Agricultural pests.*

Pet therapy. Pet therapy. Animal assisted therapy. Pet facilitated therapy. *Choose from:* dog(s), cat(s), pet(s), bird(s), animal(s), Eden Alternative, Edenizing *with:* therapy, nursing home(s), long term care. *Consider also:* companion animal program(s). *See also* Alternative medicine; Human-animal relationships; Pets; Psychotherapeutic techniques.

Petit mal epilepsy. Petit mal epilepsy. Epilepsy petit mal. Minor epilepsy. Akinetic petit mal. Pyknolepsy. Absence seizure(s). *Choose from:* absence(s) *with:* seizure(s), spell(s), petit mal, epilep(sy,tic). *See also* Epilepsy.

Petroglyphs. Petroglyph(s). Rock-carving(s). Rock art. Art rupestre. Palaeolithic rock-art. Petrogram(s). *Choose from:* carving(s), inscription(s), engraving(s) *with:* rock(s), stone(s), sandstone. *Consider also:* prehistoric, Neolithic, Bronze Age, stone-age *with:* carving(s), inscription(s), engraving(s). *See also* Cave paintings; Carving (decorative arts); Cuneiform; Hieroglyphics; Iconography; Pictography; Prehistoric art; Prehistoric sculpture; Written communications.

Pets. Pet(s). Animal companion(s). *Choose from:* domestic(ated), tame(d), housebroken, home raised, home reared, housetrained, house trained, companion *with:* dog(s), cat(s), animal(s). *Consider also:* human animal bonding, animal therapy, pet therapy, cat(s), dog(s),

parakeet(s), parrot(s), monkey(s), cockatiel(s), pet mice, goldfish(es), tropical fish(es). *See also* Animals; Cats; Dogs; Domestic animals; Human-animal relationships; Pet therapy.

Petting. See *Sexual foreplay.*

Peyote. See *Mescal (cactus).*

Phallic stage. Phallic stage. *Choose from:* phallic *with:* stage, phase. *Consider also:* phallic character. *See also* Psychosexual development.

Phallus. See *Penis.*

Phantom limb. Phantom limb(s). *Consider also:* post-amputation pain. *Choose from:* phantom *with:* hand(s), foot, feet, bod(y,ies), pain, itch(ing). *Consider also:* breast phantom phenomenon. *See also* Amputation; Body image disturbances.

Pharmacies. Pharmac(y,ies). Pharmaceutical establishment(s). Chemist shop(s). Apothecar(y,ies). Drugstore(s). Druggist(s). Prescription counter(s). Prescription sale(s). Fill(ed,ing) prescription(s). *See also* Prescription drugs; Pharmacists.

Pharmacists. Pharmacist(s). Druggist(s). *Choose from:* pharmac(y,eutical) *with:* worker(s), staff, personnel. *See also* Pharmacies; Professional personnel.

Pharmacogenomics. Pharmacogenomic(s). *Choose from:* snip(s), SNP(s), single nucleotide polymorphism(s), DNA *with:* drug(s), pharmaceutical(s), chip(s). *Consider also:* agro-pharmaceutical(s). *See also* Bioethics; Designer drugs; Gene mapping; Genetic research; Hereditary diseases; Medical ethics; Pharmacogenomics; Pharming.

Pharmacotherapy. See *Drug therapy.*

Pharming. Pharming. Barnyard biotechnology. Gene pharming. Molecular pharming. Transgenetic(s). Transgen(e,es,ic,s). *Choose from:* transgenic, biofactor(y,ies), genetically modified, biopharm(ed,ing), cross-species transplant(s) *with:* organism(s), plant(s), animal(s), bull(s), rabbit(s), sheep, goat(s), banana(s), fruit(s), tobacco, potato(es). *Consider also:* agro-pharmaceutical(s), bio-pharm(ed,ing), genetic pollution. *See also* Cloning; Genetic engineering; Genetic research; Pharmacogenomics; Reproductive technologies; Xenotransplantation.

Phased retirement. See *Flexible retirement.*

Phencyclidine. See *Hallucinogens.*

Phencyclidine abuse. See *Substance abuse.*

Phenomena, periodic. See *Periodicity.*

Phenomena, social. See *Social facts.*

Phenomena, unexplained. See *Extrasensory perception; Near death experi-*

ences; Occultism; Parapsychology; Witchcraft.

Phenomenological psychology. Phenomenological psychology. Psychological phenomenology. Phenomenal analysis. Psychophenomenolog(y,ical). *Choose from:* phenomenolog(y,ical), quotidian perspectives, every day, daily life *with:* psycholog(y,ical,ically), human sciences, psychoanalytic(al,ally). *See also* Existential psychology; Irreducibility; Metacognition; Phenomenology; Philosophical anthropology; Reflexivity.

Phenomenology. Phenomenolog(y,ic,ical, ically,ists). *Choose from:* Edmund Husserl, Max Scheler, Merleau Ponty, Alfred Schutz. *Consider also:* existentialism, dasein, daseinsanalytic, arugamama, intentionality, meaning(s), intuition. *See also* Critical theory; Existential psychology; Irreducibility; Personalism; Phenomenological psychology; Philosophical anthropology; Philosophy.

Phenomenology, psychological. See *Phenomenological psychology.*

Phenotypes. Phenotyp(e,es,ic,ically). Genetic(ally) related(ness). Immuno-phenotyp(e,es,ical). *Consider also:* famil(y,ial) *with:* resemblance(s), trait(s), pattern(s). *Consider also:* genotype(s), somatotype(s), biotyp(e,es,ing), inbred, inbreeding, genetic marker(s). *See also* Atavism (biology); Genetics.

Pheromones. Pheromon(e,es,al,ally). *Choose from:* sex *with:* attractant(s), odorant(s). Conspecific chemical cue(s). External chemical message(s). *See also* Animal mate selection; Animal scent marking; Animal sex behavior; Aphrodisiacs.

Philanderers. Philanderer(s). Womanizer(s). Flirt(s). Adulterer(s). Debaucher(s). Swinger(s). Woman chaser(s). Profligate(s). *See also* Womanizers.

Philanthropy. Philanthrop(y,ic,ist,ists). Charit(y,ies,itable). Donat(e,ed,ions). Donor(s). Corporate giving. Benefactor(s). Giv(e,ing) to need(y,iest). Charitable giving. Charitable gift(s). Neediest cases fund(s). Voluntary contribution(s). Contribut(e,ed,ing) funds. Charitable foundation(s). Bequest(s). Altruis(m,istic). Benevolen(t, ce). Beneficen(t,ce). Humanitarian. Public spirited. *Consider also:* foundations, backer(s), patron(s), supporter(s). *See also* Art patronage; Benefactors; Charitable trusts; Charities; Donations; Generosity; Giving; Magnanimity; Nonprofit organizations; Volunteers.

Philately. Philatel(y,ic,ically,ist,ists). Stamp collecting. Commemorative postage stamp(s). *Choose from:* collect(ed,ing, ion,or,ors), study(ing) *with:* stamp(s), stamped envelope(s). *Consider also:* postage stamp(s) *with:* cancellations, cover(s), design(s). *See also* Hobbies.

Philippine Islands cultural groups.
Philippine Islands cultural group(s). Filipino(s). *Choose from:* Philippine(s), Basilan Islands, Batanes Islands, Cuyo Archipelago, Leyte, Luzon, Mindanao [Mondanao], Mindoro, Palawan, Panay, Sulo Archipelago *with:* indigenous, native, population(s), people(s), ethnic group(s), minority group(s), populace, tribe(s), resident(s), inhabitant(s). *Consider also:* Aeta, Apayos, Bagobos, Bisayas, Gaddang, Hanunoo, Ifugaos, Igorots, Ilokos, Ilongot, Isinay, Kalinga, Mangyans, Manobos, Moro, Negritos, Pangasinans, Quianganes, Subamos, Sulu, Tagalog, Tinguianws, Tirurayes, Yakan, Yogads. *See also* Cultural groups; Culture (anthropology); Culture change; Culture contact; Malayo-Polynesian languages; Oceania; Southeast Asia.

Philology. See *Linguistics.*

Philosophers, medieval. See *Medieval philosophers.*

Philosophical anthropology. Philosophical anthropolog(y,ical). Natural man. Homo ferus. Feral child(ren). Wild m(an,en). *Consider also:* philosophical psychology, philosophy of action, Max Scheler, Helmuth Plessner, natural goodness, moral monstrosit(y,ies), common humanity, cultural universal(s), natural value(s), innately human, noble savage(s). *See also* Animal nature of man; Anthropocentrism; Fallibility; Human nature; Humanism; Humanity; Mind body problem; Natural law; Phenomenological psychology; Phenomenology; Psychological anthropology; Soul.

Philosophy. Philosoph(y,ers,ical). Study of truth. Fundamental belief(s). Underlying theor(y,ies). Philosophical doctrine(s). *Consider also:* absolutism, aesthetics, agnosticism, animism, Aristotelian(ism), asceticism, atheism, behaviorism, cosmology, determinism, dialectics, dualism, egalitarianism, epistemology, ethics, existentialism, fatalism, free will, functionalism, gnosticism, hedonism, hermeneutics, historicism, holism, humanism, idealism, instrumentalism; logic, Marxism, materialism, metaphysics, mysticism, naturalism, neoplatonism, nihilism, nominalism, ontologism, pacifism, phenomenalism, phenomenology, Platonism, pluralism, pragmatism, rationalism, reductionism, relativism, scholasticism, semiotics, spiritualism, teleology, Thomism, transcendentalism, utilitarianism, utopia(s), vitalism, voluntarism. *See also* Act (Philosophy); Analysis (Philosophy); Animism; Asceticism; Chain of being; Classes

(logic); Conceptionalism; Dialectics; Disposition (Philosophy); Dualism; Egalitarianism; Epistemology; Essence (philosophy); Ethics; External world (Philosophy); Fatalism; Form (philosophy); Hedonism; Hermeneutics; Humanism; Idealism; Ideologies; Instrumentalism (philosophy); Interest (ethics); Irrationalism (philosophy); Logic; Logical positivism; Marxism; Medical philosophy; Medieval philosophers; Metaphysics; Mysticism; Naturalism; Nihilism; Pacifism; Peripatetics; Phenomenology; Political philosophy; Pragmatism; Rationalism; Realism; Reductionism; Religion; Renaissance philosophy; Scholasticism; Semiotics; Social philosophy; Speech act theory; Teleology; Theology; Voluntarism (philosophy).

Philosophy, medical. See *Medical philosophy.*

Philosophy, modern. See *Deconstruction; Egalitarianism; Empiricism; Ethics; Existentialism; Humanism; Logocentrism; Phenomenology; Political philosophy; Postmodernism; Pragmatism; Realism; Reductionism; Semiotics; Social philosophy; Voluntarism (philosophy).*

Philosophy, moral. See *Ethics.*

Philosophy, political. See *Political philosophy.*

Philosophy, renaissance. See *Renaissance philosophy.*

Philosophy, social. See *Social philosophy.*

Philosophy of language. Philosophy of language. Linguistic philosophy. Philosophical linguistics. *Consider also:* philosophical grammar, philosophical semantics. *See also* Linguistics; Semantics; Semiotics.

Philosophy of life. See *Worldview.*

Philters, love. See *Aphrodisiacs.*

Phobia, cat. See *Cat phobia.*

Phobia, insect. See *Insect phobia.*

Phobia, pain. See *Pain phobia.*

Phobia, school. See *School phobia.*

Phobia, snake. See *Snake phobia.*

Phobia, social. See *Social phobia.*

Phobia, spider. See *Spider phobia.*

Phobias. Phobia(s). Phobic disorder(s). Phobic neuros(is,es). Morbid anxiety. Dread. Horror. Fear(ful). Panic. Anxious. Acarophob(ia,ic). Acoustico-phob(ia,ic). Acerophob(ia,ic). Acrophob(ia,ic). Acluphob(ia,ic). Achluophob(ia,ic). Aerophob(ia,ic). Agoraphob(ia,ic). Agyiophob(ia,ic). Aicmophob(ia,ic). Aichmophob(ia,ic). Aidophob(ia,ic). Aidsphob(ia,ic). Ailurophob(ia,ic). Algophob(ia,ic).

Amathophob(ia,ic). Amaxophob(ia,ic). Amychophob(ia,ic). Androphob(ia,ic). Anemophob(ia,ic). Anginaphob(ia,ic). Anginophob(ia,ic). Anginophob(ia,ic). Antlophob(ia,ic). Anthropophob(ia,ic). Anthrophob(ia,ic). Apeirophob(ia,ic). Aphephob(ia,ic). Apiphob(ia,ic). Aquaphob(ia,ic). Arachnophob(ia,ic). Asthenophob(ia,ic). Astraphob(ia,ic). Astrapophob(ia,ic). Atephob(ia,ic). Aulophob(ia,ic). Autodysosmo-phob(ia,ic). Automimophob(ia,ic). Automysophob(ia,ic). Auroraphob(ia,ic). Autophob(ia,ic). Autocsopophob(ia,ic). Aviophob(ia,ic). Bacillophob(ia,ic). Bathophob(ia,ic). Batrachophob(ia,ic). Barophob(ia,ic). Basiphob(ia,ic). Batophob(ia,ic). Ballistophob(ia,ic). Belonephob(ia,ic). Blatophob(ia,ic). Bromidrosiphob(ia,ic). Brontophob(ia, ic). Cancerphob(ia,ic). Cancerophob(ia, ic). Carcinophob(ia,ic). Cardiophob(ia, ic). Carniphob(ia,ic). Cenophob(ia,ic). Chromophob(ia,ic). Chromatophob(ia, ic). Chrono-phob(ia,ic). Climaco-phob(ia,ic). Clithrophob(ia,ic). Claustrophob(ia,ic). Claustroxensco-pophob(ia,ic). Cheimaphob(ia,ic). Chionophob(ia,ic). Chromatophob(ia,ic). Chromophob(ia,ic). Cometophob(ia,ic). Computerphob(ia,ic). Counterphob(ia, ic). Cryophob(ia,ic). Cynophob(ia,ic). Coprophob(ia,ic). Corticophob(ia,ic). Cibophob(ia,ic). Crystallophob(ia,ic). Chrematophob(ia,ic). Cremnophob(ia, ic). Catagelophob(ia,ic). Coitophob(ia, ic). Chionophob(ia,ic). Climacophob(ia, ic). Cyberphob(ia,ic). Cypridoophob(ia, ic). Cypriphob(ia,ic). Decidophob(ia,ic). Dromophob(ia,ic). Demophob(ia,ic). Dysmorphophob(ia,ic). Demon(ia,ic). Demonoman(ia,ic). Demonophob(ia,ic). Dentalphob(ia,ic). Dentophob(ia,ic). Dikephob(ia,ic). Destrophob(ia,ic). Dermatosiophob(ia,ic). Dermatophob(ia, ic). Dermatozoophob(ia,ic). Domo-phob(ia,ic). Doraphob(ia,ic). Dysmor-phob(ia,ic). Dysmorphophob(ia, ic). Dysppsychophob(ia,ic). Eikosi-phob(ia,ic). Eremophob(ia,ic). Eremiophob(ia,ic). Ereuthophob(ia,ic). Ergophob(ia,ic). Eritrophob(ia,ic). Erotophob(ia,ic). Erythrophob(ia,ic). Esophob(ia,ic). Entheophob(ia,ic). Electrophob(ia,ic). Emetophob(ia,ic). Entomophob(ia,ic). Eurotophob(ia,ic). Formphob(ia,ic). Galeophob(ia,ic). Gatophob(ia,ic). Geneticophob(ia,ic). Genetophob(ia,ic). Genophob(ia,ic). Gephrophob(ia,ic). Gerontophob(ia,ic). Gynephob(ia,ic). Gynophob(ia,ic). Graphophob(ia,ic). Gymnophob(ia,ic). Hedonophob(ia,ic). Heliophob(ia,ic). Hemophob(ia,ic). Hematophob(ia,ic). Heterophob(ia,ic). Hodophob(ia,ic). Homophob(ia,ic). Homosexphob(ia,ic). Horror feminae. Hydrophob(ia,ic). Iatrophob(ia,ic). Icosaphob(ia,ic). Ictophob(ia,ic). Idosophob(ia,ic). Idrosophob(ia,ic). Interphob(ia,ic).

Jinnophob(ia,ic). Kainophob(ia,ic). Kainotophob(ia,ic). Kakorrhapio- phob(ia,ic). Kathisophob(ia,ic). Kenophob(ia,ic). Kinesophob(ia,ic). Kleptophob(ia,ic). Kopophob(ia,ic). Lactophob(ia,ic). Leprophob(ia,ic). Litigaphob(ia,ic). Locophob(ia,ic). Lyssophob(ia,ic). Maieusiophob(ia,ic). Malingerophob(ia,ic). Math phob(ia,ic). Mathophob(ia,ic). Monophob(ia,ic). Monotophob(ia,ic). Musophob(ia,ic). Mycophob(ia,ic). Mysophob(ia,ic). Necrophob(ia,ic). Neophob(ia,ic). Nikephob(ia,ic). Nosophob(ia,ic). Nyctophob(ia,ic). Ochlophob(ia,ic). Odontophob(ia,ic). Ophidiophob(ia,ic). Ophob(ia,ic). Opiophob(ia,ic). Ornithophob(ia,ic). Osmophob(ia,ic). Panphob(ia,ic). Panophob(ia,ic). Parasitophob(ia,ic). Parturiphob(ia,ic). Pathophob(ia,ic). Pavor scleris. Pedagophob(ia,ic). Phagophob(ia,ic). Pharmaphob(ia,ic). Pharmacophob(ia, ic). Phobophob(ia,ic). Phonophob(ia,ic). Photophob(ia,ic). Phrenophob(ia,ic). Phytophob(ia,ic). Ponophob(ia,ic). Pseudoagoraphob(ia,ic). Pseudophob(ia, ic). Psychotheraphob(ia,ic). Ptophob(ia,ic). Pyrophob(ia,ic). School phob(ia,ic). Scriptophob(ia,ic). Sclerophob(ia,ic). Scopophob(ia,ic). Selenophob(ia,ic). Sitophob(ia,ic). Skoptophob(ia,ic). Social phob(ia,ic). Sociophob(ia,ic). Spermatorrhea- phob(ia,ic). Statiscophophob(ia,ic). Symbiophob(ia,ic). Syphilophob(ia,ic). Taphophob(ia,ic). Technophob(ia,ic). Tecnophob(ia,ic). Thalassophob(ia,ic). Thanatophob(ia,ic). Thermophob(ia,ic). Toxiphob(ia,ic). Toxicophob(ia,ic). Trichophob(ia,ic). Triskaidekaphob(ia, ic). Venereophob(ia,ic). Vermiphob(ia, ic). Vigintophob(ia,ic). Vomitophob(ia, ic). Xenophob(ia,ic). Zoophobia. *See also* Anxiety; Cat phobia; Fear; Insect phobia; Pain phobia; School phobia; Social phobia; Snake phobia; Spider phobia.

Phonemes. Phoneme(s,ic,ics,ically). Phonological unit(s). Speech sound(s). Morphophon(ic,emic). Phonological coding. Allophon(e,es,ic). Fricative(s). *Consider also:* consonant(s), vowel(s). *See also* Language; Phonetics; Speech; Suprasegmentals.

Phonetics. Phonetic(s,al,ally). *Consider also:* phonic(s), morpheme(s), phonem(e,es,ic), phonolog(y,ical), plosive(s), fricative(s), vowel(s), consonant(s), syllable(s), word(s), phonetic unit(s), spoken language(s), speech sound(s). *See also* Articulation (speech); Closure (phonetics); Lan- guage; Phonemes; Speech.

Phonological stress. See *Inflection.*

Phonology, lexical. See *Lexical phonology.*

Photographers. Photographer(s). Camera(man,men,woman,women). Paparazz(o,i). News camera(s). Camerist(s). Photographist(s). Photoist(s). Photojournalist(s). *Consider also:* street photographer(s). *See also* Journalists; Photojournalism; Workers.

Photography. Photograph(s,ic,ed,ers,y). Photo(s). Daguerrotype(s). Ferrotype(s). *Consider also:* pictorial, picture(s), slide(s), photoreproduction, photobio- graphy, polaroid, camera(s), microfilm- ing, motion picture(s), holography, photogrammetry, photomicrography, photofluorography. *See also* Audiovisual communications; Candid photography; Copies; Films; Illustrated books; Photojournalism; Representation (likeness).

Photography, candid. See *Candid photography.*

Photography, satellite. See *Aerial recon- naissance.*

Photojournalism. Photojournalis(m,t,ts,tic). Journalistic photograph(er,ers,y). *Choose from:* news, press, report(s,age), stor(y,ies) *with:* photograph(,er,ers,y), photo(s). *Consider also:* documentar(y, ies). *See also* Candid photography; Documentary theater; Journalism; Photographers; Photography; War news.

Photopic stimulation. Photopic stimula- tion. Photostimulation. *Choose from:* photopic, photic, light, daylight, flash(es), illumination, glare *with:* stimul(i,us,ation), exposure, intensit(y, ies). *See also* Visual stimulation.

Phrases. Phrase(s,eology). Clause(s). Word sequence(s). Anaphor(a). *See also* Conditionals; Language; Sentences.

Phratries. See *Clans.*

Phrenology. Phrenolog(y,ical). Craniology. Skull conformation. Skull asymmetr(y, ies). *See also* Physiognomy; Somato- types.

Phylogeny. Phylogen(y,ic,esis,etic,etically). *Choose from:* evolution(s,ary) *with:* population, species. *See also* Creation- ism; Darwinism; Evolution; Prehistoric people.

Physical abnormalities. Physical abnormalit(ies,y). Congenital(ly) handicap(s,ped). Deformit(y,ies). *Choose from:* congenital, birth, neonatal, fetal, amniogenic *with:* disorder(s), defect(s), deformit(y,ies), malform(ed, ation,ations), deform(ed,ity,ities), handicap(s,ped,ping), impair(ed,ment, ments), anomal(y,ies). Freak(s). Congenital asymmetr(y,ies). Fetal disease(s). Hereditary disease(s). Genetic defect(s). Teratogen(esis,icity). Teratolog(y,ical). Monster(s). *See also* Cleft palate; Congenitally handicapped; Disability; Drug addicted babies; Drug induced abnormalities; Hereditary diseases; Human abnormalities; Physical disfigurement; Severely handicapped infants; Teratology.

Physical abuse. See *Abusive parents; Battered women; Child abuse; Corporal punishment; Cruelty; Elder abuse; Emotional abuse; Family violence; Flagellants and flagellation; Marital rape; Police brutality; Rape; Sadism; Sexual abuse; Sexual sadism; Sexual violence; Spouse abuse; Terrorism; Torture; Violence.*

Physical agility. Physical agility. Agil(e,ity). High level motor skill(s). Dexterity. *Consider also:* speed, quick(ness), flexib(le,ility), nimble(ness), mobil(e,ity), physical abilit(y,ies), supple(ness), sports abilit(y,ies), athletic abilit(y,ies), well coordinated. *See also* Awkwardness; Motor development; Motor coordination; Physical dexterity.

Physical aging. See *Physiological aging.*

Physical anthropology. Physical anthropolog(y,ists). Anthropometr(y,ic). Craniometr(y,ic). Osteolog(y,ical). Osteometr(y,ic). Craniolog(y,ical). Paleontolog(yical). Paleodontolog(y, ical). Paleopatholog(y,ical). Ectomorph(y,ic). Endomorph(y,ic). Mesomorph(y,ic). Study of hominids. Forensic anthropolog(y,ists). Somatolog(y,ic). *Consider also:* biometr(y,ic), medical genetics, human evolution, human fossils. *See also* Age determination by skeleton; Age determination by teeth; Animal nature of man; Animal remains (Archaeology); Archaeology; Cultural anthropology; Medical anthropology; Human remains (archaeology); Paleontology; Paleopathology; Plant remains (archae- ology).

Physical appearance. See *Personal appearance.*

Physical attractiveness. See *Attractiveness.*

Physical characteristics. Physical characteristic(s). Physique(s). Physiol- ogy. Somatotype(s). Anatom(y,ical). *Choose from:* body *with:* height, weight, shapes, proportion(s), type(s), character- istics, size(s), build, composition, mass, measures. Physiognomy. Physical feature(s). Anatomical difference(s). Physical appearance. Physiological variables. Posture. Obesity. Under- weight. Overweight. Anthropometric data. Body mass. Anthropometric characteristics. Anthropometric measures. Endomorph(y,s). Meso- morph(y,s). Actomorph(y,s). *Consider also:* age, sex, race. *See also* Age differences; Attractiveness; Awkward- ness; Body height; Body weight; Characteristics; Demeanor; Facial features; Gender differences; Personal beauty; Physical agility; Physical dexterity; Physical disfigurement; Physical fitness; Physical maturity; Physical strength; Physically handicapped; Physiognomy; Physique; Qualities; Racial differences.

Physical comfort. Physical(ly) comfort(able). Content(ed). Ease. Rested. Soothed. Relieved. Relax(ed,ation). Untroubled. Cheerful. Undisturbed. Complacent. Placid. Quiet. Restful. Tranquil. Serene. Peaceful. Restored. Refreshed. Without care. *Consider also:* quality of the environment, thermal comfort. *See also* Comfortableness; Environment; Ergonomics; Furniture; Satisfaction; Spatial organization.

Physical condition. See *Disease susceptibility; Health; Health problems; Physical fitness.*

Physical contact. Physical(ly) contact(ing). Bod(y,ily) contact. Touch(ed,ing). Physical interaction(s). Hit(ting). Physical intimacy. Caress(ed,ing). Physically intimate. Physical involvement. Tactile. Strok(e,ing). Pet(ted,ting). Rub(bing). Fondl(e,ing). Jostl(e,ed,ing). Push(ing). Shov(e,ed,ing). Slap(ped, ping). Punch(ed,ing). Swat(ted,ting). Spank(ed,ing). Pok(e,ed,ing). Strik(e,ing). Smite. Nudg(e,ed,ing). Nuzzl(e,ing). Massage. Cuddl(e,ing). Embrac(e,ed,ing). Hug(ged,ging). Pat(ted,ting). Snuggl(e,ed,ing). *See also* Childrearing; Intimacy; Massage; Personal space; Sexual foreplay; Sexual intercourse; Sexuality; Social contact; Spatial behavior; Sports.

Physical development. Physical development. *Choose from:* physical, biological, motor, neural, neuromotor, organ, anatomical, prenatal, psychomotor, sexual, body, physiological *with:* development, growth, maturation. *See also* Age differences; Body height; Body weight; Developmental stages; Laterality; Menarche; Physical characteristics; Physical maturity; Physical strength; Prenatal development.

Physical dexterity. Physical dexterity. Deft(ness). Nimble(ness). Agil(e,ity). Quick(ness). Adept(ness). Sleight. Quick handed. Dexterous. *Consider also:* physical, manual, digital, bimanual, hand, motor, finger(tip), psychomotor, manipulative *with:* dexterity. *See also* Motor coordination; Motor development; Physical agility; Psychomotor development.

Physical disabilities. See *Disability; Physically handicapped.*

Physical disfigurement. Physical(ly) disfigure(d,ment). *Choose from:* physical(ly), facial(ly), body, bodily, limb(s) *with:* disfigure(d,ment), malform(ed,ation), mutilat(ed,ions), deformit(y,ies), deformed, anomal(y,ies), blemish(es), disfigure(d,ment), defect(s), marred, scarred, blemish(ed,es). *Consider also:* birthmark(s), leprosy, acne, spina bifida, hydrocephalus, dwarfism, stoma, cleft lip(s), cleft palate(s). *See also* Disability; Hereditary diseases; Human abnormalities; Injuries; Physical abnormalities; Ritual disfigurement; Severely handicapped infants.

Physical education. Physical education. *Choose from:* movement, physical, athletic, endurance, strength *with:* training, education. *Consider also:* gymnastics, calisthenics, physical activity program(s), exercise, physical conditioning, physical fitness program, athletics, aerobics, isometrics, weight training. *See also* Adapted physical education; Athletic participation; Dance education; Exercise; Physical fitness; Sports.

Physical education, adapted. See *Adapted physical education.*

Physical endurance. See *Endurance.*

Physical examinations. See *Health examinations.*

Physical exercise. See *Exercise.*

Physical fitness. Physical(ly) fit(ness). Endurance. Wellness. Hard(y,iness). Health(y,iness). Heart(y,iness). Work capacity. Muscular(ly) power(ful). Muscle power. Muscularity. Sinewy. Vigorous(ness). Viril(e,ity). Ablebodied. Robust(ness). Sturd(y,iness). *Choose from:* physical(ly), bod(y,ies) *with:* fit(ness), strong, strength, capacity, condition, power(ful), robust, health(y), tough(em,ened,ening). *Consider also:* abled, physical normalcy, physical(ly) normal(ity). *See also* Exercise; Fortitude; Physical agility; Physical strength.

Physical growth. See *Physical development.*

Physical handicaps. See *Physically handicapped.*

Physical handicaps, attitudes toward. See *Attitudes toward physical handicaps.*

Physical health. See *Health.*

Physical illness. See *Illness.*

Physical illness, attitudes toward. See *Attitudes toward physical illness.*

Physical maturity. Physical maturity. *Choose from:* physical, biological, motor, neural, anatomical, prenatal, psychomotor, sexual, body, physiological *with:* matur(e,ity), ripe(ness), adulthood. *See also* Physical development.

Physical mobility. Physical(ly) mobil(e,ity). Ambulat(e,ing,ory,ion). Locomotion. Walk(ed,ing). Gait. Wander(ed,ing). Movab(le,ility). *See also* Architectural accessibility; Disability; Frail Elderly; Mobility aids.

Physical punishment. See *Corporal punishment.*

Physical restraint. Physical(ly) restrain(t, ed). *Choose from:* restrict(ed,ing,ion), limit(ed,ing,ation,ations), restrain(t,ed, ing), curtail(ed,ing) *with:* movement(s), mobility, environment(s), motion, activit(y,ies). *Consider also:* immobiliz(e,ed,ing,ation), held secure(ly), straightjacket(s), caged, tether(ed,ing), muzzled, leash(ed), swaddling, corral(s,ed), handcuffed, imprisoned, trapped, shackle(s,d), siderail(s), side rail(s), restraining snare(s), headholder(s), restraining device(s). *See also* Control; Immobility; Motor activity; Trapping; Treatment.

Physical strength. Physical strength. *Choose from:* physical, muscular, hand(s), arm(s), grip, handgrip, leg(s), limb(s), physiological *with:* strength, endurance, power(ful). *Choose from:* lifting, physical, workload, physiological *with:* capacit(y,ies). *Consider also:* fitness, brawn, stamina, brute force. *See also* Exercise; Physical fitness.

Physical stress. See *Physiological stress.*

Physical therapy. Physical therap(y,ies, eutic). Exercise therap(y,ies). Physiotherap(y,ies,eutic). Rehabilitative therap(y,ies). *Consider also:* physiatr(y, ic,ics), physical medicine, balneolog(y, ical), diathermy, electrotherap(y,ies), heliotherap(y,ies), hydrotherap(y,ies), massage(s). *See also* Rehabilitation.

Physical trauma. See *Injuries.*

Physically handicapped. Physical(ly) handicap(ped,s). Physical disabilit(y,ies). Physically disabled. Parapleg(ia,ic). Quadripleg(ia,ic). Wheelchair athlete(s). Wheelchair(s). Cane(s). Crutch(es). Brace(s). *Choose from:* motor, mobility, orthopedic(ally), locomotor, physical(ly), postural *with:* disabilit(y,ies), disabled, handicap(s,ped), impair(ed, ments), anomal(y,ies), defect(s). *Consider also:* amput(ee,ees,ation, ations), cleft palate(s), artificial limb(s), polio(myelitis), muscular dystrophy, multiple sclerosis, spinal cord injur(ed,y,ies), cerebral palsy. *See also* Congenitally handicapped; Disability; Drug induced abnormalities; Frail Elderly; Injuries; Physical abnormalities; Physical disfigurement; Quadriplegia.

Physician assisted suicide. See *Assisted suicide.*

Physician impairment. Physician impairment(s). *Choose from:* addicted, troubled, distressed, impair(ed,ment, ments), disabled, alcoholic, chemically dependent, mentally ill, exploitive, abusive, problem drinking, substance abuse, suicidal, addicted *with:* physician(s), doctor(s), MD's, surgeon(s), psychiatrist(s), intern(s), medical student(s), medical profession(al,s). *See also* Alcoholism; Mental illness; Physicians; Substance abuse; Suicide.

Physician patient relations. Physician patient relation(s,ship). Hippocratic oath. *Choose from:* practitioner(s), physician(s), doctor(s), clinician(s) *with:* client(s), patient(s) *with:* relation(s,ship), compliance, cooperation, teamwork, assistance, helping, support, involvement, distance, rapport, interaction(s), covenant(s), role(s), trust, agreement(s), distrust, attitude(s), perception(s), communication(s), influence(s). *See also* Assisted suicide; Bioethics; Client relations; Euthanasia; Malpractice; Medical ethics; Medical philosophy; Patient rights; Patients; Physicians; Physicians role; Professional ethics; Quackery; Sexual exploitation; Unethical conduct.

Physicians. Physician(s). Doctor(s). Clinician(s). MD(s). Medical practitioner(s). Medical school graduate(s). Medical profession. General practitioner(s). Allergist(s). Anesthesiologist(s). Cardiologist(s). Dermatologist(s). Endocrinologist(s). Gastroenterologist(s). Gynecologist(s). Hematologist(s). Internist(s). Nephrologist(s). Neurologist(s). Neurosurgeon(s). Obstetrician(s). Oncologist(s). Pathologist(s). Pediatrician(s). Psychiatrist(s). Radiologist(s). Rheumatologist(s). Surgeon(s). Urologist(s). *Consider also:* hospitalist(s). *See also* Family physicians; Professional personnel.

Physicians, family. See *Family physicians.*

Physicians assistants. Physicians assistant(s). *Choose from:* physician(s), anesthesia, surgeon(s), ophthalmic, pediatric *with:* assistant(s), extender(s). *Consider also:* feldsher(s), midwi(fe, fery,ves), nurse practitioner(s). *See also* Allied health personnel.

Physicians role. Physician(s) role. *Choose from:* role(s), responsibilit(y,ies), perception(s), status, dut(y,ies), stereotype(s), expected behavior *with:* physician(s), pediatrician(s), medical profession, doctor(s), general practitioner(s), surgeon(s), psychiatrist(s). *See also* Physician patient relations; Physicians; Roles.

Physics. Physics. Energy state(s). *Consider also:* acoustics, aerophysics, astrophysics, biophysics, calorimetry, doppler effect, electricity, electronics, gravitation, kinetics, lubrication, magnetics, mechanics, microphysics, motion, physical concepts, Newtonian dynamics, nuclear physics, optics, oscillometry, physicists, psychophysics, radiation, rheology, thermal conductivity, thermodynamics. *See also* Big bang theory; Cations; Sciences.

Physiognomy. Physiognom(y,ies). *Choose from:* temper(ament), character, mind. *with:* face(s), countenance, facial expression, facial feature(s), guise, contour(s) of face, visage, mazard, demeanor. *See also* Cephalometry; Phrenology; Physical characteristics; Physique; Somatotypes.

Physiological aging. Physiological aging. Aging process. Aging bod(y,ies). Age related difference(s). Degenerative disease(s). *Choose from:* elderly, aging, old, aged, retirement, senior citizen(s), gerontological, geriatric, age related *with:* physical change(s), physiological process(es), hearing loss(es), vision loss(es), sensory impairment(s), osteoporosis, physical declin(e,ing), cerebral blood flow, psychophysiolog(y, ical), sexual dysfunction(s). *See also* Aging; Decline; Deterioration; Developmental stages; Elderly; Frail Elderly; Loss of function; Psychological aging.

Physiological correlates. Physiological correlate(s). *Choose from:* physiological, physical, somatic, biological, psychophysiological, blood pressure, heart rate, EEG, sexual, respiratory, pain, hormonal, metabolism, etc. *with:* correlat(e, es,ed,ing,ion,ive), reciprocal(ly) relat(ionship,ed), corresponding, invariabl(y,e) accompan(ied,iment), causal(ly) relat(ionship,ed). *See also* Biological factors; Comorbidity; Sex factors; Symptoms.

Physiological mental disorders. See *Organic mental disorders.*

Physiological psychology. Physiological psychology. Biobehavioral. Psychophysical. *Choose from:* biological, physiological, physical, somatic *with:* determin(ation,ant,ants), correlate(s), bas(is,es) *with:* mental, psycholog(y, ical), behavior(al), emotion(s,al). *Consider also:* psychophysiolog(y,ic), biological psychiatry, psychoacoustics, psychophysics, psychopharmacology, habituation, psychobiology, neuropsychology. *See also* Biological factors; Evolutionary ethics; Psychobiology; Psychophysiology; Sociobiology.

Physiological stress. Physiological(ly) stress(es,ed,ors). Physiological stresses. *Choose from:* physiological(ly), immobilization, physical, heat, cold, temperature, thermal, pressor, immersion, surgical, food deprivation, isometric, acceleration, exercise, noise *with:* stress(es,ed,ors), strain(s). *Consider also:* pain(ful), foot shock(s), footshock(s), stress induced analgesia, tail pinch, electric shock(s), distress(ed), tension, overstrain(ed), overwork(ed), overtax(ed,ing), breaking point. *See also* Acceleration effects; Burnout; Deprivation; Environmental effects; Environmental pollution; Environmental stress; Physiological correlates; Psychological

stress; Repetitive motion disorders; Sick building syndrome; Social stress; Thermal acclimatization.

Physique. Physique(s). Somatotype(s). *Choose from:* body *with:* height, weight, shape(s), proportion(s), type(s), characteristic(s), size(s), build, composition, mass, measure(s). Physiognomy. Height. Weight. Physical features. Anatomical difference(s). Physical appearance. Physiological variable(s). Posture. Obesity. Underweight. Overweight. Physical characteristics. Body mass. *Choose from:* anthropometric *with:* data, characteristics, measure(s). *Consider also:* endomorph(y,s), mesomorph(y,s), ectomorph(y,s). *See also* Body height; Body weight; Physical characteristics; Physical strength; Physiognomy; Somatotypes.

Phytogeography. Phytogeograph(y,ical). Plant geograph(y,ical). *Choose from:* plant(s,ae), vegetation(al), botan(y,ical), flora, *with:* geograph(y,ical), altitudinal distribution, topographical limitations, climatic limitations, biogeograph(y,ical), distribution pattern(s), region(s,al) distribution, species distribution, endemi(c,cally,city,sm, native. *Consider also:* vegetation ecology. *See also* Agricultural ecology; Animal environments; Biogeography; Biological diversity; Geographic distribution; Geographic regions; Habitat; Natural environment; Plants (botanical); Rainforests; Sustainable development.

Phytoremediation. See *Decontamination; Rejuvenation; Restoration ecology.*

Piano, player. See *Player piano.*

Pica. Pica(e,tio). Pagophagia. Geophagia. Trichophagia. *Choose from:* craving(s), eat(ing,en), ingest(ed,ing,ion) *with:* abnormal, perver(ted,sion), lead, dirt, paint, clay, laundry starch, nonnutritive. *See also* Lead poisoning; Toxic substances.

Pick's disease. Pick(s) disease. Circumscribed cortical atrophy. Lobar sclerosis. *Consider also:* presenile *with:* psychosis, dementia. *See also* Presenile dementia.

Picketing. Picket(ing,s,ed). Demonstrat(ed, ing,ions). March(es,ed,ing,er,ers). Carr(y,ied,ying) placard(s). Protest(s, ing,er,ers,ion,ions). Strik(e,es,ing,er,ers). Crowd gather(ed,ing). Mass demonstration(s). Resister(s). Picket line(s). Walkout(s). *Choose from:* hold(ing), held *with:* rall(y,ies), demonstration(s), march(es). *See also* Boycotts; Social action; Social demonstrations; Strikes.

Picking, cherry. See *Biased selection.*

Picnics. Picnic(s). Eat(ing) outdoors. Cookout(s). Barbecue(s). Eat(ing) on the lawn. Clambake(s). Roast hotdogs. Toast marshmallows. Camping out. *See also* Festivals; Recreation.

Pictography. Pictograph(s,y). Picture writing. Pictogram(s). Logograph(s). Ideogram(s). Rebus writing. *Consider also:* petroglyph(s), petrogram(s), rock art, phonogram(s). *See also* Cave paintings; Cuneiform; Hieroglyphics; Iconography; Petroglyphs; Visual communication; Written communications.

Pictorial stimuli. Pictorial stimuli. *Choose from:* pictorial, picture(s), drawing(s), sign(s), visual, color *with:* stimul(i,us, ation), recall, recognition, judgment(s), memory, naming, identification. *See also* Visual stimulation.

Picture writing. See *Pictography.*

Pictures, motion. See *Motion pictures.*

Pidgin languages. Pidgin(s,ize,ized, ization). Pidgin English. Patois pidgin. Pidgin French. Expanded pidgin(s). West African Pidgin English. Tok Pisin. First generation pidgin. *Consider also:* foreigner talk, trade language(s). *See also* Creoles; Culture contact; Language maintenance; Language shift; Language varieties; Languages in contact; Lingua franca; Loan words; Nonstandard English; Trade languages.

Piercing, body. See *Body piercing.*

Piers. Pier(s). Wharf. Wharves. Dock(s). Harbor facilit(y,ies). Landing(s). Quay(s). Mooring place(s). Marina(s). Drydock(s). *See also* Harbors; Ports; Ships; Shipping industry.

Piety. Pietis(m,t,ts,tic,tically). Pious(ness). Devout(ness). Religious(ness). Saintliness. Sanctity. Sanctifi(ed,cation). Righteous(ness). Faithful(ness). Blessed. Covenanted. Devotion. Fidelity. *Consider also:* dutiful(ness), Godl(y, iness), hol(y,iness), prayerful, reveren(cing,tial). *See also* Filial piety; Religiosity; Spirituality.

Piety, filial. See *Filial piety.*

Pigments. Pigment(s,ed,ation,ary). Color(ing,ation). Chroma(tic). Dye(s). Paint(s). *Consider also:* carotene, melanin. *See also* Animal coloration; Dyes and dyeing.

Pilgrimages. Pilgrim(s,ages). Hajj. *Choose from:* journey(s), pilgrimage(s), visit(s,ed,ing), procession(s) *with:* shrine(s), holy place(s), Eleusis, Delphi, Benares, Puri, Allahabad, Ganges, Mt. Tai, Uji-yamada, Taisha, Temple at Jerusalem, Mecca, Kerbala, Jerusalem, Bethlehem, Nazareth, Rome, Santiago de Compostela, Canterbury, Holy land(s), Walsingham, Glastonbury, Loreto, Montserrat, Fatima, Lourdes, Ste Anne d'Auray, Einsiedeln, Czestochowa, Croagh-Patrick, Saint Patrick's Purgatory, Sainte Anne de Beaupre, Guadalupe Hidalgo. *Consider also:* crusade(s), supplicant(s). *See also* Crusades; Quests; Religious practices; Religious rituals; Shrines.

Pill, abortion. See *Abortifacients; Medical abortion.*

Pill, morning after. See *Emergency contraception.*

Pillage. Pillag(e,ed,ing). Loot(ed,ing). Plunder(ed,ing). Take booty. *Consider also:* ravag(e,ed,ing), depredat(e,ed,ing), desecrat(e,ed,ing), despoil(ed,ing,ment), devastat(e,ed,ing), devour(ed,ing), sack(ed,ing), lay waste, ransack(ed,ing), spoliat(e,ed,ing,ion), vandal(ize,ized, ism). *See also* Archaeological thefts; Art thefts; Destruction of property; Vandalism.

Pillarization. Pillariz(ed,ation). Verzuiling. *Consider also:* network(s) of organizations, social movement(s), coalition(s), complex(es), interweaving, consociationalism, aggregate(s), mutually related organizations, vertically integrated social groups, related organizations, ideological affiliation(s). *See also* Coalescence; Coalitions; Coalition formation.

Piloerection. Piloerect(ion,or). Pilomot(ion, or). Hair raising. Goose flesh. Gooseflesh. Cutis anserina. *See also* Responses; Thermal acclimatization.

Pimps. Pimp(s). Procurer(s). Procuress(es). Panderer(s). White slaver(s,y). Solicitor(s). Madam(s). *See also* Prostitution; Sex industry; Trafficking in persons.

Pink collar workers. See *Clerical workers.*

Pioneer life, frontier. See *Frontier and pioneer life.*

Pioneering. Pioneer(ing,s). Vanguard. Avant garde. Groundbreak(ing). Forefront. Forerunner(s). Cutting edge. State of the art. Precursor(s). Spearhead(ing). Pathfinder(s). Scout(s). Advance guard. Explor(ation,ations,ing,ers). Innovat(ion, ions,ing,ors). Discover(y,ies,ing,ers). *See also* Frontier and pioneer life; Frontier thesis; Pioneers.

Pioneers. Pioneer(s). Early settler(s). Pilgrim(s). Frontiers(man,men). Backwoods(man,men). Early colonist(s). Homesteader(s). Early immigrant(s). *Consider also:* discoverer(s), explorer(s), pathfinder(s), scout(s), trailblazer(s), leader(s). *See also* Discoveries (geography); Explorers; Frontier and pioneer life; Frontier thesis; Pioneering; Quests; Scientific expeditions; Scientists; Spanish explorers.

Pipelines, gas. See *Gas pipelines.*

Pipes, tobacco. See *Tobacco pipes.*

Piracy (at sea). Piracy. Pirat(e,es,ing). *Choose from:* holdup(s), robber(y,ies), hijack(ers,ing), commandeer(ed,ing), maraud(ers,ing), brigand(s,age), buccaneer(s,ing) *with:* ship(s), sea, boat(s), ocean, liner(s), schooner(s), freighter(s), vessel(s), yacht(s). *Consider also:* Achille Lauro, privateer(s). *See also* Capture at sea; Hijacking; Privateers; Seizure of ships.

Piracy (copyright). Piracy (copyright). Pirated edition(s). *Choose from:* pirat(ed,ing), piracy, illegal copying, illegal copies, counterfeit(ed,ing,er,ers), copyright violation(s), fake, bootleg(ged, ging) *with:* edition(s), software, book(s), textbook(s), database(s), information, CD(s), video disk(s), digital, television program(s), movies. *See also* Copyright; Counterfeiting; Intangible property; Plagiarism; Property rights.

Pirate radio broadcasting. Pirate radio broadcast(s,ing). Offshore radio broadcast(s,ing). Radio pirate(s). *Choose from:* pirate(d), offshore, rebel, nonlicensed, unlicensed, illegal, renegade *with:* radio, broadcast(s,ing, er,ers), station(s), transmitter(s), transmission(s), airwaves, channel interference. *Consider also:* Radio Free Berkeley, Kids Discovery Radio, microradio, micro-caster(s). *See also* Alternative radio broadcasting; Broadcast journalism; Broadcasting; Broadcasting stations.

Pitch discrimination. Pitch discrimination. *Choose from:* pitch, frequenc(y,ies), ton(e,es,al), chord(s) *with:* discriminat(e, ed,ing,ion), match(ed,ing), differentiat(e, ed,ing,ion), detect(ed,ing,ion), select(ed, ing,ion), identif(y,ied,ication). *See also* Auditory perception; Auditory threshold.

Pitch (frequency). Pitch. *Choose from:* sound(s), tone(s), voice(s), acoustic, signal(s) *with:* frequenc(y,ies), intensit(y,ies). *Consider also:* voice quality, pure tone(s). *See also* Auditory perception; Tuning.

Pitch perception. Pitch perception. *Choose from:* pitch, frequenc(y,ies), ton(e.es,al), chord(s) *with:* perception, perceiv(e,ed, ing), recogni(ze,zed,zing,tion), calculat(e,ed,ing,ion), sensitivity. *See also* Auditory perception.

Pity. Pit(y,ying,ied). Commiserat(ed,ing, ion). Compassion(ate). Sympath(y,etic). Condolence(s). *Consider also:* sorrowful(ly), regretful(ly), lamentab(le, ly), feel sorry for, weep for, grieve for, have mercy upon, contemptuous sorrow. *See also* Compassion; Consolation; Emotions; Mercy; Regret; Sentimentality; Sympathy.

Place disorientation. Place disorientation. *Choose from:* place(s), spatial, space(s), location(s,al), pilot(s), ward(s) *with:* disorient(ed,ing,ation). *Consider also:* wandering behavior. *See also* Consciousness disorders.

Place of business. Place(s) of business. *Choose from:* business(es), corporation(s), compan(y,ies), store(s), factor(y,ies), shop(s) *with:* address(s), location(s), box number(s), site(s). *Consider also:* email address(es). *See also* Headquarters relocation; Home office; Office buildings; Place of residence; Plant relocation; Workplaces.

Place of residence. Place of residence. Residential location(s). Legal address(es). Street address(es). *Choose from:* home(s), residen(ce,ces,tial), dwelling(s), house(s), apartment(s) *with:* address(s), location(s), number(s). *Consider also:* box number(s), street name(s), zipcode(s), email address(es). *See also* Housing; Place of business.

Placebos. Placebo(s). Bogus. Dumm(y,ies). *See also* Drug therapy; Sham surgery.

Placement (of a dependent person). Place(d,ment). Custody. Transfer(red). Commit(ment,ted). Admit(ted). Admission(s). Room assignment. Assigned place(s). Dispositional alternative(s). Adopt(ed,ing,ion). *Consider also:* foster placement, permanent placement, deinstitutionalization, boarding home(s), readmission, hospitalization, institutionalization. *See also* Boardinghouses; Child custody; Deinstitutionalization; Foster home care; Hospitalization; Institutionalization (persons).

Placement, educational. See *Educational placement.*

Placement, job. See *Personnel placement.*

Placement, personnel. See *Personnel placement.*

Places, imaginary. See *Imaginary places.*

Places, public. See *Public places.*

Places, sacred. See *Sacred places.*

Places of worship. Places of worship. Religious building(s). Church(es). Synagogue(s). Chapel(s). Temple(s). Parish house(s). Cathedral(s). Minster(s). Abbey(s). Monaster(y,ies). Convent(s). Kirk(s). Meeting house(s). Sanctuar(y,ies). Shrine(s). House(s) of prayer. House(s) of God. House(s) of worship. Tabernacle(s). Mosque(s). Place(s) of pilgrimage. Sacred tomb(s). Basilica(n). Holy See. Consecrated building(s). *Consider also:* sacred, holy, consecrated *with:* land(s), cit(y,ies), ground(s), site(s). *See also* Basilicas; Chapels; Churches; Community churches; Mosques; Religious buildings; Religious institutions; Sacredness; Sanctuaries; Shrines; Synagogues; Temples.

Plagiarism. Plagiar(ism,ize,ized,ing). Forge(ry,ries,rer,rers). Copyright violation(s). Copyright infringement. Lacking proper acknowledgement.

Borrow(ed,ing) from speech(es). Lack(ed,ing) credit for quote(s). Without credit(ing) source(s). Unattributed quot(e,es,ation,ations). Unattributed borrowing. Literary theft(s). Literary piracy. *Choose from:* steal(ing), stolen, unattributed, borrow(ed,ing) *with:* text(s), quot(e,es,ation,ations), phrase(s), manuscript(s). *See also* Cheating; Intangible property; Journalistic ethics; Literary ethics; Literary forgeries and mystifications; Piracy (copyright); Quotations; Writing (composition).

Plague. Plague(s). Black death. Bubonic plague. Pestis fulminans. Pestis major. Pasturella pestis. Plague bubonica. Oriental plague. Pest plague. Pneumonic plague. Septicemic plague. Pestilence(s). *See also* Epidemics.

Plainsong. Plainsong. Cantus planus. *Consider also:* plainchant. *See also* Antiphons; Chants; Gregorian chants; Hymns.

Planes, war. See *Military airplanes.*

Planets, life on other. See *Extraterrestrial life.*

Planned communities. Planned communit(y,ies). Residential development. *Choose from:* plan(ned,ning,s), design(ed,ing), develop(ed,ing,ment), redevelop(ed,ing,ment), propos(e,ed,ing,al,als), master-plan(ned,ning,s) *with:* communit(y,ies), neighborhood(s), campus(es), resort(s), residential area(s), business district(s), commercial center(s), landmark(s), downtown, real estate. *See also* Community (geographic locality); Community development; Local planning; New towns; Real estate development; Suburban development; Urban fringe.

Planned economies, centrally. See *Centrally planned economies.*

Planned parenthood. See *Birth control; Family planning.*

Planning. Plan(s,ned,ners,ning). Setting goal(s). Setting objective(s). Formulat(e,ed,ing,ion) objective(s). Strategic planning. Establishing framework(s). Developing check list(s). Priority setting. Design(ing). Draft(s,ing). Blueprint(s). Scenario(s). Futures research. Counterplan(s). Masterplan(s). Delphi technique(s). Futuriz(e,ed,ing). Land use decision(s). Expectation(s). Prognosticat(e,ed,ion,ions). Prepar(e, ing) program(s). Predict(ed,ions). Propos(e,als,ition,itions). Plot(s,ted, ting). Prearrange(d,ment,ments). Strateg(y,ies). Scheme(s). *See also* Architecture; Career goals; Designs; Diagrams; Disaster planning; Educational plans; Environmental design; Facility design and construction; Family planning; Financial planning; Future; Goals; Health planning; Implementation;

Language planning; Life plans; Local planning; Logistics; Long range planning; Management planning; Military planning; Needs assessment; Operations research; Patient care planning; Policy making; Priorities; Regional development; Research design; Retirement planning; Short term planning; Social planning; State planning; Strategies; Urban planning.

Planning, career. See *Career change; Career development; Career goals; Career ladders; Occupational choice; Occupational interests; Vocational guidance; Vocational maturity.*

Planning, city. See *Urban planning.*

Planning, community. See *Local planning.*

Planning, disaster. See *Disaster planning.*

Planning, economic. See *Economic planning.*

Planning, environmental. See *Environmental design.*

Planning, estate. See *Estate planning.*

Planning, family. See *Family planning.*

Planning, financial. See *Financial planning.*

Planning, government. See *State planning.*

Planning, health. See *Health planning.*

Planning, language. See *Language planning.*

Planning, local. See *Local planning.*

Planning, long range. See *Long range planning.*

Planning, long term planning. See *Long range planning.*

Planning, management. See *Management planning.*

Planning, military. See *Military planning.*

Planning, national. See *State planning.*

Planning, patient care. See *Patient care planning.*

Planning, population. See *Population policy.*

Planning, regional. See *Regional development.*

Planning, research. See *Research design.*

Planning, retirement. See *Retirement planning.*

Planning, short term. See *Short term planning.*

Planning, social. See *Social planning.*

Planning, state. See *State planning.*

Planning, strategic. See *Strategic planning.*

Planning, town. See *Urban planning.*

Planning, urban. See *Urban planning.*

Planning, workforce. See *Workforce planning.*

Plans. Plan(s). Scheme(s). Arrangement(s). Scale drawing(s). Floor plan(s). Design(s). Plot(s). Blueprint(s). Map(s). Pattern(s). Draft(s). Outline(s). Sketch(es). Layout(s). Chart(s). Diagram(s). Prototype(s). Archetype(s). Model(s). *See also* Diagrams; Educational plans; Employee incentive plans; Lesson plans; Life plans; Planning.

Plans, educational. See *Educational plans.*

Plans, employee incentive. See *Employee incentive plans.*

Plans, employee stock ownership. See *Employee stock ownership plans.*

Plans, lesson. See *Lesson plans.*

Plans, life. See *Life plans.*

Plans, marketing. See *Marketing plans.*

Plant closings. Plant clos(ings,ure). Plant(s) shutdown(s). Clos(e,ing) office(s). Phasing out plant(s). Factory closing(s). Close down plant(s). Suspend(ed,ing) production. Fail(ed,ing) industr(y,ies). *Choose from:* clos(e,ed,ing), bankrupt(cy), lock(ed) out, out-of-service, padlocked, shutdown(s), shut(ting) down, phas(e,ing) out, fail(ing,ure,ures), ceas(e,ed,ing), terminat(e,ed,ing,ion, ions), relocat(e,ed,ing,ion,ions), discontinu(e,ed,ing) *with:* plant(s), factor(y,ies), shipyard(s), mill(s). *Consider also:* deindustrialization, dislocated worker(s). *See also* Deindustrialization; Depression (economic); Dislocated workers; Factories; Headquarters relocation; Organizational dissolution; Organizational survival; Personnel termination; Plant relocation; Severance pay; Technological unemployment; Turnaround management; Unemployment.

Plant cover. See *Vegetation.*

Plant cultivation. Plant cultivation. *Choose from:* plant(ae,s,ing,ings), crop(s), herb(age,s), flower(s,ing), tree(s), flora, vegetation, vegetable(s), vine(s), berr(y,ies), fruit(s), grass(es), etc. *with:* cultivat(e,ed,ing,ion), maintenance, maintain(ed,ing), restor(e,ed,ing,ation), weed(ing, plough(ed,ing), dig(ging), dug, garden(ed,ing), nurser(y,ies), compost(ed,ing), mulch(ed,ing), till(ed,ing,age). *See also* Agriculture; Crops; Cultivated Plants; Forestry; Gardening; Plant introduction; Plants (botanical).

Plant domestication. See *Cultivated plants.*

Plant drugs. See *Herbal medicine; Medical botany.*

Plant folklore. Plant folklore. Plant lore. Herbal lore. *Choose from:* plant(ae,s,ing, ings), herb(al,s), flower(s,ing), petal(s), leaf, leaves, seed(s), berr(y,ies), tree(s), flora, vegetable(s), vine(s), weed(s), grass(es) *with:* folklore, lore, tale(s), myth(s), fable(s), legend(s), artifact(s),

superstition(s), tradition(s), riddle(s), proverb(s), stor(y,ies), music, song(s), art, remed(y,ies), healer(s), belief(s), custom(s). *See also* Alternative medicine; Ayurvedic medicine; Chinese medicine; Ethnobotany; Folk culture; Folklore; Herbal medicine; Mescal (cactus); Oriental medicine; Plants (botanical); Psychotropic plants; Quackery; Shamanism; Traditional medicine.

Plant genetics. Plant genetics. *Choose from:* plant(s), flower(s), agricultural, crops *with:* genetic(s,ally), gene(s), RNA, DNA, genomic(s), genome(s). *See also* Agricultural engineering; Biotechnology; Genetic engineering; Genetics; Plants (botanical).

Plant geography. See *Phytogeography.*

Plant introduction. Plant introduction. *Choose from:* plant(ae,s,ing,ings), herb(age,s), flower(s,ing), tree(s), flora, vegetation, vine(s), weed(s), grass(es) *with:* introduc(e,ed,ing,tion), import(ed,ing,ation), arriv(e,ed,ing,al, als), acquisition(s), foreign origin *Consider also:* non-native plant(s), alien plant(s), non-indigenous plant(s), *See also* Bioinvasion; Cultivated Plants; Plant cultivation; Plants (botanical).

Plant lore. See *Plant folklore.*

Plant relocation. Plant relocation. *Choose from:* plant(s), factor(y,ies), manufacturer(s), facilit(y,ies), mill(s), foundr(y,ies) *with:* relocat(e,ed,ing,ion), new location(s), change(d) address, move(d), moving. *See also* Headquarters relocation; Factories; Migration of industry; Place of business; Plant closings; Relocation.

Plant remains (archaeology). Archaeological plant remains. Archaeobotan(y,ical). Paleoethnobotan(y,ical). *Choose from:* plant(s,ae), flower(s,ing), wood, flora, vegetation, botan(y,ical), grass(es), leaf(y, leaves, squash(es), acorn(s), seeds, berr(y,ies), maize, pollen, farming, cereal(s), legume(s), conifer(s), angiosperm(s), *with:* archaeobotan(y, ical), prehistoric, early, ancient, mid-Holocene, longterm burial, radiocarbon dating, macroremains, artifacts, fossil(s,ized), antiquity, bronze age, iron age, stone age, ice age, neolithic, paleolithic, Quaternary Period, Jurassic, Pleistocene. *See also* Animal remains (archaeology); Archaeological chemistry; Archaeology; Fossils; Paleoecology; Paleontology; Physical anthropology; Plants (botanical).

Plant succession. Plant succession. Grass-to-forest succession. Succession planting. *Choose from:* grassland(s), plant(s,ing,ings), grazing management, tree(s), forest(s) *with:* succession(al,s), species replacement(s), invasion, restoration, postfire changes. *Consider*

also: crop rotation. *See also* Agricultural ecology; Conservation of natural resources; Crops; Deforestation; Environmental protection; Forest conservation; Plants (botanical); Reclamation of land; Reforestation; Restoration ecology; Soil conservation; Tree planting.

Plantation songs. See *Afro-American music.*

Plantations. Plantation(s). Landed estate(s). Farmstead(s). *Consider also:* hacienda(s), squire(s), tenant encomienda, farmer(s), sharecropp(er, ers,ing), latifund(ia,ismo,ium,ist,ists). *See also* Agrarian societies; Agrarian structures; Feudalism; Land reform; Peasants; Peonage; Sharecropping; Slavery.

Planting, tree. See *Tree planting.*

Plants (botanical). Plant(ae,s,ing,ings). Houseplant(s). Vegetable(s). Herb(age,s). Flower(s). Shrub(s). Tree(s). Flora. Vegetation. Botan(y,ical). Legume(s). Vine(s). Seedling(s). Lawn(s). Bush(es). Weed(s). Grass(es). Leaf(y). Leaves. Berr(y,ies). *Consider also:* bryophyta, lycopodophyta, clubmosses, sphenophyta, horsetails, filiciniphyta, ferns, cycadophyta, gingkophyta, coniferophyta, angiospermophyta, monocotyledonae, dicotyledonae, rose(s), dais(y,ies), corn, etc. *See also* Agriculture; Bark peeling; Crops; Cultivated Plants; Edible plants; Flowers; Food; Forestry; Grasses; Mescal (cactus); Natural resources; Phytogeography; Plant cultivation; Plant folklore; Plant genetics; Plant introduction; Plant remains (archaeology); Plant succession; Poisonous plants; Psychotropic plants; Raw materials; Trees; Vegetation.

Plants, cultivated. See *Cultivated plants.*

Plants, edible. See *Edible plants.*

Plants, electric power. See *Electric power plants.*

Plants, industrial. See *Factories.*

Plants, medicinal. See *Herbal medicine; Medical botany.*

Plants, nuclear power. See *Nuclear power plants.*

Plants, poisonous. See *Poisonous plants.*

Plants, psychotropic. See *Psychotropic plants.*

Plastic surgery. See *Reconstructive surgery.*

Platforms, political. See *Political platforms.*

Play. Play(ed,ing). *Choose from:* ludic, play *with:* behavior(s), activit(y,ies). Homo ludens. *Consider also:* playful(ly), fun, jest(ed,ing), amusement(s), pastime(s), recreation, lighthearted(ness), diversion(s), entertainment, make-believe, frolic(king), romp(ing). *See also* Adult games; Children's games; Childhood play development; Doll play; Imagination; Leisure activities; Play therapy; Playgrounds; Recreation; Toys.

Play development, childhood. See *Childhood play development.*

Play, doll. See *Doll play.*

Play therapy. Play therapy. *Choose from:* play, recreation(al), game(s), puppet(s,ry) *with:* therap(y,ies,eutic), rehabilitat(e,ed,ing,ion), diagnos(is,es, tic), psychotherap(y,ies,eutic), desensitiz(e,ed,ing,ation). *See also* Psychotherapy.

Play, word. See *Word play.*

Player piano. Player piano(s). Pianola(s). Reproducing player piano(s). *Consider also:* Duo-Art, Fonola, Phonola, Welte Mignon, player organ(s). *See also* Automatic instruments; Musical instruments.

Playgrounds. Playground(s). *Choose from:* play(ing), recreational, sports, game(s) *with:* area(s), environment(s), facilit(y, ies), setting(s), space(s), field(s). *Consider also:* park(s), school ground(s), school yard(s), sand lot(s), tot lot(s), baseball diamond(s), basketball court(s), tennis court(s). *See also* Facilities; Recreation; Recreation areas; School sports.

Playhouses. See *Theater.*

Playing, role. See *Role playing.*

Plays. See *Drama; Theater.*

Plays, medieval. See *Medieval drama.*

Plays, miracle. See *Miracle plays.*

Plays, morality. See *Morality plays.*

Plays, mystery. See *Liturgical drama.*

Plays, passion. See *Passion plays.*

Plays, television. See *Television plays.*

Playthings. See *Toys.*

Plea bargaining. Plea bargain(ed,ing). Negotiated plea(s). Plea negotiation(s). Charge bargaining. Bargained justice. Pre-trial argument(s). *See also* Alternatives to incarceration; Arrests; Contempt of Court; Criminal investigations; Criminal proceedings; Defense (verbal); Judicial decisions; Sentencing; Trial (law); Verdicts.

Pleading, equity and procedure. See *Equity pleading and procedure.*

Pleading insanity. See *Insanity defense.*

Pleasure. Pleasur(e,es,able,ing). Enjoy(ed, ing,ment,able). Joy(ful,fulness,ous). Fun. Pleasant(ness). Satisf(y,ied,action). Gratif(y,ied,ying). Hedon(ism,istic,ic). Fulfill(ed,ing,ment). Content(ed,ment). Recreation(al). Merriment. Joll(y,ity).

Delight(ed,ing,ful,s). Zest(y,iness). Celebrat(e,ed,ing,ation). Happ(y,iness). *See also* Anhedonia; Enjoyment; Euphoria; Happiness; Hedonic damages.

Pleasure, inability to experience. See *Anhedonia.*

Plebiscite. See *Referendum.*

Plundering. See *Pillage.*

Plural marriages. See *Polygamy.*

Plural societies. Plural societ(y,ies). Heterogeneous societ(y,ies). Multi-national state(s). Consociational democrac(y,ies). Proportional democrac(y,ies). Fragmented societ(y,ies). *Consider also:* social pluralism, cultural pluralism. *See also* Assimilation (cultural); Biculturalism; Cultural identity; Cultural pluralism; Ethnic groups; Linguistic minorities; Melting pot; Multicultural education; Multilingualism; Pluralism; Racial diversity; Social integration; Separatism.

Pluralism. Plural(ity,ism,ist,istic). Heterogeneity. Diversity. Diffuse(d) power. Decentraliz(e,ed,ing,ation). Distribut(ed, ing,ion) power. Multiple elites. Countervailing theor(y,ies). Rival elite(s). Multiculturalism. Biculturalism. Pluriculturalism. Cultural accomodation. Religious pluralism. Plural(istic) societ(y,ies). Melting pot. Multicultural societ(y,ies). *See also* Cultural pluralism; Melting pot; Monadology; Monism; Plural societies; Political power; Racial diversity.

Pluralism, cultural. See *Cultural pluralism.*

Plurality of worlds. Plurality of worlds. Possible worlds. Other worlds. *Choose from:* plurality. possib(le,ility,ilities), outside the solar system, beyond the Earth, orbiting stars *with:* world(s), planet(s). *Consider also:* other planetary systems, extraterrestrial life, intelligent life in the solar system, intelligent life outside the solar system. *See also* Extraterrestrial environment; Extraterrestrial life; Extraterrestrial space; Interplanetary voyages; Space exploration.

Plutocracy. See *Oligarchy; Power elite; Ruling class.*

PMS. See *Premenstrual syndrome.*

Pneuma. Pneum(e,a,atology). Anima. Animus. Elan vital. Psyche. Spiritual being(s). Vital force(s). Neum(e,ic). *Consider also:* ethereal, spirit, soul. *See also* Animism; Essence; Soul; Vitalism.

Poaching. Poach(ed,ing.es). Steal(ing) game. Deerjack(ed,ing). *Choose from:* illegal(ly), unlawful(ly) *with:* hunt(ed, ing), fish(ed,ing). *See also* Deer; Duck hunting; Fowling; Game and game birds; Game laws; Game protection; Hunting.

Poems. See *Poetry.*

Poems, symphonic. See *Symphonic poems.*

Poesies. See *Poetry.*

Poetic unity. See *Unity (Literature).*

Poetics. Poetic(s). *Choose from:* poet(s,ry), poem(s), vers(e,es,ification) *with:* theor(y,ies,etical), doctrine(s), practice(s), principle(s), aesthetic(s), technique(s), criticism. *See also* Alliteration; Imagery; Metaphors; Meter (poetry); Poetry; Theories; Unity (Literature).

Poetry. Poet(s,ry). Poem(s). Poet(ic,ics, ical). Poes(y,ies). Haiku. Verse(s). Versif(y,ied,ication). Rhym(e,es,ed,ing). Couplet(s). Sonnet(s). Song(s). Hymn(s). Couplet(s). Eleg(y,ies). Limerick(s). Ballad(s,ry). Psalm(s). Lyric poe(try,ms). Ghazal(s). Ghazel(s). Quatrain(s). Rubai. *Consider also:* iambic pentameter, dactylic meter, villancico(s), etc. *See also* Alliteration; Children's poetry; Concrete poetry; Dramatic poetry; Elegiac poetry; Elegies; Epigrams; Erotic poetry; Experimental poetry; Folk culture; Folk literature; Haiku; Historical poetry; Humorous poetry; Idyll; Latin laudatory poetry; Laudatory poetry; Literary parallels; Literature; Lyrical poetry; Medieval poetry; Meter (poetry); Narrative poetry; Nature literature; Occasional verse; Onomatopoeia; Oral reading; Pastorales; Poetics; Poets; Prosody; Psychopoetry; Renaissance poetry; Rhymes; Skaldic poetry; Stanzas; War poetry.

Poetry, children's. See *Children's poetry.*

Poetry, concrete. See *Concrete poetry.*

Poetry, devotional. See *Devotional poetry.*

Poetry, dramatic. See *Dramatic poetry.*

Poetry, elegiac. See *Elegiac poetry.*

Poetry, epic. See *Epic literature.*

Poetry, erotic. See *Erotic poetry.*

Poetry, experimental. See *Experimental poetry.*

Poetry, folk. See *Folk poetry.*

Poetry, historical. See *Historical poetry.*

Poetry, humorous. See *Humorous poetry.*

Poetry, Latin laudatory. See *Latin laudatory poetry.*

Poetry, laudatory. See *Laudatory poetry.*

Poetry, love. See *Love poetry.*

Poetry, lyric. See *Lyric poetry.*

Poetry, medieval. See *Medieval poetry.*

Poetry, meter. See *Meter (poetry).*

Poetry, narrative. See *Narrative poetry.*

Poetry, pastoral. See *Pastorales.*

Poetry, renaissance. See *Renaissance poetry.*

Poetry, Scaldic. See *Skaldic poetry.*

Poetry, Skaldic. See *Skaldic poetry.*

Poetry, therapeutic use of. See *Psychopoetry.*

Poetry, war. See *War poetry.*

Poetry, wedding. See *Epithalamia.*

Poets. Poet(s). Bard(s). Minnesinger(s). Troubador(s). Versifier(s). Minstrel(s). Jongleur(s). Sonneteer(s). Balladeer(s). Lyricist(s). Elegist(s). Rhymester(s). Payadore(s). *Consider also:* goliard(s). *See also* Minnesinger; Minstrels; Poetry; Troubadour; Trouvere.

Point of view (literature). Point(s) of view (literature). Narrative perspective(s). Narrative voice(s). Literary persona. Voice of the narrator. *Consider also:* second person narrative(s), third person narrative(s), through the eyes of. *See also* Autobiography; First person narrative; Literature; Narratives; Perspective taking; Self report; Storytellers; Subjectivity.

Points, reference. See *Reference points.*

Points, turning. See *Turning points.*

Poison control centers. Poison control center(s). *Choose from:* poison(s,ing), toxicology, pesticide(s), toxic substance(s) *with:* control center(s), information center(s), emergency service(s), medical service(s), network(s). *See also* Health facilities.

Poisoning. Poison(ing,ings,ed,ous). Toxicos(is,es). Toxicity. Toxic substance(s). Arachnidism. Argyria. Botulism. Favism. Narcosis. Thyrotoxicosis. Ergotism. Lathryism. Septicemia. Ichthyosarcotoxism. Tyrotoxicosis. Githagism. Sitotoxism. Allantiasis. Plumbism. Locoism. Mytilotoxism. Tetraodontoxism. Tabacosis. Bromatotoxism. Tetraodontoxism. Intoxication(s). Venom(s,ous). Venen(osus,ate). Snakebite(s). Spiderbite(s). Bee sting(s). Wasp sting(s). *Consider also:* alcohol(ic), akee, barbiturate, blood, cadmium, carbon disulfide, carbon monoxide, carbon tetrachloride, cheese, dural, elasmobranch, fluoride, forage, food, fugu, gas, gossypol, gymnothorax, lead, loco, meat, mercury, milk, mussel, plant(s), puffer, Renghas, salmon(ella), saturnine, sausage, scombroid, selenium, shellfish, tetrachlorethane, tetraodon, tobacco, trinitrotoluene *with:* poison(ing, ings,ed,ous), toxicos(is,es), toxic(ity). *See also* Food poisoning; Hazardous materials; Hazardous wastes; Lead poisoning; Poisonous plants; Pollution control; Toxic substances; Toxic torts.

Poisoning, food. See *Food poisoning.*

Poisoning, lead. See *Lead poisoning.*

Poisonous animals. Poisonous animal(s). *Choose from:* poison(ous), venom(ous) *with:* animal(s), fish(es), snake(s), lizard(s), reptile(s). *Consider also:* arachnida, poisonous spider(s), viper(s), snakebite(s). *See also* Animal aggressive behavior; Animal defensive behavior; Poisonous plants; Reptiles; Snake handling.

Poisonous gases. Poison(ous) gas(es). *Choose from:* poison(s,ous), toxic, pathogenic, noxious *with:* gas(es), fume(s), inhal(e,ed,ation), emission(s), vapor(s). *Consider also:* carbon monoxide, motor vehicle exhaust gas, refrigerator gas(es), chlorine, ether, chloroform, nitrous oxide, pesticide(s), insecticide(s), volcanic gas(es), fungicide(s). *See also* Chemical warfare; Gas; Hazardous materials; Hazardous wastes; Poisons; Toxic inhalation; Toxic substances.

Poisonous plants. Poisonous plant(s). *Choose from:* poison(s,ous), pathogenic(ity), toxic(ity), lethal, fatal, harmful, hazardous *with:* plant(s), mushroom(s), berr(y,ies), flower(s), vine(s), fruit(s), leaf, leaves, stalk, weed(s), blossom(s), alkaloid(s). *Consider also:* daffodil(s), dieffenbachia, English ivy, philodendron, lily of the valley, poison Ivy, poison oak, poison sumac, castor bean(s), etc. *See also* Edible plants; Hazardous materials; Plants (botanical); Poisoning; Poisons; Poisonous animals; Toxic substances.

Poisons. Poison(s,ous,ed,ing). Venom(s, ous). Toxin(s). Toxic substance(s). Toxicolog(y,ic,ical). Pesticide(s). Toxic(ity,osis,ants). Toxic agent(s). Herbicid(e,es,al). Solvent(s). Envenomat(e,ed). Endotoxin(s). Lethal dose(s). Fatal drug(s). Rodenticide(s). Ecotoxicolog(y,ical). Harmful substance(s). Hazardous material(s). Toxic chemical(s). Toxic compound(s). Virulent. Noxious. Viperous. Mephitic. *Choose from:* poison(ous), venom(ous), toxic(ity), lethal, fatal, noxious, harmful, hazardous *with:* substance(s), agent(s), dose(s), drug(s), substance(s), material(s), chemical(s), compound(s), waste(s), contaminant(s), solvent(s). *Consider also:* specific poisons by name, alcoholic poisoning, argyria, spider bites, bee stings, cadmium poisoning, carbon tetrachloride poisoning, ergotism, fluoride poisoning, food poisoning, gas poisoning, lead poisoning, mercury poisoning, asbestos, agent orange, PCBs, etc. *See also* Hazardous materials; Hazardous wastes; Herbicides; Pesticides; Poisoning; Poisonous animals; Poisonous gases; Poisonous plants; Toxic substances.

Polar regions. See *Antarctic Regions; Arctic regions.*

Polarity. Polar(ity). Opposit(e,es,ion). Contrar(y,iety). Contradict(ed,ing,ion, ions,ory). Antithes(is,es). Antithetical(ly). *Consider also:* antipod(al,ean), antipole, converse(ly), counter, diametric(al,ally), revers(e,ed, ing,al), antagonis(m,tic). *See also* Antonyms; Polarization; Resistance.

Polarization. Polariz(e,ed,ing,ation). Polar force(s). Polemic(s). Dividing. Divisiveness. Alienating. Polarity. *Consider also:* cleavage, extremism, factionalism, partisanship, radicaliz(e,ed,ing,ation), pillariz(e,ed,ing,ation), bipolarity. *See also* Alignments; Confrontation; Dialectics; Extremism; Factionalism; Partisan; Pillarization; Polarity; Polemics; Social cleavage; Schism; Social segmentation.

Polemics. Polemic(s,ist,ists,al). Polemiciz(e, ed,es,ing). Polemiz(e,ed,es,ing). Polemist(s). Disputant(s). Disputation(s, al). Refut(e,ed,ing,ation). Engag(e,ed, ing) in controversy. Debat(e,ed,ing, er,ers). Contention(s). Argument(s, ative,ation). *See also* Arguments; Debate; Extremism; Pillarization; Polarization; Political attitudes; Refutation; Schism.

Police, international. See *International police.*

Police, secret. See *Secret police.*

Police brutality. Police brutality. Unexplained jail death(s). *Choose from:* police(men,man,women,woman), patrol(men,man,women,woman), guard(s) *with:* brutal(ity,izing,ize,ized), misconduct, abuse(s,d), beat(en,ing, ings), massacre(s,d), complaint(s), human rights violation(s), violence, use of force, excessive force, deadly force, unnecessary force, manhandl(e,ed,ing), attack(ed,s,ing), murdered, harass(ed, ment), improper arrest(s), shooting(s), shootout(s), mistreat(ed,ment), wounded, tortured, stun gun(s), tear gas, bullet(s), cattle prod(s). *See also* Arrests; Law enforcement; Law enforcement personnel; Missing persons; Police community relations; Police questioning; Political crimes; Political prisoners; Political violence; Prison violence; Torture; Violence.

Police community relations. Police community relation(s,ship,ships). *Choose from:* police, police(man,men, woman,women), sheriff(s), law enforcement personnel, traffic officer(s), cop(s), detective(s), police officer(s) *with:* citizen(s), communit(y,ies), neighborhood(s), local(ity,ities), local area(s), town(s), village(s), parish(es), precinct(s), suburb(s,an) *with:* relation(s,ship,ships), involv(e,ed,ing, ement), reaction(s), cooperation, public relations, image(s). *Consider also:* neighborhood patrol(s), street patrol(s).

See also Civil supremacy over the military; Citizen participation; Crime prevention; Criminal investigations; Fear of crime; Law enforcement; Military civilian relations; Police brutality; Public support; Surveillance of citizens.

Police dogs. Police dog(s). *Choose from:* police *with:* dog(s), canine(s). *Consider also:* sniff search(es), K-9 patrol. *See also* Crime prevention; Detectives; Dogs; Drug and narcotic control; Substance abuse detection.

Police personnel. Police(men,man,woman, women). Law enforcement personnel. Gendarme(s). Cop(s). Security guard(s). Officer(s) of the peace. Officer(s) of the law. Traffic officer(s). Law officer(s). Sheriff(s). Armed guard(s). Detective(s). *Choose from:* police, public safety *with:* personnel, patrol(s), officer(s), guard(s), deput(y,ies). *Choose from:* shore, school, neighborhood *with:* patrol(s), watch(es). *See also* Crime prevention; Police community relations; Correctional personnel; Correctional system.

Police questioning. Police question(s,ing, ed). *Choose from:* police, arresting officer(s), right to counsel, Miranda, right to remain silent *with:* question(s, ing,ed), quiz(zed,zing), interrogat(e,ed, ing,ions,atory), interview(ed,ing), cross examin(e,ed,ing,ation), direct examin(e, ed,ing,ation,ations), elicit(ed,ing) testimony, entrapment(s), elicit(ed,ing) confession(s), lineup technique(s). *See also* Arrests; Bill of Rights; Civil rights; Criminal investigations; Due process; Police brutality; Search; Search and seizure.

Police records. Police record(s). *Choose from:* police, sheriff(s), arrest, conviction, criminal, FBI, law enforcement *with:* report(s), record(s), data, blotter(s), register(s), testimony, information, file(s), note(s), correspondence. *Consider also:* criminal histor(y,ies). *See also* Biographical data; Records; Surveillance of citizens; Testimony.

Policies, news. See *News policies.*

Policy. Polic(y,ies). Regulation(s). Principle(s). Objective(s). Guideline(s). Rule(s). Official rule(s). Plan(s) of action. Line of conduct. Practice(s). Plan(s). Manual(s). Treat(y,ies). Manifesto(s,es). *Consider also:* public, health, administrative, discipline, educational, financial, foreign, interdistrict, personnel, school, welfare, transportation, regulatory, land use, immigration, housing, environmental, affirmative action, agricultural, budgetary, business, civil rights, economic, criminal justice, energy *with:* polic(y, ies), regulation(s), guideline(s), rule(s), plan(s), manual(s). *See also* Administrative policy; Energy policy; Environmental law; Environmental policy; Family

policy; Fiscal policy; Foreign policy; Goals; Health policy; Housing policy; Labor policy; Language policy; Law (legal philosophy and theory); Military policy; Monetary policy; News policies; Personnel policy; Policy analysis; Policy evaluation; Policy implementation; Policy making; Population policy; Public policy; Regulations; Science policy; Standards; Welfare policy.

Policy, administrative. See *Administrative policy.*

Policy, broadcasting. See *Broadcasting policy.*

Policy, demographic. See *Population policy.*

Policy, economic. See *Balanced budget; Budget deficits; Capitalism; Collectivism; Economic planning; Fiscal policy; Market economy; Monetary policy; Nationalization; Private enterprise; Privatization; Public debt; Socialism.*

Policy, energy. See *Energy policy.*

Policy, environmental. See *Environmental policy.*

Policy, family. See *Family policy.*

Policy, fiscal. See *Fiscal policy.*

Policy, foreign. See *Foreign policy.*

Policy, government. See *Public policy.*

Policy, health. See *Health policy.*

Policy, housing. See *Housing policy.*

Policy, information. See *Information policy.*

Policy, investment. See *Investment policy.*

Policy, labor. See *Labor policy.*

Policy, language. See *Language policy.*

Policy, linguistic. See *Language policy.*

Policy making, foreign. See *Foreign policy making.*

Policy, mass media. See *Mass media policy.*

Policy, military. See *Military policy.*

Policy, monetary. See *Monetary policy.*

Policy, naval. See *Military policy; Sea power.*

Policy, personnel. See *Personnel policy.*

Policy, population. See *Population policy.*

Policy, public. See *Public policy.*

Policy, science. See *Science policy.*

Policy, social. See *Energy policy; Family policy; Fiscal policy; Foreign policy; Government policy; Health policy; Housing policy; Labor policy; Language policy; Population policy; Public policy; Welfare policy.*

Policy, transportation. See *Transportation policy.*

Policy, welfare. See *Welfare policy.*

Policy analysis. Polic(y,ies) analys(is,es). Environmental impact statement(s). *Choose from:* polic(y,ies), program(s), regulation(s), principle(s), objective(s), guideline(s), rule(s), plan(s) of action, line(s) of conduct, practice(s), plan(s), manual(s), treat(y,ies) *with:* analysis, assess(ed,ing,ment), functional analysis, process theory, impact(s), model(s), efficiency, effectiveness, evaluat(e,ed, ing,ion), alternative(s), option(s), goal(s), objective(s), premise(s), values, ideolog(y,ies), cost-benefit, decision criteria, priorit(y,ies), optimum, debate(s), deliberation, negotiation, stud(y,ies), feasibility, legality, timing, satisficing, systems analysis, systems theor(y,ies), problem assessment, monitoring, input-output analysis, dynamics, cybernetics, feedback. *Consider also:* policy analysis *with:* rational comprehensive, incremental, mixed scanning, per se decision rules, financial, budgeting, decision trees, simulation. *See also* Policy; Policy evaluation.

Policy evaluation. Policy evaluation. *Choose from:* polic(y,ies), rule(s), regulation(s), plan(s), program(s), treat(y,ies) *with:* evaluat(e,ed,ing,ion), accountab(le,ility), responsib(le,ility), cost effective(ness), equity, fair(ness), efficiency, impact(s), goal displacement, outcome(s), effect(s), review(s,ed,ing), performance, pretest, posttest, criteria. *See also* Policy; Policy analysis.

Policy formation. See *Policy making.*

Policy implementation. Polic(y,ies) implement(ed,ing,ation). *Choose from:* polic(y,ies), program(s), regulation(s), principle(s), guideline(s), rule(s), plan(s) of action, line of conduct, plan(s), manual(s), treat(y,ies) *with:* implement(ed,ing,ation), design(ed,ing), decision making, participat(ion,ory), consolidation, discretion, coordinat(e,ed, ing,ation), enforc(e,ed,ing,ement), develop(ed,ing,ment), establish(ed,ing, ment), plan(ning,ned), operations, service delivery, backward/forward mapping, administrative distance, directive(s), compliance, decision path(s), agenda(s), monitor(ing), innovation, shap(e,ing), shift(ing), clearance, linkage(s). *Consider also:* outcomes, strategic planning, bending rules. *See also* Administration; Administrative procedures; Implementation; Legislation; Policy making; Public policy; Regulations.

Policy making. Polic(y,ies) making. *Choose from:* polic(y,ies), regulation(s), principle(s), objective(s), guideline(s), rule(s), plan(s) of action, line of conduct, practice(s), plan(s), manual(s), treat(y, ies) *with:* mak(e,ing), formulat(e,ing), form(ation), chang(e,ed,ing), becom(e,ing), setting, develop(ed,ing, ment), establish(ed,ing,ment), plan(ning,ned), innovation, shap(e,ing), design(ed,ing), shift(ing), sunset. *Consider also:* strategic plan(s,ning), bend(ing) rule(s). *See also* Administrators; Councils; Criteria; Decision making; Enactment; Foreign policy making; Governing boards; Legislation; Planning; Policy; Policy implementation; Precedence; Priorities; Public policy; Strategies.

Politeness. See *Social skills.*

Political action. Political action. Political process(es). Politic(ized,ization,s). Political action committee(s). PAC(s). Redemocratization. *Choose from:* politic(s,al), partisan, party, vot(ing,ers), citizen(ry,s), elector(ate,al), grassroots, congress(men,women,ional), legislat(ive, ors,ure), senator(s,ial) *with:* action, activ(ity,ism), advocacy, agitation, coalition(s), reform, demonstration(s), militan(cy,t), dissent(ers), process(es), movement(s), campaign(s), change(s), conflict(s), force(s), influence(s), development(s), mobilization, behavior, leadership, control, manipulation, maneuvering, relationship(s), decision making, involvement, participation, strateg(y,ies), role(s), support, tactics. *Consider also:* power formation, building consensus, playing politics, voting, elections, statesmanship, party platform(s), diplomacy, influence peddling, lobbying, civil disobedience, etc. *See also* Activism; Civil disobedience; Collective action; Interest groups; Lobbying; Mobilization; Political attitudes; Political behavior; Political movements; Political participation; Political power; Social action; Social legislation; Protest movements; Social reform; Voting behavior.

Political action committees. See *Interest groups.*

Political activism. See *Activism; Advocacy; Interest groups; Lobbying; Militancy; Political action; Populism; Protest movements; Social action; Social reform.*

Political advertising. Political advertis(ing, ements). Polispot(s). Political spot(s). Political ad(s,vertisements,vertising). Mudslinging. Campaign commercial(s). *Choose from:* political, election, politician(s), primar(y,ies), mayoral, presidential, senat(e,orial), gubernatorial, congress(ional), party, candidate(s) or names of specific candidates *with:* sound bite(s), publici(ty,ze,zed,zing), ad(s,vertising,vertisements), commercial(s), promotion(s,al). *See also* Advertising; Comparative advertising; Musical ads; Political broadcasting; Political campaigns; Political platforms; Push-polling; Slogans.

Political affiliation. Political affiliation. Political party identification. Partisan(ship). *Choose from:* political, sociopolitical, partisan, party, voter(s), Republican(s), Democrat(ic,s), left wing, right wing, liberal, conservative, radical, constituenc(y,ies) *with:* affiliat(e,ed,ion), identit(y,ies), identification, member(s, ships), preference(s), alignment(s), faction(s), support, grouping(s). *See also* Partisan; Political attitudes; Political parties; Politics; Sectarianism.

Political agitation. See *Social agitation.*

Political assassination. See *Assassination.*

Political asylum. Political asylum. Asylum for rebel(s). Fugitive(s). Safe haven(s). Defect(ed,or,ors). Sanctuary. Escape(d) from persecution. Resettled rebel(s). Soviet emigres,etc. Fled. Escaped from. Refuseniks. Boat people. Haven(s). *Choose from:* political, diplomatic *with:* refug(e,es,ees), exile(s). *Consider also:* stay(s) of deportation, exterritoriality, extraterritoriality, extradit(e,ed,ion), repatriat(e,ed,ing,ion), Temporary Safe Haven Act, underground railroad. *See also* Authors in exile; Deportation; Emigrants; Forced migration; Illegal aliens; Immigration; Political defection; Purges; Refugees; Right of asylum.

Political attitudes. Political attitude(s). Political perception(s). Political party identification. Political opinion(s). *Choose from:* political, sociopolitical, partisan, party, voter(s), Republican(s), Democrat(ic,s), left wing, right wing, liberal, conservative, radical *with:* attitude(s), consciousness, rationale, alignment(s), dissent, preferences, thinking, choice(s), opinion(s), interest(s), ideolog(y,ies), loyalt(y,ies), intention(s), orientation(s), view(s), perception(s), support, tolerance, alienation, values, outlook(s), inclination(s), bent, bias, prejudice(s). *Consider also:* politicalization. *See also* Apathy; Dissent; Dissidents; Extremism; Left wing; McCarthyism; Political action; Political affiliation; Political conservatism; Political ideologies; Political liberalism; Political myths; Political philosophy; Political radicalism; Political socialization; Public opinion; Public opposition; Right wing politics; Voters; Voting behavior.

Political authoritarianism. See *Authoritarianism (political).*

Political ballads. Political ballad(s). *Choose from:* politic(s,al,ally), election, president(ial) campaign(s), candidate(s), Democrat(s,ic), Whig(s), political part(y,ies), political campaign(s), partisan(s), social commentary *with:* ballad(s), song(s), singer(s), music(al, ally), tune(s), ditt(y,ies), lyric(s,ism), songwriter(s), dirge(s), minstrel(s), folksong(s), sheet music, bandstand(s),

verse(s). *Consider also:* songsters, "Happy Days Are Here Again." *See also* Military music; Music; Patriotic music; Protest songs.

Political behavior. Political behavior. Political action. Politic(ized,ization,s). Democratiz(e,ed,ing,ation). Redemocratiz(e,ed,ing,ation). Student politics. *Choose from:* politic(s,al,ally), elector(al,ate), partisan, party, vot(ing, ers), grassroots, congress(men,women, ional), legislat(ive,ors,ure), senator(s, ial), presiden(t,cy,tial) *with:* action, activ(ity,ism), advocacy, agitation, alignment(s), alliance(s), apath(y,etic), campaign(s), change(s), conflict(s), consciousness, coalition(s), reform, demonstration(s), discourse, debate(s), dynamics, militan(cy,t), dissent(er,ers), process(es), movement(s), influence(s), development(s), mobilization, behavior, leadership, control, manipulation, maneuvering, relationship(s), decision making, involvement, participation, process(es), quiescen(t,ce), ritual(s), recruitment, solidarity, strateg(y,ies), role(s), socialization, support, tactics, tradition(s), violence. *Consider also:* lobbying, loyal opposition, power formation, building consensus, citizenship, voter turnout, playing politics, voting, elections, statesmanship, party platform(s), party formation, diplomacy, influence peddling, lobbying, civil disobedience, etc. *See also* Civil disobedience; Interest groups; Political action; Political campaigns; Political culture; Political defection; Political movements; Political participation; Political revolutions; Political violence; Voters; Voting behavior.

Political bosses. Political boss(es). Party boss(es). Machine politics. Political machine(s). Political elite(s). City hall. Boss rule. Tammany Hall. *Consider also:* William Marcy Tweed, Boss Tweed, Jim Pendergast, Frank Hague, James Michael Curley, Richard J. Daley. *See also* Elected officials; Corruption in government; Local politics; Oligarchy; Political elites; Political parties; Political patronage; Political power; Power elite; Urban politics.

Political broadcasting. Political broadcast(s,ing). *Choose from:* broadcast(s, ing), telecast(s), television, radio, cable program(s), cable news, media coverage, prime time, network news, local news, interviews, documentar(y,ies), docudrama(s) *with:* fairness doctrine, equal time, First Amendment, Washington bureau(s), political, candidate(s), propaganda, jamming. *Consider also:* Radio Marti, Radio Free Europe, Radio Liberty, Voice of America. *See also* Political advertising; Political campaigns; Political candidates; Political parties; Propaganda.

Political campaigns. Political campaign(s). Candidate(s) expenditure(s). Political rhetoric. Solicit vote(s). Photo op(portunity,portunities). Incumbent advantage(s). Campaign(ing) for office. Campaign strateg(y,ies). Presidential coattails. Electioneer(ing). Take to the stump. Stand(ing) for office. Run(ning) for office. Throw hat in the ring. Barnstorm(ed,ing). *Choose from:* political, election, politician(s), primar(y, ies), mayoral, presidential, senat(e,orial), gubernatorial, congress(ional), party, candidate(s), incumbent(s) *with:* campaign(ing,s), ad(s,vertising), race(s), nominating convention(s), platform(s), commercial(s), contribution(s), stump(ed,ing), whistlestop(s), market(ed,ing), promotion(s,al), debate(s), ran, run(ning). *See also* Advocacy advertising; Campaign debates; Campaign finance reform; Defamation; Election districts; Elections; Interest groups; Musical ads; Negativism; Political advertising; Political broadcasting; Political candidates; Political contributions; Political parties; Political platforms; Political rhetoric; Push-polling; Scandals; Voter participation.

Political candidates. Political candidate(s). *Choose from:* political, election, re-election, Democratic, Republican, Socialist, etc., presidential, gubernatorial, congressional, senatorial, mayoral *with:* candidate(s), candidacy, campaign(s,ing), nominee(s), challenger(s), contender(s), run(ning), ran for office, governor, president, congress, mayor, etc. *Consider also:* politician(s), office seeker(s), front runner(s), dark horse, political hopeful(s), Seek(ing) office, stand(ing) for office. *See also* Candidates; Elections; Political campaigns; Political parties; Political platforms; Primaries; Voters.

Political cartoons. See *Political humor.*

Political conservatism. Political(ly) conservat(ive,ism). Rightist. Traditionalis(m,t). Right wing. Moral majority. New right. Bubba vote. Neoconservatis(m,t,ts). Sociopolitically conservative. Conservatism. Religious right. Christian politics. Republican right. Radical right. Political right. Law and order. Fundamentalis(m,t). *Choose from:* conservative, traditional, right wing, neoconservative *with:* ideolog(y, ies), candidate(s), values, movement(s), perspective(s), opinion(s), viewpoint(s), orientation, attitude(s), vot(e,ers,ing), polic(y,ies), politics, doctrine(s). *Consider also:* authoritarianism, diehard, oppos(e,ed,ing) change, orthodox(y,ness), preserv(e,ed,ing) the status quo, resist(ed,ing,ance) change, reactionary, Tory, Birchism, hunkerism, rightism, redneck(s). *See also* Absolut-

ism; Anti-intellectualism; Anti-environmentalism; Antiabortion movement; Religious fundamentalism; Right wing politics; McCarthyism; Traditionalism; Witch hunting.

Political contributions. Political contribution(s). Soft money. Hard money. *Choose from:* part(y,ies), Democratic National Committee, DNC, Republican National Committee, RNC, GOP, candidate(s), officeholder(s), incumbent(s), political(ly) *with:* fund(s, raising), contribution(s), contributor(s), PAC(s), Political action committee(s), special interest(s), support(ed,ing,er,ers), brib(e,es,ed,ing), underwrit(er,ers,ten), donat(e,ed,ing,ion,ions), donor(s), present(s), gift(s), honorari(a,um), gratuit(y,ies). *See also* Advocacy advertising; Campaign finance reform; Campaign funds; Contributions; Giving; Interest groups; Political campaigns; Political ethics.

Political crimes. Political crime(s). Political offense(s). Political offender(s). President(ial) misdeed(s). *Choose from:* political(ly), politician(s), politically motivated, dissenter(s), rebel(s), dissident(s), refusenik(s) *with:* kill(ings), disappearance(s), desaparecid(a,o,os), tortur(e,es,ed,ing), offense(s), illegal arrest(s), detain(ed,ment), imprison(ment), trial(s), persecution, oppression, prisoner(s), offender(s), abuse, payoff(s), patronage, fraud, corruption. *Consider also:* state terror, Amnesty International, torture of civilian(s). *See also* Corruption in government; Government investigations; Missing persons; Political asylum; Political defection; Political prisoners; Political violence.

Political culture. Political culture(s). Political climate(s). Political values. *Choose from:* politic(s,al,ally,ian,ians), sociopolitic(s,al,ally), government(al,s), legislat(ive,ure,or,ors), voter(s), elector(ate,al), constituen(cy,cies), partisan, political part(y,ies), presidential, congress(ional,men,man,women, woman), senat(e,or,orial) *with:* culture(s), subculture(s), climate(s), consciousness, behavior pattern(s), belief(s), myth(s,making), ethos, philosoph(y,ies), ideolog(y,ies), style(s), creed(s), code(s), ethic(al,s), environment(s), socialization, norm(s). *See also* Cultural conflict; Cultural pluralism; Political socialization.

Political defection. Political defector(s). Desert(ed,er,ers). Political refug(ee,ees). Renegade(s). Political(ly) disillusion(ed, ment). Political exile(s). Fugitive(s). Defect(ed,ors). Escape(d) from persecution. Resettled rebel(s). Soviet emigre(s),etc. Fled. Escaped from. Refusenik(s). Boat people. *See also* Apostasy; Authors in exile; Citizenship;

Disillusionment; Dissent; Dissidents; International relations; Loyalty; Political asylum; Political crimes; Refugees; Right of asylum; Schism.

Political demonstrations. See *Social demonstrations.*

Political dissent. Political dissent(er,ers). Anti-establishment. Dissident(s). Political radical(s). Revolutionar(y,ies). Foe(s) of regime. Political nonconformist(s). Politically suspect. Refusenik(s). Political activist(s). Political reformer(s). Nationalist dissent. Draft resister(s). Anti-government. Anti-apartheid. *Choose from:* political(ly) *with:* dissent(er,ers), opposition, opponent(s), protest(er,ers), satire, dissident(s), radical(s), revolutionar(y, ies), rebel(s,lion,lions), nonconformist(s), suspect(s), extremist(s), uprising(s), resist(ance,er,ers), defiance, unrest, reactionar(y,ies), counterrevolutionar(y,ies), demonstrat(or,ors), activis(m,ts), reformer(s), discontent(ed, ment), dissatisf(ied,ation). *See also* Anti-government radicals; Counterrevolutions; Dissent; Peasant rebellions; Political attitudes; Political crimes; Political ideologies; Political repression; Political stability; Political prisoners; Political violence; Protest movements; Social movements; Social reform.

Political dynamics. See *Political stability.*

Political elections. See *Elections.*

Political elites. Political elite(s). Political party leader(s). Political party elite(s). Party central committee. Presidium. Power broker(s). Kingmaker(s). Campaign financier(s). Head(s) of state. Supreme leader(s). Caudillo(s). Dictator(s). Fuhrer(s). Labor union leader(s). Elected political officeholder(s). Campaign manager(s). Elected executives. President(s). Governor(s). Mayor(s). Cabinet member(s). Diplomats. Legislator(s). Wielder(s) of legitimate power. Tribal chief(s). Hereditary ruler(s). *Choose from:* power, governing, ruling, dominant *with:* elite(s), class(es), group(s), caste(s), faction(s). *Choose from:* political, political party, interest group, governing, military, administrative, national, bureaucratic *with:* leader(s), lobbyist(s), elite(s), chair(man,men,woman,women, person,persons). *Consider also:* political influence, clout, aristocrac(y,ies). Civil religious hierarch(y,ies). *See also* Chiefs; Elected officials; Elites; Elitism (government); Governing boards; Governors; Hegemony; Legislative bodies; Military regimes; Monarchy; Oligarchy; Political bosses; Power elite; Political leadership; Political power; Power structure; Presidents; Priests and priestly classes (anthropology); Privelege; Ruling class.

Political ethics. Politic(s,ally) ethic(al,s). *Choose from:* elected representative(s), mayor(s,al), politician(s), elected official(s), candidate(s), judge(s), government official(s), federal official(s), state official(s), public officer(s), government employee(s), Congress, Parliament, prime minister(s), governor(s), congress(men,man,women, woman), senator(s), lobbyist(s), president(s,ial), Pentagon, incumben(t,ts, cy), lawmaker(s), politic(s,ians,al,ally) *with:* ethic(s,al), integrity, accountability, honest(y), principle(s,d), moral(s,ity), responsibility, conscience, conscientious(ness), trustworth(y,iness), truth(ful,fulness), openness, fidelity, incorruptib(le,ility). *Consider also:* political terms *with:* abuse(d,s), alter(ed,ing) evidence, alter(ed,ing) record(s), bilk(ed,ing), bribe(s,ry), buy(ing) Pentagon, buy(ing) vote(s), campaign slander, cocaine, collusion, concealment, conflict(s) of interest, conspiracy, corrupt(ing,ed), coverup(s), criminal behavior, cronyism, defraud(ing), divert(ed,ing) fund(s), divert(ed,ing) government property, embezzle(ment), ethical question(s), forger(y,ies), fraud(ulent), gift(s), honorar(ia,ium), illegal contribution(s), illegal(ities,ity), immoral(ity,ities), improper(ly), impropriet(y,ies), insensitivity, junket(s), kickback(s), lax ethics, libel, lining pocket(s), loophole(s), malfeasance, misappropriation(s), misconduct, misdeed(s), misdemeanor(s), mismanagement, misuse, mudslinging, no show employee(s), oversight(s), patronage, perjur(e,y), pilfer(ed,ing), political plum(s), profiteering, questionable behavior, racketeer(s,ing), revolving door, RICO, scam(s), scandal(s), shred(ding) document(s), skirt(ing) law(s), sleaz(e,y), smear tactic(s), smuggl(e,ed,ing), special tie(s), tarnished reputation, unethical, unlawful(ly), violation(s), wrongdoing(s). *See also* Conflict of interest; Corruption in government; Ethical practices; Ethics; Financial disclosure; Interest groups; Legitimacy of governments; Misconduct in office; Moral obligation; Natural law; Political bosses; Political crimes; Political obligation; Professional ethics; Social ethics; Unethical conduct.

Political extremism. See *Extremism.*

Political fiction. Political fiction. *Choose from:* political(ly), politic(s,ian,ians), White House, mayor(s,al), president(s, ial), senat(e,or,ors,orial), gubernatorial, governor(s), congress(es,ional) *with:* novel(s), fiction(al), story(line), stories, thriller(s), myster(y,ies). *See also* Antiheroes; Fiction; Heroes; Historical fiction; Nonfiction novel; Novels; Political fiction; Politicians.

Political forecasting. Political forecast(s, ing). *Choose from:* political, election(s), presidential race(s), gubernatorial race(s), candidate(s), voter(s) *with:* poll(s,ed,ing,ster,sters), risk assessment(s), forecast(s,ing), postdiction(s), predict(ing,ion,ions), conjectur(e,ed, ing), future trend(s), probabilit(y,ies), prognos(is,es,tics), prognosticat(e,ed, ing,ion,ions), prophe(cy,cies,sy,tic), prospect(s), outlook(s), projection(s). *Consider also:* exit poll(s). *See also* Elections; Future of society; Prediction.

Political geography. Political geography. *Choose from:* politic(s,al), nationalism, electoral, election(s), voting, voter(s), power *with:* geograph(y,ic), spatial, territorial, regional, map(s), location(s), district(s), ward(s), redistrict(s,ed,ing), gerrymandering, north south, east west. *See also* Annexation; Borderlands; Boundaries; Economic geography; Election districts; Geographic determinism; Geopolitics; Historical geography; Poverty areas; Regionalism; Territorial expansion; Territorial issues; Territorial waters; Territoriality.

Political humor. Political humor. *Choose from:* political(ly), politics, politician(s), president(ial), congress(ional), Washington, Democrat(s), Republican(s), GOP, White House, oval office, governor(s), legislator(s), legislature(s) *with:* humor(ous), satir(e,ical) humorist(s), comedian(s), comic(s), joke(s), wit(ty,tiness), parod(y,ies,ied), caricatur(e,es), cartoon(s). *See also* Caricatures; Cartoons; Humor; Humorous poetry; Satire.

Political ideologies. Political ideolog(y,ies, ical). Political philosoph(y,ies). Political theor(y,ies). Political value(s). *Choose from:* politic(s,al,ally,ian,ians), sociopolitic(s,al,ally), government(al,s), legislat(ive,ure,or,ors), voter(s), elector(ate,al), constituenc(y,ies), constituent(s), partisan, political part(y,ies) *with:* ideolog(y,ies,ical), belief(s), thought, thinking, orientation, ideal(s), weltanschauung(en), world view(s), concept(s), myth(s,making), philosoph(y,ies), creed(s), code(s), ethic(al,s), theor(y,ies). *Consider also:* anarchism, authoritarianism, capitalism, colonialism, communism, conservatism, corporatism, democracy, despotism, elitism, extremism, fascism, feudalism, imperialism, individualism, internationalism, liberalism, materialism, Marxism, militarism, nationalism, neutralism, nihilism, pacifism, patriotism, populism, radicalism, separatism, socialism, syndicalism, theocratism, totalitarianism. *See also* Anti-government radicals; Anarchism; Authoritarianism (political); Capitalism; Communism; Corporatism; Despotism; Elitism (government); Extremism; Fascism; Feudalism; Gerontocracy; Imperialism; Individualism; Liberalism; Marxism; Militarism; Nationalism; Neutrality; Nihilism; Nonviolence; Pacifism; Patriotism; Political conservatism; Political liberalism; Political radicalism; Populism; Progressivism; Regionalism; Schism; Sectarianism; Separatism; Social thought; Socialism; Theocracy; Totalitarianism.

Political issues. Political issue(s). *Choose from:* political, sociopolitical, party, partisan, election, candidate(s), congress(ional), legislative, platform(s), public, civic, civil, grassroots, government(al), federal, state, bipartisan, national, citizen(s), electorate, voter(s) *with:* issue(s), position(s), problem(s), discussion(s), debate(s), controvers(y, ies,ial), concern(s), question(s), promise(s), agenda, plank(s), pledge(s), question(s), topic(s), contention(s), crux, dispute(s), difference(s). *See also* Controversial issues; Political campaigns; Political platforms; Public opinion; Voting behavior.

Political leadership. Political leader(s,ship). *Choose from:* politic(s,al), democratic, national, congressional, president(ial), party, government(al) *with:* leader(s, ship), executive(s), hero(es), *Consider also:* bully pulpit, changing of the guard, politician(s), president(s,ial), speaker(s) of the house, ruling class(es). *See also* Authority (power); Change agents; Charisma; Command (of troops, ships, etc.); Leadership; Opinion leaders; Political elites; Politicians; Responsibility (answerability).

Political legitimacy. See *Legitimacy of governments.*

Political liberalism. Political(ly) liberal(ism,ity,ization,s). Neoliberal(ism, s). New left. Neoliberalism. Left liberal(s). Progressivism. Progressive force(s). Political left. Sociopolitically liberal. Forward looking. Reformist. Left wing. Leftist. *Choose from:* liberal(s, ism,ity) *with:* doctrine(s), ideolog(y,ies), values, movement(s), perspective(s), view(s), politic(s,al), rhetoric, action, influence(s), agenda(s). *Consider also:* middle of the road, liberal world view(s), radical, independent, freedom of choice, unprovincial(ism). *See also* Abortion rights movement; Civil rights organizations; Feminism; Left wing; Liberation theology; Political attitudes; Progressivism; Reform.

Political loyalty. See *Loyalty; Loyalty oaths; Patriotism.*

Political machines. See *Political bosses.*

Political majorities. See *Majorities (political).*

Political movements. Political movements. Student politics. *Choose from:*

politic(s,al), vot(ing,ers), citizen(ry,s), elector(ate,al), grassroots, underground *with:* activis(m,ts), advocacy, agitation, coalition(s), reform, demonstration(s), militan(cy,t), dissent(ers), movement(s), mobilization, involvement, ideolog(y, ies), participation, support. *Consider also:* ethnic revival(s,ism), ethnonationalism, power formation, building consensus, playing politics, voting, elections, statesmanship, party platform(s), counter-revolution(ary, aries), populis(t,m), moral majority, ecopolitics, new left, new right, people power, black power, bund(s), influence peddling, lobbying, civil disobedience. *See also* Activism; Antifascist movements; Autonomy (government); Black power; Civil disobedience; Decolonization; Dissent; Interest groups; Labor movements; Liberation theology; Lobbying; Men's movement; Nazism; Peace movements; Peasant rebellions; Political action; Political behavior; Political reform; Politics; Protest movements; Rebellions; Reform; Regional movements; Resistance movements; Revolution; Social change; Social movements; Suffrage movement; Youth movements.

Political murder. See *Assassination.*

Political myths. Political myth(s,ology, ologies). *Choose from:* politic(s,al), official, partisan, governmental, national, factional, historical, voter(s), Republican(s), Democrat(ic,s), left wing, right wing, liberal, conservative, political part(y,ies) *with:* myth(s,ology, ologies,making), assumption(s), stereotyp(e,ed,ing), rhetoric, misconception(s), belief(s), premise(s), idees fixes, misguided notion(s), oversimplification(s), label(s), old fear(s), old complaint(s), nostalgia, symbol(s), slogan(s), fable(s). *Consider also:* collective memory, conspiracy theor(y,ies), party line, historical assumption(s), geostrategic definition(s), ethnohistorical definition(s). *See also* Common culture; Cultural knowledge; Mythology; Patriotism; Political attitudes; Political rhetoric; Political socialization; Political symbolism; Propaganda; Slogans.

Political obligation. Political obligation(s). *Choose from:* political, citizen(s,ry), civil, associative, communal *with:* obligation(s), oblig(e,ed), obligat(e,ed, ory), requir(e,ed,ing,ement,ements), dut(y,ies), responsibilit(y,ies). *Consider also:* civic dut(y,ies), citizen-state relation(s,ship). *See also* Citizen participation; Citizenship; Civil disobedience; Legitimacy of governments; Moral obligation; Political ethics Social contract; Social responsibility.

Political opinions. See *Political attitudes.*

Political oratory. See *Political rhetoric.*

Political participation. Political participation. Citizen participation. Collective action. Mass participation. Community action. Citizen interest groups. Participatory democracy. Local politics. Role of residents. Popular sovereignty. *Choose from:* citizen(s), public, community, taxpayer(s), grassroots, voter(s), resident(s), elect(ion,orate), local *with:* politic(s,al,ally), respons(e,iveness), action, appeal(s), movement(s), empowerment, power, involv(e,ed,ing, ement), participat(e,ed,ing,ion,ory), cooperat(e,ed,ing,ion), action, mobiliz(e,ed,ing,ation), turnout(s), registration, support(ed,ing), protest(s,ed,ing). *See also* Citizen participation; Elections; Local politics; Political parties; Political self determination; Popular sovereignty; Protest movements; Public policy; Voting.

Political parties. Political part(y,ies). Splinter part(y,ies). Minor part(y,ies). Third part(y,ies). *Choose from:* Democrat(s,ic), Independent(s), Republican(s), Tor(y,ies), Whig(s), Labour, Conservative *with:* part(,ies). *Choose from:* party, partisan *with:* affiliation(s), preference(s), member(s, ships), machine(s), platform(s), convention(s), discipline, boss(es), activist(s), factionalism, realignment, reform, system(s), competition, loyalty. *Choose from:* political *with:* sector(s), contingent(s), caucus(es), primar(y,ies), bloc(s), league(s), faction(s), affiliation(s), machine(s). *Consider also:* partisanship, independent voter(s), minority part(y,ies). *See also* Elections; Majorities (political); Partisan; Political affiliation; Political attitudes; Political campaigns; Political candidates; Political ideologies; Political movements; Political participation; Political platforms; Political power; Preference voting; Schism; Social democracy; Third parties (United States politics).

Political patronage. Political patronage. Porkbarrel. Political hir(e,es,ing). Partisan appointment(s). Spoils system. Political plum(s). Clubhouse politics. Senatorial courtesy. Trading jobs for favor(s). Political favor(s). Clientelism. Sinecure(s). *Choose from:* politician(s), elected official(s), government official(s), Federal official(s), State official(s), public officer(s), government employee(s), Congress, Parliament, prime minister(s), governor(s), congress(men,man,women,woman), senator(s), lobbyist(s), president(s,ial), Pentagon, department of., candidate(s), judge(s), political *with:* patronage, cronyism, kickback(s), no-show employees, special tie(s). *Consider also:* politician(s), official(s), governor(s), president(s), congress(men,man,women,

woman), senator(s) *with:* appointment(s), employment, job(s), contract(s), license(s), franchise(s), honor(s), benefit(s) *with:* friend(s), supporter(s), relative(s), family member(s), nepotism. *See also* Corruption in government; Military patronage; Patronage; Political bosses.

Political persecution. Political persecution. Political(ly) persecut(ed,tion). Suppression of political activit(y,ies). *Choose from:* politic(s,al,ally), government(al), dissent(er,ers), protest(s,er,ers), demonstrat(or,ors,ion,ions), partisan(s), civilian(s), citizen(s), activist(s) *with:* persecut(ed,ion,ory), torture(d), torment(ed), crackdown, imprison(ed, ment,ments), jail(ed), martyr(s,dom), slave camp(s), punish(ing,ment,ments), atrocit(y,ies). *Consider also:* amnesty, political asylum, political refuge(e,es), political violence, exile(d,s), mass killings, secret police, labor camps, political repression, Gulag, human rights abuse(s), secret trial(s), state terror, genocide, tyranny, censorship, blacklist(ed,ing), politicide(s), state repression, human rights violations, state terrorism. *See also* Blacklisting; McCarthyism; Persecution; Political repression; Political violence; Secret police.

Political philosophy. Political philosoph(y, ies). Political doctrine(s). Political ideolog(y,ies,ical). Political theor(y,ies). Political values. *Choose from:* politic(s, al,ally,ians), sociopolitic(s,al,ally), government(al,s), legislat(ive,ure,ors), voter(s), elector(ate,al), constituen(cy, cies), partisan, political part(y,ies) *with:* ideolog(y,ies,ical), doctrine(s), belief(s), thought, thinking, orientation, ideal(s), myth(s,making), philosoph(y,ies), creed(s), code(s), ethic(al,s), theor(y,ies). *Consider also:* anarchism, capitalism, colonialism, collectivism, communism, conservatism, corporatism, democracy, despotism, elitism, extremism, fascism, federalism, feudalism, imperialism, individualism, internationalism, liberalism, materialism, Marxism, militarism, nationalism, neutralism, nihilism, pacifism, patriotism, populism, radicalism, separatism, socialism, syndicalism, theocracy, totalitarianism. *See also* Philosophy; Political attitudes; Political ideologies; Political systems; Social thought; Theocracy.

Political platforms. Political platform(s). *Choose from:* political, election, politician(s), congress(ional), party, Republican(s), Democrat(ic,s) *with:* platform(s), plank(s), position(s), campaign promise(s), principle(s), polic(y,ies). *See also* Campaign debates; Political advertising; Political campaigns; Political candidates; Political issues; Political parties; Political rhetoric.

Political power. Political(ly) power(s,ful, fulness). Divine right of king(s). Consent of the governed. *Choose from:* politic(s,al,ally,ian,ians), sociopolitic(s, al,ally), citizen(s,ry), vot(er,ers,ing), government(al), legislat(ive,or,ors,ure), congress(ional,men,man,women,woman), gubernatorial, governor(s), elector(al, ate), grassroots, senator(s,ial), presiden(t,cy,tial) *with:* control(led,ling), dominan(ce,t), strong, strength, authority, self determination, command(ing), efficac(ious,iousness,y), willpower, influen(ce,cing,tial), empower(ing,ment), coerc(ion,ive), imperial, Machiavellian(ism), hierach(y, ies), compliance, master(ing), domination, carte blanche, clout, ascendan(t,cy), poten(cy,t), supremacy, might(y,iness), force(ful,fulness), overpower(ed,ing), impregnability, asymmetrical relation(s, ships), asymmetrical interaction, power structure, leadership, powerless(ness), dependen(t,cy), constraint, exploit(er, ers,ation). *See also* Black power; Civil disobedience; Delegation of powers; Divine right of kings; Executive powers; Interest groups; Legislative bodies; Legislative powers; Lobbying; Political bosses; Political elites; Political movements; Power elite; Ruling class; Separation of powers; Voters.

Political prisoners. Political prisoner(s). Jailed activist(s). Prisoner(s) of conscience. Disappeared people. Desaparecido(s). *Choose from:* jail(ed), detention, detain(ed,ee,ees,ing,ment), confine(d,ment), custody, taken prisoner, arrest(s,ed,ing), held, imprison(ed,ment, incarcerat(ed,ion), labor camp(s), abduct(ed,ing), persecut(ed,ing,ion), repression, Gulag *with:* activist(s), dissident(s), refusenik(s), radical(s), separatist(s), revolutionar(y,ies), political opponent(s), anti-government demonstrator(s), human rights supporter(s), rebel(s), opposition group(s), protester(s), resister(s), rights activist(s). *See also* Arrests; Missing persons; Oppression; Political repression; Preventive detention.

Political processes. Political process(es). Politics. *Choose from:* politic(s,al), partisan, party, vot(ing,ers), congress(men,women,ional), legislator(s), senator(s,ial) *with:* process(es), action, structure(s), consequence(s), movement(s), campaign(s), candidate(s), machination(s), opinion(s), change(s), conflict(s), influence(s), development(s), repression, mobilization, behavior, leadership, control, manipulation, maneuvering, relationship(s), decision making, reform, involvement, solution(s), opposition, negotiation(s), participation, strateg(y,ies), role(s), tactic(s,al). *Consider specific processes such as:* majority rule, majority control,

power formation, building consensus, playing politics, voting, elections, statesmanship, party platform(s), realpolitik, diplomacy, influence peddling, governance, legislation, lobbying. *See also* Elections; Majorities (political); Political action; Political campaigns; Political issues; Political participation; Political parties; Political representation; Political revolutions; Voting.

Political protests. See *Activism; Civil disobedience; Dissent; Dissidents; Nonviolence; Political defection; Political dissent; Political radicalism; Political revolutions; Political violence; Protest movements; Protesters; Social action; Social demonstrations; Social unrest.*

Political purges. See *Purges.*

Political radicalism. Political radical(s, ism). Radicaliz(e,ed,ing,ation). Radical left. Radical right. Political extremis(m, ts). Extraparliamentary. Revolutionar(y,ies). Radical political movement(s). Radical movement(s). Extreme right. Extreme left. Rebel(s,lion,lious). Insurgen(cy,t). Insurrection. Seditious. Iconoclasm. Terroris(t,m). Iconoclastic. Underground. Freethinking. Avantgarde. Nonconformist(s). Anarchistic. Agitator(s). *See also* Agitators; Anarchism; Extremism; Iconoclasm; Left wing; Political attitudes; Protest songs; Right wing politics.

Political reform. Political reform(s). *Choose from:* political, regime(s), constitutional, legal, state, government(al) *with:* reform(s), change(s), restructur(e,ed,ing), revis(e,ed,ing,ion, ions), democratiz(ed,ing,ation), improv(e,ed,ing,ment,ments), reform(s, ed,ing), reorganiz(e,ed,ing,ation), reconstruct(e,ed,ing,ion), transform(ed, ing,ation,ations), transition(al,s), innovat(e,ed,ing,ion,ions), renew(al,ed, ing), regenerat(e,ed,ing,ion), revolution(s), cleanup(s), purge(s), bloodletting(s) shift(s), progress, upheaval, liberalization, restructur(e,ed, ing,ion). *Consider also:* clean government, open election(s). *See also* Campaign finance reform; Civil rights; Corruption in government; Democratization; Elections; Land reform; Political action; Political movements; Progress; Reform; Social movements; Social reform.

Political refugees. See *Political asylum; Refugees.*

Political representation. Political representation. One person one vote. One man one vote. Elected representative(s). Democratic representation. Indirect republican form of government. Representative government. Representative democracy. Delegated authority.

Legislative power(s). Legislature(s). Overrepresent(ed,ation). Underrepresent(ed,ation). *See also* Apportionment; Delegation of powers; Legislative bodies; Legislative powers; Voting.

Political repression. Political(ly) repress(ed,ion). Repressive state apparatus. Berlin wall. Iron curtain. Bamboo curtain. Totalitarian(ism). Authoritarian(ism). Despot(ism). Dictator(ships). *Choose from:* political, state, government, military, totalitarian, authoritarian, despotic, dictator(ial), official *with:* repress(ed,ive,ion,ions), oppress(ed,ive,ion,ions), control, subjection, forcible restrain(t,ed), constrain(ed,t), stifl(e,ed,ing), curb(ed,ing), subdue(d), limit(ed,ing), containment, pacification, quell(ed,ing), arrest(s), subjugat(ed,ion), restrict(ed, ing). *See also* Authoritarianism (political); Civil supremacy over the military; Censorship; Dictatorship; Exploitation; Information policy; McCarthyism; Military civilian relations; Oppression; Persecution; Political persecution; Political prisoners; Refugees; Social unrest; Totalitarianism; Tyranny.

Political revolutions. Political revol(t,ts, ution,utions). Revolutionar(y,ies). Political protest(s,ers). War(s) of liberation. War(s) of national liberation. Insurgen(t,ts,cy). Political riot(s). Revolutionary process(es). Civil strife. Overthrow of government. American revolution. French revolution. Russian revolution. Cultural revolution. Uprising(s). Rebel(s,lions). Guerrilla movement(s). National liberation. Overthrow of colonialism. Insurrection. Divide and rule. Class struggle(s). Eighteenth brumaire. Mutin(y,ies). Sedition. Putsch. Maoism. *Consider also:* revolutionary, rebel, liberation, protest *with:* leader(s), movement(s), coalition(s), change(s), uprising(s), insurrection(s), struggle(s). *See also* Assassination; Civil war; Guerrillas; Internal security; Liberation theology; National fronts; Peasant rebellions; Political self determination; Protest movements; Provisional government; Revolutionary ballads and songs; Secession; Separatism; Social movements; Terrorism.

Political rhetoric. Political rhetoric. Party line. *Choose from:* political, politician(s), congress(ional), political part(y,ies), Republican(s), GOP, Democrat(ic,s), president(ial), congress(ional), governor(s), states(men,man,women,woman), Washington, White House, oval office, candidate(s), incumbent(s) *with:* rhetoric(al,ally), speech(es,making), oratory, oration(s), speak(ing), debate(s), preach(ed,ing), rebuttal(s), argument(s), sound bite(s). *Consider also:* political language, political communication(s), political discourse. *See also* Oratory; Persuasion; Political campaigns; Political myths; Political platforms; Propaganda; Rhetoric; Slogans; Speeches (formal discourse).

Political rights. See *Bill of rights; Civil rights; Human rights; Political self determination.*

Political satire. See *Political humor.*

Political scandals. See *Corruption in government.*

Political self determination. Political self determination. Government(al) autonom(y,ous). Nonalignment. Decoloniz(e,ed,ing,ation). Free election(s). Home rule. National liberation. Separatism. Independence. Self determination. Sovereign nation. Autarky. Autarchy. Autochthon(y,ous). Nationalism. *Choose from:* nation(al), government(s), state(s), countr(y,ies), political *with:* autonom(y,ous), independen(t,ce), self-legislating, sovereign(ty), free(dom), self govern(ment,ing), self determination. *See also* Autonomy (government); Decolonization; Democratization; Freedom; Nationalism; Political revolutions; Popular sovereignty; Secession; Separatism; Sovereignty.

Political socialization. Political socialization. Formation of political consciousness. Political attitude formation. Encouraging political participation. Internalization of political values. Political mobilization. Ideological indoctrination. *Choose from:* form(ing, ation), develop(ing,ment), encourag(e, ing,ement), socializ(ing,ation), internaliz(e,ed,ing,ation), transmi(t, ssion), acquir(e,ed,ing), indoctrinat(e,ed, ion) *with:* political attitude(s), political consciousness, political values, ideolog(y,ies,ical), party, partisan, politic(s,al). *Choose from:* accept(ance) or respect *with:* political authority. *Choose from:* party membership, political involvement, political campaign(s) *with:* effect(s). *Consider also:* voter registration drives, building party loyalty, conform(ity,ing) to political culture, political manipulation. *See also* Brainwashing; Citizenship education; Indoctrination; Political attitudes; Political myths; Progressivism; Socialization.

Political songs. See *Political ballads.*

Political stability. Political stability *Choose from:* political, democratic, democrac(y, ies), regime(s), government(s), order *with:* stability, stabl(e,ization), instability, unstable, chang(e,ed,ing), destabiliz(e,ed,ing,ation), volatil(e,ity), dynamic(s), cohes(ion,ive,iveness). *Consider also:* constitutionalism, balance of power, legitimate authority,

political order. *See also* Consensus; Economic stability; Legitimacy of governments; Political dissent.

Political symbolism. Political symbolism. *Choose from:* political(ly), national(ism), party, president(ial), congress(ional), governor(s), state(s) *with:* symbol(s,ic,ism), emblem(s), insignia(s), flag(s), icon(s), pennant(s), banner(s), flag(s). *Consider also:* political gesture(s), Republican elephant(s), Democrat donkey(s), state flower(s), state bird(s). *See also* Emblems; Flags; National emblems; Political myths; Slogans; Symbolism.

Political systems. Political system(s). Political economic system(s). Ecopolitical system(s). Sociopolitical system(s). Democratic system(s). Political structure. Political environment. Political condition(s). Colonialism. Nazism. Fascism. Democracy. Totalitarian(ism). Imperialism. Oligarch(y,ies). Polyarch(y,ies). Monarch(y,ies). Republic(s). Federation(s). Confederation(s). *Consider also:* capitalism, communism, socialism, technocrac(y,ies). *See also* Aristocracy; Chiefs; Constitution (legal); Democracy; Dictatorship; Empires; Gerontocracy; Government; Ideologies; Legislative bodies; Monarchy; Oligarchy; Political ideologies; Political philosophy; Polyarchy; Primitive government; Republics; Separation of powers; Social philosophy; Society; Technocracy.

Political violence. Political(ly) violen(t,ce). Civil disorder(s). Assassin(ate,ating, ation). Coup(s) d'etat. Terror(ists,ism, ize,izing). Rebel(ling,led,lions). Guerrilla(s). Internal disorder. Holy war(s). State terror. Molotov cocktail(s). *Choose from:* politic(s,al,ally), government(al), secret police, dissent(er,ers), protest(s,er,ers), partisan(s), civil, citizen(s) *with:* mob(bed,bing), assault(ed,ing), stab(bed,ing), riot(s,ed, ing), beat(en,ing,ings), bomb(ed,ing, ings), incendiar(y,ies), dangerous(ness), atrocit(y,ies), tortur(e,ed,ing), knifing(s), fighting, vandal(s,ize,ism), attack(s,ed, ing), armed conflict(s), loot(ed,ing), pillag(e,ed,ing), plunder(ed,ing), ravag(e,ed,ing), destruct(ion,ive), brute force, rap(e,ed,ing), injur(e,ing), harm(ed,ing,ful), murder(s,ing,ous), bloodthirsty, disorderly. *Consider also:* Guernica, Beirut, Northern Ireland, Palestinian(s), Mau Mau, South Africa(n) *with:* uprising(s), rebellion(s), riot(s,ed,ing), war(s) of rebellion, civil war(s). *See also* Anti-government radicals; Anarchism; Assassination; Authoritarianism (political); Capitalism; Civil war; Communism; Corporatism; Counterinsurgency; Coups d'Etat; Despotism; Dissent; Elitism (govern-

ment); Extremism; Fascism; Feudalism; Genocide; Gerontocracy; Guerrilla warfare; Guerrillas; Imperialism; Individualism; Liberalism; Marxism; Militarism; Military regimes; Nationalism; Neutrality; Nihilism; Nonviolence; Pacifism; Patriotism; Peasant rebellions; Police brutality; Political conservatism; Political liberalism; Political persecution; Political prisoners; Political radicalism; Political repression; Populism; Prison violence; Purges; Regionalism; Revolution; Riots; Schism; Sectarianism; Separatism; Social unrest; Socialism; Terrorism; Torture; Totalitarianism.

Political wit and humor. See *Political humor.*

Politicians. Politician(s). Congress(men, man,woman,women). Elected official(s). Elected public official(s). Incumbent(s). Lame duck(s). Lawmaker(s). Legislator(s). Mayor(s). Member(s) of Congress. Member(s) of Parliament. Office holder(s). Party leader(s,ship). Politico(s). Presidential ambition(s). President(s). Prime minister(s). Representative(s). Senator(s). States(men,man,women,woman). *Choose from:* political *with:* candidate(s), communicator(s), contender(s), figure(s), hero(es), hopeful(s), leader(s,ship), life, office seeker(s). *See also* Elected officials; Legislative bodies; Local officials and employees; Political bosses; Political candidates; Political fiction; Political leadership; Statesmen.

Politics. Politic(al,ally,s). Partisan. Voter(s). Grass roots. Electorate. Electoral. Political philosophy. Political science. Political attitude(s). Political process(es). Special interest group(s). Political action committee(s). Student activism. Statesmanship. *Choose from:* politic(al, ally,s), politician(s), voter(s), partisan *with:* involvement, education, factor(s), aspect(s), influence(s), process(es), activity, power, strateg(y,ies), campaign(s), pressure(s), activis(,ts), behavior, part(y,ies), leader(s). *See also* Class politics; Elections; Geopolitics; Government; Ideological struggle; Interest groups; Left wing; Legislation; Legislative bodies; Legislative processes; Local politics; Lobbying; Majorities (political); Political action; Political behavior; Political bosses; Political campaigns; Political candidates; Political elites; Political ethics; Political issues; Political movements; Political parties; Political power; Political representation; Political socialization; Politicians; Right wing politics; Urban politics; Voting behavior; Voters.

Politics, class. See *Class politics.*

Politics, community. See *Local politics.*

Politics, local. See *Local politics.*

Politics, machine. See *Political bosses.*

Politics , municipal. See *Local politics.*

Politics, organizational. See *Organizational politics.*

Politics, partisan. See *Political parties.*

Politics, right wing. See *Right wing politics.*

Politics, urban. See *Urban politics.*

Politics, world. See *International relations.*

Polling. See *Opinion polls.*

Polling, push. See *Push-polling.*

Polls, opinion. See *Opinion polls.*

Pollutants, environmental. See *Environmental pollutants.*

Pollution. See *Acid rain; Agricultural chemicals; Air pollution; Atmospheric contamination; Carcinogens; Contamination; Environmental effects; Environmental impacts; Environmental pollutants; Environmental pollution; Environmental protection; Environmental stress; Food contamination; Greenhouse effect; Hazardous wastes; Herbicides; Industrial wastes; Medical wastes; Noise (sounds); Nuclear waste; Oil spills; Pesticides; Pollution control; Sewage; Sick building syndrome; Tobacco smoke pollution; Waste disposal; Waste to energy; Waste spills; Waste transport; Water pollution.*

Pollution, air. See *Air pollution.*

Pollution, air syndrome. See *Sick building syndrome.*

Pollution, environmental. See *Environmental pollution.*

Pollution, tobacco smoke. See *Tobacco smoke pollution.*

Pollution, water. See *Water pollution.*

Pollution control. Pollut(e,ed,ants,ing,ion) control. Superfund. Resource conservation and Recovery Act. Reus(e,ed,ing, able,ables). Recycl(e,ed,ing,able,ables). Returnable beverage container(s). *Choose from:* pollut(e,ed,ants,ing,ion), environmental exposure, pesticide residue(s), waste product(s), litter(ed,ing), contaminat(ed,ing,ant, ants), dirt(y), soot(y), smok(e,ing,y), unhealthy condition(s), unhygienic, exhaust(s), dust(s), smog, ozone, heavy metal(s), nuclear waste(s), toxic metal(s), tobacco smoke, toxic chemical(s), carbon monoxide, emission(s), acid rain, herbicide(s), effluent(s), incinerat(ors,ion), trash, spill(s), toxic(ity), carcinogen(s,ic), hazard(ous) *with:* control(led,ling,s), abat(e,ed,ing,ement), regulat(e,ed,ing,ory,ion,ions), manag(e, ed,ing,ement), prevent(ed,ing,ion), remediat(e,ed,ing,ion), audit(ed,ing,s),

minimiz(e,ed,ing,ation), disposal, protect(ed,ion,ing), polic(y,ies). *See also* Air pollution; Alternative energy; Conservation of natural resources; Containers; Containment of biohazards; Decontamination; Drinking water; Earth; Ecology; Environment; Environmental pollutants; Environmental pollution; Environmental protection; Environmental stress; Environmentalism; Medical wastes; Nuclear safety; Nuclear waste; Oil spills; Quality of life; Recycling; Restoration ecology; Tobacco smoke pollution; Waste disposal; Waste to energy; Water pollution; Water purification; Water reuse.

Polyamory. Polyamor(y,ous,ist,ists). Polyamour(y,ous,ist,ists). Polyfidelity. Non-monogam(y,ous). Nonmonogam(y,ous). Loving more. Multipartner relat(ing,ion,ionship). Multiple partner(s,ed). *Consider also:* open marriage(s). *See also* Group marriage; Polyandry; Polygamy; Polygyny.

Polyandry. Polyandr(y,ous,ic,ist,ists). Two husband(s). More than one husband. Anticipatory levirate. *Choose from:* attenuated polyandry, adelphic polyandry, fraternal polyandry. *See also* Polyamory; Polygamy; Polygyny.

Polyarchy. Polyarch(y,ies,ical). Multiplicity of elites. *Consider also:* particracy, pluralist(ic) democrac(y,ies), shared power, democratic pluralism, social balance of power. *See also* Political elites; Political power; Political systems.

Polydipsia. Polydips(ia,ic). Excessive thirst. Excessive drinking. Induced hyperdipsia. Schedule induced drinking. Food related hyperdipsia. *See also* Operant conditioning.

Polyfidelity. See *Polyamory.*

Polygamy. Polygam(y,ous,ist,ists). Polygyn(y,ous,ist,ists). Polyandr(y,ous, ist,ists). Bigam(y,ous,ist,ists). Co-wife. Cowife. Co-wives. Cowives. Multiple wives. Group marriage(s). Cenogam(y, ous,ist,ists). Plural marriage(s). *See also* Alternative family forms; Marriage; Monogamy; Polyamory; Polyandry; Polygyny; Serial polygamy.

Polygamy, serial. See *Serial polygamy.*

Polygenism. See *Evolution.*

Polyglot. See *Multilingualism.*

Polygraphs. See *Lie detection.*

Polygyny. Polygyn(y,ous,ist,ists). Plural wives. Co-wife. Multiple wives. Sororal polygyny. *Consider also:* polygam(y, ous,ist,ists), bigam(y,ous,ist,ists). *See also* Polyamory; Polyandry; Polygamy.

Polymorphisms, single nucleotide. See *Single nucleotide polymorphisms.*

Polytheism. See *Paganism.*

Polytheism (pantheism). See *Pantheism (polytheism).*

Pongidae. See *Apes.*

Pools, car. See *Car pools.*

Pools, insurance. See *Insurance pools.*

Poor. See *Homeless; Low income; Lower class; Poverty; Women living in poverty.*

Poor, near. See *Low income.*

Pop art. Pop art. Neo-Dada(ism,ist,ists). *Consider also:* Andy Warhol, Roy Lichtenstein, Claes Oldenburg, Peter Blake, Richard Hamilton. *See also* Arts; Dadaism; Modern art; Popular culture; Surrealism.

Popular culture. Pop(ular) culture. Mass culture. Masscult. Mass taste(s). Pop art. Lowbrow. Popular media. Popular music. Bourgeois culture. Popular press. Pop chart(s). Contemporary culture. Middle class culture. Middle class values. Working class culture. *Consider also:* rock 'n roll, Beatles, Rolling Stones, rock culture, circus(es), paperback(s), teddy bear(s), kitsch, juke box(es), punk, popular song(s), comic book(s), popular science, designer jeans, garage sale(s), screen image(s), professional sports, soap opera(s), greeting card(s), break dancing, fotonovela(s), movie(s), folk culture, country music, folk music, thriller(s), jazz, slang, melodrama, music hall(s), comed(y,ies). *See also* Arts; Avant-garde; Bawdy songs; Bluegrass music; Blues (music); Circus performers; Collages; Convenience Foods; Countercultures; Country and western music; Cultural literacy; Cybercafes; Cybercommunities; Cyberpunk culture; Decorative arts; Depravity; Detective and mystery television programs; Disco music; Eating establishments; Electronic instruments; Electronic music; Entertainers; Entertainment; Extreme sports; Fashions; Fads; Fiction; Folk culture; Happening (art); Heavy metal (music); Horror tales; Jazz; Jazz dance; Junk food; Mass media; Mass media effects; Mass media violence; Mass society; Materialism; Music; Musical ads; Pop art; Popular literature; Popular music; Public opinion; Soap operas; Social thought; Sports; Styles; Television; Television plays; Television programs; Western fiction; Winter sports; Youth culture.

Popular literature. Popular literature. Popular fiction. Popular press. Dime novel(s). Street literature. Romance novel(s). Mystery stor(y,ies). Serial novel(s). Pocket book(s). Mass market paperback(s). Penny dreadful(s). Potboiler(s). Roman a clef. Fan magazine(s). Scandal sheet(s). *Choose from:* lowbrow, kitsch(y), middlebrow, popular, bourgeois, science fiction, fantasy, mystery, horror, romance, military *with:* fiction, literature, reading, book(s), edition(s), E-text, publishing. *Consider also:* comic book(s), photoplay edition(s). *See also* Ballads; Horror tales; Mass media; Popular culture; Tabloids.

Popular music. Popular music. Pop music. Popular song(s). Hit tune(s). Top tune(s). Hit parade. Hit song(s). Top 40. *Consider also:* Stephen Foster, Jerome Kern, Irving Berlin, George Gershwin, Cole Porter, Richard Rodgers, Vaudeville, nickelodeon(s), Tin Pan Alley, Leroy Anderson, Kingston Trio, Peter, Paul and Mary, Bob Dylan, Joan Baez, rock and roll, Elvis Presley, the Beatles, Rolling Stones, Bing Crosby, Frank Sinatra, Doris Day, Nat King Cole, Louis Armstrong, etc. *See also* Afro-American music; Ballads; Big band; Disco music; Folk music; Heavy metal (music); Jazz; Musicals; Popular culture; Rhythm and blues; Rock and roll; Rock music.

Popular songs. See *Popular music.*

Popular sovereignty. Popular sovereignty. Legitimate political authority. Government accountability. Govern(ed,ing, ment) by consent. Consent of the governed. Democra(cy,tic). *See also* Autonomy (government); Democracy; Political self determination; Sovereignty.

Popularity. Popular(ity). *Choose from:* social(ly) *with:* desirab(le,ility), approval, esteem(ed), acceptab(le,ility), recognition. Pop chart(s). Popularity rating(s). Interpersonal attraction. Attribut(e,ed,ing,ion) positive trait(s). Personal prestige. Sociometric status. Admired. High social status. Widespread acceptance. Well-liked. Well-received. Beloved. Adored. Celebrated. Celebrit(y, ies). Renown(ed). Lioniz(ed,ation). Acclaim(ed). Idoliz(e,ed,ing,ation). Hero(es). *See also* Friendship; Peer relations; Prestige; Social acceptance; Social desirability; Social status.

Population. Population(s). Populace. Inhabitant(s). Resident(s). People. Folk. Census. Depopulat(e,ed,ing,ion). Occupant(s). Head count. Demograph(y,ic). Overpopulat(ed,ing,ion). Community sample. Community survey. General public. Citizen(s,ry). *See also* Birthrate; Capitation fee; Citizens; Demographic changes; Demography; Emigration; Family planning; Fertility; Geographic distribution; Geographic mobility; Heterogeneity; Homogeneity; Immigration; Indigenous populations; Inhabitants; Migration; Mortality rates; Population characteristics; Population decline; Population growth; Social density; Voters.

Population (statistics). Population(s). Subject population(s). Sample(s).

Respondent(s). Survey respon(ses, dents). Subpopulation(s). Universe(s). Sampling. Distribution. Confidence interval(s). Confidence level(s). Census(es). Statistical area(s). Geographic distribution. National sample(s). Local sample(s). *See also* Research design; Sampling; Statistical data.

Population, farm. See *Agricultural workers; Rural population.*

Population, rural. See *Rural population.*

Population, urban. See *Urban population.*

Population, world. See *World population.*

Population change. See *Demographic changes.*

Population characteristics. Population characteristics. *Choose from:* population, demographic, census *with:* characteristic(s), profile(s), data, variable(s), type(s), pattern(s), factor(s), background(s). *See also* Age groups; Characteristics; Cohort analysis; Demography; Group composition; Health transition; Population; Qualities; Races; Sex ratio; Socioeconomic status.

Population control. Population control. *Choose from:* population, fertility, birth rate *with:* control(led,ling), regulat(e, ed,ing,ion), limit(ed,ing,ation,s), disincentive(s). *Consider also:* antinatalist polic(y,ies), zero population growth. *See also* Birth control; Family planning; Population policy; Zero population growth.

Population decline. Population decline. Depopulat(e,ed,ing,ion). Outward migrat(e,ed,ing,ion). *Choose from:* fertility, population, tax base, resident(s), birth rate(s), demographic, size(s) of famil(y,ies) *with:* declin(e,ed,ing), shrink(ing), losing, migrat(e,ed,ing, ion,ions), falling, below replacement level. *See also* Emigration; Family planning; Fertility decline; Population control; Population policy; Zero population growth.

Population density. Population density. *Choose from:* populat(e,ed,ing,ion,ions) *with:* density, dense(ly), concentrat(e,ed, ing,ion,ions), distribution, size, imbalance(s), growth, depression, count, reduction, dynamic(s), intensity, diffusion, dispersion. *Consider also:* species distribution, overpopulation, crowding, sparsely populated, community size, demography, personal space. *See also* Community size; Crowding; Demography; Environmental effects; Overpopulation; Privacy.

Population distribution. Population distribution. *Choose from:* population, inhabitant(s), resident(s), people, occupant(s), demograph(y,ic) *with:* distribut(ed,ion), concentration(s), deconcentration, change(s), dispersion,

mobility, migration(s), redistribution, model(s), pattern(s). *Consider also:* internal migration, migration pattern(s), residential mobility, urbanization pattern(s), settlement pattern(s), rural urban distribution. *See also* Anthropogeography; Demographic changes; Geographic distribution; Internal migration; Land settlement; Migration; Migration patterns; Population characteristics; Relocation; Residential patterns; Rural population; Settlement patterns; Sex ratio; Urban population; World population.

Population dynamics. Population dynamics. *Choose from:* population, demograph(y,ic,ics) *with:* dynamics, change(s), cycle(s), fluctuation(s), stability, stable, unstable, instability, movement(s), trend(s). Survivorship. Life tables. Demographic rate(s). *Consider also:* population growth, birth rate, migration, population distribution, fertility, mortality, family mobility, relocation. *See also* Birthrate; Demographic changes; Emigration; Fertility; Geographic mobility; Health transition; Immigration; Migration patterns; Mortality rates.

Population explosion. See *Population growth; Overpopulation.*

Population genetics. Population genetics. Anthropogenetic(s). *Choose from:* genetic(s), evolution, evolv(e,ed,ing), heredit(y,ary,able), breeding, inbreeding, outbreeding, inherit(ed,ing,able,ability), Mendelian, allele(s), gene pool(s), genetic distance(s), genetic affinit(y,ies), genealog(y,ical), immunogenetic(s), cytogenetic(s), hybrid(s,ization), natural selection, survival of the fittest, Darwinism, phenotype(s), genotype(s) *with:* population(s), demograph(y,ic), subpopulation(s), ethnic(ity), rac(e,ial), blood group(s), anthropolog(y,ical), human difference(s), indigenous, polymorphism. *See also* Anthropogeography; Evolution; Genetics.

Population growth. Population growth. *Choose from:* population, demograph(ic, y), birth rate(s), fertility *with:* grow(th, ing), ris(e,ing), expand(ed,ing), increase(s,d), explosion, exploding, Malthusian. *Consider also:* fecundity, fertility rate(s), overpopulat(ed,ion), population bomb, pronatalism. *See also* Birthrate; Boom towns; Demographic changes; Family size; Fertility; Malthusian theory; Overpopulation.

Population growth, zero. See *Zero population growth.*

Population mobility. See *Migration.*

Population planning. See *Population policy.*

Population policy. Population polic(y,ies). Demographic policy. Population debate. Population planning. Population project(s). Sterilization polic(y,ies). Population redistribution polic(y,ies). Migration polic(y,ies). Immigration polic(y,ies). Naturalization act of 1952. Immigration act of 1965. Political measures to increase population. Government regulation of procreation. *Choose from:* population, fertility, pronatalist, demographic, migration, immigration, family planning, birth control, sterilization, procreation *with:* polic(y,ies), law(s), regulation(s), legislation. *Consider also:* eugenics. *See also* Abortion; Birth control; Eugenics; Family policy; Malthusian theory; Overpopulation; Policy; Population control; Social legislation; Zero population growth.

Population redistribution. See *Internal migration.*

Population statistics. See *Census; Population (statistics).*

Population surveillance. See *Surveillance of citizens.*

Population surveys. See *Demographic surveys.*

Population transfer. Population transfer(s, red,ring). *Choose from:* population, resident(s), refugee(s), individual(s), famil(y,ies), people(s), nomad(s), communit(y,ies), citizen(s) *with:* transfer(s,red,ring), resettl(e,ed,ing, ement), uproot(ed,ing), deport(ed,ing, ation,ations), exil(e,ed,ing), military conscription, forced sedentarization, transplant(ed,ing). *Consider also:* population movement(s), removed from their homelands. *See also* Deportation; Emigration; Homeless; Immigration; Migration; Refugees; Relocation.

Population turnaround. See *Return migration.*

Populations, indigenous. See *Indigenous populations.*

Populations at risk. See *High risk persons.*

Populism. Populis(m,t). *Consider also:* People's party, Narodniks, Land and Freedom party, People's Will, Black Distribution, Social Credit party, peasant part(y,ies), moral majority, anti-intellectualism. *See also* Anti-intellectualism; Interest groups; Masses; Political action; Political ideologies; Protest movements.

Pornography. Porn(o,ographic,ography). Smut. Centerfold(s). Dirty picture(s). Explicit(ly) sexual stimuli. Pictures of sexual act(s). X-rated. Sin strip(s). Strip joint(s). Peep show(s). Exotic danc(ing,er,ers). Sexually oriented advertising. Indecen(t,cy). Bawdy. Lewd. Obscen(e,ity). Hustler magazine.

Pos(e,ed,ing) nude. Sex shop(s). Cheesecake. Dial-a-porn. Playboy. Penthouse. Raree show(s). Peep show(s). *Choose from:* obscen(e,ity), indecen(t,cy), licentious, adult, X-rated, erotic, suggestive, nude, sex oriented, porn(o,ographic,ography), salacious, explicit sex, sensual(ly), bawdy, pedophilic, sexually provocative, hard core, prurien(t,ce) *with:* picture(s), movie(s), film(s), grafitti, video(s), literature, book(s), book(s,stores), periodical(s), show(s), magazine(s), material(s), radio, club(s), art, poetry, poem(s), riddle(s), joke(s), doggerel, stor(y,ies), verse(s), advertis(ments,ing), theater(s), telephone(s), phone(s), 900 number(s). *Consider also:* strip joint(s), erotic club(s), massage parlor(s), topless bar(s). *See also* Censorship; Cybersex; Depravity; Erotica; Images of women; Indecent communications; Information policy; Obscenity; Prurience; Publications; Sex offenses; Sexism; Sexual deviations; Sexual exploitation; Vulgarity.

Portents. See *Omens.*

Portfolio workers. See *Contract labor.*

Portraits. Portrait(s,ure). Likeness(es). Pictorial representation(s). Painting(s). Bust(s). Death mask(s). Cameo(s). *See also* Arts; Busts; Coin portraits; Photography.

Portraits, coin. See *Coin portraits.*

Portrayal, media. See *Media portrayal.*

Ports. Port(s). Seaport(s). Port facilit(y,ies). *Consider also:* shipyard(s), harbor(s,age), dry dock(s), torpedo station(s), anchorage, home port(s). *See also* Coast defenses; Dry docks; Harbors; Navy yards and naval stations; Piers; Ships.

Position, social. See *Social status.*

Positions, applications for. See *Job applicants.*

Positive evidence. Positive evidence. Direct evidence. Eye witness testimony. Proof positive. *Consider also:* expert witness(es), sufficient evidence. *See also* Circumstantial evidence; Extenuating circumstances; Evidence; Sufficient evidence; Witnesses.

Positive reinforcement. Positive reinforcement. Praise. Reward(s,ed). Earned approval. *Choose from:* appetitive, food, token(s) *with:* condition(ed,ing), reinforc(e,ed,ing,ement). *Consider also:* positive feedback. *See also* Flattery; Praise; Reinforcement.

Positive sanctions. Positive sanctions. Endors(e,ed,ing,ment). Authoriz(e,ed, ing,ation). Countenance. Permission(s). Permit(ted,ting). Validat(ed,ing,ion). Accreditat(ed,ing,ion). Certif(y,ied, ication). Legaliz(e,ed,ing,ation).

Consent(s). Imprimatur. Stamp of approval. Reward(s). Confirm(ed,ing, ation). Reinforc(e,ed,ing,ement). Ratif(y,ied,ication). Underwrit(e,ing, ten). Acquiesc(e,ing,ent). Support(ed, ing). Approv(e,ed,al). Consent(ed,ing). *See also* Approval; Certification; Legalization of drugs; Reinforcement.

Positive transfer. Positive transfer. *Choose from:* transfer *with:* learning, training. *Consider also:* crossover effect, cross modal transfer. *See also* Transfer (learning).

Positivism. See *Empiricism.*

Positivism, logical. See *Logical positivism.*

Possession. See *Ownership.*

Possession, demonic. See *Spirit possession.*

Possession, spirit. See *Spirit possession.*

Possessions. See *Personal property.*

Possessiveness. Possessive(ness). Greed(y, iness). Grasp(ed,ing). Cling(ing). Jealous(y,ness). Control(led,ling). Domineer(ing). Overprotective(ness). Mistrust(ing,ful). Distrust(ing,ful). *See also* Father child relations; Jealousy; Misers; Mother child relations; Overprotection; Parent child relations; Selfishness (stingy); Sexual violence; Spouse abuse.

Possibilities. Possibilit(y,ies). Feasib(le, ility). Likelihood. Potentialit(y,ies). Practibilit(y,ies). Probab(le,leness,ility). Prospect(s). Workab(le,ility). Favorable odds. Favorable chance. Realizab(le, ility). Attainab(le,ility). *See also* Barriers; Constraints; Contingency; Opportunities.

Possible art. See *Conceptual art.*

Possible worlds. See *Plurality of worlds.*

POSSLQ. See *Cohabitation.*

Post-baby boom generation. Post-baby boom generation. Twentysomething(s). Generation X. Generation Xer(s). GenX. Xer(s). Baby buster(s). Baby boomlet(s). Boomerang bab(y,ies). Baby Bust Generation. 18-29 years old. Under 30. Born 1965 to 1977. *See also* Baby boom generation; College students; Generation gap; Young adults.

Post-Communism. Post-Communis(m,t). Excommunist(s). Postcommunist democratization. Post-Deng Xiaoping. Post-Soviet. End of the cold war. *Consider also:* transition to a capitalist economy, Yeltsin, etc. *See also* Countries in transition; Decommunization; Democratization; Market economy; Nationalism; Privatization.

Post-Impressionism. Post-Impressionis(m, t,ts). Postimpressionis(m,t,ts). Neo-Impressionis(m,t,ts). Divisionism. Pointillism. *Consider also:* Paul Cezanne, Paul Gauguin, Vincent van

Gogh, Georges Seurat, Paul Signac, etc. *See also* Expressionism (art); Impressionism (art); Modern art.

Post-object art. See *Conceptual art.*

Post traumatic stress disorders. Post traumatic stress disorder(s). *Choose from:* combat, battle, trauma(tic), repatriation, survivor(s), posttrauma(tic), post- trauma(tic), post-Vietnam, accident, war, delayed stress, veterans, trauma induced, concentration camp(s), prisoner(s) of war *with:* neuros(is,es), stress disorder(s), amnesia, emotional sequelae, psychological effect(s), trichotillomania, psychoneuros(is,es), psychopathology, psychological aftereffect(s), conversion hysteria. *Consider also:* combat disorder(s), repatriation syndrome, survivor syndrome, post Vietnam syndrome, shell shock(ed). *See also* Anxiety disorders; Concentration camp syndrome; Emotional trauma; Stress reactions; Survivors; War victims.

Post-viral fatigue syndrome. See *Chronic fatigue syndrome.*

Postal psychotherapy. Postal psychotherap(y,ies). Correspondence therap(y,ies). *Choose from:* postal, correspondence, mail *with:* psychotherap(y,ies,eutic), therap(y,ies,eutic), advice, counsel(ed,ing). *See also* Letters (correspondence); Psychotherapy; Written communications.

Postal service. Postal service(s). *Choose from:* mail, postal, courier *with:* service(s), deliver(y,ies). *Consider also:* post office(s), express mail, overnight deliver(y,ies), overnight mail. Postage stamp(s). Post Office(s). Universal Postal Union. Rural free delivery. *See also* Letter carrier(s); Letters (correspondence); Mail room; Public services.

Posters. See *Broadsides.*

Postgraduate students. Postgraduate student(s). Postdoctoral student(s). *Consider also:* intern(s). *See also* Students.

Postgraduate training. Postgraduate training. *Choose from:* postgraduate, continuing, postdoctoral *with:* education, training, retraining. *See also* Continuing education.

Postindustrial societies. Postindustrial societ(y,ies). Postindustrialism. Advanced industrial democrac(y,ies). Neoindustrial societ(y,ies). Information societ(y,ies). Postmaterialism. *Choose from:* post-economic, post-capitalist, post-maturity, post-modern, technetronic, technocratic *with:* societ(y,ies). *Consider also:* service econom(y,ies). *See also* Complex societies; Community networks (computer); Deindustrialization; Industrial societies; Information

society; Teledemocracy; Urbanization; Western society.

Postmodernism. Postmodern(ism,ity,ist, ists). Post-modern(ism,ity,ist,ists). Postmodern thought. Postmodern aesthetic(s). Postmodern consumer society. *Consider also:* hypermodernism, eclectic(ism), pastiche(s), parod(y,ies), antihero(es), antinovel(s), magic realism, relativity of meaning(s), simulacr(a,um), new wave cinema, discontinuity, disembodiment, decenter(ed,ing), fragment(ed,ation), ambigu(ous,uity,uities), intertextual(ity), self-reflexivity, indetermina(cy,teness), satir(e,ical), iron(y,ic,ical), Jacques Derrida, Michel Foucault, Jean-Francois Lyotard, Jean Baudrillard, Umberto Eco, etc. *See also* Absurd; Alienation; Anti-science movement; Critical theory; Deconstruction; Experimental literature; Experimental poetry; Fragmentation (experience); Indeterminism; Intertextuality; Irony; Literary movements; Logocentrism; Modern architecture; Modern civilization; Patchwork; Relativism; Satire; Surrealism.

Postnatal care. Postnatal care. *Choose from:* postnatal, after delivery, postpartum, perinatal, neonat(e,es,al) *with:* care, nursing. *See also* Bottle feeding; Breast feeding; Postnatal period; Pregnancy.

Postnatal depression. See *Postpartum depression.*

Postnatal period. Postnatal period. Puerperium. *Choose from:* postpartum, postnatal, puerperal *with:* period. *See also* Postnatal care; Postpartum depression; Pregnancy.

Postoperative care. Postoperative care. *Choose from:* postoperative, postsurgical, following surgery, after surgery *with:* care, treatment(s), nutrition, management, followup, nursing, monitoring. *See also* Nursing care; Postoperative complications; Posttreatment followup.

Postoperative complications. Postoperative complication(s). *Choose from:* postsurgical, surgery, surgical, postoperative, postcardiotomy, postgastrectomy, amputation(s), tonsillectom(y,ies), appendectom(y,ies), cholecystectom(y, ies), hysterectom(y,ies), colostom(y,ies), vasectom(y,ies), pericardiotom(y,ies), etc. *with:* pain, seizure(s), complication(s), mortality, psychosis, symptom(s), dysfunction, side effect(s), delirium, shock, infection(s), dehiscence. *See also* Postoperative care.

Postpartum depression. Postpartum depression. Baby blues. *Choose from:* postpartum, puerperal, postnatal, maternity, antenatal, post childbirth, childbirth related *with:* depression(s), mood change(s), mood swing(s),

mood(y,iness), blue(s), emotional disturbance(s), psychos(is,es), psychotic, adjustment, stress(es), distress(es), mental illness(s). *See also* Postnatal period; Depression (psychology).

Posts, military. See *Military bases; Garrisons.*

Postsurgical complications. See *Postoperative complications.*

Posttesting. Posttest(s,ed,ing). *Choose from:* post *with:* test(s,ed,ing), measur(e,ed,es,ing), questionnaire(s). Posttrial(s). *Consider also:* retest(ed,ing, s), repeated measure(s). *See also* Measurement; Test taking.

Posttraumatic stress disorders. See *Post traumatic stress disorders.*

Posttreatment followup. Posttreatment followup. Aftercare. Catamnes(sis,tic). Relapse prevention. *Choose from:* posttreatment, postsurgical, posthospital, postdischarge, postoperative *with:* followup(s), follow up(s), following up, monitoring, assessment(s). *Consider also:* patient(s), therap(y,ies), treatment(s), psychotherap(y,ies), medical, surgical, outpatient(s) or specific treatments or therapies *with:* followup(s), follow up(s), following up. *See also* Postoperative complications; Treatment outcome.

Postulates. Postulate(s). Axiom(s). Principle(s). Theorem(s). Truth(s). Presupposition(s). Premise(s). Assumption(s). Proposition(s). Precept(s). Supposition(s). Hypothes(is,es). *See also* Assumptions; Axioms; Dictums; Hypotheses; Hypothetical; Research methods; Researcher expectations.

Posture. Posture(s). Stance. Pose. Postur(e,al,ing). Body tilt(ed,ing). Bearing. *Consider also:* kinesic(s), equilibrium reaction(s), head righting, tilt reaction(s), prone, semiprone, inclined position(s), standing tall, standing erect, body position(s), orthosta(sis,tic,tism), supine, slouch(ed, ing), reclin(ed,ing), head erect, body attitude(s). *See also* Body language; Physique; Posture in worship.

Posture, liturgical. See *Posture in worship.*

Posture in worship. Posture in worship. *Choose from:* worship(ped,ping), religio(us,n), pray(er,ers,ing,ed), monastic, ritual(ly) *with:* posture(s), bow(ed,ing) head(s), physical(ly) lower(ed,ing), stand(ing), stood, kneel(ed,ing). *See also* Body language; Posture; Prayer; Religious behavior; Religious rituals.

Postures, threat. See *Threat postures.*

Pot, melting. See *Melting pot.*

Potential, achievement. See *Achievement potential.*

Potential, human movement. See *Human potential movement.*

Potential dropouts. Potential dropout(s). High risk student(s). *Choose from:* potential, prone, likel(y,ihood), predict(ed,ing,ion,ions,or,ors), tendenc(y,ies), intention(s), intend(ed, ing), forecast(ed,ing) *with:* dropout(s), drop(ped,ping) out, school leav(ing,er, ers), leav(e,ing) school, client withdrawal, discharge(s) against medical advice. *See also* High risk persons; Patient dropouts; Student dropouts.

Potential employment. See *Employability.*

Potentiation, drug. See *Drug interactions.*

Potions, love. See *Aphrodisiacs.*

Potpourri. See *Patchwork.*

Pottery. Pottery. Clayware. Earthenware. *Choose from:* clay, earthen, ceramic *with:* vessels, cup(s), plate(s). *Consider also:* pot(s,ting,ter,ters,tery), stoneware, ceramic(s). *See also* Antiquities (objects); Ceramics; Collectibles; Crafts; Pre-Columbian art.

Poultry. Poultry. Chick(s,en,ens). Hen(s). Rooster(s). Fowl(s). Pullet(s). Capon(s). Turkey(s). Duck(s). Goose. Geese. Gosling(s). Gander(s). Pheasant(s). Guinea fowl(s). Dove(s). Pigeon(s). *Consider also:* gallinacea, natatores, columbidae. *See also* Animals; Birds; Chickens; Cocks.

Poverty. Poverty. Poor. Indigen(t,ce, cy). Low income(s). Impoverish(ed,ment). Welfare famil(y,ies). Disadvantage(d, ment). Homeless(ness). Vagran(t,ts,cy). Lower class. Low status. Low socioeconomic status. Need(y,iness). Economic disadvantagement. Economic(ally) insecur(e,ity). Economic plight(s). Economic(ally) depress(ed,ion). Slum(s). Ghetto(es). Privation. Destitut(e,ion). Penniless(ness). Pauper(s,ize,ized,izing,ization). Penur(y,ious,iousness). Impecunious. Economic hardship. Poverty area(s). Underprivileged. Beggar(s). *See also* Adversity; Almshouses; Antipoverty programs; Developing countries; Disadvantaged; Economic dependence; Economic underdevelopment; Hardships; High risk borrowers; Homeless; Indigence; Low income; Minimum wage; Poverty areas; Relative deprivation; Underclass; Unemployment; Vagrants; Women living in poverty.

Poverty, feminization of. See *Women living in poverty.*

Poverty, urban. See *Urban poverty.*

Poverty, women living in. See *Women living in poverty.*

Poverty areas. Poverty area(s). Tenement(s). Skid row. Bowery. Slum(s). Shantytown(s). Inner cit(y,ies). Milieu of poverty. Depressed area(s). Redlin(e,ed,ing). Ghetto(es,ization). Appalachia. Low income area(s). Street corner district(s). Favela(s). *Choose from:* low income, poor, poverty, depressed, transitional, ethnic, Black, minority, disadvantaged, segregated, redlined, declining *with:* area(s), count(y,ies), communit(y,ies), neighborhood(s), school district(s), barrio(s). *See also* Disadvantaged; Environmental racism; Geographic distribution; Human ecology; Inner cities; Minority groups, Political geography; Poverty; Racial segregation; Slums.

Poverty programs. See *Antipoverty programs.*

Power. Power(s,ful,fulness). Control(led, ling). Dominan(ce,t). Strong. Strength. Authority. Self determination. Command(ing). Efficac(y,ious,iousness). Willpower. Influen(ce,es,ed,cing,tial). Social control. Interpersonal control. Empower(ed,ing,ment). Coerc(ion,ive). Machiavellian(ism). Omnipoten(ce,t). Command(ed,ing) the situation. Tak(e,en,ing) charge. Took charge. Hierach(y,ies). Gain(ed,ing) compliance. Master(ing). Dominat(e,ed,ing,ion). Carte blanche. Clout. Ascendan(t,cy). Poten(cy,t). Supremacy. Imperial(ism, istic). Might(y,iness). Force(ful,fulness). Overpower(ed,ing). Impregnab(ility,le). Asymmetrical relation(s,ships). Asymmetrical interaction. Power structure(s). Pecking order(s). Divine right(s). Consent of the governed. *Choose from:* associative coordination, hierarchical coordination *with:* leadership. *Consider also:* political, Black, individual, legitimate, moral, traditional, charismatic, rational, legal, hereditary, arbitrary, competitive *with:* power. *Consider also:* perceived control, locus of control, perception(s) of control, balance of power, checks and balances, constraint, dominance - dependence relation(s), proactive - reactive relation(s), exploiter(s). *See also* Authority (power); Bargaining power; Black power; Carte blanche; Coercion; Conflict; Dominance; Dominance subordination; Family power; Formal social control; Influence; Informal social control; Leadership; Mana; Omnipotence; Organizational power; Personal independence; Political bosses; Political power; Politicians; Politics; Power elite; Power sharing; Power structure; State power.

Power (authority). See *Authority (power).*

Power, abuse of. See *Abuse of power.*

Power, air. See *Air power.*

Power, atomic. See *Nuclear energy; Nuclear power plants.*

Power, balance of. See *Balance of power.*

Power, bargaining. See *Bargaining power.*

Power, black. See *Black power.*

Power, community. See *Community power.*

Power, corporate. See *Organizational power.*

Power, family. See *Family power.*

Power, gray. See *Gray power.*

Power, judicial. See *Judicial power.*

Power, military. See *Military power.*

Power, naval. See *Sea power.*

Power, nuclear. See *Nuclear energy.*

Power, organizational. See *Organizational power.*

Power, parental. See *Family power.*

Power, political. See *Political power.*

Power, purchasing. See *Purchasing power.*

Power, sea. See *Sea power.*

Power, social. See *Power.*

Power, state. See *State power.*

Power, water. See *Water power.*

Power, wind. See *Wind power.*

Power elite. Power elite(s). Governing elite(s). Political elite(s). Mover(s) and shaker(s). Interlocking directorate(s). National elite(s). Oligarch(y,ies). Dominant group(s). Corporate power. Political party leader(s). Directorate(s). Board(s) of director(s). Executive(s). Boss(es). Top management. Presidium. Power broker(s). Kingmaker(s). Power behind the throne. Head(s) of state. Ruling faction(s). Dominant class(es). Labor union leader(s). Elected political officeholder(s). Wall streeter(s). Elected executive(s). Wielder(s) of power. Ruling elite(s). Tribal chief(s). Hereditary ruler(s). Civil religious hierarch(y, ies). Plutocrac(y,ies). *Choose from:* corporate, political, party, financial, banking, military, organization(al), administrative, bureaucratic, managerial, govern(ment,ing) *with:* leader(s,ship), elite(s), hierarch(y,ies), chair(men,man, woman,women), chairperson(s), executive(s), clique(s), in-group(s). *See also* Economic elites; Elites; Elitism (government); Leadership; Oligarchy; Opinion leaders; Political bosses; Political elites; Political power; Power structure; Ruling class.

Power plants, electric. See *Electric power plants.*

Power plants, nuclear. See *Nuclear power plants.*

Power sharing. Power sharing. Codetermination. *Choose from:* power, control(s,led,ling), govern(ance,ment, ing) *with:* shar(e,ed,ing), participat(ive, ory), collaborat(e,ed,ing,ive,ion), collective(s). *Consider also:* coalition government(s), advisory committee(s). *See also* Alliances; Coalitions; Collective security; Control; Cooperation; Cultural pluralism; Egalitarian families; Employee ownership; Employee stock ownership plans; Empowerment; Federations; Governing; Industrial democracy; International alliances; Mergers; Participative decision making; Participative management; Partners; Power; Preference voting; Separation of powers; Social justice; Stability; States' rights; Worker control; Worker participation.

Power structure. Power structure(s). Locus of power. Power relation(s,ship,ships). Decision making authority. Pecking order(s). Power broker(s). Dominance dependence relation(s,ship,ships). Superordinat(e,ion). *Choose from:* power, decision making, authority, control, influence *with:* structure(s), hierarch(y,ies), directorate(s), model(s), centraliz(ed,ation), decentraliz(ed,ation), channel(s), pyramid(s), stratif(ied, ication). *See also* Administrators; Authority (officials); Corporate control; Elites; Dominance subordination; Elected officials; Elites; Elitism (government); Governing boards; Heads of state; Interlocking directorates; Legislative bodies; Management structures; Managers; Middle level managers; Organizational politics; Organizational structure; Power elite; Political elites; Presidents; Priests and priestly classes (anthropology); Privilege; Ruling class; Social stratification.

Powerlessness. Powerless(ness). Impotent. Weak(ness,nesses). Incapable. Inability. Futil(e,ity). Ineffective(ness). Useless(ness). Alienat(e,ed,ing,ion). Estrange(d,ment). Dissociat(ed,ion). Hopeless(ness). Meaningless(ness). Disaffected. Dispossessed. Emasculat(ed,ion). Disaffiliat(ed,ion). Dehumaniz(ed,ation). Social detachment. Kafkaesque. *Consider also:* anomie, rootless(ness), helplessness, psychological deprivation, depersonalization, unrelatedness. *See also* Abjection; Alienation; Apathy; Deprivation; Disengagement; Existentialism; Hopelessness; Learned helplessness; Noninvolvement; Oppression; Pessimism; Political repression; Social isolation.

Powers, delegation of. See *Delegation of powers.*

Powers, discretionary. See *Discretionary powers.*

Powers, executive. See *Executive powers.*

Powers, governmental. See *Governmental powers.*

Powers, legislative. See *Legislative powers.*

Powers, separation of. See *Separation of powers.*

Practical experience. Practical experience. Clinical experience. Internship(s). Office practice. Supervised farm practice. Apprenticeship(s). Preceptor program(s). Practicum(s). Field experience. Fieldwork education. Mentorship(s). Clerkship(s). Extern(ship,ships). Extramural training. Extramural experience. Practice teaching. *See also* Expertise; Fieldwork; Internships.

Practical theology. Practical theology. Responsible grace. Missiological pastoral care. Practical ontology. *Consider also:* practical philosophy, moral theology. *See also* Casuistry; Ethics; Exclusivity (Religion); Good works (theology); Liberation theology; Relativism; Religious beliefs; Theology.

Practice (repetition). Practic(e,ed,es,ing). Experience. Training. Drilling. Pattern(ed) drill(s). Repetition(s). Rehearsal(s). Rehears(e,ed,ing). Repeated sessions. Review(ed,ing). Reinforc(e,ed,ing,ement). Exercise(s,d). Stud(y,ied,ying). Workout(s). Warm-up(s). *See also* Repetition; Rote learning; Teaching methods.

Practice, massed. See *Massed practice.*

Practice, private. See *Private practice.*

Practices (methods). Practice(s). Praxis. Custom(s). Method(s). Procedure(s). System(s). Routine(s). Habit(s). Convention(s). Mode of operation. *See also* Best practices; Implementation; Management methods; Methods; Performance; Protocols.

Practices, best. See *Best practices.*

Practices, corrupt. See *Bribery; Cheating; Computer crimes; Conflict of interest; Consumer fraud; Corruption in government; Covert; Doping in sports; Embezzlement; Falsification (scientific); Fraud; Industrial espionage; Kickbacks; Political crimes; Price fixing; Professional ethics; Product tampering; Quackery; Racketeering; Unethical conduct; Scientific misconduct; White collar crime.*

Practices, ethical. See *Ethical practices.*

Practices, feeding. See *Feeding practices.*

Practices, flexible workplace. See *Flexible workplace practices.*

Practices, management. See *Management methods.*

Practices, religious. See *Religious practices.*

Practices, unfair trade. See *Restraint of trade.*

Practicum supervision. Practicum supervis(ion,or,ors). Preceptor(s,ship). *Consider also:* supervis(ion,or,ors) *with:*

trainee(s), clinical training, student therapist(s), student teacher(s), extern(s,ships), field experience. *See also* Field experience programs; Internships.

Practitioner patient relations. See *Physician patient relations; Professional client relations.*

Practitioners, family. See *Family physicians.*

Practitioners, nurse. See *Nurse practitioners.*

Pragmatism. Pragmat(ic,ism,ists). Practical(ity). Experience based. Utilitarian. Practica(l,lity,lities,ble). Realistic. Unsentimental. Unromantic. *See also* Instrumentalism (philosophy); Philosophy.

Praise. Prais(e,ed,es,sing). Approval. Social reinforcement. Social approval. Verbal reinforcement. Extol(ling,led). Laud(ed,ing). Commend(ed,ing,ation, ations). Acclaim(ed,ing). Testimonial(s). Flattery. Applause. Recommend(ed,ing, ations). Pay tribute. Eulogiz(e,ed,ing). Compliment(s,ed,ing). *Choose from:* positive *with:* appraisal, comment(s), statement(s), feedback. *See also* Commendation; Eulogies; Flattery; Positive reinforcement; Tribute.

Praxis. See *Practices (methods).*

Prayer. Prayer(s). Pray(ed,ing). Worship. Supplicat(e,ed,ion,ing). Supplicant(s). Spiritual exercise(s). Say(ing) grace. Spiritual practice(s). Communion. Conscious(ness) of God. Evensong. Mattins. Tephill(ah,oth). Tefil(ah,oth). Salat. Devotional practice(s). Devotion(s). Supplication(s). *Choose from:* communicat(e,ed,ing,ion), commun(e,ed,ing) *with:* God. *Consider also:* station(s) of the Cross, meditat(e,ed,ing,ion), liturg(y,ies,ical), laying on of hands, psalm(s), psalter(s), hymn(s), intercessory petition(s), suffrage(s). *See also* Antiphons; Blessing; Books of hours; Devotional poetry; Grace at meals; Incantations; Invocation; Meditation; Moslem prayer; Posture in worship; Prayerbooks; Religious commitment; Religious experience; Religious life; Religious rituals; Saints; Spiritual exercises; Spiritual gifts; Spirituality; Worship.

Prayer, houses of. See *Places of worship.*

Prayer, Moslem. See *Moslem prayer.*

Prayerbooks. Prayerbook(s). Prayer book(s). Book of Common Prayer. Missal(s). Mass book(s). Euchology(y, ion). Lectionar(y,ies). Breviar(y,ies). Gospel book(s). Siddur(im). *Consider also:* Psalter(s). *See also* Books; Books of hours; Liturgical book(s); Prayer; Religious literature; Sacred books.

Pre-Columbian art. Pre-Columbian art(s,ist,ists). *Choose from:* pre-Columbian, Olmec, Maya(n), Toltec, Aztec, Mixtec, Zapotec, Inca(n), Pre-Inca(n), Paracas, Nazca(n), Mochica, Tiahuanaco, etc. *with:* sculpture(s), architectur(e,al), carv(ed,ing,ings), painting(s), fresco(es), pyramid(s), temple(s), gold(work), jewel(s,ry), turquoise, mosaic(s), pottery, featherwork, textile(s), ceramic(s), figurine(s), terracotta, metalwork. *See also* Pottery; Prehistoric art; Prehistoric sculpture; Primitive art.

Pre-Columbian empires. Pre-Columbian empire(s). Ancient American civilization(s). *Choose from:* pre-Columbian, prehispanic, Andean, meso-America(n), Mesoamerica(n), native American *with:* civilization(s), chiefdom(s), empire(s), dynast(y,ies), kingdom(s), culture(s), nation(s), tribe(s). *Consider also:* Aztec(s,an), Inca(s,an), Maya(s,an), Olmec(s), Zapotec(s,an), etc. *See also* African empires; Algonquian languages; Andean-Equatorial languages; Asian empires; Central America; Central American native cultural groups; Civilization; Cultural history; Culture contact; Dynasties; Eskimo-Aleut languages; GE-Pano-Carib languages; Historical periods; Hokan-Siouan languages; Indigenous populations; Macro-Chibchan languages; Macro-Otomanguean languages; Nadene languages; North American native cultural groups; Penutian languages; South America; South American native cultural groups; Traditional societies; Uto-Aztecan languages; Vikings; Western civilization; World history.

Preachers. Preacher(s). Minister(s,ial,ing). Ministry. Pastor(s). Parson(s). Reverend. Ministerial student(s). Priest(s). Clergy(women,woman,men,man). Seminarian(s). Seminary student(s). Divinity student(s). Chaplain(s). Cleric(als,s). Ecclesiastic(s). *See also* Clergy; Preaching; Religious personnel.

Preaching. Preach(ed,ing). Sermoniz(e,ed, ing). Pulpitry. *Consider also:* moraliz(e, ed,ing), religious harangue(s), evangeliz(e,ed,ing,ation), exhort(ed, ing,ation). *See also* Clergy; Lay religious personnel; Preachers; Sermons.

Preadolescence. See *Puberty.*

Precapitalist societies. See *Traditional societies.*

Precedence. Precedence. Rank. Seniority. Preeminen(t,ce). Suprem(e,acy). Primacy. Priorit(y,ies). Privilege(s). First order of business. Predominan(ce,t). *See also* Choice behavior; Choices (alternatives); Decision making; Goals; Policy making; Priorities; Privilege; Social dominance; Superior subordinate relationship.

Precepts. See *Aphorisms; Axioms; Cliches; Creeds; Doctrines.*

Precocious development. Precocious development. Precocity. Pubertas praecox. *Choose from:* precocious, advanced, accelerated *with:* development, maturation, puberty, intellect(ual, ually). *Consider also:* early *with:* development, maturation, reading, reader(s). *See also* Developmental stages; Physical development; Precocious puberty; Psychogenesis.

Precocious puberty. Precocious puberty. Pubertas praecox. *Choose from:* puberty, pubertal, sexual, menarche *with:* precocious, precocity, premature. *Consider also:* congenital adrenal hyperplasia. *See also* Precocious development; Puberty.

Precognition. Precognition(s). Precogniz(e, ant). Precognitive. Ouija board(s). Clairvoyan(t,ce). ESP. Extrasensory perception. Preconscious perception. Telepath(y,ic). *See also* Extrasensory perception; Omen.

Predatory animals. Predatory animal(s). Predator(s). Predation. *Consider also:* carnivore(s), big cat(s), mountain lion(s), wildcat(s), lynx(es), cheetah(s), bobcat(s), bear(s), wolf, wolves, coyote(s), wolverine(s), lynx(es), hyena(s), shark(s), predatory songbird(s), hawk(s), shrike(s), falcon(s), owl(s), eagle(s). *See also* Animal aggressive behavior; Animals; Birds of prey; Parasites; Predatory behavior; Territoriality; Wolves.

Predatory behavior. Predatory behavior. Predatory activit(y,ies). Predation. Prey catching. Predator(s,ial). Plunder(ed, ing). Forag(e,ed,ing). Prey-predator interaction. Prey selection. Depredat(or, ory,ion). Intraspecific aggression. Kill(ing) and consuming animal(s). Prey catching response(s). *See also* Animal aggressive behavior; Animal foraging behavior; Predatory animals.

Predelinquent youth. Predelinquent youth. Predelinquen(t,ts,cy). *Choose from:* delinquency *with:* prone(ness), risk(s). *Consider also:* dependent-neglected, need of supervision, runaway(s), dropout(s), disruptive, behavior problem(s), socially deviant, maladjusted, status offender(s), subculture(s) *with:* youth(s), adolescent(s), teenager(s), child(ren), 8th grader(s), 9th grader(s), juvenile(s), minor(s). *Consider also:* delinquency prevention. *See also* Adolescence; Children; Deviant behavior; Juvenile delinquency; Potential dropouts.

Predestination. See *Fatalism; Fate.*

Predicables (Logic). See *Predicate (Logic).*

Predicate (Logic). Predicat(e,ed,ing,ion). Predicable(s). Praedicabilia. *Consider also:* quinque voces. *See also* Categories (philosophy); Logic.

Predictability. Predictab(le,ility). Likelihood. Risk identification. *Choose from:* predictive validity, measure(ment) of potential. *Consider also:* probabilit(y,ies), predictor(s). *See also* Fluctuations; Predictive validity; Reliability.

Prediction. Predict(ed,ing,ion,ive,or,ors, ability). Prognos(is,ticate,tication). Forecast(s,ed,er,ing). Prophe(sy,tic). Fore(tell,told). Foresee(n,ing). Foresight. Prescience. Estimat(e,ing) likelihood. Augury. *Consider also:* second sight. *See also* Divination; Impending; Omen; Oracles; Predictability; Probability; Prophets; Self fulfilling prophecy.

Predictive validity. Predictive validity. *Consider also:* predict(ive,ion,ions) *with:* valid(ity), reliab(le,ility), useful(ness). *See also* Predictability; Prediction.

Predisposition. Predispos(e,ed,ing,ition, itions). High risk(s). Predictab(le,ly). Vulnerab(le,ility). Susceptib(le,ility). Prone(ness). Precondition(s). Family histor(y,ies). Patient histor(y,ies). Variable(s) influencing. Correlate(s). Tend(ing,ency) toward. Inclin(e,ed,ing, ation,ations). Antecedent(s). Determining tendenc(y,ies). Likel(y,ihood,iness). Liab(le,ility). Propensit(y,ies). Family incidence. Background factor(s). Predilection(s). Proclivit(y,ies). *Choose from:* associated, related, inherit(ed,ing) *with:* tendenc(y,ies), trait(s), weakness(es), strength(s). *Consider also:* attitude(s), mind set(s), mental set(s). *See also* Attitudes; Disease susceptibility; Disposition (Philosophy); Expectations; Family history; Generational cycle of child abuse; High risk persons; Premorbidity; Researcher bias; Set (psychology).

Preening. Preen(ed,ing). Groom(ed,ing). Body care. Plum(e,ed,ing). Arrang(e,ed, ing) feather(s). Trim(med,ming). Primp(ed,ing). *Consider also:* uropygial gland. *See also* Animal grooming behavior; Birds.

Prefaces. See *Introductions.*

Preference, occupational. See *Occupational choice.*

Preference, vocational. See *Occupational choice.*

Preference measures. Preference measure(s). *Consider also:* preference(s), choice(s), preferred object(s) *with:* measure(s), scale(s), inventor(y,ies), test(s), schedule(s). *See also* Measurement; Preferences.

Preference voting. Preference voting. Single transferable vote. Preferential voting. Instant runoff(s). *Consider also:*

multiple preference voting, Voters' Choice Act, proportional voting system(s). *See also* Coalitions; Elections; Political parties; Power sharing; Proportional representation; Strategic alliances; Third parties (United States politics).

Preferences. Preference(s). Choice(s). Prefer(able,red). Like(s). Dislike(s). Lik(e,ing). Desir(e,ed,able,ing). Choos(e,ing). Perceived desirability. Attract(ed,ive,ion,iveness). Favorite. First choice. Popular(ity). Select(ed). Favor(ed,ite). Taste(s). *See also* Aesthetic preferences; Attitudes; Choice behavior; Favoritism; Food preferences; Occupational choice; Preferred rewards; Residential preferences; Royal favorites; Sexual preferences; Trade preferences; Wants.

Preferences, aesthetic. See *Aesthetic preferences.*

Preferences, food. See *Food preferences.*

Preferences, housing. See *Residential preferences.*

Preferences, residential. See *Residential preferences.*

Preferences, sex. See *Sexual preferences.*

Preferences, sexual. See *Sexual preferences.*

Preferences, trade. See *Trade preferences.*

Preferential treatment. Preferential treatment. VIP treatment. Favoritism. Preferential admission standard(s). Special treatment. Racial preference(s). Preferential hiring. *Consider also:* tax break(s), partiality, most favored, quota(s). *See also* Affirmative action; Elites; Favoritism; Privilege; Privileges and immunities; Royal favorites.

Preferred rewards. Preferred reward(s). *Choose from:* prefer(red,ence,ences), choice(s), chosen, desir(ed,able,ability), attractive(ness) *with:* reward(s), prize(s). *See also* Preferences; Reward.

Pregnancies, senior. See *Senior pregnancies.*

Pregnancy. Pregnan(t,cy,cies). Gestation(al). Prenatal. Obstetric(s,al). Expectant mother(s). Expectant parent(s). Superfetate. Primigravid(a,as). Cyesis. Gravid(a,ism,ity). Parturient(s). *With:* child. *See also* Birth; Childbirth training; Conception; False pregnancy; Fertilization; Fetus; Labor (childbirth); Prenatal care; Prenatal development; Postnatal care; Postnatal period; Pregnancy rate; Reproductive technologies; Sexual reproduction; Teenage mothers; Unwanted pregnancy.

Pregnancy, adolescent. See *Teenage mothers.*

Pregnancy, false. See *False pregnancy.*

Pregnancy, teenage. See *Teenage mothers.*

Pregnancy, unwanted. See *Unwanted pregnancy.*

Pregnancy rate. Pregnancy rate(s). Farrowing rate(s). *Choose from:* pregnancy, conception(s), fecundity, fertility, fertilization, insemination *with:* rate(s), ratio(s), expectation(s), trend(s), data, projection(s), pattern(s). *Consider also:* reproductive efficiency, litter size(s), twinning rate(s). *See also* Birthrate; Fertility; Pregnancy; Vital Statistics.

Prehension. Prehension. Reach(ing)-to-grasp. Grip(s,ped,ping). Grasp(s,ed,ing). Tak(e,en,ing) hold. Seiz(e,es,ed,ing). *Consider also:* prehensil(e,ity). *See also* Motor coordination.

Prehistoric agriculture. Prehistoric agricultur(e,al). *Choose from:* prehistoric, ancient, archaeological, early, fossil(s), primitive, bronze age, iron age, stone age, neolithic, pre-neolithic, paleolithic *with:* subsistence econom(y, ies), diet (s), maize, agricultur(e,al), livestock, rice, cultivat(e,ed,ion), animal(s), crop(s), food(s,stuff,stuffs), farm(s,ing). *See also* Cultivated Plants; Ethnoarchaeology; Prehistoric people; Primitive agriculture; Primitive food.

Prehistoric art. Prehistoric art. Paleoart. Cave painting(s). Prehistoric figurine(s). *Choose from:* prehistoric, ancient, archaeological, early nonliterate, fossil(s), primitive, bronze age, iron age, stone age, mesolithic, neolithic, pre-neolithic, paleolithic, Cro-Magnon *with:* art(istic), drawing(s), depiction(s), image(s), engraving(s), rock engraving(s), paint(ed,ing,ings), carving(s), figure(s), decoration(s), representation(s). *Consider also:* cave paintings *with:* Altamira, Font de Gaume, Lascaux, Les Combarelles, Niaux Cave, Les Trois Frères, Chauvet. *See also* Cave paintings; Carving (decorative arts); Petroglyphs; Pre-Columbian art; Prehistoric people; Prehistoric sculpture.

Prehistoric commerce. Prehistoric commerce. *Choose from:* prehistor(y,ic), hunter gatherer(s), bronze age, iron age, stone age, neolithic, paleolithic *with:* commerce, trad(e,ed,ing), sale(s), procurement, exchange(s), reciprocity. *See also* Hunting and gathering societies; Prehistoric people; Prehistoric transportation; Primitive agriculture; Primitive fishing; Primitive industries; Traditional societies.

Prehistoric diseases. See *Paleopathology.*

Prehistoric ecology. See *Paleoecology.*

Prehistoric fishing. See *Primitive fishing.*

Prehistoric people. Prehistoric people(s).

Prehistoric man. Neanderthal(s). Neandertal(s). Telanthropus. *Choose from:* Solo, Rhodesian, Mt. Carmel, Cro-Magnon, Grimaldi, Boskop, Wadjak, Boxgrove, Tollund, Lindow *with:* man, men, people(s), human(s). *Choose from:* prehistoric, early, primitive, bronze age, iron age, stone age, ice age, copper age, neolithic, paleolithic, mesolithic *with:* man, men, woman, women, people(s), human(s), hominid(s), homo sapiens, population(s). *Consider also:* prehuman(s), cave art, prehistoric venus(es), hunter-gatherer(s), Acheulian culture, Aurignacian culture, lake dweller(s), Magdalenian culture, Megalithic monuments, Mousterian culture, Paleo-Indian(s), prehistoric iceman. *See also* Archaeology; Bog bodies; Bone implements; Bronze age; Ethnoarchaeology; Kitchen middens; Mesolithic period; Paleolithic period; Paleopathology; Physical anthropology; Prehistoric agriculture; Prehistoric art; Prehistoric commerce; Prehistoric sculpture; Prehistoric transportation; Primitive fishing; Prehominids; Primitive industries; Stone implements; Souterrains; World history.

Prehistoric sculpture. Prehistoric sculpture(s). *Choose from:* prehistoric, ancient, archaeological, early, bronze age, iron age, stone age, mesolithic, neolithic, pre-neolithic, paleolithic *with:* sculpture(s), clay engraving(s), fertility figure(s), terracotta, carving(s), glyptic sculpture(s), bronze(s), bas-relief, statue(s,tte,ttes). *Consider also:* Benin bronze(s), *See also* Cave paintings; Carving (decorative arts); Petroglyphs; Pre-Columbian art; Prehistoric art; Prehistoric people; Sculpture.

Prehistoric transportation. Prehistoric transportation. *Choose from:* prehistor(y, ic), homo erectus, hunter gatherer(s), bronze age, iron age, stone age, neolithic, paleolithic *with:* transport(ed, ing,ation), sail(ed,ing), boat(s), road(s), migrat(ed,ion,ions), route(s), forag(e, ed,ers), ranging. *See also* Hunting and gathering societies; Prehistoric commerce; Prehistoric people; Primitive industries; Traditional societies; Transportation.

Prehominids. Prehominid(s). Australopithe(cines,cus). Meganthropus. Zinjanthropus. Pithecanthropines. Pithecanthropus erectus. Sinanthropus pekingensis. Homo erectus. Atlanthropus. Telanthropus. Neanderthaloid(s). Africanthropus njarasensis. Homo neanderthalensis. *Choose from:* arcanthropic, paleoanthropic, neanthropic, Java, Peking, Eyassi, Challean, Heidelberg, Swanscombe, Steinheim *with:* man, men, women, woman, people. *See also*

Archaeology; Physical anthropology; Prehistoric people.

Prejudice. Prejudic(e,ed,ial). Intoleran(ce,t). Racial(ly) bias(ed). Anti-semit(ic,ism). Antisemit(ic,ism). Discriminat(e,ed,ing, ion). Racis(m,t). Lack of tolerance. Sexis(m,t). Ageis(m,t). Stereotyp(e,es, ing). Bias(es,ed). Ableism. Handicapism. Heightism. Stigmatiz(e,ed,ing,ation). Inequality. Ethnic attitude(s). Negative perception of minorit(y,ies). Ingroup. Outgroup. Chauvinis(tic,m). Ethnocentric(ism). Xenophob(ia,ic). Bigot(ed,ry,s). *See also* Age discrimination; Antisemitism; Bias; Bigotry; Anti-Americanism; Attitudes toward the aged; Attitudes toward handicapped; Attitudes toward homosexuality; Attitudes toward mental illness; Attitudes toward mental retardation; Attitudes toward physical handicaps; Attitudes toward physical illness; Ethnocentrism; Exclusivity (Religion); Fanaticism; Hostility; Inequality; Intergroup relations; Intolerance; Male chauvinism; Misanthropy; Minority groups; Nationalism; Otherness; Puritanism; Racism; Religious prejudice; Sex discrimination; Sexism; Social attitudes; Social discrimination; Social distance; Social problems; Stereotyping; Tolerance; White supremacy movements; Xenophobia.

Prejudice, racial. See *Racial attitudes; Racism.*

Prejudice, religious. See *Religious prejudice.*

Prejudice motivated crimes. See *Hate crimes.*

Prekindergarten. See *Preschool education.*

Preludes. Prelud(e,es,ial). Praeludi(a,um). Praeludium(s). Preambel(en). Vorspiel(en), Preludio(s). Preambul(a, um). Praeambul(a,um). Prelud(er,ieren). Curtain raiser(s). *Consider also:* tiento(s), toccata(s), ricercar(s), fantasia(s), arpeggiata(s), tastata(s), entrada(s). *See also* Improvisation (music); Introduction; Overtures (music).

Premarital counseling. Premarital counseling. *Choose from:* premarital, prenuptial, pre-marriage, engaged couple(s) *with:* counseling, guidance, problem solving, advice, preparation, enrichment, education. *See also* Counseling; Couples therapy; Covenant marriage; Family therapy.

Premarital intercourse. See *Premarital sexual behavior.*

Premarital sexual behavior. Premarital sex(ual,uality). Premarital intercourse. Cohabitation. Sexual revolution. Shotgun wedding(s). Premarital pregnanc(y,ies). Unwed mother(s). Fornication. Bundling. Gueesting.

Nonmarital sex. Casual sex. Fornicat(e, ed,ing,ion). *Choose from:* premarital, unmarried, engaged couple(s) *with:* sex(ual,uality), behavior(s), intercourse, relations, permissive(ness), conception, coitus, contraception, cohabitation. *Consider also:* teen(age), adolescen(t,ce) *with:* sex(ual,uality). *See also* Adolescence; Birth control; Cohabitation; Extramarital relations; Human courtship; Promiscuity; Sexual behavior surveys; Sexual ethics; Sexual foreplay; Sexual intercourse; Sexual partners; Sexual permissiveness, Sexually transmitted diseases; Single mothers; Single person; Social dating; Virginity.

Premature birth. See *Premature infants.*

Premature ejaculation. Premature ejaculat(ion,ors). Ejaculatio praecox. *Consider also:* ejaculat(ion,ions,ory) *with:* problem(s), disturbance(s), disorder(s), prematur(e,ity), impairment(s). *See also* Impotence; Orgasm; Sexual function disorders.

Premature infants. Premature infant(s). Prematurity. Early birth. Born before term. *Choose from:* premature, preterm *with:* infant(s), bab(y,ies) child(ren), newborn(s), fetus(es), neonate(s). Early birth. Born before term. *Consider also:* gestational age, premature labor, tiny newborn(s), very low birth weight. *See also* Birth weight; Infant mortality; Infant small for gestational age; Newborn infants; Prenatal development; Very low birth weight infants.

Premenstrual syndrome. Premenstrual syndrome. Premenstrual tension. PMS. *Choose from:* premenstrual, premenstruation *with:* tension(s), anxiet(y,ies), syndrome(s), symptom(s,atology), edema, affective symptom(s), affective syndrome(s), mood(s), bloat(ed,ing), distress(es). *See also* Menstrual cycle; Menstrual disorders; Menstruation.

Premenstrual tension. See *Premenstrual syndrome.*

Premiums. Premium(s). Frequent flyer program(s). Coupon(s). Trading stamp(s). Bonus(es). *See also* Prizes.

Premorbidity. Premorbid(ity). Anamnes(is,tic). Prepsychopathic. Prepsychotic. *Choose from:* pre-existing, preadmission, prior, prone(ness), propensity, risk *with:* symptom(s), disease(s), illness(es). *See also* Disease susceptibility; High risk persons; Onset (disorders); Patient history; Predisposition.

Prenatal care. Prenatal care. Obstetrics. *Choose from:* prenatal, pregnan(t,cy), obstetric(s,al), expectant mother(s), childbirth *with:* health care, medical service(s), preventive medicine, class(es), preparation. *Consider also:* perinatology, Lamaze. *See also* Health

care; Health promotion; Health services; Postnatal care; Primary prevention; Pregnancy.

Prenatal development. Prenatal development. Fetal development. Embryonic stage(s). Fetal maturity. Stage(s) of gestation. Gestational age. Gestation(al) stage. *Choose from:* prenatal, fetal, embryonic, gestation(al), fetus(s), newborn(s), intrauterine, in utero, foetal *with:* development(al), grow(th,ing), age(s), stage(s), maturation, matur(e,ing,ity), weight(s). *Consider also:* blastula, gastrula, blastocyst(s), blastomere(s), cleavage stage ovum, embryo, fetus. *See also* Birth weight; Embryology; Fetal alcohol syndrome; Fetus; Pregnancy; Premature infants; Prenatal care; Very low birth weight infants.

Prenuptial contracts. See *Marriage contracts.*

Preoccupied *with:* sex. See *Erotomania.*

Preparation, employment. See *Employment preparation.*

Preparation, food. See *Food preparation.*

Preparedness, disaster. See *Disaster planning.*

Preparedness, emergency. See *Disaster planning.*

Preschool children. Preschool child(ren). Toddler(s). Preschooler(s). Two to five year old(s). 2-5 year old(s). Kindergartener(s). *Choose from:* preschool, nursery school, kindergarten *with:* child(ren), student(s), pupil(s). *Consider also:* early childhood. *See also* Child day care; Child development; Developmental stages; Early childhood development; Preschool education.

Preschool education. Preschool education. *Choose from:* preschool, prekindergarten, head start, early education, nursery school(s), infant school(s). *Consider also:* early childhood *with:* education, program(s), class(es), curriculum, playgroup(s), student(s), pupil(s). *See also* Elementary education; Preschool children.

Preschool teachers. Preschool teacher(s). *Choose from:* preschool, kindergarten, prekindergarten, early childhood, Headstart, nursery school *with:* teacher(s), educator(s). *See also* Preschool education; Teachers.

Prescience of God. See *Omniscience of God.*

Prescription drugs. Prescription drug(s). *Choose from:* prescription, prescribed, generic, controlled *with:* drug(s), medicine(s), medication(s), remed(y,ies). *Consider also:* controlled substance(s), drugs by name. *See also* Analgesia; Antidepressive agents; Appetite depressants; Drugs; Narcoanalytic drugs; Non-prescription drugs; Prescription fees; Tranquilizers.

Prescription fees. Prescription fee(s). *Choose from:* prescription(s), prescribed drug(s), medication(s) *with:* fee(s), price(s), charge(s), cost(s), bill(s), expense(s). *See also* Fees; Health expenditures; Prescription drugs.

Presence (attendance). See *Attendance (presence).*

Presence of God. Presence of God. God's presence. *Choose from:* God, deity, divin(e,ity), divine other, the Lord, divine being, infinite majesty, Jesus, Yahweh, Yahveh, Allah, almighty *with:* presen(t,ce), hidden(ness), hiding, exist(ed,ing,ence), absen(t,ce), manifest(ed,ing,ation). *Consider also:* death of God. *See also* Attributes of God; Christianity; Death of God (theology); Deism; Faith; God concepts; Immanence of God; Jehovah; Judaism; Knowledge of god; Meaninglessness; Oneness of God; Pantheism (universal divinity); Religious experience; Theism; Theophany.

Presenile dementia. Presenile dementia. Senium praecox. Presbyophren(ia,ic). Atrophic dementia. Abiotrophic atrophic dementia. *Choose from:* presenile, praesenile, premature, progressive *with:* dementia, sclerosis. *Consider also:* Alzheimer(s) disease, Jakob Creutzfeldt syndrome, Pick(s) disease, senile dementia. *See also* Organic mental disorders; Senile dementia.

Presentation, self. See *Self presentation.*

Presentations. Presentation(s). Present(ed, ing). Appearance(s). Debut(s,ed,ing). Demonstration(s). Display(s,ed,ing). Enactment(s). Exhibit(ed,ing,ion,ions). Exposition(s). Performance(s). Portrayal(s). Rendition(s). Unveil(ed, ing,ings). (e,ed,es,ing,ion,ions). *Consider also:* pitch(ing,ed,es). *See also* Campaign debates; Debate; Enactment; Lectures and lecturing; Product introduction; Public speaking; Theater.

Presents. See *Gifts.*

Preservation. Preserv(e,ed,ing,ation,ative). Protect(ed,ing,ion). Conserv(e,ed,ing, ation). Safeguard(ed,ing). Sav(e,ed,ing). Keep(ing). Kept. Retain(ed,ing). Sustain(ed,ing). Maintain(ed,ing). Maintenance. Perpetuat(e,ed,ing,ion). Shield(ed,ing). Prevent(ed,ing,ion). *See also* Change; Conservation of natural resources; Cultural maintenance; Environmental protection; Environmentalism; Food preservation; Forest conservation; Land preservation; Maintenance; Modernization; Natural environment; Neighborhood preservation; Obsolescence; Pollution control; Prevention; Preventive maintenance;

Protection; Shelters; Shore protection; Soil conservation; Tree planting; Quality of life; Survival; Water conservation; Wildlife conservation; Wildlife sanctuaries.

Preservation, food. See *Food preservation.*

Preservation, land. See *Land preservation.*

Preservation, neighborhood. See *Neighborhood preservation.*

Preservice teachers. Preservice teacher(s). *Choose from:* preservice, prospective, student *with:* teacher(s). *See also* College students.

Presidential campaigns. See *Political campaigns; Elections.*

Presidents. President(s). Chief executive(s). CEO(s). Chief of state. Commander in chief. *Consider also:* White House, Oval Office, George Washington, John Adams, Thomas Jefferson, James Madison, James Monroe, John Quincy Adams, Andrew Jackson, Martin Van Buren, William Henry Harrison, John Tyler, James K. Polk, Zachary Taylor, Millard Fillmore, Franklin Pierce, James Buchanan, Abraham Lincoln, Andrew Johnson, Ulysses S. Grant, Rutherford B. Hayes, James A. Garfield, Chester A. Arthur, Grover Cleveland, Benjamin Harrison, William McKinley, Theodore Roosevelt, William Howard Taft, Woodrow Wilson, Warren G. Harding, Calvin Coolidge, Herbert C. Hoover, Franklin D. Roosevelt, Harry S. Truman, Dwight D. Eisenhower, John F. Kennedy, Lyndon B. Johnson, Richard M. Nixon, Gerald R. Ford, James E. Carter, Ronald W. Reagan, George H. W. Bush, William J. Clinton. *See also* Administrators; Authority (officials); Chief executive officers; Chiefs; Executive branch (government); Executive powers; Heads of state; Monarchy; Power elite; Power structure; Ruling class.

Press. See *News media.*

Press, alternative. See *Alternative press.*

Press, free and fair trial. See *Freedom of the press; Fair trial; Trial (law).*

Press, freedom of the. See *Freedom of the press.*

Press agents. Press agent(s). Publicist(s). Press secretar(y,ies). Press aide(s). Media spokesperson(s). Celebrity publicist(s). PR firm(s). Press officer(s). Communications director(s). Press representative(s). *See also* Press conferences; Public relations; Publicity; Spin doctors; Spokespersons.

Press conferences. Press conference(s). News conference(s). Press briefing(s). *Consider also:* reporter(s) *with:* interview(s,ed,ing), exchange(s), conference(s). *See also* Announcements;

News coverage; News media; News policies; Newspapers; Opinion leaders; Press agents.

Press coverage. See *News coverage.*

Presses, little. See *Little presses.*

Pressure. Pressure(s). Strain(s). Tension(s). Stress(ing,es). Distress(ed,ing). Urgen(t,cy). Insisten(ce,t). Persist(ent). Compulsion(s). Compel(ling). Constrain(ing). Force(d,ing). Stretch(ed,ing). Intens(e,ity). Hardship(s). Burden(ed). Overburden(ed). Afflict(ed,ion). *See also* Hypertension; Social pressure; Stress.

Pressure, blood. See *Blood pressure.*

Pressure, high blood. See *High blood pressure.*

Pressure, social. See *Social pressure.*

Pressure groups. See *Interest groups; Lobbying.*

Pressure sensation. Pressure sensation. *Choose from:* press(ure) *with:* sensation(s), sensing, sensitivity, adapt(ed,ing,ation), stimulation, perception. *See also* Sensation; Somatic delusions.

Prestation (anthropology). See *Ceremonial exchange.*

Prestige. Prestig(e,ious,iousness). Honor(ed). Renown(ed). Influential. Esteemed. Public esteem. Social recognition. Public recognition. Popular(ity). High ranking. Pre-eminen(t,ce). Prominen(t,ce). Eminen(t,ce). Celebrit(y,ies). Notable(s). Hero(es,ine,ines). Dignitar(y,ies). Respected. Admired. Social position. Top rank(eding). First rate. Lionized. *See also* Admiration; Awards; Famous people; Glory; Goodwill; Honored (esteem); Leadership; Occupational status; Privilege; Recognition (achievement); Reputation; Social desirability; Social status.

Presumption of death and absence. See *Absence and presumption of death.*

Presuppositions. See *Postulates.*

Pretenses, false. See *Fraud.*

Pretesting. Pretest(ed,ing). Initial evaluation(s). *Consider also:* preliminary *with:* trial(s), evaluation(s), test(s,ed,ing), assessment(s). Trial period(s). Tryout(s). Pre-employment questionnaire(s). *See also* Assessment; Tests; Evaluation.

Pretrial release. See *Bail.*

Prevailing wages. Prevailing wage(s). Frequently occuring wage(s). *Consider also:* Davis-Bacon Act, wage averaging, wage survey(s), prevailing minimum wage(s), union wage(s). *See also* Cheap labor; Equity (payment); Income inequality; Labor costs; Labor economics; Labor laws; Labor market; Living standards; Minimum wage; Wage differentials; Wages.

Prevalence. Prevalen(t,ce). Number of cases. Universality. Frequency. Extent. Extensive. Rampant. Global(ly). Nationwide. Occurrence. Spread. Widespread. Distribution. Patterns of use. Trend(s). Epidemic. Ubiquitous(ness). Seasonal fluctuation(s). Seroprevalence. Disease outbreak(s). Space time clustering. Attendance. Birth rate(s). Dropout rate(s). Enrollment rate(s). Morbidity rate(s). Mortality rate(s). Rates of. *Consider also:* incidence, epidemiolog(y,ic,ical). *See also* Crime rates; Distribution (apportion); Epidemics; Fluctuations; Frequently; Marriage rates; Mortality rates; Rates; Transience; Unemployment rates.

Prevention. Prevent(ed,ing,ion,ive). Deterren(t,ts,ce). Prophyla(ctic,xis). Precaution(ary,s). Preventative(s). Safety measure(s). Protect(ion,ions,ive). Shield(ed,ing,s). Screen(ing,ed,s). Immuniz(e,ed,ing,ation,ations). Innoculat(ed,ion,ation,ations). Safeguard(s, ed,ing). *Consider also:* prepared(ness), curb(ed,ing), control(led,ling), reduc(e,ed,tion), eliminat(e,ed,ing,ion), holistic health, antismoking, early diagnosis, early detection, early intervention(s), early warning(s). *Choose from:* accident(s), delinquency, dropout(s), crime(s), fire(s), disaster(s), flood(s,ing), illness(es) *with:* prevent(ed,ing,ion). *See also* Accident prevention; Child abuse prevention; Conservation of natural resources; Crime prevention; Deterrence; Early intervention; Environmental protection; Fire prevention; Pollution control; Preservation; Preventive medicine; Preventive psychiatry; Primary prevention; Safety; Sanitation; Suicide prevention; War prevention.

Prevention, accident. See *Accident prevention.*

Prevention, child abuse. See *Child abuse prevention.*

Prevention, crime. See *Crime prevention.*

Prevention, disease. See *Health; Holistic health; Mental health; Preventive medicine; Prevention; Quality of life; Sanitation; Well being.*

Prevention, fire. See *Fire prevention.*

Prevention, primary. See *Primary prevention.*

Prevention, primary mental health. See *Preventive psychiatry.*

Prevention, suicide. See *Suicide prevention.*

Prevention, war. See *War prevention.*

Prevention of floods. See *Flood control.*

Preventive detention. Preventive detention. *Choose from:* preventive, probable cause, reasonable suspicion, suspect(s), dangerous(ness) *with:* detention, custody, detain(ed,ing,ee,ees), on remand, quarantin(e,ed,ing), arrest(s), den(y,ied,ial,ying) bail, incarcerat(e,ed, ing,ion), behind bars, imprison(ed,ing, ment). *Consider also:* investigative detention, detention for interrogation. *See also* Arrests; Bail; Crime prevention; Defendants; Detention; Imprisonment; Offenders; Political prisoners.

Preventive health services. See *Preventive medicine; Preventive psychiatry; Primary prevention.*

Preventive maintenance. Preventive maintenance. *Choose from:* prevent(ive, on), preventative, renew(ed,ing,al,als), repair(ed,ing) *with:* maintenance, maintain(ed,ing), care, checklist(s). *Choose from:* prevent(ive,on), preventative, maintenance, protect(ion,ive) *with:* service(s), tip(s), polic(y,ies), strateg(y,ies). *Consider also:* replacement polic(y,ies), winteriz(e,ed,ing, ation), rust protectant(s), weatherproof(ed,ing), diagnostic program(s), annual inspection(s). *See also* Appliance repair; Equipment failure; Maintenance; Preservation; Product life cycle; Service contracts.

Preventive medicine. Preventive medicine. Prophyla(ctic,xis). Health(y,ful,). Wellness program(s). Hygien(e,ic). Immuniz(e,ed,ing,ation,ations). Vaccinat(e,ed,ing,ion,ions). Early detection. Dental checkup(s). Mammogra(m,ms,phy,phies). Pap smear(s). Chest X-ray(s). *Choose from:* prevent(ed,ing,ion,ions,ive), eradicat(e,ed, ing,ion) *with:* disease(s), illness(s), epidemic(s). *Choose from:* prevent(ive, ion,ed,ing), prophylactic, health oriented, wellness *with:* medicine, medical, dental, health service(s), care, examination(s), screening(s), diagnosis, treatment(s), health maintenance, health training, hygien(e,ic), intervention(s), check-up(s), checkup(s), detection. *Consider also:* nutrit(ion,ious), diet(s), exercise(s). *See also* Diet; Disease susceptibility; Early intervention; Hygiene; Immunity; Lifestyle; Maternal health services; Natural foods; Patient education; Primary prevention; Preventive psychiatry; Public health; Risk; Sanitation; Screening; Vaccinations.

Preventive psychiatry. Preventive psychiatry. *Choose from:* prevent(ive,ion), prophylaxis, screen(ed,ing), early detection, early intervention *with:* psychiatr(y,ic), mental health, mental disorder(s), neuros(is,es), mental illness(es), psychos(is,es), emotional disorder(s). *Consider also:* primary mental health prevention. *See also* Early intervention; Preventive medicine; Primary prevention; Suicide prevention.

Prey, birds of. See *Birds of prey.*

Price, bride. See *Bridewealth.*

Price control. Price control(s). *Choose from:* price(s), rent(s) *with:* control(led, ling,s), regulat(e,ed,ing,ion,ions), polic(y,ies), reform(s), stabiliz(e,ed,ing, ation), minimum(s), ceiling(s), fair trade, rollback(s), valorization, fix(ed,ing) support(s,ed,ing). *See also* Inflation (economics); Economic planning; Economic stabilization; Price trends.

Price fixing. Price fixing. Fix(ed,ing) price(s). Conscious parallel action(s). *Choose from:* collus(ive,ion), rig(ged, ging), stabiliz(e,ed,ing,ation), maintenance, maintain(ed,ing), fix(ed,ing) *with:* price(s), bid(s). *Consider also:* price leadership, administered price(s). *See also* Antitrust law; Cartels; Monopolies; Restraint of trade; White collar crime.

Price regulation. See *Price control.*

Price supports. See *Price control.*

Price supports, agricultural. See *Agricultural price supports.*

Price trends. Price trend(s). *Choose from:* price(s), cost(s), charge(s) *with:* trend(s), cycle(s), fluctuation(s), pattern(s), swing(s), surge(s), rall(y,ies), fall(s,ing), fell, downturn(s), plung(e,ed,ing), movement(s). *See also* Business cycles; Economic stabilization; Inflation (economics); Price control; Production consumption relationship.

Prices. Pric(e,es,ing). Amount paid. *Consider also:* rate(s), cost(s), charg(e, es,ed,ing), fee(s), overcharg(e,es,ed,ing), market value(s), markup, appraised value(s), valuation. *See also* Costs; Expenditures; Face value; Finance; Gratis; Inflation (economics); Living standards; Market value; Payments; Purchasing power; Supply and demand.

Prices, agricultural. See *Agricultural prices.*

Pride. Pride. Proud. Overconfiden(t,ce). Boast(s,ing,ful). Face saving. Smug(ness). *Choose from:* self *with:* praise, superior(ity), admir(ing,ation), approbation, love, adulation, esteem, respect, satisf(action,ied). *Consider also:* conceit(ed), vanity. *See also* Ego; Egoism; Self assessment; Self concept; Self esteem; Self respect; Snobs and snobbishness.

Priestesses. See *Female spirituality; Holy women; Nuns; Priests; Women religious.*

Priestly classes and priests (anthropology). See *Priests and priestly classes (anthropology).*

Priests. Priest(hood,s). Priestess(es). Seminarian(s). Bishop(s). Archpriest(s). Church father(s). Priestly ministry. Men in religious orders. Pope(s). Cardinal(s).

Monsignor(s). Dean(s). Catholic clergy(men,man). Jesuit(s). Episcopal clergy(men,man,women,woman). Archbishop(s). Reverend. Prelate(s). Vicar(s). Parson(s). Chaplain(s). *See also* Clergy; Fathers of the church; Holy men; Ministers; Monasticism; Ordination; Priests and priestly classes (anthropology); Rabbis; Religious councils and synods; Religious leadership; Religious personnel; Shamanism.

Priests and priestly classes (anthropology). Priests. Priestly class(es). Alafin(s). Angakok(s). Brahman(s). Taura. Uijatao(s). Yomta(s). *See also* Chiefs; Religious councils and synods; Religious leadership; Religious personnel; Shamanism; Traditional societies.

Primacy effect. Primacy effect(s). Law of primacy. Primacy recency phenomonon. *Consider also:* recency effect, serial position effect(s). *See also* Learning.

Primal therapy. Primal therapy. *Choose from:* primal *with:* therapy, scream, theory, scene(s), experience, pain. *See also* Psychotherapeutic techniques; Psychotherapy.

Primaries. Primar(y,ies). Caucus(es). Super delegate(s). *Choose from:* campaign(s), race(s), run(ning), ran *with:* nomination. Preliminary contest(s). *Consider also:* open primar(y,ies), closed primar(y,ies), blanket primar(y,ies), crossover primar(y,ies). *See also* Elections; Contests; Political candidates.

Primary education. Primary education. Kindergarten. First grade. Second grade. Third grade. *Consider also:* primary *with:* grade(s), school(s), education. *See also* Elementary education; Elementary school students; Elementary schools.

Primary groups. Primary group(s). Face-to-face group(s). Famil(y,ies). Intimate group(s). Informal group(s). Support group(s). *Choose from:* primary, close, intimate *with:* group(s), neighbor(s). *Consider also:* friend(s), rural communit(y,ies), clique(s), peer group(s), kin(ship,folk). *See also* Cliques; Family; Friendship; Interpersonal relations; Peers; Primary relations; Significant others; Traditional societies.

Primary health care. Primary health care. *Choose from:* primary *with:* care, health service(s), physician(s), health team. *Consider also:* general practitioner(s). *See also* Health care; Health examinations; Health promotion; Health services; Preventive medicine; Preventive psychiatry; Primary prevention.

Primary mental health prevention. See *Preventive psychiatry.*

Primary prevention. Primary prevention. Disease prevention. *Choose from:* preventive *with:* medicine, psychiatry, mental health, measure(s), care, program(s), practice(s). *Consider also:* immuniz(e,ed,ing,ation), innoculat(e,ed, ing,ion), vaccinat(e,ed,ing,ion), precaution(s,ary), prophyla(xis,ctic), risk reduc(e,ed,ing,tion), health promotion, sanitary measure(s). *Choose from:* early *with:* diagnos(is,es), detect(ed,ing,ion), intervention(s), identification. *See also* Health care; Health examinations; Hygiene; Prevention; Preventive medicine; Preventive psychiatry; Sanitation; Screening; Vaccinations.

Primary products. See *Raw materials.*

Primary reinforcement. Primary reinforce(ment,ments,r,rs). Primary reward(s). *Consider also:* unconditioned, tangible, concrete, direct, edible *with:* reward(s), reinforce(ment, ments,r,rs). *See also* Conditioning (psychology).

Primary relationships. Primary relation(s, ship,ships). *Choose from:* primary, personal, close, intimate *with:* relation(s, ship,ships), involvement(s), commitment(s). *Consider also:* mutual love. *See also* Family; Family relations; Friendship; Interpersonal relations; Peer relations; Primary groups; Significant others; Sociability; Social cohesion; Social contact; Social interaction; Social support.

Primary school students. Primary school student(s). 1st grader(s). 2nd grader(s). 3rd grader(s). First grader(s). Second grader(s). Third grader(s). *Choose from:* primary school, primary grade(s), primary level *with:* student(s), child(ren), pupil(s). *See also* Elementary school students; Primary schools.

Primary schools. Primary school(s). *Choose from:* primary *with:* school(s), grade(s). Lower grades. *Consider also:* grade one, grade two, grade three, first grade, second grade, third grade. *See also* Elementary schools; Primary school students.

Primates. Primat(e,es,ology,ological). Pongid(ae,s). Pongo. Hominid(ae,s). Hominoid(ae,s). Paleoprimatology. Anthropoid(s). Australopithecus. Australopithecine. Homo erectus. Human(s). Man. Ape(s). Gibbon(s). Orang-utan(s). Orangutan(s). Gorilla(s). Monkey(s). Baboon(s). Macaque(s). Chimpanzee(s). Tamarin(s). Marmoset(s). Anthropoidea. Callithricid(ae). Callithrix. Saguinus. Cebid(ae). Alouatta. Aotus-trivirgatus. Cebus. Saimiri. Cercopithecid(ae). Cercopithecus. Cercopithecus-aethiops. Colobus. Erythrocebus-patas. Macaca. Macaca-fascicularis. Macaca-mulatta. Macaca-nemestrina. Macaca-radiata. Papio. Theropithecus-gelada. Chimpansee-troglodytes. Gorilla-gorilla. Hylobates. Pongo-pygmaeus. Prosimii.

Lemurid(ae). Lemur. Lorisid(ae). Potto galagos. Galago. Tupaiid(ae). Tupaia. *Consider also:* indridae, avahia, indri, simpoona, loris, pan, tarsiid(ae), tarsier, cynomolgus, daubentoniid(ae). *See also* Animals; Apes; Vertebrates.

Primitive agriculture. Primitive agriculture. Traditional farm(s,ing,er,ers). First European farmer(s). Early rice cultivation. *Choose from:* primitive, traditional, earl(y,iest), native, fossil(s,ized), ancient, pre-Neolithic, Neolithic, indigenous *with:* agricultur(e,al), farm(s,ing,er,ers), crop(s), grain(s), rice, diet(s), food gathering, food preparation, domesticat(ed,ing,ion) animal(s), cultivat(e, ed,ing,ion) soil. *See also* Agrarian societies; Pastoral societies; Prehistoric agriculture; Prehistoric commerce; Traditional societies.

Primitive architecture. Primitive architecture. Tribal architecture. Traditional architecture. *Choose from:* primitive, tribal, Mayan, Toltec, African, prehistoric, archaeolog(y,ical), etc. *with:* architectur(e,al), dwell(ing,ings,er,ers), build(ing,ings,er,ers), hut(s), shelter(s), living site(s), habitat(s), house(s). *See also* Ancient architecture; Antiquity (time); Archaeology; Architectural styles; Excavations (Archaeology); Extinct cities.

Primitive art. Primitive art(s,work,works). Naive art(s,work,works). Pre-Columbian art(s,work,works). Unsophisticated art(s,work,works). *See also* Expressionism (art); Folk art; Pre-Columbian art; Prehistoric art.

Primitive fishing. Primitive fishing. *Choose from:* primitive, prehistoric, archaeolog(y,ical), traditional, earl(y,iest), native, pre-literate, non-literate, origins, fossil(s,ized), pre-Neolithic, Neolithic, indigenous *with:* fishing, fish catch(es), catch(ing) fish, fish catching. *See also* Fishing; Hunting and gathering societies; Prehistoric commerce; Prehistoric people; Primitive food; Primitive hunting; Subsistence hunting.

Primitive food. Primitive food(s). Paleo-diet(ary). Paleonutrition. *Choose from:* primitive, archaeolog(y,ical), prehistoric, ancient *with:* crop(s), foods(s), diet(s, ary), rice, cake(s), fish, seed(s), nut(s), grain(s), pollen(s), plant(s), edible. *Consider also:* origins of agriculture, domestication of animals, domestication of plants. *See also* Cultivated Plants; Traditional societies; Prehistoric agriculture; Primitive fishing; Primitive hunting; Subsistence economy; Subsistence hunting.

Primitive government. Primitive government(s). *Choose from:* primitive, tribal, tribe(s), indigenous *with:* government(s), governing bod(y,ies), politic(s), political system(s). *See also* Chiefs; Priests and priestly classes (anthropology); Traditional societies.

Primitive hunting. Primitive hunting. *Choose from:* primitive, prehistoric, early, Cro-Magnon(s), ice age, neanderthal(s), neandertal(s), fossil(s), Plains Indian(s), archaeological, paleolithic, hominid(s) *with:* hunt(er,ers, ing,ed), weapon(s,ry), archery, arrow(s), bow(s), spear(s), spearpoint(s), kill(e, ing,s), trap(s,ped,ping). *Consider also:* bison hunting, bison jump(s). *See also* Hunting and gathering societies; Primitive fishing; Primitive warfare; Subsistence hunting.

Primitive industries. Primitive industr(y, ies). Primitive tool(s). *Choose from:* industr(y,ies), assemblage(s) *with:* artifact(s). *Choose from:* primitive, prehistoric, paleolithic, pre-industrial *with:* material culture, technolog(y,ies, ical), tool(s), stone implement(s), bone implement(s), handax(es), cleaver(s). *See also* Prehistoric commerce; Prehistoric people; Prehistoric transportation; Traditional societies.

Primitive man. See *Prehistoric people; Prehominids.*

Primitive medicine. See *Traditional medicine.*

Primitive people. See *Prehistoric people; Prehominids.*

Primitive societies. See *Traditional societies.*

Primitive warfare. Primitive war(fare). *Choose from:* primitive, tribal, prehistoric, ancient *with:* war(fare), conflict(s), massacre(s), strife, murder(s), civil war(s), opponent(s), enmity. *Consider also:* primitive fortification(s), ethnic murder(s). *See also* Hunting and gathering societies; Primitive hunting; War.

Principals. See *Educational administrators.*

Principals, school. See *School principals.*

Principle, economy. See *Occam's razor.*

Principles. Principle(d,s). Moral law(s). Rule(s) of conduct. Golden rule. Ten commandment(s). Universal truth(s). Basic(s). Natural law(s). Moral code(s). Ethics. Ethical code(s). Fundamental(s). Fundamental law(s). Axiom(s,atic). Rule(s). Precept(s). Formula(s). Theorem(s). Proposition(s). Postulate(s). Theor(y,ies). *See also* Canons; Deduction; Edicts; Ethics; Fundamental; Generalities; Ideologies; Natural law; Occam's razor; Propositions; Rules (generalizations); Standards; Synthesis; Theories; Values.

Printers marks. Printers mark(s). Printers emblem(s). Printers device(s). Printers monogram(s). *Consider also:* colophon(s). *See also* Book imprints; Books; Colophons; Emblems.

Printing. Print(ing,ers,ed,shops). Typograph(y,ic). Typeset(ting). Offset. Lithograph(y). *Consider also:* engraving(s), graphic art(s), etching(s), printmaking, desktop publishing. *See also* Books; Engraving; Etching; Graphic arts; Publications; Written communications.

Printing (handwriting). Printing. Lettering. Handlettering. Calligraph(y,ic). Printscript. Uncial script(s). Block letter(s,ed,ing). *See also* Handwriting; Written communications.

Printing, block. See *Block printing.*

Priorities. Priorit(y,ies). Preference(s). Preferential rating(s). Precedence(s). Primacy. Prerogative(s). Superiority. Influence(s). Choice(s). Eminence. Urgen(t,cy). *See also* Choice behavior; Choices (alternatives); Decision making; Goals; Needs; Needs assessment; Planning; Policy making; Precedence; Resource allocation; Short term planning; Social values; Triage.

Prison camps. See *Concentration camps.*

Prison culture. Prison culture. Prisoniz(ation,ed). *Choose from:* inmate(s), prison(ers), imprison(ed, ment), offender(s), convict(s), incarcerat(ed,ion), jailhouse *with:* code(s), folkway(s), more(s), norm(s), customs, life, culture, climate(s), extremism, social system(s), mentalit(y,ies), psychology, social structure, pecking order(s), social relation(s,ships), societ(y,ies), criminalization, clique(s), effect(s), subculture(s), socialization, contraculture, contra-culture, attitude change(s), famil(y,ies), conformity, stratification, solidarity, community, value system(s), adaptation pattern(s), coping strateg(y,ies), attitude(s). *See also* Correctional institutions; Correctional personnel; Prisonization; Prison psychosis; Subcultures.

Prison discipline. Prison(er,ers) discipline. *Choose from:* prison(er,ers), inmate(s), jail(s), captive(s), prison(s), correctional institution(s), penitentiar(y,ies) *with:* disciplin(e,ary), behavioral control(s), correct(ed,ing,s,ion,ions), restrain(t,ed, ing), rebuk(e,ed,ing). *Consider also:* solitary confinement. *See also* Discipline; Prisoners; Punishment.

Prison guards. See *Correctional personnel.*

Prison inmates. See *Prisoners.*

Prison personnel. See *Correctional personnel.*

Prison psychosis. Prison psychos(is,es). *Consider also:* Ganser syndrome, prison neuros(is,es), chronophobia. *See also* Prison culture; Prisonization; Psychoses.

Prison violence. Prison violence. *Choose from:* prison(s,er,ers), penitentiar(y,ies), jail(s), correctional institution(s), reformator(y,ies) *with:* violen(t,ce), riot(s,ed,ing), mob(bed,bing), assault(ed, ing), stab(bed,ing), beat(en,ing,ings), bomb(ed,ing,ings), incendiar(y,ies), dangerous(ness), atrocit(y,ies), tortur(e, ed,ing), knifing(s), fight(s,ing), vandal(s, ize,ism), attack(s,ed,ing), armed conflict(s), loot(ed,ing), pillag(e,ed,ing), plunder(ed,ing), ravag(e,ed,ing), destruct(ion,ive), brute force, rap(e,ed, ing), injur(e,ing), harm(ed,ing,ful), murder(s,ing,ous), bloodthirsty, disorderly, hostage(s). *See also* Correctional institutions; Police brutality; Political violence; Prisons; Prisonization; Riots; Torture.

Prisoners. Prisoner(s). Hostage(s). Convict(s). War captive(s). Incarcerated. Committed to training school(s). *Choose from:* inmate(s) *with:* jail(s), prison(s), correctional institution(s), penitentiar(y, ies). *Consider also:* institutionalized person(s), parolee(s), exprisoner(s). *See also* Alternatives to incarceration; Correctional institutions; Imprisonment; Offenders; Parole; Prison culture; Prison discipline; Prisoners' rights; Prisoners' writings; Prisonization; Prison psychosis; Prisoners of war.

Prisoners, political. See *Political prisoners.*

Prisoners of war. Prisoner(s) of war. War captivity. POW(s). Survivor(s) of war camp(s). *Choose from:* prisoner(s), prison camp(s), captiv(e,es,ity), captured *with:* war(s,time), battle(s), Korean conflict, WWI, WWII, World War I, World War II, Vietnam, military, combat, guerrilla(s). *Consider also:* concentration camp prisoner(s), USS Pueblo crew member(s), hostage(s), missing in action, MIA(s), Geneva Convention. *See also* Captivity; Concentration camps; Hostages; International offenses; Military capitulations; Missing in action; Prisoners; War; War crimes; War victims.

Prisoners' rights. Prisoner(s) right(s). *Choose from:* prisoner(s), inmate(s), jail(s), penitentiar(y,ies), POW(s) *with:* civil right(s), civil liberties, constitutional right(s), personal security, self government, union(s), transfer(s), medical service(s), dental service(s), psychiatric service(s), right to treatment, conjugal visit(s), remedial education, legal advice, grievance(s). *Consider also:* Geneva Convention. *See also* Civil rights; Prisoners.

Prisoners' writings. Prisoner(s) writing(s). *Choose from:* prisoner(s), prison(s), inmate(s), imprisoned, jail(s,ed), gulag, POW(s) *with:* writing(s), letter(s), autobiograph(y,ies), narrative(s), poetry, poem(s), novel(s), memoir(s), diar(y,ies). *Consider also:* speaking from the dock. *See also* Authors; Prisoners; Writers; Writing (composition).

Prisonization. Prisoniz(ation,ed). *Choose from:* inmate(s), prison(s,er,ers), imprison(ed,ment), offender(s), convict(s), incarcerat(ed,ion), jail(s,house) *with:* personality change(s), psychology, mentalit(y,ies), co-opt(ed,ing,ation), adapt(ed,ing,ation), code(s), folkway(s), more(s), norm(s), custom(s), life, culture, climate(s), extremism, social system(s), social structure, pecking order, social relation(s,ships), societ(y, ies), criminaliz(e,ed,ing,ation), regiment(ed,ing,ation), clique(s), effect(s), subculture(s), socializ(e,ed,ing,ation), contraculture(s), contra-culture(s), attitude change(s), famil(y,ies), conform(ed,ing,ity), stratif(ied,ication), solidarity, community, value system(s), coping strateg(y,ies), attitude(s). *Consider also:* prison psychos(is,es), prison neuros(is,es). *See also* Imprisonment; Prison culture; Prison psychosis; Prison violence; Socialization.

Prisons. Prison(s). Correctional facilit(y, ies). Correctional institution(s). Corrective institution(s). Penal institution(s). Penal colon(y,ies). Death row. Guardhouse. Brig(s). Penitentiar(y,ies). House(s) of detention. Detention center(s). Jail(s,house,houses). Gaol(s). Prison cell(s). Reformator(y,ies). Correctional school(s). Borstal(s). *Consider also:* Bastille, Tower of London, Sing Sing, Devil's Island, Alcatraz, Dannemora, etc. *See also* Alternatives to incarceration; Concentration camps; Correctional institutions; Correctional system; Imprisonment; Juvenile detention homes; Maximum security facilities; Penal reform; Prisonization; Prison culture; Prison violence; Prisoners; Prisonization; Reformatories; Refugee camps.

Prisons, open. See *Alternatives to incarceration.*

Privacy. Priva(cy,te,teness). Confidential(ity). Behind closed doors. Secre(cy,t, ts,tiveness). Refus(e,al) to divulge. Privy. Anonym(ous,ity). Refus(e,ed, ing,al) to disclose. Discretion. Intimacy. Intimate(ness). Seclud(e,ed). Seclusion. Reserved(ness). Covert. Off limits. Concealed. Hidden. Sequest(er,ering, ered,ration). Solitar(y,iness). Solitude. Cloister(s,ed). Conceal(ed,ing). *See also* Anonymity; Civil rights; Computer security; Confidential communications; Confidential records; Confidentiality; Interpersonal relations; Invasion of privacy; Online privacy; Personal space; Physician patient relations; Private sphere; Privileged communications; Right of privacy; Secrecy; Solitude.

Privacy, invasion of. See *Invasion of privacy.*

Privacy, medical. See *Medical privacy.*

Privacy, online. See *Online privacy.*

Privacy, right of. See *Right of privacy.*

Privacy laws. Privacy law(s). Disclosure laws. Privacy Act of 1974. 1986 Privacy Act. Data Privacy Act. Fair Health Information Practices Act. Video and Library Privacy Protection Act of 1988. *Choose from:* privacy, private, personal data, personal affairs, medical data, medical record(s), wiretap(s,ping), privileged information, tax return(s) *with:* access(ed,ing), confidential(ity), disclosure, incursion(s), protect(ion), eavesdrop(ped,ping) *with:* law(s), legislative proposal(s), bill(s), Supreme Court decision(s), constitutional right(s), polic(y,ies), legal provision(s), regulat(e, ed,ing,ion,ions), litigat(e,ed,ing,ion, ions), legislat(e,ed,ing,ion). *See also* Civil rights; Computer security; Confidential communications; Confidential records; Confidentiality; Cyberlaw; Invasion of privacy; Laws; Medical privacy; Online privacy; Patient rights; Privileged communications; Right of privacy; Secrecy; Surveillance of citizens.

Private, going. See *Privatization.*

Private agencies. Private agenc(y,ies). *Choose from:* private, voluntary, charitable, for-profit, non-profit, nongovernment(al) *with:* agenc(y,ies), foundation(s), organization(s), center(s), clinic(s), association(s), bureau(s), institution(s). *See also* Agencies; Nonprofit organizations; Private sector.

Private enterprise. Private enterprise. Private sector. Privatiz(e,ed,ation). Privatis(e,ed,ation). Private hands. Open market(s). Private business(es). Commercial interest(s). Capitalis(t,ts,m,tic). Profit making. For profit. Profit motive. Commercializ(e,ed,ing,ation). Business organization(s). Entrepreneur(s,ial, ialism). Free enterprise. Enterprise culture. Private investor(s). Private industry. Private ownership. Private capital. Private good(s). *Choose from:* private(ly), commercial, capitalis(t,ts,tic, m), profitmaking, privatiz(e,ed,ation), corporate *with:* hands, own(ed,ership), enterprise, agenc(y,ies), organization(s), firm(s), foundation(s), investment(s), monopol(y,ies), good(s), fund(ed,ing), indust(ry,ries), institution(s). *See also* Business; Economic competition; Entrepreneurship; Free trade; Market economy; Private sector; Privatization; Profit motive.

Private languages. See *Secret languages.*

Private practice. Private practice. *Choose from:* private, solo, independent *with:* practice. *See also* Delivery of services; Health care.

Private schools. Private school(s). *Choose from:* private, parochial, Catholic, proprietary, nonpublic, independent, religious(ly) affiliat(ed,ion), Protestant, Christian, Jewish, Lutheran, Baptist, Seventh Day Adventist, Fundamentalist, boarding, religious, privately supported, exclusive, prep(aratory) *with:* school(s), high school(s), academ(y,ies), institutions of higher education. *See also* Colleges; Educational vouchers; Religious education; School choice; Schools.

Private sector. Private sector. Privatiz(e,ed, ation). Private enterprise. Private business(es). Commercial interest(s). Capitalis(t,ts,m,tic). Profit making. Profit motive. Commercializ(e,ed,ing, ation). Business organization(s). Entrepreneur(s,ial,ialism). Free enterprise. Private investor(s). *Choose from:* private(ly), commercial, capitalis(t,ts,tic,m,), profitmaking, privatiz(e,ed,ation), corporate *with:* developer(s), hands, power, financed, interest(s), own(ed,ers,ership), enterprise, agenc(y,ies), organization(s), firm(s), foundation(s), investment(s), monopol(y,ies), good(s), fund(ed,ing), indust(ry,ries), institution(s). *See also* Business; Entrepreneurship; Market economy; Private enterprise; Privatization; Public sector.

Private sphere. Private sphere(s). *Choose from:* private, household, domestic, personal, home, women's, woman's *with:* sphere(s), domain(s), forum(s), space(s), work, world(s), life. *Consider also:* homelife, homebod(y,ies), traditional female role(s), personal identit(y,ies), privacy, family life, foot binding, harem(s), hidjab, seclud(e,ed, ing), seclusion, totem center(s), right of asylum. *See also* Gender identity; Harems; Home environment; Privacy; Public sphere; Purdah; Sex discrimination; Sex roles; Sexism; Sexual division of labor; Veiling of women.

Privateers. Privateer(s,ing). Letter(s) of marque. *Consider also:* armed ship(s), pirate ship(s), sea rover(s), corsair(s). *See also* Capture at sea; Hijacking; Piracy (at sea); Revenge; Seizure of ships.

Privately owned. See *Private enterprise.*

Privatization. Privatiz(e,ed,ing,ation). Denationaliz(e,ed,ing,ation). Commercializ(e,ed,ing,ation). Marketiz(e,ed, ing,ation). Decommuniz(e,ed,es,ing, ation). Overprivatiz(e,ed,ing,ation). Dismantl(e,ed,ing) state run enterprise(s). *Choose from:* sell(ing), take over *with:* state owned, federal(ly) owned, government owned, national, state asset(s), public(ly) owned. *Choose from:* return(ed,ing), restor(e,ed,ing), transfer(red,ring), conversion, convert(ed,ing) *with:* government, federal, state *with:* private, free enterprise, open market. *Choose from:* private(ly), commercial *with:* prison(s), mail delivery, postal system(s), school(s), garbage removal, street repair(s), park(s), wilderness, wildland(s). *Consider also:* debureaucratiz(e,ed,ing,ation), shrink(ing) government, public choice economics, voucher system(s), private sector contract(s,ing), open(ed,ing) market(s), assigned service provider(s), go(ing) private, purchas(e,es,ed,ing) service(s), contract(ed,ing) service(s), competitive bidding, Reaganism, Thatcherism. *See also* Capitalism; Contracting out; Countries in transition; Decommunization; Downsizing; Educational vouchers; Industrial enterprises; Labor economics; Minimal government; Nationalization; Post-communism; Profit motive; Private enterprise; Private sector; Privatized pension systems; Public sector; School choice.

Privatized pension systems. Privatized pension system(s). *Choose from:* privatiz(e,ed,in,ation), pay-as-you-go, privately managed, individually owned, Chilean *with:* retirement account(s), pension system(s), social security, retirement annuit(y,ies). *See also* Income; Pensions; Privatization; Retirement; Retirement income; Retirement planning; Savings.

Privilege. Privilege(s,d). Overadvantag(e,es,ed,ing). Unearned benefit(s). Prerogative(s). Perquisite(s). Birthright(s). Favored. Unaccountable. Not liable. Exempt(ed). Immun(e,ity,ities). Excused. Protected. Indulged. Dispensation(s). Preferential treatment. Special advantage(s). *See also* Elites; Elitism (government); Occupational status; Political elites; Power elite; Power structure; Precedence; Preferential treatment; Prestige; Privileges and immunities; Ruling class; Social dominance; Social status.

Privileged communications. Privileged communication(s). Confidential(ity,ly). Secre(t,ts,cy). Confid(ed,ing). Right of privacy. Strict(est) confidence. Inaccessible record(s). Entrusted *with:* confidence(s). *Choose from:* confidential, secret, privileged, private, privy *with:* information, communication(s), record(s), source(s). *See also* Anonymity; Confidential records; Physician patient relations; Privacy; Privacy laws.

Privileges and immunities. Privilege(s) and immunit(y,ies). *Choose from:* diplomatic, congressional, governmental, judicial, congressional, presidential *with:* immunit(y,ies), privilege(s). *Consider also:* privileged communication(s), patient confidentiality, confidentiality of source(s), immunity from prosecution, franking privilege(s), mailing privilege(s), shield law, absolution, exonerat(e,es,ed,ing,ion), special treatment. *See also* Diplomats;

Elected officials; Exemption (law); Preferential treatment; Privilege.

Privileges and immunities, diplomatic. See *Diplomatic privileges and immunities.*

Prizes. Prize(s). Award(s). Honor(s). Prizewinner(s). Medal(s). Blue ribbon(s). Medalist(s). Citation(s). Knighthood. Order of the Garter. Honorary degree(s). Certificate(s) of merit. Honorary membership(s). Certificate(s) of recognition. Gold key(s). Nobel prize(s). Pulitzer prize(s). Grand Prix. Laureate(s). Accolade(s). Cordon Bleu. Highest honor(s). Phi Beta Kappa. Summa cum laude. Magna cum laude. *See also* Awards; Fellowships (educational); Incentives; Literary prizes; Performance; Prestige; Recognition (achievement); Scholarships (educational); Reward.

Prizes, literary. See *Literary prizes.*

Pro-choice. See *Abortion rights movement.*

Proactive inhibition. Proactive inhibition. Prior learning effect(s). *Choose from:* proactive *with:* inhibit(ed,ing,ion), interfer(e,ed,ing,ence). *Choose from:* anterograde effect(s) *with:* learn(ed,ing), acquisition. *See also* Interference (learning).

Probability. Probab(ility,ilities,ilism,le). Poisson distribution. Normal distribution. Bayes theorem. Bayesian(ism). Uncertainty. Risk factor(s). Stochastic model(s). Markov chain(s). Risk assessment. Estimate risk(s). Prediction. Toss(ed,ing) coin(s). Roll(ed,ing) die. Gaming odds. Likel(y,ihood). Reasonable doubt. Reason to suspect. Prospect(s). Law of averages. Chance. Odds. Statistical inference. Binomial distribution. Law of large numbers. Random(ness). Central limit theorem. Gauss Markov theorem. Lotter(y,ies). *See also* Chance; Estimation; Expectations; Game theory; Predictability; Prediction; Predictive validity; Probability judgment; Probability theory; Quantitative methods; Reliability; Risk assessment; Sampling; Statistical inference; Statistical significance; Stochastic processes.

Probability, response. See *Response probability.*

Probability judgment. Probability judgment. *Choose from:* probabilit(y,ies), probabilistic, likelihood, risk(s), uncertain(ty), odds *with:* judgment, assessment(s), estimat(e,ed,ing,ion,ions), rating(s), predict(ed,ing,ion,ions). Gambling decision(s). *See also* Judgment; Probability; Probability learning; Risk assessment.

Probability learning. Probability learning. *Choose from:* probabilit(y,ies), probabilistic *with:* learn(ed,ing), comprehen-

sion. *See also* Learning; Probability; Probability judgment.

Probability theory. Probability theory. *Choose from:* probability, uncertainty, chance *with:* theor(y,ies,em). *Consider also:* central limit theorem, law(s) of large numbers, law of average(s), stochastic process(es), approximation method(s), statistical probability, Bayes(ian) theor(y,ies,em). *See also* Probability; Theories.

Probation. Probation(ary,er,ers,ed). Work release offender(s). Under supervision of court. Probated delinquent(s). Probated felon(s). Sentenc(e,ed,ing) to community service. *Consider also:* temporary contract(s), pretenure, trial period(s), initial appointment(s), testing period(s), academic probation, probationary period(s). *See also* Academic probation; Alternatives to incarceration; Criminal rehabilitation; Imprisonment; Law enforcement; Parole; Sentencing.

Probation, academic. See *Academic probation.*

Probation officers. Probation officer(s). *Choose from:* probation, community corrections, juvenile court *with:* officer(s), worker(s), staff, counselor(s), personnel, volunteer(s). *Consider also:* parole officer(s), probation supervision. *See also* Correctional personnel; Parole officers.

Problem, mind body. See *Mind body problem.*

Problem drinking. Problem drinking. Binge drink(er,ers,ing). Chronic(ally) drunk(en,enness). Chronic drinker(s). *Choose from:* drink(ing,er,ers), drunk, alcohol, liquor, intoxicat(ed,ion) *with:* problem(s), escape, dyssocial, excess(ive), abuse(rs,ing), thymogenic, dependen(t,cy), misuse, related, offense(s). *Consider also:* alpha, reactive, symptomatic *with:* alcoholism. *See also* Alcoholism; Drinking behavior; Drunk driving.

Problem solving. Problem solving. Reason(ed,ing). Strateg(y,ies). Solving problem(s). Problem schema(s). Concept utilization. Solution(s) to problem(s). Troubleshooting. Problem resolution. Solution achievement. *Consider also:* game theory, hypothesis testing, tactic(s). *See also* Brainstorming; Cognitive processes; Conflict resolution; Crisis intervention; Crisis management; Coping; Decision making; Divergent thinking; Evaluation; Help seeking behavior; Heuristics; Improvisation; Information seeking; Intuition; Inventions; Logical thinking; Problems; Reasoning; Research methods; Scientific method; Search strategies; Strategies; Systems analysis; Word games.

Problem solving, anagram. See *Anagram problem solving.*

Problem solving, group. See *Group problem solving.*

Problems. Problem(atic,s). Puzzle(s). Riddle(s). Conundrum(s). Enigma(tic). Gordian knot(s). Question(s). Quandar(y,ies). Dilemma(s). Predicament(s). Impasse(s). Bone of contention. Subject of dispute. Mind boggl(ing,er,ers). Labyrinth(s). Hidden meaning(s). Plight(s). Perplex(ed,ing,ity). Issue(s). Obstacle(s). Cris(is,es). Disorder(s). Challenge(s). Multi-problem(s). Barrier(s). Trouble(s). Constraint(s). Limitation(s). Difficult(y,ies). *See also* Adjustment (to environment); Barriers; Conflict; Constraints; Crises; Difficulties; Disorders; Limitations; Problem solving.

Problems, administrative. See *Administrative problems.*

Problems, behavior. See *Behavior problems.*

Problems, community. See *Community problems.*

Problems, economic. See *Economic problems.*

Problems, emotional. See *Emotionally disturbed.*

Problems, family. See *Family problems.*

Problems, financial. See *Economic problems; Poverty.*

Problems, health. See *Health problems.*

Problems, international. See *World problems.*

Problems, social. See *Social problems.*

Problems, theoretical. See *Theoretical problems.*

Problems, world. See *World problems.*

Procedure, administrative. See *Administrative procedure.*

Procedure and pleading, equity. See *Equity pleading and procedure.*

Procedures. See *Legal procedures; Methods; Selection procedures.*

Procedures, civil. See *Civil procedures.*

Procedures, court. See *Legal procedures.*

Procedures, grievance. See *Employee grievances.*

Procedures, legal. See *Legal procedures.*

Procedures, selection. See *Selection procedures.*

Proceedings, criminal. See *Criminal proceedings.*

Process, due. See *Due process.*

Process, judicial. See *Adjudication; Due process; Legal procedures.*

Process, labor. See *Labor process.*

Process psychosis. Process psychos(is,es). Process schizophrenia. Nuclear schizophrenia. Dementia praecox. Malignant psychos(is,es). *See also* Psychoses; Schizophrenia.

Processes, cognitive. See *Cognitive processes.*

Processes, copying. See *Copying processes.*

Processes, group. See *Group processes.*

Processes, intersensory. See *Intersensory processes.*

Processes, legislative. See *Legislative processes.*

Processes, mental. See *Cognitive processes.*

Processes, perceptual motor. See *Perceptual motor processes.*

Processes, personality. See *Personality processes.*

Processes, political. See *Political processes.*

Processes, psychotherapeutic. See *Psychotherapeutic processes.*

Processes, social. See *Social processes.*

Processes, stochastic. See *Stochastic processes.*

Processes, therapeutic. See *Therapeutic processes.*

Processess, psychomotor. See *Perceptual motor processes.*

Processing, data. See *Data processing.*

Processing, electronic data. See *Electronic data processing.*

Processing, human information. See *Human information storage.*

Processing, image. See *Image processing.*

Processing, information. See *Information processing.*

Processing, order. See *Order processing.*

Processions. Procession(s,al,als). Cortege(s). Parade(s). Cavalcade(s). Motorcade(s). March(es). Viceregal entrance(s). Triumphal entr(y,ies). Pageant(s,try). Pilgrimage(s). *See also* Crusades; Expeditions; Marches; Pilgrimages.

Proclamations. See *Manifesto.*

Procrastination. Procrastinat(e,ed,ing,ion). Postpon(e,ed,ing,ement). Delay(ed,ing). Defer(red,ring,ment). Procrastinator(s). Irresolute(ness). Dilatory. Lag(ged,ging). Dawdl(e,ed,ing). Temporiz(e,ed,ing). *See also* Delays; Habits; Hesitation; Motivation; Passiveness; Time utilization.

Procreation. Procreat(e,ive,ion,or,ors). Propagat(e,ed,ing,ion). Beget(ting). Begot. Begat. Reproduc(e,ed,tion). Spawn(ed,ing). Conceive(d).

Engender(ed,ing,ment). Generat(e,ed, ing). Proliferat(e,ed,ing). Giv(e,ing) birth. Gave birth. *See also* Birth; Sexual reproduction.

Procurement, government. See *Government procurement.*

Produce, farm. See *Farm produce.*

Product, gross national. See *Gross national product.*

Product discontinued. Product discontinued. *Choose from:* product(s), commodit(y,ies), goods *with:* discontinu(e,ed, ing,ance), ceased production, suspen(d, de,ding,sion), cessation. *Consider also:* out-of-print, out-of-stock. *See also* Consumer goods; Defunct; Durable goods; Product life cycle; Product recall; Products.

Product introduction. Product introduction. *Choose from:* product(s), commodit(y,ies), goods *with:* introduc(e,ed, ing,tion), announc(e,ed,ing,ment), bring(ing) out, brought out, present(e,ed, ing,ment), inaugurat(e,ed,ing,ion), usher(ed,ing) in, roll(ed) out. *See also* Inauguration; Inventions; Presentations; Product development; Product life cycle; Products; Technological innovations.

Product labeling. Product labeling. *Choose from:* product(s), package(s), ingredient(s), material(s), content(s), merchandise, drug(s), food *with:* label(s,ing), insert(s), identification, list(s,ing), information, expiration date(s). *See also* Consumer protection; Corporate social responsibility; Marketing; Product warranty; Products.

Product liability. Product liabilit(y,ies). Warranty coverage. Lawsuit(s) against producer(s). Product recall(s). Manufacturer(s) liabiiity. Suit against manufacturer(s). *Choose from:* product(s), invention(s), device(s), equipment, merchandise, goods, services or product by name *with:* adverse health effect(s), liable, liabilit(y,ies), defect(s,ive), substandard, injur(ed,ious), seek(ing) damage(s), hazard(s,ous), recall(s), lawsuit(s), claimant(s). *See also* Consumer fraud; Consumer protection; Imperfection; Negligence; Product labeling; Product recall; Product tampering; Products; Quality control.

Product life cycle. Product life cycle(s). *Choose from:* product(s), durable good(s) *with:* life cycle(s), lifetime(s), normal lives, normal life, life span(s), life extension. *Consider also:* product durability. *See also* Obsolescence; Preventive maintenance; Product introduction; Product discontinued; Products.

Product recall. Product recall(s). Recall(ed, ing) car(s),etc. Call(ed,ing) back. *Choose from:* stop(ping,ped), suspend(ed,ing), suspension *with:*

sale(s), deliver(y,ies), marketing, using, usage. Offer(ed,ing) free replacement(s). *See also* Defunct; Product discontinued; Products; Quality control.

Product safety. Product safety. *Choose from:* product(s), invention(s), device(s), equipment, merchandise, goods, service(s), drug(s) or product by name *with:* safe(ty), guarantee(s), reliab(le, ility), quality control, quality assurance, regulat(e,ed,ing,ion), standard(s,ize,ized, izing,ization), monitor(ed,ing), inspect(ed,ing,ion), approv(e,ed,ing,al). *See also* Consumer fraud; Consumer protection; Guarantees; Product labeling; Product liability; Product recall; Product tampering; Products; Quality control; Safety.

Product tampering. Product tampering. Consumer terrorism. *Choose from:* tamper(ed,ing), poison(s,ed,ing), taint(ed,ing), lac(ed,ing), cyanide, ground glass, sabotag(e,ed,ing), damag(e,ed,ing), meddl(e,ed,ing), adulterat(e,ed,ing), needle(s), razor blade(s), contaminat(e,ed,ing) *with:* product(s), produce, goods, equipment, capsule(s), tablet(s), Tylenol, candy, tea bag(s), Excedrin, baby food, cheese, grape(s), apple juice, fruit juice(s), orange juice, etc. *See also* Product liability; Products; Quality control; Sabotage.

Product warranty. Product warrant(y,ies). Product guarant(y,ies,ee,ees). Warranty coverage. Lemon law(s). *Choose from:* product(s), invention(s), device(s), equipment, merchandise, goods, service(s) or product by name *with:* warrant(y,ies), guarant(y,ies,ee,ees). *Consider also:* product reliability. *See also* Consumer fraud; Consumer protection; Product labeling; Product liability; Product recall; Product safety; Product tampering; Products; Quality control.

Product development. Product development. Develop(ing,ment) product(s). Test product(s). Prototyp(e,es,ing). Technological(ly) develop(ed,ing). New product(s). Technological advance(s). New device(s). Research and development. Product design(s). Industrial design(s). Introduc(ed,ing) product(s). New version(s). Product innovation(s). *See also* Inventions; Product introduction; Products; Research; Scientific development; Technological innovations.

Production. Production. Productiv(e,ity). Productive(ness). Growth. Producing. Output(s). Yield(s). Fruitful(ness). Prolific. Contribution(s). Effective(ness). Efficien(cy,t). High performance. Performance indicator(s). Publication rate(s). *Consider also:* Gross National Product, GNP, Gross Domestic Product, GDP, fertil(e,ity), inventive(ness), creativ(ity,eness), imaginative(ness),

resourceful(ness), manufactur(e,ed,ing). *See also* Business cycles; Consumption (economic); Economic conditions; Economic dependence; Economic development; Economic indicators; Economic statistics; Industrial capacity; Industrial efficiency; Industrial expansion; Industrial production; Industry; Labor process; Offshore production (foreign countries); Production consumption relationship; Productivity; Subsistence economy.

Production, industrial. See *Industrial production.*

Production, mass. See *Mass production.*

Production, offshore foreign countries. See *Offshore production (foreign countries).*

Production capacity. See *Industrial capacity.*

Production consumption relationship. Production consumption relationship. Product(s) market equilibrium. Consumption production relationship. Supply and demand. Production relations. *Consider also:* overproduction, shortage(s), aggregate supply. *See also* Aggregate economics; Commodities; Consumer behavior; Consumption (economic); Demand; Economic conditions; Luxuries; Market economy; Prices; Production; Price trends; Supply and demand; Supply side economics.

Production control. Production control. *Choose from:* production, operations, output, manufacturing *with:* control(led, ling), plan(ning,ned), rout(e,ed,ing), schedul(e,ed,ing), dispatch(ed,ing), inspect(ed,ing,ion). *See also* Factories; Factory automation; High technology industries; Industrial capacity; Industrial efficiency; Industrial production; Labor aspects of technology.

Productivity. Productiv(e,ity). Productive(ness). Man-hour output. Output input ratio. Production. Producing. Output(s). Yield(ing,s). Fruitful(ness). Prolific. Contribution(s). Effective(ness). Efficien(cy,t). High performance. Performance indicator(s). Publication rate(s). *Consider also:* fertil(e,ity), inventive(ness), creativ(ity,eness), imaginative(ness), resourceful(ness). *See also* Accountability; Achievement; Cost effectiveness; Economic statistics; Economic underdevelopment; Effectiveness; Employee productivity; Industrial efficiency; Organizational effectiveness; Production; Quality of working life; Quotas; Resourcefulness; Scientific management; Time utilization.

Productivity, agricultural. See *Agricultural productivity.*

Productivity, employee. See *Employee productivity.*

Products. Product(s). Item(s) produced. Product line(s). Goods. Services. Merchandise. Yield(s). Output(s). Outcome(s). Crop(s). By-product(s). Fruit. Result(s). Opus. Masterpiece(s). Consequence(s). Effect(s). Proceeds. Turnout. Creation(s). Invention(s). Work(s) of art. Musical composition(s). *See also* Commodities; Consumer goods; Crops; Durable goods; Inventions; Marketing; Patents; Prices; Product discontinued; Product introduction; Product life cycle; Sales; Trade.

Products, animal. See *Animal products.*

Products, dairy. See *Dairy products.*

Products, macaroni. See *Pasta.*

Products, primary. See *Raw materials.*

Products, quality of. See *Quality control.*

Products, staple. See *Raw materials.*

Products, waste. See *Recycling; Salvaging; Waste to energy.*

Profane. See *Everyday Life; Secularization.*

Profanity. See *Obscenity.*

Professional achievement. See *Occupational success.*

Professional associations. See *Professional organizations.*

Professional certification. Professional(ly) certif(ied,ication). *Choose from:* professional(s), practitioner(s), lawyer(s), attorney(s), social worker(s), pharmacist(s), therapist(s), dentist(s), nurse(s), physician(s), doctor(s), counselor(s), clinician(s), psychotherapist(s), caseworker(s) *with:* certif(ied,ication), accredit(ed,ation), licens(e,es,ed), degree(s). *Consider also:* pass(ed,ing), admit(ted) *with:* bar, board. *See also* Accreditation; Law societies; Licenses; Occupational qualifications; Professional development; Professional organizations; Professional personnel; Professional standards.

Professional client relations. Professional client relation(s,ship). *Choose from:* professional(s), practitioner(s), lawyer(s), attorney(s), social worker(s), pharmacist(s), therapist(s), dentist(s), nurse(s), physician(s), doctor(s), counselor(s), clinician(s), psychotherapist(s), caseworker(s) *with:* client(s), patient(s) *with:* relation(s,ship), rapport, interaction(s), covenant(s), role(s), trust, agreement(s), distrust, attitude(s), perception(s), communication(s), influence(s). *See also* Client rights; Clients; Communication (thought transfer); Confidential communications; Confidential records; Customer relations; Dentist patient relations; Impaired professionals; Interprofessional relations; Investor relations; Nurse patient relations; Parent school relations; Physician patient relations; Police community relations; Professional ethics; Professional family relations; Professional liability; Professional malpractice; Sexual exploitation; Student teacher relations; Unethical conduct.

Professional communication. See *Professional literature.*

Professional competence. Professional competence. *Choose from:* professional(s), practitioner(s), lawyer(s), attorney(s), social worker(s), pharmacist(s), librarian(s), teacher(s), therapist(s), dentist(s), nurse(s), physician(s), doctor(s), counselor(s), clinician(s), psychotherapist(s), caseworker(s) *with:* competen(t,ce,cy, cies), skill(s), expert(ise,ness), knowledge, qualification(s), proficien(t,cy), experience. *See also* Ability; Competence; Educational background; Performance; Professional certification; Professional development; Professional education; Professional standards.

Professional consultation. See *Consultation.*

Professional corporations. Professional corporation(s). *Choose from:* incorporat(e,ed,ing,ion), corporation(s) *with:* profession(s,al), medical practice, veterinary practice, dental practice. *See also* Corporations; Professional liability; Professional personnel.

Professional development. Professional development. *Choose from:* professional(s), career(s), staff, faculty, practitioner(s), lawyer(s), attorney(s), social worker(s), pharmacist(s), librarian(s), teacher(s), therapist(s), dentist(s), nurse(s), physician(s), doctor(s), counselor(s), clinician(s), psychotherapist(s), caseworker(s) *with:* develop(ed,ing,ment), growth, professionalization, professional socialization, relicens(ed,ing), recertif(ied,ication), retrain(ed,ing), advanced study, postdoctoral, continuing education. *Consider also:* inservice, refresher *with:* course(s), training, learning. *See also* Career change; Career development.; Continuing education; Employment history; Inservice teacher education; Inservice training; Job rotation; Law societies; Mentors; Occupational aspirations; Professional certification; Professional education; Professional literature; Professional personnel; Professional socialization; Staff development.

Professional education. Professional education. *Choose from:* profession(al, s), graduate, career(s), practitioner(s), architect(s,ure,ural), lawyer(s), attorney(s), legal, social work(er,ers), pharmacist(s), librarian(s), teacher(s), therapist(s), dentist(s), nurse(s), physician(s), doctor(s), medical,

counselor(s), clinic(al,ian,icians), psychotherapist(s), casework(er,ers), theological *with:* study, educat(e,ed,ing, ion), course(s), degree(s), train(ed,ing), learn(ed,ing), curricul(a,um), preparation, intern(s,ship,ships), clerkship(s). *See also* Adult education; Art education; Art schools; Business education; Career education; Continuing education; Graduate education; Inservice teacher education; Inservice training; Law societies; Medical education; Nursing education; Postgraduate training; Professional development; Psychiatric training.

Professional employees. See *Professional personnel.*

Professional ethics. Professional ethic(s). Helsinki declaration. Hippocratic oath. Professional code(s). Humane concern(s). *Choose from:* professional(s, als), physician(s), doctor(s), dentist(s), experimenter(s), lawyer(s), attorney(s), teacher(s), professor(s), instructor(s), social worker(s), nurse(s), dentist(s), psychologist(s), psychiatrist(s), pediatrician(s), librarian(s), clergy, auditor(s), accountant(s), advertiser(s), journalist(s), drug trial(s), experiment(s, ation), research *with:* humane, ethic(s,al), moral(s,ity), immoral(ity), deception, obligation(s), integrity, accountability, honest(y), principle(s), code(s), openness, fidelity, conscience, conscientious(ness), conflict of interest, trust(worthy,worthiness), truth(ful, fulness), incorruptib(le,ility), unethical(ly), improper, misdeed(s), misconduct, conflict(s) of interest, malpractice, bribe(s,ry), sex(ual,ually) abuse(s,d), corrupt(ion), alcoholi(c,sm), drug abuse(rs), violat(e,ed,ing,ions), illegal(ity,ities), impropriet(y,ies), collusion, scandal(s), breach of confidence, fraud(ulent), unlawful(ly), sleaz(e,y), unprofessional, breach of decorum, corporate raider(s), withholding information, accept(ance) of gift(s), overbill(ed,ing), cheat(ed,ing), wrongdoing(s), nepotism, unscrupulous(ness), trust violation(s), inappropriate conduct, falsif(y,ying,ied,ication), extortion, illegal dumping, tamper(ed,ing) false claim(s), false expense(s), false advertising, price manipulation, sexual misconduct, tax evasion, financial irregularit(y,ies), kickback(s), illegal contribution(s), mishandling funds, defraud(ed,ing). *See also* Codes of ethics; Corruption in government; Deception; Falsification (scientific); Fraud; Investor relations; Journalistic ethics; Judicial corruption; Legal ethics; Malpractice; Medical advertising; Medical ethics; Ministerial ethics (clergy); Nursing ethics; Political crimes; Political ethics; Professional malpractice; Quackery; Research ethics;

Scandals; Scientific misconduct; Sexual harassment; Unethical conduct.

Professional family relations. Professional family relation(s,ship). *Choose from:* professional(s), practitioner(s), lawyer(s), attorney(s), social worker(s), pharmacist(s), therapist(s), dentist(s), nurse(s), physician(s), doctor(s), counselor(s), clinician(s), pediatrician(s), psychotherapist(s), caseworker(s) *with:* famil(y,ies), relative(s), home(s), parent(s), child(ren), mother(s), father(s), grandparent(s), grandmother(s), grandfather(s), brother(s), sister(s), sibling(s) *with:* teamwork, cooperation, assistance, relation(s,ship), interaction(s), rapport, support, involvement, covenant(s), role(s), trust, agreement(s), distrust, attitude(s), perception(s), communication(s), influence(s). *See also* Family influence; Professional client relations.

Professional identity. Professional identit(y, ies). *Choose from:* professional(s), socioprofessional, practitioner(s), lawyer(s), attorney(s), social worker(s), pharmacist(s), therapist(s), dentist(s), nurse(s), physician(s), doctor(s), counselor(s), clinician(s), psychotherapist(s), caseworker(s), teacher(s), professor(s), librarian(s), accountant(s) *with:* identit(y,ies), identification, orientation(s), socialization, role concept(s), value(s), model(s), reference group(s). *See also* Professional image; Professional orientations; Professional socialization; Social identity.

Professional image. Professional image(s). Professionalism. Occupational image(s). *Choose from:* profession(s,al), occupation(s,al), physician(s), attorney(s), dentist(s), nurse(s), librarian(s), teacher(s), etc. *with:* image(s), stereotype(s), prestige, status, portrayal, visibility, professionalism, public perception, misperception(s), professional identity, media image(s), popular image(s), professional pride, role(s). *See also* Occupational status; Professional client relations; Professional family relations; Professional identity; Social identity.

Professional isolation. Professional isolation. Collegial isolation. *Choose from:* professional(s), collegial, faculty, teacher(s), provider(s), staff *with:* isolat(e,ed,in,ion), lack of support, lack of communication, lack of interaction, sex discrimination, individualism. *See also* Alienation; Faculty development; Interprofessional relations; Isolation; Professional socialization; Social isolation; Working conditions.

Professional journals. See *Professional literature.*

Professional liability. Professional liability. Professional accountability. Professional responsibility. Patient sue(d,s). Liability to patient(s). Professional malpractice. *Choose from:* profession(al,s,als), physician(s), doctor(s), lawyer(s), attorney(s), law firm(s), professor(s), dentist(s), psychologist(s), psychiatrist(s), pediatrician(s), teacher(s), social worker(s), nurse(s), librarian(s), clergy, auditor(s), accountant(s), advertiser(s), press, journalist(s) *with:* negligen(t,ce), liab(le,ility), iatrogenic, unethical, improper, immoral(ity), misdeed(s), misconduct, conflict of interest, malpractice, bribe(s,ry), sexu(al,ally), abuse(s,d), corrupt(ion), alcoholi(c,sm), drug abuse(s), violation(s), illegal(ities), impropriet(y, ies), collusion, scandal(s), breach of confidence, fraud, unlawful(ly), sleaz(e,y), unprofessional behavior, breach of decorum, withholding information, acceptance of gift(s), overbill(ed,ing), cheat(ed,ing), wrongdoing, nepotism, unscrupulous, trust violation(s), inappropriate conduct, falsif(y,ying,ication), extortion, illegal dumping, tampering, false claim(s), false expense(s), false advertising, price manipulation(s), sexual misconduct, tax evasion, financial irregularit(y,ies), kickback(s), illegal contribution(s), mishandling funds, defraud(ed,ing). *See also* Accountability; Impaired professionals; Negligence; Professional ethics; Professional malpractice.

Professional licensing. See *Professional certification.*

Professional literature. Professional literature. *Choose from:* science, scientific, literary, research, scholarly, serious, professional *with:* communication(s), journal(s), newsletter(s), book(s), review(s), publication(s), article(s), literature, report(s), proceeding(s), bulletin(s), yearbook(s), serial(s), monograph(s), dissertation(s), periodical(s), magazine(s). *See also* Addendum; Literature; Professional development; Professional education; Scholarly periodicals.

Professional malpractice. Professional malpractice. *Choose from:* profession(al, s,als), physician(s), doctor(s), lawyer(s), attorney(s), law firm(s), professor(s), dentist(s), psychologist(s), psychiatrist(s), pediatrician(s), teacher(s), therapist(s), social worker(s), nurse(s), librarian(s), clergy, auditor(s), accountant(s), advertiser(s), press, journalist(s) or others *with:* harass(ed, ing,ment), negligen(t,ce), liab(le,ility), iatrogenic, unethical, improper, immoral(ity), misdeed(s), misconduct, conflict of interest, malpractice, bribe(s,ry), sexu(al,ally), abuse(s,d), corrupt(ion), alcoholi(c,sm), drug abuse, violation(s), illegal(ities), impropriet(y, ies), collusion, scandal(s), breach of

confidence, fraud, unlawful(ly), sleaz(e,y), unprofessional behavior, breach of decorum, withhold(ing) information, withheld information, acceptance of gift(s), overbill(ed,ing), cheat(ing), wrongdoing, nepotism, unscrupulous, trust violation(s), inappropriate conduct, falsif(y,ying, ication), extortion, illegal dumping, tamper(ed,ing), false claim(s), false expense(s), false advertising, price manipulation(s), sexual misconduct, tax evasion, financial irregularit(y,ies), kickback(s), illegal contribution(s), mishandl(ed,ing) fund(s), defraud(ed, ing). *See also* Deception; Ethics; Falsification (scientific); Fraud; Impaired professionals; Professional ethics; Professional liability; Quackery; Research ethics; Scientific misconduct.

Professional organizations. Professional organization(s). *Choose from:* professional(s), medical, legal, physician(s), lawyer(s), social work(ers), teacher(s), librar(y,ies,ian,ians), educator(s), statistic(s,ian,ians), anthropolog(y,ist, ists), architect(s,ure,ural), psycholog(y, ical,ist,ists), sociolog(y,ical,ist,ists), political scien(ce,tist,tists), histor(y,ical, ian,ians), scien(ce,tific,tist,tists), chemi(cal,istry,ist,ists), biolog(y,ical, ist,ists) or others *with:* organization(s), association(s), societ(y,ies), affiliation(s), academ(y,ies), council(s), fraternit(y,ies), league(s). *See also* Archaeological societies; Associations (organizations); Law societies; Professional certification; Professional development; Professional education; Professional personnel; Professional socialization; Scientific societies; Societies (organizations).

Professional orientations. Professional orientation(s). *Choose from:* professional(s), socioprofessional, practitioner(s), lawyer(s), attorney(s), social worker(s), pharmacist(s), therapist(s), dentist(s), nurse(s), physician(s), doctor(s), counselor(s), clinician(s), psychotherapist(s), caseworker(s), teacher(s), professor(s), librarian(s), accountant(s) or others *with:* attitude(s), perspective(s), orientation(s), outlook(s), commitment(s), culture, norm(s), more(s), profile(s), ethic(s), identit(y,ies), identification(s), socialization, role(s), values, model(s), reference group(s). *See also* Professional identity; Professional socialization; Professionalism.

Professional patient relations. See *Professional client relations.*

Professional personnel. Professional personnel. Professional(s,ization). *Choose from:* professional *with:* employee(s), staff, women, woman, men, man, person(s), people, degree(s). *Consider also:* white collar worker(s),

lawyer(s), nurse(s), social worker(s), teacher(s), etc. *See also* Accountants; Administrators; Architects; Archivists; Artists; Attorneys; Businessmen; Clergy; Computer experts; Consultants; Counselors; Dentists; Engineers; Faculty; Foreign professional personnel; Gold collar workers; Impaired professionals; Intellectual life; Journalists; Knowledge workers; Librarians; Mental health personnel; Musicians; Occupational status; Occupations; Pharmacists; Physicians; Professional client relations; Professional family relations; Professional identity; Professional socialization; Professional women; Psychiatrists; Psychologists; Research personnel; Scientists; Social workers; Teachers; Therapists; Vocations; White collar workers; Writers; Yuppies.

Professional personnel, foreign. See *Foreign professional personnel.*

Professional socialization. Professional socialization. *Choose from:* professional(s), socioprofessional, practitioner(s) or specific professions by name *with:* socialization, identit(y,ies), identification, orientation(s), role(s), attitude(s), values, model(s), reference group(s), expectation(s), consciousness. *See also* Professional identity; Professional isolation; Professional organizations; Professional orientations; Professional personnel.

Professional standards. Professional standard(s). *Choose from:* profession(al,s), clinical, educational, judicial, physician(s), psychologist(s), social worker(s), psychotherapist(s), therapist(s), psychiatrist(s), lawyer(s), treatment provider(s), mental health service(s) or other professions by name *with:* standard(s), accountab(le,ility), competenc(e,y,ies), certif(ied,ication), principle(s), quality assurance, values, norm(s), qualification(s), peer review, accredit(ed,ing,ation), guideline(s), code(s) of conduct, licens(e,ed,ing,ure), accredit(ed,ing,ation), certif(y,icd, ication), regulation(s), ethic(s,al). *See also* Professional certification; Professional competence; Professional development; Professional education; Professional ethics; Professional socialization; Professionalism.

Professional status. See *Occupational status.*

Professional training. See *Professional education.*

Professional women. Professional wom(an, en). Wom(en,an) professional(s). Female professional(s). Businesswom(en,an). Career women. Congresswom(en,an). *Choose from:* woman, women, female(s) *with:* professional(s), professionalization, professional degree(s), advanced degree(s), professional school graduate(s), professionally trained, accountant(s), academi(a,c,cs), administrator(s), architect(s), artist(s), athletic coach(es), attorney(s), chiropractor(s), clergy, counselor(s), dentist(s), doctor(s), engineer(s), entrepreneur(s), executive(s), expert(s), faculty, information scientist(s), journalist(s), lawyer(s), librarian(s), managerial personnel, mathematician(s), musician(s), nurse(s), midwi(fe,ves), optometrist(s), president(s), pharmacist(s), physician(s), planner(s), psychologist(s), psychotherapist(s), practitioner(s), professor(s), research director(s), researcher(s), scientist(s), senator(s), social scientist(s), social worker(s), statistician(s), supervisory personnel, teacher(s), therapist(s), technical personnel, veterinarian(s), writer(s) or other professions by name. *See also* Family work relationship; Females (human); Labor market segmentation; Professional personnel; Working women.

Professional workers. See *Professional personnel; Professional women.*

Professionalism. Professionalism. Professionalization. *Choose from:* professional(s), socioprofessional or name of specific profession *with:* competenc(y,ies), attitude(s), relationship(s), socialization, code(s), ethic(s), role(s), value(s), skill(s), knowledge, commitment(s), perspective(s), association(s), autonom(y,ous), identit(y,ies), identification, jurisdiction, qualification(s), credential(s), status, control. *See also* Professional identity; Professional orientation; Professional socialization.

Professionalization. See *Professional socialization; Professionalism.*

Professionals, impaired. See *Impaired professionals.*

Professionals, legal. See *Legal professionals.*

Professions. See *Occupations; Professional personnel.*

Professions, health. See *Allied health personnel; Health occupations; Nurses; Physicians.*

Professions, medical. See *Allied health personnel; Health occupations; Nurses; Physicians.*

Professors. See *Faculty.*

Proficiency. See *Competence.*

Proficiency, language. See *Language proficiency.*

Profiles. See *Biographical data.*

Profiles (measurement). Profile(s). *Choose from:* trait(s) *with:* pattern(s), organization. *Consider also:* composite score(s),

configuration(s), typolog(y,ies). *See also* Analysis; Measurement.

Profiling, racial. See *Harassment; Racism; Stereotyping; Street harassment.*

Profit motive. Profit motive(s). Monetary incentive(s). Production bonus(es). Profit objective(s). Bottom line. For profit. Mercenar(y,ies). Acquisitive(ness). Profitmaking. Capitalis(m,t, tic). Free enterprise. Private ownership. Corporate ownership. Free trade. Free market. Bourgeois political economy. Private enterprise. Capital accumulation. Profit system(s). Economic competition. Market econom(y,ies). Entrepreneurial(ism). Private investment(s). *Consider also:* commercializ(e,ed,ing,ation), commodif(y,ied,ication), Protestant ethic, laissez faire government, competitive econom(y,ies). *See also* Businessmen; Capitalism; Economic attitudes; Economic competition; Economic man; Entrepreneurship; Marketing; Monetary incentives; Motivation; Privatization; Profitability; Profits.

Profit sharing. Profit sharing. Gainsharing. *Choose from:* profit(s), gain(s), equity *with:* sharing. Performance linked pay. *Consider also:* employee stock ownership, ESOPs. *See also* Employee incentive plans; Employee motivation; Monetary incentives; Worker participation.

Profitability. Profitab(le,ility,albeness,ably). Advantageous(ness). Cost effective(ness). Earning(s). Gainful(ly). Fruitful(ly). Lucrative. Moneymaking. Remunerative. Reward(s,ed,ing). Well-paying. Valuable. Worthwhile. *See also* Business; Capital (financial); Dividends; Gains; Income; Investments; Monetary incentives; Profits; Profit motive; Stock Exchange; Wealth.

Profits. Profit(able,ability,making,s). Profit margin(s). Markup(s). Earn(ed,ing,ings). Windfall(s). Income(s). Revenue(s). Break even. High(ly,est) paid. Bottom line. Receipt(s). Lucrative. Remunerat(ion,ive). Proceeds. Gain(s). Excess gain(s). Surplus(es). *Consider also:* rate of return, interest rate(s), return on investment(s), long-term growth, short-term growth, capital gain(s), shareholder value, value creation, payback period(s). *See also* Business; Capital (financial); Dividends; Gains; Income; Investments; Monetary incentives; Profitability; Profit motive; Stock Exchange; Wealth.

Profoundly mentally retarded. Profound(ly) mental(ly) retard(ed,ation). *Choose from:* profound(ly) mental(ly) *with:* retard(ed,ation,ates), handicap(s, ped), deficien(t,cy,cies). *Consider also:* IQ below 25, custodial mental(ly) retard(ed,ation). *See also* Custodial care; Mental retardation.

Prognosis. Prognos(is,tic,es,tication). Clinical assessment. *Consider also:* predict(ed,ing,ion), forecast(s,ing), prospect(s) *with:* vulnerability, outcome(s), rehabilitation, failure(s), survival, illness, disease(s), recover(y), treatment efficacy, terminal, death, mortality, morbidity. *See also* Diagnosis; Medical history taking; Patient history; Symptoms.

Program development. Program development. *Choose from:* program(s), service(s), seminar(s), course(s), campaign(s), project(s), practice(s), plan(s), agenda(s), undertaking(s), strateg(y,ies), schedule(s), plank(s), platform(s) *with:* develop(ed,ing,ment), evolution, evolv(e,ed,ing), expansion, expand(ed,ing), progress(ed,ing,ion), strengthen(ed,ing), further(ed,ing), perfect(ed,ing), enrich(ed,ing), advanc(e,ed,ing), promot(e,ed,ing,ion), exten(d,ded,sion). *See also* Program evaluation; Program implementation; Programs.

Program evaluation. Program evaluation. *Choose from:* evaluat(e,ed,ing,ion), measur(e,ed,es,ing), review(ed,ing), assess(ed,ing,ment), monitor(ing), analy(sis,ses), success, effectiveness, impact(s), efficacy, critique(s,d), appraisal(s), quality *with:* program(s), service(s), seminar(s), campaign(s), project(s). *See also* Course evaluation; Educational programs; Program development; Program implementation; Program proposals; Quality control; Self evaluation (groups); Treatment outcome.

Program implementation. Program implement(ed,ing,ation). *Choose from:* program(s), service(s), seminar(s), course(s), campaign(s), project(s), practice(s), plan(s) *with:* implement(ed, ing,ation), design(ed,ing), decision making, dissemination, participat(ion, ory), coordinat(e,ed,ing,ation), enforc(e,ed,ing,ement), develop(ed,ing, ment), establish(ed,ing,ment), operation(s), service delivery, backward/ forward mapping, administrative distance, directive(s), compliance, decision path(s), agenda(s), monitor(ing), innovation, shap(e,ing), shift(ing), clearance, linkage(s). *See also* Creators; Delivery of services; Founding; Logistics; Program development.

Program music. Program(matic) music. Programmusik. Musique a programme. *Consider also:* program symphon(y,ies), symphonic poem(s), concert overture(s), character piece(s), tone poem(s), tondichtung(en), rhapsod(y,ies). *See also* Absolute music; Music; Symphonic poems.

Program proposals. Program proposal(s). *Choose from:* program(s), project(s) *with:* proposal(s), funding request(s), grant application(s), plan(s), proposed, proposition(s), recommendation(s). *See also* Grants; Program development; Program evaluation; Program implementation; Programs.

Program symphony. Program(matic) symphon(y,ies). Descriptive symphon(y, ies). Poematic symphon(y,ies). *See also* Program music; Symphonic poems.

Programed instruction. Programed instruction(s). *Choose from:* programmed, programed, computer assisted *with:* instruction(s,al), textbook(s), text(s), learning, course(s), text(s), study aid(s), tutor(s,ed,ing), curricul(a,um), teach(ing), education(al). *Consider also:* autoinstructional, interactive *with:* instruction(al,s), learning, textbook(s), text(s), course(s). *See also* Computer assisted instruction; Educational technology; Feedback; Individualized instruction; Language laboratories; Teaching methods.

Programming (broadcast). See *Broadcasts.*

Programming, neuro-linguistic. See *Neuro-linguistic programming.*

Programs. Program(s). Project(s). *Consider also:* service(s), seminar(s), course(s), campaign(s), project(s), plan(s) of action, practice(s), plan(s), agenda(s), order of business, outline(s), scheme(s), design(s), blueprint(s), draft(s), sketch(es), undertaking(s), proposition(s), procedure(s), strateg(y,ies), schedule(s), plank(s), platform(s). *See also* After school programs; Antipoverty programs; Deinstitutionalization; Delivery of services; Educational programs; Employee assistance programs; Field experience programs; Food services (programs); Government programs; Home visiting programs; Income maintenance programs; Literacy programs; Medical assistance; Mental health programs; National health programs; Outreach programs; Participation; Program development; Program evaluation; Program implementation; Services; Unemployment relief; Workfare.

Programs, after school. See *After school programs.*

Programs, antinuclear. See *Nuclear weapons non-proliferation.*

Programs, antipoverty. See *Antipoverty programs.*

Programs, assistance. See *Antipoverty programs; Employee assistance programs; Food services (programs); Government programs; Medical assistance; Outreach programs; Public welfare; Social programs.*

Programs, detective and mystery television. See *Detective and mystery television programs.*

Programs, educational. See *Educational programs.*

Programs, employee assistance. See *Employee assistance programs.*

Programs, field experience. See *Field experience programs.*

Programs, food distribution. See *Food services (programs).*

Programs, food services. See *Food services (programs).*

Programs, government. See *Government programs.*

Programs, home visiting. See *Home visiting programs.*

Programs, income maintenance. See *Income maintenance programs.*

Programs, intern. See *Internships.*

Programs, literacy. See *Literacy programs.*

Programs, mental health. See *Mental health programs.*

Programs, mutual help. See *Self help groups.*

Programs, national health. See *National health programs.*

Programs, outreach. See *Outreach programs.*

Programs, poverty. See *Antipoverty programs.*

Programs, social. See *Social programs.*

Programs, television. See *Television programs.*

Programs, universal health. See *National health programs.*

Programs, welfare. See *Antipoverty programs; Food services (programs); Income maintenance programs; Medical assistance; Public welfare; Social agencies; Social programs; Social services; Unemployment relief; Workfare.*

Progress. Progress(ion). Achievement. Cutting edge. Breakthrough(s). State of the art. Leading edge. Mov(e,ing) forward. Advanc(e,es,ed,ing,ment). Making headway. Continuing. Ongoing. Further(ed,ing,ance). Gain(ing,s). Grow(ing,th). Improv(e,ed,ing,ement). Develop(ed,ing,ment,ments,al). Upgrad(e,ing). Perfect(ing,ion). Enrich(ed,ing,ment). Enhanc(e,ed,ing, ment,ments). Restor(e,ed,ing,ation). Economic growth. Moderniz(e,ed,ing, ation). Industrializ(e,ed,ing,ation). *Consider also:* meaningful change(s), perfectibility of man. *See also* Change; Development; Economic development; Evolution; Improvement; Modernization; Political reform; Reform; Regression (civilization); Scientific development; Scientific discoveries; Scientific

revolutions; Social change; Social stability; Revolution.

Progress, social. See *Culture change; Industrialization; Modernization; Progress; Social change; Social Darwinism; Social development; Social processes.*

Progress, societal. See *Culture change; Industrialization; Modernization; Progress; Social change; Social Darwinism; Social development; Social processes.*

Progress, technological. See *Technological progress.*

Progressive relaxation therapy. Progressive relaxation therapy. *Choose from:* progressive muscle relaxation, systematic relaxation therapy. *Consider also:* relaxation *with:* training, technique(s), therap(y,ies), exercise(s), practice(s), treatment(s). *See also* Hypnotherapy; Muscle relaxation; Relaxation; Relaxation training.

Progressive taxes. Progressive tax(es,ing,ation). *Choose from:* progressive, ability to pay, income, personal expenditure(s), consumption, inheritance, gift, estate, sales, capital gains, luxur(y,ies), sin *with:* tax(es,ing,ation). *Consider also:* tax exempt(ion,ions) *with:* dividend(s), capital gain(s). *See also* Income redistribution; Tax deductions; Taxes.

Progressivism. Progressiv(e,es,ism). Neoliberal(s,ism). New liberal(s,ism). Reform liberal(s,ism). Social liberal(s,ism). *See also* Democracy; Humanistic education; Humanitarianism; Humanization; Individualism; Left wing; Liberalism; New Deal; Political ideologies; Political liberalism; Political socialization; Social values; Utilitarianism; Welfare state.

Prohibited books. See *Blacklisting; Censorship.*

Prohibition. Prohibit(ed,ing,ion). Interdict(ion,ive,or,ory). Disallow(ed, ing,ance). Proscrib(e,ed,ing). Proscription. Outlaw(ed,ing,ry). Reject(ed,ing, ion). *See also* Ban; Blacklisting; Boycotts; Embargo; Forbidden; Taboo; Veto.

Projection (psychological). Projection. Projective identification. *Choose from:* project(ed,ing,ive) *with:* counteridentification, attribution(s), pattern(s), response(s), hostil(e,ity), guilt, anger, countertransference. *Consider also:* allopsychosis, scapegoat(s,ed,ing), idea(s) of reference, externaliz(ed,ing, ation). *See also* Defense mechanisms; Displacement (psychology); Scapegoating.

Projection, self. See *Self presentation.*

Projective techniques. Projective technique(s). Projective personality measure(s,ment). Projective attitude measure(s,ment). *Choose from:* projective *with:* technique(s), test(ing,s), technic(s), measure(s,ment). *Consider also:* association measure(s), Bender Gestalt Test, Blacky Pictures Test, Childrens Apperception Test, Color Pyramid Test, Draw a Person, Draw a Family, Franck Drawing Completion Test, Holtzman Inkblot Technique, Holtzman Inkblot Test, House-tree-person Technique, Human Figures Drawing, Incomplete Man Test, ink blot test(s), onomatopoeia and images test(s), Rorschach Test, Rosenzweig Picture Frustration study, Rotter Incomplete Sentences Blank, Senior Apperception Test, storytelling test(s), Szondi Test, Tasks of Emotional Development; Thematic Apperception Test, Zulliger Z Test. *See also* Ink blot tests; Personality; Personality measures.

Projects, housing. See *Public housing.*

Proletarianization. Proletarianiz(e,ed,ing, ation). *Consider also:* class interest(s), class consciousness, worker militancy, unioniz(e,ed,ing,ation), degrading class structure, proletarian attitude(s), deprofessionaliz(e,ed,ing,ation), de-skill(ed,ing), lower(ed,ing) skill requirement(s). *See also* Class consciousness; Embourgeoisement; Lower class attitudes; Mass production; Proletariat; Social mobility; Work simplification; Working class.

Proletariat. Proletar(iat,ian). Lower class(es). Low(er,est) socioeconomic. Impoverished. Inner city neighborhood. Rural family life style. Poor(est). Low(er,est) SES. Low income. Working class. Poverty. Low status. Disadvantaged. Peasant. Working man. Low(er, est) social status. Low(er,est) status. Blue collar worker(s). Plebeian. Common people. Common man. Untouchable(s). Manual labor(ers). Wage earner(s). *See also* Class conflict; Class consciousness; Common people; Low income; Lower class; Working class.

Prolife. See *Antiabortion movement.*

Proliferation, nuclear. See *Nuclear proliferation.*

Prologue. See *Introduction.*

Promiscuity. Promiscu(ity,ous,ousness). Don Juan(ism). Licentious(ness). Sexual(ly) permissive(ness). Wanton(ness). Sleeping around. Swinging. Lewd(ness). Lascivious(ness). Libertine. *Consider also:* prostitution, sexual(ly) delinquen(t,cy), loose(ness), lax(ness), unrestrained, immodest, unchaste, indecent, debauched, dissipated. *See also* Deviant behavior; Extramarital relations; Hypersexuality; Premarital

sexual behavior; Prostitution; Sexual ethics; Sexual permissiveness.

Promises. Promis(e,es,ed,ing). Pledg(e,es, ed,ing). Vow(s,ed,ing). Covenant(s). Guarantee(s,d,ing). Warrant(y,ies). Word of honor. Swear(ing). Sworn. Oath(s). *See also* Agreement (document); Guarantees; Oaths; Treaties; Trustworthy; Truth.

Promote, foster. See *Foster (promote).*

Promoters. Promoter(s). Booster(s). Backer(s). Press agent(s). Publicist(s). Public relations. Spokes(person,man, men,woman,women). Advertiser(s). Supporter(s). Advocate(s). Proponent(s). Championing. Lobbyist(s). *See also* Advertising; Advocacy; Lobbying; Promotion (business); Public relations; Spin doctors.

Promotion (business). Promot(e,ed,ing, ion). Attempt(s,ed,ing) to sell. Populariz(eed,ing,ation). Endors(e,ed,ing,ement). Advocat(e,ed,ing). Boost(ed,ing). *Consider also:* sponsor(ed,ing,ship), back(eding). *See also* Advertising; Advertising campaigns; Advertising agencies; Advocacy; Advocacy advertising; Client attitudes; Comparative advertising; Customer relations; Promoters; Propaganda; Public opinion; Public relations; Publicity; Spokespersons.

Promotion (occupational). Promot(e,ed, ing,ion). *Choose from:* occupation(al), labor, work, job(s), career(s), employment, vocational, employee(s), staff, faculty, teacher(s), personnel, worker(s) *with:* promot(e,ed,ing,ion,ional), advance(d,ment), upgrad(e,ed,ing). *Consider also:* career ladder(s), fast track(s,er,ers), professional development. *See also* Career goals; Career ladders; Career mobility; Employment opportunities; Occupational aspirations; Occupational status; Occupational success; Salaries.

Promotion, employee. See *Promotion (occupational).*

Promotion, health. See *Health promotion.*

Promotion, industrial. See *Industrial promotion.*

Promotion, job. See *Promotion (occupational).*

Promotion, personnel. See *Promotion (occupational).*

Prone, coronary behavior. See *Coronary prone behavior.*

Proneness, accident. See *Accident proneness.*

Pronunciation. Pronunciation. Pronounc(e, ed,ing). Articulat(e,ed,ing,ion,ory). Elocution. Enunciat(e,ed,ing,ion). Diction. Phonat(e,ion). Manner of speaking. Spelling sound correspon-

dence. Vowel production. *Choose from:* word(s), syllab(le,les,ic), speech, phonological *with:* stress(ed,ing), accent(s,ed). *See also* Articulation (speech); Articulation disorders; Child language; Speech; Speech characteristics; Speech intelligibility.

Propaganda. Propagand(a,ize,ized,izing, ist,ists,istic). Indoctrinat(e,ed,ing,ion). Thought reform. Brainwash(ed,ing). Greenwash(ed,ing). Persuasive communication. Advertis(e,ed,ing,ement, ements). Agitprop. Political communication(s). Persuasion technique(s). Promulgat(e,ed,ing,ion). Proselyti(sm,ze,zing). *Consider also:* promoting view(s), putting a spin, spin machine(s), spin doctor(s), mass communication(s), thought control, credibility gap(s). *See also* Advertising; Brainwashing; Communications research; Controversial literature; Deception; Declarations; Indoctrination; Information dissemination; Malinformation; Mass media; Mass media effects; Media portrayal; Partisan; Persuasion; Political myths; Political rhetoric; Promotion (business); Public opinion; Public relations; Social agitation; Social influences; Social unrest; War news.

Properties (characteristics). See *Characteristics; Qualities.*

Property (land). See *Government property; Land (property); Land ownership; Ownership; Personal property; Real estate.*

Property, abandoned. See *Abandoned property.*

Property, community. See *Common ownership.*

Property, cultural. See *Cultural property.*

Property, destruction of. See *Destruction of property.*

Property, enemy. See *Enemy property.*

Property, government. See *Government property.*

Property, industrial. See *Industrial property.*

Property, intangible. See *Intangible property.*

Property, intellectual. See *Intangible property.*

Property, literary. See *Copyright.*

Property, offenses against. See *Property crimes.*

Property, personal. See *Personal property.*

Property, public. See *Public property.*

Property crimes. Property crime(s). Theft. Thieve(s,ry). Shoplift(er,ers,ing). Vandal(s,ism). Breaking and entering. Aircraft hijacking. Armed robbery.

Arson. Burglar(y,ies). Loot(ed,ing). Vandal(s,ism). Joyriding. *Choose from:* art, auto(s,mobiles), vehicle(s), good(s), credit card(s), propert(y,ies), possession(s), radio(s), television(s), valuable(s) *with:* theft, steal(th,ing), stole(n), burglar(s,y), thie(f,ves), hijack(ed,ing,ers). *Consider also:* poach(ing,ed,er,ers). *See also* Arson; Booty (International law); Burglary; Crime; Enemy property; Personal property; Property rights; Robbery; Theft; Trespassing; Vandalism.

Property rights. Property rights. Right of private property. Owners right(s). Rights of owner(s,ship). Copyright(s). Land right(s). Patent(s). *See also* Civil rights; Copyright; Intangible property; Ownership; Patents; Piracy (copyright); Property crimes; Real estate; Trespassing.

Property values. Property value(s). *Choose from:* real estate, land(s), propert(y,ies), house(s), farm(s), farmland(s), home(s), lot(s), realty, acreage, building(s), tract(s), holding(s), parcel(s), manor(s), site(s), shopping center(s), strip mall(s), plantation(s), estate(s), ranch(es) *with:* value(s), market value(s), worth, cost(s), apprais(e,ed,al,ing), price(s), valuation, assess(ed,ing,ment), demand. *See also* Housing costs; Housing market; Land speculation; Land values; Site selection; Valuation.

Prophecy. Prophecy. Prophet(s). Inspired utterance(s). Inspired declaration(s). Inspired revelation. Prophe(sy,tic). Precognition. Fore(tell,told). Foresee(n). Foresight. Prescience. Predict(ed,ing, ion). Prognosticat(e,ed,ing,ion). Forecast(s,ed,er,ers,ing). Foreknowledge. Presentiment. Second sight. Clairvoyan(t,ce). Fortunetelling. Divination. *See also* Apocalypse; Apocalyptic literature; Divination; Messiahs; Millenarianism; Omniscience of God; Prediction; Prophets; Religious beliefs; Self fulfilling prophecy; Will of God.

Prophecy, self fulfilling. See *Self fulfilling prophecy.*

Prophets. Prophet(s,ess). Forecaster(s). Augur(s). Fortuneteller(s). Oracle(s). Visionar(y,ies). Astrologer(s). Diviner(s). Prognosticator(s). Seer(s). Sibyl(s,lic,line). *See also* Apocalypse; Apocalyptic literature; Divination; Forecasting; Messiahs; Millenarianism; Oracles; Prophecy; Prediction; Religious beliefs; Self fulfilling prophecy.

Prophylaxis. See *Prevention.*

Propitiatory rites, fetal. See *Fetal propitiatory rites.*

Proportional representation. Proportional representation. Proportional electoral system(s). Single transferable vote.

Consider also: one man one vote. *See also* Delegates; Delegation of powers; Election districts; Elections; Legislative bodies Preference voting; Representatives.

Proportionality. Proportional(ity). Well proportioned. Symmetr(y,ical). Balanced. Harmonious(ly). Commensur(ate, able). Apportioned. *Consider also:* congru(ity,ous), analogous(ly), equivalen(t,ce), comparab(le,ility). *See also* Beauty; Dimensions; Harmonization; Size.

Proposals, program. See *Program proposals.*

Propositions. Proposition(s). *Consider also:* hypothes(is,es,etical,ize), postulate(s), explanation(s), inference(s), theor(y,ies,ems), model(s), construct(s), generalization(s), generalizability, paradigm(s), assumption(s), presumption(s), thesis(es), conclusion(s), deduction(s), interpretation(s), premise(s), principle(s). *See also* Deduction; Hypotheses; Inference; Paradigms; Postulates; Theories.

Proprietary medicines. See *Non-prescription drugs.*

Proprietary schools. See *Private schools.*

Proprioception. Propriocept(ion,ive,or,ors). Equilibrium. Kinesthe(tic,sis,sia). Internal orientation. *See also* Equilibrium; Muscular sense.

Prose. Prose. Fiction. Nonfiction. Literature. Autobiograph(y,ies,ical). Biograph(y,ies, ical). Stor(y,ies). Text(s). Narrative(s). Essay(s). Expository passage(s). Discursive writing. Composition(s). Written excerpt(s) Written passage(s). Everyday language. Written in natural language. *See also* Essays; Literature; Writing (composition).

Prosecution. Prosecut(e,ed,ing,ors,ion). Proceed(ings) against. Criminal proceeding(s). Legal proceeding(s). Seek(ing) redress. Sue(d). Lawsuit(s). *Consider also:* indict(ed,ing,ment), take(n) to court. *See also* Arrests; Competency to stand trial; Criminal proceedings; Defendants; Defense (verbal); Evidence; Expert testimony; Forensic medicine; Forensic psychiatry; Indictments; Judicial decisions; Law enforcement; Plea bargaining; Sentencing; Trial (law); Verdicts; Witnesses.

Proselytism. Proselyt(e,ism,ize,ing). Conver(t,ted,ting,sion). Induce(d,ment) to change. Persua(de,ded,sion) to change. *Consider also:* recruit(ed,ing, ment), neophyte(s). *See also* Evangelistic work; Evangelists; Missionaries; Religious advertising; Religious conversion; Salvation.

Prosocial behavior. Prosocial behavior. Social interest. Shar(e,ed,ing).

Smil(e,ed,ing). Kind(ness). Altruis(m, tic). Helpful(ness). Positive social action(s). Donor(s). Friendl(y,iness). Willing(ness) to compromise. Social(ly) involve(d,ment). Prosocial(ity). Reciproc(al,ity). Empath(y,ic). Concern for other(s). Unselfish(ness). *Consider also:* supportive, helping, responsible, outgoing *with:* behavior. *Consider also:* social minded(ness), social mindful(ness). *See also* Affective behavior; Altruism; Assistance; Brotherliness; Charitable behavior; Community involvement; Cooperation; Favors; Friendship; Group consciousness; Kindness; Love; Magnanimity; Sharing; Pacifism; Peace movements; Peace negotiations; Socially responsible investing; Trusting; Trustworthy; Unselfishness.

Prosody. Prosod(y,ic). Versif(y,ied,ication). Metrical structure. *Consider also:* iambic pentameter, dactylic hexameter. *See also* Meter (poetry); Poetry; Stanzas.

Prospective studies. Prospective stud(y,ies). *Choose from:* prospective, planned *with:* stud(y,ies), survey(s), clinical trial(s), experiment(s,al,ation), investigation(s). *See also* Research design.

Prostheses. Prosthe(ses,sis,thetic). Bioprosthe(ses,sis,thetic). Implant(s). Intraocular lense(s). *Choose from:* artificial, prosthetic, replace(ment) *with:* leg(s), hand(s), joint(s), hip(s), eye(s), larynx(es), limb(s), blood vessel(s), heart valve(s), knee(s), lense(s), mandibular, maxillofacial. *See also* Amputation; Devices; Mobility aids; Self help devices.

Prostitution. Prostitut(e,es,ion). Massage parlor(s). Entertainment girl(s). Harlot(s). Whore(s). Streetwalker(s). Call girl(s). Hooker(s). Lad(y,ies) of the evening. Oldest profession. Pander(ing). *Consider also:* call boy(s), street hustler(s), bar hustler(s), camp follower(s). *See also* Brothels; Courtesan(s); Disorderly houses; Female offenders; Organized crime; Pimps; Promiscuity; Sex industry; Sex offenses; Sexual ethics; Sexual exploitation; Trafficking in persons; Victimless crimes.

Protagonist. Protagonist(s). Principal character(s). Champion(s). Hero(es,ine, ines). Lead character(s). Leader(s). *See also* Antiheroes; Fiction; Heroes.

Protagonists. See *Heroes.*

Protection. Protect(ed,ing,ion). Defense. Preserv(e,ed,ing,ation). Conserv(e,ed, ing,ation). Safeguard(ed,ing). Safekeeping. Defend(ed,ing). Guard(ed,ing). Secure(d). Shield(ed,ing). Shelter(ing, ed). Invulnerab(le,ility). Impregnab(le, ility). Security. Precaution(s,ary). Immun(e,ity). Buffer(ed,ing). Safety zone(s). *See also* Bicycle helmets; Civil defense; Consumer protection; Convoys; Crisis intervention; Environmental protection; Fortification; Foster (promote); Foster home care; Law enforcement; Preservation; Protective services; Safety; Security; Self defense; Shore protection; Trade protection.

Protection, consumer. See *Consumer protection.*

Protection, environmental. See *Environmental protection.*

Protection, game. See *Game protection.*

Protection, nature. See *Conservation of natural resources.*

Protection, shore. See *Shore protection.*

Protection, trade. See *Trade protection.*

Protectionism. See *Trade protection.*

Protective services. Protective service(s). Guardian(s,ship). Escort service(s). Mistreatment identification. Advoca(cy, tes). Defender(s). *Choose from:* impaired, weak, vulnerable, helpless, elderly, child(ren), disabled, handicapped, retarded *with:* protect(ed,ing, ion), advoca(tes,cy), ombuds(men,man, woman,women), defen(se,ders,ded,ing), guard(ed,ing,ianship), security, shield(ed,ing), shelter(s,ing,ed), safety, intervention(s). *See also* Advocacy; Community health services; Community mental health services; Consumer protection; Crisis intervention; Drug enforcement; Detectives; Emergency services; Health services; Home care services; Maternal health services; Mental health services; Occupational health services; Patient advocacy; Preventive medicine; Preventive psychiatry; Primary prevention; Relief services; Student health services; Supportive services.

Proteins, blood. See *Blood proteins.*

Protest, separation. See *Attachment behavior; Separation anxiety.*

Protest literature. Protest literature. *Choose from:* protest(er,ers), resistance, anti-establishment, anti-war, antiwar, opposition, suffrage, anti-slavery, abolitionis(t,ts,m), revolutionary, leftwing, New Left, political action, street rall(y,ies), consciousness raising, freedom, sociopolitical, class struggle(s), social concern(s), strike(s,r,rs), rebellion(s), social movement(s), solidarity, animal rights, Green movement, dissent, militan(t,cy), feminis(t,m), subversive *with:* novel(s), essay(s), writing(s), literature, text(s), published work(s), satire, poetry, poem(s), drama fiction(al). *See also* Literature; Protest movements; Protest songs; Protesters.

Protest movements. Protest movement(s). Social protest(s). Political protest(s). *Choose from:* activ(ism,ist,ists), protest(s,er,ers), movement(s),

insurgen(cy,t,ts), revolt(s), reform, picket(ed,s,ing), uprising(s), violen(t,ce), militan(cy,ce,t,ts), organized against, strik(ing,ers,es), general strike(s), dissen(t,ting,ter,ters,sion), petition(s, ing), riot(ing,s), struggle(s), sympathizer(s), opposition, mobiliz(ed,ing, ation), resist(ed,ing,ance,er,ers), collective action, boycott(s) *with:* animal rights, animal welfare, anti-nuclear, veteran(s), handicapped, anti-war, civil liberties, civil rights, reproductive rights, right to life, abortion, anti-abortion, death penalty, apartheid, pacifism, nuclear power, environmental(ism,ist, ists), green(s), elderly, senior citizen(s), student(s), citizens rights, public rights, drunk(en) driving, MADD, religious liberty, homosexual rights, lesbian rights, gay rights, anti-rac(ism,ist,ists), cruise missile(s), Corsicans, Croatians, farmers, Irish, Northern Ireland, NIMBY, youth, tax(es), non-align(ed,ment), women(s), Indian(s), Native American(s), homeless, etc. *See also* Abortion rights movement; Activism; Animal rights movement; Anti-fur protests; Anti-government radicals; Antiabortion movement; Antinuclear movements; Antismoking movement; Civil disobedience; Civil disorders; Civil rights organizations; Disability rights movement; Dissent; Gray power; Homosexual liberation movement; Hunger strikes; Militancy; Nonviolence; Political action; Political movements; Political participation; Political violence; Populism; Protest literature; Protest songs; Protestors; Radical movements; Social action; Social conflict; Social criticism; Social demonstrations; Social unrest; Student demonstrations; Suffrage movement; Women's groups; Women's rights.

Protest movements, war. See *Peace movements.*

Protest songs. Protest song(s). *Choose from:* protest(er,ers), anti-establishment, anti-war, socially relevant, abolitionist(s), suffrage, anti-slavery, revolutionary, leftwing, New Left, political action, street rall(y,ies), consciousness raising, freedom, sociopolitical, class struggle(s), social concern(s), strike(s,r, rs), rebellion(s), social movement(s), solidarity *with:* ballad(s), music, song(s), singing, chorus(es), folksong(s), chant(s), tune(s), ditt(y,ies), anthem(s), recording(s), dirge(s), melod(y,ies), sheet music. *Consider also:* protest poetry, Woody Guthrie, Pete Seeger, Bob Dylan, etc. *See also* Demonstrators; Folk songs; Labor movements; Labor songs; Political ballads; Political radicalism; Protest literature; Protest movements; Protesters; Revolutionary ballads and songs; Songs.

Protestant ethic. Protestant ethic. Protestant work ethic. Work ethic. Puritan ethic. Work value(s). Dedicate(d,ion) to hard work. Value(s) of work. Calvinism. *Consider also:* salvation through work(s), salvational anxiety, achievement motivation, individualism, deferred gratification. *See also* Achievement need; Protestantism; Puritanism; Stoicism; Work values.

Protestant reformation. Protestant reformation. Rise of Protestantism. Reformation. *Consider also:* Humanism, Diet of Worms, Confession of Augsburg, Calvinism, Act of Supremacy (1534), John Wyclif, John Huss, Martin Luther, Huldreich Zwingli, John Calvin, John Knox, Henry VIII. *See also* Protestantism; Religious movements; Roman Catholicism.

Protestantism. Protestant(ism,s). Amish. Puritan(s). Church of England. Calvinism. Lutheran(s). Presbyterian(s). Puritan(s,ism). Baptist(s). Episcopal(ian, ians). Methodist(s). Anglican(s). Mennonite(s). Mormon(s). Pentecostalis(m,ts). United Church of Christ. Anabaptist(s). Congregational(ist,ists, ism). Seventh Day Adventist(s). Fundamental(ist,ists,ism). Quaker(s). Society of Friends. Wesleyanism. Zwinglianism. Huguenot(s). Dutch Reform. Amish. Hutterite(s). Evangel(icals,istic,ism). Jehovah's Witness(es). *Consider also:* Pietis(m,t,ts), Great awakening, Evangelis(m,t,ts,tic). *See also* Christianity; Evangelists; Protestant reformation; Religious denominations; Religious fundamentalism; Religious movements; Religious revivals; Social gospel.

Protesters. Protester(s). Protestor(s). Demonstrator(s). Agitator(s). Civilian unrest. Uprising(s). Rioter(s). Rebel(s). Refusenik(s). Hunger strike(s,r,rs). Insurrectionist(s). Mob(s). Public demonstration(s). Sit-ins. Rall(y,ies). March(es). Strike(s). Walkout(s). Boycott(s). Self-immolation. *Choose from:* civil, nonviolent *with:* demonstration(s), confrontation(s), disorder(s). *See also* Activism; Agitators; Boycotts; Dissent; Dissidents; Hunger strikes; Nonviolence; Political violence; Protest literature; Protest movements; Protest songs; Rebels; Social action; Social demonstrations; Social unrest; Student demonstrations.

Protests, political. See *Activism; Civil disobedience; Dissent; Dissidents; Nonviolence; Political defection; Political dissent; Political radicalism; Political revolutions; Political violence; Protest movements; Protesters; Social action; Social demonstrations; Social unrest.*

Protests, student. See *Student demonstrations.*

Protocols. Protocol(s). Code(s) of behavior. Conventional practice(s). Conventional usage(s). Custom(s,ary,arily). Diplomatic code(s). Decorum. Formalit(y,ies). Good form. Good manners. Rules of behavior. Rules of conduct. Set of convention(s). *See also* Diplomatic etiquette; Etiquette; Manners; Practices (methods).

Provenance. Provenance. Provenience. Source(s). Place of origin. Derivation. Pedigree(s). Lineage. Background. Foundation(s). Inception. History of ownership. Birthplace. *See also* Beginning; Home ownership; Land ownership; Ownership; Personal property.

Provenience. See *Provenance.*

Proverbs. See *Aphorisms; Folklore.*

Providers, Internet service. See *Internet service providers.*

Provincialism. See *Localism.*

Proving grounds. Proving ground(s). Firing range(s). *Choose from:* weapon(s,ry), cannon artillery, ordnance *with:* test(ing) range(s), test(ing) space(s). *Consider also:* vehicle test system(s), road test(s,ing). *See also* Military bases; Military weapons; Weaponry.

Provisional government. Provisional government(s). *Choose from:* provisional, interim, temporary, transitional, acting *with:* government(s), legislature, presiden(t,ts,cy), head(s) of state. *See also* Constitution (legal); Coups d'Etat; Executive branch (government); Government; Legislative bodies; Legitimacy; Martial law; Military regimes; Political revolutions; Purges.

Proxemics. Proxemic(s). Interpersonal distance(s). Interpersonal space(s). Territoriality. Crowd(ed,ing). Touch(ing). Breathing room. Personal space. Space bubble(s). Distal(ly). Proxim(al,ity). *Choose from:* spatial *with:* arrangement(s), behavior(s), habit(s). *Choose from:* flight, fight, intimate, personal, public, interpersonal, social *with:* distance(s), zone(s). *Choose from:* sociofugal, sociopetal *with:* space(s). *Choose from:* primary, secondary, public *with:* zone(s), territori(y,es). *See also* Crowding; Life space; Nonverbal communication; Privacy; Social interaction; Spatial behavior; Territoriality.

Proximity of family. Proximity of famil(y,ies,ial). *Choose from:* famil(y,ies,ial), kin(folk), relative(s), sib(ling,lings,ships), parent(s), child(ren), offspring, spouse(s), husband(s), wives, wife, sister(s), brother(s), mother(s), father(s), grandparent(s), grandfather(s), grandmother(s) *with:* proximity, near-by, nearby, out-of-state, long distance,

location, geographic(al,ally) distan(t,ce), absen(ce,t). *See also* Commuting (travel); Dual career families; Family life; Family members; Family work relationship; Long distance caregivers; Long distance marriages; Parental absence.

Prudence. Pruden(ce,t,tly). Cautious(ness). Careful(ness). Discreet(ness). Discretion. Sagaci(ous,ousness,ity). Astute(ness). Foresight(ed,edness). Practical wisdom. Good judgement. Forethought. Precaution(s). Clearsighted(ness). Perspicac(ous,ousness, ity). Shrewdness. Frugal(ity). Thrift(y, iness). *See also* Cardinal virtues; Common sense; Frugality; Thriftiness; Virtue; Wisdom.

Prudishness. See *Desexualization; Sexual inhibitions.*

Prurience. Prurien(ce,t). Lascivious(ness). Lewd(ness). Lecherous(ness). Satyric(al). Concupiscen(t,ce). Salacious(ness). Debauch(ed,ery). Carnal. Sensual(ly,ity). Erotic(ism). Shameless(ness). Perver(ted,sion). Degenerate(d). Lustful(ness). *Consider also:* bawdy, unwholesome interest(s), unusual sexual desire(s). *See also* Adult entertainment; Bawdy songs; Obscenity; Pornography; Scatology; Vulgarity.

Psephology. See *Elections.*

Pseudonyms. Pseudonym(ous,s). Alias(es). Assumed name(s). False name(s). Pen name(s). Nom de plume. Nom de guerre. Professional name(s). Stage name(s). Fictitous name(s). Concealed identit(y, ies). False passport(s). False identification. False papers. Nickname(s). Unnamed source(s). Refus(e,ed,ing) to be identified. *Consider also:* AKA, anonym(s). *See also* Anonymity; Authors; Disputed authorship; Literature; Literary forgeries and mystifications.

Pseudonyms and anonyms. See *Anonymity.*

Pseudopregnancy. Pseudopregnanc(y,ies). Pseudocyesis. *Choose from:* spurious. false *with:* pregnanc(y,ies). *See also* Conversion disorder; Pregnancy.

Pseudoretardation. Pseudoretard(ed,ation). Pseudomental deficienc(y,ies). Pseudofeebleminded(ness). Six-hour retarded child(ren). *See also* Cultural deprivation; Psychosocial deprivation.

Pseudoscience. See *Occultism.*

Psyche. See *Mind.*

Psychedelic drugs. See *Hallucinogens; Narcotics; Street drugs.*

Psychedelic experiences. Psychedelic experience(s). *Choose from:* psychedelic, hallucinogen(s,ic), psychotomimetic, LSD, methylene dioxy amphet-

amine, dipropyltryptamine *with:* state(s), flashback(s), subjective effect(s), high(s), experience(s). *See also* Altered states of consciousness; Drug addiction; Drug withdrawal; Hallucinations; Hallucinogens; Substance induced organic mental disorders; Substance induced psychoses.

Psychiatric aides. Psychiatric aide(s). *Choose from:* psychiatric *with:* helper(s), assistant(s), attendant(s), auxiliar(y,ies), aide(s), trainee(s). *See also* Allied health personnel; Mental health personnel.

Psychiatric clinics. Psychiatric clinic(s). *Choose from:* psychiatr(ic,y), mental health, psychotherapy, child guidance, neuropsychiatric *with:* clinic(s), center(s), dispensar(y,ies), ambulatory care, outpatient facilit(y,ies). *See also* Clinics; Community mental health services; Mental health services; Outpatient treatment; Outpatients; Walkin clinics.

Psychiatric commitment. Psychiatric commitment. *Choose from:* compulsory, involuntar(y,ily), court order *with:* institutionaliz(ed,ing,ation,ations), hospital admission(s), hospitaliz(ed,ing, ation,ations). *Consider also:* commit(ted,ting,ment) *with:* mental(ly), psychiatric, psychotic, insan(e,ity), involuntary, voluntary. *See also* Alternatives to institutionalization; Deinstitutionalization; Detention; Hospitalization; Institutionalization (persons); Involuntary (unwilling); Patient admission; Patient discharge; Sentencing.

Psychiatric disorders. See *Cognition disorders; Mental illness.*

Psychiatric education. See *Psychiatric training.*

Psychiatric emergency services. Psychiatric emergency service(s). *Choose from:* psychiatric, mental health, suicide(s), rape(s), psycho(tic,sis), crisis *with:* emergency service(s), emergency room(s), crisis center(s), hotline(s), phone counselor(s), crisis intervention. *See also* Crisis intervention; Emergency services; Help lines (telephone); Psychological debriefing; Rape crisis counseling; Suicide prevention.

Psychiatric hospitalization. Psychiatric hospitalization. Admission to state hospital(s). Involuntary psychiatric treatment. *Choose from:* psychiatric, mental(ly), schizophren(ia,ic), hallucination(s), psycho(tic,sis,ses), depress(ed,ion), manic *with:* hospitaliz(ed,ation), inpatient(s), admission(s), commit(ted,ment), readmission(s), readmit(ted,ting). *See also* Alternatives to institutionalization; Deinstitutionalization; Hospital environment; Hospitalization; Hospitalized children; Institutionalization (persons); Patient discharge; Psychiatric commitment; Psychiatric hospitals.

Psychiatric hospitals. Psychiatric hospital(s). *Choose from:* psychiatric, mental, psychotherapeutic *with:* hospital(s), ward(s), institution(s). Sanitorium(s). Sanitarium(s). Hospital(s) for mentally ill. Hospital(s) for the insane. Hospitals for the mentally handicapped. Asylum(s). Madhouse(s). Bedlam. State mental hospital(s). *See also* Halfway houses; Maximum security facilities; Psychiatric hospitalization; Psychiatric patients; Residential facilities; Sanatoriums; Therapeutic community.

Psychiatric patients. Psychiatric patient(s). Psychiatric inpatient(s). *Choose from:* mental, psychiatric, neuropsychiatric, mentally ill, schizophrenic, insane, psychotherapy, mental hospital(s), depressed, manic, neurotic *with:* patient(s), inpatient(s), outpatients, client(s). *See also* Alternatives to institutionalization; Community mental health services; Deinstitutionalization; Insanity defense; Mental illness; Mentally ill offenders; Psychiatric clinics; Psychiatric commitment; Psychiatric hospitalization.

Psychiatric services. See *Mental health services; Psychiatric clinics; Psychiatric social work.*

Psychiatric social work. Psychiatric social work. Mental health work(ers). *Choose from:* psychiatric, mental health, mental illness *with:* social work(ers), social casework, social service. *See also* Community mental health services; Mental health services; Psychiatric clinics.

Psychiatric social workers. Psychiatric social worker(s). Psychiatric case-worker(s). Psychiatric care worker(s). *See also* Allied health personnel; Psychiatric social work; Social workers.

Psychiatric training. Psychiatric training. *Choose from:* psychiatrist(s), psychiatr(y,ic), mental health, psychoanalytic *with:* education, train(ed,ing), study, course(s), residen(t,ts,cy), intern(s,ship,ships), clerkship(s), class(es), instruct(ed,ing,ion), curricul(a,um). *See also* Cotherapy; Graduate education; Higher education; Postgraduate training; Psychoanalysis.

Psychiatrists. Psychiatrist(s). Neuropsychiatrist(s). Psychoanalyst(s). Psychiatric team(s). *Choose from:* member(s) *with:* American Academy of Child Psychiatry, Canadian Psychiatric Association, American Psychiatric Association. *Consider also:* psychiatric consult(ant,ants,ation), psychiatric candidate(s), psychiatr(y,ic) physician(s), psychiatr(y,ic) resident(s). Special(ist,ists,izing) in psychiatry. *See*

also Physicians; Psychoanalysts; Psychologists; Psychotherapists.

Psychiatry. Psychiatry. Neuropsychiatry. Orthopsychiatry. *Choose from:* social, transcultural, adolescent, child, community, preventive, primary prevention, forensic, geriatric, military, biological *with:* psychiatry, neuropsychiatry. *Consider also:* psychiatric nursing, psychoanalysis, psychosomatic medicine. *See also* Cross cultural psychiatry; Forensic psychiatry; Preventive psychiatry.

Psychiatry, cross cultural. See *Cross cultural psychiatry.*

Psychiatry, folk. See *Shamanism; Traditional medicine.*

Psychiatry, forensic. See *Forensic psychiatry.*

Psychiatry, preventive. See *Preventive psychiatry.*

Psychic trauma. See *Emotional trauma.*

Psychoacoustics. Psychoacoustic(s,al). *Choose from:* psychophysical *with:* tone suppression, tuning, scaling. *See also* Acoustics; Auditory perception; Echolocation; Hearing; Psychophysiology; Tuning.

Psychoanalysis. Psychoanaly(sis,ses,tic, tical,tically). Psycho-analytic(al). Psychoanalytic therap(y,ies). Dream analys(is,es). Freudian analys(is,es). *Consider also:* psychoanalytic theor(y,ies). *See also* Abreaction; Catharsis; Dream interpretation; Dreams; Mental illness; Oedipus complex; Psychoanalytic interpretation; Psychoanalytic theory; Psychotherapy; Self understanding; Unconscious (psychology).

Psychoanalysts. Psychoanalyst(s). *Consider also:* psychoanaly(tic,tically,sis) *with:* psychiatrist(s), psychotherapist(s), therapist(s). *See also* Psychiatrists; Psychoanalysis; Psychologists.

Psychoanalytic interpretation. Psychoanalytic interpretation(s). Psychoanalytic literary criticism. Psychohistor(y,ical). Psychobiograph(y,ical). *Choose from:* psychoanalytic, dream, Adlerian, Freudian, Jungian, psychiatric, psychological *with:* interpretation(s), analys(is,es), observation(s), reinterpretation(s), approach(es), symbol(s,ism). *See also* Dream interpretation; Dreams; Psychoanalysis; Psychoanalytic theory; Symbolism; Unconscious (psychology).

Psychoanalytic theory. Psychoanalytic theor(y,ies). *Consider also:* psychoanaly(tic,sis), Freud(ian), Jung(ian) *with:* theor(y,ies,etical), concept(s). *See also* Psychoanalysis; Psychoanalytic interpretation; Theories.

Psychoanalytical therapy. See *Psychoanalysis.*

Psychobiology. Psychobiolog(y,ic,ics,ical). Psychophysiolog(y,ical). Biopsychosocial. Biological psychiatry. Behavioral biology. Physiological psychology. *Choose from:* biolog(y,ical), neurolog(y, ic,ical,ically), neurophysiological(ly), physiological(ly), physiology, neuroscience, genetic(s,ally), biochemical(s, ally), biochemistry, neurobiological(ly), physical(ly), nervous system, brain, hormone(s), neural *with:* mental(ly), psychiatr(y,ic), psycholog(y,ical,ically), personality, mood(s), behavior(s,al), psycho(sis,ses,tic), neuro(sis,ses,tic), depression(s), mania(s).

Psychodiagnosis. Psychodiagnos(is,es,tic). *Choose from:* psychiatric, personality, psychopatholog(y,ical), psychological, emotional, schizophren(ia,ic), depress(ed,ion), mental, neuros(es,is), neurotic, psychos(es,is), psychotic, behavior(al), psychoneurotic *with:* diagnos(tic,es,is), assess(ed,ing,ment), clinical judgment(s), classif(y,ying,ied), classification, label(led,ling), label(ed,ing), evaluat(e,ed,ing,ion), detect(ed,ing,ion), identification, predict(ed,ion), screen(ed,ing), rat(ed,ing). *Consider also:* MMPI score(s). *See also* Diagnosis; Interviews; Medical history taking; Patient history; Psychodiagnostic typologies; Psychological interview; Psychological tests.

Psychodiagnostic typologies. Psychodiagnostic typolog(y,ies). *Choose from:* psychodiagnostic, psychiatr(y,ic) *with:* typolog(y,ies), taxonom(y,ies), classification(s). *Consider also:* DSM-III. *See also* Labeling (of persons); Psychodiagnosis.

Psychodrama. Psychodrama(tic,tics,s). Psychotheatr(e,es,ic,ics). Sociodrama(tic,tics,s). Psychodance. Psychoopera. Psychoeducational drama. Dramatic play. Physiodrama(tic,tics,s). Axiodrama(tic,tics,s). Psychomusic. Hypnodrama(tic,tics,s). *Choose from:* drama(s,tic,tics) *with:* therap(y,ies,eutic), psychotherap(y,ies,eutic). *See also* Group psychotherapy; Psychomedia; Role playing.

Psychodynamics. Psychodynamic(s). *Choose from:* psychological, behavioral, emotional, sociopsychological, psychosocial *with:* dynamics, interplay, process(es), mechanism(s), correlate(s). *See also* Cognitive development; Group dynamics; Interpersonal relations; Motivation; Personality; Social behavior; Social interaction; Symbiotic relations.

Psychogenesis. Psychogen(esis,etic,ic). Psychopathogen(esis,etic,ic). *Choose from:* psychological, psychic, psyche, emotional, personality *with:*

predisposition(s), predispos(e,ed,ing), precipitating factor(s), cause(s), early development, early memor(y,ies), origin(s,ated,ating). *See also* Adolescent development; Adult development; Age differences; Behavior development; Child development; Childhood play development; Cognitive development; Delayed development; Development; Developmental stages; Early childhood development; Emotional development; Euthenics; Human development; Infant development; Intellectual development; Language development; Moral development; Motor development; Perceptual development; Personality development; Physical development; Prenatal development; Psychomotor development; Psychosexual development; Psychosocial development; Sexual maturation; Speech development.

Psychogenic pain. Psychogenic pain. *Choose from:* psychophysiolog(y,ical), psychogenic, psychic, functional, psychosomatic *with:* pain(s,ful), ache(s), headache(s), backache(s), discomfort. *Consider also:* factitious disorder(s), hypochondria(c,cal,sis), conversion neuros(is,es). *See also* Chronic pain; Conversion disorder; Hypochondriasis; Psychophysiologic disorders; Somatoform disorders.

Psychohistory. Psychohistor(y,ical). Psycho-histor(y,ical). Histoire psychologique. Psychohistorian(s). Psychoanalytic interpretation of history. *Consider also:* psychobiograph(y,ies, ical), historical psychodynamics. *See also* Biography; Cultural history; Historical biography; Historical perspective; Historical research; History; Life history; National characteristics; Psychoanalytic interpretation.

Psychokinesis. Psychokines(is,ia). Defective inhibition(s). Impulse insanity. *See also* Impulse control disorders.

Psychokinesis (parapsychology). Psychokine(sis,tic). Telekine(sis,tic). PK. *Consider also:* poltergeist(s), psi, telepath(y,ic). *See also* Extrasensory perception; Parapsychology.

Psycholinguistics. Psycholinguistic(s). *Choose from:* psycholog(y,ical), neuropsycholog(y,ical), cognit(ive,ion) *with:* language(s), linguistic(s), verbal behavior(s). *Consider also:* language development. *See also* Bilingualism; Ethnolinguistics; Generative grammar; Language acquisition; Language disorders; Linguistic interference; Linguistics; Metalanguage; Multilingualism; Sociolinguistics; Speech errors; Thinking.

Psychological adaptation. See *Emotional adjustment*.

Psychological aging. Psychological aging. *Choose from:* elderly, aging, old, aged,

retirement, senior citizen(s), gerontological, geriatric *with:* social, psychosocial, psychological, emotional, interpersonal *with:* development(s,al), stage(s), matur(e,ed,ing,ation), transition(s). *See also* Aging; Decline; Deterioration; Developmental stages; Elderly; Frail Elderly; Life change events; Life cycle; Life experiences; Life review; Life stage transitions; Lifelong learning; Maturation; Physiological aging.

Psychological anthropology. Psychological anthropology. *Choose from:* psycho-log(y,ical), personalit(y,ies), cognit(ion, ive), self, psychiatry, psychoanalysis, human nature, mental(ly,ity), emotion(s,al,ally) *with:* anthropolog(y, ical), culture, social construction, social cognition, socialization. *Consider also:* ethnopsychiatry, culture-and-personality. *See also* Behavior development; Cultural anthropology; Culture (anthropology); Culture specific syndromes; Ethnolinguistics; Ethnopsychology; Ethnospecific disorders; Philosophical anthropology.

Psychological assimilation. See *Assimilation (psychology)*.

Psychological association. See *Association (psychology)*.

Psychological authoritarianism. See *Authoritarianism (psychological)*.

Psychological conditioning. See *Conditioning (psychology)*.

Psychological debriefing. Psychological debriefing(s). Psychological defusing(s). Crisis debriefing(s). *Choose from:* debrief(ed,ings), defus(e,ed,ings) *with:* emotional(ly), psychological(ly), victim(s), crisis, trauma(s,tic), disaster(s), emergenc(y,ies). *Consider also:* postdisaster psychosocial intervention(s). *See also* Assistance in emergencies; Counseling; Crisis intervention; Disaster recovery; Disaster relief; Emotional crisis; Interviews; Psychiatric emergency services; Rape crisis counseling.

Psychological depression. See *Depression (psychology)*.

Psychological desensitization. See *Desensitization (psychology)*.

Psychological development. See *Behavior development; Cognitive development; Emotional development; Enlightenment (state of mind); Human development; Human potential movement; Intellectual development; Language development; Moral development; Personality development; Psychomotor development; Psychosexual development; Psychosocial development; Self actualization; Socialization*.

Psychological distress. Psychological(ly) distress(ed). Anguish(ed). Emotional(ly) stress(ed). Mental(ly) stress(ed). Posttraumatic stress. *Choose from:* psychosomatic, psychophysiological(ly), psychiatric, mental(ly), emotional(ly) *with:* distress(ed,ing). *Consider also:* burnout, depression, worr(y,ied), unhappy, combat reaction(s), status insecurity, high level of stress, strain(s), malaise, bereavement, psychological stress(es,ed), emotional cris(es,is). *See also* Emotional crisis; Emotional trauma; Pain; Pessimism; Psychological stress; Suffering.

Psychological endurance. Psychological endurance. Chutzpah factor. Feist(y,iness). *Choose from:* coping, emotional, psychological *with:* endurance, strength(s), resource(s), hard(y,iness), resistance, resilience, invulnerab(le,ility), survival. *See also* Emotional maturity; Emotional stability; Fortitude; Hopefulness; Optimism; Patience; Psychological well being; Stress reactions.

Psychological interview. Psychological interview(s). *Choose from:* psychological, psychodiagnostic, clinical, psychotherapeutic *with:* interview(s,ed,ing). *See also* Interviews; Medical history taking; Psychodiagnosis.

Psychological needs. Psychological need(s). *Choose from:* individual, existential, psychological, emotional, psychosocial, interpersonal, personal(ity), social, approval, human contact(s), information, power, approval, support, achievement, structure, affect(ive,ion), privacy, personal space, recognition, dependency, belong(ing), affiliation, comfort(ing), give, status, self fulfillment, self actualization, security, stimulation, adventure *with:* need(s), motivation(s). *Consider also:* deficiency motivation. *See also* Achievement need; Affection; Affiliation motivation; Delay of gratification; Emotional security; Goal orientation; Humanization; Individual needs; Need satisfaction; Needs; Needs assessment; Personal independence; Personal space; Recognition (achievement); Security; Self actualization; Sex drive.

Psychological phenomenology. See *Phenomenological psychology*.

Psychological repression. See *Repression (defense mechanism)*.

Psychological stress. Psychological(ly) stress(ed). Anxiety. Anxious. Tension(s). Ego stress. Separation anxiety. Eustress. Life change(s). Sleep disturbance(s). Defensive reaction(s). *Choose from:* emotional(ly), mental(ly), psychosomatic, psychophysiological(ly), psychosocial, psychological, life, neuropsychic, nervous, psychobiochemical *with:* stress(ed), pressure(s), anxiet(y,ies), tension(s), reaction(s), disturbance(s). *Consider also:* burnout, depression, worr(y,ied), unhappy, combat reaction(s), status insecurity, high level of stress, strain(s), malaise, bereavement, psychological distress, emotional cris(es,is), psychiatric distress, anguish(ed), posttraumatic stress. *See also* Anguish; Burnout; Caregiver burden; Coping; Deprivation; Mental fatigue; Occupational stress; Physiological stress; Psychological distress; Psychological endurance; Tensions.

Psychological tests. Psychological test(s,ing). *Choose from:* psychological, self concept, neuropsychological, behavior(al), emotional, ego strength, personality, psychometric, inkblot, Rorschach, projective, attitude, anxiety, creativity, intelligence, association, aptitude, perceptual, preference *with:* test(s,ing), measure(s,ment), scale(s), assessment(s), questionnaire(s), rating(s), batter(y,ies), questions, survey(s), score(s), evaluation(s), examination(s), checklist(s), score(s), inventor(y,ies), schedule(s). *Consider also:* psychometrics. *See also* Aptitude tests; Intelligence tests; Perceptual measures; Personality measures; Projective techniques; Questionnaires; Tests.

Psychological warfare. Psychological war(fare). Psywar. *Choose from:* psychological *with:* war(fare), terror(ism,ist,ists). *Consider also:* propaganda, brainwash(ed,ing), thought control, undermin(e,ed,ing) morale, induced fear, theatrical violence, intimidation, involuntary conversion. *See also* Brainwashing; Intimidation; Propaganda; Terrorism.

Psychological well being. Psychological well being. Morale. High self esteem. Self confident. Fully functioning person(s). *Choose from:* subjective, mental(ly), psychologic(al,ally), emotional(ly), psychosocial(ly) *with:* health(y), well being, satisfaction, happ(y,iness). *Consider also:* generativity, creativity. *See also* Emotional maturity; Emotional stability; Happiness; Mental health; Morale; Optimism; Psychological endurance; Self efficacy; Self esteem; Well being.

Psychologically abused men. Psychologically abused men. Emotionally abused men. *Choose from:* male(s), men, man, husband(s), father(s), grandfather(s), widower(s) *with:* psychological(ly) abuse(d), emotionall(ly) abuse(d), belittl(e,es,ed,ing), shame(d), victimization, scapegoat(ed,ing), threaten(ed, ing) withdrawal of love, emotional abandonment, negative labeling, humiliat(e,es, ed,ing). *Consider also:* sexually abused men. *See also* Emotional abuse; Insensitivity; Psychosocial deprivation; Scapegoating; Sexual abuse; Verbal abuse.

Psychologists. Psychologist(s). *Choose from:* psychology *with:* major(s), professional(s), professor(s), graduate(s). neuropsychologist(s). American Psychological Association member(s). *Consider also:* school psychologist(s), clinical psychologist(s), educational psychologist(s), experimental psychologist(s), industrial psychologist(s), social psychologist(s). *See also* Industrial psychologists; Psychiatrists; Psychotherapists.

Psychologists, industrial. See *Industrial psychologists.*

Psychology. Psycholog(y,ical,ically,ists). *Consider also:* adolescent psychology, applied psychology, behaviorism, child psychology, clinical psychology, cognitive psychology, community psychology, comparative psychology, consumer psychology, counseling psychology, depth psychology, developmental psychology, educational psychology, engineering psychology, ethnopsychology, experimental psychology, Freudian psychology, forensic psychology, geriatric psychology, gestalt psychology, humanistic psychology, individual psychology, industrial psychology, Jungian psychology, mathematical psychology, medical psychology, metapsychology, military psychology, neuropsychology, pediatric psychology, physiological psychology, psychoacoustics, psychometrics, psychopathology, psychophysiology, school psychology, social psychology. *See also* Applied psychology; Cognitive psychology; Comparative psychology; Criminal psychology; Educational psychology; Engineering psychology; Environmental psychology; Experimental psychology; History of psychology; Humanistic psychology; Individual psychology; Industrial psychology; Military psychology; Physiological psychology; Psychobiology; Psychohistory; Psychopathology; Psychopharmacology; Psychophysiology; Social psychology; Sport psychology.

Psychology, abnormal. See *Psychopathology.*

Psychology, animal. See *Animal psychology.*

Psychology, applied. See *Applied psychology.*

Psychology, cognitive. See *Cognitive psychology.*

Psychology, comparative. See *Comparative psychology.*

Psychology, criminal. See *Criminal psychology.*

Psychology, educational. See *Educational psychology.*

Psychology, engineering. See *Engineering psychology.*

Psychology, environmental. See *Environmental psychology.*

Psychology, existential. See *Existential psychology.*

Psychology, experimental. See *Experimental psychology.*

Psychology, genetic. See *Genetic psychology.*

Psychology, gestalt. See *Gestalt psychology.*

Psychology, history of. See *History of psychology.*

Psychology, humanistic. See *Humanistic psychology.*

Psychology, individual. See *Individual psychology.*

Psychology, industrial. See *Industrial psychology.*

Psychology, mass. See *Mass psychology.*

Psychology, military. See *Military psychology.*

Psychology, phenomenological. See *Phenomenological psychology.*

Psychology, physiological. See *Physiological psychology.*

Psychology, race. See *Ethnopsychology.*

Psychology, self. See *Self psychology.*

Psychology, social. See *Social psychology.*

Psychology, sport. See *Sport psychology.*

Psychology of language. See *Psycholinguistics.*

Psychomedia. Psychomedia. Teleconsultation. *Choose from:* psychotherap(y,ies, eutic), therap(y,ies,eutic), psychodrama *with:* radio, television, broadcast(s,ed, ing), multimedia. *See also* Psychodrama; Role playing; Television.

Psychometrics. Psychometric(s). *Choose from:* psychometric, psychological, personality, behavior, trait(s), intelligence, interest(s), aptitude(s), abilit(y, ies) *with:* test(s,ing), examination(s), questionnaire(s), rating scale(s), inventor(y,ies), instrument(s), measuring device(s), measure(s). *See also* Intelligence tests; Personality measures; Psychological tests; Quantitative methods; Test interpretation; Tests.

Psychomotor agitation. Psychomotor agitation. Restless(ness). Agitat(ed,ion). Akathis(ia,ic). Acathis(ia,ic). Handwringing. Kathisophob(ia,ic). *Choose from:* psychomotor *with:* agitat(ed,ion), excit(ed,ation,ement), activat(ed,ion). *See also* Agitation; Attention deficit disorder; Attention span; Concentration difficulties; Hyperkinesis; Motor activity; Psychomotor disorders; Restlessness.

Psychomotor development. Psychomotor development. Neuromaturation(al). *Choose from:* psychomotor, neuropsychological *with:* development(al), learning, test score(s), performance, skill(s). *Consider also:* marksmanship, object manipulation, perceptual motor coordination. *See also* Child development; Motor coordination; Motor development; Perceptual development; Physical agility; Physical development; Physical dexterity; Speech development.

Psychomotor disorders. Psychomotor disorder(s). *Choose from:* psychomotor, motor behavior, neuromotor *with:* disorder(s), late development, disturbance(s), deficit(s), retard(ed, ation), handicap(ped,s), impairment(s), disease(s). *Consider also:* hyperactiv(e, ity), tic(s), automatism, Tourette(s). *See also* Apraxia; Ataxia; Attention deficit disorder; Automatism; Catalepsy; Cataplexy; Catatonia; Developmental disabilities; Hyperkinesis; Psychomotor agitation.

Psychomotor processess. See *Perceptual motor processes.*

Psychomotor skills. See *Motor skills; Psychomotor development.*

Psychoneuroimmunology. Psychoneuroimmunolog(y,ic). Psychological influence(s) on immunity. Psychoimmunolog(y,ic). Psychoimmunolog(y, ic). *Choose from:* stress(es,ed) *with:* immun(e,ity), immunosuppression, neuroendocrine, neurohormonal. *Consider also:* neuroimmunomodulation, psychobiology, psychooncology, healing response(s), mindbody, mindbody. *See also* Disease susceptibility; Etiology; Meditation; Mind body problem; Psychobiology; Psychophysiologic disorders; Relaxation training.

Psychoneuroses. See *Neuroses.*

Psychopathic personality. See *Antisocial personality disorder.*

Psychopathology. Psychopatholog(ical, y,ies). Mental disease(s). Pathological defense(s). Pathopsycholog(y,ical). Psychopath(ic). Sociopath(ic). Abnormal psychology. Emotional illness(es). Mental illness(es). Insanity. *Choose from:* patholog(ical,y,ies), dysfunction(s,al,ally), disorganiz(ed,ation) *with:* psychosocial, mental(ly), emotional(ly), personality, psychological, psychiatric. *See also* Affective disorders; Antisocial personality disorder; Emotionally disturbed; Dementia; Hallucinations;

Mental illness; Neuroses; Personality disorders; Psychoses; Sexual deviations.

Psychopathy. See *Affective disorders; Antisocial personality disorder; Cognition disorders; Mental illness; Personality disorders.*

Psychopharmacology. Psychopharmacolog(y,ical). Neuropharmacolog(y,ical). Pharmacological psychiatry. Neuropsychopharmacolog(y,ical). Pharmacopsychiatr(y,ic). Psychopharmacogenetic(s). Psychopharmacotherap(y, ies,eutic). *Consider also:* psychotropic, psychopharmacological, narcotherapeutic, psychoactive, antipsychotic, neuroleptic *with:* drug(s), medication(s), substance(s), agent(s). *See also* Antidepressive agents; Drugs; Hallucinogens; Narcoanalytic drugs; Narcotics; Tranquilizers.

Psychophysiologic disorders. Psychophysiologic disorder(s). Somatization reaction(s). Organ neuros(is,es). Illness(es) without organic cause. Somatopsychic disorder(s). Dermatopsychosomatic(s). *Choose from:* psychophysiologic(al), psychosomatic, psychogenic, somatopsychic, functional, psychoneuroimmunologic *with:* disorder(s), illness(es), disease(s), pain, reaction(s). *See also* Alexithymia; Anorexia nervosa; Arthritis; Asthma; Bulimia; Causality; Conversion disorder; Disorders; Dysmorphophobia; Etiology; Factitious disorders; Functional hearing loss; Hyperphagia; Hypersensitivity; Hyperventilation; Hypochondriasis; Hysterical anesthesia; Hysterical paralysis; Hysterical vision disturbances; Illness; Infertility; Malingering; Mental illness; Migraine headaches; Mind body problem; Obesity; Premenstrual syndrome; Psychobiology; Psychogenic pain; Psychogenesis; Psychoneuroimmunology; Psychophysiology; Sexual function disorders; Sick role; Somatoform disorders.

Psychophysiological habituation. See *Habituation (psychophysiology).*

Psychophysiology. Psychophysiolog(y,ical). *Choose from:* psycholog(y,ical), emotional(ly), mental(ly), anxiety, anxious(ness), mood(s), relax(ed,ing, ation), meditat(e,ed,ing,ion,ive) *with:* appetite, arousal, biofeedback, blushing, reaction time(s), reflex(es), biofeedback, electrodermal, galvanic skin response, heart rate, pulse rate, body temperature, blood pressure, vasomotor, respiration. *Consider also:* psychobiolog(y,ical), physiological psychology, psychophysical, psycho-physiolog(y,ical), psychomotor, psychosomatic, psychoneuroimmunolog(y,ical), habituation, somatopsychic(s). *See also* Causality; Conversion disorder; Functional hearing loss; Habituation (psychophysiology);

Hysterical anesthesia; Hysterical paralysis; Hysterical vision disturbances; Mind body problem; Mind-body relations (metaphysics); Psychobiology; Psychogenesis; Psychogenic pain; Psychoneuroimmunology; Psychophysiological disorders.

Psychopoetry. Psychopoetry. *Choose from:* poet(ry,ic), poem(s), epic(s), verse(s) *with:* therap(y,ies,eutic), heal(ed,ing), wisdom, treatment, stress management, mental health, counseling. *See also* Art therapy; Bibliotherapy; Psychotherapy; Poetry; Self help.

Psychoses. Psychos(is,es). Psychotic disorder(s). Insan(e,ity). Psychoticism. Mentally ill. Mental illness(es). Deranged. *Consider also:* psychiatric disorder(s), altered consciousness, pseudopsychos(is,es), schizophren(ia,ic), behavioral breakdown(s), cataton(ia,ic), man(ia,ic), delirium tremens, hallucinat(e,ed,ing,ion,ions), hallucinosis, autism, echolalia, Capgras(s) syndrome, organic mental disorder(s), parano(ia,id), folie-a-deux. *See also* Acute psychosis; Alcoholic hallucinosis; Alcoholic psychoses; Borderline personality disorder; Capgras's syndrome; Childhood psychosis; Culture specific syndromes; Delirium; Experimental psychosis; Hallucinations; Hallucinosis; Organic psychoses; Paranoid schizophrenia; Process psychosis; Psychosis of association; Reactive psychosis; Schizophrenia; Senile dementia; Substance induced psychoses; Symbiotic infantile psychosis.

Psychoses, alcoholic. See *Alcoholic psychoses.*

Psychoses, drug induced. See *Substance induced psychoses.*

Psychoses, organic. See *Organic psychoses.*

Psychoses, senile. See *Senile dementia.*

Psychoses, substance induced. See *Substance induced psychoses.*

Psychoses, toxic. See *Substance induced psychoses.*

Psychosexual behavior. See *Sex behavior.*

Psychosexual development. Psychosexual development. *Choose from:* psychosexual, sexual(ity), preadolescent, adolescent, pubescen(t,ce), gender identity, sexual behavior, heterosexual, homosexual, prehomosexual, sexual identity, sexual orientation *with:* development(al,ally), matur(e,ed,ing, ation), differentiat(e,ed,ing,ion). *Consider also:* anal stage, latency period, oral stage, phallic stage, genital phase, menarche, puberty. *See also* Adolescent development; Emotional development; Gender identity; Menarche; Psychosocial development;

Puberty; Sex behavior; Sexual attitudes; Sexual maturation.

Psychosexual disorders. See *Sexual deviations; Sexual function disorders.*

Psychosexual dysfunction. See *Sexual function disorders.*

Psychosis. See *Psychoses.*

Psychosis, acute. See *Acute psychosis.*

Psychosis, childhood. See *Childhood psychosis.*

Psychosis, chronic. See *Chronic psychosis.*

Psychosis, collective. See *Mass hysteria.*

Psychosis, exotic. See *Culture specific syndromes; Ethnospecific disorders.*

Psychosis, experimental. See *Experimental psychosis.*

Psychosis, involutional. See *Involutional psychosis.*

Psychosis, prison. See *Prison psychosis.*

Psychosis, process. See *Process psychosis.*

Psychosis, reactive. See *Reactive psychosis.*

Psychosis, symbiotic infantile. See *Symbiotic infantile psychosis.*

Psychosis, traumatic. See *Reactive psychosis.*

Psychosis of association. Psychos(is,es) of association. *Choose from:* shared paranoid disorder(s), psychic infection(s), familial mental infection(s), reciprocal insanity, influenced psychos(is,es), mystic paranoia. *Choose from:* communicated, induced, infectious, double, triple *with:* insanity, schizophrenia, psychos(is,es), paranoi(a,d). *Choose from:* folie *with:* induite, simultanee, imposee, communique, double, double forme, beaucoup, deux, trois, quatre, cinq. *See also* Mass hysteria; Social contagion.

Psychosocial deprivation. Psychosocial deprivation. Emotional(ly) depriv(ed, ation). Affect hunger. *Choose from:* psychosocial(ly), affective, psychic, emotional(ly), social(ly), socioenvironmental, affection(al), maternal(ly), cultural(ly), sociocultural(ly) *with:* depriv(ed,ation), impoverish(ed,ment), isolat(ed,ion), lack(s,ed,ing), acrescentism, marginaliz(e,ed,ation), disadvantage(d,ment), retard(ed,ation), handicap(s,ped), deficit(s), neglect(ed), abandon(ed,ing,ment). *Choose from:* love, affection, friend(s,ship) *with:* depriv(ed,ation), lack(s,ed,ing). *Choose from:* wild, wolf, feral *with:* child(ren). *Consider also:* sensory deprivation, affective separation, masked deprivation, cultural deprivation, homeless(ness), lonel(y,iness), underprivileged. *See also* Abandoned children; Anaclitic depression; Child neglect; Cultural deprivation; Failure to thrive (psychosocial);

Loneliness; Maternal deprivation; Pseudoretardation; Psychologically abused men; Psychosocial mental retardation; Parental absence; Social isolation; Socially handicapped.

Psychosocial development. Psychosocial development. *Choose from:* psychosocial, personality, childhood play, psychosexual, emotional, identity, sociocognitive, social cognitive, social competence, altruism, verbal, affective, interpersonal skill(s) *with:* development, growth. *Consider also:* socialization. *See also* Childhood play development; Emotional development; Emotional maturity; Engenderment; Moral development; Object relations; Personality development; Psychosexual development; Social maturity; Social skills; Socialization.

Psychosocial failure to thrive. See *Failure to thrive (psychosocial).*

Psychosocial mental retardation. Psychosocial mental retardation. *Choose from:* psychosocial(ly), cultural familial, socio-affective, social(ly) *with:* retard(ed,ation), dwarfism, mental deficienc(y,ies). *Consider also:* maternal, cultural, sensory, psychosocial *with:* depriv(e,ed,ation). *See also* Borderline mental retardation; Cultural deprivation; Mental retardation; Psychosocial deprivation.

Psychosocial needs. See *Psychological needs.*

Psychosocial readjustment. Psychosocial readjustment(s). *Choose from:* psychosocial, psychological, social, post-hospital, sociovocational, hospital discharge *with:* re-adaptat(ed,ing,ion), adapt(ed,ing,ation), readjust(ed,ing, ment), adjust(ed,ing,ment), resocializ(e, ed,ing,ation), rehabilitat(e,ed,ing,ion), recover(ed,ing,y), reentry, reintegrat(ed, ing,ion). *See also* Adjustment (to environment); Alcohol rehabilitation; Deinstitutionalization; Drug rehabilitation; Institutional release; Patient discharge; Post traumatic stress disorders; Psychosocial rehabilitation; Rehabilitation; Remotivation therapy.

Psychosocial rehabilitation. Psychosocial rehabilitation. *Consider also:* psychosocial, socioenvironmental, vocational, social, post-hospital, sociovocational, post-release, post-discharge, post-war *with:* rehabilitat(ed,ing,ion), reentry, readjust(ed,ing,ment), aftercare, resocializ(e,ed,ing,ation), reintegrat(e,ed, ing,ion), recover(y). *Consider also:* widowhood, loss(es), physical limitation(s), disabilit(y,ies), illness(es), death(s) *with:* adjust(ed,ing,ment). *Consider also:* therapeutic social club(s), therapeutic communit(y,ies), redefin(e,ed,ing,ition) self, normalization, psychological recovery. *See also*

Deinstitutionalization; Institutional release; Parole; Patient discharge; Psychosocial readjustment; Rehabilitation counseling; Self help books; Self help groups; Therapeutic social clubs; Vocational rehabilitation.

Psychosomatic disorders. See *Psychophysiologic disorders.*

Psychosurgery. Psychosurg(ery,ical). *Consider also:* thalamotom(y,ies), leukotom(y,ies), lobotom(y,ies), gyrectom(y,ies), leucotom(y,ies), topectom(y,ies), thalamotom(y,ies), hypothalamotom(y,ies), lobectom(y,ies), hemispherectom(y,ies), pulvinotom(y, ies). *See also* Organic mental disorders.

Psychotherapeutic breakthrough. Psychotherapeutic breakthrough(s). *Choose from:* psychotherap(y,ies,eutic), therap(y,ies,eutic), psychoanaly(tic,sis) *with:* breakthrough(s), turning point(s), insight(s), resolution(s), resolv(e,ed,ing). *See also* Insight; Psychotherapeutic processes; Psychotherapeutic techniques; Turning points.

Psychotherapeutic imagery. Psychotherapeutic imagery. Guided imagery. *Choose from:* imagery, imaging, mental image(s, ry), visualization *with:* heal(ed,ing), intervention(s), treat(ed,ing,ment,ments), psychotherap(y,ies,eutic), therap(y,ies, eutic), relax(ed,ing,ation), pain(ful), disorder(s). *Consider also:* guided visualization, imaginal flooding therapy. *See also* Alternative medicine; Hypnosis; Imagination; Psychotherapy; Relaxation training; Third-force therapy.

Psychotherapeutic outcomes. Psychotherapeutic outcome(s). *Choose from:* psychotherap(y,ies,eutic), therap(y,ies, eutic), casework, counsel(ed,ing), psychoanaly(sis,tic) *with:* outcome(s), result(s), effective(ness), responsive(ness), success(ful), fail(ed,ing,ure), improvement(s), terminat(ed,ing,ion), change(s), satisf(ied,action), anxiety reduction, stress reduction, adjust(ed, ment), recidivism. *See also* Patient dropouts; Psychotherapeutic processes; Recovery; Recidivism; Relapse; Remission; Treatment efficacy; Treatment outcome; Termination of treatment.

Psychotherapeutic processes. Psychotherapeutic process(es). *Choose from:* psychotherap(y,ies,eutic), therap(y,ies, eutic), psychoanaly(sis,tic), casework, counseling, therapist patient, psychotherapist patient, counselor client *with:* process(es), insight(s), breakthrough(s), resistance, transference, interaction(s), technique(s), relation(s,ship,ships), contact(s), progress. *Consider also:* acting out, catharsis, abreaction, countertransference, transference. *See also* Communicative psychotherapy; Countertransference; Insight; Psychotherapeutic breakthrough; Psychotherapeutic outcomes; Psychotherapeutic resistance; Psychotherapeutic techniques; Self disclosure; Self talk; Therapeutic processes.

Psychotherapeutic resistance. Psychotherapeutic resistance. Negative treatment response. Negative therapeutic reaction. Client resistance. *Choose from:* resistan(ce,ces,t), impasse(s), obstruct(ed,ing,ion,ions), counter-resistance, stalemate(s), blind spot(s), scotomization *with:* psychoanaly(tic, tical,sis), psychotherap(y,ies,eutic), analytic, treatment, therap(y,ies,eutic), hypnotherapy, transference. *Consider also:* epinosic, id, repression, superego *with:* resistan(ce,ces,t). *See also* Patient dropouts; Psychotherapeutic breakthrough; Psychotherapeutic processes; Psychotherapeutic techniques.

Psychotherapeutic techniques. Psychotherapeutic technique(s). *Choose from:* psychotherapeutic, therapeutic, psychoanalytic, psychiatric, counseling, casework *with:* technique(s), method(s), approach(es), intervention(s), strateg(y,ies), procedure(s). *Consider also:* aromatherapy, autogenic training, cotherapy, directed reverie therapy, dream analysis, mutual storytelling, paradoxical technique(s), psychodrama, free association(s), role playing, pet therapy, hypnotherapy, play therapy. *See also* Age regression (hypnotic); Aromatherapy; Autogenic therapy; Client centered therapy; Cotherapy; Directed reverie therapy; Music therapy; Mutual storytelling technique; Paradoxical techniques; Pet therapy; Primal therapy; Psychodrama; Psychotherapeutic breakthrough; Psychotherapeutic processes; Psychotherapeutic resistance; Psychotherapy; Rational emotive psychotherapy; Reality therapy; Relaxation training; Role playing; Self help books; Self help groups; Self talk.

Psychotherapeutic transference. See *Transference (psychology).*

Psychotherapist attitudes. Psychotherapist attitude(s). *Choose from:* psychotherapist(s), therapist(s), counselor(s), analyst(s), psychoanalyst(s), mental health professional(s), psychologist(s), psychiatrist(s), social worker(s) *with:* attitude(s), opinion(s), bias(es), perception(s), mindset, sensitivity, expectation(s), expectanc(y,ies), preconception(s), preconceived, belief(s), attribution(s), stereotyp(e,es, ing), prejudice(s). *See also* Attitudes; Psychotherapists; Psychotherapy training; Therapist attitudes; Therapist role.

Psychotherapists. Psychotherapist(s). Psychoanalyst(s). Hypnotherapist(s). Therapist(s). Counselor(s). Psychiatrist(s). *Consider also:* social worker(s), caseworker(s), psychiatric nurse(s), group therapy leader(s), psychotherapy team(s), cotherapists, cotherapy team(s), clinical psychologist(s), psychotherapy practitioner(s). *See also* Psychiatrists; Psychoanalysts; Psychologists; Psychotherapist attitudes; Social workers.

Psychotherapy. Psychotherap(y,ies,eutic). Psychological intervention(s). Casework. Counsel(ed,ing). Emotional support. Dream analysis. Free association. Transference. Abreaction. Catharsis. *Choose from:* behavior(al), blue collar, child, conjoint, experiential, expressive, marital, milieu, nondirective, persuasion, poetry, reconstructive, relationship, Rogerian, semantic, supportive, talk(ing) *with:* psychotherap(y,ies,eutic), therap(y,ies,eutic). *Consider also:* aromatherapy, autogenic training, autosuggestion, biofeedback, desensitization, dream analysis, holding therapy, neurolinguistic programming, psychotherapeutic counseling, relaxation training. *See also* Analytical psychotherapy; Aromatherapy; Art therapy; Autogenic therapy; Aversive therapy; Behavior modification; Bibliotherapy; Brief psychotherapy; Child guidance; Client centered therapy; Cognitive therapy; Communicative psychotherapy; Cotherapy; Dance therapy; Directed reverie therapy; Encounter groups; Existential therapy; Family therapy; Feminist therapy; Geriatric psychotherapy; Gestalt therapy; Group psychotherapy; Holistic health; Hypnotherapy; Implosive therapy; Individual psychotherapy; Insight therapy; Marathon group therapy; Milieu therapy; Multiple psychotherapy; Music therapy; Neuro-linguistic programming; Paradoxical techniques; Pastoral care; Play therapy; Postal psychotherapy; Primal therapy; Psychoanalysis; Psychodrama; Psychopoetry; Psychotherapeutic imagery; Psychotherapeutic processes; Psychotherapeutic techniques; Rational emotive psychotherapy; Reality therapy; Recreation therapy; Self help groups; Sensitivity training; Social work; Socioenvironmental therapy; Therapeutic community; Telephone psychotherapy; Transactional analysis.

Psychotherapy, analytical. See *Analytical psychotherapy.*

Psychotherapy, brief. See *Brief psychotherapy.*

Psychotherapy, child. See *Child guidance.*

Psychotherapy, collaborative. See *Multiple psychotherapy.*

Psychotherapy, communicative. See *Communicative psychotherapy.*

Psychotherapy, geriatric. See *Geriatric psychotherapy.*

Psychotherapy, group. See *Group psychotherapy.*

Psychotherapy, individual. See *Individual psychotherapy.*

Psychotherapy, multiple. See *Multiple psychotherapy.*

Psychotherapy, postal. See *Postal psychotherapy.*

Psychotherapy, rational emotive. See *Rational emotive psychotherapy.*

Psychotherapy, short term. See *Brief psychotherapy.*

Psychotherapy, telephone. See *Telephone psychotherapy.*

Psychotherapy, time limited. See *Brief psychotherapy.*

Psychotherapy training. Psychotherapy training. *Choose from:* psychotherapist(s), psychoanalyst(s), therapist(s), counselor(s), social worker(s), caseworker(s), psychiatric nurse(s), clinical psychologist(s), psychotherapy practitioner(s), mental health professional(s), psychiatrist(s) *with:* education(al), train(ed,ing), supervis(ed,ion), professional development, instruc-tion, trainee(s), intern(s,ship,ships). *See also* Cotherapy; Psychotherapist attitudes; Psychotherapy.

Psychotic depressive reactions. See *Major depression.*

Psychotic disorders. See *Psychoses.*

Psychotomimetic drugs. See *Hallucinogens.*

Psychotropic drugs. See *Antidepressant agents; Designer drugs; Hallucinogens; Narcoanalytic drugs; Narcotics; Street drugs; Tranquilizers.*

Psychotropic plants. Psychotropic plant(s). *Choose from:* psychotropic, mind altering, consciousness altering, psychoactive, disorientation, hallucination(s) *with:* plant(s), seed pod(s), seed(s), root(s), stem(s), flower(s,ing), blossom(s), leaves, acorn(s), mushroom(s), cactus(es), popp(y,ies), fruit(s). *Consider also:* coca plant(s), medicinal plant(s), jimson weed, peyote. *See also* Alternative medicine; Ethnobotany; Folk culture; Folklore; Hallucinogens; Herbal medicine; Medical anthropology; Medical botany; Mescal (cactus); Plant folklore; Plants (botanical); Shamanism; Traditional medicine.

Puberty. Pubert(y,al). Menarche. Pubescen(t,ce). Emerging sexuality. Preadolescen(t,ce). Early adolescence. Preteen(s). Tweenie(s). *Consider also:* postpubert(y,al), prepubescen(t,ce), prepubert(y,al). *See also* Adolescence; Initiation rites; Life cycle; Life stage transitions; Menarche; Psychosexual development; Rites of passage; Sexual maturation.

Puberty, delayed. See *Delayed puberty.*

Puberty, precocious. See *Precocious puberty.*

Puberty rites. See *Rites of passage; Puberty.*

Pubescence. See *Psychosexual development; Puberty.*

Public, general. See *General public.*

Public, going. See *Going public.*

Public administration. Public administration. Public sector. Social administration. *Choose from:* public polic(y,ies), public program(s) *with:* execution, enforcement, implementation, analysis. *Choose from:* public, government(al) *with:* administration, management, leadership, enterprise, employ(ment, ees,ers), official(s), bureaucra(cy,cies,ts), welfare, infrastructure(s), department(s), agenc(y,ies), board(s), commission(s), advisory committee(s), service, budget(s,ing), decision making, ethics, problem solving, power, resources, personnel, revenue(s). *See also* Administration; Administrative agencies; Administrative responsibility; Bureaucracies; Cities; Civil service; Government agencies; Infrastructure (economics); Public officers; Public policy; Public sector; Public services.

Public art. Public art. Mural art. Lobby art(work,works). Outdoor painting(s). *Consider also:* monument(s), memorial work(s), public sculpture(s), gallery art, statue(s), fresco(es), fountain(s), mural(s). *See also* Arts; Cultural property; Municipal art; Mural painting and decoration; Sculpture; Street art.

Public assistance. See *Antipoverty programs; Food services (programs); Medical assistance; Public welfare; Social agencies; Social programs.*

Public attitudes. See *Public opinion.*

Public baths. Public bath(s). *Choose from:* public, municipal, city, neighborhood , community *with:* bath(s), bathhouse(s), bathing, sento(s), sauna(s), hammam(s). *See also* Capitols; Commons; Facilities; Public buildings; Public places.

Public behavior. Public behavior. Street behavior. *Choose from:* public, public place(s), audience(s), public context(s) *with:* behavior, talk(ing), display(s,ed), conversation(s), discourse, smoking, drinking, drunk(en,enness), lewd(ness), interaction(s), presentation(s), conduct, performance(s), misbehavior. *See also* Anonymity; Deviant behavior; Sociability; Social behavior.

Public buildings. Public building(s). Publically owned building(s). Municipal building(s). Federal building(s). State building(s). State capitol(s). Public school building(s). Town hall(s). Public place(s). Open to the public. City hall(s). Public librar(y,ies). Post office(s). Fire station(s). Courthouse(s). Capitol building(s). *See also* Arenas; Auditoriums; Buildings; Concert halls; Public baths; Public places; Public spaces; Public property.

Public confidence. See *Public support.*

Public debt. Public debt. *Choose from:* national, federal, public, U.S., government, external, foreign *with:* debt(s), deficit(s), indebted(ness). Government borrowing. Deficit spending. Government bond(s). Gramm-Rudman-Hollings deficit reduction law. Country creditworthiness. Public indebtedness. Government liabilit(y,ies). Balance of payment(s). Public spending. Deficit spending. *Choose from:* credit rating, credit standing *with:* names of countries, states, cities. *See also* Balance of payments; Budget deficits; Budgets; Debt-for-nature swap(s); Debt moratoriums; Debts; Economic crises; External debts; Government expenditures; Government finances; Public finance; Wasteful; World economy.

Public domain. See *Public goods; Public lands.*

Public employees. See *Civil service; Elected officials; Government personnel.*

Public enterprises. See *Public sector.*

Public expenditures. See *Government expenditures; Public finance.*

Public figures. Public figure(s). Famous people. Famous person(s). Pop star(s). Notable(s). Personage(s). Dignitar(y,ies). Prominent people. Prominent public official(s). Celebrit(y,ies). Well known people. Hero(es). Heroine(s). Eminent. Preeminent. Esteemed. Respected. Renowned. Celebrated. Big name(s). Noted. Fame. Distinguished. Venerable. Acclaimed. Immortalized. Luminar(y, ies). Prestigious. Protagonist(s). Superhero(es). Movie idol(s). Movie star(s). Sports figure(s). Cult of personality. First lad(y,ies). Oscar winner(s). Nobel prize winner(s). VIP(s). *See also* Entertainers; Presidents; Politicians; Royalty.

Public finance. Public financ(e,es,ing). General Accounting Office. Office of Management and Budget. Federal Reserve System(s). *Choose from:* public, government, state, county, city, municipal, military, school *with:* financ(e,es, ing,ial), budget(s,ing), expenditure(s), encumbrance(s), fiscal, fund(s,ing), tax(es,ing), revenue(s), payroll(s), payment(s), tariff(s), cost(s), debt(s), deficit(s), borrow(ing), account(s,ing), user fee(s), appropriation(s), audit(s,ing, ors), grant(s), trust fund(s), subsid(y,ies). *Consider also:* revenue sharing, sales tax(es), income tax(es), value added tax(es), sumptuary tax(es), sin tax(es), set-aside(s), intergovernmental transfer(s). *See also* Cost control; Cost recovery; Fiscal federalism; Fiscal policy; Government expenditures; Government subsidization; Public debt; Taxes.

Public folklore. Public folklore. *Choose from:* public sector, public policy, government(s,al), bureaucra(t,ts,tic, cy,cies) *with:* folklore, folk art, lore, myth(s), cultur(e,al), belief(s), tradition(s,al,ally). *See also* Bureaucracies; Culture (anthropology); Government personnel; Occupational folklore; Organizational culture.

Public good. Public good. Public interest. Common good. Common welfare. Collective good. General welfare. National interest(s). Public benefit. Public purpose(s). Utilitarianism. Pareto optimum. *Choose from:* public, general, common, collective *with:* interest, good, welfare, interest(s), benefit. *See also* Collective consciousness; Collectivism; Democracy; Sharing; Utilitarianism.

Public goods. Public goods. Collective goods. Commonly owned. Publicly owned. Community owned. Free goods. Public domain. *Consider also:* communal, public park(s), public television, village commons, conjoint interest(s), environmental protection, air quality, water quality, public health. *See also* Collectivism; Nationalization; Public good; Public lands; Public sector; Public services.

Public health. Public health. World Health Organization. Department(s) of health. Health department(s). Surgeon General. International health organization(s). National health service(s). National health organization(s). Center(s) for Disease Control. National Institutes of Health. *Choose from:* public, community, social, society *with:* health, hygiene, epidemiology. *Consider also:* health planning, occupational medicine, social medicine, zoonoses, communicable disease control, consumer product safety, decontamination, environmental pollution, health education, sanitation. *See also* Drainage; Environmental pollution; Epidemics; Health services; Morbidity; Occupational diseases; Occupational health services; Occupational safety; Sanitation; State medicine; Toxic substances; Vaccinations; Waste disposal; World health.

Public housing. Public housing. Housing support. Public apartment house(s). *Choose from:* hous(ing,e,es), apartment(s), dwelling(s) *with:* government, public, low-income, federal, city, state, community, council, subsidized. *Consider also:* housing project(s). *See also* Affordable housing; Civic improvement; Housing policy; Public services; Rental housing; Tenants; Urban renewal.

Public inquiries. See *Government investigations.*

Public interest. See *Public good.*

Public lands. Public land(s). Commons. *Choose from:* public(ly), state, government(ally), federal(ly), communal, community, common, town(ship), county, Indian, trust, public domain, eminent domain *with:* land(s), property, tract(s), area(s), holding(s), upland(s), park(s), landholding(s), rangeland(s), farmland(s), woodland(s), grassland(s), pasture(s), coastland(s), beach(es), swamp(s), wetland(s), wilderness, reservation(s), preserve(s), territor(y,ies). *See also* Collectivism; Land (property); Public goods; Public spaces; Rangelands; Right of pasture.

Public meals. See *Group meals.*

Public meetings. Public meeting(s). *Choose from:* public, open, town hall, local government, sunshine law(s) *with:* meeting(s), conference(s), hearing(s), gathering(s), assembl(y,ies), session(s), debate(s), forum(s), fora, discussion(s). *Consider also:* public deliberation, stakeholder participation, direct meeting(s), Sunshine Act, freedom of information, deliberative democracy. *See also* Access to information; Conferences; Debate; Local government; Religious gatherings; Social demonstrations.

Public morality, offenses against. See *Victimless crimes.*

Public officers. Public officer(s). *Choose from:* public, government, federal, state, local, municipal, county, city, town, cabinet *with:* officer(s), official(s), authorities. *See also* Civil service; Elected officials; Government personnel; Local officials and employees; Public administration;.

Public officials. See *Elected officials; Government personnel.*

Public opinion. Public opinion. Opinion poll(s). Interview(s) *with:* man in the street. Voice of the people. Will of the people. Wishes of the majority. Exit poll(s). Straw poll(s). *Choose from:* public, citizen(s), community, voter(s), man in the street, people(s), readership, consumer(s), viewer(s), listener(s), popular, social, societal, majority, minority *with:* attitude(s), opinion(s), view(s), response(s), brief(s), resistance, preference(s), understanding, acceptance, satisfaction, dissatisfaction, opposition, poll(s), mindset, interest(s), reaction(s), concern(s), support, perceive(s,d), awareness, perception(s), perspective(s), stereotype(s), commentar(y,ies), referend(a,um),

sympath(y,ies,ize,ized,izing), condemn(ed,ing,ation), expectation(s), ambivalence, conception(s), random sample(s). *See also* Citizenship; Community attitudes; Consensus; Credibility; Defamation; Dissent; General public; Gossip; Honored (esteem); Ideologies; Liberty of conscience; Mass media effects; Media portrayal; Moral attitudes; Opinion polls; Polarization; Political attitudes; Promotion (business); Propaganda; Popular culture; Public opposition; Public policy; Public relations; Public support; Recognition (achievement); Reputation; Rumors; Scandals; Social attitudes; Social unrest; War news.

Public opinion research. See *Opinion polls.*

Public opposition. Public opposition. *Choose from:* public, citizen(s), community, voter(s), man in the street, people(s), readership, consumer(s), viewer(s), listener(s), social, societal, majority, minority *with:* oppos(e,ed,ing), opposition, resist(ed,ing,ance), dissatisfaction, antagonis(m,ed,ing), hostil(e, ity), defiance, disagree(d,ing,ment), voted down, dissent(ing), contradict(ory), object(ed,ing), refus(e,ed,ing). *See also* Dissent; Polarity; Public opinion; Public support.

Public order. Public order. Civility. Rule of law. Social order. Public safety. Safe street(s). Public security. Sidewalk behavior. Neighborhood order. Low(er) crime rate(s). Peaceful public demonstration(s). *See also* Breach of the peace; Decency; Everyday life; Formal social control; Norms; Peace; Quality of life.

Public participation. See *Citizen participation.*

Public perceptions. See *Public opinion.*

Public places. Public place(s). Public librar(y,ies). Public restroom(s). Public meeting room(s). *Consider also:* restaurant(s), church(es), bar(s), school(s), store(s), supermarket(s), theater(s), shopping mall(s). *See also* Arenas; Auditoriums; Concert halls; Public baths; Public buildings; Public spaces.

Public policy. Public polic(y,ies). Government polic(y,ies). Social polic(y,ies). *Choose from:* public, government(al), federal, state, congressional, national, Washington, social, city, county *with:* polic(y,ies), decision(s), principle(s), guideline(s), control, regulation(s), rule(s), law(s). *Consider also:* regulatory, redistributive, distributive, constituent *with:* polic(y,ies). *See also* Administrative law; Administrative policy; Energy policy; Family policy; Fiscal policy; Foreign policy; Future of society; General public; Health policy;

Housing policy; Immigration law; Investment policy; Labor policy; Language policy; Legislation; Military policy; Monetary policy; Policy analysis; Policy evaluation; Policy implementation; Policy making; Political participation; Social legislation; Transportation policy; Welfare policy.

Public property. Public property. *Choose from:* government(al), federal(ly), national(ly), state, county, city, public(ly) *with:* property, land(s), building(s), park(s), garden(s), own(ed,ership), facilit(y,ies). *See also* Public buildings; Public goods; Public lands; Public spaces.

Public records. See *Government records.*

Public relations. Public relations. Community relations. Fund raising appeals. Publicity. Manipulat(e,ed,ing) public opinion. Public appeals. Respond(ed, ing) to public pressure. Community institutional relations. Interinstitutional relations. Campaign(s,ing). Advertisement(s). News media relations. Publicity. Press release(s). Image building. Creat(ing) public image(s). Promot(e,ed, ing) public awareness. *Choose from:* promotion(al) *with:* materials, awareness, program(s). *Choose from:* public service *with:* advertising, announcement(s), message(s). *See also* Advertising; Advocacy; Advocacy advertising; Business ethics; Client attitudes; Customer relations; Corporate social responsibility; Investor relations; Manifesto; Mass media; Press agents; Promotion (business); Propaganda; Public opinion; Publicity; Spin doctors; Spokespersons.

Public relief. See *Public welfare.*

Public response. See *Social response.*

Public schools. Public school(s). Secular school(s). *Consider also:* public education. *See also* Community services; Elementary schools; High schools; Private schools; Public services; School choice; Schools.

Public sector. Public sector. Public enterprise(s). Nationaliz(ed,ation). State run. *Choose from:* national(ized), government(al), federal, state, county, city, municipal, local, town, public, civil service, socialized *with:* sector(s), sphere(s), organization(s), own(ed, ership), control(led), facilit(y,ies), financed, fund(ed,ing,s), administration, service(s), good(s), enterprise, economy, institution(s), operat(ed,ions), produc(ed,tion), planning, personnel, employee(s), official(s), executive(s), bureaucra(cy,ts), administrator(s), worker(s). *See also* Government property; Nationalization; Private sector; Privatization; Public administration; Public services; Public works; State role.

Public service. See *Civil service; Elected officials; Government personnel; Volunteers.*

Public services. Public service(s). Public enterprise(s). *Choose from:* national(ized), government(al), federal, state, county, city, municipal, local, town, public, civil service, socialized *with:* access, amenit(y,ies), transit, transportation, service(s), shelter(s), facilit(y,ies), hospital(s), park(s), health service(s), medical service(s), utilit(y,ies), housing, school(s), police, prison(s), highway(s), fire department(s), civil defense, environmental protection, welfare, zoning. *See also* Community services; Emergency services; Government agencies; Government aid; Government publications; Human services; Law enforcement; Postal service; Public administration; Public goods; Public sector; Public schools; Public transportation; Public utilities; Welfare state.

Public spaces. Public space(s). Public area(s). Public property. Public square(s). Public park(s). Sidewalk(s). Pedestrian space(s). Social area(s). *Choose from:* public, urban, downtown, open, pedestrian, parking *with:* space(s), area(s), land(s), lot(s), property, square(s), park(s). *Consider also:* playground(s), walkway(s), road(s), highway(s). *See also* Public buildings; Public lands; Public places; Public property; Public sphere.

Public speaking. Public speaking. Speech(es). Toastmaster(s). Master of ceremonies. Orat(ion,ions,or,ors). Sermon(s). Lecture(s). *Choose from:* verbal, group, public *with:* presentation(s), address(ed,ing,es). *See also* Ad lib; Audience analysis; Debate; Forensics (public speaking); Lectures and lecturing; Oral communication; Persuasion; Presentations; Rhetoric; Speech; Speech anxiety; Speeches (formal discourse).

Public speaking, addresses. See *Lectures and lecturing.*

Public sphere. Public sphere(s). *Choose from:* public, societal, social, political, business, community, collective, man's, men's *with:* sphere(s), domain(s), forum(s), space(s), world(s), life. *Consider also:* democratic participation, commodification, consumer culture(s), citizenship. *See also* Gender identity; Private sphere; Public spaces; Sex roles; Sexism; Sexual division of labor; Worldview.

Public support. Public support. Popular support. Popularity rating(s). Approval rating(s). Voice of the people. Will of the people. Wishes of the majority. Elected by an overwhelming majority. Unanimously elected. Favored by most people. Landslide victory. Mandat(e,es, ed,ing). *Choose from:* public, citizen, community, voter(s), man in the street, people(s), readership, consumer(s), viewer(s), listener(s), social, societal, majority, minority *with:* confidence, favorable attitude(s), positive opinion(s), positive response(s), preference(s), acceptance, satisfaction, interest(s), support(ed,ing), acclaim(ed), popular(ity), back(ed,ing), endorse(d,ment), approval. *See also* Community attitudes; Public opinion; Police community relations; Political attitudes; Public opinion; Public opposition; Resistance; Social response.

Public support (financial). See *Antipoverty programs; Fiscal federalism; Government aid; Government financing; Government programs; Government subsidization; Medical assistance; Public welfare.*

Public transportation. Public transportation. *Choose from:* public, mass, urban, inter-urban, local, commuter *with:* train(s), transportation, transit. *Consider also:* rapid transit, bus(ses), subway(s), trolley(s), light rail transit, taxi(s,cabs), jitney(s), streetcar(s), cable car(s). *See also* Air transportation; Automobiles; Commuting (travel); Mass transit; Public services; Railroads; Transport workers; Transportation policy; Urban development; Urban sprawl.

Public utilities. Public utilit(y,ies). Public power authority. Telephone compan(y, ies). *Choose from:* public *with:* utilit(y,ies), power, gas, electric(ity), water. *See also* Alternative energy; Conservation of natural resources; Communications media; Electric utilities; Energy conservation; Energy consumption; Energy costs; Energy generating resources; Energy policy; Sanitation; Water conservation; Water pollution; Water power; Water purification; Water safety; Water supply.

Public welfare. Public welfare. Public assistance. The dole. Workfare. Medicare. Medicaid. Food stamp(s). Food bank(s). Food relief. Safety net. Antipoverty program(s). Entitlement program(s). Unemployment compensation. Unemployment benefit(s). Aid to Families *with:* Dependent Children [AFDC]. Old Age Assistance [OAA]. Supplemental Security Income [SSI]. Social Security. Survivors Insurance. Black lung benefit(s). Special Supplemental Food Program for Women, Infants and Children. Temporary Disability Insurance. Veterans benefit(s). Unemployment insurance. Head Start. Public relief. Work relief. *See also* Antipoverty programs; Community health services; Community mental health services; Food services (programs); Humanitarianism; Medical assistance; Public housing; Social agencies; Social programs; Social services; Welfare policy; Welfare recipients.

Public works. Public works. *Choose from:* public, government, state, federal, civil *with:* works, construction, infrastructure, project(s). *See also* Government property; Infrastructure (economics); Public administration; Public goods; Public property; Public sector.

Public worship. See *Church attendance; Worship.*

Publications. Publication(s). Edition(s). Issue(s). Magazine(s). Book(s). Serial(s). Periodical(s). Review(s). Digest(s). Newsletter(s). Yearbook(s). Monograph(s). Newspaper(s). Journal(s). Bulletin(s). Gazette(s). Tabloid(s). Flier(s). Handbill(s). Circular(s). Copyrighted work(s). Proceeding(s). Paperback(s). Catalog(s). Pamphlet(s). Broadside(s). Comic book(s). Government document(s). *Choose from:* published, printed *with:* communications, media, material(s), bibliograph(y,ies), translation(s). *See also* Audiovisual communications; Authors; Book reviews; Books; Broadsides; Bulletins; Censorship; Community newspapers; Continuation; Copyright; Documentation; Documents; Government publications; Information dissemination; Journal articles; Journalism; Library acquisitions; Literary criticism; Literature; Malinformation; Manuscripts; Mass media; News media; Newspapers; Periodicals; Pornography; Printing; Publishing; Readership; Records; Reference materials; Telecommunications; Written communications.

Publications, government. See *Government publications.*

Publicists. See *Press agents.*

Publicity. Publici(ty,ze,zing). Public relations. Advertis(ing,ements). Ads. Announcing. Broadcasting. Proclaiming. Displaying. Placard(s). Poster(s). Public notice(s). Public announcement(s). Commercial(s). Junk mail. Spotlight. Limelight. Hype. Promot(e,ing). Retail promotion(s). Promotional material. Promotion campaign(s). Campaign to promote. Handbills. Propagand(a,ize). Bumper sticker(s). Business theatre. *See also* Advertising; Communication (thought transfer); Information dissemination; Mass media; Press agents; Promotion (business); Public relations; Telecommunications.

Publicity, government. See *Government publicity.*

Publicly financed. See *Government financing.*

Publishers. Publisher(s). Publishing house(s). Publishing compan(y,ies). *See* *also* Alternative press; Art publishing; Bookselling; Book industry; Editors; Little presses.

Publishing. Publish(ed,ing,ers). Print(ed,ing). Disseminat(e,ed,ing). Circulat(e,ed,ing,ion). *Consider also:* publishing house(s), book industry, book trade, magazine industry, publishing compan(y,ies), bookbind(ing,ers), booksell(ing,ers), book price(s), copyright, little magazine(s), newsletter(s), newspaper(s). *See also* Art publishing; Best sellers; Book covers; Books; Copyright; Electronic publishing; Information dissemination; Little presses; Mass media; Printing; Publications; Transmission of texts; Written communications.

Publishing, art. See *Art publishing.*

Publishing, desktop. See *Desktop publishing.*

Publishing, electronic. See *Electronic publishing.*

Publishing, online. See *Electronic publishing.*

Pubs. See *Restaurants.*

Pulling, hair. See *Hair pulling.*

Punched card systems. Punched card system(s). *Consider also:* McBee, Hollerith, perforated record, punch(ed), data processing, keypunch(ed), edge punched, 80 column *with:* card(s). *See also* Data processing.

Punishment. Punish(ed,ing,ment). Censure(d). Retaliat(e,ed,ing,ion). Footshock(s). Shock(s). Electric shock(s). Peniten(ce,ts). Penalt(y,ies). Reproof. Aversive control. Reprimand(s,ed,ing). Negative evaluation. Aversive stimulation. Restitution. Retribution. Correct(ed,ing,ion). Overcorrect(ed,ing,ion). Sentenc(e,ed,ing). Punitive(ness). Admonish(ed,ing). Chastis(e,ed,ing,ment). Disciplin(e,ed,ing). Castigat(e,ed,ing,ion). Forfeit(ure). Imprison(ed,ing,ment). Negative consequence(s). Aversive procedure(s). Solitary confinement. Rebuk(e,ed,ing). Bread and water. Contingent electric shock(s). Spank(ed,ing). Penaliz(e,ed,ing,ation). Demerit(s). Fine(s,d). Admonition(s). Chasten(ed,ing). Scold(ed,ing). *Consider also:* retributivism, capital punishment. *See also* Alternatives to incarceration; Censure; Child discipline; Clemency; Coercion; Corporal punishment; Death penalty; Detention; Deterrence; Disapproval; Employee discipline; Flagellants and flagellation; Forfeiture; Formal social control; Future punishment; Informal social control; Life sentence; Negative reinforcement; Penalties; Political repression; Prison discipline; Punitiveness; Reprisals; Sentencing; Torture; Vigilantes.

Punishment, capital. See *Death penalty.*

Punishment, corporal. See *Corporal punishment.*

Punishment, endless. See *Future punishment.*

Punishment, future. See *Future punishment.*

Punishment, physical. See *Corporal punishment.*

Punitiveness. Punitive(ness). Punitory. Penaliz(e,ed,ing). Punish(ed,ing,ment). Corrective. Correction(s,al). Disciplin(e,ary). Retaliat(e,ed,ing,ory). Revenge(ful,fulness). Retribut(ive,ion). Vindictive(ness). *Consider also:* vengeance, vengeful(ly,ness), harsh(ly,ness), severe(ly,ness) *with:* disciplin(e,ed,ary), penalt(y,ies), punish(ed,ment). *See also* Child abuse; Child discipline; Corporal punishment; Death penalty; Employee discipline; Punishment; Reprisals.

Puns. Pun(s,ning). Play(s) on words. Equivoque(s). Wordplay(s). Equivocal word(s). Double-entendre. Bon mot(s). Equivocation(s). *Consider also:* witticism(s). *See also* Double meanings; Jokes; Word games; Word play.

Pupil teacher relationship. See *Student teacher relations.*

Pupils. See *Students.*

Puppets. Puppet(s,ry). Marionette(s). Fantoccin(i,o). Puppenspiel. Hand puppet(s). Finger puppet(s). String puppet(s). *Consider also:* Howdy-Doody, Charlie McCarthy, Mortimer Snerd, Punchinello, Punch and Judy. *See also* Children's theater; Doll play; Dolls; Toys.

Puppets, string. See *Puppets.*

Purchasing. Purchas(e,es,ed,ing). Procur(e,ed,ing,ment). Acquir(e,ed,ing). Acquisition(s). Buy(ing). Bought. Shop(ping). Shopaholi(c,cs,sm). Military contract(s). Defense contract(s). Cooperative contract(s,ing). *Consider also:* spending, mortgage(s), ordering by mail, mail order(s), retail. *See also* Acquisition; Advertising; Bartering; Brand loyalty; Brand names; Consumer behavior; Consumer expenditures; Consumer goods; Consumer society; Consumption (economic); Deals; Earnest money; Discounts; Economic exchanges; Library acquisitions; Marketing; Ownership; Retailing; Sales; Trade.

Purchasing power. Purchasing power. Purchasing capacity. Value of money. Value of the dollar. *Consider also:* price index(es), exchange rate(s), real income, income power. *See also* Cost of living; Costs; Currency speculation; Devaluation (of currency); Income; Inflation (economics); Living standards; Prices.

Purdah. Purdah. Pardah. Hijab. Hidjab. *Consider also:* veil(s,ed), seclusion, seclud(e,ed,ing) *with:* woman, women, harem(s), menage(s). *See also* Hinduism; Islam; Private sphere; Sex discrimination; Sex roles; Sexism; Sexual inequality; Sexual division of labor; Sexual oppression; Veiling of women.

Purge binge syndrome. See *Bulimia.*

Purges. Purg(e,es,ed,ing). Expel(led,ling). Expulsion(s). Exterminat(e,ed,ing). Exil(e,ed,ing). Displac(e,ed,ing,ement). Liquidat(e,ed,ing,ation). Remov(e,ed,ing,al) from office. Clean sweep. Weed(ed,ing) out. Sweep out. Clean house. Cleanup(s). Depos(e,ed,ing,ition). Reshuffled. Blood bath(s). Show trial(s). Political upheaval(s). Remov(e,ed,ing) from post(s). Shakeup(s). Ouster(s). Oust(ed,ing). Deport(ed,ing,ation). *See also* Assassination; Coups d'Etat; Political violence; Provisional government; Revolution; Right of asylum.

Purges, political. See *Purges.*

Purification, water. See *Water purification.*

Purification rites. Purification rite(s). *Choose from:* purification, purif(y,ied,ing), purity, cleansing, ablution(s), washing(s) *with:* ritual(s,ized), rite(s), symbol(s,ic), tradition(al,s), ceremon(y,ies), practice(s). *Consider also:* baptism(s), ghusl, mikveh. *See also* Ceremonies; Festivals; Purity; Religious mysteries; Religious rituals; Ritual purity.

Puritan ethic. See *Protestant ethic.*

Puritanism. Puritan(ical,ism). Priggish(ness). Strait-laced. Stiffnecked. Austere(ness). Ascetic(ism). Abstinen(t,ce). Intoleran(t,ce). Narrow-minded(ness). *Consider also:* Calvinist doctrine(s), zealot(s,ry), punitive(ness), moral reprimand(s). *See also* Moral attitudes; Prejudice; Protestant ethic; Social values.

Purity. Purity. Pure. Purified. Unadulterated. Clean(ness,liness). Spotless(ness). Immaculate(ness). Unsoiled. Untarnished. Unblemished. Unstained. Stainless(ness). Untainted. Taintless(ness). Antiseptic. Steril(e,ity). Asep(tic,sis). Unalloyed. *See also* Authenticity; Harmlessness; Innocence; Integrity; Morality; Purification rites; Ritual purity; Simplicity; Virginity.

Purity, ritual. See *Ritual purity.*

Purposes. See *Function; Goals; Intentionality; Teleology.*

Purposive accidents. Purposive accident(s). *Consider also:* intentional accident(s), paraprax(ia,is). *See also* Accident proneness; Accidents.

Purposiveness. See *Intentionality*.

Push-polling. Push-Poll(s,ing,ster,sters). Negative phone-bank operation(s). *Choose from:* telephone survey(s), pollster(s), poll(s,ed,ing), political polling, survey(s) of voters, public-opinion survey(s), phone bank(s), canvass potential voters, *with:* negative comment(s), attack(s,ed,ing), partisan, innuendo(s), distort(ed,ing,ion,ions), lie(s), lying, phony organization(s), unethical(ly), promot(e,ed,ing) cause, bogus question(s), sleaz(e,y,iness), rumor(s), whisper campaign(s), smear, biased, misleading, half truth(s), mudslinging, false information, damaging information, derogatory question(s), decept(ive,ion), unethical, misrepresent(ed,ing,ation), mean-spirited, exaggerated assertion(s). *Consider also:* suppression phone bank(s), political telemarketing, scare phoning, pseudo-poll(s). *See also* Data collection; Defamation; Opinion polls; Political advertising; Political campaigns; Surveys.

Push technology. Push Technology. Webcast(ing). Pointcast(ing). Netcast(ing,er,ers), Multicast(ing,er,ers). *Choose from:* automatic(ally) *with:* deliver(ed,ing), distribut(e,ed,ing), send(ing), deploy(ed,ing,ment), upgrad(e,ed,ing), broadcast(ing), transmit(ted,ting), streaming, channelling, narrowcast(ing) *with:* information, data, software, Web, World Wide Web, Internet, net, news. *Consider also:* push vendor(s), push product(s), PointCast, e-mail, multicast(ing), spam(med,ming), unsolicited e-mail. *See also* Electronic journals; Electronic mail; Electronic publishing; Internet (computer network); Junk email; Online harassment; Teleconferencing.

Pyromania. Pyromania(c,cs). Incendiarism. *See also* Arson; Fire setting behavior; Impulsiveness; Personality disorders.

Q

Quackery. Quack(s,ery). Fraud in medicine. *Choose from:* fraud(ulent), unqualified, charlatan(s), bogus, imposter(s), hoax(s), parapsychological, unprov(en,ed) *with:* medicine(s), medical, physician(s), doctor(s), healer(s), remed(y,ies), treatment(s). *Consider also:* nostrum(s), snake oil, therapeutic cult(s). *See also* Alternative medicine; Anti-science movement; Fraud; Medical ethics; Nostrums; Plant folklore; Sham surgery; Therapeutic cults; Traditional medicine; Unethical conduct.

Quadriplegia. Quadriplegi(a,c). Tetraplegi(a,c). Locked-in syndrome. Tetraparesis. *See also* Injuries; Physically handicapped; Spinal cord injuries.

Quadruplets. Quadruplet(s). *Consider also:* Hellin's law, multiple birth(s). *See also* Multiple births.

Quakers. Quaker(s,ism). Society of Friends. *Consider also:* George Fox, William Penn, American Friends Service Committee, Service Council of the British Society of Friends. *See also* Protestantism.

Qualifications. Qualification(s). Qualif(y, ying,ied). Requirement(s). Prerequisite(s). Abilit(y,ies). Skill(s). Experience(d). Competen(ce,cy,cies). Attainment(s). Background. Knowledge. Judgment. Eligibility. Prepared(ness). Readiness. Proficiency. Fluency. *See also* Ability; Academic degrees; Achievement; Aptitude; Certification; Employment history; Experience (background); Job requirements; Occupational qualifications; Performance; Reputation; Requirements; Skill; Work skills.

Qualifications, employment. See *Employability; Occupational qualifications.*

Qualifications, job. See *Occupational qualifications.*

Qualifications, occupational. See *Occupational qualifications.*

Qualifications, work. See *Occupational qualifications.*

Qualitative analysis. See *Qualitative methods.*

Qualitative methods. Qualitative method(s, ologies). Descriptive method(s,ologies). Open-ended question(s). Biographical material(s). Use of life histories. Hermeneutics. Participant observation. Historical research. Fieldwork. Interview(s,ing). Descriptive account(s). *Choose from:* qualitative, descriptive, biographical *with:* data, technique(s), analys(is,es), research, stud(y,ies),

method(s,ologies), approach, variable(s). *Consider also:* nominal scale(s), classificatory scale(s). *See also* Case studies; Data collection; Ethnography; Fieldwork; Interviews; Participant observation; Quantitative methods; Research methods; Verstehen.

Qualitative research. See *Qualitative methods.*

Qualities. Qualit(y,ies). Characteristic(s). Character. Propert(y,ies). Attribute(s). Trait(s). Feature(s). Peculiarit(y,ies). Oddit(y,ies). Idiosyncras(y,ies). Singularit(y,ies). Nature. Gift(s). Talent(s). *Consider also:* abilit(y,ies), capabilit(y,ies), eccentric(ity,ities), virtue(s). *See also* Characteristics; Client characteristics; Community characteristics; Cultural characteristics; Demographic characteristics (of individuals); Employee characteristics; Family characteristics; National characteristics; Physical characteristics; Population characteristics; Residence characteristics; Sex characteristics; Speech characteristics; Student characteristics; Teacher characteristics; Therapist characteristics.

Quality. Quality. Excellen(t,ce). Superior(ity). Value. Eminen(t,ce). Preeminen(t,ce). Distinction. Great(ness). Fine(ness). Worth(y). Perfection. High standard(s). Best. *See also* Accountability; Accreditation; Accuracy; Achievement; Criteria; Environmental protection; Evaluation; Excellence; Failure; Living standards; Perfection; Performance; Quality control; Quality of health care; Quality of life; Quality of working life; Standards; Success; Supererogation.

Quality assurance. See *Quality control.*

Quality control. Quality control. *Choose from:* quality, accuracy, safety *with:* control, ensur(e,ed,ing), responsibility, assurance, criteria, assess(ment,ed,ing), requirement(s), management, reliability, evaluat(e,ed,ing,ion), test(s,ed,ing), inspect(ed,ing,ion), standard(s). *Consider also:* detect(ed,ing,ion) fault(s,y), product standardization, quality circle(s), consumer safeguard(s), industry regulation, industry standards, product reliability, Pareto chart (s). *See also* Accountability; Accreditation; Certification; Debugging; Electronic data interchange; Flawless; Food laws and legislation; Imperfection; Industrial engineering; Operations research; Organizational effectiveness; Organizational objectives; Participative management; Performance; Pretesting; Program

evaluation; Product liability; Product recall; Product tampering; Quality; Reliability.

Quality of health care. Quality of health care. *Choose from:* quality, adequa(cy, te), standard(s), checklist(s), inadequa(cy,te), sufficien(t,cy), satisfaction, effective(ness), norm(s), accountab(le, ility), assess(ed,ing,ment), peer review(s) *with:* health care, nursing care, patient care, surg(ery,ical), medic(al,ine), nursing, primary care, ambulatory care, homecare, treatment(s), therap(y,ies, eutic), caregiving, social service(s). *See also* Accountability; Health care; Medical care.

Quality of life. Quality of life. Wellness. Well being. Social support. Social justice. Health(y,iness). Per capita income. Lifestyle(s). Life situation assessment. *Choose from:* life, living, survival *with:* quality, standard(s), satisf(ying,action), cost(s), style(s), product(ive,ivity). *See also* Alternative lifestyles; Appropriate technologies; Austerities; Basic needs; Comfortableness; Community development; Consumption (use); Deprivation; Disadvantaged; Ecology; Economic conditions; Energy consumption; Environmental protection; Environmental stress; Evaluation; Everyday life; Family life; Holistic health; Humanization; Life (biological); Life expectancy; Life satisfaction; Life space; Lifestyle; Living conditions; Living standards; Natural foods; Productivity; Public order; Quality of working life; Restoration ecology; Social class; Social conditions; Social environment; Social indicators; Social problems; Socioeconomic status; Social values; Technological progress; Technology; Technology and civilization; Values; Wealth; Well being.

Quality of products. See *Quality control.*

Quality of working life. Quality of work(ing) life. Work life quality. QWL. Working condition(s). Job tension(s). Work environment(s). Job enrichment. Work culture. *Choose from:* quality of life, humaniz(e,ed,ation,ing), enrich(ed,ing,ment), satisfaction *with:* work, factor(y,ies), workplace(s), worklife, job(s), labor, employ(ees, ment), office(s). Employee satisfaction. Occupational ergonomics. Occupational health. Work stress. Employee centered production. *See also* Careers; Employee assistance programs; Employee concerns; Employment; Humanization; Industrial psychology; Job enrichment;

Job satisfaction; Labor aspects of technology; Labor management relations; Labor unions; Life satisfaction; Occupational adjustment; Occupational diseases; Occupational exposure; Occupational neuroses; Occupational roles; Occupational safety; Occupational stress; Occupations; Organizational climate; Organizational development; Productivity; Quality of life; Sick building syndrome; Superior subordinate relationship; Technological progress; Technological unemployment; Technology; Technology and civilization; Working conditions.

Quantification. See *Measurement; Quantitative methods.*

Quantitative analysis. See *Quantitative methods.*

Quantitative methods. Quantitative method(s,ology,ologies). Quantif(y,ied, ying,ication). Ordinal data. Rank order scale(s). Interval scales. Aggregate data. *Choose from:* quantitative, quantifiable, numerical, statistical, linear, multivariate, psychometric, factor, regression, mathematical, inferential, sociometric, probabilistic *with:* assessment(s), scale(s), method(s,ology,ologies), analys(is,es), research, stud(y,ies), technique(s), model(s), index(es), test(s). *Consider also:* econometric(s), cliometric(s), psychometric(s). *See also* Analysis; Data collection; Empirical methods; Frequency distribution; Mean; Measurement; Median; Models; Probability; Qualitative methods; Research design; Research methods; Sampling; Scientific method; Statistical bias; Statistical correlation; Statistical data; Statistical inference; Statistical norms; Statistical significance; Statistical tables; Validity.

Quantitative research. See *Quantitative methods.*

Quantity. Quantit(y,ies). Amount(s). Measure(s). Share(s). Portion(s). Quota(s). Dos(e,es,ages). Allotment(s). Apportionment(s). Allowance(s). Number(s). *Consider also:* bulk, bundle(s), expanse(s), load(s), lot(s), magnitude(s), mass(es), volume(s). *See also* Measurement; Size.

Quarrels, literary. See *Literary quarrels.*

Quasi-firms. See *Adhocracies; Boundaryless organizations; Contract services; Contracting out; Independent contractors; Virtual organizations.*

Query. See *Questioning.*

Questioning. Question(ing,ed). Quer(y,ying,ied). Quiz(zed,zing). Interrogat(e,ed,ing,ion,ions,atory). Inquir(e,ed,ing,y,ies). Interview(ed,ing, s). Cross examin(e,ed,ing,ation,ations). Direct examin(e,ed,ing,ation,ations). *Choose from:* question(s), quer(y,ies) *with:* ask(ed,ing), pos(e,ed,ing), put(ting). *Consider also:* questionnaire(s), elicit(ed,ing) testimony. *See also* Cognitive processes; Curiosity; Guessing; Information seeking; Inquiry (theory of knowledge); Interviews; Police questioning; Questionnaires; Uncertainty

Questioning, police. See *Police questioning.*

Questionnaires. Questionnaire(s). *Consider also:* interview schedule(s), delphi technique, data form(s), set(s) of questions, mail(ed) survey(s), inventor(y,ies), data collect(ing,ion) instrument(s), checklist(s), batter(y,ies) of questions, self report(s), evaluation form(s), opinionnaire(s). *See also* Attitude measurement; Data collection; Fieldwork; Interviews; Library surveys; Measurement; Opinion polls; Questioning; Research; Surveys.

Quests. Quest(s,ed,ing). Search(ed,ing). Explor(e,ed,ing,ation). Inquir(y,ed,ing). Pursuit(s). Pursu(e,ed,ing,al,ance). Seek(ing). Sought. *Consider also:* delv(e,ed,es,ing), inquest(s), inquisition, investigat(e,es,ed,ing,ion), prob(e,ed,es, ing), research(es,ed,ing). *See also* Adventure; Challenge; Crusades; Expeditions; Investigations; Pilgrimages; Pioneers; Scientific expeditions; Search; Tourism; Travel.

Quiet. See *Silence.*

Quietude. See *Silence; Solitude.*

Quintuplets. Quintuplet(s). *Consider also:* Hellin's law, multiple birth(s). *See also* Multiple births.

Quislings. See *Collaborators; Traitors.*

Quodlibets. Quodlibet(s). Farrago(es). Ensalada(s). Messanza(s). Misticanza(s). Centone(s). Incatenatura(s). *See also* Arrangement (Music); Centos; Patchwork.

Quotas. Quota(s). Share(s). Portion(s). Part(s). Division(s). Apportion(ed,ing, ment,ments). Allotment(s). Proportion(s). Percentage(s). Goal(s). *See also* Affirmative action; Criteria; Goals; Mathematical concepts; Productivity; Standards.

Quotas, import. See *Trade protection.*

Quotations. Quotation(s). Quot(e,es,ed, ing). Cit(e,ed,ing,ation,ations). Epigraph(s). Excerpt(s,ed,ing). Exemplif(y,ied,ication). Repeat(ed,ing). Give instance(s). Illustrat(e,ed,ing,ion). *See also* Epigraphs; Excerpts; Indirect discourse; Influence (literary, artistic, etc.); Plagiarism.

Quotient, intelligence. See *Intelligence quotient.*

R

Rabbinical literature. Rabbinic(al) literature. *Consider also:* Midrash, Talmud, Babylonian Talmud, Jerusalem Talmud, Rashi commentaries on Talmud, Maimonides commentaries on Torah, Mishneh Torah, Gemarah, [Gemara], gaonic [geonic] literature, Haggadah, [Aggadah], Halacha [Halakha, Halakah], Hekhaloth-Merkabah texts, Merkava, Mekhilta of Rabbi Ishmael, Mishnah, Responsa. *See also* Bible; Deities; God concepts; Jewish literature; Jewish law; Judaism; Rabbis; Religious literature.

Rabbis. Rabbi(s,nic,nical,nate). Jewish spiritual leader(s). *See also* Clergy; Judaism; Ordination; Rabbinical literature; Religious councils and synods; Religious leadership; Religious personnel.

Race. See *Races.*

Race, arms. See *Arms race.*

Race, Australoid. See *Australoid race.*

Race, Caucasian. See *Whites.*

Race, human. See *Humanity.*

Race, mixed adoption. See *Interethnic families.*

Race, Mongoloid. See *Mongoloid race.*

Race, Negro. See *Blacks.*

Race attitudes. See *Racial attitudes; Racism.*

Race awareness. Race awareness. Racial consciousness. *Choose from:* race, racial(ly), racis(m,t,ts), black(ness), white(ness), African American(s), Afro-American(s), ethnic(ally), Asian American(s), Anglo(s), people of color, Native American(s) *with:* aware(ness), conscious(ness), allegiance, disallegiance, semiconscious undercurrent(s), internaliz(e,ed,ing,ation). *Consider also:* racial interest group(s), white awareness training, race traitor, race politics, white revisionism, anti-racism, interracialism. *See also* Biculturalism; Ethnic identity; Race relations; Racial attitudes; Racial differences; Racial identity; Social consciousness.

Race bias. See *Racial attitudes; Racism.*

Race discrimination. See *Racial segregation; Racism.*

Race discrimination. See *Racial attitudes; Racial segregation; Racism.*

Race psychology. See *Ethnopsychology.*

Race relations. Race relations. Racial relation(s,ships). Interracial. Racism. Apartheid. Desegregat(ed,ion). Jim crow(ism). Separate but equal.

Integrat(ed,ion). Racist(s). Biracial. Reverse discrimination. Minority relations. Intermarriage(s). *Choose from:* racial, interracial, Black White *with:* relation(s,ships), perception(s), bias(es), inequalit(y,ies), socializ(e,ed,ing,ation), contact(s), friendship(s), marriage(s), domination, tension(s), discrimination, integrat(ed,ion), violence, hostilit(y,ies), harmony, social acceptance, equality, problem(s), reaction(s), conflict(s), interaction, attitude(s). *Consider also:* intergroup relations, civil rights, White flight. *See also* Apartheid; Black community; Black power; Blacks; Consciousness raising activities; Cross cultural competency; Cultural cooperation; Cultural pluralism; Cultural sensitivity; Ethnic differences; Ethnic relations; Intergroup relations; Interracial marriage; Minority groups; Race awareness; Races; Racial attitudes; Racial diversity; Racial integration; Racial segregation; Racially mixed; Racism; Social Darwinism; Whites.

Races. Race(s). Racial heritage. Racial stock(s). Racial group(s). Racial classification(s). Racial origin(s). Racial group membership. Colored population(s). White population(s). Black(s). White(s). Caucasian(s). Negroid. Negro(es). Mongoloid(s). Nonwhite(s). Australoid(s). Oriental(s). Asian(s). European stock. European ancestry. Amerindian(s). American Indian(s). Racial trait(s). Racial inheritance. *Consider also:* Eurasian(s), Native American(s), African American(s), Mulatto(es), Mestizo(s). *See also* Australoid race; Blacks; Cultural groups; Ethnic groups; Ethnicity; Eugenics; Genetics; Indigenous populations; Majority groups; Minority groups; Mongoloid race; Nature nurture; Pacific Islanders; People of color; Physical anthropology; Physical characteristics; Race relations; Racial attitudes; Racial differences; Racial identity; Racial integration; Racial segregation; Racially mixed; Racism; Whites.

Races, mixed. See *Interethnic families; Intermarriage; Interracial marriage; Racially mixed.*

Races, native. See *Aborigines; African cultural groups; Australoid race; Central American native cultural groups; Indigenous populations; Mongoloid race; North American native cultural groups; Oceanic cultural groups; South American native cultural groups; Traditional societies.*

Racial animus. See *Racism.*

Racial attitudes. Racial attitude(s). Racism. Racial jokes. Racial slurs. Bigotry. Rainbow coalition. White supremacy. Apartheid. Jim Crow(ism). White rightist(s). Fascis(m,t,ts). Nazi(s,ism). Neonazi(s,ism). Neofascis(m,t,ts). Hatemonger(s). Good race relations. Racial equality. Racial harmony. *Choose from:* race(s), racial, Black(s), Negro(es), Eskimo(s), Asian(s), Coloured(s), American Indian(s), Native American(s), Canada native(s), Oriental(s), Chinese, Japanese, Korean, Vietnamese, White(s), Aborigin(es,al) *with:* stereotyp(e,es,ing), prejudic(e,ed), hatred, bias, intolerance, exclud(e,ing,ed), exclusion, oppress(ed,ion), mindset, racis(m,ts), backlash, ethnocentrism, toleran(t,ce), sensitiv(e,ity), liberality, understanding, open-minded(ness), harmony, good-will. *See also* Cultural sensitivity; Dysconscious racism; Ethnic differences; Moral attitudes; Race awareness; Race relations; Racial differences; Racial diversity; Racial identity; Racism; Stereotyping.

Racial crossing. See *Racially mixed.*

Racial differences. Racial difference(s). *Choose from:* race(s), racial, Negro(es,oid), White(s), Caucasian(s), Asian(s), Mongoloid *with:* characteristic(s), profile(s), variation(s), variance, patterns, differences, unique(ness), variabilit(y,ies), styles, contrast(s), comparison(s), deviation(s), divergen(ce), discrepan(cy,cies), disparit(y,ies), distinction(s), inequalit(y,ies), nonconformit(y,ies). *See also* Assimilation (cultural); Biculturalism; Ethnic differences; Ethnocentrism; Individual differences; Intercultural relations; Interethnic families; Interracial marriage; Nature nurture; Physical characteristics; Race awareness; Races; Racial attitudes; Racial diversity; Racial identity; Racial integration; Racially mixed; Social attitudes; Stereotyping.

Racial discrimination. See *Racial attitudes; Racial segregation; Racism.*

Racial diversity. Racial diversity. Racial(ly) mix(ed). Multi-racial. Rainbow coalition. *Choose from:* race(s), racial(ly), interracial *with:* diversity, heterogene(ity,ous,ousness), mix(ed, ing), integrat(e,ed,ing,ion), diversif(y, ied,ying,ication), dissimilarit(y,ies), variation(s), variability. *See also* Cultural diversity; Cultural pluralism; Desegregation; Heterogeneity; Melting pot; Plural societies; Pluralism; Racial attitudes; Racial integration.

Racial equality. See *Affirmative action; Social equality; Social equity; Social justice.*

Racial equity. See *Affirmative action; Social equality; Social equity; Social justice.*

Racial groups. See *Races.*

Racial heritage. See *Races.*

Racial identity. Racial identity. *Choose from:* race, racial(ly), black, African, African American, Afro-American, white, caucasian, Asian, Asian American, Native American *with:* identity, consciousness, identification, pride, homophily, ethnocentrism, descent, bloodline(s). *Consider also:* blackness, whiteness, Africanity, cultural identity. *See also* Afrocentrism; Black power: Ethnic identity; Ethnicity; Identity; Race awareness; Racial attitudes; Racial differences; Self concept; Social identity.

Racial integration. Racial integrat(ed,ion). Desegregat(ed,ion). School desegregation. School integration. Racial transition. Racial(ly) integrat(ed,ion). Racial(ly) mix(ed). Biracial. Multiracial. Interracial. Increased minority participation. School busing. Nonsegregated. Open to all races. Nonracialism. *See also* Access; Affirmative action; Civil rights; Desegregation; Interethnic families; Interracial marriage; Plural societies; Race relations; Racial diversity; Racially mixed; School integration; Tokenism.

Racial prejudice. See *Racial attitudes; Racism.*

Racial profiling. See *Harassment; Racism; Stereotyping; Street harassment.*

Racial relations. See *Race relations.*

Racial segregation. Racial segregation. Hypersegregation. Separate but equal. White supremac(y,ists). Apartheid. Jim Crow(ism). White rightist(s). White flight. Blockbusting. Redlining. Anti-busing. *Choose from:* racial(ly), Black(s), Negro(es), Eskimo(s), Asian(s), Coloured(s), American Indian(s), Native American(s), Canada native(s), Oriental(s), Chinese, Japanese, Korean, Vietnamese, Aborigin(es,al) *with:* discriminat(e,ed,ing,ion,ory), exclud(e,eding), exclusion, oppress(ed, ion), segregat(e,ed,ion), separatis(m,ts), separation, inequality, distance. *Choose from:* residential, housing, school, de facto *with:* segregat(ed,ing,ion), inequality. *See also* Apartheid; Civil rights; De facto; Occupational segregation; Race relations; Racial integration; Racism; Residential segregation; School integration; School segregation.

Racial stocks. See *Races.*

Racially mixed. Racially mixed. Biracial(ity). Mixed blood. Mestizo(s). Mulatto(es,s). Mixed ancestry. Mixed descent. Creole(s). Hispano-Indians. Mixed population(s). Racial mixture(s). Eurasian(s). Hybrid(s). Cholo(la,s). Half-breed. Half-caste. Arafura. Octoroon(s). Quadroon(s). *Consider also:* miscegenation, amalgamation, cross-racial, racial crossing, racial passing, excolored, pass(ed,ing) for white. *See also* Desegregation; Interethnic families; Interracial marriage; Pacific Islanders; People of color; Races; Racial diversity; Racial integration.

Racing, bicycle. See *Bicycle racing*

Racism. Racis(m,t,ts). Racialis(m,t,ts). Racial discrimination. Racial profiling. Racial hatred. Apartheid. School segregation. Hypersegregation. Separate but equal. Ku Klux Klan(smen). Jim Crow(ism). *Choose from:* White, Caucasian, Black *with:* supremac(y,ists), right(ists), flight, backlash, extremist(s). *Choose from:* Black(s), Negro(es), Eskimo(s), Asian(s), Coloured(s), American Indian(s), Native American(s), Canada native(s), Oriental(s), Chinese, Japanese, Korean, Vietnamese, Aborigin(es,al), Hispanic(s), Latino(s), nonwhite(s), minority group(s), racial(ly), race(s), people of color, Caucasian(s), White(s) *with:* discriminat(e,ed,ing,ion), prejudic(e,ed), hatred, bias, intolerance, exclu(ded,sion), tension(s), killing(s), oppress(ed,ion), segregat(e,ed,ion), polariz(ed,ation), backlash, ethnocentrism, sterotyp(e,es, ed,ing), inequality, degradation, joke(s), slur(s). *Consider also:* bigot(ed,ry), hatemonger(s), hate group(s), cross burning(s), fascis(m,mo,ts), nazi(s,ism), neo-nazi(s,sm), neo-fascis(m,ts), Peronis(m,t,ts). *See also* Affirmative action; Anti-government radicals; Antisemitism; Apartheid; Black Muslims; Black power; Dysconscious racism; Employment discrimination; Environmental racism; Ethnocentrism; Eurocentrism; Hate crimes; Hate groups; Labor market segmentation; Lynching; Nazism; Oppression; Prejudice; Race relations; Racial segregation; Residential segregation; School segregation; Sexism; Social discrimination; Stereotyping; Tribalism; White supremacy movements.

Racism, dysconscious. See *Dysconscious racism.*

Racism, environmental. See *Environmental racism.*

Racketeering. Racket(s,eer,eers,ing). Organized crime. Rig(ged) bid(s). Extortion(ist,ists). Extort(ed,ing). Bribe(s,ry). Shakedown(s), RICO. Threatening letter(s). Death threat(s). Blackmail(ed,ing,er,ers). Ransom. Protection money. Payment(s) for protection. Vote buying. Sting operation(s). Payoff(s). Money laundering. Loan shark(s). Embezzl(ing,ement). Fraud(ulent). Smuggl(e,ed,ing). Defraud(ed,ing). Kickback(s). Corrupt(ed,ing,ion). *See also* Crime; Drug trafficking; Fraud; Money laundering; Organized crime; Smuggling.

Radar, ground penetrating. See *Ground penetrating radar.*

Radiation. See *Nuclear accidents; Nuclear safety; Nuclear warfare; Nuclear waste; Nuclear winter.*

Radical environmentalism. See *Deep ecology.*

Radical history. Radical history. Social protest history. *Choose from:* histor(y, ian,ians,iography) *with:* radical(ism), social protest, expos(e,ed,ing,ure) injustice(s). *See also* Dissidents; Historians; Historiography; Radical movements.

Radical movements. Radical movement(s). Radical(s,ism,ization). Extremis(m,ists). Revolutionar(y,ies). Rebel(s,lion,lious). Insurgent(s). Terroris(m,t,ts). Counter culture. Radical feminism. New left. Left activist(s). Liberation arm(y,ies). Draft resister(s). Radical theatre. Radical therap(y,ies). True believer(s). Students for a Democratic Society. Chicago Eleven. Jacobin(s). *Choose from:* radical, revolutionary, extremist, insurgent, rebel(s), protest, militan(t,cy) *with:* movement(s), organization(s), group(s), societ(y,ies), crusader(s), religio(us,n,ns). *See also* Extremism; Left wing; Political radicalism; Protest movements; Radical history; Right wing politics; Social movements; Student demonstrations; Terrorism.

Radicalism, political. See *Political radicalism.*

Radicals, anti-government. See *Anti-government radicals.*

Radio broadcasting, alternative. See *Alternative radio broadcasting*

Radio broadcasting, offshore. See *Pirate radio broadcasting.*

Radio broadcasting, pirate. See *Pirate radio broadcasting.*

Rage. Rage(ful). Enraged. Wrath(ful). Fur(y,ious). Berserk. *Consider also:* anger, hostil(e,ity). *See also* Anger; Emotions; Hostility; Jealousy.

Rage, air. See *Air rage.*

Rage, road. See *Road rage.*

Ragtime. See *Afro-American music.*

Railroads. Railroad(s). Railway(s). Train(s). Locomotive(s). Rail line(s). *Choose from:* passenger, transport, freight, local, limited, diplomatic, express, supply, excursion, commuter(s), troop, boat, mail *with:* train(s). *Consider also:* Amtrak, Orient Express, Delaware and

Hudson, Canadian Pacific, etc. *See also* Public transportation; Transport workers; Transportation; Transportation policy; Yuppie hobos.

Rain, acid. See *Acid rain.*

Rainfall. Rainfall. Precipitation. *Consider also:* rainstorm(s), heavy rain(s), raindrop(s), rainy season(s), monsoon rain(s). *See also* Floods; Weather.

Rainforests. Rainforest(s). Rain forest(s). Tropical forest(s). Jungle(s). Amazon forest(s). *See also* Deforestation; Ecological imperialism; Environmental protection; Fire ecology; Forest conservation; Forestry; Old growth forests; Phytogeography; Slash burn agriculture; Trees.

Rainforests, tropical. See *Rainforests.*

Raising, fund. See *Fund raising.*

Raising money. See *Fund raising.*

Ranches. Ranch(es,o,os,ing). Livestock farm(s). Cattle farm(s). *See also* Cattle industry; Farms; Right of pasture.

Random. Random(ness). Random allocation. Randomiz(ed,ation,ing). Random(ly) allocat(ed,ion). Random sampl(e,es,ing). Random subject selection. Random allotment. Random numbers. Due to chance. Pure(ly) chance. Equal chance of inclusion. Random basis. Unpredictab(le,ility). *See also* Causality; Chance; Chaos; Sampling.

Range, home. See *Home range.*

Rangelands. Rangeland(s). Stock range(s). *Choose from:* range(s), graz(e,ed,ing), cattle, deer, horse(s), stock, livestock *with:* land(s), district(s), ecosystem(s), yard(s), plains. *Consider also:* meadow(s), prairie(s), pasture(s), range management, ranches. *See also* Grazing lands; Home range; Land (property); Open spaces; Public lands; Right of pasture; Rural areas, Rural land.

Ranges, stock. See *Grazing lands; Rangelands.*

Rank, academic. See *Academic rank.*

Ranking. Rank(s,ed,ing). Position(s). Standing(s). Strat(a,um). Status(es). Grade(s). Level(s). Location(s). Degree(s). *Consider also:* stratif(y,ied, ication), hierarch(y,ies,ical), sort(ed,ing), order(ed,ing), categoriz(e,ed,ing,ation), classif(y,ied,ication), prioritiz(e,ed,ing, ation). *See also* Measurement; Scaling; Status.

Ranking (social). See *Social stratification.*

Rape. Rap(e,ed,ist,ists,ee,ees). *Consider also:* sexual(ly) *with:* molest(ed,ation), assault(ed), coerc(ed,ion), forc(ed,ing, ible), violat(ed,ing,ion,ions). *Consider also:* statutory rape, rape victims, homosexual rape. *See also* Acquaintance rape; Antisocial behavior; Battered women; Child abuse; Crime; Incest; Marital rape; Rape crisis counseling; Reproductive rights; Sex offenders; Sex offenses; Sexual abuse; Sexual harassment; Statutory rape; Victimization.

Rape, acquaintance. See *Acquaintance rape.*

Rape, date. See *Acquaintance rape.*

Rape, domestic. See *Marital rape.*

Rape, marital. See *Marital rape.*

Rape, spouse. See *Marital rape.*

Rape, statutory. See *Statutory rape.*

Rape, wife. See *Marital rape.*

Rape crisis counseling. Rape crisis counseling. *Choose from:* rape(s,d), sexual(ly) abuse(d) *with:* crisis intervention, counseling, treatment, care. *See also* Acquaintance rape; Battered women; Counseling; Crime prevention; Crisis intervention; Marital rape; Psychological debriefing; Rape; Sexual abuse; Sexual assault; Sexual harassment; Shelters; Spouse abuse; Victimization.

Rape drugs. Rape drug(s). Date rape drug(s). Rohypnol. Roofies. Flunitrazepam. Gammahydroxybuterate. GHB. *Consider also:* Mickey Finn, knockout drop(s), chloral hydrate, chloryl alcohol. *See also* Acquaintance rape; Drugs; Drug use; Drug overdoses.

Rapport. Rapport. Affinit(y,ies). Rapprochement. Understanding. Agreement. Concordance. Like mindedness. Unison. Amicability. Harmon(y,ious). Interpersonal compatibility. Similarit(y,ies). Complementarity. Compatib(le,ility). Complementary need(s). Congruence of cognitive style(s). Congruent role expectations. Best friend(s). Similar likes and dislikes. Similarities between partners. Interpersonal congruence. Interpersonal attraction. Accord. Congruency between personalities. Similar opinions. Match of personal styles. Cognitive style matching. Felicity. Mutuality. Consensus in dyads. Closeness. *See also* Friendship; Interpersonal attraction; Interpersonal compatibility; Interpersonal relations; Intimacy; Trusting.

Rare books. Rare book(s). Old book(s). Antique book(s). Antiquarian book(s). Rare childrens book(s). Gutenberg Bible(s). Incunabula. Scarce book(s). First edition(s). Fine book(s). Limited edition(s). *See also* Antiquarian booksellers; Antiques; Bestiaries; Books; Book collecting; Book imprints; Book ornamentation; Books of hours; Collectibles; Exotica; Illumination of books and manuscripts; Incipits; Incunabula; Printers marks.

Rate. See *Payments; Rates; Values.*

Rate, birth. See *Birthrate.*

Rate, heart. See *Heart rate.*

Rate, learning. See *Learning rate.*

Rate, pregnancy. See *Pregnancy rate.*

Rates. Rate(s). Occurrence(s). Frequenc(y,ies). Distribution. Statistics. Trend(s). Table(s). Pattern(s). *Consider also:* periodicity, iteration(s), reiteration(s). *See also* Crime rates; Fertility; Frequently; Judicial statistics; Marriage rates; Measurement; Mortality rates; Statistical data; Unemployment rates.

Rates, crime. See *Crime rates.*

Rates, death. See *Mortality rates.*

Rates, fatality. See *Mortality rates.*

Rates, marriage. See *Marriage rates.*

Rates, mortality. See *Mortality rates.*

Rates, unemployment. See *Unemployment rates.*

Ratification. Ratif(y,ied,ying,ication). Approv(e,ed,ing,al). Confirm(ed,ing, ation). Authoriz(e,ed,ing,ation). Formal(ly) sanction(s,ed,ing). Endors(e, ed,ing,ement). Validat(e,ed,ing,ation). Consent(s,ed,ing). *See also* Confirmation; Legislative processes.

Ratio, sex. See *Sex ratio.*

Rational choices. Rational choice(s). Rational decision(s). Rational man. Pareto(s) optimality. *See also* Choice behavior; Decision making; Discretion; Evaluation; Judgment; Objectivity; Rationality; Reasoning; Utilitarianism.

Rational emotive psychotherapy. Rational emotive psychotherapy. Cognitive restructuring. *Consider also:* cognitive, rational *with:* behavior(al), emotive *with:* counseling, psychotherap(y,ies), therap(y,ies). *See also* Behavior modification; Cognitive therapy; Psychotherapeutic techniques; Psychotherapy.

Rationalism. Rationalis(m,t,ts). Doctrine of innate ideas. Self evident premises. *Consider also:* neo-Platonis(m,t,ts). *See also* Deism; Irrationalism (philosophy); Natural theology; Philosophy; Reason; Scholasticism.

Rationality. Rational(ity). Goal oriented. Adapt(ed,ing,ation) means to ends. Adapt(ed,ing,ation) action to values. Logic(al). Reason(able). Game theory. Deduction. Syllogism. *Choose from:* rational, logical *with:* opinion(s), belief(s), choice(s), action(s), behavior. *Consider also:* pragmatic, commonsense, sensible, well-advised, satisficing, plausible. *See also* Beliefs; Equitability; Intentionality; Irrational beliefs; Objectivity; Rational choices; Rationalization (sociology); Reasoning.

Rationalization (defense mechanism).
Rationaliz(ed,ing,ation,ations).
Intellectualiz(ed,ing,ation). Justif(y,ied,
ication). Rationale(s). Excuse(s).
Alibi(s). Explain away. Explanation(s).
See also Blame; Defense mechanisms;
Denial (psychology); Guilt; Neutraliza-
tion; Scapegoating; Shame.

Rationalization (sociology). Rationaliz(e,
ed,ing,ation). Commodif(y,ied,ication).
Mathematiz(e,ed,ing,ation). Iron cage.
Calculated. Calculability. Means ends.
Rational legal(istic). Utilitarian(ism).
Regulat(e,ed,ing,ion). Technocratiz(e,
ed,ing,ation). Commercializ(e,ed,ing,
ation). *Choose from:* rational(ly,ity,ize,
ized,izing,ization) *with:* planning,
organiz(ed,ing,ation), foundation(s),
Weber(s,ian), technolog(y,ical).
Consider also: efficien(t,cy), profit
motive, cost benefit, instrumentali(sm,
ty), demystif(y,ied,ying,ication),
dehumaniz(e,ed,ing,ation). *See also*
Bureaucratization; Capitalist societies;
Dehumanization; Industrial societies;
Instrumentalism (philosophy); Labor
process; Modernization; Profit motive;
Rationality; Scientific management;
Secularism; Secularization; Technocracy.

Rationing. Ration(ed,ing). Allocat(e,ed,ing,
ion,ions). Mandatory cutback(s).
Quota(s). Allowance(s). Allot(ed,ment,
ments). Apportion(ed,ment,ments).
Consider also: prioritiz(e,ed,ing,ation),
triage. *See also* Allocation; Health care
rationing; Priorities; Triage.

Rationing, health care. See *Health care
rationing.*

Rationing, medical care. See *Health care
rationing.*

Raw materials. Raw material(s). Primary
product(s). Staple product(s). *Choose
from:* raw, unfinished, uncut, unprocessed, nonprocessed, semifinished,
natural, crude, primary, agricultural
with: material(s), goods, resource(s),
product(s), commodit(y,ies), timber,
bauxite, etc. *Consider also:* agricultural
product(s), raw wool, crude oil, etc. *See
also* Coal; Commodities; Industry;
Natural resources; Plants (botanical);
Resources; Trees.

Razor, Occam's. See *Occam's razor.*

Reaction, dyssocial. See *Dyssocial
reaction.*

Reaction, escape. See *Escape reaction.*

Reaction, fugue. See *Fugue reaction.*

Reaction, neurotic depressive. See
Neurotic depressive reaction.

Reaction, startle. See *Startle reaction.*

Reaction formation. Reaction formation.
Reversal formation. *Consider also:*
superego, repressed impulse(s), impulse

negation, repression, obsessive compulsive neurosis, disgust, shame. *See also*
Disgust; Defense mechanisms.

Reaction time. Reaction time(s). *Choose
from:* react(ed,ing,ion), response(s) *with:*
time(s), rate(s), lag(s), speed(s),
delay(s,ed,ing). *Consider also:* refractory period(s). *See also* Conceptual
tempo; Response parameters.

Reactionary. See *Conservative; Traditionalism.*

Reactions. See *Responses.*

Reactions, anniversary. See *Anniversary
reactions.*

Reactions, crisis. See *Stress reactions.*

Reactions, drug adverse. See *Drug effects.*

Reactions, psychotic depressive. See
Major depression.

Reactions, stranger. See *Stranger reactions.*

Reactions, stress. See *Stress reactions.*

Reactive attachment disorder. Reactive
attachment disorder. Attachment
disorder syndrome. *Consider also:*
separation disorder(s). *See also*
Attachment behavior; Failure to thrive
(psychosocial); Separation Anxiety.

Reactive depression. Reactive depression.
Reaction depression. Depressive
episode(s). *Choose from:* reactive(ly),
reaction(s), situation(al), endoreactive,
secondary, anniversary *with:*
depression(s), depress(ed,ive). *See also*
Anniversary reactions; Major depression; Neurotic depressive reaction.

Reactive disorders, child. See *Child
reactive disorders.*

Reactive inhibition. Reactive inhibition.
Choose from: reactive, conditioned,
retroactive *with:* inhibition. *Consider
also:* fatigue, nonresponse, aversive
motivational condition. *See also*
Inhibition (psychology).

Reactive psychosis. Reactive psychosis.
Bouffee delirante. Delirious reaction(s).
Choose from: reactive, traumatic,
psychogenic, hysterical, postpartum,
post-traumatic *with:* psychos(es,is),
schizophrenia, deliri(um,ous),
paranoi(a,as,d), mani(a,as,ic). *See also*
Psychoses.

Readability. Readab(lity,le). *Choose from:*
read(ing) material(s), printed material(s),
book(s), text(s,books), document(s)
with: easy, ease, comprehensib(le,ility),
simplif(y,ied,ication), familiar(ity),
difficult(y), intelligib(le,ility), cohesion,
coherence, interest level(s), meaning-
ful(ness), complex(ity), legib(le,ility),
white space. *See also* Children's
literature; Reading; Reading comprehension; Reading interests.

Readership. Reader(s,ship). Reading
audience(s). Book market(s). Market for
journal(s). Booklover(s). Bibliophile(s).
Subscriber(s). *See also* Audiences;
Books; Fans (persons); Internet traffic;
Literary societies; Periodicals; Viewers.

Readiness, military. See *Military readiness.*

Readiness, reading. See *Reading readiness.*

Readiness, school. See *School readiness.*

Reading. Read(s,ing,ers). Liter(acy,ate).
Choose from: comprehen(d,ding,sion),
understand(ing), understood *with:*
print(ed), written. Reading aloud.
Choose from: basal, beginning, braille,
content, corrective, critical, directed,
early, functional, independent, individualized, music, oral, recreational,
remedial, silent, speed, story, sustained
with: reading. *Consider also:* brows(e,
ed,ing). *See also* Advance organizers;
Books; Children's literature; Dyslexia;
Literacy; Oral reading; Reading ability;
Reading achievement; Reading comprehension; Reading disabilities; Reading
education; Reading materials; Reading
readiness; Reading skills; Reading tests;
Remedial reading; Silent reading;
Storytelling; Textbooks; Vocabulary;
Word recognition.

Reading, oral. See *Oral reading.*

Reading, remedial. See *Remedial reading.*

Reading, silent. See *Silent reading.*

Reading ability. Reading abilit(y,ies).
Litera(te,cy). Illitera(te,cy). *Choose
from:* read(ing,er,ers) *with:* abilit(y,ies),
comprehension, development,
skill(s,ed), level(s), poor, low, slow,
beginning, good, able, precocious, fast,
competent, normal, cababilit(y,ies),
rate(s), speed, style(s), comprehension.
See also Academic achievement;
Reading achievement; Reading disabilities; Reading readiness; Reading skills;
Verbal ability.

Reading achievement. Reading achieve-
ment(s). *Choose from:* read(ing,er,ers),
literacy *with:* achieve(d,ment(s),
attainment(s), proficien(t,cy), skill(s),
success, accuracy, parity, progress,
score(s), improvement, development,
score(s), improvement. *See also*
Academic achievement; Academic skills;
Achievement gains; Reading; Reading
ability; Reading tests.

Reading aloud. See *Oral reading.*

Reading comprehension. Reading
comprehension. *Choose from:* reading,
text(s), printed material(s), text(s),
stor(y,ies), paragraph(s), sentence(s)
with: comprehension, comprehend(ed,
ing), understand(ing), understood. *See
also* Readability; Reading; Reading
skills; Verbal comprehension; Word
recognition.

Reading disabilities. Reading disabil(ity, ities). Dyslex(ia,ic). *Choose from:* read(ing,ers) *with:* disabil(ity,ities), disabled, impair(ed,ment), disorder(s, ed), deficit(s), difficult(y,ies), problem(s), retard(ed,ation), slow, poor. *Consider also:* Illiter(ate,acy). *See also* Alexia; Dyslexia; Educational diagnosis; Language disorders; Learning disabilities; Reading; Reading ability; Remedial reading.

Reading education. Reading education. *Choose from:* reading, literacy *with:* education, instruct(ion), teach(ing), learn(ed,ing), achievement, class(es), program(s), train(ed,ing). *See also* Curriculum; Reading; Remedial reading; Whole language approach.

Reading interests. Reading interest(s). *Choose from:* reading, books, literature, fiction *with:* interest(s,ed,ing), preference(s), attitude(s), for pleasure, favorite(s), enjoy(ed,ing,able,ment). *Consider also:* reading habits, love of reading. *See also* Library users; Literacy programs; Readability; Reading materials.

Reading materials. Reading material(s). *Choose from:* reading *with:* material(s), series, text(s,book,books), workbook(s). Remedial reader(s). Primer(s). Childrens book(s). Junior reading book(s). Literary classic(s). Children(s) literature. Large type material(s). Basal reader(s). Talking book(s). *Choose from:* basal, McGuffey *with:* reader(s), series. *See also* Bibliotherapy; Books; Children's literature; Instructional media; Newspapers; Periodicals; Publications; Readability; Reading; Reading interests; Teaching; Teaching materials; Text structure; Textbooks.

Reading readiness. Reading readiness. Prereading. Literacy play. *Choose from:* readiness, predictor(s), early, preschool(er,ers) *with:* read(ing), writing. Pre-readiness skill(s). Learn(ed,ing) the alphabet. *See also* Reading; Reading ability; School readiness.

Reading skills. Reading skill(s). *Choose from:* reading *with:* rate(s), speed, comprehension, abilit(y,ies), accura(te,cy), level(s), development, achievement, performance, fluency. *Consider also:* litera(te,cy), good reader(s), poor reader(s). *See also* Adult literacy; Basic skills; Literacy; Minimum competencies; Reading ability; Reading comprehension; Reading tests; Word recognition.

Reading tests. Reading test(s). *Choose from:* reading, literacy *with:* test(s), evaluation(s), measure(ment,s), assessment, diagnos(tic,sis), score(s), batter(y,ies), exam(s,ination,ions), instrument(s), subtest(s), essay question(s). *See also* Achievement tests; Language tests; Reading; Reading achievement; Reading comprehension; Reading skills; Verbal tests.

Readings, selected. See *Selected readings.*

Readjustment. See *Adjustment (to environment).*

Readjustment, psychosocial. See *Psychosocial readjustment.*

Readmission, patient. See *Patient readmission.*

Real estate. Real estate. Real property. Land(s). Propert(y,ies). House(s). Farm(s). Farmland(s). Home(s). Lot(s). Realty. Acreage. Building(s). Apartment house(s). Plat(s). Plot(s). Tract(s). Holding(s). Parcel(s). Manor(s). Site(s). Plantation(s). Estate(s). Ranch(es). Freehold. Territor(y,ies). Townhouse(s). Condominium(s). Single family. Multi-family. Dwelling(s). *See also* Home ownership; House buying; Housing; Housing market; Land (property); Land ownership; Land speculation; Landlords; Ownership; Property rights; Property values; Real estate closings; Real estate development; Valuation; Zoning.

Real estate closings. Real estate closing(s). Transfer(red,ring) title(s). Clos(e,ing) title(s). Pass(ed,ing) title(s). *Consider also:* real estate settlement(s), real estate sale(s). *See also* Economic exchanges; House buying; Real estate; Sales.

Real estate development. Real estate development. Land development. *Choose from:* real estate, land, property, building(s), house(s) *with:* develop(ed, ing,ment), improv(e,ed,ing,ement, ements), invest(ed,ing,ment,ments), reinvest(ed,ing,ment,ments), moderniz(e, ed,ing,ation), plan(s,ned,ning), progress, redevelop(ed,ing,ment), revitaliz(e,ed, ing,ation), rezon(e,ed,ing), transform(ed, ing,ation), zon(e,ed,ing). *See also* Boom towns; Community development; Growth management; Land use; Local planning; New towns; Planned communities; Real estate; Zoning.

Realism. Realis(m,t). Universal(s). Platonism. Common sense philosophy. *Choose from:* direct, critical, epistemological, logical, naive, nominal, perceptual, Platonic *with:* realis(m,t,ts). *Consider also:* reality, realist(s,ic), neorealis(m,t,ts), commonplace, natural law, naturalis(m,t,ts), fidelity to nature, exact portrayal(s), socialist realism, chosism technorealis(m,t,ts). *See also* Artistic styles; Epistemology; Historical realism; Idealism; Literature; Materialism; Modern literature; Naturalism; Philosophy; Realism in art; Reality; Sociological theory.

Realism, historical. See *Historical realism.*

Realism, magic art. See *Magic realism (art).*

Realism, magic Literature. See *Magic realism (Literature).*

Realism, socialist in art. See *Socialist realism in art.*

Realism in art. Realis(m,t,ts,tic) in art. Representational art. Veris(m,t). *Choose from:* realis(m,t,ts,tic), representational, veris(m,t,ts), literal(ness), radical utopian empiricism, naturalistic *with:* art(ist,istic), figuration, portrait(s), painting(s), painter(s), landscape(s), still life(s), woodcut(s), etching(s), watercolor(s), drawing(s). *Consider also:* conceptual realis(m,t,ts), figurative art. *See also* Artistic styles; Arts; Genres (art); Historical realism; Figurative art; Magic realism (art); Naturalism; Realism; Socialist Realism in Art; Surrealism

Reality. Real(ity,ities,ism,ness,lly,istic). Actual(ly,lity). Experien(ce,tial). Truth. Truly. Fact(s,ual). Tangib(le,ility). Valid(ity). Verit(y,ies). Substantial(ity, ness). Authentic(ity). Debunk(ed,ing). Demythologiz(e,ed,ing). Empiric(al, ism). Positivism. Sense data. *See also* Beliefs; Demythologization; Fantasies (thought disturbances); Feasibility; Form (philosophy); Imagination; Metaphysics; Ontology; Phenomenology; Philosophy; Realism; Reality testing; Reality therapy; Social reality; Truth.

Reality, social. See *Social reality.*

Reality, social construction of. See *Social facts; Social meaning; Social reality.*

Reality, virtual. See *Virtual reality.*

Reality testing. Reality test(s,ing). Test(ing) reality. *Choose from:* reality, delusion(s), real event(s), unreality, pretense(s) *with:* test(s,ing), orientation, cognitive investigation, shock, monitor(ing), confront(ing,ation), processing, experience(e,ed,es,ing), presentation, differentiat(e,ed,ing). *See also* Cognitive processes; Mental illness; Personality processes; Reality.

Reality therapy. Reality therapy. Reality treatment. *Choose from:* reality *with:* therap(y,ies,eutic), treatment(s), orientation(s), session(s), training, program(s), psychotherap(y,ies,eutic). *See also* Behavior modification; Child discipline; Counseling; Demythologization; Psychotherapeutic techniques; Psychotherapy; Reality; Self actualization; Self concept; Social reinforcement.

Realization, self. See *Self actualization.*

Reapportionment. See *Apportionment.*

Reared at home, mentally retarded. See *Home reared mentally retarded.*

Rearing, child. See *Childrearing.*

Reason. Reason(s). Explanation(s). Justification(s). Rationale(s). Rationaliz(e,ed,ing,ation). Argument(s).

Proof(s). Logical inference(s). Deduction(s). Deductive thought. *Consider also:* sufficient reason(s). *See also* Common sense; Natural theology; Rationalism; Reasoning; Revealed theology; Wisdom.

Reason, sufficient. See *Reason; Sufficient evidence.*

Reasonableness. Reasonable(ness). Moderate(ness). Rational. Sensible. Even-handed(ness). Fair(ness). Candid. Sincer(e,ity). Impartial(ity). Dispassionate. Impersonal. Unbiased. *See also* Moderation; Personality traits; Rationality.

Reasoning. Reason(ed,ing). Think(ing). Verbal processing. Logical thought. Infer(ences). Representational abilit(y,ies). Logical knowledge. Problem solving. Abstract thinking. Abstract thought. Formal reasoning. Concept formation. Judgment. Problem solving. Conceptualization. Analog(y, ies,ical). Cognitive skill(s). Deduct(ive, ion). Inductive. Categoriz(ing,ation). Critical thinking. Formal thought. Abstract(ion,ing). Complex thought. Rationality. Reasoning task(s). Analytical thought. Logical processes. Generalization(s). *See also* Abstraction; A priori; A posteriori; Analogical reasoning; Cognitive processes; Complexity; Concept formation; Critical thinking; Deduction; Dialectics; Fallacies; Hypothesis testing; Induction; Inference; Intelligence; Intuition; Irrational beliefs; Judgment; Judgment (logic); Logic; Moral reasoning; Postulates; Problem solving; Rational choices; Rationality; Reason; Thinking.

Reasoning, abstract. See *Abstraction; Reasoning.*

Reasoning, analogical. See *Analogical reasoning.*

Reasoning, moral. See *Moral reasoning.*

Reassignment, sexual. See *Sex change.*

Reassurance. See *Assurances.*

Rebellions. Rebel(led,ling,lion,lions). Rebel(s). Mutin(y,ies). Civil strife. Political mobilization. Strike(s,rs). Revolt(s). Revolution(s). Anti-colonialism. War(s) of liberation. War(s) of national liberation. Guerrilla movement(s). National liberation movement(s). Overthrow of colonialism. Class struggle(s). Agrarian socialist movement(s). Landless movement(s). Social banditry. Sedition. Putsch. Maoism. Belligeren(t,ts,cy). Civil war(s). *Consider also:* revolutionar(y, ies), liberation movement(s), protest(s, er,ers), insurgen(t,ts,cy), riot(s), strife, revolution(s), uprising(s), rebel(s,lion, lions,liousness), overthrow, insurrection(s), resistance, radical(s,ization), mobiliz(e,ed,ing,ation), struggle(s), Mau

Mau rebellion. *See also* Anti-government radicals; Civil war; Decolonization; Guerrilla warfare; Guerrillas; Internal security; Liberation theology; National fronts; Peasant rebellions; Political movements; Political violence; Rebels; Resistance; Resistance movements; Revolution; Revolutionary ballads and songs; Riots; Separatism; Social agitation; Social unrest; Terrorism.

Rebellions, peasant. See *Peasant rebellions.*

Rebellious behavior. See *Rebelliousness.*

Rebelliousness. Rebellious(ness). Anticonformity. Resist(ed,ing,ance,ant) authority. *Consider also:* recalcitran(t, ce), refractory, defian(t,ce), incorrigible, obstreperous(ness), instigator(s). *See also* Antisocial behavior; Deviance; Nonconformity (personality); Personality traits.

Rebels. Rebel(s). Insurgent(s). Insurrectionist(s). Revolutionar(y,ies). Mutineer(s). Agitator(s). Anarchist(s). Seditionist(s). Malcontent(s). Young turk(s). *Consider also:* traitor(s), protestor(s). *See also* Anti-government radicals; Change agents; Civil disobedience; Countercultures; Dissidents; Dissent; Guerrillas; Heresy; Protestors; Rebellions; Religious dissenters; Traitors; Treason.

Recall. Recall(ed,ing). Memor(y,ies,ize, ization). Elicit(ed,ing) past experience. Recollect(ed,ing,ion). Remember(ed, ing). Short term memory. Chunking. Hypermnesia. Reminisc(e,ed,ing,ences). *See also* Free recall; Reminiscence; Retention (psychology); Verbal memory; Visual memory.

Recall, free. See *Free recall.*

Recall, product. See *Product recall.*

Recall of government officials. Recall of government official(s). Recall vote. Recall drive. Removal of public office holder(s). Remove(d) from office. *Choose from:* recall(ed,ing,s), oust(ed, er), impeach(ed,ment), call(s,ed,ing) for resignation, dismiss(ed), remov(e,ed, al,ing), pressure to resign *with:* office holder(s), politician(s), elected official(s), legislator(s), judge(s), congressm(an,en), congresswom(an,en), senator(s), elected representative(s), lawmaker(s), member(s) of Congress, mayor(s), town supervisor(s), governor(s), lieutenant governor(s), president(s), vice president(s), premier(s), prime minister(s), member(s) of parliament, member(s) of the board of education, county supervisor(s), county executive(s), county legislator(s), city manager(s), member(s) of the house of commons, city council(man,men, woman,women), assembly(man,men,

woman,women). *Consider also:* retention election(s). *See also* Elections; Elected officials; Political processes.

Receivable and payable accounts. See *Accounts payable and receivable.*

Receivership. See *Bankruptcy.*

Recession. Recession(s). Stagflation. Negative economic growth. Minidepression. Bear market. Disinflation. Financial crises. Market crises. Market slump. Falling dollar. Slow economic growth. High unemployment. Decession(s). *Choose from:* economic, econom(y,ies) *with:* stagnat(e,ing,ation), slowdown(s), downturn(s), declin(e,ed, ing), falter(ed,ing), contract(ed,ing, ion,ions), slump(s), hard times, downswing. *Consider also:* decession(s). *See also* Business cycles; Decline; Depression (economic); Economic conditions.

Recessive genes. Recessive gene(s). *Choose from:* gene(s,tic,tically), trait(s), characteristic(s), mutation(s), inheritance, transmission *with:* recessive(ness). *See also* Genetics.

Recidivism. Recidivis(m,t,ts,tic). Recidiv(es,al). Relaps(e,ed,ing). Repeater(s). Repeat(ed) visit(s). Rearrest(ed,s). Repeat offender(s). Return(ed) to prison. Parole failure(s). Recurren(t,ce). Parole violat(or,ors,ion). Repetitive offense(s). Readmission(s). Probation revocation. Returnee(s). *Consider also:* post release behavior, recovery rate(s), repetition of crime(s). *See also* Antisocial behavior; Behavior disorders; Behavior patterns; Career criminals; Delinquents; Deviant behavior; Imprisonment; Institutionalization (persons); Offenders; Prevention; Recurrence; Relapse.

Recipients, welfare. See *Welfare recipients.*

Reciprocity. Reciproc(al,ate,ation,ity,ities). Mutual(ity). Interdependen(t,cy). Interchangeab(le,ility). Retaliat(e,ed, ing,ion). Retribution. Respond(ed,ing). Complementar(y,ity). Exchang(e,ed,ing). Social exchange(s). Symbio(sis,tic). *See also* Ceremonial exchanges; Cooperation; Exchange theory; Feedback; Reprisals; Sharing; Social behavior; Social contract; Social exchange; Symbiotic relations.

Recitative. Recitative(s). Rezitativ. Recitativo. *Consider also:* text setting, stile rappresentativo, stile recitativo, recitativo semplice, recitativo secco, recitativo accompagnato, recitativo stromentato, recitativo obbligato, arioso. *See also* Librettos; Narrative poetry.

Reclamation. See *Recycling.*

Reclamation of land. Reclamation of land. *Choose from:* reclaim(ed,ing), reclamation, restor(e,ed,ing,ation), replant(ed,

ing), replenish(ed,ing), re-establish(ed, ing), sav(e,ed,ing), renew(ed,ing), return(ed,ing) *with:* land(s), woodland(s), forest(s), swamp(s,land), pasture(s), desert(s), field(s), wood(s), marsh(es), jungle(s), rain forest(s), propert(y,ies), acreage. Reforest(ed,ing, ation). Arrest(ed,ing) deforestation. *See also* Forest conservation; Forestry; Irrigation; Land (property); Land preservation; Land use; Landfill; Plant succession; Reconstruction; Recycling; Reforestation; Restoration ecology; Salvaging; Shore protection; Shorelines; Soil conservation; Soil degradation; Soil erosion; Submerged lands; Tree planting; Wilderness.

Recluses. See *Social isolation.*

Recognition (achievement). Recogni(zed, izing,tion). Approval. Esteemed. Professional standing. Privilege(s). Promotion(s). Reward(s,ing). Incentive(s). Token(s). Payoff(s). Praise(d). Bonus(es). Merit pay. Honorari(a,um). Prize(s). Reinforcement. Positive feedback. Encouragement. Recompense. Acknowledgement(s). Award(s). Accolade(s). Troph(y,ies). Oscar(s). Emmy(s). Decoration(s). Medal(s,lions). Recompense. Honor(s,ed). Appreciation. Renown. Special attention. *See also* Achievement; Admiration; Awards; Commendation; Compensation (payment); Emphasis; Evaluation; Festschriften; Honored (esteem); Incentives; Literary prizes; Morale; Prestige; Privilege; Promotion (occupational); Reputation; Reward; Self esteem; Status.

Recognition, employee. See *Employee recognition.*

Recognition, pattern. See *Pattern recognition.*

Recognition, word. See *Word recognition.*

Recollection. See *Recall.*

Reconciliation. See *Conflict resolution.*

Reconnaissance, aerial. See *Aerial reconnaissance.*

Reconstituted families. See *Remarriage; Stepfamily.*

Reconstruction. Reconstruct(ed,ing,ion). Rebuil(t,d,ding). Restor(e,ed,ing,ation). Remodel(ed,ing). Rehabilitat(e,ed,ing, ion). Renovat(e,ed,ing,ion). Repair(ed, ing). Renew(ed,ing,al). Modernization. Reorganiz(e,ed,ing,ation). Recondition(ed,ing). Reformulat(e,ed,ing,ion). *Consider also:* Marshall Plan, European Recovery Program. *See also* Natural disasters; Reclamation of land; Social disorganization; Urban renewal; War.

Reconstructive surgery. Reconstructive surgery. Plastic surgery. Cosmetic surgery. Breast augmentation. Breast implant(s). Breast reduction. Blepharoplast(y,ic). Chemexfoliation. Dermabras(ive,ion). Lipectom(y,ies). Mammaplast(y,ic). Oculoplast(y,ic). *Choose from:* reconstruct(ive,ion), plastic, cosmetic *with:* surg(ery,ical). *Choose from:* soft tissue(s), ligament(s) lip(s) *with:* augmentation, reconstruction. *See also* Beauty culture; Cosmetics; Surgery.

Records. Record(ed,s,keeping). Credential(s). Account(s). Will(s). Worksheet(s) Birth certificate(s). Death certificate(s). Registr(y,ies). Chart(s). Check list(s). Checklist(s). Report(s). Document(s,ed,ation). Log(s). Chartbook(s). Signed agreement(s). Data reporting. Form(s). Certificate(s). Register(s). Ship(s) log(s). Diar(y,ies). Logbook(s). Deed(s). Catalog(s). Meeting minutes. Transcript(s). Transaction(s). Contract(s). Receipt(s). Report card(s). *Choose from:* attendance, case, confidential, payroll, student, birth, death, church, dental, medical, hospital, nursing *with:* record(s). *See also* Academic records; Archives; Cartularies; Certificates; Chronicles; Confidential records; Documents; Chronology; Government records; Medical records; Narratives; Nursing records; Police records; Publications; Records management; Registries; Scientific records; Student records; Wills.

Records, academic. See *Academic records.*

Records, confidential. See *Confidential records.*

Records, government. See *Government records.*

Records, medical. See *Medical records.*

Records, nursing. See *Nursing records.*

Records, police. See *Police records.*

Records, public. See *Government records.*

Records, scientific. See *Scientific records.*

Records, student. See *Student records.*

Records control. See *Records management.*

Records management. Record(s) management. Record(s) control. Recordkeeping. Information storage. Archiv(e,es,ing). *Choose from:* managing, manage(d, ment), keep(ing), filing, file(d), retain(ed,ing), retention, system(s), administration, preservation, conservation, control(led,ling), archiv(e,es,ed, ing), stor(e,ed,ing,age), retain(ed,ing), retention, keep(ed,ing), weed(ed,ing), destroy(ed,ing), shred(ded,ding), destruction, process(ed,ing), microfilm(ed,ing), catalog(ed,ing), classif(y, ied,ying) *with:* record(s), document(s), information, data, file(s), manuscript(s), paperwork. *See also* Archives; Government records; Information processing; Records.

Recovery. Recover(y,ed). Cured. Healed. Return(ed) to health. Regain(ed,ing) health. Reviv(e,ed,ing,al). Rehabilitat(e, ed,ing,ion). Resuscitat(e,ed,ing,ion). Recuperat(e,ed,ing,ation). Convalescence. Rejuvenat(e,ed,ing,ion). *See also* Convalescence; Disaster recovery; Disorders; Illness; Mental illness; Postoperative care; Postoperative complications; Posttreatment followup; Recovery rooms; Rehabilitation; Remission; Sick role; Sobriety; Spontaneous remission; Treatment outcome.

Recovery, cost. See *Cost recovery.*

Recovery, disaster. See *Disaster recovery.*

Recovery, economic. See *Economic stabilization; Economic well being.*

Recovery, resource. See *Recycling.*

Recovery rooms. Recovery room(s). Postoperative intensive care unit(s). *Choose from:* recovery, postoperative, resuscitation *with:* room(s), unit(s). *See also* Postoperative care; Recovery.

Recreation. Recreation(al). Sport(s). Hobb(y,ies). Play(ing). Leisure activit(y,ies). Game(s). Entertainment. Adventure. Outdoor game(s). Pleasure. Free time activit(y,ies). *Consider also:* art collecting, bicycling, biking, dart games, camping, card games, model trains, nature walks, backpacking, chess, tennis, wilderness, dancing, baseball, basketball, football, judo, swimming, sailing, parasailing, windsurfing, skateboarding, traveling, vacationing, picnic(s,king), theme park(s). *See also* Athletic participation; Billiard parlors; Camping; Childhood play development; Children's games; Clubs; Dance; Doll play; Enjoyment; Entertainment; Gambling; Hobbies; Holidays; Leisure activities; Leisure time; Martial arts; Outdoor life; Parks; Recreation areas; Recreation therapy; Recreational facilities; Relaxation; Sports; Television; Tourism; Toys; Travel; Vacations.

Recreation areas. Recreation(al) area(s). Park(s). Picnic area(s). Youth center(s). Forest preserve(s). Gymnasium(s). Playground(s). Hiking trail(s). Zoo(s). National park(s). State park(s). Theme park(s). Wilderness. Resort(s). Tourist area(s). Camp(s,grounds). Beach(es). Parkland(s). *Choose from:* recreation(al), play, athletic, sports, picnic *with:* area(s), setting(s), ground(s), site(s), field(s), center(s). *See also* Amusement parks; Beaches; Community centers; Recreation; Recreational facilities; Parks; Playgrounds; Urban planning.

Recreation therapy. Recreation(al) therapy. Therapeutic recreation. *Choose from:* activity, hobb(y,ies), recreation(al), diversional, play(ing), game(s), bicycling, biking, wilderness, art, painting, music, danc(e,ing), poetry, movement, equine, riding, puppetry, swimming, sport(s), running, skiing, excursion(s), scuba diving, theater, theatre, camping, gardening, judo, skating, jogging, walking, hiking, tennis, golf, archery, handball *with:* therap(y,ies, eutic), rehabilitat(ion,ive). *Consider also:* total-push therapy. *See also* Art therapy; Dance therapy; Music therapy; Play therapy; Psychotherapy; Recreation; Therapeutic camps.

Recreational facilities. Recreation(al) facilit(y,ies). Recreation(al) center(s). Sport(s) facilities. Hobb(y) center(s). Playing fields. Game room(s). Entertainment center(s). Bicycle path(s). Dart board(s). Camp(s). Camping facilit(y, ies). Campground(s). Nature trail(s). Tennis court(s). Ballroom(s). Baseball field(s). Basketball court(s). Football field(s). Swimming pool(s). Bowling alley(s). State park(s). National park(s). Town park(s). Holiday resort(s). *See also* Billiard parlors; Camping; Common lands; Community centers; Land use; Libraries; Museums; Nature trails; Parks; Playgrounds; Recreation; Recreation areas; Resorts; Tourism.

Recreations, literary. See *Literary recreations.*

Recruiting, labor. See *Personnel recruitment.*

Recruitment, job. See *Personnel recruitment.*

Recruitment, military. See *Military recruitment.*

Recruitment, personnel. See *Personnel recruitment.*

Recruitment, teacher. See *Teacher recruitment.*

Recurrence. Recurren(ce,ces,t,ing). Recur(ring,red). Reoccurren(t,ce). Reoccur(ring,red). Relaps(e,es,ed,ing). Persisten(t,ce). Repeat(ed,ing). Repetition(s). Recidivis(m,t,ts). *Consider also:* reoperation(s), intermittent, cycl(e,es,ical), alternation, re-enact(ed,ing,ment), restor(e,ed,ing, ation), renovat(e,ed,ing,ation), renaissance, parallel(s,ism), duplicat(e,ed, ing,ion), natural regularit(y,ies), dialectic(s,al), revolution(s). *See also* Chronic disease; Recidivism; Relapse; Remission; Repetition.

Recycling. Recycl(e,ed,ers,es,ing,able, ables,ability). Material(s) recovery. Resource recovery. Source separation. Source reduction. Bottle bank(s). Can bank(s). Gasif(y,ying,ication). Compost(ed,ing). Degradable. Biodegradable. Waste to energy. Waste product(s). *Choose from:* sewage, waste(s), refuse, garbage, can(s),

bottle(s), container(s), trash, sludge, newspaper(s), cardboard, beverage container(s), high density polyethylene, plastic(s), polyethyelene terephthalate, scrap, water, asphalt *with:* recycl(e,ed, ers,ing,able), recover(y,able), gasif(y, ying,ication), conver(t,ted,ting,sion), utiliz(e,ed,ing,ation), fertilizer(s), bioreclamation, reclamation, reclaim(ed,ing), reus(e,ed,es,ing,able), return(able,ing,ed), rehabilitat(e,ed,ing, ion), treatment, redemption, redeem(ed, ing). *Consider also:* blue box(es). *See also* Alternative energy; Conservation of natural resources; Containers; Environmental pollutants; Environmental pollution; Environmental protection; Environmentalism; Nonrenewable resources; Organic farming; Reclamation of land; Renewable resources; Scrap materials; Sewage as fertilizer; Sewage disposal; Solid waste; Water reuse; Waste to energy.

Recycling, waste. See *Recycling*

Redemption (theology). Redemption. Redeem(ed,ing,er,ers). Deliverance. Spiritual fulfillment. Moral vision. Spiritual(ly) transform(ed,ing,ation). *See also* Atonement; Faith; Good works (theology); Grace (theology); Immanence of god; Messiahs; Salvation; Spiritual formation.

Redesign, job. See *Job design.*

Redevelopment. See *Neighborhood change; Urban renewal.*

Redistribution. See *Land reform; Income redistribution.*

Redistribution, income. See *Income redistribution.*

Redistribution, population. See *Internal migration.*

Redistricting. See *Apportionment.*

Redlining. Redlin(e,ed,ing). Housing discrimination. *Choose from:* rac(e,ial), minorit(y,ies), discriminat(e,ed,ing,ion), bias, segregat(e,ed,ing,ion) *with:* housing, mortgage(s), real estate, loan(s), home(s), house(s), insurance, zoning, siting, home credit. *Consider also:* Fair Housing Act, Community Reinvestment Act. *See also* Housing; Loans; Residential segregation; Zoning.

Reduction, cost. See *Budget cuts; Cost control; Saving.*

Reduction in force. See *Involuntary retirement; Mandatory retirement; Personnel termination; Plant closings.*

Reductionism. Reduction(ist,istic,ism). Atom(ist,istic,ism). Elementarism. *Consider also:* simplif(y,ying,ied, ication), oversimplif(y,ying,ied,ication). *See also* Behaviorism; Determinism; Holism; Philosophy.

Redundancy. Redundan(t,cy). Superflu(ity, ous). Profus(e,ion). Abundan(t,ce). Word(y,iness). Verbos(e,ity). Lavish(ness). Overflowing. Redound. Excess(ive,iveness). Repetitive(ness). *See also* Effectiveness; Function; Excess; Surplus.

Reengineering. Reengineer(ed,ing). Re-engineer(ed,ing). Restructur(ed,ing). Redesign(ed,ing). Reinvent(ed,ing,ion). Transform(ed,ing). *Consider also:* reform(ed,ing), consolidat(ed,ing,ion), reus(e,ed,ing,able,ability), workflow solution(s), rightsiz(e,ed,ing), downsiz(e,ed,ing), outsourc(e,ed,ing). *See also* Contracting out; Decentralization; Devolution; Downsizing; Industrial efficiency; Merger integration; Organizational structure; Reorganization; Turnaround management.

Reentry, work. See *Work reentry.*

Reentry students. Reentry student(s). Mature student(s). Nontraditional student(s). Adult student(s). Midlife student(s). Returning student(s). Reentering student(s). Re-entry student(s). Reentry wom(an,en). Wom(an,en) returning to college. Nontraditional undergraduate(s). Returning wom(en,an) student(s). Older student(s). *See also* Adult students; Attendance (presence); College students; Continuing education; High school students; Nontraditional education; Student dropouts.

Reentry women. Reentry women. *Choose from:* return(ed,ing,s), reenter(ed,ing,s), re-enter(ed,ing), re-entran(t,ts,ce), reentran(t,ts,ce), restart(s,ing) *with:* women, woman, female(s), mother(s), homemaker(s). *Consider also:* displaced homemaker(s). *See also* Career breaks; Displaced homemakers; Retraining; Skills obsolescence; Work reentry.

Reference, frame of. See *Frame of reference.*

Reference books. See *Reference materials.*

Reference groups. Reference group(s). *Choose from:* psychological identification, normative reference group(s), comparative reference group(s), relative deprivation, subjective frame of reference, group norm(s), group values, group influence(s). *Consider also:* like status, significant other(s), spouse(s), famil(y,ies), peer(s), peer group(s), contemporar(y,ies), friend(s), social network(s), neighbor(s), colleague(s), classmate(s), co-worker(s), cohort(s), playmate(s), companion(s), partner(s), associate(s), gang(s). *See also* Associates; Collaborators; Colleagues; Groups; Identification (psychology); Inner directed; Interpersonal relations; Interprofessional relations; Other directed; Peer influences; Peers; Relative deprivation; Self concept; Significant others; Social identity; Social psychology; Social support networks; Social values; Socialization.

Reference materials. Reference material(s). *Choose from:* reference *with:* material(s), book(s), source(s), collection(s). *Consider also:* abstract(s), almanac(s), atlas(es), bibliograph(y,ies), catalog(s), dictionar(y,ies), director(y, ies), discograph(y,ies), encyclopedia(s), filmograph(y,ies), glossar(y,ies), handbook(s), guide(s), index(es), thesaur(i,us), yearbook(s). *See also* Abstracts; Atlases (geographic); Bibliography; Dictionaries; Directories; Encyclopedias; Information services; Instructional media; Libraries; Library materials; National bibliography; Publications.

Reference points. Reference point(s). Anchor(s). *See also* Reference values.

Reference values. Reference values. Norm(s). Normative data. Typical performance(s). *Consider also:* normal(ity) *with:* range(s), value(s), distribution(s), curve(s), limit(s), variation(s). *Choose from:* reference *with:* range(s), interval(s). *Choose from:* standard, uniform, index, reference, normative *with:* value(s). *See also* Norms; Reference points.

Referendum. Referend(a,um,ums). Direct legislation. Referr(al,ed) to electorate. Referr(al,ed) to voters. Voter approval. Voter rejection. Submit to popular vote. Plebiscite(s). *See also* Elections; Enactment; Legislation; Voting.

Referral. Referral(s). Refer(red,ring). Second opinion(s). *Consider also:* consultation(s), endorsement(s), recommend(ed,ing,ation,ations). *See also* Consultants; Consultation; Delivery of services; Information dissemination; Professional personnel; Remote consultation; Specialists.

Refinancing. Refinanc(e,ed,ing). Recapitaliz(e,ed,ing,ation). Renegotiat(e,ed,ing) mortgage(s). Second mortgage(s). Debt reacquisition. Re-fund(ed,ing). Interest rate swap(s). *See also* Debt moratoriums; Debts; Home ownership; Loans.

Reflectiveness. Reflective(ness). Contemplative. Meditat(ive,ing,ion). Ponder(ed,ing). Cogitat(e,ed,ing,ive). Ruminat(e,ed,ing). Pensive(ness). Preoccupied. Engrossed. *See also* Delay of gratification; Impulsiveness; Personality traits.

Reflex. Reflex(es). Chemoreflex(es). Baroreflex(es). Startle reaction. Gag(ged,ging). Blink(ing). Involuntary response(s). Achilles jerk(s). Areflexia. Chin jerk(s). Knee jerk(s). *Consider also:* galvanic skin response, piloerection, nystagmus, ocular accomodation.

See also Involuntary (automatic); Orienting responses; Startle reaction.

Reflex, orienting. See *Orienting reflex.*

Reflexivity. Reflexiv(e,ity). Refer(ring) to itself. *Consider also:* reflexive role taking, looking glass self, reflexive sociology, humanistic sociology. *See also* Ethnomethodology; Phenomenological psychology; Phenomenology; Subjectivity.

Reflexotherapy. Reflexotherap(y,ies,eutic). Acureflexotherap(y,ies,eutic). Neuroreflexotherap(y,ies,eutic). *Choose from:* reflex *with:* therapy, acupuncture. *See also* Therapy; Treatment.

Reforestation. Reforest(ing,ed,ation). Forest regenerat(ing,ion). *Choose from:* forest(s), timber, tree(s) *with:* reclaim(ed,ing), reclamation, renew(al,ing), restor(ed,ing,ation). *Consider also:* tree planting(s), forest planting(s), seeding tree(s), forest management, controlled forest burning. *See also* Conservation of natural resources; Deforestation; Environmental protection; Forest conservation; Plant succession; Reclamation of land; Restoration ecology; Soil conservation; Soil erosion; Tree farms; Tree planting; Trees.

Reform. Reform(s). Change(s). Restructur(e,ed,ing). Revis(e,ed,ing,ions). Improv(e,ed,ing,ments). Reorganiz(e, ed,ing,ation). Remodel(ed,ing). Reconstruct(ed,ing,tion). Transform(ed, ing,ation,ations). Transition(s). Perfect(ed,ing,ion). Innovat(e,ed,ing, tion,tions). Revis(e,ed,ing,ion). Reclaim(ed,ing). Reclamation. Recast(ed, ing). Uplift(ed,ing). Reshap(e,ed,ing). Rejuvenat(e,ed,ing,ion). Renew(al,ed, ing). Redistrict(ed,ing). Rehabilitat(e, ed,ing,ation). Regenerat(e,ed,ing,ion). Revolution(s). Cleanup(s). New Deal. Purge(s). Bloodletting(s). Cultural revolution. Depose leader(s). Vote(d) out of office. Perestroika. *Consider also:* social democracy. *See also* Development; Educational reform; Improvement; Land reform; Military reform; Penal reform; Political movements; Political reform; Progress; Social movements; Social reform; Strategies; Welfare reform.

Reform, campaign finance. See *Campaign finance reform*

Reform, educational. See *Educational reform.*

Reform, health care. See *Health care reform.*

Reform, land. See *Land reform.*

Reform, law. See *Law reform.*

Reform, military. See *Military reform.*

Reform, penal. See *Penal reform.*

Reform, political. See *Political reform.*

Reform, school. See *Educational reform.*

Reform, social. See *Social reform.*

Reform, welfare. See *Welfare reform.*

Reformation, Protestant. See *Protestant reformation.*

Reformatories. Reformator(y,ies). Borstal(s). *Choose from:* juvenile(s), minor(s), adolescent(s), teenage(r,rs,d), children *with:* correctional institution(s), training school(s), detention center(s), reform school(s), correctional facilit(y,ies), incarceration, correctional education. *See also* Correctional institutions; Juvenile detention homes; Prisons; Residential facilities.

Reformers. See *Activists.*

Refraction, light. See *Light refraction.*

Refractory. Refractory. Resistan(t,ce). Unresponsive(ness). Unmanageable. Obstinate(ness). Obstinacy. Stubborn(ness). *See also* Chronic disease; Chronic pain; Chronic psychosis; Imperviousness; Stubbornness.

Refrain (music). Refrain(s). Kehrreim(e). Ripresa(s). Estribillo(s). *Consider also:* repetend(s), ritornello(s), chorus(es), burden(s), repeated phrase(s), repeated verse(s), recurrent theme(s). *See also* Choruses; Folk songs; Leitmotiv; Repetition; Themes.

Refuge. See *Shelters; Wildlife sanctuaries.*

Refugee camps. Refugee camp(s). *Choose from:* refugee(s), defector(s), fugitive(s), escapee(s), undocumented immigrant(s) *with:* camp(s), compound(s), internment, asylum, center(s). *See also* Concentration camps; Displaced persons; Prisons; Refugees; War victims.

Refugees. Refugee(s). Deportee(s). Wetback(s). Defect(ed,or,ors,ion). Brain drain. Territorial asylum. Political asylum. Escapee(s). Escap(e,ed,ing) persecution. Displaced person(s). Emigre(s). Exile(s,d). Seek(ing) refuge. Sought refuge. Resettle(d,ment). Fugitive(s). Boat people. Boat person(s). Expatriate(s). Alien(s). Stateless(ness). Expelled from country. *Consider also:* repatriation, deport(ed,ing,ation). *See also* Acculturation; Authors in exile; Diaspora; Deterritorialization; Emigrants; Foreign labor; Foreign professional personnel; Foreign students; Foreign workers; Foreigners; Homeland; Homeless; Immigrants; Immigration law; Land settlement; Migrants; Migration; Political defection; Political asylum; Population transfer; Refugee camps; Relocation; Religious refugees; Right of asylum; Statelessness; Undocumented immigrants; War; War victims; World problems.

Refugees, political. See *Political asylum; Refugees.*

Refugees, religious. See *Religious refugees.*

Refuges. See *Shelters.*

Refuse. See *Wastes.*

Refuse disposal. See *Waste disposal.*

Refuse utilization. See *Alternative energy; Recycling; Sewage as fertilizer; Waste to energy.*

Refutation. Refut(e,ed,ing,ation,ational). Disprov(e,ed,ing). Disproof. Rebut(ted, ting,tal). Contradict(ed,ing,ion). Discredit(ed,ing). Confut(e,ed,ing,ation). Controvert(ed,ing). Disconfirm(ed,ing). Invalidat(e,ed,ing,ation). *See also* Arguments; Contradictions; Dialectics; Polemics.

Regeneration (theology). Regeneration. Rebirth. Reborn. Born again. Self renewal. Gift of Holy Spirit. Receiv(e, ed,ing) sacrament(s). *See also* Evangelical revival; Faith; Great awakening; Rejuvenation; Religious conversion; Religious revivals; Repentence; Salvation.

Regimen compliance, medical. See *Patient compliance.*

Regimes, military. See *Military regimes.*

Region, Mexican American border. See *Mexican American border region.*

Region, Pacific. See *Pacific region.*

Regional development. Regional development. Regional planning. Regionalization. *Choose from:* regional, interregional, county, multi-county, subnation(s,al), subregion(s,al), macroregion(s,al), metropolitan, area(wide,s), state(wide), multi-state, interstate, provincial, multi-province, territorial, intergovernmental, multinational *with:* compact(s), cooperation, coordinat(e, ed,ing,ion), plan(s,ned,ning), model(s), design(ed,ing), goal(s), develop(ed, ing,ment), redevelop(ed,ing,ment), polic(y,ies), decision making. *Consider specific services such as:* pollution control, highway(s), transportation, water conservation, historic preservation, infrastructure planning, spatial management, growth management, river basin commissions, port authorities, solid waste disposal. *Consider also:* European Economic Community, EEC, Tennessee Valley Authority, TVA, Appalachian Commission, etc. *See also* Development; Economic development; Economic history; Geographic regions; Infrastructure (economics); Regional government; Regional movements; Rural development; Rural industries; Rural land; State planning; Urban development.

Regional dialects. See *Dialects.*

Regional differences. Regional difference(s). Regional variation(s). *Choose from:* regional, cross-regional, interregional, county, cross-county, inter-county, area, state, cross-state, inter-state, provincial, interprovincial, cross-province, territorial, national, cross-national, international *with:* differen(ce,ces,tials,tiation), variation(s), diversity, diversification, compar(itive, ability), comparison(s), inequalit(y,ies), disparit(y,ies), discrepan(t,cy,cies), contrast(s), uniqueness, distinct(ions, iveness), heterogeneity, dissimilarit(y, ies), unequal. *Consider specific comparisons such as:* sunbelt vs frostbelt, northeast compared to middlewest, etc. *See also* Borderlands; Boundaries; Differences; Ethnic differences; Geographic regions; Racial differences; Rural urban differences.

Regional government. Regional government. *Choose from:* regional, subnational, interregional, multi-county, metropolitan, area(wide,s), multi-state, interstate, multi-province, territorial, intergovernmental, multinational *with:* government(s,al), authorit(y,ies), minister(s), council(s), autonomy. *See also* Regional development; Municipal government.

Regional labor workers. See *Migrant workers.*

Regional movements. Regional movement(s). Regionalism. Pan-Africanism. *Choose from:* regional, homeland, ethnoregional *with:* movement(s), union(s), sharing, unification, consolidation, integration, alliance(s), federation(s), confederation(s), league(s), coalition(s), change(s), consortium, mobilization, compact(s), treat(y,ies), struggle(s). *Consider also:* revol(t,ts, ution,utions), anti-colonialism, war(s) of liberation, war(s) of national liberation, nationalism, guerrilla movement(s), national liberation movement(s), overthrow of colonialism, class struggle(s), agrarian socialist movement(s), landless movement(s). *See also* Geographic regions; Nationalism; Pan-Africanism; Political movements; Regional development; Regionalism; Social movements; State.

Regional planning. See *Regional development.*

Regionalism. Regionalis(m,t). Regional movement(s). Regionaliz(e,ed,ing,ation). Subregional(ism,ist). Pan African(ism). Pan American(ism). *Choose from:* regional, homeland(s), ethnoregional, interdistrict, interstate, intercity, interprovincial, intergovernmental *with:* council(s), commission(s), cooperation, movement(s), union(s), sharing, unification, consolidation, integration, alliance(s), federation(s), confederation(s), league(s), coalition(s),

change(s), consort(ia,ium), mobilization, compact(s), treat(y,ies). *Consider also:* regional port authorit(y,ies), federal district(s), river basin commission(s), council(s) of government(s), regional planning commission(s), North Atlantic Treaty Organization, NATO, Warsaw Treaty Organization, Warsaw Pact, European Community, European Free Trade Association, Benelux, Latin American Integration Association, Central American Common Market, Council of Mutual Economic Assistance, Organization of American States, Council of Europe, Arab League, Organization of African Unity, Association of Southeast Asian Nations, ASEAN. *See also* Deterritorialization; Devolution; Geographic regions; International organizations; Interorganizational networks; Interstate cooperation; Localism; Nationalism; Political geography; Political ideologies; Separatism; Social attitudes.

Regions. See *Areas; Geographic regions.*

Regions, antarctic. See *Antarctic Regions.*

Regions, arctic. See *Arctic Regions.*

Regions, arid. See *Arid lands.*

Regions, geographic. See *Geographic regions.*

Regions, polar. See *Antarctic Regions; Arctic regions.*

Registers, criminal. See *Police records.*

Registries. Registr(y,ies). Register(s). Record(s). Reporting system(s). Central register(s). Central registr(y,ies). Registration data. Record(s,ed,ing) of accident(s). Biometr(y,ic). Patient registration. Case registration. Roll call. Roll(s). Roster(s). Guestbook(s). Catalogue(s). Catalog(s). Inventor(y,ies). List(s). Roster(s). Census(es). Director(y,ies). Tall(y,ies). Docket(s). Calendar(s). Poll(s). Passenger list(s). *See also* Records.

Regression (civilization). Regression. Dark age(s). *Choose from:* civilization, great powers, modern society, superpowers *with:* decaden(t,ce), degenerat(e,es,ed, ing,ion), collaps(e,ed,ing), fall(en,ing), fail(ed,ing,ure), moral(ly) declin(e,ed, ing), social breakdown, apocalyptic expectation(s), eschatolog(y,ical), millenarian(ism), doom(ed), demoraliz(e,ed,es,ing,ation). *Consider also:* civil disturbances, end of the world, end of civilization. decaying cities, increasing crime, ruthless ruling class(es), economic collapse, environmental degradation, ecological catastrophe(s). *See also* Anomie; Decadence; Decline; Deterioration; Devolution; Environmental degradation; Future of society; Moral conditions; Progress; Social change; Social Darwinism; Social disorganization.

Regression (defense mechanism).
Regress(ion,ive,ed). Narcissis(m,tic).
Choose from: regress(ive,ion),
childish(ness) *with:* behavior, mental
activit(y,ies), adaptive, patholog(y,ical),
ego, psychotic. Childhood ego state(s).
Consider also: transference. *See also*
Defense mechanisms.

Regression, age hypnotic. See *Age
regression (hypnotic).*

Regressive taxes. Regressive tax(es,ing,
ation). *Choose from:* regressive *with:*
sales, personal, real property, excise,
value-added *with:* tax(es,ing,ation).
Consider also: tax(es,ing,ation) *with:*
food(s), medicine(s). *See also* Income
inequality; Taxes.

Regret. Regret(s,ted,ting,ful). Deplor(e,ed,
ing,able). Repent(ed,ing,ant,ance).
Bemoan(ed,ing). Bewail(ed,ing).
Lament(ed,ing,ation). Griev(e,ed,ing).
Mourn(ed,ing). Sorrow(s,ing,ful).
Deprecat(e,ed,ing,ion). Disapprov(e,
ed,ing). Remorse(ful,fully). Contrit(e,
ion). *See also* Apologies; Penitents; Pity;
Repentence.

Regulation. Regulat(e,ed,ing,ion,ory).
Control(led,ling). Interven(e,ed,ing,
tion). Officiat(e,ed,ing). Limit(s,ed,ing).
Set(ting) standard(s). Govern(ed,ing).
Price control(s). Quality control(s).
Standardiz(e,ed,ing,ation). Accountab(le,
ility). Law(s). Ordinance(s). Inspect(ed,
ing,ion). Supervis(e,ed,ion). Oversee(n,
ing). Protection(ism). Superintend(ed,
ing). Administer(ed,ing). Direct(ed,ing).
Censor(ed,ing,ship). Ban(s,ned,ning).
Enforc(e,ed,ing) rule(s). *See also*
Accountability; Censorship; Certifica-
tion; Electronic data interchange;
Facility regulation and control; Formal
social control; Informal social control;
Law (legal philosophy and theory);
Laws; Licenses; Price control; Quality
control; Uniformity.

Regulation, foreign trade. See *Foreign
trade regulation*

Regulation, government. See *Government
regulation.*

Regulation, self. See *Self management
(individual), Self monitoring.*

Regulation and control, facility. See
Facility regulation and control.

Regulations. Regulation(s). Rule(s).
Ordinance(s). Law(s). Statute(s).
Decree(s). Order(s). Command(s).
Prescription(s). Prohibition(s).
Restraint(s). Restraining order(s).
Subpoena(s). Warrant(s). Enactment(s).
Edict(s). Ruling(s). *See also* Banking
law; Edicts; Environmental law;
Environmental policy; Regulation;
Laws.

Regulations, antitrust. See *Antitrust law.*

Regulations, environmental. See *Environmental law; Environmental policy.*

Regulations, federal. See *Government
regulation.*

Regulations, health care. See *Health
policy.*

Regulations, international travel. See
International travel regulations.

Regulatory commissions, independent.
See *Independent regulatory commissions*

Rehabilitation. Rehabilitat(e,ed,ing,
ive,ion). Re-educat(e,ed,ing,ion).
Retrain(ed,ing). *Consider also:* physical
therapy, reintegration, correctional
treatment, habilitat(e,ed,ing), convalescence, recovery, halfway house(s). *See
also* Adjustment (to environment);
Alcohol rehabilitation; Basic education;
Basic skills; Behavior modification;
Cognitive restructuring; Counseling;
Criminal rehabilitation; Deinstitutionalization; Disability; Disadvantaged;
Disease; Drug rehabilitation; Emotionally disturbed; Injuries; Intervention;
Occupational therapy; Patients; Physical
therapy; Physically handicapped;
Psychosocial rehabilitation; Recovery;
Rehabilitation centers; Rehabilitation
counseling; Rehabilitation counselors;
Retraining; Self care; Self help; Social
support networks; Social work; Special
education; Student dropouts; Therapeutic camps; Therapeutic community;
Therapeutic processes; Therapeutic
social clubs; Victimization; Vocational
rehabilitation.

Rehabilitation, alcohol. See *Alcohol
rehabilitation.*

Rehabilitation, cognitive. See *Cognitive
rehabilitation.*

Rehabilitation, correctional. See *Criminal
rehabilitation.*

Rehabilitation, criminal. See *Criminal
rehabilitation.*

Rehabilitation, drug. See *Drug rehabilitation.*

Rehabilitation, psychosocial. See *Psychosocial rehabilitation.*

Rehabilitation, vocational. See *Vocational
rehabilitation.*

Rehabilitation centers. Rehabilitation
center(s). *Choose from:* rehabilitation
with: center(s), agenc(y,ies), setting(s),
home(s), clinic(s), facilit(y,ies),
hospital(s). *Consider also:* alcoholism,
delinquency, addiction(s) *with:* treatment
center(s), halfway house(s). *See also*
Boardinghouses; Employment of
persons with disabilities; Group homes;
Housing; Mental health services; Milieu
therapy; Rehabilitation; Sheltered
housing; Sheltered workshops; Therapeutic community.

Rehabilitation counseling. Rehabilitation
counseling. *Choose from:* counseling,
social work, casework *with:* rehabilitation, rehab, handicap(s,ped), disabilit(y,
ies), disabled, blind, alcohol(ic,ics,ism),
ex-addict(s), ex-offender(s), prisoner(s),
delinquent(s). *Consider also:* vocational
rehabilitation. *See also* Adjustment (to
environment); Alcohol rehabilitation;
Drug rehabilitation; Employment of
persons with disabilities; Rehabilitation;
Rehabilitation centers; Sheltered
workshops; Therapeutic community;
Vocational guidance; Vocational
rehabilitation.

Rehabilitation counselors. Rehabilitation
counselor(s). *Choose from:* rehabilitation, rehab *with:* counselor(s),
psychologist(s), professional(s),
practitioner(s). *Consider also:* alcoholism counselor(s), alcohologist(s). *See
also* Counselors; Rehabilitation.

Rehearsal. Rehears(e,ed,ing,al). Drill(ed,
ing). Practic(e,ed,ing). Warm(ed,ing) up.
See also Experiences (events); Familiarity; Overlearning; Practice (repetition).

Reification. Reif(y,ied,ication). Commodity
fetishism. *Consider also:* objectification,
dereif(y,ied,ication). *See also* Alienation;
Marxism.

Reimbursement, tuition. See *Tuition
reimbursement.*

Reimbursement mechanisms. Reimbursement mechanism(s). *Choose from:*
capitation, third party, provider(s),
vendor, case mix, patient centered, direct
apportionment *with:* payment(s),
reimbursement(s). *See also* Cost
recovery; Educational vouchers; Tuition
reimbursement.

Reincarnation. Reincarnat(e,ed,ing,ion).
Gilgul. Transmigrat(e,ed,ing,ion)
soul(s). Prior life. *Consider also:*
Karma, pre-existence, preta(s), twice
born, once born, recurr(ing,ent) death,
redeath, punar mrtyu, moksha, Atman,
spiritual rebirth, sukshma sarira, astral
body, rebirth, metempsychos(is,es). *See
also* Ancestor worship; Buddhism;
Heaven; Hell; Hinduism; Immortality;
Karma; Rejuvenation.

Reinforcement. Reinforc(e,ed,es,er,ers,ing,
ement). Reward(s,ed,ing). Positive
feedback. *Consider also:* incentive(s),
punishment, timeout, token econom(y,
ies), knowledge of result(s), reinforcement schedule(s), enhancement of
response, praise. *Choose from:* negative,
positive, social, verbal, differential,
external, internal, fixed-interval, fixed-
ratio, variable-interval, variable-ratio,
monetary, nonverbal, preferred, primary,
secondary, self *with:* reward(s),
reinforc(e,ed,ing,ement). *See also*
Autoshaping; Behaviorism; Behavior
modification; Biofeedback; Conditioning (psychology); Delay of gratification;

Encouragement; Extinction (psychology); Feedback; Fixed interval reinforcement; Learning; Monetary rewards; Motivation; Negative reinforcement; Nonverbal reinforcement; Operant conditioning; Positive reinforcement; Praise; Preferred rewards; Primary reinforcement; Punishment; Reinforcement amounts; Reinforcement schedule; Reward; Secondary reinforcement; Self reinforcement; Self stimulation; Social reinforcement; Teaching methods; Token economy; Variable interval reinforcement; Verbal reinforcement; Vicarious experiences.

Reinforcement, fixed interval. See *Fixed interval reinforcement.*

Reinforcement, negative. See *Negative reinforcement.*

Reinforcement, nonverbal. See *Nonverbal reinforcement.*

Reinforcement, positive. See *Positive reinforcement.*

Reinforcement, primary. See *Primary reinforcement.*

Reinforcement, secondary. See *Secondary reinforcement.*

Reinforcement, self. See *Self reinforcement.*

Reinforcement, social. See *Social reinforcement.*

Reinforcement, variable interval. See *Variable interval reinforcement.*

Reinforcement, verbal. See *Verbal reinforcement.*

Reinforcement amounts. Reinforcement amount(s). *Choose from:* amount(s), percentage, size, magnitude, reduc(e,ed, ing,tion), increas(e,ed,ing), small(er), large(r), number, density *with:* reinforcement(s), reinforcer(s), reward(s). *See also* Reinforcement.

Reinforcement schedule. Reinforcement schedule(s). *Choose from:* schedul(e,es, ed,ing), fixed interval(s), delay(s,ed,ing), variable interval(s), continuous, intermittent, rate(s), frequency, spac(e,ed,ing), fixed time(s) *with:* reinforcement, reinforcer(s), food presentation. *See also* Fixed interval reinforcement; Reinforcement; Variable interval reinforcement.

Rejection (psychology). Reject(ed,ion,ing). Refus(e,ed,ing,al). Rebuff(ed,ing). Avoid(ed,ance,ing). Shun(ned,ning). Ignor(e,ed,ing). Spurn(ed,ing). Renounc(e,ed,ing). Disown(ed,ing). Exclu(de,ded,ding,sion). Derogat(e,ed, ing,ion). Ostracis(m,ed). *Consider also:* den(y,ying,ied,ial) of gratification. *See also* Acceptance; Alienation; Anger; Interpersonal relations; Ostracism; Resentment; Resistance; Social acceptance; Social attitudes; Social behavior; Social isolation; Social

response; Stigma; Unwanted children; Unwanted pregnancy; Withdrawal (defense mechanism).

Rejection, social. See *Ostracism; Rejection (psychology); Resentment; Resistance; Social isolation; Stigma; Withdrawal (defense mechanism).*

Rejuvenation. Rejuvenat(e,ed,ing,ion). Reviv(e,al). Renew(ed,ing,al). Resuscitat(e,ed,ing,ion). Regenerat(e,ed, ing,ion). Revitaliz(e,ed,ing,ation). Rebirth. Born again. Refurbish(ed,ing). Re-energiz(e,ed,ing). Restor(e,ed,ing, ation). *Consider also:* bioremediat(e,ed, ing,ion), phytoremediat(e,ed,ing,ion). *See also* Corporate retreats; Enlightenment (state of mind); Evangelical revival; Healing; Modernization; Regeneration (theology); Reincarnation; Relaxation; Religious experience; Religious revivals; Salvation; Spiritual exercises; Urban renewal.

Relapse. Relaps(e,ed,ing). Recurren(t,ce). Recidivis(m,tic). Reactivat(e,ed,ing,ion). Resum(e,ed,ing). Reoccur(ed,ing,ence). Revolving door(s). *See also* Disorders; Illness; Mental illness; Postoperative complications; Posttreatment followup; Recidivism; Recurrence; Treatment outcome.

Relations. Relation(ship,s). Related(ness). Interrelation(ship,s). Interrelated(ness). Abuse. Absence. Acceptance. Affair(s). Affiliation(s). Affinit(y,ies). Aggression. Alliance(s). Association(s). Attachment(s). Attraction(s). Bond(s,ing). Care. Cause effect. Closeness. Cohesiveness. Collaborat(e,ed,ing,ion,or,ors). Comfort(ing). Communicat(e,ed,ing, ion). Compatib(le,ility). Conflict(s). Connection(s). Consult(ed,ing,ation, ations). Contingen(t,cy,cies). Cooperat(e, ed,ing,ion). Correlat(e,ed,ion,ions). Dependen(t,ce,cy). Depriv(e,ed,ing, ation,ations). Disciplin(e,ed,ing). Discord. Dispute(s). Distance. Distrust. Dynamics. Empathy. Expect(ed,ing, ation,ations). Feedback. Feeling(s). Fight(ing). Friend(s,ship,ships). Guilt. Help(ed,ing,er,ers). Hierarch(y,ies,ical). Incest(uous). Independen(t,ce). Influence(s). Interaction(s). Interactive. Interconnect(ed,ion,ions). Interdependen(t,ce). Intervention(s). Intima(te,cy). Involve(d,ment). Jealous(y). Kinship. Lov(e,ed,ing,er,ers). Liaison(s). Link(s,ed,ing,age,ages). Mutual(ity). Negotiation(s). Nurtur(e,ed,ing,ance). Overprotect(ed,ion,ive). Partner(s,ship, ships). Participat(e,ed,ing,ion). Permissive(ness). Play(ed,ing). Presence. Prosocial. Rapport. Ratio(s). Reject(ed, ing,ion,ions). Rebell(ious,iousness,ion). Reciproc(al,ity). Reference. Response(s). Rival(s,ry). Role(s). Solidarity. Social(ity). Stab(le,ility). Support(ed, ing,ive). Symbio(sis,tic). Sympath(y, etic). Team(s,work). Tension(s).

Trust(ed,ing). Understand(ing). Understood. Unity. *Consider also:* oedip(al,us), oedip(al,us), electra *with:* conflict(s), complex(es). *Consider also:* fathering, mothering, parenting. *See also* Church state relationship; Class relations; Classification; Client relations; Community institutional relations; Cultural relations; Customer relations; Dentist patient relations; Ethnic relations; Extramarital relations; Family life; Family relations; Family work relationship; Father child relations; Friendship; Gay couples; Heterosexual relationships; Homosexual relationships; Human ecology; Human relations training; Intercultural relations; Interdepartmental relations; Intergenerational relations; Intergovernmental relations; Intergroup relations; International relations; Interpersonal relations; Interprofessional relations; Intimacy; Labor management relations; Landlord tenant relations; Marital relationship; Marital sexual behavior; Marriage; Military civilian relations; Mother child relations; Networks; Nurse patient relations; Object relations; Parent adolescent relations; Parent child relations; Parent school relations; Peer relations; Physician patient relations; Police community relations; Primary relationships; Production consumption relationship; Professional client relations; Professional family relations; Public relations; Race relations; Researcher subject relations; Secondary relationships; Sibling relations; Social contact; Social interaction; Social life; Stability; Student teacher relations; Superior subordinate relationship; Symbiotic relations.

Relations, adult child. See *Parent child relations.*

Relations, Black White. See *Race relations.*

Relations, class. See *Class relations.*

Relations, client. See *Client relations.*

Relations, community institutional. See *Community institutional relations; Public relations.*

Relations, cultural. See *Cultural relations.*

Relations, customer. See *Customer relations.*

Relations, dentist patient. See *Dentist patient relations.*

Relations, doctor patient. See *Physician patient relations.*

Relations, domestic. See *Family relations.*

Relations, domestic. See *Domestic relations.*

Relations, employee. See *Labor management relations; Superior subordinate relationship.*

Relations, ethnic. See *Ethnic relations.*

Relations, extramarital relations. See *Extramarital relations.*

Relations, family. See *Family relations.*

Relations, father child. See *Father child relations.*

Relations, female male. See *Heterosexual relationships.*

Relations, foreign. See *International relations.*

Relations, human. See *Interpersonal relations.*

Relations, industrial. See *Labor management relations.*

Relations, intercultural. See *Intercultural relations.*

Relations, interdepartmental. See *Interdepartmental relations.*

Relations, interethnic. See *Ethnic relations.*

Relations, intergenerational. See *Intergenerational relations.*

Relations, intergovernmental. See *Intergovernmental relations.*

Relations, intergroup. See *Intergroup relations.*

Relations, interinstitutional. See *Interinstitutional relations.*

Relations, international. See *International relations.*

Relations, international economic. See *Balance of payments; Colonialism; Dependency theory (international); Embargo; Exports; Foreign aid; Foreign investment; Foreign trade regulation; Foreign exchange; Imports; International division of labor; International economic integration; International economic organizations; International relations; Multinational corporations; Trade protection; World economy.*

Relations, interpersonal. See *Interpersonal relations.*

Relations, interprofessional. See *Interprofessional relations.*

Relations, interracial. See *Race relations.*

Relations, investor. See *Investor relations.*

Relations, Jewish-Arab. See *Jewish-Arab relations.*

Relations, labor management. See *Labor management relations.*

Relations, landlord tenant. See *Landlord tenant relations.*

Relations, male female. See *Heterosexual relationships.*

Relations, marital. See *Marital sexual behavior.*

Relations, military civilian. See *Military civilian relations.*

Relations, mind-body metaphysics. See *Mind-body relations (metaphysics).*

Relations, mother child. See *Mother child relations.*

Relations, nurse patient. See *Nurse patient relations.*

Relations, object. See *Object relations.*

Relations, opposite sex. See *Heterosexual relationships.*

Relations, parent adolescent. See *Parent adolescent relations.*

Relations, parent child. See *Parent child relations.*

Relations, parent school. See *Parent school relations.*

Relations, parent teacher. See *Parent school relations.*

Relations, peer. See *Peer relations.*

Relations, physician patient. See *Physician patient relations.*

Relations, police community. See *Police community relations.*

Relations, practitioner patient. See *Physician patient relations; Professional client relations.*

Relations, professional client. See *Professional client relations.*

Relations, professional family. See *Professional family relations.*

Relations, professional patient. See *Professional client relations.*

Relations, public. See *Public relations.*

Relations, pupil teacher. See *Student teacher relations.*

Relations, race. See *Race relations.*

Relations, researcher subject. See *Researcher subject relations.*

Relations, sexual. See *Sexual intercourse.*

Relations, shareholder. See *Investor relations.*

Relations, sibling. See *Sibling relations.*

Relations, social. See *Church state relationship; Class relations; Ethnic relations; Intergroup relations; Interpersonal relations; Peer relations; Race relations; Social contact; Social interaction.*

Relations, symbiotic. See *Symbiotic relations.*

Relations, teacher parent. See *Parent school relations.*

Relations, training human relations. See *Human relations training.*

Relations, union management. See *Labor management relations.*

Relations, vendor. See *Vendor relations.*

Relationship, church state. See *Church state relationship.*

Relationship, consumption production. See *Production consumption relationship.*

Relationship, family work. See *Family work relationship.*

Relationship, man nature. See *Human ecology.*

Relationship, marital. See *Marital relationship.*

Relationship, nature man. See *Human ecology.*

Relationship, parent adolescent. See *Parent adolescent relations.*

Relationship, parent child. See *Parent child relations.*

Relationship, parent school. See *Parent school relations.*

Relationship, parent teacher. See *Parent school relations.*

Relationship, patient doctor. See *Physician patient relations.*

Relationship, production consumption. See *Production consumption relationship.*

Relationship, pupil teacher. See *Student teacher relations.*

Relationship, student teacher. See *Student teacher relations.*

Relationship, superior subordinate. See *Superior subordinate relationship.*

Relationship, teacher student. See *Student teacher relations.*

Relationships, heterosexual. See *Heterosexual relationships.*

Relationships, homosexual. See *Gay couples.*

Relationships, homosexual. See *Homosexual relationships.*

Relationships, human-animal. See *Human-animal relationships.*

Relationships, personal. See *Family life; Friendship; Gay couples; Heterosexual relationships; Homosexual relationships; Interpersonal compatibility; Interpersonal relations; Intimacy; Marital relationship; Parent child relationship; Primary relationships; Social life.*

Relationships, primary. See *Primary relationships.*

Relationships, secondary. See *Secondary relationships.*

Relationships, sexual. See *Couples; Extramarital relations; Gay couples; Heterosexual relationships; Intimacy; Marital relationship; Marriage; Premarital sexual behavior; Sexual partners; Spouses.*

Relationships, strategic global. See *Strategic alliances.*

Relative deprivation. Relative deprivation. Relative poverty. Equity comparison(s). Conception of deprivation. *Consider also:* reference group(s). *See also* Deprivation; Expectations; Poverty; Perceptions; Reference groups; Self concept; Socioeconomic status.

Relatives. See *Family members.*

Relativism. Relativ(e,ism,ist,istic,ity, ization). Relative value(s). Situation(al) ethics. Relative morality. Referential parameter(s). Historicism. *Choose from:* cultural, ethical, moral *with:* relativ(ity, ism), pluralism, nonabsolutism, diversity. *Consider also:* relative, situation(al), subjectivism *with:* standard(s), importance, truth(s), morality, ethic(s), judgment(s). *Consider also:* antinomian(ism), historical skepticism, historical subjectivism, subjective history, conceptual realism, rhetorical realism. *See also* Absolutism; Casuistry; Cultural relativism; Dogmatism; Ethics; Exclusivity (Religion); Existentialism; Historical realism; Knowledge; Liberalism (Religion); Multicultural education; Postmodernism; Practical theology; Sociology of knowledge; Undecidability.

Relativism, cultural. See *Cultural relativism.*

Relativism, ethical. See *Relativism.*

Relativism, moral. See *Relativism.*

Relaxation. Relax(ed,ing,ation). *Choose from:* releas(e,ed,ing), discharg(e,ed, ing), reduc(e,ed,ing,tion) *with:* tension(s), stress(es). *Consider also:* meditation, rest(ed,ing). *See also* Autogenic therapy; Corporate retreats; Enjoyment; Leisure activities; Massage; Meditation; Muscle relaxation; Progressive relaxation therapy; Recreation; Rejuvenation; Relaxation training; Yoga.

Relaxation, muscle. See *Muscle relaxation.*

Relaxation therapy, progressive. See *Progressive relaxation therapy.*

Relaxation training. Relaxation training. *Choose from:* relaxation, stress reduction *with:* training, technic(s), technique(s), therapy, treatment, exercise(s), instruction(s). *Consider also:* progressive, deep, directed imagery, cue controlled, therapeutic *with:* relaxation. *Consider also:* meditat(e,ed,ing,ion), yoga, zen, trance(s). *See also* Anxiety; Autogenic therapy; Behavior modification; Biofeedback; Biofeedback training; Desensitization (psychology); Hypnotherapy; Hypertension; Meditation; Muscle relaxation; Progressive relaxation therapy; Psychotherapeutic imagery; Relaxation; Stress management; Therapy.

Relearning. Relearn(ed,ing). Reacquisition. Learn(ed,ing) again. *Choose from:* recovery *with:* learning, memory, function(s). *Consider also:* retrain(ed, ing), refresher course(s). *See also* Learning; Memory.

Release, institutional. See *Institutional release.*

Release, pretrial. See *Bail.*

Relevance. Relevan(ce,t). Pertinen(t,ce). Bearing. Connect(ed,ion). Pertain(ing). Appurtenan(t,ce). Germane(ness). Apropos. Fitting. Congruous. Applicab(le,ility). Opportun(ness). Related(ness). Allied. Akin. Appropriate(ness). Suited. Suitab(le,leness, ility). *See also* Accountability; Career education; Culturally relevant pedagogy; Curriculum development; Educational needs; Educational objectives; Effectiveness; Effects; Future of society; Goals; Influence; Needs; Nontraditional education; Values; Vocational education.

Reliability. Reliab(le,ility). Dependab(le, ility). Responsib(le,ility). Stab(le,ility). Honorable. Trustworth(y,iness). Constancy. Loyal(ty). Upright. Faithful(ness). Unfailing. Sincer(e,ity). Devot(e,ed,ion). Honest(y,ly). Authentic(ity). Steadfast(ness). Fidelity. Safe(ty). Secur(e,ity). Truth(ful). Conscientious(ness). Careful(ness). Infallib(le,ility). Believab(le,ility). Credib(le,ility). Assur(ed,ance,ances). Guarantee(s,ing,d). Warrant(ed,eed). Unquestionable. Indisputable. Incontestable. *See also* Accuracy; Assurances; Correlation; Errors; Expectations; Experimental replication; Fault tolerant computing; Forecasting; Frequency distribution; Interrater reliability; Measurement; Performance; Predictability; Prediction; Predictive validity; Probability; Quality control; Quantitative methods; Relevance; Research methods; Risk; Sampling; Statistical data; Test reliability; Validity.

Reliability, interobserver. See *Interrater reliability.*

Reliability, interrater. See *Interrater reliability.*

Reliability, test. See *Test reliability.*

Reliance, self. See *Personal independence.*

Relics. Relic(s). Artifact(s). Antique(s). Heirloom(s). Remembrance(s). Keepsake(s). Memento(s). Souvenir(s). Token(s). Troph(y,ies). *Consider also:* reliquar(y,ies). *See also* Antiquities (objects); Art objects; Ceremonial objects; Collectibles; Miniature objects; Religious articles.

Relief, disaster. See *Disaster relief.*

Relief, food. See *Food relief.*

Relief, international. See *Disaster relief; Emergency services; Food relief; International organizations; Relief services; Rescue.*

Relief, pain. See *Analgesia.*

Relief, public. See *Public welfare.*

Relief, unemployment. See *Unemployment relief.*

Relief, work. See *Work relief.*

Relief services. Relief service(s). *Choose from:* emergenc(y,ies), disaster(s), catastrophe(s), hurricane(s), tornado(es), flood(s), storm(s), earthquake(s), famine(s), survivor(s) *with:* service(s), work, relief, crisis intervention, rescue, Red Cross, Red Crescent, humanitarian, nursing, care, health service(s), shelter(s), help(ing), intervention, respon(d,ded,se,ses). *Choose from:* relief, crisis intervention, rescue *with:* service(s), work. *See also* Disaster relief; Disasters; Emergency services; Food relief; Public welfare; Rescue; Social services; Survivors; Unemployment relief; Work relief.

Religion. Religion(s). Faith(s). Religiosity. Ecumenical council. Ecumenical movement. Interfaith. Divine. Ecclesiastical. Gospel(s). Hymn(s). Interreligious. Liturg(y,ies,ical). Missionar(y,ies). Spiritual values. Spiritual beliefs. Stigmatization. Theolog(ical,y). *Choose from:* religious, spiritual *with:* affiliation(s), attitude(s), belief(s), behavior, ceremon(y,ies), conversion(s), doctrine(s), dogma(s), education, fundamentalism, literature, music, movement(s), mysticism, orthodox(y), revival(s,ism), ritual(s), tradition(s). *See also* Ancestor worship; Animism; Antinomianism; Apostasy; Beliefs; Bible; Celibacy; Church attendance; Church membership; Church music; Church state relationship; Clergy; Creationism; Cultural activities; Deities; Folklore; Freedom of religion; Functionalism; God concepts; Heresy; Holy men; Holy women; Humanities; Martyrs; Meditation; Messiahs; Messianic movements; Millenarianism; Missionaries; Mysticism; Mythology; Nontheistic religion; Pantheism (universal divinity); Philosophy; Places of worship; Prayer; Priests; Priests and priestly classes (anthropology); Rabbinical literature; Religions; Religiosity; Religious advertising; Religious affiliation; Religious attitudes; Religious behavior; Religious beliefs; Religious buildings; Religious communities; Religious conversion; Religious cults; Religious cultural groups; Religious denominations; Religious dialogues; Religious doctrines; Religious education; Religious experience; Religious fundamentalism; Religious literature; Religious movements; Religious personnel;

Religious practices; Religious prejudice; Religious revivals; Religious rituals; Sacredness; Sacrificial rites; Saints; Sects; Secularization; Sin; Spiritualism; Spirituality; Syncretism; Theology; Totemism; Traditionalism; Worship.

Religion, freedom of. See *Freedom of religion.*

Religion, goddess. See *Goddess religion.*

Religion, natural. See *Natural theology.*

Religion, nontheistic. See *Nontheistic religion.*

Religion, offenses against. See *Offenses against religion.*

Religion, separatism. See *Religious dissenters.*

Religions. Religion(s). Faith(s). Anabaptist(s). Anglican(s). Animism. Apocalyp(se,tic). Atheis(m,tic). Bahais(m,ts). Baha'i faith. Baptist(s). Bonpo. Brahman(s,ism). Buddhis(m,t, ts). Catholic(s,ism). Christian(s,ity). Christian Science. Confucian(ism). Disciples of Christ. Deis(m,t,ts). Episcopal(ian,ians). Evangelical(s,ism). Fundamentalis(m,ts). Greek Orthodox. Hebrew(s). Hindu(ism). Hutterite(s). Islam(ic). Jainis(m,t,ts). Jehovahs witness(es). Jew(s,ish). Judai(c,sm). Judeo. Lutheran(s). Manicheism. Methodis(m,ts). Mennonite(s). Monotheis(m,tic). Mormon(s). Moslem(s). Muslim(s). Nagualism. Pagan(s,ism). Pantheis(m,t,ts,tic). Pentecostal(s). Presbyterian(s). Polytheis(m,t,ts,tic). Protestant(s,ism). Quaker(s). Roman Catholic(s,ism). Russian Orthodox. Shaker(s). Shaman(ism). Shinto(ism). Sikh(s,ism). Spiritual(ism,ist,ists). Sweden Borgian(ist,ists,ism). Syncretism. Tantrism. Taois(m,t,ts). Theis(m,ts,tic). Unification church. Unitarian(s,ism). Zen Buddhis(m,t,ts). Zoroastrian(ist,ists, ism). *See also* Ancestor worship; Animism; Atheism; Bahaism; Beliefs; Buddhism; Christianity; Church state relationship; Hinduism; Islam; Jainism; Judaism; Millenarianism; Missionaries; Messianic movements; Nontheistic religion; Paganism; Protestantism; Religion; Religious beliefs; Religious cults; Religious cultural groups; Religious denominations; Religious fundamentalism; Roman Catholicism; Sects; Shamanism; Shintoism; Spiritualism; Taoism; Zen Buddhism; Zoroastrianism.

Religions, new. See *Cults.*

Religiosity. Religiosity. Spirituality. Religious(ness). Spiritual journey(s). Religious experience(s). Born again. Faith development. Spiritual wellbeing. Believer(s). Piet(y,ism). *Choose from:* religious, spiritual, church, temple,

Christian, Jewish, Hindu, Islamic, Moslem, Protestant, Catholic *with:* affiliation(s), allegiance, attitude(s), belief(s), behavior, commit(ment,ted), consciousness, conversion(s), devotion, doctrine(s), dogma(s), education, fundamentalism, growth, ideolog(y,ies), identification, involvement, maturity, mysticism, orientation, orthodox(y), participation, upbringing, revival(s,ism), ritual(s), tradition(s), witness(ed,ing,es). *See also* Church attendance; Female spirituality; Piety; Prayer; Religious behavior; Religious beliefs; Religious commitment; Religious experience; Religious fundamentalism; Religious life; Sacredness; Secularization; Spiritual gifts; Spirituality.

Religious, women. See *Women religious.*

Religious accommodation. Relig(ion, ious,osity) accommmodation(s). *Choose from:* relig(ion,ious,iosity), sabbath, Sunday(s), Saturday(s), Friday(s) *with:* work, workplace, job(s), employe(e,es, r), labor, occupation(s,al), schedul(e,es, ing), reasonable accommodation(s). *See also* Cultural pluralism; Melting pot; Religious prejudice.

Religious advertising. Religious advertis(ing,ement,ements) Tele-evangelism Televangelism. *Choose from:* religious, church(es), temple(s), Christian(s,ity), Baptist(s), Protestant(s), Presbyterian(s), Methodist(s), Episcopalian(s), Catholic(s), Evangelis(m,t,ts,tic), God, Billy Graham *with:* advertis(e,ed,ing,ement,ements), sell(ing), telemarket(ed,ing,er,ers), ad(s,man,men), commercial(s), market(ed,ing). *See also* Advertising; Church attendance; Proselytism; Religious behavior; Religious conversion; Religious fundamentalism.

Religious affiliation. Religious affiliation(s). Churchgoing. *Choose from:* religious, church(es), temple(s), parish, Buddhist, Christian(s), Jew(s,ish), Hindu, Islamic, Moslem(s), Baptist(s), Protestant(s), Presbyterian(s), Methodist(s), Episcopalian(s), Catholic(s) *with:* affiliation(s), commit(ment,ted), conversion(s), identification, involvement, member(s, ship), participat(e,ed,ing,ion). *See also* Church attendance; Church membership; Religion; Religions; Religiosity; Religious behavior; Religious beliefs; Religious practices.

Religious art. Religious art. *Choose from:* religio(us,n), theolog(y,ical), God(s), sacred, spiritual(ity), holiness, holy, divin(e,ity), Biblical, Talmudic, Buddhist, Christian, Hindu, Jewish, Islamic, Protestant, Catholic, etc., *with:* art, fresco(es), drawing(s), aesthetic(s), carving(s), painting(s), architecture, mosaic(s), monument(s), sculpture. *See also* Arts; Christian art.

Religious articles. Religious article(s). Religious object(s). *Choose from:* religious, church, sacred, holy, saintly, Christian, Jewish, Islamic, Hindu, Buddhist *with:* article(s), object(s), monument(s), souvenir(s), replica(s), miniature(s), statue(s), relic(s), token(s), symbol(s), cop(y,ies). *Consider also:* cross(es), rosar(y,ies), mezuz(a,as,ah, ahs,ot), reliquar(y,ies). *See also* Ceremonial objects; Chalices; Christian art; Christian symbolism; Crosses; Figurines; Material culture; Relics; Religious rituals.

Religious attitudes. Religious attitude(s). Religiosity. Spirituality. Religiously committed. Religious(ness). Religiously minded. Believer(s). *Choose from:* religious, spiritual, church, temple, Buddhist, Christian, Jewish, Hindu, Islamic, Protestant, Catholic *with:* attitude(s), belief(s), commit(ment,ted), consciousness, conversion(s), devotion, doctrine(s), dogma(s), education, fundamentalism, mindset, identification, involvement, mysticism, opinion(s), orientation, orthodox(y), outlook(s), preference(s), perspective(s), prejudice(s), reaction(s), response(s), tolerance, upbringing, revival(s,ism), value(s), view(s). *Consider also:* seculariz(e,ed,ing,ation). *See also* Attitudes; Cultural values; Female spirituality; Moral attitudes; Prayer; Religiosity; Religious beliefs; Religious doctrines; Religious fundamentalism; Religious prejudice; Spirituality; Tolerance; Worship.

Religious awakening. See *Enlightenment (state of mind); Religious experience.*

Religious behavior. Religious behavior. Piet(y,ism). Hymn(s). Pray(ing,ers). Worship. *Choose from:* religious, spiritual, church, temple, synagogue, Buddhist, Christian, Jewish, Islamic, Protestant, Catholic, Baptist, Episcopalian, Presbyterian, Methodist *with:* activit(y,ies), adherence, affiliation(s), ascetic(ism), attendance, behavior(s), conversion(s), devotion(s,al), involvement, life, observance(s), membership, participation, practice(s), sacrifice(s), upbringing, revival(s,ism), ritual(s), tradition(s), worship. *See also* Asceticism; Church attendance; Church membership; Posture in worship; Prayer; Proselytism; Religiosity; Religious advertising; Religious affiliation; Religious commitment; Religious conversion; Religious practices; Religious revivals; Religious rituals; Sacredness; Sacrificial rites; Worship.

Religious beliefs. Religious belief(s). Religiosity. God concept(s). Sin. Original sin. Gospel(s). Divine revelation. Theolog(y,ies,ical). Biblical literalism. *Choose from:* religious, spiritual, sacred, theolog(y,ical),

Biblical, Talmudic, Buddhist, Christian, Hindu, Jewish, Islamic, Protestant, Catholic, etc., *with:* belief(s), concern(s), concept(s), creed(s), doctrine(s), dogma(s), education, fundamentalism, literature, mysticism, orthodox(y), stigmatization. *Consider also:* dharma, karma, orthodoxy, syncretism. *See also* Agnosticism; Asceticism; Atheism; Attitudes; Attitudes toward death; Attributes of God; Bible; Creationism; Cults; Death of God (theology); Deism; Ethics; Exclusivity (Religion); Existentialism; Fatalism; Forgiveness; God concepts; Grace (theology); Heresy; Immanence of god; Irreligion; Millenarianism; Morality; Mysticism; Occultism; Oneness of God; Pantheism (polytheism); Pantheism (universal divinity); Practical theology; Prophets; Religiosity; Religious affiliation; Religious doctrines; Religious education; Religious fundamentalism; Religious literature; Religious practices; Religious prejudice; Revealed theology; Sacred animals; Sacredness; Salvation; Sin; Snake handling; Spirituality; Superstitions; Theism

Religious brotherhoods. See *Holy men; Monasticism; Religious communities.*

Religious buildings. Religious building(s). Church(es). Synagogue(s). Chapel(s). Temple(s). Church(es). Chapel(s). Parish house(s). Cathedral(s). Minster(s). Abbey(s). Monaster(y,ies). Convent(s). Kirk(s). Meeting house(s). Sanctuar(y, ies). Shrine(s). House(s) of prayer. House(s) of God. Tabernacle(s). Place(s) of worship. Mosque(s). Place(s) of pilgrimage. Sacred tomb. Holy See. *Choose from:* sacred, holy *with:* land(s), cit(y,ies), ground(s), site(s). *See also* Abbeys; Architecture; Auditoriums; Basilicas; Chapels; Churches; Mosques; Places of worship; Sacred places; Synagogues; Temples.

Religious ceremonies. See *Religious rituals.*

Religious colloquies. See *Religious disputations*

Religious commitment. Religious commitment. Faith in God. Religiousness. Religiosity. *Choose from:* religious, Christian, Jewish, Confucian, Islamic, Muslim, Moslem *with:* allegiance, identification, life, belief(s), faith, behavior, involvement. *Consider also:* koinonia, communion, born again, religious observance, spirituality. *See also* Church attendance; Female spirituality; Prayer; Religiosity; Religious behavior; Religious life; Spiritual gifts; Spirituality.

Religious communities. Religious communit(y,ies). Lamaser(y,ies). Priorate(s). Cloister(s). Monaster(y,ies). Monastic seminar(y,ies). Convent(s).

Nunner(y,ies). Abbey(s). Prior(y,ies). *See also* Convents; Monasticism; Religious cultural groups; Religious life.

Religious conflict. See *Sectarian conflict.*

Religious conversion. Religious conversion. Convert(s). Reborn. Rebirth. Catechumen(s). Proselyt(e,ize,ized,ism). Bapti(ze,zed,sm). Rebapti(ze,zed,sm). Chang(e,ed,ing) religion(s). Missionization. Religious transformation. Christianization. Religious recruitment. Paganiz(ing,ation). *Choose from:* religious, Christian(ity), Jewish, Moslem, Buddhist, Hindu *with:* conver(t,ted,sion), new adherent(s), new believer(s), new member(s), born again, neophyte(s), change(s) of heart. *Consider also:* evangeliz(ing,ation), missionary activit(y,ies). *See also* Apostasy; Change; Crusades; Evangelical revival; Evangelistic work; Missionaries; Proselytism; Regeneration (theology); Religions; Religious advertising; Religious behavior; Religious beliefs; Religious gatherings; Religious revivals; Salvation; Syncretism.

Religious councils and synods. Religious council(s). Synod(s,al). Curia(l). *Choose from:* religious, bishops, archbishop(s), church(es), ecclesiastical, Christian, clergy, diocesan, Vatican, Jewish, ecumenical, oecumenical, Presbyterian, Episcopal, Church of England, Methodist, etc. *with:* council(s), conference(s), synod(s), assembl(y,ies), meeting(s), regional organization(s), ruling bod(y,ies). *Consider also:* episcopac(y, ies), presbyter(y,ies). *See also* Canons; Christian leadership; Clergy; Fathers of the church; Jewish law; Ecclesiastical courts; Ordination; Papacy; Priests; Priests and priestly classes (anthropology); Religious disputations; Religious gatherings; Religious leadership.

Religious cults. Religious cult(s). Charismatic sect(s). New religious movement(s). New religion(s). Marginal religious movement(s). Deviant religion(s). Controversial religion(s). Religious sect(s). Protestant sect(s). Christian commune(s). Spiritual communit(y,ies). Nativistic movement(s). Ras Tafari. Shaker(s). Survivalism. Spiritualist cult(s). Holy Spirit movement. Millenialism. Scientology. Jonestown. New religion(s). Church of the Cosmic Liberty. Jesus Movement. Church of the Sun. Meher Baba. Maharaji Ji. Unification Church. Moonie(s). Reverend Moon. Sun Myung Moon. Universal Church of the Kingdom of God. Bhagwan Shree Rajneesh. Kirpal Light Satsang. Evangelical(s). Santeria Cult. Afro-Cuban Church of Santerian Faith. Movement of Spiritual Inner Awareness.

Christian Patriots Defense League. Divine Light Mission. Love Israels Church of Armageddon. Hare Krishna. Children of God. Jews for Jesus. Nation of Islam. Pentacostalism. Pentecostal Church Movement. Church of the Subgenius. Voodoo. Religious communes. New mysticism. New Orientalism. Cargo cult(s). Witch cult(s). Satan worship. Devil worship. Fundamentalist sect(s). *Consider also:* millennium cult(s), deprogramming. *See also* Cargo cults; Charisma; Countercultures; Devils; Dolmen; Messianic movements; Millenarianism; Mysticism; Unification Church; Religion; Religions; Religious behavior; Religious cultural groups; Religious fundamentalism; Religious movements; Religious rituals; Sects; Snake handling; Syncretism; Witchcraft; Worship.

Religious cultural groups. Religious cultural group(s). Religious communit(y, ies). Religious group(s). *Choose from:* ethnic church(es), Seventh Day Adventist(s), Shaker(s), Zionist(s), Ashkenazi(c,m), Sephardi(c,m), Chassid(im,ic), Hassid(im,ic), Huguenot(s), Karaite(s) [Karaism], Mormon(s), Ras Tafari, Mennonite(s), Sikh(s), Sunni(s,tes), Hannafis, Hanbalite(s), Malakis, Shafiite(s), Shiite(s), Druz(e,ean) [Drus(e,ian)], Ismailite(s), Ithna 'Ashariyah. *See also* Buddhism; Christians; Cultural values; Culture (anthropology); Ethnic groups; Hinduism; Islam; Judaism; Minority groups; Places of worship; Protestantism; Religions; Religious beliefs; Religious communities; Religious cults; Religious denominations; Religious movements; Religious revivals; Religious rituals; Roman Catholicism; Secularization; Subcultures; Taoism.

Religious debates. See *Religious disputations.*

Religious denominations. Religious denomination(s,al,alism). Sect(s). Church(es). Religious bod(y,ies). Ecclesiastical bod(y,ies). Confessional famil(y,ies). Religious affiliation(s). Adventist(s). African Methodist Episcopal. Anabaptist(s). Anglican(s). Armenian church. Baptist(s). Buddhis(t, m). Catholic(s,ism). Christian Scien(ce, tist,tists). Church of the New Jerusalem. Christian(ity,s). Congregational(ism, ists). Conservative Judaism. Coptic Church. Disciples of Christ. Eastern Orthodox Church. Episcopal(ians). Evangel(ism,ical,icalism,s). Fundamentalis(t,m). Hind(i,u,us,ism). Huguenot(s). Hussite(s). Hutterite(s). Islam(ic). Jacobite Church. Jehovahs witness(es). Jew(s,ish). Judai(c,sm). Lutheran(s). Mennonite(s). Methodis(m, t,ts). Mohammedan(s,ism). Moravian Church. Mormon(s). Moslem(s).

Muslim(s). Nestorian Church. Orthodox Judaism. Pentecostal(s,ism). Presbyterian(s). Protestant(s,ism). Quaker(s). Reform Judaism. Reformed Church(es). Roman Catholic(s,ism). Russian Orthodox Church. Shaker(s). Shinto(ism). Sweden Borgian(ism). Uniate(s). Unitarian(s). Universalis(m, ts). Zen Buddhis(t,m). *See also* Christianity; Cults; Independent churches; Religions; Religious cults; Religious cultural groups; Religious institutions; Sectarianism; Sects.

Religious dialogues. Religious dialogue(s). *Choose from:* religious, interfaith, interreligious, Jewish Christian, interdenominational, theolog(y,ies,ical), theonomous, scripture(s), faith(s) *with:* dialogue(s), discussion(s), conversation(s). *See also* Christianity; Ecumenical movement; Intercommunion; Interdenominational cooperation; Social movements.

Religious discrimination. See *Religious prejudice.*

Religious disputations. Religious disputation(s). *Choose from:* religious, congregation(s), Jewish, Christian, church(es), theolog(y,ical), Biblical, Talmudic, Buddhist, Christian, Hindu, Jewish, Islamic, Protestant, Catholic, etc. *with:* colloqu(y,ies), debate(s), disput(e, es,ation,ations), argument(s,ation), conflict(s), quarrel(s), dissension, polemics, controvers(y,ies,ial). *See also* Arguments; Conflict; Controversial issues; Debate; Disputes; Religious councils and synods; Sectarian conflict.

Religious dissenters. Religious dissent(er, ers). Catholic dissenter(s). *Choose from:* religious, religion(s), Christian, Catholic, Protestant, Jewish, Muslim, Moslem, Islamic, Buddhist *with:* dissident(s), dissent(er,ers,ing), heretic(s), nonconformist(s), separatis(m,t,ts). *Consider also:* religious refugee(s). *See also* Dissent; Heresy; Liberty of conscience; Nonconformity (personality); Rebels; Religious refugees.

Religious doctrines. Religious doctrine(s). Gospel(s). *Choose from:* religious, church, theological, ecclesiastic(al) *with:* doctrine(s), teaching(s), instruction, dogma(s), tenet(s), belief(s), canon(s), ideolog(y,ies), text(s), principle(s). *See also* Apologetics; Canons; Ideologies; Deities; Ethics; Philosophy; Religions; Religious beliefs; Religious fundamentalism; Religious literature; Revealed theology; Schism; Theology.

Religious doubt. See *Agnosticism; Uncertainty.*

Religious drama. Religious drama(s). Assumption play(s). *Choose from:* religious, passion, sacred, Christmas, Easter, Bibl(e,ical), Buddhis(m,t),

church *with:* drama(s), play(s), theatre(s), theater(s), folktheatre. *See also* Drama; Liturgical drama; Medieval drama; Miracle plays; Morality plays; Religious rituals.

Religious education. Religious education. Sunday school(s). Cateche(sis,ses,tics, tical). Catechism(s). *Choose from:* religious, church, parochial, theolog(y, ical), Christian, Jewish, Judai(c,sm), Hebrew, Hasidic, Kabbalah, Talmudic, Catholic(ism), Protestant, Episcopal(ian), Presbyterian, Methodist, Islamic, Koranic, Biblical, Quaker, Baptist, etc. *with:* education(al), instruction(al), indoctrination, development, textbook(s), training, school(s), college(s), academ(y,ies), seminar(y,ies), course(s). *Consider also:* catechumen(s). *See also* Church state relationship; Clergy; Medieval education; Moral education; Private schools; Religions; Religious beliefs; Religious literature; Spiritual exercises; Spiritual formation; Seminarians; Seminaries.

Religious experience. Religious experience(s). *Choose from:* religious, God, spiritual, divine, angel(s), saint(s) *with:* experienc(e,ed,ing,s), response(s), awakening, encounter(s,ed,ing), respond(ed,ing), realiz(e,ed,ing,ation, ions), transcend(ed,ing,ent,ence), mystic(ism,al,s), vision(s), miraculous, miracle(s), state(s), revelation(s), light, consciousness, phenomen(a,on), event(s), trance(s), voice(s), power(s). *Consider also:* born again. *See also* Enlightenment (state of mind); Healing; Knowledge of god; Meditation; Mysticism; Prayer; Presence of God; Rejuvenation; Religiosity; Salvation; Spiritual exercises; Spiritual formation; Spiritual healing; Spiritualism; Spirituality; Theophany.

Religious facilities. See *Religious buildings.*

Religious festivals. See *Festivals; Holidays.*

Religious films. Religious film(s). *Choose from:* religio(us,n), theolog(y,ical), God(s), evangelical, prayer(s), sacred, spiritual(ity), holiness, holy, divin(e,ity), Easter, Christmas, Hannukah, Passover, Ramadan, priest(s), salvation, saint(s), Bibl(e,ical), Gospel stor(y,ies), Buddhist, Christian, Hindu, Jewish, Islamic, Protestant, Catholic, Vatican, Moses, Jesus, Buddha, Mohammed(an), etc. *with:* film(s), feature film(s), movie(s), cinema(s), screenplay(s), motion picture(s), video(s), videocassette(s), cinematograph(y,ic,ically), Hollywood, documentar(y,ies). *See also* Film adaptations; Films; Religious literature.

Religious freedom. See *Freedom of religion.*

Religious fundamentalism. Religious fundamentalis(m,ts). Fundamentalist school(s). Creationism. Billy Graham.

Evangel(ism,ists,ical). Born again Christian(s). *Choose from:* literal(ly), infallib(le,ility) *with:* Bible, Biblical, scripture(s). *Choose from:* fundamental(ism,ist), conservative, traditional(ism, ist), orthodox *with:* believer(s), baptis(m,t,ts), church(es), religion(s), militant(s), religious, Protestant(s,ism), Catholic(s,ism), Jew(s,ish), Moslem(s), Muslim(s), Islam(ic). *Consider also:* Assembly of God, Pentacostal(ism), Creationism, Jesus People, Jesus Movement, religious conservative(s), religious right, right wing Christian(s), Christian right, moral majority, old time religion, religious orthodoxy, Orthodox Jew(s,ish), televangelism, tele-evangelism, Dakwah, militant Sikh(s), Confucian revivalist(s), Pentecostal(s,ism,ist,ists), Roman Catholic traditionalis(m,t,ts), Taliban. *See also* Absolutism; Anti-intellectualism; Creationism; Evangelists; Exclusivity (Religion); Infallibility; Islam; Islamic fundamentalism; Jewish law; Millenarianism; Protestantism; Religions; Religiosity; Religious advertising; Religious revivals; Sects; Spiritual healing; Sunday legislation; Theocracy; Traditionalism.

Religious gatherings. Religious gathering(s). *Choose from:* church, religious, evangelical, Bibl(e,ical), pentecostal(s,ism), baptism *with:* gathering(s), meeting(s), assembl(y,ies), rall(y,ies), convocation(s), communal picnic(s), communal dinner(s), collective worship. *Consider also:* tent meeting(s), camp meeting(s), Promise Keepers. *See also* Evangelical revival; Messianic movements; Public meetings; Religious conversion; Religious councils and synods; Religious movements; Religious revivals; Salvation.

Religious groups. See *Monasticism; Religions; Religious cults; Religious cultural groups.*

Religious healing. See *Spiritual healing.*

Religious holidays. See *Holidays.*

Religious institutions. Religious institution(s). *Choose from:* religious, denominational, sectarian, ecclesiastical, Jewish, Catholic, Protestant, Christian, Islamic, Hindu, Buddhist *with:* institution(s), organization(s), association(s), fellowship(s), group(s). *Consider also:* monaster(y,ies), cloister(s). *See also* Churches; Convents; Ecumenical movement; Mosques; Nonprofit organizations; Places of worship; Religious denominations; Sacred places; Sects; Synagogues; Temples.

Religious intermarriage. See *Intermarriage.*

Religious laity. See *Lay religious personnel.*

Religious leadership. Religious leader(s, ship). *Choose from:* religious, spiritual, church(es), ecclesiastical, clergy, diocesan, ecumenical, oecumenical, denominational, sectarian, Presbyterian, Episcopal, Church of England, Methodist, Catholic, Christian, Protestant, Jewish, Islamic, Hindu, Buddhist etc. *with:* leader(s,ship), authorit(y,es), mentor(s), guide(s), counselor(s), teacher(s). *Consider also:* Vatican, cardinal(s), archbishop(s), bishop(s), pope(s), priest(s), minister(s), rabbi(s), mullah(s), imam(s). *See also* Apostles; Christian leadership; Clergy; Fathers of the church; Guru; Lay religious personnel; Leadership; Papacy; Priests; Priests and priestly classes (anthropology); Religious councils and synods; Rabbis.

Religious liberty. See *Freedom of religion.*

Religious life. Religious life. Religious lives. *Choose from:* religious(ly), religiosity, devout(ly,ness), saintly, spiritual(ity), contemplative, righteous(ness), humane, caring, inspirational *with:* life(style), living, way of life. *Consider also:* spiritual sustenance. *See also* Abstinence; Asceticism; Contemplative orders; Convents; Friars; Holy men; Holy women; Inspiration; Meditation; Monasticism; Monks; Nuns; Prayer; Religiosity; Religious commitment; Religious communities; Spirituality; Women religious.

Religious literature. Religious literature. Bibl(e,ical). Koran. Qur'an. Alcoran. Talmud(ic). Torah. Pentateuch. Midrash. Haggadah. Siddur. Mishnah. Sefer Bahir. Zohar. Missal(s). Liturg(y,ies). Book of Common Prayer. Prayerbook(s). Hymnal(s). Bhagavata Purana. Bhagavad Gita. Upanishads. Vedas. Sutras. Sastra. Shastra. Tantra. Avesta. Zend-Avesta. Tripitaka. Dhammapada. Agamas. Granth Adigranth. Eddas. Scripture(s). Old Testament. New Testament. Epistle(s). Gospel(s). Book of Mormon. Meditation(s). Prayer(s). Hagiograph(y,ies). Lives of Saints. Biblical concordance(s). *Choose from:* religious, Bahai, Christian, Protestant, Catholic, Jewish, Islamic, Buddhist, Confucian, Taoist, Zen, Zoroastrian, church, biblical, rabbinic(al), devotional, evangelical, liturgical, theological, papal, patristic, eschatological *with:* reading(s), writing(s), book(s), literature, commentar(y,ies), fable(s), legend(s), fiction, poetry, poem(s), publication(s), tract(s), title(s), text(s). *See also* Apocalyptic literature; Apologetics; Bible; Canons; Christian symbolism; Devotional poetry; Fall of man; Literature; Liturgical books; Prayerbooks; Rabbinical literature; Religious beliefs; Religious doctrines; Religious education; Religious films; Revealed theology; Sacred books; Sacredness; Sermons; Theology.

Religious movements. Religious movement(s). Spiritual movement(s). Charismatic Christian(s). Messian(ic, ity,ism). *Choose from:* religious, spiritual, ecumenical, fundamentalist, Christian, evangelical, sacred, parareligious *with:* activis(m,t,ts), movement(s), revival(s,ism), sect(s), cult(s), association(s), fellowship(s). *Consider also:* Scientology, Divine Light, Jews for Jesus, Jesus Movement, Krishna, New Age, Perfect Liberty Kyodan, Pentecostal(s,ism), Rastafari, Bagwan Shree Rajneesh, Renunciate Hermitage, Social Gospel, Spiritual Frontiers, Sri Narayana Dharma Paripalana, Umbanda, Unification Church, Way International. *See also* Bahaism; Charisma; Creationism; Ecumenical movement; Great awakening; Messianic movements; Millenarianism; Protestant reformation; Religious beliefs; Religious communities; Religious cultural groups; Religious cults; Religious fundamentalism; Religious gatherings; Religious revivals; Secularization; Social movements; Zionism.

Religious music. Religious music. *Choose from:* religious, church(es), synagogue(s), temple(s), cantor(s), liturgical, gospel, worship, sacred, scriptural, ecclesiastical, sabbath, Jewish, Christian, Baptist, Lutheran, Congregational, Methodist, Protestant, etc. *with:* choir(s), chorus(es), tune(s), music(al,ally,ian,ians), song(s), chant(s), aria(s), anthem(s), antiphon(s), cantata(s), motet(s), bell-ringing, psalter(s), singing, sung. *Consider also:* psalm(s), alleluia(s), plainsong, hymn(s), laude, leisen, shofar(s), cantillation, Missinai tune(s), Nusah. *See also* A cappella singing; Bells; Cantatas; Chants; Church music; Dirges; Funeral music; Hymns; Jewish music; Motets; Music.

Religious mysteries. Religious myster(y, ies). *Choose from:* religious(ly), Madonna, Mary, Marian, Jesus, holy, faith, pilgrim(s), millennium, Eleusinian *with:* myster(y,ies), apparition(s), visionar(y,ies), phenomen(a,on), miracle(s), miraculous(ly), mystical(ly), metaphysic(s,al), above reason. *Consider also:* Eucharist(ic), transubstantiat(e,ed, ing,ion,al,ally). *See also* Exorcism; Liturgical drama; Miracle plays; Morality plays; Mother goddesses; Oracles; Purification rites; Religious rituals; Transubstantiation.

Religious nonconformists. See *Religious dissenters.*

Religious objects. See *Religious articles.*

Religious orders. See *Contemplative religious orders; Military religious orders; Monasticism; Monks; Nuns.*

Religious orders, military. See *Military religious orders.*

Religious orthodoxy. See *Religious fundamentalism.*

Religious persecution. See *Anti-Catholicism; Antisemitism; Hate crimes; Offenses against religion; Religious prejudice; Religious refugees.*

Religious personnel. Religious personnel. Nun(s). Monk(s). Clergy(men,man, woman,women). Priest(s). Minister(s). Rabbi(s). Chaplain(s). Pastor(s). Preacher(s). Ministry. Women religious. Religious communit(y,ies). Religious career(s). Deacon(s). Parish priest(s). Priestess(es). Abbot(s). Bishop(s). Archbishop(s). Pope(s). Cantor(s). Church choir(s). Seminarian(s). Saint(s). Prophet(s). Missionar(y,ies). Evangelist(s). Pilgrim(s). Imam(s). *Choose from:* religious, church, synagogue, temple, mosque, spiritual, seminary *with:* personnel, staff, leader(s), teacher(s), board member(s), order(s), brotherhood(s), occupation(s), healer(s), hierarch(y,ies). *See also* Abbots; Abstinence; Asceticism; Chaplains; Clergy; Evangelists; Fathers of the church; Holy men; Holy women; Lay religious personnel; Ministers; Missionaries; Monasticism; Monks; Nuns; Preachers; Priests; Priests and priestly classes (anthropology); Rabbis; Sacredness; Saints; Seminarians; Women religious.

Religious personnel, lay. See *Lay religious personnel.*

Religious practices. Religious practice(s). Pray(ed,ing,er,ers). Bapti(sm,ize,izing, ized). Monastic(ism). Observ(e,ed,ing) Sabbath. Religiosity. Sermon(s). Sacrament(s,al). Eucharist. Liturg(y, ical). Piet(y,ism). Reborn. Rebirthing. Born again. Sabbath. Shabbat. Tithing. Faith healing. Salvation. Dervish ritual. *Choose from:* religious, sacred, church, synagogue, temple, Christian, Jewish, Moslem, Hindu, Taoist, Buddhist *with:* practice(s), custom(s), rite(s), ritual(s), worship, vow(s), observance(s), ceremon(y,ies), tradition(s), celebration(s), service(s), symbol(s), reliquar(y,ies), participation, holiday(s), possession, confirmation, attendance, object(s), holiday(s), fast(s,ing), fiesta(s), communion, wedding(s), confession(s,al), meditation, ascetic(ism), ecstasy, life, devotion(s). *See also* Asceticism; Ceremonial objects; Church attendance; Confirmation; Glossolalia; Jewish law; Meditation; Monasticism; Mysticism; Prayer; Purification rites; Religious affiliation; Religious behavior; Religious beliefs;

Religious rituals; Sabbath; Sacrificial rites; Spiritual healing; Worship; Yoga.

Religious prejudice. Religious prejudice(s). Interreligious strife. Religiocentric(ism). Pogrom(s). Holocaust. Jewish question. *Choose from:* religious, faith based, interreligious, holy, Catholic(s), Jew(s,ish), Protestant(s), Hindu(s), Islam(ic), Muslim(s), Moslem(s), Baha'i(s), sabbath, Christian(s), Buddhist(s) *with:* prejudice(s), bias(es), stereotype(s), bigot(s,ry,ed), persecut(e, ed,ing,ion), victim(s,ize,ized,izing), discriminat(e,ed,ing,ion), intoleran(t,ce), conflict(s), oppress(ed,ion), minorit(y, ies), hostil(e,ity,ities). *Consider also:* anti-religious, anti-Catholic(ism), anti-Jewish, anti-Semitic, anti-Protestant(ism), anti-Papism, Mozarabic Christian(s). *See also* Anti-Catholicism; Antisemitism; Bigotry; Church state relationship; Exclusivity (Religion); Freedom of religion; Hate crimes; Offenses against religion; Prejudice; Religious accommodation; Religious beliefs; Sacrilege; Social discrimination.

Religious refugees. Religious refugee(s). *Choose from:* religious, Catholic(s), Protestant(s), Puritan(s), Quaker(s), Huguenot(s), Jew(s,ish), Muslim(s), Moslem(s), Christian(s), Buddhist(s), Moor(s), heretic(s), reformation, inquisition *with:* refugee(s), defect(ed, or,ors,ion), seek(ing) asylum, escapee(s), escap(e,ed,ing) persecution, emigre(s), emigration(s), exile(s,d), seek(ing) refuge, sought refuge, resettle(d,ment), migrat(e,ed,ing,ion,ions), migrant(s), wander(ed,ing), fugitive(s). *See also* Freedom of religion; Refugees; Religious dissenters; Tolerance.

Religious revivals. Religious revival(ism, ists,s). Charismatic Christian(s). Charismatic religious movement(s). Born again. Rebapti(sm,ze,zed,zing). Muscular Christianity. Laestadian(ism). Evangelism. Evangelical movement(s). Pentecostal(s,ism). Prayer meeting(s). *Choose from:* Christian, Islamic, religious, spiritual, fundamentalist, evangelical, pentecostal, faith, church(es) *with:* revival(ism,ists,s), resurgence(s), charismatic, revitalization, renaissance, born again, reborn, renewal, renew(ing), conversion(s), mobilization, inspiration. *Consider also:* Billy Graham crusade(s), pilgrimage(s). *See also* Evangelical revival; Evangelists; Great awakening; Islam; Messianic movements; Protestantism; Regeneration (theology); Rejuvenation; Religions; Religious conversion; Religious cultural groups; Religious gatherings; Religious movements; Salvation.

Religious right. See *Religious fundamentalism.*

Religious rituals. Religious ritual(s). Sacrament(als,s). Baptism(s). Christening(s). Anointing of the sick. Confirmation. Bar Mitzvah(s). Bat Mitzvah(s). Foot washing. Lord's Supper. Seder(s). Marriage(s). Funeral(s). Mourning. Ordination. Penance. Prayer(books,beads). Dharma. Tanunaptra. Fasting. Firewalking. Kneeling. Genuflection. Prostration. Incense. *Choose from:* Buddhist, Christian, Jewish, Hind(u,i), Islamic, Moslem, Muslim, religious, spiritual, fundamentalist, evangelical, pentecostal, faith, church(es), sacred *with:* ritual(s), rite(s), ceremon(ial,y,ies), dut(y,ies), danc(es,ing), worship, practice(s), devotions, liturg(y,ies). *Consider also:* religious symbolism, ritual ecstasy, Ramadan. *See also* Absolution; Antiphons; Baptism; Blessing; Burials; Ceremonies; Church attendance; Church music; Churching of women; Confession; Confirmation; Crosses; Death rituals; Dolmen; Festivals; Funeral rites; Grace at meals; Holidays; Invocation; Liturgical drama; Liturgy; Masses (music); Moslem prayer; Ordination; Pilgrimages; Places of worship; Posture in worship; Prayer; Purification rites; Religious articles; Religious behavior; Religious cultural groups; Religious drama; Religious fundamentalism; Religious mysteries; Religious practices; Rites of passage; Ritual disfigurement; Ritual purity; Sacred songs; Sacrificial rites; Secret societies; Sermons; Shamanism; Shrines; Spiritual healing; Syncretism; Weddings; Worship; Yoga.

Religious schools. See *Private schools.*

Religiousness. See *Religious commitment.*

Relocation. Relocat(e,ed,ing,ion). Re-establish(ed,ing,ment). Re-hous(e,ed, ing). Resettl(e,ed,ing,ement). Resituat(e, ed,ing). Displac(e,ed,ing,ement). Transfer(red,ring). Translocat(ed,ing, ion). *Consider also:* plant closing(s), dispers(ed,ing),ion), diaspora, population redistribution, leav(e,ing) home, evict(ed,ing,ion,ions), repatriat(e,ed,ing, ion), extradit(e,ed,ing,ion), expulsion, expel(ling,led), transmigrat(e,ed,ing, ion), evacuat(e,ed,ing,ion), white flight, brain drain, migrat(e,ed,ing,ion,ions), deport(ed,ing,ation), immigrat(e,ed,ing, ion), emigrat(e,ed,ing,ion). *See also* American Indian territories; Career mobility; Civic improvement; Diaspora; Dismissal of staff; Emigrants; Employee transfers; Employee turnover; Geographic mobility; Headquarters relocation; Homeland; Homeless; Housing; Involuntary retirement; Job applicants; Job search; Labor migration; Land reform; Land settlement; Migration; Migration of industry; Migration patterns; Personnel termination; Place of residence; Plant closings; Plant

relocation; Population distribution; Population transfer; Refugees; Residences; Residential mobility; Rural to urban migration; Severance pay; Tenant relocation; Urban renewal; Urban to rural migration.

Relocation, headquarters. See *Headquarters relocation.*

Relocation of employees. See *Employee transfers.*

Relocation of industry. See *Migration of industry.*

Relocation, plant. See *Plant relocation.*

Relocation, tenant. See *Tenant relocation.*

REM dream deprivation. REM dream deprivation. *Choose from:* REM, sleep *with:* depriv(ed,ation), loss. *See also* Deprivation; REM dreams.

REM dreams. REM dream(s). Rapid eye movement dream(s). *Choose from:* rem *with:* dream(s,ing), recall. *See also* Dreams; REM dreams; REM sleep.

REM sleep. REM sleep. Paradoxical sleep. *Choose from:* REM, rapid eye movement, fast wave, desynchronized, activated *with:* sleep. *See also* REM dreams; Sleep.

Remains, animal archaeology. See *Animal remains (archaeology).*

Remains, human archaeology. See *Human remains (archaeology).*

Remains, plant archaeology. See *Plant remains (archaeology).*

Remains, skeletal. See *Animal remains (archaeology); Human remains (archaeology); Skeleton.*

Remarriage. Remarriage(s). Remarr(y,ied, ing). Marr(y,ied) again. Rewed(ded). Stepfamil(y,ies). Multiple marriages. Multiple families. *Choose from:* second, third, serial *with:* marriage(s), mate(s), spouse(s), wife, wives, husband(s). *Consider also:* step, reconstituted, blended, multimarriage, remarried *with:* famil(y,ies). *See also* Annulment; Divorce; Former spouses; Marriage timing; Stepfamily; Widowhood.

Remedial education. Remedial education. Remedial teaching. Remediation. Tutor(ed,ing). Reading clinic(s). Learning improvement program(s). Learning assistance program(s). *Choose from:* remedial *with:* education, mathematics, reading, writing, instruction, program(s), course(s), work. *See also* Compensatory education; Learning disabilities; Peer teaching; Remedial reading; Special education.

Remedial reading. Remedial reading. *Choose from:* remedial, corrective, remediation, tutor(ed,ing), clinic(s) *with:* reading, reader(s). *See also* Dyslexia; Educational placement; Learning disabilities; Reading education; Remedial education.

Remedies, home. See *Herbal medicine; Non-prescription drugs; Nostrums; Quackery; Traditional medicine; Vitamin therapy.*

Remedies, natural. See *Naturopathy.*

Remember names, inability to. See *Anomia (inability to remember names).*

Remembering. See *Reminiscence; Retention (psychology).*

Reminiscence. Reminiscen(ce,ces,t). Reminisc(e,ed,ing). Life review. Autobiographical memor(y,ies). Recollection(s). Recall(ed,ing). Remembrance(s). Reliv(e,ed,ing). Retrospect(ion). Nostalgi(a,c). Memoir(s). Look(ing) back. Remember(ed,ing). Guided autobiograph(y,ies). Liv(e,ing) in the past. Think(ing) about the past. Dwell(ing) in the past. *See also* Autobiography; Early memories; Forgetting; Nostalgia; Oral history; Recall; Retention (psychology).

Remission. Remission(s). *Choose from:* remission, abat(e,ed,ing,ement), disappear(ed,ance), diminution, lessen(ed,ing), diminish(ed,ing) *with:* symptom(s). *See also* Disorders; Mental illness; Recovery; Recurrence; Relapse; Spontaneous remission; Symptoms; Treatment outcome.

Remission, spontaneous. See *Spontaneous remission.*

Remorse. See *Repentence.*

Remote consultation. Remote consultation. Teleconsult(ation,ing). *Choose from:* remote, distance, telephone, long distance, telecommunications, interactive video, fax, e-mail, internet, electronic highway, wired *with:* consult(ing,ed,ation,ative), interview(s, ed,ing), diagnos(tic,e,ed,ing,is,es), therap(y,ies,eutic), advice, advisory, interpret(ed,ing,ation). *Consider also:* telementor(ed,ing), e-mail reference. *See also* Consultation; Distance education; Help lines (telephone); Referral; Telemedicine; Telephone psychotherapy.

Remotivation therapy. Remotivation therap(y,ies). *Choose from:* remotivat(e, ed,ing,ion), reality *with:* therap(y,ies, eutic), psychotherap(y,ies,eutic), activit(y,ies), program(s). *Consider also:* bridge(s) to reality. *See also* Psychotherapy; Reality therapy.

Remuneration. See *Compensation (payment).*

Renaissance. Renaissance. 14th century. Fourteenth century. 15th century. Fifteenth century. 16th century. Sixteenth century. 17th century. Seventeenth century. Reformation.

Counter-Reformation. Neo-Classical period. Tudor. *Choose from:* rise, growth, development *with:* commercialism, humanism, neoclassicism, the Reformation, beginning of scientific method. Enlightenment period. *Consider also:* late medieval period, 14th to 17th centuries, emergence of nation state(s). *Consider also:* rebirth, renewal, revival. *See also* Classicism; Cultural history; Historical periods; Humanism; Humanists; Medieval theology; Middle ages; Renaissance; Renaissance literature; Renaissance music; Renaissance philosophy; Renaissance poetry.

Renaissance literature. Renaissance literature. *Choose from:* Renaissance, 1430-1600, 15th century, fifteenth century, 16th century, sixteenth century, 17th century, seventeenth century, Reformation, Elizabethan, early Stuart, Counter-Reformation, neo-Latin, neo-Greek, neo-Classical, Tudor *with:* devotional literature, chronicle(s), memoir(es,s), literary, sonnet(s), drama, fiction, allegor(y,ies,ical), writing(s), panegyric(s), biograph(y,ies). *Consider also:* ars moriendi, Roman del la Rose, Le Morte D'Arthur, Michel de Montaigne, Miguel de Cervantes, John Milton, Christopher Marlowe, William Shakespeare, Desiderius Erasmus, John Colet, Thomas More, etc. *See also* Classicism; Cultural history; Humanism; Humanists; Literature; Medieval literature; Renaissance; Renaissance music; Renaissance philosophy; Renaissance poetry.

Renaissance music. Renaissance music. *Choose from:* Renaissance, 1430-1600, 16th century, sixteenth century, Reformation, Counter-Reformation *with:* mass(es), motet(s), canzon(a,e), ricercar, intabulation, chanson(s), madrigal(s), music(al,ally,ian,ians), ballad(es), rondeau(x), composer(s). *Consider also:* John Dunstable, Guillaume Dufay, Gilles Binchois, Burgundian school, Matteo da Perugia, Johannes Ockeghem, Jacob Obrecht, Josquin Desprez, Giovanni Pierluigi da Palestrina, William Byrd, Orlando di Lasso [Orlandus Lassus], Tomas Luis de Victoria, etc.. *See also* Basse danse; Frottola; Lauda; Medieval music; Middle ages; Motets; Music; Renaissance; Renaissance literature; Renaissance poetry.

Renaissance philosophy. Renaissance philosophy. Renaissance humanism. *Choose from:* Renaissance, 1430-1600, 15th century, fifteenth century, 16th century, sixteenth century, 17th century, seventeenth century, Reformation, Elizabethan, early Stuart, Counter-Reformation, neo-Latin, neo-Greek, neo-Classical, Tudor *with:* philosoph(y,ies, ical,er,ers), political theor(y,ies), humanis(m,t,ts), philosophy of nature,

Platonis(m,t,ts). *Consider also:* Protestant Reformation, Albertus Magnus, St. Thomas Aquinas, St. Bonaventure, John Duns Scotus, Niccolò Machiavelli, Sir Francis Bacon, Thomas Hobbes, René Descartes, Desiderius Erasmus, Sir Thomas More, Michel de Montaigne, Baruch (Benedict) de Spinoza, Giordano Bruno. *See also* Classicism; Cultural history; Humanism; Medieval logic; Medieval philosophers; Medieval theology; Philosophy; Renaissance; Renaissance literature.

Renaissance poetry. Renaissance poe(try, m,ms). *Choose from:* Renaissance, 1430-1600, 15th century, fifteenth century, 16th century, sixteenth century, 17th century, seventeenth century, Reformation, Counter-Reformation, neo-Latin, neo-Greek, neo-Classical, Tudor *with:* poe(try,m,ms), sonnet(s), madrigal(s), pastoral(s), epigram(s), lyric(s,ism), eleg(y,ies), ottava rima, ode(s), sonnet(s). *Consider also:* individual authors such as: Torquato Tasso, Giovanni Batista Guarini, Pierre de Ronsard, Edmund Spenser, Christopher Marlowe, Michael Drayton, William Shakespeare, George Chapman, John Donne, Ben Jonson, John Skelton, etc. *See also* Poetry; Renaissance; Renaissance literature; Renaissance music.

Renewable resources. Renewable resource(s). Renewable energy. *Consider also:* wood, solar, geothermal, ocean thermal, hydroelectric, water, hydropower, biomass, synthetic fuel(s), methanol, sustainab(le,ility). *See also* Alternative energy; Conservation of natural resources; Energy generating resources; Fuel; Natural resources; Nonrenewable resources; Recycling; Restoration ecology; Solar energy; Sustainable development; Tree planting; Wind power; Waste to energy; Water power.

Renewal, urban. See *Urban renewal.*

Renown. See *Famous people.*

Rent control. Rent control. *Choose from:* apartment(s), rent(al,als,ed,er,ers,s) *with:* control(led), decontrol, fixed rate, regulat(e,ed,ing,ion), set rate, deregulat(e,ed,ing,ion). *Consider also:* Rent stabilization. *See also* Affordable housing; Housing costs; Rental housing.

Rent strikes. Rent strike(s). *Choose from:* rent(s) *with:* strike(s), withhold(ing), withheld. *See also* Landlord tenant relations; Resident councils.

Rental housing. Rental housing. Leas(ing,es,ed). Rent(s,al). Sublet(ting). *Consider also:* tenan(ts,cy), rented apartment(s), rent control, boarder(s), boarding house(s), single room occupancy, lodger(s), letting room(s), rentier(s), landlord(s), leasehold interest(s), leasee(s), leasor(s). *See also* Affordable housing; Housing; Landlords; Landlord tenant relations; Leasing; Public housing; Rent control; Tenants.

Renters. See *Tenants.*

Renunciation. Renunciat(ion,ive,ory). Renounc(e,ed,ing,ement). Relinquish(ed, ing,ment). Repudiat(e,ed,ing,ation). Self denial. Disavow(ed,ing,al). Abnegat(e, ed,ing,ion). Abdicat(e,ed,ing,ion). Resign(ed,ing,ation). Ced(e,ed,ing). Ceas(e,ed,ing). Cessation. Retract(ed, ing,ion). Defect(ed,ing,ion). Disown(ed,ing). Eschew(ed,ing). Forbear(ing). *See also* Abdication; Abstinence; Ceding; Self denial; Self sacrifice.

Reorganization. Reorganiz(ed,ing,ation, ations). *Choose from:* re-establish(ed, ment), chang(e,es,ed,ing), develop(ed, ment,ing), innovat(e,ed,ing,ion,ions), redesign(ed,ing), reform(ed,ing), retrench(ed,ing,ment), restructur(e,ed, ing) turnaround(s), recapitaliz(e,ed,ing, ation), reshap(e,ed,ing), reshuffl(e,ed, ing), transform(ed,ing,ation), grow(th, n,ing), downsiz(e,ed,ing), rightsizing, democratiz(e,ed,ation), merg(e,ed,ing, er,ers), reconstruct(ed,ing,ion), remodel(led,ling), transition(s), reconstitut(e,ed,ing,ion), centraliz(e,ed, ing,ation), decentraliz(e,ed,ing,ation), evolv(e,ed,ing), evolution(ary), revolutionary, revolutioniz(e,ed,ing), alter(ed,ing,ion,ions), renew(ed,al,als, ing), moderniz(e,ed,ing,ation) *with:* organization(s,al), business(es), compan(y,ies), corporat(e,ion,ions). *Consider also:* reconfigurable organization(s). *See also* Centralization; Change agents; Contracting out; Cooptation; Decentralization; Devolution; Downsizing; Merger integration; Mergers; Organizational change; Organizational development; Organizational dissolution; Organizational structure; Organizations; Reengineering.

Repair, appliance. See *Appliance repair.*

Reparations. Reparation(s). War debt payment(s). Restitution. Victim compensat(e,ed,ing,ion). Right(ed,ing) wrong(s). Mak(e,ing) amends. Mak(e,ing) good. Made amends. Made good. Recompense. Redress(ed,ing). Atone(d,ment). Retribution. Indemni(ty, ification). Repayment(s). Requit(e,ed,al). Pay(ed,ing) claim(s). *Consider also:* community service *with:* offender(s), settlement, remuneration. *See also* Alternatives to incarceration; Claims; Costs; Damages; Restitution; Restorative justice.

Repatriation. Repatriat(e,ed,ion). Return migrant(s). Return migration. Reverse migration. Population turnaround. Migration loop(s). Returnee(s). *Choose*

from: displaced person(s), population, migrat(ion,ory,ing), migrant(s), exile(s), emigrant(s), expatriate(s) *with:* revers(al, e,es,ing), turnaround, loop(s), return(ed, ing). *Consider also:* extradit(e,ed,ing, ition), resettl(e,ed,ing,ement). *See also* Displaced persons; Emigration; Expatriates; Immigrants; Immigration; Migration; Political asylum; Refugees.

Repeal. Repeal(ed,ing). Annul(led,ling, ment). Abrogat(e,ed,ing,ion). Revok(e,ed,ing). Revocation. Rescind(ed,ing). Abolish(ed,ing,ment). Cancel(led,ling,lation). *See also* Annulment; Cancellation; Disclaim; Legislative processes; Nullification.

Repentence. Repenten(t,ce). Remorse(ful, fully). Peniten(t,ce). Contrit(e,ition). Aton(e,ed,ing,ement). Regretful(ly). Apologetic(ally). Apolog(y,ies). Sorry. Rueful(ly). Conscience stricken. Guilt ridden. Chastened. *See also* Apologies; Atonement; Confession; Guilt; Penitents; Regeneration (theology); Regret; Sin; Spiritual exercises.

Repetition. Repetition(s). Repeat(ed,ing). Iterat(e,ed,ing,ion,ions). Reiterat(e,ed, ing,ion,ions). *Consider also:* ingeminat(e,ed,ing), renew(ed,ing), recount(ed,ing), rehears(e,ed,ing), hash(ed,ing) over, recapitulat(e,ed,ing), rehash(ed,ing), restat(e,ed,ing), retell(ing), echo(es,ed,ing), duplicat(e, ed,ing), reproduc(e,ed,ing), cop(y,ies, ied,ying), ditto, imitat(e,ed,ing), recur(red,ring), return(ed,ing), revert(ed,ing), mirror site(s). *See also* Experimental replication; Grade repetition; Practice (repetition); Recurrence; Refrain (music).

Repetition, compulsive. See *Compulsive behavior.*

Repetition, grade. See *Grade repetition.*

Repetitive motion disorders. Repetitive motion disorder(s). Repetitive task injur(y,ies). Cumulative trauma. Cumulative stress injur(y,ies). *Consider also:* carpal tunnel syndrome. *See also* Hazardous occupations; Occupational diseases; Occupational safety; Physiological stress.

Replevin. See *Restitution.*

Replication, experimental. See *Experimental replication.*

Report, self. See *Self report.*

Reporters. See *Journalists.*

Reporting, fairness and accuracy in. See *Fairness and accuracy in reporting.*

Reporting, mandatory. See *Mandatory reporting.*

Reporting, trial. See *Court news.*

Reporting centers, day corrections. See *Day reporting centers (corrections).*

Reports, annual. See *Annual reports.*

Reports, case. See *Case studies.*

Reports, financial. See *Financial statements.*

Representation, collective. See *Collective representation.*

Representation (likeness). Represent(ed, ing,ation). Likeness. Portray(ed,ing,al). Depict(ed,ing,ion). Delineat(e,ed,ing, ion). Cop(y,ied,ing). Description(s). Reproduction(s). Interpretation(s). Imitation(s). Impersonation(s). Present(ed,ing,ation). Symboliz(e,ed, ing,ation). Pictorialization(s). *See also* Arts; Copies; Description; Media portrayal; Photography.

Representation, political. See *Political representation.*

Representation, proportional. See *Proportional representation.*

Representation in management (employee). See *Employee ownership; Industrial democracy; Participative management; Worker control; Worker participation.*

Representational art. See *Realism in art.*

Representative government. See *Democracy.*

Representatives. Represent(ed,ing, ative,atives,ation). Emissar(y,ies). Envoy(s). Diplomat(s). Congress(men, man,women,woman). Senator(s). Member(s) of Parliament. Agent(s). Deput(y,ies). Surrogate(s). Prox(y,ies). Broker(s). Intermediar(y,ies). Mediar(y,ies). Substitute(s). Delegate(s). Middlem(an,en). Minister(s). Ambassador(s). *See also* Advocacy; Brokers; Diplomats; Legislative bodies; Legislators; Messengers; Political representation; Spokespersons.

Repression (defense mechanism). Repress(ed,ing,ion,ions,ive). Anticathex(is,es). Anticathex(is,es). Ego resistance. Suppress(ed,ing,ion). Ward(ed,ing) off. Den(y,ied,ial). Unconscious feeling(s). Banish(ed,ing) from consciousness. *Consider also:* after-expulsion, afterexpulsion. *See also* Avoidance; Sublimation; Suppression (defense mechanism).

Repression, political. See *Political repression.*

Repression, psychological. See *Repression (defense mechanism).*

Repression sensitization. Repression sensitization. *Consider also:* defensiveness, defensive style(s), defensive response(s), intellectualiz(ing,ation), obsessive behavior, ruminative worry(ing), den(y,ial) anxiety, rationalization. *See also* Personality traits.

Reprisals. Reprisal(s). Retaliat(e,ed,es, ing,ion,ions). Reveng(e,ed,ing,eful). Retribution. Redress(ed,ing). Counterblow(s). Counterattack(s,ed,ing). Requital(s). Vindicat(e,ed,ing,ion). Quid pro quo. *Consider also:* vendetta(s), reparation(s). *See also* Hate crimes; Feuds; Punishment; Punitiveness; Reciprocity; Restitution; Revenge; Social exchange.

Reproduction, cultural. See *Cultural capital; Dominant ideologies; Social reproduction.*

Reproduction, human. See *Human reproduction.*

Reproduction, sexual. See *Sexual reproduction.*

Reproduction, social. See *Social reproduction.*

Reproductive rights. Reproductive right(s). Right to choose. Right to make reproductive choice(s). Right to make procreative decision(s). *Choose from:* right(s), empower(ed,ing,ment), status, women's role *with:* choos(e,ing), decid(e,ing), mak(e,ing) decision(s), determin(e,ing), information, adequate facilities, health care *with:* birth control, hav(e,ing) children, spacing children, matern(al,ity), contraception, reproduct(ion,ive), sexuality, sterilization, abortion, *Consider also:* reduc(e,ed,ing) unwanted pregnanc(y, ies), safe motherhood, maternal health service(s), nutrition program(s), prenatal care, postnatal care, protect(ed,ing,ion) pregnant worker(s), right to decide how to live, women's equality, women's rights. *See also* Abortion; Battered women; Birth control; Contraception; Family planning; Human rights; Involuntary sterilization; Marital rape; Rape; Rights; Sex discrimination; Sex information; Sexual abuse; Social justice; Unwanted pregnancy; Women's rights.

Reproductive technologies. Reproductive technolog(y,ies). Artificial procreation. Assisted reproduction. *Choose from:* reproduct(ion,ive), infertility, subfertility, procreation, insemination *with:* technolog(y,ies,ical), technique(s), biotechnolog(y,ies,ical), therap(y,ies), treatment(s), technic(s), artificial(ly). *Consider also:* surrogate mother(s, hood), in-vitro fertilization, embryo freezing, embryo transfer(s), sperm bank(s), fertility drug(s), noncoital reproduction, fetal imaging, fetal monitoring, genetic engineering, ovarian hyperstimulation, transfer of zygote(s), transfer of gamete(s), intrafallopian transfer(s), gamete donor(s), test tube bab(y,ies), extracorporeal fertilization. *See also* Artificial insemination; Birth; Cloning; Eugenics; Fertility enhancement; Fertilization; Fertilization in vitro;

Genetics; Pharming; Pregnancy; Sexual reproduction; Sperm banks; Surrogate mothers.

Reptiles. Reptil(e,es,ia,ian). Cotylosauria. Loricata. Mesosauria. Pelycosauria. Pterosauria. Rhynchocephalia. Squamata. Testudinata. Therapsida. *Consider also:* snake(s), turtle(s), lizard(s), loricate(s), frog(s), crocodile(s), alligator(s), toad(s). *See also* Amphibia; Endangered species; Poisonous animals; Sacred animals; Turtles; Vertebrates.

Republics. Republic(s,anism). Elected government(s). Representative government(s). Elected representative government(s). Accountab(le,ility) *with:* people, electorate. *See also* Democracy; Political systems.

Republics, former Yugoslav. See *Former Yugoslav republics.*

Repugnance. Repugnan(ce,cy,t). Revulsion. Repuls(ive,ion). Distaste(ful). Disgust(ed). Offensive(ness). *Consider also:* abomination, abhorren(ce,t), avers(ive,iveness,ion), detest(ed,ing, ation), hat(e,ed,ing), hatred, horror, nausea(ting), loath(ed,ing,some). *See also* Aversion; Contempt; Disgust; Hate; Horror.

Reputation. Reput(able,e,ed,ation). Well-known. Good name. Bad name. Renown. Prominence. Prestige. Respect(able,ability,ed). Public esteem. Personal honor. Eminent. Preeminent. Credibility. *Consider also:* rating(s), standing, status, popular image. *See also* Admiration; Attribution; Credibility; Defamation; Honored (esteem); Integrity; Prestige; Public opinion; Qualifications; Recognition (achievement); Requirements; Scandals; Social attitudes; Social status.

Requiem. See *Funeral rites.*

Requirements. Requirement(s). Qualification(s). Qualif(y,ying,ied). Prerequisite(s). Provision(s). Stipulat(e, ed,ing,ion,ions). Requisite. Mandatory. Demanded. Compulsory. Obligatory. Binding. Necessitated. Indispensable. Essential. Precondition(s). *See also* Ability; Basic education; Caloric requirements; Certification; Courses; Credentialism; Educational background; Job requirements; Minimum competencies; Needs; Occupational qualifications; Performance standards; Qualifications; Reputation; Residence requirements; Skill; Work experience.

Requirements, caloric. See *Caloric requirements.*

Requirements, job. See *Job requirements.*

Requirements, residence. See *Residence requirements.*

Requirements, work. See *Job requirements.*

Rescue. Rescu(e,ed,ing). Salvag(e,ed,ing). Recover(y,ed,ing). Preserv(e,ed,ing, ation). Redeem(ed,ing). Redemption. Sav(e,ed,ing). *See also* Accidents; Bailouts; Crisis intervention; Disaster relief; Emergency services; Relief services; Safety; Salvaging; Shelters.

Rescue operations, search and. See *Disaster relief; Relief services.*

Research. Research(ed,ing,er,ers). Experiment(ed,ing,al,ation,s). Control groups(s). Data collection and analys(is,es). Replicat(ed,ing,ion,ions). Drug trial(s). Clinical trial(s). Empiric(al,ism). Examin(e,ed,ing, ation,ations). *Choose from:* scientific, controlled, laboratory, empirical *with:* inquir(y,ies), probe(d,s), result(s), endeavor(s), method(ology,ologies,s), investigat(ed,ing,or,ors,ion,ions), achievement(s). *Consider also:* statistical stud(y,ies), use stud(y,ies), pilot project(s), research design(s). *See also* Action research; Agricultural research; Animal studies; Archaeological surveying; Biased sampling; Case studies; Cohort analysis; Communications research; Control groups (research); Cross cultural comparisons; Data analysis; Data collection; Data interpretation; Dependent variables; Discoveries (findings); Economic research; Empirical methods; Endowment of research; Error analysis; Evaluation; Experiment controls; Experiment volunteers; Experimental epilepsy; Experimental games; Experimental instructions; Experimental neurosis; Experimental psychology; Experimental psychosis; Experimental replication; Experiments; Feasibility studies; Fieldwork; Followup studies; Genetic research; Group research; Hypothesis testing; Independent variables; Information; Interdisciplinary approach; Interviews; Inventions; Investigations; Literary research; Longitudinal studies; Market research; Measurement; Methods; Models; Null hypothesis testing; Observation; Operations research; Organizational research; Opinion polls; Panel studies; Placebos; Population (statistics); Prospective studies; Psychometrics; Qualitative methods; Quantitative methods; Questionnaires; Random; Research applications; Research design; Research ethics; Research methods; Research personnel; Research subjects; Research support; Researcher bias; Researcher expectations; Researcher subject relations; Retrospective studies; Sampling; Sciences; Scientific development; Scientific discoveries; Scientific knowledge; Scientific method; Scientific revolutions; Secondary analysis;

Sociometric technics; Statistical bias; Statistical correlation; Statistical data; Statistical inference; Statistical norms; Statistical significance; Statistical tables; Surveys; Technological innovations; Technology assessment; Technology transfer; Theories; Theory verification; Time and motion studies.

Research, action. See *Action research.*

Research, advertising. See *Advertising research.*

Research, agricultural. See *Agricultural research.*

Research, animal. See *Animal studies.*

Research, communications. See *Communications research.*

Research, consumer. See *Market research.*

Research, control groups. See *Control groups (research).*

Research, economic. See *Economic research.*

Research, endowment of. See *Endowment of research.*

Research, genetic. See *Genetic research.*

Research, group. See *Group research.*

Research, historical. See *Historical research.*

Research, literary. See *Literary research.*

Research, market. See *Market research.*

Research, operations. See *Operations research.*

Research, organizational. See *Organizational research.*

Research, public opinion. See *Opinion polls.*

Research, qualitative. See *Qualitative methods.*

Research, quantitative. See *Quantitative methods.*

Research, scientific. See *Research.*

Research applications. Research application(s). Applied research. *Choose from:* research, scientific result(s), scientific achievement(s), finding(s), innovation(s) invention(s) *with:* appli(ed,cation,cations), implement(ed, ing,ation), diffusion, disseminat(e,ed, ing,ion), impact(s), utiliz(e,ed,ing,ation), transfer(s,ring,red), product(ion,ivity). *See also* Adoption of ideas; Applied psychology; Diffusion of innovation; High technology industries; Research; Technological innovations; Technology; Technology transfer.

Research bias. See *Research design; Researcher bias; Researcher expectations; Researcher subject relations.*

Research design. Research design(s). Experimental design(s). *Choose from:*

research, experiment(s,al), control, analytic instrument(s), questionnaire(s), quasiexperiment(s,al) *with:* design(s), framework(s), guide(s), outline(s), plan(s,ning). *Consider also:* double blind method(s), random allocation, between groups design, followup-stud(y,ies). *See also* Control groups (research); Dependent variables; Experiment controls; Experiments; Hypothesis testing; Independent variables; Interviews; Models; Observation methods; Participant observation; Participants; Posttesting; Pretesting; Qualitative methods; Quantitative methods; Research; Research methods; Researcher bias; Sampling; Scientific method; Scientific models; Statistical significance; Surveys; Theoretical problems; Theory verification.

Research ethics. Research ethic(s). *Choose from:* experiment(al,ation,s), research(er, ers), laborator(y,ies), SS, subject(s), case stud(y,ies), survey(s), participant observation *with:* ethic(s,al), informed consent, human rights, Helsinki Declaration, confidentiality, privacy, misrepresent(ed,ing,ation), falsif(y, ied,ication), fraud, deception, deceit, deceiv(e,ed,ing), exploit(ed,ing,ation), security, safety, qualification(s), moral(s, ity), human welfare, animal welfare. *See also* Bioethics; Falsification (scientific); Medical ethics; Medical philosophy; Patient rights; Physician patient relations; Professional ethics; Researcher subject relations; Scientific misconduct; Social epistemology; Value neutral; Value orientations; Unethical conduct

Research methods. Research method(s, ology,ologies). *Choose from:* research, experiment(s,al), scientific, empirical, qualitative, quantitative *with:* method(s, ology,ologies), procedure(s), technique(s), approach(es), condition(s), design(s). *Consider also:* replication, data collection, data analys(is,es), sampling, survey(s), case stud(y,ies), ex post facto research. *See also* Biased sampling; Case studies; Cohort analysis; Content analysis; Control groups (research); Cost analysis; Data analysis; Data collection; Data interpretation; Deduction; Documentation; Empirical methods; Ethnomethodology; Evaluation; Experiment controls; Experiments; Experimental instructions; Experimental replication; Factor analysis; Falsification (scientific); Fieldwork; Focus groups; Heuristics; Historical research; Historiography; Hypotheses; Hypothesis testing; Induction; Interdisciplinary approach; Interviews; Measurement; Models; Observation methods; Participant observation; Problem solving; Qualitative methods; Quantitative methods; Research design; Research subjects; Reliability; Sampling; Scientific method; Scientific models;

Self report; Statistical significance; Surveys; Theory formation; Theory verification; Validity; Value neutral.

Research personnel. Research personnel. Researcher(s). Scientist(s). Investigator(s). Participant observer(s). Experimenter(s). *Consider also:* research, scientific, R&D, laboratory, survey *with:* director(s), assistant(s), personnel, womanpower, manpower, worker(s), staff, interviewer(s), office(s), team(s), scholar(s), scientist(s), manager(s), confederate(s), technician(s), fieldworker(s). *See also* Biologists; Participant observation; Professional personnel; Psychologists; Research ethics; Researcher bias; Researcher expectations; Researcher subject relations; Scientists.

Research planning. See *Research design.*

Research reviews. See *Reviews.*

Research subjects. Research subject(s). Human subject(s). Animal subject(s). Control subject(s). SS. *Choose from:* research, experiment(al,s), drug trial(s), clinical trial(s), case stud(y,ies), control group(s), survey(s) *with:* subject(s), respondent(s), informant(s), interviewee(s), object(s), participant(s), laboratory animal(s), sample(s), universe. *See also* Experiment controls; Experiment volunteers; Human subjects (research); Informed consent; Patient rights; Research ethics; Research methods; Researcher subject relations; Respondents.

Research support. Research support. Sponsored research. *Choose from:* research, R&D *with:* grant(s,smanship), fellow(s,ship,ships), support(ed,ing), subsid(y,ies,ization), sponsor(ed,ship), fund(s,ing), financ(ed,ing). *See also* Endowment of research; Financial support; Research.

Researcher bias. Researcher bias(es). *Choose from:* researcher(s), experimenter(s), observer(s), investigator(s), examiner(s), ethnographer(s), scientist(s), interviewer(s) *with:* bias(es,ed), influenc(e,es,ed,ing), effect(s), distort(ed,ing,ion,ions). *See also* Bias; Biased sampling; Falsification (scientific); Objectivity; Predisposition; Research design; Research ethics; Researcher expectations; Researcher subject relations; Scientific misconduct; Social epistemology; Value neutral.

Researcher expectations. Researcher expectation(s). *Choose from:* researcher(s), experimenter(s), observer(s), investigator(s), examiner(s), ethnographer(s), scientist(s), interviewer(s) *with:* expectation(s), expectanc(y,ies), prediction(s), preconceiv(e,ed,ing), preconception(s), prejudg(e,ed,ing), prejudgement(s), prejudice(s). *See also* Expectations;

Prediction; Researcher bias; Self fulfilling prophecy.

Researcher subject relations. Researcher subject relations. Experimenter effects. *Choose from:* researcher(s), experimenter(s), observer(s), interviewer(s), fieldworker(s) *with:* respondent(s), SS, subject(s) *with:* effect(s), relation(s,ship, ships), transference, cooperation, ethics, morality, interaction(s), communication(s), expectation(s), feedback, involvement, rapport, rejection, response(s), role(s), trust. *See also* Experiment volunteers; Research ethics; Research personnel; Research subjects; Sexual exploitation.

Researchers. See *Research personnel.*

Resemblance. Resemblance(s). Resembl(e, ed,ing). Semblance(s). Likeness(es). Similar(ity,ities). Similitude. Simile(s). Identical(ness). Analogous(ly,ness). Corresponding(ly). Alike(ness). Comparab(le,ility). Equivalen(t,cy). Approximation(s). Affinit(y,ies). Duplicat(e,es,ed,ing,ion). Facsimile(s). Cop(y,ies). Replica(s). Look alike(s). *See also* Differences; Similarity; Similes; Uniformity.

Resentment. Resent(ful,ed,ing,ment). Take umbrage. Pique(d). Indigna(nt,tion). Offend(ed,ing). Insult(ed,ing). Outrag(e, ed). Affront(ed). Hostil(e,ity). Mad. Ang(ry,er). Rage. Animosit(y,ies). Animus. Antagon(ism,istic). Ill will. Grudg(e,ing). Begrudg(e,ed,ing). Spite(ful). Contempt(uous). Enmity. Hatred. Hat(e,ed,ing). Dislik(e,ed,ing). Disaffect(ed,ion). Embittered. Revenge(ful). *See also* Air rage; Alienation; Anger; Hate; Hate crimes; Hostility; Jealousy; Negativism; Rejection (psychology); Road rage; Scapegoating; Tensions; Threat; Violence.

Reservations, Indian. See *American Indian territories.*

Reserves, forest. See *Forest reserves.*

Resettlement. See *Relocation.*

Residence, matrilocal. See *Matrilocal residence.*

Residence, patrilocal. See *Patrilocal residence.*

Residence, place of. See *Place of residence.*

Residence, virilocal. See *Patrilocal residence.*

Residence characteristics. Residence characteristic(s). *Choose from:* residen(tial,ce,ces), home(s), dwelling(s), housing, domicile(s), apartment(s), condo(s,minium,miniums) *with:* characteristic(s), rural, suburban, urban, condition(s), age, location(s), floorplan(s), size(s), type(s), high rise, single family, multiple family, two-

family, two-story, three-bedroom. *See also* Characteristics; Neighborhoods; Qualities; Residences; Residential preferences.

Residence requirements. Residence requirement(s). *Choose from:* resid(e,ing,ence,ency,ent,ents) *with:* requir(e,ed,ing,ements), law(s), rule(s), regulation(s). *Consider also:* bona fide residen(ts,cy), legal residen(ts,cy), ban(ned,ning) nonresident(s). *See also* Absentee voting; Place of residence.

Residences. Residence(s). Living quarter(s). Dwelling(s). Abode(s). Habitation. Quarters. Lodging(s). Living accomodation(s). Living space(s). Home(s). House(s). Cottage(s). Apartment(s). Tenement(s). Flat(s). Domicile(s). Barrack(s). Dormitior(y,ies). Mansion(s). Farmhouse(s). *See also* Community (geographic locality); Demography; Households; Housing; Matrilocal residence; Migration; Neighborhoods; Patrilocal residence; Place of residence; Relocation; Rental housing; Residential mobility; Residential patterns; Residential preferences; Residential segregation; Workplaces.

Resident councils. Resident council(s). *Choose from:* resident(s), tenant(s), inmate(s), patient(s) *with:* council(s), committee(s), representation, participation. *See also* Landlord tenant relations; Rent strikes; Tenants.

Resident satisfaction. See *Community support.*

Residential care. See *Residential treatment.*

Residential change. See *Residential mobility.*

Residential development. See *Planned communities.*

Residential displacement. See *Relocation.*

Residential facilities. Residential facilit(y,ies). Hostel(s). Sheltered accommodation(s). Halfway house(s). Community living arrangement(s). Dwelling(s). Home(s). Dormitor(y,ies). Apartment(s). Flat(s). Group home(s). Residence(s). *Choose from:* residential, sheltered, inpatient *with:* facilit(y,ies), school(s), center(s), hotel(s), institution(s), accommodation(s), setting(s). *Consider also:* institutional *with:* residence(s), setting(s), living arrangement(s), accommodation(s). *See also* Assisted living; Boarding schools; Boardinghouses; Correctional institutions; Group homes; Halfway houses; Housing; Institutional homes; Institutionalization (persons); Juvenile detention homes; Nursing homes; Orphanages; Psychiatric hospitals; Reformatories; Rehabilitation centers; Residential treatment; Retirement communities; Sanatoriums; Skilled nursing facilities.

Residential mobility. Residential mobility. Relocat(e,ed,ing,ion). Geographic mobility. Wander(ed,ing,er,ers). Mov(e,ed,ing). Chang(e,ed,ing) residence(s). Chang(e,ed,ing) address(es). Resettl(e,ed,ing,ement). Population turnover. Depopulat(e,ed, ing,ion). Transferred employee(s). Ecological mobility. Migrat(e,ed,ing, ion). Emigrat(e,ed,ing,ion). Immigrat(e, ed,ing,ion). Emigrant(s). Immigrant(s). Migrant(s). *See also* Community (geographic locality); Geographic mobility; Housing; Internal migration; Migration; Neighborhoods; Relocation; Residences; Residential patterns.

Residential patterns. Residen(ce,tial) pattern(s). Housing pattern(s). *Consider also:* suburban racial composition, migratory redistribution, redlining, residential differentiation, housing class, housing discrimination, ecological structure, residential segregation, residential integration, de facto segregation, residential subdivision(s), neighborhood(s), population distribution, census tract(s), residential density, housing density, urban homesteading, equal housing opportunit(y,ies). *See also* Commuting (travel); Demography; Exclusive neighborhoods; Housing; Housing market; Land settlement; Land subdivisions; Migration; Migration patterns; Neighborhoods; Place of residence; Population distribution; Racial segregation; Racial integration; Relocation; Residential mobility; Residential segregation; Rural to urban migration; Settlement patterns; Urban to rural migration.

Residential preferences. Residential preference(s). *Choose from:* residen(ces, tial), housing, living, location(s,al) *with:* preference(s), choice(s), option(s), satisfaction(s). *See also* Cohabitation; Community attitudes; Exclusive neighborhoods; Housing; Residences; Residential segregation.

Residential segregation. Residential segregation. Redlining. Blockbusting. White flight. Ghetto(es). Hyperghettoiz(e,ed,ing,ation). Ethnic neighborhood(s). Black neighborhood(s). White neighborhood(s). De facto segregation. *Choose from:* residen(tial,ce,ces), housing, neighborhood(s), communit(y, ies), landlord(s), tenant(s) *with:* discriminat(e,ed,ing,ion), exclud(e,ed, ing), exclus(ive,ion), segregat(e,ed,ion), separatis(m,t,ts). *Consider also:* housing class(es), Fair Housing Act, Housing and Community Development Act of 1974. *See also* Desegregation; Ethnic neighborhoods; Exclusive neighborhoods; Housing; Housing market; Poverty areas; Racial integration; Racial segregation; Racism; Redlining; Residential preferences.

Residential treatment. Residential treatment. *Choose from:* resident(s,ial), inpatient(s), institutional, hospital, ward *with:* treat(ed,ing,ment,ments), care, therap(y,eutic), rehabilitat(ed,ing,ion). *See also* Hospitalization; Residential facilities.

Residents. Resident(s). Tenant(s). Occupant(s). Dweller(s). Citizen(s). Voter(s). Taxpayer(s). Ratepayer(s). Native(s). Settler(s). Inhabitant(s). Inmate(s). Squatter(s). *Consider also:* patient(s). *See also* Citizens; Community (geographic locality); Neighborhoods; Neighbors; Rural population; Tenants; Urban population; Voters.

Residual schizophrenia. Residual schizophren(ia,ias,ic,ics). Interepisodic schizophren(ia,ias,ic,ics). *See also* Schizophrenia.

Resignations. Resign(ed,ing,ation,ations). Abdicat(e,ed,ing,ion,ions). Retir(e,ed, ing,ement,ements). Step(ping) down. Quit(ting). *See also* Abdication; Attrition; Career breaks; Career change; Career mobility; Ceding; Employee turnover; Employment history; Job security; Labor market; Labor mobility; Labor supply; Personnel termination; Retirement.

Resistance. Resistan(ce,t). Resist(ing,er, ers). Noncomplian(ce,t). Confront(ed, ing,ation). Oppos(e,ed,ing,ition). Countermovement(s). Dissen(t,sion). Discord. Rebel(s,ling,lion). Defian(t,ce). Negativism. Civil disobedience. Antagonis(m,t,ts). Opponent(s). Underground. Refus(e,ed,ing,al). Repulse(d). Insurgen(t,ts,cy). Insubordinat(e,ed,ion). Mutin(y,ies). Sedition. Insurrection(s). Revolt(s). Uprising(s). Strike(s). Protest(s,er,ers). Demonstrat(ed,ing,ion,ions). Boycott(s). Struggle(s). Sabotage. *Consider also:* obstacle(s), barrier(s), red tape, imped(e,ed,ing,iment,iments). *See also* Acceptance; Approval; Change; Civil disobedience; Conflict; Countermovements; Dissatisfaction; Dissent; Guerrillas; National fronts; Peasant rebellions; Polarity; Public opposition; Public support; Rejection (psychology); Resistance movements.

Resistance, nonviolent. See *Nonviolence.*

Resistance, passive. See *Nonviolence.*

Resistance, psychotherapeutic. See *Psychotherapeutic resistance.*

Resistance movement, Islamic. See *Islamic resistance movement.*

Resistance movements. Resistance movement(s). Partisan resistance. *Choose from:* resistance, underground, anti-nazi, anti- communist, antifascis(t,m,mo), opposition, partisan(s) *with:* movement(s), conspirac(y,ies), mobiliz(e,ed,ing,ation,ations), hideout(s), secret societ(y,ies), activis(m,t,ts), forces, insurrection(s), rebellion(s). *Consider also:* underground railroad(s), freedom fighter(s), revolutionary group(s). *See also* Anti-apartheid movement; Antifascist movements; Guerrillas; Liberation movements; National fronts; Nativistic movements; Political movements; Rebellions; Resistance; Revolution; Secret societies; Underground;

Resistance to disease. See *Immunity.*

Resistance to government. See *Civil disobedience; Civil disorders; Conscientious objectors; Decolonization; Demonstrators; Guerrillas; Islamic Resistance Movement; National fronts; Nonviolence; Peasant rebellions; Political action; Protest movements; Resistance; Revolution; Social demonstrations; Separatism.*

Resisters, draft. See *Draft resisters.*

Resolution, conflict. See *Conflict resolution.*

Resolution, dispute. See *Dispute settlement.*

Resorts. Resort(s). Hotel(s). Motel(s). Inn(s). Lodge(s). Hostel(s). Tourist attraction(s). Tourist house(s). Bed and breakfast. Guest house(s). Camp(s, ground,grounds). Amusement park(s). Beach(es). Ski lodge(s). Spa(s). Cabin(s). Roadhouse(s). Motor court(s). Chalet(s). Dude ranch(es). *See also* Health resorts; Recreational facilities; Tourism.

Resorts, health. See *Health resorts.*

Resource allocation. Resource allocation. *Choose from:* resource(s), scarce resource(s), land, energy, time, suppl(y,ies), staff, personnel, equipment, medicine(s), food, water, fund(s,ing), money *with:* allocat(e,ed,ing,ion,ions), exchang(e,ed,es,ing), distribut(e,ed, ing,ion), maldistribut(e,ed,ing,ion), ration(ed,ing), decision(s), partition(ed, ing), politics, divid(e,ed,ing), division, transfer(red,ring,s), compet(e,ed,ing, ion), fair(ness), just, equit(y,able), allot(ed,ing,ment), appropriat(e,ed,ing, ion,ions), apportion(ed,ing,ment,ments), shar(e,ed,ing), disseminat(e,ed,ing,ion), budget(ed,ing). *Consider also:* triage. *See also* Administration; Allocation; Appropriations (set aside); Budgets; Capital (financial); Cost effectiveness; Delivery of services; Equity (payment); Expenditures; Financial management; Needs assessment; Priorities; Resource management; Resource stress; Resources; Sustainable development; Wills.

Resource management. Resource management. *Choose from:* conservation, protection *with:* energy, soil, water, resource(s). Organic farming. Organic agriculture. Wildlife refuge(s). Habitat protection. Forever wild. Environmental defense. Recycling. Efficient use of resources. Land use planning. *Choose from:* manag(e,ed,ing,ment), plan(ned, ning), control(led,ling), allocat(e,ed,ing, ion,ions), development, sav(e,ed,ing), incentive(s), conserv(e,ing,ation), preserv(e,ed,ing,ation), defend(ing,er, ers), protect(ed,ing,tion), maintain(ed, ing), maintenance, safeguard(ing), monitor(ing), reclaim(ed,ing), reclamation, reforest(ed,ing,ation), restor(e,ed, ing,ation), replant(ed,ing) *with:* soil, water, air, energy, atmosphere, biosphere, ecosystem(s), land, natural resource(s), woodland(s), timber(land, lands), rain forest(ry,s), swamp(s), wetland(s), desert(s), marsh(es), jungle(s), wildlife, animal(s), mammal(s), bird(s), species, plant(s), tree(s), fish(es), reptile(s). *See also* Alternative energy; Conservation of natural resources; Efficiency; Energy conservation; Energy consumption; Energy generating resources; Land use; Natural resources; Nonrenewable resources; Pollution control; Recycling; Renewable resources; Resource allocation; Resources; Soil surveys; Sustainable development.

Resource recovery. See *Recycling.*

Resource stress. Resource stress(es). Environmental stress(es). Deforestation. Pollut(e,ed,ing,ion). Crowd(ed,ing). Overcrowd(ed,ing). Inefficient use of resource(s). *Choose from:* stress(es,ed, ing), shortage(s), deplet(e,ed,ing,ion), degrad(e,ed,ing,ation), crowd(ed,ing), overcrowd(ed,ing), overgraz(ed,ing), slash and burn, overpopulat(ed,ing,ion), pollut(ed,ing,ion) *with:* energy, food, soil, water, ozone layer, ecosystem(s), resource(s), air, atmosphere, biosphere, land, natural resource(s), woodland(s), timber(land), rain forest(ry,s), swamp(s), wetland(s), desert(s), marsh(es), jungle(s), wildlife, animal(s), mammal(s), bird(s), species, plant(s), tree(s), fish(es), reptile(s). *See also* Crowding; Deforestation; Environmental degradation; Environmental pollution; Environmental stress; Greenhouse effect; Overpopulation; Slash burn agriculture; Soil conservation; Soil degradation; Soil erosion; Water pollution.

Resource teachers. Resource teacher(s). *Choose from:* resource, reading, media, music *with:* teacher(s), specialist(s), consultant(s). *See also* Teachers.

Resourcefulness. Resource(ful,fulness). Adaptab(le,ility). Inventive(ness). *Consider also:* coping, help seeking, self control, locus of control, interpersonal competence, creativ(e,ity), astute(ness). *See also* Common sense; Creative thinking; Productivity.

Resources. Resource(s). Suppl(y,ies). Reserve(s). Cache(s). Asset(s). Goods. Collective wealth. Natural wealth. Mineral(s). Material(s). *See also* Alternative energy; Assets; Capital (financial); Conservation of natural resources; Constraints; Development; Economic resources; Energy generating resources; Environment; Equipment; Facilities; Financial support; Health resources; Human resources; Marine resources; Natural resources; Needs; Nonrenewable resources; Organizations; Ownership; Raw materials; Renewable resources; Resource allocation; Resource management; Scarcity; Services; Technology; Tools; Waste to energy.

Resources, conservation of natural. See *Conservation of natural resources.*

Resources, economic. See *Economic resources.*

Resources, energy generating. See *Energy generating resources.*

Resources, health. See *Health resources.*

Resources, human. See *Human resources.*

Resources, marine. See *Marine resources.*

Resources, natural. See *Natural resources.*

Resources, nonrenewable. See *Nonrenewable resources.*

Resources, renewable. See *Renewable resources.*

Resources development, water. See *Water resources development.*

Respect. Respect. Deference. Esteem(ed). Honor(ed). High(ly) regard(ed). Admir(e,ed,ing,ation). Venerat(e,ed, ing,ion). Rever(e,ence). Homage. Praise(d). Approv(e,ed,al). Approbation. Appreciat(e,ed,ing,ion). *See also* Admiration; Honored (esteem); Human dignity; Interpersonal relations; Reputation; Self esteem; Self respect; Social behavior.

Respect, self. See *Self respect.*

Respectability. See *Decency.*

Respiration, artificial. See *Artifical respiration.*

Respiratory care units. Respiratory care unit(s). *Choose from:* respirat(or,or,ors, ory,ion) *with:* intensive care, therapy unit(s). *Consider also:* mechanical ventilatory assistance. *See also* Hospitals.

Respiratory system. Respiratory system(s). Larynx(es). Glottis. Vocal cords. Laryngeal cartilage(s). Laryngeal mucosa. Laryngeal muscle(s). Lung(s). Bronchi. Pulmonary alveoli. Nose(s). Nasal bone(s). Nasal cavit(y,ies). Nasal mucosa. Nasal septum. Nasopharynx. Turbinate(s). Concha nasalis. Paranasal sinus(es). Pleura. Trachea. *See also* Human body.

Respite care. Respite care. *Choose from:* respite *with:* care, service(s), program(s). *Consider also:* caregiver support, adult day care. *See also* Care of the sick; Caregivers; Chronic disease; Disability; Home care; Home care services.

Respondents. Respondent(s). Informant(s). Interviewee(s). Subject(s). Participant(s). Households surveyed. *Consider also:* response rate(s), nonrespon(se,ses,dent, dents). *See also* Data collection; Interviews; Questionnaires; Research subjects; Surveys.

Response, community. See *Social response.*

Response, galvanic skin. See *Galvanic skin response.*

Response, public. See *Social response.*

Response, social. See *Social response.*

Response bias. Response bias. Over-report(ed,ing). Underreport(ed,ing). Response order bias(es). Response shift bias(es). Reporting bias(es). Nonattitude(s). *Choose from:* response(s), answer(s), performance, item(s), test score(s), nonresponse(s), report(s,ed,ing), survey(s) *with:* bias(ed,es), unreliab(le,ility), inaccura(cy,te), inconsisten(t,cy), error(s). *See also* Measurement; Predisposition; Researcher bias; Statistical bias; Test bias; Test taking.

Response duration. Response duration. *Choose from:* response(s), persistence, reflex(es), keypeck(s) *with:* duration, sustain(ed,ing), long, short. *See also* Response parameters.

Response frequency. Response frequency. *Choose from:* response(s), responding, reflex(es), keypeck(s) *with:* frequen(t,cy, cies), rate(s), decrease(s,d), delay(s,ed, ing), decrement(s), interval(s), inter-response, time(s), speed, schedule(s). *See also* Response parameters.

Response generalization. Response generalization. *Choose from:* general-iz(ed,ing,ation) *with:* response(s), learning, conditioning. *See also* Response parameters.

Response interference. Response interfer-ence. *Choose from:* response(s) *with:* interference, suppress(ed,ing,ion), inhibit(ed,ing,ion). *See also* Interference (learning); Responses.

Response latency. Response latency. Interresponse time(s). *Choose from:* response(s), reflex(es), reaction(s) *with:* laten(t,cy), delay(s,ed,ing), time(s), speed, strength. *See also* Response parameters.

Response parameters. Response parameter(s). *Choose from:* response(s), reflex(es), reaction(s) *with:* parameter(s), criteria, time(s), frequen(cy,cies), amplitude, duration, latency, probabilit(y,ies), variabilit(y,ies), set(s), generalization(s). *See also* Interresponse time; Reaction time; Response duration; Response frequency; Response generali-zation; Response latency; Response probability; Response variabilty; Responses.

Response probability. Response probabil-ity. *Choose from:* response(s), reaction(s), reflex(es) *with:* probabilit(y,ies), probabilistic, model(s), prediction. *See also* Probability; Response parameters.

Response variability. Response variability. *Choose from:* response(s), reflex(es), reaction(s) *with:* variab(le,ility), covariation(s), variance, pattern(s). *See also* Response parameters.

Responses. Respons(e,es,ivity,ive,iveness). Respond(ed,ing,ent,ents). React(ance, ive,ivity,ion,ions,ionary). Reflex(es). Repl(y,ies,ied). Answer(s). Rejoinder(s). Acknowledge(ment). *See also* Alarm responses; Anniversary reactions; Burnout; Conditioned responses; Conditioned suppression; Conditioning (psychology); Dyssocial reaction; Emotional responses; Escape reaction; Feedback; Galvanic skin response; Interaction; Mediated responses; Orienting responses; Reaction time; Response interference; Response parameters; Shock; Social response; Startle reaction; Stimuli; Stranger reactions; Stress reactions; Uncondi-tioned responses.

Responses (liturgical). Response(s). Responsive reading(s). Litan(y,ies, ia,iae). Responsorial singing. Liturgical dialogue(s). *Choose from:* invok(e,ed, ing), invocation(s), supplication(s), petition(s), versicle(s) *with:* respon(d, ded,ding,ive,e,es,sorial). *Consider also:* responsor(y,ies,ia,ium). *See also* Choral music; Liturgy.

Responses, alarm. See *Alarm responses.*

Responses, conditioned. See *Conditioned responses.*

Responses, emotional. See *Emotional responses.*

Responses, mediated. See *Mediated responses.*

Responses, orienting. See *Orienting responses.*

Responses, unconditioned. See *Uncondi-tioned responses.*

Responsibilities. See *Duties; Obligations.*

Responsibility (answerability). Responsib(le,ility). Accountab(le,ility). Liab(le,ility). Answerab(le,ility). Brought to account. Bring(ing) to account. *See also* Accountability; Authority (officials); Consumer protection; Corporate social responsibility; Duties; Ethics; Fiduciary responsibility; Filial responsibility; Integrity; Leadership; Liability; Malpractice; Moral authority; Moral obligation; Obligations; Personal independence; Political leadership; Professional liability; Professional malpractice; Social behavior; Social responsibility.

Responsibility, administrative. See *Administrative responsibility*

Responsibility, community. See *Corporate social responsibility.*

Responsibility, corporate social. See *Corporate social responsibility.*

Responsibility, diminished. See *Insanity defense.*

Responsibility, fiduciary. See *Fiduciary responsibility.*

Responsibility, filial. See *Filial responsibility.*

Responsibility, legal. See *Liability*

Responsibility, ministerial government. See *Ministerial responsibility (government).*

Responsibility, moral. See *Moral obligation.*

Responsibility, social. See *Social responsibility.*

Responsible (socially), investing. See *Socially responsible investing.*

Responsories. See *Responses (liturgical).*

Rest. Rest(ed,ing). Work break(s). Coffee break(s). Lie down. Nap(ped,ping,s). Rest(ing) period(s). Relax(ed,ing,ation). Catnap(s). *Consider also:* bed-rest, sleep, repose, slumber(ed,ing), doz(e,ed,ing), siesta(s), recess(es), time off, inactivity, pause(s). *See also* Dormancy; Inactivity; Relaxation; Sleep; Work rest cycles.

Rest, day of. See *Sabbath.*

Restaurants. Restaurant(s). Cafeteria(s). Cafe(s). Coffee shop(s). Coffeehouse(s). Diner(s). Tavern(s). Pub(s). Brewpub(s). Lunchroom(s). Luncheonette(s). Eating place(s). Eating establishment(s). Eating house(s). Delicatessen(s). Lunch counter(s). Lunchroom(s). Buffet(s). Pizzeria(s). Grill(s). Steakhouse(s). Tearoom(s). Snack bar(s). Fast food outlet(s). *See also* Bars; Coffee houses; Cybercafes; Eating establishments.

Restitution. Restitution. Victim compensation. Replevin. Replev(y,ying,ied,iable). Seisin. Seizin. Mak(e,ing) amends. Mak(e,ing) good. Recompense. Reparation(s). Redress. Atonement. Retribution. Indemni(ty,ification). Repayment. Requital. *Consider also:* war debt payment(s), community service *with:* offender(s), settlement, remunera-

tion. *See also* Alternatives to incarceration; Compensation (payment); Correctional system; Criminal justice; Offenders; Reparations; Reprisals Restorative justice; Sentencing; Victimization; War damage compensation; War victims.

Restlessness. Restless(ness). Dysphor(ia,ic). Psychomotor agitation. Akathis(ia,ic). Akathes(ia,ic). Kathisophob(ia,ic). Acathis(ia,ic). Akatiz(ia,ic). Acathiz(ia,ic). Agitat(ed,ion,ional). Behavioral excitement. Fidget(ed,ing,y). Unrest. Excite(d,ment). Inability to concentrate. Concentration disturbance(s). Uneas(y,iness). Restive. Jumpy. Nervous(ness). Unsettled. Perturbed. Disturbed. Distracted. *See also* Agitation; Concentration difficulties; Hyperkinesis; Motor activity; Psychomotor agitation; Symptoms.

Restoration ecology. Restoration ecology. Bioremediat(e,ed,ing,ion). Phytoremediat(e,ed,ing,ion). *Choose from:* restor(e,ed,ing,ation), rehabilitat(e,ed,ing,ion), revitaliz(e,ed,ing,ation), recover(y,ed,ing), decontaminat(e,ed,ing,ation), remediat(e,es,ed,ing,ion), reclaim(ed,ing), reclamation, cleanup(s), clean(ed,ing) up, *with:* ecosystem(s), ecolog(y,ical), habitat(s), river(s,ine), lake(s), wetland(s), ground water, waterway(s), public land(s), soil(s), species. *Consider also:* reintroduc(e,ed, ing,tion) native species, manag(e,ed, ing,ement) of ecological integrity. *See also* Agricultural ecology; Conservation of natural resources; Containment of biohazards; Decontamination; Ecosysytem management; Environment; Environmental protection; Environmentalism; Forest conservation; Irrigation; Land preservation; Neighborhood preservation; Organic farming; Plant succession; Pollution control; Quality of life; Reclamation of land; Reforestation; Renewable resources; Soil conservation; Tree planting; Wildlife conservation; Wildlife sanctuaries.

Restorative justice. Restorative justice. Restorative sentencing. Restorative service sanction(s). Reparative justice. Victim-offender reparation(s). Victim-offender mediation. *Choose from:* offender(s), criminal(s), delinquent(s) *with:* restorat(ive,ion,ions), rectify(ing) wrong(s), compensat(e,ed,ing,ion) damage(s), reparat(ive,ion,ions), mak(e,ing) redress, seek(ing) forgiveness, victim compensation. *Consider also:* Navajo Peacemaker Courts, community service. *See also* Alternatives to incarceration; Criminal rehabilitation; Deinstitutionalization; Parole; Reparations; Restitution; Sentencing; Volunteers.

Restraint, emotional. See *Emotional control.*

Restraint, judicial. See *Judicial restraint*

Restraint, physical. See *Physical restraint.*

Restraint of trade. Restraint of trade. Unfair trade practice(s). *Choose from:* restrict(ive), limit(s,ed,ing), barrier(s), imped(e,ed,ing,iment,iments) *with:* trade, business practice(s), competit(ive, iveness,ion). *Consider also:* monopol(y, ies), price fixing, collus(ion,ive), vertical restraint(s). *See also* Antitrust law; Injustice; Monopolies; Price fixing; Trade.

Restraints. Restrain(ed,ing,t,ts). Constraint(s). Contain(ment). Control(led,ling). Deter(rence,rent). Hold back. Barrier(s). Restrict(ed,ing, ions). Limit(ed,ing,ations). Control(led, ling). Disciplin(e,ed,ing). Repress(ed, ing,ion). Inhibit(ed,ing,ion). Stifl(e,ed, ing). Suppress(ed,ing,ion). *See also* Access to education; Access to information; Architectural accessibility; Barriers; Boundaries; Constraints; Development; Emotional control; Freedom; Inhibition (psychology); Laws; Limitations; Needs; Opportunities; Physical restraint; Problems; Resources; Restrictions.

Restrictions. Restrict(ed,ing,ion,ions). Confin(e,ed,ing,ement). Restrain(ed,ing, t,ts). Limit(ed,ing,ations). Delimit(ed, ing,ations). Constraint(s). Barrier(s). Control(led,ling). Disciplin(e,ed,ing). Repress(ed,ing). Inhibit(ed,ing). Stifl(e,ed,ing). Suppress(ed,ing). Taboo(s). *See also* Barriers; Constraints; Formal social control; Laws; Limitations; Regulations; Restraints; Taboo.

Restructuring. See *Reorganization.*

Restructuring, cognitive. See *Cognitive restructuring.*

Results. Result(ant,s). Effect(s). Consequen(t,ces). Outcome(s). Sequel(ae). Repercussion(s). Aftereffect(s). Product(s). By-product(s). Backlash. Outgrowth. Side effect(s). Reaction(s). Aftermath. Response(s). Impact(s). Eventualit(y,ies). Conclusion(s). Harvest(s). *Consider also:* evaluation. *See also* Accountability; Consequences; Drug effects; Educational attainment; Educational objectives; Effectiveness; Effects; Failure; Followup studies; Knowledge of results; Longitudinal studies; Program evaluation; Psychotherapeutic outcomes; Treatment efficacy; Treatment outcome; Sequelae; Success.

Results, knowledge of. See *Knowledge of results.*

Resuscitate, orders do not. See *Do not resuscitate orders*

Retailing. Retail(er,ers,ing). Retail industry. Retail outlet(s). Merchant(s). Vendor(s). Shop(s). Store(s). Supermarket(s). Direct sale(s). Discount house(s). Fast food chain(s). Department store(s). Shopping mall(s). Shopping center(s). *See also* Advertising; Brand names; Business; Consumer behavior; Consumers; Department stores; Discount stores; Discounts; Loyalty cards; Market research; Marketing; Merchants; Purchasing; Sales; Sales personnel; Second hand trade; Shopping centers; Stores; Street vendors; Trade.

Retaliation. See *Reprisals.*

Retardation, attitudes toward mental. See *Attitudes toward mental retardation.*

Retardation, borderline mental. See *Borderline mental retardation.*

Retardation, mental. See *Mental retardation.*

Retardation, mild mental. See *Educable mentally retarded.*

Retardation, psychosocial mental. See *Psychosocial mental retardation.*

Retarded, educable mentally. See *Educable mentally retarded.*

Retarded, education of mentally. See *Education of mentally retarded.*

Retarded, home reared. See *Home reared mentally retarded.*

Retarded, institutionalized. See *Institutionalized mentally retarded.*

Retarded, mentally. See *Mental retardation.*

Retarded, profoundly mentally. See *Profoundly mentally retarded.*

Retarded, severely mentally. See *Severely mentally retarded.*

Retarded, trainable mentally. See *Trainable mentally retarded.*

Retarded speech development. Retarded speech development. *Choose from:* delayed, slow, retard(ed,ation) *with:* speech, language, articulation, talking, phonological(ly). *See also* Delayed development; Language delayed; Speech development; Speech disorders.

Retention (psychology). Retention. Memor(yize,ized,izing). Retain(ed,ing). Reminiscen(t,ce). Remember(ed,ing). Recogni(ze,zed,zing,tion). Recall(ed, ing). Recollection(s). Memoriz(e,ed,ing, ation). Learn(ed,ing). Response persistence. *See also* Advance organizers; Cues; Extinction (psychology); Forgetting; Habituation (psychophysiology); Interference (learning); Learning; Memory; Mnemonic learning; Primacy effect; Recall; Redundancy; Reminiscence; Retention measures; Rote learning.

Retention measures. Retention measure(s). *Choose from:* retention, recall, recognition, memory *with:* measure(s,ment),

scale(s), assessment(s), batter(y,ies), questionnaire(s), test(s,ed,ing), task(s), score(s). *See also* Measurement; Retention (psychology).

Retirement. Retir(e,ed,ee,ees,ing,ement). Pension(ed,er,ers). Annuitant(s). Discontinue(d) work(ing). Preretirement. Postretirement. Withdraw(al) from workforce. Disengagement. Superannuat(ed,ion). *Choose from:* early, flexible, involuntary, voluntary, mandatory, compulsory *with:* retir(e,ed, ees,ing,ement). *Consider also:* over 65, over sixty five, 70 plus, seventy plus. *See also* Age discrimination; Aged 80 and over; Attitudes toward the aged; Early retirement; Elderly; Employee turnover; Employment history; Flexible retirement; Involuntary retirement; Job security; Leisure time; Life stage transitions; Mandatory retirement; Pensions; Personnel policy; Personnel termination; Privatized pension systems; Retirement communities; Retirement income; Retirement planning; Status; Unemployment; Workers.

Retirement, compulsory. See *Involuntary retirement; Mandatory retirement.*

Retirement, early. See *Early retirement.*

Retirement, flexible. See *Flexible retirement.*

Retirement, forced. See *Involuntary retirement; Mandatory retirement.*

Retirement, involuntary. See *Involuntary retirement.*

Retirement, mandatory. See *Mandatory retirement.*

Retirement, phased. See *Flexible retirement.*

Retirement benefits. See *Pensions; Retirement income.*

Retirement communities. Retirement communit(y,ies). *Choose from:* retirement, life care, senior, adult, long term care, LTC, sheltered, age segregated *with:* housing, home(s), center(s), living facilit(y,ies), communit(y,ies), village(s), residen(ces,tial), new town(s), subdivision(s). *See also* Assisted living; Boardinghouses; Group homes; Life care; New towns; Nursing homes; Retirement; Sheltered housing.

Retirement housing. See *Retirement communities.*

Retirement income. Retirement income. Pension(s). Social security. Annuit(y, ies). Pension plan(s). Old age assistance. Keogh plan(s). Independent retirement account(s). IRA(s). *Consider also:* retir(e,ed,ee,ees,ing,ement), superannuat(e,ed,ion), postretirement *with:* pay, benefit(s), system(s), income, savings, investment(s), plan(s), nest egg(s). *See also* Annuities; Compensation (pay-

ment); Deferred compensation; Employee benefits; Financial planning; Military pensions; Pensions; Privatized pension systems; Retirement; Retirement planning; Salaries; Wages.

Retirement planning. Retirement plan(s,ning,ned). *Choose from:* retirement, preretirement *with:* plan(s,ning,ned), prepar(e,ed,ing,ation). *See also* Deferred compensation; Financial planning; Pensions; Privatized pension systems; Retirement; Retirement income.

Retraining. Retrain(ed,ing). Refresher course(s). Recertif(y,ied,ication). Re-entry train(ed,ing). Occupational rehabilitation. Re-educat(e,ed,ing,ion). Re-skilling. *Consider also:* train(ed,ing), new skill(s) *with:* mid-career, mid-life, retiree(s), older worker(s), ex-offender(s), laid-off, displaced, dislocated, re-entry. *See also* Adult education; Career breaks; Continuing education; Dislocated workers; Displaced homemakers; Inservice training; Occupations; Reentry women; Rehabilitation; Skill learning; Skills obsolescence; Work reentry.

Retreat, military. See *Military retreat.*

Retreats. See *Artists' colonies; Sanctuaries; Vacation houses.*

Retreats, corporate. See *Corporate retreats.*

Retreats, management. See *Corporate retreats.*

Retribution. See *Punishment; Restitution.*

Retrieval, automated information. See *Automated information retrieval.*

Retrieval, online information. See *Automated information retrieval.*

Retrieval systems, information. See *Automated information retrieval.*

Retroactive inhibition. Retroactive inhibition. Retroaction. *Choose from:* retroactive, latent, prior knowledge *with:* inhibit(ed,ing,ion), interference, effect(s). *See also* Interference (learning).

Retrospective studies. Retrospective stud(y,ies). *Choose from:* retrospective, case control *with:* stud(y,ies), analys(is,es), survey(s), trial(s), control(s). *See also* Research.

Return migration. Return migra(nts,tion). Repatriat(e,ion). Reverse migration. Population turnaround. Migration loop(s). Reoccup(y,ying,ied,ation). Returnee(s). Homeland(s) movement. *Choose from:* population, migrat(ion, ory,ing), migrant(s), exile(s), emigrant(s), expatriate(s) *with:* revers(al,e,es,ing), turnaround, loop(s), return(ing). *See also* Migration; Repatriation; Urban to rural migration.

Reunification. See *Armistices; Peace negotiations; Unification.*

Reunions, family. See *Family reunions*

Reuse, water. See *Water reuse.*

Revealed theology. Revealed theology. Divine revelation(s). *Consider also:* Divine will, mysteries of faith, revealed knowledge, revealed truth(s), Heilsgeschichte theology, Covenantal theology. *See also* Antinomianism; Attributes of God; Creationism; Creeds; Disclosure; Dogma; Faith; God concepts; Immanence of God; Natural theology; Reason; Religious beliefs; Religious doctrines; Religious literature; Theology; Theophany; Will of God.

Revelation. See *Disclosure.*

Revelation, self. See *Self disclosure.*

Revenants. See *Ghosts.*

Revenge. Reveng(e,eful,efulness,ing). Venge(ance,ful). Aveng(e,ed,ing). Retaliat(e,ed,ing,ion,ory). Punitive(ness). Retribution. Reprisal(s). Exact(ing) satisfaction. Vendetta(s). Blood feud(s). Death feud(s). Unforgiving. *Consider also:* vindicat(e,ed,ion). *See also* Hate; Hate crimes; Feuds; Privateers; Punishment; Punitiveness; Reprisals; Restitution; Shrunken heads.

Revenue. Revenue(s). Income(s). Earning(s). Amount earned. Yield(s). Salar(y,ies). Rate(s) of return. Remunerat(ion,ive). Compensat(e,ed, ing,ion). Payment(s) received. Wage(s). Interest earned. Family allowance. Earned money. Receipt(s). Profit(s). Proceeds. Gains. Honorar(ia,ium). Annuit(y,ies). Pension(s). Subsid(y,ies). Stipend(s). Recompense. Paycheck(s). Monetary reward(s). Monetary allowance(s). *See also* Budgets; Capital (financial); Compensation (payment); Economics; Expenditures; Finance; Gross national product; Income distribution; Income inequality; Informal sector; Living standards; Low income; Money; Pensions; Profits; Salaries; Saving; Taxes; Wages; Wealth.

Reverie, directed therapy. See *Directed reverie therapy.*

Reversal, role. See *Role reversal.*

Reversal, sex. See *Sex change.*

Reversal learning. Reversal learning. *Choose from:* shift, reversal *with:* learning, stud(y,ies). *See also* Discrimination (psychology); Learning.

Reverse discrimination. Reverse discrimination. *Choose from:* preferential treatment, undeserving advantage *with:* protected class(es), minorit(y,ies), women. Bakke decision. *See also* Affirmative action; Age discrimination; Attitudes toward handicapped; Equal education; Equal job opportunities;

Racial segregation; Racism; Sex discrimination; Sexism; Social discrimination.

Review, life. See *Life review.*

Review, peer. See *Peer review.*

Reviews. Review(s). Overview(s). History of development. Comparison of views. Critical survey(s). Critique(s). Survey(s) of work. *Choose from:* research, information, literature, state of the art *with:* review(s), analy(sis,ses), comparison(s), summar(y,ies,ization), survey(s). *See also* Art criticism; Book reviews; Evaluation; Literary criticism.

Reviews, book. See *Book reviews.*

Reviews, literature. See *Book reviews; Literary criticism; Reviews.*

Reviews, research. See *Reviews.*

Revisionism. Revision(ist,ists,ism). Critical reinterpretation. Doctrin(e,es,al) innovation(s). Rewrit(e,ing) history. *Consider also:* deviation(ist,ists,ism), here(sy,sies,tical). *See also* Communism; Marxism; Socialism.

Revitalization. See *Enlightenment (state of mind); Religious conversion; Religious revivals; Salvation; Urban renewal.*

Revival, classic. See *Classic revival*

Revival, evangelical. See *Evangelical revival.*

Revival, gothic. See *Gothic revival.*

Revivals, religious. See *Religious revivals.*

Revolts. See *Rebellions.*

Revolution. Revolution(s,ary). *Choose from:* fundamental, basic, radical, large scale, sweeping, complete, macrostructure(s), paradigm(s) *with:* transformation(s), change(s), restructur(ed,ing), replacement(s). Chang(e,es,ed,ing) in power structure. *Choose from:* social, political, cultural, industrial, urban, computer, scientific, technological, nonviolent, peaceful, peasant, palace, permanent *with:* revolution(s). *Consider also:* coups d'etat, overthrow(n,ing), war(s) of national liberation, revolt(s), rebellion(s), insurgenc(y,ies). *See also* Activism; Anti-government radicals; Change; Civil war; Conflict resolution; Coups d'Etat; Cultural conflict; Developing countries; Dissent; Economic change; Founding fathers; Future of society; Guerrillas; History; Ideological struggle; Industrialization; Marxism; National fronts; Paradigms; Peasant rebellions; Political ideologies; Political movements; Political revolutions; Political violence; Rebellions; Resistance movements; Scientific revolutions; Sexual revolution; Social action; Social change; Social reform; Technological progress; Terrorism; Theory formation; Underground; Violence; War; World problems.

Revolution, industrial. See *Industrialization.*

Revolution, sexual. See *Sexual revolution.*

Revolution, social. See *Revolution.*

Revolutionary ballads and songs. Revolutionary ballad(s). Revolutionary song(s). *Choose from:* revolution(ary), rebel(s,lion), insurrection(ist) *with:* ballad(s), music, song(s), singing, chorus(es), folksong(s), chant(s), tune(s), ditt(y,ies), anthem(s), recording(s), melod(y,ies), hymn(s). *Consider also:* Yankee Doodle, Marseillaise, the Internationale, etc. *See also* Civil war; Folk songs; Guerrillas; Labor songs; Peasant rebellions; Political revolutions; Protest songs; Rebellions; Songs.

Revolutionary movements. See *Decolonization; Guerrillas; National fronts; Nationalism; Nativism; Patriotism; Peasant rebellions; Political self determination; Protest movements; Radical movements; Separatism; Social movements.*

Revolutions, political. See *Political revolutions.*

Revolutions, scientific. See *Scientific revolutions.*

Revolutions, technological. See *Scientific revolutions.*

Reward. Reward(s,ing). Incentive(s). Token(s). Payoff. Praise. Gratif(y,ied,ication). Bonus(es). Merit pay. Honorari(a,um). Prize(s). Reinforcement. Positive feedback. Encouragement. Recognition. Recompense. Acknowledgement. Award(s). Accolade(s). Troph(y,ies). Oscar(s). Emmy(s). Grammy(s). Tony(s). Decoration(s). Medal(s,lions). Honor(s,ed). *See also* Awards; Compensation (payment); Deferred compensation; Delay of gratification; External rewards; Glory; Hunting trophies; Incentives; Internal rewards; Meritocracy; Monetary rewards; Motivation; Positive sanctions; Preferred rewards; Recognition (achievement); Self reinforcement; Social closure; Social exchange; Social reinforcement; Token economy.

Rewards, external. See *External rewards.*

Rewards, internal. See *Internal rewards.*

Rewards, job. See *Employee benefits; Compensation (payment).*

Rewards, monetary. See *Monetary rewards.*

Rewards, preferred. See *Preferred rewards.*

Rhetoric. Rhetoric(al,ian,ians). Orator(y, ical,s). Oration(s). Eloquen(t,ce). Expressive(ness). Elocution. Command of word(s). Forceful speaker(s). Persuasive communication. Powerful argument(ation,s). Glib(ness). *Choose from:* insincer(e,ity), false, showy, grandiloquent, declamatory, persuasive, convincing *with:* speech, expression, words, speaker(s). *See also* Apologetics (Rhetoric); Closure (Rhetoric); Debate; Discourse; Discussion; Eloquence; Language; Lectures and lecturing; Oratory; Persuasion; Political rhetoric; Propaganda; Public speaking; Speech; Speeches (formal discourse).

Rhetoric, political. See *Political rhetoric.*

Rhymes. Rhym(e,es,ed,ing). Verse(s). Limerick(s). Jingle(s). Ditt(y,ies). Versif(y,ying,ied,ication). *See also* Children's poetry; Nursery rhymes; Poetry.

Rhymes, nursery. See *Nursery rhymes.*

Rhythm. Rhythm(s,ic,os,us,e). Ritmo(s). Tempo(s). Temporal flux(es). Metric cycle(s). Musical beat(s). Metric accent(s). Caden(ce,ces,cy,tial). Drum beat(s). Recurring sequence(s). *Consider also:* metronome(s), accent(uation), puls(e,ed,ing,ation), throb(bed,bing), syncopat(ed,ion). *See also* Biological rhythms; Cadence; Dance; Marches; Meter (poetry).

Rhythm, alpha. See *Alpha rhythm.*

Rhythm and blues. Rhythm and blues. Rhythm 'n' blues. R 'n' B. *Consider also:* the Ravens, the Orioles, the Drifters, the Coasters, urban blues. *See also* Afro-American music; Disco music; Heavy metal (music); Popular music.

Rhythm method. Rhythm method. Ovulation method. Temperature method. Safe period. Billings method. Temperature rhythm method. *Consider also:* natural *with:* family planning, birth planning, birth regulation, birth control. *See also* Birth control; Contraception; Family planning.

Rhythms, biological. See *Biological rhythms.*

Rhythms, circadian. See *Biological rhythms.*

Right, new. See *Right wing politics.*

Right, religious. See *Religious fundamentalism.*

Right and wrong, sense of. See *Conscience.*

Right of assembly. Right of assembly. Freedom to protest. Freedom of assembly. Right to protest. Public forum doctrine. Right of association. Constitutional protection of parade organizers. *Consider also:* right to free speech, First Amendment right(s). *See also* Bill of Rights; Freedom of speech.

Right of asylum. Right of asylum. *Choose from:* right(s), polic(y,ies), law(s), adjudication, standard(s), Board of Immigration Appeal(s), requirement(s), petition(s) *with:* asylum, sanctuary, seek(ing) refuge. *Consider also:* underground railroad, diplomatic asylum, humanitarian immigration, sanctuary movement. *See also* Authors in exile; Deportation; Forced migration; Illegal aliens; Immigration; Political asylum; Political defection; Purges; Refugees.

Right of pasture. Right of pasture. *Choose from:* common, right(s), permit(s), public land(s), lease(s) *with:* pasture(s, land,lands), grazing, forag(e,ing), rangeland(s). *Consider also:* Taylor Grazing Act, pastoral leasehold(s). *See also* Agricultural laws and legislation; Cattle industry; Grazing lands; Home range; Land (property); Open spaces; Public lands; Ranches; Rangelands; Rural areas, Rural land.

Right of privacy. Right of privacy. Privacy right(s). Privacy issue(s). Confidentiality. Confidential record(s). Personal space. Privileged communication(s). Patient privacy. Student privacy. Privacy act of 1974. Privacy legislation. *Choose from:* priva(cy,te,teness), confidential(ity), privy, anonym(ity,ous), seclusion, solitude *with:* right(s,ful), legitima(cy,te), entitle(d), deserv(e,ed, ing). *See also* Bill of Rights; Civil rights; Confidential communications; Confidential records; Confidentiality; Eavesdropping; Electronic eavesdropping; Human rights; Libel; Online privacy; Patient rights; Physician patient relations; Privacy; Privacy laws; Search and seizure; Student rights; Surveillance of citizens.

Right to die. Right to die. Death with dignity. Living will(s). Rational suicide. Hemlock society. Brophy case. Quinlan case. Conroy case. Nancy Cruzan case. *Choose from:* right(s) *with:* die, choose death, terminally ill, suicide, voluntary death, terminate treatment(s), euthanasia. *See also* Assisted suicide; Euthanasia; Human rights; Life extension; Life support care.

Right to know. See *Freedom of information.*

Right to life. See *Antiabortion movement.*

Right to work. Right to work. *Consider also:* open shop(s). *See also* Union shop.

Right wing politics. Right wing politics. Right wing. Moral majority. New right. Ultraright. Right wing extremis(m,ts). New Christian right. Religious right. Christian politics. Neoconservat(ism, ive). Republican right. Radical right. Political right. Law and order. Fundamentalis(m,t). Political(ly) conservat(ive,ism). Right(ism,ist,ists).

Traditionalis(m,t). Sociopolitically conservative. Conservatism. *Choose from:* conservative, traditional, right wing, neoconservative *with:* ideolog(y, ies), candidate(s), values, movement(s), perspective(s), opinions, viewpoint(s), orientation, attitudes, vot(e,ers,ing), polic(y,ies), politics, doctrine(s). *Consider also:* authoritarianism, diehard, oppos(ed,ing) change, orthodox(y,ness), preserving the status quo, resist(ance) to change, reactionary, Tory, Birchism, Hunkerism, redneck(s), bigot(s,ry), McCarthyism. *See also* Anti-environmentalism; Conservative; Extremism; Left wing; McCarthyism; Political conservatism; Politics; Traditionalism; Vigilantes.

Rights. Right(ful,s). Libert(y,ies). Freedom(s). Independence. Autonomy. Self govern(ing,ment). Citizenship. Self-determination. Prerogative(s). Perquisite(s). Just claim(s). Entitle(d, ment,ments). Birthright(s). Authorized. Sanctioned. Deserving. Immunit(y,ies). Exemption(s). License(s,d). Benefit(s). Priorit(y,ies). Carte blanche. Laissez faire. Latitude. Enfranchise(d,ment). Legitimate. *See also* Animal welfare; Bill of Rights; Carte blanche; Children's rights; Civil rights; Claims; Client rights; Freedom; Freedom of information; Freedom of religion; Freedom of speech; Freedom of the press; Human rights; Law (legal philosophy and theory); Legal rights; License agreements; Moral obligation; Obligations; Parent rights; Patient rights; Political self determination; Property rights; Reproductive rights; Right of privacy; Right to die; Right to work; Social justice; Voting rights; Women's rights.

Rights, abortion movement. See *Abortion rights movement.*

Rights, animal. See *Animal welfare.*

Rights, Bill of. See *Bill of Rights.*

Rights, children's. See *Children's rights.*

Rights, civil. See *Civil rights.*

Rights, civil movement. See *Civil rights organizations.*

Rights, client. See *Client rights.*

Rights, equal for women. See *Women's rights.*

Rights, gay. See *Homosexual liberation movement.*

Rights, human. See *Human rights.*

Rights, individual. See *Bill of rights; Civil rights; Human rights.*

Rights, legal. See *Legal rights.*

Rights, maternal. See *Parent rights.*

Rights, natural. See *Human rights.*

Rights, parent. See *Parent rights.*

Rights, parental. See *Parent rights.*

Rights, paternal. See *Parent rights.*

Rights, patient. See *Patient rights.*

Rights, political. See *Bill of rights; Civil rights; Human rights; Political self determination.*

Rights, prisoners'. See *Prisoners' rights.*

Rights, property. See *Property rights.*

Rights, reproductive. See *Reproductive rights.*

Rights, student. See *Student rights.*

Rights, voting. See *Voting rights.*

Rights, women's. See *Women's rights.*

Rights, workers'. See *Workers' rights.*

Rights associations, human. See *Abortion rights movement; Activism; Anti-apartheid movement; Antiabortion movement; Black power; Civil disobedience; Civil rights organizations; Disability rights movement; Gray power; Homosexual liberation movement; Interest groups; Labor movements; Peace movements; Political movements; Protest movements; Social movements; Suffrage movement; Women's groups; Women's rights; Youth movements.*

Rights for women, equal. See *Women's rights.*

Rights movement, disability. See *Disability rights movement.*

Rights organizations, civil. See *Civil rights organizations.*

Rights violations, human. See *Medical ethics; Oppression; Political prisoners; Political repression; War crimes.*

Rigid personality. Rigid personalit(y,ies). Inflexib(le,ility). Intoleran(t,ce). Dogmat(ic,ism). Tradition bound. Authoritarian(ism). Moralistic. Prejudice(d). Einstellung. Mental set(s). Mindless(ly,ness). *Choose from:* closed, literal, narrow, single *with:* mind(ded, dedness). *Choose from:* rigid(ity), inflexib(le,ility) *with:* personalit(y,ies), mindset(s), mind-set(s), thinking, habit(s), learner(s), behavior(s,al). *See also* Authoritarianism (psychological); Dichotomous thinking; Dogmatism; Personality traits.

Rigidity. See *Rigid personality.*

Ringing, change. See *Change ringing*

Riots. Riot(ing,er,ers,s). Crowd action. Civil disorder(s). Rebel(s,lion,lions). Brawl(s,ed,ing). Street fight(s,ing). Institutional disturbance(s). Violent crowd(s). Angry mob(s). Insurrection(s). Hooligan(s,ism). Loot(ed,ing). Mob law. Mob rule. Mobocrac(y,ies). Vigilante rule(s). Mayhem. Collective violence. Unlawful assembly. Rac(e,ial) war(s).

Pogrom(s). *Consider also:* racial disorder(s), lynching. *Choose from:* ghetto, street, mob(s), crowd(s), rac(e,ial), social, institution(s,al), stadium(s), prison(s) *with:* disorder(s), rebel(s,lions), revolt(s), fight(s,ing), disturbance(s), uprising(s), angry, anger, insurrection(s), loot(ed,ing), violence, unlawful, war(s), lynch(ed,ing). *See also* Aggression; Civil disorders; Collective behavior; Conflict; Confusion (disarray); Crowds; Political violence; Prison violence; Rebellions; Social unrest.

Risk. Risk(y,s,iness). Chance. Speculat(ive, ion). Gambl(e,ing). Venture. Risk/ benefit. Risky shift. Uncertain(ty,ties). Jeopard(y,ize). Adventur(e,ous,ousness). Danger(ous,ousness). Hazard(ous, ousness). Liab(le,ility). Insecur(e,ity). Vulnerab(le,ility). Precarious(ness). Life threatening. *Consider also:* probabil(ity, istic), play odds, long shot, tak(e,en,ing) chance(s), speculat(e,ed,ing,ion), daredevil(s), thrill seeking, risk factor(s). *See also* Chance; Cost effectiveness; Decision making; Entrepreneurship; Game theory; Hazards; Insurance; Prediction; Probability; Reliability; Risk assessment; Risk management; Risk taking; Security; Social behavior; Threat.

Risk, high borrowers. See *High risk borrowers.*

Risk, high persons. See *High risk persons.*

Risk analysis. See *Risk assessment.*

Risk assessment. Risk assessment. *Choose from:* risk(y,s,iness), chance(s), uncertain(ty,ties), danger(s,ous,ousness), hazard(s,ous,ousness), liabilit(y,ies), vulnerabilit(y,ies) *with:* assess(ed,ing, ment,ments), identif(y,ied,ication), analys(is,es), perception(s), judgment(s), predict(ed,ing,ion,ions), probab(le, ility,ilities), likelihood. *See also* Evaluation; Forecasting; Risk.

Risk management. Risk management. *Choose from:* risk(s), hazard(s), danger(s), error(s), uncertain(ty,ties), vulnerab(le,ility,ilities) *with:* manage-ment, prevent(ed,ing,ion), cut(ting), reduc(e,ed,ing,tion), control(led,ling), hedg(e,ed,ing), eliminat(e,ed,ing). *Consider also:* hedge fund(s), safety, warning(s), risk assessment. *See also* Asset management; Pension fund management; Risk; Safety.

Risk taking. Risk taking. Gambl(e,ed,er, ers,ing). Bet(s,ting). *Choose from:* play(ed,ing) *with:* odds, horse(s), market(s). Speculat(e,ed,ing,ion). Daredevil(s). Long shots. Thrill seeking. Ventur(e,ed,ing). Brinksmanship. *Choose from:* risk(s,y), chance(s), dangerous sport(s) *with:* tak(e,en,ing), attitude(s), preference(s), decision(s), choice(s), cautious(ness), shift(s). *See also* Adventure; Extreme sports;

Gambling; Needle sharing; Risk; Sensation seeking; Social behavior; Speculation.

Rites. See *Rituals.*

Rites, birth. See *Birth rites.*

Rites, fetal propitiatory. See *Fetal propitiatory rites.*

Rites, funeral. See *Funeral rites.*

Rites, initiation. See *Initiation rites.*

Rites, marriage. See *Weddings.*

Rites, puberty. See *Rites of passage; Puberty.*

Rites, purification. See *Purification rites.*

Rites, sacrificial. See *Sacrificial rites.*

Rites of passage. Rite(s) of passage. Rites de passage. Passage rite(s). Status passage. Sacrament(s). Graduation(s). Bar Mitzvah. Bat Mitzvah. Bas Mitzvah. Christening(s). Baptism(s). Wedding(s). Funeral(s). *Choose from:* rite(s), ceremon(y,ies), celebration(s), ritual(s) *with:* passage(s), transition(s), puberty, initiation(s), birth(s), marriage(s), death(s), separation(s), transition(s), incorporation, conversion(s), transform-ation(s), confirmation(s), bedtime, parting(s). *Choose from:* liminal(ity) *with:* phase(s), period(s), entit(y,ies), state(s). *Consider also:* funerary ritual(s). *See also* Birth rites; Circumci-sion; Confirmation; Female circumcision (ritual); Funeral rites; Initiation rites; Life stage transitions; Puberty; Religious rituals; Ritual disfigurement; Rituals; Taboo; Traditions; Weddings.

Ritual disfigurement. Ritual disfigurement. Ritual(istic) scarification. *Choose from:* ritual(istic), cultural(ly), custom(s), symbolic, satanic *with:* disfigur(e,ed,ing, ement), mutilat(e,ed,ing,ion), tattoo(s,ed,ing), scarif(y,ied,ication), cicatriz(e,ed,ing,ation), wound(s), filing teeth, pierc(e,ed,ing). *Consider also:* ritual(istic) abuse(s), genital mutilation. *See also* Body art; Body piercing; Female circumcision (ritual); Initiation rites; Physical disfigurement; Religious rituals; Rites of passage; Torture; Violence.

Ritual murder. See *Human sacrifice.*

Ritual objects. See *Ceremonial objects.*

Ritual purity. Ritual purity. Theology of purity. *Choose from:* ritual(ized,istic), ceremonial(ly), pray(ed,ing,er,ers), sanctif(y,ied,ying,ication), sacrifical *with:* pur(e,ity), purif(y,ied,ying,ication), sexual abstinence, celiba(te,cy), bath(ed,ing), abstention, abstain(ed,ing), ascetic(ism), kashrut(h), kosher, mikveh, clean(liness). *Consider also:* trans-form(ed,ing,ation) of unclean(ness), ritual impurit(y,ies), lustrat(e,ed,ing, ation). *See also* Contamination;

Purification rites; Purity; Religious rituals; Scapegoating; Symbolism; Taboo; Virginity.

Rituals. Ritual(ized,s). Rite(s). Symbolic behavior. Formal behavior. Formalit(y, ies). Nicet(y,ies). Tradition(al,s). Ceremon(y,ies). Celebration(s). Fiesta(s). Festival(s). Carnival(s). Masquerade(s). Funeral practice(s). Feast(s). Feast day(s). Mardi Gras. Coronation(s). Ritual healing. Mourning. Wake(s). Funeral(s). Shower(s). Communion(s). Observance(s). Liturg(y,ies). Sacrament(s). Potlatch(es). Cult practice(s). Gift giving. Handshak(e,ing). Bowing. Kneeling. Genuflect(ing,ion). *See also* Cannibalism; Ceremonies; Culture (anthropology); Customs; Death rituals; Festivals; Gift giving; Human sacrifice; Holidays; Mythology; Religious rituals; Rites of passage; Symbolism; Traditional societies; Traditions; Weddings.

Rituals, death. See *Death rituals.*

Rituals, religious. See *Religious rituals.*

Rivalry. Rival(s,ry). Competit(ion,or,ors). Compet(e,ed,ing). Opponent(s). Oppos(e,ed,ing,ition). Antagonis(m,t,ts). Jealous(y). Vie(d). Vying. Contend(ed, ing,er,ers). Conflict(s). Contest(ed,ing, ant,ants). Challeng(e,ed,er,ers,ing). One-upmanship. *See also* Challenge; Competition; Competitive behavior; Conflict; Disputes; Interpersonal relations; Jealousy; Literary quarrels; Sibling relations; Social behavior.

Rivers. River(s). Stream(s). Tributar(y,ies). Creek(s). Brook(s). Rivulet(s). *Consider also:* estuar(y,ies). *See also* Floods; Geopolitics; Inland water transportation; International rivers; Oceans; Stream channelization; Streams; Territorial waters; Tides; Water levels; Water pollution; Water transportation.

Rivers, international. See *International rivers.*

Road rage. Road rage. Violent road behavior. Aggressive driv(ing,er,ers). *Choose from:* hostil(e,ity), rage, enraged, anger, aggress(ive,ively,ion, ions,or,ors), hostile, violen(ce,t), reckless(ly), argument(s), fight(s,ing), shout(ed,ing), gesticulat(e,ed,ing), physically threaten(ed,ing), obscenit(y,ies), fury, assault(s,ed,ing), shoot(ing,ings), gun(s), harass(ed,ing, ment,ments), *with:* driv(e,er,ers,ing), motor(ing,s), motorist(s), highway(s), freeway(s), traffic jam(s), automotive, automobile(s), car(s), road(s). *Consider also:* frustration, stress, impatien(t,ce) *with:* driv(e,er,ers,ing), motor(ing,s), motorist(s), highway(s), freeway(s), traffic jam(s), road(s), violator(s). *See also* Aggression; Air rage; Anger; Antisocial behavior; Automobile driving; Belligerency; Driveby crimes;

Highway safety; Hostility; Impatience; Resentment; Violence.

Roads. Road(s). Street(s). Highway(s). Turnpike(s). Thruway(s). Freeway(s). Parkway(s). Road(s,ways). Express-way(s). Toll road(s). Route(s). Interstate highway(s). Superhighway(s). Thoroughfare(s). Causeway(s). Access road(s). Arterial(s). Traffic route(s). Boulevard(s). Freeway(s). Autobahn. Frontage. *See also* Automobiles; Crossroads; Highway safety; Highways; Transportation.

Robbers, brigands and. See *Bandits.*

Robbery. Rob(ber,bers,bery). Theft(s). Thie(f,ves,vry). Fraud(ulent). Steal(ing). Stole(n). Burglar(y,s). Shoplift(ing,er, ers). Pilfer(age,ed,ing). Hold up. Held up. Heist(s). Embezzl(e,ing,ement, er,ers). Misappropriat(ed,ing,ion,ions). Purse snatching. Mugg(er,ers,ed,ing, ings). Bootleg(ging,ger,gers). Larcen(y, ous). Poach(ing,er,ers). Plunder(ed,ing). Swindl(e,er,ers,ing). Pira(te,tes,cy). Ripoff(s). Hijack(ing,er,ers). Kidnap(ped,ping,per,pers). *See also* Assault (personal); Bandits; Booty (International law); Burglary; Crime; Grave robbing; Larceny; Theft; Thieves.

Robbing, grave. See *Grave robbing.*

Robotics. Robot(s,ic,ics,ically,ization). Cybernated. Domotic(s). Automated assembl(y,ies). Automatically guided. Multirobot(ic,s). Automated manufacturing. Unmanned vehicle(s). Factory automation. Autonomous land vehicle(s). Autonomous vehicle(s). Telerobot(ic,ics,s). Automaton(s). *Consider also:* animatron(ic,ics), knowbot(s,ics), cobot(s,ics), microbot(s,ics). *See also* Artificial intelligence; Automation; Bionics; Cybernetics; Factory automation; Man machine systems.

Rock and roll. Rock and roll. Rock 'n' roll. *Consider also:* Elvis Presley, Jerry Lee Lewis, Everly Brothers, Chuck Berry, Little Richard, Fats Domino, Paul Anka, Frankie Avalon, Beach Boys, etc. *See also* Afro-American music; Disco music; Heavy metal (music); Popular music; Rock music; Rock musicians.

Rock art. See *Cave paintings; Carving (decorative arts); Petroglyphs.*

Rock carvings. See *Petroglyphs.*

Rock drawings. See *Cave paintings; Petroglyphs.*

Rock engravings. See *Petroglyphs.*

Rock music. Rock music. *Choose from:* jazz, art, folk, country, progressive *with:* rock. *Consider also:* punk music, punk rock, alternative-rock, grunge sound, postpunk, punk grunge, new wave, rock videos, Jefferson Airplane, Rolling Stones, Grateful Dead, Jefferson

Starship, Beatles, Sex Pistols, etc. *See also* Afro-American music; Disco music; Heavy metal (music); Popular music; Rock and roll; Rock musicians.

Rock musicians. Rock musician(s). Rock star(s). *Choose from:* rock *with:* musician(s), singer(s), songwriter(s), group(s), band(s), bandleader(s), performer(s), guitarist(s), star(s), Hall of Fame. *Consider also:* rocker(s), Rolling Stones, Grateful Dead, MTV, Elvis Presley, The Beatles, etc. *See also* Heavy metal (music); Musicians; Rock and roll; Rock music.

Rocking, body. See *Body rocking.*

Rods, divining. See *Divining rods.*

Rogues. Rogue(s). Knave(s). Scapegrace(s). Rascal(s). Wastrel(s). Villain(s). Miscreant(s). Blackguard(s). Scoundrel(s). *Consider also:* lowlife, roper(y,ipe), good-for-nothing, blighter(s), bounder(s), ringer(s), impostor(s), charlatan(s), bad guy(s), trickster(s). *See also* Antisocial behavior; Bandits; Deviant behavior; Offenders; Tricksters.

Role, counselor. See *Therapist role.*

Role, father. See *Father child communication; Father child relations; Parent role; Paternal behavior.*

Role, female. See *Gender identity; Images of women Sex roles.*

Role, male. See *Gender identity; Sex roles.*

Role, men's. See *Gender identity; Sex roles.*

Role, mother. See *Maternal behavior; Maternal love; Mother child communication; Mother child relations; Parent role.*

Role, parent. See *Parent role.*

Role, physicians. See *Physicians role.*

Role, sick. See *Sick role.*

Role, state. See *State role.*

Role, therapist. See *Therapist role.*

Role, woman's. See *Gender identity; Sex roles.*

Role, women's. See *Gender identity; Sex roles.*

Role ambiguity. Role ambiguit(y,ies). Roleless(ness). *Choose from:* role(s), function(s), dut(y,ies), status, position(s) *with:* ambigu(ity,ous,ousness), ambivalen(t,ce), overlap, diffusion, lack of definition, stress, multiplicity. *See also* Occupational roles; Role conflict; Roles; Self concept; Social identity; Status inconsistency.

Role attitudes, sex. See *Sex role attitudes.*

Role changes. Role change(s). *Choose from:* role(s), function(s), position(s), status, duties *with:* change(s), transition(s), discontinuit(y,ies). *See also*

Adult development; Life stage transitions; Midcareer change; Midlife crisis; Roles.

Role conflict. Role conflict(s). Multiple role involvement. Dual commitment(s). Contradictory role(s). Conflicting image(s). *Choose from:* role(s), interrole, multiple role(s), double role(s), dual role(s), dual career(s), dual profession(s), dual function(s), dual position(s) *with:* strain(s), stress(es,or,ors), demand(s), conflict(s,ing), spillover, ambiguit(y,ies), problem(s), incongruen(t,ce,cy,cies), confusion, discrepan(t,cy,cies), inconsisten(t,cy, cies), incompatibilit(y,ies), distress(es), overload(s), balancing. *Consider also:* career home conflict(s), working mother(s), work family role(s), work family conflict(s), role related problem(s), role reversal, role sharing, role distance, househusband(s), unemployed father(s). *See also* Alienation; Ambivalence; Caregiver burden; Conflict; Conflict of interest; Family work relationship; Internal conflict; Role ambiguity; Roles; Self concept; Self congruence; Sex roles; Social identity; Status inconsistency; Working women.

Role expectations. Role expectation(s). *Choose from:* role(s), position(s), job(s), *with:* expect(ed,ation,ations), norm(s), demand(s), function(s), dut(y,ies), concept(s,ion,ions), definition(s), attribution(s), stereotype(s,d), image(s), perception(s). *Consider also:* professional socialization, expected behavior, role profile(s), ideal(ized) role, role orientation. *See also* Expectations; Role perception; Roles.

Role identity, sex. See *Gender identity.*

Role models. Role model(s). *Consider also:* role identif(y,ied,ication), role identit(y,ies), mentor(s), behavior modelling, imitation, ego ideal, exemplar(s,ism), professional socialization, significant other(s), hero(es), idol(s), role ideal(ization). *See also* Example; Identification (psychology); Imitation; Mentors; Moral authority; Occupational roles; Observational learning; Sex roles; Role perception; Roles; Social influences; Significant others; Socialization.

Role orientations, sex. See *Gender identity; Sex role attitudes; Sexual orientation.*

Role perception. Role perception. Perception of responsibilit(y,ies). *Choose from:* role(s), function(s), dut(y,ies), status, position(s), *with:* perceiv(e,ed,ing), perception(s), attitude(s), concept(s,ion, ions), view(s), definition(s), identif(y, ied,ication), identit(y,ies), stereotype(s), image(s). *Consider also:* professional identit(y,ies), professional socialization, role expectation(s). *See also* Identification (psychology); Perspective taking;

Role expectations; Role playing; Role taking; Roles; Self actualization; Stereotyping.

Role playing. Role play(ing). Sociodrama(s, tic). Socio-drama(s,tic). Roleplay(ing). Behavioral rehearsal(s). Simulated famil(y,ies). *Choose from:* role(s) *with:* play(ing), game(s), portrayal(s), enact(ed,ing,ment,ments), rehearsal(s), accept(ed,ing,ance), act(ing), performance. *Consider also:* dramaturg(y,ic, ical,ically). *See also* Childhood play development; Group dynamics; Psychodrama; Perspective taking; Psychotherapy; Role perception; Role taking; Roles; Simulation games; Teaching methods.

Role reversal. Role reversal. *Choose from:* role(s), function(s), dut(y,ies), status, position(s) *with:* reversal(s), inconsistenc(y,ies). *Consider also:* pathological nurturance, househusband(s). *See also* Role ambiguity; Role conflict; Roles.

Role satisfaction. See *Job satisfaction; Life satisfaction.*

Role taking. Role taking. *Choose from:* emotional, interpersonal, social *with:* understanding, perception, cognition. *Choose from:* role(s), perspective(s), view(s,point,points) *with:* tak(e,en,ing). *Consider also:* empath(y,ic), verstehen. *See also* Egocentrism; Perspective taking; Role perception; Role playing; Roles.

Role transitions. See *Life stage transitions; Role changes.*

Roles. Role(s). Social position(s). Expected behavior(s). Social function(s). Professional function(s). Position in pecking order. Professional position. Status. Identit(y,ies). Purpose(s). Social position. Dut(y,ies). *Consider also:* stereotype(s), images(s), socialization, persona(s). *See also* Ascription; Behavior; Division of labor; Family roles; Function; Individuals; Life stage transitions; Norms; Occupational roles; Parent role; Parenthood; Physicians role; Role ambiguity; Role changes; Role conflict; Role expectations; Role models; Role perception; Role playing; Role reversal; Role taking; Sex role attitudes; Sex roles; Sexual division of labor; Sick role; Social status; Social types; State role; Therapist role.

Roles, conjugal. See *Family roles; Sex roles; Sexual division of labor.*

Roles, family. See *Family roles.*

Roles, gender. See *Sex roles.*

Roles, marital. See *Family roles; Parent role; Sex roles; Sexual division of labor.*

Roles, occupational. See *Occupational roles.*

Roles, sex. See *Sex roles.*

Roles, social. See *Roles.*

Roles, work. See *Occupational roles.*

Roman and Greek games. See *Greek and Roman games.*

Roman Catholicism. Roman Catholic(ism). Vatican. Pope. Ultramontane. Papacy. Papal. Rosar(y,ies). *Choose from:* Catholic *with:* church(es), archbishop(s), bishop(s), priest(s), clergy, nun(s), parish(s), diocese(s), mass(es), Eucharist. Latin rite. Council of Trent. Sacrament(s). Apostolic succession. Jesuit(s). *Consider also:* Ignatius of Antioch, Thomas Aquinas, Alphonsus Liguori, Pius XII, John XXIII, Paul VI, John Paul II. *See also* Christianity; Clergy; Confession; Contemplative orders; Excommunication; Monasticism; Papacy; Priests; Protestant reformation; Religions; Religious affiliation; Religious communities; Religious personnel; Saints.

Roman law. Roman law(s). *Choose from:* Roman(s), Rome, plebeian(s), praetor(s,ium), Latin *with:* law(s), legal system, edict(s), formulary, juristic writing(s). *Consider also:* Twelve Tables, legis actio(nes), jus civile, jus gentium, jus honorarium, judex, Theodosian code, Breviary of Alaric, Corpus Juris Civilis, classical law, Lex Romana Visigothorum, Justinian's codification. *See also* Ancient literature; Antiquity (time); Codes (rules); Laws; Legal procedures; Rule of law.

Roman, nouveau. See *Nouveau roman.*

Romance languages. Romance language(s). Romanic language(s). Catalan. Dalmatian. French: Canadian French, Haitian, Creole, Louisiana French, Old French. Galician. Italian: Tuscan, Old Italian. Moldavian. Portuguese: Brazilian Portuguese, Old Portuguese. Provencal. Old Provencal. Romanic: Friulian, Ladin, Romansh, Romanian [Roumanian, Rumanian], Sardinian. Spanish: American Spanish, Philippine Spanish, Judeo Spanish [Ladino, Sephardic], Old Spanish. *Consider also:* Italic language(s). *See also* Italic non-romance languages; Language; Languages (as subjects); Western Europe.

Romances, gothic. See *Gothic romances*

Romantic love. Romantic love. Eros. Roman(ce,tic). Beloved. Amorous(ness). Sentiment. Tenderness. Ador(e,ing, ation). Lover(s). Intima(cy,te). Infatuat(ed,ion). *Consider also:* romantic, conjugal, heterosexual, homosexual, puppy, courtly, adolescent *with:* love, attraction, attachment(s), involvement(s), feeling(s). *See also* Affection; Forms of affection; Human courtship; Love; Love letters; Love poetry; Love songs; Love stories.

Romanticism. Romanticis(ts,m). Romantic ideal. Romantic movement. Romantic school. *Consider also:* neo-romantic(ism,ists), folk-oriented nationalism, anti-formalism. *See also* Artistic styles; Literary movements; Literature; Music.

Rondo. Rondo(s). Episodic form(s). *Consider also:* rondeau(x), sonata-rondo. *See also* Music.

Room, mail. See *Mail room.*

Roommates. Roommate(s). Room mate(s). Suite mate(s). *Choose from:* residential, domestic *with:* dyad(s,ic), triad(s,ic), partnership(s). Liv(e,ing) together. *See also* Cohabitation.

Rooms, clean. See *Clean rooms.*

Rooms, delivery. See *Delivery rooms.*

Rooms, operating. See *Operating rooms.*

Rooms, recovery. See *Recovery rooms.*

Roots, grass. See *Citizen participation; Community involvement; Community power; Community support; Local government; Local politics; Neighborhood associations; Populism.*

Rope. Rope(s). Line(s). String(s). Cord(s). Knot(s). Wire rope(s). Jump(ing) rope(s). Skip(ping) rope(s). Nylon rope(s). Leather rope(s). Nylon rope(s). Plastic rope(s). Braided rope(s). *Consider also:* cable(s). *See also* Sisal hemp.

Rotation, circulation. See *Circulation (rotation).*

Rotation, job. See *Job rotation.*

Rote learning. Rote learning. Memoriz(e, ed,ing,ation). Parrot(ed,ing). Verbatim. *Choose from:* rote, drill *with:* learn(ed, ing), task(s). Learn(ed,ing) by heart. *See also* Learning; Practice (repetition); Primacy effect; Retention (psychology); Serial learning.

Routes, sea. See *Trade routes.*

Routes, trade. See *Trade routes.*

Royal favorites. Royal favorite(s). *Choose from:* royal(ty), court, king(s), queen(s), prince(s), princess(es) *with:* patronage, favorit(e,es,ism), partial(ity), preference(s), nepotism, pet(s). *See also* Favoritism; Monarchy; Nepotism; Preferences; Preferential treatment; Privilege; Royalty.

Royal patronage. See *Royal favorites.*

Royal supremacy. Royal supremacy. Supremacy of the King. *Choose from:* king(s,dom), royal(ty), monarch(s,y,ies), queen(s), prince(s), throne, ruler(s), crown(s), potentate(s) *with:* suprem(e, acy), preeminen(t,ce), predominan(t,ce), power, authority, omnipoten(t,ce), ascendan(t,cy), dominion, masterdom, preponderan(ce,cy), prepoten(t,ce,cy),

sovereign(ty). *See also* Divine right of kings; Emperor worship; Monarchy; Royalty; Sovereignty.

Royalty. Royal(ty). Monarch(s,y). King(s). Queen(s). Aristocracy. Emperor(s). Royal family. Titled person(s). Heir(s) to throne. Royal heir(s). Crown prince(s). Prince(s,ess,esses). Duke(s). Duchess(es). Peerage. Emir(s). Sultan(s). Her Majesty. Royal house. Throne. Czar(s). Tsar(s). Kaiser(s). Caesar(s). Earl(s). Noble ancestry. Nobility. Noble(man,men). Pharoah(s). Shah(s). Royal couple. Sovereign(s). Dynast(y,ies). Royal line. Marquis(es). Marquess(es). Viscount(s). Baron(s). *See also* Aristocracy; Eminence; Emperor worship; Monarchy; Palaces; Royal favorites; Royal supremacy.

Rubber industry. Rubber industry. *Choose from:* rubber, latex(es), india rubber, caoutchouc *with:* industr(y,ies,ial), manufactur(e,er,ing,ed), compan(y,ies), process(es,ed,ing), produc(e,ed,er,ers, ing,tion), firm(s), vulcaniz(e,ed,es,ing, ation), corp(oration,orations), import(ed, ing,s), export(ed,ing,s), market(s). *Consider also:* Goodyear Tire and Rubber, recycled rubber, rubber hose(s), rubber chemistry, rubber goods, artificial rubber, reclaimed rubber, tire industry. *See also* Automobile industry; Industry.

Rubbish disposal. See *Waste disposal.*

Ruined cities. See *Extinct cities.*

Ruins. Ruin(s,ation). Remains. Remnant(s). Wreck(s,age). Debris. Detritus. Vestige(s). *Consider also:* relic(s), fossil(s), remainder(s). *See also* Debris; Extinct cities; Fragments; Historic sites.

Rule, boss. See *Boss rule.*

Rule, home. See *Home rule.*

Rule, indirect government. See *Indirect rule (government).*

Rule, M'Naghten. See *Insanity defense.*

Rule, McNaughton. See *Insanity defense.*

Rule of law. Rule of law. Supremacy of law. *Consider also:* Stare decisis. *See also* Due process; Justice; Legal procedures; Legal system; Roman law.

Ruler worship. See *Emperor worship.*

Rulers, kings and. See *Aristocracy; Emperors; Monarchy; Oligarchy; Ruling class.*

Rules (generalizations). Rule(s). Generaliz(e,ed,ing,ation,ations). Generalit(y,ies). Classification(s). Principle(s). Inference(s). Law(s). General statement(s). Categoriz(e,ed, ing,ation,ations). *Consider also:* invariable rule(s), empirically verifiable hypothes(is,es), *See also* Canons; Codes (rules); Cognitive generalization; Generalities; Hypotheses; Laws; Norms;

Principles; Social norms; Theories.

Rules, codes. See *Codes (rules).*

Rules, social. See *Social norms.*

Ruling class. Ruling class(es). Dominant class(es). Ruling clique(s). Mandarin(s, ate). Hegemon(y,ies). Political elite(s). Power elite(s). Head(s) of state. Intelligentsia. Oligarch(y,ies). Owning class(es). Upper class(es). Corporate class(es). Establishment(s). Civil religious hierarch(y,ies). Plutocrac(y, ies). *See also* Aristocracy; Chiefs; Elites; Elitism (government); Governing boards; Government; Heads of state; Interlocking directorates; Monarchy; Oligarchy; Political elites; Political power; Power elite; Power structure; Privilege; Social class; Social status; Social stratification; Upper class.

Rumors. Rumor(ed,s,monger,mongers). Bruited about. Gossip(ed,ing). Hearsay. Grapevine(s). Whispering campaign(s). Mud slinging. Scandal(s). Scuttlebutt. *See also* Announcements; Conversation; Defamation; Gossip; Gossip sites; Labeling (of persons); Libel; Messages; Political campaigns; Public opinion; Reputation; Rumors; Scandals; Scapegoating; Trivia; Truth; Witch hunting.

Runaway parents. See *Desertion.*

Runaway slaves. See *Fugitive slaves.*

Runaways. Runaway(s). Run(ning) away. Ran away. Flee(ing). Fled. Tak(e,ing) flight. Took flight. Desert(ing,er,ers). Escap(ing,ee,ees). Break(ing) away. Living on the street. Abscond(ing,ed,er, ers). Pushout(s). Throway(s). Truant(s). Fugitive(s). *Choose from:* runaway(s), homeless, missing, street, out-of-home, status offender(s) *with:* child(ren,hood), kid(s), youth, teenager(s), adolescen(t,ts, ce). *See also* Desertion; Deviant behavior; Family relations; Homeless; Juvenile delinquency; Military desertion; Missing persons; Parent child relations; Single parent family; Student dropouts; Truancy.

Running. Run(ning). Ran. Jog(ging,ged). Trot(ted,ting). Canter(ed,ing). Gallop(ed,ing). Sprint(ed,ing). Foot race(s). Marathon race(s). Pacer(s). Dash(ed,ing). Mile race(s). Treadmill(s). Wheelrunning. Triathlon(s). *See also* Athletic participation; Physical education; Physical fitness.

Rural architecture. See *Farmhouses.*

Rural areas. Rural area(s). Hinterland(s). Small town(s). Prairie(s). Hamlet(s). Ranch(es). Farm(s). Countryside. Village(s). Small communit(y,ies). Hometown(s). Nonmetropolitan. Unincorporated area(s). *Choose from:* rural, outlying, isolated, remote, peasant, farm(ing), agricultural, wilderness, unsettled, forest, pastoral, mountain(s, ous), sparsely populated, *with:* environment(s), area(s), setting(s), region(s), communit(y,ies), school district(s), town(s), region(s), territor(y, ies), count(y,ies). *See also* Agrarian societies; Agricultural collectives; Farming; Farms; Geographic regions; Hinterland; Metropolitan areas; Pastoral societies; Rangelands; Right of pasture; Rural communities; Rural development; Rural education; Rural health; Rural housing; Rural industries; Rural land; Rural mental health; Rural population; Rural to urban migration; Rural urban differences; Rural women; Rural youth; Small farms; Towns; Urban fringe; Urban to rural migration.

Rural communities. Rural communit(y,ies). Small town(s). Village(s). Small communit(y,ies). Hometown(s). Hick town(s). Crossroad(s). Hamlet(s). Main street. Rural habitat. *Choose from:* rural, outlying, isolated, remote, peasant, mountain, farm(ing), agricultural, wilderness, pastoral *with:* communit(y, ies), school district(s), town(s), settlement(s), village(s), burg(s). *See also* Community (geographic locality); Community (social); Farm life; Peasants; Rural areas; Rural conditions; Rural population; Rustic life.

Rural conditions. Rural condition(s). Country life. *Choose from:* countryside, rural, Australian bush, outback, hinterland(s), agrarian, frontier town(s), small village(s), fishing communit(y, ies), farm(s,ing), remote area(s), sparsely populated area(s) *with:* condition(s), situation(s), circumstance(s), poverty, wealth, prosperity, health, welfare, population, people, life, culture, society, social organization. *See also* Country life; Rural population; Rural communities.

Rural development. Rural development. Land reclamation. *Choose from:* rural, agricultur(e,al), farm(s,land,lands), agrarian, village(s), developing countr(y,ies), third world, hinterland(s), countryside *with:* moderniz(e,ed,ing, ation), mechaniz(e,ed,ing,ation), electrif(y,ied,ication), power generat(or,ors,ion), reform(s), reclaim(ed,ing), industrializ(ed,ing, ation), irrigat(e,ed,ing,ation), plan(s,ned,ning), building, built, construct(ed,ing,ion), improv(ed,ing,ement, ements), progress, evolution, evolv(ed, ing), gain(ed,ing), technolog(y,ies,ical), grow(th,ing), expan(d,ding,sion), develop(ed,ing,ment,ments), agribusiness(es), commercializ(e,ed, ing,ation), transform(ed,ing,ation). *See also* Agribusiness; Agricultural assistance; Agricultural diversification; Agricultural extension; Agricultural mechanization; Community develop-

ment; Development; Economic development; Electrification; Growth management; Irrigation; Land reform; Land use; Modernization; Regional development; Rural areas; Rural industries; Rural land; Sustainable development; Urban development.

Rural education. Rural education. One room schoolhouse(s). *Choose from:* rural, small town, country, long distance, Indian reservation(s) *with:* educat(ed, ing,ion), teacher(s), school(s,house, houses), student(s), pupil(s), course(s), grade(s), kindergarten(s), class(es,room, rooms), learner(s), school district(s), high school(s), junior high school(s), middle school(s), elementary school(s). *See also* Agricultural extension; Rural areas; Schools.

Rural electrification. See *Rural development.*

Rural environments. See *Rural areas.*

Rural health. Rural health. Agricultural workers disease(s). *Choose from:* rural, peasant, farm(ing), agricultural, pastoral, small town, agrarian, country, Appalachia(n) *with:* health, hygiene, medicine, medical, disease(s), disorder(s), morbidity, mortality, nutrition, illness(es), hospital(s), sanita(ry,tion), cancer, tuberculosis, malnutrition, hookworm, accident(s), epidemiolog(y,ical), epidemic(s), quality of life. *See also* Agricultural workers disease; Community health services; Community mental health services; Rural areas; Rural mental health.

Rural housing. Rural hous(e,es,ing). *Choose from:* rural, small town, outlying, isolated, remote, peasant, mountain, farm(ing), agricultural, wilderness, pastoral *with:* hous(e,es,ing) home(s), cottage(s), dwelling(s), residence(s), homestead(s), trailer(s), mobile home(s). *Consider also:* farmhouse(s). *See also* Farm life; Farmhouses; Housing; Rural areas; Rural population.

Rural industries. Rural industr(y,ies). *Choose from:* rural, countryside, agrarian, village(s), township(s), hinterland(s) *with:* industr(y,ies,ial), enterprise(s), manufacturing, small business(es), family firm(s), small firm(s). *See also* Agribusiness; Agricultural mechanization; Economic development; Electrification; Modernization; Regional development; Rural areas; Rural Development; Sustainable development.

Rural land. Rural land(s). Farmland(s). Rangeland(s). Wetland(s). Woodland(s). *Choose from:* rural, agricultural, farm(ing), forest(s) *with:* land(s), area(s), region(s). *Consider also:* right to farm, deforestation, rain forest, *See also* Agribusiness; Agricultural diversifica-

tion; Growth management; Hinterland; Land reform; Land use; Rangelands; Regional development; Right of pasture; Rural areas; Rural Development.

Rural life. See *Country life.*

Rural mental health. Rural mental health. *Choose from:* rural, peasant, farm(ing), agricultural, pastoral, small town, agrarian, country, Appalachia(n) *with:* mental, emotional, psychiatric, psychological, psycho(ses,sis,tic), neuro(ses,sis,tic), alcoholi(c,ism), schizophren(ia,ic), depress(ive,ion), drug abuse(rs), substance abuse(rs), substance dependence, drug dependence. *See also* Mental health; Rural areas; Rural health.

Rural population. Rural population(s). Villager(s). Homesteader(s). Residents of small communit(y,ies). *Choose from:* rural, peasant, farm(ing), agricultural, pastoral, small town, agrarian, country *with:* population(s), dweller(s), resident(s), inhabitant(s), occupant(s), worker(s), adult(s), child(ren), men, women, people, person(s), famil(y,ies), youth, communit(y,ies), congregation(s), student(s), folk, demography, citizen(s,ry). *See also* Agricultural workers; Demography; Family farms; Groups; Internal migration; Population; Population distribution; Population growth; Residents; Rural areas; Rural communities; Rural conditions; Rural housing; Rural to urban migration; Rural urban differences; Rural women; Rural youth; Urban population; Urban to rural migration.

Rural to urban migration. Rural to urban migration. Rural urban migrant(s). Back to the city. Peasant migra(nt,nts,tion). Squatter(s). Rural out migration. Rural urban turnaround. Farm migration(s). Rural exodus. Urbanization. Farm to city migration. *Consider also:* interregional migration(s). *See also* Internal migration; Metropolitan areas; Migration; Rural areas; Rural population; Urban population; Urban to rural migration; Urban sprawl; Urbanization.

Rural urban differences. Rural urban differences. *Choose from:* rural, hometown(s), hinterland(s), small town(s), ranch(es), farm(s), village(s), countryside, nonmetropolitan, outlying area(s), isolated area(s), remote area(s), peasant(s), farm(ing), agricultural area(s), wilderness, unsettled area(s), forest(s), pastoral region(s), sparsely populated *with:* urban(ized,ization), cit(y,ies), municipal(ity,ities), metropolitan *with:* differen(ce,ces,tials), contrast(ed,ing,s), compar(ison,isons, ative,ability), discrepanc(y,ies), dissimilar(ity,ities), disparit(y,ies), distinct(ions,iveness), inequalit(y,ies), variation(s). *See also* Differences; Gemeinschaft and gesellschaft;

Lifestyle; Metropolitan areas; Regional differences; Rural areas; Urbanism.

Rural women. Rural women. *Choose from:* rural, hometown(s), hinterland(s), small town(s), ranch(er,ers,es), farm(er,ers, ing), village(s,r,rs), peasant(s), agricultur(e,al), pioneer(s,ing), country *with:* women, woman, female(s), wife, wives, housewi(fe,ves), homemaker(s), mother(s), daughter(s), sister(s), aunt(s), grandmother(s). *See also* Females (human); Rural areas; Rural population.

Rural youth. Rural youth. 4-H group(s). Future farmer(s). *Choose from:* rural, hometown(s), hinterland(s), small town(s), ranch(er,ers,es), farm(er,ers, ing), village(s,r,rs), peasant(s), agricultural, 4-H, country *with:* youth, young adult(s), teenager(s), adolescen(t,ts,ce), young men, young women, juvenile(s), young people, high school student(s). *See also* Rural areas; Rural population; Young adults.

Rustic life. Rustic life. Pastoral scene(s). Country life. Simple life. Rural life. *See also* Country life; Farm life; Idyll; Rural communities.

S

Sabbath. Sabbath. Day of worship. Day of rest. Friday. Saturday. Sunday. Lord's day. Seventh day. *See also* Holidays; Leisure time; Religious practices; Time; Work rest cycles.

Sabotage. Sabotage(d). Saboteur(s). Treachery. Subvers(ion,ive). Mischief. Wreck(ed,ing). Computer virus(es). Letter bomb(s). Arson(ists). Spanner in the work(s). Ecotage. Cybotage. *Choose from:* deliberate(ly), purposely, intentionally *with:* contaminat(e,ed,ing), damag(e,ed,ing), disabl(e,ed,ing), undermin(e,ed,ing). *Choose from:* terroris(t,ts,m) *with:* attack(s), bomb(s). *Choose from:* tamper(ed,ing) *with:* brakes, food, pill(s), bottle(s). *See also* Arson; Computer crimes; Defacement; Espionage; Product tampering; Terrorism; Vandalism.

Sacred animals. Sacred animal(s). *Choose from:* sacred, revered, worship(ed,ped), venerated, religious belief(s), religious significance, gods, divine incarnation(s) *with:* animal(s), bear(s), jackal(s), wolves, antelope(s), cat(s), ibis(es), boar(s), turtle(s), cow(s). *See also* Animism; Human-animal relationships; Pantheism (polytheism); Pantheism (universal divinity); Personification; Reptiles; Religious beliefs; Totemism.

Sacred books. Sacred book(s). *Choose from:* sacred, holy, consecrated, devotional, church(ly), spiritual(ity), venerated, religious *with:* book(s), text(s), writing(s), literature. *Consider also:* Bible(s), Koran, Talmud, Torah, apocryphal book(s), New Testament, Old Testament, Lindisfarne Gospels. *See also* Apocalyptic literature; Books of hours; Liturgical books; Prayerbooks; Religious literature; Sacred songs; Sacredness.

Sacred meals. Sacred meal(s). *Choose from:* sacred, ritual, ceremonial, sacrificial *with:* meal(s), supper(s), feast(s), eating and drinking, break(ing) bread. *Consider also:* seder(s), Lord's supper, agape, thanksgiving meal(s), Eucharist. *See also* Dinners and dining; Fasting; Festivals; Grace at meals; Holidays.

Sacred places. Sacred place(s). *Choose from:* sacred, holy, venerated, consecrated, hallowed *with:* place(s), land(s), cit(y,ies), ground(s), site(s), space(s), domain(s). *Consider also:* reliquar(y, ies), altar(s), ark(s), bema, bima(h). *See also* Chapels; Churches; Mosques; Religious buildings; Religious institutions; Sanctuaries; Shrines; Spiritual exercises; Synagogues; Temples.

Sacred songs. Sacred song(s). Hymn(s,al, als). *Choose from:* sacred, religious, gospel, holy, devotional, church(ly), spiritual(ity), liturgical *with:* song(s), lyric(s), chant(s), melod(y,ies), tune(s), refrain(s), chorus(es), response(s). *See also* Devotional poetry; Religious rituals; Sacred books; Sacredness; Songs.

Sacredness. Sacred(ness). Sacral(ize,ized, izing,ization). Hol(y,iness). Saint(ed,ly, hood). Religious. Revere(d). Reverence. Consecrate(d). Dedicate(d). Sanctif(y, ied). Blessed. Hallowed. Purified. Sanctity. Sacrosanct. Enshrined. Beatified. Anointed. Divine revelation. Scriptural authority. Venerated. *See also* Apotheosis; Holy men; Holy women; Mana; Places of worship; Religious beliefs; Religious literature; Religious personnel; Sacred books; Sacred songs; Saints; Secularization; Shrines.

Sacrifice, animal. See *Animal sacrifice.*

Sacrifice, self. See *Self sacrifice.*

Sacrifices, human. See *Human sacrifice.*

Sacrificial rites. Sacrificial rite(s). Ritual killing(s). *Choose from:* sacrific(ial,e,es, ed), offering(s), oblation(s), immolation, renounc(e,ed,ing), consecrat(e,ed,ing) *with:* ritual(ized,s), rite(s), symbol(ic, ism), tradition(al,s), ceremon(y,ies,ial), celebration(s), practice(s), feast(s), event(s), healing, mourning, funeral(s). *Consider also:* cult(s,ic), human, blood, killing(s), child(ren), food, drink, incense, animal(s), first born, scapegoat(s) *with:* sacrific(ial,e,es,ed), offering(s), oblation(s). *Consider also:* communion. *See also* Animal sacrifice; Austerities; Abstinence; Cannibalism; Deities; Human sacrifice; Paganism; Religious rituals; Self sacrifice; Worship.

Sacrilege. Sacrileg(e,ious,iously,iousness). Profan(e,ed,ing,ation,eness,ity,ities). Blasphem(y,ies,ous). Desecrat(e,ed,ing, ion). *Choose from:* violat(e,ed,ing,ion), debas(e,ed,ing,ement), disrespectful(ly), dishonor(ed,ing), defil(e,ed,ing,ement), despoil(ed,ing,ment), pillag(e,ed,ing), irreveren(t,ce), mock(ed,ing,ery) *with:* sacred, holy, sacrament(s), hallowed, consecrated. *Consider also:* irreveren(t, ce), heres(y,ies), heretic(al,ally), impiet(y,ies), curs(e,ed,ing). *See also* Blasphemy; Hate crimes; Heresy; Offenses against religion; Religious prejudice; Taboo.

Sadism. Sadis(m,t,ts,tic). Sadomasochis(m, tic). Sexual aggression. Sexual cruelty. De Sade. Tortur(e,ed,ing) victim(s). Vampirism. *See also* Cruelty; Cruelty to animals; Flagellants and flagellation; Masochism; Sexual deviations; Sexual sadism; Sexual violence; Torture.

Sadism, sexual. See *Sexual sadism.*

Sadness. Sad(ness). Sorrow(ful). Unhapp(y,iness). Grief. Griev(e,ed,ing). Grievous(ness). Melanchol(y,ia). Cheerless(ness). Discourag(ed,ing, ement). Dishearten(ed,ing). Downhearted. Doleful(ness). Gloom(y). Bleak(ness). Woe(ful,fulness). Miserable. Depress(ed,ing,ion). Despondent. Low spirits. Brokenhearted. *See also* Bereavement; Depression (psychology); Emotions; Loss (psychology); Moodiness.

Sadomasochism. See *Masochism; Masochistic personality; Sexual sadism; Sexual violence.*

Safeguards. Safeguard(s). Buffer(s). Bulwark(s). Defense(s). Escort(s). Guard(s). Password(s). Precaution(s). Precautionary measure(s). Firewall(s). Shield(s). *See also* Safety; Safety devices.

Safety. Safe(ty,r). Hazards management. Security measure(s). *Choose from:* hazard(s), risk(s), danger(s), threat(s) *with:* manag(e,ed,ing,ement), mitigat(e,ed,ing,ion), control(led,ling), prevent(ed,ing,ion), precaution(s,ary), protect(ed,ing,ion), warning(s), reduc(e,ed,ing,tion). *Consider also:* fire(s), disaster(s), safety, accident(s), crime(s), burglar(s), emergenc(y,ies) *with:* drill(s), control(led,ling), prevent(ed,ing,ion), precaution(s,ary), protect(ed,ing,ion), warning(s), reduc(e,ed,ing,tion), alarm(s), signal(s,ling), patrol(s). *See also* Accident prevention; Accident proneness; Accidents; Aviation accidents; Aviation safety; Consumer protection; Crime; Crime prevention; Equipment safety; Fire; Fire prevention; Harmlessness; Hazards; Health promotion; Highway safety; Injuries; Nuclear safety; Occupational exposure; Occupational safety; Personal injuries; Product safety; Rescue; Risk management; Safeguards; Safety devices; Sanitation; Security; Traffic accidents; Vulnerability; Water safety.

Safety, air. See *Aviation safety.*

Safety, aviation. See *Aviation safety.*

Safety, equipment. See *Equipment safety.*

Safety, highway. See *Highway safety.*

Safety, industrial. See *Industrial accidents; Occupational health services; Occupational safety.*

Safety, job. See *Occupational safety.*

Safety, nuclear. See *Nuclear safety.*

Safety, occupational. See *Occupational safety.*

Safety, product. See *Product safety.*

Safety, traffic. See *Highway safety.*

Safety, water. See *Water safety.*

Safety, work. See *Occupational safety.*

Safety devices. Safety device(s). Protector(s). Fire alarm(s). *Choose from:* safety, protective *with:* equipment, device(s), clothing, belt(s), helmet(s), shield(s), glasses, vest(s). *Consider also:* ear protector(s), warning signal(s), warning device(s), reflector(s), headlight(s), mask(s), seat belt(s), air bag(s), bulletproof vest(s), bulletproof glass. *See also* Devices; Hazards; Safeguards; Safety; Seat belts; Security measures.

Sagas. Saga(s). Old Norse stor(y,ies). Epic(s). Edda(s). Legend(s). Roman fleuve. *Consider also:* kings' saga(s), Iceland(ic,er,ers) saga(s), legendary saga(s), Morkinskinna, Fagrskinna, Heimskringla, Volsunga saga. *See also* Chronicles; Folklore; Legends; Narratives; Oral history.

Sailing. Sail(ed,ing). Cruis(e,es,ed,ing). Set(ting) sail. Voyage(s) at sea. Boat trip(s). Put(ting) to sea. Hoist(ing) sail. Rais(e,ed,ing) sail. Mak(e,ing) sail. Leav(e,ing) port. *See also* Cruising; Marine accidents; Sailing ships; Seafaring life; Water transportation.

Sailing ships. Sailing ship(s). Sailing vessel(s). Sailboat(s). Tall ship(s). Clipper(s). Schooner(s). Sloop(s). *Consider also:* yawl(s), ketch(es), yacht(s), cutter(s), frigate(s). *See also* Historic ships; Naval architecture; Sailing; Shipbuilding; Ships; Vikings; Warships.

Sailors. Sailor(s). Seam(an,en). Matriner(s). Seafarer(s). Petty officer(s). Bluejacket(s). Boatswain(s). Bosun(s). Coxswain(s). Helmsm(an,en). Steersm(an,en). First mate(s). Limey(s). *Consider also:* skipper(s), navigator(s), pilot(s), midshipm(an,en). *See also* Blue collar workers; Boatmen; Enlisted military personnel; Seafaring life.

Sailors' songs. See *Sea songs.*

Saints. Saint(hood,ly,s). Venerated person(s). Hagiograph(y,ies). Canoniz(ed,ation). Sanctification. Angel(s). Patron saint(s). *Consider also:* Virgin Mary, Blessed Virgin, St. Joseph, St. Francis, St. Peter, St. Paul, St. Luke, St. John, St. Nicholas, St. Anne, St. Christopher, St. James, St. George, St. Thomas Aquinas, St. Andrew, St. Patrick, St. Stephen, St. Anthony, St. Denis, St. Thomas a Becket, St.

Augustine, etc. *See also* Apotheosis; Hagiography; Holy men; Holy women; Martyrs; Prayer; Religious personnel; Roman Catholicism; Sacredness; Worship.

Salaries. Salar(y,ies). Earning(s). Bonus(es). Paycheck(s). Wage(s). Stock option(s). Compensation. Sick pay. Income. Remuneration. Pension(s). Pension plan(s). Minimum wage. Fringe benefit(s). Postretirement increase plan(s). Merit increase(s). Merit system(s). Fringe(s). Stipend(s). Emolument(s). Honorari(a,um). Monetary reward(s). *See also* Bonuses; Compensation (payment); Compensation management; Employee benefits; Income; Labor costs; Promotion (occupational); Retirement income; Wages.

Sales. Sale(s). Sell(ing). Sold. Transfer(red, ring) ownership. Transfer(red,ring) title(s). Change of ownership. Auction(s, ed,ing). Vend(ing,ition). Resale(s). Trafficking. Deal(ing). Peddl(e,ing). Commerce. *Consider also:* consultative selling. *See also* Advertising; Auctions; Business; Consumption (economic); Deals; Discounts; Economic exchanges; Marketing; Order processing; Orders (business); Purchasing; Real estate closings; Retailing; Shopping centers; Stores; Trade.

Sales, direct. See *Direct marketing.*

Sales, garage. See *Secondhand trade.*

Sales agents. See *Sales personnel.*

Sales personnel. Sales personnel. Salespeople. Seller(s). Merchant(s). Account executive(s). Salesperson(s). Salesm(en,an). Saleswom(an,en). Salesclerk(s). Salesgirl(s). Real estate broker(s). Car dealer(s). *Choose from:* sales, retail *with:* personnel, worker(s), clerk(s), agent(s), representative(s), people, manager(s), person(s), associate(s), broker(s), employee(s), staff, department(s), force. *See also* Businesspersons; Merchants; Retailing; Street vendors; Traveling sales personnel; White collar workers.

Sales personnel, traveling. See *Traveling sales personnel.*

Sales strategies. See *Marketing strategies.*

Sales, yard. See *Secondhand trade.*

Saloons. See *Bars.*

Salutations. Salut(e,es,ed,ing,ation,ations). Greeting(s). Hail(ed,ing). Hello(s). Welcoming remark(s). Present(ed,ing) arms. Pay(ing) tribute. Paid tribute. Pay(ing) honor. Paid honor. *Consider also:* handshake(s), embrac(e,ed,ing). *See also* Gift baskets; Letters (correspondence).

Salvaging. Salvag(e,ed,ing). Salvor(s). Reclaim(ed,ing). Reclamation. Remodel(led,ling). Rescu(e,ed,ing). Recondition(ed,ing). Reus(e,ed,es,ing). Waste product(s). *Choose from:* retriev(e,ed,ing), recover(ed,ing), refloat(ed,ing), rais(e,ed,ing) *with:* ship(s), treasure(s), vessel(s), barge(s), wreck(s), ruin(s). *Consider also:* underwater excavation, rehab, salvage value(s). *See also* Collectibles; Reclamation of land; Reconstruction; Recycling; Rescue; Treasure.

Salvation. Salvation. Saved. Born again. Enlighten(ed,ment). Transcend(ence, ing). Nirvana. Religious conversion. Deliverance. Redemption. Liberation. Emancipation. Rebirth. Regeneration. Soteriolog(y,ical). *See also* Baptism; Emancipation; Enlightenment (state of mind); Forgiveness; Grace (theology); Infant salvation; Messiahs; Messianic movements; Personal independence; Redemption (theology); Regeneration (theology); Religious conversion; Religious experience; Religious gatherings; Religious revivals; Sin; Spiritual exercises; Spiritual formation.

Salvation, infant. See *Infant salvation.*

Samaritans, good. See *Good samaritans.*

Same sex. Same sex. Suigenderism. *Consider also:* homoerot(ism,icism,ic), homosexual(ity), homogenital(ity). *See also* Gender identity; Homosexuality; Sexual preferences.

Same species. See *Conspecific.*

Samoyedic languages. Samoyedic language(s). Nenen. Ngasan. Selkup. Yenen. *See also* Central Asia; Eastern Europe; Language; Languages (as subjects).

Sampling. Sampl(e,ed,ing). *Choose from:* sample(s), respondent(s) *with:* select(ed,ing,ion), determination of size, random, composition, distribution, representative(ness). *Consider also:* probability, nonprobability, quota, systematic random, stratified *with:* sample(s). *Consider also:* statistical inference. *See also* Biased sampling; Data collection; Enumeration; Experiments; Probability; Quantitative methods; Random; Research design; Research methods; Statistical bias; Statistical data; Surveys; Verification.

Sampling, biased. See *Biased sampling.*

Sanatoriums. Sanator(ia,ium,iums). Sanatar(ia,ium,iums). Convalescent home(s). Health spa(s). *Consider also:* asylum(s), infirmar(y,ies), health resort(s), special hospital(s). *See also* Hospitals; Nursing homes; Psychiatric hospitals; Residential treatment.

Sanctification. See *Saints.*

Sanctions, negative. See *Negative sanctions.*

Sanctions, positive. See *Positive sanctions.*

Sanctions, social. See *Formal social control.*

Sanctity. See *Sacredness.*

Sanctuaries. Sanctuar(y,ies). Haven(s). Refuge(s). Shelter(s). Retreat(s). Asylum(s). *Consider also:* holy place(s), shrine(s), sanct(a,um,ums), sacred ground(s), national park(s). *See also* Cultural property; Forest reserves; Homeless shelters; Places of worship; Sacred places; Sanctuary gardens; Shrines; Wildlife sanctuaries.

Sanctuaries, wildlife. See *Wildlife sanctuaries.*

Sanctuary gardens. Sanctuary garden(s). *Choose from:* garden(s,ing), backyard(s), back yard(s), yard(s), wooded setting(s), horticulture, plant(s,ing,ings), natural area(s), landscap(e,ed,ing), vegetation, flower(s), lawn(s), wildflower(s), native plant(s) *with:* sanctuar(y,ies), personal oas(is,es), haven(s), refuge(s), retreat(s), hideaway(s), secret, preserve(s). *Consider also:* pleasure garden(s). *See also* Animal environments; Birds; Flowers; Gardening; Gardening to attract wildlife; Gardens; Landscape architecture; Natural environment; Natural monuments; Nature worship; Sanctuaries; Wildlife conservation; Wildlife sanctuaries.

Sanitation. Sanitation. Hygien(e,ic,ics). Clean(ing,liness). Disinfect(ed,ing, ant,ants). Bactericid(e,es,al). Antibacterial. Antifungal. Fungicid(e,es,al). Sanitary engineering. *Choose from:* sanita(ry,tion) *with:* condition(s), facilit(y,ies), service(s), practice(s), measure(s), engineering, drainage, waste disposal, inspection(s), standard(s), technology. *Choose from:* sewage, wastewater, effluent(s), groundwater *with:* treat(ed,ing,ment), purif(y,ied, ication), disposal, technology, plumbing, decontaminat(e,ed,ing,ion), hygien(c,ic), safe(ty). *Consider also:* drinking water, swimming pool(s) *with:* quality, pot(able,ility), treat(ed,ing,ment), purif(y,ied,ication), filtration, filter(ed,ing), decontaminat(e,ed,ing, ion), chlorinat(e,ed,ing,ation), hygien(e,ic), safe(ty). *Consider also:* toilet facilities, refuse disposal, garbage disposal, waste disposal, water supply, food inspection. *See also* Decontamination; Disease; Drainage; Epidemics; Food inspection; Hand washing; Health; Health behavior; Hygiene; Occupational safety; Prevention; Public health; Safety; Sewage; Sewage disposal.

Sanitoriums. See *Asylums; Hospitals; Psychiatric hospitals.*

Satan. See *Devils.*

Satellite photography. See *Aerial reconnaissance.*

Satiation. Satiat(ed,ion,iety). Sate(d). Surfeit(ed). Glut(ted,ting). Cloy(ed,ing). Gorg(e,ed,ing). Pall(ed,ing). *Consider also:* gratif(y,ied,ication), fulfill(ed,ing, ment), full(ness). *See also* Appetite; Fulfillment; Hunger, food deprivation; Motivation; Obesity.

Satire. Satir(e,ic,ical,ically,ize,ized,izing). Wit(ty,tiness). Iron(y,ies,ic,ical). Sarcas(m,tic). Mock(ed,ing,ery). Ridicul(e,ed,ing). Caricatur(e,ed,ing). Parod(y,ying,ies). Burlesque. Travesty. Cartoon(s,ed,ing). Lampoon(ed,ing). Trenchant. *See also* Cartoons; Comedians; Comics; Derision; Figurative language; Humor; Irony; Literature; Parody; Political humor; Postmodernism; Scatology.

Satire, political. See *Political humor.*

Satirical songs. Satirical song(s). *Choose from:* satir(e,ical,izing), parod(y,ies,ing), lampoon(ed,ing), iron(y,ic), ridicul(e,ed, ing), spoof(s,ed,ing), mock(ed,ing) *with:* ballad(s), song(s), folksong(s), ditt(y,ies). *See also* Humorous songs; Songs.

Satisfaction. Satisf(y,ying,ied,action). Bliss(ful). Comfort(able). Content(ed, ment). Delight(ed). Fulfill(ing,ed,ment). Gratif(y,ied,ication). Glad(ness). Happ(y,iness). Morale. Meaningful(ness). Opinion(s). Orgasm(s,ic). Peace of mind. Peak experience(s). Pleasure. Pride. Rating(s). Relief. Self-efficacy. Values. Well-being. Enjoy(ed, ing,ment). *See also* Comfortableness; Enjoyment; Happiness; Job satisfaction; Life satisfaction; Marital satisfaction; Need satisfaction; Needs; Physical comfort; Quality of life; Quality of working life; Self esteem; Sexual satisfaction; Success; Well being.

Satisfaction, career. See *Job satisfaction.*

Satisfaction, community. See *Community support.*

Satisfaction, consumer. See *Consumer satisfaction.*

Satisfaction, customer. See *Consumer satisfaction.*

Satisfaction, employment. See *Job satisfaction.*

Satisfaction, job. See *Job satisfaction.*

Satisfaction, life. See *Life satisfaction.*

Satisfaction, marital. See *Marital satisfaction.*

Satisfaction, need. See *Need satisfaction.*

Satisfaction, occupational. See *Job satisfaction.*

Satisfaction, personal. See *Personal satisfaction.*

Satisfaction, resident. See *Community support.*

Satisfaction, role. See *Job satisfaction; Life satisfaction.*

Satisfaction, sexual. See *Sexual satisfaction.*

Satisfaction, work. See *Job satisfaction.*

Saving. Sav(e,ed,ing). Stockpil(e,ing). Hoard(ing). Accumulat(e,ed,ing). *Consider also:* thrift(y,iness), frugal(ity), economical. *See also* Accumulation; Collecting mania; Frugality; Habits; Hoarding; Lifestyle; Savings; Thriftiness.

Savings. Savings. Nest egg(s). Cash reserve(s). Stockpile(s). Accumulation(s). Net worth. *Consider also:* personal wealth, capital, savings account(s). *See also* Assets; Banking; Capital (financial); Finance; Financial planning; Income; Investments; Privatized pension systems; Saving; Wealth.

Scaldic poetry. See *Skaldic poetry.*

Scale , attitude. See *Attitude measurement.*

Scale, economies of. See *Economies of scale.*

Scale, geological time. See *Geological time scale.*

Scales. See *Scaling.*

Scales, musical intervals and. See *Musical intervals and scales.*

Scaling. Scal(e,es,ed,ability,ing). *Choose from:* nominal, ordinal, interval, equal interval, ratio, multidimensional, continuous *with:* scal(e,es,ing). *Consider also:* measure(s,ments), rank(s,ed,ings), rating(s), scor(e,es,ing). *See also* Measurement; Multidimensional scaling; Ranking; Tests.

Scaling, multidimensional. See *Multidimensional scaling.*

Scandals. Scandal(ize,ized,ous,ousness,s). Disgrace(d,ful). Malign(ed). Dishonor(ed). Disrepute. Defam(e,ed, ing,atory,ation). Infam(y,ous). Libelous. Shocking. Shame(d,ful). Chagrin(ed). Slander. Discredit(ed,ing). Offensive to propriety. Immorality. Misdeed(s). Wrongdoing(s). Transgression(s). Misconduct. Misbehavior. Impropriet(y, ies). Corruption. *See also* Corruption in government; Defamation; Depravity; Gossip; Immorality; Improprieties; Libel; Ministerial ethics (clergy); Political campaigns; Public opinion; Reputation; Rumors; Scapegoating; Sensationalism; Tabloids; Trivia; Unethical conduct.

Scandals, political. See *Corruption in government.*

Scapegoating. Scapegoat(s,ing). Target(s) of propaganda. Blam(e,ed,ing). Butt of abuse. Fall guy(s). Whipping boy(s). Witch hunt(ing,s). Demoniz(e,ed,ing, ation). *Consider also:* displace(d,ment), diver(t,sion), repress(ed,ion) *with:* aggression, frustration, hostilit(y,ies). *See also* Blame; Defamation; Derogation; Denial (psychology); Denunciation; Displacement (psychology); Emotional abuse; Guilt; Hostility; Labeling (of persons); McCarthyism; Neutralization; Political campaigns; Projection (psychological); Psychologically abused men; Public opinion; Rationalization (defense mechanism); Reputation; Ritual purity; Scandals; Stereotyping; Stigma; Witch hunting; Witchcraft trials.

Scarcity. Scarc(e,ity,ities). Shortage(s). Deprivation. Famine(s). Drought(s). Lack(s,ing) provision(s). Insufficien(t, cy). Inadequa(te,cy). Deficien(cy,t). Paucity. Sparse(ness). Scant(y,iness). Meager(ness). Destitut(e,ion). Short suppl(y,ies). Poverty. Dearth. *See also* Consumption (economic); Consumption (use); Deprivation; Commodities; Economic conditions; Economic problems; Famine; Inadequacy; Medically underserved areas; Natural disasters; Resource allocation; Resource stress; Resources; Priorities; Shortages; Triage.

Scatology. Scatolog(y,ical,ia). Scat. *Choose from:* scatolog(y,ical,icals), excrement(s, al), excretion, latrine(s), faecal, fec(al, es), defecat(e,ed,es,ing,ion,ions), pervers(e,ity), coprophil(ia,ias,ic), shit(ted,ting), priv(y,ies), pott(y,ies), stool(e,es,s), watercloset(s), toilet(s), bathroom(s), turd(s), coprophil(ia,ous), ordure, droppings, dung, anal eroticism, scatophag(ia,ic) *with:* interest(s), preoccup(ied,ation,ations), obsess(ed, ion,ions), mind, thought(s), tendenc(y, ies), humor, irony, pun(s), comic, imagery, poe(try,m,ms), analog(y,ies), treatise(s), social commentar(y,ies), satir(e,ic,ical), litera(ry,ature), text(s,ual, ually), subject(s), mock encom(ia,ium, iums), treatise(s), tract(s). *Consider also:* excremental vision, excremental esthetic, new emetics. *See also* Absurd; Bawdy songs; Coprophagia; Cybersex; Indecent communications; Irony; Literature; Obscenity; Prurience; Satire; Sexual deviations; Vulgarity.

Scenarios. See *Forecasting.*

Scenery. See *Landscape.*

Scenery, natural. See *Landscape.*

Scent marking, animal. See *Animal scent marking.*

Scepticism. See *Uncertainty.*

Schedule, reinforcement. See *Reinforcement schedule.*

Schedules, flexible work. See *Alternative work patterns; Personnel scheduling; Work load; Work schedules; Workday shifts; Worktime.*

Schedules, learning. See *Learning schedules.*

Schedules, school. See *School schedules.*

Schedules, work. See *Work schedules.*

Schedules and appointments. See *Appointments and schedules.*

Scheduling, personnel. See *Personnel scheduling.*

Schism. Schism(s,atic). Discord(ant). Split(ting,s). Faction(s,alism). Disharmon(y,ious). Separat(e,ed,ing, ism). Disunity. Dissiden(t,ts,ce). Heretic(s,al). Dissension. *See also* Apostasy; Dissent; Dissidents; Extremism; Factionalism; Partisan; Polarization; Political defection; Political ideologies; Political parties; Religions; Religious fundamentalism; Religious movements; Sectarianism; Social cleavage; Social conflict; Social unrest.

Schizoid. Schizoid(ia,ism). Schizotyp(al,ic). Schizophrenic personality type. Schizothyme(s). Shut-in personality. *See also* Personality disorders; Schizophrenia.

Schizophrenia. Schizophren(ia,ic,ics). Dementia praecox. Schizophrenic disorder(s). Late paraphrenia. Schizoid. Hebephren(ia,ic). Heboid. Heboidophren(ia,ic). Schizophrenosis. *Choose from:* catatonic, childhood, disorganized, paranoid, acute, chronic, hebephrenic, nuclear, process, pseudopsychopathic, pseudoneurotic, simple, undifferentiated, borderline, compensation, ambulatory, latent, mixed, residual, postemotive *with:* schizophren(ia,ic,ics). *Consider also:* schizophrenogenic, schizophreniform disorder(s), schizoaffective disorder(s), schizoaffective psychos(is, es), schizotaxia, toxiphrenia. *See also* Anhedonia; Autism; Catalepsy; Catatonic schizophrenia; Childhood schizophrenia; Depersonalization disorder; Disorganized schizophrenia; Fragmentation (schizophrenia); Latent schizophrenia; Paranoid schizophrenia; Psychoses; Residual schizophrenia; Schizoid; Schizophrenic language; Schizophrenogenic family; Schizotypal personality disorder; Undifferentiated schizophrenia.

Schizophrenia, catatonic. See *Catatonic schizophrenia.*

Schizophrenia, childhood. See *Childhood schizophrenia.*

Schizophrenia, disorganized. See *Disorganized schizophrenia.*

Schizophrenia, hebephrenic. See *Disorganized schizophrenia.*

Schizophrenia, latent. See *Latent schizophrenia.*

Schizophrenia, paranoid. See *Paranoid schizophrenia.*

Schizophrenia, residual. See *Residual schizophrenia.*

Schizophrenia, undifferentiated. See *Undifferentiated schizophrenia.*

Schizophrenic fragmentation. See *Fragmentation (schizophrenia).*

Schizophrenic language. Schizophrenic language. Schizophrenese. Autoecholalia. Cataphasia. Verbigeration. Aboiement. *Choose from:* schizophren(ic,ia) *with:* speech, language, verbal behavior, incoheren(t,ce). *See also* Schizophrenia; Language disorders; Speech disturbances.

Schizophrenogenic family. Schizophrenogenic famil(y,ies). *Choose from:* schizophrenogenic, schizophrenic transaction(s) *with:* famil(y,ies), parent(s), mother(s), father(s), relative(s), sibling(s). *See also* Childhood schizophrenia; Double bind interaction; Family problems; Family relations; Father child relations; Fear of closeness; Mother child relations.

Schizotypal personality disorder. Schizotypal personality disorder(s). *Choose from:* schizotypal, schizoadaptation *with:* disintegrat(ed,ion), decompensat(ed,ion), compensat(ed, ion), personalit(y,ies), disorder(s). *See also* Personality disorders; Schizoid.

Scholarly journals. See *Scholarly periodicals.*

Scholarly periodicals. Scholarly periodical(s). *Choose from:* scholarly, learned, academic *with:* periodical(s), journal(s). *See also* Periodicals; Professional literature.

Scholarly societies. See *Professional organizations.*

Scholarly writing. See *Scholarship.*

Scholars. Scholar(s). Philosopher(s). Savant(s). Professor(s). Sage(s). Man of letters. Intellectual(s). Learned person. Pedant(s). Pedagogue(s). Well-read person. Well-educated person. Author(s). Student(s). Renaissance man. *See also* Academic ability; Academic achievement; Academically gifted; Authors; College teaching; Faculty; Historians; Intellectual life; Intelligentsia; Scholarship; Scientists; Students.

Scholarship. Scholar(ly,ship). Erudition. Formal learning. Intellectualism. Knowledge(able). Wisdom. Author(s,ship). *Choose from:* scholarly, learned, academic *with:* writing(s). publication(s), work(s). *See also* Academic achievement; Dissertations;

Historiography; Intelligentsia; Knowledge; Research; Scholars; Wisdom; Writing (composition).

Scholarships (educational). Scholarship(s). Fellowship(s). Assistantship(s). Training support. Stipend(s). Student loan(s). Educational award(s). Tuition grant(s). Scholarship loan(s). Educational financial assistance. *Consider also:* tuition voucher(s), school federal aid, school financial assistance. *See also* Awards; Educational vouchers; Fellowships (educational); School choice; Student financial aid; Tuition reimbursement.

Scholastic achievement. See *Academic achievement.*

Scholastic aptitude. See *Academic aptitude.*

Scholastic theology. See *Scholasticism.*

Scholasticism. Scholasticis(m,t,ts). Scholastic theology. *Consider also:* St. Anselm, St. Thomas Aquinas, neo-scholasticism, neo-platonism, nominalis(m,t,ts). *See also* Casuistry; Medieval literature; Medieval philosophers; Medieval theology; Peripatetics; Philosophy; Rationalism; Theology.

Scholia. Scholi(a,um,ums). Scholastic marginali(a,um,ums). Marginal commentar(y,ies). Marginal annotation(s). *See also* Ancient literature; Antiquity (time); Commentaries; Exegesis; Incunabula.

School, programs after. See *After school programs.*

School absenteeism. See *Absenteeism.*

School adjustment. School adjustment. *Choose from:* school(s), student(s), classroom(s), college(s) *with:* adjust(ed, ing,ment), maladjust(ed,ing,ment), adapt(ed,ing,ation), adaptive behavior, readjust(ed,ing,ment), orient(ed,ing, ation). *See also* Adjustment (to environment); School orientation; School readiness; Student attitudes; Student personnel services.

School administrators. See *Educational administrators.*

School admission criteria. School admission criteria. *Choose from:* school(s), college(s), universit(y,ies) *with:* admission(s), entrance, matriculation, enrollment *with:* examination(s), criteria, standard(s), requirement(s), test score(s), polic(y,ies). *See also* Academic standards; Access to education; Admissions; Criteria.

School attendance. School attendance. Student persistence. *Choose from:* school, class(es), college, educational *with:* persistence, attend(ed,ing,ance), absence(s), dropout(s), truan(t,ts,cy), refusal, absent(eeism). *See also* Absenteeism; Academic persistence;

Access to education; Attendance (presence); Potential dropouts; Reentry students; School expulsion; School suspension; Student dropouts; Truancy.

School boards. School board(s). Board(s) of education. School district agenc(y,ies). *Consider also:* board(s) of trustees, board(s) of directors, school committee(s), governing board(s), regents. *See also* Educational administration; Governing boards; School management; Trustees.

School choice. School choice(s). Educational choice(s). *Choose from:* school(ing), educational *with:* choice(s), selection, market approach(es), quasi-market(s), alternatives. *Consider also:* school voucher(s), charter school(s), public aid to parochial school(s), education savings account(s), tuition tax credit(s), homeschooling, magnet school(s), open enrollment. *See also* Educational vouchers; Private schools; Privatization; Public schools; Scholarships (educational); Schools; Tuition reimbursement.

School clubs. School club(s). After-school club(s). Campus association(s). *Choose from:* school(s), student(s), campus *with:* club(s), fraternit(y,ies), sororit(y,ies), social group(s), fellowship(s), societ(y,ies), organization(s). *Consider also:* glee club(s), homemaker(s) club(s), science club(s), youth club(s), key club(s), science club(s), student group(s), Phi Beta Kappa, honor societ(y,ies), brotherhood(s), sisterhoods(s), hermandades. *See also* Extracurricular activities; Fraternities; School newspapers; School sports; Sororities; Student activities.

School counseling. School counseling. *Choose from:* educational, school, student(s), pupil(s), classroom(s) *with:* counseling, guidance, advis(e,ed,ing), therapy. *Consider also:* guidance counseling. *See also* Educational counseling; Educational diagnosis; School counselors; Student personnel services; Vocational guidance.

School counselors. School counselor(s). *Choose from:* school, college, university, education(al), student services *with:* counselor(s), guidance personnel. *Consider also:* guidance counselor(s). *See also* Counselors; School counseling; Student personnel services.

School desegregation. See *School integration.*

School discipline. School discipline. *Choose from:* school(s), student(s), pupil(s), classroom *with:* disciplin(ary,e, ed,ing), correction(s), reprimand(s,ed, ing), punish(ed,ing,ment,ments), enforc(e,ed,ing,ement), obedien(t,ce), rules of conduct, behavior(al) control, sanction(s), regulation(s). *See also* Child

discipline; Classroom environment; Discipline; Nonpunitive approach (discipline); School expulsion; School suspension.

School dropouts. See *Student dropouts.*

School enrollment. School enrollment. *Choose from:* enroll(ed,ing,ment), matriculat(e,ed,ing), enter(ed,ing), entry, entrance, register(eding), registration(s), roster(s) *with:* school(s), student(s), college(s), universit(y,ies), educational institution(s). *Consider also:* register(ed,ing) for class(es). *See also* Access to education; Admissions; Attendance (presence); Course load; Student dropouts.

School environment. See *Educational environment.*

School expulsion. School expulsion(s). *Choose from:* school(s), student(s), pupil(s), class(es,room,rooms) *with:* expulsion(s), expel(led,ling), forced withdraw(al), terminat(e,ed,ing,ation, ations), dismiss(ed,ing,al), disciplinary removal. *Consider also:* pushout(s), school suspen(d,ded,ding,sion). *See also* Academic failure; Academic probation; Child discipline; School attendance; School discipline; School suspension; Student dropouts.

School facilities. See *Educational facilities.*

School health services. See *Student health services.*

School integration. School integration. Increas(e,ed,ing) minority enrollment. School busing. Bussed students. Integrated student body. *Choose from:* integrat(e,ed,ion), desegregat(e,ed,ion), biracial, multiracial, interracial, racially mixed *with:* school(s), college(s), universit(y,ies), education, classroom(s). *Consider also:* Brown vs. Board of Education. *See also* Access; Equal education; Desegregation; School segregation; Racial diversity; Racial integration; Racial segregation.

School leavers. See *Student dropouts.*

School management. See *Educational administration; School boards.*

School meals. School meal(s). *Choose from:* school(s) *with:* meal(s), lunch(es), breakfast(s), food service(s), cafeteria(s), feeding program(s), milk program(s). *See also* Child nutrition; Diet; Food services (programs); Hunger, food deprivation; Nutrition.

School newspapers. School newspaper(s). *Choose from:* school(s), student(s), scholastic *with:* newspaper(s), journalis(m,t,ts), publication(s), periodical(s), paper(s), magazine(s). *Consider also:* student home page(s), school homepage(s) student reporter(s). *See also* Extracurricular activities; School clubs; Student activities.

School orientation. School orientation. *Choose from:* school(s), student(s), fresh(men,man), new faculty *with:* orientation(s), welcome program(s). *See also* Adjustment (to environment); Educational counseling; School counseling; Student personnel services.

School parent relationship. See *Parent school relations.*

School performance. See *Academic achievement.*

School phobia. School phob(ia,ias,ic,ics). Pedagophob(ia,ias,ic,ics). *Choose from:* school, preschool *with:* phob(ia,ias,ic, ics), refusal, anxiet(y,ies), fear(s,ful), avoid(ed,ing,ance). *See also* Anxiety; Mathematics anxiety; Phobias; Separation anxiety; Student teacher relationship; Test anxiety.

School principals. School principal(s). Principal(s) of school(s). Assistant principal(s). Principalship. School administrator(s). Headmaster(s). *See also* Educational administration; Educational administrators; School boards.

School readiness. School readiness. *Choose from:* school, kindergarten, first grade, learning *with:* read(y,iness), prepared(ness), maturity. *See also* Cognitive development; Educational placement; Emotional development; Learning ability; Physical development; Reading readiness.

School reform. See *Educational reform.*

School schedules. School schedule(s). *Choose from:* school(s), academic, education(al) *with:* schedul(e,es,ing), block schedul(e,es,ing), double session(s), flex(ible) schedul(e,es,ing), extended day(s), extended-time scheduling, half day(s), time block(s), alternate day(s), *Consider also:* innovative time schedule(s), longer school day(s). *See also* Appointments and schedules; Academic environment; Educational innovations; Educational reform; Extended school year Lesson plans; Organizational innovation; Work schedules.

School segregation. School segregation. Segregated school(s). *Choose from:* segregat(ed,ing,ion), separate, apartheid, exclusion(ary) *with:* school(s), college(s), universit(y,ies), education(al), classroom(s). *Consider also:* separate but equal, Plessy v. Ferguson, Brown v. Board of Education. *See also* Apartheid; Racial segregation; Racism; School integration; Schools.

School societies. See *School clubs.*

School sports. School sport(s). *Choose from:* school(s), extracurricular, student(s), after-school, fresh(men,man), sophomore(s), junior(s), senior(s),

eighth grader(s), etc. *with:* sport(s), team(s), athlet(e,es,ic,ics), gymnastic(s), baseball, bowling, boxing, cricket, fencing, field hockey, foot races, football, karate, handball, high jump, hockey, lacrosse, martial arts, racquetball, racing, rugby, swimming, soccer, softball, squash, track, tennis, volleyball, wrestling. *See also* Extracurricular activities; Playgrounds; School clubs; Sports; Student activities.

School superintendents. See *Superintendents.*

School suspension. School suspension. *Choose from:* suspen(d,ded,ding,sion), dismiss(ed,al,ing), temporary forced withdrawal *with:* school(s), student(s), pupil(s), fresh(man,men), sophomore(s), junior(s), senior(s). *See also* Child discipline; School attendance; School discipline; School enrollment; School expulsion; Student dropouts.

School truancy. See *Truancy.*

School violence. School violence. *Choose from:* school(s), schoolyard(s), classroom(s), playground(s), student(s), youth *with:* massacre(s), shooting(s), shot, kill(s,ed,ing,ings), violen(t,ce), bomb(s,ed,ing,ings), slaying(s), gun(s), semiautomatic(s), weapon(s). *See also* Gun control; Harassment; Mass media violence; Sports violence; Violence; Students.

School vouchers. See *Educational vouchers.*

School year, extended. See *Extended school year.*

Schoolbooks. See *Textbooks.*

Schoolchildren. Schoolchild(ren). *Choose from:* school student(s), pupil(s), kindergartener(s), first grader(s), second grader(s), third grader(s), fourth grader(s), fifth grader(s), sixth grader(s), etc. *See also* Children; Elementary school students; High school students; Preschool children.

Schooling, home. See *Home schooling.*

Schools. School(s). Academ(y,ies). Kindergarten(s). Preschool(s). Seminar(y,ies). College(s). Universit(y,ies). Educational institution(s). Educational system(s). Training institute(s). Institution(s) of higher learning. Education(al) center(s). *See also* Admissions; Boarding schools; Correspondence schools; Curriculum; Educational administration; Educational programs; Elementary schools; Graduate schools; High schools; Institutional schools; Junior high schools; Medical schools; Military schools; Nongraded schools; Nontraditional education; Nursery schools; Primary schools; Private schools; Public schools; School boards; School choice; School enrollment; School integration; School

principals; Students; Teachers; Teaching; Traditional schools.

Schools, alternative. See *Nontraditional education.*

Schools, art. See *Art schools.*

Schools, boarding. See *Boarding schools.*

Schools, church. See *Private schools.*

Schools, correspondence. See *Correspondence schools.*

Schools, elementary. See *Elementary schools.*

Schools, flight. See *Flight schools.*

Schools, free. See *Nontraditional education.*

Schools, graduate. See *Graduate schools.*

Schools, grammar. See *Elementary schools.*

Schools, high. See *High schools.*

Schools, inclusive. See *Inclusive education.*

Schools, institutional. See *Institutional schools.*

Schools, junior high. See *Junior high schools.*

Schools, medical. See *Medical schools.*

Schools, military. See *Military schools.*

Schools, nongraded. See *Nongraded schools.*

Schools, nursery. See *Nursery schools.*

Schools, parochial. See *Private schools.*

Schools, primary. See *Primary schools.*

Schools, private. See *Private schools.*

Schools, proprietary. See *Private schools.*

Schools, public. See *Public schools.*

Schools, religious. See *Private schools.*

Schools, secondary. See *High schools.*

Schools, single sex and. See *Single sex schools.*

Schools, traditional. See *Traditional schools.*

Schools, vocational. See *Vocational education.*

Science, cognitive. See *Cognitive science.*

Science, soil. See *Soil science.*

Science anxiety. Science anxiety. *Choose from:* science(s), geology, biology, physics, chemistry *with:* anxiet(y,ies), anxious(ness), fear, aversion(s), apprehensive(ness), apprehension(s), avoid(ed,ing,ance), phob(ic,ia,ias), disabilit(y,ies), stress(es). *See also* Anxiety; Computer anxiety; Computer illiteracy; Educational background; Mathematics anxiety; School phobia; Sciences; Test anxiety.

Science avoidance. See *Science anxiety.*

Science policy. Science polic(y,ies). *Choose from:* scien(ce,tific), research, technolog(y,ies,ical), medicine, medical, R & D, biolog(ists,ical), chemist(s,ry), physic(ists,s), geolog(y,ists), meteorolog(y,ists) *with:* polic(y,ies), regulation(s), guideline(s), rule(s). *See also* Policy; Research; Scientific development; Scientists.

Sciences. Scien(ce,ces,tific,tists). *Consider also:* technolog(y,ical), research(er,ing), bod(y,ies) of knowledge, discipline(s). Behavioral science(s). Biological science(s). Information science. Natural science(s). Physical science(s). Social science(s). Space science(s). Veterinary science(s). *Consider also:* acoustics, anatomy, anthropology, astronomy, biochemistry, biology, biophysics, botany, chemistry, communications, computer science, criminology, demography, electronics, engineering, environment design, epidemiology, ethology, genetics, geography, geology, mathematics, medicine, neuroanatomy, neurobiology, neurochemistry, neuroendocrinology, neurology, neuropsychiatry, neuropsychology, neurosciences, orthopsychiatry, pharmacology, physics, physiology, political science, psychiatry, psychobiology, psycholinguistics, psychology, psychopharmacology, psychophysics, psychophysiology, radiology, sociology, zoology. *See also* Astronomy; Environmental sciences; Experimental biology; Medical sciences; Paramedical sciences; Science policy; Scientific community; Scientific development; Scientific discoveries; Scientific knowledge; Scientific method; Scientific revolutions; Social sciences; Technology; Theoretical orientation; Theories.

Sciences, behavioral. See *Social sciences.*

Sciences, environmental. See *Environmental sciences.*

Sciences, human. See *Social sciences.*

Sciences, life. See *Life sciences.*

Sciences, medical. See *Medical sciences.*

Sciences, paramedical. See *Paramedical sciences.*

Sciences, social. See *Social sciences.*

Scientific associations. See *Scientific societies.*

Scientific communication. See *Professional literature; Scientific language.*

Scientific community. Scientific community. Invisible college(s). *Choose from:* scien(tific,ce), research, technical, engineering *with:* communit(y,ies), association(s), organization(s), elite(s), scholar(s), consensus, expert(s), specialist(s), leader(s), investigator(s), worker(s), researcher(s). *Consider also:* scientist(s), scientific researchers. *See*

also Brain drain; Community (social); Elites; Intellectual life; Intelligentsia; Networks; Scientific societies; Scientists; Technology transfer.

Scientific development. Scientific development. *Choose from:* scien(ce,tific), technical, technological, research, engineering, biolog(y,ical), chem(istry, ical), physics, geolog(y,ical), etc. *with:* develop(ed,ing,ment,mental), accumulat(e,ed,ing,ion), revolution(s), history, cooperation, matur(e,ed,ing,ity), expan(d,ded,ding,sion), improv(e,ed,ing, ment), exten(d,ded,ding,sion), progress(ed,ing,ion), further(ing,ance), spread(ing), advanc(es,ed,ing,ement). *Consider also:* sociology of science. *See also* Economic development; Progress; Science policy; Scientific discoveries; Scientific knowledge; Scientific revolutions; Research; Technological innovations; Technological progress.

Scientific discoveries. Scientific discoveries. *Choose from:* scien(ce,tific), technical, technological, research, engineering, biolog(y,ical), chem(istry, ical), physics, geolog(y,ical), etc. *with:* discover(y,ies), finding(s), invention(s), innovation(s), uncover(ing), breakthrough(s), conclusion(s), result(s), answer(s). *See also* Discoveries (findings); Discovering; Medical innovations; Patents; Research; Scientific development; Scientific expeditions; Scientific knowledge; Scientific revolutions; Technological innovations; Technological progress.

Scientific equipment. Scientific equipment. *Choose from:* scientific, science, technological, technical, biological, chemical, physics, geological, astronomical, etc. *with:* equipment, instrument(s,ation), apparatus, component(s), tool(s), utensil(s), device(s). meter(s), recorder(s), aid(s), computer(s), etc. *Consider also:* medical equipment, specific instruments by name. *See also* Electronic equipment; Equipment; Technological innovations; Technology; Tools.

Scientific errors. Scientific error(s). Scientific inaccurac(y,ies). *Choose from:* scien(ce,ces, tific), experimenter(s), experiment(s), research(er,ers) *with:* error(s), mistake(s,n), inaccura(cy,cies, te), incorrect(ly,ness), erroneous(ly), discrepan(cy,cies), fallac(y,ies,iousness), anomal(y,ies), miscalculat(e,ed,ion,ions), omission(s), omit(ted), irregularit(y,ies), misidentif(ied,ication), false negative reaction(s), false positive reaction(s), bogus, illogic(al,ally). *See also* Errors; Fallibility; Falsification (scientific); Illogical; Incorrect.

Scientific expeditions. Scientific expedition(s). *Choose from:* scientific, research, polar, biotechnical, biological,

naturalist(s), underwater, oceanic *with:* expedition(s), venture(s), safari(s), journey(s), travel(s), quest(s). explorer(s), exploration(s), voyage(s), safari(s). *See also* Expeditions; Pioneers; Quests; Scientific discoveries; Travel.

Scientific falsification. See *Falsification (scientific).*

Scientific fraud. See *Falsification (scientific).*

Scientific institutions. See *Scientific societies.*

Scientific instruments. See *Scientific equipment.*

Scientific knowledge. Scientific knowledge. *Choose from:* scien(ce,tific), technical, technological, research, engineering, biolog(y,ical), chem(istry,ical), physics, geolog(y,ical), etc. *with:* knowledge, expert(ise,ness), cognizance, erudition, sophistication, awareness, comprehension, understanding, insight, inform(ed, ation), wisdom, know-how, learning, scholarship, proficiency, accomplishments. *See also* Inquiry (theory of knowledge); Mathematical ability; Research; Scientific discoveries; Scientific method; Scientific revolutions; Scientists; Technology; Technology transfer.

Scientific language. Scientific language. *Choose from:* scientific, science(s), technolog(y,ies,ical), research, technical *with:* language, terminolog(y,ies,ical), term(s), vocabular(y,ies), lingo, definition(s), communication(s). *See also* Communication (thought transfer); Professional literature.

Scientific literature. See *Professional literature.*

Scientific management. Scientific management. Taylor(ism,ist,ian). Fordism. *Consider also:* rationalization of production, mass production, deskilling, assembly lines, neo-Taylorist. *See also* Automation; Division of labor; Job design; Job evaluation; Labor process; Labor management relations; Mass production; Productivity; Proletarianization; Rationalization (sociology).

Scientific method. Scientific method(ology, s). Empiric(al,ism). *Choose from:* scien(ce,tific), research *with:* method(ology,s), concepts, principles, theor(y,ies), model(s), paradigm(s), theoretical bas(is,es), premis(es), hypothes(is,es), experiment(s,ing,ation), data, deduct(ion,ive), generalization(s). *See also* Covering laws; Deduction; Empirical methods; Experiments; Explanation; Induction; Inquiry (theory of knowledge); Objectivity; Sciences; Research; Theories.

Scientific misconduct. Scientific misconduct. Unprofessional conduct. *Choose from:* scien(ce,tific,tists), research, biomedical, medical, physician(s) *with:* misconduct, fraud(ulence,ulent), charlatan(s), deceit(ful), deceiv(e,ed, ing), decept(ion,ive), dishonest(y), fak(e,ed,ery,ing), false claim(s), false data, falsif(y,ied,ication), factifudging, fudg(ed,ing), forger(ies,y), hoax(es), imposter(s), lying, misappropriat(e,ed, ing,ion,ions), misrepresent(ed,ing,ation), phony, quack(ery,s), subterfuge(s), unsubstantiated claim(s), ethics charge(s), unethical, uncorroborated. *See also* Deception; Falsification (scientific); Physician patient relations; Professional client relations; Quackery; Researcher subject relations; Scandals; Sexual harassment; Unethical conduct; White collar crime.

Scientific models. Scientific model(s). *Choose from:* scientific, research, technical, physic(s,al), natural, biological, chemical, geological, sociological, psychological, economic(s), etc. *with:* model(s), prototyp(e,es,ical), paradigm(s), archetyp(e,es,ical), sample(s), standard(s), pattern(s), design(s), simulat(ion,ions,or,ors), replica(s). *See also* Anatomic models; Animal testing alternatives; Biological models; Causal models; Examples; Mathematical models; Models; Operations research; Research design; Research methods; Simulation; Structural models; Systems analysis; Theories.

Scientific records. Scientific record(s). *Choose from:* scientific, science, technological, technical, biological, chemical, physics, geological, astronomical, etc. *with:* record(s), histor(y,ies), file(s), data. *See also* Medical records; Nursing records; Records.

Scientific research. See *Research.*

Scientific revolutions. Scientific revolutions. *Choose from:* scien(ce,tific), technical, technological, research, information, computer, microelectronic, space, microcomputer, automation *with:* revolution(s,ary,izing,ize), transition(s), dialectics, progress, development, evolution(ary). *See also* Economic development; Information; Microcomputers; Modernization; Progress; Scientific development; Scientific discoveries; Scientific knowledge; Research; Technological change; Technological innovations; Technological progress; Technological unemployment; Technology; Technology and civilization; Theories.

Scientific societies. Scientific societ(y,ies). *Consider also:* scien(ce,tific), engineering, medical, research, technolog(y,ical),

environment(al) *with:* association(s), organization(s), societ(y,ies), fraternit(y,ies), council(s). *See also* Professional organizations; Scientific community; Societies (organizations).

Scientific writing. See *Technical writing.*

Scientists. Scientist(s). Scientific culture. Scientific researcher(s). *Choose from:* scien(tific,ce), laboratory, research *with:* career(s), personnel, staff, majors, expert(s), specialist(s), leader(s), investigator(s), worker(s), assistant(s). *Consider also:* social scientist(s), natural scientist(s), chemist(s), biologist(s), physicist(s), biochemist(s), astronomer(s), geneticist(s), geologist(s), meteorologist(s), sociobiologist(s), information scientist(s), astronomer(s). *See also* Biologists; Brain drain; Expert testimony; Experts; Geneticists; Intellectual life; Research personnel; Sciences; Scientific community.

Scores, cutting. See *Cutting scores.*

Scoring, musical. See *Orchestration.*

Scrambling, data. See *Cryptography.*

Scrap materials. Scrap material(s). Scrap(iana). Waste material(s). Leftover(s). Remainder(s). Leavings. Discard(s,ed). Throwaway(s). Junk. Remnant(s). Second-hand. Hand-me-down(s). Shard(s). Fragment(s). *Consider also:* recycl(e,ed,ers,es, ing,able,ables,ability). *See also* Fragments; Litter (waste); Recycling; Solid waste; Waste to energy.

Scratching. Scratch(ed,ing). Excoriat(e,ed, ing,ion). Abrad(e,ed,ing). Scrap(e,ed, ing). Chaf(e,ed,ing). Rub(bed,bing). *Consider also:* itch(es,ed,ing). *See also* Habits.

Screening. Screen(ed,ing). Identif(y,ied,ing) risk. Evaluat(e,ed,ing,ion). Predict(ed, ing,ion) success. Prognostic test(s). Readiness test(s). Entrance examination(s). Admission test(s). Routine test(s,ing). Routine admission test(s,ing). Diagnostic test(s). Prehospitalization examination(s). Casefinding. Preadmission assessment(s). Candl(e,ed,ing). Handicap identification. Chest X-ray(s). Mammograph(y,ies). Pap smear(s). Wassermann test(s). *See also* Biochemical markers; Diagnosis; Disability evaluation; Educational measurement; Educational placement; Genetic screening; Indicators (biology); Job applicant screening; Mass screening; Personnel selection; Selection tests.

Screening, genetic. See *Genetic screening.*

Screening, health. See *Mass screening.*

Screening, job applicant. See *Job applicant screening.*

Screening, mass. See *Mass screening.*

Screenwriters. See *Authors; Scriptwriting.*

Scribes. Scribe(s). Inscriber(s). Transcriber(s). Copyist(s). Scrivener(s). *Consider also:* clerk(s), stenographer(s). *See also* Manuscripts; Medieval literature; Medieval manuscripts; Writers.

Scriptwriting. Scriptwrit(er,ers,ing). *Choose from:* script(s), motion picture(s), television, play(s) *with:* author(s,ship), writer(s), adapt(ed,ing,er, ers,ation). *Consider also:* screenwriter (s), playwright(s) *See also* Authors; Dramatists; Writers.

Sculpture. Sculptur(e,ed,es,ing). Plastic art(s). Scrimshaw. *Choose from:* clay, wood, marble, stone, rock(s), metal(s) *with:* sculpt(ed,s,ing), model(ed,ing), carv(e,ed,ing). *Consider also:* monument(s), statu(e,es,ary), waxwork(s), ceramic(s). *See also* Arts; Carving (decorative arts); Ceramics; Medieval sculpture; Municipal art; Prehistoric sculpture; Public art; Statues.

Sculpture, medieval. See *Medieval sculpture.*

Sculpture, prehistoric. See *Prehistoric sculpture.*

Sea, capture at. See *Capture at sea.*

Sea, collisions at. See *Collisions at sea.*

Sea power. Sea power. Seapower. Gunboat diplomacy. *Choose from:* sea(s), maritime, naval, nav(y,ies), nautical, ship(s), fleet(s), gunboat(s), submarine(s), aircraft carrier(s), destroyer(s), battleship(s), shore base(s), torpedo(es), seamen *with:* power(s,ful), control(led,ling), strength, presence, show force(s), blockade(s), offensive(s), security, armament(s), strateg(y,ies,ic), geopolitic(s,al), territorial, weapon(s,ry), supremacy, diplomacy. *See also* Aerial warfare; Aircraft carriers; Assault (battle); Coast defenses; Combat; Invasion; Military operations; Military power; Military readiness; Military strategies; Naval strategy; Navy yards and naval stations; Shipping industry; Ships; Troop strength; Warships.

Sea routes. See *Trade routes.*

Sea songs. Sea song(s). Shant(y,ies). Chant(y,ies,ey,eys). Boatmen's song(s). *Choose from:* sea, sailor(s), ship(board), rowing, sailing, nav(y,ies,al), nautical *with:* song(s), ballad(s), ditt(y,ies), tune(s). *See also* Folk songs; Seafaring life; Work songs.

Seafaring life. Seafar(ing,er,ers). Whal(er,ers). Fisher(man,men,women, woman). Sailor(s). Shipmaster(s). Mariner(s). Sea(man,men). *Choose from:* nav(y,al), Merchant Marine, Coast Guard, oceangoing, seagoing *with:* career(s), life. *Consider also:* marine biolog(ist,ists), pirate(s). *See also*

Boatmen; Marine accidents; Sailing; Sailors; Sea songs.

Seafood. Seafood. Shellfish. Lobster(s). Clam(s). Crab(s,meat). Fish chowder(s). Clam chowder(s). Shrimp. Scallop(s). Oyster(s). Squid. Octopus. Mussel(s). Calamari. *Consider also:* salmon, flounder, cod, trout, etc. *See also* Diet; Fish as food; Fishes; Food; Mariculture.

Seamen. See *Sailors.*

Seaports. See *Ports.*

Search. Search(ed,es,ing). Seek(ing). Sought. Hunt(ed,ing). Investigat(e,ed, ing). Explor(e,ed,ing,ation). Look(ed, ing). Examin(e,ed,ing,ation). Frisk(ed,ing). Rummag(e,ed,ing). Perus(e,ed,ing). Scrutiniz(e,ed,ing, ation). Track(ed,ing). Inspect(ed,ing, ion). *Consider also:* urine, hair, breath, DNA *with:* sample(s), test(s,ed,ing). *See also* Help seeking behavior; Information seeking; Job search; Police questioning; Quests; Search and seizure; Search strategies.

Search and rescue operations. See *Disaster relief; Relief services.*

Search and seizure. Search and seizure. Visit(ation) and search(ed,ing). Sting operation(s). *Consider also:* frisk(ed,ing), drug test(s,ing), search(es), search warrant(s), raid(s,ed,ing), visit(s,ing,ation) *with:* arrest(ed,ing), confiscat(e,ed,ing,ion), seiz(e,ed,ing, ure), forfeit(ed,ing,ure). *Consider also:* no-knock warrant(s), RICO seizure(s), canine search(es), warrantless search(es), police obtained evidence, Fourth Amendment. *See also* Arrests; Criminal investigations; Drug and narcotic control; Forfeiture; Law enforcement; Police dogs; Police questioning; Right of privacy.

Search firms, executive. See *Executive search firms.*

Search strategies. Search strateg(y,ies). *Choose from:* search(ing), boolean, research, information-seeking *with:* strateg(y,ies), tactic(s). *Consider also:* search(ing) *with:* technique(s), procedure(s), scheme(s), profile(s), term(s), key(s). *See also* Access to information; Automated information retrieval; Information seeking; Problem solving; Search.

Seas, freedom of the. See *Freedom of the seas.*

Seashore. See *Beaches; Shorelines.*

Seasonal affective disorder. Seasonal affective disorder(s). Seasonal mood disorder(s). Seasonal depression. Winter depression. *Choose from:* season(s,al, ality), winter, summer, autumn, fall, spring, weather, holiday(s), Christmas, daylight, melatonin *with:* affect(ive), depress(ive,ion,ions), suicid(es,al), mood(s,y,iness), psycho(sis,ses,tic), malaise, blues, melanchol(y,ia), schizoaffective. *See also* Affective disorders; Anniversary reactions; Biological rhythms; Cyclothymic disorder; Depression (psychology); Depressive disorder; Holiday depression; Neurasthenia; Seasonal variations; Seasons.

Seasonal labor. See *Migrant workers; Temporary employees.*

Seasonal unemployment. Seasonal unemployment. *Choose from:* season(s,al,ality), winter, summer, autumn, fall, spring, vacation(s), harvest(s,ing), holiday(s) *with:* unemploy(ed,ment,able), laidoff, laid off, layoff(s), out of work, jobless(ness), idle(d) worker(s), unwaged. *See also* Disguised unemployment; Dislocated workers; Dismissal of staff; Migrant workers; Temporary employees; Transience; Underemployment; Unemployment; Unemployment rates; Unemployment relief; Workforce planning.

Seasonal variations. Seasonal variation(s). *Choose from:* season(s,al,ally,able), spring(like,ly), summer(like,ly), autumn(like,ly), winter(like,ly), wintry *with:* variation(s), variab(le,ility), fluctuat(e,ed,ing,ion,ion(s), change(s, ability), cycle(s), adjustment(s). *See also* Biological rhythms; Climatic changes; Fluctuations; Hibernation; Holiday depression; Seasonal affective disorder; Seasons; Variations.

Seasonal workers. See *Migrant workers; Temporary employees.*

Seasons. Season(al,s). Summer(time). Summer solstice. Haying time. Spring(time). Vernal equinox. Sowing time. Vernal season. Autumn. Fall. Harvest time. Autumnal equinox. Winter(time). Time of the year. Snowtime. Winter solstice. Wet season. Dry season. Rainy season. Cold months. *See also* Biological rhythms; Seasonal affective disorder; Seasonal variations; Temperature effects; Weather.

Seat belts. Seat belt(s). Seatbelt(s). Safety belt(s). Car restraint(s). Safety seat(s). Lap belt(s). Shoulder belt(s). Automobile child restraint(s). *See also* Safety devices.

Secession. Secession(ism,ist,ists). Seced(e, ed,ing). Separatist(s). Withdraw(al). Gain independence. Win independence. Liberation. Separate from. Sever(e,ed, ing) ties. Break(ing) away. Breakaway republic(s). Independence movement(s). *See also* Peasant rebellions; Political self determination; Separatism.

Seclusion. See *Social isolation.*

Second careers. See *Career change; Career mobility; Career patterns; Life stage transitions.*

Second hand trade. Second hand trade. Flea market(s). Garage sale(s). Yard sale(s). *Choose from:* second hand, swap, resale, thrift, used goods, used book(s), junk *with:* market(s), auction(s), retail(er,ers,ing), store(s), outlet(s), shop(s), dealer(s). *See also* Antiquarian booksellers; Auctions; Bartering; Retailing.

Second language education. Second language education. Foreign language education. *Choose from:* second language(s), foreign language(s), bilingual, Spanish, French, Russian, etc. *with:* education, course(s), program(s), immersion program(s), language laborator(y,ies), lesson(s), instruction, teaching, learning, acquisition; skill(s), proficien(t,cy), competence, achievement, comprehension, performance, vocabulary, conversational ability. *Consider also:* TEFL, TESL, ESL. *See also* Area studies; Bilingual education; Language acquisition; Language transfer (language learning); Multilingualism; Second languages; Whole language approach.

Second language learning. See *Second language education.*

Second languages. Second language(s). Foreign language(s). Non-native language(s). *Consider also:* bilingual, Spanglish. *See also* Bilingual education; Creoles; Language; Language planning; Language shift; Languages (as subjects).

Second marriages. See *Remarriage.*

Second opinion. See *Referral.*

Second order language. See *Metalanguage.*

Secondary analysis. Secondary analysis. Published data. Secondary source(s). Re-analysis. Archival data. *See also* Archives; Data collection; Resources.

Secondary education. Secondary education. *Choose from:* secondary *with:* grade(s), school(s), program(s). High school(s). Prep(aratory) school(s). College preparation. Pre-college. Grade(s) 9-12. Grades nine through twelve. Junior high school(s). Ninth grade. Tenth grade. Eleventh grade. Twelfth grade. *See also* Adult education; High schools; Junior high schools; Vocational education.

Secondary gains. Secondary gain(s). Epinos(ic,is). *See also* Sick role.

Secondary reinforcement. Secondary reinforcement. *Choose from:* secondary, token, conditioned *with:* reinforcement, reinforcer(s), reward(s), stimul(i,us). *Consider also:* second order conditioning. *See also* Conditioning (psychology); Reinforcement.

Secondary relationships. Secondary relation(s,ship,ships). Categorical contact(s). *Choose from:* secondary, impersonal, business, personal *with:* relation(s,ship,ships), contact(s). *See also* Acquaintances; Interpersonal relations; Peers; Social contact; Social distance; Social interaction.

Secondary school students. See *High school students.*

Secondary school teachers. See *High school teachers.*

Secondary schools. See *High schools.*

Secondhand booksellers. See *Antiquarian booksellers; Second hand trade.*

Secrecy. Secrecy. Secret(e,s,ive,iveness, ness). Back-channel(s). Censor(ed,ing, s,ship). Classified information. Clandestine(ness). Conceal(ed,ing, ment). Confidential(ity). Covert(ness). Coverup(s). Cryptography. Dissemb(le, led,ling). Dissimulat(e,ed,ing,ion). Evasive(ness). Evasion. Furtive(ness). Hide. Hidden. Hiding. Insider trading. Low profile(s). Money laundering. Off the books. Prevent(ed,ing) disclosure. Priva(cy,te). Privileged commun- ication(s). Privileged information. Sly(ness). Sneak(y,iness). Stealth(y, iness). Subterfuge. Suppress(ed,ing). Surreptitious(ness). Unbetrayed. Uncommunicated. Undercover. Unreported. Untold. With(hold,held). *See also* Classified information; Clandestinity; Confidential communica- tions; Confidentiality; Cryptography; Deception; Espionage; Government secrecy; National security; Privacy; Privacy laws; Secret languages; Secret societies; Trade secrets.

Secrecy, government. See *Government secrecy.*

Secret codes. See *Cryptography.*

Secret languages. Secret language(s). Cipher system(s). *Consider also:* private language(s), pig latin, secret handshake(s), encrypt(ed,ing,ion), speaking in tongues, enigma code, etc. *See also* Cryptography; Secrecy; Secret societies.

Secret police. Secret police. State security police. Tsarist political police. *Consider also:* reign(s) of terror, police state(s), Stasi, Staatssicherheitsdienst, Fontanka, Securitate, Operation Condor, Gestapo, NKVD, Vecheka, Cheka, KGB, Komitet Gosudarstvennoy Bezopasnosti. *See also* Eavesdropping; Espionage; Intelligence service; Military intelligence; Political persecution; Subversion; Surveillance of citizens; Undercover operations.

Secret societies. Secret societ(y,ies). *Choose from:* clandestine, secret, undercover, underground *with:* societ(y,ies), club(s), fraternit(y,ies), sororit(y,ies), brotherhood(s), sisterhood(s), alliance(s), federation(s), league(s), organization(s), association(s), guild(s). *Consider also:* Rosicrucians, Camorra, Carbonari, Eastern Star, Masons, Shriners, Freemasons, Oddfellows, Ku Klux Klan, Skull and Bones secret society, Black Hand, Mafia, Molly Maguires. *See also* Anti-government radicals; Associations (organizations); Confraternities; Cults; Religious rituals; Resistance movements; Secrecy; Secret languages; Societies (organizations); Underground.

Secretaries. Secretar(y,ies). Stenogra- pher(s). Steno(s). Typist(s). Clerical personnel. Secretarial personnel. Support staff. Support occupation(s). *Consider also:* clerk(s), receptionist(s), typing pool(s), secretarial staff, girl friday(s), pink collar worker(s), administrative assistant(s), executive assistant(s). *See also* Clerical workers.

Secrets, official. See *Censorship; Classified information; Government secrecy; News policies.*

Secrets, state. See *Censorship; Classified information; Government secrecy.*

Secrets, trade. See *Trade secrets.*

Sectarian conflict. Sectarian conflict(s). Religious conflict(s). *Choose from:* sectarian, religious, denominational, interdenominational *with:* conflict(s), disagreement(s), dispute(s). *See also* Conflict; Religious disputations.

Sectarianism. Sectarian(ism,ization). Parochial(ism). Faction(s,al,alism). Partisan(ship). Denomination(al,alism). Hyperorthodox. Doctrinaire. Extremis(m,ts). Cult(ish). *See also* Bias; Ethnocentrism; Factionalism; Partisan; Political affiliation; Political ideologies; Religious denominations; Schism; Social attitudes; Social contact; Traditionalism; Tribalism; Worldview.

Sector, industrial. See *Industry.*

Sector, informal. See *Informal sector.*

Sector, private. See *Private sector.*

Sector, public. See *Public sector.*

Sects. Sect(s). Early Christian(s). Shaker(s). Jehovah's Witnesses. Pentacostal(s). Early Quaker(s). Early Methodist(s). Adventist(s). Early Christian Scientist(s). Nativistic movement(s). Schismatic(s). Sectarian movement(s). Flagellant group(s). *Consider also:* denominalization, cult(s), part(y,ies), faction(s), counterculture(s). *See also* Churches; Countercultures; Cults; Jewish sects; Religious cults; Religious denominations; Religious fundamental- ism; Religious institutions; Snake handling.

Sects, Jewish. See *Jewish sects.*

Secularism. Secularis(m,t,tic). Secular humanis(m,t,ts,tic). Secular societ(y,ies). Utilitarian value(s). Worldl(y,iness). Nonspiritual(ity). *Choose from:* indifferen(ce), reject(ed,ing,ion), exclud(e,ed,ing), exclusion *with:* religion(s), religious consideration(s), religious value(s), church(es). *Consider also:* materialis(m,tic), temporal(ity). *See also* Anticlericalism; Church state relationship; Rationalization (sociology); Secularization.

Secularization. Secular(ism,ize,ized, ization). Secular societ(y,ies). Utilitarian value(s). De-Christian(ize,ized,ization). Profan(e,ation). Desanctif(y,ied,ying, ication). Here(sy,tical). Desacraliz(e,ed, ation). Rational(ism,ize,ized,ization). *Choose from:* disavowal, abandon(ed, ing,ment), reject(ed,ing) *with:* relig(ious,ion), church, synagogue. *Consider also:* invisible religion, atheism, death of God, nonbeliever(s), disenchant(ed,ment), separation of church and state, secular humanism. *See also* Anticlericalism; Church state relationship; Churches; Creationism; Death of God (theology); Liberalism; Liberalism (religion); Modernization; Rationalization (sociology); Religions; Religious beliefs; Religious cultural groups; Religious fundamentalism; Religious movements; Sacredness; Secularism; Social processes.

Securities. See *Investments.*

Securities, electronic trading. See *Electronic trading (securities).*

Securities dealers. See *Stock brokers.*

Security. Assur(ed,ance,ances). Carefree. Confiden(t,ce). Certain(ty,titude). Certif(y,ied,ication). Conserv(e,ed, ation). Corroborat(e,ed,ion). Custody. Defended. Dependab(le,ility). Fortif(y,ied,ication). Guarantee(s,d). Guard(ed,ianship). Haven(s). Impregnab(le,ility). Immun(e,ity,ities). Inner strength(s). Insur(e,ed,ing,ance). Invulner(able,ability). Permanent employment. Preserv(e,ed,ation). Protect(ed,ive,ion). Reassur(ed,ing, ances). Refuge(s). Reliab(le,ility). Secur(e,eness,ity). Safe(ty). Sense of belonging(ness). Stab(le,ility). Support(ed). Sure(ty). Salvation. Safekeeping. Sanctuar(y,ies). Shelter(ed,s). Safeguard(s,ed). Shield(ed,ing). Steadfast(ness). Tenure(d). Trust(worthy,worthiness). Unassail(able,ability). Unperturbed. Untroubled. Undistressed. Verif(y,ied,ication). Warrant(y,ies,ed). *See also* Affiliation motivation; Autonomy (government); Belongingness; Certainty; Control; Crime prevention; Durability; Economic security; Emotional security; Fear; Fortification; Group feeling; Individual needs; Job security; Law enforcement; National security; Personal independence; Protection; Risk; Safety; Security measures; Social acceptance; Stability; Threat; Trusting; Vulnerability.

Security, collective. See *Collective security.*

Security, economic. See *Economic security.*

Security, emotional. See *Emotional security.*

Security, internal. See *Internal security.*

Security, job. See *Job security.*

Security, national. See *National security.*

Security facilities, maximum. See *Maximum security facilities.*

Security guards. Security guard(s). Sentry(y,ies). Sentinel(s). Watch(man, men). Shore patrol(s). Bodyguard(s). Building guard(s). Watchdog(s). *See also* Law enforcement personnel.

Security measures. Security measure(s). *Choose from:* security, safety, protect(ion,ive) *with:* system(s), guard(s), procedures, lock(s), personnel, force(s), device(s). *Consider also:* alarm systems, safeguard(s), police protection, loss prevention, theft prevention, guard(s,ing), vault(s), safety deposit box(es), safe(s), closed circuit television, surveillance, crime protection, protecting property, lighting, fence(s), exit control(s), monitoring, detector(s), armored car(s), staybolt(s), deadbolt(s), warning system(s), barrier(s), personnel detector(s), computer security, intrusion detection, fire protection, data security, anti-virus, anti-viral. *See also* Crime prevention; Fences; Fire prevention; Network backup; Preventive medicine; Preventive psychiatry; Risk management; Safety devices; Seat belts; Vaccinations.

Seduction. Seduc(e,ed,ing,tion,ement). Attract(ed,ing,ion,ions). Allur(e,ed,es, ing). Entic(e,ed,es,ing). Beguil(e,ed,es, ing). Captivat(e,ed,es,ing). Charm(ed, s,ing). Titillat(e,ed,es,ing). *Consider also:* lead(ing) astray, tempt(ed,s,ing), lur(e,ed,es,ing), bewitch(ed,ing), enraptur(e,ed,es,ing), inveigl(e,ed,ing, ement). *See also* Eroticism; Interpersonal influences; Persuasion; Sex customs; Temptation.

Seekers, status. See *Status Seekers.*

Seeking, information. See *Information Seeking.*

Seeking, novelty. See *Sensation Seeking.*

Seeking, sensation. See *Sensation Seeking.*

Seeking, thrill. See *Extreme sports; Risk taking; Sensation Seeking.*

Seeking assistance. See *Help Seeking behavior.*

Seeking behavior, health. See *Health; Health promotion; Holistic health; Mental health; Preventive medicine; Preventive psychiatry; Primary prevention; Quality of life; Well being.*

Seeking behavior (help seeking). See *Help Seeking behavior.*

Seers. See *Occultism.*

Segmentation, labor market. See *Labor market segmentation.*

Segmentation, market. See *Market segmentation.*

Segmentation, social. See *Social segmentation.*

Segregated housing. See *Residential segregation.*

Segregation, educational. See *School segregation.*

Segregation, housing. See *Residential segregation.*

Segregation, job. See *Occupational segregation; Labor market segmentation.*

Segregation, neighborhood. See *Residential segregation.*

Segregation, occupational. See *Occupational segregation.*

Segregation, racial. See *Racial segregation.*

Segregation, residential. See *Residential segregation.*

Segregation, school. See *School segregation.*

Seizure, search and. See *Search and seizure.*

Seizure of ships. Seizure of ship(s). *Choose from:* hijack(ed,ing), hostage(s), pira(cy,te,tes), captur(e,ed,ing), holdup, hold up, held up, commandeer(ed,ing), take possession, took possession, overpower(ed,ing), takeover(s) *with:* ship(s), boat(s), freighter(s), barge(s), tugboat(s), submarine(s), destroyer(s), frigate(s), oceanliner(s), cruiseship(s), cruiser(s), tanker(s), vessel(s), cargo(es), sailboat(s), catamaran(s), ketch(es), yawl(s), schooner(s), yacht(s), steamship(s), ferryboat(s), ferr(y,ies). *Consider also:* Achille Lauro. *See also* Capture at sea; Hijacking; Piracy (at sea); Privateers; Shipping industry; Ships.

Seizures, epileptic. See *Epileptic seizures.*

Selected readings. Selected readings. Antholog(y,ies,ize,ized,izing). Compilation(s). Compendium(s). *Consider also:* select(ed,ion,ions), collect(ed,ion,ions) reading(s), writing(s), work(s). *See also* Anthologies; Literature.

Selection, animal mate. See *Animal mate selection.*

Selection, biased. See *Biased selection.*

Selection, book. See *Book selection.*

Selection, employee. See *Personnel selection.*

Selection, human mate. See *Human mate selection.*

Selection, job. See *Occupational choice.*

Selection, natural. See *Darwinism.*

Selection, personnel. See *Personnel selection.*

Selection, site. See *Site selection.*

Selection procedures. Selection procedure(s). *Choose from:* selection, decision making, screen(ed,ing), allocat(e,ed,ing,ion), hiring *with:* procedure(s), test(s), basis, criteria, process(es), polic(y,ies), guideline(s), method(s,ology,ologies), technique(s), practice(s), rule(s), program(s), formula(s), system(s). *Consider also:* review(ed,ing) credential(s). *See also* Choices (alternatives); Criteria; Decision making; Employment interviews; Human mate selection; Job applicant screening; Personnel selection; Selection tests.

Selection tests. Selection test(s). Qualifying examination(s). Scholastic aptitude test(s). Graduate record examination(s). *Choose from:* select(ing,ion), screening, admittance, admission(s), entry, licensing *with:* test(ing,s), inventor(y, ies), examination(s), procedure(s), interview(s), measure(s), scale(s), formula(s). *See also* Screening; Measurement.

Selective attention. Selective attention. *Consider also:* control(led,ling), focus(ed,sed,ing,sing), single channel, selective(ly), direct(ed,ing,ion), filter(ed,ing), screen(ed,ing) *with:* attent(ion,ive), attending, aware(ness). *See also* Altered states of consciousness; Attention; Awareness; Concentration; Distractibility; Distraction; Divided attention; Monitoring; Vigilance.

Selective breeding. Selective breeding. *Choose from:* select(ive,ively,ion,ed,ing) *with:* breed(ing), bred, inbreed(ing), inbred, genetic(s), crossbreed(ing), crossbred. *See also* Animal breeding; Animal domestication; Eugenics; Reproductive technologies.

Self, idealized. See *Idealized self.*

Self accusation. Self accusat(ion,ions,ory). Feeling worthless(ness). Intropunitive(ness). Mea culpa. *Consider also:* self *with:* accusation, blam(e,ed,ing), derogat(ing,ion). *See also* Blame; Denunciation; Depression (psychology); Guilt; Pessimism; Self debasement; Self hate.

Self actualization. Self actualiz(ed,ing, ation). Growth motivation. Self generated growth. *Choose from:* self, personal, inner, spiritual *with:* actualiz(ed,ing,ation), realiz(ing,ation), development, growth, motivation, utilization, transcenden(t,ce), reclamation, regenerat(e,ed,ion), renew(al), discovery, transformation. *Consider also:* anagogic tendenc(y,ies), self consistency, humanistic psychology, B cognition, B love. *See also* Aspirations; Enlightenment; Help seeking behavior; Human potential movement; Behavior development; Careers; Gestalt therapy; Humanistic education; Job satisfaction; Individualism; Individuals; Intellectual development; Life change events; Life satisfaction; Life stage transitions; Marital satisfaction; Mental health; Morale; Need satisfaction; Personal independence; Personality; Personality development; Reality therapy; Role perception; Self concept; Self congruence; Self culture; Self efficacy; Self evaluation; Self expression; Self help; Self knowledge; Sensitivity training; Spiritual exercises; Spiritual formation; Values.

Self administration. Self administ(ered, ration). Automedicat(e,ed,ing,ion). Self medicat(e,ed,ing,ion). *Choose from:* self *with:* administ(ered,ration), inject(ed, ing,ion,ions). *Consider also:* patient(s) *with:* use, misuse, compliance. *See also* Non-prescription drugs; Patient compliance; Patient education; Patient participation; Self care.

Self annihilation. See *Self destructive behavior; Self hate; Self inflicted wounds; Self mutilation; Suicide.*

Self assessment. Self assessment. *Choose from:* self *with:* assessment(s), evaluation(s), acceptance, devaluation, deprecat(ing,ion), rating(s), appraisal, punish(ing,ment), esteem, derogation, effacement, dynamism, concept. *See also* Metacognition; Reminiscence; Self concept; Self efficacy; Self esteem; Self evaluation; Self knowledge; Self management (individual); Self monitoring; Self perception; Self report; Social comparison; Sensitivity training; Transactional analysis.

Self awareness. See *Self perception.*

Self blame. See *Self accusation.*

Self care. Self care. *Choose from:* self, home *with:* monitor(ed,ing), examination, administ(ered,ration), treat(ed, ing,ment), help, care, injection(s), catheteriz(ed,ing,ation), dialysis, check(ed,ing), medication, measur(e,ed, ing,ement), bathing, feed(ing), dress(ing), groom(ing). *Consider also:* continuous ambulatory peritoneal dialysis. *See also* Activities of daily living; Aftercare; Ambulatory care; Body

care; Child self care; Coping; Rehabilitation; Self administration; Self help; Self help devices; Self neglect; Skill learning.

Self care, child. See *Child self care.*

Self centeredness. See *Egocentrism.*

Self concept. Self concept(s). *Choose from:* self *with:* concept(s), image(s), identity, sense, congruence, esteem, assessment, depiction, perceived, perception, rating(s), evaluat(ion,ive), portrait(s), awareness, acceptance, appraisal, attribution(s). *Consider also:* ideal self, personal identity, looking glass self. *See also* Aspirations; Body image; Defense mechanisms; Delay of gratification; Depersonalization disorder; Ego; Egocentrism; Egoism; Ethnic identity; Ethnicity; Extraversion (psychology); Gender identity; Gestalt therapy; Honor (integrity); Humanistic education; Identification (psychology); Identity; Idealized self; Images; Locus of control; Morale; Personality; Perspective taking; Pride; Racial identity; Pride; Reference groups; Relative deprivation; Role ambiguity; Role conflict; Role expectations; Self actualization; Self assessment; Self congruence; Self efficacy; Self esteem; Self knowledge; Self perception; Self respect; Shame; Social identity.

Self confidence. See *Pride; Self assessment; Self concept; Self efficacy; Self esteem.*

Self congruence. Self congruence. Level of self awareness. Actual self vs ideal self. Body self split. *Choose from:* self *with:* congruen(t,ce), incongruen(t,ce), congruity, ideal, expectation(s), alienation, perception, consisten(t,cy), inconsisten(t,cy), concept. *Choose from:* self concept, self image, self perception, self ideal *with:* congruen(t,ce), discrepanc(ies,y), conflict(s), disturbance(s), inconsisten(t,cy). *Consider also:* status inconsistency, role conflict(s). *See also* Attitudes; Behavior; Cognitive dissonance; Role conflict; Self actualization; Self concept; Self knowledge; Status inconsistency.

Self consciousness. Self conscious(ness). Ill at ease. Ashamed(ly). Bashful(ly). *See also* Body awareness; Egocentrism; Egotism; Embarrassment; Narcissism; Self concept; Self debasement; Self efficacy; Self esteem; Self hate; Self monitoring; Self report; Shame.

Self control. Self control. *Choose from:* self, internal, ego, impulse(s), feeling(s), urge(s), act(s), personal, anger, hostility *with:* control(led,ling), discipline, manag(e,ed,ing,ement), restrain(t,ed, ing), monitor(ed,ing), master(y,ed,ing), overcontrol(led,ling), regulat(e,ed, ing,ion). *Consider also:* abstinence, impulse control, willpower, resist(ed,ing) temptation(s), delay of gratification, inhibit(ed,ions),

repress(ed,ion,ions), internaliz(e,ed, ing,ation) of responsibility, internal locus of control, internal control, inner directed. *See also* Abstinence; Behavior modification; Behavior problems; Biofeedback; Cognitive restructuring; Compliance; Defense mechanisms; Delay of gratification; Emotional maturity; Inhibition (psychology); Inner directed; Metacognition; Mental discipline; Personal independence; Personality traits; Resistance; Self culture; Self denial; Self efficacy; Self management (individual); Self sacrifice.

Self culture. Self culture(d). *Choose from:* self, personal *with:* culture(d), develop(ed,ment), enhancement, instruction, cultivation, educat(ed,ion), discipline(d), creat(ed,ion). *Consider also:* wellness program(s), self-directed learning, homeschool(ed,ing). *See also* Mental Discipline; Mnemonic learning; Self actualization; Self control; Self management (individual).

Self debasement. Self debas(ement,ed,ing). Self abas(ement,ed,ing). Low self esteem. *Choose from:* self *with:* deprecat(e,ed,ing,ion), degrad(e,ed,ing), demean(ed,ing), disparag(e,ed,ing, ement), derogat(e,ed,ing,ion), devalu(e,ed,ing), effacement. *See also* Defense mechanisms; Derogation; Guilt; Pessimism; Self accusation; Self defeating behavior; Self hate; Shame.

Self deception. Self deception. *Choose from:* self, oneself, myself, himself, herself , themselves *with:* decept(ion, ive), deceit(ful), deceiv(e,ed,ing,ing), lying to, delud(e,ed,ing), delusion(s), denial(s). *Consider also:* denial of anger, faking, impression management, conscious biasing, self-discrepancy. *See also* Artificiality; Authenticity; Deception; Faking; Hypocrisy; Malingering; Self knowledge.

Self defeating behavior. Self defeating behavior. Self destructive(ness). Self handicapping. Counterproductive(ness). *Choose from:* self defeating, masochistic, abasive, self destructive, counterproductive *with:* behavior(s), personality disorder(s), motivation, tendenc(y,ies). *Consider also:* fear(ed,ing) or avoid(ed,ing,ance) *with:* success. *See also* Fear of success; Self debasement; Self fulfilling prophecy; Pessimism; Self destructive behavior.

Self defense. Self defense. Victim response(s). Victim resistance. Rape prevention. Martial art(s). Neighborhood watch. Judo. Karate. Jujitsu. Aikido. Fighting back. Street smart. Hatpin(s). Foil(ed) attempt. Mace. Carry gun for protection. Watchdog(s). Defense technique(s). Self preservation. Defense against intruder(s). Put up a fight. *Choose from:* self, yourself, oneself, herself, himself, personal, home, neighborhood, wom(an,en) *with:* defense(s), defend(ed,ing), protect(ed,ing,ion). *See also* Armor; Crime prevention; Extenuating circumstances; Justification (law); Martial arts; Security measures; Victimization; Violence.

Self denial. Self denial. Self sacrific(e,ed, ing). Self abnegat(e,ed,ing,ion). Self depriv(e,ed,ing,ation). Selfless(ness). Unselfish(ness). Altruis(m,tic). Self restraint. Abstemious(ness). Abstinen(t, ce). Asceticism. Martyr(s,dom). *Choose from:* avoid(ed,ing,ant), renunciation, renounc(e,ed,ing) *with:* pleasure(s), enjoyment. *Consider also:* self effac(ing,ement), self blam(e,ing), fast(ed,ing). *See also* Abstinence; Renunciation; Self control; Self sacrifice.

Self designing organizations. See *Organizational change.*

Self destructive behavior. Self destructive behavior. *Choose from:* self *with:* harm(ed,ing,ful), destruct(ion,ive), destroy(ed,ing), violen(ce,t), injur(e,ed, ing,ious), immolat(e,ed,ing,ion), mutilat(e,ed,ing,ion), handicap(ped, ping), inflict(ed,ing), abus(e,ed,ing,ive), punish(ed,ing,ment), shoot(ing), stab(bing). *Consider also:* parasuicid(e, es,al), suicid(e,es,al), overdos(e,es,ed, ing). *See also* Antisocial behavior; Attempted suicide; Behavior disorders; Death instinct; Deviant behavior; Head banging; Masochism; Personality disorders; Self control; Self hate; Self inflicted wounds; Self mutilation; Substance abuse; Suicidal behavior; Suicide; Suicide victims.

Self determination (individual). See *Inner directed; Personal independence.*

Self determination (national). See *Autonomy (government); Freedom; Political self determination; Popular sovereignty.*

Self determination, patient. See *Advance directives; Consumer directed care; Human rights; Informed consent; Patient rights; Right to die; Termination of treatment.*

Self determination, political. See *Political self determination.*

Self directed learning. See *Individualized instruction.*

Self direction (psychology). See *Inner directed; Personal independence.*

Self discipline. See *Self control.*

Self disclosure. Self disclos(ure,ing). Self express(ion,ive). Self reported. Self revelation. Disclosure reciprocity. Transparent self. Open(ness). Open communication. Show(ed,ing) feeling(s). Display(ed,ing) emotion(s).

Expressive(ness). *See also* Anonymity; Communication (thought transfer); Confidentiality; Counseling; Disclosure; Intimacy; Psychotherapy; Self expression; Self help.

Self education. Self educat(ed,ion). Self taught. *Choose from:* self, independent *with:* instruct(ed,ion), taught, teaching, learning, study, educat(ed,ion). *Consider also:* correspondence course(s), programmed learning, programed learning, programmed instruction, programed instruction. *See also* Active learning; Adult education; Correspondence schools; Individualized instruction; Language laboratories; Lifelong learning; Personal independence.

Self efficacy. Self efficacy. *Choose from:* self, personal *with:* efficacy, confidence, competenc(e,y,ies), trust, expect(ed,ing, ation,ations). *Consider also:* empower(ed,ing,ment). *See also* Achievement; Behavior development; Effectiveness; Empowerment; Expectations; Individualism; Metacognition; Optimism; Personal independence; Self actualization; Self control; Self esteem; Self evaluation; Self perception.

Self employment. Self employ(ed,ment). Owner operated. Own business(es). Home business(es). *Consider also:* consultant work, consultan(cy,cies), entrepreneur(s,ial). *See also* Business; Careers; Employment; Employment opportunities; Entrepreneurship; Home based businesses; Microenterprise; Small businesses.

Self esteem. Self esteem. Morale. *Choose from:* self, personal *with:* esteem, satisf(ied,action), confiden(t,ce), respect, worth, dignity, accept(ing,ance), regard, love, affirm(ing,ation), adequacy, efficacy, positive attribution, actualiz(ing,ation), concept(s), perception, image, definition, validation. *Consider also:* personal autonomy, well being. *See also* Assertiveness; Attribution; Cognitive dissonance; Egoism; Happiness; Honor (integrity); Honored (esteem); Human dignity; Interpersonal relations; Narcissism; Personality traits; Recognition; Respect; Satisfaction; Self concept; Self confidence; Self congruence; Self debasement; Self efficacy; Self esteem; Self evaluation; Self hate; Self knowledge; Self presentation; Sensitivity training.

Self evaluation. Self evaluation. *Choose from:* self, personal, oneself, own *with:* evaluat(ed,ing,ion), assess(ed,ing,ment, ments), rat(ed,ings), scor(ed,ing), monitor(ed,ing), analysis, report(ed,ing), interpret(ed,ing,ation), estimat(e,ed,es, ing,ion,ions), apprais(ed,ing,al), description(s), describ(e,ed,ing), stud(y,ies), predict(ed,ing,ions). *See also* Evaluation; Metacognition; Peer review;

Reminiscence; Self actualization; Self assessment; Self concept; Self efficacy; Self esteem; Self management (individual); Self monitoring; Self report; Sensitivity training; Social comparison; Transactional analysis.

Self evaluation (groups). Self evaluation program(s). *Choose from:* self, internal, performance *with:* evaluat(ion,ive), assess(ed,ing,ment,ments), appraisal, administered *with:* stud(y,ies), program(s), review(s). *Consider also:* institutional self stud(y,ies), organizational internal review, organizational self study. *See also* Evaluation; Needs assessment; Organizational effectiveness; Policy making; Program evaluation.

Self examination. See *Examination of conscience.*

Self expression. Self express(ive,iveness, ion). *Choose from:* self, oneself, yourself, herself, himself, personal, individual, emotional *with:* express(ive, iveness,ion). *Consider also:* responsive(ness), expressivity, communicative(ness), eloquence. *See also* Art therapy; Assertiveness; Catharsis; Communication (thought transfer); Conversation; Creativity; Dance therapy; Eloquence; Emotionality; Individualism; Journalism; Movement therapy; Music therapy; Nonverbal communication; Personal independence; Self actualization; Self disclosure; Self presentation; Transactional analysis.

Self fulfilling prophecy. Self fulfilling prophec(y,ies). *Choose from:* pygmalion, expectancy, Rosenthal *with:* effect(s). *Consider also:* looking glass self. *See also* Attitudes; Attribution; Expectations; Labeling (of persons); Motivation; Prophets; Prediction; Self congruence; Social reinforcement; Stereotyping; Teacher expectations.

Self government. See *Autonomy (government); Freedom; Political selfdetermination; Popular sovereignty.*

Self hate. Self hate. *Choose from:* self *with:* hate, hatred, despis(e,es,ed,ing), dislik(e,ed,es,ing), blam(e,ed,es,ing). *See also* Self accusation; Self consciousness; Self debasement; Self destructive behavior; Self esteem; Shame; Suicide.

Self help. Self help. Self directed stress reduction. Intensive journal process. Bibliotherapy. *Choose from:* self, himself, herself, themselves, autonomous *with:* guidance, help(ing), chang(e,es,ed,ing), monitor(ed,ing), reinforc(e,ed,ing,ement), counseling, treatment(s), management, analysis, relaxation training, instruction, assertiveness training, desensitization, care, therapy. *See also* Behavior modification; Bibliotherapy; Biofeedback; Help seeking behavior; Lifelong learning; Psychopoetry; Rehabilitation; Self actualization; Self disclosure; Self help books; Self help devices; Self help groups; Self management (individual); Self monitoring; Social support networks.

Self help books. Self help book(s). Personal guide(s). *Choose from:* personal, self-help, self improvement, inspirational, consumer, do-it-yourself *with:* book(s), guide(s), literature. *See also* Biblio-therapy; Books; Self help.

Self help devices. Self help device(s). *Choose from:* self help, disabled, handicapped, self feeding, mobility, helping, reading, writing, communication *with:* device(s), aid(s), tool(s), product(s), technolog(y,ies,ical), machine(s), computer aid(s). *Consider also:* speech synthesizer(s), communication board(s), transfer board(s), transfer commode seat(s), toileting device(s), mouthstick(s), standing frame(s), wheelchair(s), crutch(es), cane(s), prosthes(is,es), spoon plate(s), orientation aid(s), writing mouthpiece(s), hearing aid(s), captioned television. *See also* Communication aids for handicapped; Devices; Disability; Mobility aids; Prostheses; Self care; Self help.

Self help groups. Self help group(s). Self help movement. *Choose from:* mutual *with:* aid, support, help, assistance. *Choose from:* self help, therapeutic social, support, ex-patient(s) *with:* group(s), program(s), club(s), network(s). *Consider also:* parents groups, Recovery Inc., Parents Without Partners, Parents Anonymous, Mothers Anonymous, Gamblers Anonymous, Alcoholics Anonymous, Al Anon, Schizanon, Recovery, Inc., peer counseling, peer tutoring, La Leche League, weight loss groups, widows group(s), organizations of patients and families, associations of patients and families, women's group(s). *Choose from:* group(s), societ(y,ies), organization(s), association(s) *with:* lung disease, heart disease, cancer, Parkinson's, Alzheimer's, mastectomy, etc. *See also* Alcohol rehabilitation; Drug rehabilitation; Group psychotherapy; Help seeking behavior; Helping behavior; Parent help groups; Peer counseling; Self help; Social support networks; Women's groups.

Self hypnosis. See *Autohypnosis.*

Self identification. See *Identification (psychology).*

Self image. See *Self concept.*

Self improvement literature. See *Self help books.*

Self incrimination. Self incriminat(ing,ion). Confess(ed,ing,ion,ions). Plead(ing) guilty. *Choose from:* admission, admit(ted,ting) *with:* crime(s), misdemeanor(s), misdeed(s). *Consider also:* fifth amendment, right to silen(t,ce). *See also* Bill of Rights; Civil rights; Confession; Due process; Legal procedures; Trial (law).

Self indulgence. Self indulgen(t,ce). Me generation. Hedonis(m,tic). Pleasure seeking. Unrestrain(t,ed). Intemperance. La dolce vita. Fast living. Greed(y, iness). *Choose from:* self, personal, impulse *with:* indulgen(t,ce), overindulgen(t,ce), gratif(y,ied,ing, ication). *Consider also:* onanism. *See also* Impulsiveness; Masturbation; Need satisfaction; Selfishness (egocentric).

Self inflicted wounds. Self inflicted wound(s). Auto-aggression. *Choose from:* wrist(s) *with:* cut(ting), slash(ed, ing). Lip biting. *Choose from:* self *with:* inflicted, wound(s), biting, cutting, injur(y,ies,ious), aggress(ion,ive), destruct(ion,ive), puncturing, excoriat(ing,ion), abus(e,ive), assault, mutilat(ing,ion). *See also* Attempted suicide; Head banging; Injuries; Self destructive behavior; Self mutilation; Suicidal behavior.

Self instruction. See *Individualized instruction.*

Self interest. Self interest(ed). Own interest(s). Selfish(ness). Self seeking. Self concerned. Nimby. Not-In-My-Backyard. Narrow concern(s). Narrow interest(s). Self advocacy. Self-absorption. Self-absorbed. Egoistic(ally). Selfish motivation(s). Self centered(ness). *Consider also:* greed(y,iness), self-gratification. *See also* Altruism; Economic man; Egotism; Hedonism; Individualism; Monetary incentives; Selfishness (egocentric); Selfishness (stingy); Wants.

Self knowledge. Self knowledge. Reflexiv(e,ely,eness,ity). Reflectiv(e,ely, eness,ity). *Choose from:* self, oneself, himself, herself, themselves *with:* know(ledge,n,ing), aware(ness), understand(ing), understood, insight(s), reflection, discovery. *Consider also:* self image, self concept(ion), self esteem self deception. *See also* Aspirations; Attribution; Body awareness; Gender identity; Insight; Self actualization; Self assessment; Self concept; Self congruence; Self deception; Self efficacy; Self esteem; Self monitoring; Self perception; Self report; Self understanding; Social identity.

Self love. See *Egotism; Narcissism; Self respect.*

Self management (individual). Self management. Autoregulat(e,ed,ing,ion). *Choose from:* self, internal, personal, life, time, habit(s) *with:* manag(e,ed, ing,ement), regulat(e,ed,ing,ion), control(led,ling), initiat(e,ed,ing,iative), plan(ned,ning), restrain(t,ed,ing), govern(ed,ing), direct(ed,ing,ion). *See also* Behavior modification; Cognitive therapy; Mental discipline; Self control; Self culture; Self efficacy; Self help; Self reinforcement.

Self management (industrial). See *Industrial democracy; Worker control; Worker participation.*

Self mastery. See *Self control.*

Self medication. Self medicat(e,ed,ing,ion). Automedication. *Choose from:* self, yourself *with:* medicat(e,ed,ing,ion), administration, administered, treat(ed,ing,ment), prescrib(e,ed,ing), inject(ed,ing,ions). *Consider also:* self care, home remed(y,ies), over-the-counter drug(s), OTC drug(s), nonprescription medicine(s). *See also* Herbal medicine; Home care; Non-prescription drugs; Patient education; Self care.

Self monitoring. Self monitor(s,ed,ing). *Choose from:* self *with:* monitor(s,ed, ing), record(ed,ing), report(s,ed,ing), observation(s), measurement(s), measur(e,ed,ing), check(ed,ing), rat(ed,ing), aware(ness), regulat(ed,ing, ion), control(led,ling), correct(ed,ing, ion), referenc(ed,ing), focused attention. *Consider also:* metacognit(ive,ion), mindful(ness), home monitor(s,ed,ing). *See also* Behavior modification; Cognitive therapy; Self evaluation; Self help; Self knowledge; Self management (individual); Self report.

Self mutilation. Self mutilat(ed,ing,ion). Automutilat(ed,ing,ion). Autotomia. Autoaggress(ion,ive). *Choose from:* self, auto *with:* mutilat(ed,ing,ion), immolat(e,ed,ing,ion), inflicted, surgery, injur(y,ies,ed,ing,ious), aggression, destruct(ion,ive), emasculat(ed,ing,ion), castrat(ed,ing,ion), biting, abus(e,ive), excoriat(e,ed,ing,ion), destructive behaviour. *Consider also:* head banging, cut(ting) wrist(s), slash(ed,ing) wrist(s), factitial illness(es), morsicatio buccarum, morsicatio laborium, Munchhausen syndrome. *See also* Behavior disorders; Emotionally disturbed; Self destructive behavior; Self hate; Self inflicted wounds; Suicide.

Self neglect. Self neglect. *Choose from:* self, personal care, themselves *with:* neglect(ed,ing), uncared for, ungroomed, unwashed, unbathed, uncombed, disheveled. *Consider also:* loss of the will to live, domestic squalor, personal squalor, lack of care, squalor syndrome, Diogenes syndrome. *See also* Activities of daily living; Apathy; Body care; Depression (psychology); Elder abuse; Emotional abuse; Hygiene; Self care; Social isolation.

Self perception. Self perception. Metacognit(ion,ive). Body image. Ego. Identity. *Choose from:* self, oneself *with:*

perception, perceived, acceptance, efficacy, aware(ness), attribution, construing, referenc(ed,ing), recognition, focus, image, consciousness, affirm(cd,ing,ation), understanding, report, evaluation, knowledge, congruence, esteem, assessment, comparison(s). *See also* Aspirations; Attribution; Body awareness; Gender identity; Personality; Reference groups; Self actualization; Self assessment; Self concept; Self congruence; Self efficacy; Self esteem; Self knowledge; Self monitoring; Self presentation; Self report; Social identity.

Self presentation. Self presentation. Presentation of self. *Choose from:* image management, self definition, good manners, dramaturg(y,ical), self conscious(ness), ingratiat(e,ed,ing,ion), going public, out of the closet, expressive behavior, self expression, persona, social facade(s). *Consider also:* self projection. *See also* Assertiveness; Impression management; Self concept; Self esteem; Self expression; Social interaction; Social perception.

Self projection. See *Self presentation.*

Self psychology. Self psycholog(y,ical). Self-representation(s). Self-referen(t,ce). *Choose from:* self, ego, oneself *with:* aware(ness), referen(ce,t), rever(y,ies), unconscious, fantas(y,ies). *Consider also:* Heinz Kohut, excessive focus on oneself, excessive need(s) for approval, excessive need(s) for self-gratification, ego psycholog(y,ical), intersubjectiv(e, ity), hyperreflexiv(e,ity), self-self object, psychic reality, omnipotent thinking. *See also* Ego; Egocentrism; Narcissism; Selfishness (egocentric).

Self realization. See *Self actualization.*

Self regulation. See *Self management (individual), Self monitoring.*

Self reinforcement. Self reinforcement. *Choose from:* self *with:* reinforc(ed,ing, ement), reward(s), administ(ered,ration), manage(d,ment), deliver(y,ed), regulat(ed,ing,ion), modification, approv(al,ing,ed). *See also* Self management; Self stimulation.

Self reliance. See *Personal independence.*

Self report. Self report(ed,ing,s). *Choose from:* self, patient, personal, subjective *with:* report(ed,ing,s), assess(ed,ing, ment), recollect(ed,ing,ion,ions), estimat(e,ed,es,ing,ion), account(s), presentation(s), inventor(y,ies), narrative(s), disclos(e,ed,ing,ure). *Consider also:* remembrance(s), journal(s), diar(y,ies). *See also* First person narrative; Point of view (literature); Self evaluation; Self knowledge; Self monitoring; Self perception.

Self respect. Self respect. Pride. *Choose from:* self, personal *with:* respect, relian(t,ce), assurance, esteem, confiden(t,ce), sufficiency, worth, dignity, accept(ing,ance), affirm(ing, ation), adequacy, efficacy, positive attribution, actualiz(ing,ation), validat(e,ed,ing,ion. *See also* Pride; Self concept; Self confidence; Self efficacy; Self esteem; Self perception.

Self revelation. See *Self disclosure.*

Self sacrifice. Self sacrific(e,ing). Self renunciation. Self den(y,ying,ial). *Choose from:* self, oneself, himself, herself, themselves *with:* sacrific(e,ing), renunciation, den(y,ying,ial), abnegat(e, ed,ing), surrender(ed,ing), yield(ed,ing), relinquish(ed,ing,ment). *Consider also:* unselfish(ness). *See also* Abstinence; Celibacy; Martyrs; Renunciation; Sacrificial rites; Self control; Self denial; Sexual abstinence; Temperance; Unselfishness.

Self stimulation. Self stimulat(e,ed,ing,ion, ory,or,ors). *Consider also:* self *with:* arousal, injection, stirring, administration. *See also* Masturbation; Operant conditioning; Reinforcement; Self reinforcement.

Self sufficiency, economic. See *Autarky.*

Self talk. Self talk. *Choose from:* inner, self *with:* talk, speech, statement(s), questioning, voice(s). *See also* Psychotherapeutic techniques.

Self transcendence. See *Commitment (emotional); Enlightenment (state of mind).*

Self understanding. Self understanding. *Choose from:* self, introspective *with:* understanding, aware(ness), insight(s), knowledge. *See also* Introspection; Enlightenment (state of mind); Psychoanalysis; Self knowledge.

Self worth. See *Self esteem.*

Selfishness (egocentric). Selfish(ness). Self seeking. Self centered. Self interest(ed). Self gratification. Ego-centered. Egocentric. Egoistic. Egotistic(al,ally). Self indulgent. Self concerned. Narcissis(m,tic). Self serving. Vanity. Vain. Conceit(ed). Arrogan(ce,t). *See also* Egocentrism; Narcissism; Personality traits; Self indulgence; Self interest; Self psychology.

Selfishness (stingy). Selfish(ness). Sting(y,iness). Greed(y,iness). Grasping. Hoarding. Avaricious(ness). Ungenerous(ness). Possessive(ness). Uncharitable(ness). Penny pinching. Miser(ly,liness). Parsimonious(ness). *See also* Meanness; Misers; Personality traits; Possessiveness; Self interest.

Selling. See *Sales.*

Semantic differential. Semantic differential. Bipolar(ity) *with:* semantic variables. Adjective scale(s). *Choose from:* semantic *with:* analysis, distance, differentia(l,tion). *See also* Attitude measurement; Measurement; Personality measures.

Semantics. Semantic(s,al,ally). Semasiolog(y,ical). Semolog(y,ical). Word meaning(s). *Choose from:* meaning(s), sense *with:* language, linguistic. Lexicology. *Consider also:* meaning relation, sense relation, synonymy, antonymy. *See also* Antonyms; Etymology; Grammar; Homonyms; Intertextuality; Liar paradox; Linguistics; Metaphors; Philosophy of language; Semiotics; Verbal meaning; Vocabulary; Words.

Semasiology. See *Semantics.*

Semeiotics. Scc *Semiotics.*

Semi arid lands. See *Arid zones.*

Semi-skilled workers. See *Blue collar workers.*

Seminarians. Seminarian(s). *Choose from:* seminary, theolog(y,ical), pastoral *with:* intern(s), candidate(s), student(s). *See also* Religious personnel; Students.

Seminaries. Seminar(y,ies). *Choose from:* divinity, rabbinical, religious, theological, church related, clergy *with:* school(s), academ(y,ies), college(s). *See also* Colleges; Religious education.

Semiotics. Semiotic(s). Semeiotic(s). Semiolog(y,ical). Semiosis. Sign(s, ification,ifiers). Symbol(s,ic,ization). Resemiosis. Iconic communication. Iconicity. *Consider also:* pragmatics, semantics. *See also* Aporia; Hermeneutics; Intertextuality; Language; Linguistics; Philosophy of language; Semantics; Sex symbolism; Symbolism; Verbal communication.

Semitic languages. Semitic language(s). Akkadian: Babylonian, Assyrian, Nuzi Akkadian. Canaanite: Old Canaanite, Moabite, Phoenician, Punic, Ugaritic, Hebrew, Israeli Hebrew. Aramaic: Biblical, Palestinian, Syriac, Mandean, Neo-Syriac, Arabic, Classical Arabic, Arabian Arabic, Iraqui Arabic, Syrian Arabic, Egyptian Arabic, Western Arabic, Maltese, Andalusian, Southern Arabic, Himyaritic, Sabaean. Ethiopic: Geez, Tigre, Tigrinya, Amharic, Abyssinian. *Consider also:* Hamito-Semitic language(s). *See also* African cultural groups; Hamitic languages; Language; Languages (as subjects); Middle East; North Africa.

Senates. See *Legislative bodies.*

Senators. See *Legislators.*

Senescence. See *Aging; Elderly.*

Senile dementia. Senile dementia. Senil(e,ity). Primary degenerative dementia. Senile deterioration. Senile delirium. Presbyophrenia.

Psychogeriatric. Chronic organic brain syndrome. Progressive supranuclear palsy. *Consider also:* psycho(sis,ses,tic), dementia(s) *with:* geriatric, old age, elderly, multi-infarct, senil(e,ity). *See also* Aging; Alzheimer's disease; Cognition disorders; Mental confusion; Mental illness; Organic mental disorders; Presenile dementia; Wandering behavior.

Senile psychoses. See *Senile dementia.*

Senility. See *Senile dementia.*

Senior citizens. See *Elderly.*

Senior pregnancies. Senior Pregnanc(y,ies). Senior maternity. Pregnant after menopause. *Choose from:* elder(ly,s), menopaus(al,e), older, perimenopausal, postmenopaus(al,e), senior(s), over 50, over 55 *with:* assisted reproduction, birth(ing,s), birth mother(s), birthmother(s), childbearing, maternity, mother(hood,s), pregnan(cies,cy,t). *See also* Biological clocks; Childbearing age; Late childbearing; Maternal age.

Seniority. Senior(ity). *Consider also:* preferred *with:* ranking(s), standing(s), station(s), status(es). *See also* Academic rank; Academic tenure; Aging; Career change; Employment history; Job security; Occupational tenure; Personnel termination; Promotion (occupational); Work experience.

Sensation. Sensation(s). Sensory. Senses. Sense organs. Somatosensory. Sensitiv(e,ity). Subjective estimate(s). Feeling. *Consider also:* percept(ual,ion), hearing, pain, proprioception, kinesthesis, smell, taste, temperature, thermal sensitivity, touch, vision. *See also* Attention; Awareness; Auditory perception; Discrimination (psychology); Extrasensory perception; Illusions (perception); Intersensory processes; Monitoring; Perceptual discrimination; Pressure sensation; Sense datum; Sensory thresholds; Subliminal stimulation; Tactual perception; Visual perception.

Sensation, pressure. See *Pressure sensation.*

Sensation seeking. Sensation seek(ing,ers). *Choose from:* sensation(s), stimulus, thrill(s), excitement, stimulation, arousal, risk(s), novelty *with:* seek(ing, ers), desire, need(s), taking. *Consider also:* venturesome(ness), curiosity, boredom, hedonism, skydiv(ing,er,ers), bungee jump(ing,er,ers), bungie jump(ing,er,ers), bungy jump(ing,er,ers), base jump(ing,er,ers), canyoning. *See also* Extreme sports; Personality traits; Risk taking.

Sensationalism. Sensationalis(m,istic). Sensationaliz(e,ed,ing). Melodrama(tic). Lurid(ness). Oversentimental(ity). Mawkish(ness). Shock value. Yellow journalis(m,ist,ists). Scandal coverage. Media feeding frenzy. Media circus. Splashy news. Trash journalis(m,ist,ists). *Consider also:* banner headline(s). *See also* Journalistic ethics; Gossip; Gossip sites; Libel; Literary ethics; Mass media; Newspapers; Scandals; Surprise; Tabloids; Trivia.

Sense, common. See *Common sense.*

Sense, muscular. See *Muscular sense.*

Sense datum. Sense dat(a,um). Sens(um,a). Sense impression(s). *See also* Sensation.

Sense of humor. Sense of humor. Humorous(ness). Funny bone. Ability to laugh at oneself. Humorous style. Wit(ty,tiness). Droll. Mischievous(ness). Playful(ness). Frolicsome. Humor score(s). Humor appreciation. *Consider also:* cartoonist(s), gagwriter(s), perception of humor, humor assessment, humor-related trait(s). *See also* Comedians; Ethnic wit and humor; Fools and jesters; Humor; Laughter.

Sense of right and wrong. See *Conscience.*

Sense of smell, loss of. See *Anosmia.*

Sense organs. Sense organ(s). Sensory organ(s). Sensory system(s). *Choose from:* ear(s) *with:* external, canal, middle, tympan(i,ic), labyrinth, cochlea(r). *Choose from:* eye(s) *with:* cornea(l), iris, pupil, lens, retina(l). Nose(s). Olfactory cell(s). Taste buds. Sensory neuron(s). *Consider also:* afferent neurons, sense receptor(s). *See also* Anatomy; Ear; Eye; Human body.

Senses. See *Sensation.*

Sensitivities, multiple chemical. See *Multiple chemical sensitivities.*

Sensitivity (personality). Sensitiv(e, eness,ity). Responsiv(e,eness,ivity). Discriminating. Oversensitiv(e,eness, ity). Thin skinned. Irritab(le,ility). Hypersensitiv(e,eness,ity). Kind-hearted(ness). Tender(ness). Gentle(ness). Sympath(y,etic). Empath(ic,y,etic). Compassion(ate). Intuitive. Perceptiv(e,ity,eness). Insightful(ness). *See also* Personality traits.

Sensitivity, cultural. See *Cultural sensitivity.*

Sensitivity training. Sensitivity training. T group(s). Human relations training. Erhard Seminar Training. *Choose from:* sensitivity, growth, human relations, interpersonal, empathy, social skills, relations skills, couples, race relations, assertive(ness), consciousness raising, interpersonal competence *with:* training, group(s), technique(s), skills, treatment, workshop(s). *See also* Communication skills; Consciousness raising activities; Encounter groups; Group dynamics; Group psychotherapy; Human relations training; Interpersonal relations; Marathon group therapy; Marital enrichment; Personnel training; Self actualization; Self esteem; Self evaluation; Social skills training.

Sensitization, repression. See *Repression sensitization.*

Sensory adaptation. Sensory adaptation. *Choose from:* sensory, sensorimotor, perceptual, ocular, oculomotor, olfactory, binocular, monocular, auditory, acoustic, hearing, loudness, darkness, contrast, taste, vision, visual, motion, touch, tact(ile,ual) *with:* adapt(ed,ing, ion), orient(ed,ing,ation), reflex(es), response(s), plasticity. *See also* Adaptation; Habituation (psychophysiology); Light adaptation; Orienting reflex; Orienting responses; Thresholds.

Sensory defensiveness. Sensory defensiveness. *Choose from:* sensory, tactile, noise, auditory, light, touch *with:* defensiveness, sensitiv(e,ity), hypersensitiv(e,ity), supersensitiv(e,ity). *Consider also:* poor balance feedback. *See also* Attention deficit disorder; Defensive; Perceptions; Perceptual defense; Stereotyped behavior.

Sensory deprivation. Sensory deprivation. *Choose from:* sensory, perceptual, visual(ly), vision, sight, light, monocular, binocular, auditory, hearing, sound(s), acoustic, stimul(i,us,ation), touch, tact(ile,ual) *with:* depriv(e,ed,ing, ation). *Consider also:* isolation, psychosocial mental retardation, blindfold(s,ed), dark rear(ed,ing), hood rear(ed,ing), diffusing goggles, white noise. *See also* Deprivation; Sensory loss.

Sensory development. See *Perceptual development.*

Sensory feedback. Sensory feedback. *Choose from:* sensory, kinesthetic, perceptual, visual(ly), auditory, tact(ual,ile) *with:* feedback, cue(s), reinforcement. *Consider also:* proprioncept(ion,ive), biofeedback, peripheral feedback. *See also* Feedback; Muscular sense; Perceptual stimulation.

Sensory integration. Sensory integration. Multisensory integration. *Choose from:* sensory, multisensory, perceptual, visual-motor, auditory, visual, sensorimotor, sight, touch, hearing, taste, smell *with:* integrat(ed,ing,ion,ions), interaction(s), functioning. *Consider also:* interhemispheric communication, balance control, eye-hand interaction(s). *See also* Child development; Perceptual development; Perceptual motor coordination; Perceptual motor learning; Sensory loss; Spatial ability.

Sensory loss. Sensory loss(es). *Choose from:* sensory, vision, hearing, sight, smell, olfactory, taste *with:* loss(es), deficit(s), lose, lost, decreased ability, impair(ed,ments), diminish(ed,ing), incapacit(y,ies), deficienc(y,ies), fail(ing), defect(s,ive), absen(t,ce). *Consider also:* ageus(ia,is,tia), numb(ed,ness). *See also* Blindness; Deafness; Disability; Incapacitation; Sensory deprivation; Sensory integration.

Sensory systems. See *Sense organs.*

Sensory thresholds. Sensory threshold(s). *Choose from:* sensory, visual, pain, taste, touch, tact(ile,ual), sensation, olfactory, sensitivity, differential *with:* threshold(s), limen(s), level(s). *Consider also:* subliminal stimulation, sensitivity, sensory adaptation, negative adaptation, just noticeable difference(s). *See also* Sensation; Taste (food); Temperature perception; Thresholds.

Sentence, life. See *Life sentence.*

Sentence comprehension. Sentence comprehension. *Choose from:* sentence(s), syntactic *with:* comprehen(d,ding,sion), understand(ing), understood, process(ed,ing), interpret(ed,ing,ation), discrimination, verif(y,ied,ication), meaning(s), recall, memory. *See also* Verbal comprehension.

Sentence structure. Sentence structure. *Choose from:* senten(ces,tial) *with:* structur(e,es,al), complex(ity), ambiguous(ness), ambiguity, simpl(e,icity), context(s,ual), part(s), pars(e,ed,ing), phrase(s). *See also* Conditionals; Text structure.

Sentences. Senten(ce,ces,tial). Intrasentence. Intersentential. Kernal sentence(s). *Consider also:* phrase(s), pars(e,ed,ing). *See also* Conditionals; Discourse analysis; Grammar; Imperative mood; Language; Sentence structure; Writing (composition).

Sentencing. Sentenc(ing,e,es,ed). Presentence. Penalty scaling. Apply(ing) penalt(y,ies). Remand(ing,ed). Commit(ted,ment) to correctional institution. *Choose from:* reduced, death, harsh, punitive, indeterminate, determinate, prison, arbitrary *with:* sentenc(ing, ed,es). Fine(s,d). Prison term(s). Punish(ed,ing,ment,ments). Jail(ed,ing). Going to prison. Sent to jail. Criminal sanctions. *Consider also:* plea bargaining. *See also* Adjudication; Alternatives to incarceration; Court judges; Court opinions; Death penalty; Defendants; Evidence; Criminal proceedings; Criminals; Imprisonment; Institutionalization (persons); Judicial decisions; Judicial discretion; Juries; Law enforcement; Legal procedures; Life sentence; Plea bargaining; Penalties; Prisoners; Prisons; Probation; Psychiatric commitment; Punishment; Restitution; Restorative justice; Trial (law); Verdicts; Witnesses.

Sententiae. See *Aphorisms; Axioms; Cliches; Creeds; Dictums; Doctrines.*

Sentimentality. Sentimental(ity,ism). Emotional(ism,ity). Emotive(ness). Melodrama(tic). Maudlin(ism,ness). Overemotional. *Consider also:* pathos, romantic(ism). *See also* Emotionality; Emotions; Pity.

Separation anxiety. Separation anxiety. *Choose from:* separation, abandonment, deprivation *with:* anxiet(y,ies), anxious(ness), fear(s), worr(y,ies), nightmare(s), distress, overanxious, nostalgia, response(s), conflict(s), crisis, reaction(s). *Consider also:* maternal deprivation, school phobia(s), homesick(ness), fear of object loss, separation protest. *See also* Anxiety disorders; Attachment behavior; Reactive attachment disorder; School phobia; Stranger reactions.

Separation individuation. See *Individuation.*

Separation, marital. See *Marital disruption; Marital separation.*

Separation of church and state. See *Church state relationship.*

Separation of powers. Separation of powers. Checks and balances. Separated powers. Division of powers. Shared powers. Advise and consent. Advice and consent. *Choose from:* administrative, presiden(t,ts,tial,cy,cies), executive, veto, judicia(l,ry,ries), Supreme Court, legislat(ive,ure,ures), Congress(es,ional) *with:* power(s), authority, responsibilit(y, ies). *Consider also:* War Powers Resolution, judicial independence. *See also* Delegation of powers; Discretionary powers; Executive powers; Executive branch (government); Governmental powers; Judicial activism; Judicial power; Legal system; Legislative bodies; Legislative powers; Political power; Power sharing; State power.

Separation protest. See *Attachment behavior; Separation anxiety.*

Separatism. Separat(ism,ists,istic). Schism(atic,s). Sece(de,ding,ssion). Segregat(e,ed,ing,ion). Cleavage(s). Regionalism. Racial segregation. School segregation. Hypersegregation. Separate but equal. Apartheid. Jim Crow(ism). American Indian reservation(s). *Consider also:* independence, autonomy, sovereignty, separation, nationalism, self-determination, exclus(ive,ivity, iveness,ion,ionary). *See also* Anti-government radicals; Apartheid; Guerrilla warfare; Indian territories; National fronts; Nationalism; Occupational segregation; Peasant rebellions; Plural societies; Political ideologies; Political self determination; Racial segregation; Residential segregation; Regionalism; School segregation; Secession.

Separatism (religion). See *Religious dissenters.*

Separatist movements. See *Anti-government radicals; Decolonization; Guerrillas; Liberation movements; National fronts.*

Sepulchral monuments. Sepulchral monument(s). *Choose from:* sepulchr(e,es,al), funer(al,eal,ary), memorial, commemorative, mortuary, epitaph(s) *with:* monument(s), bust(s), statue(s), urn(s). *Consider also:* pyramid(s), sarcophag(i,us,uses), grave marker(s), headstone(s), gravestone(s), tombstone(s), memorial plaque(s), entomb(ed,ment), mausoleum(s), soldiers monument(s). *See also* Burials; Cemeteries; Grave goods; Monuments.

Sequelae. Sequel(ae). Continuation(s). Continuance(s). Succession(s). Chain of events. Suplement(s). Progression. Sequen(ce,ces,tial). Series. Subsequent development(s). *Consider also:* aftereffect(s), aftermath, outgrowth, consequence(s), eventualit(y,ies), issue(d), outcome(s), result(s), upshot, fallout, aftertaste, afterglow, result(s). *See also* Consequences; Continuation; Effects; End; Epilogues; Externalities; Means ends; Results; Spinoffs.

Sequential learning. Sequential learning. *Choose from:* sequen(tial,ce,ces,cing), successive, hierarch(y,ies,ical) *with:* learn(ed,ing), retention, processing, recall(ed,ing), cue(s,d,ing), acquisition. *See also* Learning; Mastery learning.

Seraphim. See *Angels.*

Serfs. See *Peasants.*

Serial killers. See *Serial murderers.*

Serial learning. Serial learning. *Choose from:* serial, sequential *with:* learning, memory, recall, recognition, retention. *Consider also:* successive association(s). *See also* Learning; Verbal learning; Verbal memory.

Serial murderers. Serial murder(er,ers). Serial killer(s). *Choose from:* serial, multiple, spree(s) *with:* murder(er,ers), killers(s), slaying(s). *Consider also:* methodological killer(s), Unabomber. *See also* Homicide; Offenders.

Serial music. Serial music. Serialism. Serial technique. Atonality. Twelve tone music. *Consider also:* dodecaphonic music, Schoenberg(ian). *See also* Electronic music; Twentieth century Western art music.

Serial polygamy. Serial polygamy. Tandem polygamy. Sequential marriages. *Consider also:* sequential monogamy. *See also* Marriage; Polygamy.

Seriousness. Serious(ness,ly). Serious

minded(ness). Staid. Reflective(ness). Pensiv(e,eness,ity). Somber. Solemn(ity). Sober(ness). Purposeful(ness). *See also* Personality traits.

Sermons. Sermon(s). Homil(y,ies). Preach(ed,ing,ings). Televangelis(t,ts,m). Worship service(s). *Choose from:* religious, Sunday morning *with:* discourse(s), talk(s), message(s), speech(es). *See also* Clergy; Evangelists; Parables; Preaching; Religious literature; Religious rituals.

Servants. See *Domestic service.*

Servants, civil. See *Civil service; Government personnel.*

Service, civil. See *Civil service.*

Service, community. See *Restorative justice; Volunteers.*

Service, compulsory military. See *Military draft.*

Service, domestic. See *Domestic service.*

Service, intelligence. See *Intelligence service.*

Service, military. See *Military service.*

Service, postal. See *Postal service.*

Service, public. See *Civil service; Elected officials; Government personnel; Volunteers.*

Service contracts. Service contract(s). *Choose from:* service, repair(s), maintenance *with:* contract(s), guarantee(s,d,ing), warrant(y,ies), package(s). *Consider also:* independent service organization(s), ISO(s), underwriter(s), extended warrant(y,ies). *See also* Appliance repair; Brand loyalty; Client relations; Consumer satisfaction; Customer relations; Customer service; Guarantees; Maintenance; Preventive maintenance; Vendor relations.

Service industries. Service industr(y,ies). Service work(s,er,ers,ing). *Choose from:* transportation, retail trade, insurance, real estate, banking, financ(e,ial), child care, food, entertainment, recreation, hotel, laundry, cleaning, barber, beauty shop, legal, engineering, medical, health, domestic, automobile, repair *with:* industr(y,ies), business(es), service(s). *See also* Accounting; Banking; Beauty shops; Deindustrialization; Domestic service; Hospitality industry; Industry; Insurance; Postindustrial societies; Real estate; White collar workers.

Service providers, Internet. See *Internet service providers.*

Servicemen. See *Military personnel.*

Services. Service(s). Advanc(e,ed,ement, ing). Assistance. Aid. Benefit(s,ting,ted). Boost(ed,ing). Car(e,ed,ing). Commodit(y,ies). Cooperat(e,ing,ion).

Contribut(e,ed,ing). Deliver(y,ies). Furnish(ed,ing). Further(ed,ing). Help(ed,ing). Maintain(ed,ing). Outreach. Promot(e,ed,ing,ion). Provid(e,ed,ing). Relief. Serv(e,ed,ing). Suppl(ier,ied,y,ying). Sustain(ed,ing). *Consider also:* agenc(y,ies), center(s), charit(y,ies), clinic(s), crisis intervention, information dissemination, hot lunch(es), hotline(s), housing, program(s), referral(s), shelter(s), system(s), testing, treatment, utilit(y,ies). *See also* Access to education; Access to information; Advocacy; Agencies; Alternatives to institutionalization; Child health services; Clinics; Community mental health services; Community services; Consultants; Contract services; Delivery of services; Diagnostic services; Drug information services; Eligibility determination; Emergency services; Food services (programs); Health services; Health services misuse; Health services needs and demand; Home care services; Homemaker services; Human services; Information services; Library services; Maternal health services; Mental health services; Occupational health services; Personal health services; Program implementation; Programs; Protective services; Psychiatric emergency services; Public services; Relief services; Resources; Social services; Social support networks; Student health services.

Services, alternative. See *Alternatives to institutionalization.*

Services, child care. See *Child care; Child caregivers; Child day care; Corporate day care.*

Services, child health. See *Child health services.*

Services, community. See *Community services.*

Services, community health. See *Community health services.*

Services, community mental health. See *Community mental health services.*

Services, contract. See *Contract services.*

Services, customer. See *Customer services.*

Services, delivery of. See *Delivery of services.*

Services, diagnostic. See *Diagnostic services.*

Services, drug information. See *Drug information services.*

Services, emergency. See *Emergency services.*

Services, food programs. See *Food services (programs).*

Services, health. See *Health services.*

Services, health care. See *Health services.*

Services, health needs and demand. See *Health services needs and demand.*

Services, home care. See *Home care services.*

Services, homemaker. See *Homemaker services.*

Services, human. See *Human services.*

Services, indigenous health. See *Traditional medicine.*

Services, industrial health. See *Occupational health services.*

Services, information. See *Information services.*

Services, library. See *Library services.*

Services, maternal health. See *Maternal health services.*

Services, mental health. See *Mental health services.*

Services, military. See *Armed forces.*

Services, occupational health. See *Occupational health services.*

Services, online. See *Information networks.*

Services, outplacement. See *Outplacement services.*

Services, personal health. See *Personal health services.*

Services, preventive health. See *Preventive medicine; Preventive psychiatry; Primary prevention.*

Services, protective. See *Protective services.*

Services, psychiatric. See *Mental health services; Psychiatric clinics; Psychiatric social work.*

Services, psychiatric emergency. See *Psychiatric emergency services.*

Services, public. See *Public services.*

Services, relief. See *Relief services.*

Services, school health. See *Student health services.*

Services, social. See *Social services.*

Services, student health. See *Student health services.*

Services, student personnel. See *Student personnel services.*

Services, supportive. See *Supportive services.*

Services, welfare. See *Antipoverty programs; Food services (programs); Income maintenance programs; Medical assistance; Public welfare; Social agencies; Social services; Social programs; Unemployment relief; Workfare.*

Services misuse, health. See *Health services misuse.*

Servicewomen. See *Military personnel.*

Servitude. Servitude. Bondage. Enslave(d,ment). Enthrallmnt. Peon(age). Serf(dom,hood). Servility. Slave(s,ry). Thrall(dom). Impressment. Vassal(s,age). *See also* Oppression; Peasants; Slavery.

Set (psychology). Set(s). Einstellung. Determining tendenc(y,ies). Propensit(y,ies). *Consider also:* expect(ancy,ancies,ation,ations), expected effect(s), anticipat(e,ed,ing, ion,ions), suggest(ing,ion,ions,ive), fixed behavior(al) pattern(s), cognitive set(s), response set(s). *See also* Attitudes; Expectations; Predisposition.

Set, mind. See *Attitudes; Predisposition; Set (psychology).*

Set aside, appropriations. See *Appropriations (set aside).*

Setting, goal. See *Goal orientation.*

Setting fires, behavior. See *Fire setting behavior.*

Settlement, dispute. See *Dispute settlement.*

Settlement, land. See *Land settlement.*

Settlement patterns. Settlement pattern(s). *Choose from:* settlement(s), resettlement(s), resettl(e,ed,ing), plantation(s), homestead(s), colon(y,ics) *with:* pattern(s), scheme(s), distribution, dispers(ed,ion,al). *Consider also:* residen(tial,ce) preference(s). *See also* Colonization; Human settlements; Immigrants; Land settlement; Migration; Migration patterns; Population distribution; Residential patterns.

Settlement patterns, land. See *Settlement patterns.*

Settlements, collective. See *Collective settlements.*

Settlements, human. See *Human settlements.*

Settlements, marriage. See *Marriage settlements.*

Settlements, social. See *Social settlements.*

Settlers. Settler(s). Pioneer(s). Immigrant(s). Homesteader(s). Colonist(s). Colonizer(s). Squatter(s). Founding father(s). Backwoods(man, men). Frontiers(men,man,women, woman). *See also* Colonization; Frontier and pioneer life; Frontiers; Homesteading; Immigrants; Land settlement.

Severance pay. Severance pay. Dismissal pay. Termination pay. *Consider also:* golden parachute(s), outplacement service(s). *See also* Dismissal of staff; Involuntary retirement; Job search; Outplacement services; Personnel termination; Plant closings; Relocation.

Severely handicapped infants. Severely handicapped infant(s). *Choose from:* infant(s), newborn(s), neonate(s), bab(y,ies) *with:* abnormalit(y,ies), handicapped, retard(ed,ation), Down(s) syndrome, brain damaged, congenital disorder(s), spina bifida, birth injur(y,ies), defect(s,ive), disabled, seriously ill, malformed, monster(s). *See also* Birth injuries; Congenitally handicapped; Drug addicted babies; Disability; Infants; Mental retardation; Physical abnormalities; Physical disfigurement; Severely mentally retarded; Severity of disorder; Teratology.

Severely mentally retarded. Severely mentally retarded. Severely retarded. *Choose from:* severe(ly), profound(ly), custodial *with:* mental(ly) retard(ed, ation), mental(ly) handicap(ped), mental(ly) deficien(t,cy). IQ 20-34. Imbecile(s). *See also* Disability; Mental retardation; Severely handicapped infants; Severity of disorders.

Severity of disorders. Sever(e,ely,ity) of disorder(s). *Choose from:* sever(e,ely, ity), acute, mild(ly,ness), serious(ly, ness), intens(e,ity), level(s), degree(s), status *with:* disorder(s), disabilit(y,ies), complaint(s), symptom(s), affliction(s), infection(s), impairment(s), disabilit(y,ies), ill, illness(es). *See also* Acute disease; Acute psychosis; Chronic disease; Chronic pain; Chronic psychosis; Diagnosis; Disability; Disability evaluation; Disease; Disorders; Mental illness; Prognosis.

Sewage. Sewage. Wastewater(s). Waste water(s). Effluen(t,ce). Liquid refuse. Waste liquid(s). Liquid waste(s). Waste fluid(s). Urban runoff(s). Contaminated water. Night soil. Organic waste(s). Fecal pollution. Sewer discharge(s). Sewer water. Liquid manure. Pig slurr(y,ies). Animal waste(s). Municipal waste(s). Sludge(s). *See also* Drainage; Industrial wastes; Sanitation; Sewage as fertilizer; Sewage disposal; Solid waste; Waste disposal; Waste to energy; Wastes; Water pollution.

Sewage as fertilizer. Sewage as fertilizer. *Choose from:* sewage, manure(s), wastewater(s), waste water(s), sludge(s), liquid waste(s), organic waste(s), liquid manure, pig slurr(y,ies), animal waste(s) *with:* fertilizer(s), recycl(e,ed,ing), crop production, soil, agricultur(e,al). *See also* Animal products; Organic farming; Recycling; Waste spills; Water purification; Water reuse.

Sewage disposal. Sewage disposal. Septic tank(s). Sewer(s). Sewage system(s). Sewerage system(s). *Choose from:* sewage, sewer(s,age), wastewater(s), waste water(s), effluen(t,ts,ce), liquid refuse, waste liquid(s), liquid waste(s), waste fluid(s), municipal waste(s), sludge(s) *with:* dispos(e,ed,ing,al), purif(y,ied,ying,ication), treatment, dump(ed,ing), ocean dumping, discharg(e,ed,es,ing). *Consider also:* sewage, sludge *with:* primary treatment, secondary treatment, tertiary treatment. *See also* Drainage; Recycling; Sanitation; Sewage; Waste disposal; Waste to energy; Waste transport; Wastes; Water purification; Water pollution; Water reuse.

Sewing. Sew(s,n,ing). Stitch(ed,ing). Seam(ing,ed). Bast(e,ed,ing). Hem(med,ming). *Consider also:* embroider(ed,ing), smock(ed,ing). *See also* Clothing workers; Fabrics; Fancy work; Fibers.

Sex. See *Animal sex behavior; Demographic characteristics (of individuals); Gender identity; Sex behavior; Sex characteristics; Sex ratio; Sexual intercourse.*

Sex, Internet. See *Cybersex.*

Sex, nonconsensual. See *Sexual coercion.*

Sex, online. See *Cybersex.*

Sex, oral. See *Oral sex.*

Sex, preoccupied with. See *Erotomania.*

Sex, same. See *Same sex.*

Sex attitudes. See *Sexual attitudes.*

Sex attractants. Sex attractant(s). *Choose from:* odor(s), secretion(s), taint(s), scent(s), chemosignal(s), attractant(s) *with:* genital, sex(ual), female(s), vaginal, ear gland, anogenital, preputial. *Consider also:* pheromon(e,es,al,ally), contact aphrodisiac(s), chemical attract(ion,ant,ants), social chemosignal(s). *See also* Animal mate selection; Animal sex behavior; Pheromones.

Sex behavior. Sex(ual) behavior. Coitus. Copulat(e,ed,ing,ion). Orgasm(s,ic). Lovemaking. Adulter(y,ous). Romantic relationship(s). Lovers. Romance. Male female relation(s). Courtship. Fellatio. Cunnilingus. Sodomy. *Choose from:* sex(ual), psychosexual, heterosexual, homosexual, bisexual *with:* behavior(s), interaction(s), satisfaction, affair(s), activity, intimacy, practice(s), relations, functioning, intercourse, performance. *Consider also:* automanipulation, masturbat(e,ing,ion), self pleasuring, contraceptive behavior, extramarital relations, prostitution, sexual abstinence, bisexuality, dyspareunia, penile erection(s), eroticism, exhibitionism, fetishism, frigidity, homosexual(ity), hypersexual(ity), impotence, incest, lesbianism, nocturnal emission(s), pedophilia, petting, premarital intercourse, premature ejaculation(s), promiscuity, sexual function disturbance(s), sexual masochism, sexual sadism, vaginismus, rutting. *See also* Animal sex behavior; Extramarital relations; Human courtship; Hypersexuality; Masturbation; Oral sex; Orgasm; Premarital sexual behavior; Sex customs; Sexual abstinence; Sexual abuse; Sexual arousal; Sexual asphyxia syndrome; Sexual behavior surveys; Sexual ethics; Sexual exploitation; Sexual foreplay; Sexual intercourse; Sexual masochism; Sexual sadism; Sexual satisfaction; Sodomy.

Sex behavior, animal. See *Animal sex behavior.*

Sex bias. See *Sexism.*

Sex change. Sex change(s). Sexual identity change(s). *Choose from:* sex, gender, genital, male female, female male *with:* reassignment, change(s), reversal(s), transformation(s), conversion(s), modif(y,ied,ying,ications). *Consider also:* transsexual(ism), sexual metamorphos(is,es). *See also* Metamorphosis; Transsexualism.

Sex characteristics. Sex characteristic(s). *Choose from:* sex(es), gender(s), male(s), female(s) *with:* characteristic(s), typical, differen(ce,ces,tial), dimorphism. *See also* Characteristics; Gender differences; Sex differentiation (embryogenetic).

Sex counseling. See *Sex therapy.*

Sex crimes. See *Sex offenses.*

Sex customs. Sex custom(s). *Choose from:* sex(ual), seduc(e,ed,ing,tion), lovemaking, lover(s), erotic, intimacy, courtship, eros, libid(o,inal), dating, premarital, marital *with:* custom(s,ary, arily), ceremon(y,ies), cultur(e,al), ethic(s,al), practice(s), value(s), viewpoint(s), taboo(s), myth(s), moral(s,ity). *See also* Norms; Seduction; Sex behavior; Taboo.

Sex differences, human. See *Gender differences.*

Sex differentiation (embryogenetic). Sex differentiation. *Choose from:* sex(ual), testicular, gonad(s,al) *with:* morphogenesis, differentiation. *Consider also:* prenatal sexual development, sex determination. *See also* Embryology; Sex characteristics.

Sex discrimination. Sex discrimination. Sex(ism,ist). Sex bias(es,ed). Discrimination against women. Glass ceiling(s). Sticky floor(s). Treated as sex object(s). Male stronghold(s). All-male military academ(y,ies). *Choose from:* female(s), women, woman, sex(ual), gender, girl(s), feminin(e,ity), men, man, male(s) *with:* inequality, inequit(y,ies), discrepanc(y,ies), unfair, discriminat(e, ed,ing,ion), prejudic(e,ed,ial), bias(ed,es), stereotype(s), stratification, segregat(ed,ion), chauvinism, intolerance, harassment. *Consider also:* Title IX, affirmative action, sex equity. *See also* Affirmative action; Age discrimina-

tion; Attitudes toward homosexuality; Coeducation; Civil rights; Equal education; Equal job opportunities; Equity (payment); Feminism; Gender differences; Gender identity; Harems; Images of women; Income inequality; Injustice; Labor market segmentation; Private sphere; Purdah; Reproductive rights; Reverse discrimination; Sexism; Sexual division of labor; Sexual exploitation; Sexual harassment; Sexual inequality; Sexual oppression; Single sex schools; Social discrimination; Veiling of women; Wage differentials; Working women; Women's rights.

Sex disorders. See *Sexual deviations; Sexual function disorders.*

Sex drive. Sex(ual) drive(s). Libid(o,inal). Lust(ful). Hypersexual(ity). Genital arousal. Penile erection(s). *Choose from:* sex(ual), erotic, psychosexual *with:* drive(s), desire(s), feeling(s), arous(e,ed,ing,al), pleasure, responsive(ness), interest, motiv(e,es,ated), tension(s), intent(ion), attract(ed,ing,ion). *See also* Libido; Sexual arousal; Sexuality.

Sex education. Sex education. *Choose from:* sex(uality), contracept(ive,ion), marriage, pregnancy, sexually transmitted disease(s), STD(s), AIDS, venereal disease(s), syphilis, gonorrhea, herpes *with:* education, course(s), program(s), information, learn(ed,ing), knowledge, workshop(s), teaching, advice. *See also* Birth; Contraception; Ethics; Family planning attitudes; Menarche; Sex information; Sexual ethics; Sexual maturation; Sexuality; Sexually transmitted diseases.

Sex equity. See *Affirmative action; Social equality; Social equity; Social justice.*

Sex factors. Sex factor(s). *Choose from:* sex, gender, male female, intersexual *with:* aspect(s), bas(is,es), constraint(s), characteristic(s), correlate(s), context(s), component(s), comparison(s), consideration(s), determinant(s), determin(ed,ing,ation), difference(s), dimension(s), dynamic(s), effect(s), element(s), explanation(s), factor(s), influence(s), implication(s), impact(s), obstacle(s), pattern(s), similarit(y,ies), variable(s). *See also* Biological factors; Determinism; Factors; Personality correlates; Physiological correlates; Social factors; Sociocultural factors; Socioeconomic factors.

Sex identity. See *Gender identity.*

Sex industry. Sex industry. Trafficking of women. Sex tour(s,ism). Sex oriented business(es). Sex shop(s). Adult business(es). Topless club(s). Topless bar(s). Pornographic shop(s). Sex service(s). Sex trade. Peep show(s). Commercial sex. Sex sector. *See also*

Cybersex; Exploitation; Pimps; Pornography; Prostitution; Sexual abuse; Sexual exploitation; Trafficking in persons.

Sex information. Sex information. Facts of life. *Choose from:* sex(ual,uality), contracept(ion,ive), birth control, marriage, pregnancy, venereal disease(s), syphilis, gonorrhea, herpes, AIDS, sexually transmitted disease(s), STD(s) *with:* information, manual(s), guide(s), handbook(s), book(s), textbook(s), knowledge, data, fact(s,ual), awareness, advice column(s). *See also* Contraception; Information; Reproductive rights; Sex education; Sexually transmitted diseases.

Sex instruction. See *Sex education.*

Sex manuals. See *Sex information.*

Sex offenders. Sex offender(s). Sexual offender(s). Sexual predator(s). Sexual psychopath(s). Child molester(s). Rapist(s). *Choose from:* abuser(s) perpetrator(s), abusive famil(y,ies), delinquent(s), offender(s), predator(s), criminal(s), recidivis(t,ts), molester(s), murderer(s), killer(s), sadist(s) *with:* sexual(ly), rape(s,d), *Consider also:* voyeur(s), incestuous father(s). *See also* Acquaintance rape; Antisocial behavior; Battered women; Child abuse; Crime; Deviant behavior; Female offenders; Incest; Indecent exposure; Male offenders; Marital rape; Mentally ill offenders; Offenders; Perpetrators; Rape; Sex offenses; Sexual abuse; Sexual harassment; Victimization.

Sex offenses. Sex offense(s). *Choose from:* sex(ual,ually) *with:* offense(s), crime(s), molest(ed,ing,ation), misconduct, abus(e,ed,ing), forc(e,ed,ing), assault(s,ed,ing,ive), violen(t,ce), aggress(ive,iveness,ion), harrass(ed,ing, ment), delinquency. *Consider also:* rap(e,ed,es,ing), paraphilia(s), prostitut(e,es,ion), incest(uous), pedophil(e,es,ia,ias), exhibitionism, child seduction, stalk(ed,ing,er,ers), pornograph(y,ic), voyeurism. *See also* Incest; Indecent exposure; Online harassment; Pornography; Rape; Sex offenders; Sexual abuse; Sexual assault; Sexual harassment; Sexual exploitation; Sexual misconduct; Sexual violence.

Sex oriented businesses. See *Sex industry.*

Sex oriented periodicals. See *Pornography.*

Sex preferences. See *Sexual preferences.*

Sex ratio. Sex ratio(s). Distribution of sexes. *Choose from:* sex *with:* ratio(s), distribution, proportion. *Choose from:* ratio(s), distribution, proportion *with:* male(s), men, boy(s) *with:* female(s), women, girl(s). *See also* Population distribution.

Sex reversal. See *Sex change.*

Sex role attitudes. Sex role attitude(s). *Choose from:* sex role(s), gender role(s), female role(s), male role(s), masculin(e, ity), feminin(e,ity) *with:* expectation(s), stereotype(s,d), stereotyping, attitude(s), typing, perception(s), ideolog(y,ies), orientation(s), conflict(s), identit(y,ies), belief(s), values, norms, conceptions, attribution(s). *Consider also:* sex stereotypes. *See also* Attitudes; Attitudes toward homosexuality; Men's movement; Sex roles; Sex stereotypes; Stereotyping.

Sex role identity. See *Gender identity.*

Sex role orientations. See *Gender identity; Sex role attitudes; Sexual orientation.*

Sex roles. Sex role(s). *Choose from:* sex(ual), gender, masculin(e,ity), feminin(e,ity), male, female, man(s), men(s), woman(s), women(s), mother(s), father(s), daughter(s), son(s) *with:* role(s), behavior, function(s), dut(y,ies), purpose(s), expectation(s), expected behavior, image(s); identit(y,ies), orientation, identification, traits, stereotype(s), appearance(s). *See also* Androgyny; Bisexuality; Dual career families; Egalitarian families; Family roles; Family work relationship; Females (human); Femininity; Gender differences; Gender identity; Harems; House husbands; Housewives; Images of women; Labor market segmentation; Males (human); Masculinity; Nontraditional careers; Occupational segregation; Private sphere; Public sphere; Purdah; Role conflict; Role models; Sex discrimination; Sex role attitudes; Sex stereotypes; Sexual division of labor; Sexual inequality; Sexism; Shared parenting; Social norms; Stereotyping; Working women.

Sex stereotypes. Sex stereotype(s). *Choose from:* sex(ual), gender, masculin(e,ity), feminin(e,ity), male, female, man's, woman's, mother(s), father(s), daughter(s), son(s), macho *with:* stereotyp(es,ing), typ(e,ed,ing), depict(ed,ion), social representation, image(s), label(s), myth(s), expectation(s), expected behavior(s). *See also* Beauty culture; Females (human); Gender differences; Gender identity; Idealization of women; Images of women; Labor market segmentation; Male chauvinism; Males (human); Nontraditional careers; Occupational segregation; Private sphere; Public sphere; Purdah; Sex discrimination; Sex role attitudes; Sex roles; Sexism; Sexist language; Sexual inequality; Social discrimination; Stereotyping; Veiling of women.

Sex surveys. See *Sexual behavior surveys.*

Sex symbolism. Sex(ual,uality) symbol(s,ism,ist,ists,ic,ics,izing,ize,ization).

Choose from: sex(ual,uality), Freudian, erotic(a), male, masculin(e,ity), man, female, feminin(e,ity), woman, phall(ic,us), androcentri(c,sm), carnal, lesbian(ism), homosexual(ity), heterosexual(ity), gender, lust, cock, penis, vulva, gang rape, bride capture *with:* symbol(s,ism,ist,ists,ic,ics, izing,ize,ization), latent content, represent(s,ed,ing,ation,ations), image(s,ry), metaphor(s,ical), ritual(ly) depict(ed,ing,ion,ions), motif(s), interpretation(s), icon(s). *See also* Allusions; Christian symbolism; Dream interpretation; Expressionism (Art); Figurative language; Iconography; Images; Meaning; Metaphors; Mythology; Semiotics; Sexist language; Social meaning; Symbolism.

Sex therapy. Sex(ual) therap(y,ies). *Choose from:* sex(ual), anorgasm(ia,ic), sexual dysfunction(s), sexual disorder(s), sexual phobia(s), erectile dysfunction(s), ejaculatory dysfunction(s), marital problem(s), retarded ejaculation, premature ejaculation, sexual conflicts, sexual enhancement, anhedonia, frigidity, dyspareunia *with:* therap(y,ies), counseling, therap(y,ies), treatment(s), psychotherapy. *Consider also:* sexual surrogate therapy, sexual rehabilitation, orgasmic reconditioning, masturbatory training. *See also* Couples therapy; Family therapy; Marital therapy; Sexual function disorders.

Sex trade. See *Sex industry.*

Sexism. Sex(ism,ist). Sex discrimination. Sex bias(es,ed). Discrimination against women. Sex object(s). Male chauvinis(m,t,ts). *Choose from:* female(s), women, woman, sex(ual), gender, girl(s), feminin(e,ity) *with:* inequality, inequit(y,ies), discrepanc(y, ies), unfair, discriminat(e,ed,ing,ion), prejudic(e,ed,ial), bias(ed,es), stereotype(s), stratification, segregat(ed,ion), chauvinism, intolerance, harassment. *See also* Androcentrism; Anti-government radicals; Feminism; Gender differences; Harems; Images of women; Labor market segmentation; Male chauvinism; Misogyny; Occupational segregation; Oppression; Prejudice; Private sphere; Public sphere; Purdah; Racism; Sex discrimination; Sex role attitudes; Sex roles; Sex stereotypes; Sexist language; Sexual division of labor; Sexual exploitation; Sexual harassment; Sexual oppression; Sexual inequality; Women's rights; Veiling of women.

Sexist language. Sexist language. *Choose from:* sex(ism,ist), he/man, macho, patriarchal, sex bias(es,ed), gender bias(es,ed), paternal(istic), male oriented, male chauvinis(m,t,ts), sexually oppressive, male centered, phallocentric *with:* language, speech,

speaking, pronoun(s), noun(s), verb(s), title(s), name(s), pronomial, term(s,inology), label(s,ling), rhetoric, word(s), definition(s), symbol(s), metaphor(s). *Consider also:* microinequit(y,ies), phallogocentrism, phallocentrism. *See also* Language; Language usage; Nonsexist language; Sex stereotypes; Sex symbolism; Sexism; Social meaning.

Sexual abstinence. Sexual(ly) abstinen(t, ce). Celiba(cy,te). Midcycle abstinence. Sexual(ly) inactiv(e,ity). Sexless marriage. Ascetic(ism). Sexual continence. Chas(te,tity). Sexual self denial. Postpartum abstinence. Temperature rhythm method of birth control. Sexual deprivation. Apareunia. *See also* Celibacy; Contraception; Sex behavior; Self sacrifice.

Sexual abuse. Sexual(ly) abuse(d). Sexual(ly) harass(ed,ment). Lecherous(ness). Intimate remark(s). Seduction attempt(s). Pedophil(ia,iacs, es). Sex offense(s). Incest(uous). Exhibition(ists,ism). Child pornography. Child prostitution. Rap(e,ed,ing). Moral offense(s). *Choose from:* sex(ual,ually), gender *with:* abus(ive,ers,ed), harass(ed,ing,ment), harass(ed,ing, ment), unwanted attention, comment(s), intimidat(e,ed,ing,ion), threat(en,ening, s), advance(s), approach(es), remark(s), exploit(ed,ive,ing,ation), proposition(s), molest(ation,ing), intimations, attempt(s), coercion, innuendo(s), request(s), pass(es), unwelcome behavior, unsolicited behavior. *Consider also:* harass(ed,ing,ment) *with:* women, girl(s), boy(s), child(ren). *Consider also:* anatomically correct doll(s). *See also* Acquaintance rape; Antisocial behavior; Battered women; Child abuse; Elder abuse; Family violence; Female circumcision (ritual); Incest; Molested children; Psychologically abused men; Rape; Reproductive rights; Sex offenders; Sex offenses; Sexual assault; Sexual deviations; Sexual exploitation; Sexual harassment; Sexual misconduct; Sexual violence; Statutory rape; Trafficking in persons; Victimization.

Sexual arousal. Sexual arousal. Erotic(ally,ize,ized,izing,ization). Pelvic vasocongestion. Penile erection(s). Aphrodisia(c,cs). Aphrodisioman(ia,ic). *Consider also:* sexual(ly), erotic(ally) *with:* arous(al,ability,ed,ing), excit(e,ed,ing,ement), stimulat(ing,ion), reaction(s), interest(s), desire(s), respons(e,es,ive,ivity,iveness), receptiv(e,eness,ity). *See also* Eroticism; Libido; Masturbation; Orgasm; Sex behavior; Sex drive; Sexual intercourse; Sexual fantasies; Sexual foreplay.

Sexual asphyxia syndrome. Sexual asphyxia syndrome. Autoerotic asphyxiation. Autoerotic death(s).

Erotized hanging(s). *Choose from:* autoerotic(ism), auto erotic(ism), sexual masochism, sexual arousal, sexual activit(y,ies), erotic(ism), masturbat(e, ed,ing,ion) *with:* asphyxia(s,ting,tion), death(s), fatal(ity,ities), suicide(s), hanging(s), dangerous(ness). *See also* Death; Masturbation; Sexual deviations.

Sexual assault. Sexual(ly) assault(ed). Rape(d). Incest(uous). *Choose from:* sexual(ly), courtship, date, marital, wife, spouse(s) *with:* aggression, molest(ed, ation), assault(ed), murder(s), attack(ed,er,ers,ing), violen(t,ce), victimiz(e,ed,ing,ation), coerc(e,ed, ing,ion), forc(e,ed,ing,ible), violat(e,ed, ing,ion,ions). *See also* Acquaintance rape; Assault (personal); Rape; Sexual abuse; Sexual exploitation; Sexual harassment; Sexual misconduct; Sexual violence; Victimization.

Sexual attitudes. Sexual attitude(s). *Choose from:* attitude(s), belief(s), concern(s), opinion(s), opposition, modest(y), mores, knowledge, permissive(ness), prejudice(s), awareness, conservatism, guilt, romanticism *with:* sex(ual,ually, uality), heterosexual(ly,ity), psycho-sexual, homosexual(ly,ity), lesbian(ism), erotic(ism), virgin(s,ity). *See also* Attitudes; Misogyny; Moral attitudes; Sex behavior; Sex role attitudes; Sexual maturation.

Sexual behavior. See *Sex behavior.*

Sexual behavior, marital. See *Marital sexual behavior.*

Sexual behavior, premarital. See *Premarital sexual behavior.*

Sexual behavior surveys. Sexual behavior survey(s). Sex survey(s). *Choose from:* HIV related behavior(s), pregnanc(y,ies), sex(ual), psychosexual, heterosexual, homosexual *with:* behavior(s), interaction(s), satisfaction, affair(s), activity, intimacy, practice(s), relations, functioning, intercourse, custom(s), risktaking, sexually transmitted disease(s), STD(s) *with:* research stud(y,ies), survey(ed,s,ing), poll(s,ed, ing). interview(s), questionnaire(s), sampl(e,es,ing), public opinion research, data collectionself-report measure(s). *Consider also:* Masters and Johnson, Kinsey report. *See also* Attitude measurement; Data collection; Extra-marital relations; Human courtship; Premarital sexual behavior; Sex behavior; Social surveys; Surveys.

Sexual coercion. Sexual(ly) coerc(ed,ing, ion,ive). *Choose from:* sexual(ly,ity), rape(s,d), kissi(ed,ng), hug(ged,ging), touch(ed,ing) breast(s), touch(ed,ing) genital(s), oral intercourse, oral sex, anal intercourse, vaginal intercourse *with:* coerc(ed,ing,ion,ive), demand(ed,ing), nonconsensual, duress, threat(en,ening, ened), intimidat(e,es,ed,ing,ion,ions),

forc(e,ed,ing), aggressor(s). *Consider also:* sexual advances, date rape. *See also* Acquaintance rape; Coercion; Intimidation; Online harassment; Sexual consent; Sexual exploitation; Sexual harassment Victimization.

Sexual consent. Sexual consent. *Choose from:* consen(t,sual,sually), concur(red, ring,rence), acquiescen(t,ce), complian(t, ce), agree(d,ing,ment), assent(ed,ing), permission, permit(ted,ting), voluntar(y,ily), willing(ly,ness), yield(ed,ing) *with:* sex, sexual activity, sexual intercourse. *See also* Acquain-tance rape; Consent (law); Sexual coercion; Sexual permissiveness.

Sexual delinquency. See *Promiscuity; Sexual offenses.*

Sexual desire. See *Sexual arousal.*

Sexual desire, inhibited. See *Sexual inhibitions.*

Sexual development. See *Psychosexual development; Sexual maturation.*

Sexual deviations. Sexual deviation(s). *Choose from:* sexual(ly), psychosexual(ly) *with:* deviation(s), deviate(s), devian(ce,t,ts), disorder(s), masochis(m,t,ts,tic), sadis(m,t,ts,tic), perversion(s), aberrant, aberration(s), psychopath(s,ology), abnormal(ity,ities), homicide(s), offender(s), molester(s), phobia(s). *Consider also:* bestiality, exhibitionis(m,t,ts), fetish(ism), frottage, toucheurism, incest, pedophil(e,es,ia, iac,iacs), transvest(ite,ites,ism), voyeur(s,ism), erotoman(ia,ic), sodom(y,ized), homosexual(ity), necrophil(ia,ic), nymphoman(ia,iac), bisexual(ity). *See also* Autoerotic death; Deviance; Deviant behavior; Exhibition-ism; Fetishism; Flagellants and flagella-tion; Incest; Indecent exposure; Mental illness; Oedipus complex; Paraphilias; Pedophilia; Pornography; Scatology; Sex behavior; Sex offenses; Sexual abuse; Sexual asphyxia syndrome; Sexual masochism; Sexual sadism; Sexuality; Sodomy; Transsexualism; Transvestism; Voyeurism.

Sexual discrimination. See *Labor market segmentation; Male chauvinism; Sex discrimination; Sexism; Sexual division of labor; Sexual inequality.*

Sexual division of labor. Sexual division of labor. Conjugal role(s). Domestic division of labor. Household division of labor. Provider role(s). Homemaker role(s). Dual labor market(s). Occupa-tional sex segregation. Mommy track(s). Unpaid household labor. Job ghetto(es,s). Glass ceiling(s). Sticky floor(s). Female intensive occupation(s). Fifth world. *Choose from:* sexual, gender, famil(y,ies), parent(s,al), conjugal, domestic, household *with:* division of labor, division of work,

subdivi(sion,ding) work, task(s), sharing work, specialization, work roles, housework. *Consider also:* marital symmetry. *See also* Affirmative action; Comparable worth; Division of labor; Dual career families; Dual economy; Egalitarian families; Employment discrimination; Equity (payment); Family power; Family roles; Family work relationship; Gender differences; Harems; Homemakers; House husbands; Housekeeping; Housewives; Income inequality; Labor economics; Labor market segmentation; Marriage contracts; Nontraditional careers; Occupational roles; Occupational segregation; Private sphere; Public sphere; Purdah; Sex discrimination; Sex roles; Sexism; Sexual inequality; Shared parenting; Social equality; Veiling of women; Wage differentials; Working women.

Sexual dysfunction. See *Sexual function disorders.*

Sexual equality. See *Affirmative action; Comparable worth; Equity (payment); Fairness; Nonsexist language; Sex discrimination; Sexual division of labor; Sexual inequality; Social equality; Social equity.*

Sexual equity. See *Affirmative action; Social equality; Social equity; Social justice.*

Sexual ethics. Sexual ethic(s). *Choose from:* sex(ual,ually,uality), dating, premarital, extramarital, homosexual, lesbian, heterosexual, lover(s), mate(s), spouse(s), fornicat(e,ed,ing,ion), mak(e,ing) love, lovemaking, adulter(y, ous), incest(uous) *with:* ethic(s,al), moral(s,ity), immoral(ity), deception, obligation(s), integrity, accountability, honest(y), principle(s), code(s), openness, fidelity, conscience, conscientious(ness), conflict of interest, trust(worthy,worthiness), truth(ful, fulness), unethical(ly), improper, misdeed(s), misconduct, conflict(s) of interest, violat(e,ed,ing,ions), illegal(ity,ities), impropriet(y,ies), scandal(s), breach of confidence, unprofessional, breach of decorum, cheat(ed,ing), wrongdoing(s), unscrupulous(ness), trust violation(s), inappropriate conduct. *See also* Birth control; Chastity; Ethics; Extramarital relations; Feminist ethics; Morality; Premarital sexual behavior; Promiscuity; Sex behavior; Sex education; Sexual permissiveness; Social dating; Unethical conduct.

Sexual excitement. See *Sexual arousal.*

Sexual exploitation. Sexual(ly) exploit(ed,ing,er,ation,ative). Sexploit(ed,ation). Sex tourism. Snuff film(s). Peep show(s). Sex ring(s). Statutory rape(s). Child porn(ography).

Kiddie porn(ography). Indecent libert(y,ies). *Choose from:* sex(ual,ually, ualization) *with:* misus(e,ed,ing), victim(s,izing,ize,ized,ization,izations), slave(s,ry), oppress(ed,ing,ion). *Choose from:* child(ren), teen(age,aged, ager,agers), adolescen(t,ts,ce) *with:* prostitut(e,ed,ion). *Consider also:* anatomically correct doll(s), good touch bad touch. *See also* Acquaintance rape; Cybersex; Harems; Incest; Indecent communications; Malinformation; Marital rape; Molested children; Pedophilia; Physician patient relations; Pornography; Professional client relations; Prostitution; Researcher subject relations; Sex industry; Sexual abuse; Sexual assault; Sexual coercion; Sexual harassment; Sexual misconduct; Sexual violence; Statutory rape; Trafficking in persons; Unethical conduct.

Sexual fantasies. Sexual fantas(y,ies). Sexual phantas(y,ies). *Choose from:* sexual(ly), erotic(a,ism), masturbat(e,ed, ing,ion,ory), rape, seduct(ory,ive), coit(us,al), courtesan, hetaeral *with:* imagination, daydream(s,ing), fantas(y,ies), phantas(y,ies). *See also* Eroticism; Femmes fatales; Masturbation; Sexual arousal.

Sexual foreplay. Sexual foreplay. Sex(ual) play. Forepleasure. Kiss(ed,ing). Fondl(e,ed,ing). Strok(e,ed,ing). Petting. Necking. Spooning. Courtship behavior. Premarital sexual behavior. *See also* Human courtship; Premarital sexual behavior; Sex behavior; Sexual arousal.

Sexual freedom. See *Sexual permissiveness*.

Sexual function disorders. Sexual function disorder(s). *Choose from:* sex(ual,ually), psychosexual, coital, erection(s), erectile, ejaculat(ion,ory), copulatory, orgasm(s,ic) *with:* disorder(s), problem(s), dysfunction(al,s), conflict(s), disturbance(s), difficult(y,ies), disinterest(ed), inadequa(te,cy), incompeten(t,ce). *Consider also:* apareunia, anorgasm(ia,ic,y), inorgasmic. *See also* Disorders; Dyspareunia; Frigidity; Impotence; Orgasmic dysfunction; Premature ejaculation; Sexual inhibitions; Vaginismus.

Sexual harassment. Sexual harassment. Lecher(s,ous,ousness). Seduction attempt(s). Office affair(s). *Choose from:* sex(ual,ually), women, woman, gender *with:* harass(ed,ing,ment), harrass(ed, ing,ment), unwanted attention, abuse(d), grop(e,ed,ing), overture(s). *Choose from:* sex(ual,ually) *with:* workplace, work setting, office(s), comment(s), intimidation, threat(en,ened,s), advance(s), approach(es), exploitation, proposition(s), invitation(s), molest(ation,ing), intimation(s),

attempt(s), coercion, affair(s), innuendo(s), pass(es), unwelcome behavior, unsolicited behavior. *Choose from:* intimate, vulgar, obscene, suggestive *with:* gesture(s), remark(s). *See also* Abusive parents; Acquaintance rape; Antisocial behavior; Cybersex; Harassment; Incest; Indecent communications; Intimidation; Invective; Molested children; Online harassment; Rape; Sex discrimination; Sex offenders; Sex offenses; Sexual abuse; Sexual assault; Sexual coercion; Sexual exploitation; Sexual misconduct; Sexual violence; Stalking; Street harassment; Unethical conduct; Verbal abuse; Victimization.

Sexual identity. See *Gender identity*.

Sexual inequality. Sex(ual) inequalit(y,ies). Sex(ual) inequit(y,ies). Gender inequal(ity,ities). Sexual stratification. *Choose from:* female(s), women, woman, sex(ual), gender, girl(s), feminin(e,ity) *with:* inequality, inequit(y,ies), exploit(ed,ing,ation), discrepanc(y,ies), unfair, discriminat(e, ed,ing,ion), stratification, segregat(ed, ion). *Consider also:* patriarch(y,al), male dominat(ed,ion), sex discrimination, sex(ism,ist), sex bias(es,ed), discrimination against women, treated as sex object(s). *See also* Affirmative action; Androcentrism; Attitudes toward homosexuality; Civil rights; Egalitarian families; Equal education; Equal job opportunities; Equity (payment); Family roles; Females (human); Gender differences; Income inequality; Inequality; Labor market segmentation; Males (human); Nontraditional careers; Occupational segregation; Private sphere; Public sphere; Sex discrimination; Sex role attitudes; Sex roles; Sexism; Sexual Division of Labor; Sexual oppression; Social discrimination; Social equality; Social equity; Wage differentials; Working women.

Sexual inhibitions. Sexual inhibit(ed,ion, ions). Prud(ery,ish,ishness). Victorian values. Sex(ual) guilt. Inhibited sexual desire(s). *Choose from:* sex(ual), libidinal, orgasm(ic) *with:* block(ed,s), hangup(s), restrain(t,ed), repress(ed,ion, ions). *Consider also:* narrow-minded, puritanical, straight-laced, strait-laced, demure, over(ly)-modest(y). *See also* Attitudes; Desexualization; Sexual function disorders.

Sexual intercourse. Sexual intercourse. Coit(al,us,ion). Copulat(e,ed,ing,ion). Sexual relations. Mat(e,ed,ing). Fornicat(e,ed,ing,ion). Mak(e,ing) love. Lovemaking. Adulter(y,ous). *Consider also:* coitus interruptus, dyspareunia, extramarital intercourse, incest, premarital intercourse, rape, sex(ual) behavior. *See also* Dyspareunia; Extramarital relations; Incest; Marital

sexual behavior; Orgasm; Premarital sexual behavior; Rape; Sex behavior; Sexual arousal; Sexual foreplay; Sexual permissiveness; Sexual reproduction; Sexual satisfaction; Sexuality.

Sexual liberation. See *Sexual permissiveness*.

Sexual masochism. Sexual(ly) masochis(m,t,tic). *Choose from:* sexual(ly), erotic(ism,ally), heterosexual(ly), autoerotic(ally,ism), homosexual(ly), paraphilia(s), coitus, masturbation *with:* masochis(m,t,tic), asphyxia, self punish(ed,ing,ment), sadomasochis(m,t,tic), bondage, flogging, flagell(ation,antism), humiliat(e,ed,ing,ion), restrain(ed,t), tortur(e,ed,ing), submission, punish(ment), torment(s), whip(ped, pings), spanking(s). *See also* Fetishism; Flagellants and flagellation; Masochism; Sexual asphyxia syndrome; Sexual deviations; Sexual sadism.

Sexual maturation. Sex(ual,ually) matur(e,ing,ation,ity). Pubert(y,al). Adolescent development. Menarch(e, eal). Pubescen(t,ce). *Choose from:* reproductive, genital, ovarian, sex(ual,ually), sexuality, psychosexual *with:* development, matur(e,ed,ing, ation). *See also* Adolescent development; Menarche; Psychosexual development; Puberty.

Sexual misconduct. Sexual misconduct. *Choose from:* sexual(ly), sex, bedroom(s), premarital, extramarital *with:* misconduct, scandal(s,ous,ously), reprehensible behavior, misdeed(s), misbehavior, transgression(s), naught(y,iness), indiscre(et,tion,tions), misdemeanor(s), affair(s). *See also* Extramarital relations; Immorality; Sex offenses; Sexual abuse; Sexual assault; Sexual exploitation; Sexual harassment; Sexual permissiveness; Unethical conduct.

Sexual oppression. Sex(ual) oppression. *Choose from:* female(s), women(s), woman(s), sex(ual), gender, girl(s), feminin(e,ity) *with:* oppress(ed,ing,ion), dominat(e,ed,ing,ion), servitude, subordinat(e,ed,es,ing,ation), subjugat(e,ed,ing,ion), inequality, inequit(y,ies), trivializ(e,ed,ing,ation), paternalis(m,tic), patriarch(y,ies,al), powerless(ness), learned helplessness, self sacrific(e,es,ing), exploit(ed,ing, ation), objectif(y,ied,ication), repress(ed,ing,ion), discrepanc(y,ies), unfair(ly), de-sexualiz(e,ed,ing,ation), discriminat(e,ed,ing,ion), stratification, segregat(ed,ion). *Consider also:* machismo, primogeniture, polygyny, male dominat(ed,ion), sex discrimination, sex(ism,ist), sex bias(es,ed), discrimination against women, sex object(s). *See also* Androcentrism;

Battered women; Harems; Images of women; Labor market segmentation; Male chauvinism; Misogyny; Occupational segregation; Oppression; Patriarchy; Purdah; Sex discrimination; Sexism; Sexist language; Sexual Division of Labor; Sexual harassment; Sexual inequality; Spouse abuse; Veiling of women; Women living in poverty.

Sexual orientation. Sexual orientation(s). *Choose from:* sex(ual), gender, homosexual(s,ity), lesbian(s), gay(s), androgyn(y,ous), bisexual(s,ity), feminin(e,ity), masculin(e,ity), male(s), female(s), man(s), men(s), woman(s) women(s) *with:* role(s), identit(y,ies), orientation(s), identification, stereotype(s), appearance(s), image(s), traditional, nontraditional, expectation(s), expected behavior, conformity, nonconformity, lifestyle(s), preference(s). *See also* Androgyny; Bisexuality; Gender differences; Gender identity; Heterosexuality; Homosexuality; Identification (psychology); Lesbianism; Male homosexuality; Self concept; Sex roles; Sex stereotypes; Sexual preferences; Social identity.

Sexual partners. Sex(ual) partner(s). Lover(s). Mate(s). Consort(s). Sexual histor(y,ies). *Choose from:* partner(s), contact(s), couple(s), wife, wives, husband(s) *with:* sex(ual), homosexual, cohabiting. *Consider also:* spouse(s), significant other(s). *See also* Cohabitation; Couples; Extramarital relations; Gay couples; Heterosexual relationships; Intimacy; Premarital sexual behavior; Significant others; Spouses.

Sexual permissiveness. Sexual(ly) permissive(ness). *Choose from:* sex(ual,ually), dating, premarital, extramarital, homosexual, lesbian, heterosexual *with:* permissive(ness), freedom, liberation. Open marriage(s). Bundling. Free love. Situational ethics. Double standard(s). Promiscu(ity, ousness). Prosex(ual,uality) ideolog(y,ies). Casual sex. *Consider also:* wife, wives, husband(s), spouse(s), mate(s) *with:* swap(ped,ping). *See also* Extramarital relations; Premarital sexual behavior; Promiscuity; Sex behavior; Sexual consent; Sexual ethics; Sexual misconduct.

Sexual perversions. See *Paraphilias; Sexual deviations.*

Sexual preferences. Sexual preference(s). Erotic preference(s). Sexual minorit(y,ies). Sexual variation(s). Alternat(e,ive) sexual preference(s). Sexual orientation(s). Sex role orientation(s). *Consider also:* heterosexual(ly,s,ity), opposite sex, homosexual(ly,s,ity), gay, homoerotic, lesbian, bisexual(ly,s,ity), intersexual *with:* preference(s), relationship(s),

attraction, interaction(s), intimacy, lover(s), roman(tic,ce,ces), choice(s), desir(e,ability). *See also* Bisexuality; Gender identity; Homosexuality; Heterosexuality; Lesbianism; Male homosexuality; Sexual orientation; Sexuality.

Sexual reassignment. See *Sex change.*

Sexual relations. See *Sexual intercourse.*

Sexual relationships. See *Couples; Extramarital relations; Gay couples; Heterosexual relationships; Intimacy; Marital relationship; Marriage; Premarital sexual behavior; Sexual partners; Spouses.*

Sexual reproduction. Sexual reproduction. *Choose from:* reproductive, sexual *with:* function(s), competition(s), behavior(s), activit(y,ies). *Consider also:* procreation, sexual selection, courtship, breed(ing), fertil(ity,ization), insemination, mating, conception, pregnan(t,cy), birth, whelping, calving, foaling, parturition. *See also* Animal breeding; Animal mate selection; Animal sex behavior; Artificial insemination; Birth; Conception; Fertility enhancement; Fertilization; Fertilization in vitro; Genetics; Pregnancy; Reproductive technologies; Sex behavior; Sexual intercourse; Surrogate mothers.

Sexual revolution. Sexual revolution. *Choose from:* sex(ual,ually,uality), abortion(s), contracept(ion,ive,ives), dating, premarital, extramarital, homosexual *with:* revolution(s,ary), freedom, liberat(e,ed,ing,ion), emancipat(e,ed,ing,ion). *Choose from:* sex(ual,ually,uality), abortion(s), contracept(ion,ive,ives), dating, premarital, extramarital, homosexual *with:* attitude(s), standard(s), norm(s), value(s) *with:* chang(e,es,ed,ing), evolution, evolv(e,ed,ing), liberaliz(e,ed,ing,ation). *See also* Extramarital relations; Moral attitudes; Premarital sexual behavior; Sexual permissiveness.

Sexual sadism. Sexual(ly) sadis(m,tic). Sexual(ly) violen(t,ce). Sado-masochism. Algolagnia. *Choose from:* sadis(m,tic), sadomasochis(m,tic), violen(t,ce), tortur(e,ed,ing), bondage *with:* sex, sexual(ly), psychosexual(ly), erotic(ism), homosexual(ly), rape(s,d), fetish(s,ism), pedophil(ia,iac,ias), voyeur(ism), perversion(s), devian(t,ts,ce). *See also* Fetishism; Flagellants and flagellation; Sadism; Sexual deviations; Sexual masochism; Sexual violence.

Sexual satisfaction. Sexual(ly) satisf(y,ying,ied,action). *Choose from:* sex(ual,ually), sexuality, coit(us,al), lovemaking, fellatio, cunnilingus, kissing, sexual foreplay, sexual intimacy, heterosexual, homosexual, intercourse,

masturbat(e,ed,ing,ion) *with:* satisf(y,ying,ied,action), pleasur(e,able), enjoy(ed,ing,ment), joy(ful), delight(ful), fulfill(ed,ing,ment), happ(y,iness), climax(es), climactic, peak(s), orgas(m,ms,mic,tic), *See also* Intimacy; Love; Orgasm; Sex behavior; Sexual intercourse.

Sexual violence. Sexual(ly) violen(ce,t). *Choose from:* sexual(ly), courtship, date(s), wife, wives, spouse(s), husband(s), mate(s) *with:* violen(t,ce), assault(ed,ive,ing), victimiz(e,ed,ing, ation), attack(s,ed,ing), homicid(e,es,al), forced, harass(ed,ing,ment), abus(e,ive), killer(s), killing(s), murder(s,er,ers). *Consider also:* rap(e,ed,ing), marital rape(s), incest(uous), pedophil(e,es,ia, iacs). *See also* Acquaintance rape; Antisocial behavior; Battered women; Child abuse; Elder abuse; Family violence; Jealousy; Marital rape; Mass media violence; Possessiveness; Rape; Sex offenses; Sexual abuse; Sexual assault; Sexual exploitation; Sexual harassment; Spouse abuse; Television violence.

Sexuality. Sexualit(y,ies). Libid(o,inal). Seductive(ness). Eros. Eroticism. Lustful(ness). Sex(y,iness). Phall(ic,os). Pheromone(s). Don Juan(s). Femininity. Masculinity. *Choose from:* sexual(ly), gender, genital, erotic, homosexual(ly), heterosexual(ly), psychosexual(ly) *with:* express(ion,iveness), intent(ions), identit(y,ies), drive(s), fulfill(ed,ing, ment), excitation, functioning, character. *See also* Bisexuality; Cohabitation; Gender differences; Gender identity; Heterosexuality; Homosexuality; Hypersexuality; Extramarital relations; Frigidity; Incest; Intimacy; Libido; Love; Personality traits; Pornography; Psychosexual development; Sex behavior; Sex drive; Sex role attitudes; Sexual deviations; Sexual intercourse; Sexual preferences; Transsexualism.

Sexuality, compulsive. See *Hypersexuality.*

Sexuality, human. See *Sexuality.*

Sexually transmitted diseases. Sexually transmitted disease(s). Sexual transmission of disease(s). *Choose from:* sexual(ly) *with:* acquired, transmitted, transmissible, transferred, communicable, health hazard(s). AIDS. HIV infection(s). Venereal disease(s). VD. Venereological disease(s). Syphil(is,itic). Clap. Gonorrhea. Chancre. Chancroid. Social disease(s). Granuloma inguinale. Lymphogranuloma venereum. Lues venerea. CNS lues. Chlamydia. Herpes genitalis. Genital herpes. Genital wart(s). *Choose from:* acquired *with:* immune deficiency, immunodeficiency, immunologic deficiency *with:* syndrome. *Consider also:* crab lice, honeymoon cystitis. *See also* AIDS; Female genital disorders; Gonorrhea; Herpes genitalis;

Male genital disorders.

Sham disorders. See *Factitious disorders.*

Sham surgery. Sham surgery. Phony operation(s). Surgery as placebo. See also *Placebos; Quackery.*

Shamanism. Shaman(s,ic,ism,istic). Priest-doctor(s). *Choose from:* ritual(s), folk *with:* heal(ing,er,ers), cathar(sis,tic), remed(y,ies), treatment(s). *Consider also:* symbolic heal(ing,er,ers), ritual trance(s), sorcer(y,er,ers), diviner(s), exorcis(m,t,ts), seance(s), magician(s), folk psychotherapy, indigenous practitioner(s), medicine men, nangarri, native healer(s), obeah(s), curander(o,os, ismo). *See also* Cross cultural psychiatry; Culture specific syndromes; Cults; Divination; Ethnopsychology; Folk culture; Magic; Plant folklore; Priests and priestly classes (anthropology); Psychotropic plants; Religious beliefs; Religious rituals; Spiritual healing; Supernatural; Traditional medicine; Traditional societies.

Shame. Shame(d,ful,fully). Ashamed. Blush(ed,ing). Embarrass(ed,ment). Scotophob(ia,ic). Scopophob(ia,ic). Abashed. Shamefaced. Chagrin(ed). Contrit(e,ion). Humiliat(e,ed,ion). Disgrac(e,ed). Self conscious(ness). *Consider also:* guilt(iness), feel(ing) guilty, penitent, conscience stricken. *See also* Anxiety; Anxiety disorders; Blame; Conscience; Denial (psychology); Embarrassment; Emotions; Examination of conscience; Guilt; Honor (integrity); Humiliation; Morality; Neutralization; Rationalization (defense mechanism); Self consciousness; Self debasement; Self hate; Sin.

Shanties. See *Sea songs.*

Shantytowns. See *Slums.*

Share, market. See *Market share.*

Sharecropping. Sharecrop(per,pers,ping). Cropsharing. Tenant farm(ers,ing). Metay(er,age) system. *Consider also:* peasant household production, feudalism, semi-feudalism, precapitalist production, bataidar(s). *See also* Feudalism; Land tenure; Peonage; Plantations; Slavery; Tenant farmers.

Shared housing. See *Group homes.*

Shared paranoid disorder. See *Psychosis of association.*

Shared parenting. Shared parenting. Co-parenting. Parenting together. *Choose from:* shar(e,ed,ing), equal(ity), joint *with:* parent(ing,hood), childrearing, child rearing, parent(al) responsibilit(y, ies), parent(al) task(s), parent(al) dut(y,ies), parent(al) role(s), caregiver(s), child care, nurtur(e,ance,ing), toilet training, child discipline, mothering, fathering. *Consider also:* joint custody. *See also* Egalitarian families; Family

roles; Childrearing; Parent adolescent relations; Parent child relationship; Sex roles; Sexual division of labor.

Shared services. Shared service(s). Shared Hospital Services. *Choose from:* shar(e,ed,ing), cooperative, communal, interagency, partnership(s) *with:* service(s), program(s), responsibilit(y, ies), resource(s). *Consider also:* work(ing) together, superhospitals, group purchasing organization(s), group purchase(s), shared catalog(ing). *See also* Alliances; Contracting out; Subcontracting.

Shared work. See *Alternative work patterns.*

Shareholder relations. See *Investor relations.*

Sharing. Shar(e,ed,ing). Social(ly) interdependen(t,ce). Altruis(m,tic). Prosocial behavior. Contribut(e,ed,ing, ion,ions). Donat(e,ed,ing,ion,ions). Generous. Generosity. Acts of kindness. Participat(e,ed,ing,ion). Unselfish(ness). Take part. Partak(e,ing). Turn taking. Cooperative(s). Communal(ity). *See also* Altruism; Charitable behavior; Cohousing; Communes; Cooperation; Cost sharing; Favors; Generosity; Helping behavior; Interpersonal relations; Kindness; Prosocial behavior; Reciprocity; Social behavior; Social exchange; Social interaction.

Sharing, cost. See *Cost sharing.*

Sharing, job. See *Alternative work patterns; Work sharing.*

Sharing, needle. See *Needle sharing.*

Sharing, power. See *Power sharing.*

Sharing, profit. See *Profit sharing.*

Sharing, work. See *Work sharing.*

Sheep. Sheep. Lamb(s). Ewe(s). Ram(s). *Consider also:* ovis, jumbuck, mutton. *See also* Animals; Cattle; Herders; Livestock; Mammals; Wool industry.

Sheets, balance. See *Financial statements; Financial data.*

Shell shock. See *Combat disorders; Post traumatic stress disorders.*

Shelter. See *Housing.*

Sheltered housing. Sheltered housing. Residential care home(s). Residential alternative(s). *Choose from:* sheltered, supportive, assisted, senior(s), retirement, disab(led,ility,ilities), handicap(s,ped), custodial, domiciliary *with:* home(s), house(s), housing, residence(s), residential setting(s), living, commune(s), living center(s), accomodations, facilit(y,ies). *Consider also:* dormitor(y,ies), halfway house(s), board and care home(s). *See also* Adult foster care; Boardinghouses; Group homes; Homeless shelters; Homes for

the elderly; Noninstitutionalized disabled; Retirement communities; Sheltered workshops; Shelters.

Sheltered workshops. Sheltered workshop(s). *Choose from:* sheltered, rehabilitation, disability, disabled, retarded, handicapped, blind, protected *with:* workshop(s). *See also* Attitudes toward handicapped; Disability; Disabled workers; Employment of persons with disabilities; Employer attitudes; Employment discrimination; Equal job opportunities; Rehabilitation centers; Rehabilitation counseling; Sheltered housing; Vocational rehabilitation.

Shelters. Shelter(s). Refuge(s). Asylum(s). Haven(s). Sanctuar(y,ies). Transitional living center(s). Network of abused women. Crisis shelter(s). Humane Society. ASPCA. ASPCC. SPCA. Society for the Prevention of Cruelty to Animals. Society for the Prevention of Cruelty to Children. Salvation Army. Red Cross. American Humane Association. Animal shelter(s). Rape crisis center(s). YWCA. Animal pound(s). Sheltered care. Cit(y,ies) of refuge. Totem center(s). *Consider also:* group home(s), temporary housing. *See also* Animal welfare; Asylums; Battered women; Crisis intervention; Emergency services; Halfway houses; Help lines (telephone); Homeless; Homeless shelters; Orphanages; Rape crisis counseling; Rescue; Sheltered housing; Victimization; Wildlife sanctuaries.

Shelters, crisis. See *Shelters.*

Shelters, homeless. See *Homeless shelters.*

Shift, language. See *Language shift.*

Shift, linguistic. See *Language shift.*

Shift work. See *Workday shifts.*

Shifting, cost. See *Cost shifting.*

Shifts, workday. See *Workday shifts.*

Shintoism. Shinto(ism). *Consider also:* Kami, Kami-no-michi, Kojiki, Nihongi, Yengishiki. *See also* Ancestor worship; Religions.

Shipbuilding. Shipbuild(ing,er,ers). Marine architecture. *Choose from:* build(ing), built, design(ed,ing), construct(ed,ing, ion), reconstruct(ing,ion) *with:* ship(s), schooner(s), battleship(s), trawler(s), showboat(s), boat(s), yacht(s). *Consider also:* shipyard(s). *See also* Dry docks; Historic ships; Naval architecture; Sailing ships; Ships.

Shipping industry. Shipping industry. Steamship line(s). *Consider also:* freighter(s), tanker(s), merchant ship(s), container ship(s), merchant(man,men), merchant marine, maritime industry, marine service, marine transportation. *See also* Cargo; Carriers (shipping);

Containers; Dry docks; Earth; Exports; Freight; Imports; Longshoremen; Oceans; Piers; Sea power; Ships; Territorial waters; Trade routes; Transport workers; Transportation.

Ships. Ship(s). Aircraft carrier(s). Barge(s). Battleship(s). Boat(s). Brigantine(s). Catamaran(s). Clipper ship(s). Cruiser(s). Cruiseship(s). Destroyer(s). Destroyer tender(s). Ferr(y,ies). Fishing smack(s). Freighter(s). Ketch(es). Oceanliner(s). Riverboat(s). Sailboat(s). Schooner(s). Sloop(s). Steamship(s). Submarine(s). Supply ship(s). Tanker(s). Tinclad(s). Tugboat(s). Trawler(s). Vessel(s). Whaling ship(s). Yacht(s). Yawl(s). *See also* Aircraft carriers; Boats; Collisions at sea; Cruising; Dry docks; Harbors; Historic ships; Marine accidents; Naval architecture; Ports; Sailing ships; Sea power; Seizure of ships; Shipbuilding; Shipping industry; Warships.

Ships, historic. See *Historic ships.*

Ships, sailing. See *Sailing ships.*

Ships, seizure of. See *Seizure of ships.*

Shipwrecks. See *Marine accidents.*

Shock. Shock(s,ed,ing). Footshock(s,ed, ing). Postshock. Preshock. Crush syndrome. Blow. Trauma(tic,tized). Bombshell. Stun(ned). Startl(e,ed,ing). *Consider also:* cardiogenic, septic, surgical, traumatic, hemorragic *with:* shock(s,ed,ing). *See also* Culture shock; Electroshock; Emotional trauma; Injuries; Shock therapy; Stress; Surprise.

Shock, culture. See *Culture shock.*

Shock, electric. See *Electroschock.*

Shock, shell. See *Combat disorders; Post traumatic stress disorders.*

Shock therapy. Shock therapy. *Choose from:* electroconvulsive, electric convulsive, shock, electroshock *with:* therap(y,ies), treatment(s). *Consider also:* ECT, electric sleep, electro-hypnosis. *See also* Aversive therapy; Electrosleep treatment; Shock.

Shoes and boots. See *Boots and shoes.*

Shoes, ballet. See *Ballet shoes.*

Shop, closed. See *Closed shop.*

Shop, open. See *Open shop.*

Shop, union. See *Union shop.*

Shoplifting. Shoplift(ing,ers). Pilfer(age). Purloin(ed,ing). Filch(ed,ing). *Choose from:* retail, shop(s), store(s), employee(s), customer(s), merchandise, goods *with:* theft, steal(ing), stolen. *See also* Behavior disorders; Crime; Elderly offenders; Juvenile delinquency; Larceny; Theft; Thieves.

Shoppers. See *Clients.*

Shopping. See *Purchasing.*

Shopping centers. Shopping center(s). Galleria(s). *Choose from:* shopping, retail *with:* arcade(s), center(s), mall(s), complex(es), plaza(s). *Consider also:* department store(s), marketplace(s), superstore(s), strip mall(s), cybermall(s), mallpark(s). *See also* Consumer society; Consumers; Department stores; Embourgeoisement; Mass society; Merchants; Retailing; Stores.

Shops, beauty. See *Beauty shops.*

Shore protection. Shore protection. *Choose from:* shore(s), shoreline(s), shore line(s), shoreland(s), coast(s,al), shorefront(s), beach(es), seashore(s), coastline(s), waterfront(s), beachfront(s), riverfront(s), seaside(s), oceanside(s), oceanfront(s), lakeshore(s), coastal zone(s), coastal resource(s), coastal area(s), coastal propert(y,ies), wetland(s), salt marsh(es) *with:* protect(ed,ing,ion), dike(s,d), conserv(e,ed,ing,ation), conservancy, management, erosion control, preserv(e,ed,ing,ation), sav(e,ed,es,ing), barrier(s), land use planning, regulat(e,ed,ing,ion), restor(e,ed,ing, ation), engineer(ed,ing). *Consider also:* barrier island(s), barrier beach(es), breakwater(s), jett(y,ies), groin(s), dune(s), sea wall(s), seawall(s), beach nourishment, estuar(y,ies,ine), littoral sand transport. *See also* Beaches; Conservation of natural resources; Dikes (engineering); Earth; Ecology; Environmental protection; Island ecology; Islands; Land preservation; Natural environment; Natural resources; Reclamation of land; Shorelines; Soil conservation; Soil erosion; Submerged lands; Tides; Water levels; Wildlife conservation.

Shorelines. Shoreline(s). Shore line(s). Coast(s,al). Shorefront(s). Beach(es). Shore(s). Oceanfront(s). Oceanside(s). Seashore(s). Seaside(s). Beachfront(s). Coastline(s). Waterfront(s). Riverfront(s). Lakeshore(s). *Consider also:* coastal *with:* zone(s), resource(s), area(s), propert(y,ies), wetland(s), salt marsh(es), dockland(s), tidewater area(s), river bank(s). *See also* Beaches; Boundaries; Coast defenses; Island ecology; Islands; Reclamation of land; Shore protection; Stream channelization; Submerged lands; Territorial waters; Tides; Wetlands.

Short stories. See *Anecdotes.*

Short term memory. Short term memory. *Choose from:* iconic, short term, recent, immediate, working *with:* memory, recall, retention. *See also* Iconic memory; Memory.

Short term planning. Short term plan(s,ning). *Choose from:* short term, immediate future, one year, 5 year, seasonal, month(ly), week(ly), daily

with: plan(s,ned,ning), goal(s), objective(s), forecast(s,ed,ing). *Consider also:* middle range plan(s,ning). *See also* Goals; Implementation; Long range planning; Management planning; Priorities; Strategies.

Short term psychotherapy. See *Brief psychotherapy.*

Shortages. Shortage(s). Scarcit(y,ies). Running out. Food cris(is,es). Panic buying. Panic stockpiling. Lack of reserve(s). Curtailed production. Unavailab(le,ility). Ration(ed,ing). Material deprivation. Bread line(s). Soup kitchen(s). Underserved. Drought(s). Famine(s). Conservation measure(s). Insufficien(t,cy). Meager. *Choose from:* scant, short, low, dwindl(e,ing) *with:* suppl(y,ies). *See also* Commodities; Consumption (economic); Deprivation; Economic problems; Famine; Natural disasters; Resource allocation; Resources; Scarcity; Supply and demand.

Shows, trade. See *Trade shows.*

Shrines. Shrine(s). Temple(s). Tabernacle(s). Sacred place(s). Hallowed place(s). Place(s) of worship. Place(s) of pilgrimage. Sacred tomb(s). Holy cit(y,ies). Holy ground(s). Holy place(s). Holy site(s). Sacred ground(s). House(s) of prayer. Sanctuar(y,ies). House(s) of God. Altar(s). Sacrificial stone(s). Stupa(s). *Consider also:* Eleusis, Delphi, Benares, Puri, Allahabad, Ganges, Mt. Tai, Uji-yamada, Taisha, Temple at Jerusalem, Mecca, Kerbala, Jerusalem, Bethlehem, Nazareth, Rome, Santiago de Campostela, Holy Lands, Loreto, Montserrat, Fatima, Lourdes, Auray, Einsiedeln, Czestochowa, Croagh-Patrick, Saint Patrick's Purgatory, Sainte Anne de Beaupre, Guadelupe Hidalgo. *See also* Cultural property; Martyrs; Pilgrimages; Places of worship; Religious rituals; Sacred places; Sacredness; Sanctuaries; Temples.

Shrunken heads. Shrunken head(s). Tsantsa(s). Tsantza(s). *Choose from:* shrink(ing), shrank, shrunk(en), preserv(e,ed,ing,ation), mummif(y,ying, ied,ication) *with:* human head(s), tattooed head(s). *Consider also:* pickled head(s), headhunting, cannibalism, cabeza(s) reducida(s). *See also* Cannibalism; Feuds; Human sacrifice; Revenge; Superstitions; Talisman; Tribalism.

Shutdowns. See *Plant closings.*

Shutdowns, factory. See *Plant closings.*

Shyness. Shy(ness). Diffiden(t,ce). Self conscious(ness). Bashful(ness). *Consider also:* social anxiety, social introversion, wary, wariness, withdrawn, socially inhibited, social inhibition(s), social avoidance, communication apprehension. *See also* Anxiety;

Introversion; Inhibition (psychology); Interpersonal relations; Personality traits; Social anxiety; Social isolation; Social phobia; Timidity.

Siamese twins. Siamese twins. Conjoin(t,ed) twins. Thoracopagus twins. Double fetal monster. Pygopagus twins. *See also* Twins.

Sibling relations. Sibling relation(s,ships). *Choose from:* sib(s,ling,ship), brother(s), sister(s), twin(s) *with:* relation(s,ships), rival(s,ry,ries), closeness, interaction(s), support, communication, participation, rejection, acceptance, expectations, dynamics, pattern(s), involvement, attitude(s), guilt, behavior, dependence, independence. *See also* Birth order; Family relations; Siblings; Stepfamily.

Siblings. Sib(s,ling,lings,ship). Brother(s). Sister(s). Twin(s). Litter mate(s). Triplet(s). Quadruplet(s). Quintuplet(s). *Consider also:* birth order, first born, eldest child(ren), youngest child(ren), middle child(ren). *See also* Birth intervals; Birth order; Brothers; Daughters; Family characteristics; Family life; Family members; Family size; Half siblings; Heterozygotic twins; Kinship; Monozygotic twins; Multiple births; Sibling relations; Siamese twins; Sisters; Sons; Twins.

Siblings, half. See *Half siblings*.

Sick building syndrome. Sick building syndrome. SBS. Air pollution syndrome. Tight building syndrome. *Choose from:* air quality, passive smoking, smoke, carbon monoxide, aerosol(s), dust, mold(s), harmful vapor(s), air pollut(ed,ing,ion,ants), air contaminat(ed,ing,ion), air contaminant(s) *with:* headache(s), fatigue, insomnia, eye irritation(s), irritability, depression, impaired judgment, visual disturbance(s), hearing disturbance(s), seizure(s), memory disturbance(s) *with:* building(s), work environment, working condition(s), room(s), office(s). *See also* Air pollution; Environmental effects; Environmental pollutants; Environmental pollution; Environmental stress; Hazardous occupations; Hypersensitivity; Multiple chemical sensitivities; Occupational exposure; Occupational safety; Occupational stress; Physiological stress; Quality of working life; Working conditions.

Sick, care of. See *Care of the sick*.

Sick leave. Sick leave(s). Medical leave(s). Sick day(s). *See also* Absenteeism; Employee benefits.

Sick role. Sick role. Illness behavior. Patient role. Pregnant role. Disability behavior. *Choose from:* role(s), behavior(s), adjustment(s), adapt(ed,ing,ation,ations), coping, acceptance, response(s), compliance *with:* illness, sick(ness),

patient(s), rehabilitation, medical recommendations, health care, illness, health problems, pain. *Consider also:* sociology of illness. *See also* Illness; Patient participation; Patients; Physician patient relations; Secondary gains.

Sickness. See *Illness*.

Sickness, altitude. See *Altitude sickness*.

Sickness, motion. See *Motion sickness*.

Side effects (drugs). See *Drug effects*.

Siege warfare. Siege warfare. *Choose from:* siege(s), blockad(e,es,ed,ing), besiege(d), encircle(d,ment), cut(ting) off suppl(y,ies) *with:* war(fare), battle(s), fight(s,ing), fought, combat, resist(ed,ing,ance), fort(s,ress,resses), fortification(s), walled town(s). *See also* Defense (Military science); Fortification; Military strategies.

Sight. See *Vision*.

Sight, loss of. See *Blindness*.

Sighted, partially. See *Partially sighted*.

Sign language. Sign language. Manual sign(s). Interpreting for hearing impaired. Ameslan. ASL. American sign language. *Choose from:* sign(ed), manual *with:* language, English, alphabet(s), communication, lexicon. *See also* Language; Manual communication.

Signatures. Signature(s). Countersign(ed, ing,ature,atures). Autograph(s). Signed by author(s). Inscribe(d). Inscription(s). John Hancock. *Consider also:* endors(e,ed,ing,ement), underwrit(ten, ing), trademark(s), brand name(s), label(s). *See also* Autographs; Cursive writing; Digital signatures; Endorsement; Forgery; Handwriting; Inscriptions.

Signatures, digital. See *Digital signatures*.

Significance, statistical. See *Statistical significance*.

Significance tests. See *Statistical significance*.

Significant others. Significant other(s). Spouse(s). Primary relationship(s). Close confidant(s,es). Significant people. Intimates. Close friend(s). Family member(s). Boyfriend(s). Girlfriend(s). Partner(s). Consort(s). *See also* Couples; Family relations; Friendship; Gay couples; Heterosexual relationships; Identification (psychology); Interpersonal relations; Marital relationship; Mentors; Peers; Reference groups; Role models; Self concept; Sexual partners; Sibling relations; Socialization; Spouses.

Silence. Silen(t,ce). Quiet. Still(ness). Soundless. Noiseless. Hushed. Inaudible. *Consider also:* tranquil, peaceful, muted. *See also* Noise (sounds); Nonverbal communication; Solitude.

Silent reading. Silent reading. *Choose from:* silent(ly), sub-vocal *with:* read(ing,er,ers). *See also* Inner speech; Oral reading; Reading.

Silviculture. See *Forestry*.

Similarity. Similarit(y,ies). Resemb(le,led, ling,lance). Likeness(es). Alike(ness). Look alike(s). Duplicat(e,es,ed,ing,ion). *See also* Agreement; Attitude similarity; Conformity (personality); Differences; Resemblance; Similes; Social cohesion; Social conformity; Uniformity.

Similarity, attitude. See *Attitude similarity*.

Similes. Simile(s). Analog(y,ies,ous). Likeness(es). Semblance(s). Similarit(y,ies). Similitude(s). Resemblance(s). *Consider also:* metaphor(s), affinit(y,ies), alike(ness), comparison(s). *See also* Imagery; Metaphors; Resemblance; Similarity.

Simplicity. Simplicity. Simple(ness). Uncomplicated. Clarity. Clear(ly,ness). Lucid(ity). Limpid(ity). Uncompounded. Explicit(ly,ness). Unmistakab(le,ly,ness). Intelligib(le,ility). Decipherab(le,ility). Pure(ly,ness). Purity. Legib(le,ility). Distinct(ly,ness). Direct(ly,ness). Explicit(ly,ness). *Consider also:* unadorn(ed,ment), unornament(ed, ment), unembellish(ed,ment), sparse(ly,ness), artless(ness), guileless(ness), forthright(ly,ness), candor, candid(ly,ness). *See also* Harmlessness; Innocence; Lifestyle; Purity.

Simplification, work. See *Work simplification*.

Simulation. Simulat(ed,ing,ion,ions). Model(s,ed,ing). Monte Carlo method(s). Role playing. Management game(s). Mock trial(s). Psychodrama(tics). Sociodrama(tic,tics). Rehearsal(s). Mock interview(s). Mock jur(y,ies). Moot court(s). Laboratory analog(s). Flight trainer(s). *Consider also:* laboratory condition(s), controlled environment(s), artificial intelligence, artificial life, a-life, alife, mathematical model(s). *See also* Animal testing alternatives; Artificial intelligence; Artificiality; Biological models; Cybernetics; Example; Flight simulation; Game theory; Heuristics; Mathematical models; Models; Role playing; Scientific models; Simulation games.

Simulation, flight. See *Flight simulation*.

Simulation games. Simulation game(s). *Choose from:* simulat(ed,ion), role playing, stochastic *with:* game(s). *Consider also:* management game(s), educational game(s). *See also* Game theory; Simulation.

Simultaneum. See *Interdenominational cooperation*.

Sin. Sin(ful,fully,fulness,ned,s,ner, ners,ning). Err(ed,ing). Evil(ness). Error of ways. Misdeed(s). Wrongdoing(s). Guilt(y,iness). Crime(s). Debt(s). Transgression(s). Trespass(es). Immoral(ity). Mea culpa. Vice(s). Unrepentant. Stray(ed,ing). Rebel(led,ling,lion) against God. *Consider also:* cardinal, chief, mortal, original, deadly, capital, venial, unforgivable, besetting, voluntary, involuntary, external, internal *with:* sin(s). *Consider also:* sin(s) of weakness, sin(s) of omission, sin(s) of comission, blasphem(e,ed,y,ous), idolatry, adultery, murder, anger, avarice, envy, gluttony, laziness, lust, pride. *See also* Casuistry; Confession; Cursing; Depravity; Evil; Fall of man; Forgiveness; Guilt; Morality; Penitents; Religious beliefs; Repentence; Shame; Salvation; Taboo.

Sincerity. Sincer(e,ity). Authentic(ity). Genuine(ness). Open(ness). Honest(y). Ingenuous(ness). Guile(less). Upright(ness). Undeceptive. Straightforward. Incorruptib(le,ility). Uncorrupt. Candid(ly). Candor. Frank(ness). Honorable. Unpretentious(ness). Earnest(ness). Trustworthy. *See also* Honesty; Personality traits; Simplicity; Truth.

Singers. Singer(s). Vocalist(s). Baritone(s). Bass(es). Soprano(s). Mezzo-soprano(s). Contralto(s). Alto(s). Tenor(s). Countertenor(s). Vocal artist(s). Soloist(s). Chorister(s). Cantor(s). Chanteuse(s). *Choose from:* choir, chorus, gleeclub *with:* member(s), boy(s), girl(s). *Consider also:* minstrel(s), crooner(s), choir(s), chorus(es), precentor(s), chanter(s), hymner(s), caroler(s), diva(s), prima donna(s), Grammy winner(s), rock star(s), castrat(o,i), coloratura(s). *See also* Artists; Choirs (music); Choral music; Choral singing; Choral societies; Choruses; Ensembles; Minnesinger; Minstrels; Opera singers; Singing; Troubadour; Trouvere.

Singers, opera. See *Opera singers.*

Singing. Sing(s,ing,en). Sang. Sung. Vocaliz(e,ed,ing,ation). Croon(ed,ing). Serenad(e,ed,ing). Chant(ed,ing). *Consider also:* voice training, Sprechstimme, Sprechgesang, yodel(ed,led,ing,ling). *See also* A cappella singing; Choral singing; Folk songs; Part songs; Singers; Songs; Voice.

Singing, choral. See *Choral singing.*

Single fathers. See *Single parent family.*

Single men. See *Bachelors; Single person.*

Single mothers. Single mother(s,hood). Unwed mother(s,hood). *Choose from:* unwed, single, unmarried, exnuptial, premarital, out-of-wedlock, divorced *with:* mother(s,hood), parent(s,hood), pregnan(t,cy), adolescent mother(s), birth(s), abortion applicant(s), primapara, multipara. *See also* Abortion applicants; Divorced people; Female headed households; Illegitimacy (children); Mother child relations; Mothers; Parental absence; Single parent family; Teenage mothers; Unmarried women; Unwanted pregnancy.

Single nucleotide polymorphisms. Single nucleotide polymorphism(s). SNP(s). Snip(s). *Consider also:* genetic determinant(s), genetic instruction(s), nucleotide(s), DNA, phenotype(s), genotype(s), genetic marker(s) *with:* health(y), disorder(s), disease(s). *See also* Bioethics; Gene mapping; Genetic research; Hereditary diseases; Medical ethics; Pharmacogenomics; Pharming.

Single parent family. Single parent famil(y,ies). Parental absence. Single parent(s,hood,ing). *Choose from:* single parent, one parent, fatherless, motherless, father absent, mother absent, broken, female headed, incomplete *with:* famil(y,ies), home(s). *Choose from:* solo, lone, single, divorced, abandoned, widowed, unsupported, unmarried, unwed *with:* parent(s,ing), mother(s), father(s). *See also* Child custody; Divorce; Divorced people; Family characteristics; Family size; Family stability; Female headed households; Parental absence; Parenthood; Single mothers; Single person.

Single person. Single person(s). Bachelor(s,hood). Singles. Unmarried. Never married. Nonmarried. Out-of-wedlock. Unwed. Spinster(s,hood). Spouseless. Old maid(s). *Choose from:* single, unmarried, bachelor, solo, divorced, lone, alone *with:* person(s), people, man, men, woman, women, parent(s), male(s), female(s), adult(s), life(style), status, mother(s), father(s). *Consider also:* widow(s,ers), divorcee(s), living alone, wom(an,en) alone, m(en,an) alone, lone wom(an,en), lone m(an,en). *See also* Bachelors; Cohabitation; Divorce; Divorced people; Living alone; Marital separation; Marital status; Premarital sexual behavior; Sex behavior; Single mothers; Single parent family; Social dating; Unmarried women; Virginity; Widowhood.

Single room occupancy hotels. Single room occupancy hotel(s). SROs. Slum hotel(s). Welfare hotel(s). *Consider also:* homeless, inner city, central city, elderly *with:* hotel(s), tenement(s), boarding house(s), shelter(s). *See also* Boardinghouses; Homeless; Poverty areas; Skid row; Slums; Tenants.

Single sex schools. Single sex school(s). *Choose from:* single sex, girls only, boys only, gender specific, all female, all male *with:* school(s), class(es,room,rooms), program(s), college(s), educational institution(s). *See also* Access to education; Children's rights; Coeducation; Egalitarianism; Equal education; Equal job opportunities; Feminism; Nonsexist education; Sex discrimination; Social equality; Social equity.

Single women. See *Single person; Unmarried women.*

Sinistrality. See *Laterality.*

Sino-Thai languages. Sino-Thai language(s). Chinese language(s). Mandarin (North Chinese). Kiangsi dialect(s). Central Coast Chinese (Shanghai, Ningpo, Hangchow). South Chinese (Foochow, Amoy-Swatow, Cantonese, Hakka). Thai. Thai (Siamese). Thai-Laos. Shan. Karen. *Consider also:* Sino-Tibetan language(s), Manchu, Hmong, Miao Yao language(s), Kam Tai language(s), Tibeto Burman language(s). *See also* Far East; Language; Languages (as subjects); Southeast Asia.

Sisal hemp. Sisal hemp. Agave sisalana. *Consider also:* henequen, agave fourcroydes, cord(age), twine. *See also* Rope.

Sisters. Sister(s,ly,hood). Sororal. Female sibling(s). Female twin(s). *See also* Brothers; Females (human); Half siblings; Sibling relations; Siblings; Sorority membership.

Sit-ins. See *Social demonstrations.*

Sit-ins. See *Civil disobedience; Demonstrators; Social demonstrations.*

Site selection. Site selection. *Choose from:* select(ed,ing), plan(s,ned,ning), choos(e,ing), chosen, acquisition, acquir(e,ed,ing) *with:* site(s), location(s,al), homesite(s), building lot(s), acreage. *Consider also:* location criteria. *See also* Facility design and construction; Land (property); Land values; Land use; Property values.

Sites, gossip. See *Gossip sites.*

Sites, historic. See *Historic sites.*

Sites, looting of archaeological. See *Archaeological thefts.*

Situation ethics. See *Relativism.*

Situational therapy. See *Milieu therapy; Socioenvironmental therapy; Therapeutic communities.*

Size. Size(s). Magnitude. Length. Breadth. Large(r,st). Small(er,est). Long(er,est). Short(er,est). Tall(er,est). High(er,est). Wide(r,st). Narrow(er,est). Big(ger,est). Little(r,st). Fat(ter,test). Thin(ner,nest). Tin(y,ier,iest). Huge. Weight(s). Weigh(ed,ing). Height(s). Bulk(y,ier,iest). Dimension(s). Extent.

Amount(s). Heav(y,ier,iest). Volume(s). Quantit(y,ies), Range(s). Scope. Expanse(s). *See also* Body height; Body weight; Capacity; Community size; Dimensions; Family size; Group size; Health facility size; Organization size; Proportionality; Size perception; Small businesses; Small farms; Small groups.

Size, body. See *Body size.*

Size, community. See *Community size.*

Size, family. See *Family size.*

Size, group. See *Group size.*

Size, health facility. See *Health facility size.*

Size, market. See *Market size.*

Size, organization. See *Organization size.*

Size perception. Size perception. *Choose from:* size(s), quantit(y,ies), length, width, breadth, distance(s), volume, weight, height *with:* perception, discriminat(e,ed,ing,ion), judgment(s), perceiv(e,ed,ing), estimat(e,es,ed,ing, ion). *See also* Size; Perception.

Size of farms. Size of farm(s). Farm size(s). *Choose from:* size(s,d), small(er,est), large(r,st), big(ger,gest) *with:* farm(s,stead,steads), ranch(es). *See also* Family farms; Farms.

Skaldic poetry. Skaldic poe(try,m,ms). Scaldic poe(try,m,ms). Skald(s). Scald(s). Old Norse court poe(try,m,ms). Drottkvaett. Drapa. *Choose from:* Skaldic, Scaldic *with:* poe(try,m,ms), verse(s). *See also* Medieval poetry; Poetry; Troubadour; Vikings.

Skeletal remains. See *Animal remains (archaeology); Human remains (archaeology); Skeleton.*

Skeleton. Skeleton(s). Skeletal structure(s). Bone structure(s). *Consider also:* bones, backbone(s), spine(s), vertebra(e). *See also* Animal remains (Archaeology); Frames (physical); Human remains (archaeology).

Skeleton, age determination by. See *Age determination by skeleton.*

Skepticism. See *Uncertainty.*

Sketchbooks. See *Drawing books.*

Sketches, character. See *Character sketches.*

Sketches, literary. See *Essays.*

Skid row. Skid row. *Choose from:* skid row(s), homeless(ness), Bowery, gospel mission(s), city mission(s), rescue mission(s), Salvation Army, soup kitchen(s), flophouse(s). *See also* Homeless; Inner cities; Poverty areas; Shelters; Single room occupancy hotels; Skid row alcoholics; Slums; Vagrants.

Skid row alcoholics. Skid row alcoholic(s). Skid row population. Dissolute person(s). *Choose from:* skid row(s),

homeless(ness), bowery *with:* alcoholic(s), bum(s), panhandler(s), drunk(s), inebriate(s), drinking. *See also* Alcoholism; Homeless; Skid row; Vagrants.

Skill. Skill(ed,ful,fulness,s). Proficien(t,cy, cies). Dexterity. Competenc(e,y). Expertise. Expert(ness). Mastery. Adept(ness). Capabilit(y,ies). Deft(ness). Effectiveness. *See also* Ability; Area of knowledge; Basic skills; Communication skills; Driving skills; Expertise; Fine motor skills; Gross motor skills; Language proficiency; Mathematics skills; Minimum competencies; Motor skills; Occupational qualifications; Perceptual skills; Performance; Reading skills; Skill learning; Skilled workers; Skills obsolescence; Social skills; Training; Work skills.

Skill development. See *Skill learning.*

Skill learning. Skill learning. *Choose from:* skill(s), proficien(cy,cies), competenc(e,y), expertise, expert(ness), capabilit(y,ies) *with:* learn(ed,ing), develop(ed,ing,ment), acquisition, acquir(e,ed,ing), generaliz(e,ed,ing, ation), master(ed,ing,y), achievement, maintain(ed,ing), maintenance, train(ed,ing). *See also* Fine motor skills; Gross motor skills; Perceptual skills; Social skills training; Skill; Upskilling.

Skilled labor. See *Skilled workers.*

Skilled nursing facilities. Skilled nursing facilit(y,ies). Extended care facilit(y,ies). *Choose from:* skilled care, skilled nursing *with:* facilit(y,ies), unit(s), setting(s), nursing home(s). *See also* Nursing homes.

Skilled workers. Skilled worker(s). Crafts(men,man,person,persons). Artisan(s). *Choose from:* skilled, trained, educated *with:* worker(s), labor(er,ers), workforce, personnel, staff, employee(s), help, manpower, occupation(s), job(s), trade(s). *Consider also:* carpenter(s), electrician(s), plumber(s), mason(s), bench worker(s), crane worker(s), technician(s), mechanic(s), machinist(s), journeym(en,an), journey worker(s), construction worker(s), forem(en,an), machinist(s), roofer(s), auto body repairm(an,en), craft worker(s), floor layer(s), glazier(s), locomotive engineer(s), repairm(en,an), watchmaker(s). *See also* Blue collar workers; Industrial personnel; Unskilled workers; Work skills.

Skills. See *Skill.*

Skills, academic. See *Academic skills.*

Skills, basic. See *Basic skills.*

Skills, communication. See *Communication skills.*

Skills, driving. See *Driving skills.*

Skills, employee. See *Work skills.*

Skills, fine motor. See *Fine motor skills.*

Skills, gross motor. See *Gross motor skills.*

Skills, information. See *Information skills.*

Skills, interpersonal. See *Social skills.*

Skills, job. See *Work skills.*

Skills, language. See *Language proficiency.*

Skills , life. See *Basic skills; Communication skills; Coping; Social skills; Work skills.*

Skills, management. See *Managerial skills.*

Skills, managerial. See *Managerial skills.*

Skills, mathematics. See *Mathematics skills.*

Skills, motor. See *Motor skills.*

Skills, perceptual. See *Perceptual skills.*

Skills, psychomotor. See *Motor skills; Psychomotor development.*

Skills, reading. See *Reading skills.*

Skills, social. See *Social skills.*

Skills, work. See *Work skills.*

Skills obsolescence. Skills obsolescence. *Choose from:* skill(s), expertise, craft(s), competenc(y,ies), training *with:* obsolescen(ce,t), obsolete, outdated, outmoded, out of date. *Consider also:* jobless(ness), unemploy(ed,ment) *with:* automat(e,ed,ion), robotic(s), computer(s,ized,ization). *See also* Defunct; Information literacy; Reentry women; Technological change; Technological progress; Technological unemployment; Work reentry; Work skills.

Skills training, social. See *Social skills training.*

Skin. Skin. Epiderm(is,al). Derm(is,al). Epithel(ial,ium). *Consider also:* cutaneous, cuticle. *See also* Anatomy; Body covering (Anatomy); Human body.

Skin response, galvanic. See *Galvanic skin response.*

Slander. See *Libel.*

Slang. Slang. Jargon. Buzzword(s). Argot. Epithet(s). Dirty word(s). Lingo. Profanit(y,ies). Graffiti. Swear(ing). Obscene language. Fad word(s). Colloquial language. Colloquialism(s). Nickname(s). Double entendre. Taboo word(s). Cheating term(s). Gambling term(s). Vernacular. Slanguage. Idiom(s,atic). Newspeak. Gayspeak. Nonstandard vocabular(y,ies). Africanism(s). Black English. Patois. Shoptalk. Vulgarism(s). Legalese. Street talk. Street language. Jive. Rap(ping). *See also* Colloquial language; Dialects; Epithets; Ethnolinguistics; Idioms; Language; Language usage; Language varieties; Nonstandard English; Subcultures; Vocabulary.

Slanted news. See *Media portrayal.*

Slash burn agriculture. Slash burn agriculture. Slashburn(ing). Swidden. Shifting cultivator(s). Jhuming. *See also* Deforestation; Ecological imperialism.

Slaughterhouses. Abattoir(s). Slaughterhouse(s). Butcher(s,y). Meat pack(ers,ing). Meat handler(s). Meatworks. *See also* Animal industry; Animal products; Food; Food inspection; Food supply; Meat industry.

Slave trade. Slave trade(r,rs). Trade in slaves. Slave dealer(s). African slaver(s). Slave ship(s). *See also* Maritime law; Slavery.

Slavery. Slave(ry,s,holding). Slavehold(ing, ers). Bondage. Bonded labor. Involuntary servitude. Enslave(d,ment). Serf(s,dom). Peon(s,age). Encomienda(s). Unfree labor. *Consider also:* slave trade, sell(ing) child(ren), Emancipation Proclamation, manumission, underground railroad, slavocracy, indentured servant(s), bondservant(s), impressed seam(en,an), white slave trade, traffick(ed,ing) in women, forced labor, domestic servitude, enthrallment, thralldom, vassal(s,age). *See also* Abolitionists; Black family; Blacks; Captivity; Civil rights; Exploitation; Forced labor; Freedom; Freedmen; Fugitive slaves; Harems; Human rights; Liberation theology; Oppression; Ownership; Peonage; Plantations; Racism; Servitude; Sharecropping; Sexual oppression; Slave trade; Trafficking in persons.

Slaves, freed. See *Freedmen.*

Slaves, fugitive. See *Fugitive slaves.*

Slaves, manumission of. See *Emancipation.*

Slaves, runaway. See *Fugitive slaves.*

Slavic languages. Slavic language(s). East Slavic: Byelorussian, Russian, Ukrainian. South Slavic: Bulgarian, Macedonian, Old Church Slavonic, Serbo-Croatian, Slovenian. West Slavic: Czech, Kashubian, Polabian, Polish, Slovak, Sorbian (Wendish). *See also* Eastern Europe; Language; Languages (as subjects).

Sleep. Sleep(ing,y,iness). Slept. Asleep. Slumber(ed,ing). Oversleep(ing). Overslept. Drows(y,iness). Somnolen(t,ce). Nap(ped,ping,s). Sleeper(s). Sleep wake state(s). NREM. REM. Rest(ed,ing). Narcosis. *Consider also:* dream(s,ing), repose, siesta(s), soporific(s). *See also* Dormancy; Dreams; Fatigue; Hypersomnia; Narcolepsy; Nightmares; NREM sleep; REM dream deprivation; REM dreams; REM sleep; Sleep apnea; Sleep

deprivation; Sleep disorders; Sleep onset; Sleep stages; Sleep talking; Sleep treatment; Sleep wake cycle; Sleepwalking.

Sleep, NREM. See *NREM sleep.*

Sleep, REM. See *REM sleep.*

Sleep apnea. Sleep apnea. Central alveolar hypoventilation. Ondine(s) curse. Primary alveolar hypoventilation. Sleep disordered breathing. *Choose from:* apnea, apneic, apnoea, respiratory disturbance(s), periodic respiration *with:* central, obstructive, sleep(ing), hypersomnia. *Consider also:* Pickwickian syndrome. *See also* Sleep disorders; Sudden infant death.

Sleep deprivation. Sleep deprivation. Fatiguing vigil. *Choose from:* sleep(ing), slept *with:* depriv(e,ed,ing,ation), restricted, lack(ed,ing), loss, lose, losing, decreas(e,ed,ing). *Consider also:* sleeplessness. *See also* Sleep; Sleep disorders.

Sleep disorders. Sleep disorder(s). *Choose from:* sleep wakeful(ness) *with:* disorder(s), disturbance(s), paralysis, onset disturbance(s), problem(s), terror(s), seizure(s), hypoxaemia, paroxysmal, epilepsy. *Consider also:* dyssomnia, hypersomnia, insomnia, narcolepsy, somnambulism, sleepwalking, night terror(s), pavor nocturnus, nightmare(s), nocturnal myclonus, Ekbom(s) syndrome, Kleine Levin syndrome, Kleine Levin Critchley syndrome. *See also* Consciousness disorders; Hypersomnia; Hypnagogic hallucinations; Insomnia; Night terror; Nightmares; Sleep apnea; Sleep deprivation.

Sleep onset. Sleep onset. Drows(y,iness). Fall(ing,en) asleep. Sleep(y,iness). Presleep. Nap(s,ped,ping). Hypnagogic. Sleep *with:* induc(e,ed,ing,ement, ements). *See also* Sleep; Sleep stages.

Sleep stages. Sleep stage(s). *Choose from:* sleep *with:* stage(s), REM, NREM, slow wave, fast wave, cycle(s), synchronized, desynchronized, orthodox, paradoxical, stage I, stage II, stage III, stage IV, stage 1, stage 2, stage 3, stage 4, stage one, stage two, stage three, stage four, firststage, second stage, third stage, fourth stage. *Consider also:* drows(y,iness), sleep state(s). *See also* Sleep; Sleep onset; Sleep wake cycle.

Sleep talking. Sleep talking. Somniloquy. Sleeptalking. *Choose from:* sleep *with:* talk(ed,ing), utterance(s), verbalization, mutter(ed,ing), mumbl(e,ed,ing), speak(ing), speech. *See also* Consciousness disorders; Sleep.

Sleep terror. See *Night terror; Nightmares.*

Sleep treatment. Sleep treatment(s).

Prolonged narcosis. *Choose from:* sleep, rest, electrosleep *with:* therap(y,ies, eutic), cure(s). Bedrest. Narcotherap(y,ies). *See also* Drug therapy; Electrosleep treatment; Narcotherapy; Sleep.

Sleep wake cycle. Sleep wake cycle. Sleep rhythm(s). *Choose from:* sleep(ing), slept *with:* wak(e,ing,fulness) *with:* cycle(s), pattern(s), rhythm(s), circadian. *See also* Biological rhythms; Sleep; Wakefulness.

Sleepwalking. Sleepwalk(ing,ers). Somnambulis(m,tic,t,ts). Hypnobades. Hypnobat(ia,ic,s). Noctambulat(e,ed,ing, ion,er,ers). Nocturnal wander(ings,er, ers). Nocturnal ambulatory automatism. *See also* Consciousness disorders; Sleep disorders.

Slips of the tongue. See *Speech errors.*

Slogans. Slogan(s). Motto(es). Byword(s). Logo(s). Tagline(s). Catchphrase(s). Cliche(s). Catchword(s). *Consider also:* acronym(s), buzzword(s), shibboleth(s). *See also* Advertising; Aphorisms; Axioms; Epigrams; Folklore; Political advertising; Political myths; Political rhetoric; Political symbolism.

Sloth. See *Laziness.*

Slow learners. Slow learner(s). *Choose from:* slow, mentally handicapped, poor *with:* learn(er,ers,ing), reader(s), student(s). *Choose from:* low *with:* intelligence, IQ, abilit(y,ies). *Choose from:* borderline, mild(ly) *with:* mental(ly), intellectual(ly) *with:* retard(ed,ation), backward, deficien(cy,t). *Consider also:* learning disabled, reading disabilit(y,ies), educable mentally retarded. *See also* Educable mentally retarded; Education of mentally retarded; Learning disabilities; Mental retardation.

Slums. Slum(s). Poverty area(s). Skid row. Bowery. Shantytown(s). Inner cit(y,ies). Tenement(s). Milieu of poverty. Depressed area(s). Redlin(ed,ing). Ghetto(es,ization). Appalachia. Low income area(s). Street corner district. Barrio(s). Favela(s). Neglected urban building(s). Colonia(s). *Choose from:* low income, poor, poverty, depressed, transitional, ethnic, Black, minority, disadvantaged, segregated, redlined *with:* area(s), count(y,ies), communit(y, ies), neighborhood, school district(s). *See also* Inner cities; Poverty; Poverty areas; Skid row; Urban environments; Urban poverty; Urban renewal.

Slurs. See *Defamation; Derogation; Invective; Libel.*

Small businesses. Small business(es). Small scale industr(y,ies). Mini-enterprise(s). Microenterprise(s). Micro-enterprise(s). Micro-industr(y,ies). Sole proprietor(s). Electronic cottage(s). Cottage industr(y,ies). *Choose from:* small(er,est), micro, home grown, home based, independent, mom and pop *with:* business(es), enterprise(s), industr(y,ies), retail(er,ers), production, operation(s), store(s), shop(s). *Consider also:* embroiderer(s), artisan workshop(s). *See also* Business Incubators; Digital money; Digital signatures; E-commerce; Emerging markets; Entrepreneurship; Family businesses; Franchises (commercial); Home based businesses; Microenterprise; Minority businesses; Organization size; Self employment; Start up business; Street vendors; V-commerce; Women owned businesses.

Small farms. Small farm(s). Smallholder(s). Minifund(ia,ismo). Croft(ing,er,ers). *Choose from:* small(er,est), small scale, independent, truck, subsistence, peasant, family *with:* farm(s,er,ers,ing), agricultur(e,al). *See also* Agrarian structures; Agricultural mechanization; Agriculture; Family farms; Farming; Farms; Part time farming.

Small for gestational age, infant. See *Infant small for gestational age.*

Small groups. Small group(s). Minigroup(s). Dyad(s,ic). Triad(s,ic). *Choose from:* small(er,est), face-to-face, primary, three-person, conversational *with:* group(s), committee(s), jur(y,ies), panel(s). *See also* Cliques; Dyads; Triads; Group dynamics; Group norms; Group size; Groups; Interpersonal relations; Size; Social behavior; Social cohesion; Social interaction; Sociometric technics.

Small towns. See *Towns.*

Smell. See *Odor discrimination.*

Smell, inability to. See *Anosmia.*

Smell, loss of sense of. See *Anosmia.*

Smiling. Smil(e,es,ers,ing,ingly). Grin(ned,ning). Friendly expression. Pleasant countenance. Pleasant appearance. Happy facial expression. Agreeable expression. Beam(ed,ing). *Choose from:* look(ed,ing) *with:* pleased, happy, contented, cheerful. *Consider also:* laugh(ter,ing), joyous(ness), cheerful(ness). *See also* Cheerfulness; Facial expressions; Laughter; Nonverbal communication; Social skills.

Smog. See *Air pollution.*

Smoke, environmental tobacco. See *Tobacco smoke pollution.*

Smoke pollution, tobacco. See *Tobacco smoke pollution.*

Smoking. Smok(e,ed,er,ers,ing). *Choose from:* snuff, tobacco, cigarette(s), nicotine, pipe(s), cigar(s) *with:* habit(s,ual), addict(s,ed,ion,ions), use(s,d), using, dependen(t,ce), abuse(r,rs), consum(e,ed,ing,ption).

Consider also: smoker(s), smoking, tobacco use disorder(s), chain smoking, chronic smoking, snuff. *See also* Antismoking movement; Cancer; Carcinogens; Cigarette industry; Cigarettes; Drug use; Habits; Health; Smoking cessation; Tobacco habit; Tobacco industry; Tobacco pipes; Tobacco smoke pollution.

Smoking, passive. See *Tobacco smoke pollution.*

Smoking, tobacco. See *Smoking.*

Smoking cessation. Smoking cessation. *Choose from:* smok(e,ed,ing,er,ers), tobacco, pipe(s), cigar(s,ette,ettes), nicotine *with:* cessation, ceas(e,ed,ing), fading, reduc(e,ed,ing,tion,tions), withdraw(al), quit(ting), treatment(s), control(led,ling), hypno(sis,tic,tics), replac(e,ed,ing,ement,ements), stop(ped,ping), modif(y,ied,ying, ication), avoid(ed,ing,ance), abstain(ed,ing), abstinence. *See also* Drug rehabilitation; Smoking; Tobacco habit.

Smuggling. Smuggl(e,ed,ing). Contraband. Customs violation(s). Carrying undeclared item(s). Conceal(ed,ing) undeclared item(s). Gunrunning. Bootlegging. Black market. *Choose from:* illegal(ly), clandestine *with:* import(s,ed,ing), ship(ped,ments), wildlife, wild animal(s), export(ed,s, ing), flow(s), landing(s), traffick(ing), divert(ed,ing), arms transfer(s), trade. *Consider also:* mule(s). *See also* Crime; Drug and narcotic control; Drug enforcement; Drug trafficking; Money laundering; Organized crime; Racketeering; Stowaway.

Snake handling. Snake handl(e,ed,er,ers, ing). *Choose from:* snake(s), serpent(s), reptile(s), viper(s) rattlesnake(s), cobra(s), python(s) *with:* tak(e,en,ing) up, handl(e,ed,er,ers,ing), captur(e,ed, ing), hold(ing), held, fondl(e,ed,er, ers,ing), caress(ed,ing). *Consider also:* snake charmer(s). *Consider also:* Church of God With Signs Following. *See also* Poisonous animals; Religious beliefs; Religious cults; Sects; Snake phobia.

Snake lore. Snake lore. *Choose from:* snake(s), pit viper(s), serpent(s), cobra(s), python(s), rattlesnake(s), copperhead(s), water moccasin(s), boa constrictor(s), massasauga(s), fer-de-lance(s), bushmaster(s), blacksnake(s), etc. *with:* lore, folklore, folk tale(s), stor(y,ies), anecdote(s), mytholog(y, ical), legend(s), superstition(s), fable(s). *Consider also:* animal lore. *See also* Animal lore; Animals; Bestiaries; Folklore; Mythical animals; Mythology; Superstitions; Traditional medicine.

Snake phobia. Snake phobia. Ophidio-

phobi(a,c). *Choose from:* snake(s), reptile(s), viper(s), serpent(s) *with:* phobi(a,as,c), dread(ed,ing), fear(s,ful), avoid(ed,ing,ant,ance), aversion, afraid, anxiety, anxious(ness). *See also* Phobias; Snake handling.

Sniffing, glue. See *Inhalant abuse.*

Snobbishness, snobs and. See *Snobs and snobbishness.*

Snobs and snobbishness. Snob(s,bish, bishness,bery,bism). Ostentatious(ness). Snoot(y,iness). Pretentious(ness). Haught(y,incss). Uppish(ness). Supercilious(ness). Pompous(ness). Pomposity. *Consider also:* exclusiv(e, ity), sophisticat(ed,ion), status seeker(s), affectation(s), social climber(s), vain, vanity, boastful(ness). *See also* Conceit; Egoism; Egotism; Idealized self; Narcissism; Personality traits; Pride.

Soap operas. Soap opera(s). Soaps. Telenovela(s). *Consider also:* daytime drama(s), televised drama(s), television serial(s). *See also* Mass media; Popular culture; Television; Television plays; Television programs.

Sobriety. Sobriety. *Choose from:* alcohol(ic, ism), liquor, drinking *with:* abstain(ed, ing), abstinen(t,ce), remission, recover(y,ing). *Consider also:* alcoholics anonymous. *See also* Alcohol drinking attitudes; Alcohol rehabilitation; Alcoholism; Detoxification; Recovery.

Sociability. Sociab(le,ility). Friendl(y,iness). Gregarious(ness). Perceptive(ness). Affiliation motivation. Amicab(le,ility). Polite(ness). Neighbor(ly,liness). Good manner(s,ed). Congenial(ity). Charming. Affab(le,ility). Good neighbor(s). Outgoing. Goodnature(d). Agreeab(le, ility). Genial(ity). Cordial(ity). Courteous(ness). Courtesy. *Consider also:* interpersonal, social(ly) *with:* competence, awareness, skill(s), oriented, intelligence, responsive(ness), sensitivity. *See also* Affiliation motivation; Gregariousness; Interpersonal relations; Peer relations; Personality traits; Primary groups; Public behavior; Social activities; Social behavior; Social contact.

Social ability. See *Social skills.*

Social acceptance. Social acceptance. Popular(ity). Sociometric status. High status. Assimilation. Social success. Well-liked. Highly regarded. Respected. Social(ly) integrat(ed,ion). Social distance. Approbation. Affirm(ed,ation). Recognition. Belonging(ness). *Choose from:* social(ly), interpersonal, peer, group, community *with:* accept(ed,ance, ability), relations, regard, status, validation, position, standing, reception, attraction, inclusion, tolerance, approval, disapproval, neglect(ed). *See also* Admiration; Admissions; Affiliation motivation; Approval; Approval need; Belongingness; Inclusion; Interpersonal relations; Needs; Popularity; Rejection (psychology); Social approval; Social behavior; Social distance; Social nearness; Social response; Stigma.

Social action. Social action. Community action. Interest group(s). Dissent(er,ers). Demonstration(s). Demonstrator(s). Political(ly) act(s,ion,ive,ism). Reform organization(s). Reform movement(s). Advocacy. Boycott(s). Agitat(ion,or,ors). Counter-movement(s). Sit-ins. March(es,er,ers). Picket(s,ed,ing). Rights group(s). Political participation. Political protest(s,er,ers). Student protest(s,er,ers). Sociopolitical activism. Protest group(s). Student activism. *Choose from:* social, community, citizen, voluntary, workers *with:* action, movement(s), reform(s), demonstration(s), participat(e,ion), protest(s,er,ers), militan(cy), dissent, activis(m,t,ts), involvement, participation, crusade(s), march(es), response(s). *See also* Action research; Activism; Advocacy; Affirmative action; Boycotts; Charities; Citizen participation; Civil disobedience; Civil rights organizations; Collective action; Community involvement; Community power; Contributions; Dissent; Humanitarianism; Ideological struggle; Ideologies; Intervention; Political action; Political issues; Protest movements; Revolution; Social agitation; Social attitudes; Social change; Social goals; Social legislation; Social movements; Social problems; Social processes; Social reform; Social responsibility; Socially responsible investing; Society; Strikes; Student demonstrations; Volunteers; Youth movements.

Social action (sociological). Social action(s). Human action(s). Human interaction. Social actor(s). *See also* Social behavior.

Social activities. Social activit(y,ies). *Choose from:* dinner part(y,ies), cocktail part(y,ies), picnic(s), garden part(y,ies), church supper(s), potluck supper(s), bingo game(s), christening(s), wedding(s), funeral(s), wake(s), reception(s), sport(s), bowling, card game(s), dancing, athletic participation, baseball, basketball, football, tennis, fair(s), festivit(y,ies), festival(s), celebration(s), club(s), voluntary association(s). *See also* Dinners and Dining; Friendship; Leisure activities; Play; Sociability; Social dating; Social life.

Social adaptation. See *Acculturation; Adaptation; Interpersonal relations; Social adjustment.*

Social adjustment. Social adjustment. Adaptive behavior(s). Social survival skill(s). Psychosocial functioning.

Socializ(e,ed,ing,ation). Resocializ(e,ed,ing,ation). *Choose from:* social(ly), psychosocial, school, community, postdivorce, relocation, family, interpersonal, posthospital, deinstitutionalization *with:* adjust(ed,ing,ment), maladjust(ed,ment), adapt(ed,ing,ation), readjust(ed,ing,ment), functioning level, coping, well adapted, survival skill(s). *See also* Adjustment to environment; Alienation; Coping; Defense mechanisms; Emotional adjustment; Extraversion (psychology); Introversion; Interpersonal relations; Peer relations; Psychosocial readjustment; Social behavior; Social conformity; Social development; Social influences; Social isolation.

Social agencies. Social agenc(y,ies). Social service(s). Charit(y,ies). Council of community services. *Choose from:* social, public, child care, welfare, social work, casework, health, health planning, sociopsychological, community, charitable, helping, foster care, referral, day care, mental health, counseling, homemaker, protective, supportive *with:* service(s), service organization(s), institution(s), agenc(y,ies). *See also* Charities; Community health centers; Information services; Nongovernmental organizations; Public welfare; Social services; Social work.

Social agitation. Agitat(ed,ion,or,ors). Arous(ed,al). Commotion. Disturbance(s). Demonstration(s). Excit(ed,ation). Insurrection(s). Insurgen(t,ce,cy,cies). Incite(ed,ment). Mutin(y,ies,ous). Restless(ness). Turbulen(t,ce). Turmoil. Upheaval. Unrest. Rebel(s,lion,lions,lious,liousness). *See also* Activism; Agitators: Demagogues; Mobilization; Peasant rebellions; Persuasion; Political action; Propaganda; Rebellions; Social action; Social change; Social movements; Social unrest; Student demonstrations.

Social alienation. See *Alienation.*

Social anthropology. See *Cultural anthropology.*

Social anxiety. Social anxiety. Stage fright. Performance anxiety. Self conscious(ness). Stranger reaction(s). Social insecurity. Withdrawn. Social(ly) anxious(ness). Embarrass(ed,ment). Interpersonal anxiety. Shy(ness). Heterosocial anxiety. Social situational anxiety. Discomfit(ure). Abash(ed). Timid(ity). Bashful(ness). *See also* Anxiety disorders; Fear; Shyness; Social interaction; Social isolation; Social phobia; Speech anxiety.

Social approval. Social approval. Recognition. Credential(s,ing). Popular(ity). High(ly) regard(ed). Halo effect. Legitimat(e,ed,ing,ion). Endors(e,ed,ing,ment). Perceived legitimacy. Positive feedback. Approval from others.

Favorable impression(s). Well liked. Deemed acceptable. Esteemed. Admired. Recommended. Good reference(s). Approbation. Kudos. Honored. Respected. *Choose from:* peer, social(ly), community *with:* approval, recognition, validation, valued, accept(ed,ance), rating(s), desirability, support, reinforcement. *Consider also:* charisma, charm(ing), ingroup(s). *See also* Acceptability; Criticism; Glory; Likability; Popularity; Social acceptance; Social reinforcement.

Social areas. See *Public spaces.*

Social attitudes. Social attitud(e,es). Public opinion. *Choose from:* social, societal, public, community, sociopolitical *with:* attitud(e,es), opinion(s), feeling(s), preference(s), bias(ed,es), compassion, perspective(s), beliefs, stereotype(s), acceptance, rejection, stigma, view(s,point,points), reaction(s), response(s), image(s), mindset(s), prejudic(ed,es), values, expectation(s), fear(s), hope(s), dissatisf(ied,action), perception(s). *Consider also:* anti-intellectual(ism), worldview(s), homophob(ic,ia), egalitarian(ism), sense of (in)justice, cosmopolitan(ism), ethnocentri(c,sm), localism, regionalism, traditionalism, ageism, alienation, altruis(m,tic), elitis(m,t), racis(m,t) anti-semiti(c,sm), sexis(m,t), handicap-pedism. *See also* Attitudes; Acceptance; Activism; Alienation; Altruism; Apathy; Approval; Attitudes; Attitudes toward handicapped; Attitudes toward homosexuality; Attitudes toward mental illness; Attitudes toward mental retardation; Attitudes toward physical handicaps; Attitudes toward physical illness; Attitudes toward the aged; Beliefs; Community attitudes; Consciousness raising activities; Cosmopolitan; Dissent; Egocentrism; Elitism (government); Ethnocentrism; Hidden curriculum; Ideologies; Impression formation; Localism; Moral attitudes; Nativism; Optimism; Ostracism; Otherness; Pessimism; Political attitudes; Political socialization; Prejudice; Public opinion; Racial attitudes; Racism; Regionalism; Rejection (psychology); Reputation; Scandals; Sectarianism; Sexism; Social action; Social change; Social consciousness; Social desirability; Social development; Social distance; Social environment; Social influences; Social nearness; Social perception; Social values; Tolerance; Traditionalism; Worldview.

Social awareness. See *Social consciousness.*

Social background. Social background(s). *Choose from:* social(ly), societal, sociocultural, socioeconomic, sociopolitical, economic, cultural, ethnic, political, community, national, public, sociological, class, collective, common, city, urban, rural, suburban *with:* background(s), antecedent(s), experience(s), histor(y,ies,ical), past, factor(s), setting(s), conditions, framework(s), environment(s), climate(s). *See also* Early experiences; Educational background; Family background; Parental background; Social class; Social conditions; Social influences; Socioeconomic status.

Social behavior. Social behavior(s). Sociosexual behavior. Socializ(e,ed, ing,ation). Classroom behavior. Zoosocial behavior. *Choose from:* social(ly), prosocial, interpersonal *with:* behavior(s), role(s), graces, functioning, competence, assertive(ness), responsive(ness), response(s), interaction(s), activit(y,ies), helpful(ness), generosity, kindness, outgoing, extrover(t,ted,sion), introver(t,ted,sion), shyness, withdrawing, acceptance, adjustment, approval, dating, demonstration(s), drinking, facilitation, perception(s), reinforcement, skills. *Consider also:* courtship, division of labor, dominance, dissent, disengagement, generosity, interpersonal communication, kindness, mass behavior, maternal behavior, meanness, persecution, praise, stinginess, thoughtfulness. *See also* Acceptance; Activism; Advocacy; Aggression; Alliances; Altruism; Ambivalence; Anger; Anomie; Antisocial behavior; Approval; Arguments; Assertiveness; Assistance; Attachment behavior; Attack; Attribution; Bargaining; Behavior; Behavior development; Behavior problems; Charitable behavior; Collective behavior; Competitive behavior; Compliance; Conflict; Conformity (personality); Conversation; Cooperation; Countercultures; Criticism; Crowding; Deception; Deviant behavior; Disengagement; Dissent; Dominance subordination; Double bind interaction; Egalitarianism; Emotions; Encouragement; Exchange theory; Eye contact; Facilitation; Favors; Formal social control; Friendship; Gambling; Group discussion; Group dynamics; Group norms; Group participation; Group performance; Help seeking behavior; Helping behavior; Hostility; Impression management; Informal social control; Institutionalization (social); Interpersonal attraction; Interpersonal compatibility; Interpersonal influences; Interpersonal relations; Interviews; Involvement; Kindness; Leadership; Leadership style; Machiavellianism; Manipulation; Mass behavior; Militancy; Negotiation; Nonverbal reinforcement; Norms; Nurturance; Obedience; Organizational behavior; Ostracism; Participation; Peace; Peer influences; Peer relations; Personal space; Praise;

Privacy; Prosocial behavior; Public behavior; Race relations; Reciprocity; Rejection (psychology); Resistance; Respect; Responsibility (answerability); Riots; Risk taking; Rivalry; Sharing; Small groups; Sociability; Social acceptance; Social adjustment; Social approval; Social behavior disorders; Social change; Social conformity; Social contagion; Social dating; Social demonstrations; Social desirability; Social discrimination; Social drinking; Social equity; Social facilitation; Social facts; Social influences; Social interaction; Social perception; Social pressure; Social reinforcement; Social responsibility; Social skills; Social support; Social support networks; Sociobiology; Sociometric technics; Stranger reactions; Student behavior; Teamwork; Territoriality; Threat postures; Transactional analysis; Trusting; Verbal reinforcement; Victimization; Violence; War.

Social behavior disorders. Social behavior disorder(s). Behavior(al) problem(s). Antisocial emotional disorder(s). Dangerous behavior. Social withdrawal. Socially dangerous action(s). Social(ly) inadequa(te,cy). *Choose from:* behavior(al), conduct *with:* problem(s), disorder(s), antisocial, dangerous(ness), deviant, withdraw(al,n), aggressive(ness), maladjusted, inadequa(te,cy), deficit(s), maladaptive, criminal, delinquent, predelinquent, disturbance(s), dyssocial behavior. *See also* Acting out; Aggression; Antisocial behavior; Behavior disorders; Cheating; Child abuse; Child behavior disorders; Child neglect; Crime; Deception; Elder abuse; Fire setting behavior; Incest; Juvenile delinquency; Rape; Runaways; Sexual abuse; Sexual harassment; Shoplifting; Theft; Torture; Vandalism; Violence.

Social benefits. See *Externalities; Social impact.*

Social bias. See *Age discrimination; Attitudes toward handicapped; Attitudes toward homosexuality; Attitudes toward mental retardation; Attitudes toward mental illness; Attitudes toward physical handicaps; Attitudes toward physical illness; Attitudes toward the aged; Bias; Bigotry; Ethnocentrism; Male chauvinism; Misanthropy; Nationalism; Prejudice; Racism; Sex discrimination; Sexism; Social discrimination; Xenophobia.*

Social bond. See *Social cohesion.*

Social breakdown syndrome. Social breakdown syndrome. Disability syndrome. Deteriorat(ing,ion) of social abilit(y,ies). Desocialization. Institutionalism. Institutional neuros(is,es). *Consider also:* social distress syndrome, social environmental breakdown, loss of

social support, lack of social support, social disintegration, dysfunctional famil(y,ies), chronic sick role. *See also* Alienation; Anomie; Demoralization; Depersonalization disorder; Learned helplessness; Regression (defense mechanism).

Social casework. See *Social work.*

Social change. Social change(s). *Choose from:* social, societ(al,y,ies), sociocultural, institution(al,s), famil(ial,ies), intergenerational, cultural, sociopolitical, social beliefs, mores, norms, socioeconomic, role(s), status(es) *with:* moderniz(e,ed,ing,ation), urbaniz(c,cd, ing,ation), national(ization,ism), independence, internationalism, restructuring, reconstruction, innovation(s), chang(e,es,ed,ing), gap(s), dissolution, transition(s), dynamic(s), process(es). *Consider also:* moderniz(e,ed,ing,ation), urbaniz(e,ed, ing,ation), nationalism, internationalism, generation gap, cross generational change(s), culture war(s), westernization, expanding world(s), shrinking world(s), industrialization, third wave, information age, changing values, urbanization, universalization, future shock. *See also* Action research; Activism; Assimilation; Change agents; Community change; Community development; Cooptation; Critical theory; Cultural lag; Cultural transformation; Culture change; Democratization; Desegregation; Economic change; Economic development; Fads; Fashions; Future of society; Generation gap; Industrialization; Modernization; Organizational change; Organizational development; Organizational survival; Peaceful change; Political movements; Progress; Regression (civilization); Revolution; Social action; Social agitation; Social attitudes; Social behavior; Social conditions; Social conflict; Social Darwinism; Social development; Social disorganization; Social equilibrium; Social history; Social impact; Social influences; Social integration; Social legislation; Social movements; Social planning; Social processes; Social programs; Social reform; Social structure; Social stability; Social unrest; Society; Technological change; Technology and civilization; Traditionalism; Urbanization.

Social class. Social class(es). Socioeconomic class(es). Social stratification. Social position. Social rank. Perceived class. Class status. Class origin. Class level. Class identification. *Consider also:* social, socioeconomic, sociocultural, economic, occupational, upper, middle, lower, working, capitalist, proletariat, owning, propertied, intellectual, administrative, managerial, petty bourgeois, manual, non-manual, intermediate *with:* class(es), rank(s), level(s), strat(a,um). *Consider also:* feudal *with:* estate(s), lord(s), vassal(s), knight(s). *See also* Caste system; Class analysis; Class conflict; Class consciousness; Class differences; Class formation; Class identity; Class identity; Class mobility; Class politics; Class relations; Class society; Class stratification; Disadvantaged; Elites; Family work relationship; Income; Income inequality; Lower class; Middle class; Otherness; Poverty; Quality of life; Ruling class; Social background; Social closure; Social distance; Social factors; Social immobility; Social mobility; Social order; Social stratification; Social structure; Socioeconomic status; Subcultures; Upper class; Working class.

Social cleavage. Social cleavage(s). Cultural cleavage(s). Ethnic cleavage(s). Factionali(sm,ize,ized,izing). Polariz(e,ed,ing,ation). Separatism. Value cleavage(s). Social segmentation. Fragment(ed,ing,ation). Schism(s). Pillarization. Segregation. *See also* Cliques; Cultural pluralism; Dissent; Factionalism; Pillarization; Polarization; Political dissent; Schism; Separatism; Social cohesion; Social conflict; Social segmentation; Social stratification; Subcultures.

Social climate. See *Social environment.*

Social closure. Social closure. *Choose from:* closed-class system(s), caste(s), exclusionary code(s), estate system, closed circle(s), clos(ed,ing) access. *See also* Boundary maintenance; Caste system; Labor market segmentation; Opportunities; Social class; Social discrimination; Social environment.

Social clubs, therapeutic. See *Therapeutic social clubs.*

Social cohesion. Social cohesion. Group cohesion. Conformity to group norm. Ingroup(s). Leader endorsement. Ingroup bias. Team building. Teamwork. Groupthink. Gemeinschaft. Consensus of values. Male bond(s,ing). Camaraderie. Togetherness. *Choose from:* group(s), social, societal, neighborhood, ethnic, famil(y,ies), ingroup(s), unit(s), department(al), trib(al,e,es), team(s), staff, national, state(s) *with:* bond(s), cohes(ion,iveness), commonality, unity, unification, cooperation, coorientation, conformity, interdependence, integration, knitted(ness), well knit, closely knit, consensus, solidarity, reintegration, reciproc(al,ity), mutual support, morale, spirit. *See also* Anomie; Assimilation (cultural); Belongingness; Collective representation; Community (social); Community feeling; Consensus; Cooptation; Group consciousness; Group dynamics; Group feeling; Group norms; Groups; Labor songs; Organiza-

tional dissolution; Primary groups; Similarity; Small groups; Social cleavage; Social disorganization; Social environment; Social equilibrium; Social identity; Social integration; Social interaction; Social order; Social processes; Society.

Social community. See *Community (social).*

Social comparison. Social comparison. Comparison with other(s). Self other contrast(s). Interpersonal comparison(s). Social cognition. Social cognitive orientation. Intrapersonal feedback. Defensive projection(s). *Choose from:* self, oneself *with:* compari(tive,sons), appraisal, assessment, evaluation(s), prediction(s), efficacy, criticism. *See also* Comparison; Peer influences; Reference groups; Self evaluation; Self monitoring; Social influences.

Social competence. See *Social skills.*

Social conditioning. See *Attitude formation; Conditioning (psychology); Learned behavior; Learned helplessness; Social learning; Socialization.*

Social conditions. Social conditions. *Choose from:* social, societ(y,ies,al), community, sociocultural *with:* conditions, unrest, order, environment, dynamics, situation(s), problem(s). *Consider also:* human ecology, cultural ecology. *See also* Community attitudes; Dissatisfaction; Dissent; Economic conditions; Life satisfaction; Living conditions; Moral conditions; Quality of life; Social change; Social conflict; Social criticism; Social development; Social environment; Social factors; Social impact; Social justice; Social movements; Social structure; Social unrest; Society; Socioeconomic factors; Unemployment.

Social conflict. Social conflict(s). *Choose from:* social, economic, societal, class, ethnic, sociopolitical, peasant, cultural, international, ideological, religious *with:* conflict(s), revolution(s), controvers(y, ies), factionalism, disagreement(s), oppos(e,ed,ing,ition), disput(e,es,ed, ing), confront(ed,ing,ation), rival(s,ry), struggle(s), dissen(t,sion), tension(s), divisive(ness), cris(is,es), disorder(s), unrest. *Consider also:* war(s), argument(s), riot(s), feud(s). *See also* Civil disorders; Class politics; Class relations; Coalition formation; Cultural conflict; Disputes; Dissent; Dissidents; Feuds; Factionalism; Intergroup relations; Organizational dissolution; Polarization; Protest movements; Schism; Sectarianism; Social change; Social cleavage; Social conditions; Social criticism; Social disorganization; Social movements; Social order; Social problems; Social stress; Social unrest.

Social conformity. Social conformity.

Conform(ing,ism,ists,ity). Social traditionalism. Social compliance. Peer influence(s). Obedien(t,ce). Allegiance. Conventional(ity). Orthodox(y). Social convention(s). Traditional(ism). Customary. Established usage. *See also* Conformity (personality); Embourgeoisement; Peer influences; Social influences; Traditionalism.

Social consciousness. Social(ly) conscious(ness). *Choose from:* social(ly), sociopolitical(ly), political(ly), community, public, societal, sociocultural, interracial, racial, ethnic, minority, socioeconomic, national, international *with:* conscious(ness), aware(ness), sensitiz(ed,ing), sensitiv(e,ity), concern(ed), conscience, conscientious(ness), comprehension, perception(s). *Consider also:* class consciousness, gender consciousness, false consciousness. *See also* Class consciousness; Consciousness raising activities; Political behavior; Race awareness; Social perception; Social values; Worker consciousness.

Social construction of reality. See *Social facts; Social meaning; Social reality.*

Social contact. Social contact(s). *Choose from:* social, interpersonal, neighborhood, community, interracial, intergroup, interethnic, interfaith *with:* contact(s), relation(s,ships), interaction(s), attachment(s), bond(s), friend(s,ships), link(s), exposure, proximity, communications, cooperation, association(s), network(s). *Consider also:* club(s), friendship(s), companionship, affiliation(s), subculture(s). *See also* Associations (organizations); Community (social); Community networks; Culture contact; Group participation; Intergroup relations; Interpersonal relations; Loneliness; Neighbors; Organizational affiliation; Ostracism; Physical contact; Primary groups; Secondary relationships; Sociability; Social interaction; Social isolation; Social life; Social support networks; Spatial behavior; Visits.

Social contagion. Social contagion. Social epidemic(s). Emotional contagion. *Choose from:* spread, contagion, communicat(e,ed,ing,ion), pervasive(ness), pervad(e,ed,ing) *with:* mood(s), thought(s), behavior(s). *Consider also:* rumor(s), fad(s), bandwagon effect, craze(s). *See also* Accomplices; Collective behavior; Collective suicide; Copycat crime; Copycat suicide; Crowds; Fads; Mass behavior; Mass hysteria; Messianic movements.

Social context. See *Social environment.*

Social contract. Social contract(s). *Choose*

from: social, Locke(an), Hobbes(ian), Rousseau(ian) *with:* compact(s), contract(s,arian,arianism), covenant(s). *Consider also:* moral theory, just society, consent of the governed, Le Contrat social. *See also* Human rights; Legitimacy of governments; Moral obligation; Political obligation; Reciprocity; Social ethics; Social exchange; Social justice.

Social control. See *Formal social control; Informal social control.*

Social control, formal. See *Formal social control.*

Social control, informal. See *Informal social control.*

Social costs. See *Externalities; Social impact.*

Social criticism. Social criticism. Prophetic tradition. Counterculture(s). Dissident(s). Anti-establishment. Loyal opposition. Critical sociology. Humanistic sociology. *Choose from:* social, political, sociopolitical, establishment, status quo *with:* critic(s,ical,ism,izing), dissent(er,ers), radical(s,ism), protest(s,er,ers), dissatis(fied,action), oppos(e,ed,ing,ition), dialectic(s,al), adversar(y,ies,ial). *See also* Activism; Advocacy; Chattering class; Commentators; Countercultures; Criticism; Dissent; Dissidents; Protest movements; Social conditions; Social conflict; Social disorganization; Social reform; Social theories.

Social Darwinism. Social Darwinism. Darwin(ian,ism). Survival of the fittest. *Consider also:* social, cultural, biosocial, sociobiological *with:* evolution(ary), selection(ism), progress. *Consider also:* biopolic(y,ies), Nazism, eugenics. *See also* Competition; Culture change; Eugenics; Evolutionary ethics; Fascism; Evolution; Genetics; Imperialism; Race relations; Regression (civilization); Social change; Social development; Territorial expansion.

Social dating. Social dat(e,ed,es,ing). Steady date(s). Going steady. Romantic relationship(s). Courtship. Boyfriend(s). Girlfriend(s). First date(s). *Choose from:* dat(e,ed,es,ing), premarital *with:* behavior, relation(s,ships), stage, couple(s), dyad(s), adolescen(t,ce). *See also* Couples; Friendship; Human courtship; Interpersonal relations; Premarital sexual behavior; Sexual ethics; Social behavior; Social interaction; Social life.

Social democracy. Social democra(cy,tic, ts). *Choose from:* reform(ism), democratic change(s), change(s) through democratic process(es), revisionism, socialism. *See also* Collectivism; Democracy; Industrial democracy; Political ideologies; Political parties;

Socialism; Welfare state.

Social demonstrations. Social demonstration(s). Sit-in(s). Strike(s). Love-in(s). March(es). Picket(s,ed,ing). *Choose from:* social, civil, street, student, political, public, citizen(s), nonviolent, anti-, campus, collective, civil rights, peace, mass *with:* demonstrat(ed,ing,ion,ions,ors), protest(s,ing,er,ers), barricad(e,ed,es, ing), march(es,ed,ing), picket(s,ed,ing), strike(s), disobedience. *Consider also:* public assembl(y,ies,ing), activis(m,t,ts), rall(y,ies,ing), riot(s,ed,ing). *See also* Activism; Boycotts; Civil disobedience; Civil disorders; Collective behavior; Demonstrators; Hunger strikes; Political participation; Protesters; Protest movements; Public meetings; Social action; Social behavior; Social agitation; Social movements; Strikes; Student demonstrations.

Social density. Social density. Crowd(ed, ing). Proximity. Interaction intensity. Social privacy. Dispersal. Number of occupants. Occupancy. Density. Crowded condition(s). Overcrowd(ed, ing). Personal space. Seating arrangements. Interpersonal distance. Living space. High density housing. Highrise apartment(s). *Choose from:* social, population, spatial, interaction, sidewalk, occupant, pedestrian, urban, residential, interpersonal, housing *with:* density, proximity, intensity, overcrowding, crowd(ed,ing), congest(ed,ion), spacing, closeness, distance. *See also* Crowding; Overpopulation; Personal space; Social environment.

Social deprivation. See *Cultural deprivation; Psychosocial deprivation.*

Social desirability. Social desirability. *Choose from:* social(ly), interpersonal *with:* desirab(le,ility), valued, acceptab(le,ility), esteem(ed), admir(e,ed,ation), attract(ive,ion), approv(ed,ing,al). *Consider also:* social status, attribution, prestige, sociometric status, popularity. *See also* Acceptability; Acceptance; Admiration; Approval; Attractiveness; Expectations; Honored (esteem); Personal beauty; Personality traits; Peer relations; Popularity; Prestige; Social acceptance; Social approval; Social attitudes; Social behavior; Social influences; Social nearness; Social values; Socioeconomic status; Sociometric technics.

Social determinism. See *Determinism; Social factors; Socioeconomic factors.*

Social development. Social development. Moderniz(ed,ing,ation). New social thinking. Social change. Green revolution. Industrializ(ed,ing,ation). New social structure(s). Democratiz(ed,ing, ation). *Choose from:* social, societ(y,ies,al), cultural, socioeconomic,

third world, fourth world, national, living conditions *with:* develop(ed,ing, ment), evolv(e,ed,ing), evolution(ary), progress, advance(s), transition(s), improvement(s), growth, change(s), rising expectation(s). *See also* Culture change; Developing countries; Economic development; Industrialization; Least developed countries; Less developed countries Modernization; Progress; Social change; Social conditions; Social Darwinism; Social processes.

Social development (individual). See *Emotional maturity; Psychosocial development; Social maturity; Social skills; Socialization.*

Social disadvantagement. See *Cultural deprivation; Disadvantaged; Psychosocial deprivation.*

Social discrimination. Social discrimination. Prejudiced treatment. Unequal treatment. Jim Crow(ism). Chauvinis(m, t,ts). Classis(m,t,ts). Class prejudiced. Intoleran(t,ce). Marginaliz(e,ed,ing, ation). Microinequit(y,ies). Outcaste(s). Ageis(m,t,ts). Ableis(m,t,ts). Racis(m,t, ts). Sexis(m,t,ts). Bigot(s,ed,ry). Apartheid. Homophob(ia,ic). Heterophob(ia,ic). Xenophob(ia,ic). *Choose from:* social, ethnic group(s), minorit(y,ies), race, racial, Black, Asian, gender, sex, homosexual, gay, lesbian, age, class(es), educational, ethnic, housing, religious, reverse *with:* discriminat(e,ed,ing,ion), imbalance(s), injustice(s), exclusion, bias(es,ed), exclud(e,ed,ing), ostracism, ostraciz(e, ed,ing), unequal treatment, intimidat(e, ed,ing,ion), unfair(ly,ness). *Consider also:* stereotypes, labelling, labeling, bias, prejudice. *See also* Affirmative action; Age discrimination; Antisemitism; Apartheid; Attitudes toward handicapped; Attitudes toward homosexuality; Attitudes toward mental retardation; Attitudes toward mental illness; Attitudes toward physical handicaps; Attitudes toward physical illness; Attitudes toward the aged; Bigotry; Caste system; Civil rights; Dominated cultures; Employment discrimination; Ethnocentrism; Exclusivity (Religion); Hate crimes; Hate groups; Injustice; Labor market segmentation; Male chauvinism; Misanthropy; Nativism; Oppression; Persecution; Prejudice; Racial attitudes; Racial segregation; Racism; Religious prejudice; Residential segregation; Reverse discrimination; Separatism; Sex discrimination; Sexual division of labor; Sexual inequality; Sexual oppression; Sexism; Subjugation; Xenophobia.

Social diseases. See *Sexually transmitted diseases.*

Social disorganization. Social disorganization. Criminogenic. Anomie. Pathogenic social processes. *Choose from:* social(ly), societal, community, group *with:* disorganiz(ed,ation), deviance, disintegrat(e,ed,ing,ion), breakdown, patholog(y,ical), dissolution, chaos, disrupt(ion,ive), fragmentation, demoraliz(ed,ing,ation). *See also* Anomie; Chaos; Civil disorders; Confusion (disarray); Crime; Decadence; Deviance; Fragmentation (experience); Norms; Organizational dissolution; Reconstruction; Regression (civilization); Social change; Social conflict; Social criticism; Social equilibrium; Social norms; Social order; Social processes; Social structure; Social unrest; Socioeconomic factors.

Social distance. Social distanc(e,ing). Social separat(eness,ion). Affective detachment. Interpersonal distance. Sociometric status. Sociometry. Marital distance. Interanimal distance. *Choose from:* social, cultural, sociocultural, crosscultural, socioreligious, interpersonal, intergroup, intercultural, group(s), status(es), caste(s), psychological *with:* distanc(e,ing), exclusion, inequality, separat(eness,ion), difference(s). *Consider also:* avoidance, social status difference(s), social space(s), remoteness, linguistic politeness, outsider(s), social(ly) isolat(ed,ion), emotional distance, estrange(d,ment), stigmatized, prejudice, otherness, stereotypical attitude(s). *See also* Contempt; Isolation; Marginality (sociological); Ostracism; Otherness; Prejudice; Secondary relationships; Social acceptance; Social attitudes; Social class; Social integration; Social interaction; Social isolation; Social nearness; Social status; Social stratification; Social structure; Sociometric technics; Stereotyping; Tolerance.

Social dominance. Social(ly) dominan(t, ce). Dominance hierarch(y,ies). Caste(s). Social(ly) position. Social ranking. *Choose from:* dominan(t,ce), hierarch(y,ies,ical) *with:* social(ly), group, community, society, status, relationship, subordinat(e,ion). *Consider also:* social, power *with:* rank(s,ing), status, structure, precedence. *See also* Aggression; Authoritarianism (psychological); Authority (power); Coercion; Dominated cultures; Dominance subordination; Dominant ideologies; Elites; Hegemony; Informal social control; Formal social control; Power; Power elite; Power structure; Precedence; Privilege; Superior subordinate relationship.

Social drinking. Social drinking. *Choose from:* social, part(y,ies), occasional, moderat(e,ion), normal, average, pub(s), beer parlor(s), cocktail lounge(s), bar(s) *with:* drink(ing,ers), alcohol consumption, use of alcohol. Cocktail part(y,ies).

Happy hour(s). Wine and cheese part(y,ies). Winetasting(s). Three martini lunch(es). *See also* Alcohol drinking; Drinking behavior; Drinking customs; Drinking songs; Drunk driving; Problem drinking; Social behavior.

Social dynamics. See *Dynamics; Group dynamics; Intergroup relations; Population dynamics; Social change; Social interaction; Social processes.*

Social ecology. See *Human ecology.*

Social elites. See *Elites.*

Social engineering. Social engineering. *Consider also:* social technology, social intervention, behavioral engineering, social reform, social planning, applied sociology. *See also* Social change; Social planning; Social reform.

Social environment. Social environment(al, s). Crowding. Isolation. *Choose from:* social, psychosocial, socioenvironment(al), sociocultural, cultural, supportive, interpersonal, hostile *with:* environment(al,s), area(s), climat(e), setting(s), situation(s), context(s), atmosphere(s), ecolog(y,ies,ical). *Consider also:* school environment(s), classroom environment(s), commune(s), communit(y,ies), ghetto(es), home environment(s), kibbutz(im), neighborhood(s), poverty area(s), rural environment(s), school environment(s), suburban environment(s), town(s), urban environment(s), working condition(s), social support network(s), public place(s), prison environment(s), hospital environment(s), ward atmosphere, cocktail part(y,ies), etc. *See also* Academic environment; Adjustment (to environment); Architectural accessibility; Classroom environment; Communes; Community (geographic locality); Community (social); Community networks; Cultural conflict; Cultural deprivation; Educational environment; Formal social control; Home environment; Informal social control; Family life; Neighborhoods; Organizational climate; Organizational culture; Poverty areas; Psychosocial deprivation; Quality of life; Social attitudes; Social background; Social closure; Social cohesion; Social conditions; Social density; Social equity; Social factors; Social history; Social indicators; Social influences; Social integration; Social isolation; Social life; Social pressure; Social structure; Social support networks; Social values; Sociocultural factors; Subcultures; Working conditions.

Social epistemology. Social epistemology. *Choose from:* epistemolog(y,ical), epistemic(ally) justif(ied,ication), truth seeking, knowledge seeking *with:* social dimension(s), social force(s), social factor(s), social pressure(s). *Consider also:* ontological gerrymandering,

reliabilism, social definition(s). *See also* Epistemology; Feminist criticism; Inquiry (theory of knowledge); Knowledge; Research ethics; Researcher bias; Sociology of knowledge.

Social equality. Social equality. Egalitarian(ism). Equality principle. Distributive justice. Social justice. Just world. Affirmative action. Women's liberation. Status equilibration. *Choose from:* racial, sex(ual), role, gender, age, disabilit(y,ies) *with:* equality, equity, fair(ness). *Choose from:* equal *with:* access, education, right(s), protection, status, opportunit(y,ies). *See also* Affirmative action; Civil rights; Coeducation; Comparable worth; Egalitarian families; Egalitarianism; Equal education; Equal job opportunities; Equality before the law; Equity (payment); Ethnic relations; Fairness; Gender differences; Human rights; Inequality; Multicultural education; Nonsexist language; Race relations; Sexual inequality; Single sex schools; Social discrimination; Social justice; Social equity; Social integration; Wage differentials.

Social equilibrium. Social equilibrium. Social stability. Social order(liness). Social harmony. *Choose from:* group(s), social, societal, community, neighborhood, ethnic, famil(y,ies), trib(al,e,es), team(s), staff, national, state(s) *with:* harmon(y,ious), stability, stable, continuity, static, homeostat(is,ic), unanimity, equanimity. *See also* Functionalism; Social cohesion; Social disorganization; Social order; Social stability; Sociocultural factors; Socioeconomic factors; Stability; Systems theory.

Social equity. Social equity. Equitable treatment. Equitable allocation(s). Fair(ness). Proportional(ity) of allocation(s). *Choose from:* equit(y,able), inequit(y,able), power balance, fair(ness), even-handed(ness), justice, impartial(ity), neutral(ity), objectivity, toleran(t,ce), reciprocity, equality *with:* social, society, gender, sex, dyad(ic,s), couple(s), relationship(s), spouse(s), triad(ic,s), famil(y,ies), marriage(s), marital, conjugal, friend(s,ships), business(es), employment, promotion(s). *Consider also:* equalitarian, egalitarian, democra(tic,cy). *See also* Affirmative action; Civil rights; Coeducation; Comparable worth; Egalitarian families; Egalitarianism; Equal education; Equal job opportunities; Equality before the law; Equity (payment); Ethnic relations; Fairness; Human rights; Inequality; Justice; Multicultural education; Nonsexist language; Race relations; Sexual inequality; Single sex schools; Social discrimination; Social equality; Social justice; Social integration; Wage differentials.

Social ethics. Social ethics. Social obligation(s). Golden rule(s). Moral imperative(s). Moral obligation(s). *Choose from:* social, community, humanity, future generations, interpersonal, heritage, health, education, culture, equality, freedom, peace, tolerance, solidarity *with:* ethic(s,al), obligation(s), integrity, accountability, honest(y), principle(s,d), moral(s,ity), responsibility, conscience, conscientious(ness), openness, fidelity, incorruptib(le,ility), unethical. *Consider also:* promot(e,ed,ing,ion) peace, spiritual heritage, commitment to sharing, social covenant(s). *See also* Altruism; Bioethics; Ethics; Moral obligation; Morality; Political ethics; Social justice; Social contract; Social philosophy; Social responsibility; Social values; World citizenship.

Social evolution. See *Culture change; Evolutionary ethics; Social change; Social Darwinism; Social development; Sociobiology; Progress.*

Social exchange. Social exchange(s). *Choose from:* social, interpersonal, resource(s), symbol(s,ic), favor(s) *with:* exchange(s), reward(s), cost(s), reciprocity, bargaining power. *Consider also:* interpersonal transaction(s), sexual exchange(s), symbolic interaction(ism, ist,ists), interpersonal bargaining, reparation(s), retribution. *See also* Ceremonial exchanges; Cooperation; Exchange theory; Reciprocity; Reprisals; Reward; Sharing; Social behavior; Social contract; Social interaction; Symbiotic relations.

Social facilitation. Social facilitation. Social increment(s). Social decrement(s). Nondirective leadership. *Choose from:* social, interpersonal, group, peer, audience *with:* facilitat(e,ed, ing,ion), reinforcement, leadership, support, influence, effect(s), encourag(e,ed,ing,ement). *Consider also:* interstimulat(e,ed,ing,ion). *See also* Facilitation; Leadership; Foster (promote); Social behavior; Social influences; Social reinforcement.

Social factors. Social factor(s). Sociogenic. *Choose from:* common, city, class, collective, community, cultural, economic, ethnic, gender, group, interpersonal, minority, national, peer, political, public, racial, religious, rural, sociological, social(ly), societal, sociocultural, socioeconomic, sociopolitical, sociological, suburban, urban *with:* aspect(s), basis, background(s), cause(s), condition(s), constraint(s), characteristic(s), change(s), correlate(s), context(s), component(s), consideration(s), determinant(s), determin(ed,ing,ation), difference(s), dimension(s), dynamic(s), effect(s),

element(s), explanation(s), factor(s), force(s), influence(s), implication(s), indicator(s), impact(s), mechanism(s), obstacle(s), pattern(s), precondition(s), process(es), similarit(y,ies), setting(s), variation(s). *See also* Biological factors; Determinism; Factors; Nature nurture; Personality correlates; Physiological correlates; Psychosocial development; Sex factors; Social background; Social class; Social conditions; Social environment; Social influences; Social mobility; Social planning; Socialization; Society; Sociocultural factors; Socioeconomic factors.

Social facts. Social fact(s). Social phenomen(a,on). *Consider also:* social, sociological, demographic *with:* marker(s), dat(a,um). *See also* Facts; Social behavior; Social interaction; Social reality.

Social forces. See *Social factors.*

Social fragmentation. See *Social disorganization.*

Social function. See *Function; Functionalism.*

Social geography. See *Human ecology; Human geography.*

Social goals. Social goal(s). *Choose from:* common, collective, community, group, national, political, public, social(ly), societal, sociocultural, socioeconomic, sociopolitical, policy *with:* goal(s), objective(s), aim(s), campaign(s), purpose(s), intent(ions), mission(s), hope(s), dream(s), expectation(s), target(s), aspiration(s). *See also* Goals; Public policy; Social institutions; Social legislation.

Social gospel. Social gospel. *Choose from:* social, inner cit(y,ies), urban, sociology, social welfare *with:* gospel, God's mission, faith, apostle, church(es), Christianity, Protestant(ism). *Consider also:* urban ministry, social Christianity, Christian socialism, Christian sociology, Washington Gladden, Josiah Strong, George D. Herron, Richard T. Ely, doctrine of environment. *See also* Christianity; Protestantism; Social reform.

Social groups. See *Groups.*

Social hierarchy. See *Dominance subordination; Hierarchy; Social dominance; Superior subordinate relationship.*

Social history. Social history. Sociohistor(y, ies,ical). Social memor(y,ies). Sociological histor(y,ies). Societal history. History of society. *Choose from:* histor(y,ies, ical) *with:* social, societ(y,ies,al), intellectual, everyday life. *Consider also:* oral histor(y,ies), collective memor(y,ies). *See also* Cultural knowledge; Culture (anthropology); Family history; Historiography; History;

Holidays; Intellectual history; Lifestyle; Local history; Oral history; Social change; Social environment; Sociocultural factors; Socioeconomic factors; Sociology; Traditionalism.

Social hygiene. See *Public health.*

Social identity. Social identity. Personal identity. Counteridentification. *Choose from:* social, group, cultural, subcultural, ethnic, racial, professional, class, ego, self, sex role, gender *with:* identit(y,ies), identification, role(s), consciousness. *See also* Affiliation motivation; Anonymity; Class identity; Cosmopolitan; Ethnic identity; Ethnocentrism; Group identity; Identity; Interpersonal relations; Localism; Professional identity; Racial identity; Reference groups; Self concept; Self knowledge; Social cohesion; Social perception.

Social immobility. Social immobility. Social fixity. Caste system(s). Rigid class system(s). *See also* Caste system; Immobility; Social mobility; Social processes.

Social impact. Social impact(s). *Choose from:* collective, community, cultural, economic, group, interpersonal, national, political, public, racial, religious, ethnic, rural, sociological, social(ly), societal, sociocultural, socioeconomic, sociopolitical, sociological *with:* impact(s), implication(s), effect(s), consequence(s), result(s), outcome(s), aftermath, side effect(s), reaction(s), response(s), outgrowth, by-product(s), repercussion(s), product(s). *See also* Economic indicators; Externalities; Quality of life; Social change; Social conditions; Social indicators; Socioeconomic factors; Technological progress; Technological unemployment; Technology and civilization.

Social indicators. Social indicator(s). Social index(es). *Choose from:* indicator(s), index(es), measure(s,ment), correlate(s), inventor(y,ies), indices, statistics, table(s), data *with:* social climate, socio-economic development, quality of life, standard of living, social progress, socioeconomic condition(s), social development, social life, sociological, macrosocial, QWL, quality of working life. *See also* Birthrate; Crime rates; Economic indicators; Future of society; Indexes (indicators); Life satisfaction; Living standards; Income; Life expectancy; Marriage rates; Mortality rates; Prediction; Quality of life; Social change; Social environment; Social impact; Social problems; Sociocultural factors; Socioeconomic factors; Statistical data; Trends; Unemployment rates.

Social inequality. See *Inequality.*

Social influences. Social influence(s).

Crowd psychology. Peer influence(s). Social anchoring. *Choose from:* social(ly), prosocial, interpersonal, peer, group, societal, sociocultural, socioeconomic, sociopolitical, cultural, community, sociological, class, collective *with:* influence(s), pressure(s), factor(s), approval, criticism, praise, prejudice(s), taboo(s), loyalt(y,ies), values, norm(s), determinant(s), consensus, facilitation, standard(s), force(s), conformity. *See also* Authority (power); Criticism; Cultural values; Embourgeoisement; Ethics; Facilitation; Formal social control; Groups; Informal social control; Interpersonal influences; Mass media effects; Mentors; Moral conditions; Opinion leaders; Peer influences; Political socialization; Popularity; Population growth; Power elite; Prejudice; Prestige; Propaganda; Reputation; Reference groups; Role models; Social adjustment; Social approval; Social attitudes; Social background; Social behavior; Social change; Social comparison; Social conformity; Social desirability; Social development; Social environment; Social facilitation; Social factors; Social integration; Social movements; Social norms; Social pressure; Social reinforcement; Social status; Social stratification; Social theories; Social values; Socialization; Society; Sociocultural factors; Socioeconomic factors; Subcultures; Superstitions; Taboo; Traditionalism.

Social innovation. See *Social change.*

Social institutions. Institution(s). Regular social practice(s). Social organization(s). Kinship system(s). System(s) of social roles and norms. Culture complex(es). Court system(s). *Consider also:* economic, political, religious, cultural, educational, economic, legal, government(al), political, stratification *with:* institution(s), system(s), organization(s). *See also* Churches; Courts; Education; Family; Foundations (organizations); Government; Hospitals; Institutionalization (social); Law (legal philosophy and theory); Libraries; Marriage; Norms; Organizations; Religions; Schools; Social order; Social structure; Society; Traditions.

Social integration. Social(ly) integrat(ed, ion). Assimilat(e,ed,ing,ion). Acculturat(ed,ion). Multicultural acceptance. Equal rights. Desegregat(ed,ion). Melting pot. *Choose from:* group(s), social, cultural, societal, intercultural, multicultural, interethnic, interracial, interfaith, interreligious, subcultures *with:* cooperation, unity, interdependence, integration, reintegration, mainstream, harmony. *See also* Acculturation; Activism; Affirmative action; Anti-apartheid movement; Assimilation (cultural); Civil rights; Civil rights

organizations; Common culture; Cultural cooperation; Culture change; Desegregation; Diversity; Ethnic groups; Ethnic relations; Equal education; Equal job opportunities; Immigrants; Indigenous populations; Intercultural communication; Intercultural relations; Interethnic families; Intergroup relations; Intermarriage; Interracial marriage; Mainstreaming; Melting pot; Multicultural education; Nativism; Peaceful change; Plural societies; Race relations; Racial diversity; Racial integration; School integration; Social change; Social class; Social cohesion; Social discrimination; Social distance; Social environment; Social equality; Social influences; Social problems; Social processes; Social segmentation; Socialization; Subcultures; Tokenism.

Social intelligence. See *Social maturity; Social skills.*

Social interaction. Social interaction. Negotiation(s). Social situation(s). Social distance. Sociability. Socializ(e, ed,ing,ation). Conversation(s). Cooperation. Solidarity. Affiliation. Friendship. Kinship. Marriage. Rapport. Group unity. Argument(s). Assistance. Bargaining. Charitable behavior. Collective behavior. Conversation. Cooperation. Double bind interaction. Encouragement. Eye contact. Communication. Compatibility. Sharing. Peer relations. *Choose from:* social, interpersonal, prosocial, heterosocial, peer, group, interprofessional, neighborhood, community *with:* interact(ion,ional, ions,ing), exchange(s), behavior, relationship(s), role(s), conflict(s), confrontation(s), encounter(s), play, involvement, mutual(ity), participation, functioning, network(s,ing), performance(s), influence(s), process(es), bond(s,ing), activit(y,ies), attraction, discussion(s). *See also* Aggression; Arguments; Assertiveness; Assistance; Bargaining; Charitable behavior; Collective behavior; Community (social); Conflict; Conflict resolution; Conversation; Cooperation; Double bind interaction; Emotions; Encouragement; Ethnomethodology; Exchange theory; Eye contact; Forgiveness; Friendship; Gift giving; Group composition; Group discussion; Group participation; Group performance; Help seeking behavior; Helping behavior; Impression formation; Impression management; Interpersonal attraction; Interpersonal compatibility; Interpersonal influences; Interpersonal relations; Interviews; Loneliness; Negotiation; Participation; Peace; Peer relations; Personal space; Physical contact; Primary groups; Psychodynamics; Riots; Rivalry; Self monitoring; Self presentation; Sharing; Small groups; Social anxiety; Social behavior; Social cohesion; Social

contact; Social dating; Social distance; Social facts; Social life; Social nearness; Social perception; Social processes; Social support networks; Teamwork; Victimization; Violence; War.

Social interest. See *Community feeling; Group feeling; Prosocial behavior.*

Social introversion. See *Introversion.*

Social isolation. Social(ly) isolat(ed,ion). Socioenvironmental isolation. Lonel(y,iness). Alone(ness). Social(ly) depriv(ed,ation). Seclu(ded,sion). Hermit(s). Recluse(s). Asocial(ity). Liv(e,ing) alone. Friendless(ness). Estrange(d,ment). Separat(ed,ion) from friends. Separat(ed,ion) from family. Solitar(y,iness). Confine(d,ment). Outsider(s). Outcaste(s). *Consider also:* alienat(ed,ion), anom(ie,ic), lonelyhearts, withdrawn, private sphere(s), purdah. *See also* Acceptance; Affiliation motivation; Alienation; Anomie; Asceticism; Deprivation; Disadvantaged; Disengagement; Indian territories; Indigenous populations; Interpersonal relations; Introversion; Isolation; Living alone; Loneliness; Marginality (sociological); Maternal deprivation; Ostracism; Otherness; Paternal deprivation; Professional isolation; Rejection (psychology); Self neglect; Shyness; Social adjustment; Social anxiety; Social contact; Social distance; Social environment; Social integration; Social segmentation; Social processes; Society; Solitude; Withdrawal (defense mechanism).

Social issues. See *Controversial issues; Political issues; Social movements; Social problems.*

Social justice. Social justice. Equal opportunit(y,ies). Equal protection. *Consider also:* equal(ity,itarianism), egalitarian(ism), fair(ness), just(ness), just world, impartial(ly,ity), even handed(ness), toleran(t,ce), unbiased, unprejudiced, disinterested, equit(y, able), human rights, civil rights. *See also* Affirmative action; Civil rights; Comparable worth; Egalitarianism; Equal education; Equal job opportunities; Equality before the law; Equity (payment); Fairness; Global inequality; Human rights; Impartiality; Inequality; Justice; Multicultural education; Power sharing; Reproductive rights; Social contract; Social ethics; Social equality; Social equity; Social goals; Social reform; Social responsibility; Socially responsible investing; Society.

Social learning. Social learning. *Choose from:* social, psychosocial, interpersonal, informal, submissiveness, assertiveness, powerlessness *with:* learn(ed,ing), condition(ed,ing). *See also* Attitude formation; Consciousness raising activities; Imitation; Imprinting (psychology); Inhibition (psychology); Learned helplessness; Nonverbal learning; Observational learning; Peer influences; Reference groups; Role models; Significant others; Social reinforcement; Socialization; Subcultures.

Social legislation. Social legislation. *Choose from:* social, pension(s), welfare, health care, family, elderly, dependent(s), low income, patient(s), civil rights, disability rights, gay rights, affirmative action, education *with:* legislation, ballot initiative(s), law(s), bill(s), mandate(s), incentive(s), statut(e,es,ory), rationing, *Consider also:* social contract(s), social polic(y,ies), public polic(y,ies), GI Bill of Rights, Servicemen's Readjustment Act of 1944, Civil Rights Act of 1964, Americans With Disabilities Act, etc. *See also* Family policy; Health policy; Housing policy; Intervention; Labor laws; Labor standards; Labor policy; Land reform; Legislation; Penal reform; Political action; Population policy; Public policy; Social action; Social change; Social goals; Social problems; Social reform; Social responsibility; Welfare reform; Welfare policy.

Social life. Social life. Friend(s,ship). *Choose from:* social, interpersonal, community, shared *with:* life, interaction(s), relation(s,ships), custom(s), activit(y,ies), participation, support, contacts, dating, network(s). *See also* Anniversaries and special events; Ceremonies; Everyday life; Family life; Festivals; Friendship; Interpersonal attraction; Interpersonal relations; Life satisfaction; Lifestyle; Popularity; Social contact; Social dating; Social development; Social environment; Social interaction; Society.

Social loafing. Social loafing. Loafing by group member(s). *Consider also:* shirker(s), uncooperative(ness), slacker(s), malinger(ers), truant(s), sponger(s), neglector(s), deadbeat(s), noncontributor(s). *See also* Alienation; Group dynamics; Group participation; Group performance; Group processes; Laziness; Social parasites; Work groups.

Social maladaptation. See *Adjustment disorders; Dyssocial reaction; Maladaptation; Maladjustment.*

Social marginality. See *Marginality (sociological).*

Social maturity. Social(ly) matur(e,ity). *Choose from:* psychosocial(ly), interpersonal, socioemotional, social(ly) *with:* matur(e,ity), development, competence, skill(s). *Consider also:* social age, social intelligence. *See also* Adjustment (to environment); Age groups; Emotional maturity; Personal

independence; Personality traits; Physical characteristics; Self control; Social skills; Socialization; Vocational maturity.

Social meaning. Social meaning(s). *Choose from:* social, cultural, collective, connotative *with:* meaning(s), definition(s), construct(s). *See also* Collective representation; Meaning; Sex symbolism; Sexist language; Social facts; Social processes; Social reality; Symbolism.

Social medicine. Social medicine. Sociomedical. Medical sociology. Social bas(e,is,es) of health. *Choose from:* social *with:* medicine, medical, hygien(e,ic), pediatric(s), health. *Consider also:* socially transmitted disease(s). *See also* Health occupations; Medical model; Medical sociology.

Social mobility. Social mobility. Social flexibility. Status competition. Cross(ing) class lines. *Choose from:* marr(y,ying,iage) *with:* high(er) status. Status seeker(s). Loss of status. Change(s) in social status. *Choose from:* social, sociocultural, social class, upward(ly), status, occupational, socioeconomic, downward(ly), intragenerational *with:* mobil(e,ity), immobil(e,ity), destination, aspiration(s), achiev(e,ed,ing,ement), advancement, attainment, improvement(s), opportunit(y,ies), transition(s). *See also* Access to Education; Achievement; Aspirations; Career mobility; Class mobility; Demography; Educational attainment; Elites; Embourgeoisement; Generation gap; Geographic mobility; Intergenerational mobility; Proletarianization; Social class; Social factors; Social processes; Social status; Social stratification; Socioeconomic status; Status attainment; Status seekers.

Social mobilization. See *Consciousness raising activities; Mobilization; Social agitation.*

Social morphology. See *Social structure.*

Social movements. Social movement(s). Abolitionis(m,t,ts). Activist(s). Avant garde. Black power. Consciousness raising group(s). Counterculture(s). Countermovement(s). Demonstrator(s). Environmentalis(m,t,ts). Feminis(m,t,ts). Pacifis(m,t,ts). Prohibitionis(m,t,ts). Protester(s). Reformer(s). Social protest(s). Social action. Social activism. Student activism. Suffragette(s). Zionis(m,t,ts). *Choose from:* abolitionist, abortion, anti-abortion, anti-apartheid, anti-illiteracy, anti-lynching, anti-nuclear, anti-suffrage, anti-war, Black, civil rights, collective, conservative, consumer, ecological, ecumenical, emancipation, empowerment, environmental, feminist, gay rights, homophile, labor, lesbian, liberation, mass, men's,

nationalist, peace, peasant, pacifist, populist, prohibitionist, protest, radical, reform, religious, revolutionary, social(ist), student(s), suffrage, rights, temperance, underground, women(s), worker(s) *with:* movement(s), activis(m,t,ts), resistance, part(y,ies), group(s), campaign(s), mobilization, sect(s), boycott(s). *See also* Abortion rights movement; Activism; Antiabortion movement; Black Muslims; Black power; Change agents; Civil disobedience; Civil rights; Civil rights organizations; Coalition formation; Collective behavior; Countermovements; Ecumenical movement; Environmentalism; Feminism; Gray power; Homosexual liberation movement; Human rights; Interest groups; Labor movements; Men's movement; Millenarianism; Nazism; Peace movements; Peasant rebellions; Political movements; Political participation; Political reform; Protest movements; Radical movements; Religious dialogues; Religious movements; Social action; Social agitation; Social change; Social conditions; Social demonstrations; Social goals; Social influences; Social problems; Social processes; Social programs; Social reform; Suffrage movement; Women's groups; Women's rights; Youth movements.

Social nearness. Social(ly) near(ness). *Choose from:* social(ly), cultural(ly), interpersonal(ly), sociophysical(ly), sociocultural(ly) *with:* close(ness), related(ness), inclusion, similar(ity,ities), integrat(ed,ion), congregation(s), attachment(s). *Consider also:* relationship building, social integration interpersonal attachment, comradery, fraternity, similar attitude(s), physical(ly) close(ness), ingroup(s), equal status contact, kinship ties, peer acceptance. *See also* Belongingness; Interpersonal relations; Intimacy; Multicultural education; Social acceptance; Social attitudes; Social desirability; Social distance; Social interaction; Sociometric technics.

Social needs. See *Affiliation motivation; Individual needs; Psychological needs.*

Social networks. See *Networks; Social support networks.*

Social networks, boundary spanning. See *Boundary spanning; Interorganizational networks.*

Social norms. Social norm(s). Behavior standard(s). Moral norm(s). Rules of order. Role norm(s). Relationship rule(s). Polite(ness). Nondeviant. Social(ly) appropriate(ness). Privacy norm(s). *Choose from:* social, cultural, community, group *with:* norm(s), convention(s), rule(s), regularit(y,ies), expectation(s), assumption(s). *See also*

Fashions; Folkways; Formal social control; Group norms; Informal social control; Laws; Norms; Peer influences; Reference groups; Reference values; Rules (generalizations); Sex roles; Social conformity; Social influences; Social institutions; Social values; Stereotyping; Taboo; Traditions.

Social obligation. See *Social ethics.*

Social order. Social order. Rule enforcement. Law and order. *Choose from:* social, community, societ(y,ies,al) *with:* order(ing), regulation, stability, conformity, control, normality, organization. *See also* Cargo systems; Community (social); Informal social control; Formal social control; Law enforcement; Social disorganization; Social equilibrium; Social cohesion; Social cohesion; Social conflict; Social institutions; Social stability; Social structure; Social theories.

Social organization. See *Caste system; Occupational segregation; Oppression; Organizational structure; Political elites; Political repression; Power elite; Power structure; Racial segregation; Residential segregation; Social cleavage; Social reality; Social stratification; Social structure.*

Social parasites. Parasit(e,ic,ical,ically). Sycophant(s). Toad(y,ies). Leech(es). Spong(e,er,ing). Obsequious flatterer(s). Freeloader(s). Lounge lizard(s). Deadbeat(s). Cadger(s). Moocher(s). *Consider also:* laz(y,iness), dependen(t, cy), exploit(s,ed,ing,ive), self-seek(ing, er,ers), servil(e,ity), opportunis(m,tic), scrounger(s). *See also* Dependency (personality); Exploitation; Laziness; Machiavellianism; Manipulation; Social loafing.

Social participation. See *Group participation; Involvement; Prosocial behavior.*

Social perception. Social perception. Person perception. Interpersonal perception. Attribution(s). *Choose from:* social(ly), interpersonal *with:* perception(s), perceived, perspective(s), impression(s), opinion(s), conception(s), sensitivity, view(s), awareness, attitude(s), cognition. *Consider also:* stereotyping, bias, socioempath(y,etic). *See also* Anonymity; Attribution; Consciousness raising activities; Credibility; Cynicism; Empathy; Halo effect; Impression formation; Impression management; Labeling (of persons); Likability; Perception; Perceptions; Popularity; Public opinion; Role perception; Self presentation; Social attitudes; Social behavior; Social comparison; Social identity; Social interaction; Social types; Social reality; Stranger reactions.

Social phenomena. See *Social facts.*

Social philosophy. Social philosoph(y,ies). Sociophilosophical. Philosoph(y,ies) of human nature. *Choose from:* social, society, community *with:* philosoph(y, ies), ideolog(y,ies), logic, ethics, aesthetics, metaphysics, epistemology. *See also* Philosophy; Social ethics; Social theories; Social thought; Social values; Society; Verstehen.

Social phobia. Social phobia. Shy(ness). Self conscious(ness). Agoraphob(ia,ic). *Choose from:* social(ly), psychosocial *with:* phob(ia,ic), anx(iety,ious, iousnesss), fear(s), avoidance, panic, stress. *See also* Agoraphobia; Introversion; Phobias; Shyness; Social anxiety.

Social planning. Social planning. *Choose from:* common, city, collective, community, cultural, economic, environment(al), group, interpersonal, national, political, public, rural, social(ly), societal, sociocultural, socioeconomic, sociopolitical, sociological, suburban, urban *with:* plan(s,ned,ning), design(s, ed,ing), blueprint(s), renewal. *See also* Disaster planning; Economic planning; Environmental design; Health planning; Language planning; Local planning; Population policy; Regional development; Social change; Social factors; Social reform; Society; State planning; Urban planning.

Social policy. See *Energy policy; Family policy; Fiscal policy; Foreign policy; Government policy; Health policy; Housing policy; Labor policy; Language policy; Population policy; Public policy; Social legislation; Welfare policy.*

Social position. See *Social status.*

Social power. See *Power.*

Social pressure. Social pressure(s). Lobb(y,ies). Pressure group(s). Interest group(s). Public demand(s,ing). Social movement(s). Public sentiment(s). *Choose from:* social, public, community, political, majority, minority, popular, societal, people(s), citizen(s,ry), voter(s), peer(s), neighborhood *with:* pressur(e,es, ed,ing), demand(s,ed,ing), outcry, oppos(e,ed,ing,ition), reject(ed,ing,ion), resist(ed,ing,ance), antagonis(m,tic), mandate(s), insisten(t,ce), support(ed, ing), appeal(s,ed,ing), clamor(ed,ing), opinion(s), power, arousal, norm(s), influence(s), conform(ing,ity). *See also* Community attitudes; Deterrence; Informal social control; Peer influences; Public opinion; Social conformity; Social environment; Social influences; Society; Uniformity.

Social problems. Social problem(s). *Choose from:* social, community, societ(y,ies,al), psychosocial, sociocultural, socioeconomic, neighborhood, sociological *with:* issue(s), problem(s), illness(es), risk situation(s), question(s), dilemma(s), dispute(s). *Consider also:* abortion, alienation, arms race, civil disorders, civil liberties, civil rights, deinstitutionalization, desegregation, divorce, draft, dropouts, drug abuse, energy, environment, equal rights, euthanasia, homosexual rights, housing, illegitimacy, incest, inflation, integration, legal reform, peace, pollution, population problem(s), poverty, prostitution, race relations, riot(s), substance dependence, suicide, theft, unemployment, war, welfare, women's rights. *See also* Alcoholism; Crime; Deprivation; Disasters; Drug addiction; Economic problems; Family conflict; Family violence; Hazards; Homeless; Inequality; Juvenile delinquency; Labor disputes; Overpopulation; Political issues; Poverty; Prejudice; Public policy; Racism; Refugees; Sexism; Social conflict; Social discrimination; Social disorganization; Social justice; Social legislation; Social movements; Social reform; Social work; Sociological jurisprudence; Substance abuse; Unemployment; World problems.

Social processes. Social process(es). Group process(es). Social change. Cultural change. *Consider also:* social differentiation, democratization, social evolution, sociocultural evolution, cultural development, racial conflict, social transition, social progress, unionization, social inventions, cultural exchange, social disintegration, social catastrophe. *See also* Acculturation; Anomie; Assimilation (cultural); Bureaucratization; Class conflict; Class formation; Coalition formation; Cultural evolution; Deindustrialization; Embourgeoisement; Equity (payment); Future of society; Group formation; Immigration; Industrialization; Institutionalization (social); Mediation; Migration; Modernization; Organizational change; Organizational development; Peace; Polarization; Political processes; Proletarianization; Refugees; Secularization; Social action; Social change; Social cohesion; Social conflict; Social development; Social disorganization; Social factors; Social integration; Social isolation; Social mobility; Social movements; Social reality; Social segmentation; Social stratification; Social structure; Socialization; Sociocultural factors; Socioeconomic factors; Society; Suburbanization; Urbanization; War.

Social programs. Social program(s). Antipoverty program(s). Food bank(s). Safety net. Community development program(s). *Choose from:* antipoverty, entitlement, welfare, community, public, outreach, shelter, food, hunger, employment, housing *with:* program(s), service(s). *See also* Antipoverty programs; Income maintenance programs; Program implementation;

Social progress. See *Culture change; Industrialization; Modernization; Progress; Social change; Social Darwinism; Social development; Social processes.*

Social psychology. Social psycholog(y,ical). Sociopsycholog(y,ical). Psychosocial. Sociobehavioral. Psychosociolog(y,ical). Social context psychology. *Consider also:* social behavior, social interaction, group psychology, psychology of small groups, group behavior, group processes, interpersonal relations. *See also* Applied psychology; Mass psychology; Psychology.

Social reality. Social realit(y,ies). Social construction of reality. Reality construction. Social fact(s). Social phenomen(a, on). *Consider also:* worldview(s), weltanschauung(en), social(ly) defin(ed,itions), associative meaning(s), shared symbol(s,ic), cultural meaning(s), sociology of knowledge. *See also* Demythologization; Everyday life; Family life; Moral conditions; Reality; Social facts; Social meaning; Social processes; Social reproduction; Social theories; Society; Worldview.

Social reform. Social reform(s). Social engineering. Constitutional change(s). Democratiz(e,ed,ing,ation). Cultural revolution. Depos(e,ed,ing) leader(s). Vote(d) out of office. Progressivism. Tax reform. Prison reform. *Choose from:* social, sociopolitical, constitutional, legal, societ(al,y,ies), public, state, government(al), institutional, system(s) *with:* change(s,), restructur(e,ed,ing), revis(e,ed,ing,ion,ions), democratiz(ed, ing,ation), improv(e,ed,ing,ment,ments), reform(s,ed,ing), reorganiz(e,ed,ing, ation), reconstruct(e,ed,ing,ion), transform(ed,ing,ation,ations), transition(al,s), innovat(e,ed,ing,ion, ions), renew(al,ed,ing), regenerat(e,ed, ing,ion), revolution(s), cleanup(s), purge(s), bloodletting(s). *Consider also:* social democracy, perestroika, glasnost, impeach(ed,ing,ment). *See also* Affirmative action; Land reform; Law reform; New Deal; Political action; Political ideologies; Political reform; Revolution; Social action; Social change; Social goals; Social gospel; Social justice; Social legislation; Social movements; Social planning; Social problems; Social processes; Social programs; Social responsibility; Society; Welfare reform.

Social reinforcement. Social reinforcement. *Choose from:* social(ly), interpersonal, peer(s) *with:* reinforc(e,ed,ing,ement, ements), support, consequence(s), positive feedback, reward(s), recogni-tion. *Consider also:* social support, praise, approval, reassur(e,ed,ing,ance), positive social consequence(s), applau(d,ed,se), acclaim(ed,ing), compliment(s), flatter(ed,ing,y), plaudit(s), kudo(s). *See also* Awards; Behavior modification; Delay of gratification; Encouragement; Eye contact; Facilitation; Feedback; Foster (promote); Honored (esteem); Motiva-tion; Nonverbal reinforcement; Peer influences; Praise; Punishment; Reward; Social approval; Social influences; Social learning; Verbal reinforcement.

Social rejection. See *Ostracism; Rejection (psychology); Resentment; Resistance; Social isolation; Stigma; Withdrawal (defense mechanism).*

Social relations. See *Church state relation-ship; Class relations; Ethnic relations; Intergroup relations; Interpersonal relations; Peer relations; Race relations; Social contact; Social interaction.*

Social reproduction. Social reproduction. Reproduction of labor power. Capitalist reproduction. Self perpetuat(ion,ing). Cultural reproduction. *See also* Cultural transmission; Social reality; Social structure; Socialization; Society.

Social response. Social respons(e,es,ivity, ive,iveness). *Choose from:* social, societal, public, communit(y,ies) *with:* respons(e,es,ivity,ive,iveness), react(ance,ive,ivity,ion,ions,ionary), repl(y,ies,ied), resist(ed,ing,ance), accept(ed,ing,ance), reject(ed,ing,ion), support(ed,ing). *See also* Acceptance; Collective behavior; Crises; Dissent; Labeling (of persons); Negative sanctions; Positive sanctions; Public opinion; Public opposition; Public support; Rejection (psychology); Social acceptance; Social approval; Stranger reactions.

Social responsibility. Social respon-sibilit(y,ies). *Choose from:* common, city, citizen(s,ship), class, collective, community, constituent(s), corporate, electorate, group, interpersonal, national, political, public, social(ly), societal *with:* responsibilit(y,ies), obligation(s), dut(y,ies), liabilit(y,ies), accountab(le, ility), answerab(le,ility). *See also* Citizen participation; Citizenship; Community involvement; Corporate social responsi-bility; Ethics; Helping behavior; Humanitarianism; Leadership; Negli-gence; Political obligation; Social action; Social behavior; Social ethics; Social justice; Social legislation; Social services; Socially responsible investing; State intervention; State role; Volunteers.

Social responsibility, corporate. See *Corporate social responsibility.*

Social revolution. See *Revolution.*

Social roles. See *Roles.*

Social rules. See *Social norms.*

Social sanctions. See *Formal social control.*

Social sciences. Social science(s). Human science(s). Behavioral science(s). Social research. Geisteswissenschaft(en). Study of social phenomena. Social theor(y,ies). Scientific study of society. *Consider specific social science disciplines by name for example:* child psychology, clinical psychology, community development, community psychology, comparative psychology, consumer psychology, counseling psychology, criminology, cultural anthropology, developmental psychology, environment design, forecasting, gerontology, human geography, international studies, jurisprudence, linguistics, neuropsychol-ogy, political science, political sociol-ogy, population dynamics, sociology, urban sociology. *See also* Academic disciplines; Anthropology; Applied psychology; Cognitive psychology; Comparative psychology; Criminal psychology; Demography; Economics; Educational psychology; Engineering psychology; Environmental psychology; Experimental psychology; Geography; History; History of psychology; Humanistic psychology; Individual psychology; Industrial psychology; Law (legal philosophy and theory); Medical sciences; Military psychology; Physi-ological psychology; Psychology; Social psychology; Social studies; Sociobiol-ogy; Sociology; Sport psychology; Theoretical orientation; Theories; Topography.

Social segmentation. Social segmentation. Subgroup(s). Subdiv(isions,iding). Cleavage. Stratification. Faction(s). Segregat(e,ed,ing,ion). Denomination(s). Social differentiation(s). Societal differentiation(s). Pillarization. Verzuiling. *Consider also:* role insula-tion, group formation, polarization, coalition(s). *See also* Anomie; Factional-ism; Group formation; Intergroup relations; Labor market segmentation; Polarization; Political movements; Social cleavage; Social integration; Social isolation; Social stratification; Social structure; Specialization; Subcultures.

Social services. Social service(s). Charit(y, ies). Council of community services. *Choose from:* social, child care, welfare, social work, casework, health, health planning, sociopsychological, commu-nity, charitable, helping, foster care, referral, day care, mental health, counseling, homemaker, protective, supportive *with:* service(s), service organization(s), institution(s), agenc(y,ies). *See also* Adult day care; Adult foster care; Antipoverty programs; Assistance; Caregivers; Child day care; Community services; Emergency

Public policy; Public welfare; Social change; Social movements; Social reform; Social services.

services; Foster home care; Government programs; Group homes; Health services; Hospices; Human services; Humanitarianism; Long term care; Mental health services; Public welfare; Social agencies; Social programs; Social responsibility.

Social settlements. Social settlement(s). Social work settlement(s). Settlement house(s). Neighborhood union(s). Neighborhood center(s). Community Center(s). Neighborhood gild(s). *Consider also:* settlement work, settlement school(s), Young Women's Christian Assn (YMCA) women's center(s), Henry Street Settlement; Hull House. *See also* Black community; Ethnic neighborhoods; Immigrants; Social work.

Social skills. Social skill(s). Polite(ness). Good manners. Diploma(cy,tic). Assertion skill(s). Poise. Articulate(ness). *Choose from:* social, interpersonal, personal life, relationship, relationally, heterosocial, psychosocial *with:* skill(s), abilit(y,ies), competenc(e, ies,t), aware(ness), sensitivity, problem solving skill(s), cognition, intelligence. *See also* Ability; Assertiveness; Communication skills; Consciousness raising activities; Extraversion (psychology); Gregariousness; Interpersonal relations; Manners; Personality traits; Popularity; Prosocial behavior; Psychosocial development; Reality therapy; Sensitivity training; Shyness; Smiling; Social adjustment; Social attitudes; Social behavior; Social maturity; Social skills training; Socialization; Tact; Teamwork.

Social skills training. Social skill(s) training. *Choose from:* social skill(s), interpersonal skill(s), assertiveness, sensitivity, social awareness, social competenc(e,ies), community living, interpersonal problem solving *with:* skill development, training, workshop(s). *See also* Alcohol rehabilitation; Assertiveness training; Behavior modification; Consciousness raising activities; Drug rehabilitation; Human relations training; Sensitivity training; Skill learning; Social skills.

Social stability. Social stability. *Choose from:* social, societ(y,ies), communit(y, ies), nation(s,al) *with:* stab(ility,le), continuity, resilien(t,ce), strength(s), intact(ness), well-being, dependab(le, ility), durab(le,ility), endur(ing,ance), cohesion, cohesive(ness), invulnerab(ility,le), permanen(t,ce), preserv(e,ed,ation), reliab(le,ility), secur(e,ed,ity), solidarity. *See also* Economic security; Family stability; Legitimacy of governments; Progress; Social change; Social equilibrium; Social order.

Social statistics. See *Census; Social indicators; Vital statistics.*

Social status. Social status. Socioeconomic status. SES. Status ranking. Status differentiation. Class status. Class identification. Socioeconomic background. Dominance rank. Income level. *Choose from:* social, socioeconomic, psychosocial, high, low, minority, welfare, class, sociometric, occupational, achieved, ascribed *with:* status, position, standing, rank. *Consider also:* life chances, life-styles. *See also* Ascription; Cargo systems; Caste system; Disadvantaged; Elites; Hierarchy; Initiation rites; Life satisfaction; Lower class; Marginality (sociological); Marital status; Middle class; Occupational status; Otherness; Peers; Popularity; Prestige; Privilege; Quality of life; Reputation; Roles; Self concept; Social class; Social distance; Social influences; Social mobility; Social stratification; Social structure; Socioeconomic status; Status attainment; Status inconsistency; Status seekers; Upper class.

Social stratification. Social stratification. Social class structure(s). Horizontal and vertical social structure(s). Social class(es). Social rank(s). Occupational prestige ranking(s). Social strat(a,um). Hierarch(y,ies) of social strata. Status differentiation(s). Social inequalit(y,ies). Microstratification. Class division(s). Status division(s). Ranking of statuses. Caste system(s). Caste(s). Dual labor market(s). *Consider also:* sex(ual), gender, school, age, economic, racial *with:* stratification. *See also* Boundaries; Cargo systems; Caste system; Class analysis; Class society; Class stratification; Elitism (government); Functionalism; Income inequality; Power structure; Social class; Social distance; Social mobility; Social segmentation; Social status; Social structure; Socioeconomic status; Socioeconomic factors; Wealth.

Social stress. Social stress(es). Strained relationship(s). Interpersonal conflict(s). Social coping. Societal pressure(s). Stresses of unemployment. Social instability. Stress situation(s). Social discomfort. Just-in-time society. *Choose from:* social, collective, psychosocial, psycho-social, territorial, interpersonal, acculturative, family, crowding, interactional, group, role, psychocultural, situational, status, mobility *with:* stress(ed,es,ors,ful), strain(ed,s), pressure(s,d), discomfort, tension(s), cris(is,es), distress(ed,), anxiety. *See also* Burnout; Interpersonal conflict; Psychological stress; Role conflict; Stress.

Social structure. Social structure. Social pattern(s,ing). Hierarchical structure. Social stratification. Social order. Caste system. *Choose from:* role(s), class,

community, communication, socioeconomic, group, power, organizational, neighborhood, population, social, influence, sociometric *with:* structure(s), organization, categories, hierarch(y,ies), system(s), network(s), pattern(s), relationships, stratification, order. *See also* Agrarian structures; Boundaries; Cargo systems; Caste system; Categories (philosophy); Civil society; Center and periphery; Centrality; Class analysis; Class society; Community structure; Dominance subordination; Elites; Family characteristics; Family roles; Formal social control; Functionalism; Group structure; Hierarchy; Informal social control; Kinship; Lower class; Majority groups; Middle class; Occupational segregation; Occupational structure; Organizational structure; Organizations; Power structure; Racial segregation; Residential segregation; Sexual division of labor; Social change; Social class; Social cleavage; Social conditions; Social disorganization; Social distance; Social environment; Social institutions; Social order; Social processes; Social reproduction; Social segmentation; Social status; Social stratification; Social theories; Society; Structure; Upper class.

Social studies. Social studies. *Choose from:* social studies, social science(s), societal issues, history, global, historical geography, geography, local history, civics, world history, citizenship, cultural heritage *with:* studies, curriculum, teaching, course(s), education, instruction, training, learning. *See also* Anthropology; Area studies; Civics; Economics; Geography; History; Social sciences.

Social support. Social support. *Choose from:* social, interpersonal, informal, community, friend(ship), peer(s), kin, famil(y,ial) *with:* support, resource(s), bond(s), tie(s), network(s), aid, reinforcement. *Consider also:* close friend(s), social network(s), supportive context(s), safety net(s). *See also* Affiliation motivation; Assistance; Caregivers; Consciousness raising activities; Cooperation; Counseling; Cybercommunities; Donations; Employee assistance programs; Encouragement; Family relations; Friendship; Helping behavior; Human services; Humanitarianism; Interpersonal relations; Primary groups; Reference groups; Rehabilitation; Self help groups; Social agencies; Social behavior; Social environment; Social interaction; Social support networks.

Social support networks. Social support network(s). Support group(s). Social network(s,ing). Support system(s). Community support. Family support system(s). Peer support. Group support.

Social reinforcement network. Personal network(s). Self help group(s). Mutual aid. *Choose from:* social, human service, community, conjugal, family, peer, personal, interpersonal, self help, psychosocial *with:* network(s,ing), support system(s), support group(s). *See also* Assistance; Caregivers; Community churches; Consciousness raising activities; Cooperation; Counseling; Donations; Family relations; Friendship; Helping behavior; Human services; Humanitarianism; Reference groups; Rehabilitation; Social agencies; Social responsibility; Social services; Social work; Social workers; Self help; Self help groups; Social interaction; Social support.

Social surveys. Social survey(ed,s,ing). Election stud(y,ies). Market research. *Choose from:* social, crime, income, population, opinion(s), economic, socioeconomic, famil(y,ies), household(s), employment, social condition(s), sociological *with:* survey(ed,s,ing), poll(s,ing), telephone interview(s), mailed questionnaire(s), telephone sampling, opinion research, data collection. *See also* Data collection; Demographic surveys; Health survey(s); Library surveys; Market research; Nutrition surveys; Opinion polls; Questionnaires; Sexual behavior surveys; Social Indicators; Surveys.

Social system. See *Social structure.*

Social theories. Social theor(y,ies). *Choose from:* social, action, balance, biosocial, communication, conflict, contagion, convergence, critical, evolutionary, exchange, game, information, learning, middle range, systems, sociological *with:* theor(y,ies,etical), paradigm(s). *Consider also:* dialectical materialism, Marxism, organicism, functionalism, structuralism, etc. *See also* Behavior theories; Critical theory; Dependency theory (international); Dialectical materialism; Exchange theory; Functionalism; Game theory; History of psychology; History of the family; Ideologies; Malthusian theory; Materialism; Middle range theories; Rules (generalizations); Social change; Social criticism; Social Darwinism; Social environment; Social influences; Social order; Social philosophy; Social reality; Social structure; Socialization; Society; Sociological theory; Systems theory; Teleology; Theory formation; Theory verification; Theories; Voluntarism (philosophy); World systems theory.

Social thought. *Choose from:* social, social issue(s), social reality, culture, society *with:* thought, analysis, perspective(s), belief(s), interpret(e,ed,ing,ation,ations), myth(s,making), theor(y,ies). *Consider also:* moral thought, traditional belief(s). *See also* Intellectual history; Liberalism;

Political philosophy; Political ideologies; Popular culture; Public opinion; Social philosophy.

Social trends. See *Fads; Popular culture; Trends.*

Social types. Social type(s). Town character(s). Personage(s). Eccentric(s). *Consider also:* snob(s), highbrow(s), grand dame(s), gentlemen, playboy(s), hippie(s), streetpeople, etc. *See also* Categorization; Ideal types; Labeling (of persons); Roles; Social perception; Stereotyping.

Social understanding. See *Verstehen.*

Social unrest. Social unrest. Instability. Unstable condition(s). Ethnic conflict(s). Social protest(s). *Choose from:* social, civil(ian), political, societal, community, neighborhood, public, citizen(s,ry), urban, ethnic, racial, intergroup *with:* unrest, tension(s), instability, unstable, conflict(s), protest(s), agitat(ed,ion,or, ors), discontent, arous(ed,al), commotion(s), disturbance(s), demonstration(s), excit(ed,ation), insurrection(s), insurgen(t,ce,cy), incite(ed,ment), rebel(s,lion,lions, lious,liousness), restless(ness), turbulen(t,ce), turmoil, upheaval, unrest, violence, cris(is,es), shakeup(s). *See also* Civil disorders; Dissent; Intergroup relations; Protest movements; Public opinion; Rebellions; Schism; Social agitation; Social conditions; Social conflict; Social demonstrations; Social disorganization; Tensions.

Social usage. See *Etiquette.*

Social values. Social(ly) valu(e,es,ed,ing, ation). *Choose from:* social, sociocultural, societ(al,y,ies), group, cultural, traditional, middle class, bourgeois, social class, moral, materialistic, work, interpersonal, political, democratic, egalitarian, religious *with:* valu(e,es, ation), norms, undervalu(e,es,ed,ing, ation), devalu(e,es,ed,ing,ation), ethics, attitude(s), ideal(s), ideolog(y,ies,ical), mores, beliefs. *Consider also:* puritan ethic, value conflict(s). *See also* Aesthetics; Altruism; Anomie; Beliefs; Censorship; Civilization; Conservative; Critical theory; Cultural values; Egalitarianism; Ethnic values; Formal social control; Human dignity; Humanitarianism; Ideologies; Individualism; Informal social control; Information policy; Liberalism; Moral authority; Moral conditions; Morality; Norms; Peer influences; Personal values; Political attitudes; Political ideologies; Prestige; Priorities; Progressivism; Protestant ethic; Puritanism; Quality of life; Reference groups; Social attitudes; Social change; Social consciousness; Social desirability; Social environment; Social ethics; Social goals; Social influences; Social justice; Social norms;

Social philosophy; Social reality; Socialization; Society; Technology assessment; Traditionalism; Work values.

Social welfare. See *Antipoverty programs; Charities; Food service (programs); Medical assistance; Outreach programs; Public welfare; Social agencies; Social services; Social programs.*

Social withdrawal. See *Autism; Introversion; Social isolation; Withdrawal (defense mechanism).*

Social work. Social work. Casework. Case work. Group work. Child care work. Social service(s). Protective service(s). Social agenc(y,ies). Social welfare service(s). *Choose from:* school, medical, psychiatric, group, family *with:* social work. *See also* Charities; Counseling; Criminal justice; Family therapy; Group work; Health services; Helping behavior; Intervention; Mental health services; Psychiatric social work; Public welfare; Rehabilitation; Social settlements; Social agencies; Social services; Social support networks; Social workers.

Social work, psychiatric. See *Psychiatric social work.*

Social workers. Social worker(s). Caseworker(s). Child care workers. Social service worker(s). Case worker(s). Social agency staff. Welfare worker(s). Community worker(s). Case aide(s). School social worker(s). Parole officer(s). Probation officer(s). *Consider also:* caseload. *See also* Caregivers; Counseling; Counselors; Law enforcement personnel; Mental health personnel; Professional client relations; Psychiatric social workers; Psychologists; Rehabilitation counselors; Social work; Vocational counselors.

Social workers, psychiatric. See *Psychiatric social workers.*

Social zone. See *Proxemics.*

Socialism. Socialis(m,t,tic). Commun(e,al). Left(ist). Common ownership. Centrally planned econom(y,ies). *Consider also:* Fabian(ism), utopian(ism), Marx(ian,ist), Owen(ism,ite,ites), Fourier(ism), people's democrac(y,ies), labor movement, egalitarian(ism). *See also* Agricultural collectives; Capitalism; Centrally planned economies; Collectivism; Communes; Communism; Employee ownership; Guild socialism; Industrial democracy; Marxism; Political ideologies; Revisionism; Social democracy; Utopias; Welfare state.

Socialism, guild. See *Guild socialism.*

Socialist realism in art. Socialist realism in art. *Choose from:* socialist realism, Soviet, propagand(a,istic), Stalin, state-mandated style(s), communis(m,t,ts), totalitarian *with:* art(ist,istic), figuration, mural(s), portrait(s), painting(s), painter(s), landscape(s), still life(s), woodcut(s), etching(s), watercolor(s), drawing(s), sculpture(s), pastel(s). *See also* Artistic styles; Arts; Genres (art); Figurative art; Magic realism (art); Naturalism; Realism; Realism in art; Surrealism.

Socialization. Socializ(e,ed,ing,ation). Cultural conditioning. Social conditioning. Enculturat(ion,ive). Attitude formation. Process of cultural transmission. Role learning. Resocializ(e,ed, ing,ation). *Choose from:* conform(ity,ed, ing), internaliz(e,ed,ing,ation), learn(ed,ing), develop(ed,ing), acquir(e,ed,ing) *with:* expectation(s), mores, norm(s,ative), moral(s), rule(s), value(s), attitude(s), mutual respect, recipro(cal,city), social behavior, social attitude(s), social consciousness, value(s), role(s). *See also* Adjustment (to environment); Assertiveness training; Attitude formation; Child development; Childrearing; Cognitive dissonance; Compliance; Consciousness raising activities; Cultural transmission; Education; Engenderment; Ethnicity; Group identity; Hidden curriculum; Identification (psychology); Ideologies; Imitation; Individuals; Learning; Peer influences; Personality; Political socialization; Prisonization; Professional socialization; Reference groups; Religious education; Role models; Significant others; Social conformity; Social integration; Social learning; Social maturity; Social processes; Social reproduction; Social skills; Social theories; Social values; Subcultures.

Socialization, political. See *Political socialization.*

Socialization, professional. See *Professional socialization.*

Socialized medicine. See *National health programs; State medicine.*

Socially deviant behavior. See *Deviant behaviors.*

Socially disadvantaged. See *Cultural deprivation; Disadvantaged; Psychosocial deprivation.*

Socially handicapped. Socially handicapped. Socially deprived. Disadvantaged. *Consider also:* low income, poverty, disabilit(y.ies), development delay(s), low socioeconomic background(s), minorit(y,ies) social inequality. *See also* Disadvantaged; Marginality (sociological); Psychosocial deprivation.

Socially responsible investing. Socially responsible invest(ing,ment,ments). *Choose from:* socially responsible, sustainable development, green *with:* invest(ing,ment,ments), fund(s,ing). *See*

also Citizen participation; Corporate social responsibility; Ethics; Prosocial behavior; Social action; Social justice; Social responsibility.

Societal change. See *Social change.*

Societal progress. See *Culture change; Industrialization; Modernization; Progress; Social change; Social Darwinism; Social development; Social processes.*

Societies (organizations). Societ(y,ies). Association(s). Organization(s). League(s). Club(s). Council(s). Board(s). Fraternit(y,ies). Sororit(y,ies). Men's group(s). Women's group(s). Federation(s). Alliance(s). *Consider also:* professional, medical, national, voluntary, interorganizational, scientific, honor, alumni *with:* association(s), organization(s), societ(y,ies). *See also* Art societies; Associations (organizations); Clubs; Confraternities; Law societies; Literary societies; Professional organizations; Scientific societies; Youth organizations.

Societies, agrarian. See *Agrarian societies.*

Societies, agricultural. See *Agrarian societies.*

Societies, archaeological. See *Archaeological societies.*

Societies, art. See *Art societies.*

Societies, bourgeois. See *Bourgeois societies.*

Societies, capitalist. See *Capitalist societies.*

Societies, choral. See *Choral societies.*

Societies, complex. See *Complex societies.*

Societies, folk. See *Traditional societies.*

Societies, herding. See *Pastoral societies.*

Societies, historical. See *Historical societies.*

Societies, humane. See *Shelters.*

Societies, hunting and gathering. See *Hunting and gathering societies.*

Societies, industrial. See *Industrial societies.*

Societies, journeymen. See *Guilds.*

Societies, law. See *Law societies.*

Societies, literary. See *Literary societies.*

Societies, musical. See *Musical societies.*

Societies, nonindustrial. See *Traditional societies.*

Societies, pastoral. See *Pastoral societies.*

Societies, plural. See *Plural societies.*

Societies, postindustrial. See *Postindustrial societies.*

Societies, precapitalist. See *Traditional societies.*

Societies, primitive. See *Traditional societies.*

Societies, scholarly. See *Professional organizations.*

Societies, school. See *School clubs.*

Societies, scientific. See *Scientific societies.*

Societies, secret. See *Secret societies.*

Societies, student. See *School clubs.*

Societies, traditional. See *Traditional societies.*

Society. Societ(y,ies,al). Nation state(s). Social formation(s). Human race. Civilization. Communit(y,ies). Gesellschaft. Mankind. Humankind. Nation(s). State(s). Tribe(s). Body politic. Commonwealth. General public. *Consider also:* agrarian, pastoral, bourgeois, capitalist, civil, class, communist, complex, industrial, liberal democratic, mass, modern, plural, postindustrial, socialist, traditional, western, eastern *with:* communit(y,ies), societ(y,ies,al), nation(s), state(s). *See also* Agrarian societies; Bourgeois societies; Capitalist societies; Civilization; Class society; Classless society; Community (social); Complex societies; Consumer society; Countries; Cultural groups; Culture (anthropology); Future of society; Groups; Humanity; Hunting and gathering societies; Industrial societies; Mass society; Modern society; Pastoral societies; Plural societies; Postindustrial societies; Social action; Social change; Social cohesion; Social conditions; Social factors; Social goals; Social indicators; Social influences; Social institutions; Social integration; Social isolation; Social justice; Social life; Social philosophy; Social planning; Social pressure; Social processes; Social reality; Social reform; Social reproduction; Social stratification; Social structure; Social theories; Social values; Sociocultural factors; Socioeconomic status; Sociology; Technology and civilization; Traditional societies; Western society.

Society, civil. See *Civil society.*

Society, class. See *Class society.*

Society, classless. See *Classless society.*

Society, consumer. See *Consumer society.*

Society, contemporary. See *Modern society.*

Society, future of. See *Future of society.*

Society, information. See *Information society.*

Society, mass. See *Mass society.*

Society, modern. See *Modern society.*

Society, open. See *Democracy.*

Society, western. See *Western society.*

Sociobiology. Sociobiology. Sociobio-logical(ly). Psychological evolution. Evolution of social behavior. Biosocial. Biopsychosocial. Biocultural. Biopolitical. Nature nurture. *Choose from:* biolog(y,ical), Darwin(ian,ism), genetic, evolution *with:* social, psycholog(y,ical), behavior, personality. *Consider also:* neo-Darwinism. *See also* Animal nature of man; Behavioral genetics; Biosocial; Biological drives; Biological factors; Darwinism; Environmental determinism; Evolution; Evolutionary ethics; Genetic psychology; Genetics; Psychobiology; Social behavior; Sociology.

Sociocentrism. See *Ethnocentrism.*

Sociocultural factors. Sociocultural factor(s). Social cultural factor(s). *Choose from:* community, cultural, ethnic, gender, minority, national, racial, religious, ritual, symbolic, rural, sociological, social(ly), societal, sociocultural, sociological, sociolinguistic, anthropological, ethnographic, ethnological *with:* aspect(s), basis, background(s), cause(s), condition(s), constraint(s), characteristic(s), change(s), correlate(s), context(s), component(s), consideration(s), determinant(s), determin(ed,ing,ation), difference(s), dimension(s), dynamic(s), effect(s), element(s), explanation(s), factor(s), influence(s), implication(s), indicator(s), impact(s), mechanism(s), obstacle(s), pattern(s), precondition(s), process(es), similarit(y,ies), setting(s), variation(s). *See also* Biological factors; Birth rites; Civilization; Cross cultural comparisons; Cultural deprivation; Cultural groups; Cultural issues; Cultural relativism; Culture (anthropology); Culture change; Death rituals; Determinism; Environmental effects; Ethnic identity; Ethnic values; Ethnicity; Ethnography; Ethnology; Family characteristics; Initiation rites; Kinship; Personality correlates; Physiological correlates; Psychosocial deprivation; Races; Rites of passage; Social conditions; Social environment; Social factors; Social history; Social influences; Social processes; Society; Socioeconomic factors; Sociolinguistics; Weddings; Western civilization.

Sociodrama. See *Psychodrama; Role playing.*

Socioeconomic factors. Socioeconomic factor(s). Social economic factor(s). *Choose from:* socioeconomic, economic, social class *with:* aspect(s), bas(is,es), background(s), cause(s), condition(s), constraint(s), characteristic(s), change(s), correlate(s), context(s), component(s), consideration(s), determinant(s), determin(ed,ing,ation), difference(s), dimension(s), dynamic(s), effect(s), element(s), explanation(s),

factor(s), influence(s), implication(s), indicator(s), impact(s), limit(s), mechanism(s), obstacle(s), pattern(s), precondition(s), predisposition(s), process(es), similarit(y,ies), setting(s), variation(s), variable(s). *Consider also:* income, earnings, poverty, indigen(t,cy), disadvantage(d,s,ment), advantage(d,s, ment), wealth, privilege, social class, social status, upper class, middle class, lower class, educational status, educational background, employment, unemployment, family status, occupation, socioeconomic status, SES. *See also* Determinism; Economic conditions; Environmental determinism; Factors; Living standards; Social background; Social conditions; Social disorganization; Social equilibrium; Social factors; Social indicators; Social influences; Sociocultural factors; Socioeconomic status; Stratification.

Socioeconomic status. Socioeconomic status. SES. SEG. Social class(es). Social strat(a,um). Social status. Life chances. Life-styles. Economic class(es). *Choose from:* socio-economic, socioeconomic *with:* group(s), class(es), level(s). *Choose from:* manual, skilled, non-professional, semi-skilled, unskilled *with:* worker(s), labor. *Consider also:* professional(s), employer(s), manager(s), middle manager(s), junior executive(s), capitalist(s), landowner(s), upper class, middle class, lower class, working class. *See also* Career mobility; Class differences; Demographic characteristics (of individuals); Disadvantaged; Economic elites; Educational attainment; Family socioeconomic status; Income; Income inequality; Low income; Lower class; Middle class; Middle income level; Poverty; Quality of life; Relative deprivation; Social background; Social class; Social desirability; Social mobility; Social status; Social stratification; Socioeconomic factors; Society; Stratification; Upper class; Upper income level; Wealth.

Socioeconomic status, family. See *Family socioeconomic status.*

Socioenvironmental therapy. Socioenvironmental therapy. Sociopsychotherap(eutic,y,ies). Sociotherap(eutic, y,ies). *Choose from:* socioenvironmental, milieu, social, situational *with:* therap(y,ies,eutic), psychotherap(y,ies, eutic). *Consider also:* therapeutic communit(y,ies), group psychotherap(y, ies), family therap(y,ies), psychodrama, role playing, sensitivity training, encounter group(s). *See also* Milieu therapy; Therapeutic communities.

Sociolinguistics. Sociolinguistic(s). Sociolinguistic(s). Ethnolingusitic(s). Sociology of language. Dialect stud(y,ies). Language planning. *Choose*

from: language(s) *with:* culture, society. *Consider also:* language(s), linguistic *with:* minorit(y,ies), variet(y,ies), variation, planning, sociolog(y,ical). *See also* Areal linguistics; Bidialectalism; Bilingualism; Code switching; Dialects; Diglossia; Ethnolinguistics; Grammar; Hermeneutics; Language; Language maintenance; Language planning; Language policy; Language shift; Language usage; Language varieties; Linguistics; Monolingualism; Multilingualism; Native language; Nonstandard English; Psycholinguistics; Sociocultural factors; Socioeconomic status; Sociology; Speech communities.

Sociological factors. See *Social factors; Sociocultural factors; Socioeconomic factors.*

Sociological jurisprudence. Sociological jurisprudence. Sociological litigation. *Choose from:* law(s),legal, jurisprudence, judicial, justice, litigation, court decision(s) *with:* sociological effect(s), social phenomena, social context, sociological school, sociological knowledge. *Consider also:* sociological justice, legal sociology. *See also* Crime prevention; Criminal justice; Judicial decisions; Social problems; Sociology.

Sociological theory. Sociological theor(y,ies,etical,ems). *Choose from:* sociolog(y,ical), social, sociopsychology(y,ical), socioeconomic, sociocultural, sociopolitical, cultural, biosocial, sociobiolog(y,ical) *with:* theor(y,ies, etical,ems), axiom(s,atic), conclusion(s), codification(s), construct(s), deduction(s), explanation(s), formalization, general(ity,ization,izations, izability), hypothes(is,es,etical,ize), inference(s), interpretation(s), metatheor(y,ies,etical), model(s), postulate(s), proposition(s), paradigm(s), thes(es,is), analog(y,ies), antinom(y,ies), assumption(s), concept(ual,s), derivation(s), dialectic(s,al), framework(s), ideal types, interpretation(s), metaphor(s,ical), philosoph(y,ies), presumption(s), premise(s), principle(s), symbol(s,ic), typolog(y,ies). *Consider also:* Chicago school, Frankfurt school, functionalis(m,t), Marxis(m,t), metasociolog(y,ies,ical), neo-positivism, positivism, realism, symbolic interactionism, structuralis(m,t), middle range theories, social action theory, systems theory, teleolog(y,ical), conceptual paradigms, classificational paradigms, analogical paradigms, formal paradigm(s). *See also* Dependency theory (international); Exchange theory; Gemeinschaft and gesellschaft; Game theory; Malthusian theory; Middle range theories; Paradigms; Psychoanalytic interpretation; Psychoanalytic theory; Realism; Social theories; Sociology; Systems theory; Teleology; Verstehen; Voluntarism (philosophy).

Sociology. Sociolog(y,ical,ists). *Choose from:* social *with:* research, theor(y,ies), science(s). *Consider also:* cultural anthropology, sociobiology, social psychology, psychosociology, sociography, demography, criminology, sociometric(s). *See also* Critical theory; Demography; Ethnomethodology; Human ecology; Medical sociology; Social history; Sociological jurisprudence; Social psychology; Social sciences; Social theories; Society; Sociobiology; Sociolinguistics; Sociology of knowledge; Sociological theory.

Sociology, medical. See *Medical sociology.*

Sociology of knowledge. Sociology of knowledge. Social determinant(s) of knowledge. Sociology of science. *Consider also:* historical epistemology, historicism. *See also* Concepts; Epistemology; Hidden curriculum; Ideologies; Intellectual history; Knowledge; Phenomenology; Relativism; Scientific knowledge; Social epistemology; Social meaning; Social reality; Undecidability.

Sociometric technics. Sociometric tech(nique,niques,nic,nics). Sociogram(s). Sociomet(ry,rics). *Choose from:* sociometric *with:* test(s), status, choices, measure(s,ment), analys(is,es), structure(s), grouping(s). *Consider also:* group interaction, social status, social distance, peer preference(s) *with:* test(s), measure(s,ment), analys(is,es), scale(s), questionnaire(s). *See also* Group dynamics; Group structure; Intergroup relations; Small groups; Social behavior; Social distance; Quantitative methods.

Sociopathic personality. See *Antisocial personality disorder.*

Sociotherapy. See *Socioenvironmental therapy.*

Sodalities. See *Confraternities.*

Sodomy. Sodom(y,ize,ized,ites). Anal intercourse. Buggery. Cochone(s). Coitus analis. Coitus in ano. *Consider also:* bestiality. *See also* Homosexuality; Sex behavior; Sexual deviations; Sexual intercourse; Zooerasty.

Software (computers). Software. Firmware. Computer program(s). Computer instruction(s). Shareware. Freeware. Beta version(s). *See also* Computer industry; Computers; Debugging; Hardware (computers).

Soil conservation. Soil conservation. Arrest(ed,ing) deforestation. Reforest(ed,ing,ation). Contour plowing. No-till planting. Crop rotation. Interplant(ed,ing). Erosion control. Flood control. Preserv(e,ed,ing) ecosystem(s). Conserv(e,ed,ing) rain forest(s). Sav(e,ed,ing) redwood(s). Forest management. *Choose from:*

sav(e,ed,ing), conserv(e,ed,ing,ation), preserv(e,ed,ing), irrigat(e,ed,ing,ation), protect(ed,ing,tion), maintain(ance), quality control, safeguard(ing), monitor, reclaim(ed,ing), reclamation, restor(e,ed,ing,ation), replant(ed,ing), replenish(ed,ing), re-establish(ed,ing), return(ed,ing), retention *with:* soil(s), topsoil, land(s), woodland(s), forest(s), swamp(s,land,lands), wetland(s), pasture(s), desert(s), wasteland(s), field(s), wood(s), marsh(es), jungle(s), rain forest(s), propert(y,ies), acreage, ecosystem(s). *See also* Agricultural chemicals; Agricultural diversification; Agriculture; Arable land; Conservation of natural resources; Desertification; Ecology; Environmental protection; Environmentalism; Forestry; Forest conservation; Irrigation; Land preservation; Land use; Natural resources; Plant succession; Reclamation of land; Reforestation; Resource stress; Restoration ecology; Shore protection; Soil degradation; Soil erosion; Soil fertility; Soil science; Soil surveys; Tree planting.

Soil degradation. Soil degradation. *Choose from:* soil(s), topsoil, dirt, earth *with:* degrad(e,ed,ing,ation), nutrient(s) loss(es), saliniz(e,ed,ing,ation), acidif(y,ied,ication), deteriorat(e,ed,ing,ion), radioactiv(e,ity), pollut(e,ed,ing,ion), contaminat(e,ed,ing,ion). *See also* Agricultural chemicals; Agricultural diversification; Agricultural mechanization; Arable land; Desertification; Land preservation; Land use; Reclamation of land; Resource stress; Slash burn agriculture; Soil conservation; Soil erosion; Soil fertility; Soil science; Soil surveys.

Soil erosion. Soil erosion Soil eros(ion, ional,ive). Runoff. Landslide(s). Soil loss(es). Degraded soil(s). Gull(y,ies). Desertif(y,ied,ication). Sand storm(s). Soil blow(n,ing). Overgraz(e,ed,ing). Sediment transport. Soil degrad(ed, ation). *Choose from:* wind, water, land(s), soil(s), cropland(s), topsoil(s), earth *with:* erosion, erod(e,ed,ing), degrad(e,ed,ing,ation), denud(e,ed,ing, ation), weather(ed,ing), wash(ed,ing) away, wear(ing) away. *Consider also:* shore damage, channel morphology, watershed sediment, storm damage, beach erosion, shore current(s), littoral current(s), flood control, agricultural sediment. *See also* Agricultural mechanization; Arable land; Arid lands; Conservation of natural resources; Desertification; Environmental protection; Irrigation; Land preservation; Land use; Landfill; Natural resources; Reclamation of land; Reforestation; Resource stress; Shore protection; Soil conservation; Soil science; Soil surveys; Tree planting.

Soil fertility. Soil fertility. *Choose from:* soil(s), topsoil, dirt, earth *with:* nutrient(s), fertiliz(e,ed,ing,er,ers), organic, nitrogen, manure, productivity, mulch(ed,ing), lim(e,ed,ing), agrochemical, yield(s). *Consider also:* tillage, humus, nutritional aspect(s), organic matter. *See also* Agricultural chemicals; Agricultural diversification; Arable land; Fertility (farming); Soil conservation; Soil degradation; Soil science; Soil surveys.

Soil science. Soil science. Pedolog(y,ic, ical). Paleopedolog(y,ic,ical) *Choose from:* soil(s), mud(s) *with:* science, research, taxonom(y,ies,ic), classification system(s), model(s), field stud(y,ies). *Consider also:* soil(s), mud(s), clay(s) *with:* form(ing,ation) factor(s), geograph(y,ic), hydraulic properties, attribute(s), water retention, moisture, drainage, percolation, seepage, permeab(le,ility), absorption, physics, temperature, mechanics, texture(s), bulk, density, sample(s), erosion, stabiliz(e,ed, ing,ation), conservation, composition. *See also* Agricultural research; Soil conservation; Soil degradation; Soil erosion; Soil fertility; Soil surveys.

Soil surveys. Soil survey(s,ing). *Choose from:* soil(s) *with:* survey(s,ing), map(s,ping), profile(s), description(s), correlat(e,es,ed,ing,ion,ions), soil classif(y,ied,ing,ication,ications), interpretive table(s), laboratory analy(sis,ses), evaluat(e,ed,es,ing, ion,ions), report(s), quantitative information, data. *Consider also:* soil taxonomic identification. *See also* Agricultural research; Resource management; Soil conservation; Soil degradation; Soil erosion; Soil fertility; Soil science.

Solar access. Solar access. *Choose from:* solar, sunlight *with:* access, easement(s), permit(s), entitlement(s), ordinance(s), restrictive covenant(s). *See also* Light sources; Solar energy.

Solar energy. Solar energy. Solar photovoltaic cells. Passive solar. *Choose from:* solar, photovoltaic, sun(light) *with:* energy, power, heat(ed,ing), hot water, furnace(s), cooker(s), cell(s), collect(or,ors,ion), technology, alternative(s), conversion, architecture, panel(s), thermal, electric, retrofit(s). *See also* Alternative energy; Climate; Energy conservation; Energy generating resources; Energy policy.

Soldiers. See *Military personnel.*

Solid waste. Solid waste(s). Waste material(s). Garbage. Refuse. Trash. Litter. Rubbish. Junk. Compost(ed,ing). Ash(es). Sweepings. Dregs. Dust. Leavings. Landfill. Discard(ed,ing,s). Offal. Sludge. PCBs. Polychlorinated biphenyls. Debris. Remains. Rubble.

Wreckage. Abandoned car(s). Biodegradable(s). Non-biodegradable(s). *Choose from:* waste *with:* matter, product(s), paper, yard, stream. *See also* Clutter; Debris; Environmental pollutants; Environmental pollution; Environmental protection; Hazardous wastes; Landfill; Recycling; Scrap materials; Toxic substances; Waste disposal; Waste to energy; Waste transport.

Solidarity. See *Social cohesion.*

Soliloquy. See *First person narrative.*

Solipsism. Solipsis(m,tic). *Consider also:* subjective idealism, egois(m,tic). *See also* Egocentrism; External world (philosophy); Narcissism; Subjectivity.

Solitude. Solitude. Solitar(y,iness). Quietude. Seclud(e,ed,ing). Seclusion. Isolat(e,ed,ing,ion). Alone(ness). Reclusion. Reclus(e,ive,iveness). Hermit(s,ry). Priva(cy,te). *Consider also:* detach(ed,ment), separate(ness), quarantine(d), lonel(y,iness), lonesome(ness). *See also* Disengagement; Isolation; Isolation (defense mechanism); Living alone; Loneliness; Privacy; Silence; Social isolation.

Solmization. Solmiz(e,ed,ing,ation). Solmis(e,ed,ing,ation). *Consider also:* Guidonian system, Bebiz(e,ed,ing,ation), Boced(e,ed,ing,ation), Damen(e,ed, ing,ation), Bob(e,ed,ing,ation), Jam(e,ed,ing,ation), Jale method, Tonwart system, Tonic sol-fa notation. *See also* Musical intervals and scales; Musical theory.

Solution achievement. See *Problem solving.*

Solvent abuse. Solvent(s) abus(e,ed,er, ers,ing). *Choose from:* benzine, toluol, carbon tetrachloride, naptha, amyl nitrite, nitrous oxide, gas(oline), glue, cleaning fluid(s), laughing gas *with:* abus(e,ed,er,ers,ing), misuse(d,r,rs), sniff(ed,ing,er,ers), inhal(e,ed,ing). *See also* Inhalant abuse; Street drugs; Substance abuse; Toxic inhalation.

Solving, anagram problem. See *Anagram problem solving.*

Solving, problem. See *Problem solving.*

Solving problems, group. See *Group problem solving.*

Somatic delusions. Somatic delusion(s). Somatopsychic delusion(s). *Choose from:* false belief(s), delusion(s,al), exaggerated idea(s) *with:* body, bodily, somatic. *Consider also:* autopsychic delusion(s), somatic hallucination(s). *See also* Body image disturbances; Delusions.

Somatic therapies. Somatic therap(y,ies). Organic therap(y,ies). *Choose from:* electroacupuncture, aversive conditioning, fasting, progressive relaxation,

running, jogging, muscle relaxation, osteopathy. *Choose from:* orthomolecular, convulsive, electroconvulsive, vitamin, megavitamin, touching, massage, relaxation, electroconvulsive, electric convulsion, electroshock, megavitamin, vitamin, tactile, orthomolecular, shock *with:* therap(y,ies). *See also* Acupuncture; Biofeedback; Electrosleep treatment; Narcotherapy; Progressive relaxation therapy; Psychopharmacology; Psychosurgery; Vitamin therapy.

Somatic types. See *Somatotypes.*

Somatoform disorders. Somatoform disorder(s). Hypochondria(c,cal,sis). Mind body disorder(s). Psychogenic pain. *Choose from:* conversion *with:* neuros(is,es), disorder(s). *Choose from:* hysterical *with:* anesthesia, paralysis, vision disturbance(s). *Choose from:* Briquet(s) *with:* syndrome, disease, hysteria. *See also* Conversion disorder; Functional hearing loss; Hypochondriasis; Hysterical paralysis; Mind-body relations (metaphysics); Psychogenic pain; Psychophysiologic disorders.

Somatology. See *Physical anthropology.*

Somatopsychic disorders. See *Psychophysiologic disorders.*

Somatopsychics. See *Psychophysiology.*

Somatotypes. Somatotype(s). Physique(s). Constitutional type(s). *Choose from:* body, morphological *with:* type(s), build, composition. *Consider also:* brachymorphic, endomorph(s,ic), ectomorph(s, ic), mesomorph(s,ic), obes(e,ity), thin(ness), asthenic, hypersthenic, leptosome, athletic, dysplastic, hypervegetative, megalosplanchnic, pyknic, phlegmatic, phthisic, cerebral, sterile, Kretschmer's, Sheldon's, Carus' *with:* type(s), typolog(y,ies). *See also* Personal appearance; Personality; Phrenology; Physiognomy; Physique.

Somnambulism. See *Sleepwalking.*

Sonata da camera. Sonata da camera. Chamber sonata(s). Court sonata(s). Trio sonata(s). Tratteniment(i,o) da camera. Concert(i,o) da camera. Alettament(i,o) per camera. *See also* Sonata da chiesa.

Sonata da chiesa. Sonata(s) da chiesa. Church sonata(s). Trio sonata(s). *See also* Sonata da camera.

Song cycle. Song cycle(s). Liederkreis(e). Liederzykl(us,en). *See also* Part songs; Songs.

Songbooks. Songbook(s). Song book(s). Hymnal(s). Partbook(s). Tunebook(s). Tune book(s). *Consider also:* song(s), glee(s), catch(es), round(s), madrigal(s), folksong(s), ballad(s), chant(s), chorale(s), hymn(s), psalm tune(s), lovesong(s), laud(e,a,es,as), cantigua(s), chanson(s), lied(er) *with:*

compendium(s), book(s), sheet music, collection(s), compilation(s), antholog(y,ies). *See also* Books; Songs.

Songs. Song(s). Glee(s). Catch(es). Round(s). Folksong(s). Ballad(s). Ballata(s). Chant(s). Chorale(s). Hymn(s). Lovesong(s). Laud(e,a,es,as). Cantigua(s). Chanson(s). Lied(er). *Consider also:* cant(i,us), cantio(nes), caccia(s), cancion ranchera, madrigal(s), Christmas carol(s), paean(s). *See also* Ballads; Bawdy songs; Border ballads; Cantatas; Choral music; Drinking songs; Erotic songs; Folk songs; French songs; German songs; Humorous songs; Hymns; Labor songs; Lyrics; Music; Noels; Part songs; Protest songs; Revolutionary ballads and songs; Sacred songs; Satirical songs; Sea songs; Singing; Songbooks; Song cycle; Stanzas; Student songs; Textless vocal works; Work songs.

Songs, African American. See *Afro-American music.*

Songs, battle. See *War songs.*

Songs, bawdy. See *Bawdy songs.*

Songs, boatmen's. See *Sea songs.*

Songs, children's. See *Children's songs.*

Songs, Christmas. See *Noel.*

Songs, college. See *Student songs.*

Songs, cradle. See *Lullabies.*

Songs, drinking. See *Drinking songs.*

Songs, erotic. See *Erotic songs.*

Songs, folk. See *Folk songs.*

Songs, French. See *French songs.*

Songs, German. See *German songs.*

Songs, Hebrew. See *Jewish music.*

Songs, humorous. See *Humorous songs.*

Songs, Jewish. See *Jewish music.*

Songs, labor. See *Labor songs.*

Songs, love. See *Love songs.*

Songs, marriage. See *Epithalamia.*

Songs, national. See *Patriotic music.*

Songs, part. See *Part songs.*

Songs, plantation. See *Afro-American music.*

Songs, political. See *Political ballads.*

Songs, popular. See *Popular music.*

Songs, sacred. See *Sacred songs.*

Songs, sailors'. See *Sea songs.*

Songs, satirical. See *Satirical songs.*

Songs, sea. See *Sea songs.*

Songs, student. See *Student songs.*

Songs, war. See *War songs.*

Songs, wedding. See *Epithalamia.*

Songs, work. See *Work songs.*

Songs and ballads, revolutionary. See *Revolutionary ballads and songs.*

Songsters. See *Political ballads.*

Sons. Son(s). *Choose from:* male *with:* child(ren), offspring, descendant(s). *Consider also:* grandson(s), boy(s). *See also* Males (human); Children; Parent child relationship; Sibling relations; Siblings.

Soothsaying. See *Divination; Oracles.*

Sophistication. Sophisticat(ed,ion). Worldl(y,iness). Savoir faire. Knowledgeable. Experienced. Urban(e,ity). Suave(ness). Tact(ful,fulness). Finesse. *Consider also:* elegan(t,ce), stylish(ness), gracious(ness), good taste, tasteful(ness), decorum, poise(d). *See also* Catholic (universality); Civilized; Cosmopolitan; Elegance; Experience (background); Styles.

Sophistry. See *Casuistry; Deception; Fallacies.*

Sophrosyne. See *Temperance.*

Sorcery. See *Voodooism; Witchcraft.*

Sorcery trials. See *Witchcraft trials.*

Sororities. Sororit(y,ies). Greek letter societ(y,ies). Greek organization(s). Greek membership. Fraternal organization(s). Greek system. *Consider also:* sisterhood(s), fraternit(y,ies). *See also* Associations (organizations); Clubs; Fraternities; School clubs; Societies (organizations).

Sorrow. See *Grief.*

Soteriology. See *Salvation.*

Soul. Soul(s). Essence. Spirit. Vital spirit. Animating spirit. Psyche. Ego. Heart of the matter. Courage. Heroism. Idealism. Breath of life. Atman. *Choose from:* essential, immortal, inner, true, divine *with:* nature, self, spirit, spark. *Consider also:* pneuma, vital force. *See also* Animal nature of man; Animism; Attitudes toward death; Death; Death rituals; Essence; Essence (philosophy); Ghosts; Immortality; Mind; Personality; Philosophical anthropology; Pneuma; Religious beliefs; Salvation; Spirit possession; Spirits.

Soul music. Soul music. *Consider also:* soul jazz, Ray Charles, James Brown, Aretha Franklin, Stevie Wonder, Otis Redding, etc. *See also* Afro-American music; Gospel music.

Sound localization. Sound localization. *Choose from:* sound(s), noise(s), auditory *with:* localiz(e,ed,ing,ation), position(ed,ing), orientation, estimat(e,ed,ing,ion) distance(s), estimat(e,ed,ing,ion) direction. *See also* Auditory perception; Noise (sounds); Perceptual stimulation; Sensory feedback.

Sound perception. See *Auditory perception.*

Sound symbolism. See *Onomatopoeia.*

Sound systems, high fidelity. See *High fidelity sound systems.*

Sounds (noise). See *Noise (sounds).*

Sounds, nature. See *Nature sounds.*

Source identification, news. See *Attribution of news.*

Sources. Source(s). Origin(s,ation,ator, ators). Provenience. Provenance. Genesis. Beginning(s). Root(s,age, stock). Derivation(s). *Consider also:* fount(s,ain,ainhead), inception(s), well(s,head,spring,springs), birthplace(s), author(s,ed,ship), antecedent(s), determinant(s). *See also* Causality; Evidence.

Sources, light. See *Light sources.*

Souterrains. Souterrain(s). Fogous. Pictish house(s). *Choose from:* underground, below ground *with:* chamber(s), pit(s), depositor(y,ies), silo(s), passage(s,way, ways), storage cellar(s). *See also* Archaeology; Prehistoric people; Primitive architecture.

South America. South America(n). Argentin(a,ian). Bolivia(n). Brazil(ian). Chile(an). Colombia(n). Ecuador(ian). Guyan(a,ese) [British Guiana]. Paraguay(an). Peru(vian). Surinam(e, ese) [Dutch Guiana, Netherlands Guiana, Netherlands New Guinea, Dutch New Guinea]. Uruguay(an). Venezuela(n). *Consider also:* French Guian(a,ese,an), South Georgia(n), Falkland Islands [Islas Malvinas]. *See also* Andean-Equatorial languages; Caribbean; Central America; Central American native cultural groups; GE-Pano-Carib languages; Latin Americans; Macro-Chibchan languages; South American native cultural groups.

South American Indians. See *South American native cultural groups.*

South American native cultural groups. South American cultural group(s). South American Indian(s). South American Amerind(s). *Consider combining names of countries:* Argentin(a,ian) Bolivia(n), Brazil(ian), Chile(an), Colombia(n), Ecuador(ian), Guyan(a,ese), Paraguay(an), Peru(vian), Surinam(e,ese), Uruguay(an), Venezuela(n) *with:* Indian(s), native(s), indigenous, Native American(s), Mestizo(s). *Consider names of specific groups, for example:* Alacaluf, Arawak, Aymara, Araucanian, Baniwa, Carib, Cayapo, Chibcha, Chimu, Colorado, Guarani, Incas, Jivaro, Kanamari, Kraho, Makiritare, Mapuche, Mochica, Motilones, Nazca, Ona, Panoa, Piaroa, Paracana, Pauo, Puelches, Quechua, Shirishana, Tehuelches, Ticuna, Terena, Trio, Tupi guarani, Waorani, Warao,

Xavante, Yahgan, Yanomama. *See also* Andean-Equatorial languages; Cargo systems; Central American native cultural groups; Cultural groups; Culture (anthropology); Culture change; Culture contact; Eskimo-Aleut languages; Ethnic groups; GE-Pano-Carib languages; Hunting and gathering societies; Indigenous populations; Macro-Chibchan languages; North American native cultural groups; Pre-Columbian empires; South America; Traditional societies.

South Asia. South Asia(n). Bangladesh(i) [East Pakistan(i)]. Bhutan(ese). India(n). Nepal(ese,i). (Islamic Republic of) Pakistan(i) [West Pakistan(i)]. Sri Lanka(n) [Ceylon(ese)]. *Consider also:* (Republic of) Maldives, British Indian Ocean Territory. *See also* Central Asia; Dravidian languages; Far East; Indian (India) cultural groups; Indo-Iranian languages; Indonesian cultural groups; Middle East; Southeast Asia; Southeast Asian cultural groups.

Southeast Asia. Southeast Asia(n). Indochin(a,ese). Union of Myanmar [Burm(a,ese)]. (Republic of) Indonesia(n) [Netherlands East Indies, Dutch East Indies]. Kampuchea(n) [Cambodia(n), French Indochin(a,ese), Cochin-China, Cochin-Chine]. Lao(s,tian) [French Indochin(a,ese), Cochin-China, Cochin-Chine]. Malaysia(n). Papua New Guinea(n). (Republic of the) Philippine(s). Singapore(an). Thai(s,land) [Siam(ese)]. (Socialist Republic of) Vietnam(ese) [North Vietnam(ese), South Vietnam(ese), French Indochin(a,ese), Cochin-China, Cochin-Chine]. (Republic of) the Philippines [Philippine Islands]. *Consider also:* Malay Archipelago, Malay Peninsula, Peninsular Malaysia, Malaya, Borneo, Brunei (Darussalam), Sabah, Sarawak, Pacific Rim. *See also* Annamese-Muong languages; Far East; Indonesian cultural groups; Malayo-Polynesian languages; Mon-Khmer languages; Oceania; Pacific region; Philippine Islands cultural groups; Sino-Thai languages; South Asia; Southeast Asian cultural groups; Tibeto-Burman languages.

Southeast Asian cultural groups. Southeast Asia(n) cultural group(s). Indochin(a,ese). Mon-Khmer. *Choose from:* Indo-Chin(a,ese), Union of Myanmar [Burm(a,ese)], Kampuchea(n) [Cambodia(n), French Indochin(a,ese), Cochin-China, Cochin-Chine]; Lao(s,tian) [French Indochin(a,ese), Cochin-China, Cochin-Chine]; Malaysia(n), Singapore(an), Thai(s,land) [Siam(ese)], (Socialist Republic of) Vietnam(ese) [North Vietnam(ese), South Vietnam(ese), French Indochin(a,ese), Cochin-China, Cochin-Chine], Malay(a,an), Malaysia(n),

Tonkin(ese) *with:* indigenous, native(s), population(s), people, ethnic group(s), minority group(s), populace, tribe(s), resident(s), inhabitant(s). Burma, *Consider also:* names of specific groups, for example: Chin, Kachin, Karen, Lahu, Mergui, Mon, Palaung, Shan, Wa. Thailand, *consider also names of specific groups, for example*: Akha, Chaobon, Chaonam, Haw, Karen, Khon Muang [Lannathai, Phuthai, Thai Isan, Yuon], Khmu, Lahu, Lawa, Lisu, Miao [Meo], Mon, Pattani Malays, Thai Islam, Thai Malay, T'in, Yao, Yumbri [Mrabri, Phi Tong Luang, Ma Ku]. Indochina, *consider also names of specific groups, for example:* A'dham, Arap, Alak, Alakong, Bahnar, Bla, Blo, Bohnam, Brao, Bru, Budip, Budeh, Bulach, Bulo, Chaobon, Chong, Chrau, Churu, Cua [Khua], Epan, Golar, Habau, Halang, Ho Drong, Hodrung, Hre, Hroy [Bahnar Chams], H'wing, Jeh, Jre, Jo Long, Kasseng, Katang, Katu, Kayong, K'drao, Khmu, Koho, Kpa, Kui, Lamet, Loven, Ma, M'dur, Moi-Kha, Mon-Khmer, Monom, Mnong, Muong, Mru, Nha-Heun, Ngeh, Oy, Pacoh, Pear, Phnong [Pnong], Raglai, Rengao, Rhade, Roh, Saoch, Sedang, Sesan, So, Stieng, Tau-Oi, Tolo, To Sung. Malaya, *consider also names of specific groups, for example:* Jakun, Malays, Orang laut, Sakai, Semang, Senoi, Sea Gypsies. General area, *consider also names of specific groups, for example:* Black Thai, Chuang, Dioi (Chung-chia), Garo, Khasi, Mon, Moi-Kha, Nhang, Nicobarese, Nung, Puthai, Red-Thai, Sakai, Tho, Shan-Thai, Tung, White Thai. *See also* Annamese-Muong languages; Far East; Indian (India) cultural groups; Indonesian cultural groups; Malayo-Polynesian languages.; Mon-Khmer languages; Oceania; Oceanic cultural groups; Philippine Islands cultural groups; Sino-Thai languages; South Asia; Southeast Asia; Tibeto-Burman languages.

Sovereignty. Sovereign(ty). Suzerain(ty). Overlord(s). Kingship. Preeminen(t,ce). Supreme power. Royal supremacy. Supremacy of the king. *Consider also:* ascendan(t,cy), dominan(t,ce), dominat(ing,ion), dominion, master(ship,dom), prepoten(t,ce,cy), seignority. *See also* Autonomy (government); Divine right of kings; Monarchy; Political self determination; Popular sovereignty; Royal supremacy.

Sovereignty, popular. See *Popular sovereignty.*

Space, extraterrestrial. See *Extraterrestrial space.*

Space, life. See *Life space.*

Space, outer. See *Extraterrestrial space.*

Space, personal. See *Personal space.*

Space, work. See *Working space.*

Space, working. See *Working space.*

Space exploration. Space explor(e,ed,ing,ation). Sealed cabin ecology. Weightlessness. Spaceflight. Spaceship. Biosputnik. Sputnik. Soyuz. Cosmos. Salyut. Kosmos. Challenger. Spacelab. Space medicine. Biosatellite(s). Space biology. Space station. Spacecraft. Space technology. Spacefaring. Cosmonaut(s). Astronaut(s). Trip(s) to the moon. Voyager. Apollo mission(s). Space program. *Choose from:* space, extraterrestrial, planetary, interplanetary, lunar *with:* explor(e,ed,ation), flight(s), travel, mission(s), expedition(s), probe(s), shuttle(s), satellite(s). *See also* Aerospace industries; Aerospace medicine; Aerospace personnel; Astronauts; Interplanetary voyages; Plurality of worlds; Space law; Terraforming.

Space flight. See *Space exploration.*

Space law. Space law(s). *Choose from:* extraterrestrial, satellite(s), spaceflight, spacecraft, spaceship(s), space station(s), space based, space shuttle(s), space colon(y,ies,ization), outer space, outerspace, planet(s,ary), lunar, mar(s,tian), interplanetary, astrobusiness, geostationary, SDI, strategic defense initiative(s) *with:* law(s), legal(ity,ities), treat(y,ies), convention(s), agreement(s), regulation(s), sovereign(ty), property right(s), human right(s). *See also* Law (legal philosophy and theory); Space exploration.

Space perception. Space perception. *Choose from:* spatial, space(s), visuospatial, depth, distance(s), form(s), pattern(s), stereoscopic, size(s) *with:* abilit(y,ies), percept(ion,ual), perceiv(e, ed,ing), recognition, discriminat(e,ed, ing,ion), distort(ed,ing,ion), sense. *See also* Depth perception; Spatial ability.

Space stations. Space station(s). Space colon(y,ies,ization). Geostationary. Space based. Manned mission(s). *Choose from:* space, extraterrestrial, outerspace, orbit(s,ed,ing) *with:* satellite(s), station(s), industrial facilit(y,ies), construction, commercializ(e,ed,ing,ation). *Consider also:* spacecraft, spaceship(s), astrobusiness. *See also* Astronauts; Space exploration; Space law; Space suits; Spacecraft.

Space suits. Space suit(s). Spacesuit(s). Anti-g suit(s). Adeli-92. Extravehicular space suit(s). Entry suit(s). Escape suit(s). *Choose from:* space, astronaut(s), extravehicular, pressurized *with:* clothing, glove(s), suit(s). *See also* Astronauts; Clothing; Space stations.

Space technology. See *Space exploration; Spacecraft.*

Space time clustering. Space time cluster(s,ing). Time space cluster(s,ing). Temporal spatial cluster(s,ing). Geographic cluster(s). Regional cluster(ed,ing). Cluster(ed,ing) over time. *See also* Time.

Spacecraft. Spacecraft. Space satellite(s). Space technology. Space colon(y,ies). Aerospace technology. Space shuttle(s). Skylab. Aerospace satellite(s). Space vehicle(s). Aerospace vehicle(s). Apollo 11. Challenger. Spacelab. Space station(s). Voyager. Mariner. Mars rover. Mars probe. Vega. Sputnik. Giotto. Re-entry vehicle(s). Galileo mission. Mars mission. Venera. Moon orbiter. Viking. Salyut. Space platform(s). Pathfinder. Sojourner. Rover. *Consider also:* star war(s). *See also* Astronauts; Space exploration; Space law; Space stations.

Spacecraft environment. See *Extraterrestrial environment.*

Spaceflight. See *Space exploration.*

Spaces, open. See *Open spaces.*

Spaces, public. See *Public spaces.*

Spacing, birth. See *Birth intervals.*

Span, attention. See *Attention span.*

Span, life. See *Life expectancy.*

Spanish American literature. See *Latin American literature.*

Spanish Americans. See *Hispanic Americans; Latin Americans.*

Spanish explorers. Spanish explorer(s). *Choose from:* Spanish, *with:* explorer(s), discoverer(s), expedition(s), exploration(s). *Consider also:* Juan Ponce de Leon, Hernando de Soto, etc. *See also* Discoveries (geography); Explorers; Pioneers.

Spanning, boundary. See *Boundary spanning.*

Spare time. See *Leisure time.*

Spasm. Spasm(s). Involuntary muscle contraction(s). Muscle cramp(s). *Consider also:* myoton(ia,ic), trismus, spastic(ity), spasmogenic, vasospas(m, ms,tic,ticity), pylorospasm(s), cardiospasm(s), blepharospasm(s). *See also* Convulsions; Pain; Symptoms.

Spatial ability. Spatial abilit(y,ies). *Choose from:* spatial, visuospatial, directional, locational, orientation *with:* problem solving, abilit(y,ies), judgment, cognition(s), sense, skill(s). *See also* Ability; Cognitive processes; Sensory integration; Space perception; Spatial imagery.

Spatial analysis. See *Spatial organization.*

Spatial behavior. Spatial behavior. Territoriality. Crowding. Proxemics. Body boundar(y,ies). Privacy. Spatialization. Distancing. Proximity.

Spacing. Zon(e,ed,es,ing). Use(s) of space. Body buffer zone(s). Touch(ed,ing). *Choose from:* spatial *with:* behavior, skill(s), learning, memory, orientation, segregation. *See also* Interaction; Personal space; Physical contact; Proxemics; Social contact; Working space.

Spatial distribution. See *Spatial organization.*

Spatial imagery. Spatial image(s,ry). *Choose from:* spatial, space(s), depth, form(s), distance(s), map(s) *with:* image(s,ry), mental representation(s), imagin(e,ed,ing), reasoning, visualiz(e, ed,ing,ation), concept(s). *See also* Cognitive mapping; Imagery; Spatial ability; Spatial memory; Spatial organization.

Spatial memory. Spatial memory. *Choose from:* spatial, space(s), map(s), diagram(s), spatiotemporal, visuospatial, locational *with:* memory, learn(ed,ing), recall, recognition, retention. *See also* Cognitive mapping; Eidetic imagery; Memory; Spatial imagery.

Spatial organization. Spatial organization. Space organization. Spatial analysis. Environmental scale. Spacing. Seating distance. Midline(s). Meridian(s). Boundar(y,ies). Displace(d,ment). Map(ped,ping). Environmental organization. Floorplan(s). Geometric. Spatial arrangement. Rearrangement. Positioning. *Choose from:* spatial, space, territor(y,ial) *with:* organization, analysis, dimension(s), spread, distribution, separation, configuration, parameters, location, context, sequencing, definition(s), utilization, relation(s, ships), position(s), boundar(y,ies), position(s), transformation. *See also* Cognitive mapping; Facility design and construction; Space perception; Spatial imagery.

Spatial perception. See *Space perception.*

Speak, inability to. See *Aphasia; Speech disorders; Speech disturbances.*

Speaking. See *Debate; Eloquence; Lectures and lecturing; Oral communication; Oratory; Preaching; Public speaking; Rhetoric; Vocalization; Voice.*

Speaking, public. See *Public speaking.*

Special education. Special education. *Choose from:* mental(ly) retard(ed, ation), gifted, emotionally disturbed, handicapped, disabilit(y,ies), deaf, blind, impair(ed,ment,ments), learning disabled, special needs *with:* class(es), education, physical education, program(s), curriculum, tutor(ed,ing), school(s,ing). *Consider also:* special school(s,ing), special class(es), remedial education, adapted physical education. *See also* Ability grouping; Access to education; Adapted physical education;

Behavior modification; Disability; Early intervention; Educational placement; Exceptional persons; Gifted; Housebound; Individual needs; Individualized instruction; Intervention; Labeling (of persons); Mainstreaming; Rehabilitation; Remedial education; Special education students; Therapy.

Special education students. Special education student(s). *Choose from:* special education, special needs *with:* student(s), pupil(s). *Consider also:* exceptional, handicapped, disabled, disabilit(y,ies), LD, learning disabilit(y,ies), impair(ed,ment), retard(ed,ation), disorder(ed), disturbed *with:* student(s), pupil(s). *See also* Special education; Students.

Special events and anniversaries. See *Anniversaries and special events.*

Special interest groups. See *Interest groups; Lobbying; Political movements; Women's groups.*

Specialists. Specialist(s). Expert(s). Authorit(y,ies). Consultant(s). Connoisseur(s). Master(s). Professional(s). Scholar(s). *See also* Advisors; Connoisseurs; Consultants; Expert testimony; Experts; Gold collar workers; Professional personnel; Scholars; Specialization.

Specialization. Specializ(e,ed,ing,ation). Specialty choice. Career specialization. *Choose from:* college, academic *with:* specializ(e,ed,ing,ation), major(s,ing), department(s), concentration(s). *Consider also:* domain of knowledge. *See also* Area of knowledge; Aspirations; Complex societies; Complexity; Curriculum; Differences; Division of labor; Occupational choice; Occupations; Particularism; Professional education; Social segmentation; Specialists; Work.

Specialization, academic. See *Specialization.*

Species, endangered. See *Endangered species.*

Species, exotic. See *Exotic species.*

Species, same. See *Conspecific.*

Species specific. See *Conspecific.*

Species differences. Species difference(s). Difference(s) between species. *Consider also:* names of species *with:* "vs" such as gorillas vs macaques, doves vs pigeons, etc. *Choose from:* phyletic, phylogenetic, strain, taxonomic, subspecies, species *with:* differen(t,ce, ces,tials,tiation), divers(e,ity), variation(s), deviation(s), compar(itive, ison,isons,ability), diverg(e,ed,ing,ence), dissimilar(ity,ities), distinct(ion,ions, iveness), variance, variabilit(y,ies), specificity, correlates, factor(s). *See also* Animals; Genetics.

Specific, species. See *Conspecific.*

Specifications, job. See *Job requirements; Personnel specifications.*

Specifications, personnel. See *Personnel specifications.*

Specimens. Specimen(s). Sample(s). Example(s). Exemplar(s). *Consider also:* instance(s), typical case(s), exemplification(s), slide(s), biological culture(s) *See also* Benchmarks; Examples.

Spectator violence. See *Sports violence.*

Spectators. Spectator(s). Audience(s). Observer(s). Viewer(s). Eyewitness(es). Bystander(s). Witness(es). *Consider also:* onlooker(s), watcher(s), sightseer(s), beholder(s), crowd(s). *See also* Athletic participation; Audiences; Groups; Sports fans; Sports violence.

Spectators, sports. See *Sports fans.*

Specters. See *Apparitions; Ghosts.*

Speculation. Speculat(e,ed,ing,ion,or,ors). Speculative purchas(e,es,ing). Risk taking. Tak(e,en,ing) risk(s). *Consider also:* defensive investment(s), letter stock(s), venture capital fund(s), hedging, arbitrage(ur,urs). *See also* Currency speculation; Junk bonds; Land speculation; Risk taking; Speculators; Stock exchange; Stock options.

Speculation, currency. See *Currency speculation.*

Speculation, land. See *Land speculation.*

Speculators. Speculator(s). Day trader(s). *Consider also:* investor(s), gambler(s), play(ed,ing) the market. *See also* Capitalists and financiers; Speculation; Stockholders.

Speech. Speech. Speak(ing,ers). Spoken. Verbal(ly,ize,ized,ization). Voice(s). Pronounce(d). Pronunciation. Phon(etics,ation,ology). Inflection. Utter(ed,ing,ance,ances). Vocal(ize, ized,izing,ization). Inton(e,ed,ate, ation,ational). Articulat(e,ed,ing,ion). Talk(ed,ing). Convers(e,ed,ing,ation). Discourse. Public speaking. Baby talk. Whisper(ed,ing). *Choose from:* verbal, oral *with:* behavior, communication, fluency. *Choose from:* speech *with:* inner, subvocal, compression, intelligib(le,ility), compressed, filtered, characteristics, pause(s), pitch, processing, rate(s), rhythm. *Consider also:* language skills, linguistic(ally,s), lingual, bilingual(ism), monolingual(ism), multilingual(ism), ethnolinguistic(s), dialect(s), gramma(r,tical), word(s), sentence structure, vocabular(y,ies), rhetoric(al), psycholinguistic(s), communicative ability. *See also* Articulation (speech); Direct discourse; Discourse; Fluency; Indirect discourse; Inner speech;

Intonation (phonetics); Language; Language acquisition; Language disorders; Language shift; Language usage; Linguistics; Oral reading; Phonetics; Pronunciation; Public speaking; Rhetoric; Self talk; Speech acts; Speech anxiety; Speech characteristics; Speech development; Speech disturbances; Speech errors; Speech intelligibility; Speech perception; Speech therapy; Verbal ability; Verbal communication.

Speech, articulation. See *Articulation (speech).*

Speech, figures of. See *Figurative language.*

Speech, free. See *Freedom of speech.*

Speech, freedom of. See *Freedom of speech.*

Speech, inability. See *Aphasia; Speech disorders; Speech disturbances.*

Speech, inner. See *Inner speech.*

Speech, loss of. See *Aphasia; Speech disorders; Speech disturbances.*

Speech act theory. Speech act theory. Pragmatics. *Consider also:* illocutionary act(s), performative utterance(s), performativity. *See also* Instrumentalism (philosophy); Intentionality; Philosophy.

Speech acts. Speech act(s). Speech event(s). Illocutionary act(s). Locutionary act(s). Perlocutionary act(s). Utterance(s). *See also* Communication (thought transfer); Discourse analysis; Meaning; Speech; Verbal communication.

Speech anxiety. Speech anxiety. *Choose from:* speech, communication, speaking, telephone(s), talking *with:* anxiety, anxious(ness), apprehens(ion,ive, iveness), inhibition(s), reticence, fear(s,ful). *Consider also:* stage fright. *See also* Anxiety disorders; Communication disorders; Public speaking; Social anxiety; Stage fright.

Speech characteristics. Speech characteristic(s). *Choose from:* speech, fluency, verbal, conversation(s,al), voice(s,d), vocal, utterance(s) *with:* characteristic(s), intelligib(le,ility), accent(s), disfluenc(y,ies), articulation, propert(y,ies), bizarre(ness), qualit(y,ies), style(s), harsh(ness), soft(ness), loud(ness), schizophrenic, stutter(ed,ing), impair(ed,ment,ments), disorder(s). *See also* Articulation (speech); Characteristics; Inflection; Intonation (phonetics); Pronunciation; Speech intelligibility.

Speech communities. Speech communit(y, ies). Language communit(y,ies). Linguistic communit(y,ies). Common mother tongue. Shared linguistic system(s). *Consider also:* language regime(s), dialect speaker(s). *See also*

Areal linguistics; Cultural identity; Creoles; Dialects; Ethnic groups; Ethnolinguistics; Language maintenance; Languages in contact; Linguistic geography; Linguistic minorities; Nationalism; Sociolinguistics.

Speech development. Speech development. *Choose from:* speech, babbling, vowel(s), fluency, language, verbal, conversation(s,al), phonological, grammar, grammatical, articulation, pronunciation *with:* development(al), acquisition, learn(ed,ing), emergence. *See also* Cognitive development; Language development; Motor development; Physical development; Psychogenesis; Psychomotor development; Retarded speech development.

Speech development, retarded. See *Retarded speech development.*

Speech disorders. Speech disorder(s). *Choose from:* speech, speaking, verbal, voice, velopharyngeal, neurolinguistic, phonological *with:* disorder(s,ed), deficit(s), impair(ed,ment,ments), impediment(s), retard(ed,ation), deficienc(y,ies), dysarthr(ia,ic), dysprax(ia,ic), aprax(ia,ic), dysfunction(s,al), disabled, disabilit(y,ies), handicap(ped,s), delayed, disturbance(s), problem(s), insufficien(t,cies), difficult(y,ies), anomal(y,ies). *Consider also:* aglossia, dyslalia, allolaia, alalia, palilalia, alogia, misarticulation, hypernasality, disfluen(t,cy), cleft palate(s), delayed speech, stuttering, anomia, aphasia, mutism, dysphonia, speechless(ness), esophageal speech, tracheoesophageal speech, alaryngeal speech, cleft palate. *See also* Apraxia; Articulation disorders; Cleft palate; Communication disorders; Dysarthria; Language disorders; Mutism; Retarded speech development; Speech therapy; Stuttering; Voice disorders.

Speech disturbances. Speech disturbance(s). *Consider also:* aboiement, acataphas(ia,ic), akataphas(ia,ic), agitophas(ia,ic), agitolalia, syntactical aphasia, agramma(tism,ta,taphasia, tologia), agrammalogia, aphas(ia,ic), aphras(ia,ic), acalcul(ia,ic), dyssymbol(y,ia). *See also* Aphasia; Communication disorders; Schizophrenic language; Speech disorders.

Speech errors. Speech error(s). Freudian slip(s). Slip(s) of the tongue. Paraprax(is,es,ia,ias). *Consider also:* disordered phonology, speech disfluenc(y,ies), speech fragmentation. *See also* Errors; Faux pas; Linguistic interference; Psycholinguistics; Speech.

Speech events. See *Speech acts.*

Speech handicapped. See *Speech disorders.*

Speech intelligibility. Speech intelligibility. *Choose from:* speech, speaker(s), sound(s) *with:* intelligib(le,ility), understandab(le,ility). *See also* Articulation (speech); Articulation disorders; Pronunciation; Speech characteristics.

Speech perception. Speech perception. *Choose from:* speech, linguistic, spoken word(s) *with:* perception, discriminat(e,ed,ing,ion), recognition, comprehension. *See also* Auditory perception; Lipreading; Word recognition.

Speech therapy. Speech therapy. *Choose from:* speech, articulation, voice, stuttering *with:* therap(y,ies), remediation. *Consider also:* speech training. *See also* Communication disorders; Speech disorders; Treatment.

Speeches (formal discourse). Speech(es). Address(es). Acceptance speech(es). Benediction(s). Formal discourse(s). Allocution. Lecture(s). Oration(s). Valedictory address(es). Closing words. Introduction(s). Narration(s). Sermon(s). After dinner speech(es). *See also* Eulogies; Last words; Lectures and lecturing; Oratory; Political rhetoric; Public speaking; Rhetoric; Tribute.

Speeches, dedications. See *Commemoration.*

Speed, acceleration. See *Acceleration (speed).*

Speed, hurry. See *Hurry (speed).*

Spells. See *Incantation; Magic; Spirit possession; Voodooism.*

Spending, consumer. See *Consumer expenditures.*

Spending, defense. See *Defense spending.*

Spending, defense. See *Defense spending*

Spending, government. See *Government expenditures.*

Sperm banks. Sperm bank(s,ing). Cryosperm bank(s,ing). *Consider also:* sperm *with:* stor(e,ed,age,ing), preserv(e,ed,ing,ation). *See also* Fertilization in vitro; Reproductive technologies; Tissue banks.

Sphere, private. See *Private sphere.*

Sphere, public. See *Public sphere.*

Spheres of influence. Sphere(s) of influence. Sphere(s) of hegemony. Bloc(s). *Consider also:* superpower dominance, satellite countr(y,ies), puppet state(s), colonial expansion, Monroe Doctrine, containment, domino theory, Eisenhower Doctrine, satrap(y,s). *See also* Balance of power; Borderlands; Center and periphery; Colonialism; Cultural imperialism; Dependency theory (international); Dominance; Geopolitics; Hegemony; Imperialism; International alliances; Lobbying.

Spider phobia. Spider phobia(s). Arachneophob(ia,ic). Arachnophob(ia, ic). *Consider also:* acarophob(ia,ic). *See also* Phobias.

Spiderbites. Spiderbite(s). Arachnidism. Spider bite(s). Loxoscelism. Tarantism. *Choose from:* spider(s), scorpion(s), black widow(s), loxosceles reclusa, *with:* bite(s), bitten, sting(s), stung, envenomation. *See also* Insect bites and stings.

Spies. See *Espionage*.

Spills, oil. See *Oil spills*.

Spills, waste. See *Waste spills*.

Spin doctors. Spin doctor(s,ing). Spindoctor(s,ing). Spin control master(s). Media consultant(s). *Consider also:* public relations personnel, public relations official(s), spokesperson(s), press secretar(y,ies). *See also* Manipulation; Press agents; Promoters; Public relations; Spokespersons.

Spinal cord injuries. Spinal cord injur(y,ies). *Choose from:* spinal cord, cervical spine, vertebra(e) *with:* injur(y,ies,ed), trauma(tic), shock(s), compression. *See also* Nervous system; Paraplegia.

Spinoffs. Spinoff(s). Spin-off(s). Spun off. Outgrowth. By-product(s). Derivative(s). Descendant(s). Offshoot(s). *Consider also:* subsidiar(y,ies), branch(es). *See also* Consequences; Sequelae; Subsidiaries.

Spinster. See *Single person*.

Spirit. See *Awareness; Conscious (awake); Enthusiasm; Morale; Pneuma; Soul*.

Spirit, communal. See *Community feeling*.

Spirit possession. Spirit(ual,s) possession. Possession cult(s). Black magic. Tarantism. Candomble. Jinetigi. Demon(ic) possession. Religious possession. Voodooism. *Choose from:* spirit(s), sprite(s), apparition(s), fair(y,ies), elves, elf, pixie(s), leprechaun(s), gnome(s), ghost(s), genie(s), jinni, dybbuk(s), dibbuk(s), supernatural being(s), daemon(s), demon(s) *with:* possess(ed,ion), enchant(ed,ing,ment,ments), spell(s), trance(s). *See also* Devils; Demons; Elves; Evil; Evil eye; Fairies; Folk literature; Folklore; Ghosts; Good spirits; Trance; Witchcraft.

Spirits. Spirit(s). Sprite(s). Apparition(s). Fair(y,ies). Elves. Elf. Imp(s). Pixie(s). Leprechaun(s). Gnome(s). ghost(s). Genie(s). Hobgoblin(s). Jinn(i,s). Djin(n,ni). Dibbuk(s). Dybbuk(s). Supernatural being(s). Daemon(s). Demon(s). Phantom(s). Ghoul(s). Spook(s). Angel(s). Banshee(s). Specter(s). Succub(a,ae,i,us). *See also* Ancestor worship; Animism; Demons;

Devils; Ghosts; Soul; Spirit possession; Spiritualism; Succubus; Supernatural; Water spirits.

Spirits, evil. See *Devils*.

Spirits , good. See *Good spirits*.

Spirits, water. See *Water spirits*.

Spiritual direction. Spiritual direction. *Choose from:* spiritual(ity), Biblical, religious *with:* direction(s), study, teaching(s), authority, guidance, advice, advisor(s), authority, focus, mentor(s,ed,ing). *Consider also:* spiritual teacher(s), guru(s), pastoral counsel(or,ors,ing). *See also* Clergy; Guru; Mentors; Moral authority; Spiritual formation; Spirituality; Wise person.

Spiritual exercises. Spirit(ual) exercise(s). Spiritual pursuit(s). Meditat(e,ed,ing, ion). Purif(y,ied,ication). Sattvification of consciousness. Pray(ed,ing,er,ers). *Choose from:* remold(ed,ing), reshap(e,ed,ing), restructur(e,ed,ing), transform(ed,ing,ation), disciplin(e,ed, ing) *with:* spirit(s,ual,ually), mental process(es), mind, conscious(ly,ness), soul(s). *Consider also:* spiritual growth, attend(ed,ing) religious service(s), religious exercise(s), program(s) for spiritual awareness, affirmation(s), kything. *See also* Enlightenment (state of mind); Meditation; Prayer; Religious education; Religious experience; Rejuvenation; Repentence; Sacred places; Salvation; Self actualization; Spiritual formation.

Spiritual formation. Spirit(ual) form(ed, ing,ation). Spiritual growth. Evok(e, ed,ing) the spirit. *Choose from:* nourish(ed,ing,ment), grow(th), develop(ed,ing,ment), form(ed,ing, ation,ative), foster(ed,ing), awaken(ed, ing), regenerat(e,ed,ing,ion) *with:* spirit(uality), virtuous(ness), righteous(ness). *See also* Enlightenment (state of mind); Inspiration; Moral development; Redemption (theology); Religious education; Religious experience; Salvation; Self actualization; Spiritual direction; Spirituality.

Spiritual gifts. Spiritual gift(s). Charism(s,ata). Charismatic touching. Extraordinary power(s). Power of healing. *Choose from:* gift(s), power(s) *with:* spiritual, Christian, Pentecostal(s, ism), Holy Spirit. *Consider also:* spiritual significance, grace of God, gift of tongues, spirit baptism. *See also* Female spirituality; Miracles; Prayer; Religiosity; Religious commitment; Religious fundamentalism; Spirituality.

Spiritual growth. See *Spiritual formation*.

Spiritual healing. Spiritual healing. Faith healing. Spiritual healing. Divine healing. Indigenous heal(ing,ers). Laying on of hands. Messianic healer(s).

Christian Scien(ce,tists). Shaman(s,ism). *Choose from:* divine, faith, ritual, charismatic, spiritual(ist), traditional, totemic, touch, prayer(s), symbolic, magic(al), psychic, shaman(s,istic), cult(s), mental(ly) *with:* heal(ed,ing, er,ers), cure(d,s), curing, restor(e,ed, ing,ation). *Consider also:* divine intervention. *See also* Cultural therapy; Feminist therapy; Healing; Miracles; Religious experience; Religious fundamentalism; Religious practices; Shamanism; Spiritual gifts; Therapeutic cults; Traditional medicine; Witchcraft.

Spiritual life. See *Spirituality*.

Spiritual mentors. See *Clergy; Guru; Mentors; Moral authority; Spiritual direction; Wise person*.

Spiritualism. Spiritualis(m,t,ts). Spiritism. Spirit phenomena. Spirit reading(s). Spirit healing(s). *Choose from:* communication *with:* medium(s), psychic, dead. *See also* Divination; Ghosts; Occultism; Parapsychology; Spirits; Spiritual healing; Supernatural; Superstitions.

Spirituality. Spirituality. Spiritual growth. Spiritually minded. Spiritual life. Pious(ness). Righteous(ness). Saintl(y,iness). Hol(y,iness). Devout(ness). Prayerful. Mindful(ness). Religiosity. Godl(y,iness). *Choose from:* spiritual, religious, contemplative *with:* life, growth, well-being, experience(s), values, direction(s), maturity. *Consider also:* idealis(tic,m), anagogic, uplifting, reveren(cing,tial), pietis(m,t,ts,tic, tically). *See also* Female spirituality; Inspiration; Meditation; Personalism; Personality traits; Piety; Prayer; Religiosity; Religious beliefs; Religious commitment; Religious life; Spiritual direction; Spiritual formation; Spiritual gifts.

Spirituality, female. See *Female spirituality*.

Split personality. See *Multiple personality*.

Spoils system. See *Political patronage*.

Spokespersons. Spokesperson(s). Spokes(man,men,woman,women). Press agent(s). Public relations officer(s). Official representative(s). Surrogate(s). *Consider also:* attorney(s), lawyer(s). *See also* Press agents; Promotion (business); Public relations; Representatives; Spin doctors.

Sponsored housing, government. See *Public housing*.

Sponsorship. Sponsor(s,ed,ing,ship). Patron(s,age). Endors(ing,ed,ement). Recommend(ing,ed,ation). Advoca(cy,tes). Proponent(s). Aegis. Backing. *Consider also:* grant(s), support(ed,ing), fund(s,ing), subsid(y,ies,ization), financ(ed,ing), cosigner(s), ensurer(s), guarantee(s,d). *See also* Assistance; Financial support; Grants; Immigration; Patronage.

Spontaneity. Spontan(city,cous,cousness). Natural(ly,ness). Unaffected. Enthusias(m,tic). Effortless(ly,ness). Zest(y,ful). Uncontrived. Extemporaneous(ly). Impetuous(ly, ness). Direct(ness). Unrehearsed. Unforced. Impulsive(ly,ness). Capricious(ly,ness). Inspir(ed,ation). Unpremeditated. Nonpurposive. Nondeliberate. *Consider also:* reflex action(s). *See also* Ad lib; Brainstorming; Compulsive behavior; Emotional responses; Exploratory behavior; Impetuous; Impulsiveness; Instinct; Intuition; Surprise.

Spontaneous abortions. See *Miscarriages.*

Spontaneous generation. Spontaneous(ly) generat(ed,ion). Spontaneous emergence of life. *Choose from:* life, biological substances *with:* spontaneous(ly) *with:* appear(ed,ing,ance), emergence, arose *Consider also:* origins of life, nascent life, abiotic chemistry, first building blocks of life, protometabolism, synthesis of life. *See also* Creationism; Evolution; Life (biological).

Spontaneous remission. Spontaneous remission. *Choose from:* symptom(s), spontaneous(ly) *with:* arrest(ed), recover(y), remission(s). *Consider also:* episodic disorder(s). *See also* Recovery; Therapy; Treatment.

Sport psychology. Sport psychology. *Choose from:* sport(s), athlet(e,es,ic,ics), sports(women,woman,men,man), basketball player(s), baseball player(s), tennis player(s), wrestler(s), swimmer(s), golfer(s), etc., olympics, coach(es) *with:* psycholog(y,ies,ical), motivat(e,ed,ing,ion), personalit(y,ies), attribution(s), attitude(s), expectanc(y, ies), competitive(ness), psychosocial characteristic(s), stress(es), personal construct(s). *See also* Applied psychology; Challenge; Extreme sports; Sports.

Sports. Sport(s,ing,smanship). Athletic(s). Gymnastic performance(s). Sports(man, woman,men,women). Athlete(s). Olympic(s). *Consider also:* archery, baseball, bodysurfing, bicycling, boardsurfing, boardsailing, bowling, boxing, canoeing, contact sports, cricket, cycling, diving, equestrian, fencing, field hockey, foot races, football, golf(ing), gymnastic(s), handball, high jump, hockey, horseriding, horseback riding, ice skating, jogging, judo, karate, lacrosse, lifting weights, martial arts, mountaineering, mountain climbing, parasail(ing,or,ors), polo, racquetball, racing, rugby, roller skating, racing cars, running, squash, sledding, skateboard, surfing, swimming, skiing, skating, scuba, snowmobile, soccer, softball, squash, track, tennis, tumbling, volleyball, waterskiing, weightlifting, windsurfing, wrestling. *See also* Aeronautical sports; Amateurs; Aquatic sports; Archery; Athletes; Athletic participation; Ball games; Baseball clubs; Bicycle racing; Bicycle touring; Bullfights; Challenge; Cockfighting; Competition; Contests; Duck hunting; Drugs in athletics; Extreme sports; Fowling; Greek and Roman games; Horse sports; Hunting; Leisure activities; Outdoor life; Physical contact; Popular culture; Recreation; School sports; Sport psychology; Sports fans; Sports medicine; Sports violence; Water safety; Winter sports.

Sports, aeronautical. See *Aeronautical sports.*

Sports, aquatic. See *Aquatic sports.*

Sports, doping in. See *Drugs in athletics.*

Sports, extreme. See *Extreme sports.*

Sports, horse. See *Horse sports.*

Sports, school. See *School sports.*

Sports, winter. See *Winter sports.*

Sports fans. Sports fan(s). Sports spectator(s). *Choose from:* sport(s), baseball, football, golf, tennis, soccer, olympics *with:* fan(s), spectator(s), viewer(s), crowd(s), enthusiast(s), supporter(s), addict(s), regulars, devotee(s), watcher(s), buff(s). *See also* Audiences; Fans (persons); Spectators; Sports; Viewers.

Sports medicine. Sports medicine. *Choose from:* sport(s), athletic(s), athlete(s), badminton, baseball, basketball, bicycl(e,es,ed,ing,ist,ists), big league(s), boating, bowl(er,ers,ing), boxing, cricket, cycl(e,ed,ing,ist,ists), div(e,ed, ing,er,ers), football, golf, gymnast(s,ic), handball, hang glid(e,ing,er,ers), hockey, horseback riding, jockey(s), jog(ging, ger,gers), karate, little league(s), mountain climbing, oars(man,men), parachut(e,es,ist,ists), pole vault(ed,ing, er,ers), pugilistic, racketball, racquetball, racecourse(s), racehorse(s), rac(ed,ing), rowing, rugby, run(ning,ner,ners), scuba, ski(ed,ing,er,ers), snowmobile(s), soccer, spelunk(ing,ed,er,ers), sprint(ed,ing,er, ers), swim(ming,mer,mers), tennis, track and field, weight lift(ed,ing,er,ers), wrestl(ed,ing,er,ers) *with:* accident(s,al), back problem(s), cardiac, cardiovascular, concussion(s), diet(s,etic), disease(s), disorder(s), dop(e,ed,ing), drug(s), endurance, energy, exhaust(ed,ion), fatalit(y,ies), first aid, fracture(s), hearing loss(es), heat stroke(s), health(y,iness), heart rate, hernia(s), hypertens(ive,ion), injur(y,ies,ed), lesion(s), loss of sight, medical, medicine, nutrition(al), orthopedic, physician(s), physiolog(y,ical), ruptur(e,ed,es,ing), safety, sick(ness), sprain(ed,ing,s), strain(ed,s), stress(es), therap(y,ies,eutic), trauma(s,tic), treat(ed,ing,ment), weight gain(s), weight loss(es). *Consider also:* bowlers thumb, tennis elbow, tennis leg, swimming pool ear, swimmers nose. *See also* Athletes; Athletic participation; Exercise; Injuries; Medical care; Physical education; Physical fitness; Physical therapy; Preventive medicine; Sport psychology.

Sports participation. See *Athletic participation.*

Sports spectators. See *Sports fans.*

Sports violence. Sports violen(t,ce). *Choose from:* spectator(s), crowd(s), audience(s), fan(s), mob(s), soccer, football, hockey *with:* mob(bed,bing), riot(s,ed,ing), disorder, hooligan(s,ism), aggressive(ness), aggressive behavior, assault(ed,ing), beat(ing,en), danger- ous(ness), knifing(s), switchblade(s), fighting, gang wars, vandal(s,ize,ism), loot(ed,ing), destruct(ion,ive), injur(e,ing), harm(ed,ing), disorderly, drunk(enness). *See also* Extreme sports; Mass media violence; School violence; Spectators; Sports; Violence.

Sportsmanship. See *Fairness.*

Sportsmen. See *Athletes.*

Sportswomen. See *Athletes.*

Spouse, death of. See *Widowhood.*

Spouse abuse. Spouse abuse. Conjugal crime. Wifebeating. Family violence. Domestic violence. Husband abuse. Abusive husbands. Marital rape. *Choose from:* spouse(s), women, wife, wives, conjugal, husband(s), home, famil(y,ies), domestic, mother(s), mate(s), marital *with:* abuse(d,rs), abusive, battered, battering, beating, assault(ed,ing), rape, crime(s), violen(t,ce), stress, crisis, victim(ization), verbal abuse, mental cruelty. *See also* Battered women; Child abuse; Cruelty; Elder abuse; Family violence; Husbands; Jealousy; Marital rape; Marriage; Possessiveness; Sexual abuse; Sexual violence; Wives.

Spouse rape. See *Marital rape.*

Spouses. Spouse(s). Wife. Wives. Conjugal. Husband(s). Mate(s). Marital. Marriage partner(s). Groom(s). Bride(s). Bridegroom(s). Consort(s). Nupturient(s). *Choose from:* married, wed(ded), marital *with:* people, person(s), man, men, woman, women, female(s), male(s), couple(s), partner(s). *See also* Authors' spouses; Couples; Divorce; Family; Family life; Family members; Homemakers; Housewives; Human mate selection; Husbands; Kinship; Marital relationship; Marriage; Married students; Parents; Significant others; Widowhood; Wives.

Spouses, authors'. See *Authors' spouses.*

Spouses, corporate. See *Corporate spouses.*

Spouses, former. See *Former spouses.*

Spouses, military. See *Military families.*

Sprawl, urban. See *Urban sprawl.*

Spread, language. See *Language spread.*

Spying. See *Electronic espionage; Espionage; Industrial espionage; Intelligence service.*

Squad, death. See *Death squad.*

Squatters. Squatt(ers,ing). Trespasser(s). Illegal shantytown(s). Living in unoccupied house(s). Occupy(ing) vacant building(s). Spontaneous settlement(s). Spontaneous shelter. Shantytown(s). Illegally settled. Tent town(s). Cardboard camp(s). Unauthorized housing. Informal land acquisition. *Consider also:* barriad(s,a) gecekondus, favela(s), displaced person(s), homeless(ness). *See also* De facto; Homeless; Homeless shelters; Homesteading; Housing; Land settlement; Occupancy.

Stabbing. Stab(bed,bing). Knifing. *Choose from:* knife, knives, machete(s), switchblade(s), bayonet(s) *with:* slash(ed,ing), wound(s,ed,ing), attack(ed,s,ing), impal(ed,ing), slit, cut(s), thrust(ing). *See also* Violence.

Stability. Stab(ility,le). Abiding. Balanced. Calm(ness). Changeless. Continuity. Dependab(le,ility). Durab(le,ility). Endur(ing,ance). Even temper(ed, ament). Easygoing. Equanimity. Equilibrium. Firm(ness). Fixed. Guarantee(s,d). Immob(le,ility). Immun(e,ity). Immutab(le,ility). Impregnab(le,ility). Invulnerab(ility,le). Permanen(t,ce). Preserv(e,ed,ation). Reliab(le,ility). Resilien(t,ce). Secur(e,ed,ity). Steadfast. Stead(y,iness). Solid(ity,ness). Impassive. Unchanging. Unmoved. Unexcitable. Unflappable. Uninterrupted. Unperturbed. Unvarying. Unswerving. Unyielding. *See also* Change; Control; Cooptation; Durability; Economic stability; Emotional stability; Family stability; Instability; Permanent; Power sharing; Relations; Security; Social equilibrium; Uniformity.

Stability, economic. See *Economic stability.*

Stability, emotional. See *Emotional stability.*

Stability, family. See *Family stability.*

Stability, political. See *Political stability.*

Stability, social. See *Social stability.*

Stabilization, economic. See *Economic stabilization.*

Staff. See *Personnel.*

Staff, dismissal of. See *Dismissal of staff.*

Staff, hospital. See *Allied health personnel; Health occupations; Medical staff; Nursing staff; Physicians.*

Staff, medical. See *Medical staff.*

Staff, nursing. See *Nursing staff.*

Staff, support. See *Support staff.*

Staff development. Staff development. *Choose from:* staff, faculty, personnel, employee(s), worker(s), inservice, on-the-job *with:* develop(ed,ing,ment), train(ed,ing), improv(e,ed,ing,ement), continuing education, growth, refresher(s), orientation, upgrad(e,ed, ing). *See also* Continuing education; Faculty development; Inservice teacher education; Inservice training; Organizational development; Personnel training; Professional development.

Stage, anal. See *Anal stage.*

Stage, oral. See *Oral stage.*

Stage, phallic. See *Phallic stage.*

Stage, world as a. See *Theatrum Mundi.*

Stage band. See *Big band.*

Stage design. Stage design. *Choose from:* stage *with:* design(s,ed,ing,er,ers). *Consider also:* stage *with:* setting(s), scenery, scene painting, lighting, machinery, props. *See also* Theater.

Stage fright. Stage fright. Stage jitters. Speech anxiety. Speech fright. Speechphobic. *Choose from:* stage, public speaking, speech(es), communication *with:* anxiety, fright(en,ened,ening), fear, phobi(a,c), apprehens(ion,ive). *See also* Anxiety; Anxiety disorders; Performance anxiety; Speech anxiety.

Stage of life. See *Theatrum mundi.*

Stage transitions, life. See *Life stage transitions.*

Stages, developmental. See *Developmental stages.*

Stages, life. See *Ages of man; Human life cycle; Life cycle; Life stage transitions.*

Stages, sleep. See *Sleep stages.*

Staining and painting, glass. See *Glass painting and staining.*

Stains, blood. See *Blood stains.*

Stalking. Stalk(ed,ing,er,ers). Obsessional follow(ing,er,ers). Cyberstalk(ed,ing,er, ers). *Choose from:* trail(ed,ing), surveillance, spy(ing), follow(ed,ing) *with:* victim(s), women, woman, men, man. *Choose from:* harass(ed,ing,ment), threaten(ed,ing), unwanted, menacing *with:* incident(s), approach(es), phone call(s), mail, communication(s), letter(s), electronic mail. *See also* Battered women; Erotomania; Family violence; Obsessive love; Online harassment; Sexual harassment; Street harassment; Victimization.

Stammering. See *Stuttering.*

Stamp collecting. See *Philately.*

Stand trial, competency to. See *Competency to stand trial.*

Standard, classic. See *Classic (standard).*

Standard, gold. See *Gold standard.*

Standard of living. See *Living standards.*

Standards. Standard(s,ize,ized,izing, ization). Specification(s). Norm(s,ative). Normal value(s). Criterion referenced measure(s). Index(es). Criteria. Principle(s). Model(s). Pattern(s). Exemplar(y). Prototype(s). Rule(s). Principle(s). Guideline(s). Yardstick(s). Gauge(s). Benchmark(s). *See also* Academic standards; Accreditation; Achievement; Benchmarks; Certification; Criteria; Credentialing; Eligibility determination; Ethics; Evaluation; Excellence; Failure; Labor standards; Laws; Living standards; Measurement; Models; Norms; Perfection; Performance standards; Principles; Professional standards; Qualifications; Quality control; Quotas; Residence requirements; Requirements; Success; Tests; Validity; Values.

Standards, academic. See *Academic standards.*

Standards, accounting. See *Accounting standards.*

Standards, labor. See *Labor standards.*

Standards, living. See *Living standards.*

Standards, performance. See *Performance standards.*

Standards, professional. See *Professional standards.*

Stanzas. Stanza(s,ic). Stanzaic composition. Stanzaic verse. Verse paragraph(s). *Consider also:* strophe(s), stave(s), *See also* Meter (poetry); Poetry; Prosody; Songs.

Staple products. See *Raw materials.*

Start up business. Start up business(es). Startup(s). *Choose from:* start(ed, ing,up), launch(ed,es,ing), open(ed,ing), found(ed,ing), creat(e,ed,ing,ion), establish(ed,ing), new, venture capital, emerging *with:* business(es), restaurant(s), compan(y,ies), firm(s). *Consider also:* initial public offering(s), enter(ed,ing) market(s), new franchise(s), business plan(s). *See also* Business incubators; Creators; Entrepreneurship; Founding; Small businesses; Venture capital.

Startle reaction. Startle reaction(s). *Choose from:* startl(e,ed) *with:* reaction(s), reflex(es), response(s), reactiv(e,ity), stimuli, effect(s), respond(ed,ing), elicit(e,ed,ing), induc(e,ed,ing, ement, ements), blink(s,ed,ing), eyeblink(s). *See also* Alarm responses; Reflex.

Starvation. Starv(e,ed,ing,ation). Famine(s). Food shortage(s). Hung(er, ering,ry,riness). Malnourish(ed,ment). Malnutrition. Protein deficien(cy,t). Vitamin deficien(cy,t). Calorie deficien(t,cy). Inadequate diet. Lack of food. Poor diet. Semistarv(ed,ing,ation). Scarce food. Undernourish(ed,ment). Undernutrition. Food deprivation. Feed restriction. Food deprived. Restricted food. Restricted calories. Food scarcity. Famish(ed,ment). *Consider also:* hunger strike(s). *See also* Famine; Hunger, food deprivation; Hunger strikes; Malnutrition; Suffering.

State (national). See *Countries.*

State, adult ego. See *Emotional maturity.*

State, Corporate. See *Corporate state.*

State, heads of. See *Heads of state.*

State, individual and the. See *Individual and the state.*

State, vegetative. See *Vegetative state.*

State, welfare. See *Welfare state.*

State aid. See *Government aid.*

State capitalism. State capitalism. State monopoly capitalism. *Consider also:* state, federal, government, public *with:* intervention, investment(s), subsidiz(ed,ing,ation), regulat(ed,ing, ion), enterprise(s). *Consider also:* post-capitalism, nationalization, state ownership *with:* market econom(y,ies). *See also* Capitalism; Government regulation; Government subsidization; Welfare state.

State church relationship. See *Church state relationship.*

State dependent learning. State dependent learning. *Choose from:* state dependent, drug effect(s), drugged, alcohol, intoxicat(e,ed,ing,ion) *with:* learn(ed, ing), memory, retention, memory deficit(s), recognition, recall(ed,ing), acquisition. *See also* Learning.

State employees. See *Civil service; Government personnel.*

State farms. See *Agricultural collectives.*

State finances. See *Government finances.*

State government. State government(s). *Consider also:* California, Vermont, etc. *with:* govern(ed,ing,ment,ments,mental), legislature(s), governor(s), assembl(y, ies), senate(s), senator(s), representative(s), commission(s), department(s), agenc(y,ies), elected official(s), bureaucrac(y,ies). *See also* Governors; Government; Government personnel; Local officials and employees; State planning; State power; State role; States' rights.

State intervention. State intervention. *Choose from:* state, government, federal, official *with:* authoriz(ed,ing,ation), censor(ed,ship), control(led,ling), directive(s), intervention, inspect(ed,ing, ion), licens(ed,ing,ure), polic(y,ies), price control(s), protection(ism), regulat(ed,ing,ion), role(s), sanction(s), standard(s), subsid(y,ies,ization), wage control(s). *See also* Community involvement; Government regulation; Intervention; Social responsibility; State role.

State medicine. State medicine. National health service(s). British national health service. *Choose from:* state, socialis(m, tic,ed), socialized, national, government(al), public or names of countries having national health services such as Canada, England, etc. *with:* medicine, medical care, medical service(s), health care, health service(s). *See also* Health care; Health insurance; Health planning; Health policy; Health services; National health programs; Public health.

State mental hospitals. See *Psychiatric hospitals.*

State of mind, enlightenment. See *Enlightenment (state of mind).*

State officials. See *Elected officials; Government personnel.*

State planning. State plan(ned,ning). Statism. *Choose from:* state, national, federal, government(al), central(ized), socialist *with:* plan(s,ning), design(s), objective(s), goal(s), projection(s), outline(s). *See also* Centrally planned economies; Disaster planning; Economic planning; Local planning; Planning; Regional development; Social planning; State; State role; Urban planning.

State power. State power(s). *Choose from:* national, state, government(al), federal, public, official, imperial *with:* control(led,ling), dominan(ce,t), authority, command, influen(ce,cing, tial), coerc(ion,ive), domination, supremacy, might(y,iness), force(ful,fulness), control(led,ling), overpower(ed,ing), impregnability, constraint, power(s), intervention. *Consider also:* statism, garrison state, states rights, military power, secret police. *See also* Authority (officials); Censorship; Compulsory participation; Formal social control; Governmental powers; Hegemony; Imperialism; Nationalization; Political power; Political repression; Power; State; State intervention; State role; States' rights; Surveillance of citizens.

State role. State role(s). *Choose from:* state, government, federal, official *with:* authority, function(s), responsibilit(y, ies), response(s), protection, intervention, role(s). *See also* Roles; Social responsibility; State; State intervention; State planning; State power.

State secrets. See *Censorship; Classified information; Government secrecy.*

Statelessness. Stateless(ness). Loss of citizenship. *Consider also:* displaced person(s), political refugee(s), expatriat(e,es,ion), permanent tourist(s), non-citizen(s), wartime relocation, without a country, denaturaliz(e,ed,ing, ation). *See also* Citizenship; Deportation; Displaced persons; Refugees.

Statements. See *Assertions.*

Statements, financial. See *Financial statements.*

States (national). See *Countries.*

States (national) by name. See *Antarctic regions; Arctic Regions; Caribbean; Central America; Central Asia; Eastern Europe; Far East; Middle East; North Africa; North America; Oceania; South America; South Asia; Southeast Asia; Sub-Saharan Africa; Western Europe.*

States, emotional. See *Emotional states.*

States, multi-national. See *Plural societies.*

States, newly independent. See *Countries in transition.*

States of consciousness, altered. See *Altered states of consciousness.*

States' rights. States' rights. Powers reserved to the states. Tenth Amendment, 11th Amendment. *Consider also:* state sovereignty, confederation(s), dual sovereignty, new federalism. *See also* Confederalism; Federalism; Governmental powers; Intergovernmental relations; Power sharing; State power; State role; Unitarism.

Statesmen. States(men,man,women, woman). Political leader(s,ship). Veteran lawmaker(s). Solon(s). Lawmaker(s). Lawgiver(s). Head(s) of state. President(s). Prime minister(s). Vice president(s). Cabinet member(s). Governor(s). Supreme Court justice(s). *See also* Diplomats; Elected officials; Politicians.

Stations, broadcasting. See *Broadcasting stations.*

Stations, naval and navy yards. See *Navy yards and naval stations.*

Stations, space. See *Space stations.*

Statistical bias. Statistical bias. Systematic errors. Attrition effect(s). Self selected sample. *Choose from:* bias(ed) *with:* sampl(es,ing), statistic(s,al), data, specification, test(s), nonresponse, survey(s), selectivity, regression effect, test items, selection. *See also* Bias; Errors; Quantitative methods; Research design; Sampling; Test bias; Validity.

Statistical correlation. Statistical correlation. *Consider also:* linear regression, nonlinear regression, phi coefficient, point biserial correlation, rank difference correlation, rank order correlation, tetrachoric correlation. Pearson product moment correlation coefficient, canonical correlation(s), linear relationship, nonlinear relationship. Intercorrelational. Correlat(e,ed,es,ing, ions,ional). Linear function. Statistical association method(s). Part(ial) correlation. Multiple correlation. Measure(s) of association. *Consider also:* specific measures of association such as: tau, Spearman's rho, gamma. *See also* Construct validity; Dependent variables; Factor analysis; Independent variables; Measurement; Statistical data; Statistical inference; Statistical significance.

Statistical data. Statistical data. *Consider also:* survey, longitudinal, rank order, ordinal, nominal, hierarchical, interval, aggregate, ratio *with:* data. *See also* Data collection; Economic statistics; Financial data; Statistical correlation; Statistical norms; Statistical significance.

Statistical inference. Statistical inference. Inferential statistics. Non-parametric method(s). Bayesian inference. Statistical generalization(s). *See also* Causal models; Correlation; Estimation; Factor analysis; Forecasting; Hypotheses; Hypothesis testing; Inference; Probability; Quantitative methods; Sampling; Statistical data; Statistical significance.

Statistical norms. Statistical norm(s). Response norm(s). Group difference(s). Normal distribution(s). *Consider also:* IQ test(s), standardized test(s). *See also* Norms; Statistical data.

Statistical significance. Statistical significance. Statistically significant. Significance test(s). *Consider also:* t test, F test, chi square(d) test, non-parametric, sampling distribution, normal distribution, confidence interval(s), type I error(s), type II error(s). *See also* Factor analysis; Hypothesis testing; Measurement; Probability; Research design; Statistical correlation; Statistical inference.

Statistical tables. Statistical table(s). Kendall's table of exact probabilities. Table(s) of confidence intervals. General expectancy table(s). Table of critical values. T distribution. F distribution. Chi square distribution. Table(s) of normal distribution. *See also* Statistical data.

Statistics, economic. See *Economic statistics.*

Statistics, judicial. See *Judicial statistics.*

Statistics, market. See *Market statistics.*

Statistics, population. See *Census; Population (statistics).*

Statistics, social. See *Census; Social indicators; Vital statistics.*

Statistics, vital. See *Vital statistics.*

Statues. Statu(e,es,ed,ing). Statuar(y,ies). Sculptured likeness(es). *Consider also:* statuette(s), figurine(s), acrolith(ic), caryatid(s), xoanon(s). *See also* Monuments; Sculpture.

Statuettes. See *Figurines.*

Status. Status(es). Rank(s,ing). Hierarchical position(s). Income level(s). *Choose from:* status(es), position(s), standing(s), rank(ing,ings), grade level(s). *Consider also:* occupational prestige, importance, station in life, life chance(s), life style(s), lifestyle(s), seniority, role(s), class(es), situation(s), marginal(ity,ize, ized,izing,ization), role(s). *See also* Differences; Hierarchy; Marital status; Occupational tenure; Ranking; Seniority; Social status; Social stratification; Stratification.

Status, class. See *Social status.*

Status, educational. See *Educational attainment.*

Status, employment. See *Employment status.*

Status, family socioeconomic. See *Family socioeconomic status.*

Status, health. See *Health status.*

Status indicators, health. See *Health status indicators.*

Status, inherited. See *Ascription.*

Status, job. See *Occupational status.*

Status, marital. See *Marital status.*

Status, occupational. See *Occupational status.*

Status, professional. See *Occupational status.*

Status, social. See *Social status.*

Status, socioeconomic. See *Socioeconomic status.*

Status attainment. Status attainment. Achieved status. *Choose from:* status(es), position(s), standing(s), rank(ing,ings), level(s), promotion(s) *with:* achieve(d,ment), attain(ed,ment), earned. *Consider also:* degrees earned, nouveau riche. *See also* Attainment; Elites; Occupational status; Social mobility; Social status; Status inconsistency; Status seekers.

Status inconsistency. Status inconsistenc(y, ies). *Choose from:* status(es), role(s), lifestyle(s), standing(s), hierarchical, profession(s), function(s), position(s) *with:* incongruen(t,ce,cy,cies), incongruit(y,ies), discrepan(t,cy), inconsisten(t,cy,cies), incompatibilit(y, ies), ambiguit(y,ies), disequilibrium. *See also* Alternative lifestyles; Role ambiguity; Role conflict; Self congru-

ence; Social status; Status attainment; Status seekers.

Status of women. See *Women's rights.*

Status seekers. Status seeker(s). Social climber(s). Upward(ly) mobil(e,ility). Nouveau riche. Opportunist(s). Aspiration(s). Ambitious(ness). *See also* Reference groups; Social mobility; Status attainment; Status inconsistency.

Status symbols. See *Consumer society; Luxuries.*

Statutes. Statute(s). Law(s). Rule(s). Regulation(s). Legal requirement(s). Legislation. Code(s). Legal polic(y,ies). Act(s). Legal prohibition(s). State restriction(s). Constitutional right(s). Constitutional amendment(s). Legal code(s). Civil code(s). *Consider also:* legal *with:* aspect(s), issue(s), context(s), decision(s), sanction(s), position(s). *See also* Constitution (legal); Enactment; Laws; Legislation.

Statutory rape. Statutory rape. *Choose from:* sexual intercourse, sexual relations, seduc(e,ed,ing,tion) *with:* under age, under the age of consent, under 16, under 17, under 18. *See also* Acquaintance rape; Adolescence; Child abuse; Rape; Sexual abuse; Sexual exploitation; Victimization.

Stay, length of. See *Length of stay.*

Stealing. See *Burglary; Kleptomania; Larceny; Property crimes; Robbery; Theft.*

Steel and iron workers. See *Iron and steel workers.*

Stem family. Stem famil(y,ies). Famille-souche. Two-generation famil(y,ies). Three-generation famil(y,ies). *See also* Extended family; Nuclear family; Patriarchy.

Stepfamily. Stepfamil(y,ies). Step famil(y,ies). Stepfather(s). Stepparent(s). Stepmother(s). Step mother(s). Step parent(s). Step father(s). Stepchild(ren). *Choose from:* blended, reconstituted, multiple marriage, remarried, multiple *with:* famil(y,ies). *See also* Biological family; Extended family; Family characteristics; Family life; Family relations; Half siblings; Kinship; Nuclear family; Remarriage.

Stereognosis. Stereognos(is,tic). Ability to judge shape or form by touch. *Choose from:* tactile *with:* recognition, discrimination, spatial resolution, perception. *Consider also:* asterognosis, stereoacuity. *See also* Tactual perception.

Stereotyped attitudes. See *Stereotyping.*

Stereotyped behavior. Stereotyp(ed,ic,ical) behavior. Stereotypy. *Choose from:* stereotyped *with:* behavior(s), gnawing, sniffing, response(s), respond(ed,ing), movement(s). *Consider also:* repetitive action(s), circling behavior, turning behavior, rotary movement(s), body rocking, head banging, autoecholalia, autoechopraxia. *See also* Animal behavior; Animal parental behavior; Animal sex behavior; Instinct; Sex roles; Social norms; Symptoms.

Stereotypes, gender. See *Sex stereotypes.*

Stereotypes, sex. See *Sex stereotypes.*

Stereotyping. Stereotyp(ing,ical,es,ed). Stereotyped thinking. Prejudice(d,s). Gender stereotype(s). Stigma(tized). Label(s,ed,ing). Label(led,ling). Typif(y,ied,ication). Cultural image(s). Minority role(s). Racial profiling. *Choose from:* stereotyp(e,es,ed,ing,ical), label(s,ing), image(s), mindset(s), perception(s), expectation(s), expectanc(y,ies), devalu(e,ed,ing,ation), type(cast,d), attribution, character-ization(s), caricature(s), social categoriz(e,ed,ation) *with:* sex(ual), gender, women, woman, female(s), men, man, male(s), ethnic, rac(e,ial), Black(s), Hispanic(s), mental(ly) ill(ness), old age, old(er) people, elder(s,ly), handicap(s, ped), disab(led,ility,ilities), minorit(y, ies), homosexual(s,ity), teacher(s), politician(s). *Consider also:* attribution, demoniz(e,ed,ing,ation), social categori-zation, social bias, chauvin(ism,istic). *See also* Age discrimination; Antisemitism; Attitudes toward handicapped; Attitudes toward homo-sexuality; Attitudes toward mental illness; Attitudes toward mental retardation; Attitudes toward physical handicaps; Attitudes toward physical illness; Attitudes toward the aged; Bias; Categorization; Characterization; Ethnic slurs; Ethnocentrism; Expectations; Ideal types; Images; Images of women; Jokes; Labeling (of persons); Nonsexist language; Otherness; Prejudice; Racism; Role perception; Scapegoating; Self fulfilling prophecy; Sex role attitudes; Sex stereotypes; Sexism; Sexist language; Social discrimination; Social distance; Social identity; Social types; Tribalism.

Sterility. See *Childlessness.*

Sterilization (sex). Steriliz(e,ed,es,ing, ation). Castrat(e,es,ed,ing,ion). Eunuch(oid,ism). Ovariectom(y,ies). Emasculat(e,ed,es,ing). Geld(ed,ing). Alter(ed,ing). Desexualiz(e,ed,ation). Asexualiz(e,ed,ation). Vasectom(y,ies). Hysterectom(y,ies). Tubal ligation(s). Neuter(ed,ing). Orchidectom(y,ies). Gonadectom(y,ies). Spay(ed,ing). Oophorectom(y,ies). Ovariotom(y,ies). Salpingectom(y,ies). *Consider also:* capon(s), gelding(s), steer(s). *See also* Birth control; Desexualization; Eugen-ics; Family planning; Involuntary sterilization; Male castration.

Sterilization, forced. See *Involuntary sterilization.*

Sterilization, involuntary. See *Involuntary sterilization.*

Stigma. Stigma(tized,tization,ta). Spoiled identit(y,ies). Inferiorized. Discredit(ed, able). Deviant identit(y,ies). Outcast(s). Loss of status. Scapegoat(ing,s). Social prejudice(s). Label(ed,s,ing). Negative image(s). Branded. Castigat(e,ed,ion). Untouchable(s). Marginaliz(e,ed,ing, ation). *See also* Coping; Deviance; Humiliation; Labeling (of persons); Ostracism; Otherness; Rejection (psychology); Scapegoating; Social acceptance; Stereotyping.

Stillbirths. See *Infant mortality.*

Stimulants. Stimulant(s). Elevating drug(s). Caffeine. Appetite Stimulant(s). Neurochemical stimulation. Meth. Cineole. Phenolphthalein. Provigil. No-doz. Amphetamine. Aphrodisiac(s). Bemegride. Benzphetamine. Dextroam-phetamine. Doxapram. Ephedrine. Mazindol. Methamphetamine [methedrine, bombit, crank, crystal, meth, speed, methylphenidate]. Methylphenidate. Nikethamide. Pemoline. Phenmetrazine. Phentermine. Picrotoxin. *Consider also:* amphetamine(s). *See also* Drugs in athletics; Hallucinogens; Street drugs.

Stimulation, olfactory. See *Odors.*

Stimulation, perceptual. See *Perceptual stimulation.*

Stimulation, photopic. See *Photopic stimulation.*

Stimulation, self. See *Self stimulation.*

Stimulation, subliminal. See *Subliminal stimulation.*

Stimulation, tactile. See *Tactual stimula-tion.*

Stimulation, tactual. See *Tactual stimula-tion.*

Stimulation, taste. See *Taste stimulation.*

Stimulation, visual. See *Visual stimulation.*

Stimuli. Stimul(i,us). Cue(s). Stimulant(s). *Consider also:* stimulation, exposure, presentation, input(s), reinforce(r,rs, ment), incentive(s), inducement(s), provocation, impetus, enticement(s). *See also* Behaviorism; Conditioning (psychology); Cues; Deprivation; Desensitization (psychology); Motiva-tion; Perception; Pictorial stimuli; Psychophysiology; Redundancy; Responses; Temptation; Verbal stimuli; Unconditioned stimulus.

Stimuli, pictorial. See *Pictorial stimuli.*

Stimuli, verbal. See *Verbal stimuli.*

Stimulus, unconditioned. See *Uncondi-tioned stimulus.*

Stings and bites. See *Bites and stings.*

Stings and bites, insect. See *Insect bites and stings.*

Stochastic processes. Stochastic process(es). *Choose from:* stochastic, Markov, Gaussian, Wiener *with:* process(es), structure(s), model(s), analys(is,es), dynamics, mechanism(s), quantification, theory. *See also* Math-ematical models; Probability.

Stock brokers. Stock broker(s). Stockbroker(s). Securities dealer(s). *Choose from:* stock, securities, floor, street, over-the-counter *with:* broker(s), dealer(s), agent(s). *Consider also:* stockjobber(s), market maker(s), stock exchange specialist(s). *See also* Businesspersons; Brokers; Dealers; Electronic trading (securities); Stock exchange.

Stock exchange. Stock exchange(s). Securities exchange(s). Stock market(s). Bourse(s). *Consider also:* Wall street, American Stock Exchange, New York Stock Exchange, Tokyo Stock Ex-change, NASDAQ, Chicago Board Options Exchange; London Stock Exchange, British Stock Exchange, etc. *See also* Business cycles; Dividends; Electronic trading (securities); Futures market; Going public; Investments; Junk bonds; Profitability; Profits; Specula-tion; Stock brokers; Stockholders.

Stock market. See *Stock exchange.*

Stock options. Stock option(s). Put option(s). Call option(s). Puts and calls. Index option(s). Long-term equity anticipation securit(y,ies). *Consider also:* put spread, call spread, pay-later put, stop-loss order(s), equity option(s), warrant(s). *See also* Business cycles; Dividends; Investments; Speculation; Stockholders.

Stock ownership. See *Employee stock ownership plans; Investments; Stock-holders.*

Stock ownership plans, employee. See *Employee stock ownership plans.*

Stock ranges. See *Grazing lands; Range-lands.*

Stockholders. Stockholder(s). Shareholder(s). *Choose from:* stock(s), share(s), equity *with:* owner(s,ship), hold(er,ers), held, investor(s), bearer(s). *See also* Capitalists and financiers; Corporations; Dividends; Electronic trading (securities); Equity (financial); Family corporations; Going public; Investments; Investor relations; Speculators; Stock exchange; Stock options.

Stockpiling. See *Accumulation; Storage; Warehouse.*

Stocks. See *Investments.*

Stocks, racial. See *Races.*

Stoicism. Stoic(ism,al,ally). Self-control(led). Dispassion(ate,ately). Passionless(ness). Unimpassioned. Indifferen(t,ce). Unexcitab(le,ility). Imperturbab(le,ility). Long suffering. Uninterested. Apath(y,etic,etically). Impassiv(e,eness,ity). Insensib(le,ility). *Choose from:* den(y,ied,ial), suppress(ed, ing,ion), control(led,ling), lack(ed,ing), indifferen(t,ce) *with:* emotion(s,al,ally), feeling(s), sympath(y,ies,etic). *Consider also:* insensitiv(e,ity), unresponsiv(e, eness,ity), personal restraint, propriet(y,ies). *See also* Asceticism; Endurance; Isolation (defense mechanism); Patience; Protestant ethic.

Stone age, middle. See *Mesolithic period.*

Stone carving. See *Carving (decorative arts).*

Stone implements. Stone implement(s). Stone technolog(y,ies). Microlithic tool(s). *Choose from:* stone(s), rock(s), flint, lithic, sandstone, soapstone, granite, limestone, slate, shale, lava(s), quartz(ite), chert, obsidian, volcanic glass *with:* implement(s), artifact(s), flake(s,d), arrowhead(s), arrow head(s), tool(s,making), technology, mortar(s), pestle(s), bladelet(s), baking, boiling, hook(s), nut(s), point(s), axe(s), cleaver(s), pick(s), adze(s), scraper(s), chopper(s), hammer(s), blade(s,let,lets), burin(s), awl(s), knife, knives. *See also* Artifacts; Bone implements; Prehistoric people; Tools; Weaponry.

Stoppages, work. See *Strikes.*

Storage. Storage. Container(s). Tank(s). Stockpile(s). Warehouse(s). Storage media. Optical disk(s). Hard disk(s). Floppy disk(s). Storage site(s). Grain house(s). Silo(s). Cache(s). Safe deposit vault(s). Armor(y,ies). Storehouse(s). Storage place(s). Repositor(y,ies). Depositor(y,ies). Grain elevator(s). *See also* Accumulation; Automated information storage; Containers; Depositories; Facility design and construction; Food storage; Human information storage; Inventory management; Warehouse.

Storage, automated information. See *Automated information storage.*

Storage, food. See *Food storage.*

Storage, human information. See *Human information storage.*

Stores. Store(s). Market(s,places). Shop(s). Marketplace(s). Factory outlet(s). Supermarket(s). Emporium(s). Boutique(s). Retail outlet(s). Drugstore(s). Mart(s). Outlet(s). Thriftshop(s). Concession(s). *Choose from:* department, retail, discount, chain, specialty, factory *with:* store(s). *Consider also:* retail, shopping *with:* plaza(s), center(s), mall(s). *See also* Consumers; Department stores; Discount stores; Discounts; Facilities; Merchants;

Retailing; Sales; Shopping centers.

Stores, department. See *Department stores.*

Stores, discount. See *Discount stores.*

Stories, adventure. See *Adventure stories.*

Stories, ghost. See *Ghost stories.*

Stories, love. See *Love stories.*

Stories, short. See *Anecdotes.*

Stories, western. See *Western fiction.*

Storms. Storm(s,y). Blizzard(s). Rainstorm(s). Turbulent conditions. Tornado(s,es). Thunderstorm(s). Cloudburst(s). Deluge(s). Downpour(s). Torrent(s,ial). Gale wind(s). Heavy wind(s). Cyclone(s). Dust storm(s). Hailstorm(s). Hurricanes. Monsoon(s). Typhoon(s). Rainstorm(s). Sandstorm(s). Twister(s). Snowstorm(s). Squall(s). Windstorm(s). *Consider also:* northeaster(s), cordonazo(s), snow flurr(y,ies). *See also* Catastrophes; Natural disasters; Weather; Weather control; Weather forecasting.

Storytellers. Storyteller(s). Story teller(s). Teller(s) of tales. Yarn spinner(s). Yarnspinner(s). Folklorist(s). *Choose from:* myth(s), legend(s), lore, folklore, folk tale(s), folk literature, children's literature, kiddie literature, yarn(s) *with:* teller(s), keeper(s), historian(s). *Consider also:* raconteur(s), bard(s), minstrel(s). *See also* Narratives; North American Native Cultural Groups; Oral history; Point of view (literature); Storytelling.

Storytelling. Storytell(er,ers,ing). Story tell(er,ers,ing). *Choose from:* tell(ing), told, teller(s), spin(ning), spun, spinner(s) *with:* stor(y,ies), tale(s), yarn(s), anecdote(s). *See also* Narratives; Oral history; Oral reading; Storytellers; Verbal communication.

Stowaway. Stowaway(s). Stow away. Unregistered passenger(s). *Choose from:* sneak(ed,ing), hid(e,ing,den), secreted *with:* aboard, ship(s), plane(s), jet(s), liner(s), boat(s), train(s), vehicle(s). *See also* Smuggling; Travel.

Strain. See *Conflict; Stress.*

Stranger reactions. Stranger reaction(s). *Choose from:* strange situation(s), stranger(s), unfamiliar, unknown *with:* fear, reaction(s), frighten(ed,ing). *See also* Attachment behavior; Emotional responses; Familiarity; Fear; Separation anxiety; Social perception; Xenophobia.

Strangers. Stranger(s). Nonacquaintance(s). Unknown person(s). Outsider(s). Intruder(s). Alien(s). Foreigner(s). Newcomer(s). John Doe. Jane Doe. *Consider also:* xenosis, xenophobia. *See also* Assimilation (cultural); Foreigners; Newcomers; Social response; Xenophobia.

Strategic alliances. Strategic alliance(s). Joint venture(s). Strategic global relationship(s). International strategic alliance(s). Strategic marketing alliance(s). Strategic business alliance(s). Strategic network(s). Coopetition. Co-opetition. Satellite organization(s). *Choose from:* strategic, organizational, mutual incentive(s), mutual benefit(s), mutual reward(s), equity stake(s), share(d) risk(s), pool(ed) resource(s), *with:* alliance(s), partner(s,ship,ing), working relationship(s), collaboration, cooperat(e,ed,ing,ion,ive). *Consider also:* partner(ing,ship) agreement(s), networked organization(s), interfirm cooperation, licensing agreement(s), buyer-supplier partnership(s), reciprocal code-sharing, high tech collaboration, client contractor partnership(s), common platform(s), seamless service(s), alliance partner(s), cooperative working relationship(s), cooperative contract(s). *See also* Alliances; Affiliation (businesses); Boundary spanning; Coalitions; Cobranding; Consortia; Contracting out; Industrial cooperation; Joint ventures; License agreements; Mergers; Organizational development; Preference voting; Subcontracting; Teaming; Virtual organizations.

Strategic global relationships. See *Strategic alliances.*

Strategic management. Strategic management. Strategic leadership. Strategic planning. Corporate strateg(y,ies). Competitive strateg(y,ies). Strategic cost management. *Consider also:* resource management, long term approach(es), portfolio strategy, corporate mission, goals and objectives, strategic thinking, strategy development. *See also* Chaos management; Corporate mission; Decision support systems; Growth strategies; Institutional mission; Long range planning; Management decision making; Management information systems; Management planning; Management structures; Military strategies; Organizational objectives; Organizational change; Strategic planning; Strategies.

Strategic networks. See *Strategic alliances.*

Strategic planning. Strategic plan(ning,s). Strategic analys(is,es). Strategic design(s). Strategic perspective(s). *Choose from:* developing, finding, setting, shaping, formulat(e,ed,ing,ion) *with:* strateg(y,ies), purpose(s), direction(s), destin(y,ies), goal(s) *with:* organization(s), business(es), corporat(e,ion,ions), compan(y,ies). *Consider also:* building sustainable growth, scenario-driven planning, market-driven strateg(y,ies), management strateg(y,ies). *See also* Corporate mission; Institutional mission; Long range planning; Organizational objectives; Strategic management.

Strategies. Strateg(y,ies,ize,ized,izing). Game plan(s). Management plan(s). Master plan(s). Strategic plan(s). Tactic(s). Scheme(s). Approach(es). Plot(s,ting,ted). *Consider also:* scenario(s), angle(s), design(s), maneuver(s,ed,ing). *See also* Change; Cognitive processes; Coping; Guessing; Learning; Management planning; Market strategies; Military strategies; Planning; Policy making; Problem solving; Reform; Short term planning; Strategic management.

Strategies, anti takeover. See *Anti takeover strategies.*

Strategies, growth. See *Growth strategies.*

Strategies, management. See *Management methods.*

Strategies, marketing. See *Marketing strategies.*

Strategies, military. See *Military strategies.*

Strategies, sales. See *Marketing strategies.*

Strategies, search. See *Search strategies.*

Strategies, survival. See *Coping.*

Strategy, naval. See *Naval strategy.*

Stratification. Stratif(y,ied,ication). Strat(a,um). Hierarch(y,ies). Layer(ed,s). Graded status(es). Ability grouping(s). Economic cleavage(s). Economic segment(s,ation). Class structure(s). Social structure(s). Social class(es). Social rank(s). Ranking(s). Status differentiation(s). Microstratification. Class division(s). Class distinction(s). Status division(s). Ranking of statuses. Caste system(s). Caste(s). Dual labor market(s). *See also* Class stratification; Classification; Groups; Hierarchy; Inequality; Social class; Social stratification; Socioeconomic factors; Socioeconomic status; Status; Structure.

Stratification, class. See *Class stratification.*

Stratification, social. See *Social stratification.*

Stream channelization. Stream channelization. *Choose from:* stream(s,let,lets,flow), channel(s), river(s), freshet(s), brook(s), creek(s), waterway(s), tributar(y,ies), bayou(s) *with:* channeliz(e,ed,ing,ation), alter(ed,ing,ation,ations), bank stabilization(s), modif(y,ied,ication), straighten(ed,ing), dredg(ed,ing), geomorphic process(es), widen(ed,ing). *See also* Canals; Channels (hydraulic engineering); Rivers; Shorelines; Streams.

Streams. Stream(s,let,lets,flow). River(s). Freshet(s). Brook(s). Creek(s). Tributar(y,ies). Bayou(s). *Consider also:*

kill(s), rill(s), rivulet(s), runnel(s), watercourse(s), arroyo(s), gull(y,ies), estuar(y,ies), inlet(s). *See also* Canals; Channels (hydraulic engineering); Floods; Rivers; Stream channelization; Water levels.

Street art. Street art(s). Art in the square. Urban mural(s). Barricadeart(s). Outdoor art(s). Sidewalk art(s,show,shows). Window art(s). *Choose from:* art, painting(s), pastel(s), chalk(s) sculpture(s), drawing(s), poster(s), vignette(s), galler(y,ies), mural(s) *with:* outdoor, street, urban, public, market square(s), window(s), subway(s). *Consider also:* graffiti art, people's art, sgraffito. *See also* Arts; Cultural property; Graffiti; Municipal art; Mural painting and decoration; Public art; Sculpture.

Street children. Street child(ren). Street kid(s). *Choose from:* street(s), sidewalk(s), homeless, vagrant(s), abandoned *with:* child(ren), gang(s), youth, teenager(s), juvenile(s), minor(s), boy(s), girl(s). *See also* Abandoned children; Child neglect; Homeless children.

Street drugs. Street drug(s). Rock cocaine. Crack cocaine. Glue sniffing. *Choose from:* street, illicit, illegal, counterfeit, smuggled *with:* drug(s), tablet(s), heroin, cocaine, marijuana, marihuana, mescaline, methaqualone. *Consider also:* amobarbital [amytal, blue angels, blue devils, blue velvet, blues, lilly], amobarbital/secobarbital [Tuinal, Christmas trees, double trouble, rainbows, tooies], amphetamines [speed], amphetamine sulfate [Benzedrine, A's, beans, bennies, cartwheels, crossroads, jelly beans, hearts, peaches, whites], amphetamine sulfate/amobarbital [Dexamyl, greenies], amyl nitrite [amys, pears, snapper, poppers], atropine, barbiturate(s) [barbs, candy, dolls, goofers. peanuts, sleeping pill(s)], biphetamines, cleaning fluid [naptha, scrubwomans kick], cocaine [basuco, basuko, bazuco, bazuko, coke, crack(head,heads), methyl benzoyl ecgonine, bernies, big C, flake, freebase, free base, happy dust, ice,snow], dexamyl, dextroamphetamine sulfate [Dexedrine, brownies, Christmas trees, dexies, hearts, wakeups], elixir Terpin Hydrate [schoolboy, blue velvet], heroin [black tar, black stuff, H, hard stuff, horse, junk, skag, smack, diacetylmorphine, diamorphin, acetomorphine], hydromorphone [Dilaudid, lords], lysergic acid diethylamide [LSD, ergot fungus, acid, pink wedges, sandos, sugar cubes, lysergide, Delysid], laughing gas, mescaline [mesc, peyote, barf tea, big chief, lophophora, mescal buttons, trimethoxyphenethylamine, cactus], methamphetamine hydrochloride

[methedrine, bombit, crank, crystal, meth, speed, methylphenidate], methadone hydrochloride [Dolophine, dollys, amidone], methaqualone [Quaalude, ludes, sopors], morphine [dope, M, Miss Emma, morpho, white stuff], nembutal, nitrous oxide [laughing gas, nitrous], numorphan, opi(um,ates,ods) [PG, licorice], oxymorphone [Numorphan, lords], paregoric, pentobarbital [Nembutal, nebbies, yellow bullets, yellow dolls], phencyclidine [Sernyl, angel dust, PCP, peace pills], phenobarbital [Luminal, phennies, purple hearts], psilocin [psilocyb(c,in, business man's acid, magic, mushroom], robitussin [robby], secobarbital [Seconal, pink lady, red devils, reds, seccy, pinks], Tetrahydrocannabinoids [cannabis, sinsemilla, ganja, bhang, charas, kif, hasach, grass, hay, hashish, hemp, joints, marijuana, marihuana, mary jane, pot, reefer(s), rope, smoke, tea, tetrahydrocannibinol, weed, Acapulco gold, Panama red], 2CB, 2CB, 2CB. THC. *See also* Designer drugs; Drug and narcotic control; Drug lords; Drug trafficking; Drugs; Gateway drugs; Hallucinogens; Medical marijuana; Narcotics; Needle sharing; Stimulants; Substance abuse.

Street harassment. Street harassment. *Choose from:* street(s) *with:* harass(ment,ing,ed,er,ers), hassl(e,es,ed,ing). Girl watch(er,ers,ing). Wolf whistl(e,es,ed,ing). Catcall(s). Street remark(s). Racial profiling. *Consider also:* ogl(e,ed,es,ing), lecher(s,ous,ousness), gawk(s,ed,ing). *See also* Harassment; Invective; Sexual harassment; Stalking; Verbal abuse.

Street people. See *Homeless.*

Street traffic. Street traffic. *Choose from:* street(s), road(s), avenue(s), boulevard(s), thoroughfare(s), highway(s) *with:* traffic, congest(ed,ion), peak hour(s), jam(s), crowded(ed,ing), overcrowd(ed,ing). *See also* Highway safety; Traffic accidents.

Street vendors. Street vendor(s). Market women. Higgler(s). Peddler(s). Hawker(s). Pushcart salesm(en,an). Pushcart entrepreneur(s). Huckster(s). Mobile food unit(s). Peanut stand(s). Popcorn stand(s). Ice cream truck(s,stand,stands). Shoeshine kiosk(s). Newsstand(s). Outdoor concession(s,aire,aires). Hot truck(s). Cold truck(s). Hawking ware(s). *See also* Retailing; Sales personnel; Small businesses; Women merchants.

Street vernacular. See *Slang.*

Streetpeople. See *Homeless.*

Streets. Street(s). Road(s,way,ways). Avenue(s). Boulevard(s). Thoroughfare(s). Highway(s). Lane(s).

Alley(s). Route(s). Arter(y,ies). Concourse(s). Parkway(s). *Consider also:* corridor(s), driveway(s), walkway(s). *See also* Crossroads; Highways; Street traffic.

Strength, attitude. See *Attitude strength.*

Strength, physical. See *Physical strength.*

Strength, troop. See *Troop strength.*

Stress. Stress(es,ed,ful,ors,ability). Tension(s). Strain(s). Pressure(s). Eustress. Technostress. Distress(ed,ing, ful). Anxiet(y,ies). Anxious(ness). Stress reaction(s). *Consider also:* life, psychological, physiological, social, occupational, environmental, subjective *with:* stress(es,ed,ful,ors,ability), distress(ed,ing). *Consider also:* life change event(s), life change(s), burnout, burned out, burn out, burnt out. *See also* Ambiguity; Anxiety; Burnout; Coping; Crises; Crowding; Deprivation; Disasters; Disease; Distress; Endurance; Environmental stress; Family crises; General adaptation syndrome; Hypertension; Identity crisis; Info fatigue syndrome; Life change events; Mental fatigue; Natural disasters; Occupational stress; Organizational crises; Physiological stress; Psychological stress; Shock; Social stress; Stress management; Stress reactions; Surprise; Threat.

Stress, environmental. See *Environmental stress.*

Stress, job. See *Occupational stress.*

Stress, occupational. See *Occupational stress.*

Stress, phonological. See *Inflection.*

Stress, physical. See *Physiological stress.*

Stress, physiological. See *Physiological stress.*

Stress, psychological. See *Psychological stress.*

Stress, resource. See *Resource stress.*

Stress, social. See *Social stress.*

Stress disorders, post traumatic. See *Post traumatic stress disorders.*

Stress management. Stress management. Autogenic training. Autogenic therap(y, ies). *Choose from:* stress(es), type A behavior, anger, hassle(s), anxiety, tension(s) *with:* management, training, inoculat(e,ed,ing,ion), cop(e,ed,ing), reduc(e,ed,ing,tion), biofeedback, relax(e,ed,ing,ation), resist(ed,ing,ance), control(led,ling), alleviat(e,ed,ing), interven(e,ed,ing,tion), self hypnosis, prevention, monitor(ed,ing), program(s), support system(s). *See also* Adjustment (to environment); Behavior modification; Catharsis; Cognitive techniques; Coping; Counseling; Crisis management; Health education; Meditation; Relaxation training; Self help groups;

Stress; Symptoms.

Stress reactions. Stress reaction(s). *Choose from:* stress(s,ful), crisis, crises, distress, trauma(tic), post-traumatic, disaster(s), catastrophe(s), near death *with:* response(s), reaction(s), psychophysiolog(y,ic), result(s,ing), impact(s), effect(s), sequelae, aftermath, aftereffect(s). *See also* Coronary prone behavior; Neurasthenia; Post traumatic stress disorders; Psychological endurance.

Strike damage. Strike damag(e,ed,ing,s). *Choose from:* strike(s,er,ers), picket(s,ed, ing,er,ers) *with:* liab(le,ility,ilities), violen(t,ce), damag(e,ed,ing,s), mutilat(e,ed,ing,ion), wreck(ed,ing), vandal(ism,ize,ized,izing). *See also* Damage; Strikes; Vandalism.

Strikes. Strik(e,es,ing). Industrial action(s). Job action(s). Work stoppage(s). Labor unrest. Walkout(s). Downer(s). Picket line(s). Picket(s,ed,ing). Work slowdown(s). Sickout(s). Lockout(s). *Choose from:* general, quickie, labor, wildcat, sympathy, economic, illegal, secondary, jurisdictional *with:* strik(e,es, ing). *Consider also:* Taft Hartley Act, boycott(s), work stoppage(s), strikebreaker(s), work by the book. *See also* Arbitration; Boycotts; Collective bargaining; Labor disputes; Labor force; Labor management relations; Lockouts; Negative sanctions; Picketing; Rent strikes; Student demonstrations.

Strikes, hunger. See *Hunger strikes.*

Strikes, rent. See *Rent strikes.*

String puppets. See *Puppets.*

Strip mining. Strip min(e,es,ed,ing). *Choose from:* open-pit, opencast, surface *with:* mine(s), mining. *Consider also:* pit(s), quarr(y,ies). *See also* Coal mines and mining; Natural resources.

Strippers. See *Nudity.*

Strips, film. See *Film strips.*

Striving. See *Aspirations.*

Stroke. See *Cerebral hemorrhage.*

Structural imperatives. Structural imperative(s). Imperative(s) of compatibility. *See also* Functional imperatives.

Structural models. Structural model(s). Manikin(s). Moulage(s). Replica(s). Dumm(y,ies). *Choose from:* structur(e, al), anatomic(al), molecular, three dimensional, wax, plaster *with:* model(s), simulat(ion,ions,or,ors). *See also* Models; Scientific models; Structure.

Structure. Structur(al,e,es,ation,alism). Arrangement. Boundar(y,ies). Centraliz(ed,ing,ation). Channel(s). Cluster(s,ed,ing). Complex(ity). Compos(ed,ition). Component(s).

Configur(ed,ing,ation). Constellation(s). Construct(ed,ing,ion). Decentraliz(ed, ing,ation). Destructur(ation,alization). Foundation(s). Format(ion). Heterogeneity. Hierarch(y,ies,ical). Homogeneity. Leaderless(ness). Makeup. Model(s). Morpholog(y,ies). Network(s). Order(ed,ing). Organiz(e,ed,ing,ation). Organizational design. Organizational form(s). Pattern(s). Polariz(e,ed,ing, ation). Position(ed,ing). Profile(s). Pyramid(s). Refigur(e,ed,ing,ation). Restructur(ed,ing). Rigid(ity). Segment(ed,ing,ation). Stratif(y,ied, ication). Strat(a,um). Substructure(s). Typolog(y,ies). *See also* Agrarian structures; Classification; Clusters; Cognitive structures; Community structure; Components; Designs; Family characteristics; Form (aesthetics); Frames (physical); Group structure; Groundwork; Hierarchy; Morphology; Occupational structure; Organizational structure; Power structure; Sentence structure; Social stratification; Social structure; Stratification; Structural models; Systems; Text structure.

Structure, class. See *Social stratification; Social structure.*

Structure, community. See *Community structure.*

Structure, corporate. See *Organizational structure.*

Structure, family. See *Family characteristics.*

Structure, group. See *Group structure.*

Structure, occupational. See *Occupational structure.*

Structure, organizational. See *Organizational structure.*

Structure, power. See *Power structure.*

Structure, sentence. See *Sentence structure.*

Structure, social. See *Social structure.*

Structure, text. See *Text structure.*

Structures, agrarian. See *Agrarian structures.*

Structures, cognitive. See *Cognitive structures.*

Structures, data. See *Data structures.*

Structures, garden. See *Garden structures.*

Structures, management. See *Management structures.*

Struggle, class. See *Class conflict.*

Struggle, ideological. See *Ideological struggle.*

Stubbornness. Stubborn(ness). Obstinate(ly). Headstrong. Self-willed. Contrar(y,iness). Pervers(e,ity). Balk(y,iness). Uncooperative(ness). Refractor(y,iness). Recalcitran(t,ce).

Defian(t,ce). Contumac(y,ious,iously). Dogged(ly). Relentless(ness). Unrelenting(ly). Incorrigib(le,ility). Persisten(t,ce). *Consider also:* contempt of court, cantankerous(ness), orner(y, iness), unyielding, adamant(ly,ine), inflexib(le,ility). *See also* Imperviousness; Passive aggressive personality disorder; Personality disorders; Refractory.

Student achievement. See *Academic achievement.*

Student activism. See *Youth movements.*

Student activities. Student activit(y,ies). Extracurricular activit(y,ies). *Choose from:* student(s), pupil(s), after-school, fresh(men,man), sophomore(s), junior(s), senior(s), eighth grader(s), etc. *with:* activit(y,ies), involvement, community service, volunteer work, part(y,ies), sports, athletic participation, festivit(y,ies), festival(s), celebration(s), club(s), voluntary association(s). *See also* Extracurricular activities; Friendship; Leisure activities; Play; School clubs; School newspapers; School sports; Social activities; Social dating; Social life; Student newspapers and periodicals; Student rights.

Student attitudes. Student attitude(s). *Choose from:* student(s), pupil(s), undergraduate(s), freshmen, sophomore(s), junior(s), senior(s), schoolchild(ren) *with:* attitude(s), apathy, opinion(s), feeling(s), preference(s), bias(ed,es), perspective(s), belief(s), satisf(y,ied,action), accept(ed,ing,ance), reject(ed,ing,ion), mindset(s), view(s,point,points), response(s), reaction(s), resist(ed,ing, ance), prejudic(e,ed,es), intoleran(t,ce), toleran(t,ce), expectation(s), dissatisf(y,ied,action), perception(s), dislike(s), like(s). *See also* Attitudes; Classroom environment; Student behavior; Student characteristics; Student motivation; Students.

Student behavior. Student behavior. *Choose from:* student(s), pupil(s), classroom, schoolchild(ren), undergraduate(s), upperclassmen, freshmen, sophomore(s), junior(s), senior(s) *with:* behavior, conduct, performance, habit(s), adjustment, assertiveness, attachment(s), autism, communication, competitive(ness), cooperative(ness), competition, cooperation, disobedience, drinking, drug use, hyperactiv(e,ity), imitat(e,ed,ion,ive), inhibit(ed,ing,ion, ions), leadership, misbehavior, participation, persistence, physical activit(y,ies), response(s), risk taking, self control, smoking, sociability, socializ(e,ed,ing, ation), social behavior, spontaneity, social conformity, social dominance, substance abuse. *See also* Behavior;

Child discipline; Due process; Student attitudes; Student characteristics; Student teacher relations; Students.

Student characteristics. Student characteristics. Characteristics of students. Personal qualities of students. *Choose from:* characteristics, trait(s) *with:* student(s), pupil(s), schoolchild(ren), school child(ren), learner(s), undergraduates, freshmen, sophomore(s), junior(s), senior(s). *Consider also:* personality, gender, exceptional, disabilit(y,ies), handicapped, gifted, marital status, family background, behavior patterns, personality traits, status, age, race, religion, place of residence, grade, urban, rural, etc *with:* student(s), pupil(s), school child(ren), learner(s), undergraduate(s), freshmen, sophomore(s), junior(s), senior(s). *See also* Academic ability; Academic achievement; Academic aptitude; Academic skills; Characteristics; Student attitudes; Student behavior; Student motivation; Students.

Student clubs. See *School clubs.*

Student demonstrations. Student demonstration(s). Student protest(s). *Choose from:* student(s), college(s), universit(y,ies), campus(es) *with:* sit-in(s), love-in(s) demonstrat(ed,ing,ion, ions,ors), protest(s,ing,er,ers), barricad(e,ed,es,ing), march(es,ed,ing), picket(s,ed,ing), strike(s), disobedience, activis(m,t,ts), rall(y,ies,ing), rebel(s,led,ling,lion,lions), unrest, riot(s,ed,ing). *See also* Boycotts; Civil disobedience; Civil disorders; Demonstrators; Protest movements; Protesters; Radical movements; Social action; Social agitation; Social movements; Strikes; Students; Youth movements; Youth organizations.

Student dropouts. Student dropout(s). *Choose from:* school, student(s), college, education *with:* dropout(s), leaver(s), drop(ped,ping) out, discontinue(d), quit(ting). Failure to graduate. Interrupted education. Noncompletion of education. *Consider also:* academic failure, expulsion, disqualification, out of school youth, suspension, withdrawal from school. *See also* Academic failure; Attendance (presence); Attrition; Potential dropouts; Reentry students; Rehabilitation; Retraining; Runaways; School expulsion; School suspension; Truancy; Withdrawal (defense mechanism).

Student financial aid. Student financial aid. Scholarship(s). Training support. *Choose from:* student(s), education(al), training, tuition *with:* subsid(y,ies), fellowship(s), financial aid, assistantship(s), support, stipend(s), loan(s), award(s), grant(s), financial assistance. *Consider also:* tuition

voucher(s), school federal aid, school financial assistance. *See also* Access to education; Assistance; Educational vouchers; Eligibility determination; Fellowships (educational); Financial support; Grants; Loans; Needs assessment; Scholarships (educational); School choice; Student personnel services; Students; Tuition reimbursement.

Student health services. Student health service(s). *Choose from:* school(s), student(s), college(s), universit(y,ies) *with:* health service(s), clinic(s), health screening, medical checkup(s), health program(s), medical service(s), health plan(s), health care, primary care, wellness program(s), immuniz(e,ed,ing, ation,ations), vaccinat(e,ed,ing,ion,ions), innoculat(e,ed,ing,ion,ions), eye test(s,ing), vision test(s,ing). *See also* Health education; Health services; Mental health services; Student personnel services; Students; Vaccinations.

Student motivation. Student motivation(s). *Choose from:* student(s), pupil(s), academic, educational, learning *with:* motivat(e,ed,ing), motivation(s,al), motive(s), ambition(s), intent(ion,ions), ambitious(ness), initiative(s), goal(s), incentive(s), interest(ed,s), aspir(e,ed, ing,ation,ations), cognitive dissonance, achievement need(s), achievement motivation, intrinsic motivation, fear of success, fear of failure, temptation(s). *See also* Academic aspiration; Achievement need; Active learning; Aspirations; Student attitudes; Student characteristics; Students.

Student movements. See *Social movements; Youth movements.*

Student newspapers and periodicals. Student newspaper(s). Student periodical(s). *Choose from:* school, student(s), college(s), universit(y,ies), campus(es) *with:* newspaper(s), newsletter(s), periodical(s), yearbook(s), magazine(s), journalism. *See also* Newspapers; Periodicals; Student activities.

Student periodicals. See *Student newspapers and periodicals.*

Student personnel services. Student personnel service(s). Pupil personnel service(s). *Consider also:* student(s), undergraduate(s), school(s), college(s), universit(y,ies) *with:* counseling, guidance, placement service(s), psychological service(s), mental health service(s). *See also* Counseling; Educational counseling; Mental health services; School counseling; Student financial aid; Student health services; Vocational guidance.

Student protests. See *Student demonstrations.*

Student records. Student record(s). *Consider also:* student(s), school(s), pupil(s), academic *with:* record(s), report card(s), transcript(s), achievement information, evaluation report(s). *See also* Confidential records; Records; Students.

Student rights. Student rights. *Choose from:* student(s), campus(es), pupil(s), schoolchild(ren) *with:* right(s), civil liberties, due process, freedom of speech, equal education, justice, privacy rights, First Amendment rights, Constitutional rights. *See also* Academic freedom; Children's rights; Equal education; Human dignity; Human rights; Legal rights; Parent rights; Right of privacy; Student activities.

Student societies. See *School clubs.*

Student songs. Student(s) song(s). College song(s). Fight(ing) song(s). Sports song(s). Team song(s). Team chant(s). Alma mater(s). Drinking song(s). Fraternity song(s). Sorority song(s). School anthem(s). School hymn(s). *Consider also:* rugby cheer(s). *See also* College students; Drinking songs; High school students; Songs.

Student teacher relations. Student teacher relation(s,ship). Classroom interaction(s). *Choose from:* student(s), pupil(s), student body, schoolchild(ren), school population, student population *with:* faculty, teacher(s), teaching staff, professor(s), instructor(s), schoolmaster(s) *with:* relation(s,ship), interaction(s), cooperation, conflict(s), discipline, dispute(s), expectation(s), feedback, friendship, compatib(le,ility), bond(s,ing), helping, hostility, influence(s), perception(s), caring, interpersonal behavior, attachment, rapport, rejection, role(s), partnership(s), support, trust, understanding. *Consider also:* student rating(s), teacher expectation(s), teacher attitude(s), student attitude(s). *See also* Classroom environment; Educational malpractice; Grading (educational); Interpersonal relations; Mentors; Professional ethics; Students; Teacher evaluation; Teacher expectations; Teachers.

Students. Student(s). Pupil(s). Student body. School youth. School enrollee(s). Child(ren) in school. Schoolchild(ren). Freshmen. Sophomore(s). Junior(s). Senior(s). School population. College men. College women. Schoolgirl(s). Schoolboy(s). Student population. Incoming class. Person(s) attending school. Seventh grader(s), etc. Classmate(s). Learner(s). *See also* Absenteeism; Academic achievement; Academic aptitude; Adult students; Business students; Classroom environment; College students; Education students; Educational attainment; Educational opportunities; Educational plans; Elementary school students; Fellowships (educational); Foreign students; Graduate students; High school students; Intermediate school students; Junior college students; Junior high school students; Married students; Medical students; Middle school students; Nursery school students; Nursing students; Postgraduate students; Preschool children; Primary school students; Reentry students; Scholarships (educational); School violence; Schools; Special education students; Student activities; Student attitudes; Student behavior; Student characteristics; Student demonstrations; Student dropouts; Student motivation; Student teacher relations; Teacher expectations; Truancy; Vocational school students.

Students, adult. See *Adult students.*

Students, business. See *Business students.*

Students, college. See *College students.*

Students, education. See *Education students.*

Students, elementary school. See *Elementary school students.*

Students, foreign. See *Foreign students.*

Students, graduate. See *Graduate students.*

Students, high school. See *High school students.*

Students, intermediate school. See *Intermediate school students.*

Students, junior college. See *Junior college students.*

Students, junior high school. See *Junior high school students.*

Students, kindergarten. See *Preschool children.*

Students, married. See *Married students.*

Students, medical. See *Medical students.*

Students, middle school. See *Middle school students.*

Students, nursery school. See *Nursery school students.*

Students, nursing. See *Nursing students.*

Students, postgraduate. See *Postgraduate students.*

Students, primary school. See *Primary school students.*

Students, reentry. See *Reentry students.*

Students, secondary school. See *High school students.*

Students, special education. See *Special education students.*

Students, university. See *College students.*

Students, vocational school. See *Vocational school students.*

Studies, animal. See *Animal studies.*

Studies, area. See *Area studies.*

Studies, case. See *Case studies.*

Studies, ethnic. See *Ethnic studies.*

Studies, feasibility. See *Feasibility studies.*

Studies, followup. See *Followup studies.*

Studies, longitudinal. See *Longitudinal studies.*

Studies, panel. See *Panel studies.*

Studies, prospective. See *Prospective studies.*

Studies, qualitative. See *Qualitative methods.*

Studies, quantitative. See *Quantitative methods.*

Studies, retrospective. See *Retrospective studies.*

Studies, social. See *Social studies.*

Studies, time and motion. See *Time and motion studies.*

Study, comparative. See *Comparative study.*

Study, foreign. See *Foreign study.*

Study abroad. See *International educational exchange.*

Study habits. Study habits. *Choose from:* study(ing), notetaking, homework *with:* habit(s), approach(es), skill(s), strateg(y,ies), method(s). *See also* Behavior patterns.

Stupas. See *Shrines.*

Stuttering. Stutter(ing,ers). Stammer(ing). *Consider also:* disfluen(t,cy,cies). Speak haltingly. *See also* Speech disorders.

Style, cognitive. See *Cognitive style.*

Style, leadership. See *Leadership style.*

Style, learning. See *Cognitive style.*

Style, life. See *Lifestyle.*

Style, literary. See *Literary style.*

Style, management. See *Leadership style; Management methods.*

Style, perceptual. See *Perceptual style.*

Style, supervisory. See *Leadership style.*

Styles. Style(s). Styl(ish,istic). Flair. Fashion(s,able). Good taste. Bad taste. Avant-garde. Mode(s). Modish(ness). Sophisticated. Refined. Cultured. Cosmopolitan. Suave. Panache. Manner(s). Vogue. Fad(s). *See also* Clothing; Customs; Elegance; Fads; Fashions; Popular culture; Sophistication.

Styles, architectural. See *Architectural styles.*

Styles, artistic. See *Artistic styles.*

Styles, communication. See *Communication styles.*

Stylistics. Stylistic(s). Linguostylistic(s). Stylostatistic(s,al). Stylometr(y,ical). Phonostylistic(s). *Consider also:* general stylistics, literary stylistics, applied stylistics, style(s) of grammar. *See also* Linguistics.

Sub-Saharan Africa. Angola(n) [Portuguese West Africa(n)]. Benin(ese) [Dahomey]. Botswana [Bechuanaland]. Burkina Faso [Upper Volta]. Burundi(an) [Ruanda-Urundi]. Cameroon(ian) [Cameroun, Cameroons]. Cape Verde(an). Central African Republic [Central African Empire, Ubangi-Shari]. (Republic of) Chad(ian) [Tchad(ian), French Equatorial Africa(n)]. Cote d'Ivoire. [Ivory Coast, Ivorian]. (Federal Islamic Republic of the) Comoros. Congo [Republic of Zaire, Belgian Congo, Congo Free State, Democratic Republic of the Congo]. Congo Republic [People's Republic of the Congo(lese), French Congo, Middle Congo]. Djibouti(an) [French Somaliland, French Territory of the Afars and Issas]. Equatorial Guinea(an) [Spanish Guinea]. Eritrea [Ethiopia]. Ethiopia(n) [Abyssinia(n)]. Gabon(ese) (Republic) [Gabun]. Gambia(n). Ghan(a,ian) [Gold Coast, Ashanti]. Guinea(n) [French Guinea]. Guinea Bissau [Portuguese Guinea]. Kenya(n). Lesotho [Basutoland]. Liberia(n). Madagasca(r,n) [Malagasy Republic]. Malawi(an,s) [Nyasaland]. (Republic of) Mali(an) [French Sudan]. (Islamic Republic of) Mauritania(n). Mauriti(us,an). Mozambi(que,cen) [Portuguese East Africa, Mocambique]. Namibia(n) [German Southwest Africa, South West Africa, South Africa]. Niger(ien) [French West Africa]. (Federal Republic of) Nigeria(n). Rwanda(n). Sao Tome(an) and Principe. Senegal(ese). Seychelles. Sierra Leone. Somalia(n) (Democratic Republic). (Republic of) South Africa(n) [Union of South Africa]. Swaziland. Tanzania(n). (Republic of) Togo(lese) [Togoland]. Uganda(n). Zambia(n) [Northern Rhodesia]. Zimbabwe(an) [Southern Rhodesia(n), Rhodesia(n). *Consider also:* Kongo, Saint (St.) Helena, Madeira. *See also* African Cultural groups; African empires; Anti-apartheid movement; Apartheid; Benue-Niger languages; Chad languages; Kwa languages; Mandingo (Mande) languages; Middle East; Niger-Congo languages, Atlantic (Western); North Africa; South Asia; Voltaic (Gur) languages.

Subconscious. Subconscious(ly,ness). Subliminal(ly). Suppressed. Repressed. Latent. Preconscious(ness).

Fantasm(s,ic). Inner self. Collective unconscious. Dim(ly) aware(ness). *See also* Psychoanalysis; Psychoanalytic interpretation; Psychoanalytic theory; Subliminal; Subliminal stimulation.

Subcontracting. Subcontract(ing,ed,or,ors). Outsourc(ed,ing). *Consider also:* strategic industrial sourcing, industrial procurement. *See also* Adhocracies; Border industries; Contracting out; Labor economics; Labor market; Shared services; Virtual organizations.

Subcultures. Subcultur(e,es,al). Micro culture(s). Subsociet(y,ies). Cultural subgroup(s). Counterculture(s). Societal subsystem(s). Hippie(s). Moonie(s). Gyps(y,ies). Sexual minorit(y,ies). *Consider also:* hyphenated American(s), Korean American(s), Korean-American(s), Italian American(s), Italian-American(s), Polish American(s), Polish-American(s), etc. *Choose from:* freak, drug, counter, flower, youth, homosexual, motorcycle, street, prison *with:* subcultur(e,es,al), subgroup(s), culture(s), generation, subsystems, gang(s), societ(y,ies). *See also* Acculturation; Assimilation (cultural); Camp (aesthetics); Countercultures; Cross cultural comparisons; Cultural groups; Cultural identity; Cultural issues; Cultural pluralism; Cultural values; Cults; Culture (anthropology); Ethnic groups; Ethnic neighborhoods; Ethnic relations; Intercultural communication; Minority groups; Needle sharing; Prison culture; Religious communities; Religious cults; Religious cultural groups; Slang; Social class; Social environment; Social influences; Social integration; Social segmentation; Socialization.

Subdivisions, land. See *Land subdivisions.*

Subject analysis. See *Content analysis.*

Subject headings. Subject heading(s). Subject index term(s). Subject term(s). Index term(s). Descriptor(s). Uniterm(s). Classified heading(s). Subheading(s). Subject entr(y,ies). Subject concept(s). Subject device(s). Subject authorit(y,ies). Facet(s). *Consider also:* thesaur(i,us,uses). *See also* Catalogs; Controlled vocabulary; Vocabulary.

Subject researcher relations. See *Researcher subject relations.*

Subjective knowledge. See *Subjectivity.*

Subjectivism. See *Subjectivity.*

Subjectivity. Subjectiv(e,ity,ism,ively). Intersubjectivity. Subjectiviz(e,ed,ing, ation). Self-conscious(ness). Subjective knowledge. *Consider also:* personal perspective, inner feeling(s), subject-object, phenomenal, phenomenology, private experience. *See also* Bias; Cultural relativism; Experience (background); Individuals; Objectivity;

Personality; Personality traits; Point of view (literature); Reflexivity; Solipsism.

Subjects, experimental. See *Research subjects.*

Subjects, human research. See *Human subjects (research).*

Subjects, research. See *Research subjects.*

Subjugation. Subjugat(e,ed,ing,ion). Dominat(e,ed,ing,ion). Domineer(ed, ing). Overrul(e,ed,ing). Tyranniz(e,ed, ing). Oppress(ed,ing,ion). Coloniz(e,ed, ing,ation). *See also* Colonization; Forced labor; Oppression; Slavery.

Sublimation. Sublimat(ion,e,ed,es,ing,ory). Symbolic expression(s). *Choose from:* externaliz(e,ed,ing,ation), diver(t,sion) *with:* instinct(s,ual), impulse(s). *Consider also:* desexualiz(e,ed,ing, ation). *See also* Repression (defense mechanism).

Subliminal. Subliminal(ly). Hidden message(s). Secondary message(s). Below threshold (limen) of conscious perception. Below threshold of recognition. Below recognition level. *Consider also:* weak stimuli, subliminal fringe of excitation, stimuli *with:* summation, aggregation. *See also* Subconscious; Subliminal stimulation.

Subliminal stimulation. Subliminal stimulation. *Choose from:* subliminal *with:* stimul(i,us,ate,ating,ation), perception, auditory input, arousal, presentation, activation, auditory cue(s), psychodynamic(s), motion picture(s). *See also* Subconscious; Subliminal.

Submarine archaeology. See *Underwater archaeology.*

Submerged lands. Submerged land(s). *Choose from:* submerged, underwater, offshore, outer continental *with:* land(s), beach(es). *Consider also:* continental shelf, coral reef(s). *See also* Conservation of natural resources; Environmental protection; Island ecology; Islands; Land preservation; Reclamation of land; Shore protection; Shorelines; Underwater archaeology; Wetlands.

Submission. Submiss(ion,ive). Subordinat(e,ed,ing,ion). Obedien(t,ce). Follower(s,ship). Powerless(ness). Deferen(ce,tial). Subaltern. Inferiority. Inferior status. Servil(e,ity). Yield(ed, ing). Meek(ness). Docil(e,ity). Complian(t,ce). *See also* Dependency (personality); Dominance; Inequality; Obedience; Passiveness; Powerlessness; Social status; Superior subordinate relationship.

Submissive behavior. See *Obedience; Submission.*

Submissiveness. See *Obedience.*

Subordinate superior relationship. See *Superior subordinate relationship.*

Subordination, dominance. See *Dominance subordination.*

Subsidiaries. Subsidiar(y,ies,ily). Auxiliar(y,ies). Supplementary. Ancillar(y,ies). Accessor(y,ies). Adjuvant. Contributor(s,y). Subservient. *Consider also:* operating unit(s), backup(s), branch(es), division(s,al), minor role(s), tributar(y,ies). *See also* Affiliation (businesses); Ancillaries; Branch operations; Holding company; Multinational corporations; Spinoffs; Subsidiary management.

Subsidiary management. Subsidiary management. *Choose from:* subsidiar(y, ies), branch(es), division(s,al) *with:* manag(e,ed,ing,ement), managerial, strateg(y,ies,ic), plan(ned,ning,s), administrat(ive,or,ors). *See also* Affiliation (businesses); Branch operations; Management methods; Multinational corporations; Offshore production (foreign countries); Organizational effectiveness; Subsidiaries.

Subsidies. Subsid(y,ies,ized,izing,ization). Grant(s). Stipend(s). Allowance(s). Honorari(a,um). Gratuit(y,ies). Pension(s). Entitlement(s). Subvent(ed, ing,ion,ions). *Choose from:* financial *with:* support, assistance, aid. *Choose from:* government, federal, public, congressional, state, county, city, local, taxpayer(s) *with:* underwrit(e,ing, ten), financ(ed,ing), support(ed,ing), tax break(s), tax writeoff(s), bailout(s), bail(ing) out, pork barrel(ing), sponsor(ed,ing,ship), aid, investment(s), fund(ed,ing,s), price support(s), loan(s), pay(ing) the bill, picking up the tab, scholarship(s), assistance. *See also* Financial support; Government financing; Government subsidization; Grants; Loans; Payments.

Subsidization, government. See *Government subsidization.*

Subsidized housing. Subsidized housing. *Choose from:* subsid(y,ies,ized), allowance(s) *with:* housing, rent(s,al). Rent rebate(s). *See also* Affordable housing; Government subsidization; Housing; Housing costs; Public housing.

Subsistence economy. Subsistence econom(y,ies). *Choose from:* subsistence, traditional, peasant, marginal, underdevelop(ed,ment), self-sufficient, natural *with:* econom(y,ies), farm(s,er, ers), crop(s), agriculture, horticulture, work, production, technolog(y,ies). *Consider also:* small farm(s,er,ers), pastoralism, pastoral societ(y,ies). *See also* Bartering; Developing countries; Economic underdevelopment; Nomads; Poverty; Primitive food; Subsistence hunting; Traditional societies.

Subsistence hunting. Subsistence hunting. Hunt(ing) for food. *Choose from:* hunt(ing,er,ers), trapp(er,ers,ing),

fish(ing), wildlife, game, harvests, wild food(s), Moose, caribou, whale(s), duck(s), etc. *with:* subsistence, traditional use(s), indigenous people. *Consider also:* hunting customs of indigenous people, subsistence harvest(s,ing), marine mammal harvest(s), subsistence lifestyle(s), native hunt(ing,er,ers). *See also* Hunting; Hunting and gathering societies; Primitive fishing; Primitive food; Primitive hunting; Subsistence economy; Traditional societies.

Substance abuse. Substance abus(e,ed,ers, ing). Drug abus(e,ed,ers,ing). Heroin(omania,omaniac). Narcoti(sm, icism). Toxicoman(ia,ias,iac,iacs,iacal). Polytoxicoman(ia,ias,iac,iacs,iacal). Dual addiction(s). *Choose from:* substance(s), drug(s), heroin, caffeine, cocaine, crack, narcotic(s), amphetamine(s), sedative(s), alcohol, barbiturate(s), solvent(s), polydrug(s), analgesic(s), tranquilizer(s), marihuana, marijuana, cannabis, phencyclidine, PCP, inhalant(s) *with:* abus(e,ed,er, ers,ing), dependen(t,ce,cy,cies), overdos(e,ed,ing), habit(s,uate,uated, uating,uation), habitual(ly), overus(e,ed,ing), misus(e,ed,ing), polymorphic use(r,rs), toleran(t,ce), addict(s,ed,ing,ion). *See also* Addiction; Alcoholism; Alcohol rehabilitation; Behavior disorders; Designer drugs; Detoxification; Drug addicted babies; Drug addiction; Drug rehabilitation; Drug use; Drugs; Drugs in athletics; Eating disorders; Gateway drugs; Hallucinogens; Inhalant abuse; Narcotics; Needle sharing; Self destructive behavior; Solvent abuse; Street drugs; Substance abuse detection; Substance dependence; Substance use disorders; Toxic inhalation; Tranquilizers.

Substance abuse detection. Substance abuse detection. *Choose from:* illegal substance(s), cocaine, crack, narcotics, illicit drug(s), street drug(s), heroin, amphetamine(s), alcohol, polydrug(s), marihuana, marijuana, cannabis, phencyclidine *with:* detect(ed,ing,ion), test(ed,ing), screen(ed,ing), determin(e, ed,ing), identif(y,ied,ication), urin(e,ary, alysis). *See also* Crime prevention; Drug and narcotic control; Law enforcement; Police dogs; Substance abuse.

Substance abuse, testing for. See *Substance abuse detection.*

Substance dependence. Substance dependence. Sedativism. Polydrug addiction(s). Dual addiction(s). Multiple addiction(s). Drug habituation. Drug addiction(s). Chemical dependency. *Choose from:* substance(s), drug(s), narcotic(s), ethanol, morphine, opiate(s), polydrug(s), sedative(s), tranquilizer(s), heroin, cocaine, crack, phencyclidine, PCP, cannabis, marijuana or names of

specific drugs *with:* dependen(t,ce,cy, cies), overdependen(t,ce,cy,cies), abus(e,ed,ing,er,ers), addict(s,ed,ion, ions,ing,ive), habituat(e,ed,ion,ing), habit(s,ual), toleran(ce,t). *Consider also:* toxicomania. *See also* Addiction; Alcoholism; Drug addiction; Drug use; Emotional dependence; Gateway drugs; Substance abuse.

Substance induced organic mental disorders. Substance induced organic mental disorder(s). *Choose from:* substance(s), drug(s), alcohol(ic,ism), atropine *with:* intoxicat(ed,ion), withdrawal syndrome(s), deliri(a,um), hallucination(s), mental disorder(s), brain syndrome(s). *See also* Alcoholic dementia; Alcoholic hallucinosis; Alcoholic psychoses; Drug withdrawal; Psychedelic experiences; Substance induced psychoses.

Substance induced psychoses. Substance induced psychos(is,es). *Choose from:* toxic(ity), alcohol(ic,ism), amphetamine(s), belladonna, benzodiazepeine, benzhexol, bromide, cannabis, chloral hydrate, cimetidine, cocaine, cortisone, crack, diet(s,etic), drug(s), hallucinogen(s), imipramine, isoniazid, paraldehyde, pharmacotoxic, phencyclidine, procarbazine, propanolol, pseudoephedrine, solvent(s), theophylline, thiocyanate, toluene, tricyclics *with:* psychos(is, es), psychotic, disorientation. *Consider also:* alcohol amnestic disorder, acarophobia, formication. *Choose from:* lilliputian, diminutive visual, microptic *with:* hallucination(s). *See also* Alcoholic dementia; Alcoholic hallucinosis; Alcoholic psychoses; Alcoholism; Drugs; Drug addiction; Psychoses; Substance induced organic mental disorders.

Substance use disorders. Substance use disorder(s). Drug use disorder(s). Gasoline inhalation. Solvent intoxication. Glue snorting. Glue inhalation. Solvent encephalopathy. Phencyclidine intoxication. Arecaidinism. Chew(ed, ing) betel. Drug induced neurological pathology. *Choose from:* drug(s), substance(s), narcotic(s), alcohol, heroin, cocaine, crack, phencyclidine, cannabis, marijuana, marihuana, morphine, tobacco, opiate(s), solvent(s), glue, toluene *with:* use, usage, abuse, disease(s), dependen(t,ce,cy), disorder(s), crav(e,ed,ing,ings), addict(s,ed, ion,ions,ing,ive), overdependen(t,ce,cy). *See also* Alcoholism; Drug addiction; Drug induced abnormalities; Drug withdrawal; Gateway drugs; Impulse control disorders; Inhalant abuse; Substance abuse; Substance dependence; Substance induced organic mental disorders; Substance induced psychoses; Substance withdrawal syndrome.

Substance withdrawal syndrome.
Substance withdrawal syndrome.
Choose from: substance(s), alcohol,
drug(s), opiate(s), heroin, cocaine,
marijuana *with:* withdrawal, discon-
tinu(e,ed,ing,ance), abstinence *with:*
syndrome(s), problem(s), delirium,
effect(s), aftereffect(s). *Consider also:*
detox(ify,ified,ification), cold turkey. *See
also* Detoxification; Drugs; Drug
addiction; Drug rehabilitation; Hallucinogens; Narcotics; Street drugs;
Substance abuse; Substance dependence.

Substances, abuse of. See *Alcoholism;
Drug addiction; Solvent abuse;
Substance abuse.*

Substances, toxic. See *Toxic substances.*

Substitution, import. See *Import substitution.*

Subterranean economy. See *Informal
sector.*

Subterranean voyages. See *Voyages to the
otherworld.*

Suburban development. Suburban
development. Suburbaniz(e,ed,ing,
ation). *Choose from:* suburb(s,an,ia),
satellite town(s), bedroom communit(y,
ies), commuter communit(y,ies) *with:*
annex(ed,ing,ation), building, construction, develop(ed,ing,ment), design(ed,
ing), evolution, evolv(e,ed,ing), expan(d,
ding,sion), exten(d,ded,ding,sion),
further(ed,ing), gain(s,ing), grow(n,th,
ing), improv(e,ed,ing,ement,ements),
invest(ed,ing,ment,ments), reinvest(ed,
ing,ment,ments), moderniz(e,ed,ing,
ation), plan(s,ned,ning), progress,
reconstruct(ed,ing,ion), regenerat(e,ed,
ing,ion), redevelop(ed,ing,ment),
renew(al,ed,ing), spread(ing), revitaliz(e,
ed,ing,ation), rezon(e,ed,ing),
transform(ed,ing,ation), zon(e,ed,ing).
See also Community development;
Commuting (travel); Planned communities; Suburbanization; Urban fringe;
Urban sprawl.

Suburban growth, controlling. See *Growth
management.*

Suburban mental health. Suburban mental
health. *Choose from:* mental health,
psycho(tic,sis,ses), mental(ly)
ill(ness,nesses), neuro(tic,sis,ses),
emotional(ly) disturb(ed,ance,ances),
alcohol(ic,ism), schizophren(ia,ic,ics),
drug abuse, behavior problem(s),
alienat(e,ed,ing,ion) *with:* suburb(s,an),
satellite town(s), dormitory area(s),
bedroom communit(y,ies), urban fringe.
See also Mental health; Suburbs.

Suburbanization. Suburban(ized,izing,
ization). Urban suburban migration.
Exurbaniz(ed,ation). *Consider also:*
urban, cit(y,ies), metropolitan *with:*
deconcentrat(ed,ion), decentraliz(ed,
ation, dispers(ed,ion), commuter(s). *See
also* Suburban development; Suburbs;

Urban to rural migration; Urbanization.

Suburbs. Suburb(s,an,ia,anized,anizing,
anization). Exurban(ite,ites). Exurbia.
Bedroom communit(y,ies). Commuter
communit(y,ies). Split level trap.
Nonmetropolitan. Nonurban. Dormitory
area(s). Satellite town(s). Satellite
communit(y,ies). Suburbanite(s). Urban
fringe(s). Outside city limit(s). Suburban
sprawl. *See also* Annexation; Community (geographic locality); Commuting
(travel); Geographic regions; Inner
cities; Metropolitan areas; New towns;
Suburbanization; Urban environments;
Urban fringe; Urban sprawl; Urban to
rural migration.

Subventions. See *Subsidies.*

Subversion. Subvers(ion,ionary,ive,
iveness). Subvert(ed,ing). Overthrow(n).
Un-American Activities. McCarran
Walter Act. Fifth column. Corrupt(ing,
ion) loyal(ty,ties). *Consider also:*
treason, sedition, sabotage, coup d'etat,
undermin(ed,ing), overturn(ed,ing),
insurrection, insurgent(s), traitor(s,ous),
underground. *See also* Espionage;
Intelligence service; Traitors; Treason;
Secret police; Undercover operations.

Subways. Subway(s). *Consider also:*
underground rapid transit, underground
rail, metrorail, BART, MTA, BMT, IRT,
METRO, CTA, etc. *See also* Commuting
(travel); Mass transit.

Success. Success(ful). Succeed(ed,ing).
Achiev(e,ed,ment,ing). Promot(e,ed,ing,
ion). Satisf(y,ied,action). Attain(ed,ing,
ment). Goal attain(ed,ment). Realiz(e,ed,
ing) ambition(s). Prosper(ed,ing).
Accomplish(ed,ment,ments). Pro-
gress(ed,ing,ion). Advanc(ed,ement,ing).
Fruitful(ness). Well-paying. Reward(ed,
ing). Upward mobility. *Choose from:*
occupational, professional, job, career,
educational *with:* success(ful),
attain(ed,ment), achiev(ed,ment,ments,
ing), promot(ed,ing,ion), accomplish(ed,
ment,ments), progress(ed,ing,ion),
advanc(ed,ement,ing), reward(s,ed,ing).
See also Academic achievement;
Achievement; Achievement gains;
Achievement need; Aspirations;
Comfortableness; Competence; Defeat;
Educational attainment; Effectiveness;
Evaluation; Excellence; Expectations;
Failure; Fear of success; Goal orienta-
tion; Goals; Improvement; Motivation;
Occupational success; Organizational
effectiveness; Overachievement;
Perfection; Performance; Prestige;
Psychotherapeutic breakthrough;
Psychotherapeutic outcomes; Quality;
Satisfaction; Standards; Treatment
efficacy.

Success, fear of. See *Fear of success.*

Success, occupational. See *Occupational
success.*

Succession. See *Inheritance.*

Succession, plant. See *Plant succession.*

Succubus. Succub(a,ae,i,us). Unholy
temptress(es). Snow witch(es). Witch-
moon(s). Blackjade(s). Hellspawn(s).
Red vex(es). Soul burner(s). *Consider
also:* incub(i,us,uses). *See also* Demons;
Devils; Images of women; Nightmares;
Spirits; Water spirits.

Sucking behavior. Sucking behavior.
Suck(ed,ing). *Consider also:* nursing
behavior, neonatal feeding reflex(es).
See also Weaning.

Suckling animals. See *Newborn animals.*

Sudanic languages. Sudanic language(s).
Chari-Nile (Macro-Sudanic) languages,
eastern group: Nubian dialects, Nilotic
dialects, Dinka, Masai, Watutsi. Chari-
Nile (Macro-Sudanic) languages, central
group: Bagirmi, Mangbetu, Nile-
Nubian. Fur. Koman: Gule, Koma,
Uduk. Maban: Maba. Saharan: Daza,
Kanuri, Teda. Songhai. *See also* African
cultural groups; Language; Languages
(as subjects); North Africa.

Sudden infant death. Sudden infant
death(s). Crib death(s). Cot death(s).
SIDS. *Choose from:* infant(s), infancy
with: sudden death(s), sleep apnea. *See
also* Death; Infant mortality.

Suffering. Suffer(ed,ing). Afflict(ed,ing,
ion,ions). Anguish(ed). Anxiet(y,ies).
Ache(s). Aggravat(e,ed,ing). Agitat(ed,
ion). Agon(y,ies,ized,izing). Deject(ed,
ion). Depress(ed,ion). Desolat(ed,ion).
Discomfort(ed,ing). Discontent(ment).
Distress(ed,ing,ful). Disturb(ed,ing).
Disquiet(ening). Emotional trauma(s).
Fearful(ness). Grief. Griev(e,ed,ing).
Heartache(s). Malaise. Miser(able,y,ies).
Ordeal(s). Pain(ful,fulness). Torment(s,
ed,ing). Uneas(y,iness). Woe(s).
Worr(y,ies,ied). Vex(ed,ing,ation).
Wretched(ness). *See also* Distress;
Emotions; Grief; Pain; Patience;
Psychological distress; Starvation;
Torture; Tragedy.

Sufficient evidence. Sufficient evidence.
Weight of evidence. *Choose from:*
sufficien(t,cy), adequate, satisfactory,
credible, warrant(ed,ing) conviction
with: evidence, reason(s), cause.
Consider also: probable cause(s),
substantial evidence, relevant evidence.
See also Circumstantial evidence;
Evidence; Indictments; Justification
(law); Positive evidence; Withholding
evidence.

Sufficient reason. See *Reason; Sufficient
evidence.*

Suffrage. Suffrage. Voting right(s). Political
rights. Entitled to vote. Voting age.
Multilingual ballot(s). Franchise.
Enfranchise(d,ment). Fifteenth amendment. Nineteenth amendment.

Participat(e,ion) in political process. Electoral participation. *See also* Civil rights; Suffrage movement; Voting rights; Women's rights.

Suffrage movement. Suffrage movement(s). Suffragette(s). Suffragist(s). National Woman Suffrage Association. American Woman Suffrage Association. National American Woman Suffrage Association. National Woman's Party. Woman's Rights Convention. Women's Liberal Associations. Primrose League. 19th Amendment. Nineteenth Amendment. *Consider also:* Elizabeth Cady Stanton, Lucretia Mott, Susan B. Anthony, Lucy Stone, Abby Kelley Foster, Angelina Emily Grimke, Sarah Moore Grimke, Anna Howard Shaw, Carrie Chapman Catt, Alice Paul, Lucy Burns, Sheffield Female Political Association, Women's Social and Political Union, Lydia Becker, Barbara Bodichon, Emily Davies, Dr. Elizabeth Garrett Anderson, Mrs. Henry Fawcett, Emmeline Pankhurst. *See also* Civil disobedience; Feminism; Political movements; Social movements; Suffrage; Women's groups; Women's rights.

Suffrage, woman. See *Suffrage; Suffrage movement; Voting rights; Women's rights.*

Suggestion. Suggestion. *Consider also:* autogenic training, persuasive communication, suggestib(le,ility), hypnotic susceptibility, autosuggestion, post hypnotic suggestion, expectation(s), hypnotherapy. *See also* Expectations; Hypnotic susceptibility; Self fulfilling prophecy; Teacher expectations.

Suicidal behavior. Suicidal behavior(s). Suicide related behavior(s). *Choose from:* suicid(e,es,al,ality), self destructive, self harm(ful,fulness,ing,ed) *with:* behavior(s), manifestation(s), note(s), call(s,ed,ing,er,ers, prone(ness), risk(s), vulnerab(le,ility), factor(s), ideation, thought(s). *Consider also:* jump(s,ed, ing) from bridge(s), drug overdose(s), etc. *See also* Attempted suicide; Drug overdoses; Self destructive behavior; Self inflicted wounds; Suicide; Suicide prevention; Suicide victims.

Suicide. Suicid(e,es,al). Self immolation. Self annihilation. Hara-kiri. Seppuku. Hunger strike(s). Kamikaze. Suttee. Died by own hand. *Choose from:* self, oneself *with:* harm(ed,ing), destruct(ion, ive), hurt(ing), injur(y,ious), poison(ed, ing), kill(ed,ing), starv(e,ed,ing), dangerous, disembowel(ed,ment), murder(ed,ing). *Consider also:* overdose(s), parasuicid(e,es,al). *See also* Attempted suicide; Behavior disorders; Collective suicide; Copycat suicide; Death; Death instinct; Drug overdoses; Mortality rates; Self destructive

behavior; Self mutilation; Suicidal behavior; Suicide prevention; Suicide victims; Teenage suicide.

Suicide, assisted. See *Assisted suicide.*

Suicide, attempted. See *Attempted suicide.*

Suicide, collective. See *Collective suicide.*

Suicide, copycat. See *Copycat suicide.*

Suicide, physician assisted. See *Assisted suicide.*

Suicide prevention. Suicide prevention. *Choose from:* suicid(e,es,al), parasuicid(e,es,al) *with:* prevent(ed,ing, ion,ive), aware(ness), intervention(s), recognition, crisis line(s), hotline(s), hot line(s), help line(s), Samaritan(s). *See also* Attempted suicide; Crisis intervention; Prevention; Suicidal behavior; Suicide; Suicide victims.

Suicide, teenage. See *Teenage suicide.*

Suicide victims. Suicide victim(s). Suicides. *Choose from:* suicide(s) *with:* victim(s), mortalit(y,ies), fatalit(y,ies), completed, successful(ly). *See also* Attempted suicide; Collective suicide; Copycat suicide; Death; Death instinct; Drug overdoses; Mortality rates; Self destructive behavior; Suicidal behavior; Suicide; Suicide prevention; Teenage suicide; Victimization.

Suits, space. See *Space suits.*

Sum games, non zero. See *Non zero sum games.*

Sunday legislation. Sunday legislation. Blue law(s). *Choose from:* sabbath, Sunday(s) *with:* law(s), labor, closing(s), legislation. *See also* Church state relationship; Religious fundamentalism; Traditionalism.

Superego. Superego. Super ego. Unconscious conscience. Conscience. Morality. Ego ideal. *Consider also:* interego, sphincter morality, guilt, shame, moral development, inner directed. *See also* Conscience; Examination of conscience; Guilt; Moral development; Moral judgment; Morality; Repression (defense mechanism); Shame; Sublimation; Values.

Supererogation. Supererogation. Supererogatory act(s,ion,ions). Perform(ed, ing) more than required. Beyond the call. More than the minimum. Extra mile. Act(s,ed,ing,ion,ions) beyond morality's call. Beyond normal practice(s). Exceeding minimum(s). Do(ing) more than necessary. Beyond role description(s). Outside the commandments. Beyond expectation(s). *Consider also:* scrupulosity, surplus works, extraordinary effort(s). *See also* Accountability; Duties; Excellence; Moral obligation; Obligations; Quality.

Superheroes. See *Heroes.*

Superhighway, information. See *Information highway.*

Superintendents. Superintendent(s). Assistant superintendent(s). School administrator(s). School district administrator(s). *Consider also:* director(s), over *See r(s), supervisor(s), manager(s). See also* Administrators; Educational administrators; School boards; School principals.

Superintendents, school. See *Superintendents.*

Superior subordinate relationship. Superior subordinate relationship. Office hierarch(y,ies). Office politics. Workplace discipline. Manage(rial,ment) style. *Choose from:* superior(s), boss(es), manager(s), administrator(s), supervisor(s), employer(s), leader(s), executive(s), director(s), chair(women, woman,men,man,person,persons), coordinator(s), superintendent(s), fore(man,men), captain(s), dean(s), president(s), department head(s), principal(s) *with:* subordinate(s), employee(s), staff, personnel, underling(s), servant(s), civil servant(s), laborer(s), secretar(y,ies), typist(s), clerk(s), crafts(men,man), white collar worker(s), member(s), assistant(s) relation(s,ship), interaction(s), authority, cooperation, conflict(s), control, discipline, dispute(s), expectation(s), feedback, friendship, helping, hierarch(y,ies,ical), hostility, problem(s), influence(s), leadership, organizational structure, paternalism, rapport, rejection, role(s), support, trust, understanding, working life. *See also* Dominance; Dominance subordination; Interpersonal relations; Labor management relations; Leadership; Management functions; Management methods; Managerial skills; Obedience; Organizational culture; Organizational structure; Paternalism; Patronage; Personnel management; Precedence; Quality of working life; Supervision; Working conditions.

Superiority, emotional. See *Emotional superiority.*

Supermarkets. See *Stores.*

Supernatural. Supernatural(ism). Astral projection. Astral travel. Astrology. Amulet(s). Apparition(s). Black magic. Cabal(a,ism). Chakra(s). Cosmology. Clairvoyan(t,ce). Deathbed vision(s). Daimon(ism,ology). Demon(ic,ology). Demon possession. Devil(s). Divination. Divining rod(s). Dowsing. Duende(s). Dracula cult. Dybbuk(s). Earth ray(s). ESP. Extrasensory perception. Extrasensible. Exorcis(m,t). Fortune telling. Firewalking. Flying saucer(s). Ghost(s). Hobgoblin(s). Haunted house(s). Haunting. Horoscop(e,y). Human aura. Hex(es). Jinx(es).

Incantation(s). Kirlian photography. Levitation(s). Magic(al). Medium(s). Mental healing. Mystic(al,ism,s). Near death experience(s). Necromancy. Out of body. Obe. Obeah. Occult(ism). Orgone energy. PSI. Paranormal. Parapsycholog(y,ical). Pseudoscientific. Parapsychosomatic(s). Phantom(s). Possession trance(s). Precognition. Psychic(al,s). Psychic healing. Psychokine(sis,tic). Psychophotograph(y,ic). Poltergeist(s). Radiesthesia. Reincarnation. Seance(s). Shamanis(m, tic). Spirit possession. Spiritualis(m,tic). Survival after death. Telekine(sis,tic). Telepath(y,ic). Thaumaturgy. Voodoo. Werewol(f,ves). Witchcraft. *See also* Apparitions; Divination; Evil eye; Fetishism; Ghosts; Hallucinations; Magic; Mana; Miracles; Occultism; Parapsychology; Shamanism; Spirit possession; Spirits; Spiritualism; Superstitions; Uncanniness; Voodooism; Witchcraft.

Superrealism. See *Surrealism.*

Superstitions. Superstit(ion,ions,ious, iousness). Supernatural belief(s). Amulet(s). Astrolog(y,ical). Black magic. Dracula cult(s). Demonolog(y, ical). Exorcis(m,t,ts). Evil eye. Fascinum. Hobgoblin(s). Hex(es). Jinx(es). Old wives tale(s). Occult(ism). Sorcery. Shamanism. Talisman. Vampire(s). Voodoo. Werewol(f,ves). Witchcraft. *Consider also:* supernatural, magic(al), demon(ic,ological), extrasensible, occult *with:* belief(s), thinking, premise(s), idea(s). *See also* Attitudes; Beliefs; Evil eye; Divination; Folk culture; Folklore; Ghost stories; Ghosts; Groundless; Haunted houses; Irrational beliefs; Magic; Mermaids; Religious beliefs; Shrunken heads; Snake lore; Spiritualism; Supernatural; Taboo; Talisman.

Supervision. Supervis(ion,ory,or,ors). Supervisory method(s). Computer surveillance. Stewardship. Office hierarch(y,ies). *Choose from:* office(s), workplace(s), shopfloor(s), assembly line(s), sweatshop(s) *with:* control, authority, disciplin(e,ing,ary), expectation(s), feedback, management, motivation. *Choose from:* manage(rial, ment), supervisory *with:* method(s), practice(s), principle(s), style(s), model(s), skill(s), technique(s), system(s), philosoph(y,ies), strateg(y,ies). *Consider also:* span of control, managerial grid, personnel management, delegation of authority, delegation of responsibility, satisficing, accountability, task organization, code(s) of ethics, merit system(s), human relations program(s). *See also* Administration; Coordination (interpersonal); Job performance; Leadership; Leadership style; Management functions; Management methods; Personnel

management; Practicum supervision; Superior subordinate relationship; Workers.

Supervision, practicum. See *Practicum supervision.*

Supervisor employee interaction. See *Superior subordinate relationship.*

Supervisors. See *Managers; Superintendents.*

Supervisory style. See *Leadership style.*

Supplies, military. See *Military supplies.*

Supply, food. See *Food supply.*

Supply, labor. See *Labor supply.*

Supply, medical personnel. See *Medical personnel supply.*

Supply, money. See *Money supply.*

Supply, personnel. See *Human resources; Labor supply; Manpower.*

Supply, water. See *Water supply.*

Supply and demand. Supply and demand. Price war(s). Oversuppl(y,ied). Production quota(s). Overabundance. Supply side. *Choose from:* price(s), suppl(y,ies), quota(s) *with:* demand, consumption. *Consider also:* tight supply, falling demand, falling prices, shortage(s), market system, market economy. *See also* Aggregate economics; Bartering; Business cycles; Costs; Demand; Economic change; Economic competition; Economic exchanges; Economics; Exchange; Inflation (economics); International trade; Labor market; Labor supply; Market economy; Market value; Marketing; Markets; Prices; Production consumption relationship; Productivity; Purchasing; Socioeconomic factors; Supply side economics; Trade.

Supply side economics. Supply side economics. Supply-side theory. Supply sider(s). Neoclassical economics. Trickle down. Reduc(e,ed,ing) marginal tax rate(s). Cut(ting) marginal tax(es). Cut(ting) capital gains tax(es). Laffer curve. *Choose from:* lower(ed,ing), reduc(e,ed,ing), cut(ting) *with:* marginal tax(es), income tax(es), capital gains tax(es). *Consider also:* capital accumulation, regressive taxation, voodoo economics, dynamic scoring. *See also* Aggregate economics; Business cycles; Capital (financial); Economic change; Economics; Inflation (economics); Market economy; Production consumption relationship; Supply and demand; Taxes.

Support, child. See *Child support.*

Support, community. See *Community support.*

Support, domestic. See *Alimony; Dependent parents; Family assistance; Family budgets; Filial responsibility; Food services (programs); Public welfare.*

Support, financial. See *Financial support.*

Support, life care. See *Life support care.*

Support, public. See *Public support.*

Support, public financial. See *Antipoverty programs; Fiscal federalism; Government aid; Government financing; Government programs; Government subsidization; Medical assistance; Public welfare.*

Support, research. See *Research support.*

Support, social. See *Social support.*

Support, training. See *Training support.*

Support networks. See *Social support networks.*

Support networks, social. See *Social support networks.*

Support staff. Support staff. Administrative assistant(s). *Choose from:* support, pink collar, clerical *with:* staff, personnel, occupation(s). *See also* Assistants; Clerical workers; Entourage; Secretaries; White collar workers.

Support systems. See *Financial support; Social support; Social support networks.*

Support systems, decision. See *Decision support systems.*

Supportive services. Supportive service(s). *Choose from:* support(ive), attendant(s), aide(s), practical nurse(s), day care, foster care, home health, homemaker(s), meal(s), respite care, visiting nurse(s) *with:* service(s), program(s). *See also* Alternatives to institutionalization; Community services; Consumer directed care; Emergency services; Food services; Health services; Home care services; Homemaker services; Long distance caregivers; Social services; Relief services.

Supports, price. See *Price control.*

Suppositions. See *Postulates.*

Suppression (defense mechanism). Suppress(ed,ing,ion). Conscious(ly) inhibit(ed,ing,ion). *Consider also:* avoidant thinking, denial, den(ied,ying) memor(y,ies), shutting away memor(y,ies). *See also* Forgetting; Repression (defense mechanism).

Suppression (political). See *Political repression.*

Suppression, conditioned. See *Conditioned suppression.*

Supranationalism. See *Internationalism.*

Suprasegmentals. Suprasegmental(s). Prosodic analys(is,es). Prosodic phonology. *Consider also:* stress, tone, intonation. *See also* Inflection; Intonation (phonetics); Phonemes.

Supremacy, royal. See *Royal supremacy.*

Supremacy, White groups. See *White supremacy movements.*

Supremacy movements, white. See *White supremacy movements.*

Supremacy of law. See *Rule of law.*

Supremacy of the king. See *Royal supremacy; Divine right of kings; Sovereignty.*

Supremacy over the military, civil. See *Civil supremacy over the military.*

Suprematism. Suprematis(m,t,ts). Suprematiz(m,t,ts). *Consider also:* Casimir Malevich, New Realism. *See also* Constructivism; Modern architecture; Modern art.

Surgery. Surger(y,ies). Surg(ery,ical). Surgical procedure(s). Surgical operation(s). Microsurg(ery,ical). *Consider also:* chirurgy, trephin(e,ed, ing,ation), organ transplantation, dissect(ed,ing,ion), laparoscop(y,ies), tonsillectom(y,ies), cholecystectom(y, ies), mastectom(y,ies), etc. *See also* Abortion; Ambulatory surgery; Amputation; Dental surgery; Fetal surgery; Heart surgery; Reconstructive surgery; Vasectomy.

Surgery, ambulatory. See *Ambulatory surgery.*

Surgery, cosmetic. See *Reconstructive surgery.*

Surgery, dental. See *Dental surgery.*

Surgery, fetal. See *Fetal surgery.*

Surgery, heart. See *Heart surgery.*

Surgery, plastic. See *Reconstructive surgery.*

Surgery, reconstructive. See *Reconstructive surgery.*

Surgery, sham. *Sham surgery.*

Surplus. Surplus(ses,age). Excess. Superabundan(t,ce). Glut(ted,ting). Overstock(s,ed,ing). Oversuppl(y,ies,ied). Overabundan(t,ce). Overflow(ing). Plethora(s). Superfluit(y,ies). Surfeit(s). *Consider also:* remainder(s), remnant(s), residue(s), extra(s), redundan(t,ce,cy). *See also* Excess; Redundancy.

Surplus labor. See *Labor supply; Unemployment.*

Surprise. Surpris(e,ed,ing). Astonish(ed, ment,ing). Astound(ed,ing). Amaz(e,ed, ing,ingly,ement). *Consider also:* flabbergast(ed), unforeseen, unexpected(ly), unanticipated, sudden(ly). *See also* Impetuous; Sensationalism; Shock; Spontaneity; Stress.

Surrealism. Surreal(ism,istic,ity). Surrealis(me,mo,mus,te,tes,tische). Veristic surrealist(s). Superrealis(m,ti, tis). *Consider also:* fantastic art, magic realism, pop art, automatic writing, stream of consciousness, theater of the absurd, Andre Breton, Paul Eluard, Salvador Dali, Yves Tanguy, Max Ernst,

Louis Aragon, Antonin Artaud, Aime Cesaire, Rene Char, Rene Crevel, Robert Desnos, Julien Gracq, Michel Leiris, Benjamin Peret, Francis Picabia, Raymond Queneau, Philippe Soupault, Tristan Tzara. *See also* Abstract art; Assemblage (Art); Avant-garde; Concrete art; Concrete poetry; Dadaism; Magic realism (art); Pop art; Postmodernism; Realism in art; Socialist realism in art.

Surrender. See *Military capitulations.*

Surrogate mothers. Surrogate mother(s, hood). Host mother(s). Surrogate parent(s,ing). Pregnancy by proxy. Gestational mother(s). Surrogate birth(s). Surrogate bab(y,ies). Biological mother(s). *Choose from:* surroga(te,cy), host, proxy, gestational, uterine, hir(ed,ing), biological *with:* mother(s), parent(s,ing), pregnancy, birth(s), motherhood, baby, babies. *See also* Artificial insemination; Cloning; Fertilization in vitro; Pregnancy; Reproductive technologies; Sexual reproduction.

Surveillance, electronic. See *Electronic eavesdropping.*

Surveillance, population. See *Surveillance of citizens.*

Surveillance of citizens. Population surveillance. Domestic spying. Security file(s) on private citizen(s). Police spy(ing). Police spie(s,d). Monitoring political group(s). Investigation(s) of dissident(s). Police surveillance. Cellular scanner(s). Home audio surveillance. FBI files. FBI harassment. Big brother. *Choose from:* e-mail, voice-mail, cellular telephone(s), population, domestic, citizen(s), dissident(s), political group(s), private lives, demonstrator(s), resident(s), member(s), dissenter(s), protester(s), resister(s), opposition *with:* surveillance, FBI, spy(ing), spie(d,s), monitor(ed,ing), investigat(e,ed,ing, ion,ions), eavesdrop(ped,ping), phone tap(ped,ping,s). *See also* Aerial reconnaissance; Bill of Rights; Civil rights; Civil supremacy over the military; Cyberlaw; Dissent; Eavesdropping; Electronic eavesdropping; Freedom of speech; Governmental powers; Government records; Identification cards; Intelligence service; Internal security; Invasion of privacy; Martial law; Military civilian relations; Military intelligence; National security; Online privacy; Political dissent; Police community relations; Police records; Privacy laws; Right of Privacy; Secret police.

Surveying. See *Surveys.*

Surveying, archaeological. See *Archaeological surveying.*

Surveying, land. See *Land surveying.*

Surveys. Survey(ed,s,ing). Poll(s,ed,ing). Telephone interview(s). Mail(ed,ing) questionnaire(s). Telephone sampl(e,es, ing). Public opinion research. Election stud(y,ies). Market research. Data collection. *See also* Archaeological surveying; Attitude measurement; Comparative study; Data collection; Enumeration; Feasibility studies; Fieldwork; Health care surveys; Health surveys; Interviews; Investigations; Library surveys; Market research; Measurement; Needs assessment; Nutrition surveys; Opinion polls; Public opinion; Push-polling; Questionnaires; Research methods; Sampling; Sexual behavior surveys; Social surveys.

Surveys, consumer. See *Market research.*

Surveys, demographic. See *Demographic surveys.*

Surveys, health. See *Health surveys.*

Surveys, health care. See *Health care surveys.*

Surveys, library. See *Library surveys.*

Surveys, market. See *Market research.*

Surveys, nutrition. See *Nutrition surveys.*

Surveys, population. See *Demographic surveys.*

Surveys, sex. See *Sexual behavior surveys.*

Surveys, sexual behavior. See *Sexual behavior surveys.*

Surveys, social. See *Social surveys.*

Surveys, soil. See *Soil surveys.*

Survival. Surviv(e,ed,ing,al,or,ors). *Consider also:* rescued, saved, near death, found alive, outdoor living skill(s), endur(ed,ing,ance), saved life, lifesaving, self preservation. *See also* Accidents; Child mortality; Civil defense; Coping; Death; Disaster relief; Disasters; Environmental protection; Genocide; Hazards; Health policy; Holocaust; Infant mortality; Longevity; National security; Natural disasters; Organizational survival; Outdoor life; Overpopulation; Preservation; Widowhood.

Survival, organizational. See *Organizational survival.*

Survival strategies. See *Coping.*

Survivor syndrome. See *Concentration camp syndrome; Post traumatic stress disorders.*

Survivors. Survivor(s,ship). Outliv(e,ed, ing). Outlast(ed,ing). Surviv(e,ed,ing). Those remaining. Remain(ed,ing) alive. *See also* Beneficiaries; Concentration camp syndrome; Post traumatic stress disorders; Relief services; Survivors benefits.

Survivors benefits. Survivors benefit(s). *Choose from:* survivor(s), widow(er,ers,s), surviving spouse(s), death *with:* benefit(s), pension(s), annuit(y,ies), beneficiar(y,ies). *See also* Beneficiaries; Estate planning; Life insurance; Survivors.

Susceptibility, disease. See *Disease susceptibility.*

Susceptibility, hypnotic. See *Hypnotic susceptibility.*

Suspense. Suspense(ful,fully,fulness). Excit(e,ed,ing,ement). Uncertain(ty,ies). Anticipat(e,ed,ing,ion). *Consider also:* anxiet(y,ies), apprehens(ive,ion), undecided, myster(y,ies), crime fiction, sleuth(s). *See also* Anticipation; Anxiety; Detective and mystery television programs; Ghost stories; Gothic romances; Haunted houses; Horror films; Horror tales.

Suspension, school. See *School suspension.*

Suspicion. Suspic(ion,ious,iousness). Distrust(ful,fulness). Skeptic(al,ism). Unbelief. Disbelief. Mistrust(ing,ful, fulness). Misgiving(s). Doubt(s,ing, ed,ful). Dubious(ness). Discredit(ed, ing). Suspect(ed,ing). *See also* Distrust; Doubt; Emotions; Jealousy; Trusting; Uncertainty.

Sustainable development. Sustainable development. Sustainable progress. Sustainable agriculture. Sustainable forestry. Sustainable land use(s). Sustainability. Ecodevelopment. Resource stewardship. Input-conserving technolog(y,ies). Appropriate technolog(y,ies). Bioeconomic model(s). Restorative economics. *Choose from:* economic growth, economic development, regional development, agricultural production, food production, full employment, output, infrastructure, prosperity *with:* ecological(ly), environment(al,ally), resource(s) *with:* sustainab(le,ility), balanc(e,ed,es,ing), tradeoff(s), optimal allocation(s), quality, renewable, self sustaining. *Consider also:* environmental limit(s), limit(s) to growth, permaculture, permanent agriculture, energy self sufficient, self sufficient housing, biological diversity. *See also* Agricultural ecology; Alternative energy; Appropriate technologies; Arid regions agriculture; Biological diversity; Bioregionalism; Community development; Debt-for-nature swap(s); Developing countries; Economic development; Conservation of natural resources; Environmental protection; Growth management; Infrastructure (economics); Organic farming; Phytogeography; Renewable resources; Resource management; Resource stress; Rural development; Rural industries; Transportation policy; Urban development; Zero emissions vehicles.

Swallowing air. Swallow(ed,ing) air. Aerophagia. Air swallowing. Nervous eructation. *See also* Habits.

Swamps, marshes and. See *Wetlands.*

Swapping, mate. See *Extramarital relations.*

Swaps, debt-for-nature. See *Debt-for-nature swaps.*

Swearing. See *Cursing; Oaths.*

Sweatshops. Sweatshop(s). Sweat shop(s). Sweated industr(y,ies). Sweating system(s). *Choose from:* labor, garment worker (s), factory worker (s), garment factor(y,ies), garment industry *with:* child labor, underage, low wage(s), less than minimum wage, unfair practice(s), abusive practice(s), indentured labor, illegal(ity,ities), inhuman(e) condition(s), harsh working condition(s), cheap(er) labor, 16 hour day(s), 80 hour week(s), long hours. *See also* Cheap labor; Child labor; Clothing workers; Exploitation; Foreign workers; Garment industry; Labor market; Oppression; Overwork; Trafficking in persons; Workers' rights; Working conditions.

Sweetheart deals. See *Conflict of interest.*

Sweethearts. See *Couples.*

Swimming. Swim(ming,mer,mers). Swam. Div(e,ing). *Consider also:* water sport(s), back, breast, side, butterfly, crawl *with:* stroke(s). *See also* Aquatic sports; Diving; Drowning; Recreation; Sports.

Switching, code. See *Code switching.*

Syllables, nonsense. See *Nonsense syllables.*

Symbiotic infantile psychosis. Symbiotic infantile psychos(is,es). *Consider also:* anaclitic depression, separation anxiety. *See also* Childhood psychosis; Childhood schizophrenia; Mother child relations; Psychoses; Symbiotic relations.

Symbiotic relations. Symbiotic relation(s, ship,ships). Symbio(sis,tic,tics). Symbiontic. Interdependen(t,ce,cy). Fruitful interaction(s). Synerg(y,ism, istic). Mutual(ly) dependen(t,ce,cy). Commensal(ism). *Consider also:* symbiotic psychos(is,es), symbiotic infantile psychos(is,es), psychos(is,es) of association, co-dependen(t,ce,cy), folie a deux. *See also* Attachment behavior; Complementary needs; Cybernetics; Interaction; Interdependence; Interpersonal relations; Man machine systems; Psychodynamics; Reciprocity; Social exchange; Technology.

Symbolism. Symbol(s,ism,ist,ists,ic,ics, izing,ize,ization). Graphic representation(s). Emblem(s,atic). Blissymbolic(s). *Consider also:* psychoanalytic interpretation(s), icon(s), latent content, represent(s,ed,ing,ation, ations), image(s,ry), metaphor(s,ical), ritual(ly) depict(ed,ing,ion,ions), motif(s), semiotic(s), semiology, poster child(ren), icon(s). *See also* Allusions; Arts; Christian symbolism; Collective representation; Communication (thought transfer); Dream interpretation; Emblems; Expressionism (Art); Figurative language; Iconography; Images; Language; Literature; Meaning; Metaphors; Political symbolism; Ritual purity; Rituals; Scapegoating; Semiotics; Sex symbolism; Symbolist movement; Visual communication.

Symbolism, Christian. See *Christian symbolism.*

Symbolism, political. See *Political symbolism.*

Symbolism, sex. See *Sex symbolism.*

Symbolism, sound. See *Onomatopoeia.*

Symbolist movement. Symbolist movement. *Consider also:* Stephane Mallarme, Paul Verlaine, Arthur Rimbaud, Jules LaForgue, Henri de Regnier; Gustave Kahn; Emile Verhaeren, Georges Rodenbach, Jean Moreas, Francis Viele-Griffin, Joris-Karl Huysmans, Maurice Maeterlinck, Vladimir Sergeyevich Solovyov, Aleksandr Blok, Vyacheslav Ivanovich Ivanov, Fyodor Sologub, Andrey Bely, Nikolay Gumilov. *See also* Aestheticism; Decadence (Literary movement); Literary movements; Symbolism.

Symbols, status. See *Consumer society; Luxuries.*

Sympathy. Sympath(y,etic,izing). Condolence(s). Solace. Consol(e,ed,ing,ation). Pity. Compassion(ate). Commiserat(ed, ing,ion). Compassion(ate). Comfort(ed, ing). Considerate(ness). Thoughtful(ness). Solicitous(ness). Kindl(y, iness). Shar(e,ed,ing) pain. *See also* Compassion; Consolation; Emotions; Empathy; Interpersonal relations; Pity; Tact.

Symphonic poems. Symphonic poem(s). Tone poem(s). Symphonische Dichtung. Poeme symphonique. *Consider also:* program music. *See also* Leitmotiv; Music; Overtures (music); Program music.

Symphony, program. See *Program symphony.*

Symposia. Sympos(ia,ium,iums). Colloqu(ia,ium,iums). Conference(s). Panel discussion(s). Round table(s). Convocation(s). Assembl(y,ies). *Consider also:* congress(es), convention(s), institute(s), meeting(s), seminar(s), workshop(s), proceedings. *See also* Conferences; Continuing education; Professional organizations.

Symptoms. Symptom(atic,s). Characteristic(s). Feature(s). Indicat(or,ors, ion,ions). Sign(s). Prodrome(s). Manifest(ed,ing,ations). Syndrome(s). Evidence. *See also* Acting out; Affective symptoms; Anhedonia; Anorexia nervosa; Behavior disorders; Body rocking; Catalepsy; Catatonia; Coma; Comorbidity; Convulsions; Delirium; Depersonalization disorder; Diagnosis; Disorders; Disease susceptibility; Distractibility; Early intervention; Fatigue; Fecal incontinence; Fever; Frigidity; Headache; Health; Hemorrhage; Hyperkinesis; Hyperphagia; Hypersexuality; Hypersomnia; Hyperventilation; Hypothermia; Illness; Insomnia; Migraine headaches; Nausea; Obesity; Pain; Physiological correlates; Restlessness; Scratching; Shock; Spasm; Stress management; Syncope; Tic; Trembling; Urinary incontinence; Vertigo; Vomiting.

Symptoms, affective. See *Affective symptoms.*

Synagogues. Synagogue(s). Temple(s). Shul(s). Schul(s). House(s) of worship. *See also* Judaism; Places of worship; Religious institutions; Sacred places.

Synchronism. Synchron(ism,ic,icity,ous). Simultane(ous,ousness,ity). Concurren(t, ce). Coinstantaneous(ness). Isochron(al, ism,ous). Parallel. Concomitan(t,ce). Coinciden(t,ce). *Consider also:* synesthesia. *See also* Comparative linguistics; Context; Harmonization; Historical perspective; Historiography; Linguistics.

Syncope. Syncop(e,al,ic). Faint(s,ed,ing). Blackout(s). *Choose from:* los(e,ing,t), loss *with:* consciousness. *Consider also:* pass(ed,ing) out, knock(ed,ing) out. *See also* Blood pressure; Shock; Symptoms; Unconsciousness; Vertigo.

Syncretism. Syncret(ic,ism,istic). Fusion. Physiognomic thinking. *Consider also:* eclectic(ism), synthes(es,is), reconciliation of beliefs. *See also* Cults; Paganism; Religions; Religious behavior; Religious conversion; Religious rituals; Taoism; Zen Buddhism.

Syndrome, acquired immunodeficiency. See *AIDS.*

Syndrome, air pollution. See *Sick building syndrome.*

Syndrome, amnesic. See *Amnesic syndrome.*

Syndrome, attachment disorder. See *Reactive attachment disorder.*

Syndrome, binge purge. See *Bulimia.*

Syndrome, Capgras. See *Capgras syndrome.*

Syndrome, chronic fatigue. See *Chronic fatigue syndrome.*

Syndrome, concentration camp. See *Concentration camp syndrome.*

Syndrome, Downs. See *Downs syndrome.*

Syndrome, fetal alcohol. See *Fetal alcohol syndrome.*

Syndrome, Ganser. See *Ganser syndrome.*

Syndrome, general adaptation. See *General adaptation syndrome.*

Syndrome, Gulf war. See *Gulf war syndrome.*

Syndrome, housewife's. See *Housewife's syndrome.*

Syndrome, info fatigue. See *Info fatigue syndrome.*

Syndrome, information fatigue. See *Info fatigue syndrome.*

Syndrome, Korsakoff's. See *Alcohol amnestic disorder.*

Syndrome, Munchausen. See *Factitious disorders.*

Syndrome, post-viral fatigue. See *Chronic fatigue syndrome.*

Syndrome, premenstrual. See *Premenstrual syndrome.*

Syndrome, sexual asphyxia. See *Sexual asphyxia syndrome.*

Syndrome, sick building. See *Sick building syndrome.*

Syndrome, social breakdown. See *Social breakdown syndrome.*

Syndrome, substance withdrawal. See *Substance withdrawal syndrome.*

Syndrome, survivor. See *Concentration camp syndrome; Post traumatic stress disorders.*

Syndromes, culture specific. See *Culture specific syndromes.*

Synergism, drug. See *Drug interactions.*

Synergy. Synerg(y,ism). *Consider also:* combined effect(s), enhanc(e,ed,ing, ement,ements,er,ers), joint effort(s). *See also* Combinations; Connectivity; Cooperation; Sharing; Teamwork.

Synesthesia. Synesthe(sia,tic,te,tes). Synaesthe(sia,tic,te,tes). Colour(ed) hearing. Color(ed) hearing. Tast(e,ed, ing) color(s). Hear(d,ing) color(s). *Consider also:* intersensory effects, tone colour relationships, photism(s), concomitant sensations. *See also* Illusions (perception); Onomatopoeia; Perception.

Synods and councils, religious. See *Religious councils and synods.*

Synthesis. Synthe(sis,ses,tic,size,sized, sizing). Dialectical unity. Fusion. Merg(e,ed,ing). Amalgam(ate,ated,ating, ation). Integrat(e,ed,ing,ation). Unif(y,ied,ying). Unification. Unified theor(y,ies). Unified general theory. *Choose from:* unified, comprehensive, integrated *with:* theor(y,ies). *See also* Cognition; Cognitive processes; Comparative study; Dialectics; Knowledge; Principles.

Synthetic drugs. See *Designer drugs.*

System, cardiovascular. See *Cardiovascular system.*

System, caste. See *Caste system.*

System, correctional. See *Correctional system.*

System, digestive. See *Digestive system.*

System, endocrine. See *Endocrine system.*

System, factory. See *Factory system.*

System, gastrointestinal. See *Digestive system.*

System, judicial. See *Legal system.*

System, legal. See *Legal system.*

System, metayer. See *Sharecropping.*

System, nervous. See *Nervous system.*

System, penal. See *Correctional system.*

System, respiratory. See *Respiratory system.*

System, social. See *Social structure.*

System, spoils. See *Political patronage.*

Systematic desensitization. See *Desensitization (psychology).*

Systems. System(s). Subsystem(s). Ecosystem(s). Biosystem(s). Macrosystem(s). Microsystem(s). *Choose from:* related *with:* definitions, assumptions, propositions, functions. *Consider also:* network(s), complex unity, interacti(ve,ion), interdependen(t,ce), totalit(y,ies), coherent unification, universe(s), interwoven, interconnected, interrelationship, interrelated parts, overall structure(s), sum total, hierarch(y,ies), general theor(y,ies), totalit(y,ies). *See also* Cardiovascular system; Caste system; Correctional system; Computers; Connectivity; Digestive system; Endocrine system; Expert systems; Legal system; Man machine systems; Management information systems; Multi-institutional systems; Nervous system; Networks; Number systems; Patient identification systems; Philosophy; Political systems; Punched card systems; Respiratory system; Social support networks; Structure; Systems analysis; Systems theory; User friendly systems.

Systems, accounting. See *Accounting systems.*

Systems, billing. See *Billing systems.*

Systems, cargo. See *Cargo systems.*

Systems, chaotic behavior in. See *Chaotic behavior in systems.*

Systems, data transmission. See *Data transmission systems.*

Systems, decision support. See *Decision support systems.*

Systems, expert. See *Expert systems.*

Systems, feedback control. See *Cybernetics; Feedback; Robotics.*

Systems, filing. See *Files and filing; Records management.*

Systems, geographic information. See *Geographic information systems.*

Systems, high fidelity sound. See *High fidelity sound systems.*

Systems, human machine. See *Man machine systems.*

Systems, information retrieval. See *Automated information retrieval.*

Systems, interactive computer. See *Interactive computer systems.*

Systems, man machine. See *Man machine systems.*

Systems, management information. See *Management information systems.*

Systems, multi-institutional. See *Multi-institutional systems.*

Systems, number. See *Number systems.*

Systems, patient identification. See *Patient identification systems.*

Systems, political. See *Political systems.*

Systems, privatized pension. See *Privatized pension systems.*

Systems, punched card. See *Punched card systems.*

Systems, sensory. See *Sense organs.*

Systems, support. See *Financial support; Social support; Social support networks.*

Systems, therapeutic. See *Alternative medicine.*

Systems, user friendly. See *User friendly systems.*

Systems, worker machine. See *Man machine systems.*

Systems analysis. Systems analys(is,es). Functional systems theory. System(s) theoretic(al) model(s). Computer simulation. System simulation. Systems approach. Network analysis. Systems dynamics simulation. *Consider also:* task analysis, operations research. *See also* Analysis; Cost effectiveness; Decision making; Man machine systems; Management information systems; Mathematical models; Needs assessment; Organizational effectiveness; Problem solving; Relevance; Scientific models; Systems; Systems theory; Task performance and analysis.

Systems theory. System(s) theor(y,ies, etical). Cybernetic(s). General system(s) theor(y,ies). Queuing theory. *Choose from:* system(s), microsystem(s), macrosystem(s) *with:* perspective(s), concept(s), theor(y,ies,etical), approach(es), dynamic(s), model(s). *See also* Context; Cybernetics; Decision making; Functionalism; Holism; Management information systems; Models; Planning; Problem solving; Social equilibrium; Sociological theory; Systems; Systems analysis; Teleology; Theories.

Systems theory, world. See *World systems theory.*

T

T groups. See *Sensitivity training*.

Tablature. Tablature(s). Tabulatur(en). Intavolatura. Tabulatura. Cifra. *Consider also:* guitar alfabeto(s). *See also* Music.

Tables, statistical. See *Statistical tables*.

Tableware. Tableware. Dinnerware. Table setting(s). Tablesetting(s). Cutlery. Flatware Eating utensil(s). Table settings. Silverware. Kitchenware. Glass(es,ware). *Consider also:* earthenware, creamware, stoneware, hollowware, pottery, corncob holder(s), fork(s), knives, knife, spoon(s), plate(s), bowl(s), pitcher(s), tabletop item(s), crockery, tureen(s), chopstick(s), dish(es), china. *See also* Dinners and dining; Eating establishments; Hardware.

Tabloid newspapers. See *Tabloids*.

Tabloids. Tabloid(s). Entertainment magazine(s). Checkbook journalis(m, t,ts). Yellow journalism. Scandal sheet(s). *Consider also:* paparozzi, poison(ed) pen(s), sensational stor(y,ies), sensational(ism), paying for stor(y,ies), New York Post, New York Daily News, National Enquirer, National Examiner, Boston Herald, Chicago-Sun Times, London Sun, The Star, etc. *See also* Journalistic ethics; Gossip; Gossip sites; Libel; Mass media; Newspapers; Popular literature; Scandals; Sensationalism.

Taboo. Taboo(s,ed). Tabu(s,ed). Ban(ned, ning). Proscribe(d). Forbid(den). Prohibit(e,ed,ing,ion,ions). *Consider also:* unclean(liness), sacred(ness), holy, holiness. *See also* Animism; Cannibalism; Cross cultural psychiatry; Customs; Ethnology; Forbidden; Incest; Intermarriage; Prohibition; Rites of passage; Ritual purity; Sacrilege; Sex behavior; Sex customs; Sin; Superstitions; Traditions; Words.

Tact. Tact(ful,fully,fulness). Diplomacy. Savoir faire. Finesse. *Consider also:* poise(d), courtesy, gallantry; politie(ness), smooth(ness), suav(e,ity), urban(e,ity), adroit(ness), perceptive(ness), sensitiv(e,ity), grace, thoughtfulness good manners. *See also* Diplomacy; Etiquette; Social skills; Sympathy.

Tactics, minor and drill. See *Drill and minor tactics*.

Tactile defensiveness. See *Sensory defensiveness*.

Tactile stimulation. See *Tactual stimulation*.

Tactual displays. Tactual display(s). Tactile display(s). Braille. Tangible graph(s).

Tangible line(s). *Choose from:* tactile, vibrotactile *with:* diagram(s), display(s), aid(s), letter(s), pattern(s), information, map(s,ping), identification. *See also* Tactual stimulation.

Tactual perception. Tactual perception. *Choose from:* tactual, tactile, cutaneous, tactuo-spatial, tactuospatial, touch, vibrotactile, haptic *with:* perception, recognition, communication, discrimination, sensation(s), sense, sensibility, identification, coding. *See also* Stereognosis; Texture perception; Vibrotactile thresholds.

Tactual stimulation. Tactual stimulation. Touch(ed,ing). Manual tracing. Face touching. Tickl(e,ed,ing). *Choose from:* tactual, tactile, cutaneous, tactuo-spatial, tactuospatial, touch, vibrotactile, haptic *with:* stimul(i,us,ate,ated,ating,ation), cue(s), contact, communication, prompt(s), information, input(s), aid(s). *See also* Perceptual stimulation; Tactual stimulation.

Takeover defense. See *Anti takeover strategies*.

Takeovers, corporate. See *Corporate acquisitions; Mergers*.

Takeovers, hostile. See *Hostile takeovers*.

Taking, perspective. See *Perspective taking*.

Taking, risk. See *Risk taking*.

Taking, role. See *Role taking*.

Taking, test. See *Test taking*.

Taking history, medical. See *Medical history taking*.

Taking history, patient. See *Medical history taking*.

Talent. See *Ability*.

Tales, fairy. See *Fairy tales*.

Tales, horror. See *Horror tales*.

Talisman. Talisman(s,ic,ically). Amulet(s). Juju(s). Periapt(s). Phylacter(y,ies). Scarab(s). Zemi(s). *Consider also:* good-luck piece, lucky horshoe(s), good luck charm(s). *See also* Ancient jewelry; Fetishism; Jewish mysticism; Magic; Shrunken heads; Superstitions.

Talk, baby. See *Baby talk*.

Talk, self. See *Self talk*.

Talking, sleep. See *Sleep talking*.

Talking therapies. See *Psychotherapy*.

Talks, peace. See *Peace negotiations*.

Taming. See *Animal domestication*.

Tampering, product. See *Product tampering*.

Tampering, witness. See *Witness tampering*.

Tanks, think. See *Think tanks*.

Tantrums. Tantrum(s). Tantrum behavior. Temper tantrum(s). Screaming fit(s). Explosive children. Violent temper(s). Outburst(s). Disruptive behavior. Violent temperament(s). Rage. *See also* Behavior disorders.

Taoism. Tao(ism,ist). Lao Tzu. Chuang Tzu. Huai Nan Tzu. Wu Wei. Neo-Taoism. School of dark learning. Hsuan-hsueh. Nonbeing. Hsiao-yao. Lieh Tzu. *See also* Asian empires; Pantheism (universal divinity); Religions; Syncretism.

Tapping, finger. See *Finger tapping*.

Target marketing. Target market(s,ing). *Choose from:* target *with:* audience(s), group(s), market(s,ing), consumer(s). *See also* Advertising; Direct marketing; Market development; Market research; Market segmentation; Marketing; Marketing plans; Marketing strategies; Markets

Tariffs. Tariff(s). Customs dut(y,ies). Import tax(es). Schedule of charge(s). *Consider also:* retaliatory dut(y,ies, tariff war(s), most favored nation clause. *See also* Imports; International trade; Nontariff trade barriers; Taxes; Trade protection.

Task analysis. See *Task performance and analysis*.

Task complexity. Task complexity. Complexity of task(s). Task difficulty. *Choose from:* task(s), problem(s) *with:* complex(ity), difficulty, level(s), characteristic(s), content, demand(s), factor(s), competing. *See also* Complexity; Task performance and analysis; Tasks.

Task performance and analysis. Task performance and analysis. *Choose from:* task(s), work(load), productivity, performance, efficiency *with:* analy(sis,ses), measur(e,ed,ing), evaluat(e,ed,ing,ion), stud(y,ies,ying), improv(e,ed,ing,ement,ements), monitor(ed,ing), track(ed,ing). *Consider also:* time and motion studies, work simplification, evaluat(e,ed,ing,ion) efficiency, performance difference(s). *See also* Cognitive processes; Content analysis; Job performance; Systems analysis; Task complexity; Tasks; Work simplification.

Tasks. Task(s). Chore(s). Job(s). Dut(y,ies). Assignment(s). Lesson(s). Exercise(s).

Errand(s). Homework. Responsibilit(y,ies). Mission(s). Routine(s). *See also* Division of labor; Job descriptions; Occupational roles; Occupational structure; Task complexity; Task performance and analysis; Work; Work load.

Tasks, household. See *Housekeeping.*

Tasks, work. See *Tasks.*

Taste (food). Tast(e,es,ed,ing). Flavor sensitiv(e,ity). Flavor preference(s). Gustatism. *Choose from:* flavor, food, gustatory *with:* sensitivity, aversion, preference(s), palatability, stimulation, perception, discrimination, tast(e,es,ed, ing). *Consider also:* electrogustomet(ry,ic,er,ers), taste bud(s), taste perception, taste threshold(s). *See also* Sensory thresholds; Taste perception; Taste threshold.

Taste, literary. See *Literature appreciation.*

Taste perception. Taste perception. *Choose from:* taste, flavor(s,ed,ing,ings), salt(y,iness), gustatory, sweet(ness), sucrose, saccharin, sugar, sour(ness), bitter(ness) *with:* perception, recogniz(e, ed,ing), recognition, discriminat(e,ed, ing,ion,ions), reactiv(e,ity), reaction(s), sensation(s), sense, sensibility, identification, preference(s), palatab(le,ility), unpalatab(le,ility). *See also* Odor discrimination; Taste (food); Taste threshold.

Taste stimulation. Taste stimulation. *Choose from:* taste(s), flavor(s,ing,ings), gustatory, salt(y,iness), sour(ness), bitter(ness), sweet(ness), sugar, saccharin, sucrose *with:* stimul(i,us,ated, ating,ation), present(ed,ing,ation), exposure, irritation(s), irritant(s), cue(s), information, input(s). *See also* Perceptual stimulation; Taste (food).

Taste threshold. Taste threshold(s). *Choose from:* taste *with:* threshold(s), submodalit(y,ies), synergism, papillae, acuity, sensitivit(y,ies), reactiv(e,ity), perception, sense, recognition. *Consider also:* electrogustometr(y,ic,er,ers), salt threshold(s), sucrose threshold(s). *See also* Sensory thresholds; Taste (food).

Tastes. See *Preferences.*

Tax deductions. Tax deduct(able,ability,ion, ions). *Choose from:* tax(es,ation), rate(s) *with:* credit(s), subsid(y,ies), shelter(s, ed), avoid(ed,ing,ance), relief, exile(s), refund(s), exempt(ion,ions), write-off(s), adjustment(s). *Consider also:* tax haven(s). *See also* Abatement; Income; Tax exemption; Tax evasion; Tax opportunities; Taxes.

Tax evasion. Tax evasion. *Choose from:* tax(es), IRS, internal revenue, toll(s), tariff(s), surtax(es) *with:* evasion, evad(e,er,ers,ing), fraud(ulent), avoid(ed,ing,ance), cheat(ed,ing,s),

dodge(s,er,ers), exile(s), expatriate(s), refus(e,ed,ing,al), violat(e,ed,ing,ion, ions,er,ers), illegal(ity,ities), falsif(y,ying,ied,ication), defraud(ed, ing), fail(ed,ing,ure), conspirac(y,ies), delinquen(t,cy,cies). *Consider also:* tax shelter(s), tax haven(s), violat(e,ed,ing, ion) tax exempt status, conceal(ed,ing) income, illegal tax loss(es), money laundering. *See also* Crime; Tax deductions; Tax exemption; Tax opportunities; Taxes.

Tax exemption. Tax exemption(s). Tax free. Tax deduct(ible,ion,ions). *Choose from:* tax(es,ing,ation), customs, tariff(s), IRS, Internal Revenue Service, dut(y,ies), lev(y,ies,ied), surtax(es), toll(s) *with:* exempt(ion,ions), break(s), relief, loophole(s), exclusion(s), not-for-profit, nonprofit, charitable institution(s). *Consider also:* tax credit(s). *See also* Exemption (law); Tax deduction; Tax evasion; Tax opportunities; Taxes.

Tax opportunities. Tax opportunit(y,ies). Tax benefit(s). Tax credit(s). *Choose from:* tax(es,ation) *with:* deduct(ible,ion, ions), investment initiative(s), savings initiative(s), *Consider also:* tax relief, nontaxable IRA contribution(s), Lifetime Learning Credit, College Expenses Tax Credit. *See also* Tax deductions; Tax exemption; Tax evasion; Taxes.

Taxation. See *Taxes.*

Taxes. Tax(es,ing,ation,able). IRS. Internal Revenue Service. Dut(y,ies). Lev(y,ies,ied). Tariff(s). Surtax(es). Toll(s). Revenue(s). Impost(s). Progressive tax(es). Regressive tax(es). Value added tax(es). *Choose from:* tax(es,ed, ing,ation) *with:* assessment, base, credit, deed, deferred, dodge(s), evasion, exempt(ed,ing,ion,ions), foreclosure, haven(s), lien(s), polic(y,ies), rate(s), reform(s), shelter(s). *Choose from:* capital gains, estate, excise, federal, fuel, gas(oline), general, gift, income, inheritance, local, luxury, sales, school, sin, state, property, use *with:* tax(es). *Consider also:* taxpayer(s), assessed valuation, custom(s). *See also* Capitation fee; Finance; Fiscal policy; Government finances; Income; Ownership; Progressive taxes; Public finance; Public policy; Regressive taxes; Supply side economics; Tariffs; Tax deductions; Tax exemption; Tax evasion; Tax opportunities.

Taxes, progressive. See *Progressive taxes.*

Taxes, regressive. See *Regressive taxes.*

Taxonomies. Taxonom(y,ies,ic,ical). Typolog(y,ies,ical). Classification system(s). Subtyp(e,es,ed,ing). Classif(y,ying,ication). Hierarchical organization. Hierarchical tree(s). Categoriz(e,ed,ing,ation). Categorical representation(s). Taxometric. Clustering

program(s). Class analysis. Logical type(s). Ideal type(s). Grouping. *Consider also:* chain of being. *See also* Classification; Coding; Hierarchy; Labeling (of persons); Occupational classification; Stratification; Structure; Types.

Tay Sachs disease. Tay Sachs disease. Gangliosidosis GM2. GM2 gangliosidosis. GM2 ganglioside. Amaurotic famil(y,ial) idiocy. *See also* Hereditary diseases; Mental retardation.

Taylorism. See *Scientific management.*

Teacher attitudes. Teacher attitude(s). *Choose from:* teacher(s), schoolteacher(s), schoolmaster(s), professor(s), faculty, instructor(s), educator(s) *with:* attitud(e,es,inal), acceptance, attribution(s), aversion(s), belief(s), bias(ed,es), dissatisf(ied,action), dislike(s), expectation(s), feeling(s), labeling, labelling, like(s), outlook, opinion(s), orientation(s), perception(s), preference(s), personal values, perspective(s), mindset, permissiveness, prejudic(ed,es), reaction(s), rejection, satisfaction, standpoint, stereotypes, value(s), view(s), viewpoint(s), worldview(s). *See also* Attitudes; Student teacher relations; Teacher characteristics; Teacher evaluation; Teacher expectations; Teacher personality; Teachers.

Teacher characteristics. Teacher characteristic(s). *Choose from:* teacher(s), instructor(s), faculty, educator(s), professor(s), schoolteacher(s) *with:* characteristic(s), personal qualit(y,ies), style(s), effectiveness, authoritarianism, dogmatism, credential(s), attractiveness, stereotype(s), personality, talented, masculinity, feminity, bias(es), warmth, coldness, indifference, genuine(ness), sincer(e,ity), insincer(e,ity), empath(y,etic), intelligen(t,ce), sensitiv(e,ity), insensitiv(e,ity), personality, experience, orientation, gender, disabilit(y,ies), handicap(s,ped), gifted, family background, income, place of residence, ethnic(ity), nationality, religion, health status, behavior patterns, qualit(y,ies), trait(s), profile(s), socioeconomic status, marital status, sexual preference, age, race, religion, educational level, urban, rural. *See also* Characteristics; Individual differences; Student teacher relations; Teacher attitudes: Teacher expectations; Teacher personality; Teachers; Teaching; Qualities.

Teacher education, inservice. See *Inservice teacher education.*

Teacher evaluation. Teacher evaluation. Teacher effectiveness evaluation. Teacher rating(s). *Choose from:* teacher(s), schoolteacher(s), instructor(s), faculty, professor(s), coach(es) *with:* effectiveness, teaching problem(s), performance *with:* evaluat(e,ed,ing,ion), assess(ed,ing, ment), rating(s). *See also* Course evaluation; Faculty development; Personnel evaluation; Student teacher relations; Teacher attitudes; Teacher characteristics; Teaching.

Teacher expectations. Teacher expectation(s). Expectation(s) of teachers. *Choose from:* teacher(s) *with:* labeling, labelling, attribution(s), expect(ed,ation, ations), prediction(s), expectanc(y,ies). *Consider also:* looking glass self. *See also* Self fulfilling prophecy; Student teacher relations; Teacher attitudes; Teacher characteristics.

Teacher parent relationship. See *Parent school relations.*

Teacher personality. Teacher personality. *Choose from:* teacher(s), instructor(s), faculty, educator(s), professor(s), schoolteacher(s) *with:* personalit(y,ies), personal characteristic(s), personal qualit(y,ies), authoritarian(ism), creativity, creative(ness), extraver(t,ted, sion), easygoing, neurotic(ism), expressive(ness), cooperative(ness), dogmat(ic,ism), masculinity, femininity, bias(es), warmth, coldness, indifferen(t, ce), genuine(ness), sincer(e,ity), insincer(e,ity), empath(y,ic), pedantic, intelligen(t,ce), sensitiv(e,ity), insensitiv(e,ity), adaptab(le,ility), sociab(le,ility), humor(ous,ousness), formal(ity), rigid(ity), self aware(ness), toleran(t,ce), trusting, suspicious(ness), assertive(ness), independen(t,ce). *See also* Personality traits; Teacher characteristics; Teachers.

Teacher pupil relationship. See *Student teacher relations.*

Teacher recruitment. Teacher recruitment. *Choose from:* teacher(s), faculty, professor(s), educator(s), instructor(s), schoolteacher(s) *with:* recruit(ed,ing, ment), hir(e,ed,es,ing), select(ed,ing, ion), job offer(s). *See also* Personnel management; Personnel recruitment; Teachers.

Teacher student interaction. See *Student teacher relations.*

Teacher student relationship. See *Student teacher relations.*

Teacher tenure. See *Academic tenure.*

Teachers. Teacher(s). Facult(y,ies). Academ(e,ia,ics). Academic status. Academic staff. Teaching staff. School staff. Academic personnel. School master(s). Schoolmaster(s). Schoolteacher(s). University teaching staff. Professoriate. Professor(s). Instructor(s). Dean(s). Don(s). Academician(s). Educational personnel. Educator(s). Coach(es). Headmaster(s). Headmistress(es). Mentor(s). *See also*

Academic rank; Academic tenure; Elementary school teachers; Faculty; Faculty development; High school teachers; Junior high school teachers; Parent school relations; Preschool teachers; Preservice teachers; Resource teachers; Student teacher relations; Teacher attitudes; Teacher characteristics; Teacher evaluation; Teacher expectations; Teacher personality; Teacher recruitment; Teaching; Teaching methods.

Teachers, college. See *Faculty.*

Teachers, elementary school. See *Elementary school teachers.*

Teachers, high school. See *High school teachers.*

Teachers, junior high school. See *Junior high school teachers.*

Teachers, preschool. See *Preschool teachers.*

Teachers, preservice. See *Preservice teachers.*

Teachers, resource. See *Resource teachers.*

Teachers, secondary school. See *High school teachers.*

Teachers, University. See *Faculty*

Teaching. Teach(ing). Taught. Educat(e,ed, ing,ion,ional). Lectur(e,ed,ing). Coach(ed,ing). Course(s). Didactic(s, ism). Directed learning. Drill(ed,ing). Educational process(es). Indoctrinat(e, ed,ing,ion). Initiat(e,ed,ing,ion). Instruct(ed,ing,ion,ional). Orient(ing, ed,ation). Pedagog(y,ic,ical). Preceptor(ship). Retrain(ed,ing). Seminar(s). Teach(ing). Train(ed,ing). Tutor(ed,s, ing). *See also* Bilingual education; College teaching; Computer assisted instruction; Course evaluation; Directed discussion; Discovery learning; Educational field trips; Educational television; Group instruction; Home schooling; Individualized instruction; Instructional media; Lecture method; Lectures and lecturing; Lesson plans; Nondirected discussion method; Open classroom method; Peer teaching; Programed instruction; Reading materials; Teacher characteristics; Teachers; Teaching materials; Teaching methods.

Teaching, college. See *College teaching.*

Teaching, peer. See *Peer teaching.*

Teaching materials. Teaching material(s). *Choose from:* teaching, classroom, instructional, curriculum, educational, study *with:* material(s), media, guide(s). *Consider also:* classroom librar(y,ies), textbook(s), workbook(s), advance organizer(s), instructional film(s), laboratory manual(s), learning module(s), programmed instruction(al), protocol material(s), student developed

material(s), teacher developed material(s), audio-visual aid(s). *See also* Educational technology; Library materials; Teaching; Reading materials.

Teaching methods. Teaching method(s). *Choose from:* teaching, instruction(al), educational *with:* method(s), technique(s), practice(s), procedure(s), system(s), module(s), approach(es), mode(s), model(s), process(es). *See also* Advance organizers; Audiovisual instruction; Computer assisted instruction; Directed discussion; Discovery learning; Educational field trips; Educational television; Fieldwork; Group instruction; Individualized instruction; Lecture method; Lesson plans; Mastery learning; Nondirected discussion method; Nontraditional education; Open classroom method; Peer teaching; Practical experience; Practice (repetition); Practicum supervision; Programed instruction; Role playing; Teaching; Teaching materials; Whole language approach.

Team, nursing. See *Nursing team.*

Team, patient care. See *Patient care team.*

Teaming. Teaming. Team(ed) up. Form(ed,ing) team(s). Form(ed,ing) group(s). Team based structure(s). *Consider also:* collaborat(e,ed,ing,ion), partner(s,ship,ships), teamwork, joint venture(s), task force(s). *See also* Adhocracies; Alliances; Affiliation (businesses); Coalitions; Cobranding; Consortia; Cooperation; Mergers; Organizational development; Strategic alliances; Teamwork; Teams; Virtual organizations.

Teams. Team(s). Crew(s). Aircrew(s). Work group(s). Committee(s). Collaborator(s). Partnership(s). Troupe(s). Compan(y, ies). Gang(s). Squad(s). Corp(s). Band(s). Brigade(s). Collective(s). *See also* Groups; Nursing team; Teaming; Teamwork.

Teamwork. Teamwork. Work group(s). Teamplay(er,ers). Combined action. Work(ing) together. *Choose from:* team(s), group(s), unit(s), brigade(s), collective(s) *with:* work, spirit. *Choose from:* team(s) *with:* build(ing), approach(es). *Consider also:* quality circle(s), alliance(s), cooperat(e,ed,ing, ive,ion), coalition formation, collaborat(e,ing,ion), join(ed,ing) forces, collusion, unite(d) effort(s), joint action. *See also* Combinations; Cooperation; Group decision making; Interdisciplinary approach; Peer relations; Social behavior; Teaming; Teams.

Teasing. Teas(e,ed,ing). Torment(e,ed,ing). Bedevil(ed,ing). Bother(ed,ing,some). Pester(e,ed,ing). Bug(ged,ing). Hassl(e,ed,ing). Vex(ing). Provok(e,ed, ing,ation). Taunt(ed,ing). Name calling. Gib(e,ed,ing). *Consider also:* mak(e,ing) fun of, clown(ed,ing), scoff(ed,ing), derid(e,ed,ing), jeer(ed,ing, sneer(ed,ing), flout(ed,ing). *See also* Antisocial behavior; Derision; Harassment; Intimidation; Verbal abuse.

Technica, memoria. See *Mnemonic learning.*

Technical assistance. Technical assistance. *Choose from:* transfer(ring,red,ence), aid(ed,ing), assist(ed,ing,ance), export(ed,ing), diffusion *with:* technical skill(s), expertise, consultant(s), technolog(y,ical). *Consider also:* technology transfer, agricultural assistance, development aid, foreign assistance, technical cooperation, appropriate technolog(y,ies), Peace Corps. *See also* Appropriate technologies; Arms transfers; Community development; Consultants; Consultation; Developed countries; Developing countries; Economic development; Financial support; Human resources; International cooperation; International educational exchange; International relations; Technical information; Technical personnel; Technological progress; Technology transfer.

Technical information. Technical information. *Choose from:* technical, industrial, technological, scientific, sci-tech *with:* information(al), data, fact(s), report(s), text(s), communique(s), document(s), blueprint(s), book(s), letter(s), manuscript(s), source(s), knowledge. *Consider also:* technical librar(y,ies). *See also* Information; Technical assistance; Technical writing.

Technical innovations. See *Technological innovations.*

Technical personnel. Technical personnel. Technician(s). Technical worker(s). Engineering officer(s). Radio operator(s). Electric components operator(s). Technologist(s). Computer operator(s). Electrician(s). *Choose from:* technical *with:* personnel, worker(s), officer(s), employee(s), operator(s), staff. *Consider also:* engineer(s), industrial personnel, scientific personnel, mathematician(s), scientist(s). *See also* Consultants; Human resources; Technical assistance; Technocracy.

Technical writing. Technical writing. *Choose from:* technical, scien(ce,tific), research, American Chemical Society, American Institute of Physics, training manual(s), *with:* writ(ing,er,ers), author(s), manuscript(s), editor(s,ial), style manual(s), report(s,ing). *Consider also:* medical writing, science news, specification writing, technical correspondence, technical manual(s), scholarly writing, technical English. *See also* Technical information; Writing (composition).

Technicians. See *Technical personnel.*

Technicians, emergency medical. See *Emergency medical technicians.*

Technics, sociometric. See *Sociometric technics.*

Technique, mutual storytelling. See *Mutual storytelling technique.*

Techniques, cognitive. See *Cognitive techniques.*

Techniques, management. See *Management methods.*

Techniques, paradoxical. See *Paradoxical techniques.*

Techniques, projective. See *Projective techniques.*

Techniques, psychotherapeutic. See *Psychotherapeutic techniques.*

Technocracy. Technocra(cy,cies,tic, t,ts,tization). Rule by technician(s). *Consider also:* role of expert(s), technological utopianism, high tech(nology) society, Deus ex machina. *See also* Dehumanization; Meritocracy; Oligarchy; Political systems; Rationalization (sociology); Technical personnel.

Technological change. Technological change(s). Moderniz(e,ed,ing,ation). *Choose from:* technolog(y,ies,ical), technical, industrial, engineering, manufacturing, sociotechnical, biotechnical, computer(s,ized,ization), automat(e,ed,ing,ion), microcomputer(s), robot(s,ic) *with:* change(s), changing, advance(s), progress, development(s), transformation(s), new, innovation(s), forecast(s,ing), revolution(s). *See also* Agricultural mechanization; Automation; Culture change; Dislocated workers; Economic change; High technology industries; Industrialization; Information; Inventions; Modernization; Public policy; Scientific discoveries; Scientific revolutions; Social change; Skills obsolescence; Technological forecasting; Technological innovations; Technological progress; Technological unemployment; Technology assessment; Technology transfer.

Technological forecasting. Technological forecast(s,ing). *Choose from:* technolog(y,ies,ical), technical, innovation(s), research *with:* forecast(s,ing), forecaster(s), Delphi stud(y,ies), vision(s), estimate(s), predict(ed,ing,ion,ions), scenario(s), trend(s), futurist(s), future, the year 2100, the year 2050, etc. *Consider also:* Star Trek, Ecotopia, greenhouse effect, fusion energy, clean burning hydrogen, fusion reactor(s), space colon(y,ies), extraterrestrial population(s), expert system(s), high speed rail system(s), automated highway system(s), intelligent transportation system(s), exploration of Mars. *See also* Future of society;

Inventions; Technological change; Technological innovations; Technological progress; Technological unemployment; Technology; Technology and civilization; Technology assessment; Technology transfer.

Technological innovations. Technological innovation(s). Moderniz(e,ed,ing,ation). *Choose from:* technolog(y,ies,ical), technical, industrial, engineering, manufacturing, sociotechnical, biotechnical, computer(s,ized,ization), automat(e,ed,ing,ion), microcomputer(s), robot(s,ic) *with:* innovat(ive,ion,ions), breakthrough(s), emerging, forecast(s,ing), advance(s), progress, development(s), discover(y, ies), finding(s), new, alternative, new generation, fifth generation. *See also* Adoption of ideas; High technology industries; Industrialization; Intangible property; Inventions; Medieval technology; Medical innovations; Patents; Product development; Product introduction; Research; Scientific development; Scientific discoveries; Scientific equipment; Scientific revolutions; Technological change; Technological forecasting; Technological progress; Technology.

Technological progress. Technological progress. Electrification. Moderniz(e,ed, ing,ation). *Choose from:* technolog(y,ies, ical), technical, industrial, engineering, manufacturing, sociotechnical, biotechnical, computer(s,ize,ized, ization), automat(e,ed,ing,ion), microcomputer(s), robot(s,ic) *with:* achievement(s), breakthrough(s), cutting edge, leading edge, state-of-the-art, discover(y,ies), advance(s), progress, emerging, development(s), invention(s), new, innovation(s), forecast(s,ing), revolution(s). *See also* Adoption of ideas; Appropriate technologies; Cybernetics; Economic development; Future of society; Inventions; Medieval technology; Modernization; Quality of life; Quality of working life; Scientific development; Scientific discoveries; Scientific revolutions; Technical assistance; Technological change; Technological innovations; Technological forecasting; Technological unemployment; Technology; Technology and civilization; Technology assessment; Technology transfer.

Technological revolutions. See *Scientific revolutions.*

Technological transfer. See *Technology transfer.*

Technological unemployment. Technological(ly) unemploy(ed,ment). *Choose from:* skill(s) *with:* obsolescen(t, ce), obsolete. *Choose from:* automation, microcomputer(s), computer(s,ized, ization), technical change(s), deskill(ed,ing), deskill(ed,ing), new methods, labor saving, labor augmenting *with:* unemploy(ed,ment,able), layoff(s), jobless(ness), idle(d) worker(s), out of work. *See also* Labor aspects of Technology; Personnel termination; Plant closings; Skills obsolescence; Technological change; Technological forecasting; Technological progress; Technology and civilization.

Technologies, appropriate. See *Appropriate technologies.*

Technologies, reproductive. See *Reproductive technologies.*

Technology. Technolog(y,ical,ically,ies). Biotechnolog(y,ical,ically,ies). Machine(s). Device(s). Equipment. Cytotechnolog(y,ies). Instrument(ation, s). Technic(s). Deus ex machina. Appropriate technolog(y,ies). Industrial arts. Apparatus. Assembly line(s). Mechaniz(e,ed,ing,ation). Mechanis(e, ed,ing,ation). Engineer(ed,ing). Bioengineer(ed,ing). Man machine. Automation. Mechanics. Cybernetics. Hydraulics. Refrigeration. Reprography. *Choose from:* technical, industrial, technological *with:* development(s), progress, advance(s). *See also* Aerospace industries; Agricultural mechanization; Appropriate technologies; Automation; Biotechnology; Culture (anthropology); Cybernetics; Economics; High technology industries; Industry; Inventions; Labor aspects of technology; Labor process; Medieval technology; Research applications; Resources; Sciences; Scientific equipment; Scientific knowledge; Scientific revolutions; Spacecraft; Technical assistance; Technological change; Technological forecasting; Technological innovations; Technological progress; Technology and civilization; Technology assessment; Technology transfer; Telecommunications; Tools; Western society.

Technology, educational. See *Educational technology.*

Technology, high industries. See *High technology industries.*

Technology, labor aspects of. See *Labor aspects of technology.*

Technology, medieval. See *Medieval technology.*

Technology, military. See *Military technology.*

Technology, push. See *Push technology*

Technology, space. See *Space exploration; Spacecraft.*

Technology, workplace effects. See *Labor aspects of technology.*

Technology and civilization. Technology and civilization. Technostress. Technostress. *Choose from:* technolog(y,ies, ical), high technolog(y,ies), high tech,

advanced technolog(y,ies), satellite(s), new technolog(y,ies), biotechnolog(y,ies, ical), smart machine(s), laptop(s), fax machine(s), television, video(s), videotape(s), videocassette(s), laser(s), microwave(s), semiconductor(s), robot(s,ic,ics), supersonic transport(ation), jet(s), airplane(s), plane(s), technocra(cy,cies,t,ts,tic,tized, tization), electronic(s), microelectronic(s), Silicon Valley, micro-chip(s), computer(s), microcomputer(s), industrial(ized,ization), manufacturing, combustion engine, steam engine, telecommunication(s), railroad(s), automobile(s), telephone(s), electricity, running water, sanitation, radio(s), movie(s), cinema(s), typewriter(s), washing machine(s), freezer(s), electric iron(s) *with:* civilization, social institution(s), societ(y,ies,al), man(kind), men, woman(kind), women, people, human being(s), human need(s), social change(s), values, terroris(m,t,ts), famil(y,ies), child(ren), employment, unemployment, social progress. *See also* Agricultural mechanization; Alienation; Automation; Computers; Dehumanization; Environmental stress; History; Industrialization; Information society; Labor aspects of technology; Medieval technology; Modernization; Postindustrial societies; Quality of life; Quality of working life; Skills obsolescence; Social change; Technological forecasting; Technological unemployment; Technology; Teledemocracy; Western society.

Technology assessment. Technology assessment. *Choose from:* technolog(y,ies,ical), technical, industrial, engineering, manufacturing, sociotechnical, biotechnical, computer(s), microcomputer(s) *with:* assess(ed,ing,ment,ments), impact(s), effect(s), evaluat(e,ed,ing,ion,ions), efficac(y,ious), safety, benefit(s), risk(s), reassess(ed,ing,ment,ments), apprais(e,ed,ing,al), cost(s), social cost(s), ethic(s,al). *See also* Appropriate technologies; Ergonomics; Ethics; Scientific discoveries; Social impact; Social values; Technological change; Technological forecasting; Technological progress; Technology; Technology transfer.

Technology development. See *Product development; Scientific development; Scientific discoveries; Scientific revolutions; Technological change; Technological innovations; Technological progress.*

Technology transfer. Technolog(y,ical) transfer. *Choose from:* technical, industr(y,ies,ialization), equipment, computer(s), microcomputer(s), innovation(s), research result(s), skills, expertise, consultant(s),

technolog(y,ies,ical), technical assistance, *with:* export(s,ed,ing,ation), transfer(ence), diffusion, import(ed,ing, ation), introduc(e,ed,ing,tion), propagat(e,ed,ing,ion), disseminat(e,ed, ing,ation), shar(e,ed,ing), universaliz(e, ed,ing,ation), globaliz(e,ed,ing,ation), international flow(s), piracy. *Consider also:* intermediate technolog(y,ies), appropriate technolog(y,ies), agricultural assistance, development aid, foreign assistance, technical cooperation. *See also* Adoption of ideas; Appropriate technologies; Arms transfers; Automation; Communications research; Diffusion of innovation; Distribution channels; Economic development; High technology industries; Industrialization; Information dissemination; Innovations; Inventions; International cooperation; Marketing; Modernization; Patents; Research; Research applications; Scientific community; Scientific development; Scientific knowledge; Technical assistance; Technological forecasting; Technological progress; Technology; Technology and civilization; Technology assessment.

Teenage fathers. Adolescent father(s). *Choose from:* adolescen(t,ce), teen(s,age) *with:* father(s,hood,ing), male parent(s). *See also* Adolescence; Marriage age; Pregnancy; Teenage mothers.

Teenage mothers. Teenage mother(s,hood). Adolescent mother(s,ing,hood). Babies having babies. *Choose from:* adolescen(t,ce), teen(s,age,aged,ager, agers), early, student(s), minor(s), high school(s) *with:* mother(s,ing,hood), pregnan(t,cy,cies), parent(ing,hood), childbearing, high school, illegitma(cy, te), conception, primigravida(s), birth(s), childbirth(s), primipara(s), bab(y,ies). *See also* Adolescence; Expectant mothers; Marriage age; Pregnancy; Prenatal care; Teenage fathers.

Teenage pregnancy. See *Teenage mothers.*

Teenage suicide. Teenage suicide(s). *Choose from:* teen(s,age,ager,agers), adolescen(ce,t,ts), youth(s), minor(s), high school student(s) *with:* suicid(e,es, al), hunger strike(s), self destruct(ion, ive), self injur(y,ious), overdose(s), kill(ed,ing) themselves. *See also* Adolescence; Attempted suicide; Death instinct; Drug overdoses; Gateway drugs; Self destructive behavior; Suicide; Suicide victims.

Teenagers. See *Adolescence; High school students; Junior high school students; Puberty; Teenage fathers; Teenage mothers.*

Teeth, age determination by. See *Age determination by teeth.*

Teeth grinding, nocturnal. See *Bruxism.*

Telecommunications. Telecommun-ication(s). Broadcast communication(s). Electronic communication(s). Signal service(s). Microwave relay system(s). Wire communication(s). Television consultation(s). Electronic newsletter(s). Electronic publishing. Electronic mail. Telegraph(ic,y). Remote communication(s). Telecopier(s). Long distance transmission. Teleconferenc(e,es,ing). Viewdata. Prestel. Telephone(s). Teletype. Teletypewriter(s). Televoice. Television. Radio. Radar. Telephone(s). Communications media. Communications satellite(s). Fax machine(s). Facsimile transmission. Videotex. Dataphone. Closed circuit television. Cable television. Connectivity. *See also* Audiovisual communications; Communications media; Computer networks; Connectivity; Cyberlaw; Data transmission systems; Electronic mail; Electronic publishing; Long distance telephone companies; Teleconferencing; Telemedicine; Telephone; Television.

Telecommuting. See *Home based businesses; Small businesses.*

Teleconferencing. Teleconferenc(e,es, ed,ing). Electronic discussion group(s). Virtual meeting(s). Electronic conference(s). Desktop conferenc(e,es, ing). *Choose from:* virtual, electronic, multicast, Internet *with:* conferenc(e,es, ing), discussion group(s), meeting(s). *Consider also:* electronic whiteboard(s), NetMeeting, Multicast Backbone, M Bone, group conferencing, videoconferenc(e,ed,ing), workgroup computing, collaborator(y,ies), computer conferencing. *See also* Conferences; Interactive video; Push technology; Telecommunications.

Teledemocracy. Teledemocracy. Tele-democracy. Electronic town meeting(s). Electronic democracy. Wired democracy. Electronic vot(e,es,ing). *Consider also:* electronic ballot(s), vot(e,es,ed,ing) by computer, computeriz(e,ed,ing,ation) of voting, cyberactiv(ist,ists,ism), tele-lobby, teleparticipat(e,ed,ing,ion), electronic referend(a,um), telereferend(a, um), telepolling, electronic bulletin board(s), talk radio. *See also* Community networks (computer); Ballots; Information highway; Interactive computer systems; Modern civilization; Postindustrial societies; Information society; Technology and civilization; Virtual reality; Voter participation; Voting.

Telemarketing. Telemarket(er,ers,ing). Cold calling. Cold call selling. *Choose from:* telephone *with:* selling, sales, marketing, advertising, solicitation(s), scam(s), fraud(s,ulent). *Choose from:* home shopping, direct marketing, *with:* interactive, technolog(y,ies), electronic, television, telephone. *Consider also:* interactive home shopping, telescam(s), 900 number(s), mail order(s). *See also* Advertising; Advertising campaigns; Database marketing; Direct mail advertising; Direct marketing; Marketing; Marketing strategies; Orders (business).

Telemedicine. Telemedic(ine,al). Telehealth. *Choose from:* remote, distance, telephone, phone, long distance, telecommunications, interactive video, fax, e-mail, internet, electronic highway, wired *with:* medic(al,ine), health, consult(ing,ed,ation,ative), diagnos(tic,e, ed,ing,is,es). *Consider also:* teledermatolog(y,ical), teleradiolog(y,ical), telepatholog(y,ical), telenursing, telepsychiatr(y,ic), tele-medical, tele-advisory, tele-surg(ery,ical,ically), telecardiolog(y,ical), telemedical record(s). *See also* Delivery of services; Distance education; Remote consultation; Telecommunications.

Teleology. Teleolog(y,ical). Consequen-tialism. *Consider also:* final cause(s), end purposes, shaped by purpose(s), vitalism, end time thinking. *See also* End; Ends; Epistemology; Functional-ism; Goals; Millenarianism; Metaphys-ics; Natural theology; Social theories; Sociological theory; Systems theory.

Telepathy. Telepath(y,ic). Mind reading. Thought transference. ESP. Clairvoyan(t,ce). Precognition. Extra sensory perception. *See also* Extrasen-sory perception; Parapsychology.

Telephone. Telephone(s). Phone(s). Dial access. Bell system. Long distance call(s). Transtelephone. Tele-monitoring. WATS lines. Dial systems. Sprint. MCI. AT&T. Dataphone(s). *Consider also:* cellular phone(s), car phone(s). *See also* Conversation; Long distance telephone companies; Telecommunications; Telephone psychotherapy.

Telephone, help lines. See *Help lines (telephone).*

Telephone companies, long distance. See *Long distance telephone companies.*

Telephone psychotherapy. Telephone psychotherapy. *Choose from:* telephon(e,ed,ing), phone(s,d) *with:* counsel(ed,ing), therap(y,ies,eutic), psychotherap(y,ies,eutic), psychiatric service(s). *See also* Crisis intervention; Help lines (telephone); Psychotherapy; Remote consultation; Telephone.

Television. Televis(ed,ing,ion). TV. Telly. *Choose from:* airborne, color, overhead, broadcast, cable, closed circuit, commercial, educational, public, satellite, network, UHF, VHF *with:* television. *Consider also:* video. *See also* Broadcasts; Cartoons; Detective and mystery television programs; Documen-tary theater; Educational television;

Journalism; Mass media; Mass media effects; Mass media violence; Networks; News coverage; News media; Popular culture; Soap operas; Telecommunica-tions; Television plays; Television programs.

Television, cable. See *Cable television.*

Television, educational. See *Educational television.*

Television coverage. See *News coverage.*

Television drama. See *Television plays.*

Television effects. See *Mass media effects.*

Television plays. Television play(s). Television drama(s). Soap opera(s). *Choose from:* television, TV *with:* play(s), drama(s), script(s), serial(s), adaptation(s). *See also* Detective and mystery television programs; Mass media violence; Popular culture; Soap operas; Television; Television programs.

Television programs. Television program(s). Television serial(s). Talk show(s). Comedy program(s). Cooking show(s). Game show(s). *Choose from:* children(s), docudrama(s), nature, quiz, religious, sitcom(s), situation comed(y,ies), fantas(y,tic), horror, infomercial(s), miniseries, mini-series, science fiction, science, documentar(y, ies), soap opera(s), business, evening news, news magazine, prime time, etc. *with:* TV, televis(ed,ion), TV, program(s), show(s). *Consider also:* telethon(s), television adaptation(s). *See also* Cartoons; Detective and mystery television programs; Documentary theater; Educational television; Infomercials; Journalism; Mass media; Mass media effects; Mass media violence; Networks; News coverage; News media; Popular culture; Soap operas; Television; Television plays.

Television programs, detective and mystery. See *Detective and mystery television programs.*

Television serials. See *Television programs.*

Television violence. See *Mass media violence.*

Telling, fortune. See *Divination.*

Temperament. Temperament(s,al,ally). Even tempered. Bad tempered. Good natured. Kind(ly). *Choose from:* even, hot, nasty, bad, good, kind, sweet *with:* tempered, natured, disposition. *Choose from:* emotional(ly) *with:* stable, stability, unstable, instability, volatil(e,ity). *Choose from:* personality, psychological *with:* trait(s), dimension(s), profile(s), type(s), characteristic(s). *See also* Personality; Personality traits.

Temperance. Temperance. Alcohol free. Alcohol control. Dry state(s). Teetotal(er,ers,ism). Sobriety.

Sophrosyne. *Choose from:* alcohol, liquor, drinking *with:* abstinence, prohibition(ist,ists). *Consider also:* moderation, self restraint, self control, refrain(ed,ing), forbear(ance), desist(ance), abstention, nonindulgen(t, ce), abstemious(ness), continence, austerity, asceticism, self denial, self abnegation. *See also* Abstinence; Alcohol drinking; Alcoholism; Cardinal virtues; Drunkenness; Moderation; Self sacrifice; Sobriety; Temperance movements.

Temperance movements. Temperance movement(s). Friends of temperance. Crusade against alcohol. Eighteenth amendment. Prohibitionis(m,t,ts). *Consider also:* Father Theobald Mathew, John Bartholomew Gough, Women's Christian Temperance Union, W.C.T.U., Anti-Saloon League, Frances Elizabeth Willard, Carry Nation, Susan B. Anthony. *See also* Alcohol drinking; Alcoholism; Drunkenness; Social movements; Temperance.

Temperature, body. See *Body temperature.*

Temperature effects. Temperature effect(s). *Choose from:* temperature, heat, hot(ter), cold(er,est), cool(ness,er), climat(e,ic), thermal, warm(th) *with:* effect(s), reaction(s), response(s), induced, adapt(ed,ing,ation,ations) or specific effects such as activ(e,ity), dorman(t,cy), aggressive(ness), nest building, hibernat(e,ed,ing,ion). *See also* Acclimatization; Adjustment (to environment); Atmospheric conditions; Body temperature; Environmental pollution; Heat; Heat effects; Hibernation; Seasons; Thermal acclimatization.

Temperature perception. Temperature perception. Thermosensitiv(e,ity). Thermoreception. Thermoperception. *Choose from:* temperature, heat, cold, climate, thermal, warm(th) *with:* sens(e,ation), perception, subjective evaluation, rating, subjective experience, detect(ed,ing,ion), discriminat(e,ed,ing, ion), feel(ing,ings), felt, comfort, estimat(e,ed,ing,ion), threshold(s). *See also* Body temperature; Sensory thresholds.

Temples. Temple(s). House(s) of prayer. House(s) of worship. Synagogue(s). Stupa(s). Dagoba(s). Pagoda(s). Tope(s). Pantheon(s). Ambalam(s). *See also* Churches; Mosques; Places of worship; Religious institutions; Sacred places; Shrines; Synagogues.

Tempo, conceptual. See *Conceptual tempo.*

Temporary employees. Temporary employee(s). Temp(s). *Choose from:* temporar(y,ily), transient, contingent, contract, nonpermanent, summer, leased, fly-by-night *with:* employee(s), employment, personnel, workforce, operator(s), staff, manpower, worker(s),

work force, office force, labor force, labor(er,ers), crew(s), hired help, secretar(y,ies). *Consider also:* part-time employee(s), moonlighting, labor pool(s). *See also* Alternative work patterns; Contract labor; Employees; Migrant workers; Seasonal unemployment; Temporary help services; Transience.

Temporary help services. Temporary help service(s). Temporary employment agenc(y,ies). Temp(s). *Choose from:* temp(orary), transient, contingent, contract, nonpermanent, summer, leased, migrant *with:* employee(s), employment, personnel, operator(s), staff, manpower, worker(s), work force, office force, labor force, labor(er,ers), crew(s), help, secretar(y,ies) *with:* agenc(y,ies), service(s). *Consider also:* outsourcing, independent contractor(s), contingent staffing arrangement(s), tempnapping, employment externalization. *See also* Employment agencies; Independent contractors; Temporary employees.

Temptation. Temptation(s). Enticement(s). Allur(e,ed,ing,ement,ements). Seduc(e, ed,ing,tion,tions). Beguil(e,ed,ing, ement,ements). Induc(e,ed,ing,ement, ements). Lur(e,ed,ing). Forbidden fruit(s). *Consider also:* compulsive urge(s), impulsiv(e,ity), increased desire, compulsion(s). *See also* Incentives; Motivation; Seduction.

Tenancy, farm. See *Tenant farmers.*

Tenant farmers. Tenant farm(ers,ing). Crofting. Sharecrop(per,pers,ping). Cropsharing. *Consider also:* peasant household production, feudalism, semifeudalism, precapitalist production, rented land, bataidar(s), hacienda(s), plantation(s), latifund(ia,ismo), campesino(s). *See also* Farming; Feudalism; Peasants; Sharecropping.

Tenant landlord relations. See *Landlord tenant relations.*

Tenant relocation. Tenant relocation. *Choose from:* tenant(s), lessee(s), leaseholder(s), renter(s), roomer(s), boarder(s), lodger(s), sharecropper(s), dweller(s), occupant(s), inhabitant(s) *with:* relocat(e,ed,ing,ion), oust(ed,ing), expel(led,ling), terminat(e,ed,ing,ion) lease(s), left, leav(e,ing), move(d), moving, displac(e,ed,ing,ement), evict(ed,ing,ion,ions). *See also* Eviction; Landlord tenant relations; Rental housing; Tenants.

Tenants. Tenan(ts,cy). Lessee(s). Leaseholder(s). Renter(s). Roomer(s). Boarder(s). Lodger(s). Sharecropper(s). *Consider also:* rent(ed,al) apartment(s), rent control, boarding house(s), letting room(s), rentier(s), landlord(s), rental housing, leas(ing,es,ed), rent(s,al), sublet(ting), dweller(s), occupant(s), inhabitant(s). *See also* Affordable

housing; Housing; Landlord tenant relations; Landlords; Leasing; Public housing; Rent strikes; Rental housing; Resident councils; Tenant relocation.

Tendencies. Tendenc(y,ies). Inclination(s). Propensit(y,ies). Proclivit(y,ies). Tend(ed,ing). Lean(ed,ing). Bent. Prone(ness). Verging. Like(ly,liness). Susceptab(le,ility). Predispos(ed,ition). Predilection(s). Trend(s). Drift(ed,ing). Penchant(s). *See also* Analysis; Change; Disposition (Philosophy); Trends; Development; Forecasting; Indexes (indicators); Quantitative methods; Social indicators; Time.

Tender, legal. See *Money*

Tenements. See *Slums.*

Tension, premenstrual. See *Premenstrual syndrome.*

Tensions. Tension(s). Tense(ness). Anxiet(y, ies). Anxious(ness). Sense of urgency. Mistrust(ed,ing,ful). Nervous(ness). Fearful(ness). Apprehens(ion,ions, iveness). Dread(ed,ing). Misapprehension(s). Impatien(t,ce). Fear(s). Distress(ed,ing). Mental stress(es,ed,ful, or,ors). Strain(s). Pressure(s). Agon(y, ies,ized,izing). *Consider also:* life(style,styles), psychological, physiological, social, occupational, environmental, subjective *with:* suffer(s,ed,ing), stress(es,ed,ful,or,ors, ability), distress(es,ed,ing), strain(s). *See also* Anxiety; Crises; Emotions; Hostility; Impatience; Intergroup relations; Interpersonal relations; Psychological stress; Social conflict; Social unrest; Threat.

Tenure, academic. See *Academic tenure.*

Tenure, faculty. See *Academic tenure.*

Tenure, job. See *Occupational tenure.*

Tenure, land. See *Land tenure.*

Tenure, occupational. See *Occupational tenure.*

Tenure, teacher. See *Academic tenure.*

Tenure of office. Tenure of office. Term of office. *Consider also:* term limit(s,ation, ations), rate of turnover, tenure ceiling(s), limited tenure, congressional term(s), second term(s), third term(s), single term(s), lame duck. *See also* Elected officials; Occupational tenure.

Teratology. Teratolog(y,ic,ical). Fetal malformation(s). Major malformation(s). Monster(s). *Consider also:* teratogen(s, ic,esis), mutagen(ic,esis), birth defect(s), craniofacial defect(s), limb defect(s), cleft palate(s), micrognathia, micromelia, congenital malformation(s), dysmorphogene(tic,sis), developmental anomal(y,ies), skeletal dysplasia(s). *See also* Congenitally handicapped; Drug induced abnormalities; Human abnormalities; Physical abnormalities; Severely handicapped infants.

Term of office. See *Tenure of office.*

Terminal care. Terminal care. Hospice(s). *Choose from:* terminal(ly) ill(ness, nesses), dying, terminal patient(s), terminal condition(s), death, end stage, terminally sick *with:* palliative(s), care, help(ing), communicat(e,ed,es,ing), treat(ed,ing,ment), assist(ance,ed,ing), comfort(ed,ing), hospitaliz(ed,ing,ation), counsel(ed,ing). *Consider also:* euthanasia, life prolong(ed,ing,ation), palliative care, futile care. *See also* Advance directives; Care of the sick; Death; Dying; Euthanasia; Health care; Hospices; Right to die; Terminal illness; Thanatology.

Terminal care facilities. See *Hospices.*

Terminal illness. Terminal illness(es). End stage(s). Near death. Moribund. Deathbed. Declining. Expiring. *Choose from:* terminal(ly), dying, last, final, advanced, fatal, mortal(ly) *with:* ill(ness,nesses), disease(s), patient(s), condition(s), sick(ness,nesses), wound(s, ed). *Consider also:* life threatening illness(es), life prolongation, prolong(ed, ing) life, hospice(s), terminal care, last rite(s). *See also* Assisted suicide; Death; Dying; Euthanasia; Hospices; Illness; Right to die; Terminal care; Thanatology.

Terminals, hazards of video display. See *Hazards of video display terminals.*

Termination, employee. See *Personnel termination.*

Termination, employment. See *Personnel termination.*

Termination, personnel. See *Personnel termination.*

Termination, treatment. See *Termination of treatment.*

Termination of treatment. Terminat(e,ed, ing,ion) of treatment. *Choose from:* abandon(ed,ing), attrition, cessation, ceas(e,ed,ing), discharg(e,ed,ing), discontinu(ance,e,ed,ing), end(ed,ing), forego, forgo, interrupt(ed,ing,ion,ions), noncompliance, taper(ed,ing), terminat(e,ed,ing,ion), withdraw(al,n, ing), withhold(ing), withheld *with:* care, resuscitat(e,ed,ing,ion), treat(ed,ing, ment,ments), therap(y,ies,eutic), medication(s), rehabilitation, psychotherap(y,ies,eutic), diet(s), detoxification, tube feeding(s). *Consider also:* do not resuscitate, DNR, living will(s). *See also* Advance directives; Counseling; Do not resuscitate orders; Health care utilization; Interruption; Length of stay; Patient compliance; Patient discharge; Patient dropouts; Treatment outcome; Treatment withholding.

Terminology. Terminolog(y,ies,ical). Nomenclature. Taxonom(y,ies). Classification(s). Designation(s). Name(s). Word usage. Term(s). Descriptor(s). Definition(s). Language construct(s). Keyword(s). Phras(e,es,ing, eology). Subject heading(s). Vocabular(y,ies). Qualifier(s). Adjective(s). Noun(s). Categor(y,ies). Jargon. Buzzword(s). Code word(s). Label(s). Slang. Acronym(s). Expression(s). Name(s). Eponym(s). Index term(s). Abbreviation(s). Antonym(s). Pseudonym(s). Shoptalk. Vernacular. *Consider also:* lexical paradigm(s). *See also* Catchwords; Cliches; Communication (thought transfer); Controlled vocabulary; Definition (words); Language; Literary terms; Metalanguage; Verbal communication; Vocabulary; Words.

Terms, literary. See *Literary terms.*

Terraforming. Terraform(ed,ing,er,ers). Engineering planetary environment(s). Planetary engineering. Worldscap(ed, ing). *Consider also:* ecopoesis, ecopoiesis, manned landing(s), human colonization, geoengineering, coloniz(e,ed,ing,ation) Mars. *See also* Interplanetary voyages; Plurality of worlds; Space exploration.

Terrain. See *Topography.*

Territorial boundaries. See *Boundaries.*

Territorial claims. See *Territorial issues.*

Territorial expansion. Territorial expansion. *Choose from:* land(s), territor(y,ies,ial), area(s), turf, border(s), region(s,al), waterway(s), maritime, marine resource(s), right-of-way, jurisdiction(al), zone(s), countries by name such as Kuwait, Sudetenland, Gaza *with:* annex(ed,ing,ation), claim(s), expansion, coloniz(e,ed,ing,ation), occup(y,ying,ied,ation), invad(e,ed,ing), invasion, disput(e,ed,ed,ing), spoils of war, grab(bed,bing). *Consider also:* manifest destiny, irredent(a,ism,ist,ists), frontier thesis, Turner thesis. *See also* Acquisition of territory; Aggression; Annexation; Borderlands; Boundaries; Boundary maintenance; Colonialism; Deterritorialization; Geopolitics; Imperialism; Political geography; Social Darwinism; Territorial issues; Territoriality.

Territorial issues. Territorial issue(s). Territorial dispute(s). Border talk(s). *Choose from:* land(s), territor(y,ies,ial), area(s), turf, border(s), region(s,al), waterway(s), maritime, marine resource(s), right-of-way, jurisdiction(al), zone(s), annex(ed,ing,ation) *with:* dispute(s,d), fight(s,ing), sovereignty, negotiat(e,ed,ing,ion,ions), claim(s), debat(e,ed,es,ing), talk(s,ed, ing), controvers(y,ies,ial), discuss(ed, ing,ion), issue(s), question(s), legal

problem(s). *Consider also:* irredent(a,ism,ist,ists). *See also* Annexation; Border wars; Borderlands; Boundaries; Boundary maintenance; Claims; Geopolitics; Historic geography; Political geography; Territorial expansion; Territorial waters; Territoriality.

Territorial waters. Territorial water(s). Sea boundar(y,ies). 12 mile limit(s). 200 mile limit(s). *Choose from:* waterway(s), maritime zone(s), marine resource(s), sea(s), ocean(s), Northwest passage, Arctic water(s), straits, offshore land(s), continental shelf, fisher(y,ies), fishing water(s), fishing zone(s), offshore mineral(s), offshore oil *with:* sovereignty, exclusive, territorial, boundar(y, ies), claim(s), jurisdiction(al), delimit(ed,ing,ation), dominion, juridical status. *Consider also:* law of the sea, cod war(s), coastal zone(s). *See also* Borderlands; Boundaries; Coast defenses; Fisheries; Geopolitics; International rivers; Island ecology; Islands; Marine resources; Maritime law; Maritime war; Oceans; Offshore factories (floating); Offshore oil; Political geography; Rivers; Shipping industry; Shorelines; Submerged lands; Territorial issues; Territoriality.

Territoriality. Territorial(ity). Habitat selection. Territorial song(s). *Choose from:* habitat, territor(y,ies,ial), home range, personal space, nest(s) *with:* select(ed,ing,ion), boundar(y,ies), mark(ed,ing,ings), behavior, aggression, defense, choice, relations, maintenance. *Consider also:* scent, urine *with:* marking(s). *Consider also:* personal distance, personal space. *See also* Animal aggressive behavior; Animal courtship behavior; Animal dominance; Animal foraging behavior; Animal scent marking; Behavior; Borderlands; Borders; Boundaries; Boundary maintenance; Geopolitics; Habitat; Home range; Personal space; Political geography; Predatory animals; Social behavior; Territorial expansion; Territorial issues; Territorial waters.

Territories, American Indian. See *American Indian territories.*

Territories, Indian. See *American Indian territories.*

Territory, acquisition of. See *Acquisition of territory.*

Terror, night. See *Night terror.*

Terror, sleep. See *Night terror; Nightmares.*

Terrorism. Terror(ist,ists,ism,ize,ized, izing). Narcoterror(ism,ist,ists). Hijack(ing,er,ers). Skyjack(er,ers,ing). Assassinat(e,ed,ing,ions). Kidnap(ped, pings). Bomb(ing,ings). Bomb threat(s). Hostage(s). Piracy. Firebomb(ed,ing, ings). Incendiar(y,ies,ism). Plant(ed,ing) bomb(s). Throwing grenade(s). Molotov cocktail(s). Guerrilla war(fare). Bomb plot(s). Nuclear blackmail. Macro terror. Violence. Assassin(s). Homemade bomb(s). Sky pirate(s). Inflight crime(s). Sabotage. Saboteur. Death squad(s). Reign of terror. Jihad. Armed fundamentalist(s). Unconventional warfare. *Consider also:* Jacobins, Baader Meinhof, IRA, Irish Republican Army, Omega 7, FALN, Croatian liberation forces, FLN, BOKA, Irgun, Fedayeen, Red brigade, PLO, Mujahidin, Mujahedeen, Aum Shinrikyo, Abu Nidal, Ramzi Ahmed Yousef, Osama bin Laden, Osama bin Muhammad bin Awad Bin Laden, National Islamic Front, etc. *See also* Agitators; Anti-government radicals; Antisocial behavior; Aggression; Assassination; Crime; Guerrilla warfare; Guerrillas; Hijacking; Hostages; Internal security; Intimidation; Mail bombs; Piracy (at sea); Police brutality; Political revolutions; Psychological warfare; Radical movements; Revolution; Sabotage; Seizure of ships; Torture; Violence; War crimes; World problems.

Test anxiety. Test anxiet(y,ies). *Choose from:* test(s), exam(s,ination,inations) *with:* anxiet(y,ies), stress(es), phob(ia,ias,ic), fear(s), anxious(ness), distress(ed,ing), apprehens(ion,ive, iveness). *Consider also:* school anxiety. *See also* Anxiety; Computer anxiety; Mathematics anxiety; Science anxiety; School phobia; Test taking; Tests; Testwiseness.

Test bias. Test bias(es,ed). *Choose from:* bias(es,ed), cultur(e,al) test bias, unfair, racial imbalance, slant(ed) *with:* test(s,ing), item(s), scale(s), measure(s, ment), assessment(s), exam(s,inations), question(s), questionnaire(s), quiz(zes), instrument(s). *See also* Bias; Culture fair tests; Ethnic groups; Social discrimination; Test construction; Test interpretation; Test validity; Testwiseness.

Test construction. Test construction. *Choose from:* test(s,ing), item(s), scale(s), measure(s,ment), assessment(s), exam(s,inations), question(s), questionnaire(s), quiz(zes), instrument(s) *with:* construct(ed,ing,ion,ions), develop(ed, ing,ment,ments), design(ed,ing), build(ing), built, creat(ed,ing), adapt(ed,ing,ation,ations). *See also* Content analysis; Criterion referenced tests; Culture fair tests; Factor analysis; Pretesting; Scaling; Task performance and analysis; Test bias; Test reliability; Test validity.

Test interpretation. Test interpretation. *Choose from:* test(s,ing), item(s), scale(s), measure(s,ment), assessment(s), exam(s,ination,inations), question(s), questionnaire(s), quiz(zes), instrument(s) or test by name *with:* interpret(ed,ing, ation,ations), reinterpret(ed,ing,ation,

ations), analy(sis,ses,ze,zed,zing), refinement(s). *See also* Culture fair tests; Data interpretation; Criterion referenced tests; Psychometrics; Test bias; Test reliability; Test validity.

Test marketing. Test market(s,ing). Market test(s). Test(ed,ing) new product(s). Test commercial(s). *Consider also:* computer simulations, pretest(ed,ing) *with:* market(s), product(s). *Consider also:* focus group(s), direct-mail survey(s), telemarketing, flier(s). *See also* Consumer behavior; Market research.

Test reliability. Test reliability. *Choose from:* test(s,ing), item(s), scale(s), measure(s,ment), assessment(s), exam(s,inations), question(s), questionnaire(s), quiz(zes), instrument(s) or test by name *with:* reliab(le,ility), accuracy, accurate, shortcoming(s), dependab(le,ility), critical review(s), consisten(t,cy), stability, stable, valid(ity), comparability, equivalent(s), equivalence. *See also* Criterion referenced tests; Culture fair tests; Test bias; Test construction; Test interpretation; Test validity.

Test taking. Test taking. *Choose from:* test(s,ing), exam(s,ination,inations), questionnaire(s) *with:* tak(e,ing), took, perform(ed,ing,ance), complet(e,ed,ing, ion), exposure. *See also* Cheating; Guessing; Response bias; Test anxiety; Testwiseness.

Test validity. Test validity. *Choose from:* test(s,ing), item(s), scale(s), measure(s, ment), assessment(s), exam(s,inations), question(s), questionnaire(s), quiz(zes), instrument(s) or test by name *with:* valid(ity), standardiz(ed,ation), discriminant analysis, specificity, equivalent(s), review(s,ed). *See also* Construct validity; Factor analysis; Measurement; Predictive validity; Test construction; Test interpretation; Test reliability; Testwiseness.

Testimony. Testimon(y,ies,ial). Witness(es) statement(s). Testif(y,ying,ied). Attest(ed,ing). Under oath. Affidavit(s). Depos(e,ed,ition,itions). Testified in court. *Choose from:* expert, legal, court, sworn, eyewitness *with:* testimony, hearing(s), witness(es). *Consider also:* state's evidence. *See also* Affidavit; Allegations; Assertions; Cross examination; Deposition; Expert testimony; Lie detection; Trial (law); Witness tampering; Witnesses.

Testimony, expert. See *Expert testimony.*

Testing, drug. See *Substance abuse detection.*

Testing, genetic. See *Genetic screening.*

Testing, group. See *Group testing.*

Testing, hypothesis. See *Hypothesis testing.*

Testing, individual. See *Individual testing.*

Testing, null hypothesis. See *Null hypothesis testing.*

Testing, reality. See *Reality testing.*

Testing alternatives, animal. See *Animal testing alternatives.*

Testing for ability. See *Ability identification.*

Testing for substance abuse. See *Substance abuse detection.*

Tests. Test(s). Assay(s). Assessment(s). Audit(s). Batter(y,ies). Checklist(s). Checkup(s). Diagnostic(s). Essay question(s). Evaluation(s). Exam(s, ination,inations). Instrument(s). Inventor(y,ies). Measure(ment,s). Midterm(s). Pretest(s). Posttest(s). Questionnaire(s). Quiz(zes). Rating(s). Scale(s). Schedule(s). Screening(s). Score(s). Subtest(s). Trial(s). *Consider also:* medical tests such as: autops(y,ies), biop(sy,sies), urinalysis, radioimmune assay(s), etc. *See also* Achievement tests; Aptitude tests; Criterion referenced tests; Culture fair tests; Diagnostic tests; Entrance examinations; Essay tests; Evaluation; Forced choice tests; Health examinations; Indexes (indicators); Ink blot tests; Intelligence tests; Inventories; Language tests; Measurement; Nonprojective personality measures; Occupational tests; Perceptual measures; Performance tests; Personality measures; Preference measures; Psychological tests; Reading tests; Retention measures; Selection tests; Standards; Statistical significance; Test bias; Test construction; Test interpretation; Test reliability; Test validity; Verbal tests.

Tests, achievement. See *Achievement tests.*

Tests, aptitude. See *Aptitude tests.*

Tests, criterion referenced. See *Criterion referenced tests.*

Tests, culture fair. See *Culture fair tests.*

Tests, diagnostic. See *Diagnostic tests.*

Tests, employment. See *Occupational tests.*

Tests, essay. See *Essay tests.*

Tests, forced choice. See *Forced choice tests.*

Tests, ink blot. See *Ink blot tests.*

Tests, intelligence. See *Intelligence tests.*

Tests, language. See *Language tests.*

Tests, multiple choice. See *Forced choice tests.*

Tests, occupational. See *Occupational tests.*

Tests, performance. See *Performance tests.*

Tests, personality. See *Personality measures.*

Tests, psychological. See *Psychological tests.*

Tests, reading. See *Reading tests.*

Tests, selection. See *Selection tests.*

Tests, significance. See *Statistical significance.*

Tests, verbal. See *Verbal tests.*

Testwiseness. Testwise(ness). Test wise(ness). Test taking skill(s). Test taking strateg(y,ies). *See also* Guessing; Incidental learning; Intentional learning; Problem solving; Test anxiety; Test bias; Test taking; Test validity.

Text structure. Text structure(s). *Choose from:* text(s,ual) *with:* arrangement(s), format(s), structure(s), page size(s), paragraph sequence(s), position of illustration(s), organization, composition, spacing, construction. *See also* Prose; Reading materials; Sentence structure; Verbal communication.

Textbooks. Textbook(s). Workbook(s). Text(s). Method(s) book(s). Education(al) book(s). Primer(s). Required reading(s). Supplementary book(s). School book(s). Schoolbook(s). Reader(s). Handbook(s). Workbook(s). *Consider also:* classroom material(s). *See also* Books; Children's literature; Instructional media; Reading materials; Texts.

Textile industry. Textile industry. *Choose from:* textile(s), fabric(s), cloth, yarn, knit(ting), weav(e,ing,er,ers) *with:* industr(y,ies,ial), design(ed,ing,er,ers), manufactur(e,ed,ing), loom(s), mill(s), dye(s,d), process(es,ed,ing), produc(e, ed,ing,tion), compan(y,ies). *See also* Industry; Knit goods industry; Manufacturers; Weaving; Wool industry.

Textile workers. Textile worker(s). *Choose from:* textile(s), sweatshop(s), knitting, weaving, clothing, needle, suit *with:* worker(s), unionist(s), union member(s). *Consider also:* mill worker(s). *See also* Clothing workers; Garment industry; Knit goods industry; Textile industry.

Textless vocal works. Textless vocal work(s). Vocalise(s). Vocalizzi. Voice(s) without text. Solfeg(e,eggio,ietto). *Consider also:* melisma(s,tic), humming. *See also* Music; Songs.

Texts. Text(s). Guide(s). Textbook(s). Reader(s). Manual(s). Instructional material(s). Handbook(s). Guideline(s). Workshop outline(s). Curriculum guide(s). Guidebook(s). Workbook(s). Resource book(s). Practice program(s). Drill exercise(s). Exercise book(s). Book(s) of exercises. Learning module(s). Introductory material(s). Teaching material(s). Great book(s). Primer(s). Treatise(s). Policybook(s). Laboratory manual(s). *See also* Content analysis; Guidebooks; Guidelines; Handbooks; Literary research; Manuscripts; Texts.

Texts, transmission of. See *Transmission of texts.*

Texture perception. Texture perception. *Choose from:* perception, judgement(s), discrimination *with:* texture(s). *See also* Tactual perception; Visual perception.

Thanatology. Thanatolog(y,ical). Thanatogenesis. Thanatopsychology. *Choose from:* study, science *with:* death, dying, dead, died, postmortem. *See also* Death; Dying; Hospices; Terminal care; Terminal illness.

Thanatos. See *Death instinct.*

Thanks, appreciation. See *Gratitude.*

Theater. Theater(s). Theatre(s). Playhouse(s). Theatrical play(s). Drama(tic,tics,turgy,turgical,turgically). Playwrit(e,es,ing). Dramatic production(s). Dramatic presentation(s). Dramatic reading(s). Dramatic activit(y,ies). Creative dramatics. Radio play(s). Stage play(s). Theatrical(s). Comed(y,ies). Script(s). Traged(y,ies). Opera(s,tic). Performing arts. Burlesque. Summer stock. Kabuki. *See also* Acting; Actors and actresses; Amateur theatricals; Arts; Audiences; Auditoriums; Ballet production; Burlesque; Comic operas; Commedia dell'arte; Concert halls; Cultural activities; Dance; Drama; Drama festivals; Dramatists; Experimental theater; Films; Folk drama; Improvisation (acting); Jewish drama; Little theater; Method (acting); Miracle plays; Morality plays; Musicals; Opera; Presentations; Stage design; Theatrum mundi; Tragedy; Traveling theater.

Theater, children's. See *Children's theater.*

Theater, community. See *Little theater.*

Theater, documentary. See *Documentary theater.*

Theater, experimental. See *Experimental theater.*

Theater, little. See *Little theater.*

Theater, medieval. See *Medieval drama.*

Theater, traveling. See *Traveling theater.*

Theatre, children's. See *Children's theater*

Theatre, documentary. See *Documentary theater.*

Theatricals, amateur. See *Amateur theatricals.*

Theatrum mundi. Theatrum mundi. Theatre of the world. Le theatre du monde. Schauwplatz der Welt. Stage of life. World as a stage. *See also* Drama; Theater.

Theft. Theft(s). Thief. Thieve(s,ry). Steal(ing). Stole(n). Burglar(y,s). Rob(bed,bing,ber,bers,bery). Shoplift(ing,er,ers). Pilfer(age,ing). Heist(s). Hold up. Held up. Embezzl(e,ing,ement,er,ers). Misappropriat(ed,ing,ion). Purse snatching. Mugg(er,ers,ed,ing). Bootleg(ging,ged). Larcen(y,ous). Plagiar(ize,ized,izing,ism). Poach(ing,ed,er,ers). Plunder(ed,ing). Swindl(e,er,ers,ing). Pirate(s). Piracy. Ripoff(s). Hijack(ing,ers). Kidnap(ped,ping,pers). *See also* Antisocial behavior; Archaeological thefts; Art thefts; Behavior disorders; Booty (International law); Burglary; Crime; Larceny; Robbery; Shoplifting; Thieves; White collar crime.

Thefts, archaeological. See *Archaeological thefts*

Thefts, art. See *Art thefts.*

Theism. Theis(m,ts,tic). Personal God. God the father. Monotheis(m,ts,tic). Deis(m,ts,tic). Polytheis(m,ts,tic). *Consider also:* panentheis(m,ts,tic), trinit(y,arian,arianism). *See also* Attributes of God; Deism; God concepts; Oneness of God; Presence of God; Religious beliefs; Theology; Theophany.

Themes. Them(e,es,atic). Thema(s). Tema(s). Main idea(s). Topic(s). Subject(s). Motif(s). Main argument(s). Keynote(s). Recurrent pattern(s). *See also* Concepts; Leitmotiv; Refrain (music).

Theocracy. Theocra(cy,cies,tic,tically). Theonom(y,ies,ic,ous). Religious nationalism. Christian nationalism. Biblical state(s). *Choose from:* rul(e,ed,ing), govern(ed,ing), dominat(e,ed,ing,ion), political agenda(s), government(s), law(s). *with:* clergy, priest(s), divine guidance, God, Islamic, Christian. *Consider also:* religious ruler(s), Christianiz(e,ed,ing, ation), Islamiciz(e,ed,ing,ation), Deseret, deontological law(s), divine king(s), theo-conservativ(e,es,ism). *See also* Absolutism; Church state relationship; Divine right of kings; Political ideologies; Political philosophy; Religious fundamentalism.

Theological belief. See *Faith.*

Theological disputations. See *Religious disputations.*

Theological education. See *Religious education.*

Theological virtues. Theological virtue(s). Christian virtue(s). Supernatural virtue(s). Faith. Hope. Charity. *Consider also:* agape, sanctifying grace. *See also* Cardinal virtues; Charity; Faith; Hopefulness; Virtue.

Theology. Theolog(y,ies,ical,ians). Theological opinion(s). Gospel(s). Hermeneutic(s). Theodicy. *Choose from:* religious, divine, Christian, Jewish, Islamic, Hindu, Protestant, Catholic *with:* thought, opinion(s), principle(s), truth(s), doctrine(s), dogma(s), creed(s).

See also Black theology; Ethics; Feminist theology; Freedom (theology); God concepts; Liberation theology; Metaphysics; Medieval theology; Natural theology; Philosophy; Practical theology; Religious beliefs; Religious doctrines; Religious literature; Revealed theology; Scholasticism; Theism.

Theology, Black. See *Black theology.*

Theology, death of God. See *Death of God (theology).*

Theology, feminist. See *Feminist theology.*

Theology, liberal. See *Liberalism (Religion).*

Theology , liberation. See *Liberation theology.*

Theology, medieval. See *Medieval theology.*

Theology, natural. See *Natural theology.*

Theology, practical. See *Practical theology.*

Theology, revealed. See *Revealed theology.*

Theology, scholastic. See *Scholasticism.*

Theomachy. Theomachy. Combat myth. *Choose from:* cosmic, heavenly, primordial, gods *with:* strife, rebel(ling,lion), battle(s), combat. *See also* Combat; Deities; Mythology.

Theophany. Theophan(y,ies,ic). Appearance(s) of God. *Choose from:* manifestation(s), appear(ed,ing,ance, ances) *with:* God(s), deit(y,ies), divin(e,ity), Christ. *Consider also:* religious revelation(s), prophetic vision(s), transfiguration, epiphan(y,ies), incarnation. *See also* Attributes of God; God concepts; Immanence of God; Knowledge of god; Presence of God; Religious experience; Revealed theology; Theism.

Theoretical interpretations. Theoretical interpretation(s). *Choose from:* theor(y,ies,etical,ems), axiom(s,atic), general(ity,ization,izations,izability), metatheor(y,ies,etical), model(s), postulate(s), proposition(s), paradigm(atic,s), dialectic(s,al), framework(s), model(s), ideal type(s), philosoph(y,ies,ical), premise(s), principle(s), typolog(y,ies), psychoanalytic, psychological, sociological, anthropological, legalistic *with:* interpret(ed,ing,ation,ations), analy(sis, ses), critique(s). *Consider also:* hermeneutic(s), biblical exegesis. *See also* Exegesis; Psychoanalytic interpretation; Theories.

Theoretical orientation. Theoretical orientation(s). Ideolog(y,ies). School(s) of thought. *Choose from:* theoretical, philosophical, eclectic *with:* orientation(s), foundation(s), principle(s), model(s), paradigm(s),

position(s), premise(s), background, trend(s), viewpoint(s), approach(es). *See also* Sciences; Social sciences; Psychotherapy; Theories; Therapist characteristics.

Theoretical problems. Theoretical problem(s). *Choose from:* theor(y,ies, etical,em,ems), axiom(s,atic), construct(s), deduction(s), general(ity, ization,izations,izability), hypothes(is,es, etical,ize,ized,izing), inference(s), metatheor(y,ies,etical), model(s), postulate(s), proposition(s), paradigm(atic,s), thes(es,is), assumption(s), concept(s), dialectic(s,al), framework(s), ideal type(s), philosoph(y,ies), presumption(s), premise(s), principle(s), typolog(y,ies) *with:* critic(al,ism,s), lacunae, critique(d,s), conflict(ing), problem(s,atic), debate(s,d), reformulation. *See also* Hypothesis testing; Research design; Theories; Theory formation; Theory verification.

Theories. Theor(y,ies,etical,ems). Axiom(s, atic). Conclusion(s). Construct(s). Deduction(s). Explanation(s). Generalization(s). Hypothes(is,es,ize, ized,izing). Hypothetical(ly). Inference(s). Interpretation(s). Metatheor(y, ies,etical). Model(s). Postulate(s). Proposition(s). Paradigm(s). Thes(es,is). *Consider also:* analog(y,ies), antinom(y, ies), assumption(s), concept(s), dialectic(s,al), framework(s), ideal type(s), metaphor(s,ical), philosoph(y, ies), presumption(s), premise(s), principle(s), symbol(s,ic), typolog(y,ies). *See also* Adaptation level theory; Atomism; Behavior theories; Concepts; Dependency theory (international); Exchange theory; Game theory; Generalities; Gestalt theory; History of psychology; Hypotheses; Hypothesis testing; Hypothetical; Ideal types; Ideologies; Information theory; Knowledge; Learning theories; Literary theory; Malthusian theory; Middle range theories; Models; Personality theories; Poetics; Postulates; Principles; Probability theory; Propositions; Psychoanalytic theory; Research; Rules (generalizations); Sciences; Scientific method; Scientific models; Scientific revolutions; Social Darwinism; Social sciences; Social theories; Sociological theory; Systems theory; Theoretical interpretations; Theoretical orientation; Theoretical problems; Theory formation; Theory verification.

Theories, behavior. See *Behavior theories.*

Theories, learning. See *Learning theories.*

Theories, middle range. See *Middle range theories.*

Theories, personality. See *Personality theories.*

Theories, social. See *Social theories.*

Theory, adaptation level. See *Adaptation level theory.*

Theory, big bang. See *Big bang theory.*

Theory, critical. See *Critical theory.*

Theory, exchange. See *Exchange theory.*

Theory, game. See *Game theory.*

Theory, gestalt. See *Gestalt theory.*

Theory, information. See *Information theory.*

Theory, international dependency. See *Dependency theory (international).*

Theory, literary. See *Literary theory.*

Theory, Malthusian. See *Malthusian theory.*

Theory, musical. See *Musical theory.*

Theory, probability. See *Probability theory.*

Theory, psychoanalytic. See *Psychoanalytic theory.*

Theory, sociological. See *Sociological theory.*

Theory, speech act. See *Speech act theory.*

Theory, systems. See *Systems theory.*

Theory, world systems. See *World systems theory.*

Theory formation. Theory formation. *Choose from:* theor(y,ies,etical,em,ems), axiom(s,atic), construct(s), deduction(s), general(ity,ization,izations,izability), hypothes(is,es,etical,ize,ized,izing), inference(s), metatheor(y,ies,etical), model(s), postulate(s), proposition(s), paradigm(atic,s), thes(es,is), assumption(s), concept(s), dialectic(s,al), framework(s), ideal type(s), philosoph(y, ies), presumption(s), premise(s), principle(s), typolog(y,ies) *with:* form(ed,ing,ation), formulat(e,ed,ing, ion), develop(ed,ing,ment), construct(ed, ing,ion). *See also* Cognition; Concept formation; Discoveries (findings); Heuristics; Hypotheses; Hypothesis testing; Research methods; Scientific revolutions; Theoretical problems; Theories; Theory verification.

Theory verification. Theory verification. *Choose from:* theor(y,ies,etical,em,ems), axiom(s,atic), construct(s), deduction(s), general(ity,ization,izations,izability), hypothes(is,es,etical,ize,ized,izing), inference(s), metatheor(y,ies,etical), model(s), postulate(s), proposition(s), paradigm(atic,s), thes(es,is), assumption(s), concept(s), dialectic(s,al), presumption(s), premise(s), principle(s) *with:* verif(y,ied,ication), test(s,ed,ing), confirm(ed,ing,ation), support(ed,ing), fail(ed,ing,ure) to support, review(s,ed, ing), evaluat(e,ed,ing,ion), validat(e,ed, ing,ion). *See also* Hypothesis testing; Theories; Theory formation.

Therapeutic camps. Therapeutic camp(s). *Choose from:* therapeutic, psychotherapeutic, rehabilitat(ive,ion), resocializ(e, ed,ing,ation), weight reduction *with:* camp(s,ed,ing), daycamp(s), wilderness program(s). *Consider also:* Outward Bound program(s). *See also* Camping; Milieu therapy; Recreation therapy; Therapeutic community.

Therapeutic community. Therapeutic communit(y,ies). *Choose from:* therapeutic, psychotherapeutic, rehabilitat(ion,ive), treatment, supportive *with:* milieu, communit(y,ies), substitute famil(y,ies), environment(s). *Consider also:* milieu program(s), homelike environment(s), total-push therap(y,ies), Gheel colony, surrogate famil(y,ies). *See also* Group psychotherapy; Milieu therapy; Psychotherapy; Therapeutic camps.

Therapeutic cults. Therapeutic cult(s). *Choose from:* treatment, healing, health, therapeutic, psychotherapeutic, medicin(e,al), medical, nutrition(al) *with:* cult(s), sect(s). *Consider also:* homeopathy, medical fad(s), faith healing, hydropathy, folk medicine. *See also* Anthroposophy; Cults; Naturopathy; Quackery; Spiritual healing; Vegetarianism.

Therapeutic outcome. See *Treatment outcomes.*

Therapeutic processes. Therapeutic process(es). Therapeutics. *Choose from:* therapeutic, therap(y,ies), treatment, healing, supportive *with:* process(es), interaction(s), relationship(s), regimen(s). *Choose from:* doctor, dentist, nurse, physician, staff, counselor *with:* patient(s), client(s) *with:* interaction(s), relationship(s), facilitat(e,ed,ing,ion), support, rapport, involvement, warmth, genuineness, empathy, mutual respect. *Consider also:* cure(s), mind body technique(s), acupuncture, antipyretic(s), bed rest, chelation therapy, chemotherapy, diet therapy, drug therapy, electrotherapeutic(s), fluid therapy, gene therapy, hemodialysis, homeopath(y,ic), hormone therapy, immunotherapy , injection(s), intravenous therapy, oral medication(s), orthomolecular therapy, palliative treatment, placebo(s), medicine(s), psychotherapy, radiation therapy, respiratory therap(y,ies), self medication, speech therapy, stimulant(s), x rays, pharmaceutical(s). *See also* Client education; Psychotherapeutic outcomes; Psychotherapeutic processes; Termination of treatment; Treatment outcome.

Therapeutic social clubs. Therapeutic social club(s). *Choose from:* social therapeutic, sociotherapeutic, psychosocial *with:* club(s). *Consider also:* support group(s). *See also* Psychosocial rehabilitation.

Therapeutic systems. See *Alternative medicine.*

Therapeutic use of poetry. See *Psychopoetry.*

Therapeutics. See *Therapeutic processes.*

Therapies, organic. See *Somatic therapies.*

Therapies, somatic. See *Somatic therapies.*

Therapies, talking. See *Psychotherapy.*

Therapist attitudes. Therapist attitude(s). *Choose from:* rehabilitation professional(s), clinician(s), physical therapist(s), occupational therapist(s), *with:* attitude(s), belief(s), opinion(s), reaction(s), expectation(s), perception(s), judgment(s). *See also* Allied health personnel; Attitudes; Psychotherapist attitudes; Therapist characteristics; Therapist role.

Therapist characteristics. Therapist characteristic(s). *Choose from:* therapist(s), psychotherapist(s), analyst(s), psychoanalyst(s), counselor(s), psychiatrist(s), psychologist(s), social worker(s), caseworker(s), psychiatric nurse(s) *with:* characteristic(s), personal qualit(y,ies), warmth, cold(ness), indifferen(t,ce), genuine(ness), sincer(e,ity), insincer(e,ity), empath(y, etic), intelligen(t,ce), sensitiv(e,ity), insensitiv(e,ity), personality, effective(ness), experience, orientation, gender, disabilit(y,ies), handicap(s,ped), gifted, family background, income, place of residence, ethnic(ity), nationality, religion, health status, behavior patterns, qualit(y,ies), trait(s), profile(s), socioeconomic status, marital status, sexual preference, age, race, religion, educational level, urban, rural. *Consider also:* patient therapist *with:* compatib(le, ility), complementarity. *See also* Characteristics; Therapist attitudes; Theoretical orientation; Qualities; Therapists.

Therapist patient interaction. See *Psychotherapeutic processes; Therapeutic processes.*

Therapist personality. See *Therapist characteristics.*

Therapist role. Therapist role(s). *Choose from:* therapist(s), psychotherapist(s), analyst(s), psychoanalyst(s), counselor(s), psychiatrist(s), psychologist(s), social worker(s), caseworker(s), psychiatric nurse(s) *with:* role(s), status(es), image(s), perception(s), function(s), dut(y,ies), position(s). *See also* Psychotherapist attitudes; Roles; Therapist attitudes; Therapists.

Therapists. Therapist(s). Psychotherapist(s). Counselor(s). Analyst(s). Psychiatrist(s). Psychoanalyst(s). Caseworker(s). Social Worker(s). Occupational therapist(s). Physical therapist(s). Speech therapist(s). *See also* Allied health personnel; Lay therapists; Professional personnel; Psychiatrists; Psychologists; Psychotherapy; Therapy; Therapist attitudes; Therapist characteristics; Therapist role.

Therapists, lay. See *Lay therapists.*

Therapy. Therap(y,ies). Treat(ed,ing,ment). Therapeutic care. Aftercare. Remed(y,ies). *Consider also:* analgesi(a,c), acupuncture, surgery, intervention(s), pain relief, rehabilitation, psychotherapy, detoxification, diet(s), prescription(s), hospitalization(s), nursing. *See also* Aftercare; Alcohol rehabilitation; Art therapy; Autogenic therapy; Aversive therapy; Behavior modification; Bibliotherapy; Client centered therapy; Cognitive therapy; Convulsive therapy; Counseling; Crisis intervention; Cultural therapy; Dance therapy; Dental care; Detoxification; Diagnosis; Directed reverie therapy; Drug rehabilitation; Drug therapy; Exercise therapy; Existential therapy; Family therapy; Feminist therapy; Gestalt therapy; Group counseling; Group psychotherapy; Health services; Helping behavior; Holistic health; Home care; Hospices; Hospitalization; Implosive therapy; Informed consent; Insight therapy; Interdisciplinary treatment; Marathon group therapy; Marital therapy; Milieu therapy; Movement therapy; Music therapy; Occupational therapy; Orthomolecular therapy; Outpatient treatment; Patient compliance; Patient history; Patient rights; Physical restraint; Physical therapy; Play therapy; Postal psychotherapy; Posttreatment followup; Primal therapy; Primary health care; Progressive relaxation therapy; Psychoanalysis; Psychosocial readjustment; Psychosocial rehabilitation; Psychotherapeutic outcomes; Psychotherapeutic processes; Psychotherapeutic techniques; Psychotherapy; Quality of health care; Reality therapy; Recreation therapy; Reflexotherapy; Rehabilitation; Relaxation training; Remotivation therapy; Sensitivity training; Sex therapy; Shock therapy; Social work; Socioenvironmental therapy; Spontaneous remission; Speech therapy; Spiritual healing; Spontaneous remission; Stress management; Termination of treatment; Therapists; Therapeutic camps; Therapeutic community; Therapeutic cults; Therapeutic processes; Therapeutic social clubs; Third-force therapy; Treatment efficacy; Treatment outcome; Vitamin therapy.

Therapy, activity. See *Recreation therapy.*

Therapy, art. See *Art therapy.*

Therapy, autogenic. See *Autogenic therapy.*

Therapy, aversive. See *Aversive therapy.*

Therapy, behavior. See *Behavior modification.*

Therapy, client centered. See *Client centered therapy.*

Therapy, cognitive. See *Cognitive therapy.*

Therapy, convulsive. See *Convulsive therapy.*

Therapy, correspondence. See *Postal psychotherapy.*

Therapy, couples. See *Couples therapy.*

Therapy, cultural. See *Cultural therapy.*

Therapy, dance. See *Dance therapy.*

Therapy, directed reverie. See *Directed reverie therapy.*

Therapy, drug. See *Drug therapy.*

Therapy, electroconvulsive. See *Shock therapy.*

Therapy , environmental. See *Milieu therapy; Socioenvironmental therapy; Therapeutic communities.*

Therapy, exercise. See *Exercise therapy.*

Therapy, existential. See *Existential therapy.*

Therapy, family. See *Family therapy.*

Therapy, feminist. See *Feminist therapy.*

Therapy, gestalt. See *Gestalt therapy.*

Therapy, group. See *Group counseling; Group psychotherapy.*

Therapy, humanistic. See *Human potential movement; Humanistic psychology; Third-force therapy.*

Therapy, implosive. See *Implosive therapy.*

Therapy, industrial. See *Occupational therapy.*

Therapy, insight. See *Insight therapy.*

Therapy, marathon group. See *Marathon group therapy.*

Therapy, marital. See *Marital therapy.*

Therapy, marriage. See *Marital therapy.*

Therapy, milieu. See *Milieu therapy.*

Therapy, movement. See *Movement therapy.*

Therapy, music. See *Music therapy.*

Therapy, natural. See *Naturopathy.*

Therapy, nondirective. See *Client centered therapy.*

Therapy, occupational. See *Occupational therapy.*

Therapy, orthomolecular. See *Orthomolecular therapy.*

Therapy, pet. See *Pet therapy.*

Therapy, physical. See *Physical therapy.*

Therapy, play. See *Play therapy.*

Therapy, primal. See *Primal therapy.*

Therapy, progressive relaxation. See *Progressive relaxation therapy.*

Therapy, psychoanalytical. See *Psychoanalysis.*

Therapy, reality. See *Reality therapy.*

Therapy, recreation. See *Recreation therapy.*

Therapy, remotivation. See *Remotivation therapy.*

Therapy, sex. See *Sex therapy.*

Therapy, shock. See *Shock therapy.*

Therapy, situational. See *Milieu therapy; Socioenvironmental therapy; Therapeutic communities.*

Therapy, socioenvironmental. See *Socioenvironmental therapy.*

Therapy, speech. See *Speech therapy.*

Therapy, third-force. See *Third-force therapy.*

Therapy, vitamin. See *Vitamin therapy.*

Thermal acclimatization. Thermal acclimatization. *Choose from:* thermal, temperature, polar, cold, winter, heat, hot, warmth, summer, arctic, tropical *with:* acclimatiz(e,ed,ing,ation), acclimat(e,ed,ing,ion), adapt(ed,ing, ation), endurance, reaction(s), response(s), adjust(ed,ing,ment). *See also* Acclimatization; Adaptation; Atmospheric conditions; Environmental stress; Heat; Physiological stress; Temperature effects; Thermoregulation.

Thermoregulation. Thermoregulat(e,ed, ing,ion,ory). *Choose from:* temperature(s) *with:* regulat(e,ed,ing,ion), control(led,ling). *Consider also:* thermogen(esis,ic,etic). *See also* Body temperature; Hypothermia; Thermal acclimatization.

Thesis, frontier. See *Frontier thesis.*

Thieves. Thieves. Thief. Bandit(s). Brigand(s). Burglar(s). Robber(s). Kleptomaniac(s). Pilferer(s). Rifler(s). *Consider also:* pillager(s), marauder(s), thug(s), pirate(s), corsair(s), privateer(s), smuggler(s), poacher(s), holdup men, cattle rustler(s), highwayman, pickpocket(s), shoplifter(s), swindler(s). *See also* Antisocial behavior; Burglary; Crime; Larceny; Robbery; Shoplifting; Theft; White collar crime.

Thin. See *Thinness.*

Think tanks. Think tank(s). Brain trust(s). Scientific advisor(s). Brainstorming. *Consider also:* World Policy Institute, Institute for Policy Research, Trade Policy Research Centre, Institute for International Economics, American Enterprise Institute for Public Policy Research, Institute for Policy Studies, Heritage Foundation, Hoover Institution, Rand Corporation, Institute for Religion and Democracy, Center for East and West Trade Policy, New Directions for News, Chicago Institute for Architecture and Urbanism, Institute for Policy Studies, International Institute of Communications, Institute for Strategic Studies, Manhattan Institute for Policy Research, Reason Foundation, Worldwatch Institute, Brookings Institute. *See also* Advisors; Consultants; Experts; Scientists.

Thinking. Think(ing). Thought(s). Analy(sis,ses,tical). Believ(e,ed,ing). Cogitat(e,ed,ing,ion). Cognit(ive,ion, ions). Cognitive process(es). Comprehen(d,ded,ding,sion). Conceiv(e,ed,ing). Concept formation. Conception(s). Conceptual(ize,ized,izing,ization,izations). Conflict resolution. Conscious(ness). Consider(ed,ing). Creativ(e,ity,eness). Critical thinking. Decision making. Deduct(ion,ive). Encod(ed,ing). Envisag(e,ed,ing). Epistemology. Hypothesiz(e,ed,ing). Idea(s,tion). Induct(ion,ive). Infer(red,ring,ence,tial). Intuition. Judgment process(es). Knowledge. Language processing. Learn(ed,ing). Memory. Mental activit(y,ies). Mental performance. Mental process(es). Metacognition. Perception. Problem solving. Reason(ed, ing). Reflect(ed,ing,ion,ions). Speculat(e,ed,ing,ion,ions). Theoriz(e,ed, ing). Understand(ing). *See also* Abstraction; Association (psychology); Autistic thinking; Cognitive processes; Concepts; Conflict resolution; Creativity; Critical thinking; Decision making; Deduction; Dichotomous thinking; Divergent thinking; Imagination; Induction; Inference; Intuition; Learning; Logical thinking; Magical thinking; Mind; Problem solving; Psycholinguistics; Reasoning.

Thinking, artificial. See *Artificial intelligence.*

Thinking, autistic. See *Autistic thinking.*

Thinking, creative. See *Creative thinking.*

Thinking, critical. See *Critical thinking.*

Thinking, dichotomous. See *Dichotomous thinking.*

Thinking, divergent. See *Divergent thinking.*

Thinking, logical. See *Logical thinking.*

Thinking, magical. See *Magical thinking.*

Thinness. Thin(ness). Emaciat(ed,ion). Underweight. Undernourish(ed,ment). Slim(ness). Underdeveloped. Lean(ness). Low weight. Low birth weight. Slight. Light(weight). Skinny. Anorexic. Cachectic. Hypotroph(y,ic). Lithe. Svelte. Gaunt. Fleshless. Lank(y). Bony. Rawboned. Scrawny. Puny. Underfed. *See also* Anorexia nervosa; Body image; Body weight; Diet; Malnutrition; Nutrition disorders.

Third-force therapy. Third-force therap(y,ies). Humanistic therap(y,ies). *Consider also:* rational, imagery, experiential *with:* therap(y,ies), psychotherap(y,ies). *Consider also:* bioenergetics. *See also* Client centered therapy; Existential therapy; Gestalt therapy; Primal therapy; Psychotherapeutic imagery; Psychotherapy; Reality therapy; Transactional analysis.

Third parties (United States politics). Third part(y,ies). 3rd part(y,ies). Minor part(y,ies). New political part(y,ies). *Consider also:* American Labor Party, Green Party, Reform Party, Conservative Party, Libertarian Party, Taxpayers' Party, New Party, Independence Party, grassroots activist(s), nonvoting majorit(y,ies), fusion politics. *See also* Citizen participation; Coalitions; Majorities (political); Political parties; Preference voting.

Third party payments. See *Reimbursement mechanisms.*

Third world. See *Developing countries.*

Thirst. Thirst(y,iness). Dry mouth. Dry throat. *Consider also:* dehydrat(e,ed, ing,ion), water depriv(e,ed,ing,ation), hypernatremia, dipsia, polydipsia, hypodipsia, water intake. *See also* Drinking (water, fluids); Motivation; Water deprivation.

Thought. See *Thinking.*

Thought, computer. See *Artificial intelligence.*

Thought, free. See *Free thought.*

Thought, social. See *Social thought.*

Thought content. See *Cognitions.*

Thought control. See *Brainwashing.*

Thought disturbances. Thought disturbance(s). *Choose from:* thought(s), thinking, cognition(s), cognitive, consciousness *with:* disturbance(s), disorder(s), demented, pathological, bizarre, abnormal, broadcast(ing), deprivation, block(ed,ing), derail(ed, ment), intrusive, ruminative, disorganiz(ed,ation), echoing, obstruction, pressure, schizophren(ia,ic). *Consider also:* verbigeration, paralogia, word salad(s), delusion(s). *See also* Amnesia; Autistic thinking; Clutter; Cognition disorders; Consciousness disorders; Delusions; Fantasies (thought disturbances); Fragmentation (schizophrenia); Fugue reaction; Judgment disturbances; Magical thinking; Memory disorders; Mental confusion; Obsessions; Overinclusion; Perseveration.

Thought disturbances (fantasies). See *Fantasies (thought disturbances).*

Thought transfer. See *Communication (thought transfer).*

Thraco-Illyrian languages. Thraco-Illyrian languages. Albanian. Illyrian. Thracian. *See also* Eastern Europe; Language; Languages (as subjects).

Thraco-Phrygian languages. Thraco-Phrygian languages. Armenian. Classical Armenian. Phrygian. *See also* Eastern Europe; Language; Languages (as subjects).

Threat. Threat(s,en,ened,ening). Counterthreat(s). Intimidat(e,ed,ing,ion). Menac(e,ed,ing). Peril(s,ous). Risk(s). Hazard(s,ous). Danger(s,ous). Jeopard(y,ize,ized,izing). Imperil(ed, ing). *Consider also:* warning(s), omen(s), caution(s,ed,ing,ary). *See also* Aggression; Anxiety; Conflict; Crises; Danger; Dangerous behavior; Dangerousness; Hazards; Hostility; Omen; Punishment; Risk; Security; Stress; Tensions; Threat postures; Vulnerability.

Threat postures. Threat(ening) posture(s). *Choose from:* threat(s,en,ened,ening), intimidat(e,ed,ing,ion), anti-predator, agonistic, offensive, bluff, appetitive *with:* posture(s), display(s), encounter(s), behavior(s). *Consider also:* gunboat diplomacy. *See also* Animal aggressive behavior; Predatory behavior; Social behavior; Threat.

Threats, bomb. See *Bomb threats.*

Threshold, auditory. See *Auditory threshold.*

Threshold, taste. See *Taste threshold.*

Threshold determination. Threshold determination(s). *Choose from:* threshold(s) *with:* determin(e,ed,ing, ation,ations), detect(ed,ing,ion), estimat(e,ed,ing,ion), assess(ed,ing, ment), measurement(s). *See also* Thresholds.

Thresholds. Threshold(s). Differen(ce,tial) limen. Just noticeable difference(s). Least noticeable difference(s). Weber Fechner law. Weber's law. Edge(s). *Choose from:* differential, auditory, critical flicker fusion, olfactory, pain, vibrotactile, visual *with:* threshold(s). *Consider also:* dark adaptation, sensory adaptation. *See also* Auditory threshold; Pain perception; Perceptual measures; Sensory adaptation; Sensory thresholds; Taste threshold; Threshold determination; Vibrotactile thresholds; Visual thresholds.

Thresholds, pain. See *Pain perception.*

Thresholds, sensory. See *Sensory thresholds.*

Thresholds, vibrotactile. See *Vibrotactile thresholds.*

Thresholds, visual. See *Visual thresholds.*

Thriftiness. Thrift(y,iness). Frugal(ity). Economiz(e,ed,ing). Parsimon(y,ious, iousness). Scrimp(ed,ing). Miser(ly, liness). Penur(y,ious,iousness). Sting(y,iness). *See also* Abstinence; Anal personality; Frugality; Orderliness; Prudence; Saving.

Thrill Seeking. See *Extreme sports; Risk taking; Sensation* See *king.*

Thrive, failure to psychosocial. See *Failure to thrive (psychosocial).*

Thugs. Thug(sery,gish,gee). Gangster(s,ism, dom). Desperado(s,es). Bandit(s). Ruffian(s). Assassin(s). Killer(s). Racketeer(s). Hoodlum(s). Hooligan(s, ism). Roughneck(s). Rowd(y,ies). Cutthroat(s). Gunm(an,en). Mobster(s). Killer(s). *See also* Bandits; Career criminals; Crime; Delinquents; Offenders; Perpetrators.

Tibeto-Burman languages. Tibeto-Burman languages. Tibetan: Standard Tibetan, Lepcha, Newari, Kachin, Naga, Bodo. Burman: Standard Burmese, Burmese dialects, Miao, Yao. *See also* Language; Languages (as subjects); Southeast Asia; Southeast Asian cultural groups.

Tic. Tic(s). Mimic spasm(s). Habit spasm(s). Maladie des tics. *Consider also:* tic douloureux, trigeminal neuralgia, habit contraction(s), twitch(es,ing), tiquer, severe eye blink(s,ing), Tourette(s), blepharospasm(s). *See also* Symptoms.

Tides. Tide(s). Tidal current(s). Tidal wave(s). Tidewater(s). Tide race. Rip tide. Neap tide. High tide(s). Low tide(s). Ebb tide. Flood tide. Ris(e,ing) and fall(ing) of water. *Consider also:* intertidal, current(s), drift(s,ed,ing), flood(s), flux(es), fluctuat(e,es,ed,ing, ion,ions), flowing stream current(s), ocean wave(s), waters of the ocean. *See also* Beaches; Fishing; Marine ecology; Oceans; Rivers; Shore protection; Shorelines; Water levels.

Tightrope performers. See *Aerialists.*

Timber. Timber(land,lands). Wood(s,land, lands). Lumber. Kindling. Pulpwood. Firewood. Tree(s). *Consider also:* forest(s), weald(s). *See also* Deforestation; Forest conservation; Forest fires; Forest ecology; Forest reserves; Forestry; Lumber industry; Old growth forests; Trees.

Time. Tim(e,ed,es,ing). Interval(s). Periodicity. Delay(s). Long term. Short term. Season(s,al). Length of task. Length of acquaintance. Overtime. Chronolog(y,ical). Duration(s). Tempo. Sequential. Pace(d). Pacing. Schedule(s). Wait(ed,ing). Timeout. Intermittent. Recovery period(s). Before. During. After. Prolonged. Epoch(s). Era(s). AM. PM. Hours. Clock(s). Daylight saving. Metronome. Timekeeping. Past. Present. Future. Today. Tomorrow. Yesterday. Time lapse. Temporal distance. Telling time. Interminable. Half life. Periodicity. Postoperative period(s). Time factor(s).

Interresponse time(s). Fourth dimension. *See also* Age differences; Calendar; Chronology; Clocks and watches; Dawn; Daytime; Evolution; Future orientation; Horology; Interresponse time; Leisure time; Limitations; Nautical astronomy; Reaction time; Sabbath; Space time clustering; Time and motion studies; Time factors; Time measurement; Time perception; Time periods; Time perspective; Time utilization; Trends; Work rest cycles.

Time, cognition of. See *Time perception.*

Time, free. See *Leisure time.*

Time, geological. See *Geological time.*

Time, interresponse. See *Interresponse time.*

Time, leisure. See *Leisure time.*

Time, reaction. See *Reaction time.*

Time, spare. See *Leisure time.*

Time allocation. See *Time utilization.*

Time and motion studies. Time and motion stud(y,ies). *Choose from:* time *with:* motion, work, utilization, activit(y,ies), use, movement *with:* stud(y,ies), analysis, measur(ed,ing,ement,ements). *See also* Management methods; Performance; Scientific management; Time; Time factors; Time measurement; Time utilization.

Time budget. See *Time utilization.*

Time disorientation. Time disorientation. *Choose from:* time, temporal *with:* disorient(ed,ing,ation), distort(ed,ing, ion), disturbance(s). *See also* Consciousness disorders; Time.

Time estimation. See *Time perception.*

Time factors. Time factor(s). Chronolog(y,ies,ical). Long term. Short term. Past. Present. Future. *Choose from:* time *with:* duration, delay(s), interval(s), elapsed, frequenc(y,ies), lapse(s), period(s), utiliz(ed,ation), allocat(ed,ion). *Choose from:* tim(e,ing) *with:* aspect(s), bas(is,es), background(s), cause(s), condition(s), constraint(s), characteristic(s), change(s), correlate(s), context(s), component(s), consideration(s), determinant(s), determin(ed,ing,ation), difference(s), dimension(s), dynamic(s), effect(s), element(s), explanation(s), factor(s), influence(s), implication(s), indicator(s), impact(s), limit(s), mechanism(s), obstacle(s), pattern(s), precondition(s), predisposition(s), process(es), similarit(y,ies), setting(s), variation(s), variable(s). *See also* Conceptual tempo; Delays; Historical periods; Planning; Reaction time; Time; Time and motion studies; Time measurement; Time utilization.

Time horizon. See *Time utilization.*

Time limited psychotherapy. See *Brief psychotherapy.*

Time management. See *Time utilization.*

Time measurement. Time measurement. Time telling. Track(ed,ing) time. Keep(ing) track of hours and minutes. Horolog(y,e,ical). Chronograph(y). Temporal specification(s). *Consider also:* timer(s), clock(s), watch(es), sundial(s), chronometer(s), timepiece(s), US Naval Observatory master clock, calendar(s), calendar date(s), punch clock(s), time zone(s). *See also* Calendar; Chronology; Clocks and watches; Horology; Time; Time and motion studies; Time factors; Time measurement; Time utilization.

Time perception. Time perception. Timekeeping. Mental chronometry. Cognition of time. *Choose from:* time, temporal, interval(s), past, future, duration(s) *with:* perspective, perception, perceived, estimat(e,ed,ing,ion), judgment(s), differentiation, orient(ed, ation), error(s), disorganiz(ed,ation), discriminat(e,ed,ion), disorient(ed,ation), comparison(s), comprehension, distort(ed,ions), subjective. *See also* Clocks and watches; Perception; Time; Time perspective.

Time periods. Time period(s). Centur(y, ies). Era(s). Epoch(s). Ages. Interim. *Choose from:* time, historical, year *with:* period(s), span, interval(s). *Consider also:* second(s), minute(s), hour(s), day(s), week(s), month(s), year(s), aeon(s), lifetime(s), decade(s), generation(s). *See also* Antiquity (time); Chronology; Generations; Historical periods; History; Middle ages; Modern society; Prehistoric people; Renaissance; Time.

Time perspective. Time perspective. Internal clock(s). *Consider also:* time, temporal, future, present, past *with:* experience(s), urgency, structuring, order, conceptualization, orientation(s), expectation(s), subjective sense, optimism, recall, recollect(ed,ing,ion, ions), centered(ness). *See also* Time; Time percption.

Time scale, geological. See *Geological time scale.*

Time utilization. Time utilization. *Choose from:* time *with:* utiliz(ed,ing,ation), wast(e,ed,ing), use(s,d), using, management, structur(e,es,ed,ing), budget(s,ed, ing), allocat(e,ed,ing,ion), schedul(e,ed, es,ing), organization, polic(y,ies). *Consider also:* time saving, time horizon, efficien(t,cy,cies). *See also* Agenda; Leisure time; Management planning; Productivity; Time; Utilization; Work rest cycles.

Timidity. Timid(ity,ness). Timorous(ness). Hesitant. *Consider also:* fearful(ness), lack(ing) courage, indecisive(ness), war(y,iness). *See also* Hesitancy; Personality traits; Shyness.

Timing, first birth. See *First birth timing.*

Timing, marriage. See *Marriage timing.*

Tipping. Tip(ped,ing,s). Gratuit(y,ies). Service charge(s). *See also* Baksheesh; Bribery; Compensation (payment); Gratuities; Monetary rewards.

Tiredness. See *Fatigue.*

Tissue banks. Tissue bank(s). *Choose from:* tissue(s), blood, eye(s), sperm, bone(s), skin, liver(s), nipple(s), organ(s), cryosperm *with:* bank(s,ing). Eyebank(s). Spermbank(s). Skinbank(s). *Consider also:* kidney transplant center(s). *Consider also:* organ donation(s), donor(s). *See also* Anatomical gifts; Dead bodies; Health facilities; Living donors; Organ transplantation; Sperm banks; Tissue donors.

Tissue donors. Tissue donor(s). *Consider also:* blood, tissue, organ(s), bod(y,ies), eye(s), kidney(s), renal, bone marrow, cadaver, fetal organ(s), corneal, brain dead *with:* donor(s), donation(s). *See also* Anatomical gifts; Blood donors; Dead bodies; Living donors; Organ transplantation; Tissue banks.

Titled persons. See *Royalty.*

Titles, land. See *Land ownership.*

Tobacco farms. Tobacco farm(s,ing,er,ers). *Choose from:* tobacco *with:* farm(s,ing, er,ers), plantation(s), crop(s), culture, grower(s), acreage, cooperative(s). *See also* Agribusiness; Cigarette industry; Farming; Tobacco industry.

Tobacco habit. Tobacco habit(s). Nicotine dependence. Heavy smok(er,ers,ing). Tobacco addiction. *Choose from:* tobacco, cigarette(s), smok(e,ed,ing), nicotine *with:* habit(s,ual,ually), dependence, addict(ed,ion), abuse. *Consider also:* tobacco chewing. *See also* Antismoking movement; Cancer; Carcinogens; Cigarette industry; Cigarettes; Dangerous behavior; Drug use; Habits; Health; Smoking; Smoking cessation; Tobacco industry; Tobacco pipes; Tobacco smoke pollution.

Tobacco industry. Tobacco industry. Big tobacco. *Choose from:* tobacco, cigarette(s), cigar(s), smoking *with:* industr(y,ial), agriculture, manufacture(r, rs), distribution, sales, compan(y,ies), corporat(e,ion,ions), business(es). *Consider also:* Brown and Williamson, Philip Morris, Camels, etc. *See also* Cigarette industry; Industry; Smoking; Tobacco farms; Tobacco habit; Tobacco pipes.

Tobacco pipes. Tobacco pipe(s). Hookah(s). Hooka(s). Hooqqa(s). Hubble-bubble(s). Hukah(s). Hukkah(s). Narghile(s).

Nargileh(s). Nargile(s). Water pipe(s). Meerschaum pipe(s). *Consider also:* smoking paraphernalia. *See also* Smoking; Tobacco habit; Tobacco industry; Tobacco smoke pollution.

Tobacco smoke, environmental. See *Tobacco smoke pollution.*

Tobacco smoke pollution. Tobacco smoke pollution. Passive smok(e,er,ers,ing). Second hand smok(e,er,ers,ing). Involuntary smoking. Environmental tobacco smoke. *Choose from:* smok(e,ed,ing), smoker(s), cigarette(s), tobacco *with:* pollut(e,ed,ing,ion), passive, involuntary, workplace(s), worksite(s), home(s), exposure, environment(al). *See also* Air pollution; Antismoking movement; Carcinogens; Environmental pollutants; Occupational exposure; Sick building syndrome; Smoking; Tobacco habit; Tobacco pipes.

Tobacco smoking. See *Smoking.*

Together, living. See *Cohabitation.*

Togetherness. See *Belongingness; Brotherhoods; Community feeling; Group consciousness; Fellowship; Group feeling; Social cohesion.*

Toilet training. Toilet train(ed,ing). *Choose from:* toilet, cleanliness, dry bed, bowel control, bladder control *with:* train(ed, ing), learn(ed,ing), retrain(ed,ing), reinforc(e,ed,ing,ement). *Consider also:* training pants, toileting. *See also* Childrearing.

Token economy. Token econom(y,ies). *Choose from:* token(s) *with:* econom(y, ies,ics), program(s), reinforcement, reward(s), contingent use(s), therapeutic, behavior change(s), incentive(s), system(s), cost response(s). *Consider also:* secondary reinforcement. *See also* Behavior modification; Operant conditioning; Reward.

Tokenism. Tokenism. Token woman. Token women. Token Black(s). Minimal compliance. *Consider also:* hypocrisy, hypocritical, lip service. *See also* Affirmative action; Equal education; Equal job opportunities; Equity (payment); Hypocrisy; Racial diversity; Racial integration; School integration; Social integration.

Tokharin languages. Tokharin language(s). Tokharian A (Turfanian). Tokharian B (Kuchean). *See also* Far East; Language; Languages (as subjects).

Tolerance. Toleran(t,ce). Tolerat(e,ed,ing, ation). Unprejudiced. Liberal. Unbigoted. Openminded(ness). Broadminded(ness). Dispassionate. Democratic. Impartial(ity). Nonpartisan(ship). Neutral(ity). Unbiased. Unslanted. *Consider also:* overtoleran(t,ce), intoleran(t,ce), forbear(ing,ance), patien(t,ce), moderate, accepting,

sympathetic, charitable, uncomplaining, compassionate, lenien(t,cy). *See also* Academic freedom; Attitudes; Ethics; Liberty of conscience; Moderation; Openmindedness; Patience; Permissiveness; Personality traits; Political attitudes; Prejudice; Public policy; Religious attitudes; Religious beliefs; Religious refugees; Social attitudes; Social distance; Tolerance for ambiguity; Values.

Tolerance, drug. See *Drug tolerance.*

Tolerance for ambiguity. Tolerance for ambiguity. *Choose from:* toleran(t,ce), accept(ed,ing,ance), tolerat(e,ed,ing) *with:* ambiguity, ambiguous(ness), uncertain(ty), novelty, complexity, incongruity, inconsistency. *See also* Personality; Tolerance.

Tolerant of faults, computing. See *Fault tolerant computing.*

Toleration. See *Tolerance.*

Tonadilla escenica. See *Interludes (music); Opera.*

Tone deafness. Tone deaf(ness). Ason(ia,ic). *See also* Hearing disorders.

Tone, muscle. See *Muscle tone.*

Tongue, mother. See *Native language.*

Tongue, slips of the. See *Speech errors.*

Tonic immobility. Tonic immobility. *Consider also:* immobil(ity,ized,izing, ization), cataleptic-like *with:* behavior(al), response(s), reflex(es), defensive, psychological stress(es), fear(ful), alarm(ed). *Consider also:* feign(ed,ing) *with:* death. *See also* Alarm responses; Animal defensive behavior; Immobility.

Tool industry, machine. See *Machine tool industry.*

Tools. Tool(s). Implement(s). Utensil(s). Instrument(s). Machine(s). Device(s). Contrivance(s). Apparatus. Appliance(s). Mechanism(s). Gear. Equipment. Gadget(s). *Consider also:* artifact(s), adze(s), ard(s), arrow(s), arrowhead(s), awl(s), ax(es), bar(s), bit(s), bec-de-flute(s), blade(s), bow(s), brace(s), cam(s), can-opener(s), chisel(s), coup-de-poing(s), crank(s), crowbar(s), dibble(s), endscraper(s), fishhook(s), gouge(s), grattoir(s), graver(s), hack(s), hammer(s), harpoon(s), hoe(s), hook(s), jack(s), keo-phay, knife, knives, lathe(s), leister(s), lever(s), lissoir(s), loom(s), mano(s), needle(s), net(s), pail(s), pestle(s), plane(s), plow(s), plumb(s), plummet(s), pulley(s), rake(s), rigging, saw(s), scoop(s), scraper(s), screw(s), screwdriver(s), shovel(s), shuttle(s), sickle(s), sledge(s), sledgehammer(s), slug(s), spade(s), spanner(s), spear(s), spearhead(s), tackle, tumbler(s), weapon(s), wheel(s), widget(s), wrench(es). *See also* Appliances;

Artifacts; Bone implements; Clocks and watches; Devices; Equipment; Hardware; Labor process; Machine tool industry; Machinery; Material culture; Medieval technology; Resources; Scientific equipment; Stone implements; Technology; Weaponry.

Top level managers. See *Administrators.*

Topography. Topograph(y,ical). Microtopograph(y,ical). Altimetr(y,ic). Contour map(s,ping). Terrain representation. *Choose from:* map(ped,ping,s), represent(ed,ing,ation), chart(s), delineation *with:* relief, terrain, landform(s), landscape(s), elevation(s), surface, contour(s), feature(s), seafloor. *See also* Demography; Earth; Earthwork; Geography; Landscape; Oceans; Social sciences.

Torts, toxic. See *Toxic torts.*

Torture. Tortur(e,ed,ing). Cruel(ty). Abus(e,ed,ing). Mutilat(e,ed,ing,ion). Terror(ism,ize,ized,izing). Torment(ed, ing). Flagellat(e,ed,ing,ion). Beat(en, ing). Flog(ged,ging). Molest(ed,ing, ation). Mistreat(ed,ing,ment). Maltreat(ed,ing,ment). Martyr(ed,ing). Persecut(e,ed,ing,ion). Crucif(y,ied,ying, ixion). Human shield(s). Harass(ed, ing,ment). *Consider also:* violent crime(s), hostage(s), activity deprivation. *See also* Antisocial behavior; Child abuse; Coercion; Cruelty; Family violence; Flagellants and flagellation; Hostages; Human rights; Kidnapping; Persecution; Political violence; Prison violence; Punishment; Punitiveness; Ritual disfigurement; Sadism; Sexual sadism; Spouse abuse; Victimization; Violence.

Totalitarianism. Totalitarian(ism). Tyrran(y,ies,ical,ize). Total state control. Dictator(s,ial,ship). Repress(ion,ive). Despot(ic,ism). Fascis(m,t). Nazi(s,sm). Maoism. Human rights abuse(s). Authoritarian(ism). Extreme regimentation. Autocra(cy,tic). Monopoly of power. Monolithic power. *Consider also:* thought control, big brother, Stalinist Russia, Orwell's 1984. *See also* Authoritarianism (political); Caciquism; Communism; Democracy; Dogmatism; Despotism; Dictatorship; Fascism; Military regimes; Nazism; Oppression; Political attitudes; Political power; Political prisoners; Political repression; Tyranny.

Totemism. Totemis(m,t,tic). Totem(ic,ite). Totem pole(s). *Consider also:* family emblem(s), clan emblem(s), sacred object(s). *See also* Animism; Cannibalism; Ceremonial objects; Clans; Emblems; Religions; Sacred animals.

Touch. Touch(ed,ing). *Choose from:* tactual, tactile, vibrotactile, haptic, dichaptic. *Consider also:* somatesthe(sia,tic), proprioception(ion,ive), cutaneous sense, tickl(e,ing), physical contact. *See also* Forms of affection; Massage; Physical contact; Tactual displays; Tactual perception.

Touching. See *Physical contact.*

Touching (handling). See *Handling (touching).*

Toughmindedness. Toughminded(ness). Tough-minded(ness). *Consider also:* realistic, skeptical, materialistic, fatalistic, pessimistic. *See also* Pragmatism; Realism.

Touring, bicycle. See *Bicycle touring.*

Tourism. Touris(m,t,ts,tic). Tour(ed,ing). Tour guide(s). Tourist trade. Travel agen(t,ts,cy,cies). Ecotourism. Travel industry. *Consider also:* vacation(s,ers,ing), traveler(s), excursion(s), cruise(s), resort(s). *See also* Business travel; Camping; Caravans; Destination; Hotels; International travel regulations; Quests; Recreation; Recreational facilities; Transportation; Travel; Travel literature; Travel writing; Travelers; Vacations.

Towers. Tower(s). Minaret(s). Spire(s). Steeple(s). Obelisk(s). Pagoda(s). Pyramid(s). Farm silo(s). Tall structure(s). Grain Elevator(s). *Consider also:* clock tower(s), bell tower(s), campanile(s), belfr(y,ies), carillon(s), water tower(s). *See also* Buildings; High buildings; Modern architecture.

Town planning. See *Urban planning.*

Towns. Town(s). Village(s). Small communit(y,ies). Hamlet(s). Crossroad(s). Small cit(y,ies). Township(s). County seat(s). Pueblo(s). Kraal(s). Burg(s). Thorp(s). Shtetl(s). Smalltown(s). Settlement(s). Oasis communit(y,ies). *Consider also:* new, boom, small, hick, little, jerkwater *with:* town(s). *See also* Boom towns; Cities; Community size; Company towns; New towns; Social environment.

Towns, boom. See *Boom towns.*

Towns, company. See *Company towns.*

Towns, ghost. See *Extinct cities.*

Towns, industrial cities and. See *Industrial cities and towns.*

Towns, mill. See *Industrial cities and towns.*

Towns, mining. See *Mining towns.*

Towns, new. See *New towns.*

Towns, small. See *Towns.*

Toxic inhalation. Toxic inhalation. Sick building(s). Glue sniffing. Solvent inhalation. Solvent abuse. Inhalant abuse. Sniffing glue. *Choose from:* sniff(ed,ing), inhal(e,ed,ing,ation), abus(e,ed,ing) *with:* carbon monoxide, rug shampoo, iodine, smoke, toxic, paint(s), fume(s), chemical(s),

solvent(s), glue, toluene, benzine, toluol, carbon tetrachloride, naptha, amyl nitrite, nitrous oxide, gas(oline), glue vapor(s), cleaning fluid(s), laughing gas, correction fluid, thinner(s). *See also* Air pollution; Inhalant abuse; Poisonous gases; Sick building syndrome; Solvent abuse; Substance abuse.

Toxic psychoses. See *Substance induced psychoses.*

Toxic substances. Toxic substance(s). Poison(s,ous,ed,ing). Venom(s,ous). Toxin(s). Pesticide(s). Toxic(ity,osis, ant,ants). Herbicid(e,es,al). Solvent(s). Envenomat(e,ed,ing,ion). Endotoxin(s). Exotoxin(s). Lethal dos(e,es,age,ages). Rodenticide(s). Ecotoxicolog(y,ical). Virulent. Noxious. Viperous. Mephitic. *Choose from:* poisonous, venomous, toxic, lethal, fatal, noxious, harmful, hazardous *with:* substance(s), agent(s), dose(s), dosage(s), drug(s), substance(s), material(s), chemical(s), compound(s), waste(s), contaminant(s), solvent(s). *Consider also:* alcohol poisoning, argyria, spider bite(s), bee sting(s), cadmium poisoning, carbon tetrachloride poisoning, ergotism, fluoride poisoning, food poisoning, gas poisoning, lead poisoning, mercury poisoning, asbestos, agent orange, PCBs, etc. *See also* Air pollution; Environmental impacts; Environmental pollutants; Environmental pollution; Hazardous materials; Hazardous wastes; Herbicides; Industrial wastes; Medical wastes; Pesticides; Poisoning; Poisonous gases; Poisonous plants; Poisons; Solid waste; Toxic torts; Waste disposal; Waste to energy; Waste transport; Water pollution.

Toxic substances damage, liability for. See *Toxic torts.*

Toxic torts. Toxic tort(s). Liability for toxic substance(s) damage. *Choose from:* toxic(ity), hazardous substance(s), dangerous goods, poison(ous,s) *with:* injur(y,ed,ing,ious), damag(e,es,ed,ing), wrong(ful,s,ed), liabilit(y,ies), liable. *See also* Damages; Poisoning; Toxic substances.

Toxic wastes. See *Hazardous wastes.*

Toy industry. Toy industry. *Choose from:* toy(s), game(s), doll(s), miniature train(s), electronic games, kiddie computer(s) *with:* industry, business(es), compan(y,ie), product(s,ion), acquisition(s), trade, retailer(s), shop(s), store(s), shelf space, brand(s), market share, firm(s), market educational learning aid(s), competitor(s), research and development. *Consider also:* Hasbro, Mattel, Toyland, Toys 'R' Us, Early Light, Playskool, Fisher Price, etc. *See also* Children's games; Dolls; Educational toys; Industry; Toys.

Toys. Toy(s). Plaything(s). Doll(s). Game(s). Swing(s). Sandbox(es). Hula

hoop(s). Crib mobile(s). Matchbox car(s). Football(s). Basketball(s). Teddy bear(s). Model train(s). Miniature railroad(s). Boomerang(s). Stuffed animal(s). *Consider also:* Furby(s), Lego block(s), Cabbage patch kid(s), Ninja turtle(s), Lincoln log(s). *See also* Childhood play development; Children's games; Dolls; Educational toys; Miniature objects; Play; Puppets; Recreation; Toy industry.

Toys, educational. See *Educational toys.*

Trace, memory. See *Memory trace.*

Track and field. Track and field. *Consider also:* long jump(s,ing), high jump(s,ing), broad jump(s,ing), high jump(s,ing), track race(s), hammer throw(s,ing), track meet(s), decathlon, 100 meter run, high hurdle(s), pole vault(ed,ing,s), shot put, discus throw(ing), javelin throw(ing). *See also* Athletic participation; Running.

Tracking (education). Tracking. Streaming. Track system. Flexible progression. Ability grouping. *Choose from:* stratif(ied,ication) *with:* class(es), learning, program(s). *Consider also:* college preparatory, vocational *with:* class(es), program(s), school(s). *See also* Ability grouping; Academic achievement; Nongraded schools.

Tracking, visual. See *Visual tracking.*

Tracts. See *Broadsides; Land (property).*

Trade. Trad(e,ed,ing). Commerce. Relations of exchange. Export(s,ing,ed). Monetary exchange(s). Buy(ing). Sell(ing). Purchas(e,es,ed,ing). Sale(s). Import(s, ed,ing). Export(s,ed,ing). Vend(ed,ing). Bargain(ing). Peddl(e,ing). Retail. Economic system(s). Commercialism. Consumption. Market(s,ing). Business transaction(s). Merchandising. Barter(ed,ing). Economic exchange(s). Exchange(s). Swap(ped,ping,s). Monetary trade. Monetary exchange(s). Non-monetary trade. Non-monetary exchange(s). Trade without money. Exchange of goods. Hidden economy. Cashless transaction(s). Informal economy. Countertrade. Counterpurchas(es,ing). Contratrade. Compensation goods. Trafficking. *See also* Balance of trade; Bartering; Business; Center and periphery; Commodities; Consumption (economic); Drug trafficking; Economics; Exports; Finance; Free trade; Harmonization (trade); Imports; International economic organizations; International trade; Market economy; Marketing; Markets; Nontariff trade barriers; Products; Purchasing; Restraint of trade; Retailing; Sales; Second hand trade; Supply and demand; Trade preferences; Trade protection; Trade routes; Trade shows; World economy.

Trade, balance of. See *Balance of trade.*

Trade, book. See *Bookselling; Publishing.*

Trade, drug. See *Drug trafficking.*

Trade, free. See *Free trade.*

Trade, fur. See *Fur trade.*

Trade, grain. See *Grain trade.*

Trade, grocery. See *Grocery trade.*

Trade, international. See *International trade.*

Trade, military. See *Arms trade; Defense spending; Government procurement; Military budget; Military market; Military industrial complex.*

Trade, restraint of. See *Restraint of trade.*

Trade, second hand. See *Second hand trade.*

Trade, sex. See *Sex industry.*

Trade, slave. See *Slave trade.*

Trade, wool. See *Wool industry.*

Trade adjustment assistance. See *Trade protection.*

Trade agreements. See *Commercial treaties.*

Trade and factory waste. See *Industrial wastes.*

Trade associations. Trade association(s). Trade group(s). Local business association(s). *Choose from:* trade, manufacturers, business *with:* association(s), group(s), council(s), societ(y,ies). *Consider also:* chamber(s) of commerce, Association of American Railroads, Chemical Manufacturers Association, Society of the Plastics Industry, Edison Electric Institute, Fertilizer Institute, Chemical Manufacturers Association, European Shippers Council, American Bankers Association, etc. *See also* Affiliation (businesses); Cartels; Employers associations; Guilds; Interest groups; Interorganizational networks; Oligopolies; Trade protection; Labor unions.

Trade barriers. See *Nontariff trade barriers; Tariffs; Trade protection.*

Trade barriers, nontariff. See *Nontariff trade barriers.*

Trade cycles. See *Business cycles.*

Trade harmonization. See *Harmonization (trade).*

Trade language, Mobilian. See *Mobilian trade language.*

Trade languages. Trade language(s). Lingua(e) franca(s,e). Commercial tongue(s). Commercial dialect(s). *Consider also:* business English, international language(s). *See also* Creoles; International languages; Lingua franca; Loan words; Mobilian trade language; Pidgin languages.

Trade practices, unfair. See *Restraint of trade.*

Trade preferences. Trade preference(s). Duty free. *Choose from:* trade, export(s,ed,ing), import(s,ed,ing), tariff(s), customs dut(y,ies) *with:* preferen(tial,ce,ces), duty-free, duty free, discriminatory. *Consider also:* generalized system of preferences, retaliatory dut(y,ies, tariff war(s), most favored nation clause. *See also* Custom unions; Free trade; Trade.

Trade protection. Trade protection. Protectionis(m,t). Neo-mercantilis(m,t, ts). Mercantilis(m,t,ts). Import quota(s). Import dut(y,ies). Trade barrier(s). Restrict(ing,ion,ions,ed) import(s). Customs dut(y,ies). Unfair trade practice(s). Export subsid(y,ies,ization). Tariff(s). Hawley Smoot Tariff Act. Trade adjustment assistance. *Choose from:* import(ed,ing,ation,s), trade *with:* protectionis(m,t), quota(s), dut(y,ies), barrier(s), restrain(t,ed,ing), restrict(ing, ions,ed), tariff(s), limit(ed,ing,s,ation, ations), sanction(s), curb(s,ed), block(ed,ing,s), retaliat(e,ed,ing,ion). *Consider also:* foreign trade practice(s), trade polic(y,ies), open trade, free trade, GATT, General Agreement on Tariffs and Trade, European Community, European Union, Common Market, NAFTA, North American Free Trade Agreement, European Free Trade Association, EFTA, Uruguay Round. *See also* Autarky; Commercial treaties; Foreign trade regulation; Import substitution; Imports; International economic integration; International trade; Negative sanctions; Nontariff trade barriers; Tariffs; Trade; Trade associations.

Trade regulation, foreign. See *Foreign trade regulation.*

Trade routes. Trade route(s). Shipping route(s). Commercial route(s). Strait(s). Sea lane(s). Sea route(s). Overland route(s). *See also* Shipping industry; Trade.

Trade secrets. Trade secret(s). Trade secrecy. *Choose from:* competit(or,ors, ive), business *with:* secret(s), intelligence. Intellectual propert(y,ies). Confidential information. Proprietary information. *Consider also:* copyright(s), patent(s). *See also* Competitive intelligence; Copyright; Industrial espionage; Intangible property; Patents.

Trade shows. Trade show(s). Trade fair(s). *Choose from:* trade, industry, small business, vendor(s) *with:* show(s), fair(s), exhibit(ion,ions,or,ors), expo(sition,sitions). *Consider also:* world's fair(s). *See also* Aeronautical museums; Bibliographical exhibitions; Commerce; Exhibits; Museums; Trade; Traveling exhibitions; Traveling sales personnel.

Trade unions. See *Labor unions.*

Trade zones, foreign. See *Foreign trade zones.*

Trade zones, free. See *Foreign trade zones.*

Trademarks. Trademark(s). *Consider also:* trade name(s), logo(s), brand name(s), label(s), designer label(s), trade dress, service mark(s). *See also* Advertising; Brand loyalty; Brand names; Hallmarks; Market research; Product labeling; Retailing.

Trades, needle. See *Garment industry.*

Trading securities, electronic. See *Electronic trading (securities).*

Tradition, literary. See *Influence (literary, artistic, etc.).*

Tradition, oral. See *Oral tradition.*

Tradition directed. See *Traditionalism.*

Traditional behavior. See *Folkways.*

Traditional healers. See *Shamanism; Traditional medicine.*

Traditional medicine. Traditional medicine. Ethnomedic(al,ine). Ethnopharmacolog(y,ical). Folk remed(y,ies). Witch doctor(s). Medicine men. Shaman(s, ism). Snake oil. Spring tonic. Healing through meditation. Folk concepts in psychiatry. Curander(os,ismo). Acupuncture. Barefoot doctor(s). Medicina tradicional. *Consider also:* traditional, folk(lore), primitive, indigenous, native, tribal, aboriginal, shaman(s,ic), faith, ritual(s,istic), cult(s), meditation, herbal *with:* medicine(s), remed(y,ies), medical practice(s), psychiatr(y,ic), heal(ing,er, ers), tonic(s), treatment(s), therap(y, ies,eutic). *See also* Alternative medicine; Ayurvedic medicine; Biopiracy; Chinese medicine; Ethnobotany; Folk culture; Folklore; Herbal medicine; Humoralism; Medical anthropology; Medical botany; Medical missions; Naturopathy; Nostrums; Oriental medicine; Paleopathology; Plant folklore; Plants (botanical); Psychotropic plants; Quackery; Shamanism; Snake lore; Spiritual healing; Tropical medicine; Vitamin therapy.

Traditional schools. Traditional school(s). *Choose from:* traditional, fundamental, structured, conventional *with:* school(s), instruction(al), teaching, education(al), curriculum, class(es), classroom(s). *See also* Back to basics; Lecture method; Nontraditional education.

Traditional societies. Traditional societ(y, ies). Tribe(s). Tribal(ism). Gemeinschaft. *Choose from:* traditional, preliterate, non-literate, primitive, indigenous, native, tribal, hunter gatherer, peasant, folk, simple, small-scale, pastoral, pre-industrial, non-industrial, pre-capitalist(ic), precapitalist(ic), archaic, nomadic, agrarian, rural, aboriginal, prehistoric, isolated *with:* societ(y,ies), communit(y,ies), clan(s). *Consider also societies by name such as:* Maori, Inuit, Masai, Yoruba, etc. *See also* Aborigines; African cultural groups; African empires; Agrarian societies; American Indian territories; Ancestor worship; Animism; Arranged marriages; Asian empires; Cargo cults; Cargo systems; Caste system; Ceremonial exchanges; Central American native cultural groups; Chiefs; Civilization; Clans; Common lands; Cultural groups; Cultural values; Culture (anthropology); Culture change; Culture contact; Customs; Developing countries; Emperor worship; Ethnic groups; Ethnography; Ethnology; Folk culture; Folk dancing; Gemeinschaft and Gesellschaft; Gypsies; Hunting and gathering societies; Indian (India) cultural groups; Indigenous populations; Indonesian cultural groups; Initiation rites; Kinship; Mana; Marriage brokers; Material culture; Modernization; Money (primitive cultures); Nomads; North American native cultural groups; Oceanic cultural groups; Paganism; Pastoral societies; Peasants; Philippine Islands cultural groups; Pre-Columbian empires; Prehistoric commerce; Prehistoric people; Prehistoric transportation; Priests and priestly classes (anthropology); Primitive agriculture; Primitive food; Primitive government; Primitive industries; Rituals; Secret societies; Shamanism; South American native cultural groups; Southeast Asian cultural groups; Subsistence economy; Subsistence hunting; Traditional medicine; Traditionalism; Tribalism; Voodooism.

Traditionalism. Traditional(ism,ist,ists, ization,ity). Old regime(s). Stable societ(y,ies). Old belief(s). Conventional(ity). Conservat(ive,iveness,ism). Conform(ity,ing). Orthodox(y,ness). Conservative ideolog(y,ies). New right. Right wing. Authoritarian(ism). Bureaucrat(ic,ism). Rightist. Resistan(t,ce) to change. Traditional morality. Conventional social attitude(s). Political right. Dogmatism. Traditional attitude(s). Conformity. Political overconformity. Establishment politics. Resistance to change. Reactionary. Ultraconservatism. Opposed to change. John Birch(ism). Tor(y,ies). Unprogressive. Die hard(s). Christian politics. Moral majority. Neoconservat(ive,ism). Fundamental(ist,ists,ism). Law and order. Oppos(e,ed,ing) change(s). *See also* Attitudes; Authoritarianism (psychological); Church state relationship; Conservative; Culture change; Embourgeoisement; Ethnicity; Political attitudes; Political conservatism; Religions; Religious fundamentalism; Sectarianism; Social attitudes; Social

conformity; Social values; Sunday legislation; Traditional societies; Traditions.

Traditions. Tradition(s). Social custom(s). Folkway(s). More(s). Myth(s). Feast(s). Rite(s). Ritual(s). Cultural heritage. Common inheritance. Unwritten law(s). Folklore. Lore. Oral history. Legend(s). Fable(s). Convention(s). Custom(ary). Orthodox(y). Observance(s). *See also* Adoption of ideas; Anniversaries and special events; Ceremonies; Behavior; Common sense; Cultural values; Culture (anthropology); Customs; Ethnography; Ethnology; Family traditions; Folk culture; Folklore; Festivals; Heritage; Laws; Norms; Rites of passage; Rituals; Social institutions; Taboo; Traditional societies; Traditionalism.

Traditions, family. See *Family traditions.*

Traffic, air accidents. See *Aviation accidents.*

Traffic, Internet. See *Internet traffic.*

Traffic, street. See *Street traffic.*

Traffic accidents. Traffic accident(s). Auto(mobile,motive) accident(s). Motor vehicle accident(s). *Choose from:* auto(mobile,mobiles,motive), car(s), driving, driver(s), motor(ist,ists), traffic, road(s,ways), bicycle, bus(ses), driv(ers,ing), car, front end(ed), rear end(ed), sideswipe(d), pedestrian, highway(s), road(s,way,ways), bus(ses), truck(s), lorr(y,ies), motorcycle(s), motor vehicle(s), moped(s) *with:* accident(s), safety, danger(s,ous), crash(ed,es,ing), death(s), casualt(y,ies), fatalit(y,ies), injur(y,ies,ed), collision(s). *See also* Accidents; Automobile driving; Highway safety; Personal injuries; Safety; Street traffic.

Traffic control, air. See *Air traffic control.*

Traffic safety. See *Highway safety.*

Trafficking, drug. See *Drug trafficking.*

Trafficking, narcotics. See *Drug trafficking.*

Trafficking in persons. Trafficking in person(s). Fleshtrade. *Choose from:* traffick(ed,ing), traffic, forcib(ly,ble) repatriat(e,ed,ing,ion), forced marriage(s), compulsory labor, forced labour, forced labor, debt bondage, sexual slavery, forced prostitution *with:* person(s), women, woman, girl(s), female(s), child(ren). *Consider also:* commercial sex work, sexual exploitation, sweatshop labor, exploit(ed,ing,ive, ative,ation) domestic service, sex industry *with:* decept(ive,ion), coerc(ive, ion), abuse(s) of authority, fraud(ulent), abduct(ed,ing,ion), lured from home(s), migrant women. *Consider also:* white slaver(s,y). *See also* Child labor; Exploitation; Forced labor; Oppression; Pimps; Powerlessness; Prostitution; Sex

industry; Sexual abuse; Sexual exploitation; Slavery; Sweatshops.

Trafficking of women. See *Sex industry; Trafficking in persons.*

Tragedy. Traged(y,ies). Serious drama(s). Tragic drama(s). Greek drama(s). Buskin(s). *See also* Adversity; Catharsis; Drama; Suffering; Theater.

Trails, nature. See *Nature trails.*

Train travel. See *Railroads; Travel.*

Trainable mentally retarded. Trainable mental(ly) retard(ed,ation). Moderate(ly) mental(ly) retard(ed,ation). Trainable retarded. Trainable retardate(s). IQ 35-49. IQ 55-40. Moderate(ly) retard(ed, ation). *Choose from:* moderate(ly) mental(ly) *with:* retard(ed,ation), impair(ed,ment,ments), handicap(s,ped), subnormal(ality,alities). *See also* Down's syndrome; Mental retardation.

Training. Train(ing,ed,ees). Apprentice(s, ship). Academic. Class(es,room,rooms). Coach(ed,ing). Course(s). Curricul(a, um). Development. Didactic(s,ism). Drill(ed,ing). Educat(e,ed,ing,ion,ional). Enrichment. Exercise(s). Grade(s). Indoctrinat(e,ed,ing,ion). Initiat(e,ed, ing,ion). Instruct(ed,ing,ion,ional). Intern(ed,ing,s,ship,ships). Learn(ed, ing). Lesson(s). Orientation. Pedagog(y, ic,ical). Preceptor(ship). Pupil(s). Renewal. Retrain(ed,ing). School(ed, ing). Scholar(ly,ship). Scholastic. Seminar(s). Student(s). Stud(y,ies). Study(ing). Teach(ing). Tutor(ed,s,ing). *See also* Animal training; Assertiveness training; Biofeedback training; Career ladders; Childbirth training; Education; Educational programs; Human relations training; Inservice training; Personnel training; Management training; Military training; Parent training; Postgraduate training; Professional education; Psychiatric training; Psychotherapy training; Relaxation training; Sensitivity training; Skill learning; Social skills training; Toilet training; Training support.

Training, animal. See *Animal training.*

Training, assertiveness. See *Assertiveness training.*

Training, biofeedback. See *Biofeedback training.*

Training, childbirth. See *Childbirth training.*

Training, human relations. See *Human relations training.*

Training, inservice. See *Inservice training.*

Training, job. See *Personnel training.*

Training, management. See *Management training.*

Training, manual. See *Manual training.*

Training, memory. See *Mnemonic learning*

Training, military. See *Military training.*

Training, occupational. See *Vocational education.*

Training, on the job. See *Inservice training.*

Training, parent. See *Parent training.*

Training, parent effectiveness. See *Parent training.*

Training, personnel. See *Personnel training.*

Training, postgraduate. See *Postgraduate training.*

Training, professional. See *Professional education.*

Training, psychiatric. See *Psychiatric training.*

Training, psychotherapy. See *Psychotherapy training.*

Training, relaxation. See *Relaxation training.*

Training, sensitivity. See *Sensitivity training.*

Training, social skills. See *Social skills training.*

Training, toilet. See *Toilet training.*

Training, worker. See *Personnel training.*

Training of children. See *Childrearing.*

Training support. Training support. *Choose from:* training, education(al), student, retraining, academic, tuition *with:* support, grant(s), subsid(y,ies), loan(s), award(s), scholarship(s), financial support, fund(ing,s), financ(ed, ing), assistantship(s), financial aid, financial assistance, allowance(s), parent financial contribution. *See also* Financial support; Training.

Trains. See *Railroads.*

Trait, aggressiveness. See *Aggressiveness (trait).*

Traitors. Traitor(s). Quisling(s). Double agent(s). Informer(s). Betrayer(s). *See also* Betrayal; Collaborators; Deception; Duplicity; Espionage; Intelligence service; R.els; Subversion; Treason; Undercover operations.

Traits, personality. See *Personality traits.*

Tramps. See *Homeless.*

Trance. Trance(s,like). Half conscious. Half aware. Half awake. Half asleep. Daze(d). Stupor(ous). Dream state(s). Swoon(ed, ing). Suspended animation. Somnolen(t, ce). Deep hypnosis. *Consider also:* profound(ly) absor(bed,ption), reverie(s), numb(ness), stupef(action, ied). *See also* Altered states of consciousness; Ecstasy; Hypnotic susceptibility; Spirit possession.

Tranquility. See *Calmness.*

Tranquilizing agents. Tranquilizing agent(s). Tranquilizer(s). Anxiolytic(s). Ataractic(s). Ataraxic(s). Tranquilo-sedative(s). *Choose from:* antianxiety, anxiety reducing, thymoleptic, hypnotic, neuroleptic, sedative, muscle relaxing *with:* drug(s), agent(s). *Consider also:* alprazolam [Xanax], hydroxyzine hydrochloride [Atarax], chlordiazep-oxide hydrochloride [Librax, Librium], chlorpromazine [Thorazine], chlorpro-thixene [Taractan], clorazepate dipotas-sium [Gen-XENE, Tranxene], diazepam [Valium], fluphenazine hydrochloride [Prolixin], haloperidol [Haldol], hydroxyzine hydrochloride [Atarax, Marax, Vistaril], lithium carbonate [Eskalith, Lithane, Lithobid], lorazepam [Ativan], loxapine [Loxitane], mep-robamate [Deprol, Equanil, Equagesic, Meprospan, Miltown], mesoridazine [Serentil], molindone hydrochloride [Moban], oxazepam [Serax], perphena-zine [Etrafon, Triavil, Trilafon], pimozide [Orap], prochlorperazine [Compazine], reserpine [Serpasil], thioridazine [Mellaril], thiothixene [Navane], trifluoperazine hydrochloride [Stelazine, Trifluoperazine]. *See also* Drug addiction; Drugs; Narcotics; Prescription drugs.

Trans-racial adoption. See *Interethnic families.*

Transactional analysis. Transaction(al) analysis. *Consider also:* interaction process(es), transaction(al), functional, ego state(s) *with:* analys(is,es), approach(es). *Consider also:* script theory. *See also* Group dynamics; Group psychotherapy; Human potential movement; Psychotherapy; Self evaluation; Self expression; Social behavior.

Transcendence, Self. See *Commitment (emotional); Enlightenment (state of mind); Religious experience.*

Transfer (learning). Transfer of learning. Transfer of training. *Choose from:* transfer(red,ring), generaliz(e,ed,ing, ation) *with:* learning, training, skill(s), rule(s), concept(s). *Consider also:* negative, positive, discrimination, aversions, meaning with transfer(red, ring). *See also* Negative transfer; Positive transfer; Skill learning; Training.

Transfer, language learning. See *Language transfer (language learning).*

Transfer, negative. See *Negative transfer.*

Transfer, population. See *Population transfer.*

Transfer, positive. See *Positive transfer.*

Transfer, technological. See *Technology transfer.*

Transfer, technology. See *Technology transfer.*

Transfer payments. Transfer payment(s). Electronic funds transfer. *Choose from:* income, payment(s), fund(s), check(s) *with:* transfer(red,ring), redistribut(e,ed, ing,ion), electronic deliver(y,ies). *Consider also:* Federal assistance, entitlement(s), grant(s), social security, payment(s) in kind, income mainte-nance, medicaid, medicare, food stamp(s). *See also* Antipoverty pro-grams; Fiscal federalism; Government financing; Government programs; Government subsidization; Income distribution; Income maintenance programs; Medical assistance; Public welfare; Social programs; Workfare.

Transference (psychology). Transference. Countertransference. Parataxic distor-tion. Transferential reaction(s). Psycho-logical rapport. Therapeutic alliance. *Consider also:* positive, negative, psychotherapeutic, narcissistic, libidinal, aggressive, libidinal-defensive, aggres-sive-defensive, anxious-defensive, floating, sibling, identification *with:* transference. *See also* Clients; Psycho-therapeutic processes; Psychotherapy.

Transference, psychotherapeutic. See *Transference (psychology).*

Transfers, arms. See *Arms transfers.*

Transfers, employee. See *Employee transfers.*

Transformation. See *Change; Develop-ment; Metamorphosis.*

Transformation, cultural. See *Cultural transformation.*

Transformation, peaceful. See *Peaceful change.*

Transhumance. Transhuman(ce,t). Transhuming cattle. *Choose from:* seasonal movement(s), herd(ed,ing), transport(ed,ing), vaquero(s), cowboy(s), shepherd(s), trail(s), route(s), path(s), drove(n) road(s) *with:* livestock, sheep, goat(s), cattle, herd(s) *with:* mountain pasture(s), lowland pasture(s), winter pasture(s), summer pasture(s), summer grazing ground(s), wintering area(s). *See also* Herders; Nomads; Pastoral societies.

Transience. Transien(ce,t). Transitor(y,ily, iness). Temporar(y,ily,iness). Ephemeral. Evanescen(ce,t). Short-lived. Momen-tar(y,ily,iness). Brevity. Brief(ly,ness). Perish(able,ability). Fugitive(ness). Impermanen(ce,t). *Consider also:* fleeting, volatil(e,ity). *See also* Fluctua-tions; Frequently; Prevalence; Seasonal unemployment; Temporary employees.

Transient workers. See *Migrant workers; Temporary employees.*

Transit. See *Transportation.*

Transit, local. See *Local transit.*

Transit, mass. See *Mass transit.*

Transition, countries in. See *Countries in transition.*

Transition, health. See *Health transition.*

Transition, lifecourse. See *Life stage transitions.*

Transition, midlife. See *Career change; Displaced homemakers; Life stage transitions; Midlife crisis.*

Transitional objects. Transitional object(s). Security blanket(s). *Choose from:* attach(ed,ment), beloved *with:* object(s), blanket(s), teddybear(s), stuffed animal(s), plush animal(s), soft toy(s). *See also* Child development; Object relations; Individuation.

Transitions, life stage. See *Life stage transitions.*

Transitions, role. See *Life stage transitions; Role changes.*

Translating and translations. Translat(e, ed,ing,ion,ions,or,ors). Interpret(e,ed,er, ers,ion,ing). Transliterat(e,ed,ing,ion). Language shift(s). English subtitle(s). Captioned performance(s). *Consider also:* deaf, machine *with:* interpret(ed, ing,ation,ations), translat(e,ed,ing, ation,ations). *See also* Bilingualism; Captions; Communication (thought transfer); Definition (words); Languages (as subjects); Linguistics; Meaning.

Translation, foreign language. See *Translating and translations.*

Translations, translating and. See *Translating and translations.*

Transmigration. See *Reincarnation.*

Transmission, cultural. See *Cultural transmission.*

Transmission, literary. See *Transmission of texts.*

Transmission, oral. See *Oral tradition.*

Transmission of culture, intergenerational. See *Generativity; Cultural transmission.*

Transmission of texts. Transmission of text(s). Literary transmission. *Choose from:* text(s), litera(ry,ture), book(s), novel(s), version(s), edition(s) *with:* spread(ing), transmission(s), publish(ed, ing), transcription(s), transcrib(e,ed,ing), render(ed,ing), treatment, emend(ed,ing, ation), delet(e,ed,ing,ion), explicat(e,ed, ing,ion,ions), translat(e,ed,ing,ion,ions), critiqu(e,es,ed,ing), correct(ed,ing,ion, ions), deriv(e,ed,ing,ion,ions), amend(ed,ing), revis(e,ed,ing,ion,ions). *See also* Cultural transmission; Distribution (delivering); Full-text databases; Literature; Publishing.

Transmission systems, data. See *Data transmission systems.*

Transmitted sexually, diseases. See *Sexually transmitted diseases.*

Transmutation of metals. See *Alchemy.*

Transnational corporations. See *Multinational corporations.*

Transplantation, organ. See *Organ transplantation.*

Transport, waste. See *Waste transport.*

Transport workers. Transport worker(s). Teamster(s). Chauffeur(s). Truck driver(s). Bus driver(s). Train crew(s). Ship crew(s). Airline employee(s). *Choose from:* air(line), ship(ping), transport(ation), railroad(s), truck(ing) *with:* worker(s), profession(al,als), occupation(s,al,ally), employee(s), pilot(s), operator(s), driver(s), crew(s). *See also* Air transportation; Cargo handling; Carriers (shipping); Ground transportation; Hazardous occupations; Longshoremen; Mass transit; Public transportation; Railroads; Shipping industry; Transportation; Water transportation.

Transportation. Transport(ed,ing,ation). Transit. Transfer(red,ring). Travel(ed, ing). Mov(e,ed,ing). Carr(y,ied,ying). Commut(e,ed,ing). Convey(ed,ing,ance). Evacuat(e,ed,ing,ion). Haul(ed,ing). Send(ing). Sent. *Consider also:* traffic, rider(s), passenger(s), commuter(s), car pool(s), bicycl(e,ed,ing), truck(ed,ing), people mover(s), moving walkway system(s), car(s), railroad(s), train(s), automobile(s), plane(s), airplane(s), airline(s), jet(s), rail line(s), ridesharing, vehicle(s), bus(ing,es), motorcycle(s), carrier(s), ship(ped,ping,ments), highways, road(s), route(s), trip(s), taxi(s,cab,cabs). *See also* Air transportation; Automobiles; Convoys; Carriers (shipping); Ground effect machines; Ground transportation; Highways; Mass transit; Prehistoric transportation; Public transportation; Railroads; Shipping industry; Tourism; Transport workers; Transportation accidents; Transportation of patients; Transportation policy; Travel; Water transportation.

Transportation, air. See *Air transportation.*

Transportation, ground. See *Ground transportation.*

Transportation, inland water. See *Inland water transportation.*

Transportation, mass. See *Mass transit.*

Transportation, prehistoric. See *Prehistoric transportation.*

Transportation, public. See *Public transportation.*

Transportation, water. See *Water transportation.*

Transportation accidents. Transportation accident(s). *Choose from:* transport(ed, ing,ation), transit, travel(ed,ing), commut(e,ed,ing,er,ers), conveyance(s), traffic, rider(s), passenger(s), bicycl(e, ed,ing), biker(s), truck(ed,ing), people mover(s), moving walkway system(s), car(s), railroad(s), train(s), automobile(s), plane(s), airplane(s), airline(s), jet(s), rail line(s), ridesharing, vehicle(s), bus(ing,es), motorcycle(s), carrier(s), ship(ped,ping,ment,ments), highways, road(s), route(s), trip(s), taxi(s,cab,cabs) *with:* accident(s), crash(es), collision(s), danger(s,ous), fatalit(y,ies). *See also* Accidents; Aviation accidents; Pedestrian accidents; Traffic accidents; Transportation.

Transportation of patients. Transport(ed, ing,ation) patient(s). *Choose from:* transport(ed,ing,ation), evacuat(e,ed, ing,ion), mov(e,ed,ing), travel(led,ling), transfer(s,red,ring), helicopter(s), ambulance(s) *with:* patient(s), wounded, sick. *See also* Patients; Transportation.

Transportation policy. Transportation polic(y,ies). *Choose from:* transport(ation), railroad(s), railway(s), traffic, mass transit, motor vehicle(s), bus service(s), passenger(s), freight, road system(s), motorway(s), expressway(s), airport(s), emission(s), road construction, fuel efficiency *with:* polic(y,ies), regulation(s), plan(s), law(s), requirement(s), standard(s), rule(s), white paper(s), objective(s). *Consider also:* Federal highway program. *See also* Energy policy; Environmental policy; Highway safety; Land use; Mass transit; Public policy; Public transportation; Railroads; Sustainable development; Transportation.

Transsexualism. Transsexual(ism,s,ity). Transgender(s,ed). Gender shift(s). Gender change(s). Gender dysphoria. *Choose from:* gender, sex differentiation *with:* dysphor(ia,ic), disturbance(s), identity confusion, disorder(s). *Consider also:* eonism, psychic hermaphroditism, epicene, metatropism, severe intersexuality, sex change(s), genital reconstruction, genital reconstructive surgery, sex reassignment, gender crossing. *See also* Bisexuality; Gender identity; Homosexuality; Lesbianism; Sexuality; Transvestism.

Transubstantiation. Transubstant(e,ed, ing,iation). Transform(ed,ing). Metamorphos(e,ed,ing). Metamorphos(is,es). *Consider also:* communion, eucharist(ic), chang(e,es,ed), commut(e,ed,ation), convert(ed,ing), conversion(s), transfigur(e,ed,ing, ation,ations), translat(e,ed,es,ing, ion,ions), transmogrif(y,ied,ication, ications), transmut(e,ed,es,ing,ation, ations), transpos(e,ed,es,ing,ition,itions). *See also* Alchemy; Change; Medieval theology; Metamorphosis; Religious mysteries.

Transvestism. Transvest(ite,ites,ism,itism). Eonism. Cross dress(ed,er,ers,ing). Homeovestism. Wear(ing) drag. Drag queen(s). In drag. Effeminate homosexual(ity). *Consider also:* female impersonator(s), male impersonator(s), alyha. *See also* Couvade; Effeminacy; Sex behavior; Transsexualism.

Trapping. Trap(ping,ed,er,ers). Entrapment. Snar(e,es,ed,ing). Mine(s). Lur(e,ed, ing). Mousetrap(s). *Consider also:* bait(ed,ing), come-on(s), decoy(ed, s,ing), entic(e,ed,ing,ement), inveigl(e, ed,ing,ement), seduc(e,ed,ing,ement), tempt(ed,ing,ation), ensnar(e,ed,ing, ement), entangl(e,ed,ing,ement), tangl(e,es,ed,ing), snag(ged,ging). *See also* Cruelty to animals; Entrapment games; Fur trade; Physical restraint.

Trashing. See *Libel.*

Trauma, birth. See *Birth trauma.*

Trauma, emotional. See *Emotional trauma.*

Trauma, physical. See *Injuries.*

Trauma centers. Trauma(tology) center(s). *Consider also:* burn(s), spinal cord injur(y,ies), acute accident(s), critical(ly) injur(y,ies,ed) *with:* center(s), unit(s). *See also* Emergency services; Medical care.

Traumatic neurosis. See *Post traumatic stress disorders.*

Traumatic psychosis. See *Reactive psychosis.*

Traumatic stress disorders, post. See *Post traumatic stress disorders.*

Travel. Travel(ed,led,ing,ling,ers,lers). Tourist(s). Journey(s,ing,ed). Tour(ed, ing,s). Trip(s). Voyage(s). Expedition(s). Cruise(s). Vacation abroad. Commut(e, ed,ers,ing). Roam(ed,ing). Wander(ed, ing). Pilgrimage(s). Migrat(e,ed,ing,ion). Rov(e,ing). Trek(ked,s). Junket(s). *See also* Automobiles; Commuting (travel); Cruising; Destination; Educational field trips; Geographic mobility; Government travel; International travel regulations; Luggage; Pilgrimages; Quests; Scientific expeditions; Stowaway; Tourism; Transportation; Travel barriers; Travel journalism; Travel literature; Travel writing; Traveling sales personnel; Vacations.

Travel (commuting). See *Commuting (travel).*

Travel, air. See *Air transportation.*

Travel, business. See *Business travel.*

Travel, government. See *Government travel.*

Travel, train. See *Railroads; Travel.*

Travel barriers. Travel barrier(s). *Choose from:* travel, transportation, transit, airline(s), bus(ses), train(s) *with:* access(ible,ibility), obstacle(s), barrier(s), restrict(ed,ion,ions). *Consider also:* travel, transportation, transit, airline(s), bus(ses), train(s) *with:* disabilit(y,ies), disabled, handicap(ped, s), blind, deaf(ness). *See also* Architectural accessibility; Entrances; Travel.

Travel industry. See *Tourism.*

Travel journalism. Travel journalis(m,t,ts). Foreign correspondent(s). Travel correspondent(s). *Choose from:* travel(ling,led,ler,lers), tour(ed,ing), overseas, abroad, on location *with:* journalis(m,t,ts), correspondent(s), advisor(s), reviewer(s), reporter(s). *Consider also:* travel writer(s). *See also* Commentaries; Journalism; Tourism; Travel; Travel writing.

Travel literature. Travel literature. Travel book(s). *Choose from:* travel, touris(t, m), ecotourism, vacation, cruise(s), excursion(s), safari(s), resort(s) *with:* literature, tourbook(s), guide(s,book, books), itinerar(y,ies), promotion(s). *Consider also:* Baedeker(s), Fodor(s), etc. *See also* Guidebooks; Tourism; Travel.

Travel regulations, international. See *International travel regulations.*

Travel to work. See *Commuting (travel).*

Travel writing. Travel writing. *Choose from:* travel(ling,led,ler,lers), tour(ed, ing), voyage(s), cruise(s), excursion(s), overseas, tourist(s), vacation(s,ed,ing), trip around the world *with:* writing, letter(s), account(s), diar(y,ies), reminiscence(s), memoir(s), journal(s), recollection(s). *See also* Adventure stories; Americans abroad; Authors' notebooks; Diaries; Electronic mail; Letters; (correspondence); Tourism; Travel; Travel journalism.

Travelers. Traveler(s). Traveller(s). Tourist(s). Voyager(s). Hiker(s). Backpacker(s). Sight-seer(s). Jet-setter(s). Passenger(s). Rider(s). *Consider also:* hitch-hiker(s), immigrant(s), migrant(s), vagabond(s), bum(s), drifter(s), tramp(s). *See also* Astronauts; Caravans; Explorers; Migrants; Tourism; Traveling sales personnel.

Travelers, commercial. See *Traveling sales personnel.*

Traveling exhibitions. Traveling exhibition(s). Road show(s). *Choose from:* tour(s,ed,ing), travel(s,ed,ing), road, cavalcade(s), pilgrimage(s), on wheel(s), moveable *with:* show(s), exhibit(s,ion,ions), collection(s), museum(s), trade show(s), circus(es), museum(s). *See also* Circus performers; Exhibits; Museums; Musicals; Trade shows; Traveling theater.

Traveling sales personnel. Traveling sales personnel. Commercial traveler(s). Traveling salesm(en,an). *Choose from:* traveler(s), traveling, field, regional *with:* salesperson(s), salesm(en,an), saleswom(an,en), representative(s). *See also* Business travel; Occupations; Sales personnel; Trade shows; Travel; Travelers.

Traveling theater. Traveling theater(s). *Choose from:* traveling, opening out of town *with:* theater(s), theatre(s), show(s). *See also* Caravans; Circus performers; Cultural events; Little theater; Theater; Traveling exhibitions; Troubadour.

Travesty. See *Parody.*

Treachery. See *Betrayal.*

Treason. Treason(able,ous). Traitor(ous,s). Sedition. Seditious(ness). Disloyal(ty). Conspir(e,ed,acy,ing) to overthrow government. Plot(ting) assassination(s). Coup(s) d'etat. Insurrection(s). Subvers(ion,ive). Insurgen(t,cy). *Consider also:* rebel(s), rebellion(s), revolution(ary,aries). *See also* Espionage; Intelligence service; Rebels; Subversion; Traitors; Undercover operations.

Treasure. Treasure(s). Riches. Wealth. Gold coins. Pieces of eight. Jewel(s,ry). Valuables. Spanish galleon. Booty. Loot. *Choose from:* valuable, invaluable, precious *with:* object(s), item(s), artifact(s), gem(s). *See also* Ancient goldwork; Antiques; Art metalwork; Beads; Booty (International law); Collectibles; Gems; Goldwork; Salvaging; Wealth.

Treaties. Treat(y,ies). Accord(s). Trade agreement(s). Pact(s). International protocol(s). Signed agreement(s). Binding agreement(s). Final agreement(s). Peace plan(s). Armistice(s). Truce(s). Cease fire. SALT I. SALT II. Compact(s). Convention(s). Settlement(s). Charter(s). Concord(at). Covenant(s). *See also* Alliances; American Indian territories; Collective security; Foreign policy; International alliances; International law; International relations; Unification.

Treaties, commercial. See *Commercial treaties.*

Treatment. Treat(ed,ing,ment). Therap(y, ies). Therapeutic care. Aftercare. Medication(s). Remed(y,ies). *Choose from:* medical, health, patient(s) *with:* care. *Consider also:* analgesi(a,c), acupuncture, surgery, intervention(s), pain relief, rehabilitation, psychotherapy, detoxification, diet(s), prescription(s), hospitalization(s), nursing. *See also* Aftercare; Convulsive therapy; Crisis intervention; Counseling; Crisis intervention; Dental care; Detoxification; Diagnosis; Drug therapy; Drugs; Electrosleep treatment; Exercise therapy; Healing; Health services; Helping behavior; Herbal medicine; Hospitalization; Iatrogenesis; Informed consent; Interdisciplinary treatment; Medical care; Medication errors; Non-prescription drugs; Outpatient treatment; Palliative treatment; Patient admission; Patient care planning; Patient compliance; Patient history; Patient participation; Patient rights; Physical therapy; Physician patient relations; Postoperative care; Posttreatment followup; Prescription drugs; Professional malpractice; Psychotherapy; Quality of health care; Reflexotherapy; Rehabilitation; Residential treatment; Therapy; Sex therapy; Shock therapy; Sleep therapy; Somatic therapies; Spiritual healing; Spontaneous remission; Termination of treatment; Treatment efficacy; Treatment outcome; Treatment withholding; Vitamin therapy.

Treatment, electrosleep. See *Electrosleep treatment.*

Treatment, interdisciplinary. See *Interdisciplinary treatment.*

Treatment, medical. See *Drug therapy; Treatment.*

Treatment, outpatient. See *Outpatient treatment.*

Treatment, palliative. See *Palliative treatment.*

Treatment, preferential. See *Preferential treatment.*

Treatment, residential. See *Residential treatment.*

Treatment, sleep. See *Sleep treatment.*

Treatment, termination of. See *Termination of treatment.*

Treatment compliance. See *Patient compliance.*

Treatment dropouts. See *Patient dropouts.*

Treatment duration. See *Length of stay.*

Treatment efficacy. Treatment efficacy. *Choose from:* treat(ed,ing,ment,ments), therap(y,ies), care, aftercare, remed(y,ies), medicine(s), medication(s), analgesi(a,c), acupuncture, surgery, intervention(s), pain reliever(s), psychotherapy, detoxification, diet(s), prescription(s), prescribed, hospitalization(s), nursing, rehabilitation *with:* efficacy, effective(ness), impact(s), outcome(s), success(ful), improvement(s), cure(s,d). *See also* Psychotherapeutic outcomes; Treatment; Treatment outcome.

Treatment outcome. Treatment outcome(s). *Choose from:* treatment(s), therap(y,ies,eutic), health care, medical procedure(s), medical intervention(s), psychotherapeu-

tic *with:* outcome(s), recover(y,ies), result(s), effective(ness), evaluation, followup, success(ful), fail(ed,ing,ure), assess(ed,ing,ment,ments), progress, performance measure(s), impact(s), aftereffect(s), side effect(s), reaction(s), response(s), consequence(s), survival, efficacy, long term effect(s). *See also* Drug effects; Iatrogenesis; Postoperative complications; Posttreatment followup; Psychotherapeutic outcomes; Psychotherapeutic processes; Recovery; Relapse; Remission; Therapeutic processes; Treatment; Treatment efficacy.

Treatment termination. See *Termination of treatment.*

Treatment withholding. Treatment withholding. Passive euthanasia. *Choose from:* treat(ed,ing,ment,ments), therap(y,ies), care, remed(y,ies), medicine(s), medication(s), resuscitat(e,ed,ing,ion), nutrition *with:* withhold(ing), withheld, withdraw(n,ing), abandon(ed,ing), stop(ped,ping), ceas(e,ed,ing), refus(e,ed,ing), discontinu(e,ed,ing), terminat(e,ed,ing,ion), cessation. *Consider also:* do not resuscitate, DNR. *See also* Advance directives; Death; Do not resuscitate orders; Dyads; Human rights; Informed consent; Patient compliance; Patient rights; Right to die; Termination of treatment; Treatment.

Tree crops. See *Tree farms; Tree planting.*

Tree farms. Tree farm(s). Pine plantation(s). Timber plantation(s). *Choose from:* tree(s), forestry, timber *with:* farm(s), plantation(s), crop(s), harvest(ed,ing). *Consider also:* agroforestry. *See also* Deforestation; Forest conservation; Forest fires; Forest ecology; Forest reserves; Forestry; Lumber industry; Tree planting; Trees.

Tree planting. Tree planting. *Choose from:* plant(ed,ing,s), replant(ed,ing,s), reintroduc(e,ed,ing,es) *with:* tree(s), woodland(s), sapling(s), forest(s). Reclaim(ed,ing) forest(s). Afforest(ed,ing,ation). Reforest(ing,ed,ation). *Consider also:* forestry, agroforestry, forest conservation, tree ordinance(s), landscaping, urban forestry, street tree(s). *See also* Conservation of natural resources; Environmental protection; Forest conservation; Plant succession; Reclamation of land; Reforestation; Restoration ecology; Soil conservation; Soil erosion; Tree farms; Trees.

Trees. Tree(s). Forest(ed,s). Wood(s). Arboretum. Timber. Woodland(s). Sapling(s). Evergreen(s). Conifer(s). *Consider also:* bamboo, birch(es), beech(es), cypress(es), dogwood(s), elm(s), fir(s), juniper(s), larch(es), maple(s), oak(s), pine(s), poplar(s), sequoia(s), sycamore(s), redwood(s), willow(s), etc. *See also* Bark peeling;

Forest conservation; Forestry; Lumber industry; Old growth forests; Plants (botanical); Rainforests; Reforestation; Timber; Tree farms; Tree planting.

Trembling. Trembl(e,ed,ing). Shak(e,en,ing). Quak(e,ed,ing). Quiver(ed,ing). Shiver(ed,ing). Shak(e,ing). Shook. Tremor(s). Tremulous(ness). *Consider also:* asterixis. *See also* Symptoms.

Trends. Trend(s). Current(s). Change(s). Declin(e,es,ed,ing). Development(s). Drift(ed,ing). Fall(en,ing). Fashion(s). Fad(s). Forecast(s). Grow(th,ing). Megatrend(s). Movement(s). Pattern(s). Projection(s). Prospect(s). Progress. Rate(s). Ris(e,en,ing). Projection(s). Shift(ing,s). Style(s). Transition(s). Tendenc(y,ies). Resurgence(s). General direction(s). *See also* Analysis; Change; Development; Employment trends; Fads; Forecasting; Future of society; Indexes (indicators); Longitudinal studies; Migration patterns; Quantitative methods; Residential patterns; Social indicators; Statistical data; Surveys; Time.

Trends, economic. See *Business cycles; Depression (economic); Inflation (economics); Recession.*

Trends, employment. See *Employment trends.*

Trends, price. See *Price trends.*

Trends, social. See *Fads; Popular culture; Trends.*

Trendsetters. See *Opinion leaders.*

Trespassing. Trespass(ed,er,ers,ing). Break-in(s). Break and enter(ed,ing). Unlawful entry. Intruder(s). Wrongful entry. Intrusion(s). Unwarranted entry. *Consider also:* encroach(ed,ing,ment), invasion(s), invad(e,ing). *See also* Property crimes; Property rights; Vandalism; Yuppie hobos.

Triads. Triad(s,ic). Three person group(s). *Consider also:* triangle(s), menage a trois. *See also* Dyads; Small groups.

Triage. Triag(ed,ing). Classif(y,ying,ied,ication) of wounded. Allocat(e,ed,ing,ion) of scarce medical resources. Priority for treatment. *See also* Allocation; Health care rationing; Health services needs and demand; Health resources; Medical care; Medically underserved areas; Priorities; Scarcity.

Trial (law). Trial(s). Prosecut(e,ed,ing,ion). Lawsuit(s). Fair hearing(s). Due process(es). Court(s) martial. Litigat(e,ed,ing,ion). *Choose from:* court(s,room,rooms), jur(y,ies), judge(s), legal *with:* proceeding(s), hearing(s), verdict(s), decision(s), indict(ed,ing,ment,ments), arraign(ed,ing,ment,ments). *See also* Arrests; Bail; Competency to stand trial; Court judges; Court news; Courts;

Criminal proceedings; Defendants; Due process; Evidence; Expert testimony; Fair trial; Indictments; Insanity defense; Instructions to juries; Judicial decisions; Juries; Law enforcement; Litigation; Offenders; Plea bargaining; Prosecution; Self incrimination; Sentencing; Testimony; Verdicts; Withholding evidence; Witnesses.

Trial, competency to stand. See *Competency to stand trial.*

Trial, fair. See *Fair trial.*

Trial, fair and free press. See *Freedom of the press; Fair trial; Trial (law).*

Trial reporting. See *Court news.*

Trials, sorcery. See *Witchcraft trials.*

Trials, witchcraft. See *Witchcraft trials.*

Tribal chiefs. See *Chiefs.*

Tribal government. See *Chiefs; Priests and priestly classes (anthropology); Primitive government.*

Tribalism. Tribalism. Neo-tribalism. Retribalis(ing,ation). Ethnic conflict(s). *Choose from:* tribe(s), tribal(ly), ethnic(ity), cultural(ly) *with:* hostilit(y, ies), rivalr(y,ies), political struggle(s), massacre(s), genocide, conflict(s), prejudice(d,s), discriminat(e,ed,ing,ion), subjugat(e,ed,ing,ion), resistance, discontent(ed), violen(t,ce), oppress(ed, ing,ion), dominat(e,ed,ing,ion), issue(s), marginaliz(e,ed,ing,ation), antagonis(m, tic). *Consider also:* tribal life, tribal custom(s), tribal danc(es,ing), tribal kingdoms, tribal societ(y,ies), cultural imperialism, cultural militant(s), deculturation, ethnocide, chauvinism, nativism, ethnocentr(c,ism), cultural competition, irredent(a,as,ism,ist,ists). *See also* Antisemitism; Black nationalism; Cultural conflict; Cultural issues; Ethnocentrism; Eurocentrism; Jingoism; Nationalism; Nativism; Nativistic movements; Racism; Sectarianism; Shrunken heads; Stereotyping; Traditional societies; White supremacy movements; Xenophobia.

Tribes. See *Aborigines; African cultural groups; Central American native cultural groups; Hunting and gathering societies; Indian (India) cultural groups; Indigenous populations; Indonesian cultural groups; Nomads; North American native cultural groups; Oceanic cultural groups; Philippine Islands cultural groups; South American native cultural groups; Southeast Asian cultural groups; Traditional societies.*

Tribute. Tribute(s). Testimonial(s). Encomium(s). Panegyric(s). Appreciation. Salutation(s). Paean(s). Show(ing) respect. Formal(ly) attest(ed,ing,ation). Hymn of praise. Enthusiastic praise. Honorary degree(s). Kudo(s).

Laud(ation). Acclaim(ed). Acclamation. Plaudit(s). Accolade(s). Commendation(s). Compliment(s). *See also* Admiration; Commemoration; Commendation; Eulogies; Flattery; Honored (esteem); Praise; Speeches (formal discourse).

Tricksters. Trickster(s). Prankster(s). Rogue(s). Inveigler(s). Deceiver(s). Hoodwinker(s). Bamboozler(s). Dissembler(s). Faker(s). *See also* Deception; Faking; Hoaxes; Jokes; Rogues.

Trills. Trill(s). Tremblement(s). Trill(er, erkette). Trill(o,i). Tremol(o,i). Gropp(o,i). Trino(s). Quiebro(s). Reyterado(s). Redobl(s). *Consider also:* pralltriller(s), schneller(s). *See also* Ornamentation (music).

Trips. See *Travel.*

Trips, educational field. See *Educational field trips.*

Triumphal arches. Triumphal arch(es). L'Arc de triomphe. *Consider also:* Soldiers' and Sailors Memorial Arch, Der Titusbogen, Arch of Titus, Arch of Septimus Severus, Arch of Constantine, Arch of Janus Quadrifrons. *See also* Commemoration; Historic sites; Medieval military history; Military history; Monuments; War; War memorials.

Trivia. Trivia(lity,lities). Useless information. Factoid(s). Minor detail(s). Minutiae. Inconsequentia(l). Insignifican(t,ce). Unimportant information. *See also* Data; Eavesdropping; Facts; Gossip; Gossip sites; Grapevine; Information; Rumors; Scandals; Tabloids.

Troop movements. Troop movement(s). *Choose from:* troop(s), cavalr(y,ies), infantr(y,ies), foot soldier(s), militia(s), division(s), regiment(s), brigade(s), gunner(s), artillery *with:* movement(s), deploy(ed,ing,ment,ments), relocat(e,ed, ing,ion), break(ing) camp, proceed(ed, ing), regroup(ed,ing), advanc(e,ed,ing), push(ed,ing), staging area(s), assault(ed, ing), attack(ed,ing). *See also* Assault (battle); Military operations; Military retreat; Military strategies; Troop strength.

Troop strength. Troop strength. Troop cut(s). *Choose from:* troop(s), cavalr(y,ies), infantr(y,ies), foot soldier(s), militia(s), division(s), regiment(s), arm(y,ies), US forces, military forces, allied forces, enemy forces *with:* strength, strong, power, weakness(es), read(y,iness) buildup(s), reduc(e,ed,ing,tion,tions). *See also* Armed forces; Balance of power; Demobilization; Manpower; Military personnel; Military power; Military readiness; Troop movements.

Tropes. See *Figurative language.*

Trophies, hunting. See *Hunting trophies.*

Tropical medicine. Tropical medicine. *Choose from:* tropic(s,al), equator(ial), hot climate(s), jungle(s), rainforest(s) *with:* medicine(s), infection(s), medical(ly), disease(s), epidemic(s), epidemiolog(y,ical), health, mortality, morbidity, pandemic(s), epidemic(s), patient(s). *Consider also:* malaria. *See also* Developing countries; Environmental effects; Environmental stress; Epidemics; Medical climatology; Medical sciences; Medically underserved areas; Traditional medicine; World health.

Tropical rainforests. See *Rainforests.*

Troubadour. Troubadour(s). Trobador(s). Trovador(es). Trovator(i). Medieval composer poet(s). *Consider also:* jongleur(s), joglar(s), Guilhem de Peitus, Jaufre Rudel, Marcabru, Bernart de Ventadorn, Giraut de Bornelh, Peire Vidal, Folquet de Marseille, Raimbaut de Vaqeiras, Gaucelm Faidit, Peirol, Raimon de Miraval, Aimeric de Peguilhan, Guiraut Riquier, etc. *See also* Courtly love; Medieval music; Minnesinger; Minstrels; Poets; Singers; Skaldic poetry; Traveling theater; Trouvere.

Trouvere. Trouvere(s). Medieval poet musician(s). *Consider also:* jongleur(s), joglar(s), Blondel de Nesle, Chastelain de Couci, Conon de Bethune, Gace Brule, Thibaut de Navarre, etc. *See also* Courtly love; Medieval music; Minnesinger; Minstrels; Poets; Singers; Troubadour.

Truancy. Truan(t,ts,cy). *Choose from:* persistent, school, student *with:* absenteeism, attendance problem(s). Refus(e,ed,ing,al) to attend school. Unjustified absence(s). *See also* Absenteeism; Attendance (presence); Deviant behavior; Runaways; School attendance; Student dropouts.

Truancy, school. See *Truancy.*

Trust (interpersonal). See *Trusting.*

Trust in God. See *Faith.*

Trustees. Trustee(s,ship). Board member(s). Governing board(s). Volunteer board(s). Regent(s). *Consider also:* guardian(s), executor(s), board(s) of directors. *See also* Administrators; Educational administration; Governing boards; School boards.

Trusting. Trust(ing,ful). Believ(e,ed,ing). Unsuspecting. Unquestioning. Confident. Sure. Convinced. Credulous. Hav(e,ing) faith. Rely(ing) upon. Depend(ing) upon. *See also* Confidence; Credulity; Optimism; Prosocial behavior; Social behavior; Trustworthy.

Trusts, charitable. See *Charitable trusts.*

Trustworthy. Trustworth(y,iness). Faithful(ness). Dependab(ility,le,leness). Reliab(ility,le,leness). Believab(ility,le, leness). Loyal(ty,ness). Credib(ility,le, leness). Responsib(ility,le,leness). Steadfast(ness). Unchanging. Enduring. Honest(y). Aboveboard. Honorable. Earnest. Straightforward. Truthful. Uncorrupt(ible). Sincer(e,ity). Upright. Upstanding. Righteous. Ethical. *See also* Honesty; Personality traits; Trusting.

Truth. Truth(ful,fulness). Reality. Actuality. Candor. Fact(ual,s). Authentic(ity). Frank(ness). Genuine(ness). Open(ness). Valid(ity). Sound(ness). Certainty. Certitude. Veracity. Verity. Honest(y). Integrity. Upright(ness). Righteous(ness). Sincer(e,ity). Straightforward(ness). *Consider also:* axiom(s, atic). *See also* Accuracy; Beliefs; Correctness; Credibility; Deception; Demythologization; Errors; Ethics; Facts; Fallacies; Honesty; Morality; Objectivity; Pragmatism; Reality; Rumors; Sincerity; Truth disclosure; Validity; Values; Verification.

Truth disclosure. Truth disclosure. *Choose from:* inform(ed,ing), disclos(e,ed,ing, ure), tell(ing), told, transmit(ted,ting), communicat(e,ed,ing), reveal(ed,ing) *with:* truth(ful,fulness), fact(s), patient(s), evidence, diagnos(is,es). *Consider also:* informed consent, right to know. *See also* Disclosure; Freedom of information; Informed consent; Patient rights; Truth; Withholding evidence.

Tuition reimbursement. Tuition reimbursement. *Choose from:* tuition, educational expense(s) *with:* reimburs(e,ed,ing, ement), waiver(s), grant(s), voucher(s), employer-support(ed), financial aid(s), scholarship(s), fellowship(s), award(s), internship(s). *Consider also:* GI Bill, employer-provided educational assistance, Pell grant(s). *See also* Cost recovery; Educational vouchers; Fellowships (educational); Reimbursement mechanisms; Scholarships (educational); School choice; Student financial aid.

Tumulli. See *Cemeteries.*

Tunebooks. See *Songbooks.*

Tunes, curtain. See *Interludes (music).*

Tuning. Tuning. Tune(d). Stimmung. Accordatura. Afinacion. *Choose from:* adjust(ed,ing), rais(e,ed,ing), lower(ed, ing) *with:* frequenc(y,ies), pitch. *Consider also:* musical pitch, tuning fork(s). *See also* Musical intervals and scales; Musical theory; Pitch (frequency); Psychoacoustics.

Tunnels. Tunnel(s,led,ling). Underground passageway(s). Burrow(s,ed,ing).

Underground road(s). Chunnel. *See also* Earthwork; Maze pathways.

Turnaround, population. See *Return migration.*

Turnaround management. Turnaround management. Corporate renewal. *Choose from:* turnaround(s), sav(e,ed, ing), salvag(e,ed,ing), comeback, retrofit(ting), revamp(ed,ing), moderniz(e, ed,ing), technology upgrade(s), debottleneck(s,ed,ing), improving performance, overhaul(ed,ing) equipment, restor(e,ed, ing) *with:* business(es), corporat(e,ion, ions), management, compan(y,ies), customer dissatisfaction, bankrupt(cy), plant(s). *Consider also:* reengineering, restructuring, crisis management. *See also* Bankruptcy; Debt management; Downsizing; Industrial efficiency; Management methods; Organizational dissolution; Organizational survival; Plant closings; Reengineering.

Turning points. Turning point(s). Watershed(s). Crossroad(s). Juncture(s). Critical period(s). Point(s) of no return. Decisive moment(s). Moment(s) of truth. Rubicon. Decisive point(s). *Consider also:* climax(es), zero hour. *See also* Contingency; Crisis; Experiences (events); Life change events; Life stage transitions; Maturational crisis; Midlife crisis; Psychotherapeutic breakthrough.

Turnout, voter. See *Voter participation.*

Turnover, employee. See *Employee turnover.*

Turnover, labor. See *Employee turnover.*

Turpitude, moral. See *Depravity.*

Turtles. Turtle(s). Terrapin(s). Tortoise(s). Testudin(idae,ata). *Consider also:* giant tortoise(s), diamondback terrapin(s). *See also* Endangered species; Reptiles; Vertebrates.

Twentieth century Western art music. Twentieth century Western art music. Contemporary music. Modern music. Electro-acoustic music. *Consider also:* neoclassical music, third stream, twelve tone music, Arnold Schoenberg, Alban Berg, Anton von Webern, Igor Stravinsky, Charles Ives, Bela Bartok, Serge Prokofie(v,f,ff), Paul Hindemith, Aaron Copland, Les six, Louis Durey, Arthur Honegger, Darius Milhaud, Germaine Tailleferre, Georges Auric, Francis Poulenc, Erik Satie, Henry Cowell, Lou Harrison, Harry Partch, Edgard Varese, Milton Byron Babbitt, Karlheinz Stockhausen, Pierre Boulez, John Cage, Morton Feldman, Earle Brown, Kryzsztof Penderecki, Gyorgy Ligeti, Luciano Berio, Lukas Foss, John Eaton, Ben Johnston, Mauricio Kagel, Frederic Rzewski, Cornelius Cardew, Steve Reich, Philip Glass, etc. *See also* Atonality; Chance composition;

Electronic music; Futurism (music); Serial music.

Twentysomethings. See *Post-baby boom generation.*

Twins. Twins. Multiple births. *Choose from:* identical, fraternal, monozygotic, dizygotic, monochorial, monochorionic, similar, biovular, binovular, dichorial, dichorionic, dissimilar, false, heterologus, hetero-ovular, two-egg, unlike, enzygotic, true, uniovular, Siamese *with:* twins. *See also* Family members; Heterozygotic twins; Monozygotic twins; Multiple births; Siamese twins; Siblings.

Twins, heterozygotic. See *Heterozygotic twins.*

Twins, identical. See *Monozygotic twins.*

Twins, monozygotic. See *Monozygotic twins.*

Twins, Siamese. See *Siamese twins.*

Two career families. See *Dual career families.*

Two income families. See *Dual career families.*

2000 (year) date conversion. See *Millennium bug.*

Type A Personality. See *Coronary prone behavior.*

Types. Type(s). Typolog(y,ies). Archetyp(e, es,ical). Classification(s). Categor(y,ies). Sort(s). Grade(s). Cluster(s). Label(s). Form(s). Genre(s). Order(s). Genus. Species. Phyl(a,um). Subspecies. Stereotype(s). Class(es). *Consider also:* denomination(s), division(s), variet(y, ies). *See also* Categorization; Classic (standard); Classification; Constructs; Film genres; Genres; Genres (art); Ideal types; Psychodiagnostic typologies; Social types; Somatotypes; Stereotyping; Taxonomies.

Types, body. See *Somatotypes.*

Types, constitutional. See *Somatotypes.*

Types, ideal. See *Ideal types.*

Types, social. See *Social types.*

Types, somatic. See *Somatotypes.*

Typologies. See *Classification; Taxonomies; Types.*

Typologies, psychodiagnostic. See *Psychodiagnostic typologies.*

Tyranny. Tyrann(y,ical,ize). Despot(s,ic, ism). Autocrat(ic,s). Dictator(s,ship). Absolutism. Tyrant(s). Absolute ruler(s). Authoritarian(ism). Totalitarian(ism). Domineer(ing). Fascis(m,t). Oppress(ion,ive). Megalomaniac(al). One man rule. Monocra(tic,cy). *See also* Abuse of power; Authoritarianism (political); Dictatorship; Despotism; Oppression; Political ideologies; Political repression; Totalitarianism.

U

Ugliness. Ugl(y,iness). Bad looking. Unsightl(y,iness). Unattractive(ness). Homel(y,iness). Distorted. Deformed. Misshapen. Blemished. Disfigured. Mutilated. *Consider also:* offensive(ness), disagreeable(ness), unpleasant(ness), distasteful(ness), displeasing, objectionable, repulsive(ness), revolting, repugnant, obnoxious(ness), nast(y,iness). *See also* Antisocial behavior; Disorderly conduct; Grotesque; Hostility.

Unbelief. See *Irreligion; Uncertainty.*

Unbelievers. See *Infidels.*

Unborn child. See *Fetus.*

Uncanniness. Uncann(y,ier,iest,ily,iness). Eerie(ness). Mysterious(ly). Weird(ly, ness). Unexplain(ed,able,ably). *Consider also:* frightening(ly), ghost(ly,liness), unearth(ly,liness), dreadful(ly,liness), gloom(y,iness), unheimlich. *See also* Apparitions; Gothicism; Horror tales; Supernatural.

Uncertainty. Uncertain(ty). Agnostic(ism). Ambigu(ity,ous,ousness). Caut(ion,ious, iousness). Doubt(s,ful,fulness). Dubious(ness). Disbelief. Distrust(ful). Hesitan(t,cy). Hesitat(e,ed,ing,ion). Improbab(ility,le,leness). Inconclusive(ness). Indefinite(ness). Indeterminate(ness). Inconsisten(t,cy). Misgiving(s). Mistrust. Perplex(ed,ity). Pyrrhonis(m,t,ts). Question(ed,ing,able). Risk(y,iness). Sceptic(al,ism). Skeptic(al,ism). Suspicion(s). Suspicious(ness). Tentative(ness). Unbelief. Unbelieving. Unclear. Unsure(ness). Unpredictab(ility, le,leness). Unforeseeable. Unsettled. Unaccountab(ility,le,leness). Unreliab(ility,le,leness). Vague(ness). Variab(ility,le). Wary. Wariness. Agnostic(ism). Suspend(ed,ing) judgment. *See also* Agnosticism; Chaos; Distrust; Doubt; Indefiniteness; Irreligion; Questioning; Suspicion.

Unconditioned responses. Unconditioned response(s). *Choose from:* unconditioned, innate, unlearned, original *with:* response(s), reflex(es). *See also* Classical conditioning; Conditioning (psychology); Responses.

Unconditioned stimulus. Unconditioned stimulus. *Choose from:* unconditioned, natural, unlearned *with:* stimul(i,us), reinforcer(s). *See also* Classical conditioning; Conditioning (psychology); Operant conditioning; Primary reinforcement.

Unconscious (psychology). Unconscious(ly,ness). Subconscious(ly,ness). Coconscious(ness). Fringes of consciousness. Preverbal thought. Suppress(ed,ion). Nonconscious. Repress(ed,ion). Bypass(ing) conscious. Subliminal. Symbolic. Fantasy level. Psychoanalytic interpretation(s). Latent meaning(s). Intuition. Levels of consciousness. *Consider also:* id, primary process(es). *See also* Death instinct; Dream interpretation; Id; Psychoanalytic interpretation.

Unconscious conscience. See *Superego.*

Unconsciousness. Unconscious(ness). Syncope. Coma(tose). Stupor. Blackout(s). Loss of consciousness. Pass(ed,ing) out. Knock(ed,ing) out. Narcosis. Insensib(le,ility). *See also* Coma; Nothingness; Syncope; Vegetative state.

Unconventional warfare. See *Guerilla warfare.*

Undecidability. Undecidability. Undecidable. Inability to choose. *Consider also:* ambivalen(t,ce), indetermin(ate,acy,ism), inconclusive(ness), groundless(ness), neither true nor false, random(ness), uncertain(ty), unprovable. *See also* Aporia; Deconstruction; Relativism; Sociology of knowledge.

Underachievement. Underachiev(ement,er, ers,ing). *Consider also:* low achiev(ement,er,ers,ing), antiachiever(s), below grade level, poor academic performance. *See also* Academic achievement; Academic failure; Academic probation; Failure; Fear of success; Grade repetition; Overachievement; Student dropouts.

Underachievement, academic. See *Underachievement.*

Underclass. Underclass. Secondary labor market. Peripheral economy. Feminized occupation(s). Ethnic labor market(s). Illegal worker(s). Reserve army of unemployed. *Consider also:* marginal population group(s). *See also* Dual economy; Homeless; Homeless shelters; Illegal aliens; Labor market segmentation; Marginality (sociological); Poverty.

Undercover operations. Undercover operation(s). *Choose from:* undercover, covert, secret, secrecy, decept(ion,ive), clandestine, concealed, hidden *with:* operation(s), activit(y,ies), arms shipment(s). *Consider also:* sting operation(s), entrapment(s), death squad(s), counterintelligence, CIA, FBI, Iran-Contra. *See also* Electronic eavesdropping; Espionage; Intelligence service; Military intelligence; Secret police; Traitors; Treason.

Underdeveloped countries. See *Developing countries.*

Underdevelopment, economic. See *Economic underdevelopment.*

Underemployment. Underemploy(ed, ment). Subemploy(ed,ment). Subempleo. Inadequate employment. *Consider also:* occupational incongr(uity,uence), overqualif(ied,ication,ications), underutiliz(ed,ation), overeducated, involuntary part-time. *See also* Alternative work patterns; Labor economics; Labor market; Labor supply; Low income; Moonlighting; Part time employment; Part time farming; Poverty; Seasonal unemployment; Unemployment; Work skills.

Undergraduate education. Undergraduate education. *Choose from:* undergraduate, college, baccalaureate, bachelor's degree, associate degree, community college, two-year college, junior college *with:* education, training, study, classes, instruction, curricul(a,um), programs. *See also* Colleges; Higher education; Universities.

Undergraduates. See *College students.*

Underground. Underground movement(s). Resistance movement(s). Guerrilla(s). *Choose from:* underground, hidden, covert, clandestine, subterranean, secret *with:* movement(s), press(es), newspaper(s), market(s), econom(y,ies), railroad(s), universit(y,ies), industr(y, ies). *Consider also:* counter-culture(s), alternative societ(y,ies), anti-war movement(s), samizdat, underground press(es), illegal econom(y,ies), black market(s), third economy, illegal worker(s), illegal immigrant(s), hidden workforce, informal sector, samizdat, tamizdat. *See also* Alternative press; Black economy; Guerrillas; Informal sector; Political movements; Rebellions; Resistance; Resistance movements; Revolution; Secret societies; War.

Underground economy. See *Black economy; Informal sector.*

Undernourishment. Undernourish(ed, ment). Malnourish(ed,ment). Malnutrition. Nutritional(ly) deficien(t,cy,cies). Starv(e,ed,ing). Protein deficien(t,cy, cies). Vitamin deficien(t,cy,cies). Calorie deficien(t,cy,cies). Inadequate diet(s). Lack of food. Poor diet(s). Semistarv(ed, ing,ation). Reduced food intake. Undernutrition. Food deprivation. Food deprived. Restricted food. Restricted calories. *See also* Anorexia nervosa;

Body weight; Diet; Hunger, food deprivation; Malnutrition; Nutrition disorders; Starvation; Thinness; Vitamin deficiency disorders.

Underprivileged. Underprivileged. Disadvantage(d,ment). Depriv(ed,ation). Socially handicapped. Unemploy(ed, able,ables). Depressed area(s). Appalachia. Ghetto(es). Health impaired. Low(er) income. Low socioeconomic status. Welfare. Inner city. Lower class. Delayed development. Skid row. Poverty. Slum(s). Shantytown(s). Retard(ed,ation). Malnourished. Malnutrition. Illiter(ate,acy). Disenfranchise(d,ment). Disfranchise(d, ment). Impoverished. Indigent. Poor. Neglected. Cultural deprivation. Powerless(ness). Downtrodden. Underclass. *Consider also:* handicapped, disabled, disabil(ity,ities), migrant worker(s), immigrant(s), minorit(y,ies), disadvantaged youth, economically disadvantaged, educationally disadvantaged, socially disadvantaged. *See also* Affirmative action; Deprivation; Disadvantaged; Living conditions; Lower class; Poverty; Poverty areas; Quality of life; Rehabilitation; Social status; Student dropouts; Welfare recipients.

Underserved areas, medically. See *Medically underserved areas.*

Understanding. Understand(ing). Comprehen(d,ded,ding,sion). Cogni(tion,zance). Wisdom. Insight. Aware(ness). Know(ing,ledge). Discern(ment,ing). Realiz(e,ed,ing,ment). Verstehen. *See also* Apperception; Comprehension; Consciousness raising activities; Empathy; Intuition; Listening comprehension; Meaning; Meaningfulness; Number comprehension; Reading comprehension; Sentence comprehension; Self understanding; Verbal comprehension; Verstehen.

Understanding, self. See *Self understanding.*

Understanding, social. See *Verstehen.*

Underwater archaeology. Underwater archaeology. Submarine archaeology. *Choose from:* underwater, marine, submarine, nautical, ship(s,wreck, wrecks), wooden vessel(s), sea, ocean floor, diving unit(s), submerged, maritime, sunken *with:* archaeolog(y, ical,ist,ists), ancient, artifact(s), ruins, wreckage(s). *Consider also:* Atlantis, sunken treasure(s), sunken ship(s). *See also* Archaeology; Cultural property; Maritime law; Submerged lands.

Underwater effects. Underwater effect(s). *Choose from:* underwater, immersion, deep sea, diver(s), diving *with:* effect(s), change(s,d), stress(es), performance(s), exposure(s), response(s), adapt(ed,ing, ation,ations), reaction(s), vision,

distort(ed,ing,ion,ions), bends. *See also* Environmental effects; Gravitational effects.

Underweight. See *Thinness; Undernourishment.*

Underworld. See *Bandits; Career criminals; Crime; Delinquents; Juvenile gangs; Offenders; Perpetrators; Serial murderers.*

Underworld voyages. See *Voyages to the otherworld.*

Underwriting. See *Insurance.*

Undeveloped countries. See *Least developed countries.*

Undifferentiated schizophrenia. Undifferentiated schizophren(ia,ic,ics). *Consider also:* mixed, latent, incipient, borderline, prepsychotic *with:* schizophren(ia,ic, ics). *See also* Schizophrenia.

Undocumented immigrants. Undocumented immigrant(s). Illegal alien(s). *Choose from:* illegal, undocumented, clandestine *with:* alien(s), immigrant(s), worker(s), border crossing(s), entry, migrant(s), migration, immigration, population, refugee(s), status, Central Americans, Mexican(s). Hidden workforce. Wetback(s). *Consider also:* Immigration Reform and Control Act, United States Border Patrol, Bracero Program, Sanctuary movement, immigration amnesty. *See also* Borderlands; Foreign workers; Illegal aliens; Immigrants; Immigration law; Labor migration; Migrant workers; Migration; Refugees.

Unemployed, hard-core. See *Hard-core unemployed.*

Unemployment. Unemploy(ed,ment,able). Laidoff. Laid off. Layoff(s). Out of work. Jobless(ness). Idle(d) worker(s). Unwaged. *Choose from:* loss, lost, lose, losing, terminat(e,ed,ing,ation) *with:* employment, job(s), career(s). *Choose from:* seek(ing), look(ing), search(ing) *with:* work, employment, job(s), career(s). *Consider also:* marginal(ly) employ(ed,ment), inadequate employment, irregular(ly) employ(ed,ment), subemploy(ed,ment), underemploy(ed, ment). *See also* Depression (economic); Discouraged workers; Disguised unemployment; Dislocated workers; Dismissal of staff; Economic problems; Employability; Employment trends; Hard-core unemployed; Job creation; Job search; Labor economics; Labor force; Labor market; Labor policy; Occupational qualifications; Personnel termination; Plant closings; Poverty; Seasonal unemployment; Social conditions; Technological unemployment; Workforce planning; Underemployment; Unemployment rates; Unemployment relief.

Unemployment, disguised. See *Disguised unemployment.*

Unemployment, seasonal. See *Seasonal unemployment.*

Unemployment, technological. See *Technological unemployment.*

Unemployment rates. Unemployment rate(s). *Choose from:* unemploy(ed, ment,able), layoff(s), out of work, jobless, idle worker(s), seek(ing) job(s), look(ing) for work, seek(ing) employment *with:* rate(s), data, figure(s), measure(s,ment), statistics. *Consider also:* employment statistics, employ(ed, ment) rate. *See also* Demography; Disguised unemployment; Economic statistics; Labor market; Seasonal unemployment; Unemployment.

Unemployment relief. Unemployment relief. *Choose from:* unemploy(ed,ment), out of work, jobless(ness), idle(d) worker(s) *with:* compensation, aid, assistance, relief, reliev(e,ed,ing), grant(s), program(s), insurance, opportunit(y,ies), workfare. *Consider also:* employment, job(s), position(s) *with:* relocat(e,ed,ing,ion), placement(s), creat(e,ed,ing,ion), training, retraining. *See also* Antipoverty programs; Food services (programs); Income maintenance programs; Medical assistance; Public welfare; Seasonal unemployment; Unemployment; Workfare.

Unethical conduct. Unethical conduct. Corrupt(ed,ing,ion). Scandal(s). Unprincipled. Unscrupulous(ness). Unprofessional. Bribe(s,d,ry). Wrongdoing(s). Deceit(ful,fulness). Crooked. Questionable. Misdeed(s). Misconduct. Conflict of interest. *Consider also:* tarnished reputation, sleaz(y,e), smuggl(ed,ing), racketeer(ing), embezzlement, perjury, conspiracy, wrongdoing(s), violation(s), forgery, illegal(ly,ity,ities), immoral(ity,ities), pilfer(ed,ing), patronage, ethical question(s), cronyism, libel, collusion, concealment, profiteering, lax ethics, criminal behavior, revolving door, questionable behavior, illegal contribution(s), vote buying, skirting law(s), loophole(s), lining pocket(s), shred(ded, ding) document(s), alter(ing) record(s), withhold(ing) information, alter(ed,ing) evidence, misdemeanor(s), malfeasance, kickback(s), misappropriation(s), divert(ed,ing) fund(s), divert(ed,ing) government property, no-show employee(s), sexual misconduct, fraud(ulent), impropriet(y,ies), unlawful(ly), payoff(s), payola, launder(ed,ing) money, deception, lying, dishonest(y). *See also* Business ethics; Cheating; Conflict of interest; Corruption in government; Deception; Falsification (scientific); Financial disclosure; Fraud; Fraudulent advertising; Impaired professionals; Improprieties; Journalistic ethics; Judicial corruption; Judicial ethics; Legal ethics; Medical ethics; Military ethics; Military offenses; Misconduct in office; Naval offenses; Ministerial ethics (clergy); Political ethics; Professional ethics; Research ethics; Scientific misconduct; Sexual ethics; Sexual exploitation; Sexual harassment; Sexual misconduct; Withholding evidence; Witness tampering.

Unexplained phenomena. See *Extrasensory perception; Near death experiences; Occultism; Parapsychology; Supernatural; Witchcraft.*

Unfair trade practices. See *Restraint of trade.*

Unfairness. See *Injustice.*

Unicity of God. See *Oneness of God.*

Unification. Unification(s). Unif(y,ying, ied). Reunification(s). Reunif(y,ying, ied). Re-unification(s). Re-unif(y,ying, ied). Enosis. Unite(d). Uniting. Incorporat(e,ed,ing). Consolidat(e,ed, ing,ion). Intergovernmental pact(s). Merger(s). Alliance(s). Amalgamat(e,ed, ing,ion,ions). Confeder(acy,acies). Confederat(e,ed,ion,ions). Coalescence(s). *Consider also:* coadunation(s), coalition(s), affiliation(s), interlocking director(ship,ships), join(ed,ing), link(ed,ing,age), coupling(s), hookup(s). *See also* Alliances; Annexation; Confederalism; Merger integration; Mergers; Treaties.

Uniformity. Uniform(ity). Homogene(ity, ous). Consisten(t,cy). Constan(t,cy). Stability. Stable. Symmetrical. Regular(ity). Stead(y,fast). Equal(ity). Well-proportioned. Unvar(ied,ying). Similar(ity,ities). Identical. Alike. Same(ness). Equivalen(t,cy). Even(ness). Conform(ity). *See also* Conformity (personality); Social conformity; Deviance; Differences; Harmonization; Norms; Regulation; Resemblance; Similarity; Social pressure; Stability.

Unilineal descent. Unilineal descent. Unilateral descent. Unilineality. *Consider also:* patrilineal descent, patrilineality, matrilineal descent, matrilineality. *See also* Cognatic descent; Kinship; Matrilineality; Patrilineality.

Union, mystical. See *Enlightenment (state).*

Union management relations. See *Labor management relations.*

Union members. Union member(s). *Choose from:* union(ized), AFL-CIO, UFW, United Farm Workers, UAW, United Auto Workers, ILWU, International Longshore Workers Union, ILGWU, International Ladies Garment Workers Union, United Mine Workers of America, teamster(s) *with:* member(s), join(ed,ing), belong(s,ing), membership(s), dues, card(s), worker(s), participation, employee(s), leader(s, ship), steward(s), activists, men, man, women, woman, officer(s), official(s). *See also* Labor unions.

Union organizing, labor. See *Organizing activities.*

Union shop. Union shop(s). Agency shop(s). Closed shop(s). Pre-entry closed shop(s). Union security clause(s). *Consider also:* Rand formula. *See also* Labor management relations; Labor unions.

Unions, custom. See *Custom unions.*

Unions, economic. See *Economic unions.*

Unions, labor. See *Labor unions.*

Unions, monetary. See *Monetary unions.*

Unions, trade. See *Labor unions.*

Unitarism. Unitarism. Unitary state(s). Centraliz(ed,ation) power. Centralized government(s). *See also* Confederalism; Federations.

Units, activity. See *Activity units.*

Units, respiratory care. See *Respiratory care units.*

Unity. Unity. Unani(mous,mity). Consensus. Harmony. Agreement. Like-minded(ness). Compatibility. Accord(ance). Concord(ance). Concurren(t,ce). Social cohesion. Group cohesion. Conformity to group norm. Ingroup(s). In-group bias. Team building. Teamwork. Groupthink. *Choose from:* group(s), social, societal, neighborhood, ethnic, famil(y,ies), ingroup(s), unit(s), department(al), trib(al,e,es), team(s), staff, national, state(s) *with:* cohes(ion,iveness), commonality, unity, unification, cooperation, coorientation, conformity, interdependence, integration, knitted(ness), well knit, closely knit, consensus, solidarity, reintegration, reciproc(al,ity), mutual support, morale, spirit. *See also* Assimilation (cultural); Collective representation; Community (social); Consensus; Cooptation; Group dynamics; Group norms; Groups; Organizational dissolution; Primary groups; Similarity; Small groups; Social cleavage; Social cohesion; Social disorganization; Social environment; Social equilibrium; Social identity; Social integration; Social order; Teamwork; Unification.

Unity (Literature). Unit(y,ies). Poetic unit(y,ies). *Choose from:* literar(y,ature), poetic, artistic *with:* unit(y,ies), symmetry, total effect, singleness, whole(s). *Consider also:* unity of action, unity of time, unity of place, unity of plot, Aristotelian rules, organic unity. *See also* Form (aesthetics); Literature; Poetics.

Unity, group. See *Social cohesion.*

Unity of God. See *Oneness of God.*

Unity of mankind. See *Brotherliness.*

Universal divinity, pantheism. See *Pantheism (universal divinity).*

Universal health programs. See *National health programs.*

Universalism. Universalis(m,t,ts,tic). Universality. Universal salvation. All inclusive(ness). Worldwide. Equal treatment. Treat(ed,ing) people equally. *Consider also:* universal law(s), multicultural societ(y,ies), multi cultural(ism), multicultural(ism), cultural diversity, multinational(ism), cosmopolitan, whole(ness). *See also* Catholic (universality); Collectivism; Equal education; Global integration; Globalization; World citizenship.

Universality. See *Catholic (universality).*

Universals, cultural. See *Cultural universals.*

Universe. Universe. Heavens. Cosmos. Milky way galaxy. *Consider also:* world, earth. *See also* Earth.

Universe, expanding. See *Expanding universe.*

Universities. Universit(y,ies). Land grant universit(y,ies). Open universit(y,ies). State universit(y,ies). Urban universit(y, ies). Universitas. Academ(e,ia,ics). Professional school(s). Graduate school(s). Graduate education. *See also* Colleges; Graduate education; Graduate schools; Higher education; Undergraduate education.

Universities, free. See *Nontraditional education.*

Universities, open. See *Nontraditional education.*

University, virtual. See *Distance education.*

University students. See *College students.*

University teachers. See *Faculty.*

Unmarried. See *Bachelors; Divorce; Marital separation; Marital status; Single mothers; Single parent family; Single person; Unmarried women; Widowhood.*

Unmarried couples. See *Cohabitation.*

Unmarried women. Unmarried women. Single mother(s). Solo mother(s). Divorcee(s). Spinster(s). Old maid(s). *Choose from:* unmarried, single, bachelor, never married, solo *with:* women, woman, female(s), mother(s). *See also* Divorce; Female headed households; Marital separation; Single mothers; Single parent family; Single person; Widowhood.

Unmet needs. Unmet need(s). Need(y, iness). Unsatisfied need(s). Greatest need(s). *Consider also:* insufficien(t,cy, cies), lack(s,ed,ing), depriv(e,ed,ing, ation), deficien(cy,cies), paucity, inadequa(te,tely,cy). *See also* Basic needs; Constraints; Delay of gratification; Deprivation; Hardships; Malnutrition; Need satisfaction; Needs; Needs assessment; Wants.

Unpaid labor. Unpaid labor. *Choose from:* unpaid, unsalaried, unrewarded, uncompensated, voluntary, volunteer *with:* labor, employee(s), personnel, workforce, staff. *Consider also:* donat(e,ed,ing) time. *See also* Cheap labor; Housewives; Volunteers; Workers' rights.

Unrelated individuals. Unrelated individual(s). Nonrelative(s). Non-kin. *Consider also:* exogam(y,ous), stranger(s). *See also* Strangers.

Unreported crimes. Unreported crime(s). *Choose from:* unreported, fail(ed,ure) to report, discrepanc(y,ies) in reporting *with:* crime(s), delinquency, criminal(s), delinquen(t,ts), vandalism, rape, arson, violence, burglar(y,s), robber(y,ies,s), illegal, unlawful, violation(s). *See also* Crime; Crime rates; Mandatory reporting; Victimless crimes.

Unrest, social. See *Social unrest.*

Unselfishness. Unselfish(ness). Generous(ly). Generosity. Unsparing(ly). Altruis(m,tic). Ungrudgin(ly). Magnanimous(ly). Philanthrop(y,ic, ically). *See also* Altruism; Generosity; Gift giving; Magnanimity; Prosocial behavior; Self sacrifice.

Unskilled workers. Unskilled worker(s). *Choose from:* unskilled, untrained, semiskilled, custodial, uneducated *with:* labor, worker(s), employee(s), personnel, operator(s), staff. *See also* Blue collar workers; Employees; Labor market segmentation; Nonprofessional personnel; Skilled workers; Work skills; Working class.

Unwanted children. Unwanted child(ren). *Choose from:* child(ren), bab(y,ies), infant(s), neonate(s), juvenile(s), offspring, son(s), daughter(s) *with:* unwanted, undesired, rejected, disinherited, disowned, abandoned, neglected, throw away. *Consider also:* unwanted, unsought *with:* pregnanc(y,ies), childbearing. *See also* Abandoned children; Child neglect; Foundlings; Rejection (psychology); Unwanted pregnancy.

Unwanted pregnancy. Unwanted pregnanc(y,ies). *Choose from:* unwanted, conflict(s), undesired, unintended, ambivalen(ce,t), inconvenient, unwelcome, untimely, unsought *with:* pregnan(t,cy,cies), conception. *See also* Abortion; Illegitimacy (children); Incest; Rape; Rejection (psychology); Reproductive rights; Single mothers; Unwanted children.

Unwed mothers. See *Female headed households; Single mothers; Single parent family.*

Unwilling (involuntary). See *Involuntary (unwilling).*

Up (computers). Up (computers). *Choose from:* computer(s), PC(s), network(s), with: up and running, functioning, connected. *Consider also:* online. *See also* Computers; Down (computers).

Upper class. Upper class(es). Power elite(s). Wealthy famil(y,ies). Elite status. Rich. Super rich. Nobility. Upper household(s). Upper income. Upper socioeconomic group(s). Upper rank(s). High(er) income(s). Wealth(y). Ruling class(es). Affluen(ce,t). Elite(s). High status. High SES. High socioeconomic status. High socioeconomic strata. High socioeconomic stratum. Higher class. High ranking. High position. Aristocra(cy,cies,t,ts,tic). Patrician. Peerage. Nobility. Nouveau riche. Well-born. Leisure class(es). Advantaged. Oligarch(y,ies). Owning class(es). Overclass(es). *See also* Economic elites; Elites; Establishment; Exclusive neighborhoods; Intelligentsia; Power elite; Ruling class; Upper class attitudes; Upper income level; Wealth.

Upper class attitudes. Upper class attitude(s). *Choose from:* upper class(es), wealthy, affluen(t,ce), dominant group(s), elit(e,es,ist), advantaged *with:* norm(s), conscious(ness), preference(s), ideolog(y,ies,ical), mindset, perception(s), values, attitude(s). *See also* Attitudes; Class consciousness; Class identity; Class politics; Lower class attitudes; Socioeconomic status; Ruling class; Upper class.

Upper income level. Upper income level. *Choose from:* high, upper *with:* socioeconomic strat(a,um), socioeconomic status. *Consider also:* affluen(t,ce), upper class, economically advantaged, wealth(y,iest), high income(s), rich, super rich, prosperous, owning class. *See also* Socioeconomic status; Upper class; Wealth.

Uprisings. See *Decolonization; Guerrillas; Liberation theology; National fronts; Peasant rebellions; Political violence; Rebellions; Resistance; Separatism; Social unrest; Terrorism.*

Upskilling. Upskill(ed,ing). Multiskill(ed, ing). Crosstrain(ed,ing). Cross-train(ed, ing). *Consider also:* reskill(ed,ing), lifelong learning. *See also* Inservice training; Skill learning; Work skills.

Upward mobility. See *Class mobility; Social mobility; Status Seekers.*

Urban areas. See *Metropolitan areas; Urban environments.*

Urban beautification. Urban beautification. *Choose from:* cit(y,ies), urban, communit(y,ies), metropolitan, downtown, waterfront area(s) *with:* beautif(y, ying,ied,ication), revitaliz(e,ed,ing, ation), well-designed, cleanup, clean(ed,ing) up, remodel(ed,ing), renovat(e,ed,ing,ion), sanitiz(e,ed, ing,ation). *See also* Brownfields; Cities; Civic improvement; Neighborhood preservation; Urban environments; Urban renewal.

Urban crime. Urban crime(s). *Choose from:* urban, cit(y,ies), metropol(itan,is), municipal(ity,ities), slum(s), ghetto(es), downtown, street(s) *with:* arrest(s), arson(ists), assassinat(e,ed,ion), assault(s,ed,ing), batter(ed,ing), blackmarket(s), Black Hand, burglar(y,ies), break in(s), child abuse, corrupt(ion), delinquen(cy,t), drug peddling, extort(ion), felon(s,ies,y), flimflam, forger(ies,y), holdup(s), homicide(s), drive-by shooting(s), drive-by(s), joyrid(e,es,ing), kidnap(ped,ping, pings), lawbreaking, lawless(ness), fraud(ulent), larcen(ous,y), Mafia, Mafioso, manslaughter, misdemeanor(s), murder(s), molest(ed,ing,ation), mug(ged,ging,gings), offense(s), offender(s), organized crime, prostitut(e, es,ion), pornograph(ic,y), pickpocket(s), racial conflict(s), rape(s), riot(ed,s,ing), robber(ies,y), racket(s), racketeer(ing), sabotage, scofflaw(s), sex offense(s), sexual abuse(s), sexual exploitation, shoplift(er,ers,ing), slay(ings), spouse abuse, theft(s), thieve(s,ry), trespass(er, ers), Unione Siciliano, unrest, vandal(s,ism), violence, white collar crime(s). *See also* Corruption in government; Crime; Driveby Crimes; Drug trafficking; Urban environments; Urban poverty; White collar crime.

Urban development. Urban development. *Choose from:* cit(y,ies), metropoli(s,tan), downtown, municipal(ity,ities), urban(ized,ization), ghetto(es), slum(s), town(s), barrio(s), business district(s), zone(s) of transition, enterprise zone(s) *with:* annex(ed,ing,ation), building, construction, develop(ed,ing,ment), design(ed,ing), evolution, evolv(e,ed, ing), expan(d,ding,sion), exten(d,ded, ding,sion), further(ed,ing), gain(s,ing), grow(n,th,ing), improv(e,ed,ing,ement, ements), invest(ed,ing,ment,ments), reinvest(ed,ing,ment,ments), moderniz(e, ed,ing,ation), plan(s,ned,ning), progress, redevelop(ed,ing,ment), spread(ing), revitaliz(e,ed,ing,ation), rezon(e,ed,ing), transform(ed,ing,ation), zon(e,ed,ing). *Consider also:* growth machine(s). *See also* Cities; Civic improvement; Community development; Economic development; Growth management;

Land use; Neighborhood change; Public transportation; Regional development; Rural development; Urban environments; Urban planning; Urban renewal; Urbanization.

Urban education. Urban education. Blackboard jungle(s). *Choose from:* urban, cit(y,ies), inner cit(y,ies), central cit(y,ies), metropol(itan,is), municipal(ity,ities), slum(s), ghetto(es), downtown *with:* school(s,ing), school district(s), universit(y,ies), college(s), education. *See also* Education; Schools; Urban environments.

Urban environments. Urban environment(s). Cit(y,ies). Ghetto(es). Inner cit(y,ies). Urbanism. SMSA. SMA. Boomtown(s). Satellite cit(y,ies). Urbanite(s). Metropolitan. Metropolis(es). Megalopolis(es). Bedroom communit(y,ies). Satellite communit(y,ies). *Choose from:* urban(ized,ization,ism), cit(y,ies), metropolitan, metropolis, slum(s), ghetto(es), downtown, municipal(ity, ities), business district(s), town(s), barrio(s) *with:* environment(s), area(s), setting(s), location(s), surrounding(s), milieu, condition(s), count(y,ies), school district(s), communit(y,ies), neighborhood(s). *See also* Air pollution; Civic improvement; Community characteristics; Crowding; Municipal art; Poverty areas; Urban beautification; Urban crime; Urban development; Urban education; Urban fringe; Urban health; Urban mental health; Urban planning; Urban population; Urban poverty; Urban renewal; Urban sprawl; Urbanization; Water pollution.

Urban fringe. Urban fringe. Urban periphery. City outskirt(s). Industrial fringe. Residential fringe. Outer city. Urban sprawl. Megalopolis. Rural urban continuum. Urbanization. Urban diffusion. Bedroom communit(y,ies). Edge cit(y,ies). Satellite cit(y,ies). Zone V. *See also* Planned communities; Rural areas; Suburbs; Urban sprawl.

Urban from rural migration. See *Rural to urban migration.*

Urban ghettos. See *Ethnic neighborhoods; Poverty areas.*

Urban health. Urban health. Urban rat control. Epidemiolog(y,ical) survey of slum(s). City health care. Sanitation in cit(y,ies). *Choose from:* urban(ized, ization), cit(y,ies), metropoli(s,tan), megalopolis, ghetto(es), slum(s), municipal(ity,ities), barrio(s), downtown(s), business district(s), town(s) or specific cities such as: Detroit, Chicago, Atlanta, Boston, Cleveland, Houston, Tucson, Minneapolis, Dallas, Washington, Baltimore, London, Tokyo, Rome, Moscow, Paris, Peking, Copenhagen, etc. *with:* health,

hygiene, medicine, medical, epidemiolog(y,ical), disease(s), disorder(s), illness(es), nutrition, mortality, morbidity, hygien(e,ic), cancer, death, sanitation, screening, accident(s), hospital(s,ization,izations), quality of life, clinic(s), public health, immuniz(e,ed,ing,ation,ations) water purification, pest control, sewage treatment. *See also* Environmental pollution; Epidemics; Urban environments; Urban mental health.

Urban mental health. Urban mental health. Mental health in cit(y,ies). Mental illness in cit(y,ies). Mental disorders in urban area(s). Psychiatric admissions in metropolitan area(s). *Choose from:* cit(y,ies), metropoli(s,tan), downtown, municipal(ity,itics), urban(ized,ization), ghetto(es), slum(s), town(s), barrio(s), business district(s), zone(s) of transition *with:* mental health, mental hygiene, mentally ill, mental illness(es), mental disorder(s), emotional(ly) disturb(ed, ance,ances), neuro(tic,sis,ses), psycho(tic,sis,ses), alcoholi(cs,sm), suicide(s), drug abuse, schizophren(ia, ic), depress(ive,ion), insan(e,ity), psychiatr(y,ic), drug abus(e,ers), substance abus(e,ers), drug dependen(ce, t), substance dependen(ce,t). *See also* Mental health; Urban environments; Urban health.

Urban planning. Urban planning. *Choose from:* city, urban, town(s) *with:* budget(ing), capital improvement, strategic planning, land use. *Choose from:* municipali(ty,ties), metropolitan, urban, city, cities, public housing, housing, communit(y,ies), neighborhood(s), local(ity,ities), regional, downtown, central business district, county, multi-county, infrastructure, town(s) *with:* plan(s,ned,ning), design(ed,ing), develop(ed,ing,ment), highway design, conservation, preservation, revitaliz(e,ed,ing,ation), redevelop(ed,ing,ment), polic(y,ies), zon(ed,ing), decision making, studies, subdivision regulation(s). *Consider specific land uses such as:* residential, industrial, commercial, business, public. *Choose from:* board(s), commission(s), board of appeals *with:* zoning, planning, historic preservation. *Consider also:* garden cities, official map(s), eminent domain, growth management. *See also* Annexation; Cities; Civic improvement; Civil engineering; Community development; Facility design and construction; Growth management; Growth strategies; Land subdivisions; Land use; Landscape architecture; Local government; Local planning; Municipal art; Neighborhood change; Public transportation; Recreation areas; Recreational facilities; Regional development; Social planning; State planning; Urban development;

Urban environments; Urbanization; Urban politics; Urban renewal; Zoning.

Urban politics. Urban politics. *Choose from:* cit(y,ies), municipal(ity,ities), urban, metropolitan, local government(s), city council(s), city manager(s), county commissioner(s), mayor(s), grass roots *with:* politic(s,al,ians), elect(ion, ions,orate), referend(a,um,ums), part(y,ies), machine(s), power, elite(s), boss(es), vot(e,ed,ing,er,ers), lobb(y,ies, ing), campaign(s,ing), pressure(s), citizen activis(m,t,ts), citizen movement(s), special interest(s), patronage, interest group(s), constituenc(y,ies), unrepresented group(s). *See also* Local government; Local politics; Political bosses; Politics; Urban planning.

Urban population. Urban population. Urban dweller(s). Urban resident(s). Urbanite(s). Resident(s) of urban area. City dweller(s). Townspeople. City folk. Urban children. Urban elderly. Cosmopolite(s). Metropolitan population. *Choose from:* cit(y,ies), metropoli(s,tan), municipal(ity,ities), megalopolis, town(s), urban(ized, ization), ghetto(es), slum(s), barrio(s), or names of specific cities *with:* population, resident(s), inhabitant(s), dweller(s), people, person(s), adult(s), child(ren), youth, occupant(s), famil(y,ies), communit(y,ies), demograph(y,ic), student(s), worker(s), folk, citizen(s,ry), birth rate(s), death rate(s), fertility, mortality, population growth, population decline, population distribrution. *See also* Civic improvement; Community size; Internal migration; Population distribution; Population growth; Rural to urban migration; Urban environments; Urban to rural migration; Urbanization.

Urban poverty. Urban poverty. Street kid(s). Streetchild(ren). Skid row. Bowery. Slum(s). Shantytown(s). Inner cit(y,ies). Ghetto(es,ization). Low rent district(s). Low income area(s). Street corner district(s). Favela(s). Colonia(s). *Choose from:* urban, cit(y,ies), metropolitan *with:* low income, poor, indigent, impoverish(ed,ment), need(y,iest), homeless(ness), underclass(es), squatter(s), shelter(s), welfare client(s), vagran(t,cy), underprivileged, poverty, depressed, disadvantaged. *See also* Environmental racism; Homeless; Inner cities; Poverty; Poverty areas; Slums; Urban crime; Urban environments.

Urban renewal. Urban renewal. *Choose from:* neighborhood(s), communit(y,ies), area(s), slum(s), ghetto(es), urban, cit(y,ies), municipal(ity,ities), metropolis, downtown, inner cit(y,ies), metropolitan, blight(ed), zone(s) of transition, names of areas such as South Bronx, etc. *with:* clear(ance), improv(e,ed,ing, ement,ements), reconstruct(ed,ing,ion), rehabilitat(e,ed,ing,ion), renew(ed,ing, al), redevelop(ed,ing,ment), revitaliz(e, ed,ing,ation), reclaim(ed,ing), reclamation, regenerat(e,ed,ing,ion), renovat(e, ed,ing,ion), restor(e,ed,ation), develop(ed,ing,ment). *Consider also:* gentrif(y,ied,ication), enterprise zone(s), model cities program. *See also* Antipoverty programs; Brownfields; Cities; Civic improvement; Community change; Community development; Enterprise zones; Housing policy; Improvement; Inner cities; Modernization; Neighborhood preservation; Poverty areas; Public housing; Relocation; Urban development; Urban environments; Urban planning; Urban population.

Urban rural differences. See *Rural urban differences.*

Urban sprawl. Urban sprawl. Megalopolis. Metropolis. Rural urban continuum. Urbanization. Urban diffusion. Urban fringe. Urban growth. Suburban growth. Bedroom communit(y,ies). Satellite cit(y,ies). Edge cit(y,ies). *See also* Metropolitan areas; Rural to urban migration; Suburbs; Urban fringe; Urban to rural migration.

Urban to rural migration. Urban to rural migration. Urban rural migrant(s). Back to the land. Gentlem(an,en) farmer(s). Urban out migration. Urban rural turnaround. Moving to the hinterland(s). Urban exodus. Ruralization. Ruralism. City to farm migration. Exurb(ia,anite, anites). Country living estate(s). *Consider also:* interregional migration(s). *See also* Migration; Migration patterns; Population distribution; Relocation; Residential patterns; Rural areas; Rural population; Rural to urban migration; Urban environments; Urban population; Urban sprawl; Vacation houses.

Urbanism. Urbanism. Metropolitan(ism). *Choose from:* urban, city, downtown, metropolitan *with:* life, culture, bias(es). *See also* Cities; Commuting (travel); Cosmopolitan; Everyday life; Lifestyle; Rural urban differences; Urban environments; Urbanization.

Urbanization. Urban(ism,ization). Urban change. City in transition. Growth of town(s). Gesellschaft. *Choose from:* urban, cit(y,ies), metropolitan, metropolis *with:* chang(e,es,ing), transition(s), grow(th,ing), rise, develop(ed,ing,ment), expansion, expand(ed,ing), migrat(ing, ion), sprawl. *Consider also:* citification, urban rural difference(s). *See also* Cities; Community change; Economic development; Industrial societies; Industrialization; Mass society; Modern society;

Modernization; Postindustrial societies; Rural to urban migration; Social processes; Suburbanization; Urban development; Urban environments.

Urinary incontinence. Urinary incontinence. Enuresis. Aconuresis. Bedwetting. Bed wetting. *Choose from:* bladder, urinary *with:* incontinen(t,ce), loss of control. *See also* Behavior disorders; Defecation; Fecal incontinence; Urination.

Urination. Urinat(e,ed,ing,ion). Micturat(e, ed,ing,ation). Micturit(e,ed,ing,ion). *Choose from:* void(ed,ing), pass(ed,ing), flow, output, continen(t,ce), incontinen(t, ce) *with:* urin(e,ary). *Consider also:* enuresis, nocturia, nycturia, aconuresis, acraturesis, diuresis. *See also* Body fluids; Urinary incontinence.

Usage, language. See *Language usage.*

Usage, social. See *Etiquette.*

Use (consumption). See *Consumption (use).*

Use, alcohol. See *Alcohol drinking.*

Use, drug. See *Drug use.*

Use, energy. See *Energy consumption; Energy costs.*

Use, land. See *Land use.*

User friendly systems. User friendly system(s). *Choose from:* user cordial, user-cordial, user friendly, user-friendly, menu driven, public access, natural language *with:* system(s), interface(s), software, computer(s), microcomputer(s). *Consider also:* end user(s), online *with:* tutorial(s). *Consider also:* high level programming language(s). *See also* Artificial intelligence; Attitudes toward computers; Automated information retrieval; Computer anxiety; Computer illiteracy; Computers; Man machine systems; Online users.

Users. See *Clients.*

Users, library. See *Library users.*

Users, online. See *Online users.*

Usury. Usur(y,ious,iousness). Loanshark(s,ing). Loanshark(s,ing). *Consider also:* pawnshop(s), easy-credit provider(s), check-cashing outlet(s), rent-to-own store(s), poverty industry, high interest rate(s), exorbitant interest rate(s), predatory lending compan(y,ies). *See also* Credit; Exploitation.

Utilitarianism. Utilitarian(ism). Benthamism. *Consider also:* pragmatism, summum bonum. *See also* Ethics; Exchange theory; Hedonism; Interest (ethics); Liberalism; Morality; Norms; Philosophy; Progressivism.

Utilities, electric. See *Electric utilities.*

Utilities, public. See *Public utilities.*

Utility costs. Utility cost(s). *Choose from:* utilit(y,ies), fuel(s), electric(ity), energy, heating, gas, oil, coal *with:* cost(s), rate(s), expense(s), expend(ed,iture, itures), price(s,d), charg(es,ed,ing), bill(s), payment(s), affordab(le,ility). *See also* Alternative energy; Cost of living; Energy consumption.

Utilization. Utiliz(e,ed,ing,ation). Usage. Use(s,d). Consum(e,ed,ption). Appl(y, ied,ication). Adopt(ed,ing). Accept(ed, ing). Employ(ed,ing,ment). Exploit(ed, ing,ation). Avail oneself. Mobiliz(e,ed, ing). Wield(ed,ing). Manipulat(e,ed,ing). *See also* Consumption (use); Health care utilization; Land use; Time utilization.

Utilization, health care. See *Health care utilization.*

Utilization, refuse. See *Alternative energy; Recycling; Sewage as fertilizer; Waste to energy.*

Utilization, time. See *Time utilization.*

Uto-Aztecan languages. Uto-Aztecan language(s). Nahuatian: Nahuatl, Tolteca-Chichimeca. Shoshonean: Comanche, Hopi, Paiute, Shoshone, Ute. Tanoan: Isleta, Jemez, Kiowa, San Ildefonso, San Juan, Santa Clara, Taos. Zuni. *See also* Central America; Central American native cultural groups; Language; Languages (as subjects); Nahuatl language; North America; North American native cultural groups.

Utopias. Utopia(s,n,ns,nism). Utopic. Utopist(s). Ideal state(s). Paradise. Millenialism. Owenite(s). Saint Simonian(s). Phalanster(y,ies). Millennial dream(s). Millenarianism. The good society. Classless societ(y,ies). Land of milk and honey. Arcadia. Brook Farm. Camelot. Celestial city. Christianopolis. City of God. Clockwork Orange. Cockaigne. El Dorado. Elysium. Erewhon. Garden of Eden. Goshen. Happy Valley. Heavenly city. Icaria. Kingdom of Micomicon. Land of Beulah. Land of Prester John. Laputa. New Atlantis. New Canaan. New Jerusalem. Oneida community. Oz. Plato(s,nic) Republic. Promised Land. Shangri-La. Walden Two. Walden II. Walden Three. Walden III. *See also* Classless society; Collectivism; Communes; Idealism; Idealists; Imaginary places; Literature; Marxism; Millenarianism; Paradise; Socialism; World history.

V

V-commerce. V-commerc(e,ial). *Choose from:* voice Internet, Voice Markup Language, VoxML, speech recognition, voice based, voice technolog(y,ies) *with:* commerc(e,ial), financial service(s), credit card activation, card replacement(s), travel planning, banking, bill payment, electronic commerce, e-commerce. *See also* Commerce; Digital money; Digital signatures; E-commerce; Electronic data interchange; Electronic mail; Information society; Internet (computer network); Small businesses.

Vacancies, job. See *Employment opportunities.*

Vacation houses. Vacation house(s). *Choose from:* vacation, summer, country, seaside, resort, recreational, second *with:* house(s), home(s), housing, cabin(s), cottage(s), condo(s,minium,miniums), camp(s), property, retreat(s), chalet(s). *See also* Artists' colonies; Country homes; Housing; Tourism; Urban to rural migration.

Vacations. Vacation(s,ing,er,ers). Excursion(s). Touris(t,ts,m). Summer visitor(s). Recreational travel. Summer holiday(s). Furlough(s). Recess(es). Rest and recuperation. Annual leave(s). *Consider also:* picnic(s), camping, beach visit(s), summer travel, term break(s), cruise(s), sight seek(ing), leave(s), absence(s), busman's holiday, rest and relaxation. *See also* Beaches; Camping; Employee benefits; Holidays; Leaves of absence; Leisure activities; Outdoor life; Recreation; Tourism; Travel; Vacation houses.

Vaccinations. Vaccin(e,es,ate,ated,ating, ation,ations). Immuniz(e,ed,ing,ation, ations). Innoculat(e,ed,ing,ion,ions). Booster shot(s). Revaccinat(e,ed,ing,ion, ions). Immunotherapy. *Consider also:* vaccine(s), flu, measles, tetanus, distemper, polio, smallpox, rabies, etc. *with:* shot(s), innoculation(s), injection(s). *See also* Disease; Epidemics; Health; Health services; Immunity; Public health; World health.

Vagabonds. See *Migrants; Vagrants.*

Vaginismus. Vaginismus. Vagina(l) spasm(s). *See also* Dyspareunia; Frigidity; Sexual function disorders.

Vagrants. Vagran(ts,cy). Homeless(ness). Vagabond(s). Rootless(ness). Gyps(y, ies). Itinerant. Loiter(er,ers,ing). Bum(s). Tramp(s). Hobo(s). Derelict(s). Beggar(s). Mendican(t,ts,cy). Panhandler(s). Beachcomber(s). Beach bum(s). Drifter(s). No visible means of support. Migrateur(s). Wanderer(s). *See also* Homeless; Homeless shelters; Illegal aliens; Marginality (sociological); Poverty.

Validity. Valid(ity,ation,ating). Verifiab(le, ility). Provab(le,ility). Authentic(ity). Accura(te,cy). Correct(ness). Factual. Legitimat(e,ion). Truthful. Cross-valid(ity,ation,ating). *Consider also:* effective(ness), useful(ness), efficien(t, cy), comparab(le,ility), quality, legitimat(e,ion), efficacious(ness), poten(t,cy), forceful(ness), strength, vigor(ous,ousness), substan(ce,tial,tive, tiveness), significan(t,ce), cogen(t,cy), credib(le,ility), believab(le,leness), persuasive(ness). *See also* Accuracy; Construct validity; Correctness; Correlation; Data interpretation; Deduction; De jure; Empiricism; Evaluation; Fallacies; Flawless; Good; Induction; Inference; Logic; Measurement; Predictive validity; Quantitative methods; Reliability; Research methods; Standards; Statistical bias; Statistical data; Test bias; Test validity; Truth.

Validity, concept. See *Construct validity.*

Validity, construct. See *Construct validity.*

Validity, predictive. See *Predictive validity.*

Validity, test. See *Test validity.*

Valuation. Valuation. Valu(ed,ing). Setting value(s). Apprais(e,ed,ing). Estimat(e,ed, ing) value(s). Revalu(e,ed,ing,ation). Assessed value(s). Overvalu(ed,ing, ation). Undervalu(ed,ing,ation). *Consider also:* fair market value(s), basis for compensation, taxable value(s), full value, fractional assessment. *See also* Appraisal; Assessment; Assets; Capitalization; Economic value; Intangible property; Land (property); Land values; Personal property; Real estate; Property values.

Value, economic. See *Economic value.*

Value, market. See *Market value.*

Value neutral. Value neutral(ity). Value free(dom). Wertfrei(heit). Value free assessment. Culture independent. Ethical(ly) neutral(ity). *Consider also:* objectiv(e,ity), rational, cultural relativism. *See also* Cultural relativism; Empirical methods; Equitability; Impersonal; Objectivity; Research ethics; Research methods; Researcher bias; Values.

Value orientations. Value orientation(s). Family values. Habits of the heart. Corporate culture. Philosophical bas(is,es). Cultural conditioning. Axiolog(y,ical). *Choose from:* value(s), ethical, ideolog(y,ies), tradition(s,al), ideal(s), meaning(s), moral, belief(s), worldview(s) *with:* orientation(s), commitment(s), transmission. *See also* Cultural relativism; Family values; Machiavellianism; Morality; Orientation; Religious beliefs; Values.

Values. Value(s). Value system(s). Mores. Tradition(s). Ideal(s). Purpose(s). Meaning(s,ful). Belief(s). Worldview(s). Life view(s). Ideolog(y,ies,ical). Priorit(y,ics). Goal(s). Intention(s). Ethic(s,al). Belief system(s). Moral basis. Perspective(s). Attitude(s). Norm(s,ative). Moral(s). Standard(s). Principle(s). Custom(s). *Consider also:* aesthetic, democratic, moral, social, ethnic, personal, social *with:* value(s). *Consider also:* axiolog(y,ical). *See also* Altruism; Beliefs; Commitment (emotional); Conscience; Cultural values; Dissent; Elitism (government); Equity (payment); Ethnocentrism; Ethics; Ethnic values; Examination of conscience; Fairness; Family values; Forgiveness; Freedom; Hidden curriculum; Honesty; Ideologies; Integrity; Judgment; Loyalty; Moral conditions; Moral development; Morality; Narcissism; Norms; Nurturance; Objectivity; Perfectionism; Personal values; Philosophy; Popular culture; Principles; Priorities; Quality of life; Relevance; Social equality; Social justice; Social values; Standards; Tolerance; Truth; Value neutral; Value orientations; Work values; Worldview.

Values, cultural. See *Cultural values.*

Values, ethnic. See *Ethnic values.*

Values, family. See *Family values*

Values, land. See *Land values.*

Values, moral. See *Ethics; Moral attitudes.*

Values, personal. See *Personal values.*

Values, property. See *Property values.*

Values, reference. See *Reference values.*

Values, social. See *Social values.*

Values, work. See *Work values.*

Vampires. Vampir(e,es,ism). Nosferatu. *Consider also:* Dracula, undead. *See also* Gothicism; Horror films; Horror tales.

Vandalism. Vandal(s,ism,ize,ized,izing). Firesetting. Juvenile destruction. Crime(s) against property. Destructive(ness). Desecrat(e,ed,ing, ion). Graffiti. Arson. Ransack(ed,ing). Plunder(ed,ing). Loot(ed,er,ers,ing). *Choose from:* damag(e,ed,ing), defac(e,es,ed,ing), mutilat(e,ed,ing,ion), tear(ing), destroy(ed,ing) *with:* property, cloth(es,ing), furnishing(s), book(s), periodical(s), building(s), wall(s), house(s), car(s). *See also* Antisocial behavior; Crime; Defacement; Destruction of property; Juvenile delinquency; Pillage; Sabotage; Terrorism; Trespassing; Victimization.

Variability, response. See *Response variability.*

Variable interval reinforcement. Variable interval reinforcement. *Choose from:* variable interval(s), paus(e,ed,s,ing), intermittent, random(ly), variation(s) *with:* reinforc(e,ed,ing,ement). *See also* Reinforcement; Reinforcement schedule.

Variables, dependent. See *Dependent variables.*

Variables, independent. See *Independent variables.*

Variations. Variation(s,al,ally). Variat(a). Variation(en). Change(s,ed). Variance(s). Fluctuation(s). Var(y,ied,ies,ying). Alter(ed,ation,ations). Modif(y,ied, ication,ications). Mutation(s). Divergence(s). Veranderung(en). *See also* Anomalies; Arrangement (Music); Biological diversity; Deviation; Diversity; Exceptions; Fluctuations; Individual differences; Orchestration; Seasonal variations.

Variations, seasonal. See *Seasonal variations.*

Varieties, language. See *Language varieties.*

Vasectomy. Vasectom(y,ies,ized). Removal of vas deferens. *Consider also:* steriliz(ed,ing,ation), castrat(ed,ing,ion) *with:* male(s), men, man. *See also* Birth control; Family planning; Male castration; Sterilization (sex); Surgery.

Vegetable materia medica. See *Medical botany.*

Vegetarianism. Vegetarian(s,ism). Lacto vegetarian(s,ism). Vegan(s). Lacto-ovo-vegetarian(s,ism). Abstain(ed,ing) from meat. Meatless. Raw foodis(m,st,sts). Rawist(s). Living foodis(m,st,sts). Natural hygienis(m,st,sts). *Consider also:* macrobiotic diet(s). *See also* Beans; Diet fads; Natural foods; Nutrition; Therapeutic cults.

Vegetation. Vegetation(al). Plant cover. Ground cover. Ground flora. Foraging patch(es). Vegetated surface(s). Herbage. Leaf area(s). Forest border(s). Grass(y) area(s). Plant growth. Plant communit(y, ies). Heathland(s). *Consider also:* vegetation mosaic, forest plot(s), woodland(s). *See also* Grasses; Grasslands; Grazing lands; Land preservation; Plants (botanical); Wetlands.

Vegetative state. Vegetative state(s). Vegetative level(s). Persistent vegetative state(s). *See also* Brain death; Coma; Unconsciousness.

Vehicle accidents, motor. See *Traffic accidents.*

Vehicles, motor. See *Motor vehicles.*

Vehicles, zero emissions. See *Zero emissions vehicles.*

Veiling of women. Veiling of women. *Choose from:* veil(s,ing) *with:* woman, women, female(s), wear(ing), worn. Parda. Sirkar. Burka(h). Chador. Social veil(s). *Consider also:* seclusion, purdah, hidjab. *See also* Gender identity; Private sphere; Sexual division of labor; Sex roles; Sexism; Sexual oppression.

Velocity. Velocit(y,ies). Speed(s). Rapid(ity). Accelerat(e,ed,ing,ion). Swift(ly,ness). Quick(ness). Miles per hour. Revolutions per minute. *Choose from:* rate(s) *with:* motion, movement, drift, rotation. *See also* Hurry (speed); Vibration.

Velocity of money. Velocity of money. *Consider also:* income velocity, velocity of circulation, demand for money. *See also* Money supply.

Vendettas. See *Feuds; Revenge.*

Vendor payments. See *Reimbursement mechanisms.*

Vendor relations. Vendor relation(s,ship, ships). *Choose from:* vendor(s), provider(s), contractor(s), discounter(s), supplier(s), merchant(s), retailer(s), trades(people,men,man), dealer(s), trader(s), jobber(s), middle(man,men) *with:* relation(s,ship,ships), polic(y,ies), agreement(s), contract(s), expectation(s), trust, acceptance, retention, satisf(y,ied, action), dissatisf(y,ied,action), partner(s, ship,ships), rapport. *See also* Client relations; Customer relations; Merchants; Service contracts.

Vendors. See *Merchants.*

Vendors, street. See *Street vendors.*

Venereal diseases. See *Sexually transmitted diseases.*

Venture capital. Venture capital(ism,ist, ists). Risk capital. Start up capital. *Consider also:* venture, entrepreneurial *with:* financ(e,ed,ing), portfolio(s). *See also* Business incubators; Capital (financial); Entrepreneurship; Founding; Start up business.

Ventures, joint. See *Joint ventures.*

Verbal ability. Verbal ability. *Choose from:* verbal, word(s), vocabulary, grammatical, language, reading, linguistic *with:* abilit(y,ies), intelligence, fluen(t,cy), aptitude(s), comprehension, performance, skill(s), proficien(t,cy), competen(t,cy,cies), development. *Consider also:* speech abilit(y,ies). *See also* Academic aptitude; Basic skills; Cognitive ability; Communication skills; Nonverbal ability; Language proficiency; Oral communication; Verbal

communication; Verbal comprehension; Verbal learning; Written communications.

Verbal abuse. Verbal(ly) abus(e,es,ed,ive, iveness). Belittl(e,ed,es,ing). Put(ting) down(s). Belittl(e,ed,ing). Humiliat(e,ed, ing,ion). Disparag(e,es,ed,ing). Caustic remark(s). Verbal(ly) obscen(e,ity,ities). Profan(e,ity,ities). Catcall(s). Namecalling. Name-calling. Backbit(e,es,ing). Back-bit(e,es,ing). Berat(e,ed,es,ing). Ridicul(e,es,ed,ing). Jeer(ed,ing,s). Taunt(s,ed,ing). *Choose from:* ethnic, racist, discriminatory *with:* remark(s), slur(s), joke(s). *See also* Derision; Emotional abuse; Ethnic slurs; Harassment; Indecent communications; Invective; Obscenity; Psychologically abused men; Sexual harassment; Street harassment; Teasing; Verbal behavior; Vulgarity. Womanizers.

Verbal behavior. Verbal behavior. Verbalization(s). *Choose from:* verbal, speech, speaking, language, conversation(al), interview(s) *with:* behavior, expression, imitation(s), participation, difficult(y,ies), problem solving, response(s), interaction(s), appropriate(ness), inappropriate(ness), skill(s), spontan(eity,eous), fluen(t,cy). *Consider also:* profanity, profane language, blasphem(y,ous). *See also* Conversation; Verbal abuse; Verbal communication.

Verbal communication. Verbal communication. Speech. Speak(ing,ers). Spoken. Verbal(ly,ize,ized,ization). Talk(ing). Voice(s). Pronunciation. Phon(etics, ation,ology). Inflection. Utter(ed,ing, ances). Vocal(ization). Articulat(e,ed, ing,ion). Talking. Pronounce. Language skills. Linguistic(ally,s). Lingual. Bilingual(ism). Monolingual(ism). Multilingual(ism). Ethnolinguistics. Dialect(s). Gramma(r,tical). Word(s). Sentence structure. Vocabular(y,ies). Rhetoric(al). Psycholinguistics. Publicspeaking. Communicative ability. Conversation. Discourse. *Choose from:* verbal, oral *with:* behavior, communication, fluency. *Choose from:* speech *with:* inner, subvocal, compression, intelligib(le,ility), compressed, filtered, characteristics, pause(s), pitch, processing, rate(s), rhythm. *See also* Articulation (speech); Communication (thought transfer); Communication skills; Conversation; Debate; Discourse; Discussion; Grammar; Handwriting; Language; Language development; Language proficiency; Letters (correspondence); Linguistics; Manual communication; Nonverbal communication; Oral communication; Reading; Semiotics; Speech; Speech acts; Storytelling; Terminology; Verbal ability; Verbal behavior; Vocabulary; Vocalization; Written communications.

Verbal comprehension. Verbal comprehension. *Choose from:* verbal(ly), vocabulary, language(s), metaphor(s), analog(y,ies), lexical, syntactic, syntax, semantic(s), idiom(s,atic), speech, linguistic(s), discourse *with:* comprehen(d,ded,ding,sion), understand(ing), interpret(ed,ing,ion,ions), cogni(tion, zance), knowledge. *See also* Listening comprehension; Reading comprehension; Sentence comprehension; Verbal ability.

Verbal defense. See *Defense (verbal).*

Verbal development. See *Language development; Speech development; Verbal learning.*

Verbal fluency. See *Fluency.*

Verbal learning. Verbal learning. *Choose from:* verbal, language(s), speak(ing), speech, talk(ed,ing), word(s), vocabular(y,ies), spelling *with:* condition(ed,ing), learn(ed,ing), storage, recognition, recogniz(e,ed,ing), memoriz(e,ed,ing), acquisition, remember(ed,ing), retention, comprehension. *See also* Advance organizers; Language acquisition; Language development; Nonverbal learning; Paired associate learning; Serial learning; Verbal ability; Verbal memory; Verbal stimuli.

Verbal meaning. Verbal meaning(s). Connot(e,ed,ing,ative,ation,ation,ations). Denot(e,ed,ing,ative,ation,ations). *Choose from:* literal, figurative, word(s), phrase(s), sentence(s) *with:* meaning(s). *Consider also:* ambigu(ity,ous), nonambigu(ity,ous), inference(s), literal(ness), impl(y,ied,ication,ications), interpret(ed,ing,ation), semantic(s), lexicology, lexicograph(y,ical,ically), metaphor(s,ical), simile(s), sense, acceptation, signif(y,ied,ication). *See also* Definition (words); Figurative language; Meaning; Semantics; Word meaning.

Verbal memory. Verbal memory. *Choose from:* verbal, lexical, sublexical, word(s), name(s) *with:* memor(y,ize,ized,izing, ization), recognition, association(s), recall(ed,ing), retrieval. *See also* Memory; Recall; Serial learning; Verbal learning.

Verbal reinforcement. Verbal reinforcement. *Consider also:* verbal, spoken *with:* reinforc(e,ed,ing,ement), feedback, reward(s), approval, conditioning, recognition. *Consider also:* positive comment(s), compliment(s), prais(e,ed, ing), commend(ed,ing,ation). *See also* Praise; Reinforcement; Social behavior; Social reinforcement.

Verbal stimuli. Verbal stimul(i,us,ation). *Choose from:* verbal, word(s), letter(s), syllable(s) *with:* stimul(i,us,ation), cue(s). *See also* Verbal learning; Visual stimulation; Word recognition.

Verbal tests. Verbal test(s). *Choose from:* verbal, English placement, language development, vocabulary, semantic categories, antonym, sentence completion, analogy, listening comprehension, reading, speech *with:* test(s), score(s), scale(s), checklist(s), rating(s), question(s), questionnaire(s). *Consider also:* essay test(s). *See also* Essay tests; Language tests; Reading tests; Tests.

Verbs. Verb(s). Predicate(s). *Choose from:* past, present, future *with:* tense. Passive voice. Action word(s). Present perfect. Pluperfect. Past perfect. *See also* Sentence structure.

Verdicts. Verdict(s). Decision(s). Judgment(s). Determination(s). Resolution(s). Settlement(s). Finding(s). Opinion(s). Ruling(s). Conclusion(s). Decree(s). Edict(s). Answer(s). Adjudication. Court decision(s). *See also* Acquittal; Criminal proceedings; Death penalty; Judicial decisions; Juries; Law enforcement; Litigation; Plea bargaining; Trial (law).

Verification. Verif(y,ied,ication). Confirm(ed,ing,ation). Proof(s). Prov(en,ing). Substantiat(e,ed,ing,ion). Assurance(s). Corroborat(e,ed,ing,ion). Establish(ed,ing,ment). Certif(y,ied, ication). Validat(e,ed,ing,ion). Authenticat(e,ed,ing,ion). Affirm(ed, ing,ation). *See also* Accuracy; Empirical methods; Evaluation; Experiments; Fact checking; Falsification (scientific); Financial audit; Hypotheses; Research design; Research methods; Sampling; Theories; Theory verification; Truth.

Verification, theory. See *Theory verification.*

Vernacular. See *Slang; Dialects.*

Vernacular, street. See *Slang.*

Verse. See *Poetry.*

Verse, occasional. See *Occasional verse.*

Versification. See *Meter (poetry); Poetry; Prosody.*

Verstehen. Verstehen. Interpretative sociology. Interpretative method(s). *Choose from:* social, interpersonal, intercultural, empathetic *with:* interpretation, understanding, insight, intuition, comprehension. *Consider also:* intellectul empathy, rapport, hunch(es), Geisteswissenschaften. *See also* Analysis; Comprehension; Empathy; Ethnomethodology; Explanation; Hermeneutics; Ideal types; Intuition; Meaning; Participant observation; Phenomenology; Qualitative methods; Role taking; Social philosophy; Social structure; Sociological theory.

Vertebrates. Vertebrate(s). Craniate(s). Agnatha. Gnathostomata. *Consider also:* alligator(s), amphibia(n,ns), animal(s), antelope(s), anthropoidea, anura, artiodactyl(e,es,a), aves, baboon(s), bat(s), bear(s), beaver(s), bird(s), blackbird(s), budgerigar(s), buffalo(es), camel(s), canar(y,ies), caribou, carnivor(e,es,a,ous), carp, cat(s), cattle, cebidae, cercopithecidae, cetacea, cheetah(s), chicken(s), chimpanzee(s), chinchilla(s), chiroptera, chondrichthyes, chordata, cichlid(s), cricetidae, crocodilian(s), crocodile(s), deer, dipodomys, dog(s), dolphin(s), dove(s), duck(s), echidna, edentata, elephant(s), feline(s), ferret(s), fish(es), fox(es), frog(s), geese, gerbil(s), goat(s), goldfish(es), gorilla(s), guinea pig(s), hamster(s), herbivor(e,es,a,ous), horse(s), hyrax(es), insectivora, hedgehog(s), kangaroo(s), lagomorpha, lemur(s), lion(s), lizard(s), marmot(s,a), marsupial(s,a), mice, mink(s), mole(s), monotremata, monkey(s), muridae, opossum(s), osteichthyes, otter(s), penguin(s), perissodactyla, pigeon(s), pig(s), pinnipedia, platypus, pongidae, porpoise(s), primate(s), prosimii, psittacine(s), quail(s), rabbit(s), rat(s), reindeer, reptile(s), robin(s), rodent(s,ia), salamander(s), salmon, sciuridae, sea gull(s), seal(s), shark(s), sheep, shrew(s), skunk(s), snake(s), squirrel(s), stickleback(s), swine, toad(s), turtle(s), walrus(es), whale(s), wolf, wolves, xenopus, etc. *See also* Animals; Camels; Deer; Elephants; Invertebrates; Mammals; Reptiles; Turtles.

Vertical organizations. See *Hierarchy.*

Vertigo. Vertig(o,inous). Dizz(y,iness). Vestibular syndrome. Vestibulopathy. Unstead(y,iness). Gidd(y,iness). *Choose from:* equilibrium, balance *with:* disorder(s), disturbance(s). *See also* Syncope; Symptoms.

Very low birth weight infants. Very low birth weight infant(s). *Choose from:* very low birthweight(s), very low birth weight(s), VLBW, extremely low birth weight, extremely premature, preterm, growth retard(ed,ation), light for date, immature *with:* infant(s), newborn(s), neonate(s), bab(y,ies). *Consider also:* fetal weight below 1000 g. *See also* Premature infants; Prenatal development; Small for gestational age.

Very old. See *Aged 80 and over.*

Vessels, drinking. See *Drinking vessels.*

Veterans. Veteran(s). Vets. GI(s). Exservice(man,men,women,woman). Readjustment act of 1944. *Choose from:* experience(d), fought, served, retired, discharged, returnee(s), former(ly), veteran(s) *with:* World war I, World war II, Korean war, Vietnam war, military, Army, Navy, Air Force, combat, Marines, captain(s), colonel(s), lieutenant(s), quartermaster(s), petty officer(s), sergeant(s), etc. *See also* Enlisted military personnel; Military officers; Military pensions; Military personnel; Military service; War; War memorials; War victims.

Veto. Veto(es,ed,ing). *Consider also:* reject(ed,ing,ion), block(ed,ing), overrul(e,ed,ing). Oppos(e,ed,ing,ition). Kill(ed,ing) bill(s). Denial(s). Interdict(ed,ing,ion). Prohibit(ed,ing, ion). *See also* Legislation; Legislative processes; Prohibition.

Vibration. Vibrat(e,ed,ing,ion,ions,ory). Resonance(s). Vibrotactile. Microvibration(s). Electrovibration(s). Vibromassag(e,ed,ing). Vibrostimulat(e,ed, ing,ion,ions). *Consider also:* reverberat(e,ed,ing,ion,ions), purr(ed,ing), puls(e,ed,ing,ation). *See also* Velocity.

Vibrotactile thresholds. Vibrotactile threshold(s). *Choose from:* vibrotactile, vibration(s), vibratory *with:* threshold(s), sensation magnitude(s), detection, perception, sensitivit(y,ies). *See also* Tactual perception; Thresholds.

Vicarious experiences. Vicarious experience(s). *Choose from:* vicarious(ly), indirect(ly) *with:* reinforce(d,ment), experience(s,d), participat(e,ed,ing,ion), emotion(s), learn(ed,ing), effect(s), arous(e,ed, ing,al), expos(e,ed,ing,ure), outlet(s), observ(e,ed,ing,ation,ations). *See also* Experiences (events); Imagination; Reinforcement.

Victimization. Victim(s,ized,ization,ology). Martyr(s). Complainant(s). Injured part(y,ies). Injured one(s). Survivor(s). Sufferer(s). Scapegoat(s). Prey. Held hostage. Robbed. *Choose from:* abused, mistreat(ed,ment), maltreated, molested, harrassed, mugged, raped *with:* child(ren), infant(s), person(s), people, elderly, man, men, woman, women. *Consider also:* restitution, aftermath, underdog. *See also* Battered women; Casualties; Child abuse; Child neglect; Debit card fraud; Crime; Cruelty; Elder abuse; Family violence; Fear of crime; Fraud; Hostages; Iatrogenesis; Incest; Malpractice; Online harassment; Perpetrators; Persecution; Personal injuries; Rape; Rape crisis counseling; Restitution; Self defense; Sex offenders; Sexual abuse; Sexual coercion; Sexual exploitation; Sexual harassment; Shelters; Stalking; Statutory rape; Suicide victims; Torture; Vandalism; Violence; Vulnerability; War victims; Witnesses.

Victimless crimes. Victimless crime(s). Crime(s) without victim(s). Non-victim crime(s). Morals offense(s). Offense(s) against public morality. *Choose from:* moral(s,ity), mores *with:* enforc(e,ed, ing,ement), legislat(e,ed,ing,ion), criminaliz(e,ed,ing,ation), offense(s). *Consider also:* prostitution, nuisance offender(s), service crime(s),

inebriat(e,ed,es,ion), pornograph(y,ic), deviance, lewdness, gambling, alcoholism, drug possession, suicide, marijuana, panhandling, vagrancy, loitering graffiti, public urination, misdemeanor(s), minor crime(s). *See also* Crime; Decriminalization; Unreported crimes.

Victims. See *Victimization.*

Victims, crime. See *Victimization.*

Victims, crimes without. See *Victimless crimes.*

Victims, suicide. See *Suicide victims.*

Victims, war. See *War victims.*

Video display terminals, hazards of. See *Hazards of video display terminals.*

Video, interactive. See *Interactive video.*

View, point of literature. See *Point of view (literature).*

Viewers. Viewer(s). Audience(s). Spectator(s). Listener(s). Attendant(s). Person(s) attend(ing). Observer(s). Witness(es). Onlooker(s). Viewing public. Watcher(s). Hearer(s). Playgoer(s). Filmgoer(s). Reading public. Readership. Theatergoer(s). Target group(s). Assemblage. *Consider also:* crowd(s), galleries. *See also* Audiences; Internet traffic; Readership; Sports fans.

Vigilance. Vigilan(t,ce). *Consider also:* arousal, attention, wakeful(ness), alert(ness), sustained attention, hypervigilan(t,ce). *See also* Attention; Attention span; Awareness; Monitoring; Selective attention.

Vigilantes. Vigilant(e,es,ism). Vigilance committee(s). Lynch mob(s). Paramilitary group(s). Citizen patrol(s). Citizen crime fight(er,ers,ing). Citizen arrest(s). Private police. Guardian angel(s). Red beret(s). *Consider also:* mob rule, lynch law. *See also* Anarchism; Criminal justice; Due process; Extremism; Law enforcement; Legal system; Lynching; Paramilitary; Punishment.

Vikings. Viking(s). Norse(men). *Consider also:* Varangian(s), Northmen, Leif Ericsson, Societas Celtologica Nordica. *See also* Antiquity (time); Pre-Columbian empires; Sailing ships; Skaldic poetry.

Villages. See *Towns.*

Violation. Violation(s). Infring(e,ed,ing, ement,ements). Encroach(ed,ing,ment, ments). Breach(ed,es,ing). Infraction(s). Transgress(ed,ing,ion,ions). Trespass(ed, ing). Illegalit(y,ies). Delinquen(t,cy). Offense(s). Misbehavior. Misdemeanor(s). Felon(y,ies). Crime(s). Dereliction(s). *See also* Crime; Illegal; Offenses.

Violations, human rights. See *Medical ethics; Oppression; Political prisoners; Political repression; War crimes.*

Violence. Violen(t,ce). Mob(bed,bing). Assault(ed,ing). Stab(bed,ing). Riot(ing,s). Batter(ed,ing). Beat(ing,en). Cosh(ed,ing). Bombing(s). Molotov cocktail(s). Incendiar(y,ies). Terroris(t,ts,m). Dangerous behavior. Dangerous(ness). Atrocit(y,ies). Tortur(e,ed,ing). Knif(e,ed,ing,ings). Switchblade(s). Fight(s,ing). Gang war(s). Terror(ism,ize,ized,izing). Vandal(s,ize,izing,ism). Life threatening behavior. Physical attack(s). Civil disorder(s). Loot(ed,ing). Pillag(e,ed, ing). Plunder(ed,ing). Ravag(e,ed,ing). Destruct(ion,ive). Brute force. Rap(e,ed,ing). Injur(e,ed,ing). Harm(ed,ing). Murder(s,ed,ing,ous). Bloodthirsty. Disorderly conduct. Assassin(ate,ated,ating,ation). Massacre(s). Pogrom(s). *Choose from:* abuse(d) *with:* adult, wife, child(ren), spouse. *See also* Aggression; Air rage; Assault (battle); Assault (personal); Battered women; Child abuse; Civil disorders; Coercion; Combat; Conflict; Corporal punishment; Cruelty; Dangerous behavior; Dangerousness; Depravity; Disorderly conduct; Elder abuse; Family violence; Flagellants and flagellation; Hostility; Marital rape; Mass media violence; Political violence; Prison violence; Rape; Revolution; Ritual disfigurement; Road rage; School violence; Self defense; Self mutilation; Sexual abuse; Sexual assault; Sexual violence; Social demonstrations; Sports violence; Spouse abuse; Stabbing; Terrorism; Torture; Victimization; War.

Violence, conjugal. See *Family violence; Battered women; Marital conflict; Spouse abuse.*

Violence, domestic. See *Family violence.*

Violence, family. See *Family violence.*

Violence, marital. See *Family violence; Marital rape; Spouse abuse.*

Violence, mass media. See *Mass media violence.*

Violence, mob. See *Riots.*

Violence, political. See *Political violence.*

Violence, prison. See *Prison violence.*

Violence, school. See *School violence*

Violence, sexual. See *Sexual violence.*

Violence, spectator. See *Sports violence.*

Violence, sports. See *Sports violence.*

Violence, television. See *Mass media violence.*

Violence in the media. See *Mass media violence.*

Virelai. Virelai(s). Chanson(s) balladee. *Consider also:* bergerette(s), formes fixes. *See also* Ballata; Formes fixes; Medieval music; Music.

Virginity. Virgin(ity,s,al). Hymen(al). Maiden(s,head,hood). *Consider also:* chast(e,ity), unwed, unmarried, pristine, unsullied, innocen(t,ce), spinster(s, hood), celiba(te,cy), unused, untried, unblemished, immaculate, Marianismo. *See also* Celibacy; Chastity; Innocence; Purity; Premarital sexual behavior; Ritual purity; Sexual intercourse.

Virilocal residence. See *Patrilocal residence.*

Virtual libraries. Virtual librar(y,ies). Library home page(s). Library homepage(s). Virtual reference desk(s). Internet reference site(s). Internet Public Librar(y,ies). *Consider also:* interactive library network(s), online librar(y,ies), digital librar(y,ies), electronic librar(y, ies), global village librar(y,ies); internet public librar(y,ie), library web page(s), library web site(s). *See also* Community networks (computer); Electronic journals; Home pages; Information society; Internet (computer network); Virtual organizations; Virtual reality.

Virtual organizations. Virtual organ-ization(s). Quasi-firm(s). *Choose from:* virtual *with:* organization(s), compan(y, ies), business(es), enterprise(s), corporation(s), factor(y,ies). *Consider also:* network organization(s), modular corporation(s). *See also* Adhocracies; Boundaryless organizations; Chaos management; Contracting out; Cybercommunities; Industrial coopera-tion; Interorganizational networks; Library cooperation; Organizational structure; Strategic alliances; Subcon-tracting; Teaming; Virtual libraries; Virtual reality.

Virtual reality. Virtual reality. *Choose from:* virtual, interactive, augmented, synthe(sis,tic), perceptually convincing *with:* reality, environment(s), world, feedback, space, interface(s). *Consider also:* realtime, cyberspace. *See also* Community networks (computer); Cybercommunities; Home pages; Information society; Internet (computer network); Online privacy; Online users; Teledemocracy; Virtual libraries; Virtual organizations.

Virtual university. See *Distance education.*

Virtue. Virtu(e,es,ous). Good(ness). Righteous(ness). Moral(ity). Creditab(le,ility). Laudab(le,ility). Meritorious(ness). Commendab(le,ility). Worth(y,iness). Praiseworth(y,iness). Saintl(y,iness). Moral excellence. Ethical(ly). Upright(ness). Integrity. Honor(able). Respectab(le,ility). High minded(ness). Decen(t,cy). Faithful(ness). Scrupulous(ness).

Responsib(le,ility). Truthful(ness). Loyal(ty). Straightforward(ness). Right conduct. *Consider also:* candor, honest(y), chastity, justice, prudence, temperance, faith, hope, charity, love. *See also* Cardinal virtues; Courtly love; Ethics; Excellence; Charity; Good; Good works (theology); Honor (integrity); Integrity; Moral development; Morality; Perfection; Prudence; Theological virtues.

Virtues, cardinal. See *Cardinal virtues.*

Virtues, theological. See *Theological virtues.*

Viruses, computer. See *Computer viruses.*

Vision. Vision. Visual(ly). Sight(ed). See(ing). Binocular interaction(s). Eyesight. *Choose from:* visual *with:* process(es), acuity, information processing, discrimination, excitation, perception, field(s). *Choose from:* color, depth, distance, form, brightness *with:* perception. *Choose from:* entoptic, binocular, monocular, stereoscopic *with:* vision. *Consider also:* phosphene(s), afterimage(s), figural aftereffect(s), flicker fusion, autokinetic illusion(s). *Consider also:* sensitivity *with:* retina. *See also* Autokinetic effect; Blindness; Color perception; Depth perception; Eye; Hysterical vision disturbances; Partially sighted; Vision disorders; Visual acuity; Visual aids; Visual discrimination; Visual feedback; Visual hallucinations; Visual masking; Visual memory; Visual perception; Visual stimulation; Visual thresholds; Visual tracking.

Vision, color. See *Color perception; Color blindness.*

Vision disorders. Vision disorder(s). Partial blindness. Legally blind. Low vision. *Choose from:* vision, visual(ly), sight, seeing, ocular, eye, ophthalmologic, oculomotor *with:* disorder(s), loss(es), handicap(s,ped), defect(s), abnormalit(y, ies), disturbance(s), deficien(cy,cies), impair(ed,ments), failing, disabilit(y,ies), diminution, limit(s,ed). *Consider also:* ametropia, strabismus, amblyopia, color blindness, diplopia, hemianopsia, scotoma, hemeralopia, nyctalopia. *See also* Blindness; Partially sighted; Vision.

Vision disturbances, hysterical. See *Hysterical vision disturbances.*

Visions. See *Mysticism.*

Visiting programs, home. See *Home visiting programs.*

Visitors. Visitor(s). Caller(s). Guest(s). Tourist(s). Patron(s). Attendee(s). *See also* Clients; Guests; Home visiting programs; Visitors to patients; Visits.

Visitors to patients. Visitor(s) to patient(s). *Choose from:* visit(ing,or,ors,ation), community contact(s), family presence,

social interaction *with:* patient(s), inmate(s), hospital(s), prisoner(s), institutionalized person(s), nursing home(s), residential home(s). *Consider also:* visit(ing,ation) *with:* hour(s), right(s), privilege(s), arrangement(s). *See also* Home visiting programs; Hospital volunteers; Visitors.

Visits. Visit(s,ation). Social call(s). Sojourn(s). Pay a call. *Consider also:* outreach. *See also* Office visits; Visitors.

Visits, office. See *Office visits.*

Visual acuity. Visual acuity. *Choose from:* visual, vision *with:* acuity, discrimina-tion, threshold(s), clear(ness), keen(ness), hyperacuity. *Consider also:* visual, form, shape(s), pattern(s), detail(s), spatial *with:* perception. *See also* Pattern recognition; Vision; Visual perception.

Visual aids. Visual aid(s). *Choose from:* visual, graphic(al) *with:* display(s), aid(s), cue(s), representation(s). *Consider also:* bulletin board(s), cartoon(s), chalkboard(s), chart(s), diagram(s), graph(s), illustration(s), map(s), photograph(s), sign(s), transparenc(y,ies), painting(s), informa-tion display(s), poster(s), road marking(s), overhead material(s), opaque display(s), drawing(s), chalkboard(s), scatterplot(s). *See also* Audiovisual materials; Cartoons; Films; Instructional media; Maps.

Visual communication. Visual communica-tion. *Choose from:* visual, graphic, pictorial, cartographic *with:* communica-tion, message(s), language, explanation(s). *See also* Graphic arts; Iconography; Pictography; Symbolism; Written communications.

Visual disabilities. See *Blindness; Partially sighted; Vision disorders.*

Visual discrimination. Visual discrimina-tion. *Consider also:* visual, vision, color(s), light, dark(ness), pattern(s), shape(s), form(s), letter(s) *with:* perception, discriminat(e,ed,ing,ion), recogni(ze,zed,tion). *See also* Vision; Visual perception; Visual tracking.

Visual disorders. See *Vision disorders.*

Visual displays. See *Visual aids.*

Visual feedback. Visual feedback. *Choose from:* visual, vision, video, videotape(d) *with:* feedback, knowledge of result(s), reinforcement. *See also* Feedback; Perceptual stimulation; Sensory feedback; Vision; Visual stimulation.

Visual hallucinations. Visual hallucin-ation(s). *Choose from:* See(n,ing), saw *with:* apparition(s), ghost(s), vision(s). *Choose from:* visual, vision(s), optical *with:* hallucinat(e,ed,ing,ion,ions,ory). *See also* Hallucinations; Perceptual disturbances; Vision.

Visual impairments. See *Blindness; Partially sighted; Vision disorders.*

Visual masking. Visual masking. *Choose from:* visual, light, flicker(ed,ing) *with:* mask(s,ed,ing). *See also* Masking; Visual stimulation.

Visual memory. Visual memory. *Choose from:* visual(ly), visuospatial(ly), spatial(ly) *with:* retention, recognition, recogniz(e,ed,ing), memor(y,ize,ized, izing,ization), encoding, recall(ed,ing), retrieval, learn(ed,ing), cuing. *See also* Memory; Pattern recognition; Recall; Vision.

Visual perception. Visual perception. *Choose from:* visual, vision, depth, color(s), space(s), distance(s), form(s), pattern(s), size(s), brightness *with:* perception, discrimination, threshold(s), acuity, recognition, sensitivity. *See also* Autokinetic effect; Color perception; Eye; Lipreading; Perception; Texture perception; Vision; Visual acuity; Visual discrimination; Visual thresholds; Visual tracking.

Visual stimulation. Visual stimulation. *Choose from:* visual, photic, pictorial, light, chromatic, dichoptic, photopic, prismatic, scotopic, stereoscopic, tachistoscopic *with:* stimul(i,us,ation), presentation(s), feedback, message(s). *See also* Color; Perceptual stimulation; Pictorial stimuli; Visual feedback; Visual masking.

Visual thresholds. Visual threshold(s). *Choose from:* vision, visual, flicker fusion, luminance, contrast, photic, optical *with:* threshold(s), sensitivit(y, ies), detect(ed,ing,ion). *See also* Light adaptation; Thresholds; Vision; Visual perception.

Visual tracking. Visual tracking. *Choose from:* visual, vision, eye(s), ocular *with:* track(ed,ing), pursuit, follow(ed,ing). *See also* Perceptual motor processes; Vision; Visual discrimination; Visual perception.

Visualization. See *Imagery.*

Visually handicapped. See *Blindness; Partially sighted; Vision disorders.*

Vital statistics. Vital statistics. *Choose from:* vital, birth(s), fertility, marriage(s), divorce(s), death(s), mortality, morbidity, suicide(s), parish, reproduction, health, life expectancy, sex ratio, census *with:* statistic(s,al), registration(s), record(s), rate(s), data, register(s), registr(y,ies), file(s). *See also* Birthrate; Census; Fertility; Life expectancy; Morbidity; Mortality rates; Pregnancy rate; Sex ratio; Suicide.

Vitalism. Vitalis(m,tic). Entelechy. Life force(s). Elan vital. Vital principle. Pous Seevitale. Vital impulse. Bergsonian evolutionism. Neovitalis(m,tic). *See also* Animatism; Libido; Pneuma; Soul.

Vitamin deficiency disorders. Vitamin deficiency disorder(s). Avitamin(osis, oses,ous). Vitamin deficien(t,cy,cies). Hypovitamin(osis,oses,ous). Scurvy. Pellagra. Beriberi. Osteomalacia. Rickets. Steatitis. Kwashiorkor. Swayback. *Choose from:* nutritional(ly), nutrient(s), protein(s), calorie(s), vitamin(s) or specific vitamins by name *with:* deficien(t,cy,cies), lack(s,ed,ing). *See also* Malnutrition; Undernourishment.

Vitamin therapy. Vitamin therap(y,ies). *Choose from:* vitamin(s), multivitamin(s), food supplement(s), megavitamin, orthomolecular, ascorbic acid, B complex, niacin, niacinamide, pyridoxine, ascorbic acid, vitamin B12, vitamin C, vitamin E, etc. *with:* supplement(s), therap(y,ies,eutic), treat(ed,ing,ment) or specific conditions, diseases or deficiencies. *Consider also:* nutriceutical(s), medical food(s). *See also* Herbal medicine; Medical foods; Nonprescription drugs; Vitamins.

Vitamins. Vitamin(s,ology). Multivitamin(s). Nutritional supplement(s,ation). Megavitamin. Food supplement(s). Diet(ary) supplement(s). Nutriceutical(s). Polyvitamin(s). *Consider also:* ascorbic acid, dehydroascorbic acid, bioflavonoid(s), esculin, flavones, quercetin, hesperidin, rutin, vitamin A, vitamin B complex, aminobenzoic acid(s), P-aminobenzoic acid, biotin, carnitine, acetylcarnitine, palmitoylcarnitine, folic acid, pteroylpolyglutamic acids, formyltetrahydrofolates, citrovorum factor, inositol, lipoic acid, nicotinic acid(s), niacin, nicotinamide, 6-aminonicotinamide, pangamic acid, pantothenic acid, pyridoxal, pyridoxamine, pyridoxine, riboflavin, thiamine, thiamine monophosphate, thiamine pyrophosphate, thiamine triphosphate, Vitamin B 12, cobamides, hydroxocobalamin, transcobalamins, vitamin D, cholecalciferols, hydroxycholecalciferols, calcifediol, dihydroxycholecalciferols, calcitriol, dihydrotachysterol, ergocalciferol, ergosterol, vitamin E, vitamin K, phytonadione, vitamin U, yeast, choline. *See also* Drugs; Vitamin deficiency disorders; Vitamin therapy.

Vocabulary. Vocabular(y,ies). Word stock(s). Word hoard. Acquisition of word(s). Word knowledge. Lexical development. Lexical competence. Word recognition. Known words. *Choose from:* active, passive *with:* vocabulary. *Consider also:* dictionar(y,ies), lexicon(s), lexicograph(y,ical,ically), thesaur(us,uses,i), glossar(y,ies), wordbook(s). *See also* Anagrams; Antonyms; Glossaries; Homonyms; Language; Language acquisition; Literacy; Neologisms; Reading; Slang; Semantics; Terminology; Verbal communication; Verbs; Word frequency; Words.

Vocabulary, controlled. See *Controlled vocabulary.*

Vocal works, textless. See *Textless vocal works.*

Vocalise. See *Textless vocal works.*

Vocalization. Vocalization(s). Vocaliz(e, ed,ing). *Consider also:* distress call(s), cry(ing), cries, laughter, subvocalization, voice(s,d), voicing, vocal, speak(ing), spoken, speech, sing(ing), sung, talk(ing), conversation(s,al), verbaliz(e, ed,ing,ation,ations), utter(ed,ing), utterance(s), babbl(e,ed,ing), chatter(ed, ing), grunt(ed,ing), sigh(ed,ing), moan(ed,ing), wail(ed,ing), shriek(ed, ing), scream(ed,ing). *See also* Animal communication; Animal vocalization; Communication (thought transfer); Crying; Infant vocalization; Laughter; Oral communication; Verbal communication; Voice.

Vocalization, animal. See *Animal vocalization.*

Vocalization, infant. See *Infant vocalization.*

Vocational adjustment. See *Occupational adjustment.*

Vocational aspirations. See *Occupational aspirations.*

Vocational choice. See *Occupational choice.*

Vocational counseling. See *Employment counseling.*

Vocational counselors. Vocational counselor(s). *Choose from:* employment, guidance, vocational, placement, vocational, occupational, rehabilitation, work adjustment, career *with:* counselor(s), specialist(s), practitioner(s), officer(s), school counselor(s), psychologist(s), personnel. *Consider also:* personnel officer(s). *See also* Counselors; Mentors; School counselors; Social workers; Vocational guidance.

Vocational education. Vocational education. Employment preparation. *Choose from:* vocational, job, employment, industrial, technical, trade, occupational, prevocational, career development, cooperative, distributive *with:* education, training, school(s), student(s), orientation, instruction, preparation, curriculum, program(s), apprenticeship(s). *See also* Apprenticeship; Business education; Career education; Cooperative education; Manual training; Occupational qualifications; Occupations; Vocational rehabilitation; Vocational school students.

Vocational guidance. Vocational guidance. *Choose from:* vocational, career, employment, occupational, midcareer, preretirement *with:* guidance, counseling, advis(ing,ment), advice, planning. *Consider also:* mentor(s). *See also* Advice; Career development; Career education; Careers; Employment preparation; Occupational aspirations; Occupational choice; School counseling.

Vocational maturity. Vocational maturity. *Consider also:* vocational, career, professional, occupational, work *with:* matur(e,ity), self-efficacy, readiness, stability, congruence, self awareness. *See also* Attitudes toward work; Career development; Decision making; Employee attitudes; Occupational adjustment; Occupational aspirations; Occupational choice.

Vocational mobility. See *Career mobility.*

Vocational preference. See *Occupational choice.*

Vocational rehabilitation. Vocational rehabilitation. *Choose from:* vocational, work, occupational *with:* rehabilitation, retraining, reeducation, therapy. Sheltered workshop(s). *Consider also:* handicap(s,ped), disabilit(y,ies), disabled, blind *with:* employ(ed,ing, ment), vocation(s,al), work(ed,ing), profession(s,al), occupation(s,al). *See also* Disability; Employment; Employment of persons with disabilities; Rehabilitation counseling; Sheltered workshops; Vocational education.

Vocational school students. Vocational school student(s). *Choose from:* vocational, cooperative, education, distributive, occupational, prevocational, technical, trade, industrial *with:* student(s). *See also* Vocational education.

Vocational schools. See *Vocational education.*

Vocations. Vocation(s). Occupation(s,al). Career(s). Employment. Job(s). Work. Calling(s). Lifework. Livelihood. Work(er) role(s). Trade. Business(es). Work activity. Paid work experience. Occupational status. Vocational interest(s). Work history. Worker function(s). Employment status. Self employed. White collar job(s). *See also* Careers; Occupations; Professional personnel.

Voice. Voic(e,es,ed,ing). Vocal(ize,ized, izing,ization). Utterance(s). Phonat(ion, ory). Intonation. Sing(ing). *See also* Communication (thought transfer); Crying; Infant vocalization; Inflection; Intonation (phonetics); Oral communication; Singing; Vocalization.

Voice disorders. Voice disorder(s). Aphon(ia,ic). Dysphon(ia,ic). Hoarse(ness). *Choose from:* phonation, voice, vocal, vocal cord(s) *with:* disorder(s), abnormal(ity,ities), dysfunction(s,al), falsetto, quality deviation(s), laryngectom(y,ies), tremor(s). *See also* Speech disorders.

Volition. Volition(al). Will power. Free will. Self control. Self determination. Intent(ion). Willing(ness). Purposive(ness). Purpose(ful,fully). Conat(us,ive,ion,ional). *Consider also:* determinism, individual power, voluntary movement, voluntary activity, striv(e,ing). *See also* Action; Awareness; Choice (psychology); Choice behavior; Decision making; Freedom; Freedom (theology); Indeterminism; Intentionality; Mind; Voluntarism (philosophy).

Voltaic (Gur) languages. Voltaic (Gur) languages. Dagomba. Dogon. More (Moshi). Senufo. *See also* African cultural groups; Language; Languages (as subjects); Sub-Saharan Africa.

Voluntarism (philosophy). Voluntarism. *Consider also:* free will, individual choice, psychologism. *See also* Determinism; Freedom (theology); Indeterminism; Philosophy; Social action (sociological); Social theories; Sociological theory; Systems theory; Volition.

Voluntarism (social). See *Volunteers.*

Voluntary associations. Voluntary association(s). *Choose from:* voluntary *with:* association(s), organization(s), group(s), membership(s), participation. *See also* Associations (organizations); Civil society; Clubs; Confraternities; Groups; Nongovernmental organizations; Professional organizations; Societies (organizations); Youth organizations.

Voluntary health agencies. Voluntary health agenc(y,ies). *Choose from:* voluntary, nonprofit, charitable, volunteer *with:* health, medical *with:* agenc(y,ies), organization(s). *Consider also:* Red Cross, American Heart Association, American Cancer Society, American Lung Association, Samaritans, Mental Health Association, Easter Seal Society, March of Dimes, Tuberculosis Society, etc. *See also* Health resources; Nonprofit organizations; Volunteers.

Volunteer military personnel. Volunteer military personnel. Enlistee(s). Voluntary enlistment(s). Volunteer military force(s). *Choose from:* volunteer, voluntary, recruit(s) *with:* Army, Air Force, Navy, Marines, Marine Corps, Coast Guard, military. *See also* Enlisted military personnel; Military personnel.

Volunteers. Volunteer(s,ing,ism). Community service. Voluntary worker(s). Civic participation. Civic life. Communitarian(ism). Civic activism. Voluntarism. Peace Corps worker(s). Donate(d) time. Contribute(d) time. Contribute(d) services. Hospital auxiliar(y,ies). Junior League. Candystriper(s). Big Brother program(s). Big Sister program(s). Lay worker(s). *Choose from:* volunteer, voluntary, Peace Corps, VISTA, unpaid, contributed, donated *with:* worker(s), service, subject(s), tutor(s), participation, organization(s), personnel. *See also* Activism; Altruism; Ancillaries; Charities; Contributions; Donations; Experiment volunteers; Fire departments; Hospital volunteers; Human services; Nonprofit organizations; Participation; Restorative justice.

Volunteers, experiment. See *Experiment volunteers.*

Volunteers, hospital. See *Hospital volunteers.*

Vomiting. Vomit(ed,ing,s,us). Emes(ia,is). Hatemes(ia,is). Hyperemesis gravidarum. Regurgit(e,ed,ing,ation). Retch(ed,ing). Autemes(ia,is). Throw(ing) up. Motion sickness. Morning sickness. Radioemes(ia,is). *See also* Gastrointestinal disorders; Nausea; Symptoms.

Voodooism. Voodoo(ism,istic). Candomble. Zombi. Hoodoo(ism,istic). Vodun. Vodou. Occult(ism). Sorcer(ers,y). Amulet(s). Black magic. Black art. Demon(ic,ology). Demon possession. Devil(s). Hex(es). Jinx(es). Incantation(s). Magic(al). Mystic(al,ism,s). Necromancy. Obiism. Obeah(ism). Possession trance(s). Spirit possession. Supernatural(ism). Thaumaturgy. Spell(s). Witchcraft. *See also* Ancestor worship; Conjuring; Cursing; Evil; Evil eye; Incantations; Magic; Occultism; Spirit possession; Supernatural; Traditional societies; Water spirits; Witchcraft.

Vote. Vote(s). Suffrage. Ballot(s). Franchise. Voting right(s). *See also* Suffrage; Voting rights.

Voter participation. Voter participation. Vote(s) cast. *Choose from:* elector(al, ate), vot(ing,er,ers), polls *with:* action(s), activ(ity,ism), alignment(s), alliance(s), behavior, coalition(s), consensus, control, demonstration(s), debate(s), decision making, drive(s), dynamics, dissent(ers), indifference, influence(s), involv(ed,ing,ement), leadership, malaise, mobiliz(ed,ing,ation), manipulation, militan(cy,t), movement(s), opposition, participat(e,ed,ing,ion), register(ed,ing), registration, process(es), recruitment, solidarity, strateg(y,ies), support(ed,ing), tactic(s), turnout. *See also* Political action; Political advertising; Political affiliation; Political participation; Teledemocracy; Voters; Voting behavior.

Voter turnout. See *Voter participation.*

Voters. Voter(s). Electorate. Taxpayer(s). Constituen(t,ts,cy,cies). Citizen(s). Balloter(s). *See also* Ballots; Citizens; Elections; Majorities (political); Primaries; Political attitudes; Political behavior; Political candidates; Political power; Voter participation; Voting.

Voting. Vot(e,ed,ing). Cast(ing) ballot(s). Ballot(ing). Poll(s). Plebiscite(s). Referendum. Political franchise. *See also* Absentee voting; Ballots; Citizenship; Civil rights; Democracy; Election law; Elections; Political action; Political participation; Political representation; Referendum; Voters; Voting behavior; Voting rights.

Voting, absentee. See *Absentee voting.*

Voting, preference. See *Preference voting.*

Voting behavior. Voting behavior. *Choose from:* voting, voter(s), electorate, electoral *with:* behavior, decision(s), preference(s), participation, position(s), pattern(s), record(s), turnout, support, opposition, volatility, reason(s), choosing, choice(s), survey(s), opinion(s), realignment, dealignment. *Consider also:* candidate preference, issue voting, party voting, nonvoting, election outcome(s), political behavior, voter registration, Condorcet(s) paradox, psephology. *See also* Elections; Opinion polls; Political attitudes; Politics; Voting.

Voting rights. Voting right(s). Suffrage. Political rights. Entitled to vote. Voting age. Multilingual ballot(s). Franchise. Enfranchise(d,ment). Fifteenth amendment. Nineteenth amendment. Participat(e,ion) in political process. Electoral participation. *See also* Civil rights; Elections; Ombudsmen; Suffrage; Voting.

Vouchers, educational. See *Educational vouchers.*

Vouchers, school. See *Educational vouchers.*

Vowels. Vowel(s). Semivowel(s). Vocoid(s). Diphthong(s). *See also* Alphabets.

Vows. Vow(s). Oath(s). Promise(s). Pledge(s). *See also* Promises.

Vows, marriage. See *Weddings.*

Voyages, interplanetary. See *Interplanetary voyages.*

Voyages, subterranean. See *Voyages to the otherworld.*

Voyages, underworld. See *Voyages to the otherworld.*

Voyages to the otherworld. Voyage(s) to the otherworld. Subterranean voyage(s). *Choose from:* subterranean, otherworld, underworld(s), Hell, infernal, netherworld(s), Osirian, underground, centre of the Earth, world of the dead

with: voyage(s), journey(s), epic(s), quest(s), odyssey(s). *See also* Afterworld; Hell; Imaginary places.

Voyeurism. Voyeur(s,ism,istic). Peeping tom(s). Scopophil(ia,ic). Scoptophil(ia, ic). *Consider also:* ecouteur(ism). *See also* Exhibitionism; Sexual deviations.

Vulgarity. Vulgar(ity,ness,ism). Indecen(t, cy). Obscen(e,ity,eness). Lewd(ness). Filth(y,iness). Salac(ity,ious,iousness). Vile(ness). Foul(ness). *Consider also:* unsophisticat(ed,ion), rude(ness), crude(ness), boorish(ness), crass(ness), ill bred, brutish(ness), shameless(ness). *See also* Antisocial behavior; Bawdy songs; Blasphemy; Cybersex; Epithets; Erotic songs; Indecent communications; Malinformation; Obscenity; Pornography; Prurience; Scatology; Verbal abuse.

Vulnerability. Vulnerab(le,ility). High risk. At risk. Exposed. Unprotected. Unguarded. Unprepared. Defenseless(ness). Helpless(ness). Susceptib(le,ility). Prone(ness). Predispos(e,ed,ing,ition). Unresist(ing,ant). Easily wounded. Assailable. Easy mark(s). Gullib(le, ility). Life threatening condition(s). *See also* Credulity; Disease susceptibility; High risk persons; Risk; Safety; Security; Threat; Victimization.

W

Wage, minimum. See *Minimum wage.*

Wage differentials. Wage differential(s). *Choose from:* compensation, pay(ed, ing,ment,ments), reward(s), income, allocation(s), distribut(e,ed,ing,ion,ions), salar(y,ies), wage(s), earning(s) *with:* differential(s), difference(s), disparit(y, ies), inequit(y,ies,able), injustice(s), inequality, unequal, unfair(ness), two-tier, gap(s), discrimination. *See also* Cheap labor; Comparable worth; Employment discrimination; Equity (payment); Income inequality; Prevailing wages; Sexual division of labor; Sexual inequality; Social equity.

Wage earners. Wage earner(s). Bread-winner(s). Bread winner(s). Head(s) of household(s). Wage labor(er,ers). *See also* Dual career families; Employees; Female headed households; Salaries; Self employment; Working women; Workers.

Wagers. See *Betting; Gambling.*

Wages. Wage(s). Income(s). Earning(s). Salar(y,ies). Remunerat(ion,ive). Compensation. Family allowance. Earned money. Payment(s) received. Recompense. Paycheck(s). Monetary reward(s). Emolument(s). Piece rate(s). *See also* Bonuses; Cheap labor; Compensation (payment); Employee benefits; Income; Income distribution; Income inequality; Labor costs; Living standards; Living conditions; Minimum wage; Prevailing wages; Retirement income; Salaries; Wage differentials; Workers' rights.

Wages, prevailing. See *Prevailing wages.*

Waiting lists. Wait(ing) list(s). Waitlist(ed, ing). Queue(s,d). Queuing. *Choose from:* waiting *with:* line(s), time(s), period(s). Stand(ing) on line. *See also* Allocation; Distribution (apportion); Scarcity.

Waitperson. Waitperson(s). Waiter(s). Waitress(es). Waitron(s). Headwaiter(s). *Consider also:* steward(s), butler(s), wine steward(s), busboy(s), bartender(s), maitre d'. *See also* Eating establishments;.

Wake sleep cycle. See *Sleep wake cycle.*

Wakefulness. Wakeful(ness). *Consider also:* insomnia(c,cs), awake(n,ned,ning), unable to sleep, inability to fall asleep, phase shift, sleep wake disruption(s). *Consider also:* agrypnotic(s). *See also* Sleep deprivation; Sleep disorders; Sleep wake cycle.

Walk-in clinics. Walk-in clinic(s). *Choose from:* walk-in, community based, storefront *with:* clinic(s), treatment center(s), crisis intervention center(s), information and referral, medicine, medical, doctor(s), physician(s). *Consider also:* medical mall(s), medical plaza(s), urgicenter(s), McDoctor, DocInABox, Walkin Medical Care, suburban outpatient center(s). *See also* Ambulatory care; Ambulatory surgery; Clinics; Community health services; Community mental health services; Crisis intervention; Emergency services; Outpatient treatment; Outpatients; Psychiatric clinics.

Walking. Walk(ed,s,ing,er,ers). Ambulat(e, ed,ing,ion,ory). Promenade(s). Stroll(ed, ing). Rambl(e,ed,ing). Travel on foot. Perambulat(e,ed,ing,ion). *Consider also:* mobility, wander(ing,ers), pedestrian(s), strid(e,ing), march(ed,ing), peram-bulat(e,ed,ing,ion), pac(e,ed,ing), tread, saunter(ed,ing), hik(e,ed,ing), tramp(ed, ing), gait(s). *See also* Exercise.

Waltz. Waltz(es,ing,ed). Walz(er,en). Valse(s). Valz(er). *Consider also:* danza tedesca. *See also* Ballroom dancing; Dance.

Wanderers. See *Nomads; Vagrants.*

Wandering behavior. Wandering behavior. *Choose from:* wander(ed,ing), pacing, ambulation *with:* aimless(ness), Alzheimer(s), demented, confus(ed,ion). *See also* Alzheimer's disease; Cognition disorders; Mental confusion; Senile dementia.

Wants. Want(s). Desiderat(e,a). Desir(e,es, ed,ing). Crav(e,es,ed,ing). Willful(ness). Demand(s,ed,ing). Pursu(c,cd,ing,it). Yearn(es,ed,ing). Wish(ed,ing) for. Wish list(s). Covet(s,ed,ing). Longing(s). Hankering(s). Sexual energy. *Consider also:* erotomania, erotic feeling(s), hung(er,ry,riness). *See also* Motivation; Needs; Preferences; Self interest; Unmet needs.

War. War(s,fare,ring,time). Armed conflict(s). Belligeren(t,ts,cy). Civil strife. Civil war(s). International aggression. Guerrilla attack(s). Revolution(s). Jihad(s). Holy war(s). Battle(s). Military struggle(s). Combat(s). Invasion. Invad(e,ed,er, ers,ing). Occupied territor(y,ies). Conquer(ed,er,ers,ing). Air raid(s). Blitzkrieg. *Consider also:* nuclear, thermonuclear, holy, biological, chemical, environmental, psychological *with:* war(s,fare). *Consider also:* specific wars by name: Korean conflict, World War I, World War II, Russian Revolu-tion, Thirty Years War, Desert Storm, etc. *See also* Aerial warfare; Aggression; Armed forces; Assault (battle); Attack (Military science); Balance of power; Belligerency; Biological warfare; Borderlands; Chemical warfare; Civil defense; Civil war; Cold war; Combat; Combat disorders; Conflict; Crimes against peace; Defense (Military science); Defense spending; Disarma-ment; Feuds; Foreign policy; Guerrilla warfare; Guerrillas; Gulf war syndrome; History; Imperialism; International alliances; International conflict; International relations; Invasion; Just war doctrine; Militarism; Military draft; Military history; Military offenses; Military operations; Military personnel; Military planning; Military readiness; Military retreat; Military service; Military strategies; National fronts; National security; Nuclear warfare; Nuclear weapons; Patriotism; Peace; Peace movements; Peace negotiations; Peasant rebellions; Political violence; Primitive warfare; Prisoners of war; Psychological warfare; Rebellions; Reconstruction; Refugees; Resistance; Revolution; Sea power; Terrorism; Treaties; Triumphal arches; Under-ground; Veterans; Violence; War crimes; War memorials; War news; War prevention; War victims; Weapons of mass destruction; World problems.

War, cold. See *Cold war.*

War, justification of. See *Just war doctrine.*

War, maritime. See *Maritime war.*

War, prisoners of. See *Prisoners of war.*

War atrocities. War atrocit(y,ies). *Choose from:* war(s,time), military, soldier(s), Nazi(s), Japanese, Turkish, My Lai, US, Vietnam, rebel(s), fascist(s), government force(s) *with:* atrocit(y,ies), atrocious(ness), massacre(s,d), attack(s,ed,ing) civilian(s), disappearance(s), human rights violation(s), mistreat(ed,ing,ment), heinous(ness), monstrous(ness). *Consider also:* germ warfare. *See also* Atrocities; Ethnic cleansing; Genocide; Massacres; War crimes; War victims.

War attitudes. War attitude(s). *Choose from:* war(s,fare), cold war, battle(s), combat, armed conflict(s), revolution(s), Vietnam, World War II, etc. *with:* consensus, attitude(s) toleran(t,ce), protest(ed,ing,er,ers), oppos(e,ed,ing, ition), support(ed,ing,er,ers), shock(ed, ing), mourn(ed,ing), point(s) of view, public opinion, dislik(e,ed,ing), hawk(s,ish), dove(s), accept(ed,ing, ance), patriot(ic,ism). *Consider also:* antiwar, war resister(s), prowar, warmonger(ing,ers). *See also* Conscientious objectors; Jingoism; Just war doctrine; Militarism; Neutrality; Noncombatants; Pacifism; Patriotism; Peacemovements; War news; War prevention.

War crimes. War crime(s). Genocid(e,al). *Choose from:* war(s) *with:* crime(s), criminal(s), atrocit(y,ies), victim(s). *Choose from:* Nuremberg, Tokyo *with:* tribunal(s), principles, judgment(s), trial(s). *Consider also:* crimes against peace, crimes against humanity. *See also* Biological warfare; Chemical warfare; Depravity; Ethnic cleansing; Genocide; Holocaust; International offenses; Military law; Military offenses; Naval offenses; Nazism; Prisoners of war; War; War atrocities; War victims.

War damage compensation. War damage compensation. War claim(s). *Choose from:* war(s), revolution(s), military activit(y,ies) *with:* damage(s), recover(y,ed), environmental cleanup(s), reimbursement, restitution, reparation(s), compensat(e,ed,ing,ion). *See also* Compensation (payment); Restitution; War victims.

War doctrine, just. See *Just war doctrine.*

War memorials. War memorial(s). *Choose from:* war(s), veterans, battle(s,field, fields), Marine Corps, Army, Navy, sailor(s), soldier(s), Armed Forces, Vietnam, Korean War, Civil War, Revolutionary War, Great War, World War I, World War II, Battle of Normandy, Iwo Jima, Gettysburg, etc. *with:* memorial(s), monument(s), pilgrimage(s), commemorat(e,ed,ing, ion), consecrat(e,ed,ing,ion), dedicat(e,ed,ing,ion), plaque(s). *Consider also:* Tomb of the Unknown Soldier. *See also* Commemoration; Historic sites; Medieval military history; Military history; Monuments; Triumphal arches; Veterans; War; War victims.

War neuroses. See *Combat disorders.*

War news. War news. Helicopter journalis(m,t,ts). *Choose from:* war(s), battleground(s), military decision(s), military operation(s), military action(s), bombing(s), troop movement(s), military frontline(s), air raid(s), troop maneuver(s), ceasefire(s) *with:* public information policy, press coverage, columnist(s), cover stor(y,ies), headline(s), footage, media, journalis(m,t,ts,tic), newspaper(s), radio, television, TV, broadcast(s,ing,er,ers), news agenc(y,ies), wire service(s), press, periodical(s), magazine(s), reporting, reporter(s), newspeople, newspaper(s), newsroom(s), newsweekl(y,ies), columnist(s), CBS, New York Times, portray(ed,ing,al,als), depict(ed,ing, ion,ions), coverage, lack of coverage, propagand(a,ize,ized,izing,ist,ists), censor(ed,s,ing,ship). *See also* Censorship; Editorials; Fairness and accuracy in reporting; Mass media; Media portrayal; News coverage; Photojournalism; Propaganda; Public opinion; War; War attitudes.

War pensions. See *Military pensions.*

War planes. See *Military airplanes.*

War poetry. War poetry. War poem(s). *Choose from:* war(time), battle(s), soldier(s,y), sailor(s), cannon ball(s), hydrogen bomb(s), sword(s), bomb(s, ing,ings,ardment), bullet(s), gun(s), arm(y,ies), battle(s), battlefield(s), bloodshed, combat, conquering legions, gunboat(s), victor(y,ies), carnage, troops, drummer boy(s), warrior(s), Civil War, World War I, First World War, World War II, Second World War, Korean War, Vietnam War, Persian Gulf War, Boer War(s) *with:* poe(m,ms,try), ballad(s), verse(s). *Consider also poems by title, for example:* "In Flanders Fields," "The Charge of the Light Brigade," "The Breaking of Nations," etc. *Consider also authors of war poetry for example:* Alfred Lord Tennyson, Siegfried Sassoon, Walt Whitman, Wilfred Owen, etc. *See also* Epic literature; Epitaphs; Folk poetry; Heroes; Historical poetry; Patriotism; Poetry; War songs.

War prevention. War prevention. *Choose from:* maintain(ed,ing), preserv(e,ed,ing) *with:* peace. *Choose from:* war(s), military conflict(s), regional conflict(s), outbreak(s), surprise attack(s) *with:* prevent(s,ed,ing,ion), deter(red,rent, rents,rence,ring), avoid(ed,ing,ance), reduc(e,ed,ing) risk(s), eliminat(e,ed,ing, ion) risk(s), remov(e,ed,ing) threat(s). *Consider also:* nonproliferation, arms limitation(s), summit meeting(s), strategic balance(s), reciprocated disarmament, defensive shield(s), disarm(ed,ing) first strike(s). *See also* Arms control; Balance of power; Crimes against peace; Deterrence; Disarmament; International relations; Just war doctrine; National security; Nuclear weapons non-proliferation; Peace; Peace movements; Peace negotiations: Peaceful change; Peaceful coexistence; Peacekeeping forces; Treaties; War; War attitudes.

War protest movements. See *Peace movements.*

War songs. War(time) song(s). *Choose from:* war(time), battle, soldier(s,y), patriotic, Civil War, World War I, World War II, Korean War, Vietnam War Persian Gulf War, resistance, martial *with:* music, song(s), tune(s), ditt(y,ies), lyric(s), musical motif(s), tattoo(s), fanfare(s), melod(y,ies). *Consider also:* Star Spangled Banner, A Long Way to Tipperary, Over There, Le Chant des Partisans, etc. *See also* Janissary music; Marches; Militarism; Patriotic music; War poetry.

War syndrome, Gulf war. See *Gulf war syndrome.*

War victims. War victim(s). *Choose from:* war, combat, battle(s), landmine(s), napalm, soldier(s), military, troop(s), Holocaust, civil war(s), atomic bomb, Hiroshima, Nagasaki, Vietnam, Korean conflict, World War II, World War I, Desert Storm, Bosnia, Kosovar, etc. *with:* victim(s), wound(s,ed), killed, murdered, raped, casualt(y,ies), refugee(s), trauma(s,tic,tically), maim(ed,ing), concentration camp(s), tortured, crime(s). *Consider also:* displaced persons, war relief. *See also* Casualties; Disability; Displaced persons; Military offenses; Post traumatic stress disorders; Prisoners of war; Refugee camps; Refugees; Restitution; Veterans; Victimization; War; War atrocities; War crimes; War damage compensation; War memorials.

Warehouse. Warehouse(s). Wholesale establishment(s). Stockroom(s). Storage site(s). Storehouse(s). Storage place(s). Distribut(ion,ing) center(s). Depot(s). Stockpile(s). Barn(s). Repositor(y,ies). Depositor(y,ies). Grain elevator(s). *See also* Distributors; Storage.

Warfare, aerial. See *Aerial warfare.*

Warfare, air. See *Aerial warfare.*

Warfare, biological. See *Biological warfare.*

Warfare, chemical. See *Chemical warfare.*

Warfare, gas. See *Chemical warfare.*

Warfare, germ. See *Biological warfare.*

Warfare, guerilla. See *Guerilla warfare.*

Warfare, medieval. See *Medieval military history.*

Warfare, nuclear. See *Nuclear warfare.*

Warfare, partisan. See *Guerrilla warfare.*

Warfare, primitive. See *Primitive warfare.*

Warfare, psychological. See *Psychological warfare.*

Warfare, siege. See *Siege warfare.*

Warfare, unconventional. See *Guerilla warfare.*

Warm blooded. Warm blooded. Homoio-therm(al,y,s,ic). *See also* Animals.

Warming, global. See *Atmospheric contamination; Greenhouse effect.*

Warmups. See *Exercise.*

Warnings. Warn(ed,ing,ings). Caveat(s). Admonition(s). Caution(s). Forewarn(ed, ing). Distress signal(s). Warning label(s). *See also* Animal defensive behavior; Communication thought transfer; Danger.

Warranty, product. See *Product warranty.*

Warriors. See *Heroes; Military personnel.*

groundwater, wastewater, sewage *with:* purif(y,ying,ied,ication), chlorinat(e,ed, ing,ion), filter(ed,ing), desalinat(e,ed, ing,ion), desalinization, denitrification, treat(ed,ing,ment), boil(ed,ing), soften(ing,er,ers), remov(e,ed,ing,al) impurit(y,ies), remov(e,ed,ing,al) chemical(s), etc. *See also* Drinking water; Environmental protection; Sewage as fertilizer; Sewage disposal; Water pollution; Water reuse; Water safety; Water supply.

Water resources development. Water resources development. *Choose from:* water, groundwater, freshwater, streamflow, instream flow, river basin *with:* management, supply, resource(s), allocat(e,ed,ing,ion,ions), withdraw(ing, al,als), control(led,ling) *with:* project(s), development, implementation, plan(s,ned,ning), strateg(y,ies). *Consider also:* dam(s), irrigation system(s), hydropower, flood control, reservoir(s). *See also* Flood control; Irrigation; Water banking; Water conservation; Water power; Water supply.

Water reuse. Water reuse. *Choose from:* water(s), freshwater, drinking water, tapwater, saltwater, rainwater, groundwater, wastewater, sewage *with:* reus(e,ed,es,ing), recycl(e,ed,es,ing), reclamation, reclaim(ed,ing). *See also* Recycling; Sewage as fertilizer; Sewage disposal; Water pollution; Water purification.

Water safety. Water safety. *Choose from:* water, swimming, sailing, boat(s,ing), canoe(s), sailboat(s), diving, pool(s), ship(s), motorboat(s), underwater, scuba, yacht(s), aquatic, surf, surfboard(s,ing) *with:* safety, accident prevention, rescue(d,s), rescuing, first-aid, lifesaving, lifeguard(s). *See also* Accident prevention; Safety; Sports.

Water spirits. Water spirit(s). Water sprite(s). Naiad(s,es). Nereid(s). *Choose from:* water(y), marine, aquatic, saltwater, sea(s), ocean(s), fishtailed, waterfall(s), dew, rainbow(s), river, fish *with:* spirit(s), sprite(s), siren(s), nymph(s), divinit(y,ies), deit(y,ies). *Consider also:* Rusalk(i,a), Ondine, Undine, Poseidon, Neptune, Nereus, Oceanid(s), Mamma Wata, Mammy Water, Lasiren, Lasyrenn, lwa, Oshun, Yemoja, Ezili. *See also* Animism; Mermaids; Mythology; Spirits; Succubus; Voodooism.

Water supply. Water supply. Drought(s). *Choose from:* water(s), groundwater, freshwater, lakewater *with:* level(s), resource(s), suppl(y,ies), availab(le,ility), allocation(s), scarc(e,ity), shortage(s), protect(ed,ing,ion), abundan(t,ce), reserve(s). *Consider also:* reservoir(s), aquifer(s), river(s), lake(s), pond(s) *with:* level(s), dry, flood(s,ed,ing). *Consider*

also: well(s), artesian well(s), water shed(s), public water system(s), municipal water system(s). *See also* Aqueducts; Divining rods; Drinking water; Water banking; Water conservation; Water levels; Water pollution; Water purification; Water resources development; Water reuse; Water safety.

Water transportation. Water transport(ation). Sail(ed,ing). *Choose from:* sea, water, river(s), lake(s), ocean(s,ic), marine *with:* transport(ed,ing,ation), travel(ed,ing), ship(ped,ping), transit, carry(ing), carried. *Consider also:* barge(s), tanker(s), cargo ship(s), Merchant Marine. *See also* Boats; Canals; Cruising; Ground effect machines; Inland water transportation; Sailing; Shipping industry; Ships; Transport workers; Travel.

Water transportation, inland. See *Inland water transportation.*

Water witching. See *Divining rod.*

Waterfronts. See *Shorelines.*

Waters, territorial. See *Territorial waters.*

Watersheds. See *Turning points.*

Way of life. See *Lifestyle.*

Weakness. See *Asthenia; Debility.*

Wealth. Wealth(y,iest). Rich(es,est). Affluen(t,ce). Well-to-do. Fortune. Millionaire(s). Billionaire(s). Decamillionaire(s). Tycoon(s). Magnate(s). Worth millions. High income. Upper class. Jet set. Upper income level. Prosperous. Deep pockets. Blue book(s). Social register(s). Opulen(t,ce). *See also* Accumulation; Capital (financial); Class identity; Consumption (economic); Dual economy; Economic elites; Gross national product; Income; Income distribution; Investments; Living standards; Luxuries; Money; Money (primitive cultures); Ownership; Poverty; Prestige; Privilege; Profitability; Profits; Social class; Socioeconomic status; Upper class; Upper income level; Ruling class.

Weaning. Wean(ed,ing). Introduc(e,ed,ing) solid food. *Consider also:* stop(ped, ping), ceas(e,ed,ing), cessation, transfer *with:* breast feeding, infant nursing. *See also* Breast feeding; Bottle feeding; Eating; Sucking behavior.

Weaponry. Weapon(ry,s). Military hardware. Warhead(s). Gun(nery,s). Armament(s). Firearm(s). Ammunition. Antiaircraft system(s). Artillery. Arm(s,ed,ing). Arsenal. Arrow(s). Assault rifle(s). Assault weapon(s). Ballistic(al,s). Bastinado(s). Bazooka(s). Bomb(s). Bow and arrow(s). Cannon(s). Carbine(s). Catapult(s). Club(s). Crossbow(s). Cruise missile(s). Cudgel(s).

Dagger(s). Fire ball(s). Grenade(s). Gunpowder. Gunshot. Halberd(s). Handgun(s). Howitzer(s). Kris(s). Lantaka(s). Letter bomb(s). Longbow(s). Machete(s). Machine gun(s). Macahuitl(s). Marriwirri(s). Mere(s). Missile(s). Molotov cocktail(s). Munition(s). Musket(s,ry). Patriot missile(s). Pistol(s). Poniard(s). Revolver(s). Rifle(s). Rocket(s,ry). Scud missile(s). Shotgun(s). Sling(s). Small arms. Spear(s). Submachine gun(s). Switchblade(s). Sword(s). Tomahawk(s). Tomahawk missile(s). Uzi(s). Wadd(y,ies). *See also* Armor; Artillery; Ballistic missiles; Bombs; Firearms industry; Hardware; Land mines; Military weapons; Proving grounds; Self defense; Stone implements.

Weapons, incendiary. See *Incendiary weapons.*

Weapons, military. See *Military weapons.*

Weapons, nuclear. See *Nuclear weapons.*

Weapons non-proliferation, nuclear. See *Nuclear weapons non-proliferation.*

Weapons of mass destruction. Weapons of mass destruction. WMD. *Choose from:* chemical, biological, nuclear *with:* weapon(s), attack(s), war(fare), agent(s), threat(s,en,ened,ening), terroris(m,t,ts). *Consider also:* cyber attack(s), landmine(s), toxic cocktail(s). *See also* Atomic bomb; Biological warfare; Chemical warfare; Cyber attacks; Genocide; Gulf war syndrome; International offenses; Military weapons; Nuclear warfare; Nuclear weapons; War.

Weather. Weather. Atmospheric condition(s). Meteorological condition(s). Prevailing wind(s). *Consider also:* meteorolog(y,ic,ical, ically,ist,ists), temperature(s), humidity, barometric pressure, wind(s,y), windstorm(s), storm(s), gale(s), hurricane(s), tropical storm(s), thunderstorm(s), rain(y,s,fall), snow(ed,ing), snowstorm(s), drought, clear weather, sunny, cloudy, breezy, squall(s), blizzard(s), typhoon(s), tornado(es), twister(s). *See also* Atmosphere; Atmospheric temperature; Earth; Ecology; Environmental effects; Geographic regions; Natural disasters; Rainfall; Seasons; Storms; Weather control; Weather forecasting.

Weather control. Weather control. Seed(ed,ing) cloud(s). Cloud Seed(ing). Rainmak(er,ers,ing). Rain-mak(er,ers, ing). *Choose from:* weather, atmospheric condition(s), meteorological, rain, hail(s,storm,storms), storm(s), wind(s,y), windstorm(s), hurricane(s), thunderstorm(s), rainstorm(s), snowstorm(s), drought, squall(s), blizzard(s), typhoon(s), tornado(es) *with:* control(led,ling), modif(y,ied,ication, ications), suppress(ed,ing,ion), diver(t,ting,ted,sion,sions). *See also* Storms; Weather.

Weather forecasting. Weather forecast(s, ing,er,ers). *Choose from:* weather, atmospheric conditions, meteorolog(ical,ist,ists), temperature, humidity, barometric pressure, wind(s,y), windstorm(s), storm(s), gale(s), hurricane(s), flood(s,ing), thunderstorm(s), rain(y,s), rainstorm(s), snow(ed,ing), snowstorm(s), drought, clear weather, fair weather, sunny, cloudy, breezy, squall(s), blizzard(s), typhoon(s), tornado(es) *with:* forecast(ed,ing), warn(ed,ing,ings), predict(ed,ing,ion,ions), watch(es). *Consider also:* weather *with:* report(s,ed,ing), service(s). *See also* Forecasting; Storms; Weather.

Weaving. Weav(ing,er,ers). Wove(n). Loom(s). Warp. Weft. Braid(ed,ing). Plait(ed,ing). Interlac(e,ed,ing). *Consider also:* basketweaving, basket weaving, basketry, textile making, knit(ted,ing). *See also* Artisans; Crafts; Guilds; Textile industry; Wool industry.

Wedding poetry. See *Epithalamia.*

Wedding songs. See *Epithalamia.*

Weddings. Wedding(s). Marriage rite(s). Marriage ritual(s). Marriage ceremon(ies,y). Wedding ceremon(ies, y). Nuptial(s). Holy matrimony. Matrimon(y,ial). Bride(s). Bridal. Bridegroom(s). Espousal(s). Elopement(s). Holy wedlock. Unit(e,ed, ing) in marriage. Confarreatio. *Consider also:* marriage *with:* ceremon(y,ies), rite(s), ritual(s), vow(s), festivit(y,ies). *Consider also:* bridal chamber(s), newlywed(s), epithalam(ium,iums,ion, ia,ic). *See also* Epithalamia; Marriage; Marriage customs; Marriage rates; Religious rituals; Rites of passage; Rituals.

Wedlock. See *Marriage.*

Week, work. See *Worktime.*

Weight, birth. See *Birth weight.*

Weight, body. See *Body weight.*

Weight control. Control(led,ling) weight. Weight loss program(s). Therapeutic fast(ing). Diet(er,ers,ing). Reducing diet(s). Maintenance diet(s). Dietary restraint. Overeaters Anonymous. Weight Watchers. Behavioral weight loss. Reducing calories. *Choose from:* weight, obes(e,eness,ity), overweight, fat(ness), thin(ness), anorex(ia,ic) *with:* control(led,ling), reduc(e,ed,ing,tion), therapy, regulat(ed,ing,ion), diet(s,ing), maintenance, restrain(t,ed,ing), surgery, intervention, treatment, management. *See also* Body weight; Calories (food); Diet; Diet fads; Exercise; Obesity; Thinness; Weight gain; Weight loss.

Weight gain. Gain(ed,ing) weight. *Choose from:* becom(e,ing), became *with:* overweight, obese, fat, corpulen(t,ce), plump, heavy. Fat(ness,ten,tenning). Excess weight. Weight problem. Weight increase(s). Grow(ing) fat. Putting on weight. *See also* Body weight; Calories (food); Diet; Diet fads; Obesity; Thinness; Weight control; Weight loss.

Weight lifting. Weight lift(ing,er,ers). Weightlift(ing,er,ers). Lift(ing) weight(s). Pump(ed,ing,s) iron. Bodybuild(ing,er,ers). Body build(ing,er, ers). Strength training. Weight training. *See also* Exercise; Exercise therapy.

Weight loss. Weight loss. Weight management. Anorex(ia,ic). Decreased body mass. Fast(ing). Diet(ed,ing). Dieter(s). Reducing diet(s). Weight control. Dietary restraint. *Choose from:* reduc(e,ed,ing), restrict(ed,ing) *with:* calories, diet, eating. *Choose from:* weight, pounds *with:* loss, los(e,ing), lost, shed, dropped, reduc(e,ed,ing,tion). *Consider also:* phenfen, phentermine fenfluramine, appetite suppressant(s), diet pill(s). *See also* Anorexia nervosa; Body weight; Calories (food); Diet; Diet fads; Malnutrition; Obesity; Thinness; Undernourishment; Weight control.

Weight perception. Weight perception. Barognosis. *Choose from:* weight(s), heaviness *with:* perception, perceiv(e, ed,ing), aware(ness), recognition, discriminat(e,ed,ing,ion), concept(s,ion), judgment(s), judg(e,ed,ing), evaluat(ed, ing,ion), assess(ed,ing,ment). *Consider also:* gravimetric. *See also* Perception.

Weightlessness. Weightless(ness). *Consider also:* space flight, zero gravity, microgravity, micro-gravity. *See also* Environmental effects; Extraterrestrial environment.

Welfare, animal. See *Animal welfare.*

Welfare, child. See *Antipoverty programs; Child day care; Child health services; Child support; Family assistence; Public welfare.*

Welfare, general. See *Public good.*

Welfare, maternal. See *Maternal welfare.*

Welfare, personal. See *Well being.*

Welfare, public. See *Public welfare.*

Welfare, social. See *Antipoverty programs; Charities; Food service (programs); Medical assistance; Outreach programs; Public welfare; Social agencies; Social services; Social programs.*

Welfare policy. Welfare polic(y,ies). *Choose from:* welfare, public assistance, social insurance, public relief, workfare, social security, medicare, medicaid, food stamp(s), antipoverty, entitlement, unemployment, Old Age Assistance [OAA], Supplemental Security Income [SSI], Aid to Families with Dependent Children [AFDC] *with:* polic(y,ies), ideolog(y,ies), guideline(s), law(s), legislation, regulation(s). *See also* Family policy; Housing policy; Low income; Public policy; Social legislation; Welfare reform; Welfare state.

Welfare programs. See *Antipoverty programs; Food services (programs); Income maintenance programs; Medical assistance; Public welfare; Social agencies; Social programs; Social services; Unemployment relief; Workfare.*

Welfare recipients. Welfare recipient(s). Welfare roll(s). Welfare poor. Welfare dependency. *Choose from:* welfare, public assistance, dole, workfare, food stamp(s), AFDC, aid to families with dependent children, old age assistance, supplemental Security Income, SSI, special supplemental food program, WIC *with:* mother(s), household(s), recipient(s), famil(y,ies), dependen(t,ts, cy), client(s), patient(s), unemployed. *See also* Benefits (compensation); Dependents; Disadvantaged; Income maintenance programs; Poverty; Public welfare; Unemployment relief; Workfare.

Welfare reform. Welfare reform. *Choose from:* welfare, public assistance, medicaid, food stamp(s), antipoverty program(s), entitlement program(s), unemployment compensation, unemployment benefit(s), Aid to Families with Dependent Children, AFDC *with:* reform(s,ed,ing), work incentive(s), tougher eligibility, streamline(e,ed,ing), reduc(e,ed,ing) benefit(s). *See also* Social legislation; Welfare policy; Welfare state; Workfare.

Welfare services. See *Antipoverty programs; Food services (programs); Income maintenance programs; Medical assistance; Public welfare; Social agencies; Social services; Social programs; Unemployment relief; Workfare.*

Welfare state. Welfare state(s). Cradle to grave. Nanny state. *Consider also:* welfare capitalism, interventionist state(s), liberal democratic societ(y,ies), social democratic state(s). *See also* Liberalism; Progressivism; Public policy; Public services; State; State capitalism; Welfare policy; Welfare reform.

Well being. Well being. Wellbeing. Happ(y, iness). Health(y,iness). Prosper(ity, ousness). Mental(ly) health(y). Satisf(ied,ying,action,actions). Confiden(t,ce). Hopeful(ness). Zest(y). Well(ness). Fulfill(ed,ment). Content(ed,ment). Meaningful(ness). Gratif(ied,ying,ication). Robust(ness). Vigor(ous,ness). Good fortune. *Consider* *also:* abled, physical normalcy, physical(ly) normal(ity). *See also* Adjustment (to environment); Comfortableness; Coping; Deprivation; Fortitude; Happiness; Health; Holistic health; Individual needs; Life satisfaction; Lifestyle; Mental health; Mindbody relations (metaphysics); Morale; Natural foods; Needs; Preventive medicine; Preventive psychiatry; Psychological well being; Quality of life.

Well being, economic. See *Economic well being.*

Well being, economic individuals. See *Austerities; Basic needs; Consumption (use); Deprivation; Disadvantaged; Everyday life; Living conditions; Living standards; Quality of life; Socioeconomic status; Wealth.*

Well being, psychological. See *Psychological well being.*

Wellness. See *Health; Holistic health; Hygiene; Mental health; Physical fitness; Preventive medicine; Primary prevention; Quality of life; Well being.*

Weltanschauung. See *Worldview.*

Wertfreiheit. See *Value neutral.*

West Altaic languages. West Altaic language(s). Bulgaric: Chuvash, Volga-Kama Bulgar. Turkic: Iranized Uzbek, Chaghatay, Old Uighur, Kok Turkic, New Uighur, Turkish, Ottoman Turkish, Osmanli, Azeri, Azerbaijani, Turkoman (Turkomenian), Kazan Tatar, Kipchak, Karaim, Crimean Tatar, Kazakh, Karakalpak, Noghay, Kirgiz, Soyon, Abakan, Oyrot, Tuva, Yakut. *See also* Eastern Europe; Central Asia; Language; Languages (as subjects).

West Indies. See *Caribbean.*

Western and country music. See *Country and western music.*

Western art music, Twentieth century. See *Twentieth century Western art music.*

Western civilization. Western civilization. *Choose from:* western, occidental, Judeo-Christian, Indo-European, Medieval, European, North American, industrial(ized) *with:* civilization(s), culture(s), nation(s), philosoph(y,ies), world, thought, values, tradition(s), music, song(s), literature, art(s), empire(s), dynast(y,ies), kingdom(s). *See also* African empires; Asian empires; Christianity; Civilization; Cultural history; Culture (anthropology); Developed countries; Eurocentrism; Industrial societies; Judaism; North America; Pre-Columbian empires; Sociocultural factors; Western Europe; Western society.

Western Europe. Europe(an). Andorra(n) [Andorra la Vella]. Austria(n) [Osterreich]. Belgi(um,ian) [Belgique, Belgie]. Cypr(us,iot). Denmark [Danish]. England [English]. Finland [Suomi, Finnish]. France. (Federal Republic of) Germany [Deutschland, West Germany, German Democratic Republic, East Germany]. Greece [Hellas, Ellas]. Iceland. (Republic of) Ireland [Hibernia(n), Irish Free State, Eire]. Ital(y,ian) [Italia]. Liechtenstein(er). Luxembourg(er) [Luxemburg(er)]. Malta [Maltese]. Monaco. Netherland(s,er) [Nederland(er), Holland, Dutch]. Norway [Norge, Norwegian]. Portugal [Portuguese]. Scotland [Scot(s,tish)]. Spain [Espana, Spanish]. Sweden [Sverige, Swedish]. Switzerland [Suisse, Schweiz, Svizzera, Helvetia, Swiss]. Turkey [Ottoman Empire]. Vatican City [Citta del Vaticano]. *Consider also:* Azor(es,ean,ian), Canary Islands [Islas Canarias], Channel Islands [Faeroe Islands [Faroes(e), Faero(erne,ese)], Gibraltar, Great Britain, Hebride(s,an) [Western Isles, Outer Hebrides, Inner Hebrides], United Kingdom of Great Britain and Northern Ireland, Lapland(er) [Lapp(s)], Mediterranean Islands, Scandinavia(n), Wales, Baltic state(s), Estonia(n), Latvia(n), Lithuania(n), San Marin(o,ese). *See also* Baltic languages; Celtic languages; Eastern Europe; Finno-Ugric languages; Germanic languages; Greek languages; Italic non-romance languages; Middle East; North Africa; Romance languages; Western civilization; Western society.

Western fiction. Western fiction. Western stor(y,ies). *Choose from:* western, old west, American west, Zane Grey, American frontier, cowboy(s) *with:* fiction, stor(y,ies), novel(s), legend(s,ary), literature. *See also* Adventure stories; Country and western music; Fiction; Heroes; Novels; Popular culture.

Western society. Western societ(y,ies). Western nation(s). Western power(s). European Economic Community. Developed countr(y,ies). First world. Industrial(ized) countr(y,ies). Developed nation(s). Industrial(ized) world. Industrial power(s). Industrial(ized) democrac(y,ies). Industrial societ(y,ies). Modern civilization(s). *Choose from:* western, north Atlantic, developed, industrial(ized), advanced, urbanized, bourgeois, capitalist, modern *with:* countr(y,ies), nation(s), state(s), societ(y,ies), world, communit(y,ies). *See also* Bourgeois societies; Capitalist societies; Consumer society; Developed countries; Industrialized societies; Modern society; Mass society; North America; Popular culture; Postindustrial societies; Technology and civilization; Western civilization; Western Europe.

Western stories. See *Western fiction.*

Western world. See *Western civilization; Western society.*

Wetlands. Wetland(s). Tidal marsh(es). Marsh(es,land,lands). Bottomland(s). Flood plain(s). Floodplain(s). Bog(s). Swamp(s). Salt marsh(es). Coastal zone(s). Pond(s). *See also* Arid lands; Drainage; Geographic regions; Grasslands; Grasses; Land preservation; Shore protection; Shorelines; Submerged lands; Vegetation.

Wetting, bed. See *Urinary incontinence.*

Whiskey industry. See *Liquor industry.*

Whistle blowing. Whistleblow(ers,ing). *Choose from:* blow(ers,ing), blew *with:* whistle(s). Disclos(e,ed,ing,ure). Informer(s). Informant(s). Speak(ing) out. Go(ing) public. *Choose from:* reveal(ed,ing), leak(s,ed,ing), report(ed,ing) *with:* fact(s), information, news, fraud, corruption, illegal(ity,ities). *Consider also:* dissent, leak(s) to the press, employees right to free speech. *See also* Corruption in government; Government secrecy; Information leaks; Informers; Misconduct in office.

White Black relations. See *Race relations.*

White collar crime. White collar crime(s). Antitrust violation(s). Black market(s). Blackmail(ed,ing). Bogus invoice(s). Breach(es) of contract. Bribe(s,ry). Cheat(ed,ing). Computer crime(s). Conflict(s) of interest. Copyright violation(s). Corrupt practice(s). Counterfeit(ed,ing). Coverup(s). Economic crime(s). Embezzle(d,ment). Environmental crime(s). Fencing stolen property. Fix(ed,ing) price(s). Price fixing. Illegal business practice(s). Illegal competition. Illegal employment. Illegal pollution. Industrial espionage. Industrial theft(s). Insider trading. Irregular business practice(s). Kickback(s). Launder(ed,ing) money. Misconduct in politics. Occupational crime(s). Overbill(ed,ing). Overcharg(e, ed,ing). Payoff(s). Phony accident claim(s). Pilferage. Ponzi scheme(s). Pyramid sale(s). Scam(s). Securities theft(s). Sweetheart contract(s). Tax evasion. Unethical practice(s). Waste public funds. *Consider also:* bureaucrat(s,ic), business, corporat(e, ion), employee(s), executive(s), industrial, occupational, white collar, politics, environmental, official(s) *with:* corrupt(ed,ing,ion), offense(s), fraud(ulent), illegal(ality,alities), theft(s), steal(ing), stolen, crim(e,es,inals,inality), offender(s), dishonest(y), deceptive practice(s), misconduct, conspiracy, defraud(ed,ing), falsif(y,ied,ication, ying), receiving stolen good(s), scandal(s), misdeed(s), unethical. *See also* Collusion; Computer crimes; Corruption in government; Crime;

Electronic eavesdropping; Financial disclosure; Fraud; Industrial espionage; Judicial corruption; Thieves.

White collar workers. White collar worker(s). Office worker(s). *Choose from:* white collar, new collar, office, salaried, management, managerial, administrative *with:* worker(s), employee(s), job(s), occupation(s), staff, personnel. *Consider also:* bank officer(s), executive(s), business(man, men,woman,women), manager(s), accountant(s), clerical worker(s), secretar(y,ies). *See also* Blue collar workers; Clerical workers; Managers; New middle class; Occupational classification; Occupations; Paraprofessional personnel; Professional personnel; Sales personnel; Service industries; Working class.

White noise. White noise. *Consider also:* white(n,ning,ned), random, background, pink *with:* noise(s). *Consider also:* whitening speech, noise masking, screen(ed,ing) noise(s), sound machine(s). *See also* Noise (sounds); Perceptual stimulation.

White people. See *Whites.*

White supremacy movements. White supremacy movement(s). White power group(s). Aryan Nation(s). Christian Identity Movement. Neo-Nazi(s,sm). Skinhead(s). The Order (Organization). White Liberation Movement. Posse Comitatus. White Aryan Resistance. The Covenant, the Sword and the Arm of the Lord. Order of the Silent Brotherhood. Afrikaner Resistance Movement. White freedom movement. White Patriot Party. Bruder Schweigen Strike Force II. Schweigen Order II. Falang(e,ists). Peronis(m,t,ts). Ku Klux Klan. Christian Coalition. Identity Believer(s). Identity Religion. *Consider also:* hate group(s), cross burning(s), fascis(m,mo,ts), paramilitary group(s). *See also* Antiabortion movement; Anti-government radicals; Antisemitism; Apartheid; Ethnocentrism; Eurocentrism; Hate crimes; Hate groups; Lynching; Militias; Nazism; Oppression; Paramilitary; Prejudice; Racism; Tribalism.

Whites. White(s). Caucasian(s). Anglo(s). Anglo American(s). Caucasian race. Caucasoid race. White race. Caucasian student(s). White student(s). WASP(s). White Anglo Saxon Protestant(s). European(s). European stock. European ancestry. European descent. *Consider also:* ofay(s). *See also* Ethnic groups; Race relations; Races; Racial differences; Racially mixed.

Whole language approach. Whole language approach. Holistic literary approach. Integrated approach(es) to learning. *Consider also:* literature-based reading program(s), literature-based

language arts program(s). *See also* Reading education; Second language education; Teaching methods.

Wholeness. See *Perfection.*

Wholism. See *Holism.*

Wholistic health. See *Holistic health.*

Whorehouses. See *Brothels.*

Widowhood. Widow(s,er,ers,ed,hood). Dowager(s). *Consider also:* spouse(s), husband(s), wife, wives, conjugal(ly), mate(s) *with:* loss, los(e,ing), death, dead, died, bereave(d,ment), mourn(ed, ing,er,ers), surviv(ed,ing,al,or,ors). *See also* Caregiver burden; Death; Displaced homemakers; Elderly; Life stage transitions; Marital disruption; Marital status; Marriage; Parental absence; Remarriage; Single parent family; Spouses; Survival.

Wife. See *Wives.*

Wife abuse. See *Spouse abuse.*

Wife battering. See *Battered women; Spouse abuse.*

Wife lending. Wife lending. Hospitality prostitution. *Choose from:* lend(ing), hospitality *with:* wife, wives. *See also* Customs.

Wife rape. See *Marital rape.*

Wild animals. Wild animal(s). Wildlife. *Choose from:* wild, undomesticated, nondomestic, untamed, feral, native, ferine, forest, jungle, wilderness, endangered *with:* animal(s), beast(s), mammal(s), bird(s), rodent(s), reptile(s), specie(s). *Consider also:* aardvark(s), antelope(s), agouti(s), baboon(s), bat(s), beaver(s), chimpanzee(s), chipmunk(s), coyote(s), deer, dolphin(s), elephant(s), fox(es), gorilla(s), hyena(s), kangaroo(s), lemur(s), mink(s), monkey(s), opossum(s), porpoise(s), seal(s), squirrel(s), wolf, wolves. *See also* Animals; Coyotes; Deer; Mammals; Nature sounds; Vertebrates; Wolves.

Wilderness. Wilderness. Wilds. Forever wild. Jungle(s). Rainforest(s). Rain forest(s). Wasteland(s). Barren(s). Wild and scenic. Land preserve(s). Wetland(s). Marsh(es). Grassland(s). Woods. Woodland(s). Forest(s). Timberland(s). Swamp(s,lands). Desert(s). *Choose from:* uninhabited, unexplored, remote, pristine, virgin, undeveloped, preserved *with:* country, territory, area(s), land(s), forest(s), place(s), wood(lands,s). *Consider also:* wildlife, nature, game, animal(s), bird(s) *with:* preserve(s), habitat(s), refuge(s), sanctuar(y,ies), area(s). *Consider also:* national park(s), natural monument(s), state park(s). *See also* Conservation of natural resources; Earth; Ecology; Environment; Environmental pollution; Environmental protection; Environmen-

talism; Habitat; Natural areas; Natural environment; Natural monuments; Nature sounds; Open spaces; Parks; Preservation; Reclamation of land; Wildlife sanctuaries.

Wildlife, gardening to attract. See *Gardening to attract wildlife.*

Wildlife conservation. Wildlife conservation. Wildlife corridor(s). *Choose from:* wild animal(s), wildlife, habitat(s), wilderness, wildflower(s), forest(s), rainforest(s), wetland(s), desert(s), jungle(s), ecosystem(s), biological diversity, endangered specie(s) or species by name such as: alligator(s), baboon(s), bat(s), beaver(s), bird(s), chimpanzee(s), chipmunk(s), coyote(s), deer, dolphin(s), elephant(s), fox(es), gorilla(s), kangaroo(s), Karner blue butterfly, lemur(s), mammal(s), manatee(s), mink(s), monkey(s), opossum(s), porpoise(s), reptile(s), seal(s), snail darter(s), squirrel(s), tortoise(s), waterfowl, wolf, wolves *with:* conserv(e,ed,ing,ation), preserv(e,ed,ing,ation), protect(ed,ing, ion), maintain(ed,ing), maintenance, recover(y,ies,ed,ing), defend(ing,ed), defense, sav(e,ed,ing), preserve(s), refuge(s), sanctuar(y,ies). *See also* Birds; Conservation of natural resources; Coyotes; Ecosystem management; Endangered species; Environmental protection; Food chain; Forest conservation; Gardening to attract wildlife; Habitat; Land preservation; Restoration ecology; Sanctuary gardens; Shore protection; Wildlife sanctuaries; Wolves.

Wildlife sanctuaries. Wildlife sanctuar(y, ies). Forever wild. *Choose from:* wildlife, nature, endangered species *with:* sanctuar(y,ies), refuge(s), area(s), preserve(s), reserve(s). *Consider also:* animal park(s), haven(s), game preserve(s), State park(s), National park(s), National forest(s), Nature Conservancy. *See also* Animal environments; Birds; Conservation of natural resources; Endangered species; Environmental protection; Forest reserves; Game and game birds; Game protection; Gardening to attract wildlife; Habitat; Natural areas; Natural environment; Old growth forests; Parks; Restoration ecology; Sanctuaries; Sanctuary gardens; Shelters; Wilderness; Wildlife conservation.

Will. See *Volition.*

Will, free. See *Volition.*

Will, general. See *General will.*

Will, liberty of the. See *Freedom (theology); Volition.*

Will, loss of. See *Loss of will.*

Will of God. Will of God. God's will. *Choose from:* God, divine, almighty, Lord's *with:* will, purpose(s), act(s), caus(e,es,ed,ing,ation). *Consider also:* divine revelation(s). *See also* Attributes of God; Judgment of God; Omnipotence; Prophecy; Revealed theology.

Willpower. See *Self control.*

Wills. Will(s). Living will(s). Last will. Bequeath(ed,ing). Bequest(s). Testament(ary). *See also* Financial support; Future interests; Records; Resource allocation.

Wills, living. See *Advance directives; Do not resuscitate orders; Right to die; Termination of treatment; Wills.*

Wind power. Wind power. Windmill(s). Wind machine(s). *Choose from:* wind *with:* energy, power, machine(s), catcher(s), sail(s). *See also* Alternative energy.

Wine. Wine(s). Enology. Oenology. *Consider also:* sherry, port, burgundy, champagne, chablis, beaujolais, claret, reisling, sauterne, winer(y,ies), vineyard(s), viniculture, or names of specific grapes such as Concord, etc. *See also* Alcoholic beverages; Liquor industry.

Wing, left. See *Left wing.*

Winter, nuclear. See *Nuclear winter.*

Winter depression. See *Seasonal affective disorder.*

Winter sports. Winter sport(s). *Choose from:* winter, Christmas(time), December, January, February, snow, ice *with:* sport(s), athlet(e,es,ic,ics), Olympic(s). *Consider also:* figure skat(e,ed,ing), skiboard(ing), snowshoe(s,ing), bobsled(s,ding), luge(ing), ice hockey, ice fish(ing), iceboat(s,ing), skis, skiing, sled dog rac(e,es,ing), sleigh(s,ed,ing), snowboard(s,ing), snowmobil(e,es,ing), snowshoe(s,ing), toboggan(s,ed,ing), ski bik(e,es,ing), winter carnival(s). *See also* Athletes; Popular culture; Sports.

Wiretapping. See *Electronic eavesdropping.*

Wisdom. Wisdom. Wise(ness). Sagac(ity,ious,iousness). Sage(ness). Perceptive(ness). Discern(ing,ment). Common sense. Clear thinking. Intelligen(ce,t). Astute(ness). Sound thinking. Good judgment. Clearheaded(ness). Prescien(t,ce). Rational(ity). *Consider also:* wicca. *See also* Experience (background); Judgment; Knowledge; Prudence; Reason; Wise person.

Wise person. Wise person(s). Sage(s). Savant(s). Philosopher(s). Guru(s). Malim(s). *Choose from:* learned, wise, experienced *with:* man, men, woman, women, person(s), people. *Consider also:* wicca, teacher(s), mentor(s). *See also* Advisors; Guru; Mentors; Spiritual direction; Wisdom.

Wit and humor, ethnic. See *Ethnic wit and humor.*

Wit and humor, political. See *Political humor.*

Witch hunting. Witch hunt(s,ing). *Choose from:* witch(es), heretic(s), dissenter(s) *with:* persecut(e,ed,ing,ion), burn(t,ed, ing), auto-da-fe, hang(ed,ing,ings), drown(ed,ing,ings), dunk(ed,in,insg), inquisition, trial(s), execut(ed,ion,ions). *See also* Defamation; Gossip; Inquisition; Libel; Labeling (of persons); McCarthyism; Persecution; Political campaigns; Public opinion; Reputation; Rumors; Scandals; Scapegoating; Witchcraft trials.

Witchcraft. Witch(es,craft). Occult(ism). Amulet(s). Black magic. Curse(s,d). Demon(ic,ology). Demon possession. Devil(s). Dracula cult(s). Exorcis(m,t,ts). Ghost(s). Hobgoblin(s). Haunted house(s). Haunt(ed,ing). Hex(es). Jinx(es). Incantation(s). Magic(al). Mystic(al,ism,s). Necromancy. Obe. Obeah. Possession trance(s). Ritual killing(s). Satan(ism). Secret divination. Sorcer(y,ers). Spirit possession. Supernatural(ism). Thaumaturgy. Warlock(s). Werewol(f,ves). Wicca. Wizard(s,ry). *See also* Cults; Demons; Devils; Evil; Evil eye; Fairies; Fetishism; Folk literature; Folklore; Ghosts; Good spirits; Magic; Occultism; Parapsychology; Spirit possession; Spiritual healing; Supernatural; Witches.

Witchcraft trials. Witchcraft trial(s). Sorcery trial(s). *Choose from:* witchcraft, sorcer(y,er,ers), witch(es), demonic possession *with:* trial(s), prosecut(e,ed, ing,ion,ions), tribunal(s), accus(e,ed,ing, ation,ations), witness(ed,ing,es), testified against. *Consider also:* witch(es,craft) *with:* execut(e,ed,ing,ion,ions) hunt(s), confession(s), lynch(ed,ing,ings). *See also* Exorcism; Heresy; Misogyny; Persecution; Scapegoating; Witch hunting.

Witches. Witch(es). Sorceress(es). Hecate(an). *Consider also:* wicca, coven(s), crone(s). *See also* Witchcraft.

Witching, water. See *Divining rod.*

Withdrawal (defense mechanism). Withdraw(al,n,ing). *Consider also:* disengag(e,ed,ing,ement), avoid(ed,ing, ance), retract(ed,ing), retir(e,ed,ing), detach(ed,ing,ment), distanc(e,ed,ing), runaway behavior, retreat(ed,ing), turn(ed,ing) away, preoccup(y,ied,ation, ations), disinterested, aloof(ness). *Consider also:* elective mutism, autis(m,tic). *See also* Autism; Defense mechanisms; Introversion; Social isolation; Student dropouts.

Withdrawal, drug. See *Drug withdrawal.*

Withdrawal, social. See *Autism; Introversion; Social isolation; Withdrawal (defense mechanism).*

Withdrawal delirium, alcohol. See *Alcohol withdrawal delirium.*

Withdrawal syndrome, substance. See *Substance withdrawal syndrome.*

Withholding, treatment. See *Treatment withholding.*

Withholding evidence. Withhold(ing) evidence. Withheld evidence. *Choose from:* withhold(ing), withheld, fail(ed,ing,ure) to disclose, omit(ted, ting) to disclose, stifl(e,ed,ing), destroy(ed,ing), destruction *with:* evidence, document(s), record(s), information. *Consider also:* suppress(ed, ing,ion) of evidence. *See also* Affidavit; Contempt of Court; Corruption in government; Circumstantial evidence; Deposition; Evidence; Fair trial; Government secrecy; Justice; Legal procedures; Obstruction of justice; Sufficient evidence; Trial (law); Truth disclosure; Unethical conduct; Witness tampering; Witnesses.

Witness tampering. Witness tampering. *Choose from:* witness(es) *with:* tamper(ed,ing), meddl(e,ed,ing), interfer(e,ed,ing,ence), promise(s), threat(s,en,ened,ening), persuad(e,ed, ing), persuasion(s), entreat(y,ies), bribe(s,ry), corrupt(ed,ing,ion). *See also* Affidavit; Bribery; Corruption in government; Deposition: Obstruction of justice; Testimony; Unethical conduct; Withholding evidence; Witnesses.

Witnesses. Witness(ed,es,ing). Eyewitness(es). Observer(s). Onlooker(s). Spectator(s). Viewer(s). Surveillant(s). Bystander(s). Participant observer(s). Watcher(s). Lineup identification. Testimonial(s). Child(ren's) testimony. Expert testimony. Testifier(s). Deponent(s). Beholder(s). Hearsay. *See also* Affidavit; Circumstantial evidence; Cross examination; Defendants; Deposition; Evidence; Expert testimony; Positive evidence; Testimony; Trial (law); Withholding evidence; Witness tampering.

Witnesses, Jehovah's. See *Jehovah's Witnesses.*

Wives. Wives. Wife. Bride(s). Housewife. Housewives. Cowives. Coverture. *Choose from:* married, spouse(s) *with:* woman, women, female(s), mother(s). *See also* Homemakers; Husbands; Marital relationship; Mothers; Spouse abuse; Spouses.

Wives, executives'. See *Corporate spouses.*

Wives, farmers'. See *Rural women.*

Wolves. Wolves. Wolf. Canis lupus. Canis rufus. Timber wol(f,ves). Gray wol(f,ves). Red wol(f,ves). Arctic wol(f,ves). Holarctic wol(f,ves). *Consider also:* coyote(s), jackal(s). *See also* Animals; Coyotes; Predatory animals; Wild animals; Wildlife conservation.

Woman. See *Females (human)*.

Woman, ideal. See *Idealization of women*.

Woman suffrage. See *Suffrage; Suffrage movement; Voting rights; Women's rights*.

Woman's role. See *Gender identity; Sex roles*.

Womanism. Womanis(m,t,ts,h). *Consider also:* Black, Africana, Afrikana, of color *with:* womanis(m,t,ts), feminis(m,t,ts). *See also* Blacks; Black family; Feminism; People of color.

Womanizers. Womanizer(s). Woman chas(er,ers,ing). Philander(er,ers,ing). Lecher(s,ous,ousness). Gigolo(s). Rapper(s). Hustler(s). Casanova(s). Don Juan(s). Lothario(s). Bluebeard(s). Sex addict(s,ion). *See also* Philanderers; Verbal abuse.

Women. See *Females (human)*.

Women, battered. See *Battered women*.

Women, career. See *Dual career families; Professional women; Working women*.

Women, churching of. See *Churching of women*.

Women, employed. See *Dual career families; Professional women; Working women*.

Women, equal rights for. See *Women's rights*.

Women, farm. See *Rural women*.

Women, fear of. See *Fear of women*.

Women, holy. See *Holy women*.

Women, idealization of. See *Idealization of women*.

Women, images of. See *Images of women*.

Women, market. See *Street vendors; Women merchants*.

Women, married. See *Wives*.

Women, pauperization of. See *Women living in poverty*.

Women, professional. See *Professional women*.

Women, reentry. See *Reentry women*.

Women, rural. See *Rural women*.

Women, single. See *Single person; Unmarried women*.

Women, status of. See *Women's rights*.

Women, trafficking of. See *Sex industry; Trafficking in persons*.

Women, unmarried. See *Unmarried women*.

Women, working. See *Working women*.

Women criminals. See *Female offenders*.

Women in male dominated occupations. See *Nontraditional careers*.

Women living in poverty. Women living in poverty. Pauperization of women. Feminization of poverty. Welfare famil(y,ies). *Choose from:* female(s), wom(en,an), mother(s), maternal, feminine, feminiz(e,ed,ing,ation) *with:* poverty, poor, indigen(t,ce,cy), low income(s), unemploy(ed,ment), underemploy(ed,ment), impoverish(ed, ment), disadvantage(d,ment), homeless(ness), destitut(e,ion), pauper(s,ize, ized,izing,ization), vagran(t,ts,cy), low status, low socioeconomic status, economic(ally) need(y,iness), hardship(s), economic(ally) insecur(e,ity). *Consider also:* fatherless famil(y,ies). *See also* Battered women; Cheap labor; Disadvantaged; Hardships; Home economics; Homeless; Labor market segmentation; Low income; Poverty; Sex discrimination; Sexism; Sexual inequality; Sexual oppression; Single parent family; Wage differentials.

Women merchants. Women merchant(s). Market wom(en,an). Women traders. *Choose from:* wom(en,an), female(s) *with:* merchant(s), trader(s), commercial enterprise(s), entrepreneur(s), food seller(s), vendor(s). *See also* Merchants; Street vendors; Women owned businesses.

Women of color. See *People of color*.

Women owned businesses. Women owned business(es). *Choose from:* women, woman, female(s) *with:* entrepreneur(s, ship). *Choose from:* women, woman, female(s) *with:* own(ed,ing,er,ers, ership), head(s,ed,ing), president(s), proprietor(s,ship,ships) *with:* business(es), enterprise(s), firm(s), compan(y,ies), corporation(s), factor(y,ies), industr(y,ies), retail(er,ers), production, operation(s), store(s), shop(s). *Consider also:* microenterprise(s). *See also* Beauty shops; Entrepreneurship; Family businesses; Home based businesses; Microenterprise; Minority businesses; Professional women; Self employment; Small businesses; Working women; Women merchants.

Women religious. Women religious. Priestess(es). Nun(s). Clergywom(an, en). *See also* Female spirituality; Holy women; Nuns; Religious life;.Religious personnel.

Women's groups. Women(s) group(s). Suffragette(s). Sororit(y,ies). Sisterhood(s). *Choose from:* women(s), woman(s), feminis(t,m), lesbian, wives, mothers *with:* group(s), club(s), union(s), league(s), council(s),

committee(s), congress(es), alliance(s), auxiliar(y,ies), organization(s), association(s), movement(s). *Consider also:* National Organization for Women, Women's Health Network, La Leche League, League of Women Voters. *See also* Females (human); Feminism; Groups; Interest groups; Self help groups; Suffrage movement; Women's rights.

Women's liberation. See *Women's rights*.

Women's movement. See *Feminism; Political movements; Social movements; Suffrage movement; Women's groups; Women's rights*.

Women's rights. Women(s) rights. Women(s) movement. Women(s) liberation. Feminis(m,t,ts). Sexual equality. Title IX. Equal Rights Amendment. Affirmative action. Comparable worth. Sex Discrimination Act of 1975. Maternal rights. Neofeminist(s). Profeminist(s). Nineteenth Amendment. Womens Educational Equity Act. *Choose from:* women(s), woman(s), female(s), girl(s), sex, gender, mother(s), wives, daughter(s), lesbian(s) *with:* rights, movement, liberation, equality, equal rights, equal protection, consciousness raising, affirmative action, status, stereotype(s), bias, civil rights, discrimination, equity, comparable worth, fair(ness), inequit(y,ies), prejudice(s), equal pay, exploit(ed,ing,ation), equal employment opportunities. *Consider also:* abortion rights, freedom of choice, reproductive freedom. *See also* Abortion laws; Affirmative action; Civil rights; Comparable worth; Females (human); Feminism; Gender differences; Human rights; Men's movement; Nonsexist language; Ombudsmen; Reproductive rights; Sex role attitudes; Sexism; Social equality; Social equity; Social movements; Suffrage; Suffrage movement; Women's groups.

Women's role. See *Gender identity; Sex roles*.

Women's work. See *Family roles; Labor market segmentation; Sex roles; Sexual division of labor*.

Wood carving. See *Carving (decorative arts)*.

Wood industry. See *Lumber industry*.

Woodcutters. See *Lumbermen*.

Woodlands. See *Forestry*.

Wool industry. Wool industry. *Choose from:* wool(s,en,ens), shearless wool, fleece(s), yak hair, camel's hair, mohair, cashmere, boucle, sheep, knitting yarn(s), sweater(s) *with:* industry, trade, product(s,ion), producer(s), produc(e,ed, ing), farmer(s), grower(s), harvest(s,ed, ing), mill(s), market(s), manufacturer(s), export(s), price(s). *See also* Animal products; Fabrics; Sheep; Textile industry; Weaving.

Wool trade. See *Wool industry.*

Word association. Word association(s). *Consider also:* word(s), verbal, synonym(s), adjective(s), noun(s), keyword(s) *with:* association(s), associat(e,ed,ive), related, paired associate(s). *See also* Cognitive processes; Paired associate learning.

Word blindness. See *Alexia.*

Word deafness. Word deafness. Auditory aphasia. *See also* Aphasia.

Word frequency. Word frequenc(y,ies). *Choose from:* word(s), noun(s), adjective(s), verb(s), adverb(s), pronoun(s), synonym(s), antonym(s), epithet(s), lexical, name(s), term(s) *with:* frequenc(y,ies), frequently used, occurrence(s). *See also* Language.

Word games. Word game(s). Language game(s). *Choose from:* word(s), linguistic, language *with:* game(s). *Consider also:* acrostic(s), crossword puzzle(s), anagram(s), Scrabble, brain twister(s), word puzzle(s). *See also* Anagrams; Anagram problem solving; Entertainment; Hobbies; Literary recreations; Problem solving; Puns; Word play.

Word history. See *Etymology.*

Word meaning. Word meaning(s). Semantic(s). Lexical meaning(s). *Choose from:* word(s), term(s), noun(s), verb(s), pronoun(s), adjective(s), adverb(s) *with:* definition(s), connotat(ive,ion,ions), denotat(ive,ion, ions), sense(s), significance, signif(y, ying,ied,ication), acceptation. *See also* Definition (words); Language.

Word play. Word play. Pun(s,ning). Riddle(s). Verbal play. *See also* Entertainment; Hobbies; Puns; Word games.

Word recognition. Word recognition. *Choose from:* word(s), term(s), lexical *with:* recogni(tion,ize,ized,izing), identif(y,ied,ying,ication), process(ed, ing), comprehen(d,ded,ding,sion). *See also* Reading skills; Speech perception; Words.

Words. Word(s,ing). Phonetic unit(s). *Consider also:* homophone(s), grapheme(s), noun(s), verb(s,al,iage), adjective(s), adverb(s), pronoun(s), name(s), heteronym(s), synonym(s), antonym(s), polyphone(s), term(s), morpheme(s), etymon(s), verbal symbol(s), loanword(s), password(s). *See also* Affixes; Antonyms; Etymology; Grammar; Homonyms; Language; Neologisms; Semantics; Vocabulary; Vowels; Word recognition.

Words, last. See *Last words.*

Words, loan. See *Loan words.*

Work. Work(ed,ing). Toil(ed,ing). Labor(ed,ing). Exert(ed,ing,ion). Effort(s). Endeavor(s). Strain(ed,ing). Work load. Workload. Physical work(ing). Drudgery. Slav(e,ed,ing,ery). Handwork. Piecework. Housework. Spadework. *Consider also:* efficiency, industrious(ness), diligence. *See also* Alternative work patterns; Attitudes toward work; Diligence; Employment; Family work relationship; Housekeeping; Job performance; Job requirements; Labor force; Labor process; Occupational aspirations; Occupational classification; Occupational structure; Quality of working life; Specialization; Tasks; Teamwork; Work experience; Work groups; Work humanization; Work load; Work rest cycles; Work schedules; Work simplification; Work skills; Work values; Workday shifts; Worker control; Worker participation; Workers; Working conditions.

Work, attitudes toward. See *Attitudes toward work.*

Work, evangelistic. See *Evangelistic work.*

Work, family relationship. See *Family work relationship.*

Work, fancy. See *Fancy work.*

Work, farming out. See *Contracting out.*

Work, group. See *Group work.*

Work, journey to. See *Commuting (travel).*

Work, overtime. See *Overtime work.*

Work, part time. See *Part time employment.*

Work, psychiatric social. See *Psychiatric social work.*

Work, right to. See *Right to work.*

Work, shared. See *Alternative work patterns.*

Work, shift. See *Workday shifts.*

Work, social. See *Social work.*

Work, travel to. See *Commuting (travel).*

Work, women's. See *Family roles; Labor market segmentation; Sex roles; Sexual division of labor.*

Work and family life, balancing. See *Dual career families; Family work relationship; Working women.*

Work at home. See *Home based businesses.*

Work attitudes. See *Attitudes toward work; Employee attitudes.*

Work design. See *Job design.*

Work environment. See *Organizational climate; Organizational culture; Working conditions.*

Work ethic. See *Protestant ethic.*

Work experience. Work experience. Years worked. Years of experience. Seniority. Career stage(s). Length of service. Level of job skills. *Choose from:* work(er), job(s), employee(s), professional, employment, clerical, nonprofessional, preprofessional, manager(ial,s), staff *with:* experience, years, background, senior(ity), inexperienced, novice, qualifications, history, beginning, entry level, veteran(s), longevity. *See also* Apprenticeship; Attitudes toward work; Career patterns; Employability; Employment history; Job requirements; Occupational qualifications; Work; Work reentry.

Work family relationship. See *Family work relationship.*

Work force. See *Labor force.*

Work groups. Work group(s). Workgroup(s). Quality circle(s). *Choose from:* work(er,ers) *with:* group(s), team(s), unit(s), crew(s), gang(s), brigade(s), division(s), subgroup(s), subunit(s). *Consider also:* teamwork. *See also* Group dynamics; Human relations training; Social loafing; Work; Work humanization.

Work hazards. See *Agricultural workers disease; Black lung disease; Hazardous materials; Hazards of video display terminals; Industrial accidents; Multiple chemical sensitivities; Occupational diseases; Occupational exposure; Occupational neuroses; Occupational safety; Occupational stress; Repetitive motion disorders; Sick building syndrome.*

Work history. See *Employment history; Work experience.*

Work hours. See *Alternative work patterns; Personnel scheduling; Work load; Work schedules; Workday shifts; Worktime.*

Work humanization. Work humanization. Humaniz(e,ed,ing,ation) work. *Choose from:* work(ing,er,ers), job(s), task(s), labor, employee(s) *with:* humaniz(e,ed, ing,ation), meaningful(ness), purposeful(ness), empower(ed,ing, ment), human dimension, rehumaniz(e, ed,ing,ation), theory Y, theory Z, self actualiz(e,ed,ing,ation), humanis(m,tic), human factor(s). *Consider also:* ergonomics. *See also* Attitudes toward work; Employee assistance programs; Human relations training; Humanization; Job satisfaction; Labor process; Quality of working life; Work; Work groups; Working conditions.

Work load. Work load(s). Workload(s). Caseload(s). *Choose from:* work(ing), teaching, job, case, faculty, task(s) *with:* load(s), assignment(s), assigned, hours, overload, schedule(s,d). *See also*

Alternative work patterns; Backlog; Course load; Division of labor; Job descriptions; Job performance; Overtime work; Personnel scheduling; Workday shifts; Work schedules; Working conditions; Worktime.

Work measurement. Work measurement. *Choose from:* work, output, productivity, performance, operations *with:* measur(e,es,ement,ements,ing), test(s,ing), criteria, assess(ed,ing,ment, ments), monitor(s,ed,ing), evaluat(e,ed, ing,ion,ions). *Consider also:* quality control, quality circle(s), supervis(e,ed, ing,ion). *See also* Measurement; Work.

Work orientations. See *Attitudes toward work; Occupational adjustment; Professional orientations.*

Work patterns, alternative. See *Alternative work patterns.*

Work qualifications. See *Occupational qualification(s).*

Work reentry. Work reentry. Work re-entry. *Choose from:* return(ed,ing,s), reenter(ed,ing,s), re-enter(ed,ing), re-entran(t,ts,ce), reentran(t,ts,ce), restart(s,ing) *with:* work, workplace(s), workforce, labor force, labor market, job market, employment. *Consider also:* updat(e,es,ed,ing) job skill(s). *See also* Career breaks; Displaced homemakers; Reentry women; Retraining; Skills obsolescence; Work.

Work relief. Work relief. *Choose from:* welfare, public assistance, dole, food stamp(s), antipoverty program(s), entitlement program(s), unemployment compensation, unemployment benefit(s), Aid to Families with Dependent Children [AFDC], Supplemental Security Income [SSI] *with:* job(s), employ(ed,ing,ment), work incentive(s), work(ed,ing), training. *Consider also:* workhouse(s). *See also* Unemployment relief; Workfare; Welfare reform.

Work requirements. See *Job requirements.*

Work rest cycles. Work rest cycle(s). *Choose from:* work(ing), labor *with:* rest(ing), leisure *with:* period(s), cycle(s). *Consider also:* coffee break(s), pac(ed,ing) work, work break(s), flextime, work(ing) schedule(s), work shift(s), sabbatical(s). *See also* Work; Work schedules; Working conditions.

Work roles. See *Occupational role(s).*

Work safety. See *Occupational safety.*

Work satisfaction. See *Job satisfaction.*

Work schedules. Work schedules. *Choose from:* work, task(s), dut(y,ies), job(s), personnel, employee(s), labor *with:* schedul(e,es,ed,ing), rotat(e,ed,ing), cycle(s), shift(s), hour(s), timing, pac(e,ed,ing), time allocat(ed,ion,ions). *Consider also:* flextime, flexitime. *See*

also Alternative work patterns; Overtime work; Personnel scheduling; School schedules; Work load; Work rest cycles; Workday shifts; Worktime.

Work schedules, flexible. See *Alternative work patterns; Personnel scheduling; Work load; Work schedules; Workday shifts; Worktime.*

Work sharing. Work sharing. Worksharing. *Choose from:* work, job(s), position(s), staff line(s), appointment(s), dut(y,ies), responsibilit(y,ies), schedule(s) *with:* shar(e,ed,ing), split(ting). *Consider also:* work time reduction(s), shorten(ed,ing) hours, part-time work, phased retirement. *See also* Alternative work patterns; Job sharing; Part time employment; Temporary employees.

Work simplification. Work simplification. *Choose from:* job(s), task(s), work, duties, function(s), process(es) *with:* simplif(y,ied,ication), redesign(ed,ing), restructur(ed,ing). *Consider also:* Taylorism, Fordism, de-skill(ed,ing), scientific management. *See also* Automation; Cost effectiveness; Job design; Job evaluation; Productivity.

Work skills. Work skill(s). Employee(s) skill(s). Vocational skill(s). Job skill(s). *Choose from:* employee(s), vocational, job(s), marketable, technical, clerical, labor, professional, teaching, work, operator, occupational, white collar, blue collar, secretarial, business, managerial, agricultural, business, manpower, computer *with:* skill(ed,s), abilit(y,ies), competenc(e,y,ies), knowledge, familiar(ity), experience(d), capabilit(y, ies), capacit(y,ies). *Consider also:* employability, job obsolescence, manpower development. *See also* Employability; Employment; Executive ability; Job knowledge; Job requirements; Labor market; Managerial skills; Occupational classification; Occupational qualifications; Occupational status; Skill; Underemployment; Upskilling; Work; Workers.

Work songs. Work song(s). Worksong(s). Arbeitslied(er). *Choose from:* work(ing), rowing, labor, prison(er,ers), train(s), fishing, spinning, quilting, camp, wobbl(y,ies) *with:* worksong(s), song(s), lyric(s), ballad(s), melod(y,ies), tune(s), chant(s), shant(y,ies), ditt(y,ies), refrain(s), chorus(es). *Consider also:* slave(ry) song(s). *See also* Folk songs; Part songs; Sea songs; Songs.

Work space. See *Working space.*

Work stoppages. See *Strikes.*

Work tasks. See *Tasks.*

Work values. Work values. Work ethic. *Choose from:* value(s), ethic(s), meaning(ful,s), commitment, importance, involvement, belief(s), interest, expectations, motivation, myth(s),

ideolog(y,ies), ideal(s), aspiration(s) *with:* work(ing), career(s), job(s), employment, employee(s), staff, worker(s), profession(s,al), occupation(s,al), vocation(s,al). *Consider also:* attitude(s) toward work, workahol(ism,ic), work satisfaction. *See also* Attitudes toward work; Job satisfaction; Occupational aspirations; Professional orientations; Professionalism; Protestant ethic; Work.

Work week. See *Worktime.*

Workbooks. See *Teaching materials; Textbooks; Texts.*

Workday shifts. Workday shift(s). Shiftwork. Flexshift(s). Rotating work schedule(s). Nightshift(s). *Choose from:* workday, day, night, evening, work(ed, ing), schedule(s), rotat(e,ed,ing,ion), swing *with:* shift(s). *See also* Alternative work schedules; Daytime; Overtime work; Personnel scheduling; Work load; Work schedules; Working conditions; Worktime.

Worker attitudes. See *Employee attitudes.*

Worker consciousness. Worker consciousness. *Choose from:* working class, worker(s), proletaria(t,n), crafts(men,man,women,woman), millworker(s), labor(ers), employee(s) *with:* awareness, perception(s), consciousness, solidarity, sensitiz(e,ed,ing, ation). *See also* Class consciousness; Class politics; Labor movements; Social consciousness; Working class; Workers.

Worker control. Worker control. Democratic work organization. Industrial self management. Autonomous work group(s). Self managed firm(s). Workplace democracy. *Choose from:* employee(s), worker(s) *with:* self manage(d,ment), participation, cooperative(s), control, ownership. *Consider also:* worker capitalists, profit sharing, gainsharing, industrial democra(cy,tize,tized,tizing,tization), participatory decision making, democratic workplace, participation team(s), power sharing, managing cooperatively, codetermination, worker managed, humanistic management, workplace participation, participative team(s), theory Z, participative ownership, employee ownership, employee stock ownership, kibbutz(im), mondragon, syndicalism. *See also* Control; Employee ownership; Employee stock ownership plans; Industrial democracy; Power sharing; Worker participation.

Worker machine systems. See *Man machine systems.*

Worker ownership. See *Employee ownership.*

Worker participation. Worker participation. Participat(ive,ory) management. Participative decision making. Team management. *Choose from:* employee(s), worker(s), labor, worksite, shopfloor, workplace *with:* involvement, participat(ory,ive,ion), cooperative(s), consultat(ive,ions), ownership, self management, represent(ed,ing,ation), democra(tic,cy), egalitarian(ism). *Consider also:* works council(s), works committee(s), quality circle(s), profit sharing, gainsharing, industrial democra(cy,tization), participatory decision making, democratic workplace, participation team(s), power sharing, managing cooperatively, codetermination, worker managed, humanistic management, workplace participation, participative team(s), theory Z, participative ownership, economic democracy. *See also* Employee stock ownership plans; Industrial democracy; Labor management committees; Participation; Participative decision making; Participative management; Power sharing; Worker control.

Worker training. See *Personnel training.*

Workers. Worker(s). Apprentice(s). Cadre(s). Child labor. Coworker(s). Crew(s). Employee(s). Functionar(y,ies). Hired help. Human resource(s). Labor force. Labor supply. Laborer(s). Manpower. Nonprofessional(s). Occupational group(s). Office force. Operator(s). Proletaria(n,t). Personnel. Practitioner(s). Paraprofessional(s). Professional(s). Sales force. Staff. Subordinates. Troop(s). Wage earner(s). Working class. Workforce. Work force. Workm(en,an). Breadwinner(s). *Choose from:* employed, civil service, working, hired *with:* woman, women, men, man, people, group(s), males, female(s), person(s), civilian(s). *Consider also:* air traffic controller(s), accountant(s), attorney(s), administrator(s), agricultural personnel, artisan(s), autoworker(s), baker(s), barber(s), bricklayer(s), butcher(s), blue collar worker(s), bookkeeper(s), carpenter(s), cabinetmaker(s), caseworker(s), church worker(s), civil servant(s), caregiver(s), clerk(s), clergy, consultant(s), computer programmer(s), crafts(man,men, women,woman), craftsperson(s), craftspeople, designer(s), driver(s), director(s), domestic servant(s), editor(s), engineer(s), electrician(s), faculty, farmworker(s), firefighter(s), glassworker(s), guard(s), government employee(s), health personnel, hairdresser(s), home economist(s), journey(men,man), librarian(s), machine operator(s), mason(s), mechanic(s), military personnel, nurse(s), pink collar worker(s), pipefitter(s), plumber(s), police officer(s), photographer(s), pilot(s), programmer(s), press(men, man), sales(men,man,women,woman), salespeople, salesperson(s), secretar(y,ies), shipbuilder(s), steam fitter(s), stevedore(s), teacher(s), technician(s), trainer(s), truck driver(s), typist(s), waiter(s), waitperson(s), waitress(es), white collar worker(s), etc. *See also* Agricultural workers; Attitudes toward work; Beauty operators; Blue collar workers; Cheap labor; Child labor; Civil service; Clerical workers; Clothing workers; Construction workers; Craft workers; Disabled workers; Discouraged workers; Dislocated workers; Displaced homemakers; Electronics industry workers; Employee assistance programs; Employee ownership; Employees; Employment; Enterprises; Foreign workers; Government personnel; Health manpower; Homemakers; Human resources; Industrial workers; Job performance; Job satisfaction; Journalists; Labor disputes; Labor force; Labor management relations; Labor market; Labor movements; Labor policy; Labor supply; Labor unions; Lumbermen; Man machine systems; Migrant workers; Occupational roles; Occupational structure; Occupational tenure; Occupations; Pensions; Personnel management; Professional personnel; Quality of working life; Retirement; Seniority; Skilled workers; Supervision; Temporary employees; Unskilled workers; Wages; Work; Work skills; Worker consciousness; Workers' rights; Working class; White collar workers; Working women.

Workers, agricultural. See *Agricultural workers.*

Workers, automobile industry. See *Automobile industry workers.*

Workers, blue collar. See *Blue collar workers.*

Workers, clerical. See *Clerical workers.*

Workers, clothing. See *Clothing workers.*

Workers, construction. See *Construction workers.*

Workers, contingent. See *Temporary employees.*

Workers, contract. See *Independent contractors.*

Workers, craft. See *Craft workers.*

Workers, disabled. See *Disabled workers.*

Workers, discouraged. See *Discouraged workers.*

Workers disease, agricultural. See *Agricultural workers disease.*

Workers, dislocated. See *Dislocated workers.*

Workers, displaced. See *Dislocated workers.*

Workers, dock. See *Longshoremen.*

Workers, electronics industry. See *Electronics industry workers.*

Workers, factory. See *Industrial workers.*

Workers, farm. See *Agricultural workers.*

Workers, fishery. See *Fishery workers.*

Workers, foreign. See *Foreign workers.*

Workers, gold collar. See *Gold collar workers.*

Workers, government. See *Civil service; Government personnel.*

Workers, guest. See *Foreign workers.*

Workers, health care. See *Health manpower.*

Workers, industrial. See *Industrial workers.*

Workers, iron and steel. See *Iron and steel workers.*

Workers, knowledge. See *Knowledge workers.*

Workers, manual. See *Blue collar workers.*

Workers, migrant. See *Migrant workers.*

Workers, migratory. See *Migrant workers.*

Workers, office. See *Clerical workers; White collar workers.*

Workers, pink collar. See *Clerical workers.*

Workers, portfolio. See *Contract labor.*

Workers, professional. See *Professional personnel; Professional women.*

Workers, psychiatric social. See *Psychiatric social workers.*

Workers, regional labor. See *Migrant workers.*

Workers, seasonal. See *Migrant workers; Temporary employees.*

Workers, semi-skilled. See *Blue collar workers.*

Workers, skilled. See *Skilled workers.*

Workers, social. See *Social workers.*

Workers, textile. See *Textile workers.*

Workers, transient. See *Migrant workers; Temporary employees.*

Workers, transport. See *Transport workers.*

Workers, unskilled. See *Unskilled workers.*

Workers, white collar. See *White collar workers.*

Worker's rights. Worker(s) right(s). *Choose from:* worker(s), labor, employee(s) *with:* right(s), freedom(s). *Consider also:* freedom of association, freedom from discrimination, freedom from child labor, freedom from forced labor, International Labor Organization convention(s), Universal Declaration of Human Rights. *See also* Cheap labor; Child labor; Exploitation; Forced labor; Labor movements; Labor policy; Labor unions; Minimum wage; Sweatshops;

Unpaid labor; Wages; Workers; Working conditions.

Workfare. Workfare. Wage stop. *Choose from:* welfare recipient(s) *with:* work(ing), employ(ed,ment). *See also* Work relief; Welfare reform.

Workforce, itinerant. See *Migrant workers.*

Workforce planning. Workforce planning. *Choose from:* workforce, human resources, labor force, employee(s), qualified worker(s), skilled worker(s), unskilled laborer(s), staff, personnel, unemployment *with:* forecasting need(s), plan(ned,ning), implementing diversity, supply and demand, oversupply, shortage(s). *Consider also:* Workforce 2000, Workforce 2020. *See also* Attrition; Business cycles; Demographic changes; Economic development; Employment forecasting; Employment opportunities; Employment trends; Future; Future of society; Labor economics; Labor supply; Personnel management; Seasonal unemployment; Unemployment.

Working class. Working class. Proletar(iat, ian). Laborer(s). Laboring class(es). Lower class(es). Low(er,est) socioeconomic. Peasant(s). Working man. Low(er,est) status. Low(er,est) status. Blue collar. Plebeian. Common people. Common man. Manual labor(ers). Wage earner(s). Wage labor(ers). Working poor. Campesino(s). Subordinate class(es). Underclass. Factory worker(s). *Consider also:* middle class. *See also* Blue collar workers; Capitalist societies; Class politics; Embourgeoisement; Employees; Industrial workers; Labor force; Labor movements; Labor supply; Lower class; Marxism; Masses; Middle class; Migrant workers; Peasants; Proletarianization; Proletariat; Skilled workers; Social class; Unskilled workers; White collar workers; Workers.

Working conditions. Work(ing,place,site) condition(s). Work life. Work rest cycle(s). Organizational climate. Hawthorne effect. Worker eyestrain. Working underground. Work week length. Workday shift(s). Sweatshop(s). *Choose from:* work(ing,ers), employ(ees,ment), work(life,shop, place,site), shopfloor, job(s), office(s), occupation(al), factor(y,ies) *with:* conditions, climate, environment(s,al), setting(s), safety, design, exposure, ergonomic(s,ally), humaniz(e,ed,ing, ation), hazard(ous,s), danger(ous,s), noise, context, space, stress(ed,or,ors, ing), life, comfort, discomfort, quality, design, enrichment, culture, burnout, risk(s). *See also* Agricultural workers disease; Corporate social responsibility; Ergonomics; Hazardous occupations; Industrial engineering; Industrial fatigue; Job descriptions; Job enrichment; Job performance; Job satisfaction;

Labor management relations; Labor laws; Labor standards; Living conditions; Man machine systems; Management methods; Noise levels (work areas); Occupational diseases; Occupational exposure; Occupational safety; Occupational stress; Organizational climate; Organizational culture; Overtime work; Personnel management; Personnel policy; Professional isolation; Quality of working life; Sick building syndrome; Superior subordinate relationship; Sweatshops; Work; Work humanization; Work load; Work rest cycles; Work schedules; Work simplification; Workday shifts; Worker control; Worker participation; Workers' rights; Working space; Workplaces; Worktime.

Working day. See *Alternative work patterns; Personnel scheduling; Work load; Work schedules; Workday shifts; Working conditions; Worktime.*

Working hours. See *Alternative work patterns; Personnel scheduling; Work load; Work schedules; Workday shifts; Working conditions; Worktime.*

Working life, length of. See *Length of working life.*

Working life, quality of. See *Quality of working life.*

Working mothers. See *Dual career families; Family work relationship; Female headed households; Professional women; Working women.*

Working space. Working space(s). Workspace(s). *Consider also:* office(s), work(ing), workstation(s), workplace(s) *with:* space(s), spatial, area(s), room(s), arrangement(s), design(s,ed), layout, setting(s), dimension(s), environment, placement, use pattern(s), traffic flow(s), structure(s), landscaping. *See also* Spatial behavior; Working conditions.

Working women. Working wom(en,an). *Choose from:* wom(en,an), female(s), mother(s,hood), maternal, wife, wives, childbirth, fertility, pregnan(t,cy,cies) *with:* employ(ed,ees,ment), work(ed,ing, ment), career(s), labor force, work force, occupation(s,al), wage earn(er,ers,ing), entrepreneur(s,ial), vocation(s,al), profession(s,al), job(s). *Consider also:* mommy track(s), maternity leave(s). *See also* Affirmative action; Alternative work patterns; Comparable worth; Displaced homemakers; Dual career families; Dual economy; Egalitarian families; Employment; Equal education; Equal job opportunities; Equity (payment); Family work relationship; Female headed households; Female intensive occupations; Females (human); Feminism; Home based businesses; House husbands; Income inequality; Labor force; Labor market segmentation; Nontraditional careers; Occupational roles; Occupational segregation;

Occupational status; Professional women; Rural women; Sex role attitudes; Sex roles; Sexual division of labor; Shared parenting; Single parent family; Wage differentials; Work reentry; Workers; Women living in poverty; Women's rights.

Workingmen's associations. See *Guilds; Labor unions.*

Workload. See *Work load.*

Workmen. See *Workers.*

Workmens compensation. Workmens compensation. *Choose from:* worker(s), workmen(s) *with:* compensation. *Consider also:* compensation *with:* disabled worker(s), injured worker(s), disability insurance, work injur(y,ies). *See also* Employee benefits; Financial support; Health insurance; Insurance; Unemployment relief.

Workouts. See *Exercise.*

Workplace effects of technology. See *Labor aspects of technology.*

Workplace practices, flexible. See *Flexible workplace practices.*

Workplaces. Workplace(s). Worksite(s). Work(ing) environment(s). Work situation. Office(s). Workshop(s), Shopfloor. Factor(y,ies). Work setting(s). Industrial setting(s). Electronic cottage(s). Assembly line(s). Mill(s). Foundr(y,ies). Plant(s). Laborator(y,ies). Stockyard(s). Shipyard(s). *See also* Commuting (travel); Enterprises; Factories; Home based businesses; Occupational safety; Office buildings; Sheltered workshops; Place of business; Work; Working conditions.

Workplaces, home. See *Home based businesses.*

Works, good theology. See *Good works (theology).*

Works, public. See *Public works.*

Works, textless vocal. See *Textless vocal works.*

Works of art, lost. See *Lost works of art.*

Works of music, lost. See *Lost works of music.*

Workshops, sheltered. See *Sheltered workshops.*

Workstations. Workstation(s). Workspace(s). Desk(s). Cubicle(s). Office(s). Lagoon(s). Hotdesk(s,ing). Locker(s). *Consider also:* desktop(s), Sun workstation(s). *See also* Desktop publishing; Ergonomics.

Worktime. Work(time,day,week,load). Work week length. Workday(s). Work(ing) hours. Worklife scheduling. *Choose from:* work(ing) *with:* week(s), hour(s), schedul(e,es,ing), load(s), patterns. 39 hour week. 40 hour week.

37 1/2 hour week. Office hours. Four day week. *Consider also:* work sharing, job sharing, flextime, flex-time, flexitime, flexible working hours, maximum hours worked, overtime, part time work, full time work. *See also* Alternative work patterns; Part time employment; Personnel scheduling; Work load; Work schedules; Workday shifts; Working conditions.

Workweek, compressed. See *Alternative work patterns.*

World, borderless. See *Globalization.*

World, external philosophy. See *External world (philosophy).*

World, fifth. See *Labor market segmentation; Sex discrimination; Sexual division of labor; Sexual inequality.*

World, first. See *Developed countries.*

World, fourth. See *Least developed countries.*

World, life. See *Everyday life.*

World, one. See *Globalization.*

World, third. See *Developing countries.*

World, western. See *Western civilization; Western society.*

World as a stage. See *Theatrum Mundi.*

World citizenship. World citizen(s,ship). Citizen(s) of the world. World community. *Consider also:* globecentrism, global village, United Nations Charter, Universal Declaration of Human Rights, Nuremberg Principles, Bills of Rights, etc. *See also* Citizenship education; Curriculum change; Deep ecology; Cross cultural competency; Deterritorialization; Globalization; Information highway; Information society; Interdependence; International education; International law; Internationalism; Multicultural education; Pantheism (universal divinity); Social ethics; Universalism; World health; World population; World problems; World systems theory.

World economy. World economy. *Choose from:* world, supranational, international, multinational, transnational, global, worldwide, universal, cross-national, United Nations *with:* econom(ic,y,ies), depression(s), inflation(s), stock market(s), currenc(y, ies), monetary, interest rate(s), debt(s), business cycle(s), business condition(s), trade, financial, macroeconomics. *See also* Agricultural colonies; Center and periphery; Colonialism; Common currency; Common markets; Dependency theory (international); Economic assistance; Economic competition; Economic conditions; Economic dependence; Economic development; Economic dualism; Economic history; Economic planning; Economic re-

sources; Economic underdevelopment; Exports; External debts; Global inequality; Global integration; Globalization; Harmonization (trade); Imports; Foreign aid; International division of labor; International economic organizations; International relations; Multinational corporations; Offshore production (foreign countries); Oligopolies; Public debt; Trade; Trade preferences; Trade protection; World history; World systems theory.

World health. World health. *Choose from:* world, international, transnational, global, worldwide, universal, cross-national, United Nations *with:* health, medical, medicine, disease(s), epidemiolog(y,ies,ical), epidemic(s), innoculat(e,ed,ing,ion,ions), sanitation, hygiene, nutrition. *See also* Disease; Epidemics; Famine; Global integration; Health; Health indices; Hygiene; Life expectancy; Health indices; Health status indicators; Health surveys; Infant mortality; Internationalism; Medical geography; Morbidity; Mortality rates; Nutrition surveys; Public health; Sanitation; Tropical medicine; Vaccinations; World citizenship.

World history. World history. Universal history. Human history. *Choose from:* world(wide), universal, human, global, recorded, transcivilizational, international *with:* histor(y,ical,ically). *See also* African empires; Ancient geography; Antiquity (time); Asian empires; Chain of being; Civilization; Colonialism; Cultural history; Economic history; Historical geography; Historical periods; Industrialization; Internationalism; Military history; Nationalism; World economy.

World order. See *Globalization; International cooperation; International economic integration; International law; International organizations; International relations; World economy; World problems.*

World politics. See *International relations.*

World population. World population(s). *Choose from:* world(wide), international, global, earth, foreign, United Nations, UNESCO *with:* populat(ed,ion,ions), inhabit(ed,ant,ants), people(s), census, depopulat(ed,ion), demograph(y,ic), overpopulat(ed,ion), migration(s), immigration(s), emigration(s), fertility, mortality, birth rate(s), death rate(s), Malthusian, population distribution, overcrowd(ed,ing). *See also* Demography; Global integration; Internationalism; Malthusian theory; Overpopulation; Population distribution; Population growth; World citizenship; Zero population growth.

World problems. World problems. *Choose from:* supranational, international,

multinational, transnational, global, worldwide, universal, cross-national, United Nations *with:* problem(s), cris(is,es), famine(s), disease(s), destabiliz(e,ed,ing,ation), disorder(s), depression(s), inflation(s), drought(s), tension(s), warfare, militarization, epidemic(s), terrorism, pollution, greenhouse effect, AIDS, overpopulation, population explosion, poverty, hunger, human rights, boundary dispute(s). *See also* Bioinvasion; Disarmament; Economic problems; Economic underdevelopment; Environmental pollution; Famine; Global integration; Human rights; Hunger, food deprivation; International relations; Internationalism; Overpopulation; Poverty; Problems; Refugees; Social problems; Terrorism; War; World citizenship.

World systems theory. World system(s) theor(y,ies,ist,ists). Capitalist world system. *Choose from:* world, international(ization), global(ization), intersocial, transnational *with:* system(s), network(s) *with:* theor(y,ies,etical), perspective(s), model(s). *Consider also:* Immanuel Wallerstein, postinternational theor(y,ies). *See also* Capitalism; Center and Periphery; Dependency Theory; Developing Countries; Exploitation; Global inequality; Globalization; Internationalism; Market economy; World citizenship; World Economy.

Worlds, plurality of. See *Plurality of worlds.*

Worlds, possible. See *Plurality of worlds.*

Worldview. Worldview(s). World view(s). Weltanschauung(en). Belief system(s). World outlook(s). Philosophy of life. Outlook on life. Cultural ethos. *Choose from:* philosophy, view(s), belief(s), perception(s), outlook(s), judgment(s), purpose(s), meaning(s) *with:* world, life, human nature, existence. *Consider also:* social realit(y,ies), cultural myth(s), ultimate realit(y,ies), cosmolog(y,ies), weltschmerz, religious commitment(s), just world belief(s), utopian(ism), anthropomorphism, cosmolog(y,ies), spiritualism. *See also* Afrocentrism; Attitudes; Beliefs; Catholic (universality); Civilized; Common sense; Context; Cultural knowledge; Culture (anthropology); Cynicism; Ethnocentrism; Eurocentrism; Hermeneutics; Ideologies; Intellectual history; Lifestyle; Optimism; Perceptions; Pessimism; Sectarianism; Social attitudes; Social reality; Values; Zeitgeist.

Worry. Worr(y,ied,ing). Worrisome. Anx(iety,ieties,ious). Distress(ed,es). Angst. Miser(y,ies). Fret(ted,ting). Agon(y,ies,ize,ized,izing). Perplexed. Mental anguish. Apprehens(ion,ive, iveness). Vex(ed,ation). Woe(s). *See also* Anxiety.

Worship. Worship(ped,ping,pers). Pray(er,ers,ing). Prayer meeting(s). Religious experience(s). Offertory ritual(s). Mass. Vespers. Devotions. Invocation. Supplication. Beatification. Benediction. Veneration. Evensong. Matins. Eucharist. Holy Communion. Deification. *Choose from:* religious, divine, church, temple *with:* ritual(s), reverence, devotions, service(s), ceremon(y,ies). *See also* Ancestor worship; Apotheosis; Blessing; Church attendance; Cults; Deities; Fetishism; Invocation; Liturgy; Masses (music); Moslem prayer; Nature worship; Places of worship; Prayer; Religions; Religious beliefs; Religious behavior; Religious rituals; Religious practices; Sacrificial rites; Saints.

Worship, ancestor. See *Ancestor worship.*

Worship, emperor. See *Emperor worship.*

Worship, freedom of. See *Freedom of religion.*

Worship, nature. See *Nature worship.*

Worship, places of. See *Places of worship.*

Worship, posture in. See *Posture in worship.*

Worship, public. See *Church attendance; Worship.*

Worship, ruler. See *Emperor worship.*

Worth, comparable. See *Comparable worth.*

Worth, monetary. See *Economic value.*

Worth, self. See *Self esteem.*

Wounds. See *Injuries.*

Wounds, self inflicted. See *Self inflicted wounds.*

Wrecking. See *Demolition.*

Wrecks. Wreck(s,age,ages). Shipwreck(s). Jalop(y,ies). Total(ly) ruin(ed,ation). Clunker(s). Ruin(s). Broken remains. Hulk(s). Rubble. *See also* Accidents; Debris; Demolition; Marine accidents.

Writer's block. See *Blocking.*

Writers. Writer(s). Author(s,ship). Composer(s). Compiler(s). Novelist(s). Narrator(s). Dramatist(s). Screenwriter(s). Poet(s). Essayist(s). Lyricist(s). Pamphleteer(s). Biographer(s). Journalist(s). Reporter(s). Playwright(s). Chronicler(s). *Consider also:* publication credit, byline(s), plagiarism, written anonymously, literary scholar(s), literary critic(s,ism). *See also* Authors; Autographs; Biographers; Composers; Dramatists; Editors; Intellectual life; Journalists; Literary prizes; Literary quarrels; Literature; Poets; Prisoners' writings; Professional personnel; Publications; Publishing; Scribes; Scriptwriting; Writing (composition).

Writing. Writing. Handwrit(ten,ing). Scribbl(e,ed,ing). Inscrib(e,ed,ing). Sign(ed,ing). Autograph(ed,ing). Penmanship. Print(ed,ing). Typewritten. Typ(e,ed,ing). Graphem(e,es,ic). Shorthand. Cursive writing. *See also* Autographs; Cursive writing.

Writing (composition). Writing(s). Writ(e,es,ten), Correspondence. Letter(s). Manuscript(s). Prepar(e,ed, ing) for publication. Journal entr(y,ies). Tak(e,n,ing) notes. Caption(ed,s).

Literary composition(s). Journalism. Abstracting. Playwriting. Authorship. *Choose from:* expository, descriptive, creative, news, technical *with:* writing(s). *See also* Editing; Language; Minimum competencies; Prisoners' writings; Technical writing; Writers.

Writing, academic. See *Scholarship.*

Writing, cursive. See *Cursive writing.*

Writing, learned. See *Scholarship.*

Writing, nature. See *Nature literature.*

Writing, picture. See *Pictography.*

Writing, scholarly. See *Scholarship.*

Writing, scientific. See *Technical writing.*

Writing, technical. See *Technical writing.*

Writing, travel. See *Travel writing.*

Writings, prisoners'. See *Prisoners' writings.*

Written communications. Written communication(s). Written word. *Choose from:* written, printed, handwritten *with:* communication(s), expression(s), language, instruction(s), feedback, paper(s), summar(y,ies), message(s), word(s), report(s), media, stor(y,ies). *Consider also:* correspondence, letter(s), script(s), text(s), essay(s), diar(y,ies), manuscript(s), memo(s), newsletter(s), newspaper(s), thes(is,es), dissertation(s), book(s), journal(s). *See also* Abbreviations; Compendiums; Cuneiform; Hieroglyphics; Iconography; Language; Letters (correspondence); Manuscripts; Petroglyphs; Pictography; Postal psychotherapy; Visual communication.

X

Xenophobia. Xenophob(e,es,ia,ic). *Choose from:* fear(ful), hatred, prejudice(d), suspicious, discriminat(ed,ion) *with:* foreign(er,ers), immigrant(s), alien(s), stranger(s). *See also* Anti-government radicals; Ethnic cleansing; Jingoism; Militias; Nativism; Nationalism; Patriotism; Social discrimination; Stranger reactions; Strangers; Tribalism.

Xenotransplantation. Xenotransplant(ion). Xenograft(s,ed,ing). Xenoplast(y,ic). Heterograft(s,ed,ing). Heterologous graft(s,ed,ing). Heteroplastic graft(s,ed,ing). Heteroplast(y,ic). Heterotransplant(ed,ing,ion). Cross-species transplant(s,ation). *See also* Biotechnology; Organ transplantation; Pharming.

Y

Y2K Problem. See *Millennium bug.*

Y2K bug. See *Millennium bug.*

Yahweh. See *Jehovah.*

Yard sales. See *Secondhand trade.*

Yards, navy and naval stations. See *Navy yards and naval stations.*

Year, extended school. See *Extended school year.*

Year 2000 date conversion. See *Millennium bug.*

Yoga. Yog(a,i,ic,in). Hatha Yoga. Raja Yoga. Kundalini Yoga. Patanjali Yoga. *Consider also:* tantrism, mantra(s), pranayama, sutra(s). *See also* Exercise; Hinduism; Religious practices; Relaxation.

Young adults. Young adult(s). Youth. College student(s). *Choose from:* 17-24 years, 18-30 years, 18-25 years, 18-26 years, 18-32 years, 18-35 years, etc. College age. Young worker(s). Student generation(s). Early adulthood. Graduate student(s). Young married couple(s). Young women. Young woman. Young man. Young men. *See also* Adolescence; Adult; Adult development; Age groups; College students; Graduate students; Human life cycle; Life stage transitions; Marriage timing; Married students; Postbaby boom generation; Postgraduate students; Sex behavior; Single person; Youth culture; Yuppies.

Young animals. See *Animal offspring.*

Young people. See *Adolescence; Young Adults.*

Youth. See *Adolescence; Young Adults.*

Youth, predelinquent. See *Predelinquent youth.*

Youth, rural. See *Rural youth.*

Youth associations. See *Youth organizations.*

Youth clubs. See *Youth organizations.*

Youth culture. Youth culture. *Choose from:* youth, adolescen(ce,t,ts), teen(s,age,ager,agers), young adult(s,hood), high school student(s), college student(s) *with:* cultur(e,es,al), fad(s), fashion(s), dress, style(s), lifestyle(s), subculture(s), counterculture(s), value(s), music, concert(s), worldview(s). *Consider also:* punk(s), skinhead(s), deadhead(s). *See also* Adolescence; Countercultures; Culture (anthropology); Lifestyle; Popular culture; Young adults; Youth movements; Youth organizations.

Youth movements. Youth movement(s). Counterculture. Flower generation. *Choose from:* student(s), youth, young adult(s), teen(s,age,aged,ager,agers), adolescen(t,ts,ce) *with:* movement(s), group(s), activis(m,ts), societ(y,ies), culture, subculture(s), protest(s,er,ers), revolt(s), demonstrator(s), participation, dissident(s), new left, politic(s,al), political(ly) correct(ness), resistance, sect(s). *See also* Activism; Countercultures; Political movements; Protest movements; Social action; Social movements; Student demonstrations; Youth culture.

Youth organizations. Youth organization(s). Youth club(s). *Choose from:* youth, student(s), young adult(s), teen(s,age,aged,ager,agers), adolescen(t,ts,ce), girls, boys *with:* organization(s), club(s), association(s), group(s), program(s). *Consider also:* Outward Bound, 4-H, Future Farmers, Girl Scouts, Boy Scouts, Big Brothers, Big Sisters, etc. *See also* Adolescence; Clubs; Juvenile gangs; Organizations; Student demonstrations; Youth culture.

Youthful. Youthful(ness). Girlish(ness). Boyish(ness). Youngish(ness). Freshness. Light hearted(ness). Vigor(ous,ousness). Buoyant. Optimis(m,tic). Cheerful(ness). Sophomoric. Childish(ness). Infantile. Immatur(e,ity). Inexperienced. Uninitiated. Naive(te). Innocen(t,ce). Undeveloped. *Consider also:* agerasia. *See also* Age differences; Cheerfulness.

Yugoslav republics, former. See *Former Yugoslav republics.*

Yuppie hobos. Yuppie hobo(s). Recreational hobo(s). Train hopper(s). *Consider also:* freighthop(pers,ping). *See also* Railroads; Trespassing; Yuppies.

Yuppies. Yupp(y,ies). Young urban professional(s). Young upwardly mobile professional(s). Young professional(s). Yapp(y,ies). Dink(s). Occupationally successful young adults. Young managers. *Consider also:* bupp(y,ies). *See also* Career mobility; Professional personnel; Young adults; Yuppie hobos.

Z

Zealots. Zealot(s,ry). Zealous(ness). Fanatic(s,al). True believer(s). Enthusiast(s). Bigot(s). Junkie(s). Fiend(s). Extremist(s). *Consider also:* disciple(s), follower(s), partisan(s), sectar(y,ies), supporter(s). *See also* Absolutism; Enthusiasts; Extremism; Fanaticism.

Zeitgeist. Zeitgeist. Spirit of the time(s). Spirit of the age. Climate of opinion. Mood of the period. Intellectual climate. Temper of the time(s). Esprit du siecle. Esprit du temps. *Choose from:* intellectual, moral, cultural *with:* climate, spirit, mood. *Consider also:* common intellectual presupposition(s), common forms of sensibility, mental climate, historism. *See also* Context; Cultural history; Historical perspective; Historiography; Ideologies; Periodization; Worldview.

Zen Buddhism. Zen Buddhism. *Choose from:* Zen *with:* koan, meditation, Buddhis(m,t,ts), exercise(s), Soto, Rinzai. *Consider also:* satori, sunyata, Mahayana Buddhism, dhyana, ch'an, prajna, Bodhidharma, Hui Neng, Sengtsan, Dogen. *See also* Buddhism; Meditation; Religion; Religious affiliation.

Zero economic growth. Zero economic growth. Steady state econom(y,ies). *Choose from:* econom(y,ies), economic *with:* equilibrium, zero growth, control(led,ling) growth, limited growth, growth moratorium, stationary state, steady state. *See also* Economic conditions; Economic planning; Economic stabilization.

Zero emissions vehicles. Zero emissions vehicle(s). ZEVs. Non-polluting car(s). Non-polluting vehicle(s). No-emissions vehicle(s). Solectria car(s). Clean-burning fuel(s). Non-polluting engine(s). *Consider also:* electric car(s), electric vehicle(s). *See also* Alternative energy; Automobiles; Environmental protection; Motor vehicles; Sustainable development.

Zero population growth. Zero population growth. ZPG. One child famil(y,ies). Limit(ed,ing) reproduction. Zero pop growth. Fertility control. Delayed parenthood. Voluntary childlessness. Reduced fertility. *Choose from:* fertility, population, birth rate(s), size(s) of famil(y,ies) *with:* limit(ed,ing), declin(e,ed,ing), stationary, cut(ting), falling, equilibrium, optimal size, below replacement level. *See also* Family planning; Population control; Population policy; World population.

Zionism. Zionis(m,t,ts). Jewish national movement. Israeli sympathizer(s). Emigrat(e,ed,ing,ion) to Israel. *Consider also:* Aliyah. *See also* Judaism; Social movements.

Zone, social. See *Proxemics.*

Zone management, coastal. See *Shore protection.*

Zones, enterprise. See *Enterprise zones.*

Zones, foreign trade. See *Foreign trade zones.*

Zones, free trade. See *Foreign trade zones.*

Zoning. Zon(ed,ing). Regulat(e,ed,ing) land use(s). Restrict(ed,ing) land use(s). *Consider also:* community planning, zonal differentiation, deed restriction(s), regionalization, enterprise zone(s), setback(s), variance(s). *See also* Enterprise zones; Growth management; Land use; Real estate; Real estate development; Suburbs; Urban planning.

Zoo animals. Zoo animal(s). *Choose from:* zoo(s,logical), captivity, caged *with:* animal(s), mammal(s), reptile(s), bird(s), lion(s), tiger(s), elephant(s) or other animals by name. *Consider also:* menager(y,ies), circus animal(s). *See also* Animals; Captivity; Endangered species; Environmental enrichment (animal culture); Exotic species; Wild animals.

Zooarchaeology. See *Animal remains (archaeology).*

Zooerasty. Zooerast(y,ia). Bestiality. Zoophilia. *See also* Sodomy.

Zoroastrianism. Zoroastrian(s,ism). Mazdaism. Ahur Mazda. Ohrmazd. Zoroaster. Avesta. Amesha spentas. Parsis. *See also* Religions.

Appendix A: Putting Searches in Context

To put your search in the right context, it may be necessary to define a broad subset of a database. Some systems, such as Lexis-Nexis Academic Universe, begin the search process by having the user select a broad category in which to conduct the search. Other systems, such as Northern Light, organize the results of a search by broad subject categories, allowing you to select the results from subject areas of interest. Some databases have subject codes that you can use to limit a search to specified categories.

A caution concerning broad subject category codes should be noted. Some databases assign only one or two broad subject codes to each item, usually to those items that have the subject as a primary focus. Some items that discuss the subject may not have the code assigned. If you are trying to broaden your search, you may need to enrich your strategy with additional terms. On the other hand, limiting your results to a particular subset can effectively refine your search. In the following section, broad category searching on selected databases using several different systems is described and illustrated.

Dissertation Abstracts on DIALOG

In *Dissertation Abstracts*, each citation is assigned only one or two subject categories (called descriptors) chosen from the *DAI [Dissertation Abstracts International] Subject Classification Scheme* by the author. The category assigned to a citation reflects the major focus of the dissertation. Examples of some DAI descriptors are: " Political science, general," "American studies," "Economics, general," "Political science, international law and relations," "Education, higher," "Sociology, social structure and development," "Sociology, ethnic and racial studies," and "Sociology, criminology and penology." For a complete list of subjects, see the *Dissertation Abstracts* database documentation.

The following searches are examples of a search using a free-text term put in context by combining it with *DAI* descriptors in File 35: *Dissertation Abstracts Online* on the DIALOG system. The first search is for the word "conviction" (truncated and limited to the title field) and illustrates the meaning of the word when it is combined with the descriptor "Religion."

File 35:Dissertation Abstracts Online 1861-1999/Apr
(c) 1999 UMI

Set Items Description
--- ----- -----------

?s conviction?/ti
    S1   71   CONVICTION?/TI

?s s1 and religion/de
      71 S1
   33370 RELIGION/DE
  S2   12 S1 AND RELIGION/DE
Titles retrieved include the following:

FUNDAMENTAL **CONVICTIONS** AND THE NEED FOR JUSTIFICATION (RATIONALITY, RELATIVISM)

NEW ENGLAND PURITAN EDUCATIONAL **CONVICTION** DURING THE SEVENTEENTH AND EIGHTEENTH CENTURIES (SEVENTEENTH CENTURY, EIGHTEENTH CENTURY)

EXPERIENCES OF WOMEN WITH STRONG RELIGIOUS **CONVICTIONS** WHO ENDURED AND TERMINATED ABUSIVE MARITAL RELATIONSHIPS

PROPHESYING DAUGHTERS: NINETEENTH-CENTURY BLACK WOMEN PREACHERS, RELIGIOUS **CONVICTION** AND RESISTANCE

The same term combined with the descriptor "Criminology" produces results in which the word "conviction" has a quite different meaning, as the following search illustrates.

?s s1 and criminology/de
      71 S1
   7101 CRIMINOLOGY/DE
  S3   8 S1 AND CRIMINOLOGY/DE
Titles retrieved include the following:

AN EMPIRICAL INVESTIGATION OF THE RELATIONSHIP BETWEEN ALCOHOL AND DRUG-RELATED MOTOR VEHICLE **CONVICTIONS** AND PILOT FLYING PERFORMANCE (DRUNK DRIVING)

THE EFFECTIVENESS OF VOIR DIRE AS A SAFEGUARD AGAINST ERRONEOUS **CONVICTION** RESULTING FROM MISTAKEN EYEWITNESS IDENTIFICATION (MISTAKEN IDENTIFICATION)

THE SIGNIFICANCE OF RELATIONSHIPS WITH IMPORTANT MALE "OTHERS" IN THE FIRST **CONVICTION** OF FEMALE OFFENDERS (OFFENDERS)

Arts & Humanities Search on FirstSearch

The *Arts & Humanities Search* has broad subject categories assigned to source journals. A limited number of categories is assigned to each journal. Each journal is assigned at least one subject code and up to a maximum of four. Each citation is coded to indicate the subject category of the *journal* in which it was published. Obviously, categorizing articles by the journals in which they are published rather than by the subject of the articles themselves means that the codes may retrieve some irrelevant material and may not retrieve all relevant material. Examples of some of the codes are "Architecture," "Arts & humanities, general," "History," "Language & linguistics," "Religion," "Literary reviews," and "Literature."

Truncation and wild cards are not available in FirstSearch, although plurals can be searched. A search for "harmonization," which on another system would be truncated as "harmoniz," is here searched as "harmonization or harmonized." Searching it in the subject field (su:) and combining it with the journal subset (js=) for "music" looks like this:

> Database= Arts & Humanities Search
> | Search= js="music" and su:(harmonization or
> harmonized)
> Results= 8 records |

Titles retrieved include the following:

THEORY AND AESTHETICS OF **HARMONIZATION** OF EXOTIC TUNES IN THE EARLY 20th CENTURY.

ELEMENTARY JAZZ **HARMONIZATION**.

THE 2-VOICE FRAMEWORK AND ITS **HARMONIZATION** IN ARCADELT 'FIRST BOOK OF MADRIGALS' (16TH-CENTURY HARMONY).

LISZT **HARMONIZATION** OF LINEAR CHROMATICISM.

If the search had not been limited to citations from music journals, a total of 26 citations would have been retrieved as shown by the following search.

> Database= Arts & Humanities Search
> | Search= (harmonization or harmonized)
> Results= 26 records |

Some of the titles retrieved from other subject areas, in which "harmonized or harmonization" have a different meaning, are:

THE RECEPTION OF ENGLISH WORDS IN THE FRENCH PRESS-PROPOSITIONS FOR THE **HARMONIZATION** OF ENGLISH LOANWORDS.

HARMONIZATION OF EDUCATION AND TRAINING-PROGRAMS FOR LIBRARY, INFORMATION AND ARCHIVAL PERSONNEL.

COLERIDGE 'BIOGRAPHIA LITERARIA' - EXTRAVAGANTLY MIXED GENRES AND THE CONSTRUCTION OF A **HARMONIZED** CHAOS.

HARMONIZATION TO MEET THE CHALLENGE OF CHANGE.

PsycLIT on SilverPlatter, WebSPIRS Version 3.1.

Numeric codes are also used to assign items to broad subject areas of *PsycINFO*, the online database and *PsycLIT*, the CD-ROM database. Generally, only one category representing the main subject is assigned to an item. In some cases, a secondary code is also assigned. Categories include such areas as "personality" (category 3100); "treatment and prevention" (category 3300); and "developmental psychology" (category 2800). Categories are further subdivided into subsets. For example, "developmental psychology" is divided into "cognitive and perceptual development (category 2820) and "psychosocial & personality development (category 2840). Both can be retrieved by searching for the abbreviated form "28" in the classification category field. A complete list of the codes is published in the *Thesaurus of Psychological Index Terms*. For the format used by your system, consult your system manual.

This search of *PsycLIT* (1996-1999/03) on SilverPlatter shows the difference in the results retrieved when the word "conviction" (truncated and limited to titles) is combined with category 3236 (Criminal Behavior and Juvenile Delinquency) as compared to when it is combined with category 3120 (Personality Traits and Processes).

The search looks like this:

Search	Results
#1 (conviction*) in TI	15
#2 cc=3236	1188
#3 cc=3120	3968
#4 #1 and #2	4
#5 #1 and #3	3

Titles retrieved with the criminal behavior code include the following:

Handgun purchasers with misdemeanor *convictions*.

Prior misdemeanor *convictions* as a risk factor for later violent and firearm-related criminal activity among authorized purchasers of handguns.

Temperamental and familial predictors of criminal *convictions*.

Temperamental and familial predictors of violent and nonviolent criminal *convictions*: Age 3 to age 18.

Titles retrieved with the personality traits code include the following:

A review of the IPC Questionnaire for *Conviction* Control (IPC).

Conviction management: Lessons from hypnosis research about how self-images of dubious validity can be willfully sustained.

Attitude *conviction*: A self-reflective measure of attitude strength.

Searching the World Wide Web using Northern Light

Northern Light is a sophisticated Web search engine that sorts search results into folders representing concepts or types of sites and automatically displays a sample of the most highly ranked titles. A search for the word "Harmonization" on Northern Light returned 32,731 items that were organized by the system into Custom Search Folders with the following titles:

Search Current News
Special Collection documents
Highways, roads & pavements
Transportation safety
Building standards & codes
National Technical Information Service
(NTIS) (report)
Building materials
Structural engineering
International trade
Air pollution
Law
Nuclear waste
Satellite technology
all others. . .

By selecting a folder, you focus and limit your search results to a specific area. For example, by selecting the folder for "International trade," the results above were reduced to 1,892 items. Titles of the highest ranking results retrieved include the following:

___Report of the FDA Task Force on International Harmonization.

___Countdown to Osaka: Asia-Pacific Economic Cooperation or Confrontation?

___Harmonization of Standards and Regulations: Problems and Opportunities for the U. . .

___International Harmonization of Standards: Done with or without Us.

Used judiciously, broad subject category codes can enhance natural language computer searching.

References

Arts & Humanities Search, 1980- . FirstSearch. Online from OCLC.

Dissertation Abstracts Online. University Microfilms International, 1861- . Online from DIALOG.

Northern Light, online at <http://www.nlsearch.com/>.

PsycLIT. Washington, DC: American Psychological Association, 1967- . On SilverPlatter, WebSPIRS Version 3.1.

Appendix B: British Spellings

British spellings may be important if the database you are searching has international coverage. British spellings have not been included in the records in this volume; however, they may be of importance in some searches. The following general models of letter combinations can be used to retrieve both U.S. and British spellings.*

US	British	Example
ction	xion	connection/connexion
dg	dge	judgment/judgement
e	ae,oe	eolian/aeolian, ecology/oecology
er	re	theater/theatre
ize	ise	organize/organise
l	ll	leveling/levelling
or	our	humor/humour
s	c	defense/defence

*Gove, William Babcock, ed. *Webster's Third New International Dictionary of the English Language Unabridged.* Springfield, MA: G.&C. Merriam, 1976.

Selected Sources Used to Compile This Thesaurus

Concepts and terms were derived from both online and printed sources. In some cases, more than one edition of a source was used so more than one edition is listed.

Abercrombie, Nicholas; Hill, Stephen, et al. *The Penguin Dictionary of Modern Sociology*. London: Penguin Books, 1988.

ABI/Inform. CD-ROM edition. Louisville, KY: UMI/Data Courier, 1985- . On CD-ROM from UMI.

Ageline. Online edition. Washington, DC: American Association of Retired Persons, 1978- . On CD-ROM from SilverPlatter.

Agricola. Online edition. Beltsville, MD: National Agricultural Library, 1970- . Online from DIALOG.

America History & Life. Online from DIALOG, file 38. Santa Barbara, CA: ABC-CLIO, Inc., 1964- .

Arts & Humanities Search. Online edition. Philadelphia: Institute for Scientific Information, 1980- . Online from FirstSearch.

Arts & Humanities Search [Online]. Available from DIALOG, file 439. Philadelphia: Institute for Scientific Information, 1980- .

Black, Henry Campbell, *Black's Law Dictionary*. St. Paul, MN: West Publishing Company, 1990.

Boudon, Raymond; Bourricaud, Francois. *A Critical Dictionary of Sociology*. Chicago: University of Chicago Press, 1989.

Bridgwater, William; Kurtz, Seymour, eds. *The Columbia Encyclopedia*. New York: Columbia University Press, 1963.

The Cambridge Dictionary of Philosophy. Cambridge: Cambridge University Press, 1995.

Campbell, Robert Jean. *Psychiatric Dictionary*. NewYork: Oxford University Press, 1981.

Capek, Mary Ellen S., ed. *A Women's Thesaurus*. New York: Harper & Row, 1989.

Colby, Anita Y. *Thesaurus of Linguistic Indexing Terms*. San Diego: Sociological Abstracts, c1992.

Cole, Steven W., ed. *Religion Indexes: Thesaurus*. Chicago: American Theological Library Association, 1987.

The Columbia Dictionary of Modern Literary and Cultural Criticism. Joseph Childers and Gary Hentzi, eds. New York: Columbia University Press, 1995.

A Concise Dictionary of Business. New York: Oxford University Press, 1990.

Crim, Keith, ed. *The Perennial Dictionary of World Religions*. New York: Harper & Row, 1989.

Crystal, David. *A Dictionary of Linguistics and Phonetics*. Oxford: Blackwell, 1997.

DeVries, Mary Anne. *Business Thesaurus*. New York: Barron's, 1996.

Dictionary of Multicultural Education. Carl A. Grant and Gloria Ladson-Billings, eds. Phoenix, AZ: Oryx Press, 1997.

Dissertation Abstracts Ondisc. CD-ROM edition. Ann Arbor, MI: UMI, 1985- . On CD-ROM from UMI.

ERIC. Online edition. Rockville, MD: ERIC Processing and Reference Facility, 1966- . Online from DIALOG.

ERIC. CD-ROM edition. Rockville, MD: ERIC Processing and Reference Facility, 1966- . On CD-ROM from SilverPlatter.

Expanded Academic Index. Foster City, CA: Information Access Company, 1991- . Online from DIALOG.

Goldenson, Robert M., ed. *Longman Dictionary of Psychology and Psychiatry*. New York: Longman, 1984.

Harvey, Van Austin. *A Handbook of Theological Terms*. New York: Macmillan, 1964.

Hays, Terence E., ed. *Encyclopedia of World Cultures*, Vol. II: *Oceania*. Boston: G.K. Hall, 1991.

Historical Abstracts. Online edition. Santa Barbara, CA: ABC-CLIO, 1973- . Online from DIALOG.

Humanities Index. New York: H.W. Wilson Company, 1994-1996.

IAC National Newspaper Index. Online edition. Belmont, CA: Information Access Company, 1979- . Online from DIALOG.

INFO-SOUTH Latin American Information System. Coral Gables, FL: Institute of InterAmerican Studies, North-South Center, Graduate School of International Studies, University of Miami, 1988- . Online from DIALOG.

Knowles, Elizabeth and Julia Elliott. *The Oxford Dictionary of New Words*. New York: Oxford University Press, 1997.

Laird, Charlton. *Webster's New World Thesaurus*. New York: New American Library, 1975.

Levy, Ronald. *The New Language of Psychiatry: Learning and Using DSM-III*. Boston: Little, Brown and Company, 1982.

Library of Congress, Cataloging Policy and Support Office. *Subject Headings Weekly Lists*. <http://lcweb.loc.gov/catdir/cpso/wls.html>.

Library of Congress, Subject Cataloging Division. *Library of Congress Subject Headings*. Washington, DC: Library of Congress, 1996.

Linguistics and Language Behavior Abstracts. Online from DIALOG, file 36. San Diego: Sociological Abstracts, Inc., 1973- .

Little, William. *The Oxford Universal Dictionary on Historical Principles*, 3rd ed. Prepared by William Little, H.W. Fowler, and J. Coulson; revised and edited by C.T. Onions. Oxford: The Clarendon Press, 1955.

MLA Bibliography. On CD-ROM from SilverPlatter. New York: Modern Language Association of America, 1981- .

Magazine Index. Online edition. Belmont, CA: Information Access Company, 1959- . Online from DIALOG.

Meadows, A.J.; Gordon, M.; Singleton, A. *The Random House Dictionary of New Information Technology.* New York: Random House, 1982.

Medline. Online edition. Bethesda, MD: National Library of Medicine, 1966- . On CD-ROM from SilverPlatter.

Merriam Webster's Encyclopedia of Literature. Springfield, MA: Merriam Webster, 1995.

National Library of Medicine Staff. *Medical Subject Headings, Annotated Alphabetic List.* Bethesda, MD: National Library of Medicine, 1986-1998.

The New Harvard Dictionary of Music. Don Michael Randel, ed. Cambridge, MA: Belknap Press of Harvard University Press, 1986.

The New Princeton Encyclopedia of Poetry and Poetics. Alex Preminger and T.V.F. Brogan, eds. Princeton, NJ: Princeton University Press, 1993.

The New York Times on the Web. <http://www.nytimes.com/>.

Newspaper Abstracts Thesaurus. Ann Arbor, MI: UMI, 1988.

The Oxford Dictionary of Art. Ian Chilvers and Harold Osborne, eds. Oxford: Oxford University Press, 1997.

Philosopher's Index. Online from DIALOG, file 57. Bowling Green, OH: Philosophy Documentation Center, Bowling Green University, 1940- .

Physician's Desk Reference. Montvale, NJ: Medical Economics Company, 1992.

Plano, Jack C. *The Public Administration Dictionary.* Santa Barbara, CA: ABC-Clio, 1988.

Plano, Jack C.; Olton, Roy. *The International Relations Dictionary.* Santa Barbara, CA: ABC-Clio, 1982.

Plano, Jack C.; Riggs, Robert E., et al. *The Dictionary of Political Analysis.* Santa Barbara, CA: ABC-Clio, 1982.

PsycINFO [Online]. Available from DIALOG, file 11. Washington, DC: American Psychological Association, 1967- .

PsycLIT. CD-ROM edition. Washington, DC: American Psychological Association, 1974- . On CD-ROM from SilverPlatter.

Public Affairs Information Service. Online edition. New York: Public Affairs Information Service, 1972- . Online from SilverPlatter.

Public Affairs Information Service. CD-ROM edition. New York: Public Affairs Information Service, 1972- .On CD-ROM from SilverPlatter.

Public Affairs Information Service. *PAIS Subject Headings.* New York: Public Affairs Information Service, 1984.

Random House Webster's College Dictionary. New York: Random House, 1991.

Ritter, Harry. *Dictionary of Concepts in History.* Westport, CT: Greenwood Press, 1986.

Rodale, Jerome Irving. *The Synonym Finder.* Emmaus, PA: Rodale Press, 1978.

Rosenberg, Jerry M. *Dictionary of Business and Management.* New York: John Wiley & Sons, 1983.

Rosenberg, Jerry M. *Dictionary of Business and Management.* New York: John Wiley & Sons, 1993.

Rosenberg, Jerry M. *Dictionary of International Trade.* New York: John Wiley & Sons, 1994.

Scott, David Logan. *Wall Street Words.* Boston: Houghton Mifflin, 1988.

Sills, David L., ed. *International Encyclopedia of the Social Sciences.* [New York]: The Macmillan Company and The Free Press, 1968.

Social SCISEARCH(r). Online edition. Philadelphia: Institute for Scientific Information, 1972- . Online from DIALOG.

Sociofile. CD-ROM edition. San Diego: Sociological Abstracts, 1974- . On CD-ROM from SilverPlatter.

Sociological Abstracts. San Diego: Sociological Abstracts, 1963- . DIALOG, file 37. San Diego: Sociological Abstracts, Inc., 1963- .

TechEncyclopedia. <http://www.techweb.com/encyclopedia/>.

Theodorson, George A.; Theodorson, Achilles G. *Modern Dictionary of Sociology.* New York: Thomas Y. Crowell, 1970.

Thesaurus of Aging Terminology. Washington, DC: American Association of Retired Persons, 1986.

Thesaurus of ERIC Descriptors, 11th ed. Phoenix, AZ: Oryx Press, 1986.

Thesaurus of ERIC Descriptors, 12th ed. Phoenix, AZ: Oryx Press, 1990.

Thesaurus of ERIC Descriptors, 13th ed. Phoenix, AZ: Oryx Press, 1995.

Thesaurus of Psychological Index Terms. Washington, DC: American Psychological Association, 1988.

Thesaurus of Psychological Index Terms. Arlington, VA: American Psychological Association, 1991.

Thesaurus of Psychological Index Terms. Washington, DC: American Psychological Association, 1994.

Thesaurus of Sociological Indexing Terms. San Diego: Sociological Abstracts, Inc., 1986.

Thesaurus of Sociological Indexing Terms. San Diego: Sociological Abstracts, Inc., 1989.

Tulloch, Sara. *The Oxford Dictionary of New Words.* New York: Oxford University Press, 1991.

Winick, Charles. *Dictionary of Anthropology.* Towota, NJ: Littlefield Adams, 1977.

Winthrop, Robert H. *Dictionary of Concepts in Cultural Anthropology.* New York: Greenwood Press, 1991.

Wolman, Benjamin B. *Dictionary of Behavioral Science.* New York: Academic Press, Inc, 1989.

Sara D. Knapp is coordinator of the Computer Search Service at the University Library, University at Albany, State University of New York. Her articles have appeared in *Online*, *Database*, *The Reference Librarian*, *Behavioral and Social Sciences Librarian*, *Journal of Educational Technology Systems*, *The Journal of Academic Librarianship*, *RQ*, and *Library Quarterly*. She is a founder and past chair of the Machine-Assisted Reference Section (MARS) of the Reference and Adult Services Division of the American Library Association (ALA). Knapp was the 1984 recipient of ALA's Isadore Gilbert Mudge Citation for distinguished contributions to reference librarianship and was also a recipient of the SUNY Chancellor's Award for Excellence in Librarianship.